READER'S DIGEST ILLUSTRATED GUIDE TO

AUSTRALIAN PLACES

Editing, design and cartography by Reader's Digest (Australia) Pty Ltd

First edition, first revise
Published by Reader's Digest (Australia) Pty Ltd
26-32 Waterloo Street, Surry Hills, NSW 2010

National Library of Australia cataloguing-in-publication data:

Reader's Digest illustrated guide to Australian places

Includes index.
ISBN 0 86438 399 1.

1. Australia – Guidebooks. I. Title: Illustrated guide to Australian places.
919.40463

Imagesetting by Wysiwyg Design Pty Ltd, Sydney
Colour separation by Colourscan Overseas Co. Pte Ltd, Singapore
Printing and binding by Toppan Printing Co. (S) Pte Ltd, Singapore

Front cover: Approaches to Sheffield, near Mount Roland, Tasmania.
Back cover, top to bottom: Victoria Dock, Hobart;
Euchra Valley rainforest, east Gippsland;
Kosciusko National Park;
Emu Point, the Kimberley.
End papers: False Pera Head, northern Cape York.
Page 1: Rainbow Valley, near Alice Springs.
Page 3: Bathurst, New South Wales.
Page 5: Purnululu National Park, east Kimberley.
Page 7: Karri forest, Margaret River, Western Australia.

READER'S DIGEST ILLUSTRATED GUIDE TO

AUSTRALIAN PLACES

READER'S DIGEST, SYDNEY

CONTRIBUTORS

The publishers would like to thank the following people for their contributions to this book:

History Consultants

David Carment, BA, PhD
Associate Professor in History, Northern Territory University

Cathie Clement, PhD, MPHR
Consulting Historian, National Heritage

Ian Elliot, MPHR
Consulting Historian, Wildtrax Australia

Alan Frost, MA, MA PhD, FRHists, FAHA
Professor of History, La Trobe University

Peter A. Howell, MA, PhD, FRHists
Associate Professor, History, The Flinders University of South Australia

Associate Professor S.M. Jack, MA, BLitt (Oxon), DipEd UNE, FRHS

W. Ross Johnston, BA, PhD, LLB, MA
Associate Professor, History Department, University of Queensland

Clive Moore, BA, PhD
Senior Lecturer, History Department, University of Queensland

---

Principal writers

Lesley Dow
Deborah Guyon
Robert Irving
Margaret McPhee
Anne Matthews
Peter Prineas
Tullio Rubinich
Judith Simpson

Other writers

Ann Atkinson
Baiba Berzins
Greg Callaghan
Linda Donaldson
Bary Dowling
Bob Engich
Alan Frost
Meredith Hall
Bill Hornadge
Mary Rennie
Yani Silvana
Murray Thompson
Susan Tomnay
Paul Tyson
David Underhill
Rosy Whelan

INTRODUCTION

MAPS AND atlases help you to find places, but they do not show you what places look like or if there is a story behind the dot on the map.

Illustrated Guide to Australian Places does what an atlas does but goes much further by telling the stories an atlas cannot tell. Here are one hundred and seventy-eight detailed maps that locate more than twenty-five hundred places. Each map sets the scene for comprehensive portraits of cities, towns and hamlets, as well as natural landmarks.

Persistent and comprehensive research revealed that most places have either some interesting geographical features or a history worth relating; and of course many have both. For this book is about people too. It includes Aborigines' special places and traces the course of European expansion and the building of a nation. *Illustrated Guide to Australian Places* is a practical reference book, but it is also a book designed to give the pleasure of discovering Australia to all its readers. □

THE EDITORS

CONTENTS

HOW TO USE THIS BOOK

ILLUSTRATED GUIDE TO AUSTRALIAN PLACES divides Australia into 178 regions, each region based on two major population centres. Places of interest in each region – towns, national parks and other public reserves or geographical features – are given entry numbers; numbers run numerically throughout the book from 1 to 2551. All towns with more than 500 people are described, along with many other smaller settlements of historical, geographical or tourist interest.

Landmarks such as historic buildings, monuments, parks and gardens, and places of interest within or near a town, are treated as sub-entries and listed after the main entry. Major cities and outstanding geographical features such as the Great Dividing Range, Arnhem Land and the Murray and Murrumbidgee river system are separated out and treated as two- or four-page special features.

Finding a region

To find a particular region, refer to the key diagram at the beginning of each state section (see example, right). States are in the following order: New South Wales, Victoria, Queensland, South Australia, Western Australia, Tasmania and the Northern Territory. Regions shown on the diagram are linked by a number to the list opposite which lists their book page number.

Using the maps

Two maps accompany each region. A small locator map in the top, left-hand corner of the page highlights the region in its state context and acts as a bridge between the key diagram and the colour map showing the region in detail. All major places described have an entry number which is repeated on the coloured maps in easy-to-read, black panels. As well as the entries, maps display national parks, outstanding landmarks, railway routes and major roads with distances between towns. Page numbers of adjoining maps are cross-referenced in red. Symbols used are explained in the panel at top right.

Finding a place

The book's numerical-order listing system makes looking for a specific place easy. Simply refer to the index on page 690 where place names and entry numbers are given together in **bold** type, as they appear in the book.

Populations

Populations are never static so for the sake of consistency the population figure given in *italics* at the end of each town of more than 500 people is the latest figure available from the Australian Bureau of Statistics at the time of publication, rounded out to the nearest multiple of five.

Festivals

Major local festivals have been listed under some town entries with the month or time of month – early, mid- or late – when they are celebrated. This is a guide only and festivals and their exact dates are best confirmed with local authorities as cancellations or date changes sometimes occur. □

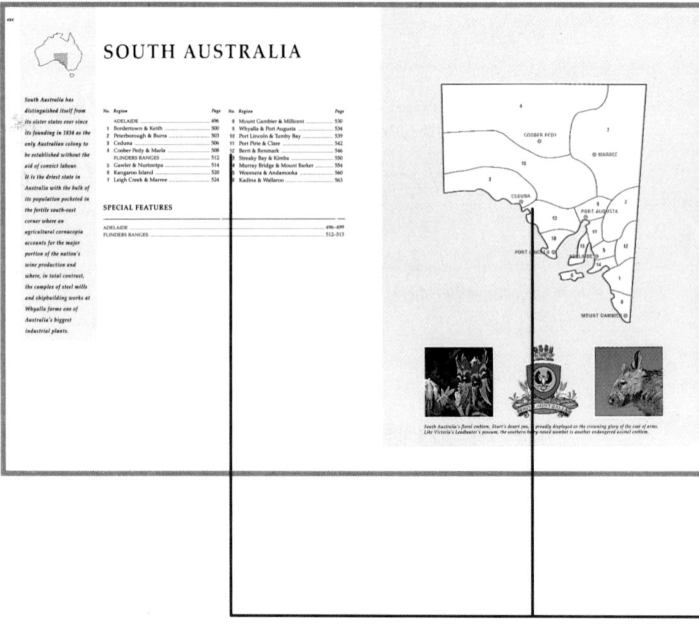
SOUTH AUSTRALIA
SPECIAL FEATURES

To find a region, refer to the key diagram (above right). Each region is cross-referenced to the list at left which gives its name and page number. Turn to the page, where a small locator map accompanies the main, detailed map.

Places are listed alphabetically with an entry number. To find the location of a place, simply look for its entry number in a black panel on the map.

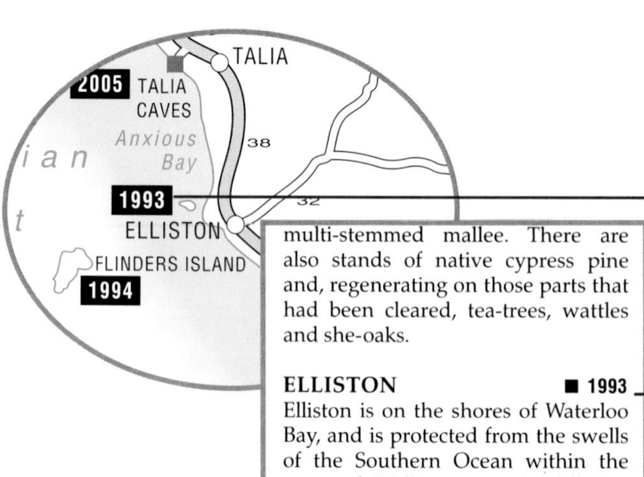
TALIA
2005 TALIA CAVES
Anxious Bay
38
1993
32
ELLISTON
FLINDERS ISLAND
1994
multi-stemmed mallee. There are also stands of native cypress pine and, regenerating on those parts that had been cleared, tea-trees, wattles and she-oaks.
ELLISTON ■ 1993
Elliston is on the shores of Waterloo Bay, and is protected from the swells of the Southern Ocean within the arms of Wellington and Wellesley points – a naming spree of natural features here in 1865 celebrated the fiftieth anniversary of the British victory over Napoleon's forces in the Battle of Waterloo (appropriately, Wellington and Wellesley were brothers in fact as well as in arms). It is generally accepted that the town,

Map legend

Highways	
Unsealed highways	
Other roads (sealed)	
Other roads (unsealed)	

(Generally, distances under four kilometres have not been included.)

Vehicular track	
Walking track	
Railway	

(Due to curtailment of many rail services, some lines may carry goods traffic only.)

State boundary

*Centres of population**

- Regional centres
- 3000 or more people
- 500–3000 people
- less than 500 people

* Based on Australian Bureau of Statistics figures available at time of publication.

National and state parks and reserves

Aboriginal land

Prohibited area

Lake

River

Dry or intermittent lake

Swamp (inland)

Swamp (river)

Symbols

- ▲ Mountain
- □ Man-made feature
- ■ Natural feature
- ✱ p 000 Adjoining map page reference

Abbreviations

Beach	Bch
Conservation Park	Cons. Pk
Creek	Ck
Developmental Road	Develop. Rd
Head	Hd
Highway	Hwy
Island/s	I./Is
Lake	L.
Lookout	Lkt
Mount	Mt
Mountain	Mtn
National Park	N.P. or Nat. Pk
North	Nth
Park	Pk
Peak	Pk
Point	Pt
Range/s	Ra./Ras
Reserve	Res.
Reservoir	Resvr
River	R.
Road	Rd
South	Sth
State Recreation Area	Rec. Area

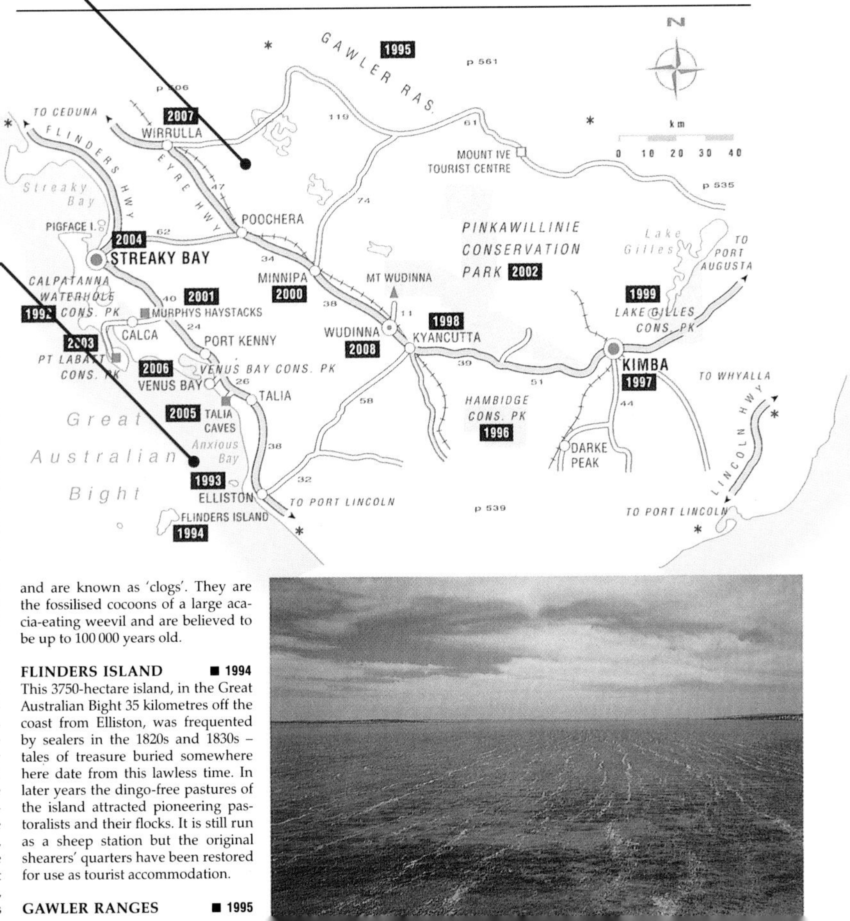

550 SOUTH AUSTRALIA

Streaky Bay & Kimba

Since the 1860s, the upper Eyre Peninsula has grown much of South Australia's wheat. In contrast, a series of arid-land parks protects examples of its plants and animals while outcrops of mound-shaped rocks dot the flat landscape.

CALPATANNA WATERHOLE CONSERVATION PARK ■ 1992
The extensive system of salt lakes protected in this park fill with winter rains but, in the long hot summers, can dry to shimmering salt pans. They are fringed by low-growing semi-succulent plants, and surrounding them on sandy and stony ridges is an area of semi-arid scrub which is characteristic of the west coast of South Australia. In particular this includes salt paperbark and the multi-stemmed mallee. There are also stands of native cypress pine and, regenerating on those parts that had been cleared, tea-trees, wattles and she-oaks.

ELLISTON ■ 1993
Elliston is on the shores of Waterloo Bay, and is protected from the swells of the Southern Ocean within the arms of Wellington and Wellesley points – a naming spree of natural features here in 1865 celebrated the fiftieth anniversary of the British victory over Napoleon's forces in the Battle of Waterloo (appropriately, Wellington and Wellesley were brothers in fact as well as in arms). It is generally accepted that the town, though, was named for a local, Miss

and are known as 'clogs'. They are the fossilised cocoons of a large acacia-eating weevil and are believed to be up to 100 000 years old.

FLINDERS ISLAND ■ 1994
This 3750-hectare island, in the Great Australian Bight 35 kilometres off the coast from Elliston, was frequented by sealers in the 1820s and 1830s – tales of treasure buried somewhere here date from this lawless time. In later years the dingo-free pastures of the island attracted pioneering pastoralists and their flocks. It is still run as a sheep station but the original shearers' quarters have been restored for use as tourist accommodation.

GAWLER RANGES ■ 1995

The ranges were sighted by explorer Edward Eyre on his 1839 trek from Streaky Bay back east across the top of the peninsula which now bears his name. He named them for the Governor of South Australia, George Gawler. The area had been known to the Aborigines for thousands of years and within the ranges Yantanabie Historic Reserve protects an Aboriginal quarry where material for tools was obtained.

HAMBIDGE CONSERVATION PARK ■ 1996
This park preserves a large area of undisturbed arid country, an important example used in evaluating the impact of past land use in similar areas, and in understanding the processes which form various desert-region landscapes.

The scrub-covered limestone and sand ridges of Hambidge, rising usually six to twelve metres, run roughly parallel in a north-east, south-west direction. In the highest part of the park, at Prominent Hill, they are a towering sixty to ninety metres high. In the depressions and clay pans between the ridges grow tall mallees, and on the dune crests there are cypress pines. Its mammals include creatures which have adapted to the harsh desert life so that they can conserve moisture and survive climatic extremes. Among them are the fat-tailed dunnart, its tail a storehouse of food, Mitchell's hopping mouse and the western pigmy possum; there is even a possibility that the rare brush-tailed rat kangaroo exists in the park.

KIMBA ■ 1997
Kimba serves one of the major wheat regions in South Australia. European land use here dates from the 1870s, when sheep runs were taken up. Agricultural development dates from the early 1900s when the dense mallee was cleared and wheat and barley planted. The town was proclaimed in 1915. *Population 795*

KYANCUTTA ■ 1998
Kyancutta lies at the waterless heart of the Eyre Peninsula, a tiny township which serves the surrounding agricultural community. It came into being in 1917 when settlement here became possible due to the arrival of

THE SPREAD OF SETTLEMENT

Four hundred years ago, intimations of a great south land provoked the curiosity of imaginative European sailor-adventurers. The fragmentary outlines on the charts they made were gradually put together, and by the middle of the seventeenth century the known portions of Australia's vast coastline had formed into a tantalising, half-completed jigsaw puzzle.

Britain was the only nation to express any real interest in the great south land, despite William Dampier's reports of an impossibly bleak and barren west coast and no reports at all of the east. But to James Cook and Joseph Banks, who in 1770 were the first to touch the eastern shores, the land seemed full of bright promise. Their favourable reports led to the first settlement, motivated by the twin imperatives of dumping British convicts and establishing a strategic British presence in the South Pacific.

Two hundred years later, Australia had been an urbanised nation for more than a century. It is now characterised by eight capital cities, seven of them on the coastal rim and one not far inland. The bridging of the great distances between these centres, reflecting the continent's great size, has been a compelling factor in its development. The sequence of town settlement, and the permanence and primacy of those eight capitals, make the choice of their initial location particularly intriguing: though all the sites were determined before the surrounding countryside had been fully explored. The seeming infallibility of their founders' insight is part of the fascinating pattern of the Australian jigsaw.

At first there was just the single colony of New South Wales. Colonial expansion radiated from Sydney and until the 1820s was limited to Norfolk Island (1788), Coal River (Newcastle) (1801) and Van Diemen's Land (1804) all of them convict settlements. Bathurst and the crossing of the Great Dividing Range symbolised the first big push westward, in 1815.

Then, as though to expand horizons, meet new demands, satisfy curiosity and improve security, colonists gained new footholds in key positions on the remoter edges of the continent over the next twenty years.

- Van Diemen's Land became Tasmania in 1825 and the port town of Hobart its capital.
- Swan River, the first non-convict colony in Australia, was established in 1829 after the visit of the French explorer Dumont d'Urville to King George Sound three years earlier in 1826.
- Melbourne began as the barely legal creation of the Port Phillip Association. On its behalf John Batman 'purchased' 243 000 hectares of land from the Aborigines in 1835 and a city was born.
- South Australia, settled around the 1836 Torrens River town named for William IV's con-

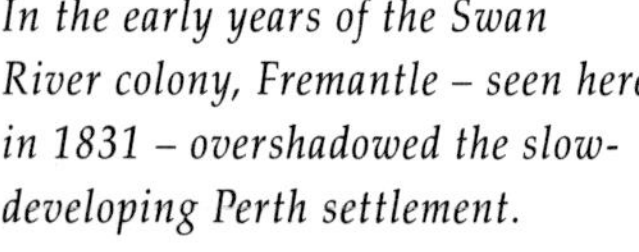

In the early years of the Swan River colony, Fremantle – seen here in 1831 – overshadowed the slow-developing Perth settlement.

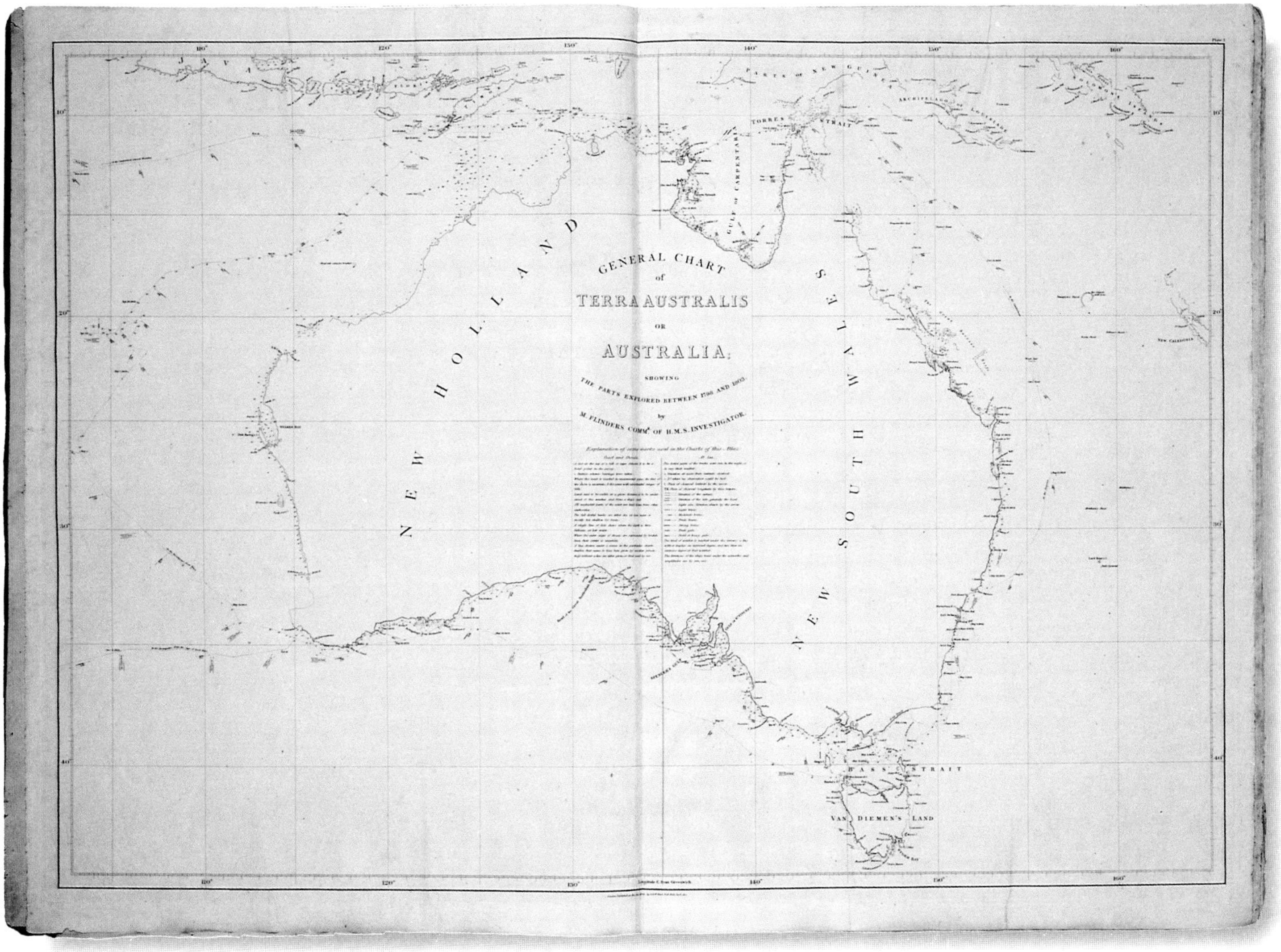

GENERAL CHART of TERRA AUSTRALIS OR AUSTRALIA: SHOWING THE PARTS EXPLORED BETWEEN 1798 AND 1803, by M. FLINDERS COMMR. OF H.M.S. INVESTIGATOR.

sort, was an experimental venture of agricultural adventurers. The greenbelt-encircled capital of Adelaide was sited just inland from its port.

- Moreton Bay was at first a hated place of convict punishment. Nearly all the convicts were withdrawn by 1839 and teams began surveying the land for free settlement. Its chief town was named after Governor Brisbane.

All of these settlements became separate colonies and the pattern of spread was clear. The site of Darwin – at first called Palmerston – was surveyed in 1869 and the town itself followed. It has been argued that its location, establishing a British presence on the northern coastline, was strategic, as Perth's had been.

Finally, in 1911, the site of Canberra, the 'bush capital', was settled on – ten years after the colonies had federated into a Commonwealth.

Movement inland from the perimeter

The same forces that drove the explorers who opened up the inland also motivated the developers. The wonder of an unknown hinterland, strategies of colonial expansion and personal possession, the discovery and exploitation of hinted natural resources, the mastering of long-distance communication and difficulties of drought and flood – these were the kinds of challenges savoured by those who now sought security or fame or fortune.

The earliest needs were crops and grazing land, to feed the struggling settlements. In the search for arable land beyond Parramatta, the Hawkesbury-Nepean River area was explored from 1789 and the splendid Hunter River and its fertile land was soon discovered. Camden, first viewed as early as 1795, was soon settled and named by John Macarthur after an English patron and there, on Macarthur's farm, the foundation stones of a great wool industry were laid. Across Bass Strait the plains of the Coal River estuary near Richmond, in Van Diemen's Land, were the 'granary of Australia' for a decade or so around the 1820s, before the western plains of New South Wales came into production.

The area now called New England was first explored by the Surveyor-General John Oxley in 1818 when he crossed the Warrumbungle Range and the Liverpool Plains. In 1827, the explorer

In 1804, a year after Matthew Flinders circumnavigated Australia, the chart above was published and the continent's true shape was shown for the first time. One-hundred-and-nine years later, in March 1913, Australia's fifth Governor-General, Lord Denman, officiated at the naming ceremony of the national capital (below).

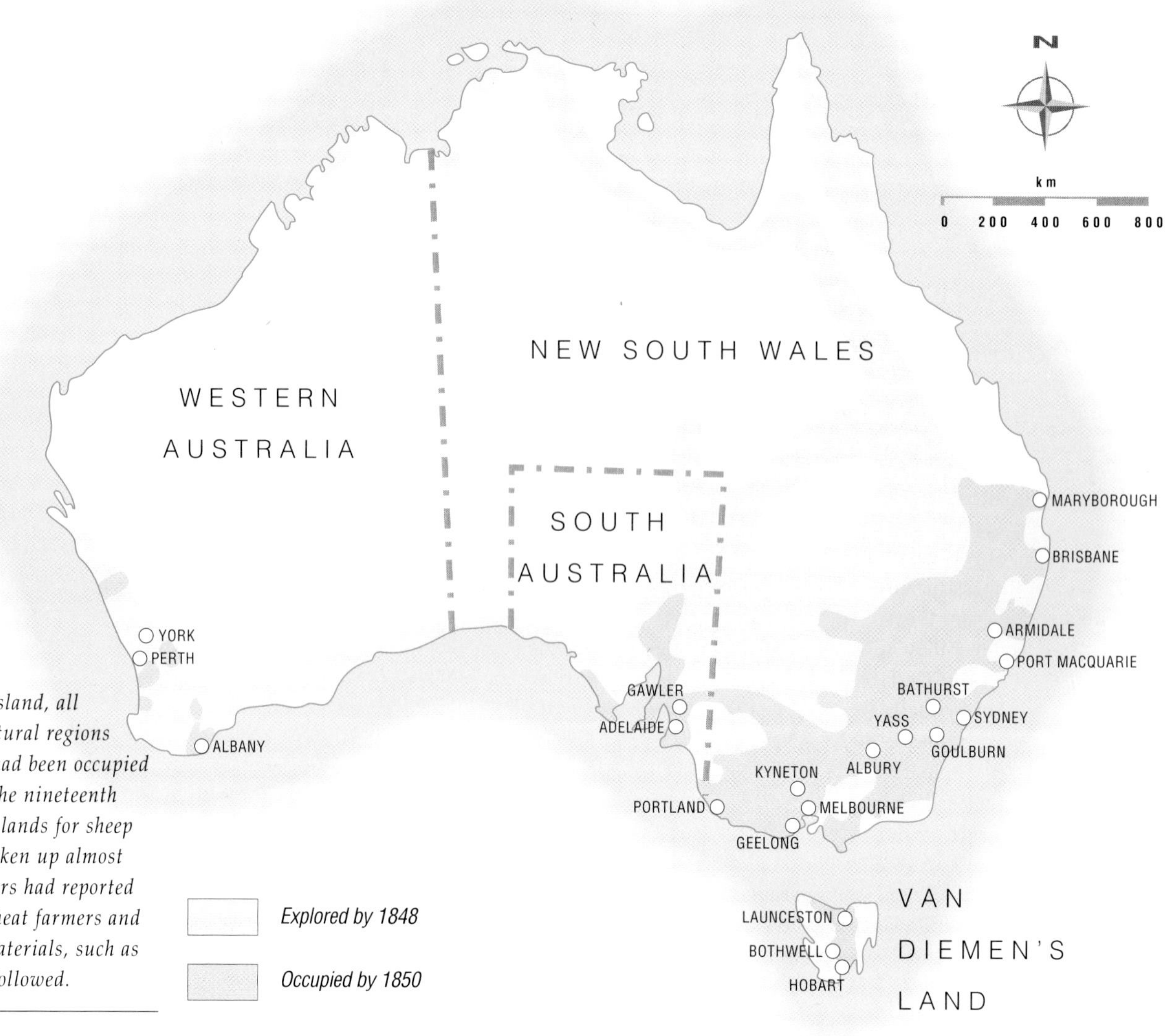

N

km

0 200 400 600 800

NEW SOUTH WALES

WESTERN AUSTRALIA

SOUTH AUSTRALIA

MARYBOROUGH

BRISBANE

ARMIDALE

PORT MACQUARIE

BATHURST

SYDNEY

YASS

GOULBURN

ALBURY

YORK

PERTH

ALBANY

GAWLER

ADELAIDE

KYNETON

PORTLAND

MELBOURNE

GEELONG

VAN DIEMEN'S LAND

LAUNCESTON

BOTHWELL

HOBART

Explored by 1848

Occupied by 1850

Except for Queensland, all the major agricultural regions of modern times had been occupied by the middle of the nineteenth century. Grazing lands for sheep and cattle were taken up almost as soon as explorers had reported their findings; wheat farmers and those after raw materials, such as timber and coal, followed.

By 1900, timber-getters had blazed trails deep into the hardwood forests of northern New South Wales (below) and Queensland.

he crossed from south to north through a district later to be occupied by towns such as Barraba. In what was to become Queensland, the real impetus for development was provided by the early explorers' push westward from New England to the fertile Darling Downs. Responding to glowing reports of its possibilities, squatters began swarming on to the downs in 1840.

On the Southern Tablelands, the intrepid John Oxley established a cattle station near Bargo. Charles Throsby, doctor and farmer, settled nearby at Bong Bong in 1819 and explored the area near what is now Canberra, and in 1823 the discovery of the Monaro Plains attracted squatting communities of wool producers, with Goulburn acting as a kind of frontier camp. The town's location soon made it a service centre for the whole of south-east Australia. The region that became the Riverina was explored by Charles Sturt during his Murrumbidgee expedition in

John Oxley's 1818 expedition into western New South Wales was a spur to pastoral development; the expedition's artist depicted the Warrumbungle Range (left), the last barrier to the Liverpool Plains.

1828. After Gundagai was gazetted in 1838, squatters migrated to that fertile area, most of them from the plains west of Sydney.

When the Hunter Valley was opened up in the 1820s, the settlers moved their produce of wheat and potatoes to Sydney by water. Then, in a cycle to be repeated in many parts of Australia, the crop-farmers were replaced by squatters, who in turn gave way to farmers again later in the century. Further north, when convicts were moved to Port Macquarie in 1823 they were made to cut cedar from forests on the Hastings River.

Private loggers soon followed, keen to supply timber for building in the Sydney area. The cedar-getters worked their way still further north: to the Macleay River by 1837, the Clarence by 1838 and the Richmond in the 1840s. Eventually, small ports developed for shipping the valuable hardwood logs to Sydney; some became important towns. Many which started as timber ports have now become major tourist centres, such as Byron Bay. Coffs Harbour was once Australia's largest timber port.

Extending the influence of Sydney further south-west, Hamilton Hume and William Hovell crossed the Murray at what is now Albury in 1824. The first sheep runs were taken up in 1834–35. Increasing movement from Sydney to Melbourne led to the formation of a village at the river crossing there and a punt was installed in the 1840s. When Victoria was separated from New South Wales in 1851, Albury was the obvious place to establish a customs post. Hamilton Hume also explored the Yass region and eventually settled there, at Cooma Cottage, beside the highway that now bears his name. In western New South Wales, the Darling River was explored by Charles Sturt in 1829 and its junction with the Murray was found. The new Surveyor-General, Thomas Mitchell, explored the Darling between Bourke and Menindee in 1835 and built Fort Bourke as a stockade against hostile Aborigines. Further south, the overlanders came, droving their cattle from New South Wales to South Australia. Wentworth became a settlement in the 1840s and was soon one of Australia's busiest river ports, handling wool from New South Wales for shipment to South Australia.

The northern thrust of pastoral exploration beyond Brisbane, into the central tablelands of Queensland, commenced in the early 1850s. Charles and William Archer, advised by the explorer Ludwig Leichhardt of the possibility of a large river flowing into Keppel Bay, reached and named the Fitzroy River near Rockhampton in May 1853. They had established 'Gracemere' station there by 1855 which still thrived as a working property in the twentieth century. By the early 1860s a great northern land rush had spread into the wide 'waste lands of the crown'.

The Aborigines resisted fiercely and frontier warfare went on for twenty years. Still further north, John Lort Stokes put the name 'Plains of Promise' on an otherwise empty map, but the climate and terrain of the Cape York peninsula meant that its potential was to go unrealised for many years. Explorers crossed and re-crossed Queensland's enormous west-central region in a series of expeditions from 1845, when Charles Sturt ventured into the colony's arid south-eastern corner. As elsewhere, the explorers were followed close behind by the squatters and stockmen, though settlement remained very sparse for many years.

Away over on the Indian Ocean side, many Swan River settlers soon became disenchanted with Perth. They moved east, and in Western Australia's first spread of settlement, the Avon Valley towns of York, Northam and Beverley were laid out. A Spanish Benedictine mission was founded at New Norcia in the 1840s, to work among the Aborigines.

Most major wheat-growing areas were established by the 1880s and flour mills like this one at Chiltern in Victoria were rural landmarks.

Audacious cattle-droving operations from the east and the south had turned large sections of the Northern Territory's semi-arid lands into a vast cattle run by the 1880s. Small, self-contained settlements centred on homesteads such as 'Spring Vale' (above).

John McDouall Stuart was the first European to explore the desperately dry, desert-bound centre of the continent, in 1860. The real attractions of the sparsely populated region did not start to be developed for more than a century.

Unlocking the riches

With the growth of intercolonial and international markets, the expansive potential of wheat, meat and wool was realised. Soon coal, gold and a host of other minerals were being won, requiring big capital, the development of extensive transport networks and manufacturing and, as well, the founding of more settlements for those actually working the resources.

For a while after the establishment of Adelaide, the good agricultural land in the south-east of South Australia became the main providore to the rest of the continent, giving prominence to Port Adelaide, from where grain was exported. Wheat was even ferried from small ports along Gulf St Vincent to the bigger port. Inland, small farms and bullock-waggon connections led to the growth of numerous small towns. In the Adelaide hills, some stone flour mills still survive, relics of the days when 'Adelaide' flour was known all round the continent.

In the Hunter Region of New South Wales, by contrast, it was dairying that first gave small-scale farmers a secure base, producing butter and cheese. Norco – the North Coast Company – was factory-producing butter from 1895. Cattle and sheep were taken north to the New England and north-west slopes area in the 1830s, from the Hunter area on to the tablelands. And as in so many other areas, the graziers profoundly disrupted the Aboriginal way of life, interfering with water and food supplies – they were dismissive of most aspects of Aboriginal culture. The culmination of unrest there was the Myall Creek massacre, near Bingara.

One hundred years after European settlement began Australia was riding well and truly 'on the sheep's back' and shearers, such as these men with hand shears photographed in central Queensland in the 1890s, figured fondly and often in popular legend.

But the real cattle country of Australia is further north. The cattlemen moved into the Rockhampton region in the 1860s, displacing the sheep flocks already there. Before long, the supremacy of wool and gold, the two commodities on which the region was founded, was overtaken by beef and coal. Lakes Creek meatworks, established in 1871 in Rockhampton, became the largest export works in the Southern Hemisphere.

Leases were taken up in about 1883 in the isolated Ord River and Upper Fitzroy basins, in the Kimberley of Western Australia. They were stocked with cattle from the Northern Territory by graziers such as the Duracks. The problem of great distances from markets and supplies was partly overcome by establishing meat processing works at Wyndham in 1919 and Broome in 1941, for transporting the refrigerated meat by sea.

The big cattle stations of the Northern Territory have endured for a century despite problems such as remoteness and the low carrying capacities of the land.

Sheep, like cattle, require large areas of pasture and so, as Australia developed, grazing land moved further away from the earlier towns, new centres often being set up to cater for the handling and processing of wool. Transport terminals such as seaports and river towns became important components in the settlement pattern.

The largest of the early pastoralists was the Australian Agricultural Company while individual sheep graziers became known as 'squatters'. Well into the 1840s the term was applied with considerable disrespect, for often the squatter fought, with dubious legality, to buy out and eliminate small landholders, thereby amassing large holdings for sheep runs. Only gradually did the term become the respectable equivalent of 'pastoralist'.

Squatters took up large pastoral holdings in the Western District of Victoria in the 1830s and 1840s. The land owned by the Henty brothers, who helped to settle the Port Phillip District, extended inland from Portland to the Casterton district. Townships followed: Geelong in 1837, Portland in 1840, Warrnambool in 1846. Darling River frontages below Bourke were taken up for sheep by about 1860, the river towns being part of the transport route to South Australian ports. Thargomindah, in the dry and isolated west-central region of Queensland, was a stopover for carriers taking wool to Bourke for transport down the Darling. In the 1890s, Charleville had 500 bullock teams passing through in each wool season to link the sprawling sheep stations with the rail terminus at Cunnamulla.

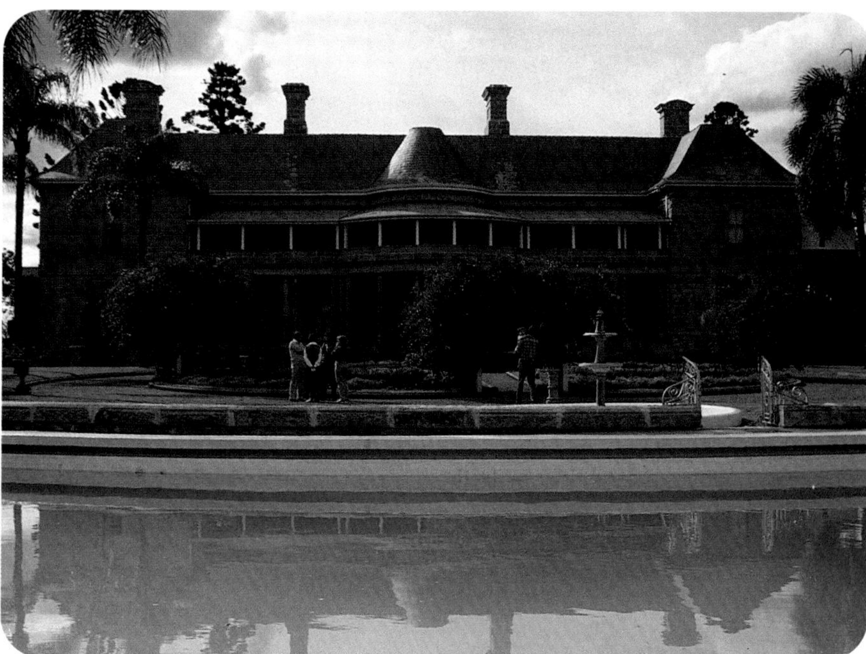

Grand homesteads on sheep stations the size of European principalities reflected the then seemingly boundless prosperity of the wool industry; Jimbour House in the Darling Downs originally had 120 000 hectares attached.

In 1830, the human population of the north of Tasmania, centred on Launceston, was less accurately known than the sheep population, which was calculated at 340 000. The squatters and their flocks were the basis of settlement in central Queensland in the early 1850s. When the north coast region of Queensland was thrown open for settlement in 1861, pastoralists following in Leichhardt's footsteps swiftly carved the interior into 'runs'. Settlements on the coast, initially established to service this pastoral hinterland, flourished even more with the discovery and exploitation of minerals.

Allan Cunningham's observations about the lush, open woodlands of the Darling Downs quickly attracted pastoral settlers. By 1860, there were thirty-three stations in the region from Dalby to Warwick and a hundred pastoral leases on the Western Downs. The squatters – known colloquially as the 'pure merinos' – established an elite landed gentry of considerable wealth and large estates. They dominated regional and state politics and sometimes tried to recreate a way of life modelled on that of the British aristocracy.

The woolshed at 'Jondaryan' (see *Dalby & Oakey*), with eighty-eight shearers' stands, typifies the kind of building needed for shearing the huge numbers of sheep. Toowoomba is one of the cities most importantly owing its present prominence to wool. Further south, Victorian squatters entered the Riverina area, already occupied by many New South Welshmen, in the 1850s. From there, wool transport for London markets was much cheaper by steam coaster to the port of

By 1848, thirty-five years after Launceston was laid out, Brisbane Street was at the centre of a spacious, thriving, commercial centre serving the farmers and graziers of Tasmania's northern hinterland.

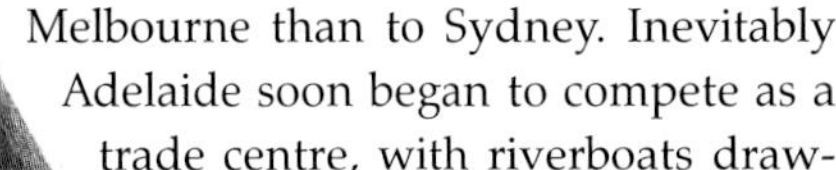

The rest is history...Edward Hargraves used this cradle – a device he brought from the California goldfields – to wash the gravel of an Ophir Creek in 1851 and make Australia's first major payable gold find.

Melbourne than to Sydney. Inevitably Adelaide soon began to compete as a trade centre, with riverboats drawing Riverina goods westwards along the Murray. The south-east of South Australia, in contrast with the plains and hills around Adelaide, was pastoral country. Many of the district's first settlers came from western Victoria which is part of the same geographical region.

The squatters acquired large freehold estates and built mansions upon them. They sometimes used the 'dummying' method – substituting stooges as land buyers – to subvert the intention of the South Australian legislation of the 1870s aimed at encouraging selection.

Coal and gold: the first mineral boom

Australia's settlements based on coal were quite different in character from those that resulted from wheat and wool. With the large number of workers required to operate mines and the industries that the fuel source attracted they often developed into substantial towns rather than regional service centres.

The coal seams underlying the Hunter Valley have made that region the major mining and electricity-generating field of New South Wales and an important area of manufacturing. Even when the penal station began in 1801, it was called Coal River. After a state of quiet following the moving of convicts, Newcastle began to prosper from coal in the 1840s. Ores have been smelted there since 1851.

From 1849, rich coal seams in the Illawarra district provided the base on which metal extraction and iron and steel fabrication industries could be established. Port Kembla became the dominant port, then an important steel centre.

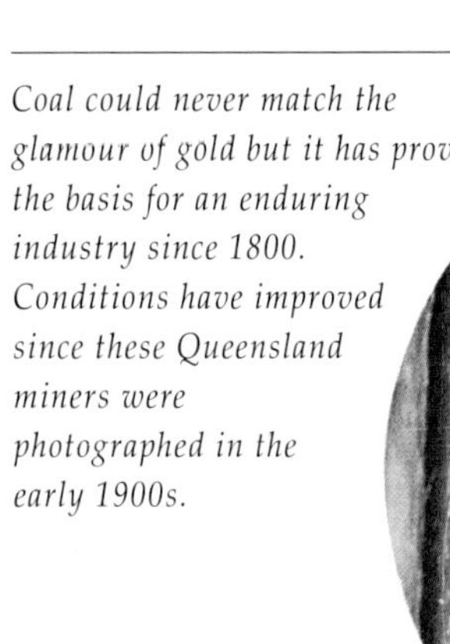

Coal could never match the glamour of gold but it has provided the basis for an enduring industry since 1800. Conditions have improved since these Queensland miners were photographed in the early 1900s.

Coal deposits were uncovered along the banks of the Brisbane and Bremer rivers about 1843. Ipswich was the centre of coal operations and large numbers of Welsh miners arrived. Coal winning there lasted until the 1960s. The 'good coal' found by Leichhardt in 1845 was the first indication of what became the immense Bowen Basin coal beds of central Queensland, exploited mainly since the 1960s when a massive export trade to Japan commenced. Coalmining began in Gippsland late in the nineteenth century, at Korrumburra, and black coal was mined at Wonthaggi from 1906 to 1968, the town being established by the government specifically to house miners. Open-cut mining of brown coal began in the La Trobe Valley in 1916 and continues today, the chief towns of the valley being Morwell, Moe and Yallourn.

Tasmania, on the other hand, has employed water for power generation longer than any other state. Hydro-electric power began there at Great Lake in 1916 and has become the major source of electricity. In Queensland, the Tully Falls hydro-electric scheme opened in 1935 and was enlarged in 1959 to supply Cairns and Townsville. The Snowy Mountains Hydro-electric Scheme was launched after the Second World War, for the generation of electricity and the expansion of irrigation. The dramatic scheme, which employed a large migrant workforce, harnessed the headwaters of one of Australia's largest river systems and, in the process, made new towns in the snowfields, thereby promoting a new industry, tourism. The nearby Kiewa hydro-electric sheme in the Victorian Alps, created the new town of Kiewa.

The discovery of gold was the most dramatic of all the stimuli to Australian development in the nineteenth century. The gold fever that resulted formed an unstoppable tidal wave of diggers and instant wealth, the crest of which, rising in Victoria and New South Wales in the 1850s and 60s, moved on up to Queensland in the 70s and 80s, and then across the continent to Western Australia in the 1890s. Gold seekers flooded into Australia from many parts of the world and the population quickly multiplied.

Scores of new towns sprang up and the swelling cities on the seaboard became bigger and wealthier. At almost the same time Queensland, South Australia and Victoria became self-governing colonies and the first railways and large industries began to appear. Society was transformed. The gold rushes made waves of

The large, centrally located work force required to exploit ore deposits provided a speedy stimulus to town development; less than 8 years after the spectacular 1883 Broken Hill find, a local hotel offered drinkers the comforts of electric fans and lighting.

technology too. First came superficial alluvial mining, which made the winning of gold look deceptively simple. Strikes in remote or isolated places, without back-up services, caused a resurgence of simple, pioneer-style building as miners put up their shanty villages. The ingenuity of local diggers was legendary. Gold towns such as Gulgong, Hill End, Clunes, Castlemaine, Maldon and Gympie housed rushes of immigrants from Britain, the United States and China.

There were eventually elaborate and more permanent mining systems in which the deeper seams were mined with heavy equipment driven by steam power, a method that needed great capital resources. These brought overseas money as well as immigrants and helped generate a financial and building boom. Bendigo and Bathurst typify the cities that grew out of these conditions, while Geelong, Williamstown, Port Fairy and Townsville owe their development as seaports to the wealth of gold.

The great social and financial upheaval began with the discovery of gold in 1851 at what became known as the Ophir goldfield, in New South Wales. Then followed the Turon rush, centred on Sofala. In the same year rushes occurred in Clunes, Buninyong, Ballarat, Castlemaine and Bendigo in Victoria. Lambing Flat (Young) and Lachlan (Forbes) followed in the 1860s, Gulgong and Hill End in the 1870s and Peak Hill in the 1880s. Prospectors came from around the world and for a time gold and the men seeking it dominated life and the economy as the thousands of diggers were provisioned, outfitted and entertained. Roads were built and the influx of new people encouraged a newer and, in time, less rigid social atmosphere.

Some areas settled by pastoralists were afterwards transformed by gold. Braidwood, established in 1824, blossomed into a major centre when gold was found there in 1851. The Araluen rush in the same year gave Moruya a brief taste of glory as a goldfields port. Rushes at Kiandra, 1859, Bermagui, 1880, and Pambula, 1890, stimu-

Few parts of Australia were unaffected by the waves of migration set off by the gold rushes. These men were among the thousands who set up camp near Gympie in the 1870s.

Gold fever was all pervasive in the 1870s and Chinese and European miners sometimes travelled from goldfield to goldfield by steamer. A busy below-decks scene was depicted by the Australian Sketcher *in 1880 (right).*

lated townships further south, but all faded rapidly. Gold quickly transformed the Central Highlands of Victoria from a pastoral area with about seventy squatters into a bustling, booming region with thousands of diggers.

Gold was responsible for the 'instant' town. Many of these places – Sofala, Stuart Town (Ironbark), Cornishtown, Coolgardie – died or dwindled. Some towns survived the decline of their goldfields and became commercial centres – Young and Parkes are examples. In Beechworth, which sprang up in 1852, gold mining remained a major industry until the 1920s. The large number of Chinese miners – there were about 3000 in 1857 – meant that Beechworth had the largest Chinese population outside Melbourne until the early twentieth century. Several hundred Chinese temples, built in various parts of Australia, owe their presence to the Chinese diggers and many of these temples survive as exotic mementoes of the gold rush.

The waves of gold discovery moved northwards to Queensland in 1867, when Gympie became a flourishing mining centre with a population of 25 000. Its peak production was in 1903.

Gympie was built on gold and in 1896, 30 years after the first discovery, it was a flourishing town with a suburban landscape punctuated by mine-shafts.

An iron-foundry at Maryborough serviced the Gympie field. Charters Towers field was discovered in 1872 and became one of Queensland's most productive, with a population of 26 000; when the gold ran out, the city all but died, but Townsville, its port, continued to flourish.

In the Rockhampton district, gold mining began in 1858 with a rush in the Canoona district. Rockhampton soon became a big river port and many other similar but smaller townships were established. By far the most important event was the Morgan brothers' exploitation of rich gold in the ironstone south-west of Rockhampton. They called it Mount Morgan and by the 1890s it was the richest single goldmine in the world. Its population peaked at 16 000 early in the twentieth century; soon afterwards gold was supplanted as the main commodity of the area by beef and coal. Many squatters made fortunes supplying the diggings with such things as stock, grain, meat and horses for transport.

No place was too remote and no discomfort too great to bar the seeker after gold. In 1869, Richard Daintree found payable gold in the headwaters of the Gilbert River in the far north of Queensland and for the next forty years an incredible blend of humanity captivated by the possibility of striking it rich moved from strike to strike. The biggest was the Palmer River in 1872. In fact, the real 'explorers' of the peninsula were the fossicker and the miner, bringing towns, roads and railways to the area. In Western Australia, strikes at Coolgardie in 1892 led to the establishment of Australia's greatest goldfield at nearby Kalgoorlie. As the surface gold ran out, the mining companies moved in to exploit the deeper reefs and towns grew around the wealthy mines. This brought about some amazing engineering feats not only in mining operations but also in such imaginative ventures as the pipe-line which brought water hundreds of kilometres from the coast, bestowing permanence on the settlements. The Perth–Fremantle region, as the outlet serving the western goldfields, prospered and underwent its own financial boom, at the very same time that the eastern cities, which had burgeoned during their own earlier rushes, now crashed financially.

By the standards of Victoria or Queensland, the Northern Territory gold rush of 1872–74 was a miserable affair which ended almost as soon as it began. Gold finds in the MacDonnell Ranges, however, attracted other, more permanent settlers: pastoralists. Stuart Town took shape in 1888 and became Alice Springs in 1933. The rush further north brought a permanent settlement, Pine Creek, whose district in the 1880s had a population of 30 000, with a Chinatown of 2000. Many of the Chinese miners were the forbears of those who have helped to give Darwin its modern cosmopolitan air. In Tasmania, though the 'rushes' were less spectacular than on the mainland, it was mining wealth which financed the rebuilding of Launceston in the late nineteenth and early twentieth centuries before the mines in the surrounding district began to fade.

The great ore discoveries

Copper ores were discovered in the red earth at Cobar in 1870, leading to mining leases and the establishment of the town in 1871. Earlier, copper had been discovered near Adelaide, at Kapunda, in 1842, at Burra in 1845 and Angaston in 1846. Ore deposits were limited and so the settlements in these places did not prosper; but Port Wakefield was laid out primarily to serve the Burra mine. After copper was found in the Eyre and Yorke peninsula regions the populations of Wallaroo, Moonta, and Kadina reached 30 000 by the turn of the century. There was a rush of Cornish miners and the trio of towns became known as Little Cornwall. Copper was also discovered near Geraldton in Western Australia, in 1852 and at Mount Lyell in Tasmania, in 1895.

1911: disembarking at Fremantle at the end of a long sea voyage and the start of a new life. In the four years before the First World War, more than 150 000 assisted-passage immigrants arrived in Australia.

Often, several different minerals were found in the one area. The silver-lead-zinc deposits around Broken Hill, found by Charles Rasp in 1883, were the richest then known in the world. They led to the establishment of Australia's largest company, BHP, in 1885. The transfer of BHP's lead-smelting operations to Port Pirie in 1898 led to a resurgence of that town; it is now South Australia's second city. Silver gave its name to Silverton, near Broken Hill, but its heyday was short-lived and it is now a ghost town.

The first mining boom in Tasmania began when James 'Philosopher' Smith discovered tin deposits at Waratah in 1872. His Mount Bischoff mine was described as 'a mountain of solid tin', the world's richest tin mine. It closed in 1935 but mining was revived in 1981. In the 1870s, tin mining around Emmaville in New South Wales, made it too one of the world's main tin sources; long after it declined, open-cut mining was revived in the 1960s.

Recent indications of new underground riches have been the vast copper, uranium and gold

The gold rush stimulated the growth of Queensland's string of coastal ports, and the ensuing success of the cattle industry – the butchery at left was photographed in Mackay in 1896 – confirmed the ports' key role in the quick sea route to market.

Rum was a popular drink in the colonies and distilleries sprang up soon after sugarcane cultivation began in Queensland; a popular brand of the spirit (right) has been produced at Beenleigh since 1884.

deposits discovered in South Australia on Roxby Downs Station in 1976, and the Elura copper, lead and zinc mine, in western New South Wales, which began production in 1983.

In the middle of the twentieth century, new settlements continued to develop in unlikely places as long-term projects opened up on huge deposits of iron ore – and bauxite. The desolate, sun-blistered Hamersley Range, ignored for generations, was estimated in the 1960s to contain enough iron to feed all the blast furnaces in the world for at least one hundred years. Japanese industrialists signed contracts that involved gigantic deliveries of high-grade ore for several generations. Mount Tom Price open-cut mine was complemented by the modern, purpose-built company towns of Newman, Dampier, Tom Price, and Shay Gap.

Rutile sands have been mined at the Gold Coast, Stradbroke Island and Moreton Island, in Queensland; but mining was prevented at Fraser Island on environmental grounds. Uranium, always a controversial resource, was discovered near Mount Isa at Mary Kathleen, in the Gulf Country, where it was worked until 1963. The mine reopened in 1976, finally closing again in 1982. The major new mining settlement of the Northern Territory is Jabiru, focal point for the uranium mines of the East Alligator River basin. Much further away, linked to the outside world only by sea and air, as though waiting in the wings for the curtain to rise on a new era of communication and development, are the bauxite mine and alumina refinery on the Gove Peninsula and the manganese mine on Groote Eylandt. Both of these are strands of a modern, technological enterprise in the heart of a vast body of Aboriginal land. Mount Isa, with its enormous resources of silver and lead, remains one of Australia's most important mining complexes; northern Australia's largest and most cosmopolitan inland city grew up to service the mine and its workers.

Weipa, on Cape York, now has one of the world's largest bauxite mines. Aluminium smelting started at George Town, Tasmania, in 1955.

Until the turn of the century, more than 50 000 South Sea Islanders – many of them kidnapped into virtual slavery by 'blackbirders' – provided the indentured labour that worked the Queensland sugar plantations. The indenture system was outlawed by the new Federal Parliament in 1901.

In modern times, there are still towns that grew up or were developed purposely to service industries. Elizabeth is a 'new town' outside Adelaide named for Queen Elizabeth. It was founded in 1954 for planned residential and industrial development following the establishment there of a major motor-vehicle plant. Kununurra in Western Australia was established in the early 1960s to house and cater for workers on the Ord River Dam project which was planned to encourage intensive development of the Kimberley region.

Permanent settlers: tilling the soil

Aside from the development of the great grain-growing belts, peculiar climatic qualities resulted in certain regions of Australia being developed specifically for particular crops. Sugarcane came to Queensland as early as the 1860s. The industry started at Ormiston, now part of Brisbane, and a short-lived cane cutting and boiling works was established in 1864. A plantation style of farm development, with indentured South Sea Island labourers, was adopted.

Beenleigh had a sugar mill in 1867 and within a few years there were thirty mills in the district, usually situated by a river. A steamer which went from mill to mill treating the residue of the cane harvest had a rum distillery on board. Sugar growing spread northward to the warmer climes around Maryborough and Bundaberg and soon Bundaberg rum became famous. Sugar cultivation in New South Wales was established on the Clarence, Richmond and Tweed rivers in the 1870s. In all of these areas, small pockets of building eventually grew into towns.

Mackay typifies the development of a town based on sugar production. Sugar was grown in the region from 1865 and employed island labourers from the 1860s until 1906. There were sixteen sugar mills in 1874 but with concentration of the industry, there were only four by 1984. An artificial deep-water harbour was created in 1939 when a large sugar terminal, the first in the Southern Hemisphere, was built. As with the gold rush, immigrants sometimes came to work these crops, forming the foundation stones of the multiculturalism of later years. Woolgoolga in northern New South Wales has a large Sikh community, descended from Punjabi migrants who worked on the Queensland canefields before moving south to grow bananas. The Sikh temple at Woolgoolga was the first in Australia.

Wine-growing was one of Australia's earliest agricultural activities, Governor Phillip having brought vines with him on the First Fleet. The first vines of the Hunter River Valley were planted in the 1820s at Branxton while the vineyards of the Barossa Valley were founded largely by German migrants in the 1840s and 1850s. Hahndorf ('Hahn's village') was settled in 1839 by German families and the village was named for the captain of the ship that brought them from Europe. Tanunda was another wine settlement, its first vines being grown in 1847. German Lutherans also moved out from the well-established farming communities in South Australia to investigate and settle new localities in the Wimmera and Mallee in Victoria – for example Dimboola – where they became small-scale farmers during the 1860s and 1870s.

The Neuchatel Vineyard was established at Geelong in 1842 by Swiss settlers, at the suggestion of Governor LaTrobe and wines were produced by 1845. Many Germans settled there in the 1850s and more vineyards were planted. At Rutherglen, in north-eastern Victoria, vines were planted with attendant wineries in 1851. The Victorian industry was all but wiped out by the

In the days before mechanised transport, a convoy of mill-bound rail waggons drawn by horses carries a load of sugarcane along a line built through the rainforest west of Mackay.

The miners who flocked to the infant Coolgardie in 1890 were carried by Cobb & Co.; by 1896 the gold they won was being transported to the coast by rail.

Phylloxera virus in the 1870s and took almost one hundred years to recover.

Griffith and Leeton, New South Wales towns established by government initiative early in the twentieth century as soldier-settlement centres on the canals of the Murrumbidgee Irrigation Areas, now symbolise not only ambitious and varied wine production, but also the settlement of a new wave of immigrants, particularly after the Second World War. As a result, the spread of settlement once again assumes a different pattern. In Western Australia, the Margaret River area near Perth typifies a modern wine-growing phenomenon. Strains of grapes and growing techniques have been developed so that wines can now be produced in many places hitherto thought to be unsuitable.

Pioneer attempts at cotton growing were temporarily successful in the 1860s when the American Civil War interrupted supplies to the British mills. There was a resurgence in the 1920s at Wee Waa, on the north-western slopes of New South Wales and in other places, such as Moree, after the Second World War. Wee Waa eventually blossomed into the centre of Australia's major cotton-growing district.

A crop of a different kind that stimulated settlement in the sparsely populated north of Western Australia were the pearl oysters found at Broome in the 1860s. The town founded by that industry was one of two in the Kimberley area of Western Australia to be declared ports as early as 1883. It became one of the world's leading pearling centres, at one time notorious for the 'blackbirding' of Aborigines to become divers. Pearling based on the port of Darwin attracted a mix of Malay, Indonesian, Filipino and Japanese divers, some of whom stayed on to settle after the industry collapsed, helping to further enrich the city's colourful racial mix.

Shortly after the First World War, a new 'clean' industry totally unlike any other and with effects that were less easy to discern began to make its presence felt. Tourism had arrived, and since the 1920s, has changed many settlements from places of erstwhile simplicity into busy holiday destinations. The Gold Coast, formerly a spread of coastal hamlets, has been transformed by a spontaneous and dynamic urban amalgamation into Queensland's second biggest city. Such holiday resort development has been repeated at Noosa–Maroochydore on the Sunshine Coast and the islands of Moreton Bay – Bribie and

In 1930, the potent symbol of the Sydney Harbour Bridge (opposite) symbolised distance conquered, as modern air, sea and rail transport brought Australia's cities closer together. Migrant numbers were overwhelmingly British in 1910 when this fine body of cloth-capped English workers (right) posed on the dock at Liverpool with a placard proudly announcing their intended destination and occupation.

Stradbroke. The once-remote 'Red Centre' is now an important tourist region based on Alice Springs and reaching to Uluru.

Linking it all together

The transport networks of roads, rivers, railroads and airways, connecting thousands of centres of settlement, marvellously illustrate the final coming together of the many different strands of the spread of settlement. They symbolise the gradual closing of the enormous distances that have always restricted development. The early explorers, travelling huge distances on foot and on horseback, are now admired for their often incredible drive and tenacity. But following their discoveries each wave of settlement enlarged even more the lucrative potential of expansion.

Australia's first 'high road' was the track from Sydney to Parramatta. Governor Macquarie made it the first toll road and from then on highways induced rapid expansion. Settlement in fact became so rapid, particularly in the gold rushes, that road construction could not keep up. After the advent of the railway, road construction concentrated upon getting people and goods to and from the rail centres. Where there were no railways, horse-drawn coach services offered speedy if sometimes less than comfortable transport – the most famous of the coaching companies was Cobb & Co. which ran a service from Sydney to Bathurst as early as 1862.

Stock droving formed the basis for many roads and towns. Dubbo, for instance, was an important stopping place on the long stock route south to Victoria. On the coast and in 'the mountains', the rise of fashionable resort towns made it possible for the better-off settlers from the Northern Hemisphere to escape the summer heat. Mount Macedon, Mount Wilson and Mount Lofty were the equivalents of the hill towns so popular with Britons in India. The Blue Mountains and Phillip Island were other early resorts promoted by road transport. These and many others like them became early tourist attractions.

With the coming of the automobile came better roads and the setting-up of main roads authorities. Then, during the Second World War, defence considerations accelerated road construction. The Stuart Highway from Alice Springs to Darwin was bitumenised in 1943 as one strategic route, while a substantial road was built from Tennant Creek into Queensland. After the war, roads such as these helped encourage mineral exploration and tourism in the arid interior.

With the advent of steam power, cargo vessels assumed a crucial importance and focussed attention on the long inland rivers. The Murray and Darling became busy arteries, carrying enormous loads of wool and other produce. Mannum in South Australia developed into an important river port after the first paddle steamer, *Mary*

A festive crowd was on hand to see the first sod turned for the construction of New South Wales' first railway line at Redfern in 1850. The engineer adopted the British gauge for the line instead of the Irish measure which had already been chosen in Adelaide and Melbourne and so began one of Australia's most disruptive transport inconsistencies.

Ann, commenced operations in 1853. It was at the end of the road from Adelaide and the riverboats transported wheat from eastern Mount Lofty Ranges upstream to Victoria and New South Wales. The port of Echuca, established in 1854, was Australia's largest river port in the 1880s. Its wharfage, still surviving, typifies the amazing variation in river heights in dry and wet seasons.

Mildura was another important Murray River port, but for slightly different reasons. Alfred Deakin invited George and William Chaffey to develop an irrigation system for the area. The first irrigation water was pumped in 1887, closer settlement began in 1888 and the first fruit for drying was harvested and the first wine made in 1891. The whole district became known as 'Sunraysia' after the First World War.

The first railway line to open was that run by a private company from Melbourne to Sandridge (Port Melbourne) in 1854. Lines to the eastern and northern suburbs of Melbourne began in the late 1850s, stimulating rapid metropolitan expansion. Sydney's first line, from Redfern to Granville – effectively Sydney–Parramatta – was operational by 1855. Sydney's suburban lines also began almost immediately afterwards and likewise promoted phenomenal residential growth. Because of the great difficulty of making railways show a profit in a sparsely populated country, the colonial governments soon took over nearly all the lines, realising that rail transport would speedily open up new farming regions. There was a dramatic expansion as railway systems snaked their way all over the map – from a mere forty kilometres of line in 1860 to more than twenty thousand kilometres by 1900.

With the completion of the rail zig-zags of Lapstone and Lithgow, in 1869, the mountain barrier to rail communication from Sydney to the west was overcome, just as the road barrier was earlier. The line reached Bathurst in 1876 and Dubbo in 1881. Thus began the decline of coach transport. Rail networks provided a dramatic solution to the problem of access by farmers to the lucrative markets of the capital cities and their overseas shipping wharves. The line to Bourke opened in 1885, to Brewarrina in 1901 and to Menindee in 1919, signalling the decline of the Darling River trade. The last riverboats travelled to Bourke in 1931.

Non-agricultural industries were now part of the railway scene as well. Large-scale movements of coal, iron and steel brought much greater importance to centres like Lithgow, Wollongong and Newcastle. Communication networks, first of roads and then of railways, nearly always extended along the routes taken by the early settlers. Thus the railway reached Tamworth in 1878, Armidale in 1883, and the link to Brisbane in 1888 – all of them along already well-travelled routes.

The railways settled the destiny of the Riverina – whether to be a satellite of Melbourne or Sydney – by anchoring most of the region to Sydney. The line from Melbourne reached Wodonga in 1873 and was extended to Albury in 1883 to meet the Sydney line, connected two years earlier. Yet, as had happened elsewhere across Australia, the tracks on each side of the border were of different widths and thus both passengers and goods had to change trains. Queensland, Western Australia and the Northern Territory had all adopted narrow-gauge systems which complicated cross-border linkages until relatively recent years. With the completion of the standard-gauge line from Sydney to Perth in 1969, Parkes, along with Port Augusta, became one of several important inland rail centres.

Because of the long distances between the main centres of population aviation has played an important part in Australia's modern history. Since the Second World War, air travel has boomed and there are now more than 1700 airports and airfields which help tie the strands of a far-flung population. Internal airways may not have directly established new settlements but they have helped significantly to confirm the bustling urban centres which resulted from the gradual but steady, 200-year spread of settlement across a vast continent. □

Despite the problems of vast distances and differing rail gauges, a sophisticated network of rail and port linkages – such as on the Brisbane wharves (left) – made Australia a major exporter of food and raw materials by the 1920s.

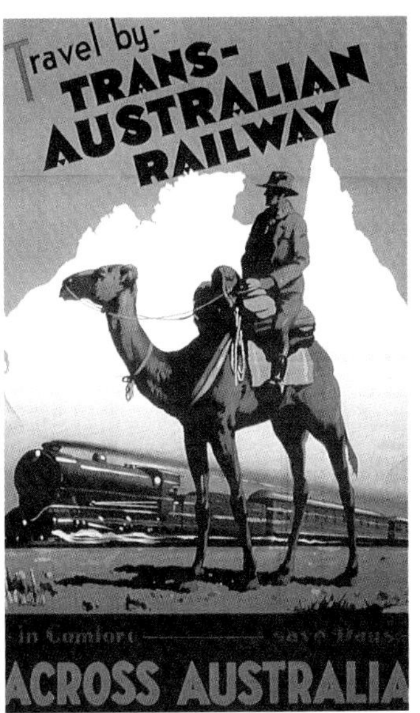

In the 1940s, well before the days of mass air travel, colourful railway promotional posters juxtaposed a romantic image of the outback with a streamlined depiction of modern rail transport.

NEW SOUTH WALES

New South Wales, where Australia's colonisers first stepped ashore, has the largest population of any state, claiming just over a third of the national total of 17 million. The majority of these inhabitants live along the coast, with more than eighty per cent concentrated in the vast metropolitan zone formed by the neighbouring cities of Sydney, Newcastle and Wollongong. The original colony absorbed half the continent as well as Tasmania, but the successive establishment of new colonies reduced the founding state to its present ten-per-cent share of the mainland.

SPECIAL FEATURES

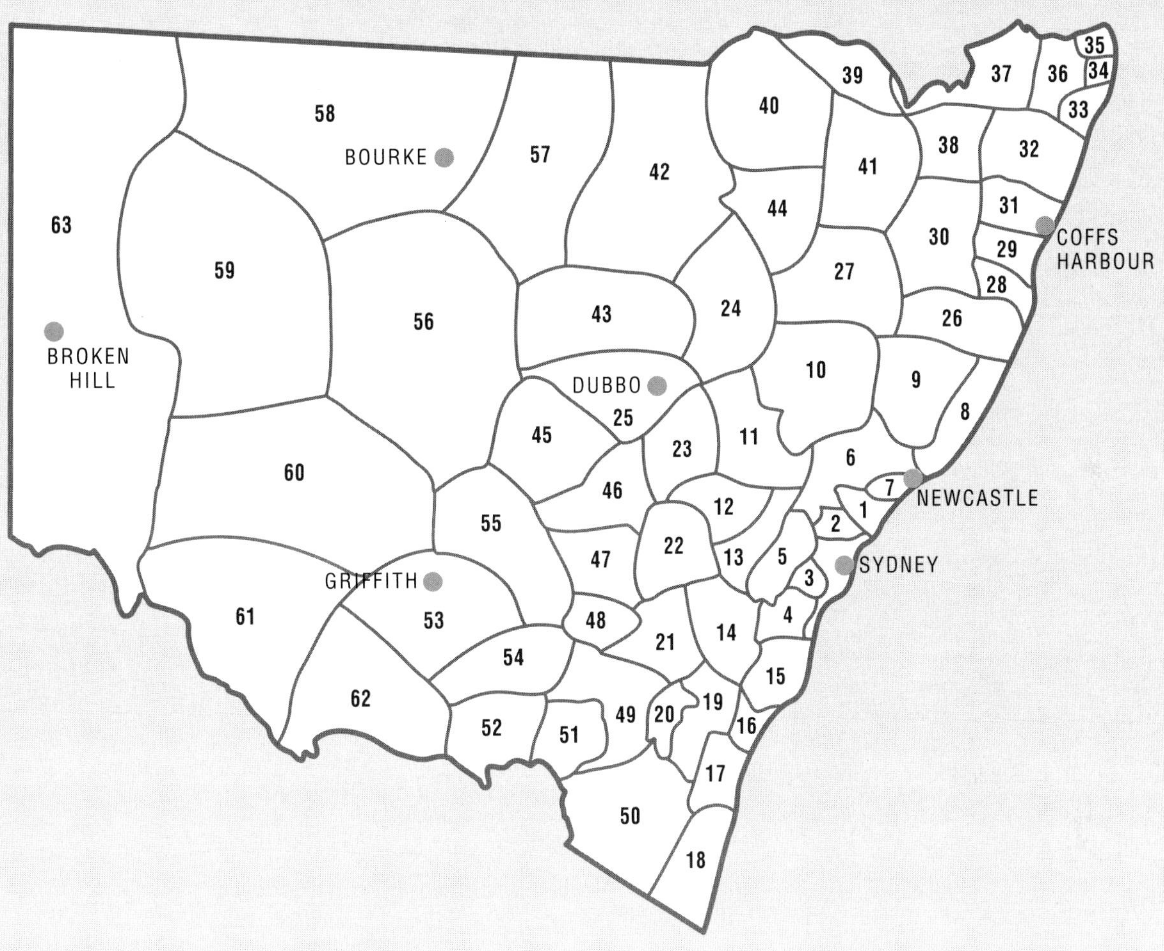

The waratah and the kookaburra are the plant and bird emblems of New South Wales. The British lion and the Australian kangaroo proudly surmount the coat of arms' motto: 'Newly risen, how bright thou shinest'.

SYDNEY

Despite 200 years of urban sprawl, the heart of Sydney – ever held in a jealous embrace by its huge metropolitan hinterland – still lies firmly locked in the sparkling network of intimate coves, inlets and bays that stretch between the 'Heads' and the Harbour Bridge.

Sydney, capital of New South Wales, the first seaport and city of Australia, entered its third century in 1988 to the accolade of 'international city'. With its aggressive, city-centre skyline and comfortable, front-stalls suburbs focused on the brilliant natural harbour of Port Jackson, together with the accompanying great leap of the Harbour Bridge and the dreamy white sculpture of the Opera House, Sydney's origins as an urban jail are not obvious.

The inner metropolitan area spreads over an undulating lowland but the city's eastern edge faces out to the Pacific Ocean with a bulwark of dramatic, yellow-orange sandstone cliffs and a string of dazzling beaches. To the north and south, the suburbs climb confidently onto heath-covered sandstone plateaux between deep, tree-filled gorges cut by streams.

Sydney sprawls west across the rolling Cumberland Plain and nibbles at the banks of the Nepean-Hawkesbury River and the steep escarpment of the mountains which give the city its cobalt blue backdrop. But the harbour has long held the dress-circle attraction. In the nineteenth century, the grandest homes in the eastern suburbs were sited to take advantage of the harbour. William Wentworth had established his gracious Vaucluse House as early as 1803, while Potts Point and Darling Point became the favoured locations for wealthy merchants' mansions in the 1830s. In *Emerald City,* playwright David Williamson makes the point that Sydney is still obsessed with its harbour view. The obsession is reflected in the prices of Sydney real estate. Houses and flats with 'harbour views' are sought after and homes with an 'absolute water frontage' change hands for millions of dollars.

Even in the 'back stalls' of the western suburbs, prices are high compared to similar areas in other cities. This contributes to Sydney's preoccupation with real estate and with money in general. It is not a new development, as Charles Darwin noted in 1836: '...everyone complained of the high rents and difficulty in procuring a house'. He added: '...the whole population, poor and rich, are bent on acquiring wealth.'

In Sydney, when all else fails there is always the beach. Egalitarian Bondi retains its peculiar charm.

The western side of the central Sydney, commercial district ridge runs down to the edge of the spectacularly redeveloped goodsyards at Darling Harbour.

Sydney's beaches have also powerfully influenced the city's people. There are almost forty ocean beaches strung along nearly sixty kilometres of coastline between Broken Bay and Port Hacking and more within the harbour. The suburban beaches gave birth to the surf-lifesaving movement with rituals and a tradition that are distinctively Australian. Facing the intense blue of the Pacific and cradled between bold, sandstone bluffs the beaches are a strong attraction to the city's millions and have helped to spawn an urban culture marked by hedonism, a relaxed morality, the honouring of sporting achievement and the sanctity of the weekend.

It is remarkable, considering Sydney's outstanding site, how little planning went into its selection. Coming halfway round the world only to reject the dimly known Botany Bay, Captain Phillip moved the First Fleet north to Port Jackson, a place that was not known at all, except for the name given to it by Captain Cook. Anxious to disembark his human cargo after the long voyage, Phillip sailed into Port Jackson on 26 January 1788, found a good stream of water at Sydney Cove – a small bay on the south shore fringed with sand, swamp mahoganies, swamp oaks and tea-tree – and decided this was the spot.

Phillip made a plan for a future city. Spacious in conception, it provided for streets sixty metres wide with a main street running straight in a south-westerly direction; but the next governor, Hunter, put a church in the middle of the plotted route. In the meantime, a bullock track straggled along the ridge west of the cove to become George Street, Sydney's main thoroughfare. Other narrow, winding tracks grew into streets and Phillip's plan was consigned to history.

Sydney's urban design owes more to a later governor, Lachlan Macquarie, who viewed the settlement at the time of his arrival as 'emerging out of infantile imbecility'. At the end of his term Sydney comprised over a thousand buildings including many in stone and brick. Among the best were those designed by his prolific convict architect Francis Greenway. Fine examples of the work of Greenway still to be seen include St James' Church and Hyde Park Barracks at Victoria Square, the Government House Stable – now the Conservatorium of Music – and at South Head, the Macquarie Lighthouse. Parts of the old 'Rum Hospital', built in Macquarie's time, now survive as Parliament House and the Old Mint Museum in Macquarie Street.

For most of its first thirty years, Sydney was a lesser town than its western appendage, Parramatta, the inland agricultural centre where Old Government House, the nation's oldest public building, still stands. The towns were joined by the Parramatta Road. Travellers on the road risked attack from Aborigines up to 1820 and by bushrangers as late as 1840. By the 1960s, the attacks were more of an aesthetic nature, with the way west consisting of many kilometres of garish advertising and strings of car saleyards.

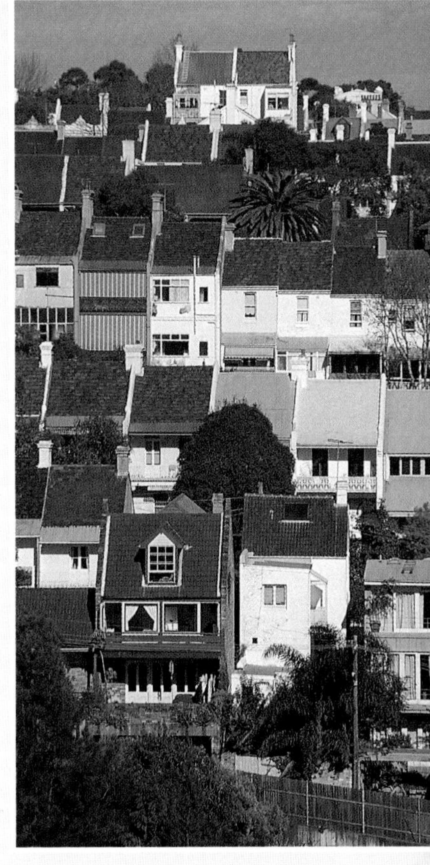

The stacked Victorian terraces of Paddington inspired a continuing inner-city restoration boom.

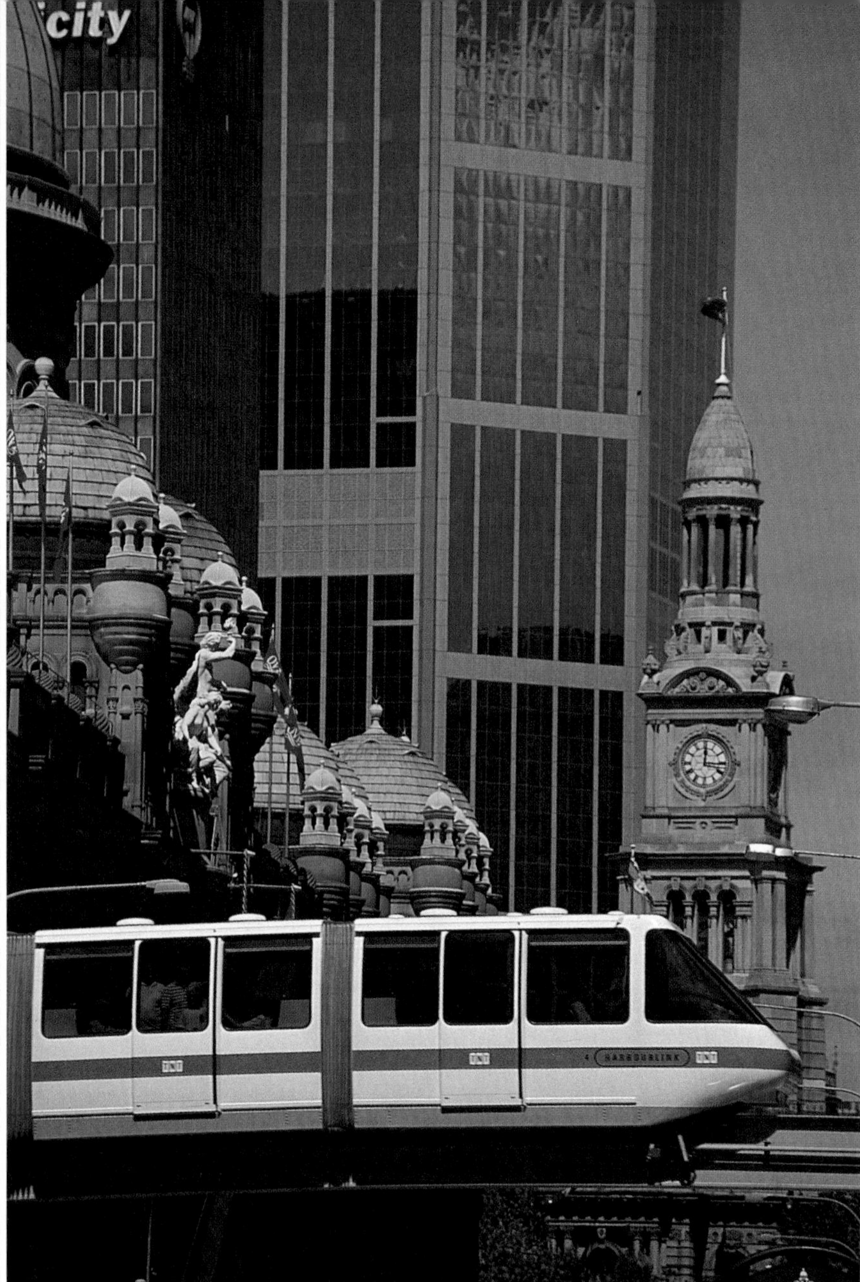

The old and the new jostle – often uncomfortably – for prominence in Sydney. The juxtaposition of the sleekly futuristic monorail and a glass skyscraper with the elaborate Victoriana of the Town Hall and the Queen Victoria Building makes for a scene typical of the city's rich architectural cocktail mix.

Sydney's population of more than 3.6 million is not large in a world of mega-cities, but the city sprawls over an area as great as London which has twice the population; it has twice the area of Beijing with its ten million people, and about five times the area of Rome. Until the end of the 1960s the city was strongly centralised. The railway and tramway systems converged on the central business district between Circular Quay and Central Station, feeding workers and shoppers to its office buildings and large department stores. The motor car and the building of freeways has complicated the pattern and encouraged the growth of huge suburban commercial centres.

The city centre is now less important as a shopping district but continues as the commercial heart. Its natural meeting with the harbour at Circular Quay is baulked by the irritating bulk of the two-deck Cahill Expressway and railway, built in the 1950s, while the western side falls away steeply to container wharves, 'recycled' roofed piers and the rejuvenated dockland of Darling Harbour. The Royal Botanic Gardens and the green spaces of the Domain and Hyde Park contain the city centre on the east, while the sandstone bulk of Central Station guards the southern approaches. Filling this six square kilometres is a brash, 'Manhattan' complex of tall, concrete and glass office blocks soaring up from cramped and often awkwardly shaped sites.

A closer look at the city, especially above the footpath awnings, reveals the sandstone, brick and moulded cement facades of those Victorian and Edwardian buildings which have so far escaped the demolisher's hammer. Wonderful examples of the city's Victorian heritage remain, including the Sydney Town Hall, St Andrew's Cathedral, the General Post Office in Martin Place, the Lands Department building in Bridge Street, St Mary's Cathedral and the very fine Queen Victoria Building which has been given renewed life as an elegant shopping arcade. Built in the honey-coloured local sandstone and displaying sculpture, great copper domes, stained glass, spires and elaborate decoration, these buildings give character and contrast to the glass-walled canyons of the city centre.

The commercial centre continues south through the cinema strip, and becomes somewhat seedier, but in the Haymarket area the contrasting form and colour of Sydney's large and bustling Chinatown with its countless restaurants and small shops provides an exotic retail boost. Beyond Railway Square the glamorously named Broadway runs up to Parramatta Road and the inner fringe of the vast stretch of the western suburbs. Here stands the tower of the University of Technology and the Victorian Gothic architecture of the University of Sydney.

The Rocks on the western side of Sydney Cove, now Sydney's main tourist district, was

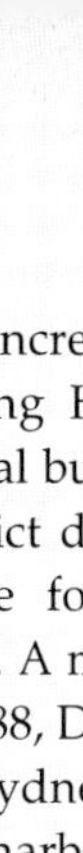

The restored maritime buildings of The Rocks are the hub of a tourist zone equally popular with locals.

where the early convicts were driven to seek shelter. It grew into a seamy, waterfront neighbourhood full of pubs, lodging houses, brothels and warehouses, making Sydney one of the toughest ports in the world. This lawless place was as far as possible ignored by the authorities until an outbreak of bubonic plague in the early 1900s compelled them to step in. The Rocks continued life mainly as a depressed residential area. In the early 1970s, a controversy erupted over government plans to demolish most of its historic terrace houses and commercial buildings to make way for a wall of skyscrapers.

Saving The Rocks became a *cause célèbre* and helped to draw world attention to Sydney's 'green bans', the union-led movement in which workers withheld their labour on social and environmental grounds. Saved from the developers, The Rocks enjoys a new life as an expression of the city's past history and present cultural life. Here, the Argyle Bond Store, with its cobblestoned courtyard, old brick walls and massive hardwood beams, has become an elegant display case for Australian-made products.

Port Jackson was quickly appreciated by early mariners for its space, its natural protection from weather and its deep, near-shore anchorages. As a working port, it gave the city its start in life and its prosperity but it is gradually letting go of its old occupation to become a tourist attraction. The white sails of racing yachts, the weekend ferry trip to Manly – 'seven miles from Sydney and a thousand miles from care' – or the shorter crossings to the diversions of Taronga Zoo Park and to Luna Park have long been synonymous with Sydney Harbour's role as a playground.

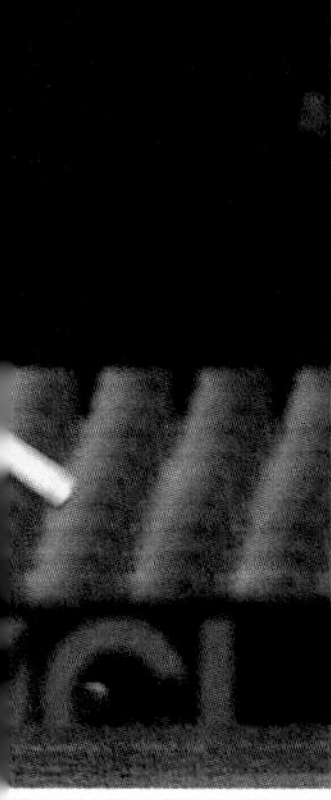

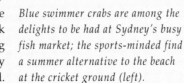

Blue swimmer crabs are among the delights to be had at Sydney's busy fish market; the sports-minded find a summer alternative to the beach at the cricket ground (left).

The increasing importance of this role has seen Darling Harbour on the western fringe of the central business district transformed from a near-derelict dockyard and rail goods terminal into a centre for exhibitions, conventions and recreation. A major tourist attraction since its opening in 1988, Darling Harbour's fifty-five hectares hold the Sydney Aquarium, the Chinese Gardens and the harbourside Festival Marketplace. Darling Harbour is linked to the city centre by the old Pyrmont Bridge and a futuristic monorail loop which runs along several city streets on a rail raised above traffic and pedestrians on steel pillars.

The Opera House is popularly viewed as the major physical manifestation of culture in Sydney but the city's cultural life is really much more dispersed. The Seymour Centre near Sydney University and the Wharf Theatre, an ingeniously converted timber wharf on the harbour west of the bridge, both offer drama as do some twenty other live theatre venues. The Art Gallery of New South Wales on the eastern side of the Domain and the Museum of Contemporary Art at Circular Quay display art from all cultures and there are many private galleries particularly in the restored historical precincts of Paddington and The Rocks. The Australian Museum, opposite Hyde Park, exhibits a natural science and environmental collection and the Powerhouse Museum in Ultimo – inside a cavernous old electricity-generating building – displays Australian social history and technology.

Cruise ships such as the QEII uphold Sydney Cove's nostalgic role as the embarkation point for 'overseas'.

Sydney's most spectacular and controversial building, the Opera House, now challenges the Harbour Bridge as the city's icon. The two structures are the grand, popular portals of an urban area that now extends along road and rail corridors almost as far as it can go into the south, west and north-west. This expansion has sparked much vigorous questioning about the city's future and has brought calls for more 'urban consolidation' with housing of medium density which migelp conserve surviving strips of green belt.

Gosford & Woy Woy

Despite the often inaccessible nature of its hinterland, the region of lakes and golden beaches between Sydney and Newcastle – in modern times a playground for both cities – was one of the earliest regions to attract exploration by Australia's first white settlers.

AVOCA BEACH ■ 1
The southern, or Erina Peninsula section of the Central Coast is largely centred around Avoca and its attendant settlements. The small resort sits comfortably between its lake and its beach of the same name with North Avoca just a short walk away across the lake's sandbar – like most of the coastal resorts of this region it has a relaxed, unpretentious air. Despite the gradual displacement of rural pursuits by new manufacturing industry and the pressures of a growing population, the Central Coast remains one of Sydney's and Newcastle's main holiday and retirement destinations, where ordinary people can still afford a two-week annual breather in a camping and caravan park or a holiday flat.

The first white man to settle here was an Irish army officer called John Moore. He sailed up the coast from Sydney to take up 280 hectares of land in 1830 and soon had a garden of date palms and wine grapes growing around his house. Moore called his property 'Avoca' after the Avoca River in his native County Wicklow. *Population 2920*

BATEAU BAY ■ 2
The long-established, lakeside holiday resorts of The Entrance, Long Jetty and Bateau Bay have slowly merged together so that instead of three settlements that came to life in the summer there is now one large town stretching along the broad spit that forms the south-eastern edge of Tuggerah Lake.

Today's Bateau Bay used to be Boat Harbour; its tight semi-circle of beach loosely enclosed by reefs and Crackneck and Yumbool Points on the landward sides provided a relatively safe landing place for long boats in the days when the fastest way to get here from Sydney was by ship. *Population 7310*

BOUDDI NATIONAL PARK ■ 3
Bouddi (pronounced Boody) is the smallest of the four national parks which form an insulating, olive-green crescent of bushland around the south-eastern perimeter of the Central Coast. Like most coastal parks of the Sydney region, it has a wooded hinterland, with occasional pockets of rainforest, and a dramatically contrasting oceanside fringe of windswept heathland.

Campers and bushwalkers have a choice of surf and protected beaches between the broad rock platforms and imposing bluffs, along the spectacular coastline, all of which can be viewed from lookouts. Bouddi National Park's special feature is its marine extension which protects a 280-hectare section of the water beyond the park's coastline and provides a fishing-free domain for snorkellers and skin-divers.

BRISBANE WATER NATIONAL PARK ■ 4
At first glance Brisbane Water looks like the first in the series of shallow lakes that dot this coastal fringe almost all the way to Port Macquarie. In fact, it is a large inlet hemmed in on all sides by rugged hills with an 'S-bend' entrance to the sea so narrow that on small-scale maps it is hardly distinguishable.

The waterway and the 14 000-hectare national park which shares its name have distinguished vice-regal connections: the first European to enter the inlet was Governor Phillip, in 1788, and in 1825 it was named after the Governor of the time, Sir Thomas Brisbane. Given the region's future as a weekend playground for Sydneyites it is ironic that Governor Phillip's visit was a fairly dismal occasion. Desperate for farmland to help feed the struggling colony at Sydney Cove, he led a party in a whaleboat up the coast to Broken Bay in the early autumn of 1788 (see *Richmond & Windsor*). More than 200 years later, Brisbane Water is a magnet for water sports enthusiasts due to being well sheltered from the open sea; fishing is almost compulsory here as the rocky or muddy, mangrove-lined shore, which keeps most swimmers at bay, provides a perfect marine breeding ground.

A large part of the inlet's western side remains unchanged, preserved in the national park. The sandstone plateau of the park is sliced in three by the creeks which have worn their way through to the wider waters of the Hawkesbury River, leaving in their wake gullies filled with rainforest, and above, eucalyptus woodland and heathland.

BUDGEWOI ■ 5
Surrounded on three sides by water, Budgewoi township has inevitably grown beyond the narrow isthmus on which it sprang up and has spread in the only direction possible – westward. To the north and south are the lakes, Munmorah and Budgewoi, and to the east, a few score metres across another isthmus, the Pacific Ocean.

When John Slade came to this then very isolated region in 1828 it was inhabited by the Awabakal Aborigines and he used their word for 'young grass' or 'decayed weed' – *pudgeway* – as the name for his cattle farm. Within a couple of years postal officials had turned Pudgeway into 'Podgewoy' and when another settler bought Slade's farm it became 'Budgeaway'. By the 1860s 'Budgewoi' was the variation most commonly used. *Population 1450*

COPACABANA ■ 6
Like Avoca Beach and Terrigal to the north, Copacabana and its neighbour MacMasters Beach have grown together to become to all intents and purposes one settlement with a common beach and divided by a lagoon

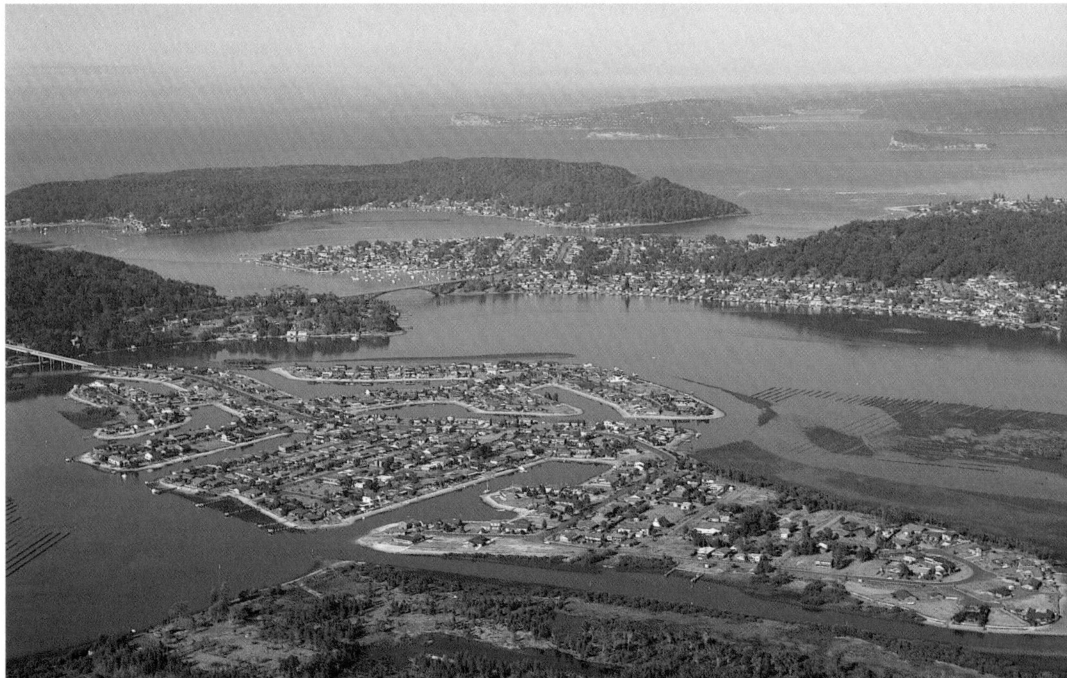

The southern settlements of the Central Coast cluster eagerly around the inlets of the lake-like Brisbane Water.

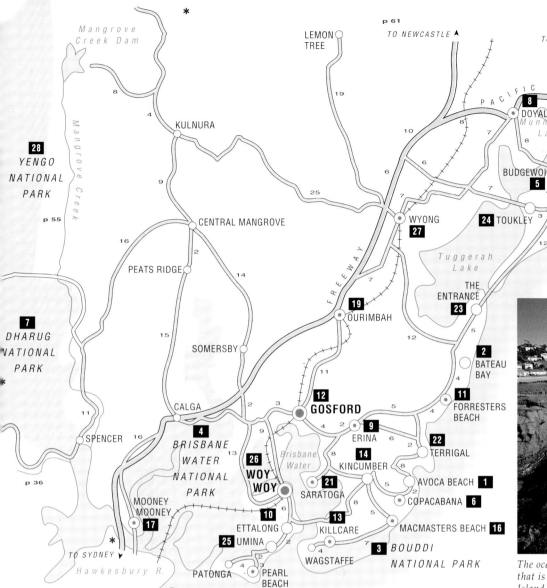

The ocean front at Avoca presents a scene that is repeated – complete with Norfolk Island pines and a peaceful lagoon behind the coastal ridge – all along this coast.

outlet which occasionally slices the strand in half. You can walk from one to the other across the beach but by car you face a ten-kilometre journey.

Despite its exotic, Latin American name this expanding residential zone with an enviable location on the headland above MacMasters Beach, bears little resemblance to its namesake in Rio de Janeiro apart from its proximity to the sea. The Copacabana headland is the most easterly between Sydney and Norah Head and the spectacular views up and down the coast make any explanation for the popularity of the Central Coast quite unnecessary. *Population 2180*

DHARUG NATIONAL PARK ■ 7

Dharug is the westward extension of the chain of parks which reserves so much of the bushland along the Hawkesbury River's tidal zone. Bushwalkers and picnickers who follow the old Great North Road – built by convicts and once the main road north out of Sydney – which delineates the park's eastern perimeter will find several entrances which will lead them into a 14 000-hectare untouched wilderness of steep ridges and deep gullies where the thick, warm temperate rainforest contrasts with the grassy swampland along the river and the open, eucalyptus woodland above.

DOYALSON ■ 8

As a road junction settlement, Doyalson has always been important to travellers; today motorists still pause for petrol and refreshments before heading off in one of three possible directions. North is the old Pacific Highway and a leisurely route – between coastal and lake waters – to Newcastle or the wine country of the Hunter Valley, west is the link to the Sydney–Newcastle Freeway and the speedy route to both metropolitan centres, and east is the holidaymaker's road to relaxation and Budgewoi Lake. *Population 1020*

ERINA ■ 9

Improved roads and the ubiquitous motor car have turned most centres between Broken Bay and Tuggerah Lake into satellite suburbs of Gosford but Erina, set midway between the coast's many attractions and Brisbane Water, still remains a semi-rural, residential area where most commercial development has been restricted to the main road.

The region is largely open country today, a result of early Sydney's need for firewood and building timbers. The timber-getters moved into what was known – appropriately – as Woodport in the 1830s; they loaded their vessels at Erina Creek and set off for Sydney Harbour on the outgoing tide. All around Brisbane Water there was similar activity for the next sixty years wherever a boat or a ship could get close enough to shore for loading to take place. A poem by George Fletcher, a shire health inspector in the early days, recalls the day when '…We counted up a hundred ketches as they laid in Melville's Bay…'. Melvilles Bay was the old name for a small cove east of Gosford. *Population 2330*

ETTALONG ■ 10

The famous French actress Sarah Bernhardt paid a social visit to Ettalong during her visit to Australia in 1891; her comments, if any, went unrecorded but she was a distinguished trailblazer for the many thousands of Sydney workers who have made an annual pilgrimage to enjoy a few weeks' swimming and fishing at this relaxed resort.

Ettalong stands guard at the ocean entrance of the channel leading into Brisbane Water and long before Miss Bernhardt's visit this place was being visited by the crews of the timber boats (see Erina) who came ashore for freshwater while waiting for the tide to carry them over Half Tide Rocks. They called the location Doherty's Hole after the depression from which they took their water but 'Ettalong', after an Aboriginal word meaning 'place for drinking', became the official appellation thanks to the Surveyor-General, Thomas Mitchell, who had a policy of using Aboriginal names over those of European origin. *Population 3770*

FORRESTERS BEACH ■ 11
Today's Forresters Beach area bears little resemblance to the twenty-two hectares of timbered land purchased by Robert Forrester in 1861 as a home for himself and his new bride...but there are remnants of vegetation to give some idea of what this region looked like 130 years ago. The northern half of the beach is still backed by scrubby sandhills, hiding the residential development behind them, while a few kilometres inland, ten hectares of rainforest valley has been preserved in 'The Ferneries' and are inhabited by kangaroos, emus and wild birds as well as peacocks. *Population 1830*

GOSFORD ■ 12
The commercial and residential centre of the Central Coast, Gosford sits in a commanding position at the head of Brisbane Water, began its life as two settlements – one government and one private, and for twenty years private enterprise led the way. Settlers followed timber-getters into the region in the 1820s and in 1822 an enterprising tea merchant called Samuel Peek began selling allotments as part of a private township at today's East Gosford. The administration of Governor Gipps did not catch up until 1839 when a site north of Peek's land was surveyed and dubbed 'Gosford' by the Governor, without explanation.

It was not until the 1850s that the two towns began to merge; Peek's development lost its prominence and it was many years after that before historians came up with an explanation for the Governor's choice of name. Gipps had served in Canada with the Earl of Gosford for two years before coming to New South Wales and it seems he was honouring his old colleague.

The hardwood trees dragged out of the hills provided excellent ships timbers and with a sheltered waterway to work in, shipbuilders soon established a secondary industry in the Brisbane Water region which continued well into the twentieth century. In the 1880s, many large landholdings were subdivided into smaller farms and orchards of citrus trees proliferated on the land cleared by the timber industry.

The Gosford region remained a relatively isolated outpost where growth was slow...until a railway bridge was thrown across the Hawkesbury River in 1889. Not only did the agricultural and timber industries suddenly flourish but the forerunners of today's tourists began to frequent the region. The door to Gosford and its sister settlements to the east was finally flung wide open after the Second World War when a road bridge complemented the railway bridge and put the Hawkesbury River punt out of business.

Since then electrification of the railway line and a modern freeway which lacks the time-consuming kinks of the old Pacific Highway have made Gosford a dormitory suburb of Sydney; more than 8000 of its residents commute to the state capital every day. *Population 128 960*

Pearl of the coast: the bush and the beach combine to make Pearl Beach the stuff of urban dwellers' dreams.

KILLCARE ■ 13
Killcare is one of the strategically placed residential regions which sit at the narrow end of the Erina Peninsula with views to the ocean on one side and the entrance to Brisbane Water on the other. In welcome contrast to the beaches to the north, the ocean beaches here are backed by the natural bushland of the Bouddi National Park (see entry).

'Killcare' was the name given to the estate which offered land for sale here in 1916. The unofficial name, typical of the comical 'Dunromin' or 'Restawhile' type of nomenclature popular at the time, fell into common use but was not officially gazetted by the Geographical Names Board until 1972. *Population 1730*

KINCUMBER ■ 14
Kincumber sits at the head of an almost completely enclosed, and thus very sheltered, inlet near the entrance to Brisbane Water. It was the sheltered waters which encouraged settlement here in the 1830s making Kincumber the oldest permanent village on Brisbane Water; it eventually became a centre for shipbuilding, with at least four yards working in the 1860s.

The name has been used since the 1820s, first as King Coimba Creek and becoming Kingcumba before finally settling at the present spelling. *Population 6200*

LAKE MUNMORAH ■ 15
Lake Munmorah is the smallest of the four Central Coast lakes between Sydney and Newcastle (For Lake Macquarie, the largest, see *Lake Macquarie*) and it and the town of the same name on its northern shores are named after an Aboriginal word meaning 'stones for grinding seeds'. The town is probably best known for one of the region's major employers, the giant Lake Munmorah power station which dominates the landscape on a man-made canal between the lake and Budgewoi Lake. *Population 2230*

MACMASTERS BEACH ■ 16
Like many beaches along this coast, MacMasters is backed by a lagoon which periodically – after heavy rain – bursts through the sand barrier to the ocean. MacMasters Beach and Copacabana (see entry) would be one if it were not for the intermittent channel between them.

The name commemorates the Scottish MacMaster family all twelve of whom settled on 270 hectares of land here in 1838. *Population 680*

MOONEY MOONEY ■ 17
Even though the deep, broad waters of the lower Hawkesbury were spanned by a railway bridge in 1889, it was not until 1945 that motorists taking the coast road north out of Sydney were able to do so without having to rely on a punt to ferry them from one bank to the other. Before the road bridge was built, Mooney Mooney, was the unloading point for the service's two punts, which became the bane of weekend motorists who sometimes had to wait four hours as the punts ploughed slowly back and forth. *Population 510*

NORAVILLE ■ 18
Observations of Aboriginal life by early settlers and their difficulty in finding accurate phonetic renderings of Aboriginal words have given Noraville, Norah Head, and the nearby Lake Munmorah names which are the same, but different! All were named after an Aboriginal grinding or sharpening stone called a 'morah' or a 'norah' depending on the ear of the colonial listener; to the north 'morah' was the preferred version, while Noraville was named after the latter word.

Unlike its neighbours Budgewoi and Toukley, Noraville is an ocean rather than a lake town. Beneath the gaze of the lighthouse and in the protected lee of the headland, there are numerous rocky coves and small beaches which gradually lengthen into the broad curve of Lakes Beach. *Population 1350*

OURIMBAH ■ 19

This small village which began its life as a timber town is one of the oldest settlements north of Brisbane Water. Ourimbah had its own school by 1864 but the village's rural serenity was shattered when the railway line from Newcastle arrived in the late 1880s, its course set straight through the school yard. In the name of progress, the school had to be moved. Peace has returned to Ourimbah with the Sydney–Newcastle Freeway carrying most of the traffic which used to run through the main street. *Population 950*

PEARL BEACH ■ 20

Pearl Beach was created for weekend retreats; this unspoiled and relatively isolated scattering of houses has nothing to offer but peace and quiet and relaxing walks along the shore. The headlands of Broken Bay keep the sandy shore calm most of the time and the whole locality is protected from the outside world by the surrounding bushland of the Brisbane Water National Park.

The township's residential area

Citrus growing and Gosford-Wyong are synonymous; in 1929 a third of the state's crop came from here.

was cleared and its timber used for shipbuilding in the nineteenth century and in the 1920s the land was subdivided as the 'Pearl Beach Estate'. A selection of local street names shows that the real estate company, having started with 'pearl', took the idea of 'theme' developments to its dizzy limits: the result is Diamond and Onyx Roads; Emerald and Opal Avenues; and the suitably alliterative Pearl Parade and Coral Crescent. *Population 500*

SARATOGA ■ 21

Despite the residential development of the seventies and eighties, Saratoga, with 180-degree views over Brisbane Water, remains a peaceful, waterside retreat. Customers were tempted with free beer and a brass band to sales of subdivided rural land here in 1906. By 1911 there were enough residents to justify a post office but the then name of Mount Pleasant had already been adopted elsewhere in Australia so a list of seven names was submitted to the postal authorities who finally settled on Saratoga, after the town of Saratoga Springs in the United States. *Population 2950*

TERRIGAL ■ 22

Nature and man have combined to make Terrigal one of the most popular beach resorts of the Central Coast; a friendly place of the sort where most Australians spend at least one summer holiday during their youth. The air is always salty and a stately row of Norfolk Island pine trees provides a backdrop to the yellow crescent of the beach, dividing it from the busy shopping centre.

The protective arm of Broken Head, with its spectacular bluff known as The Skillion – which juts out into the ocean like a launching pad – protects the southern end of the beach and provides a small boat harbour, while the lagoon behind the beach is a still-water fishing and swimming haven. These natural attractions, combined with Terrigal being only a short bus ride from Gosford, have encouraged commercial development here since the turn of the century. Today's multi-storey resort hotels are the descendants of the first guesthouses, built here in 1902; a daily bus service operated to Gosford in 1911 and by the 1920s Terrigal was a fashionable resort. *Population 6730*

THE ENTRANCE ■ 23

The Entrance is exactly that...the town is named after the break in the shoreline where the waters of Tuggerah Lake overflow into the sea. There were many other early names but the eminently descriptive present name was officially adopted in 1911. The scattering of small centres around the lake entrance, once the preserve of the retired and the annual holidaymaker have grown and joined together in one large 'suburb'.

The attractions that provided customers for the first guesthouse in 1895 remain the same, the shallow, weedy lake is abundantly full of fish and prawns and on the ocean side there are rock pools around the headlands flanking beaches which seem to go on forever...Tuggerah Beach stretches for eight kilometres before bumping into Norah Head. *Population 4130*

TOUKLEY ■ 24

Toukley is a roughly triangular shaped settlement which has the best of both worlds. Facing the spit of land that separates Budgewoi and Tuggerah Lakes, it has placid lakes

Despite urbanisation Wyong retains much of its rural character.

north and south and to the east the ocean beach of Norah Head. With water never more than a few minutes away in any direction, Toukley is one of the most popular fishing spots of the Central Coast. It was originally dubbed with the rather whimsical name of Toukley-Oukley. *Population 6730*

UMINA ■ 25

Once a modest, relatively secluded settlement looking to sea through the entrance to Broken Bay, Umina has become part of the residential sprawl that has turned Woy Woy, like its big brother Gosford to the north, into a dormitory suburb of Sydney. The electrification of the railway line and the construction of a bridge across the narrowest part of the Brisbane Water entrance channel in 1974 boosted the population but did not entirely change the character of what is still a peaceful retreat – appropriately, Umina is thought to be an Aboriginal word for 'place of sleep'. *Population 14 090*

WOY WOY ■ 26

Like many Central Coast settlements, Woy Woy is almost completely surrounded by water, with its two major approach roads crossing Brisbane Water and only the railway line approaching from the landward side. The town is one of the oldest in the region, with the first land grants having been made in 1794. The unusual name, sometimes a source of amusement to non-Woy Woyites, is said to come from an Aboriginal word meaning 'much water'.

Shipbuilding and oyster-farming were the main local industries for many years but urban development and its accompanying pollution have put paid to most of the oyster leases. For a brief time, tunnelling was Woy Woy's major industry and helped put the settlement on the map: in 1886–87, engineers built Australia's longest railway tunnel here as the Sydney–Newcastle railway line pushed its way through the rugged Central Coast hinterland. The nineteen-million bricks used to line the 1768-metre tunnel arrived by boat at the specially built Brick Wharf; leftovers were used in local buildings.

Modern Woy Woy is a part of a rapidly growing satellite residential zone of Sydney (see Umina and Gosford). *Population 9390*

WYONG ■ 27

Wyong is the commercial and administrative centre of the northern section of the Central Coast. Timber, dairy farming and citrus growing, once the major industries, now take second place to the light manufacturing industries which have become established with the improvement of transport to Sydney and Newcastle.

With the construction of the Sydney–Newcastle railway line in 1889 Wyong developed in much the same way as Gosford, as a resort in its own right and a jump-off point for the delights of the nearby coast. Wyong still attracts holidaymakers and those seeking a rural retreat but as with Gosford, speedier rail transport and a modern freeway have also put it within relatively easy commuter-reach of the capital to the south. *Population 4870*

YENGO NATIONAL PARK ■ 28

This vast wilderness is one of the 'new breed' of national parks; at approximately 140 000 hectares it is ten times the size of Dharug or Brisbane Water National Parks and is to all intents and purposes exactly as it was when the First Fleet arrived – except for the absence of its original human inhabitants. The rugged sandstone hills and ridges which render most of the region inaccessible and unsuitable for farming – and have thus ensured its preservation – are a challenge for expert bushwalkers, but only the very experienced should apply; there are no facilities and water must be carried in.

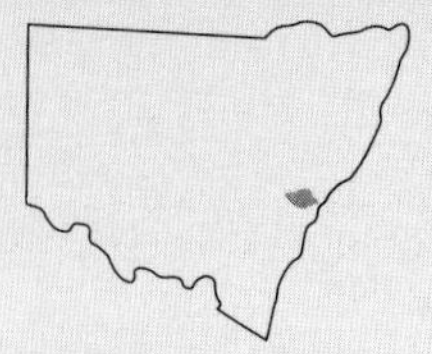

Richmond & Windsor

After two hundred years of European farming history, the Hawkesbury River district still helps to feed Sydney as well as filling its modern role as one of the city's favourite domains for recreation.

CATTAI ■ 29
Despite its proximity to the urban sprawl of Sydney, Cattai's peaceful location away from main highways and its surround of farms, parklands and forests means that the district has managed to retain its relatively rural atmosphere.

The settlement grew around Cattai farm, an estate granted to Thomas Arndell, assistant surgeon on the First Fleet, in 1798. The entire original grant of 364 hectares is now permanently protected as Cattai National Park. Today its public picnic grounds, remnant bushland and open grazing lands along the banks of the Hawkesbury River, make the Cattai district a peaceful and popular breathing space and recreation destination for the people of Sydney's sprawling north-western suburbs.

CATTAI NATIONAL PARK The two-storey Georgian farmhouse built by the Arndell family in 1821 is the main historic attraction at Cattai National Park. Also to be found in the park is the old mill _– dating from 1806 and reputed to be the oldest industrial site in Australia – bushwalking tracks, barbecue areas with free firewood and numerous children's playgrounds. The nearby Mitchell Park includes a field studies centre and a rainforest walk.

EBENEZER ■ 30
The group of free settlers who arrived in Port Jackson aboard the *Coromandel* in 1802 settled this region together and although not all the group were Presbyterians their voluntary subscriptions made possible the sandstone Presbyterian (now Uniting) church (1809) which stands today as the oldest place of worship in Australia. Despite appearances, the entry porch was not added until 1929! The farmers did not forget their old ship – the church stands at the end of Coromandel Road.

FREEMANS REACH ■ 31
Named after the stretch of the Hawkesbury it overlooks, between Richmond and Windsor, Freemans Reach is a small rural residential locality. Overlooking the nearby Bushells Lagoon is 'Reibeycroft', a colonial farmhouse topped by a roof studded with dormer windows, built in 1825 for the daughter and son-in-law of Mary Reibey, the celebrated emancipated convict who became one of Sydney's leading businesswomen. *Population 1380*

GLENORIE ■ 32
Dural, now an outer Sydney suburb, once spawned a rash of offspring 'Durals', christened North, Upper, Middle and Little. As time passed, most of them chose their own names, North Dural becoming Glenorie in 1894. Although residential development has increased since the 1950s, market gardens, and the nurseries for which the region is famous help maintain a semi-rural atmosphere. *Population 800*

GLOSSODIA ■ 33
This residential village, mainly occupied by people who work in the Richmond–Windsor area, received its botanical name (*Glossodia* is the scientific name of a genus of orchid-like native flowers) in 1922 in place of the equally colourful but more down-to-earth Currency Creek. The original epithet referred to the 'currency lads and lasses' – the popular, nineteenth-century way of describing first generation Australians of European background. Those of British birth were, by way of contrast, referred to as 'sterling'. *Population 2510*

HAWKESBURY RIVER ■ 34
A few kilometres downstream of Wisemans Ferry, the graceful bend in the river where the Hawkesbury turns east and heads for the sea is known as Trollope Reach, after the English author Anthony Trollope – perhaps an unconscious gesture of gratitude to a man who raised the historic river to the international league when he praised it in the same breath as the Rhine and the Mississippi. The Hawkesbury may lack the length and breadth of the other two rivers but its role in the early history of European settlement makes it just as important to Australians (see box).

KURRAJONG ■ 35
The former Pansy Junction – where a now-defunct railway line terminated – is a pleasant village where a quiet location off the main highway has helped encourage the development of cafes and tearooms, antique and craft shops, museums and galleries. The name – Curry Jung and Corrygong were but a few of the early versions applied to the settlement – is an Aboriginal word also applied commonly to several species of native flowering eucalyptus trees. *Population 1090*

KURRAJONG HEIGHTS ■ 36
After Kurrajong, Bells Line of Road, the distinctively named alternative route to the Great Western Highway into the Blue Mountains, ascends steeply, providing some spectacular views of the coastal plain and the distant, jagged peaks of Sydney on the way to Kurrajong Heights. The quaint village is similar to its larger sister at a lower altitude, with the addition of several historic churches and guesthouses and a post office which was prefabricated in England before being shipped to Australia. *Population 640*

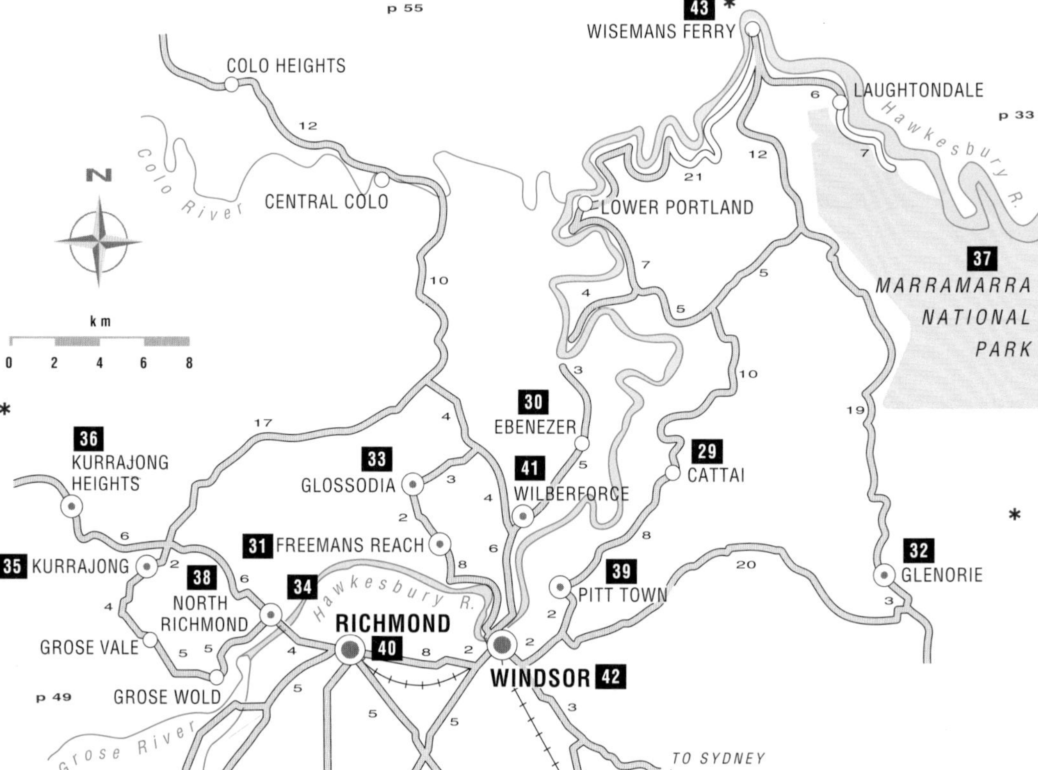

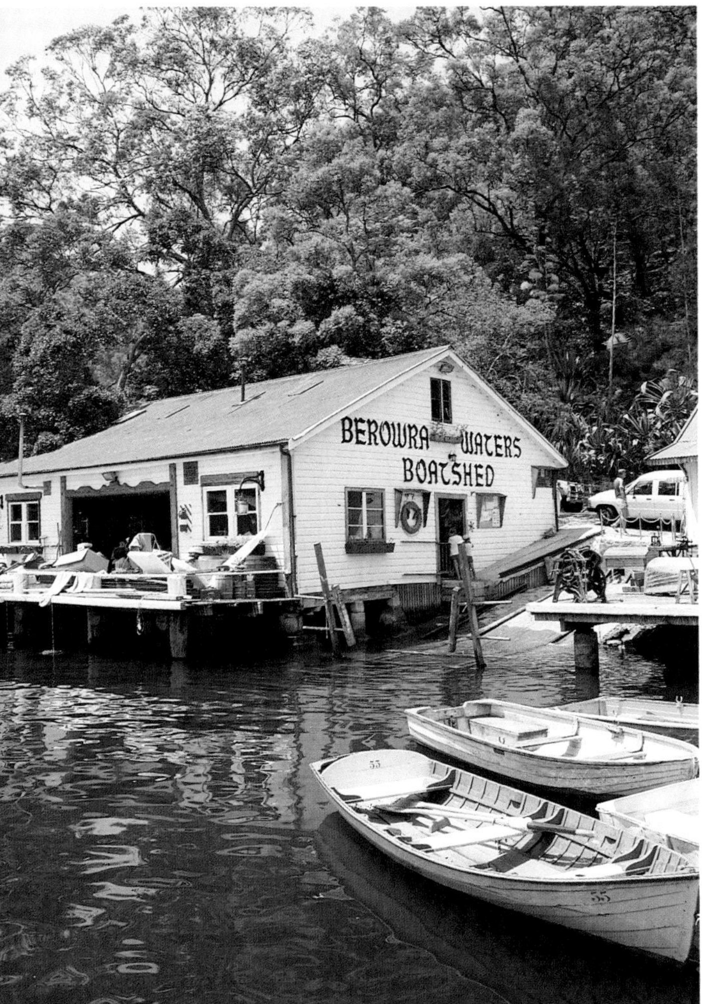

The lower Hawkesbury is the scene of much messing about in boats.

This giant Hercules is part of the large fleet of transport aircraft at Richmond – the RAAF's oldest base.

Solomon Wiseman, of Wisemans Ferry fame, built Cobham Hall – now part of a hotel – in 1826.

MARRAMARRA NATIONAL PARK ■ 37

Many summertime pleasure-seekers know the Hawkesbury River best for the spectacular beauty of its tidal reaches, between Wisemans Ferry and the entrance to the sea at Broken Bay. Here is a water-lover's paradise protected on both banks, all the way to the sea, by thousands of hectares of national parkland.

The mangrove forests, rugged, eucalypt woodlands and ferny rainforest gullies on the southern shore are part of the 12 000-hectare Marramarra National Park, probably the least developed of the several Hawkesbury parks, where the wilderness remains as it was when Governor Phillip passed by in his longboat 200 years ago. A river bend at the eastern end of the park, known as Gentlemans Halt, marks the place where Phillip and his men came ashore.

NORTH RICHMOND ■ 38

This 'suburb' of Richmond on the western bank of the Hawkesbury is a modern business and residential centre. On the western outskirts of the town are Belmont Cottage, an 1840s Georgian brick dwelling that has been converted into a shop, and the central feature of the former 'Belmont Park' estate, a majestic Victorian mansion with a grand, sweeping driveway and gatehouse, all now part of the St John of God Hospital complex. *Population 3090*

PITT TOWN ■ 39

The first permanent, planned settlements in Australia outside Sydney were on the Hawkesbury, and while the city has been largely overwhelmed by the twentieth century, the towns of the flood plain still recognisably have their origins in the early 1800s.

Twelve years after farming started on the Hawkesbury banks, the river rose and a disastrous flood swept through the region; in order to avoid loss of life and property in future disasters Governor Lachlan Macquarie organised the settlement into five towns on safe, high ground – quickly to become known as the 'Macquarie Towns' – in 1810.

Pitt Town, along with Richmond, Wilberforce and Windsor (see entries) survives, while Castlereagh has faded into history. It was named after the English politician William Pitt and like Wilberforce has retained its rural charm.

Despite the subdivision of old properties and the ever-westward spread of population, vegetables are still grown here for the Sydney market, particularly on the fertile, low-lying land which reflects the rural English origins of its first farmers by being known colourfully as Pitt Town Bottoms. *Population 630*

RICHMOND ■ 40

Richmond and Windsor are the largest surviving Macquarie Towns (see Pitt Town) and although the former may have been overshadowed by the latter's early growth as the region's administrative centre, its tree-lined streets and fine collection of Georgian and early Victorian buildings give it a special character of its own.

When Governor Phillip reached the Hawkesbury's junction with the Grose River in 1789 (see box), he surveyed the river's surrounds from a hill he dubbed Richmond Hill after the Duke of Richmond. The town which took the same name has since managed to accommodate the establishment of an agricultural college, a giant RAAF base and, by the river, extensive sand and gravel extraction works, while remaining the modest business centre of a fruit- and vegetable-growing and dairying district. *Population 9310*

HAWKESBURY AGRICULTURAL COLLEGE Australia's first institution of 'higher learning' to concentrate on agricultural teaching and research was established on the southern edge of the town in 1891. The college, now part of the University of Western Sydney – Hawkesbury, is centred around a large, rambling 1920s administration block and what is probably Australia's largest stable complex – built in the pre-tractor days of 1896, the vast timber building in the shape of a hollow square originally housed a small army of draught horses.

'HOBARTVILLE' This Georgian brick mansion on a low rise in a peaceful rural setting of paddocks and trees was constructed in 1828 and the surrounding verandah 'skirt' of columns and slate roof added later.

ST PETER'S CHURCH The old brick church (1837–41) with its square tower and timber spire, its adjoining rectory (1847) and the churchyard opposite are typical of the dozen or so 'heritage' sites in or around Richmond which testify to the town's historic past.

RAAF BASE A flying school was operating on the edge of Richmond as early as 1912. An aviation school was established in 1916 and in 1927 this became an Air Force base.

WILBERFORCE ■ 41

Wilberforce is a small village on a ridge above the northern end of the Hawkesbury River flood plain; named after the eighteenth-century anti-slavery campaigner William Wilberforce; it remains the most modest of the remaining Macquarie Towns (see Pitt Town).

Although there are few notable colonial buildings in the village proper the 'Australiana' pioneer village has a variety of old buildings which have been saved from dereliction and re-erected in a natural grouping of dwellings, shops and 'public' buildings.

The village centres around Rose Cottage (1811–16), the oldest timber house in Australia still on its original site and probably the oldest house to be continuously occupied by one family, the descendants of the builder, Thomas Rose, having lived there until 1961. *Population 1700*

WINDSOR ■ 42

This is the premier settlement of Governor Macquarie's five towns (see Pitt Town). Established in 1810, it was planned around a village square, became an administrative centre for the region, and probably retains more colonial buildings than any other town in Australia.

The first settlers called the place Green Hills; after 200 years the surrounding flood plains are still verdantly green and Windsor continues as a major regional centre of a mixed farming district although modern development has meant that many historic buildings survive as stylish islands in a sea of commercial and private architectural mixes.

The river – and then the open sea – remained the major goods route from Windsor to Sydney for many years and vessels plied the waters until the 1880s, six years after the railway reached the town. Periodic flooding has often meant disaster for local farmers and some riverside farmland has been given over to turf-growing – there have been more than fifty severe floods in the last 100 years, the worst being the 1867 inundation when the river rose to almost twenty metres.

The jewels in Windsor's architectural crown are the almost perfectly proportioned St Matthew's Anglican Church (1817–20) and the court house (1822), both works of the former convict architect Francis Greenway, but there are at least forty other 'heritage' buildings worthy of inspection. *Population 10 560*

MACQUARIE ARMS HOTEL The 'Arms' is Australia's oldest pub, even if it has not operated as one continuously since it was built at the express request of Governor Macquarie in 1811. Present-day travellers can still refresh themselves while admiring the building's best features, such as the entrance doorway and the graceful cedar staircase.

THE DOCTOR'S HOUSE The red-brick and sandstone terrace (1844) is so-called because doctors have lived in one part or other of the building since 1876. It overlooks the river and the old village square.

PENINSULA HOUSE AND OBSERVATORIES The Peninsula House residence (1844) has a neatly skirted verandah lined with flagstones supporting highly decorative, cast-iron columns. The attendant brick observatories were added in the late 1870s by the internationally recognised astronomer John Tebbutt who was born in Windsor ten years before his now-famous home was built.

WISEMANS FERRY ■ 43

There could be no more no-nonsense, descriptive name than this. Wisemans Ferry is exactly that, a sleepy scattering of commercial buildings – including a charming old pub – sitting above a bend in the Hawkesbury where a ferry – nowadays a cable-operated vehicle punt – established by a Mr Wiseman ferries cars and trucks across the water.

Solomon Wiseman was a convict who had worked on the River Thames in London; after eleven years penal servitude he was pardoned and set himself up as an inkeeper on the Hawkesbury in the mid-1820s – a few years later he began operating his ferry service – now the oldest such service in Australia. It was a wise choice of location – Wiseman prospered when the ferry became the river crossing for the first major road north out of Sydney. And this despite the fact that he was obliged to carry government loads at no charge.

WISEMANS FERRY HOTEL This popular watering hole was once Solomon Wiseman's house (1826). Originally it faced the river – thus the arrangement of semi-circular steps fanned out on the verandah's northern side.

St Matthew's graveyard at Windsor predates the church by ten years.

THE RIVER THAT SAVED A COLONY

Thanks largely to the rugged and unfarmable shoreline of its lower reaches, large stretches of the Hawkesbury still appear much as they did when a desperate Governor Phillip (inset, above) led his party this way. Modern explorers aboard the Lady Hawkesbury *(above) can retrace Phillip's journey without the hardships of longboat travel.*

FIVE weeks after establishing a fragile colony on the banks of a creek in the middle reaches of Sydney Harbour, Governor Arthur Phillip ventured northwards out of his isolated South Pacific haven to explore the next break in the coastal cliffs. On entering Broken Bay he found and briefly explored the mouth of a river which he named Hawkesbury after Lord Hawkesbury, President of Trade and Plantations in London.

Fourteen months later, in June 1789, the need for good farmland to help feed the less than happy settlement at Farm Cove drove Phillip back to the Hawkesbury River and this time he took his longboat all the way up the constantly winding river to its origin, where the Grose and Nepean Rivers join forces near present-day Richmond. Beyond the tidal reaches he found what he wanted – a fringe of flood plains with relatively level countryside beyond.

In 1794 a group of farming families were settled near the site of Windsor and within a few years the Hawkesbury district had overtaken Parramatta as the bread basket of the colony, producing about three-quarters of its flour and reducing the dependence on supply ships from England. When better grainlands were found beyond the mountains to the west, the Hawkesbury plains continued to produce vegetables and fruit for the Sydney market and despite periodic flooding, still do so today.

By accidents of history and geography the plains which fed the first colonists are still partly farmland, although parklands and other recreational facilities occupy many former paddocks – the Hawkesbury is probably one of Australia's busiest water-skiing corridors. Close settlement has bypassed the region as Sydney's sprawl occurred to its south, swallowing the Parramatta farmlands, and spreading to Penrith at the base of the Blue Mountains as it followed the main route to the west. To the north-east, beyond Wisemans Ferry, the other half of the river is flanked by rugged hillsides of dense bushland, most of it protected within large national parks. □

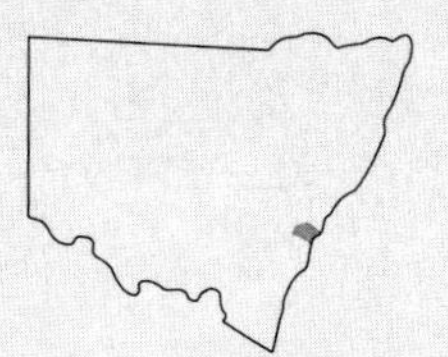

Campbelltown & Camden

Sydney's south-west is the site of one of the fastest growing satellite urban regions in Australia. In the early days of settlement this was part of the city's food bowl; it now provides homes and employment for Sydney's burgeoning population.

APPIN ■ 44

Appin was named by Governor Macquarie in 1811 after the small village in Scotland where his second wife Elizabeth was born. The first land grant was made a year later to Andrew Hume, father of Hamilton Hume, the explorer. A monument which marks the start of the sixteen-week journey by Hume and William Hovell to Port Phillip in 1824, stands on the roadside just outside Appin where their trailblazing journey started.

Skirmishes between the settlers and the Dharawal Aborigines on the banks of the Nepean River in 1816 led Macquarie to order troops into the 'infested area'. At Appin troops open-fired on a group of Aborigines, killing fourteen men, women and children, and many more are thought to have leapt to their deaths over Cataract Gorge.

In 1838, a coach service between Sydney, Liverpool, Campbelltown, Appin and the new southern coast townships began running and by 1850 Appin was described as a 'little straggling village amongst gum trees...inhabited mostly by Irish and with two opposition inns'. The road leading into Appin, conveniently flat, was used as a racecourse.

Appin has come a long way since those days and is now part of the Three-City Regional Plan whereby Campbelltown, Camden and Appin will be major regional centres for a population of half a million people by the early twenty-first century. *Population 1010*

CAMDEN ■ 45

The first 'Europeans' to move into the area around Camden after settlement were four bulls and two cows – the entire stock of Sydney Cove cattle – which went missing and were discovered by Aborigines grazing near the Nepean River in 1795. The area around Camden was therefore named the Cowpastures and the progeny of these cattle were jealously guarded for many years until Governor Brisbane ordered them shot in 1824 as inferior stock.

Despite its original name, Camden is better known for its sheep than for cattle. In 1805, John Macarthur was given two large land grants around the present-day town of Camden on to which he moved his sheep, including the colony's first merinos, and with that the Australian wool industry was born. The town on part of Macarthur's land was surveyed in 1836 and named Camden, after Lord Camden, Secretary of State for the Colonies.

Designated part of what town planners call the Macarthur Growth Centre in 1973, Camden is one of the key regional centres for an area where the population is expected to double within the next thirty years. *Population 8440*

CAMDEN PARK MANSION This house is one of Australia's great mansions; it was designed by John Verge for Macarthur and was not completed until after the wool pioneer died.

CAMPBELLTOWN ■ 46

Situated between the valleys of the Nepean and Georges Rivers, Campbelltown – first settled by wheat growers such as James Ruse to provide bread for Sydney – is probably the fastest growing urban centre in Australia. The first development plan in 1951 proposed that Campbelltown should be a satellite town of 30 000 beyond the late, lamented green belt then surrounding Sydney. By the mid-1960s, when the population was already around 20 000, future projections rose to 40–50 000 and by the late 1960s projected population figures for the region had soared to an estimate of 200 000.

Such growth was not always predictable; in 1823 the Government Architect pronounced gloomily that Campbelltown (named by Governor Macquarie after his wife's maiden name, Campbell) 'is so ill supplied with water it would not be advisable to recommend more buildings' – this at a time when the new township had one church, a schoolhouse and a few bark huts.

But by 1827, the first coach service from Sydney to Campbelltown was operating. By 1850, the demand for seats was so great that bookings had to be taken. The arrival of the railway line in 1855 greatly cut the time for the journey. *Population 148 300*

FISHER'S GHOST Frederick George Fisher was murdered by a neighbour and lay, buried and undetected, for four months until his ghost appeared to point to his grave beside what is now Fisher's Ghost Creek. The Festival of Fisher's Ghost is celebrated for two weeks every year with parades, music and a flypast of aircraft among other events. The

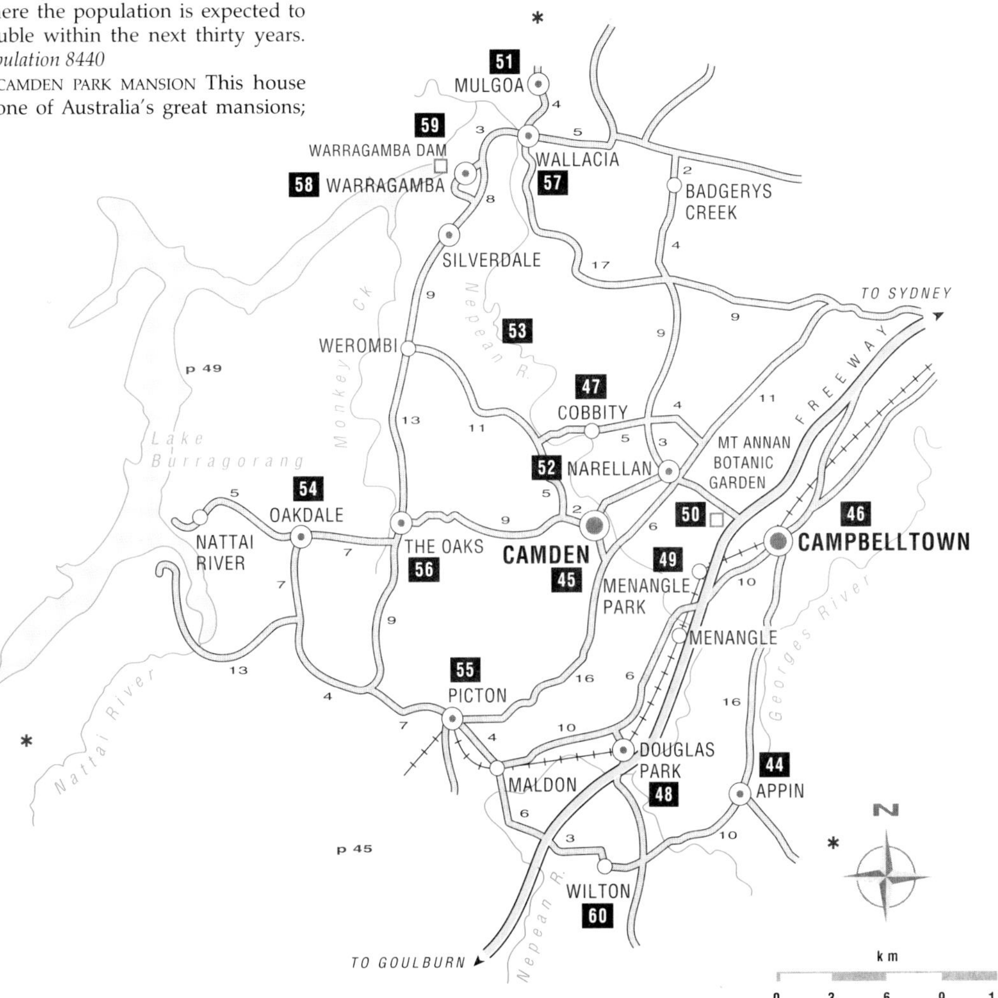

members of the Ghoul League, formed in the 1950s, watch for the unfortunate Fisher's reappearance.

COBBITY ■ 47

Although the name may suggest a village in rural England, the original spelling of 'Kobbaddee' points to an Aboriginal origin. The first settler here was Thomas Kent who was given a land grant at Cobbity in 1810.

The village developed around a number of old homesteads, most of them largely unchanged since the mid-nineteenth century. Oran Park Motor Racing is the only event that disturbs the peace of this historic rural village. *Population 146 000*

HEBER CHAPEL This small, simple Georgian brick building was named after Bishop Heber, whose exceedingly large diocese of Calcutta included Australia. Built by Thomas Hassall, the Anglican Parson appointed to Cowpastures (Camden), the Chapel was consecrated by Samuel Marsden in 1828 and is still used as a meeting hall.

DOUGLAS PARK ■ 48

Douglas Park was the spot where Frances Barallier's unsuccessful attempt to cross the Blue Mountains in 1802 nearly foundered before it began. Six hundred head of cattle in several herds tried to bar his way...possibly they knew his efforts were to be in vain.

Douglas Park is situated at the junction of the Cataract and Nepean Rivers, with access to some spectacular deep river gorges and recreation areas. *Population 630*

ST MARY'S TOWERS (known formerly as 'Parkhall') The original homestead was built for the Surveyor-General Thomas Mitchell. The foundation stone was laid in 1842 although the house was not completed until 1845.

'MORETON PARK' This privately owned house was built in 1865 or earlier on land granted to Jean Baptiste D'Arrietta, a Spanish free settler who had a vineyard there. The round windowless brick building in the garden was originally designed to be a chapel.

MENANGLE PARK ■ 49

The word 'manhangle' or 'menangle' meaning 'place of swamps' was used by the local Aborigines to describe this area but now Menangle Park is associated more with horses than with swamps.

The village has stables, stud farms, the National Equestrian Centre, and Menangle Park Raceway where trotting events are held. The raceway is second only to Harold Park in inner Sydney for trotting and is also used for the regular local Sunday markets. The National Equestrian Centre, on 130 hectares of conveniently flat land, required little work before polo playing could start. The centre has accommodation for 400 horses and in addition to polo and polocrosse, regular dressage competitions and local pony club events are held there.

As suburbia looms offstage, sheep continue to graze the historic pastures around Campbelltown and Camden.

MOUNT ANNAN BOTANIC GARDEN ■ 50

This 400-hectare botanic garden, built as a Bicentennial project and opened in 1988 will come as something as a surprise to those expecting a traditional European-style garden with green lawns and geometrically shaped flower beds. Mount Annan, an annexe of the Royal Botanic Gardens, in Sydney, is a 'state of the art' plant collection which demonstrates a new awareness of the value of Australia's plants. This huge expanse of open farmland is the largest botanic garden in Australia dedicated to the preservation of native plants.

Visitors may stroll at their leisure along walking tracks through planned 'woodlands' which incorporate theme gardens of bottlebrush, wattle and banksia. A spectacular four-hectare terraced garden at the centre of the site, contains families of Australian plants arranged to highlight their relationship with each other. There are also areas within the garden where the region's original open woodland is being regenerated and where rare and endangered species are preserved.

Eventually 25 000 native plant species will be collected at Mount Annan. A visitors' centre houses a permanent exhibition; barbecue areas and refreshments are available.

MULGOA ■ 51

William Cox, who built the road across the Blue Mountains (see *Lithgow & Oberon*), was the first to be given a land grant around Mulgoa. His son Edward Cox built the elegant 'Fernhill' mansion at Mulgoa from stone quarried on the property. Irish stonemasons were brought out to work on the house, which took four years to build. *Population 540*

NARELLAN ■ 52

Narellan was the first site to be surveyed for a town in the Camden (Cowpastures) district but remained uninhabited for many years because of the lack of water. Narellan was probably named after the nearby property 'Naralling', owned by the explorer William Hovell.

Once a water supply was laid on the town began to grow. John Oxley's Kirkham Stables at Narellan then had multiple functions being used as men's quarters and even as a court house. Narellan is noted for its horsebreeding with many local horse studs having operated for over a hundred years. *Population 2690*

NEPEAN RIVER ■ 53

When, in 1789 Watkins Tench crossed 'a river nearly as broad as the Thames at Putney' at what is now Penrith, it was not immediately apparent that the river was the upper reaches of the Hawkesbury River and so it was named the Nepean after Sir Evan Nepean, Secretary to the Admiralty.

Later explorations, starting with the investigations of Governor Phillip from the coast, gradually identified the route of the river from where it rises west of Wollongong, past Camden to Wallacia where it joins the Warragamba River. At this point it becomes part of the Hawkesbury although the name Nepean River is retained until the meeting with the Grose River, near Richmond, from where the Hawkesbury name takes over.

In order to protect government cattle at Cowpastures (Camden) passes were required for many years to cross the Nepean River. Two constables were posted at Bird's Eye Bend on the Nepean to watch for unauthorised crossing by potential cattle thieves. The first bridge across the Nepean was Cowpastures Bridge (1826) at Camden. It opened as a toll bridge in 1827...but crossing the bridge on the Sabbath was banned. In later years more bridges were built and ferry services also operated.

From the early nineteenth century when an Irishman called Patrick Curry sold water drawn from the Nepean for two shillings a wooden cask, the Nepean has been used to supply water for the Sydney region. A drought in 1902 dried up the river and the resulting water shortage in Sydney quickly prompted the first proposals for dam building; the six dams in the Upper Nepean catchment were constructed between 1907 and 1960.

OAKDALE ■ 54

The Oakdale Lookout used to offer spectacular views of the Burragorang Valley but since the building of the Warragamba Dam in 1960, all that changed – the views are still spectacular but now they are of the man-made Lake Burragorang.

Oakdale is also noted for its below-the-ground activities – coal from Oakdale is transported by rail to Port Kembla from where it is shipped overseas.

Despite the coal mine, Oakdale is primarily a rural village with orchards growing peaches, plums, nectarines, apples, oranges, pears and grapes. *Population 780*

PICTON ■ 55

The first land grant at Stonequarry (Picton) was made in 1822 to Major Henry Antill whose property was named 'Jarvisfield' after Jane Jarvis, Governor Macquarie's first wife. The homestead on the property has been 'recycled' and is now the clubhouse for the Antill Park Golf Club.

The name Picton was not used until 1845 when Governor Brisbane gave the name to Stonequarry and two other villages amalgamated with it. Brisbane had served under General Sir Thomas Picton at Waterloo and named the town in honour of this military hero.

The coming of the railway in 1863 contributed greatly to the town's development and the station master's residence, the station, the first viaduct and the gatehouse, which still stand in Picton, all date from this period. The first railway tunnel was used for growing mushrooms when it became redundant in 1919 and was used by the army during the Second World War for storing cannon shells.

Picton was not only a major junction on the Sydney rail line, from 1863 but was also a coach stop on the Old South Road. After the ride over the Razorback Range between Camden and Picton the sight of the Razorback Inn must have been a welcome one. Apart from its many inns Picton also had a creamery (1899), and a feather and fur factory (1920) which made tippets, boas and feathered cockades for the slouch hats of the Mounted Lancers.

Picton today is a town of beautiful parks and historic landmarks..and a brewery based in the George IV Inn that brews 'real ale' in the traditional German manner. *Population 2120*

THE OAKS ■ 56

John Warby, the government herdsman at Cowpastures (Camden), was the first European to enter the area around The Oaks. Something of a local explorer, he blazed a track from Cowpastures to Prospect for which he was rewarded with a land grant of 260 acres in 1816.

On the road to Lake Burragorang, The Oaks is well aware of its historical heritage and the Wollondilly Heritage Centre in the village devotes its displays to the history of Burragorang Valley and the Cowpastures. *Population 1370*

ST MATTHEW'S CHURCH Convict labour was used to fell the trees and cut the slabs used in this old timber church. The shingled roof on the original 1838 church was later replaced with an iron roof. The simple parish church is one of the oldest buildings of its type still in use. The churchyard is steeped in history, containing as it does, the graves of many of the early settlers including Suzzanah Mileham, a descendant of Captain Cook.

Future champions of the show ring and the polo field – or polocrosse as here – practise their horseback skills at the modern National Equestrian Centre at Menangle.

The Warragamba Dam transformed a narrow valley into this vast lake.

WALLACIA ■ 57

Situated at the junction of the Nepean and Warragamba Rivers, Wallacia was originally called, appropriately enough, Riverview. A local resident called Wallace volunteered his house as a depot for letters and when a permanent postal service was started the local post office assumed the name of 'Wallace' in honour of the unofficial postmaster. In 1905 the postal authorities mooted a name change to avoid confusion with another post office of the same name and the residents successfully petitioned for the name Wallacia.

The small farms of modern Wallacia now share their location with a growing number of modern housing estates. *Population 840*

BENTS BASIN STATE RECREATION AREA The recreation area has been the site of a favourite swimming hole for generations. The Bents Basin's rugged gorges, river rapids and sandy beaches harbour a variety of rare native plants and are now controlled by the National Parks and Wildlife Service.

WARRAGAMBA ■ 58

With the construction of the giant Warragamba Dam (see entry) the scenery around Warragamba has changed dramatically – what was land is now water. There is a dam information centre at Warragamba and the small village is a starting point for bushwalkers and those enjoying the recreational facilities of Lake Burragorang.

The village population can relax in the knowledge that the nearby dam is designed to handle what the statisticians refer to as 'the thousand-year flood' – an inundation of Noah's flood-like proportions – with special spillway training walls that rise forty-three metres above the normal water level to protect the village and its surrounding countryside from any possible devastation. *Population 1530*

WARRAGAMBA DAM ■ 59

The sheer size of Warragamba Dam is difficult to envisage but its reservoir is larger in area and in the length of its foreshores than Sydney Harbour. At its deepest point the water is 105 metres deep compared with the greatest depth in Sydney Harbour, a mere 47 metres. The water held by the dam is three and a half times the volume of the water in the harbour. Not only is Warragamba Dam the largest and most important dam in the Sydney region it is one of the world's largest water supply dams, impounding over two million megalitres of water.

The dam was opened in 1960. The water in the vast reservoir, now called Lake Burragorang after the valley that it flooded, is then delivered to Prospect Reservoir by gravitation through twenty-seven kilometres of piping.

The size of the dam has not seemed to daunt the short- and long-finned eels that reach maturity in the Warragamba Reservoir. The five-centimetre long baby eels, or elvers, wriggle along a small stream from where they are spawned and then cross a road, scale a concrete wall and slither down an embankment to complete their life cycle in the man-made reservoir.

WILTON ■ 60

One of the early roads in the district passed through what became Wilton village. Large grants around Wilton were made to Thomas Mitchell whose residence 'Parkhall' (see Douglas Park) lay between Wilton and Douglas Park.

Wilton now offers access to the Cordeaux Dam and to the winery opposite it. The Sydney Parachute and Skydiving Centre at Wilton is the largest sports parachute school in the Southern Hemisphere and some 16 000 jumps are made over the village each year.

WOLLONGONG

Like Newcastle but to the south, Wollongong stands in polite attendance to the larger Sydney, the three cities constantly threatening to coalesce into one vast megalopolis. Such an event would deprive one of the world's airiest, greenest industrial centres of its character.

Wollongong spreads over a coastal lowland that reaches its widest point near Albion Park and tapers northwards to end in the sea cliffs of Sydney's Royal National Park. Its urban area undulates across shallow valleys with rivers running down to the sea and barred by sand dunes into forming lagoons such as Lake Illawarra.

Bordering Wollongong on the west is a steep forested escarpment rising up to 660 metres, with the two landmark peaks of Mount Keira and Mount Kembla jutting out as eastern outliers. The city is trapped between the escarpment's sandstone crests and a striking coastline of alternating headlands and beaches facing the Pacific Ocean and the Five Islands off Port Kembla.

Flagstaff Point, north of the city centre, provides the southern arm of Wollongong's pretty harbour.

With the municipality of Shellharbour, on the south shore of Lake Illawarra, Wollongong's population is approximately 211 500, making it Australia's seventh largest city. There are panoramic views of Wollongong from Mount Keira, from the Bulli Lookout above Thirroul and from Sublime Point overlooking Austinmer. From these points, hills and bush screen the view to the west so that nothing can be seen of the mine headworks and reservoirs of the tableland country which extends westward to the Great Divide in the guise of the southern highlands. But to the east, and far below, Wollongong is laid out. It sprawls up and down the narrow Illawarra coastal strip and only the timely interruption of the aforementioned escarpment, pushing east to meet the sea, stops the city from eventually merging with Sydney's southern limits.

Unlike Newcastle, which serves as a focus for the rich Hunter Valley, the rural centres of Wollongong's hinterland are separated from the city by the ever-present escarpment and they tend to look forward on the brighter lights of Sydney. Thus Wollongong has developed as a local rather than a regional commercial centre. Perched on its narrow coastal strip, it has satisfied itself with its coal mines, its heavy industries, its port and its superb recreational attractions.

Obliterated by the city's spread, only occasional, solitary cabbage tree palms recall the rainforest of the coastal plain. Peter Cunningham, an early visitor, thought that '...the tall fern, cedar and cabbage trees; the numerous creeping vines, climbing up and throwing their fragrant tassels of flowers downwards from the tops of the less lofty trees...make you fancy yourself transported to some far distant tropical region'. The need for new pastures brought settlers here but there was also interest in the coal seams. In 1834, the Colonial Secretary approved a plan for the town of Wollongong – the name is derived from an Aboriginal word for 'sound of the sea'.

In spring, elegant waratahs bloom on the escarpment which dictates Wollongong's elongated shape.

Wollongong's port started life with the cedar trade and later loaded coal; a harbour was established by 1844. Relieved by the development of Port Kembla of any pressing economic need to expand any further, Wollongong Harbour has retained its nineteenth-century scale, and with its pleasure craft and fleet of fishing boats, is one of the city's most picturesque places.

When the writer D.H. Lawrence stayed at Thirroul in the 1920s it was a village, just one of a string of modest settlements along the Illawarra coast. In the early 1930s, the combined population of these communities was about 45 000. But change was on the way...people poured into the Illawarra between 1947 and the 1970s, creating a more or less continuous string of 'suburbs' that are mainly post-war in character, although Wollongong was proclaimed a city in 1942.

Heavy industry was attracted to this region in the early 1900s by its high-grade coal; by the end of the 1970s the city had Australia's largest steelworks and one of the world's largest blast furnaces. Industry has concentrated south of the city centre around Port Kembla, which has grown into Australia's sixth largest port. Despite Port Kembla's industrial muscle, Wollongong has continued as the business and administrative centre and the site of the major retail complexes. In the 1980s, it consolidated its position with imaginative developments including the Wollongong City Mall, a new library and the Performing Arts Centre. The green campus of the University of Wollongong plays an important role in the city's efforts to diversify. □

The same waters that support the mighty ore carriers nudging into Port Kembla wash onto Wollongong Beach next door where lifesaving is no longer an all-male domain.

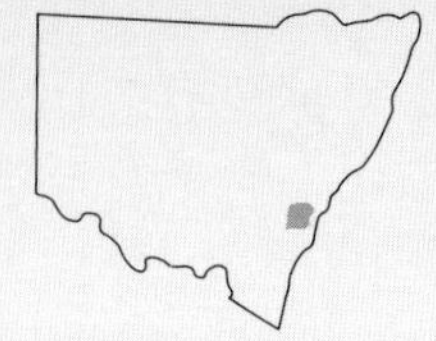

Bowral & Moss Vale

The altitude of the Southern Highlands has blessed it with four clearly defined seasons and the many Northern Hemisphere plants – both horticultural and agricultural – which thrive in the invigorating climate have led to the region being called the mountain garden of New South Wales and 'nature's art gallery'.

AVON RESERVOIR ■ 61

The Avon River, a tributary of the Nepean River, was dammed in 1927 as part of the upper Nepean catchment system. Between 1907 and 1960 six major reservoirs – Avon, Nepean, Cataract, Cordeaux, Woronora and Warragamba – were built to provide almost two-and-a-half million megalitres of water storage.

The seventy-three metre high concrete bulk of the Avon Dam holds back a reservoir of some two hundred and fifteen thousand megalitres used to supply the taps of the South Coast, Wollongong and Port Kembla. The dam wall has been classified by the National Trust as a site of architectural significance.

BARGO ■ 62

John Price, a servant of Governor Phillip, and one of the small group of Europeans first to pass through Bargo, kept a detailed journal in which he recorded on 26 January 1798 '...I shot a bird about the size of a pheasant, but the tail of it very much resembles a peacock'. This first written record of a lyrebird is commemorated in a plaque on the old Hume Highway at Bargo.

By 1815 the land around Bargo was being used for grazing by at least two European settlers – John Oxley and William Moore. Known as 'Barago' by the local Aborigines, the name Bargo was used by the settlers and this was adopted by Governor Macquarie who visited it in 1815.

The local forest, known as 'Bargo Brush', provided an ideal cover for bushrangers and the road to Bargo became notorious for its hold-ups. James Crookwell, who shot a police constable during an escape attempt in the Bargo Brush, was sent to the gallows in 1866.

Now a quiet rural village, Bargo is a sanctuary, no longer for bushrangers, but for wild animals at the Wirrimbirra Sanctuary and the Merigal Dingo Education Centre, which cares for wild dingoes and works for the official reclassification of the dingo as a dog rather than vermin. *Population 2150*

WIRRIMBIRRA SANCTUARY The sanctuary is administered by the Stead Foundation, co-founded by well-known botanist and author Thistle Y. Harris in memory of her husband David Stead. It is devoted to the study of natural systems, native plants and environmental education. There are guided nature trails and a school with two full-time teachers at the sanctuary.

BERRIMA ■ 63

When the Surveyor-General of the colony, Thomas Mitchell, camped on the site of Berrima in 1829 he described it as ideal for a town, 'on a fine, romantic part of the Wingecarribee River'. When the Great South Road was built through Berrima in 1836, the town's prominence in the region grew and many of Berrima's famous buildings date from this time.

But in 1850, the district court was moved from Berrima to Goulburn and in 1867 the railway line bypassed Berrima; thereafter the town ceased to grow.

Berrima is now the only preserved Georgian village of its period in New South Wales and is listed as a 'heritage' site. The Berrima bypass road, built in 1988, allows the tranquillity and history of Berrima to be enjoyed without the risk to life and limb which used to be prevalent when the heavy vehicles using the old Hume Highway thundered through the village. *Population 720*

BERRIMA JAIL Built between 1835 and 1839 the jail was considered by authorities at the time to be the 'finest and most commodious building of its type in the colony', although the description in *Robbery under Arms* of 'the largest, most severe, the most dreaded of all the prisons in New South Wales' would seem more accurate from the point of view of the inmates. From 1866, half of any sentence over five years had to be served in Berrima Jail...the first nine months in silence. During the First World War the jail was used for enemy aliens and was then closed. Reopened in 1949, it has been used as a rehabilitation centre for young offenders.

Berrima was one of the first towns in Australia to receive the accolade 'historic village'. The bull's head (right) is part of a now dry horse trough in the wall of the 1839 jail.

BONG BONG ■ 64

According to legend, Bong Bong was originally known as 'Toom Boong' or 'Boong Boong' meaning 'many watercourses', 'many frogs'...or 'human buttocks' – as with many places with Aboriginal names, it could be that the original inhabitants, having been dispossessed of their land, at least had the last laugh by the straight-faced bequeathing of vulgar names to be adopted by European settlers. This was the first village in the Southern Highlands to be surveyed, in 1821. Although intended to be the principal town of the district, the Great South Road was rerouted through Berrima and Bong Bong reverted to being 'the potato field' supplying this staple food for the Sydney region. The well known Bong Bong picnic races are, in fact, held in Bowral.

BOWRAL ■ 65

Bowral is the commercial centre for a district where grazing, dairy farming and stud cattle properties are still the major industries, as they were when the town was first settled.

The explorer and Surveyor-General, John Oxley, was granted 2000 hectares in and around Bowral in 1825 and it was on part of this land that the township grew with the coming of the southern railway line in 1867. Initially a construction camp for those working on the railway, Bowral grew rapidly in the late 1860s and, with its lack of humidity and varied scenery, was a favourite holiday retreat for the gentry of Sydney. Still a retreat for those wishing to escape the hustle of Sydney, Bowral has been home to many writers including Arthur Upfield, the creator of the Aboriginal detective Napoleon Bonaparte (Bony). One of Upfield's characters describes Bowral rather unkindly as a '...smallish, four-pub town. Three policemen. Five hundred yapping dogs'.

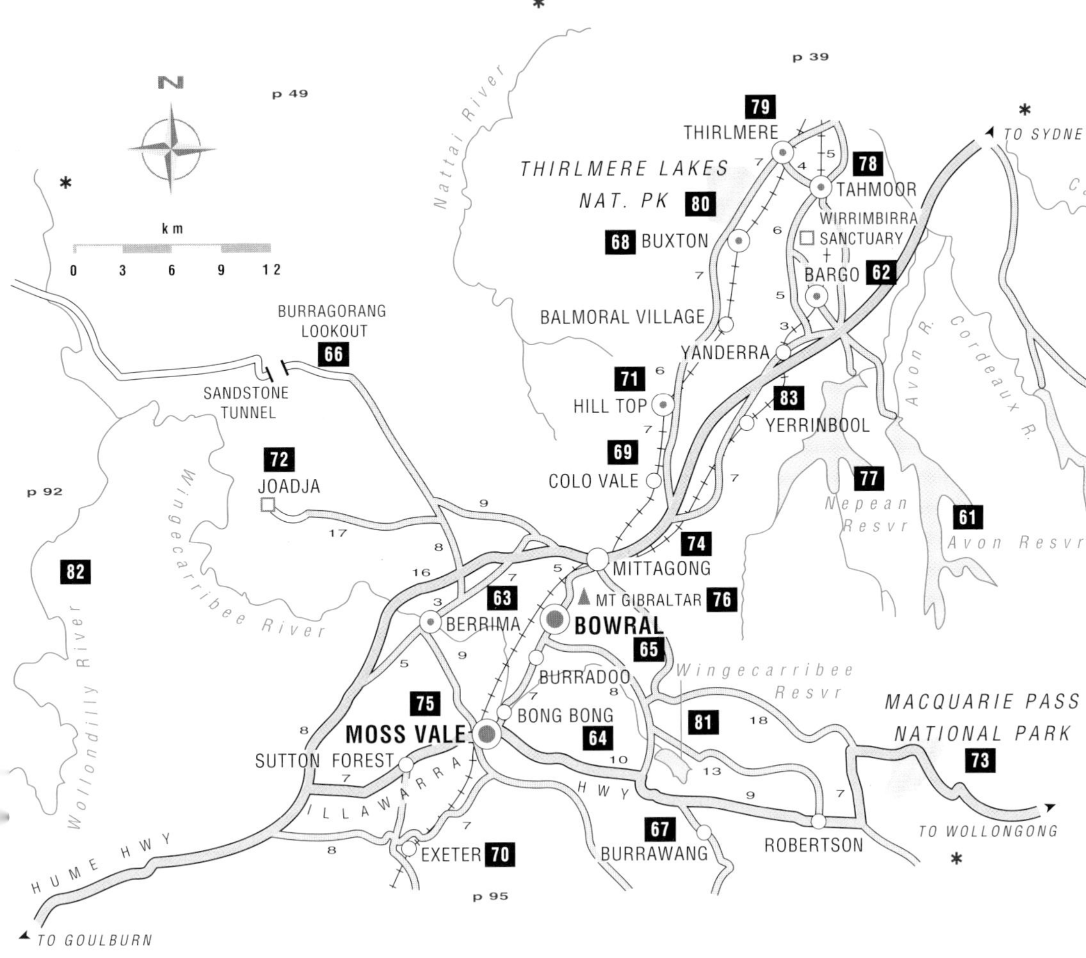

However, Bowral's most famous son is undoubtedly the cricketing great Don Bradman who scored his first century here while playing, at the age of twelve, for Bowral High School. *Population 7930*

BRADMAN MUSEUM Opposite Don Bradman's old childhood home, this museum of Australia's cricketing history was opened in 1989 in Sir Donald Bradman's presence. Cricketing memorabilia ranges from an oak cricket bat of the 1750s to the helmet worn by Allan Border during the 1989 Ashes series.

WINGECARRIBEE HOUSE Built in 1857 for Henry Molesworth Oxley, this single-storey house, made of timber and iron, was pre-fabricated in England and erected on the site at Bowral where it still stands.

FESTIVALS Jazz Festival, November; Tulip Time Festival, Spring.

BURRAGORANG LOOKOUT AND SANDSTONE TUNNEL ■ 66

The commanding views from Burragorang Lookout, with its rugged setting among steep gorges leading down to the Wollondilly River, have long made it a favourite stopping place for those on the road from Mittagong to Wombeyan Caves.

As early as 1900, to encourage the infant tourist industry, the local authorities attempted to make the Wombeyan Caves more accessible by building a narrow coach road between Mittagong and the caves.

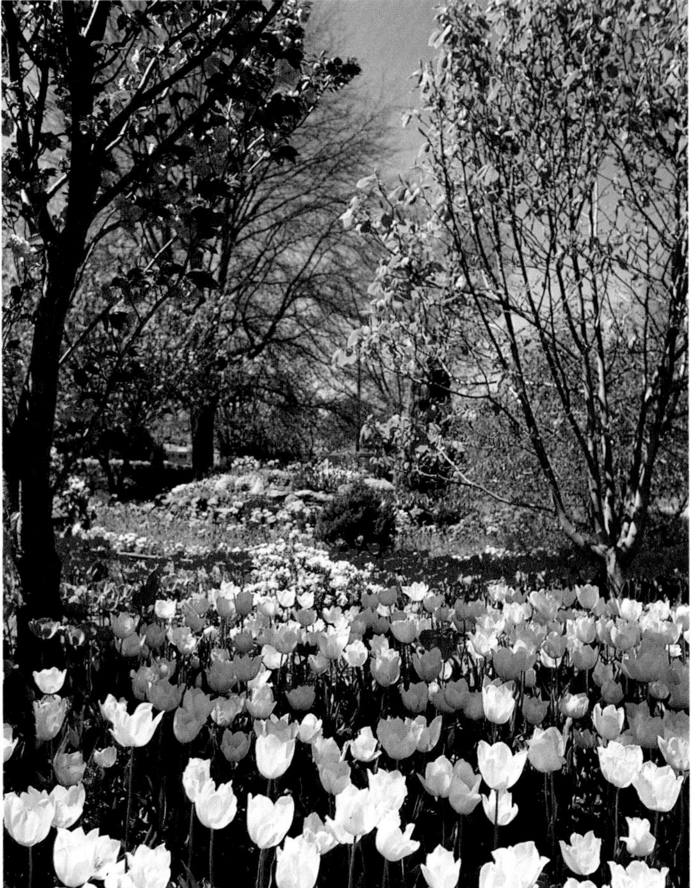

In spring, garden lovers flock to Bowral's public parks; the town's frosty winters bring out the best in tulips and other cool-climate bulbous plants.

Halfway along the road a tunnel was cut through a sandstone ridge and opened in 1900. The one-vehicle wide tunnel is still in use (see *Goulburn & Crookwell*).

BURRAWANG ■ 67

Originally a timber town built on private land, Burrawang was first settled in the 1860s and by the 1880s was an important settlement with its own debating club, school of arts and a vigilance committee. Rain delayed the consecration of the church, built in 1886, and it was finally consecrated 100 years later. Highly coloured tales of bunyips in the nearby Wingecarribee swamp were once told with relish by early settlers.

BUXTON ■ 68

The main event in this rural village is the Annual Buxton Village Fair, the high point of which is a mock bushranger attack on the steam train which makes a trip through the village on that day.

Founded in 1882, Buxton is on the loop line from Picton to Mittagong and is bypassed by the main railway line. *Population 1010*

COLO VALE ■ 69

Until recently a rural village at the foot of the mountains, and the most southerly of all the small stations bypassed by the main rail line and 'stranded' on the Picton–Mittagong loop line, Colo Vale is now a growing residential area.

The name Colo comes from an Aboriginal word for 'a hill formed by a flow of volcanic rock'. The name was first used in 1837 by a settler who purchased land there and named his property Colo. With its rich volcanic soils Colo Vale grew steadily in the late nineteenth century so that by the early 1890s the settlement had a church, a store and a butcher's shop. A school was opened in 1911 and in the 1920s a number of English immigrants settled in Colo Vale to farm poultry. *Population 690*

EXETER ■ 70

In 1822 James Badgery arrived in what is now Exeter with 103 cows.

Until 1889 they remained almost the sole inhabitants but in that year the first subdivisions of land took place and other settlers began to arrive. When the railway line came through the village was known as Badgery's Siding but was later named nostalgically after Exeter in England because of its English greenness which was enhanced by the many deciduous trees brought by the early settlers.

Many of the buildings in Exeter date from last century, among them St Aidan's Anglican Church with its beautiful stained glass windows; a tiny fragment of stone from St Peter's Cathedral in Exeter, England is on display.

HILL TOP ■ 71

As the name implies, there is a steep gradient up to Hill Top, which was exploited by bushrangers. As the trains on the old southern railway line puffed at almost a walking pace up the steep slope to Hill Top, a bushranger had ample opportunity to hop on the train, relieve the passengers of their valuables and step off before the alarm was sounded, all without risk to life or limb.

Hill Top is the site of a twenty-four metre railway cutting, the deepest cutting in mainland Australia. Three men were killed in an explosion during blasting of the cutting and their names, carved into a rock face alongside the railway track, are preserved in perpetuity. Hill Top is now, as ever, a quiet country village, mainly residential and surrounded by unspoiled bushland. *Population 920*

CAVE CREEK A walking track from Hill Top to Cave Creek leads to a small cave through which the creek passes...but which bushwalkers are advised not to follow. Near the cave entrance is some black wattle, which was used in the making of rustic wattle and daub houses in the early days of settlement.

JOADJA ■ 72

Now a ghost town and on private property, Joadja was once a thriving shale-oil mining and refining town. In 1903, competition from imported kerosene from the United States, the increasing competition from electricity and the high cost of running the unsubsidised rail line from the mine site to Mittagong led to the premature closure of the mine.

A fire swept through the ghost town in 1906 destroying all the timber dwellings built for the mainly Scottish miners. Now all that remains at Joadja are the old stone church and schoolhouse, a row of stone-built miners' cottages and the remains of the shale oil workings including the kilns and flues.

MACQUARIE PASS NATIONAL PARK ■ 73

The park stands on the Illawarra escarpment that rises abruptly from the coastal plain to a height of 700 metres. The Illawarra Highway passes through Macquarie Pass National Park in a series of hairpin – and hair-raising – bends.

The park has remnants of subtropical rainforest, wet eucalyptus forest, woodland and scrubland, and these varied habitats support an impressive diversity of animal and birdlife.

Parts of the park were logged in the nineteenth century but some of these logged areas, including areas of the now rare red cedar, are regenerating. Old logging trails, spectacular waterfalls, rapids and more tranquil swimming holes make the park a popular recreational spot.

The Southern Highlands' altitude benefits orchardists as well as gardeners: a cold winter 'crisps' the fruit which follows the spring blossoms.

MITTAGONG ■ 74

Sitting in a natural amphitheatre formed by Mounts Gibraltar (see entry) and Alexandra, Mittagong was once a favourite staging point for passenger coaches on the road to Goulburn; although no longer horse-drawn, tourist coaches still use Mittagong as a resting and watering place for their passengers.

The first Europeans to explore the Mittagong region in 1798 were John Wilson, a former convict and John Price, a servant of Governor Phillip. The main purpose of their journey from the Camden district was to lead a self-selected group of convicts to prove, once and for all, that China – and presumably, freedom – did not lie in that direction.

The first pig iron was produced in Australia at the Fitzroy ironworks in Mittagong in 1848 from local bog iron ore deposits smelted with charcoal. Articles made from Mittagong iron ore were exhibited at the Paris Exhibition in 1854. Unlike Moss Vale and Bowral, therefore, Mittagong – originally called New Sheffield after the town in England from where most of the ironworkers came – was already well established by the time the railway line was opened in 1867.

With the opening of the railway line the town's name was changed to Mittagong meaning 'little mountain' or 'many dogs'. The contribution of the ironworkers has not been forgotten; there is a memorial to them in Ironmines Oval with a sign stamped on the first cold-rolled sheet of stainless steel produced in Australia. *Population 5670*

LAKE ALEXANDRA Lake Alexandra is a man-made lake one kilometre from the centre of Mittagong. Originally it was constructed as a dam to supply water for the engines hauling coal to the Fitzroy iron works. At the foot of Lake Alexandra is a nature reserve and the starting point for a number of bush walks.

STURT CRAFT WORKSHOPS Set up in 1941 by Winifred West, founder of the girls' school Frensham (also in Mittagong), the workshops operate as an artistic community. The workshops exhibit and sell a wide range of craftwork created by resident or associated artists as well as running craft classes.

MOSS VALE ■ 75

A naval surgeon turned grazier called Charles Throsby was possibly the first European to see what is now Moss Vale – he was certainly the first to receive a land grant there. The town, however, was not named after him but after Jemmy Moss, a herdsman employed by Throsby and one of the oldest residents when the town was named in the 1860s.

Moss Vale is the headquarters of Wingecarribee Shire, which includes Bowral, Mittagong and Moss Vale as well as the surrounding rural area. Moss Vale Showground is now host to agricultural shows, rodeos, and stock and cattle sales for the surrounding district, which is famous for its horse, beef and dairy cattle studs. The annual Moss Vale Agricultural Show held in March attracts many who are heading for the Royal Easter Show in Sydney at that time of the year. *Population 5690*

TUDOR HOUSE SCHOOL The novelist, Patrick White, spent his schooldays here '...far enough away from Sydney to foment terror in the heart of a timid, introspective child' he wrote later. The school moved in 1901 to the house just outside Moss Vale, which had been built by a son-in-law of Charles Throsby.

THROSBY PARK HOUSE Built in 1834 by Charles Throsby, a nephew of the original Charles Throsby, Throsby Park House has remained in the Throsby family although it is now administered by the National Parks and Wildlife Service. Major restoration work was completed in 1990.

MOUNT GIBRALTAR ■ 76

Mount Gibraltar, between Bowral and Mittagong, is the highest point between the Illawarra coast and the Great Dividing Range. It rises to 863 metres above sea level and on clear days the mountain provides views as far as Sydney and the Blue Mountains to the north and north-west, the Cuckbundoon Range to the south-west, and Mount Keira, above Wollongong, to the east.

The local Aboriginal name for the hill was 'Bowrell' meaning 'high' but it was referred to as Mount Gibraltar by the local stockmen and may have been given this name by John Oxley who, with his naval background, possibly noted its similarity to the Rock of Gibraltar in the Mediterranean. When Bowral, the settlement at the foot of the mount, was named, the stockmen's name stuck and Mount Gibraltar is now known locally as 'the Gib'.

Originally much of Mount Gibraltar was freehold land but in 1921 the then Mayor of Bowral, Joshua Stokes, presented twenty-five hectares to the people of Bowral as a reserve. The north, west and south faces are used for the quarrying of microsyenite, commonly called trachyte, a hard, durable, fine-grained light grey stone, volcanic in origin. A telecom repeater station now surmounts the top of Mount Gibraltar.

NEPEAN RESERVOIR ■ 77

This is the only reservoir in the upper Nepean catchment that results from a dam on the Nepean River itself. The reservoir is impounded by an eighty-one-metre-high concrete dam and holds over eighty thousand megalitres of water.

The dam area is open to the public and recreational facilities at the reservoir include picnic areas, barbecues, gardens and children's playgrounds.

TAHMOOR ■ 78

Tahmoor was an Aboriginal name for 'bronzewing pigeon'and the name was used by one of the larger landowners in the area, James Crispe, when he built his residence Tahmoor Park House in 1824. The house, of weatherboard on stone foundations, later became an inn for travellers on the Great South Road.

Although bypassed by the Hume Highway, Tahmoor is still on the

Some of the Wollondilly River's water, seen here in spate near Mittagong, flows from Sydney's taps after being stored in Lake Burragorang.

main rail line from Picton to Mittagong, which has contributed to its fairly recent growth from a small rural village to a developing residential area. *Population 3410*

THIRLMERE ■ 79

This rural village was originally called 'Redbank' and how or when the name Thirlmere, a lake in Cumberland in northern England, came to be used is uncertain.

The original Southern Railway from Picton ran through Thirlmere and contractors used hand drills and gunpowder to blast their way into the sandstone ridges around the town. Thirlmere railway station is classified by the National Trust and the only trains now passing through it are the occasional excursion steam trains which run from Sydney to Thirlmere on the old loop line.

The coming of the railway was the most significant influence on Thirlmere and it is appropriate that, in 1975, the Rail Transport Museum was moved from Sydney to its present site at Thirlmere. *Population 1590*

RAIL TRANSPORT MUSEUM With financial support from the New South Wales State Rail Authority, as well as corporate and individual sponsorship, this unique museum has a long-term lease of railway property at Thirlmere. There are fifty steam, electric and diesel locomotives, carriages and waggons on permanent display along with many smaller items of railway memorabilia which attract over 100 000 visitors each year.

THIRLMERE LAKES NATIONAL PARK ■ 80

The five 'hanging' lakes in this park were formed at a bend in an ancient river valley, which was uplifted over two million years ago, isolating the lakes from the river's main drainage system. Mud and sedges then broke up the body of water into the five lakes there today.

The five narrow, interconnecting freshwater lakes average a mere three metres deep and are seven metres at their deepest. Lake Nerrigorang (from an Aboriginal name for 'shaky ground'), Lake Baraba ('tall sedges') and Lake Gandangarra (from a local tribal name) are overgrown with waterweed; Lake Werri Berri (a tribal name) is used for power boating and Lake Couridjah ('nectar from banksias') is for swimmers and canoeists.

The naturalist George Caley visited the lakes in 1802 and commented on the tall sedges and unusual flora. A rare waterlily known as the wooly frogmouth and a species of sponge found only in this area are now protected within the boundaries of the 630-hectare park. Microscopic plant and animal life in the lakes supports mosquito fish, gudgeons and catfish. The park is used for scientific research and education as well as recreational pursuits.

WINGECARRIBEE RESERVOIR ■ 81

Various spellings of Wingecarribee have been used since Governor Macquarie's day – he himself used the name 'Winge Karrabee' in 1816. The official spelling now used is the name given by John Oxley, then Surveyor-General, to his property in the district, which was also used by his successor Thomas Mitchell in his map of the district in 1834. The name is generally thought to mean 'waters to rest beside'.

Wingecarribee Reservoir was built in 1974 as part of the Shoalhaven River catchment. The increase in population in Sydney and Wollongong made the Shoalhaven Scheme a necessity. Water is now transferred from the Shoalhaven to Wingecarribee Reservoir by means of three pumping stations, two of which also generate hydro-electricity. The water is then fed from the Wingecarribee Reservoir, which can hold up to 33 500 megalitres of water to the giant Nepean and Warragamba Reservoirs by means of existing watercourses.

The earth and rockfill dam on the Wingecarribee River is seventeen metres high and over a thousand metres long.

WOLLONDILLY RIVER ■ 82

Originally called Wallandilli from an Aboriginal word meaning 'water trickling over rocks', the Wollondilly River trickles on to greatness since it represents the start of the 480-kilometre long Hawkesbury-Nepean River system.

Rising east of Crookwell, the Wollondilly flows south and then east through Goulburn (the only major settlement on its banks) before setting its course in a northwards direction for its rendezvous with the waters of Lake Burragorang.

In its upper reaches the Wollondilly flows through a landscape of gently undulating agricultural land before plunging into deep gorges in the middle section and finally coming to an enforced halt in the vast artificial lake created by the mighty Warragamba Dam (see *Campbelltown & Camden*) – exciting journey for what starts as a little trickle.

YERRINBOOL ■ 83

Yerrinbool and the neighbouring Yanderra are small apple-growing villages on the old Hume Highway. Enterprising orchardists capitalise on their position by setting up roadside stalls to sell their produce. The owner of one orchard at Yerrinbool sometimes 'rents' trees to customers who pay an annual fee – $50 in 1991 – for picking rights to the fruit borne on their tree.

Yerrinbool railway station was opened in 1919 and with this stimulus, the small community attracted a school, store and sawmill by the early 1920s. *Population 600*

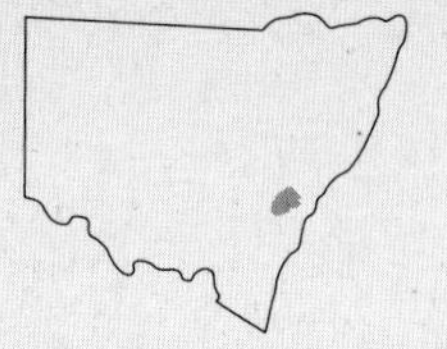

Katoomba & Blaxland

The major transport routes over the Blue Mountains are like time-lines, crowded with historic sites and haunted with memories of the dramatic events that mark the history of these hard-won thoroughfares.

BELLS LINE OF ROAD ■ 84

The intriguingly named Bells Line of Road follows a route plotted by Archibald Bell, the younger – one of the early landowners in the district – in 1823 and is still the only alternative to the Great Western Highway route over the Blue Mountains; the highway winds over almost the same course trudged in 1813 by Blaxland, Wentworth and Lawson, the first men to cross the mountains.

Closely following the original path explored by Bell, the modern road runs from Windsor to Lithgow, following the ridge of Kurrajong Heights and after passing Mounts Tomah and King George, connects with the Great Western Highway at Lithgow. For a long time, Bells Line was used only as a stock route and it was not until the Second World War that a road was built for strategic purposes. The sealed road in use today was constructed to relieve the traffic on the main highway.

Bells Line of Road passes the Mount Tomah annexe of the Sydney Royal Botanic Gardens and is sometimes known as the 'Garden Route' over the mountains. Unlike the heavily trafficked main highway, it passes through a combination of sparsely settled country landscapes and bushland, thus offering quite a different, but not uninteresting view of the spectacular mountain landscape.

BLACKHEATH ■ 85

Some of the most awe-inspiring scenery in the Blue Mountains is to be found near the pretty resort town of Blackheath – the highest town in the mountains The nearby Govetts Leap (see entry) and Evans Lookout offer breathtaking views of the Grose Valley (see entry) and the sentimentally named Bridal Veil Falls (not to be confused with the Bridal Veil Falls at Leura) which plunges in a milk-white column of water, 190 metres to the valley floor, making it the longest single-drop fall in the mountains.

For a very brief time the site of Blackheath was known as Hounslow – both names were chosen by Governor Macquarie. On his journey from Sydney to inspect the site of Bathurst in 1815, Macquarie camped in the area and wrote in his journal: '...It having rather a wild heath-like appearance, I have named it Hounslow'. Sixteen days later, on his return from Bathurst, he camped again at the same spot and, forgetting that he had already named it, wrote in his journal: '...This place having a black, wild appearance I have this day named it Black-Heath'.

The establishment of an inn in the early 1830s made Blackheath a popular stopping place for travellers and in the 1840s a large convict stockade was constructed. The little settlement bloomed after the opening of the railway in 1869 and the area became readily accessible to Sydneysiders who had already begun to use the mountains for recreational purposes. Today, Blackheath is well known for its comfortable guesthouses and annual rhododendron festival held in November. *Population 3750*

FESTIVALS Rhododendron Festival, November.

BLAXLAND ■ 86

Much of the history and development of the Blue Mountains can be traced through the gradual evolution of the railway line, construction of which commenced in 1867. The first station platforms were placed next to or near roadside inns and were named after them. In time, settlements grew around these stations and eventually developed into the townships of today. Blaxland was originally known as Wascoes after John Outrim Wascoe, proprietor of the nearby Pilgrim Inn on Lapstone Hill. The change was made in 1879 when an increased awareness of the Blue Mountains' tourist potential prompted the renaming of three railway stations after the three mountain explorers, Blaxland, Wentworth and Lawson.

Today, Blaxland is essentially a commuter suburb of Sydney – a part of the broad urban corridor flanking the main highway and railway as they follow the steep ridges to the top of the plateau. *Population 6880*

BLUE MOUNTAINS NATIONAL PARK ■ 87

The huge wilderness area that makes up the Blue Mountains National Park – some 245 719 hectares – takes in some of the most ruggedly spectacular terrain in Australia. Sliced in two by the east-west scar of the Great Western Highway, there is a constant tug-of-war along this urban strip between the desire to preserve the untouched bushland and the developmental demands of increasingly populated residential areas.

The distinctive blue haze that has earned the Blue Mountains its name is caused by slowly evaporating droplets of eucalyptus oil in the air. The dense eucalypt forests in the valleys and ridges constantly disperse these fine droplets into the atmosphere. The droplets, together with fine dust particles suspended in the air, cause the sun's rays to be scattered more evenly, intensifying the usual light refraction phenomenon which causes distant objects to appear blue.

Dominating the rural landscape from the Southern Highlands to the Hunter Valley, the Blue Mountains are in fact, not mountains at all – but the ridges of a monumental sandstone plateau. The deep gorges plunging waterfalls and wandering valleys of today are the result of millions of years of erosion by wind and water. From the 1860s, the Blue Mountains was for many people a peaceful haven away from the city. Botanists and naturalists were interested in the area throughout the nineteenth and early twentieth centuries but a concerted effort to create a national park did not come until the 1930s, with the efforts of the pio-

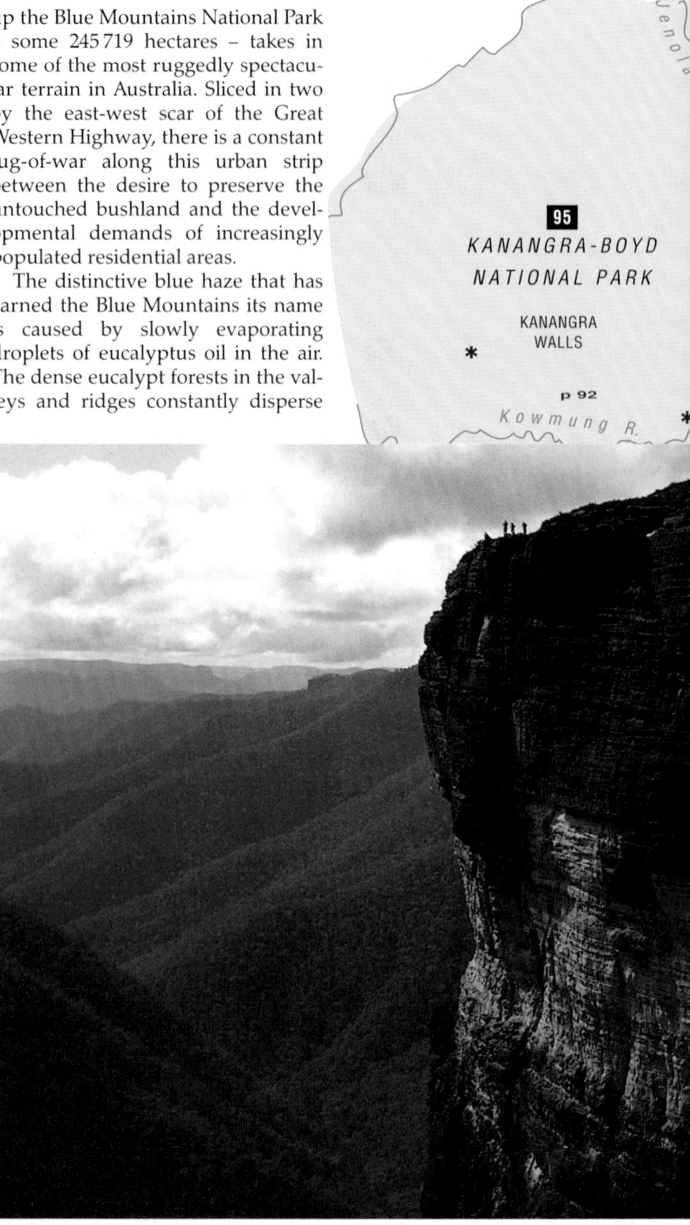

The Kanangra Walls – complete with a 'blue' mountain haze – form the western edge of the relentlessly eroded plateau of the Blue 'Mountains'.

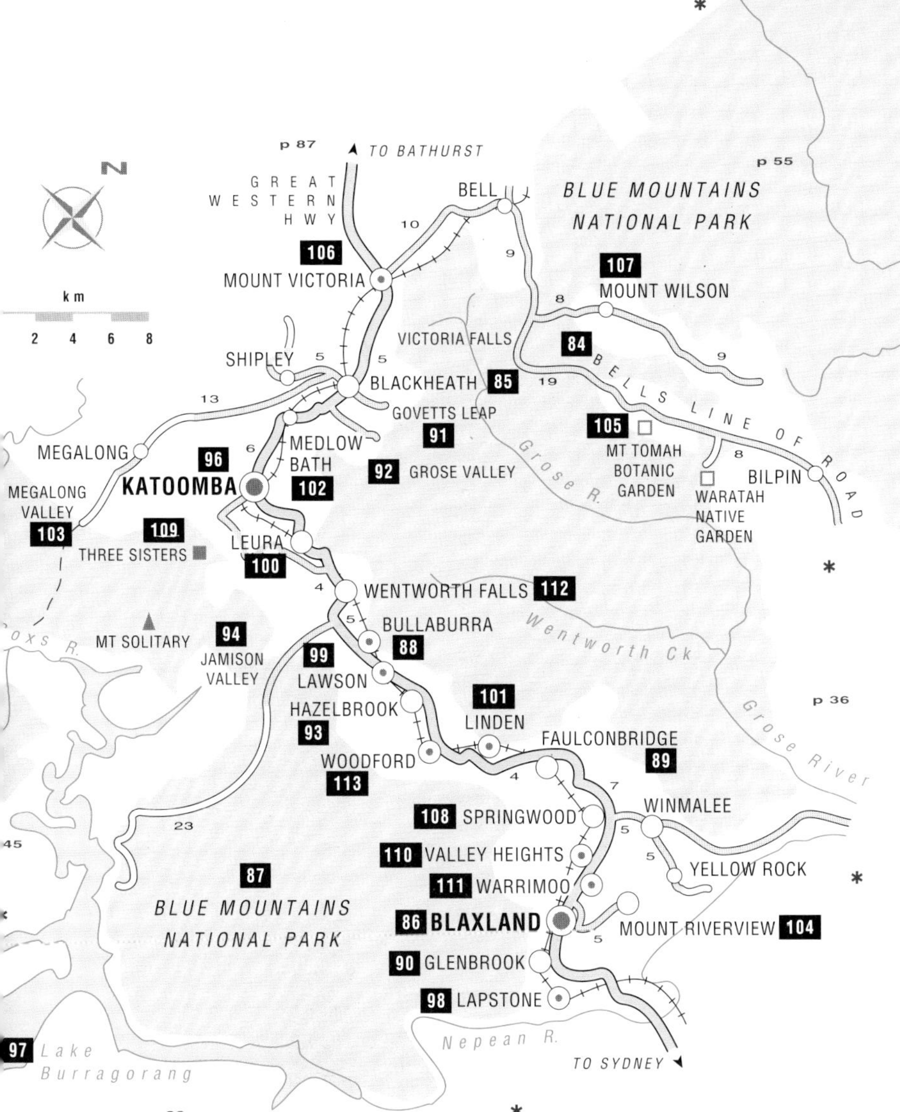

Images and forms that scandalised one generation are now on display to another at the former Blue Mountains home of the artist Norman Lindsay.

Almost 1000 metres above the humid coastal plain a Japanese maple thrives at the Mount Tomah garden.

neer conservationist Miles Dunphy. The Blue Mountains National Park was finally gazetted in 1967.

In recent years, some conservation groups have argued that the park should be nominated for World Heritage listing, mainly because of its ancient gorges and cliffs which are much older than the more famous Grand Canyon of the United States.

BULLABURRA ■ 88

Sir Henry Parkes originally owned land in the area, giving it the name Village of Colridge. Later, a real estate company developed the site as 'Bullaburra', an Aboriginal word said to mean 'blue sky'.

Blaxland, Wentworth and Lawson passed through the area on their expedition over the Blue Mountains in 1813 and the site of one of their camps is thought to lie near the town. *Population 940*

FAULCONBRIDGE ■ 89

Sir Henry Parkes, the founder of Australian Federation and five times Premier of New South Wales, had his main residence at Faulconbridge – a little town he named after his mother, Martha Faulconbridge. His grave is near the railway station and adjacent to the Prime Ministers' Avenue of Oaks in Jackson Park – a peaceful, commemorative corridor where every prime minister (or their nearest surviving relative) has planted an oak tree since the park was created in 1933. The nearby Norman Lindsay Gallery and Museum was once the home of the controversial artist and writer. *Population 3390*

NORMAN LINDSAY GALLERY AND MUSEUM Norman Lindsay was an enthusiastic artist, author and opponent of wowsers. His home and studio in Chapman Parade is now a National Trust property displaying a large collection of memorabilia and examples of his work.

GLENBROOK ■ 90

As with many of the towns and villages in the lower Blue Mountains, Glenbrook commenced life as a stop on the old Lapstone Zig-Zag Railway. Initially known as Watertank, the railway stop was just that – a place where water was piped from nearby Glenbrook Lagoon into storage tanks for the steam engines that arduously chugged up the Zig-Zag line. The construction of a crossing loop in 1847 led to the renaming of the stop as Wascoe's Siding, after the licensee of the nearby Pilgrim Inn. A passenger platform that was erected in 1877 prompted yet another name change, this time to Brookdale. This successive name-changing finally ceased in 1879 when Glenbrook was adopted over all other comers.

The nearby Lennox Bridge – an essential link in Surveyor-General Mitchell's original highway across the mountains – is the oldest stone arch bridge on the Australian mainland. David Lennox, whose name is inscribed in the keystone, was commissioned to design and build the bridge with the aid of twenty convicts whom he first had to instruct in the artful craft of stonemasonry. Completed in 1833, less than twelve months after work began, the bridge was part of the route that carried all traffic bound for the west until 1926, when a new deviation was built along an abandoned, but still useful, railway line. Still in continuous use more than 150 years later, Lennox Bridge is a working tribute to the man who designed it. *Population 5090*

RED HANDS CAVE This Aboriginal site near the Glenbrook entrance to the Blue Mountains National Park, takes its name from the natural ochre hand prints and hand stencils lining the cave walls.

GOVETTS LEAP ■ 91

The dramatic legend of Govetts Leap tells of an escaped convict-turned-bushranger named Govett who, pursued by troopers, found himself trapped on the edge of a 300-metre cliff. Preferring death to capture, he wheeled his horse around and together they leapt over the edge. The real story behind the name is much more prosaic – in fact, the place takes its name from the colonial Assistant Surveyor, William Govett, who discovered it in 1831.

GROSE VALLEY ■ 92

The first explorer of this densely wooded valley surrounded by craggy edges was William Paterson, who led an expedition up the Grose River in September 1793, thinking it might be a gateway into the interior. It was not – as his party discovered after portaging their boats around five waterfalls within the first sixteen kilometres. Sixty years passed before the valley was broached again – this time with a view to building a railway line that would connect with a tunnel through Darlings Causeway to Hartley on the western side of the Blue Mountains. A preliminary survey conducted by the Royal Engineers in 1857 revealed how rough the valley terrain was, so a track along its length was created to make further survey work easier. The Engineers Track, as it became known, took much longer than anticipated to complete. Forty-nine labourers and ten surveyors worked on the project for almost three years – at the end of which the Grose Valley was deemed an unsuitable railway route and a line constructed elsewhere! The track is rarely used nowadays and much of it has been erased over the years by flood and fire.

HAZELBROOK ■ 93

Hazelbrook is surrounded by the natural splendours of the mountains and has long been a popular holiday resort. Close to the township are a number of colourfully named waterfalls such as Horseshoe, Glow Worm Nook and Fairy Falls. Like many of the lower-mountain towns, Hazelbrook has, to some extent, become a commuter suburb of Sydney as the broad, urban corridor flanking the main highway and railway line spreads ever further west of the state capital. *Population 4130*

JAMISON VALLEY ■ 94

The naval surgeon and pioneer pastoralist Sir John Jamison was one of the party that accompanied Governor Macquarie on his historic 1815 journey to Bathurst along the road that Cox had just completed. During the journey, Macquarie named many of the geographical features in the Blue Mountains and on reaching the area known as Weatherboard Hut (now Wentworth Falls), came upon a high tableland overlooking a vast valley. He renamed the valley Jamison Valley for his companion and also gave Jamison's name to the creek that runs beside the valley.

KANANGRA-BOYD NATIONAL PARK ■ 95

Kanangra-Boyd National Park protects a wild and rugged wilderness and is the southernmost of the 'Blue Mountains' group of national parks. The views from Kanangra Walls Plateau – the central and dominant feature of the Kanangra-Boyd National Park – are among the finest in the Blue Mountains region. The sheer cliffs that line the flanks of the plateau jut out to expose the geological history of the area in a striking way. A number of spectacular waterfalls cascade from the weathered plateau through narrow canyons into the depths of Kanangra Gorge. The broad Boyd Plateau, an impressive granite dome varying from 1100 to 1200 metres high, lies in the northwest region of the park and supports a number of rare animal and plant species. The magnificent wilderness qualities of Kanangra-Boyd National Park have made it very popular with bushwalkers, who have christened many of the rugged peaks with vividly descriptive names such as Cloudmaker, Stormbreaker and the ominous-sounding Paralyser.

KATOOMBA ■ 96

To most people, Katoomba is synonymous with the Blue Mountains and it is certainly the region's residential and commercial centre. The town straddles the ridge along which the road and railway run to the western plains, surrounded by some of the most impressive landscapes in the district. The milk-white columns of numerous waterfalls spill over the nearby valley cliffs which are dotted with lookouts offering magnificent views of the sheer sandstone walls – hence the name Katoomba which is a corruption of the Aboriginal word, *godoomba* meaning 'falling water' or 'coming together of many streams'.

Katoomba began life in 1876 as a railway platform with the robust name of 'Crushers' – a reference to the nearby quarries that supplied ballast for the railway extension constructed between Wentworth Falls and Lithgow in 1869 – but was renamed Katoomba the following year. Prior to this, land in the area of the present town was used as a pound for cattle from the western plains being driven to the Sydney markets. The magnificent location and ready access to prime points of tourist interest soon saw Katoomba develop into a major holiday resort for annual vacations, a position it enjoyed for the next sixty years. In 1882, the elegant Carrington Hotel was built – it was the first tourist hotel in the Blue Mountains and is still a focal point of the town.

In 1889, Katoomba was declared a municipality, the first township in the mountains to gain such a status. After the Second World War, the surge in car ownership made the mountain towns much more accessible to day trippers, and brought about a decline of the great hotels. Nowadays, a resurgence of interest in the mountains as a readily accessible holiday retreat, has resulted in many of the old hotels and guesthouses enjoying a new lease of life. *Population 8300*

ECHO POINT A concrete viewing-platform extends beyond the cliff edge at Echo Point to give unsurpassed though to some, vertiginous views of a few of the best-known and most frequently photographed natural formations in the mountains, including the Three Sisters, the Megalong and Jamison Valleys (see entries) and Narrow Neck Peninsula.

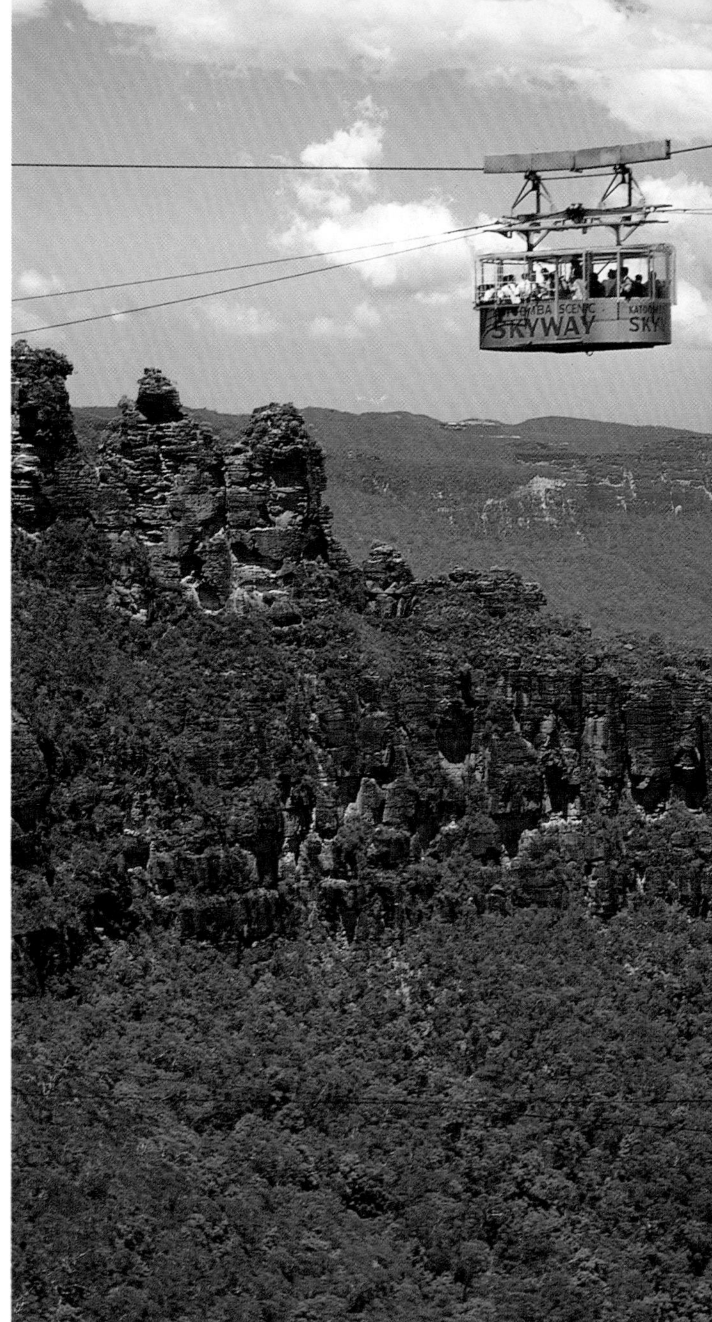

A cable-car gives intrepid tourists a different angle on some old favourites.

EXPLORERS' TREE Only the stump of this historic blackbutt, into which William Lawson carved his initials in 1813, has survived as a reminder of the trio's landmark journey across the Blue Mountains. It is located on Pulpit Hill, just outside Katoomba.

PARAGON RESTAURANT This famous restaurant and chocolate shop in Katoomba's main street is one of the most sumptuously finished Art Deco buildings in Australia. Established by the Simos family in 1916, the Paragon has been renowned since the 1920s for its handmade chocolates and confectionery. Consisting of three main rooms, all of which are classified by the National Trust, the cafe has cosy timber-panelled booths that depict scenes from Greek mythology, leadlight display cabinets and a cocktail bar that once boasted the first sprung dance floor in Australia.

SCENIC RAILWAY A sign proclaims the scenic railway at Katoomba as 'the steepest incline railway in the world'. The 'carriages' plunge almost vertically 250 metres down a 410-metre track through a lush, tree-clad gorge into the trough of the Jamison Valley. Constructed in the 1880s, the track was originally used for hauling coal skips from the valley floor.

SCENIC SKYWAY Installed in 1957, the Scenic Skyway was the first passenger carrying horizontal cableway in the Southern Hemisphere. Leaving the cliff edge near Orphan rock, the cable-car crosses the Jamison Valley offering a spectacular birds-eye view of the Three Sisters, Katoomba Falls and the rugged valley floor, 300 metres below.

THE CARRINGTON HOTEL This grand old hotel with its lofty ceilings, intricate leadlight glass and graceful colonnaded verandah, embodies all the graciousness of a bygone era. Opened in 1882, it was the first tourist hotel built in Katoomba. Now classified by the National Trust, it was originally called the Great Western Hotel, but was renamed The Carrington in 1886 in honour of the Governor of New South Wales, Lord Carrington, who made the hotel his mountain retreat. During its early years, Katoomba had the hotel to thank for its water and electricity supply, both of which were provided initially for the hotel and by default, the rest of the town.

LAKE BURRAGORANG ■ 97

Lake Burragorang is the largest city water supply reservoir in Australia, having nearly four times the capacity of Sydney Harbour and covering 7500 hectares of land as compared with the harbour's 5700 hectares. The lake is in the southern section of the Blue Mountains National Park and was created in 1960 with the completion of the Warragamba Dam (see *Campbelltown & Camden*) near the junction of the Warragamba and Nepean Rivers. The huge body of water impounded by the dam was named Lake Burragorang after the valley it submerged. Despite its size, the Lake provides only a part of Sydney's water needs, though its water also generates electricity at a power station at Warragamba.

LAPSTONE ■ 98

The sudden increase in steepness of the ascent at Lapstone has always presented a problem in the construction of transport routes along the spinal ridge of the Blue Mountains. Seven routes have been constructed since Cox's original convict road in 1814–15, including four roads, two railway lines and a railway deviation constructed in 1891. Approaches to tackling the steep ascent at Lapstone Hill often showed great ingenuity – in particular that used by John Whitton, Engineer-in-Chief for the New South Wales Railways – in the construction of the first railway line over the Blue Mountains in 1867.

Whitton decided upon zig-zags, which were much cheaper to construct than a tunnel. The Lapstone Hill Zig-Zag Railway was constructed in the form of a simple letter 'Z', with two reversing points. Trains had to shunt forward along the first part, reverse up the next, and shunt forward up the final leg to reach the hill top. In this way the train ascended a height which would have been an impossible climb on a conventional railway line.

The zig-zag method of railway construction had its limitations however, especially with the introduction of more powerful locomotives able to pull much longer trains that could not be accommodated within the zig-zag dead ends. Consequently, the Lapstone Zig-Zag Railway fell into disuse when a tunnel was constructed through part of Lapstone Hill in 1891. This infamous railway deviation lasted only until 1913. The tunnel was 800 metres long with no ventilation, and the noxious build-up of smoke and steam often meant near suffocation for the passengers and crews. Nowadays the tunnel is used for growing mushrooms and the zig-zag railway is a signposted walking track. *Population 1110*

KNAPSACK BRIDGE This colossal viaduct built in 1867 to leap a deep gully at Knapsack Creek was originally the first part of the zig-zag railway up Lapstone Hill – now it carries motor traffic as part of the Great Western Highway. Designed by John Whitton, the huge sandstone structure consists of seven arches spanning a total length of more than 120 metres. The viaduct was acquired by the Department of Main Roads and opened as a road bridge in 1926.

Bushwalkers follow a rough track to gaze on the gentle drop of Kalang Falls – fed by rainfall on the heights of Kanangra Plateau.

LAWSON ■ 99

Lawson was originally a railway platform named, of all things, Blue Mountains – a fact which may have prompted early visitors to expect a profusion of natural attractions at their doorstep.

The platform was one of the first stopping places on the railway line over the mountains built in 1867 and took its name from a nearby inn.

As a tribute to William Lawson, the surveyor in the party of three that successfully crossed the range in 1813, the platform was renamed Lawson in 1879.

By the 1880s, a number of boarding houses were established near the station and Lawson became a popular resting place for frail invalids for whom the mountain air was generally considered to be a beneficial tonic. *Population 2230*

LEURA ■ 100

Leura has developed into a true village maintaining a quite separate identity from Katoomba – despite being connected to that town by the Cliff Drive that snakes along the edge of the Jamison Valley. The town came into existence with the opening of Leura Railway Station in 1891 – the name is said to be an Aboriginal word meaning 'lava', relating to the large number of volcanic stones found in the area. Central to the modern village is the Leura Village Mall, a restored shopping street reminiscent of the 1920s, lined with turn-of-the-century buildings decorated in traditional heritage colours which house an eclectic mix of galleries, craft and gift shops, antique shops, tea rooms and restaurants.

Another historically significant street is Olympian Parade. The street borders the brink of the Jamison Valley and in the early 1900s was the address of a hospital specialising in the treatment of tuberculosis. The hospital was established by Matron Robison whose husband had been treated – unfortunately at too late a stage to effect a cure for his affliction – at a sanitorium in Europe. Matron Robison returned to Australia confident that the altitude and crisp air of the Blue Mountains would provide a recuperative environment for tuberculosis patients in Australia.

Leura's proximity to Katoomba, combined with the natural splendour of its mountain setting, has made the town a very popular resort and convention centre. The nearby Leura Cascades and Gordon Falls Reserve are two of the most visited locations in the area. *Population 3620*

EVERGLADES GARDENS Planted in the 1930s and now owned by the National Trust, the prettily named Everglades Gardens were designed by Paul Sorenson, generally agreed to be Australia's finest exponent of cold-climate landscape architecture. European-style sandstone terraces step down the steep terrain and paths wind through gardens planted with native plants as well as imported species, and a watercourse runs into a grotto pool.

LEURALLA This historic mansion in Olympian Parade is considered by many to be one of the finest buildings in the Blue Mountains. Within its sumptuous Art Deco interior is a collection of nineteenth century Australian art and historical objects as well as what is believed to be Australia's biggest collection of toys and railway memorabilia.

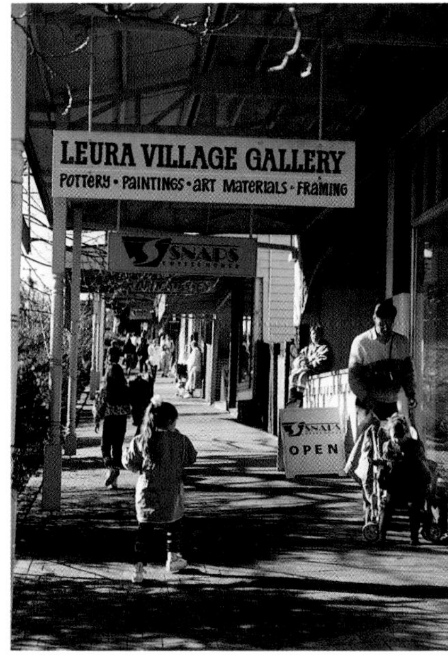

The atmosphere of the Blue Mountains' heyday is suggested most strongly in Leura where civic pride helps balance 'gentrification' and commercial practicalities.

LINDEN ■ 101

Caley's Repulse, King's Cave and Donohoe's Headstone all figure in the rich history of the Linden area.

Many journals of early explorers and travellers refer to the pile of stones known as Caley's Repulse, on the ridge at Linden, but the reason for its existence and its original location is a mystery. The cairn is named after early explorer, George Cawley, though there is no evidence to suggest that he was ever in the area, so it is highly unlikely that he built it. A popular theory held by some historians, that the mound of stones was created by Aborigines, offers yet another explanation.

The present cairn was constructed by members of the Australian Historical Society in 1912, to commemorate the famous triumvirate's (the explorers Blaxland, Lawson and

The name and architecture of the 'Hydro' is redolent of a bygone age when turn-of-the century customers came to 'take the waters' in the European fashion. The crisp mountain air is considered sufficient tonic these days.

Wentworth) crossing of the Blue Mountains nearly a century before.

The story surrounding King's Cave and Donohoe's Headstone is livelier. The 'headstone' is located near the path leading to King's Cave. According to local legend, Donohoe was a constable who met an unfortunate end when shot by a bushranger named King. King's connection with the cave is very vague and it is more likely that the cave's name comes from the King's Own Regiment who used it as a shelter when guarding convict road-builders.

The modern township of Linden grew up around the railway station that was opened in 1874. Various names were given to the platform including Seventeen Mile Hollow, Linden Tank, Henderson's Platform and finally, Linden – after the nearby Linden Lodge. *Population 1000*

MEDLOW BATH ■ 102

One of the most extravagant buildings in the Blue Mountains area is located in the tiny village of Medlow Bath – the grand old Hydro Majestic Hotel. The site was originally the home of Edward Hargraves – whose extensive publicity of the discovery of gold near Bathurst triggered Australia's first gold rush – and after his death in 1891 the Belgravia Hotel was constructed on land next to his house. Ten years later, Mark Foy (of the Mark Foy's retail store in Sydney) purchased the Belgravia, Hargraves' house and the cottage between the two buildings, and combined them into an establishment offering the very latest hydropathic therapies from Europe. Operating from about 1903, this continental-style sanitorium was responsible for the renaming of the nearby railway station as Medlow Bath, from plain 'Medlow', to indicate the fashionable 'spa' nature of the hotel complex.

Despite the popular notion of the Blue Mountains as a healthy environment where visitors could 'take the waters', the treatments offered did not draw much public response and the buildings were converted to a tourist hotel offering the more Australian leisure pursuits of tennis and bushwalking.

MEGALONG VALLEY ■ 103

Megalong is an Aboriginal word meaning 'the valley under the cliff'. Thomas Jones, a collector of plants and animals, made the first recorded European foray into the valley in 1818, but land was not taken up by settlers until 1838. The Aborigines and white settlers co-habited in the valley quite peacefully – a rare example of racial harmony at the time.

J.B. North operated mines in the Megalong and Jamison Valleys in the 1880s and 1890s and a thriving little settlement soon sprang up in the Megalong Valley to service the burgeoning industry. When the mines closed, much of the settlement was dismantled and a bushfire in 1904 consumed all that remained. More durable materials were used in the reconstruction of buildings in the district when the track from Blackheath was improved.

MOUNT RIVERVIEW ■ 104

The thick crust of towns and villages that clusters around the highway that follows the narrow ridge through the Blue Mountains is increasingly the target of people seeking a better lifestyle in the relaxed mountains communities. Although the inexorable creep of urban development has linked many of the older towns into an almost continuous urban strip, lateral development onto the surrounding slopes has been largely limited by the all-embracing, magnificent wilderness of the Blue Mountains group of national parks. Mount Riverview is a typical example of this urban spill-over, having developed as a residential annexe of Blaxland (see entry). *Population 3410*

MOUNT TOMAH BOTANIC GARDEN ■ 105

Mount Tomah Botanic Garden was established as a cool-climate garden by the Sydney Royal Botanic Gardens in 1988 as a bicentennial project. The gardens are seen as a scientific and recreational resource, with walking tracks meandering through a mist forest, rhododendron collection, rock garden and an old-world formal garden, where special emphasis has been placed on Northern Hemisphere plants which will not grow – and in general, have not been grown – along the temperate Australian coastline.

MOUNT VICTORIA ■ 106

Mount Victoria was the first headquarters of tourism in the Blue Mountains, offering day trips by horse-drawn vehicles to a number of tourist attractions. Inns sprang up throughout the district before the arrival of the railway, and the dawn of the age of tourism at the end of the nineteenth century heralded a burst in building activity as the demand for boarding houses and private summer residences intensified. The village of the 1990s offers a door to Australia's colonial past with a number of old sandstone and weatherboard buildings housing antiques, crafts and tearooms. Only two buildings in historic Station Street are under 100 years old. Mount Victoria was a renowned refreshment stop along the railway line until well into the twentieth century and now a museum is housed in the old railway refreshment rooms built in 1872. *Population 720*

MOUNT WILSON ■ 107

Probably owing to its geographic remoteness, the native bushland of the Mount Wilson area remained untouched until well into the latter half of the nineteenth century. But as the mountains' popularity as an escape from the hurly burly of life on the coastal plain below increased, so too did developmental pressure on areas beyond the narrow strip of settlement that flanked the railway line. From the 1870s onwards, Mount Wilson became the retreat of wealthy coastal dwellers who sought respite from the summer heat in the cool mountain clime. The rich volcanic soils and plentiful rainfall encouraged these early mountain residents to plant gardens reminiscent of those at 'home'. Mount Wilson is now famous for its large, English-style gardens with deciduous trees set in curious contrast to the giant eucalypts and tree-ferns of the native bushland. Many of the gardens are open to the public in spring and autumn when the trees are dressed in their brightest colours.

SPRINGWOOD ■ 108

Governor Macquarie's journal entry of 27 April 1815, written on his way to Bathurst, reads: 'We...halted at three o'clock in a pretty wooded Plain near a Spring of very good fresh water...I have named it Spring-Wood'. This is the oldest named town in the Blue Mountains. In 1816–17, Governor Macquarie set up a military post in the locality. This isolated post consisted of '...a weatherboard commodious barrack and guard house...having a kitchen garden enclosed with a fence for the use of the soldiers', and was erected on a site already cleared by Cox's party during the construction of his road.

With the extension of the railway across the Blue Mountains in 1867, Springwood became a popular location for the building of country homes where the more affluent of the coastal dwellers could escape the bustle of life on the coastal plains. Now, it has become the commercial centre of the eastern slopes of the Blue Mountains. *Population 6830*

THREE SISTERS ■ 109

Reaching out starkly from the sheer rock face of the cliffs at Katoomba, these instantly recognisable, multi-coloured rock pillars symbolise the Blue Mountains more than any other natural formation in the region. An Aboriginal legend from the Dreamtime gives a vivid explanation of the origin of this unusual rock formation as a drama involving three sisters: Gunedoo, Meenhi and Wimlah. They

BREAKING AWAY FROM SYDNEY COVE: COX'S ROAD TO BATHURST

When George Evans was given the task of plotting a road over the Blue Mountains in 1813, he reported upon his return to Emu Plains early the next year that a dozen men 'might clear a good road in three months for a cart to travel over the mountains'. Governor Macquarie was delighted by this assessment and immediately nominated William Cox, a former soldier who settled on a farm near Windsor, to oversee construction of the first road across the Blue Mountains, starting at Penrith and ending at Bathurst on the edge of the western plains.

It was a daring enterprise: thirty husky convicts took only six months to clear a carriageway through the thick bush of the rugged sandstone ridges which in places rise to over 1000 metres. When the 161-kilometre road with its 12 bridges was completed, all the convicts were rewarded with a pardon.

Precipitous as the 1832 Victoria Pass may be, its avoidance of Mount York was an improvement on Cox's perilous descent to the plains.

'Westward Ho!' might have been the title of Augustus Earle's somewhat idyllic 1820s depiction of pioneers wending their way over the Blue Mountains on Cox's road under a soft, European sky.

The road became the fledgling colony's lifeline as a steady flow of settlers began to flow westwards and the bounty of the pastoralists' labours was hauled back to the coast. Although Cox's road was an impressive feat of determination and endurance, it was hardly built for comfort. In 1822, one suffering traveller recorded her arduous journey along Cox's road thus: ...Our cart had now three bullocks...but we were worse off than ever...At length we came to a hill so steep it seemed we could never get up it. We alighted...in front it was almost perpendicular; behind was a valley so deep the eye could hardly distinguish the trees at the bottom...' Despite occasional traffic delays, the modern-day traveller ensconced in a 'horseless carriage' has comparatively little to complain about – the smooth black ribbon of the Great Western Highway to Bathurst still follows for much of its length the track taken by the original convict route. □

and their father, Tyawan, lived happily in the Blue Mountains, afraid only of the bunyip who lived in a deep hole nearby. To keep his daughters safe whilst he hunted for food each day, Tyawan left them on a high ledge. Soon after his departure one morning, a large centipede suddenly appeared on the ledge surprising one of the sisters who reacted defensively, throwing a rock that crashed down into the valley below awakening the fearsome bunyip.

The highly enraged creature lumbered towards the three sisters and Tyawan, hearing their cries, quickly pointed his magic bone and turned them to stone to protect them. The thwarted bunyip turned and chased Tyawan who transformed himself into a lyrebird. Unfortunately, in the excitement of the moment he lost his protective, magic bone. He scratched around looking for it everywhere, unable to turn himself or his daughters back into human form until it was found. The cry of the lyrebird may still be heard today as Tyawan searches unceasingly for his bone.

Horticultural artifice has transformed the upper slopes of Mount Wilson into a European landscape.

VALLEY HEIGHTS ■ 110

The thirty-two-kilometre stretch of railway line between Valley Heights and Katoomba is the steepest and fastest-climbing railway in Australia with a rise in altitude of almost 700 metres between the two stations. Typical of many of the lower-mountain towns, Valley Heights grew up around a railway platform built in 1875 to service the private residence of the Colonial Treasurer, the Hon. Geoffrey Eagar. *Population 1190*

WARRIMOO ■ 111

The site of Warrimoo first appeared on the map in 1881 when a small wooden platform named Karabar was erected close to the present site of the railway station. But it was rarely used and closed a few years later. It was not until 1918 that the 'proper' Warrimoo Station was built, taking its name from the Aboriginal word for 'eagle'. The original Warrimoo Station building burned down in the disastrous bushfires of December 1951 and was rebuilt in 1957. *Population 2210*

WENTWORTH FALLS ■ 112

Wentworth Falls was named in honour of William Charles Wentworth, one of the trio of explorers who crossed the Blue Mountains in 1813. The area was first known as The Weatherboard, after the inn that was built there in the 1830s. The town received its present name in 1879, when the station was renamed Wentworth Falls. The town provides access to many lookouts, walking tracks and waterfalls, including the falls after which the town is named. *Population 5000*

YESTER GRANGE Hidden away in a bush and parkland setting overlooking the Jamison Valley and above Wentworth Falls, this elegant Victorian country home was built in the 1870s by the timber firm of Goodlet & Smith for its managing director, Captain John Smith. The gracious house is now a Victoriana museum, gallery and restaurant.

WOODFORD ■ 113

One of the most interesting historical features of the tiny township of Woodford is the National Trust property, Woodford Academy (1828). The sandstone Georgian buildings which occupy the inn built in 1833. A succession of licensees developed the property over the ensuing years but with the arrival of the railway in the late 1860s, much of the road traffic and custom dwindled and the inn was purchased by Albert Fairfax for use as a residence. He renamed the former inn, 'Woodford' and the railway platform located close to the inn changed from Buss's Platform to Woodford soon after. *Population 700*

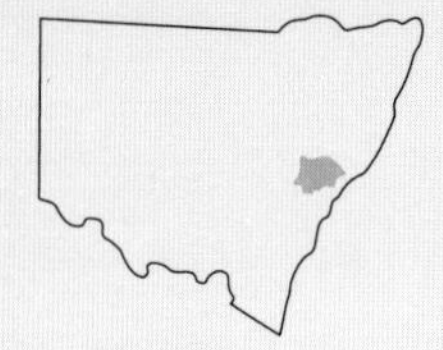

Maitland & Cessnock

When the search for good farmland outside the environs of Sydney drew explorers to the valley of the Hunter River little did they realise that they had struck the jackpot; the agricultural bounty of the Hunter, enhanced by its enviable reputation as a wine-growing area, continues, while its rich coalfields once fuelled the establishment of many of the nation's first secondary industries.

ABERMAIN ■ 114

Abermain, Aberdare, Cardiff, Stanford Merthyr and Pelaw Main...the nationality of the men who came to the lower and mid-Hunter to work the underground mines is not hard to establish. When the production of coal spread upstream from the coast to the Maitland–Cessnock region at the turn of the century the mine proprietors recruited labour from the 'old country': they imported experienced mine workers from the valleys of Wales and in turn, these immigrants brought their proud Welsh names with them.

Mining began at Abermain in 1903 and the pits produced coal for more than seventy years before becoming economically unviable. Transport difficulties put paid to plans to start mining in 1886 after the region's main coal seam was found to extend here, but by 1903 – with mines opening up in more than half-a-dozen locations – the private, coal-carrying railway lines had expanded far enough afield to include Abermain.

Today the mines are quiet and the descendants of the miners – Welsh and otherwise – make a living in the open air as dairy or poultry farmers and in the timber-getting and sawmilling industries connected with the large state forests of this region. *Population 2320*

BELLBIRD ■ 115

One of the first sightings of the giant Greta coal seam that was to form the basis of this region's major industry for seventy years was made near Bellbird. In the 1820s, a military officer surveying the route of the Great North Road out of Sydney noticed coal outcrops near here and made a sketch of them. In the 1850s, the Reverend W.B. Clarke, a pioneer geologist and gold discoverer, noticed coal seams in the Bellbird–Cessnock area. Eventually Bellbird was to have two collieries and they achieved the distinction of being based on the only mines in this region to be worked into the 1990s. The spread of population in recent years has turned Bellbird into a southern suburb of Cessnock.

The mines were to provide employment and relative prosperity but they also figured in one of Australia's worst mining tragedies. In 1923 an explosion and subsequent fire at the Bellbird Colliery killed 20 men; an hour earlier, just before a shift change, there were 500 men underground. *Population 2690*

BOLWARRA/ BOLWARRA HEIGHTS ■ 116

The site of these small residential centres on the northern outskirts of Maitland was once famous for the thick forests of cedar which grew along the river. In 1818, Governor Macquarie visited what was known as 'the cedar ground' where gangs of convicts cut down the red cedar trees and hauled the logs to the river where they were floated to Newcastle. Within twenty years most of the highly prized red cedar trees had gone. By then, the district's original settler, John Brown, had named it Bolwarra, an Aboriginal word meaning 'flash of light'. *Population 1920*

BRANXTON ■ 117

Branxton is one of a string of small townships strung out between Singleton and Maitland – nowadays dormitory suburbs of the larger centres – that have existed here since European settlement began in the 1840s. What was originally Black Creek became Branxton in 1848 when local landowners subdivided their acres and developed a small village on the edge of the flood plain that marks Branxton's eastern perimeter. A large part of Branxton was built on the extensive 'Farmborough' estate owned by William Bowen and within twenty years it had its own steam-driven mill, post office and, for those of the 500 residents wishing to improve their minds, a Mechanic's Institute.

Coal mining began at nearby Anvil Creek in 1868 and for many years Branxton, like its neighbours, was a coal town. Agriculture and winemaking are more important now – the nearby Wyndham Estate vineyards mark the northern edge of the Pokolbin wine-growing district. *Population 1860*

'DALWOOD' Only a few kilometres north-east of Branxton is the homestead known as 'Dalwood', occupied by George Wyndham in 1830 and now part of the Wyndham Estate vineyards. With its massive Doric columns and loggia below a standard gable roof, the sandstone building is a strange mixture of colonial domestic and Greek Revival design. A colonial administrator, James Busby, obtained vine-cuttings from Europe which were planted at 'Dalwood'and elsewhere in the Hunter.

CESSNOCK ■ 118

Cessnock's main business used to be mines and vines. Now there are only two coal mines still operating in the region: the open-cut 'Pelton' and the underground 'Ellalong'. The latter has flourished so that one of the main industries today is catering for the many visitors who come to see the Pokolbin district vineyards.

Coal was mined by convicts at Newcastle as early as 1801 but it was another ninety years before the first colliery was established at Cessnock. The first vines were planted in the 1820s and commercial vineyards were established in the mid-1850s but, rather like the mines, it was to be another 100 years before winemaking was to realise its promise.

The first settlers to take up land here were the Scottish brothers John and David Campbell who used their inheritance to set themselves up on a grant of 2500 acres called 'Cessnock' after a Scottish castle. The property was subdivided in 1853 and the village that grew up took its name.

The end of village life was signalled by the results of a survey by the distinguished geologist Edgeworth David in 1886 which showed that a broad and deep seam of coal – called the Greta seam after the town of the same name – extended from Cessnock to Muswellbrook. Within twenty years of the first mine opening – at Richmond Vale in 1891 – the population had risen from just under 200 to more than 8000. Mines proliferated as the coalfields of the lower Hunter fuelled the infant iron and steel industry in Newcastle; the product of the coalfields later became important in electricity generation and as a valuable export.

Mining company towns were often constructed conveniently close to the pit-head and a string of towns south of Cessnock owe their existence to such beginnings. Despite being hard-hit by the Great Depression of the 1930s, the mines were an important local industry until the 1950s when they went into a gradual decline as the readily and economically accessible coal became worked out. Engineering, light industry, timber milling, dairying, mixed farming and the enthusiastic and successful cultivation of the grape – together with its attendant tourist industry – have supplanted underground activity as the Cessnock region's economic base. *Population 17 900*

POKOLBIN Since the 1950s the only thing the winemakers and the colliery operators have had in common is that both industries have maintained their historic relationship in the Hunter Valley by both becoming well established in the Upper Hunter region (see *Muswellbrook & Scone*). As the mines in the Cessnock district declined, the wine industry came of age with a vigorous revival.

Fanned out to Cessnock's northwest and centred around the hamlet of Pokolbin are the vineyards and the rich volcanic soil which produce the wines, particularly the red wines, the region has become so famous for. Early plantings in this 'traditional' winegrowing region were largely inspired by the colonial government in an effort to replace the ubiquitous demon rum with more 'civilised' table wines. A German settler, Henri Bouffier, planted Cessnock's first vineyard in 1866; in 1882 his and other Hunter wines won medals at a French exhibition.

Economic depressions, wars and cheap imported wine dealt the Hunter wine industry various body blows in the twentieth century so that by 1947 there were only 500 hectares still under cultivation. Then in the 1960s, what the government had tried to encourage 100 years before began to happen of its own accord as Australians discovered the pleasures of table wines; today there are more than 2000 hectares of wine grapes in the Pokolbin region and tourists flock to the district's forty-odd vineyards to take advantage of cellar door wine tastings and sales.

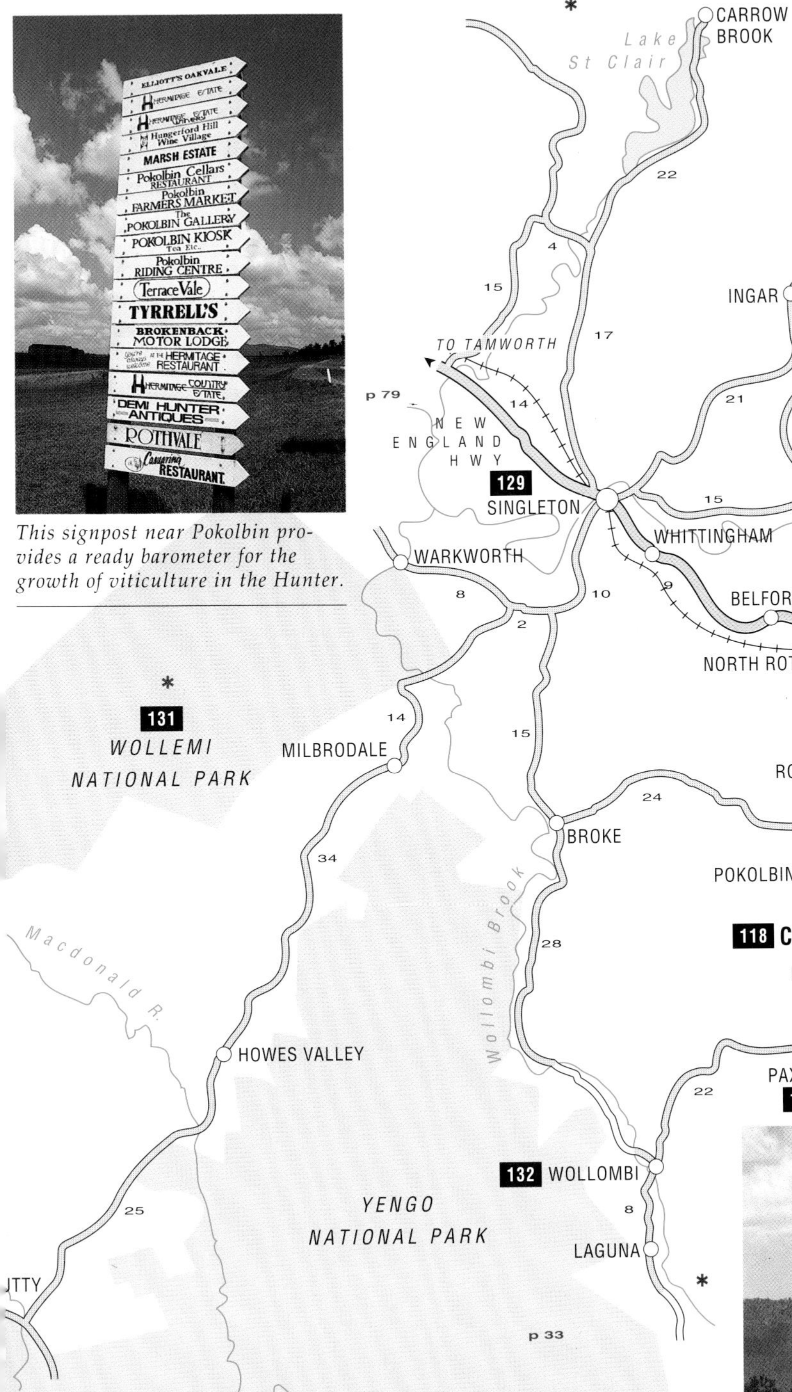

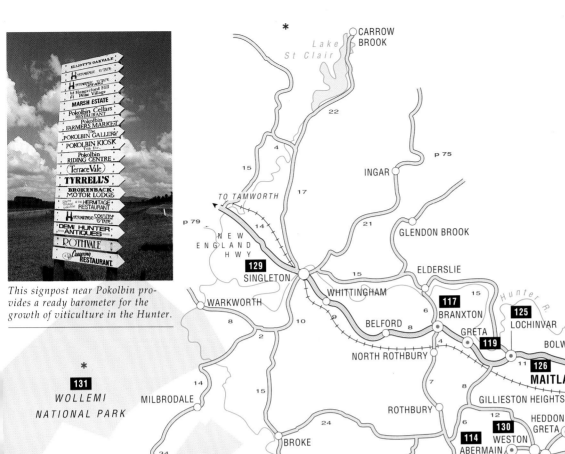

This signpost near Pokolbin provides a ready barometer for the growth of viticulture in the Hunter.

GRETA ■ 119

The streets of Greta were laid out as early as 1842 but it was not until the late 1860s when coal mining began at Anvil Creek that the hamlet, without realising it, found itself cast in an historic role as one of the earliest lower Hunter coal towns. After the true extent of the giant coal seam named after the town was revealed by survey in 1886 (see Cessnock) mining boomed and in 1907 there were ten collieries in this region.

Little trace of the mining days is left; the giant poppet heads that sat over the mineshafts were dismantled when the pits were closed down and Greta has reverted to its previous role as the commercial centre of a mixed farming and dairying district. *Population 1550*

HEDDON GRETA ■ 120

South-east of Greta, two other mines of the early 1900s spawned the towns of Heddon Greta and East Greta (now Gillieston Heights). With the closure of the pits after a half-century reign, these rural residential centres have become largely dormitory suburbs of Maitland and Cessnock.

The two 'Gretas' were among the first coal towns to be established along the Maitland–Cessnock axis and set the pattern for development of the coalfields southwards to Paxton. *Population 910*

HEXHAM ■ 121

Hexham has always been an important crossroads; as the starting point for the New England Highway it is

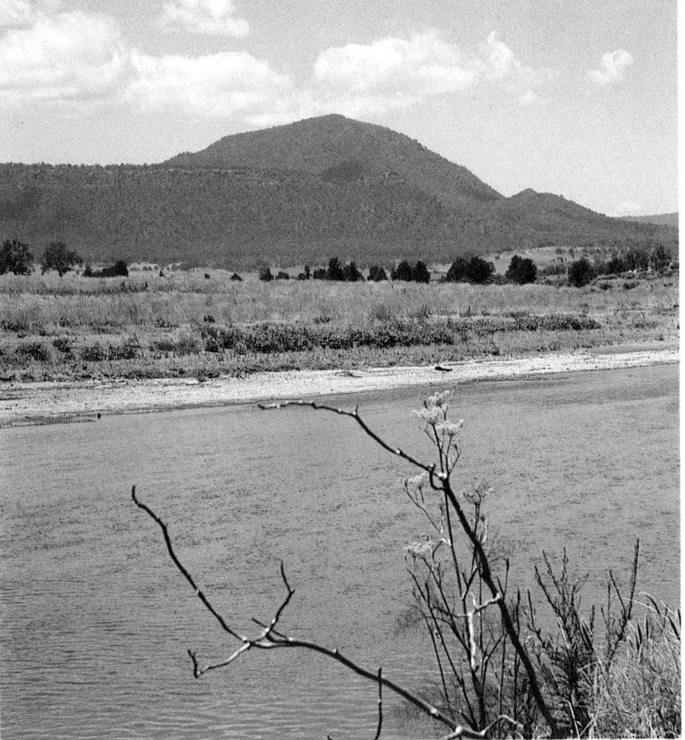

The Hunter River, shown here in its lower reaches, is the lifeblood of its broad valley; the flood plains have been cultivated for more than 150 years.

Encouraged by irrigation when the rainfall is inadequate, rows of famously productive grapevines form wavy lines as they follow the countours of the undulating landscape to clothe the Hunter Valley in orderly patterns of green. The first vineyard was planted in the 1830s (see p. 59).

the gateway to the northwest of New South Wales as well as being the doorstep of the north coast. Here the Pacific Highway crosses the Hunter River and the northbound traveller finally leaves behind the metropolitan conglomeration of Wollongong, Sydney and Newcastle .

KEARSLEY ■ 122

Despite its modest size, this residential centre on the eastern outskirts of Cessnock once lent its name to the shire council which adjoined the original Cessnock Municipal Council area. In 1956, the Kearsley Shire Council which administered more than 6700 square kilometres of the surrounding countryside – and once had the distinction of being the only local government body in Australia to be under the control of Communist councillors – was amalgamated with the Cessnock Council to form what was eventually to become known as the City of Greater Cessnock. *Population 520*

KURRI KURRI ■ 123

The Kurri Kurri Hotel says more than a thousand words could say about the history of Kurri Kurri – the name comes from an Aboriginal word for 'first'. When the grandiose building was erected Kurri Kurri was, if not first, then certainly near the top as one of the largest, fastest growing towns in New South Wales.

The town was laid out on Crown Land in 1902 and being almost exactly midway between Maitland and Cessnock was in the very middle of the network of coal mines – to become known as the South Maitland coalfield – that was being established at the same time. Business boomed and the boundless confidence of businessmen of the time is exemplified in the brash and ornately decorated exterior of the hotel – it was completed within twelve months of the town's establishment and has elaborate brackets which decorate the verandahs on the first two floors while the windows on the top floor are framed by broad, two-tone, brick arches. Along with the hotel there was a commercial centre and family cottages to cater for a population of about 1300.

When the mines started to close an aluminium smelter moved in to fill the gap in 1969 and this, together with agriculture, sawmilling, fruitgrowing and dairying, has helped maintain Kurri Kurri's prominence in the region. *Population 5830*

RICHMOND MAIN COLLIERY Industrial archaeologists will one day have reason to be grateful to the Cessnock Council for ensuring that at least a few of the old pithead building complexes remain as they were in the heyday of the coalmining industry. Richmond Main, a few kilometres south of Kurri Kurri on the Wyong Road, dates back to 1900 and has been presrved very much as it was when it closed down in the 1960s.

LARGS ■ 124

Hidden away on the road between Maitland and Morpeth, Largs lays claim to being the longest established centre of learning in the state. The public school has been in operation since 1849 and before that was the site of a Presbyterian Church school for eleven years. The original schoolhouse – a farmer's slab hut with a shingle roof – has been preserved as a museum of colonial schooling.

The hamlet's early Presbyterian connections are also evident in the shape of the privately owned Georgian residence known as Dunmore House, built in 1833 by the brother and mother of John Dunmore Lang, the first Presbyterian clergyman in New South Wales.

LOCHINVAR ■ 125

The attractions of the Hunter Valley were not lost on early settlers who were quick to take up land grants in the region. Within a little more than thirty years after the arrival of the First Fleet at Sydney Cove fine houses were being constructed as the centrepieces of rural estates. In 1821, twenty years before the village of Lochinvar was established on a subdivided estate of the same name, convicts built a handsome Georgian house for Thomas Winder, named, appropriately,'Windermere'. According to local legend, Winder is credited with being the first man to plant grapes in the Hunter. The house, for a time the residence of the Blue Mountains explorer W.C. Wentworth, was gutted by fire in 1884 but was rebuilt and part of the building is now a museum open to the public by appointment only.

MAITLAND ■ 126

The alluvial flats of the lower Hunter River were a magnet for early settlers but the river which produced the silted fertile flats also prevented Maitland from achieving the greatness once predicted for the city. Not only did the flood-prone river keep early Maitland divided in two, it eventually silted up to such an extent that the possibility of the town becoming a regional centre to rival Sydney faded and finally disappeared altogether when the railway went first to Newcastle.

But the town thirty-five kilometres upstream from the river's mouth *did* become the major commercial and residential centre for the Hunter Valley, where industry and agriculture have always enjoyed a peaceful coexistence. It all began with the Warraruah and Awabakal Aborigines who also coexisted here for thousands of years. European exploration of the region began in 1801 and within a few years the cedar-getters had arrived to establish the new colony's first export industry – timber. As in many other coastal regions of eastern Australia, the timber men, having hacked their way through the thick scrub, literally blazed the trail for those who came after.

In 1819, Governor Macquarie opened up the Hunter region for settlement and within four years two infant towns had sprung up to flank the bend in the river – Wallis's Plains (later West Maitland) and 'the Camp', on the site of an old cedargetter's camp (later East Maitland). As a junction for tracks leading into the interior and only a day's journey from the coast, the location was a popular watering hole with grog shanties doing a roaring business. The best known 'publican' was a colourful, twice-transported convict called Molly Morgan whose sixty-four-hectare land grant provided the site for a large part of Maitland.

By 1824 there was a regular steam packet service downriver to Newcastle and the government had been petitioned to establish a new town away from the flood-prone flats; thus 'Maitland' was proclaimed in 1833 and was the cause of such confusion that it had to be labelled 'East' to distinguish it from old, 'West' Maitland, one-and-a-half kilometres away. Despite its occasionally damp location, West Maitland forged ahead of its new twin and the twain did not meet until 1944 when commonsense prevailed and the municipalities of East and West Maitland and the old port of Morpeth (see entry) were combined into one urban entity.

Maitland is still a centre for the open-cut coal mining industry of the upper Hunter Valley and the development of tourism and a number of secondary industries has helped maintain its pre-eminence in the Hunter region. The city is also distinguished by being the home of New South Wales' oldest provincial newspaper – the *Maitland Mercury*, founded in 1843 – and the venue for the world's first speedway race – at the 1925 agricultural show.

Maitland is graced with a large number of architecturally distinguished buildings – authority and law and order are represented in the old 'government' town of East Maitland while to the west there is a concentration of private buildings ranging from large mansions to colonial cottages. *Population 43 210*

'CINTRA' 'Cintra' is a time capsule which preserves a long-vanished style of living. Built 1880, this grand mansion typifies the prosperity of the period; by 1887 the Victorian economic 'boom' was in full swing and the owners felt impelled to add a second wing consisting of a billiard room, servants' quarters and extra bedrooms thus giving the rendered brick building thirty-one rooms, including the attic and the cellar

GROSSMAN HOUSE This 1860 Georgian-style house – now a museum and the adjoining Brough House (1860) – now an art gallery – form part of an impressve nineteenth-century precinct with the nearby St Mary's Anglican Church (1860) and Rectory (1881) which dominates the city's skyline.

'ABERGLASSYN' This elegantly symmetrical, two-storey Regency house built of stone in 1840–42 was obviously planned as a solid base for a large country estate. The cellars are flagged and vaulted, there are marble fireplaces in the reception rooms and a cantilevered stone staircase swirls upward behind the front door towards a dome.

'ROSENEATH' The then Victoria Inn first opened its doors to customers in 1845. The building, one of the earliest two-storey buildings in East Maitland, has twelve-paned windows with shutters and handsome cedar joinery.

WALKA WATER WORKS This complex, with its handsome, two-tone brickwork buildings, at Oakhampton just north of Maitland, provided a hygienic water supply to the Lower Hunter region from 1887 to 1925. After some years as a temporary power station, the building remained empty until 1984 when it was restored and opened to the public as an example of Victorian industrial architecture and engineering. Within grounds used as a picnic area, there is an Italianate pumphouse with an elegant chimney, a reservoir, boiler house and settling tanks and filter beds used to clean water pumped from the Hunter River.

COURT HOUSE, JAIL AND POLICE STATION In a section of East Maitland where historic buildings abound, this 'law and order' grouping forms an interesting self-contained precinct. As often happened in young settlements, the jail, with its gatehouse and cells flanked by twin, two-storey administrative buildings went up first, in the mid-1840s; it is regarded as one of the finest colonial buildings in Australia. The court house came later (1866) and the fine police station was completed in 1880.

FESTIVALS Hunter Valley Steamfest (steam trains), April.

MORPETH ■ 127

Once an important river port, the town of Morpeth was subject to few modern intrusions when the river trade faded away and the brick and mellowed stone buildings remain almost exactly as they were at the turn of the century. As a result, the whole township has been classified by the National Trust and is covered by a permanent conservation order.

This early grape-crusher has been preserved for posterity; museums in the lower Hunter pay special attention to the region's wine-growing heritage.

From the 1820s this location – originally known as Green Hills – operated as a funnel for the produce of the rich Hunter region; the *Sophia Jane* blazed a trail for steamers when she chugged up the river in 1831 and from then on there was no turning back. In 1834 the 'New Town of Morpeth' was founded by the pioneer E.C. Close and was soon the major provincial port of the New South Wales coast – until trains and trucks supplanted the ships which plied back and forth to Sydney.

By the turn of the century, the bustling town where such famous Australian commercial names as Arnotts and W.H. Soul Pattinson had their start was in decline; the last steamer made its run to Sydney in 1931 and Morpeth became a peaceful, rural backwater which was amalgamated with Maitland in 1944. Today, in place of river traders, there are tourists who come to visit the past in the form of Morpeth's treasure chest of colonial architecture.

PAXTON ■ 128

Near the southern limits of the Cessnock coalfields, a pit was dug south-west of what was to become Paxton township – today a small rural crossroads, but for forty years until the 1960s a mining centre based around the productive Stanford Main No.2 pit. In a sea of green farmland, the giant mine buildings, probably the best preserved coalmine complex in Australia and classified by the National Trust as worthy of preservation, still stand around the Stanford pit – a substantial monument to the coalminers of this region and a concrete reminder of the industry which ruled its fortunes for so long. *Population 560*

SINGLETON ■ 129

In dozens of caves and overhangs of the Hunter Valley's sandstone ridges and escarpments the region's Aboriginal inhabitants have left their calling cards. At Milbrodale, south-west of Singleton, stencils of tools and a large, red-ochre painting of a huge, spirit being are reminders of the Hunter's pre-European heritage.

The world of the Aborigines was first broached by Europeans in 1819 when the need to find a land route between Sydney and the fertile plains west of Newcastle resulted in expeditions from Windsor pushing outward into unexplored territory. The chief constable at Windsor, John Howe, was the first to lead a party into the upper reaches of the Hunter in 1819; he returned with a large party in 1820 and reported in great detail to Governor Macquarie that he saw some of the '...finest country as imagination can farm and on both sides of the river for up to forty miles...and I may add a very good road for cattle may be made at trifling expense.'

The members of the expedition were rewarded for their efforts with land grants in the region they had opened up; Benjamin Singleton was quick to take up his ninety hectares and had the enterprise to open an inn, The Barlow Mow, near a ford across the Hunter River not far from today's Singleton bridges. The alluvial flood plains were soon producing crops of wheat and maize for the other settlers and Singleton, a miller by trade, set up a flour mill in 1829 as well as operating a punt at the busy crossing that would soon bear his name.

In the 1830s, Benjamin Singleton subdivided his property and sold town allotments so that twenty years after the region's discovery there was a town of Singleton with 400 people and 90 houses. Singleton continued to be the town's benefactor for many years; when a school was built at Whittingham, south of the town, he ploughed a furrow for three kilometres through the bush for the school-less children of Singleton to follow to their education. Mr Singleton's mill doubled as a court house until the grinding of the machinery became too distracting for justice to be done in peace so he built a proper court house and lock-up in the town in 1841.

Wheat and tobacco provided a secure agricultural base for Singleton and today vegetable-growing, dairying and grape cultivation are complemented by timber milling and a variety of light industries; the nearby army training camp provides an economic stimulus as do the tourists who come in growing numbers but economic security here is underwritten mainly by the large open-cut coal mines which feed almost six-million tonnes of coal a year to the giant Bayswater and Liddell power stations (see *Muswellbrook & Scone*), making Singleton the state's largest producer of open-cut coal. The power station is hard to miss – the giant 'jars' of its 132-metre-high cooling towers are at the receiving end of a mammoth conveyor belt which spirits coal ten kilometres across country from mine to boiler.

Buildings of particular interest include the railway station, the court house (not Benjamin Singleton's original building), All Saints Church and its attendant buildings, the Club House Hotel and the showground pavilion and rotunda. Outside Singleton, the grand mansion called Minimbah House is typical of the grandiose 'boom-style' architecture employed in the building of large homesteads on the great pastoral estates of the late nineteenth century.

The two-storey, sandstone and brick Minimbah House, less modest than most Australian country houses, is built on a scale to compare with the grandest of Southern mansions. With its forty-five rooms surrounded on three sides by broad verandahs and a central, three-storey tower capped by a segmented dome, it is clearly meant to be master of all it surveys. *Population 11 860*

The Wollombi Post Office – the ground floor was built in 1823 – had a ringside view of the busy parade of Hunter-bound settlers for fifty years.

WESTON ■ 130

Weston owes more to coal than most mining towns in the once intensively mined Maitland–Cessnock–Singleton triangle – it was established as a private town specifically to serve the Hebburn No.1 mine. Weston came about when the colliery owners purchased land from a farmer, James Weston, in 1903 in order to expand the infant Hebburn village which was developing around the mine.

With the passing of the underground mining industry, Weston has become a small service centre and a residential area for those who travel to work in larger towns such as Kurri Kurri or Cessnock. *Population 3210*

WOLLEMI NATIONAL PARK ■ 131

This is the second largest national park in New South Wales, protecting a vast wilderness of almost 490 000 hectares. The park contains what is probably Australia's largest continuous, untouched area of natural forest and although facilities are being developed bushwalkers are advised to stick to old fire trails unless they are experienced and know how to be self-sufficient.

Broadly speaking, the park covers the catchment areas of the Colo, Wollemi, Wolgan and Capertee Rivers, the first of these believed to be the last, major unpolluted waterway in the state. This wild region of steep ridges and narrow valleys joins with the Blue Mountains National Park to the south and the Goulburn River National Park to the north to form a broad chain of protected bushland behind the heavily settled central coastal regions of New South Wales. Access to the park is from several points along the Putty Road between Singleton and Windsor or near Bilpin on the Bells Line of Road – after that you are on your own as apart from aforementioned fire trails there are no made roads or tracks of any consequence in the park.

WOLLOMBI ■ 132

In the days when the settlers at Sydney Cove were breaking away from their coastal haven and striking inland, Wollombi's future looked assured. As a midway station on one of the first trails blazed into the Hunter Valley from Sydney through Windsor it was ideally placed to serve a busy stream of traffic to the newly discovered farmlands.

But by the 1880s the Great North Road had been superseded by rail and sea transport and all roads led to Newcastle; the early inland routes northward became backroads and their settlements were bypassed not only by traffic but by commercial development as well. The twentieth-century traveller who ventures off the highway reaps the benefit of the time-warp which has occurred here; Wollombi is probably the most charming of the string of small villages along the alternative route to the Hunter Valley vineyards. Grouped on a high rise with views over the Wollombi River valley and presided over by the business-like, two-storey post office with its deep verandahs, the township's thirty-odd honey-coloured stone buildings have seen few changes in 150 years.

COURT HOUSE AND CHURCH The simple St John the Evangelist church building (1846–49) and the nearby court house (1866 – now the Endeavour Museum) together with the police station (1846) form an interesting colonial grouping.

PUBLIC SCHOOL Like most of Wollombi's old buildings, the 1881 school house, with its common-sense Victorian addition of a teacher's house is made of sandstone.

INDUSTRY'S FUEL AND VINTAGE WINES: THE CONTRASTING BOUNTY OF A VALLEY OF PLENTY

Among all of the deep valley systems running down to the coast of eastern Australia, the Hunter Valley is extraordinary for the extent of its inland penetration. Broad floodplains and lowlands reach all the way from Muswellbrook and Denman, a distance of about 150 kilometres. Over such an expanse there are significant variations in of rainfall and temperature.

And while the valley walls rise with similar steepness on each side, the ranges behind them are differently formed. To the north the Mount Royal Range – where the Hunter River begins near Barrington Tops – is of relatively recent volcanic origin. To the south, the Hunter Range is an outcrop of ancient Hawkesbury sandstone. So the soil of the plains varies in composition, producing a diversity both in natural vegetation and in the cultivated plants that it sustains.

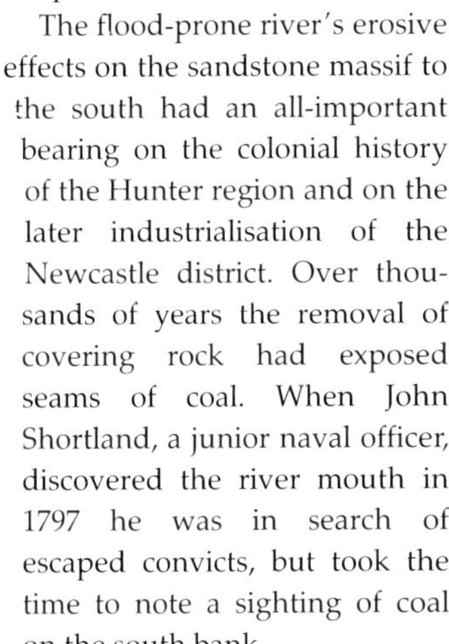

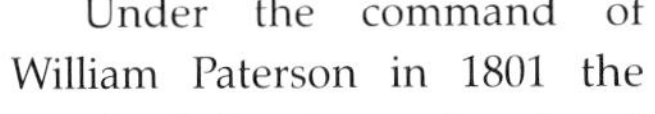

James Busby (1801–71) came to Australia in 1824 with his father John, the builder of Sydney's first proper water supply.

The flood-prone river's erosive effects on the sandstone massif to the south had an all-important bearing on the colonial history of the Hunter region and on the later industrialisation of the Newcastle district. Over thousands of years the removal of covering rock had exposed seams of coal. When John Shortland, a junior naval officer, discovered the river mouth in 1797 he was in search of escaped convicts, but took the time to note a sighting of coal on the south bank.

Under the command of William Paterson in 1801 the harbour and much of the river were charted and samples of coal were taken back to Sydney. A settlement was established in 1804 and exports of coal began in 1814, with a shipment to India exchanged for a cargo of rum. For about twenty years convicts who offended a second time in Sydney were sent to 'King's Town' on the Hunter. The mines were handed over in 1825 to the Australian Agricultural Company, which renamed the settlement Newcastle.

Coalmining spread south to the shores of Lake Macquarie but took on its greatest importance early in the twentieth century with the exploitation of vast fields of coking coal in the Maitland–Cessnock district. This led to the opening in 1915 of BHP's steelworks at Stockton, and consequently to heavy engineering and shipbuilding industries. Contemporary mining is concentrated mostly on open-cast deposits farther up the valley in the Singleton-Muswellbrook district. Nearly three-quarters of the electricity used in New South Wales comes from the Hunter region and huge chimneys and transmission pylons have become its most commanding landmarks.

Steam-powered trading vessels plied the Hunter from the 1830s, carrying goods for tran-shipment to coastal ships at Morpeth. Early roads passing over the river had drawbridges to allow for this traffic, which thrived until a railway bridge spanned the Hawkesbury River (see *Gosford & Woy Woy*) in 1888, providing a direct and speedy freight route between the Hunter Valley and Sydney. This railway line linked with a local line, built in 1853 from Newcastle to Maitland by private owners and was later extended under the government's management to the towns of Singleton, Murrurundi and finally Tamworth.

The craft of the cooper – making barrels in the traditional fashion – has all but vanished from the Hunter, but cooperages survive in the Barossa Valley.

Wine-making, pioneered in the Hunter Valley in the 1830s, has had a steadily increasing impact on the landscape and regional economy – not least because vineyard tastings and cellar-door sales have become a tourist attraction. No-one is sure who planted the valley's first commercially successful crop, but the prime mover was unquestionably a public-spirited Scot called James Busby (see Branxton). Having studied viticulture in France, Busby in 1830 published an instruction manual for growing wine grapes in Australian conditions. In 1832 he brought hundreds of vine cuttings from France and Spain, planting them on his riverside property. A year later Busby had departed to become British resident administrator in New Zealand, but he authorised the distribution in his absence during the next few seasons of no fewer than 20 000 cuttings to other landowners. Busby's zeal was matched by James King who promoted co-operative efforts to enlarge plantings and improve quality. □

Busby's legacy: a bumper harvest of purple grapes in the Hunter Valley means good news for lovers of the region's powerful red wines.

Lake Macquarie

Although geographically not part of the Hunter River system, the Lake Macquarie region – with a population greater than the city of Newcastle – has become established as a centre for industry, tourism and burgeoning residential development, closely linked with the fortunes of the 'steel city' and the Hunter.

AVONDALE ■ 133
Avondale has been a Seventh Day Adventist estate since 1897 when Avondale College was founded. The college offers tertiary education to Seventh Day Adventists in the South Pacific region. Two of the original buildings – Bethel Hall and a three-storey weatherboard dormitory – still stand on the campus whose most recent building is a large modern church built in 1985. The college has its own flying school and airstrip.

Also on the estate is the church's Sanitarium Health Food Company, which manufactures a number of well known breakfast cereals and vegetable protein foods. When the factory was built in 1934 it was one of the most advanced of its time although initially transport was less than 'advanced' since products from the factory were transported down Dora Creek by horse-drawn barge.

In addition to the college and factory, the 325-hectare estate now has primary and high schools and a retirement complex. *Population 1630*

BELMONT ■ 134
The first European to settle in what was to become Belmont was Reverend Lancelot E. Threlkeld of the London Missionary Society. Threlkeld laid the foundations of the pioneering Bahtabah mission for the local Awabakal Aborigines in 1828 but the mission soon experienced financial problems and the situation was not helped by the confrontation between Threlkeld and the controversial clergyman and wool industry pioneer Samuel Marsden over funding. The mission at Belmont was eventually closed although Threlkeld was to make a second attempt at Toronto (see entry).

A second, more commercial, venture established in Belmont was also unsuccessful. Thomas Williamson, aware of the advantages to be gained from the settlement's proximity to the port town of Newcastle, opened a guesthouse called 'Belmont' and offered inducements such as boat rides on the lake to his guests from Newcastle. The poor condition of the roads, however, deterred potential tourists but the settlement, which had been known as Williamsons now adopted the name Belmont, after his failed guesthouse.

By the 1880s Belmont was a thriving settlement, with such industries as a timber mill, a coal mine, and some small farms and orchards, including one that successfully grew pineapples for a number of years.

Improvement in the Pacific Highway, which passes right through the town has been the main factor in the growth of Belmont. As well as being the centre for the Lake Macquarie Yacht Club and a commercial centre for smaller settlements strung along the eastern shore of Lake Macquarie, Belmont is very much part of the southwards suburban and industrial growth of Newcastle. *Population 6030*

BLACKSMITHS ■ 135
Blacksmiths is at the southern end of the stretched out arch of Nine Mile Beach and its surfing beach is home to the Swansea–Belmont Surf Lifesaving Club and the Royal Volunteer Coastal Patrol – neither activity being normally associated with the culture of lakeside communities.

The town has an Aboriginal Culture Centre set up by the Bahtabah Aboriginal Land Council. Aboriginal art and artefacts from all around Australia are displayed and sold at the centre. *Population 5970*

BONNELLS BAY ■ 136
The first land grants in Bonnells Bay were made in 1884 but when the first subdivisions were put up for sale three years later there was little interest. Bonnells Bay's rough racecourse was a favourite spot for picnic races but did not seem attractive for permanent settlement. The land was readvertised after the Second World War and a number of lots were purchased including one that became a shopping centre. The population of Bonnells Bay grew to its present size after the building of Eraring Power station in 1984. *Population 1610*

BOOLAROO ■ 137
The town was first settled in 1829 and the first colliery was opened in the 1830s. Transport for the new settlement was a problem and was to remain so for some years. To get to any of the settlements on the lake necessitated a horseback ride along rough tracks or a combination of horse and punt. For some years an enterprising Chinese settler at nearby Cockle Creek operated a punt that he hauled across the lake on ropes attached to trees on each side.

As early as 1895 the Sulphide Corporation plant started operating at Boolaroo and is now a substantial part of the district's economy, being one of the largest single employers on the lake. The company produces zinc alloy products, lead, sulphuric acid and cadmium.

Boolaroo has also starred, slightly disguised, as 'Boomaroo', in the novels *Jack Rivers and Me* and *Good Mates* written by Paul Radley in the 1980s. *Population 4820*

BRIGHTWATERS ■ 138
One of the earliest land grants in Brightwaters was made to Joseph Marshall, the owner of a Sydney brewery. Marshall tinned and marketed fish caught in Lake Macquarie. He also planted sugar cane, which was processed at his sugar mill on Mill Lane before being sent to his brewery in Sydney.

Transport in the early days was by horse and dray to Morisset and Cooranbong or by water across the lake. The first bus service in Brightwaters began in 1955 – but only schoolchildren could be transported leaving the permanent settlers over school age to make their own arrangements. *Population 410*

COORANBONG ■ 139
A number of settlers in and around the area of what was called 'Dora Creek Crossing' on the trail between Brisbane Waters and Maitland were recorded as early as 1828. 'Kaurumbung' said to mean 'water over rocks' was the name given by the first of these settlers, Percy Simpson, to his 890-hectare grant.

When a small timber town grew up on part of this grant in the 1860s, the name adopted was Cooranbong. Timber felled in the Watagan Mountains was dragged by bullock teams to Cooranbong where it was sawn into sleepers, shingles or pit props at one of the town's five sawmills. The sawn timber was then transported by steamboat down Dora Creek, which had to be widened to allow the timber boats to turn.

The pioneering settlement at Cooranbong was expected to remain the major settlement on the western shores of the lake but the coming of the railway line in the 1880s brought an end to that prominence. The railway bridged Dora Creek at the settlement of the same name and left Cooranbong some kilometres west of the rail line.

Off the railway line, off the lakeshore and too far for city-fatigued Novocastrians to commute to, Cooranbong is now a quiet town that has been spared Newcastle's inexorable urban sprawl. *Population 1370*

DORA CREEK ■ 140
Dora Creek is one of only two large creeks running into Lake Macquarie – Cockle Creek near Boolaroo (see entry) being the other.

Early settlers were drawn to the creek since the valley and tributaries

Fishing is the most popular recreation at Lake Macquarie where just about everyone owns a boat.

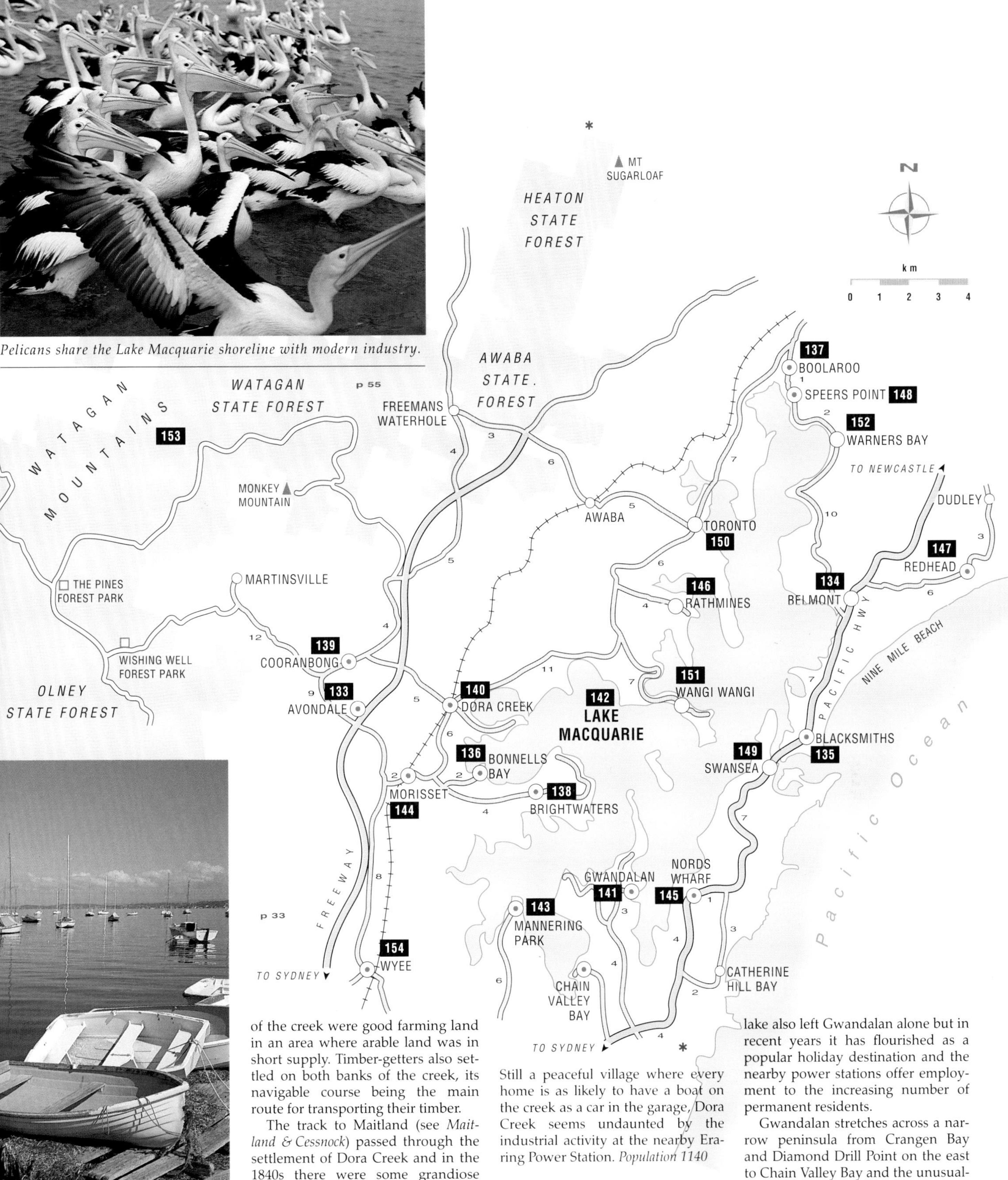

Pelicans share the Lake Macquarie shoreline with modern industry.

of the creek were good farming land in an area where arable land was in short supply. Timber-getters also settled on both banks of the creek, its navigable course being the main route for transporting their timber.

The track to Maitland (see *Maitland & Cessnock*) passed through the settlement of Dora Creek and in the 1840s there were some grandiose plans for the track to become a road; the land would be subdivided for further settlement and a new township called Newport would be born. The track remained as it was and so did Dora Creek. Even after the railway line was built in 1887 Dora Creek did not boom.

Still a peaceful village where every home is as likely to have a boat on the creek as a car in the garage, Dora Creek seems undaunted by the industrial activity at the nearby Eraring Power Station. *Population 1140*

GWANDALAN ■ 141

Located on the southern end of Lake Macquarie, furthest from Newcastle, Gwandalan remained until recently relatively quiet and unknown – its Aboriginal name meaning 'place of peace' being quite appropriate. The post-war boom in tourism on the lake also left Gwandalan alone but in recent years it has flourished as a popular holiday destination and the nearby power stations offer employment to the increasing number of permanent residents.

Gwandalan stretches across a narrow peninsula from Crangen Bay and Diamond Drill Point on the east to Chain Valley Bay and the unusually named Frying Pan Point on the west. North of Gwandalan the peninsula narrows dramatically to Point Wolstoncroft, the longest finger of land jutting into Lake Macquarie. The reserve of untouched woodland at Point Wolstoncroft is a protected area. Further south, the residential

Like most Lake Macquarie towns Swansea could hardly have an environment more suitable for aquatic pursuits.

settlement of Chain Valley Bay occupies the far south-eastern corner of the lake. *Population 3110*

LAKE MACQUARIE ■ 142

Sent in 1800 to the newly discovered Hunter River at Newcastle to take on a load of coal, Captain Reid mistakenly entered the channel at Swansea (see entry) where Lake Macquarie meets the Pacific Ocean. For many years thereafter Lake Macquarie was known to the Europeans as 'Reid's Mistake' although the Aborigines knew it as Awaba.

Lake Macquarie is the largest seaboard lake in Australia. Flooding an area of 110 square kilometres and with 150 kilometres of foreshore, it could fill Sydney Harbour four times. The lake, affected to some degree by tides, contains salt water and many of the fish within it are small ocean species. Described by Captain John Bingle in 1821 as '...serene and still; solitude reigned, no tree disturbed, no trace of white man's civilisation and all in its natural wild state' the lake's abundant natural resources of timber, coal and fish and its potential for recreation have changed it drastically. Poet Donald Moore described the same lake in 1980 as:

> *...the unquiet waters among the*
> *Saturday/Sunday crowds*
> *of herons cats and outboards*
> *inboards and followers on skis.*

MANNERING PARK ■ 143

The small township of Mannering is closely linked to the nearby Vales Point Power station, which was the largest of the power stations on the lake until usurped by Eraring which was built in the 1980s.

The building of the modern community centre at Mannering Park was an exercise in co-operation among the various elements that make up the permanent community. The centre was built by volunteer labour and funded by the shire council, the Joint Coal Board, the progress association and local fundraising. *Population 2260*

MORISSET ■ 144

One of the few nineteenth-century settlements on the western shores of the lake, Morisset was laid out in 1887 primarily to serve Cooranbong after the railway bypassed the latter. In fact the settlement was named 'Cooranbong' for a few weeks until it was renamed in honour of Lieutenant Colonel James Morisset, who had been military commandant at Newcastle from 1818 until 1823. A mental asylum and psychiatric hospital was established at Morisset in 1909 and still operates. Morisset now serves the surrounding district of lakeside settlements on the Morisset Peninsula, which has seen a boom in residential development in the last thirty years. Its accessibility by train has also seen its development as a holiday destination. The stationmaster's residence, built in 1887 and now classified by the National Trust acts as a reminder of the importance of a train service to Morisset's development. *Population 1050*

NORDS WHARF ■ 145

A quiet little backwater with large open areas of water and bushland, Nords Wharf has thus far escaped much of the development that has irrevocably changed settlements further north, not least because it is a few kilometres off that well beaten track – Pacific Highway.

Despite its name, Nords Wharf is not as attractive to boating enthusiasts as other settlements but it does possess a grassy, shaded shore...and wooden-fenced swimming baths. A ferry used to bring miners from the northern part of the lake to a point near Nords Wharf from which they could walk to nearby Catherine Hill Bay, now an historic mining village. *Population 780*

RATHMINES ■ 146

Rathmines sits across the water of Kilaben Bay from Coal Point, notable as the site of the first coal mine on Lake Macquarie. Rathmines was the site for the first (and last...it was not successful) attempt at grapegrowing on the lake. Lake Macquarie's settlements were to owe more to what came from under the ground than for what could be grown above it.

During the Second World War Rathmines was the site for the largest flying boat base in Australia. From 1939 all Catalina crews were trained at RAAF Rathmines and some 3000 officers passed through Rathmines in the war years. Several hangars and the flying boat ramp, a boon to boat launchers, still remain although the station closed in 1961 and most of the site is now derelict.

The wartime interlude and those who served here are commemorated in Catalina Park where there is a stone memorial topped by a propeller. *Population7330*

REDHEAD ■ 147

On the coast but not 'out on a limb', Redhead is very much part of Lake Macquarie and its history, marking the northern boundary of the Lake Macquarie City Council.

In 1887 the Lambton Scottish Australian Mining Company opened the Ryhope Colliery, later known as the Lambton Colliery, in Redhead. When ownership was transferred to BHP in 1932 it became the first fully mechanised mine in Australia. There have been major alterations to the colliery since then but some of the original buildings dating back to 1887 have been retained.

Less urbanised than a number of the neighbouring settlements on this part of the lake, Redhead is the most popular – and the most exposed – of the beaches on the long stretch of Nine Mile Beach. It is obvious from the red rocks on the cliffs above the beach where the town got its name. A favourite spot for hang gliders, Redhead has also been the centre of sand mining activity on Nine Mile Beach. The discovery of the minerals rutile and zircon in the sands of the beach led to a flurry of activity here. *Population 6440*

SPEERS POINT ■ 148

After the Shire of Lake Macquarie was proclaimed in 1906, the first council meeting was held at Teralba, across Cockle Bay from Speers Point. Eight years later the shire's administrative headquarters had moved to Speers Point and permanent Council Chambers were built. The original building became too small and now houses another public body – the Engineers Department.

The history of Speers Point goes back to 1888 when one of the original settlers, William Speers, was persuaded by the government to sell part of his land for use by residents of Newcastle's coalmining suburbs. Speers Point became the site for sailing and sculling regattas, camping and company picnics. After the establishment of a steam tram service from Newcastle, Speers Point became even more popular for recreation and holidays. *Population 4820*

SWANSEA ■ 149

When Captain William Reid sailed his schooner *Martha* into the navigable entrance to Lake Macquarie at Swansea in 1800, he thought he was at the entrance to the Hunter River. The site of Captain Reid's mistake was described as 'a salt water inlet about five leagues to the southwards of the (Hunter) river, having a small island at its entrance' and represents the first recorded description of Swansea Heads.

The first land grant around Swansea was made in 1833 and by the next year a salt works had been established. With the opening of the first mine on the lake, Threlkeld's Ebenezer mine at Coal Point, a wharf was built at Swansea to transport coal. The winding entrance to the

Native grass trees give a primeval appearance to the reserve at Point Wolstoncroft, near Gwandalan.

lake at Swansea and the sandbar were to prove ongoing problems in Swansea's development. Delays and groundings of ships trying to enter led to dredging and widening in the late nineteenth century but competition – or jealousy – from Newcastle proved a stumbling block as big as the sandbar and the entrance was never capable of taking ocean-going vessels. Even the infant shipbuilding industry at Swansea ran into problems as the lake and channel proved too shallow for building the ever-larger vessels that were required.

The decision in 1887 to build the railway line down the west side of the lake, however, affected Swansea's position as the only access to and exit from the settlements that had sprung up around Lake Macquarie. But the town's proximity to Newcastle and its prime position for both lake and sea fishing guaranteed its survival and continued development. The commercial fishing industry is still centred here and the days of Novocastrian 'weekenders' at Swansea have given way to a population of permanent residents who commute up the Pacific Highway to Newcastle. *Population 7980*

TORONTO ■ 150

When Reverend Lancelot Threlkeld gave up his mission at Belmont (see entry), he persuaded Governor Darling to grant him 520 hectares at what the local Aborigines called Derambambah ('narrow neck of land'). From 1830 to 1841 he ran an Aboriginal mission there but his activities were much wider than those of a missionary and student of the Awabakal language and culture. He came across coal on the peninsula south of Toronto and opened his Ebenezer Mine there in 1840 after the monopoly on coal production enjoyed by the Australian Agricultural Company was broken. By the time his Ebenezer Estate was sold in 1844 for 3450 pounds sterling, it comprised the mission buildings, a dairy farm, an orchard, the coal mine, two ships, punts, jetties and miners' huts.

The establishment of the town of Toronto had to wait, however, until the resale of the Ebenezer Estate in the 1880s to a land investment company interested in developing a tourist resort. The world champion sculling races were being held in Australia that year and the then world champion Edward Hanlon hailed from Toronto, which was chosen as the name for the town.

A steam tramway that ran from Fassifern to Toronto provided transport initially. Horse-drawn carriages as well as a variety of steam engines were used on the tramline. By the early twentieth century the tramway had been taken over by the Railway Department and the tramline converted to a branch rail line on which a mixture of trams and trains were run. On large company picnic days up to twenty trains would arrive in Toronto from Newcastle and in 1920 the Prince of Wales (who was later crowned King Edward VIII) arrived the same way on his visit to Toronto. Now the commercial centre for the western shore of the lake, Toronto is very much part of Newcastle's suburban sprawl while still retaining a great deal of the attractiveness of its earlier years. *Population 11 600*

WANGI WANGI ■ 151

The name of this small town comes from an Aboriginal word said to mean 'place of night owls' and is pronounced 'wonjee wonjee'. The peninsula on which the town now stands was granted to Edward Gostwyck Cory in 1831 but had been used before European settlement by the Awabakal Aborigines as a base for hunting, fishing and launching canoes to take them to the sacred site of Pulbah Island, the largest island on the lake.

As early as 1897 a large reserve was declared at Wangi Wangi Point and despite the walking tracks and lookouts within the bushland reserve a koala colony has survived although the cattle thieves who used to seek refuge there are long gone.

Wangi Wangi was the site of the first of the coal-fired power stations to be opened on Lake Macquarie and the colliery at Wangi Wangi now supplies some of the millions of tonnes of coal required for the furnaces at Eraring power station.

The painter William Dobell, who won the Archibald prize on three occasions, lived for thirty years in what is now Dobell Drive. His home has been retained as much as possible as the working artist's home that it was and many of his paintings are on display there. *Population 7330*

WARNERS BAY ■ 152

Warners Bay was known officially as Cockle Bay when it was founded although the local inhabitants preferred the name associated with the first settler in the area. Jonathon Warner was granted 520 hectares around the town in 1829 and the two-storey timber house he built on the hill overlooking his land survived until the 1930s. As District Magistrate Warner travelled to and from Gosford frequently and must have known this part of Lake Macquarie as well as anyone...except the displaced Awabakal Aborigines. On his property, and with the aid of convict labour, Warner ran an orange orchard and a small coal mine with a loading jetty in Warners Bay. *Population 6250*

WATAGAN MOUNTAINS ■ 153

The Watagan Mountains form the western boundary of the Lake Macquarie Basin but the 'mountains' might more properly be called hills since the highest point is Mount Heaton at 487 metres. More widley known is the smaller elevation – Mount Sugarloaf (411 metres) which rewards visitors to its summit with spectacular views of the long stretch of coast...and good television reception from the transmitter on its peak. Although the Watagan Mountains may appear from the coast as a single range they are in fact a complex of intersecting ranges that spread westwards until they meet the Great Dividing Range.

The natural forests cloaking the Watagan Mountains have attracted timber-getters since the 1830s when cedar – much prized for its building applications – was felled and transported to Lake Macquarie's sawmills. In 1916 the Forestry Commission took responsibility for the forests on the Watagan Mountains, which now form an almost continuous corridor of state forests.

As a source of quality hardwood the Watagan State Forests are hard to beat. Turpentine for marine pilings; blackbutt for mining timbers, sleepers and construction;tallowwood for flooring; she-oak for roofing shingles, and the highly prized red cedar explain why the early settlers' interest in the timber-rich mountains has been adopted by the Forestry Commission with more of an eye to regeneration than they ever envisioned might be necessary.

WYEE ■ 154

A stockyard was established at Wyee in the 1830s but the establishment of a large sawmill in the 1870s and the necessary infrastructure of a wharf to transport the sleepers, encouraged permanent settlement. The coming of the northern railway line through the town further boosted settlement.

Too far south to encourage commuters from Newcastle and too far off Lake Macquarie to encourage the holidaymakers that have made the lake their haven, Wyee's population remain small although the coal mine which supplies the power stations at Vales Point and Wangi Wangi ensures employment for those who live in Wyee. *Population 1070*

The sometimes misty 'mountains' of Watagan have been a source of hardwood timber for more than 150 years.

NEWCASTLE

As Australia's major provincial city, Newcastle is a great survivor; weathering the ups and downs of heavy industry, it has maintained the recreational asset of its beautiful waterways.

Newcastle is Australia's sixth largest city, the bustling capital of the wine-growing Hunter Valley region and – according to locals – Australia's best kept secret. The views from the heights at Merewether and Blackbutt Reserve or closer in at The Obelisk in King Edward Park suggest that they could be right. There are fine vistas taking in the city and its surroundings: the suburbs falling gently to the river where solid commercial and public buildings gather near the mouth of the Hunter River.

Newcastle was built on the foreshore of a deep natural harbour and this maritime environment would shape the city's commercial and physical identity. With a coastline fringed by wide, sandy beaches, Lake Macquarie to the south and Port Stephens to the north, more than 80 per cent of Newcastle's 262 000 residents live less than 30 minutes from ocean, lake or bay.

The chance discovery of coal by escaped convicts in 1791 in the vicinity of what is now Newcastle set the course for the city's early settlement and development. In 1797, Lieutenant John Shortland, in pursuit of yet more desperate escapees from Sydney, came upon the river which he named for Governor Hunter. Close by he too found a rich seam of coal. Two years later, before a settlement was established, coal was being sent to Sydney. Hunter's successor, Governor King, decided to establish a town at what was then known as 'Coal River' and Newcastle became the second European settlement on the mainland. For twenty years it was a brutal jail for troublesome convicts who were sent from Sydney and put to work mining coal, cutting cedar and burning shells for lime. The town was declared 'free' in 1823 and the convicts were transported to the new purgatory at Port Macquarie.

The city's industrialisation took off in the 1880s and at the turn of the century its population had increased almost seven-fold to 55 000 by which time it had enjoyed formal recognition as a city for well over a decade. By 1913, the Broken Hill Proprietary company was rolling steel at Waratah and the city's reputation for coal, iron

Newcastle's southern hinterland is trimmed by a hilly escarpment, necessitating tall aerials in suburbia. At the mouth of the Hunter (below) – for 70 years the industrial heart of Australia – another day ends.

and steel was well established. Many of the suburbs, including Merewether, Hamilton and Wallsend, started life as isolated pit towns that were to be gradually absorbed by the city's sprawl.

Although the mining of coal, its export, and its use in electricity generation and iron and steel making are still important, the economy of modern Newcastle has diversified from its traditional base and is sustained by providing goods and services in many fields including, amongst others, education, health, bulk handling technology, engineering, environmental management, horse breeding and a wide range of manufacturing industries. Industry aside, the city remains the commercial, administrative and cultural centre of the richly productive Hunter Valley and its surrounding districts.

Convicts and coal were inextricably linked in Newcastle's founding; the first export was to Bengal in 1799.

The harbour is the second largest in Australia, handling over 1000 vessels a year and annually exporting more than 35 million tonnes of goods; as well, the harbour's traditional workaday appearance has undergone significant transformation. Reclamation and redevelopment of vast areas of abandoned industrial waterfront for commercial and recreational use is breathing new, invigorating life into Newcastle's cityscape. The Foreshore, a 17-hectare harbourside park opened by Queen Elizabeth in 1988, is one example. This will link the harbour with the business district and a planned 60-hectare redevelopment of disused railway goods yards incorporating a three-kilometre waterfront stretch.

With its considerable and often dramatic history as a city born of a new colony's desperate need for raw materials, Newcastle's urban fabric offers plenty of interest and despite an earthquake in 1989 many of its original buildings still stand. The magnificent red-brick Christ Church Cathedral built in 1885, the recently refurbished picture-palace style Civic Theatre, the restored Customs House and the Trades Hall Building – which represents many years of trades union struggle on the coal fields – are diverse examples of the city's heritage. One of the best known historic sites is Fort Scratchley, with its colonnade, massive walls, and moat, built in the 1880s. It owes its existence to fears of a Russian invasion which excited nineteenth-century Australia from time to time. Although the Russians showed no interest in it, shots were fired from Fort Scratchley in 1942 at a Japanese submarine which surfaced to shell the city. The Fort houses a maritime and military museum.

Captain Cook first sighted Nobbys Head, now the site of a Navigational Signal Station, in 1770.

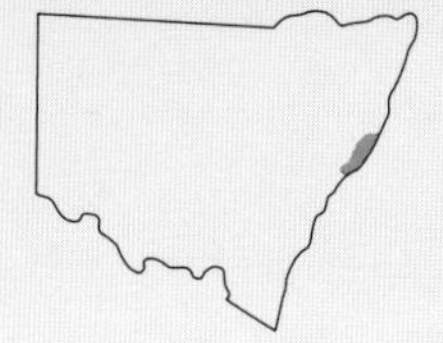

Taree & Nelson Bay

This region of inland lakes and rivers with less-than-easy entrances from the open sea, has proved remarkably resistant to industrial development. Tourism is the only major new industry to have taken hold in a region where timber and fishing have provided the economic base since European settlement.

ANNA BAY ■ 155

Until 1896, Anna Bay was known to European settlers as 'Hannah Bay' after the *Hannah*, which was shipwrecked there. The bay was also the site of another tragic accident that took the life of the earliest settler in the area, Captain William Cromarty. Cromarty, his elder son, a local Aborigine and a servant launched a small boat through the surf at One Mile Beach (Anna Bay) in 1838 and all four drowned when the waves overturned their boat.

Another pioneering family in the area was the Blanch family whose son Charlie supplied meat from his home at Anna Bay to settlements in Port Stephens (see entry). His butcher's boat was to set a precedent and for many years 'store boats' were a common sight delivering produce to their customers in the area.

But the settlement at Anna Bay, unlike many settlements around Port Stephens, was not totally dependent on water transport. In 1906 the much-travelled track from Nelson Bay to Stockton through Anna Bay was gazetted as a main road. Even by the 1920s, however, this 'main road' was still a relatively primitive thoroughfare and the drivers of the daily car service along the road had to lay logs over the swampy and sandy sections around Anna Bay in order to get through.

Anna Bay was also the site of the first school on the southern side of Port Stephens. The original school, with twenty-six pupils was opened in 1879...in a paddock. By 1886, with too few pupils, the school shared a half-time teacher with the school at Nelson Bay. But the problem of low enrolments still existed in 1910, when a new school was built to replace the white-ant ridden old school building...once again the initial enrolment was twenty-six.

Now a busy holiday resort, the settlement at Anna Bay is situated strategically between Port Stephens and Newcastle. *Population 1460*

BOOTI BOOTI STATE RECREATION AREA ■ 156

On the narrow strip of coastal land running between the two headlands of Cape Hawke and Charlotte Head stands Booti Booti State Recreation Area. The area is bounded to the east by the ocean and to the west by Wallis Lake. Booti Booti, which boasts secluded beaches and lakeside picnic spots, offers opportunities for surfing, fishing, sailing, camping and walking. From the headlands there are views of the coast and a vista west across Wallis Lake to the Great Dividing Range. In the open woodlands and patches of rainforest, there is a wide variety of vegetation from eucalypts and she-oaks to ferns, orchids and coloured fungi. Almost one third of Australia's known wild bird species can be seen within the recreation area.

BULAHDELAH ■ 157

Bulahdelah, from an Aboriginal word meaning 'meeting of the waters', sits on the Myall River surrounded by five state forests. The river and the forests were what attracted the original European settlers. Timber felled in the forests was brought by bullock teams down to the Myall River (see entry) where it was loaded onto flat-bottomed boats and transported to Port Stephens...the journey taking three weeks!

By the late nineteenth century settlers other than timber-getters were moving into the town and relations between the two groups were not always without problems. In 1866, the fully loaded punt *Bullah-Deelah* sank to the bottom of the river just outside the town and suspicion of foul play fell on the long-established cedar-getters who resented the encroachment on their territory by new settlers.

Despite the logging activity in the area, a magnificent flooded gum (*Eucalyptus grandis*) still stands in the Bulahdelah State Forest. Known locally as 'The Grandis' the seventy-six metre high tree is the tallest tree in New South Wales and is thought to be 400 years old.

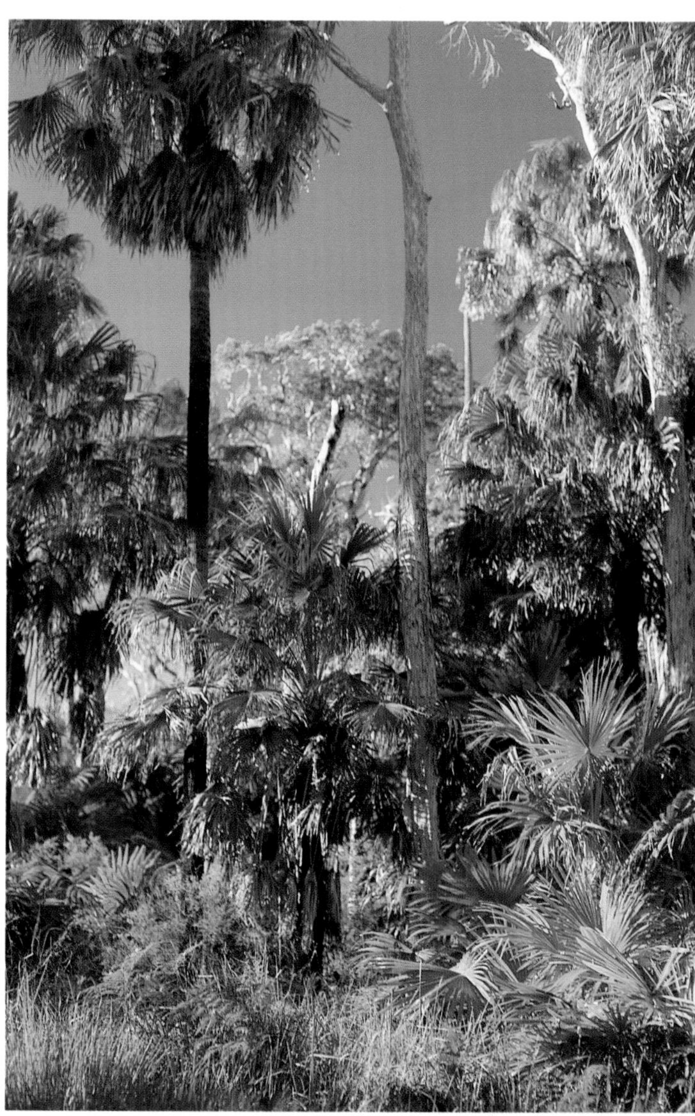

The beauty of this cabbage tree palm forest in the State Recreation Area at Booti Booti belies the bureaucratic severity of the park's official appellation.

Bulahdelah is a favourite starting point for boating trips around the Myall Lakes (see entry) into which the Myall River opens. Since the 1950s, when the Pacific Highway was routed through Bulahdelah, access to the Myall Lakes along the highway and Lakes Way, just north of the town, has also been opened up.

Bulahdelah figures prominently in Les Murray's 'The Bulahdelah–Taree Holiday Song Cycle' and the town retains various memorials of its past; the former Court House still stands high above the river bank; the old Plough Inn, used as a Cobb & Co. staging post, is still in use; and a full-sized recreation of an early timber train runs on the Bulahdelah Logging Railway. *Population 1100*

ALUM MOUNTAIN Named after the alunite deposits found there, this prominent hill was worked for eighty years from the late nineteenth century. It was the only known above-ground deposit of alunite in the world; the phosphate produced here was used in paper and dyes. In addition to the old mine workings, mineral specimens and orchids can still be found at the site.

CROWDY BAY NATIONAL PARK ■ 158

The national park stretches along the coast from Diamond Head in the

'he unspoiled beaches of Crowdy Bay National Park come to ı end where Diamond Head juts into the blue Pacific.

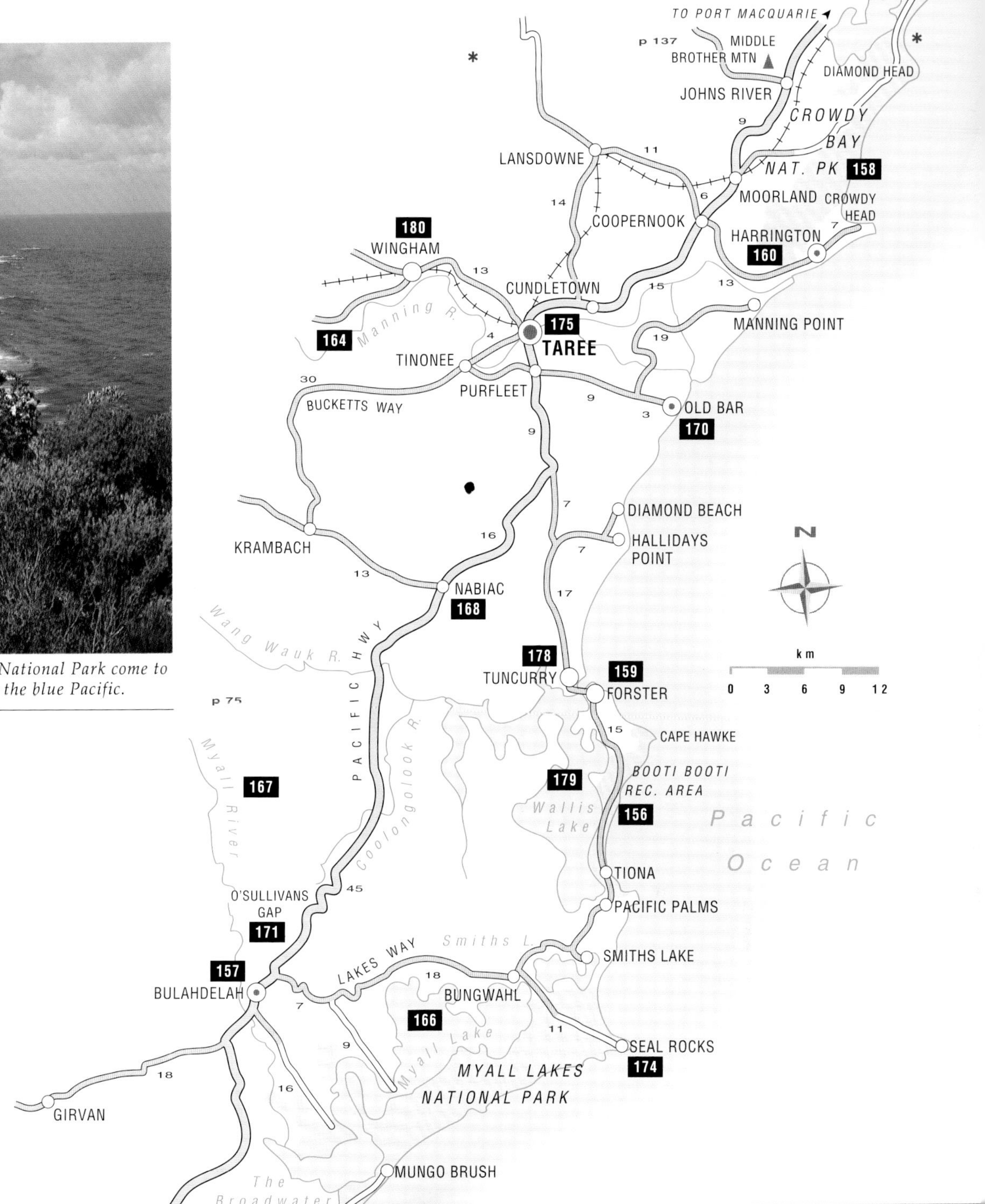

ıorth to Crowdy Head in the south.)iamond Head was given the name ›f Indian Head by Captain Cook, vho saw Aborigines on the head-and; the shiny quartz crystals found ı the rocks gave rise to the more ecent name. Crowdy Head has a ighthouse, dating from 1879, and ›oth headlands offer spectacular 360-legree views from the coast to the nountains behind.

The park contains beaches, coastal agoons, swamps and cliffs within its '412 hectares. It is well known for its pectacular pink-flowered boronias, Christmas bells, flannel flowers and paper daisies and is also host to over ›ne hundred species of birds. In addition to the rare eastern grass owl, here is a colony of black-necked wans, a species usually found only ı northern Australia.

There are some interesting dune ormations running parallel to the coast, which are evidence of ancient,

Fishing boats still seek the shelter of Forster's breakwater but most commercial fishing is based at nearby Tuncurry.

At first glance, the contemplative boat owner in this pastoral-marine scene on the banks of the Myall Lakes could be taken for a bargee in old Europe.

prehistoric shorelines. Unusual eroded rock formations jutting out into the ocean are a feature of the cliff base. The author Kylie Tennant, who wrote *The Man on the Headland*, had a hut built for her near Diamond Head by the 'man' of the title, Ernie Metcalfe. She donated the hut and surrounding land to the National Parks and Wildlife Service in 1976 and her gift is commemorated in Kylie's Hut and Kylie's Beach, favourite spots within the park.

FORSTER ■ 159

According to Captain Cook's log of 11 May 1770 he sighted and named Cape Hawke, the headland south of Forster after Baron Hawke, a British naval hero. For a hundred years after this sighting, the district around Forster remained the undisturbed home of the Worimi and Birpai Aborigines. The site of the town, on part of the Australian Agricultural Company's huge one-million-acre grant, was surveyed in 1869. The proposed settlement on the south side of the entrance to Lake Wallis was to have been called 'Minimbah' but by the time the town was gazetted in 1870 the name had been changed to Forster, after William Forster, Secretary for Lands. The early settlers devoted themselves to timber-getting, shipbuilding and fishing. The timber industry is now declining and the shipbuilding industry came to an end after the Second World War during which the last vessels were built at Forster for the Ministry of Munitions. Commercial fishing is still carried on although Forster's twin town across the water, Tuncurry (see entry), is the major centre for the local industry.

The first school was built in 1870, the year the town was gazetted and the first schoolmaster, a graduate of Cambridge University, taught for fees of threepence per week or donations of meat and potatoes.

Sitting between Wallis Lake and the ocean, Forster's climate is semi-tropical with cabbage tree palms growing wild. The annual Spring Festival in October celebrates the importance of the oyster farms on Wallis Lake and the blessing of the fishing fleet is part of the colourful celebrations. Forster attracts scuba divers to its readily accessible coral outcrops while nearby Pebbly Beach draws marine scientists in search of fossils. *Population 9520*

FESTIVALS Forster–Tuncurry Spring Festival, October.

HARRINGTON ■ 160

Harrington was named by John Oxley who first surveyed the area in 1818 and later recommended it as a possible site for the Australian Agricultural Company. He named the newly discovered entrance to the Manning River 'Harrington Lake' under the mistaken impression that it was a coastal lagoon.

Susceptible to flooding and silting, the notorious bar at Harrington was, and still is, unpredictable – ships entering the Manning River at this point required the services of a pilot. The small town of Harrington grew up around the pilot station and the graves of those whose ships foundered, the latest in 1941, can be seen on Pilot Hill.

Harrington became a port for cedar, maize and farm produce from settlements further upriver. A breakwater was built in 1894 from stone quarried at nearby Crowdy Head, the stone being transported by means of a specially built railway that ran the six kilometres from quarry to breakwater.

Despite the dangers to ships attempting to enter the river mouth, modern Harrington makes the most of its safe boating and swimming spots. In an area known for its heavy surf, the estuarine beach at Harrington is not only safe, it is situated at the part of the river where the muddy brown river waters and mangrove-lined banks are transformed into blue waters and yellow sand. *Population 1410*

HAWKS NEST ■ 161

This small town on the northern shore of Port Stephens is far less developed and busy in the summer months than other towns in the area despite its many physical advantages. It sits on the Myall River, which leads into the Myall Lakes, and at the southern end of a forty-kilometre-stretch of ocean beach. The view from Yacaaba Head behind which the town sits, offers spectacular views of the coast, the offshore islands of Cabbage Tree and Broughton (both bird-breeding sanctuaries and the inland lakes and rivers.

In the early days of settlemen Hawks Nest was an important centr for this timber and shipbuilding district before Nelson Bay (see entry achieved dominance. The first hote in this district was at Hawks Nes so-called because of a large tree i the hotel grounds, which was use as a navigational marker and wa also a favourite nesting place fo hawks. The first school in the are opened at Hawks Nest in 1878 an pupils from Tea Gardens were rowe across the narrow strip of the Mya River in the *Schooler*.

Now a quiet fishing village fo most of the year, Hawks Nest i closely linked to Tea Gardens and th two towns host the annual Mya Prawn Festival. The festival include a prawn-eating competition wher one competitor with his eyes on th record books managed to consume hearty one kilogram of shelle prawns in five minutes and six seconds. *Population 1250*

FESTIVALS Myall Prawn Festiva March.

KARUAH ■ 16

The Karuah River on which the village stands was named 'Clyde' b Lachlan Macquarie but the inhabitants stuck to the Aboriginal nam for the river and named the settlement Karuah meaning 'native plun tree'. There is still a substantia Aboriginal population in and aroun Karuah.

The first settlement in the distric was at nearby Carrington where th Australian Agricultural Company established its headquarters – movin eighty settlers, more than seven hundred sheep, fifteen horses an twelve head of cattle into Carringto in 1826. The timber getters aroun Karuah and those who farmed th oysters or dredged the shells fron the riverbank for burning to mak lime, were dependent on the settlement at Carrington for supplies With the departure of the Australia Agricultural Company in the 1840 and the development of other settlements nearer the ocean entrance t Port Stephens, Kuruah languished.

This small village on the Pacifi Highway is the northern entry poin to the Shire of Port Stephens, and i renowned for its high-quality oysters. *Population 840*

'TAHLEE' The sandstock brick hom of the first three Australian Agricultural Company commissioner still stands in extensive ground across the water from Karuah. Ther have been various additions since i was built in 1826, including the timber reception room and ballroon some distance from the house, bot of which feature white marble chimney pieces and mirrors. A stone an brick slipway in the grounds wa

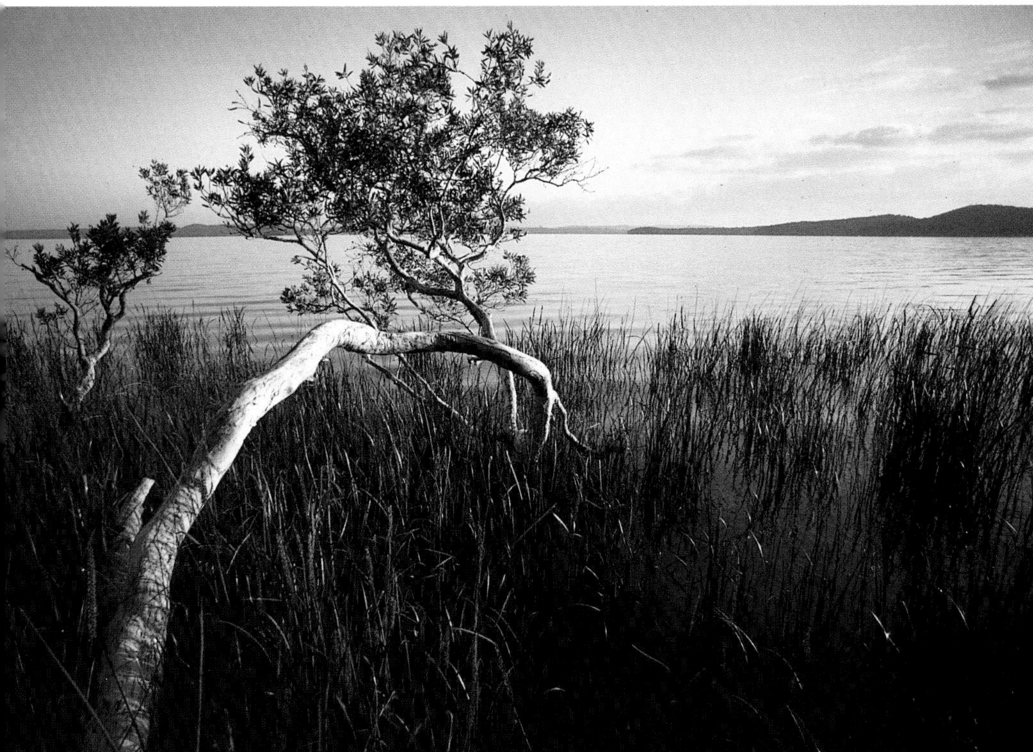

The charm of the four waterways which make up the lakes of Myall is due largely to the fact that the seagrass-fringed shoreline has remained almost completely free of development.

used to build and launch the eccentrically spelt *Caruah*, the first steamer built in Port Stephens.

LEMON TREE PASSAGE ■ 163

Lemon Tree Passage is on the Tillgerry Peninsula, which juts into the sea from the southern shore of Port Stephens. On the east of the town is the shallow, mangrove-covered Tillgerry Creek, which has some of the area's largest oyster leases. A short distance offshore, opposite the slipway and marina sits Bull Island. To the west is Tanilba Bay on which the historic Tanilba House is situated.

The town was named by early settlers who found what they thought were lemon trees growing on the point – the origin of the lemon-like trees remains a mystery. Lemon Tree Passage provided the only alternative to steamer transport to the rapidly developing city of Newcastle in the early 1900s. Passengers arrived in the town by boat to be picked up by a horse and cart, which made the regular journey to Raymond Terrace and Newcastle.

Like many of the towns on the southern shores of Port Stephens there has been a boom in the last twenty years in the number of permanent residents and tourists in Lemon Tree Passage. *Population 4930*

TANILBA HOUSE Built in 1831 for Lieutenant William Caswell, Tanilba House, a fourteen-roomed homestead was built by convicts from locally mined porphyry stone and quartz. There is even a small stone jail beneath the house. A stone gateway and wall, topped by bollards from the First World War battleship HMAS *Sydney*, was added by a later owner as was the unusual small temple in the grounds.

MANNING RIVER ■ 164

Prior to European settlement the region around the Manning River was home to a number of tribes of Aborigines. Near the food-rich shores of the river estuary, camp sites and kitchen middens were many.

Named by John Oxley in 1818, the river marked the northern boundary of the Australian Agricultural Company's land grant and also the northern perimeter of Governor Darling's 'limits of location' for legal settlement. The squatters and cedargetters who were attracted to the banks of the Manning River ignored this prohibition.

The river rises in the Great Dividing Range and a number of tributary streams and rivers including the Myall, Barrington, Gloucester and Cooplacurripa join the Manning on its 150-kilometre passage to the sea. From Wingham to Taree, the two major towns on its banks, the river is slow-moving and tranquil as it passes through dairy country. Beyond Taree the river changes to become punctuated by plantations of mangroves, mudflats and a confusion of twists, turns and channels.

The flood-prone delta system, a complex maze of channels separated by river islands, enters the sea at Harrington (see entry). Numerous old river channels and lagoons mark previous courses of the river across the flood plains. The complex estuary and ever-changing sandbars which make the river difficult to approach from the sea have discouraged the economic development that occurred around more accessible rivers such as the Hunter.

MEDOWIE ■ 165

Medowie's history is linked with that of the Hunter and Port Stephens but it has neither the coal and industry of the Hunter nor the tourism which stimulates Port Stephens.

The earliest settlers in Medowie, Robert Campbell and a Welshman Daniel James, did much to pioneer the fruit-growing that is still carried on in the district. The soil was very swampy and drainage work was necessary before the first fruit trees could be planted. Fruit has been supplied to Newcastle from Medowie ever since.

Medowie – believed to come from a local Woromi Aboriginal word meaning' place of tall trees' – stands near the Grahamstown Dam which provides water storage for Newcastle and other urban regions of the Lower Hunter. Although the waters of the dam are not available for recreational purposes, a small park on the edge of the lake is a popular picnic spot.

The population of Medowie is growing rapidly with many homes occupied by RAAF personnel from the nearby Williamtown airforce base. *Population 3260*

MYALL LAKES ■ 166

The Myall Lakes are the largest fresh-brackish water system in New South Wales. Although there is only one lake, four bodies of water in the system – Bombah Broadwater, Two Mile Lake, Boolambayte Lake and the Myall Lake – have been given names. All four lakes are relatively shallow, brown-water lakes and the first three are slightly salty.

The name Myall is believed to come from a local Aboriginal word meaning 'small, silver grey wattle tree' and until the arrival of Europeans the Lakes were home to the Worimi and Birpai Aborigines. In a short while the number of Aborigines diminished rapidly...as did the tall stands of trees around the lakes. The heavy commercial traffic in the waterways of the lake system declined as the timber ran out so that by the 1940s there were only a few fishermen working the area. Settlement around the lakes is still sparse and road access is limited.

Between the lakes and the ocean lies a belt of sand dunes, the mining of which in 1960 sparked a conserva-

Beneath the speeding traffic on the modern bridge which leaps the Myall River near Hawks Nest live the prawns for which this region is famous.

The lighthouse-keeper's compound at Sugarloaf Point looks down on the tiny village of Seal Rocks.

tion controversy that led to the declaration of the region as a national park in 1972.

MYALL LAKES NATIONAL PARK The quartzite dune system, up to 120 metres high, that separates the lakes from the ocean is unique in Australia and represents past changes in sea level. Myall Lakes National Park now covers more than 31 000 hectares that include not only the dunes but 10 000 hectares of lakebed, surrounding land, coastal beaches and offshore islands including Broughton Island, a reserve and breeding site for an estimated 200 000 shearwaters.

MYALL RIVER ■ 167

Rachel Henning described the Myall River in a letter to her sister in 1866 as '...very beautiful in its own way, not very wide but very deep so that the great timber punts can go up and down and the banks shut in by dense forest so that you cannot see any light through'. Pleasure boats of all shapes and sizes can now be seen in the river instead of timber boats.

The Myall River is separated into two distinct sections by the southernmost of the Myall Lakes–Bombah Broadwater. The Upper Myall rises east of the Craven State Forest and passes between the Myall River and Bulahdelah State Forests before reaching Bombah Boardwater. Only four small villages and the town of Bulahdelah (see entry) stand on the banks of the Upper Myall.

After exiting on the south shore of Bombah Broadwater the river runs parallel to the coast until it broadens at an area called Pull for Nothing Bay before entering Port Stephens between Tea Gardens and Hawks Nest, the only two settlements of any size on the Lower Myall.

NABIAC ■ 168

This way-station on the Pacific Highway, named for an Aboriginal word meaning 'wild fig tree', has a modern claim to fame as the birthplace of the noted poet Les A. Murray. Murray, who has received widespread critical praise for poetry which vividly describes the spiritual relationship of black and white rural Australians with the land, was raised on a dairy farm in the nearby Bunyah district.

NELSON BAY ■ 169

The first written record of the name Nelson Bay appears in Captain Philip King's chart of 1845 but whether the Nelson after whom the town is named was Horatio Nelson or the *Lady Nelson*, which brought Governor and Lady Macquarie to the area in 1818 is unknown.

The first non-Aboriginals in the Nelson Bay district were groups of Chinese fishermen who dried, salted and cured their catch which was sent for sale to their compatriots on the goldfields, to Chinese merchants in Sydney or back to China. One of the ongoing problems of European fishermen around Nelson Bay was how to get their catch fresh to markets. An attempt in 1880 to ice the catch failed and it is only since 1956 with the building of the storage and processing facilities of the Fishermens Co-operative that freshly caught fish has been successfully exported from Nelson Bay.

One of the earliest European settlers to arrive in Nelson Bay was Thomas Laman, fisheries inspector and customs officer, who joined Mr Glover, keeper of the Port Stephens Inner Light in the two-family population at Nelson Bay in the 1870s. Land around the tiny settlement was surveyed around the same time so that by 1886, when the Sea Breeze Hotel opened, Nelson Bay could boast a population of thirty. Access to and from Nelson Bay was by sea only although Magnus Cromarty, surviving son of William Cromarty, drowned at Anna Bay (see entry), did blaze a makeshift track through virgin bush south of Nelson Bay with his spring cart, the first wheeled vehicle in the district.

It was the coming of the vessel HMAS *Assault* to Port Stephens and Nelson Bay during the Second World War that finally gave the town the boost to development it had long awaited. Military Camps and depots at Nelson Bay were provided with mains water, electricity and a reasonable road. After the war Nelson Bay 'inherited' the base hospital, the camp buildings (later used as a migrant centre) and the upgraded facilities installed for the combined operations training.

With post-war prosperity came tourism and Nelson Bay became the main town on Port Stephens. A Fish Culture Research Station (researching prawn and oyster farming) and an aquarium, reflect the continuin importance of the Pacific Ocea waters in the scheme of things here *Population 6770*

OLD BAR ■ 17

When John Oxley visited the are around Old Bar he named the wate behind the bar 'Farquhar's Lake' mistaking it for a coastal lagoon rathe than the ocean's southern inlet to th Manning River. Later exploration revealed the complex delta area wit its two channels, three islands and bar as notorious as the one at Harrington (see entry). Shifts in th position of the sandbar since the lat 1980s mean the former estuary ha now become the enclosed coasta lagoon that Oxley thought it was.

Old Bar is now a thriving settlement and was one of the fastes growing communities in th Manning River valley during th 1988 housing boom. As the locatio of the nearest surfing beach to Taree Old Bar, together with Mud Bishop Reserve on the Manning River, and number of river islands, offers a interesting mixture of recreationa possibilities to tourists and resident alike. *Population 1990*

MITCHELLS ISLAND A number of wal king tracks and roads run across thi island, which has rich dairy pastures a small state forest and ten kilometres of sandy ocean beach. Aborigina shell middens are still visible. Unlik most of the other islands on this par of the Manning River, Mitchell Island and its neighbour Oxle Island are shale outcrops not alluvia soil deposits.

O'SULLIVANS GAP ■ 17

The Pacific Highway, which nov runs through the Bulahdelah Stat Forest also provides access to th O'Sullivans Gap Nature Reserve When 270 hectares was first set asid in 1940 to protect some fine stands o eucalypts and rainforest, this sectio of the highway was not completed There is now a roadside rest area a the reserve, which has been expand ed to encompass 320 hectares o carefully logged forest.

Within the Meyers Range, O'Sullivans Gap varies in height from 45–250 metres. Flooded gums up t sixty metres in height, weeping myrtles and Bangalow palms in th rainforest gullies can be seen on th thirty-minute walk through th reserve. Lace monitor lizards, koalas

At Taree, the Manning River flows placidly through an agricultural landscape before enveloping the town on two sides; here the broad waters provide the perfect venue fo Taree's annual aquatic festival each Easter. A few kilometres downstream the Manning broadens into an intricate delta as it seeks three separate exits to the sea.

quolls, possums of several species and diamond pythons are just a few of the animals to inhabit the reserve.

PORT STEPHENS ■ 172

Port Stephens was sighted, described and named (after Sir Philip Stephens, Secretary to the Admiralty) but not entered by Captain Cook in 1770. The first Europeans to enter the Port were a group of five convicts who escaped from Parramatta in 1790, four of them being found five years later living with the local Aborigines.

The next Europeans to visit Port Stephens were also escaped convicts – William Bryant, his wife Mary, their two very young children and seven companions. In 1791 this group made an extraordinary epic journey from Sydney to Timor in a six-oared fishing ketch. All survived the journey but were discovered in Timor and, from their depositions, it was revealed that Port Stephens was one of the harbours they visited during their amazing voyage.

The first official legal visit to Port Stephens had to wait until 1795 when Deputy Surveyor Grimes was sent to complete a survey of the port…which did not impress him.

Port Stephens, the drowned valleys of the Karuah and Myall Rivers, stretches twenty-four kilometres inland from two prominent headlands. The entrance to the port has been likened to the entrance to the port at Rio de Janeiro. The first lighthouse was built in 1862 on Point Stephens, which was then a peninsula linked to the mainland by a spit, swept away in 1891. The striking four-level tower of white-painted Sydney sandstone stands forty-two metres above the high-water mark. Initially powered by kerosene, then acetylene gas (1922) and electricity (1942), the light is now automatic. A second Inner Lighthouse was built in 1872 on Nelson Head inside Port Stephens. From the octagonal tower three kerosene lamps shone through separate windows. It too is now automatic.

Port Stephens has the distinction of being the only port on this part of the east coast totally devoid of industrial development…although there have been plenty of schemes to change this. In 1911, as part of decentralisation, a naval base and railway connection from the port to the main northern railway line was mooted. Land was resumed for this purpose by the government and retained until the 1960s. Two major modern cities were planned and got as far as the drawing board – one metropolis was planned for Pindimar and another for North Arm Cove designed by Walter Burley Griffin who designed the city of Canberra. By 1924 these ambitious plans had been dropped on the basis that two major overseas ports – Newcastle and Port Stephens – so close together would be unworkable. Industrial plants such as oil refineries, coal loaders and a steel plant were also proposed for this region throughout the forty years up to 1967.

Today's holidaymakers would happily acknowledge that the truly successful development to occur here has been Port Stephens' post-war tourist boom.

FESTIVALS Game Fishing Festival, February.

RAYMOND TERRACE ■ 173

Raymond Terrace sits at the junction of two rivers – the Hunter and the William and it was the exploration of the former that brought Colonel William Paterson to survey the area officially called 'First Branch of the Coal River' in 1801. He renamed the area Green Hills and it is not certain when or by whom the town was named Raymond Terrace although by 1812 on Lachlan Macquarie's first visit that was the name used. The cedar around what was to become the town site was fe.lled and floated down the Hunter River, which at that time passed right through the town, to Newcastle. By 1831 a steam ship was making the first downriver journey to Newcastle before heading south to Sydney.

The first land grant, in 1828 was made to merchant James King who ran cattle, grew wheat and planted vines from France, Spain and Portugal as well as operating a pottery on his property. After the first land sales in 1838, Raymond Terrace became an important wool-shipping port for wool from New England but the boom was to be shortlived.

A major flood in 1850, the death of King and the change in the course of the Hunter caused by silting brought a temporary end to Raymond Terrace's growth. In 1904, the population of the town was 300 adult males. By 1927 the days of Raymond Terrace's position as a port were over when the last loads of timber were shipped to Newcastle.

Since 1937 when Raymond Terrace was merged with the Shire of Port Stephens – of which it is now the administrative centre – Raymond Terrace has seen a renaissance as a residential centre. Many of its newer inhabitants come from nearby Williamtown RAAF base. Despite restrictions on swimming and fishing, Grahamstown Dam, north-east of the town, is a popular location for sailing, boating and water skiing. *Population 11 160*

SEAL ROCKS ■ 174

Seal Rocks basks in the shadow of Sugarloaf Point where the 130-year-old lighthouse still flashes a warning of the rocky shoreline – some of these rocks break the ocean's surface several kilometres out to sea and provide a winter sundeck for the fur seals after which the village is named. This isolated collection of cottages, caravan park and store with matching beaches facing north and

A foreshore park on the embankment at Tea Gardens typifies the relaxed atmosphere of this town on the western side of the Myall River Bridge (see p. 69).

south marks the north-eastern limits of the Myall Lakes National Park.

TAREE ■ 175

Before the arrival of the first European settler in 1829, the region around Taree was home to the Birpai Aborigines. The name for the town comes from a Birpai word meaning fruit of the wild fig tree. The descendants of the original Birpai people still live at Purfleet, south of Taree; life on the old reserve there in the 1950s and 60s was poignantly described in Ella Simon's 1978 book *Through my Eyes*.

William Wynter, a retired paymaster of the Royal Navy was granted land here in 1829 or 1831 and he named his property 'Tarlie'. His first schooner, used to transport timber from his cedar leases, was called *Taree*. It was this name that was chosen by his son-in-law Henry Flett for the private town laid out on the Wynter estate. At the first land sale in Taree in 1854 forty lots of forty hectares were sold and Taree became one of a number of timber shipping points on the Manning River. In addition to timber, the flat-bottomed boats known as droghers took farm and dairy produce down the Manning and returned with stores for the new town.

By the time Taree was declared a municipality in 1885 it had superseded the official government town of Wingham as the region's main centre and this dominant position was confirmed when the northern railway line was extended to Taree, not Wingham, in 1913.

Taree is now the commercial and manufacturing centre of the Manning Valley, a district of dairying, timber, mixed farming and fishing. Host to the annual Aquatic Festival and Australian Power Boat Titles at Easter, it still contains reminders of its past not only in the street names given to the town by Henry Flett but in buildings such as the old Court House and Protestant Hall both built in the late 1800s and still standing. *Population 16 300*

FESTIVALS Manning River Aquatic Festival, Easter.

TEA GARDENS ■ 176

The village sits at the mouth of the Myall River, on the quieter, less tourist-oriented shore of Port Stephens. Tea Gardens was so named after a failed experiment by the Australian Agricultural Company to grow tea there. Until 1970 and the building of the 'Singing Bridge' between Tea Gardens and the larger settlement at Hawks Nest, a ferry used to transport passengers across the Myall River.

The first timber mill in Port Stephens was established in 1920 just outside Tea Gardens. Paddle-wheel punts brought logs from Bulahdelah via the Myall Lakes to the mill. Some of the hardwood milled here was used on the Transcontinental railway line across the Nullarbor Plain and – in a rather different environment – for construction work along the waterfront at Vancouver in Canada.

Now a favourite entry point to the Myall Lakes, Tea Gardens is a small settlement with oyster leases, boat moorings and a fishing co-operative. *Population 680*

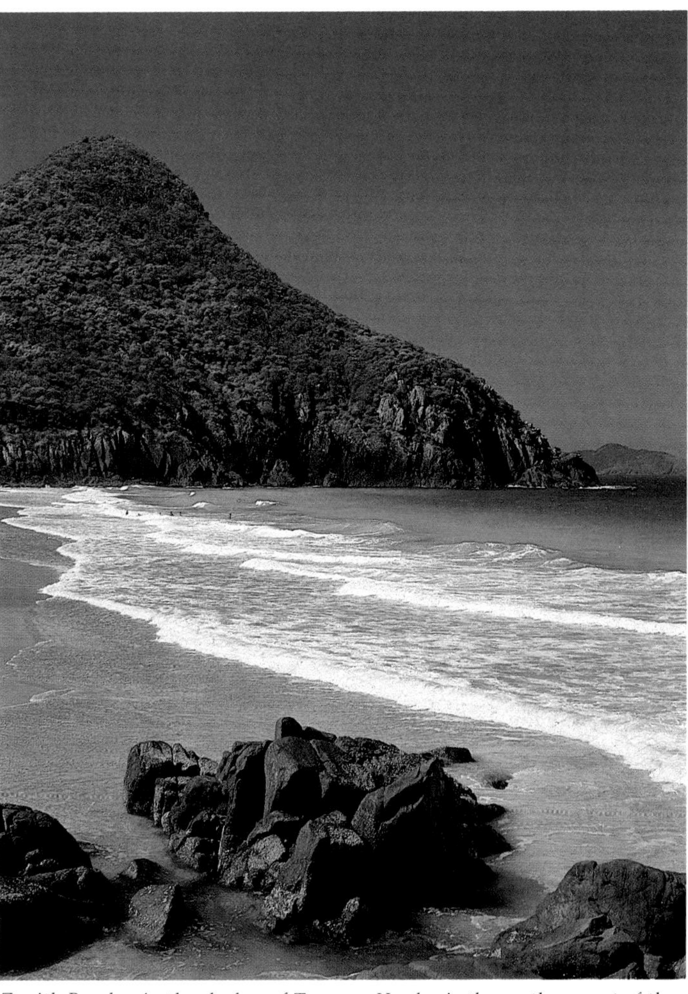

Zenith Beach – in the shadow of Tomaree Head – is the northernmost of the four compact beaches that line the blunt end of the Nelson Bay peninsula.

TOMAREE NATIONAL PARK ■ 177

This small (896 hectare) national park covers a narrow coastal strip running from south of Tomaree Point almost to Anna Bay. Bird life is everywhere with many ocean and heathland birds as well as fairy penguins making this their home.

Unfortunately, the bitou bush, an invasive, introduced South African weed threatens some of the native vegetation and the fragile ecology has been damaged by World War II defence emplacements and the activities of trail-bike riders.

TUNCURRY ■ 178

For many years after the township of Forster was laid out, Tuncurry, on the other side of Cape Hawke Harbour, was known as 'North Forster'. By 1875 most of the residents, however, used the Aboriginal name for the district Tuncurry apparently meaning 'plenty of fish' although it was only in the 1890s that the name was officially recognised.

Punts and ferries were used to transport passengers and goods between the two townships until the bridge was opened in 1959. One ferryman carried a spare pair of oars for the use of any obliging and energetic passenger. Sulkies were loaded onto punts with their wheels in the water on either side and the horse in the water ahead of the punt.

Fishing has been the mainstay of Tuncurry since the pioneer fishermen, immigrants from Lipari in Sicily, formed the basis for the trawling industry. Transport was always a problem until 1947 when the Wallis Lake Fishermen's Co-operative was founded – with an official capital of only seventeen pounds sterling – and the 'co-op' now uses its own transport to get one of New South Wales' most bountiful catches of fish, prawns, crabs and lobster to market. *Population 5020*

WALLIS LAKE ■ 179

Wallis Lake is the last of the chain of lakes that stretch up the coastline north of Sydney. The lake is fed by four rivers – the Wallamba, the Wang Wauk, Coolangolook and Wallingat – which act as spawning grounds for many of the fish species found in the lake. There is an outlet to the ocean between Forster and Tuncurry, the only major settlements around the shoreline of this waterway.

Within the seventy-eight square kilometres of lake there are over thirty river islands, including the oddly named Yahoo Island, and a number of these are now nature reserves. Wallis Lake is world famous for its succulent oysters which are grown on the 600-odd oyster leases, and exports go to Hawaii, Hong Kong, Malaysia and Tahiti as well as to Australia's capital cities.

GREEN CATHEDRAL At Tiona, on the lakeside, stands an open-air church of the Reorganised Church of the Latter Day Saints. Palm trees form the roof, large logs the seating and a stone altar stands almost in the water of the lake. Dedicated in 1941 the church is designed for private worship and meditation although annual public services are also held in the Green Cathedral.

WINGHAM ■ 180

Wingham is named after a seventh-century village of the same name in Kent, England. The town is very English in style, built round a village common, and was the first official town to be laid out in the Manning Valley in 1843. Many of the buildings around the 'common' are now listed as 'heritage' items and include hotels, the post office and a butcher shop. Other less conventional memorials have been installed on the common more recently; a huge, 400-year-old brush-box log, weighing approximately 30 tonnes, commemorates the bicentennial of Captain Cook's voyage of 1770 and the shell of a Vampire jet-fighter plane was put in place to commemorate the fiftieth anniversary of the RAAF.

Timber was first taken out through the embryo settlement of Wingham, the highest navigable place on the Manning River, in 1842 and the remains of the old wharf can still be seen. The moving of government offices to Taree in 1900 and the coming of the railway to Taree in 1913 led to a decline in Wingham's status as the 'official' centre on the Manning. *Population 4410*

WINGHAM BRUSH A seven-hectare area of 'Wingham Brush' has been preserved near the centre of Wingham. The brush is so thick that light hardly penetrates...but flying foxes do, in their thousands, at certain times of the year. Moreton Bay figs, vines, orchids, ferns and subtropical plants flourish in this isolated zone of pre-settlement bushland.

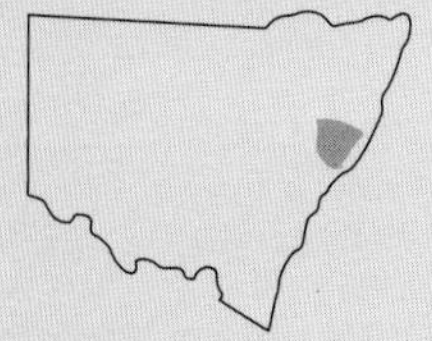

Gloucester & Dungog

Although the densely wooded ranges of the mid-north coast no longer resound to the chop of the timber-getter's axe, modern hardwood-logging operations continue to play a vital role in the region's economy. The well-watered river valleys nourish a pastoral industry dominated traditionally by dairying.

ALLYN RIVER ■ 181

The protected forests of the Barrington and Gloucester Tops area north-west of Dungog, are the origin of the Allyn River headwaters. The river winds through the Allyn Valley meeting the Paterson River near the village of Vacy, north of Maitland.

A scenic forest drive follows the course of the river's headwaters through Chichester State Forest and is the starting point for numerous walking trails through forest parks adjacent to the river. Mount Allyn Forest Park preserves dark patches of ancient negrohead beech – some up to 1000 years old – and is the location of the circular Burraga Swamp – a one-hectare swamp surrounded by towering rainforest. A lookout in the area of the river's headwaters provides spectacular views across the Williams River valley to the east and the Allyn River valley to the west.

BARRINGTON TOPS NATIONAL PARK ■ 182

The two linked plateaux – Barrington and Gloucester Tops – that crown the heavily forested Barrington Tops National Park are subject to the whims of a capricious climate that can bring mist rolling over the basalt-domed plateaux prior to a deluge of rain to be followed by a clear spell, and then another downpour in quick succession. Snowfalls occur fairly often from autumn to spring though a snow storm can blow in suddenly even during the warm months. The park covers most of the catchment area for the Hunter and Manning Rivers – the two main river systems that drain to the coast, nourishing the valleys below. The plateaux fall steeply away from a maximum height of 1555 metres and vegetation is highly diversified as a result of the varying altitudes and soil types.

Snow gums, peat bogs, sub-alpine grassland and a mosaic of gorges, waterfalls and fast-running streams dominate the upper regions, while the deep gullies and ravines below the plateaux support a community of Antarctic beech. Sheltered stands of subtropical rainforest flourish in the moist and warm valleys below the cliff line and eucalypt forests are widespread throughout the park. The rainforests which the park protects, have been accepted as part of the eastern coast World Heritage rainforest zone.

Walking is the main activity with trails taking in most of the park's impressive landforms, highland lookouts and forest areas. One of the park's most popular bushwalking trails follows part of the Link Trail from Gloucester Tops before descending to the Barrington Guest House – a rambling old ranch-style home built from the surrounding timber in 1926 and now a guest house for visitors to the park.

The park is named after Robert Barrington Dawson, son of the first agent of the Australian Agricultural Company (see Gloucester) which oversaw the first settlement in the Gloucester district in the 1890s.

BOORAL ■ 183

The small township of Booral was once at the hub of the giant Australian Agricultural Company's (see Gloucester) most significant and successful crop-growing area. The town is located on the Karuah River which in the early days before the arrival of the railway and reliable road transport , was the only transport link between Booral, Stroud, Port Stephens and the Sydney produce markets.

The old Booral wharf, a large sandstone structure on the eastern bank of the Karuah River, was built by the Australian Agricultural Company to facilitate the movement of goods between these small settlements. Two other major company buildings remaining in the town are Booral House and St Barnabas' Anglican Church.

Booral House has a commanding, lofty position atop a gently rising slope on the eastern bank of the Karuah River. The house was built by convict labour in 1831 as a company manager's residence and with its shuttered French windows, unusual six-panel main doors and recessed front verandah, is regarded as a house of great architectural and historical importance.

The fine old sandstone Anglican Church was originally situated behind Booral House, but was dismantled and carefully rebuilt on its present site in 1873 when a road was constructed through the area.

BUCKETTS WAY ■ 184

Navigable waterways were the main transport links between the Australian Agricultural Company's (see Gloucester) settlements during the early years of their development. But by 1840, a trail pioneered in the 1830s had developed into a rough track that ran from Raymond Terrace (see *Taree & Nelson Bay*) to settlements in the company's Port Stephens Estate. This track, that by 1857 continued on to Port Macquarie and Kempsey, preceded the present-day Bucketts Way – an alternative, sealed route to the Pacific Highway that passes through green, pastoral valleys. Bucketts Way branches off the highway south of Booral, passing through that village and continuing on to Stroud and Gloucester before linking up with the main highway again at Taree.

CHICHESTER DAM ■ 185

Chichester Dam is in the upper part of the Williams River catchment area, at the junction of the Chichester and Wangat Rivers. The 22 300 megalitres of water impounded by the dam forms a lake bounded around most

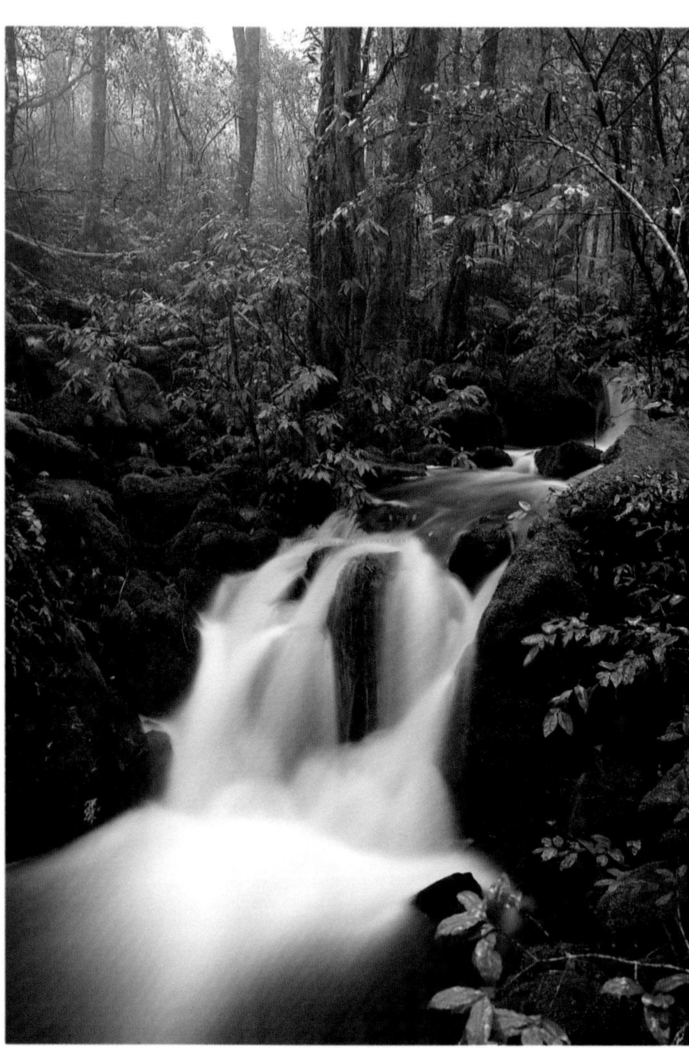

The constantly replenished streams of the Barrington Tops plateau rush from the escarpment forests to water the Hunter and Manning valleys.

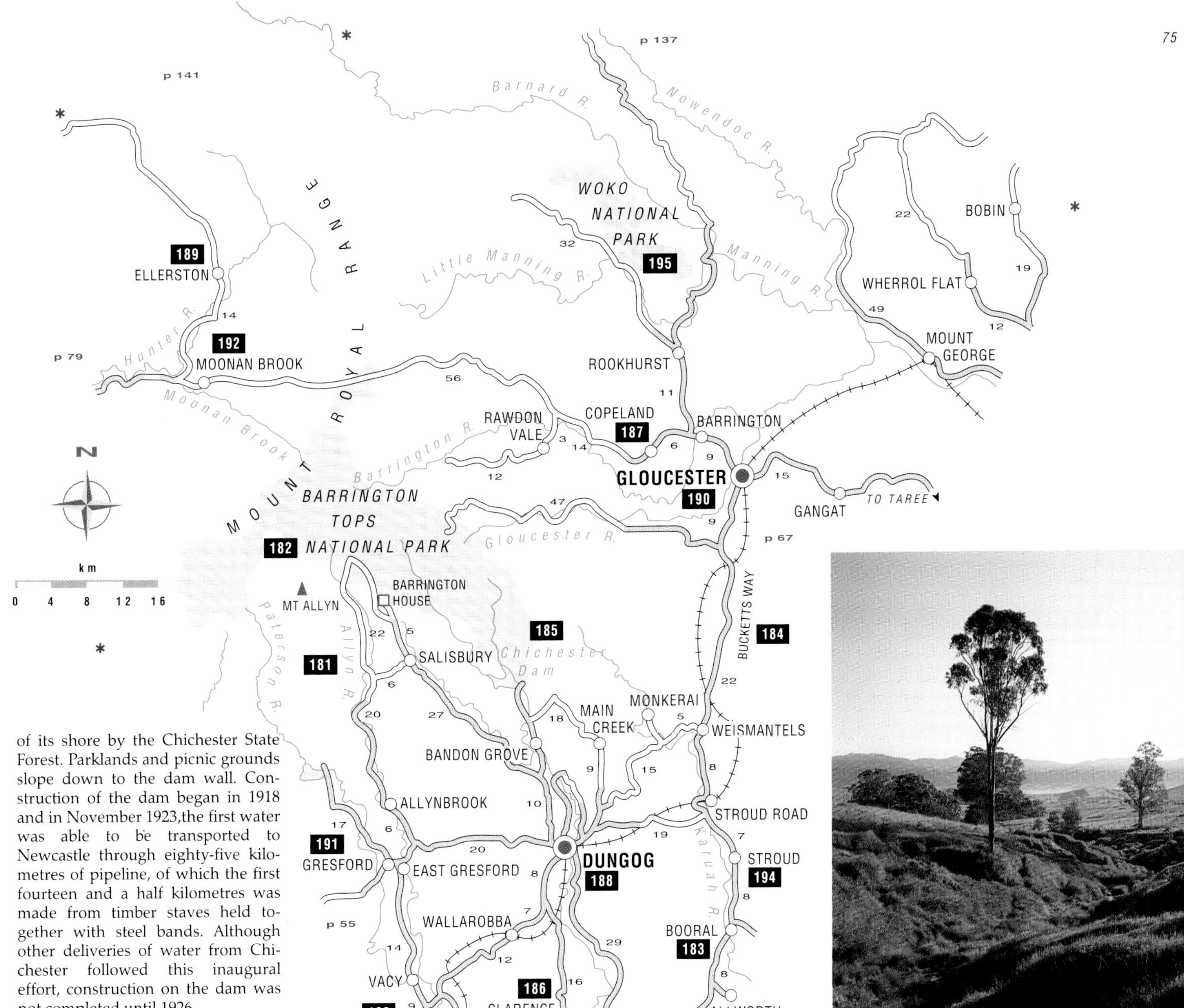

Pastoral activity has flourished in the Barrington Tops valleys for 160 years.

of its shore by the Chichester State Forest. Parklands and picnic grounds slope down to the dam wall. Construction of the dam began in 1918 and in November 1923,the first water was able to be transported to Newcastle through eighty-five kilometres of pipeline, of which the first fourteen and a half kilometres was made from timber staves held together with steel bands. Although other deliveries of water from Chichester followed this inaugural effort, construction on the dam was not completed until 1926.

CLARENCE TOWN ■ 186

When the explorer John Oxley came through the Williams River valley in 1818, he noted that 'the best hardwoods in the world were growing there'. Timber-getters were quick to follow in his footsteps, establishing a camp beside the river and harvesting the valley's blue gum forests. The huge harvest of logs coupled with a wide and navigable river, soon expanded the timber camp into a shipping port – named Clarence Town in 1826 after the Duke of Clarence who was to become King William IV.

Although land was taken up for farming in the 1820s, the fledgling town was built around the timber industry, and Williams River valley timber became the basis of the New South Wales ship-building industry, 'the nursery of its steamship trade'. In 1831, the first wholly Australian-built steamship, *William IV*, was launched at Clarence Town, the town locals giving it the apt, if somewhat irreverent nickname, 'Puffing Billy'. By 1890, flour mills, tobacco factories, a tannery, hotels and stores were part of the busy river town's thriving commercial life. But a combination of factors in the last decade of the nineteenth century, including taxes imposed on the tobacco industry, an economic depression, four consecutive years of floods and the arrival of rail transport, slowed growth considerably. The death knell to progress came early in the 1900s when a fire raced through the town. Luckily a number of the pre-1860 buildings survived and today Clarence Town retains much of the history and character of its early shipping-port origins. *Population 650*

COPELAND ■ 187

A few scattered houses, a School of Arts, a weathered, wooden church, an old Public School and the remains of batteries – used to crush gold-bearing ore – overgrown with lantana and blackberries, are all that remain of this once thriving gold-mining town. In its heyday during the 1880s and 1890s, Copeland was a lively town with a population of 3000. But when the gold yield dwindled so did the population and the area reverted to primary production.

Alluvial gold was first discovered in the valley in about 1872 by former cedar-getters who, having almost completely logged the Hawkesbury, Illawarra, Shoalhaven and Hunter River districts by the 1850s, had turned their attention from timber to gold. The diggings were originally known as the Back Creek or Barrington diggings but after an inspection by the Minister for Mines, Henry Copeland, the name was changed in his honour.

After the initial discovery of alluvial gold, increased production came with the discovery and working of quartz reefs in the area. The industry peaked in 1879 with The Mountain Maid – discovered three years earlier – producing more gold than any other mine in the field.

DUNGOG ■ 188

The town of Dungog was established as a military post in 1834 in a vain effort to help rid the settlements of the Williams River valley of the pestilence of bushrangers. Twenty-five years later, bushranging activities in northern New South Wales were more prevalent than ever, dominated by the infamous hold-up man, Frederick Ward, also known as Captain Thunderbolt. Thunderbolt's nefarious activities in the valley, which were reported regularly in the *Maitland Mercury*, so outraged settlers in the area that a demand for his immediate capture was made to the police. The bushranger was a master at eluding his pursuers and he found sanctuary in south-eastern Queensland for some months before resuming his illegal activities in New South Wales. He was eventually shot and killed at Uralla (see *Armidale & Uralla*) in 1870.

Cedar-getting was the primary industry of the first settlers in the Dungog area but by 1848, agriculture was well developed, with tobacco, cereal crops and vineyards thriving in the fertile valley – a contrast to today's principal industries which include dairying, cattle-raising, hardwood timber-cutting, sawmilling and tourism. Dungog is now one of the main access routes to Barrington Tops National Park. Australian cricket hero Doug Walters was born and raised on a dairy farm just outside the town.

Dungog is a corruption of the Aboriginal word *tunkok* meaning 'a clear hill'. *Population 2190*

ELLERSTON ■ 189

The tiny settlement of Ellerston came into being in the 1830s as an outstation of 'Belltrees' (see *Muswellbrook & Scone*), a large and historic pastoral property located in the upper reaches of the Hunter River. As an outstation, Ellerston formed a vital supply and communication link between the head station and the stock runs situated over the nearby Mount Royal Range.

GLOUCESTER ■ 190

Gloucester is located at the junction of the Avon, Gloucester and Barrington Rivers in a valley fringed by a range of unusual monolithic hills called The Bucketts – from an Aboriginal word meaning 'big rocks'. East of the town lies the Mograni Range, whilst to the north, a backdrop of hills and valleys stretches into the distance. The town's proximity to several spectacular and well-patronised national parks – including the Barrington Tops National Park (see entry) – and numerous state forest reserves has prompted the development of a substantial tourist industry that operates compatibly alongside the region's agriculturally based activities.

The first European explorer to pass through the Gloucester district was the government surveyor, Henry Dangar, in early 1826. Later that year he was followed by Robert Dawson, chief agent for the Australian Agricultural Company – a giant enterprise which had raised one million pounds in England and received more than 400 000 hectares of Crown land in New South Wales to develop the pastoral, agricultural and mineral resources of the colony. Dawson was highly impressed with the area, writing in his diary that the countryside presented 'romantic scenery like a species of enchantment'. The company soon managed to establish a chain of sheep stations in the region – none of them highly successful ventures – and by the early 1830s settlers had established small farms along the Barrington River on land leased from the company, west of the present town.

Modern Gloucester stands on what was the head station of the Gloucester Estate – a 81 000-hectare parcel of land owned by the Australian Agricultural Company which was purchased by the Gloucester Estate Company in 1899 and promptly subdivided by its new owners for closer settlement. By 1900, beef cattle, dairying, mixed-farming and harvesting of the region's rich timber resources had brought economic stability to the area and Gloucester developed as the centre of this agricultural activity.

Today, a modern cattle saleyard continues to hold regular sales, and milk processed at the local cooperative plant supplies a variety of dairy products for both Sydney and Newcastle. *Population 2460*

GLOUCESTER COTTAGE Built in 1830, this former Australian Agricultural Company cottage and its surrounding paddocks formed an important outstation on Bucketts Way – the original north coast road – that for a time was to all intents and purposes the hub of the company's rich farmland holdings.

GRESFORD/ EAST GRESFORD ■ 191

The twin towns of Gresford and East Gresford occupy an area of land between the Allyn and Paterson Rivers. The history of their settlement can be traced to the early 1820s, when explorers and cedar-getters travelled to the upper reaches of the Hunter and its tributaries opening the way for settlers who took up large grants of Crown Land along the Paterson and Allyn Rivers.

The earliest crops grown were wheat, corn, turnips and tobacco. Grapes were also cultivated by each small settlement for the production of local wines. At that stage, there were no roads to the region and goods were taken by pack-horse or bullock waggon to Morpeth (see *Maitland & Cessnock*) – the main river port of colonial New South Wales – then by boat to Newcastle and then another boat to Sydney. Later, dairying and citrus orchards became popular agricultural ventures.

The ready supply of quality timber in the area led to development of a substantial sawmilling industry with a number of sawmills producing dressed cedar, ironbark, blue gum, mahogany and turpentine for the local market. Today, the area is best known for its cattle, although dairying is still carried out on a small scale and trees are still felled and hauled out of the hills.

In recent years, many of the original large properties in the region around the two towns have been subdivided and taken up by people seeking a change from city life.

Only a few kilometres from the 'Tops' rainforests, sub-alpine plants thrive.

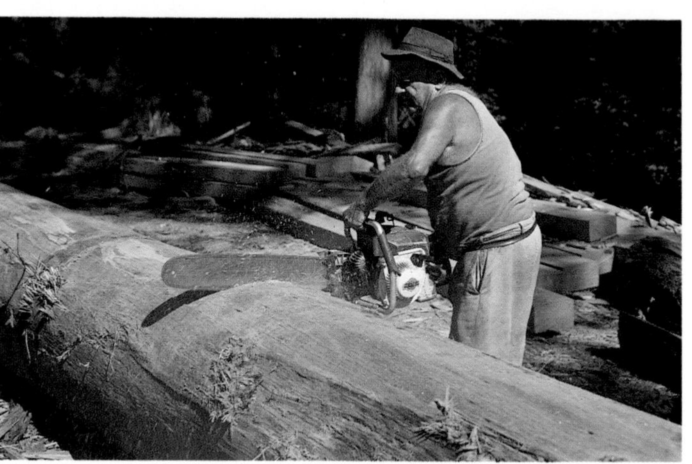

Hardwoods in the state forests still provide a challenge for Dungog loggers.

MOONAN BROOK ■ 192

Ninety years ago, the tiny settlement of Moonan Brook was known as 'The Denison' and was the heart of the Denison goldfields. Now only a few scattered cottages remain as evidence of its brief importance.

According to one local legend, the name Moonan Brook comes from a local Aboriginal word meaning 'difficult to accomplish'.

PATERSON ■ 193

The Paterson plains were opened to settlement in 1812 with the issuing of permits to ex-convicts. By 1818, the eight farms established in the area were exporting grain to Sydney. Permits were again issued in 1817 to 1818 and by 1820, twelve farms existed on the Paterson. During the 1820s the pattern of settlement in the Hunter Valley was enhanced by a system of government land grants to wealthy British immigrants – a settlement pattern reflected in the legacy of stately old homes evident throughout the region. The town of Paterson grew up on a land grant that had been issued to Susannah Ward, a soldier's widow who had 242 hectares at the head of the navigable stretch of the Paterson River – a very valuable location in the early years of settlement before the construction of roads and bridges .

In 1833 Mrs Ward agreed to exchange her land grant – called 'Cintra' – on the west side of the river for land on the east so that a town and port could be established. The settlement soon became a busy trading post and port funnel through which settlers and traders poured. Small boats carrying produce and timber from the area connected with paddle steamers bound for the markets of Sydney and overseas.

During its heyday, Paterson was a thriving industrial centre with a shipyard, sawmill, a number of flour mills, various storehouses and the offices of the then very important Hunter River Steam and Navigation Company. The arrival of the railway in 1911 inevitably killed the steamer trade and as the river shipping business declined, so did Paterson. The township has taken on a new lease of life as an increasing number of city workers take up small allotments and commute to larger towns nearby.

The graveyard near the historic St Paul's Anglican Church, where many of the district's pioneers are buried, contains the particularly ornate grave of the Reverend James Jennings Smith. The Reverend Jennings Smith – said to have been chosen as a tutor to Princess Victoria, a position he declined – was the illegitimate son of King George IV and Sara Jennings. A finely wrought, stained-glass window bearing Jennings Smith's family coat of arms commemorates the esteemed Reverend and is a feature of the church.

'TOCAL' The homestead on the former 'Tocal' estate, just south of Paterson, is one of Australia's most interesting Georgian houses. Framed by immense fig trees and set in established gardens, the house was built in 1840 and is surrounded by architecturally significant outbuildings including an unusual barn constructed from local timber in 1850 and designed by the leading colonial architect, Edmund Blacket.

'Tocal' became well known first as a vineyard, then as a stud for Herefords and thoroughbred horses. The estate is now the site of the C.B. Alexander Agricultural College, built in the 1960s by the Presbyterian Church with a bequest from the last owner after whom it is named – though Alexander's vision had been the construction of a farmhouse for destitute and orphaned children of the protestant faith. The unusual design of the college combines an Oriental appearance with European-style cloisters and a striking central chapel bearing a thrusting spire that appears to shoot directly from the ground. The design was inspired by the shape of one of the homestead's historic barns.

Like many provincial, historic public buildings, the 1884 Stroud Post Office survives almost exactly as built.

STROUD ■ 194

Every year in July, the quiet country town of Stroud is enlivened by one of the world's most unusual and eccentric sporting competitions – the international brick and rolling-pin throwing contest. This unconventional event is held between the townships of Stroud in England, the United States, Canada and Australia. The first brick-throwing contest was held in 1960 between the American and English Strouds after it was discovered that both towns had brickworks in common.

In 1961, the existence of the other two Stroud townships was discovered and thus began the contest between the four Strouds. In 1962, a rolling-pin competition was introduced for women – at the suggestion of Stroud, Australia – and since then all rolling pins used in the contest have been made in Australia and shipped overseas so that all contestants compete on an equal basis.

Unlike most colonial settlements, Stroud did not evolve piecemeal – it is believed to have been the first company town in Australia and one of three towns planned by the Australian Agricultural Company (see Gloucester) for its Port Stephens holdings. Robert Dawson, the company's chief agent, chose a site in the company's Port Stephens Estate for the development of a town, to be known as Stroud because of the area's striking resemblance to the Cotswold countryside around the original Stroud in England. Dawson recorded his vivid and glowing impressions of the Karuah Valley in an 1831 book called *The Present State of Australia:* 'As we passed on this day towards a small river, the country suddenly became exceedingly beautiful and picturesque, consisting of low undulating hills, with only as much timber as was necessary to perfect the beauty of a finely broken and varied country. I thought, at the time, I had never beheld so sweet a spot…'.

For some years, Stroud was the company's Australian headquarters and the most important settlement in its Port Stephens estate. In the original layout of its streets and the style of its buildings, it was reminiscent of a traditional English village, but the passage of time has seen the passing of much of that quality.

By 1832 the town had its own saddlers, tailors, gardeners and a wheelwright. A reorganisation of the agricultural company's operations in 1849 made subdivisions of land available for private purchase and by the late 1850s the company's interests had moved away from the coast to the Liverpool Plains and the Peel River area. When the company moved its headquarters to Sydney in 1856, significant development in the town came to a halt.

Nowadays, Stroud is a pleasant country town well-endowed with old sandstone buildings and historic sites that remain as testimony to the Australian Agricultural Company's influence. *Population 540*

ST JOHN'S ANGLICAN CHURCH Built by convicts in 1833, St John's Church still has its fine original cedar furnishings and stained-glass windows. Bricks made from local clay contribute to its highly original design. The legendary bushranger, Captain Thunderbolt, is said to have been married in the church.

STROUD HOUSE This convict-built residence is probably the most stately of the Australian Agricultural Company's many buildings. Built in 1834 and extended in 1838, the house was used originally as a guest house for various company commissioners on visits to the district. In those days, the convict servants had their living quarters in the building's cellars.

The Bank of Australasia moved into the building in 1882 and the handsome structure was not used as a private residence again until 1926 when the bank moved into purpose-built premises.

FESTIVALS International brick and rolling-pin throwing contest, July.

WOKO NATIONAL PARK ■ 195

Much of Woko National Park is mountainous terrain which forms part of the watershed between the Little Manning and Barnard Rivers. The park is located north-west of Gloucester (see entry) and protects three types of rainforest: dry, subtropical and warm temperate. The leafy rainforest canopy resounds with cries of the park's prolific birdlife while the humid lower levels are home to the earth-bound brush turkey. Soaring rock faces provide the homes for a complex mosaic of orchids, stag and elkhorns while the forests abound with large trees such as rosewood, black booyong, Moreton Bay fig and the potentially harmful giant stinging tree. Former farmland along the banks of the Little Manning River is now used as camping sites.

Muswellbrook & Scone

This region, richly endowed with natural resources, stretches from the wineries and coal mines of the Upper Hunter to the sheep, horse and cattle studs beneath the Liverpool Ranges. Through this still thinly populated area of small settlements ran the route travelled by those heading for New England.

ABERDEEN ■ 196

In 1824, surveyor Henry Dangar camped at this spot, which offered him his first views of the Liverpool Range and a ford across the Hunter River. One of the earliest landowners in the region, Thomas Potter Macqueen, petitioned the governor in 1838 for a township at 'Segenhoe Ford' to be laid out, partly on government land and partly on his own land. The new town was named Aberdeen after George Gordon,the fourth Earl of Aberdeen. The oldest building in the town, Segenhoe Inn, was built by Macqueen the year before the town was laid out.

By 1870, with the opening of the railway from Muswellbrook (see entry), the population of Aberdeen had grown to over 100 in a town with its own post office, lock-up and steam mill. The lock-up was considered necessary because any flooding at the ford would force impatient teamsters to camp in the town and displays of unruly behaviour were not unknown. The old mill, built in 1840 still stands, the oldest of its kind in Australia.

But Aberdeen's fortunes could not rely indefinitely on its chance geographical position as a convenient river crossing. In 1892 the town's major employer, the Australian Meat Cutting and Freezing Company, exported its first 14 000 sheep carcasses. The company was one of the first in Australia to operate a freezing works. Many of the early twentieth century buildings in Aberdeen were built by or for the company including the standardised housing that utilised 'ripple iron' for external walls. *Population 1800*

'BELLTREES' ■ 197

This property, long considered one of the leading pastoral estates in New South Wales, has been in the hands of the White family since 1853. Patrick White, the acclaimed writer, belonged to one branch of the family and 'Belltrees' appeared lightly disguised as 'Kudgeri' in his book *The Eye of the Storm*.

The land on which the 'Belltrees' property stands was granted in 1831 to H.C. Sempill, one-time manager of Potter Macqueen's nearby 'Segenhoe'. It was Sempill who named the property 'Belltrees' after the English estate owned by a distant relative Lord Sempill. The property was also owned briefly by W.C. Wentworth before being leased and then bought by James White in 1853.

The present two-storey homestead was built for James White in 1907 although part of the original house, a slab cottage, chapel and shearing shed date from an earlier period.

DENMAN ■ 198

Until 1853 the private village of Merton stood on William Ogilvie's land on the opposite bank of the Denman River from the present town. In that year 'Merton Village Reserve' was gazetted on government-surveyed land. The name was changed almost immediately to Denman and by 1861 most of the inhabitants of Merton had moved across the river to the new village. On the main stock route from the Upper Goulburn, Denman quickly became a cattle-buying centre and later a service centre for the surrounding district. Ogilvie's cottage (1823) is a reminder of the first landowner as is the name of the main street in Denman. Ogilvie Street's early twentieth century buildings, with distinctive verandahs out over the footpath, were destroyed by fire in 1928 and rebuilt.

Denman is still known for its dairy and hay production but in modern times horse and cattle studs, coal mining and wineries can be added to that list. One of the three wineries, Rosemount Estate, was first planted in 1855, went out of production in the early twentieth century, and was replanted in 1968. *Population 1440*

GOULBURN RIVER NATIONAL PARK ■ 199

The Aborigines used the Goulburn River on their route from the western plains to the coast. Hand stencils, paintings, camp sites and scarred trees within the park provide evidence of these ancient journeys.

The park, established in 1983, covers 70 000 hectares. The Goulburn River, rising twenty kilometres west of the park in the Great Dividing Range, cuts a spectacular ninety-kilometre gorge through the sandstone of the park. Cliffs honeycombed by caves and sandstone ridges eroded by many small streams are characteristic of the western section of the park. The semi-arid eastern section of the park has a number of basalt-capped ridges and sparse vegetation.

LAKE GLENBAWN ■ 200

A dam for flood mitigation, irrigation and water supply on the Upper Hunter was first mooted in 1939 and the site at Glenbawn chosen. Work on the dam had to wait until 1946 when the then Premier, William McKell turned the first sod. With competition from other postwar construction, and despite a large project to house workers at Glenbawn, the dam was not completed until 1958 when it was opened by another Premier, J.J. Cahill.

A drought combined with a boom in Hunter valley coal mining in the 1980s brought the water in the dam to a dangerously low eight percent of capacity and enlargement work was undertaken. The water of the dam now extends into the foothills of the Mount Royal Range and, since its opening, has been a major recreational facility for the district.

HUNTER VALLEY MUSEUM OF RURAL LIFE Opened in 1966 at Lake Glenbawn, the museum houses pioneer relics in two octagonal halls and an outdoor display area. Exhibits from the pioneer settlements in the Hunter Valley and the penal settlement at Newcastle range from cheese presses, marble baths and a grand piano to leg shackles, convict beds and an anvil from Maitland on which Les Darcy, the boxer, worked.

LAKE LIDDELL ■ 201

The lake is the cooling pond for Liddell Power Station and certain parts of it are reserved specifically for Electricity Commission use. A recreation area on the northern foreshores

At the heart of the 'Belltrees' estate is its homestead, the archetypal, gracious hub of a sheep-grazing property.

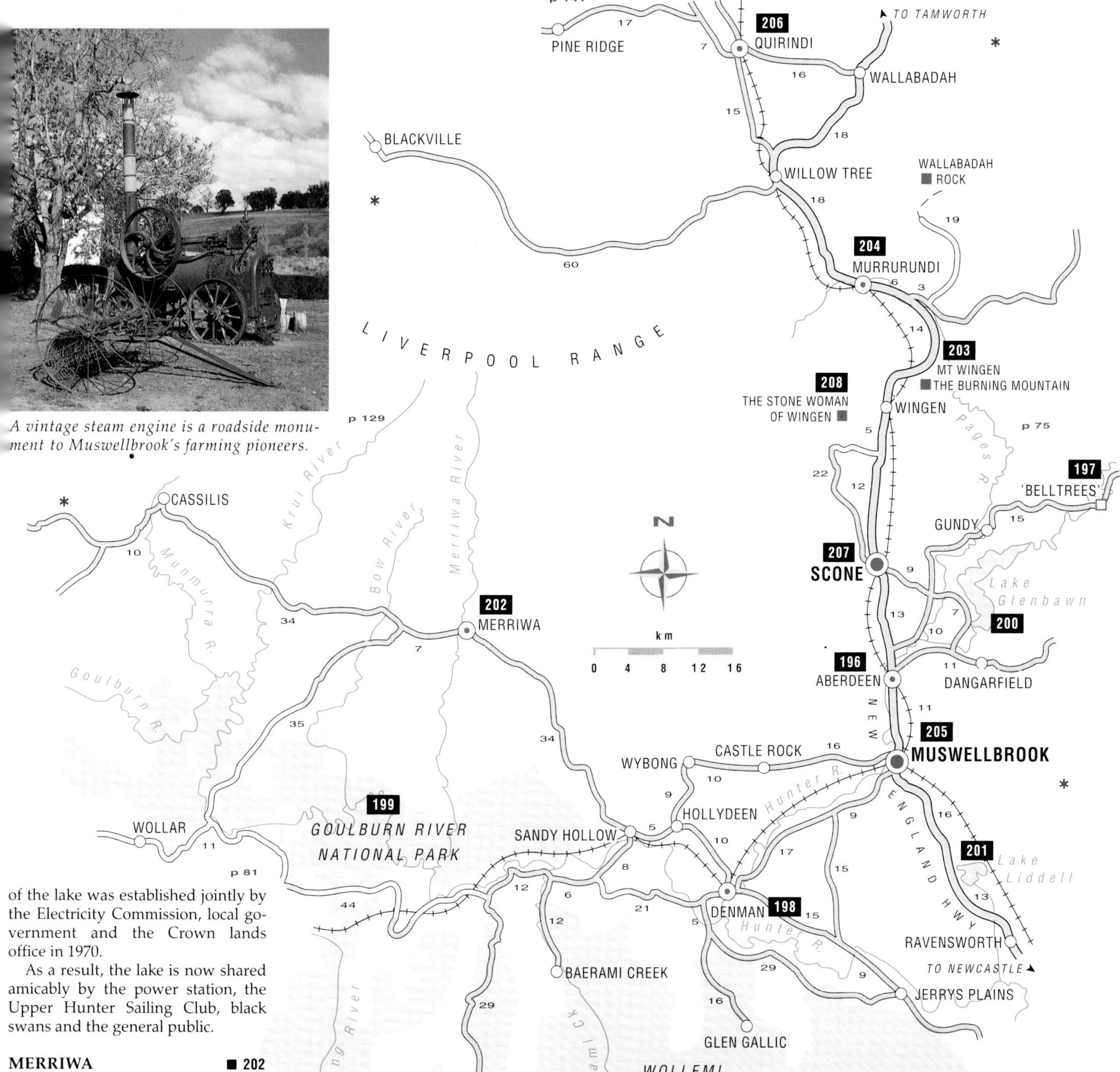

A vintage steam engine is a roadside monument to Muswellbrook's farming pioneers.

of the lake was established jointly by the Electricity Commission, local government and the Crown lands office in 1970.

As a result, the lake is now shared amicably by the power station, the Upper Hunter Sailing Club, black swans and the general public.

MERRIWA ■ **202**

The site of this village, by the well-watered banks of the Merriwa River, was a favourite Aboriginal camping ground. Noted for its grass seed, which was pounded to make flour, the name Merriwa or Gummum Plains was bestowed on the area by the original inhabitants.

Allan Cunningham was probably the first European to camp at the site in 1823 on his explorations of an inland route through the Liverpool Range. By the time Cunningham's route though the Liverpool Range was attracting a growing number of pioneers and travellers, the small settlement of Merriwa was already established in a prime position straddling the route.

Merriwa is a centre for a district of horse and sheep studs which also produces cattle, wool, fat lambs, wheat and lucerne. *Population 960*

MOUNT WINGEN (BURNING MOUNTAIN) ■ **203**

Wingen, from an Aboriginal word meaning 'fire', was thought to be an active volcano by the early settlers. In fact, thirty metres below the surface, a coal seam has been burning for over five thousand years. The initial spontaneous combustion has been fed by oxygen from the surface seeping through cracks and fissures in the rock caused by slumping of the rock strata. The seam is burning at the rate of one metre per year in a southward direction.

The mountain, with its sulphurous fumes, smoke, and temperatures up to 350°C, is accessible by a walking track through private land.

MURRURUNDI ■ **204**

Murrurundi is a short form of *murrumdoorandi* meaning 'place where the mists sit' or 'nestling in a valley'. It is the most northerly town in the Hunter Valley and lies in a narrow valley in the Liverpool Range. The early settlers brought fine merino sheep to Murrurundi, which now has a reputation for sheep, beef cattle and thoroughbred horse studs.

Being on the track to New England and, later, the terminus for the New England railway boosted the township's progress. The bushranger Ben Hall spent his childhood here and his mother is buried in the Roman Catholic cemetery. Members of the infamous Jewboy Gang, who committed many of their crimes in the Hunter region, were finally captured at Murrurundi. *Population 980*

FESTIVAL Bushman's Carnival, early October.

MUSWELLBROOK ■ **205**

Henry Dangar, sent in 1824 to survey land in the region and reserve portions of it for the government, was the first European to see Muscle Creek, which still runs through

Muswellbrook. The town was planned and gazetted in 1833 as 'Muscle Brook' apparently – despite the spelling – because of the small shellfish in the creek. By 1838 it was known to those who lived there as Muswellbrook, the Post Office also used that name despite objections from the Lands Office, and even the railway platform got a new sign in 1890 with the amended spelling. The controversy, however, was not officially settled until 1949.

The town had some high-profile settlers including Colonel William Dumaresq, Private Secretary to Governor Darling and hero of Waterloo, and the Honourable Francis Forbes, first Chief Justice of New South Wales. Their properties – 'St Heliers', 'Skellatar' and 'Edinglassie' – were to dominate the town's early history. By 1845 the township had extended south of Muscle Creek to absorb the private 'Forbestown' on the estate of Frances and David Forbes, which thereafter was known as South Muswellbrook.

Dairying became an important industry with the town providing milk for the Hunter Valley and the surplus going to the Oak dairy products factory in the town. The first coal was found in 1908 and open-cut mines around Muswellbrook now provide fuel for the local Bayswater and Liddell power stations as well as for export to Japan. The largest of these open-cut mines was established at Drayton in 1983.

Aspects of the town's more recent history can be found in Donald Horne's book of his childhood in Muswellbrook, *The Education of Young Donald*, and in a bicentennial tapestry of the valley and the township at the Muswellbrook Regional Art Gallery. *Population 15 820*

ST ALBANS ANGLICAN CHURCH (1864) Designed by Sir George Gilbert Scott, who sent a hundred drawings from England, the actual building of the church was supervised by Horbury Hunt. The Gothic revival church was built on the site of a previous church and the later additions of the bell-tower and picket fence were made to Hunt designs.

FESTIVAL Upper Hunter Wine Festival, October.

QUIRINDI ■ 206

Sitting on a plateau above the Liverpool Plains, Quirindi has the rich black soil of the plains and good underground water supply making it ideal for the growing of grain, seed and vegetable crops including magnificent sunflowers.

Even before the town was gazetted, the area around Quirindi was used as a stopping point for bullock drays and travellers heading north and west. By 1830 a number of squatters had taken up land on the nearby plains including George Loder at Quirindi station and by the 1840s an inn and some huts for teamsters had been built near Loder's property.

For some time after the town was laid out in 1856 various spellings such as 'Cuerindi' and 'Kuwherhindi' were used before the current spelling stuck. There are various interpretations of the name ranging from 'place of many possums' or 'place where fish breed' to 'dead tree on mountain top'.

Quirindi remained small until the railway arrived in 1877 and the wool, wheat, fat lambs, sheep and cattle, for which the district is now well known, could be taken to markets. From 1893 polo, for which Quirindi is also famous, was played on Quirindi Racecourse, which also hosts the Quirindi Rodeo, the Quirindi Cup and other regular race meetings each year.

An early hotel in the town called 'Who'd A Thought It' is commemorated in the nearby lookout, which still uses the unusual name…as well as offering 360-degree views of the town and district. *Population 2830*

SCONE ■ 207

Most of those who came to Scone in the 1820s were passing through on their way to the newly opened pastures on the Liverpool Plains. Scone Lagoon was a handy place to camp before tackling the Liverpool Range.

The township was laid out in the 1830s and named 'Invermein' after the large property of Dr William Carlyle, the region's first permanent settler; another local resident, Hugh Cameron, suggested that the town be named Scone after the town in Scotland where the Scottish kings were crowned in ancient times. When Bishop Broughton came to the village in 1840 to consecrate the churchyard, he was appalled by the 'great insensitivity prevailing' as to religious duties…but he was a lone English cleric in a stronghold of Scottish settlers.

Many of Scone's old buildings survive including the flour mill built in 1861 (now the RSL Club), the first store (now a private home), the lock-up (now a museum) and the court house. There is also a monument to John Graham, an employee in Dangar's store who became the first person to be murdered by the notorious Jewboy Gang (see Murrurundi).

Scone has a reputation as one of the world's leading thoroughbred and horse-breeding centres hence the handsome mare and foal sculpture by Gabriel Sterk that stands in the town. *Population 3330*

COURT HOUSE/OLD COURT THEATRE The original section of the court house was designed by Mortimer Lewis and built of handmade bricks in 1849 – it is now the 'green room' of the Court Theatre. The front verandah links with the 1882 section of rendered and painted brick with a gable roof.

FESTIVALS Polo Carnival, September; Bushman's Carnival, November; Thoroughbred Week, May.

STONE WOMAN OF WINGEN ■ 208

South-west of Wingen and on the other side of the New England Highway from Mount Wingen stands the Stone Woman of Wingen sometimes known as the Wingen Maid. When viewed from Dry Creek, the unusual rock formation, rising to 660 metres above sea level, resembles a seated woman with a bunch of flowers at her breast. This type of flat-topped, steep-walled (mesa) formation is unusual in Australia; such formations are commonly seen in the semi-arid parts of the south-western United States.

The Stone Woman of Wingen is now contained within a 700-hectare nature reserve, one of the few areas of natural bushland in an extensively cultivated district.

As with most large rivers in Australia, the flow of the Hunter is not left to chance but is controlled by the release of water from Lake Glenbawn (below).

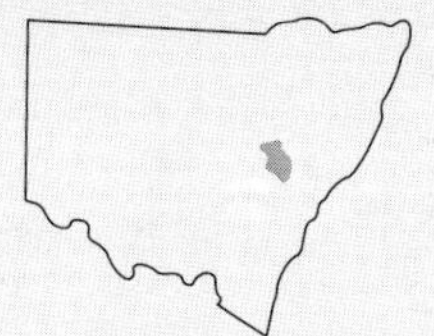

Mudgee & Gulgong

This fertile region on the western slopes of the Great Dividing Range, where the ghosts of the gold rush still hover, is noted for its fine wines. This is also Lawson country, where Henry Lawson spent his childhood, and it provides the setting for many of his poems and stories.

Memories of the gold rush and the antics of Lawson's friendless 'loaded dog' haunt the old Budgee Hotel.

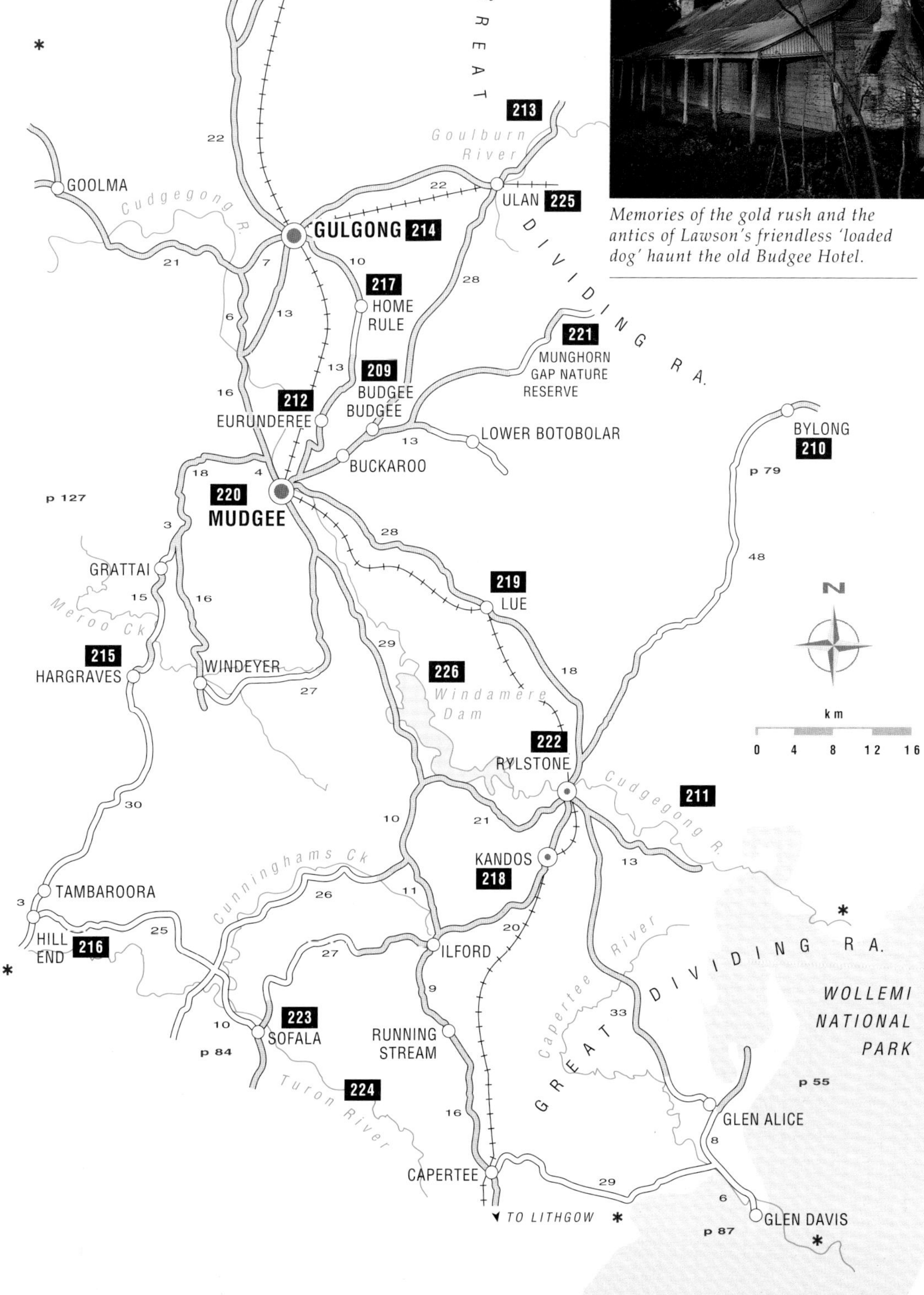

BUDGEE BUDGEE ■ 209

Less than ten kilometres out of Mudgee, the old wine shanty at Budgee Budgee was the ideal resting place and watering hole for teamsters, drovers and gold miners during the gold rush days. There is still a hotel on the site of the original inn, built in 1861 of timber slabs with a shingle roof. This is reputedly the 'small hotel or shanty on the creek not far from the claim', described in Henry Lawson's classic tale of 'The Loaded Dog'.

BYLONG ■ 210

The lush, secluded Bylong Valley was described in glowing terms by a keenly observant writer for the *Maitland Mercury* in 1884: '...instead of that worn out look common on the lower Goulburn, the Bylong country appeared actually green, and how it preserves that colour, even in a dry season, is a mystery'.

Bylong was settled in the late 1820s by John Tindale, a former convict, and his son John Richard, who were granted extensive tracts of land in the region by the Governor, Sir Thomas Brisbane. Later generations of the Tindales ran a thoroughbred stud at their property 'Bylong' and were among the first to import racehorses to Australia.

CUDGEGONG RIVER ■ 211

A tributary of the Macquarie River system, the Cudgegong rises in the Great Dividing Range near Rylstone and flows into the Lake Burrendong west of Mudgee. The much-sought-after Mudgee lucerne grows on the fertile flats along the Cudgegong River, which gets its name from the Aboriginal word for 'red clay'.

When the explorer Allan Cunningham made his first attempt at finding an alternative inland route from Bathurst out to the Liverpool Plains, the Cudgegong River was the scene of his undoing. His packhorses bolted while he was camping on the riverbank and he was forced to walk the 110 kilometres back to Bathurst.

A worse fate befell Dr Belinfante, the local doctor, when, in 1874, his buggy was swept from a ford across the rain-swollen river. Although the jury returned a verdict of accidental death they censured the government for not erecting a bridge across the river. The Belinfante Bridge still serves as a monument to the much-respected doctor.

EURUNDEREE ■ 212

Henry Lawson was six months old when he arrived in 1867 at this small settlement, called at that time Pipeclay. It was not until 1876 that the name was changed to Eurunderee, thought to mean 'lone tree'. In that year twenty-seven boys (including Henry Lawson and his brother Charles) and eighteen girls enrolled at the school at Eurunderee, featured in Henry Lawson's 'The Old Bark School':

It was built of bark and poles, and
the floor was full of holes
Where each leak in rainy weather
made a pool;
And the walls were mostly cracks
lined with calico and sacks–
There was little need for windows
in the school.

The leaky old school at Eurunderee was replaced in 1878 by a new slab structure built by Henry Lawson's father but little remains now of the school or of the Lawson home, one kilometre away. Only a chimney and a plaque, unveiled by Lawson's widow, mark the site of the Lawson house on what is now Henry Lawson Drive.

GOULBURN RIVER ■ 213

The local Aborigines used the Goulburn River on their journeys from the western plains to the coast but it was not until 1821 that the first Europeans, in a party led by Lieutenant William Lawson, saw the river. Lawson named the river after Henry Goulburn who was at that time Britain's Under-Secretary for War and the Colonies.

Described by the explorer Allan Cunningham, who crossed the river at Ulan where the Goulburn rises, as 'a small reedy stream,' the river meanders in an easterly direction through a series of spectacular sandstone gorges before it joins the Hunter River between Muswellbrook and Singleton.

GULGONG ■ 214

Gold was first discovered in the area around Gulgong in 1852 but it was not until Tom Saunders found 120 pounds worth of gold at Red Hill in April 1870 that the gold rush really began. Within two months there were 500 diggers at Red Hill and the nucleus of a town built up around them and was named Gulgong from an Aboriginal word for 'deep waterhole'. The population rose rapidly to 8000 by the end of 1870 and to a peak of 20 000 in 1872 when Gulgong was referred to rather generously as 'the hub of the world'. By 1880 it was all over but as the diggers moved on Gulgong was spared the fate of many other goldrush settlements that rapidly became ghost towns.

Gulgong is one of Australia's best documented and best preserved towns from the nineteenth-century, gold-mining era. Most significant for the preservation of these historic times were the photographs of the elegantly named Henry Beaufoy Merlin who was commissioned by Bernard Holtermann to photograph Hill End and Gulgong in the early 1870s. An exhibition of these photographs was mounted overseas to encourage immigration and the photographs then disappeared for many years until the perfectly preserved negatives were found in a Sydney suburban shed in 1951. It is these photos of Gulgong which appear on the original $10 note and which have been used to guide the restoration of some of the buildings in Gulgong.

The iron-lace balconies on the almost unaltered buildings, the hitching posts and horse troughs in Mayne Street and the superb collection in the Pioneers Museum make a visit to Gulgong like a step back into history. *Population 2040*

FESTIVALS Henry Lawson's Birthday Celebrations, June.

HARGRAVES ■ 215

The oldest of the Mudgee–Gulgong gold towns and part of the original Turon field, Hargraves was named after Edward Hargraves who, although not the first to discover gold, was the first to publicise and promote his discovery. In July 1851 'Kerr's hundredweight', containing 1272 ounces of gold, was discovered at Hargraves and for twenty-five years Hargraves boomed. Now a quiet little village with a combined store and post office, it is difficult to imagine its 'roaring days'.

HILL END ■ 216

During the 1870s Hill End was one of the largest inland towns in Australia; now it is almost a ghost town with a tiny population which survives on mixed farming and tourism.

During the 1850s and 1860s Hill End was an outpost of the much more successful alluvial goldmining settlement Tambaroora until the discovery in 1872 of the Holtermann and Beyers specimen – the largest single piece of reef gold-bearing material ever mined.

Time stands still in Hill End, where the ghosts of the gold rush dwell.

The distinctively flavoured honey produced from the Mudgee region's hives is a major money-earner.

Mudgee's richly Gothic St Mary's Church is one of the most noble places of worship in western NSW.

Tambaroora was a town
When Hill End was a pup.
Tambaroora'll be a town
When Hill End's buggered up.

was the chant taken up by the jealous miners at Tambaroora but they were dreadfully wrong – the alluvial gold ran out and Tambaroora died. Hill End meanwhile boomed, with over 200 companies, some selling worthless shares in worthless mines, attracted to the area.

In 1873, one visitor to Hill End described the well laid out town with 'straight streets and well built stores and business premises, four churches and parsonages, three banks, two newspapers, a public school and a hospital' (now a museum). He forbore to mention the more than fifty hotels, of which only one, the Royal Hotel now remains.

By 1875 the gold was petering out, the miners drifting away and businesses closing; by the 1880s Hill End was a ghost town. There have been attempts to revive gold mining in the area such as the Hawkins Hill mine founded by Cornish miners in the 1950s but such attempts have been short-lived. Hill End was proclaimed an historic site in 1967 and is ably administered by the National Parks and Wildlife Service.

HOME RULE ■ 217

Named by Irish miners to remind themselves and others of their demands for home rule for Ireland, this village is the O'Connell Town in Rolf Boldrewood's book *The Miner's Right*. Home Rule survives on its kaolin mine, which still provides the raw material used for the manufacture of porcelain pottery.

KANDOS ■ 218

Kandos owes its wealth primarily to cement and coal, sited as it is on a prehistoric lake rich in coal, shale and limestone. After coal was first successfully mined from beneath Coomber Melon Mountain ('Mount Baldy') in 1913 the NSW Coal, Lime and Cement Company was formed. The new settlement was named 'Candos', formed from the names of the directors of the first board of the company, but to avoid confusion with the town of Chandos in South Australia, the name was changed to Kandos in 1915.

Coal has been extracted from beneath Coomber Melon Mountain since 1913 and cement has been produced here since 1916 – Kandos cement was used in the construction of the Sydney Harbour Bridge. *Population 1520*

PRESBYTERY The attractive Spanish-style presbytery was constructed by volunteer labour during the Depression of the 1930s.

LUE ■ 219

The original name for this small village was Dungaree. At one time a thriving settlement and intended to become even larger because of its position on the route to the Hunter Region, Dungaree failed to live up to its planned future. The surrounding countryside was too harsh and the village was moved lock, stock and barrel in 1884 to accommodate the new railway line. After this move the village was renamed Lue and is now a rural settlement dependent on sheep and cattle farming.

MUDGEE ■ 220

Mudgee, from an Aboriginal word *moothi* meaning 'nest among the hills', was the second European settlement west of the great Dividing Range – Bathurst being the first. There was no exploration north of Bathurst until 1821 when James Blackman became the first European to explore the district. It was, however, his brother John and Lieutenant William Lawson who reached the actual site of Mudgee itself in November 1821. The first European settlers, George and Henry Cox, were followed by a few others of pioneering spirit but the settlement did not grow very rapidly because of the problems involved in crossing the Great Dividing Range. The township, laid out by Robert Hoddle who was to provide the same service for central Melbourne fourteen years later, was finally declared a municipality in 1860.

The secret of Mudgee's survival as a thriving rural centre lies in the sheer diversity of its local produce, which includes wool, fat lambs, beef, cereal crops, lucerne, vegetables and wine. *Population 7450*

WINERIES The first vines were planted in Mudgee in 1855 and the first wine made commercially three years later. One of the three original vineyards – Roth – is still in business in Mudgee. Until the 1960s Mudgee was known for its ports and muscats but there are now over 350 wines that carry the words 'Certified Mudgee Appellation Wine', Mudgee being one of the first areas in Australia to adopt the certification-appellation system used in Europe. Over 500 hectares of vines have been planted by more than 20 twenty wine-grape growers although wineries in Mudgee are small, and likely to remain so, since the large areas of land required by major commercial operators are not available. Because of Mudgee's high altitude, grapes are harvested, and the annual wine festival celebrated, later in the year than in the Hunter Valley.

RAILWAY STATION An excellent example of a Victorian country railway station with its delicate cast-iron work and a beautiful cedar waiting room. The opening of the railway station in 1884 was celebrated with a Grand Ball...in the engine shed.

POST OFFICE Designed by the Colonial Architect Alexander Dawson and built of stuccoed brick in 1862, this post office was one of the first major country post offices in New South Wales. The clocktower still awaits its clock!

ST MARY'S ROMAN CATHOLIC CHURCH The church was built in three stages between 1857 and 1911, when the octagonal steeple was finally added. St Mary's incorporated sections of the original slab church and with its Gothic exterior and Byzantine interior, it is one of the most beautiful churches in the region.

LAWSON PARK The park commemorates the connection between Henry Lawson and this region. Lawson's parents - Peter Larsen and Louisa Albury - were married in Mudgee and Henry Lawson's birth was registered there. The park, on the banks of the Cudgegong River, now has an Olympic swimming pool but in Lawson's day a small weir held back the water to create Mudgee's swimming hole. The original changing rooms now house the park staff's gardening equipment.

FESTIVALS Wine Festival, September.

MUNGHORN GAP NATURE RESERVE ■ 221

Munghorn Gap Reserve is the second oldest declared nature reserve in New South Wales and, at 3200 hectares, is one of the largest faunal reserves in the state. Dissected from east to west by the Great Dividing Range, most of the reserve is open forest and woodland but there are areas of sandstone outcrops and caves, and some former grazing properties are also included within the boundaries of the reserve. The woodland is noted for the colonies of koalas which inhabit its grey gums, and its great variety of bird species.

RYLSTONE ■ 222

The first houses in Rylstone were clustered at the junction of the Cudgegong River and Tongbong Creek, a favourite camping spot for shepherds. The site was first surveyed in 1842 and in 1885 graduated from village to town status.

Mounted police were stationed in Rylstone from as early as 1849 and presumably were responsible for the security of 'Captain Thunderbolt' (Frederick Ward) who spent the night there in 1861 on his way from Mudgee to Bathurst under police escort to stand trial for horse stealing.

The first survey for an extension to the rail line between Capertree and Mudgee nominated a route via Ilford but, fortunately for the survival of Rylstone, the route was changed to run through Kandos and Rylstone. Opened in 1884, Rylstone railway station was built by Henry Lawson's father and stands today with very few changes. *Population 720*

SOFALA ■ 223

Sofala, named after the similarly named gold-producing district of Portuguese East Africa, was one of the major centres on the Turon field with, according to some estimates, a population of 30 000 Europeans and Chinese in the 1850s–1860s.

In addition to the usual abundance of hotels, Sofala was host to Ashton's Circus and to the Turon Cup, in which 'Captain Starlight' rode the winning horse...collecting and disappearing with his prize money before the local troopers were able to collect their wits.

Sofala is now small and peaceful with a narrow main street almost enclosed on both sides by old wooden buildings, some of them survivors from the gold boom days.

TURON RIVER ■ 224

The Turon River, rising near Portland, flows 110 kilometres until it joins the Macquarie River, south of Hill End. It flows through agricultural land and, in the upper sections, passes through hills up to 900 metres above sea level. At Sofala there is a handwrought iron bridge that was painstakingly dismantled from the Fish River at Bathurst and re-erected over the Turon.

Finds of alluvial gold in the Turon River and its tributaries only three weeks after the first gold in Australia was found at Ophir started the rush to the Turon field.

ULAN ■ 225

Coal from Ulan is now carried by a rail link from the mine site but the railway has been a stop-and-start project. In 1936, as the amount of coal from the mine increased, a rail line to Ulan was begun but abandoned in 1949. It was not until 1982 that a rail link to the mine site was finally completed and the mine now ships millions of tonnes of steaming coal to Japan each year.

WINDAMERE DAM ■ 226

The earth and rockfill dam on the Cudgegong River was begun in 1974 and opened by Neville Wran, then Premier of New South Wales, in 1984. The dam holds 368 000 megalitres of water which is used for irrigation, local coal-based industrial development and town water.

Named after the property 'Windamere' on which the dam wall was built, the dam drowned the site of the township of Cudgegong, but not until after all the buildings in Cudgegong had been relocated or demolished. The old tracks and roads leading down to the water's edge are the still visible and rather eerie reminders of what once lay beneath the surface of the dam.

The Windamere Dam waters the green banks of the Cudgegong up to its junction with the Macquarie River where the Burrendong Dam takes over.

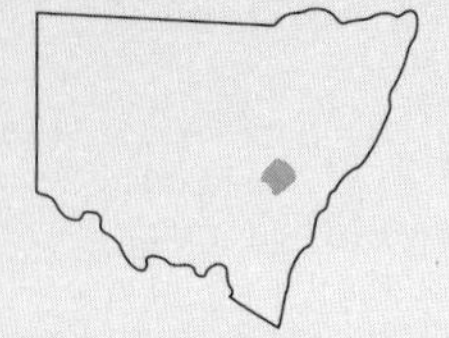

Orange & Bathurst

When Blaxland, Lawson and Wentworth finally broached the barrier of the Great Dividing Range in 1813, they opened a route to the 'sweeping plains' beyond that led to the first inland settlement in Australia. Forty years later, the central west region became the site of Australia's first gold rush.

The trail-blazing George Evans (left) returned to the western plains three times after his 1813 expedition.

BATHURST ■ 227

Bathurst is Australia's oldest inland settlement, a gracious city of wide, tree-lined streets, historic houses, fine public buildings and an abundance of open squares, parks and monuments – a dignified contrast to Bathurst's other image as the site of the internationally known motor-racing circuit at Mount Panorama.

The city lies on the western slopes of the Great Dividing Range, surrounded by fertile pastoral country. Assistant Surveyor-General George Evans was the first European to set foot in the area in 1813, praising the plains that opened out before him as 'the handsomest country I ever saw' – a comment that boded ill for the Wiradjuri Aborigines who inhabited the area. The Aborigines' weapons were no match for the firearms of the European settlers and clashes over land usually resulted in high casualties for the blacks. When Governor Macquarie traversed the new road over the Blue Mountains (see *Katoomba & Blaxland*) in 1815 to select the site for a future town, he choose the name Bathurst – after Earl Bathurst, British Secretary of State for the Colonies.

As the only substantial settlement over the ranges, Bathurst was the natural starting point for most of the exploration that opened up the west and south-west of the country. The town developed quite slowly at first, retarded by several years of drought and the consequent rural recession of the 1840s. The real impetus to growth came in 1851 with the discovery of gold in the area – an event that sparked off the first gold rush in Australia and made Bathurst the thriving centre of the western region.

By 1862, Bathurst had fifty hotels serving a population of about 5000 people – and not surprisingly, an increase in drunkenness and major crime. Gold was also the lure which brought the bushranger Ben Hall and his gang to raid the town in September 1863 in an unsuccessful attempt to steal a racehorse.

The increase in population and wealth prompted a surge in building activity which saw the construction of many of the grand public and commercial buildings which stand today, most outstanding of which is the court house – a Victorian classical building completed in 1880 that is one of Australia's finest examples of Victorian public architecture.

In 1861 the well-established town became the national headquarters for the famous Cobb & Co. coach business. When the gold yields began to dwindle, Bathurst continued to prosper as a solid commercial centre with a firm economic base in the district's rich pastoral industry. Steady expansion into secondary industries since the Second World War – including food canning, engineering and furniture manufacturing – has seen the town's role as an important rural centre greatly augmented, though an ambitious, joint federal and state government decentralisation scheme to develop Bathurst–Orange as a combined regional centre, failed to achieve its early projected levels of population and economic growth and had virtually ground to a halt by the mid-1980s. The Bathurst–Orange Development Corporation, formed in 1973 to administer development of the region, disbanded in December 1990. *Population 30 010*

ABERCROMBIE HOUSE Located eight kilometres from the centre of town, this huge baronial-style mansion of

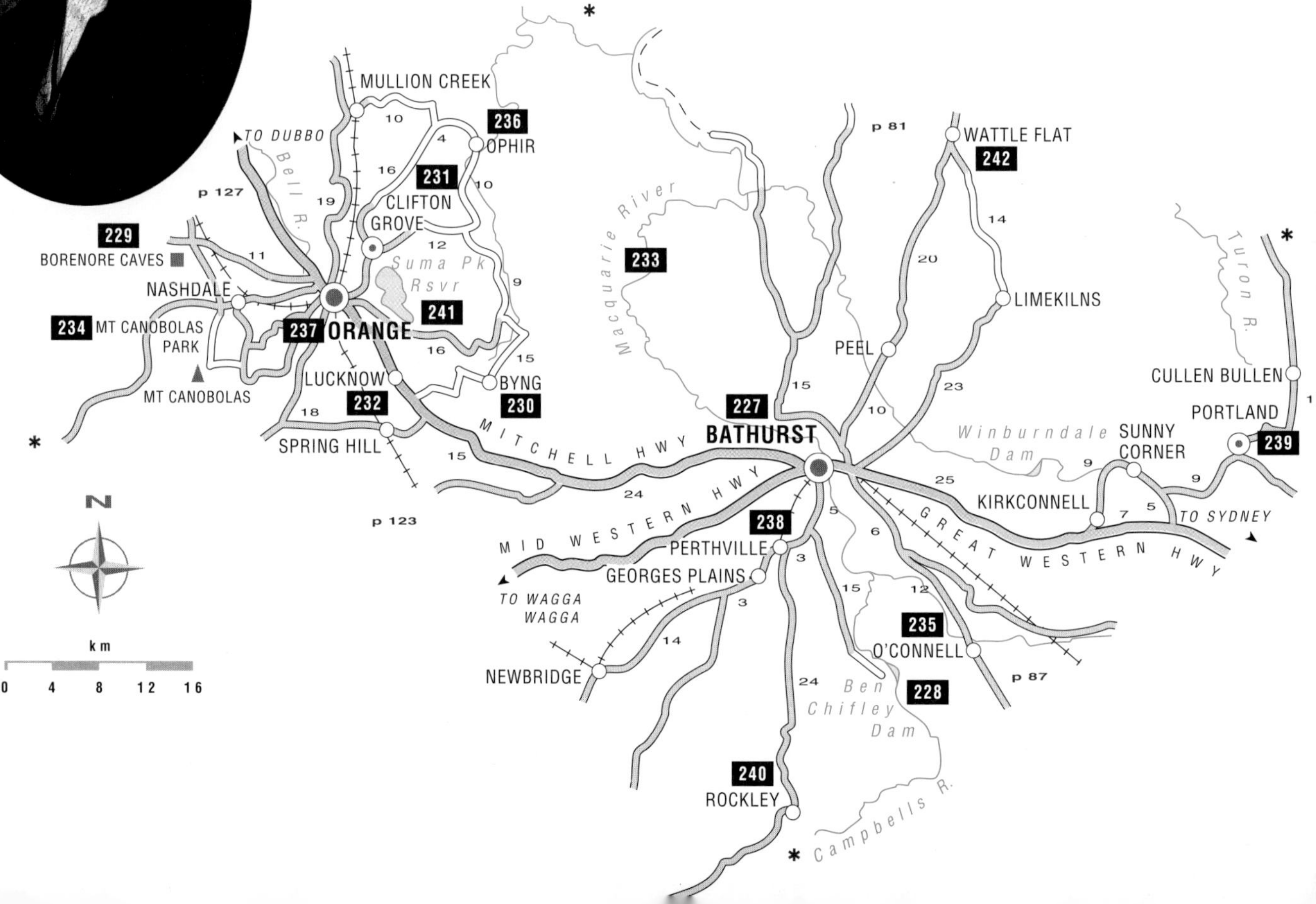

The 1880 Bathurst Court House – completed three years after its flanking wings – has an imperial grandeur that symbolises Victorian confidence...

the late 1870s was built for the son of the former Lieutenant-Governor of New South Wales.

BEN CHIFLEY'S COTTAGE On Busby Street, the cottage was home to Ben Chifley, the engine driver who became Prime Minister of Australia from 1945 to 1949.

HOLY TRINITY CHURCH In the nearby village of Kelso, this church – completed in 1835 – was not only the first Anglican church to be erected in Australia's inland, but the first in Australia to be consecrated.

MOUNT PANORAMA RACING CIRCUIT This internationally known racing circuit is the site of Australia's biggest motor-car racing event, held every year on the first weekend in October.

OLD GOVERNMENT HOUSE At the rear of George Street, the house is the only brick building remaining of those built in 1821 for Governor Macquarie's farewell visit to Bathurst – it is also the oldest brick building west of the Macquarie River.

SIR JOSEPH BANKS NATURE RESERVE Atop Mount Panorama, this nature reserve has magnificent views of the city and surrounding district.

BEN CHIFLEY DAM ■ 228

Bathurst's water supply comes from the Ben Chifley Dam – named after the former Australian Prime Minister – located about seventeen kilometres south-east of Bathurst on Campbells River. The dam has a catchment area covering almost 1000 square kilometres, and was completed in 1955.

BORENORE CAVES ■ 229

Over countless years, the currents of Boree Creek have steadily dissolved the soft limestone outcrop that borders the creek, carving out a series of deep caves and tunnels that extend for about five kilometres along its length. A signposted walking trail runs from the Arch Cave and follows Boree Creek through the picnic area to Tunnel and Verandah caves. The cave formations are part of a 121-hectare reserve that was dedicated in 1959, creating a haven for native plants and animals. River she-oaks line the banks of the creek, white and yellow box proliferate on the crests and hillslopes, ribbon gum and blackwood wattle nestle in the gullies, while native animals such as kangaroos, wallabies and the rare spotted tiger quoll – once called the native cat – inhabit the entire area.

BYNG ■ 230

Winding lanes edged with English-style hawthorn hedges, and historic homes nestled into green valleys are amongst the old-world elements that make up the peaceful township of Byng. The town was originally known as Cornish Village, after the Cornish pioneers who settled the area. The foundations of the fertile Orange district's successful and varied fruit-growing industry were laid here, though ironically, the first trees brought from Cornwall by George Hawke over 100 years ago, all died.

CLIFTON GROVE ■ 231

The area that Clifton Grove occupies, just outside Orange, was originally the site of two properties 'Clifton Grove' and 'Banjo'. The land is now a rural estate, planned and developed in the 1970s by the former Canobolas Shire Council for people wanting rural living with city amenities. The Clifton Grove Homestead – a Georgian-style cottage built in 1841 – still exists within the estate and is classified by the National Trust.

Clifton Grove's chief claim to fame is its association with the nearby birthplace of A.B. 'Banjo' Paterson at Narambla Station. The old homestead was destroyed by fire many years ago and the station is now a public reserve. An obelisk on Ophir Road, inscribed with a verse from Paterson's much-recited bush ballad, 'Clancy of the Overflow' marks the site where this famous Australian poet was born in 1864. *Population 630*

LUCKNOW ■ 232

The year 1851 marked the beginning of gold fever in Australia with the first official discovery of payable gold at Ophir near Bathurst (see entries), followed closely by the second major gold strike at Lucknow – called Wentworth Mine before receiving its Indian name. From 1851 to 1927, just over fourteen tonnes of gold was mined from the Lucknow area – with production peaking in 1895 – and it was not until 1954 that mining ceased. Today, the mines are flooded and the numerous mullock heaps and mining relics scattered around the place are silent reminders of the town's industrious past.

MACQUARIE RIVER ■ 233

The Macquarie River was discovered in 1813 by the explorer George Evans who named it after Governor Lachlan Macquarie – the Aborigines who inhabited the area knew the river as *wambool* or *wammerawa*. Its discovery greatly intrigued the Governor and his surveyors – where did this broad river flow? Its headwaters were known to rise on the western slopes of the Great Divide, south of Bathurst, and from there flow in a generally north-west direction, not towards the coast, but inland, possibly to a vast interior sea.

The legend of an inland sea had enthralled many Australian explorers for years and in 1817, Macquarie appointed Surveyor-General John Oxley to lead an expedition to trace the full course of the river. Initially, the party made good progress but as they moved northwards, the river became increasingly narrow, then diffuse and marshy. Despite this, Oxley was '...sanguine in my expectations of soon entering the long sought for Australian sea'. But his optimism was not rewarded and on 30 June, he was forced to concede defeat – the river was in flood, its waters spreading rapidly across the plains, and the safety of the party was in jeopardy.

MOUNT CANOBOLAS PARK ■ 234

Mount Canobolas Park is a popular nature reserve on the upper slopes of Mount Canobolas – an ancient and extinct volcano formed about twelve million years ago and at 1395 metres, the highest peak between the Blue Mountains and the Indian Ocean.

...as does the grand facade of the 1895 Bank of New South Wales.

The park and mountain take their distinctive name from the Aboriginal words *coona* meaning 'shoulder' and *booloo* meaning 'two', referring to the mountain's twin peaks – Old Man and Young Man Canobolas. The slopes below the native bushland reserve are given over to state forest densely planted with radiata pine. A scenic road – Thomas Mitchell Way – through Glenwood State Forest leads to the summit of Mount Canobolas and traces the route of the Surveyor-General, Thomas Mitchell, who first climbed to the peak in 1835.

O'CONNELL ■ 235

The village of O'Connell – historic and well-preserved enough to be classified by the National Trust – is graced with several mellow, red-brick and stone buildings including a fine Anglican church constructed in 1865–66. The village was established in the early nineteenth century along the first road west of the Blue Mountains and was an important stopping place for settlers awaiting the opening of country west of Bathurst (see entry). The population of O'Connell swelled briefly during the wild days of the 1850s gold rush but now all is quiet, the major routes over the mountains having bypassed the little settlement long ago.

OPHIR ■ 236

Ophir no longer exists as a village, but ranks as an important historical site as the first place where payable gold was discovered in Australia. Two lucky prospectors, William Tom and John Lister, discovered just over 100 grams of the precious metal in April 1851 – a discovery that triggered an unprecedented gold rush. Today the Ophir region remains undisturbed as part of a flora and fauna reserve, though fossicking is still a popular pastime with alluvial gold and gemstones still to be found.

The Labour Day long weekend draws a small army of car-racing enthusiasts to Mount Panorama.

ORANGE ■ 237

Orange does have a fruit connection, but it's not oranges – in fact, Orange grows apples, cherries, pears and peaches – with half the New South Wales apple crop coming from the district's rich volcanic soils. The origin of the name has nothing at all to do with the citrus fruit – Orange was named by Major Thomas Mitchell (after William, Prince of Orange who later became the King of the Netherlands), who was a fellow aide-de-camp for the Duke of Wellington during the Spanish Peninsula War.

The city is located on the eastern slopes of the extinct volcano Mount Canobolas amidst the rolling hills and green valleys of the central tablelands. Historic churches, well-established parks and respectable public buildings give Orange a look of prosperity. The area surrounding the city is abundantly fertile, producing not only apples, but a wide variety of other fruits and vegetables as well as wool, cattle, sheep, pigs, fodder crops and sunflower seeds. Orange is also home to substantial secondary industries including New South Wales' largest electrical appliance manufacturer, woollen mills, wool-scouring works, cherry-brining works and cordial factories.

The site where the developed city of Orange now stands was in earlier days known as Blackman's Swamp. The village of Orange was not proclaimed until 1846, though pioneer stockmen had settled the district well before then. A huge impetus to the early development of the village and district came not from agriculture however, but the discovery of gold reefs at nearby Ophir and Lucknow (see entries) in 1851 which heralded Australia's first gold rush. Thousands of people flocked to the diggings but although the major gold deposits were exhausted within a few years, Orange was already well established as an important agricultural centre. For more than forty years Orange has hosted the annual Australian National Field Days – an internationally recognised event that brings farmers flocking to Orange to see the most impressive exhibition of agricultural machinery in Australasia.

In the early 1970s Orange was selected to become the focus of a scheme to promote decentralisation and regional development. This Bathurst–Orange Growth Centre scheme enjoyed some initial success but the cities have not expanded as originally expected. *Population 29 640*

BOWEN TERRACE Built in 1876 and in pristine condition, this building presents a rather incongruous sight – an inner-city terrace house in a New South Wales provincial centre.

Fields of oil-rich sunflowers – a relatively new crop in the central west.

COOK PARK European trees – some planted during the 1860s – a bandstand erected in 1908 which still has its original gaslight fittings and a begonia conservatory built in 1938 combine to make this beautiful park at the end of Summer Street a popular place for strolling or just sitting.

PUBLIC SCHOOL Located in Kite Street, the spire and steeply pitched roof of this historic building give it the appearance of a church rather than a school.

FESTIVALS Banjo Paterson Festival, February; Bloom and Blossom Festival, October.

PERTHVILLE ■ 238

Towards the end of the nineteenth century, the village of Perthville was simply known as Queen Charlotte's Vale after the creek that ran alongside the main thoroughfare between Bathurst and the Lachlan River. Like all early roads, the Vale Road was extremely rough due to the heavy traffic of laden bullock and horse drays. It was just a matter of time before a settlement sprang up near Vale Creek to cater for the weary bullockies and coach travellers. The fledgling settlement was proclaimed a village and given the official name of Perth in 1855. It was not until 1908 that the village was given its present name of Perthville, to avoid confusion with Perth in Western Australia. *Population 390*

PORTLAND ■ 239

The existence of a very large deposit of limestone was the initial spur to settlement in the Portland area. From the late 1870s limestone from the area was important in the development of the Lithgow coal industry and from the 1890s, growth of the small settlement was linked to the development of the cement manufacturing company situated on the considerable limestone deposit. The town takes its name from the cement works – the limestone was a reminder of the well known stone quarried at Portland in the south-west of England. Modern Portland is the centre of a rural district which produces wool, fat lambs and prime cattle for both local and Sydney markets. *Population 2060*

ROCKLEY ■ 240

Rockley is a charming old-world village nestled in a hollow between two hills. It is classified by the National Trust as an historic village and has a large number of fine old buildings grouped around the town park, reminiscent of an English village green.

SUMA PARK RESERVOIR ■ 241

Suma Park Reservoir has flooded the site of the first land settlement in the Orange area. Damming the waters of Fredericks Valley Creek north-east of Orange, this concrete, gravity-arch structure was constructed in 1962, though the site was originally considered – along with two additional alternatives – as the second water-supply dam for the municipality in about 1905. This early proposal was rejected because of the site's closeness to the old gold-mining town of Lucknow (see entry). At the time there was a possibility that the mines might re-open and create a pollution problem if a water supply was to be located downstream. Mining operations finally ceased in Lucknow in 1954 and the reservoir was finished eight years later.

WATTLE FLAT ■ 242

The tiny village of Wattle Flat is typical of the many gold settlements that once flourished in the Turon goldfields area. The village was surveyed in 1886 and at that time boasted a population of about 2000 – a figure that took in both the village and district. By 1880, the population had sharply declined as the goldfields, depleted of the precious ore, held no other attraction.

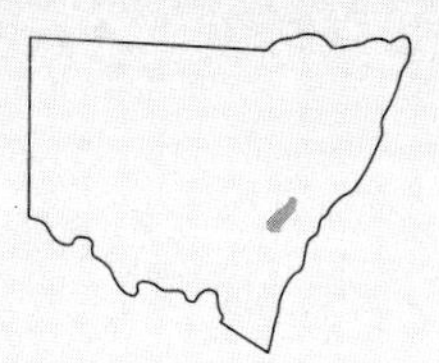

Lithgow & Oberon

The dramatic discovery of a breathtaking system of water-carved catacombs beneath the mountains and the challenge of equally breathtaking engineering feats above them ensure this rugged region's place in the history books.

BOWENFELS SOUTH ■ 243

Bowenfels South's history, as a staging post in the days when Cobb and Co. coaches rattled along the road to the west, is readily illustrated by the number of old inns which still stand in this hamlet on the southern edge of Lithgow. Two private residences, 'Ben Avon' and 'Fern-hill', are former wayside hostelries which provided for the needs of weary travellers between the 1840s and the 1860s, until the arrival of the railway.

The railway age is in turn commemorated by the dignified Gothic Revival station master's residence and the handsome railway station (1869), both well maintained and used as a restaurant and visitors' information centre respectively.

COXS RIVER ■ 244

The river which marks the western boundary of the Blue Mountains was also one of the major factors in the creation of the spectacular gorges and valleys which bring tourists flocking to the region.

The worn-down plateau known as the Blue Mountains has been eroded and sliced over thousands of years by rivers large and small, but mainly the Coxs, the Nepean and the Grose. Coxs River rises to the north-west of Lithgow and snakes its way through valleys on the west of the Great Dividing Range, collecting water from scores of creeks and smaller rivers and eventually depositing it in Lake Burragorang where the giant Warragamba Dam holds it in storage for the pipelines of Sydney.

Coxs River is named after William Cox, a former soldier who settled on a farm near Windsor and who was nominated by Governor Macquarie to oversee construction of the first road across the Blue Mountains, starting at Penrith and ending at Bathurst on the edge of the western plains. It was a daring enterprise: Cox and thirty convicts took only six months to clear a usable carriageway through the thick bush of the rugged sandstone ridges which in places rise to over 1000 metres. When the 161-kilometre road was completed in 1815 all the convicts were pardoned.

FISH RIVER ■ 245

The Fish River is nothing if not aptly named; in 1813, the explorer and surveyor George Evans – surveying a road across the Blue Mountains in the wake of the crossing by Blaxland, Wentworth and Lawson – became the first white man to see the waterway and commented '...if we want a fish it is caught immediately; they seem to bite at any time'. To the delight of anglers, they are still biting: the native freshwater fish now compete with the introduced trout and salmon which thrive in the cold mountain waters and are fair game for fishermen – as long as they cast their lines between October and May only, and throw back tiddlers under twenty-five centimetres!

The Fish rises in the state forest-clad ranges south of Oberon along the edge of the Great Dividing Range and runs north to form Lake Oberon, the source of the town's water supply. After meandering through broad valleys it turns westward south of Tarana and goes on to join with Campbells River in forming the Macquarie, one of the major rivers of the western plains.

HARTLEY ■ 246

Hartley is a ghost town with a difference – the resident ghosts have the best maintained habitations of any deserted township in Australia. Early settlers who used the newly built road across the Blue Mountains (see Coxs River) and descended from the heights along the precipitous, hard-won western pass were quick to settle the valley in which they found themselves. By the 1840s, Hartley was a thriving settlement, part of a region that was to become famous for its fruit, particularly apples. The decline of the charming little village began in 1868 when the railway came over the mountains and parted company with the road at Mount Victoria, thus bypassing Hartley and effectively consigning it to history. But the buildings survived, and in 1972 the precinct was placed under the care of the National Parks and Wildlife Service as an historic site. Seventeen of the nineteen old buildings in the village are publicly owned and all are lovingly maintained in near-original condition.

Other survivors of Hartley's heyday include 'Old Trahlee' Cottage, 'Ivy Cottage', St Bernard's Church, the former Royal Hotel and Collit's Inn, a roadside hostelry built in 1823 at Hartley Vale, seven kilometres by road to the north-east. Several old inns and farmhouses still stand at Little Hartley, the first settlement to greet exhausted travellers after the bumpy mountain crossing.

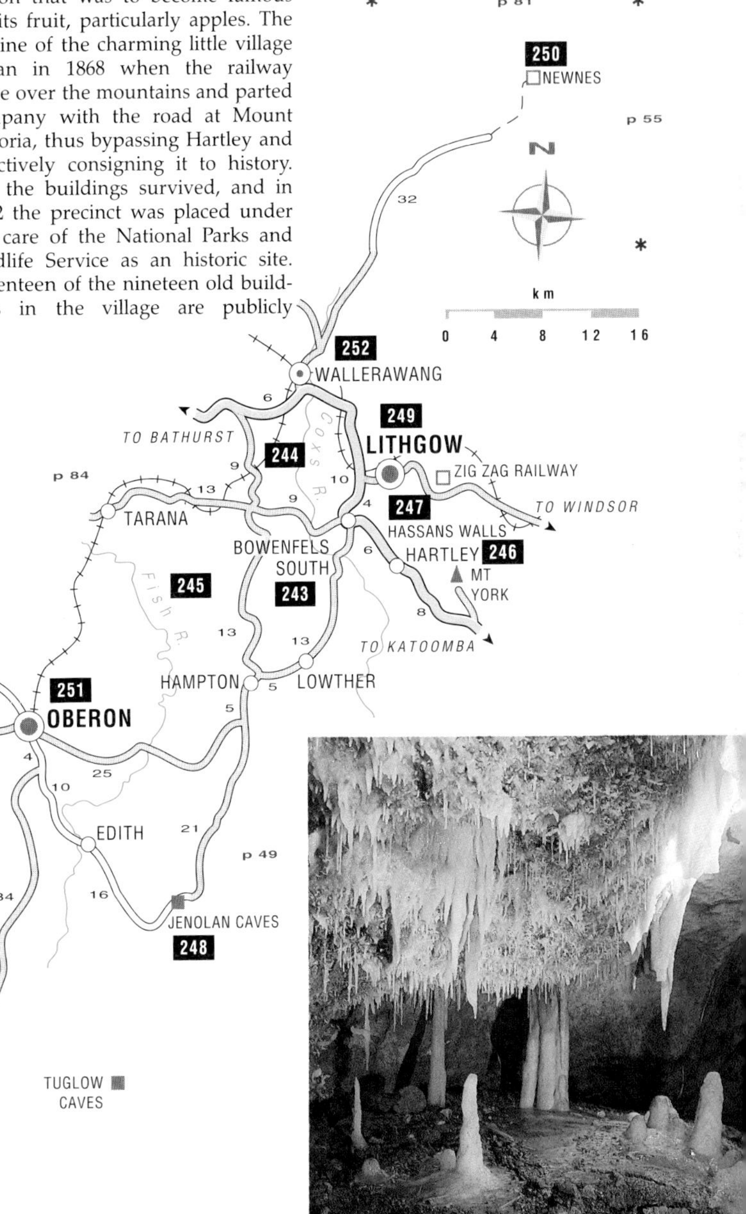

Artfully positioned electric lights reveal the wonders of the Jenolan underworld to best advantage.

THE MIGHTY ZIG-ZAG : A STONE AND STEEL HIGHWAY TO THE PLAINS

FIFTY-FIVE years after men walked over the Blue Mountains, the railway snaked its way up to the western edge of the plateau at Mount Victoria. The problem was how to take sleepers and rails down the precipitous cliff faces which barred the way to the plains beyond, with their rich farming and grazing lands.

When no contractor was found to build a three-kilometre tunnel, the chief railway engineer, John Whitton, decided to construct a system of cuttings, embankments and viaducts down the mountainside. The first zig-zag had been completed in 1867 and climbed Lapstone Hill on the eastern ascent – this project's seven-arch Knapsack Viaduct set the standard for what was to come. The Great Zig-Zag was constructed between 1866 and 1869 and follows roughly the shape of an elongated letter 'S' with three gracefully arched stone viaducts leaping deep ravines where the cliff face simply falls away. Most of the line follows a one in forty-two gradient, with this ratio being increased to a mighty one in sixty-six at dead ends to slow down the trains. Huge amounts of explosive were used to clear the way for cuttings; a ceremony was made of one occasion when the Governor's wife used an electric button to set off a charge which dislodged more than 40 000 tonnes of rock, much to the delight of the onlookers.

When the line came into service trains were shunted back and forth, sometimes with slowly chugging engines at both ends, as they negotiated the seventy-metre descent along the side of the mountain on two-and-a-half kilometres of line; the project was lauded around the world as an engineering triumph.

Sixteen years after the Great Zig-Zag fell into disuse its inspirational predecessor – the Knapsack Viaduct on the eastern side of the mountains – succumbed to progress and became a busy road bridge.

The march of time and technology eventually overtook the zig-zag and in 1910 it was replaced by a ten-tunnel deviation line which went through the mountainside rather than over it. Whitton's engineering masterpiece escaped the Knapsack Viaduct's indignity of becoming a roadway but the metal rails were removed and the bush moved back in...until 1974 when steam enthusiasts began operating a service for tourists. Seven old locomotives with period carriages now pay regular tribute to the engineers of long ago as they chug up and down the old line, occasionally tooting their distinctive whistles just for the sake of nostalgia. □

HASSANS WALLS ■ 247

The best views of the western edge of the Blue Mountains and south into the Jenolan Valley and its state forest is from the Hassans Walls lookout, five kilometres south of Lithgow. The cliffs of this spectacular, rubble-lined escarpment which rises to 1130 metres, are believed to have received their exotic name from Governor Lachlan Macquarie because of their similarity to a section of the Eastern Ghats in southern India – where he was stationed as a young soldier – known as the Walls of Hassan.

JENOLAN CAVES ■ 248

After a sometimes hair-raising drive along a road clinging to the steeply sided ridges of a spur of the Great Dividing Range, intrepid travellers to Jenolan Caves are rewarded with a view of the bitumen road surface disappearing into the black, gaping maw of the twenty-four-metre high Grand Arch. The spectacular introduction to Jenolan Caves is matched by what is on offer underground – although the faint-hearted and the claustrophobic should perhaps have second thoughts.

The broad belt of limestone at the bottom of the Jenolan Valley has been eroded over many centuries by the river of the same name and many other, smaller watercourses with the result that the region is honeycombed with cave systems of all sizes – there are at least 300 caves at Jenolan alone. The rivers dissolved the calcium carbonate in the limestone and, after the cave system was formed, the same process, occurring at a much slower rate through rainwater seepage, caused the formation of weird and wonderful shapes in the underground world.

The Aborigines called the caves 'binoomea' meaning 'holes in the hill'. The first white man to stumble across this natural wonder understandably kept it a secret; according to local legend the holes in the hill provided the perfect hiding place for an escaped convict turned bushranger named James McKeown. When his pursuers tracked him down in the unexplored wilderness in 1838 they found a farm plot and a hideout in a cave now known as McKeown's Hole. The fugitive was captured and from then on the caves began to draw a steadily growing number of curious sightseers. Charles and James Whalan, who helped capture McKeown, explored the caves and Charles eventually led guided tours although the caves were not officially opened to the public until 1866.

Early visitors here had to earn their pleasure; a buggy trip over a rough road from Oberon took them to the top of the caves hill and a night was spent in the shelter of the Grand Arch before exploration with lamp or candle began. Modern travellers have the benefit of electric illumination and central heating in the Federation-style Caves House – there is no town here and this huge, old-fashioned resort hotel, built between 1898 and 1918 provides the only accommodation in the middle of what is still a wilderness. The 'house' has taken on a new lease of life and scuttled its country-hotel image with an energetic sprucing up of the premises and its cuisine so that 'old-fashioned' now refers only to the charm of the building.

The arches in the mountainside – Grand Arch, the Devil's Coachhouse and Carlotta Arch – may be explored at any time and there are guided tours of one-and-a-half to two hours of the nine 'dark' caves – these subterranean sorties are thoughtfully graded according to the number of steps to be climbed. A 'strenuous' cave may have 1300!

LITHGOW ■ 249

The western foothills of the Blue Mountains plateau are an unlikely setting for Australia's first industrial settlement, but Lithgow can justifiably lay claim to the title. Nowadays a thriving regional centre for light industry, including the Commonwealth-owned small arms factory, and an important coal-mining city,

Almost fifty years after the Great Zig-Zag line was abandoned in favour of a system of tunnels – better able to handle the increasingly longer and more frequent, westward-bound goods trains – the mountain valleys echoed once again to the urgent sound of whistles as restored locomotives introduced a new generation to steam.

Lithgow may not have been the first settlement established after the crossing of the mountains but it is the first major town the westward-bound traveller comes upon.

Coal first put Lithgow on the map but it was not until the arrival of the railway line in 1869 that secondary industry began to develop apace: meat chilling works, brick and pottery works and, most dramatically, an ironworks that produced Australia's first steel in 1900. It appeared that a thriving steel industry might develop; a second furnace opened in 1913, and the steel plant and rolling mills operated until the late 1920s when they were transferred to Port Kembla. Today, above a network of undergound tunnels, the crumbling ruins of the powerhouse and some slag are part of a park which marks one of Australia's most historic industrial sites. *Population 11 970*

ZIG-ZAG RAILWAY AND VIADUCTS The railway, via the Zig-Zag track down the western escarpment of the Blue Mountains, made Lithgow, and in return railway enthusiasts – from Lithgow and elsewhere – breathed new life into the old line sixty years after it was abandoned (see box).

ESKBANK HOUSE Thomas Brown, the man credited with the discovery of the Lithgow coal seam, built this single-storey sandstone residence in 1842. A broad roof covers a verandah on three sides and there are covered courtyards enclosed by two narrow wings. The house is filled with period furniture and one courtyard is a pioneer's museum with photographs and artefacts illustrating the region's mining history.

POTTERY KILN SITE The kiln site is another industrial remnant which tells much about Lithgow's early days. The kilns were first fired in 1875 and for more than twenty years produced large quantities of terracotta pipe, bricks and glazed pottery; the old kiln, claystore and brick warehouse can still be seen, while nearby, in the old buggy shed of the Pottery Estate, a potter continues to fashion pots from the local clay.

FESTIVALS Biennial Festival of the Valley in November of even-numbered years.

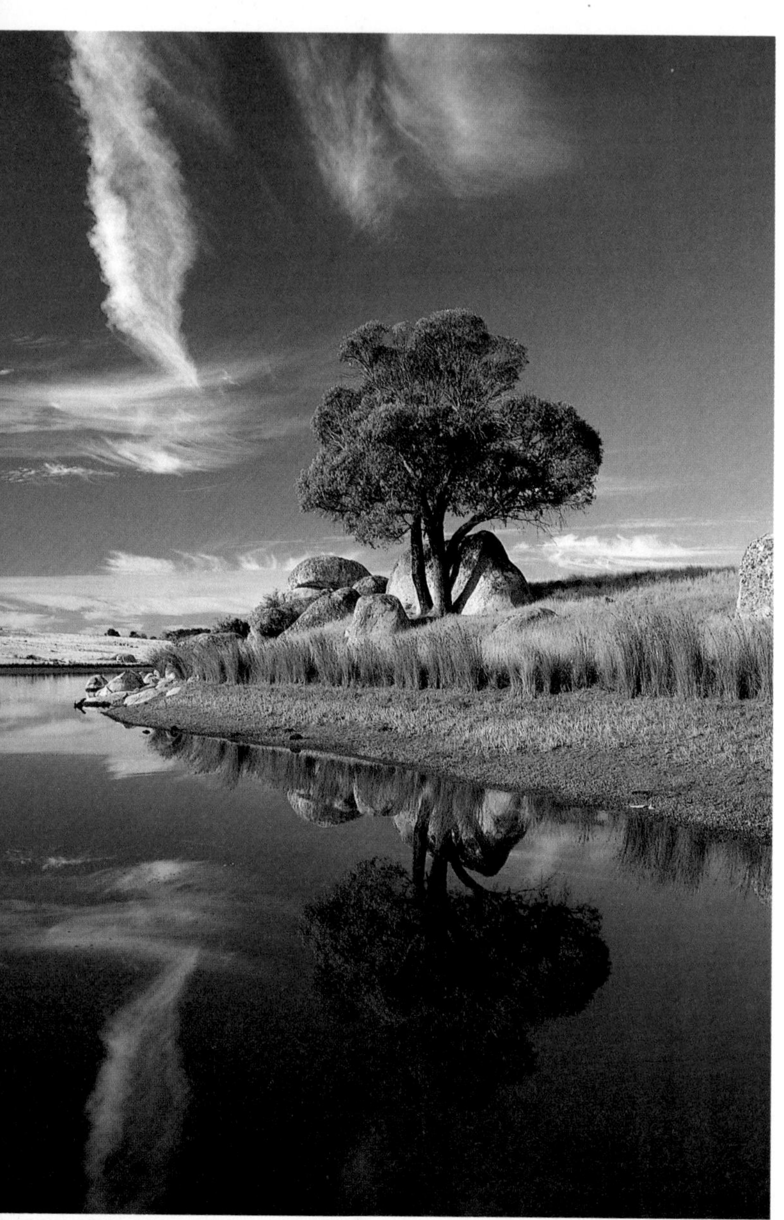

Lake Oberon, behind the Fish River Dam, provides not only a reliable water supply but also a peaceful location for fishing and sailing.

NEWNES ■ 250

Hidden away in the Wolgan Valley, Newnes is a mining ghost town where the old hotel remains as the only sign of life. From 1903 until 1924 this was a busy centre for the production of oil from shale and the old workings can still be seen across the local creek. Tunnels connected the town with the main western railway line but although some shale was hauled out for gas production, most of it was processed on site and the oil refined for lighting or lubrication. Glen Davis, another shale mining town in the nearby Capertee Valley, suffered a similar fate and a museum there records the story of the oil extraction industry.

GLOW-WORM TUNNEL The largest of the tunnels built through the mountainside to service Newnes is not deserted – it has been occupied by a huge colony of glow worms. The road into the steep hills above the town passes through the spectacular forests of the Wollemi National Park where a short walk ends in the entrance to the tunnel. Visitors are advised to enter quietly with the aid of a torch and then turn it off to see the myriad insect lights shining on the walls.

OBERON ■ 251

If it had not been for the writings of William Shakespeare the residents of this true mountain town (elevation: 1177 metres above sea level) might still be living in Bullock Flats. In the early 1860s, forty years after settlement began in this district, the town was surveyed near a region known as Bullock Flats; a sensitive local resident quickly sought inspiration from Shakespeare's *A Midsummer Night's Dream* and suggested Oberon, the name of the king of the fairies, as a more felicitous name. In later years, a nearby hamlet called Fish River Creek followed suit and opted for the name of Oberon's wife, Titania, as did a motel in modern Oberon.

Gold, silver and copper ore were mined here in the early days and although fossicking remains a popular recreation, Oberon's business is the milling of timber from the nearby state forests and the manufacture of particle board. The bracing climate is excellent for the production of large crops of vegetables such as Brussels sprouts, broccoli and potatoes.

As well as the gem and precious metal fossickers who roam the local countryside, some man-made amendments to the landscape attract other visitors. Lake Oberon, the result of a dam on the Fish River (see entry) – and most other local waterways – are well stocked with fat trout, and the state forests of the introduced radiata pine are equally well stocked with wood mushrooms between early summer and autumn. Novice mushroom fossickers are advised to pack a field guide in order to avoid the dreaded toadstool!

Jenolan Caves House – all the comforts of civilisation in the middle of a rugged, 2400-hectare wilderness.

Fossickers after exotic architecture will find an art-deco gem in Oberon's main street in the form of the former Malachi Gilmore Hall, now used as a wool store. The hall was constructed in 1936-7 and its pastel-coloured, stucco facade, studded with glass bricks, has been maintained in all the glory of its original Hollywood picture-palace style. *Population 2240*

WALLERAWANG ■ 252

The convenience of the Lithgow coal seam and the growing need for electric power put Wallerawang on the map. A variety of grazing and agricultural activities are pursued in the surrounding valleys but the giant 1000 megawatt power station dominates the region, an incongruously industrial sight in such a rural setting.

The station was opened in 1959 and its slim, pencil-shaped timber cooling towers and one futuristic concrete tower soar above the waters of the dammed Coxs River (see entry), which are used to remove heat from the steam which has been utilised to turn the plant's four giant turbo-generators. The chilly mountain lakes which have been created behind the dams – Wallerawang and Lyell – mean that this hilly region 900 metres above sea level has facilities for fishing, boating and other water sports equal to any coastal town. *Population 2060*

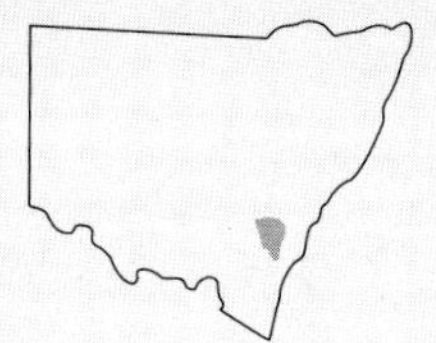

Goulburn & Crookwell

The Goulburn Plains and their adjacent tablelands, once famous as the domain of some of Australia's most notorious bushrangers, have another more noble heritage based on a history of remarkable pastoral achievements.

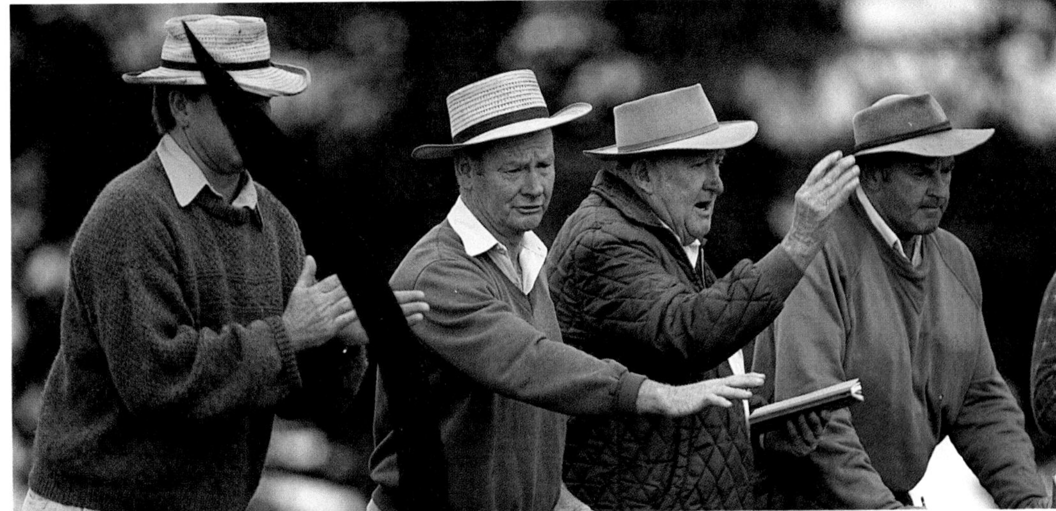

The level of bidding at the Goulburn sale [illegible] provides a barometer for the state of the rural economy.

BINDA ■ 253

The Binda settlement was gazetted as a town in 1851, some years before the neighbouring and now larger town of Crookwell. Named after an Aboriginal word meaning 'deep water', it was used as a watering hole for the bullock teams travelling from Goulburn to the recently opened Tuena goldfields.

The old Flag Hotel, now the post office, was the scene of a legendary 'bail up' by Ben Hall and his gang during the Christmas celebrations of 1864. The entire population of the village was either already in the inn or forced into it by the gang who ordered that the dance in progress should continue.

For a small village Binda has a number of old buildings of a quality more usual in larger towns. St James Church of England, built in 1864 on land belonging to Captain William Hovell, the explorer, is built of bluestone and quartzite.

BREADALBANE ■ 254

Pronounced 'bred-al-ben', this village was named in 1820 by Governor Lachlan Macquarie after the Brea[illegible]albane Mountains, west of Pe[illegible] his native Scotland. By 18[illegible] [illegible]urveyor-general was [illegible] report progress on [illegible]uth Road whe[illegible] Bong Bong to [illegible] Plains was practicable [illegible]eady for carriages'.

By 1836 there was even a local Argyle Hunt group, which met at 'Rossiville', home of the former Corsican soldier and prominent local citizen F.N. Rossi, and hunted the recently introduced fox to Breadalbane and back again. But not all the activity in and around Breadalbane was as socially acceptable as fox hunting. In the 1860s the landlord of the Lodge's Inn at Breadalbane was jailed for being an accomplice to Ben Hall and his gang and for receiving goods stolen by the gang. While in jail in Goulburn awaiting trial, his inn was the scene of a shoot out between Ben Hall's gang and the local police.

BUNGONIA STATE RECREATION AREA ■ 2[illegible]

Bungonia village, at the entran[illegible] the recreation area, was once [illegible] important than Goulburn as [illegible]ct commercial and business [illegible] The decision in 1833 to rerou[illegible] Great South Road through [illegible]rn and bypass the village [illegible] demise.

Bungonia S[illegible]eation Area covers alm[illegible]ectares and is the larg[illegible] recreation area in New [illegible] Wales. Bounded by the wa[illegible] the Shoalhaven River and B[illegible]nia Gorge, its official designa[illegible] is relatively new although the spectacular landscape has attracted visitors and walkers for many years.

Bungonia Gorge, also known as the 'Grand Canyon', has nearly vertical walls 300 metres high. One unbroken rockface of 275 metres is the highest in New South Wales. A huge pile of house-sized limestone boulders has choked the lower end of the gorge.

JERRARA FALLS These spectacular falls are best viewed from Adams Lookdown…especially after rain. The name Jerrara comes from an Aboriginal word meaning 'place where eels sleep or rest'.

COLLECTOR ■ 256

Although the name of this small village looks European it is in fact an a[illegible]ion of an Aboriginal word '[illegible]dar' or 'colegdor' thought to [illegible] 'place of pelicans'.

[illegible]llector and the road leading [illegible] it were the scenes of a number [illegible] bushranger attacks. The most seri[illegible]us attack came after Ben Hall and his gang bailed up fifty people on the Collector Road then rode into the village and robbed the store and Kimberley's Inn. Constable Samuel Nelson decided to take the gang on singlehanded and was shot down just outside the inn. There is a memorial to Nelson outside the inn, now called the Bushranger Hotel.

Collector had five hotels by the 1880s…and two cemeteries. The village was used as a gathering place for bullock teams that formed themselves into bullock trains or convoys before tackling the bushranger-ridden roads.

CROOKWELL ■ 257

Crookwell is well known for its bracing climate and, at 885 metres above sea level, has some snow in most winters. The majority of New South Wales' seed potatoes come from Crookwell, which also has a reputation for excellent merino wool – the famous 'golden bale' that was sold in 1964 at 1800 pence a pound came from Crookwell. Orchards around the town have been growing apples, pears and cherries for over a hundred years and trout fishing has also been established since last century. The first rainbow and brown trout on the mainland were released into the Wollondilly River in 1888 and trout fishing is available in many of the waterways around Crookwell.

The town was originally called Kiamma, a fairly common Aboriginal place name meaning 'good fishing ground' but by the time the town was gazetted in 1860 the name had been changed to match that of the nearby river, Crookwell. The river is thought to have got its name either from a bullocky's description of the local water supply as 'a crook well' or from the birthplace of one of the region's first settlers William Stephenson in Crookhall, County Durham.

Beneath the thick cement fleece of Goulburn's 'Big Merino' a stairway leads to its viewing-window eyes.

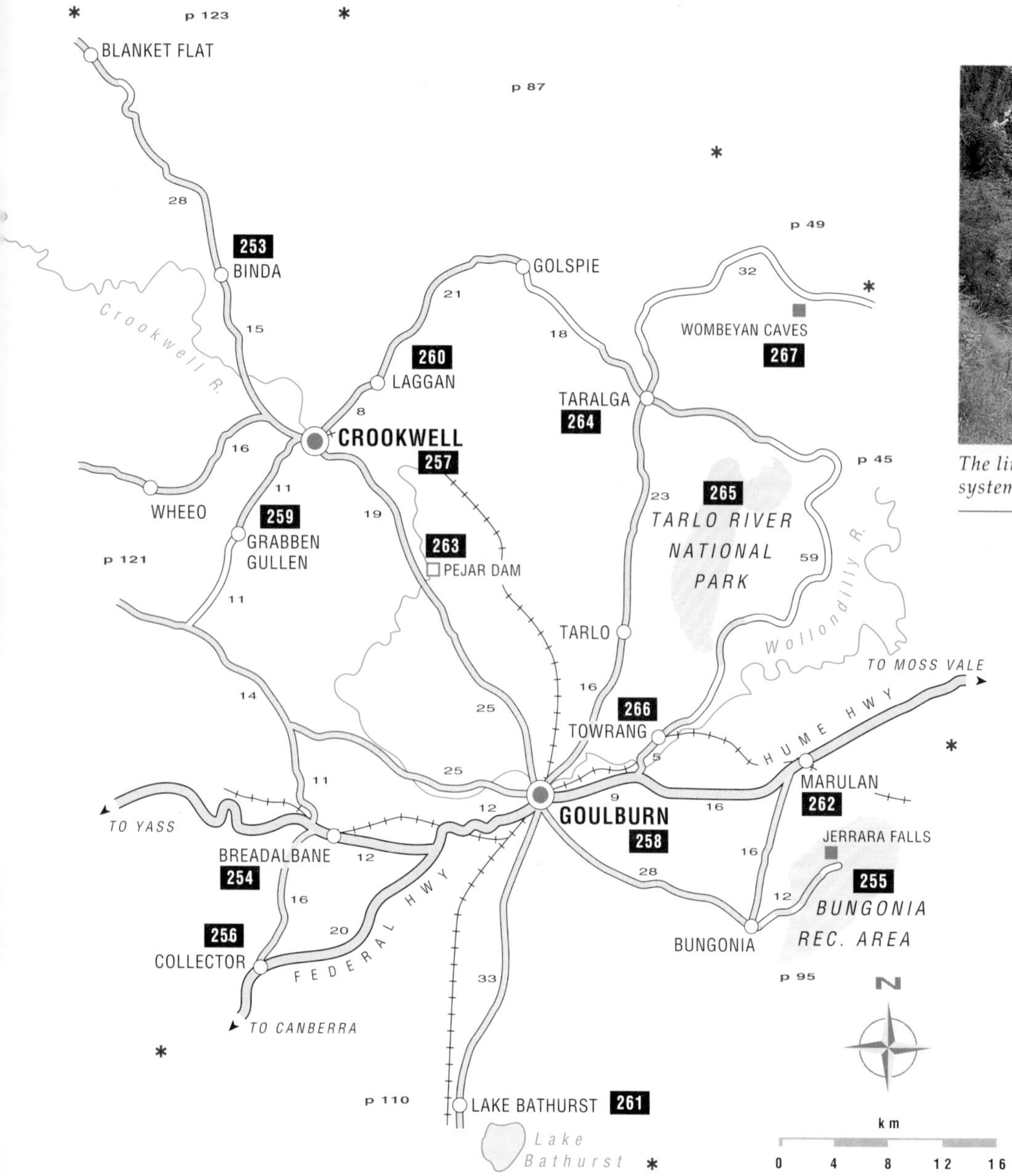

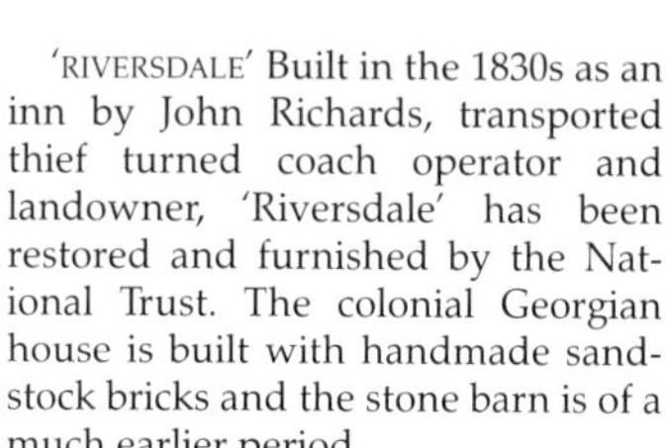

The limestone belt which produced the Jenolan Cave system also gave birth to Wombeyan's Victoria Arch.

A tunnel through the mountainside sets the mood for visitors on the approach road to Wombeyan Caves.

Stephenson's flour mill, built of random rubble bluestone in 1871, still stands and is now used as a commercial clubhouse. *Population 1970*

GOULBURN ■ 258

Goulburn was gazetted in 1833 as a garrison town with two main purposes: to guard the convicts in the stockade at nearby Towrang (see entry) and to act as a centre for police action against bushrangers in the southern region of the state. By 1836 the town of Goulburn had 'a courthouse of slabs covered with bark, a lock-up house, a few huts occupied by the mounted police and constables, a cottage of roughly cut timber and a small inn affording tolerable accommodation'.

From the early days the township was noted for its wheat, wool and stock breeding. By the 1860s wheat growing had moved further west but Goulburn's reputation for wool and livestock continued to expand with the city's wool sales remaining as the only such sales still held at a venue outside the state capital cities.

In 1864 the Anglican See of Goulburn was created and Goulburn became the last town in the British Empire to be created a city by Royal Letters Patent. There followed the boom years in its development. As the southern terminus of the rail line from Sydney, Goulburn acted as a staging centre for the transfer of goods and passengers further south or west. Many of the best known buildings in Goulburn were built between the 1860s and the 1880s.

The Great Depression of the 1920s and 1930s had a strong impact on Goulburn and since the Second World War growth in Goulburn has been slower than in most other Australian cities. It remains the centre of a strong pastoral district and has retained a rich architectural heritage from the nineteenth century including two cathedrals, the old jail and court house and many fine homesteads. *Population 24 000*

'RIVERSDALE' Built in the 1830s as an inn by John Richards, transported thief turned coach operator and landowner, 'Riversdale' has been restored and furnished by the National Trust. The colonial Georgian house is built with handmade sandstock bricks and the stone barn is of a much earlier period.

ST SAVIOUR'S CATHEDRAL Designed by Edmund Blackett in 1874, the Cathedral was dedicated in 1884. St Saviour's is one of two cathedrals in Goulburn and one of the most magnificent white sandstone cathedrals in Australia.

GOULBURN BREWERY Bradley's Goulburn Brewery was built in 1835 and operated as a brewery under a number of different owners until it was closed in 1929 by the then owner, Tooths. Restoration work on the brewery began in 1982 and the brewery is now the only surviving pre-Federation brewery.

ROCKY HILL WAR MEMORIAL Built by public subscription in 1923 to commemorate the men from the Goulburn district who served in the First World War, the War Memorial – on a craggy rise on the city's eastern outskirts – is one of Goulburn's major landmarks and is lit up at night. Standing twenty metres high it has a rotating beacon on the top and a viewing platform from which there are spectacular views of the city. The fifteen-metre square base houses a military museum.

FESTIVALS Lilac City Festival, early October.

GRABBEN GULLEN ■ 259

Known to the locals as 'Grabby', the name Grabben Gullen comes from a Wiradjuri Aboriginal word meaning 'small water'. A cairn of stones and more than 200 trees from eleven species of eucalypt have been planted to commemorate the Wiradjuri Aborigines whose traditional land the village was built on.

Gold was discovered at Grabben Gullen in the 1850s but it is sapphires for which the village is now best known. A public fossicking area is located on Sapphire Road. Now skirted by the main road, Grabben Gullen is a small village with a declining population, a few houses and a hotel which was an inn in the old sapphire mining days.

LAGGAN ■ 260

Named after Loch Laggan in northern Scotland, Laggan had 300 people in 1866 and the *Goulburn Herald* was moved to declare that 'Laggan promises ere long to outstrip many old established townships'. The population of this small village is, however, now less than half what it was in 1866 although some of the buildings from Laggan's heyday can still be seen and the village's two old mill buildings are still in use.

LAKE BATHURST ■ 261

The first European to see Lake Bathurst, called 'Bundong' by the local Aborigines, was the Deputy Surveyor-General, James Meehan, on his exploration with Hamilton Hume in 1818. The lake was the site of the first Christian service in the south of the new colony when Reverend Robert Cartwright preached to Governor Macquarie and his entourage at the lakeside in 1820.

The lake, which has a number of creeks running into it but none exiting is prevented from seeping into the swampy Milwaree Ponds, on the west of the lake, by a naturally formed bank of gravel that has built up. The gravel was quarried for railway ballast from the 1880s and a spur rail line was built from the village of Lake Bathurst to the lakeside for transporting the ballast.

MARULAN ■ 262

Originally laid out as a private township called Mooroowoolen, the name Marulan was adopted, almost by default, in 1878. The local postmaster at Mooroowoolen applied for a date stamp for his post office and was told to use the old one from Marulan Camp post office, which originally operated four kilometres south of Mooroowoolen but had since closed.

From its early days Marulan was a staging post for bullock teams and coaches on the road from Sydney to Goulburn. Joe Peters, one of the first ticket-of-leave men to be granted land in the County of Argyle, as the district around Goulburn was called, succeeded in holding up progress on the building of this main road to allow him to establish a new hotel at Marulan when it became apparent that his old hotel would be bypassed by the road.

Although the country around Marulan was not ideal grazing land, it had other assets. Limestone and marble have long been quarried here. Marulan marble varies in colour from pure white to jet black and was used for flooring in the early Sydney University buildings.

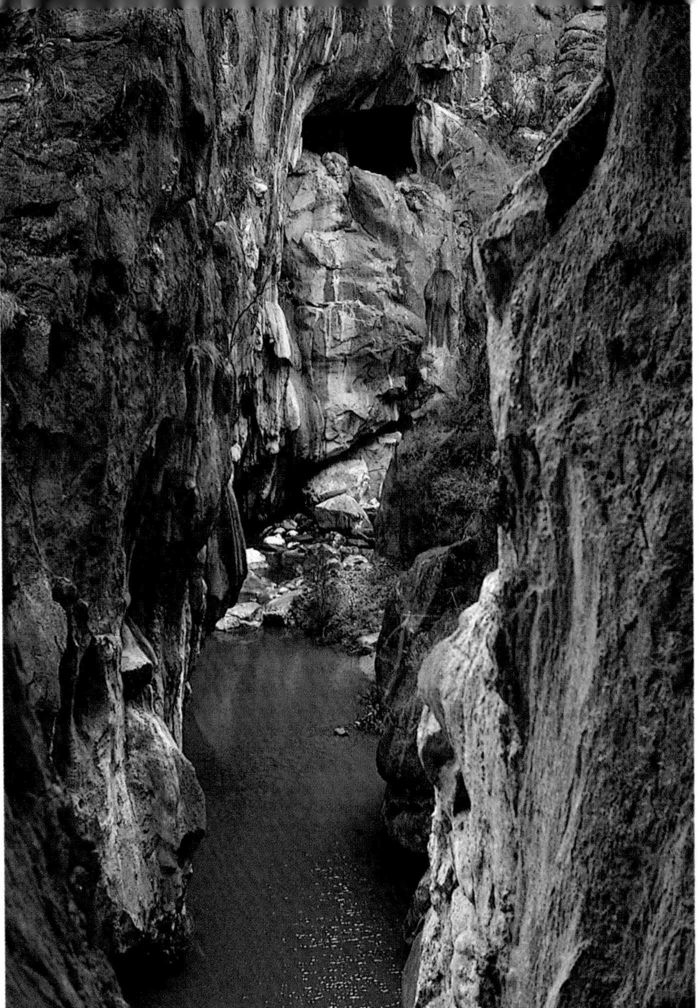

Over time, Mares Forest Creek has dissolved the limestone of this ridge to form a narrow gorge, its walls lined with inaccessible cave pockets.

PEJAR DAM ■ 263

The dam is an important recreational facility as well as providing a solution to the recurrent water problems of Goulburn. Completed in 1979 at a cost of eight million dollars, the dam was filled with water by 1984.

The rock and earth-filled barrier across the Wollondilly River downstream of where it is joined by Pejar Creek, stands 24 metres high, 380 metres long and has a catchment area of 140 square kilometres.

The dam is one of the prime fishing spots in an area noted for its trout fishing. Every year the local Crookwell Fishing Club releases fingerlings from its hatchery into the dam and nearby streams.

TARALGA ■ 264

This small farming town was first settled in the 1820s, the year after Charles Throsby passed through on his way from Moss Vale to Bathurst. One of the earliest settlers here was Lachlan Macalister who was in charge of the mounted police on the Goulburn Plains and who was wounded in a gun fight with Bold Jack Donahoe's gang of bushrangers.

The oldest building in the village is the former Commercial Hotel, nowadays a private residence. 'Richlands', the old homestead of the pioneering Macarthur family, also still stands and the property maintains its reputation for breeding fine merino sheep.

FESTIVALS Taralga Rodeo, January.

TARLO RIVER NATIONAL PARK ■ 265

Fifty-two kilometres of the length of the Tarlo River and part of the Cookbundoon Range are enclosed within what will eventually be a 12 000-hectare national park.

Rugged landforms and waterbird habitats characterise Tarlo River National Park with at least three species of wild duck nesting at different sites within the park.

Although proclaimed in 1982, access to the park is limited since permission is required to cross the surrounding private land and there are, as yet, no public walking tracks.

TOWRANG ■ 266

From an Aboriginal word meaning 'shield', Towrang was the largest penal settlement in southern New South Wales from 1837 to 1843 and was the main reason for the development of the town of Goulburn. The Towrang Stockade was a construction camp of convicts guarded by a detachment of the regiment garrisoned at Goulburn.

There were two groups of convicts in the stockade: light-sentence men, serving less than seven years, who minded horses, drove bullock teams and felled trees and the 'iron gang' of convicts serving longer sentences, who built roads, bridges and culverts. All wore a distinctive yellow and black uniform and were guarded by soldiers with fixed bayonets. In 1838 there were seventy men in irons and twenty-one men out of irons, some of whom, despite the irons and military guard, escaped into the bush and turned to bushranging in the surrounding district.

In addition to the Towrang Bridge built by the prisoners in 1839 there is a partly excavated and restored powder magazine and faint traces of the foundations of the stockade buildings to remind people of Towrang's early history

WOMBEYAN CAVES ■ 267

The word Wombeyan means 'caves in the hills' or, so some say, 'gigantic water rat' and the Wombeyan Caves are a prominent feature in the Dreamtime stories of the local Gandungara Aborigines. The holes or entries into the cave system were made by Mirragen, the mythical catman, in his pursuit of Guangatch who was part-fish and part-reptile. When Guangatch took refuge in the caves, Mirragen, who was loath to enter, dug holes in the crumbly limestone and inserted his fish spears to force Guangatch into the open.

The first Europeans to visit the caves included John Oxley and John Macarthur who visited them in 1828. The caves have been open to the public since 1865.

Five caves are open to the public: Wollondilly Cave, with regular guided tours, has spectacular flowstones; Kooringa, the smallest of the caves, and Mulwaree have restricted tours; Fig Tree Cave is for those who want to be their own guides and was closed for forty years until 1968 to protect the coloured shawls and massive broken stalactite formations; Junction Cave has regular guided tours and the superb shawls in the cave include 'Chalker's Blanket' named after Charles Chalker the first caretaker of the caves.

The Southern Tablelands has another extensive cave complex at Bungonia which is rather less accessible than Wombeyan Caves but the two systems have many fascinating formations known technically as speleotherms, in common. The best known speleotherms are stalactites, which drop from the roof of a cave, and stalagmites, which build up from the floor of a cave.

Compared with Wombeyan Caves with its stairs, handrails and accessibility to tourists of all ages, Bungonia Caves are wild, largely unknown and only for the true speliologist prepared to tackle the flimsy ladder drops, rope descents and occasional claustrophobic squeezes.

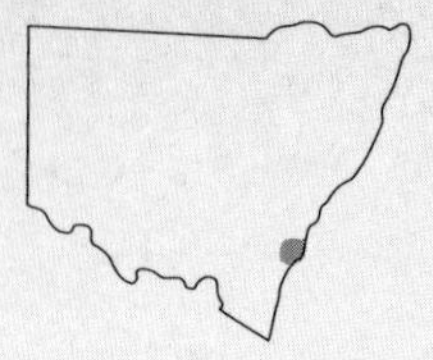

Nowra & Kiama

Beyond Wollongong–Port Kembla, the Sydney-centred urban sprawl quickly gives way to a pleasantly rural, unspoiled coastline punctuated by golden beaches and sandy estuaries and extending almost all the way to Port Phillip Bay.

BERRY ■ **268**

The modern, handsome 'town of trees' – as Berry likes to style itself – began as a sawmilling camp called Broughton Creek in about 1825. But the reason for its existence goes back further than that.

In the early 1820s a merchant called Alexander Berry sailed from Sydney on board the *Snapper* in search of land for settlement. In 1822, Governor Brisbane granted Berry and his partner Edward Wollstonecraft 4000 hectares and 100 convicts to work the property. Berry established his 'Coolangatta' property – the name was based on the Aboriginal 'cullingatty' meaning 'splendid view' – on a hillside near the mouth of the Shoalhaven River (see Shoalhaven Heads).

It was with this background that the timber-getters settled at Broughton Creek, ten kilometres inland from Seven Mile Beach, three years later. Over the years as the cedar ran out and cattle and agricultutre became the mainstay of the property, Berry purchased more land and the estate grew to more than 16 000 hectares but the Village of Broughton Creek was a village and little more than an outstation of the Coolangatta headquarters for many years.

In 1858, the 'local' newspaper, published in Kiama, reported that '...there is a good water power mill – idle – a commodious school house without an incumbent. No church – no store – no post office. Shades of Shakespeare – nothing'. Better times were ahead and by the late 1860s there was a post office, a store, a tannery *and* there was an incumbent in the school. After Alexander Berry died in 1873 his younger brother David promoted the establishment of a properly surveyed township at Broughton Creek and in 1889, the year after his death, the old sawyer's settlement was renamed 'Berry' in his honour.

The care taken in laying out the town provided an inspiration for its administrators who, late in the nineteenth century, saw that the streets were lined with a selection of deciduous European trees which provided a legacy of leafy streets for today's residents. Proper planning has also left a large part of the original townscape intact with colonial buildings still in good order and in use.

The nature of the rural landscape around Berry, along with the rest of the New South Wales southern coast, has changed in recent years; dairying is still important along with a variety of agricultural or horticultural pursuits – such as turf farming – and with the growth of large regional centres such as Nowra and improved transport the town has become a major residential and retirement centre. The nurturing of the town's appearance and its historic connections – the main street with its antique shops, and cafes and regular commercial buildings shows how charm and advertising can live side by side – have boosted tourism and Berry is an important watering-hole for travellers on the Princes Highway. *Population 1570*

HISTORY MUSEUM The former bank building looks more like a church than a temple of commerce with its steeply stepped, Dutch-style gables, tall, narrow windows and bonded brickwork. It was built in 1886 and restored and transformed into a museum in 1971.

COURT HOUSE The 1891 court house – with a coat-of-arms ennobling its front wall above a portico of columns and decorative ironwork – along with the old post office and the solidly respectable bank buildings of the Victorian era provides the unchangeable, historic hub around which the rest of the town revolves.

BOMADERRY ■ **269**

Bomaderry and Nowra started out as separate settlements but ever since they were linked by a bridge over the Shoalhaven River they have grown closer and closer together so that today the two names are simply linked with a hyphen to indicate the merging of the Nowra–Bomaderry residential and commercial zones into one urban region.

Like many towns in this region Bomaderry began as a small settlement on the Berry estate (see Berry) but, like Berry, its informal, 'organic' growth was controlled by the introduction of a formal plan in 1891 by the trustees of the estate. Twenty years before the two townships had joined to form one of the first municipal councils in the area so that when the Minister for Works arrived to open the Nowra Bridge in 1881 he was met by the mayor of Broughton Creek (later Berry)–Bomaderry as well as the mayor of Nowra. After a speech and the breaking of a bottle of champagne on the steel truss bridge – at 340 metres the longest constructed by the Public Works Department – the official party walked across the new roadway to a light luncheon in Nowra followed by a steamboat cruise of the river's lower reaches.

Bomaderry's trump card, which gave a major boost to its position as a regional industrial centre was its connection with Sydney...in other words, the railway, which as fate and a shortage in the railway authority's budget would have it, came to a sudden halt on the northern bank of the Shoalhaven in 1893 and has never proceeded any further. Poor roads meant that commerce had relied traditionally on ships to take goods to the Sydney markets so the introduc-

The high ground of the Budderoo National Park gives rise to many waterways; the waters of Lyrebird Falls help replenish the Minnamurra River.

tion of the railway was an economic stimulus to the town which suddenly found itself the railhead. In its first year the tiny station's ticket office sold more than 1100 tickets, this at a time when the population of Nowra was little more than 2000.

During the 1960s and early 1970s, the traffic flow over the old iron bridge more than doubled and in 1980 it was joined by a sleek, modern structure of reinforced concrete which now carries the northbound traffic between the interlinked centres. *Population 5640*

BOMADERRY CREEK WALKING TRACK

Several walks, ranging from one to three hours in length, can be taken through the relatively flat bushland of the belt of Crown Land that surrounds the winding waterway of Bomaderry Creek. Points of interest, such as the sandstone rock walls, caves and overhangs along the bank, are signposted.

BUDDEROO NATIONAL PARK ■ 270

The Minnamurra Falls, where the river of the same name pours over a fifty-metre drop on the edge of the Illawarra escarpment, are the star attraction of this small park which takes in a region of varied rainforest below the falls. Ferns, orchids and staghorns cling to the giant figs and other rainforest trees at the well-watered base of the falls, while above, on the top of the plateau, open, eucalypt forest and heathland provide colour in the spring. Landslides have been known to cut the short track which affords a bird's eye view of the waterfall and its narrow gorge so visitors are advised to check with the National Parks and Wildlife Service before setting out. There is no camping in the park.

BUNDANOON ■ 271

'Lovely Bundanoon, STAY!
Have you seen our beauteous sights,
verdant gorges, craggy heights?
Have you heard the lyrebird call,
seen the sparkling waterfall?
If not, then awhile here stay
and see them all without delay.'

So ran the large sign which greeted visitors to Bundanoon at the turn of the century when the sleepy southern highlands town was in the process of becoming the guesthouse capital of Australia – eventually it became so popular that there were more than sixty guesthouses in operation between the wars.

There were no guesthouses for the first European visitors, a group of escaped convicts who passed this way as early as ten years after the First Fleet's arrival. An official party despatched by Governor Macquarie in 1818 and which included the explorer Hamilton Hume passed this way while surveying a route to Jervis Bay; one of the group, Charles Throsby, who was later granted 400 hectares in the region by the governor, is said to have noted the Aboriginal word 'bantanoon', meaning 'deep gullies'.

Exploration led to settlement and slowly a hamlet began to grow; Jumping Rock, a few kilometres from the present town, was the first settlement; later, the site of present-day Bundanoon was known as Jordan's Crossing, after a district pioneer. Today's version of the Aboriginal name heard by Charles Throsby was not adopted until 1881. By the 1870s, coal mining, stone quarrying and timber milling were the major industries apart from farming until the 1890s when Sydneysiders realised that the Blue Mountains was not the only place they could reach by a short steam-train journey for some invigorating 'mountain' air.

Once upon a pre-car time, this platform was crowded with excited holiday-makers every weekend.

Bundanoon's success as a holiday town was based largely on the fact that in the days before freeways and the family car, it was too far away for a day-trip but its location was also all-important. The town sits on the south-eastern edge of a spur plateau of the Great Dividing Range known as the southern highlands. At 680

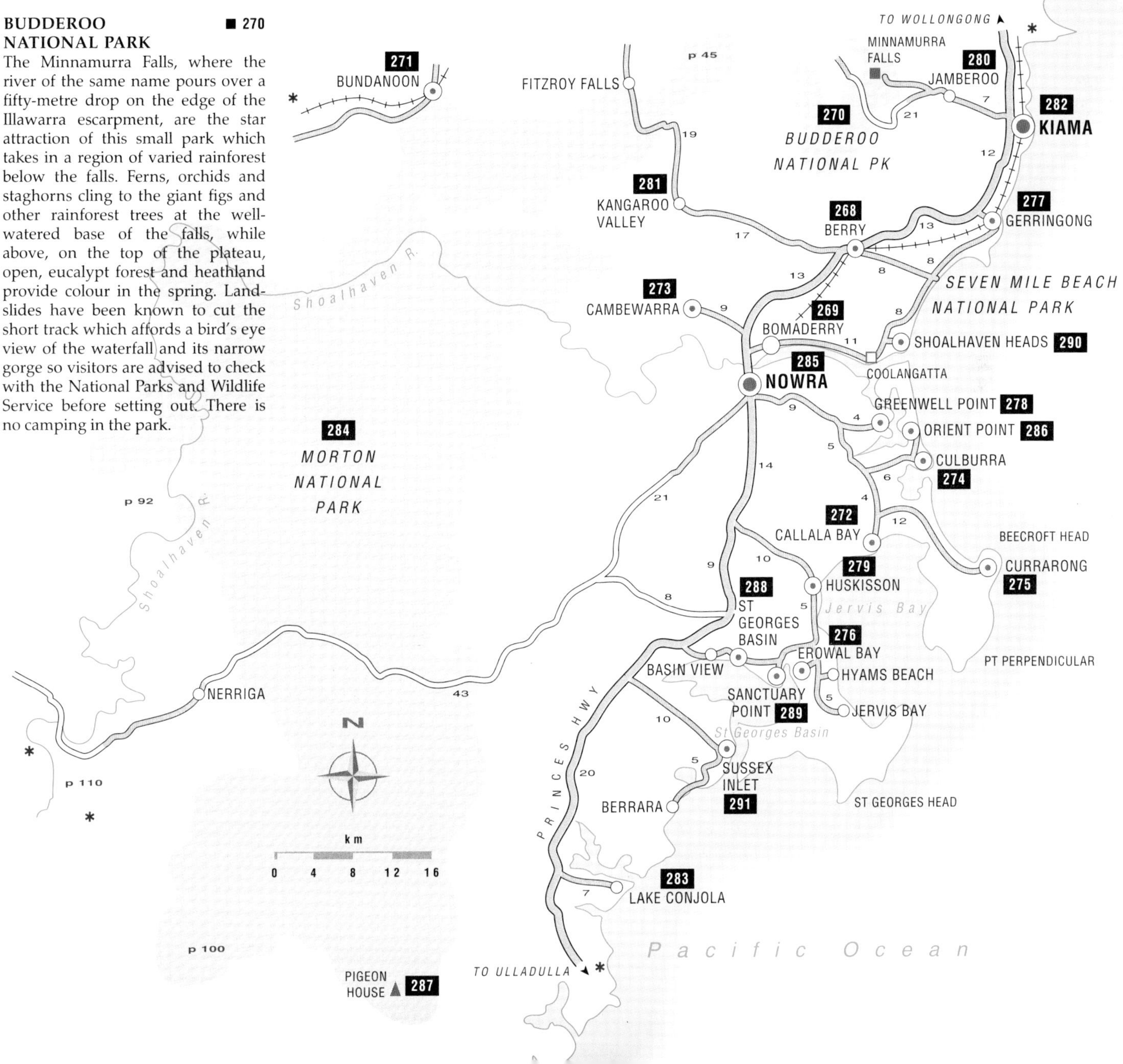

The turrets-without-a-castle of Kangaroo Valley's Hampden Bridge look slightly ill at ease in the bush.

In Kiama, the houses of the state's only timber terrace have been restored and put to work as shops.

metres above sea level the air is crisp, the seasons distinct and the views – from the ragged plateau escarpment of ravines such as the Grand Canyon, Bellbird Forest and Fairy Bower and out to the valleys of the Shoalhaven and Kangaroo Rivers – are often breathtaking.

For several generations of Sydney people the town was a jolly, egalitarian resort ideal for honeymoons, long weekends and family holidays where the main attractions were bush walking, horse riding, bicycle riding, tennis and community singing. Huge seven-seater charabancs or a large cart known as 'the sociable', where passengers sat knee-to-knee, met guests at the railway station. Today most of the guesthouses have gone but the train – albeit on a much-reduced schedule – still runs and exploring on foot, horseback or by bicycle remain the main preoccupations of modern travellers many of whom come to enjoy the delights of the rugged Morton National Park (see entry). Although much of the native tree cover has gone from the farmland, the exotic, deciduous trees planted along streets and around farm-property perimeters last century have now reached majestic maturity. *Population 1510*

FESTIVALS Brigadoon Festival, April.

CALLALA BAY ■ 272

This popular holiday township is the most northerly of the modest Jervis Bay settlements and its sheltered, deep-water moorings and wide launching ramp make it a mecca for boat-owners.

Just south of the town the generous white-sand curve of Callala Beach sweeps all the way down the bay's north-western side to Huskisson. The first European known to tramp the sands was the explorer and surveyor, George Evans, who called it Honeysuckle Beach after the honeysuckle-like flowers of native plants he noticed along the beach fringe. By the early 1840s, when settlement had begun, the present name took hold and because of the coincidentally similar pronunciation of an Aboriginal and an Irish word credit for its origin must be shared – it could be from the town of Calala in Ireland – the birthplace of a local convict – or 'kallalla' – an Aboriginal word for 'fish'! *Population 1380*

CAMBEWARRA ■ 273

The coachwood and Illawarra flame trees, which thrive along the slopes of the Great Dividing Range's eastern perimeter and explode brilliant red when in flower, are responsible for the name of this upland township. In 1830, one of the first settlers here called his farm Cumbewarra Farm after a marriage of two Aboriginal words meaning 'mountain of fire' – a reference to the spring colour of the native forests.

The Cambewarra Mountain Lookout, several kilometres to the east of the town and at the end of a worthwhile ten-kilometre detour off the Princes Highway, provides one of the most spectacular coastal views in Australia; at an altitude of almost 680 metres it can be wreathed in mist even in summer as warm air pushed by onshore Pacific breezes rises up the mountainside. *Population 700*

CULBURRA ■ 274

Culburra–Orient Point is the common administrative label for this modern holiday resort which has incorporated the small settlement of Crookhaven into a well-developed seaside 'suburb' of the City of Shoalhaven. The 'hammerhead' peninsula of Orient Point is a waterlover's paradise with its long, blunt eastern side facing the Pacific Ocean, the estuary of the Crookhaven River on the northern and western sides and, beyond the peninsula's narrow neck, the prawn-infested waters of the inlet known as Wollumboola Lake.

'Culburra', said to be an Aboriginal word meaning 'sand', was first used about 1920 when subdivision of the original farming properties began – today the beach is a popular surf beach with Nowra's inhabitants. The locality is historically important to Aborigines and the descendants of the original Dharawal people were once housed in a settlement at Orient Point. *Population 3130*

CURRARONG ■ 275

Currarong nestles comfortably within the protective southern arm of the Shoalhaven Bight, with the windswept heathland of the Beecroft Peninsula between it and the often wild seas to the east. One victim of these seas was the steamship *Merimbula* which foundered on a reef just to the east of the township in 1928 and rusts there to this day; to the west is a broad sweep of protected beach. The track along Beecroft Peninsula runs through a sea of wildflowers in the spring and culminates in a cliff-top vantage point with spectacular views out to sea and 'in' to Jervis Bay. *Population 570*

EROWAL BAY ■ 276

This pleasant backwater on the shores of St Georges Basin has all that is required to relax in this part of the world – a beach, a boat ramp and a grocery store to provide the wherewithal of a hearty breakfast in the unlikely event that the fish are not biting! The village is named after 'Errowel', the property developed on one of the first land grants made in the area, in 1835.

GERRINGONG ■ 277

Like many a township of Australia's eastern coast, Gerringong was founded as a harbour town and for many years it was an important shipping point for timber, usually cedar, which the energetic cedar-getters were anxious to despatch to the markets of Europe and Asia. The coming of the railway in the 1880s spelled the end for the coastal steamers and today pastures grazed by fat dairy cattle have replaced the forests and holiday-makers fish and snorkel where a sturdy jetty once groaned under the weight of giant logs.

Despite the pressures of tourism, the village has retained much of its nineteenth-century character with the preservation of buildings such as 'Alne Bank', a 140-year-old, homestead with a stone barn and the simple, whitewashed Roman Catholic church known as St Mary's, Star of the Sea. The town functions as a service centre for a number of smaller beach resorts along this stretch of coast. *Population 2480*

GREENWELL POINT ■ 278

Greenwell Point has the honour of overlooking the estuary of two rivers – the short-lived Crookhaven and, to its north, the more important but not always readily navigable Shoalhaven. Until the turn of the century, by which time the railway was the speediest form of transport, Greenwell Point enjoyed more than fifty years as a major port of the Shoalhaven River region. The district's produce was ferried to the river mouth by shallow-draught vessels – cedar logs were floated or towed – and loaded aboard steamers bound for Sydney.

Since then flathead, bream, snapper and a multitude of other fish have provided the village's living; the commercial fishing fleet ties up by the grassy shoreline and the amateur anglers cast their lines off the popular jetty or any unoccupied rock. Oyster fanciers are said to visit here just to taste the succulent local bivalves. *Population 1130*

HUSKISSON ■ 279

The British Colonial Secretary after whom Huskisson is named is remembered less for the perpetuation of his name by this main service centre and entry point for the Jervis Bay area than for the rather bizarre way in which he met his death. Only a few years after the tiny settlment was named after him, William Huskisson was in conversation with – of all people – the Duke of Wellington at the opening of the Liverpool to Manchester railway line when he was run down and killed by George Stephenson's recently invented steam engine, the 'Rocket'.

Huskisson was an established settlement by the 1840s and its sheltered position by the mouth of the Currambene Creek encouraged the eventual development of a successful boat building industry; the boat builders's craft is remembered by a maritime museum and working dock where pride of place goes to the former Sydney Harbour ferry *Lady Denman* which was returned to Huskisson after being 'retired' from service. *Population 3050*

JAMBEROO ■ 280

European settlers became well established in the lush forests of the Jamberoo Valley by the 1820s; the first land grant was made in 1817. By the 1840s, a private village had been established to service the needs of the local farmers who were harvesting the valley's hardwoods and establishing grazing properties. The paddocks they created are still grazed by fat dairy cattle and the tiny village seems little disturbed by the passage of time. The cluster of old buildings includes several stone churches and the 1876 stone school house; slightly grander, and classified by the National Trust, are the old homesteads of Minnamurra House – built about 1840 and believed to be the oldest house in the Illawarra region – and the Georgian-style Terragong House, built in the late 1850s. *Population 700*

FESTIVALS Folk Festival, March.

KANGAROO VALLEY ■ 281

No greater compliment can be paid to the beauty of this tranquil, pastoral haven other than to record that

The sands of Jervis Bay – protected by the Beecroft Peninsula with its Point Perpendicular lighthouse – are said to be among the whitest in the world.

the compilers of the New South Wales National Trust inventory of all that is worth preserving were unable to restrain themselves to listing just the Kangaroo Valley township's old buildings – they deemed the whole valley worthy of classification.

This lush river valley with its rye grass pastures which give it a perennially green appearance is part of the 'skirt' of the Great Dividing Range and lies in the shadow of the escarpment protected within Morton National Park (see entry). When the first settlers appeared in the early 1820s the region was known as Kangaroo Ground and the animals were said to abound but within twenty years they had moved on to make way for farms and cattle paddocks.

Part of the valley's charm is that apart from the exit point where the meandering Kangaroo River departs from the valley it helped create it is almost completely surrounded by tall hills; the eastern approach through the Macquarie Pass is particularly spectacular but from all directions the arriving traveller is greeted by the sudden appearance of breathtaking vista. At the township of Kangaroo Valley the river is crossed by a majestic, Mediaeval-style, stone suspension bridge with two castellated towers on either side. The bridge was completed in 1898 – just in time as it happened. Five days after it opened the old timber bridge was washed away by a sudden flood. A museum near the 1848 bridge records the lives of the early settlers.

KIAMA ■ 282

The heavily indented coastline where Kiama faces the sea provided the ideal location for a man-made harbour in the days of steam and sail, when travelling over the water was the only practical way of harvesting the produce of the rich southern coastal regions. Ships which sheltered in the little bay before the harbour was built in 1876 were prey to fierce south-easterly gales...as the poet Henry Kendall recorded in his poem 'Kiama', it was a place where '*...foam-flecked crags with surges chill, and rocks embraced of cold-lapped spray*'.

The first known European to shelter here and view the 'chill surge' of the famous blow-hole was the navigator George Bass who stopped off in his whaleboat in 1797 and noted that the blow-hole made a 'most tremendous noise'. Cedar-getters were using the bay to move out their logs by 1815; by 1831 the thickly forested hinterland had been surveyed and a year later houses started to appear. The streets of the town that was planned in 1837 and gazetted in 1839 were laid out in Sydney with little regard for local topography with the result that some of them ran straight up steep inclines that defeated even the strongest horse with a cart in tow!

As in most coastal regions of New South Wales, dairying prospered and the bay began to fill with ships carrying milk products and – in the 1880s – blue metal, particularly from the huge Bombo quarry. In 1876 a proper, excavated harbour was opened and the busy shipping traffic was able to tie up in complete safety. By the 1890s fresh milk was going to Sydney on the new rail service and gradually the port lost much of its traffic although the blue metal boats continued to ply the sea until the last run was made in 1963. Nowadays commercial fishing boats and pleasure craft tie up at the historic piers, where the sea still surges up to the breakwater wall.

Kiama – named for an Aboriginal word 'kiarama-a', meaning 'where the sea makes a noise' – is the major

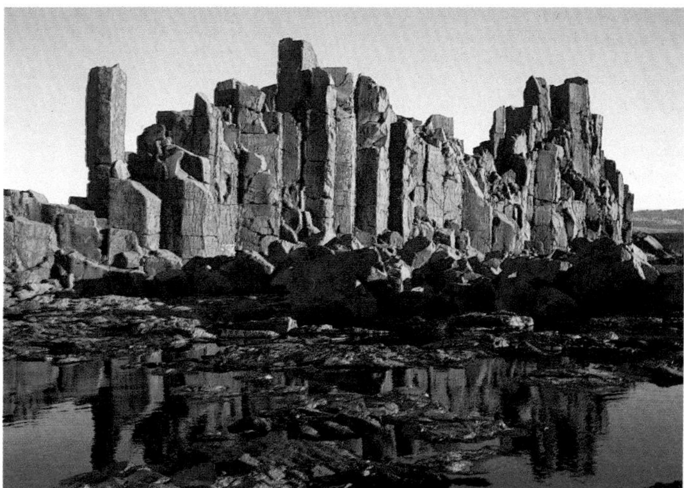

Blue metal quarry workings, such as Kiama's Bombo (above), were spurred by the deteriorating state of early Sydney's easily worn sandstone paving.

The Kangaroo Valley's evergreen scenic attractions have earned it a place on the 'national estate' list.

town in the stretch of coast between Wollongong and Nowra as well as being a relaxed holiday destination; the indentations in the Kiama coast contain many pleasant beaches as well as a small bay. *Population 10 630*

BLOW-HOLE The ever-restless ocean which created the blow-hole is gradually proving its undoing. The famous attraction which threw a spectacular plume of spray up to sixty metres into the air when the seas were high is gradually losing its force. But although the action of the sea has widened the blow-hole's underwater tunnel, thus reducing its water-pressure, a strong south-easterly swell can still produce a violent watery eruption.

POST OFFICE The brightly painted, rather Italianate 1878 post office with its distinctive three-storey square tower is like a colourful exclamation mark at the centre of the business district on the corner of Manning and Terralong streets.

TERRACE HOUSES The only timber terrace in New South Wales not to have fallen to the demolisher's hammer stands in Collins Street on the edge of the shopping centre. The restored cottages, built to house quarry workers more than one hundred years ago, have been restored and now attract tourists with their craft shops, cafes and galleries.

FESTIVALS Jazz Festival, February; Seaside Food and Wine Festival, October.

LAKE CONJOLA ■ 283

Conjola is the label affixed to a number of landmarks in the region including a small township on the Princes Highway, once a postal village, a state forest, and Conjola Lake, a coastal lake which drains to sea past tall sandhills as well as a much smaller, lagoon-like, enclosed lake, called Lake Conjola, to avoid confusion! The lake was once known as Cunjurong, from the Aboriginal name Cundjuhrong, and this name still applies to the village on the northern arm of the lake's mouth.

MORTON NATIONAL PARK ■ 284

Running a close second to the Blue Mountains string of parks for the sheer rugged beauty of a spectacularly worn landscape comes this vast area of bushland, the first link in an almost unbroken chain of parks between Bundanoon and Bega.

At more than 154 000 hectares this is one of the largest national parks in New South Wales as well as one of the most rugged – the comparison with the Blue Mountains region is not made lightly. This park preserves another long, narrow stretch of the Great Dividing Range's ragged eastern fringe.

Like the Blue Mountains, the northern part of the park is a deeply worn sandstone plateau where the views into the valleys from the Bundanoon region (see entry) while not as well known, certainly rival those of the traditional tourist magnets at Katoomba and Blackheath. The Bundanoon section is well endowed with walks and lookouts; to the east there is a visitor's centre at Fitzroy Falls, possibly the park's star attraction. Picnic and camping facilities are provided here, where the Yarrunga Creek obligingly plunges more than eighty metres over a cliff to form the falls. The lesser known but still spectacular Lady Hordern Falls, Twin Falls and Belmore Falls can be reached from here.

The southern section of the park is largely wilderness made up of a series of valleys, ridges and ravines formed by the action of rivers such as the Kangaroo, Shoalhaven and Clyde as they wormed their way through the sandstone to the coast. In the eucalypt forests that clothe these hillsides small animals and birds abound while in the more open areas, such as the heathland zones, there are the endangered swamp parrot and eastern bristle bird together with grey kangaroos and red-necked and swamp wallabies. The relative isolation and ruggedness of the southern section makes it advisable for visitors contemplating an expedition into this area to contact the Nowra park office before setting out.

GLOW WORM GLEN Of the many park attractions readily accessible from Bundanoon, this is the only one where visitors are advised to come after dark and armed with a torch to find their way. Within the deep shelter of a large rock overhang, the larvae of the fungus-gnat – wedged into crevices and cracks – give off a strange, blue luminescence. Visitors are asked to keep to made paths and not disturb the environment.

NOWRA ■ 285

With the almost irresistible distractions of a holiday playground coastline out of sight fifteen kilometres away to the east Nowra has become the commercial and administrative centre of the southern New South Wales coastal region. The original township of Nowra has merged with the settlement of Bomaderry to form the modern urban region of Nowra–Bomaderry (see Bomaderry) where a number of light industries thrive on the industrial estates around the urban fringes.

As in most coastal regions, after explorers had nibbled around the edges – the Shoalhaven River was explored as early as 1805 – the cedar-getters moved in to log the forests. This venture set an historical pattern as timber – along with dairying – has been a major local industry ever since and there are at least ten state forests in this region where native hardwoods are logged. The Forestry Commission office in Nowra advises travellers on the bushwalking and picnicking facilities available in the region's forests.

Settlement began in earnest in the 1820s, fanning out slowly from Alexander Berry's pioneering farm at Coolangatta (see Berry). By 1851 there were enough people to justify a proposal for a township and before long the residents'physical and spiritual needs were being catered for by a hotel, bakery, church and school – officialdom made its presence felt later, for when the first town blocks were offered for sale in 1856 it was discovered that the official planners had not reserved spaces for government or administrative buildings.

Preceding the arrival of the railway at Bomaderry by twelve years – and even more important in terms of local development – was the spanning of the Shoalhaven River by a bridge in 1881 (see Bomaderry). The wrought iron superstructure was manufactured in the United States and delivered to the site by two schooners. After the train service to Sydney was introduced, travel to the rest of the south coast was by one of the last horse-drawn coach services to be introduced before the era of the motor car. One-hundred-and-fifty horses and forty coaches were used in the regular, five-hundred-kilometre run to Bega.

More recently significant landmarks in Nowra's history include the awarding of the World Butter Championship to the town in 1938, the establishment of an Aboriginal Cultural Centre in the town in 1977 and the proclamation of the City of Shoalhaven with Nowra as its headquarters in 1976. *Population 21 930*

NAVAL AVIATION MUSEUM The Royal Australian Navy air station, HMAS *Albatross*, is only a few kilometres from Nowra and its museum which houses restored aircraft, models of ships and aircraft and a large collection of historic photographs is open to the public.

MEROOGAL Conducted tours are held through this restored 1885 weatherboard house. The 'storybook' structure for many years the home of the unmarried or widowed women of the family which built it, houses a valuable collection of period furniture and ornamentation.

BENS WALK This five-and-a-half kilometre scenic walk follows the south banks of the Shoalhaven River and Nowra Creek before crossing the creek and returning along its northern side. It retraces part of a track established by Ben Walsh, a local benefactor who engaged unemployed men to build a pathway here in the Great Depression, and passes a number of historic landmarks and meanders through stretches of undisturbed bushland.

FESTIVALS Shoalhaven Spring Festival, November.

ORIENT POINT ■ 286

Orient Point is indivisible from its slightly larger twin Culburra – the residential streets of the two settlements occupying the Orient Point peninsula have gradually melded together over the last twenty years (see Culburra).

While Culburra looks to sea over a long surfing beach that runs up to Crookhaven Heads and its lighthouse, Orient Point faces in to the Crookhaven River estuary where the waters are plied by boats heading for the Shoalhaven River. Since the Shoalhaven estuary silted up, vessels have to pass Orient Point and turn north behind Comerong Island to enter the waterway.

The locality was originally called Caffery's Hill after a shepherd who worked here for Alexander Berry (see Berry) in the 1830s; the modern name has been in use since about 1916. *Population 3130*

PIGEON HOUSE ■ 287

Named by Captain Cook in 1770 because its silhouette suggested the shape of an English pigeon-cote, Pigeon House, at almost 720 metres high, is not only the most prominent feature of Morton National Park but the most obvious landscape feature along this stretch of coast. The two-hundredth anniversary of Captain Cook's sighting from the *Endeavour* is commemorated by a plaque on a stone pillar at Burrill Lake.

The first Europeans to climb Pigeon House were the explorer Hamilton Hume and a settler, Alexander Berry (see Berry) in 1822. The national park which surrounds the blunt-topped mountain protects the forests of the Budawang Range from Clyde Mountain in the south to Morton National Park in the north. Pigeon House is thirty kilometres by road from Ulladulla; there is a five-

The distinctive appearance of Pigeon House inspired Captain Cook to name it thus in 1770.

kilometre walk from the car park to the top, the last few metres on steel ladders erected in 1970.

The Aborigines who used rock shelters in the area called the mountain 'tytdel' or 'diddel'. Traces of shellfish have been found in these shelters and Aboriginal trails, parts of which still survive, were used by early settlers to find their way over and around Pigeon House. A distinctive local Aboriginal art style, where a charcoal outline is filled in by rubbing rough rock clean with a soft stone, has been found at a number of sites in the foothills of the Budawang Range. The location of the sites is safeguarded by the descendants of the original artists on the Jerinja Aboriginal Land Council.

Budawang National Park affords the bushwalker spectacular views, good rock climbing and tracks through a variety of lowland, rainforest and high-country vegetation types. The area is geologically complex and there is evidence of glacial activity in the Yadboro Valley and of volcanic activity at numerous mountain sites. Sea levels have been both above and below the present level and at one time waves lapped on the 'shore' of the Budawang escarpment.

ST GEORGES BASIN ■ 288

This holiday hamlet takes its name from the large body of placid water on which it sits – one of the largest coastal 'lakes' between Sydney and the Victorian border. Technically the basin is a twelve-kilometre-long, fish-filled lagoon fed by dozens of creeks and streams; the shoreline waters are little more than a metre deep for about 100 metres into the lake, making it an ideal children's swimming spot. Local names, such as Jewfish Bay, Bream Point and Bonito Point indicate that anglers are often better served here than swimmers.

Although much of the shoreline is swampy and lined by mangroves there are a number of sandy pockets, particularly around the townships, like St Georges Basin itself, that line the northern shores. Opposite the township, on the lake's far shore, the narrow channel of Sussex Inlet provides an outlet to the sea as well as defining the southern limits of the Commonwealth Territory of Jervis Bay. *Population 770*

SANCTUARY POINT ■ 289

Sanctuary Point occupies a broad, blunt headland at the eastern end of St Georges Basin and even has a 'suburb' in the adjoining residential area of St Georges Basin East. Known originally as Royal Park, it is a major jump-off point for boating and fishing excursions; Palm Beach offers ideal conditions for just about all forms of water sport (see Erowal and St Georges Basin). *Population 3840*

SHOALHAVEN HEADS ■ 290

At the end of its 320-kilometre journey from the Great Dividing Range, the Shoalhaven River glides up the town that bears its name and out to sea. After many years of having to detour to the south to reach open waters because of a vast sandbank, the river resumed its historic course in the 1980s after floodwaters forced their way through the barrier.

Geographically the centre of the Shoalhaven Bight, the township of Shoalhaven Heads also marks the southern limits of the Seven Mile Beach National Park and offers access to surf and stillwater fishing and swimming. *Population 2350*

COOLANGATTA The original settlement of the Shoalhaven district began here, on the outskirts of today's Shoalhaven Heads, where a modern tourist village has been built around some of the original buildings of Alexander Berry's homestead (see Berry). The name – given by the Aborigines to a nearby tall hill which forms a dramatic landmark– was passed on to the Gold Coast Coolangatta in tragic circumstances. Berry dubbed one of his Shoalhaven-built trading vessels the *Coolangatta* and despatched it to Moreton Bay where it was wrecked near the mouth of the Tweed River. The name of the wreck stuck to the location and as one Coolangatta faded into history it gave birth to another.

SUSSEX INLET ■ 291

At Sussex Inlet, as with many a modest coastal resort, location is all. Not only along this charming coast, but all around Australia, few new arrivals – whether pioneer settlers concerned about accessibility to sea transport or twentieth-century escapers from city life – could resist the attractions of a placid river estuary or inlet flanked by golden beaches.

Here, the inlet is also the 'outlet' which drains St Georges Basin to the sea. Strung out along the sandy banks of the little waterway, the township is technically an island owing to the construction of a canal estate and a more pleasant, aquatic environment would be hard to imagine...needless to say 'Sussex' is a fishing and boating heaven where even the rankest amateur cannot avoid success when the prawns are running. *Population 2320*

Sussex Inlet is resigned to accepting its happy fate as somewhere where nothing much ever happens.

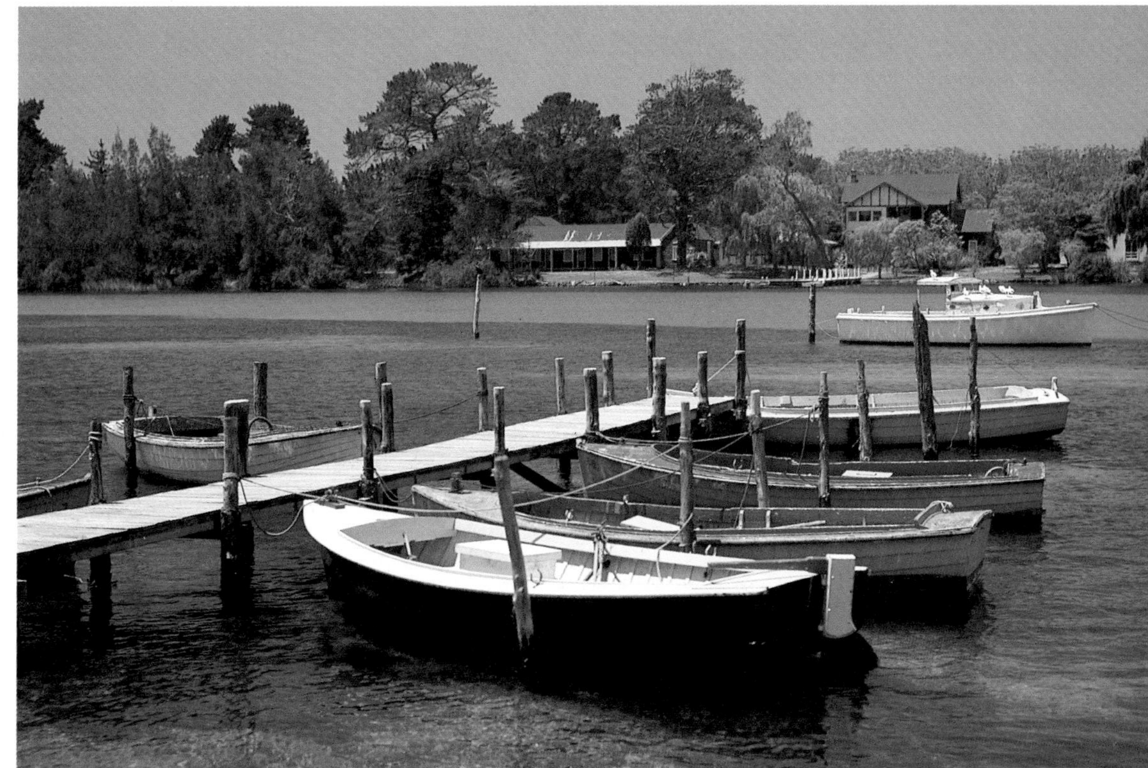

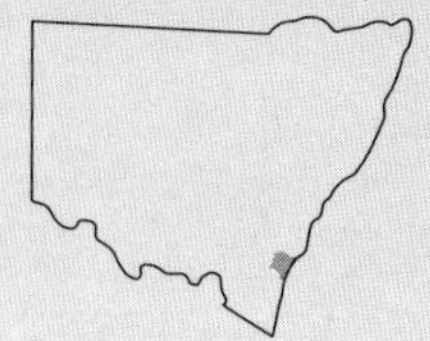

Batemans Bay & Ulladulla

'Gone fishin' ' could well be the motto of the unhurried towns of this coast where an endless string of beaches, lakes and inlets – ringed by a green belt of forests and parks – renders tourist-brochure hyperbole quite unnecessary.

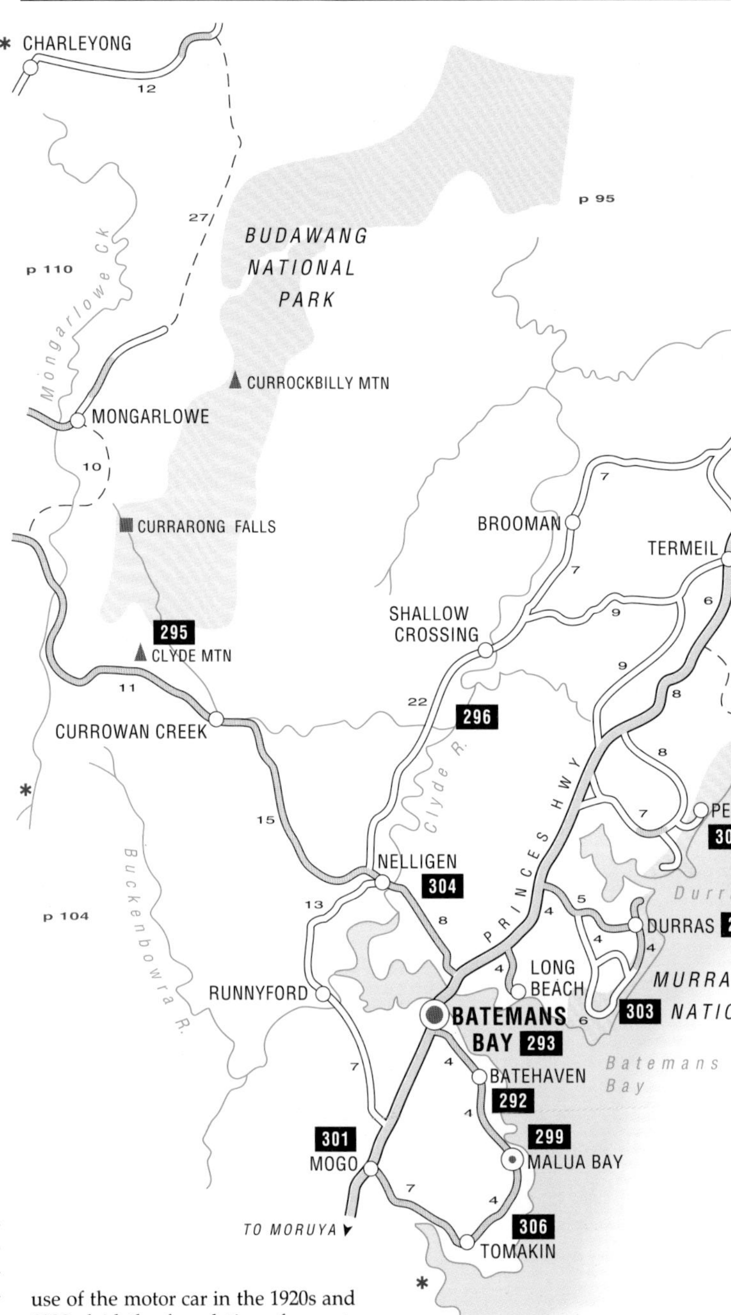

BATEHAVEN ■ **292**

Batehaven, the site of an early sawmill, sprang up as a 'suburb' of Batemans Bay after the Second World War when resorts – based around caravan parks and a few fibro cottages – and retirement devel -opments spilled southwards along this coast. Just north of the village, behind the string of sandy crescents that face the ocean, is a two-hectare area of rainforest, called Birdland.

BATEMANS BAY ■ **293**

The 'bay' at the mouth of the Clyde River – in fact a broad-mouthed inlet – was originally named Bateman Bay by Captain Cook on 21 April 1770 after Nathaniel Bateman, the captain of the *Northumberland*, a ship on which Cook had once sailed. It is sometimes referred to as 'little Canberra' because so many people from the national capital, a few hours' away, repair to Batemans Bay for weekends or their annual holidays.

Aborigines living in the area were seen by Cook in 1770 – near present-day Durras – and they assisted a party of shipwrecked sailors walking north from Bass Strait who passed by the bay in 1797 (several of the party were killed later in the journey). By 1808 their attitude had changed and they killed a group of sailors looking for water. Settlement began with the sale of land in 1841. In 1859 the township of Batemans Bay was laid out. The timber trade was profitable from the beginning but at first, Nelligen, up-stream on the Clyde River, was the focus of activity and the bay settlement grew slowly before 1870.

Until the Second World War, development here was unremarkable but steady as communications were improved; the opening of the Princes Highway in 1920 and the increasing use of the motor car in the 1920s and 1930s laid the foundations for post-war growth. This was based largely on holiday and tourist traffic but also greatly stimulated by the rapid expansion of Canberra after the war. The bridge over the Clyde was opened in 1956 by which time the town had become the centre of the local dairying and fishing industries, with a particular reputation for its oysters and crayfish. *Population 8320*

BAWLEY POINT ■ **294**

First settled in the 1890s when an isolated timber mill was built here, Bawley Point is a small holiday resort on a relatively secluded stretch of the coast. The mill burnt down in 1922.

At Murramarang Point, also called Point Upright, just south of Bawley Point, Captain Cook first sighted the Aboriginal inhabitants of Australia and an Aboriginal campsite on the point has in modern times become a protected archaeological site. Rocky ledges on the headlands provide access to the large variety of fish which feed around the low dome of rock just offshore.

CLYDE MOUNTAIN ■ **295**

Clyde Mountain is at the head of a steep pass through a low range of hills attached to the Great Dividing Range. The winding road was first surveyed in 1853 by the Surveyor-General, Sir Thomas Mitchell as part of a route linking Braidwood and its goldfields to the river port of Nelligen. Today's Capital Way from Canberra to the coast, closely follows Mitchell's original route.

The Corn Trail, a walking and riding track, winds from the top of the mountain in an 800-metre descent through virgin forest until it joins the highway about 12 kilometres down the pass at the head of the Bolero Valley. The trail dates from the 1830s when corn grown in the valley was carried over the range to the Southern Tablelands on packhorses. When Mitchell's route was opened in 1854 the original trail fell into disuse but it was reconnoitred by the army in the

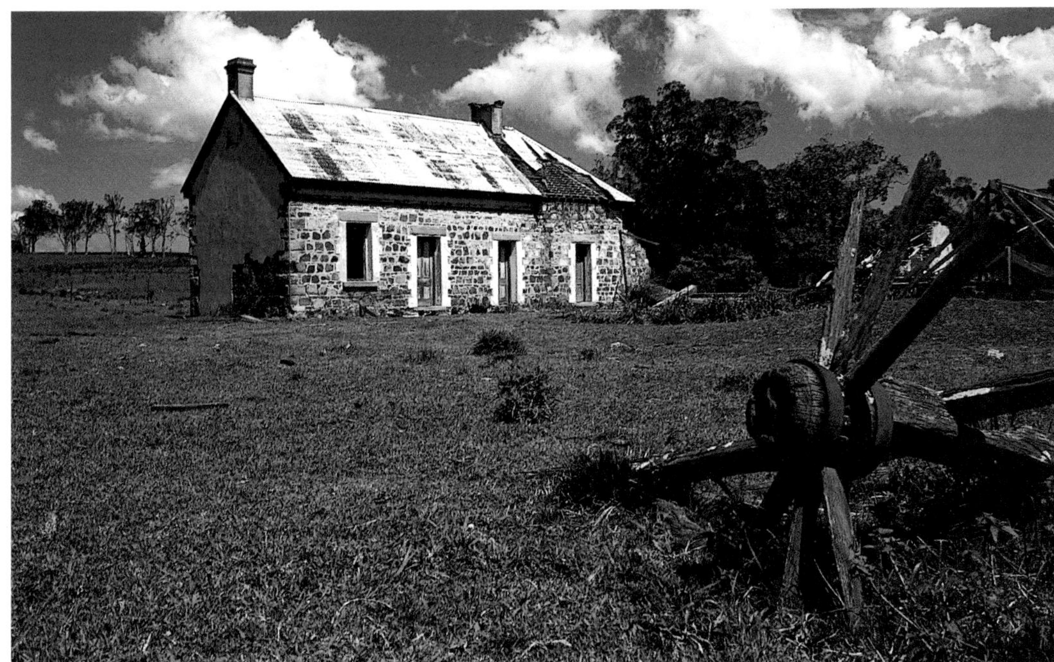
The stonemason who built Ulladulla's pier moved slightly inland to craft farmhouses like this one at Milton.

Second World War as a possible alternative route over the range.

CLYDE RIVER ■ 296

The Clyde flows to sea at Batemans Bay through a gorge, formed when the sea level was much lower than it is now and later drowned by rising water at the end of the Ice Age. Tidal influence extends almost forty kilometres upstream to Shallow Crossing and early settlers, finding the river navigable for about thirty-five kilometres, used it as their highway to the outside world.

Nelligen, fourteen kilometres upstream, was an important early port and crossing point of the Clyde. Aboriginal shelters in the headwaters of the river include several art sites, one discovered as late as 1977, as well as other remains which suggest that the region had been occupied for more than 20 000 years. The Aboriginal name for the river was Bindoo or Bhundoo.

DURRAS ■ 297

Durras, Durras Lake and Durras North, at the mouth of Durras Lake, first began to attract tourists in the 1950s although there was settlement at Durras Mountain as far back as the 1840s. Camping parks at Durras North are close to the still waters of the lake, the surf of the broad ocean beach and the wave-washed, cliff-base rock platforms so beloved of adventurous fishermen. Fishing is not a new activity here – an Aboriginal archaeological site at Durras North, estimated to be at least 500 years old, provides evidence that the varied diet of the original inhabitants was based on fishing, mutton-birding and the use of burrawang nuts.

The north head at Durras was given the name Point Upright by Captain Cook. In 1797, during a detailed exploration of Australia's south-eastern coastline, George Bass and his party entered Durras Inlet, mistaking it for Batemans Bay.

KIOLOA ■298

Kioloa names both a beachfront resort, south of Bawley Point, and a state forest accessible from Termeil Store or East Lynne by a forest drive of about fifty kilometres. This has always been timber country; after the pioneer, itinerant cedar-getters had moved on the first settlers started the serious work of harvesting the more plentiful supplies of hardwood – a job which continues to employ people here today. The first timber mill was built in 1881 at the southern end of the beach and in the early 1990s the forest was yielding about 50 000 cubic metres of timber a year. Areas for caravanning and camping are also located at the southern end of the beach.

MALUA BAY ■ 299

Malua Bay, eleven kilometres south-east of Batemans Bay, is a typical township of this low-key, holiday-oriented coastline: a good surfing and fishing beach backed by a few shops, a cluster of cottages and a reserve, in short, a perfect place for government types from Canberra to wind down. At the southern end of the bay a narrow neck of land ends in the craggy prominence of Pretty Point which affords uninterrupted 180-degree views up and down the coast and out to the offshore islands. Malua Bay and its sister towns to the south were little visited until the scenic coastal road known as George Bass Drive was completed in the 1970s. *Population 1360*

MILTON ■ 300

According to one story, Milton was named after the English poet, John Milton, but the name may also be a corruption of Milltown, a reference to early timber mills in the district. Today timber-getting is still important and along with dairying is one of the main industries in the region. One of the first settlers, John Booth, who ran a successful store, hotel and produce business, established Milton as a private township in 1860. The poet Henry Kendall, whose grandfather the Reverend Thomas Kendall was an early settler, was born in 1839 in a slab hut at a place marked by a cairn at Kirmington, five kilometres north of the town. There are a number of historic buildings including 'Danesbank' and 'Mt Airlie' on the Woodstock road, and 'Kendall Dale' and 'Whoppadilly', near Kirmington. *Population 980*

FESTIVALS Settlers Fair, October.

MOGO ■ 301

Mogo, on the Princes Highway south of Batemans Bay, sprang up in the late 1850s as a wild gold rush town. Within thirty years most of the readily accessible gold had been taken out and over the next twenty years the town's fortunes dwindled gradually but it remains a small service centre for the surrounding district. Amateur fossickers may still try their luck at an official gold-fossicking area on the nearby Tomago River. An old underground gold mine with a steam traction engine and a stamping battery is open for inspection in the town's goldfields park.

MOLLYMOOK ■ 302

Teal ducks at what is now Mollymook Creek suggested the name of Teel Creek (his spelling), for this place to the government surveyor in the 1820s. The present name may be derived from mollymawk, a name for a somewhat larger water bird. Since the 1920s Mollymook has been the main surfing beach for the towns of Milton and Ulladulla. In 1918 a six-hectare reserve was set aside behind the beach and in 1935 a surf-lifesaving club was formed. Silica and quartzite were once mined here and shipped from a wharf at Bannister Point, at the north end of the beach, to Newcastle steelworks for use in lining furnaces.

MURRAMARANG NATIONAL PARK ■ 303

This narrow coastal park, created in 1973, is a two-kilometre-wide zone of bushland divided into halves by a stretch of private property at Durras. The park extends for about twenty kilometres along the coast between Snapper Point, near Kioloa, to the north and Batemans Bay to the south. It is backed by state forests and embraces a variety of landforms and a range of forest types, including wet eucalypt forest with burrawangs, some pockets of rainforest, especially near Durras Mountain (283 metres), coastal heathland and she-oak scrub.

The park backs the coastal resorts of Pretty Beach, Pebbly Beach and Depot Beach which provide camping and caravan areas for those who

Oyster leases mark the course of early timber steamers on the lower Clyde.

As in many parts of eastern and northern Australia, coral trees are a feature of Ulladulla's shoreline.

come here for the fishing, swimming, diving and bushwalking. Kangaroos and wallabies are common and the camping areas are a second home to a number of tame animals. Other mammals and many kinds of birds can be seen in the park.

'Murramarang' was the name of the first property in the district, established in 1828. At Nundera Point, just north of Kioloa, a part of the old property now belongs to the Australian National University and is the base for a geographical and biological research station.

NELLIGEN ■ **304**

A road from Braidwood to Nelligen, about fifteen kilometres upstream along the Clyde River from Batemans Bay, was surveyed in 1828-29 and the region was thrown open for farming but there was no village until 1854. Early settlers were attracted by the timber, both cedar and hardwood, which flourished on the hillsides above the river.

The prospect of easy money hereabouts was to indirectly provide the stimulus required to form a township. After gold discoveries at Braidwood, Araluen and Majors Creek, a route over the Clyde Mountain to Nelligen was surveyed as an alternative to the two-week trip by dray from Sydney. In 1853, convicts built the first section of the road to the base of the mountain and the rest of the road was built by contractors. In the same year the first steamship was piloted up the Clyde River to Nelligen by one of the first settlers, James McCauley, to provide the final link in the transport chain between the goldfields and Sydney.

The Illawarra and South Coast Steam Navigation Company began a regular service to Sydney in 1861 and paddlewheelers were in use until 1870. By this time the gold rush was over and Nelligen had settled down as a centre for timber-getting and sawmilling. Wattlebark, used in tanneries, and oysters were other important local products. The town's business, commercial and government agencies, relied on the regular shipping service to Sydney and the ferry service over the Clyde River was also a stimulus to growth.

With improvements in road and rail transport the shipping service suffered many cutbacks until it finally stopped altogether in 1952. In 1964 the ferry carried its last load across the Clyde and was replaced by a bridge. Times were changing; a link with the early days, the old Steam Packet Hotel, reverted to residential use but a new hotel of the same name was built on a site near the approach to the bridge. Some historic buildings from the days of the steamers are preserved in the Nelligen Historic Village. The 'bushranger tree' is so named because in 1867 the Clarke brothers, a local criminal duo, were chained to it overnight before being taken to Sydney to face justice.

PEBBLY BEACH ■ **305**

Famous for its tame kangaroos, Pebbly Beach is a popular camping and picnicking spot at the southern end of Murramarang National Park (see entry). One of the earliest timber mills in the district operated here until the 1920s. On calm days, logs were sawn and taken to rocks at the north end of the beach where they were winched on board ship.

TOMAKIN ■ **306**

Tomakin, about twenty kilometres south of Batemans Bay at the mouth of the Tomago River, was a small but busy township in the late nineteenth century with a sawmill, brick kiln and boatbuilding yard. These small industries have long since faded but the twentieth-century fondness for holidays by the water has ensured Tomakin's popularity and survival. Those wishing to while away their annual holiday by a gentle stream need go no further than the camp sites on the bank of the Tomago River. Early explorers recorded 'tomaga' as the Aboriginal name for this location and the town and the river were both originally called Tomagan. The name was changed in 1880 to prevent confusion with the town of Tomago, near Newcastle. *Population 630*

ULLADULLA ■ **307**

The name Ulladulla originally applied to the area within which 'the settlement', now Milton, and 'boat harbour', today's Ulladulla, were located. The name itself appears to be a corruption of the Aboriginal names 'woollahderrah' recorded by the first surveyor in the area, or 'nullladolla' used by an early settler in 1828. The settlement was also once called Holey Dollar after the colony's unofficial coinage and this – according to one local legend – was corrupted to Ulladulla to give the town an Aboriginal-sounding name.

To the far north lived the Wandandian Aborigines, after whom the township of Wandandian is named, and to the south, the Walbangas. Excavation at a site at Burrill, just south of Ulladulla, has revealed that Aborigines lived in the area over 20 000 years ago when the sea was fifteen kilometres further east and the climate approximately 10°C cooler.

Early in the nineteenth century, settlers arrived here to harvest timber and by 1840 they were well enough established to organise the construction of a schooner. By mid-century the area was producing dairy products, still important today, and wheat, corn and vegetables. The little harbour became increasingly important to shipping and to provide a safe, enclosed berth, a stone pier was built out over a natural reef in 1869; ten years later the end of the pier was crowned with the formal adornment of a grand, iron lighthouse. The lighthouse was moved in 1889 and stands today at Warden Head, south of the harbour. The master mason who built the pier stayed on to build solid, stone houses and many of these remain as the historic buildings of nearby Milton.

Tourism was first promoted late in the nineteenth century, but it did not become important to the local economy until better roads – notably the Princes Highway – and the spread of the motor car made the area accessible to the average worker. Along with tourism, commercial fishing has developed as another important industry with many boats operated by families of Italian background.

The fishing industry was pioneered by the Puglisi family which had emigrated from the island of Lipari, near Sicily, to Wollongong in the early 1920s; in 1937 the family moved to Ulladulla where it was joined by other Italian families after the Second World War. A popular tourist attraction of the town is the annual blessing of the trawler fleet on Easter Sunday. All-year attractions include the engine from the Mitchell Bros sawmill which operated from 1929 to 1973, and is now in the grounds of the Civic Centre; a heathland reserve to the south of the town and a wildflower reserve on its western edge. *Population 7380*

FESTIVALS Blessing of the Fleet, Easter Sunday.

Many years of familiarity between campers and Pebbly Beach's 'surfing' eastern grey kangaroos has bred trust.

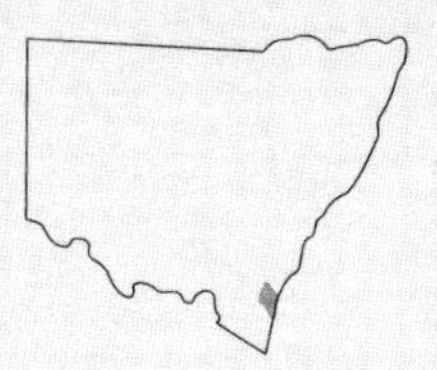

Narooma & Moruya

Game fishermen, anglers, boating enthusiasts, energetic bushwalkers and those wishing simply to catch a South Pacific roller all head for this pleasant, unspoiled rural environment with the beach-fringed coastline that so impressed Captain Cook in 1770.

BERMAGUI ■ 308

With a large well-protected harbour on Horseshoe Bay where the Bermagui River reaches the sea, Bermagui was initially developed as a seaport for the inland town of Cobargo. The name Bermagui came from an Aboriginal word meaning 'canoe with paddles'. By the second half of the nineteenth century, steamers called at the port twice a week and timber was shipped to Sydney from the town's sawmill.

Although William Tarlinton, one of the earliest settlers did dabble in whaling for a few years, the trawling industry was the town's mainstay. After Zane Grey, the American 'western' writer, came here in the 1930s and wrote of his experiences in *An American Angler in Australia*, Bermagui's reputation for game fishing was established. With record catches of a 310-kilogram black marlin and a 260-kilogram hammerhead shark, it continues to attract game fishermen. *Population 1170*

BODALLA ■ 309

Thomas Mort, a pioneer of refrigeration, founded Bodalla in the 1860s – just over a kilometre to the west of the present town – as a model agricultural village, specialising in cheese production. He was a firm but fair landowner – he immediately remitted all tenant's rents due to the disastrous floods that had just swept the region but workers had to observe strict rules: alcohol and swearing were prohibited on the estate, a 10.30 p.m. curfew was imposed and attendance at Sunday church services was compulsory. Mort's pioneering efforts established the dairying industry that became so prevalent on this part of the coast and resulted in the popular Bodalla variety of cheese which put the town on the map.

ALL SAINTS' ANGLICAN CHURCH The church, designed by Edmund Blackett and built as a memorial to Thomas Mort, was completed two years after his death. The castellated tower was added in 1901.

BROULEE ■ 310

Broulee, one of the earliest settlements in this district, was officially proclaimed in 1837 and remained the main village until Moruya (see entry) took its place.

Its sheltered port was visited by whalers, coastal shipping, and ocean-going vessels. For some time after Moruya was founded, goods were punted down the shallow Moruya River for shipping from Broulee. Since the mouth of the river enters the sea five kilometres south of Broulee, the punts had to undertake a short but hazardous sea trip. Punts would wait at the river mouth for favourable conditions and were then poled out over the sandbar, along the coast and through the gap between Broulee Island and the mainland.

Mossy Point, over the bridge across Candlagan Creek from Broulee, has a much more recent history. The short, sluggish Tomago River flows into the sea at Mossy Point past a wooden jetty and a concrete boat ramp, still one of the best places to launch a sea-going boat.

From Mossy Point Lookout, where there are views to the thick bush of Broulee Island, an anchor from the *Scotia* – wrecked off the point in 1884 – reminds sightseers of the dangers of the sea.

BROULEE ISLAND NATURE RESERVE The forty-three-hectare island, offshore from Broulee village, has steep, well vegetated cliffs where banksias, casuarinas and eucalypts provide an ideal setting for the grave of Elizabeth Malabar. Her father is thought to have been the publican of the island's inn, which was dismantled and moved to Moruya, leaving only its overgrown foundations – and Elizabeth's grave – on the island.

CENTRAL TILBA ■ 311

Apart from a classification by the National Trust in 1975 as an historic village, the twenty-five wooden buildings in Central Tilba have changed little since the town was built between 1889 and 1906.

Sitting at the foot of Mount Dromedary (see entry), Central Tilba developed during the short-lived gold rush but the inhabitants quickly turned to dairying and cheesemaking when the gold ran out.

Although there is now electricity and town water at Central Tilba, the local businesses – woodturner, leadlighter, shoemaker, saddlemaker and cheesemaking are reminiscent of the crafts and trades of a bygone era.

Above the bay, atop the Bermagui headland, is the Zane Grey Caravan Park.

DALMENY ■ 312

Situated on the coast where Lake Mummuga flows into the sea, Dalmeny has the best of both worlds. The surfing is good and fishing off the rocky headland for bream, whiting or flathead is excellent. The lake offers a calm environment for swimming. Dalmeny was named after the village of the same name in Scotland and is on part of what was the Mort family estate where some of the old houses still stand. Timber from the surrounding state forests is processed at the sawmill at Dalmeny.

There are now many large houses with extensive gardens all of which cluster around the lake or face the

Distinctive cheeses have been produced at Bodalla for more than 130 years with the town giving its name to one of Australia's best known commercial varieties.

A taxi rank of big-game boats awaits customers at Bermagui's marina.

sea with their backs firmly turned to the Princes Highway passing to the west of the town. *Population 1480*

DEUA NATIONAL PARK ■ 313

The rugged Deua Park covers more than 80 000 hectares of wilderness area stretching from Araluen in the north to Belowra Valley in the south and is dissected by the Deua River. The underground drainage systems, caves, sinkholes and gorges – known as karst – are typical of a landscape where limestone is the predominant rock. The park extends along the edge of the Monaro Plateau with the highest peaks being Big Badja (1362 metres) and Mother Woila Mountains (1180 metres).

The park's relative inaccessibility to all but the most intrepid bushwalkers and cavers, protects the park's birds and mammals from disturbance; the rare parma wallaby is one of the creatures that has been sighted here.

Permits are required to explore the caves, most of which have fragile – and therefore vulnerable – formations. The Big Hole, ninety-six metres deep with near-vertical sides, is an unusual geological formation in the Berlang area of the park.

GLASSHOUSE ROCKS ■ 314

The rocks, south of Narooma's main surfing beach, are blue-grey basalt that shines very much like glass. The story that they were named by Captain Cook because they reminded him of glasshouses is unlikely to be true since Cook's *Endeavour* was so far off the coast that he was unable to recognise that the much more dominant feature of Montague Island was, in fact, an island.

If Captain Cook had passed the Glasshouse Rocks a few million years earlier he would certainly have spotted them since they were then 1600 metres higher than they are now. The basalt rocks which resulted from volcanic activity around Mount Dromedary have been eroded to their present shape and height.

MONTAGUE ISLAND ■ 315

This part of the New South Wales coast is noted for its game fishing and Montague Island is at the centre of that reputation. But there is much more to Montague Island than the marlin and yellowfish tuna for which the waters around it are renowned.

The Aborigines called the island Baninguba and there is evidence from archaeological sites that the island was a productive hunting ground. The food sources that drew the Aborigines to the island are now protected. There are estimated to be 10 000 nesting pairs of 'little' penguins, shearwaters, crested terns and silver gulls using the island as a breeding site and it is the last place on the New South Wales coast where Australian fur seals come ashore.

The island is a granite outcrop six kilometres east of Narooma and it is thought that Captain Cook wrongly identified it as a headland. The captain of the convict ship, the *Surprise*, is probably the person who correctly identified and named it. A lighthouse has operated on the island since 1881; it was converted to solar-power in 1986, the year the island came under the management of the National Parks and Wildlife Service.

MORUYA ■ 316

Despite the reputation this region has for its beaches, Moruya, the shire headquarters, has no beach since it is six kilometres from the ocean. It sits on the Moruya River (part of the Deua River system), and extensive dredging and the building of retaining walls took place from the 1880s to allow ships to navigate the shallow river. Moruya is the port for local dairy produce, timber and oysters.

The north bank of the Moruya River used to mark the boundary of the 'Nineteen Counties' – the settled districts of the new colony beyond which squatters could only lease, not own, land. The site for the town was surveyed in 1850 and named after an Aboriginal word said to mean 'resting place of black swans' or 'a water crossing'. Moruya developed rapidly with the discovery of gold in the Araluen Valley, sixty kilometres up the Moruya River. Much of the mining traffic passed this way and the town became the major supplier of services to the goldfields until the gold ran out in the 1890s.

Another natural deposit in Moruya had a longer history – granite. Samples of the granite, first quarried in the 1860s, were sent to the Colonial Architect, James Barnet who used it for the columns of the General Post Office in Sydney. The quarry was at its most active from 1924 to 1932 when a small township grew up around it while granite was supplied for the pylons of the Sydney Harbour Bridge. When the bridge was finished, and in the middle of the Depression, the quarry closed. The Scottish stonemasons and Italian

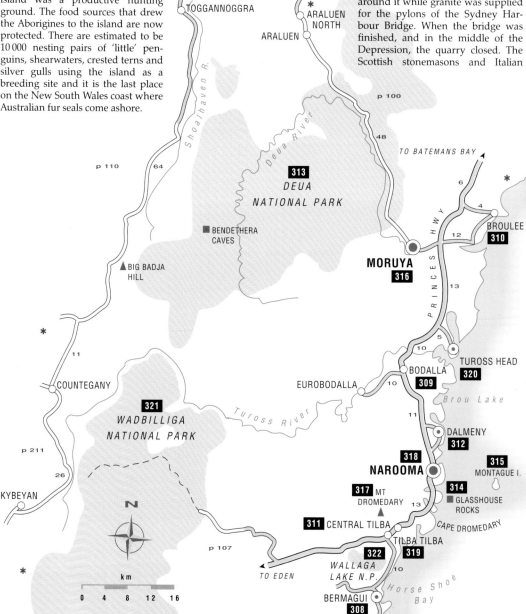

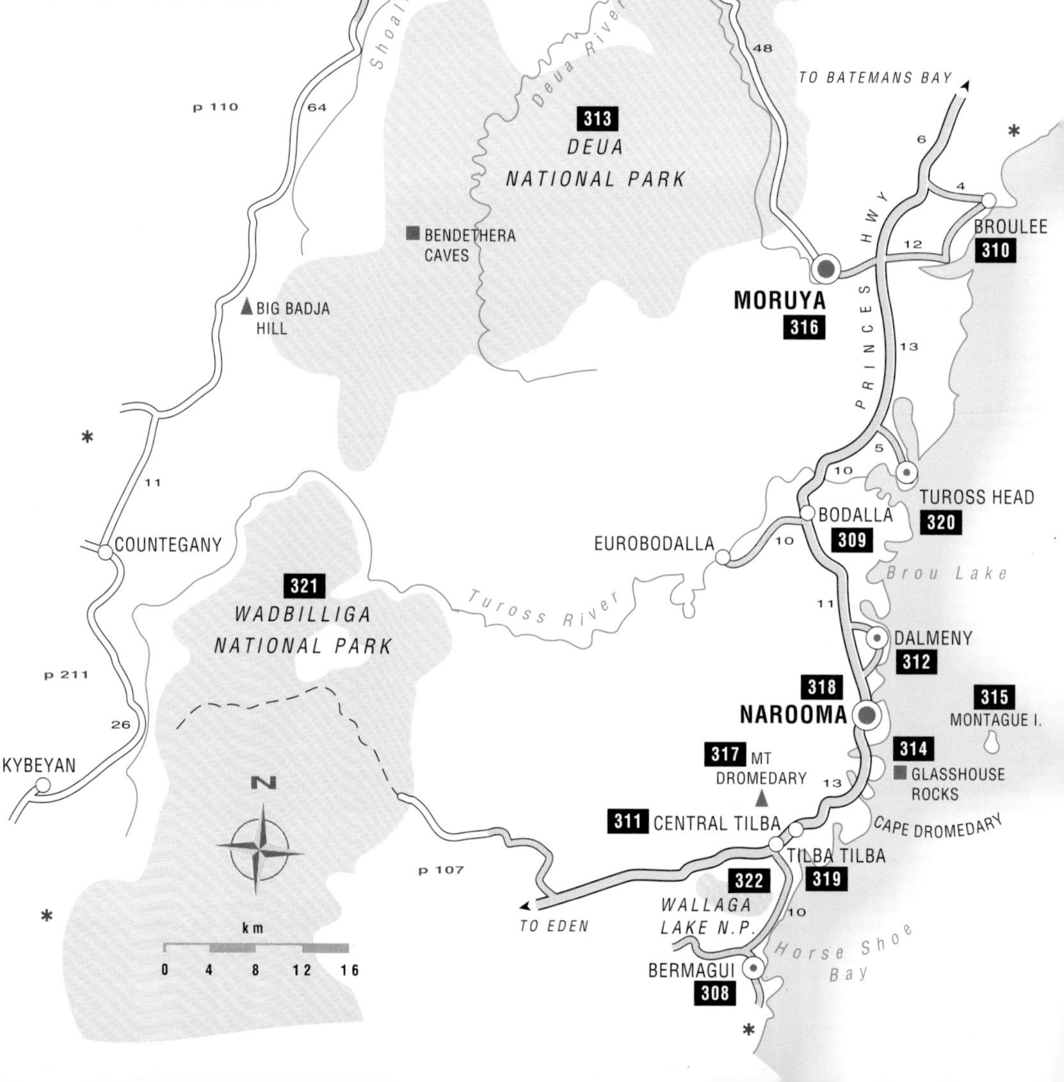

TOGGANNOGGRA
ARALUEN NORTH
ARALUEN
Shoalhaven R.
Deua River
p 100
48
TO BATEMANS BAY
p 110
64
313 DEUA NATIONAL PARK
BENDETHERA CAVES
BROULEE 310
PRINCES HWY
MORUYA 316
BIG BADJA HILL
TUROSS HEAD 320
BODALLA 309
COUNTEGANY
EUROBODALLA
Brou Lake
321 WADBILLIGA NATIONAL PARK
Tuross River
DALMENY 312
p 211
318 NAROOMA
315 MONTAGUE I.
314 GLASSHOUSE ROCKS
KYBEYAN
317 MT DROMEDARY
311 CENTRAL TILBA
CAPE DROMEDARY
TILBA TILBA 319
p 107
322 WALLAGA LAKE N.P.
TO EDEN
Horse Shoe Bay
BERMAGUI 308
km
0 4 8 12 16

craftsmen left 'Granite Town' but many of the local buildings in the area attest to the quality of Moruya granite. *Population 2520*

MORUYA HEADS The small seaside village at the mouth of the Moruya River has an historic cemetery. Constable Miles O'Grady, who was shot by a gang of bushrangers which terrorised the Araluen–Moruya area during the wild goldrush days, is buried there.

MOUNT DROMEDARY ■ 317

An isolated volcanic core rising to a height of 800 metres, the mountain was sighted and named by Captain Cook in 1770. 'We are abreast of a pretty high mountain laying near the shore which on account of its figure I named Mount Dromedary', he recorded in his log.

Alluvial gold was found on the mountain in 1853 and reef gold in 1860. By 1903 some 400 people were living on the slopes of Mount Dromedary but by 1920 it was all over. Old packhorse trails, scattered mine machinery and a memorial to Julius Saunders, the last prospector, remain as haunting reminders of the wild gold rush days.

Small mountain dams supply water to Narooma and Bermagui and part of the Bodalla State Forest which covers the mountain's flanks has been set aside as a flora reserve.

NAROOMA ■ 318

Frances Hunt who occupied land in the area in the 1840s and called his property 'Noorooma' from an Aboriginal word meaning 'sacred stone' or 'blue water', was probably the first settler in what is now called Narooma. The town site was surveyed in 1883 after several sawmills had been established. The town was named after Hunt's property but was known to most people as Narooma although this name was not officially recognised until 1972.

There was no great rush of people to the newly created township until the early twentieth century when the local timber industry developed. Timber from the Wagonga forests was cut and processed at the sawmill at Narooma. The hardwood was used for railway sleepers and local shipbuilding – complementary industries which had sprung up all along the eastern coast of Australia in the late 1800s. A thriving export industry also developed and ships taking timber out of Narooma carried fishermen and tourists on the return journey.

These passengers now represent one of the main industries in Narooma – tourism – although timber, oyster farming and fishing are also still important. *Population 3440*

UNITING CHURCH AND PARSONAGE The original wooden church, with decorated gable and picket fence was built as a Methodist Church in 1914. The timber-framed bell tower and the adjacent single-storey parsonage with its beautiful leadlight windows were built about twenty years later. The two buildings are now on the state's 'heritage' list.

TILBA TILBA ■ 319

Four kilometres south of Central Tilba and also nestling at the foot of Mount Dromedary stands the tiny village of Tilba Tilba. Richard Bate, the son of an early selector in the Tilba region, built a few houses and shops for lease on part of his property in the 1880s. The reef goldminers on Mount Dromedary moved on shortly after that and there was little need to add to the number of houses and shops already built.

The original Tilba store is still a store but is now licensed. This would not have pleased the original lessees of the neighbouring 'Greengables' who ran the house as the Tilba Tilba Temperance Hall and Guesthouse.

FESTIVALS Tilba Festival, Easter.

TUROSS HEAD ■ 320

On a narrow-necked peninsula running from Tuross Lakes to the sea, Tuross Head is almost completely surrounded by water. Early tourists came by steamer from Moruya or by coach through the Araluen Valley.

Tuross Lakes comprise Lake Tuross to the south of the peninsula and Coila Lake to the north. The lakes are a complex network of rivers, streams, channels, shallows and low islands.

Some Tuross Head streets are named after Sydney beach suburbs – Bondi, Coogee and Manly among them. The main road into town is named after Hector McWilliam, a local resident who died in 1974 at the age of ninety-seven after devoting fifty years to planting and caring for the Norfolk Island pine trees that line the road. *Population 1630*

Beneath the penguin burrows of Montague Island is the granite used for construction of Sydney's GPO.

WADBILLIGA NATIONAL PARK ■ 321

This 76 000 hectare park almost joins Deua National Park to the north. Like Deua it is a mountainous wilderness area but Wadbilliga National Park is even more inaccessible and has fewer tracks. Bushwalking here is not for the fainthearted amateur.

On the Wadbilliga Plateau, which rises to its highest point at Belowra Mountain (1337 metres) the park encompasses one of the largest undisturbed river catchments in New South Wales. Three major rivers – the Tuross, Wadbilliga and Brogo – rise here and wide, steep-sided valleys are a feature of the park where vegetation varies, according to altitude, from casuarinas through pockets of rainforest to snowgums.

TUROSS FALLS In its early stages, but still big enough to cause a considerable splash, the Tuross River – having risen in the rugged ranges to the south – makes a spectacular entry by dropping thirty-five metres over a cracked granite wall just after flowing into the park's confines.

In Central Tilba, the clock seems to have stopped at the turn of the century.

WALLAGA LAKE NATIONAL PARK ■ 322

The park covers 1141 hectares on the lake's western shores. Much of the landscape is dry open forest, with steep creek gullies and some dense rainforest understorey. The park is a haven for waterbirds such as black swans, black ducks and the blue-breasted waterhen.

Formed by several deep river valleys that were drowned by the sea, Wallaga Lake is unusual among the mostly shallow estuarine lakes of New South Wales because of its depth – over eleven metres at its deepest. Much of the sediment on the bottom of the lake was laid down 10 000 years ago.

With over one hundred kilometres of shoreline, it is possible to spend weeks exploring the numerous headlands and inlets without visiting the same one twice.

There are many Aboriginal middens around the shoreline and King Merriman Island, a sacred Aboriginal site, was the first 'Aboriginal Place' to be listed under 1979 legislation aimed at protecting and preserving such locations. Legend has it that in the Dreamtime, King Merriman, the leader of the Wallaga Tribe, used magic spears and boomerangs in a vain attempt to turn back an aggressive Victorian tribe. On defeat, King Merriman turned himself into a whirlwind and flew to Shoalhaven to warn the tribes there of the approach of the aggressors.

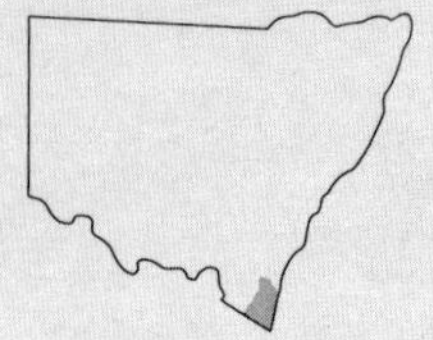

Bega & Merimbula

Far from the madding crowds of the big cities, the rural peace and tranquillity of the continent's green and pleasant south-east has been disturbed by controversy over the future of its diminishing natural timber resources.

BEGA ■ 323
When George Bass explored the area around Bega, he came by boat up the Bega River but stopped short of what was to become the site for the town. The early squatters, driven to move by drought, came overland to find alternative grazing for their cattle. On one of the largest and earliest cattle runs, 'Biggah', the town of Bega – also known briefly as Bika – was laid out in 1851. It soon became apparent that the site north of the Bega River was flood prone and the town was moved south of the river.

With the passing of two major land acts in the late 1850s, which allowed squatters to lease their land, the population grew rapidly. However, it was only after the building of the wharf at nearby Tathra in the 1860s that Bega boomed.

In addition to its large cattle runs,Bega also had farms of wheat, corn, fruit and vegetables, which were transported by sea to Sydney. When rust affected the wheat in the 1880s the dairying industry, which had been producing cheese since 1870, came to the prominence it has enjoyed ever since. The Bega Cheese factory still operates north of the river and is a testament to the efforts of these early pioneers.

Bega today is the major commercial and administrative centre for this part of the south-east coast. It sits at the junction of the Princes Highway and the Snowy Mountains Highway so that it is indeed possible to surf in the morning and ski in the afternoon…or vice versa. *Population 4200*

'JELLAT JELLAT' Just outside Bega on the Tathra road, 'Jellat Jellat' was built for the Gowing family in 1876. Inside the two-storey timber house there are panelled cedar doors and a cedar staircase.

BEMBOKA ■ 324
The village of Bemboka at the foot of Brown Mountain is an ideal stopping-off point for those travelling on the Snowy Mountains Highway from the south coast to Cooma.

A new national park was established at Bemboka in 1990, one of eight new national parks in the area set up to protect the unlogged forests in New South Wales' south-east. This rugged, scenic park encompasses areas of cool temperate rainforest and contains the rare bitter pea shrub known as *Daviesia suavolens.*

BEN BOYD NATIONAL PARK ■ 325
This 9000-hectare park, established in 1973, stretches along the coastline from Pambula Bay to Disaster Bay and is split into two sections by Twofold Bay.

The underlying rocks – red and brown shales, conglomerates and sandstones – are not only colourful but have been folded and eroded to form strangely shaped landmarks – among them the dramatic Pinnacles at Long Beach where climbing on the unstable formations is forbidden.

Vegetation ranges from coastal heathland densely covered with flowering shrubs to tall eucalypt woodland further inland. The park encompasses what was, until the mid-1950s, Broadwater State Forest pine plantation. Unfortunately, these introduced species are spread like weeds in some areas by yellow-tailed black cockatoos, which carry and drop pine cones to seed elsewhere. The rare ground parrot is also found in the park which was named after Benjamin Boyd, founder of the eponymous Boydtown (see entry).

BOYD TOWER Built in the 1840s by Benjamin Boyd as a lighthouse (which the government of the day forbade him to light) and whaling lookout, the tower still stands on the southern headland of Twofold Bay. Benjamin Boyd's name is carved at the top of the five-storey tower.

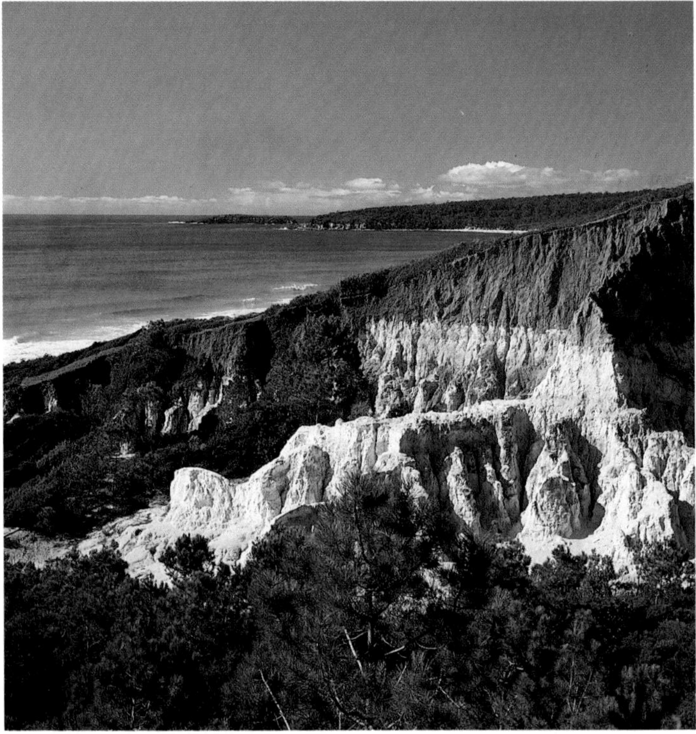

Relentless erosion of the red clay and the sand beneath has formed the never permanent, fragile shape of the Pinnacles in the Ben Boyd National Park.

BOMBALA ■ 326
A small town 750 metres above sea level in the Monaro region, Bombala sits in the picturesque valley of the Bombala River. Compared with the temperate, sea-level towns of this region, temperatures are low and can drop to below zero in winter.

Before the first squatters arrived, Bombala was home to the Ngarigu Aborigines and their word for 'meeting of the waters' was adopted as the new village's name in 1850.

The town developed slowly with a number of cattle and sheep runs in the area. However, within twenty years of this tentative settlement and the passing of the Free Selection Act, the town had become 'the best in the Monaro' and it is peppered with a large number of willows, poplars and oaks planted by these early settlers. Some of the old timber homes and the Imperial, a grand country inn, still stand.

Bombala today services a district where beef cattle, sheep and timber milling are the main industries. It has the added distinction of being one of the richest trout fishing areas in New South Wales. *Population 1400*

BOURNDA STATE RECREATION AREA ■ 327
Situated on the small coastal range between Tathra and Merimbula, the Bournda recreation area combines an unspoilt natural environment with many fine recreational facilities. The 2300-hectare park has salt and freshwater lakes, Bournda lagoon, creeks and coastal beaches.

Prawning, fishing, swimming, sailing and water skiing are available and, for 'landlubbers' there is bushwalking and birdspotting. There are over ninety species of birds in the park including little penguins, three species of albatross, peregrine falcons and three species of robin.

BOYDTOWN ■ 328
On the southern shore of Twofold Bay stands Boydtown, now a ghost town and a memorial to the grandiose plans of Benjamin Boyd. Boyd, a former London stockbroker and banker, took up pastoral land in the area and attempted to build a town that would not only rival the neighbouring official township of Eden but Sydney itself.

From 1842 to 1849 Boyd had about 500 men working for him on the buildings and jetty in Boydtown, tending his flocks, operating his whaling station or running the steamship service that he started. His empire collapsed in 1849 and he left for the California goldfields and later moved on to the Pacific Islands.

SEAHORSE INN The hotel, built by Benjamin Boyd in 1843 in a confusion of Victorian, Gothic and Tudor styles, has been restored and still operates as a hotel. Apart from the ruins of Boyd's church it is the only remnant of Boydtown's shortlived heyday still standing.

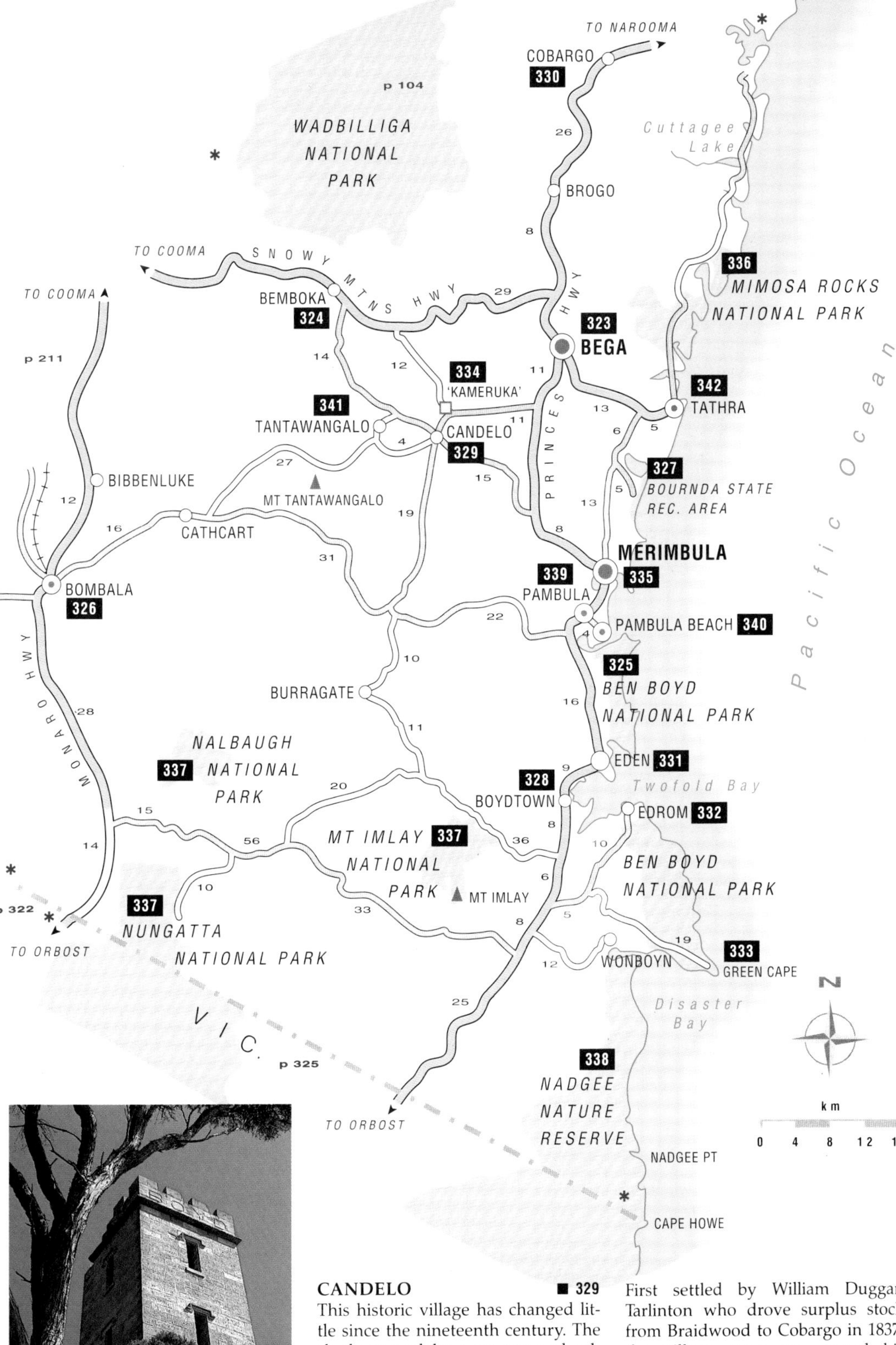

The inscription around the turret leaves no doubt as to who owned the Twofold Bay lookout tower.

CANDELO ■ **329**

This historic village has changed little since the nineteenth century. The shady verandahs, tearooms and galleries attract tourists who find a hint of a calmer, slower past.

The old Bimbaya butter factory just outside the village now houses a museum. The highlight of the collection is an array of early farm machinery relating to cheese and butter manufacture.

COBARGO ■ **330**

Fossils dating back 300 million years have been found at Cobargo but most people who visit this beautiful village are impressed by its nineteenth-century charm.

First settled by William Duggan Tarlinton who drove surplus stock from Braidwood to Cobargo in 1837, the village grew up around his 'Bredbatoura' station and, for a time was the main town in the Bermagui area. Now a quiet historic village in a dairying area with some abandoned mines, Cobargo survives primarily on tourism.

EDEN ■ **331**

The town of Eden, the main port for the southern coast of New South Wales, has one of the most strategically placed harbours on the east coast of Australia. Twofold Bay, on which Eden stands, was named by George Bass who sailed into it in an open boat in 1798 and noticed that the promontory on which the town now stands, split the bay in two.

The site of the town was chosen primarily as a base for the whaling industry (see box) although cattle and, later, timber were also shipped from the port of Eden. Cattle were exported to Van Diemen's Land and New Zealand; the hapless beasts were herded into the water and hauled along by a rope around their horns and then manhandled on to the boats in Cattle Bay by means of a leather strap around their bodies.

A brief gold rush to Kiandra in the 1850s saw a sudden boom at Eden as the diggers were shipped into Snug Cove (also named by George Bass). The first harbourmaster was appointed to cope with the sudden rush, which also saw the building of thirteen hotels in a town whose permanent population would have had problems keeping one publican in business.

From 1903 onwards, timber ships were a frequent sight at Eden and the timber industry still thrives with a sawmill at Eden and a chipmill on the south shore of Twofold Bay. Regular steamship services operated from Melbourne and Sydney right through to the 1950s. With no railway and poor road access, Eden was dependent upon coastal shipping. There is still no railway but with the improvement of the road system after the 1940s, Eden's importance as a coastal port receded.

One industry that has survived from the very early days is fishing. The boats in the large fishing fleet at Snug Cove may have become more modern over the years but the catch is still vital not only for Eden but for the fishmarkets at Sydney and Melbourne. Over 5000 tonnes of tuna, snapper, morwang, flathead, redfish, gemfish, trevally, salmon and abalone are caught by the fishing fleet off Eden each year. Some of the tuna catch is offloaded at Cannery Wharf in Cattle Bay directly to the tuna-canning factory. *Population 3280*

EDROM ■ **332**

The only major timber-chipping mill in eastern Australia opened at Edrom in 1969. It receives the lower quality timber from the neighbouring state forests. The timber is chipped by a single-blade saw and conveyed by belt to the Japanese bulk tankers sitting in the bay.

Within walking distance of the mill is Edrom Lodge, built in 1910 and now owned and operated by the Forestry Commission as a conference and education centre.

GREEN CAPE ■ **333**

The lighthouse at Green Cape stands at the southernmost point of Ben Boyd National Park on the shores of Disaster Bay. Built in 1883, the light was originally fuelled by kerosene.

The placid waters of Twofold Bay were once stained red with the blood of southern right whales (see opposite).

There is a graveyard and memorial at Green Cape to the crew of the *Ly-ee-moon* which was wrecked off Green Cape in 1886.

Henry Lawson's poem '*Did you see me sailing past?*' was written in 1910 after a visit to Disaster Bay and was supposedly penned in romantic vein for the daughter of the lighthouse keeper at Green Cape.

'KAMERUKA' ■ 334

Kameruka was originally one of the cattle stations of the Imlay brothers, the second settlers to arrive in the area. During his term of office, Governor Fitzroy stayed at 'Kameruka' and, during a hunt, succeeded in falling, together with his horse, into the river.

'Kameruka' came into the hands of the Tooth family (of Tooth's brewery) in 1854 and was run as a model dairy farm. Kameruka Estate was a prominent pioneer of cheesemaking and dairying in the region.The English-style estate on 5000 hectares is still owned by the Tooth family and the old homestead, built in 1845, the church, designed by Edmund Blackett and dedicated in 1869, and the clocktower are all still in use.

'Kameruka' runs sheep, beef and dairy cattle including one of the oldest Jersey studs in Australia but nowadays the cheesemaking operations have moved to Bega.

MERIMBULA ■ 335

At least one of Merimbula's local industries has an ancient history. The middens of old shellfish shells around Merimbula Lake on which the town stands attest to the fact that oysters were 'harvested' by the Aborigines long before the establishment of the current oyster leases for which Merimbula is famous.

Merimbula was founded as a private village and port by the Twofold Bay Pastoral Association in 1855. By 1857, the village had its own postmaster, a hotel, a butcher's shop, baker, a steam mill for flour-making and four warehouses owned by the Illawarra Steam Navigation Company. Flat-bottomed boats were used to load and unload the steamers beyond the bar until the company built a wharf in 1901. The wharf was used until 1952 and then became a glorified fishing platform until it was declared dangerous and blown up in 1979.

The first land sales and the rush to the Kiandra goldfields gave the town a boost in the 1860s. Diggers shipped into Merimbula used a track via Big Jack Mountain to the Snowy Mountains goldfields. Inevitably, inns – and bushrangers – sprang up along this track. By the time the gold ran out a new industry – maize – was there to take its place. Matthew Munn with his special millstones had arrived from Scotland and from 1868 until 1917 cornflour was manufactured at his works at Merimbula.

Although the town was gazetted in 1912, Merimbula did not develop as a tourist resort until after the 1950s with the conversion of the wartime airstrip to a civil airport and the upgrading of the bridge and causeway across the waters of Merimbula Lake. *Population 4530*

OLD SCHOOL MUSEUM The wife of the local minister, the Reverend Mr Thom, was the daughter of Henry Parkes and it is said that it was her influence on her education-oriented father that led to the school being built in 1874. The old stone building operated as a school until 1946 then fell into disrepair. It was restored in 1973 and now operates as a museum of local history.

MIMOSA ROCKS NATIONAL PARK ■ 336

Mimosa Rocks, from which the park takes its name, are the weathered remains of an ancient laval flow 350 million years old. A rise in sea level at the end of the last Ice Age isolated the rocks which now stand as an offshore stack.

The park boundaries enclose more than 5000 hectares and seventeen kilometres of coastland, providing swimming, bushwalking and camping at designated areas. Divided into two sections by the Wapengo Lake, an ancient river valley, the two sections of the park differ not only in geology but in flora and fauna.

Unlike Mimosa Rocks and the northern section of the park, which are volcanic in origin, the southern section of the park is composed mainly of sedimentary rocks. The sparse coastal heath gives way inland to heavily timbered areas, mainly eucalypts. Many species of birds including ocean albatrosses, oystercatchers, black swans, wrens and honeyeaters share the bushland with bandicoots, swamp wallabies and big sand goannas.

MOUNT IMLAY NATIONAL PARK ■ 337

This small, heavily forested park is one of three similar parks in this south-eastern corner. In addition to their recreational value to energetic bushwalkers who are prepared to tackle their comparatively inaccessible reaches, the three parks also protect areas of native forest from the woodchipping industry.

Mount Imlay National Park was dedicated in 1972 and is dominated by Mount Imlay which rises to 886 metres and has unusual alternating beds of sandstone, conglomerate and shale, which have the appearance of a giant flight of steps. Major soil erosion control has been necessary on the south-western face of the mountain because of the crumbly nature of these sedimentary layers.

A formerly unknown species of multi-trunked eucalypt, known to science as *Eucalyptus imlayensis*, and a rare waxflower previuously thought to grow only in Tasmania and at one site in Victoria have been discovered in the park.

NALBAUGH NATIONAL PARK Nalbaugh is a rugged, mountain park dominated by Wog Wog Mountain and White Rock Mountain and has few tracks or other facilities. There is an old feldspar mine, now overgrown, within the 3764-hectare park.

NUNGATTA NATIONAL PARK Larger than either Mount Imlay or Nalbaugh parks, Nungatta's 6100 hectares cover an area that stretches from the river flats of Genoa River up mountainous slopes to Nungatta Mountain. A fierce blaze which swept through the park in 1983 caused such devastation that it was the early 1990s before the bushland had properly regenerated.

NADGEE NATURE RESERVE ■ 338

Established in 1958 as a scientific reference centre and wildlife research area, Nadgee Nature Reserve covers

At Tathra, the restored wharf survives as a monument to the steam trade.

IN THE DAYS OF HARPOON AND WHALE BOAT

THOMAS RAINE financed the first whaling off Eden in 1828 and his team was soon joined by others who jumped onto this very lucrative though dangerous bandwagon. By 1847 there were two shore stations – Ben Boyd's at East Boyd and the government-sponsored shore station at Eden.

Open whaling boats operated in and around Twofold Bay and much of the mapping of this part of the coastline, with its numerous bays and inlets, was completed by these early whalers. Female southern right wales, which came into Twofold Bay to calve were the original targets of the whalers' long harpoons and great profits could be made from their thick blubber and the flexible baleen from their mouths, often called 'whalebone'. The blubber was boiled down to make oil, used for lighting and lubrication. The baleen was used to stiffen corsets and umbrellas.

By the 1840s the southern right whales had been hunted almost to extinction but a new target appeared – the sperm whale. Although it has teeth rather than baleen it was hunted for its blubber and the oil-rich organ in its huge head ; the oil that could be produced from one sperm whale made it well worth catching. Ben Boyd made 42 000 pounds sterling from sperm whales in a single year – in those days an enormous sum of money.

Bay whaling for sperm whales (above) was marginally less risky than the deep-sea slaughter depicted in an old French print (top).

The most extraordinary aspect of the whaling in Twofold Bay was the assistance offered to the whalers by a group of killer whales, a species of dolphin that is known to harass and kill whales and other creatures, such as seals, in the wild. The schools of killer whales in the waters around Eden are reported to have herded other whales into Twofold Bay and kept them at the surface to allow the whalers to harpoon them. The carcasses were then sunk to the bottom for twenty-four hours to allow the killer whales to get their grisly reward of the tongues and lips before being taken to the shore station where the blubber was stripped off and boiled in huge vats – a very smelly business.

The most famous of these 'assisting' killer whales was Old Tom who was thought to be eighty when his body was found floating in Snug Cove in 1930. The whaling industry had almost ceased ten years before that but the last whaler, George Davidson, was called on to strip and reconstruct Old Tom's skeleton, which is now in the Eden Killer Whale Museum.

Remains of the whaling industry can now be seen not only at the museum but at the Davidson Whaling Station on the southern shore of Twofold Bay and Boyd Tower where in the old days the lookout on duty would send a rider or fire a gun to alert the shore station when a whale was sighted. But the best reminder of the activities in Twofold Bay is the sighting of occasional whales returning unharassed to their traditional migration routes and calving areas. □

17 000 hectares and is one of the largest nature reserves in New South Wales. It stretches from Wonboyn Lake to the Victorian border and includes some of the most unspoilt coastline environments in the state.

The only access to the park is from the north and this has tended to deter all but the most intrepid of bushwalkers. But the long walk into the park and the effort of fording the Merrica River is worth it since inside the park are three river estuaries, five beaches, headlands and a salt lake.

Management of the park focuses on protection and propagation of wildlife species, which include red-tailed cockatoos, sea eagles and many species of wallaby.

PAMBULA ■ 339

When the first subdivisions were made in what was then called 'Pambula' (from an Aboriginal word meaning 'two waters'), the Pambula River was not only navigable but followed a different course than it does today. After major floods in 1860, the river changed to its present course and silted up. Without a navigable river, Pambula owes its survival to Merimbula, which became its port.

Syms Covington, who had sailed with Charles Darwin in the *Beagle* in the 1830s, returned to Australia in 1840 and settled at Pambula in the late 1840s He became the postmaster and later ran the first licensed inn 'The Forest Oak' in his home, built in 1856 and now a restaurant.

In the late 1880s gold was found near Pambula and although the gold rush lasted for twenty years any remnants of this activity have been swept away by bushfires which have razed the Mount Gahan and Pipeclay Creek regions.

Dairying, and the production of maize and potatoes had been the main economic activities of the district until the 1950s when tourism was added to this list. *Population 790*

PAMBULA BEACH ■ 340

This seaside residential and holiday village sits directly across from the northern point of Ben Boyd National Park (see entry). Pambula Beach is also known as Jiguma and most of its streets also have Aboriginal names. *Population 690*

TANTAWANGALO ■ 341

Until recently the name of this small village was virtually unknown but from the mid-1980s, Tantawangalo began to appear regularly in newspaper headlines in association with the disagreement between loggers and environmentalists over the fate of the south-east forests.

A proposal for eight new national parks includes one outside Tantawangalo. In addition to scenic landscapes, the new park will preserve koala habitats, and at least one threatened species of plant.

TATHRA ■ 342

The Gowing family shipped produce from their property at 'Jellat Jellat' through Kianinny Bay at Tathra from 1857. Money was offered to any master willing to bring his boat into Tathra; there was no wharf until 1862 at which stage Tathra replaced Merimbula as the port for Bega.

Tathra was surveyed in 1861 but despite the shipping activity around the wharf there were no permanent residents until 1876 so the only building was the receiving store. Passengers who arrived at Tathra, after a journey that took twenty-four hours from Sydney, were transported to the nearest accommodation at Bega. The first hotel in Tathra, the Brighton Hotel, was burnt down in 1881, the year after it was built. The Ocean View Hotel, built just seven years after this event, still stands.

A coastal watch unit was established at Tathra during the Second World War and some members witnessed the torpedo attack on the United States warship *William Dawes* which was sunk off this coast in 1942. Despite more than its fair share of floods and bushfires, and a relatively small permanent population, Tathra survived – as did the historic wharf. Marked for demolition in 1981, the wharf was saved by energetic local fundraising and a grant from the New South Wales Heritage Council. *Population 1570*

Queanbeyan & Bungendore

As a microcosm of the nation's past – explorers, pioneer farmers, gold, bushrangers, federalism and states' rights – this region has it all. The settlements have a history much longer than that of the Australian Capital Territory to which their fate is now so closely tied.

BRAIDWOOD ■ 343
The first settler in the Braidwood area was Dr Thomas Braidwood Wilson, a naval doctor and surgeon who had accompanied a number of convict transport ships to Australia and was known for his humanitarianism. By 1837, there were a sufficient number of settlers for Dr Wilson to build, at his own expense, a court house where he acted as part-time magistrate and in 1839 a petition to the government called for a town to be proclaimed on his land. The new town took the doctor's middle name; he died four years later and is buried on its outskirts.

Until the 1850s the settlers in and around Braidwood concentrated on sheep, cattle and horse breeding but in 1852 gold was found at nearby Araluen and the town changed dramatically as its population swelled. Gold diggers made the journey down from Braidwood to the Araluen goldfields hauling their supplies along the steep slope on sledges.

Inevitably, bushrangers were attracted to the district and the Clarke brothers, sometimes with, and sometimes without, Ben Hall in their company , held up the coaches plying between Goulburn, Queanbeyan and Cooma. In 1865, Tom Clarke made a speedy escape from Braidwood Jail when he leapt onto a racehorse tethered outside by an accomplice. This was not Ned Kelly country...until 1966 when Braidwood was used as the setting for the film 'Ned Kelly', starring Mick Jagger.

When the rail line was built, Braidwood, despite already having a Station Street and a Railway Hotel, was bypassed. However, many of the early Georgian buildings from Braidwood's heyday remain and the town is classified by the National Trust. *Population 980*

FESTIVALS Heritage Week, April.

BUNGENDORE ■ 344
The Aboriginal name for Bungendore's location was said to be 'bungadow' meaning 'place of gum blossom' or 'big hill rising from the plain', but when the first land was granted in 1825 the title was registered as being in the 'Parish of Bungendore'. The town was proclaimed under this name in 1837; it was later reclassified as a village.

Because of its location at the junction of roads leading to Goulburn, Queanbeyan, Braidwood and the Monaro region, Bungendore was a favourite stopping point for travellers and in its heyday had a large number of inns, hotels and sly-grog shops, a flour mill and – after the turn of the century – a rabbit freezing works as well as the usual stores, churches and schools. The coming of the railway to Bungendore in 1885 brought tourists who stayed at local guesthouses and took steamer trips on Lake George.

Bungendore's most infamous son was William Westwood, the handsome 'gentleman bushranger' often known by the nickname 'Jacky Jacky'. After numerous escapes Jacky

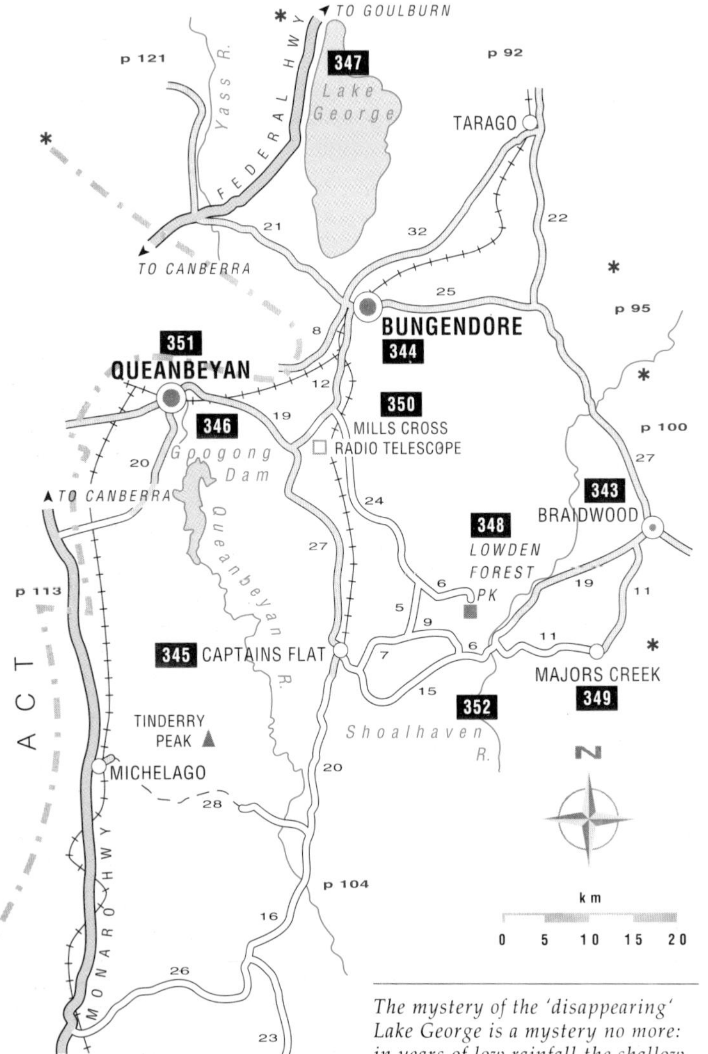

The mystery of the 'disappearing' Lake George is a mystery no more: in years of low rainfall the shallow depression which acts as a natural reservoir simply dries up...

Houses such as 'Bedervale' (left) and 'Deloraine' (above) are part of Braidwood's rich collection of Georgian and Victorian architecture. The verandah on the Georgian 'Bedervale' (1836) is a concession to climate.

Jacky was finally captured at the local Lake George Hotel and banished to Norfolk Island where he was hanged at the age of 26. His exploits are commemorated in a sound and light show in Bungendore. *Population 1150*

CAPTAINS FLAT ■ 345

The township of Captains Flat was established in 1888. As the gold at the Araluen mines ran out at about this time, many of the miners moved to Captains Flat where gold, copper, lead and zinc continued to be mined until 1901.

The mine at Captains Flat was reopened in 1937 and continued to produce mainly zinc but also lead, copper and iron pyrites, which were transported by a branch rail line to Bungendore. The mine finally closed down in 1962.

Since the 1980s, Captains Flat has evolved a new role as a dormitory town for Canberra.

GOOGONG DAM ■ 346

The lower part of the town of Queanbeyan has been flooded on eight occasions since 1852, at least twice in recent years. One of the aims of the Googong Dam, nine kilometres upstream from the town on the Queanbeyan River, was to solve this perennial flooding problem.

The earth and rock-fill dam was built in 1978 and has a fifty-nine-metre-high wall. Behind the wall, a reservoir holds 125 000 megalitres of water, which is used to supply Canberra and Queanbeyan.

LAKE GEORGE ■ 347

Governor Macquarie visited the Lake George district in 1820, the year the lake was discovered. According to Macquarie's journal, the lake was 'full of fine large ponds and lagoons of fresh water...We drank a bumper toast to the future settlers of the shores of Lake George, which name I have given to this grand and magnificent sheet of water in honour of His present Majesty'.

The 'fine large ponds and lagoons' that Macquarie saw are not permanent and the reasons for the periodic disappearance of the waters of the lake caused much speculation for years. The waters of the lake are held in a shallow basin and evaporate readily. Whether the lake is full or whether the fences on the lake bed are visible and cattle graze there, depends on the sequence of dry and wet, and hot and cold years.

Geologists say gravel terraces at the north end of the lake mean that lake levels were higher in the past. At its highest, 20 000 years ago, the lake was twice its present area and six times as deep as today's maximum of five metres. The higher levels do not mean that rainfall was greater at that time but that temperatures were cooler and evaporation less.

Since 1971, core samples have been taken from the lake bed and analysis of the pollen and charcoal in the sediments has provided the longest continuous record of vegetation history in Australia. Analysis indicates that the present eucalypt forests are only 130 000 years old and that, from the increasing frequency of fires after that time, Aborigines may have been present some 90 000 years earlier than archaeological evidence so far suggests. The Aboriginal name for the lake – 'wee-ree-waa' – is commemorated in the name of the nearby Federal electorate of Werriwa.

LOWDEN FOREST PARK ■ 348

Lowden Forest Park, controlled by the Forestry Commission, is in a zone of forest used by logging contractors as a camp site in the 1930s. There are signposted walking trails and overnight camping is permitted.

In 1952, the old waterwheel used by the contractors to charge the batteries of their logging trucks and to provide limited electricity was returned to the site, restored and in full working order.

MAJORS CREEK ■ 349

The first gold in the district was discovered here in October 1851 by a Mrs Baxter who bought land at 'Irish Corner' with the money from her find. The gold rush to Majors Creek included many Chinese miners but Mrs Baxter did not live to see what her discovery had wrought since she was crushed to death when a cart overturned on her eighteen months after her find.

By 1871, five of the eleven crushers operating in the district were sited at Majors Creek. Prosperity brought a number of hotels, a 200-pupil school, a branch of the lodge, or society, known as the Grand United Order of Oddfellows and a rapid 'sprawl' of houses south of the original village of Majors Creek.

With the gold and the diggers long gone, Majors Creek is now a small village noted for its spectacular waterfalls and Clarke's Lookout on Majors Creek Mountain.

MILLS CROSS RADIO TELESCOPE ■ 350

The Mills Cross Radio Telescope comprises two long, ground antennae that bisect each other evenly in a north–south and east–west direction. The 'Mills Cross' is named after its inventor B.Y. Mills who was employed by the CSIRO Division of Radiophysics at the time of his revolutionary invention in 1953.

The 'Mills Cross' system has been adopted internationally in radio telescopes, which are the basic tools of radio astronomy – the study of the physics of the sun and planets by collecting and analysing radio waves gathered from the heavens.

QUEANBEYAN ■ 351

In their search for the Murrumbidgee River, Joseph Wild, former convict and constable of Argyle county and his companions, James Vaughan and Charles Throsby Smith reached the confluence of the Queanbeyan and Molonglo rivers in 1820. The location became a natural stopping place for settlers crossing into the Monaro region.

By 1833, there were twelve sheep stations in the area including one owned by Edward John Eyre whose exploring began as he took his stock overland from the developing township to Adelaide. The town was proclaimed in 1838 and the Aboriginal name Queanbeyan, meaning 'clear water' used in preference to the European spellings of 'Queen Bean' and 'Quinbean' as used for local property names.

Queanbeyan's agricultural reputation was enhanced in 1901 with the release of James Farrer's 'Federation' rust-free strain of wheat to international acclaim. A memorial to Farrer was erected in the renamed Farrer Place in 1938 during Queanbeyan's centenary celebrations.

The Australian Capital Territory was originally planned to include the town of Queanbeyan but the New South Wales Government refused to cede the town, offering a similar area of land to the south of Canberra in its place. Queanbeyan's development since the establishment of Canberra has nonetheless been closely tied to that of the 'new' city next door with much of the town's trade coming *from* and much of its population commuting *to* the national capital. The railway line acts as a border between the two territories and it is possible to 'travel' interstate on a simple local shopping trip to Queanbeyan, which was proclaimed a city in 1972. *Population 23 710*

YE OLDE KENT HOUSE (1849) Built as a private home, this house had a huge ballroom on the upper floor with an ornate 'balconette' leading off French windows. Now a hotel, the building has been a court house, bank, hospital and a church for two different denominations.

SHOALHAVEN RIVER ■ 352

The Shoalhaven is the major river of the New South Wales southern coastal region and has been a vital source of water for Sydney and other centres since the first stages of the Shoalhaven water scheme of dams and reservoirs was put into operation in 1977.

The 320-kilometre-long river rises on the eastern slopes of the Great Dividing Range and cuts the first of two huge gorges as it travels through the Southern Tablelands. After passing Captains Flat, the river is joined by a number of tributaries to form a wide valley around the town of Braidwood. When the river meets Bungonia Creek east of Marulan it flows through the second deep gorge or canyon on its passage to the sea. Emerging from the hills at Tallowa Dam, the Shoalhaven crosses the coastal lowland and passes between Nowra and Bomaderry to enter the sea in a complex of lagoons and sandhills at Shoalhaven Heads.

THE CHIMNEYS Two large brick chimneys are still visible on the banks of the Shoalhaven River east of Bungonia. The copper smelter that operated here from 1900 sent out its ore by 'flying-fox' but transporting supplies in was so difficult that the mine closed in 1911.

Australian Capital Territory

Fierce rivalry between two heavyweights – Sydney and Melbourne – prompted the search for a 'neutral' zone in which to build the nation's capital. The sheep paddocks of the Limestone Plains in southern New South Wales – up till then the domain of graziers, and placed diplomatically almost midway between the two arch-rival cities – was the location chosen for the establishment of Canberra in 1908.

With three dams along its relatively short length – this is the Corin – little of the Cotter River's water is wasted.

BRINDABELLA RANGE ■ 353

The Brindabella Range, on the territory's western boundary, forms a rugged backdrop for Canberra (see p. 116). The range is a 'spur' of the Snowy Mountains Range and part of the high country traditionally popular with Aboriginal moth-hunters throughout the south-eastern highlands. Each October, millions of Bogong moths migrate from their breeding grounds in the plains of western New South Wales and southern Queensland and fly over the capital territory on their way to rest in the cool mountain ranges of the Australian Alps.

The dormant moths, clustering on the walls and crevices of caves throughout the ranges were easy prey for the Aborigines who simply scraped them off with a stick and collected them in fibre nets. The protein-rich bodies of the Bogong moths, roasted on heated stones, were the basis of great feasts as tribes gathered at the foot of the ranges for corroborees and initiation ceremonies, before moving up the slopes to plunder the caves.

CANBERRA ■ 354

Canberra – the symbolic heart of the nation – is unique among Australian capital cities in that it was created for a specific function: the business of government. Visualised by Walter Burley Griffin – the Chicago architect who won the international competition to design the city's layout in 1912 – as a European-style, high-density, people-oriented city, modern Canberra has evolved – at least to some extent - along slightly different lines. Civic pride is evident in the design of efficient and dignified, rather than grandiose, official buildings, surrounded by green and open spaces, and the Australian preference for suburban living has resulted in the growth of low-density suburbs linked by arterial roads.

Since its inception, Canberra has been lauded by its supporters and criticised by its detractors, both conceptually and physically. Heedless of the debate between these two bodies of opinion, Canberra has established itself as a convenient place for the business of government to be transacted (see p. 116). *Population 276 160*

CORIN DAM ■ 355

The Corin Dam is 912 metres above sea level near the junction of the Cotter River and Kangaroo Creek, about sixty kilometres from Canberra. The 47-metre-high earth and rock-fill dam is named after William Corin – an electrical engineer for the New South Wales Department of Works. Corin investigated a proposal that the Cotter River be used to supply both water and power for Canberra. The 'double-function' plan was rejected and the dam – completed in 1968 – now serves primarily as a reserve water supply to top up the Bendora Dam further down the Cotter River. With a storage capacity of nearly 75 000 million litres, the Corin Dam is the largest of three dams on the river.

CORIN FOREST RECREATION AREA On the Corin Dam road, Corin Forest's popular alpine recreaction area has Australia's longest bobsled slide, a winding silver trough over 800 metres long that passes through mountain forests on its way to the valley floor. During the winter months, snow blankets the ground transforming the forest into a winter sports field for the additional activities of skiing and snow tobogganing.

COTTER DAM ■ 356

Cotter Dam was Canberra's first, and principal water-supply dam until the 1960s, when construction of the larger Bendora and Corin Dams usurped its importance. Strung along the watery thread of the Cotter River, the three dams together form an important part of Canberra's water supply. Since 1967, the Cotter has been used as a standby reservoir and with the help of the nearby Cotter Pumping Station it is used to help meet peak demands for water or to alleviate drought conditions by providing a back-up supply to the Bendora pipeline service.

Construction of the Cotter Dam was completed in 1915; extensions were carried out in the early 1950s which raised the dam's height from nineteen metres to more than thirty metres and increased its capacity to over four-thousand-million litres.

The dam is named after Garrett Cotter, an Irish convict transported to Australia in 1821 for 'insurrection and firing at His Majesty's troops'. Cotter was posted as a servant to the owner of a Lake George sheep station but soon came up against the local authorities and was banished by the governor to the fringe of European settlement west of the Murrumbidgee River. There, he lived among the Aborigines, sustaining his existence by raising cattle until he was eventually pardoned and settled down south of Canberra.

HALL ■ 357

The village of Hall was one of the earliest villages in the region, together with Tharwa (see entry) at the southern end of the territory. Hall was surveyed three times before being established at its present location on the banks of Halls Creek in 1881. The village was first gazetted as Ginninderra even though another, similarly named private village already existed. The name was changed in 1885 and is thought to recall either Henry Hall, a pastoralist who ran sheep and cattle on a nearby land grant, or his cousin, Edward Smith Hall, the founder and editor of the politically orientated Sydney newspaper, the *Monitor*.

Many of the village's historic buildings are well-preserved, including St Francis Xavier's Church – a neo-Gothic building constructed of

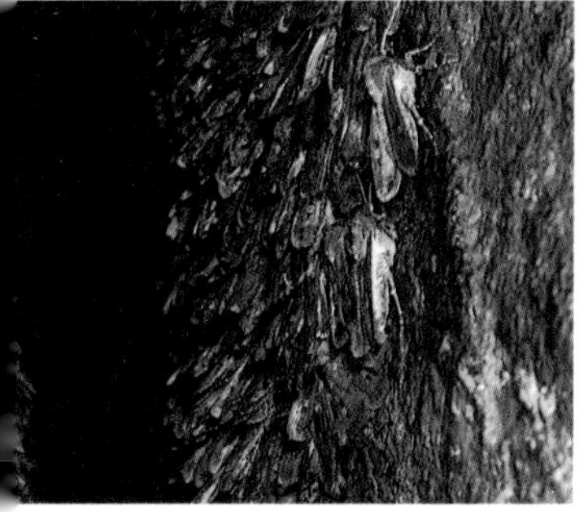

Bogong moths are an annual phenomenon in the ACT – once they even invaded Parliament House.

bluestone granite in 1910 – and Kinlyside Hall – built in 1906 and now housing an antique business – which in earlier incarnations functioned as a painting and finishing shop for a coach builder, a bootmaker's shop, a dance hall, a church and a cinema. A building near the antique shop was once owned by a bootmaker who claimed to have made the biggest boots in New South Wales. Two pennies stuck on the counter – a considerable distance apart – showed customers the impressive size of the order.

'LANYON' ■ 358

'Lanyon' homestead, on the banks of the Murrumbidgee River (see entry), recalls the Victorian tradition from which it arose – with well-established orchard, vegetable and flower gardens providing the household necessities as well as the green and pleasant centre of a successful pastoral property. The complex is one of the finest remaining examples of a colonial sheep station homestead and is on the National Trust's 'must preserve' list.

The property was established by James Lanyon, who with James and William Wright took up a land grant in the Tharwa area in 1835 and used convict labour to build the first stone cottage, complete with tiny windows and a quaint bell-tower – used to call convicts and shepherds from the fields. All the buildings are now covered with a green mantle of ivy. In 1847, the property was sold to a Scottish banker, Andrew Cunningham, who built the main homestead. This stuccoed stone-rubble house with its French doors opening onto wide and cool verandahs was the setting for a very salubrious style of living as the Cunninghams, in defiance of the harsh, bushland setting, maintained many of the refinements of upper class, Victorian England. Elegant furnishings, candelabras on the tables and liveried groomsmen were often the order of the day.

In its early days, 'Lanyon' assumed the proportions of a small, self-supporting village – the cluster of outbuildings that form a courtyard to the rear of the main homestead included a bootmaker's shop, a blacksmith's shop, jail, dairy and meathouse, coach house and stables, storeroom, and convicts' barracks. The dairy is the oldest timber building at 'Lanyon' and has log slabs joined entirely without nails. From 1860 to 1862, the homestead even had its own post office.

The Cunninghams sold 'Lanyon' in 1926 and the property changed hands twice more before the homestead was bought by the government in the early 1970s. In 1980, the fully restored 'Lanyon' was opened as a museum offering a look into Australia's colonial past, with displays of furnishings from the nineteenth and early twentieth centuries. The homestead also has a Sidney Nolan art gallery which includes many of the artist's 'Ned Kelly' paintings.

CANOE TREE A short distance from the homestead is the only well-preserved Aboriginal canoe tree found in the territory. Protected by a fence, the tree displays a long scar where Aborigines removed a large piece of bark to make a canoe.

The residence at 'Lanyon' – dating from 1859 – is flanked by a variety of farm outbuildings; the original, 1836 stone cottage is on the left.

MOLONGLO RIVER ■ 359

Early in the nineteenth century, the prominent pastoralist-explorer Dr Charles Throsby was told by the Aborigines of the Goulburn Plains, of a large lake (Lake George) and a big river (Murrumbidgee River) that existed on the plains. His appetite for the discovery of potentially rich pastoral land whetted, Throsby sent ex-convict, Joseph Wild to find these elusive bodies of water. In the course of his search, Wild discovered the Molonglo River which joins the Murrumbidgee River (see entry) near the territory's north-western boundary.

Now, the river is an integral part of the ACT scene, rising in the Great Dividing Range and flowing through undulating, sheep-grazing country and through the heart of the capital where its course has been blocked by the Scrivener Dam to create the central focus of Lake Burley Griffin (named after the city's designer).

Along its length, the river's mainly bushland corridor rings with cries of wild birds, and the numerous rocky outcrops are home to some less common creatures such as the legless lizard and the black-headed snake.

MOUNT STROMLO OBSERVATORY ■ 360

The outcrop of silver domes capping Mount Stromlo house an impressive array of powerful optical telescopes and other instruments that form the Mount Stromlo observatory and research station, operated by the Australian National University. The complex is an important centre of optical astronomy, with a battery of research telescopes used to monitor objects in deep space (see box).

MURRUMBIDGEE RIVER ■ 361

The Murrumbidgee River may not be as 'mighty' as that other great Australian waterway, the Murray River, but it does nevertheless lay claim to being the second longest river in New South Wales.

The river rises in the swampy ground of Long Plain in the northern part of Kosciusko National Park (see *Cooma & Mount Kosciusko*) and flows past Cooma before heading north. South of Yass, the Murrumbidgee starts its long journey westwards, joining the Murray River 1500 kilometres from its source. Passing across the artificial boundary of the NSW–ACT border, the Murrumbidgee runs unimpeded through the territory, carving an indelible line through rolling pasture and peaceful gorges such as Bullen Range Gorge and Red Rocks Gorge, where it is enlivened by a series of abrupt drops

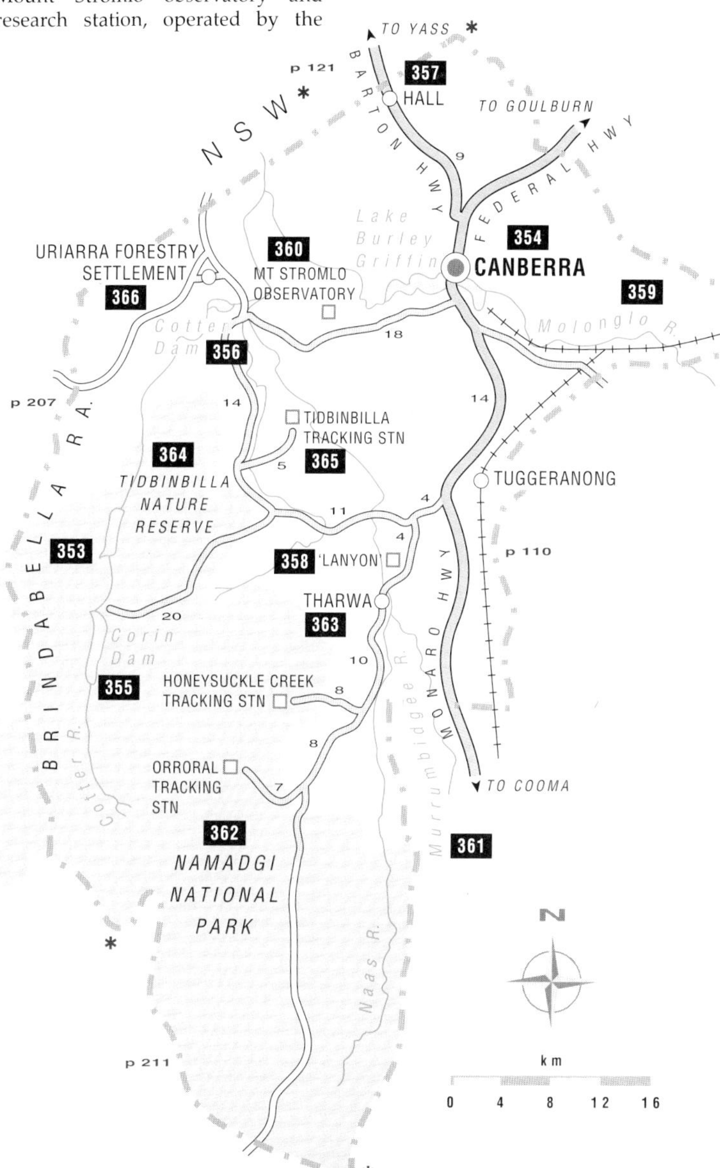

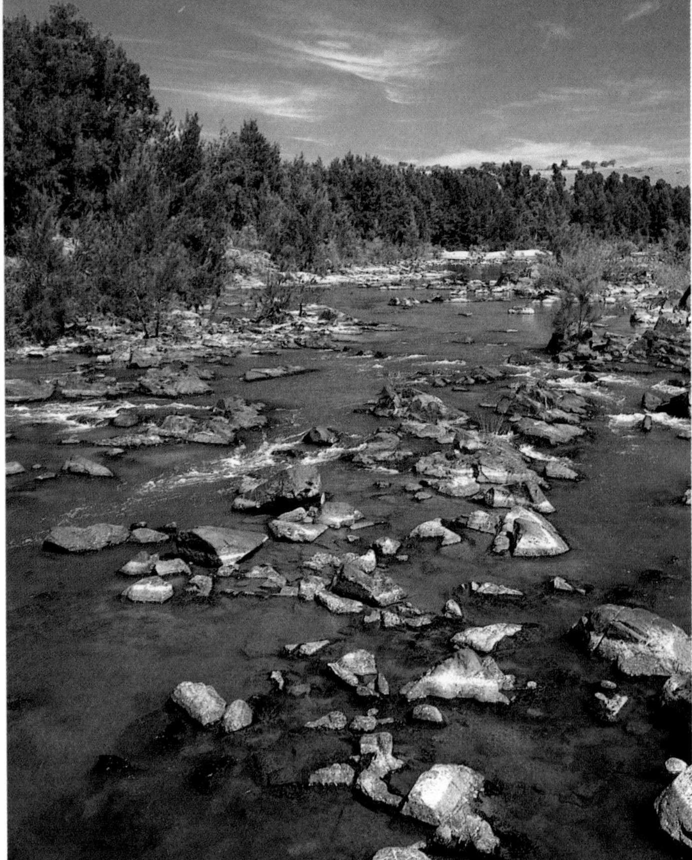
The Cotter and the Molonglo help swell the Murrumbidgee in the ACT.

that form rapids too difficult for the white-water skills of canoeists, with whom the river is popular.

Europeans first heard of the Murrumbidgee from the Aboriginal inhabitants of the Goulburn Plains. In 1820, Dr Charles Throsby, informed the governor that he was looking forward to finding 'a considerable river of salt water, called by the natives Mur-rum-bid-gee', an Aboriginal word meaning 'big river' or 'plenty of water'. His hopes were realised in April 1821, when accompanied by the ex-convict, Joseph Wild, he reached the river at a point near Pine Island, where it flows from the south-east. Their progress along the river's downstream course was cut short by 'lofty and rugged country', but Throsby's theory that the Murrumbidgee joined the Lachlan River (see *Yass & Boorowa*) further inland was later proved correct by the explorer Hamilton Hume.

FARRER MEMORIAL The grave on a hill behind 'Lambrigg' homestead (a private property) on the Murrumbidgee River is the final resting place of William James Farrer, the scientist whose experiments with wheat resulted in the development of a strain resistant to rust (a reddish-brown fungus). His discovery was a boon to farmers not only in Australia but throughout the world and his grave is preserved as a monument to his achievement.

NAMADGI NATIONAL PARK ■ 362

Spread across the south-western end of the Australian Capital Territory, Namadgi National Park is 94 000 hectares of rugged upland country occupying approximately forty per cent of the territory's area. The park was proclaimed in 1984 and is a part of what is officially described as the National Capital Open Space System – dedicated to the establishment of a range of natural environments in, and surrounding, Canberra.

The park includes a large portion of the Cotter River valley and the river's catchment area as well as the whole of the area previously known as Gudgenby Nature Reserve.

'Namadgi' is the Aboriginal name for the mountains encompassed by the park. Beautiful alpine and sub-alpine wilderness areas which are covered with snow in winter, are fully protected though other parts of the park have been developed for bush recreation with marked trails and camping and picnicking facilities. A rich variety of plant and animal communities in the park include sub-alpine and savannah woodland, wet eucalypt forests and a mosaic of sub-alpine grasslands, heaths, herb-fields, sphagnum bogs and swamps. These environments are inhabited by such creatures as the endangered broad-toothed rat, the gang-gang cockatoo – which migrates to the mountains in spring and is seen regularly in Canberra during autumn and winter – koalas, platypuses, possums and kangaroos. In late summer, the herb-fields are a colourful carpet of wildflowers.

Many Aboriginal and European heritage sites are protected within Namadgi National Park. Some stone arrangements are thought to have been constructed by Aborigines from the Canberra–Queanbeyan region for ceremonial purposes. Colourful and well-preserved Aboriginal rock paintings have been found in several rock shelters in the park, the best-known sites being at Yankee Hat, Rendezvous Creek and Nursery Swamp. Abandoned homesteads, huts, and dray routes used by miners heading for the Kiandra goldfields during the 1860s are among the leftovers from early nineteenth-century European settlement.

THARWA ■ 363

Tharwa is one of the oldest settlements in the ACT, growing up at the crossing on the Murrumbidgee River north of its junction with the Naas River, where a ford existed before Tharwa Bridge – the oldest bridge in the Australian Capital Territory – was constructed. Traffic was often bogged in the quicksands of the ford crossing and the completion of the bridge in 1895 was cause for carnival-style celebrations. The day was declared a public holiday with a parade culminating in a ribbon-cutting ceremony performed by the oldest inhabitant – Mrs Elizabeth McKeahnie. Picnics, a baby show, a cricket match and a dance followed.

In the 1891 census, Tharwa was a town of 255 people and it has remained a small village. Time is marked at the Tharwa school – built in 1912 – by a bell from the old Tuggeranong school. Part of the school's playground is said to have been an Aboriginal camping ground and the name of the village is thought to be an Aboriginal term for the nearby hill named Mount Tennent by early settlers after a bushranger.

'CUPPACUMBALONG' This historic property on the banks of the Murrumbidgee River just south of Tharwa was acquired by the Commonwealth Government in 1971 and converted into a public recreation area. Now the property houses a gallery, coffee shop, an arts and craft studio and picnic and barbecue facilities.

'Cuppacumbalong' was bought by Leopold de Salis in 1855 but the original homestead was destroyed by fire before the Second World War and the building that replaced it – though not deemed historically significant – stands as a reminder of more gracious times and was a stopover for Queen Elizabeth during her first Australian tour in 1954.

TIDBINBILLA NATURE RESERVE ■ 364

This 5510-hectare nature reserve south-west of Canberra in the mountains of the Tidbinbilla Range is an important link in the chain of parks stretching from the Australian Capital Territory to Victoria. Tidbinbilla Nature Reserve is best known for its large wildlife enclosures holding different species of kangaroos and koalas and native birds. Visitors to the reserve are able to enjoy an uninterrupted view of native animals in their natural environments. The waterbird enclosure is the result of several years' work beginning in 1976 and its five lagoons have become a wetland complex regarded as one of the finest man-made, waterbird exhibitions in the world.

Very little is known about the culture of the Aborigines who inhabited the region, though the name 'Tidbinbilla' derives from an Aboriginal word said to mean 'place of initiation', relating to the ceremony where boys were formally accepted into manhood. So far, no trace of a ceremonial ground has been found to substantiate this.

There are many bushwalking trails throughout the reserve, ranging from the paved footpaths of the wildlife enclosures to the challenging fire-trails that climb steeply through a series of habitats ranging from the native grasslands of the valley, to moist eucalypt forests sheltering ferny gullies and racing streams, on to sub-alpine forests and heaths at the higher altitudes. The 'Camel Back', leading to the ridge of the Tidbinbilla Range, is the longest and most spectacular of the reserve's fire-trails. On one side of the Camel Back, jutting peaks, ridges and the sometimes mist-filled valleys all cloaked in a dense growth of eucalypts reward

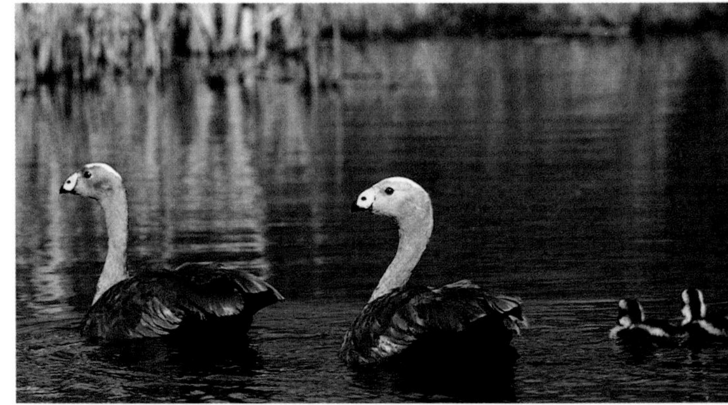
At Tidbinbilla Reserve, 'hides' allow a close-up view of Cape Barren geese.

A DRESS CIRCLE VIEW OF THE SOUTHERN CROSS

AUSTRALIA occupies a dress-circle seat for viewing the astronomical riches of the skies of the Southern Hemisphere. This propitious geographical location, combined with the country's mild climate and advanced technology, have made it a leader in world astronomy.

As early as 1910, Mount Stromlo – 782 metres above sea level – was deemed a suitable site for an astronomical observatory but regular observations of the heavens did not commence until 1925. The first instrument at Mount Stromlo was a refracting telescope donated by a Ballarat benefactor and installed in 1911 and which is now popular with amateur groups.

The futuristic domes at Mount Stromlo observatory date back as far as the 1920s; the observatory is managed by the Australian National University.

Mount Stromlo opened as a solar observatory and the reputation of the fledgling institution was established early by C.W. Allen's work on the solar spectrum – a major catalogue of the intensities of some thousands of spectral lines. By 1930 an atmospheric research station had been established on the mountain and in 1931, a seventy-six-centimetre reflecting telescope – which is still in use – was installed.

During the Second World War, the observatory did its bit for the war effort by becoming an optical munitions factory for the manufacture of gun and bomb sights and other optical devices for military use. After the war, Mount Stromlo continued as an optical astronomy observatory, but by the late 1950s it was evident that the bright nightlights of the rapidly developing city on the plains below would interfere increasingly with the observatory's efficiency, and Siding Spring Mountain near Coonabarabran in New South Wales (see *Coonabarabran & Coolah*) – now one of the world's major astronomical sites – was chosen as the site for a new, complementary observatory. Mount Stromlo has remained an important centre for spectroscopic observation, in which the light from a star is analysed and measured.

Both reflecting telescopes (using mirrors to collect light) and refracting telescopes (using lenses to collect light) are used at Mount Stromlo, though of all the research telescopes, only one – the 188-centimetre telescope – is open for public inspection. The massive, moving parts of the instrument weigh more than forty tonnes; the mirror alone is an impressive 1814 kilograms.

Looking like giant silver igloos, the outcrop of revolving domes that house the massive but delicate astronomical instruments are painted with aluminium or titanium oxide to deflect the heat of the summer sun. The domes also protect the telescopes from wind disturbance.

The 122-centimetre reflector telescope now being rebuilt as a specialised infra-red telescope was originally deemed a failure. Built in Dublin, the telescope arrived in Melbourne in 1868 and at the time was the largest equatorially-mounted telescope in the world. Unfortunately, it soon revealed serious design flaws that made it difficult to operate and maintain. Gradually, the 'Great Melbourne Telescope' fell into disuse and was finally sold as scrap to Mount Stromlo Observatory in 1945. But extensive modification and refurbishing at Mount Stromlo saved the telescope from an ignominious end and it gave good service for many years as a reflector telescope. It is expected to give many more in its latest role as an infra-red telescope. □

Mount Stromlo's 120-year-old 'Great Melbourne Telescope', was once the world's largest.

the bushwalker with wild and spectacular views, while on the other side of the ridge, valleys stripped of most of their original forest cover, are the domain of graziers.

TIDBINBILLA TRACKING STATION ■ 365

Australia has co-operated with the United States' National Aeronautics and Space Administration (NASA) in the operation of deep-space tracking stations since the late 1950s when satellites were first put into orbit. The Tidbinbilla Tracking Station is one of three such stations in Australia – all in the Australian Capital Territory – which are operated by the Department of Science and Technology on behalf of NASA.

Although the construction and operation of the tracking stations is financed by the United States, the design and construction of the station buildings and support facilities, as well as management and operation of the station, is provided by the Commonwealth Government.

The Tidbinbilla complex is dominated by two dishes – the 'little' twenty-six-metre antenna and the huge sixty-four-metre unit that weighs over 7000 tonnes – both of them highly sensitive and powerful instruments that constantly receive signals and transmit commands in the process of tracking spacecraft across hundreds of millions of kilometres of space.

The station is part of NASA's worldwide network of space-tracking and communication stations and over the years has played a crucial role in supporting many missions including the manned landings on the moon in 1969. When not devoted to NASA work, the station is also used from time to time for Australian satellite-tracking requirements and for other local scientific purposes. Its location in the Tidbinbilla Valley provides an almost ideal site for such a station, as the surrounding mountain ridges reduce radio-frequency interference from man-made sources.

URIARRA FORESTRY SETTLEMENT ■ 366

Before European settlement the Uriarra area was a gathering place for Aboriginal people, who harvested Bogong moths in the nearby mountains. The name comes from an Aboriginal word 'urayarra', the call used to summon tribal members to come to the moth feast.

The first European settlers arrived in the Uriarra area in 1838, taking up land for sheep grazing, and much of the native forest cover had been cleared by the time the grazing properties were resumed by the Commonwealth Government for the establishment of the Australian Capital Territory. The construction of a dam on the Cotter River – it would form an artificial lake to become the domestic water supply for the new city of Canberra – prompted the government to plant the land around the dam's lake with hundreds of imported Monterey pine trees – in order to maintain a 'healthy' catchment area and help preserve the quality of the water. These trees became the basis of a thriving timber industry and the reason for the establishment of the tiny Uriarra Forestry Settlement – one of several such settlements in the *Pinus radiata* – Monterey pine – plantations in the Australian Capital Territory.

CANBERRA

Canberra is one of a rare breed among the world's capital cities. The capital has no 'old' quarter, and few restored dwellings to remind the visitor of the city's past but stands as a purpose-built monument to national aspirations – and modern technology.

Canberra is a planned, formal city with its centre arranged carefully around the shores of Lake Burley Griffin. On the south shore within the 'Parliamentary Triangle', grandly monumental public buildings stand resplendent in parkland while broad avenues ceremoniously radiate and circle around them.

In contrast to the grand architectural highlights, several buildings in the nearby embassy district inject a note of whimsy with their expressions of 'archetypal' national architecture – a New Guinea 'spirit house', the horned gables of Thailand and the ornamental roofs of China.

The city's prominent hills, punctuated by the high-technology silhouette of the Black Mountain Tower, provide a backdrop of native bushland, while the central feature of Parliament House on Capital Hill, with its roof of lawns, seems to have settled right into the landscape. There is little intrusive street advertising or urban clutter, and instead of the crush of people and traffic, the visitor finds quiet, verdant spaces and rich plantings of exotic and native trees. Canberra's view to the west and south is dominated by the blue outline of the Brindabella Range and the distant shape of Bimberi Peak, often snow-flecked in winter.

Recipients of the Order of Australia medal (above) are announced in Canberra on the Australia Day and Queen's Birthday holidays. In spring, the Floriade Festival sees Commonwealth Park blossom.

The central business district at Civic, on the north shore of the lake, presents a subdued version of the high-rise office buildings, shops and plazas to be found in most cities. Beyond the city centre, Canberra's suburbs spread past the gaunt bush of Black Mountain or Mount Ainslie to the north and Red Hill to the south to the satellite centres such as Belconnen and Woden Valley. These suburbs of free-standing brick homes are green and leafy places and they remember in the names of their broad streets past worthies in Australian politics, law and public service.

With more than 270 000 people and situated in a sea of bushland and paddocks – in the federal enclave of the Australian Capital Territory – almost midway between Sydney and Melbourne, Canberra is easily Australia's largest inland city. It spreads itself in a carefully pre-arranged pattern across the valleys of the Molonglo River and Ginninderra Creek not far from where they join the Murrumbidgee River. The Molonglo was dammed in 1964 to form Lake Burley Griffin, the city's sparkling centrepiece.

At an elevation of around 600 metres and an inland location not far from the Snowy Mountains, Canberra winters can be cold and foggy, while its summers are hot. The city's remarkable plantings of exotic deciduous trees encourage many visitors to arrive in time for the impressive show of autumn colours and springtime blossoms.

Canberra is a young city, little more than eighty years old, and its beginnings and development are unlike any other Australian city. It was created as an act of national will in a place where no city would otherwise have grown. With the joining of the Australian states into a federation on 1 January 1901, the search for a federal capital began. The Australian Constitution, negotiated earlier between the states in an atmosphere of

All aspects of Australian life have come to be represented in the national capital. In the Australian Institute of Sport's futuristic dome, athletic performances are recorded and analysed.

intense – and not unexpected – Sydney–Melbourne rivalry, determined a fair compromise: the new capital city must be within New South Wales but not closer than 160 kilometres to Sydney.

The Federal Parliament sat in Melbourne while the search went on and it was not until 1908 that a site in the Yass–Canberra district was chosen by a parliamentary committee. The place was mainly open grazing country – St John's Church and schoolhouse at Reid, Lanyon Homestead at Tharwa and Blundell's Farmhouse at Russell are among the few buildings of this pastoral era still standing. In 1911, the Australian Capital Territory – forever after known as 'the ACT' – was established over some 2500 square kilometres of land earlier ceded by New South Wales to the Commonwealth. In that year also, an international competition was opened for the design of the federal capital.

Walter Burley Griffin, a Chicago landscape architect who had worked with Frank Lloyd Wright, submitted the winning design without visiting the site. Considerable controversy greeted this choice, but Griffin was allowed to pursue his design for a city based on a 'land axis' running from Mount Ainslie through Red Hill to the distant, 2000-metre Bimberi Peak. Along this axis he placed the elevated Parliament House site below his 'Capitol' – now Capital – Hill, not on it, and below that, on land falling to the shores of a planned lake, he set the major complex of government offices.

From Griffin's 'Capitol' the main thoroughfares radiated outwards to different 'suburban' centres, with lesser streets circling around each centre. A 'water axis' ran from Black Mountain through the lake intersecting the land axis at right angles and was parallelled by a third 'municipal axis' running north of the lake. Lines drawn from points along these axes to his 'Capitol' formed the 'Parliamentary Triangle'. It was a noble design, concerned with visual quality, intended to link the city to the dominant natural features surrounding it and, symbolically,

The modest concealment of Parliament House put the finishing touch to Canberra's dramatic land axis.

with the state capital cities – each of which was to have a main thoroughfare bearing its name radiating from the 'Capitol' in the city's direction.

Progress with Griffin's plan was delayed by bureaucratic resistance to his appointment to direct the design of the capital and lack of resources during the First World War. When his final plan was adopted in 1925, Griffin's contract had long since expired and he had returned to the United States. Apart from a few unrealised sketches, he designed none of Canberra's public buildings and he deplored the site chosen for the old Parliament House. Nevertheless, Canberra's grand and handsome design remains largely the handiwork of Griffin.

In Canberra, it has been possible to guide development with a firm hand as all land is owned by one body – the Commonwealth Government. Conditions have been written into leases for private or commercial lessees governing how land is to be used and developed. Several distinct periods are illustrated in the city's architecture, including the beginnings in the 1920s when Mediterranean-style stucco with red-tile roofs was favoured, as shown in the Sydney Building at the Civic complex and in the houses of old suburbs such as Griffith. For many years Canberra's development was painfully slow, earning it the dismissive snub 'seven suburbs in search of a city'. It was not until the damming of the Molonglo River and the artful creation of the artifical lake in 1961 that Griffin's vision truly became a reality.

The new Parliament House, like many other important buildings of the city, and Canberra itself, is the result of an architectural competition. Opened in 1988, it is a monumental structure but one that does not inhibit or dominate. By taking away, then recreating the profile of Capital Hill with an impression of grassed slopes climbing over the building's roof, the designers sought to preserve Griffin's idea of an unimpeded sightline from Mount Ainslie through to Bimberi Peak.

The orientation of the Parliament building's two massive, curved walls, separated by a great mall, reinforces this aim as does the transparency of the huge, metal structure supporting the central flag mast. In the time-honoured Australian tradition of mocking authority, less respectful observers noting this juxtaposition of lawn and metal have been heard to refer to the flag support as 'the sprinkler on the hill.'

Despite the capital's many monumental buildings, Canberra's most visible structure is the space-age Black Mountain Tower.

Facing Parliament House from the foot of Mount Ainslie, across the lake, is the Australian War Memorial. Opened in 1941, this domed building with its massive flanking pylons encloses a fine memorial courtyard. It also serves as a museum, housing a comprehensive display of aircraft, weapons, photographs and other exhibits recording Australia's war history.

The Governor-General's residence, 'Yarralumla', dates from 1891; it assumed its final shape in 1939.

The slope from Parliament House down to the lake is the site of several important buildings, including the 'wedding cake' old Parliament House which 'temporarily' accommodated sittings of the House of Representatives and the Senate for sixty years from 1927. Closer to the lake is the 'powerhouse' outline of the High Court building with its dramatic central foyer. Along the lake shore to the west is the neo-classical, marbled form of the National Library which, as well as maintaining a national collection of library material, houses displays of Australian photography, art and history; Captain Cook's historic journal is held here and also the expedition diary of Wills of the ill-fated Burke and Wills expedition to the continent's northern coast.

Across the road from the National Library is the Science and Technology Centre where 'hands-on' exhibits aim to give an understanding of the role of science and technology in society. Along the lake shore to the east of the High Court is the modernistic, concrete form of the National Gallery which displays the most comprehensive collection of Australian art in the country, together with European and Asian collections, and art from Oceania and other cultures.

Canberra's embassy buildings are concentrated in a 'diplomatic belt' at Yarralumla, just to the west of Capital Hill, and, as mentioned, many of them have been designed with an eye to displaying national architectural traditions. The United States Embassy building is based on an eighteenth-century Virginia mansion, the Greek Embassy, with its marble-clad colonnades, modestly echoes the Parthenon, while the Indonesian

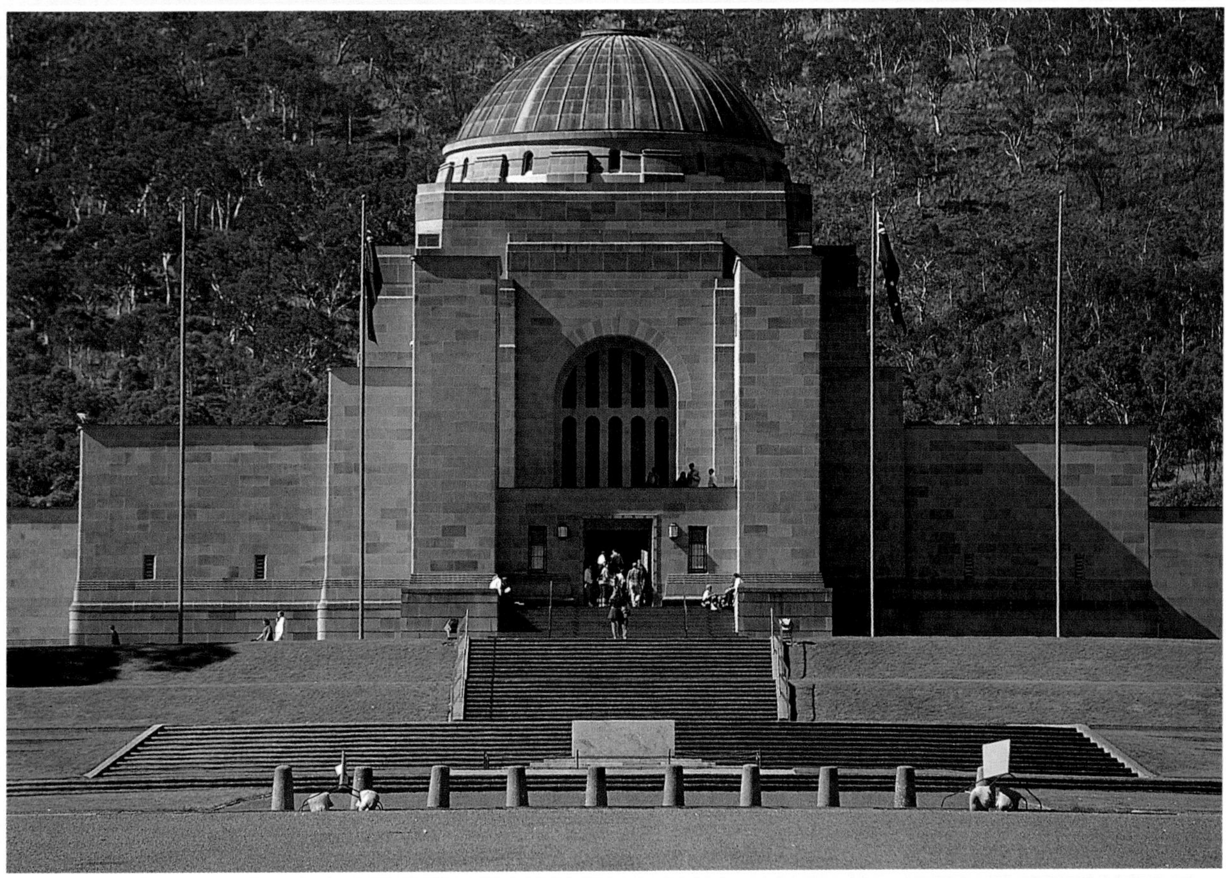

The dignified edifice of the War Memorial attracts more visitors than any other Canberra building.

Embassy presents a graceful stairway ornamented tastefully with Balinese Hindu statuary.

The attractive, water-axis lake that unites the national capital's elements bears the name of its designer and is largely given over to the city's inhabitants for recreation. The banks of Lake Burley Griffin are almost entirely parkland open to the public and cyclists can ride round most of the lake shores on a cycleway. The gracefully soaring water spout near the Commonwealth Avenue Bridge and the Carillon on Aspen Island near the Kings Avenue Bridge are the lake's decorative finishing touches.

Broad vistas of Canberra can be obtained from lookouts on Mount Ainslie, Red Hill and from the roof of the new Parliament House. Black Mountain's enormous telecommunications tower provides more sophisticated vantage points from its revolving restaurant and viewing galleries. At the foot of Black Mountain Drive are the Australian National Botanic Gardens which boast the largest collection of Australian native plants in cultivation – warm-climate plants are grown at the gardens' coastal annexe on Commonwealth land at Jervis Bay. The north-western slopes of Black Mountain are traversed by an extensive system of bushwalking tracks. □

The national coat-of-arms, rendered in many styles, decorates the entranceways of Canberra's government offices.

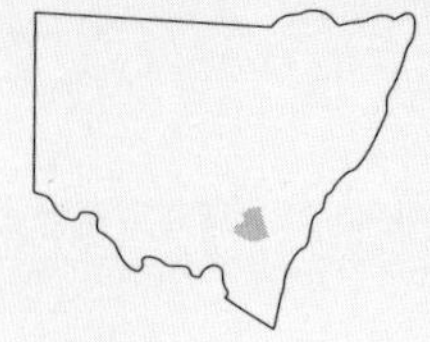

Yass & Boorowa

Harnessing the waters of the Murrumbidgee and its tributaries for irrigation has all but banished the threat of flooding in this region and provided a reliable water supply for the producers of fine wool, cereal and fruit.

BINALONG ■ 367

The village of Binalong has a long and colourful history and many nineteenth-century buildings still stand as reminders of the past. The court house, built in 1883, is the largest building in the village while the old Cobb & Co. inn – the Black Swan (1847) – is the oldest.

In 1865, Johnny Gilbert, a member of Ben Hall's gang, was shot and killed on the outskirts of the village and is buried in Binalong. There is a suspicion that his grandfather divulged his hiding place to the police and possibly interfered with Gilbert's gun, which failed to fire when the police drew their weapons. Gilbert, who had committed numerous murders and had a reputation as a 'ladies' man', was only twenty-five when he died.

Andrew Barton (Banjo) Paterson, was only a year old when Johnny Gilbert was shot. Stories about Gilbert ran rife around the local Binalong primary school, which Banjo Paterson attended from 1869 after his father took up a farm at Illalong just outside the village. According to Paterson, 'the youngest child on the Watershed can tell you how Gilbert died'. Banjo Paterson's father is buried in the local cemetery and the annual Banjo Paterson poetry awards are still held at Binalong.

BOOKHAM ■ 368

The village was originally called Bogolong but by the mid-1840s, the name Bookham was used on a map that showed the track from the Yass River to Gundagai passing through the village.

Once a staging past for Cobb & Co. coaches, Bookham is set amongst fine wool grazing country. Despite an influx of soldier-settlers in the 1950s it nowadays supports a lone general store. It is the nearest settlement to the spectacular white-water canoeing watercourse at Childowla on the Murrumbidgee.

BOOROWA ■ 369

In the 1830s, the first settlers moved on to the 'Burrua' run on the banks of what is now the Boorowa River. The name Boorowa was adopted for the town when it was gazetted in 1850 and is thought to come from an Aboriginal word meaning 'plains turkey' or 'bustard turkey'.

From its earliest days, the town of Boorowa has relied on wheat and wool for its economic survival and is now the headquarters for the shire named after it. Boorowa Shire, adjoining Yass Shire to the south and Gunning Shire to the west, stretches from south of the town of Boorowa to Lake Wyangala.

The court house, completed in 1884, still dominates the main street. The other major building is St Patrick's Catholic Church, which has an altar of beautifully crafted Italian marble. *Population 1090*

BURRINJUCK STATE RECREATION AREA ■ 370

This parcel of public land covers 1700 hectares on the western shore of the man-made Lake Burrinjuck. Over a quarter-of-a-million visitors are attracted to the parkland on the lake banks each year, partly for the recreation available on the lake – fishing (especially for trout), boating, water sports and birdwatching – and partly for the spectacular setting. The location, beneath Mount Barren Jack (600 metres) and offering views of the Brindabella Ranges to the south, is reached by a road that descends 300 metres from the plateau of the Southern Highlands through wooded hills to the shores of the lake. The last part of this road follows the old rail line used during dam construction when a large construction camp occupied some of what is now the recreation area.

GUNNING ■ 371

The village of Gunning, in the Southern Tablelands 580 metres above sea level, is on the Hume Highway and by the headwaters of the Lachlan River. Sheep, fine wool, cattle, together with some mixed farming and mining have supported the inhabitants since first settlement.

There were settlers in the area around Gunning by the early 1820s, among them Hamilton Hume and his two brothers – John Kennedy Hume and Francis Rawdon Hume. It was from Hamilton Hume's station at Gunning on 17 October 1824 that he and William Hovell set off through unknown country on their journey of exploration to Port Phillip Bay. A commemorative column and tablet were unveiled in 1924.

The town of Gunning was planned in 1838 on a site just south of the present village where a stockyard, troopers' residence and staging place were set up. By 1848, the 'town' had twenty houses, ninety-five people, Cooper's Store, the White Hart Hotel and was of substance enough to attract the unwelcome attention of Ben Hall.

Ben Hall and his gang held up the mail on Gunning Hill in 1864 and on leaving the scene of their crime came across three Gunning residents on horseback. Ben Hall proceeded to swap his old boots with the brand-new footwear worn by one of the residents! The victim was then given a guinea (twenty-one shillings) to buy another pair.

LAKE BURRINJUCK ■ 372

Lake Burrinjuck is held in place behind a 230-metre-long wall on the Murrumbidgee just below the point where two of its tributaries – the Goodradigbee and Yass rivers – join the main stream. In addition to its recreational facilities, including fishing for introduced Atlantic salmon, Lake Burrinjuck irrigates a large area and provides hydro-electric power to a generating station at Port Kembla.

Fossil evidence proves that a natural inland sea existed millions of years ago on the site of what is now the man-made Lake Burrinjuck. The name Burrinjuck was the local Aboriginal name, believed to mean 'rugged-topped mountain' but for many years after settlement the Europeans used the anglicised name Barren Jack – there was even an act of Parliament entitled the *NSW Barren Jack and Murrumbidgee Canals Construction Scheme Act 1906*.

The dam, in Barren Jack Gorge on the Murrumbidgee River, was the first major water storage and irrigation scheme in the drought-ridden Murrumbidgee Valley and was the first in a series of inland lakes designed to open the Murray–Murrumbidgee area to irrigation farming.

MURRUMBATEMAN ■ 373

Murrumbateman, with a climate similar to the Bordeaux area of France, is well known for its cool-climate wines. The once-thriving nineteenth-century wine industry eventually languished and was only re-established in the 1970s; the town now boasts several wineries.

One of the village's best known residents was Granny Davis. Having been transported for stealing a pocket watch, her wrongful conviction was overturned and she was given land in Murrumbateman where she lived until her death at the age of 113. Her grave is in the Gounyan cemetery north of Murrumbateman.

Wheat is second only to wool in the northern part of this region in the shadow of the Great Divide; in the south, vineyards are flourishing.

Wine grapes once grew in the paddocks near the Cooma Cottage stables...

...and after a 100-year interval, cool-climate wines are making a successful comeback around Yass.

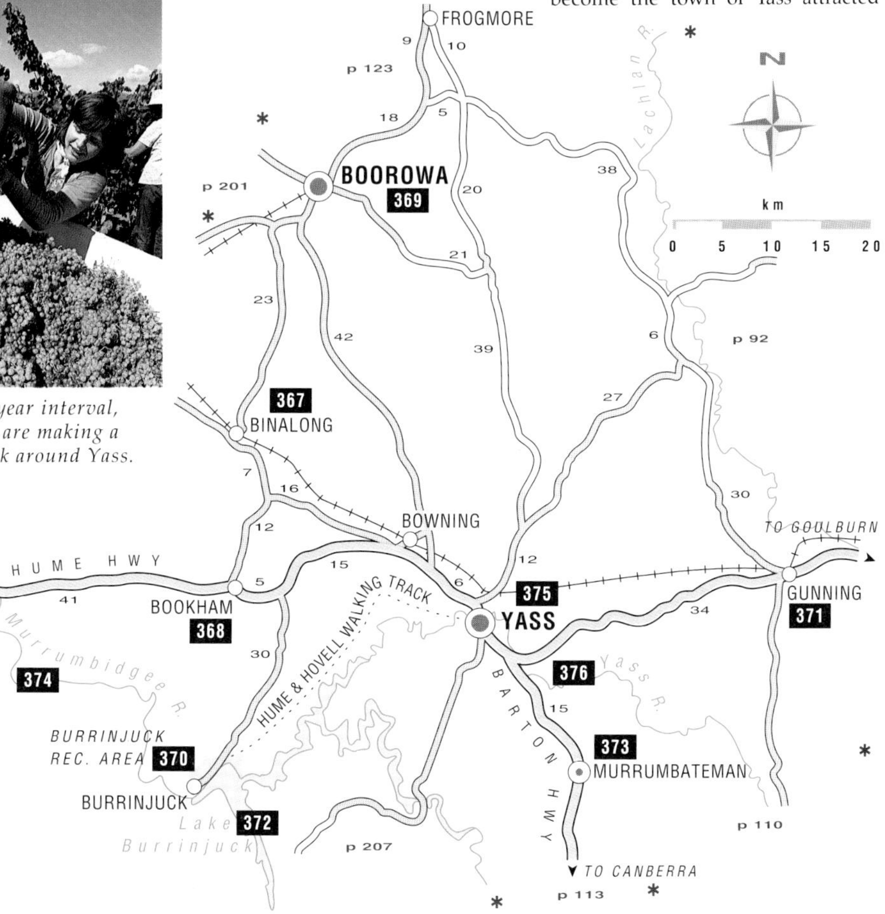

The village's annual Field Days, initiated to help hobby farmers, now attract up to 20 000 people annually. *Population 770*

MURRUMBIDGEE RIVER ■ 374

I bought a run a while ago
On country rough and ridgy
Where wallaroos and wombats grow –
The Upper Murrumbidgee.
The grass is rather scant, it's true,
But this a fair exchange is,
The sheep can see a lovely view
By climbing up the ranges.

This was the way Banjo Paterson, in his poem 'A Mountain Station' achieved the almost impossible by coming up with a rhyme for the word 'Murrumbidgee'.

Geological evidence suggests that the Murrumbidgee River (see special feature) is over 400 million years old. The existence of the 'Morumbidgee' River was known to Europeans from Aboriginal descriptions some time before it was seen by the first white man. Between 1821 and 1824 a number of explorers – Charles Throsby and Joseph Wild, Mark Currie, Hamilton Hume and William Hovell – crossed the river at various points. Hamilton Hume swam across the river with a line so that supply drays, their wheels removed, could be floated across the river.

Howevever, it was not until Charles Sturt's expedition of 1824 that the Murrumbidgee's eventual conclusion was discovered by white men. Sturt, who described the Murrumbidgee where he first saw it at Jugiong as 'wild, romantic and beautiful' took almost two months to reach the river's junction with the Murray River.

The importance of the Murrumbidgee Irrigation Area for primary production in New South Wales cannot be overemphasised. Harnessing the waters of the Murrumbidgee allowed the release of the first irrigated blocks of farmland in 1913 and started the irrigation of the 'Riverina' district from which the major proportion of the state's rice, apricots, grapes, pears and peaches come.

YASS ■ 375

In the 1820s, after the Yass Plains were discovered by Hume and Hovell, the district around what was to become the town of Yass attracted itinerant shearers, mounted troopers and a few settlers. At the river crossing, a few businesses were set up to serve those waiting to ford the river. The 'frontier' town of Yass was proclaimed in 1837 and it was here that the Port Jackson–Port Phillip mail coach terminated. The Port Phillip mail proceeded by packhorse – ten horses working in relay were used to cover the distance but the charge was 'not to exceed threepence halfpenny per mile for conveyance of the mail on horseback'.

In 1873, Yass was declared a municipality and most of the major historic buildings in the town – the court house, the school and the three oldest banks in the main street – date from around this period.

Although cattle, wheat, fruit and mining have played a part in the development of Yass, the town is best known for its superb fine wool. Charles Sturt was to record in his journal that 'sheep, I should imagine would thrive uncommonly well on these (Yass) plains' and the earliest settlers followed his suggestion. Yass fine wool – fourteen microns in thickness compared with the more usual seventeen-and-a-half microns – is world renowned.

In 1903, Yass was one of the leading contenders for the site of the national capital and although it lost out to Canberra its nearness to the federal capital has added to its strategic situation on the Hume Highway between Sydney and Melbourne and has had a bearing on its recent economic development. *Population 4830*

COMUR STREET The main street through Yass with its collection of nineteenth-century commercial buildings was listed as part of the National Estate in the 1960s.

COOMA COTTAGE Originally called 'Comur' and built by Cornelius O'Brien in 1835, Cooma Cottage with forty hectares of land was bought by Hamilton Hume in 1839. The original weatherboard cottage is still intact although almost completely hidden by later extensions.

ST CLEMENT'S ANGLICAN CHURCH (1847) Hamilton Hume was a foundation trustee of St Clement's church which was designed by Edmund Blackett. The bells in the belltower – which are still in use – were cast in Birminghan and inscribed 'We sing the Lord's song in a strange land'. It is believed to be the only full peal of bells in rural Australia.

YASS RIVER ■ 376

The short Yass River rises just west of Lake George, part of the river's old drainage system, and flows north-west through Yass, the only town on its banks, then south-west to join the Murrumbidgee River.

The name Yass comes from an Aboriginal word with a number of possible spellings – 'yarh', 'yahr' or 'yharr' – all of which mean 'running water'. The region's early explorers camped beside the river on their journeys and one, Hamilton Hume, so liked the river that he bought Cooma Cottage overlooking it.

There was a ford at Yass River from the 1820s called, appropriately enough, Mud Flat but frequent flooding led to increasingly urgent requests for a bridge. The first timber bridge across the Yass River was designed by Edmund Blackett and built in 1854. By 1865, the bridge was unsafe and construction on a new iron bridge began. When the river flooded in 1870, the original timber bridge and the partly constructed iron bridge were both swept away. The four iron pillars, all that remained, were used as the basis for the Hume Bridge, built in 1872 and replaced in 1978 by the bridge that now carries the Hume Highway across the Yass River.

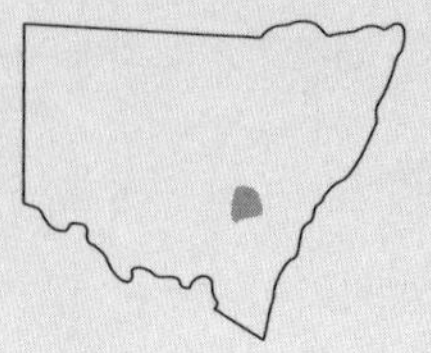

Cowra & Blayney

This part of the 'golden west' was pioneered by stockmen and developed by farmers and pastoralists. The high hills are honeycombed with caves carved by rivers and creeks, and abandoned mine shafts dug by those seeking gold, silver, copper and lead.

ABERCROMBIE CAVES ■ 377
Although the Abercrombie Caves are one of Australia's smaller cave systems, they contain one of the largest natural tunnels or arches in the world. The Grand Arch or Arch Cave is over 220 metres long, 60 metres wide in some places and the average height of its roof is 30 metres. During daylight hours, the natural light entering both ends of the tunnel creates a wonderful spectrum of colours as it bounces off the marble lining the walls.

Although the caves were not 'discovered', by Surveyor-General W.R. Davidson, until 1842, they had been known to bushrangers – and those responsible for their capture – for a number of years. One of the major bushranging incidents had in fact taken place some twelve years earlier when the Ribbon Boys, Bathurst jail escapees led by a man with a red ribbon in his hair, had a three-day gun battle with police at Abercrombie Caves. The first law-abiding tourists – six ladies and ten gentlemen, two of them knights of the realm – rode to the caves from a nearby property in 1834. After the official 'discovery' in 1842, the Governor, Sir Charles Fitzroy, visited the caves and, so the story goes, deposited a case of champagne in a grotto in Pulpit Cave.

Of the five caves leading off the Arch, perhaps the best known is the Hall of Terpsichore, named after the Greek muse of dancing and choral song. A wooden dance floor was built at the end of the nineteenth century by local gold miners and the raised floor has since been used for concerts, boxing matches, church services, weddings and christenings (using water from a creek running through the caves). The floor is Baltic pine and was imported from England – already tongue-and-grooved – either as packing cases for mining equipment or as ballast.

Bushrangers Cave, was used by Ben Hall and his cohorts as a hideout, to stash provisions or sometimes to detain prisoners or hostages. Bushranger's Stable Cave was used for their horses. There are many bushranging legends associated with Abercrombie Caves including the rumour that Frank Gardiner's gold haul from the Eugowra hold up – all 14 000 pounds sterling worth of it, in four boxes – was dumped in the caves until it could be shared but, with the jailing of Gardiner and his departure for the United States as soon as he was released, there was no opportunity to retrieve it.

The destruction of many of the stalactites in the cave system by vandals and souvenir hunters led to the appointment of a caretaker for the caves in 1888. The nature reserve surrounding the caves contains Grove Creek, the watercourse responsible for eroding the caves out of the limestone.

ABERCROMBIE RIVER ■ 378
The Abercrombie River is one of the three main tributaries of the Lachlan River (see entry). It was first sighted by a European in 1815 when George Evans, attempting to trace the Macquarie River, came instead upon the Abercrombie. Four years later, Dr Charles Throsby and his party, including three local Aborigines – Cookoogong, Dual and Bion – traced the river to the point where it met the Lachlan River. It was not, however, until 1820 that the river was named – by John Oxley who crossed this 'considerable stream'.

Rising in the mountains, north-east of Crookwell, the Abercrombie River is now dammed at Lake Wyangala (see entry). In the 1870s, it cost one shilling per head in summer and one shilling and sixpence in time of flood to be transported by ferry across the Abercrombie River near Tuena (see entry) – the crossing is nowadays free and by bridge.

BLAYNEY ■ 379
Blayney, in the valley of the Belubula River, is the centre of a rich farming and grazing area. The town is also one of the major meat-supplying centres in the region, as well as the shire headquarters. Although a study of actual winter temperatures does not bear it out, Blayney has long had the reputation of being one of the coldest towns in the state.

As early as 1821, when Blayney was called King's Plains, it was a centre for the stockmen responsible for the government herds. The area was thought to be unsuitable for permanent settlement and was reserved, until 1828, for cattle.

In 1828, a town site was reserved and, in 1843, the town, which at that time contained a mill, an inn and a few houses, was surveyed. In a letter from the Colonial Secretary in June 1843, the plan was approved for 'Blaney' and this was the name gazetted in September 1843.

The population grew quite rapidly, especially after the discovery of copper and some gold. The completion of the Bathurst–Blayney railway line and the later railway link with Cowra established Blayney as an important junction for produce going to markets in Sydney and for provisions coming into the central western region. Its position on the Mid-western Highway since the 1920s has confirmed the town's role as a regional centre. *Population 2650*

CANOWINDRA ■ 380
Canowindra, pronounced 'Canoundra', – meaning 'home' – sits by the Belubula River, surrounded by gently rolling hills. Timber- and flour-milling, buttermaking, grazing and cereal have been the mainstay of the town for most of its history although it also has a more recent reputation of a non-agricultural kind.

The town is noted for its ballooning, with more flights being made over Canowindra than anywhere else in the country. From March to November balloonists flock to the town to take advantage of ideal hot-air ballooning conditions.

In the early morning light, intrepid hot-air balloonists prepare to float up-up-and-away above the Canowindra region. The often ideal atmospheric conditions above the town – wind, but not too much of it – have made it a centre for the revival of hot-air ballooning.

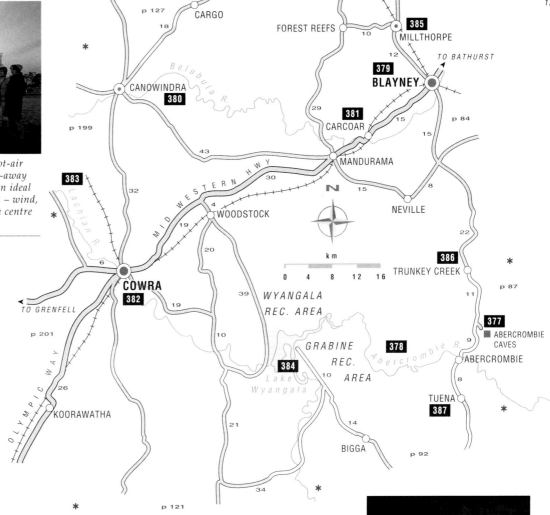

Canowindra was on the old bullock-waggon road used in the early 1800s. In 1836, five years after the first land was taken up for farming, Governor Fitzroy passed through the area; within the next few years a settlement began to develop and in 1849, the first inn – the Canowindra Inn – was built.

It was, however, the Miners' Arms or Robinson's Hotel that was the site of the 'Canowindra spree' immortalised in the poem 'The Afterlife of Bold Jack Donahue' and based on a true incident. For several days in October 1863, Frank Gardiner, Ben Hall and others, had a party where the forty residents of the village were 'shouted' free drink, food and cigars by the bushrangers; needless to say the bill was never paid.

The three-day binge – or siege, depending on your point of view – is commemorated in the Ben Hall Monument in the town. Other aspects of the town's history can be seen in the museum in Memorial Park with its exhibitions of nineteenth-century farm machinery and in the conservation area in the narrow main street where there are a number of hotels, banks and a nursing home that are now listed as 'heritage' sites.

History of a more recent, more respectable and quite different type was made at the Canowindra Hotel in the 1930s, when Kylie Tennant wrote her novel *Tiburon* there, while her husband was employed as a teacher at Canowindra Public School. *Population 1720*

CARCOAR ■ 381

Thomas Icely, with ten cross-bred lambs and a two-year-old bull bought from John Macarthur, pioneered the pastoral industry in and around Carcoar in 1831. He, along with other early settlers including William Lawson (of Blue Mountains-crossing fame), was instrumental in having the town proclaimed in 1839. A number of names such as 'Carcuan', 'Carcoon' and 'Corcoran' were used for this, the third town to be proclaimed west of the Blue Mountains. Mitchell's 'Map of the Nineteen Counties' used the name Carcoar, thought to be an Aboriginal word for 'frog' or from 'cah-co-ah', the sound of the kookaburra.

The village developed rapidly to become the 'mother town' of the Lachlan Valley and a commercial centre for the region. Bushrangers also used Carcoar as their centre and, in the 1840s, the town was threatened with martial law because of its lawlessness. Frank Gardiner worked in the village butcher's shop and saddlery for some time. The birth of Ben Hall's son at 'Flash Dan' Charter's farm just outside the village, was registered in Carcoar. Carcoar also was the scene of Australia's first recorded daylight bank hold-up in 1863 when Johnny Gilbert and John O'Meally robbed the Commercial Bank (still standing).

By the 1860s, Carcoar's heyday as a major, regional commercial centre also came to an end. From a maximum population of about 600 in the mid-1860s, the town declined as large gold discoveries were made further west and the routing of the railway line through Blayney in 1876 brought that town to prominence as the rural centre. Despite this, iron ore and cobalt mining helped keep Carcoar's name on the map.

The small valley settlement of Carcoar with its very English deciduous trees – and its very English climate, including regular snowfalls – is now classified as an historic village.

ST PAUL'S ANGLICAN CHURCH Designed by Edmund Blackett, the church was built in 1845-49 and is supposed to be a replica of a church at Plympton, in the west of England. Its tall spire, covered with shingles, dominates the village.

STOKE'S STABLE MUSEUM The convict-built stable for Thomas Icely's first overseer, Mr Stokes, was erected as a hay barn in 1849 and is the oldest building in the village. Bought by the historical society for one dollar, the stable is now a museum.

CHURCH OF THE IMMACULATE CONCEPTION The church dates back to 1867 and has a highly original and natural air-conditioning system in which air passes through the thick walls and enters the church through vents in the windowsills.

FESTIVALS Carcoar Village Fair, January; Ben Hall Festival, November.

COWRA ■ 382

Cowra is best known for the wartime 'breakout' from the Japanese prison camp based in the town (see box) but it is also an important agricultural and commercial centre for the Lachlan Valley. A large proportion of the vegetables from the Lachlan valley, and most of Australia's asparagus, is canned in Cowra.

Exotic formations such as the one above exist in the side-galleries to the Abercrombie Caves Grand Arch.

One of the earliest settlers in the district, Reverend Henry Fulton called his property 'Cowra Rocks' – an unnecessary repetition since the Aboriginal word 'coura' is thought to mean 'rocks'. A few years later, when the town was surveyed, the name Cowra was adopted.

Conditions were particularly harsh in the early years of settlement with three droughts in the 1840s that dried up the Lachlan River and a fierce flood which drowned over one

The Englishness of Carcoar's St Paul's is sabotaged only by the trees.

thousand sheep. The round trip by bullock cart with wool from Cowra to Sydney and provisions from Sydney to Cowra took three months.

As late as 1910, teams of bullocks and horses still gathered at Cowra railway station before the lines to Grenfell and Canowindra were opened and its current position at the intersection of three major highways – the Mid-western Highway, Lachlan Valley Way and Olympic Way – suggests that its importance as a freight junction remains. *Population 8420*

FESTIVALS Festival of International Understanding, March; Eisteddfod, May/June; Wine Show, July.

LACHLAN RIVER ■ 383

The Lachlan River rises near Gunning and flows in a northerly direction until it is joined by its main tributary, the Abercrombie River (see entry), east of Cowra. A dam at this confluence has formed what is now Lake Wyangala (see entry). The Lachlan River then heads in a north-westerly direction before turning south-west to join the Murrumbidgee River west of Hay.

The river has many and varied moods. Tranquil, secluded stretches give way to stretches where it meanders, cutting across itself to form ox-bow lakes (such as Lake Forbes) and fill in dry, former riverbeds. Sometimes the river is confined by tree-lined banks several metres high and at other times it flows through wide open country.

The Aboriginal name for the river was 'callara' but, after it was discovered by Europeans in 1815 and explored by John Oxley in 1817, it was named Lachlan after Governor Lachlan Macquarie. Although Oxley explored much of the river, he was eventually blocked by a huge expanse of marshes and it was left to Charles Sturt in 1830 to reach the spot where the Lachlan River joins the Murrumbidgee.

LAKE WYANGALA ■ 384

Lake Wyangala was created by damming the Lachlan and Abercrombie rivers approximately forty kilometres south-east of Cowra. The original concrete dam wall was completed in 1935 and greatly enlarged by an earth and rock-fill wall in 1971, which increased the height of the crest so that water is now stored to 400 metres above sea level.

The idea for damming at this point, primarily for irrigation and flood control, came from a local resident Don Elliott whose efforts are commemorated in Elliott's Lookout, a favourite spot for bushwalkers.

The lake is one of the best known and most popular water recreation areas in New South Wales west of the Blue Mountains. A number of species of fish – including brown and rainbow trout, Macquarie perch and cod – attract keen fishermen.

WYANGALA STATE RECREATION AREA On the north-west, or Cowra, side of the lake this recreation area is the larger of the two on its banks and also the most accessible by road. The area is 'developed' and even has a country club nearby although rough, 'away-from-it-all' camping is possible at Markham's Creek, Oaky Creek and Quartpot.

GRABINE STATE RECREATION AREA This relatively undeveloped zone of public parkland on the upper reaches of the lake is accessible by road, although slightly off the beaten track, and can also be reached by boat from the adjacent and larger Wyangala State Recreation Area.

MILLTHORPE ■ 385

The railway station for Millthorpe stands 955 metres above sea level and has the distinction of being the highest point between the Great Dividing Range and the Indian Ocean. But as well as height, the village has a distinctive history.

The village, which grew up around an old crossroads where the track from the former Blackman's Swamp (Orange) to King's Plains (Blayney) crossed the track from Flyers Creek, was known originally as Spring Grove.

This name was to remain until the railway arrived in the 1870s when, to avoid confusion with the nearby Spring Hill railway station, it was changed to Millthorpe ('mill' to celebrate the recently completed flour mill and 'thorpe', an old English word meaning village). The village was a flourishing commercial centre, initially for wheat and vegetables, and later for dairying and hay production. The coming of the railway line also saw the end of the schoolmaster's supplementary income of ten pounds a year as acting postmaster; the task being transferred to the station master.

This vintage press at 'Coombing Park', near Carcoar, once formed wool into bales.

The 1890s saw the start of the rural depression and this brought an end to Millthorpe's growth. The lack of development since the nineteenth century and, more particularly, since the First World War has ensured the preservation of many original buildings and the whole village is now 'heritage-listed'.

Once noted for its potato production – over half a million bags in a good year – Millthorpe retains the character of its early days. Its historical atmosphere, helped by residents' careful maintenance of original facades makes it a popular refreshment stop between Blayney and Orange. *Population 630*

TRUNKEY CREEK ■ 386

The village of Trunkey Creek was originally called 'Arthur' after the man who discovered the first gold-carrying quartz vein at the site of the village. The name was later changed and whether it comes from an Aboriginal word said to mean 'large kangaroo' or a shortened form of the unpronounceable Polish name of an early gold miner, is still disputed.

The gold rush to Trunkey Creek started in 1868 and at its peak the village had five hundred miners. Now all that remains are the abandoned mine shafts around the village.

TUENA ■ 387

A local minister, the Reverend Douglas, was responsible for the opening of the Tuena goldfield in 1851. On his way to perform a christening he stopped to boil a billy and turned over a stone – and found gold! The alluvial deposits lasted until 1869 and then quartz-bearing gold, copper, rubies, sapphires, silver and lead were exploited. It is hardly surprising that the Court of Petty Sessions sat at Tuena from 1865 onwards and mounted troopers were stationed there from the 1870s. The Goldfields Inn, built in 1866, must also have done a roaring trade, and the wattle-and-daub building still stands – the oldest such building known to be standing in Australia.

Despite a short-lived revival in gold mining during the Depression of the 1930s, the only 'mining' that now takes place in Tuena is during the annual Gold Rush Festival, a unique event that includes among its attractions the Australian National Goldpanning Championships. Competitors are scored on speed (bonus points if under four minutes and penalty points if over four minutes), recovery of gold (a minimum of ten pieces of gold or a 'shotty') and the cleanness of the concentrate (one penalty point for each minim of sand – equal to about a drop of water).

FESTIVAL Gold Rush Festival, Easter.

THE COWRA BREAKOUT: A WARTIME CLASH AND A PEACETIME UNDERSTANDING

As early as June 1944, there had been rumours that the 1104 Japanese in Camp B of the POW camp at Cowra would attempt to seize control of the camp and security had been tightened.

The meeting on 4 August between the Australian camp commandant and two of the Japanese camp leaders seems to have acted as a trigger for these plans. At the meeting it was revealed that, within three days, all the Japanese prisoners below NCO rank would be transferred to the prison camp at Hay. The rest of the day passed quietly but at 1.30 a.m. next morning, a bugle call was heard and the prisoners in Camp B burst out of their huts, after kicking over the braziers inside them so that the huts burst into flames behind them.

Prisoners prepare for an inspection at the Cowra prisoner-of-war camp shortly before the attempted escape.

The Japanese carried crudely improvised weapons such as baseball bats, sticks, clubs and kitchen knives that had been sharpened or serrated. They carried blankets or towels and wore baseball gloves, boot soles or even wads of toilet paper on their hands...the reasons for which became obvious as they reached the barbed wire fence. There were, in fact, three barbed-wire fences ten metres apart – the spaces beween them filled with tangled barbed wire and coils of extra barbed wire along the top or on the inside of the fences. With their primitive protection, the prisoners climbed over or under the fence while some lay across the wire so that others could use them as 'bridges'.

Two cultures and two landscapes – one formal, one not so readily tamed – come together in the tranquil setting of Cowra's Japanese garden which provides a living symbol of reconciliation.

The Cowra 'breakout' was not so much a bid for freedom or escape but was aimed at a takeover of the camp or death in the attempt since, for the Japanese, capture was a cause of great shame and guilt. The attempted takeover failed and cost the lives of 231 Japanese and four Australian soldiers.

The Australian guards died as their machine-gun emplacements were overrun or were killed outside the camp by groups of escapers. Of the Japanese who died, most were shot during the 'breakout' but there were many who died by their own hand – hanged, burned to death in blazing huts, stabbed or disembowelled with the sharpened knives from the camp canteens and, for two who managed to reach Cowra station, death came when they threw themselves under a train. Of the 378 Japanese who escaped through the perimeter fence, all were recaptured within a very short time.

In 1948, the members of Cowra RSL who had maintained the four graves of their comrades in the Australian War Cemetery, decided to take over responsibility for the upkeep of the Japanese graves as well. When the Japanese government came to make a decision, in the early 1960s, about the repatriation of the soldiers' remains, officials visited the cemetery at Cowra and were so impressed with the way the graves had been looked after that, with the cooperation of the Australian Government and local authorities, they decided to establish an official Japanese War Cemetery at Cowra. All 522 Japanese who died during the Second World War on Australian soil, at Cowra, in internment camps or during the attack on Darwin, are now buried at the official, Japanese-style cemetery at Cowra. An avenue of cherry trees now runs the five kilometres between the Australian and Japanese cemeteries.

A Japanese Garden and Cultural Centre, built on the hillside near the former camp in 1979, is similar in style to the imperial gardens at Kyoto and was designed by Ken Nakajima, a prominent Japanese landscape architect. Cowra High School runs a student exchange program with high schools in Tokyo and Nara, and the annual Lachlan Festival in Cowra has adopted 'international understanding' as a theme.

In 1991 all these efforts led to Cowra being awarded the World Peace Bell. Instead of fading into obscurity or perhaps becoming an emotional catalyst for ongoing suspicion between the two nations involved, the Cowra 'incident', unique in Australia's history, has instead led to the exact opposite. □

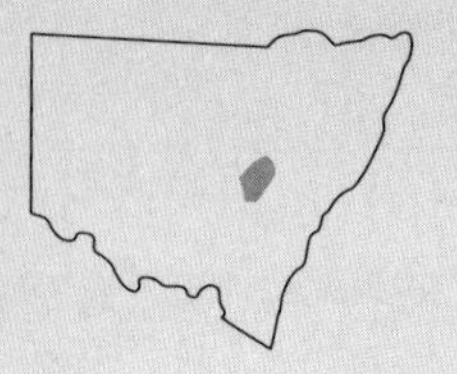

Wellington & Molong

This valley rich in natural resources, which Oxley praised in 1817, is watered by the Macquarie River and Lake Burrendong, and protected by the Catombal Ranges. It was the first area west of Bathurst to be settled by Europeans.

There is always something in flower at the Burrendong Arboretum – such as (left to right) mottlecah, blue lechenaultia, Sturt's desert rose and orange stars – where native plants from all climates are brought together.

BELL RIVER ■ 388

When John Oxley crossed the Bell River on his return journey to Bathurst in August 1817, he named this 'strong and beautiful stream' the Bell River after Brevet Major Bell of the 48th Regiment.

The Bell River has its headwaters east of Molong (see entry) and initially flows west almost to Larras Lee before turning north and flowing through Wellington to join the larger Macquarie River. On one memorable occasion, in 1955, the two rivers joined forces, banking up at Wellington, and hitting Dubbo with the largest flood in living memory. But to most locals the Bell River is the pretty river that flows through Cameron Park, one of the most attractive spots in Wellington.

BURRENDONG STATE RECREATION AREA AND ARBORETUM ■ 389

This recreation area comprises two distinct and physically separate sections – Burrendong, on the main arm of Lake Burrendong (see entry) and accessible from the Apsley–Mumbil road, and Mookerawa, on the Macquarie River arm of the lake and accessible from the old gold-rush village, Stuart Town.

In addition to the usual range of water sports and fishing (for redfin, golden perch and cod) available on the man-made lake, there are nature trails, gold fossicking, a mountain-bicycle track and a skateboard rink within the area. But the most distinctive feature of this recreation area is the Burrendong Arboretum.

Established by community efforts in 1964, the 160-hectare arboretum holds 40 000 native plants of 2000 species. The aim is to establish and protect every known species of Australian tree, shrub and plant – 10 000 species to be collected within the next 70–80 years. A unique microclimate for the cultivation of ferns and subtropical plants has been built in a gully, protected by a bush-covered structure suspended by cables that covers an area of 1400 square metres.

CUDGEGONG RIVER PARK ■ 390

On the eastern, or Mudgee, side of Lake Burrendong, Cudgegong River Park was established the year Lake Burrendong was filled. Unlike Burrendong State Recreation Area (see entry) Cudgegong River Park is not administered by the National Parks and Wildlife Service, but by trustees appointed by the Department of Land and Water Resources, who manage the facilities, including one hundred permanent caravan sites, on a non-profit basis.

LAKE BURRENDONG ■ 391

Although construction of the Burrendong Dam on the Macquarie River commenced immediately after the Second World War, for financial reasons, the dam was not completed until 1967. With a capacity of almost two million megalitres of water, the lake has a surface area of ninety square kilometres and a maximum depth of fifty metres.

One of the largest of the state's man-made water storage lakes, Lake Burrendong supplies water for irrigation of the crops – primarily cotton – of the Macquarie Valley and for flood mitigation. Flood outflows, directed by a concrete spillway, are operated by seven huge radial gates.

MACQUARIE RIVER ■ 392

The Fish and Campbell rivers join forces at Bathurst to emerge as the Macquarie River, which flows in a north-westerly direction through the towns of Wellington, Dubbo and Warren then west to join the Darling River…or dissipate in the Macquarie Marshes before reaching the Darling. This basic information on the Macquarie River was not easily won and expeditions by Evans (1813), Oxley (1817 and 1818), Sturt (1828) and finally, Mitchell (1831) were needed to unlock the secrets of the Macquarie for Europeans.

The Aboriginal name for the Macquarie River was 'wambool' said to mean 'place of a river' and the many carved trees on its banks suggest that there were a number of burial and initiation sites along its length. To Europeans, ignorant of the continent's interior, the Macquarie River was the route to the elusive inland sea or great lake, a phantom which fascinated explorers for many years.

The Macquarie Marshes, which prevented Oxley from reaching the Darling River, are the largest wetland area in the Murray–Darling system and cover 148 000 hectares with a complex of lagoons, channels and marshes that never dry up. Half of the area of the marshes has been a wildlife sanctuary since 1955.

MANILDRA ■ 393

First settled in 1830, Manildra is located on the banks of Mandagery Creek and midway between Orange and Parkes. The flour mill at Manildra, one of the largest and most modern in New South Wales, has led to Manildra becoming the location for the National Bread Show. The show attracts entries from small-scale and large commercial bread manufacturers around Australia.

Just outside Manildra lies an area known as the 'Gumble Scrub', which provides the habitat for at least one unique species of parrot.

MOLONG ■ 394

Molong, from an Aboriginal word said to mean 'all rocks', sits among the stony outcrops of the Macquarie Range. The town, on the Rural Way between Orange and Dubbo, is well known for its wheat, wool and beautiful poplar trees.

In the 1840s, Molong was a stockade and government stockyard on the route to the convict settlement at Wellington (see entry). The first land grants were made in the early 1830s to William Lee, who called his property 'Larras Lake' (the stone entrance gates can still be seen at Larras Lee) and to Reverend Samuel Marsden and his three daughters. Mary Marsden's grant adjoined the town of Molong when it was gazetted in 1847 but her homestead 'Roundhouse' is now derelict.

The first copper mine in New South Wales was opened in Molong in the 1840s but the 1870s and 1880s were the boom times for Molong and, by the start of the rural depression in 1890, Molong had the same population as it has today. Many old buildings that have been given a new lease of life – such as the historic cottage which houses the Yarn Market, the coach house of the New

Every dog has its day in Molong, where sheepdogs show their mettle at the annual NSW championships.

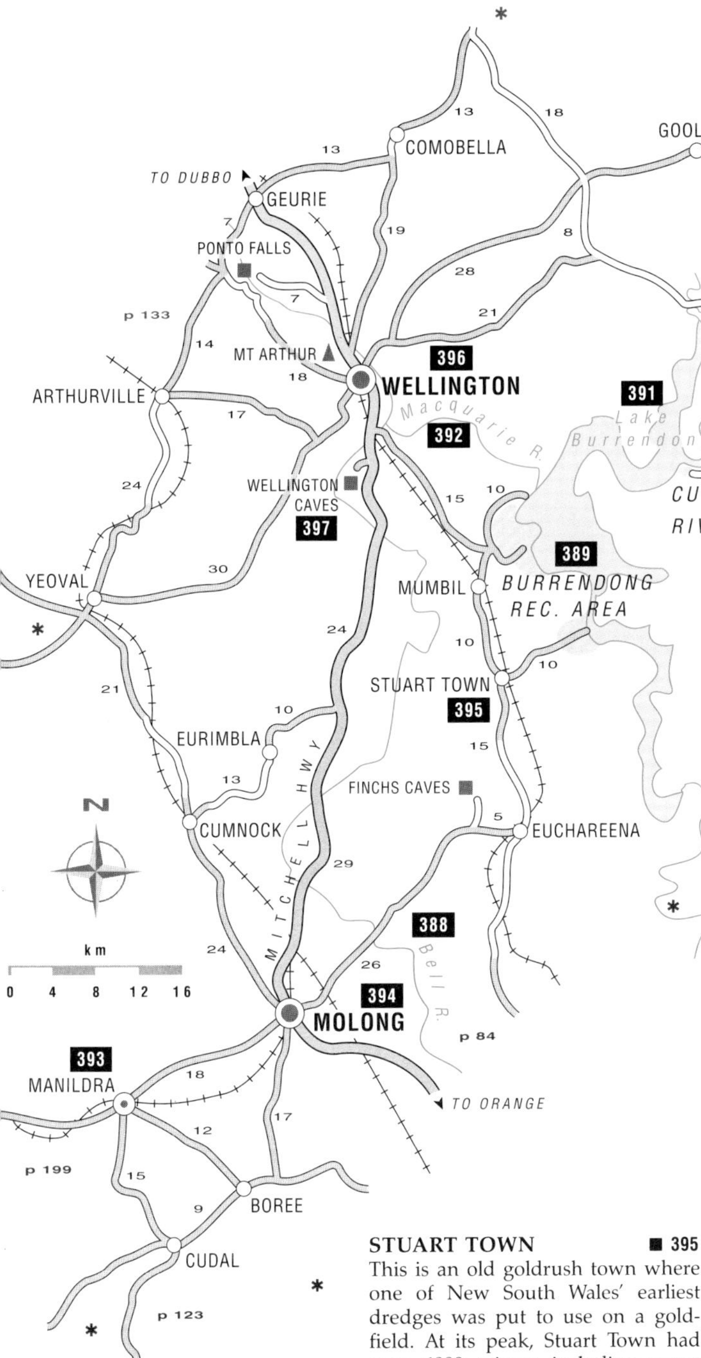

Royal Hotel, which is now a Craft and Exhibition Centre and the former Golden Fleece Hotel, now a historical museum – were constructed before 1890. *Population 1560*

YURANIGH'S GRAVE Yuranigh, who was Major Thomas Mitchell's highly respected Aboriginal guide on his 1846 exploration, died at Gamboola Station at Molong in 1850. His grave, marked by four carved trees signifying a man of great standing in the Aboriginal community, is also surrounded by a fence erected by the government at Mitchell's request. The headstone inscribed and paid for by Mitchell himself was replaced with a marble slab in 1900.

FESTIVALS Australian Sheepdog Trials (NSW Championships), March; Molong May Festival, May.

STUART TOWN ■ 395

This is an old goldrush town where one of New South Wales' earliest dredges was put to use on a goldfield. At its peak, Stuart Town had over 6000 miners including many Chinese – there are over fifty old mineshafts in the hills above the village as well as a Chinese oven. Between 1860 and 1914, when the last mine closed, over 4350 kilograms of gold were mined at Stuart Town.

Every Australian child knows the story about the man from Stuart Town...though Banjo Paterson used the old name for the town in his poem *The Man from Ironbark*. Banjo Paterson spent his childhood years in Yeoval, on the other side of the Mitchell Highway from 'Ironbarks' or Stuart Town.

WELLINGTON ■ 396

A convict settlement was founded in 1823 where Wellington now stands and the hard-worked convicts built a number of buildings including a commandant's house, a brick office, a military barracks and a log and weatherboard jail, before the settlement was abandoned in 1830.

In 1831 the abandoned government buildings were given to the Church Missionary Society for the opening of a mission for the local Aborigines. When a town was later proposed, the society objected on the grounds that this would interfere with its work and its mission. The society's view prevailed and the government approved a settlement at Newrea instead. It was not, therefore, until after the mission closed in the 1840s that a township developed on its site and was proclaimed as the town of Wellington in 1846.

The discovery of gold in the 1850s and the coming of the railway in 1880 brought growth, though not a sudden boom, to Wellington and it was during this period that many of the older buildings in the town such as the Bank of New South Wales (1883) – now the museum – and the Church of St John the Baptist(1867) were built. The first train, forced to run on rails laid under the shallow water, was hauled across the Macquarie River by horses in 1880.

Wellington today is the commercial centre for a rural district noted for its lucerne, wheat, wool and beef, and, more recently, two wineries. The town, at the junction of the Macquarie and Bell rivers, is overlooked by Mount Arthur (540 metres), which is now a nature reserve. Cameron Park makes up one side of the main street running down to the Bell River. The sunken gardens within the park are on the site of the former municipal baths and the adjoining lily pond was once the children's pool. *Population 5430*

MONTEFIORES The private town of Montefiores was established by a wealthy tea merchant on the northern side of the Macquarie River. The town was strategically placed at the point where all traffic and provisions had to cross the river. It is thought that the last known duel fought in Australia – between two drunken police magistrates, one of whom fired one shot that hit no-one – was fought in the town in 1854.

A surface area three-and-a-half times that of Sydney Harbour makes Lake Burrendong a mecca for devotees of watersports.

WELLINGTON CAVES ■ 397

Situated on Bell River, the Wellington Caves were discovered by the explorers Charles Sturt and Hamilton Hume in 1828. Cathedral Cave contains one of the largest stalagmites in the world. Known as 'The Madonna', the stalagmite rises from the floor to a height of fifteen metres and measures thirty-two metres around its base. Cathedral Cave has been open to the public since 1870.

When Rankin and Thomas Mitchell explored the Wellington Caves together in 1830 they came upon Bone Cave, so named because it contained the bones of giant, extinct animals including the diprotodon (which looks like a cross between a giant wombat and a trunkless, small-eared elephant). This discovery sent ripples of excitement throughout the scientific community when a paper on it was read to the Geological Society in London in 1831 and the cave is today reserved for scientists because of its value as a souce of information on Australia's prehistory.

In 1884 the first caretaker for the caves, James Sibbald, was appointed and it was he who discovered Gaden Cave in 1902. This cave is noted for its cave 'coral' – clusters of calcite nodules growing like short stalks out of the cave walls. Gaden Cave is the only other cave, apart from Cathedral Cave, which is open to the public. Caves no longer open to the public include Gaspipe which was closed in 1958 after very high levels of carbon dioxide were measured in its atmosphere.

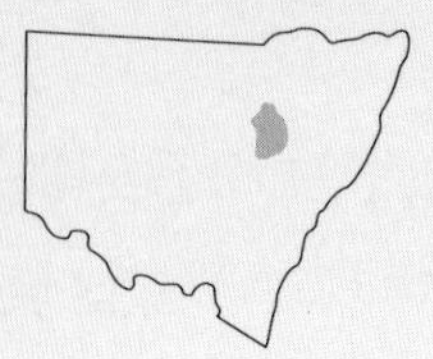

Coonabarabran & Coolah

Beyond the ancient mountains and volcanic spires of the jagged Warrumbungle Range is the flat expanse of the wheat and sheep country of central western New South Wales. The astronomical sophistication of the Siding Spring Observatory is a stark contrast to the region's rural focus.

BARADINE ■ 398

The small sawmilling town of Baradine – an Aboriginal word said to mean 'red wallaby' – owes its existence to the flat expanse of wild forest and scrubland covering almost half-a-million hectares of countryside between the Warrumbungle and the Nandewar Ranges, known as the Pilliga Scrub (see entry).

A substantial part of the Pilliga Scrub comprises state forests from which huge quantities of cypress pine and ironbark trees are culled. At the southern end of this vast area of scrub vegetation is Baradine, the commercial and population centre for the region's considerable timber production industry. *Population 660*

BINNAWAY ■ 399

Binnaway, on the banks of the sluggish Castlereagh River (see entry) was settled in the mid-1880s, and in those days was an important junction for railway lines that served the agricultural settlements of the central west. From the axis of Binnaway, railway lines radiated north-west to Gwabegar, south-west to Dubbo, east to Werris Creek and south to Mudgee. Nowadays, the town's chief activity is the fortnightly stock sales that attract buyers throughout the region, though it has a small claim to fame as the location of the film *The Shiralee*, starring Peter Finch and made in 1956. *Population 530*

THE BLACK STUMP ■ 400

A large black stump placed in a roadside rest area approximately nine kilometres north of Coolah advertises the shire's strong association with the original black stump popularised in the colloquial Australian expressions 'beyond the black stump' and 'this side of the black stump'.

Four towns spread across three states all lay claim to a 'black stump'. But of these places, the Coolah district is generally regarded as having the strongest claim on the original 'black stump' of Australian folklore – if such an object ever existed – its association with the name going back more than 120 years.

During pioneering days of teamsters, bullock waggons and Cobb & Co. coaches, the Coolah Shire was dotted with inns that catered for travellers on the long and comfortless coach routes. The best known of these was the Black Stump Wine Saloon – a busy staging post at the junction of several coach roads that was destroyed by fire in 1908. The inn took its name from the nearby 'Black Stump' run and Black Stump Creek. Today, a charred stump standing at a roadside rest area about ten kilometres north of Coolah – near the former site of the Black Stump Wine Saloon – marks the district's historical link with this symbolic reference to the nameless, nether lands of the continent's vast interior.

As a place name, the origins of the black stump are not clear, but as the mythical marker of the limits of civilisation, an explanation may be found in the Coolah Shire's account of Governor Darling's proclamation in 1826 concerning the 'limits of location ...beyond which land was neither sold nor let' nor 'settlers allowed'. In 1829 the boundary limiting the spread of settlement was described by three rivers: the Manning River in the north, the Moruya River in the south and the Lachlan River in the west. The approximate location of the 'Black Stump' run in the Coolah Shire formed part of this boundary. Inevitably, graziers encroached upon the restricted areas beyond the 'limits' and in the Coolah area, these illegal grazing areas were vaguely referred to as being 'beyond the black stump'.

CASTLEREAGH RIVER ■ 401

The great hook of the Castlereagh River rises in the Warrumbungle Range near Siding Spring Observatory, taking in the waters of the many creeks which drain the country of the Warrumbungles. From its headwaters, the river winds through Coonabarabran, Binnaway and Mendooran (see entries) before curving north-west through Gilgandra and carving a path through the extensive wheat and sheep plains that surround Coonamble, finding its final destination in the Macquarie River. The river's 550-kilometre length is broken occasionally by sandbanks that build up on the river bed and contribute to its sluggish passage, a trait noted in A.B. 'Banjo' Paterson's poem, 'The Travelling Post Office':

The roving breezes come and go, the
reed beds sweep and sway,
The sleepy river murmurs low, and
loiters on its way,
It is the land of lots o'time along
the Castlereagh.

The river was discovered by the explorer George Evans in 1818 and named after Viscount Castlereagh, the Secretary for the Colonies.

The sluggish waters of the Castlereagh, in no hurry to keep their appointment with the Macquarie River, often come to a standstill, thereby providing a haven for water birds such as black swans.

COOLAH ■ 402

Coolah has been officially recognised as the home of the original black stump, with its own pictorial postmark (see entry and above right). The black stump has been associated with the town for more than 120 years, with a sheep run, a creek and an inn – all within the district in the colonial days – bearing the name.

The Coolah area was discovered by the botanist and explorer, Allan Cunningham, in 1823. After a three-month journey from Bathurst (see *Orange & Bathurst*), Cunningham traversed the Warrumbungle Range at Pandoras Pass and was rewarded by a magnificent view of the Liverpool Plains and Coolah Valley. An interesting but unsubstantiated story has it that he was so inspired by the land's potential for settlement that he buried a bottle containing a message, which upon discovery was to be delivered to the inhabitants of Bathurst. However, the town's citizens wait in vain, for the bottle has never been found.

After Cunningham, came the early pioneers who took up land along the banks of the Coolaburragundy River and European settlement began in earnest from the 1830s. By 1848 Coolah consisted of a motley assortment of primitive, ironbark slab buildings; within thirty years these structures had been replaced by more gracious sandstone constructions, some of which still stand today. East of the town lie the dense state forests of the Coolah Tops, which have supplied hardwood – mainly stringybark – to the timber mill at Coolah since logging operations commenced in the region in 1941.

In addition to the long-established hardwood industry which supplies

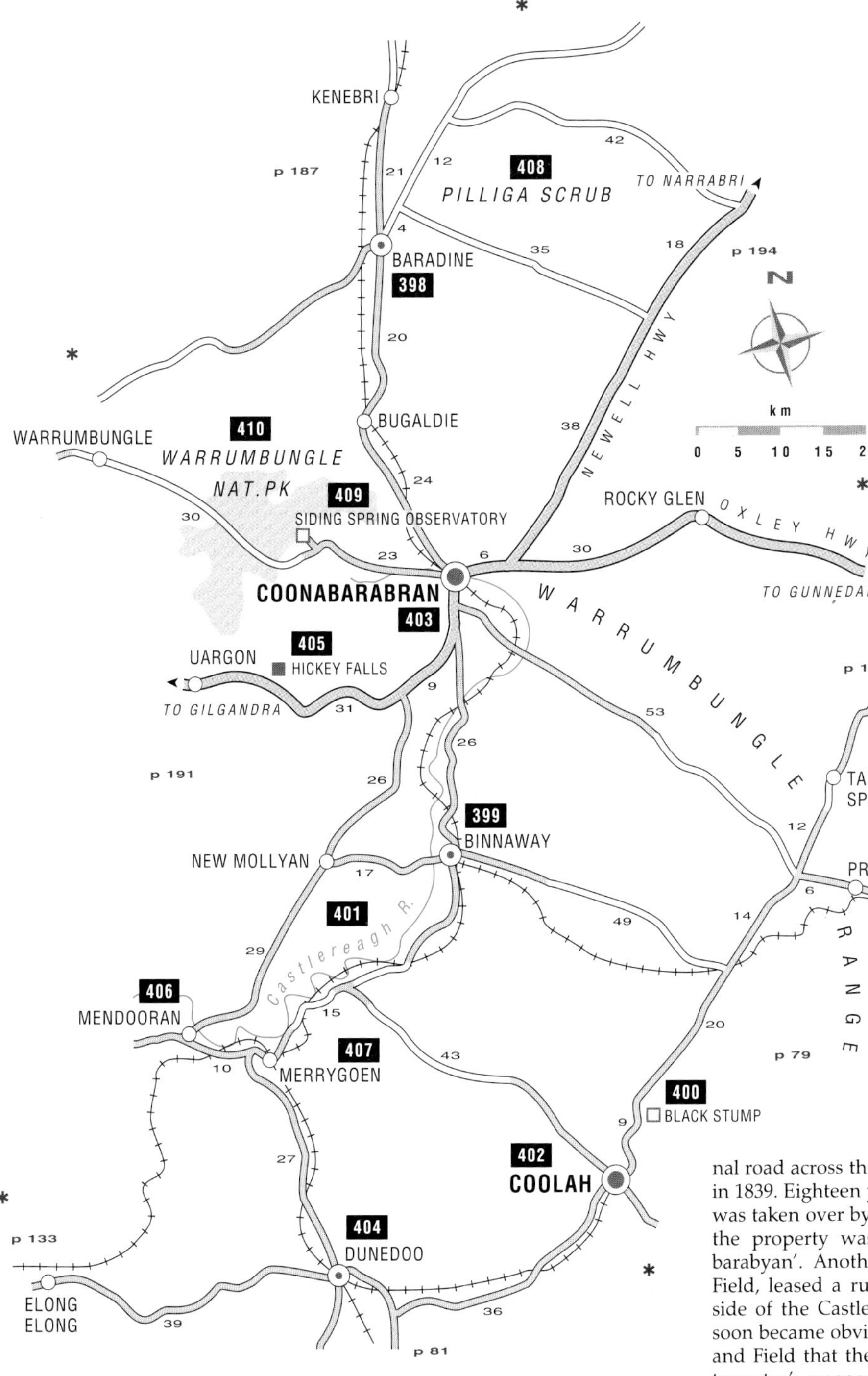

timber for general-purpose building and railway sleepers, Coolah has a substantial rural industry base which includes mixed farming, prime cattle, fat lambs and superfine wool production. *Population 890*

FESTIVALS Coolah Rodeo, Boxing Day, December.

COONABARABRAN ■ **403**

Proximity to Siding Spring Observatory and Warrumbungle National Park (see entries) gives Coonabarabran a promotional double-billing as the 'astronomy capital of Australia' and the 'gateway to the Warrumbungles'. The town sits astride the slow-flowing Castlereagh River (see entry) and is the commercial centre of a large pastoral and agricultural district. Coonabarabran is believed to be an Aboriginal word meaning 'inquisitive person'.

At the junction of two major inland highways – the Oxley and the Newell – Coonabarabran has witnessed the passing parade of traffic for more than a century. As a commodious stopping place for modern travellers using the main north-south road-route, the town carries on a tradition of hospitality that began early in the last century when teamsters loaded with wool traversed the district on their way to the markets at Newcastle and Sydney.

Like many country towns, Coonabarabran was once a squatting run for sheep and cattle. 'Cooleburbarun' was leased by George and Henry Cox – the sons of William Cox who supervised the building of the original road across the Blue Mountains – in 1839. Eighteen years later the lease was taken over by James Weston and the property was renamed 'Coolabarabyan'. Another grazier, William Field, leased a run on the northern side of the Castlereagh River and it soon became obvious to both Weston and Field that the constant traffic of teamster's waggons through the area would be profitably served by a hotel and store. The two bush inns that were erected became the centre of an early settlement.

By 1858 the little settlement had a police force but no jail. Law enforcement was somewhat primitive but effective. Persons charged with dangerous horse riding were handcuffed by a set of bullock chains to the nearest gum tree – or to a police officer for twenty-four hours! Justice was served in a more conventional fashion with the construction of a wooden lock-up and court house in 1860 – the same year that the first government land auctions were held in the district and the town was gazetted as Coonabarabran.

The railway line did not reach Coonabarabran until 1917. When it did arrive, it caused a revolution in the transport of goods, with trains proving a much more efficient mode of transport than the Cobb & Co. coaches that had served the district so well.

Wheat and wool are still the district's main industries but the natural splendour of the volcanic rock formations in the Warrumbungles and the astronomical marvel of Siding Spring Observatory (see entries) are the real drawcards for visitors to the town. *Population 2960*

DUNEDOO ■ **404**

The low hills and wide valleys of the countryside surrounding Dunedoo, are favoured with a temperate climate that makes the region a fertile ground for growing wheat, sheep and cattle. The first settlers in the district arrived in the 1830s but it was not until 1868 that the original town site was plotted and named Dunedoo – an Aboriginal word for swan – after the graceful creatures inhabiting nearby lagoons. The slow development of the little town can be charted through the growth of its services: the railway arrived in 1910; wheat silos were erected in 1936 and the town water supply was turned on in 1939. Dunedoo is favoured with an invaluable resource in the form of unlimited quantities of artesian water – even in the driest times, the town has never been short of water. *Population 830*

HICKEY FALLS ■ **405**

A roadside rest area known locally as Devil's Hole provides the parking space for visitors to Hickey Falls, a popular summer retreat with picnic facilities. The falls shower down from a rocky outcrop in the bed of Wallumburrawang Creek, which rises in the Warrumbungle National Park and flows into the Castlereagh River south-east of Gilgandra.

MENDOORAN ■ **406**

The sparsely settled and quiet village of Mendooran has the distinction of being the oldest settlement on the Castlereagh River, with a settlement thought to have existed as early as the 1840s. Of chief interest to visitors are the substantial quantities of semi-precious stones, such as agate and jasper, and petrified wood that can be found readily in the district.

ULUNGRA SPRINGS North of Mendooran on the road to Tooraweenah (see *Gilgandra & Nyngan*) are the Ulungra Springs, an inviting area where reeds and rushes bristle in the cool waters. The springs are part of the Ulungra Reserve and are often mentioned in connection with tales of early pioneers.

MERRYGOEN ■ **407**

Merrygoen's local hotel was built in 1915 with the anticipation of giving long and profitable service to the residents of the then thriving township.

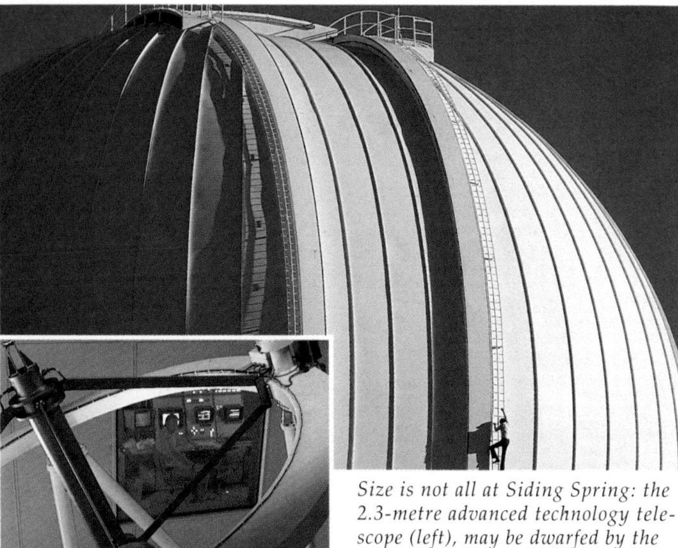

Size is not all at Siding Spring: the 2.3-metre advanced technology telescope (left), may be dwarfed by the giant dome housing the 4-metre Anglo-Australian telescope (above), but it has an array of sophisticated attachments that extend its optical range and versatility.

But the fledgling community never achieved the dimensions of a substantial town and became instead the quiet village of today.

PILLIGA SCRUB ■ 408

The Pilliga Scrub – a vast expanse of semi-arid open forest and heathland that spreads across the country north of the Warrumbungle Range – has earned a place in the history of Australian literature as the subject of an award-winning book by Eric Rolls entitled, *A Million Wild Acres* and as the setting for Kylie Tennant's book, *The Honey Flow*.

Much of the Pilliga Scrub comprises the largest state forest in New South Wales and a substantial section forms the Pilliga Nature Reserve. The dense forest is dominated by cypress pine – widely used as floor boards – with substantial tracts of narrowleaf ironbark that is used for railway sleepers and fencing timber. Aside from timber production the Pilliga State Forest is used for various purposes including honey production, grazing, recreation and as a sanctuary for the region's diverse wildlife. A network of forest drives built for timber harvesting and fire protection leads visitors along tree-lined avenues to points of interest where picnic facilities are provided.

In spring, the broom plains of the Pilliga Scrub are transformed by the blooms of a profusion of wildflowers including wattles, native daisies, flannel flowers and Darling peas.

The name Pilliga is based on an Aboriginal word believed to mean 'swamp oak'.

SIDING SPRING OBSERVATORY ■ 409

Siding Spring Observatory, with its eight telescopes tracking the movement of objects in deep space, is one of the largest and best equipped optical observatories in the world.

The observatory is owned by the Australian National University and its site – selected in 1962 as a field station for the Mount Stromlo Observatory at Canberra and overlooking Warrumbungle National Park – is free from the obfuscatory effects of light and dust pollution and enjoys a high proportion of cloudless nights, thus making it the perfect location for stellar research. By the mid-1960s, three telescopes were operating at the newly constructed observatory and in 1984 the university's largest telescope – the innovative 2.3-metre telescope, that can be enhanced to operate as a direct imaging, spectra or infra-red instrument – was introduced to the complex.

Lengthy negotiations between the Australian and British governments during the 1950s, about a jointly constructed large telescope, came to fruition in 1969 when Siding Spring Observatory was chosen as the site for the four-metre Anglo-Australian Telescope. Housed in a concrete building over fifty metres high and topped by a weighty, rotating steel dome, the telescope has become a prominent landmark in the area.

WARRUMBUNGLE NATIONAL PARK ■ 410

The awe-inspiring domes, spires and mesas of Warrumbungle National Park, jutting out from the central-west plains of New South Wales are remnants of colossal volcanic forces that gave birth to the spectacular and ancient landscape some thirteen million years ago. The explorer and Surveyor-General, John Oxley, was the first European to sight the Warrumbungles in 1818. He named the range Arbuthnot after a British civil servant. The name was later changed to Warrumbungle – an Aboriginal word said to mean 'broken, crooked mountains'. Oxley's first view of the Warrumbungles clearly impressed him and his journal account is generous in its praise, 'To the east a most stupendous range of mountains, lifting their blue heads above the horizon...' and 'From east northeast to south, the country was broken and irregular; lofty hills arising from the midst of lesser elevations, their summits crowned with perpendicular rocks, in every variety of shape and form, that the wildest imagination could paint.'

Of all the rock formations in the park, the Breadknife is the most outstanding – a ninety-metre-high sheet of igneous rock that is a mere metre thick. Rock climbers may be tempted by this slender silhouette but are forbidden the challenge of its imposing face. The park's towering spires and domes such as Crater Bluff, Tonduron Spire and The Needle, are remnants of ancient volcanoes that blocked their own throats with hard, trachyte plugs resistant to the erosive forces that have worn away their soft casing of solidified lava and ash.

Frequently described as the point where east meets west, the Warrumbungles support an extraordinary combination of plants and animals from both the dry western plains and the moist east coast. The park's rich volcanic soils are forested with eucalypts dominated by white box trees. White gum, narrowleaf ironbark and black and white cypress pine thrive on the drier sandstone soils and outcrops of volcanic rocks, while heath and snow-gum grow on the high tops. Wild fig trees create a deep green canopy in the moist gullies where ferns also flourish. In the spring, the sandstone areas come to life with colourful wildflowers.

With such a diverse range of habitats, the Warrumbungles teem with wildlife. The 180 recorded species of birds in the park includes almost one third of Australia's species of cockatoos and parrots with hundreds of brightly-plumaged rainbow lorikeets, scaly-breasted lorikeets, king parrots, crimson rosellas, blue bonnets and spotted pardalotes creating a blur of colour in the tree canopy.

The park began life as a recreation reserve in 1953 and was declared a national park two years later. Since then, it has grown steadily to its present size of just over 21 000 hectares.

Too sheer for vegetation, the once-molten Breadknife slices it way 100 metres above the Warrumbungles.

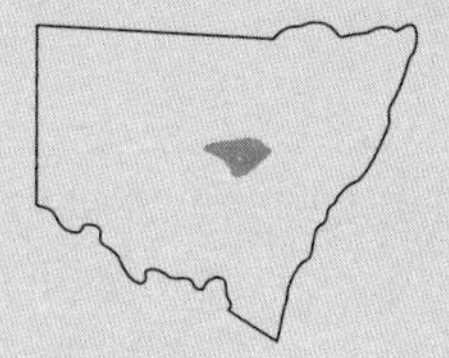

Dubbo & Narromine

In the 1880s, the push west to the central plains of New South Wales was led by the railway. Trains meant speedy transport for the wheat that was transforming the plains into a golden belt of grain which provided the economic mainstay for this region's developing communities.

BALLIMORE ■ 411

A search for coal deposits near the small town of Ballimore in the 1880s, led to the discovery of an underground spring – in fact a bore which struck artesian water – from which drinkable water has been flowing ever since. The bore is located on private property about seven kilometres north-east of Ballimore where the remains of a now defunct, bottling operation are visible in the pipes that protrude from the ground – though travellers can still stop and refresh themselves with 'spring' water.

DANDALOO ■ 412

During the dusty days of horse and carriage travel, Dandaloo was one of the biggest changing stations in New South Wales with a hotel, general store, blacksmith's shop, cafe, school and post office. But the advent of improved roads and motor transport meant a diminished role for the town and the population dwindled.

'Banjo' Paterson wrote his poems 'An Idyll of Dandaloo' and 'An Evening in Dandaloo' during the town's heyday and a somnolent account of the place is given in the opening lines of *An Idyll of Dandaloo*:

On Western plains, where shade is not,
'Neath summer skies of cloudless blue,
Where all is dry and all is hot,
There stands the town of Dandaloo
A township where life's total sum
Is sleep, diversified with rum.
Its grass-grown streets with dust are deep,
'Twere vain endeavour to express
The dreamless silence of its sleep,
Its wide, expansive drunkenness.

DUBBO ■ 413

Dubbo has long been known as the 'hub of the west' because of its geographical location as a service centre for the Orana region – an area covering a quarter of New South Wales. From 1824, the district was settled by squatters and one of them, Robert Venour Dulhunty, gave the area its name when he called his run Dubbo – supposedly after a venerable Aboriginal elder he found camped in the vicinity. Another version has it that the name is an Aboriginal word meaning 'a man's hat'. But Dubbo really came into being because a young Frenchman had a sudden attack of appendicitis!

Jean Emile de Bouillon Serisier was struck down with appendicitis during a round-the-world voyage and was put ashore in Sydney. Eventually he went to Wellington (see *Wellington & Molong*) in 1847 to establish a trading post.

Serisier quickly realised there were more possibilities further north along the Macquarie River where a large north-south trade in cattle was developing. He went downstream to where Dubbo is now located and built a crude slab store – the first commercial venture in the area.

One of Dubbo's early magistrates was Thomas Alexander Browne who supported his large family by writing and it was at Dubbo that he penned *Robbery Under Arms* using the pseudonym, Rolf Boldrewood. The novel was the most successful book published in Australia during the last century, earning Browne more than ten thousand pounds – a huge sum in those days.

Today, Dubbo is a prosperous regional service centre with one of Australia's largest saleyards operations and a widely diversified rural economy. In recent years, it has also developed as a major tourist destination largely as a result of the establishment of the Western Plains Zoo (see box). *Population 28 070*

COURT HOUSE This Victorian Classical court house located in Brisbane Street was built in 1847 and designed by the Colonial Architect, James Barnet. Remarkably, it still retains its original court-room fittings.

OLD DUBBO JAIL Solid sandstone buildings and manicured lawns surrounded by foreboding walls are the tranquil setting for a building with a chilling past. By the time the jail closed in 1966, eight men had met their end on the gallows which still stand in the main yard. The jail is thought to have been built in 1871.

FESTIVALS Country Life Expo, March; Antique Fair, July.

EUMUNGERIE ■ 414

Eumungerie is an Aboriginal word for the quandong, a native peach tree that offered much appreciated variety to the simple fare of early settlers. Now a quiet dormitory suburb of Dubbo, the small village of Eumungerie evolved from a roadside inn-cum-store known as The Coalbaggie Inn that was established in 1874. Between 1872 and 1881, various selectors took up blocks of land surrounding the inn and before long a small settlement grew up taking its name from the hotel. Development was spurred by the arrival of the railway line in 1901. The timber mill that opened by the new railway line at Coalbaggie Creek became the focus of the timber-getters and sleeper-cutters who worked the ironbark-rich plains surrounding the settlement. By the time the village was dedicated as Eumungerie in 1904 there were already several businesses in operation including a smithy, butchery, bakery and post office.

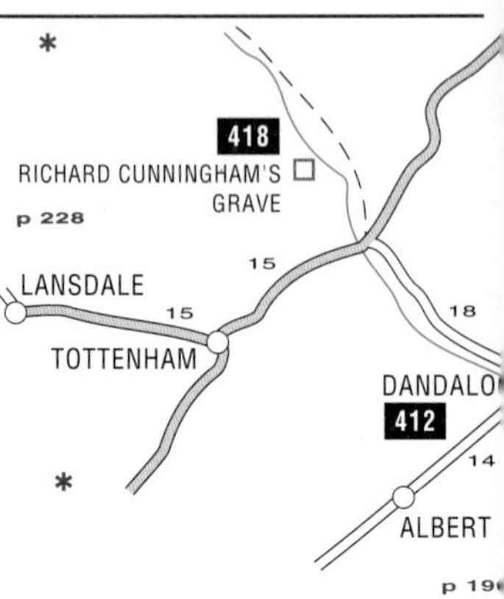

The 1881 rail bridge underlined Dubbo's importance as a junction.

GIN GIN WEIR ■ 415

Nowadays, the chief usage of the old Gin Gin Weir is recreational, with picnicking, fishing and bushwalking the most popular activities around its shores. The weir was built in 1896 for irrigation purposes but flood waters since have damaged the walls and reduced the weir's capacity to a fraction of what it was originally.

NARROMINE ■ 416

By the time the railway line reached the Narromine area in 1882, a township was already established, ready to absorb the flow of new settlers, many of whom came to make their living as wheatfarmers.

The settlement was originally the site of 'Narramine', a station established by Thomas Raine – the first settler in the district – in 1840, and later taken over by the famous explorer, William Charles Wentworth. The station was sold in 1870 and by the turn of the century, pas-

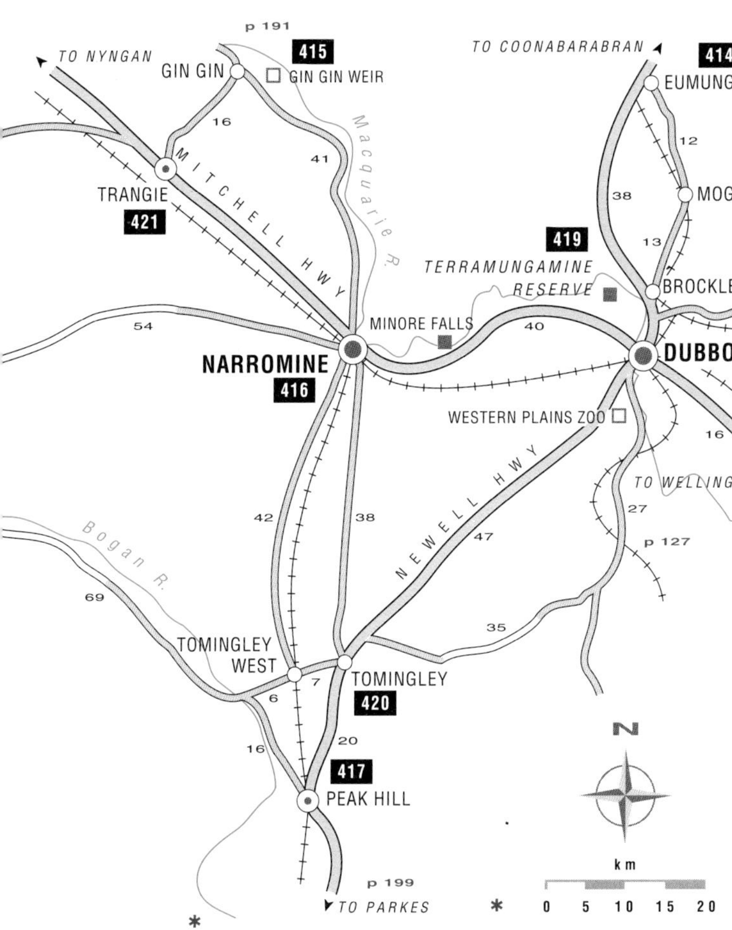

Behind Dubbo's elaborately decorated 1890 court house is a streamlined, steel-and-glass complex.

toral holdings were considerably reduced and widespread wheat cultivation predominated.

Citrus crops, for which the region is now well known, were not introduced until 1913. From 1967, the new Burrendong Dam further boosted the region's agricultural output.

Narromine is noted for its thriving gliding club and proudly accords itself the subtitle 'gliding capital of Australia'. The club operates from the huge Narromine aerodrome that during the Second World War was used by the RAAF as a training-school for pilots. *Population 3380*

PEAK HILL ■ 417

Gold was discovered north-west of Dubbo in 1883 but it was the discovery of gold at 'The Peak' in 1889 and at 'The Golden Hole' in 1890 that sparked an immense rush with people swarming to the area in the hope of striking it rich. A few months after the 'Peak' discovery, the population of the hastily laid-out town of Peak Hill had reached 10 000. A report from the 14 September 1890 issue of the *Evening News*, conveys the chaos and excitement of the rush: 'Several passenger coaches arrived today and are now laid up like the ships at Sydney, as the drivers went in for pick and shovel, and did not care to go back for passengers. All hands from the battery, from the manager downwards have become diggers. The streets are thronged with great crowds of men...' But the press reports gave a somewhat false impression – Peak Hill gold was a low grade ore; cyanide treatment made it profitable. The rush was actually short-lived as volatile miners swamped the town for a month or so before leaving for greener pastures.

The open-cut goldmine that gave birth to the town is now a tourist attraction The two massive holes that were gouged out by hand can be seen from a lookout. *Population 980*

RICHARD CUNNINGHAM'S GRAVE ■ 418

Richard Cunningham – the younger brother of well known botanist and explorer, Allan Cunningham – was appointed Colonial Botanist in 1832. Three years later he accompanied the Surveyor-General, Sir Thomas Mitchell, on an expedition into western New South Wales. At the Bogan River, south-west of today's Dandaloo, Cunningham met a violent death. Leaving the main group on 17 April to trace Mitchell's footsteps to the night's camp, Cunningham lost his way and was never seen alive again. Some time later, police arrested three Aborigines who confessed to killing the botanist. His grave site is marked by a memorial stone.

TERRAMUNGAMINE RESERVE ■ 419

This reserve is the site of the Terramungamine grinding grooves that were used by the local Aborigines for sharpening their tools and weapons. These indentations – some one-hundred-and-fifty of them – can be seen on an outcrop of rock that extends for about one hundred metres along the bank of the Macquarie River.

TOMINGLEY ■ 420

Prior to the discovery of alluvial gold at Peak Hill (see entry) in 1889, the Tomingley goldfield was regarded as the most important and promising gold discovery in this region. Quartz reefs showing gold of exceptional value were discovered in the vicinity of the Bogan River in 1881 and soon after, a township sprang up.

But by 1884 many of the quartz reefs were stripped of their gold and within another three years gold-mining operations at Tomingley were almost at a standstill – only the Myall Reefs continued to yield payable quantities of the precious ore.

TRANGIE ■ 421

The extension of the railway line from Dubbo to Nevertire (see *Gilgandra & Nyngan*) in 1882 established Trangie's place on the map. Pastoral properties throughout the region loaded their wool clips at railheads along the line and a township soon formed at Trangie, on land that was earlier part of Weemaabah Station.

Commercial enterprises sprang up in response to the steady flow of settlers to the region. In 1909, Trangie became the location for a government-funded experimental farm for the development of improved strains of wheat and the breeding of Merino sheep in the area. Cotton is now the major crop, cultivated on land watered by the Burrendong Dam irrigation network, and sorghum, maize, lucerne and safflower are also grown. *Population 990*

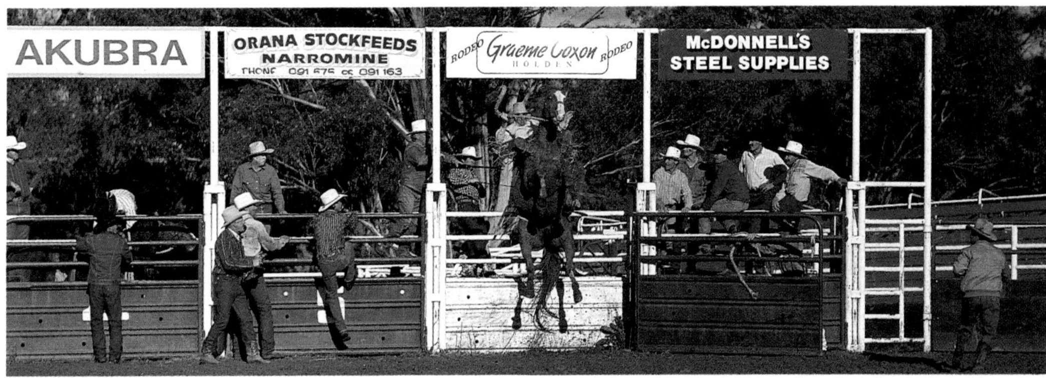

Blue jeans and bravado are the order of the day as stockmen risk life and limb on the rodeo circuit of the mid-west.

A 'FREE RANGE' ZOO, WITHOUT BARS

THE Western Plains Zoo is located near Dubbo on the undulating plains of the central west, far from the population centres of major cities – which might seem an odd location for such a major tourist attraction. But this rural setting provides the perfect accommodation for Australia's first open-range zoo which also has the distinction of being the first major zoo to be established in Australia in sixty years.

Bulldozers sculpted moats and lakes – and a large hippopotamus pond – from the plains outside Dubbo. A special fencing system keeps out unwanted animals such as dogs, cats and foxes.

Unlike many conventional zoos with their concrete enclosures, bars and wire-mesh fences, the Western Plains Zoo offers clear views of animals in settings that have been landscaped to closely resemble their natural environments. 'Natural' barriers such as moats and ditches separate the animals from the visitors, giving the animals freedom to roam through their paddocks while preventing visitors from making too close an acquaintance with the zoo's more dangerous exhibits.

The benefits of the open-range principle are many: not only is the zoo the next best thing to observing animals in the wild but the information garnered by closely studying the animals contributes to the world-wide bank of knowledge about endangered and rare species. Since it was opened in 1977, the zoo has assumed a leading role in international conservation and breeding programs. When a litter of cheetahs was born in 1987, the Western Plains Zoo was accorded the distinction of being the only zoo in Australasia to have successfully bred the animal – an achievement for which it received international acclaim. It is also the only Australasian zoo to have African elephants.

The zoo's 300 hectares of natural bushland is dissected by waterways and a six-kilometre bitumen road that meanders through enclosures holding more than 800 animals. The layout of the zoo is unusual with animals grouped in five continental zones: South America, Australia, North America, Eurasia and Africa, plus an area devoted to water birds. Some of the more exotic animals contained within these six different areas include tigers, Asiatic lions, white rhinoceroses, North American bison and the rare Przewalski horse – also known as the Mongolian wild horse. The Przewalski horse is the only remaining true wild horse in the world. It was domesticated about 5000 years ago and is the only survivor of the three wild horse species that were the ancestors of the many varieties of domestic horse we know today. Now extinct in the wild, the Przewalski horses' numbers had been reduced to less than sixty by 1959 and it owes its current population of nearly 1000 animals to breeding programs such as that conducted at Dubbo. Australia received its first Przewalski horses in 1982 when four colts and nine fillies were transported from England to their new home at the Western Plains Zoo. Since then, several other breeding populations have been established successfully elsewhere in Australia. A species coordinator ensures that all information relating to the Australian population of the horse is recorded in the Australian Species Management Plan. The ultimate aim of this and similar programs throughout the world is to preserve and propagate this very rare species for reintroduction to the land-locked plains of its Central Asian habitat.

Western Plains' 'parent' zoo at Taronga Park in Sydney had such success in breeding the tallest of all animals that a ready-made herd of giraffes moved into the plains' spacious paddocks.

An unlikely sight in the central west of New South Wales is a paddock inhabited by African elephants, four of whom came the long way – via England and a 52-day sea voyage.

The water bird area with its artificial lakes is home to a diverse assortment of swimming birds such as the pelican, black swan and Australian shelduck, grazing waterfowl including the Cape Barren goose and maned duck, and large wading birds such as the Pacific heron and sacred ibis.

The zoo's future hinges largely on its successful breeding and research programs and its usefulness as an educational, as well as recreational, facility. Strict quarantine laws forbid the future importation of certain animals that are already in the zoo. If the zoo's entire population of any of these animals was to die out, they could not be replaced.

Built at a cost of two-and-a-half-million dollars by the Zoological Parks Board of New South Wales – which also administers Taronga Zoo Park in Sydney – the Western Plains Zoo was formerly the site of a Second World War army camp for 6000 men. □

Port Macquarie & Wauchope

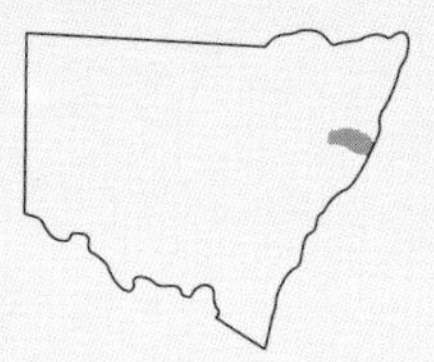

From the highlands in the west of this region, characterised by gorges and waterfalls, magnificent stands of eucalypt and lush rainforests give way to dairy pastures in the Hastings Valley and a series of lakes and estuaries on the coastal plains.

BONNY HILLS ■ 422

Slumbering under the protective gaze of Grants Head, the village of Bonny Hills is typical of the off-highway retreats which punctuate the coastline between Newcastle and Nambucca Heads. The town looks north along Rainbow Beach, all the way to Lake Cathie. *Population 1210*

CAMDEN HAVEN ■ 423

Camden Haven is a tranquil, eight-kilometre-long inlet which occurs where the Camden Haven River meets the sea. Once a shipping port for timber, maize and cattle it now lives up to its name as a peaceful haven for fishermen where anglers based in the hamlets of Laurieton, Dunbogan, and North Haven have a choice of lake, estuary or offshore fishing. Popular catches include lobsters, crabs, rock cod, bream, whiting and flathead.

The Comboyne Plateau in the Camden Haven hinterland offers fine bushwalking tracks, mountain lookouts with spectacular 190-degree coastal views and a colourful show of wildflowers in the spring.

DUNBOGAN ■ 424

Like its fellow Camden Haven fishing villages, this is a perfect base from which to hire a boat and explore the surrounding lagoons and waterways armed with a rod and line. No trace is left of the sawmill built here by Messrs Dunn and Bogan for whom the town was named. *Population 620*

ELLENBOROUGH FALLS ■ 425

Situated on the headwaters of the Ellenborough River, these falls have poured relentlessly over a sheer 157-metre drop on the edge of the New England Tableland since time immemorial – according to local legend they have never run dry. Even the most unathletic should visit the lookout near the top of the falls. A clearly defined trail leading to a viewing point of the full drop.

HASTINGS RIVER ■ 426

The Hastings River is a coastal stream that rises on the eastern slopes of the Great Dividing Range. Characterised by sandy beaches and refreshing deep pools it flows with its major tributaries, the Forbes and the Ellenborough, for about 100 kilometres to meet the sea at Port Macquarie. During the wet season from January to March the river swells and its rapids provide a challenge for adventurous canoeists and white water rafters.

The explorer John Oxley named the Hastings River in 1818 in honour of the Governor-General of India, the First Marquis of Hastings.

KENDALL ■ 427

Originally named Camden Heads this village honours the Australian poet Henry Kendall who came here in 1875 to work for a local family. The coastal bushland provided the inspiration for many of his poems, such as 'Bell-Birds' written in 1867:

Through breaks of the cedar and
sycamore bowers
Struggles the light that is love to the
flowers;
And, softer than slumber and sweeter
than singing,
The notes of the bell-birds are running
and ringing.

Kendall's six-year stay in the town is commemorated by a memorial. Modern Kendall has developed a name as a popular rural crafts centre and base for woodworkers, shoemakers, potters and others of that ilk. Norfolk Punch, a local non-alcoholic herbal brew, is exported world-wide. *Population 710*

LAKE CATHIE ■ 428

Lake Cathie is a recent phenomenon; this area of lakes, swamps and mangroves was not permanently settled until the 1930s and it was the mid-

A bird's-eye-view of Camden Haven from North Brother Mountain says more than a thousand words could express about the attractions of this coast.

Koalas live close in to the Port Macquarie urban area; a special hospital tends to sick and injured animals.

1950s before an electricity supply was laid on. Despite its spelling, the name is pronounced 'cat-eye' in line with the original name, Lake Cati, which was changed in order to avoid confusion with Cattai – a hamlet west of Sydney on the Hawkesbury River (see *Richmond & Windsor*).

In earlier times, the many food sources along the shoreline assured a thriving Aboriginal population and a number of campsites can still be identified along the coastline. Koalas live in the bushland around the town, and the local bowling club even has a reserve for the use of gumleaf-eating marsupials only. The shallow water of Lake Cathie, which is filled when the tide rises over the sandbar, provides a safe swimming spot for children. *Population 1470*

LAKE INNES NATURE RESERVE Christmas Bell Plain separates Lake Innes from the coast, taking its name from the riot of scarlet and yellow, bell-shaped flowers that bloom there in mid-summer. The native plants of the reserve are threatened by bitou bush, brought from South Africa to stabilise the sand dunes, and lantana, introduced as a garden plant in the pioneering days. These exotic plants thrive in the warm, coastal climate and the campaign to eradicate them from bushland continues.

LAURIETON ■ 429

Home to the local fishing fleet and its co-operative, Laurieton stands on the banks of the Camden Haven River at the foot of 487-metre North Brother Mountain, known locally as 'Big Brother'. The summit affords a 360-degree view of coastline, inland waterways and the hinterland backdrop of mountains.

Laurieton was originally known as Peachgrove but this was later changed in honour of Joseph Laurie who arrived in 1840 to build a sawmill. *Population 930*

LORD HOWE ISLAND ■ 430

Despite its splendidly isolated location in the Pacific Ocean, several flying hours from the mainland, the crescent-shaped Lord Howe Island is administratively part of New South Wales (see box).

MOUNT SEAVIEW ■ 431

The first European to climb this steep-sided peak near the head of the Hastings River was the explorer John Oxley. Having reached the top, it took Oxley's team 18 days to trek to the coast from its summit, a distance of about 80 kilometres. He wrote: '... it was a continual ascending and descending of the most frightful precipices, so covered with trees, shrubs and creeping vines that we were frequently obliged to cut our way through'.

Since then, path and tracks have formed so that visitors to this mountain retreat can enjoy horse riding and bushwalking in the forests, or swimming, fishing and canoeing in the nearby Hastings River.

NORTH HAVEN ■ 432

North Haven lies nearest to the Pacific of the three Camden Haven hamlets and its excellent surfing beach attracts swimmers and surfers year round. To traverse the many fishing grounds of the productive inland waterways of this region, the Aboriginal inhabitants carved canoes from tall hardwood trees, leaving scarred trunks, some of which are still visible. They fashioned the shafts of their spears from the stalks of grass trees and followed coastal streams such as the Camden Haven River to their headwaters in the scarp country as the supply of food dictated. *Population 1860*

OXLEY WILD RIVERS NATIONAL PARK ■ 433

There are at least fourteen major waterfalls in this 92 000-hectare park. Above the precipitous gorges and away from the damp subtropical rainforest that surrounds most of the the falls – particularly the tall and spectacular Wollomombi Falls (see *Armidale & Uralla*) – there are dry eucalypt woodlands and savannahs inhabited by grey kangaroos and red-necked wallabies.

Pademelons are found in rainforest pockets in the gullies, while uncommon brush-tailed rock wallabies delight visitors to Yarrowitch Gorge. Platypuses can sometimes be seen at dawn or dusk in the pools at the bottoms of the gorges, while above, wedge-tailed eagles and peregrine falcons soar, keeping an eye out for lizards and snakes.

An easy three-kilometre walk that follows the rim of the Tia Gorge provides magnificent views of the Wollombi Falls from specially constructed platforms. In addition to exhilarating bushwalking in the gorges and swimming at Tia Falls, there is rock climbing and canoeing

North Haven – with North Brother Mountain behind – lives up to its name as a tranquil retreat for fishing boats as well as people.

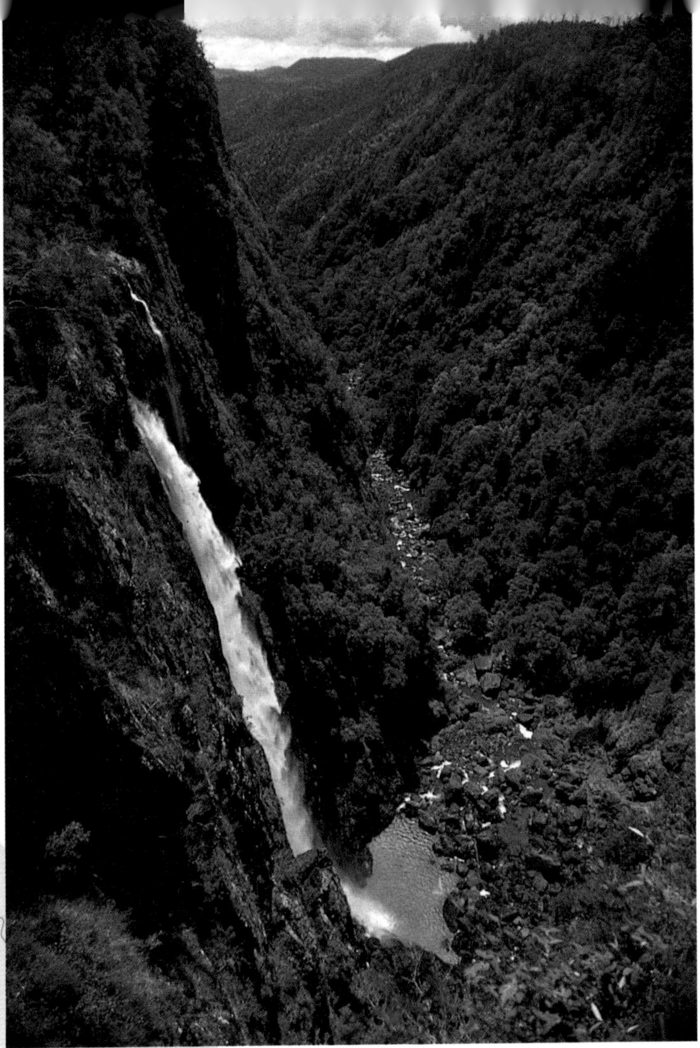

The slim plume of the Ellenborough Falls drains the Bulga Plateau.

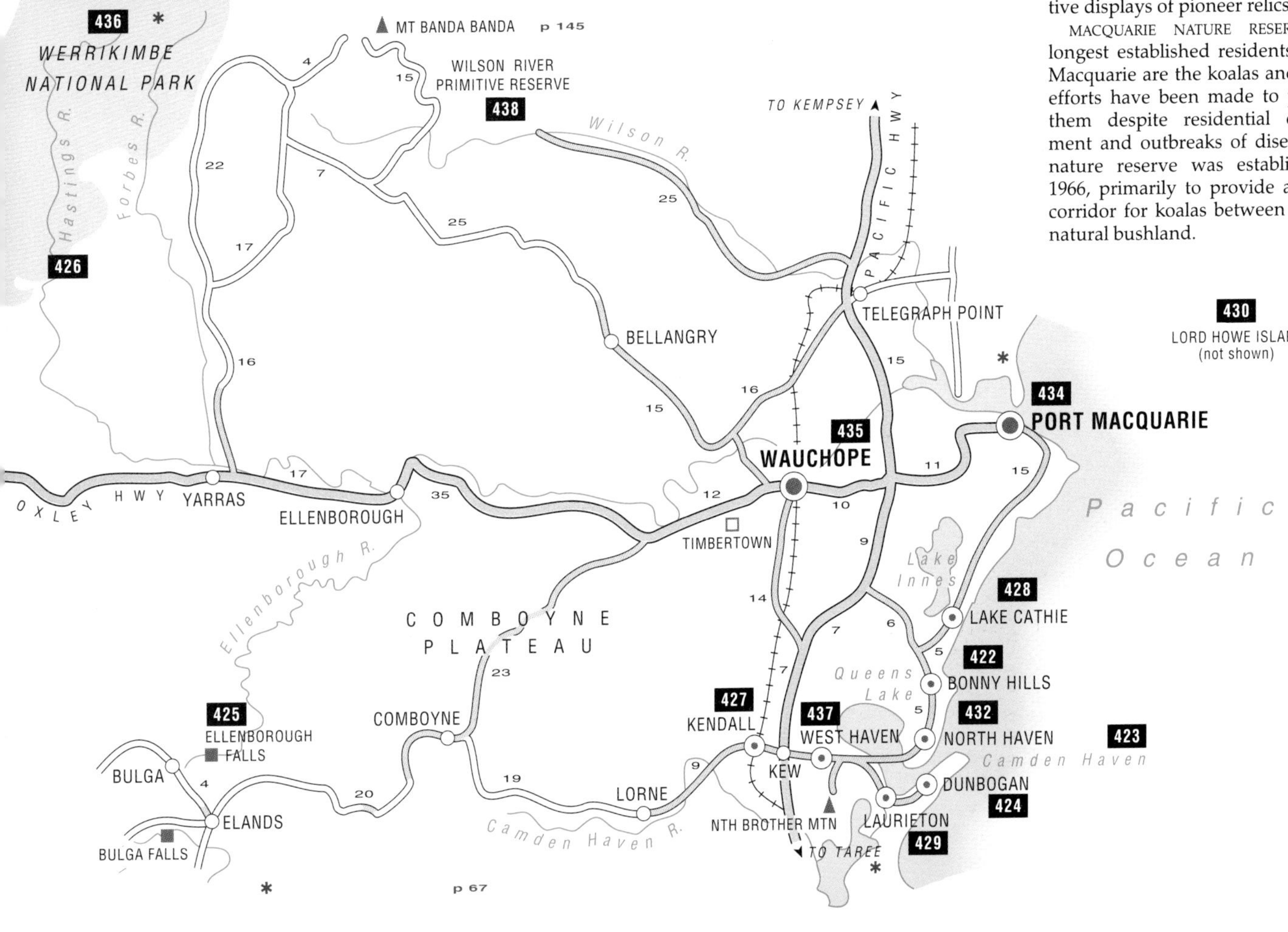

436 WERRIKIMBE NATIONAL PARK
MT BANDA BANDA p 145
WILSON RIVER PRIMITIVE RESERVE 438
TO KEMPSEY
PACIFIC HWY
Wilson R.
Hastings R.
Forbes R.
426
TELEGRAPH POINT
BELLANGRY
430 LORD HOWE ISLAND (not shown)
434 PORT MACQUARIE
435 WAUCHOPE
OXLEY HWY
YARRAS
ELLENBOROUGH
TIMBERTOWN
Pacific Ocean
Lake Innes
428 LAKE CATHIE
Ellenborough R.
COMBOYNE PLATEAU
422 BONNY HILLS
Queens Lake
425 ELLENBOROUGH FALLS
COMBOYNE
427 KENDALL
437 WEST HAVEN
432 NORTH HAVEN
423
Camden Haven
BULGA
KEW
DUNBOGAN
424
ELANDS
LORNE
BULGA FALLS
Camden Haven R.
NTH BROTHER MTN
LAURIETON
429
TO TAREE
p 67

or for those of adventurous bent, rafting the rapids of the Apsley and Macleay rivers.

PORT MACQUARIE ■ 434

Port Macquarie, at the mouth of the Hastings River, is one of the most important fishing ports on Australia's east coast as well as attracting more tourists and retired people than almost any other destination in New South Wales.

The view of this site from the sea has altered considerably since surveyor Clement Hodgkinson recorded in 1840: 'The first view from the sea of Port Macquarie is very pleasing. On entering the surf of the bar, one sees immediately beyond the last breaker, the mirror-like surface of the river extending in a long reach; whilst on the left, dark serpentine rocks protect the base of a smooth round eminence...whilst turning to the west and north-west, the eye...can trace...the windings of the valley through which the river Wilson flows...the distant ranges at the Macleay river, and the huge frowning mountain at the back of Cogo, half dissolved in blue ether'.

The Surveyor-General John Oxley was the first European to explore the area. In search of proof of an inland sea – a proposition that continued to fascinate explorers for many years – his expedition of 1818 foundered at the Macquarie Marshes and the party turned eastward, finally reaching the coast at the Hastings River estuary on 8 October where Oxley reported, '...the port abounds with fish, the sharks were larger and more numerous than I have ever before observed. The forest hills and rising grounds abounded with large kangaroos and the marshes afford shelter and support to innumerable wild fowl. Independent of the Hastings River, the whole country is generally well watered, there is a fine spring at the very entrance to the Port'. He continued, 'I named this inlet Port Macquarie in honour of His Excellency the Governor, the original promoter of these expeditions'.

Following Oxley's return to Sydney and his report to Governor Macquarie, a further expedition was made to explore the area more closely with a view to establishing a convict settlement. The findings were favourable and Port Macquarie was established as Australia's third penal and military settlement in 1821. In 1830 the area was opened to free settlers, who were lured by the promise of timber, rich farming pastures and fishing. By then the more dangerous convicts had been transported to Moreton Bay in southern Queensland or to Norfolk Island. In the 1860s and 1870s sugar cane was an important crop. *Population 27 720*

HISTORY MUSEUM This carefully restored 1830s cottage, the headquarters of the local historical society, has won several awards for its imaginative displays of pioneer relics.

MACQUARIE NATURE RESERVE The longest established residents of Port Macquarie are the koalas and special efforts have been made to preserve them despite residential development and outbreaks of disease. The nature reserve was established in 1966, primarily to provide a linking corridor for koalas between areas of natural bushland.

While the future of native forests remains the subject of a controversial debate between government, loggers and environmentalists, more peaceful days are recalled at Wauchope's Timbertown, a sawmiller's village where the transport and crafts of 1880 are recreated.

ST THOMAS' ANGLICAN CHURCH This is one of Australia's oldest churches, built by convicts in the 1820s. Its sandstone walls, almost one metre thick,the solid cedar pews and the beautiful oyster-shell mortar were all crafted from local materials.

FESTIVALS Golden Lure Game Fishing Tournament, January.

WAUCHOPE ■ 435

Named after Captain Robert Andrew Wauch's property 'Wauchope' (pronounced 'war-hope') established in 1836, this town grew up as a base for the local milling industry. Despite cutbacks in logging in recent years, Wauchope still has one of Australia's biggest and busiest timber-handling railway yards. During Wauchope's heyday in the late nineteenth century ships travelled almost twenty kilometres up the Hastings River from Port Macquarie to pick up and deliver goods. *Population 4300*

TIMBERTOWN Bullock teams, horse-drawn drays and an old steam train provide transport in this faithful recreation of a logging community of the late 1800s. This tribute to the economically important regional timber industry and its hardy pioneers is centred around a steam-operated sawmill. Timbertown is a 'working' museum where craftsmen such as woodturners and blacksmiths demonstrate their skills.

WERRIKIMBE NATIONAL PARK ■ 436

The Forbes and Hastings rivers and Kunderung Brook form an assortment of gorges, cascades and waterfalls in this 35 000-hectare wilderness as they begin their journeys to the coastal plains. The park covers the catchment zone of the Upper Hastings River and its eastern boundary is formed by the rugged Werrikimbe Range.

There is contrasting vegetation, depending on altitude and rainfall: eucalypt woodlands of coachwoods, sassafras and the unusual yellow carrabbeens with their flying buttress trunks; swamp and snowgum grasslands; boronia heathlands and 'Cobcroft's Brush', one of the largest single stands of subtropical rainforest in New South Wales. The Antarctic beech forests at the end of the North Plateau Road are estimated to be up to 1000 years old.

WEST HAVEN ■ 437

West Haven is a 'suburb' of the Camden Haven settlements (see entries) between the forests that surround North Brother Mountain and the waters of Queens Lake. A spectacular overview of the region is provided by the lookout on the top of North Brother – known locally as 'Big Brother'. *Population 800*

WILSON RIVER PRIMITIVE RESERVE ■ 438

The search for red cedar led Europeans into these lush forests in the 1890s. The reserve covers the headwaters of the Wilson River on the edge of the Banda Banda Range. Proclaimed in 1953, it protects the clear mountain waters of the river as well as a typical example of this region's once widespread subtropical rainforest, where blue gums, bangalow palms, trailing vines, elkhorns and birds-nest ferns thrive. Although most of the reserve's animal inhabitants are shy, nocturnal creatures, red-necked and swamp wallabies are occasionally seen during the day. Whip birds, brush turkeys and lyrebirds are often seen searching for food early in the morning.

LORD HOWE: ADRIFT IN THE BLUE PACIFIC

IN THE dim, distant past – about 80 million years ago – violent undersea eruptions pushed part of the seabed above the ocean's surface to create Lord Howe Island and its attendant islets.

Scientific examination of the animals and plants of this scattering of islands – Lord Howe, Balls Pyramid and the Admiralty Islands – has shown that long before the sea rose to its present level they were probably part of the same giant land mass as New Caledonia, Norfolk Island, Australia and New Zealand.

Lieutenant Henry Lidgbird Ball, commander of the First Fleet vessel, HMS *Supply*, sighted Lord Howe in 1788 while sailing from Sydney to Norfolk Island and named it after the most senior admiral in the British Navy. For many years, the only visitors to Lord Howe were passing whaling

Once an uninhabited speck in the ocean visited only by sea-weary whalers, today Lord Howe Island is a popular destination for airborne tourists who come to visit the coral-reef world of the butterfly cod (top), or perhaps attempt an ascent of the awesomely craggy heights of Balls Pyramid, twenty-three kilometres to the south-east.

ships which anchored offshore while crewmen refilled water casks from what was then thought to be the island's scanty water supply. In the early 1840s, settlers were landed on the island; the sponsors of the settlement abandoned the isolated outpost in 1847 but three families stayed on and by 1851 a self-sufficient community of sixteen rugged souls had been established.

The lack of an obvious, plentiful supply of fresh water probably saved the island from suffering the same fate as Norfolk Island (see *Ballina & Alstonville*) and being turned into an open prison for hardened convicts. The authorities in Sydney considered the possibility of establishing a penal settlement in 1834 and again twenty years later, but on both occasions the idea was dropped.

The mountainous region to the south of Lord Howe Island is dominated by Mt Gower. Climbers are rewarded with a spectacular view from its 875-metre-high summit. The summit of next-door Mt Lidgbird – (765 metres) Lieutenant Ball had to go no further than his own middle name to find a label for this landmark – is conquerable by experts only and is rarely climbed.

More than 120 bird species flourish on these islands, including the providence petrel for which this is the only remaining breeding ground, and the flightless Lord Howe Island woodhen, one of the world's rarest birds. During the summer months evening visitors to Ned's Beach are rewarded by the sight of thousands of muttonbirds returning to their burrows on the beach.

Fish of tropical and temperate waters abound in the surrounding sea and the world's southernmost coral reef, a delight to snorkellers and scuba divers, encircles the limpid water of the lagoon. Emperors and wrasse circle lazily around swimmers at Erscott's Hole inside the lagoon, while the wreck of the *Favourite* at North Bay is the home of a colourful menagerie of fish, including drummer and butterfly cod.

Chartered fishing boats provide access to Balls Pyramid, the core of an ancient volcano that rises a sheer 552 metres out of the ocean. The west face remains unclimbed, a remote and challenging goal for mountaineers from the mainland.

The Lord Howe Island group became a World Heritage Area in 1982. Tourism and the worldwide export of Kentia palm seedlings for the indoor plant trade, a business venture which began in the 1800s, provide a living for the islanders. In 1913, the government of the day appointed a special board to oversee the palm industry and regulate the island's affairs. A board, responsible to the New South Wales Minister for Lands, continues to administer the island. □

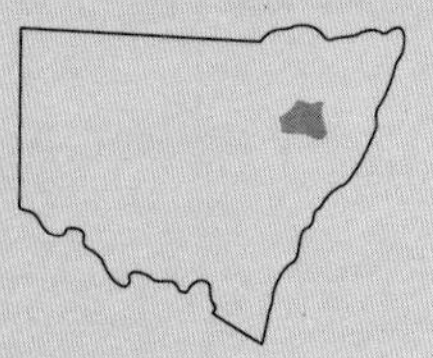

Tamworth & Gunnedah

Animal herders and pioneer farmers – stockmen, shepherds, squatters and selectors – trekked to the Liverpool Plains but it was the squatters, along with the Australian Agricultural Company, who came to dominate this region until the early years of the twentieth century.

CHAFFEY DAM ■ 439

The poetically named 'morning glory spillway' at Chaffey Dam is one of only two in Australia and is so called because of its bell-shaped contours.

In 1967, the site for the dam was selected at Bowling Point Alley, the scene of a seven-year gold rush in the 1850s. Work on the dam wall, with its distinctive red jasper, began in 1976 and was completed in 1979. The water impounded by the dam wall floods an area of 542 hectares and provides water for irrigation and for Tamworth's water supply.

Research on potential flood levels has indicated that, although the dam could handle floods much greater than any yet experienced, upgrading of the dam wall to withstand an exceptional one-in-a thousand year flood, is being investigated. Local homes have been installed with flood-warning equipment and flood-warning and evacuation procedures have been put in place downstream of the dam during this work.

CURLEWIS ■ 440

The small village of Curlewis was founded by Henry Thomas Pike, a sawmiller from Norfolk in England who was to become Mayor of nearby Gunnedah (see entry) in 1902.

Water, or the lack of it, was an ongoing problem. As late as 1950, the year before electricity was laid on to the village, the council had to desilt an old earthen dam and erect a tank from which Curlewis residents could draw water. Reticulated water came to Curlewis in 1972.

The first stock sales in Curlewis took place in 1919, and were, for many years, run by two brothers who founded a local independent stock agents' association. Sales were held in alternate weeks at Gunnedah and Curlewis until the increasing investment and modernisation of the Gunnedah stock saleyards, eclipsed Curlewis's and led to their closure. *Population 650*

'GOONOO GOONOO' ■ 441

In 1841, the Australian Agricultural Company moved the headquarters of its sheep-grazing operations in the Peel Valley from Calala (Tamworth), on the eastern boundary of its land, to 'Goonoo Goonoo', in the centre of its landholding. The name is thought to be a combination of *goon* meaning 'water' and *oo* meaning 'with' giving a translation of 'plenty of water'. An alternative suggestion is that the name comes from a word meaning 'poor country for game' – but since the company brought sheep in their thousands from their initial land grant at Port Stephens the lack of native game was probably irrelevant.

A substantial homestead was built at 'Goonoo Goonoo' and a village grew up around it. The old store and post office, woolshed, chapel and fountain still stand.

GUNNEDAH ■ 442

The respected leader of the Gunnedarr people, Cumbo Gunnerah, was buried in Gunnedah probably in the late 1700s. His bones and a section of the carved tree marking his burial site were delivered to the Australian Museum in Sydney in the late 1800s but the story of the noted Aboriginal leader was not forgotten, thanks to the book *Red Chief* (1953) by Ion Idriess. In 1984, a bronze sculpture was erected in Gunnedah in memory of Cumbo Gunnerah.

The first European to settle on the site of Gunnedah on the Namoi River (see *Narrabri & Wee Waa*) was John Johnson in 1834. His woolshed became a gathering place for those waiting to cross the river and eventually a small settlement known as 'Johnson's woolshed' or more simply 'Woolshed' grew up. The first survey of a town site in 1854 took account of the possible flooding of the Namoi River...but a severe flood in 1856 showed that the flood level had been underestimated and the town was replanned. There is a flood gauge in the centre of Gunnedah on which are recorded the flood levels over the last 150 years.

By the time the first land was sold in 1857 the nameWoolshed had been dropped in favour of Gunnedah, meaning 'place of white stones'. The white stones, however, have not survived, the white quartzite or crushed lime, was used in road construction.

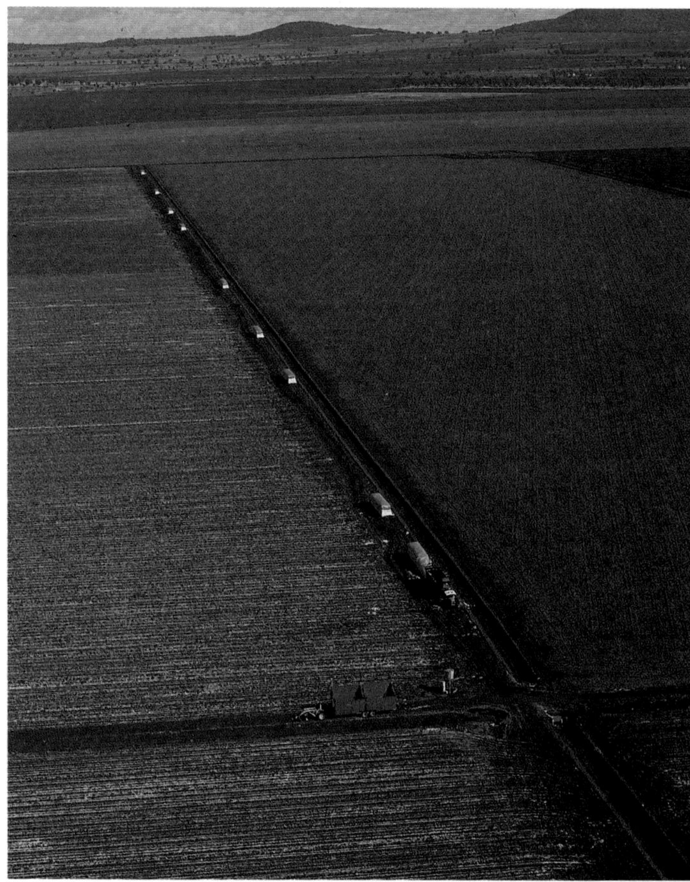

Once the exclusive domain of wheat and sheep, the rich alluvial flats of the Gunnedah distict now support cotton varieties that are particularly suited to the short growing season of the district. The cotton is planted in October, flood irrigated from December to March and picked mid-year.

The early settlers were pastoralists and wheat growers and nowadays Gunnedah town is one of the largest centres for wheat and stock sales in Australia. Some 350 000 sheep and 138 000 cattle are handled at Gunnedah saleyards annually and the large abattoir exports meat to the United States, Europe, Canada and the Middle East. The annual Ag-Quip (farm machinery) field days bring thousands of people to the town every year. More recent additions to the industries of Gunnedah have been coal mining, started in 1900 with new discoveries of high-quality coal in the 1970s and, since the 1980s, cotton. *Population 8870*

DOROTHEA MACKELLAR MEMORIAL Dorothea Mackellar's family had two

properties in the area and from 1905 to the 1930s the poet stayed intermittently at one of these, 'Kurrumbede'. The breaking of a lengthy drought in the Gunnedah district was the inspiration for her most famous poem, 'My Country'. A life-size sculpture of Dorothea Mackellar on horseback was erected in 1983 in the town.

EAST MERIDIAN Twenty-seven kilometres west of Gunnedah runs the 150-degree meridian of longitude that has, since 1895, been the measuring point for Australian Eastern Standard Time (EST), which is ten hours ahead of Greenwich Mean Time (GMT). A sundial and information board mark the site.

WATER TOWER MUSEUM The local historical museum is housed in the converted water tower that was the town's original reservoir from 1908. Exhibits are displayed on three floors and an observation roof.

PORCUPINE HILL LOOKOUT The Aborigines who used the lookout as a signal post, knew long before the tourists who now flock there that the lookout – which is surrounded by a bushland reserve – offers peerless views of an area stretching from the Nandewar Ranges to the Great Dividing Range.

FESTIVALS Gunnedah Eisteddfod, June; Ag-Quip Field Days, August.

HANGING ROCK ■ 443

Picnics at Hanging Rock are very popular pastime with locals and tourists alike...although this Hanging Rock was not the one that featured in the book and film. Hanging Rock is a treeless and forbidding rockface that overhangs a chasm and rises to 984 metres above sea level.

The great attraction for those who climbed Hanging Rock in the early 1850s was the gold to be found there. Now the big attraction for picnickers and campers is the reserve at the top of Hanging Rock where two dams built by the Mount Sheba Company in 1888 to wash or sluice mine crushings can now be used for swimming. Advice and exhibits for fossickers are also available at Hanging Rock.

KOOTINGAL ■ 444

Scheelite (the ore refined into tungsten) and molybdenite mines were worked at Betts Hill in Kootingal for some years but mining never altered the fundamental character of Kootingal – a village surrounded by horse studs, stone-fruit orchards and poultry farms. Twenty-two per cent of the state's egg production – over 250 million eggs each year – comes from the small farms at Kootingal.

One of the meanings of the Aboriginal work Kootingal is 'star' – an appropriate name for a village that now has a planetarium, housing a working model of the solar system. Kootingal has in recent years been developing as a residential suburb of Tamworth. *Population 2000*

LAKE KEEPIT ■ 445

Of the three dams on the Namoi River system – Keepit, Chaffey and Split Rock (see entries) – Keepit is the principal dam, the oldest and the only one on the Namoi River itself. Until 1927, local farmers had used artesian bores for irrigation but, during that year, the levels in the wells dropped and calls for a dam, which had started thirty years before, grew more insistent. By the time a site on the Namoi River just north-east of where it joins with the Peel River, had been selected and construction begun, World War II had also started. Construction on the dam wall was therefore delayed and Lake Keepit was not finally filled with water until 1960. Lake Keepit is named after one of the earliest properties in the district – William Sims Bell's Keepit Station, established in 1837.

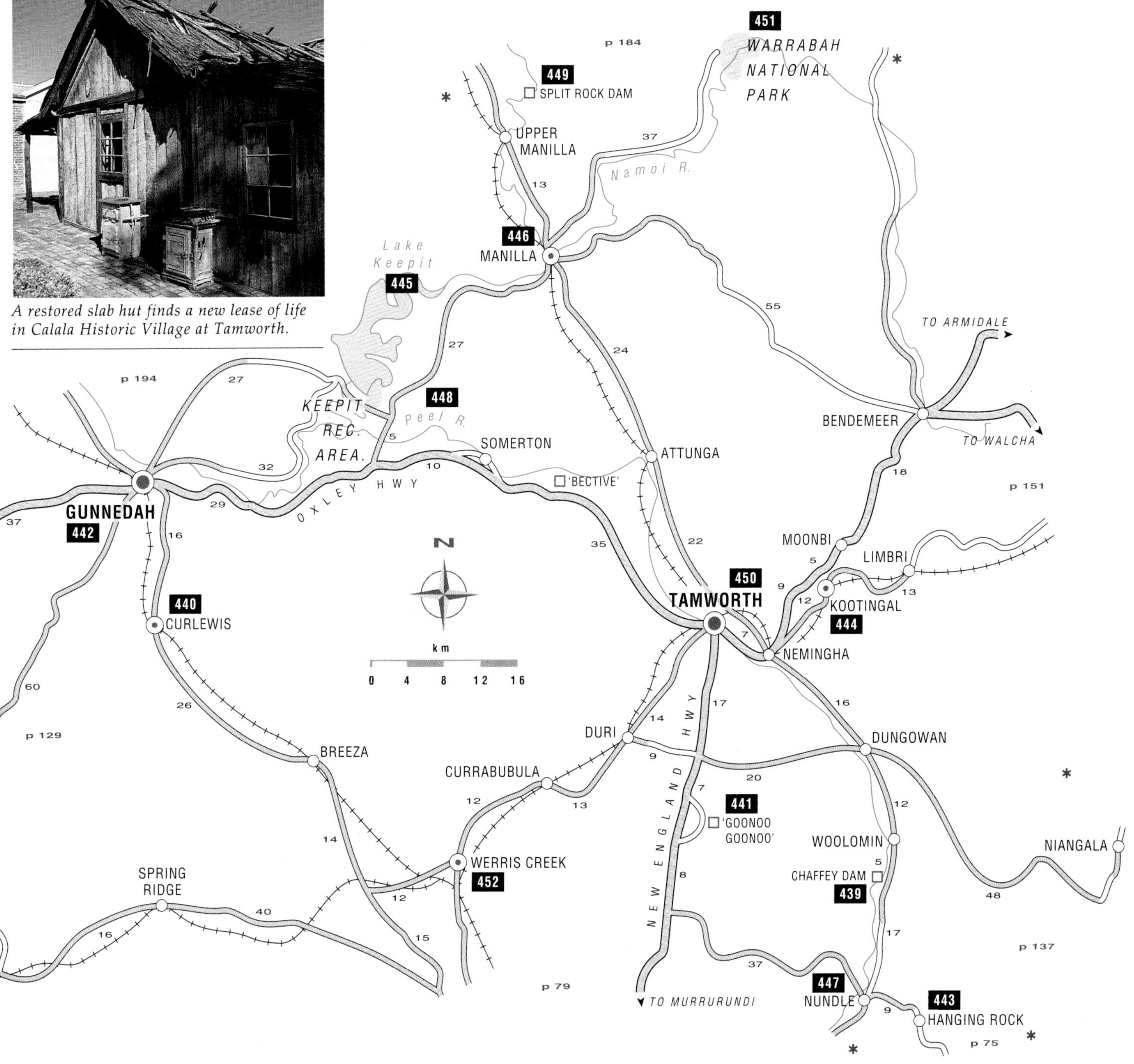

A restored slab hut finds a new lease of life in Calala Historic Village at Tamworth.

The paddocks of Tamworth produce top thoroughbreds; five national horse breeders' associations are based here.

The lake's waters are used mainly for irrigation and were instrumental in the development of the cotton industry in the Narrabri and Wee Waa region; from twenty-six hectares of cotton, production rose to twenty-thousand hectares within ten years of the dam's opening.

Incorporating 4370 hectares and 104 kilometres of shoreline, Lake Keepit offers recreation ...and an object lesson in organisational co-operation. The Department of Water Resources supervises the dam; the Electricity Commission administers the six-megawatt hydroelectric generator; the Department of Sport, Recreation and Racing operates the National Fitness Camp on the eastern foreshore; the National Parks and Wildlife Service maintains the walking tracks; the Department of Conservation and Land Management oversees the State Recreation Area on the south-western shores, which is administered locally by a Trust. The local sailing club hosts the Keepit Kool Regatta each June.

MANILLA ■ 446

George Veness built a store, wine-shop and house at the junction of the Namoi and Manilla rivers in 1853 – and the site was known simply as 'The Junction'. It was not until a post office was established and Veness was employed as the first postmaster that an official name for the settlement was required. Veness selected Manilla, which is a corruption of an Aboriginal word said to mean 'winding or round about river'.

Economic activities near the town were initially confined to grazing on large squatter runs and some quartz mining. Bushranging seems to have been confined to one visit from Captain Thunderbolt who robbed the mailman and the inn at Manilla in 1867 – leaving his packhorse behind when he was pursued by troopers.

Development in Manilla began only after the opening up of land for selection and closer settlement with the passing of the Land Acts of the 1860s; it was further boosted by the arrival of the railway in 1899. To the wool and wheat of the early twentieth century can now be added tobacco, which is successfully grown in the district. Drinkers as well as smokers have reason to know of Manilla since the town has one of the state's two meaderies, which produces a number of different types of mead as well as ordinary table honey. *Population 2110*

ROYCE COTTAGE (1884) Built by G.H. Royce, who constructed the bridge across the Namoi River at Manilla, the cottage has been restored for use as a museum.

FESTIVALS Festival of Spring Flowers, October.

NUNDLE ■ 447

This historic gold mining village on the Peel River, 776 metres up in the Liverpool Ranges, began life as a collection of tents when the first two hundred miners rushed to the area after gold was discovered in 1851. A village was approved in 1852 and surveyed the following year. A police barracks, built before the town layout was complete, and a court house built in the 1850s, contributed an air of permanence to the village.

The original court house has gone, replaced by the existing court house (now a museum) in 1880. The miners too have gone but the old water races can still be seen around the hills and fossickers can still hunt for zircons, serpentine, sapphires, green jasper and quartz crystals around Nundle, one of the best crystal areas in New South Wales.

In addition to its as yet, undepleted natural mineral resources, Nundle has a trout hatchery, two state forests and cattle, sheep and poultry farms on which it survives.

PEEL INN Built by a Mr McIlveen in 1860, the inn has been in the hands of the Schofield family since the late nineteenth century. The walls of the sandstock brick building are four bricks thick and still held together by the original sand-and-lime mortar.

PEEL RIVER ■ 448

The Surveyor-General, John Oxley, was the man responsible for changing the Aboriginal name for the river – Calala meaning 'place of battle' – to the Peel, in honour of Robert Peel, not then Prime Minister of Great Britain but Under Secretary of State for the Colonies. Oxley commented favourably on the fertility of the river valley when, the first European to do so, he crossed the Peel River during his inland exploration from Bathurst. An anchor from Oxley's *Sealark*, on Manilla Road in Tamworth, commemorates this crossing.

The Peel River rises north of the Liverpool Ranges and flows through Nundle and Tamworth before turning west to meet with the Namoi at Gunnedah. The fertility of the river valley on which Oxley commented comes from a long, narrow strip of black earth, known to geologists as *chernozem* that runs through what is otherwise basalt-dominated country. These fertile river flats now grow lucerne and vegetables but two other products – sheep and gold – dominated the river's history.

In the early 1830s, the first squatters, despite their lack of land title, set up runs on the banks of the Peel River. In 1834, the Australian Agricultural Company was granted more than 300 000 acres (122 000 hectares) of land along the Peel River from Nundle to Attunga. As the company moved its sheep on to the sixty-five kilometres of prime river frontage, the squatters on the west bank had to move out.

Gold miners rushed to the Peel River in 1851 where they set up mining operations on the east bank. The enterprising Australian Agricultural Company formed a subsidiary – the Peel River Land and Mineral Company – to exploit the gold on its own side of the river.

SPLIT ROCK DAM ■ 449

The long drought of 1965–68 and the increasing importance of cotton cultivation, which is thirstier for water than sheep and cattle, led to proposals for a third dam on the Namoi river system to add to the capacity already available at Keepit and Chaffey (see entries).

The dam wall, 66 metres high and 456 metres long, impounds 397 000 megalitres of water covering an area of 2150 hectares. The water is used for irrigation and to supplement the main storage dam at Lake Keepit. Advance orders for water are made by irrigators to the dam superintendent and three weirs help with the distribution of the water.

Split Rock Dam, which was officially opened in 1988, takes its name from a natural phenomenon – a fissured rock near the dam site – but, apart from the name, everything about Split Rock Dam is state-of-the-art technology. Water can be taken from any level within the reservoir not just from the topmost, warmer and highly oxygenated level. Air is pumped through the water to break up temperature layers and nutrient build up so that the concentration of harmful elements can be avoided.

TAMWORTH ■ 450

Tamworth, on the Peel River, 390 metres above sea level is the commercial centre of this region...and the centre of Australasian country music (see box).

The town is sited on an old ford across the river and when the Australian Agricultural Company took up its large landholding on the Peel it became a station and the company headquarters. Initially called Calala, after the Aboriginal name for the

Peel River, the private settlement on the west bank of the river was later renamed Tamworth after the town in England represented by Sir Robert Peel, British Prime Minister.

The huge amount of land held by the Australian Agricultural Company and the large runs of a few squatters was to hamper population growth in Tamworth in the latter half of the nineteenth century. Records show that, in 1884, over one million hectares of land was concentrated in only twenty-five holdings. The passing of the Robertson Land Acts in 1861, allowing for land selection on large squatting runs, the arrival of the railway in the 1870s and the expiry of a number of large leases in the 1890s all eased the situation slightly. But the single most important factor in Tamworth's population development occurred in 1909 with the compulsory resumption of 40 500 hectares of land owned by the Peel River Land and Mineral Company. Over 250 new farms were created from this resumed land.

The population of Tamworth was only 3000 when it was declared a municipality in 1876, at which time the private Australian Agricultural Company town on the west side of the river was amalgamated into the municipality. Electric street lighting was switched on in Tamworth in 1888, the first town in the Southern Hemisphere to have such a luxury provided by a municipal council. The Power Station Museum, with its fully operational steam-powered electricity-generating equipment opened on the site in 1988.

During the war an army training camp and an RAAF flying school were established at Tamworth – the RAAF causing the only break in activities at the Tamworth race track in a hundred years. After the war two enterprising businessmen took over the aerodrome and established East-West airlines whose first services flew from Tamworth to Sydney in one of two converted seven-seater Avro Ansons in 1947. A joint training college operated by Ansett and British Aerospace has been established at the 'new' (1954) airport. *Population 31 720*

CALALA COTTAGE (1875) This was the townhouse built for Philip Gidley King, grandson of Governor King, Superintendent of the Peel River Land and Mineral Company (1854–1904) and first mayor of Tamworth (1876–80). It has now been restored by the Tamworth Historical Society, as has the AA Company's original slab cottage.

FESTIVALS Australasian Country Music Festival, January; Fibre Textile Exhibition, October.

WARRABAH NATIONAL PARK ■ 451

It is very difficult to imagine as you enter this national park and see the Namoi River flowing quietly through the picnic and rest area, just how different the scene is in the rest of the park. The Namoi, and the numerous creeks which contribute their water to that of the main river, tumbles in a series of rapids from the western slopes of the tablelands. The river has cut a gorge through the granite, and its boulder-strewn water passes between cliffs and steep hillsides, which have their own share of the granite tors. This 3400-hectare park offers a river for the expert canoeist only and bush or river walks.

White and black cypress pine, Caley's ironbark, Hills red gum and monkey gum on the hillsides give way to red gums, river oaks, tea tree and bottle brush on the river banks. Most of the mammals and reptiles are difficult to spot although many, obligingly, leave their tracks on the occasional sandy beach to be found within the park.

WERRIS CREEK ■ 452

Flat land around Werries Creek or Weery's Creek, a tributary of the Mooki River, was used as a campsite by teamsters and drovers heading up the Great Northern Road. By the 1830s the first squatters arrived in the district and Weia Weia Creek Station, on whose land the town grew up, was established by 1841. It was the railway-building program of the late 1870s rather than pastoral activities that led to the foundation of the town. A railway encampment was set up at Werris Creek from about 1877 as the railway lines were built to Tamworth, Gunnedah and Breeza. The tents and temporary buildings gave way to more permanent marshalling yards and maintenance workshops and Werris Creek became the main junction of the State Rail Authority. The linked two-storey buildings of Werris Creek railway station are now 'heritage' listed. The diversion of much of the rail traffic to the coast line in the 1930s led to a decline in the number of trains passing through Werris Creek, and the advent of diesel trains in the 1960s, which led to the closure of the coal mine and the maintenance workshops, significantly reduced the importance of Werris Creek but it kept its place on the map...a new local industry had emerged.

From the early 1950s, grain bulk-handling facilities were developed in the town and, with major rebuilding of the facility in the 1970s, the town now has the largest grain storage silos in the district. *Population 1570*

THAT 'COUNTRY' SOUND WITH AN AUSTRALIAN ACCENT

No other symbol would have been as appropriate for Tamworth as the city's conspicuous 'big guitar'.

WHEN Radio 2TM's nightly 'Hoedown' program started in 1965, even its most ardent fans could have had no idea of what it would spawn. The live shows that 'Hoedown' put on every three months at Tamworth Town Hall, attracted the best of Australia's country and western singers and these singers, in turn, attracted recording companies. Tamworth became synonymous with country and western music and, with the inauguration of the Country Music Awards in 1973, the annual Australasian Country Music Festival was born.

For ten days in January, Tamworth attracts an additional population of 30 000. At 700 venues around the town – on official stages and in pubs, clubs, shopping centres, ovals and street corners – 6000 hours of live music is played. Singers, fiddlers, banjo pickers and guitarists perform for the coveted Golden Guitar Awards. Each year a new name is added to the Roll of Renown, unveiled in 1977 by Tex Morton, whose name was the first to appear on the roll of those who have made lasting and significant contributions to country music.

In true Hollywood fashion, singers leave their handprints in a Tamworth footpath.

The Hands of Fame Cornerstone at the corner of the New England Highway and Kable Avenue now has 150 famous hand prints in its concrete while the Winners Walkway commemorates all the award winners since 1973 with bronze plaques set in the pavement.

But, in addition to the official awards and artefacts in Tamworth, there are other, less official ones ranging from the Noses of Fame in Joe Maguire's Pub, where singers have performed live for forty years, to the twelve-metre-high golden guitar outside the new country music complex, where twenty wax figures of the 'greats', sculpted in Nashville, Tennessee, are displayed.

Buskers with fiddles and guitars make pedestrian feet tap in Tamworth's streets in January.

From bush bands to blue grass and from gospel to the 'Redback on the toilet seat', in a short eighteen years a new industry has been born. Meanwhile, the catalyst for all of this – the 'Hoedown' program – is now broadcast ten hours a night, seven nights a week from radio stations at Tamworth, Toowoomba and Brisbane. □

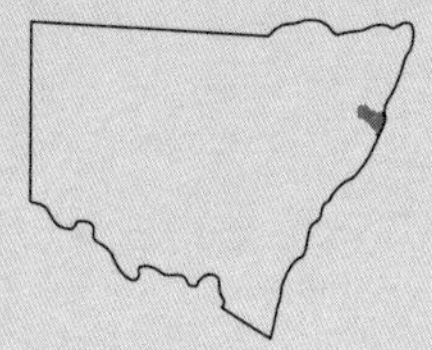

Kempsey & South West Rocks

The history and development of this region has been dominated by the life-giving artery of the Macleay River since the arrival of the early cedar-getters – their felling of the upland hardwood trees unwittingly contributed to the perennial flooding and silting of this beautiful waterway.

ARAKOON STATE RECREATION AREA ■ 453
This recreation area is one of the state's most popular, with almost one million visitors each year. The main attraction is the jail at Trial Bay but the 600-hectare playground also includes the beaches at Little Bay and Gap Beach. A walking track runs from the jail to Little Bay Beach, with its dam and waterfowl habitat, and another, steeper track leads from Little Bay Beach to Gap Beach, noted for its pockets of rainforest.

CRESCENT HEAD ■ 454
The most impressive aspect of Crescent Head is its superb physical setting. The coastline to the north and south of the town is unspoilt and runs uninterrupted from Point Plomer in the south to Hat Head in the north. Eighty per cent of this coastline is protected, with only occasional intrusions by settlements such as Crescent Head.

It is not only the coastline that is protected, but much of the land around Crescent Head is also preserved in its natural state. With Hat Head National Park (see entry) to the north, Limeburners Creek Reserve (see entry) to the south, the coastal wetlands of Goolawah Reserve between them and two state forests inland, Crescent Head sits in the middle of a sea of natural bushland.

In prehistoric times, headlands such as Crescent Head, and Racecourse, Delicate Nobby, Big Hill and Point Plomer, running south from Crescent Head, were offshore islands surrounded by seas that were at a much higher level than they are today. At the other end of the time scale, space-age minerals such as rutile and zircon were mined at Crescent Head in the 1970s; a special plant nursery propagated the greenery necessary to restore mining areas to a 'natural' state.

Crescent Head is a mecca for fishermen, hang gliders and surfers, especially those favouring the larger Malibu boards. *Population 1210*

FREDERICKTON ■ 455
A private town was established by Frederick Chapman on seventy hectares of his land at the junction of Christmas Creek and the Macleay River (see entry) in 1857. The road from Kempsey, just to the south of Frederickton, had already been surveyed and a bridge built across Christmas Creek the previous year. With a well-established track north from Frederickton to Grassy Head and the Nambucca River, and the Macleay River opening up to trade, the town was ideally placed.

The late nineteenth century saw a number of industries developing around the town: shipbuilding, a large sawmill, a sugar mill operated by the Macleay River Sugar Company, and a number of creameries. Of these, the creameries were to remain the most important. By the end of the nineteenth century there were over thirty creameries, separating stations or dairy factories in the Macleay valley; when farmers began to separate their own cream these were replaced by 1200 'dairies'. Only one of the large creameries remain at Smithtown (see entry) Frederickton's riverbank location makes it a popular stop for boating enthusiasts. *Population 830*

GLADSTONE ■ 456
Before the first bridge was built, transport between Gladstone and its sister town Smithtown across the narrow stretch of the Macleay River, was by punt – riders carrying their saddles travelling on the punt, horses swimming alongside. When the bridge was opened in 1892, a member of the official party scattered scent amongst the crowd and it was left to a local resident to break a bottle against one of the uprights.

This historic village was originally called Darkwater but, after a visit by the Governor of New South Wales, the Earl of Belmore, and his wife in 1870, the name of the village was changed to that of the governor's wife's maiden name. The old name, however, still exists since the section of Kinchela Street running between Darkwater and Macleay streets contains most of the old buildings that have resulted in a heritage listing for Gladstone.

The former Newcastle ferry Koondooloo, *on its way to a Philippines scrapyard, unexpectedly found its final resting place in Trial Bay in 1972.*

HAT HEAD NATIONAL PARK ■ 457
This crescent-shaped coastal park covers almost 6500 hectares of land from Smoky Cape in the north to Crescent Head in the south. It encompasses an incredible variety of land types from unusually high dunes, large coastal swamps and even a patch of rainforest to beaches, rocky headlands and forested hills.

The dunes, which have been built up by sea level changes and contain dune lakes, are relics of the Ice Age and have considerable scientific significance. The coastal swamps and freshwater lagoons have been created by the Macleay River as it floods the coastal plain.

Of the headlands within the park, the most interesting is Korogoro Point, an excellent site for spotting migrating humpback whales, and where a deeply eroded crevice in the rock (called the Arch) is fully exposed and explorable at low tide.

Bird life, both resident and migratory, ranges from the ducks, egrets, herons and black swans of the swamps and lagoons, through the hawks and falcons of the forested hills to the honeyeaters, flycatchers fantails, plovers and quails of the coastal heath and wildflowers.

KEMPSEY ■ 458
The Macleay River runs through Kempsey in a horseshoe shape and the main street through the town dissects this horseshoe, dividing the town into four distinct sections East, West, Central and South Kempsey, which is how the town developed and how most of the locals still see it.

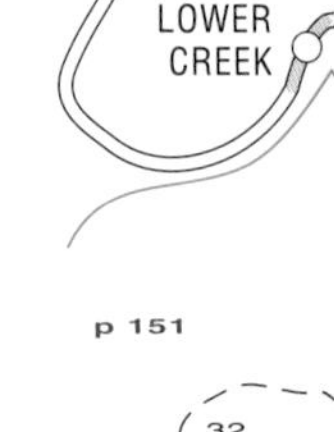

The area around Kempsey attracted cedar-getters from the 1830s and the first land grants, including one to John Verge the architect, were made in 1837. One of these land grants was bought by Kempsey's first settler and the founder of East Kempsey, Enoch Rudder. He called his homestead 'Kempsey Villa' since the area reminded him of the Kempsey Valley in the west of England. Although he arrived at his new property by boat, it did not come by the conventional route up the river from the sea but across the hills from Port Macquarie on a slide drawn by bullocks until it could be put into the water when the Macleay River was finally reached.

Rudder operated a punt service across the river and East Kempsey developed slowly as a port for timber and a centre for the squatters and pastoralists who set up along the Macleay River during the 1840s. In 1854, the government founded an official township, West Kempsey, next to Rudder's private town. In 1886, the two towns, together with two other small 'townships' on private land, were combined into the one municipality of Kempsey.

The cedar that brought the first settlers to Kempsey may be long gone but forty per cent of the poplar trees grown in Australia for use in veneering now come from Kempsey. Decentralisation has also brought a number of new, and very Australian, industries to the town, including Akubra hats, King Gee clothing and Boral bricks. The novelist Thomas Kenneally spent his childhood in Kempsey, and Burnum Burnum, the well known Aboriginal identity, spent his teenage years at the local Kinchela Aboriginal Boys Home in Kempsey. *Population 9049*

FESTIVAL Bridgestone International Off-Road Races, July.

LIMEBURNERS CREEK NATURE RESERVE ■ 459

This reserve, established in 1971, encompasses 6000 hectares of undisturbed vegetation. The diversity of the vegetation, ranging from mangrove swamps to heath-covered hills and dry open forest, is due to the large saltwater lake at the north end of the reserve, which adds the variety of its saline environment.

The reserve also has historical significance. Five to six thousand years of Aboriginal use have left behind burial sites, campsites, shell middens, a quarry for producing stone tools and one of only three fish traps in the mid-north coast.

European history has contributed the name for the reserve. Huge quantities of oyster shells were burnt in the area to produce much-needed building mortar. It is only in recent years that Limeburners Creek has once again become the site for farming oysters. The devastation to local oyster supplies caused by the limeburners has been redressed as the creek now supplies almost 90 per cent of the district's shellfish.

MACLEAY RIVER ■ 460

The Macleay River rises, as the Guyra River, in the New England Tablelands and drops down to the plain below in a number of spectacular waterfalls. It flows south-east to Kempsey then in a north-easterly direction to end its 400-kilometre journey in the Pacific Ocean at South West Rocks (see entry). The upper reaches of the river are in an isolated and mountainous wilderness. The river then passes through a middle valley of mixed farming until it reaches the broad delta where dairying is the mainstay.

The river has had a number of names from the Aboriginal 'yarrandabby', to the European 'New River', from the explorer John Oxley who considered it of 'no interest'; 'Wright River', after the original 1826 explorer Captain Samuel Wright, 'Trial River', and, finally, in 1835 the Macleay River after Alexander Macleay, Scottish-born scientist and Chief Secretary of New South Wales.

It is not only the name of the river that has changed but also its exit to the sea. Like most of the northern rivers the Macleay is prone to flooding and silting. During a flood in 1893, the river diverted through Jerseyville and pushed through the

Beyond Crescent Head's immediate surrounds of parks and reserves, well-watered paddocks have supported beef and dairy herds for over 100 years.

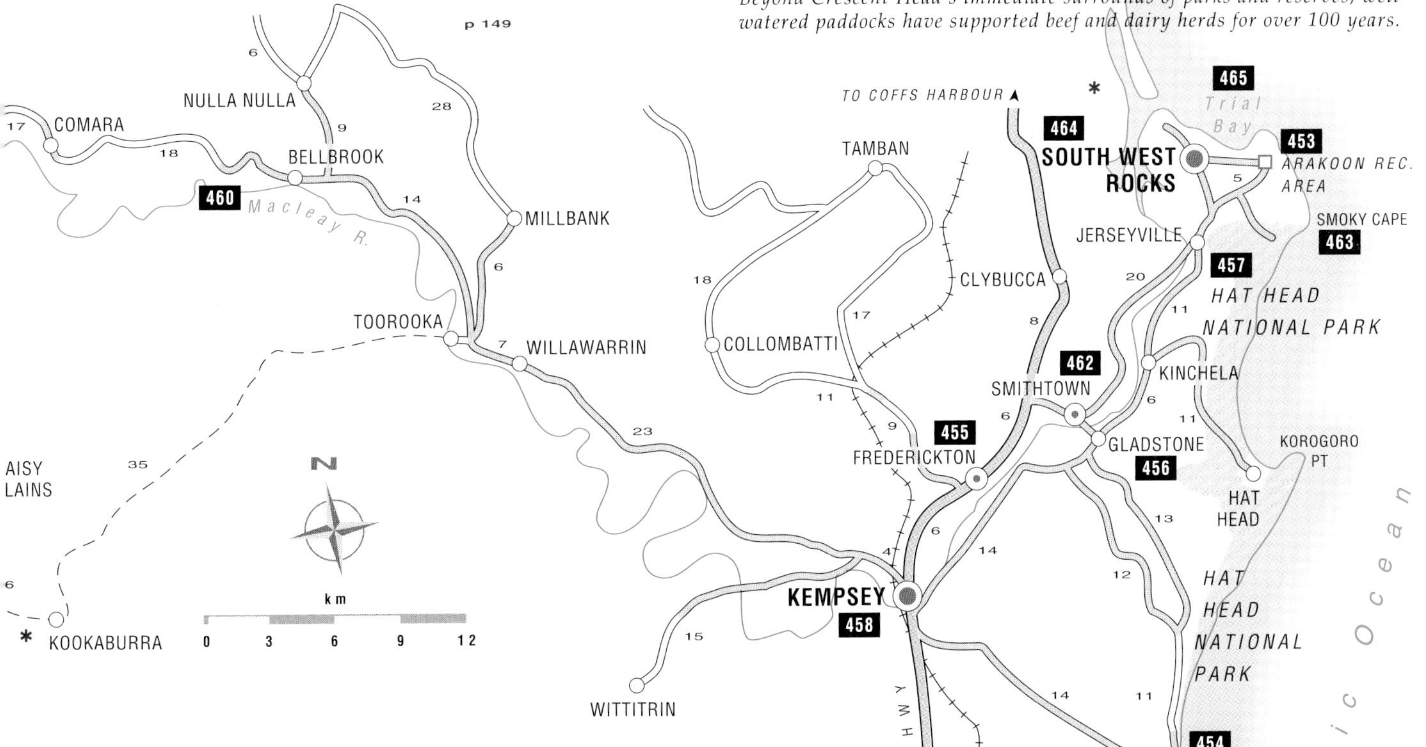

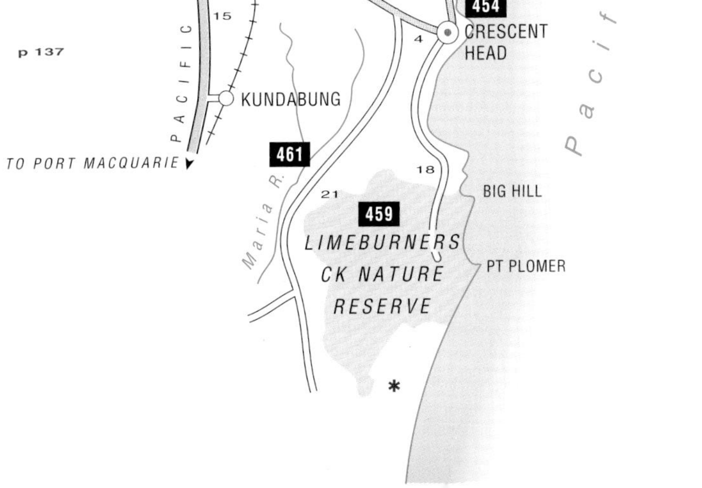

sandhills to reach the ocean at New Entrance on the northern end of Trial Bay (see entry). Work was undertaken to improve this entrance and the previous entrance at Stuarts Point and the pilot station at Grassy Head were abandoned.

The first river steamer entered the Macleay in 1858 and for eighty years the timber, vegetables and dairy produce of the Macleay Valley used the river as a major means of transport. In 1949 and 1950, however, severe flooding silted up the river to such an extent that access beyond Smithtown was impossible. Rail and road transport took over, the wharves at Kempsey lay unused and in 1954 the last North Coast Steam Navigation Company boat ran up the river.

MARIA RIVER ■ 461

The Maria River, rising south of Kempsey, flows thirty kilometres to join the Hastings River and flow with it into the Pacific Ocean at Port Macquarie. Although short and unnamed on many maps, the Maria River was of major significance for the opening of the Macleay Valley. With rumours of a new river to the north, a party set out from Port Macquarie in 1826 up the Maria River. Having rowed as far as the Maria River would take them, they then carried the boat overland for eleven kilometres until they met the Macleay River. The earliest settlers used the same route up the Maria River to where it met a track, cut by Enoch Rudder, that led them to Kempsey.

SMITHTOWN ■ 462

The first blocks of land in Smithtown were sold in 1866 and development was obviously fairly rapid since by 1886 St Patrick's Catholic Church, the largest church in the district, with seating for 700 people, was built at Smithtown. The new church, built in 1972, accommodates 275.

Since 1891 there has been a dairy at Smithtown, initially operated by the Smithtown Cooperative Dairying Company, then by the Bacchus Marsh Company and, in recent years, by Nestlé (Australia). Small steamers used to collect the milk products from the wharves – which now stand idle on the river beside the factory complex – and transport them downstream and then down the coast to Sydney. *Population 600*

SMOKY CAPE ■ 463

This headland was named Smoky Cape by Captain Cook who saw 'a great Quantity of Smoke' possibly from Aboriginal campfires on the shore. The headland rises to 140 metres above sea level and protects a beaches on either side, North Smoky Beach and South Smoky Beach. From Big Smoky Hill ('gooung', also meaning 'smoky', was the name used by the Aborigines) a freshwater waterfall drops 300 metres to North Smoky Beach. But the most distinctive feature on the cape is its lighthouse, the tallest and one of the oldest in the state and now classified by the National Trust.

The need for a lighthouse was first raised in 1873 but it was 1886 before Parliament approved funds for its design and construction. The seventeen-metre high lighthouse of octagonal shape was designed by James Barnet in 1890 but he was dismissed from his position as Colonial Architect before the lighthouse was completed. The contractor responsible for construction of the concrete lighthouse with its granite detailing, died during construction, which was then completed by his executors.

Despite these problems, the kerosene light at Smoky Cape was lit on 15 April 1891. The original kerosene light of 100 000 candelas was replaced by a kerosene lamp in 1912 that gave off 316 000 candle-power. Since 1962, the light – visible up to twenty-three kilometres away – has been powered by electricity and now produces one million candelas.

SOUTH WEST ROCKS ■ 464

This small town was originally part of the proposed township of Arakoon, subdivided in 1866. It adopted the name South West Rocks in the 1920s because the pilot's instructions to boats entering Trial Bay was to anchor 'south-west of the rocks'.

South West Rocks owes its existence to an accident of nature. When the Macleay River changed course after the 1893 flood it forced its way through the sandhills to make a new entrance to the ocean at South West Rocks. Masonry was moved in to build training walls to prevent the river from changing its mind again and the village grew up around this early twentieth-century construction site The delta area, a mass of mangrove swamps, channels, islands and creeks still silts up and changes its configuration from time to time but the river's main channel cannot deviate from its stone-walled 'canal' that directs it to the ocean at South West Rocks.

The signal station and flagstaff, together with a pilot and boatmen, were moved from Grassy Head to South West Rocks in 1902. The flagstaff was used to signal information on the safety of the bar, the depth of the water and the weather situation to boats entering Trial Bay.

In 1961 an oil terminal was sited at South West Rocks with a submarine pipeline leading from the storage tanks at Saltwater Creek to where the tankers are moored in the bay. *Population 2890*

For 20 kilometres, the unspoiled bushland of park or reserve fringes the beaches of Crescent Head.

Trial Bay jail, designed in the style of a harsh, Northern-Hemisphere stronghold appropriate to a gloomy, windswept clime, is rendered somewhat less than grim and forbidding in its sunny, bushland setting on the New South Wales north coast. Only the bare bones of the jail remain; the roof and all other readily detachable parts of the complex were sold in 1922 after which the buildings were left to decay for forty years until they began to arouse the interest of tourists.

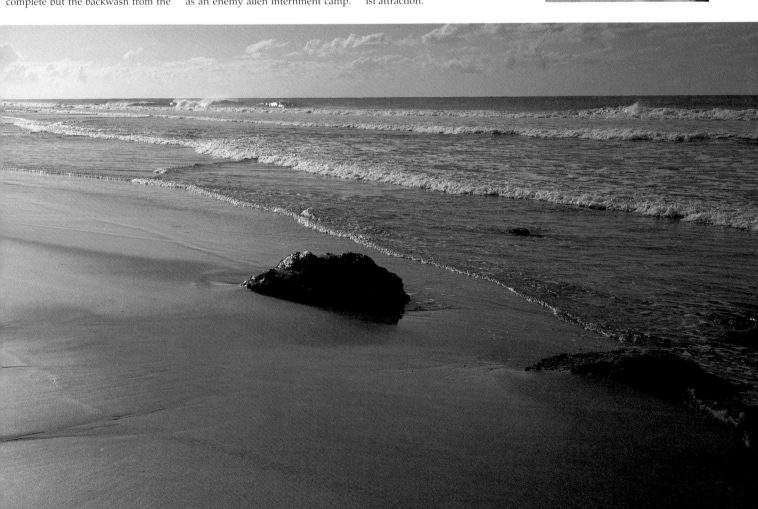

TRIAL BAY ■ 465

In 1816 the brig *Trial*, hijacked by a group of convicts from Jackson Bay, was wrecked here and gave its name to the bay and, for a while to the nearby river, later renamed Macleay. A number of other ships have been wrecked in Trial Bay including the most recent and still visible *Koondooloo*, a former Newcastle ferry, and the old showboat *Sydney Queen*, wrecked in 1972.

On tow to the Philippines, the two boats, together with a third, which sank without trace, were either cut loose from the towing vessel or broke loose and were grounded on the sands of Trial Bay. All efforts to refloat them failed and, at low tide, the superstructure of the *Sydney Queen* is visible while the *Koondooloo* lies totally exposed on the beach.

The famous jail at Trial Bay is not a relic of Australia's convict days but is a memorial to nineteenth-century enlightenment and prison reform. The prison was built as a public-works prison, the only one of its kind in the state. Construction, in the extremely hard local granite, started in 1877 and when the first wing was finished in 1886, the prisoners were moved in. Their task was to build the rest of the prison and a breakwater to make Trial Bay a safe anchorage and a 'port in a storm'.

By 1900, the rest of the prison was complete but the backwash from the Macleay River swept sections of newly built breakwater away at regular intervals. By 1902, with 300 metres of the breakwater completed, an overnight storm almost completely washed it away. The breakwater and the prison were abandoned the next year. The whaleboat ferry service that the prisoners had offered to those disembarking from steamships that could not get up the Macleay River, was sorely missed.

The prison was brought back into use from 1915 to 18 when it was used as an enemy alien internment camp. Most of the internees were German-born Australians though Germans from the Pacific Islands and a group of Buddhist monks from what was then Ceylon (Sri Lanka) were also interned at Trial Bay. At the end of the war, the internees were repatriated - the Germans had already been moved to Holsworthy, outside Sydney – and the jail was again closed.

On its spectacular site on the headland, the roofless granite building has been 're-cycled' is now enjoying a third use as a major tourist attraction.

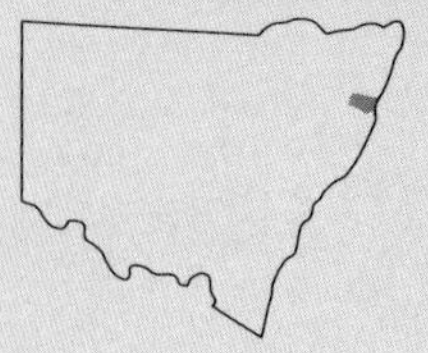

Nambucca Heads & Macksville

Though small in area and in population, this region offers a surprising variety of landscape and 'waterscape' – from the high, wilderness areas and waterfalls of two national parks, to the shifting estuaries and coastal resorts where the Bellinger and Nambucca rivers enter the ocean.

BELLINGEN ■ 466

Bellingen grew up as a service centre for the pioneer cedar-getters operating on both banks of the Bellinger River and was called 'Boat Harbour' until it was officially gazetted in 1870 as Bellingen. Billingen or Bellingen, from an Aboriginal word meaning 'cheeky fellow' or 'loudmouth', was the original name used for the Bellinger River (see entry) by Surveyor General Hodgkinson in 1841.

In addition to the timber, the town became known for its shipbuilding and, by the 1880s, for its dairy industry. In 1905, local farmers started the district's first co-operative for processing and marketing milk products and a butter factory operated in Bellingen for many years. Pigs were processed in the local bacon factory and maize and tropical fruits were later added to the list of 'exports' from Bellingen. At first, produce was carried down the Bellinger River on flat-bottomed boats but as the river became increasingly difficult to navigate, the extension of the railway line to Coffs Harbour provided a lifeline.

A small group of early twentieth-century buildings in Hyde Street, including a hotel, a ladies' hairdresser, a newsagency and a chemist, are heritage-listed. The best known and most interesting of these buildings is however, the Hammond and Wheatley Emporium, built by Bellingen resident, bridge builder and inventor, George Moore. Although Moore had invented a corn husking machine, a system for 'unifying' different rail gauges and a new type of saw, the specially designed concrete-brick-making machine he used for the construction of the emporium – the first concrete-block building in Australia – was imported from the United States.

Bellingen is perhaps best known as the birthplace of Australia's first reported quads – the Sara quads – and, in recent years as a centre for artists and craftsmen who have established a number of craft centres in the town including one in the old butter factory. *Population 2300*

FESTIVALS Bellingen Jazz Festival, August; Azalea Festival, September.

BELLINGER RIVER ■ 467

The Bellinger River rises on the Dorrigo Plateau and in the New England National Park (see entry), and waters a fertile valley – now a National Trust conservation area – on its 115-kilometre journey to the coast. It meets up with the Kalang River (previously the South Arm of the Bellinger River) near Urunga, and flows with it into the Pacific Ocean through a man-made channel.

Although it is possible that convicts on the run may have reached the Bellinger River as early as the 1820s, a stockman, William Miles, and two sawyers are usually credited with being the first Europeans to reach the river in 1841. The sawyers would certainly have been excited by what they saw.

High-quality cedar logs were soon floating down the Bellinger River, though the heaviness of some of the close-grained logs and the opportunities for timber 'rustling' (hauling an unguarded log out of the river and 'rebranding' it) added an element of risk. The largest 'raft' of logs floated down the Bellinger River was over 200 metres long and required a fleet of twenty coastal steamers to transport it to Sydney.

Paddlewheelers were later used to transport timber and regular trading ships operated in the river during the second half of the nineteenth century. Shipbuilding on the Bellinger started in the 1840s, declined in the 1850s and 1860s but was resumed, on a much smaller scale from the 1870s to the early 1900s. But the sandbar at the entrance to the Bellinger and the constant silting upstream meant that pilots, tugs and full-time dredgers were fighting a losing battle. By the 1930s the river was unnavigable to anything but small boats and canoes.

BOWRAVILLE ■ 468

Gazetted in 1870, Bowraville, like many of the settlements in the Nambucca and Bellinger valleys, boasted a steam sawmill, a butter factory and a bacon factory, for processing the three main products of the district. For some years after the Second World War, the town suffered a decline – the milk and butter factories closed and the market for local timber shrank. Without the tourism that brought wealth to the coastal towns and villages, there was little interest in, or finance for, development in Bowraville. In the long run this operated in the town's favour and Bowraville is now an urban conservation area with a streetscape of verandahs that escaped the scourge of post-war modernisation.

Bowraville, known as 'Verandah Post Town', was the setting for the Australian film *The Umbrella Woman* starring Bryan Brown, Rachel Ward and Sam Neill. The folk museum is a treasure trove of memorabilia and gadgets, including a 1902 electric belt guaranteed to cure all ills. Regular Saturday markets bring tourists from nearby Nambucca Heads – where once timber was shipped out of Bowraville to Nambucca Heads, now tourists are shipped in.

Bowraville is also the shire headquarters and its racecourse has regular meetings and an annual cup. Trees are still a vital part of Bowraville. Palms and oleanders run down the centre of High Street and, in the nature reserve on the town's perimeter, pockets of rainforest provide a habitat for lyrebirds and bush turkeys. *Population 960*

FESTIVALS Back to Bowra, October.

CATHEDRAL ROCK NATIONAL PARK ■ 469

The rock that gives the park its name is one of several huge freestanding granite boulders (tors) that are scattered around the 6529-hectare park. Like huge toys abandoned by giants, some perched precariously on top of others, these pink granite tors are the remaining hardcore of even larger boulders after 230 million years of weathering and erosion.

Cathedral Rock balances on the north face of Round Mountain (1580 metres), which is not only the highest point within the national park but is also the highest point between Canberra and North Queensland. Subsequently, the mountain's peak has a radar tracking station for aircraft flying between Sydney and Brisbane…and, despite its latitude, snow in winter.

Vegetation includes mountain and snow gums, rare pygmy cypresses, New England blackbutts, messmates and the wildflowers and mosses of the swamps around Cathedral Rock itself. Within this diverse vegetation, fly wedge-tailed eagles and a number of species of robins, thornbills and cockatoos including the rare glossy black cockatoo with the distinctive red markings on its tail.

Bushwalking – or boulder scrambling – from the two main centres at

Legal graffiti reaches artistic heights on the Nambucca Heads breakwater.

Barokee camping ground and Native Dog Creek is not for the faint hearted; a single chain is provided to haul yourself up the last boulder outcrop near the top of Cathedral Rock.

MACKSVILLE ■ 470

Macksville is on the road – and rail line – between South West Rocks and Nambucca Heads but unlike these two seaside towns it is set back from the coast and has fewer tourists, a greater diversity of industries and more of a country town atmosphere.

Macksville is divided by the Nambucca River (see entry) after which the original settlement was named in the early 1870s. It was not until 1890 that the name Nambucca or Central Nambucca was changed to Macksville after Angus Mackay and Hugh MacInally, whose land had been subdivided for the town.

Macksville was one of the first settlements on this part of the coastline and throughout the late nineteenth century was known for its regattas and sculling races. Macksville also played an important part in the development of two new, and still important regional industries. The Mid-Coast Cooperative Meat Society (Midco) was founded in 1938 with an abattoir in Macksville, the town's largest employer. The first tomatoes were shipped to the markets in Sydney from Macksville in the 1920s, laying the foundations for the Central North Coast Fruit and Vegetable Growers Association in 1926.

Steamers no longer operate from the government wharf at Macksville and the three vehicular ferries that used to transport cars from one side of the Nambucca River to the other at Macksville were replaced with a road bridge in 1931. *Population 2870*

NAMBUCCA HEADS ■ 471

The first settler in Nambucca Heads was a fisherman called Lane who, from the late 1860s, lived in a small humpy and survived on fish and the 'fares' he collected for ferrying pioneers – on their way to the Bellinger River – across the Nambucca River.

Despite the activity generated by the timber industry and an extremely active few years of shipbuilding between 1875 and 1879, the first land put up for sale found no buyers until the early 1880s. The main problem was the bar at the entrance to the Nambucca River (see entry).

Despite its position, on sea and river, loads of timber from the Nambucca Valley could not initially be shipped from Nambucca Heads but were transported overland to the Macleay River for shipping. Work on

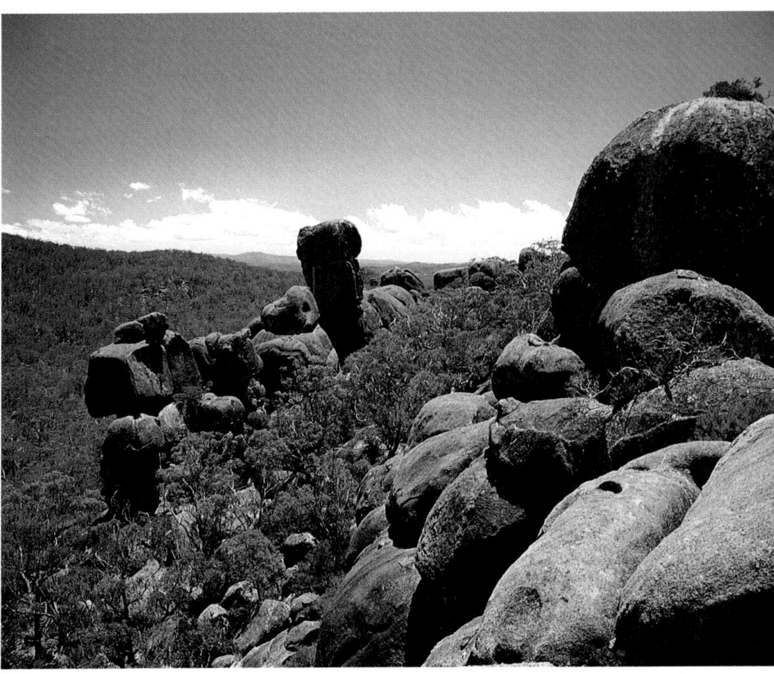

Cathedral Rock and its attendant granite outcrops – on the northern side of the Snowy Mountain Range – are a tribute to the elements' erosive powers.

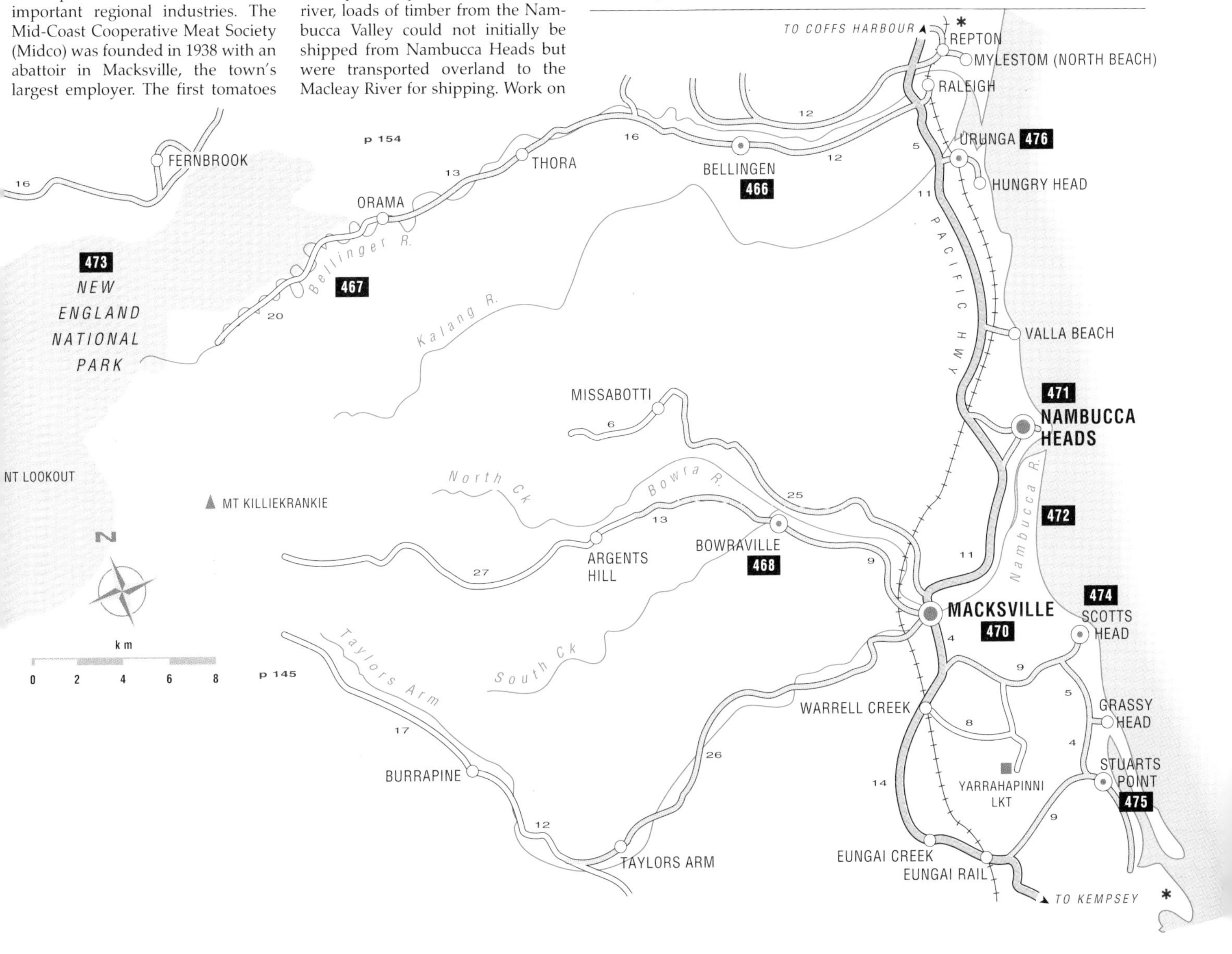

a breakwater at Nambucca Heads started in 1895 and, for several years, coastal shipping in the harbour and up river as far as Macksville was commonplace. Work on the breakwater was abandoned in the early years of this century and not reactivated until the Great Depression of the 1930s when large concrete blocks were added to the breakwater by unemployed workers. A few of these blocks, at the harbour entrance, have found a new purpose as a tourist attraction. The so-called Vee Wall is decorated with colourful, variegated graffiti, encouraged by the local government and tourist authorities.

To the timber, maize, pigs and dairy produce of the district, Nambucca Heads added bananas and, after the coming of the railway in 1923, tourists, who still flock to the town each summer. *Population 5680*

STUART ISLAND The island in the Nambucca River, joined to the mainland by a causeway, was, and still is, sacred to the Kumbainggiri Aborigines. Generations of ancestors are buried on the island as are the sacred artefacts of Ulidarra, the good spirit. From 1883 the island was an Aboriginal Reserve – until reclaimed by the Crown – the last Aborigines leaving the reserve in the 1920s. Nowadays, it is leased to the Nambucca Heads Island Golf Club.

FESTIVALS Nambucca Heads September Fest, September.

NAMBUCCA RIVER ■ 472

The river, like the town, is said to take its name from the Aboriginal word *ngambugka* meaning 'crooked river' or 'entrance to the waters'. The river starts just west of Macksville where the Bowra River meets Taylors Arm. The beer, according to the old song doesn't flow at the Taylors Arm 'pub with no beer' and neither does the water in this short, silted river that is more estuary than stream. But with its clean white sands and total lack of power boats, the river provides an excellent environment – and excellent catches – for fishermen.

NEW ENGLAND NATIONAL PARK ■ 473

This rugged park on the escarpment of the New England Tablelands owes its existence to the foresight of Phillip Wright who, in the 1920s, began working for the declaration of part of the area, which he had known since childhood, as a wilderness reserve.

In 1931 a reserve around Point Lookout was declared and by 1935 a somewhat larger area was reserved for public recreation, with a part-time ranger employed to accompany parties into the park and construct walking tracks. A huge crowd turned out for the official opening by the Governor-General, Lord Gowrie, in 1937 but the rain prevented many of them reaching Point Lookout so the ceremony was repeated down at Serpentine River...with the sun shining.

Spectacular waterfalls, frozen over in winter, tumble from the volcanic basalt peaks to the deep forested valleys. The range in altitude from 300 to 1600 metres above sea level results in a mix of vegetation that varies from the alpine to the subtropical

Unusual fauna includes the sphagnum frog, which is unique to the New England National Park. The frog burrows deep into sphagnum moss where it lays its eggs, the hatched young exiting from the burrow as fully-formed little frogs, ready to practise the distinctive soft, low growl or creak of the species. Leaf-tailed geckos, bearded lizards, water dragons, the platypuses and 2000 bent-winged bats of Platypus Creek and the increasingly rare, cat-sized – and carnivorous – spotted tail quoll are among the many inhabitants of the park.

Human visitors must appreciate the wild and rugged qualities of the park since much of it is trackless although a few walking tracks have been laid out around the lookouts at the top of the park.

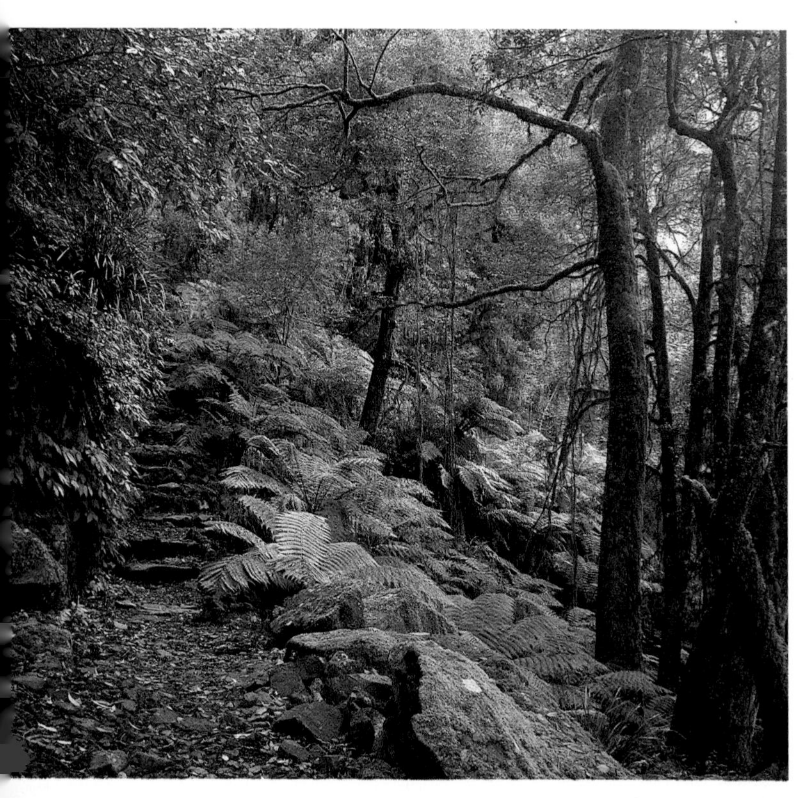

SCOTTS HEAD ■ 474

Beyond the Pacific Highway, a buffer zone of thick bushland and banana plantations preserves the tranquillity of this seaside village with its selection of small or large surfing beaches and rock-ledge surf-fishing. Walking, swimming, fishing, and boating on Warrill Creek behind the shoreline dunes are the main attractions for holiday-makers seeking an 'uncomplicated and relaxing break – as the tourist brochures say: 'the main attraction of Scotts Head is its lack of attractions'. *Population 840*

YARRAHAPINNI The branch road to Scotts Head is also the route to the Way Way State Forest and the Yarrahapinni Ecology Centre, a magnet for generations of New South Wales schoolchildren. Tourists associate the name with the spectacular lookout on the top of Mount Yarrahapinni (490 metres) in the state forest.

STUARTS POINT ■ 475

Long before Europeans arrived, the area around Stuart's Point was obviously a meeting- and eating-place for local Aborigines. The Aboriginal midden at Stuarts Point is one of the largest and most complex ever discovered. It spreads – on and off – for over two-and-a-half kilometres, at depths of up to two metres and widths up to thirty metres.

Stuarts Point was named after John Campbell Stuart who moved to the district in the 1840s searching for the ideal combination of plentiful timber and safe, deep water for his shipbuilding. By the 1870s Stuart had moved further north to open a shipyard at Nambucca Heads but his name remained.

Stuarts Point has its origins as the first wharf on the navigable Macleay River, which entered the sea at nearby Grassy Head. The government wharf, timber mill and cattle yards transformed the fledgling settlement into a bustling port...until the river changed its mind in 1893. When the Macleay River burst a new exit to the sea at South West Rocks (see *Kempsey & South West Rocks*), the effect on Stuarts Point was exactly the same as if the railway had bypassed it, especially in view of the inexplicable failure a few years earlier of the fishing industry. Abandoned by coastal shipping and fishermen, the old river entrance silted over and Stuarts Point's inhabitants turned to the fruit and vegetable growing...and 'yabbying' for which the village is well known. *Population 690*

A large portion of the eastern edge of the New England Tableland is preserved in the New England National Park where the only man-made intrusion are the pathways – here at Point Lookout – through the cool-temperate rainforest habitat of the spotted tail quoll (above).

URUNGA ■ 476

Once known as Bellinger Heads, the name Urunga meaning 'long beach' was suggested for the town by the Surveyor-General, George Evans and adopted in the early 1900s. But, in addition to the beaches such as Mylestom to the north and Hungry Head, at the original river mouth, to the south, Urunga is surrounded by water – a coastal lagoon and the ocean on its east side, the Bellinger River on its north and the Kalang River on its west. Although already rich in natural water resources, the town also has a man-made Sea Lido constructed in 1981.

From 1868 until 1933, a pilot station operated at Urunga but most of the 'shipping' around the town is now much smaller and is there for the fishing rather than the shipping of timber.

Urunga, already the largest town in what is a sparsely populated region with few settlements of any consequence inland, is now a centre for residential and tourist developments and its population is expected to increase accordingly. *Population 2670*

HONEY PLACE Visitors to the Honey Place make their entrance through a large and unusual, yellow concrete replica of a European straw beehive, which is the anteroom of the honey sampling bar and art gallery. Outside, among the beehives, is a glass observation hive through which the buzz of activity can be safely viewed.

Armidale & Uralla

Pastoral empires were established early on the prime grasslands of the New England plateau. Wealth from wool spurred the growth of a stately city and seat of learning, architecturally and culturally the richest of inland Australia.

Despite the name from homesick Britons, New England could hardly look more Australian.

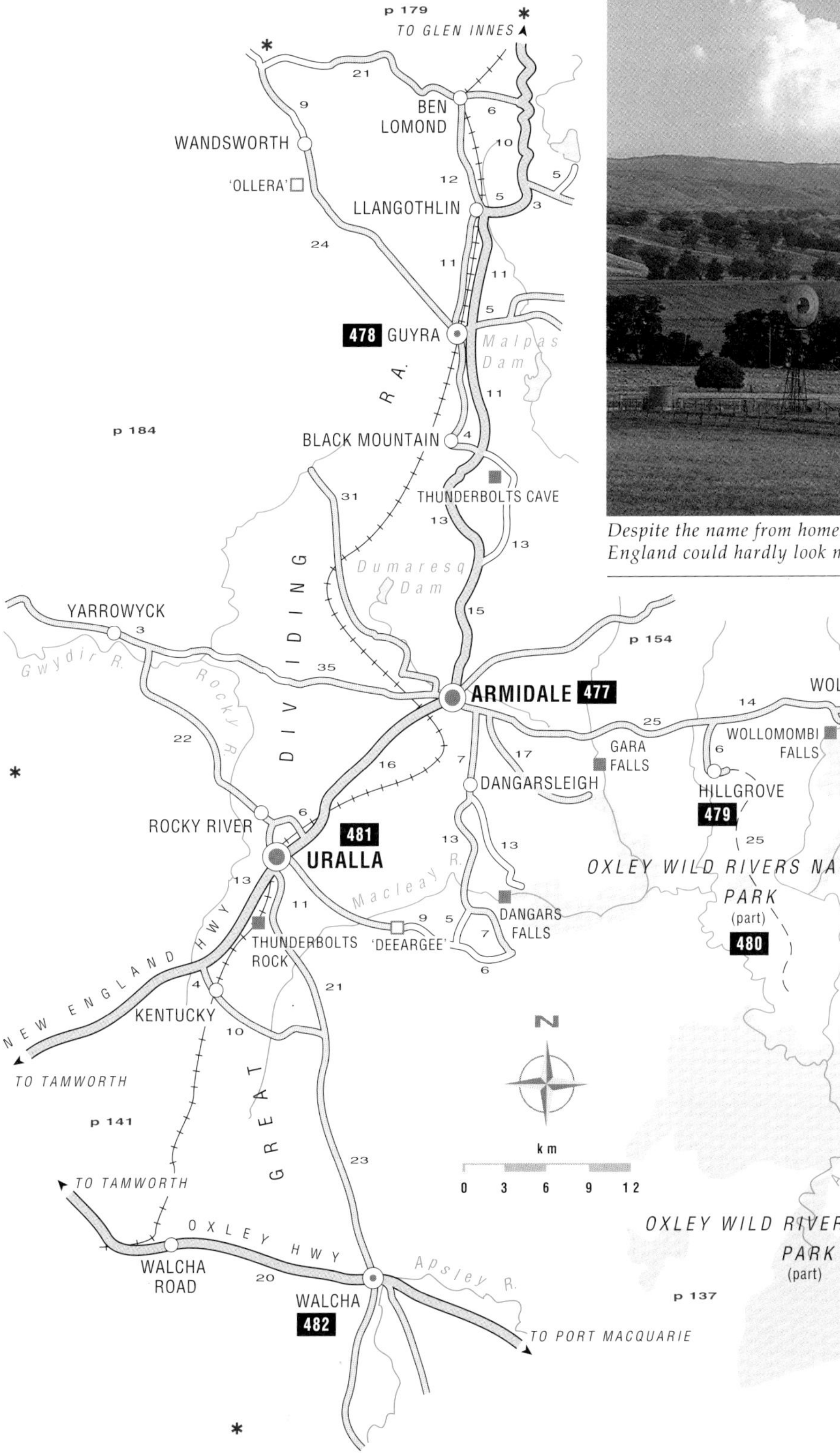

ARMIDALE ■ 477

Early this century Armidale was prominent among the inland sites considered for a federal capital. Often since, it has been the focus of periodic agitation to form a separate New England state. The city – the highest in Australia – has a grace and history that would befit a capital.

Two brothers of the Dumaresq family had already set up sheep runs at 'Saumarez' and 'Tilbuster' when a Scottish-born lands commissioner, George Macdonald, established a base beside Dumaresq Creek in 1839. He called his choice of site Armidale after the seat of his clan on the Isle of Skye. Such was the pace of pastoral growth in the region, and Armidale's suitability as a mercantile and transport centre, that it had a post office and court house by 1844 and was gazetted as a town in 1849. Urban population remained small – only 500-odd in 1851 – but the burgeoning district supported two breweries, five inns and two flour mills.

Church authorities saw an early need to set up New England administrations. Again Armidale's strategic location made it the obvious choice of see for both Anglican and Roman Catholic Bishops. St Peter's Anglican Cathedral was built between 1871 and 1878 – except for the tower, which did not come until 1938. The delaying of this finishing touch was allowed for in the structural plans of the noted architect J. Horbury Hunt, who anticipated a cut in the construction budget. This was the first Gothic-style cathedral constructed in Australia to be built entirely of brick rather than stone.

Sts Mary and Joseph's Roman Catholic Cathedral, which outdoes St Peter's in size and ornamentation and dominates the city centre, was completed in 1912. It replaced a smaller cathedral built in 1872.

Armidale was already winning a reputation as the country's finest inland seat of learning when it was proclaimed a city in 1885. This began with the establishment of boarding schools and colleges under church auspices. New England landowners increasingly placed their children in these institutions rather than send them to Sydney. Armidale Teachers' College, founded in 1928, is now a part of the University of New England. The university – at first an outpost of the University of Sydney – opened its doors in 1938, thanks to the donation of another of Horbury Hunt's buildings, the expansive 'Booloominbah' (see sub-entry) and its extensive hillside grounds on the northwestern fringe of the city. More than a quarter of the city's population works or studies at the university or depends directly on its activities. *Population 21 610*

CITY CONSERVATION PRECINCT Seven nineteenth-century buildings clustered in the centre of Armidale are individually listed by the National Trust. In the hope of preserving the overall look of the area they and some more recent grandly designed structures are embraced in a joint listing. Among the key buildings is the distinctive court house, with its many late-Victorian extensions and embellishments added to what is a simple brick design dating from 1860. Behind it is the modest sheriff's cottage (1880).

Across the street, the colonnaded front of the 1880 post office harmonises well with its neighbour, a banking house that originated in 1882 as a Lands Board office and later became the telegraph office. Perhaps most eye-catching to visitors is the richly ornamented Imperial Hotel (1890). Public areas of its spacious interior retain the decor of last century. The southern part of the precinct includes the Folk Museum, the Lands Office (1887) and the Town Hall (1882).

NEW ENGLAND REGIONAL ART MUSEUM In an ultra-modern building opened in 1983, three existing collections were brought together and added to through donations and an active policy of acquisition. The Howard Hinton collection of more than a thousand traditional Australian works was originally donated to the Armidale Teachers' College. The Chandler Coventry collection of more than 200 paintings by Sydney modernists since the 1960s was previously held in the now-superseded Armidale City Gallery, along with a city council collection of 300 more varied works.

'BOOLOOMINBAH' In 1882, grazier Frederick White bought a generous spread on Armidale's northwestern slopes and set about establishing an administrative base for his pastoral empire. The most fashionable architect of the time, the Canadian Horbury Hunt, designed the forty-five-room mansion with a grandiose entrance staircase and a labyrinth of other stairways and corridors – something to rival the stateliest of England's country homes – and it was occupied by 1888.

In 1937 White's son-in-law bought the house and 75 hectares of land from the estate and offered the property to the University of Sydney on the condition that the administrators establish a local university college. 'Booloominbah' now houses administrative offices of the University of New England.

'SAUMAREZ' Five kilometres south of Armidale, this fine late-Victorian and Edwardian country home, well maintained in its original style, is open to visitors at weekends and on public holidays in all but the mid-winter months. The two-storey house with its gardens and outbuildings was presented to the National Trust in 1984 by the White family, owners of the Armidale district's oldest sheep station.

The 'Saumarez' complex originated in 1888 as a single-storey structure of bricks baked on the site and red cedar joinery hauled from the Styx River. The upper level was added in 1906, providing for eleven bedrooms and staff quarters. Other buildings include a dairy and schoolhouse. A timber homestead previously occupied the site; some of its materials are thought to have been reused in a station hand's cottage nearby.

'Booloominbah' a prescursor of the Federation style, was as carefully designed inside as it was outside. The elaborate oak fireplace and stairway (below) is complimented by stained-glass windows (above) depicting local pastoral pursuits.

The vast bulk of 'Booloominbah', once described as 'probably the finest country house in Australia', contains a wealth of architectural elements.

GUYRA ■ 478

Graziers settled the Guyra district in the 1830s. A planned village northeast of the present site failed in the 1850s, but a settlement grew slowly at the junction of the main route north and the branch road to Inverell. In 1884, when the northern railway reached this point a commercial township developed rapidly; a town was officially proclaimed in 1885. At 1320 metres above sea level, Guyra is the highest town in New England and, subject to occasional snowfalls, styles itself the 'top of the range'town. *Population1940*

ST BARTHOLOMEW'S CHURCH A charming building of rustic simplicity, St Bartholomew's was built on donated land close to the homestead of Ollera Station, about twenty kilometres northwest of Guyra. It has been in continuous use since its completion in 1877, as has its graveyard.

MOTHER OF DUCKS LAGOON This extensive natural sanctuary for waterfowl, just south-west of Guyra, was drained early this century to create farmland and later a golf course. Despite this, some parts of the area continued to flood in very wet seasons. In the 1980s as a bicentennial project, it was decided to return as much as possible of the landscape to its original state and let nature take its course. A walkway leads from waterside picnic grounds to a viewing platform over the water, where thousands of ducks, geese, swans and wading birds can be seen from late spring to autumn.

THUNDERBOLTS CAVE Reputedly one of the hideouts of the bushranger Frederick Ward (see box), the cave is reached by a loop from the New England Highway near Guyra. It makes a pleasant picnic spot.

HILLGROVE ■ 479

Perched on the lip of a gorge that drops 600 metres to Bakers Creek, the hamlet of Hillgrove today hears mostly birdsong and the bleating of livestock. A century ago, this place resounded to the pounding of great engines and to thumping blasts from mine shafts deep in the rock below, and buzzed with the activities of nearly 4000 people.

The boomtown was founded not so much on gold – though lodes in the granite of Bakers Creek yielded plenty – as on antimony, a metal just as rare and for which there were many more uses. Employed as a hardening agent in many industrial processes, antimony in the late nineteenth century was also sought after by munitions manufacturers for the production of shrapnel shells.

During the 1890s, Australia provided up to a quarter of the global supply – and Hillgrove's smelters were the principal source. But the demand for energy to process the metal and to operate deep mining techniques called for more than the burning of wood or coal could provide. Australia's first water-driven power generator was commissioned here and Hillgrove became the first community with streets and homes lit by hydro-electricity.

Gold finds were exhausted and antimony prices declined dramatically by the 1920s. Mining companies shut down their operations and the populace drifted away. A former public school – one of three in Hillgrove's heyday, along with five churches and two banks – serves as a historical museum.

Paintings characteristic of the ancient Aboriginal culture of the New England Tablelands are on public view in a rock shelter on the western slopes of Mount Yarroyck, thirty kilometres west of Armidale. In a cavity five metres long and two-and-a-half metres deep but barely one metre high can be seen patterns of emu tracks, human stick figures and symbolic markings in orange and red. Evidence of deliberate retouching suggests that the paintings were not merely decorative but had a ceremonial importance.

OXLEY WILD RIVERS NATIONAL PARK ■ 480

Tributaries of the Macleay River plunge spectacularly from the spectacular, broken rim of the rugged New England Escarpment into narrow gorges, scattered haphazardly in a dramatically wild arc east and south of Armidale. Areas of outstanding scenic and recreational value are preserved in the disjointed sections of Oxley Wild Rivers National Park, totalling 92 000 hectares. Most are accessible from the Armidale–Dorrigo road or from Walcha.

No one should miss a view of Wollomombi Falls – at 470 metres the highest in Australia, with one sheer drop of 220 metres. The neighbouring Chandler Falls are almost as high. Continuing past them, adventurous motorists meet the upper Macleay River at Georges Creek and find the diversion of a little-known bush route that descends to the Pacific Highway at Kempsey.

Closer to Armidale, easy trips can be made to the Gara Gorge or to Dangars Falls, where delightful half-day or full-day walks can be taken. From Walcha, there is car access to another superb lookout at Budds Mare, the starting point for a long walk to the Apsley River. Other spectacular falls occur in these southern reaches of the park, the Apsley and Tia falls flow into deep gorges. While the wilderness areas of the park are fully enjoyed only by dedicated bushwalkers and canoeists, its car-access points are well endowed with public facilities.

URALLA ■ 481

When gold prospectors struck it rich at Rocky River in 1852, Samuel McCrossin struck richest of all. Two years earlier, he had established an inn where the rough track towards Bundarra left the main north road. The track eventually became a busy thoroughfare to the diggings and at the road junction – as often happened at such places – the township of Uralla sprang up quickly, with McCrossin as its leading merchant. A town was officially proclaimed on the site in 1855 and in 1859 there were three hotels, a post office,stores, a flour mill and a school.

Although miners moved on after the 1860s the town continued to prosper as the centre of a rich pastoral district unfortunately known less for the wealth of its produce than the activities of the notorious bushranger Captain Thunderbolt (see box). A remarkable number of buildings dating well back into last century can be seen on Uralla's heritage walking tour. It starts at McCrossin's Mill (1870), a massive structure of granite and brick which has been converted into a historical museum. *Population 2320*

DANGARS LAGOON NATURE RESERVE An observation hide and identification notes are provided at this bird sanctuary five kilometres south of Uralla on the Walcha road.

'DEEARGEE' WOOLSHED Astonishing architectural originality was shown by pioneering pastoralist Henry Dangar in 1851 when he designed an octagonal shearing chamber with a tiered roof like that of a truncated pagoda. The roof allowed maximum ventilation while two dozen shearers could work in a circle below, moving the sheep through with unheard-of speed. The building remains in use on 'Deeargee' (formerly part of the Dangar family's historic 'Gostwyck' property), about eleven kilometres south-east of Uralla.

WALCHA ■ 482

Walcha takes pride in having been the first area of New England settled by Europeans. The explorer John Oxley and his party camped by the Apsley River in 1818, and sheep were driven there from the upper Hunter Valley fourteen years later. The main station of the pioneering sheep run was called Wolka, said to be an Aboriginal word for 'the sun'.

In the late 1840s, the station's inn, store, post office and blacksmith's forge formed the nucleus of what almost became a private township. The government reserve, intended for a small future settlement, was extended to include these buildings so that any attempt at a private development was forestalled.

Walcha's prosperity was boosted by nearby gold discoveries in the 1870s. Timber milling and a meat industry also took on some importance. But the economic mainstay throughout the district's history has been the production of fine wool. Aerial topdressing with superphosphate was tried here for the first time in Australia in 1950. Stock-carrying capacities and the local wool clip increased dramatically.

The Tiger Moth biplane that did the job is displayed in one of the nine buildings which comprise Walcha's Pioneer Cottage and Museum complex, open at weekends and on public holidays. The rough-hewn timber slab cottage which forms the complex's centrepiece has been restored and furnished to depict the setting of a pioneering family's daily life. It is thought to date from 1858. *Population 1780*

FESTIVALS Timber Expo, September in odd-numbered years.

THUNDERBOLT: AN UNLIKELY HERO

In life, Frederick Ward was to all intents and purposes like most bushrangers – an incorrigible robber and thief who caused nothing but trouble. But in New England folklore, as the 'Thunderbolt' of the 1860s, he has become Ned Kelly and Robin Hood rolled into one. In 1988, Ward's misdeeds were glorified with a bronze equestrian statue in the centre of Uralla.

In a rampage through the region lasting nearly seven years, 'Captain Thunderbolt' notched up twenty-five mail coach robberies, more than thirty raids on homes, hotels and shops, six victimisations of itinerant traders and no fewer than eighty horse thefts. Ward does seem to have shown genuine compassion for underdogs, though a contemporary ditty took it too far:

My name is Frederick Ward,
I'm a native of this isle.
I rob the rich to feed the poor
And make the children smile.

There is no evidence that Ward had any altruistic motives for his crimes. But he was known to have relented when some of his victims showed that they could not afford to be robbed. On one occasion, he held up a band of touring musicians and took all of their money – a miserable amount. Then he commanded a roadside performance from them, handed back some of the cash and asked for the band's forwarding address. Some weeks later they received the rest of the money by post.

The son of convicts, Ward was born near Sydney in 1835 and grew up in the Hunter Valley. In 1856, he was convicted of receiving 15 stolen horses and sentenced to ten years' hard labour. He served four years on Cockatoo Island in Sydney Harbour before being paroled to work near Mudgee. There he breached his parole conditions and was sent back to the island.

After two more years, Ward escaped from the island prison by swimming across the Parramatta River; he travelled north to the countryside he knew best. Horses and food were supplied by a girl who had been his lover in Mudgee.

'Thunderbolt', a master horseman if nothing else, outran the law until 1870. Then a hawker who had been robbed at Uralla, alerted the police quickly enough for them to trap Ward near a local creek. He was shot while grappling with a constable on horseback. A heap of granite boulders by the highway south of Uralla is said to have been one of Ward's many lairs. □

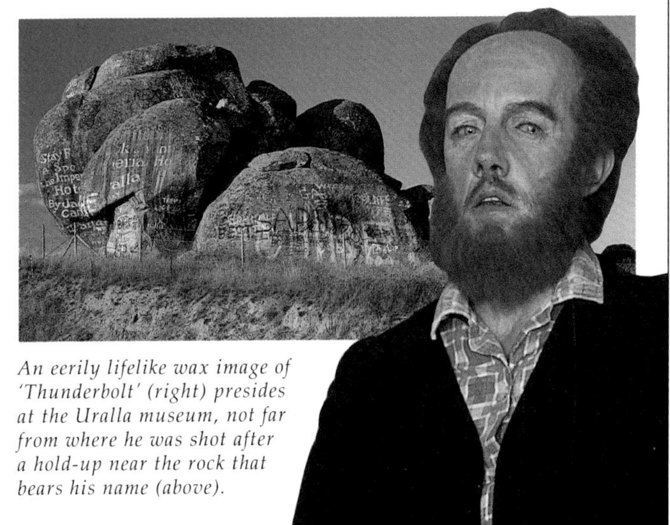

An eerily lifelike wax image of 'Thunderbolt' (right) presides at the Uralla museum, not far from where he was shot after a hold-up near the rock that bears his name (above).

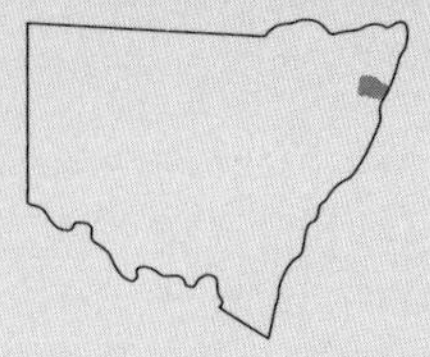

Coffs Harbour & Sawtell

The hard work of establishing towns and villages in this region was done last century, in the forests and little ports, down the mines or on struggling farms. Nowadays holiday-makers flock to sheltered beaches in a pampering climate, vowing to return again each year.

ARRAWARRA ■ 483

Arrawarra Headland's large bulk shelters Corindi Beach, sweeping eight kilometres north to Red Rock. Swimmers and anglers find ample space even at peak times. Not far up the beach, the Arrawarra township caters in a modest way for visitors, offering camping and picnic grounds and a caravan park.

An inland turn-off from the Pacific Highway just south of Arrawarra, links with the scenic Wedding Bells Forest Drive, looping back to the coast farther south at Woolgoolga or Coffs Harbour. Parts of the hilly and winding route were formed from the tracks of bullock carts – the only means of hauling out timber in the nineteenth century.

High up along Gentle Annie Road is Mary's Waterhole, one of the bullock teams' old refreshment points. Before the bullockies' intrusion it was frequented by pregnant Aboriginal women who believed that bathing in its water would ensure a trouble-free birth. *Population 1275*

COFFS HARBOUR ■ 484

Shipbuilder and trader John Korff was understandably piqued in 1861 when a port intended to be named in his honour was misspelt on Sydney survey records. He had reported a safe anchorage between South and Muttonbird Islands fourteen years before, after a southerly gale forced his ship away from the Bellinger River mouth. Korff returned later, bringing in sawyers and supplies and loading prized red cedar, and eventually became the district's pioneering settler and storekeeper.

Much earlier, Muttonbird Island had been located on the maritime chart of one of the epic voyages of colonial history. William and Mary Bryant, their two children and seven other convicts rested and feasted there in 1791, having made an audacious escape from Port Jackson in the governor's cutter. Their journey of 69

An ideal location has drawn tourists and new residents to Coffs Harbour so that, like Port Macquarie, it has become an 'urban growth centre'.

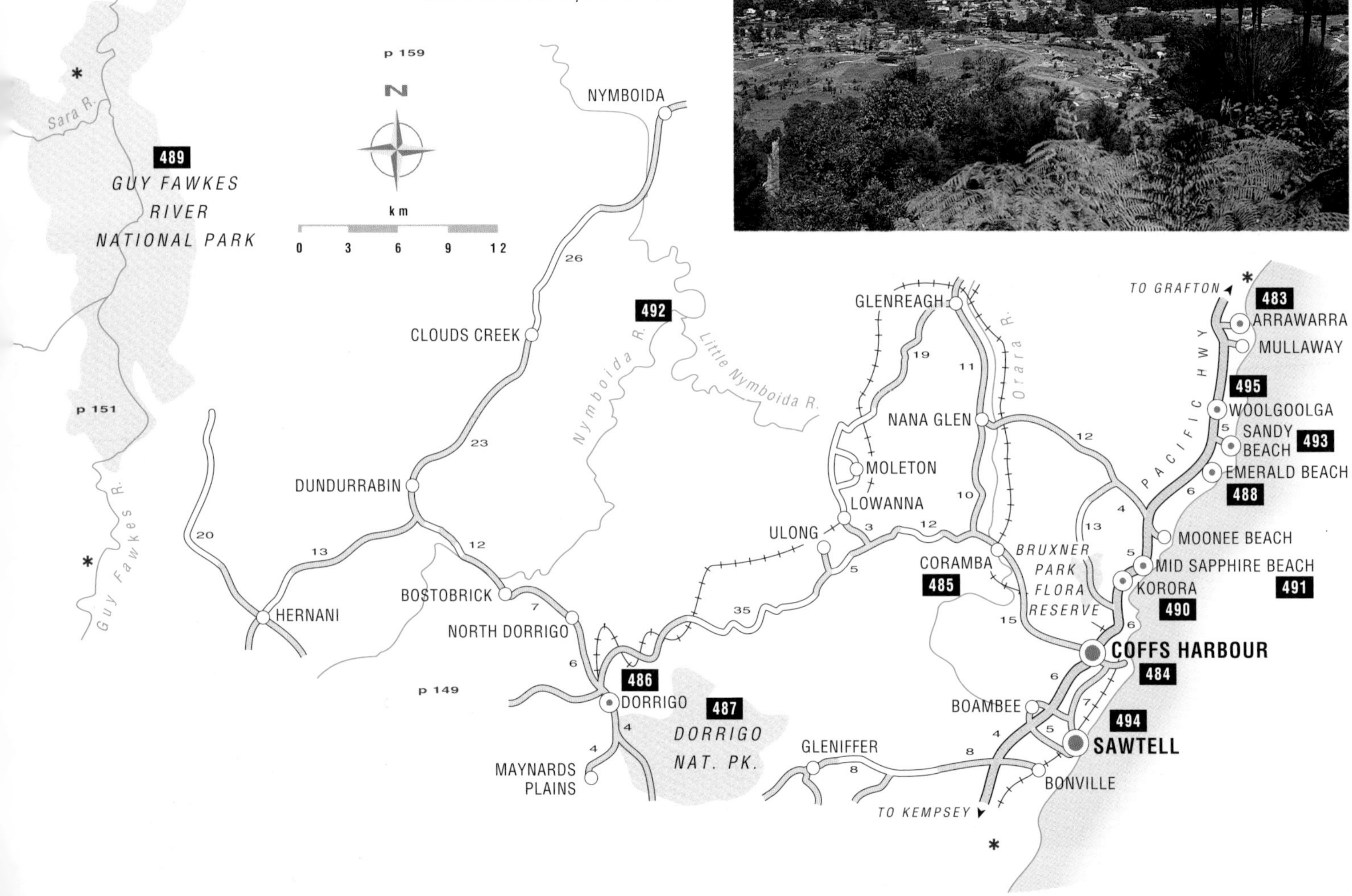

days took them to Cape York and across the Arafura and Timor Seas to Kupang, Timor – 3254 nautical miles without a single life lost.

Initially, cedar logs were rafted down the creek, then hooked to a continuous, winch-drawn cable that worked like a conveyor belt, pulling the logs to ships standing well offshore. But the 'port' lost its brief trade in 1865 when one such vessel, the *Carrywell*, was driven aground in an easterly gale and wrecked. A few years later the cedar-getters returned and timber sustained the growth in the 1870s of a village near the mouth of Coffs Creek

From around the turn of the century, farmers sowed heat-tolerant paspalum grass and introduced dairy herds. These were to be the mainstay of the district until the profitability of cultivating bananas and other fruit and vegetables became apparent in the 1930s.

A township was formally planned in 1887 and replanned in 1897. Road and rail links were expanding but the most ambitious hopes rested on the creation of a real harbour, improving on an 1890s jetty. South Island was quarried during the First World War to build the southern causeway and breakwater. Then a northern breakwater was pushed out to Muttonbird Island (see box). Although coastal shipping would gradually decline – and eventually disappear with the coming of railway freight services and road transport – the jetty was in use until the 1960s.

In spite of all its ups and downs, 'Coffs' has done better than just survive. It gained city status in 1987 and the city is part of a region with the fastest-growing population between Newcastle and the Queensland border. The white-elephant harbour has come back into its own as a base for a modern fishing fleet and for pleasure boats, reflecting the district's more recent emphasis on tourism. Taking advantage of scenic diversity and a subtropical climate, the city has excelled in tourist promotion – encapsulated in its clever 'Banana Republic' theme. *Population 20 330*

NORTH COAST REGIONAL BOTANIC GARDEN Opened in 1988 as a Bicentennial project, the garden near the centre of the city occupies an old reserve site bounded on three sides by Coffs Creek. Walks of up to an hour can be taken among well-explained subtropical trees and shrubs, including mangroves and some endangered species.

COFFS HARBOUR HISTORICAL MUSEUM Relics of Aboriginal occupation, timber-getting, early settlement, mining and coastal shipping are housed in this regional museum.

At dusk or early morning, the wallabies known as pademelons may be seen in the national parks as they emerge from the forest to feed.

CORAMBA ■ 485

Gold miners last century were a restless breed, ever-ready to move on to more promising strikes. Public servants were obliged to follow – and in Coramba's case, they took a place name with them.

The original Coramba village served mines active in the 1880s, far away on the other side of the Orara River valley to the east of Mount Coramba. As those mines petered out, new finds were being made in hills to the west of the river in the Moleton area. So the mining warden and the postmaster moved their offices to a riverside village that had sprung up in between.

Coramba was officially reborn, but ironically it soon had to play second fiddle again. In 1895 fresh discoveries were made near Mount Coramba. A new village there supported a population four times greater than that of Coffs Harbour. It even boasted electric lighting. But after only three years, and the extraction of gold worth well over a million dollars at today's prices, the lodes were exhausted but the township survived as a commercial centre.

Coramba No.2 is a pleasant spot on the back road between Coffs Harbour and Dorrigo. Appropriately it is also the key point to make for in locating the district's last fully maintained and operational old-time goldmine, George's Gold Mine.

DORRIGO ■ 486

Farming is the dominant activity on the cleared plateau surrounding Dorrigo, but a steady flow of trucks to and from the sawmill marks it still as a timber town. More than 700 metres above sea level, Dorrigo developed as the centre of the most productive rainforest logging area in New South Wales. Now it is the focus of apparently irreconcilable differences between the interests of conservationists and those of the still-important forestry industry.

The area's earliest settler called the forests the Don Dorrigo Scrub, after a Spanish general with whom he had served in the Napoleonic Wars. Unaware of this, local people later adopted a fancy that *dorrigo* was a contraction of an Aboriginal word for stringybark. If any village was so named, it is more likely Dundurrabin, north-west of Dorrigo.

The town has a small historical museum and a huge and unique collection of steam locomotives, waggons, passenger carriages and other railway memorabilia. A branch of the North Coast line ran between Glenreagh and Dorrigo from 1924 to 1972 and – despite long-running disputes about funding – volunteer railway enthusiasts have plans to reopen the line as a tourist attraction. *Population 1140*

Bananas clothe the hills along this coast; the fruit's importance is symbolised by the gaudy 'Big Banana' reclining by the roadside at Coffs Harbour.

DORRIGO NATIONAL PARK ■ 487

Waterfalls spill from all sides of a mist-shrouded amphitheatre formed by deep erosion of the New England escarpment section of the Great Dividing Range. They feed the waters of Rosewood Creek, a major tributary of the Bellinger River, which wanders among tall subtropical rainforest trees bearing ferns and orchids.

With a terrain far too daunting for old-time timber-getters, this is the finest remaining example of what was once the vast Don Dorrigo Scrub. Protected as a national park of nearly 7900 hectares, including some open country to the north-east, it is one of the jewels of the northern New South Wales World Heritage rainforest collection.

EMERALD BEACH ■ 488

Between two rocky headlands, known as Dammerels and Look at Me Now, surfboard riders delight in a long run to the tiny pocket of sand that is called Shelly Beach. Emerald Beach itself extends two kilometres to the north, Moonee Beach five kilometres to the south, providing a range of locations for swimming, angling and boating. *Population 1210*

GUY FAWKES RIVER NATIONAL PARK ■ 489

Catchments of the Guy Fawkes River and its tributaries, the Aberfoyle and Sara, are protected in an extensive park of more than 35 000 hectares. This is a wilderness area, most of it suited only to fully equipped and determined bushwalkers. Rainfall is generally low but after good summer downpours some adventurers carry in light canoes or inflatable boats to experience a ride down the narrow gorges of one of New South Wales' last truly wild rivers.

KORORA ■ 490

Steep slopes surrounding the Korora Basin provide the site for Australia's most intensive banana production. To emphasise the point, the love-it-or-hate-it 'Big Banana' symbol with its accompanying theme park assails the eyes of travellers approaching Korora from the south. The township is set close to Korora and Hills Beaches, by the calm waters in the lee of Diggers Headland.

Korora Nature Reserve occupies a rare patch of untouched hillside among the banana plantations. Its mixture of rainforest and eucalypts gives shelter and food to lyrebirds, bowerbirds and a regenerated population of koalas. Two species of pademelons have also been introduced. *Population 860*

Late spring rains on the Gibraltar Range swell the waters of the Nymboida River, heralding the start of the six-month rafting season.

MID SAPPHIRE BEACH ■ **491**
Hilly farmlands rise up almost from the back dunes of Sapphire Gardens and Mid Sapphire Beach, pushing the route of the Pacific Highway unusually close to the ocean. The two settlements with their caravan parks and camping grounds are squeezed along a narrow seaward strip. Sapphire Gardens was the site of the first known cultivation of bananas in the region. Hermann Rieck planted Fijian varieties around 1890, but his initiative and many later attempts proved financial failures. A viable industry was not established until 1929, after which banana growing steadily took over from dairying. *Population 920*

NYMBOIDA RIVER ■ **492**
White-water canoeing and rafting enthusiasts regard a plunging run down the rocky gorges of the Nymboida River as probably the most rewarding challenge to be found in New South Wales. The river originates on the highest part of the New England Escarpment, about thirty kilometres west of Dorrigo, and flows generally northward to join the Mann River and further on, the Clarence River west of Grafton. Many companies offer organised rafting trips, most starting in the vicinity of Nymboida township. The nearby power station is a major supplier of electricity to the state's northern coastal region.

SANDY BEACH ■ **493**
An Aboriginal midden – a mound of shellfish remains and other non-decaying food scraps such as fish bones – marks the southern end of Sandy Beach, where scattered European settlement began in the 1880s. Today's rural residential settlement was originally known as Sandy's Beach, after an early English settler; after subdivision in 1965 it was given the more exotic title of Diamond Head but a few years later reverted back to a version of the original name. A number of Aboriginal artefacts including axes and adzes were retrieved from the midden before the beach was sand-mined in the 1950s. *Population 1430*

SAWTELL ■ **494**
A scanty history of the Sawtell district can be traced from references to its original name, Bongil Bongil, and to Bonville, an alteration evidently intended to convey a pseudo-French gentility. A reserve for a settlement at the mouth of Bongil (Bonville) Creek was set aside as early as 1861, but for many years the area seems to have been used only for loading timber hauled from upstream and for grazing the bullock-cart teams.

Later Bonville became a minor centre for farming on land that included Sawtell. After a railway link was completed in 1925, coastal land to the north of the creek was subdivided. Sawtell received its name in 1927, in honour of the landowner.

Twin headlands enclose a surfing beach backed by parkland. Boambee Beach to the north and Bonville Beach to the south can be reached on foot. The creeks at each side of the headlands allow sheltered swimming. *Population 10 810*

FESTIVALS Sawtell Family Fun Day, New Year's Day.

WOOLGOOLGA ■ **495**
On the highest hill overlooking the seaside pleasure ground that is Woolgoolga stands a glistening white, onion-domed Sikh temple. Incongruous it may be, but far from irrelevant. It speaks for the persistence of a lonely group whose ill-paid toil contributed to the early development of the district. When sugar growing was first attempted during the 1880s, Sikhs originating in the Punjab region of India were brought from Queensland as cane cutters. Though the original sugar industry succumbed, the Sikh families held on and, in time, prospered from banana growing and other horticulture.

Woolgoolga Headland shelters a safe surfing beach and a boat ramp for anglers working near shore reefs or heading for the Solitary Islands. Visitors find ample holiday facilities close to the beach. To the south, Hearns Lake is an extensive coastal lagoon ideal for quiet fishing, swimming and canoeing. *Population 3660*

THE SECRET LIFE OF MUTTONBIRD ISLAND

COFFS HARBOUR'S northern breakwater links the mainland to a humped island as big as a racecourse, drab in colour and with an apparently barren, heath-like landscape.

Visitors can walk or drive to this untempting appendage, then spend an hour or so toiling up stairways and scuffing along dusty pathways. For their trouble they see matted, nondescript foliage, and on rocks at the seaward extremity, some pretty encrustations of lichen. Here on Muttonbird Island there is never a muttonbird to be seen – though it is home to twenty or thirty thousand of them.

During the winter months the birds, properly called shearwaters, spend all their time at sea in the Northern Hemisphere. The most numerous species, the wedge-tailed shearwater, frequents the Philippines region. The sooty shearwater feeds in waters off Japan. The short-tailed shearwater journeys as far as Alaska and Siberia.

In September, birds of all three species return to Muttonbird Island, a major breeding ground. Despite the vast distances involved, their navigational skills are undimmed as they come back each year to this same speck of land on the other side of the world. They arrive silently after nightfall, skimming the wave crests with the aid of a sea breeze.

Only some rustling in the low shrubbery betrays the presence of the muttonbirds as they creep purposefully and unerringly to the burrows of the previous seasons to start another summer of nesting and breeding. During the day, they will gather in small groups or fly out to sea alone to feed on small fish and squid, returning to their sanctuary on shore only after the sun has gone down.

By early May, all the birds will have departed, the adults of some species leaving well ahead of their fledglings for the long flight north. Disoriented by lights or blown westward by adverse winds, many immature birds become stranded on the mainland as they cannot become airborne from flat ground. The National Parks Service has simple advice for people finding a helpless shearwater: take it across to Muttonbird Island or 'just throw it off a headland' and let nature take its course. □

Each year, the migrating residents of Muttonbird Island return to the same burrow, usually occupying it with the previous season's partner.

Grafton & Yamba

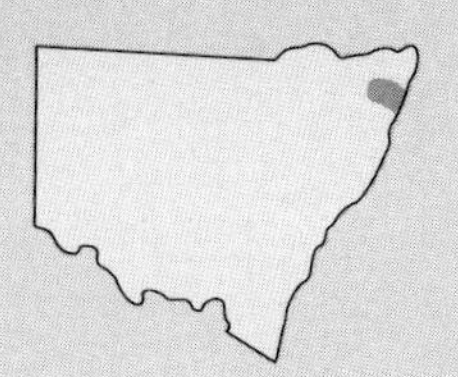

Long defying discovery by explorers, the 'big river' Clarence with its once-dangerous bar became a lifeline for agricultural development on the northern New South Wales coast. Former mercantile ports on the Clarence, particularly Grafton, are finding new vigour from tourism and fishing.

Maclean – where the Clarence River rejoins its north arm after a brief separation to embrace Woodford Island – is famous for its views of the ranges to the west and the Clarence's complex estuary to the east.

CLARENCE RIVER ■ 496

Of all the small fortunes made from the Clarence River last century, the first – and most significant – went to an escaped convict, Richard Craig, who made a chance discovery of what he called 'the big river'. He was rewarded with 100 pounds and a lenient sentence. His discovery also made a mockery of the efforts of naval explorers.

Matthew Flinders landed in the Yamba area in 1799 without realising that he was near the delta of a mighty waterway. Captain Henry Rous took a fresh look in 1827, reporting only on the bay's dangerous entrance. But in 1831 Craig, fleeing the Moreton Bay settlement where he had been sent for stealing cattle, roved far inland where he befriended the Aborigines and was able to observe not only the breadth of the waterway but also the accessibility of rich stands of red cedar.

In 1835, Craig moved to Sydney and found work with a shipbuilder and merchant, Thomas Small; a few years later, both men and a party of cedar-getters were the first to sail up the river when their schooner went as far as Woodford Island.

Surveyors and pastoralists quickly followed: the 'big river', renamed for the Duke of Clarence in 1839, was at last well and truly on the map. Navigable by ocean-going ships as far as Grafton, eighty kilometres upstream, the Clarence soon had jetties bristling from its banks.

Before the end of the decade, a brief gold rush on the upper Clarence River made traffic even busier. Sugarcane planting was beginning too, though at first with little success. Dairying and beef cattle raising followed timber as the most important industries of the Clarence until around 1870, when sugar growing took a lasting hold on the lower floodplains and islands.

Upstream, the Clarence's shifting shoals of rock and silt always called for alertness in navigation, not to mention the rivermouth bar and its nearby reef. Sometimes in southerly weather twenty ships or more had to wait to get in or out across the bar. Big islands clog the estuary of the Clarence in a manner seen nowhere else in Australia. Masses of fertile silt are separated by narrow, twisting channels, allowing a network of roads and bridgeworks. The main islands are intensively farmed for sugar, so that travellers find avenues of cane yielding to river scenes with an almost bewildering frequency.

Harwood Island is the site of the only sugar refinery and the biggest crushing mill in New South Wales. Towards the rivermouth, the waterways fringing Palmers Island and its smaller neighbours are increasingly given over to oyster and prawn farming. Upstream, Woodford Island offers a charming detour from the Pacific Highway between Maclean and Grafton.

In 1932, the Clarence was bridged by road and rail at Grafton – putting many old ferries and punts out of business. A project to build a harbour inside the northern headland at Iluka was finally abandoned in 1971. The Clarence was proclaimed a Point of First Entry for import and export in 1992. Despite the extensive and bulky breakwaters, the ocean-entrance sandbar still occasionally claims the lives of unwary seafarers. Pleasure boating enthusiasts head upstream if they are wise. As in the old days, Richard Craig's 'big river' tends to keep to itself.

SUSAN ISLAND NATURE RESERVE The upstream half of Susan Island, at Grafton, is a reserve protecting a remnant of rainforest and some areas of regeneration. More than forty tree species, including the most extensive stand of tulipwood in New South Wales, are found in an area of only twenty hectares. Up to 200 000 grey-headed flying foxes camp in the forest from spring to autumn. Access to the island is by private boat or by canoes hired from South Grafton.

GIBRALTAR RANGE NATIONAL PARK ■ 497

Scenes of arresting grandeur greet the eye from every quarter in a park of 17 000 hectares, bisected by the Gwydir Highway. Great tors of granite stud a forested plateau almost

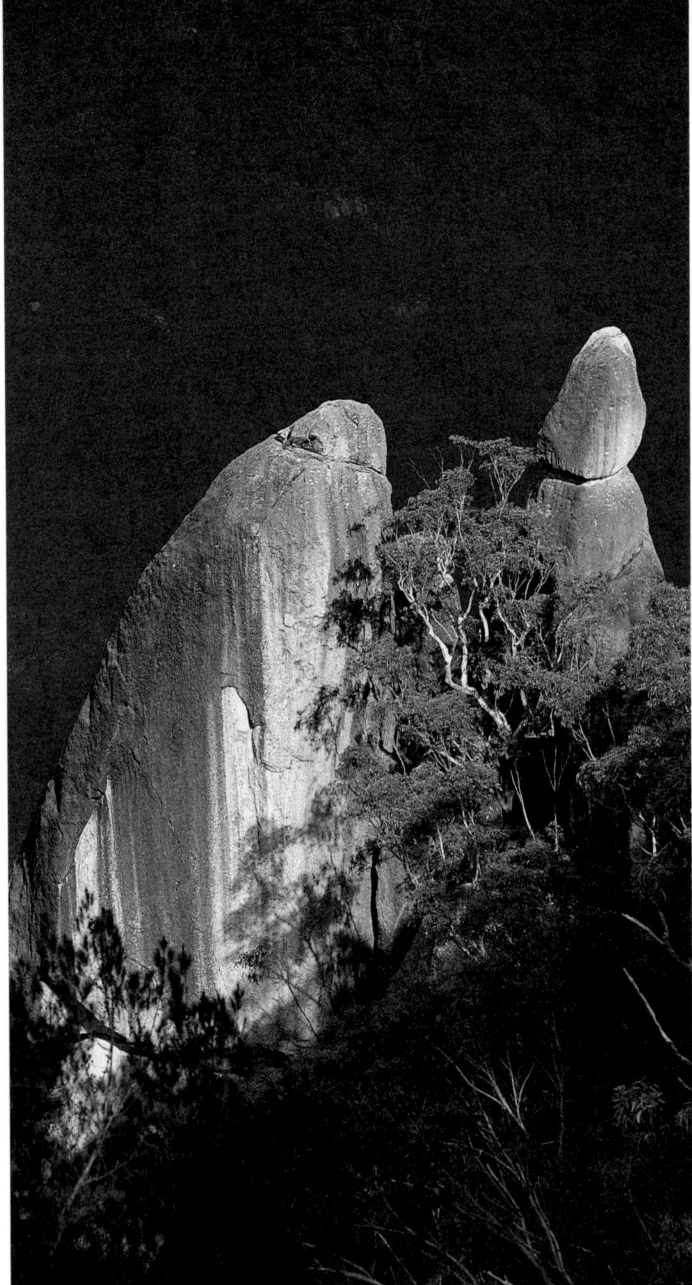

Aboriginal legend has it that the 'Needles' granite outcrop in Gibraltar Range National Park represents six sisters turned to stone by a curse.

1200 metres above sea level, while to the east the scarp of the New England Tableland drops sharply into deep gorges. The vegetation ranges from eucalypt forests – sometimes flecked with snow in winter – through heaths and swamp communities to subtropical rainforests in sheltered zones with volcanic soils. Such a variety of habitats is said to support more than 200 bird species, along with many mammals including a rare marsupial mouse and rat-kangaroo.

GRAFTON ■ 498

Travellers on the Pacific Highway through South Grafton catch only glimpses of the main part of the city across the Clarence River. Unless they interrupt their journey with a sidetrack across the high bridge, they deprive themselves of a treat. Grafton presents perhaps the most graceful urban scenes in provincial Australia. The effect of handsome homes and public buildings is enhanced by no fewer than twenty-four council-maintained parks and by unusually wide thoroughfares lined with ornamental trees. Although many colourful native species thrive here, the city is distinguished by introduced trees – above all by *Jacaranda mimosifolia* from Brazil. Festivities associated with the peak flowering of jacarandas in spring, instituted in 1934, attract thousands of visitors to the district.

A store and shipyard were established in 1839 at what became South Grafton. Pioneers simply called it 'the settlement'. When pastoralists drove flocks from New England onto the fertile floodplains of the Clarence River this became the main loading point for the shipment of their fleeces to Sydney.

The business centre for most services to agriculture on the Clarence, Grafton was accorded city status in 1883. It competed with Armidale for pre-eminence in northern New South Wales, receiving a setback when the Anglican Bishop of Armidale and Grafton decided that the New England city was more deserving of the first cathedral. Grafton people, he declared, were 'a godless lot'. Their cathedral, of locally-made, salmon-coloured bricks, was built between 1881 and 1884 to the design of the distinguished Canadian architect, J. Horbury Hunt.

Ferries and barges plied busily between the two parts of Grafton until 1932, when the double-deck road and rail bridge was completed. Its great elevation was a precaution against flooding, which disrupted the city with increasing frequency after the First World War. Levee banks, built in the 1970s and the 1990s protect Grafton proper as well as South Grafton. *Population 16 650*

CIVIC HISTORICAL BUILDINGS GROUP Eleven buildings in the heart of the city merit a group listing by the National Trust. Christ Church Cathedral has pride of place. Behind it is a church hall dating from about 1890, more homely but showing fine details of brickwork that mark it as another conception of Horbury Hunt. Of two old stuccoed brick cottages now serving as parish offices, one with a triple-doorway verandah was built in the 1850s. The court house and the former police station were built in matching style in 1881 under the design direction of Government Architect James Barnet.

GRAFTON JAIL Notorious over the years for riots, great escapes and allegation of brutality and corruption, the 1893 prison building, yard walls and governor's residence are regarded as architecturally significant

FESTIVALS Jacaranda Festival, October–November.

JUNCTION HILL ■ 499

A hill with commanding views of the surrounding countryside provided the ideal location for this rural-residential 'suburb' of Grafton, just a short distance north of the city. Its geographical position and the two roads that meet here provided a ready-made name. *Population 1110*

MACLEAN ■ 500

Overshadowed by the commercial progress of Grafton, Maclean is a slow-paced town of considerable charm. It was originally a port for shipping out timber and farm produce. Now its principal importance is as a base for prawn trawling on the lower Clarence River.

Sited where the south arm of the river emerges from its meander around Woodford Island, the settlement was first called Rocky Mouth. When a township was formally laid out in 1862 it was named after the Surveyor-General, Alister Maclean. Like him many of the pioneering farmers were Highland Scots, and in recent years the town has taken to itself the title of 'the most Scottish town in Australia'. It hosts a major Highland gathering every year and even translates some street names into Gaelic.

A leaflet guides visitors to historical buildings in the town. The Bicentennial Museum at the top of Wharf Street uses the most up-to-date display techniques to illustrate the region's development. It adjoins the historic Stone Cottage, furnished and equipped to show domestic life around the time it was built, 1879. *Population 2890*

FESTIVALS Highland Gathering, Easter; Cane Harvest Festival, late September.

NYMBOIDA NATIONAL PARK ■ 501

Tough bushwalkers and canoeists appreciate the wild beauty of a short section of the Nymboida River near its confluence with the Mann River Four-wheel-drive vehicles are recommended on the track from the Gwydir Highway, turning off forty-odd kilometres west of Grafton. The track winds through Ramornie State Forest and ends at the boundary of the park, leaving a hard slog on foot to the river.

ULMARRA ■ 502

Classified in its entirety by the National Trust, Ulmarra village is a well-preserved example of a nineteenth-century river port. Its wharf was a major loading point for farm and dairy factory produce. Old shops, now specialising in arts, crafts and antiques, attract a substantial tourist trade. A vehicular ferry crosses the Clarence between Ulmarra and Southgate.

The street-planting scheme which resulted in Grafton's famous jacarandas began 120 years ago.

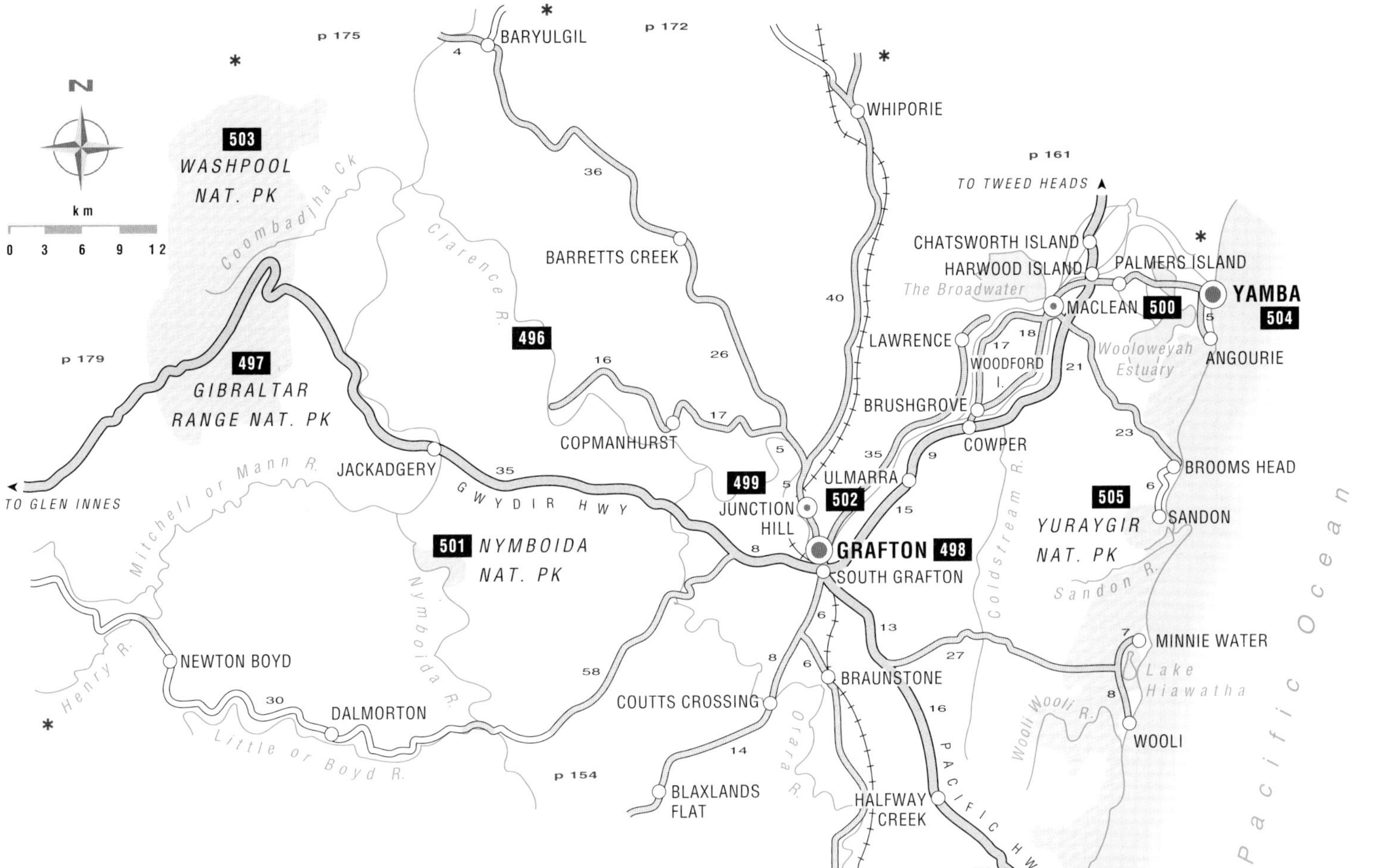

p 175
p 172
p 161
p 179
p 154

N
km
0 3 6 9 12
503 WASHPOOL NAT. PK
497 GIBRALTAR RANGE NAT. PK
496
501 NYMBOIDA NAT. PK
499
502
498
500
504
505 YURAYGIR NAT. PK
BARYULGIL
WHIPORIE
TO TWEED HEADS
CHATSWORTH ISLAND
HARWOOD ISLAND
PALMERS ISLAND
The Broadwater
MACLEAN
YAMBA
ANGOURIE
Wooloweyah Estuary
BARRETTS CREEK
LAWRENCE
WOODFORD I.
BRUSHGROVE
COWPER
COPMANHURST
JACKADGERY
TO GLEN INNES
GWYDIR HWY
ULMARRA
JUNCTION HILL
GRAFTON
SOUTH GRAFTON
BROOMS HEAD
SANDON
Sandon R.
Coldstream R.
Coombadjha Ck
Clarence R.
Mitchell or Mann R.
Nymboida R.
Henry R.
NEWTON BOYD
DALMORTON
Little or Boyd R.
COUTTS CROSSING
BRAUNSTONE
MINNIE WATER
Lake Hiawatha
Wooli Wooli R.
WOOLI
Orara R.
BLAXLANDS FLAT
HALFWAY CREEK
PACIFIC HWY
RED ROCK
CORINDI BEACH
TO COFFS HARBOUR
Pacific Ocean

WASHPOOL NATIONAL PARK ■ 503

Coombadjha Road, branching from the Gwydir Highway near the summit of the Gibraltar Range, leads to a concentration of visitor facilities on the edge of Washpool National Park. The forested and largely trackless expanse of nearly 28000 hectares reaches far to the north, where only experienced bushwalkers venture. A short walk can be taken from the Coachwood picnic area, or a ten-kilometre hike from the Coombadjha rest area, descending through warm-temperate rainforest that has earned the park World Heritage listing.

YAMBA ■ 504

Holiday-makers enjoying Yamba's modern amenities and pleasant lifestyle should spare a thought for one of the locality's first permanent residents. A hardy Canadian, Francis Freeburn, was engaged in 1854 to set up a pilot station on the headland.

When ships arrived opposite the Clarence bar, Freeburn was usually rowed out in a whaleboat to meet them. But if the seas were too rough to launch a boat he would signal the incoming ship to lower one of its own, bringing a rope close to where he waited on nearshore rocks. With the rope thrown to him and tied around his waist, Freeburn would hurl himself into the sea and be towed out to do his job.

The name Yamba was used for the town site in 1861 but settlers more often called it Woolli, while its post office remained Clarence Heads until 1881. Its harbour remains important as the base for a sizeable fishing fleet, but Yamba now is principally a holiday town with highly regarded surfing beaches. *Population 3710*

FESTIVALS Family Fishing Festival, September/October school holidays.

YURAYGIR NATIONAL PARK ■ 505

Unspoiled coastal features extend for a total of sixty kilometres along the three sections of Yuraygir National Park, making it one of the most scenically and biologically valuable conservation areas in Australia. Resort villages dotted along the coast, outside the park boundaries, meet most requirements of visitors and reduce the need for interference inside the park, except for the provision of some rest areas, nature trails and wetland boardwalks.

The northern section, formerly Angourie National Park, offers a ten-kilometre coastal walk that is often said to be the best in New South Wales. Coastal wetlands and heath predominate in the park's central section accessible by the Wooli road, and there are inland pools such as Hiawatha and Minnie Water which support abundant birdlife. High, wooded dunes back the beaches of the southern section. This was formerly called Red Rock National Park due to a prominent outcropping of red jasper at the southern end.

Ocean tides sweep 90 kilometres up the length of the Clarence and the Maclean prawn trawlers make their catches as far upstream as Ulmarra.

Of the settlements outside the park, Angourie claims most attention for the quality of its surf. Just behind the backshore north of Angourie Point is the limpid, deep Blue Pool, formed by the quarrying of rock for breakwaters at the mouth of the Clarence River. An underground spring ensures that the pool remains full of fresh water. Wooli is a holiday hamlet and commercial fishing base. It occupies a narrow spit between a long ocean beach and the waters of the Wooli Wooli River.

Ballina & Alstonville

As along the southern coast of New South Wales, the lure of the much sought-after timber of the red cedar tree brought hardy trailblazers to navigate the Richmond and the Clarence. By the 1840s, the lush river valleys were echoing to the sound of axe and saw.

ALSTONVILLE ■ 506

Alstonville, on the Bruxner Highway about midway between Lismore and Ballina, stands on a plateau surrounded by rolling ridges of red earth covered by rich green pastures and subtropical vegetation.

Alstonville's pleasant landscape was formed by huge flows of volcanic basalt which poured out of the earth's crust some thirty million years ago and covered the surface of most of the Northern Rivers region to a depth of up to 300 metres. The rim of the ancient 'Tweed Volcano' over which flowed much of this basalt is evident far to the north in the curving ridges of the Nightcap and McPherson (or Border) Ranges, while the dramatic pinnacle of Mount Warning near Murwillumbah is at its centre.

Lumley Park, almost in the centre of Alstonville, is a remnant of the 'Big Scrub', a subtropical rainforest which thrived in the deep basalt soils and high rainfall and once covered most of the Richmond River district. Victoria Park, south of Alstonville, is a nature reserve which is one of the best of the 'Big Scrub' remnants with its fine examples of white booyong, yellowwood, bumpy ash, red bean, Moreton Bay figs and other rainforest trees. It also contains the 'Big Fig Tree', so obvious a landmark on the Alstonville Plateau that it was once used as a navigational aid by coastal steamers on the north-coast run.

While the most valuable trees of the once extensive 'Big Scrub', such as red cedar, were logged for their timber, most of it was cleared away and burned by the selectors who moved into the district and took up land for farming in the 1860s and 1870s. They worked the volcanic soil to produce maize and sugar cane and as pastures for beef and dairy cattle. Sugar cane production continued around Alstonville until about the turn of the century when it was realised that this was a crop better suited to the alluvial soils and frost-free climate of the flood plains than the plateau. More recent crops include tropical fruit and macadamia nuts. Just to the east of Alstonville is the Tropical Fruit Research Station.

Most of the commercial buildings and houses here are modern, Alstonville having grown from a village into a substantial town since the 1960s. There are exceptions such as St Bartholomew's Church (1915) and the Federal Hotel (1900), with its cedar fittings and attractive verandahs. *Population 3680*

MUSEUM OF PIONEER RELICS The museum, adjacent to Lumley Park, displays horse-drawn vehicles, a bullock-drawn timber jinker and farm implements from early settler days on the Richmond River.

While neat rows of banana trees are the most obvious 'tropical' fruit at Alstonville, other, more exotic fruits are being pioneered in this region.

BALLINA ■ 507

Ballina sits beside the broad estuary of the Richmond River. The narrow course of The Canal separates it from the western shore and this is crossed easily by two bridges which carry the Pacific Highway into the town and out again. The much wider expanse of North Creek separates Ballina from East Ballina and the ocean, and this is spanned by the more substantial Missingham Bridge. Substantial breakwaters built on each side of the Richmond River mouth make the estuary safe for boating and keep the entrance clear of sandbars.

Lush, subtropical, surrounded by water and close to ocean beaches, Ballina has all the attributes of a resort town and its population swells far above its normal size during the peak tourist season. Apart from the tourist industry, Ballina makes its living from fishing, boat building, and as a service centre for the district which grows and processes sugar cane and produces tropical fruits, dairy products and beef. The town has grown strongly since the 1960s.

Captain Henry Rous of HMS *Rainbow* explored the Richmond River in August 1828, naming it after the Duke of Richmond. He entered the mouth in the ship's boat and travelled some distance upstream. At that time it was part of the territory of the Bundjalung Aborigines, Captain Rous noting many people and very substantial huts – ten metres long and two metres high – on the shore. The name of the modern town is thought to have derived from the Bundjalung word 'bullenah' meaning 'place of many oysters'; it has since been modified to Ballina, the name of a town in Ireland.

The first white settlers, who came on the scene some years after Captain Rous described the Richmond River, travelled overland from the Clarence River looking for red cedar. They were joined by cedar-getters with their families who arrived on the *Sally* in 1842 and set up camp at East Ballina with its high ground and fresh water supply. The settlement, known as Deptford was established around the saltwater lagoon of Shaws Bay and became the port for the Northern Rivers cedar trade.

Cedar-cutting camps were quickly established on tributaries of the Richmond at Uralba, Teven and Tintenbar and the logs rafted down river to be sawed and shipped out. The mood of the place and the times is evoked in the novel *They Came From the Sea* by E.V. Timms (1955) through the character of Captain Squint-eye Lush and the survivors of his foundered ship who come ashore in the 1850s.

From 1889, the government financed the building of breakwaters, North Creek Canal and a training wall in the estuary to make Ballina a safe port. The breakwaters were completed in 1911. The bridge spanning North Creek and joining Ballina to East Ballina supersedes the earlier Missingham Bridge dating from 1889 which provided access for the construction of the northern breakwater.

For decades, Ballina's main transport link was the coastal and river shipping service. Two old river vessels on display in the town are the *Richmond*, a pilot vessel that served on the river for half-a-century (behind the Pilot's Cottage in Norton Street), and the *Florrie* built in 1880 (on the banks of the Richmond River at Regatta Reserve). A railway linking the town with the North Coast line at Booyong was built during the Great Depression, but no train has run on it since 1948. *Population 14 550*

SHAWS BAY HOTEL On the waterfront at East Ballina, the hotel is the former Fenwick House, a gracious, two-storey home in the style of a Scottish manor house and built of granite with a slate roof.

COURT HOUSE Built in 1867, the court house is a well-proportioned building containing much of its original fittings and furniture. The post office was completed about 1889.

LIGHTHOUSE After many ships were lost attempting to navigate the Ballina bar, a lighthouse was built on Lighthouse Hill at East Ballina, thirty-five metres above sea level.

MARITIME MUSEUM This museum, at the Tourist Information Centre near the river in Norton Street, displays a balsa-wood raft from the 1973 Las Balsas trans-Pacific expedition. Three rafts constructed of balsa wood timbers fastened together with pegs and sisal rope, and carrying four men each, left Guayaquil in Ecuador bound for Mooloolaba in southern Queensland and reached the Australian coast 178 days later at Ballina.

FESTIVALS Oktoberfest, October.

The dramatic firing of the canefields in mid-winter clears undergrowth in preparation for a six-month harvesting period.

BROADWATER ■ 508

When Captain Henry Rous of HMS *Rainbow* sighted the Richmond River in 1828, he crossed the bar in the ship's boat and travelled upstream as far as the present site of Broadwater.

Broadwater, on the Pacific Highway between the townships of Woodburn and Wardell, is dominated by its sugar mill. The mill was opened in 1881 by the Colonial Sugar Refining company and is managed by a co-operative formed by cane growers. The mill offers guided tours for visitors on weekdays during the cane crushing season, from June to December, when it processes about 400 000 tonnes of cane.

This small town and its surrounding district is probably the best place in New South Wales to experience the sights and sounds of the sugar industry, including the dramatic firing of the cane fields, mechanical harvesters at work and the transporting of the cut cane from the fields by tractor-drawn cane trains. A 'bora' ceremonial ground west of the township was used by the Bundjalung Aborigines as recently as 1922.

BROADWATER NATIONAL PARK ■ 509

Broadwater National Park protects more than 3700 hectares of coastal sandplain, heathlands and swamp between Evans Head and Broadwater. Forested ridges further inland, which rise up to thirty metres above sea level, are ancient sand dunes which formed about 60 000 years ago when the level of the sea was higher. Coffee-rock outcrops, formed of sand and compressed organic material, can be found exposed at various places behind the beach, as in Bundjalung National Park to the south (see entry).

A road crosses the park between Evans Head and Broadwater. The Salty Lagoon track, which starts from a car park near the southern boundary of the park, takes the walker through heathlands – which flower richly in spring – with grass trees and banksias, to the swampy environs of Salty Creek where brolgas, uncommon in New South Wales, are known to breed.

The postmaster at Ballina operated from a nearby store for nine years until this post office was opened next to the court house in 1889.

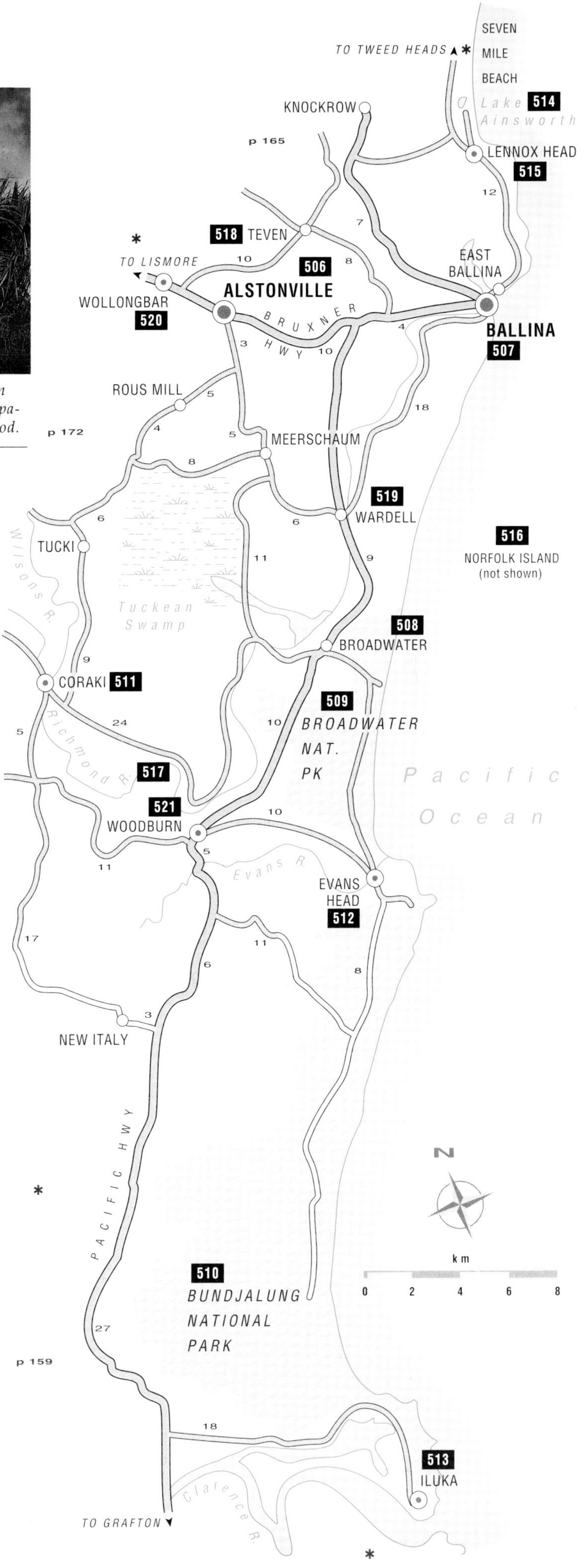

TO TWEED HEADS
SEVEN MILE BEACH
Lake Ainsworth 514
KNOCKROW
LENNOX HEAD 515
518 TEVEN
TO LISMORE
506
EAST BALLINA
WOLLONGBAR 520
ALSTONVILLE
BRUXNER HWY
BALLINA 507
ROUS MILL
MEERSCHAUM
519 WARDELL
516 NORFOLK ISLAND (not shown)
TUCKI
Wilsons R.
Tuckean Swamp
508 BROADWATER
CORAKI 511
509 BROADWATER NAT. PK
Richmond R.
517
Pacific Ocean
521 WOODBURN
Evans R.
EVANS HEAD 512
NEW ITALY
PACIFIC HWY
510 BUNDJALUNG NATIONAL PARK
N
km 0 2 4 6 8
513 ILUKA
Clarence R.
TO GRAFTON
p 165
p 172
p 159

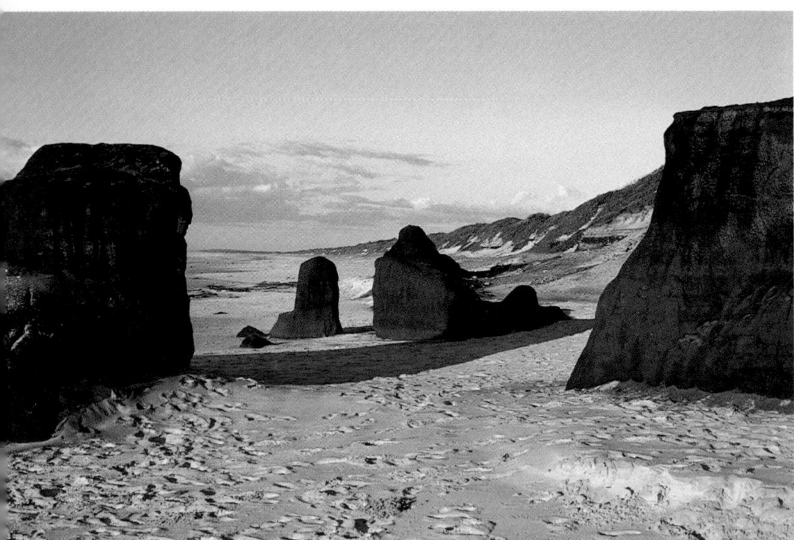

Apart from some sandmining areas, most of Bundjalung National Park remains virgin bushland. Black Rocks (left),was so-named because of its outcrops of compressed vegetable matter, known as coffee rock. Elsewhere, flowering plants including white coral heath, pink boronia and yellow dillwynia (below,left) attract nectar-eaters such as pygmy possums (below).

BUNDJALUNG NATIONAL PARK ■ 510

Bundjalung National Park, named after the Aborigines whose territory extended over this part of the coast, protects 17 500 hectares of beaches, headlands, swamp, rivers, heathland and eucalypt forest extending from near Iluka at the mouth of the Clarence River to Evans Head. The Iluka Nature Reserve abutting the southern boundary of the park contains a nowadays rare example of coastal or littoral rainforest.

Bundjalung National Park also embraces the catchment of the largely unspoilt Esk River, one of the few remaining 'wild' rivers on the New South Wales coast. Jerusalem Creek is also within the park and a 'walk-in' campsite is provided on its banks near the mouth of the creek. Camping areas accessible by vehicle are provided at Woody Head in the south, and Black Rocks on the coast about midway into the park. The northern section of the park can be reached through Evans Head.

CORAKI ■ 511

Coraki was once an important river port and the site of a shipyard established in the 1840s. Ocean-bound ships no longer call and Coraki – on the Richmond River where it is joined by the Wilson River – is now a quiet retreat on a back road between Casino and Woodburn. The peace is shattered only by the Bridge-to-Bridge Ski Classic, part of the Tea-Tree Festival, held in November.

A ferry linked the main town with South Coraki across the Richmond River until the completion in recent years of a road bridge. Coraki, with its handsome old timber homes is, like Casino, a hinterland town removed from the major tourist attractions of beach and surf and somewhat overlooked by the developmental surge which began in the sixties and dramatically altered the character of coastal towns like Ballina and Lennox Head. Coraki's main offering to the visitor is a pleasant reminder of how things once were.

The town had its beginnings in 1849 when William Yabsley, a ship builder and cedar-cutter, opened a cedar-dealer's store with sawpits and built a homestead and a wharf. This formed the nucleus of a private village. He later opened a shipyard which launched the 80-ton *Coraki* in 1858, the 180-ton *Schoolboy* (built with the help of schoolboy apprentices including his four sons) in 1864 and the 265-ton *Examiner* in 1870. The *Examiner* later came to grief on the Clarence bar, but Yabsley, not the sort of man to give up easily, gathered four bullock teams and every man he could get and spent nearly five months dragging her almost one-and-a-half kilometres across the sand to a point where the ship could be launched again into the Clarence.

The Club Hotel in Richmond Terrace (c.1880) and the Coraki Hotel are notable early buildings and still the centre of much of the town's life. Historic homes include the restored Yabsley House, now open to the public as an art gallery, guesthouse and restaurant. *Population 1100*

EVANS HEAD ■ 512

This quiet and unpretentious town of weatherboard fishermen's houses, holiday guesthouses and flats is centred on the estuary of the Evans River, between the Broadwater and Bundjalung national parks. The town's name was originally given to the headland further south, now known as Schnapper Rock, in honour of one of Captain James Cook's officers on the *Endeavour*. Chinaman's Beach to the south of the town commemorates an early gold rush dominated by Chinese, and specks of gold can still be fossicked from the beach sands.

Evans Head's growth was boosted in 1940 when it became a centre for military aerial bombing and gunnery training during the Second World War. A military airstrip was constructed and although no longer operational it is still used occasionally as a base for recreational gliding. A large section of the coast south of the town remains in use by the RAAF as a bombing range.

The boat harbour, set into the southern shore of the river estuary east of the road bridge, is protected by rock walls and at the river mouth two breakwaters of grey rock extend out to sea. Although the river mouth has a shallow bar, Evans Head is considered one of the safer harbours of this coast. Upstream the river is shallow and fringed with mangroves.

Prawn trawlers, white-hulled and draped with coloured nets, crowd into the sheltered waters of the harbour. The fleet brings in substantial catches of prawns and fish, while fishing from charter boats, the beaches, the rocks and the river is popular. Jewfish, blackfish, bream, whiting, flathead and schnapper are the main catches. *Population 2370*

ILUKA ■ 513

Like the slightly larger settlement of Yamba to the south (see *Grafton & Yamba*), this pleasant off-highway fishing village and holiday destination guards the entrance to the broad mouth of the Clarence River.

Iluka has a proud history as a fishing port; it was one of the first places on this coast where professional fishing began, settlement having begun with construction of the breakwater at the river entrance in 1862. In that year, W.A.B. Greaves, who planned the town described its site as '...a large, sandy flat covered with ferns, bloodwood, brushbox, gum trees and brush with patches of brushwood on the land behind...'

Despite the provision of a government wharf and further work on the breakwater the village was overshadowed by the larger settlement at Yamba; nowadays the large, deep-sea fishing fleet and the river prawn trawlers operate from a safe anchorage in the bay, built in 1970. For anglers, Iluka offers good seawall and estuary fishing near the town, and surf and rock fishing at nearby North Head and Woody Bluff.

ILUKA NATURE RESERVE One of the largest remaining expanses of subtropical, coastal rainforests stands in this 136-hectare reserve which runs right up to the village's residential streets. A comfortably graded walking track provides access to this jungle of water gums, vines, orchids and ferns. *Population 1800*

LAKE AINSWORTH ■ 514

Lake Ainsworth, at the northern outskirts of Lennox Head, is an unusual natural feature: a freshwater lake separated by only fifty metres or so of sand from the briny Pacific. The lake's waters are very dark in colour and this is thought to be due to staining from the roots of the tea trees which grow on its shores. The lake is a popular swimming spot and the local wisdom is that there is a unique chemistry in the water that is very good for the hair. Lake Ainsworth is also a popular venue for canoeing, sailing and wind surfing.

LENNOX HEAD ■ 515

Lennox Head, facing Seven Mile Beach and the Pacific Ocean twelve kilometres north of Ballina, is a pleasant coastal township which has grown considerably in recent years due to its attractions as a residential and resort area. From Ballina, the best approach to Lennox Head is along the coast road, with its fine views of headlands, beaches and the blue Pacific. Just before Lennox Head is the Pat Morton Lookout.

With the great sweep of Seven Mile Beach and the ocean virtually on the town's doorstep, Lennox Head offers all the expected seaside attractions of surf and sun, fishing and sailing. Lake Ainsworth (see entry), on the northern edge of the town, provides a large area of protected water for sport and recreation. There is also a reef off the southern end of Seven Mile Beach which harbours tropical fish, crustaceans and shellfish and is a popular spot for scuba diving.

Lennox Head's charm also lies in its endowment of unspoiled surrounding coastal bushland; the barrier dunes with their covering of banksias – full of honeyeaters and wattle birds when they are in bloom – are complimented by the open eucalypt forests and heathlands further inland where the dull pounding of the surf gives away to bird calls.

On the western edge of the town, there is an Aboriginal ceremonial ring or 'bora' which is fenced and open to the public. The overall diameter of the ring, formed of raised earth, is thirty-two metres making it an unusually large one. A gap in the ring on the northern side is thought to have allowed a pathway to pass to a smaller bora ring some distance away but which is no longer visible. The Bundjalung Aborigines who inhabited this area would probably have regarded this site as an important one in their religious life.

Bundjalung tradition includes a belief that long ago three brothers settled on the beach at Lennox Head and one of them, Yarbirri, thrust his spear into the sand to produce a flow of fresh water. When the tide is low, there is said to be a stain still in the place from where the water flowed.

Joseph Banks, gazing across from the deck of the *Endeavour* in 1770, saw a group of Aborigines walking along Seven Mile Beach and was amazed to note that '...not one was once observed to stop and look toward the ship; they pursued their way in all appearance entirely unmoved by the neighbourhood of so remarkable an object as a ship must necessarily be to people who have never seen one'. *Population 3040*

NORFOLK ISLAND ■ 516

The home of the famous pine tree, far to the east of that other balmy Australian territory, Lord Howe Island, has a mixed history of settlement going back even before the First Fleet – according to the latest archaeological finds (see box).

RICHMOND RIVER ■ 517

The Richmond River rises in the McPherson Range on the border between New South Wales and Queensland, a mountainous area of volcanic formation and covered with highland subtropical rainforest. After many years of controversy, logging of the rainforest ceased and this mountainous watershed of the Richmond River has been dedicated as the Border Ranges National Park.

Many tributaries flowing from the Border Ranges as far west as Mount Lindesay join to form the Richmond near the village of Wiangaree. The river then flows south past Casino, collecting tributaries from the Richmond River to the west, and turns east to Coraki where it is joined by its largest tributary, the Wilson River. After Coraki, the Richmond flows on to collect more tributaries from the Richmond Range.

The Richmond River's catchment includes some of the highest rainfall areas along this coast, including extensive areas of basalt country formed when the ancient 'Tweed Volcano', further north, expelled enormous flows of volcanic material. The river drains the major remaining areas of subtropical rainforest on the Border Ranges and the Nightcap Range, both areas now substantially protected as national parks.

In the latter part of the nineteenth century, the Richmond River became an important transport link for the region, with coastal steamers departing its waters loaded with local produce and returning with passengers and goods from Sydney. Coraki, Lismore and Casino, were in those days important ports. In 1877, Lismore received 45 steamers and 229 sailing ships and Coraki's shipyard by that time had launched vessels weighing hundreds of tonnes.

One of the regulars along the river was the freighter *Poonbar*, sixty-one metres in length and weighing over 900 tonnes. The shipping trade went into decline with the opening of the railway line to Lismore in 1932 and an increase in industrial disputes on the wharves. The spread of road transport after the Second World War was another factor and the disastrous floods of 1954 delivered the final blow.

The Richmond Mouth is barred by sand, something which caused the loss of many ships and lives in the nineteenth century, but the construction of breakwaters and other works, which commenced in 1889, eventually made the entrance in the port of Ballina reasonably safe, at least for smaller craft.

TEVEN ■ 518

Teven is a small village on Teven Creek and the disused Ballina–Booyong railway. The village had its start in the 1840s as a rough cedar-getters' camp in what was then close to the centre of 'Big Scrub'. The cedar trees were cut into logs and rafted down the creek to the Richmond River and the port at Ballina for sawing and shipping out.

Teven may be worth including in an itinerary if only because the drive there from centres such as Ballina and Alstonville is on quiet back roads and through scenery as good as any in the district. The village enjoys its pleasant valley location and makes use of this green landscape as a scenic backdrop to its all-weather, nine-hole golf course.

WARDELL ■ 519

Wardell, situated on the Richmond River and the Pacific Highway between Broadwater and Ballina, was established in 1856 as a river port and was originally known as Blackwall. It developed into an important sawmilling centre for the timber industry and later for the milling of sugar cane.

WOLLONGBAR ■ 520

Wollongbar is a smaller 'sister community' of Alstonville and is located on the Bruxner Highway about three kilometres west of the larger town. Wollongbar shares Alstonville's history as a centre for cedar-cutting and later, for the clearing of the 'Big Scrub' rainforest for farming. The region's first butter factory was established here in 1889. An agricultural research farm was started in 1894 and a research station is still operated here by the New South Wales Department of Agriculture. *Population 1270*

WOODBURN ■ 521

Woodburn is a small village on the Pacific Highway inland from Evans Head and situated on the banks of the Richmond River. The village was named by the early selectors who arrived in the area in 1866.

After 1870, Woodburn grew rapidly with the growth of the sugar cane industry and because of its location at the southernmost point on the Richmond River, which made it the port for travellers to and from the Clarence Valley and Grafton. Nowadays sawmilling is the main industry here. *Population 600*

South of the town of the same name is Lennox Head proper, preceded by the rugged shore of Boulder Beach.

NORFOLK: FROM PACIFIC 'DEVIL'S ISLAND' TO PITCAIRNERS' HAVEN

ISOLATED Norfolk Island, a tiny speck in the Pacific Ocean, is more than fifteen-hundred kilometrès east of the Australian mainland. The island's latitude approximates that of Lismore on the far north coast of New South Wales and it has a balmy, subtropical to temperate climate

The thirty-four-square-kilometre island is volcanic in origin and like its smaller neighbours, Nepean and Phillip islands, it rises from a submerged ocean ridge that runs from New Zealand north to New Caledonia. The three-hundred-metre peaks of Mount Bates and Mount Pitt dominate the island, and its sea approaches are barred by cliffs except in the south-eastern corner where the land runs down to exposed anchorages at Slaughter Bay and Emily Bay. Even here, there is a coral reef to be negotiated, inviting the appraisal of the French navigator La Perouse who thought Norfolk 'only a place fit for angels and eagles to reside in'.

Norfolk Island's reputation was such that execution – as befell the man commemmorated above – was seen by some convicts as a merciful release.

Fertile basalt soils and a good rainfall have produced a healthy endowment of plant and animal life including the handsome and justifiably famous Norfolk Island pine and big white oaks. Rainforest palms, ferns, creepers and lianes are at their best in the Mount Pitt Reserve. As on the mainland, two centuries of settlement have encouraged intruders such as lantana to mingle with the native vegetation, and introduced rabbits, livestock, cats and dogs have taken their toll.

When Captain James Cook, on the *Resolution*, logged Norfolk Island for the first time in 1774, he landed and found it uninhabited although since then stone implements and other signs of earlier and brief occupation by Polynesians have come to light. Cook thought the island a useful discovery, seeing potential in its stately pine trees for supplying ship masts and spars and in its flax plants for rope and canvas making.

While the island never kept its promise as a supplier of ship materials to the settlement at Sydney, its rich soil soon became an important source of food for the hungry parent settlement, with convicts arriving soon after Port Jackson was settled and shiploads of fresh produce going back. In 1814 the 'settlers' were moved to Tasmania and the buildings torched to prevent them being used by others. Few traces remain.

In 1825, Norfolk Island was settled again, but this time as an earthly Hell for troublesome male convicts from New South Wales who went there, in Governor Brisbane's words, 'forever excluded from all hope of return'. For the next 30 years, the island's name was synonymous with cruelty and despair. In this period the buildings which make Norfolk Island a place of such historical importance were built. Together they represent an impressive example of a British penal settlement. A common feature in the houses is their windowless walls and enclosed courtyards intended to make them defensible in the convict uprisings which occurred from time to time.

The Norfolk Island penal settlement was closed in 1855 and its miserable convicts moved to Port Arthur in Tasmania. The following year the descendants of the *Bounty* mutineers were resettled here after they had become too numerous to remain on tiny Pitcairn Island. The Pitcairners brought with them their own language: a mixture of eighteenth-century English and Tahitian which is still spoken on the Island today and known as 'Norfolk'.

A self-governing territory of Australia, Norfolk Island now makes living by issuing its own postage stamps and catering for tourists, who make use of the the duty-free attractions of the commercial town of Burnt Pine. □

Six of the almost 200 Pitcairners who emigrated to Norfolk Island in 1856 dressed in formal Victorian fashion for a portrait some years later.

Byron Bay & Mullumbimby

The Border Ranges feed this well-watered coastal strip where cedar-cutters once harvested their 'red gold'. 'Alternative' communities and hobby farms nestle in the valleys where dairy farmers pioneered the land.

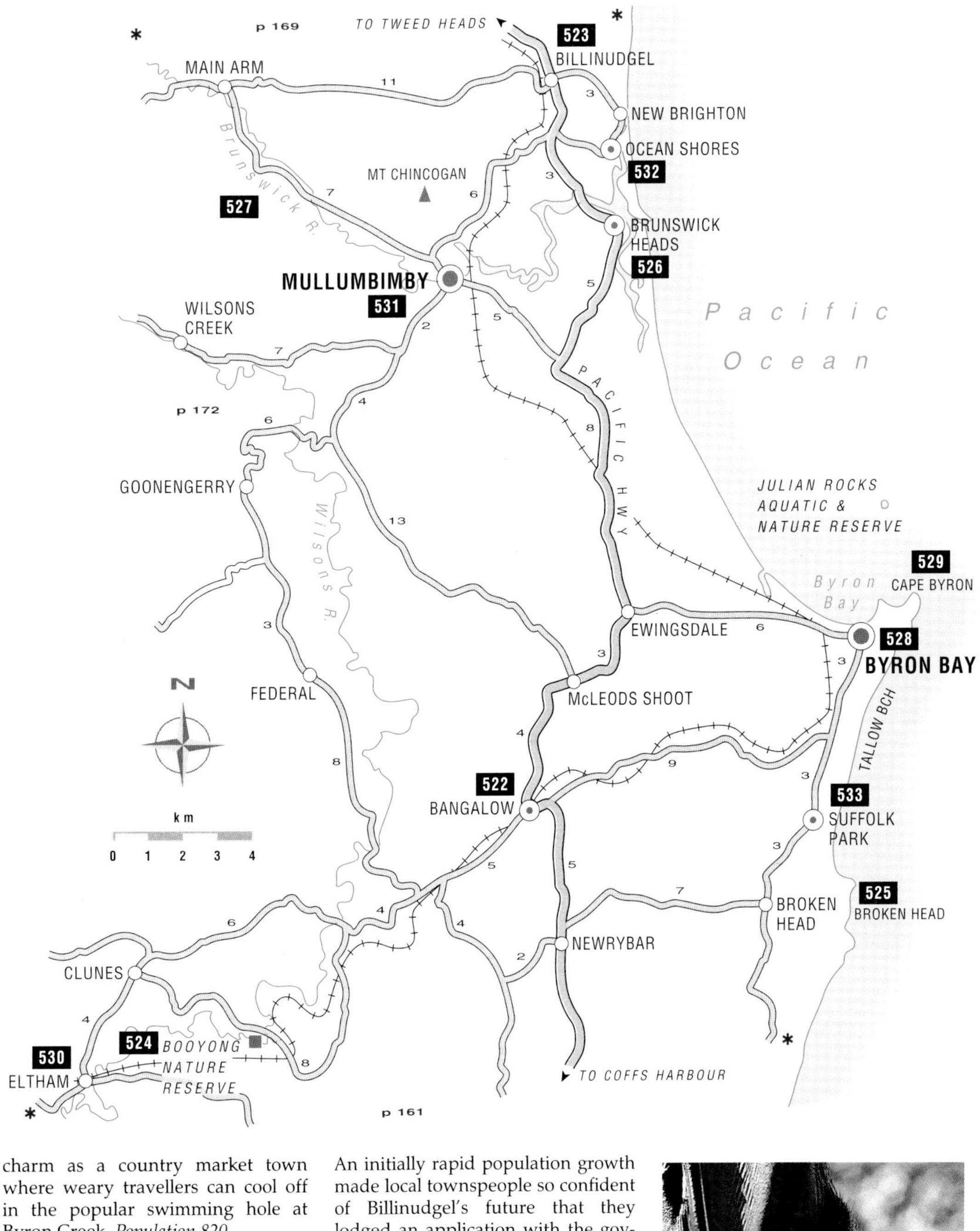

BANGALOW ■ 522

The peaceful valley in which Bangalow nestles was originally known as Byron Creek – a small tributary of the Wilson and Richmond Rivers system. It is at the northern extreme of an impenetrable rainforest dubbed 'the Big Scrub', a natural barrier of cedar, hoop pine, mahogany and tallow wood which deterred settlement until the 1880s.

Attracted by the prospect of farming the rich, red basalt soil under the Big Scrub, experienced dairy farmers from the South Coast arrived by sea with prime dairy cows to make the arduous trek through uncleared scrub. The introduction of the then new pasture grass, paspalum, which was particularly suitable for the production of creamy milk needed for butter, spurred the progress of the dairy industry. The Byron Creek Dairy Company was opened in 1893 and by 1894, with the opening of the Lismore–Byron Bay rail link, the district became a part of the rapid development of the dairy industry on the North Coast.

In 1891, a post office opened on the mail run between Byron Bay and Clunes, shops catering for the farming community evolved at the crossroads and by 1907 the name 'Bangalow' was adopted at the instigation of the post mistress whose mail was frequently lost. The name has two sources, one being the local bangalow palm tree, the other a corruption of the Aboriginal word 'bangalla' meaning 'low hill'.

By the 1950s, the town was losing business to larger rural centres, and a decline in milk production resulted in the small, regional butter factories being centralised in Lismore. Small dairy units were consolidated into larger holdings, and subtropical fruit plantations began to spring up. Bangalow has managed to retain its charm as a country market town where weary travellers can cool off in the popular swimming hole at Byron Creek. *Population 820*

BILLINUDGEL ■ 523

The exact origin of this name remains obscure, but it is thought to refer to the king parrot, this being the area where the bird was found in great numbers though today there are no records of its survival. Other possible meanings of Aboriginal origin are 'land between sea and lake' or 'meeting of the waters' – a reference to the forested slopes and the four creeks which once existed here. An initially rapid population growth made local townspeople so confident of Billinudgel's future that they lodged an application with the government to have Billinudgel declared the national capital, as well as offering it as the site for a capital city of a new state – an idea which was being promoted vigorously by the New State Movement in the 1920s. Unfortunately, these great expectations were not to be realised and Billinudgel remains a tiny village along the Pacific Highway known primarily for the New Brighton Hotel, a fine example of early Australian timber architecture.

At Booyong, a road leads into the heart of the rainforest and the home of the grey-headed flying fox.

BOOYONG NATURE RESERVE ■ 524

This flora and fauna reserve, named from the local Aboriginal word for the ironwood trees that once grew plentifully here, offers walkers a scenic amble along the banks of Wilsons River into a pocket of lush rainforest. A large bat colony shelters in the protected environment.

BROKEN HEAD ■ 525

This bush-covered headland juts out into the Pacific Ocean, dividing the wide sweeps of Tallow and Seven Mile beaches. The Broken Head Nature Reserve is an oasis of the last remnants of the coastal rainforest, and provides a tranquil escape for local bushwalkers. One walk from the caravan park leads to a steep cliff lookout with spectacular views of the Pacific stretching north and south. Another trail through the pockets of rainforest in the gullies winds down to a chain of secluded beaches. The jutting rocks off the headland, rising metres above sea level, are known as Cocked Hat Rocks or the Two Sisters Rocks. According to an Aboriginal legend, two sisters who were swimming at the beach drowned and were transformed into stone, a warning to others of the treacherous waters along of this stretch of coast.

The highway and the railway line which sweep through the middle of the town have failed to dispel the charm of Bangalow's idyllic setting.

BRUNSWICK HEADS ■ 526

This relaxed, family holiday destination offers a variety of boating, swimming, and fishing activities – all of them popular enough, and its location attractive enough, for Brunswick Heads to experience an eight-fold population increase during the peak summer season.

A good-natured Fish and Chips Festival in the early weeks of January is symbolic of Brunswick's past and present industries; the 'chips' represent the woodchips which flew when the early timber-getters were at their task while the 'fish' alludes to a major commercial activity of the present day.

The cedar-getters who set up camp at the mouth of the Brunswick River in 1849 were looking for Australian red cedar. Their itinerant lifestyle meant it was not until the late 1870s that Robert Marshall and his wife established a permanent store and hotel to cater for the large camp of timber workers. The site of the original timber structure is now occupied by the brick Brunswick Heads Hotel. Brunswick Heads remained as the hub of the cedar trade on the north coast into the 1870s. Logs were floated downriver and hauled by drays to the beaches. In a cumbersome and dangerous process known as 'surfing', bullocks would drag the lumber through the surf where it was rafted together and winched up to waiting schooners.

This audacious practice was necessitated by the treacherous sandbar which prevented large boats entering the Brunswick River. There was agitation for a breakwater, but the demand for a jetty at neighbouring Byron Bay was deemed more important. The town was again overlooked when the Lismore–Tweed rail link went through Mullumbimby because of construction problems through the swampy coastal terrain.

Despite these early obstacles, the village found its identity as a major holiday resort in the twentieth century. The government formally proclaimed the Village of Brunswick in 1885 and although it became known commonly as Brunswick Heads the name was not given the official stamp of approval until 1971.

The fish of local waters, which had always attracted anglers, also attracted commercial interest and the fishing fleet for the area was traditionally stationed at Byron Bay. The destruction of many trawlers and the collapse of the Byron Bay jetty in a 1954 storm changed the fishing scene; the fishing and prawning fleet now shelters at Brunswick Heads where a low-profile breakwater was constructed in 1960. *Population 1660*

FESTIVALS Fish and Chips Festival, January; Blessing of the Fleet, Easter Sunday.

BRUNSWICK RIVER ■ 527

While searching for navigable rivers and better grazing land for the drought-stricken farmers of Port Jackson in 1828, Captain Henry Rous noted '...another river about 8 miles N.W from Cape Byron running a W.N.W direction with a narrow and deep channel, a rocky bar at the entrance and a shallow north and south arm'.

Named Brunswick to honour the wife of King George IV, Queen Caroline of Brunswick, the river was one of the last of the northern rivers to be navigated and used to transport cedar logs. By 1840, the river mouth was surveyed and in 1849 cedar-cutters, described as 'the roughest of rough fellows, muscular as working bullocks', were camped at its mouth.

BYRON BAY ■ 528

Before the arrival of Europeans, a clearing behind today's Byron Bay Surf Life Saving Club was a place of tribal significance to the Aborigines of this region. Known as a 'cavanbah' or 'meeting place', it was a site for corroborees which brought together neighbours in a celebration of the abundance of game and seafood in this lush coastal strip. Byron Bay remains a meeting place but now there are back-packing foreigners, scuba and surfing enthusiasts and family holiday-makers as well as the rich and famous who have been tempted by the idyllic climate and the unspoilt beaches.

Soundings at the bay adjacent to Cape Byron were made in 1828 by Captain Henry Rous but it wasn't until almost fifty years later that an inn was set up on the west side of the cape for cedar-getters journeying overland from the Brunswick River to the closest settlement, Bulloona (later known as Ballina). The tough timber men moved into the Byron Bay hinterland and without rivers they developed new techniques to move logs to the ocean for shipment.

Timber was felled on the hills and slid down gullies and small valleys dubbed 'shoots'. Coopers Shoot, McLeods Shoot and Skinners Shoot still remain as landmarks today.

Construction of a large jetty into the bay in 1888 and a rail link to Lismore in 1894 put Byron Bay truly on the map. The settlement shifted to the present commercial centre around the jetty and railway, becoming officially known as Byron Bay after 1884. Refrigerated steamers shipped fresh dairy produce to the city markets from the recently established North Coast Co-operative or Norco which was supplied by the network of small farms in the hills.

In 1921, the *Wollongbar*, a cargo–passenger steamer, was ripped from its moorings and dumped on the seabed by fierce easterlies. The wreck protrudes off Main Beach today at low tide and serves as a breakwater for surfers, symbolic of Byron Bay's decline as a port. The new jetty constructed in 1929 still offered little protection from the elements and the fishing fleet was devastated twice, the second time in 1954, forcing a move to Brunswick Heads.

Thoughtful development means that modern Byron Bay has managed to avoid high-rise tourism, maintaining its country town atmosphere while absorbing a diverse service industry of restaurants, cafes, surf shops and art galleries which reflect the interests and activities of the 'new wave' of residents.

WATEGOS BEACH Between the Cape and The Pass, Wategos Beach is the only beach on the eastern seaboard that faces north; well sheltered from the wind, it is popular with surfers because of its long breakers. The beach is named after the Watego family, New Caledonian settlers who grew bananas on what is now Byron Bay's most exclusive residential area.

JULIAN ROCKS Three kilometres north of Main Beach, the twin rock outcrop known collectively as Julian Rocks was named by Captain Cook after a niece and nephew. The Aborigines had a variety of legends associated with the rocks, the most popular concerning a jealous husband spearing the canoe of his wife and her lover, and the upturned canoe turning into the rocks. The rocks are a nature reserve while the surrounding water is a spectacular marine reserve, where the tropical waters from the Coral Sea meet the cooler, temperate waters of the south. This unusual ecosystem attracts unique marine life and, in turn, the divers who come to observe it. *Population 5000*

CAPE BYRON ■ 529

Occasionally, a local marriage ceremony is held at dawn to greet the sun at the top of these steep cliffs on the most easterly point on the Australian mainland. Captain Cook, on his journey up the east coast of Australia in 1770, recorded in his journal of 15th May the sighting of native peoples and smoke near a 'tolerable high point of land'. He named it Cape Byron after Captain John Byron, the grandfather of the poet Lord Byron. The cape marks the theoretical division between the winds, currents and climate of temperate New South Wales and subtropical northern Australia.

A scenic walking trail which circles the headland gives access to seclud-

ed beaches and provides unsurpassed panoramic views both inland to the Border Ranges and out to sea.

CAPE BYRON LIGHTHOUSE Steep cliffs almost 100 metres high make the rocky headland of the cape a majestic setting for this local landmark. Both the residence and lighthouse were constructed in 1901 from concrete. The Cape Byron light remains one of seven still staffed in New South Wales and is renowned for the power of its lamp which can reach up to twenty-six nautical miles – forty-three kilometres – out to sea.

ELTHAM ■ 530

One of the earliest places settled in the 'Big Scrub' was Cowlong, adjacent to the waterway of the Wilson River and Pearces Creek. The extension of the railway from Lismore to Byron Bay resulted in a station called Eltham at Cowlong, named after a local property and this opened up the area. Today, an avenue of camphor laurel trees lines the road leading into this peaceful village.

MULLUMBIMBY ■ 531

Mullumbimby – set on the tidal stretch of the Brunswick River – is considered the capital of the Byron Shire. The town is a thriving service centre for a variety of small farms in the Brunswick Valley and has a reputation as the 'headquarters' of the alternative lifestyle culture that rose out of the 1960s hippy movement.

The name is derived from an Aboriginal word for 'small round hill' a reference to a small hill on the Goonengery Road. From the mouth of the Brunswick River, cedar-getters spread up the waterway and along the present Saddle Road and McAulays Lane to the future site of the Mullumbimby Golf Club which was cleared to provide grazing for the bullock teams which hauled timber to the coast.

This swampy patch produced a lank, swampy grass particularly palatable to the bullocks who had overdosed on salt water and sand while 'surfing' the timber out into water deep enough for it to float(see Brunswick Heads). Slightly further north, at a convenient crossing of the Main Arm, an area was reserved for a village in 1872. Within ten years, the village had been surveyed, proclaimed as Mullumbimby and Crown Land sales in the area begun.

Development as the service centre for the Brunswick Valley benefited from the decision to bypass the then larger town of Brunswick Heads in the construction of the railway line which opened in 1894. A long-term rivalry with Byron Bay resulted in the formation of a municipality here in 1908 and Mullumbimby remained an isolated administrative island of four-and-a-half square kilometres in the middle of the Byron Shire until it was incorporated into the larger body in 1980.

Mullumbimby prospered as a market town but suffered after the Second World War when a slump in the dairy and fruit industries, coupled with the closing of large employers such as the Mullumbimby timber mill, led to a downturn in land prices. It was these relatively low land prices combined with the balmy climate that attracted newcomers in the 1960s and the development of Mullumbimby as one of the early centres of the 'alternative' lifestyle. *Population 2610*

BRUNSWICK VALLEY HISTORICAL MUSEUM AND PARK Housed in the original timber post office, this local museum contains a special exhibition which pays tribute to the importance of the timber industry.

BRUNSWICK VALLEY HERITAGE PARK This award-winning parkland which stretches along the green river's edge contains species of indigenous rainforest plants, including some rare coolamon trees.

FESTIVALS Chincogan Festival, mid-September.

OCEAN SHORES ■ 532

This ambitious real estate development is set west of Marshalls Creek, which winds between New Brighton and Brunswick Heads. More than 1400 hectares of swampland were drained and reclaimed for recreational and residential use in 1969. A string of owners have proposed residential developments for the site but plans for marinas and high-rise home-unit buildings have been stalled by a series of environmental concerns. Recreational facilities such as the Ocean Shores Country Club, which provides an eighteen-hole championship golf course, are open to visitors. *Population 2800*

FESTIVALS Spring Flower Festival, August.

Cape Byron, crowned by its famous lighthouse, makes a dramatic lunge into the ocean to establish itself as Australia's most easterly point. Here, where the rays of the sun fall first each morning, herds of semi-wild goats feed on the rugged hillsides around the lighthouse which is reputed to emit one of the most powerful beams in Australia.

SUFFOLK PARK ■ 533

A few kilometres south of Byron Bay, is the self-contained holiday village of Suffolk Park. Family groups and retired people make up a residential population which prefers the more relaxed atmosphere here to the sometimes trendy bustle of Byron Bay. Situated midway along the great expanse of Tallow Beach, swimming, fishing, surfing and leisurely walks along the fine white sands of the beach are the main priority here.

Tallow sweeps in a grand arc from Cape Byron to Broken Head with a thick, foreshore scrub of banksias and casuarinas. The beach's name originates from the practice adopted by squatters in the 1860s depression of boiling down sheep for fat or tallow to make candles and soap. When the vessel *Volunteer* was wrecked off Cosy Corner in 1864, barrels of tallow were cast up on the beach. *Population 1220*

Tweed Heads & Murwillumbah

Bordered by ranges of volcanic peaks and long white sandy beaches, the streams and valleys of this well-watered region have fostered farming, fishing and tourism in and around quiet country villages. Timber-getting was the pioneer industry and pockets of the 'Big Scrub' that attracted early settlers still remain.

BILAMBIL HEIGHTS ■ 534

The small farming community of Bilambil Heights in the west Tweed area has become part of the urban sprawl into the subtropical valley of the Tweed. Largely a residential town favoured increasingly by commuters to Tweed Heads and Murwillumbah, the town has been designated as a growth area and the shire council has rezoned rural land for subdivision and further development. *Population 2020*

BOGANGAR ■ 535

The twin lures of Cabarita Beach and Cudgen Lake have made the small coastal village of Bogangar a popular holiday destination for tourists to the Tweed Coast. Watersport enthusiasts and anglers are able to choose between the lake's fresh water and the ocean for their aquatic pursuits. *Population 1540*

CONDONG ■ 536

On an idyllically rural stretch of the Tweed River, Condong is where the New South Wales Sugar and Milling Co-operative runs a large, modern mill that processes all the cane grown in the Tweed River region. The Condong mill has been in operation on this site since 1880 and is one of only three mills still working in the New South Wales Northern Rivers district.

There were about 100 mills crushing cane in this area at the peak of the sugar industry in the early 1900s. In those days, only river transport was available as no roads had been built through the thick forests. To simplify the job of transport, cane crops were planted along the river banks as some still are today.

Not much remains of the original sugar mill built by the Colonial Sugar Refinery. Nowadays, sophisticated technology has banished laborious hand-cutting, and river transport no longer plays a significant role in an industry worth about eight million dollars a year.

COOLANGATTA ■ 537

Coolangatta is best known for its beautiful stretch of sandy beach popular with board riders and body surfers. The waters are also favoured by fishermen who may be seen at sunrise and sunset fishing for bream, tailor or whiting. This southernmost of Queensland's coastal towns has, with its twin-town of Tweed Heads across the border, been the mecca of generations of holiday-makers who came to experience the glamour of Surfers Paradise and helped build the reputation of the glossy Gold Coast (see Special Feature). Despite the importance of tourism, fishing, dairy farming and fruit-growing are still major industries here.

Coolangatta was named by the region's pioneering cedar-getters for the schooner from New South Wales that foundered off the coast in 1846 (see *Nowra & Kiama*). The *Coolangatta* was sailing from Brisbane to Shoalhaven Heads and stopped here to load cedar from the mouth of the Tweed River. Gale-force winds battered the ship causing it to break away from both anchors, eventually running aground at Kirra Point. Fortunately all on board were able to swim through the surf, and managed to scramble safely ashore at Point Danger (see entry). *Population 3610*

CUDGEN ■ 538

William Guilfoyle, the distinguished horticulturalist who succeeded Ferdinand von Mueller at Melbourne's Botanical Gardens in 1873, was among the district's first successful growers of warm-climate crops such as sugar cane. By the 1870s, sugar cane and bananas were thriving in the rich volcanic soil that also nurtures the first commercial tea project in New South Wales. Researchers are now investigating the chemical properties of green tea grown here for possible use in controlling cancer.

The nearby Cudgen Lake has been extensively dredged and is now a popular location for sailing, windsurfing, waterskiing and paraflying.

FINGAL HEAD ■ 539

Fingal Head Lighthouse, built in 1872, is situated halfway along the sandspit that separates the lower Tweed region from the Pacific Ocean. Below the lighthouse is the Giants Causeway, where massive basalt columns, eroded by wind and wave action, form 'steps' to the ocean. When seas are calm, fishermen station themselves on high, flat rocks near the northern end of the causeway from where – with a little luck – they reel in kingfish, Spanish mackerel, tailor, trevally and even tuna.

COOK ISLAND NATURE RESERVE Cook Island, about 500 metres east of Fingal Point, has rocky cliffs, thick vegetation and sandy beaches and all these ingredients combined make it an ideal place for the thousands of sea birds that come here to breed. Visitors walking around the island – taking care not to disturb nests – are likely to see birds such as ospreys, sea-eagles, cormorants, crested terns and the wedge-tailed shearwater.

Ocean currents sweeping down from the Great Barrier Reef mix with more temperate southern waters in the reefs and sea around Cook Island, creating a wonderful habitat for coral and sponge gardens, turtles and a variety of tropical and southern fish. Scuba divers exploring close by the island's southern end may encounter giant Queensland groper and in January, the occasional, friendly leopard shark – some of which are three metres long.

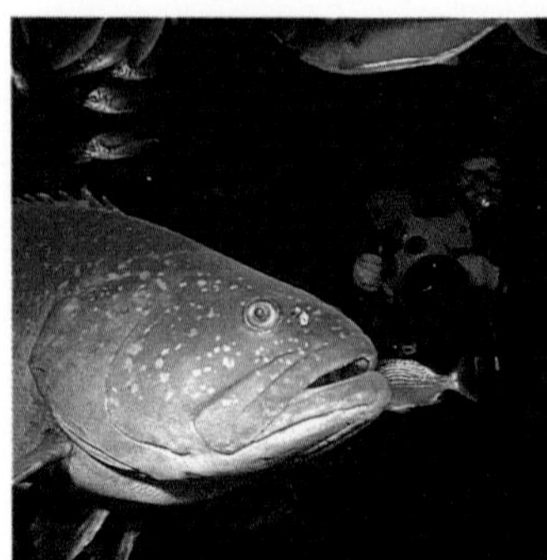

Australia's largest fish – the Queensland groper – commands respect from Cook Island divers.

MINJUNGBAL CULTURAL CENTRE ■ 540

The eight hectares of bushland that make up Minjungal Aboriginal Cultural Centre are centred around an old ceremonial bora ring about five kilometres south of Tweed Heads and commemorate the Minjungbal people who once inhabited the lower Tweed Valley. Aboriginal guides teach visitors about traditional religious and cultural aspects of life here before the arrival of Europeans. The museum displays relics such as stone tools, decorative ornaments, beads, ceremonial artefacts, boomerangs and other wooden weapons, ochres, art and craftwork.

As many as 6000 people from the Bundjalung, Kamilaroi and Wiradjuri groups once gathered for special ceremonies held in the cleared bora ground. No trace remains of the linking pathway or smaller bora ring where tribal elders carried out the ceremonial initiations of young men entering adulthood.

The trail in Ukerebagh Nature Reserve meanders through a variety of vegetation. Banksias in the eucalypt forest attract honeyeaters and colourful lorikeets while closer to the Tweed River bank, she-oaks and paperbark trees gradually give way to mangroves on the mud flats.

Extracts from the green tea grown at Madura, near Cudgen, were used in treating victims of the 1986 nuclear disaster at Chernobyl in Russia.

MOUNT WARNING NATIONAL PARK ■ 541

Mount Warning is the remnant core of Australia's largest shield volcano. More than twenty million years ago, its vast bulk extended over four thousand square kilometres, it was twice its present height and was active for three million years. The mountain is known to Aborigines as Woollumbin, said to mean 'the fighting leader' and was given its English name by Captain Cook as a literal warning to future navigators after the *Endeavour* was almost wrecked off this coast.

A steep walking track zigzags from Breakfast Creek to the summit, more than 1100 metres above. As the highest point on the east coast, this is where the sun's rays first strike the Australian mainland each day. The walk begins on the lower slopes where palms, carabeens, rosewood, blackbutt and flame trees grow in subtropical rainforests. Further up, brush box, mountain wattle and coachwood belong to the temperate rainforest while heath shrublands flourish on the exposed summit. Flower spikes of the rare northern gymea lily grow to an impressive three metres in length.

At the top, rewarding views to Nightcap National Park in the south,

Tweed Heads–Coolangatta is a town divided – the state border runs down the centre of this peninsula.

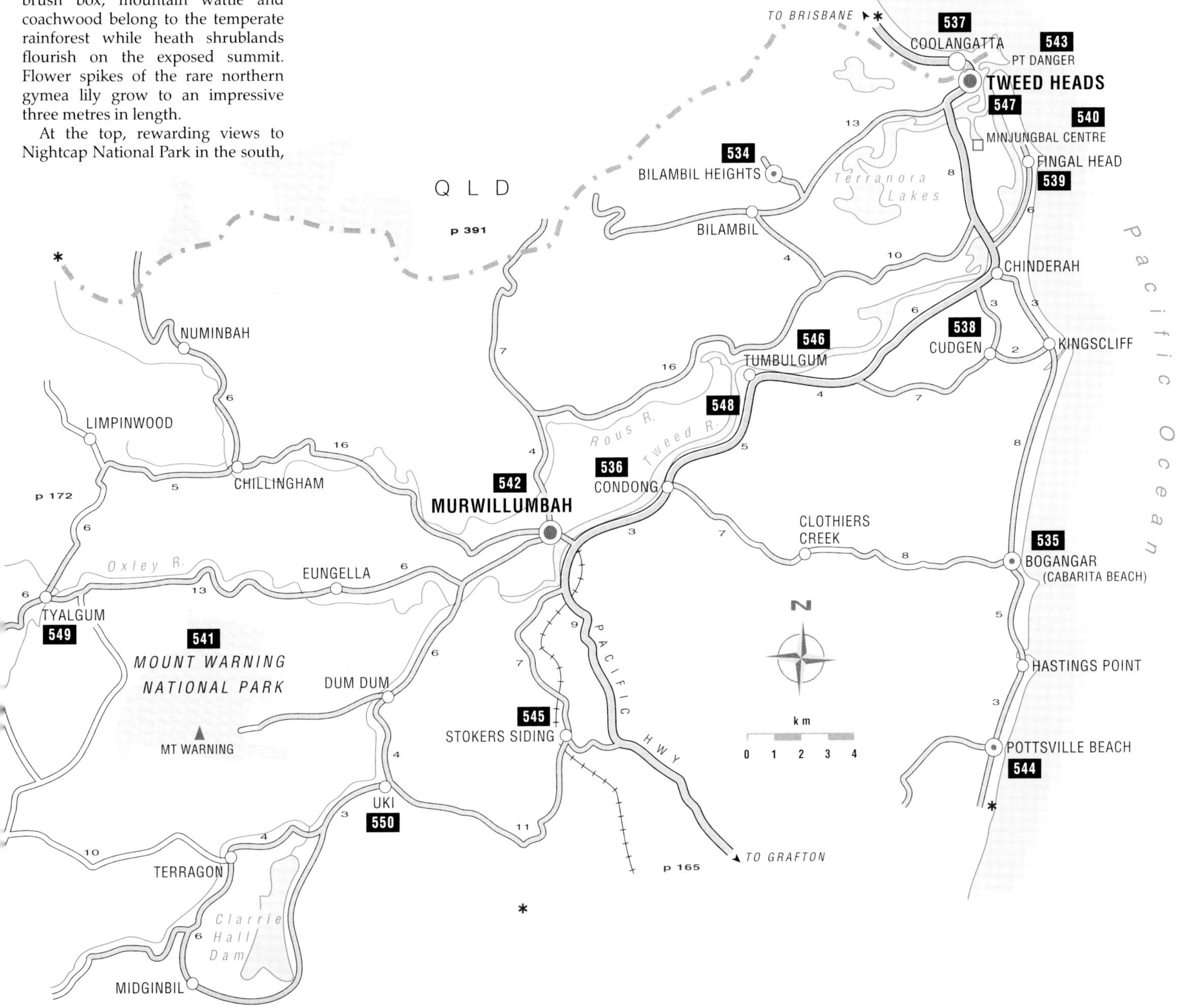

Aptly named rainbow lorikeets brighten the forest canopies of Mount Warning National Park.

the Border Ranges National Park in the west and Lamington National Park in Queensland to the northwest, show in part the outline of the ancient volcano's rim. These isolated parks have been recognised for their complex geological formation and their variety of plant and animal populations by being added to the World Heritage list in 1986.

The endangered wompoo and red-crowned pigeons feed on the fruit of rainforest trees while scrub turkeys and the endangered Albert lyrebird are ground dwellers. Most of the park's animals are nocturnal but wallabies and pademelons may be seen during the day. Summit-bound walkers should allow four hours for the return trip and are well advised to take water, raingear and warm clothing.

MURWILLUMBAH ■ 542
The McPherson Range and Mount Warning form a dramatic backdrop to Murwillumbah which was established on the banks of the Tweed River in the 1870s. In those days, the only means of crossing the river was by punt. Timber-getting and sugar-cane crushing were the district's first industries and produce was carried thirty kilometres downriver before being taken to the big-city markets.

The opening of the railway to Lismore in 1894, gave momentum to the town's development with dairy farming quickly becoming the major industry after the Norco butter factory opened at Byron Bay in 1895 and the Tweed creamery began operating in Murwillumbah two years later. Commercial banana growing began in 1910 and now macadamia nuts, tropical fruits, herbs, vegetables and beef cattle thrive on the district's rich, volcanic soil. Murwillumbah remains the terminus of the North Coast railway; plans to link the town to Tweed Heads have never been carried through.

A huge fire in 1907 destroyed most of the original town centre but the Federation-style police station and residence along with the court house survive from the early 1900s. Murwillumbah is the main service centre for the farmlands of the Tweed River valley; its proximity to the attractions of the coast – and the hinterland – has meant that tourism has developed steadily as an important industry since the 1960s.

The origin of Murwillumbah's name is open to several interpretations: the local Aboriginal dialect was the source of a number of similar-sounding words, the combination of which meant that this was either a 'place of many possums' or a 'big camping place'. *Population 8000*

POINT DANGER ■ 543
Captain Cook named Point Danger and Mount Warning in 1770 after his ship *Endeavour* almost ran aground in unexpectedly shallow waters.

Cook sailed north from here and several months later reached the Great Barrier Reef where he did run aground and was forced to dump his cast-iron ballast. Retrieved by scuba divers, it was melted down and recast as the ship's capstan and it now stands at the base of the Point Danger Captain Cook Memorial.

The world's first laser lighthouse beam was tested here at the official opening of the memorial and lighthouse in 1971. The laser has since been replaced by a more conventional electric light.

POTTSVILLE BEACH ■ 544
Located on the Moobal Creek estuary and with two council caravan parks, a store…and not much more, Pottsville Beach is a favoured holiday destination for surfing and estuary fishing enthusiasts. Nearby are the Tweed Shire Council's Bicentennial Leisure Gardens which lure the area's residents and tourists alike to wander through more than fifty hectares of savannah swamp. The gardens have a botanical theme and protect many types of vegetation that once flourished on the Tweed Coast. *Population 1290*

STOKERS SIDING ■ 545
Floods and a cyclone have helped forge a strong sense of community in the picturesque village of Stokers Siding. Backed by Mount Nullum and spectacular Mount Warning, bananas grow on the slopes and dairy cows graze in the pastures.

The old church building – now a private residence – the hall, school and general store date back to the early 1900s when Stokers Siding was an important local service centre.

In 1954, the Pacific Highway by-passed this settlement because of problems with flooding and now that the train service from Sydney to Murwillumbah no longer stops here, Stokers Siding retains a relaxed air of rural tranquillity.

TUMBULGUM ■ 546
Until 1986, when it was replaced by a bridge, a barge ferry operated here. This remnant ser.vice dated back to the beginning of the century before the advent of bridges, when Tumbulgum was known as Tweed Junction. For the Aborigines Tumbulgum meant 'the place of the meeting of the waters'. The region's first European settlements were established here and at Terranora.

For a time, Tumbulgum was a base for timber-getters. A post office was built in 1872 followed by the school, and in 1873, the town's first sugar mill opened. Author and Aboriginal-rights activist Faith Bandler was born here in 1920; one of her best-known works was the 1977 novel *Wacvie* which described the experiences of her father who was abducted from the New Hebrides by blackbirders and taken to work on the Queensland canefields.

The old Tumbulgum Hotel, built almost completely of cedar, stands as the southern landmark of the ferry crossing. The building, near the ferry terminus, dates back to the late 1800s when it served as the general store. It is a fitting testimonial to the region's timber industry, housing a woodcraft gallery that displays items fashioned from local timbers such as rosewood, hoop pine, red cedar and teak.

TWEED HEADS ■ 547
Situated strategically at the mouth of the river of the same name, Tweed Heads was once a bustling timber-shipping port. Activity centred around the estuary where brigantines, ketches, schooners and later on steamships negotiated the dangerous bar and shifting channels to bring in passengers and supplies.

Settlement began here in 1870 with the establishment of a pilot station. Before this, countless ships had come to grief including that of Captain McGregor who became the first Pilot-in-Charge. Nothing remains of the pilot station or the customs house built in 1871. The construction of breakwaters in the 1890s followed by the formation of the Commonwealth in 1901 – and the abolition of inter-colony duties – rendered both these facilities obsolete.

Tweed Heads began to develop rapidly in the 1950s and 1960s with the spread of the family car. Holidaymakers from Brisbane, Ipswich and Toowoomba flocked to the Gold Coast which had suddenly become readily accessible to the average car owner. As the Gold Coast prospered so did its component parts and Tweed Heads and Coolangatta were soon separated only by an imaginary, administrative line.

Retirement settlements and varying forms of holiday accommodation from serviced apartments to caravans bring a booming trade to the many service clubs and businesses throughout the town where tourism competes with fishing as the major money-spinner. *Population 17 380*

STOTTS ISLAND Jutting into the river between Tweed Heads and Tumbulgum is the nature reserve of Stotts Island; thickly covered with subtropical rainforest it is separated from the southern bank by a narrow channel.

RAZORBACK LOOKOUT AND OBSERVATORY HILL PARK Only three kilometres from Tweed Heads there are panoramic views of the Tweed Valley and Gold Coast from Mount Warning and the McPherson Range.

TWEED RIVER ■ 548
The system of creeks and streams that eventually forms the Tweed River is a close-knit group neatly

The dramatically jagged outline of Mount Warning stands sentinel over the rich farmlands surrounding Murwillumbah in the Tweed River Valley.

enclosed on three sides by the steep rim of the ancient Tweed volcano. The most beautiful stretches of the river are its upper reaches where Mount Warning can be seen from different angles according to bends in the river.

Once it starts to take shape as a river, the Tweed – later joined by the Oxley and Rous rivers – flows with its other tributaries for about eighty kilometres to its broad estuary at Tweed Heads.

The river is home to the region's prawning and fishing fleets; amateur anglers are catered for in the mangrove-studded estuary where bream, flathead and blackfish abound. Fishing from nearby rocks and in the surf from South Beach is also a productive occupation.

John Oxley discovered and named the Tweed River in 1823 when he sailed up the coast to investigate the Moreton Bay region. At that time the coastal lowlands of the Tweed River Valley were clad in a dense rainforest which early settlers later dubbed the 'Big Scrub'.

TYALGUM ■ **549**

Sandwiched between the Border Ranges and Mount Warning, Tyalgum lies beside the Middle Arm of the Tweed, also known as the Oxley River. Settlers established themselves in the area in the early 1900s clearing the scrub for dairy farming. Norco set up a dairy factory in Tyalgum in 1913 but closed the small enterprise seventeen years later when the company consolidated its operations in larger urban centres. Nearby creeks are a gem fossicker's paradise. Alluvial deposits contain a variety of semi-precious stones including onyx, agate and jasper. There are even 'Thunder Eggs', or spherulites, rocks of volcanic origin that sometimes contain such gemstones as agate, amethyst and chalcedony.

Tyalgum is a perfect base from which to explore the caldera of the ancient volcano. There are excellent views of nearby Mount Warning and of the Border Ranges National Park to the west. The daunting rock formation known as The Pinnacle can also be seen from here.

UKI ■ **550**

Uki was once a major dairying centre with a Norco factory operating in the village for twenty years until 1930 when the company rationalised its operations and expanded its bases in the larger urban centres. Modern Uki retains an old-fashioned air and is a service village for the surrounding region. Its unusual name is said to come from an Aboriginal word for 'an edible swamp-fern root'.

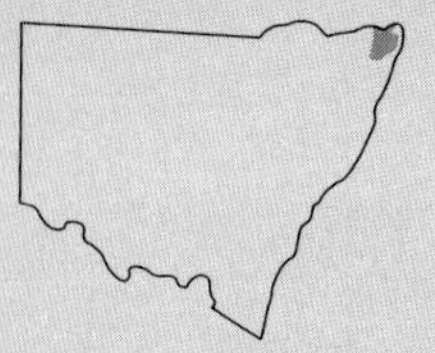

Lismore & Casino

Smallholding dairy farmers brought belated prosperity to the upper Richmond Valley, on land where pastoralist squatter families had struggled for decades. Most of the lowland 'Big Scrub' forest is gone, but a rainforest treasure house is preserved in the high country.

BORDER RANGES NATIONAL PARK ■ 551

Among the steepest, most tortuous and in some places, roughest, public roads to be found on the Australian mainland, the Tweed Range scenic drive in Border Ranges National Park rewards travellers with unforgettable views and an unusually wide sampling of rainforest types.

At least four hours of daylight should be allowed to negotiate the sixty-kilometre drive at a comfortable pace and take in the sights, and much more time to enjoy some of the many walks available. Access is from the Kyogle–Woodenbong road at Wiangaree or the alternative Kyogle–Murwillumbah road at Lillian Rock. Motorists are urged to spare their nerves and brake-linings by starting from Lillian Rock, climbing rather than descending the trickiest part of the route.

CASINO ■ 552

Few country towns dating from the 1840s have their origins so precisely indicated and their early histories as thoroughly documented as Casino. A boulder prised from the bed of the Richmond River has been set on end to mark 'the Crossing Place'. Here George Stapleton and Henry Clay, overlanding cattle and other livestock from Tenterfield, forded the river in 1840 and became the first squatters on the Richmond.

They called their spread 'Cassino', presumably after Monto Cassino in Italy. Within a year a house, several slab huts and a piggery were clustered near the ford. Cedar-getters came eagerly into the area by riverboat and a settlement sprang up just downstream at 'The Falls', where the fording shelf drops away. This natural limit to navigation became the town site, gazetted with a misspelt name in 1855. Progress was slow until closer settlement of the district came with dairying in the 1880s.

Casino's strategic position was enhanced by the completion of local railway links in the early part of this century. Thanks to indecisive planning and wrangling between the state governments, Casino became the junction where the main line from Sydney forks into Queensland – one way to what is now the Gold Coast and the other to Brisbane. The district's modern beef and dairy pro-

The carnival colours of the shopfronts in Nimbin provide a cheerful contrast to the more restrained commercial art of most country towns.

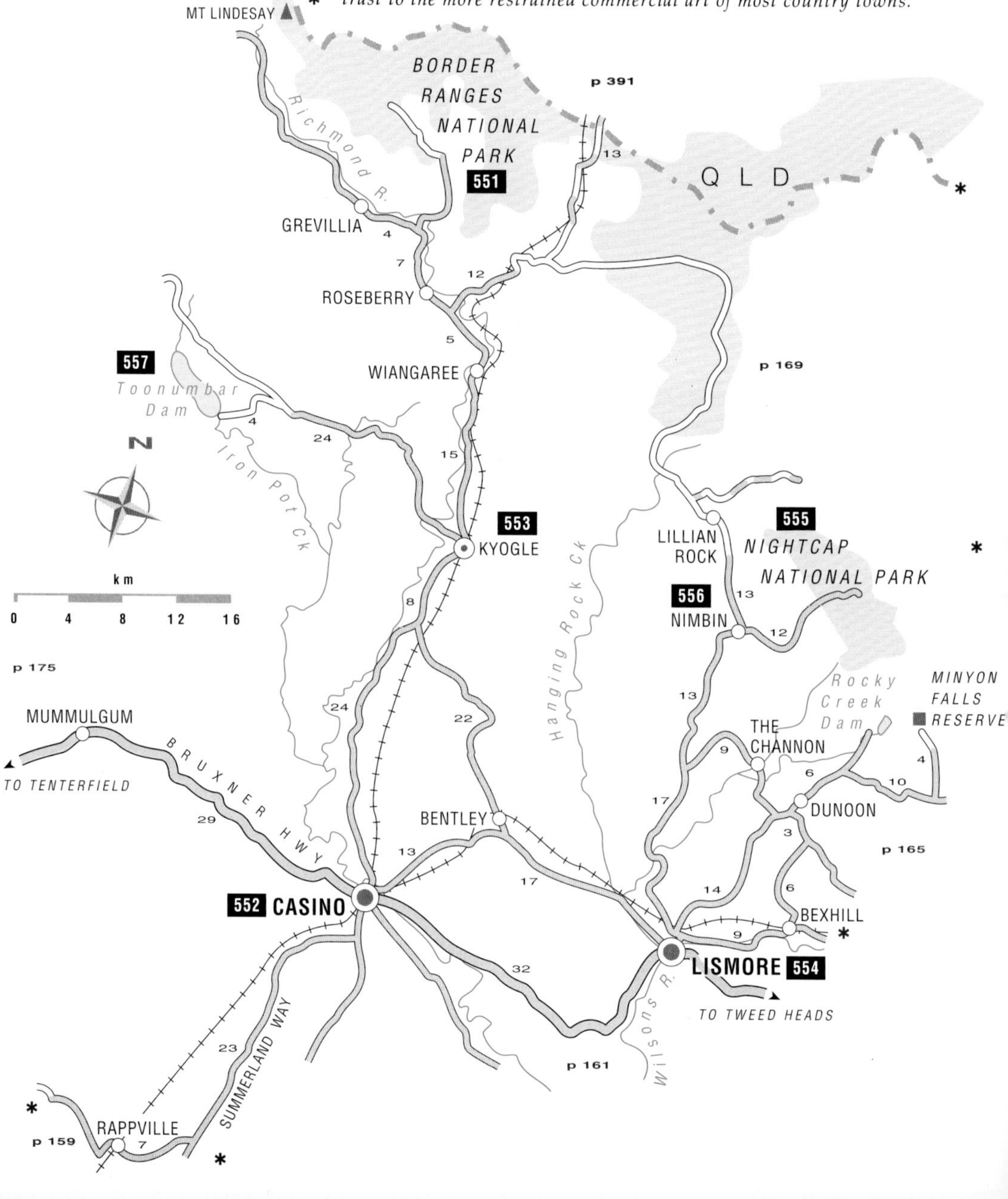

cessing industries benefit considerably from this unusual accessibility. *Population 10 170*

KYOGLE ■ 553

Lush pastures of the upper Richmond Valley and dense rainforests of the surrounding ranges are revealed from the Captain Cook Memorial Lookout halfway up Fairy Mountain (336 metres). Straddling the river at its base is Kyogle, a quiet town that was strangely slow to establish itself.

Beef-baron squatters and cedar-getters had been active in the district for about sixty years before town sites were auctioned in 1904. One of the cattle stations was for a time called Kaiu-gal, after an Aboriginal word for 'scrub turkey'. The name resurfaced as Kyogle in 1899, in an application to register a milk-collection point. By then, most of the beef-raising properties were being broken up into small holdings and restocked with dairy herds.

The opening of a butter factory in 1905 was the spur for the establishment of a town, and further growth was assured when a railway from Casino reached Kyogle in 1910. Dairying output declined after 1950, with a subsequent swing back to beef raising. Sawmilling and plywood production are also important local industries. For travellers Kyogle is a convenient base for trips along the upper Richmond and to the ranges fringing the Tweed Valley, which is bisected by the New South Wales–Queensland border. *Population 2910*

FESTIVALS Kyogle Fairymount Festival, early November.

LISMORE ■ 554

Lismore is the major centre for dairying in New South Wales. It owes most of its prosperity to planted grasslands of paspalum, introduced in 1893, and now covering much of the area where rainforests of the 'Big Scrub' used to dominate – and ultimately to the high rainfall that waters the pastures, especially in the summer months.

But the bounty of rain has had a dark side for Lismore, thanks to a restricted and ill-considered choice of town site in 1855. Where the Leycester and Wilsons creeks meet to form Wilsons River, the town was laid out on a relatively narrow floodplain, a sizable part of which was periodically subject to inundation to a depth of three metres. Again and again as a city grew, expanding up the surrounding hillsides, Lismore has been cut in two by damaging and sometimes tragic flooding.

Cedar-getters are thought to have been active upriver in the early 1840s, floating their logs down to the head of navigation at what became Lismore. The first pastoral effort, around the same time, failed because the climate was too warm for the sheep that were driven in. William Wilson took over the claim in 1844, bringing cattle. His wife named the run Lismore after an island in Scotland's Loch Linnhe where the two had spent their honeymoon.

At first, there was no rich harvest from the district, apart from the logging of the forests – which probably increased the runoff of rain and intensified flood risks in Lismore. Squatters survived the early years by boiling down the fat of their cattle for tallow, used in making soap and candles. Sugar cane was introduced in the 1860s and produced good revenues until a slump in the 1880s. By then, the big pastoral properties were being subdivided and dairying was taking hold.

Twenty small factories sprang up in the Richmond area between 1888 and 1894, by which time a railway to Murwillumbah was completed. The progress of the town from then on was assured. Lismore gained city status in 1946. Engineering and brewing now accompany dairy processing and sawmilling as major local industries while nearby farmlands are increasingly given over to specialised horticulture, producing macadamia nuts, bananas and experimental tropical fruit crops. *Population 27 250*

FESTIVALS Lismore International Festival of Friendship, August; Lismore Folk Festival, Agricultural and Industrial Show, October.

NIGHTCAP NATIONAL PARK ■ 555

Terania Creek, a conservation battleground in the late 1970s, has the best-developed visitor facilities in what, since 1983, has been Nightcap National Park. The creek is but one of hundreds of torrents rushing year-round down the forested gullies that crease the flanks of the Nightcap Range – perhaps the wettest area in New South Wales.

People keen to see what all the fuss was about, and to appreciate the quality of subtropical rainforest that has earned the park World Heritage listing, are sometimes thwarted by the flooding of causeways. Campers who do not move out quickly at the onset of heavy rains can find themselves marooned.

Strenuous walking trails lead to Tuntable Falls or Mount Matheson, linking with the old Nightcap Track. This formed part of the original packhorse route between Lismore and Murwillumbah, which used to take three days to complete.

NIGHTCAP FOREST DRIVE A remnant of the original 'Big Scrub' – the tall subtropical rainforest that once thrived on lowland volcanic soils all the way from the Richmond River to the Tweed – is seen early on a pleasant drive of an hour or so through Whian Whian State Forest. The route starts about twenty-five kilometres north of Lismore, turning onto a gravelled road just short of Rocky Creek Dam. After passing through the Big Scrub Flora Reserve it climbs the Nightcap Range and turns east to a scenic highlight at Minyon Falls.

NIMBIN ■ 556

A peaceful dairying township was catapulted into social history in 1974 after a farmer allowed his paddocks to be used for a gathering of alternative-lifestyle devotees. Many who attended the Aquarius Festival were inspired to turn their backs on city life and settle in the Nimbin district, establishing communal households and industries.

Nationwide publicity drew visitors curious to observe the ways of 'hippies', and the new settlers responded with an energetic output of arts, crafts and organically grown foodstuffs. Those remaining in the 1990s, having raised another generation of Nimbinites, are largely integrated with the long-established rural community. Little about the town seems especially unconventional by today's standards, except for the gaudy rainbow redecoration of old-fashioned buildings in the main street.

NIMBIN ROCKS An extraordinary wedge of rock, like a row of gigantic stalagmites, juts above a forest canopy three kilometres south-west of Nimbin. It was formed more than twenty million years ago, when the Tweed volcano was active. Molten material squirted up, then cooled and solidified, within a fissure in softer rock that has since disappeared through erosion. Locally called the Nimbin Needles, the formation has deep significance in Aboriginal mythology as the burial place of Nyimbinje, a spirit ancestor endowed with supernatural powers.

TOONUMBAR DAM ■ 557

Damming of Iron Pot Creek, a tributary of the Richmond River, in the early 1970s created a mecca for freshwater anglers. Bass caught in the lake behind Toonumbar Dam are claimed to average three-and-a-half kilograms. Enthusiasts from Kyogle restock the lake with small fry every year. Sailing and swimming are also popular here, along with walks in nearby rainforests.

Hardwood logs still queue for processing in this region's sawmills, but one native tree, the macadamia, is grown formally in orchards for its nuts rather than in forests.

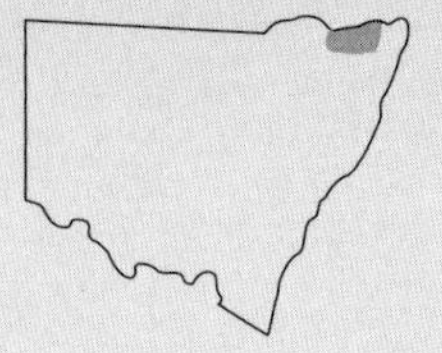

Stanthorpe & Tenterfield

Unusual geology and a bracing climate characterise the so-called 'granite belt' – unifying a region that was artificially divided by political mapmakers. Stark, timeless landforms are interspersed with flourishing orchards.

BALD ROCK NATIONAL PARK ■ 558

An enormous grey dome of deeply weathered adamellite – formed like granite but with a subtly different mineral content – rises 200 metres above a tall eucalypt forest watered by its run-off. About 750 metres long and 500 metres wide, this is the biggest granitic monolith to be seen in Australia. Echidnas nose about among a litter of smaller boulders and the flowering heaths that have colonised pockets of sandy soil where the rock is cracked. Elsewhere in this park of nearly 5500 hectares, there are woodlands and swampy gullies, giving a diversity of habitats that supports scores of bird species and many of the bigger marsupials such as grey kangaroos, wallaroos, wallabies and quolls. A walking track traverses the face of the rock and reaches the summit. The walk takes about an hour each way.

BOONOO BOONOO NATIONAL PARK ■ 559

Steep ridges flank the narrow valley of the Boonoo Boonoo River as it winds towards a spectacular waterfall, 210-metres high. A single road follows the river's tree-lined course for more than ten kilometres, offering varied scenery and access to pools in the boulder-strewn bed. The road ends at a picnic ground near a viewing platform over the falls.

GIRRAWEEN NATIONAL PARK ■ 560

Huge granitic outcroppings mark the Stanthorpe–Wallangarra district as a northern outlier of the New England Tableland. Such forms are seen nowhere else in Queensland. In Girraween National Park especially, they dominate the landscape. Broken blocks, rounded by aeons of weathering, form natural archways or pile up in ways that sometimes seem to defy gravity. The geology and peculiar vegetation of this environment are outlined in a guide to the Granite Arch Discovery Walk, a circuit taking about thirty-five minutes.

SEVERN/DUMARESQ RIVER ■ 561

Originating on the New England Tableland in the vicinity of Bald Rock, the Severn River flows west into Queensland, then generally south-westward. After its junction with Tenterfield Creek, it forms the state border almost to Goondiwindi, and is known as the Dumaresq River. Allan Cunningham, leading the first European crossing in 1827, gave it that name after the pioneering New England landholders, related by marriage to Governor Ralph Darling. Damaging floods along the Severn–Dumaresq system are mitigated by the Storm King Dam, near Stanthorpe, and by the Glenlyon Dam, on a major tributary.

STANTHORPE ■ 562

Among the highest towns in Queensland at 811 metres, Stanthorpe is consistently the coolest large population centre. Mild summertime temperatures permit southern-style horticulture, giving the district a virtual state monopoly of stone and pip-fruit growing. It is also prominent in grape and wine production. In the heyday of pastoral agriculture, the only significance of the Quart Pot crossing was as the site of an inn catering to traffic between New England and the rich, black soil plains of the Darling Downs. Prosperity came late to the district with the mining of tin, in a brief rush that started in 1872. When the rush began a private town site was hastily planned at Quart Pot. It was called Stannum – Latin for tin. The name Stanthorpe was given to an adjoining government-surveyed site; for many years the two were shown as separate entities on official maps.

Thousands of miners moved in and a settlement soon mushroomed. Just as tin prices were declining and ore was becoming scarce at the end of the decade, extra work came from railway construction. The line from Brisbane reached Stanthorpe in 1881. Eagerly awaited as a means of cutting the freight costs of the mining companies, the railway proved an unexpected boon to farmers too.

Produce from a few established Stanthorpe orchards and vineyards, speedily available on the Brisbane market, fetched premium prices. During the mid-1890s, many grazing properties were converted to fruit growing and Crown Lands were thrown open to smallholders for nominal rents. Wineries offering tastings and cellar-door sales are now Stanthorpe's leading tourist attraction. *Population 4190*

FESTIVALS Harvest Festival, February–March in even-numbered years; Granite Belt Spring Wine Festival, October.

SUNDOWN NATIONAL PARK ■ 563

Difficulty of access makes Sundown one of the least-visited of southern Queensland's national parks. Once there, the effort is worthwhile as the Severn River offers quiet pleasures for campers who book in advance. Flat, grassy sites, screened by brush

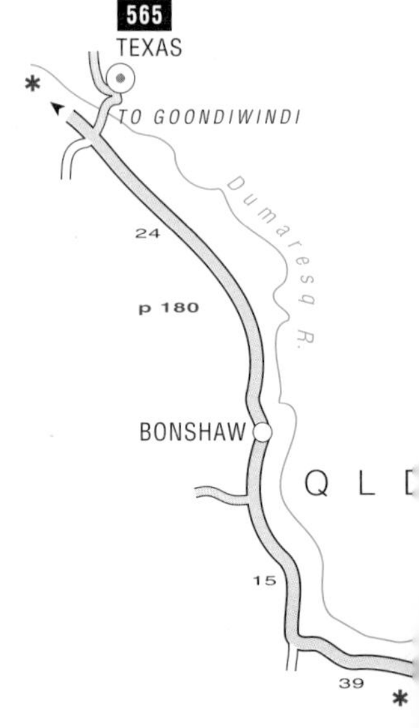

The granite belt intrudes into New South Wales most spectacularly in Bald Rock National Park where Bald Rock (left) – home to small creatures such as echidnas (above) – leaves other boulders in the shade.

fences, are provided within a stone's throw of a broad reach of clear water. Walkers can explore upstream to falls and swimming holes or accept the challenge of the valley's steep flanks.

TENTERFIELD ■ 564

Something in the crisp air of Tenterfield seems to have been conducive to political ambition in the nineteenth century. Sir Henry Parkes, five times Premier of New South Wales, was MLA for Tenterfield from 1882 to 1884 and returned there in 1889 to make the speech that earned him the title of 'Father of Federation'. Much earlier, the businessmen involved in founding Tenterfield Station, around 1840, both became colonial premiers – Sir Robert Mackenzie after moving to Queensland and Sir Stuart Donaldson in New South Wales.

Donaldson, a man of strong convictions, in 1851 took part in the last formal pistol duel in Australia, against the explorer and Surveyor-General Sir Thomas Mitchell. Honour was satisfied after three shots each were exchanged, the closest going through Donaldson's hat.

Unusual strains were put on the resources of a relatively small town during the Second World War. Thousands of soldiers poured through Tenterfield in 1942 when an emergency camp was established nearby. Unknown to the townsfolk, Tenterfield had been earmarked as a key battlefield if the Japanese should invade. It had a frontal position on the secret 'Brisbane Line', drawn between the Queensland capital and Melbourne. Overgrown tank traps and gun emplacements can still be found in woodlands off the highway, not far short of a sign indicating Thunderbolt's Hideout. A formation of boulders is said to have sheltered the bushranger Frederick Ward (see *Armidale & Uralla*), who staged some of his boldest hold-ups in the Tenterfield district. *Population 3310*

SCHOOL OF ARTS AND POST OFFICE A memorial library and museum are housed in the 1876 building where Sir Henry Parkes launched his campaign for federation of the Australian colonies. The grand post office clock tower still dominates the street scene on a nearby corner.

COURT HOUSE GROUP The court, police residences and lock-up, though built of different materials and at different times during the 1870s and 1880s, form an integrated complex of high architectural merit.

TENTERFIELD SADDLERY In an 1860s shop that was previously a bank, George Woolnough ran a saddlery business for fifty years. His grandson was the entertainer Peter Allen, who recalled their relationship in a popular ballad.

BLUFF ROCK After the murder of a shepherd in 1844, Aborigines were pursued to this granitic outcrop south of Tenterfield on the New England Highway. According to a first-hand account they were 'punished severely'. A later story has it that the fugitives were captured and thrown from the top of the rock.

TEXAS ■ 565

Tobacco crops surrounding Texas owe their existence to irrigation from the Dumaresq River. But the river has not always been a friend to the town. At a proud moment in 1890, the opening of a police station, floodwaters swept the building away, along with a hotel. Texas was largely rebuilt on its present site on high ground north of the river. The district was settled about 1840 by two brothers named McDougall. On returning from the gold rush, they found a claim-jumper. Likening the dispute that followed to a border war in the United States, they called their regained station 'Texas'. A town site was resumed from the station in the mid-1880s. *Population 820*

TOOLOOM FALLS ■ 566

Though declared as an Aboriginal site the falls, to the south-west of Urbenville, are open to the public and their surroundings make a delightful picnic area. According to Aboriginal legend, a family quarrel over water started a never-ending flood that created the Clarence River and brought the falls into existence.

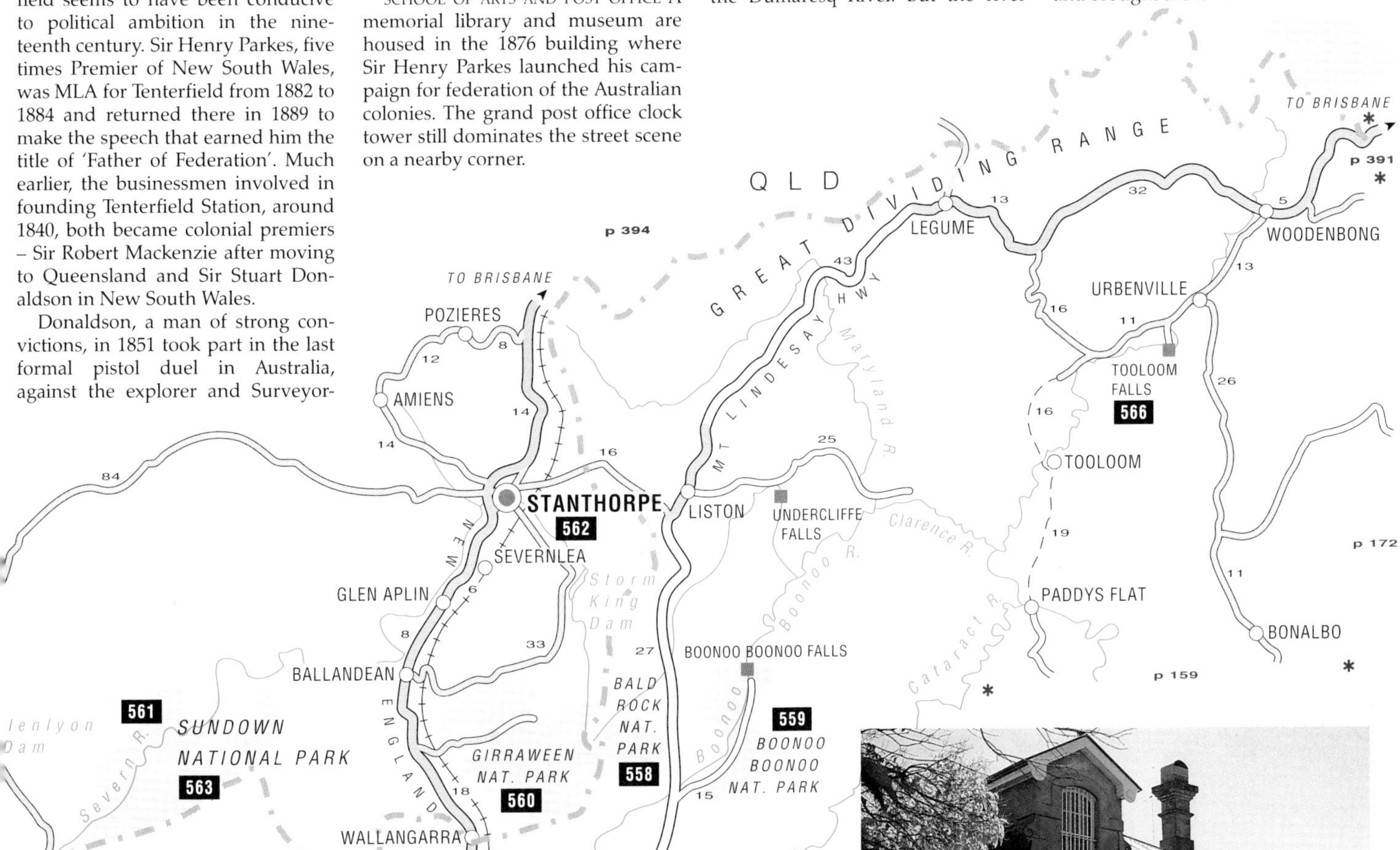

The 120-year-old Tenterfield Police Station combines with the jail and court house to form a 'law and order' complex.

THE GREAT DIVIDING RANGE

In contrast to the diminutive 'ranges' that elsewhere interrupt Australia's flat landscape horizons, the Great Dividing Range makes an audaciously dramatic, continent-long sweep.

The Great Dividing Range is an often obstructively rugged many-spurred crescent of tablelands, ranges and gorges that curves down the eastern side of the continent from Cape York in Queensland's tropical north to expire gently at the edge of the plains of western Victoria.

The corroboree frog – so named because of its strikingly 'painted' body – has webless feet and crawls around its alpine environment.

This 'mountain' range is modest compared with the Andes or the Himalayas; unlike these ranges it is not a chain of geologically young and jagged fold mountains thrown up by the clashing of great plates in the earth's crust. The Great Dividing Range is old and eroded, formed by a series of slow uplifts culminating several million years ago in the general uplift known as the 'Kosciusko epoch'. Vast sections of Eastern Australia were then raised up in a violent rearrangement to form tablelands and plateaux. Since those distant times, rivers and streams washing over these plateaux have relentlessly worn them down into a maze of blunt-topped ranges, ridges, gorges and chasms. The sheer-walled sandstone chasms of the Blue Mountains, the depths of the Apsley–Macleay gorges on the eastern edge of New England, the nearly two kilometre drop from Mount Townshend into the Geehi Valley near Khancoban: all are the patient work of gently eroding running water.

In many places, such as the Liverpool Range north-west of Newcastle, vast, volcanic outpourings of basalt covered the land. Today there are only the remnants in domed basalt peaks, like Mount Yengo north of Sydney, rising above the general height of the surrounding country. Some of the more dramatic peaks, like those of the Warrumbungles at the western extremity of the Liverpool Range, owe their existence to extinct volcanoes which have been worn away to expose vertical plugs of trachyte and other resistant volcanic rocks. During the last Ice Age the climate of the eastern highlands region was much more severe than now but it was only in the Snowy Mountains that glaciers helped to form the landscape, leaving behind the chain of glacial lakes including Lake Albina and Blue Lake.

Heavily eroded plateaux riven by deep valleys are typical of the Great Divide's coastwards sweep near Fitzroy Falls, south of Sydney.

The uplift of the highlands was so slow that some rivers such as the Cox and the Colo in the Blue Mountains, were able to keep pace – eroding down through the land at the same rate as it was rising – and have maintained their courses right through the 'mountain' barrier. For much of its length, the Great Dividing Range runs generally north–south, parting the waters which fall on its slopes between a regularly spaced skein of eastern streams descending quickly to the Pacific Ocean and the slower-paced western rivers on their long, meandering journeys inland to the Darling or Murray rivers.

It is usually not far from the east coast to the crest of the divide and so this approach to the highlands is usually obvious, marked by sudden escarpments and deep gorges. The western climb onto the divide is generally more gradual and less spectacular.

North of Canberra, the Great Dividing Range separates into two distinct divides to form an internal drainage basin. As a physical feature the 'water' divide is rather self-effacing, generally avoiding the high ridges and peaks. Most road travellers would not even be aware that they were crossing the watershed if it were not for the road signs drawing it to their attention. The Hume Highway crosses the Great Divide without much drama as does the New England Highway – there are no passes clinging precipitously to mountainsides. Only when the range approaches Mount Kosciusko does it present itself dramatically to both sides as the inhospitable barrier of the Snowy Mountains, looming up between the western-flowing Indi and Geehi rivers and the eastern-flowing Snowy.

Mount Kosciusko – a modest 2228 metres but still the eastern highland's highest point – was climbed by the Polish explorer Paul Strzelecki in 1840 and named by him for the similarity 'to a tumulus elevated in Krakow over the tomb of the patriot Kosciusko'. The slopes of Mount Kosciusko and its surrounding peaks and plateaux are some of the few sections of the 'alps' where a consistent winter snow cover for skiing is provided – nowhere is there perpetual snow.

Today, large sections of the high country in New South Wales and Victoria have been transformed by plantations of exotic radiata pine trees and all along the length of the highlands the accessible native forests are managed for timber. On the other side of the ledger, a chain of large wilderness parks has been established – often amid controversy between loggers and conservationists. In a few places with rich volcanic soils, such as the Dorrigo and Bulga plateaux, the once thick forest has been cleared for farming. The extensive New England and Monaro grasslands, snapped up in the squatters' rush, have grazed sheep and cattle since early colonial days while huge reservoirs have transformed some landscapes, especially in the Snowy Mountains. □

Whatever climatic guise the latitude dictates, the Great Dividing Range dramatically shapes the character of east-coast landscapes from the shoreline jungles of Cape Tribulation (top) to Perisher Valley's frosty heights (right) and the eroded grandeur of the Grampians (bottom).

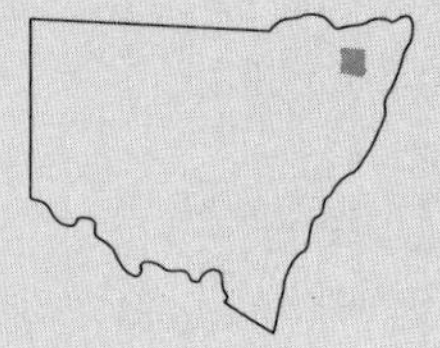

Glen Innes & Emmaville

The Glen Innes district of New England is known for its two kinds of primary produce: agriculture and livestock, and minerals and gemstones. The land has been farmed extensively since the first runs were taken up in the 1830s and mines in the area contributed greatly to making Australia one of the largest exporters of tin in the late 1800s.

BALANCING ROCK ■ 567

One of the many curiously weathered granite formations found in the Glen Innes district, the Balancing Rock is located along the New England Highway just south of Glen Innes. This giant granite boulder has been weathered away to leave a tiny base balancing on top of another smaller boulder. As it sits on private property, it must be viewed from the road or the Stonehenge Recreation Reserve, which offers its own unusual rock specimens .

Granite has been used in a number of buildings in the district, such as 'Strathbogie' homestead near Emmaville, which was made from granite quarried on the property, and the Glen Innes court house.

EMMAVILLE ■ 568

Today's small mining town was once a thriving centre, home to 4000 people, about half of whom were Chinese. The township grew after tin was discovered on nearby Strathbogie Station in 1872 and derived its original name, Vegetable Creek, from the Chinese miners who grew vegetables along the creek. The name was changed in 1882 to Emmaville in honour of Governor Augustus Loftus' wife Emma. The century-old hospital still bears the original name.

The first medical fund in New South Wales was established at Emmaville. The aim was to keep a doctor in the town to deal with the frequent accidents, and build the hospital. Lectures given at the hospital in 1891 led to the formation of the St John Ambulance Brigade.

The discovery of tin at Emmaville brought with it a flood of prospectors and set in train a succession of finds at other sites in the region. While tin was the chief metal found here, quantities of bismuth, molybdenite, tungsten, silver and wolfram were mined, but by the 1880s, mining activity had dropped off. The area is, nevertheless, still productive. Commercial operations today use large open-cut mines to reach tin deposits and gemstones.

Samples of minerals found in the area are on display at Mrs Curnow's Tin Museum in Moore Street with a gem of another sort from the old mining days: a leather bucket more than 100 years old.

Near Emmaville at Tent Hill is the old Ottery Mine established in 1920 to produce arsenic which was used in sheep and cattle dips. The mine can be inspected but visitors are warned not to touch the arsenic-covered bricks.

GLEN INNES ■ 569

Twenty years after John Oxley explored the New England region in 1818, Archibald Boyd registered the first run in today's Glen Innes district. Boyd was led to his run by the 'Beardies', two stockmen from properties north of Armidale, known by their long beards. In the following years, the Beardies turned an extra shilling showing other squatters to the best runs in what became known quaintly as the Land of the Beardies or the Beardy Plains.

Aborigines apparently did not live permanently in the area, leaving in the cold winter months. Nevertheless, there were clashes between them and the new white landholders, particularly in the early years.

The town of Glen Innes, grew out of a store operated on the 'Furracahad' property in the late 1840s. The property had passed through many owners in the financially troubled 1840s and was taken up by A.C. Mosman in 1850 who lobbied for a township to be established. Being on the route between Armidale and Toowoomba, it was considered well-positioned and was gazetted in 1852 and the first lots were sold in 1854.

In 1875, Sir Henry Parkes laid the foundation stone of the grand and elaborate Glen Innes town hall.

Mosman (after whom the Sydney suburb is named) is credited with naming the town Glen Innes after Major Archibald Clunes Innes who had owned the run in the 1840s.

Passing traffic between Armidale and Toowoomba and the discovery of tin and other minerals in the district in the 1870s ensured the town's growth in spite of the hardships of travel. By 1866, there was still no coach service; in the 1870s, a road was constructed to Grafton and in 1884 the railway reached Glen Innes.

The mining boom and the coming of the railway brought prosperity to the town, evident in many of the beautiful old buildings such as the ANZ Bank (1884) with its porch and cast-iron balconies, the town hall (1875) featuring a parapet and tower, and the ornate National Australia Bank built in 1890. The court house, built in 1874 from local granite, replaced one established in 1858 and was the scene of the trial of the Aboriginal outlaw, Black Tommy, in 1876. Black Tommy was acquitted but shot dead in a fight eighteen months later.

Today, Glen Innes is a magnet for fossickers looking for sapphires, quartz, topaz and other precious

The point of contact between Stonehenge's Balancing Rock and its support is said to be a mere 300 millimetres.

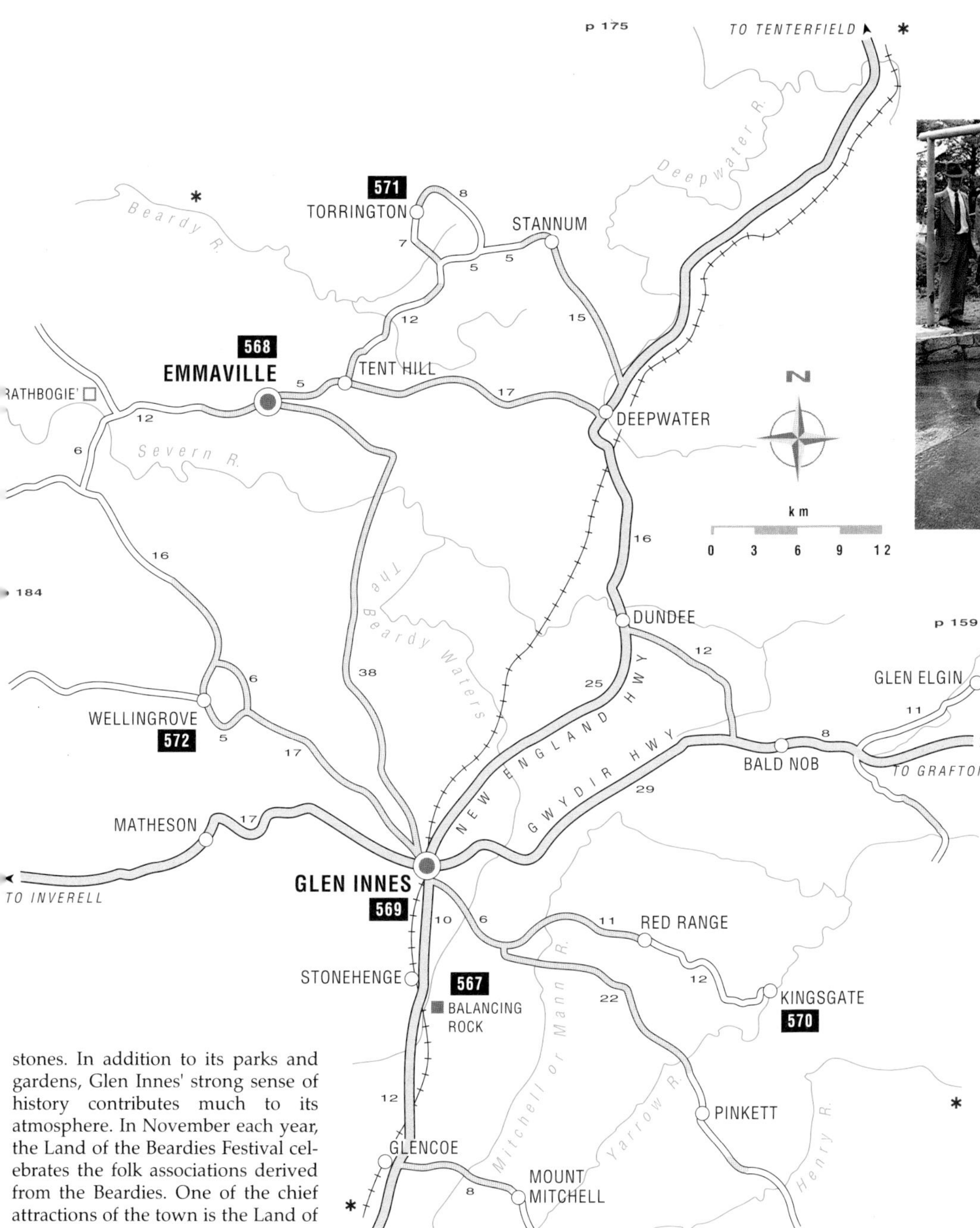

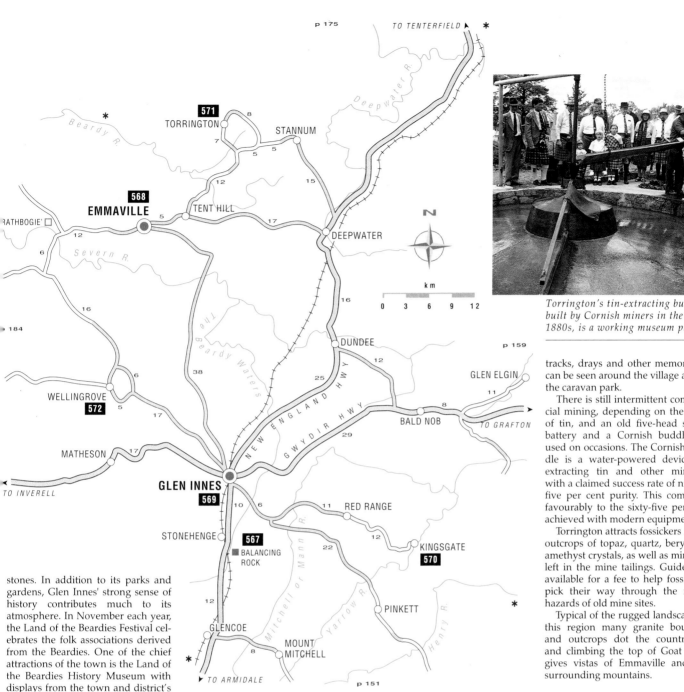

Torrington's tin-extracting buddle, built by Cornish miners in the 1880s, is a working museum piece.

stones. In addition to its parks and gardens, Glen Innes' strong sense of history contributes much to its atmosphere. In November each year, the Land of the Beardies Festival celebrates the folk associations derived from the Beardies. One of the chief attractions of the town is the Land of the Beardies History Museum with displays from the town and district's early days including an original settler's cottage. The museum is rated one of the largest and best folk museums in the state. It has a card index of 130 000 names of people who have lived in the area.

With some obvious pride many of the owners of Federation buildings in Grey Street, the main street, have repainted their buildings in their original colours. More than fifty government and business addresses in this street comprise the historic Grey Street Precinct and represent architecture dating from 1860 to 1950. Old-style street lighting has been installed along three blocks of the street, an imaginative innovation which helps underline its history.

Since its early days, the Glen Innes district has supported wool and wheat, fat-lamb, cattle, dairying and vegetable growing. Today, a large saleyard operates as well as a timber mill, a concrete pipe works and the only steam-driven brickworks in New South Wales. The steam engine is fired up mainly for displays, but has also been used to bake old-style bricks for restoration work in Sydney. *Population 6140*

MARTINS LOOKOUT The Glen Innes district has many associations with Scotland and a memorial at Martins Lookout pays tribute to the contribution that people of Celtic origin have made to Australia. The memorial of twenty-four three-metre-high stones arranged as a calendar is based on Ring Brodgar in the Orkney Islands off the Scottish coast. The Centennial Parkland's lookout provides town and countryside views.

FESTIVALS The Land of the Beardies Festival, November.

KINGSGATE MINES ■ 570

Different points around the Glen Innes district were mined chiefly for different minerals, and the mines at Kingsgate, notable for their unusual quartz pipe deposits, became Australia's chief source of molybdenite and bismuth in the early 1900s. The Kingsgate mines lie south-east of Glen Innes on the Red Range Road. Today, fossickers looking for these minerals and quartz crystals and smokey quartz try their luck in the old mine workings – there are about sixty – scattered around the land owned by a church organisation. Donations are requested to cover the cost of maintenance.

TORRINGTON ■ 571

One of the many fossicking areas in the Glen Innes district, Torrington was once a town of 2000 people producing a large supply of tin. The Torrington tin lode was discovered in 1881 and the remains of old batteries, mine shafts, old buildings, bullock tracks, drays and other memorabilia can be seen around the village and in the caravan park.

There is still intermittent commercial mining, depending on the price of tin, and an old five-head stamp battery and a Cornish buddle are used on occasions. The Cornish buddle is a water-powered device for extracting tin and other minerals with a claimed success rate of ninety-five per cent purity. This compares favourably to the sixty-five per cent achieved with modern equipment.

Torrington attracts fossickers for its outcrops of topaz, quartz, beryl and amethyst crystals, as well as minerals left in the mine tailings. Guides are available for a fee to help fossickers pick their way through the many hazards of old mine sites.

Typical of the rugged landscape of this region many granite boulders and outcrops dot the countryside and climbing the top of Goat Rock gives vistas of Emmaville and the surrounding mountains.

WELLINGROVE ■ 572

Situated twenty-odd kilometres north-west of Glen Innes, Wellingrove once rivalled it as the chief town of this part of New England. Thanks to the efforts of a local landholder, the first government offices were established at Wellingrove, but Glen Innes' position on the road between Armidale and Toowoomba, and Wellingrove's on the road to nowhere in particular, gave Glen Innes the edge. In 1854, the post office moved to Glen Innes and in 1858, the court house followed.

Today, Wellingrove is virtually a ghost town in a Crown Land fossicking area where sapphires can be found in the reddish clay which provides a surface-covering for the region's underlying granite deposits. Visitors planning to visit the fossicking area to try their luck are advised to take drinking water as there is no creek.

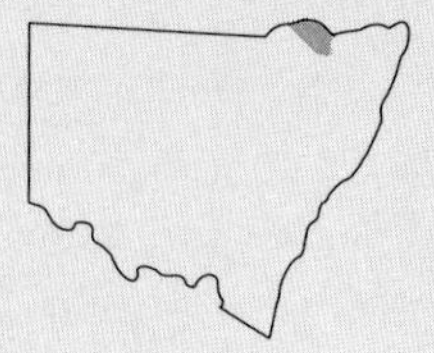

Goondiwindi & Boggabilla

This border region of wheat and cotton country has always depended on the waters of two rivers, now dammed for irrigation farming. The modern highways that run through the region follow the paths of the old stock routes from New South Wales to the Darling Downs.

BOGGABILLA ■ 573
Stockmen of old knew Boggabilla as a stopping point on the Macintyre River on the route to the Darling Downs. Now the drivers of the hundreds of trucks and semi-trailers that pass through it every day know it as the last village in New South Wales before the Queensland border. With two major highways and a railhead, Boggabilla is an important junction for traffic heading for Darwin or Brisbane and the Gold Coast.

Boggabilla and its much larger sister town on the Queensland side of the border, Goondiwindi (see entry), share responsibility for the two rivers – the Dumaresq and the Macintyre – that mark the border between the two states. The Border Rivers Commission, established in 1947, controls storage and irrigation uses of the rivers and was responsible for the new reregulating weir opened at Boggabilla in 1991. Water requested for irrigation can take ten days to travel from the dam to the irrigator and, in the meantime, the order may be cancelled, for example, if it rains. Since the water cannot be stopped or returned to the dam, it would be lost to the system without the reregulating weir at Boggabilla that catches and holds it until it is required further downstream.

Older than Goondiwindi and subject to different state laws, Boggabilla provides at least one facility that is not available on the Queensland side of the border and therefore attracts many of its citizens – a barrage of poker machines at the Boggabilla Town and Country Club. The town also offers wheat-storage facilities for the surrounding district and a hotel called the Wobbly Boot, which featured in a folk song.

In 1849, the last battle fought by Aborigines resisting white settlement in the region occurred at Boggabilla. One-hundred-and-forty years later Boggabilla TAFE College was opened to students – the majority of them Aboriginal – from a wide catchment area that includes Toomelah Aboriginal Reserve. The college is now the major provider of vocational training for Aborigines in northern New South Wales. *Population 750*

COOLATAI ■ 574
The village gets its name from the large station established in the late nineteenth century and called 'Coolootai', from an Aboriginal word said to mean 'rock adders here'. The village is unusual in this region noted for its wheat since it is the service centre of a grazing district. Coolatai's village hall and sporting complex, which offers tennis, cricket, rodeos and other horse sports, together with the local hotel, provide some social – and sporting – cohesion for those who live in surrounding properties.

DUMARESQ RIVER ■ 575
In 1827, Allan Cunningham, en route to the Darling Downs, described the river as, 'a handsome piece of water, evidently very deep' and it was Cunningham who named the river for the Dumaresq family into which Governor Darling had married. Lady Darling's three brothers, Henry who was private secretary to Governor Darling, Edward, a surveyor-general and William, a soldier and politician, were influential in early nineteenth-century Australia.

Rising on the slopes of the Great Dividing Range in Queensland, the Dumaresq River flows in a generally south-westerly direction before executing a distinctive U-turn to continue north through Texas then north-west to join the Macintyre River (see entry) thirteen kilometres east of Boggabilla. From its junction with Tenterfield Creek to its junction with the Macintyre River, it marks

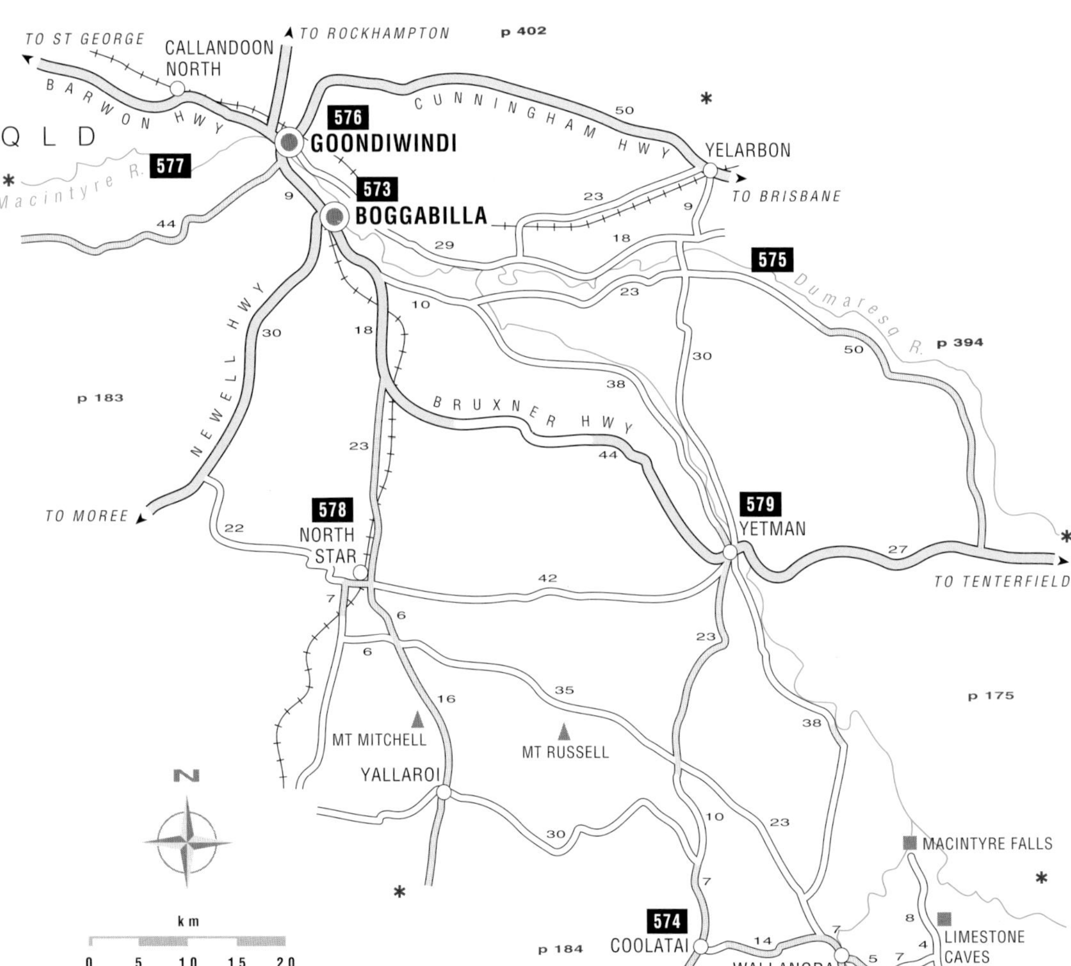

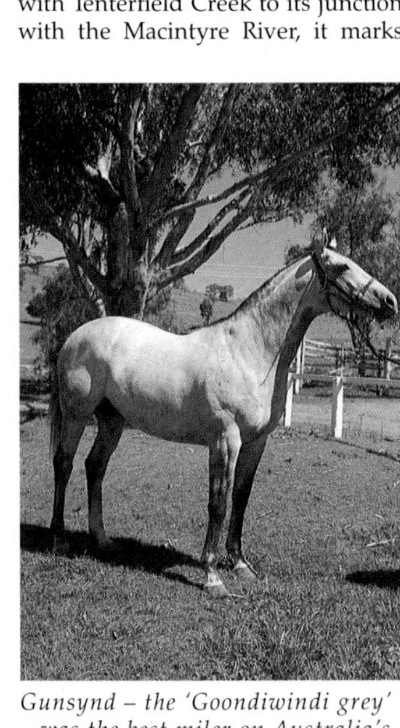
Gunsynd – the 'Goondiwindi grey' – was the best miler on Australia's racecourses during the 1970s, losing only once over that distance.

The annual cycle of wheat cultivation in the Goondiwindi–Boggabilla region begins with the preparation of the paddocks in March. The onset of rain in late April is the signal for farmers to begin sowing (below). In October-November, the ripened grain is harvested and stored in giant wheat silos.

the border between New South Wales and Queensland – elsewhere its course strictly adheres to state boundaries and never accidentally meanders into New South Wales.

GOONDIWINDI ■ 576

'Gundawinda', managed by brothers Sampson and Harry Marshall, was the first of three large stations to be established in the district between 1838 and 1846. The teamsters who brought supplies and mail from Maitland to the three stations were allowed to camp on a flat piece of land where the three properties met, while they waited – often for many weeks – for a load of wool to take on the return trip. By the early 1860s, a number of the teamsters had settled their families in more permanent accommodation on the 'free' campsite and, by 1870, a number of small businesses, including a boarding house, a private school and a Chinese market garden as well as those inevitable and essential village services – a store and blacksmith – operated in the growing settlement.

In 1888, the settlement of Goondiwindi (pronounced 'Gundawindy') came of age and was gazetted as a town and, not surprisingly, of the two possible meanings of the name – 'resting place of wild ducks' or 'droppings of ducks and shags' – the former was preferred. Few buildings remain from pre-1888 days since, in the absence of local stone, less durable timber was used in construction. However, two exceptions have withstood the test of time – Martha's Cottage (1875) built of pit-sawn and hand-dressed bush timber, and the customs house (1859).

Prior to Federation, a team of customs officers collected customs and excise duties on goods travelling interstate...the ferry across the Macintyre River at Goondiwindi, being the major border crossing in the area, made the town an ideal collection point. When the ferry was later replaced by a bridge, known as Border Bridge, a border patrol operated to prevent illegal trade and it too was housed at the customs house. With Federation in 1901, the timber building with its late nineteenth-century additions was no longer required and it became a private residence, and, in the 1970s, a folk museum.

Goondiwindi has a number of other claims to fame including the fact that the Duke of Edinburgh has played polo at the town's polo field where the Australian Gold Cup for polo was held. It also has the dubious honour of being the first town in Queensland where the once ubiquitous and devastating prickly pear was found.

Goondiwindi sits in an artesian basin topped by numerous bores in the surrounding area and there is also water-bearing gravel between ten and fifteen metres below the surface. The fertility of the farmlands surrounding Goondiwindi has made the town the largest wheat receiving depot in the Southern Hemisphere as well as a centre for beef cattle, wool and, more recently, cotton.

The cotton is picked mechanically in April and a special 'module maker' compacts it into twelve-tonne, eight-metre-long blocks that are transported to the town's Macintyre Cotton Gin; the gin operates twenty-four hours a day from April until late August or September. *Population 4330*

GUNSYND The legendary 'Goondiwindi grey' racehorse, owned by a local syndicate, won twenty-nine races and came in third in the Melbourne Cup. A statue of Gunsynd now stands near the Border Bridge.

FESTIVALS Picnic Races, early April; Spring Festival, October.

MACINTYRE RIVER ■ 577

The Aboriginal name for the river was Karaula but when Allan Cunningham crossed it in 1827, he renamed it after Peter Macintyre, the manager of Segenhoe Station (see *Muswellbrook & Scone*) who had lent him horses and drays and led him across the Liverpool Ranges. Cunningham is also supposed to have named Boobera Lagoon on the river – a place of significance to the Aborigines who lived there – after an Aboriginal tracker in his party.

Boobera Lagoon, now used for water skiing, was even then a stretch of deep permanent water in a river that was, until man intervened, a series of unconnected waterholes during the dry season. Now assured of a constant water supply by three dams, the Macintyre River flows well...at least until Goondiwindi. Murray cod weighing up to fifty kilograms have been caught in the deep waterholes there in the past.

The Macintyre River is one of the main tributaries of the Darling River system, and flows from the New England Tablelands through Inverell to just outside Boggabilla where it takes over from the Dumaresq River the function of marking the state border. The two states share responsibility for the river; the first bridge across the river at Goondiwindi was built by the Queensland government in the late 1870s while the New South Wales government shouldered its responsibility by constructing the bridge at Mungindi.

Mungindi marks the end of the Macintyre River and the start of the Barwon River (see *Coonamble & Walgett*). According to a report in the *Maitland Mercury* concerning Roderick Mitchell's journey up the two rivers in 1846, 'the settlers pushing down the Macintyre have joined issue with those pushing up the Barwon and there is no unlocated country between them' proving that the two rivers were in fact one and the same.

The Macintyre Falls drop into a picturesque gorge that allows opportunities for swimming and walking. Along the way, is a big outcropping of limestone pitted with caves, one of which can be explored without difficulty for a length of more than 500 metres. Lamps or powerful torches are needed.

NORTH STAR ■ 578

Situated in the centre of the 'golden triangle' of some of the region's largest wheat farms, the village of North Star has large storage facilities for prime hard wheat. In recent years, it has also been the centre of a successful experiment with dryland cotton, that is, cotton grown without the irrigation on demand that was thought to be vital for successful cotton growing.

Although it has no hotel and the nearest secondary school is at Warialda, North Star nevertheless has a sporting club where polo, polocrosse and other horse sports predominate.

YETMAN ■ 579

When Allan Cunningham crossed the Macintyre River in 1827, he did so near the present Yetman. The small village developed in the 1840s but the lack of roads made the transport of wool difficult so those who setttled around Yetman concentrated on cattle that were driven to Brisbane, Maitland or Sydney.

Yetman was on one of a number of tracks that linked the stations being set up along the Dumaresq and Macintyre rivers with the rest of New South Wales but the main track to Boggabilla was 'a bog in wet weather and a blacksmith's friend in the dry' so Yetman turned towards Texas in Queensland, for its own supplies. Sulkies and drays used this road, which had to be maintained by the locals inhabitants themselves since no money was supplied by either state government until 1899. The days of difficult communication have come to an end as the Bruxner Highway now speeds traffic through the town providing easy access to both Texas and Boggabilla.

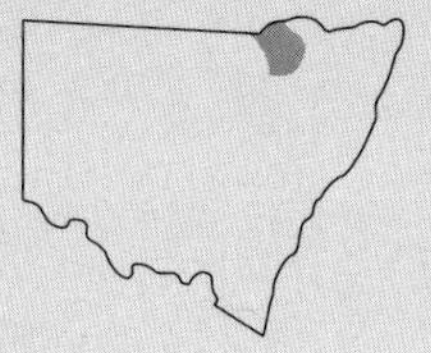

Moree & Mungindi

As in countless other parts of rural Australia, irrigation was the catalyst that revolutionised agriculture on these plains with cotton rapidly replacing wheat, sheep and wool. Beneath the surface of the black-soil plains lies another water source – the mineral-rich artesian waters tapped at Moree for therapeutic applications.

ASHLEY ■ 580

The little town of Ashley is home to two of the five ultra-modern gins in the Moree district which cater for the region's burgeoning cotton industry. The cotton is grown on the irrigated black soils of the north-west plains and is harvested from mid-April to mid-July. Visitors to the town during harvest season can observe the ginning operation in which cotton fibres are separated from the seed by a system of high speed circular saws and brushes, the lint portion is compressed into bales for transportation to the spinning mills, and the seed is collected for trucking to the crushing mills where it is processed into cotton-seed oil and cotton-seed meal.

BELLATA ■ 581

Bellata – a local Aboriginal word said to mean 'kangaroo' – is a small village on the Newell Highway south of Moree (see entry). Surrounded by grazing and farming land, the small village is notable for the nearby agate fields which are reputed to contain some of the best quality agates in New South Wales. Petrified wood and opals can also be found here.

GURLEY ■ 582

The name Gurley applies to several localities in the north-west plains of New South Wales – a creek, a pastoral station and a village. Gurley is said to originate from an Aboriginal word meaning 'creek' or it may be the Aboriginal name for a tree common to the area. The small village of Gurley, a dot on the region's pastoral landscape, was considered important enough to be made a rail stop in 1897, the year its first store opened to the public.

MEHI RIVER ■ 583

In 1975, the Geographical Names Board of New South Wales brought to an end years of confusion over the names and courses of two of the main rivers that flow across the Moree Plains to link eventually with the Darling system near Collarenebri. 'Mehi' (originally spelt 'Meei') and 'Gwydir' were interchangeable names for the same river for many years – both names having been applied to different sections of the river since European discovery in the late 1820s. The name Mehi now applies officially to the 160-kilometre-long tributary of the Gwydir River that branches off at Tareelaroi Weir and flows generally west through the Moree plains before joining the Barwon River.

Since the construction of the Copeton Dam near Inverell (see *Inverell & Barraba*), the Mehi River flows year-round; where its north-west passage meanders through Moree, the river's wooded banks have been developed as parkland.

MOREE ■ 584

Moree is at the centre of the rich, black-soil plains that stretches north to the Queensland border, south towards the Namoi River, west to Collarenebri and east towards Warialda; the fertility of this country is celebrated in the town's pictorial postmark that proudly proclaims it 'Australia's richest agricultural shire'.

From its earliest years, Moree has been the nucleus of a thriving pastoral district and irrigation of the plains since the late 1970s has dramatically changed the complexion of this rural base. The intensive agriculture of cotton growing has replaced wheat, sheep and cattle as the major industry. Moree now produces just over fifty per cent of Australia's cotton crop – enough to keep five cotton gins operating twenty-four hours a day, seven days a week during the ginning season from mid-April to mid-July. In recent years, oilseeds have been added to the growing number of different crops grown under irrigation.

Fertile black soil is not the only 'pay dirt' in Moree. Beneath the town is the liquid asset of artesian water – part of the Great Artesian Basin – which was first tapped in 1895 and yields over thirteen million litres of water every day. The Moree artesian bore was originally constructed for the purpose of irrigating an experimental farm but the mineral-rich bore water proved to be unsuitable for crop growing and became instead the invigorating health waters of the town's now famous artesian baths.

In 1851, Moree's 'founding family', the Brands, arrived and opened a general store on the banks of the river. James Brand and his wife Mary ran a successful business for five years before selling up and moving to Singleton in 1857. Two years later, Mary Brand returned, a widow, hoping to repurchase the store. Failing that, she opened another business and Moree's first inn in 1861. The following year, these few buildings – all built on Crown Land because the Lands Department had made no provision for the sale of land up until that time – became the nucleus of a new township, named after the nearby Moree Station. 'Moree' is an Aboriginal word said to mean 'water hole' or 'rising sun'.

By 1867, the town had a population of forty-three, and thirty years later the railway arrived, linking the steadily growing settlement with the coastal markets. Today, the Newell and Gwydir highways have joined the railway line as the town's main transport arteries, and the use of rail is largely restricted to freight, with buses carrying passengers .

Now the economic and cultural focus of north-western New South Wales, Moree has commemorated its founders in practical fashion with a park named after the indomitable Mary Brand who lived here until her death in 1900, and a plaque on the government building that occupies the site of the Brand Family's first store. *Population 10 060*

CEMETERY Amid the graves of Moree's pioneers is the final resting place of Edward Dickens – son of Charles Dickens – who worked in the lands office from 1900 to 1902.

LANDS OFFICE The two-storey, timber lands office building is registered by the National Trust and is a fine example of Edwardian architecture adapted to the Australian climate. The ground floor was completed in 1894 and the second storey added in 1903, partly to protect documents from floodwater. The building was severely damaged by fire in 1980 but was painstakingly restored, winning the inaugural Lachlan Macquarie Award for the 'Best Restored Building in Australia' in 1983.

MARY BRAND PARK This commemorative park on the banks of the Mehi River was once the site of the first hotel in Moree, established by Mary Brand in 1861. The park is a display area for several historic buildings including Meei Cottage – named after the original spelling of the river that runs through the town – a typical example of the cottages built in Moree during the 1890s.

MEHI WALKING TRACK The Mehi walking track meanders through the town following the course of the river after which it is named. Nearly ten kilometres in length, the track is a comfortable three-and-a-half-hour walk around the golf course and through parts of the town's residential area, taking in many historic buildings and green areas along the river bank where trees indigenous to the region grow.

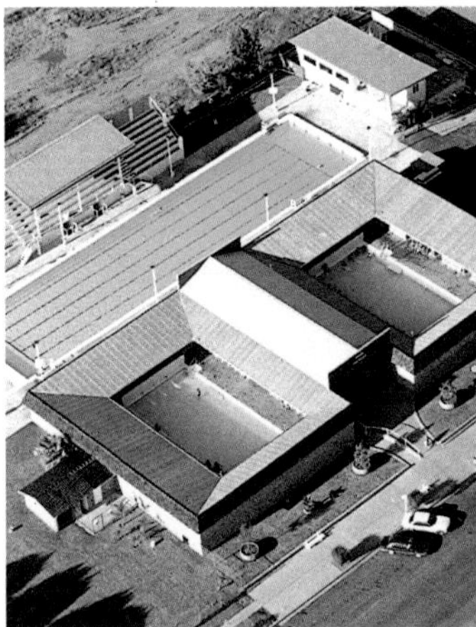

Steamy bore water gushes up 1000 metres into Moree's spa pools; near-surface water fills the Olympic pool.

MOREE SPA BATHS Thousands of visitors make the trip to Moree's 'inland health resort' each year seeking relief from a variety of nervous, rheumatic and arthritic complaints – or simply to relax – in the mineralised waters of Moree Spa Baths. Flowing from deep below the surface, the sub-artesian waters that fill the complex's two 'therapeutic' pools have been gushing out at a temperature of 41°C since the bore was struck in 1895.

FESTIVALS Festival of the Black Soil Plain, August in even-numbered years.

MUNGINDI ■ 585

Mungindi is a town divided…not by any controversial local issue but by the natural barrier of the Barwon

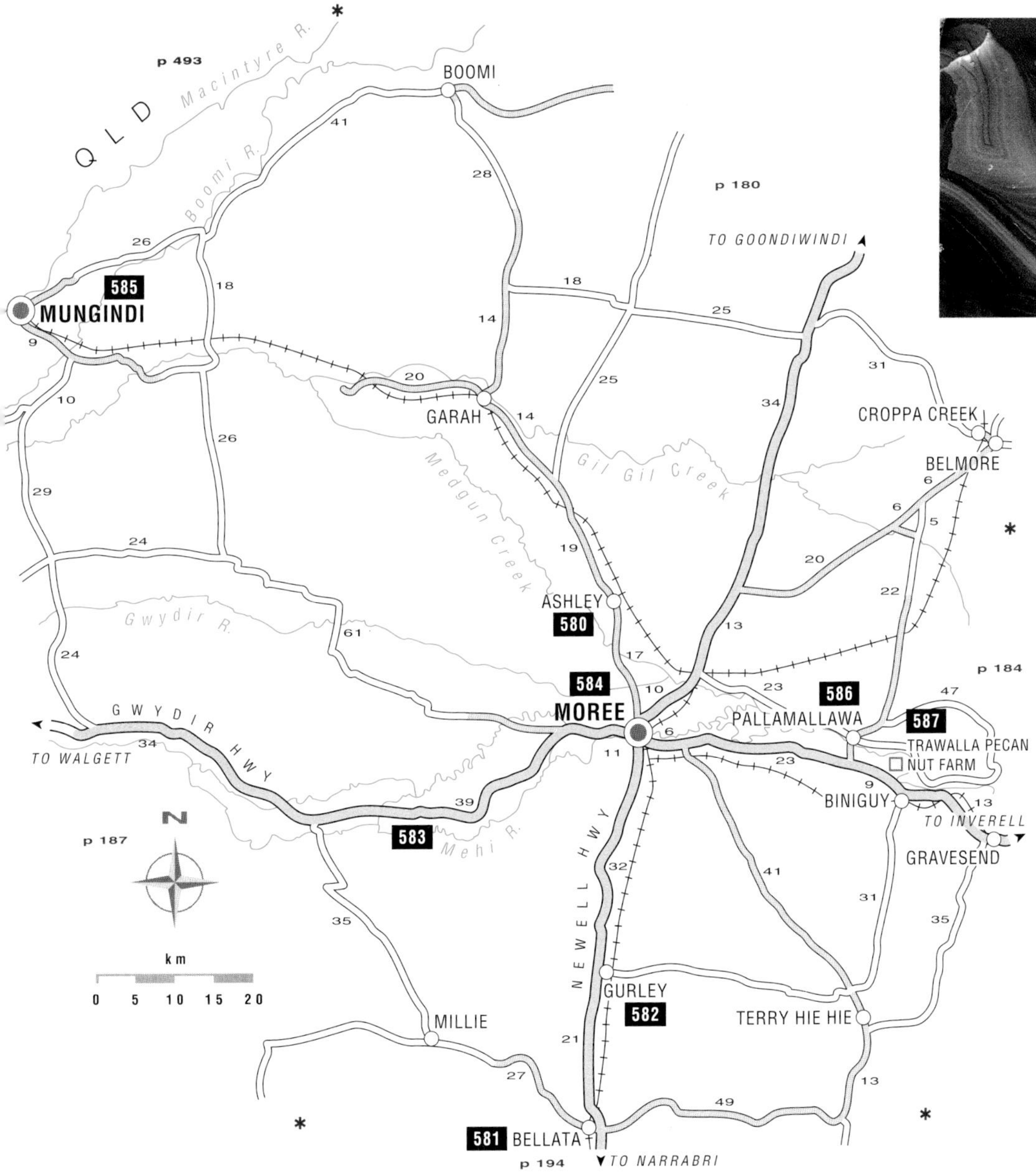

At Bellata, the intriguing, concentric bands of agates suggest their liquid, volcanic origin.

River which also marks the border between New South Wales and Queensland. This neat bisection of the town had interesting repercussions during the summer months in the years prior to Queensland's adoption of daylight saving time. In the days when Queenslanders greeted the morning sun an hour earlier than their neighbours in New South Wales, some Mungindians used the time difference to dash over the border to the local pub in Queensland and pick up an extra hour's drinking time. Others crossed the border early in the morning only to arrive at work an hour before they left home!

Mungindi is marketed as a 'sportsman's paradise' with this section of the Barwon River noted as being one of the last 'real' fishing spots along the Murray–Darling system where the angler has a chance of tagging the prized and increasingly rare 'big cod' – the Murray cod. *Population 780*

PALLAMALLAWA ■ 586

Most of the inhabitants of the small community of Pallamallawa find employment in nearby Moree or on the farm properties – such as the Trawalla Pecan Nut Farm (see entry) – in the surrounding district. The village's hotel, two general stores, primary school and police station form the nucleus of a small service centre. The Gwydir River flows through the village and is popular with local anglers.

TRAWALLA PECAN NUT FARM ■ 587

The Trawalla Pecan Nut Farm is the largest of its kind in the Southern Hemisphere, producing almost ninety-five per cent of Australia's pecan nuts. The farm was established in 1968 by an American businessman who found in the Moree Plains similar soil and climate conditions to those of his native New Mexico where the nuts are grown in great numbers. Seventy-thousand pecan nut trees thrive in the irrigated soil of what was once a relatively dry pastoral property and the farm has developed into a substantial enterprise with its own airstrip and a 'village' that houses some of the farm workers; other employees commute from the nearby villages of Pallamallawa, Biniguy and Gravesend.

Once established, these pecans – a long way from their native North America – may fruit for 200 years.

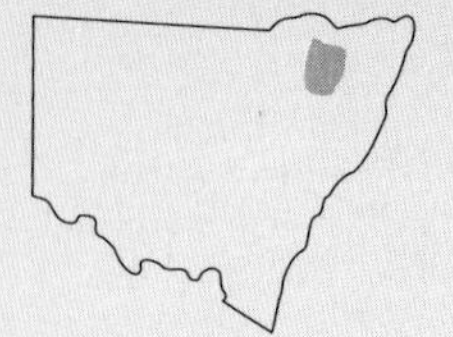

Inverell & Barraba

This region's bountiful soils yield not only pasture grasses and profitable crops but also an unusual variety of minerals. Even diamonds may be picked up along one section of the Fossickers' Way.

ASHFORD ■ 588
Lanky stands of tobacco give the farmlands surrounding Ashford an unusual appearance. Tobacco is more extensive here than in any other district of New South Wales and is harvested from January to March. The crop depends on irrigation from the Severn River, which winds through the town. Upstream, the river's flow is regulated by the Pindari Dam which has become popular for boating, waterskiing and fishing. *Population 570*

BARRABA ■ 589
Barraba has experienced more than its share of boom and bust, thanks to the complex mineralisation of the area. Fortunes in the little town on the Manilla River rose and fell on the short-lived extraction of nearby gold deposits in the 1850s and of copper in the 1890s. As recently as 1972, Barraba's hopes were buoyed anew by the opening of a $21 million chrysotile (white asbestos) mine offering employment to hundreds of people at Woodsreef, nearby to the east. Production was scarcely under way before the deadly, long-term effects of asbestos inhalation became evident and industrial demand declined. The mine ceased commercial production in 1983 and closed completely in 1985. Land values in Barraba plummeted. A few workers found employment extracting diatomite – a chalky compound used in 'pet litter' containers and insulation – but Barraba is largely dependent on a flow-on of agricultural incomes from its district. Chiefly derived from wool and wheat growing, they too have been hard hit since the late 1980s. Minerals still bring one consolation: a steady trickle of visitors follow the 'Fossickers' Way' in search of gemstones. For those who have the necessary licence, Ironbark Creek near Woodsreef is a recommended starting point. *Population 1430*

HORTON FALLS A drive of almost forty kilometres west from Barraba ascends the Nandewar Range to a spectacular twin waterfall on the Horton River.

BINGARA ■ 590
Diamond mining capital of Australia…it is hard to picture Bingara making such a claim, but in the 1880s and 1890s it could do so without fear of contradiction. More than 200 000 carats (about 40 kilograms) of diamonds came from fields west and east of the town. Most of the stones

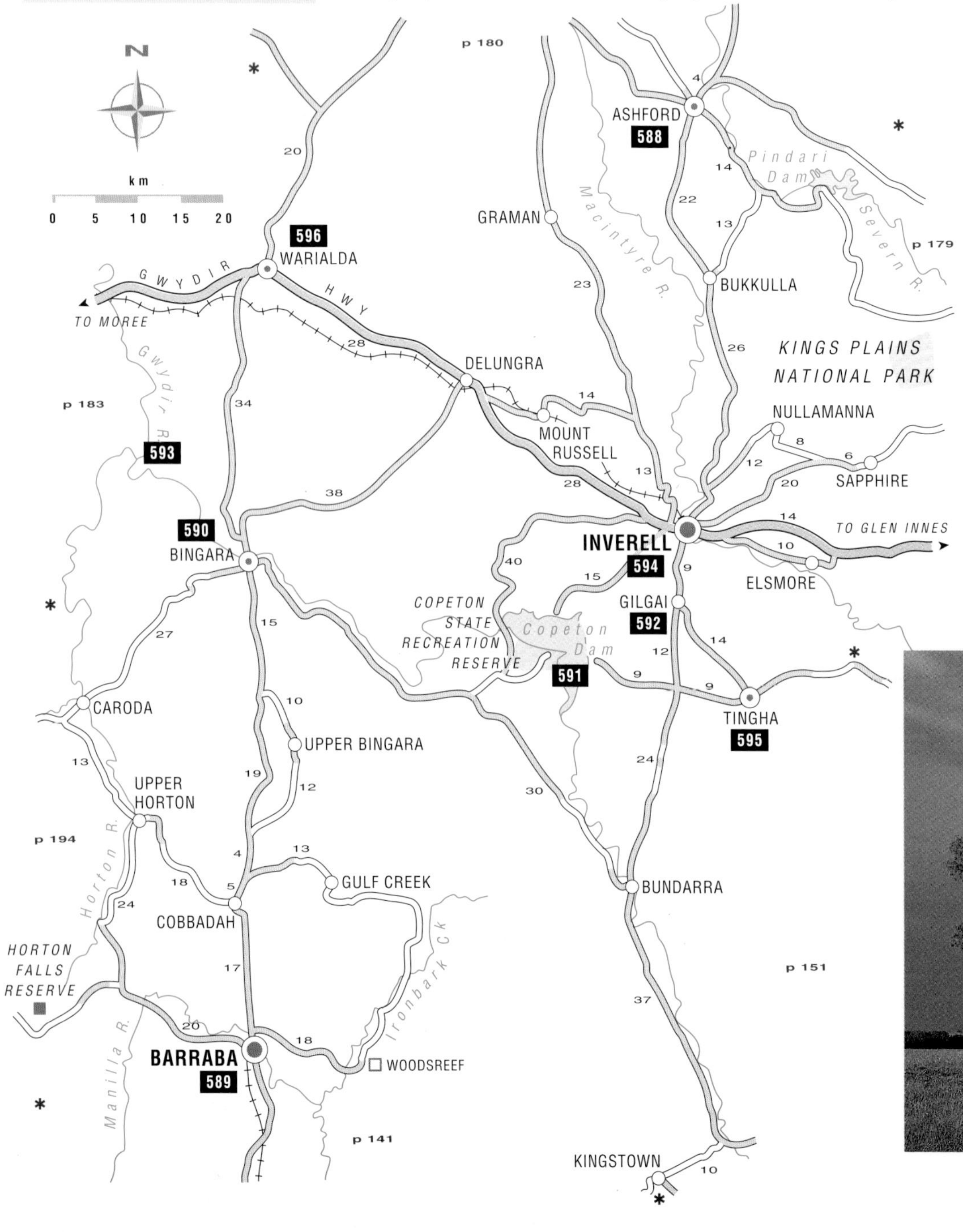

Europeans first sighted these plains in the shadow of the New England Tableland in 1827 and they have carried sheep since the early 1830s.

were small and only of industrial quality, but they brought a boost to the local economy not seen since the Upper Bingara gold rush of the early 1850s. Licensed fossickers combing the soils at designated places in the district may – with a little luck – still find diamonds – looking much like grains of rice – along with garnets, red and green jasper, serpentine and flakes of alluvial gold.

The botanist-explorer Allan Cunningham crossed the Gwydir River near Bingara in 1827, on his expedition from the Liverpool Plains to the Darling Downs. At the time, he took the river to be the Peel, realising his mistake on the way back. Squatters occupied the best grazing land in the district between 1834 and 1836, the first of them calling his run 'Bingera' from what was said to be an Aboriginal word for 'shallow crossing'.

A settlement was established by 1840, though a town site survey was not carried out until 1852, just before the discovery of gold. Most mining petered out by the end of the century but the All Nations mine, on the very edge of the town, was worked intermittently until 1948, eighty years after it opened. The New South Wales Country Women's Association was founded at the nearby 'Keira' homestead in 1922. *Population 1230*

ALL NATIONS GOLD MINE Still to be seen at the top of Hill Street, isolated in a grassy paddock, is the mine's huge, ten-headed stamper.

COURT HOUSE Unusual decorative features distinguish a handsome brick building, constructed with its rear and side offices around 1890.

SALTERS HOTEL The district historical society now occupies what is thought to have been Bingara's first inn and one of the town's first ten buildings. Its walls of cypress pine slabs, probably erected before 1860, were pit-sawn and hand-adzed, and fitted together without nails, screws or clamps.

COPETON DAM ■ 591

Completion of the Copeton Dam in 1976 brought north-western New South Wales a recreational bonus of mammoth proportions. The pent-up waters of the Gwydir River cover 4600 hectares when Lake Copeton is full. Its maximum volume is two-and-a-half times that of Sydney Harbour. Abutting the dam wall and extending from the lake's south-eastern shores, Copeton State Recreation Area comprises 900 hectares of grasslands and forest. Camping grounds, caravan parks, picnic spots and sports facilities are in heavy demand during the summer school holidays and at Easter: as many as 4000 people may use the area at one time. Power boats, sailing craft, rowing boats and swimmers share the generous expanse of water, which is stocked with golden perch (yellowbelly), Murray cod, catfish and red fin perch. Rainbow trout liberations have had limited success. Canoeists attracted to lively waters just downstream from the dam should check with the storage supervisor before launching. A release from the lake could overwhelm them.

The dam and state recreation area are about forty kilometres west and south of Inverell on a sealed road. A south-western road leads to a smaller but well-equipped recreation reserve on the northern shores of the lake. A third foreshore reserve on the eastern side is reached by an unsealed road from Tingha.

GILGAI ■ 592

Ten kilometres south of Inverell, the village of Gilgai holds a link with the earliest days of wine making in the Hunter Valley. Cuttings from vines at Dalwood, planted by George Wyndham in 1835, were brought to Gilgai by his son Charles in 1849. Generations of vintners struggled without significant success and the business collapsed after about a hundred years. Revived in 1965 – with fresh cuttings from Dalwood – the vineyard now enjoys a fair passing trade. Gilgai school, built in 1878 from bricks baked on the site, is still in use.

Joints and wooden pegs were employed to hold Salters Hotel in Bingara together; the only metal used was in the puddled – or wrought-iron – roof.

GWYDIR RIVER ■ 593

Originating from headwaters on the south-western edge of the New England Tableland, near Armidale, the Gwydir is an important tributary of the great Darling–Murray system. It flows through hilly country as far as Moree, then across the Darling Plains to join the Barwon near Collarenebri. Gorges downstream of the Copeton Dam (see entry) are difficult of access but nevertheless popular for trout fishing, canoeing and white-water rafting. Allan Cunningham, the first European to cross the Gwydir, named it in 1827 after a Welsh peer.

INVERELL ■ 594

When Scottish settlers in the Inverell district made their minds up in 1855, there was no denying them. They wanted a township at Green Swamp. A government surveyor disagreed, deciding in favour of a site farther down the Macintyre River at Byron Plains. So the protagonists of Green Swamp engaged a surveyor of their own to draw up a town plan, which they submitted with a petition to the colonial government.

To save face for the surveyor-general's office, both town sites were approved in 1858. But nothing was built at Byron Plains. Green Swamp, on the other hand, had two stores, two inns and a Presbyterian Church within a year, along with a scattering of bark huts and tents and a new name, 'Inverell'. Gaelic for 'the meeting place of swans', it came from the nearby sheep station established around 1836 by the district's first settler, Alexander Campbell. Township pioneers were the wheat growers Colin and Rosanna Ross, who in 1853 set up a store at Green Swamp as an adjunct to their homestead.

Agricultural prosperity in the surrounding district has always been the mainstay of Inverell. Exploitation of gold and diamond fields near Bingara and tin mining at Tingha brought extra economic benefits late in the nineteenth century, with continued progress assured by the completion of a branch railway line (now defunct) from Moree in 1901. Competing these days as a stopping point for travellers on New England's Fossickers' Way, Inverell likes to be known as Sapphire City. The district produces most of the world's blue sapphires, and many lesser gemstones are easily found.

A guide to permitted sites and an introduction to fossicking techniques is available at Inverell's tourist information centre, housed in an imaginatively converted water tower. Beginners are advised to try their luck at the Nullamanna Reserve, a supervised fossicking area on Frazers Creek, north-east of the town. *Population 9740*

COURT HOUSE Built in 1886, this beautifully proportioned public building of rendered brickwork, finely ornamented, brightly painted and surmounted by a tall clocktower, is a photographer's delight.

BICENTENNIAL MEMORIAL Dominating the townscape from almost any viewpoint, the memorial building with its soaring central spires is meant to be entered. Inner courtyards present a series of sensitively balanced 'walks through history that give weight not only to two hundred years of European history- but also to the district's strong Aboriginal heritage.

PIONEER VILLAGE Less than two kilometres south of Inverell on the Tingha road, various buildings from the district's early days have been relocated and restored in a bushland setting. They include a homestead, inn, woolshed, church, post office and schoolhouse, along with a display of old agricultural machinery.

GOONOOWIGALL WILDERNESS RESERVE More than 120 bird species have been observed in the sanctuary of 1680 hectares on Middle Creek, a tributary of the Macintyre River. The reserve, five kilometres south of Inverell, has limited vehicle access but offers a variety of walking trails.

FESTIVALS Sapphire City Festival, October.

TINGHA ■ 595

Shepherds had the Copes Creek district to themselves until 1870, when one of them discovered a rich deposit of cassiterite – tin oxide. Within a year, Australia's first commercial tin mines were open and a private settlement was established at what had been called Armidale Crossing. More than 6000 people flocked to the area, including 2000 Chinese. Their joss houses were Tingha's first elaborate buildings. In the early years, there were sufficient, easily accessible surface deposits for everyone to make a good living, even working without machinery as the Chinese did. Easy pickings were exhausted in the 1890s and drought added to the difficulties of deeper mining. Not quite a ghost town, Tingha remained mainly to serve the rural community. Tin dredging and mining have continued on a limited scale, the output rising and falling in response to international price fluctuations. *Population 830*

WARIALDA ■ 596

Official skulduggery gave Warialda its start, accidentally leading it to a position of regional dominance for many years. In 1840, a newly appointed Crown Lands Commissioner by the name of Edward Mayne was authorised to set up a police post on the wild north-western frontier of pastoral expansion. His choice of site, near a big waterhole of Reedy Creek, was strange: the land was already taken. It was part of a sheep run, called 'Warialda' after the Aboriginal name for the waterhole – said to mean 'place of honey'. And the run was owned by William Mayne, perhaps Edward's brother but more likely his cousin.

Commissioner Mayne bought cattle to put onto the run – without paying the standard licence fee or other government charges – just as a rural depression set in and made the stock virtually worthless. He claimed extraordinarily high expenses for his police force, evidently pocketing much of the money. Still, a court judgment went against him for non-payment of debt. Dismissing him in 1843, Governor Gipps listed a string of other misdemeanours – all of which Mayne denied. Later in the same year, Robert Mayne died and the government was left with a sheep station on its hands. In 1846, Warialda was made the permanent headquarters for regional administration. Official buildings such as a court house and post office came first, and then the beginnings of a village around 1850. Its influence limited nowadays to the administration of Yallaroi Shire, Warialda's prosperity rests heavily on the diverse agriculture of the district. *Population 1290*

COURT HOUSE This imposing gable-roofed structure of dark brick with a verandah along three sides, was completed in 1883. Two other court houses preceded it.

ELIZABETH (SISTER) KENNY MEMORIAL In the light and airy Anglican Church of St Simon and St Jude, built in the 1960s, an alcove is set aside for the christening font of Warialda's most illustrious daughter. Elizabeth Kenny, born in 1880, overcame lack of formal training to become a nursing sister and worked on troopships during the First World War. In peacetime, she took a special interest in the treatment of poliomyelitis having opened her own hospital in 1913. When an epidemic occurred in Queensland in 1932, she set up her own clinic, introducing a technique of stimulating rather than immobilising paralysed muscles. The medical establishment opposed her, and in 1938 a Royal Commission condemned her techniques. With the support of the Queensland government, Sister Kenny introduced her techniques to the United States. Her successes there quickly won official acclaim and 'Kenny clinics' were set up throughout the country.

CRANKY ROCK Just off the Gwydir Highway eight kilometres east of Warialda, Reedy Creek flows among jumbled heaps of granite boulders. Local legend has it that a Chinese gold miner, 'cranky' over some dispute, jumped to his death from the highest of the rocks. The surrounding reserve includes walking trails and a pleasant picnic area.

THE BLOODSTAINED BIRTHPLACE OF RACIAL JUSTICE

MYALL Creek Station, between Bingara (see entry) and Delungra, symbolises a turning point in Australian race relations. The cold-blooded massacre of Aborigines here in 1838 was far from unusual. But for the first time, after half a century of mounting strife, white men were punished for a crime against blacks. At the insistence of a newly installed governor, Sir George Gipps, legal force was given to an unfashionable proposition that the native people were as much human beings as the colonists.

Aborgines were welcomed and given food whenever they camped at Myall Creek. But elsewhere along the Gwydir River, towards Moree, a campaign of indiscriminate killing had started. One day, even Myall Creek was raided, this time by a party of about a dozen armed men. Most were, or had been, convicts, assigned to agricultural work; one was said to be a young member of a landowning family.

More than thirty Aborigines – mostly women and children and old men – took shelter in or near a shepherd's hut. In the absence of the station overseer the shepherd was persuaded to drive them away. They were led away on a rope and all but four or five were shot or decapitated with sabres. Fires were lit to burn at least twenty-eight bodies. Next day the raiders searched for ten or twelve other Aborigines who had fled into the bush. Whether they too were killed is unknown, but they were not seen in the district again.

The memory of the events of 1838 – depicted below left in an 1841 engraving – lingers over the peaceful Myall Creek of today (above).

On his return, the overseer discovered the burnt remains and notified the police. Governor Gipps ordered a full investigation. The men with convict backgrounds were arrested while the other member of the party retreated to one of his family's properties and was never charged.

In Sydney, the prisoners made no attempt to deny their parts in the massacre. According to Gipps, they were more than ready to plead guilty – not imagining that they could be in any jeopardy. At the urging of lawyers, hired by the owner of Myall Creek Station, they made pleas of self-defence on nine counts of wilful murder. After some confusion over the identity of an older male victim, a jury finally acquitted all the men.

Squatter society and the Sydney press were exultant. But a new trial was ordered for seven of the defendants, where they were charged with the murder of women and children. With self-defence no longer a justification, they were convicted; despite a call for mercy by a majority of jurors, the men were hanged. □

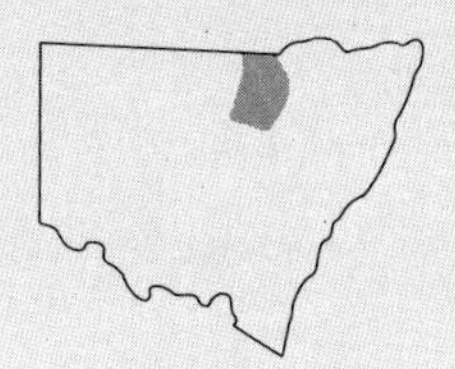

Coonamble & Walgett

River irrigation of the black soils of the north-western plains is augmented by the warm waters that gush up from the natural reservoir of the Great Artesian Basin. Pipes or open-bore drains carry water to sheep, cattle, wheat and cotton.

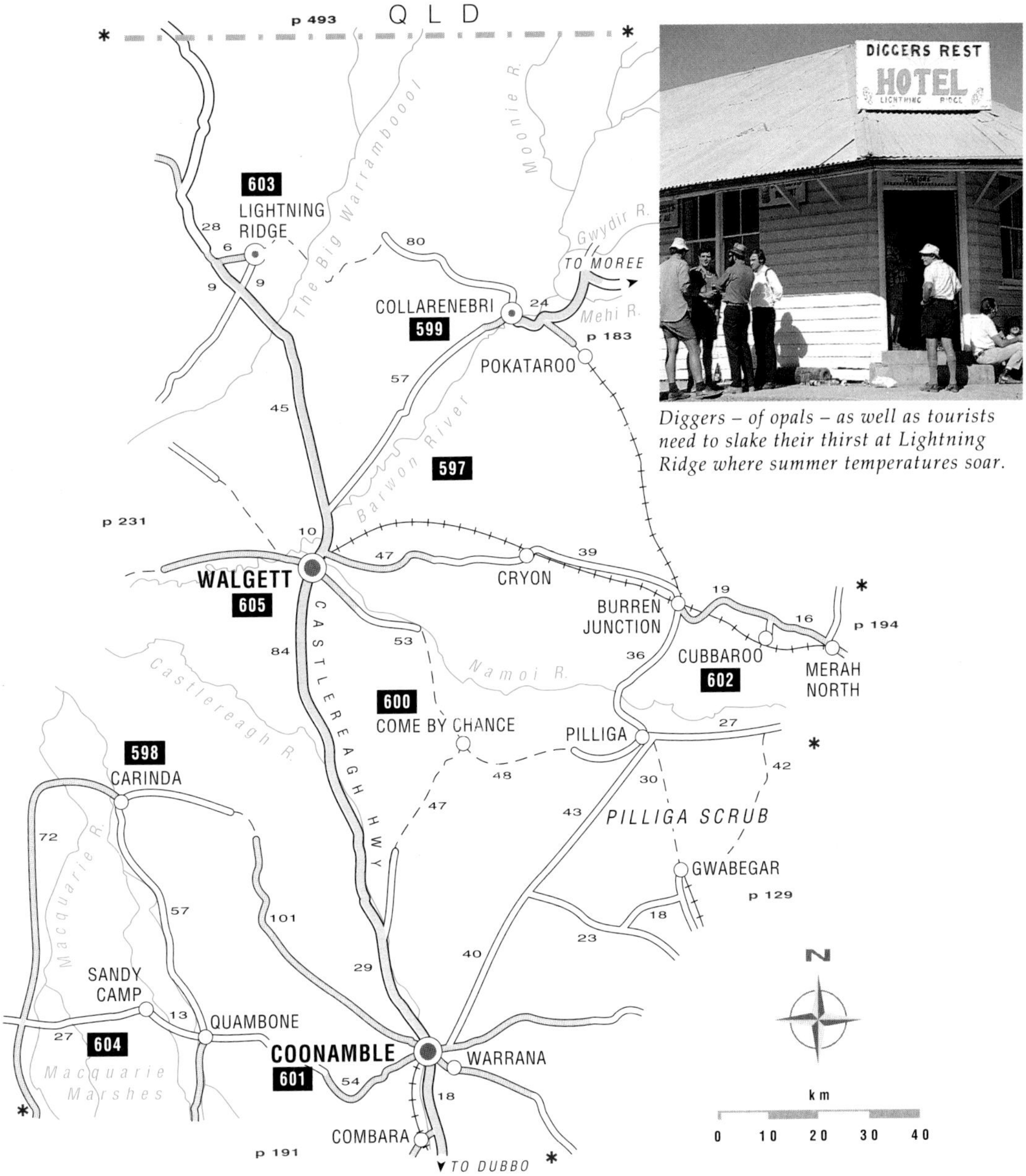

Diggers – of opals – as well as tourists need to slake their thirst at Lightning Ridge where summer temperatures soar.

BARWON RIVER ■ 597

It was not until Roderick Mitchell, Commissioner of Crown Lands and son of the explorer Thomas Mitchell, visited properties on the Macintyre and Barwon rivers in 1846, that what had long been suspected was proved correct – the Barwon River and the Macintyre River (see *Goondiwindi & Boggabilla*) are the same river under different names. The Barwon flows from Mungindi, past Collarenebri, Walgett and Brewarinna to Bourke where it meets the Darling River, passing through outback scenery and plains on which beef cattle and sheep graze or wheat and sorghum are grown.

The Aborigines, whose name for the river meant 'great, wide, awful river', built a complex series of fish traps on the Barwon; what is left of these works has been preserved and, because of their rarity, are now 'heritage' listed (see *Brewarrina & Goodooga*). In addition to the historic fish traps and the rocky rapids which occur above and below Collarenebri there are now weirs and other irrigation structures. But such blocks to river traffic were not the only problems facing those trying to navigate the Barwon River.

The rise and fall of the river level was of prime concern to the early settlers, not only for water for irrigation and domestic use but also for transport of supplies in and produce out. Information on the water level was one of the most keenly read items of the news posted daily at the post offices on the river. News of rain in southern Queensland was keenly sought since water falling there would, within weeks reach the Barwon. As in some other parts of inland Australia, it was possible to have a flood on the river while the district was in the grip of a severe dry spell and drought. From 1880 to 1912 regular steamer services ran along the Barwon from Walgett to Bourke but, in time of flood, upriver towns that normally were inaccessible would be surprised by a steamer – Collarenebri was visited (see entry) in 1879 and again in 1886 and Mungindi in 1890.

CARINDA ■ 598

The village of Carinda is a small commercial centre for a district in which the sheep, cattle and cotton are well watered by the Macquarie, Castlereagh and Barwon rivers. The first settlers to arrive in Carinda gathered around Marthaguy Creek on which the village, gazetted in 1890, stands. However, since 1896 the artesian bores which have tapped into the Great Artesian Basin have provided an alternative source of water and later settlement away from the creek was made possible. Those who live away from the creek are known as 'top enders' by the 'bottom enders' whose homes are on the creek. Many original homes are still occupied and historic woolsheds still stand but the interest of the Australian Museum has been raised by something much, much older in the form of the ancient fossil site at Carinda known as Cuddie Springs.

The large two-storey police station, acquired by default, would have been underutilised in this one-policeman village. The much larger Quirindi (see *Muswellbrook & Scone*), whose name has a very similar pronunciation was in need of a police station but the building was wrongly erected in Carinda. In the event, a smaller building served the needs of the police and in 1991, the district at last found a use for the courtroom and magistrate's study, which now serve as a waiting room and an examination room during the regular

Mountains of high-protein wheat from the north-west plains awaits transport at the Walgett railhead.

clinics held in the village by the nursing sister from Quambone.

COLLARENEBRI ■ 599

There were a number of cattle runs in the district around Collarenebri from the 1840s but the town itself grew up around a pub built by William Earl in 1859. The Squatter's Arms was built at a ford called 'The Rocks' on the Barwon River and was visited – and robbed – by Captain Thunderbolt on his only known call at Collarenebri. Thunderbolt also robbed the local store of twenty-two pounds sterling in cash and goods.

By 1867, Collarenebri, from an Aboriginal word, meaning 'place of collarin flowers' (from the coolibah tree) was designated an official stopping point on the weekly mail run from Walgett to Mingindi and was gazetted as a town the same year.

Collarenebri's main problem in the early days was transport. Although steamers plied on the Barwon River (see entry), there were only two occasions when steamers reached the town; the *Brewarinna* during the flood of 1879 and the *Bunyip* in the flood of 1886. There is a local story that the *Bunyip*, heading for Collarenebri during the big flood of 1886 strayed from the main channel and was stranded in a paddock twenty kilometres from the river. The captain and his wife stayed with the boat until it could be refloated in the next flood in 1890...by which time four children and an assortment of goats, pigs and hens had been added to the passenger list.

With the coming of the railway, the steamer service declined, but Collarenebri's transport problems continued since the nearest railhead was located on a branch line at Pokataroo to the south of the town. The Gwydir Highway now runs through the town and in fact got its name from the section of the road running from Collarenebri to Gravesend, which runs parallel to what was called the Gwydir River – nowadays, the Mehi. The nearest public transport, however, is at Walgett or Moree.

Collarenebri is the centre of a wheat- and cotton-growing district, which, unusually for an outback town, offers excellent fishing and waterskiing on the Barwon River as well as the once traditional open-air cinema. The Aboriginal cemetery just outside the town has been used for only the past eighty years but the one hundred graves, many decorated with a variety of materials, are protected. *Population 625*

FESTIVALS Collarenebri Great Raft Race, March.

COME BY CHANCE ■ 600

Come by Chance sits at the junction of two creeks – Gidginbilla Creek and Bungle Gully Creek, the official name for which is the blander Baradine Creek. There were a number of cattle runs in the district around the village from the 1850s so that by the time William Colless arrived in 1862 he thought there was little chance of stumbling across a stretch of unselected land. When he acquired the last remaining unselected plot of land, he named his station Come By Chance. Most of the village, including the post office, hotel, police station, blacksmith's, cemetery and many of the early homes were on land owned by Colless.

A bore was dug 600 metres down into the Great Artesian Basin at Come By Chance in the early 1900s, which has enabled the grazing of cattle and sheep and, more recently, the growing of cereal crops to continue. In 1991, a new project entitled Piping the Bores was launched at Come By Chance. Up to ninety-five per cent of the water from the 1200 artesian bores in New South Wales is wasted through evaporation, seepage or leakage. The new scheme, a joint effort of landowners, business and government organisations aims to cap the bores and use new heat-resistant pipes to carry the water directly where it is required, ensuring that those at the end of the line have equal access to the water.

Come By Chance was never visited by Banjo Paterson but the name intrigued him and the poet included a verse about the name in one of his ballads of the bush:

But my languid mood forsook me
when I found a name that took me;
Quite by chance I came across it –
'Come-by-chance' was what I read;
No location was assigned it,
nor a thing to help one find it'
Just an N which stood for northward
and the rest was all unsaid.

FESTIVAL Picnic Races, September.

COONAMBLE ■ 601

When George Evans crossed the Castlereagh River near Coonamble in 1817, it was in flood but when Sturt and Hume crossed it in 1829, it was in the middle of a drought. The two 'moods' of the river are still visible at Coonamble and the locals refer to it as the 'upside-down' river since, in time of drought, the dry sandy watercourse covers running water a few centimetres below the surface.

James Walker's 'Canamble' or 'Koonamble' run was probably established in the 1830s. The name comes from an Aboriginal word, goonamble, meaning 'plenty of dirt' or 'bullock dung' and, with 15 000 cattle on Walker's run, the name was certainly appropriate.

Walker's 20 000-hectare property became the centre for the district and a camping place for stockmen travelling across the plains. By 1855, an area of land on both sides of the Castlereagh River had been reserved for a proposed township. The first Coonamble postmistress was employed in 1859 and the woman in question required two guarantors in case the postage stamps with which she was entrusted should tempt her to abscond from her 'twelve-pounds per annum' position.

The mounted troopers based at Coonamble arrested Johnny Dunn, the last of Ben Hall's gang to be caught at nearby Quambone and he was held in the cells at Coonamble before being sent for trial.

Since 1903, Coonamble has been on the railway line from Dubbo, which enabled the wool clip, the original major product of the town, to reach the markets more quickly. The town is now the headquarters of one of the biggest shires in New South Wales and the centre for a wealthy pastoral and wheat-growing district, which is also noted for its sheep and cattle studs. The first bore south of the Darling was dug at Coonamble and the town's water supply still comes from four artesian bores. *Population 2890*

POLICE STATION AND STABLES MUSEUM Built in 1870, the police station is now a museum and the brick stables have changed little since they were used to house the horses of mounted troopers. Although there are now no horses, there is a register of all the horses bred in Coonamble for Tooth's Brewery drays, as well as various carts and buggies, and a side-saddle that won an award at the 1861 World Fair in London.

COURT HOUSE The court house in Aberford Street has stood on the site of the original late nineteenth-century building since 1972 and is reputed to be the first court building in New South Wales to have installed the luxury of air conditioning.

CUBBAROO ■ 602

The first squatter in Cubbaroo in 1839 was John Button who would probably be amazed to see wine grapes and cotton growing side by side in what he saw as sheep grazing country. On the railway line between WeeWaa and Walgett, Cubbaroo has become part of the booming cotton industry centred on Wee Waa and Narrabri.

Stands of river red gums line these swamps and the streams that link them throughout the no-man's-land of the Macquarie Marshes.

LURE OF THE BLACK OPAL

LIGHTNING RIDGE is the largest source of gem-quality black opals in the world. Although Jack Murray, from a station just south of Lightning Ridge may well have been the first to mine opals here in the 1880s, the start of Lightning Ridge's rapid development as opal capital of Australia and black opal capital of the world is usually credited to Charles Nettleton. Shown some surface opal by a woman in 1902, Charles Nettleton sank his shaft at 'McDonald's Six Mile Field' in 1902 and found the first officially recorded black opal the next year. Word soon got out and the opal rush was on.

Unlike other forms of mining, opals can be mined by one man…and a lot of hard work. The number of individuals who came and still come to mine at Lightning Ridge are difficult to calculate accurately. Their claims are scattered around what is to all intents and purposes a two-street town with a small permanent population. The tents of the early days on the diggings have given way to permanent miners' homes made of corrugated iron, conglomerate boulders, sandstone, mud and any other readily available material. Ingenuity is also displayed in the variety of machinery used for digging, removing the earth from the shaft, sifting it and separating the opals from the clay. The thirty-five nationalities currently working on the opal fields of this, the fastest growing town in the north-west of the state, have developed a common language…and tolerance of tourists who are permitted to 'speck, noodle the dumps or puddle the mullock while watching out for shincrackers'. □

An opal miner has used a convenient tree to stake this claim for almost 2400 square metres.

A skilled cutter and polisher transforms a raw opal into a gem.

In 1970, thirty hectares of the fertile soils watered by Pian Creek, on the Namoi River system, was planted with Shiraz grapes. Cubaroo wines can be tasted in a cellar built around an 1870s timber slab store. The grapes, picked in January, are believed to be the earliest grapes to be picked in an Australian vineyard.

LIGHTNING RIDGE ■ 603

Known locally as 'the Ridge', this small town sits in the north-western plains right in the middle of a rich opal field (see box).

Tourism is Lightning Ridge's second industry and there are walk-in and drive-in mines, an underground opal showroom and cinema, an opal bazaar and a museum – in what was a house built of beer bottles and mortar – all devoted to the story of Lightning Ridge and opal mining. *Population 1520*

MACQUARIE MARSHES ■ 604

The enormous size – 148 000 hectares – and relative inaccessibility of the Macquarie Marshes were commemorated by the Aborigines in a Dreamtime legend, and were noted by Oxley, who failed, and Sturt, who succeeded in finding a way around them. Between Carinda and Warren, the Macquarie River flows into a large natural depression, which, combined with the nature of the soil, dissipates the waters of the river into a series of channels, lagoons and swamps that never dry up.

The delicately balanced ecosystem of the Macquarie Marshes encompasses the microscopic zooplankton and phytoplankton in the waters, and the tall reeds and strange plants that have evolved to tolerate the alternating droughts and inundations of the marshes together with the species further up the food chain, which feed on them. Forty-seven species of snake, eighteen species of fish, seventeen species of amphibians and at least one-hundred-and-forty species of native and migratory birds have been recorded in the forty-eight-kilometre-long marshes. They provide the largest wetland area and the largest drought-refuge area for water birds in eastern Australia.

The building of the Burrendong Dam, which threatened to dry up the marshes in 1970 and the pollution of the marshes by runoff from nearby cotton fields, threatened the fragile ecology. An 18 000-hectare area was gazetted as a nature reserve in 1971, the marshes were given an increased priority for surplus water from the dam and a 300-metre buffer zone in which no farming was allowed will, it is hoped save the unique Macquarie Marshes.

WALGETT ■ 605

The name Walgett comes from an Aboriginal word meaning 'hollow in the ground where waters meet' – an appropriate name for the town that stands at the junction of the Barwon and Namoi rivers. A post office was gazetted at 'Wallgett on the Barwin River' in 1851 and the site for the town was surveyed in 1859 although squatters' runs in the district around the town had probably been in existence since about 1840.

In one of three poems he wrote which mentioned Walgett, Banjo Paterson described

The Barwon river that wanders down
In a leisurely manner by Walgett Town

The Barwon River was vital during Walgett's boom years of the late 1800s when steamers from Bourke and Brewarinna brought supplies to Walgett Bridge or, if the water was high enough, turned into the Namoi River and steamed into the town itself. These were the years when Walgett, the highest navigable point on the Barwon, became the 'key to the back country'. The first steamer reached the town in 1861 and from 1870 until the turn of the century the run to Walgett became as regular as the river would allow.

Katherine Susannah Pritchard describes 'Walgett perched at the end of the railway' in her autobiography and, as the terminus of the north-west rail line, Walgett became, and still is, a major stock transport centre. When the trains began chugging into the station in 1908, the days of steam-driven transport on the river were numbered; the last steamer to tie up at the wharf here was the *Wandering Jew* in 1912.

Another, slightly more contemporary author to mention Walgett was Patrick White who worked on his uncle's property in the district in 1930 and wrote in reminisences called *Flaws in the Glass* that 'at Walgett I experienced every possible seasonal change'. Walgett's fortunes have waxed and waned with these extreme seasonal changes from the drought of the 1890s, which slowed down its previously rapid development to the floods of the early 1990s, during one of which Walgett became an island for many weeks, accessible only by plane, after the waters of the Namoi and its tributaries overflowed their banks and inundated the countryside. *Population 2090*

'EUROKA' One of the largest and earliest of the runs in the district, Euroka Station's north-eastern boundary passed right through the town of Walgett. After a number of squatters and owners had worked it, 'Euroka' was bought by Fred Wolseley in 1876 and was the scene of his invention of the first known sheep-shearing machine. The new Wolseley Shearing Machine was tested at Bourke in 1888 on 184 000 sheep and eventually revolutionised shearing by offering a faster method of wool removal that resulted in fewer nicks and a better wool clip.

FESTIVAL Walgett Rodeo, August.

Gilgandra & Nyngan

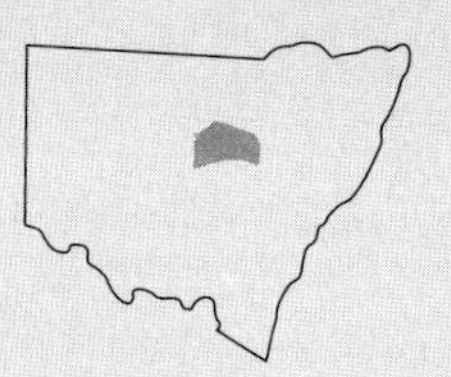

Between the fertile pastures of New England and the arid lands of New South Wales' far west, lies the land where, nature permitting, the fleece and the grain are golden. Like much of rural Australia, the central western plains are at the mercy of a drought and deluge cycle that tests the endurance of its staunchest inhabitants.

ARMATREE ■ 606

Sheep and cattle were the dominant rural industries at Armatree for more than 100 years but it was wheat that brought wealth to the region. Wheat was first sown here as early as 1838 but many years were to pass before crops were cultivated on a marketable scale. Nowadays, the former railway village which began as a makeshift campsite for men building the railway line between Gilgandra (see entry) and Coonamble in 1902 and 1903, has matured to become an important wheat storage centre.

BIDDON ■ 607

The clink of cup on saucer and the hum of conversation have replaced more rigorous activity in the barn near the historical Biddon homestead, built in 1901. The barn now houses an arts and crafts centre displaying a range of locally-made art, craftwork and preserves. Devonshire teas are served, an antique drink machine dispenses cool drinks to quench the thirst of visitors, while the elegant Biddon homestead offers bed and breakfast to those who decide to linger.

BREELONG ■ 608

The tragedy of the 'Breelong massacre' immortalised in the film *The Chant of Jimmie Blacksmith* – based on Thomas Kenneally's novel of the same name – underscores the history of this once progressive village on the banks of the Castlereagh River.

On 20 July 1900, part-Aboriginal brothers Jimmie and Joe Governor murdered four members of the Mawbey family and Helen Kerz – the school-teacher at West Breelong who boarded with them. Jimmie Governor was employed on the Mawbey property and though comparatively well educated, his status as an Aborigine debarred him from the wages he would have got as a white person and from any rights as a citizen – injustices that he felt keenly. His wife – a white woman – was subject to taunts by Helen Kerz and the Mawbey women and it is likely that their intolerant attitude was the spark that ignited the tragic sequence of events. The Mawbey family killings apparently pushed Jimmie into madness; he seemed to have seen himself as engaged in some sort of warfare and while on the run he and Joe killed several other people.

After an intensive three-month search involving more than 2000 policemen, the Governor brothers were captured, brought to trial and sentenced to death. Now, only the ruins of the homestead stand as a haunting reminder of the incident that in many respects, was the tragic culmination of a long history of Aborigine–white relationships.

Squatters took up sheep and cattle runs in the area in the 1830s and were soon followed by selectors and settlers. Typical of many small farming communities along the banks of western New South Wales rivers, Breelong grew around an inn which was also a changing station for Cobb & Co. horses, a post office, a store and for some time, the location of the only telephone in the district. The Mawbey family were the licensees of the Breelong Inn where all the Mawbey men were sleeping on the night of the massacre.

In the 1860s, a vision of Breelong as an important town on the railway line to Coonamble (see *Coonamble &*

A familiar scene in the central west – even the worthy windmill is overwhelmed by the dreadful drought.

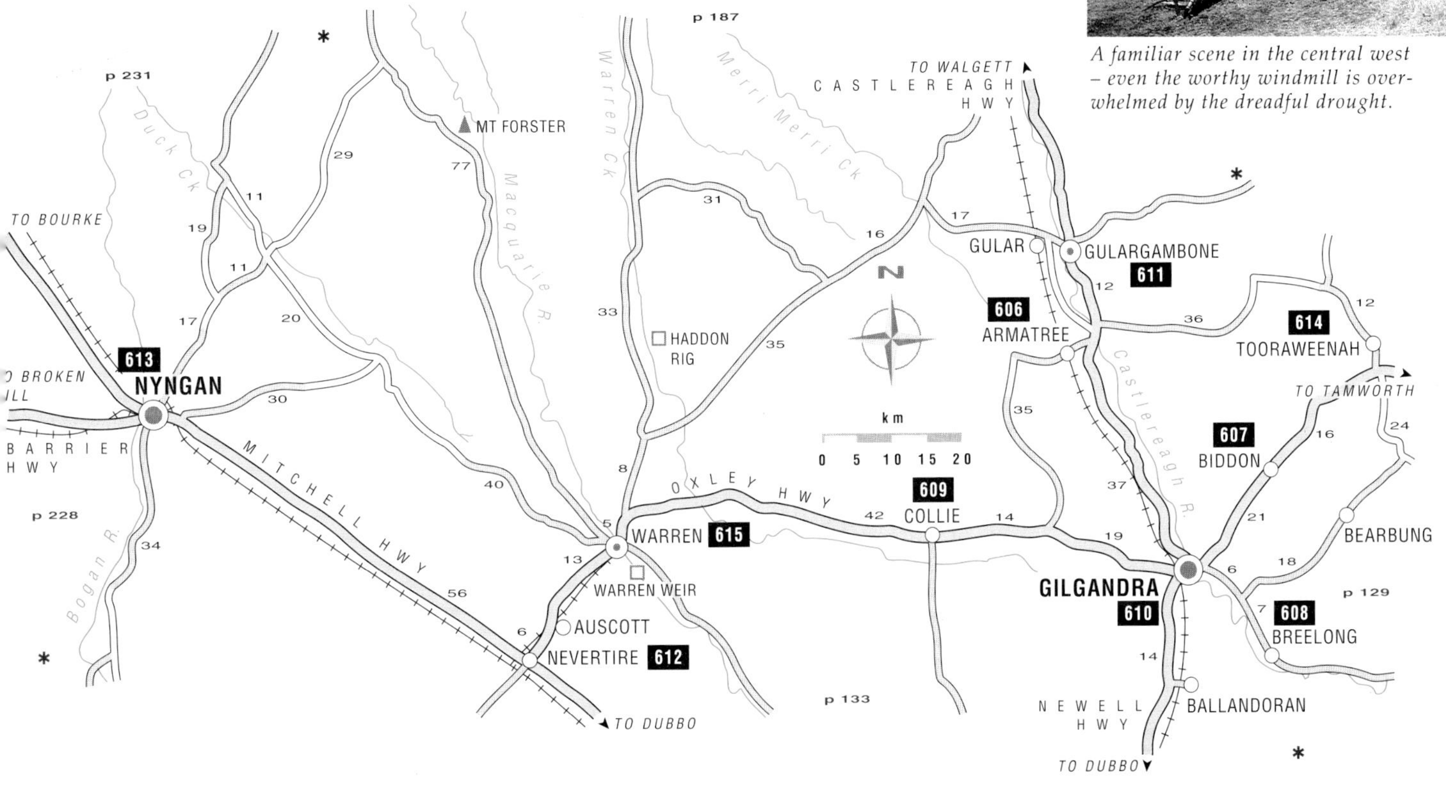

p 187
p 231
p 228
p 133
p 129
TO BOURKE
TO BROKEN HILL
BARRIER HWY
613 NYNGAN
MITCHELL HWY
MT FORSTER
HADDON RIG
Duck Ck
Bogan R.
Macquarie R.
Warren Ck
Merri Merri Ck
615 WARREN
WARREN WEIR
AUSCOTT
612 NEVERTIRE
TO DUBBO
OXLEY HWY
609 COLLIE
TO WALGETT
CASTLEREAGH HWY
GULAR
611 GULARGAMBONE
606 ARMATREE
614 TOORAWEENAH
TO TAMWORTH
607 BIDDON
Castlereagh R.
BEARBUNG
610 GILGANDRA
608 BREELONG
BALLANDORAN
NEWELL HWY
TO DUBBO
km
0 5 10 15 20

During the big wet of April 1990, helicopters took some Nyngan townsfolk to safety while livestock, marooned on 'islands', survived on bales of fodder-drop from the air.

Walgett) faded when the news came through that the proposed railway line was to be redirected through Dubbo. The ambitious town plans, which included a common, cemetery and even street-names to supplement the already existing school, inn, store, post office and sporting oval were scrapped and Breelong faded into obscurity, to be remembered now as an historic, if tragic, site.

COLLIE ■ **609**

The wayside inn near Marthaguy Creek on the Colli Run was the seed from which the town of Collie grew. Established in the 1860s, the rough bush inn and store that was a mail change for coaches on the north-east run to Quambone attracted settlers who formed the 'frontier' village of Collie. A flood in the late 1870s seems to have prompted the licensee to move the hotel to a 'drier' site where it flourished for over a century until completely destroyed by fire in 1987.

GILGANDRA ■ **610**

'Home of the Coo-ees' and 'Town of Windmills' is the description of Gilgandra given in tourist brochures. The first description is a reference to the famous Coo-ee recruiting march of the First World War. After the bloody setback of Gallipoli in 1915, recruiting drives became increasingly ineffective and the Hitchen brothers of Gilgandra came up with the idea of a 'snowballing' recruitment march from Gilgandra to Sydney. They proposed to stop in towns they passed through along the way and rally recruits with the Australian bushmen's traditional cry for help – 'Coo-ee'! The idea captured the enthusiasm of the nation and by the time the 'Coo-ees', as they became known, reached Sydney, they had enlisted 263 men, 26 of whom were from Gilgandra. The famous Coo-ee recruitment march inspired similar marches from other towns, such as the 'Kookaburras' from Tooraweenah (see entry) and resulted in a dramatic upturn in recruitment figures.

A re-enactment of the march took place on 24 October 1987. Twenty-two men marched from Gilgandra retracing the steps of the original 'Coo-ees' and reached Sydney in three weeks. The event was filmed as a documentary and shown on national television.

A scattering of windmills silhouetted against the townscape are all that remain of more than 300 that once pumped water from the sub-artesian basin for residential use during the 1950s. It wasn't until 1966 that the town developed a reticulated water supply. The few remaining windmills in Gilgandra are used by some residents for supplying garden water but most Gilgandrans now rely on the town water supply.

Though a small place, Gilgandra breeds people with big ideas. Prominently displayed in the town is a model Howard Rotavator – a farm machine with rotating blades used to break up soil in preparation for cultivation – the invention of Arthur C. Howard who developed the principal of rotavation in 1912 and worked on it for the next ten years, his efforts culminating in the mass production of the machine in Sydney in the early 1920s. Now rotary cultivators based on the original Howard design are used throughout the world.

The town was first settled in the 1830s when squatters brought their flocks to graze along the Castlereagh River (see *Coonabarabran & Coolah*). Gilgandra takes its name from a station settlement established in the 1840s that was variously known as 'Carlganda', 'Gulliganda', or 'Galganda' – all supposedly versions of an Aboriginal word said to mean 'long waterhole'. This substantial waterhole in the Castlereagh River was also the junction of two main routes through the district and it became a popular stopping place for travellers with their horses and waggon teams. A few sheep and cattle runs were taken up by selectors in the 1860s and 1870s as a result of the Robertson Land Act of 1861 and in 1866 Gilgandra's first building – the Bushman's Arms Hotel – was constructed. A post office was opened in 1867 and the settlement was finally proclaimed a village in 1888.

Wheat was introduced to the district early this century and modern Gilgandra is surrounded by fields of ripening wheat and grazing sheep, its economic base, like many rural population centres, subject to the whims of a capricious market and an often unpredictable climate. *Population 2890*

ST AMBROSE CHURCH OF ENGLAND This church owes its existence to the grateful parishioners of St Ambrose Church in Bournemouth, England, who donated 1200 pounds sterling towards its construction as thanks to the 'Coo-ees' of the First World War. The gift acknowledged the town in the British Empire with the best church and war service record.

FESTIVALS Coo-ee Festival, October.

Thomas Kenneally's novel based on the 'Breelong massacre' came to the screen in the film of the same name.

GULARGAMBONE ■ **611**

In the 1830s, land-hungry squatters with their ever-increasing and ever-hungry herds pushed further along the course of the Castlereagh River and came upon the gratifying vista of Gulargambone's sweeping grasslands. The cultivation of wheat was underway as early as 1838 and the Robertson Land Act promulgated in 1861 – designed to help small farmers by opening the old squatting runs to free selection – brought an influx of farmers and pastoralists to the district in the 1860s and 1870s. The settlement that evolved at this time, went through a variety of name changes including 'Gullengombone', 'Galargumbone', 'Gilergambone' and 'Gulergambone' until it was finally gazetted as Gulargambone in 1883.

With wide, dusty country-town-style streets planted with a variety of shade trees, modern Gulargambone has grown up at the junction of the Castlereagh River and Gulargambone Creek to become the service centre for a rich mixed farming district that lists prime cattle, Merino sheep, fat lambs and wheat as the key components of its rural-based economy. *Population 460*

NEVERTIRE ■ 612

On 28 December 1896, the habitual quietness of Nevertire, once known as Warren Pond, was shattered by a cyclone that devastated much of the town. Daunted, but not completely undone by this violent natural disruption, the locals patched their homes and public buildings and resumed their measured pace of life.

From its humble beginnings as a railhead on the western railway that reached the town in 1882, Nevertire has persisted despite considerable growing pains, drought being a regular visitor to the region. That lynchpin of all early, outback settlements – the pub – was already in existence before the town was surveyed in 1883.

In Betty Casey's poem 'Nevertire', the question, 'Have you heard of a town called Nevertire?' is both asked and answered by a weary drover:

It's right up north,
and they say its small.
There's a pub and a store,
and that's about all,
But when I get there –
right over the plain,
I know I'll never be tired again.

Today's Nevertire – where large trucks waiting to unload their haul of grain stand in place of yesterday's bullock-waggons with their cargo of wool – is still a small 'frontier' town with a pub, post office, store and petrol bowser.

NYNGAN ■ 613

The old saying, 'It never rains, but it pours' must have particular significance for the townsfolk of Nyngan who became the focus of the nation's attention during the 'big wet' of April 1990 when extensive flooding over much of central-western New South Wales prompted a mass evacuation of the town's population by helicopter, to the safety of Dubbo (see *Bathurst & Orange*).

This was not the first time that the town's stoic residents had battled rising waters. Nyngan has endured major flooding on a monotonously regular basis throughout its history. Substantial levee banks have now been built at vulnerable stretches along the town's boundary as protection against further deluges.

Having evolved as the rural service centre for the Bogan Shire – a rich agricultural and pastoral district with some of Australia's best-known Merino sheep studs – Nyngan is surrounded by some of the flattest country in the world. Kilometres of open grassland dappled with groups of sheep and cattle stretch into the distance, while improved varieties of wheat in combination with modern farming practices are transforming once marginal wheat-growing country into productive fields.

Major Thomas Mitchell passed through the area in 1835 on his way to explore the Barwon River (see *Coonamble & Walgett*) to its meeting with the Darling. He camped for a night at the present site of Nyngan, gracing the area with the name Nyingen, an Aboriginal word said to mean 'long pond of water' – a reference to the Bogan River which has now become the popular retreat of watersport enthusiasts and inland anglers. Major Mitchell made a second stop at 'Nyingen' in 1846, by which time squatters and their proliferating herds were spreading further into the apparently endless plains of central-western New South Wales. Stations were established and the construction of bush inns and stores soon followed.

Though a police station was established in the village surveyed in 1866, Nyngan was little more than a place name from 1840 to 1880 during which time the nearby twin villages of Canonba and Brownstown, on the coach-route from Dubbo to Bourke, absorbed much of the region's developmental energies.

Gazetted as a water reserve in 1865 and as a site for a future village in 1880, Nyngan stole the show from other settlements in the district when the railway line from Dubbo to Bourke was routed through the town in 1883, bypassing the formerly thriving villages of Canonba and Brownstown which, deprived of the economic advantages of a rail stop, quickly disappeared from the landscape. Nyngan became the final resting place of many of Canonba's buildings which were moved to the new town in 1883. Some of Canonba's original weatherboard houses still border the neat, tree-lined streets of Nyngan today. *Population 2310*

TOORAWEENAH ■ 614

Tooraweenah, an Aboriginal word said to mean 'home of snakes' nowadays could be more accurately described as the 'town of tranquillity'. The village is characterised by its peaceful, rural setting. Nestling in a valley on the western slopes of the Warrumbungle Mountains, Tooraweenah has streets lined with quaint buildings and an unhurried air.

Most of the land around present-day Tooraweenah was controlled by the squatter Andrew Brown who took up the Tooraweenah Run in 1837. A change in the colony's land laws in the 1880s made it possible for small farmers and pastoralists to settle on large runs previously monopolised by the early squatters and it was around this time that the settlement of Tooraweena Creek, as it was then known, came into being. A school was opened in 1884, soon followed by a hotel in 1886.

A memorial plaque located in the village common commemorates the district's war veterans and the spirited 'Kookaburras', a motley group of twenty or so men who set off from Tooraweenah on 16 January 1916 on a march to Bathurst via Mendooran, Boomely, Cobbora and Mudgee to recruit volunteers for the First World War (see Gilgandra).

In 1931, Tooraweenah was visited by the aviator Arthur Butler who landed his small aeroplane near the village during his epic flight from London to Australia and taxied to the general store to refuel! He returned to Tooraweenah seven years later to establish an inland airmail and passenger service that linked the major outback settlements with Sydney.

One of the country's most physically and mentally taxing endurance rides takes place in Tooraweenah each April. Horse-riding enthusiasts throughout Australia and from overseas come to test their mettle on the gruelling 160-kilometre trail through the Warrumbungle Mountains, hoping to win the prized Tooraweenah Endurance Ride Buckle.

WARREN ■ 615

In the winter of 1818, Captain John Oxley led an expedition to explore the course of the Macquarie River and came to a halt at the Macquarie Marshes (see *Coonamble & Walgett*), about 120 kilometres below the present site of Warren. It was assumed he had stood on the edge of a vast inland sea, a theory that was later disproved by Captain Charles Sturt's expedition in the summer of 1828–29.

Following in the footsteps of Oxley and Sturt, came the eager droves of squatters who took up vast tracts of land for grazing sheep, cattle and horses. These early pastoralists left a legacy of some of the country's finest Merino sheep studs including Haddon Rig, Egelabra and Mumblebone, all of which are located in the Warren Shire.

At the centre of all this pastoral activity, a settlement grew up and was gazetted as the town of Warren in 1861. A post office and the town's first pub, the Traveller's Rest Hotel, were established in the same year.

By the time the train steamed into Warren in 1898, over sixty different business establishments were advertised in the town's local paper.

In recent years, the shire's traditional pastoral base has changed considerably, having been supplemented by a tremendous upsurge in agricultural activity, and much land has been given over to the cultivation of crops such as wheat and oats. The construction of the Burrendong Dam on the Macquarie River in 1967 has led to even further diversification of the shire's agricultural output with cotton, grain sorghum, maize and forage crops thriving on the region's irrigated plains.

With little in the way of commercial tourist attractions, Warren still holds appeal for those who find pleasure in peaceful rural pursuits. Anglers find good catches of cod, yellow-belly and bream in the Macquarie River, while canoeists dip their oars in its waters and campers pitch their tents beside the district's many waterways. *Population 2040*

TIGER BAY WILDLIFE PARK Officially opened on Australia Day in 1988, this park just east of the town is part of a natural overflow of the Macquarie River that has been enhanced to create a wetlands refuge for the preservation of the area's diverse birdlife and aquatic flora.

FESTIVALS Merino Cup, May

Rallying to the flag are Tooraweenah's 'Kookaburras', bound for Bathurst, then the First World War.

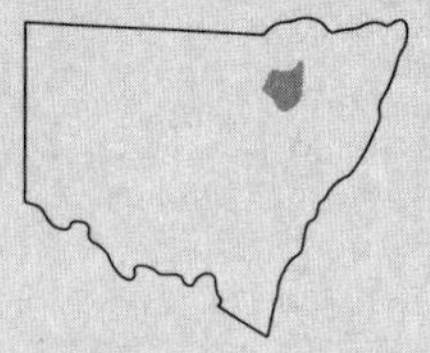

Narrabri & Wee Waa

The Narrabri Shire spans more than 14 000 square kilometres, ranging from the eerie peaks and spires of Mount Kaputar National Park to the flat, highly productive cotton fields of the Namoi Valley. In 1832, Sir Thomas Mitchell, trekked through the region in his search for the legendary inland sea.

AUSTRALIA TELESCOPE ■ 616

For twenty-four hours each day, the Australia Telescope facility at Culgoora has its 'ears' turned towards the dark depths of outer space. The radio telescope consists of five moveable dishes, twenty-two metres across, which rest on three kilometres of rail track, with a sixth placed three kilometres to the west. Each of these radio telescopes can 'listen in' to space individually, or operate as one six-kilometre-wide telescope. When linked with the sixty-four- metre telescope at Parkes, the observatory, in effect, becomes an observation device more than three hundred kilometres in diameter.

Opened as a bicentennial project in 1988, and operated by the CSIRO, the Culgoora observatory provides Australian scientists with one of the most versatile radio telescopes in the world. As well as linking in with the Parkes observatory, it can also join up with the telescope facility at Coonabarabran.

BAAN BAA ■ 617

The sleepy village of Baan Baa, with its historic pub and school house, springs into life for one special event each year – the action-packed gymkhana, held on the second Saturday in October.

The event has been run annually for over fifty years, and includes the wheat-lumpers derby, a sheaf-tossing championship, a tug-o-war and the muscle-flexing iron-man race. Participants join together afterwards for a barbecue at the local pub.

BOGGABRI ■ 618

A runaway convict called George Clark – nicknamed 'the barber' – was Boggabri's first white settler. He lived with the local Aborigines between 1826 and 1831 before being recaptured and sent to Norfolk Island. Two of the area's landmarks – Barber's Pinnacle and Barber's Lagoon – were named after him.

After hearing Clark's tales of a majestic river that supposedly spilled into a vast inland sea, Sir Thomas Mitchell explored the Boggabri area in 1832, camping within eight kilometres of the present town.

An earlier version of Boggabri was established on Gulligal lagoon, about fifteen kilometres from the present location. This was an important mail centre and Cobb & Co. stop, but it was left devastated by severe floods in 1864. After the deluge, the post office and other administrative buildings were moved to the present site of Boggabri. *Population 960*

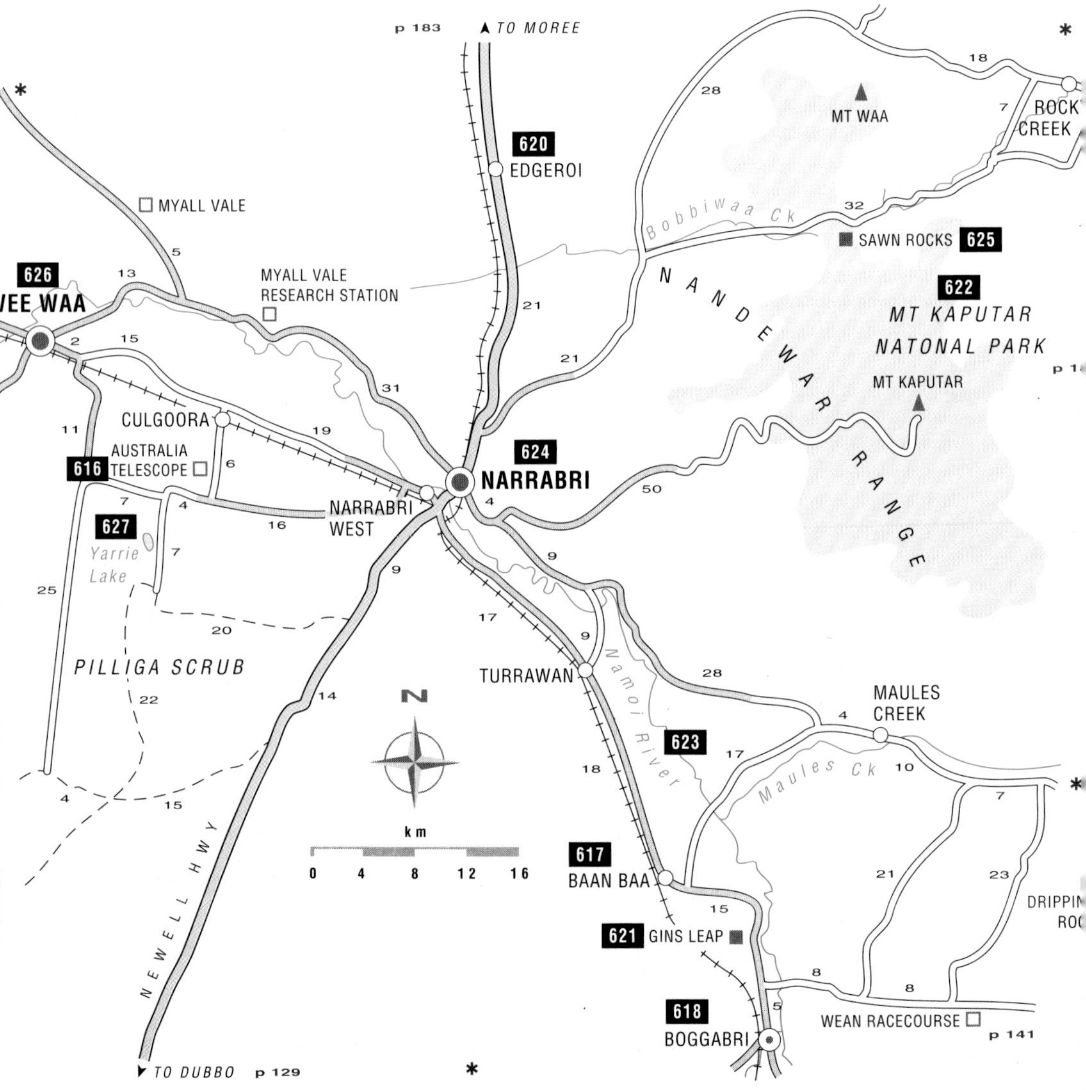

The 'full-burst' of these Namoi Valley cotton bolls means the April-May harvest is imminent.

CUTTABRI ■ 619

Cuttabri's claim to fame is its wine shanty, which, at the time of writing, had been operating in one form or another ever since it was established in about 1880. The shanty is believed to hold the second liquor licence issued in Australia. In its heyday, Cuttabri was also a stop on the Cobb & Co. coach line.

EDGEROI ■ 620

Edgeroi takes its name from an old station woolshed, the remains of which are located between Edgeroi and Bellata. The woolshed is now only a decayed relic of its former fifty-two sheep or 'stand' capacity.

Edgeroi, north of Narrabri, is one of the largest soldier-settlement subdivisions in New South Wales and came into being shortly after the Second World War.

GINS LEAP ■ 621

Legend has it that an Aboriginal girl was forced to jump to her death from the summit of Gins Leap after being chased there during a fight.

At the bottom of this sheer rock face is a vault, which contains the remains of two members of the D.W. Grover family who owned the Rock Inn, an early mail stop and changing station for Cobb & Co. coaches. Also buried here is a serving girl from the inn, who died in 1858.

MOUNT KAPUTAR NATIONAL PARK ■ 622

Often extolled as an 'ecological island' containing everything from rainforest to sub-alpine flora, the Mount Kaputar National Park is the lush remnant of a massive volcanic eruption eighteen million years ago. Mount Lindesay was probably the centre of the volcano, representing an eroded version of its former self. The park's oldest rocks go back more than two-hundred million years.

Covering more than 27 000 hectares, the Mount Kaputar National Park was established in 1959 from a reserve that had been set aside in 1925. The whole park is pockmarked by deep narrow gorges, precipitous cliffs and prominent rock formations such as Ningadhun. There are at least twenty peaks that exceed one thousand metres, including Mount Gratti, Mount Coryah and Mount Lindesay. From Mount Coryah there is an awe-inspiring view of the volcanic Yulladunida crater, considered by many to be the gem of the park.

NAMOI RIVER ■ 623

The first white man to explore the Namoi was the lone adventurer Alan Cunningham in 1827. The name of the river derives from one of two Aboriginal words: 'nynamu,' meaning 'breast', or 'ngnamai', or 'njamai', meaning 'place of the Nyamai tree'.

The Namoi River rises as the MacDonald River on the New England plateau, cutting a broad arc northwest before flowing into the Namoi River gorge. Just before it joins the gorge, the Macdonald River becomes the Namoi, flowing for about 850 kilometres past towns like Narrabri and Wee Waa.

Keepit Dam, on the Namoi River west of Tamworth, ensures year-round irrigation for the cotton, cereal and wheat fields of the lower Namoi valley. The dam was named after a sheep and cattle property that existed in the area in the 1830s.

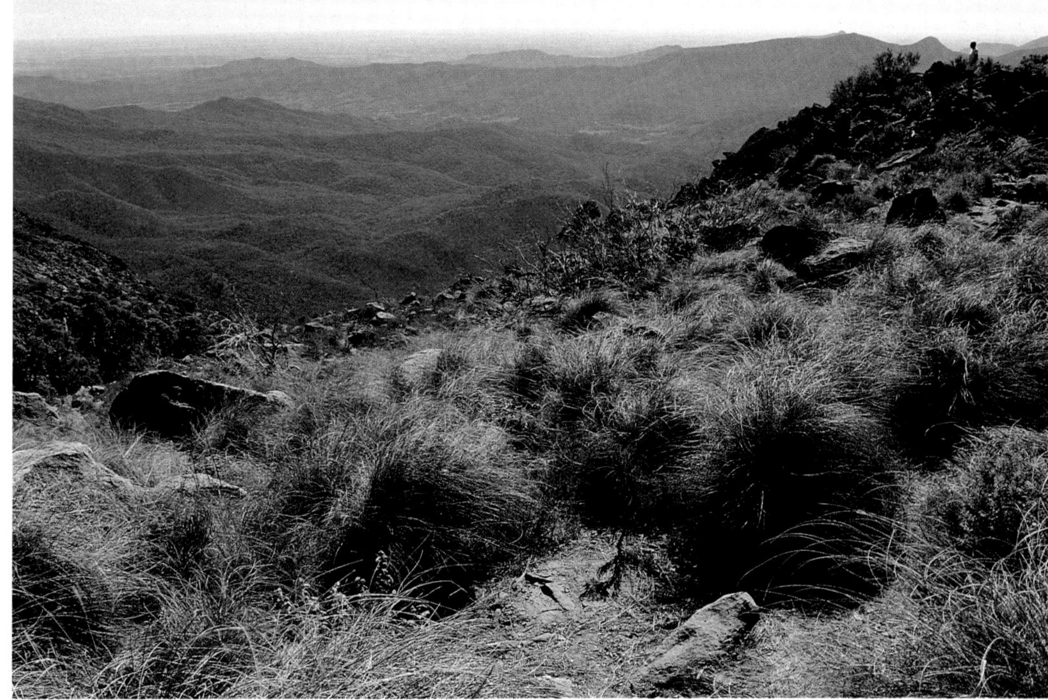

Legend has it that the 360-degree view from the top of the 1520-metre Mount Kaputar takes in almost one-tenth of New South Wales.

NARRABRI ■ 624

Nestled between the mighty Nandewar Range to the east and the Pilliga Scrub to the west, Narrabri has been described as one of the most picturesque inland towns in New South Wales. Located in the heart of the Namoi Valley, it is the second richest agricultural shire in Australia. Cotton, oilseed, cereals, wool, livestock and timber are a few of the primary industries which flourish here. The introduction of cotton in the 1960s had a dramatic impact which assured the town's financial future. Narrabri also boasts the largest oilseed mill in Australia.

Narrabri was named after an Aboriginal word said to mean 'forked stick' or 'meeting of the waters'. The first white person to reach Narrabri was probably Sir Thomas Mitchell who explored the area in 1832. Squatters moved in a year later; by the mid-1840s, another party of settlers had moved into the district and started leasing blocks of land. During the 1860s and 1870s, the town grew rapidly – a hospital was built (1864), a coach service was begun (1865) and a newspaper established (1873). The telegraph reached the town in 1869 and the railway twenty years later.

Today, Narrabri is the administrative centre of Narrabri Shire, and is one of the principal rail junctions of northern New South Wales. Three important scientific research stations are located in the district: the University of Sydney's Plant Breeding Institute and the CSIRO's Australia Telescope and Solar Observatory at Culgoora. *Population 6690*

SAWN ROCKS ■ 625

Sawn Rocks is a spectacular forty-metre-high basalt formation which resembles a series of organ pipes. This popular scenic attraction, located not far from Bingara Road, is made up of large chunks of basalt, which over thousands of years have fallen into the creek bed below, resulting in a scene that resembles the ruins of an ancient temple.

The almost perfect polygonal jointing is believed to have been caused by the very slow cooling of molten rock after volcanic activity some twenty million years ago. A picnic and barbecue area, together with a car park, are located a short walk from the site.

WEE WAA ■ 626

Wee Waa, hailed as the cotton capital of Australia, serves a rich and productive agricultural area. It has the distinction of being the first town to be developed on the Namoi River – it was originally the 'Wee Waa run,' opened up by George Hobler in 1837. Fifteen years later, the fledgling settlement was established as an administrative centre, with a constable and a Court of Petty Sessions – the magistrate came when there were sufficient cases to justify a visit. At first, neither a court house nor a jail was built, but the presence of law officers and the courts helped cement the future of the town. Wee Waa became headquarters of the Wee Waa police district, which stretched from parts of the Warrumbungle Range to the Nandewar Range. Despite this, the town's importance declined in the 1860s–70s, as various government functions were gradually transferred to Narrabri. The railway link was opened in 1903.

Cotton was first planted in the district in 1922, but it was not until the early 1960s, when an experienced American grower planted twenty-five hectares, that the industry began to flourish. Today, about 35 000 hectares – or approximately thirty per cent of Australia's cotton – are cultivated in the Namoi Valley. (The bulk of this is exported, principally to Japan and China.)

Today, Wee Waa continues to be a rural supply and service centre. Visits to the cotton fields are very popular, the best time of year to visit being in the picking and ginning season which extends from early April to the end of June.

The Cubbaroo winery, west of Wee Waa, claims to be the only property in the world to produce grapes, cotton and wheat side by side. But its wines alone are renowned for their excellence and the winery offers tastings at a licensed cellar, built around a one-hundred year-old wooden slab building. *Population 2030*

YARRIE LAKE ■ 627

Yarrie Lake is a short drive east of Wee Waa in the woodland known as the Pilliga Scrub. About one-and-half kilometres in diameter, the lake is shallow and limited to less than ten boats at a time – but remains popular for waterskiing and wind-surfing.

Condobolin & Trundle

Vast sheep runs opened up the geographical centre of New South Wales; the human population expanded in the late nineteenth and early twentieth centuries with amendments to the land laws and the discovery of gold and copper.

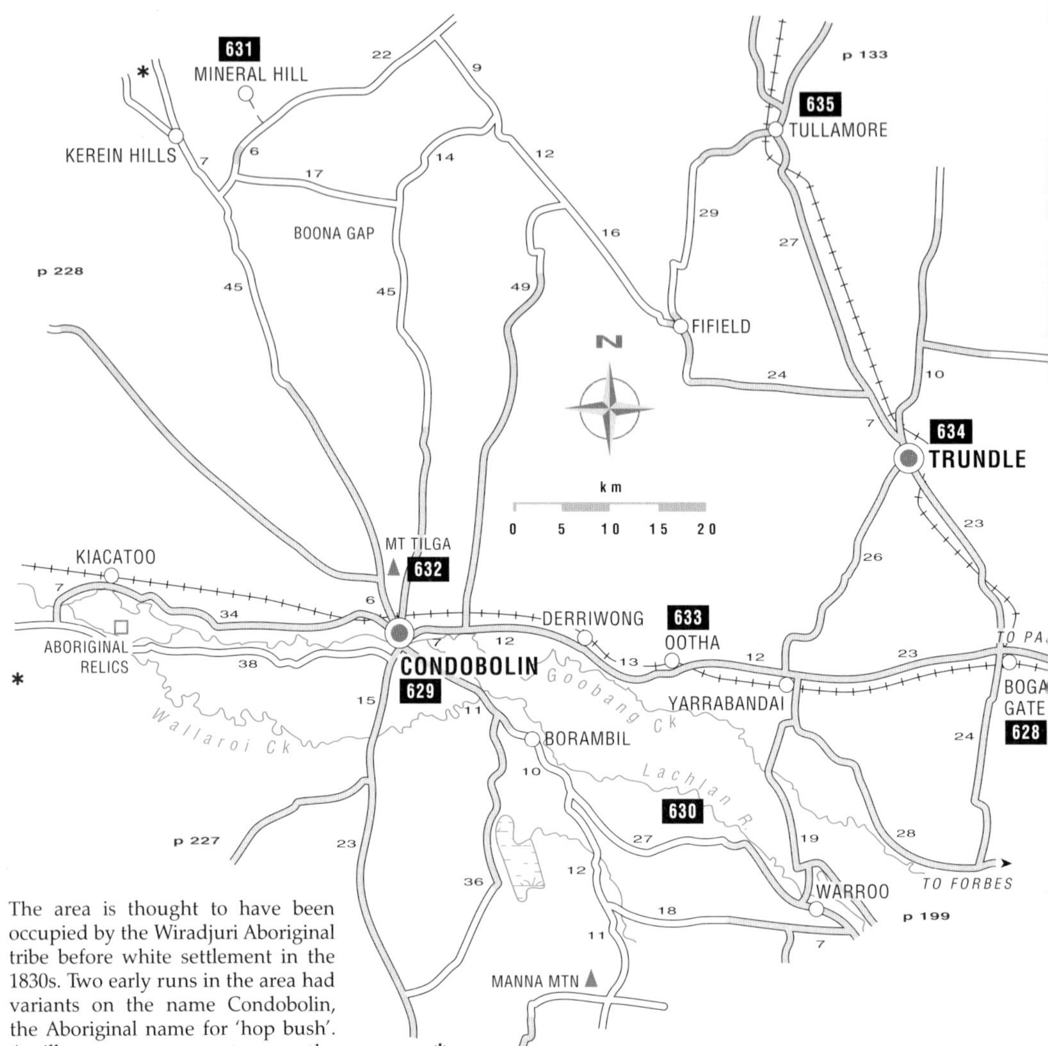

BOGAN GATE ■ 628

The gate between Burrawang and Gunningbland stations – which gave access to stock routes linking Forbes with the region known as Bogan country (after an Aboriginal word meaning 'birthplace of a great leader') – provided the name for this town. A small settlement initially grew up under a kilometre north of the gate but the town moved to its present site when the railway line was extended.

In the 1920s, its heyday, the town was graced with such amenities as a new brick-built hotel, a department store with eleven employees, stock and station agencies and a bank.

The town's population dwindled during the Great Depression when many residents moved to cities in search of work, and its importance as a commercial centre faded when motor transport was introduced.

CONDOBOLIN ■ 629

Condobolin, just under 500 kilometres by road west of Sydney, is at the geographical heart of New South Wales. Headquarters of the 15 000-square-kilometre Lachlan Shire, the town is the commercial centre for the essentially pastoral – wool, beef and wheat with some mining are the major industries here – district surrounding it.

Early explorers were John Oxley (1817), and the Surveyor-General Thomas Mitchell (1835), who suggested that the north side of Goobang Creek going west to its junction with the Lachlan – the site of Condobolin – was the most suitable for a road. Mitchell was correct in this and the railway and the main road to Condobolin follow – after much controversial discussion – this direct and usually flood-free route.

The area is thought to have been occupied by the Wiradjuri Aboriginal tribe before white settlement in the 1830s. Two early runs in the area had variants on the name Condobolin, the Aboriginal name for 'hop bush'. A village reserve was set up on the north bank of the Lachlan in 1853, and the town proclaimed six years later. For many years, Condobolin was little more than a stopping place for drovers moving cattle herds from northern and western stations to markets in Victoria.

The town took on a more permanent appearance in the 1880s, when a large landholding in the area was subdivided and sold, and copper and gold were discovered to the northwest, the gold at Overflow Station of *Clancy of the Overflow* fame.

The Great Condobolin Copper and Gold mines began operations in 1898 and continued for ten years. There is almost no commercial mining in the area today, but fossicking for gemstones, a growing tourist trade, is now allowed in some areas. Between 1898 and 1927, before the Sydney to Broken Hill line was completed, Condobolin became a major

An old barn at 'Burrawang' in the Ootha district, once part of a half-million-acre property, is based on the traditional barns of central Europe.

From the paddock, to the flour mill, to the baker...these central western farmers queue at the Bogan Gate rail junction to bring their wheat to market.

railhead for wool, wheat and sheep. In 1935, the Wyangala Dam across the Lachlan River was opened making intensive agriculture possible for a vast area (see *Cowra & Blayney*).

Condobolin became the centre for many Chinese who came to the area searching for gold in the 1800s. It was seen as a good place to settle as opportunities for farming were opening up and there were other Chinese communities at Forbes and West Wyalong. The Chinese organised workgangs for contract work such as ringbarking, fencing and dam sinking. A Chinatown of huts sprang up on both sides of the Goobang Creek, east of the town's centre, and this included a joss house (Chinese temple) with gold statues, carvings, incense burners and richly embroidered curtains. The old Chinese section of the Condobolin cemetery, which dates back to these days, has been restored

Today, Condobolin is a centre for soil conservation in the western part of the state. An agricultural research station east of the town conducts research into grains and livestock and alternative crops. To the west stand two large grain silos which hold more than two million bushels between them. Other smaller silos and a woolstore are in the centre of town. Historic buildings in the town include the court house and All Saints' Parish Church, built between 1875 and 1880.

A million-dollar sporting complex was opened in 1988, and Condobolin has become something of a centre for sport in western New South Wales. Car manufacturers such as Jaguar and Rover test their cars here and the town is the base for many major Australian car rallies. The district is also a popular location for filmmakers and productions such as *1915*, *Hunger* and *The Crossing* were shot here. *Population 3160*

ABORIGINAL GRAVE The burial place of one of the last Aboriginal leaders in the area is about forty kilometres west of Condobolin. Tribal tradition has it that he was drowned while trying to cross the Lachlan in flood. The grave, discovered by explorer John Oxley in 1817, was a cone-like mound decorated with Aboriginal paintings with low, curved mounds thought to be for seating each side of it. Although the original grave is no longer visible, the site has been marked by a copy of the Aboriginal totem which stood there. A memorial to Oxley is nearby.

A second Aboriginal site is at Manna Mountain to the south. These rock waterholes have a permanent water supply and were frequented regularly by the Aborigines of this region. There are also rocks specially grooved for sharpening tools while others are shaped for grinding seeds.

LACHLAN RIVER ■ 630

The Lachlan River, chief tributary of the Murrumbidgee River, winds for an estimated 1500 kilometres across-New South Wales.

The Wyangala Dam on the Lachlan (see *Cowra & Blayney*) has made extensive irrigation possible, particularly on the plains west of Forbes and east of Condobolin. Discovered by George William Evans in 1815, the river was later more fully explored by John Oxley who almost reached its junction with the Murrumbidgee River, but turned back because of the difficulties of crossing the low-lying, marshy country

MINERAL HILL ■ 631

When gold and copper were first discovered in the early 1900s, a village quickly grew up and thrived here. Eighty-odd years later, the open-cut mine was re-opened for a time when modern machinery made extraction an economical operation.

Another historic mining area is around the town of Fifield, west of Trundle and Tullamore. Most of Australia's magnesite, (an ore derived from magnesium and used in fertilisers, cement and insulation products) came from the Fifield mine, before it closed down in the 1980s. The hotel is the only business in Fifield, as the miners lived in neighbouring towns.

MOUNT TILGA ■ 632

Eight kilometres north of Condobolin is Mount Tilga, which has the distinction of being recognised as the geographical centre of New South Wales. A fifteen-minute climb to the summit leads to the survey mark which indicates the exact spot.

OOTHA ■ 633

The settlement of Ootha and surrounding district probably dates from 1893 when undeveloped land from the Big Burrawang Station was sold. Up until then, the area was divided between a few men with large land holdings. The first owner of the 'Burrawang' run was thought to be Thomas Kite. This and other runs were bought by Thomas Edols and William Dennis and named 'Burrawang' in the 1870s.

Christened the 'Big Burrawang' by locals, stories abound about the sheer size (around 208 000 hectares)scale and efficiency of the station. Folklore has it that the station singlehandedly supplied the town of Ootha during the 1901–02 drought, although there is little hard evidence to support this...but there is little doubt that Thomas Edols was a progressive owner and he built the first, and by far the largest, shearing shed in the district, with space for eighty shearers, and a washpool for sheep on the banks of the Lachlan.

Many of the smaller early farms in the area were not successful, and that probably helped foster the strong spirit of self-help and co-operation in residents of Ootha and nearby villages such as Derriwong. In 1910, the first agricultural bureau was formed at Ootha to help farmers exhange ideas on how to improve farming. Today, Ootha is a railway village of six or seven houses, without shops or school.

TRUNDLE ■ 634

William Cummings, an early landowner in the area, is thought to have named his run after an outer London suburb, since submerged in the urban sprawl. The namesake, however, owes its name more directly to a lagoon just below the town where the golfcourse now stands, as the first post office (1887) was known as Trundle Lagoon.

The area began to be settled after the 1884 Land Act and by the time the Goobang Shire was formed, the town had two hotels, a bank and a thriving shopping centre. A building boom followed the opening of the rail link. Wheat is still the main crop and Trundle is a very large wheat storage depot. *Population 550*

TULLAMORE ■ 635

First called Bullock Creek, this town was renamed Tullamore at the insistence of the town's hotel owner, George Tully. The town was gazetted in 1910, when the rail line was extended. Two of the first settlers in the area were Norman and Ernest Gatenby who bought a large run which they called 'Burra Burra'. At the turn of the century, Norman Gatenby bought several runs including the Jemalong Station on the Lachlan River. The privately owned homestead and quarters at 'Jemalong', are today considered worthy of preservation. Gatenby's land holdings were reduced over the years and in 1956 'Burra Burra' was subdivided for soldier settlement.

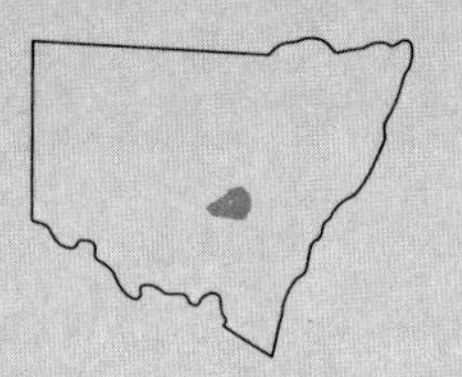

Parkes & Forbes

The Aborigines – some of whom stayed on in tribal remnants until the turn of the century – were the only people who knew this region better than Ben Hall and his mates who looked for easy pickings from the the miners who came to join the gold rush.

Lake Cowal's distinction as the largest natural lake in NSW is based on its surface area – shallow, and fed only by creeks, it contains a relatively small amount of water.

ALECTOWN ■ 636
Originally called Alec's Flat, the village was named, not after one man, but three – the Alexanders, Cameron, Patton and Whitelaw. Coincidentally, the three Alecs were the first prospectors in what proved to be a very short-lived gold boom in Alectown in the 1860s.

After the diggers moved on, Alectown became the northern boundary of one of the largest stations in the area, 'Coobang', which covered almost 30 000 hectares between Parkes and Alectown just prior to resumption of the land for closer settlement in 1884. Today, Alectown is a small village on the Newell Highway, ringed by the hills of the Cookamobil and Curumbenya ranges, and best known for the large CSIRO radiotelescope about ten kilometres south of the village (see box).

BURCHER ■ 637
Burcher missed out on the gold rushes although, in 1905, Harry Kaiser did discover a little gold in what was to become known as Kaiser's Hill. When Kaiser moved on, he left his tent behind to avoid disturbing the swallow which had nested on his tent pole. His companion Harry Leadbitter had no luck at all with gold but did find a source of pipeclay much favoured by the local housewives for whitening fireplaces.

Burcher's fortunes were founded on the railway not on gold. In 1930, a railway terminus called Euglo Siding, named after a local property called 'Euglo', meaning 'pleasant place', was built. By 1936, in the days before postcodes, complaints about mail going to Eulo in Queensland led to a change of name to Burcher, after Charles Burcher, a former owner of Euglo Station. The local farmers turned out with horses and scoops to help dig the tracks and when the railway, with the turntable on which the engines were reversed, was completed, some of the fettlers stayed on to farm. Stock destined for Flemington and Newmarket, wheat, wool and timber were sent by rail from Burcher, where wheat silos and trucking yards with regular sheep sales developed to service the district.

EUGOWRA ■ 638
When, in 1815, George Evans crossed the Lachlan River where it meets Mandagery Creek south-west of Eugowra, he marked a tree to record the occasion. The tree was later removed for safekeeping to Sydney but in 1915, to record the centenary of the event, a monument was unveiled in Eugowra – the scene of the actual crossing being too prone to flooding.

The village sits at the foot of the Eugowra Hills and has passed into the history books – and into legend – as the site of Australia's only gold escort robbery. On 15 June 1862, the gold being transported under armed guard from Eugowra to the railhead at Penrith was robbed at Escort Rock three kilometres east of Eugowra. Having waylaid two earlier teams as they passed the rock, and using their waggons as a barricade, the eight bushrangers, including Johnny Gilbert, Frank Gardiner, Johnny O'Meally and – probably – Ben Hall, hid behind the rocks.

As the Cobb & Co. mail coach came round the bend in the road to be confronted by the waggons, it slowed to a walking pace. The eight bushrangers, with blackened faces and red scarves hiding the lower part of their faces, opened fire, wounding two of the escort and causing the horses to rear, overturning the coach. After returning fire, the escort 'retired' from the scene, leaving the raiders to make off with the iron boxes and mailbags containing 14 000 pounds' worth of gold. The police weapons and coats which were taken, were a small bonus.

By 1866, the miners had moved on, the bushrangers were in prison or in their graves and the population of Eugowra had been reduced to twenty-four permanent citizens.

Modern Eugowra is a small country town on the branch rail line from Cowra with a sawmill and granite works. Only a small plaque near the Escort Rock, which is on private property, commemorates the Eugowra gold robbery. *Population 570*

FORBES ■ 639
When John Oxley passed what was to become the town site of Forbes in 1817, he named it, rather prosaically, Camp Hill. The early squatters in the 1830s knew it by the name of what was then the largest run, 'Bogabigal'. The post office originally knew it as Black Ridge and it was left to the gold miners and others who flocked to the district in 1861 to come up with a name that stuck. They chose to name the town after Sir Frances Forbes, the first Chief Justice of New South Wales who insisted that all free men were entitled to normal privileges regardless of previous status, which would doubtless have appealed to those on the goldfields.

In 1861, the year that gold was discovered in what is now the town's King George V Park, the population leapt from 124 to 30 000 but by 1863, with the rush to the New Zealand goldfields, the population had declined to 3500. Not all mining ceased, however, since as late as 1915, there were still eight mining companies operating in Forbes. By 1870, when Forbes was declared a municipality, its wealth rested primarily on sheep – 200 000 were shorn each year at one station alone. In 1872, the first sheepdog trials in Australia, and possibly in the world, were held at Forbes. Wheat was processed at local flour mills from 1872 or was transported by teams to the railway station from 1893. Fruit and vines were later added to the primary products and although the infant vines were almost wiped out by the *Phylloxera* virus in the late nineteenth century, the industry has survived.

So, too, has the historic heritage of Forbes, and a surprising number of historic buildings have been preserved despite the development that has made it one of the major towns in the Lachlan region. *Population 7550*

VANDENBERG HOTEL Originally called the Court House Hotel – in about 1880 – the Vandenberg, with its grand gardens, fountain and private coach to meet guests at the railway station catered to a different clientele from the nearby Albion Hotel, which took more money across the bar in the gold rush days than any other hotel in the colony.

LACHLAN VINTAGE VILLAGE On an eighty-hectare site on the old Britannia goldfield, the village, with its own 'population', farm animals and narrow-gauge steam railway, recreates village life during the years between 1860 and 1900.

FESTIVALS Easter Gold Rush; Harvest Festival, December.

GUNNINGBLAND ■ 640

The small village of Gunningbland was never the site of gold mining but some of the more interesting aspects of its history are indirectly related to gold. Gunningbland Station was held in the early 1840s by William Tom and his two eldest sons, who were the first to drive cattle from drought-ridden New South Wales across the Australian Alps to Gippsland. It was William Tom (junior) and his brother James who, with Lister, found gold at Ophir in 1851.

The grave of Ben Hall – shot after a three-year criminal career – remained unmarked for many years.

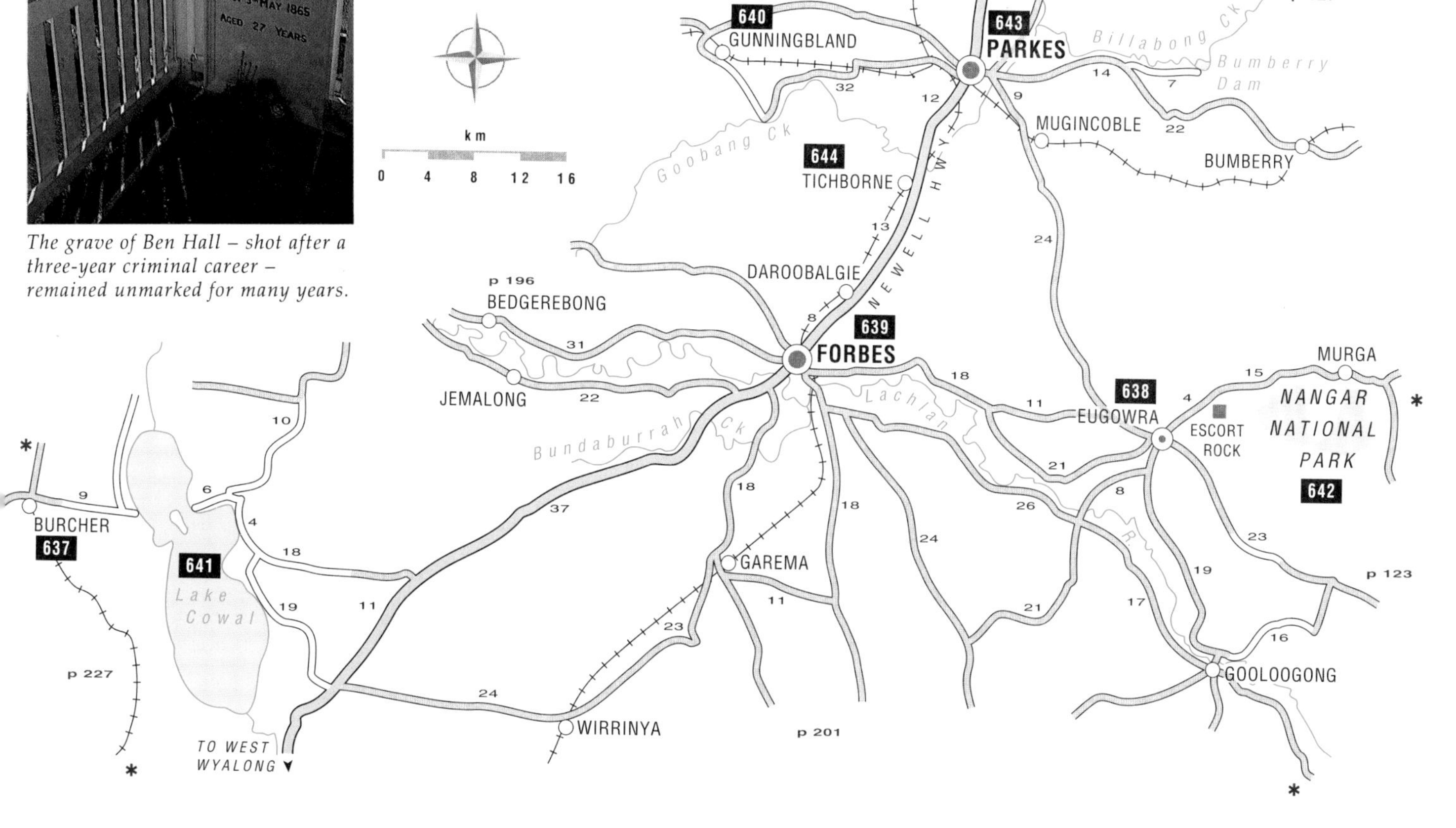

Just south of Gunningbland, on Goobang Creek, lived Mick Connolly, known to some as 'Goobang Mick', who acted as an informant for Ben Hall and his fellow bushrangers. When Ben Hall came to the Connolly home in 1865 to ask 'Goobang Mick' to withdraw money from the bank at Forbes, it was possible that Hall was intending to leave Australia. When he bedded down for the night at Goobang Creek, he was unaware that Connolly had betrayed him and that the police were already there waiting for morning. Wounded when the first shots were fired, Ben Hall begged to be killed…and there's no doubt he was – according to legend there were thirty-five bullet holes in his body.

LAKE COWAL ■ 641

Lake Cowal has the distinction of being the largest natural lake in New South Wales and the breeding ground for thousands of water birds. The branches of the dead red gums that protrude from the waters of the lake make ideal dry perches for breeding birds – and suggest that the water was much less saline in the past. The lake is now a bird 'sanctuary'…but is opened to shooters in the duck-shooting season.

It was said by the early settlers that the banks of Lake Cowal supported 'a quarter of a sheep and five thousand rabbits to the acre' and the banks, honeycombed with warrens, were netted in the 1880s. It was inevitable that such a body of water would arouse speculation about its possible use for agriculture, mining, industry and water supply. Most of these ideas came to nothing although when the lake dries up, crops such as wheat are planted in the lake bed. Lake Cowal's potential for supplying water for West Wyalong was rejected in 1895 for a number of reasons including its comparative shallowness, its propensity to dry up and the 'wild fowl excrement, weeds etc. (that) would probably choke the pipe which would be laid in the lake'.

The lake provides a natural basin for floodwater and runoff from the surrounding mountains. It is fed by a number of creeks, mainly Bland and Gorringal creeks from the south and Yeo Yeo Creek from the north. Flood-mitigation work on the Lachlan River means that floodwaters from this source no longer enter the lake as they did until 1917.

NANGAR NATIONAL PARK ■ 642

The Aboriginal name for this park means 'bold mountain' or 'red rocks' both of which are accurate descrip-

The optimism of the 'boom' years of the 1800s is reflected in Forbes' grandiose Victorian architecture.

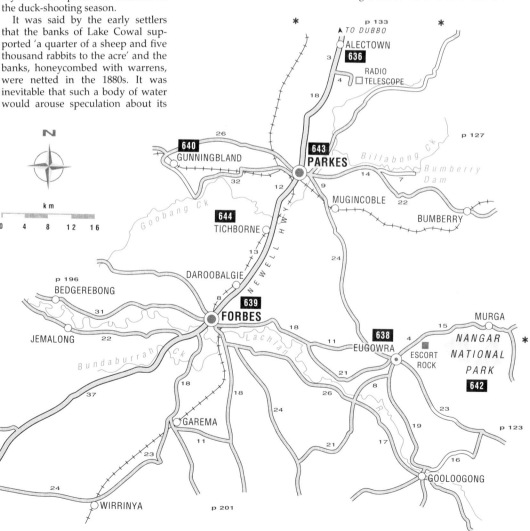

IN AN OLD SHEEP PADDOCK, AN EAR COCKED TO THE UNIVERSE

THE CSIRO'S spectacular Parkes Radio-telescope is, geographically speaking, the Alectown Radio-telescope. The small village of Alectown (see entry) north of Parkes, was chosen as the telescope site because it was accessible from Sydney, while being far enough away from the city to be free of radio-wave interference and on a flat plain not often subject to high winds.

When it was opened in 1961, the radio-telescope was the second such large telescope built (the first being Britain's Jodrell Bank). It was designed in England with advice from the highly inventive Sir Barnes Wallis, the designer of the 'Dambusters' bouncing bomb. The sixty-four-metre-diameter dish was built in Germany and put together on site during the hours of darkness – not for reasons of secrecy, but to avoid the contractions and expansions of the metal caused by changing daytime temperatures, which would compromise the accuracy of the telescope. The final cost was shared by the Commonwealth Government, and the United States-based Carnegie Corporation and the Rockefeller Foundation.

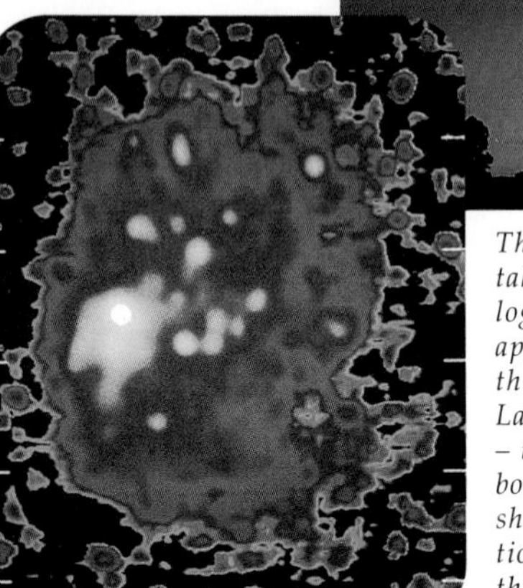

The beauties of the night sky take on a different and technological but still beautiful appearance when 'seen' through a radio-telescope. The Large Magellanic Cloud (left) – the nearest universal neighbour to earth's galaxy – is shown to be emitting radiation of different intensities by the varying colours in this 'picture' taken at Parkes.

The telescope was responsible for pinpointing the position of the first known quasar (quasi-stellar object) and has discovered a large proportion of the known pulsars (small stars that produce 'flashes' of radio waves). It also received the data from the Giotto probe sent to study Halley's comet in 1986, and from the Voyager spacecraft which 'flew' past Uranus in the same year, and Neptune in 1989. Before that, the Parkes Radio Telescope was used during a number of Apollo voyages, to monitor such things as biomedical data on astronauts in orbit.

When oxygen tanks blew up in the command module of Apollo 13, NASA receivers were installed at Parkes within six hours to re-establish weak but audible voice communications. Many of the images of the first moon landing were relayed through Parkes to an audience of 600 million television viewers in 49 countries; in return, Parkes was able to mount a display of moonrocks collected from the Sea of Tranquility by Neil Armstrong and 'Buzz' Aldrin.

It is the more specialised and less publicised technical work of the Parkes Radio-telescope in monitoring and measuring the universe which made it a pioneer facility in the 1960s. Today, it forms a major link in the 'Australia Telescope', a set of eight dishes which span 320 kilometres of New South Wales, and it takes part in telescope networks that cover the globe. □

tions of this relatively inaccessible wilderness. Nangar National Park encompasses Mount Nangar (770 metres) and the smaller eminence of Murga Mountain, which meet in a central horseshoe of cliffs. The sedimentary rocks of the cliffs include layers of shale, conglomerate, heavily rippled siltstone...and distinctive red sandstone.

Public access to the 3500-hectare park, which was gazetted in 1983, is still limited by the private properties and Nangar State Forest that surround most of it. Although the plains have been used by Aborigine and European alike, the mountainous areas have generally attracted only desperate bushrangers seeking a hideout or, in modern times, adventurous bushwalkers.

PARKES ■ 643

When Thomas Mitchell passed through this district in 1835, there were already squatters around what was to become Parkes but it remained sparsely settled until 1862 when James Pugh discovered gold at 'Currajong' just north of Parkes. A village grew up around the Currajong diggings until the reef gold ran out in 1867.

In 1871, alluvial gold was found at a number of sites south of the old Currajong diggings including 'Bushman's', which became the name of the small settlement that grew up around this second goldrush. It was during 'Bushman's' early days, that Henry Parkes, at that time Premier of the colony of New South Wales, visited the diggings and the name of the town was changed to Parkes to commemorate his visit. This second gold rush was to be more long lasting than the first, with fairly extensive mining continuing until 1914. BHP still operates two gold mines just outside the town – the most recent opened in 1994 – as well as copper mines established in the 1980s.

Even from its early days, Parkes did not rely on gold alone. The first wheat was planted, in 1865, at Currajong when the local storekeeper provided seed and expenses to Joseph Harris who supplied almost one hectare of land...and labour – the wheat was taken to Orange for milling. Since these small beginnings, Parkes has become the major wheat-storage centre for the western district with the first wheat silo opening in 1921 and the well-known Mugincoble storage facility opening in 1952. At one time the largest wooden-frame building in the Southern Hemisphere, the Mugincoble structure has been replaced by an American-style computerised wheat storage 'tank farm'.

The coming of the railway to Parkes in 1893, and the town's emergence as a major rail centre is thought to be due in part to the influence of Henry Parkes who did not forget the honour which had been bestowed upon him. The opening of the line to Broken Hill in 1927 and the completion of the standard gauge rail line to Perth in 1969 channelled even more rail traffic through Parkes, including the transcontinental Indian-Pacific train. The town's position as a major transport centre was further enhanced in 1989 when the Inland Port road–rail interchange was opened by the Premier. The new facilities allow for loads brought by road to Parkes to be offloaded straight onto flat-top rail trucks for the journey to Perth. *Population 8780*

PARKES CEMETERY Buried in the local cemetery are Ben Hall's brother, Billy Hall, who was active in the Salvation Army for many years and his son, Ben Hall, who was the court bailiff in Parkes until his death in 1938.

FESTIVALS Jazz Triduum, June; Country Music Jamboree, October.

TICHBORNE ■ 644

The intriguingly named 'Tichborne' and 'The Wapping Butcher' were two of the major goldbearing lodes near this small village. Both names were associated with the Tichborne inheritance case in the headlines at that time as a butcher from Wagga Wagga was pursuing his claim to be the missing heir to a British fortune.

The village is now a small service centre for the surrounding district and was the domain of the last known wild koalas in the region, which survived until the 1930s.

MCGUIGANS The site of an earlier gold rush just north of Tichborne, McGuigans was named after Peter McGuigan who discovered a large amount of gold in 1874 on a field long thought exhausted. Enough miners returned from Palm River in Queensland and elsewhere to support eight hotels, a brewery and a post office from late 1874 to early 1876 when the second exodus came. Even for a ghost town theres is an ultra-ghostly quality about McGuigans – hardly a reminder of the bustling gold rush days remains.

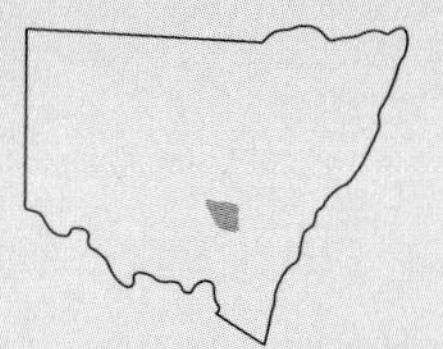

Young & Grenfell

This region of wild mountain ranges and intensively cultivated plains was the home ground of the bushranging Lachlan men. The diggings that were the birthplace of the poet Henry Lawson, and the scene of violent anti-Chinese riots have now given way to stone-fruit orchards and vineyards.

BRIBBAREE ■ 645

Steel Caldwell, one of the earliest settlers in the Bland district had a number of properties including 'Bribera' or 'Bribbaree'. He was the first settler to ringbark trees in the region...and the first to use glass in the windows of his home. John Byrne, the pioneer settler of the village of Bribaree lived with his wife and family in a more basic bag humpy when he first arrived in 1915. He built the first house in the village in 1916, the year the village was surveyed by the Lands Department.

Gold was discovered just outside Bribbaree in 1922 and the rich 'Golden Lamb' mine yielded ninety-eight ounces of gold in the first year and was then taken over by the Bribbaree Combined Company, which extracted 300 ounces from crushing in 1924.

Three of the four churches in the village sit companionably side by side separated only by their respective clergy's homes.

CARAGABAL ■ 646

The name of this small village comes from an Aboriginal word Karagbillika meaning 'to spit' and perhaps refers to the intermittent water supply in Caragabal Creek. The early settlers built unusual, leg-of-mutton-shaped tanks for water storage, often protected from evaporation by a rough shelter of saplings and bark.

Linked by the railway to Forbes and Cootamundra, Caragabal also lies on the main road from Hay to Bathurst. The first task in constructing the Mid-Western Highway in the 1930s was the construction of almost the entire road from Caragabal, west to Hay, which enhanced Caragabal's position as a small rural centre.

CONIMBLA NATIONAL PARK ■ 647

Together with Weddin Mountains and Nangar national parks, Conimbla National Park preserves what little is left of the wilderness that used to cover the central western slopes before European settlement.

The park is in two separate sections, with access provided by two different roads. The eastern section, comprising what was Kangarooby State Forest, supplemented by vacant Crown Land and leasehold land, was gazetted in 1980 and the western section, the former Yambira State Forest, was gazetted two years later.

The total area of 7590 hectares is primarily on a plateau but also contains a steep escarpment of red cliffs on the western boundary and Barabigal Mountain (621 metres) in the eastern section. Vegetation ranges from open forest and shrubs to more than 100 species of spring wildflowers. Two walking trails and two picnic areas are the park's only facilities.

GRENFELL ■ 648

In 1833, John Butler Wood, his brother Joseph George Wood and their father came to the site of what is now Grenfell from Parramatta, looking for good livestock-grazing land. Local Aborigines directed them to 'Booroodeen', meaning 'the windy place'. Their selection – and eventually the district surrounding it – was known by the slightly more anglicised name of Brundah. Sheep, cattle and horses were the mainstay of this pastoral district until 1866.

In that year, Cornelius O'Brien, one of John Butler Wood's shepherds on Brundah, discovered gold in a heap of quartz and registered his claim in Young. The local *Burrangong Argus* publicised his claim and miners poured into the area. The tent village that grew up was about to be gazetted as Emu Creek when an incident occurred at Narromine that was to change the minds of those responsible in the Surveyor-General's office. Bushrangers held up the mail coach at Narromine but as fate would have it, one of the passengers was the for-

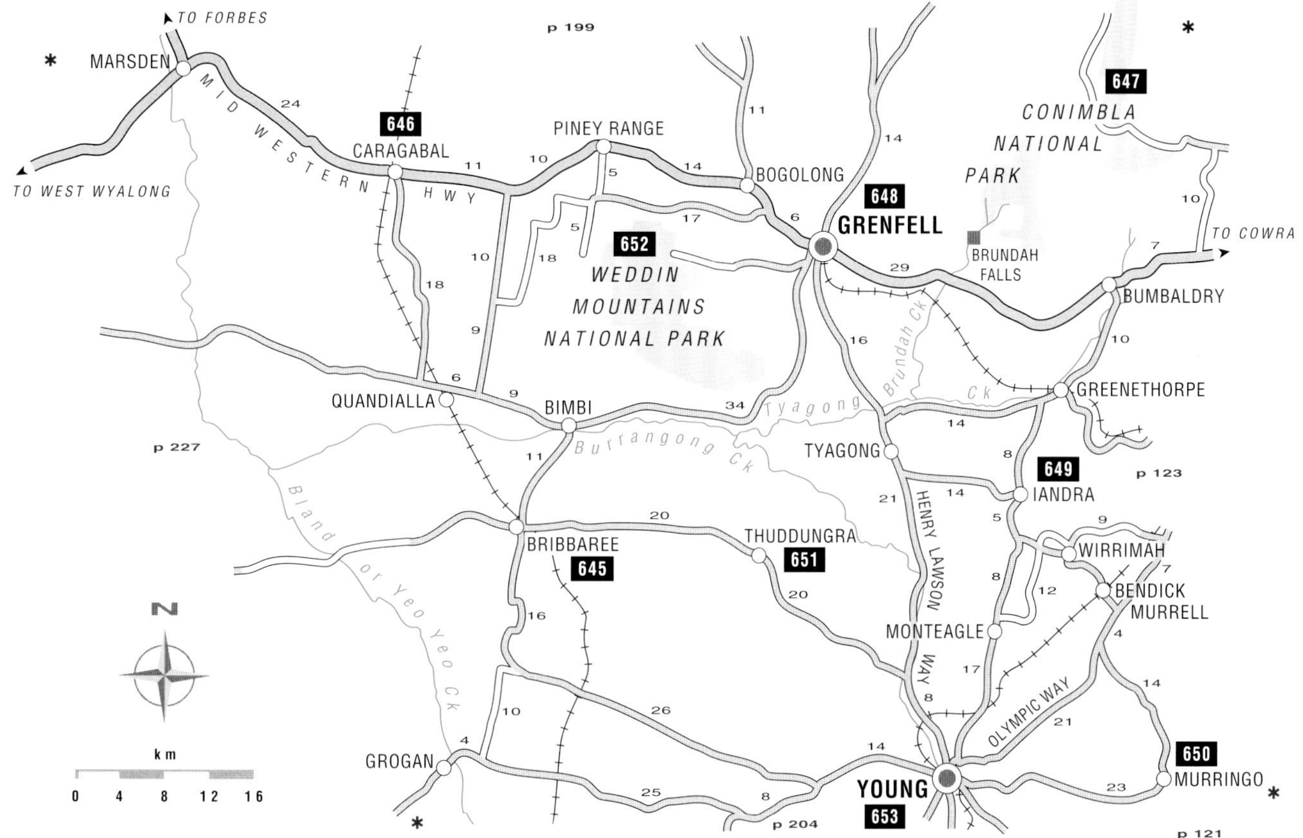

The Murringo glass artist Helmut Hiebl used two different kinds of glass, engraving one of them, to give this vase its cameo appearance.

mer Gold Commissioner and current Commissioner of Crown Lands, John Granville Grenfell, who, armed with his own gun, attempted to resist the 'bail up' and was killed in the ensuing gunfire. Emu Creek then became Grenfell. The Grenfell goldfields lasted for ten years and in that time, produced three million dollars worth of gold, including the highest production of gold in New South Wales in 1870–71. Ben Hall had taken up Wheogo Station, north-west of the town in the late 1850s. It was supposedly the persecution, wrongful arrest and consequent burning of this farm that turned the law-abiding citizen into the infamous bushranger of the early 1860s. Henry Lawson was born, quite humbly, in a tent on the Grenfell goldfields where his father Niels Hertzberg Larsen – Peter Lawson – was part-owner of a mine. He spent only the first six months of his life in Grenfell before his family moved to Eurunderee (see *Mudgee & Gulgong*) but his memorial at Grenfell, erected two years after Lawson's death in 1922, was the first of many Lawson memorials in the state. The memorial reads in part:

Though you sing of dear old Mudgee
And the home of Pipeclay Flat
You were born on Grenfell Goldfield –
And you can't get over that.

More poignant is the gravestone of the three Turland children who died of diphtheria on the road to the diggings at Forbes.

By the time the gold had run out and the diggers, including the Lawsons, had moved on, wheat had emerged as the town's main product and, despite a series of fires that devastated the original business centre on George Street, Grenfell grew and was declared a municipality in 1883 – one of the smallest municipalities in area in the state at that time. The coming of the railway in 1901 and the building of the first wheat silo in 1921 confirmed Grenfell's role as a town built to last. *Population 2040*

FESTIVALS Henry Lawson Festival of the Arts, June.

IANDRA ■ 649

Part of John Butler Wood's original Brundah Station (see Grenfell), 'Iandra' was bought by George Henry Greene in 1878 and Greene's pioneering approach to productivity was to score a number of agricultural firsts. 'Iandra' was the first property to introduce share farming to the western wheat districts; it was used for the first large-scale testing of Farrer's rust-resistant Federation strain of wheat; it was the first property to send 100 000 bags of wheat to market in one season and it was the first property to net for rabbits.

In 1891, James Huckle was to become the first sharefarmer who planted, sowed and harvested wheat on land cleared by and with seed supplied by Greene. The wheat was shared equally by farmer and landholder...except in bad years when the first five bushels (one-fifth of a cubic metre) went to the farmer and the rest was then divided equally. By 1896, almost 40 000 hectares at 'Iandra' was share farmed and other land-holders in the region followed Greene's lead. Greene built a model village at Greenethorpe to house his sharefarmers and was accused of undue influence when, during his term of office as a member of the Legislative Assembly, the Young–Grenfell railway route was redirected through Greenethorpe, from which 'Iandra' wheat was then railed.

In addition to his influence on agriculture in the region, Greene also left an unusual architectural heritage – Iandra Castle, the last of a series of homesteads. The reinforced concrete and brick 'castle' is of unusual design and was built at a cost of $100 000 by craftsmen brought from England. The fifty-seven rooms, with the luxuries of hot and cold water and exquisite panelling were never used for the lavish entertainment for which Greene built them, since he died shortly after the castle's completion. In the 1950s, the Methodist Church acquired the homestead and 350 hectares of land, which they ran for some time as the Iandra Rural Training Centre for Boys. The castle is now privately owned.

MURRINGO ■ 650

'Marengo' was originally owned by two Sydney merchants and was certainly in existence by the early 1830s when John White, walking to fetch his wife from the station, wandered off the track and was killed by wild dogs. John Scarr of Campbelltown owned 'Marengo' in 1848 when the village site was surveyed on its southern boundary where tracks to five neighbouring properties met. A brick cottage, dairy, woolshed and blacksmith's, the only buildings in the village of Murringo when it was gazetted in 1850, belonged to Scarr. The rather grandiose town plans covered a larger area than the actual village ever did since, with the establishment of Lambing Flat (Young) in the 1860s, many of the roles initially planned for Murringo were usurped by Young.

John Gilbert worked in Murringo as a stockman in the early 1860s before graduating to the more lucrative trade of bushranging. Daniel Crotty, the mailman, leaving Murringo with a packhorse of mail in 1862, was bailed up and killed by three French-speaking bushrangers who had come to the Australian goldfields from their native New Caledonia. Charles Robardy and Auguste Rivet were arrested in the Forbes goldfields soon after, but Jacques Etienne evaded capture for six years before being picked up at the Araluen goldfields.

Just as Johnny Gilbert and the three French bushrangers moved on to other pastures, so too did the majority of the travellers and diggers who journeyed through Murringo.

Some of the earliest buildings and earliest European graves in the district can still be found at Murringo. The historic village found a new use for the old blacksmith's smithy and home, as workshops for artists and craftsmen, including Helmet Hiebl, the internationally renowned glassblower and crystal designer who designed one of his native Austria's official gifts for Queen Elizabeth II.

THUDDUNGRA ■ 651

Thuddungra, from an Aboriginal word said to mean 'water rushing down', was an apt name for a settlement that grew up around Cudgell Creek, which was visited in the 1870s by the Bland squatters when the Bland or Yeo Yeo Creek dried up. The early settlers grew fruit and vegetables but had their first post office for one month only, when the publican who ran it left the village.

In 1931, a magnesite mine was established in the village and the

The countryside around Murringo was once the domain of bushrangers who preyed on the nearby goldfields.

ATTACKS ON THE CHINESE DIGGERS SETS THE STAGE FOR 'WHITE AUSTRALIA'

LONG before the late twentieth century, a volatile, multicultural Australia sprang up briefly on the busy ant-heaps that were the goldfields of the 1800s and 1860s. The largest group of 'ethnic' miners were the Chinese and they did not always have it easy.

Grievances against the Chinese on Australia's goldfields were not unique to Lambing Flat; complaints, imagined or otherwise, ranged from their 'personal habits' to their alleged misuse of scarce water but simple racism and envy of Chinese persistence and success at supposedly worked-out diggings were probably the major factors. At Lambing Flat, these grievances spilled over into a series of violent attacks on the minority Chinese population, aimed at expelling them by force from the diggings.

The dramatic clash between anti-Chinese European diggers – who rallied behind a makeshift flag (right) – and troopers in June 1861 was depicted graphically in a Sydney Mail *sketch in 1935.*

A number of increasingly widespread and violent attacks on the Chinese from November 1860 led to cavalry troops and artillery being sent to Lambing Flat in March 1861. At the same time, the Chinese were confined to an area of the diggings known as Blackguards Gully, separated from the other diggers by a furrow; the Premier of the colony promised the passage of legislation to restrict Chinese miners.

In June 1861, the miners at Lambing Flat heard that the Premier's planned legislation had failed and that 1500 Chinese had landed at Sydney, heading for Lambing Flat. Thousands of men, accompanied by a band, marched to Blackguards Gully, behind a flag made from a canvas tent flap bordered with lace and with the message 'Roll Up, Roll Up: No Chinese' embroidered on it. Using whips, sticks and knives with which pigtails and ears were cut off, the miners attacked the Chinese, burning their tents and stealing or destroying their mining equipment. Extra troops arrived, too late to protect the Chinese miners, and a number of arrests were made. Thousands of miners laid siege to the jail demanding their release and they were formally read the Riot Act.

The final result, however, was that of three ringleaders arrested only one was convicted and imprisoned. For the victims of the attacks, the result was the *Chinese Immigration Restriction Act*, which formed the basis of the later White Australia Policy.

The 'Roll Up' flag, 'lost' for many years, is now on display at the Lambing Flat Historical Museum, a tangible reminder of those less than glorious days. □

mineral was used in aircraft production during the Second World War. Since 1952, the ore, from the open-cut mine at Thuddungra, has been crushed and processed in Young.

WEDDIN MOUNTAINS NATIONAL PARK ■ 652

The name Weddin or Widden comes from an Aboriginal word meaning 'wait' or 'stay' and apparently refers to the place where young men waited prior to their initiation ceremony. Despite the name, little evidence has yet been found of Aboriginal use of the Weddin Mountain Range.

John Oxley was the first European to see the Weddin Mountains in 1817 and on his second exploration of the district, two convicts of his party, Scotchie and Witton, escaped and hid out in the mountain range...the first of a series of lawbreakers to do so. Ben Hall, John Gilbert and John O'Meally used the mountains as a hideout and a place to secret their ill-gotten gains as did other lesser known bushrangers such as Johnnie Bow whose cave along with the better known Ben Hall's Cave, are now within the park boundaries. An illicit still at Black Spring Gully, where rum was made from she-oak berries combined with potatoes and barley from the plains below, and an old saw mill add colour to the park's history.

Almost all of the crescent-shaped Weddin Mountain Range is now within the 8361-hectare national park. The ranges rise 330 metres above the cultivated farmland on the plains below and provide an 'island' of natural open forest. Within the park, isolated remnant communities of birds, reptiles and mammals survive but, without access to a wider range of animals for breeding purposes, the survival of some of these species within the park is threatened. Work on wildlife corridors and eradication of foxes, goats and rabbits within the park are underway.

Weddin National Park's primary function is conservation of flora and fauna in a wilderness area; facilities within the park are basic and include two lookouts and one or two walking tracks.

YOUNG ■ 653

When James White arrived at Burrangong Creek in the 1830s, he established a number of sheep runs including one for lambing ewes. It was on this run – Lambing Flat – that gold was found in 1860. When a number of White's stockmen were rounding up wild horses at Lambing Flat, the American cook, Alexander the Yank, recognised gold-bearing quartz from his California goldmining days...Lambing Flat changed from a pastoral idyll to a roaring, lawless goldfield. Over 20 000 miners and others flocked to Lambing Flat, including Ben Hall who sold meat to the diggers and Frank Gardiner who stole the stock that was then sold in an accomplice's butcher's shop on the diggings. Gardiner also supposedly stole the winner of the first horse race run at Lambing Flat in 1861. But it was the Chinese, not lawless bushrangers, that were to be the focus of law and order – or the lack of it – at Lambing Flat (see box).

The gold rush did not last...and neither did the name Lambing Flat since the town was gazetted as Young in 1861, the year that Sir John Young became Governor of New South Wales. Some of the foreign miners, including at least one American who planted cotton and tobacco and some Chinese who planted vegetable gardens, stayed on in Young. The most important of these was an Austrian, Nicole Jasprizza, who grafted and planted cherry trees on what was to become the largest cherry orchard in the world.

With the coming of the railway in 1885 and the addition of a fruit van to the mail train after the First World War, Young's abundant cherries and other stone fruits were processed and packed in Young. Soldier settlers added to the town's reputation as the primary source of cherries and prunes. Vines too were cultivated but this industry languished until the 1980s revival, which resulted in fourteen small commercial wineries in Young.

The old court house at Young is now a very grand assembly hall for the local high school; the old red-brick jail with its splendid iron gates is now the technical college and the annual Cherry Festival rather than the lure of gold brings people to Young. *Population 6800*

FESTIVALS Agricultural Show, September; Cherry Fest, November.

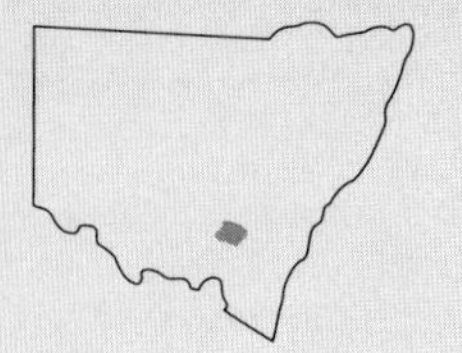

Cootamundra & Harden

The construction of Australia's first great, main-trunk railway system quickly transformed favoured towns on the south-west slopes, bringing an urban approach to commerce and secondary industry as well as sealing their positions of importance in the realm of agriculture.

BEGGAN BEGGAN ■ 654

Set in some of the finest wool-growing country in the world, this tiny village takes its name from Beggan Beggan Homestead. The homestead itself is an elegant two-storey building with an encircling single-storey verandah and gabled coach house and dates from the 1860s. It is built of brick and random rubble rendered to look like hewn stone.

BETHUNGRA ■ 655

Bethungra's Hotel Shirley, listed by the National Trust, is among the most handsome of nineteenth-century country inns. Built in 1886, it took over the stagecoach trade of rough-and-ready older hostelries that had sprung up to cater for construction workers on the Great Southern Railway during the late 1870s. Since the Second World War the railway line itself has become something of a local scenic attraction. To overcome a steep gradient that slowed traffic on the northbound track, the Bethungra spiral was built, crossing over itself and the southern line. Nearby, storage waters behind the Bethungra Dam are popular with picnickers and boating enthusiasts.

COOTAMUNDRA ■ 656

Thanks to a tree, Cootamundra has perhaps the best-known name of any country town of its size in Australia. The showy Cootamundra wattle tree (*Acacia baileyana*), originally restricted to a small area of the south-west slopes of New South Wales, has become the most widely cultivated acacia species. Silvery-grey trees up to ten metres tall produce golden balls of wintertime blossom in parks and gardens in most parts of cool-temperate of Australia. Ironically, Cootamundra's proud displays are the result of industrious planting programs. Farm clearance had made the tree's natural occurrence rare even before the town existed.

In the heroic early days of aviation, 'Coota' had another claim to national fame. Its aerodrome, established in 1920, was used almost immediately as an emergency landing place for Ross and Keith Smith when they crossed the continent after their historic England–Australia flight of nearly twenty-eight days. Cootamundra became a refuelling point for a succession of other trail-blazing aviators such as Charles Kingsford Smith, Bert Hinkler, Amy Johnson and Jean Batten.

Cootamundra was accustomed to prominence as a transport cross-roads, having been particularly well favoured by the pattern of railway development in the nineteenth century. The track from Sydney to Wagga Wagga, eventually to be the Great Southern Railway to Melbourne, reached here in 1877 and turned a mere village into a boom town. Branch lines, pushing south as far as Gundagai in 1886 and west to Temora in 1893, confirmed Cootamundra's place at the centre of an important grazing and crop-growing district. Its stockyards and abattoirs are the busiest in the region.

The Cootamundra wattle wins favour with gardeners not only because of its flowers – it is drought-resistant and grows in most soils.

Well elevated at 385 metres above sea level, Cootamundra is exposed to cold south-westerly winds in winter – sometimes bearing snow – and to hot north-westerlies in summer. The town has recorded extremes of temperature as low as 7°C and as high as 48°C. *Population 6390*

BRADMAN COTTAGE Cricket's most accomplished batsman, Sir Donald Bradman, was born in the Adams Street cottage in 1908, when it was used as a nursing home. His parents lived at Yeo Yeo, moving to Bowral on the Southern Highlands when the boy was three. The building has been restored by the shire council.

PIONEER PARK Native trees and shrubs have been regenerated in a park that commands sweeping views of Cootamundra from its southern outskirts.

RAILWAY STATION Work began about 1870 on a station that grew and grew as Cootamundra became a key junction on the Great Southern Railway. This low building of unusual design

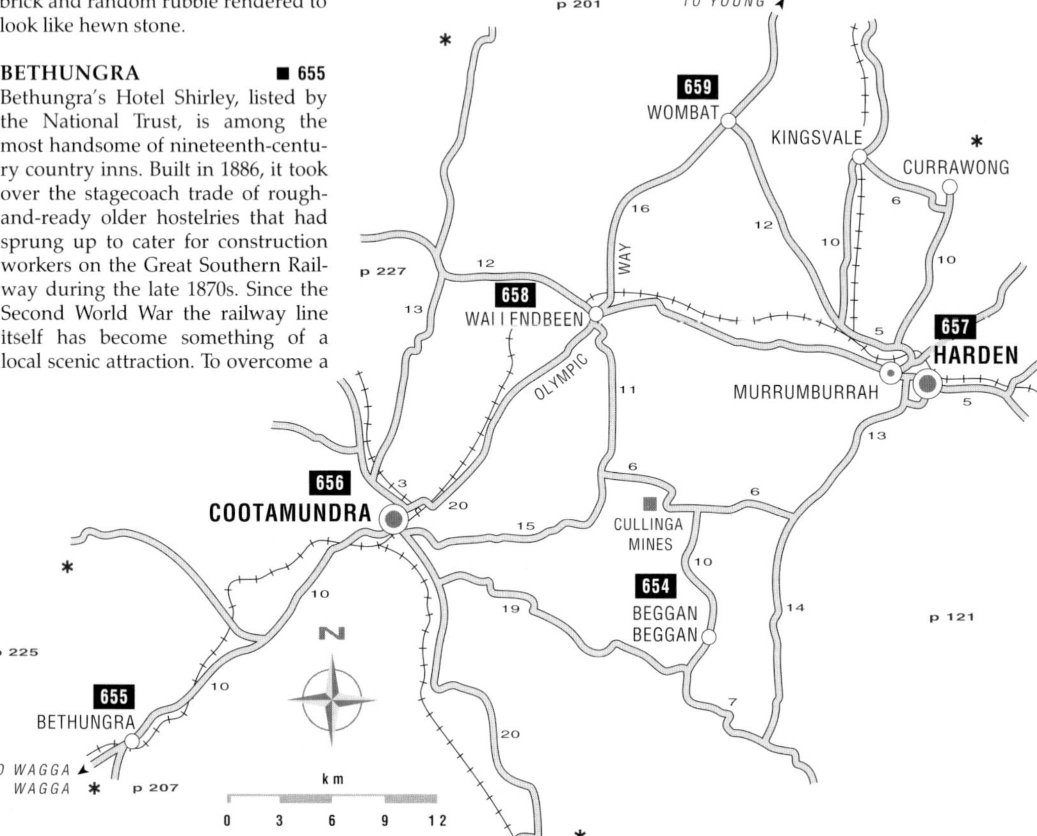

is topped by an octagonal tower. The platform is 240 metres long.

POST OFFICE The focal point of Cootamundra's townscape, this fine two-storey brick building was completed in 1881 and a slim clocktower, two storeys higher, was added in 1894. The former CBC bank building nearby was built in 1887 to harmonise with the post office design.

SCOTS CHURCH The builders of this sturdy Presbyterian church in 1878 reached back to the district's early days of settlement, reusing granite blocks from an old homestead.

BIMBADEEN COLLEGE Now in use by the Aboriginal Evangelical Fellowship for cultural and vocational instruction, Bimbadeen has a shameful past. It was built in 1887 as a district hospital, but taken over in 1911 by the Aborigines Welfare Board for the training of girls as domestic servants in wealthy white households. At the time, managers of Aboriginal reserves had a free hand in nominating anyone they wished to expel to such institutions as state wards. Children were plucked from their families without warning or spirited away without their parents' knowledge, in some cases never to be seen again. The Cootamundra Home was closed in 1968, shortly before the board was abolished.

GARDINER'S LOOKOUT An outcrop of boulders about ten kilometres south of Cootamundra on the Olympic Way are said to have been used as a vantage point by the bushranger Frank Gardiner. At Eugowra Rocks, in 1862 his gang hijacked a gold consignment worth 14 000 pounds – the biggest such robbery in New South Wales colonial history.

FESTIVALS Wattle Time, August.

HARDEN–MURRUMBURRAH ■ 657

Why what is to all intents and purposes *one* small town without any apparent division should require *two* names is a puzzle to visitors. A slipshod bureaucratic decision in 1880 is directly to blame. But underlying that is a vivid illustration of the overwhelming impact of early railway development. New lines wrought changes throughout country Australia. Few could have been as drastic as the eclipsing of Murrumburrah.

In 1877, it was a prosperous agricultural centre. Citizens rejoiced in the coming of the Sydney–Wagga Wagga railway – more so because Murrumburrah was to enjoy special importance as an engine-changing point with marshalling yards and workshops. Anticipation turned to fury when it was disclosed that while the line would pass a stone's throw from the town's slightly sloping central area, the station site had to be on an isolated stretch of flat land, nearly two kilometres away. Protesting residents were fobbed off with an unroofed passenger platform. Meanwhile 'Murrumburrah North' – to add to the confusion it was actually more to the east – was mushrooming as a railway settlement and stopover, with new hotels and shops clustering as close as they could get to the well-appointed main station.

Old and new areas had quickly merged. Murrumburrah was simply an expanded town with no reason for division. But when people living farthest from the old post office petitioned for an additional letter carrier to serve them more speedily, the authorities went one better. A second post office was built at the main station. Presumably unaware that the two offices would be within walking distance of each other, someone decided a new name was in order. He resurrected Harden (the name of the shire) from a defunct post office near Currawong, to the north.

Consequently, the main railway station was renamed Harden and the 'twin towns' came into existence, absurdly sharing a border along Lucan Street – the boundary of the two letter carriers' delivery routes. Even more absurdly, strong rivalries arose. Sporting teams did not merely decline to join forces – some even refused to play against each other. Commercial competition was just as bitter, with Murrumburrah's stores always losing ground to their counterparts to the east. Now almost all commercial activity is based in Harden; the only official building bearing the old Murrumburrah name is the 1880 court house.

Squatters drove sheep into the Harden district about 1830. Town blocks were sold in 1858 and growth was boosted by profitable gold mining until after the turn of the century. Wheat and wool growing predominate now in the mixed farming of the district. *Population 2040 (Harden 1290, Murrumburrah 750)*

HISTORICAL MUSEUM Railway memorabilia and pioneer relics can be seen at weekends and holidays.

WALLENDBEEN ■ 658

The first permanent settlers in these hills were the family of Alexander McKay, who was installed as superintendent of Wallendbeen Station in the early 1840s. The townsite was gazetted in 1877, in the same year as the arrival of the Yass–Cootamundra railway and the village developed as a district communal centre.

YANDILLA MUSTARD OIL These hills are now the centre of a thriving, export business. The crop which in spring covers the fields with a blaze of canary yellow is mustard, grown from seed specially developed for local soil and climatic conditions by CSIRO scientists. The oil from its seeds is an important ingredient in Indian cooking and the project developed because a couple who had lived in India and were unable to find their favourite oil decided to grow their own mustard. Part of the annual output of more than 90 000 litres is exported to Asia and Europe.

The 'Don' – at the crease in the 1930s when he was the nation's idol – is Cootamundra's greatest son.

WOMBAT ■ 659

Traces of mining still to be seen around Wombat attest to a short-lived gold rush. In the 1860s, the district was a hectic southern outpost of the Burrangong goldfields, centred around Young. Hundreds of diggers lived squalidly in tents and huts, spending their money in grog shanties. Substantial buildings such as the present hotel and St Matthew's Church were erected in the 1870s even as the gold was running out. Wombat's survival was secured by market gardening, first established by Chinese former diggers.

Before the land was cleared for grazing, this was the view early settlers had of the south-west slopes.

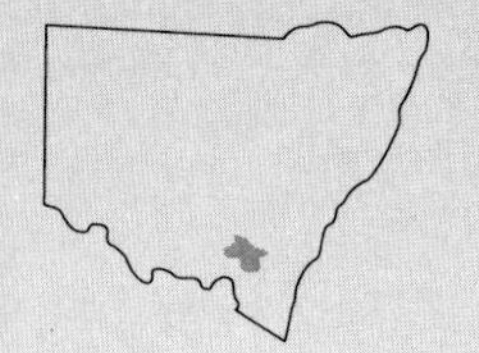

Tumut & Gundagai

The history of the Tumut – Gundagai region is the stuff of Australian legends. Opened up by the explorers Hume and Hovell, the land was farmed by squatters, picked over and at by miners, travelled by teamsters and roamed by bushrangers. The miners and bushrangers have gone but the wool and wheat farmers remain.

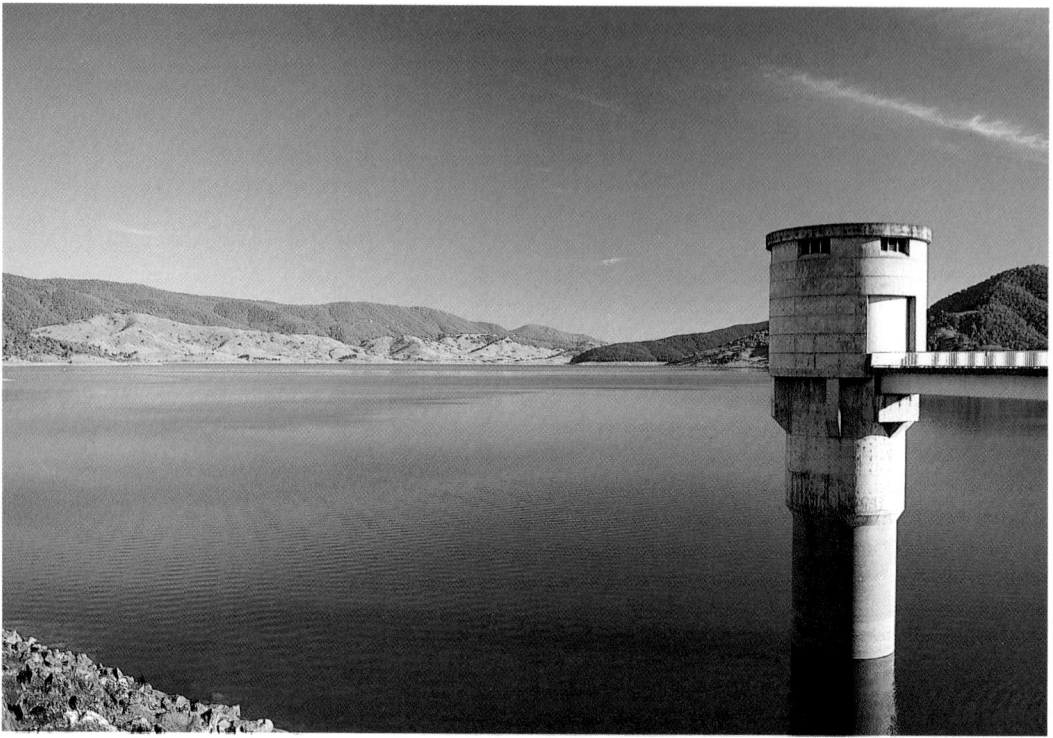

These Blowering Reservoir waters have dropped 800 metres as they generated electricity in three power stations.

ADELONG ■ 660
Set in the foothills of the Snowy Mountains, along the winding Adelong Creek, Adelong is a town with wide, tree-lined streets and a rich history. The first European landholders in the district settled in 1837, thirteen years after Hume and Hovell passed through, and the town that grew out of the closely grouped properties was first known as The Reef. The later name, Adelong, was adopted from Adelong Station, which stretched from Tumblong to Batlow – Upper Adelong was another settlement closer to Batlow.

Adelong's heyday came when a reef of gold was discovered in 1857. The town's population is said to have swelled to 20 000; mining companies moved in, machinery went into operation, and at its peak, the town produced about 12 tons of gold in five years. A tent-town known as Golden Gully sprang up along Camp Street and miners took their fun at hotels, horseraces, cock fights, and wherever else they could: local history tells the story of two doctors, whose bitter rivalry led to a duel, but whose pistols – unbeknown to them and in order to avoid serious injury being added to insult – had been filled with raspberry jam!

As the town grew, new buildings were erected and the commercial centre shifted from Golden Gully on the north side of the creek to its present location. The first church was built in 1866; the post office was established in 1870 and moved to its present building in the 1890s.

Today, a large section of Tumut Street is classified by the National Trust. The buildings, which date largely from the 1860 to 1900 period, include the Westpac Bank, the Adelong Pharmacy, the Royal Hotel and Hotel Adelong, all of which form focal points closing either end of the unusually wide street.

By the end of the Second World War, Adelong's mining days were over. The reefs were largely exhausted and the creek dredged out. For the present-day prospector, there are still gold tracings in Adelong Creek (see Adelong Falls) and plenty to see in the disused workings around the town, such as the Great Victoria Mine, which won a government award as the first mine to find payable gold beyond 800 feet (243 metres) , or the Lady Mary Mine, which filled with water before it could be mined and remains filled to this day. The town now depends on sheep and cattle farming, forestry and tourism. *Population 800*

ADELONG FALLS From this picnic spot on the outskirts of Adelong, visitors can take in views of the nearby waterfalls and the ruins of the Ritchie Gold Battery, or follow the walks that explore them. The Ritchie Gold Battery operated until the First World War, extracting gold from crushed quartz; two large waterwheels fed by water from the falls drove all the machinery, doing away with pumps and engines.

Near the old battery, along Adelong Creek, is a place set aside for fossicking. Prospectors do not need a licence to fossick in this patch about 300 metres upstream of the falls.

BLOWERING RESERVOIR ■ 661
As part of the Snowy Mountains Hydro-electric Scheme, the Snowy Mountains Authority dammed the Tumut River in 1968 creating the Blowering Reservoir and a popular location for waterskiing, sailing, boating, swimming and fishing.

The reservoir, capable of holding 1 632 400 megalitres, is the second largest in the Snowy Scheme, and the last in the series of dams in the Snowy–Tumut section before water is emptied out through the Blowering Power Station to the Murrumbidgee River for irrigation.

DOG ON THE TUCKERBOX ■ 662
Unveiled by Prime Minister Joseph Lyons in 1932, this bronze monument to the teamster's dog sits at Five Mile Creek, eight kilometres (or five miles) north of Gundagai, on the western side of the Hume Highway.

The anonymous poem of 'Bullocky Bill' first rendered the tale of the dog which did something unpleasant *in* the tuckerbox in down-to-earth, bullock-driver style: 'and the dog s[h]at in the tucker box, Five miles from Gundagai'; after Jack Moses used the words in more socially acceptable form in his poem 'Nine Miles From Gundagai' the story of the dog, the tucker box and Gundagai became a folk legend the country over.

The monument was sculpted by Frank Rusconi, who lived much of his life in Gundagai and produced the marble cathedral-in-miniature, known as Rusconi's Marble Masterpiece (see Gundagai). Another well known musical tribute to Gundagai, Jack O'Hagan's popular tune 'The Road to Gundagai', spawned a monument too. The tune was used as the theme to the long-running *Dad and Dave* radio serial, and four larger-than-life-size copper figures of Dad, Dave, Mum and Mabel now stand opposite the dog on the tucker box.

GUNDAGAI ■ 663
The many verses and songs about this town have all celebrated the teamster, the traveller and the itiner-

ant worker, who travelled the main road from Sydney to Melbourne and the Victorian goldfields, crossing the Murrumbidgee at Gundagai.

The early township grew up on the northern bank of the Murrumbidgee, and despite many inundations remained there until Australia's worst flooding disaster in 1852. When the river burst its banks one night in June, eighty-nine of the two-hundred-and-fifty inhabitants lost their lives, and a large number of stores, two hotels and thirty-four houses were destroyed. The grave of Yarri, an Aboriginal man who rescued many people in his bark canoe is in the Roman Catholic portion of the cemetery.

For safety's sake, the town was rebuilt further up the slopes of Mount Parnassus, and Sheridan Street, which had been the highest street of the old town, became the main street of the new town.

Gundagai's livelihood, nevertheless, lay with the river that divided the Sydney-Melbourne route. From around 1840 a punt operated across the Murrumbidgee, and from 1849 to 1867 when the bridge was completed – thought to be the first to use Australian-manufactured iron – a ferry shunted travellers back and forth. Briefly, in the early 1860s, Gundagai was a port in a riverboat service all the way from Adelaide.

The town had a much longer experience with worrisome bushrangers, who inevitably plagued the highway after the discovery of gold. Once a 66-ounce nugget was found, Gundagai was declared a goldfield and enjoyed two periods of production, from 1865 to 1875, then, after another find, from 1894 until 1942.

From the 1860s to 1920s, mounted troopers staffed the Gundagai police station and were kept busy by the likes of Ben Hall, Johnny Gilbert and John Dunn, and later Captain Midnight. In 1864, Gilbert shot dead police escort Sergeant Parry near Jugiong. Parry's grave is in the Gundagai cemetery, marked by a monument. After Captain Moonlight's capture some years later, he and his gang members were held in the Gundagai jail and brought to trial at the local court house. The court house, which stands in Sheridan Street, was built in 1858, with a red-cedar lined interior, but after a fire in 1942, it was replaced with local mountain ash.

A pictorial history of Gundagai life at the turn of the century is displayed in the town's Gabriel Gallery. The gallery contains hundreds of photographs taken by local doctor Charles Louis Gabriel of houses, shops, people, marriages, funerals, floods – just about everything.

Gundagai of today is a key centre serving the wool and wheat produc-

The legendary dog on the tuckerbox – in bronze – sits where bullock drivers once watered their beasts.

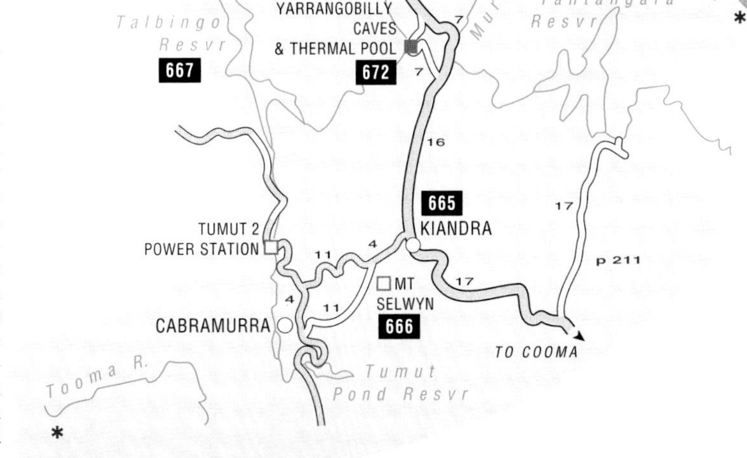

At Coolac, north of Gundagai, an 1851 coaching inn built of petrified timber still serves weary travellers as a restaurant.

The pickings may be slim these days but amateur prospectors still roam the Snowy Mountains' foothills.

ers of the district, and the fruit and vegetable growers working on the rich river flats near the town. As a traditional stopover, it has always catered for visitors, and is now a destination for gold fossickers and gem hunters, as well as canoeists who trail down the Murrumbidgee and Tumut rivers, and fishing enthusiasts attracted by the trout, Murray cod, yellow-belly and bream in the streams fed by the cool mountain water. Along with museums, historical sites, and recreation facilities, the town offers some curiosities such as sculptor Frank Rusconi's marble masterpiece, a cathedral-in-miniature made of 20 948 pieces of New South Wales marble, all cut, turned and polished by hand. It is housed in the Tourist Information Centre. *Population 2070*

JOUNAMA PONDAGE ■ 664

The forty-four-metre-high Jounama Dam, on the Tumut River just downstream of Tumut 3 Power Station, went into service in 1968 thereby creating Jounama Pondage, one of the smaller reservoirs in the Snowy Mountains Hydro-electric Scheme.

Jounama Pondage is a declared trout area where use of rod and line only is permitted. The lake also supports a colony of Murray crayfish.

KIANDRA ■ 665

Kiandra was the scene of one of Australia's most hectic, if short-lived gold rushes. In April 1860, there were 10 000 miners working the gold fields. By March 1861, the number had dwindled to 250. Kiandra is now a small village, but the evidence of the gold rush is still there in the form of abandoned houses and mines. The world's first ski club is said to have been formed in Kiandra in 1870. Skiing had been introduced by snow-bound Norwegian miners and by 1862 it was well established as a sport and races were held regularly.

MOUNT SELWYN ■ 666

Mount Selwyn, which rises 1601 metres over the mountains north of Thredbo, is a family and beginners skiing resort. Along with facilities for refreshments and ski and clothing hire, the Mount Selwyn slopes have twelve ski-lifts, including a chairlift for beginners and, for those seasons when nature doesn't oblige, snow-making facilities. The nearest place to stay is at Talbingo and Tumut to the north and Cooma and Adaminaby to the south.

TALBINGO RESERVOIR ■ 667

In service since 1972, the Talbingo Reservoir provides water, through the Talbingo Dam, to Tumut 3 Power Station. The large reservoir has a capacity of 920 550 megalitres and the dam, 162 metres high, has the tallest rock-filled wall in the Snowy Mountains Hydro-electric Scheme. Like Blowering, Talbingo Reservoir is a popular fishing spot – in the trout season, October to May, reputedly the region's best – set in scenic, wooded, mountainous country. Most fishing is by trolling from boat, which can mean a difficult journey for fishing visitors who have to travel over the rugged countryside.

TUMUT 2 POWER STATION More than two hundred metres underground, the Tumut 2 Power Station has churned out electricity since 1962 when its four 70 000-kilowatt turbo-generators went into full operation. Guided tours should resume in 1995 when renovations are complete.

TUMUT 3 POWER STATION The last of the power stations in the Snowy Mountains Scheme to be completed, Tumut 3 has the highest generating capacity at one-and-a-half million kilowatts, part of which is used to recirculate water in off-peak times from the downstream Jounama Pondage through Talbingo Reservoir for use at peak times. The above-ground power station is open daily for inspection from a viewing point.

TANTANGARA RESERVOIR ■ 668

This extensive reservoir sits on the Upper Murrumbidgee River. It went into service in 1960 as a supplementary store to the major water-store Lake Eucumbene in the Snowy Mountains Hydro-electric Scheme (see *Cooma & Mount Kosciusko*). The south lake foreshore area, part of the Kosciusko National Park, is set aside as a camping area.

TUMUT ■ 669

While close to the Snowy Mountains, Tumut is only 280 metres above sea level. The picturesque town sits on the Tumut river in fertile countryside surrounded by streams and rivers famous for their trout fishing. Poplars, elms, oaks and maples line the streets, giving the town much colour in autumn, something which is celebrated in Tumut's annual Falling Leaf Festival. A large percentage of the district's workforce is employed in the timber industry, which overtook dairying as the main industry after pine plantations were tried in 1921. Three large softwood-processing plants and several hardwood mills are located in and around Tumut. There is also a factory producing cut marble quarried just north of the town and a broom-making factory using local millet.

The first settlers to follow Hume and Hovell to the area were squatters. One of the earliest stations near the junction of the Tumut and Murrumbidgee Rivers was 'Darbalara', where the Darbalara breed of shorthorn beef cattle was bred by Thomas McAlister. In 1830, McAlister's daughter was the first white child to be born in the Tumut district.

In its earliest days, Tumut was very isolated. A bullock-team trip to Sydney and back in the 1860s took about three months and there were no regular coaches; transport was on horseback or by bullock and dray on rough bush roads and tracks.

By 1866, Tumut's population of 400 was catered for by 11 hotels! By the 1870-80 period it had eighteen hotels serving residents and the thousands of itinerant gold prospectors in the district (see Adelong). Some of Tumut's most notable buildings date from this period including the police station, built in 1874, the court house, built in 1878, and All Saints' Anglican Church, one of Edmund Blacket's rare designs in brick, built in 1875–76.

In 1903, the railway line was extended to Tumut; fifty years later the construction of the Snowy Mountains Hydro-electric Scheme (see *Cooma & Mount Kosciusko*) boosted the economy and dramatically improved communications.

Those heady days are over, and today Tumut relies on established industries and on tourism for its livelihood. The name Tumut is said to derive from an Aboriginal word meaning 'camping place by the river' and for many that is what Tumut is. Others may come to enjoy more active pleasures such as the bracing mountain walk to the nearby Thomas Boyd Trackhead, one of the major staging points along the Hume and Hovell Walking Track (see *Tumbarumba & Batlow*), taking in swimming, fishing, the magnificent-landscape and wildlife along the way. *Population 5960*

BONDO AND BILLAPALOOLA FOREST RECREATION AREAS Pine plantations now cover approximately 80 000 hectares of state forest in the Tumut district, and there are 19 000 hectares of private plantations. North-east of Tumut, a drive through the Billapaloola and Bondo State Forests shows pines of various ages and stages of harvest. Both forests have picnic and barbecue areas.

TUMUT RIVER ■ 670

The Tumut River rises near Mount Jagungal in the Snowy Mountains and more than 140 kilometres later, falling about 1800 metres through four power stations and numerous reservoirs and dams (see Talbingo Reservoir) it joins the Murrumbidgee River near Gundagai. The Tumut is the main carrier of water diverted from the Eucumbene and Tooma rivers, and the Murrumbidgee headwaters, in the Snowy-Tumut part of the Snowy Mountains Hydro-electric Scheme (see *Cooma and Mount Kosciusko*).

The river is popular with anglers and boating folk as well as being a

Tumut nestles comfortably in its picture-postcard valley, where the mountains slow the departure of the early morning mist.

'working' waterway. Trout, cod, yellow belly and silver perch are some of the fish introduced into its waters. Intrepid canoeists traverse the river from the Blowering Dam down to the Murrumbidgee, challenged by the fast flowing, cold water and sharp turn of the rapids.

WEE JASPER ■ 671

Wee Jasper, on the Goodradigbee River just before it enters Burrinjuck Dam, is a popular jump-off point to a range of activities and environments.

To the north and south are caves, including Dip, Punch-Bowl, Signature and Dogleg, and to the south is Careys Cave (see sub-entry). The Wee Jasper Valley is dotted with camping reserves, all of them taking advantage of the spectacular mountain backdrop, clear, rushing streams and Lake Burrinjuck. Two one-day return walks commence near the Fitzpatrick Trackhead. One goes through the Wee Jasper Nature Reserve, the other is to the top of Mount Jasper. The challenging Hume and Hovell Walking Track, which stretches from Gunning to Albury (see *Tumbarumba & Batlow*), also passes through the valley. A tourist camp provides caravans and cabins for those without tents, and Wee Jasper Station has accommodation in shearers' quarters.

CAREYS CAVE Just to the north of Wee Jasper, is Careys Cave. The system of seven caverns of beautiful colours and spectacular stalactites is a private tourist operation open to the public at weekends.

YARRANGOBILLY CAVES & THERMAL POOL ■ 672

The Yarrangobilly caves were first recorded in 1834 when a pioneer stockman took shelter in them during a thunderstorm. Gradually, over the following years, the 240 or so caves became a tourist attraction, famed for the variety and beauty of their calcite formations and for the cliffs, outcrops, and intriguingly weathered limestone around them. Today four caves are open to visitors, The Glory Hole, North Glory, Jersey and Jillabenan – the last name means 'dark hole' in the language of the former Aboriginal inhabitants of the Monaro region. The popular Glory Hole cave has been set up with signs to aid self-guided tours while guided inspections are conducted in the others. Near the caves are a thermal pool and spring offering all-year-round swimming in 27°C water.

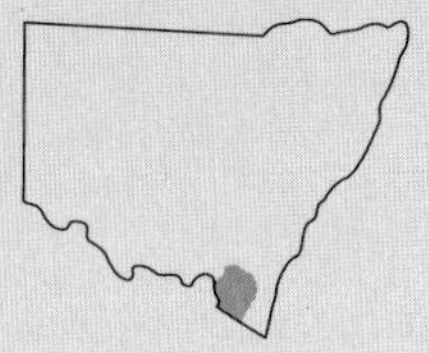

Cooma & Mount Kosciusko

The Snowy Mountains started off as inaccessible high country, used by pastoralists for their sheep and cattle. Since the Snowy Mountains Hydro-electric Scheme opened up the area, tourism has become its major industry.

ADAMINABY ■ 673
During the construction of the huge Snowy Mountains Scheme in the 1950s Adaminaby was flooded to create Lake Eucumbene and the town was moved to a new site. The move took eighteen months and more than one hundred buildings were shifted, including seventy-five houses and two churches. The churches were moved stone by stone. The lamp posts in the town square were once verandah supports for the Commercial Hotel in Old Adaminaby. Trout fishing in Lake Eucumbene or the Murrumbidgee River, both within a few minutes' drive of Adaminaby, attracts a steady flow of keen anglers to this town.

WORLD'S LARGEST TROUT Australians have a predilection for building large local icons to highlight the product or products – animal, vegetable or mineral – for which their region is most famous. Adaminaby boasts the world's largest trout. A fibreglass structure sixteen metres long, it is the work of local artist Andy Lomnici and stands in the Adaminaby Lions Club Park at the town's entrance.

FESTIVALS Trout Festival, October.

BERRIDALE ■ 674
The road to the snowfields passes through this small town situated between Cooma and Jindabyne. It is a popular spot for skiers to stay during the season since it offers cheaper accommodation than the resorts. The area was first settled in the early 1860s by William Oliver who named his property 'Berridale' after his home in Scotland. The post office opened in 1869, a blacksmith's, racing club and school in the 1880s and a bank and police station in the 1890s. A storekeeper, Andrew Anderson, planted an avenue of poplars at the turn of the century to shade his tin-shed shop. The poplars are still there and are a special feature of the town, especially around Easter time when their leaves turn autumnal gold. *Population 950*

BLUE COW MOUNTAIN ■ 675
This is the newest ski resort in New South Wales. It has been developed specifically for day visitors – it has no accommodation – and it is accessible only by a rail system through the mountain called the 'Skitube'. There are slopes catering for all levels of ski experience. In 1991, the Blue Cow resort purchased the neighbouring Guthega ski fields and the resort is now called Blue Cow Guthega.

CHARLOTTES PASS ■ 676
This ski resort was named after Charlotte Adams, who was either the daughter or wife of Philip Adams, the then surveyor-general. She had accompanied Adams to the district in 1881 and was the first European woman to climb to the top of Mt Kosciusko. There are snowgums at Charlottes Pass which is 1750 metres above sea level, and above the tree-line of about 1800 metres, anemones, snow daisies, buttercups and billy buttons bloom in summer. Here also are sphagnum bogs, home to the spectacular yellow-and-black banded corroboree frogs. The ski resort has accommodation and facilities and there are excellent slopes for beginners, and good intermediate runs.

COOMA ■ 677
The largest town in the Monaro region, Cooma is the gateway to the New South Wales ski fields and in winter the town is crowded with slopes-bound city visitors. Although it is 100 kilometres from the major resorts, many families choose to stay in Cooma for their skiing holiday because accommodation is cheaper and they can take a bus to and from the ski fields.

Cooma was gazetted in 1849, the name is said to come from the Aboriginal Coombah, meaning 'big lake' or 'open country'. Until the late 1950s, it was a sleepy town of about 2000 people which catered for the large pastoral district of the Monaro plains. But all this changed when the ambitious Snowy Mountains Hydro-electric Scheme began in 1951. The town was invaded by workers from all over Europe and the population increased five-fold to nearly 10 000 by 1965. The migrants brought with them a cosmopolitan atmosphere that the town had not experienced before and some of them settled in Cooma when the Scheme was completed. Today, Cooma remains the administrative centre of the Snowy Mountains Scheme Authority. The Scheme was completed in 1972, but by then Cooma had had another invasion – this time from skiers. The post-Second World War boom in skiing has made tourism Cooma's biggest industry now. *Population 7390*

LAMBIE STREET This is the oldest thoroughfare in Cooma and has been proclaimed an historic precinct. Many of the street's buildings have been classified by the National Trust.

MONUMENTS The Snowy Memorial was erected to the memory of the 121 people who lost their lives while working on the Scheme. In Cooma Park there is a statue of A.B. (Banjo) Patterson's 'Man from Snowy River'.

AVENUE OF FLAGS The corridor of flags in Centennial Park commemorates the workers of twenty-seven countries who helped design and build the Snowy Mountains Scheme.

AVIATION PIONEERS MEMORIAL Southern Cloud Park contains the remains of the trail-blazing aircraft 'Southern Cloud', which disappeared with six passengers and two crew in the Snowy Mountains in 1931. A worker on the Snowy Mountains Scheme found the wreckage in 1958.

DALGETY ■ 678
A small village on the banks of the Snowy River, Dalgety was once destined for greater things. In 1904, the Federal government considered it as the site of the national capital. The New South Wales government was unhappy about this proposition and the guernsey went to Canberra. The district's landscape is eerily treeless, with rolling hills and brown plains, dotted with smooth boulders which were created by soil erosion. There are records of early settlers building fires around the giant boulders in winter and when the flames flickered out, the cold night air would shatter the outside layers of the rocks as they contracted rapidly.

GUTHEGA ■ 679
The first power available from the Snowy Mountains Scheme came from Guthega – a picturesque village at the base of the Snowy Mountains main range – in February 1955. The Guthega power station was originally called Munyang. In 1991, the Blue Cow resort (see entry) purchased the Guthega ski fields and the resort reflects this union in its new name – Blue Cow Guthega. Visitors can ski in all of the area on one ticket.

When the thaw begins in spring, thousands of creeks swell with the Snowy's greatest resource, water – for power generation and irrigation.

JINDABYNE ■ 680
The old township of Jindabyne was flooded to make Lake Jindabyne and, starting in 1962, the whole town was moved to a new location on the shores of the lake. On 22 April 1967 a crowd of 7000 people said goodbye to the 140-year-old town and there was a procession of people dressed in period costume with carts, waggons and horses, who wound their

The alpine sunray – one of 60 sunray species – is now cultivated to satisfy decorators' demands for its flowers – either fresh or dried.

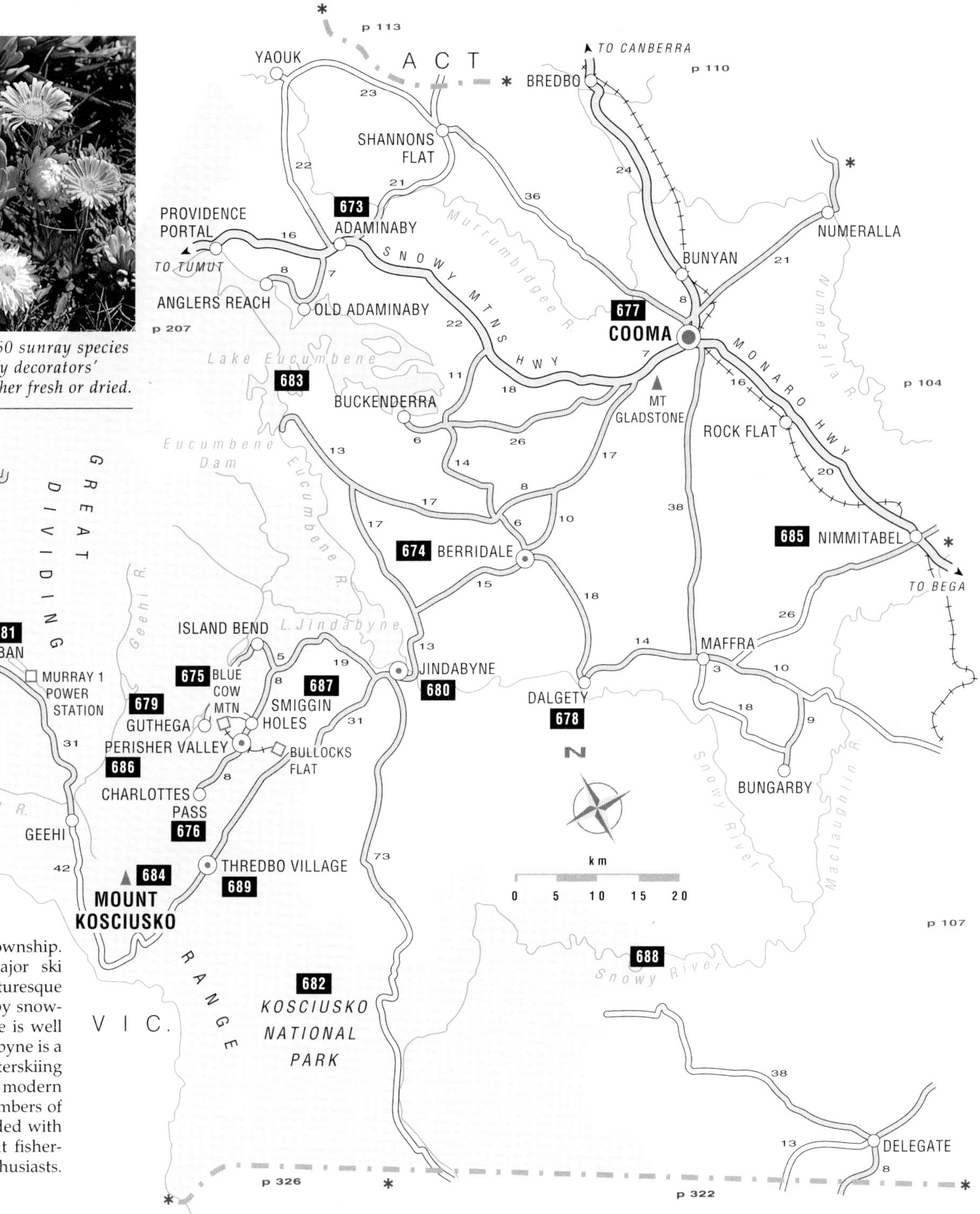

p 113
YAOUK
ACT
TO CANBERRA
BREDBO
p 110
SHANNONS FLAT
673
PROVIDENCE PORTAL
ADAMINABY
TO TUMUT
SNOWY MTNS HWY
Murrumbidgee R.
BUNYAN
NUMERALLA
Numeralla R.
ANGLERS REACH
OLD ADAMINABY
p 207
677
COOMA
Lake Eucumbene
683
MONARO HWY
BUCKENDERRA
MT GLADSTONE
p 104
ROCK FLAT
Eucumbene Dam
Eucumbene R.
GREAT DIVIDING
685
NIMMITABEL
p 214
674
BERRIDALE
TO BEGA
Geehi R.
681
KHANCOBAN
ISLAND BEND
L. Jindabyne
MAFFRA
MURRAY 1 POWER STATION
675
BLUE COW MTN
687
SMIGGIN HOLES
JINDABYNE
680
DALGETY
678
679
GUTHEGA
PERISHER VALLEY
BULLOCKS FLAT
686
Swampy Plain R.
Murray River
CHARLOTTES PASS
676
GEEHI
Snowy River
BUNGARBY
Maclaughlin R.
N
p 329
684
MOUNT KOSCIUSKO
THREDBO VILLAGE
689
km
0 5 10 15 20
p 107
RANGE
688
Snowy River
682
KOSCIUSKO NATIONAL PARK
VIC.
DELEGATE
p 326
p 322

way up the hill to the new township. In the foothills of the major ski resorts, Jindabyne is a picturesque spot with views of the nearby snow-covered mountains. The lake is well stocked with trout and Jindabyne is a popular place for sailing, waterskiing and powerboat racing. The modern township caters for large numbers of visitors. In winter it is crowded with skiers, in summer with trout fishermen and water sports enthusiasts. *Population 4600*

KHANCOBAN ■ 681
Khancoban started life as a pastoral settlement and became a construction town for the Snowy Mountains Scheme. It is the southern gateway to Kosciusko National Park, and the start of the Alpine Way, which leads to Jindabyne. The Alpine Way is a scenic, winding road which was constructed by the Snowy Mountains Authority and opened in 1956. Khancoban is close to the Murray 1 and Murray 2 Power Stations and the Murray Group Control Centre, tours of which are conducted regularly.

KOSCIUSKO NATIONAL PARK ■ 682
All the New South Wales ski resorts are within the Kosciusko National Park, attracting thousands of visitors

Not Austria or Switzerland but the Kosciusko National Park where stone is more plentiful than timber on the heath of the upper slopes and provides a ready material for simple but sturdy huts for skiers and bushwalkers.

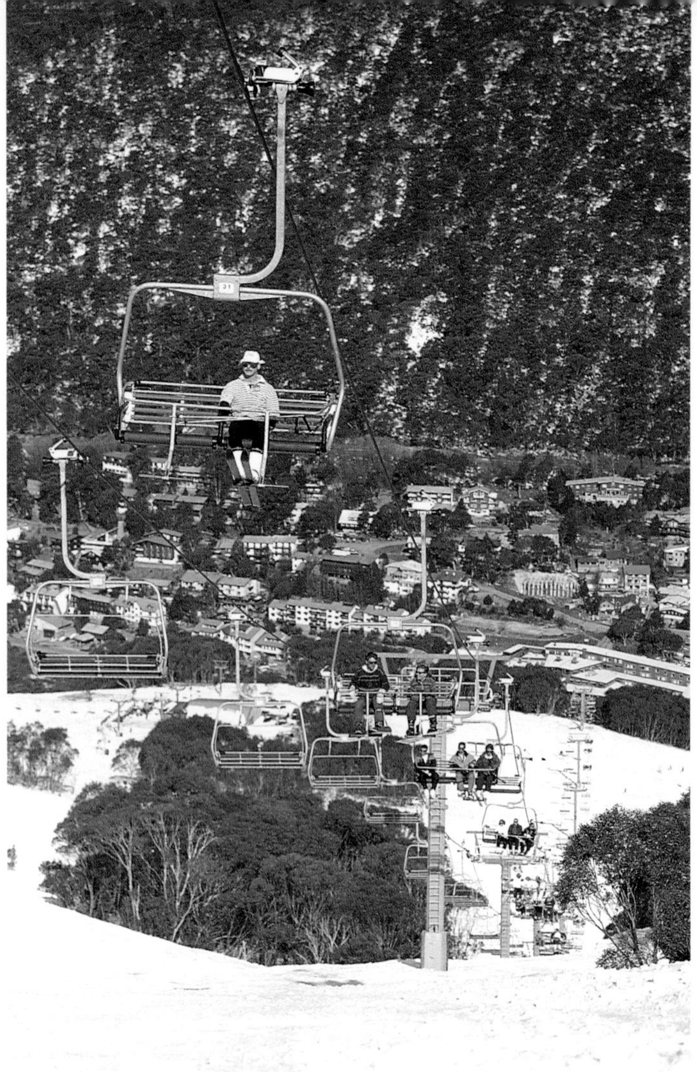

The best views in Thredbo are to be had from the chairlift which gives skiers access to the resort's 70 kilometres of ski trails. At Mount Kosciusko (right) an event is recorded: this man is clearly delighted to be – briefly – the highest person in Australia.

every winter. The park covers over six hundred thousand hectares, and even though, by world standards, the mountains are not high – Mount Kosciusko, Australia's highest mountain, at 2228 metres, is a mere hummock – there is a larger surface area of snow country here during the short winter season than in Switzerland. The giant engineering feat of the Snowy Mountains Hydroelectric Scheme is within the park too, which along with trout fishing, horseback riding, hiking, cycling and a magnificent wildflower display in summer, makes it an attractive year-round tourist destination.

The history of the park is one of politics, intrigue and vested interests. It became a state park in 1944 when it was discovered that summer grazing of sheep and cattle was altering and destroying the delicate mountain environment. Not unnaturally, the graziers were not keen to give up their leases, and erosion continued until 1963 when about 180 square kilometres surrounding the Mount Kosciusko summit were declared a Primitive Area, prohibiting human interference with the native environment. In 1967, it became a national park under the control of the National Parks and Wildlife Service of New South Wales. The authority walks a difficult tightrope, trying to maintain a balance between conservation of the environment and the demands of tourists, skiers and bushwalkers.

LAKE EUCUMBENE ■ 683

An artificial lake constructed as a reservoir for the Snowy Mountains Scheme, Lake Eucumbene holds nine times as much water as Sydney Harbour. The lake is fed by the Eucumbene River as well as by innumerable streams from the Great Dividing Range. Water is also diverted into the lake from Tantangara Dam on the headwaters of the Murrumbidgee River. A fishing haven, it contains a large number of rainbow and brown trout. Boats and fishing tackle can be hired at any of the little settlements that have sprung up along its shores. Among these are Old Adaminaby, Anglers Reach, Braemar and Buckenderra.

MOUNT KOSCIUSKO ■ 684

Paul Edmund (Count) de Strzelecki, a Polish-born explorer and geologist was the first European man to climb Mount Kosciusko, Australia's highest mountain (2228 metres). He named it after a Polish patriot, Tadeusz Kosciuszko (over time, the spelling and the pronunciation have changed).

Strzelecki had a chequered career. Born in 1797 to an aristocratic family in west Poland, his youth seems to have been spent in impulsive actions that misfired. He left Poland under the ignominious suspicion of embezzlement, travelling for several years in the Americas and Pacific islands, studying earth sciences. Reputedly a man of great charm, he arrived in Sydney in 1839 and persuaded the grazier James Macarthur to finance and accompany him on an expedition through the Alps.

He climbed Mount Kosciusko in mid-March 1840 – though opinion is divided as to whether or not he actually reached the top – after having climbed Mount Townsend three days before, believing it to be the highest peak. Strzelecki discovered areas that contained silver and coal and made a valuable contribution to the exploration of the colonies. But his scientific and anthropological work was sometimes erratic. The instruments he used for surveying were found to be inaccurate and his calculations wrong. Strzelecki settled in London in 1843 and in 1845 published his *Physical Description of New South Wales and Van Diemen's Land* for which he received a medal from the Royal Geographical Society. The National Parks and Wildlife Service recommends that only experienced hikers take the walk to the summit, and that in any season, all walkers should prepare themselves for rapid changes in weather conditions.

NIMMITABEL ■ 685

Formerly called, among other names, Nimity Bell, it is said that some long-time residents even today object to this village's present name. The settlement began in the late 1830s and by 1858 there were two hotels, a post office and a general store. A German settler, John Geldmacher, built a flour mill, but was unable to use the sails he had built for it because the regulations stated that the mill was too close to the road and the shadows of the sails might startle passing horses. He was forced to use horses to drive the mill but this was not successful and it later changed from flour to timber milling. Nimmitabel was used as a location in the film of Jon Cleary's book *The Sundowners*.

PERISHER VALLEY ■ 686

The Spencer family, pioneer settlers in the region who took up land in the 1860s are credited with naming this area Perisher Valley. One of the Spencers is also thought to have named the peak to the west of Perisher Gap 'The Paralyser'. Nowadays it is a large resort, joined to Smiggin Holes and called Perisher/Smiggins, with all the usual skiing facilities. There are slopes here for all standards. *Population 1720*

SMIGGIN HOLES ■ 687

In the nineteenth century, this was the site of a cattle camp. The name is of Scottish origin and means 'little holes', believed to refer to the shallow pools from which the cattle drank. The resort is now linked with Perisher Valley resort (see entry) and is noted for its good runs for novice and intermediate skiers.

SNOWY RIVER ■ 688

The Snowy River flows south-east from its starting point in the mountains and empties into the Tasman Sea, on the way giving its name and its waters to an audacious engineering scheme (see box).

THREDBO VILLAGE ■ 689

The Aborigines who lived in the valley near what is now Thredbo, would climb, every year, to the high country to catch the bogong moths, which were considered a great delicacy. They would light fires and have great bogong feasts. So numerous were the cooking fires that in 1846 the New South Wales Lands Department Surveyor, Thomas Townsend, noted that he could not take sights because of the great veil of smoke from the 'bogong' cooking fires.

In 1956, an ex-Czech ski instructor, then working as a hydrographer for the Snowy Mountains Authority, realised that the Thredbo area would be the perfect spot for a resort, especially since the Snowy Mountains Authority was building a road right through the valley. In 1957 the first lodge was built. *Population 2060*

THE HIGH COUNTRY, WHERE THE SKIER'S SNOW MAY DRIVE A TURBINE

SKIING is generally thought to be a relatively 'modern' sport in Australia, but in fact it was practised here well before it was adopted in the fashionable resorts of Austria or Switzerland. During the goldrush in Kiandra (see entry) snow-bound Norwegian miners introduced the alpine sport using fence palings.

The Sydney Morning Herald of 6 August 1861 reported that: 'Kiandra is a rather dreary place in winter but yet the people are not without their amusements. The roads are impassable except with snow shoes or the more novel mode of travelling on skates. These are constructed of two palings turned up at the front and about four feet long, with straps to put the feet in, and the traveller carries a long stick to balance himself and to assist him up the hill. Downhill they can go as fast as a steamer and on the level, with the aid of the pole, they can make good headway.'

Deep beneath the mountains, water from Lake Eucumbene now roars through this tunnel to turbines at Tumut 2 power station.

The pioneer skiers of Kiandra with their makeshift skis purloined from timber fences would be goggle-eyed at the thousands of ski devotees who make the pilgrimage to the snow country every winter in order to glide down the slopes on the latest streamlined, aerodynamically designed 'skates' that bear no relation to the palings. Even in their wildest dreams they could not have imagined the 'Skitube' – an underground railway system that runs from Bullocks Flat to Perisher Valley and Blue Cow Mountain, whisking skiers *through* the mountain in twenty minutes. Skiers who start out in Guthega can ski to Blue Cow and take the Skitube to Perisher Valley. In summer, tourists hire mountain bikes, take them on the train and cycle back to the terminal or to Charlottes Pass.

By 1926, when this jolly group was snapped at Mount Kosciusko, skiing had caught on.

While the holiday crowds are indulging in the breakneck, athletic thrills offered by the winter snows, all around them one of the world's most ambitious engineering schemes is putting nature to work in the interests of irrigation and power generation. The snow which thaws on the aptly named Snowy Mountains gives rise to the Murray and Murrumbidgee rivers which flow to the west of the Great Dividing Range and irrigate some of the most productive agricultural land in southern New South Wales and Victoria. Farming on these plains has always been limited by the amount of water carried by the two rivers. So it was to the Snowy River that farmers and graziers looked for an answer to their problems. At the same time its hydro-electric potential was examined, and in 1949 the Snowy Mountains Hydro-electric Authority was established for the investigation, design and construction of the dual-purpose Snowy Mountains Scheme.

The Snowy Mountains are also the birthplace of the Snowy River which once carried much of the melted snow from the eastern side of the ranges south into the Tasman Sea. The ambitious workings of the Snowy Mountains Scheme – twenty-five years in the making, it was the biggest single public project ever undertaken in Australia – divert this river through long tunnels into the Murray-Murrumbidgee system. At the same time, it generates huge quantites of electrical power (see *Tumut & Gundagai*).

In order to achieve this, dams were built, tunnels cut through rock, power stations constructed, the courses of rivers were changed and whole towns were flooded and relocated. The first dam of the Snowy River is at Island Bend and some of its waters are diverted by tunnel under the mountains. The river flows south-east from Island Bend and is joined by a number of mountain tributaries. It is dammed again at Jindabyne then flows south-east through open Monaro country before doing an about-face and heading north-west back towards the mountains. It is joined by many tributaries, and its eventual meeting with the Tasman Sea is at Marlo, near Orbost. □

At its peak in 1959, the Snowy Mountains Authority employed more than 7000 people; tent barracks housed a multi-national labour force.

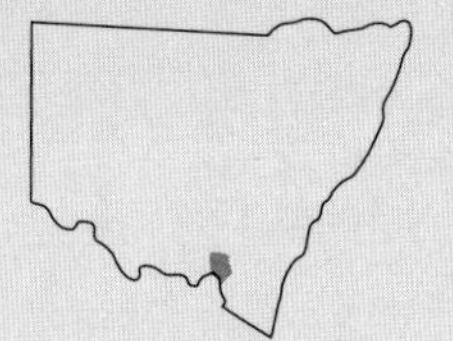

Batlow & Tumbarumba

Between the Snowy Mountains and the Murray River, there is a scenic agricultural region known in the tourist brochures as the 'Garden of the South'. It is an apt description; with its high altitude, mild summer climate and fertile soils, this region has hastened the growth of specialised and highly successful industries of forestry and fruit growing.

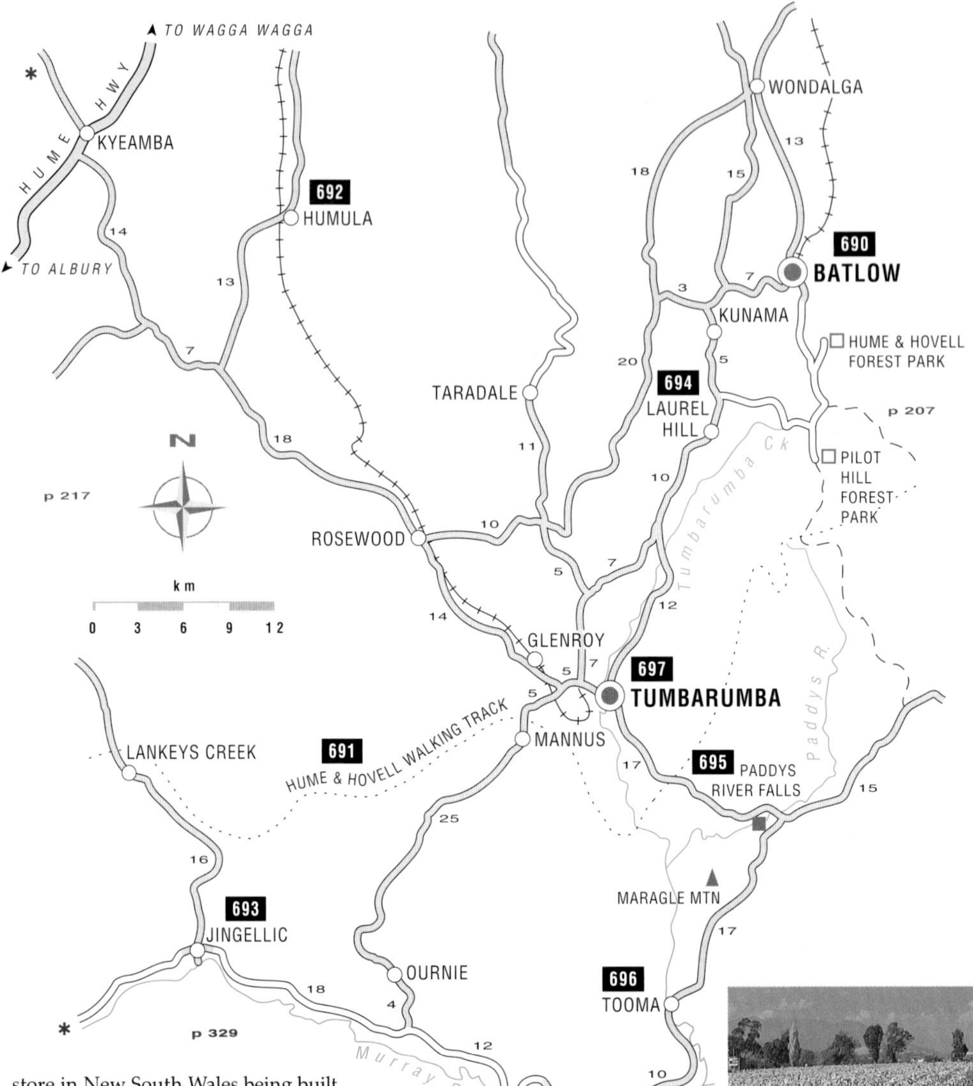

BATLOW ■ **690**

Hamilton Hume and William Hovell passed through the Batlow and Tumbarumba area, to the south-east of modern day Wagga Wagga, on their way south to the Murray River and Port Phillip in 1824. The town of Batlow, high in the Great Dividing Range, was first known as Reedy Creek but took on its present name, that of an old squatting run, in 1889. Grazing began in the 1840s, the area was surveyed in 1853, the first post office opened in 1873, and a township was proclaimed in 1910.

Alluvial gold was discovered here in 1853; several mines opened and the township grew up during the gold boom. The miners also took advantage of the region's abundant timber and, as the boom progressed, timber-getting and sawmilling developed as an offshoot of the mining industry. Chinese miners flocked into the region during this goldrush era and have left their legacy in the form of Paddys River Dam – a mainly Chinese-built earthwork, which was constructed across the river to facilitate the sluicing and washing of alluvial gold.

At 775 metres above sea-level, this region is particularly suitable for growing apples, pears, cherries and other cool-climate fruits, such as berries. Fruit and vegetable growing developed during the gold rush years and specialised fruit growing began in earnest in the late nineteenth century, with the first cool store in New South Wales being built here in 1923, and a cannery was established during the Second World War. In 1923, the railway from Sydney opened and encouraged further settlement: Batlow was on an extension of the branch line from Gundagai to Tumut, but the line proved unsuitable for heavy traffic and was eventually closed.

The town is now famous for its apples, particularly the 'Delicious' variety and the fruit industry is the major employer. Batlow still has a large cannery, as well as fruit freezing and packaging works and Australia's largest apple-handling facility. The surrounding region contains some 500 000 fruit trees in commercial orchards. Vegetables, including asparagus, are also grown, and the area has wool and beef-cattle industries. Beekeeping and horticulture are other small-scale pursuits.

There has been a forestry reserve here since 1878, with the first timber mill opening in 1880. Today, Batlow is well-known for its softwood and pine timber production (see Bago and Maragle State Forests).

Despite the opening up of the region by the Snowy Mountains Authority during the 1950s, the town is still somewhat isolated. But Batlow's proximity to the Kosciusko National Park means that tourism is important; skiers and hikers come here every year; nearby Lake Blowering provides the setting for

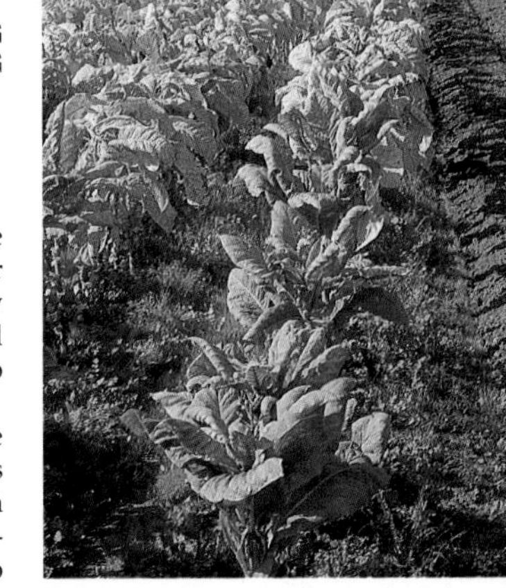

Tobacco grows at either end of the Great Dividing Range – the altitude at Tumbarumba and in Queensland ensures the necessary cool winters.

recreational activities such as fishing, sailing and waterskiing. Gold fossicking and orchard tours are also popular. *Population 1140*

FESTIVALS Apple Blossom Festival, March.

BAGO AND MARAGLE STATE FORESTS This 48 000-hectare forest outside Batlow was dedicated in 1918 and has a logging history going back to the 1870s. The vast forest is a unique blend of hardwood and softwood trees; foreign softwoods such as radiata pine were introduced in 1921 and developed further after the Second World War. The forest is the only major concentration of native alpine ash in New South Wales that is suitable for timber production.

In the northern section of the forest, historic Paddy's River Dam is now a picnic and camping spot; Buddong Falls are popular with tourists; and there is a picnic site at the Hume and Hovell Lookout – believed to be the spot from where the explorers viewed the snowy peaks to the east.

HUME & HOVELL WALKING TRACK ■ 691

Developed by the State Department of Lands as a 1988 Bicentennial project, this marked, well-made track stretches for more than 370 kilometres between Yass and Albury and follows, as closely as possible, the route taken by the explorers Hume and Hovell on their journey south in 1824. Sections of the walking track pass through the Batlow–Tumbarumba region, taking in Blowering Lake, Buddong Falls, Paddys River Dam, Burra Creek and Bago State Forest.

BURRA CREEK Explorers Hume and Hovell camped at the east and west junctions of Burra Creek in November 1824, and from 1855 onwards the area was the scene of much energetic gold and tin mining activity. The Burra Gold Fields were proclaimed in 1872 and, unlike many other workings in the area, were productive over a long period and continued to be mined until the 1930s. Sawmilling became an important activity and a mill was constructed on West Burra Creek in 1887. The site is now occupied by a tiny sawmilling settlement in the Bago State Forest.

HUMULA ■ 692

Humula today is a quiet, peaceful backwater, but for a few years from 1912 this village to the west of Batlow was the scene of lively activity while a branch railway line was constructed from Wagga Wagga and Tarcutta to Tumbarumba. The track to Humula opened in 1917.

JINGELLIC ■ 693

This small village on the New South Wales side of the Murray River was once the site of a pre-Federation border customs office. Goods and livestock were taxed here as they made their way between colonies. Today Jingellic has an exotic tree plantation, attractive river scenery, and the famous old Bridge Hotel.

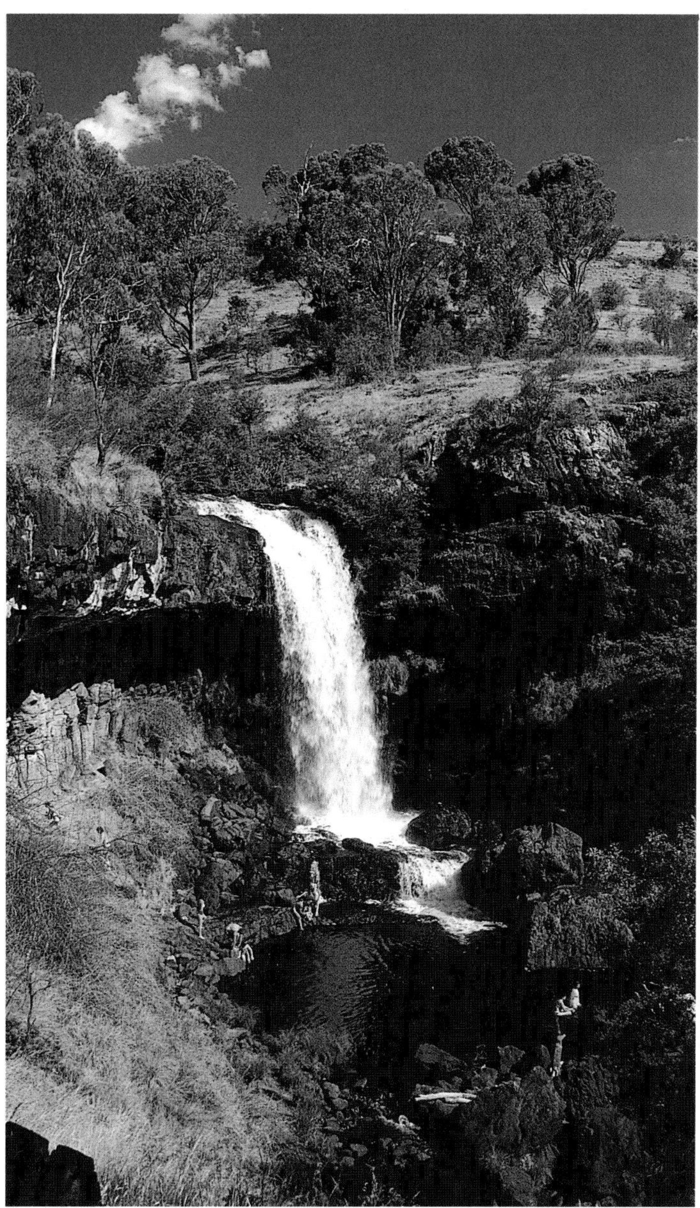

A track leads to the swimming hole where the waters of Paddys River – or Cowra Creek – make a dramatic change of level on their way to the Murray.

LAUREL HILL ■ 694

South of Batlow, this village, and the nearby mining camp at Quartzville, was once a thriving gold mining centre of more than 2000 people. Further development came through its role as a horse-changing stop on the Adelong–Tumbarumba coach route and the settlement once had a popular hotel, The Miners' Arms. Little evidence remains of these boom times, but the village still has a sawmill, handsome plantings of mature European trees and a 1908 factory that manufactures oars from alpine ash.

PADDYS RIVER FALLS ■ 695

This recreation area, to the southeast of Tumbarumba, contains a bushland reserve, the sixty metre falls, walking tracks and barbecue and picnic facilities. The creeks and dam provide an excellent habitat for trout and native fish.

TOOMA ■ 696

The small town of Tooma, set in a valley to the south of Tumbarumba, is best known for its reservoir on the Tooma River, which is fed by the Toolong River and Broadway and Bulls Head creeks. Tobacco is grown in the region, and the area's good fishing attracts many tourists.

In the 1850s, the Upper Murray's first flour mill was established at Tooma by two Scotsmen named Mair and Garland. A single-storey hotel, constructed during the 1880s, is the settlement's oldest brick building and is registered by the National Trust. According to legend, Paul Edmund de Strzelecki, the discoverer of Mount Kosciusko, first viewed the mountain from here in 1840. The site was once considered as a possible location for a national capital.

TUMBARUMBA ■ 697

The town and shire of Tumbarumba is located south of Batlow, in a sheltered valley in the western foothills of the Snowy Mountains. Known as the 'Gem of the Highlands', Tumbarumba (from an Aboriginal word, 'rumba', said to mean 'a sound' – the locals here say that the land makes a hollow sound when stamped) is at approximately 700 metres above sea-level. The local shire includes all of the Snowy Mountains Scheme west of the Great Dividing Range, and its boundary passes through Kosciusko National Park. This proximity to the mountains has brought tourism to the region.

Hume and Hovell passed this way in 1824: they crossed the nearby Tumut River in November of that year and sighted the snow-capped Snowy Mountain range from somewhere near Tumbarumba.

The first cattle graziers arrived in 1836 and soon a village began to grow up; a pastoral holding called Tombrumba Creek was gazetted in 1851. Gold was discovered here in the 1850s, leading, as so often in Australia's history, to the development of a township. As with Batlow, a large number of Chinese miners migrated into the region during this period. Bushranger Dan Morgan ventured into the area during his reign of terror, and in 1864, shot dead a policeman, Sergeant Maginnity.

Tumbarumba's court house, a brick building with timber-posted verandahs, and police station were built in the 1880s, a district hospital opened before the First World War and the railway from Wagga Wagga arrived in 1921. Time has wrought few changes here and the town has great appeal for tourists, who come to fossick for gold, zircons, rubies and sapphires; to take farm holidays, or to fish; and for the nearby Snowy Mountains' skiing. Other attractions include the Pioneer Women's Hut, a museum of domestic history, a few kilometres away at Glenroy. The museum is within the thirty-hectare Glenroy Recreation Reserve. The town also has a wool and craft centre, located in the former Tattersall's Hotel which dates from the 1880s.

Today, Tumbarumba has a diversifed agricultural economy, based on activities such as dairying, fat cattle grazing on the rich pastures, wool production, vegetable (especially potatoes and peas), apple and tobacco growing. This region is also known for its productive forestry and sawmilling industries, which have expanded considerably since a wood pulp mill was opened at Albury in 1980.

The town's New Year's Day Rodeo is one of Australia's largest rodeos and attracts riders from all over the country. *Population 1550*

FESTIVALS Tumbarumba Heritage Week, November.

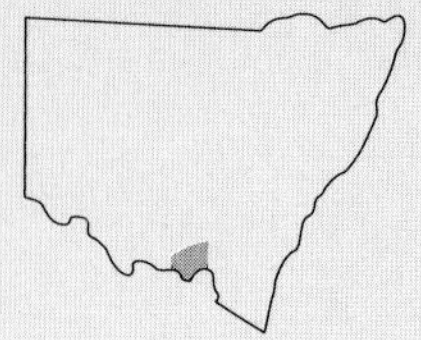

Albury & Wodonga

First explored by Hume and Hovell in 1824, the Albury–Wodonga region became the site of Australia's original government-funded National Growth Centre in 1973. Today, the twin cities are a commercial and industrial centre for the Riverina, and one of the nation's most successful experiments in decentralisation.

ALBURY ■ 698

The Wiradhuri Aborigines occupied this area long before retired sea captain William Hilton Hovell and his companion Andrew Hamilton Hume 'discovered' the Murray River on 16 November 1824. The explorers forded the river (which they named the Hume) near the present site of the Hume Weir, on their overland expedition from Sydney to Port Phillip (Melbourne). They marked two trees, one of which still stands in Albury, to commemorate their discovery.

Squatters began to follow the explorers' route and this site on the northern bank of the Murray became a popular camping spot for drovers and stockmen heading for Port Phillip with their cattle. The first cattle runs were taken up in the mid-1830s, and in 1838 an enterprising character named Robert Brown erected a slab hut to provide a store for the increasing number of travellers crossing the river. This was the first building on the site of what was to become Albury. Later that year a police post was erected and in 1839 the site was surveyed and gazetted as Albury, after a similarly named English village.

A punt crossing across the Murray River was commenced by Robert Brown in 1844, and when the era of river transport began in 1855, the riverside site proved to be critical to the town's development. Albury became a major paddlesteamer port, with links along the length of the river to South Australia. The town also became a centre for the manufacture of riverboats – the first being built in 1858. From this year onwards Albury became a vital link in the telegraph line between Sydney and Melbourne. Albury, being roughly midway between the two centres, was used as a break point in the system. Operators here took down the messages and then literally handed them over to the Victorian operators for transmission on to Melbourne.

The railway line from Sydney reached the riverlands in 1881 and in 1883, when the Sydney–Melbourne service began, Albury became the 'changeover' station for passengers – the two states' tracks remained on different gauges until 1962.

Albury is still an important pastoral centre, with an estimated five million sheep in the area, but today it is also the industrial and commercial heart of southern New South Wales. The decentralisation scheme has brought a great deal of manufacturing industry to the region. One of the largest concerns is the Albury Newsprint Mill which was established in 1981 and now produces around thirty per cent of the nation's requirements. Since 1971, new or expanding businesses have provided more than 15 000 jobs in the region and the Albury–Wodonga Development Corporation works at attracting more industrial enterprises.

Albury's urban environment has matured into one of well-established parks, gardens and tree-lined streets. Tourist attractions include the botanic gardens, the Hovell Tree – the river gum marked by William Hovell in 1824 – and many historic buildings. The city is a major inland holiday centre and, as befits an important provincial city, it boasts an 800-seater Civic Theatre, an art centre and a regional museum.

Many protected buildings remain from the 1860–85 period including the 1860 court house that was once the province of police magistrate Thomas Alexander Browne, better known as Rolf Boldrewood, author of *Robbery Under Arms*, and the splendid Victorian-Italianate railway station, opened in 1881 and classified by the National Trust. The station has the longest platform in New South Wales. *Population 39 980*

FESTIVALS Easter Hockey Carnival, April; Albury Agricultural Show, November.

Parklands, including Hovell Tree Park (above, right), line the banks of the Murray where its meandering course defines Albury's southern limits.

CULCAIRN ■ 699

This settlement north of Albury was named in 1880 by James Balfour (who was responsible for laying out the town), after his family home in England. Hume and Hovell passed through the area in 1824 and the first settlers, drawn by fertile soil and good grass cover, arrived in 1840. By 1847, four stations were gazetted as Crown Leases.

During the 1870s and 1880s, the Culcairn Shire grew rapidly thanks to the pastoral industry, and the influx of workers constructing the Sydney–Melbourne railway. Culcairn is now the centre of a shire, often known as 'Morgan Country' after the notorious bushranger, which includes the towns of Henty and Walla Walla.

Culcairn's major claim to fame is that it has Australia's largest sub-artesian domestic water supply. The thirty-nine-metre-deep, brick-lined shaft was constructed in 1926 and taps a massive underground water basin. This unlimited water supply has led to the town being noteworthy for its pleasant tree-lined streets and gardens – it was once known as the 'Oasis of the Riverina'. At least half the buildings in the main shopping street are Heritage classified and the Hotel Culcairn (1891), beside the railway station, was once the largest hostelry between Sydney and Melbourne. *Population 1180*

ETTAMOGAH ■ 700

Ettamogah is claimed – facetiously, some say – to be a local Aboriginal word for 'let's have a drink', and was once, appropriately, the name of a vineyard in the area. The famous Ettamogah pub brings to life the eccentric building of the popular cartoon feature created by artist Ken Maynard in *Australasian Post*. Nearby is Cooper's Winery, established in

Little did the explorer William Hovell know that the tree he marked in 1824 would one day be surrounded by a major city.

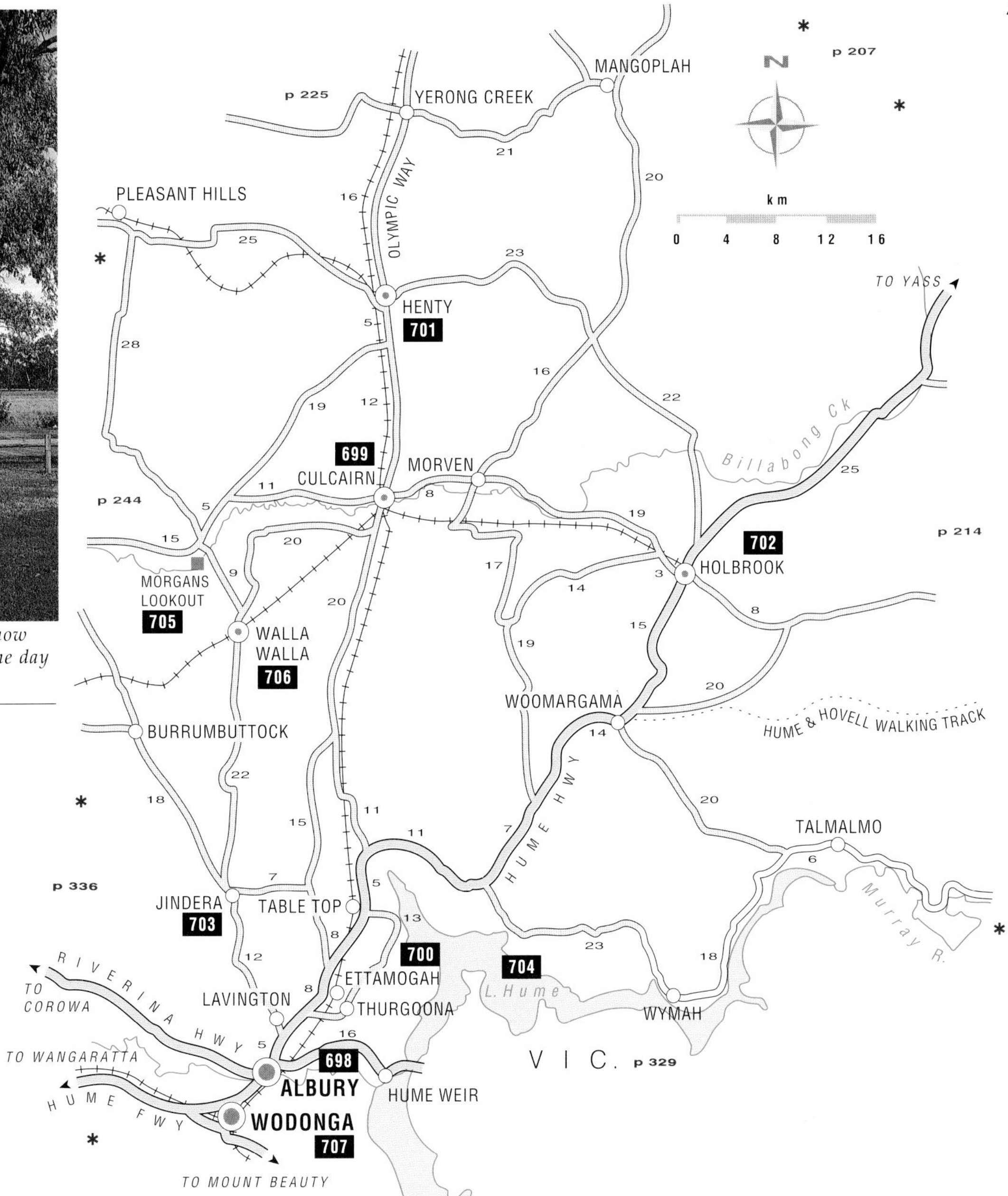

1981. Another major attraction is the Ettamogah Wildlife Sanctuary, a non-commercial operation established in 1969 by the Wildlife Conservation Society to foster an appreciation of Australian animals and plants.

MANGOPLAH
YERONG CREEK
PLEASANT HILLS
OLYMPIC WAY
HENTY 701
CULCAIRN 699
MORVEN
Billabong Ck
HOLBROOK 702
MORGANS LOOKOUT 705
WALLA WALLA 706
WOOMARGAMA
HUME & HOVELL WALKING TRACK
BURRUMBUTTOCK
HUME HWY
TALMALMO
Murray R.
JINDERA 703
TABLE TOP
ETTAMOGAH 700
L. Hume 704
THURGOONA
LAVINGTON
WYMAH
RIVERINA HWY
TO COROWA
TO WANGARATTA
ALBURY 698
HUME WEIR
VIC.
HUME FWY
WODONGA 707
TO MOUNT BEAUTY
TO YASS
km 0 4 8 12 16
p 207
p 225
p 244
p 214
p 336
p 329

HENTY ■ 701

The village of Henty, gazetted in 1888, was named for Edward Henty, a member of the famous Victorian mercantile and farming family, who leased a property in the area during the 1860s. This small settlement to the north of Albury–Wodonga was originally known as Doodle Cooma, but the name's similarity to that of Cooma in the Snowy Mountains region led to confusion and it was changed. A pastoral holding was occupied in the area by brothers John and Thomas Reighlan in 1866, and a railway siding was established here in 1885.

In 1914, a local farmer – Headlie Taylor – unveiled his remarkable invention, a time- and labour-saving mechanical header-harvester, at the town's agricultural show. The Taylor Header revolutionised the grain industry throughout the world, and modifications to his design have been made only in recent years. There is a Headlie Taylor memorial in Henty, which contains the original heading machine.

This is 'Morgan Country' and bushranger Dan Morgan shot and killed Sergeant Smyth, the leader of a troop of mounted police, on a hill west of the town in September 1864 – there is a roadside memorial to the unfortunate policeman (see box).

Henty is an agricultural centre in the Shire of Culcairn and hosts the Henty Machinery Field Days, a major three-day agricultural event, held every September. *Population 850*

HOLBROOK ■ 702

Hume and Hovell passed through this area to the north-east of Albury in 1824, but it was not until 1836 that the district was settled. John Purtell named the area Ten Mile Creek in 1838, after the nearby waterway and it was gazetted under this name in 1856. Its name was officially changed to Germanton in 1876, in honour of John Pabst, one of the early settlers and innkeeper of The Woolpack.

Anti-German feeling during the First World War led to yet another name change: this time to Holbrook, in 1915. This was in memory of British Navy Commander Norman D. Holbrook, who torpedoed a Turkish battleship from his submarine and was subsequently awarded the Victoria Cross. A model of the submarine is in the town's Commander Holbrook War Memorial Park.

The town was once a stopping place on the railway line from Sydney, but the opening of the northern line from Melbourne in 1883 diverted

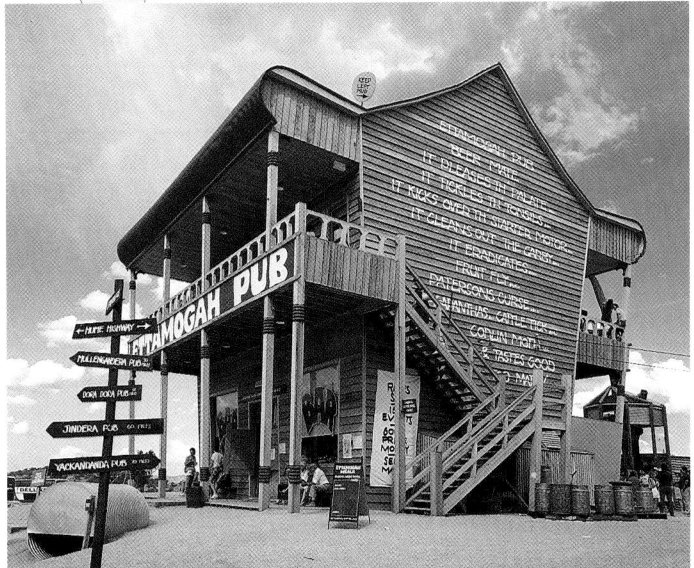

The Ettamogah pub of cartoon fame has been brought to life – complete with an alarming lean to starboard – north of Albury.

rail traffic and left Holbrook out on a limb. The modern town is located on the Hume Highway and is at the centre of a farming and grazing region which is noted for its sheep and cattle properties. *Population 1370*

JINDERA ■ 703

Originally a hamlet called Dight's Forest, which was named after John Dight, a friend of explorer Hamilton Hume, Jindera is a small village to the north-west of Albury. Settled by German Lutheran immigrants who travelled by waggon from South Australia in the 1860s in search of new farming land, it was gazetted as a town in 1869. *Population 780*

LAKE HUME ■ 704

A few kilometres east of Albury, the Hume Weir has formed one of Australia's largest man-made waterways: Lake Hume has a surface area of more than 20 000 hectares and a shoreline of 400 kilometres. The dam was built between 1919 and 1936 to provide water for the downstream Murray River irrigation system. The dam wall was later raised to provide hydro-electric power and a hydro-electric station, completed in 1957, provides power to both Victoria and New South Wales. The Hume Weir is one of four dams along the Murray and water from here serves both states for domestic, stock watering and irrigation purposes.

MORGANS LOOKOUT ■ 705

This massive white granite rock formation lies a few kilometres north of Walla Walla and was used by the infamous bushranger Dan Morgan as a lookout and hiding place. The lookout offers panoramic views over the nearby Billabong Valley and is a popular attraction for tourists.

WALLA WALLA ■ 706

Walla Walla – supposedly an Aboriginal word for 'plenty of rain' – was named after a pastoral holding which was established by a group of Lutherans who travelled in covered waggons from the Barossa Valley in the late 1860s. The Pioneer Cairn on the outskirts of town marks the spot where the families camped at the end of their six-week journey. This small township, west of Culcairn, was founded in 1869 and contains a large Zion Lutheran Church, which dates from 1924. The 1889 original granite church is nearby. The town also has an 1875 public school and St Paul's College, a major Lutheran Church school, is located just outside the town. *Population 710*

WODONGA ■ 707

Explorers Hume and Hovell crossed the Murray River near Wodonga in 1824, but the first settlers, Paul Huon and his family, did not arrive until over a decade later. Huon had heard good reports of this land on the south side of the Murray River from Hamilton Hume. The large group journeyed to the site from Goulburn in 1836. Huon took up a run here and named it 'Woodonga', an Aboriginal word for an edible nut. On his 16 500-hectare property, he built a homestead called 'Belvoir', under which name the settlement was first surveyed and gazetted in 1852.

Increasing traffic through the district – in the form of overlanders taking their stock from New South Wales to the new grazing lands around Port Phillip – led to the establishment of a police post in 1838; about the same time the Melbourne–Sydney mail service began to pass through here. During the 1840s, a small village began to grow up around the police post.

The beginning of river trade during the 1850s stimulated growth in Wodonga in the same way as it did in Albury (see entry). When Victoria and New South Wales became separate colonies in 1851, Belvoir and its New South Wales neighbour, Albury, were automatically transformed into 'border' towns. The Victorian settlement comprised 'Woodonga', plus portions of the adjacent property of 'Bonegilla'. From its pastoral beginnings, Wodonga became a thriving cattle town: for many years it held the largest cattle market between Sydney and Melbourne.

In 1861, the bridge over the Murray was opened, forging the town's historic link with Albury. In 1869, the fledgling town took on the name of the 'Woodonga' property (minus the additional 'o'). Until Federation in 1901, it was the site of a customs house for goods entering Victoria from New South Wales.

An army camp was established at nearby Bonegilla in 1940 and in 1947 this became one of Australia's largest migrant centres – more than 300 000 'new Australians' passed through the camp between 1947 and 1971.

The Rural City of Wodonga was proclaimed in 1973, in which year it also became the Victorian half of the Albury–Wodonga Growth Centre: Wodonga is now Victoria's largest provincial centre. It is linked with its sister city of Albury by the Union Bridge over the Murray. The city has a variety of manufacturing industries, one of the most successful of which is a dairy produce plant, specialising in cheeses. *Population 23 640*

In this stretch of Lake Hume, the stark, drowned eucalypts have yet to slide beneath the surface.

THE UNLAMENTED DEMISE OF 'MAD DAN'

DANIEL MORGAN – commonly known as 'Mad Dan' or 'Black Dan' – was one of Australia's most notorious and feared bushrangers. From 1863 to 1865 he terrorised travellers and station owners as he roamed the Riverina region, killing seven people and wounding more than sixty others.

Unlike some bushrangers, Morgan – shown right in an 1865 newspaper sketch – never fitted the 'Robin Hood' image and his brutality instilled a particular fear into the people of the district. There is even a school of thought that he was insane, and his behaviour was, to say the least, unpredictable. His puzzling habit of sparing some potential victims, yet arbitrarily shooting others, is perhaps best explained by this theory.

Morgan began his reign of terror in August 1863, after escaping from Melbourne's Pentridge Jail. He had received a long sentence for a petty crime and loathed the police for their harsh treatment of prisoners. The bushranger also particularly disliked squatters, one of whom he believed was responsible for his prison sentence. Among swagmen and other itinerants, Morgan was regarded as a hero, and he often evaded capture by hiding in their huts.

After the famous siege of Round Hill Station at Culcairn, on June 19 1864, when he killed two men and wounded two others, the New South Wales Government offered a reward of 1500 pounds for Morgan's capture. He went on to murder two policemen and a Chinese road worker. The persistent failure of the police to capture Morgan incensed the local population; his exploits finally came to an end when the bushranger was shot and killed during another dramatic siege at a property near Wangaratta in Victoria in April 1865. His body was briefly put on public display. The head was later amputated and sent to Melbourne University for phrenological study, but the examination revealed nothing out of the ordinary. □

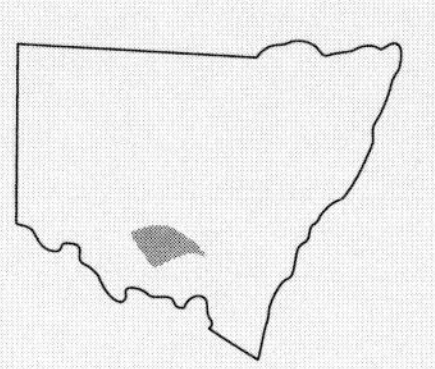

Griffith & Leeton

The fertility of this region, with the Murrumbidgee Irrigation Area at its core, is the result of a highly successful marriage between imagination and technology. The 'desolate plains' that John Oxley believed would 'never again be visited by civilised man' now support a population of 50 000 and produce the bulk of the state's rice, grapes, citrus and stone fruits.

The tree-lined streets of Griffith are greened by the same waters that bring orchards right up to the town limits.

ARDLETHAN ■ 708
Although gold was discovered at Ardlethan, it was tin around which the small town developed – together with the four sawmills the loggers kept busy. The largest open-cut tin mine in the state operated at Ardlethan and the town was second only to Tasmania in its production of tin. The mine closed in 1986.

Ardlethan, named from a Gaelic word meaning 'high or hilly', is now a centre in the irrigation zone and grain storage has replaced mining as the major industry.

CARRATHOOL ■ 709
Carrathool was a busy wool port on the Murrumbidgee River in the nineteenth century. With the coming of the railway in 1882 and consequent changes in transport patterns, it declined in importance – although it had a station, it never emerged as a major railhead for the district.

Now the main attraction of this settlement with one of the oldest police stations on the river, is Pinkers Beach, with its large trees offering shade and its muddy shallows giving way to the cool waters of one of the more scenic sections of the 'Bidgee'.

COCOPARRA NATIONAL PARK ■ 710
John Oxley passed through what is now Cocoparra National Park in 1817. It was he who named the two mountains in the southern section of the park – Mount Brogden and Mount Caley. Beneath Mount Brogden, the highest point above the surrounding plain, one of Oxley's party planted oak, peach, apricot and quince seeds to commemorate the King's Birthday. Oxley is reputed to have climbed Mount Caley from which he could see what he called 'the desolate plains', now the fertile Murrumbidgee Valley.

This national park – of more than 8350 hectares – is a wilderness area of cliffs, gullies and valleys. The Cocoparra Range, most of which is now contained within the park, rises in a narrow, steep-sided ridge – called a hogback formation – formed by millions of years of folding and tilting of sedimentary layers. One of the most spectacular of the many weathered and scenic gorges within the park is Ladysmith Glen, a thirty-three-metre gorge carved out by Jack's Creek. The western boundary of the park is formed by the old Whitton Stock Route from Melbourne to Queensland, and traces of an old bridge across Steamboat Creek used by Cobb & Co. coaches can still be seen on the road.

Dwyers mallee gums, spearwood, black cypress pine and mugga ironbark are interspersed with tea trees, lilies, grevilleas and the bright yellow acacias for which the park is best known. Over 150 species of birds, from honeyeaters and wedge-tailed eagles to peregrine falcons, and eight species of bat, including the noisy clicking mastiff bat, are found in Cocoparra. Small and large marsupials thrive…now that the feral goats have been evicted.

COLEAMBALLY ■ 711
Coleambally has a very short history. Opened in 1968 as the state's first planned town in over fifty years, it was purpose-built as an administrative and social centre for the Coleambally Irrigation Area (see entry). The town was built within a cypress pine forest on Coleambally Creek and now sits on the banks of the man-made Boona Channel or Coleambally Canal, which feeds the irrigation area.

The main crop of the surrounding district is rice, and one of the Ricegrowers' Cooperative's six mills is based in Coleambally. The up-to-date mill uses the latest technology to process the co-operative's well-known Sunwhite and Sunbrown varieties, as well as other brands for local and export markets.

Other edifices within the new town include the unusually shaped silver water tower, which resembles a giant silver wine goblet…or the tail of a rocket with its nose buried in the ground. The dragline excavator used to scrape out the irrigation canals has been preserved in the town as a memorial to this region's agricultural beginnings. *Population 580*

COLEAMBALLY IRRIGATION AREA ■ 712
The Coleambally Irrigation Area, one of nine irrigation areas administered by the Water Resources Commission of New South Wales, covers 95 000 hectares on the south side of the Murrumbidgee River. The project began in the 1950s and opened in 1968, at the same time as the Blowering Dam on which it depends (see *Cooma & Mount Kosciusko*). In winter, the Blowering Dam stores water already used upstream for electricity generation in the Snowy Mountains Hydro Scheme; in summer, the dam releases water into the Coleambally Irrigation Area – an exercise in seasonal recycling. The water, released down the Tumut River, joins the Murrumbidgee upstream of Gundagai, feeds through to the Gogeldrie Weir (see entry), which then passes the water into the main canal leading south into the irrigation area. This main canal is as wide from bank to bank as the Suez Canal.

Two hundred large farms – varying from 400 to 600 hectares – are supplied with water, primarily for rice production, although wheat, maize, soya beans, safflower and lucerne are also grown. The smaller farms usually grow fruit, including grapes, and a variety of vegetables.

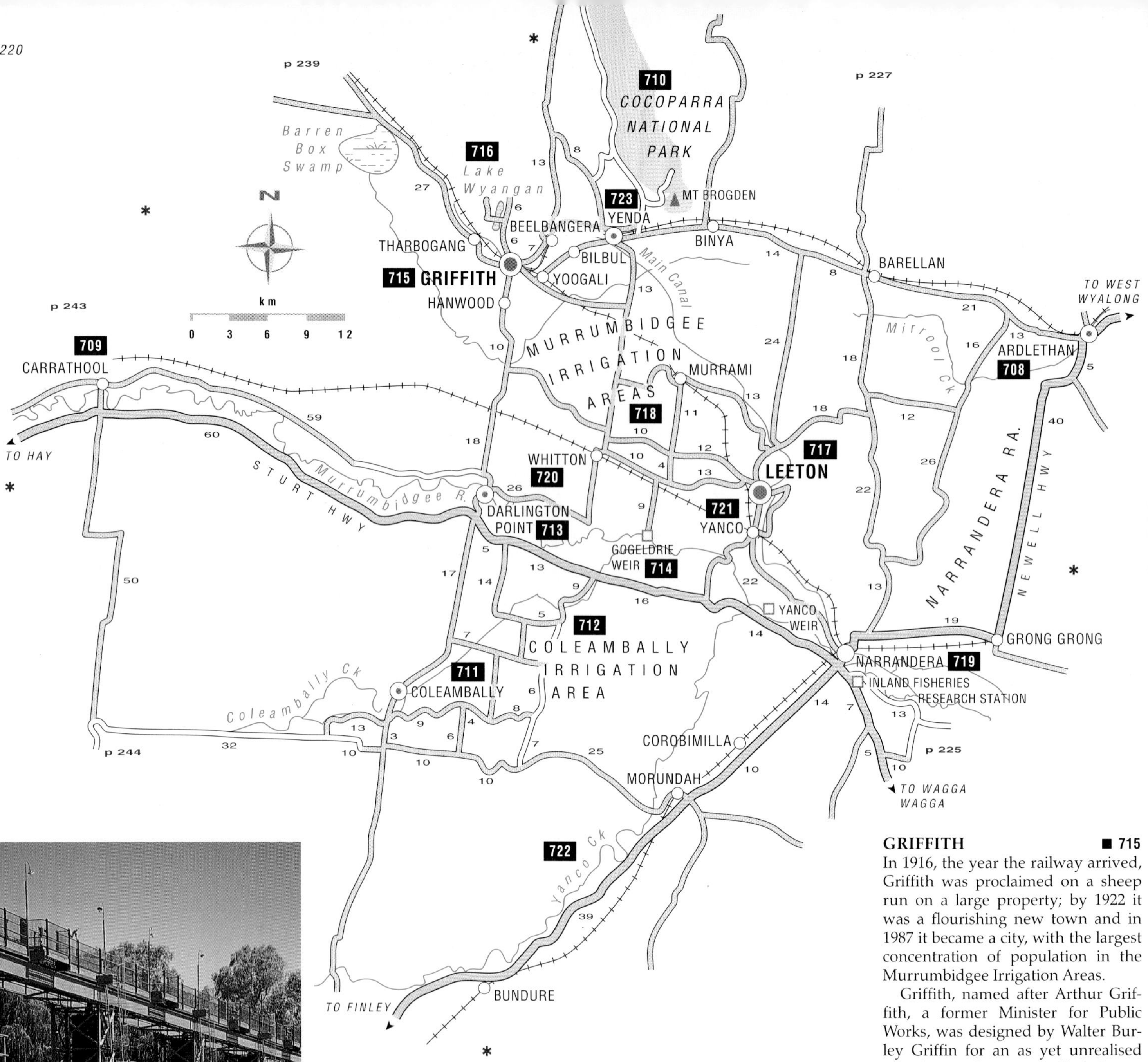

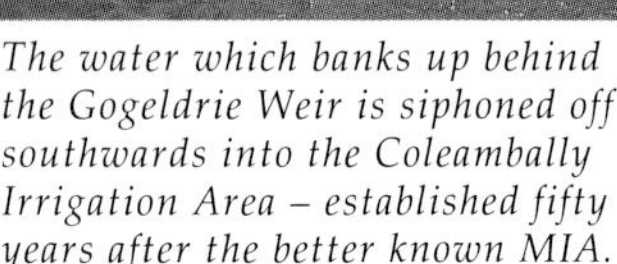

The water which banks up behind the Gogeldrie Weir is siphoned off southwards into the Coleambally Irrigation Area – established fifty years after the better known MIA.

DARLINGTON POINT ■ 713

Darlington Point is distinctive in this region for two reasons: it is an old settlement and is on the Murrumbidgee River itself rather than on a man-made canal. The small town, gazetted in 1864, grew up on a bend in the river where horses and waggons, crossing the river by punt, converged with the paddle steamers that plied this section of the river from the 1850s.

The punt was used until 1905 when a bascule bridge, which hinges upward like a drawbridge, was built across the river at Darlington Point. This bridge was replaced in 1979 by a concrete structure and the old bridge towers have now been re-erected at the local caravan park by students from the Engineering Faculty of the University of New South Wales. Periodic flooding of the Murrumbidgee has created rich alluvial soils, now used for large-scale vegetable growing and there are poultry farms as well as the more traditional sheep and cattle grazing. The town is surrounded by the river red gums of the Willbriggie State Forest and these are milled in Darlington Point's sawmill. *Population 750*

GOGELDRIE WEIR ■ 714

The name Gogeldrie is said to come from an Aboriginal word meaning 'canoe fashioned from a hollow tree' but the weir itself is a distinctively twentieth-century structure. Built as the principal diversion weir for the Coleambally Irrigation Area, it feeds water from the Murrumbidgee River south into the Boona Channel and, on occasion, diverts surplus water north through the Sturt Channel to the Murrumbidgee Irrigation Areas.

To the residents of nearby Yanco, however, the weir serves as a favourite picnic spot with waterskiing, boating and swimming downstream.

GRIFFITH ■ 715

In 1916, the year the railway arrived, Griffith was proclaimed on a sheep run on a large property; by 1922 it was a flourishing new town and in 1987 it became a city, with the largest concentration of population in the Murrumbidgee Irrigation Areas.

Griffith, named after Arthur Griffith, a former Minister for Public Works, was designed by Walter Burley Griffin for an as yet unrealised population of 30 000. Griffin's design incorporated the main canal of the Murrumbidgee Irrigation Areas into the plan of the town, and located the main commercial centre within three concentric circular roads. However, Banna Avenue, one of the straight radial roads, became the main street since the sites there were cheaper and also nearer the railway station.

Spurred by a government advertising campaign, the new citizens of the infant town came from as far afield as Italy and California and also included soldier-settlers after both wars. Italian immigrants, many of them fleeing fascism, were attracted by the type of farming – market gardening and viticulture – with which they were familiar. Now almost fifty per cent of the population is of Italian extraction and a strong Italian influence, especially on the town's restaurants and wineries, is obvious.

The first vines were planted by McWilliams in 1913, even before the

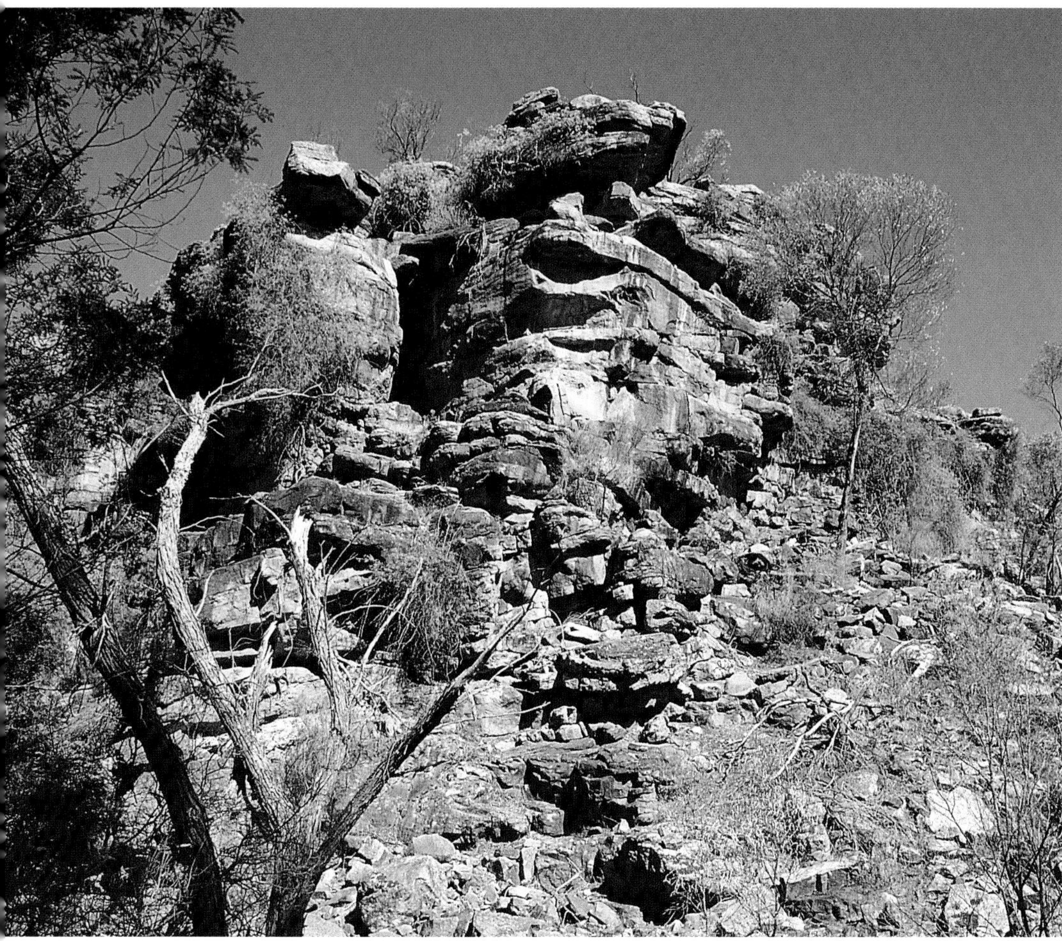

Landscapes viewed with dismay by explorers from the arid heights of Cocoparra are now greened by irrigation.

irrigation channels were complete and water had to be brought into the district by horse-drawn water tanks. McWilliams now has three wineries in the district (at Yenda, Hanwood and Beelbangera) and, with the importing of Italian viticulture techniques, especially from the 1940s onward, the region now produces approximately eighty per cent of the state's wines and twenty per cent of the national total.

Rice, citrus fruits and the nation's largest egg and poultry enterprise – started as a 'Young Farmer' project by a teenager – are the other primary products of the town, whose industries now include a large packaging facility for citrus fruits and vegetables, flour and rice mills, and canneries. *Population 13 300*

BAGTOWN While the town of Griffith was being built, construction workers stayed at a site just north-east of the town where they built temporary homes with whatever materials came to hand – primarily empty cement bags. Many were reluctant to move from the attractions of Bagtown...and Tango Joe's Cordials with its permanent 'Free drinks tomorrow' notice. But by 1922, the last residents, except those buried in the small cemetery, had moved to the new town.

HERMIT'S CAVE In the early 1930s, Valerio Riccetti on his way through Griffith, sheltered from rain in a cave in Scenic Hill above the town...and for almost ten years he never left the caves or spoke to anyone. Working at night, the reclusive Riccetti moved hundreds of tonnes of stone and used primitive tools to create rooms, a chapel, gardens, furniture and other structures and decorations in and around the caves. Hospitalised after a fall, he came to the attention of the authorities who interned him with other Italian wartime internees but his work on Hermit's Cave has been preserved.

FESTIVALS Griffith Wine and Food Festival, Easter.

LAKE WYANGAN ■ 716

Lake Wyangan is man-made and in two sections. The northern lake was formed in 1957 by the flooding of a swamp area and an old gypsum mine. The lake's southern half, once on private land, became an arboretum and wildlife refuge in 1966 and was linked with the more recent lake. A variety of birds live on the lake, including black swans, musk ducks and black-fronted dotterels.

Water levels in the lake are maintained from surplus drainage water from the Murrumbidgee Irrigation Areas and from surrounding farms. The water level in the larger, northern lake is kept reasonably constant by the pumping of water from the southern lake when necessary. This enables watersports and the activities of the sailing club and powerboat club to continue uninterrupted.

LEETON ■ 717

Surrounded by canals, weirs and irrigated fields, Leeton is the natural administrative centre of the Murrumbidgee Irrigation Areas. This garden town of tree-lined streets was the first of the Murrumbidgee Irrigation Areas' towns to be built, in 1912, to a Walter Burley Griffin design. Until the town – named after Charles Alfred Lee, the then Minister of Public Works was completed – irrigation and construction staff lived in tents arranged in 'streets' according to marital status.

The first land sales in 1913 attracted a mixture of unemployed miners, Italian immigrants and, later, returned First World War veterans. The early problems of canal seepage, waterlogging of certain land and the early experimentation with crops were successfully surmounted and Leeton now has a number of very large processing industries based on the products of the irrigation areas.

The first rice, grown near what is now the town's swimming pool, was harvested in 1924–25. By 1950, the amount of rice produced in the district was seen as a sufficient amount to justify the formation of the Ricegrowers' Cooperative, which is now the sole miller, manufacturer and marketer of rice and rice products. The co-operative built the first of its six mills in Leeton in 1951 and the town is also the headquarters of the Rice Growers' Co-operative Ltd, making it the unchallenged capital of Australia's rice industry.

A major cannery, established and operated by the state government in 1914, was purchased by fruit growers in 1935 and became the largest in New South Wales until its closure in 1994. At its peak eight hundred employees processed half a million cans of peaches, pears, apricots, plums and tomatoes every day from December to March for export to more than forty different countries.

In 1974, a number of citrus growers formed Leeton Citrus Juices Ltd and their 'Quelch' factory processes over 50 000 tonnes of fruit each year.

In addition to these major industries, Leeton boasts two wineries and a modern cheese factory where gourmet-style cheeses are produced all year round.

A major recent development was the establishment in 1991 of a 40 000 head beef cattle feedlot 14 kilometres east of Leeton. Recognised as one of the most advanced feedlot and abbatoir complexes in the world, the Rockdale Beef Cattle Feedlot employs 300 people and its products are exported to Japan, Korea and the USA. *Population 6250*

HYDRO HOTEL Built in 1919, as the headquarters for the Murrumbidgee Irrigation Areas' management team, the Edwardian building became a high-class hotel in 1924. The building was extensively refurbished in 1979 when the ballroom and its chandelier, together with a series of stained glass windows depicting the story of the Murrumbidgee Irrigation Areas, were restored to their former glory.

FESTIVALS Leeton Rice Festival, Easter of even-numbered years.

MURRUMBIDGEE IRRIGATION AREAS (MIA) ■ 718

Samuel McCaughey's irrigation experiments at North Yanco (see entry) and his campaigning were catalysts for the development of the MIA. His efforts were rewarded with a knighthood...and the resumption of his irrigated North Yanco property along with the other 270 000 hectares of ideally flat land resumed for the scheme in 1906. McCaughey's efforts would not have so effective if it had not been for the work of another Scotsman, Hugh McKinney, who had been vigorously promoting the idea of water conservation and irrigation since the early 1880s.

From the main storage dam at Lake Burrinjuck (see *Yass & Boorowa*), water flows down the Murrumbidgee River to Berembed Weir. From this weir, irrigation water – three times the daily consumption of the Sydney metropolitan area in volume – flows down a 159-kilometre main canal and into 2350 kilometres of

No patent protected the waterwheel-like Dethridge water meter and it was quickly adopted worldwide.

smaller supply channels serving 2600 farms. The journey from the dam to the farms in the irrigation area takes seven days and water distribution is controlled by channel attendants who take advance orders for water from farms within their group or division. The totals from all the divisions within the MIA are then used to calculate the amount of water that must be discharged from the dam. Where the supply channel enters a farm channel, a Dethridge wheel is installed. Invented in Victoria, the wheel has a sliding door that controls the rate of water flow and each revolution of the wheel measures a known quantity of water taken from the system.

The water in the irrigation canals first flowed in 1912 and inducements to farmers to come to the MIA included providing them with a house, sheds, fruit trees and a rebate of one-third of the fares paid by the farmer and his family. By 1914, 622 farms on 9700 hectares were irrigated; today 182 000 hectares lie within the MIA. In an effort to further publicise the MIA, Henry Lawson was paid two guineas a week and provided with a house in Leeton for a year in 1916–17 in exchange for which he was to write in praise of the MIA.

Unfortunately, despite the amount of water, the irrigation area was 'dry' as far as alcohol was concerned and the poet-in-residence had to leave the area if he wanted to visit a pub.

The original farm sizes ranged from less than a hectare to twenty-two hectares for fruit and vegetable growing but were later extended to 180–200-hectare farms to allow for the production of rice, winter cereals and vegetables. Rice-growing in Australia was pioneered in the MIA and rice is now the largest source of revenue in the region. Technological research has resulted in laser-controlled scraping machines being used to prepare rice fields in the MIA.

NARRANDERA ■ 719

The site of what was to become Narrandera, was where Charles Sturt camped in December 1829, as he set off on his exploration of the Murrumbidgee–Murray river system. The town, one of the oldest in the Riverina, developed in the 1850s on part of Narrandera Station, whose name came from the Aboriginal 'narrung durrung', meaning 'place of lizards or goannas'. The Victorian gold rush created a new market for meat and Narrandera was an ideal crossing place on the Murrumbidgee for 'meat on the hoof' being driven south from the fattening paddocks around the river. The village was officially proclaimed in 1863 and, with the arrival of the rail line from Sydney in 1881 and the line from Melbourne in 1884 combined with its prominence as a steamer port, Narrandera was to become the major town in the region – a position it retained until 1914.

The shortage of labour for the district's pastoralists, caused by the Victorian gold rushes, was solved by employing Chinese labour. During the 1880s, up to half of Narrandera's population was Chinese – among the highest concentrations of Chinese nationals in the state. Living in a self-contained community of forty or so homes with their own restaurants, hospital and joss house, the Chinese tended their orchards and vegetables on the river flats and sold the extra produce in the town.

Despite its position on the river and at the junction of the Sturt and Newell Highways, Narrandera was to be overtaken in size by the new towns of Griffith and Leeton. But unlike the two new towns, Narrandera has a longer history and many of its late nineteenth-century buildings are classified by the National Trust. Samuel McCaughey 'the father of the Murrumbidgee Irrigation Areas' is buried in the local cemetery while a Royal Doulton ceramic fountain, one of only two in the world, and a fully restored Tiger Moth – to commemorate those who came to the flying school here during the Second World War – are part of the town's more recent heritage.

In addition to the more traditional products such as wheat, wool, barley and fruit, Narrandera has become the centre for two of Australia's newer and more unusual primary products. Over eighty-five per cent of the nation's goat mohair is now grown and prepared in Narrandera before being sent off to Melbourne for auction while elsewhere in the district ostriches are being bred for their meat, skin and feathers. The first auction of ostriches in 1989 raised $750 000 for the sale of only fifty birds. *Population 4650*

INLAND FISHERIES RESEARCH STATION AND JOHN LAKE CENTRE Opened in 1962, the research station conducts research into the native fish and crustaceans of the Murray, Murrumbidgee, Lachlan and Darling rivers. Conducted tours combined with audiovisual displays provide visitors with information on the fish reference collection held in eighteen aquarium tanks, the brood and growing ponds, and the research laboratory. The fish-breeding program, which runs from October to December, provides fingerlings for sale between January and April to replenish depleted stocks.

FESTIVALS Camellia Show, August; Tree-mendous Festival, October.

WHITTON ■ 720

The original settlement in this district, in the days when teamsters and travellers passed through it on one of the main overland routes of New South Wales, was Hulong. It faded, but a nearby settlement was gazetted in 1885 as Whitton, after John Whitton, Engineer-in-Chief of the New South Wales Railways, who was credited with bringing the railway line to Whitton in the early 1880s.

The oldest town within the Murrumbidgee Irrigation Areas, Whitton was once a major centre with a court house and a number of hotels and businesses. The 1890 court house and jail now house a museum, exhibiting irrigation and farming equipment together with photographs of the development of the Murrumbidgee Irrigation Area.

Whitton's links with the new crop that arrived with the irrigation development are visible in the huge rice-storage and seed complex in the village and in the name of its only hotel – the Rice Bowl Hotel.

YANCO ■ 721

Yanco was the birthplace of the Murrumbidgee Irrigation Areas and its name is still synonymous with pioneering, dry-land agriculture.

It was on his one-and-a-half million hectares at 'North Yanco' that Samuel McCaughey, the pioneering pastoralist, began his experimentation with irrigation in 1899. Because the two creeks on his property were dry for up to twelve years at a time, McCaughey was forced to dig a series of dams, artesian wells and canals until he had around 10 000 hectares irrigated by 320 kilometres of waterways at his North Yanco property. With this background, it was only appropriate that the Murrumbidgee Irrigation Areas, should be officially opened at Yanco Regulator, the largest diversion structure in the irrigation system.

McCaughey's red-brick and sandstone homestead on 280 hectares was converted into Yanco Agricultural High School – one of Australia's leading agricultural high schools – in 1922. Yanco also has an agricultural college with a research centre on an 825-hectare site where farming and and cropping techniques honed over eighty years of dry-land irrigation experience are taught. Yanco Experimental Farm was where Australia's first rice was grown in 1919...and where ostriches were first farmed for their feathers in 1917.

As the nearby town of Leeton grew in importance, Yanco, which initially had the only railhead in the irrigation areas, went into a decline. The eight hundred Italian prisoners of war imprisoned in Yanco from 1943 to 1945 have long since gone and Yanco power station, once the most important in the district, has become a museum but the debt the region owes to this small town remains. *Population 651*

Between Narrandera and Darlington Point, the placid Murrumbidgee waters irrigate almost 300 000 of the most intensively farmed hectares in Australia.

YANCO CREEK ■ 722

The name comes from the Aboriginal word 'yanko' meaning 'the sound of running water' and, while the creek retained the original spelling for many years, the town of Yanco (see entry) opted for the more common local spelling in the late 1880s and the creek eventually followed suit with only Yanko Parish now retaining the original spelling.

When Charles Sturt started out on his exploration of the Murrumbidgee and Murray rivers in late 1829, he camped beside Yanco Creek. On his homeward journey from the Murray River in April 1830, the explorer's whaleboat, no longer required by his exhausted party, was burnt near Yanco Creek.

Following Yanco Creek from the Murrumbidgee would have led Sturt to the Murray River, since Yanco Creek is a main distributary running between the two rivers. Today, Yanco Creek, with a weir at its junction with the Murrumbidgee, runs parallel to the new man-made channel of the Coleambally Irrigation Area.

YENDA ■ 723

The name Yenda first appeared on maps in the 1870s but it was only after the Yenda–Griffith section of the main irrigation canal had been completed that this small township was officially gazetted in 1916.

Post-war soldier-settlers helped to develop the new town's fruit growing, dairying and mixed farming. Since that time, farm sizes have been increased and the agricultural scene has been varied to include citrus fruits, wheat, rice and wineries. Yenda's position on the railway is as important as its position on the main irrigation canal. This small farming township is now the main railhead for wineries at Bilbul (de Bortoli), Beelbangera (Rosetto) and Hanwood (McWilliams) as well as those in Yenda itself. *Population 920*

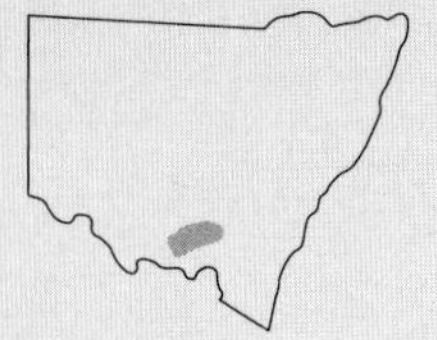

Wagga Wagga & Junee

Although gold was found and mined here in the 1850s, the real, lasting 'gold' soon proved to be the fertile soil of the plains along the slow-flowing Murrumbidgee River.This brought land-seekers in the early 1820s, even before explorer Charles Sturt journeyed up the river in a whaleboat in 1829.

COOLAMON ■ 724

Coolamon is turkey country and thousands of the birds are raised on the medium-sized farms surrounding the town. This rich pastoral area also produces wool, lamb and wheat.

'Coolamon' – once known as the 'hay and chaff capital' – refers both to a wooden vessel used by Aborigines, and waterholes of a similar shape. A cluster of waterholes on the 'Cooleman' station, established in the 1840s, was called Coolamon Holes.

The railway station which opened in 1881 was called Cowabbie Road but was changed within a week to Cooleman and in 1895 to Coolamon. *Population 1320*

FOREST HILL ■ 725

Forest Hill is an air-force town. Two Meteor jets, purchased in 1950 at the beginning of the Korean War for the 78th Fighter Wing, stand guard at the entrance to the large RAAF base in the town. Established as a School of Technical Training in 1939, the base now also includes schools of clerical and supply training, management training and technology and is the RAAF's major ground training unit with more than 1500 personnel. *Population 2480*

GALORE HILL RECREATION RESERVE ■ 726

When Henry Osborne, one of this region's early settlers climbed the only hill rising from the plains in the 1840s and said – according to legend – 'There's land enough and galore for me', he inadvertently provided a name for the hill and the town which eventually grew up nearby. The bushranger Daniel 'Mad Dog' Morgan had a hideout in caves on the side of Galore Hill, which can be reached by a walking track.

GANMAIN ■ 727

Ganmain is a major centre of the chaff industy and has a Hay Display Centre housed in a haystack-shaped building in Pioneer Park. Inside, displays of photos, a mural, machinery, and a videotape trace the history of cereal hay production in the district, showing the milling processes of sheafs, construction of haystacks and the cutting of hay into chaff.

Ganmain was the name given to a sheep run and is based on an Aboriginal word meaning 'tattooed man' though it more likely refers to men with ceremonial scars. *Population 590*

Coolamon's main street and its intersecting railway line were both laid in 1881 when station and street shared the same name, Cowabbie Road.

JUNEE ■ 728

Well-known to thousands of rail travellers – particularly children who have received lollies from Santa Claus when he passes through on Christmas Eve – Junee is the headquarters of the railway system in southern New South Wales. The railway line runs right through the middle of the town where the many late Victorian and Federation buildings bear verandahs that shade footpaths still carrying their horse-hitching rings.

Junee's elegant Renaissance-style railway station was built in 1883, five years after the line arrived, and apparently inspired the architecture of some of the town's hotels, many of which provided accommodation after the opening of the line to Hay in 1881 when Junee became an important railway town. Repair facilities were moved from Wagga to Junee in the 1880s. The circular Locomotive Round House contains a giant turntable and forty-seven repair bays and is one of the few such engine houses remaining intact.

Junee is the commercial centre of a region producing wheat, wool, wine grapes and poultry products. The Grain Handling Authority's Junee sub-terminal was constructed in 1952 and, with a capacity of 153 000 tonnes, is the largest in country New South Wales. *Population 4000*

MONTE CRISTO HOMESTEAD Set on a hill overlooking Junee, this grand, two-storey Georgian mansion was built in 1884. It has cedar fireplaces and iron-lacework verandahs as well as a collection of carriages, a working wheelwright's shop and, according to legend, a ghost.

LOCKHART ■ 729

Lockhart's commercial centre, with its wide shopfront verandahs and turn-of-the-century streetscape, has been classified by the National Trust.

In the 1860s, a Mr Green built a shanty where the road to Narrandera crossed the Brookong Creek, and the location became known as Green's Gunyah. In 1896, it was renamed Lockhart after one of the first commissioners for crown lands. The line to the town opened in 1901 and the district soon became a major wheat-growing area with bulk-handling facilities.

Lockhart's museum has a fine collection of artifacts, photographs and documents reflecting the town's pioneer days. *Population 890*

MURRAY COD HATCHERIES & FAUNA PARK ■ 730

Home to 'Big Murray', a giant Murray cod weighing more than fifty kilograms, approximately one-and-a-half metres long and believed to be over one hundred years old (as well as others of similar size), the Murray Cod Hatcheries opened in the 1970s. Several aquariums with large viewing windows enable the public to see the fish, which are not so easily spotted in the murky waters of the outdoor fish ponds. This first warm-water fish farm and hatchery in Australia provides a nation-wide fish-farming consultation service, supplying fry and fingerlings of Murray cod, golden and silver perch and catfish as well as yabbies to farmers and institutions. The hatchery can hatch one million fry at a time in its incubators.

THE ROCK ■ 731

This bluntly named township grew out of a sheep run called 'Hanging Rock' in the 1880s; the name was changed to The Rock to avoid confusion with another Hanging Rock and then amended a few years later to the more conventional Kingston. But it was too late to change...popular usage favoured the name inspired by the craggy outcrop which rises 360 metres out of the otherwise featureless plain a few kilometres to the west and The Rock prevailed. The nature reserve surrounding the original 'rock' is a popular recreation area (see sub-entry). *Population 690*

THE ROCK NATURE RESERVE The 345-hectare reserve surrounds the rocky outcrop which gave its name to the nearby town. There are open forests of grey, white and red box on the hill's lower slopes, while red gums grow higher up. Peregrine and little falcons and wedgetailed eagles find nesting sites on the ledges and in the crevices of the steeper rock faces.

WAGGA WAGGA ■ 732

Sometimes called the 'Garden City of the South' because of its parks and gardens, Wagga Wagga is the largest inland city in New South Wales, and the 'capital' of the fertile Riverina agricultural area. The Murrumbidgee River snakes through the city and members of Australia's only inland surf life-saving club patrol its beach.

Wagga is an Aboriginal word said to mean 'crow', the repetition of the word indicates the plural, so that Wagga Wagga means 'place of many crows'. The city took its distinctive name from the station first taken up by Robert Holt Best in 1832, the first land in the area to be permanently occupied by settlers.

Although land-seekers had come to the area in the 1820s, it was not explored until Charles Sturt passed through in the late 1820s; in 1836 Sir Thomas Mitchell camped where Wagga Wagga now stands. Wagga Wagga was proclaimed a town in 1849, and grew quickly with the stimulus of river-steamer transport and later, the railway, in 1878.

The Wagga economy is based on primary and secondary agricultural industries and in the early days the region was an important source of wheat for the urban market. Since then sheep and cattle have become more important; more than 34 000 animals can be handled at once in the modern Livestock Marketing Centre – the largest provincial centre in New South Wales.

Wagga is the home of institutions, such as Charles Sturt University (see sub-entry), the Soil Conservation Research Station, and the Wagga Wagga Agricultural Research Institute, established as an experimental farm in 1892. Wheat-breeding pioneer William Farrer did his research there for many years. A tree-preservation order passed by the council in 1982 has ensured the collective protection of one of the city's main assets. The thirty-kilometre Wiradjuri walking track takes in the many scenic highlights of the Wagga Wagga district, while walking routes prepared by the National Trust show off the city's many nineteenth- and early twentieth-century public buildings and private homes. *Population 53 410*

CHARLES STURT UNIVERSITY AND WINERY The university was once the Riverina-Murray Institute of Higher Education, established in 1972 and incorporating the agricultural college and the teachers college opened in 1947. Set on 600 hectares overlooking the Murrumbidgee River, the university has more than 6000 students. Among the fifty courses available, there is a viticulture course and in conjunction with this, the university enterprisingly runs its own winery to the north of the city.

LAKE ALBERT The lake is a major water recreation area for Wagga, with sailing, fishing, power boating, water skiing, canoeing and swimming. The lake was created by diverting water from Crooked Creek and Stringybark Creek into what was once a swamp. The grandly named Lake Albert Improvement League was formed in 1898 and the first weir built in 1902.

The settlement of the same name, now part of greater Wagga Wagga, was the birthplace in 1884 of Sir Thomas Blamey who had a distinguished military career, becoming the first Australian soldier to attain the rank of field-marshal.

A mind-boggling level of horse-power is stabled in Junee's Locomotive House; the engines haul the region's grain to market after harvest – a job which one farmer (below) does the traditional way.

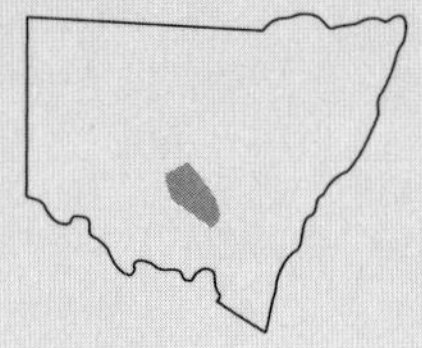

Temora & West Wyalong

Inhabited by the Aborigines in early times, the vast Bland Shire and its western environs have more recently been shaped by squatters, miners and selectors and opened up for agricultural development by the coming of the railway and other forms of modern transport.

ARIAH PARK ■ 733

Ariah Park, once known for its 'bowsers, wowsers and peppercorn trees', still has the shady tree-lined Coolamon Street and there are plans to restore the old style bowsers to the kerb. Wowsers and non-wowsers alike will find the hotel – once the home of the future Dame Mary Gilmore's family – of architectural interest. The village has changed little since its early days and is a National Trust Conservation Area; other interesting buildings include Lyons' Wool Store, Westpac Bank and the National Bank.

Nearby Lake Arbortree, a twenty-five-hectare artificial lake alongside Mirrool Creek, is popular for boating, windsurfing, waterskiing and other aquatic sports.

BARMEDMAN ■ 734

John Cartright's Barmedman Station (established in the early 1840s) gave its name to the present township. Railway records state that Barmedman is named after a Scottish village but others claim it is Aboriginal for 'a hollow-backed horse'. Neither explanation has been confirmed.

Farming has changed the landscape over the last 150 years: one pioneer settler is said to have told his family the surrounding bush was so thick he found it hard to open his penknife! Little of that original vegetation survives. First squatters grazed the land; then selectors cleared it for intensive agriculture. Rabbits had a disastrous effect on the native plants and so did the gradual spread of weeds introduced from other countries. Indigenous plants are now conserved, among them the yarran tree used for spears by Aborigines and for fence-posts and firewood by settlers.

A Mrs Treasure discovered gold at Barmedman in 1872 but it was another ten years before the fields attracted wide attention. Between November 1881 and July 1882, the *Temora Star* reported regularly on life in the thriving town.

BARMEDMAN MINERAL POOL The water problem that eventually closed the Barmedman mines is today responsible for attracting summer visitors. The workings were abandoned when it became impossible to pump out the chambers flooded by an underground stream. Excavation of a different kind began in 1951 – on a large swimming pool set in a spacious reserve. The pool is filled with mineralised, salty water from the underground stream which is recommended for aching joints.

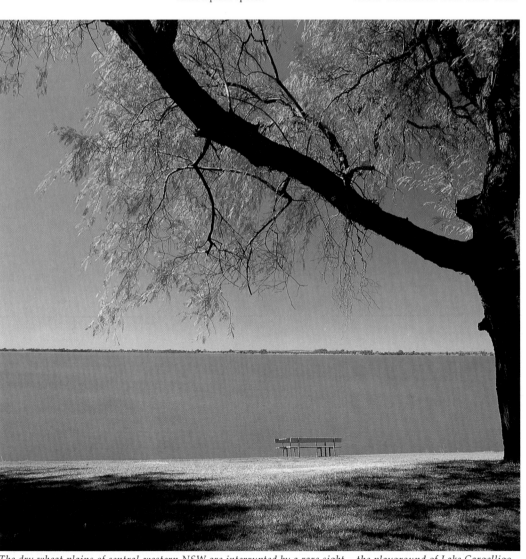

The dry wheat plains of central-western NSW are interrupted by a rare sight – the playground of Lake Cargelligo.

LAKE CARGELLIGO ■ 735

Lake Cargelligo is another old gold town that began in 1873 after Mrs Foster, the cook in a burr cutters' camp, discovered the precious mineral. Mining lasted for about ten years by which time the town had been gazetted. The opening of the railway in 1917 led to expanding agricultural interests and the lake draws watersports enthusiasts. Two other symbols of Lake Cargelligo's present economy – the saleyards and the wheat silo – stand side by side near the railway line. *Population 1260*

LAKE CARGELLIGO The explorer, John Oxley, discovered the lake in 1817 on his return from exploring the Lachlan River. He named it Regent's Lake in honour of the Prince Regent. The Surveyor-General, Sir Thomas Mitchell, who had a penchant for Aboriginal names, renamed it Cudjallagong, a variant of Cargelligo – Aboriginal for 'water'. The lake's water-storage facilities, completed in 1902, supplement downstream river flows in dry spells. The fishing is excellent and the 1440-hectare surface area large enough for the New South Wales sailing titles.

RANKINS SPRINGS ■ 736

A quiet agricultural village first sited around a spring at the foot of the Conapaira Range, this place was called Rankin after the Rankin brothers who had four selections in the district before 1866. The settlement later moved ten kilometres to its present site and the spring seems to have disappeared.

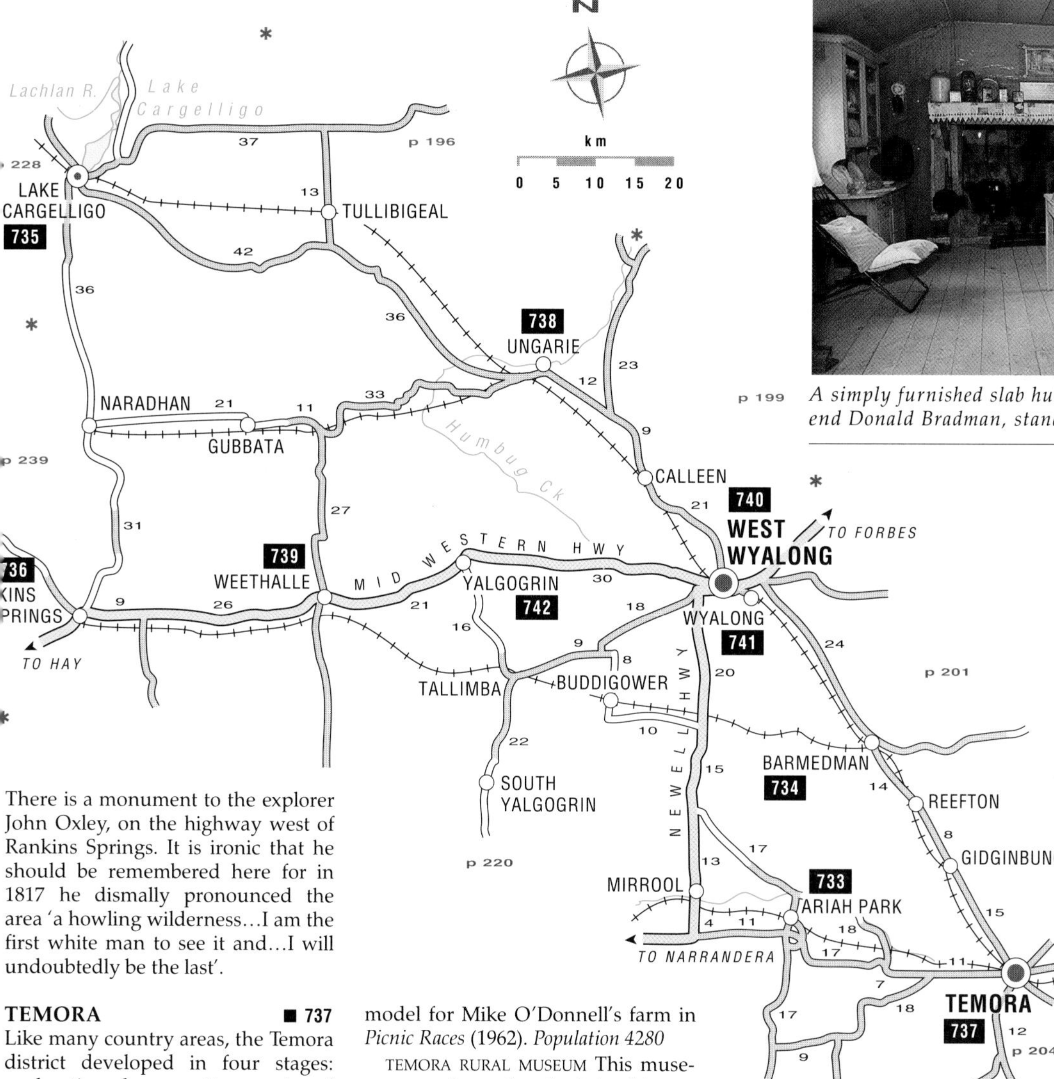

A simply furnished slab hut, the first home of the cricketing legend Donald Bradman, stands in the grounds of Temora Museum.

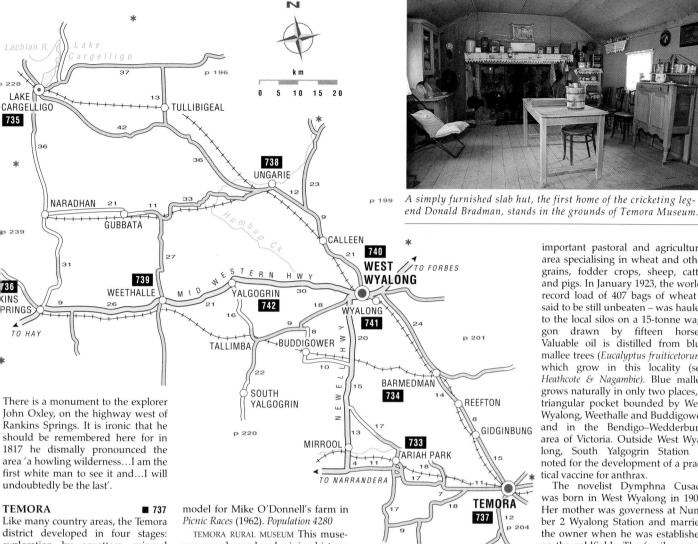

There is a monument to the explorer John Oxley, on the highway west of Rankins Springs. It is ironic that he should be remembered here for in 1817 he dismally pronounced the area 'a howling wilderness…I am the first white man to see it and…I will undoubtedly be the last'.

TEMORA ■ 737

Like many country areas, the Temora district developed in four stages: exploration by squatters, mineral exploitation, settlement by selectors and steady agricultural growth supported by roads and railway lines. Pastoralists took up large runs in the 1830s and land clearing went on for fifty years or so before gold was found. The rush peaked in the early 1880s when Temora produced half the state's yield and boasted 20 000 residents. New South Wales' largest modern-day gold mine, Paragon Gold Project, was established at Gidginbung, north of the town.

Temora – the name is from the Gaelic *teamhragh* meaning 'an eminence commanding an extensive view' – has many fine Edwardian and Federation buildings. The Shamrock Hotel (1881) which retains its lacework and timber verandah posts and Callaghan and Cowley's butcher shop with its original slate roof are particularly interesting.

Trotting is important in the region and one of the great pacers, Paleface Adios, was born and trained here. Paleface Park-Plaza, established during the bicentenary year, contains a life-size statue of the champion pacer and his driver.

The writer Dymphna Cusack (see West Wyalong) used her grandmother's dairy farm near the town as the model for Mike O'Donnell's farm in *Picnic Races* (1962). *Population 4280*

TEMORA RURAL MUSEUM This museum records rural and mining history. There is a replica of the famous Mother Shipton nugget (258 ounces) and a large collection of agricultural machinery including single-furrow and stump-jump ploughs. Sir Donald Bradman's first home, a hardwood slab cottage, has been re-erected in the grounds to house sporting memorabilia.

UNGARIE ■ 738

Ungarie, said to be an Aboriginal word for 'thigh', is the second largest settlement in Bland Shire. It lies on Humbug Creek which has a reputation for either being in flood or dry to the point of disappearing and so the district is prone to summer dust and winter mud. The first postal deliveries between West Wyalong, Ungarie and Lake Cargelligo were made by bicycle. In 1917, the railway linked the same three towns and attracted pastoral settlers.

WEETHALLE ■ 739

Weethalle is said to mean 'drink' – a reminder of the early pioneers' primary need for fresh water. Today's fortunes still depend on water and fluctuate with the grain and wool harvests. Hard times have closed some of the businesses on the main street but the general store sells almost anything from compressed gas to sewing needles. The town has good sporting amenities and a fine trotting track at the showground.

FESTIVALS Weethalle Pastoral and Agricultural Society Show, August.

WEST WYALONG ■ 740

West Wyalong is situated at the junction of the Newell and Mid Western highways. Interstate truck drivers now stop over where teamsters once rested and Cobb &Co. changed its five-horse teams - and the crooked main street still follows the route of the original teamsters' bullock track.

Gold caused a stir here too…Fred Neeld and his five sons lodged claims on George Neeld's selection in December 1893. The lode was rich and in 1899, the government geologist declared this goldfield the most productive in the colony.

Bland Shire, or 'the Levels', has its headquarters at West Wyalong. It is one of the largest local government districts in New South Wales; an important pastoral and agricultural area specialising in wheat and other grains, fodder crops, sheep, cattle and pigs. In January 1923, the world-record load of 407 bags of wheat – said to be still unbeaten – was hauled to the local silos on a 15-tonne waggon drawn by fifteen horses. Valuable oil is distilled from blue mallee trees (*Eucalyptus fruiticetorum*) which grow in this locality (see *Heathcote & Nagambie).* Blue mallee grows naturally in only two places, a triangular pocket bounded by West Wyalong, Weethalle and Buddigower and in the Bendigo–Wedderburn area of Victoria. Outside West Wyalong, South Yalgogrin Station is noted for the development of a practical vaccine for anthrax.

The novelist Dymphna Cusack was born in West Wyalong in 1902. Her mother was governess at Number 2 Wyalong Station and married the owner when he was established on the goldfields. The family moved to Sydney when the gold ran out. *Population 3460*

WYALONG ■ 741

Although Wyalong was properly surveyed and designated thus in 1884, it never had a chance to develop as a town because most of the mines and the White Tank water supply (now known as McCann Park) were at Main Camp which soon became West Wyalong. The miners refused to move and there was bitter rivalry between the towns. Public buildings were erected in Wyalong, among them the court house, which is still a showpiece. It was not until 1935 that Wyalong, Wyalong Central (the site of the railway station) and West Wyalong were officially merged by government proclamation.

YALGOGRIN ■ 742

This tiny village is affectionately called 'the Gog' by locals. Inevitably, a town sprang up after the 1893 gold strike and within four years 2000 people lived there…but as in most 'instant' gold settlements, most of them didn't stay. The year 1983 boasted another population explosion – seven became nine with the birth of twins!

Cobar & Canbelego

Sunbaked, semi-arid rangelands between the Lachlan and Darling rivers held out bleak prospects for pastoral agriculture. Searchers for permanent water chanced instead on a mineral bonanza. Four generations later, a roller-coaster mining economy is again on an upswing.

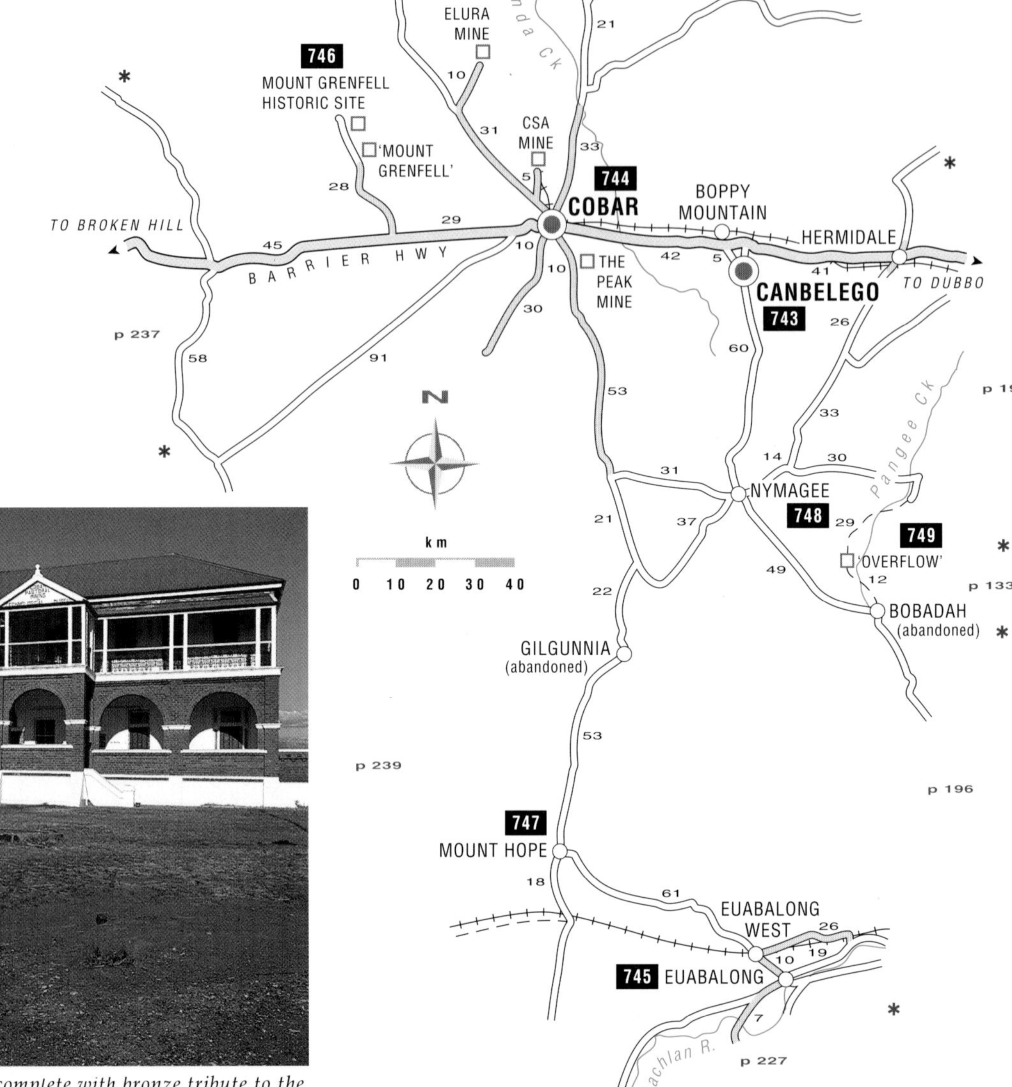

Intrepid visitors to the Cobar Museum – complete with bronze tribute to the wool industry – can descend an underground shaft into a recreated mine.

CANBELEGO ■ 743

Just off the route of the Barrier Highway, Canbelego slumbers unseen by most travellers. Time too has passed it by. But in the days before the First World War this hamlet was a bustling town serving the most productive goldfield in New South Wales. The nearby Mount Boppy mine alone yielded more than thirteen tonnes of fine gold. Its belated opening in 1901 – more than twenty years after the discovery of ore bodies and isolated nuggets – reflected not only a confusing geological structure but also the daunting costs of developing a mine and the delays forced by a long and severe drought.

Thomas Reid, who in 1896 discovered the payable lode in Boppy Mountain, was obliged to take in shareholders to explore it further. Within months, this local syndicate lost heart and sold the claim to a company that was heavily backed by British capital. Their price was a mere 800 pounds.

COBAR ■ 744

Leafy streets and green lawns in modern Cobar disguise the struggles this community has had to cope with shortages of water. These days the best vantage point from which to view the sprawling town is the top of the water filtration plant on Fort Bourke Hill, above a reservoir holding four-and-a-half million litres. To the north-west, on the opposite side of Cobar, is an even bigger reservoir of filtered water. All of this liquid bounty is piped 110 kilometres from the Bogan River, near Nyngan. The pipes were laid – one in 1966 and a second in 1983 – not simply to sustain a marginally viable town but to support the revival of mining in the district. That, in turn, has made Cobar flourish and even blossom.

It was a search for water that accidentally revealed Cobar's mineral riches. Seeking to establish a stock route, bore-sinking contractors in 1870 were led by Aboriginal guides to a waterhole near Devil's Rock, north-east of what became the town site. It turned out to be not a natural water source but a rain-collecting pit created by generations of Aborigines scraping out ochre, which they called something like *cobur*, for ceremonial body-painting. The travellers were intrigued by a rusty sediment on the bottom of the pit and blue and green stains on the sides. Samples they took were seen at a much later stage by a Cornishwoman who suggested the discolourations were caused by copper. The bore-sinkers returned as quickly as they could, lodged a mining claim and began a search for ore bodies. In 1871, a cartload of ore was hauled by bullocks to Louth and shipped down the Darling River to South Australia. Analysts at Port Adelaide found that it consisted of one-third copper.

Mines were developed rapidly on a number of leases. In 1876, the Great Cobar Company was established to amalgamate the control of the main ones. By then, a substantial township was replacing a jumble of huts and tents. The company undertook its own smelting – reducing its enormous freight costs but creating a never-ending demand for fuel. Hilly woodlands of the district were denuded to fire the smelters.

And the problems of a precarious water supply remained until Cobar gained a railway service in 1894. Tanker trains loaded with water from Nyngan came as often as once a day when necessary. Coal replaced wood in the smelting furnaces, and the mines' output was carried out at economical rates. Cobar boomed, with a population surging towards 10 000 and even had its own stock exchange trading in mining shares.

The copper bonanza was over by 1920 and much of the population drifted away. Then in the 1960s came signs of previously unknown ore bodies on the CSA leases (see subentry). Gathering a new workforce, the company settled its employees in Cobar rather than at the mine site. This example was followed by Electrolytic Zinc when it opened a mine north-west of Cobar, in the early 1980s. Houses and flats were built in the town for a commuting workforce of about 300 people. Reserves of ore at Elura, rich in lead, zinc and silver, should underpin Cobar's economy well into the twenty-first century. *Population 4140*

COBAR REGIONAL MUSEUM A handsome Edwardian building, once the headquarters of a large copper mining company, is now home to what former Governor-General, Sir Ninian Stephen, has described as 'the best museum outside a capital city'. Displays include exhibits that deal with pre-European Aboriginal culture, the domestic and working lives of pioneering settlers and all aspects of copper, gold, lead and zinc mining, including a complete site model of the recently developed Elura mine.

GREAT WESTERN HOTEL Extensive renovations during the 1980s gave Cobar's biggest hotel a split personality. Inside the hotel, which dates from 1898, accommodation and some other features were modernised. But the exterior, under a Heritage Council conservation order, was restored to its former Victorian glory. It boasts a verandah and first-floor balcony ninety metres long, exceeded among Australian pubs only by one in the West Australian town of Kalgoorlie.

CSA MINE This major base metal mine produces more than 100 000 tonnes of high-grade copper concentrate annually, making it one of the most productive mining and mineral processing operations in Australia. But this high-technology efficiency tends to mask the site's turbulent history. The deposit 12 kilometres north-west of Cobar, was discovered in 1872 and named after the birthplaces of the three founding partners – a Cornishman, a Scotsman and an Australian. By 1920 the mine had produced about 100 000 tones of ore and about 25 000 tones of lead and copper together with minor amounts of silver and gold. Disaster struck in 1920 when fire broke out in the main shaft, defying all efforts to extinguish it. The mine was sealed but the blaze continued for 16 years fuelled by the hardwood timbers of the old workings. Development of the modern mine began in the early 1960s with production commencing in 1965. The modern CSA produces annually the equivalent of what the old mine gave up in its lifetime.

COMMONWEALTH METEOROLOGICAL STATION Australia's link in a worldwide upper-atmosphere monitoring network is sited north-west of Cobar near the CSA Mine turn-off. Big balloons fitted with sensors, radio transmitters and radar reflectors are released at six-hourly intervals to report the characteristics and track the movements of high-altitude air masses. The ground station is also a major monitoring point for surface weather and flying conditions.

Surface outcrops such as these gave Cobar's pioneers tantalising evidence of the mineral riches beneath the ground.

EUABALONG ■ 745

Fishing for yellow belly and Murray cod is the chief attraction of Euabalong, which had its origins in the 1870s as a road junction and stock crossing on the Lachlan River. Its tiny public school, opened in 1889, has a proud history of racial integration. Aboriginal children were taught there from the outset and throughout the early decades of this century, in defiance of an official policy that favoured separation. The villagers stood firm again in 1919 when they resisted the pull of a new railway line between Condobolin and Roto. Trains stopped ten kilometres away at Euabalong West, where the development of a more important town could have been expected. Euabalong people remained loyal to their river, however, and the railway settlement is no more than a hamlet.

MOUNT GRENFELL HISTORIC SITE ■ 746

Deep erosion of a sandstone ridge about sixty kilometres west of Cobar created shelters that were used by the Wongaibon Aboriginal people at least as long ago as AD 200. Of seven shelters clustered around a creekbed waterhole, three contain the most impressive rock painting galleries that members of the public are able to see in New South Wales. Hundreds of small figures of animals and humans appear in a largely naturalistic style along with other motifs of symbolic significance.

Red and yellow ochre were the main colourings used, together with some white pipeclay and black ash. The pigments were moistened so that sheets of solid background colour could be applied. Most of the figures were painted finely with twig brushes, but some others were fingertip daubings. Overpaintings were frequent: poignantly, the last of them show the arrival of horses and riders.

The site is accessible by a gravel road turning from the Barrier Highway about forty kilometres west of Cobar. At least three hours are needed to make the return journey and gain a fair appreciation of the range of rock art. Picnic facilities and toilets are provided, and a five-kilometre walk can be taken to the crest of the ridge. Leaflets explain what is known of local Aboriginal culture and pre-European diet.

MOUNT HOPE–GILGUNNIA ■ 747

Twists and turns of the mining industry brought many a surprise along the now-lonely road extending south-west from Nymagee. After a shepherd discovered copper ore at Mount Hope in the 1870s, three mines in the district supported a population of about 3000. The ore smelting process was aided by the use of ironstone transported from Mount Allen, to the north. Not until 1885, when the world price of copper was depressed, did someone bother to assay the ironstone for its gold content. It was unexpectedly rich. Mount Allen became the premier mine, yielding more than 200 kilograms of gold by the turn of the century. Before then, the next rush had started, still farther north at Gilgunnia. This field produced a similar yield, about half of it from the 'Her Dream' mine. Ironically, in a region so hard pressed for rain and surface water, 'Her Dream' was dashed early this century when it was assailed by insoluble problems of underground flooding.

NYMAGEE ■ 748

One hotel survives of the five that flourished in Nymagee in the 1880s. Copper mining and gold prospects drew a population of more than 2000 to the town and the hilly district surrounding it. The main copper mine, located on the town's western outskirts, closed in 1917.

THE OVERFLOW ■ 749

Overflow Station, at the junction of two creeks beside a dusty back road that wanders north from Bobadah, is associated in some tourist literature with Banjo Paterson's famous poems 'Clancy of the Overflow' and 'The Man from Snowy River'. Such a link cannot be proved. In 1938 – nearly half a century after the poems were published – claims were made that one or other of two old stockmen had been the model for Clancy. In response, Paterson himself let it be understood that his character was imaginary. Several different grazing runs were named or nicknamed 'The Overflow' and the term was also used for seasonally inundated areas such as the Macquarie Marshes.

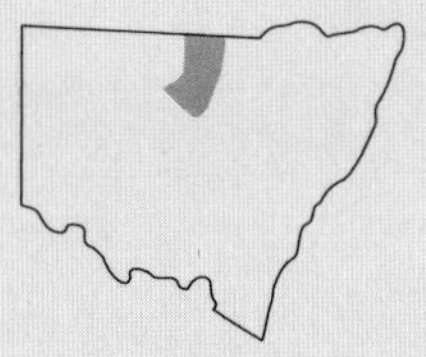

Brewarrina & Goodooga

The fortunes of the vast sheep runs of this border region depend largely on the rainfall in Queensland: it feeds the north-western rivers which come together here to give birth to the life-giving Darling.

The success of steamers such as the Brewarrina *– seen here with its wool barge in 1895 near the then port of the same name – in turning inland waterways into trade arteries ensured the survival of many isolated sheep stations.*

BOGAN RIVER ■ 750

The Bogan River is a tributary of the Darling River system, rising at Goonumbla near Parkes and flowing in a north-westerly direction to join the Barwon River about forty kilometres from Bourke. John Oxley crossed the river in 1817, although the river was named New Year's Creek by Charles Sturt around 1829. The word Bogen was mentioned by several explorers who followed the river downstream in 1833, preparing the way for the Surveyor-General Thomas Mitchell.

The river is believed to be named after a noted Aboriginal leader who lived in the area, and the name is thought to mean 'birthplace of a king'. Richard Cunningham, the botanist who was killed by Aborigines during Mitchell's 1835 expedition, is buried by the Bogan, on a property north of Tottenham.

BREWARRINA ■ 751

This riverside town, on the banks of the Barwon River (see *Coonamble & Walgett*) is the centre of a rich wool-producing district which stretches to the Queensland border. The town, established in the 1860s, was a crossing place for stock in the early days.

The same shallows that attracted the cattle herders drew the Aboriginal inhabitants long before. The Aborigines built stone traps to catch fish (see sub-entry). Brewarrina was one of the great Aboriginal meeting places of eastern Australia and in the first years of European settlement, Aborigines and whites clashed frequently, and sometimes bloodily. At Hospital Creek, white settlers massacred more than twenty men, women and children, in retaliation for the spearing of a white stockman who had taken an Aboriginal woman.

Settlement was sparse, with most of the country around Brewarrina taken up by pastoral companies with large holdings. Sheep stations such as 'Quantambone', 'Weilmoringle', 'Boorooma', 'Milroy' and 'Talwanta' were on the northern side of the Barwon River with others such as 'Merriman', 'Charlton', 'Cowga' and 'Yarrawin' on the south.

In the late nineteenth century, more than 50 000 bales of wool a year were carted into Brewarrina from surrounding stations by teamsters with bullock-, horse-, donkey- or camel-drawn waggons. Up to forty-five drivers used the 3000 hectares of the Brewarrina common to rest and feed their teams.

River transport developed as well and the town soon became famous for the prodigious wool clips loaded at its wharf and at the Brewarrina weighbridge. One super-bullock is claimed to have carried a record of 110 bales of wool into town and it was quite common for as many as twelve steamers to queue up for loading and unloading at the wharf. The remains of one steamer, the *Wandering Jew,* can still be seen in the river near the rocks where it burnt and sank.

Barwon Bridge once opened to allow paddle steamers to travel as far north along the Barwon as Mungindi. River transport was abandoned when the railway, a much speedier form of transport, was opened in 1901. Wool, sheep and cattle are still Brewarrina's main industries today. More recent crops, such as citrus and cotton, are also making an impact on the local economy. *Population 1170*

ABORIGINAL FISHERIES Just below the Brewarrina Weir are the Aboriginal Fisheries, one of the most significant Aboriginal sites in New South Wales. The fisheries are a system of stone traps in the river, designed to capture fish and they are believed to have helped feed hundreds of people during large ceremonial gatherings. The trap complex was damaged by riverboat traffic and further disturbed when the stones were rearranged to form a river crossing.

The stones, which archaeologists say were carried or dragged over great distances, were also taken from the site to be used by white settlers in buildings and roads and, as late as 1976, in the construction of the Brewarrina Weir. Since then the fisheries maze has been carefully restored using historical records and old photographs, and an Aboriginal Cultural Museum has been built nearby on the riverbank.

FESTIVALS Festival of the Fisheries, late September–early October.

BYROCK ■ 752

Byrock, the junction for road and rail lines going to Bourke or Brewarrina, was originally called Byerock. There is a waterhole nearby called Bye's rockhole, perhaps after an early family in the area. Locals have it that the name arose when bullockies talked of taking the route 'by the rock' instead of the original main road. But historians say the waterhole was a sacred Aboriginal site and a spirit called Baiame lived in the granite outcrop, which became known as Bai after him.

CULGOA RIVER ■ 753

The Culgoa River rises out of the Balonne, in south-eastern Queensland, which in turn is an extension of the Condamine. The Culgoa flows south-west through low-lying country to join the Darling above Bourke.

The 320-kilometre-long river and its fellow Darling tributaries, the Bogan, the Bokhara and the Narran all swell the network which forms the longest system of waterways – about 3700 kilometres – in Australia.

GIRILAMBONE ■ 754

The Aboriginal meaning of Girilambone is thought to mean 'place of a star' or 'place of many stars'. Aboriginal legend has it that a 'star', probably a meteorite, hit the top of Trig Hill leaving a large hole in it. The village sprang up in the 1880s after copper was found in the vicinity. It moved to its present site when the railway line was opened in 1883.

The copper mine has long since closed and the district now relies on sheep and wool but mineral exploration continues to take place.

GLENGARRY OPAL FIELD ■ 755

Opals were discovered here as early as 1905, although mining did not really get underway until the 1970s when a rich find resulted in one of the largest 'rushes' for many years – up to 200 miners worked the field. In 1987, there were 500, enough to form an association – the first of its kind in the region – to try to protect their livelihood from corporate takeovers.

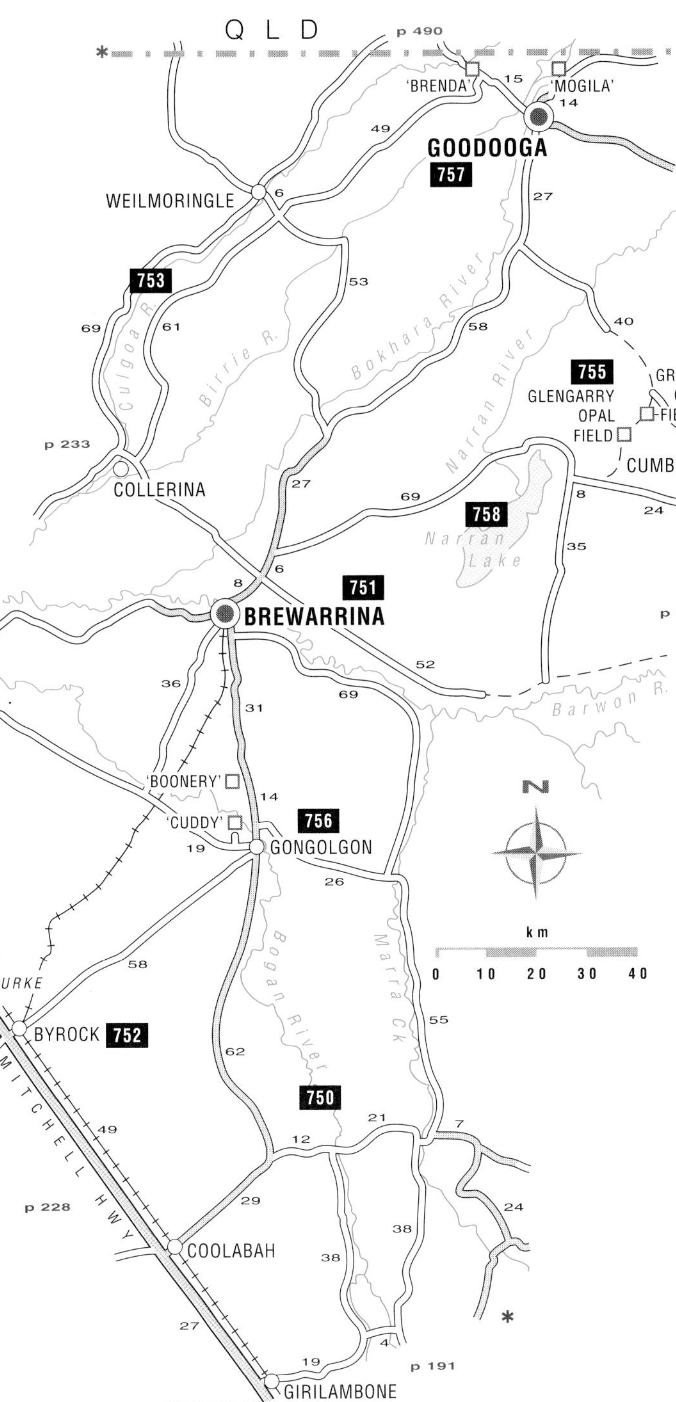

In the Barwon shallows near Brewarrina, the ravages of time and man are being erased and the Aboriginal fish trap patterns can be seen once again.

To the north-east, is the Grawin opal field where opals were first discovered in 1908 and 1920. Conditions still test even the hardy today, and visitors are advised to carry their own supply of water.

GONGOLGON ■ 756

Named after an Aboriginal word meaning 'big water hole', Gongolgan was originally a coaching station for Cobb & Co. During the 1870s, the town boasted four hotels, a police station and several shops. Since then, there has been little excitement here to match the occasion when one of the publicans captured a bushranger.

GOODOOGA ■ 757

Originally called Bokhara, a settlement began to grow here, about a kilometre from Goodooga's site, on the western banks of the Birrie River. The district was first explored in 1845 by Roderick Mitchell, son of the Surveyor-General, Thomas Mitchell.

As in the Brewarrina district, settlement was sparse and landholdings large. In the 1870s, the village of Bokhara moved to a new building site – initially a camping place for teamsters, who were the life-blood of the early settlement – east of the Bokhara river. Goodooga was also the stamping ground for the bushranger, Captain Thunderbolt – real name Frederick Ward – who was caught and convicted for horse stealing in 1856 but escaped, and hid out in the district for six months (see *Armidale & Uralla*).

A hospital and police station were built in the early 1880s and a brickworks established to provide bricks for a new store and hotel. The town remained Bokhara until 1938 when the present name was adopted.

BRENDA STATION North of Goodooga is the renowned sheep station known as 'Brenda'. Like many sheep and cattle stations it has led a chequered history. Sometime in the 1840s, Henry Adams squatted on Brenda Station, and by 1864, had branded 1000 calves. He later leased the property legally, along with eleven other stations – six in Queensland and five in New South Wales. At one time the combined area of the stations exceeded 142 000 hectares. After falling into serious financial difficulties, Adams decided to surrender his mortgages to a bishop of the Church of England in 1869. Since the bishop's death ten years later, the station has been managed by a board of trustees.

In the years that followed, 'Brenda' suffered great stock losses from the 1890 flood and the drought that followed from 1898 to 1903, and land resumptions on its Queensland side in 1896–98 substantially reduced the land holding.

Present-day 'Brenda' still straddles the state border and at more than 58 000 hectares is still a large property with earmark brands for both sheep and cattle that are widely known. Two streets in Goodooga – Brenda and Adam – take their names from the station and its connections.

NARRAN LAKE ■ 758

Narran Lake is the largest freshwater lake in New South Wales – albeit one that dries up in a drought year. The lake is part of a large depression into which the Narran River runs and its large surface area is due to the depression's shallow nature. The lake fills up when it rains in Queensland, but in dry times wheat can be seen growing in the middle of what in 'good' years is an oasis for thousands of water birds. Pelicans, ibis, black swans and ducks nest on the lake's scattered 'islands'.

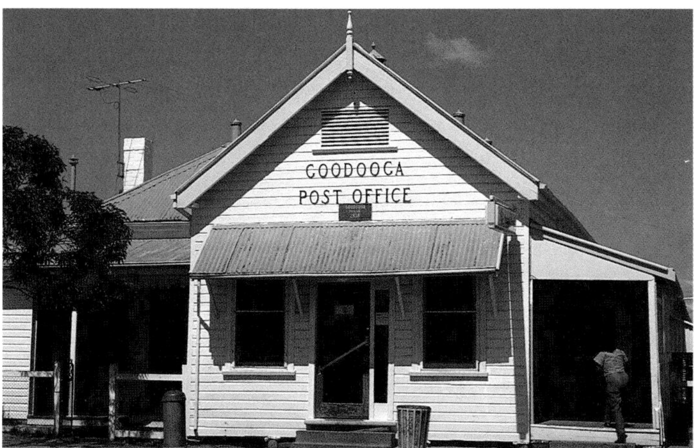

Goodooga's 1882 post office served a growing need – it was soon handling 500 letters a week, twenty times more than were posted in the late 1870s.

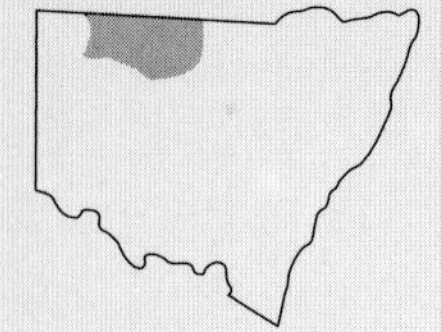

Bourke

The story of Bourke and its legendary back country is essentially the story of a river trade and a marginal pastoral industry. One inevitably declined, the other went from strength to strength. But woolgrowing no longer equates automatically with wealth – and the alternatives bring formidable problems.

BOURKE ■ 759

River red gums and coolibah trees are welcome sights in an isolated town where summer temperatures regularly exceed 40°C. Bourke is on the fringe of central Australia, with all the heat and aridity that the term implies. Yet the trees depend on flooding – a reminder of the capriciousness of the Darling River. In full flood it may spread thirty-five kilometres wide. Before levees protected the town, the river inflicted periodic havoc...but without it the town would never have existed.

Bourke was established in the early 1860s as a mercantile centre and port to serve sheep runs along the upper Darling. No significant mineral discoveries or other dramatic events have diverted it from that purpose. In 1885, while the river trade still thrived, Bourke took on new importance as a railhead. By then, artesian water bores had allowed an expansion of grazing into the forbidding country north of the river. Bourke became and still is one of the world's major centres for the transshipment of wool. Local prosperity remains tied to climatic cycles and foreign demand. Diversification into cotton planting and horticulture, dependent on irrigation from the Darling and the heavy use of fertilisers, have produced encouraging results – at a price to the health of the river that is increasingly questioned. *Population 2980*

COURT HOUSES AND POLICE STATION The elaborate court house on the corner of Oxley Street and the Mitchell Highway, opened in 1900, was the third to be built in Bourke. When the town's river trade was at its height, the building functioned as the maritime court – the farthest inland of any in Australia. Next to it the second court house, dating from 1876, is still standing. On the opposite corner the deep-verandahed police station (1889) occupies the site of the original court house.

POST OFFICE Begun as a single-storey structure in 1880, the building was extended before the end of the decade. During the disastrous flood of 1890, the upper floor served as an emergency newspaper office. Protected by its own levees, the building remained dry. A plaque on the wall marks the peak level of the flood.

HISTORICAL MUSEUM This graceful two-storey building, accommodating a pharmacy and doctor's surgery, was a medical centre between 1890 and 1920. Since the late 1970s, it has been restored by the Bourke and District Historical Society. The site was originally an allotment to the pioneer Thomas Matthews in his blacksmithing days, before he became 'King of Louth' (see entry).

BOURKE WEIR There are picnic facilities at the riverside fishing reserve downstream from the weir, which stores water for irrigation. The solid weir was built in 1941 after paddle steamers had ceased to ply the Darling. Earlier, there was a system of locks – the only ones on the river – and a weir with mobile shutters that tipped flat to allow boats and barges to pass over – now beneath the 'new' weir. The lock gates can still be seen.

NORTH BOURKE BRIDGE This is the oldest bridge in New South Wales to be built with a lifting span. A masterpiece of engineering in latticed steel, it was designed in 1878, completed in 1883 and has required minimal maintenance ever since.

FORT BOURKE STOCKADE SITE Fearing attack by Aborigines during his exploration of the Darling River in 1835, Major Thomas Mitchell ordered the building of a tree-trunk stockade to protect a stores depot. Never put to the test, the timbers of Fort Bourke were probably taken away by early settlers. A cairn marks the exact site, but no details of the construction were recorded: a 'replica' nearby was built in the 1980s largely by guesswork. The area is reached by a signposted turn-off from the Louth road.

DARLING RIVER ■ 760

The Darling River is the major waterway of the longest river system on the continent, draining a vast area of

The 17-metre 'lift' span in the North Bourke Bridge – raised by pulleys and weights – is a reminder that paddle steamers once plied these muddy waters.

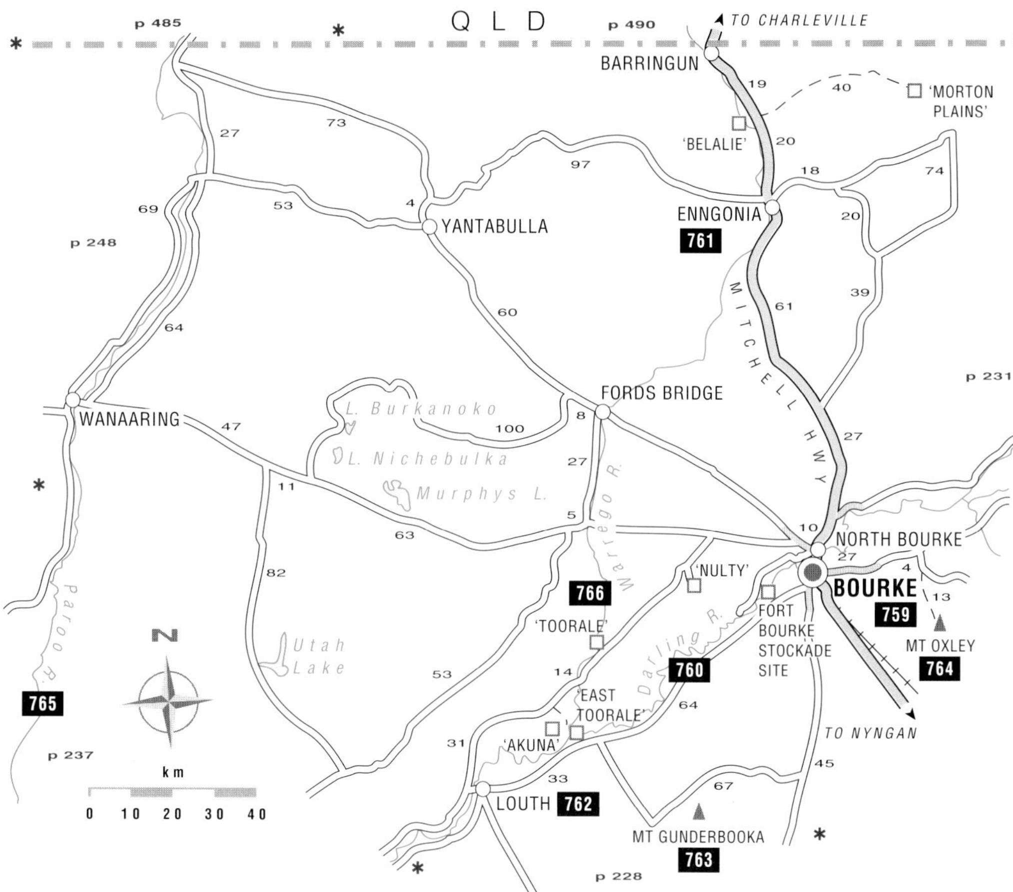

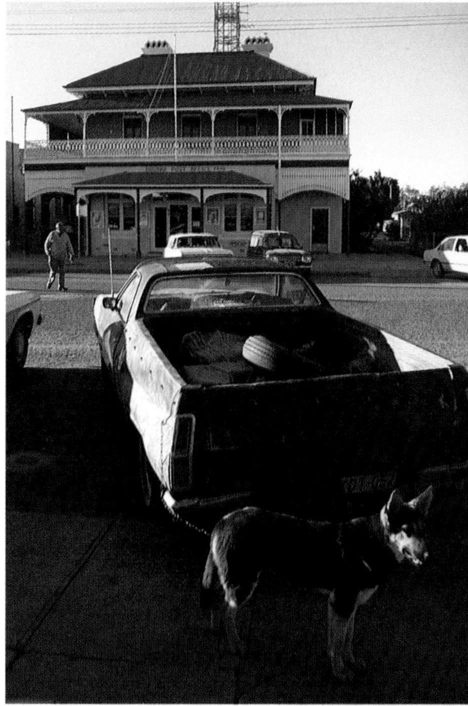

The utilitarian 'ute' and a dog – here in front of the Bourke Post Office – are often the farmer's best friends 'back o' Bourke'.

New South Wales and Queensland. It flows for approximately 2700 kilometres from its first properly identifiable source near Stanthorpe – where it is known as the Dumaresq – south-west through New South Wales to Wentworth on the Victorian border, where it links forces with its only equal, the mighty Murray (see Special Feature, pp.234-35).

ENNGONIA ■ 761

Literacy was a proud accomplishment among outback people in the late nineteenth century, and hardship and solitude were often the spurs to sensitive writing. In an odd conjunction of their careers, three distinguished bush balladists poured their thoughts onto paper from lonely sheep stations north of Bourke during the 1890s. Scots-born Will Gillespie worked as a horse-breaker at Belalie on the Warrego River. Harry 'The Breaker' Morant, who was to be disgraced and executed during the Boer War, was doing a similar job not far east at Morton Plains. It seems that both used to resort to the Barringum pub. Meanwhile Henry Lawson was working his way from Bourke to Hungerford. All three competed for space in the pages of the Sydney *Bulletin*.

Enngonia links itself romantically with an earlier era of bushranging, though this country never yielded rich pickings for outlaws. In 1868, 'Captain Starlight', whose real name was Pearson, held up the pub and shot a policeman. Eleven years later, another bushranger, Harry Law, was killed in the town. These and other incidents contributed to the character of Captain Midnight in Rolf Boldrewood's *Robbery Under Arms*.

LOUTH ■ 762

A column of granite seven metres tall dominates an old graveyard in the riverside village of Louth. More than a monument to the woman who was buried beneath, it signifies the towering ambition of her husband, Thomas Matthews. People along the Darling in the 1870s nicknamed him the 'King of Louth' or 'Old T.A.'. In fact he was its creator. For a few years his township rivalled Bourke as a port, with Mathews in control of most business activity.

Born in County Louth, Ireland, Matthews sought his fortune on the Victorian goldfields in 1856, but soon found a better living as a tradesman on outback properties. In 1865, he bought and stocked a forty-acre waterfront fragment of the 'Toorale' run and sent for his family. With their help he built a hotel and began business as a horse dealer, ferryman and contract builder. As more farmland was acquired he cut up his original holding into lots for the townsfolk of a new Louth. A wharf and bond store were built for the river trade and even though the port's prosperity was short-lived it enabled Tom Matthews to take up an 80 000-hectare sheep run and to survive in wealthy old age even after his property was eaten out by rabbits.

The somnolence of present-day Louth is shattered for one weekend in early spring, when up to three thousand people flock to an annual picnic race meeting.

MOUNT GUNDERBOOKA ■ 763

A tilted sandstone mass, jutting 300 metres above the red sandplains that reach south from the Darling River, presents unexpected scenic relief to travellers on the Bourke–Cobar road.

Seen at closer quarters, Mount Gunderbooka holds more surprises. At its foot, shaded holes in the gorge of Mullareenya Creek retain water when the rest of the countryside is parched. Aborigines knew them well: in the gorge and higher up the slope, shelters formed by erosion are painted with hundreds of small figures, mostly human and depicted in a more or less natural style.

Mount Gunderbooka was climbed by Charles Sturt early in 1829 in the hope that he would at last glimpse the much-discussed inland sea. He called the formation the Durban Range. Its later name came from a sheep run established along Gunderbooka Creek, a Darling tributary. Coincidentally, it was at the creek mouth that Sturt and Hume abandoned their exploration of the river.

MOUNT OXLEY ■ 764

Only amid a virtually featureless landscape would this flat-topped rise south of Bourke be regarded as a mountain. In 1829, Charles Sturt, leading the first European party to climb its slopes, called it Oxley's Tableland. He commemorated the exploratory achievements of John Oxley, who had died a few months earlier. From the mesa's top Sturt saw in the distance the greater eminence of Mount Gunderbooka, which so boosted his hopes that he and two companions rode there immediately.

PAROO RIVER ■ 765

Originating in the far west of Queensland, the waters of the Paroo were essential to the establishment of stock routes across the parched plains north-west of Bourke. The country was so unpromising that surveyors did not find the river until 1861. In most years, the Paroo's flow is feeble, petering out in swamps south of Wanaaring. But in exceptional seasons, floodwaters emerge from the swamps and join the Darling near Wilcannia. This causes a huge enlargement of the wetlands in the Nocoleche Nature Reserve, south of Wanaaring, where the Paroo overflow merges with the channelled floodplain of Cuttaburra Creek.

WARREGO RIVER ■ 766

Of all the far-flung rains that contribute to the vast Darling–Murray system, the northernmost are carried by the Warrego River. When it merges with the Darling south of Bourke, the Warrego completes a course of about six hundred kilometres from the Great Dividing Range in Queensland, not far south of the Tropic of Capricorn. The river was surveyed by Sir Thomas Mitchell in 1846 and quickly became a lifeline for pastoral runs that have become prime wool-growing properties.

DARLING RIVER

The Darling, the quintessential Australian inland river, follows a long, lazy and circuitous course, caring nothing for the water it loses to evaporation and seepage along the way. Its banks form a narrow oasis shaded by red gums and enlivened by the flash of wild budgerigars.

From its various sources in southern Queensland to its meeting with the Murray River near Wentworth, the stream of the Darling River is about 2800 kilometres long so it can fairly claim to be the longest waterway in Australia. Despite its length the river has no pretensions to grandeur, but it does have a certain nobility as the only major watercourse to survive a journey across the semi-arid interior.

The Darling proper originates just north of Bourke – approximately 1000 kilometres from the Murray meeting – and that it eventually makes the distance at all to join with its only rival in length is a matter of surprise as it certainly makes no rush of it, with a fall of only thirty metres over the several hundred kilometres between Bourke and Wilcannia being typical of the journey southward. Despite its unhurried approach, the river and its tributaries drain a region of more than 650 000 square kilometres, including most of western New South Wales and much of southern Queensland. Away from the river, the countryside shimmers into the far distance in a blue-grey blur of bluebush and saltbush and clumps of mallee scrub.

The Darling draws its waters from far away, with major contributions coming from the Condamine and the various channels of the Balonne in Queensland, although in very wet years even the Warrego and the Paroo will push their way through to the Darling from the state's semi-arid west. In New South Wales, the major tributaries are the Bogan, Castlereagh, Namoi, Severn, Gwydir and Macquarie rivers.

Above Wilcannia, the Darling ceases to receive tributaries and instead distributes its waters in flood channels – known as 'anabranches' – which follow a meandering course through swamps and salt flats flanked by numerous overflow lakes. The Great Anabranch which leaves the Darling below Menindee never rejoins the parent channel, flowing instead into the Murray River about fifteen kilometres west of Wentworth. Near Menindee, the western bank of the Darling opens into a series of very broad and shallow overflow lakes which complement the river for about fifty kilometres. The Menindee Lakes 'oasis' forms a minor inland sea in the form of a major water storage kept permanently full by an eighteen-metre dam on the river.

In a waterless landscape, the native water rat rarely wanders far from the banks of the Darling River.

From a mill-pond scene at Bourke, the Darling slides but gently southwards for 1000 kilometres. It was near here that European explorers first stumbled across the river.

The first recorded sighting by a European of the Darling occurred with Charles Sturt's first expedition to explore the inland rivers. In February 1829, with Hamilton Hume, Sturt saw the river and named it in honour of the then Governor of New South Wales. Considering the harsh nature of the country, settlement followed exploration with unexpected speed. When Burke and Wills arrived at Menindee on the Darling in 1860, Francis Cadell had already been operating a store there for about a year. The rapid spread of civilisation was due mainly to the river's use as a ready highway into the depths of the inland by steamers in the 1850s. The height of the trade came in the 1870s when there were about 100 steamers and barges plying the Murray–Darling system. Even Bourke, far up the Darling, was regularly serviced by flat-bottomed paddle steamers trailing strings of heavily loaded barges.

The Darling River drains much of the region of New South Wales known as the 'Western Division'. The creation of this special administrative regime followed the disastrous experience of the late nineteenth century, when overstocking combined with rabbit plagues and drought to create massive land degradation. Environmental dangers for the Darling River are no less serious today. Water quality has deteriorated to the point where in December 1991, the river suffered what some described as a 'heart attack' with more than a thousand kilometres of its length burgeoning forth with a toxic blue green 'algal' bloom, the world's largest known event of this kind. □

The life-giving arteries of the inland – the Murray (left) and the Darling – join forces at Wentworth (top). Muddy brown is the Darling's preferred colour; toxic algae, multiplying in explosive proportions, turned it into a ribbon of sickly green in 1991 (right).

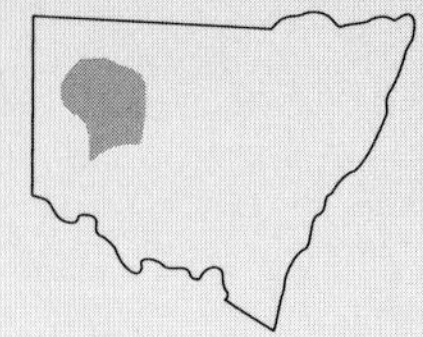

Wilcannia & White Cliffs

It took the promise of wealth from wool – produced on vast stations along the Darling – or from precious black opals to draw Europeans to this harsh land on the edge of central Australia.

COTURAUNDEE NATURE RESERVE ■ 767

To the near north-east of the Mootwingee National Park, this region of undisturbed bushland reserves 6600 hectares of the major part of the rugged Coturaundee Range as a home for an isolated group of the increasingly rare, yellow-footed rock wallaby. This marsupial is listed under the *National Parks and Wildlife Act* as: 'Fauna in Imminent Danger of Extinction'. The wallabies – previously thought to be restricted to small remnant populations in similarly arid regions of Queensland and South Australia – were first discovered here in 1966; the park was established in 1979.

MOOTWINGEE NATIONAL PARK ■ 768

This 68 900-hectare park is located to the north-west of Wilcannia and is dominated by the rugged sandstone Byngnano Range. Some of Australia's highest temperatures have been recorded in this isolated massif, which rises starkly out of the surrounding sand and gibber plains. The park was established in 1982 and is characterised by deep gorges lined with river red gums, rockpools, expanses of brown rocks and mulga trees. The fauna includes a wide variety of parrots and cockatoos, emus, red and grey kangaroos, euros and marsupial mice. There are more than 300 Aboriginal sites in the park, including Mootwingee Historic Site.

MOOTWINGEE HISTORIC SITE Situated in the Byngnano Range, the Mootwingee Historic Site comprises a wealth of Aboriginal cultural relics. The 486-hectare area is of great spiritual significance to Aboriginal people and contains superb examples of rock engravings, stencils and paintings, as well as campsites, tools and implements. Within the site there are more than twenty rockshelters, fifteen rock engraving locations and many open campsites. This concentration of relics is due to the presence of semi-permanent waterholes in the area: Aboriginal groups probably gathered here in large numbers, particularly in times of drought.

Rangers and Aboriginal guides lead towns of the site twice a week during winter months. A Cultural Resource Centre is dedicated to the preservation of Aboriginal history and mythology.

PAROO RIVER OVERFLOW ■ 769

The Paroo, an 'occasional' waterway which is more often than not dry, flows from southern Queensland to its junction with the Darling River near Wilcannia. The river's shallow nature and the flatness of the surrounding plains means that like many inland rivers, it turns its 'overflow' into a region of lakes and rich pastures – when the rains come in Queensland. Henry Lawson's poem entitled 'Paroo River' includes the line: *'But where,' said I, ''s the blooming stream?' And he replied, 'We're at it!'*

TILPA ■ 770

Tilpa sits on the west bank of the Darling River, at the junction of the Paroo and Bourke roads, north-east of Wilcannia. The colonial Surveyor-General, Major Thomas Mitchell camped near here during his 1835 expedition. Tilpa's strategic roadside position, and the fact that this was the best route during the hot summer months from Wilcannia to the Paroo River, led to the village's development; drovers used this location to herd their mobs across the Darling. The practical location was stressed in an application for a telegraph office in 1880. Tilpa sits on the flat Darling–Talyawalka floodplains, where serious flooding has been known to occur and it has been known, appropriately, as the 'Village of the Floodplain'.

During the mid-1920s the settlement was described as 'terribly tiny Tilpa' by a writer in *The Bulletin* and today it is still a mere cluster of houses around a bridge but at the centre of a region that contains many large merino sheep properties.

WHITE CLIFFS ■ 771

This small opal-mining settlement north-west of Broken Hill is named after the white shale outcrops in which the sought-after gems are found. Opals are thought to have been discovered here in 1884, but it was not until a group of kangaroo hunters came across several stones on the vast Momba Station, to the east, in 1889 that mining really took off. Samples of this find were sent to Adelaide and found to be of a high

The uninitiated could be forgiven for not recognising this as a waterway, in fact, a creek-tributary of the Paroo River – when it rains for long enough.

Not all White Cliffs' unusual dwellings are underground; this rustic hut was built during a 'rush' to nearby Poverty Flat in 1893.

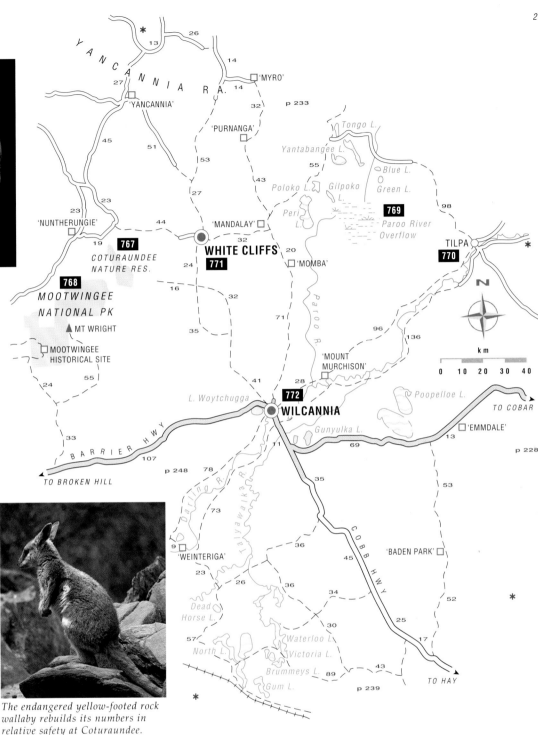

quality. The White Cliffs opal fields became the third in New South Wales, following discoveries near Bathurst and at Milparinka. Within a year, almost 600 hectares were under mining leases.

In 1897, when White Cliffs had been proclaimed a town, a piece of opal worth £8000 was found here and the ensuing publicity brought a rush of prospectors to the area: by 1899 there were 4000 people at White Cliffs. Stores and hotels - at one stage there were five - grew up to cater for the diggers' needs, and the town's first newspaper, *The Western Life*, was launched in 1897.

For more than ten years White Cliffs' opals dominated world markets, but by 1902 the field's decline had begun. A combination of the increasing rarity of the best grade opal and a glut of inferior stones, low returns and drought forced many people to leave the area. By 1914, the population plummeted to thirty but although the deposit was thought to have been almost totally exploited, opals are still hand-mined

The peculiar White Cliffs practice of living beneath the ground in abandoned hillside mine workings, which persists today, had already begun by the turn of the century. A number of businesses, including a bakery, retreated under the surface as local people saw this as a logical means of escaping the intense heat. Nowadays, there are about 140 dugouts in the town.

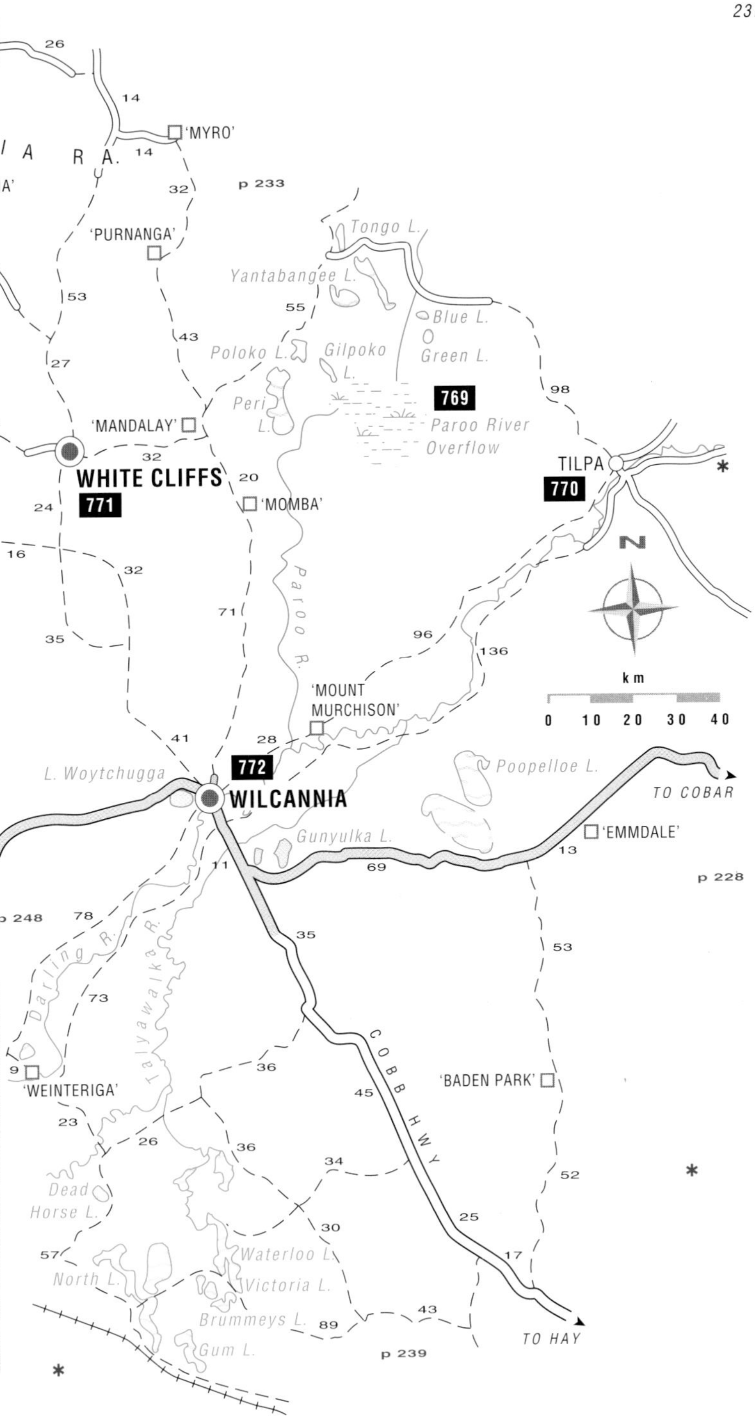

The endangered yellow-footed rock wallaby rebuilds its numbers in relative safety at Coturaundee.

The population of this isolated town varies between fifty to two hundred residents. The locals are one of White Cliffs' most intriguing features as they include a number of eccentrics, who live a modern-day pioneering lifestyle and work together as an unusually close-knit community. Many people close up their homes and diggings and move closer to the coast from December to February to escape the heat.

Tourism brings some income to White Cliffs, particularly during the cooler months, when some visitors take advantage of the unique opportunity to stay in an underground motel. Other subterranean tourist features include an art gallery and opal showrooms. Visitors can buy opals here or fossick for their own in designated areas. Another local oddity and a by-product of excavation for opals, is the 100-million-year-old fossilised skeleton of a giant reptilian marine creature called a plesiosaur, which was excavated here and is on public display.

SOLAR-ENERGY RESEARCH STATION White Cliffs is the site of Australia's first experimental solar-energy plant, which consists of fourteen computer-controlled reflectors each with a diameter of three-and-a-half metres. The station was opened in 1983 and is operated by the Broken Hill City

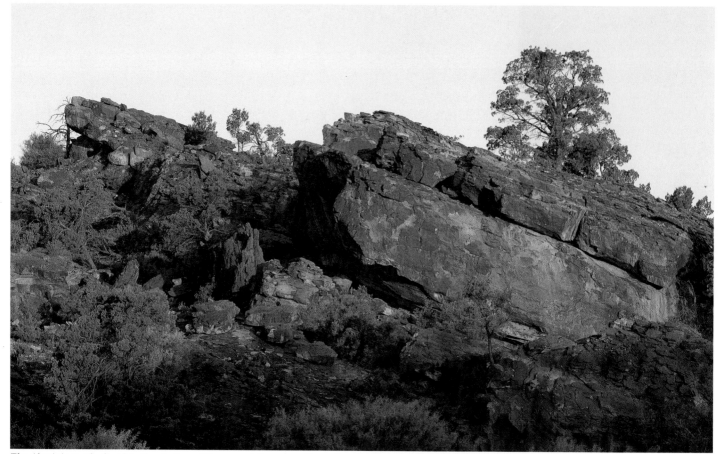

The Aborigines who lived in the shadow of the rugged Byngnano Range have left an impressive painted record of their daily and spiritual lives.

Council. It supplies electric power for street lighting, to a number of houses, and the town's public buildings.

WILCANNIA ■ 772

The Aboriginal people who had long occupied this territory before Major Thomas Mitchell, the Surveyor-General of the time, passed through on his second exploratory journey of north-west New South Wales in 1835 came off second best in their first encounter with Europeans. Despite orders not to use force against the 'natives', several Aborigines died of gunshot wounds after skirmishes with Mitchell's party.

The solar-power reflectors at White Cliffs turn 'dish upwards' at night or during strong winds.

The region remained unoccupied by Europeans until the late 1840s, when the first graziers arrived, and it was not until 1855 that settlement began in earnest. A post office, court house and a bank were established by 1860 and in 1863 a town site was selected; the only habitation here at the time was a shepherd's hut belonging to the sheep station 'Mount Murchison'. The site was officially surveyed in 1865, and a township proclaimed in the following year under the name Wilcannia – thought to be an Aboriginal word for 'a gap in a bank through which flood waters flow'.

Meanwhile, the town's location on the river proved to be vital. In 1859, a steamer reached Mount Murchison, opening the upper reaches of the river to commercial traffic. Wilcannia eventually became Australia's third largest inland port.

Wilcannia's development continued during the next two decades, hand in hand with the greatly increased wool production of north-west New South Wales. The town also became an important river crossing place for stock headed south to the Melbourne markets. During the 1870s, the town became a coaching centre for prospectors travelling to the gold, silver, opal and copper diggings in the nearby Barrier Ranges: up to twenty coaches came through Wilcannia each week.

By 1880, the town was described as 'busy and prosperous'. There were around 3000 people in the area, including Afghan camel drivers and numerous Chinese settlers. At this time, the town had thirteen hotels, and Wilcannia became known as the 'Queen City of the West'. The waterfront was a hive of activity; during 1887 alone, 222 steamers took on 26 550 tonnes of wool and other goods from the Wilcannia wharves.

During this 1880s period, the sons of two famous English novelists – Charles Dickens and Anthony Trollope – were prominent citizens in the area. Edward Dickens was employed as the manager of Momba Station, to the north of Wilcannia, and later became the district's representative in the New South Wales Parliament. Frederic Trollope worked in the Lands Department.

Although Wilcannia's heyday lasted for about fifty years, a sequence of events effectively ended the town's status as a major inland port. A succession of dry years from 1900 onwards reduced water levels, and thus access to the wharf, and the arrival of rail transport spelled the end for river transport. Railway lines from the east and the south to Broken Hill bypassed Wilcannia and wool began to leave the region through other centres. The final blow was dealt by the arrival of motor transport during the 1920s. The rotting wharves are a reminder of the town's former glory when 100 paddle steamers plied the Darling.

The town's past importance is still evident in its many fine buildings, most of which were constructed from local sandstone. St James' Church of England dates from 1875; the 1883 Athenaeum now contains Wilcannia Pioneer Museum; and the large jail and police residence were completed in 1881.

The town is a service centre for a vast cattle and sheep district. Aborigines, most of whom live on settlements by the Darling, make up about two-thirds of Wilcannia's population. As in many inland towns with large Aboriginal populations, there are often tensions between the black and white communities but positive efforts are being made to improve relations and eradicate the legacy of the violence which marked the arrival of Europeans 160 years ago. *Population 940*

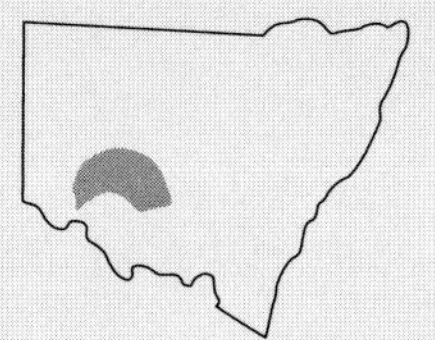

Hillston & Ivanhoe

In this region of dry lake beds, claypans and broad saltbush plains, Australia's oldest known inhabitants lived around freshwater lakes teeming with fish...and left a fossil legacy, which has led to the rewriting of the Aboriginal prehistory of the continent.

BOOLIGAL ■ 773

A theodolite – a small, tripod-mounted telescope used for surveying – is Booligal's memorial to John Oxley who passed through the future site of this Lachlan River town during his search for the inland sea.

Booligal Station appeared on maps as early as 1861 and by 1866 it was a stopover point on the overland stock route. But it was the establishment of the Cobb & Co. route from Moama on the Murray to Wilcannia on the Darling that put the small settlement on the map. The long, low California-style coaches favoured by the company in outback areas, crossed the Lachlan River at Booligal every week with passengers and mail. The government installed wells along the route and with the water supply came development. Booligal now sits on the Cobb Highway, which follows the old Cobb & Co. route.

This sheep and cattle town on a stretch of almost treeless claypan got its name from an Aboriginal word said to mean 'windy place'.

GOOLGOWI ■ 774

Goolgowi is the headquarters of Carathool Shire Council, which was established in 1906 for a population of a few hundred on a number of pastoral properties and four small villages, spread over almost twelve thousand square kilometres. Lack of rain was not the only problem for the new shire since it had neither offices, staff, equipment nor much in the way of funds.

The coming of the railway in the 1920s, the water fed through Barren Box Swamp from the extensive Murrumbidgee Irrigation Areas (see *Griffith & Leeton*), closer settlement between the two world wars and the opening of the artificial Lake Brewster (see entry) in 1948, were all vital for Goolgowi's survival.

This sheep and cattle town has one of the largest water windmills in the district and is the source of especially fine pinkish clay from clay pits just outside Goolgowi.

HILLSTON ■ 775

The Aboriginal name for the Hillston region was 'melnunni' said to mean 'red soil' and when William Hill established a hotel there in 1863, he called it the Red Bank. The name of the hotel was initially adopted as the European name for the settlement but had to be changed six years later to avoid confusion with various other Red Banks. The name of William Hill, former stockman and hotel owner, was adopted although Hill never knew the honour done to him at Hillston since he died two years before the town was renamed.

Initially there were two townships side-by-side – the official government settlement and a private township on an area of land owned by John McGee. From 1875, both townships served passing 'trade' as

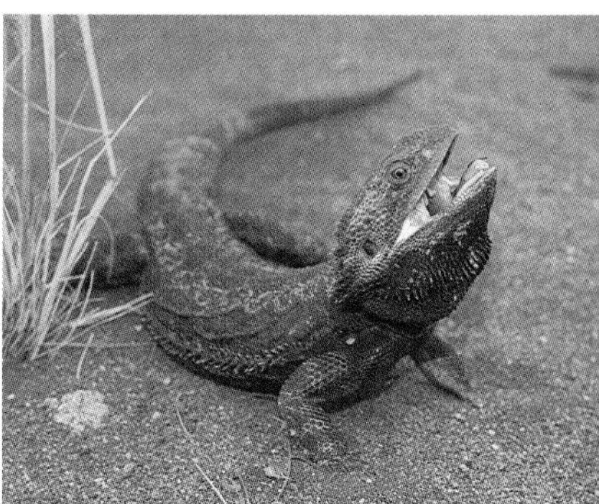

A defiant bearded dragon in the Mungo region stands his ground, not to fight, but to frighten with a fierce expression above the 'beard' – a loose flap of skin.

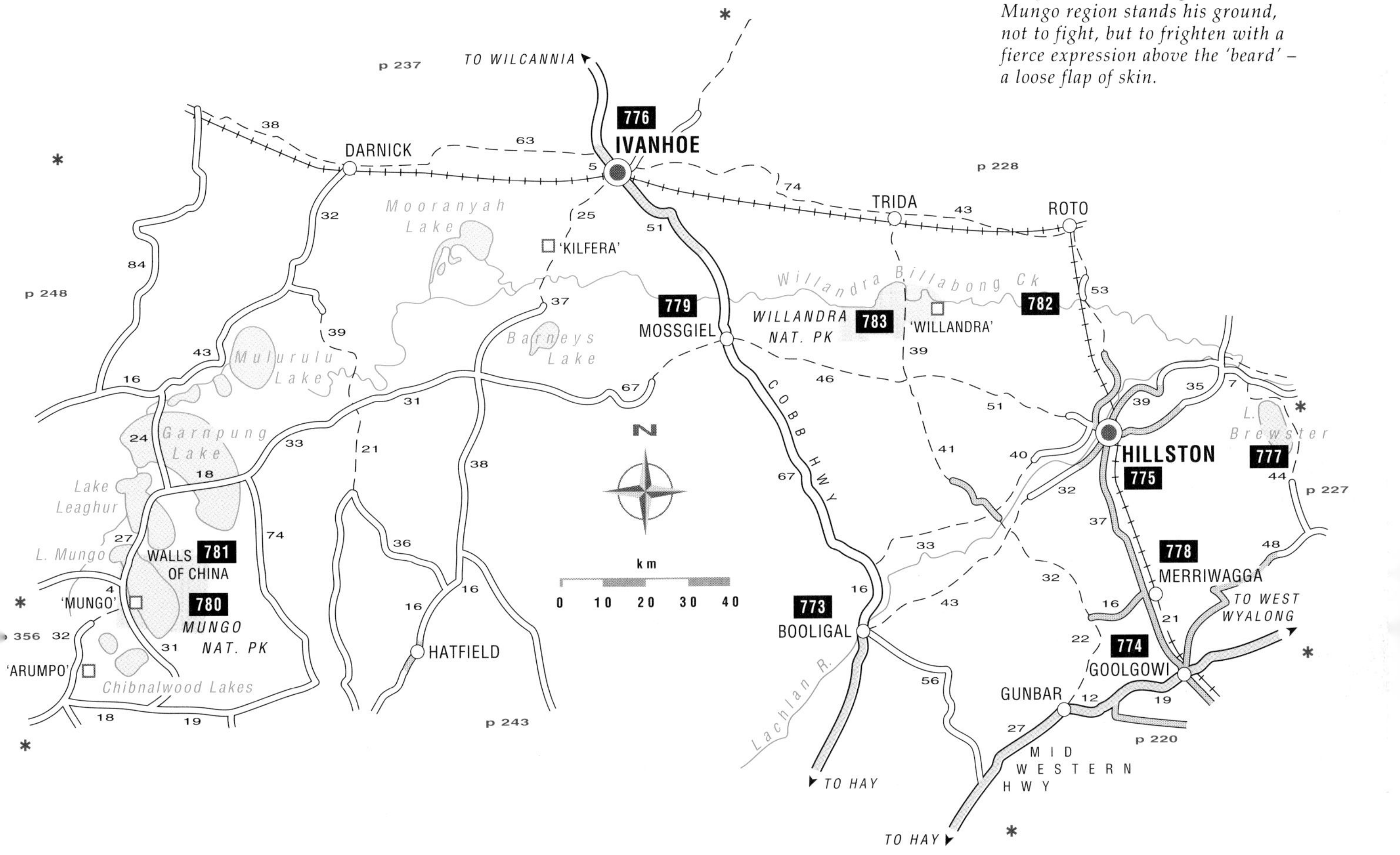

the town was a stopover on the route to Bourke, the journey from Hillston to Bourke taking four days and costing seven pounds sterling. Wool was the major local product and later, wheat, together with gold and copper discoveries, expanded the town's economic base.

Today, Hillston is seen as 'an oasis in the scrub'. Citrus fruit, orchards and vineyards, established with great success in the adjacent Murrumbidgee Irrigation Areas, spilled over into Hillston, which now boasts a productive 350-hectare citrus orchard, irrigated by an underground water supply. *Population 1030*

The Broken Hill passenger train still visits Ivanhoe twice a week – haughtily ignoring the old goods platform – but now it goes all the way to Perth.

IVANHOE ■ 776

Ivanhoe was named after the novel of the same name by Sir Walter Scott whose influence also spread to a property just south of the town in the 1860s which was called Abbotsford, the name of Sir Walter Scott's last home in Scotland.

From the early days of the town, isolation and water supply were ongoing problems. The water supply problem was solved initially by carting water by dray from Kilfera Lake, south of the town, until the government built tanks along the route of what is now the Cobb Highway. Isolation was a more difficult problem. Ivanhoe, being more than 150 kilometres from the only other town of any size in the region – Hillston – made fleeting contact with the outside world only twice a week when, from the 1880s, the Cobb & Co. coach passed through the town. It was not until the Sydney–Broken Hill railway line connected with the town in 1925 that this state of affairs was alleviated, although the roar of the Broken Hill Express as it steamed through Ivanhoe was heard at the unsociable hour of 1.30 a.m., nineteen hours after it left Sydney on Monday and Thursday mornings at 8 a.m.

LAKE BREWSTER ■ 777

Lake Brewster was named after the chief engineer responsible for creating the lake in 1952 in a natural depression just south of the Lachlan River. When the Lachlan River is running high, a weir and earth dam at a bend on the Lachlan raises the water to a level that forces it into a channel flowing into the lake. Lake Brewster covers an area of more than 6000 hectares when full and the water storage is used almost exclusively for irrigation of crops grown in the lower Lachlan Valley; the lake also holds excess floodwaters that would otherwise flood the valley.

Too shallow for such recreational activities as boating, Lake Brewster is a wildlife refuge where a number of species of waterfowl are protected. Generous rains in 1989 resulted in the lake becoming Australia's major pelican breeding site in that year.

MERRIWAGGA ■ 778

Merriwagga is one of two sites in New South Wales which lays claim to the site of the 'black stump', beyond which, or this side of which, all Australians live. The claim goes back to 1886 when, just outside the town, Barbara Blaine lit a fire one hot windy day while her teamster husband took the animals to slake their thirst at the nearby water tank. The dry grass caught fire...and so did Mrs Blaine. By the time her husband returned she was, according to his laconic description, 'just like a black stump'. The water tank, a nearby creek and swamp and the plain that stretches from Merriwagga to Gunbar all inherited the Black Stump name. Telecom too appears to stand by Merriwagga's claim since the local telephone exchange has been honoured with the name Black Stump, and in 1970 the Black Stump Picnic Area was graced with a replica of the 'black stump'.

MOSSGIEL ■ 779

In the 1860s, the Desailly brothers established a sheep run at Mossgiel, employing over three hundred men to dig wells and tanks and fence the run. Drought and a credit squeeze led to bankruptcy and the final irony – and quite likely the final straw – came when they attempted to move off the bankrupt property and were bogged in mud resulting from rain that came too late.

Drought caused the Chinese market gardeners who grew fruit and vegetables on the creek to move on three occasions...on the fourth occasion they gave up. Lack of water resulted in goats rather than cows being used locally as a source of milk and meat – unlike cows, goats do not have to be driven to water but fend for themselves.

By the 1890s, Mossgiel was a flourishing small town from which bales of wool were transported to Hay. But by 1903 it was the end for Mossgiel's thriving times. A sequence of distressing events starting with a drought and a mice plague, followed by an outbreak of typhoid, affected every home in the town and the decline continued until the 1920s when there were more empty houses than occupied ones and Mossgiel has never regained its former thriving township status.

MUNGO NATIONAL PARK ■ 780

The 28 000-odd hectares of parched country within the boundaries of Mungo National Park includes most of the Lake Mungo basin – which has

Where fish once leapt from the waters of the Willandra Lakes, the wind sculpts a moonscape from the lakebed...here and there disturbed by archaeological digs (see opposite).

WILLANDRA'S ANCIENT SANDS OF TIME

THE FOSSIL remains that led to the dry Willandra Lakes becoming one of the first sites in Australia to be registered in the UNESCO World Heritage list in 1981 were laid down up to 40 000 years ago...but the existence of this archaeological treasure trove was not discovered until the late 1960s.

In 1969, the bones of a tall, slim young woman – labelled unromantically by scientists as 'Mungo I' – were found in a burial pit originally mistaken for a fireplace. The woman had first been cremated, then her bones smashed, burnt again and reburied. The world's most ancient cremation site has been dated as approximately 25 500 years old and the excitement of this find had not died down when a further two burial sites were discovered in the vicinity. One of these revealed the body of a young man, 'Mungo III', buried with hands clasped over the top half of his body and the surrounding earth covered with powdered red ochre as part of a burial rite. This body has now been dated as 30 000 years old and has pushed back the evidence of Aboriginal occupation of Australia by thousands of years.

The evidence from Aboriginal middens and fireplaces points to a freshwater lake, which, 40 000 years ago, was a breeding ground for Murray cod, golden perch and mussels. As the waters retreated some 15–18 000 years ago, the fish poles with their bone barbs were replaced by slabs and tools used for grinding wild grass seeds into flour. Overwhelming evidence has now come to light that the Aborigines were grinding seeds at the same time as their contemporaries in the Middle East.

Other bones and remains of extinct fauna point to the existence around Lake Mungo of, among others, a three-metre-high kangaroo, a rhinoceros-sized relative of the wombat, a marsupial lion and an animal similar to the modern Tasmanian devil. By analysing layers of sediment, geologists can plot dramatic changes in climate, the environment – from fresh to salt water and vice versa – and the variations in magnetic poles over the last 50 000 years.

Most of these discoveries have been made at the site of Lake Mungo and The Walls of China. With patience, further treasure is likely to emerge from the other lakes and lunettes in the Willandra Lakes system. Meanwhile, the archaeologists showed respect for the beliefs of 'Mungo I's' descendants by handing the bones to the Aboriginal people in 1992 for reburial. □

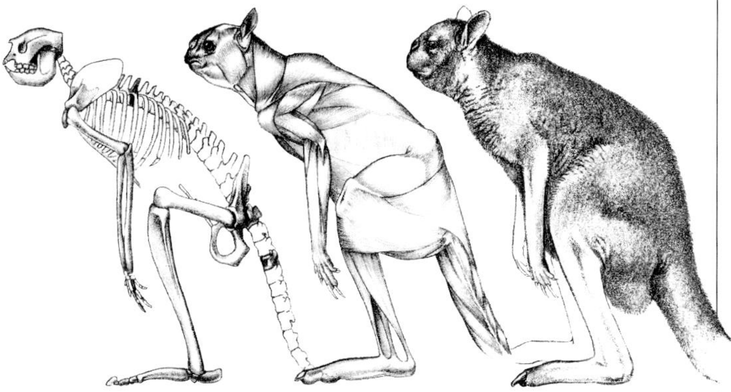

Up to 15 000 years of erosion at Lake Mungo has revealed the remains of the three-metre-tall, short-faced kangaroo (above left). Using the fossil bones, scientists have gradually reconstructed its appearance.

been bone-dry for 15 000 years – the historic sheep station on its shores, the unusual dune structures around the lake and the plains that stretch beyond the dunes.

In the section of the park within the boundaries of the former Gol Gol Station stands the Mungo Woolshed, built in 1869 by Chinese labour and the sweaty scene of the shearing of 50 000 sheep each season. In 1922, the 203 000 hectare 'Gol Gol' was broken into smaller soldier-settler blocks and on two of these – Mungo and Zanci – the Park was established in 1979. The name 'Mungo' dates only from 1922, although Lake Mungo itself was formed about 45 000 years ago and is the site of Australia's oldest fossil finds.

With an end to the environmentally damaging effects of grazing within the park in 1979, the region's unique natural vegetation – bladder saltbush on the dry lake bed, belah or leafless casuarina and mallee eucalypts on the dunes and plains – has been re-established. An variety of birds and animals including emus, orange- and white-fronted chats, pink cockatoos, reptilian species such as shinglebacks and bearded dragons, together with large red and western grey kangaroos have also returned.

WALLS OF CHINA ■ 781

On the northern and eastern shores of dry Lake Mungo, stands a twenty-five-kilometre-long, crescent-shaped dune or lunette. This lunette, estimated at 15–30 000 years old, is part of an ancient landscape, but its name dates only from the ninenteenth century when it was christened the Walls of China by – or for – the Chinese workers on Gol Gol Station.

The lunette was constructed over thousands of years as the prevailing westerly winds piled sand and other materials from the lake into the distinctive dune. As the lake gradually emptied and became more saline, clay and mud pellets from the lake bed were borne by the wind to provide a crystalline skin on the Walls of China. Wind and rain eroded what was once a forty-metre-high continuous dune into weirdly shaped pillars and other structures, creating the intriguing form of this complex, natural sculpture.

Over the years, this erosion has also exposed the lunette's internal layers of sediment and fossils, which make the Walls of China unique. All of the Willandra Lakes have similar lunettes but most of the fossil finds that led to the World Heritage listing of the Willandra Lakes (see box) were found in the Walls of China, the most extensively eroded lunette in the lakes system.

WILLANDRA BILLABONG CREEK ■ 782

In the midst of countryside characterised by clumps of saltbush and dusty claypans, the trough of Willandra Billabong Creek, offers sanctuary to cormorants, herons, ducks and a vareity of fish including yellowbelly and perch. Coolibahs, blackbox and lignum grow on the banks of this creek, which forms the northern boundary of Willandra National Park (see entry).

Willandra Billabong Creek flows west from the Lachlan River to dissipate in a series of swamps, salt flats and dry lake beds. The creek is now an intermittent stream but 45 000 years ago it was a minor branch of the Lachlan River feeding the Willandra Lakes – a once extensive network of waterways that included Mooranyah Lake, Mulurulu Lake, Garnpung Lake, Lake Leaghur, Lake Mungo and Chibnalwood Lakes – covering an area of 1000 square kilometres and supporting a diversity of wildlife. When Willandra Billabong Creek ceased to carry waters to the lakes, they dried up one by one.

WILLANDRA NATIONAL PARK ■ 783

Willandra National Park covers less than six per cent of what was once Big Willandra Station. In the late nineteenth century, 'Big Willandra' covered an area of 294 000 hectares – stretching from Hillston to Mossgiel (see entries) – and was one of the biggest merino studs in Australia. Over the years, the amount of land decreased as closer settlement and new farming practices encroached on 'Big Willandra'.

In 1972, a lease of 13 000 hectares on the western side of the park expired and was resumed as Willandra National Park. In 1975, with a donation from the Boral company, which held much of the land, the eastern section of the park including the homestead, stables, shearing complex, thatched rams' shed and several other station buildings were acquired. Although shearing still takes place in the 'Big Willandra' shearing shed, the sheep come from neighbouring properties since all grazing within the park boundaries has now ceased in an attempt to restore the saltbush and wallaby grass that covered the flat red plain in and around the park before European settlement.

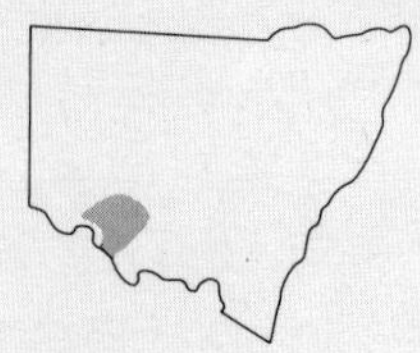

Hay & Balranald

The river towns strung along the Murrumbidgee originated as crossing points for the overlanders and grew into busy steamer ports. The sheep that wander the treeless plains have, for a century or more, produced some of the finest wool in the country. Today, the diverted waters of the rivers irrigate rice farms.

BALRANALD ■ 784

In the far south-western hinterland of New South Wales, this solid settlement was once dubbed the town 'at the very end of the line'. Balranald is on the Sturt Highway, the major road transport link between Sydney and Adelaide and it serves the surrounding rural community engaged in grain, sheep and cattle production and viniculture.

The area was first seen by Europeans in 1830 when explorer Charles Sturt made his whaleboat trip down the Murrumbidgee in 1830. Major Thomas Mitchell followed in his wake some six years later, camping at the site where Balranald now stands and on his return to Sydney whetting the appetites of land seekers with glowing reports of the 'Australia Felix' awaiting the adventurous.

Squatters and settlers were quick to act, and driving their herds and flocks before them, soon worked their way along the 'Major's Line', staking out the best land along the lifeline of the river – its permanent fresh flow watered their flocks and pastures and later provided a means of transport and trade.

The Balranald site was a fording place and the township grew from the rough huts of the hawkers and itinerant labourers who lingered here in the 1840s waiting for custom. The town was gazetted in 1851, and when riverboats came to the Murrumbidgee several years later, grew quickly into a thriving port and service centre for the settlements of the plains. In its heyday, its wharves and banks were piled high with merchandise shipped from Echuca, and thousands of bales of wool were dispatched downstream. *Population 1330*

EDWARD RIVER ■ 785

The Edward is the largest anabranch of the Murray River and flows for about 225 kilometres north and north-west after leaving the Murray south of Deniliquin. Moulamein (see entry) stands on its banks where it meets Billabong Creek. Near the small township of Kyalite (see entry) the Edward River flows into its own main anabranch, the Wakool River (see entry), which in turn rejoins the Murray upstream of the junction with the Murrumbidgee. Stevens Weir, fifteen kilometres from Deniliquin, diverts water from the Edward to irrigate the plains for rice, fodder and pasture production.

GREAT CUMBUNG SWAMP ■ 786

The Great Cumbung Swamp covers an area of more than 100 000 hectares and is the final drainage basin for the Lachlan River. Although the Murrumbidgee crosses the southern end of the swamp there is no actual junction of grand waterways and except in times of flood the flow from the Lachlan to the Murrumbidgee is quite small. The swamp is a major waterfowl breeding ground and is important for the colonies of rare freckled ducks and ibises which live in the lignum and cane grass.

HAY ■ 787

On the banks of the Murrumbidgee, near a natural crossing, and at the intersection of the Sturt, Mid Western and Cobb highways, Hay has always been an important centre of transport and communications. It was a port for the riverboats which plied these waters and was an important staging depot for Cobb & Co. coaches (see *Melton & Sunbury*).

The townsite is on the route which from the 1840s was generally taken by drovers and was one of only a handful of recognised points for the delivery of stock by squatters. It lies at a low spot on the river which allowed stock to cross and was originally known as Langs Crossing after the Lang family who took up some of the first land near here. After the discovery of gold at Bendigo in the early 1850s, there was a sharp rise in the numbers of animals needing to be moved across the river to feed the diggers of the Victorian hinterlands. In 1856, the *Sydney Morning Herald* reported that a hastily established punt here in six weeks took some 150 000 sheep and 7000 cattle heading for Melbourne across the Murrumbidgee. The town was gazetted in 1859 and its name changed to honour local parliamentarian Sir John Hay.

Cobb & Co. began a regular run to Hay in 1860 and it soon became an important part of the coaching network, with a coachbuilding factory here manufacturing both small six-seater and large, twenty-four seat coaches and a stud farm to supply the horsepower. Hay was also a riverboat town but by 1870, had lost a large share of the trade to Echuca and Deniliquin, following the extension of the railway to these towns. *Population 2820*

FESTIVALS Australia Day Surf Carnival, January.

HAY JAIL With its high brick wall and arched entry, this is a fine example of a nineteenth-century country town jail. It dates from 1879 and comprises the original cell block, kitchen and hospital wing, and part of a smaller cell block.

BISHOP'S LODGE Built in 1888 for the first Bishop of the Diocese of the Riverina, Bishop's Lodge has become a museum, exhibition gallery and conference centre. It is a unique example of a Victorian-era villa constructed with galvanised iron and insulated with sawdust, a building method typical of nineteenth-century Riverina domestic architecture.

MARKED TREE Five kilometres north of Hay, on the Mid Western Highway, is an old box tree believed to have been marked by the explorer Charles Sturt during his 1829–30 investigations of the Murray and Murrumbidgee rivers.

KYALITE ■ 788

Originally known as Wakool Crossing because of its location by the Wakool River, Kyalite was one of the earliest settlements in the area and by 1848 already had a hotel, a store, and a punt, admittedly all owned and operated by the one man, Irishman Henry Talbett. In 1860, the Burke and Wills expedition used the Wakool punt to ferry across its twenty or so tonnes of baggage.

LOWBIDGEE IRRIGATION DISTRICT ■ 789

The area known as Lowbidgee is a continuation of marshland downstream from the junction of the Lachlan and Murrumbidgee rivers in the Great Cumbung Swamp (see entry). It is now used as a flood control area which takes advantage of naturally occurring floods to spill surplus water from the lower Murrumbidgee, through Maude Weir – downstream from Hay – and Redbank Weir – upstream of Balranald – onto 50 000 hectares of surrounding, low-lying land. The pastures which result from this flooding are used to fatten stock.

MALLEE CLIFFS NATIONAL PARK ■ 790

This park was formed in 1977 to create a mallee country wildlife refuge in what is an intensive sheep and cattle grazing area.

Vegetation is largely mallee and rosewood-belah open woodland – the habitat of the mallee fowl, an unusual ground-dwelling bird which moves tonnes of sand in the construction of its mound-nest. The clearing of native scrub has severely reduced the mallee fowl's natural habitat and the bird is now considered an endangered species in New South Wales.

Access to this 57 969-hectare park, is not easy. There is no ground or surface water, and the park is likely to remain undeveloped to restrict human impact to a minimum.

MAUDE ■ 791

Fifty kilometres downstream from Hay is the tiny township of Maude, a settlement which grew up around a 'dray ford' and by the time the townsite was surveyed in 1861 the hotel where teamsters fortified themselves before attempting the crossing was already long-established.

Traffic through the town was considerable, but its growth was not. Less than two decades later, it was

described by a passing traveller as consisting of a mere four buildings, three of which were the hotel, the store and the police station, the latter manned by a solitary trooper. The only other resident, a Mr Murphy, ran both the hotel and the store.

MOULAMEIN ■ 792

This township, sited at the junction of a number of secondary roads and two waterways, the Edward River and Billabong Creek, is among the oldest in the Riverina. It was a river crossing on the early track followed by northern drovers overlanding cattle and sheep from pastures in New South Wales to the markets in Victoria, but by the 1850s, relinquished this function after the enterprising James Maiden began operating his punt upstream at the spot now known as Deniliquin. The overlanders took the shorter route bypassing Moulamein, and their tracks laid the line now followed by the Cobb Highway between the Murrumbidgee and the Murray. The town continued as a lively port; it still has an old wharf and an attractive streetscape of period buildings. Now it serves the surrounding wheat-growing district.

PENARIE ■ 793

The site of Penarie is marked by a small pub at a meeting of ways north of Balranald. It is better known as 'Homebush', the name of the hotel, and is a popular watering place. The many shearers who have passed through its doors are remembered in a mural which covers one of the bar's walls. Perhaps they included Banjo Paterson's 'Flash Jack from Gundagai' whose exploits in the area included shearing at Trida and Moulamein, as well as a spell out of work '...whalin' up the Lachlan...'. ('Whalers', common around the river country during the depressions of the 1890s and 1930s, were swagmen who camped on the riverbanks and survived by fishing and on handouts from local station owners.)

WAKOOL RIVER ■ 794

The Wakool is an anabranch of the Edward River (see entry) which it leaves to the north-west of Deniliquin to pursue its course for 345 kilometres. Just upstream of Kyalite (see entry) township it is rejoined by the Edward. The Wakool flows into the Murray at Wakool Junction. European settlement on the floodplains of the two rivers dates from the 1840s with enormous runs of up to 40 000 hectares being staked out. Stevens Weir, on the Edward River, feeds the Wakool Irrigation Area, an important rice-growing area.

YANGA LAKE ■ 795

Yanga Lake, a kidney-shaped lake about ten kilometres south-east of Balranald, is the largest permanent lake in the region and covers an area of more than thirteen square kilometres. It has sandy beaches and wide open reaches of deep water and its foreshores carry remnants of the original vegetation of the area.

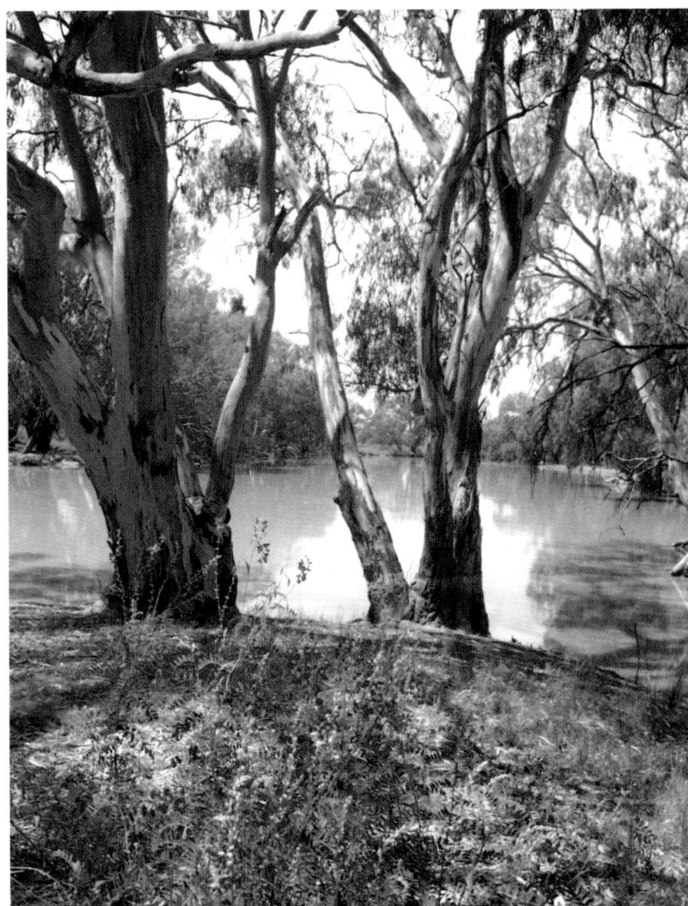

After Balranald, the hard-working, much-tapped Murrumbidgee is left in peace to run its last 80 kilometres before swelling the Murray waters.

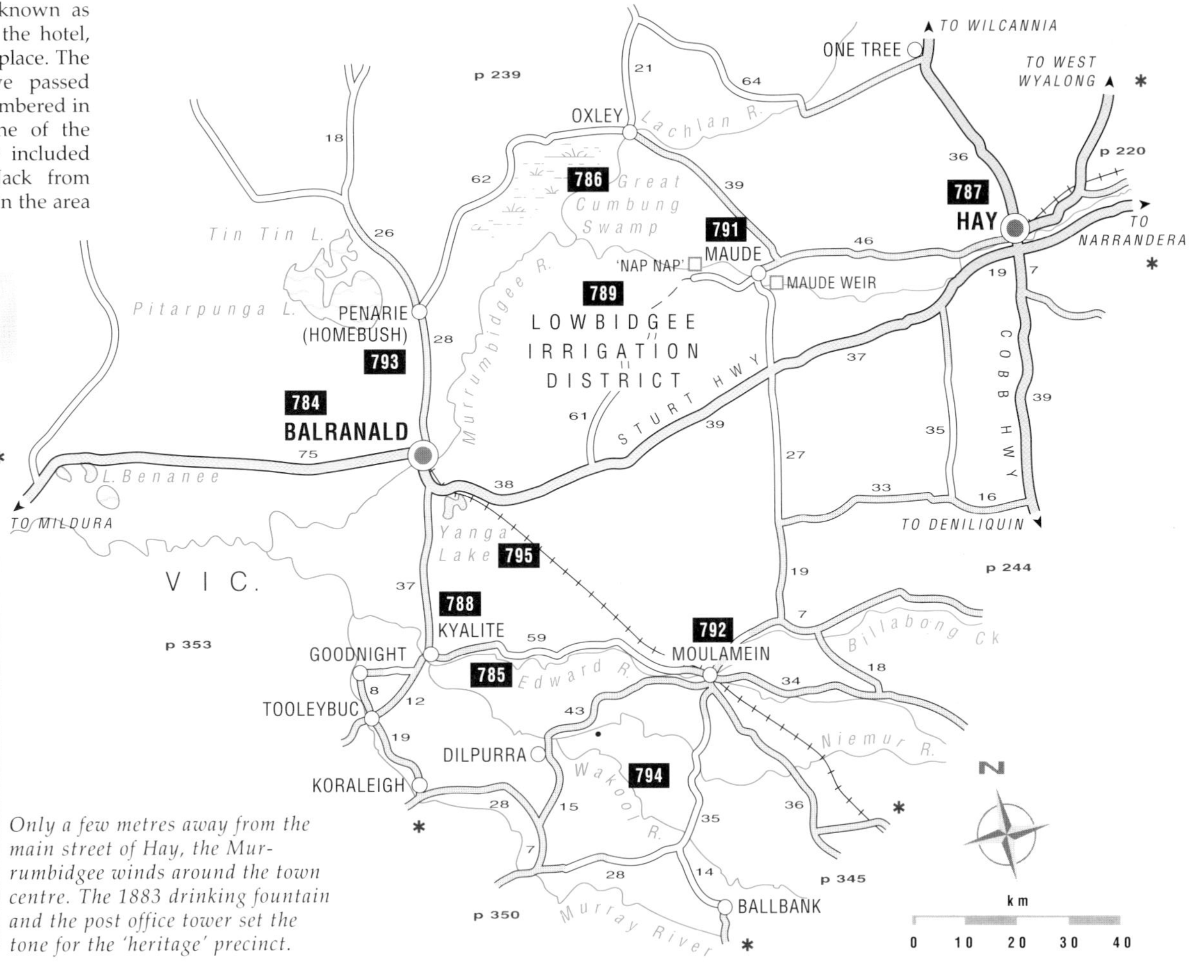

Only a few metres away from the main street of Hay, the Murrumbidgee winds around the town centre. The 1883 drinking fountain and the post office tower set the tone for the 'heritage' precinct.

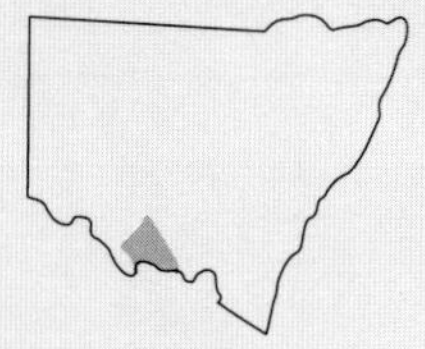

Deniliquin & Finley

Wheat and sheep take second place to rice in the southern Riverina where irrigation schemes inaugurated in the 1930s, and completed in the 1940s, have diversified agriculture. This is where the famous merino breed that once carried Australia 'on its back' came from.

BAROOGA ■ 796

Barooga is separated from its sister town, Cobram (see *Shepparton & Mooroopna*), in Victoria, by the sluggish flow of the Murray. This small farming community is surrounded by citrus and grape orchards, some of the produce of which supplies the local fruit juice factory. Handmade boomerangs – mostly crafted for the export market – are an unusual growth industry and come with a 'return guarantee'! Demonstrations are given for newcomers to the sport. *Population 840*

BERRIGAN ■ 797

Berrigan was proclaimed a village in 1890, two years after the opening of the Berrigan Hotel which still survives as the town's oldest watering hole. The town's name is believed to come from an Aboriginal word for the berrigan bush common to the region – *Eremophila longifolia*. Once the commercial and social centre for pastoralists and wheat farmers, Berrigan benefited from the introduction of irrigation in the 1930s. The construction of the Mulwala Canal in 1935, diverting water from the Yarrawonga Weir on the Murray River to the Berriquin, Denimein and Deniboota irrigation districts (see entries), has greatly diversified the region's agricultural output with citrus, rice, sorghum and grain crops now thriving in the irrigated plains. *Population 950*

BERRIQUIN IRRIGATION DISTRICT ■ 798

The greening of the riverine plains – the origin of the district name, 'Riverina' – with crops watered by irrigation has brought great agricultural diversity to the Murray Valley which during the nineteenth century was largely the domain of wheat- and wool-growers. Work on the irrigation schemes began in the 1930s and was completed in the 1940s.

The Berriquin Irrigation District, inaugurated in 1939 and administered from Finley, is one of four major irrigation districts surrounding Deniliquin (see entry) which together constitute the largest area under irrigation in Australia. The Mulwala Canal, a 120-kilometre artery branching off from the Yarrawonga Weir on the Murray River, supplies water – through a network of subsidiary channels – to more than 120 000 hectares of farmland in the Berriquin Irrigation District.

The highly prized Murray cod – Australia's largest freshwater fish – still lurks in Riverina waterways.

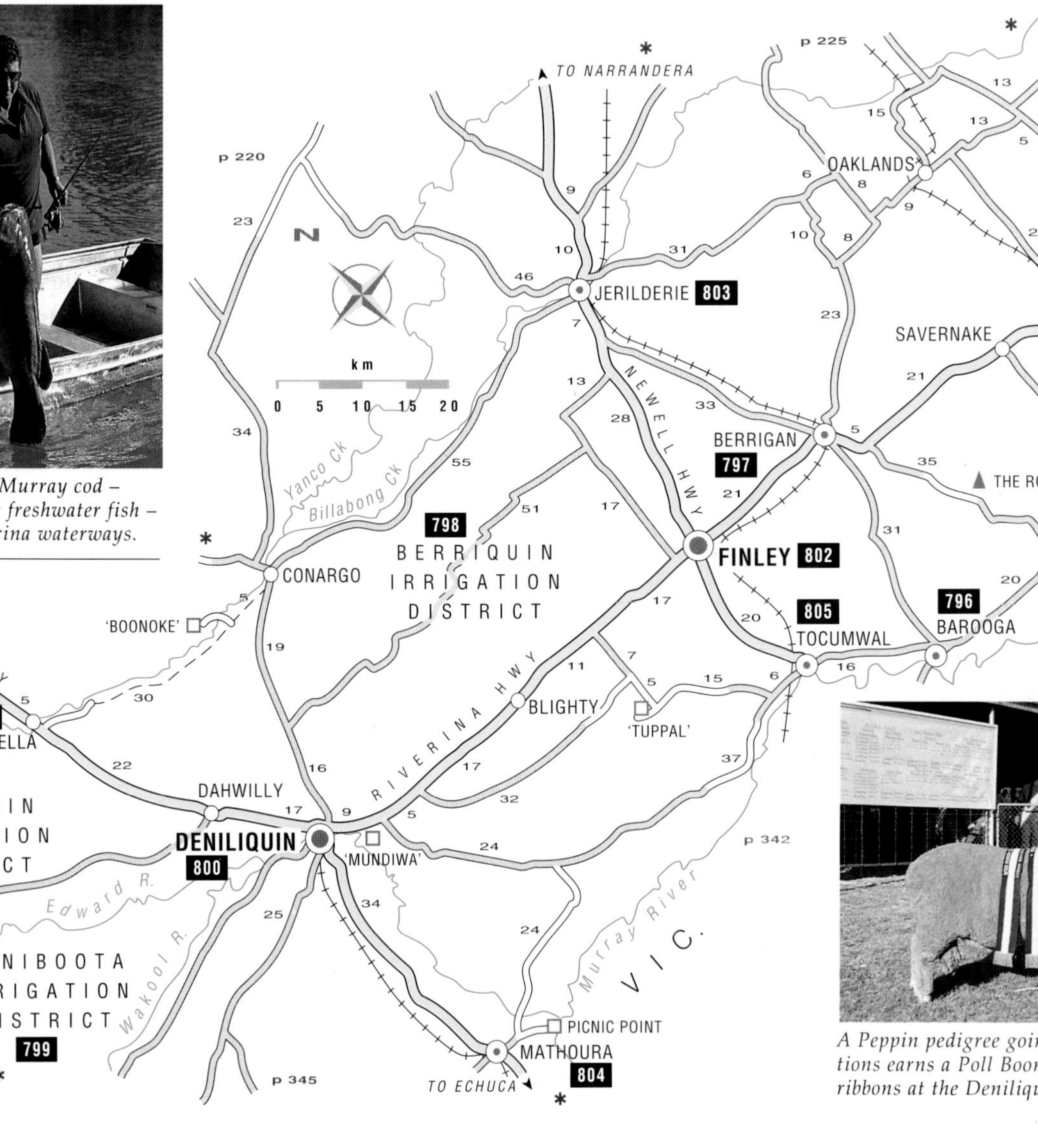

A Peppin pedigree going back many generations earns a Poll Boonoke ram handsome ribbons at the Deniliquin Show.

The rice which goes to the huge mill at Deniliquin is not sown haphazardly – the 'paddy fields' are a series of contoured bays divided by irrigation channels which keep the plants flooded to an average depth of 15 centimetres.

DENIBOOTA IRRIGATION DISTRICT ■ 799

The large Deniboota Irrigation District, one of the major irrigated areas in the riverine plains (see Berriquin Irrigation District), is nourished by the Mulwala Canal which diverts water from the Murray River. Water is piped *under* the Edward River to a network of irrigation channels by means of the Lawson Syphon, a device which diverts more water each day than is consumed daily by the city of Melbourne.

Rice is the most important irrigated grain crop in the Murray Valley with the Deniliquin–Wakool region, of which this district is a substantial part, accounting for forty-two per cent of Australia's rice production.

DENILIQUIN ■ 800

With more than 3000 hours of sunlight each year and little rainfall, Deniliquin, on the pleasant banks of the Edward River, has developed a strong outdoor orientation and is something of a sportsman's mecca in the southern Riverina. Apart from the attractions of sandy river beaches, forest drives, the prize-winning Waring Gardens which encompass an entire city block, and a river that lends itself to a wide range of watersports including waterskiing, fishing, boating and swimming, Deniliquin has the attraction of poker machines, which accounts for a steady flow of visitors to the town's registered clubs from adjacent Victoria.

The pastoral pioneer, Benjamin Boyd, took up a sheep run in the area in the early 1840s, establishing the head station – 'Deniliquin' – just six kilometres upstream from the present town. By 1847, a punt service on an early stock route was established on the Edward River and the following year, an inn opened on its northern bank. A major stock-selling town soon developed on both sides of the river at the point of convergence of three major stock routes that brought mobs of cattle from Queensland, and southern and western New South Wales for buyers from the south.

For the first six years of its official life, Deniliquin had no jail, and according to local legend, drunks and criminals of all kinds were chained to a log at the back of the town's store! This rough-and-ready state of affairs was rectified in 1856 with the construction of the town's first jail. In 1861, a bridge built across the river linked the two sides of the town and the southern side flourished, siphoning development from the northern side. The major beneficiary was John Taylor, a sometimes unconventional entrepreneur who at one time owned half the town and had a hand in many businesses. When he was jailed for fraudulent insolvency in 1870 a large part of Deniliquin was thrown into temporary bankruptcy.

Despite an influx of predominantly Victorian settlers in the 1870s and connection by a private line with the Victorian railway system in 1876 – the only other large stretch of private railway was at Silverton (see *Broken Hill & Menindee*) – the town did not come into its own until the irrigation schemes of the 1930s transformed the dry, saltbush plains and made possible both smaller holdings and agricultural diversity. Now Deniliquin is the centre of the Berriquin, Denimein, Deniboota and Wakool irrigation districts.

Though traditionally associated with the sheep industry, Deniliquin is now the location of the largest rice mill in the Southern Hemisphere and rice, fodder, oilseed and other crops grown under irrigation have joined wool as the basis of the region's prosperity. *Population 7900*

COURT HOUSE Deniliquin's most imposing building is the court house. Designed by the Colonial Architect, James Barnet, and completed in 1887, it has a magnificent main chamber which extends forward as a portico over which presides a coat of arms.

PEPPIN HERITAGE CENTRE Located in the first Deniliquin Public School (1890) in George Street, the Peppin Heritage Centre tells the story of the famous merino strain of sheep developed by the Peppin family in the 1860s. Peppin merinos graze outside the centre which displays historic photographs (see Wanganella).

RICE MILL The Australian Ricegrower's Co-operative's mill standing on the outskirts of the town is the largest in the Southern Hemisphere. The mill processes rice from the irrigation areas of the Murrumbidgee and Murray valleys and their districts and about ninety per cent of this is exported. Tours are conducted on a regular basis.

FESTIVALS Jazz Festival, Easter; Sun Festival, late January.

DENIMEIN IRRIGATION DISTRICT ■ 801

The Riverina irrigation schemes of the 1930s and 1940s changed the agricultural landscape hereabouts. Products of Murray irrigation – of which the Denimein Irrigation District is a substantial part – include fruit, vegetables, dairy produce, rice and other cereals, fodder and oilseed. But great agricultural diversity through irrigation has not been achieved without cost. One of the greatest problems facing farmers in the irrigated regions of the Murray Valley today is salinity. A combination of factors including the region's natural salinity combined with the results of fifty years of pumping for irrigation are responsible for the land's degradation. Ironically, it is estimated by some agencies that the costs of high salinity levels, in terms of lost production and salt abatement works, now exceed the original cost of installing the irrigation schemes.

FINLEY ■ 802

Finley was originally an outstation of the 'Tuppal' sheep run owned by Benjamin Boyd, and was known as the Murray Hut. This simple shepherd's hut on the junction of two overland stock routes and near an almost permanent swamp – now transformed into a popular recreational waterway – Lake Finley – was a convenient stopping place between Jerilderie and Tocumwal. As the only 'house' for miles around, the Murray Hut became something of a social centre of the district with marriages christenings and wakes conducted within its humble walls. In 1879, the hut was licensed as an inn and shortly afterwards, acquired the status of post office and bank.

During the 1870s, Francis George Finley supervised a survey of the boundaries of the squatting leases in the district and released marginal land for further settlement. Wheat cultivation was soon underway and in 1884, the Murray Hut was selected as the site for a town to be called

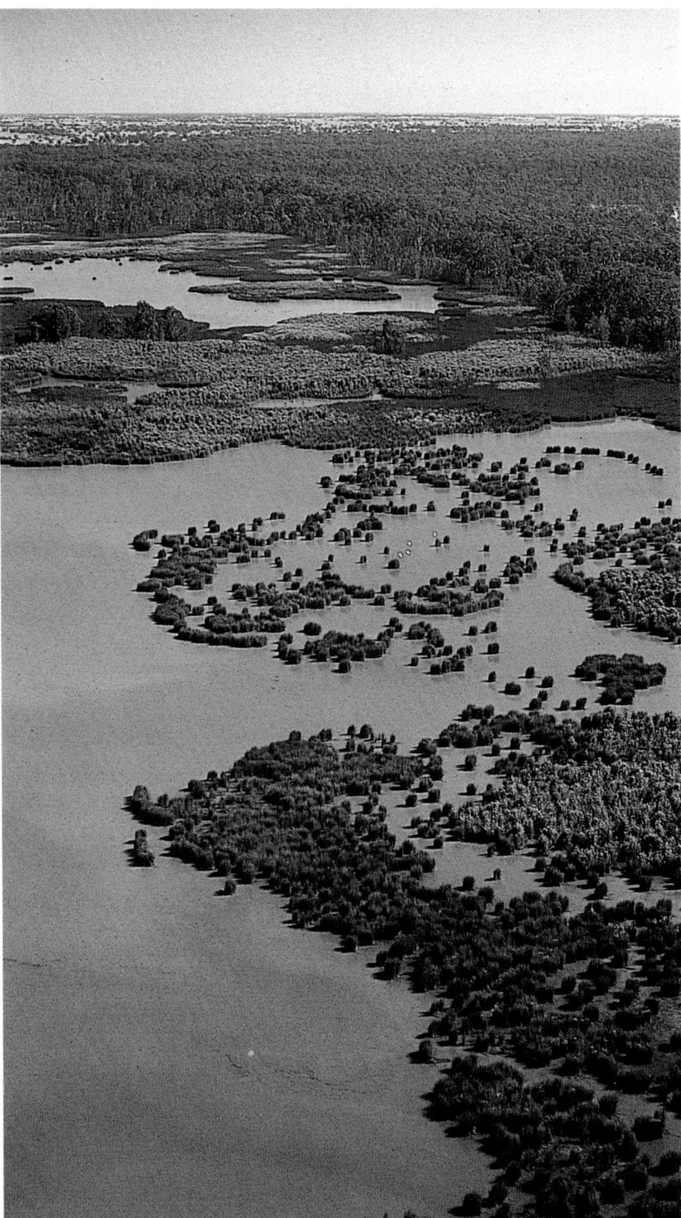

The forest between Mathoura and Echuca – here rejuvenated by the waters of Moira Lake – is the largest remaining tract of the majestic river red gum.

Ulupna though the name was later changed to Finley, after the surveyor. An influx of new settlers between 1891 and 1895 increased significantly the area of land under wheat cultivation and a further release of land in 1910 prompted another spurt in the town's growth.

In the 1930s, the region's traditional economy, based mainly on wheat and sheep, was changed irrevocably. The construction of the Mulwala Canal in 1935 brought water to the plains surrounding Finley and made possible the creation of the Berriquin Irrigation District (see entry). The rice, wool, wheat, beef cattle, dairy products and vegetables produced today, would no doubt astonish the region's pioneers. *Population 2250*

JERILDERIE ■ 803

Jerilderie derives its name from an Aboriginal word said to mean 'reedy place', probably referring to the original shoreline of Billabong Creek that runs through the town. The town is possibly best known for the Kelly gang's audacious robbery in 1879.

Riding into town on a weekend in early February, the gang treated itself to dinner at the Woolshed Hotel before capturing and locking up the town's two policemen. Two of the gang members then donned the policemen's clothes and attended a church service. After having their horses reshod, the gang held the customers of another hotel hostage while they robbed the bank and post office and cut the telegraph wires.

Before leaving, Kelly addressed his captives with a list of complaints against the Victorian Police Force. The famous 'Jerilderie letter', which elaborated on the theme of his address, was handed to a teller during the bank raid for later publication, and the gang coolly rode away, more than 2100 pounds sterling richer!

Squatters first moved into the Jerilderie district in the 1840s but it was not until the 1860s that they discovered that the short, sparse grass of the Riverland plains was much better suited to sheep than cattle, and now wool growing in one of the region's major industries.

A travelling drapery dealer, John Caractacus Powell, is credited with the establishment of the town. He opened a store on the banks of Billabong Creek in 1864. An enterprising man, he soon expanded his settlement to include a toll bridge, hotel and post office. Powell's settlement was officially proclaimed a town in 1865 and for the next thirty-five years Jerilderie – named after the cattle run on which the town was sited – developed quite rapidly as wool growing became the region's dominant industry and settlers flooded in to meet the demand for labour on sheep stations. At the turn of the century, a devastating drought brought a halt to the region's progress with many settlers forced to seek their livelihoods elsewhere.

The relatively recent introduction of irrigation schemes in the Coleambally and Berriquin districts gave the town a new impetus and now the flat plains surrounding Jerilderie are noted not only for merino studs and the production of wool but also for dairying, fat lambs, cattle, wheat, vegetables, rice and other grain crops. *Population 900*

MATHOURA ■ 804

What is believed to be Australia's largest river red-gum forest lies just east of the small town of Mathoura in the southern Riverina, providing not only the basis of the town's economy but also a majestic landscape which can be viewed close-up from the roads through the state forests. Beyond here, the forest which trims the river's edge – it cannot survive without occasional inundation – occasionally broadens to a width of almost thirty kilometres. The highly durable red-gum timber logged from the forests is used for railway sleepers, house stumps, fence-posts, bridge and wharf construction and even for house and pool decking and pergolas. Large swamps within the forest support a wide variety of water birds while kangaroos and emus inhabit the drier areas.

The town takes its name from the cattle run on which it was sited. Prior to its official recognition as a township in 1860, Mathoura was already a thriving little settlement known as Red Bank. Its location on the banks of Gulpa Creek midway between Moama and Deniliquin made the settlement a convenient stopping place on the Cobb & Co. coach run. In the late 1870s, the railway line from Moama (see *Echuca & Cohuna*) to Deniliquin was constructed, bypassing the settlement so that buildings grew up about one kilometre to the north, around the railway station that was renamed Mathoura in 1879. *Population 670*

TOCUMWAL ■ 805

From its origins as a crossing place on the Murray River, the border town of Tocumwal has developed as the main point of dispatch for produce from the irrigated areas of the Riverina, and prior to Federation, was an important customs depot. In place of the punts and ferries that transported goods and traffic over the Murray River from the early 1870s, the more solid conveyances of road and railway now rumble across the 1895 bridge which links Victoria and New South Wales. Tocumwal is an Aboriginal word said to refer to a supposedly bottomless pit in the Murray River.

Tall stands of river red gums and parks along the riverfront with sandy beaches are the backdrop for the giant fibreglass replica of a cod fish which stands in the swimming pool grounds and commemorates an ancient Aboriginal legend about the bottomless pit. A glider plane is also displayed in the town which is the site of a major gliding complex. During the Second World War, Tocumwal airfield – now a gliding base, home to three flying schools and aircraft engineering, repair and refurbishment industries – was the RAAF's largest base. Granite taken from a quarry north-west of the town now graces the facades and entrance halls of many important public buildings in Sydney, including the Sydney Opera House. *Population 1590*

WANGANELLA ■ 806

Wanganella, once a solitary homestead-turned-inn where 'the table is first rate' and the coach between Deniliquin and Hay stopped daily, was proclaimed a village in 1885 though a thriving settlement 'consisting of two inns, two blacksmiths [and] two stores' had been in existence since the mid-1860s.

The town experienced a hiatus in its march towards official village status in the early 1870s however, when it was reported to be 'not advancing'. But when development was hastened by the opening of the railway line in 1876 this prompted a building boom. Until 1909, the town was without the steadying influence of a policeman but this changed when a body was found at the back door of the Wanganella Hotel that year and Police Constable Ferris was appointed.

Wanganella rightly claims a special place in Australian history as the original breeding place of the Peppin strain of merino sheep – the foundation stock, bred in the 1860s, for most of the flocks which over almost 100 years produced the wool which carried Australia 'on the sheep's back' (see sub-entry, Deniliquin).

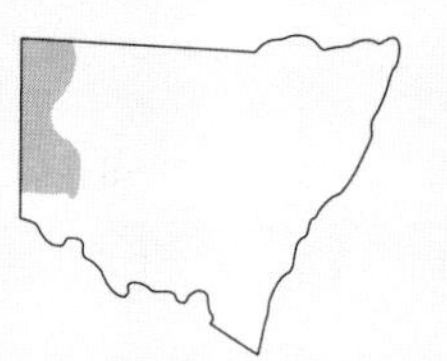

Broken Hill & Menindee

This remote north-western corner of New South Wales contains many contrasts, from the dry gibber plains and flat-topped mesas of Sturt National Park, to the vast waterways of the Menindee Lakes and the prosperous city of Broken Hill, one of the world's great mining centres.

The dead trees of Lake Menindee have a practical purpose – they are bird- and fish-breeding sites and help cut down on wave erosion of the shoreline.

BROKEN HILL ■ 807

Charles Sturt was the first European to explore this area, in 1844, and he named the high country to the north of Broken Hill 'Stanley's Barrier Range'. But the place became better known by the Aboriginal 'willyama' meaning 'hill with a broken contour' by which name it was referred to until 1886, when the township of Broken Hill was surveyed.

The mineral deposits which were to prove the future city's lifeblood were first discovered here in 1875, when Paddy Green located a silver deposit at Thackaringa, to the south-west of Broken Hill. Another find, at nearby Umberumberka, near Silverton, in 1881, led to an influx of prospectors into the area. But the most important discovery was made at Mt Gipps Station in September 1883, by Charles Rasp, a German-born boundary rider who was busy mustering sheep. His discovery of silver chlorides, which he originally believed to be tin, on the 'broken hill' turned out to be an exceptionally rich silver, lead and zinc ore deposit. From that day to this, Broken Hill has been one of the world's leading mining centres. Rasp went on to make a fortune from his find.

In 1885, the Broken Hill Proprietary Company, the original BHP, was incorporated and the Broken Hill South works opened in the same year. Broken Hill North mine also started up in the 1880s and a smelting plant began operations but since 1898, Broken Hill's smelting processes have been undertaken at Port Pirie, in South Australia.

The town on the edge of the continent's arid interior grew from 11 000 people in 1888 to some 20 000 by 1891 – and was proclaimed a city in 1907. By 1913, ten companies employed more than 8000 men in mining and mine-related industries.

Broken Hill's proximity to the South Australian border has always produced closer links between its residents and that state, rather than New South Wales: the most obvious example is that Broken Hill follows South Australian time – half an hour behind Sydney. A rail connection to Port Pirie and Adelaide has been in operation since 1887, forty years before the line arrived from Sydney. This South Australian-built line was originally destined for the nearby centre of Silverton, which overshadowed Broken Hill in the early days.

The first few years were a time of terrible hardship: diseases such as typhoid, dysentery and scarlet fever were rife; water was often rationed and the need for trees to feed the smelters led to a denuded landscape and this resulted in dust storms.

The mines claimed many lives through accidents and lung diseases and it is not surprising that pioneer industrial relations and trade-union work took place in Broken Hill. The Amalgamated Miners' Association transferred from Silverton in 1886 and a series of actions for better conditions led to the foundation of the Barrier Industrial Council in 1923. This 'parliament' of the city's trade unions is still in operation to settle any disputes with mine owners.

In the 1930s, large 'regeneration' zones around the city's outskirts were fenced to keep out animals. This, together with a post-Second World War vegetation replacement scheme, has helped reduce the dust problem and made Broken Hill a pleasant oasis in its harsh outback environment. The city has plentiful water, with local reservoirs augmented by the Menindee Lakes on the Darling River, 100 kilometres away.

The city's long-standing prosperity is evident in its exceptionally ornate late-nineteenth-century buildings, some twenty-five of which are classified by the National Trust. A prime example is the red-brick 1891 post office, with its massive tower. Other substantial buildings include the elaborately decorated town hall, which dates from 1890, the 1901 technical college and the Applied Arts and Sciences Museum.

Unlike many mining towns, which have boomed and busted, the deposits in the narrow, eight-kilometre-long ore body have yet to be exhausted. BHP ceased operations here in 1939 but mining is still carried out by other major companies. The importance of mining is evident in the city's street names: Garnet, Bromide, Sulphide, Chloride, Oxide, Iodide, Silver, Argent and Cobalt.

The Royal Flying Doctor Service's New South Wales headquarters are here, as is the School of the Air, which serves up to 80 outback children. Visitors can take surface and underground mine tours and visit the 1891 Afghan mosque – a memorial to the camel drivers who helped open up the inland. *Population 23 260*

The wind whistles through the buildings of Silverton where the ghosts of long-dead miners – and tourists – haunt the empty streets.

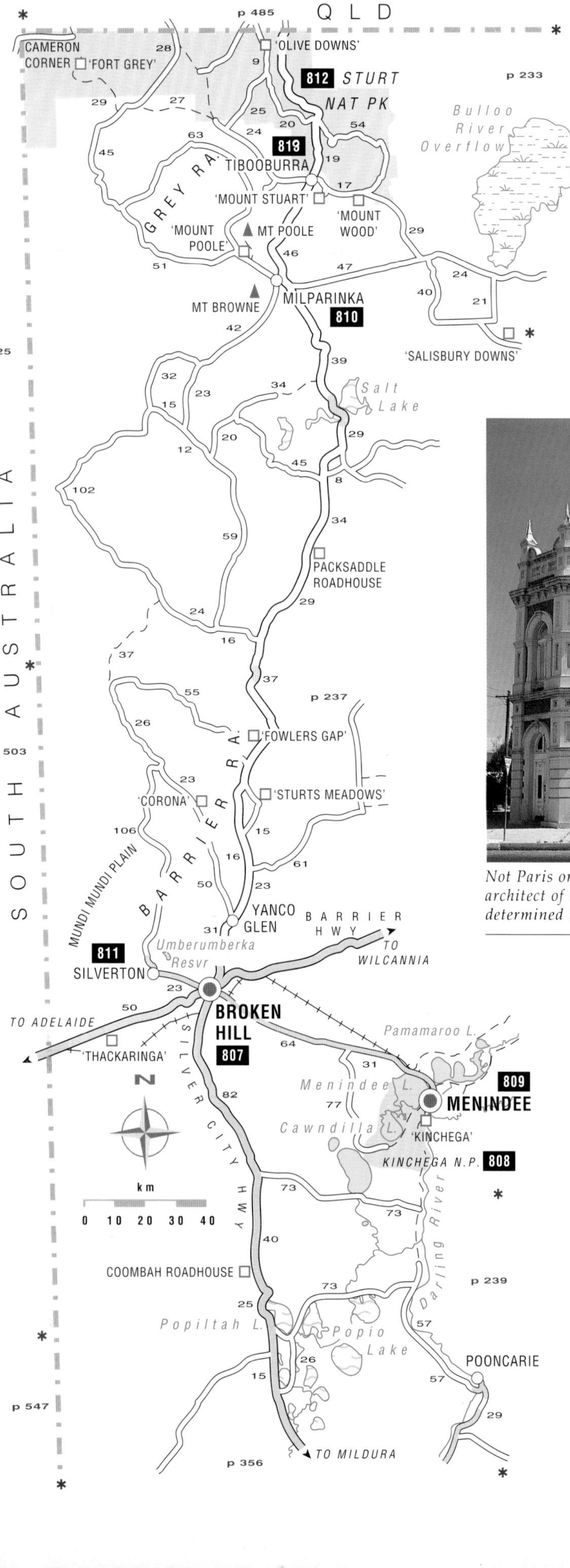

KINCHEGA NATIONAL PARK ■ 808

Dedicated in 1967, this 44 000-hectare national park adjoins the town of Menindee and was once part of vast Kinchega Station – one of this region's first sheep stations, established in the early 1850s. Kinchega contains an historic timber woolshed which belonged to the station: in its heyday, 143 000 sheep were run on the property.

Kinchega's terrain consists of red sand plains and black soil floodplains: the latter support red river gums and open forests of coolibah and black-box. In the drier regions, there is little ground cover except for dry grassland and prickly wattle.

Not Paris or Brussels but inland Australia; the architect of the 1905 Broken Hill Trades Hall was determined to make no concessions to the climate.

Turbulent winds have created a large area of lunettes, or dramatic, crescent-shaped sand dunes.

Kinchega encompasses the big lakes of Menindee and Cawndilla, as well as several smaller components of the Menindee Lakes Scheme (see Menindee), which form an ideal breeding and feeding environment for water birds. The lakes supported a substantial Aboriginal population before the coming of Europeans, and the park contains many middens, campsites, burial grounds and other relics of their culture.

MENINDEE ■ 809

The small settlement of Menindee, on the Darling River to the south-east of Broken Hill, is surrounded by the flat, dry plains that are so typical of the region. The first Europeans to visit the area were Major Thomas Mitchell, who camped here on his expedition down the Darling River 1835, and Charles Sturt. The latter used the region as a depot while on his 1844 excursions further into the interior. Burke and Wills also paused here briefly in the early stages of their epic but ill-fated 1860 journey to the north coast and some early biographers referred to the hotel here as 'a kind of club for explorers'.

Settlement of the area began in the 1850s, primarily for sheep farming, and a hotel had been established at the isolated river crossing by the late 1850s. A store was built here by Francis Cadell, the pioneer of Murray and Darling transportation, in 1859; this was followed by a post office in 1861. In 1862, the location was chosen as the site for a town, first called 'Perry' but later changed to the Aboriginal word 'menindie' (later amended to the present spelling). Although the area's first land sales were made in 1863, growth came slowly. The town's location on the Darling, combined with the boom in river transport during the 1860s and 1870s, led to its gradual development as a major wool port.

By 1881, fluctuating river levels and strong competition from Wilcannia, further upstream, meant that the town's usefulness as a port began to decline. The railway from Broken Hill reached here in 1927, and today Menindee lies on the main Indian-Pacific line from Sydney to Perth. The town contains the grave of Dost Mahomet, a cameleer on the Burke and Wills expedition, who later settled in the town.

MENINDEE LAKES Grouped around Menindee township, the lakes of Menindee, Wetherell, Pamamaroo, Cawndilla and several other, smaller waterways, make up the Menindee Lakes storage system, which was completed in 1960. Incredibly, this large expanse of water – approximately eight times the size of Sydney Harbour – lies on the edge of one of the continent's most arid regions.

In the old days, the lakes, which are connected to the Darling River by a series of creeks, would alternately fill and dry out according to river levels. Now, canals and levees store the river's excess water in the lakes, while a dam has raised the water level of the Darling by about nine metres. The waterways, which were first named 'Laidley's Chain of Ponds' by Thomas Mitchell in 1835, provide water for the city of Broken Hill – conveyed by a 100-kilometre-long pipeline. The precious liquid also provides irrigation water for the citrus fruits, grapes, cotton, barley, wheat and sunflowers as well as being the centre of a popular recreation area for the people of Broken Hill and other parts of this dry corner of New South Wales – camping, fishing, boating and waterskiing are all popular activities here.

MILPARINKA ■ 810

The town's name is based on an Aboriginal word said to mean 'water may be found here', but, ironically, it was a disastrous drought that forced Sturt to camp in the region for some six months during his 1844 expedition to locate the supposed 'inland sea'. From the permanent waterhole at Depot Glen he explored much of the surrounding countryside, and employed his men in building a stone cairn. Sturt's second-in-command, James Poole, died of scurvy here and his grave, as well the cairn, lies within the perimeters of Mount Poole Station.

Like Tibooburra, a few kilometres to the north-west, the discovery of gold – at Depot Glen in 1880 and in the following year at Mt Browne – brought prospectors into the region. Milparinka's population peaked at around 600 in the 1880s. The settlement once had three hotels, four stores, two butcher's shops, boarding houses and its own newspaper. Substantial sandstone buildings were erected during this period – the school was built in 1883, and a court house and jail in 1885 – but little now remains of these structures.

Located just off the Silver City Highway, today's Milparinka is the most isolated ghost town in New South Wales. The 1881 Albert Hotel is its only surviving, and inhabited, building. The hotel still welcomes visitors and also functions as the local store and post office.

SILVERTON ■ 811

Now a virtual ghost town which contains many 'classified' buildings, Silverton was once a booming mining town when neighbouring Broken Hill was a mere patch of unbroken ground. The reason for this prominence was the 1875 discovery of lead-silver-zinc ore at Thackaringa in the nearby Barrier Ranges. A settlement grew to serve the prospectors and comprised a store, a hotel and two boarding houses.

In 1881, the first major claim was pegged out near Silverton by John Stokie and mining operations began in 1882. The site was known under the Aboriginal name of 'umberumberka' – said to mean 'a rat hole' (see Broken Hill). The settlement was soon overshadowed by Silverton which by 1888 was serviced by a private, narrow-gauge railway from South Australia.

In the mid-1880s, the town's population peaked at around 3000 but the fields soon closed down, due to a lack of high-grade ore, and most of the population moved on to richer lodes at the recently discovered Broken Hill fields. By 1900, Silverton's residents numbered a mere 600-odd.

Silverton is now a popular tourist attraction for visitors to Broken Hill. The ruins of several substantial stone buildings remain and the 1889 jail houses a museum operated by the Broken Hill Historical Society. The film industry has also made the most of the town's wild outback scenery and many parts of Australian films such as *Mad Max, A Town Like Alice* and *Razorback*, as well as numerous commercials, have been filmed in the district. Nearby Umberumberka Reservoir, which overlooks the vast Mundi Mundi plains to the west, provides some of Broken Hill's water.

STURT NATIONAL PARK ■ 812

The name of Charles Sturt, the first European to venture this far into the interior is commemorated in this semi-desert park to the north of Tibooburra. The 344 000-hectare park has the Queensland border as its northern boundary, while its western edge is formed by the South Australian border. Cameron Corner, the bare and isolated spot where the borders of New South Wales, South Australia and Queensland meet, is located within the park. The site is named after John Cameron, who completed the first New South Wales–Queensland boundary survey in the early 1880s, and is marked by a large white post.

This is also the province of the 'Dingo Fence', the two-metre-high wire barrier that was originally erected by the Queensland government to prevent a rabbit invasion from the south, but now stops dingoes from migrating across the sheep country of three states. The fence, which runs from the Gulf of Carpentaria to the Indian Ocean, is controlled by the fiercely named Wild Dog Destruction Board and is believed to be the world's longest wire barrier (see *Quilpie & Thargomindah*).

The Sturt National Park landscape is made up mainly of floodplains, rolling stony downs, red sandhills and gibber plains studded with 150-metre-high, mesas, known locally as 'jump-ups', which rise dramatically from the plain. The silcrete stone of these mesas provided an ideal material for Aboriginal tools, and there is abundant evidence of such implements in the park.

TIBOOBURRA ■ 813

Tibooburra's main claim to fame is its location. At over 1500 kilometres north-west of Sydney, this is New South Wales' remotest town. The surrounding region is the hottest, driest and most arid area of the state – true outback country. The name is Aboriginal and, appropriately, means rocks, or heaps of boulders, as the settlement is surrounded by granite outcrops and the locality was known to the early miners as 'The Granites'.

Charles Sturt was the first European to visit the area in 1845, while Burke and Wills passed through in 1860. Gold was first discovered at nearby Mount Poole in 1867 but the most important find was at the Mount Browne field in 1881; by the following year there were approximately 1300 prospectors in the area. An 1883 visitor recorded of the miners that there were '....perhaps 1000 or more spread out with claims all over the flats. A street of shanties all selling stocks of spirits...'. It is still possible to fossick for gold at the old mine workings.

The present-day town is characterised by its wide, mostly empty streets where, it is said, children gather after a storm to collect any specks of gold washed clean by the rain! Tibooburra is the centre of a modest wool-producing area, the gateway to Sturt National Park.

Historic buildings, constructed of the local granite, include the 1888 court house, the Family Hotel, the 1890 Tibooburra Hotel and the post office – now the school residence – which dates from 1900. The nearby 'Mount Stuart' station displays a collection of Aboriginal and European relics and geological samples.

Descendants of the camels which helped establish desolate Silverton now carry tourists on 'joyrides'.

The mesas which 'jump up' to break the monotony of the gibber plains in the Sturt National Park are dignified by the title of the Grey Range.

VICTORIA

A keen desire for independence and a profound disdain for the taint of convict settlement led to the Port Phillip Bay colony's separation from New South Wales in 1851. The new colony, named in honour of the reigning monarch, was formed just in time for the social and economic upheaval of the gold rush when the population increased six-fold in ten years. Plentiful coal and oil reserves were later to make Victoria – the smallest mainland state – into one of Australia's industrial powerhouses.

SPECIAL FEATURES

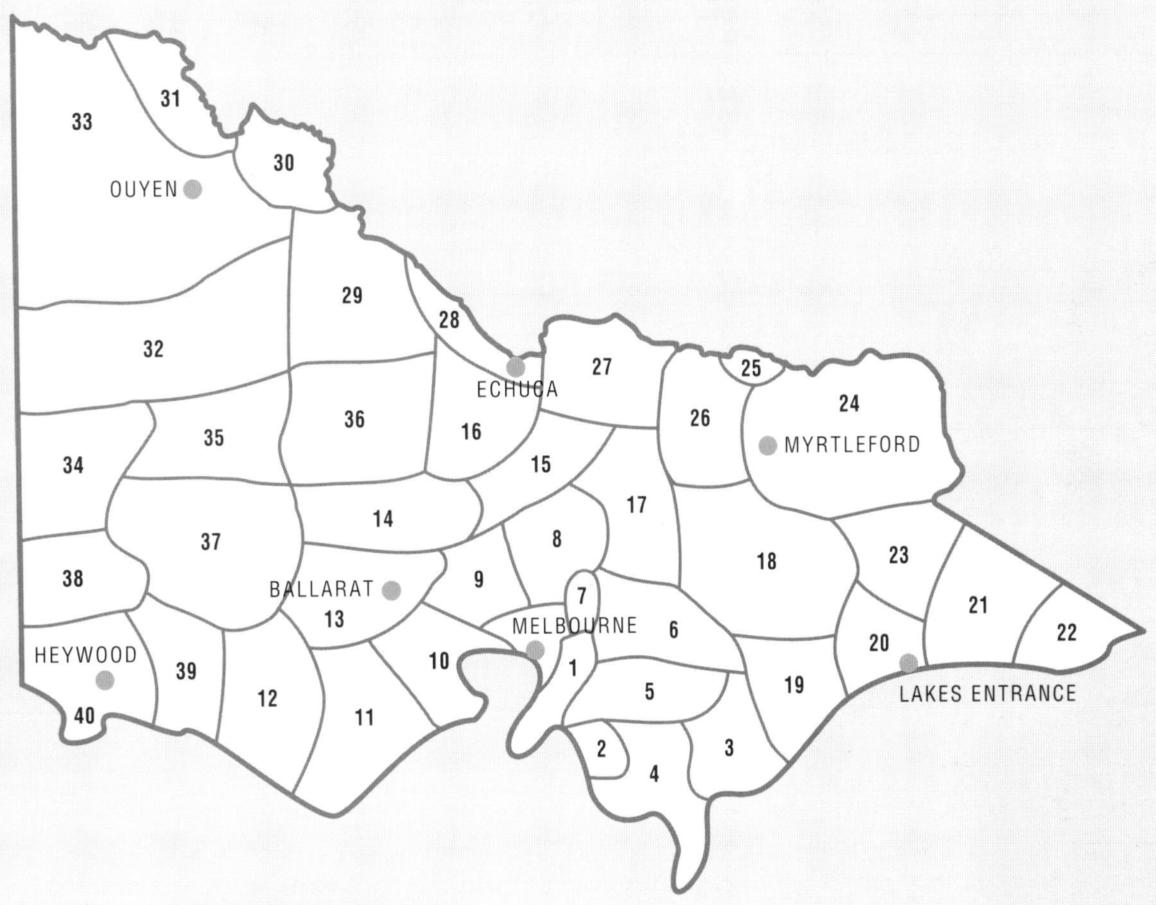

Leadbeater's possum lives nowhere else but Victoria while the state's floral emblem, the common heath (right), may be found in other parts of Australia. The stars of the Southern Cross take pride of place on the coat of arms.

MELBOURNE

Melbourne is Australia's most stylish capital: at its heart, old buildings vie with new for the visitor's attention while beyond, the tree-lined boulevards, formal parks and gardens and inner-city street life give the metropolis a decidedly continental flavour.

Gourmets delight in the veritable cornucopia of fresh produce available at Melbourne's markets.

There are two Melbournes. One is the elegant, nineteenth-century city which so favourably impresses visitors with its majestic, elm-lined avenues such as St Kilda Road and Royal Parade, quaint trams, parkland, grand public buildings, arcades and graceful, stylish housing. This city is English in character and Victorian in origin as well as in place – having been established to coincide neatly with the reign of Queen Victoria (1837–1901). The building of this city was financed by wealth from the gold boom, primary production and commerce.

The second Melbourne is of the twentieth century and international. It was made possible by post-Second World War boom and the removal of regulations on building heights, resulting in the replacement of many inner-city terraces and cottages with high-rise, low-rental housing during the 1960s. This was followed by a plethora of multi-storeyed office blocks, culminating in the glossy building extravagances of the 1980s. The marriage of these two cities is at times in conflict but more often than not it is a happy union and a 1991 international survey gave Melbourne the title of the world's 'most livable city'.

More than 276 000 people – or more than seventy one per cent of Victoria's population – live in Melbourne giving it a cosmopolitan and polyglot mix with strong ethnic communities especially of Italian, Greek and Asian origin. While Greater Melbourne is a sprawl covering some 6000 square kilometres, the central business district is orderly, compact and easily embraced as are the inner-city residential areas.

Queen Victoria has an imperial gaze forever fixed over the Yarra-side gardens that bear her name.

Melbourne's founding date is popularly accepted as 1835 when John Batman came to the banks of the Yarra River and wrote in his diary that 'this is the place for a village'. He 'purchased' about 240 000 hectares from the local Aborigines in exchange for the commonplace European goods of flour, axes, scissors, blankets and mirrors. In 1837, the city centre was surveyed in an ambitious and rigidly formal grid plan that was to reach fulfilment and go further than its originators could ever have imagined.

From mouth to source, the Yarra River and its banks form a natural haven for fauna and flora at every level, from a flyway for birds to breeding waters for tortoises, fish and even platypuses. Yarra Bend Park, about four kilometres from the General Post Office, has ancient red gums which provide a permanent home for a menagerie of native birdlife such as bright rainbow lorikeets, frogmouths and cockatoos. The Yarra is also something of a class – or 'socio-economic' – division for the city's human inhabitants. In general terms, 'south of the Yarra' – as they say in Melbourne – is more richly endowed with hills, rainfall and fertile soil and has attracted the wealth of the middle classes, whereas the areas north and west of the Yarra are flatter, drier and often given over largely to industry.

Hard by the southern city shore of this division is Australia's first botanic garden, planned in the nineteenth-century English landscape tradition but with shape and planting dictated by local topography and climate.

Adjoining the Botanic Gardens is the Kings Domain, a huge parkland containing LaTrobe's Cottage, built in 1839, which was the first Government House, and the present Italianate Government House – built in the 1870s and then regarded as the finest in the British Empire. The governor still lives there but in these egalitarian days it is open for inspection by arrangement with the National Trust. In the adjoining Domain, and dominating St Kilda Road, is the massive presence of the Shrine of Remembrance.

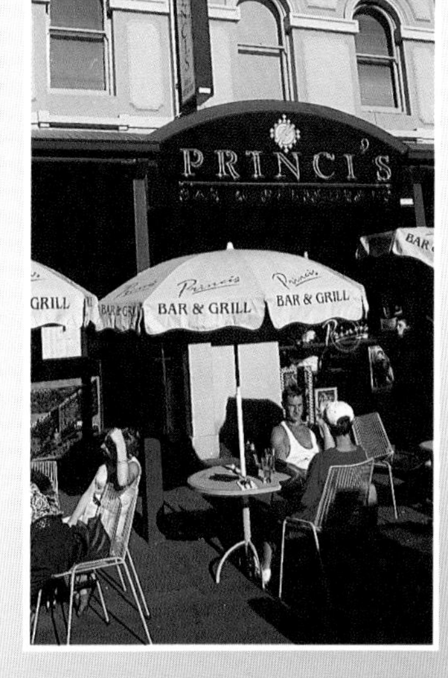

Sunrise silhouettes the Melbourne skyline overshadowing the ramparts of Flinders Street Station – with their punctuating dome and clock tower. Within a few hours the street cafes of Lygon Street (left) will be serving breakfast.

Brighton Beach's bath houses are a quaint reminder of an age when British names and habits ruled.

Many of the city's historic buildings have been classified by the National Trust and those with a penchant for Victoriana and 'heritage' matters can savour Melbourne's varied architecture on leisurely, self-guided city walks.

For city shopping, its Bourke Street Mall and environs are the home of major retailers and smart department stores but recent competition from the vast, new Melbourne Central shopping complex where a Japanese department store has opened a branch, means that Melbourne can offer shoppers a choice of stylish stores found nowhere else in Australia. Buskers in the mall include didgeridoo players, chamber music quartets, magicians, gum-leaf players and people imitating bird calls.

Collins Street has George's, a high-quality retailer, and some very exclusive and very expensive boutiques, galleries, coffee shops, tearooms and small shops selling antiques, jewellery, leather and other specialties. There are stylish, specialist shops in the historic arcades such as Block Arcade and Royal Arcade. Here the effigies of biblical Gog and Magog – the last of a race of giants descended from the thirty-three wicked daughters of Diocletian – strike out the hours on an elaborate clock. Chinatown is located in Little Bourke Street east of Swanston Street. Victoria Market sells not only fruit and vegetables but all food, art and craft, clothing and general merchandise. It can be free entertainment or hard work depending on the visitor's inclination.

Other places of interest and significance include the Victorian State Library, Museum and Planetarium, all at the corner of Latrobe and Swanston streets, Gordon House in Little Bourke Street – an early lodging house and now a place to shop and dine – the Princess' Theatre in Spring Street and the Museum of Chinese Australian History in Cohen Place. The former Royal Mint is a grand presence in William Street while St Paul's

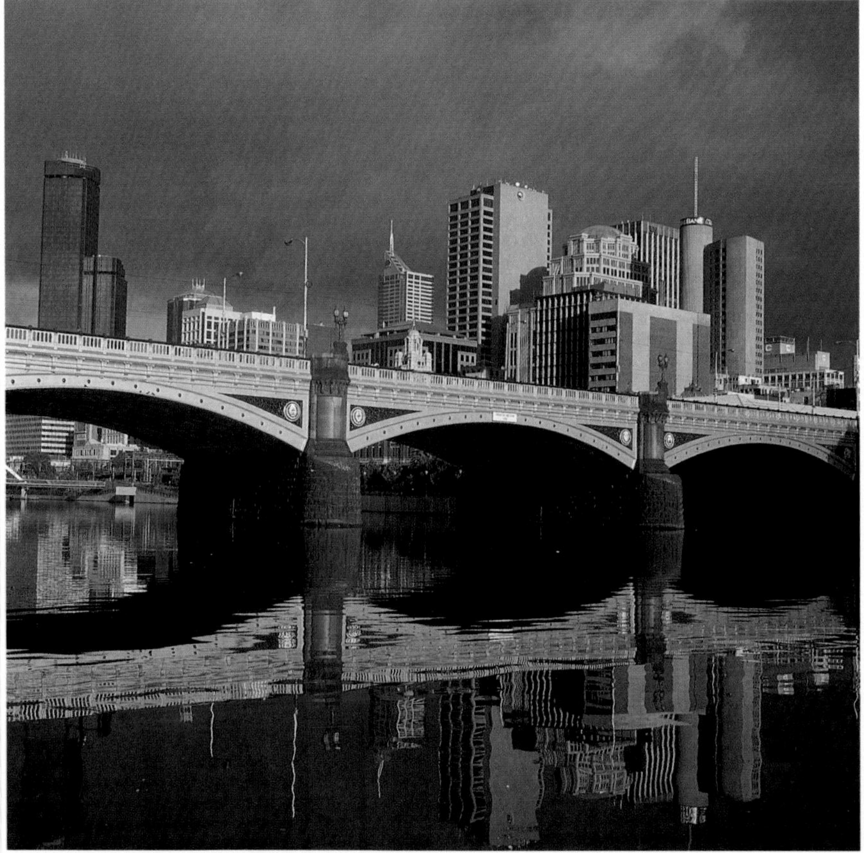

Princes Bridge is an elegant link between the commercial district and the gracious boulevard of St Kilda Road, lined by parklands and a spectacular cultural complex.

Cathedral brings dignity to the corner of Flinders and Swanston streets opposite Flinders Street Station. The Menzies-at-Rialto in Collins Street is famous for its Victorian Gothic facade and modern interior. Standing opposite each other at the intersection of Collins and Russell streets are the polychrome, brick church of St Michael's, formerly called the Independent Church, and the sandstone and limestone Scots Church. Lovers of history and architecture will be rewarded by a tour of 'Como' in South Yarra, one of the earliest and most graceful Melbourne residences still retaining extensive gardens and original furnishings dating from the 1840s. Associations which are sombre and even macabre are inevitably attached to the Old Melbourne Gaol where the notorious bushranger Ned Kelly was hung in 1880 but the building – in Russell Street opposite police headquarters – is worth a visit because of its history and its architecture.

Bustling, inner-city boulevards where street life invigorates old residential suburbs include Brunswick Street, Fitzroy, for food, books, late hours and high and low life; Chapel Street, Prahran, for similar attractions in a slightly different and richer community; Lygon Street, Carlton, for Italian style – its length is cluttered with restaurants and cafes offering Italian classics such as pasta and gelato. A strong influence here is the nearby University of Melbourne which has many significant buildings, particularly the residential colleges. The footpaths of Acland Street, St Kilda, are at times so crowded as to bring the stroller to a standstill; this street is famous for its Jewish cake shops whose cakes and pastries sometimes achieve a level of art not even found in the local galleries. There are many cafes and restaurants in nearby Fitzroy Street which also copes with a reputation for a somewhat seedy lifestyle usually equated with Sydney's Kings Cross. The best of St Kilda is free: a stroll along the pier on a Sunday afternoon after browsing through the market on the lower esplanade. Everybody strolls the pier on a sunny day. South from St Kilda are many bayside beaches including those at Frankston and the wealthy residential suburb of Mount Eliza.

Westwards, below the remarkable span of Westgate Bridge, is an inner-city wetland area that is home to breeding ibis, swans, grebes and reed warblers. With its piers and docks fretting the shoreline, historic Williamstown is less suburb than maritime village with a pretty outlook over the bay. It has a fine variety of colonial buildings such as the 1852 lighthouse and customs house as well as a maritime museum, historical museum, galleries and tourist shops.

Bourke Street boasts the only inner-city mall in Australia to double as a tram carriageway.

Comedy is a noted Melbourne strength – perhaps a result of a climate that is often invigorating compared with Sydney's sometimes enervating summers and the visitor can laugh not only during the annual comedy festival – which begins as close as possible to April Fool's Day – but on almost any day of the year at one of the many theatre restaurants. Ballet, theatre, opera and classical music performances attract the best local, interstate and international performers at venues both in the city and at the opulent Victorian Arts Centre. The Melbourne Film Festival is held annually in June while the Melbourne International Festival of the Arts – in September – covers all areas of the performing arts and has many free performances.

The vast Melbourne Cricket Ground is the hallowed birthplace of test cricket, the first England–Australia test match being played there in 1877. In winter it is also an Australian Rules football shrine where many matches of the revered ball game of southern Australia are played. Another Melbourne sporting connection which has national repercussions is the Melbourne Cup – the horse race which stops the nation for a few minutes on the first Tuesday of November. Ever since playing host to the 1956 Olympics Melbourne has been an important sporting centre and facilities at the Melbourne Sports Network include world and Olympic-class swimming and tennis venues. The tennis centre has a mechanically operated roof in case it rains…something which happens far less often than Sydneysiders, maintaining the historic Sydney–Melbourne rivalry, would care to admit. In fact, Melbourne has an average of twenty days fewer of rain a year than Sydney! □

The joyously flamboyant 1880s architecture of the Princess' Theatre owes nothing to understatement.

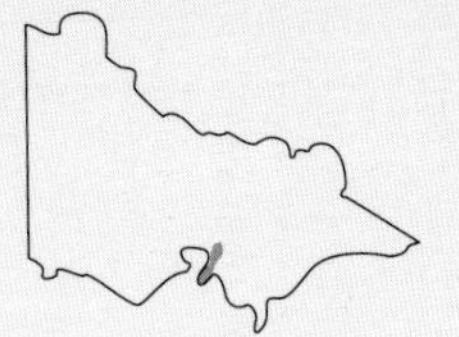

Dandenong & Mornington

From the hills of the Dandenongs to the beaches of the Mornington Peninsula, this ever-popular breathing space to Melbourne's south-east has a varied geography but shares a similar history. After timber-felling and farming came tourism – in the late-nineteenth century – and suburban intrusion in the twentieth.

ARTHURS SEAT STATE PARK ■ 814

When Matthew Flinders climbed to the top of Arthurs Seat on 27 April 1802, he was under the impression that he had anchored in Western Port. On reaching the top, he saw Western Port to the east and realised his mistake. Although Flinders was the first European to climb Arthurs Seat, it had already been named by Lieutenant John Murray who had sailed in the *Lady Nelson* into Port Phillip Bay some ten weeks earlier. He named it after a similar mount – Arthurs Seat in Edinburgh, Scotland.

Arthurs Seat State Park, previously part of Nepean State Park, was established as a separate reserve in 1988. Within its 350 hectares is Mornington Peninsula's largest area of remaining natural woodland and the extensive gardens of 'Seawinds'.

BALNARRING ■ 815

The beach resort of Balnarring is on part of what was one of a number of stations founded by brothers Alfred and Maurice Meyrick in the 1840s. The name is either of Irish origin, an adaptation of Ballymerang, or from the Aboriginal 'bael narang' meaning little gum tree. One of the smaller settlements on Western Port, Balnarring is the site of the Emu Plains craft market, held in summer, and has been home to a colony of koalas since the early 1980s. *Population 1700*

BAXTER ■ 816

Baxter's Flat was the original name given to the settlement that grew up on Captain Benjamin Baxter's Carrup Carrup Station, set up in 1840.

Now within the City of Frankston, Baxter has been home to two famous authors. Joan Lindsay, author of *Picnic at Hanging Rock*, lived in Baxter from the 1920s until her death in 1984, while Nevil Shute, author of *A Town Like Alice* and *On the Beach*, lived here for a while in the 1950s. *Population 1180*

BEACONSFIELD ■ 817

Beaconsfield, on the eastern edge of suburban Melbourne, developed as a farming township on part of Panty Gurn Gurn Station, established in 1845. The settlement was originally known as Little Berwick until the name Beaconsfield was adopted officially in 1881, the year that Benjamin Disraeli, Earl of Beaconsfield died.

The township is the centre of an orchard district where apples and lemons were grown and transported by rail to Melbourne, the urban sprawl of which has yet to take over Beaconsfield. *Population 2260*

BELGRAVE ■ 818

Belgrave stands on the south-eastern slopes of the Dandenongs, at the southern edge of the old Sherbrooke Forest Park, now part of Dandenong Ranges National Park (see entry).

Belgrave was a stop on one of the four experimental, low-cost, narrow-gauge railways built in the early 1900s to open up rural areas outside Melbourne. From 1900 to the early 1950s, steam trains ran from Ferntree Gully to Gembrook passing through Belgrave. When a landslide in 1953 blocked part of what had become a loss-making line, the line was closed.

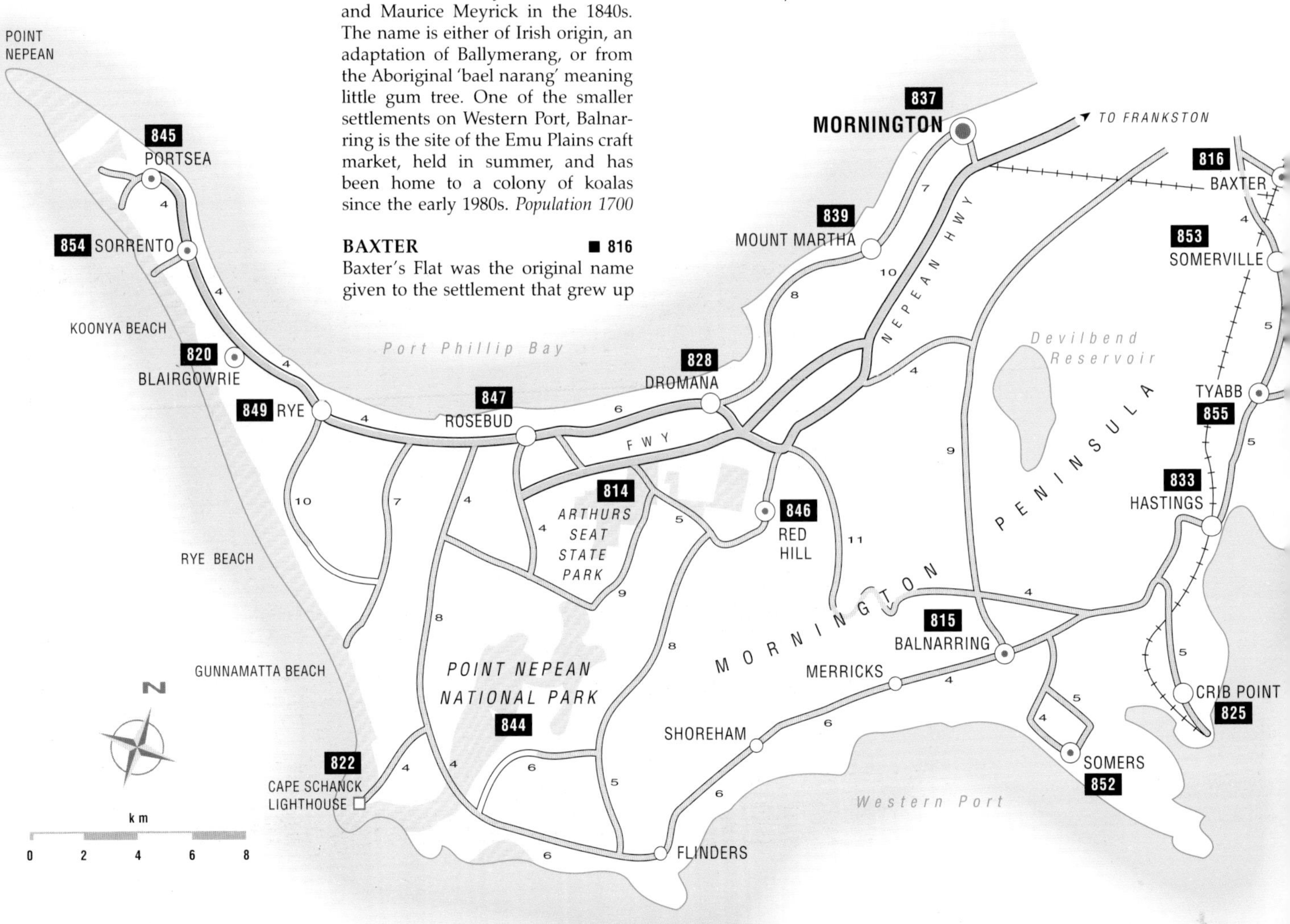

In 1962, the electrified suburban railway line was extended, reducing the time taken from Flinders Street Station to Belgrave to seventy minutes. But the charm of the historic narrow gauge line was not allowed to die. Manned by volunteers, the oldest steam locomotive in Victoria, 'Puffing Billy', runs regularly from Belgrave to Emerald Lake, a distance of thirteen kilometres. Twenty thousand tourists travel on the steam train each year…far fewer participate in the annual Great Train Race when runners on foot take on Puffing Billy. *Population 3320*

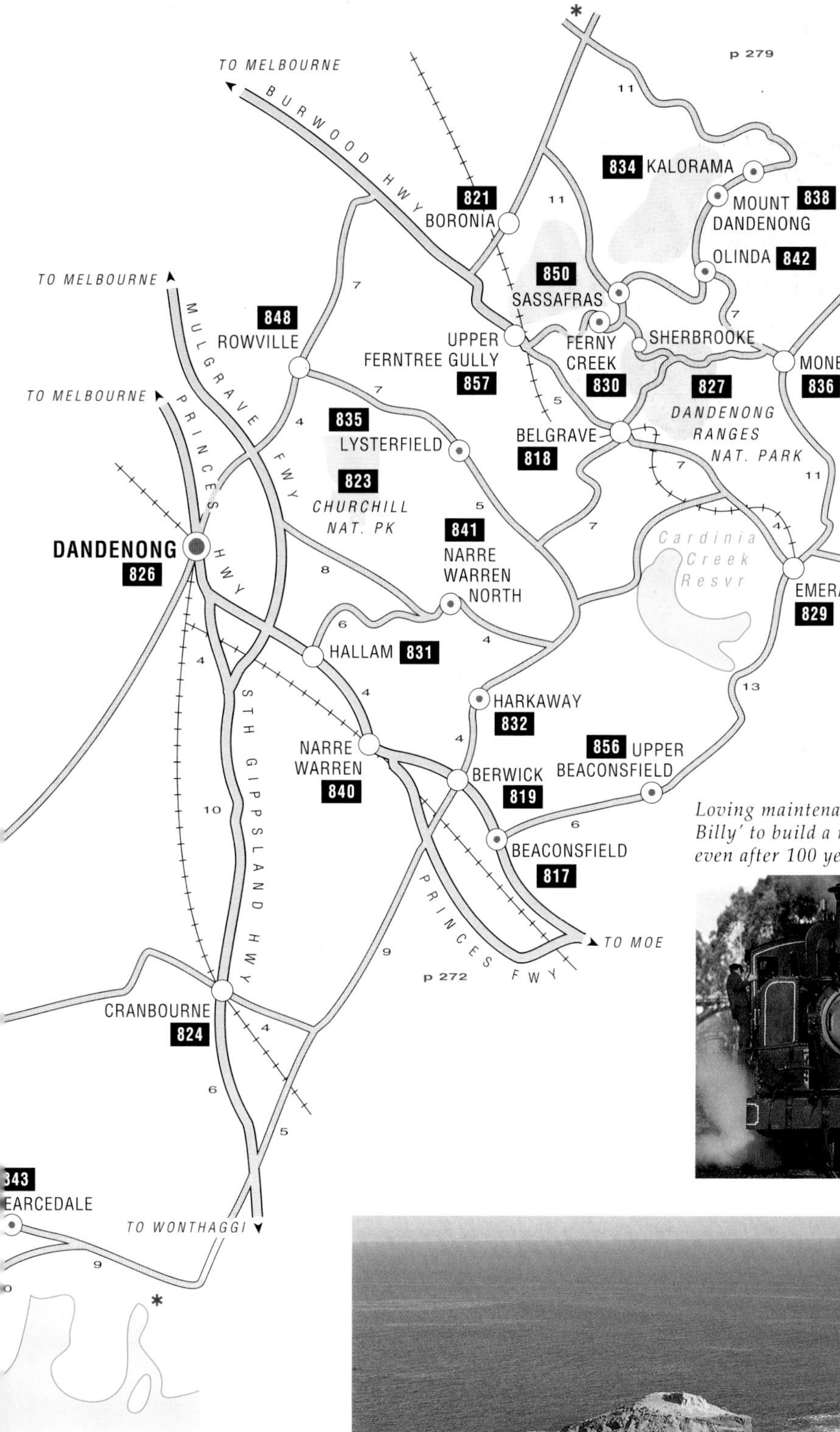

BERWICK ■ 819

In 1838, the first agricultural lease in what was then the district of Cardinia Creek was taken up by Terence O'Connor. The land on which the town grew was later sold to Captain Robert Gardiner, whose birthplace of Berwick-upon-Tweed (on the border between England and Scotland) was used as the name for the town.

Berwick Agricultural Society, set up by the local farmers in 1848, is Victoria's oldest farmers' society. The railway line from Melbourne arrived in 1877 but it took almost a hundred years before the town was absorbed into Melbourne as an outer eastern city-suburb. With its Tudor buildings, parks and reserves and well-known craft market, Berwick has retained a separate identity. *Population 10 860*

FESTIVALS Berwick Village Family Fun Day, November.

Loving maintenance allows 'Puffing Billy' to build a mean head of steam even after 100 years' service.

BLAIRGOWRIE ■ 820

On the narrow toe of the Mornington Peninsula, Blairgowrie lies on a popular stretch of coastline, running from Dromana to Portsea, but is less well known than most of the neighbouring resorts. Named after a town in northern Scotland, Blairgowrie is the site of 'Blairgowrie House'. Built of limestone in the 1870s, the single-storey villa has a square tower in the centre of four main facades each of which have different views from the elevated site. *Population 1950*

BORONIA ■ 821

Boronia, now officially part of the City of Knox on Melbourne's outer

A network of paths and boardwalks allows even the most unadventurous visitor to appreciate the windswept cliffs, rocky outcrops and historic lighthouse of Cape Schanck – at the exposed tip of Mornington Peninsula – to best advantage.

The pride of Sherbrooke Forest – the majestic ranks of 90-metre-high mountain ash trees – turn roads into green corridors lit by shafts of sunlight...

eastern edge, was, until the 1920s, a tiny settlement. In the 1920s, and particularly in the Depression years of the 1930s, cheaper land at Boronia, combined with suburban concession fares for the Melbourne workforce brought an influx of commuters.

Within a few years the settlement had a sufficient population to merit its own state school and a small community hall. By the 1980s, Boronia's modern community centre was used by an estimated 5000 people each week. *Population 20 920*

CAPE SCHANCK LIGHTHOUSE ■ 822

Cape Schanck, on the heel of Mornington Peninsula overlooking Bass Strait, was named in 1801 after Captain John Schank – inadvertently adding a 'c' to his surname – who designed the sliding keel fitted to the *Lady Nelson* (see Arthurs Seat State Park). More than fifty years later, a lighthouse was erected on the headland to mark the eastern approach to Port Phillip Bay. The lighthouse, built of local limestone, rises twenty-one metres above Cape Shanck and was completed in 1859.

CHURCHILL NATIONAL PARK ■ 823

Churchill National Park encloses just over 190 hectares of natural woodland – one of the few remaining zones of vegetation that once covered the foothills of the Dandenongs. Established in 1940 and named after Sir Winston Churchill a few years later, the park is a mere thirty-two kilometres from the centre of Melbourne. The park's black wattle and dogwood, manna gums and swamp, have survived despite the depredations of land clearing for electricity transmission lines, quarries and general urban incursion.

The fauna did not do so well and most of the animals, such as echidnas, wallabies, possums and kangaroos now found within the park's boundaries, had to be reintroduced after their populations died out.

CRANBOURNE ■ 824

The first settlers in Cranbourne were the Ruffy brothers who arrived in the district in 1836 and opened their Cranbourne Inn some time later. With the growth in the number of settlers, the town was surveyed in the 1850s and gazetted in 1861, the year after the world's largest known meteorite landed on Cranbourne. A replica of the one-and-a-half-tonne meteorite is still displayed here.

Cranbourne today is a dormitory suburb of Melbourne best known for its racecourse and as the site of an annexe of the Melbourne Botanical Gardens. *Population 23 140*

CRIB POINT ■ 825

The two Hann brothers, among the early pioneers of this area of Western Port, had their hut or 'crib' on the point, hence the name. Crib Point sits opposite French Island and regular ferries run from nearby Stony Point across Western Port to the island.

Since 1930, HMAS *Cerberus*, one of the navy's principal training establishments, has operated at Crib Point. *Population 18 040*

DANDENONG ■ 826

The heavily forested region around what is now the town of Dandenong was sighted by William Hovell in 1827 on his exploration of Western Port Bay. By 1840, much of the redgum forest had been cleared for cattle runs and there were even two hotels in Dandenong, whose name is thought to come from an Aboriginal word meaning 'high mountain'.

Dandenong was the starting point of La Trobe's 1845 expedition to Port Albert on the south-east coast and was also the starting point of the road to the rich resources of Gippsland, from 1847.

In the 1840s, an unofficial cattle market operated in a paddock in Dandenong and by the 1860s there was an official market where cattle, sheep, pigs and farm produce were auctioned. A retail market in other goods developed and in 1958, the stock market moved to new premises – Australia's largest stock market at the time – leaving the retailers the run of the old market site.

After the Second World War Dandenong became the location of an agricultural machinery works, motor assembly plants and a large housing estate, the first large post-war estate in a metropolitan region. The town's population increased threefold in the 1950s and Dandenong was declared a city in 1959. *Population 57 280*

FESTIVALS Dandenong Oktoberfest, November.

DANDENONG RANGES NATIONAL PARK ■ 827

Dandenong Ranges National Park (1920 hectares) is comparatively new, having been officially declared only in 1987, but the three sections that were amalgamated to make up the park have a much longer history.

The oldest section of the park – and the nearest to Melbourne – is Fern Tree Gully Forest. The forest was first reserved in 1882 as a sanctuary for plants and animals, attracting tens of thousands of visitors each year. From 1928 until 1987 the forest, on the slopes of One Tree Hill, was a national park in its own right – Ferntree Gully National Park.

From 1867, Sherbrooke Forest, the second section of the Dandenong Ranges National Park, was used to supply Melbourne's timber requirements but all logging came to a halt in 1930 and Sherbrooke Forest Park was declared in 1950. This section of the park is home to the mountain ash, the tallest hardwood species in the world, with specimens reaching a height of ninety metres and is also home to many lyrebirds.

...while deep in the privacy of the forest the male superb lyrebird shows his finery in a mating display.

Less accessible than the other two sections of the national park, Doongalla Forest nonetheless experienced similar depradations to Sherbrooke in the late nineteenth century with timber felling and encroachment into the remaining uncleared areas of the forest for farming. The Doongalla forest was the first governmnet purchase in 1950 as part of the 'Buy back the Dandenongs' scheme.

DROMANA ■ 828

The first European to arrive in Dromana was John Aitkin, whose ship – with a full complement of sheep – ran aground just off Dromana. An eccentric Frenchman called Simon (who gave his name to the nearby Simon's Creek) lived in a hollow log on the nearby slopes of Arthurs Seat where he is said to have survived on a diet of goanna meat! The settlement was originally called Hobson's Flat, after Edward Hobson who had one of the first cattle runs on the peninsula but, when gold was discovered near Dromana in the 1850s, the large number of Irish prospectors led to a change of name to the more Irish Dromana, after a town in Eire. *Population 5080*

FESTIVALS **Strawberry Festival, mid-January.**

EMERALD ■ 829

In the late 1850s, there was a brief gold rush at Emerald and when the prospectors moved on, the name – and the body – of one of them remained. Jack Emerald was murdered on the creek that was given his name and when the town – the oldest settlement in the Dandenongs – developed in the 1880s, it too was named Emerald after a brief life under the name 'Main Range'.

One of the early settlers, Carl Alix Nobelius, established a nursery that by the early 1900s had developed to become the largest ornamental plant and fruit tree nursery in the Southern Hemisphere. The notoriety remains – in a new form. Emerald Lake Park, a fifty-hectare leisure park with the terminus of the 'Puffing Billy' train from Belgrave (see entry) and the largest working-scale model railway in Australia now occupies part of this land. *Population 3300*

FERNY CREEK ■ 830

When it was originally settled in the late 1870s, Ferny Creek was known as either Tremont or One Tree Hill and some natural forest remains in the Ferny Creek area. On both sides of the road running through the settlement, chestnut trees were planted as a memorial to those who died in the First World War and the stretch of highway passing through Ferny Creek was renamed Anzac Avenue. *Population 1960*

HALLAM ■ 831

Named after William Hallam, a storekeeper in the early days of European settlement, Hallam is between Dandenong and Berwick (see entries) but has neither the industrial development of the former nor the residential development of the latter. As the centre of a farming district, Hallam has remained a much smaller town than either of its larger neighbours. *Population 6600*

HARKAWAY ■ 832

Off the main highway from Melbourne, Harkaway is less accessible than many other settlements in the Dandenongs and its population has grown little since the early farming days. The origin of the name is uncertain but may be linked to an English racehorse of the 1830s – although the name was not officially recorded until the late 1850s.

'The Grange' at Harkaway, built by his grandfather, became the writer Martin Boyd's home in 1948. The 'one-storied family house in the hills about 30 miles from Melbourne' was renamed but remains recognisable in Boyd's 1952 book, *The Cardboard Crown*. *Population 10 860*

HASTINGS ■ 833

First settled in the 1850s, when it was King's Creek, Hastings has a deep natural harbour, which was used by the then developing fishing industry.

Hastings is now the main town on the Western Port side of Mornington Peninsula and the site of Victoria's first decentralised industrial area at Long Island, a few kilometres from the town centre. The industrial development is well contained and Hastings is still surrounded by farms and orchards, with a new marina and a huge area of wetlands to the north. *Population 5710*

FESTIVALS Hastings Festival, February.

KALORAMA ■ 834

This resort town in the northern Dandenongs is noted for its spectacular views of the mountains and valleys as far west as Melbourne and east across Olinda Forest to Silvan Reservoir. The name of the town is Greek in origin, coming from *kalos* meaning beautiful. *Population 1190*

LYSTERFIELD ■ 835

In the southern foothills of the Dandenongs, Lysterfield, like many of the Dandenong settlements attracted those interested in culture and arts, but unlike any of the others, Lysterfield was named in 1879 after one of them, a former opera producer, William Saurin Lyster.

For over twenty years, until it burnt down in 1971, Lysterfield had its own theatre. The '1812 Theatre' was named, not for a year or even for an overture, but because, more prosaically, it sat at the junctions of Route 18 and Route 12, along which many of Lysterfield's residents now commute daily. *Population 1690*

MONBULK ■ 836

The name Monbulk comes from an Aboriginal word 'monbolloc', said to mean hiding place in the hills and it is obvious from evidence unearthed at what is now the recreation reserve in Monbulk that the town was once the site of Aboriginal corroborees. The healing powers of the natural springs at Monbulk were also known to the Aborigines.

European settlement dates from the 1890s when the Victorian Government established three official townships in the Dandenongs of which only Monbulk remains. Monbulk is known internationally for the quality of its stonefruits and berries, now processed in the Goulburn Valley, and nationally, for its flowering bulb farms, established by Dutch settlers. Tulips, gladioli, daffodils and liliums grown throughout the town, add to Monbulk's reputation as one of the most attractive towns in the Dandenongs. *Population 3840*

FESTIVALS Monbulk Mountain Festival, March; Annual Berry Festival, December.

MORNINGTON ■ 837

Matthew Flinders sailed into Mornington on the eastern shore of Port Phillip Bay in 1802. From the late 1830s, fishermen and timber-getters were the main inhabitants of the small settlement at what was then called Schnapper Point. The building of the jetty in 1857 encouraged more settlers who could ship their farm produce to Melbourne across Port Phillip Bay and by the 1860s, when the name Mornington was adopted, the market town was flourishing.

Mornington remains an attractive tourist resort as it has been since the 1880s and its deep natural harbour is still home to a scallop-fishing fleet. Nowadays, light industries, a racecourse and a museum of modern media have joined attractions such as the telegraph office, the nineteenth-century court house and the esplanade parks. *Population 19 400*

FESTIVALS Australia Day Festival, January; Tea Tree Festival, November.

MOUNT DANDENONG ■ 838

Mount Dandenong, an erosion-resistant volcanic peak, 633 metres above sea level, is the highest point in the Dandenong Ranges...and host to the transmission towers for Melbourne's television stations.

The town of Mount Dandenong is ringed by the three highest peaks in the Dandenong Ranges – Mount Dandenong itself, Barnes Lookout (625 metres) and Mount Olinda (594 metres). Despite this mountainous topography, by 1904, horse-drawn coaches were making the trip up to Mount Dandenong and, by 1922, the first motor coaches brought their tourist loads. *Population 1150*

WILLIAM RICKETTS SANCTUARY During 1935, William Ricketts, a musician turned sculptor, bought his property on Mount Dandenong and proceeded to create beautiful life-sized clay sculptures. Based on Aboriginal culture's belief of 'oneness' with the environment, the sculptures are scattered around a natural environment of trees, ferns, rocks and streams.

MOUNT MARTHA ■ 839

Mount Martha (165 metres) is one of the three highest points rising from the Mornington Peninsula and was named in honour of the wife of Captain Lonsdale, the first commandant of the settlement at Port Phillip Bay. By the 1850s, the area around and on Mount Martha, including its summit, had been cleared for grazing and the settlement on the edge of Port Phillip Bay established. But by 1929 the process was reversed when the summit was reserved as a park.

Mount Martha is a beach resort and, because it is only sixty kilometres from Melbourne, has developed into a popular outer residential area for the city. *Population 7590*

THE BRIARS This historic house was built in the 1860s by Alexander Balcombe whose father knew – and received gifts from – Napoleon Bonaparte during his imprisonment on St Helena. The house, now open to the public, still contains its Napoleonic furniture, including the old table at which Napoleon reputedly wrote his memoirs, and a secretaire with cop-

Oblivious to the objections of councils and conservationists, century-old private changing huts add a touch of Victoriana to Mornington beaches.

per medallions of Napoleon and his empress, Josephine.

NARRE WARREN ■ **840**
The name Narre Warren comes from the Aboriginal *nerre nerre warrene* believed to mean 'little hills' and was the original name given to what is now called Narre Warren North (see entry), the older of the two settlements. When the main railway line arrived in the district in 1883, the railway station was established at New Narre Warren, a few kilometres south of Old Narre Warren. Eventually New Narre Warren usurped the name Narre Warren and Old Narre Warren became Narre Warren North.

The railway station at today's Narre Warren was used by local dairy farmers and orchardists whose produce was brought by waggon for rail shipment to Melbourne. Milk was sent by early morning train to Melbourne in milk cans, which were returned empty on the afternoon train...if the guard remembered to offload them. Commuters now travel along the same line from Narre Warren into the city. *Population 13 590*

NARRE WARREN NORTH ■ **841**
This small settlement has a longer history than the City of Berwick, within whose boundaries it now lies. The first cattle run around Narre Warren North – 'Wat-Will-Roon' – was established in the late 1830s. By the 1870s, all the land in the district had been taken up and, after 1883, the farmers and orchardists transported their goods to the railway station at Narre Warren (see entry), a few kilometres to the south. Unlike the much larger Narre Warren, Narre Warren North has been less affected by Melbourne's encroaching suburbia. *Population 3420*

OLINDA ■ **842**
John Dodd, who built the first shop in the Dandenongs in 1893 and was responsible for ensuring that Olinda is the only planned settlement in the Dandenongs, also opened one of the first tearooms, now the Olinda Log Cabin Restaurant. By the time of his death in 1953, Dodd had seen the tea and scones offered to weekend travellers expanded to include Swiss fondue and Danish smorgasbords at restaurants run by the European restaurateurs who settled in Olinda.

The rhododendrons grown in the National Rhododendron Garden, a forty-hectare reserve at Olinda, were planted by the volunteers and members of the Australian Rhododendron Society from 1960 onwards. In addition to some 15 000 rhododendrons and azaleas, 3000 camellias, magnolias and ornamental shrubs are on show in the reserve, which holds an annual festival between September and November.

Named after Alice Olinda Hodgkinson, the daughter of the surveyor Clement Hodgkinson, the town's bushland environment and spectacular views have long attracted not only diners and horticulturalists but artists and craftspeople, many of whose creations are sold in Olinda's galleries. *Population 1810*

EDWARD HENTY COTTAGE Edward Henty, Victoria's first European settler, arrived in Australia in 1834 and made his fortune as a pastoralist. In 1855 a cottage was shipped from England in prefabricated sections and erected as the Henty family home in St Kilda Road, Melbourne. In 1979, the cottage was moved and re-erected in Olinda...complete with its Henty family period furniture.

FESTIVALS Spring Floral Festival, September–November.

For more than 50 years, William Ricketts used clay to interpret stories of the Aboriginal Dreamtime.

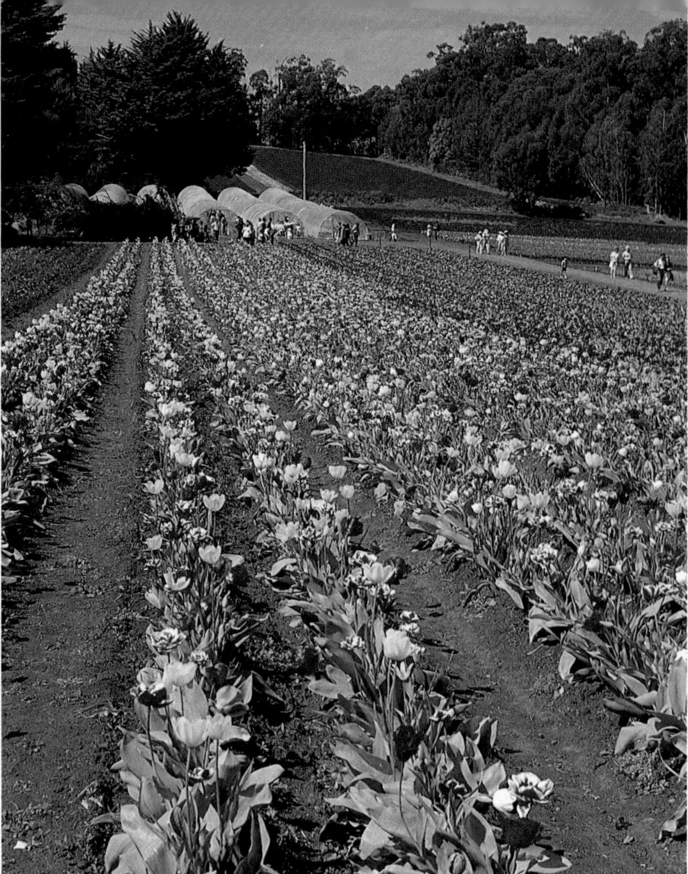

Dutch settlers who were attracted by the Dandenongs' cool winters made the Silvan–Monbulk region the centre of Australia's flower-bulb trade.

PEARCEDALE ■ **843**
Pearcedale, the busy centre of a large market gardening and fruit growing district, was named in 1907 after Nathaniel Pearce who settled on the large Lanwarrin Estate on part of which Pearcedale developed.

Berries, apples and stonefruits are not the only things to come from the fertile ground at Pearcedale. In the late 1920s, a market gardener dug up a large 'rock', which turned out to be a twenty-three-kilogram iron and nickel meteorite, part of a substantial meteorite shower to hit the area and the last specimen to be discovered. 'Meteor 12', to use its unimaginative official name, is now on display at the shire offices in Cranbourne (see entry). *Population 1920*

POINT NEPEAN NATIONAL PARK ■ **844**
This park was established in 1988 when three very different areas were combined. Point Nepean's Commonwealth land, including a quarantine centre and fortifications, had been closed to the public for more than one hundred years but in 1988 half of that land was transferred to the state government to form the nucleus of a new park. The former Cape Schanck Coastal Park and part of what had been Nepean State Park, running inland from Bushrangers Bay, formed the remainder of the new 2200-hectare national park.

The graves in the cemetery in the Port Nepean section of the park trace much of the post-settlement history of Point Nepean – pioneer settlers, those who died of fever at the old quarantine centre, those drowned in shipwrecks and the military personnel based at the various forts and barracks – manned from 1882–1945 – lie side by side. The first shots of the First World War were fired from Point Nepean – on the German freighter *Pfalz* – almost as soon as war was declared. History repeated itself at the start of the Second World War when Australia's first shot was fired on an unidentified ship – unfortunately, the vessel was discovered to be the freighter *Woniora* from the quite friendly state of Tasmania.

Separated from Point Nepean by the former quarantine centre – now the School of Army Health – is the twenty-eight-kilometre coastal fringe of the park. The peninsula coastal walk to Cape Schanck and Bushrangers Bay takes in ocean beaches, unusual rock formations and cliffs with vegetation ranging from coastal tea tree to spinifex, sand sedge and marram grass.

PORTSEA ■ **845**
James Sandle Ford, who raised cattle and horses at Portsea from 1840, was the person responsible for naming Portsea – after an area in his native town of Portsmouth in England.

In 1856, the immigrant ship *Ticonderoga* anchored at Portsea with 300 fever-stricken passengers, eighty-two of whom were to die and be buried not in graves but under the cliffs in a man-made landslide. A quarantine station at Point Nepean was built to contain future outbreaks of fever (see Point Nepean National Park).

Portsea has been popular since the nineteenth century as a holiday destination, especially with Melbourne's wealthier 'social set'. *Population 750*

RED HILL ■ **846**
Red Hill, in the rural inland of Mornington Peninsula, is the centre of a fruit-growing district with a number of vineyards. Red Hill also has one of the most successful monthly markets on the peninsula. Started on a very small scale by four local families in 1975, the market now attracts 4000 people every month, despite a 6 a.m. start! The qualifications for what may be sold are that it should have been 'made, baked, grown or bred' by the seller. *Population 2220*

FESTIVAL Red Hill Show, March; Red Hill Truck 'n' Country Music Festival, December.

ROSEBUD ■ **847**
Andrew McCrae, the first permanent settler on the Mornington Peninsula, established an extensive cattle run between Rosebud and Dromana in

1843. The McCrae homestead, built in the mid-1840s still stands north of Rosebud and has been restored to its original state, right down to details such as the furniture, paintings and household items.

The bay at Rosebud was visited by fishermen but a permanent settlement was not established until 1851. Rosebud owes its name – and possibly its existence – to the schooner *Rosebud*, which ran aground here in 1851. Rosebud today is one of the busier holiday resorts and business centres on the Mornington Peninsula. *Population 13 280*

FESTIVALS Family Fun Day Festival, November.

ROWVILLE ■ 848

In the foothills of the Dandenongs, the lush pastures and rich volcanic soils of Rowville attracted farmers – after the timber-getters had completed their work. The Rev. James Clow is thought to have been the first settler in Rowville in 1838 although the name Rowville does not appear to have been used until 1903.

Off the main road north of Dand nong, Rowville has been absorbe into the outer suburbs of Melbourn *Population 16 120*

RYE ■ 849

The limeburners, who operated on this section of the coast producing lime for building mortar, knew Rye as White Cliffs. Until the pier was built in 1860, the small community was relatively isolated. Goods being transported between Rye and Melbourne were transferred to waggons from small craft at low tide; at high tide they had to be be rowed in from boats anchored in the bay. Road transport was difficult with Arthurs Seat being a major obstacle. In 1866, part of the hillside was cut away and a track was opened around Anthonys Nose but bad weather or high tides often closed it.

Now, Rye's transport problems ai a thing of the past as the touris who flock to this beach resort, an the number of permanent residen confirm. *Population 5250*

SASSAFRAS ■ 850

When the first post office opened at Sassafras in 1894, it was named Sassafras Gully because of the number of sassafras gums with their distinctive nutmeg-smelling bark found in the area. The same year, unemployment reached such a high level in Melbourne that further land around Sassafras Cully, was opened in the hope of attracting 'selectors'.

But Sassafras, since the turn of the century, was more a tourist resort than a farming settlement. Despite its position on a particularly winding section of the road, the Sassafras guest houses, art galleries and nurseries have been attracting tourists ever since. *Population 1040*

SILVAN ■ 851

Silvan – a variation of sylvan, meaning 'forested' or 'woody' – is the centre of a flower- and fruit-growing area. The soils and climates of this still rural settlement support a number of berry farms and a large tulip farm, where children outfitted in Dutch national costume are conspicuous during the month-long tulip festival in September. *Population 790*

SILVAN RESERVOIR Upon completion in 1931, Silvan Reservoir provided half of Melbourne's water supply needs; now it does duty as a balancing storage facility, feeding water from the O'Shannassy Scheme to the much larger and more modern Cardinia Creek Reservoir. The water impounded by the forty-three-metre-high embankment covers an area of 333 hectares and is the focal point of a recreation area near the dam wall.

SOMERS ■ 852

Somers, a beach resort on Western Port, was named after Baron Somers, Governor of Victoria 1926–31. Lord Somers Boys' Camp was one of the earliest establishments in Somers and the town is still the location for an Education Department school camp, which now stands next to 'Coolart', the wetland conservation project for which Somers is now best known.

The landscaped formal gardens and lagoon, together with the mansion built by Frederick Grimwade in 1895, are now owned by the Victorian Government. In 1961, a lone pair of ibis bred on the lagoon at 'Coolart' and now 500 pairs of ibis and many other varieties of water bird breed here. *Population 880*

SOMERVILLE ■ 853

Somerville is the centre of a district noted for its horticulture and fruit growing. During the 1950s, as many as 400 nurseries operated between Somerville and Red Hill...now there are less than half that number. On the main Frankston to Flinders Road and on the main railway line from Melbourne, Somerville's importance as a residential area grew as Melbourne and Frankston grew. Since the 1970s an increasing number of industries have also been established in Somerville. *Population 5600*

SORRENTO ■ 854

Sorrento has the longest history of any settlement in Victoria and was the site of the first birth, marriage and death in the state. In 1802, Lieutenant John Murray raised the Union Jack at Point King, two kilometres west of Sorrento, to claim the land in the name of King George III.

A year later, Lieutenant-Colonel David Collins with over 300 convicts – the youngest aged only nine – marines, civil servants, free settlers and their wives and children set out from Portsmouth with two ships bound for Port Phillip Bay. His ships anchored at Sullivan Bay, on the eastern end of what is now Sorrento Beach, and the first – shortlived – settlement in Victoria was established. Within a year the settlement moved on to Tasmania...but not all those who arrived left in 1804. There are a number of graves of those who died beside the memorial to the settlement. One convict, William Buckley, escaped to live with the local Aborigines for over thirty years – an experience which is mistakenly believed to have inspired the expression 'Buckley's chance'. The phrase, which bodes the least optimistic outcome, is more likely a pun on Buckley & Nunn, a Melbourne store.

Limeburners and fishermen established a small settlement at Sorrento but the development of the village into a fashionable beach resort was largely in the hands of one man, George Coppin, a theatrical entrepreneur and businessman from Melbourne, who bought large areas of land around Sorrento in the 1870s.

The conservation of Sorrento's colourful past adds to the attractions of this beach resort and residential outpost of the much younger Melbourne, founded by John Pascoe Fawkner, the son of convict, John Fawkner, who came to Sorrento with Collins in 1802. *Population 1160*

TYABB ■ 855

The unusual name comes from an Aboriginal word thought to mean 'land of many waterholes' and Tyabb developed as an agricultural and fruit-growing area. At one of the last of the large orchards still operating in Tyabb, it is possible for visitors to view the fruit-grading, sorting and packing process and a number of nurseries also operate around the town, including one which boasts the largest display of pelargoniums – or geraniums – in Australia.

Nowadays, the section of the busy Frankston–Flinders Road that passes through Tyabb is best known for its many and varied antique shops which attract visitors from elsewhere in the peninsula and from Melbourne. *Population 1200*

UPPER BEACONSFIELD ■ 856

In the 1870s there was a brief gold rush to the area around what was to become Upper Beaconsfield but the gold-induced excitement was shortlived and the productive orchards of Upper Beaconsfield remained the mainstay of the settlement.

Off the railway line and main road, Upper Beaconsfield remained relatively untouched by the incursions of development until the 1960s and then suffered from particularly destructive bushfires in 1983. The village is now the site of the Victorian Equestrian Centre where Australia's Olympic riders train. *Population 2060*

UPPER FERNTREE GULLY ■ 857

The dense forest around Upper Ferntree Gully delayed settlement since cleared areas nearer to Melbourne were more amenable to development. By the late nineteenth century, the forest itself had become a big attraction and, as the nearest railway station to Ferntree Gully National Park – now part of the Dandenong Ranges National Park (see entry) – Upper Ferntree Gully attracted thousands of city dwellers who came to what was, and still is, the most readily accessible area of natural forest at the foot of the Dandenong Ranges.

Once the focus of a leisurely day trip by coach or steam train from Melbourne, Upper Ferntree Gully is still the gateway to the Dandenongs but is now also part of Melbourne's sprawling outer suburbia, an hour's train journey from the centre of town. *Population 3460*

The wild birds at 'Coolart' happily share the remaining 90 hectares of the old Somers estate with its mansion, outbuildings and formal gardens.

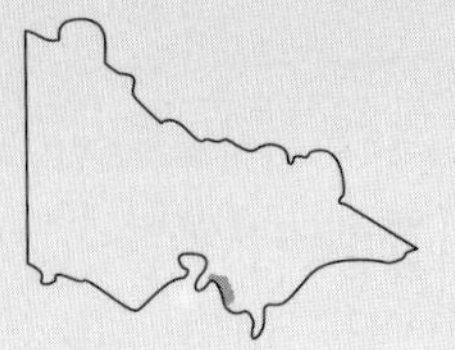

Wonthaggi & Cowes

Despite a lamentable early record of hunting and killing, much of the native fauna has returned to this coastline and its offshore islands – many species are now protected.

BASS ■ 858
This tiny village on the Bass highway was named after surgeon George Bass who discovered Western Port on 4 January 1798 and sailed a short distance up the Bass River. Samuel Anderson, after whom Andersons Inlet, is named settled here in 1835.

THE GIANT WORM EXHIBITION A roadside 'worm' ninety-one metres long and other more conventional buildings house this display. Inside, there are live giant earthworms up to three metres long and other fascinating displays of the worm's world (see *Leongatha & Korumburra*).

CAPE PATERSON ■ 859
The explorer William Hovell discovered coal at Cape Paterson shortly after landing in Corinella in 1826 and a settlement soon followed. Governor La Trobe investigated the coal seam in 1840 and concluded that it could 'scarcely be considered worth working'. Cape Paterson is known today for two contrasting beaches: sheltered Safety Beach attracts swimmers, snorkellers, beachcombers and fishing folk and surfers use the more exposed Surf Beach.

CHURCHILL ISLAND ■ 860
A part of Phillip Island until the sea level rose some 10 000 to 15 000 years ago, this fifty-seven-hectare island is now accessible by wooden bridge and keen walkers can travel its perimeter in about two hours. In 1801, Lieutenant James Grant found the soil '...easy to dig, rich and loose...' and planted Victoria's first crops: wheat, corn, peas, onions and potatoes. He called it Churchill Island to honour a friend in England who gave him the seeds. Nine months later, Lieutenant Murray returned to report: '...I never saw finer wheat or corn in my life, the straw being very nearly as large as young sugarcane'. In 1976, Churchill Island was purchased by the Victoria Conservation Trust to be developed as an historic farm complex.

CORINELLA ■ 861
Corinella is believed to be an Aboriginal word for 'running water'. A memorial cairn marks the spot – about one-and-a-half kilometres east of the present village – settled in 1826 by Captain Wright, Lieutenant Burchill, explorer William Hovell and twenty-one convicts because it was feared that the French might invade southern Australia. Captain Wright's Settlement Point was abandoned fifteen months later and the cattle turned loose (see Wonthaggi and *Leongatha & Korumburra*). Corinella later became the supply port for the French Island prison farm until it closed in 1975, and it is now a fishing and holiday resort.

COWES ■ 862
Cowes was named by the Government Surveyor, Mr Cox after the resort on the Isle of Wight in Britain and has long been a holiday retreat from Melbourne. It is the major town and administrative centre of Phillip Island Shire (see box). Cowes is reached by road across the Phillip Island Bridge or by ferry from Stony Point on the Mornington Peninsula. *Population 5350*

FRENCH ISLAND ■ 863
Captain Baudin, leader of a French scientific expedition, sailed into sheltered Western Port in 1802 and named the island *Ile de Francais*. In 1843, two enterprising colonists tried to produce barilla but heavy rains defeated them. Barilla, the ash from burnt mangroves, is rich in soda and potassium and was an ingredient in soap and glass at the time. Pastoral runs were taken up from 1850 onwards and there were unsuccessful attempts to establish salt works. During the depressed 1890s, the government subsidised six settlements, some with commendably optimistic names: Energy, Perseverance, Industrial, Star of Hope, Kiernan's and Callanan's. The bricks for the buildings were made on the island. Chicory, grown for its roots which were dried and ground up for use in coffee essence, was grown here until 1960; now islanders derive their income from sheep, cattle and dried seaweed – a valuable fertiliser.

From 1916 to 1975, an open prison was operated on French Island and public entry was restricted. McLeod Prison housed 130 farm-labouring felons. Forty per cent of the island is now state park and ferries ply from Cowes or Stony Point on Mornington Peninsula. Rare white-breasted sea eagles are sometimes seen and potoroos thrive without foxes to prey on them. Koalas have bred prolifically since they were introduced in 1874 and French Island supplies the animals to mainland parks and zoos.

GRANTVILLE ■ 864
Now another small Western Port bayside town on the Bass Highway, Grantville was once a busy pioneering seaport where settlers from the hill country received their supplies and sent out their produce. It was named for Lieutenant James Grant who followed Bass into Western Port in 1801 in the *Lady Nelson*.

INVERLOCH ■ 865
Inverloch came into being as the port for Woorayl Shire (see *Leongatha & Korumburra*) and in the early 1900s,

Pyramid Rock, near Redcliff Head, is one of a string of basalt outcrops and reefs which punctuate Phillip Island's rocky shoreline.

shipped coal from the Powlett River area to Melbourne. The town lies at the mouth of Andersons Inlet where the Tarwin River meets Bass Strait. The site was discovered by Samuel Anderson in 1840 who reported on its beauty and abundant birdlife, two things which happily are little changed 150 years later. Inverloch is surrounded by sandy beaches and reserves and is noted among anglers for its good catches of whiting. Low tide exposes the white mangrove trees at Andersons Inlet.

This region was once a productive Aboriginal hunting ground and it still contains fascinating traces of the original inhabitants. Stone scrapers and small hand tools have been found in the kitchen middens among the sand dunes bordering Venus Bay and west of Cape Paterson.

Inverloch has its own intriguing missing fortune story. In 1877, the *Avoca* was carrying a case of sovereigns from Sydney to Williamstown for shipment to England. The ship's carpenter, Martin Wiberg, extracted most of the coins so cleverly that the theft was not discovered for weeks. The police tracked him down tro Inverloch but failed to find the gold. After a few years in prison, Wiberg offered to exchange the money for his freedom. He took the police up the Tarwin River, then capsized the boat and disappeared! Years later, an Inverloch woman claimed to have seen him in Germany. Some residents are still convinced the booty is buried in the sand dunes hereabouts. *Population 2860*

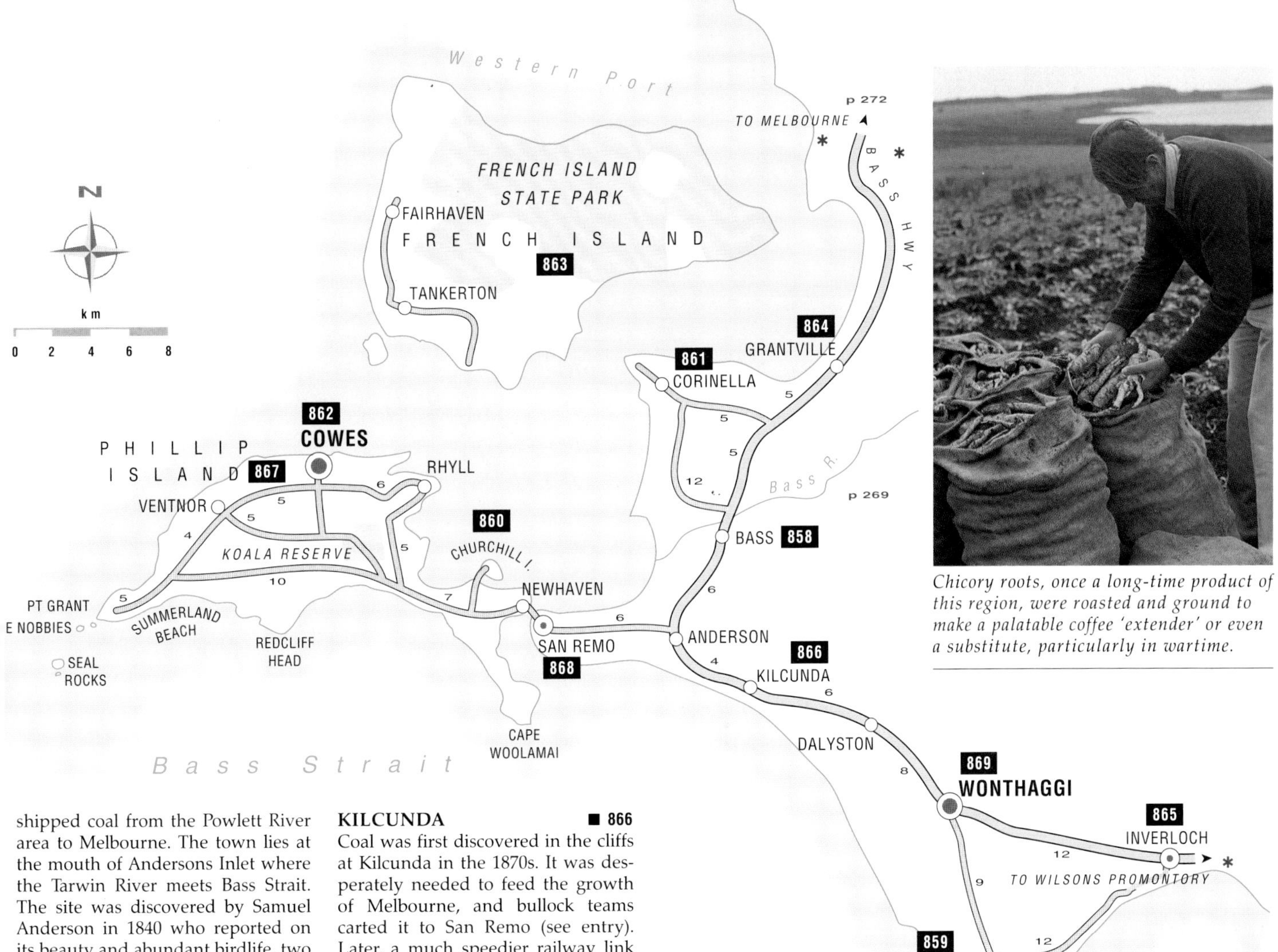

Chicory roots, once a long-time product of this region, were roasted and ground to make a palatable coffee 'extender' or even a substitute, particularly in wartime.

KILCUNDA ■ 866

Coal was first discovered in the cliffs at Kilcunda in the 1870s. It was desperately needed to feed the growth of Melbourne, and bullock teams carted it to San Remo (see entry). Later, a much speedier railway link was built and the distinctive trestle bridge carrying the now dismantled railway line from Nyora to Wonthaggi still stands on Kilcunda beach. This beach and nearby Shelly beach are popular with shell collectors.

PHILLIP ISLAND ■ 867

This is the largest of three Australian islands named after Governor Arthur Phillip – the others are near Norfolk Island, and off the north-eastern shore of Macquarie Harbour in Tasmania. Phillip Island, Victoria was originally named Snapper Island by George Bass in 1798 and was also called Grant Island. It can be reached by the Narrows Bridge linking Newhaven and San Remo or by ferry from Stony Point to Cowes. Aerial tours and flights to Melbourne take off from the island's airport (see box).

SAN REMO ■ 868

San Remo is an attractive fishing and holiday hamlet on the mainland end of the bridge to Phillip Island. The present bridge, costing about three million dollars, was opened in 1969. San Remo's fishing fleet operates far into Bass Strait and is annually blessed by the Bishop of Gippsland, usually on the first Sunday after Christmas. The steep cliffs limit access to the surrounding beaches but it is possible to walk to the Punch Bowl blowhole when the tide is low.

Like all the villages along this coastal strip, San Remo has a history based on exploration and coal. In the 1870s, it served as the port for shipping coal to Melbourne from nearby Kilcunda (see entry). *Population 670*

WONTHAGGI ■ 869

The streets of Wonthaggi are laid out on a grid pattern, a legacy from its beginnings as a well-planned state coal-mining town. The district was originally known as 'Wild Cattle Run' because of the descendants of the Corinella cattle (see entry) which were found grazing in the bush.

Serious excavation for coal began in 1908, and the next year the Victorian government opened up the coalfields because of disastrous miners' strikes in New South Wales. Within weeks of sinking the first shaft of the coal mine, a tent town sprang up with thousands of men living under canvas. Miners came from Korumburra, Outtrim and Jumbunna, some bringing their dwellings with them on bullock waggons. By the end of 1910, permanent buildings were ready for the new citizens. In a curious coincidence, Dr Sleeman, the tent town's pioneer doctor, died in 1968 just hours after the last mine was shut down.

Jack Hagan wrote a popular song: 'There's a part of my heart in Wonthaggi' and Wonthaggi's heart is these days in secondary industry, its major plants including Exacto Knitwear, Cyclone Forgings and Murray Goulburn Dairy Products. The town is also a tourist resort with easy access to Cape Paterson, Inverloch and Corinella (see entries). In July 1923, a giant whale said to be of 'awesome' size was washed up at nearby Wreck Beach. The creature's jawbone was added to the verandah of the Wonthaggi Hotel. In 1974, the verandah's posts were demolished by the council because, it said, they were 'out-of-date, backward and doomed to extinction'. A petition saved the bones which are maintained by a regular whitewashing. *Population 6450*

FESTIVALS Easter Carnival; Bass Valley Show, January.

PHILLIP ISLAND: THRILLS, SPILLS...AND PENGUINS

PHILLIP ISLAND – a region of about 10 000 hectares at the entrance to Western Port – had a busy history long before it became one of Victoria's major sporting venues and tourist attractions. The Aborigines knew it well – a kitchen midden near Forrest Caves provides evidence of a large and busy camping ground. The naval-surgeon-turned-navigator George Bass sighted the island in 1798 and soon afterwards sealers and whalers began calling in for the yearly killing season.

After feeding at sea – sometimes for over a week – Phillip Island's penguins return to their burrows.

In 1826, Captain Wright set up a military post and immediately positioned two six-pounder guns to repulse any French attempt at establishing a foothold at Port Phillip Bay but a shortage of water soon drove him away (see Corinella). In 1842, the McHaffie brothers leased the island for an annual rent of ten pounds sterling and became the first permanent settlers. Rural development was steady from 1868 onwards after selectors balloted for blocks.

Four towns with British seaside names were established at Cowes, Newhaven, Rhyll and Ventnor. The chicory industry began and the kilns used to dry the vegetables still dot the island though most are now abandoned. Chicory roots, looking rather like parsnips, were dried in the kilns, then ground to a fine powder which was blended with coffee beans. Instant coffee has lessened the demand for the product and the farmers now grow other things. Fishing from the island is particularly good and the sea yields many treasures. There are cowrie shells on the western ocean beaches and occasionally a fragile white paper nautilus is washed ashore. Eye agate, chalcedony, rock crystals, jasper and porcelainite can be found under the basalt cliffs at Kitty Miller Bay. Nearby lie the rusting remains of the SS *Speke* – the salvaged ship's bell still rings from the Uniting Church at Cowes.

Woolamai House, one of the oldest homes on Phillip Island, overlooks the Eastern Passage. The owner, John Cleeland, ran 7000 sheep, 200 Shetland ponies and several racehorses on Woolamai Station and his favourite racehorse, Woolamai won the Melbourne Cup in 1875.

Racing of a noisier and more furious kind than horse racing began on the island in 1928 when the first Australian Grand Prix championships were held over sixteen kilometres of closed public roads. The present track, completed in 1956 and improved in later years, is built to international standards and is lined regularly by enthusiastic crowds of spectators who come to thrill at the motorcycle and car racing.

Phillip Island and its offshore rocky outcrops are natural sanctuaries and the wildlife takes pride of place over everything else. Water and sea birds abound. The nightly fairy penguin parade at Summerland Beach is one of Australia's best known tourist attractions. These smallest of penguins breed elsewhere on Australian territory but nowhere are they more visible than on this beach where they come ashore at sunset and waddle to their burrows along spotlit paths. Mutton birds, once hunted in great numbers, also live here and are now protected. Each May they make an incredible journey to latitudes north of Japan for the southern winter (see *Coffs Harbour & Sawtell*).

Sealers slaughtered about 1000 fur seals a year for more than forty years and by 1860 only a hundred or so returned to breed on Seal Rocks, just off the Nobbies. With protection, their numbers have gradually built up again in modern times. They can be studied through powerful telescopes or from ferries when the water is calm. Although koalas are not native to the island – they were introduced in the 1870s – the colony has been so successful that it has helped restock habitats elsewhere in Victoria where, by the Second World War, few koalas survived. Koalas thrive on manna gums and the island reserves of these special trees are carefully and regularly replenished. □

Beyond the Blow Hole, where the ocean gouges away at Phillip Island, is The Nobbies which looks out to Seal Rocks, home to fur seals who disport themselves impervious to the elements (below).

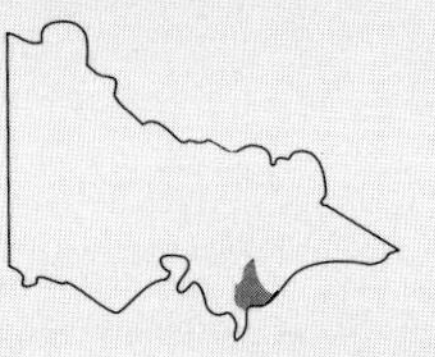

Traralgon & Morwell

The land in the shadow of the Strzelecki Ranges has been bountiful: its gold drew many to the region and the descendants of those who stayed on to farm have seen it provide coal, timber and the basis for a cornucopia of agricultural products.

ALBERTON ■ 870
This Gippsland township sprang up soon after Port Albert was discovered in 1841. Early settlers were the Martin Brothers who created a sensation in the district when they purchased an elephant to clear their land. The elephant, imported from Sri Lanka – then Ceylon – broke loose one night and its remains were found some weeks later only a short distance from the farm.

Historic buildings which remain in Alberton include the Victoria Hotel, a general store which still uses part of its original carved wooden counter and State School Number 1 – numbered not because it was the first school in the state but because it was first on the alphabetical list!

BOOLARRA ■ 871
It took four decades to settle this foothill country from 1840 when Strzelecki and his party first struggled doggedly through the rough terrain, leaving horses and equipment at a spot near here before proceeding on foot to Western Port. Selectors moved south in the late 1870s, when it was realised that the high rainfall forest of west and south Gippsland would grow good English grasses when cleared.

The town began in 1884 when a railway line from Morwell to Mirboo North was constructed and a canvas town established. Timber was one of the first industries in the area. Paling splitting was an important minor industry of the time, with thousands of palings being cut from one – usually blackbutt – tree. Trees felled from this virgin forest were huge, with one recorded as being ninety metres high with a circumference of twenty metres. One of the town's busiest industries today is the Boolarra Fish Farm, the largest goldfish farm of its kind in the Southern Hemisphere. Five different species of goldfish are produced here,to be sold all over Australia. *Population 610*

CHURCHILL ■ 872
Churchill is a satellite town of Morwell, established and named after Sir Winston Churchill in 1965, to provide housing for residents relocated from Yallourn – demolished when the open-cut mine was extended – as well as accommodation in a bush setting for those working on new development projects in the Shire of Morwell. West of the town is the Hazelwood power station – a major employer – with its giant cooling pond, the warm waters of which have turned it into a recreational spot for year-round swimming, boating and sailing. *Population 5580*

GRAND RIDGE ROAD ■ 873
This appropriately named scenic route winding along the backbone of the Strzelecki Ranges shows off the Gippsland valleys and forests to their spectacular best effect. The ranges (see *Leongatha & Kurumburra*) were named after Paul Edmund de Strzelecki, a Polish adventurer who spent twenty-two gruelling days exploring the area. The party was saved from starvation only by the hunting and survival skills of an Aborigine who accompanied them.

The 152-kilometre modern road winds through national parks such as the Tarra–Bulga National Park, rich dairy country around Mirboo and Mirboo North and affords wonderful vistas over Wilsons Promotory at Blackwarry. It takes at least a day to travel Grand Ridge Road by car…if justice is done to the breathtaking views en route.

MORWELL ■ 874
Charles Tyers, Gippsland's land commissioner, first marked out a group of sheep stations in the Morwell district around 1843.

Morwell itself, was founded in the late 1860s, at the junction of three muddy roads: the coach road to Melbourne and those leading to Morwell Bridge and Scrubby Forest station. Settlers were drawn to the area first by gold, and then the rush for land in the 1870s and 1880s when land from large stations was divided into lots for general purchase. The optimism felt by the new settlers soon faded and many were driven from the land either by inexperience or drought, flood and bushfires.

Morwell gained new prominence when the railway line was opened in the 1870s. Deposits of coal were discovered at this time, and there was a spate of mining activity. All of these

Close to its mouth, near Toora, the modest Agnes River provides a brief, frothy cascade at Agnes Falls.

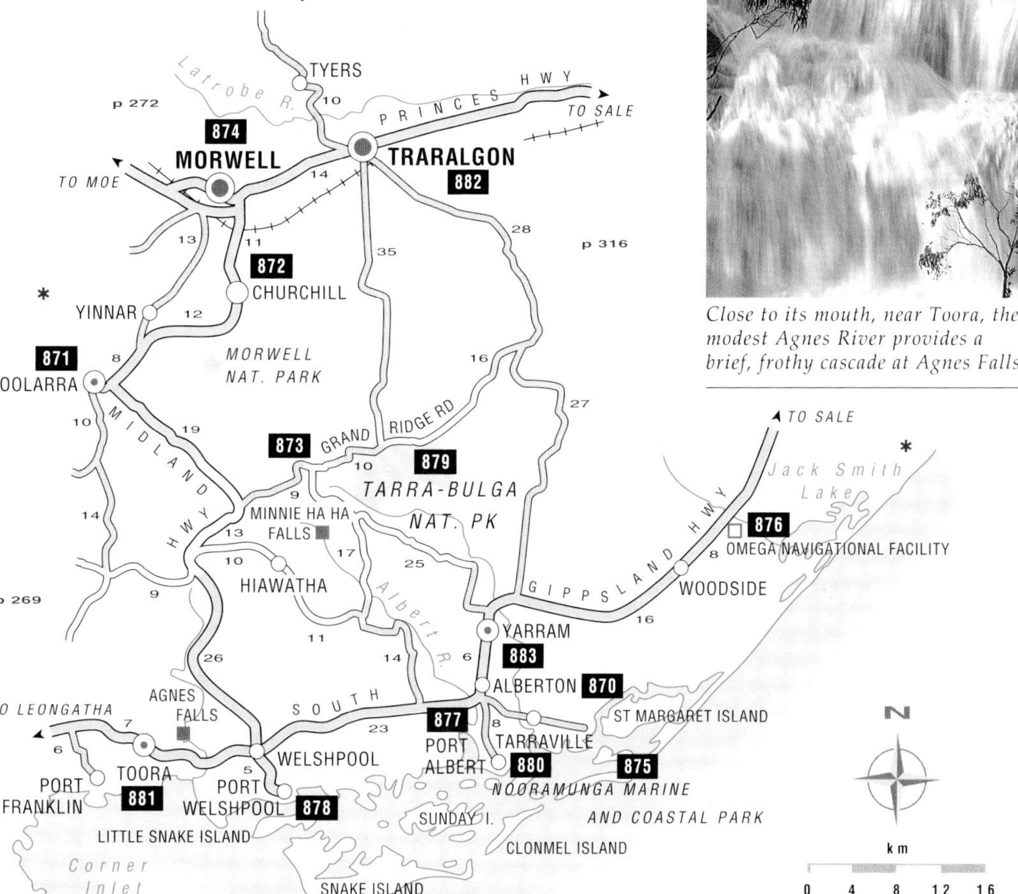

The Tarra Valley's forest of trees and giant ferns is a remnant of the vegetation which once covered the farm paddocks of the eastern Strzelecki Ranges.

ventures failed and mining was abandoned – despite predictions of limitless coalfields in Gippsland – until the 1916 coal miners' strike in New South Wales, when many of the mines were reopened. The growth of Melbourne's appetite for electricity led eventually to the development of the Morwell coalfields and, by 1923, a powerhouse.

The Morwell complex now includes the Morwell open-cut mine, the combined Morwell power station and briquette factory, two gas-turbine power stations, opened in 1979 and Hazelwood power station – the biggest in Victoria, using a phenomenal 160 000 000 litres of cooling water an hour for its steam condensors. The three-square-kilometre mine is the source of more than fifteen million tonnes of coal a year.

Beyond the mines, the countryside supports a large dairying industry, sheep- and beef cattle-raising, and crops of potatoes, millet, oats and barley. *Population 15 420*

FESTIVALS Festival of Dance, July.

NOORAMUNGA MARINE & COASTAL PARK ■ 875

The islands and mudflats of Nooramunga on the Gippsland coast are an important habitat for migratory wading birds and the establishment of the park means that their environment remains in its natural state.

Birds found here include the white-bellied sea eagle, the endangered orange-bellied parrot and the rare ground parrot.

Cattle are allowed to graze on Snake Island during the winter and return to the mainland for the summer after being herded into the sea and swimming across the channel.

OMEGA NAVIGATIONAL FACILITY ■ 876

This high-technology shipping aid, just north of the small town of Woodford, is hard to miss. The Omega Navigational Facility's tower soars to almost 430 metres and its sixteen supporting cables radiate out to cover more than twenty hectares of the surrounding countryside. The 500-tonne tower transmits signals which help aircraft and ships all over the world determine their position. There are seven such facilities scattered across the globe – in Argentina, Japan, Liberia, La Réunion, Norway, Hawaii and North Dakota on the United States mainland – to form this integrated navigational network.

PORT ALBERT ■ 877

Angus McMillan, who had earlier explored northern Gippsland and started sheep runs near the mouth of the Avon River, discovered this harbour in 1841. His search for a port in the south, so that his employer Captain Lachlan McAlister could ship livestock to Van Diemen's Land, took him to the present site of Seabank, where he carved his initials and the date on a tree before returning.

A party from the Gippsland Company – a company quickly formed after survivors from a wreck brought back glowing reports of the area – nearly beat him to it. Their camp was beside the tree McMillan had marked a fortnight earlier. Today, the town is a popular tourist attraction with its historic buildings and attractive locations for watersports.

PORT WELSHPOOL ■ 878

Port Welshpool was one of the major towns in this district before the railway was opened in the late 1870s. The railway provided an impetus for the fishing industry because fresh fish could now reach the Melbourne markets daily. Despite this, the town declined. It briefly made the headlines in 1957, when 300 whales were beached here. The town remains a popular holiday destination, a shore base for the oil rigs in Bass Strait and the mainland port for the Seacat – the fastest aluminium catamaran in the world – which connects the mainland with Tasmania.

TARRA-BULGA NATIONAL PARK ■ 879

This used to be two parks; the Bulga National Park and the Tarra National Park – named after Charlie Tarra,

Strzelecki's Aboriginal guide – until adjoining land was bought by the Victorian Government and the two parks linked together. The park is all that remains of the magnificient rain-forests which covered the eastern Strzelecki Ranges before European settlement. Lush fern gullies, mountain ash, sassafras, myrtle beech, silver wattle and blackwood provide an ideal habitat for more than 130 varieties of birds. Kangaroos, wallabies and wombats are common and platypuses, possums, bandicoots, native rats and seven species of bat inhabit the area.

TARRAVILLE ■ **880**
Once a busy stopping place on the Port Albert to Sale road, this town was one of three – Alberton, Port Albert and Tarraville – that contributed to the development of south Gippsland in the 1840s and 1850s. All three centres declined when the railway line came through. Ada Jemina Crossley, a gifted contralto and protégé of Nellie Melba, who was born here in 1874 went on to perform in the United States and before Queen Victoria. A home for elderly people in Yarram is named after her.

A creek near the town was the scene of a bloody incident in the early 1840s. After an Aboriginal boy was killed in an affray with some stockmen, an Aboriginal group retaliated by killing a white youth. The Aborigines were chased to Derriman where, according to historians, at least sixty of them were shot down.

TOORA ■ **881**
By the time Toora was settled in the 1860s, the local Aborigines had already been moved on in the wake of farms being established. It is thought that Aboriginal women and children stayed at Toora while their men went to Wilsons Promontory to take part in religious ceremonies. The town, first named Muddy Creek, grew up around a timber mill run by the Buchanan brothers. Much of the hardwood timber from Toora went to India, where it was used by the British administration as sleepers for the sub-continent's railway lines. Some of the timber also helped build early Melbourne.

One of the first piers in Melbourne is said to be made from Toora blue gum sleepers. The finished sleepers were transported by a specially built tramline across swampy flats, loaded on barges, then taken out to sea where they were loaded onto ships. Parts of the old tramline and loading facilities can still be seen.

Families came to the Toora district to farm small blocks under the Village Settlement Scheme introduced by the government during the 1892 depression. The area chosen for the scheme was called 'The Grip', after the mud which stuck tenaciously to everything it came in contact with.

The blocks of land were too small for farming and the scheme failed. The abandoned land was absorbed into large dairy farms and dairying is still the main business of modern Toora, where the Unigate Gippsland milk factory produces milk products under the brand name of Tooralac. *Population 570*

AGNES FALLS One of the highest waterfalls in Victoria is on the Agnes River, where the water drops a spectacular sixty metres. The river is dammed above the falls for use at nearby towns and farms.

This young sea eagle has taken advantage of its exclusive fishing rights at the Nooramunga Park.

TRARALGON ■ **882**
Edward Hobson, the first settler here in 1846, named this town from the Aboriginal words, 'tarra', meaning river and 'algon' meaning little fish. In spite of its namesake, the town developed as a stopping place for drovers during the gold rushes and grew in importance when the railway came in 1877. It has become the centre of an important manufacturing district since the First World War, based on the supply of cheap electric power from brown coal deposits in the area.

Loy Lang – an open-cut mine which yields 60 000 tonnes of coal a day – and its two power stations are part of one of Australia's biggest engineering projects. Other industries in the district include the large pulp and paper mill established by Australian Paper Manufacturers in the 1930s. Over half the products made by the mill come from recycled paper with the balance of raw materials coming from the forests to the north.

The Nobel prize-winner, Sir Frank Macfarlane Burnet, was born here in 1899. *Population 19 700*

YARRAM ■ **883**
This town on the banks of the Tarra river is named after the Aboriginal words, 'yarram, yarram', said to mean plenty of water. Yarram's central location in south Gippsland makes it a popular base for tourists who are heading off to enjoy the region's coastal attractions.

Those with a bent for history can inspect the old wells of a former cordial factory off the South Gippsland Highway, the court house and the Hawthorn Bank cottage, an early wattle and daub cottage in Pound Road. *Population 2210*

THE STRANGE MYSTERY OF THE MISSING CASTAWAY

PICNICKERS taking the weekend air at the bush reserve known as the White Woman's Waterhole, north of Yarram, would pause over their sandwiches if they knew of the drama that is said to have been enacted in this peaceful bushland setting one-hundred- and-fifty years ago.

In those days, the waterhole was already a gathering place – Aborigines who were said to have taken in a white woman used it and stockmen said they sighted her here. The mystery of the missing woman began in the mid-1840s with a rumour circulating in this region about a white woman supposedly held captive by Aborigines. In 1841, a group of settlers found a towel and some female clothing in an abandoned Aboriginal canoe. These were linked with the disappearance of Mrs Anna Capel, wife of a Sydney brewer, who was believed to be the only survivor of a shipwreck on the Gippsland coast. It was thought she survived in the bush by being taken under the wing of an Aboriginal group.

The rumours were so persistent that several searches were sponsored by the government to find her. White handkerchiefs were nailed to tree trunks by the searchers with a message, written in both English and Gaelic which said, 'White woman – there are fourteen armed men, partly white and partly black, in search of you. Be cautious; and rush to them when you see them near you. Be particularly on the lookout every dawn of morning for it is then that the party are in hope of rescuing you. The white settlement is towards the setting sun'.

Both searches proved fruitless. When the painted white figurehead from the wrecked vessel *Britannia* was recovered from the Aborigines, it was suggested that this was what the stockmen had glimpsed and mistakenly identified as a woman. Later, the bodies of an unidentified white woman and her child were found at Jemmys Point on the Gippsland lakes. Both were buried there, without any real attempt being made to establish the woman's identity. □

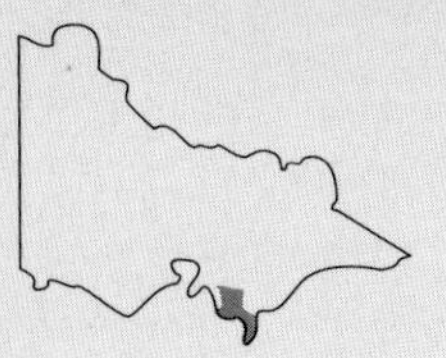

Leongatha & Korumburra

The twin magnets of arable farmland and the 'brown gold' of coal drew settlers to this scenically beautiful and agriculturally rich area of south Gippsland. At the southernmost tip of the mainland, it boasts remnants of primeval forest and, to match, the dinosaurs of the earthworm world.

South Gippsland was not always thus; dense bush made way for the lush pasture that tempts these Friesians.

FOSTER ■ 884

Originally called Stockyard Creek after a stream which yielded much alluvial gold, Foster was renamed for W.H. Foster, warden and magistrate of the south Gippsland goldfield. George Dunderdale recalled the boom days in his 1898 *The Book of the Bush* where he wrote of 'many who did not intend to dig', such as: pick-pockets, horse thieves, lawyers and claim jumpers. The jumpers wanted 'to obtain possession of the rich claim, or some part of it, and the lawyers longed for costs, and they got them'. There is a statue of a miner in Pearl Park and the old post office has been turned into a museum to display the past. Foster's fortunes now rest with dairy cows and the steady stream of tourists passing through to Wilsons Promontory and other coastal resorts.

One of south Gippsland's richest strikes was at Turtons Creek, north of Foster; the creek today is a better prospect for fishing than for panning gold. This is lyrebird country, but the elusive creatures are more likely to be heard than seen in the ferntree gullies. Looking back to the 1890s, the local businessman, writer and parliamentarian, Randolph Bedford, remembered 'the wondrous mimicry of the lyrebird – that great actor that imitates the barking of dogs and the crowing of cocks, the crack of a whip and the scream of brakes on wheels'. *Population 1080*

KORUMBURRA ■ 885

'The chief products of the 'Burra are coal, dairy produce, ferns and snakes', wrote a school teacher called Nathan Spielvogel in 1913. Dairying has proved the most lasting of his 'products'; the last coal mine closed in 1958. Korumburra – said to be an Aboriginal word for 'blowfly' – with its large cattle saleyards, is the centre of a rich dairying area and is noted for pioneering the manufacture of edible casein from milk in the 1970s.

This hilly town on the South Gippsland Highway is surrounded by good pastures cleared from dense forest which was described by Randolph Bedford as a 'wall' from which 'men of great firmness and obstinacy hacked houses and farms'. There is evidence that the Wuywurrung Aborigines lived in the area long before it was known by white settlers as 'wild cattle run' after the beasts abandoned from the Corinella convict settlement (see *Wonthaggi & Cowes*).

Although early settlers arrived about 1845, it was not until 1872 that a restless horse pawed the ground and uncovered some black coal. That is the legend; whether the horse belonged to the prospector called James Brown who is officially credited with the coal discovery is not known. Mining soon began in earnest and Korumburra peaked as a coal centre soon after the railway from Melbourne reached it in 1891. By the turn of the century, competition from New South Wales mines, strikes and fault-ridden fields had all begun to contribute to the slow but steady decline of the coal industry.

There are other, stranger things than coal beneath the surface here. There is 'believe-it-or-not' wildlife in the form of giant earthworms over three metres long, about two-and-a-half centimetres in diameter and covered in fine bristles. They generally burrow deeply but in the cool of winter come closer to the surface. These creatures have a distinctive smell; early settlers tried to feed them to their poultry without success. Live Gippsland earthworms, said to be the world's largest species, are displayed in captivity at a wormery outside Bass (see *Wonthaggi & Cowes*). *Population 2910*

COAL CREEK HISTORICAL PARK The park recreates the Korumburra of the 1890s. There is a tunnel from the Coal Creek mine, a poppet head and more than thirty restored buildings as well as an authentic wattle and daub hut from 1842.

FESTIVALS Karmai Giant Worm Festival, March.

LEONGATHA ■ 886

South Gippsland's economy has always depended heavily on dairying. Many of the gold fossickers who beat through the bush to Mount Eccles, north of Leongatha, stayed on because they were able to take up farms. They banded into small co-operatives – three or four families working together to clear the 130-hectare holdings and build rough wooden cottages; then driving in cattle from the markets at Warragul and Yarragon. The co-operative approach persisted – from 1893 to 1904, 6000 men who had been unable to find work staffed the Leongatha labour colony, clearing and farming land.

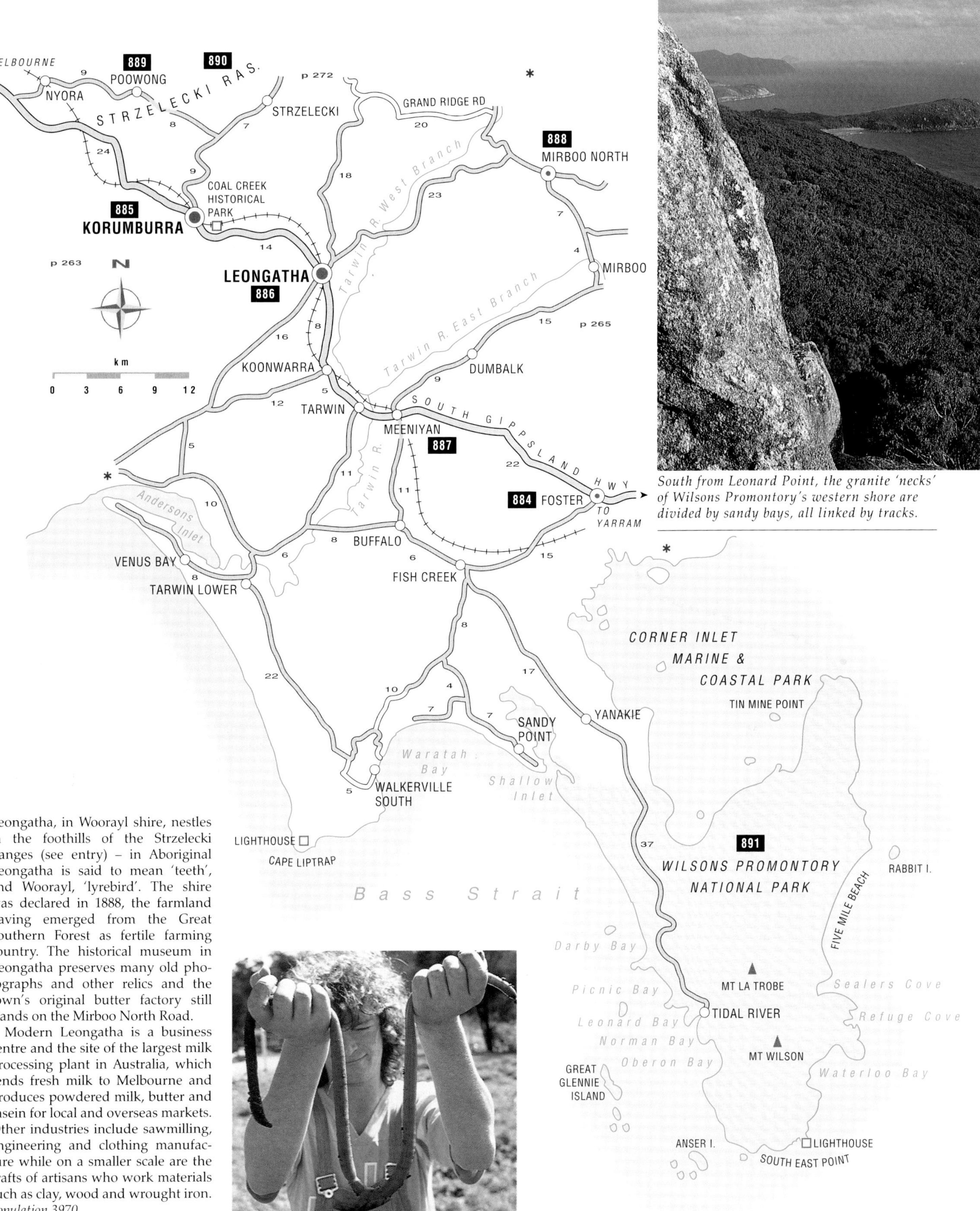

South from Leonard Point, the granite 'necks' of Wilsons Promontory's western shore are divided by sandy bays, all linked by tracks.

Even an early bird would have trouble coping with a Gippsland worm, an inhabitant of the moist hillsides of the southern Strzeleckis.

Leongatha, in Woorayl shire, nestles in the foothills of the Strzelecki Ranges (see entry) – in Aboriginal Leongatha is said to mean 'teeth', and Woorayl, 'lyrebird'. The shire was declared in 1888, the farmland having emerged from the Great Southern Forest as fertile farming country. The historical museum in Leongatha preserves many old photographs and other relics and the town's original butter factory still stands on the Mirboo North Road.

Modern Leongatha is a business centre and the site of the largest milk processing plant in Australia, which sends fresh milk to Melbourne and produces powdered milk, butter and casein for local and overseas markets. Other industries include sawmilling, engineering and clothing manufacture while on a smaller scale are the crafts of artisans who work materials such as clay, wood and wrought iron. *Population 3970*

MOSS VALE PARK This five-hectare stretch of parkland planted with European trees and shrubs is south of Leongatha along the road to the coast. It is a tranquil setting for an annual music recital in Feburary.

FESTIVALS Daffodil Festival, early September.

MEENIYAN ■ 887

Meeniyan is believed to be an Aboriginal word meaning 'moon behind the trees over the water'; the meaning is reflected in the town's logo which shows exactly that! Known locally as 'The Turning Point', Meeniyan is the junction for travellers on their way to Wilsons Promontory via Fish Creek or taking the scenic South Gippsland Highway route to Foster.

MIRBOO NORTH ■ 888

The Grand Ridge Road runs through Mirboo North. High rainfall and fertile soils have encouraged successful dairying, stockraising and potato growing. Hundreds of varieties of gladioli bloom between December and May in the Karandra Gladioli Gardens. Mirboo North is famous for its 'traditional' beers and at least five local beers are made at the Grand Ridge Brewery. One, called 'Moonshine,' is an extra strong malt beer with an alcohol content of eight-and-a-half per cent which is likened to Scottish ale. *Population 1230*

FESTIVALS St Paul's Festival, March.

POOWONG ■ 889

Poowong is another dairying town where the early settlement grew up as a centre for the surrounding land development. The 1869 Land Act provided for selection without survey and tempted many adventurous or desperate but usually inexperienced settlers to try their luck beyond the city. Their lives were all hard physical labour – tree felling and clearing scrub. Timber was used to fence pastures and build slab or log dwellings. Two kilometres west of Poowong, on a high ridge with breathtaking views, stands a rare and well-preserved example of one of these cottages built around 1880.

The sometimes controversial political journalist Wilfred Burchett came from a pioneering Poowong family and he described his boyhood in the town in his autobiography, *Passport*.

STRZELECKI RANGES ■ 890

The Strzelecki Ranges were named after the Polish explorer, Paul Edmund de Strzelecki, who led a party through these densely forested hills in 1840. Strzelecki is sometimes mistakenly credited with discovering Gippsland because he was first to report his finds but Angus McMillan was there before him and called the area 'Caledonia Australis' – Scotland in the south. Strzelecki took the liberty of changing this name to commemorate his friendship with Governor George Gipps.

The ranges rise between 300 to 500 metres and are formed of sandstone in a triangular shape, with the highway between Drouin and Sale at the base and Wilsons Promontory at the apex. Clearing began here in the late nineteenth century and it took two generations to remove the huge mountain ash trees. Soldier-farmers back from the First World War made a final attempt to tame the land but they could not use their machinery on the steep eastern slopes.

In her 1926 novel, *Robin*, Mary Grant Bruce described 'the ceaseless war against bracken fern and rabbits: paddocks littered with dry, cut ferns showed a fresh crop of green fronds starting vigorously to replace them'. The wheel soon came full circle; in the 1950s, the Forestry Commission began to acquire land for reafforestation and now there are forests of mountain ash and radiata pine.

THE GRAND RIDGE ROAD This spectacular roadway twists and turns through dramatic scenery for more than 130 kilometres from Nyora to Currajung (see *Traralgon & Morwell*). The Tarra-Bulga National Park boasts stands of original rainforest along the way (see Mirboo North).

WILSONS PROMONTORY NATIONAL PARK ■ 891

Wilsons Promontory is the most southerly point on the mainland. Shaped like a giant hook, it juts into Bass Strait to form a natural breakwater with surf pounding on the western side and sheltered beaches on the east. The mountainous windswept 'Prom' is grey granite massif composed mainly of quartz, pink and white feldspar and black mica.

Aborigines have left their kitchen middens dating back 6800 years and in the nineteenth century, hardy sealers used the promontory as a base. There was timber-cutting as well as attempts to raise cattle, and finds of tin led to a brief mining venture near Mount Hunter. Then in 1905, the greater part of the peninsula, excluding the shoreline was proclaimed a national park. The area was later extended and now covers about 49 000 hectares. Hundreds of species of flowering plants and many native animals are protected within this ruggedly beautiful sanctuary.

A casually doused billy fire in 1951 resulted in a disastrous bushfire and there are strict rules for visitors. Cars can be taken as far as Tidal River where there are tent sites and cabins. The park is crisscrossed with tracks but walks as well as camp sites must be booked at peak times. The easiest hike is the Lilly Pilly Gully nature walk; the longest track leads to the 1859 lighthouse on South East Point.

Wilsons Promontory is such a drawcard that overnight hikers must book ahead; those who make the short trek to Oberon Bay are dwarfed by the colossal cliffs.

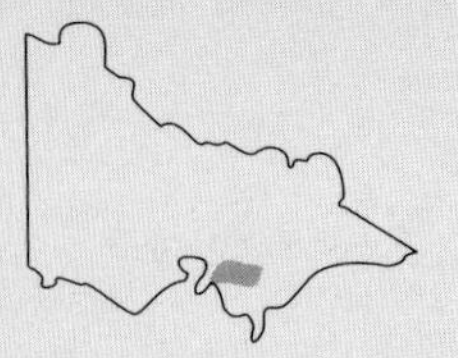

Moe & Warragul

The La Trobe Valley, holding one of the largest deposits of brown coal in the world, is the heartland of Victoria's electricity generation operations. As a contrast, there are fine cheeses and other gourmet foods to be sampled in this district, one that has long been important for dairying and agriculture.

BLUE ROCK LAKE ■ 892

This 200 000-megalitre lake, about 130 kilometres south-east of Melbourne, is contained by a dam at its southern end. Parklands have been developed for picnicking, swimming, fishing and sailing, and evidence of former mining days can be seen around the entire lake. A wide variety of birds and mammals inhabit the area including platypuses, gliders and bandicoots. Nearby is the little village of Willow Grove.

BUNYIP ■ 893

This village in the fruit-growing district of Gippsland is named after a water-dwelling monster, variously named by the Aboriginal peoples of eastern Australia. The animal was believed to prey on humans and devour them, particularly women and children. Its call was said to be a loud, booming sound. Aborigines in the eastern states have made drawings of the creature at some time or other – although no two drawings are alike. Sightings by white settlers in the nineteenth century were unable to be substantiated, and some zoologists now claim the legend of the bunyip is possibly derived from the appearance of seals, not only on the coast but inland as well.

The name Bunyeep Bunyeep or Bunyip Bunyip was given to a sheep run established here in 1851. Bunyip is also the name of a nearby river. *Population 985*

DROUIN ■ 894

Drouin, in the heart of a dairy district, is the site of one of the largest milk-processing factories in Australia. The surrounding area is known for its production of fine foods, and a sign-posted 'gourmet trail' drive draws tourists' attention to fruit and berry farms, cheese factories, a meat smokehouse, deer farms and a variety of restaurants. The Robin Hood Hotel at Drouin West, built in 1877, was once a Cobb & Co. staging post. The town is also known for the spectacular displays of red blooms which appear each summer on its street plantings of flowering gum trees. *Population 4460*

GARFIELD ■ 895

Garfield is a small central Gippsland town which serves as a commercial centre for the surrounding farming district. Until 1887, the settlement here was known as Cannibal Creek, perhaps from 'kanni' the local Aboriginal word for 'man'. It was renamed to honour United States' President James Garfield who was assassinated in 1881. *Population 680*

GEMBROOK ■ 896

This small township was once the starting point for the narrow-gauge branch line that for more than half-a-century huffed and puffed its way into the Dandenong Ranges (see box). It is surrounded by the fertile plains of a pastoral and agricultural district, and present-day industries include potato growing, sawmilling and dairying. *Population 670*

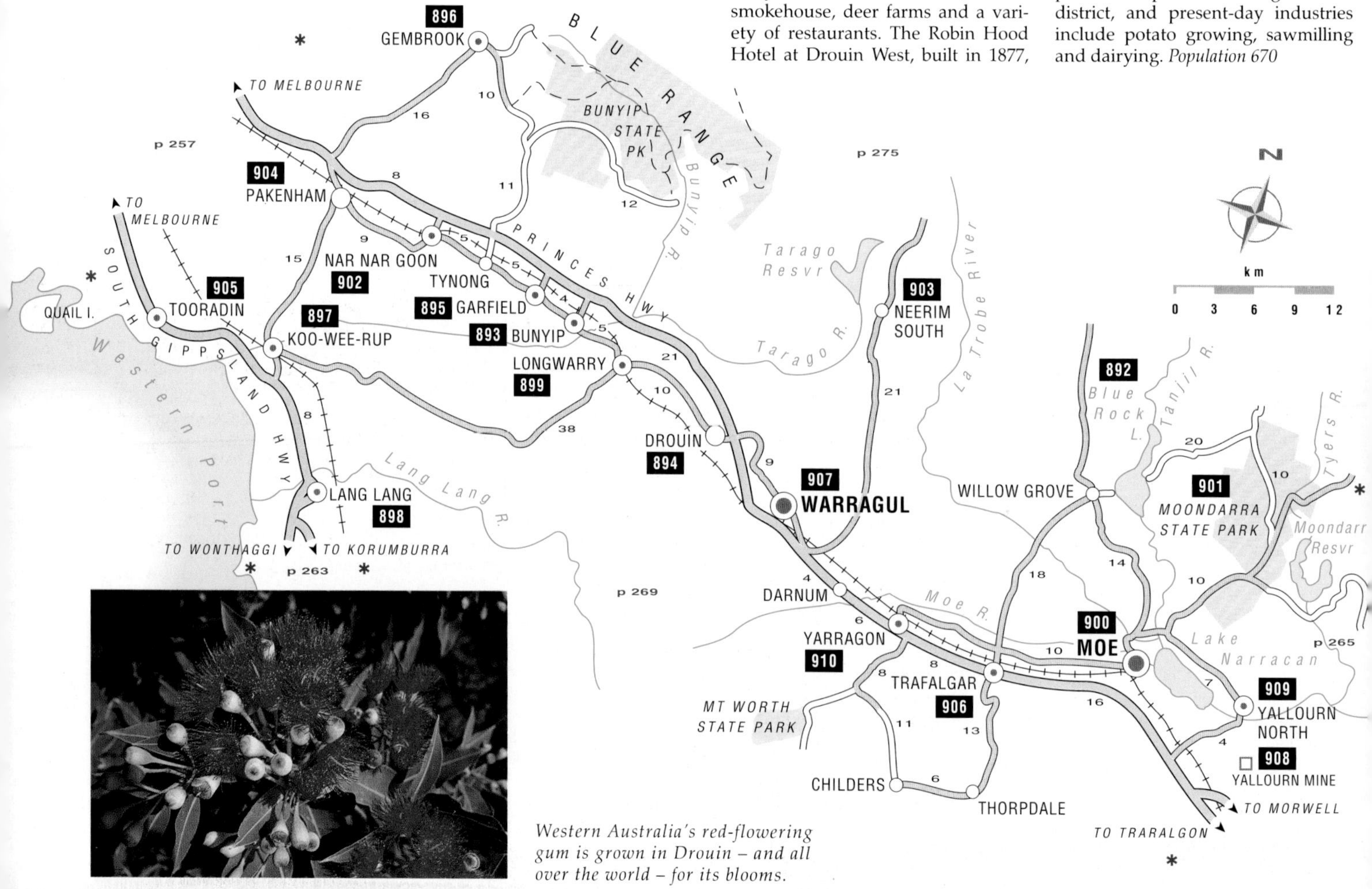

Western Australia's red-flowering gum is grown in Drouin – and all over the world – for its blooms.

The Yallourn coal mine dredges have a voracious appetite – even Yallourn township was long ago swallowed up by this 9-square-kilometre excavation.

KOO-WEE-RUP ■ **897**

The area around Koo-wee-rup was opened for settlement in the 1870s, and this small town now stands on fertile, reclaimed swampland. The name of the town is thought to be a corruption of an Aboriginal word for 'blackfish swimming'. Potatoes, vegetables – mostly for canning – and dairy farming are now the main agricultural industries carried out on this former swampland, drained by the extensive earthworks which take run-off water into Western Port. Emus, kangaroos, deer and a variety of bird life can be seen in Bayles Fauna Park, which incorporates a once-busy railway station, now surrounded by dense bushland.

Bunurong Aborigines were the inhabitants of the district when William Hovell tramped through this region – noting the Koo-wee-rup Swamp – in 1826, a year after his celebrated Sydney-Port Phillip cross-country walk with Hamilton Hume. *Population 1110*

FESTIVALS Potato Festival, March.

LANG LANG ■ **898**

This spot was originally known as Tobin Yallock and in the 1860s was the starting point of a two-metre wide pack-track, cut to encourage settlement of the hinterland, which ran from here to Moe. The track was little used, however, as it ran along the ridges, and water necessary for the team animals lay in the difficult to reach gullies. In the 1890s, the area was known both as Carrington and Proctors Plains. *Population 700*

LONGWARRY ■ **899**

Longwarry is a small agricultural township in the fine-food producing region of central Gippsland. The town founders took its name in the late 1860s from a sheep run – established in 1857 – called after an Aboriginal word said to mean 'divided waterhole'. As its name suggests, the nearby Picnic Point Reserve, by the Tarago River, is a popular recreation spot. *Population 600*

MOE ■ **900**

The meaning and origin of the name of this busy Gippsland industrial city – pronounced 'mowee' – is uncertain although many theories have been suggested. The common view is that it comes from an Aboriginal word, 'moia' or 'mouay' which is said to mean 'muddy' and referred to the Moe swamp which lay between the Great Dividing Range to the north and Strzelecki Range to the south.

In 1846, Henry Scott became the first white settler when he took up a pastoral holding of some 9000 hectares and named it Merton Rush. His holding extended from the eastern bank of Narracan Creek to the western bank of the Morwell river. In 1853, this property passed into the hands of William Robert Farley who held it as a pastoral lease until 1859. Numerous small villages had sprung up in the area by the 1870s, but it was not until the coming of the railway in 1878 that they gained any degree of permanence.

Moe is today the chief residential area for the brown coal industry of the La Trobe Valley, particularly since the town of Yallourn was reclaimed for open-cut mining. The city now includes the suburbs of Moe West, Newborough, Newborough East and Newborough North.

Brown coal from the nearby Yallourn, Morwell and Yallourn North mines is used to produce electricity at Yallourn, Morwell and the nearby Hazelwood power station. Other important industries include the processing of dairy products, textile milling, clothing manufacture and food and chemical manufacturing. *Population 17 990*

OLD GIPPSTOWN This living museum set in three hectares of parkland is a collection of old Gippsland buildings which has been developed as a pioneer village. A highlight is the McMillan Homestead from Bushy Park, the home of Angus McMillan, the explorer who opened up the Gippsland region. 'Loren', a house brought from North Melbourne, is a prefabricated iron building of a type imported during the gold-rush days, and is one of the few examples in good condition still in existence.

LAKE NARRACAN To the north – about five minutes by car from Moe – is Lake Narracan. The lake's foreshores have been set aside as parkland for picnicking, and provide a popular spot for camping, swimming, boating and waterskiing.

MOONDARRA STATE PARK ■ **901**

On the the northern edge of the La Trobe Valley, about 160 kilometres from Melbourne, is the 6000-hectare Moondarra State Park. It has extensive areas of forest and woodland with large stands of silver-tip, messmate, stringy-bark and broad-leaf peppermint. The park is also renowned for its spectacular displays of wildflowers – the most popular time to visit is spring and autumn – particularly along Sennis Road where more than fifteen species of orchid have been found. The old Moe to Walhalla railway line (see box) ran through this park. Wildlife includes koalas – which were reintroduced to this region – echidnas, bandicoots, possums, gliders and a number of reptiles.

NAR NAR GOON ■ **902**

This township is said to take its unusual name from a local Aboriginal word for 'koala', and is a reminder that the animals once lived in large numbers in the tall eucalypt forests which covered these lands in the days before European settlement. When their habitat was removed to provide pastures for dairy cattle, koala populations dwindled rapidly. *Population 630*

NEERIM SOUTH ■ **903**

Gippsland Blue cheese, Australia's only 'farmhouse' blue – where farm and factory are combined – is made here. The factory makes a variety of other farmhouse cheeses including multiple-cream bries. Visitors can watch the cheesemaking through windows and later sample the wares.

PAKENHAM ■ **904**

Pakenham is the administrative and industrial centre for the surrounding dairy, livestock and fruit growing area. The town was named after General Pakenham, a hero of the Crimean war. The district was proclaimed a shire in 1868 and it took the name Shire of Pakenham after the separation in 1973 from the city of Berwick. Pakenham is a centre for sky diving and popular 'gallops' are held regularly at the Pakenham racecourse. *Population 5850.*

FESTIVALS Yakkerboo Festival, mid-March; Agricultural Show, March.

TOORADIN ■ **905**

Built on reclaimed swampland on an inlet beside Western Port, the village of Tooradin came into existence as a small port to serve settlers on the surrounding farmlands and is now a popular spot for fishing and boating. The name – supposedly an Aboriginal word for 'monster' – refers to a creature believed to dwell in a deep hole here. *Population 670*

TRAFALGAR ■ **906**

This town, in the centre of a lush dairy district, was named after the famous naval battle off the south-western coast of Spain, where in 1805 Lord Nelson led the British to victory over the French and Spanish fleets. Trafalgar was founded in 1878 and is the headquarters of the Narracan Shire. *Population 2150*

WARRAGUL ■ **907**

William Pearson is thought to have named the first settlement here – it was known as Brandy Creek or Brandy Hot – when he flung an empty brandy bottle into a nearby stream. The Aboriginal word 'warragul' means 'wild' and the district certainly was one of the last in Victoria to be settled, as the dense bush on hills and gullies intimidated settlers looking for new land.

The first landowner was Thomas Walton who bought all of the land

Rural buildings carried in from all over Gippsland make up Old Gippstown at Moe; the iron house (centre) originally came in 'kit' form from England.

between Bunyip and Brandy Creek for forty-five pounds sterling and later declared, as the district was mostly swamp, that it 'wasn't worth forty-five pence!'.

Although a steady stream of settlers began to arrive after the passing of the 1869 Land Act the area didn't really begin to develop until the 1880s when the railway was built. The area is now the centre of a fertile fruit-growing and dairying district and a major supplier of milk to Melbourne. Some timber milling is also carried out, and other local industries include the manufacture of clothing, linen thread and rope. Warragul is also an important marketing centre for agricultural produce and livestock. There is a splendid wildflower sanctuary at Labertouche and nature reserves at Glen Cromie and Glen Nayook. *Population 8910*

MOUNT WORTH STATE PARK This state park protects nearly 1000 hectares of natural forest, some of which is a fine example of the dense forest which once covered the western Strzelecki Ranges. A major replanting program of mountain ash and mountain grey gum is now being undertaken. Lookouts give panoramic views of the La Trobe Valley and the Great Dividing Range to the north. More than ninety bird species have been recorded in the park.

DARNUM MUSICAL VILLAGE An old church, part of a complex of historic buildings off the Princes Highway, is now the resting place for a large display of antique and modern musical instruments collected by Gippsland piano-tuner Albert Fox.

YALLOURN MINE ■ 908

Yallourn lies in the heart of the La Trobe Valley, where one of the largest deposits of brown coal in the world, a belt some sixteen kilometres wide and one hundred metres or more thick, stretches for sixty kilometres. Here massive bucket-wheel dredges, twelve storeys high, scoop up 30 000 tonnes of coal a day from the vast open-cut mine. This is taken by train to fuel the numerous electricity power stations which dot the valley and supply more than ninety per cent of Victoria's power needs. Brown coal is also processed into briquettes. The mine can be viewed from the Newborough Lookout.

The huge hole that is the open-cut mine stands on the site of the former Yallourn township – a model town built to house power station and mine workers and for many years the key centre for the mining and electricity operations of the La Trobe Valley. Construction of the town – planned, owned and administered by the State Electricity Commission – began in the 1920s. It was noted for its large parks and gardens and high gabled buildings, which gave it the appearance of an English 'garden' town, and its generous provision of children's playgrounds and sportsfields. In 1969, the commission began moving residents out of the town in order to gain access to the rich coal seams on which it stood and by 1982 its demolition was complete.

YALLOURN NORTH ■ 909

North of the now-vanished Yallourn township, Yallourn North has taken over the old town's function of housing many of the mine and power house workers. The town was established in 1947 and is named after an Aboriginal word said to mean 'ever-burning'. *Population 22 340*

YARRAGON ■ 910

The township of Yarragon specialises in the wares, crafts and trimmings of bygone days. Its commercial streetscape presents a colonial front, with old buildings restored and new shops built to match. Available here are antique and reproduction furniture and fittings, craftworks and also specialist foods from the surrounding agricultural and dairying district. *Population 710*

UP HILL AND DOWN DALE BY STEAM

IN THE wake of the economic depression of the 1890s, the government of Victoria decided on a novel economy. The gauge, or width between the lines, of some of the state railway system would be halved to 76 centimetres instead of the 160-centimetre gauge already established in the colony thus reducing greatly the area of land to be cleared for track laying.

The narrow gauge was particularly appropriate for branch railways in hilly country and four such lines were eventually built – from Wangaratta along the King River Valley to Whitfield, from Ferntree Gully to Gembrook in the Dandenongs, from Moe to Walhalla in Gippsland and from Colac to Beech Ranges in the Otway Ranges.

The Gembrook line was opened in 1900 and operated until 1953, providing rail access for tourists to the Dandenongs. Of its original twenty-nine kilometres, a stretch of about six kilometres from Belgrave to the Upper Ferntree Gully terminal has been retained for special excursions, and here 'Puffing Billy' chugs and toots as in days of old from the ferns and rainforest of Sherbrook Forest to the farmlands of the valley.

The forty-kilometre Moe to Walhalla line, the last to be built, has the most spectacular setting. Its final few kilometres, cut into sheer slopes, wind around steep hillsides, and high wooden trestle bridges carry the track over fern-filled gorges. Gold mining and timber milling in the Walhalla region necessitated the building of the railway and construction began in 1904. Walhalla was brightly decorated for the occasion and a holiday declared for the opening of the line in May 1910. The railway served the area until 1944 when a dwindling population and the decline of industry led to its closure. Some sections, such as that to Erica, remained in operation until the entire line was dismantled in the 1950s. It is said that lyrebirds in the surrounding forest were able to mimic the sound of the train's whistle long after the line closed – often startling passing motorists.

Attempts were made to have some of the old track preserved as an excursion route, but unlike 'Puffing Billy' at Gembrook, it was unsuccessful, largely because of lack of resources, distance from Melbourne and the sadly neglected state of the line. The railway museum at Erica, some forty kilometres north of Moe and once a station on the line, houses steam-age memorabilia including lamps, scales and signs. □

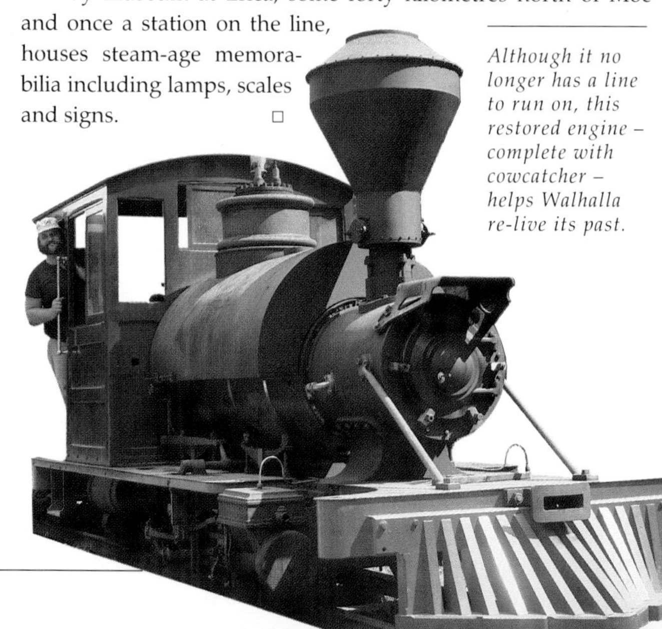
Although it no longer has a line to run on, this restored engine – complete with cowcatcher – helps Walhalla re-live its past.

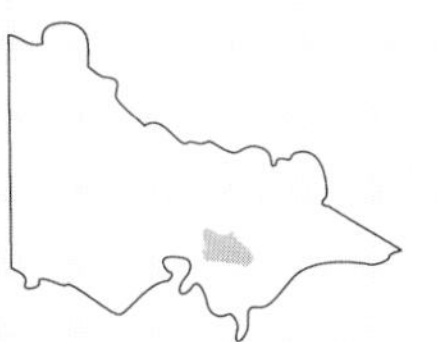

Healesville & Warburton

Much of this region was founded on gold mining during the 1850s and 1860s, but the presence of the heavily forested slopes of the Great Dividing Range led to the growth of a more enduring enterprise in the timber industry. But scenic beauty is the region's greatest asset as the many twentieth-century tourists will attest.

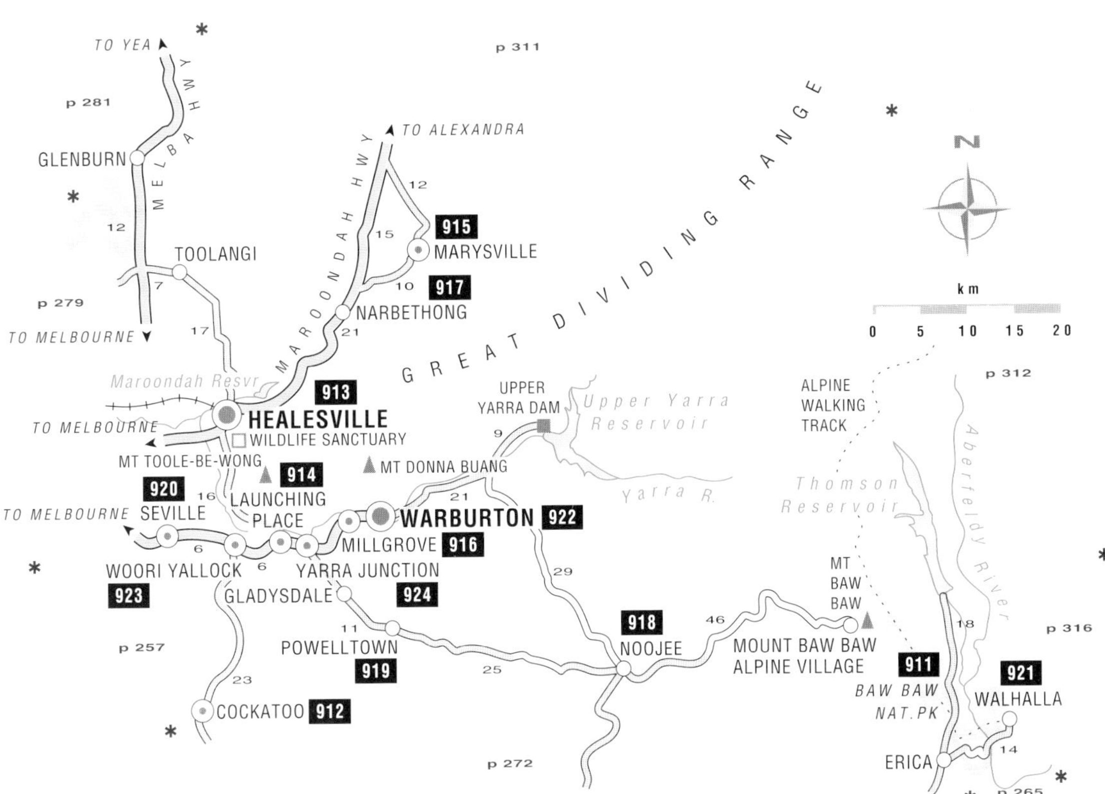

The foothills of the Great Dividing Range begin to fade out near Erica, on the fringe of the Baw Baw National Park.

BAW BAW NATIONAL PARK ■ 911

This 13 300-hectare park takes in most of the granite Baw Baw plateau, an area of heathland and forests in which gold was discovered in 1859. The Baw Baw park also contains sections of the Aberfeldy and Thomson river valleys and eight peaks. The highest point is Mt St Phillack, at 1566 metres.

From late June to early September, the park becomes a region of broad snowplains. Ski touring is popular and there are downhill skiing facilities too. Bushwalking, canoeing, fishing and horse riding are popular pursuits when the snow has melted.

The 400-kilometre Alpine Walking Track, which extends from Walhalla to the New South Wales border near Tom Groggin, crosses the national park. The track crosses some of Victoria's most rugged alpine regions, and provides a challenging trek for experienced walkers only.

MOUNT BAW ALPINE VILLAGE This ski village is a relatively modern settlement, the access road having been completed in 1963. The resort is close to the skifields and is composed mainly of ski lodges.

COCKATOO ■ 912

This village on the banks of Cockatoo Creek, between Gembrook and Emerald, was so-named by gold diggers in 1859 because of to the profusion of cockatoos here. A nearby attraction is the Bimbimbie Wildlife and Picnic Park and the region is popular with bushwalkers. *Population 2850*

Sturdy conifers act as windbreaks between fields of grape hyacinths and daffodils on a flower farm at Toolangi.

HEALESVILLE ■ 913

Healesville is blessed with the finest of locations at the junction of Grace Burn Creek and the Watts River, with the forest-clad foothills of the Great Dividing Range all around. The railway from Melbourne opened in 1889 and Healesville has been a summer resort for the city since the beginning of the century with one of the main attractions of modern times being the town's famous wildlife sanctuary.

Sheep farmers, in the late 1840s, were followed by timber cutters in the 1860s; their town was named after Sir Richard Heales, the Premier of Victoria from 1860 to 1861. Gold mining was a major preoccupation of many people from the mid-1880s to the turn of the century but since that time the main pursuits have been agricultural. Timber, cattle and vegetable- and fruit-growing are the major industries. There are also several wine-making establishments in the region, including Chum Creek Winery and Long Gully Estate.

The area has an interesting Aboriginal history and the Coranderrk Aboriginal Cemetery contains a monument to the last leader of the Yarra Yarra people. Healesville is also a popular base for bushwalkers setting out to Mount St Leonard, Badger Weir and Graceburn Weir. *Population 6260*

HEALESVILLE FAUNA PARK This internationally famous animal reserve contains more than 200 species of Australian birds, mammals and reptiles; it occupies a little-disturbed setting of gum trees and ferns. There is also a Nocturnal House which displays a variety of small animals in simulated night-time conditions. For over 50 years, the sanctuary has been involved in breeding programs for a number of endangered species, as well as research projects aimed at providing a better understanding of Australia's wildlife.

MAROONDAH RESERVOIR Just to the north-east of Healesville, this lake and the dam which made it possible came into being between 1919 and 1927 and today the reservoir supplies Melbourne with much of its water supply. The 40-metre-high dam is almost 300 metres long and is adjacent to a landscaped reserve which contains exotic and native trees, picnic areas and barbecue facilities.

TOOLANGI North of Healesville is Toolangi, the home of the poet C.J. Dennis from 1908 to his death in 1938. There is a cairn dedicated to his memory. Walks can be taken through the nearby Toolangi State Forest.

LAUNCHING PLACE ■ 914

This holiday town was one of the Upper Yarra Valley's earliest settlements, and developed as the place for gold-miners and settlers to cross the Yarra by punt. The name literally describes the location as it was then, a place for launching punts for trips either upriver to the gold diggings, or downstream to Melbourne. The settlement's Home Hotel dates from 1865, when it was a bark and slab-timber building. Visitors are drawn here by the nearby trout fishing streams, as well as for horse riding and bushwalks. *Population 1520*

HODDLES CREEK Nearby, the small town of Hoddles Creek is named after the explorer, surveyor and planner of Melbourne, Robert Hoddle, who led an expedition to the headwaters of the River Yarra in 1845. Hoddle produced the first maps of the region. The town was once a thriving gold-mining centre which boasted six hotels and contained more than 3000 miners, including many Chinese, by the turn of the century. The region now grows timber and supports orchards, vineyards and plant nurseries.

MARYSVILLE ■ 915

Located 500 metres above sea level in a narrow valley of the Great Dividing Range, Marysville was named after Mary, the wife of surveyor John Steavenson. Gold was found at nearby Cumberland Creek in 1863, when the town was established, and the site became an important provisioning and stopping place on the Yarra Track for gold prospectors on their way to the prosperous Woods Point goldfields, further east.

The Australian Hotel - now the Marysville Hotel – opened in 1863; a post office established in 1865; and a school opened in 1870. By the 1890s, the town had four hotels and in the 1920s there were twelve guesthouses. By 1914, the miners had moved on and those who remained turned to timber and cattle to earn their living. Sawmilling began in 1910 and continues, concentrating on hardwoods such as woolly butt, white mountain ash and peppermint.

Set in wooded hills, with a cool climate, Marysville has maintained its role as a resort and there are still guesthouses here, now complemented by hotels and lodges. Horse riding, golf and fishing are popular and nearby attractions include the Steavenson Falls – at more than eighty metres Victoria's tallest – and Keppels Lookout. *Population 660*

LAKE MOUNTAIN ALPINE RESERVE To the east of Marysville, this reserve contains a rich display of alpine and sub-alpine flora, particularly wildflowers, and is a popular hunting ground for botanists. The region is blanketed in snow during most of the winter months and the cross-country skiing, along marked Nordic trails, is generally considered to be some of the best outside Scandinavia! There is even tobogganing on established runs.

MILLGROVE ■ 916

Millgrove, in the Upper Yarra Shire, is just a few kilometres west of Warburton. It once had a timber mill, but the main attraction today is a trout farm, where visitors can purchase a freshly caught fish or dangle a line and hope for something even fresher! *Population 1710*

NARBETHONG ■ 917

Narbethong is on the banks of Fishers Creek, south-west of Marysville, and is said to be named after an Aboriginal word for 'a cheerful place'. It was named by the surveyor John Wrigglesworth in 1865. This region contains 'The Hermitage', a group of buildings which were erected by photographer John William Lindt in the 1890s and which have since become part of a mountain retreat surrounded by landscaped gardens.

NOOJEE ■ 918

Farming and timber milling are the main occupations at Noojee, not surprising given its location in the mountain ash forests at the junction of the La Trobe and Loch rivers. It has three times been devastated by bushfires – in 1926, 1939 and 1983. Nearby scenic attractions include the Toorongo Falls, Tarago Reservoir and Glen Nayook Reserve. Further afield lies Mount Baw Baw, and Noojee provides accommodation for the resort's overflow of skiers in winter .

POWELLTOWN ■ 919

Powelltown is named after the Powell Company's wood processing works, which were once located here. The settlement, which is surrounded by forests of mountain ash, still contains a large sawmill, but at one stage this was the site of Australia's largest timber processing plant, with timber being shipped out of the region through Yarra Junction. A web of tramlines and trestle bridges crossing rivers and streams laced the forests and were the chief means of transporting timber from the forest to the railheads or jetties.

Originally, horses pulled heavy loads of timber along these narrow-gauge, wooden tramlines but were replaced by steam engines in 1915. In their turn, steam engines and tramlines have given way to trucks and improved roads. The 1939 Black Friday bushfires which swept through the area wiped out much of the timber supply and consumed much of the old tramline network. From Powelltown there is a 36-kilometre walking track to East Warburton, which follows the path of the old timber tramlines.

THE ADA TREE This giant mountain ash north-east of Powelltown by the headwaters of the Little Ada River is the most senior of citizens in the surrounding rainforest, being estimated at 300 years old; it reaches a height of 76 metres, with a circumference of 15 metres just above the ground.

SEVILLE ■ 920

Seville is named after an early resident, Miss Seville Smith. The town lies at the centre of a fruit, berry and vine-growing area: wineries in the region include Lillydale Vineyards and Oakridge Estate. *Population 1480*

WALHALLA ■ 921

Modern Walhalla verges on being a ghost town but it once had more than 4000 residents and was the location of Victoria's richest gold mine. The discovery of alluvial gold was made by Edward Stringer and his fellow prospectors in December 1862. A gold rush began almost immediately and the source of the precious mineral, Cohens Reef, proved to be one of Australia's richest pockets of gold and was mined by several large companies for fifty years. The settlement was first named Stringers Creek, but this was changed to Walhalla in 1869, from the Walhalla Mining Co. which had named itself after the legendary, final dwelling place of the Norse gods.

The forests in the region were well utilised, providing some 34 000 tonnes of wood for the mines, and tramways were constructed to transport the timber. During the 1880s and 1890s, Walhalla had forty shops, many hotels, two banks, a post office, police station, four churches and a Mechanics Institute. A narrow gauge railway from Moe arrived in 1910 and ironically, the major mining operation, the Long Tunnel Extended Mine, closed a year later. By 1920, the population had fallen to around 250 as miners moved on.

Only a handful of people live in modern Walhalla, but the town still contains the 1865 bakery, 1886 post office, 1896 bandstand and many National Trust-listed buildings. Visitors can visit the museum, fossick for gold in Stringers Creek and fish for trout in the nearby Aberfeldy and Thomson rivers.

At the tiny hamlet of Aberfeldy a few kilometres north, is the grave of Kitty Cane, a former dance-hall girl, who ran a small grog shanty near here on her retirement. Local legend has it that on her death she was found to weigh a hefty 153 kilograms and as her pallbearers were unable to carry her into the town of Aberfeldy they buried her here instead.

WARBURTON ■ 922

Warburton is one of the Upper Yarra Valley's most popular destinations. The town was established in 1864 and named after Charles Warburton Carr, the district police magistrate. Gold was discovered here in 1859 and then again in 1863 at a site known as Yankee Jim's Creek – an event which helped maintain the gold fever for several more years.

A guesthouse was opened in Warburton in 1880 and by the turn of the century, many 'tourists' from Melbourne were visiting the town on the coaches that ran along what was then only a rough track. This influx of visitors was boosted by the arrival of the railway from Lilydale in 1901. The logging industry, based on the region's vast stands of mountain ash, had also developed by this time and at one stage as many as five trains a day, carrying both passengers and timber, left Warburton. The railway was closed down in 1965, but the timber milling industry has managed to survive. *Population 2500*

UPPER YARRA RESERVOIR This 750-hectare reservoir and its 90-metre–high dam were constructed between 1947 and 1957 and are the third largest of Melbourne's water suppliers. From its large catchment area, the reservoir's water travels through conduits to Silvan Reservoir, near Lilydale, and then to Melbourne. The surrounding Upper Yarra Reservoir Park, provides twelve hectares of tennis courts, walking trails, barbecue and picnic areas and is a popular recreation spot.

MOUNT DONNA BUANG RESERVE At an altitude of 1275 metres, Mount Donna Buang – originally known as Mount Ackerley – is snow-covered in winter, providing Melbourne with its nearest 'snow' and after good falls tobogganing is popular. In summer, the scenic reserve provides fine walking trails through the forests and spectacular views of the Yarra Valley, the Dandenongs, Cathedral Ranges and the city of Melbourne.

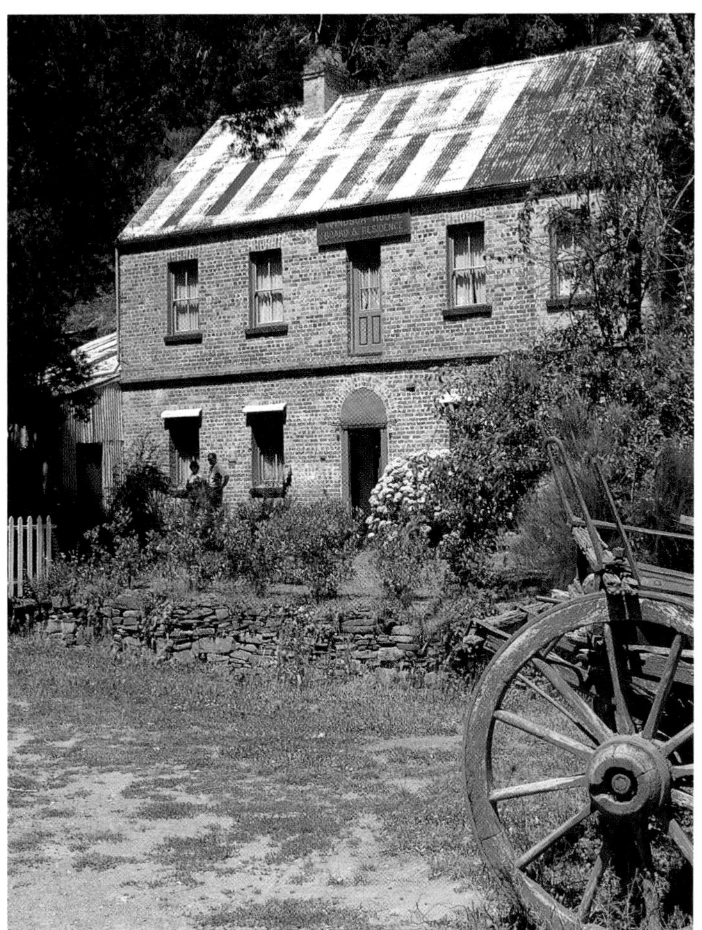

In a region where timber was plentiful, Walhalla's 1890s Windsor House guesthouse achieved instant status as the only brick building in town.

Victoria's endangered animal emblem, Leadbeater's possum, has retreated to reserves in this region.

WOORI YALLOCK ■ 923

This small township in the Upper Yarra Shire was the site of the Upper Yarra's earliest settlement. In 1838, the Ryrie family moved their cattle into the region and began planting grapevine cuttings, giving birth to the now flourishing wine industry. Woori Yallock is the centre of an orchard and farming region, its name said to come from an Aboriginal word for 'swift running creek' or 'plenty of water'. *Population 2390*

YELLINGBO STATE FAUNAL RESERVE At nearby Yellingbo, this open forest reserve is the last known sanctuary of the rare helmeted honeyeater. This endangered bird, the numbers of which have dropped to less than fifty, is found only in Victoria and is the state's bird emblem.

YARRA JUNCTION ■ 924

The place where the Little Yarra meets the Yarra River was once the centre of a massive timber industry. In its heyday, during the early years of this century, more timber passed through Yarra Junction than any other place in the world except Seattle in the United States. The timber industry still operates in the region, although on a much smaller scale, and Yarra Junction is an outlet for wood from the surrounding forests.

Today, the busy little town is also the administrative centre of the Upper Yarra Shire, and the centre of a dairying, cattle grazing and holiday district. The town's Upper Yarra Historical Society Museum contains an comprehensive display of artefacts, clothing and other remnants of the region's gold-mining and timber-cutting past. The collection is housed in the old railway station, which was originally built in 1889 at Lilydale to the west. In 1901, the building was moved to Yarra Junction, an indication of the town's importance as a link on the busy Yarra Junction-Powelltown narrow-gauge railway line. *Population 1950*

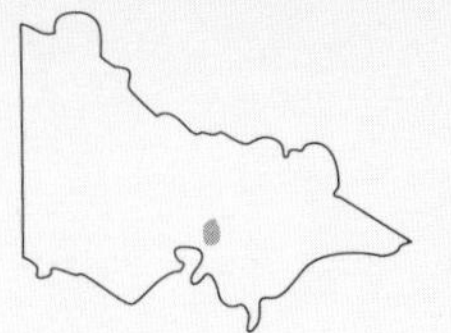

Warrandyte & Hurstbridge

The hills and rivers on the north-eastern outskirts of Melbourne, once part of a busy goldmining field, are now a leading cool-climate wine area where pastoral landscapes border thick eucalypt forests.

ARTHURS CREEK ■ 925
This small township forty kilometres north-east of Melbourne takes its name from squatter Henry Arthur, a nephew of the Lieutenant-Governor of Van Diemen's Land, Sir George Arthur. Novelist Frank Dalby Davidson lived nearby from 1948 until his death in 1970 and it was there that he wrote *The White Thorntree.*

COLDSTREAM ■ 926
Coldstream, once a rural village, is fast becoming an outer suburb of Melbourne. It is situated in a grazing and agricultural district with a long history of wine growing. St Huberts Vineyard, established by Hubert de Castella in the early 1860s had, by the 1890s, become the largest in Australia. Yeringberg Vineyard, nearby, also grew rapidly through the 1850s with the help of more than 10 000 cuttings, mostly from Bordeaux's famous Château Lafite-Rothschild.

By 1889, Yeringberg's wine was good enough to win a gold medal at the Paris Exhibition. Sadly however, by the turn of the century, these and other vineyards were falling victim not only to damaging frosts and the dreaded phylloxera virus but, more significantly, to fickle fashion, as tastes changed from table wines to fortified wines. In 1921, the last remaining vines in the Yarra Valley were uprooted and it was not until the late 1950s, with plantings in Lilydale at the Mount Mary Vineyard, that wine making returned. Coombe Cottage, retreat of Dame Nellie Melba in her later years, is in the village, but is not open to the public. *Population 2160*

HURSTBRIDGE ■ 927
The first settlement here was called Hurst's Bridge, after the Hurst family, early settlers who took up land by Diamond Creek. Henry Facey Hurst was murdered there by a bushranger in October 1866. *Population 2990*

KINGLAKE ■ 928
The surveyor and historian Alexander William Kinglake who, in 1870, surveyed the route from Queenstown across the ranges to Glenburn is commemorated in the name of this township. It boasts a house built entirely of old and modern bottles from around the world, which contains an art and antique collection. Nearby Jehosaphat Gully, in Kinglake National Park, has tracks, picnic sites and, lurking in its ferny glades, lyrebirds. *Population 580*

KINGLAKE NATIONAL PARK ■ 929
Situated on the south-western slopes of the Great Dividing Range, Kinglake is the nearest large national park to Melbourne. There are magnificent views from its ranges over rolling hills and plains down to the outskirts of the city. Eucalypt woodlands, orchids, tree ferns, parrots, lyrebirds and the forty-two-metre high Masons Falls are among the attractions which can be seen from the park's twenty-four walking tracks. Walks range from half-hour strolls to six-hour hikes. Kinglake National Park was established in 1928 and enlarged to its present three-part size of just over 11 000 hectares in 1980.

LILYDALE ■ 930
Now an outer eastern suburb of Melbourne, Lilydale, with nearby Coldstream, was one of the earliest winegrowing areas in Victoria. Vines were planted here by the Swiss brothers Paul and Hubert de Castella – the forebears of marathon runner Robert de Castella – and their fellow countryman Guillaume de Pury. Winemaking and viniculture practices brought by these Swiss pioneers had a great influence on the growth and success of the district.

Lilyvale is also Melba country. Dame Nellie's father David Mitchell, a local businessman, established a limestone quarry on the hill outside the town, had a dairy and bacon factory and also grew grapevines. The legendary singer is buried in the local cemetery – crowds lined the route of her funeral procession from Melbourne to a guard of honour at Lilyvale. The town's museum has a display of Melba memorabilia.

The town was originally named Yering after the pioneering Ryrie brothers' 'Yering' cattle run where the district's first vines were planted in 1838. Confusion surrounds the origin of the name Lilydale. It derives either from Lily, wife of Paul de Castella or from 'Lilly Dale' title of a popular contemporary song, and said to have been suggested to Government Surveyor John Hardy by his departmental superior's wife. To complicate matters further, the shire is spelt 'Lillydale'. Annual events include one of Victoria's largest machinery field days in October, and the Lilydale Show, in November.

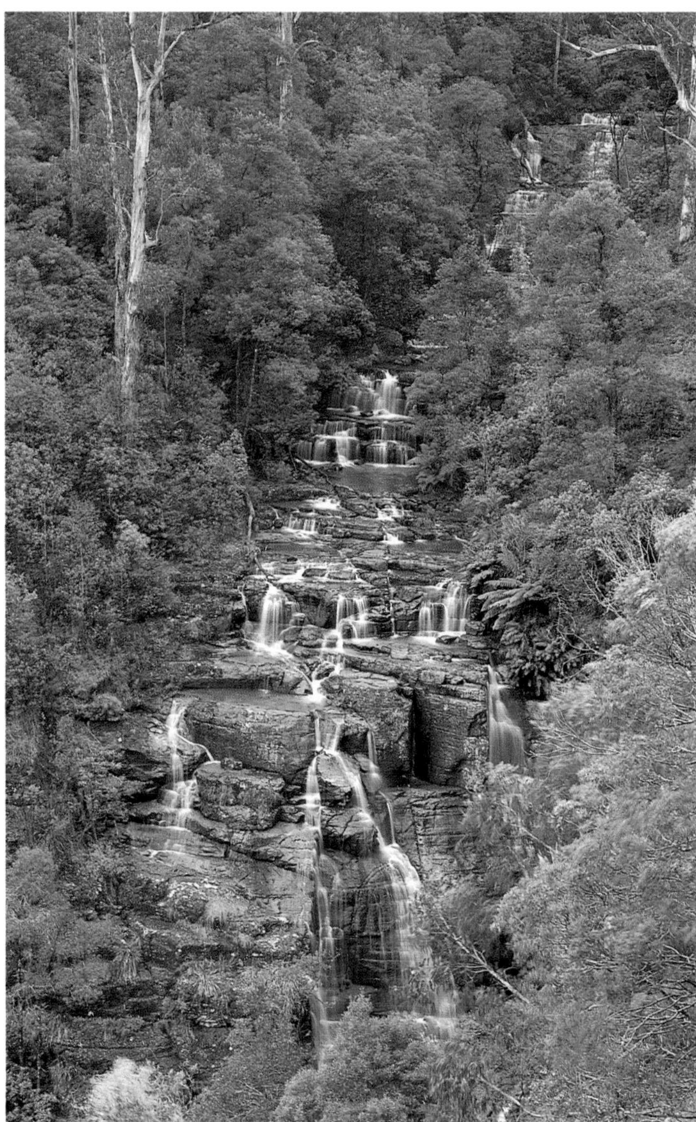

Masons Falls cascades over an extremity of the Great Divide where the range reaches out for Melbourne in the western part of the Kinglake Park.

PANTON HILL ■ 931
Panton Hill is a former goldmining town in the shire of Eltham. The town was first known as Kingstown, but this was changed to honour Joseph Anderson Panton, Goldfields Commissioner for Woods Point, Heidelberg, and Upper Yarra in 1862.

ST ANDREWS ■ 932
The atmosphere of bush and farm is still to be found in this small township in the Diamond Valley. After gold was found here in 1851, the district became known as the Caledonia Diggings, because of the number of Scots on the field. When the gold ran out, agriculture became the mainstay. In the 1960s, artists and craftspeople moved here and a community market was established. The region also has vineyards and berry farms.

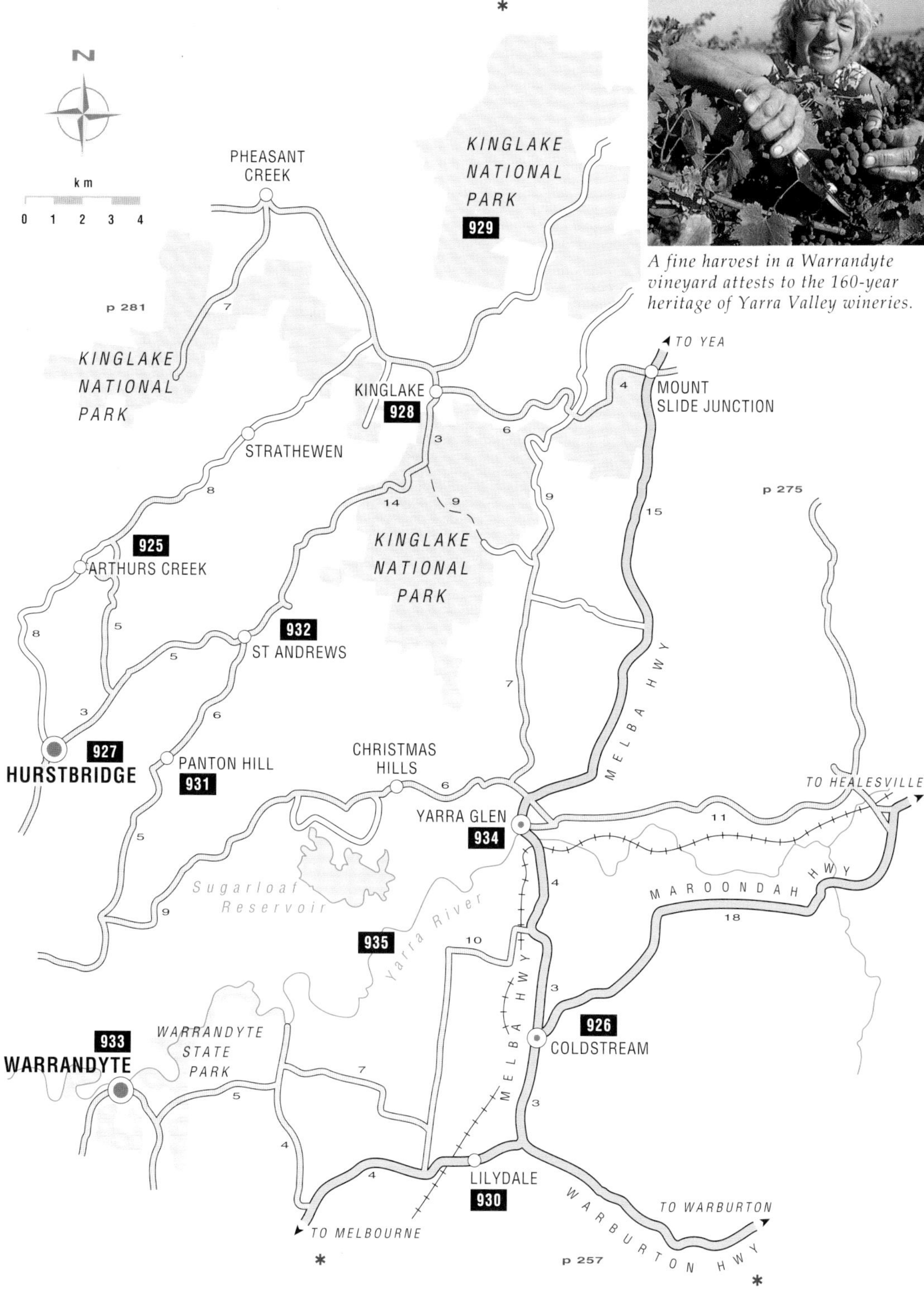

A fine harvest in a Warrandyte vineyard attests to the 160-year heritage of Yarra Valley wineries.

WARRANDYTE ■ 933

An outer eastern suburb of Melbourne on the banks of the Yarra River in the city of Doncaster and Templestowe, Warrandyte has long been known for its artists' colony. Its name, that of an early property in the area, was adopted in 1908 and comes from the local Aboriginal words for 'throw' and 'target', for in the time before European settlement this was a gathering place where boomerang and spear throwing took place. In 1852, a big corroboree took place at Pound Bend.

The first white settler was James Anderson, who established a cattle station to the west of the present town and built a hut and stockyard at the junction of the Yarra River and the creek which now bears his name. When Louis John Mitchel's party discovered gold here at the end of 1851, the area was proclaimed the first goldfield in Victoria and named the Victoria field. However the diggings which quickly sprang up continued to be known as Andersons Creek. When the shallow alluvial gold was exhausted, mining companies were formed to finance the sinking of shafts so the deep reefs could be worked. The mines continued in production until 1913. Over the years, the Warrandyte community has included a colony of artists. Clara Southern, a nineteenth-century painter and pupil of Frederick McCubbin came to live here, as did Penleigh Boyd and potter Reg Preston. *Population 7080*

WARRANDYTE STATE PARK About twenty-four kilometres from Melbourne on a meandering stretch of the Yarra River, this park offers walking tracks and canoeing. Pound Bend Tunnel (see below) and the Caledonian Mine, Warrandyte's largest, are in the park. Boilers which provided steam to operate the mine equipment can still be seen.

POUND BEND TUNNEL This tunnel, dug through 145 metres of rock at a point where the Yarra bends back upon itself, was constructed in 1870 to divert the river and allow its bed to be sluiced for gold.

FESTIVALS Warrandyte Festival, late March.

YARRA GLEN ■ 934

This small, long-established settlement is situated on one of the most attractive reaches of the Yarra and surrounded by agricultural and dairy lands. The town was known as Yarra Flats until 1889. The Grand Hotel, known for its imposing tower and balconies trimmed with wrought-iron lace, opened in 1888. Novelist Joseph Furphy was born in 1843 in a wattle-and-daub hut that stood on the site of the present Yarra Glen school. *Population 1180*

GULF STATION The homestead with outbuildings, some of which date from the 1850s, is being conserved by the National Trust as representative of nineteenth-century farm life. The homestead is not yet open to the public but the original solid timber kitchen, dairy, stables, slaughterhouse, butcher shop, schoolhouse and shearing shed may be inspected. All are made of local gum and stringybark slabs.

YARRA RIVER ■ 935

The Yarra begins its journey as a stream which rises near Mount Baw Baw in the Great Dividing Range and flows some 240 kilometres west and south-west, where it passes through Melbourne and enters the sea by the docklands of Port Phillip Bay. In pre-European times, the river was an important food source for the local Aborigines, its waters providing fish, shellfish and eels, and its fertile banks the yam daisy and a variety of mammals, reptiles and birds – and their eggs.

The first European known to have seen the river was New South Wales Surveyor-General Charles Grimes who came upon it in February 1803 and named it Freshwater Creek. The present name was given by John Helder Wedge while surveying the region for John Batman. It is believed to come from the Aboriginal words 'yarra yarra' – said to mean 'always flowing', and perhaps originally referred specifically to a fast, shallow stretch of the river where Wedge first asked its name. Had he put the question further downstream the answer might have been 'bay-ray-rung' – 'deep water'.

The river was the sole source of Melbourne's water supply for the first twenty or so years of settlement but its waters eventually became heavily polluted by sewage contamination and by clay washed down from farming and logging activities. Its upper reaches still contribute to metropolitan needs.

Craigieburn & Seymour

This region developed around the main routes north out of Port Phillip: as Cobb & Co. expanded its network so more small centres became staging posts on the forerunners of today's highways.

The meandering Goulburn River creates many billabongs and waters many hectares as it winds across Victoria.

AVENEL ■ 936

Henry Kent Hughes called his station 'Avenel' after a village in Gloucestershire in England. He gave his own name to the creek it stood beside. Township blocks were sold around 1847 and Avenel grew as a traffic halt between Melbourne and Albury and as a small farming community. When the railway opened in 1872, it became the loading point for wheat from the Goulburn valley.

Edward Kelly went to school in Avenel until he was eleven and local legend claims young Ned once rescued another boy from drowning in Hughes Creek.

Ned Kelly had to record the death of his father at Avenel court house which still stands by the highway. Another notable structure here is the six-arched, sandstone bridge across Hughes Creek (1859).

BROADFORD ■ 937

Northern Hemisphere names are sprinkled indiscriminately all over Australia reflecting the nostalgia of European pioneers. Broadford is one of them. Some records declare Ray Clark wanted to commemorate his wife's birthplace on the Isle of Skye. Others say Clark never lived at Broadford and that local residents, also natives of Skye: McDonalds, McKenzies, McLeods, McPhersons and others, gave the town its name.

The town's water supply comes from a weir in the surrounding state forest and is noted for its purity. Broadford factories process wool and manufacture clothing, confectionery and paper and there are large deposits of clay which is used to make porcelain. Mount Piper, to the west, is an extinct volcano. *Population 2220*

CRAIGIEBURN ■ 938

Craigieburn, not surprisingly, was settled by Scots too – this time from Dumfries. 'Craigie', or 'creagach', is Gaelic for craggy; the burn was Merri Creek. The Reserve Bank's note printing works are located at Craigieburn. It produced the world's first polymer-plastic currency in the form of Australia's ten-dollar note. Other local factories make bricks, steel pipes and plastics. The town has also developed rapidly as a residential area. *Population 10 100*

GOULBURN RIVER ■ 939

Victoria's most magnificent river, the 560-kilometre-long Goulburn rises in the Great Dividing Range and flows in a north-westerly direction to leave the hills at Seymour. It then flows north to Shepparton and north-west through spectacular meanders to join the Murray just east of Echuca. In 1824, William Hovell and Hamilton Hume crossed this waterway near Yea. First called the Hovell River, the name was later changed to honour the Colonial Secretary, Henry Goulburn. The river is also dammed to help make Lake Eildon and feeds Lake Nagambie behind Goulburn Weir. It irrigates the Goulburn Valley.

KILMORE ■ 940

Two strong reasons for inland settlement were fertile farmland with a good water supply and advantageous placement on a route to somewhere important – for example: a large city, port, gold or coalfield. Kilmore was a transit point between the southern coastal plains and the north. Settlers were attracted as early as 1837 and an Irishman named it for his birthplace in one of the seventeen Kilmores in Ireland.

Kilmore and Harrow – to the west – both claim to be Victoria's oldest inland town. Kilmore (meaning 'great church') has many fine stone buildings and is certainly the state's oldest Catholic parish outside Melbourne. The surrounding land still sustains agricultural and pastoral industries – wool, pigs, cattle and cottage crafts are produced locally. *Population 2620*

MERNDA ■ 941

Mernda is a tiny hamlet in the shire of Whittlesea – its name comes from an Aboriginal word 'merndi' said to mean 'earth'. The settlement was named Plenty in 1874 and then it became Morang until about 1900 when the present name was adopted. The district itself is sometimes referred to as the South Yan Yean. *Population 710*

MOUNT DISAPPOINTMENT ■ 942

In 1824, the explorers Hume and Hovell made an arduous climb of more than 800 metres to the top of Mount Disappointment hoping to see Port Phillip Bay. They recorded their feelings in the name chosen for posterity but the name was ill-chosen. Modern motoring explorers can drive a good way up the mount from any one of the surrounding townships including Kilmore, Wallan, Whittlesea, Flowerdale, Strath Creek and Broadford and then hike to the summit along a well-made track. On a clear day they will see not only the bay but also Melbourne and the Yan Yean Reservoir.

The mount and its surrounding plateau are covered in mountain ash, mountain grey gum and red stringybark. This is state forest which is logged for the timber industry and maintained for leisure purposes. Murchison Falls, where Strath Creek drops fifty metres over a cliff face, is in the north of the park.

SEYMOUR ■ 943

Seymour, named after Lord Seymour, is a busy country town at the junction of the Goulburn and Hume highways. The settlement became 'the new crossing place' on the Goulburn River from about 1843. The crossing was by punt until a bridge was built over the Goulburn in 1863. Unlucky wayfarers between Seymour and Avenel were held up by a bushranger called Power in the late 1860s. Some believe his young 'assis-

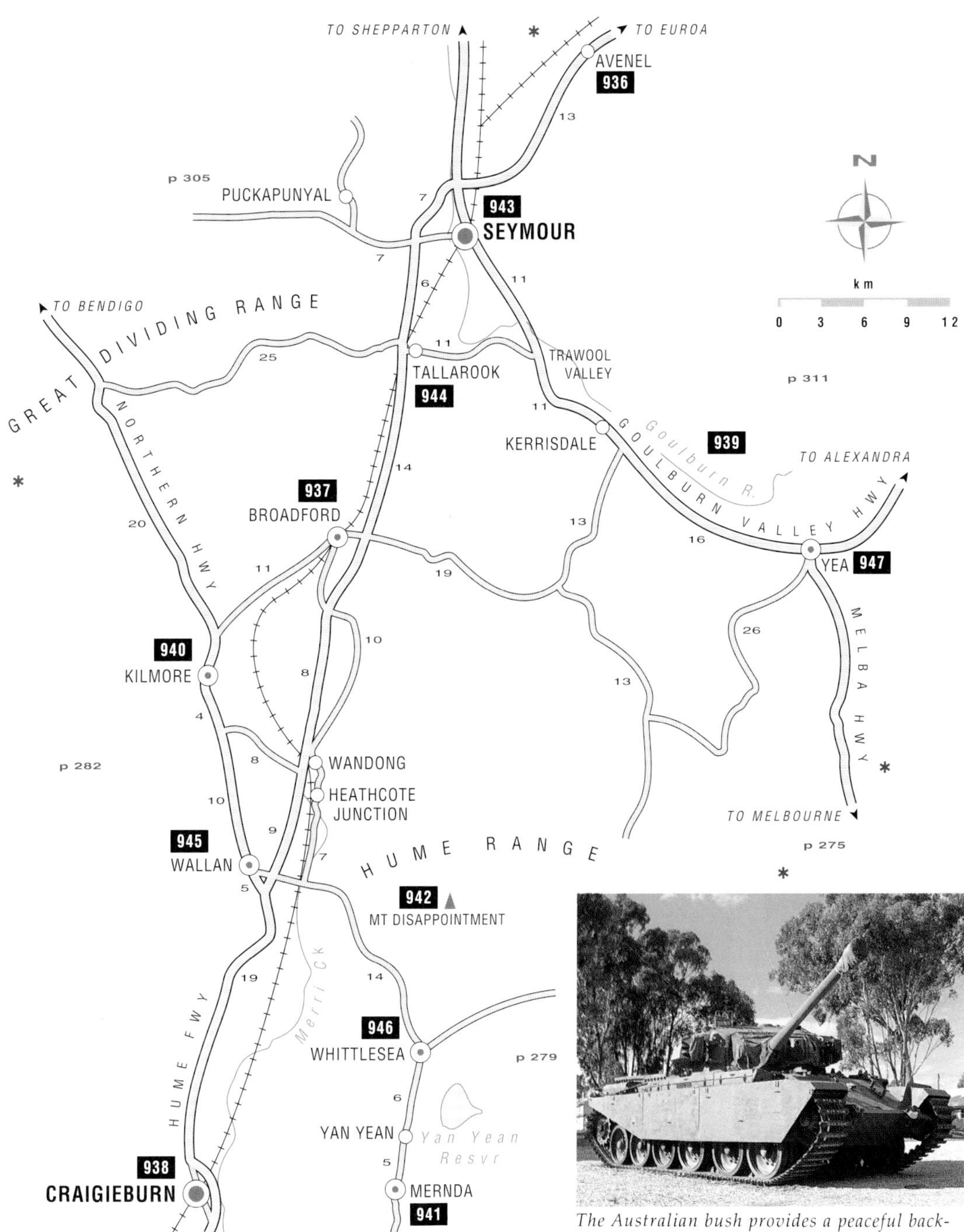

The Australian bush provides a peaceful background to the armed might of former battles at the Puckapunyal Museum.

tant' may have been Ned Kelly who was about fourteen at the time.

The Goulburn River has been both friend and foe to Seymour. Repeated flooding led to the shift of business houses from Emily Street to Station Street in the 1870s. Wool, fat lambs, beef cattle, pigs and wine are all important to Seymour's present economy. The river irrigates the market gardens, pastures and vineyards. Secondary industries include knitting and timber mills and the manufacture of a wide range of products for the building industry.

A visit and recommendation from Lord Kitchener of Khartoum in 1910 resulted in a military camp being established during the First World War. When the Puckapunyal camp was established, the Seymour–Puckapunyal area became known as 'The Home of Armour', being home to the Armoured School and the First Armoured Regiment.

Seymour's interesting buildings include the 1855 log lock-up – relocated in Kings Park – and the Royal Hotel which was the model for Russell Drysdale's famous painting 'Moody's Pub'. The disused timber trestle railway bridge nearby is one of the largest of its kind in Australia. *Population 6560*

PUCKAPUNYAL In 1939, a fully-fledged army base was opened at Puckapunyal, north- west of the town. It is one of Australia's largest bases and has had a great influence on the growth of Seymour which depends on it for many facilities. The RAAC Tank Museum displays the largest collection of armoured fighting vehicles in the Southern Hemisphere at Puckapunyal.

TALLAROOK ■ 944

Tallarook developed in the mid-1850s as a coach staging post on the Broadford-Seymour road. Its name caught the popular imagination: before and during the Second World War young Australians abroad who found themselves in tight situations might exclaim: 'Things are crook in Tallarook'. Fashions in slang change and other sayings are now current but its place in *The Dinkum Dictionary – a ripper guide to Aussie English* ensures the tiny community of Tallarook will be remembered. *McQuade's Curse*, by an unknown author, reinforces the point, and wishes a string of misfortunes on Tallarook ending with:

'May I get ague, gout and fluke
If I drink rum in Tallarook.'

WALLAN ■ 945

Despite its steep gradient, the 1838 trail blazed over the Great Dividing Range remained the route of the Sydney road until the road later known as the Hume Highway was opened in 1876. Wallan township (1853) originally catered to the needs of travellers preparing to ascend Big Hill or Pretty Sally's Hill as the diggers and carriers called it. Sally Smith (who is said to have weighed in the region of 140kg) ran an illegal shanty near its summit.

'Wallan' is Aboriginal for 'wet' and Wallan was once called Wallan Wallan – 'very wet' or 'round, flooded area'. Ned Kelly was born at nearby Beveridge in 1855 and his family's house still stands. The surrounding country supports horse breeding and training farms. *Population 2170*

WHITTLESEA ■ 946

Whittlesea is a farming district and township by the Plenty Ranges. It is probably the place where John Batman signed his worthless land treaty with the Aborigines in 1835. Later Whittlesea was named by the local surveyor who came from Whittlesea in England. The 1878 primary school is a classic example of the period of Gothic-Revival building by the Public Works Department. Nearby Yan Yean Reservoir is the oldest artificial lake in Victoria. *Population 1550*

FESTIVALS Battle of the Bands Expo, April.

YEA ■ 947

The first Europeans settlers arrived in this region in 1837 and Yea grew as a service centre for the gold mines in the 1850s but evidence suggests the Wuywurrung Aborigines knew the area long before that. The town is a meeting-place of roads from all points of the compass. There are beautiful gorges and fern gullies close to the Yea–Tallarook route and an ibis rookery at Kerrisdale.

Yea was Muddy Creek Settlement until a town was laid out in 1855 and named to remember Colonel Lacy Yea, a hero of the Crimean war. Muddy Creek eventually became Yea River. In 1908, the Trawool Water Scheme threatened to flood Yea but the proposal was abandoned.

The present-day town is the busy centre of a dairying, woolgrowing and fat lamb district. Other industries include sawmilling, an abattoir, light engineering and clothing manufacture. The district's rivers provide rewarding trout fishing – they are restocked each year with fingerlings from the Snobs Creek hatchery near Eildon. *Population 1000*

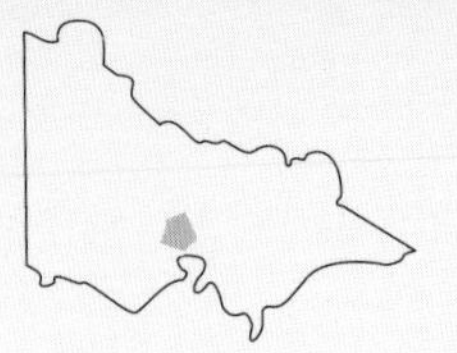

Melton & Sunbury

The spectacular rock formations and rich, productive soils of this peacefully rural part of south-central Victoria are the result of a violent prehistory of volcanic eruptions, lava deposits and glacial scouring.

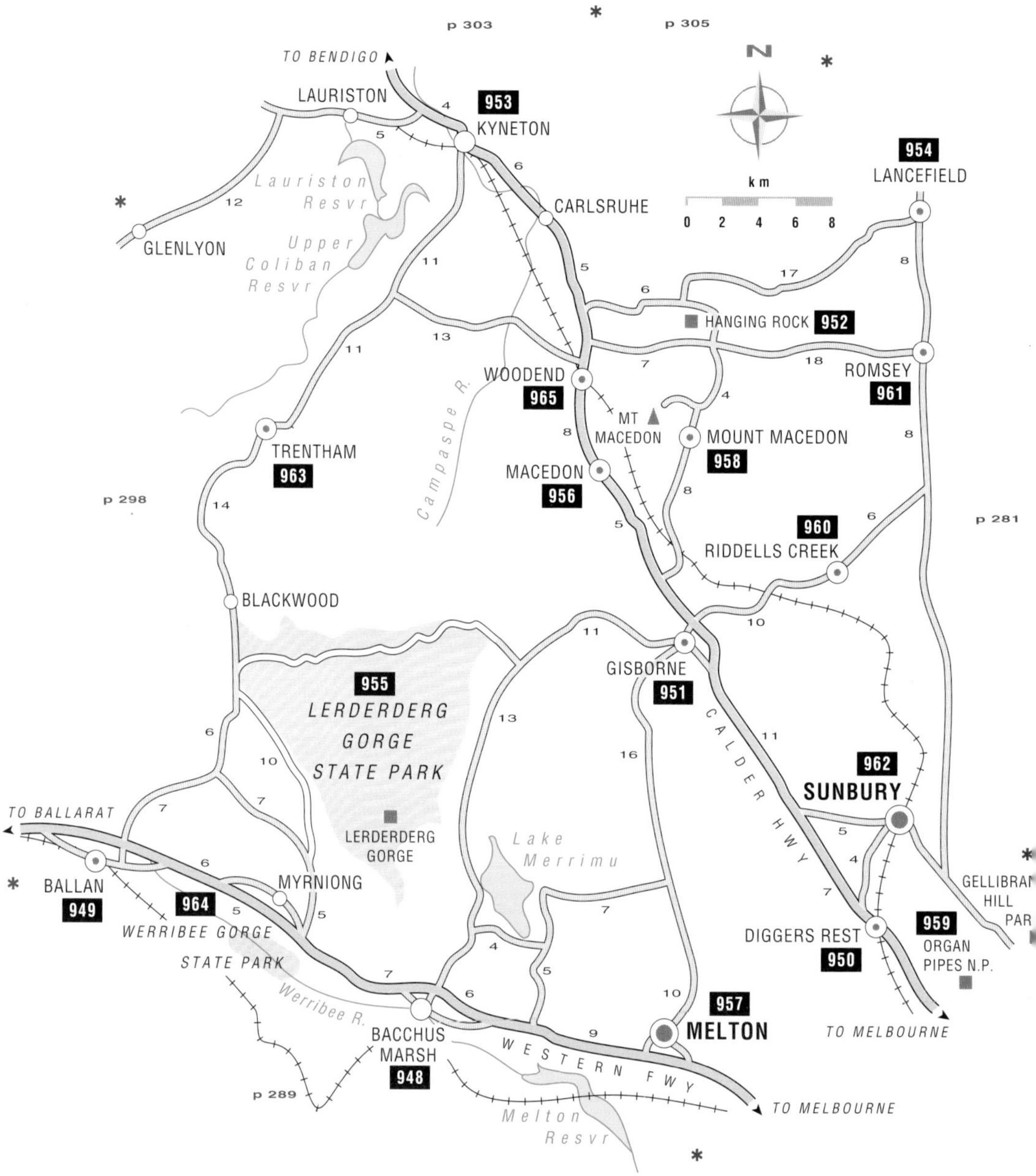

BACCHUS MARSH ■ 948
Bacchus Marsh in the shire of the same name is on the Werribee River within daily commuter distance of Melbourne. A stately avenue of trees planted in 1918 to commemorate those who served in the First World War provides a graceful introduction to the town which was named for its founder, Captain William Henry Bacchus (1838) and not 'for Bacchanalian revels under the Lerderderg willows' as writer Joan Lindsay once supposed. Captain Bacchus was also a foundation member of two prestigious Melbourne institutions, the Melbourne Club and the Melbourne Cricket Club. His two-storey, stone and brick Manor House is one of several fine buildings in Bacchus Marsh.

Today the region is known for its high-quality apples and fresh vegetables. The fertile marsh – long since drained – supports market gardens, orchards, horse studs, dairying and grazing; local manufacturing industries include various plastic goods, hardboard, firebricks, engineering equipment and clothing. Maddingley open-cut brown coal mine which supplies fuel to the Australian Paper Mills is a few kilometres south of the town centre.

The Lerderderg Stud raised the legendary Carbine, which won the 1890 Melbourne Cup carrying the heaviest weight – sixty-six kilograms – on record and in a record field of thirty-nine horses. Nearby Parwan Park is Australia's largest centre for artificially bred dairy herds.

Bacchus Marsh also has literary connections. Frank Hardy lived in Lerderderg Street until he was eighteen, Peter Carey was born here in 1943 and Sumner Locke Elliott used his memories of boyhood visits to the town in *Careful, He Might Hear You.* Joan Lindsay stayed here during the Great Depression. *Population 9700*

BALLAN ■ 949
Ballan, also on the Werribee River, is noted for its mineral springs and good trout fishing at nearby Pykes Reservoir. It is named for the Irish birthplace of an early settler and nineteenth-century Ballan followed the traditional pattern of small country towns with a hall, a Mechanics' Institute, an agricultural society and a corner pub. A freeway bypasses this peaceful village, once a staging point for coaches on the way to the goldfields. *Population 1050*

DIGGERS REST ■ 950
Diggers Rest is a rural settlement south of Sunbury (see entry) so named because diggers camped here in the 1850s on their way to the rich goldfields of central Victoria. Not surprisingly, a hotel soon opened to meet their needs. It was also the site of one of Caroline Chisholm's shelters for women travellers. Now, the area is renowned for the splendid autumnal colours of its introduced deciduous trees. *Population 1620*

GISBORNE ■ 951
In 1860, Gisborne was considered to be a boom town and boasted thirteen hotels. Like so many other places in the district, the town earned a place on the map because of the pioneer transport industry. Originally known

The wall of 'pipes' in the Organ Pipes National Park produces no music – these basalt columns are solidified lava.

The wailing cries of yellow-tailed black cockatoos echo off the massive rock formations at Hanging Rock.

as Bush Inn, coach travellers, as well as the less fortunate who had to walk, stopped here on their way to strike it rich in Forest Creek (Castlemaine) and Sandhurst (Bendigo). The town still has links with the transport business, with some residents working at nearby Tullamarine Airport. *Population 2820*

BARRINGO WILDLIFE RESERVE Deer, emus, kangaroos and wallabies roam inside this 38-hectare park which includes plenty of picnic spots and barbecue facilities.

HANGING ROCK ■ 952

'Huge boulders, originally spewed red hot from the boiling bowels of the earth, now come to rest, cooled and rounded in the forest shade' wrote Joan Lindsay in *Picnic at Hanging Rock*. Her story tells of a school excursion in 1900 from which three mysteriously never returned. In 1975, Peter Weir made a famous film of the haunting story, played out in broad daylight in the presence of the towering rock formations.

This peaceful nature reserve with its intriguing associations shelters koalas, wallabies, rosellas and rare black cockatoos. On New Year's Day and Australia Day each year the tranquillity gives way to the hoofbeats and cheers of the picnic races.

KYNETON ■ 953

Settlers arrived in the Kyneton area from 1836 onwards and soon discovered the region's quality bluestone – blue-grey or sometimes almost black in colour. There was an insatiable need for stone to build houses, bridges and railways and quarrying became a major industry in the 1850s, when the town grew as a staging post to the goldfields. In the same period Kyneton became one of Victoria's leading agricultural towns and a centre of wheat and flour production. There is an architectural exuberance about some of the old buildings – particularly the district hospital and the elaborately gabled house known as 'Ellim Eek'.

In the 1890s, Victoria's first pasteurising plant was installed in a butter and cheese factory and the malt factory was one of the largest in Australia. These industries have been replaced by knitting mills and meat works. This is the northern part of the Macedon wine producing area and Kyneton has a growing reputation for its red wines.

Freeman Cobb's coaches rattled through the town on their way to the Bendigo goldfields and the famous 'Leviathan' coach was driven from Castlemaine to Kyneton (see box). Today's motorists reach Melbourne within an hour along the much smoother Calder Highway and the Tullamarine Freeway.

Kyneton contributes generously to Victoria's 'garden state' reputation. Its eight-hectare botanical garden, stocked with European and North American deciduous trees, is said to be one of the finest outside Melbourne. *Population 3940*

KYNETON HISTORICAL CENTRE COLLECTION This extensive collection of pioneer relics is housed in an 1855 building in Piper Street, formerly a branch of the Bank of New South Wales. A drop-log cottage, originally built in 1840, has been re-erected in the grounds.

FESTIVALS Central Highlands Country Music Festival, March; Kyneton Daffodil and Arts Festival, September.

LANCEFIELD ■ 954

Lancefield is a pastoral town with tree-lined streets, old buildings and a developing vineyard. It is noted for the nearby Mount William 'quarry' where once the hard rock was levered out of the ground and trimmed into axeheads by the local Aborigines. They exchanged these for other goods with people from all over Victoria. *Population 1060*

LERDERDERG GORGE STATE PARK ■ 955

Lerderderg Gorge, a narrow, steep-sided, glaciated valley 300 metres deep, was formed about forty million years ago as a result of massive volcanic shocks in the Bacchus Marsh area. 'Although there are calm and gentle reaches, much of it is so enclosed and ridged and rugged that it is like walking through a clenched fist' writes Bary Dowling in *Exploring Australia's Southeast*. The trail that winds through the gorge is not for inexperienced bushwalkers but there are other shorter and easier tracks in the park which show off its considerable beauty.

MACEDON ■ 956

The two communities of Macedon and Mount Macedon (see entry) lie in the shadow of the mountain. When gold was discovered in 1851 at Bendigo and Castlemaine, Middle Gully (Macedon) was settled by blacksmiths, store proprietors and innkeepers who offered their essential services to the great number of travellers streaming to the goldfields. Construction workers took more than two years to drive the Northern Trunk Line through the Great Dividing Range, and Middle Gully became a railway settlement in 1861. A small Anglican church and a school were built and in 1859 the residents asked for a town survey. Two years later, Macedon was proclaimed but the station was not renamed till 1870.

The early settlers denuded the slopes of timber for pit props, railway sleepers and houses and then turned to growing fruit. By the end of 1872, the government had set up a state forest reafforestation program at Macedon which began raising trees to supply the rest of the state. Lately, the Macedon area (divided into three sub-regions) has been growing grapevines. Long slow ripening of the fruit is the key to great wines and the cool climate coupled with rich soil provide near-perfect conditions. The Macedon Ranges are pioneering European-style close plantings to resist the cold and windy conditions. When the Tullamarine Freeway was constructed, both Macedon and Mount Macedon offered Melbourne workers country living. The two towns were slowly growing until the fires came through in 1983. Since then, activity has centred on rebuilding, restoration and regeneration and the scars are gradually healing though many of the town's historical buildings have been lost forever. *Population 1240*

MELTON ■ 957

The first significant survey of Melton was made in 1837 and European settlement dates from the following year. Named after Melton Mowbray in England, the town styles itself 'Heart of the Thoroughbred Country' for its expanding horse-breeding businesses. Other activities in the district include cereal growing, fat-lamb raising and quarrying. With the constant spread of residential development, the town has become a dormitory suburb of Melbourne. *Population 29 040*

MOUNT MACEDON ■ 958

The energetic explorer Sir Thomas Mitchell was also a Greek scholar with a special interest in Alexander the Great. He named a mountain after him and on 30 September, 1836, 'steered for a bold hill to the S.E. afterwards called Mount Macedon' – for Philip of Macedonia, Alexander's father. Mitchell then named the

DR MORSE'S
PILLS

Melbourne city dwellers face only a short drive to the invigorating rural atmosphere of Bacchus Marsh where an idyllic landscape of orchards and market gardens flourishes on the drained Werribee Valley marshes.

Campaspe River for the Greek warrior's favourite mistress.

Mitchell's accounts of this beautiful and fertile region were widely published and pastoralists from the already-settled lands to the northeast and from overseas soon came to the new grazing lands, inspired by enthusiastic passages such as: 'As I stood, the first European intruder on the sublime solitude of these verdant plains, as yet untouched by flocks or herds, I felt conscious of being the harbinger of mighty changes; and that our steps would soon be followed by the men and the animals for which it seemed to have been prepared'. But there were earlier sheep runs, established after Hume and Hovell discovered Mount Macedon – Mount Wentworth to them – in 1824. The view from the summit later inspired Arthur Streeton to paint his famous landscape entitled *Australia Felix*.

The township of Mount Macedon, on the lower slopes, is famous for its clean, bracing atmosphere. When the hot summer winds blew in the city, many wealthy Melbourne families retired to the cool comfort of their Mount Macedon estates. They planted European gardens in the fertile, well-watered soil; deciduous poplars, oaks, elms, azaleas and rhododendrons decorate the streets, having returned to their former glory after the 1983 bushfires. The first of these, on 1 February, destroyed twenty-four homes and six hundred hectares in the area, the second, on 16 February, the terrible Ash Wednesday fire, killed seven people and destroyed more than four hundred homes, 30 000 hectares of forest and farmland and untold numbers of animals.

Despite the passage of time, both townships and the mountain summit are still recovering from the holocaust – many of the fine Victorian-era homes were irreparably damaged. The twenty-one-metre-high Memorial Cross, privately funded in 1935 to provide work for the unemployed and to commemorate Victorians who died in the First World War, now stands starkly at the peak, bereft of the snow gums, mountain ash and pine trees that once surrounded it. *Population 660*

ORGAN PIPES NATIONAL PARK ■ 959

The 'organ pipes' are part of a million-year-old lava deposit on the Keilor Plains which cooled into basalt and cracked to form a columnar structure – the tallest 'pipes' in the middle tapering to the shortest at

The dramatic First World War memorial cross exposed to the winds atop Mount Macedon adds a stark 21 metres to the 1000-metre-high mountain.

either end. After centuries of erosive action, the vegetation covering them has been stripped away by Jacksons Creek. Other interesting basalt formations are Rosette Rock, where the columns radiate like wheel spokes, and the Tessellated Pavement where they are worn down to ground level in hexagonal shaped basalt tiles. Land clearing and grazing in earlier years created a weed problem but the thistle and boxthorn are now under control and more than 140 native plant species have been reintroduced into the region.

RIDDELLS CREEK ■ 960

Riddells Creek is a farming village set among the paddocks to the south-east of Macedon. It took its name from the local creek which was named after John Carre Riddell who took up a run there in 1838.

The nearby homestead of 'Dromkeen' dates back to 1849 and is now a museum of children's books. It has original manuscripts and drawings and paintings for book illustrations collected from Australia, Britain, the United States and South-East Asia. *Population 1280*

ROMSEY ■ 961

Romsey is a small agricultural settlement named after an English town. The poet Vincent Buckley was born here in 1925; his father was a bush postman during the 1930s depression and Buckley recalls his Romsey childhood in his autobiography, *Cutting Green Hay (1983).* Today, the community still centres on rural pursuits and the cricket pavilion doubles as a tasting room for the local winery. *Population 2030*

SUNBURY ■ 962

Sunbury, known to the Aboriginals as 'koora kooracup', is situated on Jacksons Creek. Many of the houses built by the first European settlers are still standing – 'Rupertswood', an 1874 two-storey mansion with a tower is classified by the National Trust. Sadly, 'Emu Bottom', George Evans' homestead and the oldest in Victoria, was burned down in 1980 and now only remnants of the original homestead remain. Although the town was gazetted in 1851, the goldfields' traffic passed it by, using tracks on either side through Bulla and Diggers Rest.

Work on the Melbourne–Bendigo line began in 1858 and by January 1859 the thirty-two kilometres to Sunbury were completed. The first passengers had a strenuous journey – they had to get out to push several times because the engine lacked sufficient steam to haul its load. The forty-kilometre stretch from Sunbury to Woodend was opened in July 1861, after the Jacksons Creek viaduct was built and graded cuttings were made through the Black Forest. Trains ran between Woodend and Kyneton from April 1862.

Sunbury was a prolific wine producing area until the 1920s and viticulture has been resurrected in recent years as the southern wineries of the Macedon region have established themselves. *Population 18 530*

TRENTHAM ■ 963

'Woodside', the first pastoral run in this area, was taken up in 1837. When gold was found at Trentham in 1859, the location was known as Ogden's Forest and then in 1862 as Blue Mountain Diggings. When the gold fever cooled, serious settlers stayed on to farm. The Trewhella jack and stump grubber – a once indispensable item of farm machinery which is famous in agricultural history – had its origins in Trentham. Local industries include distilling eucalyptus oil and timber milling. *Population 630*

WERRIBEE GORGE STATE PARK ■ 964

Werribee, from the Aboriginal 'wearibi', is thought to mean both 'snake's backbone' and 'a swimming-place'. The waterway at the bottom of the deep gorge is all that remains of the glacier that gouged the rocks on its way to the sea about a million years ago. There are shales containing fossils over 500 000 000 years old and a profusion of native plants. One of these, the blue flowered dianella or flax lily, was used by the Aborigines as a spinning fibre. The cliffs at Falcons Lookout are closed to climbers for several months each year so that peregrine falcons may nest in peace.

WOODEND ■ 965

Shepherds were the first pioneers to move into the district around Woodend. Those who followed their trail often slaked their thirst here and records mention fifteen inns between Gisborne and Woodend and a number of unlicensed wine shanties. A bush hotel brought more dependable rewards than a sojourn at the diggings and the town on Five Mile Creek was a popular watering hole.

One of Victoria's few remaining sandstone bridges stands at Woodend. It was built in 1858 and spans the Djerriwarrah Creek. Since 1913, the Country Roads Board of Victoria has gradually eliminated the steep grades on this area's roads – early cars sometimes came into Woodend backwards because their forward gears were too weak to propel them up the local hills.

Woodend's industries include timber milling, farming, stock raising and the manufacture of clothing and transport trailers. *Population 2740*

William Ford's 1875 painting is thought to have inspired the famous story of the tragic picnic at Hanging Rock.

GETTING THE MAIL THROUGH IN THE DAYS OF COBB & CO.

The arrival of the mail coach in Ballarat in 1854 was the cause for some excitement; Freeman Cobb (below) relied on mail contracts for his profit.

HOOVES drumming in perfect unison, whip cracks, clattering wheels – out of the dustcloud over the rise comes a Cobb & Co. coach – surely one of the most romantic sights of the last century and one of the most welcome to news-starved inland Australians before the days of electronic communication.

The company, set up in 1853 by the American Freeman Cobb and three compatriots, began operating the following year between Melbourne and Sandridge (Port Melbourne). Of course, there were coaches before that – Australia's first real public conveyance ran weekly from Sydney through Parramatta to Windsor and Richmond in 1814. But from the time Cobb & Co. began taking passengers to the Bendigo goldfields, other coaching companies in the eastern colonies gradually faded into obscurity.

Cobb & Co.'s first coaches were imported from the United States. They were light, robust vehicles, suspended on leather straps attached at either end to iron jacks, and were reliable on the roughest roads – and the timetable was respected with frequently changed horses a feature of the Cobb & Co. service. Passengers were not so much jarred and bumped as rolled from side to side – the motion made some of them 'seasick'. Not the most comfortable of rides – one passenger complained: 'Every two or three minutes the wheel goes into a hole or over a stump with such force as it would almost throw you out of your seat'.

The touring light-opera singer, Emily Soldene, wrote graphically of her travels with Cobb & Co., her words bringing to life the rough and tumble of the ride: 'suddenly we go, down a mountain as steep as the side of a house, down into and through a rushing, roaring, tumbling, bumping, yellow river! Splash! Then with a 'houps!' 'hi!' and a big lurch, out again and up the opposite side, galloping, always galloping, breathless, the driver shouting, cracking his whip, and the horses shaking the water from their sides, tossing their heads, and jingling their harness.'

In 1859, Cobb sold the business to a fellow American, James Rutherford, who secured a monopoly on government mail contracts. He shrewdly kept the name already associated with fast and efficient service. In 1862, after the gold rush to Lambing Flat, Cobb & Co.'s headquarters moved to Bathurst in New South Wales. The company moved into Queensland in 1867 but never reached South Australia, Western Australia or Tasmania.

By 1870, 6000 horses were harnessed daily, the coaches covered 45 000 kilometres a week, the yearly income from mail subsidies was 95 000 pounds sterling and the yearly wages bill was 100 000 pounds sterling. Cobb and Co.'s other undertakings included stores, inns and factories. The 'Leviathan' was the pride of the Cobb & Co. fleet – it ran from Castlemaine to Kyneton pulled by twenty-two horses which wore pale blue rosettes over their ears. It carried up to seventy-five passengers. The driver had two or perhaps four postilions to help him with the reins. These men were local heroes and the most famous was a Tasmanian called Edward Devine – 'Cabbage-tree Ned'. In 1862, he drove the first visiting English cricket team round Australia in the comparatively diminutive 'Great Coach', drawn by twelve grey horses. At the end of the tour Ned was rewarded with a banquet and 300 sovereigns.

The drivers faced many dangers: the appalling state of the roads, fire, flood and gold-hungry bushrangers. There was an attack on Frank May in 1859 when he was driving between Broadford and Seymour in Victoria, but popular history claims there were only four fatal accidents in seventy years of service – an incredible record if true.

Cobb & Co. was inevitably destined to be overcome by the steady march of progress. Gradually, the railways took over the coastal routes and the coach network went inland where it helped to open up remote areas. The last service ran between Yeulba and Surat in Queensland in 1924 – the coach that covered the distance is now in the Queensland Museum. □

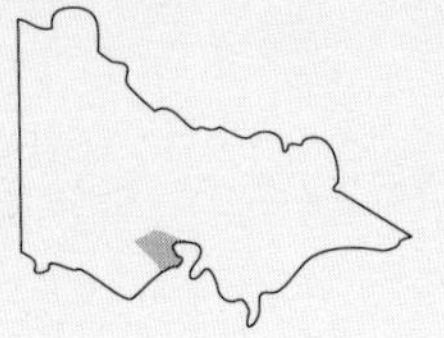

Geelong & Werribee

Newcomers in search of gold or grazing land came here from the 1830s and there is a maritime history, based around Geelong and Queenscliff, that dates back at least as far. Today, this coastline accommodates traditional holiday destinations as well as busy urban and industrial regions.

Fishing boats and wool stores along the concrete shores of inner Corio Bay symbolise Geelong's maritime history – it was once Victoria's busiest port.

ANAKIE ■ 966
To the south of the Brisbane Ranges, the hamlet of Anakie is overshadowed by three hills, known as The Anakies, which overlook the settlement. These hills were the site of a gold discovery in 1855, which led to the establishment of Steiglitz (see entry). Today, the volcanic soils of Mount Anakie support a vineyard which produces fine red or white wines. The area has a dairying and grazing history which goes back to the establishment of a station in 1842.

BANNOCKBURN ■ 967
This small township to the north-west of Geelong became the centre of Bannockburn Shire in 1864. The town, then known as Leigh Road, developed around the 1850s Somerset Hotel, beside Bruce's Creek, but during the 1860s it moved up the nearby hill to be in closer proximity to the Geelong–Ballarat railway line.

Historic buildings here include the bluestone, timber-verandahed 1863 railway station, and a lock-up which was originally constructed at nearby Lethbridge and dates from 1860. In addition to its use as a pre-trial jail, this basic brick building functioned as an overnight safehouse for gold en route to Geelong from the Ballarat goldfields. *Population 820*

BARWON HEADS ■ 968
The Barwon River enters the sea here and is flanked by the long-established holiday resort of Barwon Heads, and its neighbour across the estuary, Ocean Grove (see entry). The estuary has extensive shallow flats which provide good fishing conditions. The town has been popular with holiday anglers since 1870 – the estuary, river and surf fishing are all excellent. The sheltered river and ocean beaches also provide good swimming. Above the town there is a lookout which provides fine views of the Barwon River, Ocean Grove and the coastline. *Population 2060*

BRISBANE RANGES NATIONAL PARK ■ 969
This 1130-hectare park was designated in 1973 and contains the slate and sandstone protrusion of the Brisbane Ranges. Water erosion has created deep gorges in the rock, and the park's steep-walled Anakie Gorge is one of the area's prime attractions. The gorge reaches a depth of thirty metres in places and is accessible by walking tracks. The park is of great botanical interest – its plateau area contains some 400 species of flowering plants, including two rare grevilleas which bloom spectacularly between August and November.

CLIFTON SPRINGS ■ 970
This town, on the northern side of Bellarine Peninsula, developed as one of Victoria's most popular spa resorts during the 1880s. Mineral springs were discovered by Thomas Bales in 1870 and a pier and baths were built to cater for holiday-makers. The town is now a residential area for Geelong. *Population 5850*

CORIO BAY ■ 971
This western extension of Port Phillip Bay was first visited by Europeans in 1802 and has developed into the site of the busy Port of Geelong: the entrance to the inner harbour is marked by Point Lillias and Point Henry. The name is derived from 'coraiyo', thought to be an Aboriginal word for 'sandy cliffs'.

DRYSDALE ■ 972
Named after a Scotswoman called Anne Drysdale, a pioneer squatter who arrived here in 1843, this settlement grew up around 'Coryule', the homestead which she shared with fellow pioneer Caroline Newcomb. This National Trust sandstone mansion dates from 1849 and is the oldest building on the Bellarine Peninsula; it is also one of Victoria's finest examples of Gothic Revival domestic architecture. Drysdale was once the location for an unusual institution: the War Veterans' Home, which was established to house impoverished army and navy veterans, and modelled on the Chelsea Pensioners' Home in London. The 1891 building still stands, but is now a private residence. *Population 1410*

GEELONG ■ 973
The site of modern Victoria's second city was first visited by Europeans in 1802, when both Matthew Flinders and Lieutenant John Murray arrived in Corio Bay. The explorers Hume and Hovell reached the bay in 1824 during their overland expedition from New South Wales. It was at this time that the name Geelong became used: this came from the Aboriginal word 'jillong', which means either 'a swampy plain', or 'white seabird'.

In 1835, John Batman, repeating his experience at the head of Port Phillip Bay, acquired land in the area from Aboriginal leaders, and the first farming had begun here by 1837. A year later, survey plans were made, Geelong was declared a town, and a police station was established.

Development of the settlement progressed rapidly: a customs post was opened in 1838, and by the 1840s the town contained a post office, a general store, watch-houses, flour mills, tanneries and other small industries. Before long, Geelong contained around 8000 people, and the 1850s gold rushes increased the population dramatically. It was then that Geelong became a serious candidate for the title of Victoria's major city – a prize that was eventually won by Melbourne. Many buildings date from the second half of the nineteenth century and over 100 are classified as worthy of preservation.

Today, Geelong is a thriving commercial and industrial centre and a major port. The Port of Geelong, on Corio Bay, began life as an entry point for prospectors heading to the Victorian goldfields during the 1850s and developed into an important trading port for wool exports during the 1900s.

Flour mills, soapworks, a lime kiln and tanneries were established by the bay during the 1840s, followed by woollen mills in the 1860s and a later paper pulping plant. Important modern industries include the manufacture of automobiles, agricultural equipment, rope, chemicals, carpets, glass, fertilisers and petroleum products. The area around Geelong is a fertile farming district which supports dairying, wool production and mixed farming; there are also a number of small wineries here.

The Geelong region is Australia's eleventh largest urban centre, and includes the cities of Geelong, Geelong West and Newtown, parts of South Barwon City and the shires of Bellarine and Corio. The city also has a reputation as a cultural and educational centre. Deakin University was established on the city's outskirts in 1977 and two famous schools, Geelong Church of England Grammar School and the Geelong College are long-established, private centres of learning. Geelong is also home to the Australia's National Wool Museum, which records the nation's long association with wool production, and the Port of Geelong Authority's Maritime Museum. Nearby are the small but interesting settlements of Ceres and Fyansford, which are home to a number of buildings from the 1850s and 1860s. *Population 126 310*

BELLARINE PENINSULA This strip of coast with bay and ocean fronts, to the south-east of Geelong, is a popular holiday destination, with tourism being a major industry for towns such as Barwon Heads, Portarlington, Ocean Grove, Queenscliff and Torquay. The peninsula was used for agriculture as early as 1835 and until the 1870s the region was known as the 'granary of the colony'. In 1835, the farmers' labours were interrupted by the arrival of William Buckley – (see *Sorrento*) – who presented himself after spending thirty-two years with the Aborigines. Agriculture is still important, as is the fishing industry, based around Queenscliff and Portarlington.

HISTORIC BUILDINGS The jewel in Geelong's crown of outstanding historical buildings is the 1838 customs house which is the oldest building in Victoria; the second, much grander, customs house dates from 1856. The ornate Corio Villa was constructed in the same year, while another fine residence, the Regency-style Armytage House, dates from 1860.

Public buildings include the 1855 city hall, the Church of Christ (1858), the Classical-style Bank of Australasia (now the ANZ Bank) and the Roman Catholic Church (1864). Other handsome survivors from the nineteenth century are the 1855 'Barwon Grange', homestead fronting the Barwon River, and a number of wool stores and residences.

FESTIVALS Geelong Summer Festival, January; Australian International Air Show and Aerospace Expo, March.

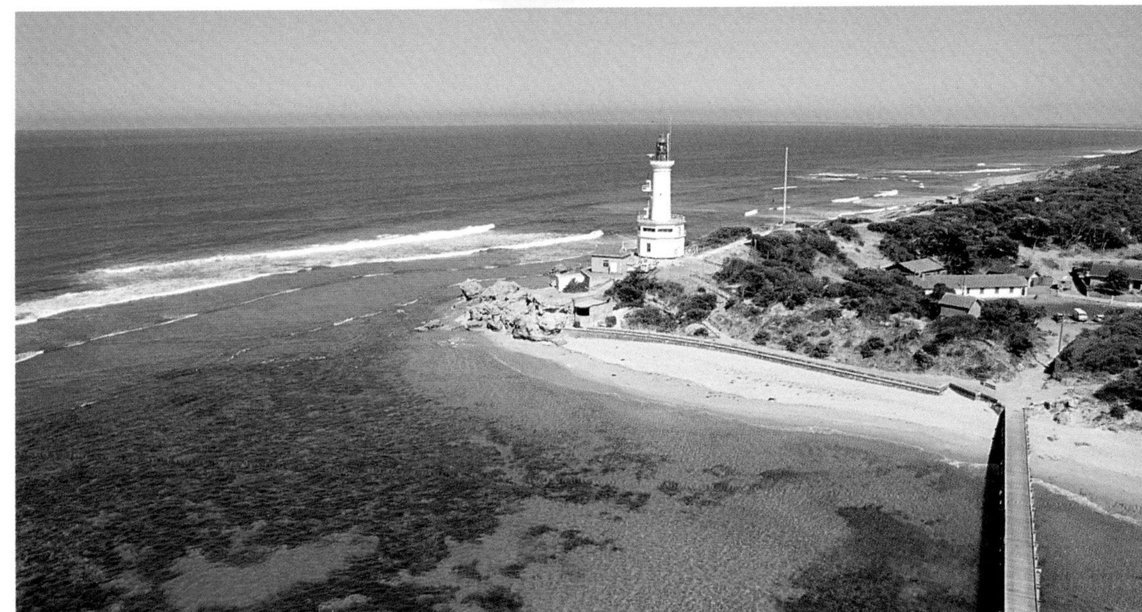

Ships 30 kilometres out to sea can navigate by the deceptively diminutive Point Lonsdale light on Port Phillip Bay.

INDENTED HEAD ■ 974

The large indentation in this coastline was named by Matthew Flinders when he sailed into Port Phillip Bay in May 1802. Flinders landed on the headland, as did John Batman, the founder of Melbourne, some 33 years later. A memorial commemorating both landings stands in the town's Batman Park. Today, this little village between Portarlington and St Leonards is a popular fishing resort. Boating, sailing and waterskiing are other pursuits which attract holidaymakers. *Population 550*

INVERLEIGH ■ 975

Located on the Leigh River and near the junction of this waterway with the Barwon, to the west of Geelong, the Inverleigh region was first settled by pastoralists in 1836. There are several historic buildings including the 1858 Anglican Church and the 1861 Presbyterian Church. There are also a number of well-maintained, pioneer-built timber structures.

LARA ■ 976

The small town of Lara, to the north of Geelong, contains a number of historic buildings. Elcho Homestead is an 1867 two-storey Gothic Revival building, while the 1860–63 'Woolloomanata' belonged to Frederick Armytage, a member of a prominen pioneering family. *Population 6320*

LEOPOLD ■ 977

Kensington was the first name of this inland Bellarine Peninsula town which was renamed Leopold in 1892 after Queen Victoria's son, the Duke of Albany. The settlement is the centre of a farming district, but also functions as a dormitory suburb for Geelong. Its main industries are a timber yard and joinery, and a plastic moulding factory. St Mark's Church on the Hill, a simple bluestone building, dates from 1862. *Population 4430*

WALLINGTON East of Leopold, the village of Wallington is surrounded by a farming district which supports orchards and strawberry farms.

MEREDITH ■ 978

This parish is named after a Tasmanian settler, Charles Meredith, and developed due to its position as the halfway point between Ballarat and

Corio Villa is a wildly imaginative prefabricated house held together by nuts and bolts; it came to Geelong from a Scottish iron foundry in 1855.

Geelong. Pastoralists, and later, gold prospectors, on their way to the Ballarat area used the settlement as an overnight stopping place. Eventually, the town was included on the Geelong–Ballarat railway line.

Planned by the government surveyor, Meredith is laid out neatly in squares, with each street bearing the name of an early pioneer. Historic buildings here are the 1862 railway station, the single-storey Meredith Shire Hall, which dates from 1878, and the 1842 Darra Homestead. This Georgian brick residence was built by Charles von Steiglitz, after whom the mining town of Steiglitz was named. Woodbourne Homestead is nearby – this dilapidated timber slab building dates from 1844. Modern Meredith lies at the centre of a high-quality wool-producing region.

OCEAN GROVE ■ 979

Linked to Barwon Heads by a bridge over the estuary, Ocean Grove is another popular holiday town which becomes very crowded in summer – the town has facilities to cater for some 15 000 campers.

The region was being farmed as early as 1836 and the town was first settled in 1854. At this time, leather tanning became an important industry, utilising the bark of the area's many wattle trees. For a time in 1887, Ocean Grove was the site for an unsuccessful experiment in alcohol-free interdenominational settlement by two American Wesleyan missionaries from Ocean Grove, New Jersey – thus the town's name. Fishing later became a major industry and Ocean Grove is still a commercial fishing port. *Population 7020*

LAKE CONNEWARRE GAME RESERVE This shallow estuarine lagoon and river region to the north of Barwon Heads has a covering of scrub, reeds, white mangroves and grasslands and forms an important link in the chain of swamps that are visited by migratory water fowl. Duck shooting is permitted here during the March to May season.

OCEAN GROVE NATURE RESERVE This 143-hectare native flora and fauna reserve, to the north of the town, represents the last large forested area on the Bellarine Peninsula. Koalas and other marsupials inhabit the reserve, and there are some 100 species of birds here, which can be observed from hides. Flora includes gum trees, banksias and orchids and there are several walking tracks through the area.

FESTIVALS Ocean Grove Community Festival, March.

POINT LONSDALE ■ 980

This is both a small resort and the name of the western headland at the entrance to Port Phillip Bay. It was named in 1837 after Captain William Lonsdale, the first police magistrate of the Port Phillip settlement. A lighthouse was built here in 1854; it was replaced by the present beacon in 1902. Point Lonsdale's Terminus Hotel dates from 1884; the old cemetery contains the graves of many colonial shipping pilots as well as other pioneers.

From the Riptide Lookout at the southern edge of the town, there is an excellent view of the heads of Port Phillip and the treacherous rip which marks the entrance to the bay.

Point Lonsdale was part of the domain of William Buckley, a convict who escaped from the Collins Settlement at Sorrento in 1803. Buckley roamed the peninsula region for some thirty-two years, living with Aborigines, before he managed to rejoin the European community and ultimately received a pardon (see Bellarine Peninsula sub-entry, Geelong). One of the hardy escaper's hideouts is believed to be Buckleys Cave, which can still be seen at the foot of Point Lonsdale Lighthouse.

PORTARLINGTON ■ 981

Located on the north side of the peninsula, the bayside holiday resort of Portarlington was established in 1851 when streets were surveyed and lots auctioned. It was developed further after the Portarlington Steam Flour Mill opened in 1857. In these years, this region was known as the 'granary of the colony'. The mill closed in 1874, but the owner, Mr T.H. Widdicombe, then utilised the building as a brick and tile works. The substantial, four-storey, sandstone mill, which was built on the site of an Aboriginal meeting ground, still stands and is under the care of the National Trust. It incorporates historical and educational displays and includes a number of Aboriginal artefacts. Other reminders of the past include the foreshore memorial to explorer Matthew Flinders, and the century-old band rotunda.

Portarlington, named in 1851 after Lord Arlington, has a fine, sheltered beach and concentrates mainly on tourism but scallop fishing, dairying, poultry farming, grazing and vegetable growing also employ local people. *Population 2550*

QUEENSCLIFF ■ 982

Queenscliff began life as a pilot station, initiated by George Tobin, as far back as 1838. Its strategic position at the entrance to Port Phillip Bay led to the establishment of pilot boats to guide ships through the dangerous waters of the rip. These boats still operate today, under the name of the Port Phillip Pilot Service.

A fishing village was established here in 1846, when the area was known as Whale Head, and later, Shortland Bluff. This latter name was dedicated to the mate of HMS *Rattlesnake*, who completed surveying work of Port Phillip in 1836. From 1840 to 1852, the area known as Shortland Bluff was a pastoral run. The town was surveyed between 1852 and 1853 and renamed by Governor Charles La Trobe in honour of Queen Victoria; a borough was proclaimed in 1863.

A telegraph station was opened in 1856, and Queenscliff later became a garrison town, as a precaution against possible Russian aggression in the post-Crimean War years. Fort Queenscliff dates from 1882 and includes a guard room and cells as well as the the 1863 'Black' Lighthouse and the original wood and brick 1852 signal station. There is also a nearby 'White' Lighthouse which, along with its black companion, forms a line by which ships navigate their way into Port Phillip Bay. Since 1946, Fort Queenscliff has been the home of the Command and Staff College – the Australian Army's officer training centre.

The railway from Geelong opened in 1879 and by the 1880s Queenscliff had become a fashionable weekend resort and many hotels were constructed during this period: the Esplanade Hotel dates from 1879, the Ozone from 1882, the Vue Grand from 1884 and the Queenscliff Hotel from 1887. There are many other historic buildings and part of the town's centre has been proclaimed a conservation area by the National Trust.

Tourism is still an important industry, but Queenscliff is also a major fishing centre, and the area produces shell grit for poultry feed. During the summer, a ferry service operates to Portsea and Sorrento at the eastern entrance of Port Phillip Bay.

Other tourist attractions include a maritime museum and the Bellarine Peninsula Railway, which is operates from the 1879 railway station. This vintage steam train and track is maintained by the Geelong Steam Preservation Society which organises passenger trips over the thirty-two-kilometre-return journey to Drysdale. *Population 3680*

Wool provided the wealth for many a Victorian pastoralist to recreate the stately homes of England; Werribee Park was a notably successful attempt.

Sturdy pilot boats such as this one are the guardians of Port Phillip Bay; the narrow entrance surges four times a day as tidal currents rush in and out.

ST LEONARDS ■ 983

Named after a coastal town in England, St Leonards first came under European influence as a source of firewood for Melbourne in the 1850s; in the 1860s it supported a large Chinese community who fished for squid, but later moved on to the Victorian gold diggings. Commercial fishing still takes place, and the town is also a thriving angling resort, providing some of Port Phillip Bay's best fishing. Catches of snapper, salmon, King George whiting, pike, yellowtail kingfish and flathead are likely here. *Population 1210*

STEIGLITZ HISTORIC PARK ■ 984

To the west of Werribee, Steiglitz was an important goldmining town from the mid-1850s until the early 1900s – the population is insignificant now, but at one stage during these boom years it peaked at around 2000. Gold was first discovered here in 1853 at Sutherlands Creek, on the land of squatters Charles and Robert von Steiglitz, who had arrived in 1847. The 1855 find of a large gold-bearing reef, by Joseph Davis and William Hooley, created a rush of hopeful diggers into the area.

The town was laid out in 1857 and by 1875 there were over 400 mines and four churches here. The fortunes of the town rose and fell repeatedly, however, and by 1896 few people remained in the region. The last Steiglitz mine closed in 1941.

Now a virtual ghost town, the streets of Steiglitz are deserted and overgrown, but the 800-hectare historic site includes the 1875 court house and an 1870 dwelling, as well as a cemetery, the remains of the 1890s Scott's Hotel and a large number of remnants of the mining era – mineshafts, mullock heaps and a powder magazine.

SWAN BAY ■ 985

Swan Bay, between Queenscliff and Edwards Point, is a shallow inlet, protected by sand spits, that contains many mud flats. The area is an important habitat for waterbirds and both Edwards Point and Duck Island are wildlife reserves.

TORQUAY ■ 986

Called Spring Creek until 1892, but later named after the seaside resort in Devon, in the west of England, this town on the southern side of the Bellarine Peninsula performs much the same role for the Geelong region. Modern Torquay is on the scenic Great Ocean Road and local businesses have been largely dependent on the tourist trade since the second half of the nineteenth century.

The town began life as a farming centre, and there was a school here as early as 1861. Tourism began in the 1880s, when James Follet opened a boarding house and constructed a bathing hut on the beach. In the latter years of the nineteenth century, Torquay also became a popular spot for Sunday school and club picnic outings. The Surf Lifesaving Club was established in 1927, after a series of drownings on Victoria's beaches.

Surfing is a particularly popular pastime here, and Torquay has become known as one of Australia's major surfing centres, a result of the ideal wave conditions at locations such as Jan Juc Beach.

International competitions are held at nearby Bells Beach, which takes its name from the Bell family, the owners of most of the land in the area during the 1840s. The Bells Easter Classic is one of the world's most important professional surfing competitions and has been conducted since 1961. The town has developed into a surfing mecca and several companies here manufacture surf boards, surfing clothing and other accoutrements of the sport.

Non-surfing tourists come to use the golf course or grass-skiing facilities or try sailing, skateboarding, windsurfing or swimming at the town's four beaches; diving and fishing, as well as simply viewing the area's rugged coastline, are other popular diversions. *Population 4890*

WERRIBEE ■ 987

To all intents and purposes an outer suburb of Melbourne, the city of Werribee is in a district first settled by Europeans in 1836 and was called Wyndham until 1884. The Werribee River, which flows into Port Phillip Bay here, was reached by Hamilton Hume and William Hovell during their 1824 exploratory journey, and this plains area has long been utilised for agriculture, especially market-gardening, grazing and dairying.

The city is most famous for Werribee Park, Victoria's finest colonial homestead, which was built by the pastoralist Chirnside family between 1873 and 1876. This sixty-room Italianate-style mansion is an opulent two-storey construction, surrounded by formal gardens that include a lake. A large part of the original grounds now belongs to Werribee State Research Farm, established in 1912, and the 1921 Point Cook RAAF Base. Between 1923 and 1972 the mansion was used as a Jesuit seminary, but Werribee Park is now government-owned and open to the public. *Population 72 230*

YOU YANGS FOREST PARK ■ 988

Just outside Lara, this 2025-hectare park is composed of ancient steep volcanic hills, cloaked with native bush and trees such as red stringybarks, river red gums and manna gums. Over 200 species of birds have been recorded here, and koalas and kangaroos also inhabit the park. The highest point, Flinders Peak, is 352 metres above sea level and was climbed by the explorer Matthew Flinders in 1802: a plaque commemorates the occasion. The peak can be reached by a walking track and there are picnic and barbecue facilities.

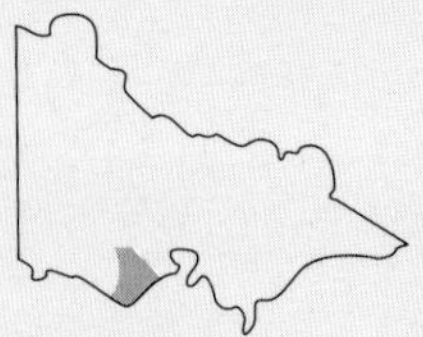

Colac & Anglesea

For over a hundred years wealthy pastoralists north of the Otway Ranges have crossed the mountains for holidays on the beaches of Victoria's south coast. Nowadays, while the tourist trade thrives in the south, the once healthy rural economy of the north faces an uncertain future.

ANGLESEA ■ 989

The beach resort of Anglesea has been a destination for Melbourne and Geelong holiday-makers since before the turn of the century, but it was the arrival of the motor car that made it a bustling resort.

Anglesea is the ideal place 'to get away from it all' and visitors flock there in the summer months to surf, swim, boat, fish, walk, drive and just appreciate the relaxed atmosphere. Fine surf beaches are perhaps the major attraction, and Anglesea is unusual in having retained the high sand dunes that were once a common feature of this coast.

The beach and rocks are also good for fishing as is the river. Originally known as Swampy Creek, the river's name was changed in 1885 to the more attractive Anglesea River. The coastal hamlet with holiday homes that grew around the popular fishing spot took its name from the river.

Flora and fauna reserves in the vicinity of Anglesea are home to a variety of plants and animals and the town is noted for its wildflowers, its birdlife, and its kangaroos, which join golfers on the local course. Many walks and drives wind through the reserves and Angahook–Lorne State Forest (see Lorne); from the various lookouts and vantage points views take in the town, ocean, Otway Range, and evidence of the district's brown coal deposits.

Coal has been mined near the town since 1959 and today an open-cut mine is operated to supply fuel for the Anglesea power station that feeds the aluminium plant in Geelong. *Population 1980*

FESTIVALS Angair – Wildflowers and Art Show, late September.

APOLLO BAY ■ 990

Apollo Bay has been a fickle haven to ships navigating the gale-wracked waters of Bass Strait. The first European visitors to the bay were sealers and whalers who sheltered there and in nearby Loutit Bay from the fierce storms that buffet the region. As traffic through Bass Strait increased, many other ships followed their example – including the schooner *Apollo* which gave the bay its name – some of them destined never to leave these waters.

The most tragic shipwreck was that of the steamer *Casino* in 1932. A regular visitor to the bay, the *Casino* capsized in heavy seas after trying to dock at the jetty. Despite heroic rescue attempts, ten people perished.

White settlement of the Apollo Bay hinterland followed the timber-getters who ranged the Otways from around 1850. The settlement first known as Middleton, then Krambruk, and not until 1898 as Apollo Bay, developed as a port for loading ships with the logs from the ranges.

Weather and conditions at the bay eventually proved too uncertain for this and by 1860 the timber trade there had ceased. Farming, fishing and tourism have taken its place, with the regional population swelling to over 30 000 in the holiday season. *Population 890*

CAPE OTWAY ■ 991

Cape Albany Otway – to use the full name – west of Melbourne, marks the entry point of vessels into Bass Strait. The cape was named by Lieutenant James Grant, who sailed through in 1800, in honour of his friend Captain Albany Otway. The similarly honoured Otway Ranges extend all the way down to the cape and apart from a rough bush track, the cape's lighthouse had to be approached by ship until 1937 when a road was built.

CAPE OTWAY LIGHTHOUSE In August 1845, the 810-tonne barque *Cataraqui* with 408 people on board struck a reef near King Island in wild storms that had blown the ship eighty kilometres off course. Seventeen of those washed overboard reached safety on the shores of the island where they were eventually found by survivors of another recent shipwreck. Together they lived off seal and wallaby meat – burying as many of the dead washed ashore as they could – until they were rescued a month later.

The captain of the *Cataraqui* had mistakenly believed he was near to Cape Otway and the disaster tragically highlighted the need for a lighthouse there – something that had been mooted four years earlier. Governor Gipps authorised the construction of Cape Otway Lighthouse, the second on the mainland, and work began in 1846. The lighthouse, made of sandstone and completed in 1848, has the distinguished record of never having broken down in more than 140 years of service. Standing on the edge of a bluff above the crashing ocean, its light can be seen twenty-two kilometres out to sea.

In was not the end of tragedy at Cape Otway, however. In 1880 *Eric the Red*, a barque loaded with goods and sailing out of New York, struck the nearby Otway Reef and broke

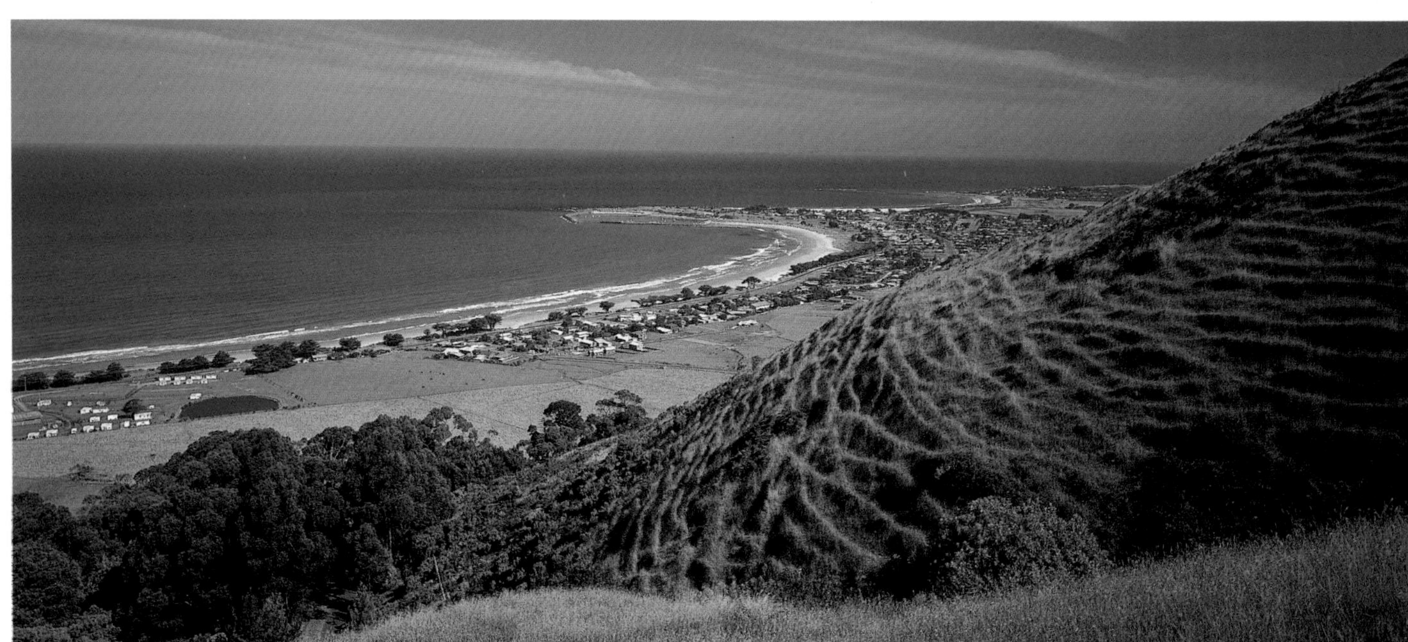

The foothills of the Otway Ranges come right down to the sea at Apollo Bay where fishing boats shelter behind the protective neck of Point Bunbury.

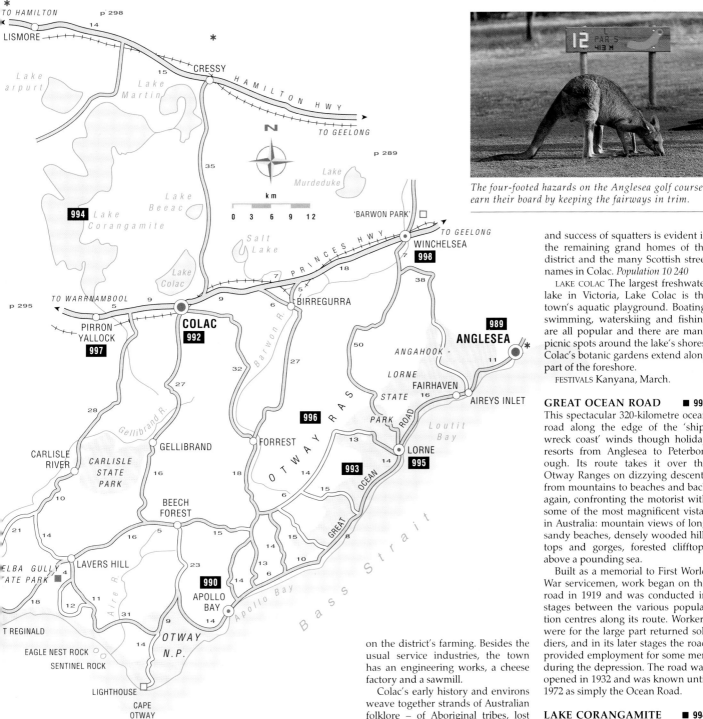

The four-footed hazards on the Anglesea golf course earn their board by keeping the fairways in trim.

up, with the loss of four men. Twenty-one survivors were rescued and debris was washed ashore as far afield as Apollo Bay and Peterborough. Timber recovered from the ship was used by some Apollo Bay residents to repair their houses. In 1881, a flashing red light was installed in the tower to alert ships to the imminence of the reef.

The reef that *Eric the Red* struck is visible from the lighthouse and one of the ship's anchors can be seen lodged firmly in the rocks below. A cemetery containing the weathered graves of shipwreck victims and lighthouse staff is nearby. The lighthouse is open to the public at certain times of the week.

COLAC ■ 992

Situated on the fertile volcanic soil of the world's third largest volcanic plain, Colac has been a pastoral and agricultural centre since Hugh Murray led a party of Van Diemen's Land squatters to the banks of Lake Colac in 1837. The good soil and relatively treeless plains of the district suited them, and since then the area has sustained dairy cattle, pigs, poultry, and the growing of vegetable crops, in particular potatoes and onions. As well, timber has long been harvested from the Otway Ranges.

The town of Colac, on the southern edge of Lake Colac, grew up from its location on the old coaching route, but its development has relied on the district's farming. Besides the usual service industries, the town has an engineering works, a cheese factory and a sawmill.

Colac's early history and environs weave together strands of Australian folklore – of Aboriginal tribes, lost explorers, pioneer timber-cutters and a wealthy squattocracy. Murray's party was not the first group of Europeans in the region. The explorers Gellibrand and Hesse, who had set out to explore the Upper Barwon region mysteriously disappeared in 1837, believed attacked by Aborigines, and searchers for them had passed through the Colac district. The inhabitants of the south banks of Lake Colac were then believed to have been the Kolakngat tribe, from whom the name Colac derives.

The district's agricultural start was helped by the arrival of large numbers of Irish settlers. Together with selectors who came after the goldrushes, the Irish settlers were often in conflict over land with the large squatter pastoralists. The supremacy and success of squatters is evident in the remaining grand homes of the district and the many Scottish street names in Colac. *Population 10 240*

LAKE COLAC The largest freshwater lake in Victoria, Lake Colac is the town's aquatic playground. Boating, swimming, waterskiing and fishing are all popular and there are many picnic spots around the lake's shores. Colac's botanic gardens extend along part of the foreshore.

FESTIVALS Kanyana, March.

GREAT OCEAN ROAD ■ 993

This spectacular 320-kilometre ocean road along the edge of the 'shipwreck coast' winds though holiday resorts from Anglesea to Peterborough. Its route takes it over the Otway Ranges on dizzying descents from mountains to beaches and back again, confronting the motorist with some of the most magnificent vistas in Australia: mountain views of long sandy beaches, densely wooded hilltops and gorges, forested clifftops above a pounding sea.

Built as a memorial to First World War servicemen, work began on the road in 1919 and was conducted in stages between the various population centres along its route. Workers were for the large part returned soldiers, and in its later stages the road provided employment for some men during the depression. The road was opened in 1932 and was known until 1972 as simply the Ocean Road.

LAKE CORANGAMITE ■ 994

The intensive volcanic activity to which the Colac area was subjected as recently as 6000 years ago has resulted in a wealth of interesting land formations. Numerous crater lakes dot the area, of which Lake Corangamite is the largest. It is also the largest lake in Victoria and its waters are three times saltier than sea water. Between Lake Colac (see Colac) and Lake Corangamite lies Red Rock Lookout atop Australia's youngest (extinct) volcano; from this point up to thirty lakes are visible.

LORNE ■ 995

For long a favourite holiday resort of the wealthy, something which has endowed the town with a certain graciousness, Lorne today is a popular tourist destination for all people

Lack of creek or river outlets means that the non-crater lakes on the volcanic plain facing Colac are up to three times saltier than the ocean.

and is within easy driving distance of Melbourne and Geelong.

Like the other beach towns on the stretch of south coast bordered by the Otway Ranges, Lorne nestles between the magnificence of the mountains and the sparkle and shine of the ocean. But it was the timber of the ranges that attracted its first residents and, for a time, Lorne was a depot for loading beached ships with felled logs for transport to Melbourne and Geelong. As timber supplies grew thin and the industry faded, fishing became – and remains – important, notwithstanding the fierceness of storms in Loutit Bay. A crane sometimes operates to lift vessels up onto the jetty during storms.

Tourist development began late in the 1860s when the grazier Mountjoy brothers extended their two-roomed house into a temperance hotel and used their horses to bring coachloads of people over the Otways on the inland roads that preceded the Great Ocean Road. Their house eventually became Erskine House which operates today as a guesthouse. Now, Lorne boasts many restaurants and old-style guesthouses. Its best known event is the annual Pier-to-Pub, the world's biggest blue-water swim that attracts up to 2500 entrants.

As well as the many, fine historic buildings, a century-old suspension bridge running from the main beach to the town contributes to Lorne's charm. On the town's southern outskirts is Teddys Lookout which gives impressive views of the coastline; to the north is the Angahook–Lorne State Park. *Population 1140*

ANGAHOOK-LORNE STATE PARK Walking tracks or leisurely drives through this 22 000-hectare park pass through spectacular terrain – Erskine Falls, Cora Lynne Cascades and gorges, peaks, cliffs and beaches too numerous to name. Some of the flora found in the forest include treeferns, wild orchids and she-oaks. Black tailed and red-necked wallabies, gliders, echidnas, possums and the poteroo also inhabit the forest. The endangered peregrine falcon breeds on the coastal cliffs.

FESTIVALS Pier-to-Pub, early January; Great Otway Classic Marathon, early June.

OTWAY RANGES ■ 996

The Otway Ranges stretch from Anglesea to Cape Otway, dropping to the waters of Bass Strait in the south and giving way to the volcanic plains of the Colac region to the north. With an average of 2000 millimetres of rain per year in their southern section, the ranges are one of the wettest areas of Victoria, and support verdant forests of tall mountain ash, blue gum, mountain grey gum, myrtle beech, with ground cover of ferns and mosses. The drier north side of the ranges is less dense.

The most rugged parts of the ranges lie to the north and the south-east, their highest point being just west of Lorne. To the south-west they are more rounded. Numerous streams and rivers tumble down the slopes and many picnic spots are located at the site of waterfalls.

A number of state and national parks – Angahook-Lorne State Park to the south-east (see Lorne), Carlisle State Park to the north-west, Melba Gully State Park to the south-west and Otway National Park around Cape Otway (see entries) – have been declared in an effort to conserve and reafforest the many logged areas of the ranges. The hardwood timbers here caught the eye of timber-getters as early as 1848, and logging flourished when the railway reached the Otways half a century later. As tall, hardwood stands were exhausted and demand dropped, logging was scaled down although it still persists in some parts. Farming and grazing made incursions into the range's northern forests early last century and remain today.

MELBA GULLY Considered one of the prettiest parts of the Otways, Melba Gully Park extends over forty-eight hectares near the town of Lavers Hill. Dense rainforest covers the area and is home to ringtail possums, walaroos and shy platypuses. Walking tracks wind through the forest and in the summer months rangers conduct guided tours at night to see the eerie light of glow-worms.

OTWAY NATIONAL PARK Extending around the east and west sides of Cape Otway, Otway National Park was proclaimed in 1981 and now includes areas that were previously Port Campbell National Park. Many of the old tramways through the park, relics of the days of logging, are used as walking tracks by visitors.

PIRRON YALLOCK ■ 997

West of Colac, along the Princes Highway at Pirron Yallock, are the floating islands, great masses of peat which have become detached from their bases and now float over a man-made lake. The 'island' description is apt – some of the masses of peat are thirty metres across and carry a thick cover of vegetation.

WINCHELSEA ■ 998

Winchelsea holds an ignominious position in the history of Australia as the first recorded place where rabbits were let loose. In 1859, a grazier, Thomas Austin, decided to import twelve pairs of rabbits for hunting, along with foxes, pheasants and quail. By 1865, 20 000 acclimatised rabbits had been killed but those that had escaped the hunter's gun were busily going about one of the world's most successful colonisations.

The Austin family arrived in the Winchelsea district in 1837 with Hugh Murray's party from Van Diemen's Land (see Colac) and were said to have been allocated their land after drawing lots with their companions. Their influence in the area was great as was their hospitality. After the opening of the new bluestone bridge in Winchelsea in 1867, the Duke of Edinburgh went to the Austin's property to shoot rabbits and stayed there so long he missed a reception held for him at Colac.

Winchelsea was first known as Barwon and developed as a stopping place on the site of a natural ford over the Barwon River. In 1851, Governor La Trobe changed its name to Winchelsea, by which time the Barwon Inn and St Thomas' Anglican church had been built, the Barwon Post Office opened; and an Aboriginal mission set up – and disbanded.

Winchelsea consolidated as more farmers came to the western districts of Victoria, and today it services the farming sector and the passing traffic on the Princes Highway. Impressive reminders of its past are to be seen in the many grand homesteads in the district built by successful pastoralists. *Population 970*

BARWON PARK HOMESTEAD The most celebrated of the historic mansions in the region, 'Barwon Park' was completed in 1871 for Thomas Austin, his third dwelling on the property.

A special ship was chartered by Austin to bring out materials from England for his new forty-two-room home; another brought out furnishings and furniture. The two-storey structure known as 'The Mansion' features a palatial timber staircase ascending magnificently from the entrance hall and intricate lace ironwork which drapes the exterior as it decorates a verandah. It became a National Trust property in 1973.

High rainfall in the southern part of the Angahook-Lorne Park accelerated the regeneration of this mountain ash forest after the 1983 bushfires.

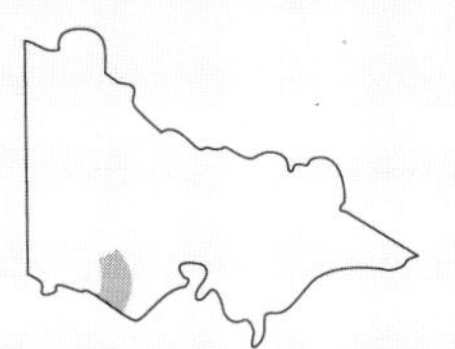

Camperdown & Terang

This is a region of starkly contrasting landscapes formed by equally contrasting forces – the rugged coastline by the action of wind and water on an ancient seabed, and the crater lakes and cones of the fertile Western District hinterland by volcanic eruption.

Nineteenth-century mariners dubbed the wild coastline guarded by the Twelve Apostles, the 'shipwreck coast'.

CAMPERDOWN ■ 999

Camperdown sits in the heart of the great volcanic plain of Victoria's Western District and is surrounded by the Crater Lakes. This is a basalt plain, the third largest in the world and the result of volcanic activity which has taken place over the past twenty million years. The town lies at the foot of Mount Leura (313 metres) an ancient volcanic cone formed when molten lava forced its way to the surface and flowed across the surrounding flat landscape.

In 1851, Government Surveyor Robert Scott, seeking a suitable spot for a town after an earlier site several kilometres to the north was deemed too marshy, was elated by the 'miles of fertile plains, hills and valleys' and the town was established in 1853. Camperdown's main street is flanked by a shady avenue of English elms planted in 1876, and dominated by a red brick clock tower, a gift in 1896 of the pioneering Manifold family, early settlers in the district, as a memorial to Thomas Manifold who was killed in a hunting accident. Another of their number is poet and folklorist John Manifold.

The dry stone walls which are a feature of the countryside were built in the 1860s by highly skilled wallers from Ireland and Scotland. A frame was used as a guide and the stones were packed between, each carefully selected to fill the required gap. The walls were set in deep trenches as a deterrent to the recently introduced rabbit pest. *Population 3320*

CRATER LAKES Lakes Bullen Merri and Gnotuk lie side by side in twin craters of the volcanic mound of Mount Bullen Merri, on the western outskirts of Camperdown. They are separated only by a narrow strip of land but their water levels differ by more than nearly fifty metres. Bullen Merri is more than eighty metres deep, and contains fresh water, while Gnotuk, some thirty metres deep, is more salty than the sea. Water from Bullen Merri can seep into Gnotuk, but for water from Gnotuk there is no escape save through evaporation, hence its high salinity.

Bullen Merri has safe swimming areas at the South Beach Reserve and in common with nearby Purrumbete, another crater lake and also a water bird sanctuary, is stocked with both trout and the rare quinnat salmon, providing some of the finest freshwater fishing in Victoria. Other crater lakes in the vicinity include Bookar and Colongulac.

PURRUMBETE HOMESTEAD The Manifold family settled on the shores of Lake Purrumbete in 1839 and in so doing founded one of the country's most long-lived squatting dynasties. Their homestead, sited on a narrow isthmus, was continuously occupied by Manifolds from 1842, when the simple bluestone and weatherboard building at its core was begun, until sold outside the family in 1983. The complex of twenty-eight rooms, plus outbuildings, is noted for its blackwood panelling, carved gallery, and especially for its murals by Walter Withers depicting pioneering scenes.

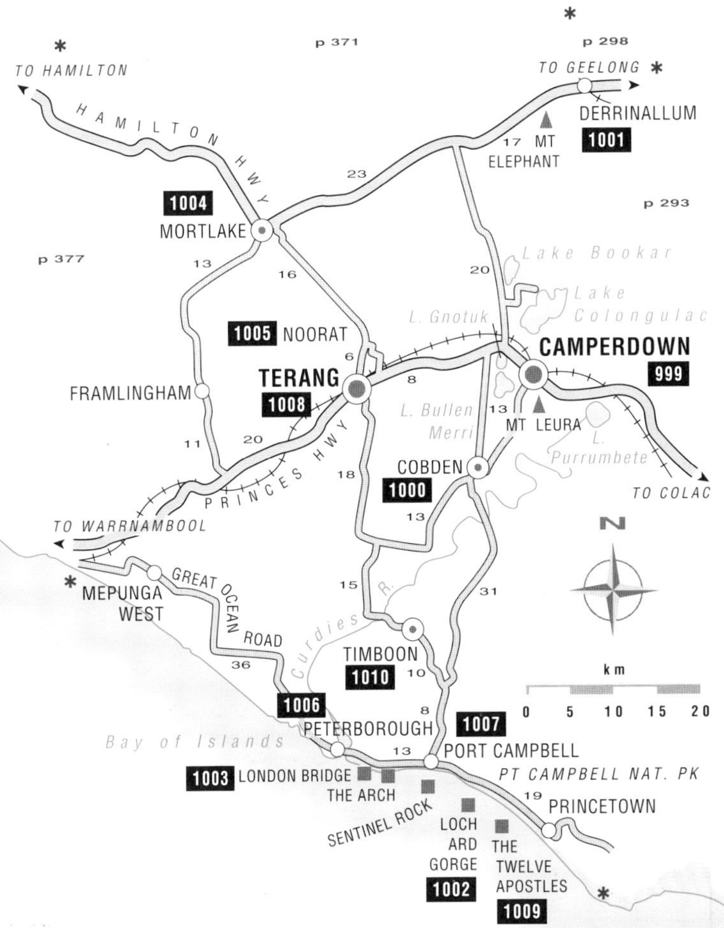

COBDEN ■ 1000

A pretty town set in grazing country south-west of Camperdown, Cobden was first known as Lovely Banks. Its present name honours the English free-trade advocate Richard Cobden. *Population 1480*

TANDAROOK RUN This land was taken up in 1840 by Daniel Curdie, a Scottish doctor who arrived in Sydney in 1839 and with his nephew overlanded cattle to Melbourne, then struck out west to these rich plains where they settled in 1840, establishing one of the Western District's earliest runs. Parts of the original cottage, built in 1843, can still be seen.

DERRINALLUM ■ 1001

The gently humped Mount Elephant (393 metres) dominates this town and is the highest of the region's volcanic cones. In January 1944, most of Derrinallum was destroyed by a major bushfire, which swept through the thick dry grass of the Western District causing appalling stock losses and turning to ash irreplaceable records and early buildings. In Derrinallum, only the Mechanics Institute, two churches and a handful of business premises survived.

When surveyed in the 1860s, the settlement here was known as Tooliorook. Its present name is that of a run taken up in 1839 and comes from an Aboriginal word meaning 'tern' or 'sea swallow', a reference to the flocks that gathered at the foot of Mount Elephant when the area was marsh. It was also a meeting place for Aborigines who gathered here when marsh birds bred and swans' eggs were plentiful.

LARRA This property on the southern and western flanks of Mount Elephant was occupied by the Currie family for more than a century. In 1844, the run was bought from John Kinross by John Lang Currie, a twenty-five-year-old farmer's son from the Scottish border country. The 1944 bushfire claimed the original Larra homestead, built one hundred years before from squared rubble scattered from the volcano, but spared its successor, a single-storey basalt structure built in 1875 and sited fortuitously close to springs which nurtured a protective screen of lush vegetation. Still standing are Larra's stone stables, with steepled bell-cote, built in 1873. The first cloth to come from Victoria's first woollen mill (in Geelong) was woven from Larra fleece.

LOCH ARD GORGE ■ 1002

In 1878, the foaming waters enclosed by these precipitous and spectacularly eroded cliffs were the scene of the tragic loss of the clipper *Loch Ard*, carrying immigrants, which shrouded in a thick mist and 'with a fearful, shuddering crash' ran aground off Muttonbird Island, several hundred metres from the mainland. Of its complement of more than fifty, only two survived. One was Tom Pearce, an eighteen-year-old senior apprentice, who swam to shore after being washed into the gorge. He heard the cries of passenger Eva Carmichael, also eighteen, who unable to swim and clinging to a broken spar, had also been washed into the gorge. He helped her to the safety of a cave (now known by her name) on the west side of the beach, gave her brandy from a case retrieved from the shore and then scaled the gorge walls to summon aid.

Eva Carmichael had lost both parents and her five brothers and sisters in the disaster and her plight moved the country deeply. This was the worst shipwreck on the Port Campbell coast. Only four bodies were recovered. They are buried in a small cemetery to the west of the gorge. The story of the tragedy is told by a plaque above the gorge close to the steps which now descend to the small beach. The anchor from the Loch Ard stands outside the visitor's centre in Port Campbell (see entry).

BLOWHOLE Water spurts from the breach in this collapsed cavern, several hundred metres inland from Loch Ard Gorge. The underground channel is some 400 metres long, 15 metres deep and 36 metres wide.

LONDON BRIDGE ■ 1003

Testimony to the power of the sea, the once double-arched rock formation of London Bridge is now an isolated span surrounded by white surf following the 1990 collapse of its landward side. Its arches were created in a few decades by waves cutting into the softer rock beneath a narrow solid headland. A collection of historic photographs at the visitor's centre in Port Campbell township shows the shaping and reshaping of the 'bridge'. Eventually the remaining archway will also be reduced to grains of sand. At nearby London Bridge Beach, artificial pipe burrows have been built to encourage the nesting of a colony of fairy penguins.

MORTLAKE ■ 1004

Mortlake stands at the foot of the volcanic cone of Mount Shadwell (200 metres) which a century-and-a-half ago marked the crossing of the ways that connected four large sheep stations. It was thus a meeting place for station hands. The first European influence here was the formation of the Mount Shadwell run in 1839; by the end of the year another five runs had been taken up. Because of its reliable springs the spot became a regular camping place for teams on their way to and from Port Fairy and Warrnambool and by the early 1850s a fledgling township existed and farming on the surrounding fertile volcanic soil was under way.

Early local farmers and pastoralists became prosperous by feeding the thousands of hopefuls who flocked to the goldfields, many of them passing through Mortlake on their way from the coast, after the 1854 discovery of the metal at Ararat. Many of Mortlake's fine bluestone buildings, including those in Shaw Street such as the post office and court house both built in 1864 date from this period of sudden prosperity. Today, the area is renowned for the quality of its wool clip and regular cattle sales are held in the town. *Population 1040*

NOORAT ■ 1005

This little township was the birthplace, in 1902, of short-story writer Alan Marshall, author of *I Can Jump Puddles*. Noorat's bluestone memorial Presbyterian Church commemorates the early Scottish settler Niel Black (see Terang). The volcanic slopes of nearby Mount Noorat (313 metres) were once a meeting place for local Aboriginal groups who traded greenstone, sandstone and animal skins. A walking track winds to the summit of the rise.

PETERBOROUGH ■ 1006

Peterborough, on the Great Ocean Road 300 kilometres west of Melbourne, is sited at the mouth of Curdies River where sandhills and beaches mark a break in the jagged cliff line which ranges east and west

By the mid-1800s, British settlers had tamed Victoria's Western District; Eugène von Guérard's 1860 painting of a homestead near Camperdown depicted a rustic scene worthy of the old country.

from the town. It offers both a fine surfing beach and the calm, broad waters of Curdies Inlet, a popular spot for fishing, swimming, sailing and sailboarding.

A settlement grew up here after the foundering in 1855 of the clipper *Schomberg* while making a record-breaking journey from Liverpool to Melbourne under the command of the flamboyant 'Bully' Hayes. Some itinerant folk who came to see the wreck or salvage its booty liked the area and stayed.

PORT CAMPBELL ■ 1007

Into an awesome and dangerous coastline is set the quiet cove of Port Campbell, the only safe anchorage in these treacherous parts. Originally called Campbell's Creek for the small stream that enters the sea here, it is named after the buccaneering Captain Alexander Campbell, one-time whaler, who is said to have traded from the tiny harbour with his ship *Condor*. By the time the coast was first surveyed in the 1840s, pastoralists were already settled on the rich hinterland and for many years the small farming community was served by this port. Its T-shaped wharf, built in 1879, is now used by the town's crayfishing fleet.

In the early 1880s, the area was the subject of one of the most extraordinary hoaxes ever perpetrated in Australia involving the supposed landing of an invading Russian fleet heading for Melbourne. The town's importance as a port declined after the arrival of the railway at nearby Timboon (see entry) in 1892. Its tiny beach is one of the few in the area safe for swimming.

PORT CAMPBELL NATIONAL PARK Comprising some 1750 hectares, this park hugs the coastal cliffs for some thirty kilometres and contains some of the wildest and most spectacular scenery in Australia. The shoreline here is in dramatic retreat. Relentlessly pounding waves and wind-whipped waters are eating into its craggy walls and pushing the coast back faster than in any other part of Australia. The remains of an ancient seabed, the sandstone and limestone of these disappearing cliffs was laid down more than twenty-five million years ago when sea levels were some 100 metres higher than at present.

Back from the precipices, the heath blanketing the headlands is home to wallabies, bandicoots and tiny birds. A two-and-a-half kilometre, self-guided 'discovery' walking track runs west from Port Campbell Creek to Two Mile Beach, a ninety-minute return walk. Brochures to the numbered signposts are available from the Visitors' Centre. The Great Ocean Road (see *Colac & Anglesea*) winds through the park on either side of Port Campbell, in many places coming within a metre or so of the cliff edge. Like the bluffs and promontories it crosses, the road too will one day be claimed by the sea.

MUTTONBIRD ISLAND Several hundred metres from the mainland, Muttonbird Island, as its name suggests, is an important breeding ground for short-tailed shearwaters, also known as muttonbirds (see *Coffs Harbour & Sawtell*). Each year they arrive with the summer to begin nesting, and when the breeding season comes to an end in April, depart on the five-to-seven-week flight to their Northern Hemisphere feeding grounds in the Bering Sea, between Alaska and Siberia. The clipper *Loch Ard* came to grief here in 1878 after hitting one of the outlying reefs of the island. It was wrecked with the loss of all but two of those aboard (see Loch Ard Gorge).

In Camperdown, the clock tower commemorates Thomas Manifold, the statue, his brother James.

TERANG ■ 1008

European settlement here began when the 'Glenormiston' run was taken up in 1839. In the following year, the property was acquired by Argyleshire Scotsman, Niel Black, whose descendants still live in the area. The first building was a shepherd's hut built at the edge of Lake Terang, now a dry basin and site of the town's sporting complex.

Black's grand home, the ground floor of which dates from 1852, now operates as the administrative offices of Glenormiston Agricultural College and, with its gardens, is open to the public. The college conducts courses in horse management and farm management, and its library and facilities are an important resource centre for the local community. The dairying lands surrounding Terang supply the district's butter factories, creameries and a powdered-milk plant. A century ago, each farm produced and was known for its own cheese. When the railway arrived in 1887, it offered a quick route to Melbourne markets for other more perishable produce, thus encouraging closer farming – a continuing trend with the influx of soldier-settlers after both world wars.

This district is also horse country and Terang has a racecourse – venue for district racing club meetings – the Dalvui Raceway for trotting races and a polo ground of international standard. *Population 4030*

THE TWELVE APOSTLES ■ 1009

The stone stacks and pillars which rise straight out of the sea east of Port Campbell were once mainland cliff front. Many of them still host coastal heath plants, relics of their recent detachment. Made of tougher stuff, the 'Apostles' have so far withstood the attack of wind and wave, but all will eventually fall to the battering of the elements. There are in fact only eight 'apostles' – some visible only at low tide – to be viewed from lookouts off the Great Ocean Road.

TIMBOON ■ 1010

Timboon is nestled in the wooded hills south-west of Camperdown on the road to Port Campbell in a dairying, wool and timber-cutting area and is known for the cheese it produces. Its name comes from the local Aboriginal word for a cutting implement made of mussel shell. A local landmark is the timber trestle bridge at Curdies Siding, built in 1892 to carry the railway line across the river and valley. It consists of twenty bush timber trestles with a sawn timber superstructure and footway, and is one of only a few railway structures of its type in Victoria. *Population 740*

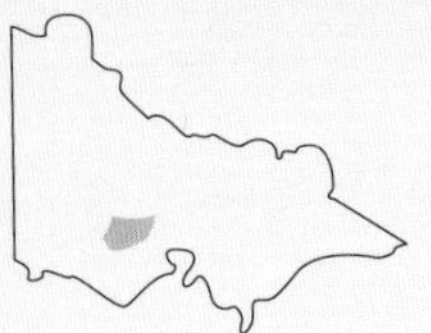

Ballarat & Daylesford

Gold! Gold! Gold! In the 1850s, dreams of fortunes in fleece changed to dreams of much greater wealth as tens of thousands flocked to the goldfields. Towns grew up wherever a find was reported; nowadays they have a different, more balanced focus.

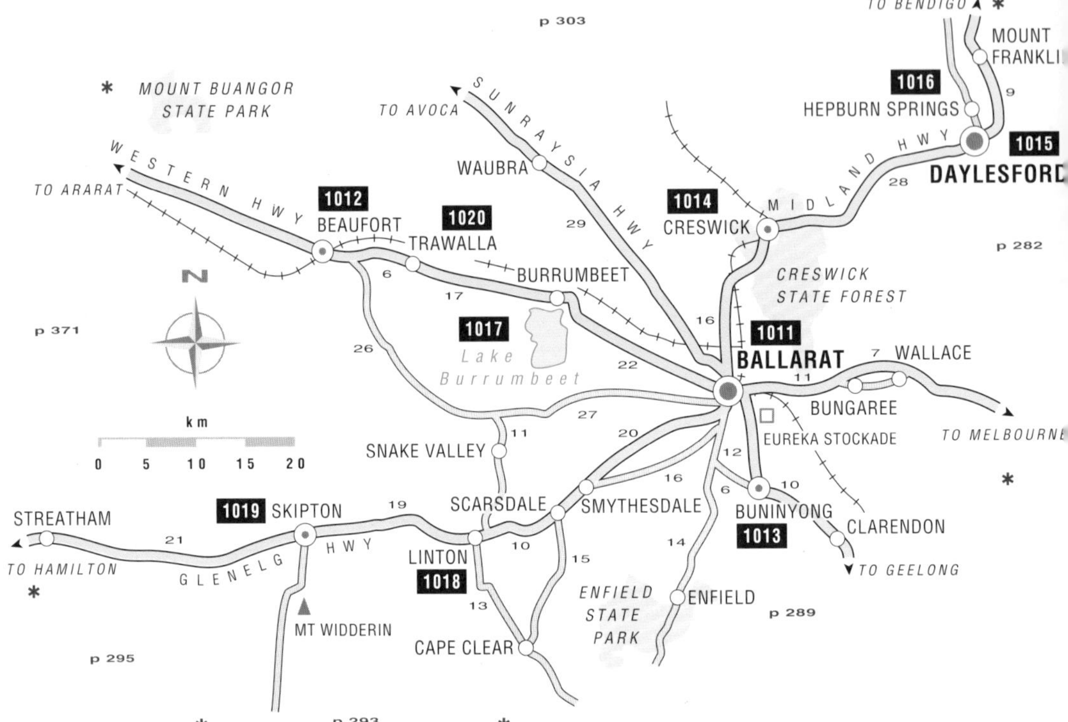

BALLARAT ■ **1011**

The name Ballarat (or Ballaarat) probably comes from two Aboriginal words – 'balla' and 'arat', which are thought to mean 'resting place'. Australia's largest inland city after Canberra lies in the southern region of Victoria's Central Highlands and has a worldwide reputation for beautiful begonias. The Western Highway approach is lined by trees for twenty-one kilometres – one tree for every enlisted soldier from Ballarat in the First World War and there is also an Arch of Victory.

Ballarat has been called 'City of Statues', the 'Historical City' and the 'Garden City' – all fitting epithets. Its golden origins are evident in the ornate, flamboyant buildings, the elaborately laid out gardens and the grand streetscapes. In 1838, pioneer squatters camped on the shores of 'Black Swamp' or 'Yuille's Swamp' where Aborigines had camped for many years before them. The site has long since been landscaped into beautiful Lake Wendouree.

Counting people was a full-time job in the nineteenth century – Victoria's population increased fourfold between 1851 and 1854. In the early 1870s, Ballarat had between 50 000 and 65 000 inhabitants and was the biggest 'gold' city the world had ever known. Royalty visited and stayed at Craig's Hotel – afterwards called Royal; Her Majesty's Theatre (1875) billed great performing artists like Dame Nellie Melba. The English novelist, Anthony Trollope, found '...a town so well-built, so well-ordered, endowed with present advantages so great in the way of schools, hospitals, libraries, hotels, public gardens'. Modern buildings such as the Ballarat Shire Offices now mix with Victorian architecture. Specks of gold or nuggets could be retrieved from alluvial deposits in creek beds by solitary prospectors. They were soon exhausted and then the going became tough. Miners began working the deeper quartz reefs in groups, usually of four – one down the hole digging, one winching the buckets of rock to the surface for crushing and panning or cradling and two cutting timber for shaft props. This was a risky method – one Ballarat digger told a parliamentary committee in 1853: 'The deep sinking is nothing more or less than a species of lottery'.

It was not all work though and the entertainment was varied. Lola Montez performed her sensational spider dance in the original Victoria Theatre to the delight of the miners who showered her with tiny nuggets. Henry Seekamp, the founding editor of the *Ballarat Times*, declared her performance indecent and the feisty Lola took to him with a horsewhip. By way of complete cultural contrast, the first recorded Australian eisteddfod was organised by Welsh miners in 1855.

The third phase of mining at Ballarat involved sinking huge shafts and working deep underground. This deep-lead method was practised by large companies which often reaped rich rewards. They brought complex machinery to the fields and employed many men. Five large nuggets, all mined in the 1850s, are among the heaviest ever found in Australia. The largest, the Welcome nugget, was eventually displayed at the Crystal Palace in London. The last company mine closed in 1918.

Though founded firmly on gold, Ballarat's future is in industry – in the factories that cure bacon and make biscuits, clothing, bricks, brake linings, ball bearings, farm machinery and house paints; in the brass and iron foundries. The city relies on tourism too – a lucrative asset to the 1990s economy. *Population 64 980*

HER MAJESTY'S THEATRE This grand Victorian theatre has been restored to its original ornate glory and is run as a commercial proposition; each Easter it attracts opera-lovers from all over Australia when it plays host to the Victorian Opera Company

BALLARAT FINE ART GALLERY Established in 1884, this gallery has the most comprehensive regional collection of Australian art. One room is devoted to works by the Lindsay family: Norman, Lionel, Percy, Ruby and Daryl. The gallery also holds the Eureka flag (see box).

MONUMENTS AND STATUARY Thomas Stoddart, a Scot who arrived around 1854, inspired Ballarat's remarkable collection of statues. By 1882, he had

Ballarat's brilliant begonias, celebrated in a festival each March, are housed in a Victorian glasshouse.

Ballarat relives the 1850s every day at Sovereign Hill where the grocery shop smells of real tea and coffee.

wealth to spend and went travelling overseas. He purchased twelve statues of Carrara marble from Genoa and sent them back to Ballarat. Other citizens made bequests such as the notable 'Flight from Pompeii', and statues on classical and religious themes or commemorations of distinguished people – Robert Burns, Adam Lindsay Gordon, Burke and Wills, Peter Lalor, Queen Victoria – and events such as Eureka Stockade.

THE OLD CURIOSITY SHOP Bricklayer, James Warwick, built the Old Curiosity Shop in 1855 and lined the walls with coloured glass, dolls' heads and other broken ornaments in intricate patterns. He gave pennies to the children who brought pieces to him.

SOVEREIGN HILL HISTORICAL PARK This living museum near Ballarat was opened in 1970 on the site of the former Sovereign Quartz Mining Company and set out to recreate the Ballarat diggings in the 1850s. The poppet head dominates the mine, while coaches clatter down the main street and the shops are open for business. Apart from seeing, it is even possible to get a feel for a bygone age by having a go at panning for gold.

FESTIVALS Begonia Festival, March; Opera Festival, Easter.

Central Ballarat: Craig's Hotel (left) and the town hall (right) flank a building missing the dome from its turret.

BEAUFORT ■ 1012

In its golden days, this small settlement in the foothills of the Pyrenees was a rough and noisy town on Yam Hole Creek; the nearby Fiery Creek diggings were exceptionally rich in shallow alluvial gold. When the mining stopped, the district reverted to sheep farming which had been started in 1838 at nearby Trawalla (see entry). The locally bred merino sheep have given the district an enviable reputation as woolgrowing country. Other local industries include cereal growing and raising fat lambs, beef cattle and pigs. Secondary industry includes a woollen mill, timber treatment plant, saw mill and engineering plant.

Brass bands were popular in the mining towns and the Beaufort band rotunda, erected in 1903 to commemorate the reign of Queen Victoria, is a classic of its time: the octagonal shape, the balcony iron lacework, the practice room underneath and the graceful clock tower are of a style adopted around the world at the turn of the century.

The year 1923 saw the first 'happy little Vegemites' when Dr C.P. Callister from Beaufort, working for the Melbourne firm Fred Walker and Co., created a spread from yeast extract, though it was not called Vegemite at first and took a few years to become something of a national icon. Other famous Beaufort sons include Prime Minister James Scullin who was born in a gate-opener's cottage at Trawalla (see entry) and the poet Bernard O'Dowd. *Population 1170*

BUNINYONG ■ 1013

Wisely they talk of wheat and wool
From Boort to Buninyong.

It is likely the people around Buninyong still chat about much the same subjects as C.J. Dennis – above – said they did, for agriculture has always been important, from the beginnings in 1838 when the Learmonth brothers pitched their tents, through to the present day.

By the time gold was found at Hiscock's Gully on 8 August 1851 and the lure of lucre pulled thousands to the area, Buninyong was already a sizeable township – the first large inland town in Victoria. And it was this discovery – recorded by the Hiscock Obelisk – that opened up the Ballarat goldfields. In the early goldrush years there were as many as eight licensed hotels in the borough – the 'Crown' claims to have the oldest continuous licence, going back to 1842, in a different building.

There were more serious establishments too – the Reverend Thomas Hastie, a Presbyterian minister, opened Victoria's first inland boarding school here in 1848. Buninyong settlers were avid readers and the Ashburner Bookselling Business began in Warrenheip Street in 1865.

The Lal Lal Falls are in the vicinity, opposite the site of the old Lal Lal racecourse. The water tumbles thirty-four metres into a sheer gorge. *Population 1630*

FESTIVALS Buninyong Gold King Festival, February.

CRESWICK ■ 1014

The Midland Highway cuts through undulating hills clothed in large pine and eucalypt plantations to Creswick which promotes itself as 'a village of pine and gold' and the 'home of forestry'. The Creswick State Forest, which covers many of the old mine workings, is surrounded by some of the most productive agricultural land in Victoria. Radiata pine from the forest is used for posts, particle board, veneering and paper pulp. Potatoes, cereals, legumes and grasses thrive in the deep, chocolate-coloured soil and a nursery of old-fashioned plants close to the town specialises in roses, lilac, lavender and herbs and old strains of fruit trees such as quinces, pomegranates, medlars and damsons.

The pyramid-shaped white mullock heaps dotted around the landscape are reminders of what went on in the past. Crushed stone from these heaps is used in abrasive household cleaners.

In 1838, Captain John Hepburn settled at Smeaton and built 'Smeaton House' in the late 1840s, a rare example of Regency style in Victoria. The boundary of his run extended as far as the present town. In 1839, W.J.T. 'Big' Clarke established the 'Bean Bean' run with the settlement on its west boundary. A few years later, John, Charles and Henry Creswick took up land on Creswick Creek but soon moved away leaving their name behind them.

Then in the early 1850s, gold was found and the town expanded in the way of so many places dependent on the precious metal – from the appalling conditions of a hastily erected tent town to buildings of substance which give Creswick its present charm. The nearby four-storeyed Smeaton Flour Mill (1862) has an attic storey in the gabled slate roof and a water wheel that weighs twenty-five tonnes. The Creswick Historical Museum displays artefacts from the past and has a spiral staircase of architectural note.

The first rush after the shallow alluvial gold peaked in 1854 with about 25 000 people in the area. The problems facing the Creswick miners were very much the same as those at Ballarat and about 200 walked there to air their grievances at the Eureka Stockade (see box).

The Australasia No. 2 mine was the scene of Australia's worst gold mine disaster when very early on 12 December 1882, forty-four men were trapped by floodwater. Some of them escaped almost immediately but over the ensuing few days twenty-two drowned or suffocated before rescuers could reach them. About 15 000 people attended the funeral at the cemetery and money was raised for the widows and children.

Norman Lindsay, born here in 1879, was but one of many distinguished sons of Creswick. Others include John Curtin, the wartime Prime Minister; Sir Alexander Peacock, three times Premier of Victoria; Sir John Northcott, a Governor of New South Wales; W.G. Spence, founder of the Australian Workers' Union; and Sir Mark Oliphant, atomic physicist and former Governor of South Australia. *Population 2390*

DAYLESFORD ■ 1015

Daylesford, originally known as Wombat or Wombat Creek, is now recognised in tourist literature as the 'spa centre of Australia' because of its location – eighty per cent of Australia's known mineral springs lie round about. There are about twenty springs within ten kilometres of the town and many more within a forty-kilometre radius. The water flows deep underground through volcanic

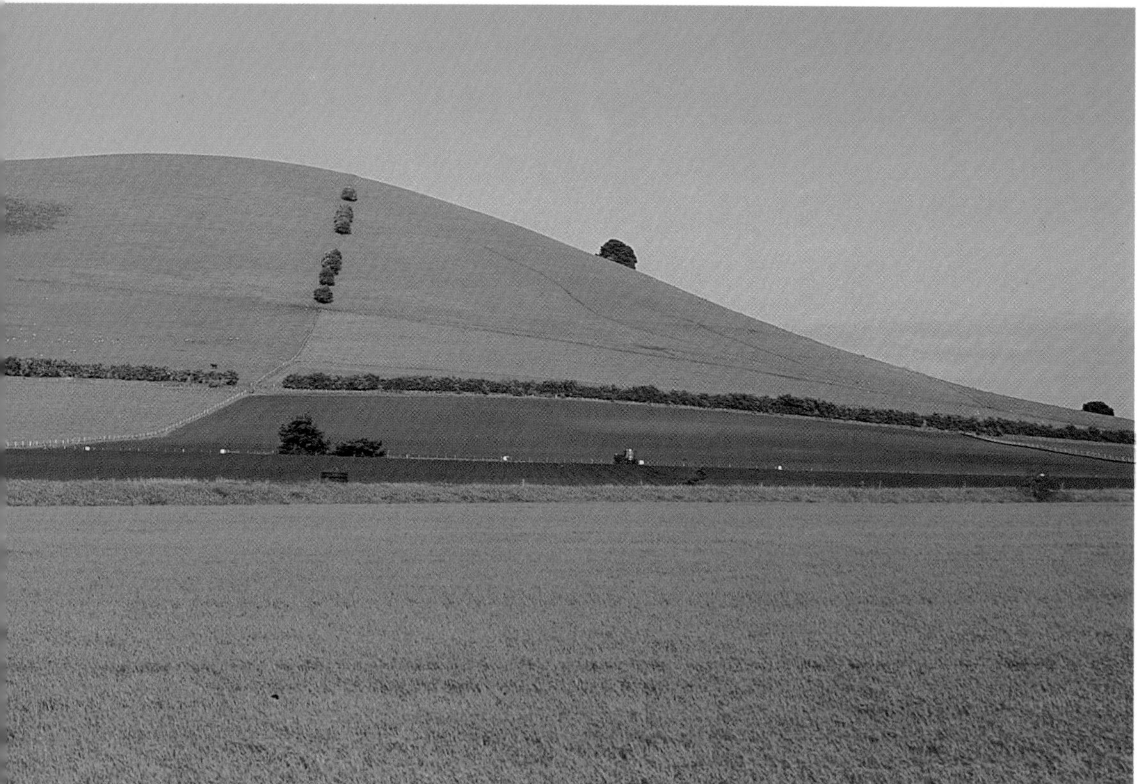

The productive, volcanic soils of the Daylesford hills contain the rich mixture of minerals that make unseen subterranean streams worth bottling when they bubble to the surface at Hepburn Springs (below).

fault lines absorbing minerals such as iron, magnesium, and sulphur, until it bubbles to the surface.

Carbon dioxide gives some spring water a natural effervescence. Such springs have long been respected for their curative properties and Daylesford and the neighbouring Hepburn Spa complex (see entry) are set up to promote health and well-being.

There are three interesting churches in Daylesford: Christ Church and St Peter's Catholic Church, both built in 1863, and St Andrew's Presbyterian Church which boasts the tower used in the long-running ABC television serial *Bellbird*.

This district also yielded that most sought after mineral of the nineteenth century. In August 1851, John Egan and others struck gold at a place called 'Jim Crow Diggings' perhaps after a popular song or from a corruption of the Aboriginal word 'jumcra'. After intense alluvial searches, quartz mining began in the 1860s and continued until the Second World War. Rubies, sapphires and other precious stones have also been found. *Population 3350*

DAYLESFORD HISTORICAL MUSEUM This building in Vincent Street dates from 1880 when it was a school of mines. Five furnaces and a twenty-five-metre chimney remain from the days when gold from the surrounding area was smelted into ingots here before being sent to Melbourne.

FESTIVALS Winter Festival, July; Highland Gathering, December.

HEPBURN SPRINGS ■ 1016

Unspoiled natural springs, which gave Hepburn Springs another focus after the gold was gone, may, in part, be a legacy of thoughtful miners; it is said the miners sometimes abandoned digging those shafts which might have sliced into the water courses. Visitors now come to 'take the waters' – to drink them or have mineral, herbal, bubble, mud or electrical baths, to relax in heated spas or be massaged and pampered. Daylesford's twin resort is named after a retired ship's captain turned drover who camped in the central highlands with his livestock in 1836 and came back to settle there a year later. John Hepburn is believed to be the first European to be taken by the beauty of the place but it is thought that the Aborigines were well aware of the bracing mountain air and therapeutic springs many years before this.

Much of Hepburn Spa's architecture is suggestive of northern Italy – thousands of Swiss Italian settlers came here in the middle of the last century. The old macaroni factory, classified by the National Trust, was built in 1859 by the Lucini brothers out of handmade bricks and has a fine hand-painted ceiling.

LAKE BURRUMBEET ■ 1017

Salty Lake Burrumbeet is the source of some of Victoria's tastiest eels which are caught in special cylindrical nets called fykes. Eels are migratory creatures: after spawning in the Coral Sea off the north coast of Queensland, the adults swim south into the waterways of the east coast and in Victoria they form the basis of an export industry (see Skipton). The lake has dried up only once in living European memory – during the great drought of 1839–41.

ERCILDOUNE HOMESTEAD This Scottish manor house, built from granite in the mid-1850s, was owned by the Learmonth brothers who took up a sheep run here in 1838. Their original split-timber dwelling is also still standing and there is an Egyptian marble wellhead which, according to legend, is two thousand years old.

LINTON ■ 1018

Less than 400 people live in and around the village of Linton today but it has a more populous and vigorous past. For instance Linton's Cricket Club, formed in 1863, frequently played Ballarat.

Mary and Joseph Linton built 'Linton Park' in 1840. They travelled from Scotland via Hobart Town and Geelong with their three small daughters. There were seven more children before Joseph was killed in a buggy accident in 1853. Gold discoveries were made in 1848 in the Wardy Yalloak–Smythsdale region (which included Linton) and in 1854 gold finds at Linton Park began the Linton Diggings and many miners – including a large Chinese contingent – sank shafts in the area. When the gold petered out, a few of the Chinese miners stayed on to establish successful market gardens.

Samuel Lewers opened a branch of the Bank of New South Wales in a tent on the diggings in June 1860. The bushranger Captain Moonlight is said to have stayed with the Lewers many times. When captured, he confessed that only the family's kindness had stopped him robbing the Linton bank.

SKIPTON ■ 1019

The Glenelg Highway runs through the small township of Skipton which stands by Mount Emu Creek surrounded by grazing land. It is the site of Australia's major eel processing centre, where the fish are frozen and sent to Germany; there is a live export trade with Hong Kong. The live eels are transported in oxygen-charged containers at a temperature of 3° Centigrade.

MOUNT WIDDERIN CAVES These long, narrow, volcanic caves south of Skipton, more accurately described as lava tunnels, were formed when tongues of lava forked out and flowed ahead of the main stream of molten rock after a prehistoric eruption here. Skipton Cave contains the largest chamber yet discovered in a lava cave in Australia.

TRAWALLA ■ 1020

This tiny settlement, east of Beaufort, is on the Western Highway beside Mount Emu Creek. Trawalla is believed to mean 'much rain' or 'wild flood water' in an Aboriginal dialect. It is on the site of the original sheep station established by Kenneth Kirkland and his brothers-in-law, James and Robert Hamilton.

Mrs Kirkland's account of life in the colonies can be found in *Chambers' Miscellany* (1845) and gives an interesting insight into the conditions of the times: 'We had neither milk nor butter at any station we were at; nothing but mutton, tea and damper, three times a day. Every meal was alike from one week to another, and from year's end to year's end. I was so sick of it, I could scarcely eat anything'. Despite these early hardships, Mrs Kirkland quickly distinguished her family's run by planting vegetables and fruit and starting a dairy. It is difficult to imagine the pioneers' privations in a region which, 150 years later, produces a wealth of farm and vineyard produce, including a fine quality champagne at the Yellowglen Winery, south-west of Ballarat.

EUREKA: THE DIGGER'S STAND FOR A FAIR GO

Peter Lalor and his compatriots rallied beneath the Southern Cross flag (top), now tattered but treasured in a Ballarat gallery.

THE BALLARAT goldfields at four o'clock in the morning on 3 December 1854 – a time and date firmly embedded in the history of Australia. The *Gold Fields Advocate* reported the events at what became known as the 'Eureka Stockade' thus: 'Sunday, 5 a.m... The events that occurred just one hour ago, which created this horrifying scene, will command a dubious place in the history of our country. At 4 a.m., as dawn paled the night sky, the stockade, built by the diggers of Eureka for their protection and fortification, was the object of a surprise attack by the military'.

What provoked this dramatic rebellion, the worst episode of civil strife in Australia's history? Captain Sir Charles Hotham, who arrived to govern Victoria in August 1854, desperately needed more money to run the colony and saw the goldfields as a potential revenue source. The police were to ensure all miners paid the monthly thirty shilling licence fee with 'on person' inspections twice a week. Some could not afford licences, others did not take them down the wet and muddy shafts.

After all, the Ballarat claims were only 3.7 metres square and sinking deep, narrow mineshafts in the seams of quartz was dangerous, time consuming and expensive, often yielding nothing but a pile of dirt, so that more and more diggers were frustrated in their attempts to make a living. The licence fee was the straw that broke the camel's back.

Late on 6 October or early next day, a miner was murdered near the Eureka Hotel. The publican, James Bentley, was suspected of killing him but the local magistrates' bench acquitted Bentley because of insufficient evidence. The miners claimed Bentley and one of the magistrates, John d'Ewes, were friends, and organised a protest meeting on 17 October after which angry men burnt the Eureka Hotel and three were arrested, charged with riot and arson and convicted.

In the meantime, Bentley was rearrested and convicted of manslaughter while d'Ewes was dismissed from his post but it was too late to appease the furious miners, who had organised themselves into the Ballarat Reform League. The *Ballarat Times* encouraged them in their four major demands to Hotham:

- the release of the three men
- the end of licence fees
- the right to vote and stand for government
- land be made available so miners could buy farms.

Hotham had already established a commission to report on goldfield conditions but he refused to order the release of the convicted men when a delegation met him on Monday, 27 November. Instead, he sent troop reinforcements to Ballarat the next day. On Wednesday, about 4000 men met at Bakery Hill and in a demonstration of defiance some burnt their licences. The government retaliated with a thorough licence search. Shots were fired at the miners and some were arrested.

The miners met again at Bakery Hill to elect Peter Lalor as their leader and hoist the Southern Cross. Tension continued to mount until the weekend by which time a stockade was built. By Saturday night only about 150 men remained on guard because they did not expect an attack on a Sunday. Four hundred troopers attacked just before dawn – the battle lasted just ten minutes. About thirty miners and five troopers were killed. Lalor took a musket ball in the shoulder and went into hiding after the fighting – his arm was later amputated.

The captured rebels were charged with high treason but the Melbourne juries refused to convict them. Lalor was never arrested; he became a member of parliament in 1855. The Eureka rebellion led to the introduction of the 'miner's right' – the payment of one pound sterling a year allowed the holder to dig for gold, vote at elections and stand for the Legislative Assembly. Over time, the miners' stand has come to symbolise a very Australian, anti-authoritarian independence of spirit. □

Thirty years after the event, an Illustrated Australian News *artist depicted the high-spirited scene outside the Melbourne court in February, 1855 when 12 of the 13 Ballarat miners charged with treason were acquitted.*

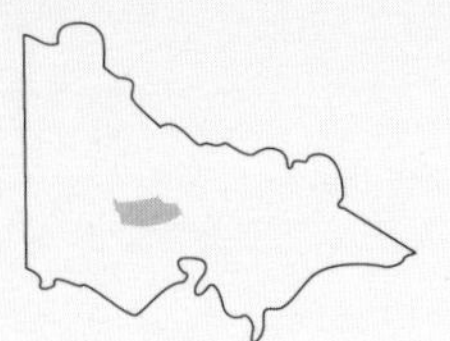

Castlemaine & Maryborough

Gold was responsible for the settlement of central Victoria and thousands came in the gold-rush years. Now there are ghost towns in a plundered landscape where visitors come to find the past.

AVOCA ■ 1021

Avoca is a former mining town at the base of the Pyrenees Range, nowadays surrounded by pastoral and agricultural land. Sheep and beef cattle are raised and grain is grown on the northern plains. Grapes from the region produce full-flavoured wines and some of the local winery labels are Mount Avoca, Chateau Remy, Summerfield, Warrenmang, Taltarni, Redbank and Dalwhinnie.

The mine shafts sunk by the diggers in the 1860s survive and a gold dredge was still working in the area up to the 1950s. Avoca's very mixed group of historic buildings include the original jail, probably the oldest chemist shop in Victoria, Primary School No. 4, Cobb & Co. stables, the court house and a house imported from Switzerland – Tunk's Residence in Dundas Street. The rock museum has meteorites, petrified wood and fossilised fish. *Population 1000*

FESTIVALS Wool and Wine Festival, late October.

CAIRN CURRAN RESERVOIR ■ 1022

The fourteen-kilometre-long Cairn Curran Reservoir holds nearly 150 000 megalitres of water which is used for irrigation, stock and domestic purposes. This artificial lake engulfed the old site of the Joyces Creek school – the school building was moved during the 1920s. The reservoir is well stocked with fish, and recreational activities include swimming, yachting, speed boating and other aquatic sports.

CARISBROOK ■ 1023

Carisbrook is a tiny hamlet just east of Maryborough. Originally Loddon Punt, it was part of an early sheep run and some of the buildings from this time or later include the town hall (1859), the jail and 'Junction Lodge'. The first grocery store is now a restaurant. *Population 560*

CASTLEMAINE ■ 1024

Once known as Forest Creek, Castlemaine began as a supply centre for the nearby Mount Alexander diggings where gold was discovered in 1851. These diggings are reputed to have been the richest shallow gold deposits ever known, with the yield in the first ten years estimated at fourteen million pounds sterling. There were few quartz reefs and the population rapidly declined when the alluvial fields were exhausted.

Some sources say that Gold Commissioner W.H. Wright, whose task it was to supervise the collection of the mining licences, called the town after his uncle, an Irish peer; others say it was named at the request of Governor La Trobe. The huge eucalyptus tree to which prisoners – often miners who had failed to pay for their licences – were sometimes chained, survives at the government camp.

Castlemaine was surveyed speedily and important buildings went up during the ten years or so of gold prosperity. The many imposing edifices include 'Buda', the home of the famous gold and silversmith, Ernest Leviny, set in magnificent gardens. There is an obelisk, erected in 1852, to mark the passage of Burke and Wills' ill-fated expedition and the former's connections with the town as a police superintendent.

Edward Fitzgerald's brewery was founded in Castlemaine and though Castlemaine Fourex is now brewed in Queensland, the modern cans are the same red and yellow as the original. Castlemaine rock – the popular, hard peppermint sweet in the same colours, first sold in 1853 – can be bought locally. The town is the centre of a fruit-growing and farming district with manufacturing interests including light engineering, woollen mills, clothing, small goods and an abattoir. *Population 6810*

CASTLEMAINE MARKET The Castlemaine Market is a truly remarkable building designed on classical lines and topped by a statue of Ceres, the Roman goddess of the harvest. It was built by local workmen during 1861 and 1862 at a cost of seven thousand pounds sterling and was a distribution point for food to all the central Victorian goldfields. It operated as a market for over 100 years. Restored in 1974, the building is now a museum.

CASTLEMAINE ART GALLERY AND HISTORICAL MUSEUM Castlemaine has one of Victoria's finest provincial art galleries, a building constructed at the height of the Great Depression. Frederick McCubbin's *Golden Sunlight* was donated by Dame Nellie Melba and there are works by Tom Roberts, E. Phillips Fox, Charles Conder, Margaret Preston and Russell Drysdale.

CASTLEMAINE AND MALDON RAILWAY The first locomotives steamed into Maldon in 1884. Ninety-two years later the Castlemaine–Maldon line was closed down but restored trains are now running again albeit with less frequency.

FESTIVALS The Castlemaine Clydesdale–Cashmere/Angora Goat–Pigeon Show, April; State Festival, early November in even-numbered years.

Castlemaine Market, lovingly restored to probably greater spick-and-span glory than its workaday, original state, once housed more than 20 vendors.

CLUNES ■ 1025

Clunes has a graceful post office tower and some fine old buildings but many of the verandahed shops are now vacant. Donald Cameron was only twenty-one when in 1839 he came with sheep and shepherds to settle in the valley. He called his run 'The Clunes' which in Gaelic means 'a pleasant place' – a well-chosen name. Tullaroop Creek watered his property and now runs through the town.

Clunes has an unique place in the history of Victoria's gold era. James Esmond arrived there from California and discovered gold on 5 July 1851 – an obelisk marks the spot. He claimed the state's first sighting, although the precious metal had been obtained secretly in the region at least a year before. An excited report appeared in the *Geelong Advertiser* on 7 July 1851: 'The long-sought treasure is at length found. Victoria is a gold country...We announce the existence of gold in the Pyrenees as a great fact...and a preface to a glorious run of prosperity in Victoria'. Within a fortnight, there were forty men at work. Both Buninyong and Ballarat (see *Ballarat & Daylesford*) attracted more early diggers but Clunes became one of the busier battery crushing areas of Victoria. It was at its peak from 1857–1881 when Cornishmen mined the deep leads with modern equipment. Esmond was a friend of Peter Lalor's and was with him both at the Eureka Stockade and in hiding in Geelong. Lalor later settled in Clunes and became chairman of the Water Commission.

The people of Clunes took the first union action in Victoria in 1873. The Lothair Mine management refused to let miners stop work at Saturday midday and they went on strike. In the ensuing 'riot', both miners and townsfolk thwarted efforts to bring in strike-breaking Chinese workers from Ballarat. *Population 850*

GUILDFORD ■ 1026

Hotels were often a measure of prosperity in the early years of the colony. It is three-quarters of a century since the Guildford area boasted seven public houses within a radius of about one-and-a-half kilometres of the township – one now remains. The Loddon River area yielded a quantity of surface gold and then mining began in earnest with tunnels driven into the hillside. When the alluvial mines shut, sluicing and bucket dredges were set up to search the river flats but once their work was over, Guildford was deserted.

HARCOURT ■ 1027

Harcourt is a small town at the foot of the steep and rocky slopes of Mount Alexander. Granite from the region was used in the construction

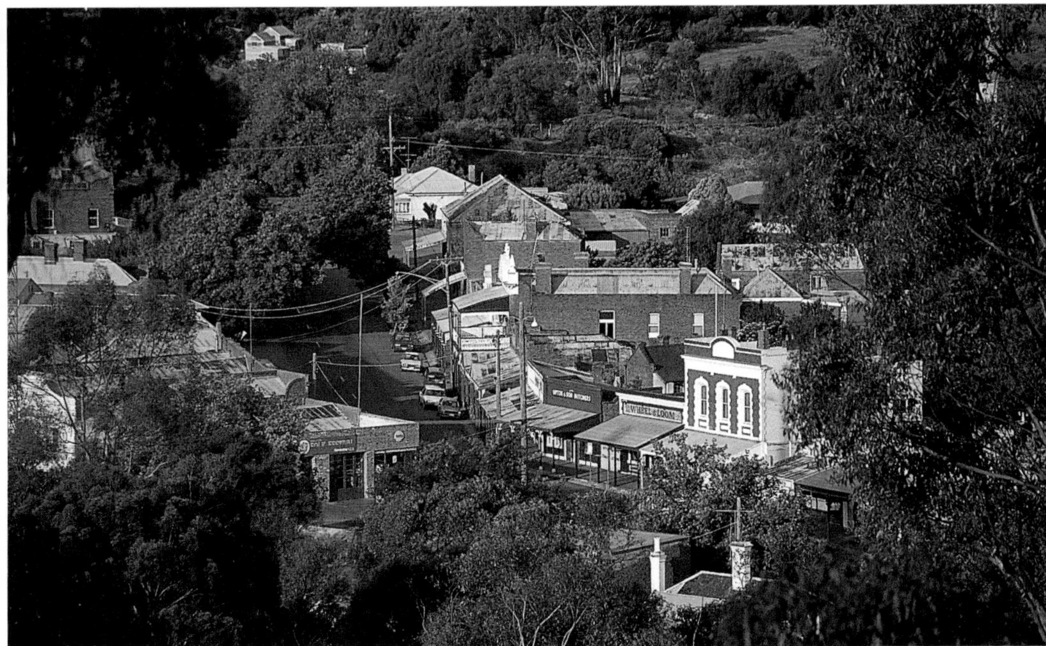

Maldon has turned lack of development to its advantage; tourists flock to see the 19th-century architecture.

A ceremonial burning tower in Maldon Cemetery incinerated offerings at Chinese diggers' funerals.

of many local war memorials and cairns, for the pedestal of the Burke and Wills statue in Melbourne and for the John Flynn Memorial in Alice Springs. Harcourt stone has also been used in the new Parliament House buildings in Canberra. The surrounding valleys produce apples and pears and the Cannie Ridge Pottery is just outside Harcourt on the Calder Highway.

MOUNT ALEXANDER This 741-metre-high eminence was named by Major Thomas Mitchell on his 1836 expedition as a 'pair' to Mount Macedon (see *Melton & Sunbury*). There are some spectacular granite rock formations in Mount Alexander State Forest including Target Rock, Dog Rocks and Eagle Rocks.

MALDON ■ **1028**

Maldon lies at the base of Mount Tarrangower and was also known as Tarrangower until 1856, when it was renamed after a town in England. The area was not a very productive alluvial goldfield but was second only to Bendigo for the richest quartz mining in the state; there were sensational deep reef finds from 1854 to 1856. Mining continued on a company basis into the twentieth century but Maldon suffered in the Great Depression; complete houses were moved to Castlemaine as the population dwindled to around 700. The amount of gold taken from Maldon is officially recorded as 2 100 000 ounces; this figure is likely to be less than the actual finds.

Maldon was hastily planned – waste was dumped in unsightly heaps and trees torn up. The shambles of the first chaotic rush to live under canvas and snatch a fortune gave way to meandering streets and buildings of diverse architectural styles and materials: wattle and daub, pisé and mud brick, weatherboard, horizontal and vertical timber slabs, brick, local ragstone and Malmsbury bluestone. Later these irregularities were recognised as potential for promoting Maldon as an attractive and, in many ways, unique place and in 1965 The National Trust declared it Victoria's first 'notable town'.

There are many buildings of interest – the old post office was home to the young Ethel (Henry Handel) Richardson while her mother was post mistress and she describes the town in *Myself When Young*. Other historical buildings include the market place turned museum (1859), the hospital (1858), Holy Trinity Church (1861), the court house (1861), police lock-up and stables (1855–1864), the Wesleyan Church and Mission Hall (1855–1863), Robert Oswald's 'Lauriston' (1866) and Abraham Bowe's cottage on the Bendigo Road. The former Royal Theatre, dating from the gold rush era, is transformed into an Old Time Music Hall on Sundays and is open to the public. Guided tours are conducted through Carman's Tunnel, a mine abandoned in 1884 after yielding only 33 ozs (935.53 grams) in the space of 2 years and 3 months. *Population 1110*

FESTIVALS Easter Carnival; Folk Music Festival, November.

MALMSBURY ■ **1029**

At the time Bendigo was booming, this small township on the Mount

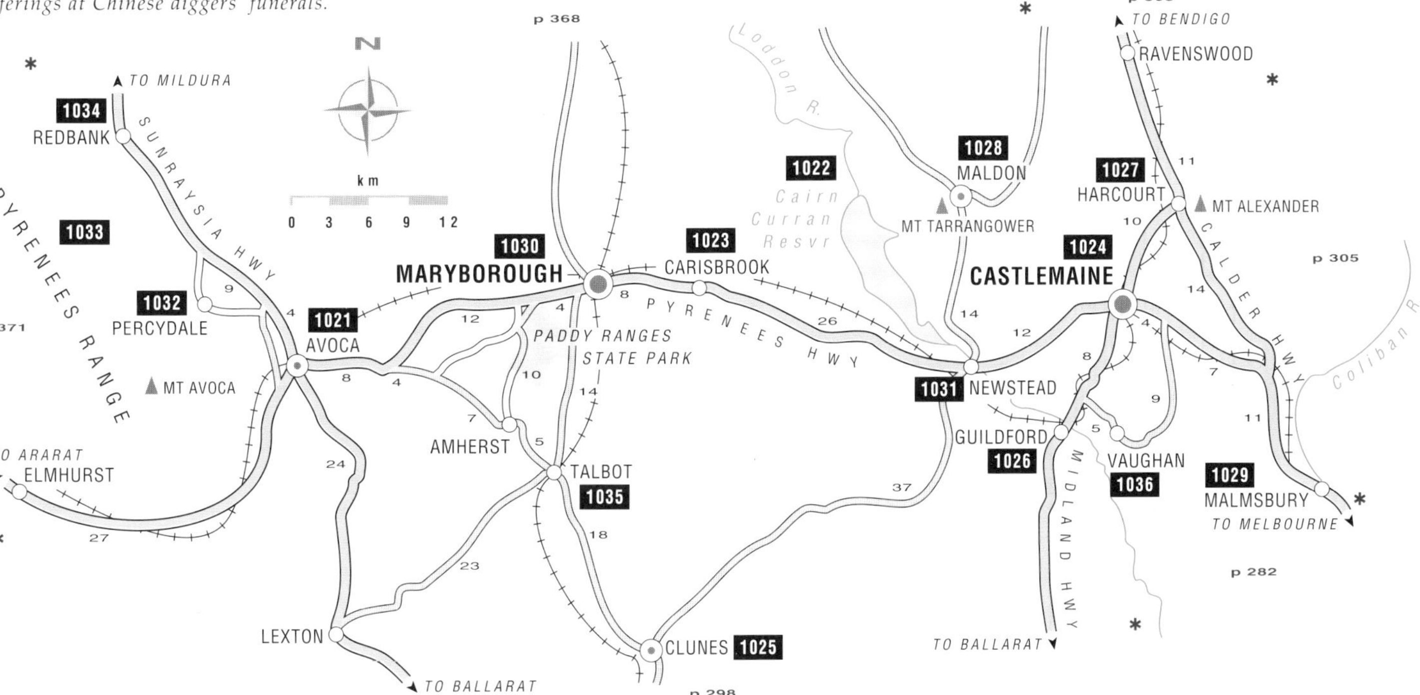

The elegant, bluestone arches of the Keystone Viaduct at Malmsbury lift the Melbourne–Bendigo railway line well above any imaginable winter flood level.

Alexander track, boasted thirteen successful goldfields. Malmsbury is a 'heritage' town, distinguished by its bluestone and local stone buildings. These include churches and cottages and the im-pressive Keystone Viaduct which carries the railway line across the Coliban River with five spans of more than eighteen metres. About 100 masons worked on the bridge and its opening in 1862 displaced the 1839 Perth bridge in Tasmania as Australia's longest stone bridge. The town's present concerns are little changed from the last century and include milling, mining, farming and stone-masonry.
Population 520

MARYBOROUGH ■ **1030**
Maryborough is a large and well-planned town on the northern slopes of the Great Dividing Range. In good seasons it produces large quantities of wheat, oats and barley and there is logging in the nearby state forests and bee-keeping and honey extraction. Secondary industries include knitting mills, joinery, printing, leather and chamois goods, steel construction and welding factories, fish processing plants, cordial and butter factories and making drills, taps and dies.

The region was first called Simsons' or Charlotte Plains. Three Scottish brothers, Hector, Donald and John, began grazing sheep there in 1839 – they are remembered by a cairn. In 1854, gold was found at White Hills and by late 1854 the population numbered around 20 000. The Maryborough Nugget, found in 1855, had a gross weight of 32 162 grams and a million ounces of gold were taken from the ground hereabouts in six years. The city's seal bears the old Biblical name Havilah which comes from the reference to the '*...land of Havilah, where there is gold; and the gold of that land is good*' in the book of Genesis. The *Maryborough Advertiser* was first published in 1855 and is one of the oldest newspapers in Australia.

The American author, Mark Twain, called Maryborough 'a railway station with a town attached'. The station building still has vestiges of its nineteenth-century glory – parquetry flooring in the booking hall, wood-panelled waiting-rooms and a 400-metre-long platform – but there are few passengers now to enjoy it. Once a busy centre linking the gold-mining towns, the demand for a rail service here has steadily declined.
Population 7620

NEWSTEAD ■ **1031**
For thousands of years before European colonists changed the face of the land, the River Yarrayne ('muddy river') connected deep waterholes where the Aboriginal people caught Murray cod. When Major Thomas Mitchell arrived in the district in September 1836 he found excellent forage for his bullocks beside 'the stream' he named the Loddon. His glowing description started a land rush from drought-stricken New South Wales. One of the best known of these early settlers was William Hunter who set up the 'Tarrangower' run in 1842. Newstead's history is inextricably connected with the river: crossing it by punt, ford or bridge; surviving floods or dredging for treasure. At first tolls were collected at Mingus' Crossing Place – an early name for the settlement – and by 1856 the coach fare from Castlemaine to Maryborough using the crossing was half-a-crown. A new concrete, bridge was opened in June 1990.

All manner of business enterprises thrived in those bygone years: blacksmiths, wheelwrights, saddle and harness shops, coachbuilders, creameries, a ginger beer factory and many butchers. The locally produced chaff, hay and grain fed thousands of hard working horses. Early Newstead had annual agricultural shows where vegetable growing and ploughing competitions were eagerly contested. The good pastoral land still supports cattle, fat lambs and wool, and cottage industries include pottery and candle-making in what was once the Co-operative Butter Factory.

PERCYDALE ■ **1032**
Gold prospectors reached Fiddlers Creek in the 1850s and some reef mines were worked. The town became Percydale in 1873 after Percy Carr – the police magistrate's son. Daly's cottage, built in 1865 from fiddleback timber, and a dairy made from locally quarried slate are still in existence. The acacia trees at the back of the cottage are reputed to have grown from seeds Mr Daly brought from Ireland.

PYRENEES RANGE ■ **1033**
The Pyrenees Range is carpeted with red stringybark and red box trees with walking tracks through to some beautiful waterfalls. The range is the natural habitat of koalas and other native species, and introduced sambar deer roam the slopes. There is a road to the summit of Mount Avoca – at an altitude of 760 metres it is the highest point of the range.

REDBANK ■ **1034**
The gold rush era fostered sudden population spurts in places where hopeful prospectors found worthwhile rewards. Towns sprang up almost overnight offering services to the miners, prospered for several years while the gold was available, and then were entirely deserted. Redbank, twenty-two kilometres to the north-west of Avoca, is one of these ghost towns.

TALBOT ■ **1035**
Talbot is a quaintly charming agricultural centre – small hobby farms became popular in the district in the 1980s. The town once thrived on the gold discovered at Back Creek (Talbot's original name) and many of the old shops are sturdily built and still stand although most of them are now closed. The main street, Scandinavian Crescent, winds along the track followed by early bullock wagons. A cluster of old sheds outside the town houses a eucalyptus still which is still in operation.

VAUGHAN ■ **1036**
Originally known as 'The Junction' because it had many roads leading to the diggings, Vaughan is another tiny township on the Loddon River surrounded by farming land in a good region for mineral springs, bush walks, swimming places, fishing and scenic drives. Gold attracted people in the 1850s and it still does – the golden colour of elms, poplars and willows on autumn days brings visitors with cameras and sketchbooks rather than picks and shovels. The settlement is named for Charles Vaughan – a member of the Legislative Council from 1856 to 1864.

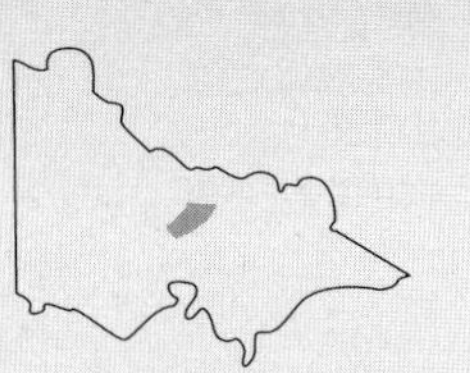

Heathcote & Nagambie

Historical and agricultural developments have left their mark on this landscape: the legacy of the gold rush of the 1850s includes solitary chimneys, scarred hillsides and outcrops of European shade trees while irrigation works have produced a profusion of artificial lakes with linking 'rivers'.

COSTERFIELD ■ 1037
At one time Costerfield was Victoria's main source of antimony – a brittle white metal used to harden lead alloys – and supplied more than ninety per cent of the state's production. Mining of both antimony and gold began here in the early 1860s. Two of the prospectors, Alan and Peniston Coster, though unsuccessful in claiming a reward for the discovery of the field, are now remembered in the name of the town. Relics of the mining days include a deserted weatherboard church, tailings and a puddling ring.

DHURRINGILE ■ 1038
The rural community of Dhurringile takes its name from the nearby property which is best known for its historic sixty-eight-roomed mansion. The house was built in 1877 by Italian tradesmen for the Winter family. 'Dhurringile's' imposing towered entrance faces onto a garden with a gracefully columned, two-tiered arcade. In 1941, it opened its stately doors as a prisoner-of-war camp for German officers and their staff, an annexe of the much larger camp at Murchison (see entry). Ironically, this military connection was to be maintained when in 1947, 'Dhurringile' was purchased by the Presbyterian Church to serve as a home for sons of deceased British ex-servicemen.

GOULBURN WEIR ■ 1039
The Goulburn Weir retains and raises the waters of the Goulburn River so that they can be diverted through three main distribution channels; the Cattanach and Stuart Murray channels carry them west to the Waranga Basin (see entry), where they supply the Goulburn River Irrigation System, and the East Goulburn Main Channel carries them to the east. The weir is a massive structure of concrete founded on bedrock, more than 200 metres long and rising fifteen metres above the river bed. Construction began in 1887 and finished three years later. Its downstream face is stepped with granite blocks quarried from nearby Mount Black Quarry – each cut with hammer and chisel to a uniform size then carted by dray twenty-five kilometres to the building site. The weir is believed to be the first major irrigation structure built in Australia and at the time was an extraordinary engineering feat.

GRAYTOWN ■ 1040
Isolated chimneys and old poppet heads mark the site of this once populous town. Payable gold was found here at Spring Creek in 1868 and within twelve months there were 20 000 eager diggers on the field. Its streets, Corbett, Mills, Wolff and Polkinghorne carried the names of the discovery party. In 1869, the township was surveyed and named, rather unimaginatively, after the local member of parliament.

The shallow alluvial deposits were exhausted within eighteen months and the hordes moved on. Water on this field was said to be so scarce that gold was washed in beer, so it was ironic that it was a flood which destroyed the town in 1870, inundating the shafts and undermining or levelling the buildings.

The site is surrounded by Rushworth State Forest (see entry) and is in the very heart of Victoria – nearby Mount Moormbool, 816 metres high and six kilometres to the north-west, is the geographical centre of Victoria.

HEATHCOTE ■ 1041
Before the discovery of gold here in late 1852, the entire area was held by squatters under annual leases. The McIvor whose name is so well perpetuated in the district is somewhat of a mystery figure. He was once thought to have been a member of Major Mitchell's party, but as there is no mention of the name in the journals of the expedition, he is more likely to have been an overseer on the station through which the creek now bearing his name ran.

Another theory put foward is that Mr McIvor was a prospector, but the name 'McIvor's Creek' was first used

Rushworth Forest's powerful wedgetail eagles provide a natural form of control for cats and rabbits.

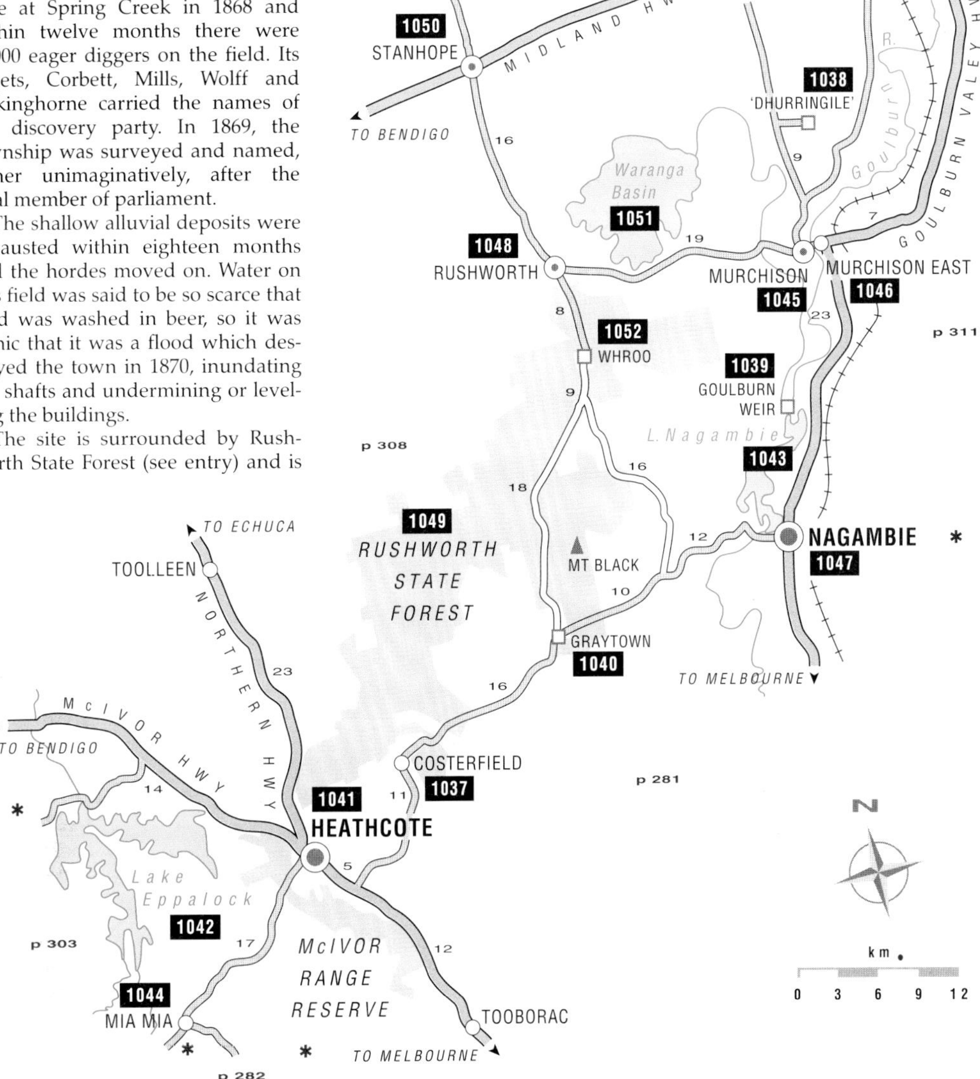

Grape juice ferments into wine here before being moved underground to mature in the Chateau Tahbilk cellars.

in 1841, more than a decade before the offical discovery of gold. Whatever his identity, he very nearly had a town named after him as well, for it was as McIvor that Heathcote was first known. It was a wild and dangerous town for the gold rush here is generally agreed to have attracted some very mean characters, with brawling, horsestealing and robbery with violence an almost daily occurrence. Within two weeks of the first strike, more than 16 000 diggers were on the field, living under canvas and trying their luck working tiny claims less than three metres square.

Stamper batteries which crushed tonnes of quartz a day to release the imprisoned veins of gold began operating here in 1856 and continued successfully for half-a-century. *Population 1510*

FESTIVALS Heathcote Show, early November.

LAKE EPPALOCK ■ 1042

Eppalock is one of Victoria's largest inland lakes, covering more than 3000 hectares with 150 kilometres of shoreline. It is the focal point of a major recreation area as well as fulfilling its principal function as an important water storage. The forty-five metre high earth and rock walls of Eppalock Weir, which block the unreliable flow of the Campaspe River, hold back waters which irrigate the farmlands of the Campaspe Valley to the north, and are piped west to supply the city of Bendigo and its region. A unique feature of the Eppalock pumphouse is the hydraulic turbines, driven by energy generated by the discharge of water into the valley, which push water uphill through the Bendigo pipeline.

LAKE NAGAMBIE ■ 1043

The waters of the Goulburn River bank up behind Goulburn Weir (see entry) to form the broad expanse of Lake Nagambie. The lake dates from the late 1880s, when the weir was built, and is unusual in that it maintains a full water level throughout the year. It is a popular location for watersports such as fishing, swimming, canoeing and boating and the river is navigable for some forty kilometres upstream of the lake.

FESTIVALS Boxing Day Rowing Regatta, December.

MIA MIA ■ 1044

In 1910, the first flight of an Australian-built aircraft was made from a paddock at Spring Plains Homestead near Mia Mia, when John Duigan, perching unprotected on the lower wing of a flimsy-looking biplane he had built himself, took to the air for a brief seven-metre hop. A memorial on the Mia Mia to Lancefield road commemorates the feat.

FESTIVALS Kite Flying Championships, April.

MURCHISON ■ 1045

Murchison had its origins in the well-intentioned but misguided Aboriginal protectorate system which entailed removing Aborigines from their lands and concentrating them in particular areas where they could be educated in western ways.

In 1839, the Goulburn River Protectorate was established on the site of what is now Murchison. The scheme was not a success and the protectorate closed down in 1850 with just a few white settlers remaining. A punt operated by local businessman Ludovic Marie crossed the river here and in 1854 the site was surveyed into township allotments. A hundred years after the founding of the protectorate another compound was sited in Murchison – the Second World War prisoner-of-war camp which was established on the western outskirts of the town. By mid-1942, it held more than 3000 Italian, German and Japanese prisoners, including survivors of the German raider *Kormorant* which had destroyed the cruiser HMAS *Sydney*. *Population 660*

DAYS MILL AND FARM This complex preserves a part of Victoria's early farming history – the only complete nineteenth-century flour mill in the state. Its power unit, an imported Cornish boiler, once drove a two-speed steam engine. The two pairs of massive grinding stones each weighing more than half a tonne gave the mill the capacity to grind some 360 kilograms of wheat an hour.

THE OSSARIO Adjoining the cemetery at Murchison is the Ossario, the solid Italian war memorial and mausoleum which holds the remains of 130 Italian prisoners of war originally laid to rest in cemeteries throughout Australia. It is constructed of Castlemaine stone, roofed with Roman tiles and contains an altar of Italian white marble.

FESTIVALS Wood Day, April.

MURCHISON EAST ■ 1046

This is wheat-growing country. Originally local mills handled the grain, but after the railway was built to Murchison East in 1880 this became a railhead where the golden harvest was bought for consignment to Melbourne. All grain was weighed with scales holding one to six bags at a time and then stacked beside the track to await transport south. Bulk handling facilities were built in 1939 and Murchison East now sprouts a cluster of silos.

NAGAMBIE ■ 1047

The township hugs the south-eastern shores of Lake Nagambie in the centre of an agricultural, pastoral and winegrowing area. A museum in the old court house and shire hall has exhibits reflecting the history of the district ranging from old coins and period dresses to steam engines and early horse-drawn vehicles. Once known as 'The Dip' because of the communal sheep dip located here, Nagambie is now called by the Aboriginal name for the lagoon

The significance of the Goulburn Weir in watering half-a-million hectares was recognised in 1913 with its depiction on the ten-shilling note.

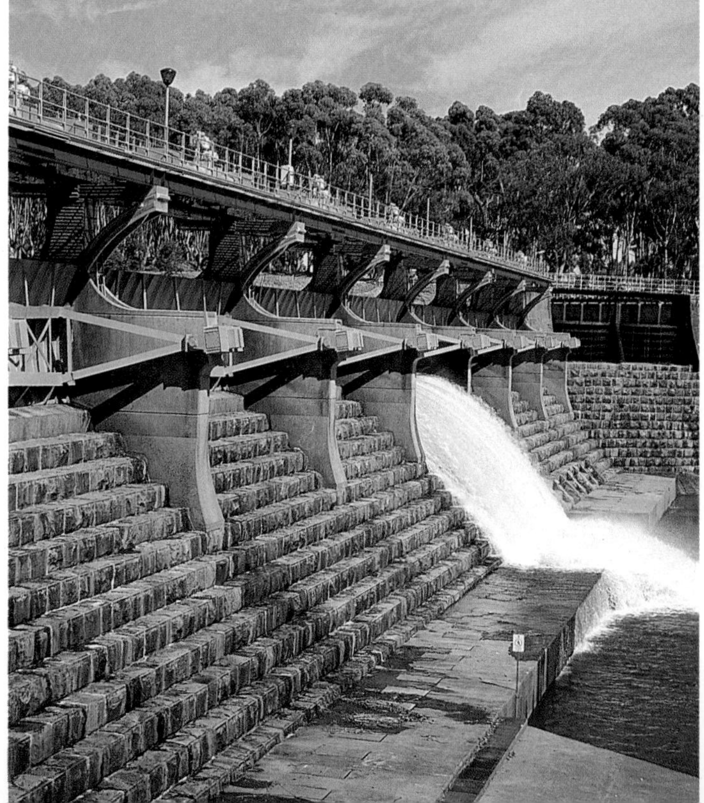

which was drowned by the waters of Lake Nagambie. *Population 1220*

FESTIVALS Boxing Day Rowing Regatta, December.

CHATEAU TAHBILK Sited on the Goulburn River near the spot where Major Thomas Mitchell crossed in 1836, this historic and picturesque winery is one of the oldest in Australia. Its underground cellars are classified by the National Trust and are open to the public for inspection, sampling and wine sales. The first vines were planted here as early as 1860. The original cellars, built in the same year, are ninety-two metres long and surmounted by a distinctive bell tower.

MITCHELTON On a bend in the river upstream of Tahbilk looms the whimsical tower of Mitchelton winery. It was built in 1969 as part of a tourist and convention centre associated with the old estate, and its encircling observation deck gives a 360-degree view of the surrounding vineyards.

RUSHWORTH ■ 1048

A large part of Rushworth town centre has been classified by the National Trust – a worthy recognition of its historic buildings which reflect the 'boom' decades following the 1850s gold rushes. This was a particularly rich alluvial field, but waterless, so it was with some difficulty that its nuggets were won. Known first as 'Dry Diggings' the settlement was named in 1854 by English writer Richard Henry ('Orion') Horne, at the time assistant gold commissioner here; this name was chosen, it is said, because he considered it a 'rush worth-while coming to', but it was more likely named after his 1852 shipboard companions Henry and Rose Rushworth.

Mining of the deep-reef gold began in 1872 and by the 1880s some fifty mines were being worked in the area. A bushfire lookout on Gawlers Hill, the site of early goldmines, gives a panoramic view of the township, Rushworth State Forest and Waranga Basin. *Population 1010*

EUCALYPTUS OIL DISTILLERY The distillery on the Whroo road, south of Rushworth, extracts oil from leaves of the local blue mallee gum. This oil is used commercially in pharmaceutical preparations such as inhalants and mouthwashes (see box).

RISSTROM'S SAWMILL Now, the only remaining sawmill of Rushworth's original seven or so mills, Risstrom's was powered by steam from an original traction engine until 1990 – it is now operated electrically.

RUSHWORTH STATE FOREST ■ 1049

This is one of the largest forests in Victoria and covers more than 24 000 hectares between Rushworth and Grayton. The predominant trees are red ironbark, grey box and yellow gum and the spectacularly colourful autumn and spring wildflower display includes wattles, grevilleas and terrestrial orchids. There is an abundance of bird and animal life, including the handsome wedgetail eagle. Included in the forest boundaries are the goldmining ghost towns of Bailieston, Angustown, Graytown and Whroo (see entries) where fossickers may still find a yellow fleck.

STANHOPE ■ 1050

The irrigated pastures here grow fodder crops and are fed from the Waranga Basin (see entry). Sir John ('Black Jack') McEwen, a long-time deputy prime minister in the governments of Sir Robert Menzies farmed cattle on the rich lands around Stanhope. He was also chairman of its dairy co-operative, now the Bonlac milk processing factory producing cheese and dried milk products. The town, formerly called Lauderdale, takes its name from the once sprawling Stanhope Station which, before it was resumed by the government for soldier-settlement blocks after the First World War, covered a large stretch of land between Seymour and Echuca. *Population 550*

FESTIVALS New Years Day Mardi Gras, January.

WARANGA BASIN ■ 1051

The reservoir was formed by the construction in 1905 of an earthen embankment more than seven kilometres long – it was enlarged to its present size in 1926 – across a natural depression referred to as Waranga Swamp or Gunn's Swamp. It is fed by water from the Goulburn Weir through the Stuart Murray Channel, cut between 1891 and 1905, and the Cattanach, opened in 1957, and has a capacity of 410 000 megalitres (see Goulburn Weir). Its main irrigation channel takes the water further west, 370 kilometres across northern Victoria, to the Wimmera and Mallee districts. Waranga is an Aboriginal word meaning 'to sing'.

WHROO ■ 1052

Nothing remains of the more than 130 buildings which once stood here save the pine and pepper trees, wells and grassy clearings which mark their sites. The goldfield opened here was dominated by Balaclava Hill, so named because gold was found here on the same day in 1854 as the battle of Balaclava in the Crimean War. It proved to be a hill of gold, its quartz threaded with the veins of six rich reefs which continued below it to a depth of some ninety metres. From 1855, it was mined by open cut, the quartz blasted out and taken by tramline for crushing.

The town has taken the Aboriginal name for the spring-fed waterhole on its southern outskirts. Whroo – pronounced 'roo' – and its weather-worn, historic relics are within the Rushworth State Forest (see entry).

THE GOOD OIL ON THE BLUE MALLEE

THE MEDICINAL value of Australia's ubiquitous eucalyptus trees was quickly recognised by the doctors of the First Fleet who used the gum exuded by the trees in the treatment of a raging outbreak of dysentry. Surgeon-General John White was soon distilling clear, golden eucalyptus oil as well, noting that the substance obtained from the peppermint gum (*Eucalyptus piperita*) was 'more efficacious in removing all cholicky complaints than...the English peppermint'.

But it was not until the 1850s, in Victoria, that commercial production of the distinctively pungent eucalyptus oil, by steam distillation, began. This followed the investigations into the medicinal properties of Australian plants by Melbourne-based English pharmacist Joseph Bosisto, encouraged and advised by the enthusiastic and multi-titled government botanist of Victoria, Baron Sir Ferdinand von Mueller.

One of the most productive species is the blue mallee gum (*E. polybractea*) found through the central and north-western parts of Victoria. This was the first species exploited commercially, and yields an oil high in eucalyptol which is used in pharmaceutical preparations. In the early days its leaves were collected by hand – Aboriginal labour was often used for this task, which is now largely mechanised – and boiled in a large iron vessel. The oil can be collected when the steam, enriched with oil vapour, is cooled. This simple distillation method dates from the Middle Ages and has been used successfully and with very few modifications by a number of small-scale eucalyptus oil distillers for nearly a century-and-a-half. In 1914, there were some two hundred eucalyptus oil stills in Victoria alone.

Oil from the blue mallee is used in preparations such as inhalants, mouth washes, cough syrups and liniments. Ironically, Australia is responsible for only five per cent of the world supply of medicinal eucalyptus oil from its native trees. Most now comes from Spain and Portugal where it is derived from the foliage of the Tasmanian blue gum (*E. globus*), another favourite of Baron von Mueller. The tree was planted in large numbers throughout southern Europe during the nineteenth century in the erroneous belief that it subdued 'malarial vapours' – this gum even came to be known as the 'fever tree' because of its real and purported medicinal properties. □

Traditional distilling is practised near Bendigo where a tank full of eucalyptus leaves (left) is filled with steam; the oil gathers in the tank.

Bendigo & Rochester

The enormous early wealth of this district came from gold which was mined extensively for nearly a century but now forest and farmland have replaced the mullock heap. The legacy of the 'boom' days is still seen in Bendigo's opulent endowment of streets lined with grand, nineteenth-century buildings.

BENDIGO ■ **1053**
Gold was first discovered on the 'Ravenswood' run near Bendigo in 1851, reputedly by Margaret Kennedy, the stationmaster's wife, but it is believed that gold was picked up along the Bendigo creek by several people around this time. It was Henry Frencham who set off the huge gold rush of the 1850s when he reported his substantial finds to the Gold Commissioner at the Forest Creek diggings.

Bendigo was to become one of the world's great gold-rush towns and certainly the greatest goldfield in Victoria, yielding 205 882 170 grams in its record year of 1856. A total of 690 000 000 grams were produced up to the 1950s when large scale mining operation ceased. At first the gold was alluvial in form – washed into gullies and stream beds by erosion – and easily accessible. It was realised later how large the Bendigo field was – 360 square kilometres, extending from Back Creek to the Whipstick Forest and from Kangaroo Flat to Huntly. There are over thirty-five reefs which run east to west and parallel to one another.

By 1853, Bendigo had a teeming gold camp, and a militant organisation was formed to campaign for the reduction of the gold licence fee to ten shillings a month and for the withdrawal of all armed forces from the goldfields. Tension on the goldfields became palpable when alluvial gold started to peter out; the arrival of thousands of Chinese to the diggings in 1854 fanned anti-Chinese feeling (see *Young & Grenfell*). A transition from alluvial to reef mining in the 1860s led to renewed prosperity but to some, the change seemed futile, unless the quartz reefs could be worked profitably.

The quartz mines eventually paid off and the wealth generated helped build new streetscapes, such as the grand Pall Mall. Operating costs of these mines were huge and eventually led to the decline of the industry, which was virtually finished by the time of the Second World War. By the 1950s only the three Deborah mines were working.

Bendigo was named after a farm hand; a fighter of some notoriety, he was given the nickname 'Bendigo' after Abednego Thompson, a famous English fighter of the time. The town was given the more respectable but far less interesting label of 'Sandhurst' by the government in 1885 but changed back to Bendigo in the 1891 after spirited public debate. Because of the rich architectural legacy of the gold rush days Bendigo is a tourist drawcard, having another attraction in its location in the middle of a growing wine-making district. *Population 57 430*

CENTRAL DEBORAH MINE Although the shaft for this mine – the last deep-reef mine in Bendigo – was sunk in 1909, the mine was not worked until the 1940s and was closed in 1956. The 411-metre-deep mine on 17 levels is now restored and is open to visitors. A 21-metre poppet head towers above ground.

JOSS HOUSE Built of handmade bricks and timber this temple is painted red, the traditional Chinese colour for strength. Two stone Kylins, or guardian beasts, stand at the entrance. Inside are thrones, altars and a rich array of banners. The joss house is now maintained by the National Trust.

DAI GUM SAN WAX MUSEUM Life-sized figures, carefully modelled and costumed and dealing with various aspects of Chinese culture and heritage – they were originally intended for a museum in Hong Kong – are displayed here. Dai Gum San means 'big gold mountain', and was the name given to the Bendigo goldfields by the Chinese miners. The museum is also the home of 'Sun Loong', which at 100 metres is said to be the world's longest ceremonial Chinese dragon. It was acquired by

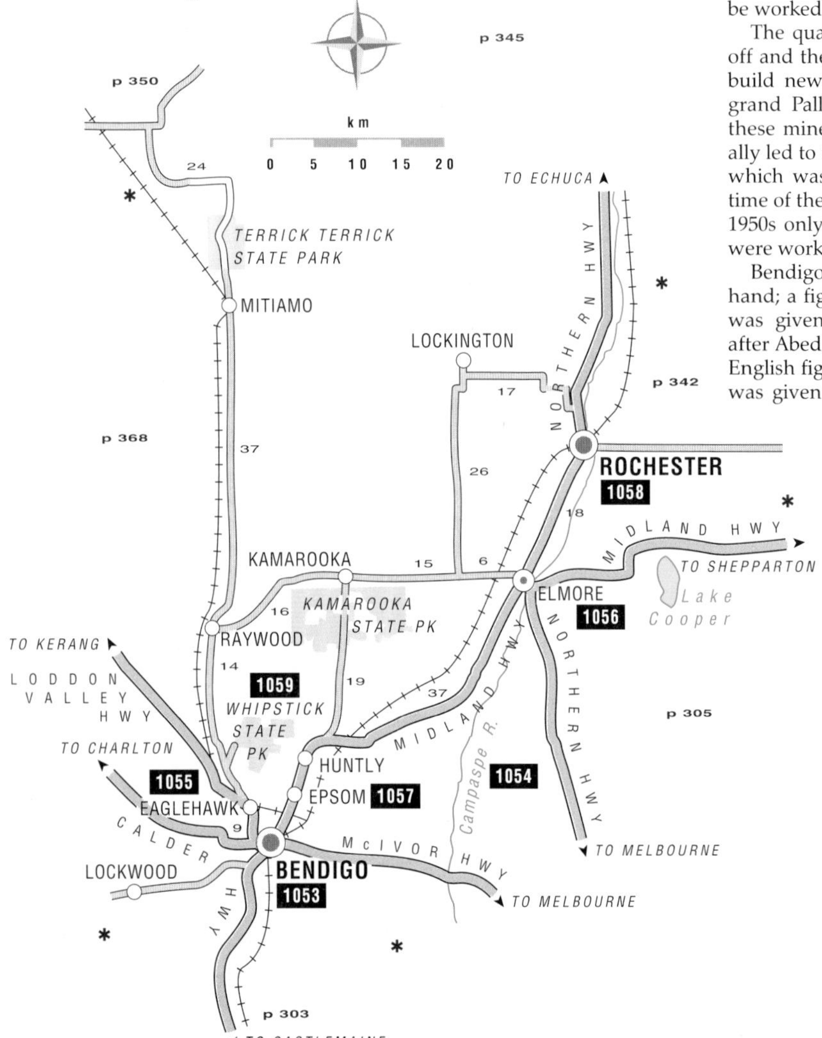

To some, these gleaming artefacts in Bendigo's Holden Museum owe as much to chrome-plating as they do to engineering.

the local Chinese community in 1970, and is a colourful feature of the Easter Festival procession.

PALL MALL Several of the city's grandest Victorian-era buildings help compose this grand streetscape. The Italianate post office (1887) and law courts (1897) were designed by W.G. Watson of the Public Works Department. Other buildings to survive not only unscathed but in a proudly restored state include the Shamrock Hotel (1897), the Beehive store (1872), the Grand United HBS building (1886), the Alexander Fountain (1881) – made from twenty tonnes of Harcourt granite – and the various banks. Near Pall Mall is View Street with a number of nineteenth-century buildings which are now classified by the National Trust.

FORTUNA This former home of a prominent mine owner is now the premises of the Army Survey and Mapping Unit. The stately mansion is noted for its fine joinery, moulded ceilings and stained-glass windows. The house is set in landscaped gardens with an ornamental lake – the last remaining of the original six.

BENDIGO ART GALLERY This gallery houses a varied collection of both Australian and European paintings. There are outstanding examples of work by members of the Heidelberg school as well as paintings by Sisley, Corot, Daubigny and Boudin. Works by Australian painters such as Lloyd Rees, Jeffrey Smart and Fred Williams are in a modern collection.

FESTIVALS Easter Fair, April.

The imposing law courts building and the adjacent formal gardens bring a European touch to central Bendigo.

CAMPASPE RIVER ■ 1054

After arising in the Great Dividing Range, seventy kilometres northwest of Melbourne, the Campaspe winds its way northward across the Murray River plains to join the Murray at Echuca. The river is part of the large Goulburn–Campaspe–Loddon system, one of the largest irrigation systems in Australia.

EAGLEHAWK ■ 1055

This historic town was the site of a gold rush in 1852 and quickly grew into a substantial town. Now a suburb of Bendigo, the town has many reminders of the mining days in buildings such as the court house, town hall and Mechanics Institute. Some of the biggest gold mines were in the Eaglehawk district and the large mullock heaps still standing today give some idea of the extent of the work done underground.

Nearby is the former mining village of Harvey Town where some of the best examples of miners' cottages can be seen. Just north of the town is the 'log lockup', one of the last in Victoria and used as recently as 1970. This unusual building is hand-made right down to its doornails.

SANDHURST TOWN, MYERS FLAT North is Sandhurst Town – not one but two recreated towns set in 324 hectares of bushland. One town shows Bendigo as it was during the gold rush, the second is a typical country town of the 1920s. A full-sized railway connects both towns.

MOHAIR FARM, LOCKWOOD Angora and Kashmir goats and Polworth and Merino sheep are bred for mohair and wool which is spun, woven and finished on this farm. Visitors can watch as yarn is produced on working nineteenth-century machinery.

FESTIVALS Arts and Dahlia Festival, late March.

ELMORE ■ 1056

Originally called Runnymede – after the island in the River Thames where the Magna Carta was signed – this rural community was first established on the other side of the Campaspe River about five kilometres from its present site. The town moved and grew rapidly when the Echuca to Bendigo railway line was completed in 1864. It remains an important centre for the surrounding rich agricultural district. For almost thirty years, Elmore has hosted a field day for agricultural machinery during the first week of October. This event attracts about 50 000 visitors over three days with farmers flying in from as far away as Queensland. *Population 750*

EPSOM ■ 1057

After trying his luck in the gold fields, George Duncan Guthrie set up the Bendigo Pottery in 1858 after recognising the superior quality of the clay at Epsom. The venture flourished until his death in 1910, when production of domestic pottery was replaced with the that of roofing tiles and pipes. Pottery for domestic use was again made in the 1970s using traditional methods, and part of the old pottery is now a museum.

The Epsom market, held each Sunday, is the largest undercover market in central Victoria.

ROCHESTER ■ 1058

An early settler of this large town on the Campaspe River was Dr John Pearson, who built a hotel here as a stopping place for the many drovers and prospectors passing through the region. Squatters moved into the area in 1844 and when the Bendigo to Echuca railway line was completed in 1854, the town grew rapidly. Today, Rochester is the centre of a thriving agricultural, pastoral and irrigation district. Australia's largest dairy products plant is located here.

Outside the town is the Campaspe Siphon, which defies gravity to take the waters of the Waranga–Mallee irrigation channel under the Campaspe River. *Population 2530*

RANDOM HOUSE This stately nineteenth-century building, Rochester's oldest, has been restored to its former glory and is open to visitors. The house is set in a landscaped garden which extends to the banks of the Campaspe River.

FESTIVALS The Rochester Agricultural Show, February.

WHIPSTICK STATE PARK ■ 1059

Red ironbark and the blue and whipstick mallee which give the park its

The 1860s Bendigo joss house, painted red to denote strength, is the oldest still in use in Australia.

name are found in abundance in this bushland reserve north of Bendigo. The name mallee is thought to derive from the sound of the recoil which occurred when early settlers attempted to flatten and clear these stands. Animals and birds found here include grey kangaroos, wallabies, galahs and mallee fowl. Several bicycle tracks wind through the forest and there are picnic areas.

EUCALYPTUS FARM The same family has been running this farm in the Whipstick Forest near Huntly for 100 years. Oil extracted from the eucalyptus trees is refined for use in pharmaceuticals, medicines, ointments, paints, and cleansers (see box, *Heathcote & Nagambie*).

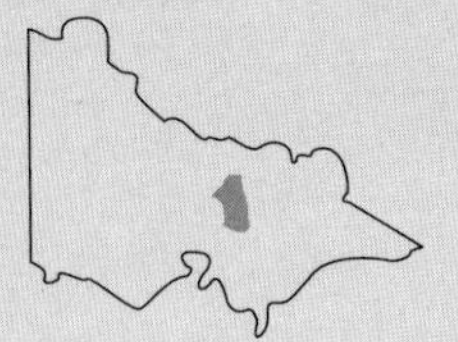

Euroa & Alexandra

Limpid valley lakes nestling beneath protective foothills and mountains have turned this region, where Ned Kelly had several hideouts, into a holiday haven for both tourist and resident alike. The lure of gold drew early settlers, and it remains one of the finest wool growing areas in Australia.

Below the ranges, at Violet Town, the cool winters make North American blueberries feel at home.

ALEXANDRA ■ 1060

The name of this farming township is probably in honour of the Victorian era Princess of Wales although three Alexanders – McGregor, Don and Luckie – found gold here in 1866, when it became known as Red Gate Diggings.

Notable buildings from the heady days of ther 1860s include the post office, law courts, library and ANZ bank. The former railway station is now a museum where a vintage steam engine and an Impulse turbine from the Rubicon hydro-electric station are displayed. Nearby are the Rouston and Rubicon falls and a nature reserve known for its spring orchid blooms. *Population 1880*

FESTIVALS Alexandra Show, November; Rotary Art Show, March–April.

CATHEDRAL RANGE STATE PARK ■ 1061

The Cathedral Range is a prominent geological feature east of the Maroondah Highway between Taggerty and Buxton with a rocky, razorback ridge that is a great attraction for bushwalkers and rockclimbers.

Tracks lead to the top of the ridge; the most popular walk is between Sugarloaf Peak and Cathedral Peak, usually with an overnight stop at the Farmyard – so named because of the lyrebirds which imitate the animals on the valley farms below.

EILDON ■ 1062

This town on the southern shores of Lake Eildon (see entry) was built in the 1950s to house workers employed on the construction of Eildon Dam. Today it is one of the most popular inland boating and fishing holiday resorts in Victoria. Nearby are Eildon State Park (see entry) and Big River State Forest, both popular camping spots. Skyline Road, a scenic route between Eildon and Fraser National Park (see entry), offers breathtaking views of Lake Eildon, the Cathedral Range and the Goulburn and Acheron valleys from several lookout points along the way. Dr James Dickson, an early settler in the area, called his station Eildon in 1838, after the three Eildon hills in Scotland, reputedly the burial place of King Arthur. *Population 770*

SNOBS CREEKS FISH HATCHERY More than two million brown and rainbow trout are bred each year at this hatchery, a few kilometres south-west of Eildon. They are fed a special diet until big enough to be released into Victoria's lakes and rivers where baited hooks wait to lure them. The scenic Snobs Creek Falls, which tumble 106 metres in a series of steps down the mountainside, are a short distance upstream.

EILDON STATE PARK ■ 1063

Three separate blocks of land, around arms of the Big and Goulburn rivers and Jerusalem Inlet, are linked by the waters of Lake Eildon to make up this 24 000-hectare park of rugged spurs and deep creeks on the lake's south-eastern shores. The scenery is spectacular. The steep-sided mountains which plunge to the flooded valley floor create a foreshore indented with many bays. The park takes in Rocky Peak (1059 metres), near Jerusalem Inlet and in the north, the Enterprise Ranges. On the slopes and ridges there is red box, broad-leaved peppermint and stringy-bark, while in the moister gullies around Jerusalem Creek blue gum forests predominate. Numerous tracks lead through the forests to the heights. Jerusalem Inlet is a well-known camping and picnicking spot.

EUROA ■ 1064

The solid colonial buildings of Euroa, dating from the mid and late nineteenth century, were meant to last and are tangible evidence of the confidence felt by the townsfolk in the future prosperity of the district. They had every reason for optimism. The town dates from the 1850s, and although it prospered by supplying the goldfields traffic, the real wealth, then as now, comes from the traditional sheep's back – the properties around here produce some of the finest wool in Victoria.

The district was first settled in the 1830s when pastoralists took up land along Seven Creeks to raise sheep and cattle. Eliza Forlonge, a far-sighted pioneer, introduced a fine wool Saxon merino flock to her property here. Sawmills were established to supply wood for mineshafts, firewood and, when the line reached Euroa, railway sleepers.

The town's other main claim to fame is its association with Ned Kelly, and it marks the southern limit of his bushranging adventures. In 1878, the Kelly gang raided the bank in Euroa and took more than two thousand pounds sterling. They also rounded up the staff of the bank and others, some thirty hostages in all, and held them prisoner at Faithfull Creek homestead. Remains of this homestead, destroyed by bushfire in 1939, can still be seen at Balmattum, a few kilometres north-east of Euroa. Contemporary reports about the raid are recorded in the Farmers' Arms Museum. *Population 2770*

SEVEN CREEKS STATION Janet Templeton took up this run in 1838, and in later years it was taken over by another woman and a relative, Eliza Forlonge, and her two sons, William and Andrew. In the late 1820s, the remarkable Mrs Forlonge spent four years in Germany learning all about the wool industry in a determined attempt to find a sheep breed both suitable for Australian conditions and acceptable to the spinners of Europe. She purchased several Saxon merino flocks, one of which was sent to Seven Creeks, the first such flock in Victoria. She died in 1859 and is buried just outside the town and close to the towering Garden Range which she could see from her homestead windows.

FESTIVALS Wool Week, October.

FRASER NATIONAL PARK ■ 1065

Much of this former grazing land on the rugged western shore of Lake Eildon has begun to regenerate since 1957 when the first portions of the park were set aside. Peppermint gum, stringybark, red box and silver wattle have returned and eastern

The waters of Snobs Creek earn their keep: after decorating a cliff face with Snobs Creek Falls, they go on to top up the ponds of a trout hatchery.

grey kangaroos, wallabies and sambar deer are among the animals which graze its 3000 hectares.

The happy combination of permanent water and open forest results in many different varieties of birds. The numerous inlets provide a habitat for cormorants, pelicans, black swans and wood duck; the timbered areas are filled with kookaburras, black-backed magpies, honey-eaters, wattle birds, gang-gang cockatoos, crimson rosellas and wedge-tailed eagles. An extensive system of walking tracks runs along the spurs and into the more remote corners and gives views over the lake and to Mount Buller. The park is a popular spot for all water sports, fishing and walking. Three camping areas cater for tents and caravans and there is a boat launching ramp.

Gold was discovered here in the late 1860s and the hills were soon covered with prospectors. Old mine shafts, waste heaps, solitary chimneys and even the remains of a tramway can be seen along some tracks. An Italian, John Merlo, after some success at gold prospecting, turned his hand to farming, and in the valley of the Delatite had a vineyard renowned for its port wine. Merlo's homestead and buildings, drowned by the waters of Lake Eildon, are now visible only when the lake is low. Italian Bay is named in his memory. The park itself honours A.J. Fraser, the first chairman of the National Parks Authority.

LAKE EILDON ■ 1066

Lake Eildon, Victoria's largest artifical lake, was created as the main storage of the vast Goulburn River Irrigation System and is a popular inland boating and fishing holiday resort. It is located on the Goulburn River immediately below its junction with the Delatite River. Its shoreline of some 500 kilometres extends south-east almost to Jamieson and north-west to Bonnie Doon and beyond. Another arm is only a few kilometres from Mansfield. Recreation facilities around the foreshores cater for sailing, water-skiing, canoeing, camping and picnicking. The lake is stocked with trout and other fish released from nearby Snobs Creek hatchery (see Eildon), making it an excellent fishing spot.

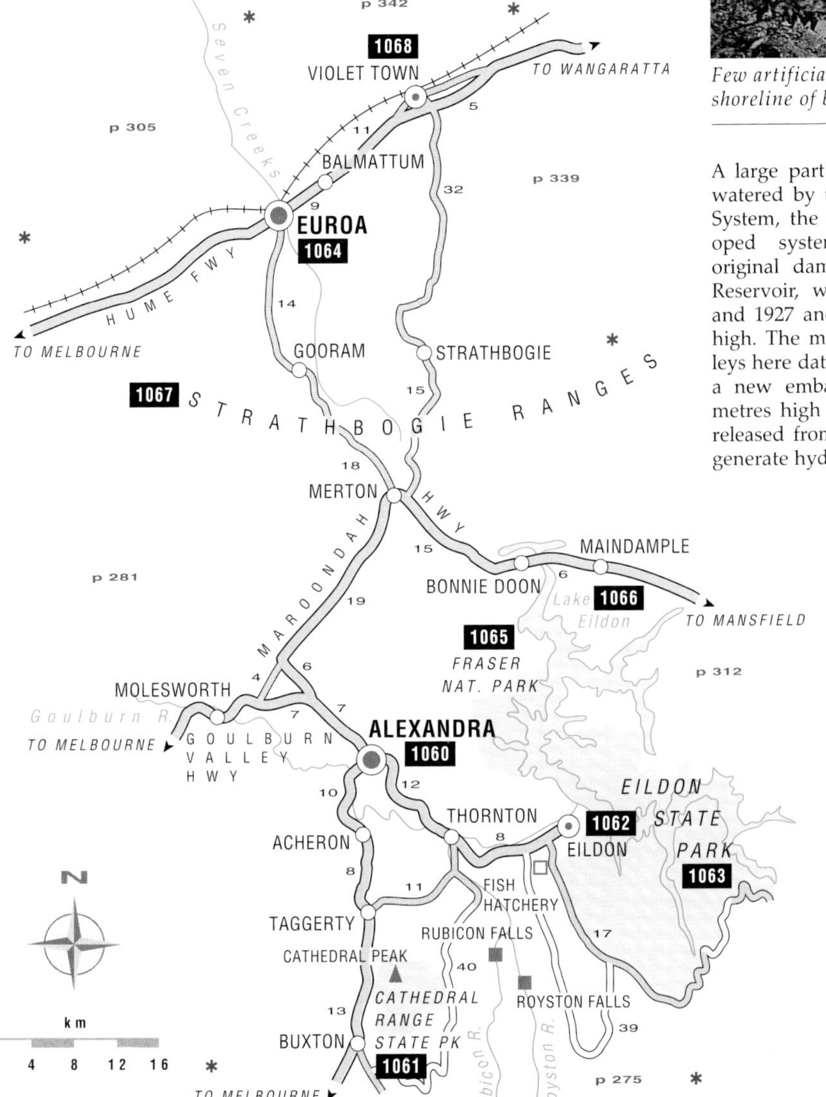

Few artificial lakes can match Lake Eildon's snaking, 500-kilometre shoreline of bays and reaches in the former valleys of the Goulburn River.

A large part of northern Victoria is watered by the Goulburn Irrigation System, the oldest and most developed system in Australia. The original dam, known as Sugarloaf Reservoir, was built between 1915 and 1927 and had a wall 44 metres high. The main flooding of the valleys here dates from the 1950s, when a new embankment almost eighty metres high was constructed. Water released from Eildon is also used to generate hydro-electric power.

STRATHBOGIE RANGES ■ 1067

From the Strathbogie Ranges, south-east of Euroa, there are commanding views over the surrounding district. This is wild and forbidding country where the Kelly gang had several hideouts and in remote reaches, even established stock-holding yards for horses stolen in New South Wales and intended for sale in southern Victoria. It says much for the Kellys' skills in bushcraft that they were able to drive mobs of unbroken horses through these steep, timbered slopes. Nearby is Polly McQuinn's Reservoir – haunted, some say, by the ghost of Polly McQuinn, who was swallowed up, with his waggon and team, by a deep waterhole in these parts.

VIOLET TOWN ■ 1068

Located between Euroa and Benalla, Violet Town is the centre of an agricultural, pastoral and dairying district. The less conventional pursuit of ostrich farming is one example of increasing agricultural diversification as farmers search for new markets. The ostrich chicks are sold for breeding and ultimately their prized skins are exported for use in high-quality leather goods. Nearer town is the Dorset Hill wildlife and game-bird park which features a wide variety of Australian native birds and animals. Historical artefacts, including an old tram from Melbourne, are also displayed. *Population 600*

Mansfield & Mount Buller

Reputations were made and lost in this high-country landscape during the wild old days of Ned Kelly raids, implacable mountain men and raucous miners seeking gold. Peaceful hamlets that were once gold towns are scattered over the hillsides where fashionable skiers come in winter and hardy bushwalkers in summer.

ALPINE NATIONAL PARK ■ 1069

More than 6400 square kilometres of Victorian high country from the Great Dividing Range near Mansfield to the New South Wales border were incorporated into this park in 1989. The park now links with Kosciusko National Park in New South Wales and its neighbour, the Namadgi National Park in the Australian Capital Territory to form a chain of protected high-country bushland. The Alpine Park is characterised by a breathtakingly beautiful landscape: mountain peaks, escarpments and high plains, such as those around Mount Feathertop, The Bluff and Bogong High Plains. More importantly, the park protects alpine and sub-alpine environments which occupy a small but vital place in the Australian landscape.

A number of plants and animals thrive here despite severe winter conditions. Of special note is the rare mountain pygmy possum, the only marsupial in the world to live exclusively in an alpine habitat and store its winter food supply. Twenty other endangered species also live in the park's precincts. Of the native plants growing here, thirty-eight are considered of national significance; twelve are found nowhere else.

The Alpine Park, the largest in Victoria, is an amalgamation of three older parks. Scenic drives - scorned by a legion of bushwalkers and cross-country skiers – link lookout points.

ALPINE WALKING TRACK ■ 1070

This challenging 400-kilometre walking track starts at Walhalla and finishes at Cowombat Flat at the New South Wales border. It was constructed in the 1970s and is now recognised as one of the finest long-distance bushwalking tracks in Australia. It also provides the spine for a system of walking tracks in Victoria's alpine region. The track generally follows the ridges through some of the highest country in Victoria and is, for the most part, remote from any settlement.

It takes about thirty days to walk the entire track but many people walk sections such as the Howqua Valley and Upper Yarra tracks which follow old mining routes. McMillans Track, cut in 1864 from Omeo to Woods Point, follows the path of the explorer Angus McMillan who tramped the ranges from 1839 to 1841 in search of new grazing lands.

Water is scarce along some sections of the track, especially in

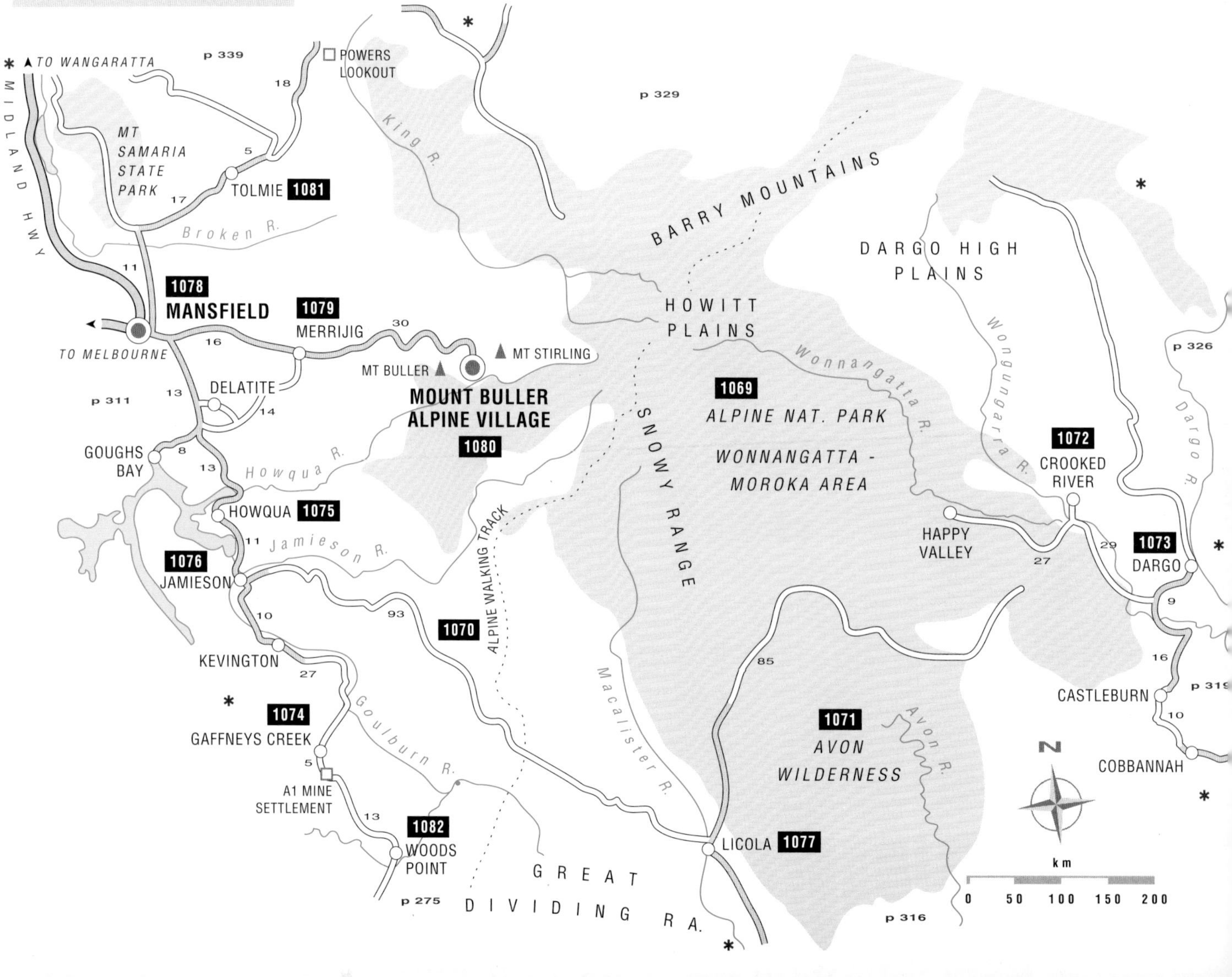

TO WANGARATTA
p 339
POWERS LOOKOUT
p 329
MIDLAND HWY
MT SAMARIA STATE PARK
TOLMIE 1081
King R.
Broken R.
BARRY MOUNTAINS
DARGO HIGH PLAINS
1078 MANSFIELD
1079 MERRIJIG
HOWITT PLAINS
TO MELBOURNE
MT STIRLING
MT BULLER
p 326
p 311
DELATITE
MOUNT BULLER ALPINE VILLAGE 1080
1069 ALPINE NAT. PARK
Wonnangatta R.
Wongungarra R.
Dargo R.
GOUGHS BAY
Howqua R.
SNOWY RANGE
WONNANGATTA - MOROKA AREA
1072 CROOKED RIVER
HOWQUA 1075
Jamieson R.
HAPPY VALLEY
1073 DARGO
1076 JAMIESON
ALPINE WALKING TRACK
1070
KEVINGTON
CASTLEBURN
p 319
Macalister R.
1074 GAFFNEYS CREEK
Goulburn R.
1071 AVON WILDERNESS
Avon R.
COBBANNAH
A1 MINE SETTLEMENT
1082 WOODS POINT
LICOLA 1077
GREAT DIVIDING RA.
p 275
p 316
N
km
0 50 100 150 200

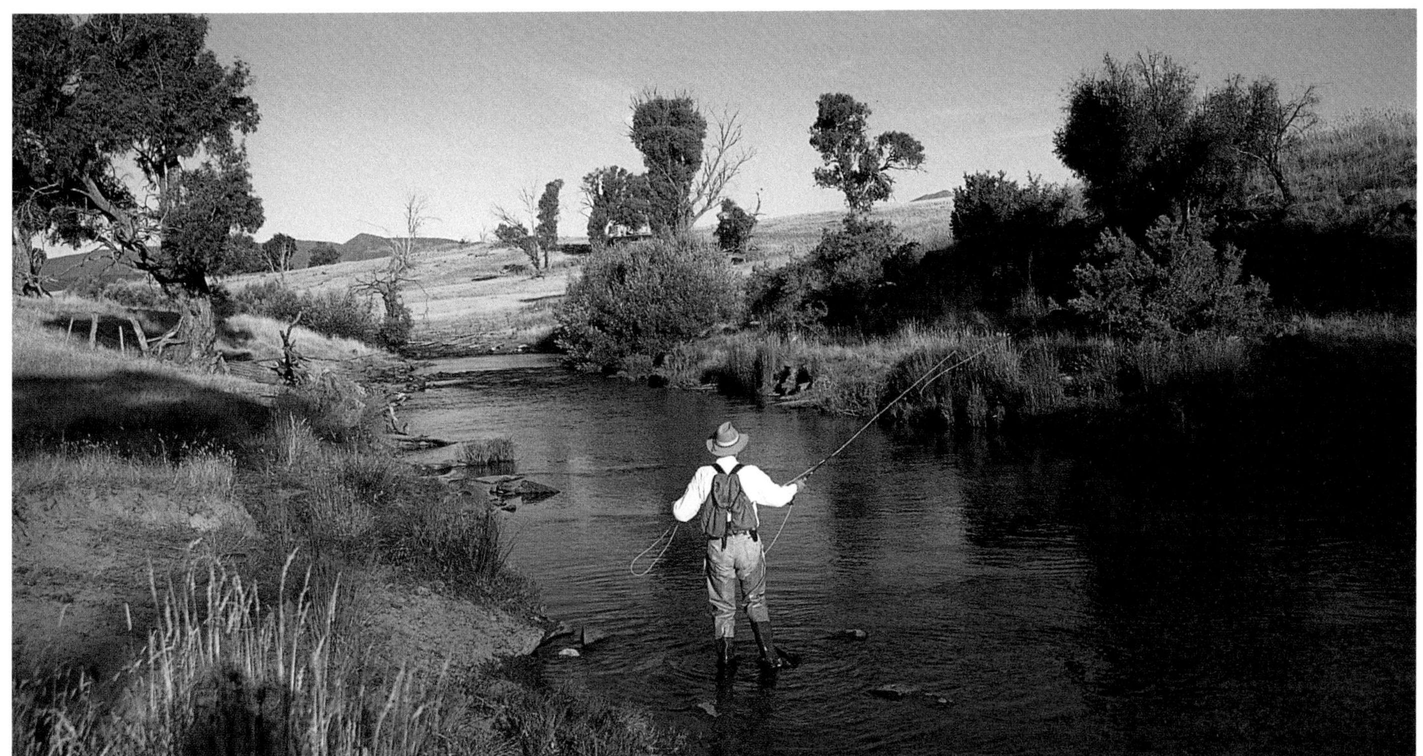

Cross-country skiing and white-water canoeing are fine, but some prefer simply to tempt the trout in the Delatite River at Merrijig by casting a fly.

summer, and park rangers recommend that a map and compass be carried for safety's sake.

AVON WILDERNESS ■ 1071
Sub-alpine woodlands, snow grass plains and mountain ash forests are found in this 40 000-hectare central Gippsland wilderness, the first to be nominated in eastern Gippsland and the second in Victoria. The area takes in the upper reaches of the Avon, Dolodrook and Turton rivers and forms the southern extremity of the Alpine National Park (see entry). Mount Wellington, at 1600 metres, is the highest 'peak'.

The high regions of the wilderness are usually snow-covered in winter while in summer, the foothills and valleys are hot and dry. Access to the western and northern sections is from Licola on the road between Heyfield and Jamieson; four-wheel-drive tracks provide access to the wilderness in several other locations. Inexperienced bushwalkers need not apply here and visitors should be adequately equipped for the rugged conditions and skilled in bushcraft. The safe minimum number for a party is four.

The year of construction was tidily bricked into this charcoal kiln which burns the waste of a Mansfield mill.

CROOKED RIVER ■ 1072
This tiny hamlet was surrounded by gold-rush towns during the boom times of the 1850s and 1860s. Probably the most spectacular of these boom-and-bust towns was to the north, at Grant. At one stage, this nugget-rich town boasted eighteen hotels but now there is only a graveyard. Mining relics such as stumping batteries, steam engines and water wheels are littered throughout the landscape. Access tracks into the Alpine National Park are along the road from Crooked River.

DARGO ■ 1073
First established as a supply centre for the goldfields in the mid-1800s, this small township is now based around a stockbreeding, sawmilling and agricultural district. To the north are the Dargo High Plains, a region of plateaux between 1200 and 1500 metres above sea level, best viewed from the scenic roadway to the east.
FESTIVALS Dargo Walnut Festival, late March.

GAFFNEYS CREEK ■ 1074
Terence Gaffney first discovered gold here in 1859, and prospectors struggled through the rugged terrain to reach the strike site. Today, the 120-year-old timber cottages they built themselves are reminders of a town once populated by more than 1000 fortune hunters. This small settlement, in the narrow Raspberry Creek Valley, still retains its original mine workings and discarded relics from the abandoned goldfields are scattered over the hills, like reminders of a long-ago battle. South of the town, is the A1 gold mine which has been operating since 1881.

HOWQUA ■ 1075
Howqua is a tiny township on the banks of the Howqua River. Greenstone outcrops used by Aborigines to make and sharpen their tools can sometimes be seen near the riverbank. A 100-metre tunnel cut in 1881 through Tunnel Spur links the Howqua River to a water race and waterwheel, and another industrial artefact, in the form of a brick chimney from a smelting furnace still stands nearby.

JAMIESON ■ 1076
The old court house is a reminder of the bustling gold town Jamieson was in the 1860s. During the boom times, the town was the centre for local gold exploration and had fourteen hotels, two breweries and a passing parade of countless prospectors.

The town today is known as a fishing spot, being at the junction of the Goulburn and Jamieson rivers and near Lake Eildon. A scenic road winds south for 135-kilometres from Jamieson to Walhalla, past old gold-mining towns and forest.

LICOLA ■ 1077
Once a timber town, Licola is now owned by the Lions Club of Victoria and is a popular holiday camp centre for children. In summer, the Licola to Jamieson road makes a particularly attractive scenic drive, winding through the Great Dividing Range to its highest point, 1558 metres above sea level. The road is closed during the winter and early spring, between June and October. Four-and-a-half kilometres north of Licola is a sign-posted track which leads to Lake Tarli Karng. This little gem of a lake, surrounded as it is by extremely steep banks, is often called the hidden lake, as it is thought not even the Aborigines knew of its existence. Further north still there are alpine plains where cattle have grazed each summer since the 1860s. Bennison's plains cover more than 400 kilometres of Victorian high country.

MANSFIELD ■ 1078
Established in the 1840s, Mansfield prospered and grew rapidly during the gold rush of the 1860s. It hit the headlines in 1878 when three policemen from Mansfield were shot dead by Ned Kelly and his gang.

The drama began with the departure from Mansfield of a posse of four policemen on Friday, 25 October. Sergeant Michael Kennedy and

Craig's Hut has not overlooked the Howitt Plains for as long as its appearance might suggest; it was built for the film Man from Snowy River.

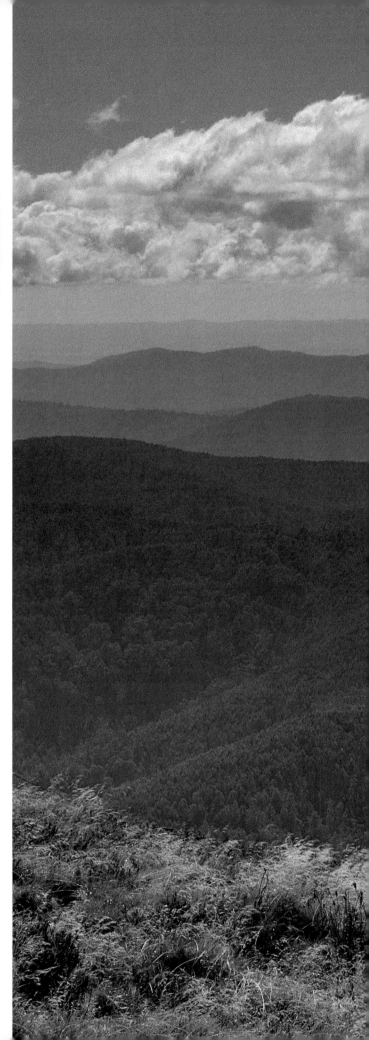

Constables Michael Scanlan, Thomas Lonigan and Thomas McIntyre set up their camp at Stringybark Creek near Tolmie, unaware they were close to the gang's hiding spot. They were ambushed by the Kelly gang the next day and, in the shootout that followed, three of the policemen were fatally wounded. Only Thomas McIntyre escaped; the bodies of his companions were recovered and buried in the Mansfield cemetery.

In 1880, a monument honouring the three policemen was erected in Main Street. Many substantial buildings from around this time still stand in Mansfield and are classified by the National Trust. The police stables, lockup, and court house have great architectural character. Today, Mansfield is at the centre of an important timber and grazing district and is a busy tourist centre.

DELATITE VINEYARD This winery just south of Mansfield started production as recently as 1982. Before this, the grapes grown here had been sent elsewhere to be crushed and processed. Wine tasting is done in a room with sweeping views of the mountains nearby.

MERRIJIG ■ 1079

The district north of this small town was the location for the film *The Man from Snowy River*. The original poem by Banjo Paterson is said to be based on 'Hellfire' Jack Clarke of Jindabyne, one of the legendary mountain cattlemen who have left a distinctive mark on the history of the entire region. Several of their high-country huts still stand and provide a useful refuge for bushwalkers when the weather is wild.

MOUNT BULLER ALPINE VILLAGE ■ 1080

Amongst the earliest European arrivals in this district were the Hearns who took up land in 1852. Later the Klingsporn family worked hard to get the Mansfield to Mount Buller Road built, opening the area to skiers, bushwalkers and other nature-lovers. Today Mount Buller has a dozen ski runs of varying levels of difficulty. Its toboggan run is probably the best known beginners' slope in Victoria.

MOUNT BULLER Because of its proximity to Melbourne, the 1806-metre Mount Buller is one of Victoria's most popular resorts. Several walking tracks start at the Alpine Village and superb views of the surrounding countryside can be seen from the top of Mount Buller itself during the three-kilometre-return summit walk. The Little Buller walk (five kilometres return) passes through snow grass plains and gum forests.

TOLMIE ■ 1081

North-east of this village noted for its potatoes and action-packed annual sports day, is Powers Lookout. The shootout between Ned Kelly and the police is said to have taken place here under the so-called 'Kelly' tree. Abseiling novices can often be seen learning the ropes on the hair-raising overhang of the lookout. To the west is Mount Samaria National Park.

WOODS POINT ■ 1082

This former gold town on the banks of the Goulburn River had the reputation of being one of the wildest towns in Victoria. During the gold rush, more than 2000 miners were served by 30 hotels, 6 banks, dance halls and a town crier. Local folklore has it that miners used to play skittles with bottles of champagne. A barmaid was said to have been given so many nuggets that she was able to retire. The town is named after Henry Wood, its first storekeeper.

A girdle of hills – such as the Blue Range (right) – makes Mansfield the gateway to the high country.

Sale & Maffra

Central Gippsland was pioneered by Highland Scots who recognised good cattle land when they saw it. They were unable to even guess at what would provide the region's modern bounty: the vast oil and gas field beneath the sea off the spectacular Ninety Mile Beach.

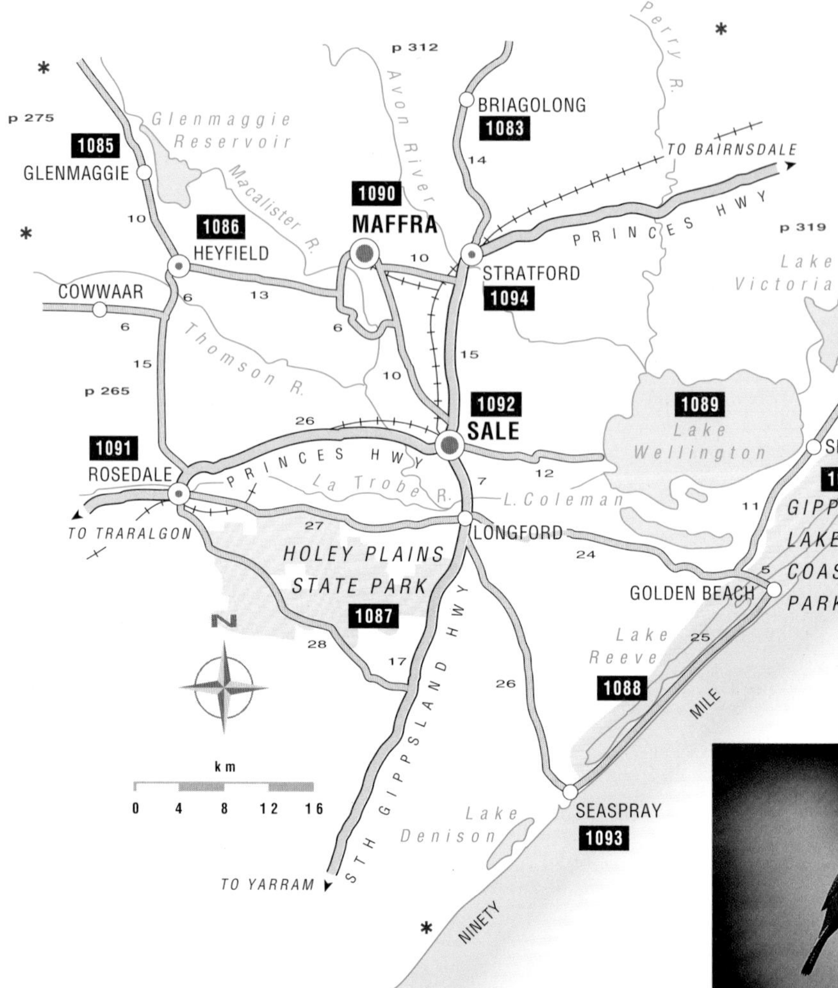

BRIAGOLONG ■ 1083

On a section of Angus McMillan's 'Bushy Park' run known as Top Plain, a small settlement was established in the 1850s and it was not until 1873 that the name was officially changed to Briagolong, from the Aboriginal 'brayakaulung', thought to mean 'men of the west', as well as the name of the local Aboriginal people.

The town has a history of distinctive industries. Timber from Briagolong paved the early streets of Melbourne and became the flooring of Australia House in London. Tobacco was grown from the late 1860s until it was killed off by disease in the 1940s; a complementary cigar factory operated for a time from the 1870s. Hops were successfully cultivated from the late 1860s until 1913.

A number of quarries, producing a distinctive and handsome honey-coloured stone once operated along Freestone Creek, which was also the scene of a brief gold rush. The first cheese factory opened in 1875 and, with the coming of the railway in 1889, two milk trains made daily deliveries from Briagolong to the dairy factories at Maffra.

In 1952, the railway line closed and by the 1960s Chester Eagle was to suggest in his book *Hail and Farewell* that this district was so untouched by at least outward signs of modern life that only the occasional road sign stood between Briagolong and the perfect setting for a turn-of-the-century film.

Population 510

GIPPSLAND LAKES COASTAL PARK ■ 1084

This long, narrow park encompasses the section of the Ninety Mile Beach running from the delightfully named Seaspray (see entry) to Lakes Entrance (see *Bairnsdale & Lakes Entrance*); the narrow spit of land separating the beach from the lakes; all of Lake Reeve (see entry) and part of the shores of Lake Victoria.

Within the 17 000-hectare park, vegetation ranges from the hairy spinifex, introduced marram grass and tea tree and banksia of the dunes to the salt-resistant species such as glasswort on the lake shores and the manna gum, shining peppermint and heathland plants of the surrounding bushland.

The park is also host to a large variety of birds – woodland, shore, ocean and migratory species. The fire-tail finch, with the distinctive red patch at the base of the tail, which features in an Aboriginal legend of the coming of fire, is found in the park. Kangaroos, possums and echidnas share the park with less common species such as the white-footed dunnart, the potoroo and the New Holland mouse, feared extinct until sighted in 1967 and now found at a few sites including Gippsland Lakes Coastal Park.

GLENMAGGIE ■ 1085

The MacFarlanes, from the Highlands of Scotland, had a number of cattle runs around the headwaters of the Thomson and Macalister rivers from the 1840s, including 'Glenmaggie'. Although gold-bearing quartz was discovered at Glenmaggie in the late 1860s, Glenmaggie's contribution to the nearby goldfields was mainly in the form of food such as beef and dairy produce. The small and relatively inaccessible settlement even had its own creamery for a short time...and a resident author, M.E. Fullerton. Born in Glenmaggie in 1868, Fullerton described her childhood at the settlement in her book *Bark House Days*.

The Glenmaggie of Fullerton's childhood has now been drowned by the waters of Glenmaggie Reservoir although three buildings – the Church of England, a hall and the Lakeside Store – were moved by bullock teams to new and higher sites before the village was inundated in 1927. The present village of Glenmaggie sits on the edge of the reservoir...but the ghostly remains of the old village can be seen in times of drought.

The distinctively coloured fire-tail finch enlivens the bushland of the Gippsland Lakes Coastal Park.

GLENMAGGIE RESERVOIR The original dam wall was built on the Macalister River between 1919 and 1927, and radial gates were installed on the spillway in the 1950s to increase the

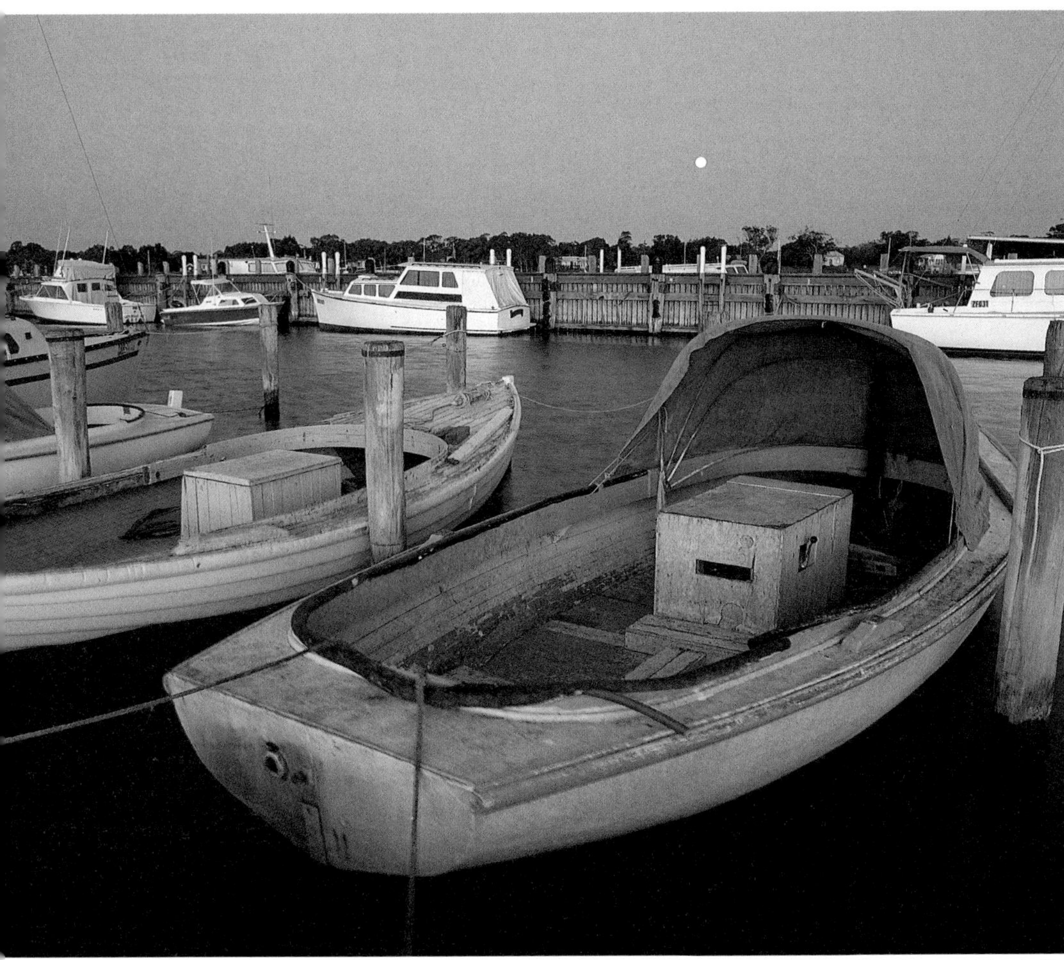

From Lake Victoria, modest amateur fishing boats have ready access to the waters of Australia's longest lake chain.

water storage capacity. Work started in 1987 to further stabilise the wall. The reservoir provides water for the 54 000-hectare Macalister Irrigation District, which supports intensive dairy farming.

HEYFIELD ■ 1086

This timber town on the banks of the Thomson River is one of the oldest settlements in the region. Around James MacFarlane's 'Heyfield' station, a small settlement sprang up in the 1840s although the township was not surveyed until 1864. Cattle, fattened in the high country, were sold at Heyfield's cattleyards but few squatters chose James MacFarlane's method of driving cattle – he did it in relative comfort from his seat in a horse-drawn gig.

When MacFarlane sold to James Tyson, the scene was set for the famous 'Battle of the Bridge'. The bridge across the river encroached on Tyson's land so he installed a locked gate across the bridge, stopping all traffic to and from Heyfield. Fuelled by free beer from a bush pub, squatters and townspeople gathered at the bridge and attempted to demolish the gate with the help of a bullock team. The law – and sheer numbers – were against Tyson who lost the battle. Mary Grant Bruce's uncle worked for Tyson and the 'Billabong' station of her children's books is thought to have been based on 'Heyfield'.

At one time there were as many as eight sawmills operating in the town and, with a major boost to the timber industry occurring after the Second World War, Heyfield eventually became the largest supplier of treated – kiln-dried – hardwood in Victoria. *Population 1610*

HOLEY PLAINS STATE PARK ■ 1087

This state park gets its name from 'Holey Plain' station, taken up by the Curlewis brothers in 1842. The land, on part of which the Park stands, was bought shortly afterwards by Edward Crooke who used it for holding cattle which were being herded from his property on the Mitta Mitta River to Port Albert. Some of the land and the original 1888 homestead have remained in the Crooke family ever since.

The park, which covers an area of almost 11 000 hectares, includes a mix of small swamps, sandy hills, open forest and heathy woodland. The region was established to provide protection for the native vegetation and is noted for its brilliant wildflower displays in spring and for such plants as the comparatively rare golden grevillea and the Gippsland grey box, which grow undisturbed within its boundaries.

LAKE REEVE ■ 1088

This long narrow lake is separated – but only just – from Ninety Mile Beach and the ocean by a very narrow spit of land. Those with boats sail across the lake and walk across the narrow peninsula to the beach. Lake Reeve – named after John Reeves, an early settler – is tidal and in dry periods extensive sandflats emerge at the edge of the lake – tourists have to be warned not to park their cars on the temporary sandflats. Although some of the land and roads around it are private property, Lake Reeve itself is part of the Gippsland Lakes Coastal Park.

In recent years, erosion of the lake shores and sand dunes has become a problem. The lake is more saline now than when the entrance to the ocean was formed in the years between 1869 and 1889 and the swamp paperbark and rushes around the lake shores are dying off, allowing further erosion of the lake shores while wind erosion is affecting the fragile dunes. The saltmarsh around Lake Reeve is an important waterfowl habitat – but wild duck and stubble quail may still be hunted in season.

LAKE WELLINGTON ■ 1089

First visited by Angus McMillan during his explorations of 1839–40, Lake Wellington is the last in the chain of four large, interconnected Gippsland Lakes, the longest chain of lakes in Australia. Fresh water flows into the lake from the Avon, Macalister and Thomson rivers while the narrow McLennan Strait connects Wellington Lake to the waters of the neighbouring Victoria Lake and eventually to the sea.

Lake Wellington remains almost completely undisturbed by housing or commercial development – Seacombe, perched at the entrance to the McLennan Straits, is the only settlement on the lake while Marlay Point on the eastern shores is popular with boating enthusiasts. As a result, Lake Wellington is more noted for its fish and other wildlife than for its human activities.

'STRATHFIELDSAYE' This large house, built on the northern shore of Lake Wellington in 1848, is the oldest continuously occupied homestead in Gippsland. The first stage was built by the property's original squatter, William Odell Raymond, and later additions were built by the Disher family who owned the home for many years before selling it to the University of Melbourne. The cannon in the garden came from a ship wrecked off the Gippsland coast and was installed 'for defence against natives' though never used.

MAFFRA ■ 1090

Referred to initially as 'Sheepfold', the official name of the town came from Mafra in Portugal where Captain Macalister, employer of Angus McMillan the pioneer of this region, spent some time during the Peninsular War which raged between 1808 and 1814.

By the 1870s, Maffra had established itself as the major cattle market in Gippsland and a future Premier of Victoria, Allan McLean, opened his stock and station agency in Maffra at that time. Although cattle have continued to be the most important product in the town's economy, Maffra was also the site of Australia's largest and, for much of the time, only, sugar beet industry. The first crops were grown and processed at the town's factory in 1897 but it was only with government assistance after 1910 that the industry managed to survive until 1946 when it was overtaken by Queensland's sugar industry. The factory office and weighbridge survive and are now used as a museum.

Maffra, with its beautiful main street gardens, is the centre of the Macalister Irrigation District which is supplied with water from the Glenmaggie Reservoir (see *Glenmaggie*). The products of the intensive dairying in the district around the town are processed at the large factory in Maffra while at the Macalister Research Farm just outside town experiments and demonstrations of improved farming practices are conducted. *Population 3880*

FESTIVALS Mardi Gras, March.

ROSEDALE ■ **1091**

Rosedale Station was named by David Parry-Okeden after his wife Rosalie in 1843 or 1844. Blind Joe, who had a hut on the creek, was possibly the first 'settler' in what was to become the town of Rosedale.

On the banks of the La Trobe River and strategically placed on the Princes Highway, Rosedale's position has always been important to its survival. Initially a staging post on the Port Albert–Sale coach route, it now offers access to central or south Gippsland, the La Trobe Valley and the slopes of the Strzelecki Ranges. A charming town with some historic buildings including the Mechanics Institute (1863) and St Mark's Church of England (1874), Rosedale is the administrative centre for a shire that includes much of the Ninety Mile Beach and the grazing and grain-growing area running from the beach to the foothills of the Great Dividing Range. *Population 1150*

'NAMBROK' On the crest of a hill, a few kilometres east of Rosedale, 'Nambrok' was built in 1864 for the pastoralist John King, grandson of Governor King. The house is a fine brick mansion incorporating a mix of architectural styles from different periods and countries. The architect is unknown but it was built by a local builder, William Allen, who was responsible for a number of the older buildings in the district and the homestead is still in private hands.

SALE ■ **1092**

Angus McMillan was the first European to explore the area around Sale and is now buried in the town's cemetery. Another Scot, Archibald MacIntosh, built a forge on the banks of Flooding Creek in 1844, and, on high ground around his forge, the settlement of Flooding Creek grew. Renamed Sale in 1850 after a British Army General, Sir Robert Henry Sale, the town soon developed as a centre for those taking up selections in the newly opened Gippsland, then as a stopover point for those heading for the Omeo and Walhalla goldfields. From 1878, Sale was the district's railhead and from the 1880s a major inland port.

The steamers and barges that once ran regularly between Melbourne and Sale have gone but the swing bridge and canal built to ease their passage remain. The swing bridge designed by John Grainger, father of the composer Percy Grainger, was built in 1883 at the junction of the La Trobe and Thomson rivers. The central span of the bridge could be swung open on eight pivot cylinders and a series of cogs and wheels. Vessels would whistle on their approach and the bridgekeeper, employed at five shillings a week and ensconced in a cottage at the bridge, opened it...up to twenty times a day at the height of shipping activity between 1880 and 1920.

The twenty-five-kilometre canal was built from Sale to the La Trobe River and from there to Lake Wellington connecting the Port of Sale to the Gippsland Lakes, Lakes Entrance and the sea. The canal also allowed supplies to be shipped right into the town rather than being offloaded at the La Trobe Wharf on the river, about five kilometres south of the town.

Sale's more recent development has been even more rapid than at the turn of the century. Since 1965, the town has been the administrative centre for Bass Strait oil and natural gas. From the oil wells in the Bass Strait, opposite Ninety Mile Beach, pipelines transport oil to the gas treatment and crude oil stabilisation plant at Longford, just south of Sale, and from there, through 190 kilometres of pipeline, to Long Island on Westernport. With the increase in population and the consequent supporting industries that have been attracted here since the 1960s, its position as the major centre in the region has been confirmed.

The English novelist Anthony Trollope visited Sale in the 1870s and described its buildings as 'generally magnificent'. Many of the buildings that Trollope saw still stand, including the council chambers built in 1863 and now a museum, the Criterion Hotel (1865) – the oldest hotel still operating in Gippsland – and the Club Hotel (1856) which was a Cobb & Co. office on the long journey to the goldfields and which was once visited by Dame Nellie Melba in the early 1900s.

Hal Porter in *The Watcher on the Cast-Iron Balcony* describes Sale as a 'provincial cathedral city set smack-flat on grassy vast plains...decorated with park-like areas of bush'. St Paul's Anglican Cathedral (1880s) and St Mary's Catholic Cathedral (1870s) still stand and the parks include a fauna park alongside the artificial Lake Guthridge, home to the Sale city emblem – the black swan – and a wildlife reserve on the 308-hectare common where handsome magpie geese have been reintroduced to share the freshwater marsh and large permanent waterhole with other water birds and numerous fish. *Population 13 860*

FESTIVALS Sale Festival, October.

The lonely artificial island of the Barracouta oil rig in Bass Strait is linked tenuously with the mainland by an underwater pipeline to Longford.

SEASPRAY ■ **1093**

This small village within earshot of the surf is one of the few settlements in this region to feel the spray of the sea off the Ninety Mile Beach. Popular in the summer months with tourists – and all year round with surf fishermen – the village of Seaspray sits just south of Lake Reeve and on the delta of Merriman's Creek. Despite the narrowness of the spit of land alongside Lake Reeve, a road runs north from Seaspray to Golden Beach, the only other accessible settlement. On a clear day, the Barracouta platform in the offshore Bass Strait oil and gas field is visible from this road.

FESTIVALS Country Fair, January.

STRATFORD ■ **1094**

In the early 1840s, William Odell Raymond drove 8000 sheep a distance of 1130 kilometres from his drought-stricken run in the Wellington Valley in New South Wales to a new run on the Avon River, which he called 'Stratford', apparently after an earlier Australian Agricultural Company run. The origin of the name has caused ongoing controversy and whether the town is named after Shakespeare's birthplace or whether it is named after Stratford St. Mary in Essex or is a distortion of 'Straight Ford' is still hotly contested. The Stratford-on-Avon Shakespeare Festival, held annually in the town, wisely does not concern itself with the argument over names.

William Raymond too was prepared to trade on the Shakespearian connection by opening a hotel called the Shakespeare Hotel on his run as early as 1847; a small settlement was already flourishing on a section of his run where the stock route forded the river – the first European child was born there as early as 1843. With the opening of the Dargo goldfields, to the north of the town, Stratford developed as a supply base. Supplies, which came by sea to Port Albert or through the Gippsland Lakes, were sent by packhorse up to the goldfields.

'At flood time imposing, no doubt, the Avon is now a stream which fails to inspire any respect' was how one visitor, the writer John Stanley James described the river in 1886 but the people of Stratford have reason to respect the Avon. The flood-prone river has extensively damaged or swept away a number of bridges at Stratford, the last time being in the 1950s. The same rushing waters that are a risk to bridges have also washed and polished stones in the river bed for thousands of years and the riverbanks at Stratford are a popular hunting ground for lapidarists searching for gemstones such as jasper and agate.

Stratford, where Aboriginal canoe trees can still be seen in the historic Knob Reserve, is the centre of a dairy and beef cattle district and the administrative centre for Avon Shire. *Population 1300*

FESTIVALS Stratford-on-Avon Shakespeare Festival, April–May; Country Music Festival, November.

Bairnsdale & Lakes Entrance

The natural barriers of mountains, dense forest, swampland and sea postponed settlement of this part of Victoria by Europeans until well into the 1840s. When they did come, overland from New South Wales, the early squatters were met with strenuous resistance from the region's Aboriginal inhabitants.

For long the main routes in and out of east Gippsland were overland from the Monaro in New South Wales, or by sea through the Gippsland lakes and rivers. It was as a trading port for the pastoral runs, small farms, timber industry, and in the 1850s and 1860s, the Omeo goldfields, that Bairnsdale developed. Steamers and boats passed through Lake King, then up the Mitchell River to Bairnsdale where they offloaded supplies and loaded produce bound for Melbourne and Sydney.

The river trade effectively ceased after the railway reached Bairnsdale in 1888, and the wharf near the old butter factory on the Bairnsdale–Paynesville Road has all but gone. The original wharf stood upstream of the present bridge but this had to be abandoned when the first bridge – dating from 1875 – was found to restrict the free passing of boats.

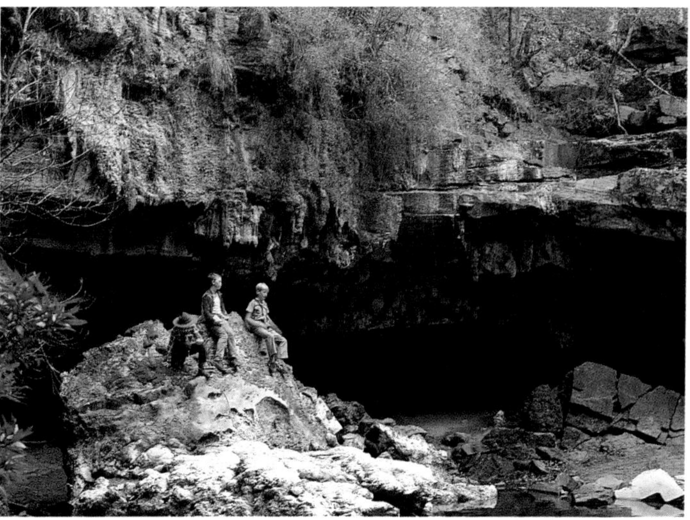

The Den of Nargun, where a malevolent Dreamtime spirit dwells beneath an eroded cliff in the Mitchell River Park, fails to scare these bushwalkers.

BAIRNSDALE ■ 1095

Many travellers on their way to the Victorian high country find themselves in Bairnsdale. Located where the Omeo Highway branches off the Princes Highway, just north of Lake King, this comfortable, rural town is nowadays heavily promoted as a tourist destination and gateway to the lakes region, with golf course, sports centre, restaurants, cultivated gardens – all the amenities of the city. It has also become a popular retirement town. But this homely image contrasts with Bairnsdale's romantic riverboat past and the district's bitter early white settlement.

The name Bairnsdale was taken from the run occupied by Archibald Macleod on the banks of the Mitchell River in the early 1840s, which he named 'Bernisdale' after his birthplace on the Isle of Skye. The corruption to Bairnsdale is said to have come after Macleod returned from a lengthy absence and was greeted by a large number of children. He is then said to have changed the name to include the Scottish 'bairn' for child!

Like most of the early settlers to the district – opened up by Angus McMillan over several expeditions between 1839 and 1841 (see *Mansfield & Mount Buller*) – Macleod was a pastoralist. Settlement was slow because of the district's remoteness, and because of Aboriginal resistance. Eventually, the Aborigines were to all intents and purposes decimated by retribution from the graziers and quickly spreading European diseases.

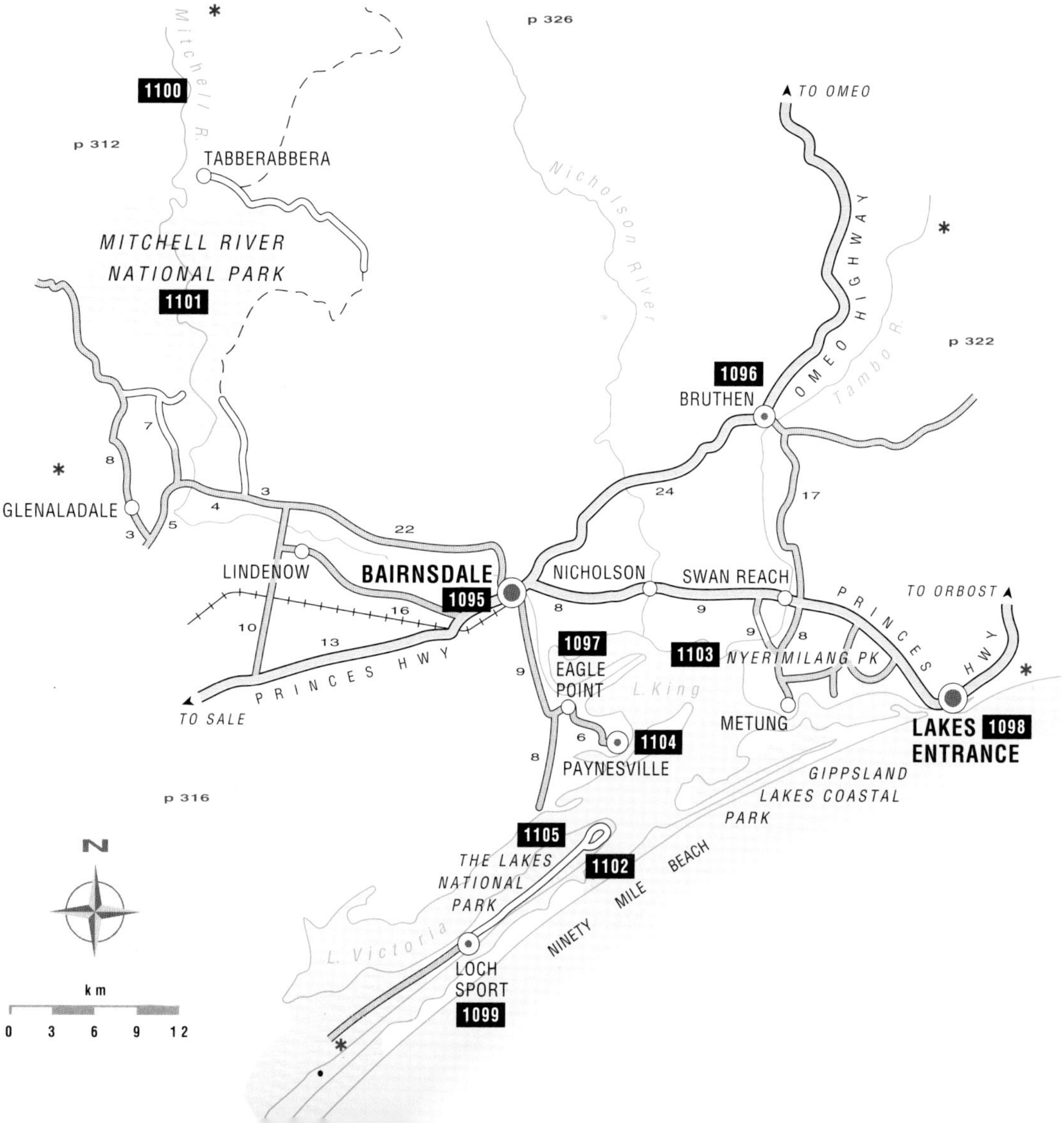

The thin yellow line of Ninety Mile Beach – 145 kilometres long – prevents the low-lying The Lakes National Park from being inundated by the sea.

The pastoralists who moved into the region prospered, and it became and continues to be a productive dairy, wool and beef-cattle area. From the 1920s, it also became a large vegetable producer, and a vegetable processing plant was located in the town. The east Gippsland region is one of Victoria's largest suppliers of timber and many mills operate around Bairnsdale. *Population 10 770*

BAIRNSDALE COURT HOUSE The court house, built between 1892 and 1893, is an elaborate structure of gables, towers and mullioned chimneys, set upon an angular, block-like body. The entrance is decorated with carvings of Australian fauna and flora, and inside there are high, wood-lined ceilings and a bench, dock and jury stalls of cedar. The building is classified by the National Trust.

MACLEODS MORASS This marshy area south of Bairnsdale has formed as a result of silt deposits from the Mitchell River in the same way as the Eagle Point silt jetties (see entry). Reached by the Paynesville Road from Bairnsdale, it is a State Wildlife Reserve. Bird boxes to encourage breeding and hides for observing the birds have been installed in strategic locations; a boardwalk runs approximately 500 metres out into the morass, which is not nearly as uninviting as its name suggests.

ST MARY'S CATHOLIC CHURCH Located in Main Street, this church is richly covered with murals depicting the Nativity, the Crucifixion and the apostles. Painted during the Great Depression by Frank Floreani, an Italian artist who studied in Turin, the ceiling of the main body of the church is decorated with various designs involving 300 to 400 angelic faces or forms, none of which are alike. The ceiling of the sanctuary shows representations of heaven, hell and purgatory, and prominently above the altar is the image of the church's patron.

FESTIVALS Marlay Point Overnight Yacht Race, March; Bairnsdale Festival, early March.

BRUTHEN ■ 1096

Bruthen is pronounced 'brewthen' and derives its name from the Aboriginal 'brewdthan' – thought to mean 'bracken' or 'place of evil spirit'. The town was an important stopover for early pioneers, and for gold seekers when the fields at Omeo, Glen Wills and Cassilis opened up. Today, it is a quiet town servicing the surrounding farms and traffic along the Omeo Highway which passes through it. Originally laid out closer to the Tambo River, Bruthen was moved further north after a flood in 1870, and the hamlet of Mossiface just to the south served as a port for traffic on the Tambo River. A flood in 1911 changed the course of the Tambo River so that it no longer flows past Mossiface which in modern times attracts attention with its restored hop kilns which date from around 1880.

Despite the connotations of its Aboriginal name, Bruthen is located in good farming country. Logging, dairying, wool growing, and crops of beans, peas and particularly maize have been successful. Attractive pockets of natural bushland remain, such as Fairy Dell Scenic Reserve west of Bruthen, which has picnic grounds and walking track set amid a temperate rainforest unique to the east Gippsland region. *Population 610*

EAGLE POINT ■ 1097

South of Bairnsdale, along the Paynesville road, lies Eagle Point, with its fine view of the Mitchell River Silt Jetties which extend nearly ten kilometres into Lake King. The jetties are believed to be formed from silt deposited by the river when it slows on reaching the lake and are considered second only to the silt jetties of the Mississippi in the Gulf of Mexico. The jetties are now being eroded and may become a chain of islands by the year 2000 if no protective measures are taken to retain them.

LAKES ENTRANCE ■ 1098

Until 1889, when a permanent entrance to the complex of lakes and rivers of east Gippsland was created, this town between the channels of North Arm and Cunninghame Arm was known as Cunninghame.

For more than thirty years, the schooners and steamers that serviced the district were forced to navigate an impermanent natural opening from the sea into the lakes at Lake Bunga. After years of discussion, work on an artificial opening finally began in 1869. Twenty years later, the opening was complete – with the help of raging storm waters that broke through the last of the sand barrier separating the lakes from the sea. The success of the artificial entrance to the lakes has not been unqualified. The fear expressed by an engineer in 1861 that a new sandbar would be created has been partly realised, and a bow-shaped bar has developed at the mouth of the entrance, on occasion causing damage to boats and preventing the fishing fleet putting to sea.

Lakes Entrance has developed into a thriving tourist destination, and supports Australia's largest fishing fleet. Snapper, tuna, flathead, shark, salmon and bream among other fish are caught in the waters, and prawns and garfish are taken from the lakes. The town is also a depot for the off-shore oil rigs in Bass Strait which can be seen in the distance from Jemmys Point on the north side of the town.

Lakes Entrance's tourist development is partly attributable to its position on the Princes Highway but its location on the water is what clinches its popularity. A footbridge across Cunninghame Arm, opened in 1937, connects the town with Ninety Mile Beach and the surf. Boating and windsurfing, amongst other sports, take place on the lakes.

Three museums of interest are the Antique Car and Folk Museum with displays of old vehicles and a variety of domestic and farm implements; the Shell Museum which has more than 80 000 shells; and the Gippsland Aboriginal Art Museum. Located a few kilometres east of Lakes Entrance, this museum is divided into nine sections showing ceremonial rites, daily activities and tools not of the historical residents of this region, but of the people who make their home in the Simpson Desert today. *Population 4620*

LAKE BUNGA Prior to the creation of the artificial entrance, water traffic passed through a natural entrance from this lake and followed Reeve's River into Cunninghame Arm, and on to Bairnsdale or Mossiface.

The unreliability of this entrance, which shifted along the sandbar, obviously proved unsatisfactory; after the new entrance was built there was a casualty: Reeve River quickly filled with sand to form the dunes and lagoon of Warm Holes.

A few kilometres to the east of Lakes Entrance, Lake Bunga provides for the quiet of lake water or the surf of Ninety Mile Beach. A nature trail from the beach through the Lake Bunga Foreshore Reserve is marked by arrows.

LOCH SPORT ■ 1099

One of the smaller resorts on the stretch of land lying between Lake Victoria and Lake Reeve, Loch Sport provides one of the most convenient roads to the Lakes National Park and parking for Ninety Mile Beach. One of the attractions of east Gippsland is the mild climate, particularly in winter, when the north-westerly winds lose much of their moisture rising over the north-east highlands and arrive warm and dry at resorts such as Loch Sport. *Population 700*

MITCHELL RIVER ■ 1100

Rising in the Dargo Plains north-west of Bairnsdale, the Mitchell River flows through steep gorges, past the rainforest and dense bush of the Mitchell River National Park, to level out in the fertile river flats just north of the town and empty into Lake King. The relatively hazardless river no longer carries steamers plying between Melbourne and east Gippsland and is used most commonly by pleasure craft touring the lakes area, or rafting in its upper reaches.

MITCHELL RIVER NATIONAL PARK ■ 1101

Located north-west of Bairnsdale on the upper reaches of the Mitchell River, this park was formerly known as Glenaladale National Park. It is mainly dry forest of red and yellow box with some kurrajong trees covering the 11 900 hectares of the park, while rainforest carpets the sides of creek and river gullies.

Along the course of Woolshed Creek lies the Den of Nargun, a cavern formed by the erosion of soil from beneath an expanse of rock. According to Aboriginal legend, the cavern is the lair of a fearsome Dreamtime figure – Nargun – who abducts unwary passers-by.

NINETY MILE BEACH ■ 1102

The long stretch of dunes and beach that forms Ninety Mile Beach is one of the least spoiled and secluded places on the crowded eastern Australian coastline. Even today, the only access to the remotest parts of the beach is by boat.

The beach extends uninterrupted from Seaspray, west of Lake Reeve, (see *Sale & Maffra*) to the artificial entrance to the Gippsland lakes created at Lakes Entrance, then beyond that to Croajingolong National Park (see *Mallacoota & Cann River*). Protected from development for much of its length by the Gippsland Lakes Coastal Park (see *Sale & Maffra*), the beach is the barrier that keeps the lakes system separate from the sea.

FESTIVALS Blessing of the Fleet; Easter. Kite Championships; November.

NYERIMILANG PARK ■ 1103

One of the smaller resorts on the Nyerimilang Homestead, built as a retreat from Melbourne in 1884. The homestead sits amid formal gardens of exotic and native trees and shrubs which give way to forested clifftops and gullies, and the marshland of Maringa Creek. The property was purchased by the Victorian Government in 1976 and has picnic facilities and walking tracks from which to observe plants and animals and take in views over the lakes. For an extra touch of 'heritage', bullockies drive a team of resident bullocks during holiday times.

PAYNESVILLE ■ 1104

Situated on the straits between Lake King and Lake Victoria, Paynesville is a resort town usually promoted as the main boating centre for the lakes. It provides moorings and boat ramps for private and commercial use and supports a sizable fishing fleet. Boats may be hired from many outlets in the town, which is a convenient departure point for the camping ground on Rotamah Island, part of The Lakes National Park and accessible by boat.

One of the most unusual buildings in the town, maintaining the nautical theme, is the church of St Peter by the Lake with its spire in the form a lighthouse, pulpit resembling the bow of a ship, and sanctuary lamp incorporating the bell of the lakes steamer *Dargo*. *Population 2440*

RAYMOND ISLAND A punt operates between Paynesville and Raymond Island, located a kilometre or so offshore from the town. The bush-covered island is home to a variety of wildlife including a colony of koalas.

FESTIVALS Flat Water Classic Windsurfing Race, November.

THE LAKES NATIONAL PARK ■ 1105

A million years ago, the Gippsland lakes area was part of a broad bay. As it forced its way in and out of the bay over thousands of years the sea deposited sands which eventually created barriers that formed the various lakes and channels, and finally the thin stretch of sand known as Ninety Mile Beach that seals them off from the ocean.

The chain of lakes cover an area of more than 400 square kilometres, forming the largest enclosed waterway system in Australia. There are three main lakes – Victoria, King and Wellington – linked to each other by narrow channels. For more than seventy years, the lakes and their tributaries – the Mitchell, La Trobe, Nicholson and Tambo rivers – served as the busy transport network for the east Gippsland district, yet they have remained a relatively undisturbed haven for much of the region's wildlife including black swans, pelicans, herons, dolphins, wallabies, koalas and wombats.

The lake and channel foreshore areas vary from protected reserves and pastoral land to urban developments – chiefly in the vicinity of Lakes Entrance, Paynesville, Loch Sport and Metung. Not all wildlife on the reserves is protected, however. Seasonal hunting in designated areas for game birds and the introduced hog deer, as well as rabbits and foxes is permitted.

The intermittent shifting of the sands which caused the natural opening from the sea to the waters of Lake Bunga to be unreliable led to the dredging of a permanent artificial opening at Lakes Entrance (see entry), which has changed the nature of the lakes. Originally fresh to brackish, the waters are now fresh only in the western part of Lake Wellington. This permanent influx of salt water has changed the vegetation, causing a decline in the growth of rushes and swamp paperbarks and an increase in salt-marsh vegetation. The opening also reduced the level of the lakes by approximately forty centimetres.

Covering almost 2400 hectares between Lake Reeve and Lake Victoria, the Lakes National Park is one of two parks and a number of reserves adjoining the Gippsland lakes. The park was first reserved in 1927 and it was expanded in 1958 and 1976.

The terrain of the Lakes National Park includes woodland and swamp as well as the lakes' dune systems, and there are a number of walking tracks marked with hides – camouflaged spots in which patient nature-lovers may wait and observe native animals. A self-guided nature walk takes visitors to Lake Reeve, and there is a picnic spot at Point Wilson, east of Loch Sport; camping is permitted on Rotamah Island, which is accessible only by boat. Of Victoria's many and varied national parks and reserves, The Lakes National Park probably has the most restrictions, prohibiting dogs and cats, horseriding and hunting, in order to maintain this peaceful, relatively undisturbed environment.

LAKE KING One of the three main bodies of water in the lakes system with Lake Victoria and Lake Wellington, Lake King is the closest of the three waterways to Bairnsdale (see entry). It is fed by the Nicholson, Tambo and Mitchell rivers and along with Lake Victoria is a popular boating and fishing place.

LAKE VICTORIA Running parallel to Ninety Mile Beach and Reeve Channel, this lake is typical of the waters of the lakes system: gentle, safe and clean. The lack of reefs and rocks attracts many boating parties, and anglers are drawn to try their luck with the sea trout, bass, leatherjacket, and red rock cod.

St Mary's Catholic Church in Bairnsdale may not rival St Peter's in size but the spectacular impact of its intricate murals is just as overwhelming.

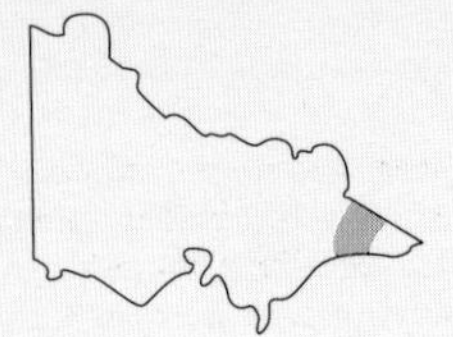

Orbost & Marlo

Victoria's 'wild' east is still largely a Snowy River wilderness, blanketed with deep forests, where the legendary waterway, celebrated in poem and film, comes to a quiet end at an almost pristine coastline just as untouched as the hinterland.

BUCHAN ■ 1106
The Buchan area was first settled in 1840. The Marston brothers travelled the Buchan–Gelantipy road in Rolf Boldrewood's novel, *Robbery Under Arms* (1881), but the district was not properly surveyed until 1899 when the government reserved the land to protect the region's cave formations from vandals. In March 1907, Frank Moon, a local prospector, found Fairy Cave – described later as 'Jenolan's rival'; Royal Cave was opened three years later. The many deciduous trees in the township put on an autumn show and Chinese brake ferns grow round the limestone outcrops. Buchan is said to come from 'buchan buchan', believed to be an Aboriginal word for a 'smoke signal expert', or 'bukkan munjie' meaning 'place of grass bags'.

BUCHAN CAVES ■ 1107
In the ancient past, 300–400 million years ago, this part of East Gippsland was covered by an ocean teeming with shellfish and coral. As the water receded, their remains formed limestone deposits which were folded and crumpled by violent movements within the earth. Later, underground rivers carved out chambers and tunnels before diverting to alternative courses. Then an infinite number of tiny calcite-bearing droplets decorated the caves with hanging stalactites, upright stalagmites, blanket 'falls' and gravity-defying helectites, which branch sideways and upwards. In places the white limestone is stained red and brown by iron oxide and green by copper.

Though the system contains about 350 caves, only two are open to the public: Royal Cave and Fairy Cave, so called because of its delicate decoration. Bones of extinct animals have been unearthed in the caves and there is evidence that people lived here long ago – tools 17 000 years old and rock engravings even older.

CABBAGE TREE CREEK ■ 1108
The village of Cabbage Tree Creek is particularly interesting to naturalists because cabbage tree palms grow in the area. They were first discovered by Baron von Mueller in 1854 and are Victoria's only indigenous palm. There are two small groups near the Cabbage Tree Creek colony and these isolated stands are more than 300 kilometres south of any other examples of the species.

CAPE CONRAN ■ 1109
Cape Conran is a rocky peninsula with sandy beaches and a carpet of sheltered bushland. The offshore fishing is excellent and the abundant marine life makes the cape a reward-

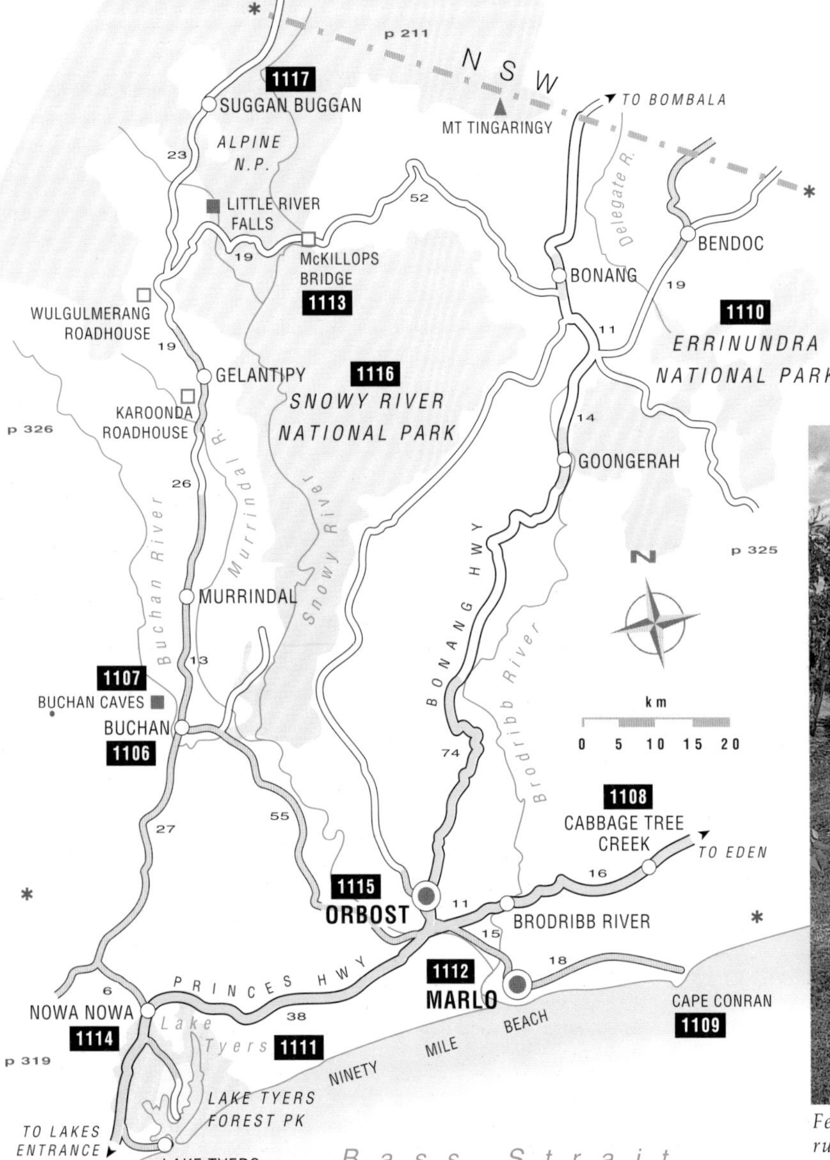

Few tourist information centres can match the quaint rusticity of the Shire of Orbost's 120-year-old slab hut.

Local hardwoods were used to march this now disused railway line across a swamp near Nowa Nowa in 1916.

ing venue for snorkellers and scuba divers. Walking and canoeing are also popular. The rare smoky mouse and ground parrot inhabit the area and nocturnal marsupials frequently raid campers' sites after dark.

ERRINUNDRA NATIONAL PARK ■ 1110

This 25 100-hectare national park, declared in July 1988, contains some of Victoria's oldest forests. Water vapour often hangs in the air and there are breathtaking waterfalls. The plateau is over 1000 metres high and there is often snow in the winter. The trees are particularly fine: majestic alpine and mountain ash, black oliveberry and white waratah which is indigenous to the area.

Sooty owls occupy hollow trees and spotted-tailed quolls and long-footed potoroos – discovered in the late 1970s at Bellbird Creek – are among the vulnerable species found within the park.

LAKE TYERS ■ 1111

According to Aboriginal legend 'the sea one day came inland to rest among the wooded hillsides and there fell asleep remaining to this day'. Lake Tyers is a sheltered waterway popular for swimming, fishing and boating; its outlet to the sea is usually closed by a sandbar and it is surrounded by forest. Nearby is the Lake Tyers Aboriginal Reserve which is the site of the first formal government land grant – in 1971 – to Aborigines in Victoria and which is home to a large Aboriginal community. The lake's birds are each associated with bringing a particular message to the Lake Tyers people: pelicans herald the arrival of a baby, white cockatoos indicate the approach of friends, black cockatoos and jays predict rain and crows warn of danger.

MARLO ■ 1112

At Marlo, the Snowy River no longer 'runs those giant hills between'; it flows gently into a large lagoon backed up by a steep bluff and cuts an outlet channel through a sandy barrier to its meeting with the sea. Lagoons are scattered among sand deposits and swamps.

Marlo was once a busy port where passengers from Melbourne disembarked to refresh themselves before going on to Orbost by boat or horse-drawn carriage. Now this tourist resort on Victoria's wilderness coast offers a well-equipped base for holiday-makers. Marlo has many fishing grounds – bass at the junction of the Snowy and Brodribb rivers, bream and luderick in coastal channels.

Marlo's name has several interpretations: perhaps after 'marloo' said to mean 'white clay' – there is some in the bluff near the jetty – or 'murloo' for 'muddy banks'. Some say the settlement was named for the French seaport or after Marlough, the Irish birthplace of an early resident.

FESTIVALS Bush Races, New Year's Day; Triathalon, January.

McKILLOPS BRIDGE ■ 1113

McKillops Bridge is a high bridge over the Snowy River – the third to be built at this crossing. The second was washed away in 1934 – a day before the official opening! Walks, white-water canoeing trips and rafting expeditions begin here. There are wide, sandy beaches and shallow river pools within easy reach of the camping ground.

NOWA NOWA ■ 1114

Nowa Nowa is a hamlet on the Princes Highway which marks the turn-off for Buchan Caves. The name is said to mean 'hill of black stones' or 'rising sun'. There is a forty-six-metre radio and repeater tower in the vicinity which has a fire-spotting cabin attached. This part of east Gippsland is rich in rare wildlife and bushfires are always a threat.

ORBOST ■ 1115

Orbost is a prosperous farming community on the Snowy River and a bustling road junction. Extravagant claims are made about the surrounding river flats – it is said they are the second richest in the world and surpassed only by the Nile Delta. Agricultural activities include dairying, raising beef cattle and growing maize and vegetables. There are timber mills and plants for packing beanseeds and freezing beans and sweetcorn. The average temperatures of Victoria's most eastern town are among the highest in the state and the tourist trade is significant to the region's economy.

The first Europeans began grazing cattle in the district in 1842 and gradually turned swamps into fertile pastures. John McLeod, from the Isle of Skye, called his run 'Orbost' which means 'winged island' in Gaelic. The Snowy River was an important transport route and a shipping company operated vessels along the waterway from 1880 to 1915. The railway came to Orbost in 1916 and electricity in the following year.

Flooding delayed the completion of a swing bridge over the Snowy River until 1890. In 1922, a timber and steel truss road and rail bridge was opened but lasted only twelve years. The Princes Highway is now raised above the flood plains with concrete supports. *Population 2520*

BALDWIN SPENCER TRAIL This 262-kilometre circuit drive begins and ends at Orbost and follows the path of the 1889 expedition led by the explorer and naturalist Walter Baldwin Spencer into east Gippsland. The trail traverses Cabbage Tree Flora Reserve and Bellbird Creek and runs up to the Errinundra Plateau (see entry). At Bendoc, high in the Great Dividing Range – where in 1867 about 500 prospectors searched the streams thoroughly for alluvial gold – Spencer found only 60 people remaining. The settlement now supports the timber industry.

BRODRIBB RIVER The Orbost region produces around twenty-seven per cent of Victoria's hardwood which is processed at about thirty regional timber mills. Some of the largest are at Brodribb River including one of the biggest hardwood sawmills in the Southern Hemisphere.

SNOWY RIVER NATIONAL PARK ■ 1116

This park borders the Snowy River and features rugged gorges, wide sandy river beaches and luxuriant lowland rainforests. The Tulloch Ard Gorge drives the river between rock walls and adventurous visitors must swim across to see what is on the other side. The Little River Gorge, two kilometres from the Little River Falls, is one of the deepest in Victoria. Some plant species are unique to the Snowy River Valley which is an important habitat for the seldom-seen brush-tailed rock wallaby. The small Gippsland water dragons – also known as Gippsland 'crocodiles' – are quite harmless.

The fifteen-and-a-half kilometre Silver Mine walking track passes by unobtrusive evidence of a brief mining period. From 1897, prospectors had high hopes of 'a great number of lodes carrying lead, silver, gold and copper of a richness fully equal to if not surpassing Broken Hill, and free from objectionable zinc'. By 1905, most had abandoned their claims. Distinctive white cypress pines can be seen from the track; the landscape is craggy and there are impressive river views and mountain vistas.

SUGGAN BUGGAN ■ 1117

This intriguing place name is linked with the Aboriginal word 'bukkan bukkan' said to mean 'bags made of grass'. William Woodhouse acquired a run in the district in 1843 and passed it to Benjamin Boyd who in turn made it the property of Edward O'Rourke in 1858. In true pioneering spirit, O'Rourke walked his wife and young children over the mountains from the Monaro district in southern New South Wales to their new home. He built the school in 1865 for his thirteen offspring and it still stands. There is dramatic mountain country between Hamilton Gap and Suggan Buggan where brumbies run free.

Stalactites rain down forever but no wind ever ripples the surface of the Font of the Gods in Buchan Caves.

Mallacoota & Cann River

Life in far east Gippsland moves in the slow lane...the happy-sounding Aboriginal place names – Mallacoota, Coopracambra and Croajingolong – are matched by the beauty of the landscape. This is a region of tranquillity with unspoilt beaches and rainforest retreats.

Embraced by the Croajingolong Park, Mallacoota intrudes upon Victoria's 'wilderness coast' to provide visitors with a few civilised, holiday comforts.

ALFRED NATIONAL PARK ■ 1118

This 2300-hectare park is the most southerly subtropical rainforest in Victoria. Outstanding scenery, dominated by three peaks over 400 metres high, can be seen from the Princes Highway which passes through the park. Despite the devastation of the 1983 bushfires which caused extensive damage to the complex balance of vegetation the bushland is slowly recovering. Epiphytic orchids and water vines grow there and more than forty fern species have been identified, including the rare oval fork fern and prickly tree fern. All five species of Victorian tree fern are found on Mount Drummer.

BEMM RIVER ■ 1119

There are fewer than fifty permanent residents in this quiet fishing hamlet on Sydenham Inlet where time stands still. 'Bemm' is thought to be an Aboriginal word for 'bend in the river'. It is sometimes called 'Bream River' because large bream are the most popular catch with anglers. Bellbirds call from the magnificent gums along the waterway which is best explored by canoe. The river supports a thriving waterfowl population and pelicans, cormorants and ubiquitous seagulls perch on the jetty. Other fish besides bream are plentiful and there are prawns in the lake in February, March and April.

CANN RIVER ■ 1120

Cann River, a small village surrounded by dairying and timber milling country, sits at the junction of the Princes and Cann Valley highways. It is an access point to a number of the region's most spectacular wilderness areas including Croajingolong and Lind national parks (see entries) and also to Point Hicks – the landmark which provided Captain Cook's first glimpse of Australia (see entry).

COOPRACAMBRA NATIONAL PARK ■ 1121

Coopracambra caters for experienced bushwalkers in search of a challenging tramp through rough wilderness country. It is a rugged and remote park of about 35 000 hectares where tetrapod footprints, possibly the oldest fossil record of land-dwelling vertebrates, have been found. The massive Gippsland grey box trees on the ridges are particularly striking. There are rare plant species watered by Murmuring, Beehive and other creeks, the waterways of Black Jack Gully, and the Genoa River, which runs through a red sandstone gorge. Coopracambra means 'kookaburra'.

CROAJINGOLONG NATIONAL PARK ■ 1122

Despite Victoria's relatively high population and intensive farming practices, nearly a third of the state is preserved natural bushland. Croajingolong's 86 000 hectares make it one of Victoria's largest national parks. Proclaimed in 1978, the park is an international Biosphere Reserve – one of many in a world-wide network. It includes mountains, lakes, rivers and Tamboon, Wingan, Mallacoota and Sydenham inlets.

The Tamboon estuary is accessible only by boat. Swan Lake is a thriving habitat for pelicans, swamp hens and blue kingfishers. Bush and beach and tall sand dunes can be explored from the mouth of the Thurra River but the surf is treacherous for swimming. Dry electrical storms are a peculiar summer phenomenon in the region.

This magnificent wilderness has three vegetation types: cool-temperate growth, soft-leaved subtropical plants and hardy species adapted to fire and drought. The rare giant trigger plant is found at Wingan Inlet where George Bass came ashore in 1797. The undisturbed environment harbours several endangered animals, among them the smoky mouse and ground parrot. Almost a third of Australia's bird species have been seen in the area including fly-catchers, lyrebirds and sea eagles. Fur seals breed on the Skerries rocks near Wingan Inlet and whales and dolphins often pass offshore.

Croajingolong is from an Aboriginal word probably meaning 'men living in the east'.

GABO ISLAND ■ 1123

This granite outcrop has an area of just over 150 hectares. The building of the Gabo Island lighthouse has been described as 'the sorriest story in the history of Australian lighthouses'. Arguments began about the site in 1846 but it was not until the *Monumental City* ran aground in 1853 with the loss of thirty-three lives, that a temporary tower was hastily erected. The keepers sounded a gong in thick fogs. In 1862, the light went on in the permanent building constructed of red granite from the site. At almost forty-seven metres high it is the second tallest coastal beacon in the country and in 1992 lost its keeper as it changed to automatic solar battery operation.

GENOA ■ 1124

Genoa is variously spelt in early writings as 'Genore', 'Jinor', 'Tinnor' and 'Jinoa'. The Aborigines pronounce it 'Jinna' which may mean 'foot' or 'track' – a plausible explanation as they made an annual trek up the Genoa River each spring in search of yams and the nutritious Bogong moth larvae.

Genoa is the last village bypassed by the Princes Highway before it enters New South Wales. It provides access to walking tracks and a steep climb to the 490-metre summit of Genoa Peak and good fishing spots.

GIPSY POINT ■ 1125

Gipsy Point lies at an idyllic location off the Genoa–Mallacoota Road at the head of Mallacoota Inlet's Top Lake, near the Genoa and Wallagaraugh rivers. The dawn mist swirls over the water and the silence is broken by the plop of rising fish and the cries of birds. It is a good place for bushwalkers, bird watchers and naturalists, for launching boats and going after flathead, mulloway and bream. Evenings are spent swapping tall stories at the local hotel.

LIND NATIONAL PARK ■ 1126

The Euchre Valley road passes through the centre of Lind National Park for five kilometres. Kanooka, blackwood and lilly-pilly tower over tree ferns and vines and in the summer months the Gippsland waratah splashes crimson across this mountainous, dense, subtropical rainforest. The park is particularly rich in bird life and wildflowers.

MALLACOOTA ■ 1127

Mallacoota, at the entrance to Mallacoota Inlet, has beauty and solitude and a diversity of water sports. It can be reached only by the road from the Princes Highway and is surrounded by a broad expanse of native bushland. Mallacoota may derive from 'mallagootha' which is an Aboriginal word for 'place of meeting' or 'come back again'; or from 'mulla' meaning 'good' or 'malla' meaning 'salt' and 'goota' meaning 'water'.

In the 1840s, a deep-sea whaling port was set up by Ben Boyd and the Imlay brothers. The early pioneers harvested wattle bark for use in tanning leather. The trees were stripped in spring through to late summer. After two weeks drying, the bagged bark was shipped to Sydney or to a tannery in Bairnsdale. Dairying was introduced and pigs were raised. Commercial fishing became important in the 1880s. Gold was found here in the 1890s but the yield was small from the local Spotted Dog mine. At the turn of the century, Mallacoota traded fish, cattle, and gold for a very short time.

E.J. Brady, author, poet and the secretary of Australia's first Socialist League, set up a camp at Captain's Point around 1909. He wanted to establish a self-sufficient colony and his guests included the writers, Louis Esson and Katherine Susannah Prichard, and artists, Arthur Streeton and Will Ashton. Henry Lawson stayed there for three months in 1910. The district now depends on fishing and tourism. Professional divers harvest oysters and abalone – an important export to Japan – from ocean beds across the sand bar. Salmon and tuna are caught off Mallacoota and there is excellent game fishing. *Population 960*

FESTIVALS Carnival, Easter.

MALLACOOTA INLET ■ 1128

The inlet is formed by Top Lake and Bottom Lake which are fed by about fourteen rivers and streams including the slow-flowing Wallagaraugh and Genoa rivers, where people-shy platypuses like to swim. The inlet and upper river can be explored by private boats or commercial cruises. The surrounding bushland is part of Croajingolong National Park where apiarists truck in their bee hives when the bloodwoods flower.

Bream and mullet inhabit the estuary and big bass live upstream where salt and fresh water meet. Huge flathead impress visiting anglers and fishy tales are rife in Mallacoota.

The flower of the Gippsland waratah is a delicate bloom when compared with the showy NSW floral emblem.

POINT HICKS ■ 1129

The obelisk at historic Point Hicks is inscribed: 'Lieutenant Captain Cook, R.N., of the 'Endeavour', first sighted Australia near this spot, which he named Point Hicks, after Lieutenant Zachary Hicks, who first saw the land, April 19 (ship's log date), April 20 (calendar date), 1770'. The actual spot recorded in the log is in fifty fathoms of water and twelve nautical miles offshore. The point was subsequently given the new name, Cape Everard, but the original name was officially restored in 1970.

In 1934, stonemasons arrived in Cape Everard to hew granite blocks and ship them to Williamstown to be made into a replica of the Captain Cook obelisk. The replica was taken to England to mark the spot where Captain Cook's cottage – since re-erected in Melbourne's Botanical Gardens – once stood.

The lighthouse on Point Hicks was officially opened in May 1890. The signal was two quick flashes every ten seconds, visible at sea for twenty-six nautical miles. At first, access to the site was by ship but now there is a road to Cann River (see entry). In 1964, kerosene power and the early clockwork mechanism were replaced by an electric motor but progress eventually caught up with this too and the light was converted to solar power during 1992 with a consequent reduction in beam.

Apart from the addition of a lighthouse and picnic facilities for day visitors Point Hicks has changed little since Captain Cook sailed by in 1770.

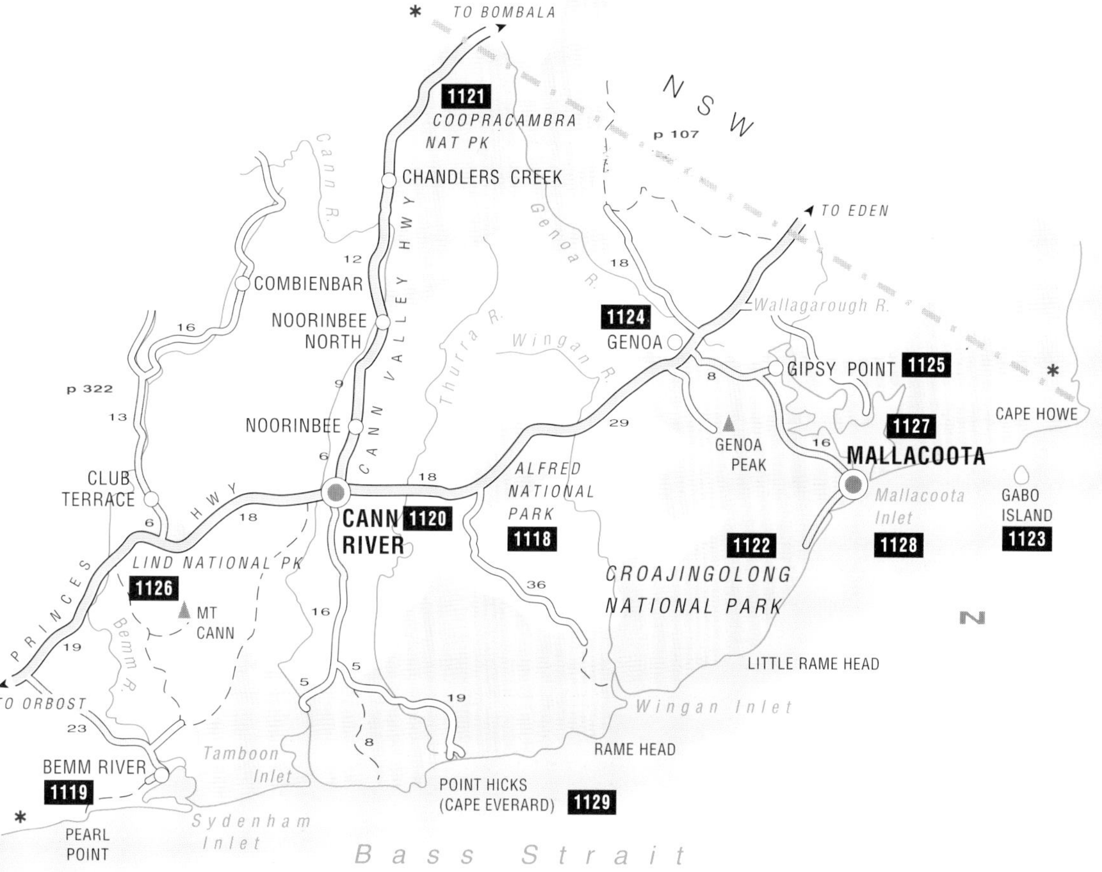

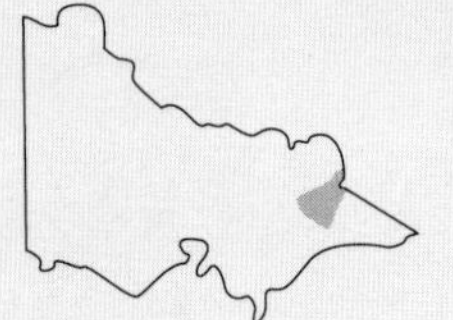

Omeo

The Omeo region was once known as the toughest goldfield in Australia – a district of high plains and wild reputations – and the early cattlemen who remained after the itinerant diggers went on optimistically to the next strike were just as hardy a band of men.

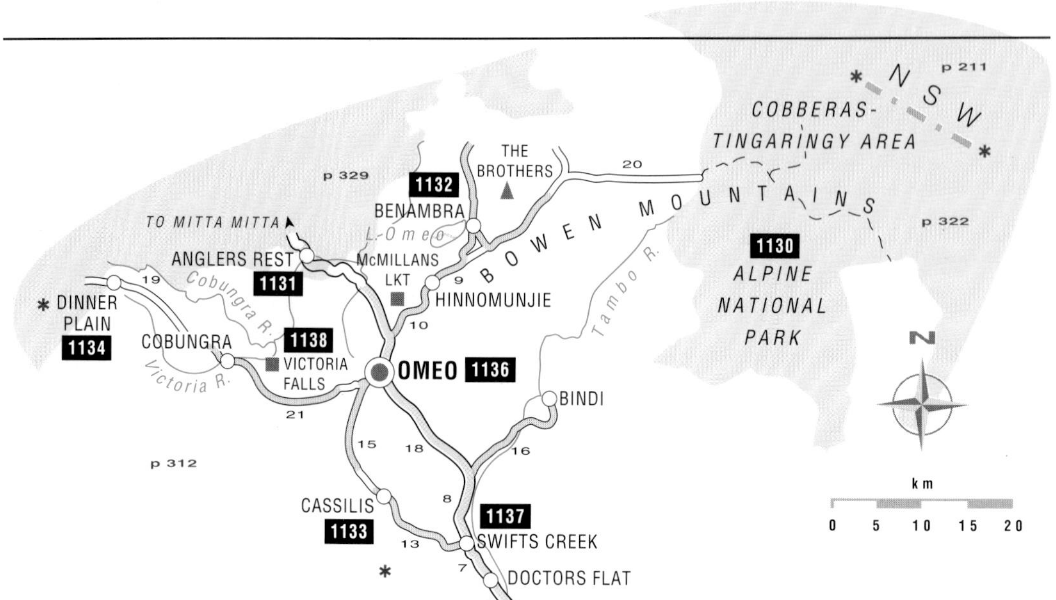

p 211
NSW
COBBERAS-
TINGARINGY AREA
THE BROTHERS
20
p 329
1132
BENAMBRA
L. Omeo
BOWEN MOUNTAINS
p 322
TO MITTA MITTA
ANGLERS REST
1131
McMILLANS LKT
9
HINNOMUNJIE
1130
ALPINE NATIONAL PARK
19
Cobungra R.
DINNER PLAIN
1134
COBUNGRA
1138
VICTORIA FALLS
Victoria R.
10
Tambo R.
OMEO 1136
BINDI
N
21
15
18
16
p 312
8
CASSILIS
1133
1137
SWIFTS CREEK
13
km
0 5 10 15 20
7
DOCTORS FLAT
10
ENSAY
1135
OMEO HWY
p 319
19
TAMBO CROSSING
TO BAIRNSDALE

ALPINE NATIONAL PARK ■ 1130

The Cobberas–Tingaringy National Park was one of three parks to be incorporated into the Alpine National Park in 1989. Its former name was taken from two of its principal mountains – Mount Cobberas (1838 metres) in the west and Mount Tingaringy (1448 metres) in the west. Features of the rugged landscape in this southern part of the park are the Snowy River Valley, one of the river's main Victorian tributaries, the Suggan Buggan River, and the upper reaches of the Murray.

Vegetation is diverse with snow gum woodlands and white-box woodlands at high altitudes and cypress pine and white-box woodland in the lower, warmer areas.

Several rare varieties of plants and animals are found here; the most readily seen creatures include the bush-tailed rock wallaby, the tiger quoll and the alpine water skink.

In 1988, a fire started by lightning ravaged 9000 hectares of the park between Willis and Mount Tingaringy and more than 50 000 hectares of the adjacent Byadbo Wilderness in Kosciusko National Park. Many tracks such as the Tingaringy Track from Hobbs Road to Mount Tingaringy had to be closed off for over a year for rebuilding.

ANGLERS REST ■ 1131

Anglers Rest, as its inviting name suggests, is a favourite camping, fishing and picnic spot near the junction of the Cobungra and Mitta Mitta rivers. The 1890 Blue Duck Inn was a stopping place between the Glen Wills and Omeo goldfields, and now is part of a local motel. Blue Duck was a colourful euphemism of the time for a pipe-dream project of an early settler who repeatedly said he was going to open a pub here but never got around to it.

An early-rising moon casts a romantic light on the paddocks surrounding Omeo, long cleared of their woodlands for use as high-quality pastures.

BENAMBRA ■ 1132

A rural township noted for its cattle, Benambra lies north-east of Omeo in the shadow of Bowen Mountains and on the southern fringe of the Alpine National Park (see entry). Early settlers were James McFarlane and the Pendergast family who settled here in 1837 and descendants of the original family still farm in the district today. McMillan's Lookout, between Omeo and Benambra, provides spectacular 360-degree views of the surrounding countryside.

CASSILIS ■ 1133

Cassilis was a boom town that grew up during the 1850s gold rush only to disappear when the gold did. It once had a population of over one thousand people, over four hundred of them Chinese, the core of a Chinese population of about 2500 which came to the region when men were said to be picking up gold from the creek beds. Parts of the Cassilis mine are still picked over by fossickers.

Brilliantly hued sands in shades of yellow, white, olive and purple mix with red clay as they spill down the old tailing mounds around the mine.

An eroded landscape at Omeo's goldmine workings is mute evidence of the feverish activity of the 1850s.

DINNER PLAIN ■ 1134

Once a stopping place for bullock teams crossing the Great Dividing Range, the name for the Dinner Plain was probably coined by hungry bullockies who walked alongside their ponderous charges, cracking their whips and urging them along with a stream of colourful language.

An alpine village stands here, its buildings based on early cattlemen's huts and constructed from traditional materials such as corrugated iron,

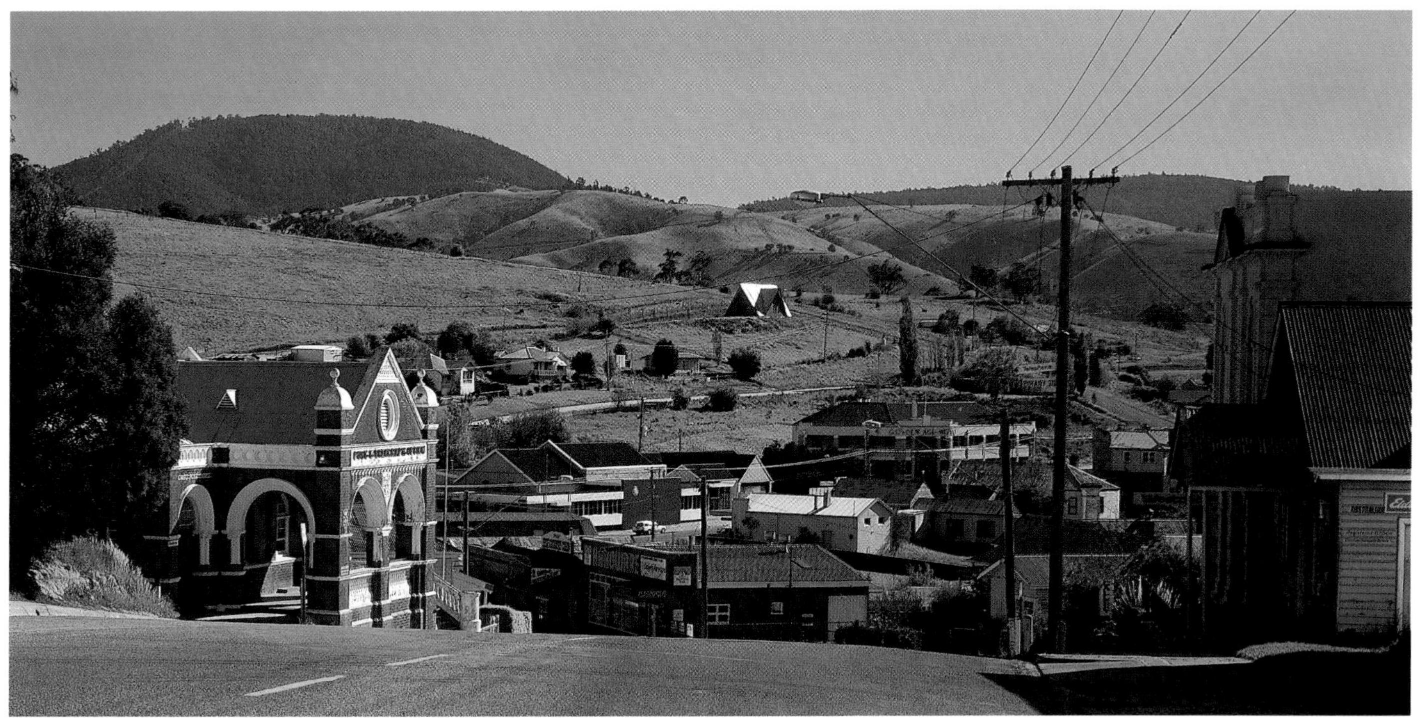

Among rolling hills, at an altitude of 643 metres, Omeo is the main south-eastern access point to the high plains country and the Alpine National Park.

timber and stone. The Dinner Plain road from Omeo has many scenic diversions such as the Kosciusko Lookout, Victoria Falls and Horse Hair Plain, so called for the horse hair which was stored there for use in whip tails and mattresses. It is now the headquarters for the Geebung Polo Club, the organisers of city versus country polo matches.

ENSAY ■ **1135**

The peaceful rural surrounds of Ensay provide the perfect setting for one of the main preoccupations in these parts: trout fishing in Haunted Stream and other creeks nearby. European settlement started with Angus McMillan who established the Numblamunjie Station here in 1839.

The station was the starting point for exploration of the region which led to the discovery of the important Gippsland shipping berth of Port Albert. The station was renamed Ensay by an early settler, Archibald McLeod, around 1843, after his wife's birthplace, an island off the coast of Scotland. The station was bought by the Hamilton family in the 1880s.

It was taken over by the Soldier Settlement Commission after the First World War but returned to the family, when T. I. Hamilton, son of the previous owner, was the successful purchaser. The family continued to farm the property until the 1950s. Tambo Crossing, to the south, is where the original Port Albert to Omeo track crossed the Tambo River.

OMEO ■ **1136**

George McKillop, James McFarlane and a Mr Livingstone first passed through this district in 1835 searching for new farmland. McFarlane's run, later called 'Omeo B', may have been Victoria's first cattle station. The station eventually passed into the hands of the Pendergast brothers, and was renamed 'Three Brothers'.

The Hinnomunjie Station, the forerunner of today's small town, was founded by Edward Crooke in 1841; he bred Thoroughbred horses for the Indian Army. The horses were shipped to India from Port Albert and the Holey Plains near Rosedale were used as a holding station before shipment.

In the 1840s, Omeo was a stopping place for squatters moving south into Gippsland in search of more land. Gold was discovered at Livingstone in 1852, but development was slow because of the rugged terrain and isolation of the area. Many diggers trekked across the Great Dividing Range from Beechwood to find the new gold strike and some of them died making the return journey.

Omeo quickly gained the reputation of being the toughest, most lawless goldfield in Australia. A substantial log jail was built soon after the police force was installed. The snowgum lockup lined with blackwood is still the official lockup in Omeo and unique in Victoria. Alexander Browne, the first magistrate of the town, later wrote hair-raising tales based on his experiences here, under the name Rolf Boldrewood.

Gold was, at first, alluvial in form, and when this began to peter out, Chinese miners took over the diggings. A second boom happened in the 1860s, when reef gold was discovered at Dry Gully, Glen Wills, Sunnyside and Cassilis. Reef mining did not last and by 1914, the mines were abandoned and the field deserted. With the decline of gold, settlers began to establish sheep and cattle runs. Since those days the Omeo cattle sales each March have become an important event, with buyers coming from all over Australia.

The town has many notable buildings, rich in local history, including the 1892 court house and the 1866 state school, which are classified by the National Trust. 'Omeo' is based on an Aboriginal word for 'mountains'. Hinnomunjie comes from 'hinnoo' which means 'no' and 'munji' meaning 'fish'.

MINE WORKINGS To the west of Omeo is the site of one of the largest hydraulic gold-sluicing operations in Australia. The artificial cliffs and tunnels were largely the work of the Chinese miners, who moved enormous amounts of earth using water. Larger rocks had to be moved by hand and the vast stone heaps, still standing, give some idea of the work involved.

THE BROTHERS Three almost identical peaks, named after the pioneer Pendergast brothers, dominate the landscape about thirty kilometres to the north-east of Omeo.

SWIFTS CREEK ■ **1137**

Timber and saw milling provide the economic base of this town, south of Omeo. Like Ensay, it is a stopping place for visitors to the district. From Swifts Creek to Omeo the road rises 300 metres and those wanting to travel on roads used for logging must get advice from the local forest officer. The town is named for an early miner's alluvial claim.

BINDI HOMESTEAD The oldest property in the Omeo district is probably Bindi Station, a few kilometres north of Swifts Creek. The historic homestead and its outbuildings are made of stone and date back to the 1850s. Both buildings have been classified by the National Trust as being worthy of preservation.

DOG'S GRAVE A cairn marking the grave of 'Boney', a bushman's dog, stands west of Swifts Creek. The grave is where the first drover's camp stood, out from the Combungra Station on the cattle run to Dargo. The dog's grave was rediscovered in 1964 by Jack Treasure, a local historian. The cairn, unveiled in 1974, has a verse penned by Jack Treasure as a tribute to all bushmen and their dogs. The first verse reads:

'He served none else but Peter Meehan
his master and his friend
A comradeship wove of the bush
to last unto the end.
Mute faith in one; a friendship bond
in rugged ranges where
A loneliness prevailed the scene
Just man and dog to share.'

VICTORIA FALLS ■ **1138**

Victoria's first hydro-electric scheme, which provided electricity for mines at Cassilis, fifteen kilometres away as the crow flies, was established at Victoria Falls. The falls – Victoria's largest – cascade down a wild gorge and are a spectacular reward for bushwalkers who trek the one hour it takes to reach them.

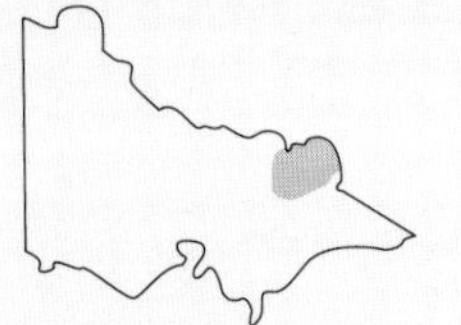

Beechworth & Myrtleford

As in so many other parts of Victoria, the lure of gold opened up this north-eastern region in the 1850s. The wealth generated in just a few decades is still reflected in the well-maintained buildings that line the main street of historic Beechworth, the region's largest town.

ALPINE NATIONAL PARK ■ 1139

There are eleven tall peaks within the Bogong Area of the vast Alpine National Park alone, including the state's highest point, Mount Bogong (1986 metres). The park was formed in December 1989 and encompasses almost 6500 square kilometres of the spectacular high country, extending along the ridge of the Great Dividing Range from Mansfield (see *Mansfield & Mount Buller*) up to the New South Wales border where it links with the Kosciusko National Park.

The park was formed through a conglomeration of existing national parks and other public land. Most of the Bogong Area is made up of high plateau – the famously spectacular Bogong High Plains – which is often under snow in winter, making it popular with cross-country skiers. Before the Alpine National Park was created, the nearby downhill ski resorts of Falls Creek and Mount Hotham were situated just outside the park's boundaries. Now, Mount Hotham is encircled by the park's extended protected areas.

In the summer, the bogs, herbfields, heathlands and grasslands of the high plains blaze briefly with the riotous colours of wildflowers. At lower altitudes where the climate is less severe, the slender, often colourfully mottled, trunks of snow gums cloak the mountain terrain. The park is home to the rare mountain pygmy possum – the only alpine marsupial in the world – thought to be extinct until it was discovered at Mount Hotham in 1966, and despite protection, still an endangered species.

Walking tracks wind along high mountain ridges, through sheltered gullies and across tumbling streams, allowing closer inspection of different aspects of the alpine wilderness. At the core of all these tracks is the Alpine Walking Track (see *Mansfield & Mount Buller*), which extends 400 kilometres through some of Victoria's finest national parks.

In the 1850s, cattlemen discovered the high plains and for many years they were used as summer pasture. Unlike the high country in New South Wales, where cattle have been banned, most of the pastureland of the Alpine National Park is still used for grazing, except for some small areas that are considered environmentally sensitive. Some of the old huts built by those pioneer graziers still stand, including Wallaces Hut near Falls Creek, which was built in 1889 and is the oldest left standing.

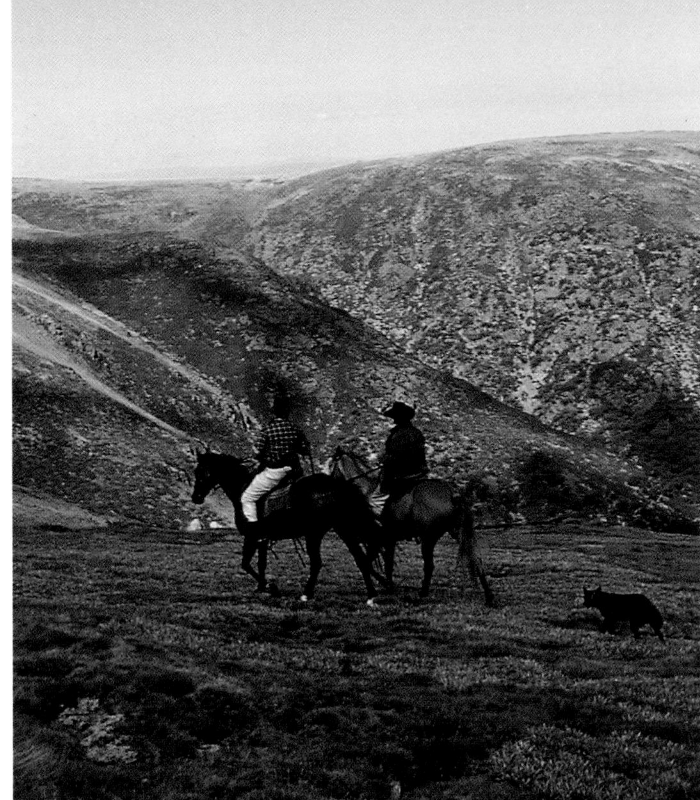

In the summer time, the mountain men still come up from their valley runs to graze cattle on the alpine meadows of the Mount Bogong high plains.

The facades of Ford Street in Beechworth have been presenting a united front since the 1870s; only the cars and the street lights jar the period effect.

BEECHWORTH ■ 1140

Beechworth is one of the best preserved of Victoria's old goldmining settlements, with wide streets lined with well-restored buildings and the National Trust has declared it a 'Notable Town' – one of only two towns in Victoria to be awarded such a distinction. The streets are lined with deciduous trees and these are particularly colourful in autumn; some – including the North American giant sequoias – were introduced by Baron von Mueller, the founder of Melbourne's Botanical Gardens.

Beechworth was established in 1852 after the discovery of gold, and was named by the government surveyor for his birthplace in England. By 1866, over 128 tonnes of gold had been extracted from the diggings in the district, and mining continued until the 1920s. The Beechworth cemetery – in which approximately 2700 early Chinese settlers are buried – boasts a number of Chinese burning towers which attest to the strong Chinese presence during the town's early days. Nowadays, Beechworth thrives on the proceeds of tourism and visitors throng the town's many historic monuments and shops on summer weekends. *Population 3250*

CARRIAGE MUSEUM The old stables, near Tanswell's Commercial Hotel – licensed since 1853 and classified by the National Trust – were built in 1859 and now contain a collection of old coaches, horse-drawn vehicles and saddlery, including one saddle that is supposed to have belonged to the bushranger 'Mad' Dan Morgan.

CHINESE BURNING TOWERS These unusual constructions in the cemetery off Sydney Road were used to make burnt offerings to the gods by relatives of Chinese workers who died on the goldfields.

NED KELLY'S CELL A cell at the rear of the town hall in Loch Street held the infamous bushranger in 1870, when he was just sixteen years old. Ned, his mother and gang members, Steve Hart and Joe Byrne, were also held at one time or another in the historic Beechworth Jail.

POWDER MAGAZINE This stone building on Gorge Road was built from

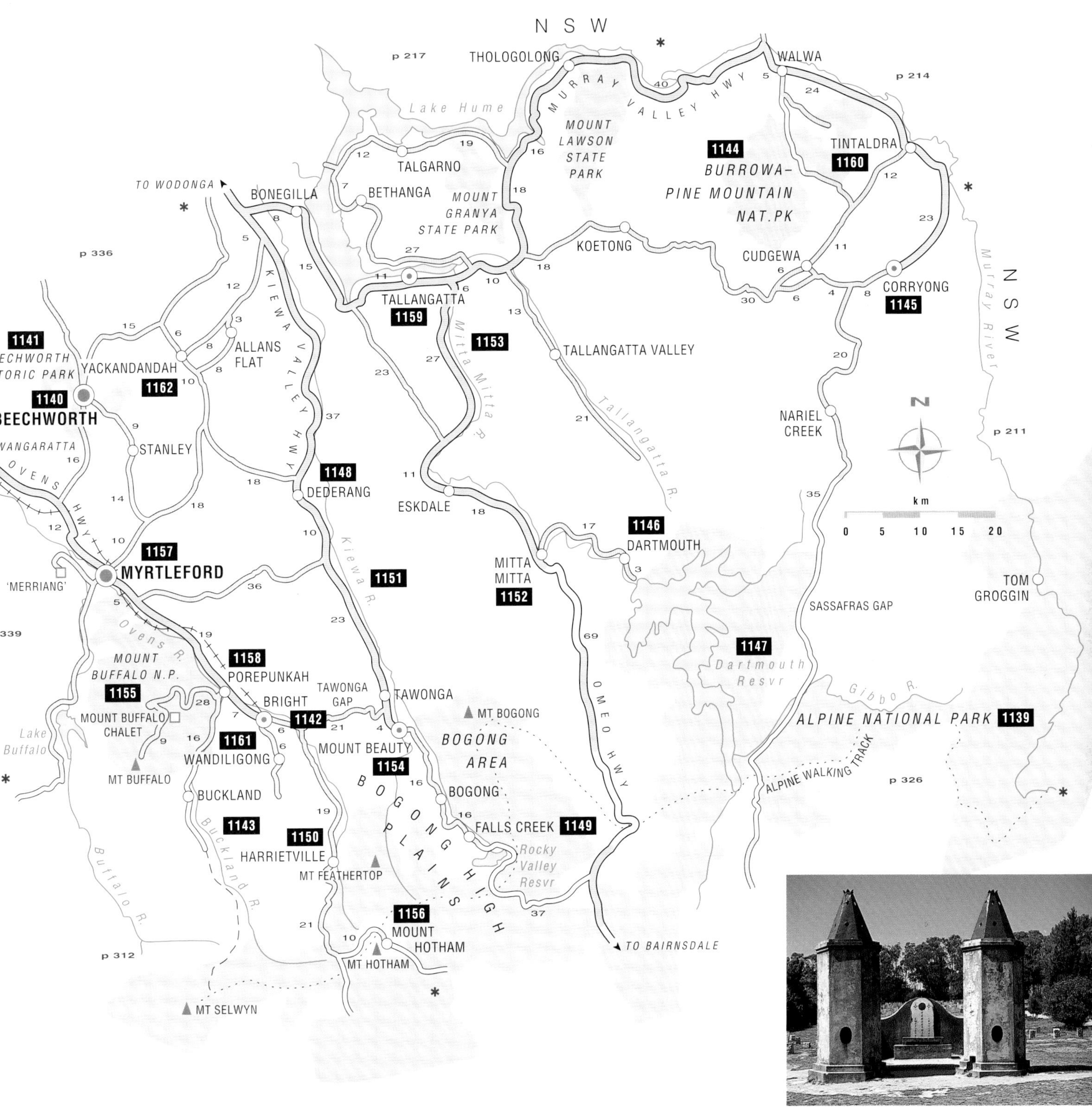

Burning towers flank a simple altar in Beechworth Cemetery – a reminder of the many Chinese diggers.

locally quarried granite in 1859 to store explosives used by miners on the goldfields. Once in ruins and a resting place for tramps – who called it the 'Menzies of the north-east' – the building is now restored.

FESTIVALS Golden Horseshoes Festival, Easter weekend.

BEECHWORTH HISTORIC PARK ■ 1141

Much of Beechworth's goldmining history is still in evidence within the magnificent natural setting of this historic park located just five kilometres from the town's post office. Self-guided walks, including the Woolshed Falls Historic Walk, encourage visitors to explore – with care – the many relics of the frantic goldmining activities of the last century. There is a veritable maze of diversion tunnels, eroded gullies and water races pockmarking the surface of the 1130-hectare park.

BRIGHT ■ 1142

The region's first settlers were pastoralists in the late 1830s, but it was the discovery of gold in the district in the early 1850s that brought people in large numbers. By 1856, Bright – which was then known as Morse's Creek – had three small timber houses and forty tents. After the gold rush was over, those who stayed on established a sawmilling industry. The shire of Bright was officially proclaimed in 1866, and at the same time the town's name was changed to honour John Bright, an English parliamentarian and social reformer.

At quite an early stage in its development, Bright became a popular tourist destination as news of the autumnal splendour of its broad avenues of European deciduous trees – planted, as in Beechworth (see entry) at the suggestion of Baron von Mueller – spread throughout Victoria. These days, Bright remains popular not only because of its trees, the colour change of which is celebrated in an annual autumn festival, but also because of its nearness to the

GOLDFIELDS HIGH-JINKS: ON A GOLD-SHOD HORSE TO PARLIAMENT

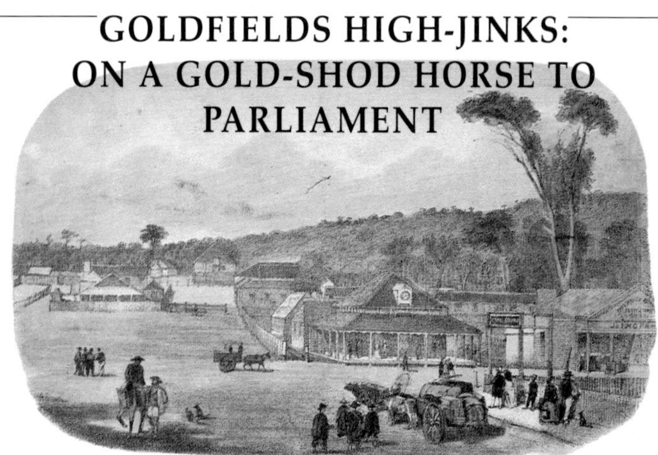

A scene of Beechworth at the time of the 'horseshoes' incident.

Of all the tales, tall and true, that tell of the rough and tumble of life on the nineteenth-century goldfields, the story of the Golden Horseshoes probably best captures the wild and colourful flavour of the time.

The diggers of the goldfields in the Ovens River Valley were split into two rival groups known as the 'Punchers' and the 'Monkeys'. The Punchers were 'dry' diggers who worked the streambanks and dry gullies. They favoured a practical garb – generally moleskins. The Monkeys, known as 'wet' miners, worked the streams. They considered themselves a superior breed to the Punchers and dressed flamboyantly in black woollen trousers, Napoleon boots, silk sashes and brightly coloured handkerchiefs. Both groups carried firearms as part of their 'costume' and outbreaks of violence were not uncommon.

The parliamentary elections of 1855 were the trigger that sparked the famous Golden Horseshoes incident. Inevitably, the Punchers and the Monkeys sponsored separate candidates to act as the representative for the Ovens Goldfields and the campaign that followed was intense and bitter.

Election day arrived in September of that year. The Monkeys, led by 'Big' Johnson, owner of the field's richest claim, marched boisterously into town, escorting their candidate, Mr Daniel Cameron, who headed the noisy procession. Upon reaching the old Vine Hotel nearly two kilometres from Beechworth, Cameron's horse was shod with solid gold horseshoes – the gold supplied especially for the occasion by 'Big' Johnson. The parade continued with supporters running alongside handing out free pannikins of beer, which were topped up by runners from the hotels. On reaching the polls, the gold-shod horse came to a halt and its luxurious horseshoes were removed, having worn down to the extent that they were one ounce (28 grams) lighter.

Against the general cacophony of rival miners imbibing free beer, rival brass bands trying to outdo each other in the music stakes and general mayhem, the two candidates appeared on the balcony of the Star Hotel, Cameron emerging as the victor of the day, his rousing campaign speech winning him the majority vote. The Punchers refused to accept this 'Monkey' victory and a poll was conducted the next day – again, Cameron was elected.

The final extravagant gesture to cap the most ostentatious event Beechworth had ever seen, was made by 'Big' Johnson, who in celebration of the win, treated the mob to a champagne shout which cost him 300 pounds sterling. □

mountains. It is the starting point for a range of walking tracks – including the Canyon Walk along Ovens River which retraces the steps of the gold-miners of the last century – through the region's invigorating high country. *Population 1880*

THE LOG LOCK-UP This historic log prison in Park Street was built in the 1870s and later moved to its present site. It is a rare example of this pioneer building technique.

FESTIVALS Bright Autumn Festival, April–May.

BUCKLAND RIVER ■ 1143

The Buckland River, which takes its name from Thomas Buckland, an early pastoralist, rises in the Great Dividing Range and flows down to meet the Ovens River at Porepunkah (see entry). In November 1853, near the present village of Buckland Lower, one of Victoria's richest alluvial goldfields was discovered by Henry Pardoe. He is reputed to have gathered 2.3 kilograms of gold on his first day there. Within weeks, thousands of people flocked to the area. Among the miners were many Chinese, and their presence eventually led to the notorious Buckland riots.

By the mid-1850s, after many diggers had been either killed or driven away by outbreaks of typhoid and sandy blight, Chinese miners outnumbered Europeans by five to one. Racial hatred spread through the valley as the Chinese – largely content to re-work the shafts and tailings abandoned by the Europeans – were regarded as parasites by the white miners who resented their 'Chinaman's luck' and their sometimes wasteful usage of precious water, and in July 1857 a decision was reached to force the Chinese to leave. At first they were allowed to go peacefully, but the situation deteriorated and many were beaten and robbed. Some 2000 Chinese miners fled from the area, and an unknown number died from wounds and exposure to the winter cold.

BURROWA–PINE MOUNTAIN NATIONAL PARK ■ 1144

Two mountainous 'blocks', vastly different in their geological make-up and linked by a narrow L-shaped corridor make up the Burrowa–Pine Mountain National Park, one of Victoria's lesser-known but botanically significant wilderness areas. Dominating the southern section of the park is the great bulk of Mount Burrowa – 1300 metres high – which is composed largely of a type of volcanic rock called Jemba rhyolite, while the smaller northern block encompasses the largely granite Pine Mountain – 1062 metres high.

The different geological substance of each mountain has resulted in quite contrasting vegetation that attracts camera-toting botanists and bushwalkers with a special interest in plants and flowers. Pine Mountain nurtures some of Australia's rarest plant species including the phantom wattle, which is studded with oval-shaped spikes of yellow flowers in late spring, and the rare Pine Mountain grevillea with its distinctive green springtime flowers. Tall, black cypress pines and kurrajongs cling to the mountain's steep, rocky sides. Mount Burrowa on the other hand, displays much greater diversity of vegetation with peppermint and gum forests covering the foothills, blue gum and fern communities in the moist gullies, candlebarks on the slopes, alpine ash in the sheltered pockets of high ground and hardy snow gums thriving on the high-altitude ridges.

CORRYONG ■ 1145

Corryong is on the edge of the High Plains – just across the border from Kosciusko National Park (see *Cooma & Mount Kosciusko*) – that were settled from the late 1830s by a hardy breed of mountain pioneers who brought their cattle to the lush alpine pastures for the spring and summer months. Today, this Upper-Murray

Autumn in Bright, and thousands of European trees and shrubs signal that the days are drawing in.

High Country still provides a fertile grazing ground for mountain cattle, sheep and dairy herds.

Ruggedly grand and climatically volatile, the high country was home to Jack Riley, who is believed to be the inspiration for the legendary horseman in Banjo Paterson's much loved ballad, *The Man from Snowy River*. Riley, who died in 1914, is now buried in the 'new' Corryong cemetery – a small pioneer cemetery dating back to the early settlement days sits unobtrusively on a hillside overlooking the valley.

Ringed by mountains and close to the upper reaches of the Murray River, Corryong has become a popular holiday destination – especially with fishermen seeking trout in the swiftly flowing rivers and streams of the high valleys, and with hang-gliders whose favourite launching site is the summit of Mount Mittamatite, which looms majestically behind this high-country town.

Folk music is Corryong's other major drawcard with thousands of nostalgic souls making a beeline for the Nariel Folk Festival Ground between Boxing Day and New Year's Day every year for a week-long indulgence in folk music, old-time dancing, storytelling around campfires and spontaneous outbreaks of musical revelry. *Population 1260*

'MAN FROM SNOWY RIVER' FOLK MUSEUM Pride of place in the museum's large collection of high-country memorabilia is a ski and snowshoe collection dating back to 1870 that includes skis used by Thomas and Elyne Mitchell, members of Australia's first Olympic ski team. At the rear of the museum, a century-old pioneer cottage from Cudgewa has been restored and furnished with period pieces.

FESTIVALS Nariel River Folk Festival, December; Corryong High Country Festival, late March.

DARTMOUTH ■ 1146

This tiny and rather isolated township was established in 1972 to house the workers constructing Australia's highest dam (see Dartmouth Reservoir). Dartmouth is now the access point for the many recreational activities offered by the man-made lake including swimming, boating, fishing and sailing. A number of walking tracks nearby provide bushwalking opportunities for those who favour drier activities.

DARTMOUTH RESERVOIR ■ 1147

Dartmouth Reservoir is the largest earth and rockfill dam in Victoria and, rising to 180 metres, the highest structure of its kind in Australia. Completed in 1979 at a cost of 139 million dollars – which was borne by the Commonwealth and states of Victoria, New South Wales and South Australia – Dartmouth reservoir impounds the waters of the Mitta Mitta River and when full, has a storage capacity of some four million megalitres.

With its 3600-square-kilometre catchment area stretching across the surrounding alpine areas of Victoria, the reservoir stores water for irrigation, stock and urban use in Victoria, New South Wales and South Australia. During dry seasons, it supplements the water stored at Lake Hume (see *Albury & Wodonga*) and augments the Upper Murray. A hydro-electric station makes use of the water's energy potential.

DEDERANG ■ 1148

The small town of Dederang has an uncluttered air, having strung its development along both sides of the main road through the area – the Kiewa Valley Highway – since the early days of nineteenth-century settlement. Surrounded by the beautiful countryside of the fertile Kiewa Valley, Dederang is best known for its annual picnic race meeting held in January each year and for its fine river fishing.

FALLS CREEK ■ 1149

Falls Creek, near the Bogong High Plains of the Alpine National Park, is Victoria's second largest ski resort and is also popular in the summertime for its mountain walks. The tiny township – little more than a collection of lodges – dates from the 1930s when members of the Ski Club of Victoria sought permission from the State Electricity Commission to occupy one-and-a-half hectares of land beside a stream called Falls Creek. The first lodge was built in the 1940s.

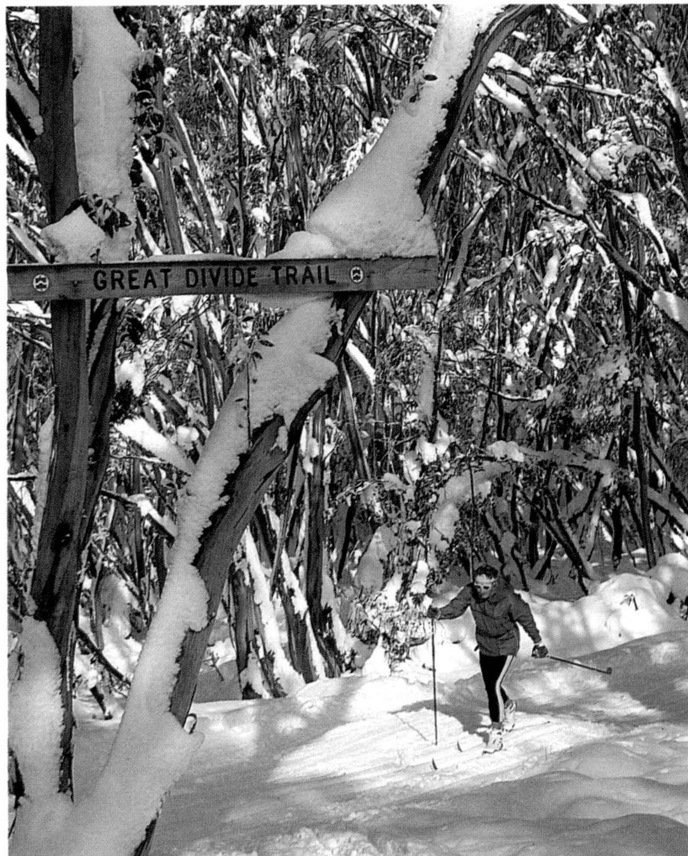

In winter, Mount Hotham's well-marked summer walking tracks make fine cross-country skiing trails for those with strong legs and plenty of energy.

HARRIETVILLE ■ 1150

Like many other towns in the district, Harrietville owes its existence to gold – it also became a transit point on the cattlemen's annual journey to and from the high plains. Discoveries were made here as early as 1853, and the makeshift settlement was given official recognition in 1879.

The last gold-miners did not leave the area until 1956, when the largest dredge in the Southern Hemisphere – the 5000-tonne *Tronoh* – ceased working on river flats near the town. This enormous machine, which needed a crew of sixty men to operate it, was dismantled into many hundreds of pieces and sent to Malaysia.

The town was named for Harriet Luke who was reputed to be the first white woman in the district.

KIEWA RIVER ■ 1151

The Kiewa River – from an Aboriginal word said to mean 'sweet water' – rises near Mount Bogong and flows 185 kilometres to join the Murray River upstream of Albury (see *Albury & Wodonga*). Its valley – known as

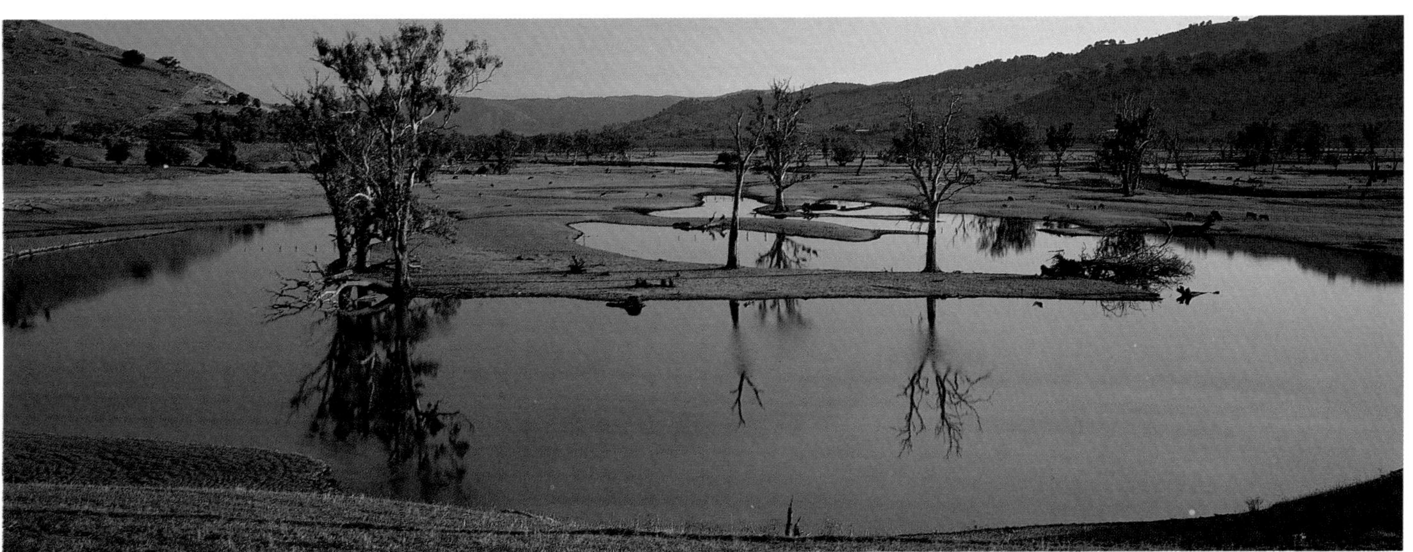

The level of a meander spawned by the Mitta River in the river valley near Tallangatta, is governed by the release of water from Dartmouth Reservoir.

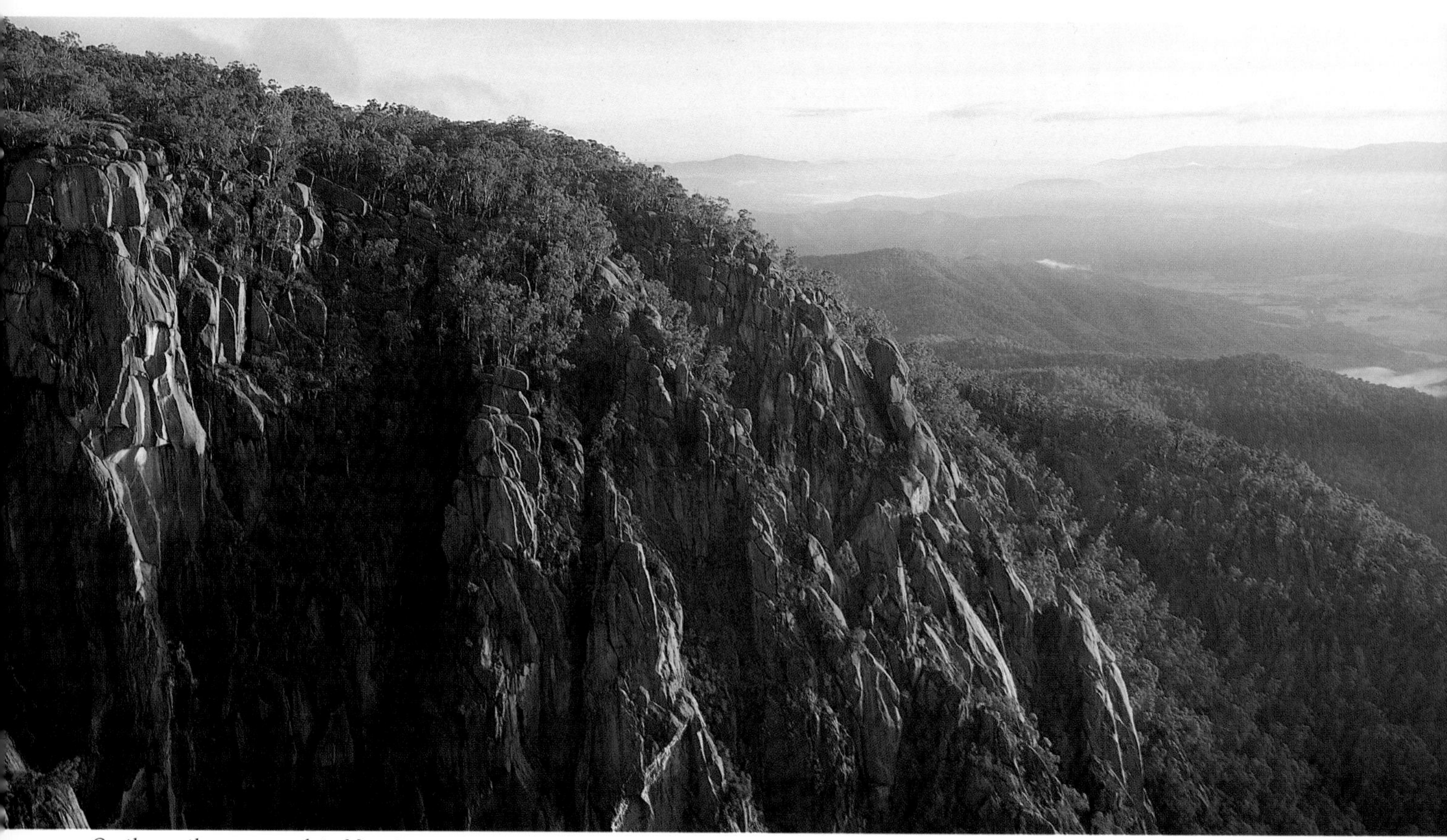

On the northern approach to Mount Buffalo, the eroded granite buttresses of The Gorge keep all but the keenest mountaineers at bay.

'marnatheran' by the Aborigines – is considered to be one of the most beautiful in north-east Victoria.

Hamilton Hume and William Hovell were the area's first white visitors, in November 1824, and the first permanent settlers arrived in the late 1830s. Then, as now, beef and dairy cattle were the valley's most important industries.

The upper reaches of the Kiewa are used to generate hydro-electric power and the townships of Mount Beauty (see entry) and Bogong were both built to house workers on the hydro-electric scheme.

MITTA MITTA ■ 1152

The site of modern-day Mitta Mitta beside the river of the same name, was settled by squatters in the late 1830s, becoming briefly populous in the 1850s, when gold was discovered on the river flats in 1852. The largest open-cut goldmine in the Southern Hemisphere was once located here. Relics of the goldmining days are still visible in the Mitta Mitta River Valley and visitors are permitted to fossick for whatever specks of the precious yellow mineral that might remain. Water-oriented folk can test their courage white-water rafting – or their patience, attempting to catch the rare Macquarie perch which swim in the Mitta Mitta River (see entry). The valley is also the habitat for plants specific to this region, such as the poverty wattle, the bear orchid and the catkin wattle.

MITTA MITTA RIVER ■ 1153

The Mitta Mitta River rises in the Victorian Alps north of Omeo (see entry) and flows for 170 kilometres in a generally northwards direction to meet with the Murray River System at Lake Hume. Before it leaves the pristine environment of the high country, the Mitta Mitta is held back by Australia's highest earth and rockfill dam at Dartmouth Reservoir (see entry). Thereafter, its flow is regulated to provide water for irrigation, stock and domestic use in three states: Victoria, New South Wales and South Australia. The rich alluvial flats of the river valley support tobacco and hop growing as well as cattle grazing, while anglers cast their lines in the river's clear running water in the hope of luring the rare and highly prized Macquarie perch, Murray cod or trout.

Hamilton Hume and William Hovell were the first Europeans to sight the river in 1824 and the name, Mitta Mitta, derives from an Aboriginal word said to mean 'little waters' or 'where reeds grow'.

MOUNT BEAUTY ■ 1154

The evocatively named Mount Beauty was established in 1947 by the Victorian Electricity Commission to accommodate workers on the Kiewa Hydro-Electric Scheme. The town takes its name from a nearby mountain which was christened by Charles Robertson, an early settler. There are spectacular views down the Kiewa Valley from the town, and also up to nearby Mount Bogong (see Alpine National Park). A large pondage, or water-holding area, created to feed the water from the hydro-electric scheme back into the West Kiewa River has become a popular recreational area for fishing, skiing and windsurfing. *Population 1840*

MOUNT BUFFALO NATIONAL PARK ■ 1155

This 31 000-hectare park established in 1898, encompasses the granite mass of Mount Buffalo – a plateau eleven kilometres long by seven kilometres wide. Dense forests clothe the slopes of the plateau, broken here and there by large, stark outcrops of bare granite. On top, tors and piles of giant rounded boulders are surrounded by sub-alpine plants.

Snow falls in winter provide relatively easy ski slopes which are popular with beginners. The entire park is criss-crossed with many clearly marked summer walking tracks and winter cross-country ski trails.

Mount Buffalo National Park has several 'first' credentials; it was the site of the country's first ski lift in the 1940s and it was the first ski resort in Australia to introduce the Arlberg technique of skiing, imported from Europe and an improvement on the older Norwegian method.

The mountain was named by the explorers Hume and Hovell during their journey from Sydney to Port Phillip in 1824 because its rounded shape reminded them of a buffalo.

EUROBIN FALLS A short track off the Mount Buffalo Road, not far from the park entrance, leads to several sets of falls that cascade in stages down steep granite slabs.

THE GORGE Immediately below the Mount Buffalo Chalet, sheer granite walls plummet more than 300 metres to the valley below. Several lookouts dotted around the rim give spectacular views towards Bright (see entry) and the surrounding countryside, and over Crystal Brook as it drops 240 metres in one dizzy leap. Rock-climbers may be seen inching their way up the many difficult routes on both sides of the gorge, and hang-glider pilots often fling themselves into space from a wooden launching ramp on the gorge's northern rim.

THE HORN At 1723 metres, the Horn is the highest point on Mount Buffalo. A walking track winds up this prominent rock pyramid on the northern edge of the plateau to give panoramic views of the park and the Victorian Alps.

MOUNT HOTHAM ■ 1156

The alpine village of Mount Hotham, situated just below the summit of the mountain it is named for, is Victoria's highest settlement.

The route from Bright (see entry), past Mount Hotham to Omeo, was pioneered by gold-miners in the late 1850s, when the mountain was generally known as Old Baldy. In 1855, Baron von Mueller, the government botanist, renamed the peak in honour of the then Governor of Victoria, Sir Charles Hotham.

Among the district's first settlers were the women who built and managed huts to accommodate miners who trudged the Mount Hotham road – the first crossing by a wheeled vehicle was not made until 1883. One of the first accommodation huts was 'Mother' Morrell's log cabin at Mount St Bernard, south-west of Mount Hotham, built in 1863.

In 1939, the buildings at Mount Hotham were destroyed in a bushfire, but they were soon rebuilt on a much larger scale.

MYRTLEFORD ■ 1157

The discovery of gold in nearby Buckland Valley in the 1850s shattered the peace of the Ovens Valley as thousands of diggers invaded the region, setting up makeshift camps along the streams and rivers from which some permanent settlements, such as Myrtleford, grew. Before the outbreak of gold-fever, the first settler in the area was John Hillas, an overlander who grazed cattle on the fertile river flats of 'Myrtle Creek' between 1837 and 1853.

Situated on the northern slopes of the Mount Buffalo range and at the junction of four waterways – the Ovens River, Buffalo River, Happy Valley Creek and Barwidgee Creek (formerly Myrtle Creek) – Myrtleford is now the centre of Victoria's thriving timber, tobacco and hop-growing district with dairying, beef cattle, and walnut groves among the region's other significant industries.

Hops were first grown to make beer for the thirsty gold-miners who frequented the hundreds of pubs that sprang up near the goldfields. The tobacco industry is also a legacy of the gold rush; many of the thousands of miners who worked the goldfields were enthusiastic smokers. The deep green pine forests that add their distinctive scent to the clear air are a more modern industry, providing the raw material for a substantial pulping and sawmilling complex in the town.

Time has seen the scars of the gold rush days fade and now the beauty of the surrounding countryside and annual events such as the Tobacco, Hops and Timber Festival in March and the Golden Spurs Rodeo on Boxing Day, entice visitors to the region. *Population 2870*

'MERRIANG' This historic, early Victorian homestead near Myrtleford is built from handmade-bricks and, as a contrast, blocks of local granite; it has seventeen rooms and has been restored by the owners.

THE PHOENIX TREE Beside the Ovens Highway on the town's western outskirts, the huge trunk and roots of an old red-gum tree felled in a flood have been carved intricately to symbolise the cycle of life and the importance of the renewal of forests throughout the world. The mythical Phoenix bird, which rises to new life from its own ashes, tops the sculpture and gives the work its name.

FESTIVALS Tobacco, Hops and Timber Festival, March; Golden Spurs Rodeo, Boxing Day.

POREPUNKAH ■ 1158

The small hamlet of Porepunkah on the junction of the Ovens and Buckland rivers is popular as a tourist destination in both summer – for bushwalking, fishing and hang-gliding from nearby Mount Buffalo – and winter, as a stopping off place for cross-country skiers making their way between the popular snowfields of Mount Buffalo, Mount Hotham and Falls Creek (see entries). The village owes its existence to the gold rushes of the 1850s and was the centre of huge dredging operations in the Ovens Valley up until 1914 when farmers, who had formed themselves into vociferous anti-dredging organisations, defeated the river-polluting 'metal monsters' that tore at the riverbanks, and reclaimed the land for agriculture.

Porepunkah's unusual name is believed to derive from two Hindu words 'pore' meaning 'wind' and 'punkah' meaning 'blower'.

TALLANGATTA ■ 1159

Like some modern day Atlantis, the 'old' township of Tallangatta – settled in the 1850s – disappeared beneath the waters of Lake Hume in 1956, when the dam wall was raised to increase the lake's capacity. When the lake waters recede, some of the old town's streets, buildings and foundations become visible. 'New' Tallangatta was relocated to its present site on the shores of Lake Hume during the 1950s and was officially opened on 29 June 1956 – only 142 of 'old' Tallangatta's 240 buildings survived the move.

Tallangatta comes from an Aboriginal word said to mean 'many trees'. *Population 1020*

FESTIVALS Arts Festival, October.

TINTALDRA ■ 1160

Tintaldra nestles beneath the Snowy Mountains on the Victorian banks of the Murray River. The village is the favoured retreat of keen anglers who fish for trout in the river. In its early days, it was a border crossing place for goods and livestock from New South Wales and a customs house was built to collect fees. The local gathering place then was the Tintaldra store and hotel, a timber and slab building constructed in 1864 that is still the centre of village life. Classified by the National Trust, the store has a craft shop and museum.

The name Tintaldra comes from an Aboriginal word thought to mean 'young man'.

Tobacco has been grown near Myrtleford for more than 130 years; these leaves are drying out before going to a cigarette factory.

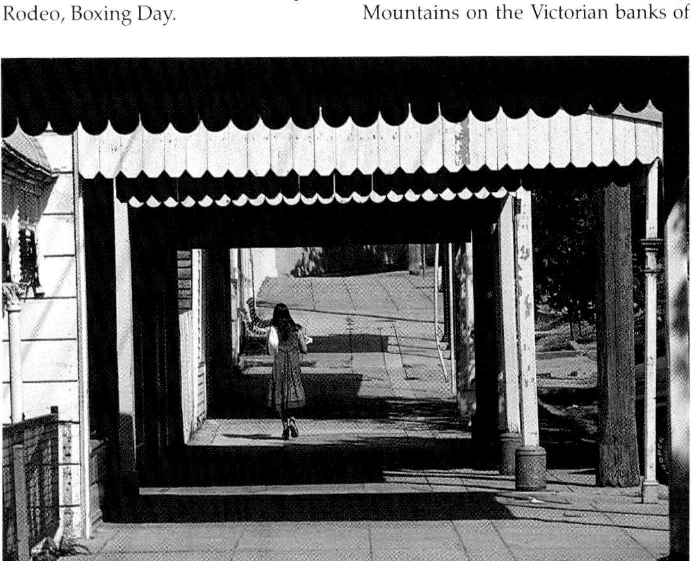

When the timber and corrugated iron verandahs of Yackandandah were built, the streets they shaded were busy and abuzz with gold-rush gossip.

WANDILIGONG ■ 1161

Wandiligong – originally known as Growlers Creek in the days when it was a goldmining settlement of 3000 people – has recovered from its mining activities of the last century and is now a tranquil and historic village surrounded by plantations of radiata pine and Douglas fir that lend their distinctive scent to the valley air. Chestnut trees, oaks and poplars planted more than a century ago and extensive apple orchards, give the town its special character and the entire valley has been given a landscape classification by the National Trust in recognition of its historic and aesthetic worth.

Wandiligong comes from an Aboriginal word said to mean 'spirit', 'ghost' or 'goblin'.

YACKANDANDAH ■ 1162

Since the early days of settlement in the last century, little has changed in this tiny hamlet ringed by hills. Wide streets shaded by grand old oak trees are lined with historic buildings that still retain the colours and trappings of their nineteenth-century origins. The main street with its verandahed shopfronts and posts is strongly reminiscent of a North American frontier town – not surprising since many of the region's early settlers were miners from Sacramento or the Klondike goldfields who had abandoned their original turf for what they hoped would be richer pickings in Australia. Today, the entire commercial district is classified by the National Trust and many of the colonial buildings house an assortment of art galleries, coffee shops, tea rooms and craft shops.

Among the town's many historic buildings is the childhood home of Sir Isaac Isaacs, the first Australian-born Governor-General, and Melville House, the home of Dr Augustus Mueller who established a winery in the town and discovered the strychnine cure for snakebite.

Gold was discovered in the Yackandandah district in 1852, just three months after the Beechworth find (see entry) and goldmining activities soon escalated from the back-breaking labour of hand tools, to the hydraulic sluicing of Yackandandah Creek by barge crews who worked the waterway twenty-four hours a day. Eventually huge bucket dredges gouged great holes in the riverbanks and river flats, reaching the deeper levels of gold and devastating the environment until operations ceased at the turn of the century. The scars are still evident today.

Wine was grown with great success in the Yackandandah area up until the late 1890s when a plant disease – *Phylloxera* – eradicated the region's entire crop. At the time, Victoria was Australia's principal wine-producing region. The disease – caused by an American grapevine louse – which devastated most of the state's vineyards, coupled with farmers' reluctance to plant resistant vines and to alter their wine-making practices, effectively called a halt to wine production in Victoria for the next seventy years.

Assured of its historic status and protected from the ravages of unrestrained commercial development, contemporary Yackandandah is the holiday destination of a continuous flow of visitors who come to savour the town's history – or its strawberry wine – fossick for gold or gemstones, fish for trout in nearby streams, or view the landscape once painted by the well-known Australian artist, Septimus Power, who looked upon Yackandandah as 'the most beautiful place in the world'.

Yackandandah comes from an Aboriginal word thought to mean 'country of hills'. *Population 600*

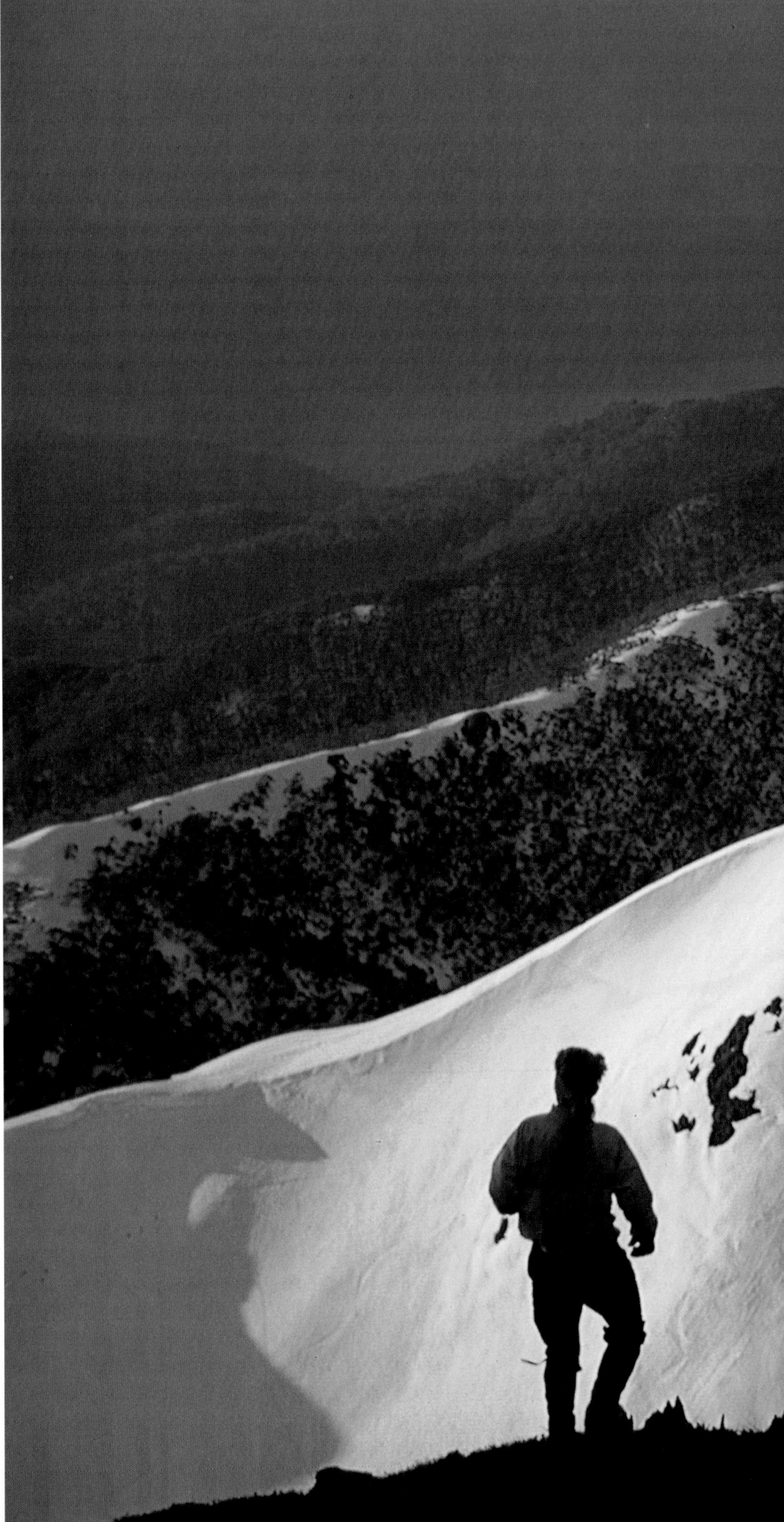

The reward for the climb to the summit of Mount Feathertop in the Bogong High Plains is this spectacular mid-winter view across the mountain's north-west spur to the Ovens Valley.

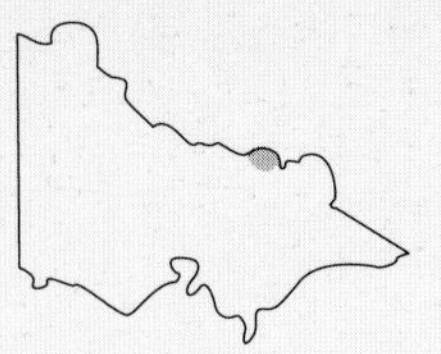

Corowa & Rutherglen

Gold was discovered, the cultivation of wine was developed and steps toward Australia's federation were made in this region. Tourism is a busy money-earner these days and the towns hereabouts fairly bristle with 'heritage' buildings.

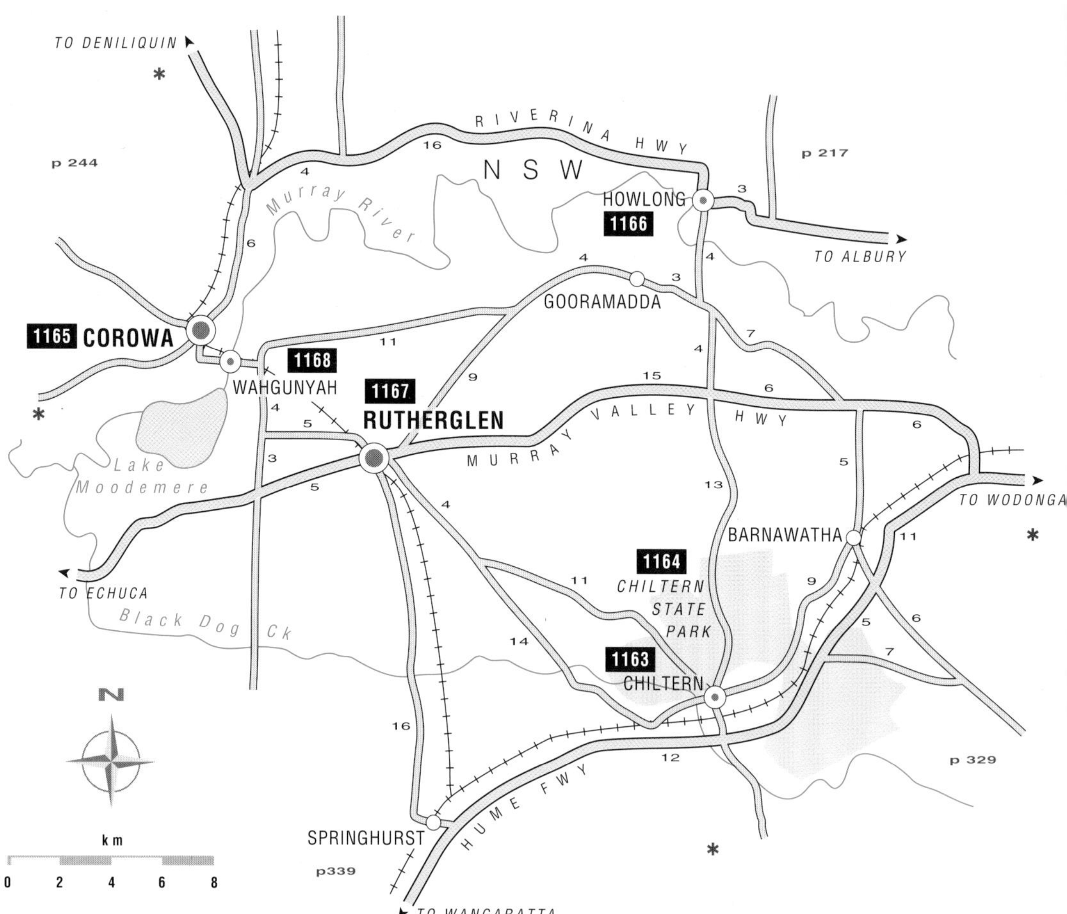

CHILTERN ■ 1163

These days an important wine town on the Hume Highway not far from the New South Wales border, Chiltern was first known as the township of Black Dog Creek, on the banks of which it stands. Overlander Joseph Hawdon apparently shot a black dingo here in the dried-up creek bed when passing through with John Hepburn in 1836. The following year, Joseph Slack took up the 'Barnawartha' run which included the present-day site of Chiltern, as well as most of the surrounding district. The next owner formed the Ullina Station on Black Dog Creek. It was transferred in 1856 to its third owner who built 'The Hermitage', which still stands today. A survey of townships in 1840 led to Black Dog township appearing on maps of the time. By 1851, the town had a hotel, stable, mail offices and several cottages. It was given the name Chiltern around 1854, most likely after the Chiltern Hills in England.

A man thought to have taken part in the Eureka Stockade rebellion, John Conness, discovered gold here in 1858 while hiding out in the district. His claim was later challenged unsuccessfully, and Conness went on to form the Prospecting Association with the idea of finding new gold-bearing leads. Chiltern gold was too deep for it to be worked successfully by individual miners or small syndicates. This did not deter small investors who formed companies to finance their reef mine ventures. A few people were lucky enough to do well, but most never saw their money again. When reef mining finally ceased, a former mine director, Dr Charles Harkin, formed the Chiltern Vineyard Company in an attempt to find work for those displaced by mine closures. He first planted vines in 1910 at the southern end of the town.

Buildings of note in Chiltern are the 1866 former Star Hotel – which has a grapevine, planted in 1867, with a 155-centimetre-circumference trunk, reputedly one of the largest in the world, in its courtyard – the Star theatre, one of the few remaining examples of an 1860s gold-rush theatre and 'Lakeview' (1870), the house immortalised by the novelist, Henry Handel Richardson. She described the house in great detail in *Ultima Thule*, giving it the name 'Barambogie'. 'Lakeview' has been fully restored by the National Trust and is a fine example of the early brick buildings of north-eastern Victoria.

The *Federal Standard* building, built about 1860, was the first printing office in this part of the state. It is also remembered for its string of strong-minded editors like George Mott and George Anderson, who helped shape residents' attitudes on local government in the district. Printing operations ceased in 1971, and the printing equipment in the refurbished building has been restored by enthusiasts. The Athenaeum and library in Conness Street is now a museum containing items of local interest. The building is painted in the original colours, with light blue walls and brown detailing.

The 1870 Chiltern railway station was the model for many stations built in other parts of Victoria. It is noted for its brickwork and cast-iron drinking fountains. The town's old-world atmosphere qualified it as the location for a Walt Disney film, *Ride a Wild Pony*, in 1974. *Population 1160*

CHILTERN STATE PARK ■ 1164

This park is formed by two blocks of land separated by the Hume Highway. A 25-kilometre scenic drive – the Chiltern Historic Drive – takes in the section of bushland to the north

Customers are requested politely not to pick the grapes from Chiltern's gnarled and aged vine.

of Chiltern. A pamphlet showing features of the drive can be picked up from a box at the beginning of the drive. Further along the Chiltern to Rutherglen road is the Donkey Hill turnoff. Still further along the road is a pioneer cemetery and the vividly-coloured earth of Magenta Mine. Around the mine landscape are giant red mullock heaps from which black ironbark trees grow. The drive finishes at the state battery near Chiltern; picnic spots are found along the way. Fine stands of native trees such as red stringybark, grey box, red ironbark and Blakely's red gum are in the park and its spring wildflowers are a byword among local people. Rare birds seen here include the turquoise parrot, regent honeyeater and the peregrine falcon.

In Chiltern, 'Lakeview's' view only briefly predates the building – Lake Anderson is a rain-filled mine subsidence.

COROWA ■ **1165**

Just across the Murray River, on the New South Wales side, is the historic town of Corowa. Charles Sturt passed through this area, first occupied by Wiradjuri Aborigines, in 1830 and 1838. The first settlers were the overlanders John Foord and John Crisp who took up the 'Wahgunyah' run which included land on the south side of the Murray River. The area really began to flourish in 1856, when river steamers were introduced along the Murray, opening up a regular and reliable transport route to markets in Melbourne. The railway replaced river transport from 1892 when the Culcairn to Corowa line was extended.

Corowa has a significant place in Australian history. Like many other colonial border towns, Corowa supported federation of the Australian colonies as a means of promoting free trade within the country. They began to campaign for a federal authority to control such matters as the mail, defence and, all-important in those days, customs duties which were then levied on all goods crossing the border from Corowa into Victoria. A Border Federation League was formed and in 1893, a major conference held in Corowa. Talks with the other colonies on fair usage of the waters of the Murray for irrigation, which culminated in the River Murray Agreement of 1915, were also held here. These historic events are commemorated in a special federation museum.

Like other centres nearby, Corowa fairly bristles with 'heritage' buildings listed as worthy of preservation. Sanger Street is lined with nineteenth-century buildings with quaint wrought-iron balconies; of particular note are the court house (1880) and railway station (1880s). The Australian painter, Tom Roberts visited a station near here in 1889, for one of his best-known paintings, *Shearing the Rams*.

River cruises past river red gums, billabongs, lakes and vineyards conjure up a whiff of the busy river traffic of earlier times. A parachutist-training school and gliding club based at the local airstrip are attractions that draw many visitors. The district is also a noted wheat- and wool-producing area. *Population 5060*

HOWLONG ■ **1166**

John Hawdon drove the first cattle overland to South Australia from Howlong. It took ten weeks for Hawdon's 325 animals to reach their destination and remarkably, he lost only four. Howlong itself was once two separate settlements – upper and lower Howlong – and was first built on land from the 'Hoolong' run. It took more than an hour to walk between the two settlements.

By 1857, the town was prosperous enough for one hotel to have both a ballroom and a concert room. Many old buildings of interest can still be seen in town, such as the 1870 Mill Hotel which is now a private home. The original horse-change station for the coach services to other parts of the colony is still on the 'Kismet' property nearby. In an echo of the days of Cobb & Co., horse-drawn caravans can be hired in Howlong for those with a taste for the life of a gypsy. *Population 1630*

RUTHERGLEN ■ **1167**

Gold was discovered and vines planted around the same time in the late 1850s and early 1860s and Rutherglen has flourished since then. Today, the town has the distinction of being the centre of the oldest wine-growing district in Australia. It was once part of 'Wahgunyah', the large stock run established between 1839 and 1841 on the south side of the Murray by the early settlers John Crisp and John Foord.

The town grew rapidly and flourished after alluvial gold was found on its western outskirts. For a time it became the largest gold rush after the Ballarat fields and the population rose to around 30 000. The first vigneron in the district, Lindsay Brown, bravely told a town meeting in 1860 that there was more gold to be gained from the first six inches below the surface than lower down. The prediction was less than accurate and mining for gold-bearing quartz continued until the 1990s; the mine's poppet head still stands outside town.

Of course, Rutherglen is best known for its wine. Many of the wineries have been in the district for more than one hundred years. Often descendants of the original founders run these wineries and any tour is as much about the history of the area as the wine. A winery walkabout weekend each year is an important local event. Many of Rutherglen's old wineries and hotels are National Trust-classified, among them the Victoria Hotel (1868) and the Mount Ophir (1891) and Olive Hill wineries (1890). There are at least five other wineries near to town. To the west is Lake Moodemere, once a Aboriginal campsite, now a wildlife reserve where fishing and swimming is permitted. *Population 1880*

FESTIVALS Wine Festival, March; Wineries Walkabout, June.

WAHGUNYAH ■ **1168**

The 'Wahgunyah' run, established by John Foord and John Crisp between 1839 and 1841 on the south side of the Murray, included the present towns of Corowa and Rutherglen. The name comes from 'wah' which is thought to be an Aboriginal word for 'big' or 'mud' and 'gunyah' meaning 'hut' or 'camp'. John Foord established a private town here in 1856 after squatters were given the right to purchase a portion of their leased land. He built a hotel, bond stores and a flour mill with workers' cottages. A paddle steamer service was operated by Foord from the mid-1850s to 1878. The port became a major supply centre for the diggings during the Rutherglen gold rush and Wahgunyah also developed into an important winegrowing centre. The first vineyard, 'Gooramadda', was established in 1851 and others followed soon after.

At the time, most vineyards in the area were named after saints, so when George Sutherland Smith established his winery he indulged in some Celtic one-upmanship and called his vineyard, All Saints. It was a boast not without foundation. The first Australian wine to be awarded a gold medal at an international exhibition in Europe was an All Saints' red at the Vienna International Exhibition in 1873. The main winery building has thick walls and battlements, and the Smith family say it is based on the Castle of May, near the founder's native village near John o'Groats in the far north of Scotland. *Population 600*

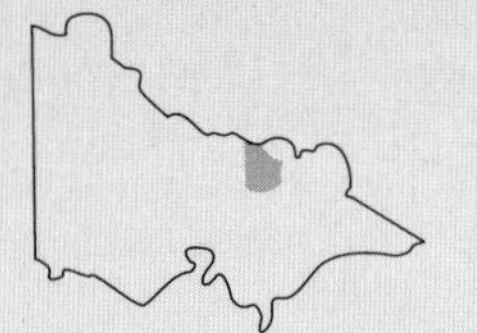

Wangaratta & Benalla

The wild bushranging activities of the Kelly gang and Dan Morgan, who roamed these hills in the 1860s, have given way to more sedate, pastoral pursuits. In modern times, this region is known for its wine, wheat, wool and textiles and also has an aeronautical connection with Australia's largest gliding fleet and a vintage aeroplane collection.

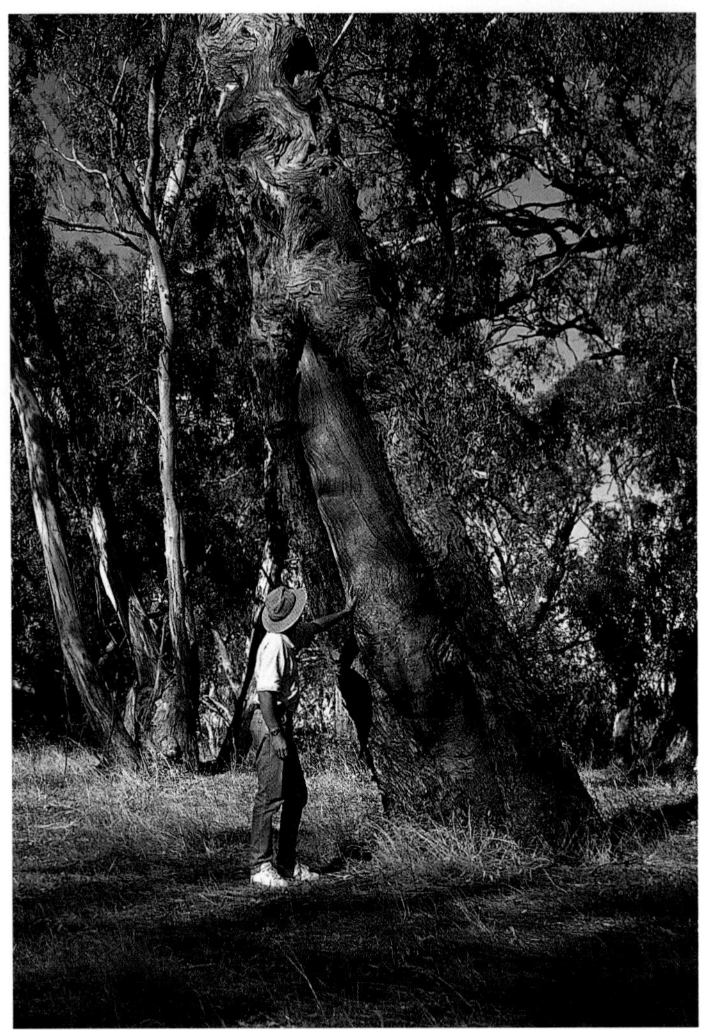

The shape of the scar on this gnarled river red gum near Mulwala indicates clearly that the bark was going to be transformed into an Aborigine's canoe.

BENALLA ■ **1169**

This is Victoria's 'City of Roses' where more than 2000 rose varieties bloom in colourful profusion from spring to early autumn. The rose garden in the Benalla Gardens was established in 1959; roses also line the highway and predominate in many private gardens throughout the town.

The 1836 crossing of Broken River by Major Thomas Mitchell and his party was marked by mishap when James 'Tally-Ho' Taylor, bugle player with the expedition, was drowned near the site of the present town. Two years later, the area was again the scene of sudden death when workers from George Faithfull's station near Wangaratta, who camped here while taking sheep and cattle further south, were attacked and killed by Aborigines whose domain they were passing through. Some of the dead were buried in a mass grave under a large red gum which came to be known as the 'Faithfull Tree'. The town site was surveyed in 1848, but there was little settlement to speak of until the late 1850s when the lure of gold sparked a general influx of population.

Benalla was headquarters for the police charged with hunting the Kelly gang and abounds with links to the bushranging past. Ned Kelly appeared four times at the red brick court house, on the first occasion in 1869 he was just fourteen. In 1880, the body of Kelly gang member Joe Byrne, retrieved from the burning Glenrowan Inn, was strung up on a door here for photographers. This door is now in the Kelly Museum in Bridge Street West, along with the witness box in which young Ned stood. The Costume and Pioneer Museum, housed in the old Mechanic's Institute, has on display the cummerbund – presented to Ned Kelly in 1864 for rescuing a young boy from drowning – which he wore under his armour at the famous Glenrowan shootout. There also is the Greta lock-up, where Kelly spent many dark hours.

In 1974, Broken River was dammed to form Lake Benalla. It is bordered by a lake walk and bush trail, and its waters are used by swimmers, small sailing craft, canoes and kayaks. The Benalla Gardens, on the banks of the lake, were opened more than a century ago as a recreation reserve. *Population 8490*

BENALLA ART GALLERY This regional art gallery houses the Ledger Collection, formed over a number of decades by L.H. Ledger, a local stock and station man. It includes many examples from the colonial period, the Heidelberg school of artists, and works from the 1900 to 1940 period. The gallery's Contemporary Collection of paintings includes works by Fred Williams, Leonard French and Margaret Preston.

STATE GLIDING CENTRE The headquarters of the Gliding Club of Victoria is located at Benalla and the fleet based here – the largest in Australia – includes high-performance, two-seater gliders, motor-gliders and single-seat competition sailplanes. The club offers gliding training, cross-country flights, and scenic joy flights and has staged national and international gliding championships.

FESTIVALS Benalla Agricultural Show, November; Benalla Rose Festival, November.

'BONTHARAMBO' ■ **1170**

Bontharambo Homestead, classified by the National Trust and on the Register of the National Estate, is a few kilometres from the Hume Highway on Boorhaman Road, north of Wangaratta. It was built in 1858 for the Reverend Joseph Docker, who in 1838, after a period as rector of Francis Greenway's St Matthew's Church at Windsor in New South Wales, undertook an eight-month overland trek to settle on these rich plains with his large family, servants, stockmen, 3000 sheep and 300 cattle. On arrival, Docker enlarged the slab hut which George Faithfull built in 1838 but abandoned soon after the massacre of some of his drovers near Benalla (see entry) – the door of this dwelling has since served the property as a garden gate.

Docker's fortunes followed the soaring price of cattle caused by the gold rush, and by the mid-1850s he was able to finance the present building, a handsome two-storey structure dominated by an eighteen-metre tower and encircled by a single-storey arcade. This grand and imposing homestead has no fewer than fourteen main rooms, including a library and billiards room; marble and the cedar staircases were imported from England, and the original furniture, much of which is still in the house, from France.

EDI ■ **1171**

In the upper valley of the King River, between Moyhu and King Valley, is the tiny settlement of Edi. At the trout farm here visitors can try their luck with rod and reel or buy freshly dressed or smoked trout. In 1878, Edi was the rendezvous point for police parties sent out to scour the country between Greta and Mansfield for the Kelly gang.

ELDORADO ■ **1172**

Eldorado stands at the head of Reids Creek Valley and it was for its welcome waters that it was named by overlander William Baker who settled here after droving stock from the drier north. Its mineral riches were unearthed later – gold was first noted in 1845 and some sluicing of the creek waters began in 1855 but it was not until the 1860s that mining of gold and tin began in earnest. At the time of its construction in 1936, the Cocks Eldorado Dredge, later to rust, disused, in its dredge pool, was the largest in the Southern Hemisphere. In its twenty years of operation it won more than 2.3 million grams of alluvial gold and some 1475 tonnes of tin from the creekbed. Fossicking for gems and panning for gold are popular activities along the banks of the creek.

GLENROWAN ■ 1173

The armour-clad Kelly gang made their last stand here in Jones's Glenrowan Inn where they held more than sixty of the townsfolk hostage while awaiting the arrival of the police train which they hoped to derail. These plans were thwarted, for the train was flagged down by a hostage and Ned Kelly, after making an other-worldly appearance in the chill morning mists in helmet, breastplate and backplate, was shot in the legs and captured. Three of the gang were killed and their hotel refuge burned to the ground by police. The town takes its name from the Rowan brothers whose Peechelba Station – scene of the death of Dan Morgan, another notorious bushranger – included the glens and slopes where the settlement grew. Wineries near

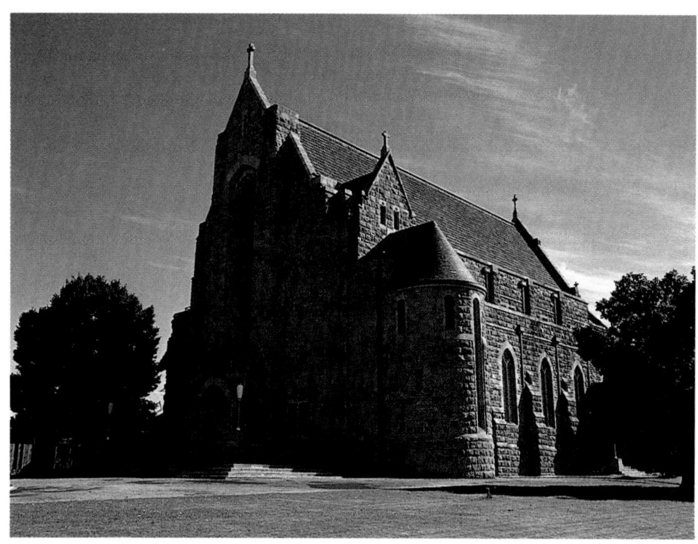

Wangaratta's Anglican Cathedral Church of the Holy Trinity has a medieval solidity that would do justice to any European cathedral town.

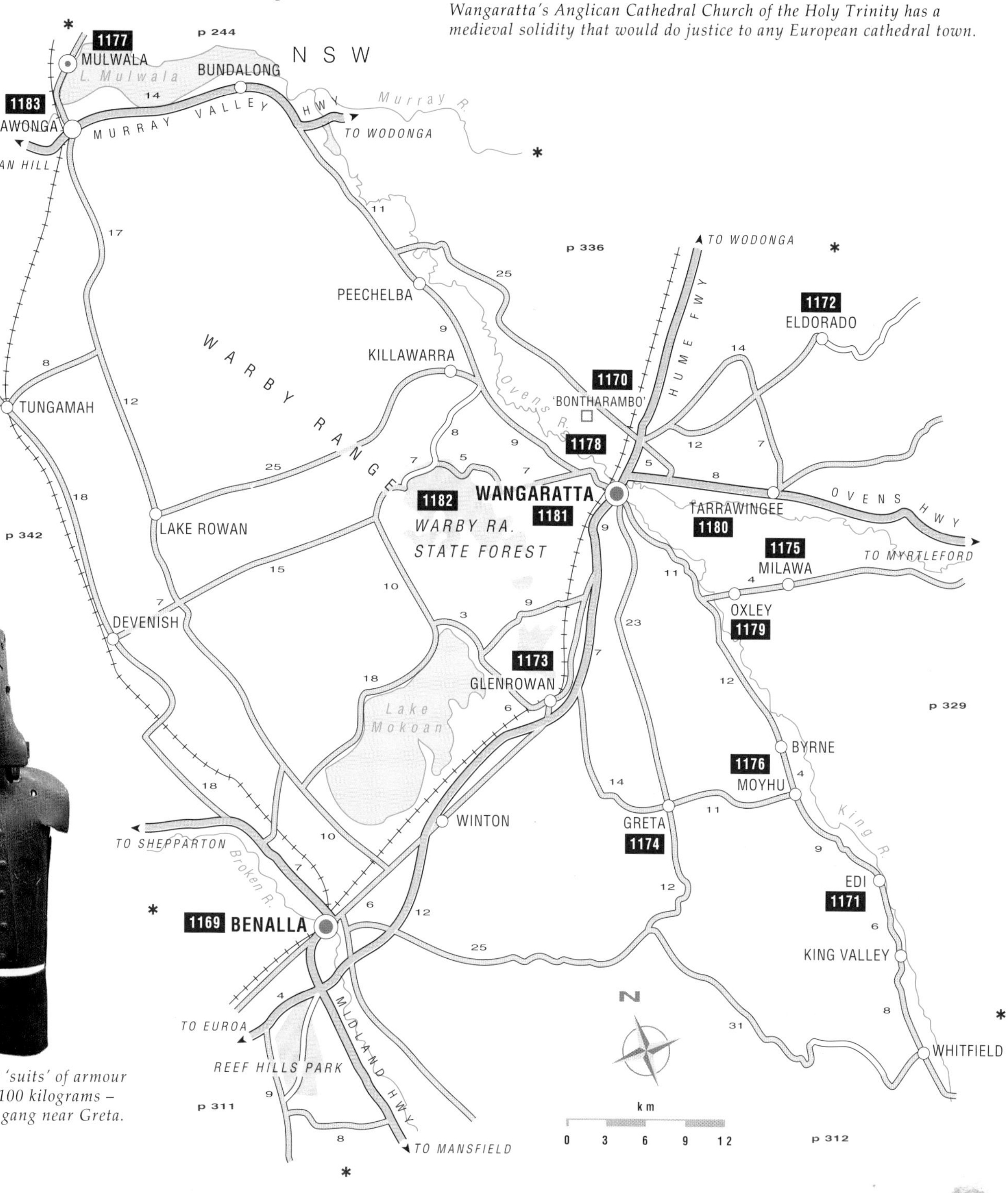

This is one of four 'suits' of armour – weighing about 100 kilograms – made by the Kelly gang near Greta.

the town, which produce full-bodied reds, include Baileys, whose first vintage dates from 1870 but which had to be re-established after the disastrous outbreak of the phylloxera disease ravaged vines in the 1880s and 1890s.

GRETA ■ 1174

During the Kelly bushranging years, Greta was a small village with a police station, hotel, smithy and store. Today, there is nothing at the crossroads but a school and a cemetery. Of the old Kelly homestead outside Greta at Eleven Mile Creek little more than the house chimneys and the slab walls of the barn still stand – they are on private property but are visible from the road.

It was to this small selection that Ellen Kelly brought her eight children after the death of her husband in 1866 and it was from here that Ned and his brothers honed their horse-riding skills and gained their intimate knowledge of the narrow valleys and steep ridges of the region. In 1870, Ellen Kelly was charged with selling liquor without a licence from the house. The armour worn by the Kelly outlaws at Glenrowan was made from ploughshares stolen in this region; the iron was heated on a large fire, probably behind the Kelly building, then flattened and shaped on a log before being riveted together. Kelly's suit and helmet protected his head and chest but left vulnerable the lower part of his body.

MILAWA ■ 1175

A three-storey brick flour mill dating from 1861 is a reminder of the days when Milawa was centre of a wheat-growing district. Brown Brothers winery was established in 1880 by the same family who ran the mill. As well as wine, the town also produces mustards and handmade cheeses.

FESTIVALS Wine and Food Festival, mid-late November.

MOYHU ■ 1176

The small township of Moyhu lies in the fertile valley of the King River. Farms on the rich river flats here produce top quality fruits, from apples to berries to wine grapes.

BYRNE HOUSE North of Moyhu township is Byrne House, one of the oldest homesteads in the district. The building has been extensively renovated and now houses a large collection of antique and period furniture as well as a gallery featuring the works of local artists.

MULWALA ■ 1177

At Mulwala, the border between New South Wales and Victoria is blurred and the towns of Mulwala and Yarrawonga (see entry), connected by bridges, blend into one urban area at the western end of Lake Mulwala. The Mulwala Canal which runs through the north of the town was constructed in 1937 and has the distinction of being the first irrigation canal in Australia. It is 120 kilometres long and draws some 8000 megalitres a day for stock and domestic irrigation.

When the explorer Charles Sturt passed through this region in 1838 he noted the large numbers of Aborigines camped on Quarry Hill, today site of the water tower. Here for thousands of years they lived well off the fish, fowl, tortoise and other game abundant in the waters and along the banks of the lagoons now covered by the lake. Within fifty years of the arrival of Europeans – as in most other districts taken up as sheep or cattle runs – they were gone from these lands. The Aboriginal name for the area was 'mulla walla', said to mean 'rain'. Modern tourist brochures promote the region as 'Sun Country'. *Population 1330*

CANOE TREE One of many 'canoe trees' in the Yarrawonga–Mulwala area stands near the lake in Kyffin's Reserve on the eastern outskirts of the town. Using stone axes, Aborigines prised the thick bark from riverside red gums to fashion into canoes and shields. This was best done in the late spring or early summer growth period when the sap flow between the bark and the core of the tree was at its strongest.

When cut, the heavy slab, a metre or more wide and up to two metres long, was laid on the ground and cut and dried to the required shape. Canoes were formed by using heavy piles of stones to force the sides together at each end – they would later be sewn together with reeds – and stout sticks in the middle to hold the sides apart. Living canoe trees are an increasingly rare link with the Aboriginal past.

The shape of the stately poplars by Lake Mulwala suggests their fate: they will be milled for use as matchsticks.

OVENS RIVER ■ 1178

The Ovens River rises on the slopes of Mount Hotham in the Victorian Alps and flows north-west for some 200 kilometres first through the narrow mountain valleys of Mount Buffalo National Park, then across the middle valley where hops are grown, to the vineyards and sheep and dairy pastures of the lower valley. Along its course the Ovens is joined by the waters of the Buffalo and the King rivers and itself joins the Murray River north of Corowa (see *Corowa & Rutherglen*).

In 1824, when explorers Hamilton Hume and William Hovell named this river after Major John Ovens, soldier, explorer and private secretary to Governor Brisbane, they noted that 'the banks and all the neighbouring country...which is extremely beautiful...consist of the finest possible soil'.

OXLEY ■ 1179

The township of Oxley grew up at a crossing over the Ovens River used by diggers on their way from Port Phillip to the Ovens Goldfields. The site was surveyed in 1857 and the first allotments auctioned; some of these are still held by descendants of the original purchasers. The township takes its name from the surrounding plains, which were named by Hume and Hovell for the Surveyor-General, John Oxley.

TARRAWINGEE ■ 1180

The scattered buildings of Tarrawingee are a reminder of the town's prosperous heyday in the 1860s and

1870s as a service centre to local selectors. Plough Inn Hotel was built in 1865 from bricks fired on the site. It was once an important coaching stop and claims Ned Kelly as a former patron. Ladson's Store, 'Carinya', was built in 1860 in anticipation of a railway link that never eventuated. It features a horseshoe-shaped cedar counter and is open to the public with many of its orignal contents on display.

WANGARATTA ■ 1181

The woollen mill established here in 1922 laid the basis for Wangaratta's famous textile industry – now Bruck Mills and Wangaratta Woollen Mills are together the largest employers in the city and offer group tours of their plants as well as direct-to-the-public shops. Major farming activities in the area include the raising of beef cattle, dairying, wool growing, the growing of wheat, fruit and wine grapes and the production of honey.

The city stands on the spot where Major Thomas Mitchell crossed the Ovens River in 1836 and where George Faithfull took up land two years later. The small settlement which grew up near Faithfull's homestead, around the punt and inn operated by William Clarke, was first known as Oven's Crossing. Its present name, that of the Faithfull property, was adopted in 1863 and comes from the Aboriginal words 'wanga', a cormorant, and 'ratta', to sit. *Population 15 980*

DAN MORGAN'S GRAVE Bushranger 'Mad' Dan Morgan's murderous reign ended when he was gunned down in 1865 at Peechelba Station, twenty kilometres north of Wangaratta. After the beard and hair were cut and torn away, his head was crudely removed and sent to Melbourne in the belief that its study might help explain the activities of brutal men such as Morgan. The grave containing his headless body is in South Wangaratta Cemetery.

AIRWORLD Said to be the world's largest collection of flying antique aircraft, this complex also contains Australia's largest collection of Holden cars, antique bicycles and vintage vehicles. It is based on the historic aircraft collection of Joe and Margaret Darge which was bought by the City of Wangaratta in 1984.

CATHEDRAL CHURCH OF THE HOLY TRINITY A city landmark, Wangaratta's magnificent cathedral church dates from a much humbler building constructed in 1856. Its timber belfry houses eight bells that were cast in England in the early nineteenth century and shipped to Wangaratta when the church they originally adorned closed. The church was given cathedral status in 1902 when Thomas Armstrong was appointed as the first Bishop of Wangaratta.

FESTIVALS ANA Athletics Carnival, January; Festival of Jazz, October.

Many of the construction materials for the Yarrawonga Weir were ferried upriver by paddle steamer in the 1930s.

WARBY RANGE STATE PARK ■ 1182

Extending north of Glenrowan for almost thirty kilometres and encompassing some 3400 hectares, this park offers a wide variety of birdlife and some panoramic views – atop Mount Glenrowan, vistas from Benalla to Wangaratta, and from the tower at Ryans Lookout, a sweeping panorama takes in the Mount Buffalo Plateau and the Victorian Alps. Black Springs is a permanent source of water throughout the year, and the Jubilee and Salisbury Falls both flow after rain.

Giant grass trees grow near Mount Warby; white cypress pine, red stringybark and grey, yellow and red box also flourish here. The ranges are named after Ben Warby who took up land here in 1844. Victoria's first orange orchards were planted in the foothills twenty years later by blacksmith James Brian – some of the original trees remain as living agricultural artefacts. Granite quarried in the ranges was used to build some of Wangaratta's churches.

YARRAWONGA ■ 1183

Yarrawonga, with its twin town Mulwala, is a popular tourist destination, for the lake here provides fishing, swimming and boating, and scenic cruises depart regularly throughout the year. On the outskirts of the towns are the Brymay poplar forests, the first of which was established in 1960 to supply timber for Redhead matches. Even eighty years after the event, Yarrawonga is probably best-known for a song composed in the trenches of France during the First World War, inspired by the cry of an injured digger, 'I'm going back again to Yarrawonga'.

The name comes from Aboriginal words meaning either 'place where the wonga pigeon nested' or 'place where the cormorant builds' and was given by Mrs Elizabeth Hume, sister-in-law of Hamilton Hume, to the run she took up in 1842 which originally stretched from Corowa downstream past the present twin towns towards Cobram. Her neighbours to the south, with whom there were several disagreements over boundaries, were the Rowan brothers (see Glenrowan). *Population 3390*

BURRAMINE HOMESTEAD Also known as 'Byramine', the homestead was built on the original Yarrawonga run in 1842 for Mrs Elizabeth Hume to the design of an English architect who intended it for erection in India. It features a large central hall, octagonal rooms and an encircling verandah. The pine used in its construction was cut nearby and the bricks were made on the site. With her nine children, Elizabeth moved here from Gunning, in New South Wales, after the murder by bushrangers of her husband John, brother of explorer Hamilton Hume. The house is classified by the National Trust and is open to the public.

LAKE MULWALA AND YARRAWONGA WEIR The 6000-hectare lake was formed in 1939 when a weir was built across the Murray to raise the water level for discharge into the Mulwala and Yarrawonga irrigation channels. The lake has a capacity of 118 000 megalitres and in places, where the Murray follows its old course across the bed, is up to twenty metres deep. The leafless limbs of a drowned red gum forest stand stark from its waters. Large numbers of trees were removed before the flooding; those left provide roosting for the prolific water-bird population and help cut down on erosion of the foreshores by breaking up waves.

FESTIVALS Burramine Gift, March; Agricultural Show, early October; Red Cross Murray River Marathon, Boxing Day.

Before he achieved notoriety, the juvenile Ned warmed himself by these fireplaces – all that remain of the old Kelly home near Greta.

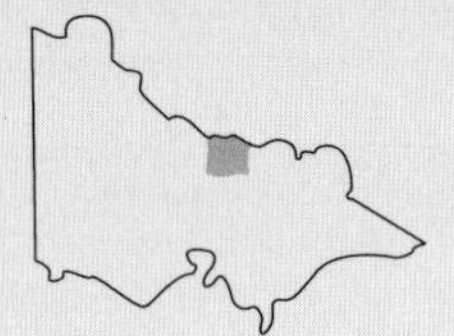

Shepparton & Mooroopna

This is a region of intensive agricultural development based on a combination of orchardists' know-how, technology and old-fashioned hard work. A local factory once processed 2 130 114 cans of fruit in one day – laid end to end they would stretch all the way from Shepparton to Melbourne.

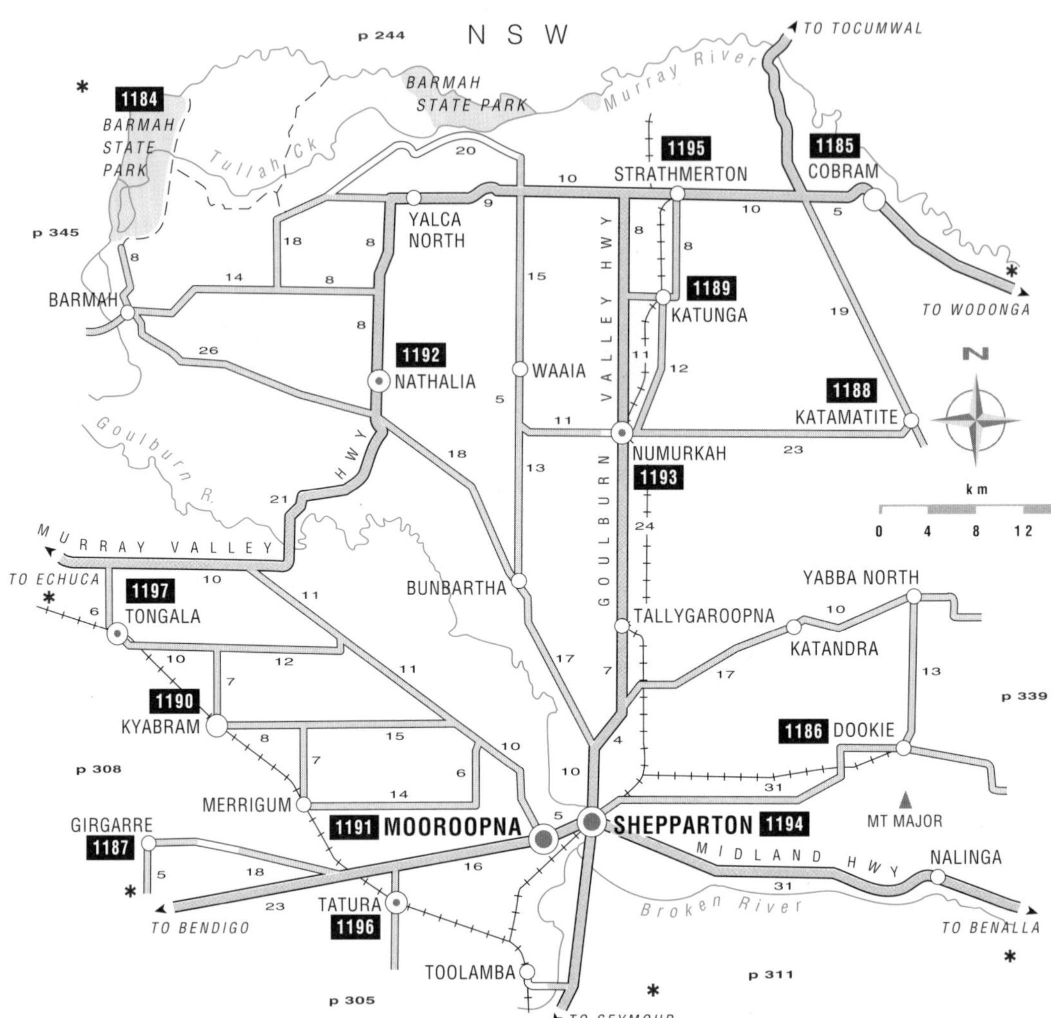

BARMAH STATE PARK ■ 1184
This 7900-hectare state park and the adjoining Millewa Forest in New South Wales are part of the great Murray River flood plain and combine to form the largest river red gum 'sanctuary' in Australia. Because of its strength and durability, the deep red, fine-textured wood is in great demand as a feature timber and for sleepers, flooring, jetties and wharves. In the early days, the felled trees were removed by barge and river steamer through canals called pontoon cuts. The Barmah Forest has 112 kilometres of Murray River frontage and is often subject to flooding – allowing this to occur here reduces the impact on towns downstream. In spring, cattle are released to graze here and then mustered together towards the end of April. Bees produce a delicious, clear honey from the blossoms of the yellow and grey box and river red gum.

Above all, the forest has special significance for the Aboriginal people who used its abundant resources for more than 40 000 years and left behind canoe trees, kitchen middens and burial grounds – the only reminders today that anyone was here before the coming of European settlers. Nearby Barmah township is a key access point to the park; recreational activities include wild pig hunting at the Glue Pot.

DHARNYA CENTRE This educational centre, a few kilometres north of Barmah township, was built as part of a multi-racial Community Employment Program and is managed by the Department of Conservation, Forests and Lands with the support of the local Aboriginal community and the Shire of Nathalia. 'Dharnya' is an Aboriginal word said to mean 'red gum'.

FESTIVALS Barmah Forest Muster, April/May.

COBRAM ■ 1185
In 1845, Octavius Phillpotts named his station after the Aboriginal word 'cobbera or 'cobramaine' for 'head', in this case, 'head station'. Cobram has a reputation for growth when other country towns are declining. It is linked by a bridge to its twin town, Barooga in New South Wales (see *Deniliquin & Finley*). Here the Murray skirts sandy beaches set among river red gums. Only wheat was grown in the area originally but agriculture diversified after the Second World War when land was allocated to 600 soldier-settlers and irrigation began from Lake Mulwala at Yarrawonga. Peaches and cream are inseparable in Cobram which has Australia's major peach orchards and the huge dairy complex, Murray Goulburn Co-operative, founded in the late 1940s by ex-servicemen dairy farmers. Other local fruits grown for canning include pears and apricots. The district grows citrus fruits, vegetables – potatoes and tomatoes – wheat, oats, barley, sunflowers, tobacco and wine grapes, and raises sheep and dairy cattle. *Population 3800*

FESTIVALS Peaches and Cream Festival, January of odd-numbered years.

DOOKIE ■ 1186
Dookie is said to have been named by surveyor J.G. Wilmot from a Singhalese word meaning 'to lament' because local settler, Mrs Turnbull, bewailed part of her property lost through his survey. The town prospered when the railway line from Shepparton opened in 1888 – nearby Cashel speedily declined and buildings from there were put on wheels and dragged by steam-traction engines to Dookie. The Cashel Experimental Farm was established in 1878 and was the forerunner of the Dookie College of Agriculture and Horticulture. The Dookie Chateau vineyards were established in the early 1880s but like other Victorian vineyards were plagued in the closing years of the century by the phylloxera disease – a root parasite.

GIRGARRE ■ 1187
'Girgarre' was the name given to one of E.W. Curr's outstations in 1844 and thought to be based on an Aboriginal word for 'sour'. The factory which once made specialty cheeses is now deserted but cheeses are still stored here and fresh district varieties can be purchased.

KATAMATITE ■ 1188

There are still many signs of Aborigines having passed the way of Katamatite: enormous mounds of ashes from their ovens, shaped stone tools and scarred trees from which were cut bark for shields or canoes. 'Katamatite' may be from an Aboriginal word 'catamateet' meaning 'of local creek', but Bill Beatty, collector of Australiana, prefers to link the name with a colourful local legend about an early settler. Returning from the inn each night he would ask his wife 'Kate, am I tight?'. Her invariable reply: 'No, just half over the Boosey'. Boosey ('gum tree') Creek is nearby.

Originally, Katamatite was part of the 'Tallygaroopna' property (see Shepparton). At this time, the only English-speaking people for hundreds of kilometres might be a shepherd and a visiting overseer. A small cross-section from early Katamatite's history shows the pattern of development for so many country places unaffected by a gold rush – the dates vary but the similar events include: 1841 first white man in the area; 1874 survey; 1876 first settlers; 1882 first church built – Wesleyan in this case – 1883 well sunk; 1884 Mechanics' Hall built, cricket team competed against Numurkah, post office handled 11 350 letters; 1885 township proclaimed; 1888 severe drought; 1889 first resident doctor – and so on.

KATUNGA ■ 1189

Katunga is said to be named after a local Aborigine. Squatters arrived in the district around the late 1830s and about twenty-five years later, settlers carted in their worldly goods on small waggons. They had drought and flood to contend with but nevertheless cleared the land for successful wheat growing. Returning soldiers from the Second World War made the area productive and efficient in dairying and fruit growing, and grape vines thrive.

KYABRAM ■ 1190

Kyabram has a large processing and canning plant to back up its bountiful fruit-growing activities. Jam, cans, clothing and agricultural machinery are also made there and dairying is important. The town's name comes from 'kiambram', thought to mean 'thick forest'. Until April 1886, the post office was called Sheridan. Kyabram West was also known as Deakin after Australia's second Prime Minister, Alfred Deakin. Kyabram has attractive public gardens and is promoted as the 'garden town of the garden state'; native flora flourishes in the fauna park in Kyabram Lake Reserve. *Population 5540*

MOOROOPNA ■ 1191

The township of Mooroopna developed in the 1850s as a punt crossing on the Goulburn River for travellers on their way to the gold diggings at Bendigo and Beechworth. Land was first offered up for sale in the region in 1860. Nowadays, the fertile, irrigated soil of the area produces mainly stone fruits which are processed at the Ardmona cannery. There are also dairying, flourmilling and sawmilling interests; the timber comes from the Barmah Forest (see Barmah State Park).

Mooroopna is said to be Aboriginal for 'ghost' or 'deep water'. Nearby, Genmill's Swamp is a wetland home to pelicans, ibis, swans, egrets, ducks and other birds. It is encircled by a five-kilometre walking track with a bird-feeding area on McFarlanes Road. The walk also includes a section of the west bank of the Goulburn River and some of the red gum forest. *Population 6500*

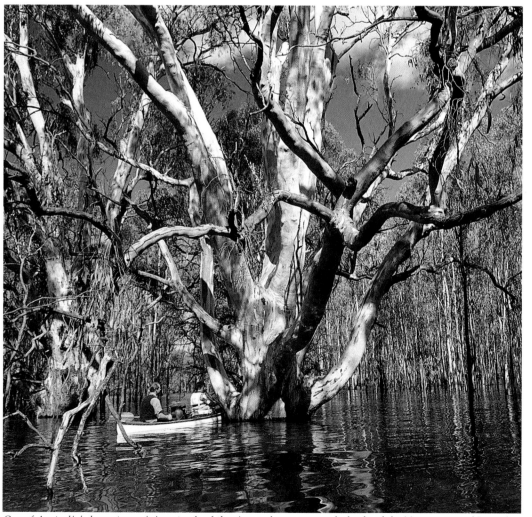

One of Australia's largest remaining stands of the river red gum grasps the banks of the Murray, east of Barmah.

Shepparton's cool winters are ideal for stone fruit; these sweet cherries are ready to go to the cannery.

NATHALIA ■ 1192

Nathalia was part of the huge 'Kotupna' run established in 1843, which was later divided into 'Kotupna' and 'Kaarimba' stations. The township, established in the late 1870s, is bisected by the meandering Broken Creek, surrounded by good agricultural land and within easy reach of the Barmah Forest. It is a tranquil place in which the main street was modelled on Sturt Street in Ballarat. The many old buildings include two of classified 'heritage' status: The Browne, Corke & Co. building – an excellent example of late nineteenth-century provincial shop architecture – and the old post office, built around 1878. Secondary industries include a dairy and a sawmill. Nathalia is said to be named after Nathalia, the Queen of Serbia – just why, nobody seems to know. *Population 1470*

NUMURKAH ■ 1193

The town was established as a support centre for land-hungry settlers who came from the northern side of the Murray River in the 1830s. Numurkah is said to mean 'war shield' in an Aboriginal dialect, but today the district pursues peaceful agricultural activities irrigated by the Murray River. Cereals, fruit, sheep and dairy and beef cattle are important and there is a sunflower oilseed industry.

The railway from Shepparton reached Numurkah in 1881 and in the same year the area was declared unsuitable for irrigation – this decision stood for nearly fifty years. The ever-turning Dethridge wheel at the Melville Street roundabout now symbolises the importance of irrigation water. This measuring device – invented in 1910 by J.S. Dethridge – records water deliveries to irrigated properties – over 15 000 Dethridge wheels operate in Victoria alone.

Numurkah was an important recruiting centre for the Second World War and many local men became prisoners of the Japanese in Singapore. When they returned, they established the Goulburn Valley Ex-Prisoners Association and planted an avenue of commemorative trees on the Tocumwal Road to Strathmerton. After the war, land was allocated to 700 veterans. *Population 3130*

FESTIVALS Mexican Festival, October.

SHEPPARTON ■ 1194

Sherbourne Sheppard, an Irishman, took up Tallygaroopna ('river of big fish') Station in 1843 after it had been abandoned by Edward Khull. It was a vast area of almost 70 000 hectares. While Sheppard was in England in 1851, his run and stock were sold to pay off debts. His solicitor advised him that the agents had no right to sell his land and suggested he repossess the property, by force if necessary. Sheppard and a group of men chopped their way into the slab hut where the Swedish overseer and the station hands had taken refuge. They surrendered and what became known as the 'Siege of Tallygaroopna' was over. Sheppard's grandson, Dr Melville Sheppard, was the first Australian to be awarded the Lister Gold Medal for surgery.

Popular usage had turned Sheppardtown into Shepparton by 1855. An earlier name was McGuire's Punt – or MacGuire, Macguire, MacQuire, Macquire or Maguire!

The 1869 Land Grant Act introduced the principle of selection before survey and marked the end of the era of huge stations in the hands of the 'squattocracy'. 'Tallygaroopna' was broken up and Shepparton saw the growth of independent, smaller farmers. Gold was not found here but discoveries at nearby Whroo (see *Heathcote & Nagambie*) meant trade and, in time, tourists for the present town which became a city in 1949.

Shepparton has a long history of European migration. The British of course, came first, and an agricultural settlement of Jewish families, most of them from eastern Europe, was founded in April 1913. Macedonians set up market gardens in the 1920s and a contingent of Albanians arrived in the 1930s. After 1944, political conditions led more Albanians to emigrate – the Shepparton group is the largest in Australia – and Italians, Yugoslavs, Greeks and others came in great numbers after the Second World War.

Kerosene lamps on iron standards once illuminated the streets of Shepparton. They were lit by a lamplighter at sundown, and burned until the fuel ran out. In 1889, gas took over and finally in October 1913, the modern wonder of electricity was switched on. But that was not to be the end of it: in 1986, Shepparton proclaimed itself 'the solar city'. This district receives the highest recorded level of sunlight in Victoria – a daily average of more than seven hours. Many electrical installations are solar powered, including some street lighting, the heating system for the city's swimming pool and parking meters in the business district.

Shepparton also counts a number of radio 'firsts' to its credit. The first Radio Australia short-wave transmitters were here and broadcasts began in 1944; radio station manager and ham operator, Bruce Wilson, made the first outside contact with the devastated city of Darwin after Cyclone Tracey struck on Christmas Eve in 1974, and in 1988, the Goulburn Valley FM station became the first country FM-stereo broadcaster. The Shepparton district, with orchards and vegetable growing, vineyards, grain crops, dairying, beef cattle, sheep and pigs, is aptly called 'the food bowl of Victoria'. Irrigation began in 1912, increasing agricultural output as well as serving dairy farmers, and before long large canning factories were established.

Apricots from this Shepparton production line may go to sixty countries.

John Hare Furphy's 1873 iron foundry, now utilised in making food-processing equipment, is the oldest company in Shepparton. Furphy's metal-bodied water carts preceded irrigation and were later used in the First World War. An army camp rumour, spread by the cart drivers, became known as the 'furphy' which has slipped into common usage. The end of the tanks were stamped with improving slogans, the most famous of these being:

'Good, better, best,
Never let it rest,
Till your good is better,
And your better – best'.

John Furphy's brother, Joseph ('Tom Collins'), wrote *Such is Life* by lamplight at Shepparton. The unique Driver Education Centre of Australia which runs defensive-driving courses and trains drivers of ambulances, fire engines and freight vehicles is based here. *Population 30 510*

MOUNT MAJOR Scenic routes for cyclists and motorists lead out of Shepparton to Mount Major which is a 377-metre-high volcanic outcrop with a commanding view of the Strathbogie and Warby Ranges, Mount Buffalo and Dookie.

CANNING FACTORIES The valleys of the Murray–Goulburn system produce about seventy per cent of Australia's canned fruit. With the introduction of irrigation in 1912, agricultural production was given a great boost and several canning factories came into existence including the Shepparton Fruit Preserving Company (SPC) in 1917 and the Ardmona Fruit Producers Co-operative at Mooroopna in 1921. Work is seasonal and thousands of itinerant workers arrive in Shepparton for the January–February fruit-picking season. In late 1990, SPC staff made industrial history by accepting a cut in wages to preserve their jobs.

FESTIVALS Goulburn Valley Regional Games, November.

STRATHMERTON ■ 1195

Strathmerton grew up around a run established by Benjamin and Edward Boyd in 1841. They coined the name from 'strath' meaning 'valley and 'Merton', the name of their family home in Scotland. Nearby 'Coonanga' homestead, built of red-gum slabs in 1866, is on the Register of the National Estate. Close to Strathmerton, the Murray twists and turns with a beach on every bend. The rare trout cod, a close relative of the Murray cod, sometimes bites but cannot be taken because it is an endangered species but the patient angler may also haul in Murray cod, bream, yellowbelly, redfin and other fish.

TATURA ■ 1196

Tatura is probably from an Aboriginal word for 'a small lagoon'. From 1836 to 1870 the 'Dhurringile' run occupied the district – the station homestead, now a prison farm, is one of the largest ever built in Australia. The surrounding district was subdivided for farming in 1870.

Tatura, promoting itself as 'water wheel country,' is a small agricultural centre in a dairying and fruit-growing region with a reputation for fine tomatoes. The town has a butter factory, a tomato processing plant, a textile factory, engineering works, saleyards and an abattoir. In the nearby Irrigation Research Institute, scientists investigate new approaches to dealing with fresh and preserved fruit, soya beans, lucerne, tomatoes and other crops. In peach-growing circles, Tatura is respected for developing the V-shaped growing trellis.

During the Second World War, internment camps were established at Tatura to house passengers from the *Dunera* – a mixed company of Austrian and German Jewish refugees, Italian and German prisoners, Germans from Iran and elsewhere and Japanese family groups. In 1947, 913 of the refugees, known as the '*Dunera* boys' were still in Australia and most of them stayed to make significant cultural, academic and economic contributions to their new nation. A museum at Tatura displays photographic and written records of the internment period and the nearby German War Cemetery has 250 graves of prisoners and internees from the two world wars, tended by the War Graves Commission. Some remains were brought from other cemeteries and reburied here in 1958. When post-war immigration began in earnest, many Germans came to settle in the region. *Population 2780*

MERRIGUM Merrigum, site of the large Carnation Milk Products factory, is said to be an aboriginal word for 'little plain'. This name dates from 1875 but the settlement was also known for a time as Harrison.

TONGALA ■ 1197

'Tongala' was the name of the squatting run managed by Edward Curr for his father in the 1840s. The town grew up around a railway siding to the south of the property and is set in some of Victoria's richest farmland – largely a result of irrigation. Tongala has a long dairying history and boasts Victoria's biggest milk-processing plant, a subsidiary of the Nestlé company, the first product of which was the popular brand of condensed milk. *Population 1060*

FESTIVALS Tent Town Festival, March in even-numbered years.

Echuca & Cohuna

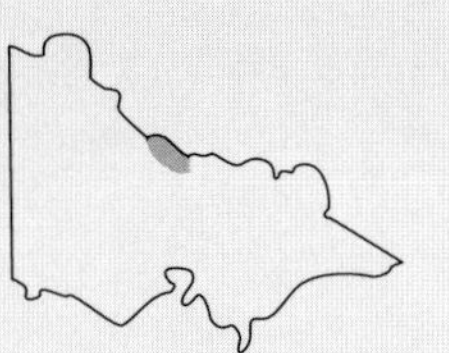

From the days when riverboats ruled the inland waterways, through the years of border squabbles and state customs duties, to the weirs and salinity problems of today's intensive irrigation, the mighty Murray and its tributaries have dominated this region where 'all the rivers run'.

BARHAM ■ 1198

Although it is on the New South Wales side of the border, Barham, like its sister town Koondrook (see entry) across the Murray, originally looked towards Melbourne rather than Sydney for its markets and development. Now best known for the citrus farms that surround it, for duck shooting and fishing, and for a complex of artifical lakes formed on a stretch of reclaimed land, Barham's history dates back to the 1840s.

When the squatter Edward Green arrived in the district in 1843 and took up his run, he named it after his wife's maiden name – Barham. Barham was, however, slower to develop than its twin, Koondrook, being on the 'wrong' side of the Murray, further from its main market and surrounded by a number of creeks and lagoons that hampered land transport. With the building of the Murray Bridge from Koondrook to Barham in 1904, the punt between the two towns became superfluous although the bridge was not without its teething problems. The central span of the bridge, lifted to allow riverboats to pass through, would sometimes jam, creating a queue of river and land transport...and a captive market for the local inns.

Transport of the district's citrus fruit, rice, wool and wheat by road is no longer a problem since the bridge span no longer lifts to allow paddle steamers to pass on their way up and down river. The town that was a 'slow starter' now has a higher population than its erstwhile larger sister, Koondrook. *Population 620*

KOONDROOK STATE FOREST Wholly within New South Wales, although the town from which it takes its name is on the Victorian side of the Murray, Koondrook State Forest is divided into two separate, but administratively amalgamated, forests – Koondrook and Perricoota.

The forest's river red gums, which require water to germinate, were able to take advantage of the ancient reshaping and rerouting of the Murray and Goulburn rivers that created the flood plain on which they now stand. Black box is the other major species within the forest but the remnants of a trial planting of pine trees during the Great Depression and an orange grove, the largest in Australia, planted in 1913, can also be seen.

The remains of an old steel barge, used to transport the timber to the sawmill, lies on the riverbed near the forest. Timber is now transported by road to the sawmill at Barham and the sawmill that stood within the forest in the 1950s and 1960s is no more.

COHUNA ■ 1199

Settled by squatters from the north side of the Murray in the early 1840s, Cohuna sits on Gunbower Creek (see entry), an anabranch of the Murray River. A bridge across the creek leads to the forests of Gunbower Island and the town has always been popular with fishermen for the variety of its fishing spots.

Cohuna, however, is even better known for its cows, which outnumber people – and possibly even the fish – having as it does the highest concentration of dairy cows per hectare of land in Australia. In addition to butter and cheese, an edible casein – the concentrated proteins from milk – was produced at the local factory for use by astronauts on the Apollo space program. But the name Cohuna also has an interna-

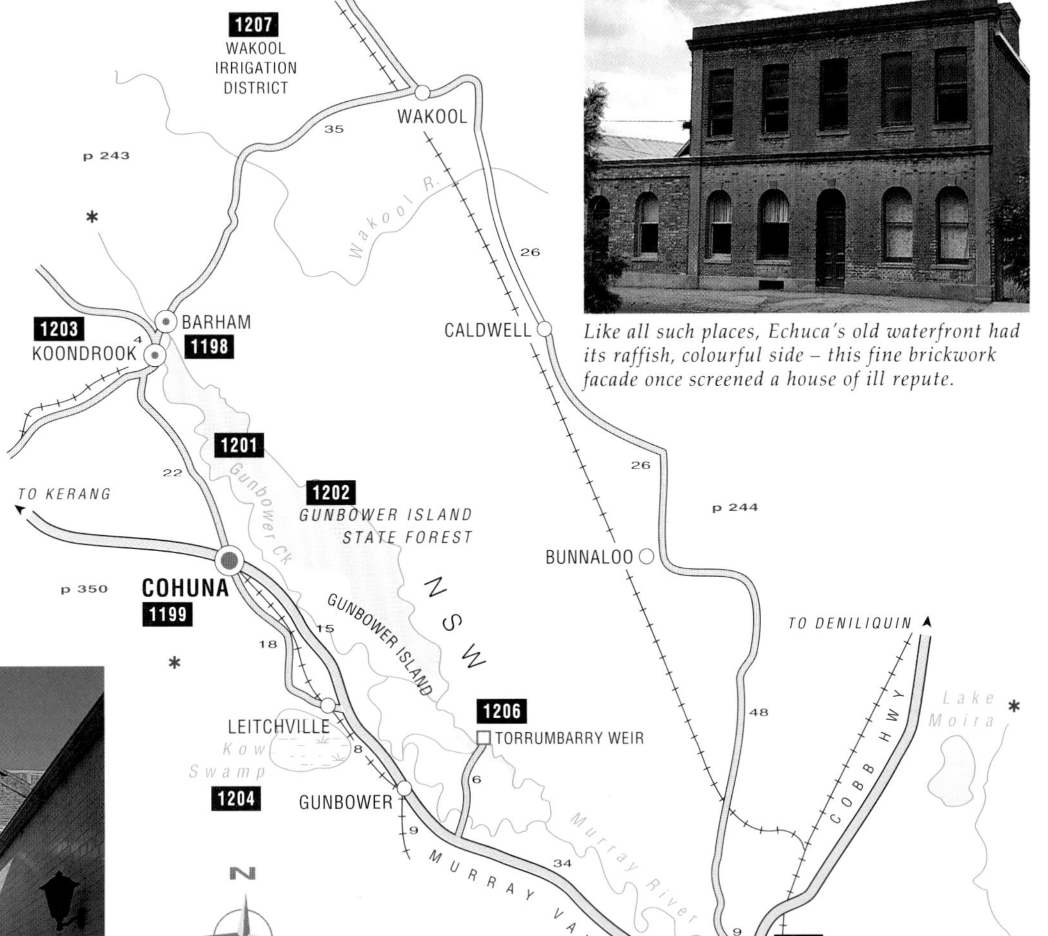

Like all such places, Echuca's old waterfront had its raffish, colourful side – this fine brickwork facade once screened a house of ill repute.

Echuca's bond store evokes the pre-Federation days when cross-Murray transactions were dutiable.

Echuca's red gum wharf has shrunk from its original one-kilometre length but the steamers still tie up by the railway line and the bond store (right).

tional association with prehistory since the first archaeological find at the nearby Kow Swamp (see entry) was dubbed the 'Cohuna Skull'.

Headworks at Cohuna were used for district irrigation before the building of the Torrumbarry Weir in the 1920s, and salinity, still a major problem in this region, was first apparent around Cohuna as early as 1911. *Population 2071*

FESTIVALS Cohuna Show, March.

ECHUCA ■ 1200

Echuca, surveyed and named in 1854 – from the Aboriginal word for 'meeting of water' – was originally known as Hopwood's Ferry after Henry Hopwood, former convict and police constable, who established a punt here in 1853. Hopwood controlled not only the punt and later a pontoon bridge but the first inn, a slab construction, which he replaced with his grand Bridge Hotel in 1859. These dual interests could be manipulated to his advantage – and to the disadvantage of James Maiden, his rival at Moama (see entry) on the other side of the Murray.

By closing the punt when it suited him, Hopwood could quite readily increase the takings at his bar as well as the demand for overnight accommodation at his hotel. But Hopwood was also an astute and determined lobbyist on Echuca's behalf, successfully persuading the Victorian government to make the town the terminus for the railway from Melbourne in 1864.

Wool and timber were exported by riverboat from Echuca from the 1850s and this shipping increased greatly after the railway came as much of the Riverina began to use Echuca as a port – the largest inland port in Australia and, in Victoria, second only to Melbourne. Within twenty years, however, the railway that had brought such large-scale development to Echuca was to contribute to its decline. As railway lines were extended to districts previously exporting through Echuca – partly because of rivalry, as each colony rushed to put in rail lines to connect wool areas with its own capital city – river trade began to decline.

As river trade dropped off, Echuca diversified from the staple products of wool, timber and leeches – for the British medical profession – to the processing of the produce of the surrounding district. Well-known brand names in the ham-canning and yoghurt and rice-processing industries are now based in Echuca together with clothing and knitting factories, a ball-bearing manufacturer and a cement pipeworks. All have played a role in keeping the town alive in the days since paddlesteamers and barges met at the Port of Echuca. A sense of the past is evoked in the town's historic buildings such as the lock-up (1867), customs house (1884), bond store (1859) and brothel – the only known former house of ill repute in Victoria to be classified by the National Trust – all still standing although with the passage of time none of them is still used for its original purpose. *Population 8410*

MUSEUMS The former police station and lock-up is now a museum exhibiting riverboat relics, including old charts, photographs…and cemetery records. The Alambee Auto and Folk Museum shelters more than thirty restored vehicles as well as pre-electric stoves, washing machines and other domestic appliances. The old bond store is now a wax museum.

WHARF The red-gum wharf at Echuca, built on three 'decks' in the 1860s to allow for changes in river level of up to ten metres, gradually fell into disrepair as the last of the riverboats left in the 1920s. In the 1940s, during a timber shortage, much of the wharf was stripped, but this process was reversed in the 1970s when restoration of the old port facilities began. Now only one-fifth of the one kilometre length that it was in its heyday, the red gum of the wharf is now grey with age but enjoying a second life as a major heritage and tourist attraction. The paddle wheelers *Pevensey*, star of the film *All the Rivers Run*, and the *Adelaide*, recommissioned by Prince Charles in 1985 and the second oldest paddle steamer still operating in the world, are tied up at the wharf.

FESTIVALS Jazz, Food & Wine Festival, February; Steam, Horse & Vintage Rally, June.

GUNBOWER CREEK ■ 1201

The name Gunbower Creek has nothing to do with guns – except in the duck shooting season – but comes from an Aboriginal word 'gambowra' thought to mean 'twisting'. The name is most appropriate since this anabranch, which leaves the Murray River just south of Torrumbarry Weir and rejoins it at Koondrook, follows a very twisted and tortuous path. A number of oxbow lakes or lagoons, now isolated from the main creek, occur at the frequent bends and the creek is forded or bridged at a number of points including Koondrook where the exotically named Condidorios Bridge spans its width.

GUNBOWER ISLAND STATE FOREST ■ 1202

With Gunbower Creek on one side and the Murray River on the other, Gunbower Island State Forest covers 20 000 hectares or 55 per cent of Gunbower Island, the remaining areas of the island being private land or public reserve. The box forest of the higher land gives way to one of Victoria's largest natural river red gum forests on low-lying land.

Driving and walking tracks crisscross the forest, home to a variety of native – and feral – fauna. In the early 1980s, an area of the wetlands of Gunbower Forest was listed as being of 'international importance'.

GUNBOWER ISLAND WILDLIFE SANCTUARY Almost half of the state forest has been declared a wildlife sanctuary, where native fauna such as kangaroos, emus and water birds – particularly ducks and quail – are protected from shooters. The sanctuary is one of the best known bird sanctuaries on the Murray with over 150 species having been sighted. In the breeding season, almost 1000 hectares of swamp within the sanctuary becomes a giant rookery.

KOONDROOK ■ **1203**

Although 192 kilometres by river from Echuca (see entry) but only 88 kilometres by road, it was the river and the river boats that were the mainstay of early Koondrook. The town developed on part of the 'Gannawarra' run, established in the 1840s, and became the centre of one of the largest redgum forest industries in Australia.

The end of the gold rush in the 1870s saw a number of settlers arriving in the district and, by the 1880s, local red gum was being used to build boats and paddle steamers at Koondrook. One of these early riverboats *Glimpse* (1886), later used as a sawmill boat at Arbuthnot's, the town's largest sawmill, still lies beneath the waters of the Murray just south of Koondrook. The paddle steamer *Melbourne*, built at Koondrook in 1914, still operates for tourists at Mildura and the *Alexander Arbuthnot* (1923) at Shepparton.

From 1889, Koondrook was indirectly linked to Melbourne via the Koondrook–Kerang tramway, a boost to its development not afforded to its sister town Barham (see entry), on the New South Wales side of the Murray River. As rail and road transport was modernised and irrigation systems developed, Koondrook was able to diversify and the town is now a centre for a number of horticultural and pastoral industries including vegetable and fruit packing, and butter and cheese manufacturing. *Population 620*

KOW SWAMP ■ **1204**

An ancient natural lake and now an artificial lake rather than a swamp, Kow Swamp is part of the Torrumbarry Irrigation system, used for off-river storage when the river is running high and as a supply reservoir for the system when irrigators' demands are at their peak. The swamp, up to three metres deep, attracts humans interested in watersports, as well as waterfowl but, since the late 1960s, the swamp has become world renowned for what it reveals about the past rather than what it offers in the present.

Around the eastern edge of Kow Swamp is a band of sand and silt from which the fossilised bones of forty men, women and children were unearthed in 1968 and 1969 – the largest burial site in the world of an era dating back 13 000 years. Radio-carbon dating suggests that the shoreline was occupied from that time until 9 500 years ago by a people whose facial and dental features were very different from the more fine-featured human remains found at Lake Mungo (see *Hillston & Ivanhoe*). Why two such very different peoples should have lived at the same time and with no obvious geographical barriers separating them is a fascinating mystery to archaeologists and anthropologists. This mystery and the amount of information on burial rites and customs that can be gleaned from the skeletal remains and quartz artefacts, have led scientists to enthusiastically declare Kow Swamp one of the most significant and exciting archaeological discoveries in recent times.

MOAMA ■ **1205**

At a crossing place on the main stock route to Melbourne, where the banks of the Murray sloped at a convenient angle, James Maiden established a punt in 1845 – eight years before his competitor and rival Henry Hopwood set up his punt on the other side of the Murray at Echuca (see entry). In 1851, Maiden's Punt officially became Moama, from the Aboriginal word 'moamay' meaning 'place of the dead' because of the burial sites in the sandhills around the settlement.

Perhaps the name had some bearing on the lack of success that Maiden and Moama had in their fierce competition with Hopwood and Echuca. There is some suggestion that the two men were known to each other before arriving on opposite banks of the Murray since Maiden was sentenced at Lent in England for burglary on the same date that Hopwood was sentenced for receiving stolen silk and their crimes may have been related. The end of the gold rush, however, brought a huge reduction in the price of the cattle, failure to Maiden and an end to the competition between the two men. As Echuca developed into a major port and railhead, Moama declined.

The New South Wales Government, hoping to gain an advantage from the increased traffic to and from the railhead at Echuca, raised its previously minimal customs duties and established a customs house at Moama in the months before the railway opened; rivalry was to characterise the relationship between the two settlements until federation. There were often squabbles over who was responsibile for bodies found in the river, depending on which bank they fell – or jumped – in from. There were legal arguments over which court house should hear a case including the classic but highly apocryphal case of a dog, kicked, so it was said, on the New South Wales side of the border but landing with most of its body on the Victorian bank. Moama's two-storey brick court house dates from these quarrelsome days. Even the 1878 bridge between Moama and Echuca caused problems since iron for the bridge was cast in Melbourne but had to be taken into New South Wales to build the northern supports of the bridge. Much time was spent by engineers and builders in Echuca trying to find a way to get the iron across the border without paying customs duty and much time was spent at Moama completing the paperwork for every dutiable piece of iron. Eventually, New South Wales refused to pay its share of the cost of building the bridge and the residents of Moama had to continue using the punt until the matter was settled.

Rivalry between the sister towns has become a thing of the past and Echuca–Moama is now the 'married' name by which the towns are known. At the restored slipway at Moama, old paddle steamers and barges are repaired and restored before being sent across to the wharf at Echuca. *Population 3220*

TORRUMBARRY WEIR ■ **1206**

Torrumbarry Weir and Lock 26 is the highest of the thirteen combined weirs and locks between Yarrawonga Weir and the mouth of the Murray – 1600 kilometres downstream. Built between 1919 and 1923 to control the level of the Murray upstream from Echuca for the benefit of river traffic and irrigators, the weir has become increasingly important for irrigation since it was opened in 1924...and far less important for steamers as modern river traffic is mainly restricted to pleasure craft.

Experiments with irrigation from the Torrumbarry Weir waters stretch back to the 1880s when David Chrystal, the owner of the 'Torrumbarry' run, began irrigating his land directly from the river. Later owners used the watercourses of Gunbower Creek and Kow Swamp combined with channels dug by horse-drawn scoops and pumps to water their land. Nowadays, the weir diverts water, by means of gravity rather than pumps, into the National Channel and from there into the complex distribution network of natural or artificial channels and lakes that supply water for the intensive dairy farming around Cohuna (see entry), mixed farming around Kerang and fruit and vegetable growing around Swan Hill (see *Swan Hill & Kerang*).

The weir provides deep, snag-free water for water sports upstream to Koondrook and the history of its river banks begins with a still visible Aboriginal canoe tree.

WAKOOL IRRIGATION DISTRICT ■ **1207**

The Wakool Irrigation District covers 200 000 hectares where rice, vegetable, fodder and pasture crops are grown and is one of four important irrigation regions on the Riverina plains. Water is diverted to the region from Stevens Weir on the Edward River, the largest anabranch of which is the Wakool River, itself the largest anabranch of the Murray River. Supplemented by water from the Mulwala Canal, Wakool Irrigation District has been transformed into one of Australia's major rice-growing areas. Its success is confirmed by the large rice-storage complex at Burraboi village, just north of Wakool.

North-west of the village of Wakool, the administrative centre for the irrigation district, there are huge evaporation ponds on both sides of the road. Like most other irrigation districts drawing on the waters of the Murray–Darling Basin, Wakool has a constant and escalating problem of shallow water tables and consequent salination of farmland. In an attempt to counteract the problem, underground water is being pumped to the surface at evaporation ponds such as these to combat the problems created by years of intensive irrigation (see *Berri & Renmark*).

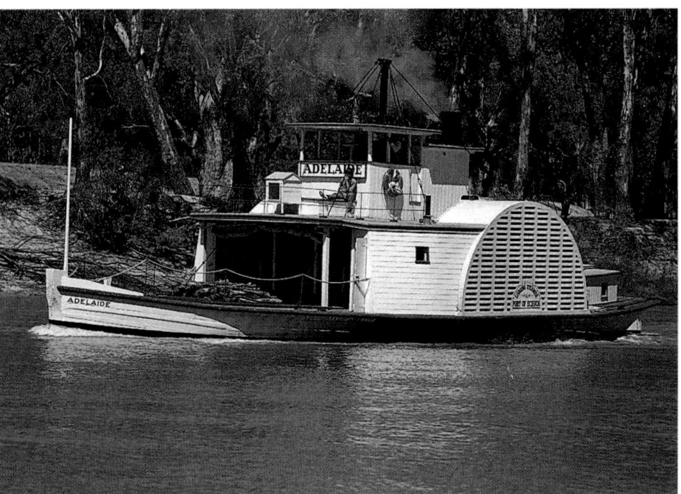

The strength of the Adelaide, *now retired, was its strength – it carried no cargo but pulled mighty loads of wool and timber to Echuca.*

MURRAY & MURRUMBIDGEE RIVERS

Two large rivers, draining from the only mountain range of any note on the world's driest continent, provide a precious lifeblood which greens the food bowls of three states.

About a third of the way along the Murray, near Echuca, a great flood plain supports Australia's largest river red gum forest; the armoured Murray crayfish also lives here.

Both the rivers which water eastern Australia's biggest irrigation food bowls rise in the Snowy Mountains between Canberra and the New South Wales–Victoria border. They wander apart, or parallel, for thousands of kilometres then join and complete their journey through South Australia to Lake Alexandrina and the sea, following a topography dictated by geology.

Or perhaps mythology…according to an Aboriginal Dreamtime legend, a man who chased a giant cod down the Murray River sang the waterway into existence and, when he caught the cod at the Murray mouth, man and fish fought so violently that their massive splashings formed Lake Alexandrina, Lake Albert and the Coorong.

The Murray once provided a home and food source for many Aboriginal peoples and there are still Aboriginal communities living along the river, such as the Yorta Yorta who have established a cultural unit and visitor education at their Dharnya Centre in the Barmah forest (see picture, below). Aboriginal shellfish middens and other food mounds, artefacts, burial sites and scarred trees where bark has been taken for shield, canoe or coolamon tell the story of Aboriginal life all along the Murray.

With the Darling, these two rivers drain a region of more than 1 063 000 square kilometres in inland Queensland, New South Wales, Victoria, the Australian Capital Territory and South Australia – about fourteen per cent of the continent or an area twice the size of France. This is the Murray–Darling Basin, one of the most significant agricultural areas in Australia.

This huge depression is a closed basin which means that *all* drainage from it will eventually, at some point, finish in the Murray, a fact central to coming to grips with the problems of salinity and pollution which have been linked to clearing of vegetation, irrigation and land use. Most of South Australia's population depends upon the Murray for domestic or industrial water.

Near its source in Victoria's alps, the Murray is a rushing, youthful stream eager for a long journey.

Commercial fishing still takes place on both rivers, the main catches being golden perch or yellowbelly while the famous Murray cod – which has been recorded at over 100 kilograms and almost 2 metres in length – is now an infrequent prize due to overfishing and the spread of European carp. The rivers, their billabongs, banks and fringing plains form a natural corridor through semi-arid country and support reptiles, mammals, crustaceans – yabbies and the Murray crayfish – fish and millions of birds. Away from the mountains and the forest's trim along the banks, the countryside is flat and, where not irrigated or flooded, semi-arid. For most of its length the waters of the Murray are technically in New South Wales; it is the southern bank which forms the border with Victoria and until recently it was necessary for Victorian anglers to have a New South Wales licence!

The Murray River – the River Murray in South Australia – is more than 2500 kilometres long and for much of its length is lined with river red gums; it forms a scene that has almost become an Australian cliché, where people boat, swim, fish or, gentled by sun, dream while the river moves quietly and red gums weep and an egret, or perhaps a heron, stands silent vigil. But this is only one picture of a river which, with a catchment largely stripped of trees – and dammed and locked along its length – is strictly regulated from its source, where it generates hydro-electric power, to its mouth where barrages prevent seawater from entering. Irrigation and other needs make demands in between on this slow journey – like most inland rivers the Murray takes its time and water may take three months to travel from source to mouth. At Mildura, it falls only fifty millimetres for each kilometre it flows; near the sea the fall is as little as sixteen millimetres to the kilometre.

The Murrumbidgee flows for 2160 kilometres from the Great Dividing Range, where its waters are diverted through the Snowy Mountains Scheme, to its junction with the Murray near Balranald. To its north, the river greens its famous irrigation area generously to produce a cornucopia of crops. West of Hay, the Lachlan River joins the Murrumbidgee which then disgorges into the Murray, sometimes strongly and swiftly, as Sturt found in 1830 when he recorded; 'Such was the force with which we had been shot out of the Morumbidgee that we were carried nearly to the bank opposite…' □

The scarlet robin brings a daring flash of vermilion to the Murray's olive and brown woodlands.

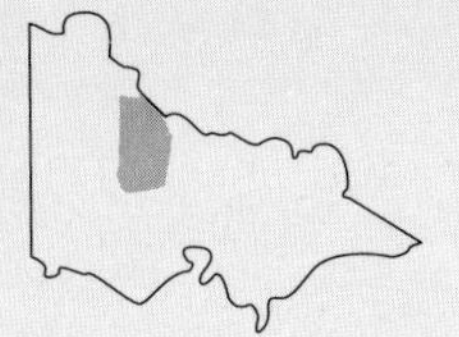

Swan Hill & Kerang

On the edge of the Mallee, as in other regions of dry-land farming, irrigation is both lifeblood and liability – soil salinity is an ever-present concern. In contrast, the Kerang wetlands are home to thousands of water birds and a playground for water sports enthusiasts.

BOORT ■ 1208

Boort is the centre of a large wheat- and wool-growing area, built beside a lake also called Boort, both after the Aboriginal word for 'smoke'. Bald Hill, where the town now stands, is believed to have been a smoke-signalling site for the Aborigines. The Boort region was settled 1843 but the town on Kinnypaniel Creek was not established until after 1870. It shifted to its present site when the railway came through in 1883. The 27 000-tonne wheat silo where harvested grain awaits transport south is a prominent landmark.

Lake Boort, sometimes called 'the Oasis of the North', is known for its prolific bird life. The road around it leads to a fauna park and the sites of Aboriginal relics. *Population 800*

KANGAROO LAKE ■ 1209

This freshwater lake is the biggest in the region and the fishing for redfin and yellowbelly is reputed to be particularly good. It is also a popular place for yachting. Gorton Drive skirts the lake and is flanked by large, graceful jacaranda trees which are said to have been planted by the father of former Prime Minister John Gorton. In spring, wildflowers colour the lake region purple and mauve.

KERANG ■ 1210

Kerang is built on the edge of a chain of wetlands taking in more than fifty lakes and swamps so it is appropriate that the town's symbol is a flying ibis. Every spring, thousands of ibis, egrets, spoonbills and herons return to the wetlands to breed. These migratory bird species are protected under international agreements between Australia, China and Japan.

At certain times of the day, the waterways are a cacophony of chatter and flapping wings – all of which can be observed from hides constructed in strategic places – particularly useful for photographers to capture the dawn ibis flight…or to watch them return at dusk, in spectacular V-shaped formations, to their nests on Second (Middle) Reedy Lake and Hirds Swamp. There are three species: the straw-necked, found only in Australia; the white ibis and the rarer glossy ibis. They are related to the sacred ibis of ancient Egypt – worshipped for its habit of devouring crop ravaging locusts.

Scientists have estimated that the 200 000 ibis, in residence from August to April on Second Reedy Lake, daily eat more than five tonnes of insects that would otherwise be eating the surrounding crops. Fourteen known species of native fish and many other birds inhabit the wetlands.

That indefatigable explorer, Major Thomas Mitchell, reached Kerang in 1836 but it was nine years before squatters followed with sheep and cattle. In 1857, Woodford Patchell set up a farm and pumped water from the Loddon River. Today's pastoral and agricultural supplies come from the Torrumbarry Weir on the Murray River (see *Echuca & Moama*) to water fat lambs, beef cattle, oil seed and lucerne crops. In 1863, Patchell managed an inn by the Loddon which became the nucleus of today's town.

The area shares a major problem with soil salinity with most of the irrigated lands of northern Victoria and southern New South Wales (see *Berri & Renmark*). The Kerang-Swan Hill Salinity Management Group is working on long-term strategies to ease the problem. *Population 4020*

LEAGHUR FOREST PARK This nearby forest of black box contains tree trunks which bear scars where the

Ibis at Reedy Lake, near Kerang, go about their business unaware that peeping toms with binoculars are watching them from the comfort of a hide on a rise at the lake's edge.

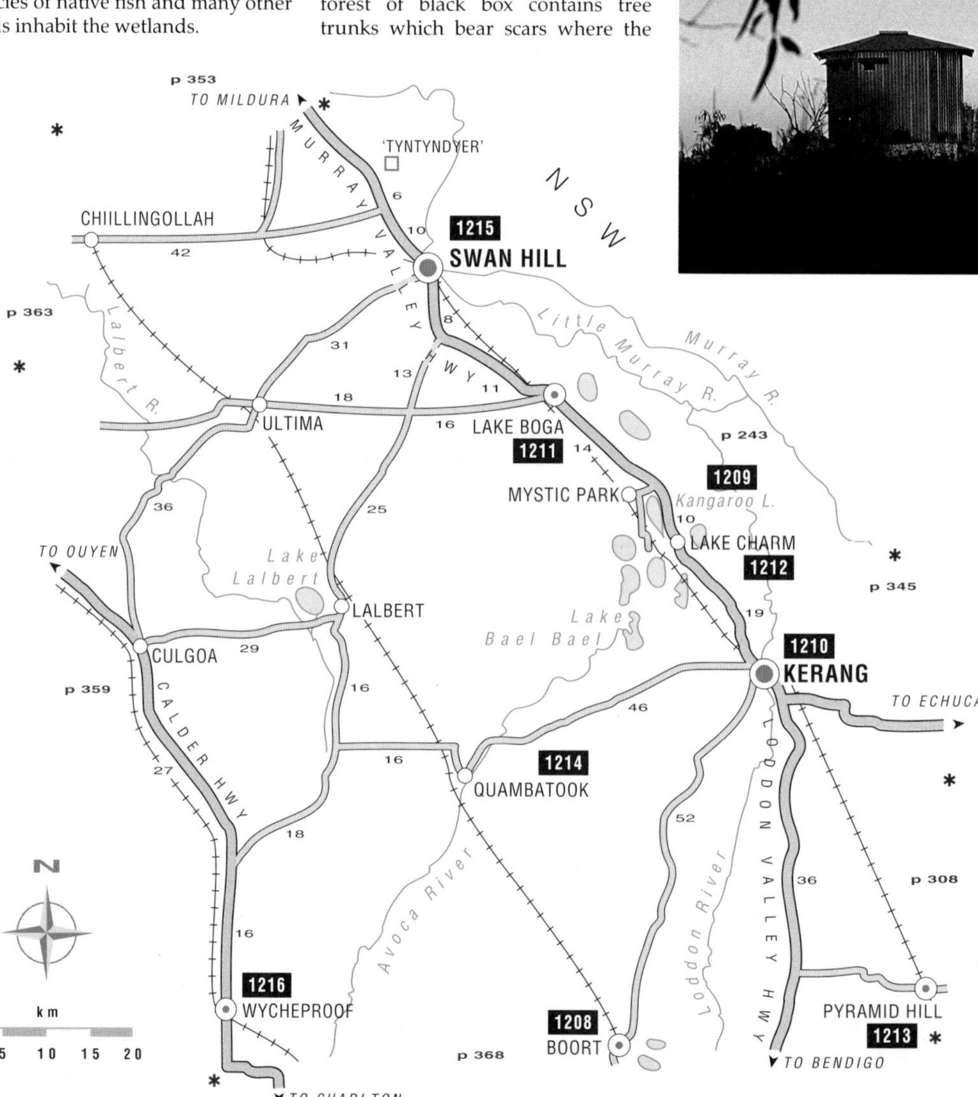

Aborigines removed bark to make canoes, shields and shelters. Steel-blade cuts on the trees show where the pioneers rested their busy axes.

LAKE BOGA ■ 1211

Lake Boga township in Swan Hill shire is the centre of a dairying, citrus fruit, cereal, and vineyard region. 'Boga' is an Aboriginal word said to mean 'big' and the broad, deepwater lake on the north-western edge of the Kerang wetlands gave the town its name.

According to Aboriginal legend a very large gum tree once grew on an island in the lake. A woman was sunning her baby on the shore when an eagle-hawk swooped down and carried the child to the island. The curlews wailed mournfully in sympathy with the mother's cries. An elder ordered the people to cut the gum trees along the shore into little pieces and throw them into the Murray and he cursed the shores of the lake – no trees have grown there since and the curlews still cry.

During the Second World War, Lake Boga was the RAAF's principal inland flying-boat base. A restored Catalina flying boat is there still. Jet skiing, waterskiing, sailing, windsurfing and para-sailing are all popular on the lake and there are scenic drives and horse-riding trails around its perimeter.

LAKE CHARM ■ 1212

The small township of Lake Charm is in the heart of the Kerang lakes area and is surrounded by agricultural land where farmers concentrate on dairy cattle and citrus fruits. Like Lake Boga, it caters to the needs of holiday-makers who come to its nearby lake for swimming, boating, waterskiing and fishing. Keen and discriminating anglers seek out the many backwaters away from the most readily accessible shoreline .

PYRAMID HILL ■ 1213

This township took its name from the tall, rocky mound – now surrounded by a golf course – labelled by Sir Thomas Mitchell and which overlooks it. The surrounding countryside is occupied mainly by stud farms and merino sheep runs. The novelist, Katharine Susannah Prichard, stayed here for a time during the First World War; her brother was a doctor in the district and she used one of his patients, a girl circus rider who had broken her back, as the model for the character 'Gina' in *Haxby's Circus*. *Population 540*

QUAMBATOOK ■ 1214

Quambatook is a small township on the Avoca River serving the district's agricultural community which distinguishes itself by hosting one of Australia's most unusual annual competitions. Modified tractors with high-powered engines come together in a battle of the giants as they compete to pull a sled weighted with 14 tonnes along a 100-metre track. The town name is from an Abo-riginal word thought to mean 'camp near water'.

FESTIVALS Australian Tractor Pull Championships, Easter Saturday.

SWAN HILL ■ 1215

Long before Sir Thomas Mitchell was kept awake all night by raucous swans, this place was part of a busy Aboriginal hunting ground. In June 1836, Mitchell noted that the nocturnal bird sounds were his reason for naming 'this somewhat remarkable and isolated feature, Swan-hill'. The town is on the Murray River on the eastern fringe of the Mallee district. It is surrounded by irrigated land producing maize, fodder crops, stone and citrus fruits and grapes. The shire of Swan Hill, with an area of 6500 square kilometres, is the largest wheat-producing municipality in Victoria. Dairy cattle, sheep and fat lambs and angora goats are raised and a large pheasant farm sends pheasants and guinea-fowl to restaurants all over Australia.

'Tyntyndyer' and 'Murray Downs' were taken up by graziers in the late 1840s. In 1847, a large punt started crossing the Murray near the site of the present bridge and remained in use until 1896. The railway arrived in 1890. Swan Hill became a city in 1965 and is now market centre for part of the southern Riverina district. There are large stock saleyards and farm machinery and polystyrene packing cases are manufactured locally. There is a memorial horse trough in Curlewis Street with a little dog trough beside it – a reminder of local philanthropist George Bills, who died in 1928. Mr Bills, who made his money patenting machinery to weave mattresses, loved animals and left his money to set up drinking troughs throughout the countries of the British Empire. Many were allotted to the Mallee towns of Swan Hill shire: Swan Hill, Chillingollah, Chinkapook, Waitchie, Robinvale, Ultima and Manangatang – where, according to legend, a rabbit was the first to slake its thirst. *Population 9360*

SWAN HILL PIONEER SETTLEMENT This open-air museum on Horseshoe Bend near Swan Hill is a working, nineteenth-century riverside settlement in re-creation. It shows the lifestyle of the riverland pioneers.

TYNTYNDYER HOMESTEAD Andrew and Peter Beveridge arrived with 350 head of cattle and built the original two-room log cabin in 1846. It was later bricked around – the first of a long and continuing line of brick veneer buildings in Australia – and became part of the larger homestead (1854) which is now classified by the National Trust. The rooms are furnished with items from the squatting era and Aboriginal artefacts are displayed in the old wine cellar. 'Tyntyndyer' is said to be an Aboriginal word for 'song of the birds'.

MURRAY DOWNS HOMESTEAD This station was probably established in 1839 by John Hawden, nephew of the famous overlander, Joseph Hawden. In 1860, Burke and Wills passed through and left a sick camel here. The homestead and its formal gardens were established by Suetonius and Charles Officer in 1866. Suetonius was a pioneer irrigator, using steam engines to pump water to his citrus groves. Murray Downs was self-supporting with its own chapel, bakery, blacksmith and, of course, shearers, drovers and rabbit and kangaroo trappers. The mansion was extended in 1888–91 by the new owners, Charles Campbell and Alfred Felton. Felton bought many works of art for the home and made a generous bequest to the National Gallery of Victoria. After 150 years, sheep, cattle and wheat are still the main business here.

WYCHEPROOF ■ 1216

The name is thought to come from two Aboriginal words: 'witchi' meaning 'rushes' and 'poorp' meaning 'head' – rushes that grow on a hilltop. Wycheproof proper has an unexpected traffic hazard: trains still run down the centre of the main street, the result of a government cost-cutting measure to save buying extra land for the railway line.

Mount Wycheproof is only forty-three metres above sea level and is registered as the smallest 'mountain' in the world. On the south side of town, Willandra Farm Museum houses a permanent exhibition of horse-drawn farm machinery and historical memorabilia. The museum, which is open on weekends and by appointment during the week, includes a rare example of a pioneer's slab hut with its original stringybark roof. *Population 780*

Murray Downs' 1860s homestead nowadays shares the architectural spotlight with a sleek golf and country club.

RIVER BOATS: THE PADDLE WHEEL TURNS FULL CIRCLE

THE FIRST person to travel the waters of the continent's largest river was the explorer Charles Sturt. In 1830, Sturt's whaleboat was pitched from the Murrumbidgee into the Murray River and he followed the waterway to the sea. Although the river was clearly navigable by shallow-draught boats, it was twenty years before steam-driven cargo vessels began to serve the squatting runs which had been taken up on both sides of the Murray since Sturt's pioneering explorations.

The P.S. Pyap *still steams regularly from the wharf at Swan Hill.*

In 1851, the South Australian government offered a 2000 pound sterling reward for the first two iron steamers of certain specifications to navigate from Goolwa to the Murray's junction with the Darling River – about 900 kilometres. The first two paddle steamers went further than required and raced all the way to Swan Hill in 1853. The *Lady Augusta* was skippered by Francis Cadell and the *Mary Ann* by William Randell. The trail-blazing *Lady Augusta* arrived just hours before her rival and soon after turned back to Goolwa. Randell went on to Moama. The *Mary Ann* did not qualify for a prize because she was too small but was consoled with 750 pounds sterling.

Sawmills near Echuca used tough little steamers like the Edwards *to tow giant red gum logs from the riverbank forests of the upper Murray.*

There were few tracks and no roads which went as deep into the hinterland as the highway of the rivers, and enterprising businessmen, particularly in South Australia, saw that money was to be made. The river boats and barges were more economical than bullock wagons and could manage heavier, bulkier loads such as machinery and roofing iron. They made it possible for fragile luxuries such as window glass and pianos to be transported inland without being shaken to pieces. Passengers too appreciated the smoother ride. Hides, tallow, chaff and wool bales were sent out from the riverside wharves. Wool from the Riverina and stations in the outback areas was 'imported' into Victoria from New South Wales and South Australia.

The hard-living steamer crews were not necessarily always experienced boatmen – station hands and swagmen were sometimes taken on too. The men took turns on six-hour shifts and slept in tiny bunks in the prow. Beer casks were often part of the cargo and no self-respecting barge-hand was without a gimlet and straw to siphon off a mugful or two for his own refreshment. By the 1860s, a regular navigation season was recognised, from about April to November, and the paddle steamers lay idle during the dry summer months.

Navigation was always tricky because the river levels fluctuated so much – when the water was low the boats might have to be hand winched from tree to tree. At times, the tops of the banks might be ten metres above the deck, sometimes they disappeared altogether in flood waters. Old chart notations indicate some of the river obstacles: 'bitch and pups', 'snaggy corner', 'rocks 2 feet under', 'clay bars in the bights'.

The heart of the river boat era was the Echuca–Swan Hill stretch where business was always brisk. By 1860, there were seventeen steamers churning up and down and trade peaked in the 1870s. At the beginning of this century, Echuca was Australia's largest inland port (see *Echuca & Cohuna*) but already the trade was declining. The railways were coming into their own and had a dramatic effect on the river ports. By 1910, the Echuca authorities had ceased to keep records of craft movements.

In the 1980s, some old vessels came back to ply a different trade – tourism. The moored museum boats at Echuca and Swan Hill evoke the bygone days and the P.S. *Pyap*, also at Swan Hill, takes visitors to Murray Downs Station twice a day. From Mildura, passenger boats ply the inland waters of the north-west on the same route as the early settlers. The new steamer *Cumberoona*, built at Albury in 1986, is modelled closely on traditional lines – the original *Cumberoona* was built in Echuca in 1866. □

The Lady Augusta *loads up at Mannum in 1864, 11 years after she won the pioneering race to Swan Hill.*

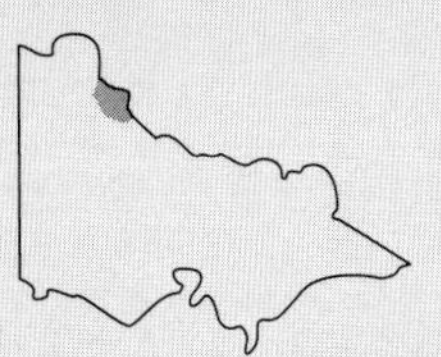

Robinvale & Nyah West

Land had to be cleared before early settlers could plant their crops, and the Mallee roller became as ubiquitous in this region as the flies and the dust. Drought and bad seasons nearly beat diggers repatriated here after the First World War, but irrigation schemes have brought to life an important wine and dried-fruit producing area.

EUSTON ■ 1217

Edmund Morey, a confident seventeen-year-old native-born Australian, squatted here on the 'Boomiaricool' run in 1846. He showed great initiative, for 'Boomiaricool' then marked the western limit of colonisation in New South Wales. Later, he purchased a portion of the Boomiaricool Station, called Euston Station. Over the years this property grew and when it was subdivided in 1946, the station had expanded to take in more than 26 000 hectares.

James Spittle and A.G. Woodhead tossed a coin to decide which half of the original station they would get. Spittle won the toss and acquired the land closest to the town of Euston – along with the two family homesteads, built sixty years apart – and Woodhead acquired the section near Lake Benanee.

Euston was a busy river port from 1850 to the turn of the century, with a large wharf and its own river ferry. There was a eucalyptus factory, boiling-down works, a wool-scouring plant, a court house with whipping post – now at the Wentworth Museum – police station and hotel. At Euston Station, 45 000 merino sheep were shorn during one season and, when shearing machines were introduced, the Euston shed installed six stands. The town declined when the river traffic began to be replaced by rail, and later road transport.

A new bridge, a railway line – that was used intermittently and then only to preserve the railway agreement between states – and a new lock on the Murray River did however give the town a new lease of life.

EUSTON WEIR At Euston Weir, fish jump their way up the fish ladder to higher water levels. The weir is surrounded by landscaped gardens and is a popular picnic spot. Water is pumped from the lock to irrigation settlements in Euston and Robinvale.

MANANGATANG ■ 1218

Manangatang comes from 'manang', an Aboriginal word for 'land' and 'kaatin', meaning 'water', possibly referring to a waterhole to the north of the present township. A Mr A.T. Creswick of the Bumbang Station had a hut built near the waterhole for his stockmen. The waterhole lies on the line of an old track, one of many used by wild animals, the Aborigines and perhaps the squatter's men, as these tracks are recorded on maps of the time.

Settlers first took up land in the Manangatang district around 1911. The 'bush' of mallee eucalypts was tamed with the 'mallee roller', a large round log or old boiler drawn by horse or bullock teams, which flattened everything in its path. The best time to roll the mallee was during the winter, in June or July, as the trees invariably grew back when rolled in the warmer months. Any

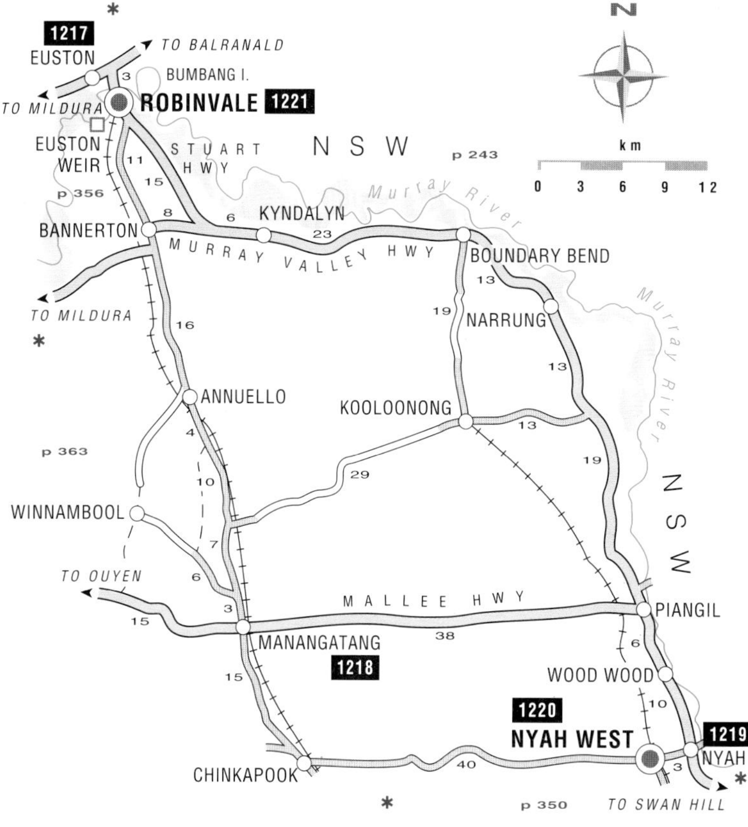

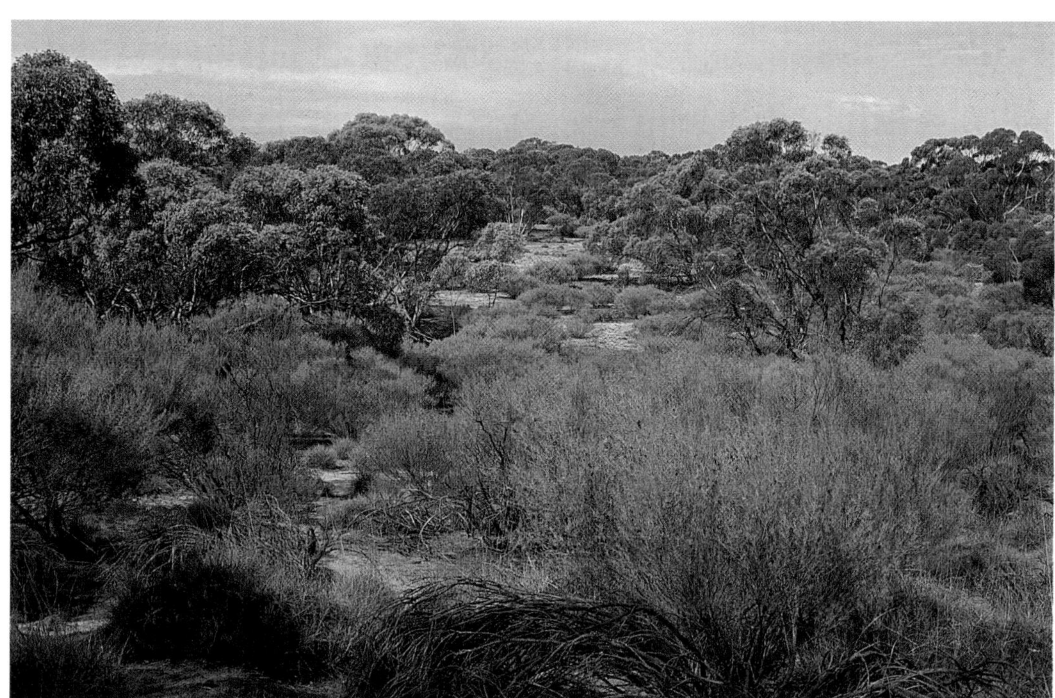
The pre-irrigation landscape around Robinvale was much like this scrubland at nearby Wandown Nature Reserve.

The enormous vacuum 'cleaner' supported by this scaffolding sucks grain into a Robinvale silo.

scrub remaining after rolling was burnt off before the first crops of wheat were planted.

Rolling started around 1908 in the Manangatang district in expectation of the settlers' arrival, and surveyed blocks were available by 1911. Town allotments were sold for between fifteen and thirty pounds sterling. The first wheat grown in Manangatang was delivered to Chillingollah Station after the 1911–12 harvest. The waggon drivers carried metal tanks on top of the wheat and brought back water on their return trip.

Many returned soldiers from the First World War took up land north of Manangatang under the Soldier Resettlement Scheme and, like the early pioneers, found the going tough, particularly in the dry years. But by the 1920s, Manangatang had changed from a canvas town to a busy commercial centre with general stores, bakers, butchers, greengrocers and an auctioneer.

A succession of bad seasons and falling world prices resulted in the establishment of the Farmers' Debt Adjustment Board in 1935. The board gave cash to creditors to the value of the farmers' assets. The farmer then had to pay over an extended period of time the amount funded by the board. Another cruel run of bad seasons, from 1938 to 1941, prompted many struggling farmers to leave the land for good, despite these assistance programs.

About this time, the Victorian government contemplated declaring the district closed to agriculture, such were the difficulties encountered by farmers over the years in what was considered by many experts to be 'marginal' land. It was finally decided under the West Mallee Settlement Areas Act to lease land to farmers north of the Manangatang–Ouyen road, and wipe all other debts to the government. Today, Manangatang is still a wheat-growing area.

NYAH ■ 1219

The Surveyor-General, Major Thomas Mitchell, led an exploration party through this district in 1836 and the tough breed of long-distance stockmen who came to be known as 'overlanders' followed his path along the Murray River in the opposite direction, when droving stock to Adelaide the same year. Among the early settlers were the Beveridge brothers who took up land here in 1846. They sold their interest to George Holloway in 1876.

The town, first named Tyntynder, was surveyed in 1892, but was renamed Nyah just two years later. Coaches carrying passengers and mail travelled through the district as early as 1860, and Nyah later became a changing station for horses.

A settlement scheme for unemployed people was started around 1893 by Sir John McIntyre, member of the Legislative Assembly for the district. He persuaded the government to subdivide blocks of land with a river frontage into 40-hectare lots to encourage more people to settle here. Later, these lots were again sub-divided into smaller, 20-hectare blocks. Leasing fees amounted to twelve shillings and eightpence for six months, on the condition that all buildings and fencing were maintained in good condition.

The relatively infertile land was difficult to farm effectively and rainfall was so irregular that water shortage was always a problem so an irrigation scheme to pump water from the Murray River was started by these pioneers in 1902. A timber-lined tunnel was built from the Murray to a twenty-one-metre-deep well at Cant's Corner, but the horse-driven pump proved ineffective. The government later installed a pump and the town had a reticulated water supply before the First World War.

Drought conditions were particularly severe from 1902 onwards and many settlers were forced to draw water from the Murray River. Many of them were to spend their time carting water in the years that followed. Probably the worst drought on record was in 1914 when the Murray ceased to flow. The Hume Weir now safeguards the water supply for irrigation in the Nyah region.

'Nyah' derives from an Aboriginal word thought to mean 'bend in the river'. The district's early pioneers called the town's location Nyah's Bend all their lives.

NYAH WEST ■ 1220

This town was known as Nyah Rail for many years until the townsfolk changed its name to Nyah West. It was first surveyed in 1914 and the first train passed through in May 1915, on its way to Piangil where the opening and celebrations were held. There was great bitterness about the route of the railway line, with the farmers winning in the end because they were the people who would be providing wheat and other goods to be transported to Melbourne.

In 1912, the area which was to become a township was still covered with mallee eucalypts and had to be cleared. There were few settlers in the district but when the rail line was built, many families had gathered there and a little store, known as Harvey's Store was built. The town is now larger than the Nyah proper township. *Population 535*

ROBINVALE ■ 1221

Scarred canoe trees and middens on Bumbang Island are clear evidence that Aborigines hunted on the banks of the Murray River and it is thought that corroborees were held regularly in the vicinity of present-day Robinvale. The Bumbang Station was first taken up in 1847 by the pioneer settler, John Grant and then sold to A.J. Creswick at the turn of the century, for large-scale wheat growing.

The town's founder, Herbert Cuttle, purchased one square mile of

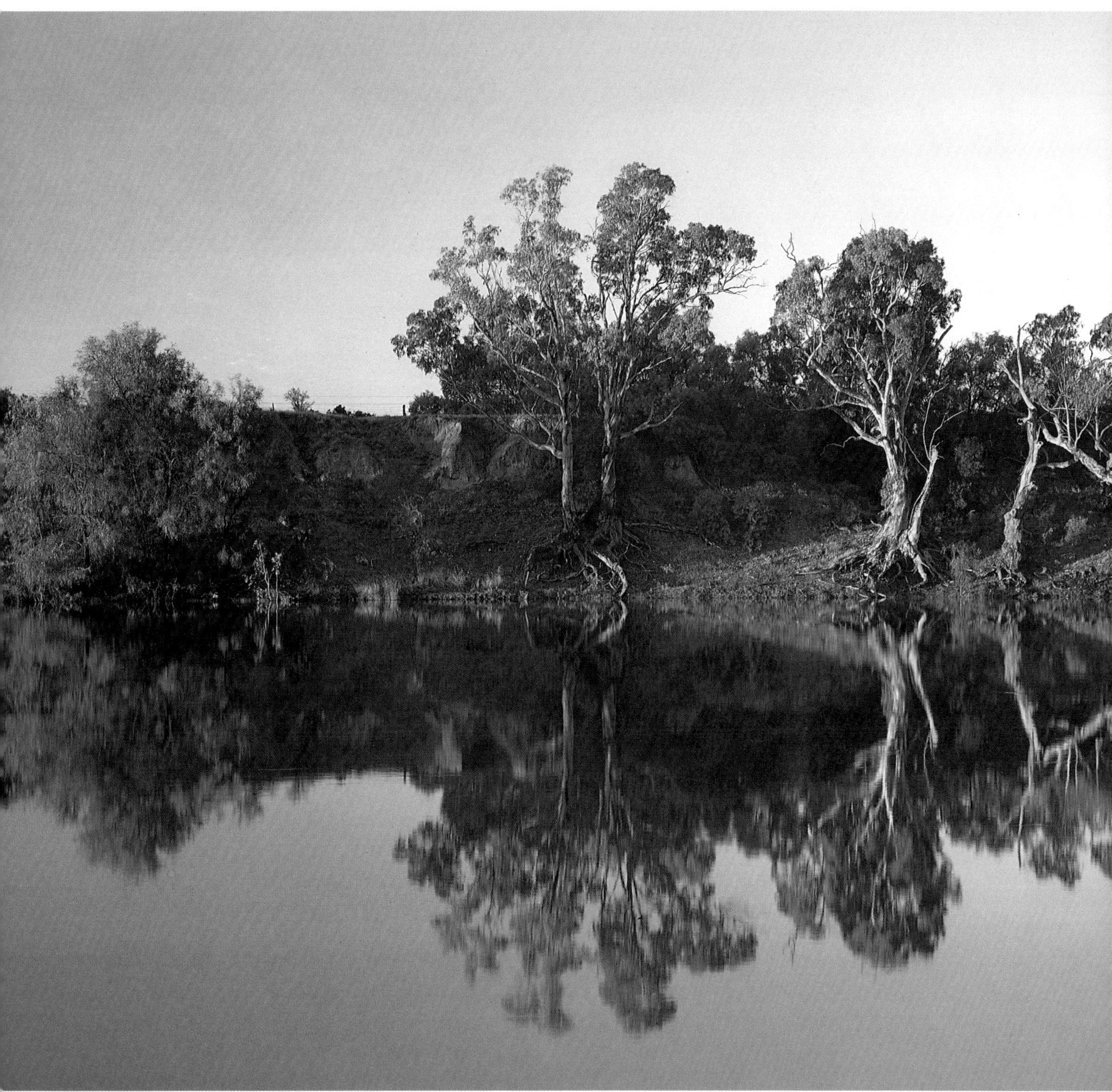

Where the sluggish Murray twists through locks and weirs at Robinvale the waters are wide and deep.

freehold land in the vicinity of Bumbang Homestead in 1912, which was later sub-divided and surveyed. The Cuttle family named the new township Robinvale in memory of their son, Second-Lieutenant George Robin Cuttle, an airman who was killed in France in 1918, towards the end of the First World War.

During the 1920s, the Cuttles built Robinsvale Homestead on the banks of the Murray River. The recently restored home is now used as a venue for private functions.. Close by is an enormous windmill, which is thought to be the largest of its kind in the Southern Hemisphere. It was constructed to supply the residents of Robinvale with domestic water.

The town grew rapidly when some 4000 hectares of land were acquired under the soldier-settlement scheme in 1947 with vines and fruit trees, particularly citrus, being planted soon after.

About the same time, a large olive plantation was bought by Herbert Cuttle. It is now the largest plantation of its kind in Australia with more than 200 hectares of olive trees producing 1500 tonnes of olives for table use and oil production.

Further south, along the Murray Valley Highway is another uncommon orchard crop in the form of a large almond plantation with more than 160 hectares planted with nut-bearing almond trees. The Robinvale Producers Co-operative in Moore Street was formed in the early 1950s. It handles over 10 000 tonnes of dried fruit from several hundred properties in the district, and is one of the biggest enterprises in the town.

Robinvale is also a wine-growing centre. The tasting room of McWilliams Wines in Moore Street is made from an early log cabin and contains items of interest from pioneering days. Local vineyards produce non-alcoholic grape juices as well as wine. *Population 1800*

Mildura & Wentworth

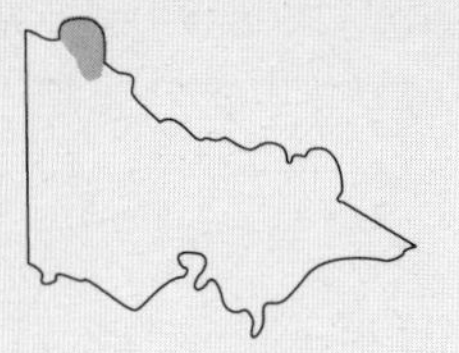

Two Canadian adventurers were the architects of the man-made oases set among the red earth of this region. The district became known as 'Sunraysia' after the First World War and it has since developed into one of the most important producers of dried fruit and wines in Australia.

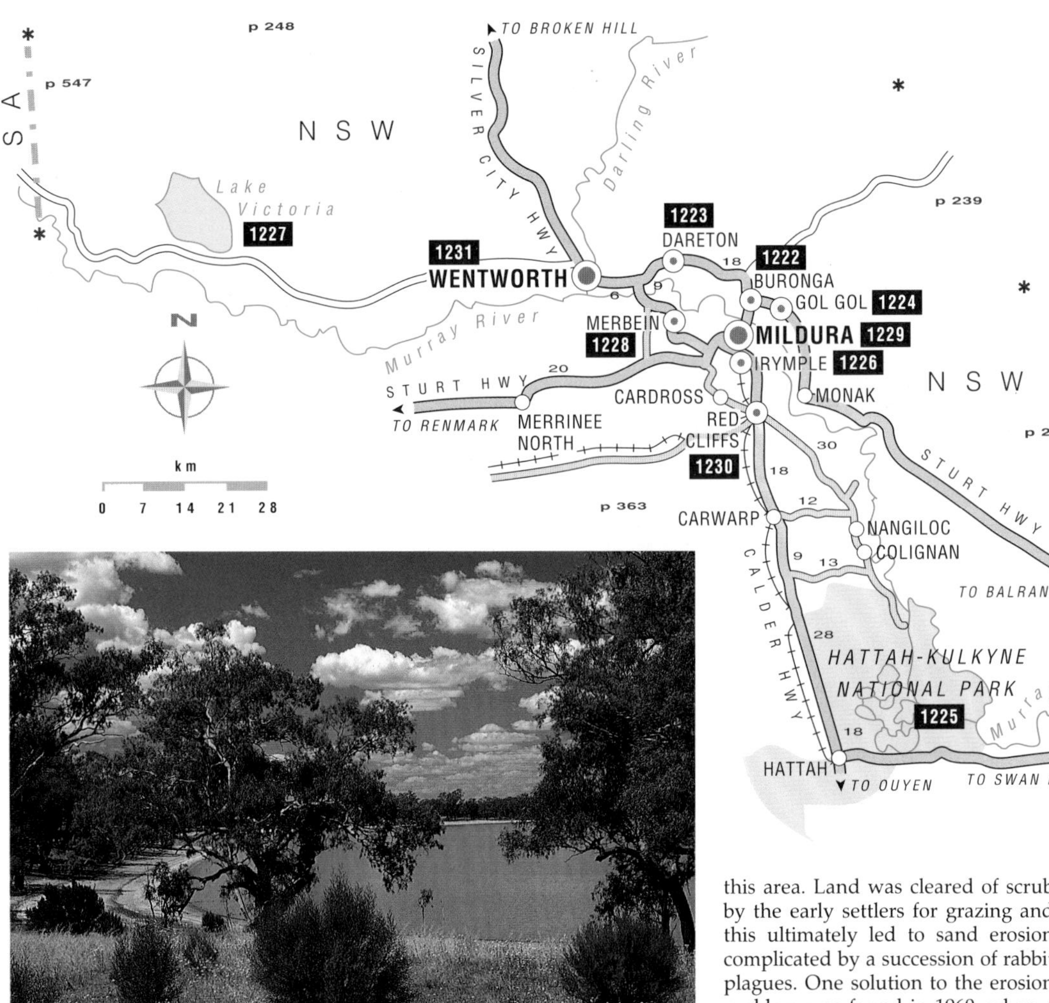

Spring showers bring poached-egg daisies into bloom around the Hattah lakes; these shallow depressions are filled by links with the Murray system.

BURONGA ■ 1222

Buronga was first established on the banks of the Murray River and from the 1850s onward it developed in tandem with Mildura. Early settlers rather unflatteringly called it 'goat town' or 'shanty town' but it nevertheless developed as the centre of a thriving vegetable-growing district. A succession of floods forced a move to higher ground, and the town was shifted away from its vulnerable spot on the riverbank to its present site. Today, a thriving river industry is based around the hiring of small pleasure craft from a marina opposite the Buronga wharf.

The town is perhaps best known for being the production centre for Stanley wine casks. The first thing to catch the attention of visitors to Buronga is a giant wine cask, the world's largest – in fact, a building disguised as a cask – a real cask of its dimensions would hold 400 000 litres! Tours of the factory show the processes involved in wine-cask production. *Population 600*

DARETON ■ 1223

This town was established when the irrigation of the Dareton–Coomealla district began in 1923. The area of the irrigation scheme was extended after the Second World War when soldiers were repatriated in 1945 under the Soldiers Land Settlement Act. It is still the centre of the Dareton-Coomealla irrigation district and an important vineyard and citrus-growing region with two fruit-packing plants on the town's outskirts. Some of the descendants of this region's original inhabitants live in the Aboriginal settlement a few kilometres to the east. *Population 650*

GOL GOL ■ 1224

Mayor Thomas Mitchell named this location 'Golgol' when he passed through the district in 1836, apparently from an Aborginal word thought to mean 'meeting place', and the site eventually became a popular river crossing point for stock drovers and camel trains on their way to market. Mail coaches changed their horses here, and the establishment of the Gol Gol Inn helped provide the impetus for this small village to become a township. Early settlers lived in huts or tents along the banks of the river. Today, Gol Gol is in the centre of a productive vineyard and orchard district, and is probably best known for its fisheries which breed yabbies for the table and several species of goldfish – not for the table. *Population 630*

HATTAH–KULKYNE NATIONAL PARK ■ 1225

Middens, pieces of shell, animals and fish bones are all that remain of the Aboriginal people who once lived in this area. Land was cleared of scrub by the early settlers for grazing and this ultimately led to sand erosion complicated by a succession of rabbit plagues. One solution to the erosion problem was found in 1960, when a native-tree replanting program and pest eradication scheme were started, and land set aside for this park.

Two main types of vegetation are found here. Around the Hattah lakes are river red gums, native grasses and water plants, while on the sand dunes and flood plains are mallee eucalypts, shrubs and grasses. The most outstanding feature of the lakes is its birdlife – many species of birds return to breed here, particularly when the lakes are in flood. Migratory birds rest here during their flight between continents. Most prominent of the 200 species of birds seen here are the natives, the mallee fowl, various water birds, emus, parrots and cockatoos.

The park gained international significance when it was declared a 'biosphere reserve' by UNESCO in 1984. Other parks with this relatively rare classification are the Everglades region and the Yellowstone National Park in the United States and

Kosciusko and Croajingolong national parks and Wilsons Promontory in Australia. A drive winds its way through some of the most scenically interesting sections of the park and there is a six-kilometre nature walk where plants, and sometimes animals, can be observed more closely than from the roadway.

IRYMPLE ■ 1226

Once part of the Mildura grazing run, an area large enough for a provincial city was initially planned for the town of Irymple. Today, the town is the centre of a citrus, dried fruit and wine-growing area. Also in the district is a horticultural research station, which has a special 'insectary' for research into local pests and disease. Popular tourist and picnic spots such as the mysteriously labelled Psyche Bend and Sandilong Park are found nearby along the Murray River. Just outside town is the Bonnonee Winery. *Population 970*

KINGS BILLABONG A popular picnic spot, this billabong twists away from the Murray River for about eight kilometres. Pelicans, swans, herons and wild duck live here and several rare species of plants are also found. At present, the billabong is used for irrigation storage and is kept permanently filled by water pumped from Psyche Bend through a channel from the northern end of the reserve.

LAKE VICTORIA ■ 1227

Lake Victoria is a 160 000-megalitre water-storage area built by the Murray–Darling Basin Commission in 1928. The lake regulates water flow to South Australia from New South Wales and Victoria, under the terms of the River Murray Water Agreement. The lake and three locks are in New South Wales although they are operated and maintained by the South Australian Engineering and Water Supply Department.

MERBEIN ■ 1228

In 1910 when William Chaffey founded White Cliffs, he named it after a Murray River landmark. The surrounding region was originally settled as a dairying district, but fruit growing is now the main primary industry. A horticultural research station established here by the CSIRO is one of the largest in Victoria. Chaffey, one of the district's first winemakers as well as being an irrigation pioneer (see box), also founded the Mildara Winery, now with its headquarters in Merbein. First named Chateau Mildura in 1910, the company was renamed Mildara Winery when it was moved from Irymple – where Chaffey's vineyard still exists – a few years later. *Population 1780*

Mischievous Major Mitchell cockatoos bear the name of the explorer who visited this region in 1836.

MILDURA ■ 1229

Mildura is an Aboriginal word for 'red rock' and accurately describes the colour of the soil in some parts of the surrounding countryside. But irrigation has provided many bright green patches to contrast with the 'red rock'; ninety-five per cent of Victoria's dried fruit and much of its wine, fresh fruit and vegetables now come from this area. About seventy per cent of Australian dried fruit production – most of it from here – is exported to Europe and Canada.

Early settlers were Hugh and Bushby Jamieson who renamed the 'Yerre Yerre' run 'Mildura' in 1858, and ran sheep and, as a precursor of what was to come with irrigation, planted vines. In a pattern all too typical in rural Australia, a series of rabbit plagues and drought ensured that the pioneering run was not always profitable.

The true architects of the district were George and William Benjamin Chaffey (see box), who were persuaded to set up an irrigation colony here by Alfred Deakin then the Victorian Minister of Water Supply and later the second Prime Minister of Australia. The city was laid out on an American-style grid pattern, with streets given numbers instead of names. Land was cleared, channels dug and pumps installed to lift water from the Murray. Settlers arrived in large numbers to take up their blocks and the community began to prosper. Many people left, disheartened, after a decade of setbacks and it wasn't until a rail link was established in 1903, and the Mildura Irrigation Trust formed, that the city began to enjoy sustained prosperity.

The paddle steamer river traffic dwindled with the introduction of the railway. The steamer era was a romantic time for the Murray River and today, several of these original boats offer chartered and regular cruises along the river for tourists. The wharf is one of the major tourist attractions in Mildura. A walk along Deakin Avenue – one of the longest streets in Australia – with its palm trees and green lawn reveals the 1915 band rotunda. The fountain – a memorial to George V – was one of two such street ornaments brought to Mildura by paddle steamer by the Chaffeys. The other fountain is now in the Grand Hotel, the former offices of the Chaffey enterprise. Mildura also has one of the biggest aviaries in Australia, a zoo with a wide range of Australian native animals, birds and reptiles, and five of Australia's best known wineries are just outside city limits. The Air Bird museum at Mildura airport displays military aircraft of different eras in various stages of restoration.

The Murray River is the location for much of Mildura's recreational activities and the city even has its own lifesaving club at Apex Park. Another unusual feature of this section of the river is the lock and weir which controls water flow and allows paddle steamers to pass from one level of the river to another. Lock Island, a wildlife sanctuary, was created when the lock was built. *Population 23 180*

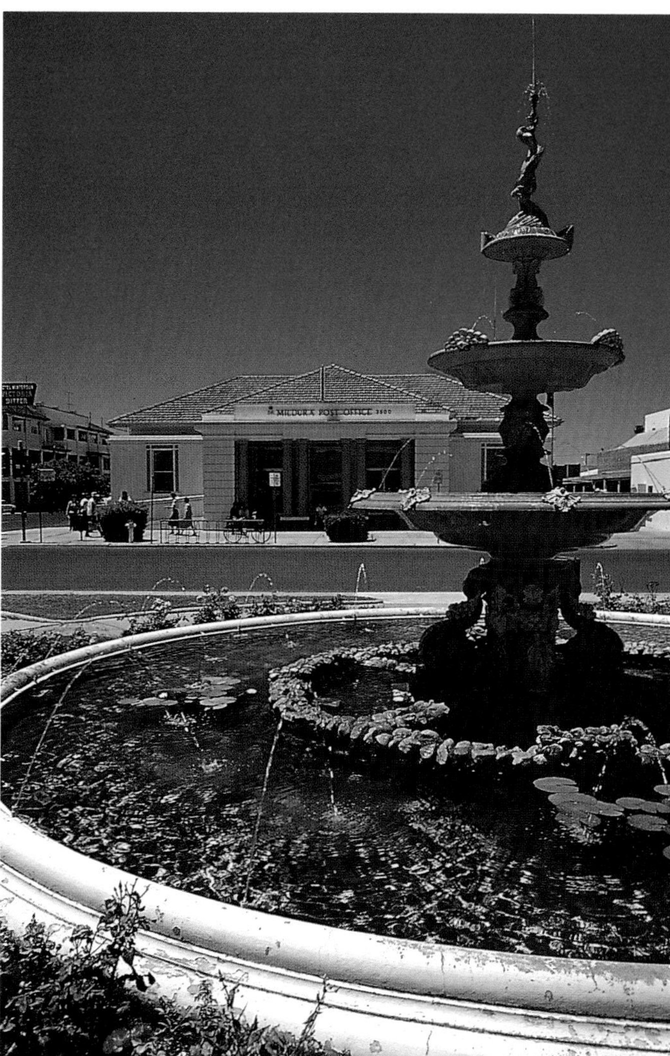

The fountain opposite Mildura's post office symbolises the importance of the water which has transformed sandy mallee scrubland into a leafy oasis.

'RIO VISTA' The Mildura Arts Centre incorporates the former home of William Chaffey, 'Rio Vista', a regional art gallery and a theatre. The 1899 Chaffey home, made from red brick from local kilns and using Murray pine and mellowed river red gum, makes a handsome museum of local history. There are Italian tiles in the hallway and stained-glass windows over the stairway. Upstairs, each room is like a miniature museum containing a variety of historical displays. There is a comprehensive collection of British and Australian paintings in the art gallery.

WORKINGMAN'S CLUB The Mildura Workingman's Club has a spectacular, ninety-one-metre-long bar in a horseshoe shape, listed in the *Guinness Book of Records* as the longest bar in the world. The bar has twenty-seven beer taps.

RED CLIFFS ■ 1230

George Chaffey first bought 6000 hectares of mallee eucalypt country for fruit growing in the 1890s, but the cliffs at the riverbank posed insurmountable problems for irrigation. The district remained virtually undeveloped until 1918 when, at the end of the First World War, approximately 700 returned servicemen were assisted by the government to clear land. The soldier-settlement scheme was one of the largest such schemes to be undertaken in Australia and led to the successful establishment a dried-fruit industry.

THE CHAFFEY BROS: ADVENTURES IN GREENING THE INLAND

THE VAST irrigation schemes of south-eastern Australia may have remained no more than planners' dreams if the potential of the Murray River had not been tapped far to the west, in the semi-arid Mallee in the 1880s. The story of how the dry scrubland was transformed into one of Australia's richest fruit- and wine-producing regions began when the Victorian Government invited the Canadian-born brothers George and W.B. (William Benjamin) Chaffey to set up an irrigation colony in Australia. The Chaffeys were known for their construction of successful irrigation works in California.

There could be no more meaningful Chaffey monument than the pump that made dreams reality in the orchards and vineyards of the Mildura district (below).

George Chaffey chose the region around what is known today as Mildura after seeing fruit trees flourishing behind a rabbit-proof fence at 'Mildura' homestead. The agreement to set aside 125 000 acres caused a storm in parliament; the Chaffeys were accused of being 'Yankee adventurers'. The project was temporarily shelved and the South Australian authorities asked the brothers to establish a colony there. Eventually, the Chaffeys signed agreements with both the South Australian and the Victorian governments, which by this time, had reappraised the project. An ambitious promotional scheme to attract settlers was launched with the Chaffeys publishing a book on the promise of Australian irrigation colonies.

Land was cleared of vegetation and many kilometres of channels dug while George Chaffey designed and ordered two triple-expansion pumping engines which were made in England. The engines caused controversy in engineering circles and many critics declared they would not work. The manufacturers refused to take responsibility for the engines and cast the Chaffey name on the engine instead of their own. As happened a number of times, time proved the audacious Chaffeys right: the pumps were installed at Psyche Bend and at Billabong and went on to pump millions of litres of water from the river each hour until they were retired in the mid-1950s.

By 1890, Mildura had 3000 residents and 2500 hectares of vines, citrus and stone fruits. A decade of setbacks followed: floods, transportation difficulties, soil salinity and the depression of the 1890s. Many settlers gave up and left the land. The Chaffeys went bankrupt and George Chaffey returned to the United States. His brother stayed on and, after a rail link was established, helped gradually guide the community back to prosperity.

Soldier-resettlement schemes after the two world wars helped provide a boost for the district and many irrigation schemes were either extended or initiated around this time. A publicity campaign after the First World War led to the whole district being given the evocative name 'Sunraysia'. The region is now Australia's most important producer of sultanas and raisins; other crops include citrus, stone fruit, avocados, melons, almonds and olives. Most of Victoria's wine comes from the Sunraysia region. □

World prices for dried fruit were high at the time, and it looked like a low-risk venture. Work gangs lived in tents and cleared twenty-eight hectares for a nursery to provide the cuttings needed for cultivation.

Mallee scrub was cleared by 'Big Lizzie', an enormous tractor with a 65-horsepower machine that was able to remove up to eight mallee stumps at a time. The large machine cleared 1500 hectares for soldier resettlement, and is permanently displayed in the town. By 1921, pumps had been installed and water began to be lifted to the cleared blocks. By the end of the decade, more than 195 kilometres of irrigation channels had been built. Around 400 megalitres of water is lifted each day by the Red Cliffs pumping station to irrigate more than 5000 hectares of land. Up to eighty per cent of this land is planted with a variety of grapevines for dried-fruit production.

Grape production in this irrigated region has proved so bountiful that it readily supports the largest winery in the Southern Hemisphere – Lindeman's Karadoc Winery – to the east of the town. *Population 2580*

WENTWORTH ■ 1231

Development of the river trade established this town at the junction of the Murray and Darling rivers. The site was settled in the 1840s, but there were only a few scattered huts around the riverbank when Captain William Randell first delivered a cargo here. By the 1850s, the town had developed into a busy inland port. In 1859, it was officially declared a town and renamed Wentworth after the New South Wales explorer and politician, William Charles Wentworth.

The new town soon became the centre of the district, with widespread commercial influence and a flourishing river trade. There was much support in Wentworth for the planned federation of the Australian colonies and Wentworth was proposed as a truly inland site for the new capital. The town was only eliminated from selection in the last round of deliberations.

Two early attempts to irrigate the surrounding district were unsuccessful, and ultimately Wentworth suffered from the expansion of Mildura (see entry) on the Victorian side of the Murray River, where the introduction of irrigation had been particularly successful (see box). A declining river boat trade and lack of a rail link to the rest of the state, also contributed to the lack of growth.

Today, the great wool barges are only used during major floods, as in 1956, although Wentworth is still the centre of an important grazing and pastoral area. A series of locks, and a new bridge across the Murray help maintain the town's position as an important junction between New South Wales and Victoria.

Wentworth has a unique tractor monument built to honor the dozens of Ferguson tractors which saved the town from the 1956 floods, together with Australia's largest collection of riverboat photographs in the Rotary Folk Museum, in a former cinema. One of the fastest ships on the Murray, the *Ruby* now sits high and dry in Fotherby Park. Cruises on other river boats run daily from the Wentworth wharf. *Population 1450*

OLD JAIL An architectural highlight of Wentworth is the old jail, built in 1881; more than a million bricks, all locally made, went into the construction of the jail which has walls forty-five centimetres thick. On display in the cells, and outside, are various items of punishment from the convict days, including stocks, a rack and a whipping stool.

Warracknabeal & Nhill

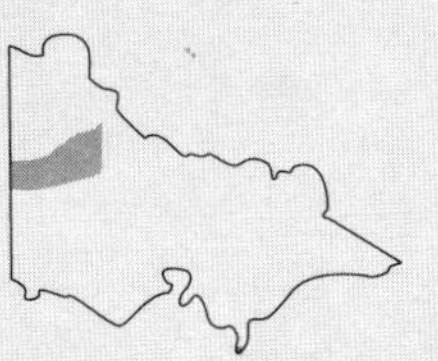

The Wimmera – wilderness and wheatfields, saltpans and artificial lakes – is a land that has always been particularly susceptible to the whims of climate...yet with persistence, the early settlers managed to transform vast tracts into rolling plains of wheat.

A sea of cereal grasses – barley and oats, but mainly wheat – dominate a typical Wimmera landscape near Rainbow.

ANTWERP ■ 1232

The first large-scale commercial distillation of eucalyptus oil in Australia began here in the early 1880s under the direction of pharmacist and research chemist Joseph Bosisto (see box, *Heathcote & Nagambie*). He chose this region on the advice of the government botanist, Baron Ferdinand von Mueller. With others, Bosisto formed the Eucalyptus Mallee Oil Company which took up the leasehold on the Antwerp Station and by mid-1882 teams of horses began carting the leaves of the mallee eucalypt into the plant. The oil distilled here was marketed under the brand name 'Emu'. The squatter Horatio Ellerman was the first European to take up land in this area, in 1846, naming his run 'Antwerp' after his birthplace in Belgium.

EBENEZER MISSION STATION In 1856, Horatio Ellerman (see above) made available some 260 hectares of his run as a mission reserve for Aborigines. This was established in 1858 by two missionaries from Germany who tended the local people, giving food and medicine to the dispossessed who readily succumbed to a variety of introduced diseases. In the forty or so years of its operation, the mission had a steady population of about fifty Aborigines. Encouraged by two local Aboriginal brothers, the people were converted to Christianity. Little remains of the settlement –

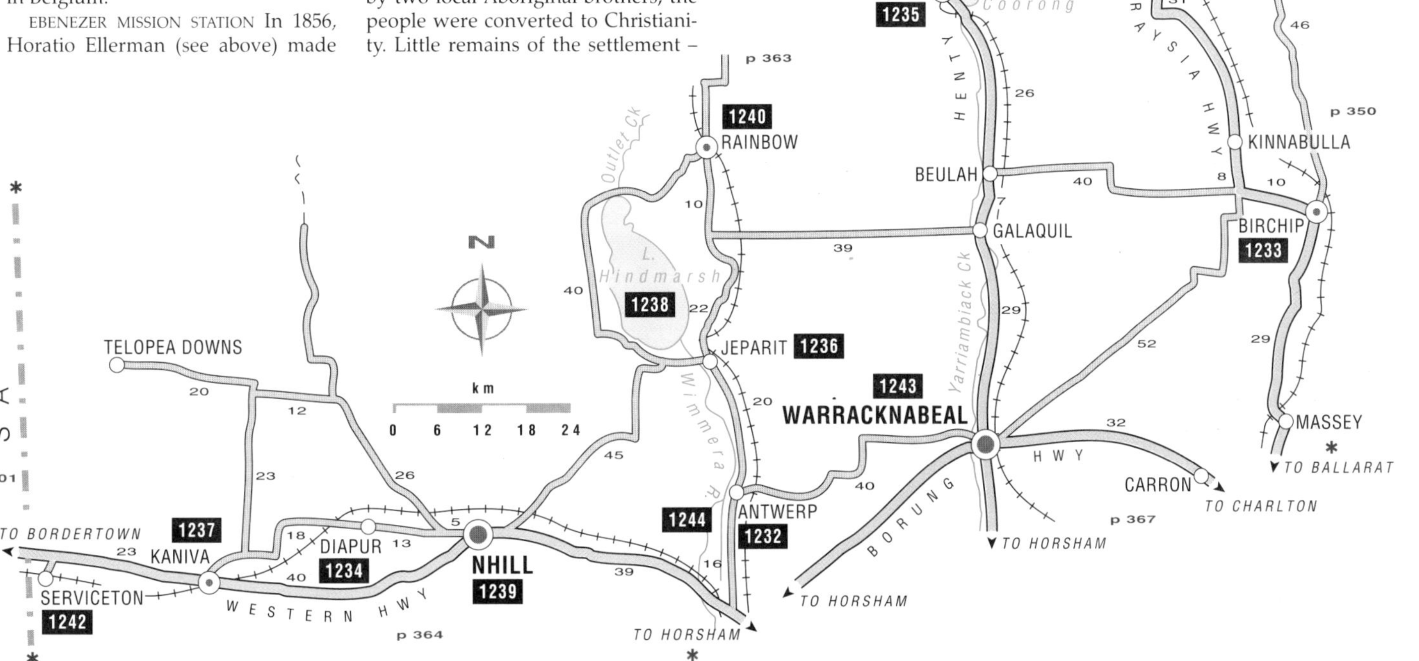

The sun that encourages Rainbow's grain crops is thoughtfully shaded from window-shoppers in the main street.

the roofless church with square bell tower rising incongruously above the mallee landscape, a storehouse, a toilet block and a cemetery containing more than eighty Aboriginal graves. The mission closed in 1904 after its numbers were severely reduced by the official exclusion of people of mixed race. The land then became available for selection.

BIRCHIP ■ 1233

Lying as it does in the dry Wimmera, it is not surprising that this town seems to be preoccupied with water. Its skyline is dominated by a twenty-nine-metre water tower and in front of the council chambers a fountain commemorating the early pioneers draws attention to the importance of water in their lives.

Birchip gets its water supply from the Grampians, carried hundreds of kilometres by the Wimmera–Mallee stock and domestic channel system, the largest gravitation irrigation system in the world. This irrigation system was constructed in the early 1900s and has proved so effective that it enables farmers to hold stock through droughts and allows towns on the waterless plains have green lawns and swimming pools. Two of the major irrigation channels intersect just north of the town.

Settlement here dates from the 1880s and grew up at the intersection of five tracks which linked early pastoral runs. 'Birchip' is a shortening of the Aboriginal word 'wirrumbirchip' – the name given to an early station nearby – and is thought to mean 'one way', a reference to the Aboriginal route from the Murray River, near Swan Hill, through this district. The town claims proudly to be 'the home of the Mallee Bull'. *Population 830*

TCHUM LAKE An artificial lake fed by the Wimmera–Mallee irrigation system, Tchum Lake offers a variety of water sports on its southern shores while on its northern shores there is a wildlife sanctuary known for its flora and birdlife.

DOG FENCE, KINNABULLA A section of the original Vermin Proof Fence still stands at Kinnabulla, north-west of Birchip. The fence was built in the mid 1880s in an attempt to stop rabbits in particular, but also feral dogs and dingoes, from moving down from the Mallee, where they were in plague proportions, into the Wimmera. It stretched from the South Australian border along the 36th parallel, past Lake Hindmarsh, and near to Birchip it turned north and ran to the Murray River, near Swan Hill. At the time, it was the longest wire-netting fence in the world and was maintained until 1949.

Bands of 'dogmen', usually accompanied by their own pack of hunting dogs trained to hunt down and kill any undesirables who breached the line, operated here, and local rabbit trappers were responsible for many tonnes of the 'underground mutton' sold on the streets of Melbourne. Another section of fence still stands near Galaquil, north of Warracknabeal, on the Henty Highway.

DIAPUR ■ 1234

The founder of one of Australia's best known retail store chains, G.J. Coles, began his business career as a storekeeper here in the early 1900s. In the 1880s, the village grew up around the dam on a sheep station, taking its name from an Aboriginal word for 'crabhole' or 'swamp'.

HOPETOUN ■ 1235

The first settler in this district was Peter McGinnis, who took up the 'Lake Corrong' run, where the town of Hopetoun now stands, in 1846. The town is named after Lord Hopetoun, the first governor-general of Australia and was a frequent visitor to the home of Edward Lascelles, who, with others, took over Lake Coorong Station in 1877.

Lascelles, often called the 'Father of the Mallee' is credited with opening up the region for settlement. He subdivided some of his run as blocks for share-farming – the tenants paid him one-third of their wheat crop – and set aside an area of rising ground near his homestead for the township. The first lots were sold in 1891. *Population 700*

HOPETOUN HOUSE Built for Edward Lascelles in 1891 and classified by the National Trust in modern times, the existing single-storey brick and limestone house replaced the original pine-slab structure which was the first homestead on the 'Lake Corrong' run. The site once had an uninterrupted view over the lake.

LAKE COORONG 'Coorong' is an Aboriginal word said to mean 'bark canoe' and on the shores of the lake was a former meeting ground where trade in mussel shells, stone axes, grinders and ochre took place. The lake is about four kilometres south-east of the town.

JEPARIT ■ 1236

A thistle-bedecked spire commemorates Jeparit's most famous son, Sir Robert Menzies, who presided over Australia's affairs as prime minister from 1939 to 1941 and, most significantly, from 1949 to 1966. The town stands on the shores of Lake Hindmarsh and boasts many pleasant swimming beaches and fishing spots. In the late 1880s, an influx of settlers from South Australia, many of them Lutherans, brought modern agricultural machinery and practices into the area, heralding a dramatic transformation in land use, from grazing to wheat growing.

WIMMERA–MALLEE PIONEER MUSEUM An open-air museum preserves a number of historic buildings from this region, including a homestead and a pine log hut from Lake Albacutya and the blacksmith's shop from Antwerp. These are complemented by farm machinery, period furnishings and antiques.

KANIVA ■ 1237

The township dates from 1881 and was known to early arrivals as Budjik, an Aboriginal word said to mean 'tomahawk'. Like Serviceton (see entry) it lay in the so-called 'Disputed Territory' with the usual dubious border activities of smuggling and police dodging occurring with regularity. The historical museum here has a large collection of items from those days. *Population 760*

BILLY-HO BUSH WALK Some ten kilometres south of Kaniva is the start of the Billy-Ho Bush Walk, a three-kilometre track through the Little Desert with numbered pegs identifying various species of desert flora.

MOOREE RESERVE This region of lagoons and tall red gums on the edge of the Little Desert (see *Edenhope & Goroke*) was much frequented by Aborigines in pre-European times as is indicated by campsite relics and the scarred trees from which bark was removed for canoes, shields and containers. Here, about twenty-five kilometres south-west of Kaniva, there are also remnants of the sheep washes and sawpits of the early pastoralists who relied on the spring in times of drought.

LAKE HINDMARSH ■ 1238

When full, this is the largest freshwater lake in Victoria with good fishing, especially for redfin, and safe sandy beaches. The lake has been known to dry up, most notably in the 1902 drought, when a water grass which was revealed on its bed was cut and fed to starving cattle. The explorer Edward John Eyre named the lake for the governor of South Australia, Sir John Hindmarsh when he came across it in 1838 while droving cattle from Melbourne to Adelaide.

Eyre had followed the Wimmera River north in the hope of finding a shorter route than this but his party was defeated by the waterless horizons beyond, and forced to retrace its steps. On the north of the lake are canoe trees cut by Aborigines. Near its southern shores is the township of Jeparit (see entry).

NHILL ■ 1239

Nhill is a small wheat town on the Western Highway, exactly halfway between Melbourne and Adelaide, which claims to have the largest single-bin grain silo in the Southern Hemisphere, its other distinction being that it was the first country town in Victoria to have its streets lit by electric light.

Nhill is the headquarters of Lowan Shire, which takes its name from the Aboriginal name for the mallee fowl (see box) which were once common across these lands and still survive in depleted numbers in nearby reserves and national parks such as Little Desert, Big Desert Wilderness and Wyperfeld (see *Ouyen*). The birds are depicted on a monument in front of the council offices and an aviary where they can be seen working on their incubation mounds in a natural bushland setting has been established at Little Desert Lodge on the southern outskirts of the town.

Poet John Shaw Neilson lived here as a young man. His cottage now stands in Shaw Neilson Park, and there is a memorial to him between here and Kaniva. 'Nhill' was the Aboriginal name given to a meeting place and corroboree ground here, and has been variously interpreted as meaning 'white mist over the water', 'place of spirits' or 'red clay'. *Population 1890*

DRAUGHT HORSE MEMORIAL Draught horses played an indispensable role in the development of the wheatlands. They pulled the rollers which flattened the mallee scrub, then the ploughs, then the reapers, and finally they hauled the bagged harvest to distant markets. The horses, bred from Scottish Clydesdales and English Sires, began to be replaced by tractors in the 1920s and within two decades a working horse team was a rare sight.

RAINBOW ■ 1240

Wheat and barley silos dominate the Rainbow skyline. The flat surrounding country grows not only good quality wheat, barley and oats but also raises sheep, wool, dairy cattle and fat lambs. The town was an important railhead in the early 1900s, and in 1909 handled more grain than any other station in Victoria.

The area was first known as 'croajabrim', the Aboriginal name for a local spring, and later as Rainbow Rise, for the bow-shaped hill to the west of the town. For thousands of years, groups of Aborigines moved across this land, reaping a seasonal harvest from country which to European eyes seemed a fruitless waste. In the old campsites are chips and flakes of rock from far-flung regions, evidence of an extensive trading network. *Population 590*

YURUNGA HOMESTEAD On the northern outskirts of Rainbow, Yurunga Homestead, from the early 1900s, is classified by the National Trust and contains a number of Edwardian fittings and antiques. A single-storey brick and limestone structure, it has an encircling cast-iron veranda and a patterned slate roof. A large underground room with a year-round temperature of 20° Centigrade was used as a retreat during heatwaves.

SEA LAKE ■ 1241

At the southern end of salty Lake Tyrrell (see *Ouyen*), Sea Lake was established in the late 1890s when the surrounding country was opened up for wheat growing. Its name is said to come from the surprise expressed by a passing bullocky at its depth being 'as deep as the sea'. *Population 800*

SERVICETON ■ 1242

Serviceton stands in what was once called the 'Disputed Territory', a strip of land claimed by both Victoria and South Australia following an inaccurate survey and the site was originally thought to be on the border. Prior to federation in 1901, customs duties had to be paid on anything that crossed into Victoria, including the buggies and waggons of travellers, but smugglers caught in the disputed strip were likely to claim that this was a no-man's-land where Victorian law did not apply.

Serviceton's railway station, built in 1889, stands over dungeons which once contained a mortuary, customs quarters and, presumably for those smugglers unable to talk their way out of arrest, prison cells. The red clay bricks for the two-storey station building were carted from Horsham. Classified by the National Trust, it now doubles as the Serviceton Hotel.

WARRACKNABEAL ■ 1243

Warracknabeal, on the banks of the Yarriambiack Creek, services a rich wheat-growing area and is noted for its historic buildings. These are identified by the 'Black Arrow' signposts of a self-drive town tour and include a solid wooden lockup, built in 1872 of red and yellow gum in the Canadian horizontal log-cabin style, the Tudor-style post office and the four-storey cylindrical water tower built for the railways in 1886.

Early settlers in the area were Andrew and Robert Scott who established their run 'Werracknabeal', in 1844. The name is usually accepted as coming from the Aboriginal word meaning 'gum trees around a hollow' or 'flooded red gums', but it has also been claimed as a combination of the Scottish family name 'Warrack' and the Gaelic word 'nabeal', meaning 'ravine'. *Population 2690*

AGRICULTURAL MACHINERY MUSEUM Dedicated to the history of wheat growing in the district, the Agricultural Machinery Museum houses a collection of equipment used on farms in the Mallee and Wimmera districts over the past hundred years. All in working order, the exhibits include a stump jump plough, a Sunshine harvester, a Ridley stripper and giant stationary engines.

WIMMERA RIVER ■ 1244

The Wimmera River rises in the Grampians, and after flowing past Horsham and Dimboola, meanders northward along the eastern edge of the Little Desert to empty into Lake Hindmarsh (see entry). After heavy rain, Lake Hindmarsh is likely to overflow into Outlet Creek, and the waters of the Wimmera once again flow along the dry bed of its ancient course to Lake Albacutya. Even more rarely it will flow further north into the system of normally dry lakes and watercourses of Wyperfeld National Park (see *Ouyen*). The river's name comes from 'woomera', an Aboriginal throwing stick.

ONE-PARENT FAMILIES IN THE MALLEE

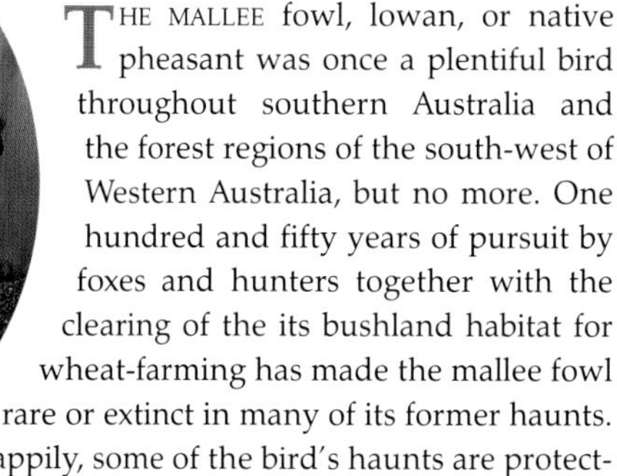

THE MALLEE fowl, lowan, or native pheasant was once a plentiful bird throughout southern Australia and the forest regions of the south-west of Western Australia, but no more. One hundred and fifty years of pursuit by foxes and hunters together with the clearing of the its bushland habitat for wheat-farming has made the mallee fowl rare or extinct in many of its former haunts. Happily, some of the bird's haunts are protected in reserves and national parks and it is still possible to see the large mounds of sand and plant matter, up to a metre high and twelve metres in circumference, which are laboriously built-up by the male bird for the female's eggs. The mound is an extremely effective incubating chamber – an essential precaution in desert regions where temperatures fluctuate widely – and may be used for many seasons.

To construct his incubator the bird scratches a hole about thirty centimetres deep which he fills with leaves and twigs. After the plant matter has been dampened by rain the bird covers it with sand and waits for the increase in temperature that comes with its decomposition. Egg-laying takes place over a week or two in spring into a hole at least forty centimetres deep in the centre of the mound. The temperature within the mound is checked regularly by the busy male, who appears to test it with his tongue and he skilfully maintains it at a constant level of about 33° Centigrade by opening and closing the mound and the judicious adding and subtracting of material.

Each day he digs to within ten or so centimetres of the eggs so that the sun can warm them. At night he re-covers them and the heat given off by the decaying vegetable matter takes over. The clutch of fifteen to twenty eggs hatch in six to eight weeks but the survival rate is very low. The chicks must first be strong enough to claw through almost a metre of sand and debris to reach the surface. There they face the threat of starvation or becoming dinner for a fox or a feral cat – for the unswerving devotion of the male parent evaporates entirely at hatching time! The chicks receive no help at all from their parents, who do not even seem to recognise their offspring, and they must wander off alone to fend for themselves.

Despite this rather offhand attitude to their offspring – another factor which does nothing to enhance the species' chances of survival in an altered environment – mallee fowls are devoted to each other and when they mate, they do so for life.

The mature birds are about the size and shape of a small turkey and have mottled black, brown and white plumage and a long broad tail. They usually spend the daylight hours roosting, well camouflaged in the shade. □

As it gains the open air from its mound-incubator – tended by a male (top) – the mallee fowl chick's only defence against carnivores is its camouflaging colour (right).

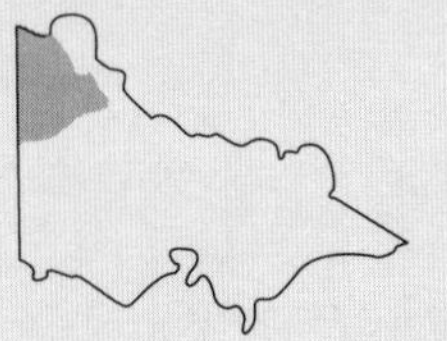

Ouyen

The Mallee that survives outside the wheat belt is a forbidding sea of grey-green scrub sprouting from undulating sandy plains and dotted with dry salt lakes. Despite appearances, it is home to an enormous variety of protected birds, animals and habitats.

BIG DESERT WILDERNESS ■ 1245
The Big Desert, the first declared wilderness area in Victoria, covers more than 100 000 hectares of semi-arid scrubland and adjoins similar large conservation areas in South Australia. Its loose, sandy soil contains almost no agriculturally useful nutrients so it was of little interest to farmers who cleared their way to its edge in the late nineteenth century but left the waterless mallee scrublands undisturbed.

Strictly speaking, this is not a desert, for most of it is densely vegetated. Its steep-sided white sand ridges, sometimes thirty metres or more high, support thick growths of broombush, silky tea-tree, desert banksia, the brilliant red-flowered correa and holly grevillea. These drought-resistant plants are superbly adapted to their environment: they protect their vulnerable leaves against moisture loss by coating them with wax or growing mats of tiny felted hairs; some have thin needle-shaped leaves to minimise the surface exposed to the sun. Mallee eucalypts occur on the deeper dunes and sandy plains.

The thin Big Desert soils are held together by big-rooted broombrushes (above) and many-stemmed mallees.

Even without a permanent supply of open water, more than ninety bird species have so far been recorded, including the rare western whipbird, the scarlet-chested parrot and the mallee fowl. With more than fifty species of snakes and lizards, the Big Desert is the most populous region in Victoria for reptiles. The little pigmy possum, extinct in other dry areas of Victoria, occurs here, as does the silky desert mouse, which inhabits the dense near-ground foliage of the tea-tree and obtains moisture from the capsules shed by the bush.

COWANGIE ■ 1246
One of the first Bush Nursing Centres in Victoria opened in Cowangie in 1918. It operated from a small stone cottage, still standing beside the Uniting Church, and brought medical help, although this might still involve a fearful waggon trip of an hour or more into town. To the north of Cowangie, a gypsum mine has operated since the 1920s. The mineral is carted to a washing plant near the town then railed to Geelong for use in the manufacture of plasters and cement.

LAKE ALBACUTYA PARK ■ 1247
Bordering the south-western section of Wyperfeld National Park this park encompasses the lake after which it is named and its shores, fringed with tall river red gums. The lake is part of the Wimmera River overflow system and fills when heavy rains breach the capacity of Lake Hindmarsh (see *Warracknabeal & Nhill*). The waters which spill into Outlet Creek flow north to Lake Albacutya. A variety of water birds frequent the lake, which takes its name from an Aboriginal word said to mean 'place of bitter quandongs', a reference to the small native fruit which grows in the area.

LAKE TYRRELL ■ 1248
This vast salt 'lake' covers some 200 square kilometres. For most of the year it is dry, leaving a thick crust of salt which is commercially harvested and sent to Geelong to be packed. Thousands of seagulls nest on the lake's many islands. The explorer Edward John Eyre, in 1838, was the first European to sight the lake.

FESTIVALS Mallee Desert Car Rally, early June.

MURRAYVILLE ■ 1249
North of Murrayville township are the Rockholes, shallow wells carved into solid rock thousands of years ago by the Aborigines. These were covered with sticks which reduced evaporation and discouraged animals from drinking but still allowed water from even a brief shower to trickle in. In this way, water was ensured when seasonal fruits bought foraging groups of food collectors to the area. Beneath the arid plains there is an abundant supply of artesian water which was first tapped by the farmers who settled here in the early 1900s. They pumped it to the surface using the windmills which now dot the region.

OUYEN ■ 1250
Ouyen lies at the crossroads of two highways in the heart of the Mallee wheat belt. This was the country skirted by explorer Major Thomas Mitchell in 1836 and who described it as 'one of the most barren regions in the world', where, when his men tried to ride into the mallee scrub the porcupine grass 'tortured the horses and tore the men's clothes'.

The first pastoral run in the district was occupied, without authority, little more than a decade later, and by the 1870s thousands of sheep and cattle grazed the surrounding plains. But when plagues of introduced rabbits reached the Mallee in the 1880s the strain on the vegetation was too great, pastures were ruined, and many farmers forced from their runs.

The town and wheat-farming date from the early 1900s. It was a hard grind – land was cleared using the 'mallee roller' (see *Mildura & Wentworth*), and water had to be carted from Mildura and the Hattah Lakes. Huge mallee roots too heavy to handle were left to rot for several years before they could be removed, and it was only the invention of the 'stump jump plough' that made sowing possible on some farms. *Population 1340*

WIRRENGREN PLAIN ■ 1251
In the days before European settlement, a large Aboriginal campsite in this area was used when infrequent heavy rains filled the dry bed of Outlet Creek and carried water beyond Pine Plains to Wirrengren on the edge of the ancient watercourse of the Wimmera (see *Warracknabeal & Nhill*). Groups from as far afield as the Grampians, the Western District, Portland and western New South Wales gathered here to trade. Evidence of their visits are the many stones found in the campsites that have been shown to come from quite different geological zones.

WYPERFELD NATIONAL PARK ■ 1252
Wyperfeld National Park protects the largest mallee forest in Australia and contains a series of usually dry lakes. More than 400 species of flowering plants grow in here, as well as the largest natural stand of broombush in Victoria.

Mallee is the name given to about twenty species of small, shrubby, drought-resistant eucalypts – as well as to the region of north-western Victoria where they predominate. The trees have multiple stems, sprouting from one large woody root. Their tangled, leaf-crowned branches form a continuous grey-green sea but, as noted in a tourist guide dating from the 1890s '...they are too stiff to move wave-like to any wind that may pass...[and make only] a sort of dry rustle, like the inarticulate murmur of many parched tongues...'

The tree is superbly adapted to the frequent bushfires sparked by dry lightning strikes that ravage the region. Its oily stems and leaves are highly combustible, encouraging the flames to strip the canopy, leaving the root system intact. Within weeks new shoots appear. To the dismay of pioneering farmers, this regenerative ability also applied when the stems were removed by hand and mallee branches sprouted among the crops.

Twenty-five million years ago, this entire region was beneath the sea. A series of lakes and rivers formed as the waters receded, and some 40 000 years ago the sand which forms long ridges, crescents and rolling dunes was blown in from the west. Today's dry rivers and lakes are relics of the wetter times and hold water only after exceptionally heavy rain, when Lake Hindmarsh overflows through Outlet Creek into Lake Albacutya, and sometimes causes it to spill into the old river course. This rare event has occurred only three or four times in the twentieth century.

Richer southern soils washed here encourage the growth of red gum

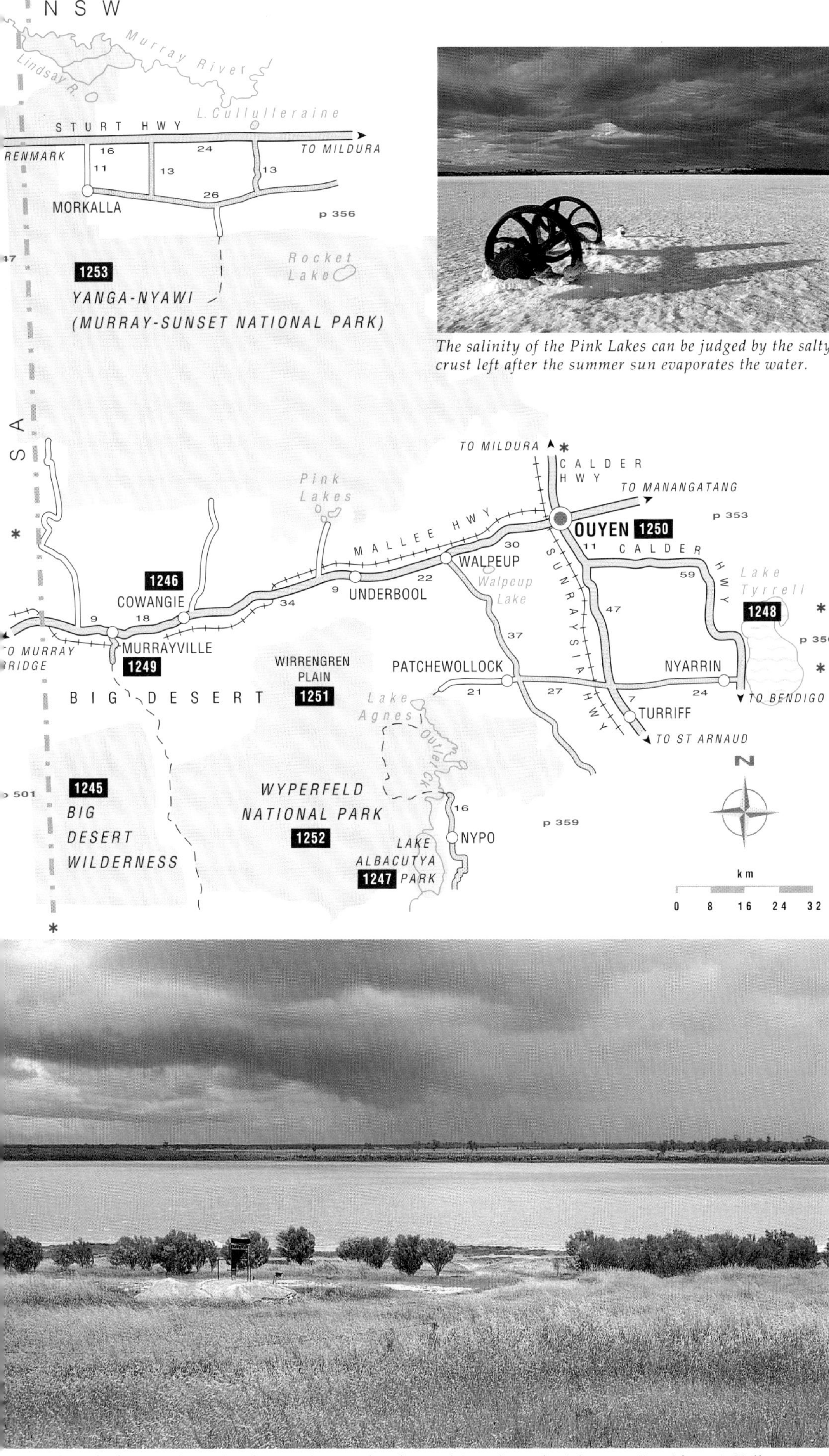

The salinity of the Pink Lakes can be judged by the salty crust left after the summer sun evaporates the water.

The alga which gives the Pink Lake its colour is elsewhere cultivated as a food dye (see Geraldton & Kalbarri*).*

and black box seedlings and the ephemeral waters attract enormous flocks of water birds. Wyperfeld is noted for its birds, of which some 200 species have so far been recorded. But the most remarkable resident is the rare mound-building mallee fowl (see *Warracknabeal & Nhill*) of which about 100 are thought now to nest in the park. In spring, honey-eaters and lorikeets feast on the nectar of flowering banksias, hakeas and grevilleas.

Huge mobs of black-faced mallee kangaroos live in the park, dozing in the shade through the heat of the day and emerging in the late afternoon to graze. It is best to visit Wyperfeld in winter or spring, as summer is very hot and dry. There are scattered reminders of settlers who in the late 1840s took up land in the area now encompassed by the park, including near the foot of Flagstaff Hill, a sad and lonely gravestone inscribed to the memory of 'Baby Cameron'.

PINE PLAINS A recent addition in the north of the park, Pine Plains has long been a popular recreation destination. It protects the most extensive stand of buloke pine in Victoria.

YANGA-NYAWI (MURRAY-SUNSET NATIONAL PARK) ■ 1253

This vast, 633 000-hectare park covers the north-western extremities of Victoria and takes in a variety of environments. In the north are the riverine plains and wetlands of the Murray and Lindsay rivers, cut by billabongs and anabranches, where forests of river red gums line the banks and Victoria's largest flower, the Murray Lily, grows. Further south are open plains of native grasslands, home to marsupials large and small, and in the west are extensive stands of blue-leafed mallee. The name is said to mean 'sunset' in the language of the Aborigines who lived in this uninhabited wilderness before the coming of Europeans.

PINK LAKES The saline waters of the Pink Lakes are coloured by the red pigment, B-carotene, which is secreted by the lake's major coloniser, the alga *Dunaliella salina*. This plant blooms in the groundwater which seeps into the lakebeds during the winter and the colour is deepest in spring. Evaporation during the summer months leaves a thick deposit of shimmering pink-tinged salt.

In the 1920s, salt was harvested using horse-drawn scrapers and tip drays to pile it at the lake's edge. There it was bagged before being carted by camel teams to railheads at Underbool and Linga for transport to Melbourne, where it was used by butchers, or to the Riverina for stock use. The lakes and saltpans are part of the Raak land zone that includes the surrounding low-lying saltbush plains, sand dunes and scattered copi (powdered gypsum) outcrops.

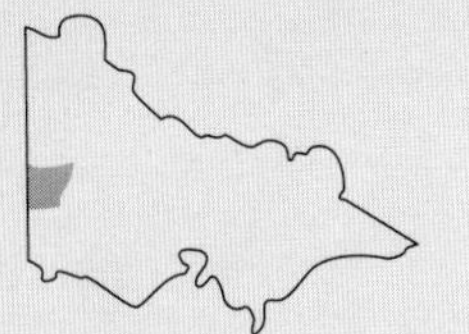

Edenhope & Goroke

The first European to stand on Mount Arapiles – today a mecca for intrepid rock-climbers – was Sir Thomas Mitchell and he thought the surrounding soil 'could scarcely be surpassed'; the bountiful wheatlands of the Wimmera have borne out this promise.

APSLEY ■ 1254

Apsley is an old pioneering pastoral township almost on the South Australian border set within stands of huge flowering gums which are at their best around February. It began as a central point for four sheep stations and was perhaps called Apsley after Apsley House in London, which the grateful British nation gave to the Duke of Wellington in 1820 for triumphing at the Battle of Waterloo. The Apsley farmers were the first in the district to introduce clover into their pastures to increase the number of sheep they could run.

Apsley's heyday was at the time of the Ballarat and Bendigo gold rushes when would-be miners passed by on their way to the diggings. The once famous Apsley Race Club slowly declined as the neighbouring towns grew. In its early years, the club boasted that Apsley prizes were second only to those at Melbourne Cup meetings. The racecourse attracted a number of notable horsemen, among them the poet, Adam Lindsay Gordon. After race meetings, the pub had to stay open all night because it was impossible to evict the hard-drinking punters!

EDENHOPE ■ 1255

In 1845, two years after William Wallace found water at Lake Wallace, the Hope brothers from Eden River in Scotland, took up a pastoral run in this district – sheep and cattle are still raised there. The town, on the shore of the lake, is the administrative and business centre for Kowree Shire where oats, lupins and wool are the main products of the land. The shire's unusual drainage system of lake basins makes up for the lack of rivers and major streams.

Edenhope is an ideal stopping-off place for excursions to nearby Mount Gambier, the Coonawarra vineyards, the caves at Naracoorte, Rocklands Reservoir, historic Harrow and the misleadingly named Little Desert National Park. The giant, green granite boulders, Bailey's Rocks, are a geological feature peculiar to the district. *Population 820*

FESTIVALS Henley-on-Lake Wallace, early February.

GOROKE ■ 1256

Goroke is a tiny town on the edge of the Little Desert, set in undulating country among big red eucalypts which help break the monotony of the flat Wimmera plains. 'Goroke' is said to be an Aboriginal word for 'magpie'. Among the historic buildings, the Georgian-style Mortat House, built in the 1860s, is an example of architecture not often seen in this western district. Present-day farmers grow wool, wheat and oats and safflower for cooking oil. Nearby Lake Charlegrark is a pleasant spot for boating and fishing.

HARROW ■ 1257

Harrow was once a bustling Cobb & Co. depot with a court house, brickworks and three hotels. Now it trades in history and lays claim to being Victoria's oldest inland settlement but this is disputed by Kilmore (see *Craigieburn & Seymour*). The surveyor Lindsay Clarke named Harrow after the English town. The Hermitage Hotel, one of several original buildings in the town, was built around 1854 and extensively renovated in the 1890s. The jail also dates from the 1850s and is a typical log lockup of the times.

Johnny Mullagh, a member of the allblack, first Australian cricket team to visit England, died in Harrow in 1891 and was buried in his cricketing gear. He is remembered by a monument there (see Lake Wallace).

LAKE WALLACE ■ 1258

William Wallace arrived at this lake in April 1843 and it was later named after him. The lake covers an area of more than 220 hectares and is 7 metres deep when full. It provides a safe haven for water birds and is also popular for water sports.

The first Australian cricket team to tour England, in 1868, was made up of Aborigines from the Edenhope and Harrow district. The players trained for about eighteen months with Tom Wills on the shores of the lake – this event is marked by a cairn in the high school grounds at Edenhope. (Tom Wills is also noted for being one of the founders of Australian Rules football.) After some match play in Victoria and New South Wales, the team, led by former Surrey professional, Charles Lawrence, sailed for England. They played forty-seven matches in the year they were away: fourteen won, fourteen lost and nineteen drawn and their score book is now in the Hamilton Institute in Victoria. The

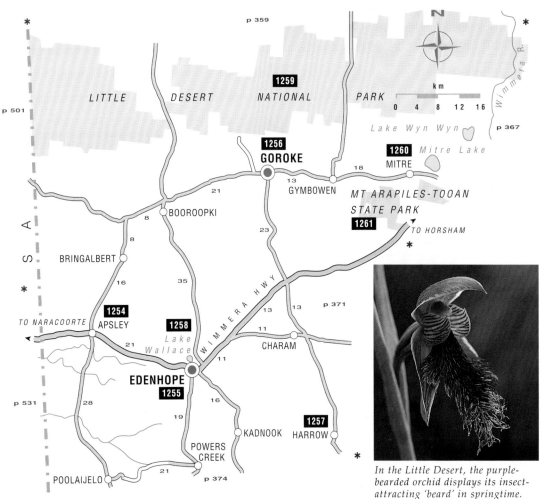

In the Little Desert, the purple-bearded orchid displays its insect-attracting 'beard' in springtime.

star all-rounder, Johnny Mullagh (see Harrow), made 1685 runs and took 241 wickets. The all-black team often demonstrated spear and boomerang throwing and contested other athletic events during matches in both Australia and England.

LITTLE DESERT NATIONAL PARK ■ 1259

The 'Little Desert' is something of a confusing misnomer – it is neither little nor a desert. The region covers an area 25 kilometres by 100 kilometres which includes the 132 000-hectare park. An arid or desert region's maximum annual quota of rain is usually set at 250mm for statistical purposes – here the average is about 400mm and the landscape supports many species of flora and fauna. There are no Sahara-like dunes but the sandy soil, poor in nutrients, disappointed the 1870s and 1880s Wimmera settlers who came in search of arable land and found what they called a 'little desert'. The terrain right up to the edge of the park has now been thoroughly cleared but the poor yield-potential saved the park region from axes and scrub rollers.

The present park is the result of an intense political, economic and conservation controversy in the late 1960s. Before that, in 1955, just over 200 hectares had been set aside as the Kiata Lowan Sanctuary to preserve fourteen mallee fowl nesting mounds. There was already interest in this rare bird which is also known as the lowan fowl (see box, *Warracknabeal & Nhill*). This reserve was enlarged to 945 hectares as the Little Desert National Park in 1968 but the government also announced plans to clear 80 000 surrounding hectares for agriculture. Wimmera people were against this, arguing that the land would only be marginal economically and that it had greater long-term value in its natural state. The government plan was abandoned at the end of 1969 and the park was increased to 35 300 hectares. Today's extended boundaries, from the Wimmera River in the east to the South Australian border, were declared in 1988.

The park, a natural wildflower garden in spring, is particularly special because the mallee flora is forever gone from the neighbouring wheatfields. There are rare and significant plants in the Little Desert's woodlands, heaths and sand plains and broombush grows on the ridges of iron rich sandstones called laterites. Showy sun orchids thrive in the Little Desert, as do the colourfully named greenhoods, bearded, red beaks, pink fingers, waxlips, donkey orchids, spider orchids and minuscule mosquito and gnat orchids.

The park is a refuge for threatened animals too, particularly the silky desert mouse – which inhabits thickets of silky teatree – Mitchell's hopping mouse and the south-western pygmy possum. Twenty-three different honey-eaters have been recorded in a bird call of over two-hundred-and-twenty species. By the middle of the day, lizards and dragons are basking in the sun and at dusk, bats wheel overhead.

MITRE ■ 1260

The hamlet of Mitre is named after the nearby rock which the Surveyor-General Thomas Mitchell thought looked like a bishop's cap. The Aborigines knew it as a sacred landmark long before his coming.

Mitre Lake is one of the twenty-seven Mitchell saw from the top of Mount Arapiles. In the 1890s, some of these lakes produced good quality salt and there was also an abundance of lime in the region. The settlers used these two industries as a reason to press for the Natimuk– Goroke rail extension. Cereals are the major crop in modern times.

MOUNT ARAPILES-TOOAN STATE PARK ■ 1261

The spectacular Mount Arapiles (369 metres) is known as the Ayers Rock of the Wimmera. It is a massive, steep-sided outcrop used as a particularly challenging climbing location with an atmosphere all its own. The climbs are graded in difficulty and have evocative names such as 'Wall of Horrors', 'Birdman of Alcatraz', 'Aftermath', 'Delirium Tremens', 'Dreadnought' and 'Anxiety Neurosis'. Hundreds of challenges for beginners through to internationally experienced climbers exist in the sandstone crags, pinnacles and gully walls and it is used as an army training area. Two short but steep walking tracks link Centenary Park and the summit, and there is a sealed road almost to the top. The views look across the Grampians, Mitre Rock and a vast expanse of flat landscape.

Sir Thomas Mitchell, eager to explore every metre of his 'Australia Felix', was almost certainly the first European to climb Mount Arapiles. Mitchell's Lookout is on the western end of the plateau and here Mitchell stood on 22 July 1836. He tackled the summit the following day. It was the anniversary of his brother's death in the Spanish Peninsular War, fighting for the British against Napoleon at the Battle of Salamanca, which raged over two hills known as Los Arapiles, in 1812.

About 500 different native plants grow in Mount Arapiles-Tooan State Park and the wildflowers are delight-

Except for the ant-like attentions of rock climbers, Mount Arapiles has changed little since Nicholas Chevalier's oil painting of 1863.

ful in spring. Some species that would normally perish in the hot, dry summer conditions are able to survive in the microclimates created by the deep, narrow gullies and cliffs. The several rare or endangered plants include rock wattle and skeleton fork-fern. The Tooan reserve supports a variety of woodland trees: black and yellow box, yellow gum, river red gum, buloke and brown stringbark. The peregrine falcon, whose numbers have been decimated by the effects of pesticides, still inhabits the region.

The bushranger Captain Melville, who operated in the district in the 1850s, said he buried his gold hoard somewhere on the mountain. He boasted to his captors that his hiding place would never be found and so far he has not been proved wrong. Many have looked for the treasure without success.

Horsham & Dimboola

Wheat and other grains have been the mainstay of this part of the Wimmera but legume crops are now being introduced. Horsham is a centre for dryland agricultural research and education. The region's dams are filled by an annual surge of water from the complex maze that is the Wimmera–Mallee irrigation scheme.

DIMBOOLA ■ 1262

The canoe trees along the riverbanks near Dimboola record human occupation long before documented history. The Aborigines cut bark from the huge gums, leaving scars in the shape of their water craft. Sheep were brought to the district in the 1840s and about thirty years later wheat farming began. Wool and wheat are still produced together with barley, field peas, chick peas, lupins and some fat lambs. Salt was once harvested from nearby Pink Lake and sent to Ballarat, Clunes, Talbot and Maryborough. The lake is named for its distinctive colouring which deepens to mauve at certain times (see *Ouyen*).

Jack Hibberd's play *Dimboola,* first staged in Melbourne in 1969 and revived in 1973, made the town famous. This short, satiric piece about an 'ocker' country wedding, has been successfully produced by companies all round Australia. The film with Bruce Spence repeating the role of bridegroom Morrie McAdam, was shot on location in Dimboola.

Hibberd may have chosen the name because he thought Dimboola had Aboriginal connotations, but in fact it is from a Singhalese word, 'dimbula', which means 'land of figs'. In 1848, only forty-eight people lived in Dimboola but it had a mail-coach link with Horsham. The original town site, 'Nine Creeks', was a popular camping place with waggoners in the early 1860s, and Matthew Joseph Edward Ternan built a store and wine shanty there. William Lloyd joined him and set up his own store and hotel. The population increased after the railway came through in 1882. Some early buildings are well preserved including Haby's cottage, the Mechanics' Institute (formerly Lowan Shire Hall) and the Dimboola Hotel. *Population 1580*

WAIL FOREST NURSERY In 1911, the Victorian Forests Commission set up a tree plantation to find species which could grow in poor soils. Sugar gums thrived and were put to use as long-lasting power poles. In 1946, the Wimmera Forest Nursery began a program to grow dry-climate native and introduced trees for shelter on the local properties. This successful venture has attracted horticultural students from Israel, Italy and England.

DONALD ■ 1263

Donald, named after a local pioneer, William Donald, lies on the Richardson River near Lake Buloke which is home to flocks of ducks. Squatters took up runs from the mid-1840s and from 1863, the town grew around the bridge over the river.

There are grain silos in the town and a recent industrial development program has established a printing works and small factories making garden and farm implements, shirts, leather goods, biscuits and fibre-glass products. Dryland farming is practised in Donald Shire and substantial amounts of legumes, including bean and lentil crops, are produced hereabouts. Donald is the centre of the Victorian Pea Co-operative which exports its products to many countries. *Population 1500*

HORSHAM ■ 1264

'Horsham sits in a plain which is as level as a floor...grey, bare, sombre, melancholy, baked, cracked, in the tedious long droughts, but a horizonless ocean of vivid green grass the day after a rain.' So wrote the visiting American author Mark Twain, in October 1895. Horsham is the unofficial capital of the Wimmera and it has been recognised as a city since 1949.

James Monckton Darlot took up land here in 1842. He met George Langlands in Melbourne in 1849 and persuaded him to set up a store and post office on the site of the present town. Darlot named the settlement after Horsham in England, where his parents lived.

This district was first developed for grazing and later by wheat growers armed with superphosphate and the 'Federation' wheat strain (see Minyip). The first flour mill was built in 1870 and by 1873, Horsham's population numbered around 300 which quintupled in four years as the town became an administrative centre. The 1879 railway link with Melbourne assisted the town's growth.

Today, this part of the Wimmera is a high-yield wheat area and produces wool, pigs and poultry. The Victorian Institute of Dryland Agriculture is at Horsham; the town also has clothing and light engineering factories. The Horsham Art Gallery houses works by Rupert Bunny, Donald Friend and John Olsen. *Population 12 550*

LONGERENONG AGRICULTURAL COLLEGE The college in Dooen was founded in 1889 and is now part of a 1000-hectare farm where a modern piggery was built in 1982. A wide range of courses equip students for modern farming including broadacre cropping, sheep husbandry, dryland development, agricultural technology, financial systems and computers in agriculture.

FESTIVALS Kanamaroo Festival, early December.

MINYIP ■ 1265

Minyip, Rupanyup and Murtoa are three small towns – in a shire with the quaint name of Dunmunkle – with a history of large-scale wheat production. In 1935, the citizens of Minyip erected a memorial to the scientist James Farrer who is justly remembered for spending twenty-five years breeding wheat strains to suit Australian conditions. Because of its high yield and tolerance of dry conditions, Farrer's most popular variety, 'Federation', was grown all over western Victoria.

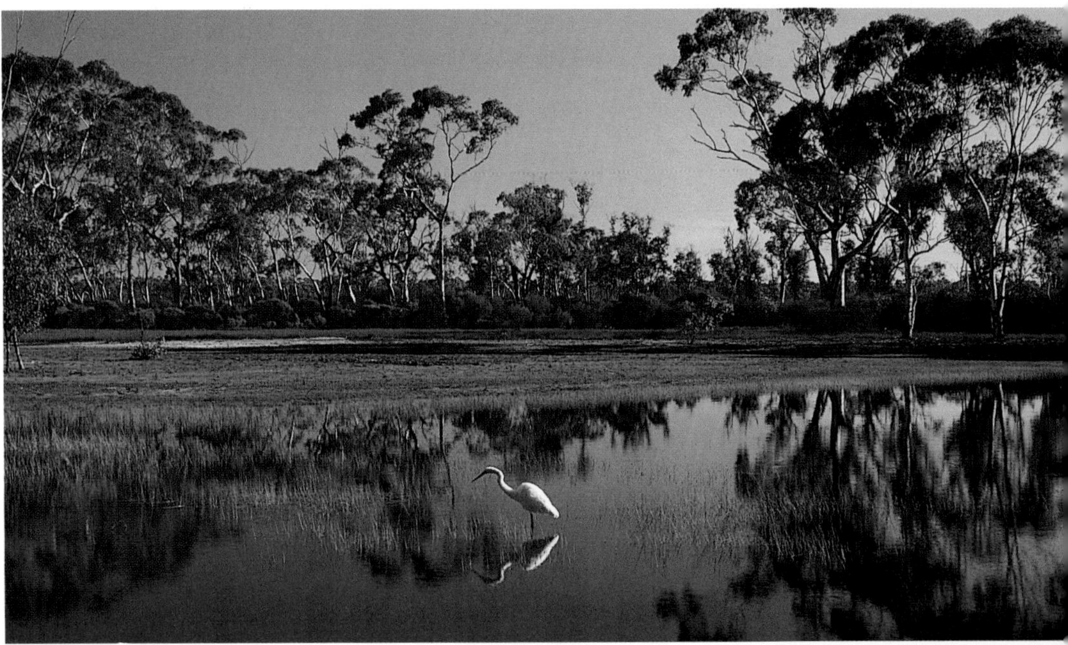

In contrast to the complex irrigation scheme which provides water to towns and farms in the arid Wimmera are the region's modest natural waterways which are a haven for waterbirds; Broughton's Waterhole is near Horsham.

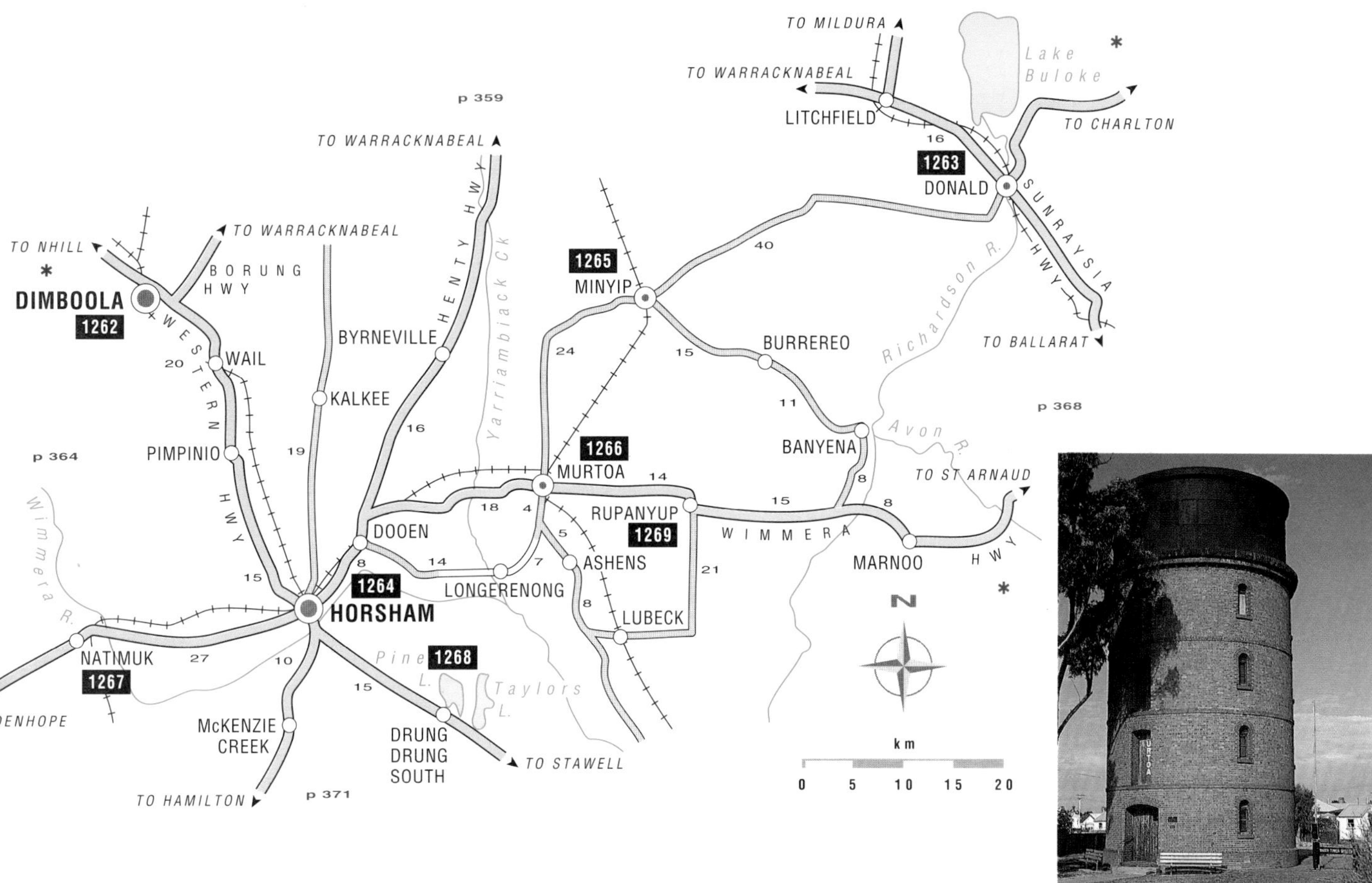

In the days of steam, engines refilled their boilers from the tank on Murtoa's stout but elegant tower.

Minyip lays claim to the first Commonwealth post office, built in 1901. St John's Lutheran Church was moved to Church Street in 1935 from Kirchheim, south-west of the town. The building is classified by the National Trust and displays lancet windows, an octagonal belfry, a nineteenth-century pipe organ and stained-glass windows. Before the settlers came, the Aborigines used to camp at Minyip – the name is said to come from 'minyup' meaning 'ashes' or 'dust' or 'monieup' meaning 'a camping place'. Minyip once also masqueraded under another name – for several years it appeared in the television series *The Flying Doctors* as 'Cooper's Crossing'. *Population 500*

MURTOA ■ 1266

Murtoa, the second town in the 'Dunmunkle triangle', lies on the edge of Lake Marma and was called 'Marma Gully' when it was part of Longerenong Station. The present name was given to the township in 1873 and is thought to be an Aboriginal word for 'home of the lizards'.

Before the railway line opened in 1878, loads of wheat from Murtoa were carted in waggons to Stawell. W.C. Thomas's flour mill began operating in 1876 and continued to grind for the next 101 years. The circular, brick, railway water tower has been a landmark in the district since 1886.

Murtoa enjoys the distinction of being the largest inland grain-receiving centre in Victoria and has two massive bulk storage sheds with a capacity of 27 000 tonnes for storing the annual harvest. The Concordia Lutheran College for training pastors and teachers was established in Murtoa in 1890 but moved to Adelaide fifteen years later. *Population 880*

NATIMUK ■ 1267

Natimuk thrived until the expansion of nearby Horsham. The town was named in 1875 after an Aboriginal word for 'little creek'. Before that, the Wilson brothers acquired three runs in the district: 'Polkemmet', 'Walmer' and 'Vectis'. Vectis Station later provided grazing paddocks for Burke and Wills' camels before they left for their ill-fated expedition into central Australia. The Wilsons were interested in horseracing and sponsored a meeting at Ballarat (see *Ballarat & Daylesford*) which founded the Victoria Amateur Turf Club in 1875.

In the 1870s, German settlers, earlier driven from their homeland by political persecution, moved from South Australia to take up selections in the Wimmera. When the Natimuk state school opened in 1875, nearly fifty per cent of the sixty-seven pupils were of German descent and German provincial styles are evident in some of the old colonial buildings; in the 1880s, some local newspapers were printed in German. Farmers in the region have diversified into legumes from the traditional crops of wheat, oats and barley.

JANE DUFF MEMORIAL This memorial, twenty kilometres west of Natimuk commemorates a 'babes in the bush' story. On an August day in 1864, Isaac Duff aged nine, his seven-year-old sister, Jane, and four-year-old Frank wandered from their timber home to play in the bush. Nine days and eight nights passed and so did hopes of finding the children alive – then King Richard, an Aboriginal tracker from Vectis Station, led the searchers to them. Isaac and Jane were unconscious and Frank was crying feebly but miraculously all three made a full recovery after careful nursing. The story of brave little Jane and her brothers was told in school readers of the time and in 1930 a schools' appeal raised money for this memorial.

MOTT'S DUMMY HUT The Victorian Selection Acts of the 1860s required people to live on their selected acres in some sort of permanent structure. David Mott's hut, which still stands west of Natimuk – having long outlived many 'real' houses – was a dummy residence aimed at increasing his family's holdings.

PINE LAKE AND TAYLORS LAKE ■ 1268

Land development was delayed in this arid region because of the shortage of water so shire councils began to construct tanks, weirs and other storage and supply works. The Wimmera–Mallee Domestic and Stock Supply System extends from the Grampians to Ouyen and Manangatang in the north, Underbool in the west and Korong Vale in the east. Open earth channels distribute the water, once a year, to the town and farm dams and many farmers graze stock in their paddocks after the grain harvest. Pine and Taylors lakes, formerly swamps, had been artificially deepened by 1923 and persist as 'balancing' storages, continuously filled from the Wimmera River and other 'upstream' reservoirs.

RUPANYUP ■ 1269

Rupanyup, by Dunmunkle Creek, is the third in the triangle of small wheat-belt centres and takes pride of place as the shire headquarters. In times past, Murtoa and Rupanyup feuded vigorously over who should administer Dunmunkle. The Shire Hall was to be moved to Murtoa but the citizens of Rupanyup, armed with picks, shovels and carpenter's tools, resisted the contractor who came to do the job. A few nights later, he stealthily removed the timber building on a large jinker. When the people of Rupanyup woke in the morning, even the tiny outbuilding was gone. The boisterous animosity between the two towns continued for years and was prone to erupt into fist fights at concerts, dances and football matches.

Early settlers called the settlement Ashen's Ten Mile Dam until 1874 when it became Karkarooc for a year and then Lallat; in 1876 it acquired its present name which is said to be from 'rubunyup' meaning 'tree by a swamp' where the local Aborigines once camped.

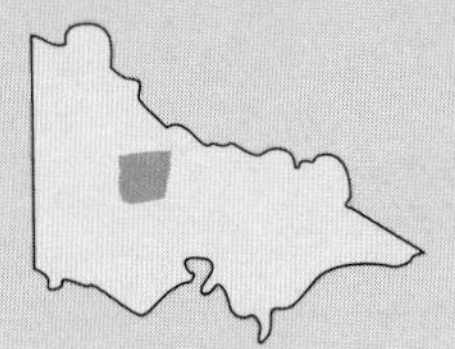

St Arnaud & Charlton

The sight and sound of metal detectors are still common in this 'golden triangle' region where gold fever never really subsided. For more than a hundred years, more – and larger – gold nuggets have been found here than in any other part of Australia.

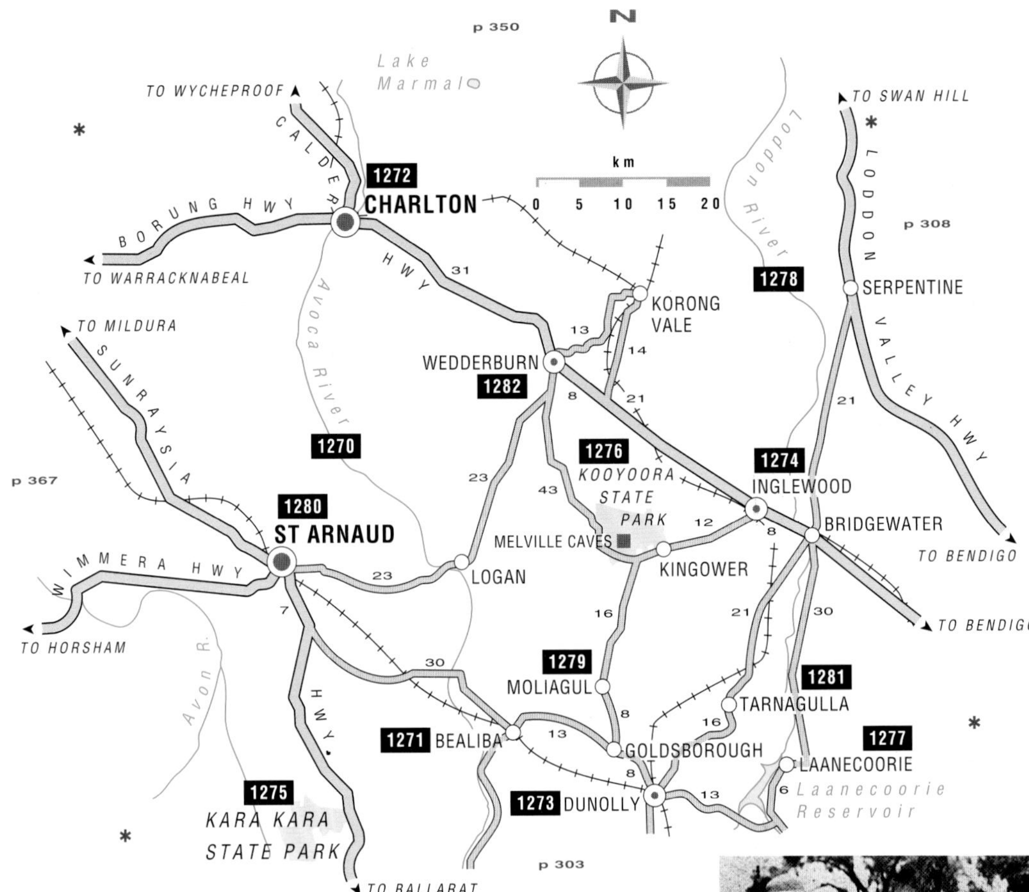

AVOCA RIVER ■ **1270**

On 10 July 1836, the Surveyor-General Sir Thomas Mitchell crossed the Avoca River east of St Arnaud and named it after the Avoca River in Ireland. The Irish Avoca rises in the Wicklow Mountains and flows into the Irish Sea, south of Dublin; the Australian Avoca has its headwaters in the Pyrenees Range and flows into Lake Bael Bael north of Kerang (see *Swan Hill & Kerang*).

One of Victoria's principal inland rivers, the Avoca flows in a generally northerly direction for 270 kilometres past the towns of Avoca and Charlton (see entry) as well as a number of smaller settlements.

BEALIBA ■ **1271**

Until 1863, Bealiba was known as Cochranes after John Cochrane who had two large runs in the area from the early 1850s. Gold was found on the most northerly of these two runs in 1856 and a small settlement developed on Cochranes Creek south of the short-lived diggings. The town was surveyed in 1863 and named Bealiba after Cochrane's home station (from the Aboriginal words 'beal', 'red gum', and 'ba', 'creek').

The railway arrived in Bealiba in 1878 and appropriately, red-gum timbers were railed from Bealiba to Melbourne. Now a small centre for a district noted for its wool, grain and vineyards, Bealiba has a cemetery which dates back to 1861, two years before the town was surveyed.

CHARLTON ■ **1272**

Charlton's most famous son was John Curtin, Prime Minister of Australia during the Second World War years of 1941 to 1945. He was educated at Charlton State School between the ages of nine and thirteen.

Although sheep played a role in Charlton's very early days, the district around the town was soon found to be ideal for wheat growing and Charlton's development has always been linked more with grain than with wool. James Malcolm and James Foreman established a flour mill apiece in the town in the 1870s...a few years after a third James, James Paterson, built the first bridge across the Avoca at Charlton. The bridge stood until 1925, as did James Foreman's flour mill. The new mill built to replace the original operated until the 1970s and still stands.

The history of wheat growing in the Charlton district is brought to life in the Golden Grain Museum, which is housed in the former Mechanics Institute, dating from 1883. On the Avoca River and at the junction of the Calder and Borung highways, Charlton has an early twentieth-century golf course designed unusually in the shape of a four-leafed clover.
Population 1180

DUNOLLY ■ **1273**

When Archibald McDougall established his run in 1849, he called it 'Dunolly' after Dunollie Castle in Scotland, the seat of the McDougall clan chiefs since the eleventh century. In 1852, gold was discovered by two Chinese prospectors on their way to Tarnagulla (see entry) and McDougall's run was soon swamped by 30 000 Chinese and European diggers. McDougall moved off his run and, in 1856, so too did the diggers. The discovery of gold a few kilometres to the south caused another mass migration and the Dunolly name moved from Old Dunolly (later renamed Goldsborough) to the new Dunolly goldfield.

More gold nuggets were found in Dunolly and the surrounding district than at any other goldfield in Australia – ten times as many as were discovered at Ballarat. Nuggets can still be unearthed around Dunolly although not many will be worth the $30 000 that was paid for a large nugget in 1976. Along Broadway, the town's main street – stretching for five kilometres in the gold-rush days but only two blocks today – are many buildings dating back to the 1850s and 1860s including the London Chartered Bank building (1867) where the famous and massive 'Welcome Stranger' nugget was weighed. In order to fit on the bank's scales the nugget had first to be broken into smaller pieces at the local blacksmith's and the anvil on which the huge nugget was broken up now takes pride of place outside the Gold-

At Moliagul, Messrs Deason and Oates re-enact the uncovering of their giant nugget with Mrs Deason and friends in supporting roles.

fields Historical Society Museum at Dunolly. Dunolly's licensed grocer where, until only a few years ago, wine was bottled on site, holds Victoria's oldest liquor licence dating back to the 1840s; when the floorboards in the shop were lifted in 1947, four forgotten boxes of gold were revealed!

Dunolly today is the centre of a rich agricultural and pastoral district where wheat, dairy produce and wool have replaced the gold on which fortunes were once made. During the Second World War, a giant, half-kilometre-long grain storage shed was built at Dunolly which became the main depot for central and northern Victoria, but it too is now a thing of the past, replaced by more conventional, cylindrical wheat silos. *Population 690*

INGLEWOOD ■ 1274

In 1859, the three Thompson brothers found gold on a forested section of Glenalbyn Station. Once known as Hall's Diggings, the name Inglewood was later given to this original find and to the second goldfield in 1860, three kilometres east of it. The simple tents, bark huts, tin shanties and more substantial buildings of Commercial Street linked old and new Inglewood, which had a population of more than 30 000 by 1860.

Between 1860 and 1880, when mining was scaled down, Inglewood had its own theatre and its own newspaper the *Inglewood Advertiser*, founded by Julius Vogel who was later to become Prime Minister of New Zealand. In 1862, it also had its own Great Fire when most of the buildings in one of the main streets were gutted and Inglewood suffered the unique deprivation of losing ten pubs in thirty minutes.

A eucalyptus distillery was established in the town in the late nineteenth century and, until recent years, the steam-distillation technique that produces the oil from blue mallee (*Eucalyptus polybractia*) had changed little since the 1850s. Inglewood is now recognised as one of the major centres in the district for the production of the oil that is used in products such as pharmaceuticals, inhalants, toothpaste and 'cough lollies' (see *Heathcote & Nagambie*).

Inglewood was the birthplace of Sir Reginald Ansett, the founder of Ansett Airways. Today, the small town is noted for waterskiing on the Loddon River and for its productive vineyards. *Population 740*

KARA KARA STATE PARK ■ 1275

This 3840-hectare state park sits on the western side of the Sunraysia Highway between Avoca and St Arnaud. The name Kara Kara, given to the shire as well as the park, derives from an Aboriginal word meaning 'gold or quartz'. There are two major water sources within the park – Teddington Reservoir and Strathfillan Creek, a tributary of the Avoca River – both of which are popular with fishermen and campers but are not suitable for swimming.

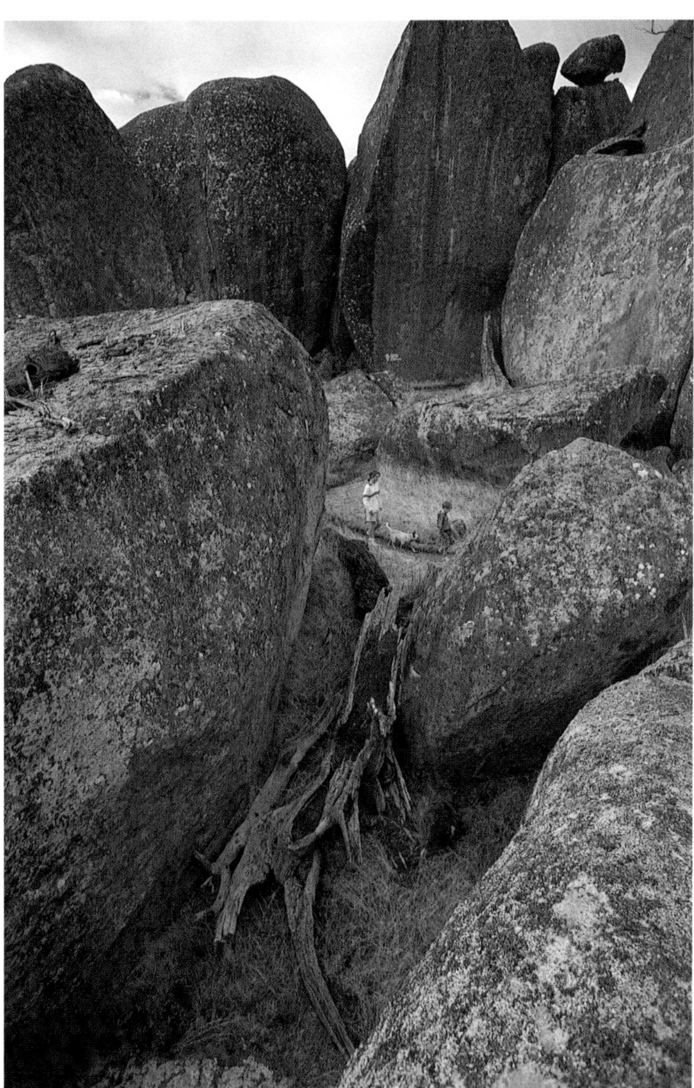

The spirits of the Aborigines and the bushrangers who sheltered there still seem to hover around the forbidding domain of Kooyoora Park's 'caves'.

KOOYOORA STATE PARK ■ 1276

The area around Mount Kooyoora in the McIntyre Ranges, was proclaimed a state park in 1985 and was the venue for that year's World Orienteering Championships. Popular with rock climbers, bushwalkers and fishermen, the state park attracts more than 10 000 visitors each year...including modern prospectors looking for gems and gold.

The Department of Conservation, Forests and Land has built a series of walking tracks within the 3590-hectare park, which encompasses the open-forest vegetation typical of north and central Victoria. This landscape is home to a score of rare or restricted plants and more than one hundred different bird species.

MELVILLE CAVES The granite outcrops on Mount Kooyoora have weathered over thousands of years to produce a complex of fissures, crevices between large tors and overhangs that were used for shelter by Aborigines and are now referred to as 'caves'. Frank McCallum, also known as 'Captain Melville', the leader of the Mount Macedon bushrangers, used the caves as one of his many hideouts. Although Melville escaped an official death sentence, he was either strangled, or hanged himself with a handkerchief while in jail.

LAANECOORIE ■ 1277

The unusual name for this small farming town came originally from the two Aboriginal words 'languy' and 'coorie', said to mean 'resting place' and 'kangaroo' respectively. First there was Langi-corrie Station in 1840 and then later, Laanecoorie when the town was officially proclaimed. The earliest Europeans in the region were described as 'three men from Yass' who had sheep runs near the Loddon River crossing at Laanecoorie.

To make the crossing less dangerous, a timber bridge was built at Laanecoorie in 1871 but when the dam wall at Laanecoorie Reservoir broke in 1909, the resulting flood washed the bridge away. Janevale Bridge, built by John – later Sir John – Monash to replace the old timber structure, was one of the earliest reinforced concrete bridges to be built in Victoria.

Laanecoorie was the site of a large blacksmith's shop where the steam-powered forge and hammer were used to build coaches and, as the gold diggers and goldfields were increasingly replaced by farmers and wheat fields, agricultural machinery such as harrows and ploughs.

LAANECOORIE RESERVOIR The first dam wall was built of earth in 1891 but after it burst in 1909, causing destructive flooding, it was rebuilt of more substantial material. The twenty-one-and-a-half-metre wall now holds back almost 8000 megalitres of water which is used for the Goulburn–Loddon Irrigation System and as town water for Dunolly, Tarnagulla and Laanecoorie.

LODDON RIVER ■ 1278

In his explorations of south-eastern Australia, Thomas Mitchell crossed the Loddon River twice and on neither occasion did he give it the name Loddon. Yarrayne, the local Aboriginal name, was the name Mitchell gave the Loddon River; he had a refreshing penchant for using what he thought were Aboriginal names over European. Renaming was obviously quickly in hand because by 1840, the first Loddon Station had appeared as a place on the river. The 392-kilometre-long river rises on the northern slopes of the Great Dividing Range, near Daylesford, and runs in a northerly direction to join the Little Murray north of Kerang.

From as early as 1857, water for irrigation was being pumped from the Loddon River at Kerang, which was and still is the major settlement on the river. Three reservoirs on the Loddon River – Laanecoorie, Cairn Curran and Tullaroop – contribute water to the Goulburn–Loddon Irrigation System. The total volume of water – some 180 000 megalitres – stored in the three reservoirs, is controlled at Loddon Weir from which the long Waranga Western Channel runs to the Goulburn River.

MOLIAGUL ■ 1279

Moliagul, despite its small size, is a two-monument village. The famous Welcome Stranger Monument (see sub-entry) commemorates the finding of the world's largest gold nugget and the other stands in memory of John Flynn, 'Flynn of the Inland', the founder of the Royal Flying Doctor Service who was born in Moliagul in 1880.

Moliagul, which derives from the Aboriginal 'moliagulk', thought to mean 'wooded hill', had its first gold rush in 1852 at Queen's Gully and was then abandoned until a second

The Loddon River's irrigating waters have been banking up into Laanecoorie Reservoir for more than 100 years.

rush in the late 1850s brought 16 000 diggers to the Little Hill goldfield. Following a third gold rush in 1861, Moliagul's fortunes were waning yet again when the finding of the huge 'Welcome Stranger' nugget in 1869 brought a fourth influx of fossickers.

Buildings still standing in Moliagul represent all four rushes. McCoy's Store was built during the first rush. The Mount Moliagul Hotel, opposite John Flynn's birthplace, dates back to the second rush of the late 1850s. The foundation stone of the Church of St Michael and All Angels, one of the state's earliest churches to be built of stone and brick, was laid by Reverend William Hall of Inglewood (see entry) in 1864. The state school was constructed in 1872 after the fourth and final gold rush and replaced the small timber school-cum-Methodist Church in which John Flynn's father taught when he first came to live in Moliagul in 1870.

Moliagul's more recent history includes the planting of a cherry orchard in the crater of the extinct Mount Moliagul volcano.

WELCOME STRANGER MONUMENT A granite obelisk, erected by the Mines Department in 1897, marks the spot where the hefty 'Welcome Stranger' nugget was found in 1869. Estimates of the nugget's net and gross weight vary from 70 000 to 78 000 grams but all sources, including the *Guinness Book of Records* agree that it was the world's largest pure gold nugget.

After fossicking in the district for seven years, Richard Oates and John Deason found the nugget among the roots of a stringybark tree a mere three centimetres below the surface. They loaded it onto a dray and took it to John Deason's hut where they burnt off the dross before carting it to Dunolly (see entry) to be weighed. The men were paid around 9500 pounds sterling for their find.

ST ARNAUD ■ 1280

Thomas Mitchell was very positive when he saw the district around St Arnaud, describing it enthusiastically in his journal as 'a country ready for the immediate reception of civilized man'...before describing his breakfast of emu eggs! By 1842, the first pastoral runs were established but it was the discovery of gold in 1855 that led to the establishment of the town. The miners who made the gold discovery attempted to keep their precious find hidden but within a few months the secret of the 'New Bendigo diggings' was out and prospectors flocked to the field.

When the village that grew up around the diggings came to be named in 1858, the Crimean War had just ended and the name of Marechal de St Arnaud, commander of the French troops in the Crimean War, was adopted. Although the initial gold rush was shortlived, deep quartz mining was an important industry in St Arnaud from 1885 to 1926. The first mine, the Lord Nelson, closed in 1915; it is now beneath the town's swimming pool. The last cyanide plant did not close down until 1950. But St Arnaud was able to survive and thrive because it was not dependent on mining alone.

After the Land Acts of the late 1860s St Arnaud became the gateway to the newly opened agricultural land of northern Victoria and a thriving centre for wool, wheat and flourmilling. These land-based pursuits, together with a large stock feed industry and a variety of light manufacturing industries from aluminium window frames to vintage car panels and eucalyptus oil to cement products have kept the attractive and historic township alive.

St Arnaud, on the eastern boundary of the Wimmera, has retained the ornamental, cast-iron lace trims now exceedingly rare in rural Victoria and has one of the state's earliest brick court houses, constructed in 1866. Napier Street which has a number of old red-brick civic buildings is now classified as a conservation area. *Population 2740*

TARNAGULLA ■ 1281

At Tarnagulla, the Poverty Mine, named after a bay in New Zealand, was anything but poor – over thirteen tonnes of gold came from the mine between 1854 and the early 1900s. The town had its own variety theatre where travelling performers put on regular shows and a bank with a gold-smelting chimney, both of which can still be seen. The cricket pitch flattened by the gold miners and on which an English professional team played, is no longer visible in the ghost village that once had a population of 20 000. The last gold from Tarnagulla came from the Poseidon Mine in 1906, the mine taking its name from that year's winner of the Melbourne Cup.

The cannon now in Memorial Park came from HMS *Nelson* to Tarnagulla in 1898 and has been fired on four occasions – the Relief of Mafeking, the 1902 coronation of Edward VII, the end of the First World War and at the 1988 Bicentennial celebrations.

WEDDERBURN ■ 1282

The Aboriginal rock carving on the mountain that the peripatetic explorer, Sir Thomas Mitchell climbed and named 'Barrabungalla' in 1836 still exists there but the cairn on the Calder Highway which commemorates Mitchell is a much more recent addition to the landscape.

Whether a Scottish shepherd by the name of Brady or another Scot, John Hunter Kerr, author of *Glimpses of life in Victoria*, made the first discovery of gold around Wedderburn in 1852 is still disputed. The goldfield was named Mount Korong, Mitchell's 'Barrabungalla' renamed, but was one of the less productive goldfields in the region. Wedderburn was surveyed in the late 1850s by William John Wills – Burke's partner in the ill-fated 1860 trans-Australia expedition – and thrived in the 1860s when the small town had as many as twenty-eight stores. The last remaining store from this period is now, appropriately, the Store Museum.

The small town has seen the rise and fall of a diversity of industries from eucalyptus factories, a cement works, a boot-uppers factory – which later became a dressing-gown factory – in the former Commercial Hotel, to brick kilns, now used to fire local pottery, and a boomerang factory, which was established in the 1970s.

But it was the post-1950s 'gold rush' that brought fame – and fortune – to sleepy Wedderburn. A large nugget – shaped like a dog and consequently named 'Golden Retriever' – was found in one lucky resident's backyard in 1950 and, within days, almost every backyard and roadside in town was being dug up. The Butterick family, who dug extensively in their backyard for three years, found three large nuggets. Three lucky schoolboys found the $50 000 'Beggary Lump' in 1979. Metal detectors became, and still are, popular with locals and tourists alike. Even the local Christmas Reef Mine has been reopened...as an art gallery in this small town where Albert Jacka, VC MC and Bar, was baptised and educated. *Population 760*

The elegant St Arnaud court house is one of a handsome group, including the old lock-up and post office, built of red brick made from local clay.

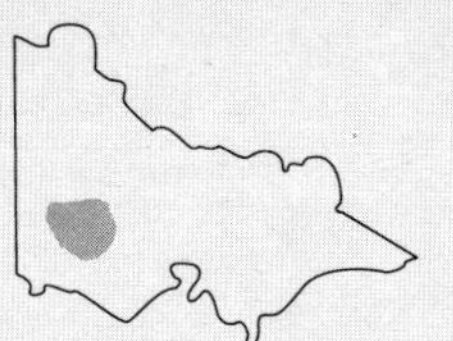

Ararat & Stawell

Some of Australia's most important examples of Aboriginal art are to be found on the rock walls of the starkly beautiful Grampians. The promise of land drew the first settlers and spelled the beginning of the end for the cave artists; the lure of gold soon drew many new inhabitants and towns began to grow.

ARARAT ■ 1283

Ararat was named by Horatio Spencer Wills, a settler who stopped here after struggling overland in 1841. He wrote, 'This is Mount Ararat, for, like the Ark, we rested here'. Gold was the flashpoint for the town's growth, and Ararat began to flourish after the precious metal was discovered at Pinky Point in 1854.

Three years were to pass before the Ararat rush began in earnest, when rich alluvial deposits of gold were discovered by some Chinese prospectors. The area was promptly named Canton Lead, although the Chinese prospectors were driven off by angry miners who mined round-the-clock to take more than 3000 ounces from the ground in less than three weeks. At the height of the rush, more than 20 000 people lived in a sprawling canvas shanty town. By the 1860s, the gold lodes were exhausted and the district once again returned to farming. Wine grapes were planted here in 1863 by Jean Pierre Trouette and Emile Blampied. By 1867, Trouette had six hectares under cultivation, and his fine wines were winning awards in Britain, France and the United States.

Historical items such as objects used by Chinese miners and Indian hawkers during the gold-mining era and a collection of Aboriginal artefacts are now housed in the Langi Morgala museum – a former woolstore in Ararat. Also of interest to the visitor are the Alexandra Gardens (1901–07) and the old post office (1861). Today, Ararat is the centre of an important agricultural, wool and wine-growing district. *Population 7630*

FESTIVALS Golden Gateway Festival, early October.

BALMORAL ■ 1284

Chinese miners once stopped here on their way to the Victorian gold fields from South Australia, where they landed to avoid Victoria's one-pound-sterling poll tax on Chinese immigrants. Today, some of the finest merino wool in the world is produced in this area. East of Balmoral, is Rocklands Reservoir, the fifth largest water storage in Victoria. The reservoir is also a popular location for watersports; the historic Glendinning Homestead (1909) is close by.

BLACK RANGE STATE PARK ■ 1285

This park in the western Grampians is often overlooked by motorists although it is well worth a visit. Rock shelters filled with Aboriginal art, imposing bluffs and cliffs and spectacular wildflowers are its main attractions. A five-kilometre return walk to the summit cairn in the south cliffs is rewarded by a panorama of the surrounding countryside.

BUNJILS CAVE ■ 1286

On one of the walls of one of these caves in the Black Ranges is an illustration of the creative being Bunjil, believed by Aborigines in this part of Victoria to be the All Father, a wise and good spirit. It was Bunjil who heated the sun which then warmed the earth, causing it to open. From its interior emerged the first men; Bunjil

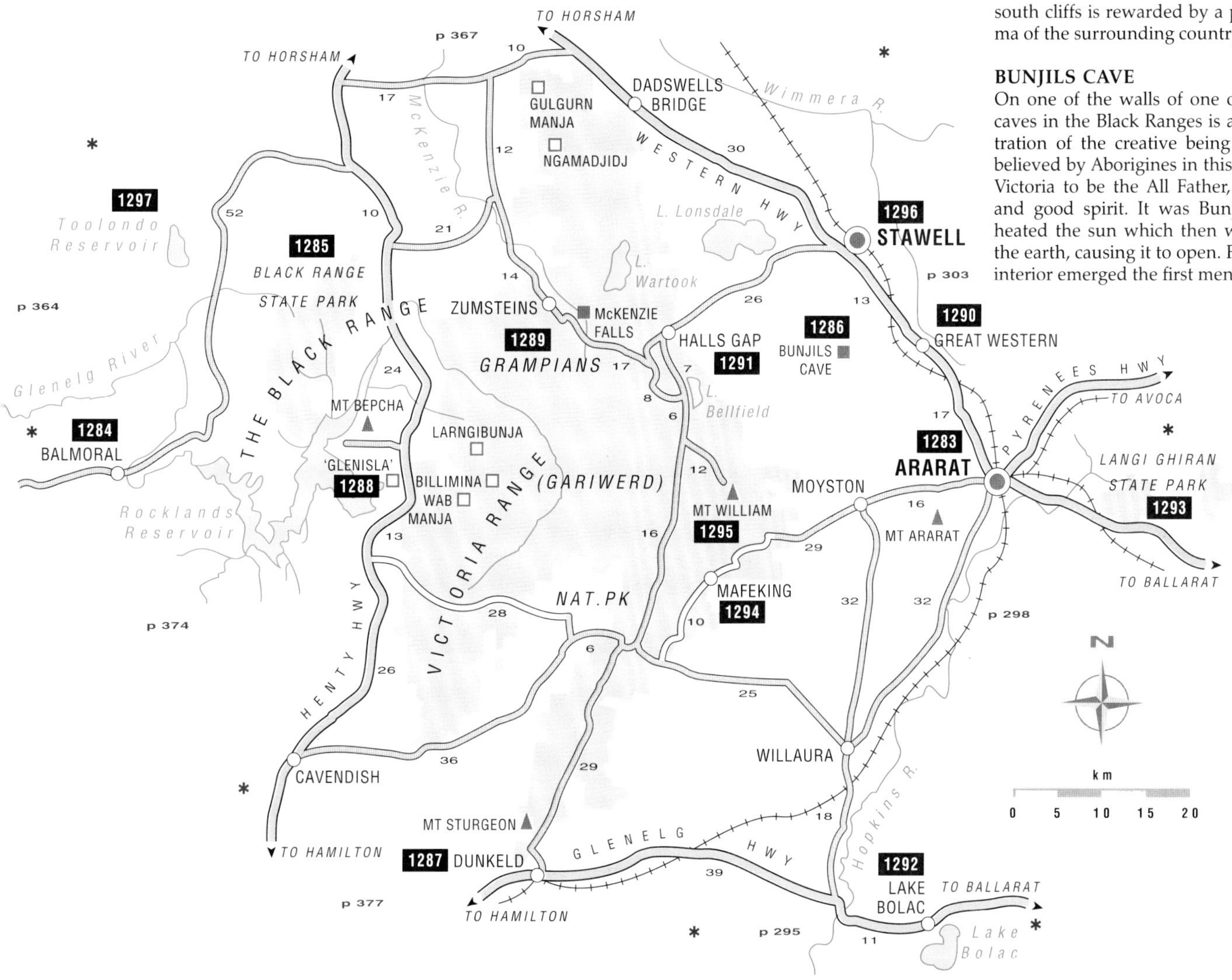

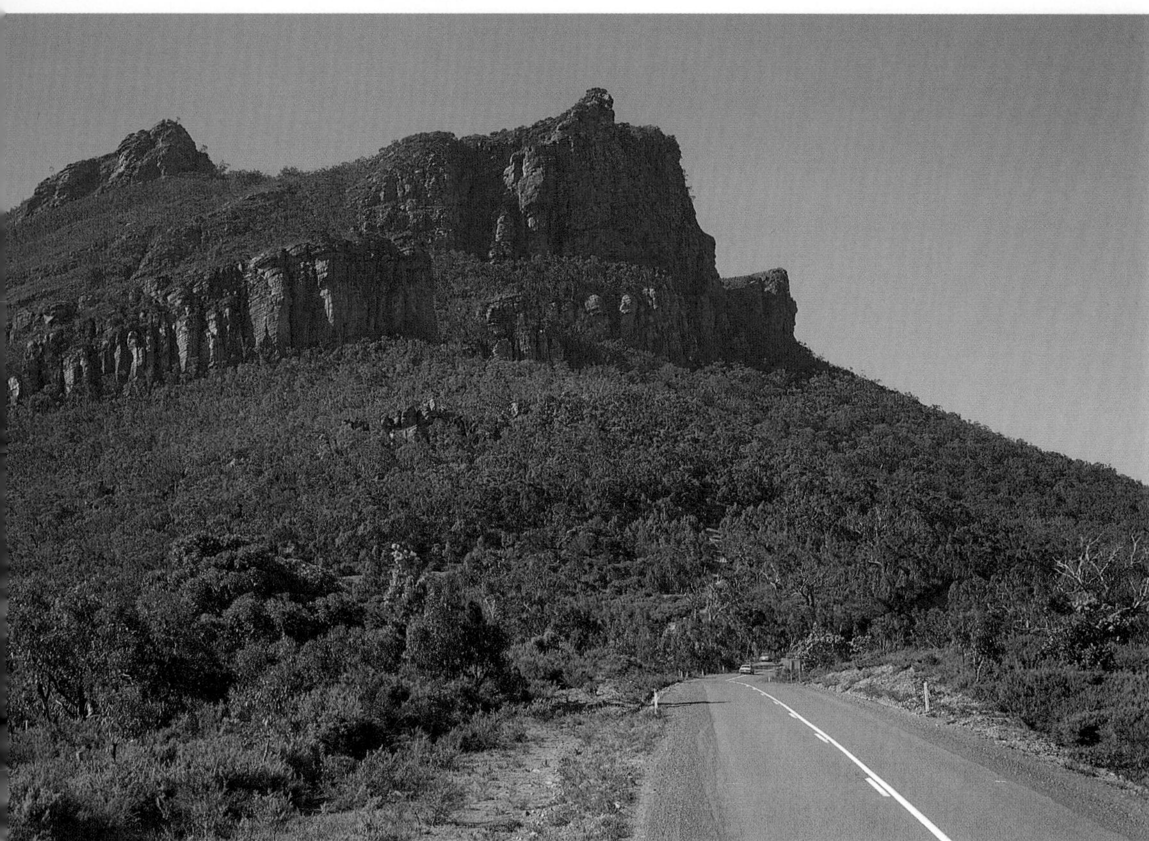

As its name suggests, Mount Abrupt is a sudden interruption to the Grampians foothills landscape near Dunkeld.

brought rain to make grass and roots grow for their nourishment, and is also credited with forming the features of the landscape. In this rock drawing, Bunjil is with his dog. The cave was found in 1957 by members of the Stawell Field Naturalists Club.

DUNKELD ■ **1287**

The explorer and Surveyor-General, Thomas Mitchell, camped for three days at the base of Mount Sturgeon in 1836 and named the two peaks here Sturgeon (590 metres), and Abrupt (830 metres). The small township which grew up in the vicinity was known as Mount Sturgeon until renamed Dunkeld by Scottish settlers nostalgic for their homeland. The town has a number of tourist shops and historic buildings including the Royal Mail Hotel (1885) and the old jail building and post office (1852).

Overseas buyers have paid record prices for the silky strands of the fine merino fleece from the farms around this town which is home to Victoria's Centre for Superfine Merino Wool.

'GLENISLA' ■ **1288**

Samuel Carter first came to 'Glenisla' around 1870, although the run had been taken up in 1843 by Hector Simpson of Charlotte Plains. Glenisla Homestead, now an historic attraction of the Western Grampians, is built of mellow pink, brown and yellow sandstone. It was half-finished when Samuel Carter was told that a road would pass through his property. After much negotiation he was able to buy the crucial stretch of road and, four years later, the homestead was finally finished. Today, it provides overnight accommodation and country-style living for visitors.

GRAMPIANS (GARIWERD) NATIONAL PARK ■ **1289**

The Grampians are a series of stark and spectacular sandstone ridges, folded into a 'cuesta' formation more than three million years ago. Cuesta is the name for an unusual landform, with steep escarpments and gently dipping slopes, which is eroded from deposits of sedimentary rock.

There are four main ranges in the Grampians: Mount William, Serra, Mount Difficult and the Victoria Ranges. Major Mitchell named these ranges after mountains in his native Scotland when passing through the area in 1836. Squatters had taken up large runs such as 'Ledcourt', near Lake Lonsdale, by 1840 and ten years later had established large homesteads such as 'Lexington', 'Barton' and the historic 'Glenisla' (see entry).

About 4000 motifs of Aboriginal rock art on the walls of secluded rock shelters throughout the Grampians have endowed them with more Aboriginal art than any other part of Victoria. Most paintings are in red ochre and the stick figures, emu tracks and hand stencils are thought to have great spiritual significance. These evocative paintings are one of the features that has made the Grampians a major tourist destination.

Some of the state's most spectacular scenery is here, and the many roads and bushwalks throughout the ranges give access to lookout points, lakes, waterfalls and wide valleys.

The major part of the Grampians became a national park in 1984, although their importance as a wildflower and wildlife sanctuary had long been recognised. Many wildflowers of the region are unique, such as the Grampian thryptomene, a delicate pink and white flowering shrub. Victoria's floral emblem, the pink heath, is one of hundreds of species which bloom on the mountain slopes in spring. The main flowering period is from June to November, although wildflowers can be seen every day of the year. Many rare and shy native animals also live in these mountains and the Grampian ranges are a stonghold for the soft-furred smoky mouse.

More than 200 species of birds are found in this 210 000-hectare parkland which adopted its alternative, local Aboriginal name in the 1990s. Emus roam on the heathlands, the wedge-tail eagle and peregrine falcon soar in the thermal air currents above Mount William, and lakes and swamps are home to a variety of waterfowl. The Grampians are the catchment for the Wimmera–Mallee domestic and stock water supply, the largest system of its kind in the world. Lake Wartook, Rocklands Reservoir, and Lake Bellfield, with a combined capacity of 336 000 megalitres, are popular recreation spots.

BRAMBUK LIVING CULTURAL CENTRE The art, clothing and tools of five Aboriginal groups from south-west Victoria are permanently displayed in this new cultural centre, two kilometres from Halls Gap. Photographs and videos of Aboriginal life and a Grampians 'soundscape' are integral to the multi-media displays.

LARNGIBUNJA SHELTER The original inhabitants of this region camped and painted images on the walls of its many rock shelters; once inaccurately given European labels, such as 'cave of fishes', these shelters are now known by descriptive, local Aboriginal names. Samuel Carter of Glenisla Station was the first to come upon painted rock shelters in 1859 while mustering his cattle in the Victoria Ranges. Numerous Aboriginal paintings are found near the picnic spot at Buandik in the Western Grampians. A ten-minute walk from Buandik goes to the Billimina shelter. A rough and slippery route, aptly known as the Goat Track, leads north from Buandik to the Larngibunja shelter. The drawings in the Larngibunja shelter were first thought to be fish but are now considered to be depictions of lizards.

NGAMADJIDJ SHELTER The Ngamadjidj shelter near Mount Zero displays white, pipe-clay paintings showing a group of twelve figures converging on two other figures in the centre who are fighting. Nearby, the Gulgurn Manja shelter is dedicated to Kartuk, the carpet snake.

ROSES GAP Roses Gap was a stopping place for the Chinese making their way to the Victoria goldfields from South Australia, where they had landed in an attempt to avoid Victoria's poll tax. A historic marker stands on the site of a police camp established to stop the influx. Today, a scenic route through Roses Gap follows the sandstone escarpments of the northern Mount Difficult Range. Briggs Bluff at the eastern entrance to the gap is named after Captain Robert Briggs who founded the 'Ledcourt' sheep run in 1840. The district is noted for its wildflowers, particularly in late winter and early spring.

WAB MANJA SHELTER The Harrop Track leads south from Buandik to the Wab Manja shelter. The cave is filled with stencilled hands, a symbol common to many Aboriginal rock shelters throughout the continent.

ZUMSTEINS Walter Zumstein, a beekeeper, set up this wildlife reserve when he returned from the First World War. Grey kangaroos are fed at dusk each evening, and black-faced mallee kangaroos occasionally appear. A walking track from Zumsteins leads to McKenzie Falls.

GREAT WESTERN ■ **1290**

Halfway between Stawell and Ararat is the little town of Great Western which gives its name to many fine Australian wines. Vines were first planted by the pioneer winemaker Joseph Best in 1866 and the district quickly established itself as a quality grape-growing area. After one intermediate change of ownership, the vineyard was sold in 1918 to the Seppelt family and is still producing some of Australia's finest table wines. Both Bests and Seppelts Great Western wineries were established after the Ararat gold rush. Ex-miners excavated enormous cellars, and millions of bottles of champagne are today maturing in more than six kilometres of underground stacking space. Seppelts Great Western vineyard was established by Joseph Best, brother of Henry, and after his death, it was acquired by Benno Seppelt. Guided tours explain the champagne-making process and afterwards wine tasting is held in the quaint old shaft house, an earthen building standing over the cellars.

HALLS GAP ■ 1291

One of the most popular sections of the Grampians, the Wonderland Forest Park, is centred around Halls Gap, a tourist centre at the base of the mountains. The town is the hub of a network of scenic drives and walking tracks, and is named after a pioneer stockman, Charles Browning Hall, who found the gap in 1840, when he followed the path taken by Aborigines across the Grampians. Hall later established three large cattle runs here. In 1969, the Boroka vineyard was established just outside town. The district is noted for its year-round wildflowers and a wildflower exhibition is held each spring.

HEATHERLIE Once the site of a quarry, Heatherlie is noted for the quality of its stone, which has been used in more than twenty buildings in Melbourne, including Parliament House and the Melbourne Town Hall. During the 1880s, it was declared a town as there were more than a hundred men working there.

Sunday wildflower expeditions by train to Heatherlie from Ararat and Stawell were once a great favourite with local people. They would jump off the train and collect wildflowers from the paddocks while waiting for the engine to take on water or coal, or while the level-crossing gates on properties were opened and shut. The quarry, north of Halls Gap along the Mount Zero Road, was closed in 1938 and is now a tourist attraction.

FESTIVALS Halls Gap Wildflower Exhibition, September–October.

LAKE BOLAC ■ 1292

A cluster of bluestone buildings on the Glenelg Highway makes up Lake Bolac, which takes its name from the nearby lake and is a popular spot for fishermen and water sports enthusiasts. Aboriginal relics such as fish traps, burial sites and middens have been found around the shores of Lake Bolac. Redfin, trout and eels are now the staple catch.

LANGI GHIRAN STATE PARK ■ 1293

This park is as intriguing as the sound of its unusual name. A lagoon lies between Mount Langi Ghiran and Mount Gorrin, the two mountains in the park. Walking tracks lead to one of the most sacred and ceremonially important Aboriginal caves in Victoria, the Cave of the Serpent on the southern slope of Mount Langi Ghiran. Here a man is depicted holding a snake, which is thought to be a sub-totem of the local Aboriginal totem, a black cockatoo. Langi Ghiran is an Aboriginal word for 'home of the yellow-tailed cockatoo'.

MAFEKING ■ 1294

A picnic area and marker are the only reminders of where this gold-rush town once stood. Gold was discovered in 1900 and thousands flocked here eager to strike it rich in the aftermath of the 1890s depression. At its height, a canvas city housed 10 000 miners, although few made their fortunes. At one stage, a nearby farm was stripped of all edible livestock and vegetables by hungry prospectors. Alluvial gold was soon exhausted and shafts for reef mining were then sunk to various depths. By 1912, the town was abandoned and bushfires in the 1960s burnt the last of the miners' huts. Overgrown pits, shafts and large, open creek beds are all that remain of the goldmining days.

MOUNT WILLIAM ■ 1295

Some of the most breathtaking views to be seen in the Grampians are from the road to Mount William (1170 metres), the highest point in the region. The summit is crowned with a small obelisk which commemorates explorer Sir Thomas Mitchell who, with four of his men, spent a night here under sub-zero conditions.

STAWELL ■ 1296

Stawell was once part of the 23 000-hectare 'Concongella' run, taken up by Dr John Blundell in 1845. It was on this station that William McLachlan, a shepherd, discovered gold in May 1853. Fabulously rich alluvial deposits were then uncovered, and the resulting gold rush, at its height, enticed 60 000 eager prospectors to the Ararat and Stawell goldfields. The alluvial gold was exhausted by the 1860s and reef mining, which involved large amounts of money and equipment, became firmly established. Goldmining was carried on profitably for another sixty years and yielded more than a million ounces of the precious metal. 'The Duke' became one of the richest mines in Victoria and mining jobs there were much sought after.

A rail link in 1876 made the town, by now quite prosperous, a frontier post for the Wimmera. Two years later, the first Stawell Gift, one of the richest foot races in the world, was staged (see sub-entry). Goldmining declined in the 1880s, but in 1886 gold was finally extracted from the elusive 'Magdala' lode. An enormous amount of capital had been poured into this operation, with little result, during the 1870s. Mining innovations such as the use of a diamond drill and dynamite to shatter the ore-laden rock eventually paid off.

Water flooding the mine shafts, poor returns and insufficient investment closed the mine in 1920, and homes were built around and on the old leases. Sixty years later, mining recommenced in the form of the Stawell Joint venture, managed by Western Mining Corporation. This time, mining was by open-cut and within six years the operation was producing more than sixty per cent of the gold extracted in Victoria.

Both tourism and the North West Woollen Mills are important economically to this region. Stawell's early days are remembered in its commercial centre with the Gold Reef Mall, the former main street and centre of the gold-rush days, the 1872 town hall which has a chiming clock and group of gold miners which is seen on the hour, and the 1873 St Patrick's Church with its altar made of Italian marble. *Population 6340*

Bunjils Cave and its depiction of a benevolent Aboriginal spirit was unknown to whites until the 1950s.

THE SISTERS Three immense granite boulders, now covered with graffiti, were named after the Levi sisters, members of an immigrant mining family which set up camp here upon its arrival at the Stawell gold diggings. During the 1860s, it was feared that the rocks might be demolished for building materials, and their preservation is due to the far-sighted action of an early settler, S.J. Davidson, who took up the land on which the boulders stood, later transferring it to the Borough of Stawell.

STAWELL GIFT This is the oldest and one of the richest foot races in the world. In early 1878, the Stawell Athletic Club was formed to organise regular events, and on Easter Monday of the same year held their first sports meeting. The first 'Gift' was run over 130 yards for a prize of twenty gold sovereigns; the distance was changed to 120 metres in 1973. Over the years, the race meeting has attracted substantial sponsorship, not only from local businesses but from nationally known corporations as well, with total prize money now in excess of 100 000 dollars.

FESTIVALS Stawell Gift, April.

TOOLONDO RESERVOIR ■ 1297

A popular trout-fishing spot, this reservoir is part of the Wimmera–Mallee water system. Remains of Aboriginal fish traps, mainly used for eeling and carbon-dated to about 1700 years ago, can be seen a few kilometres south-west of the Toolondo township.

The Grampians region is not all hills – in the valleys the paddocks are given over to fodder and wool production.

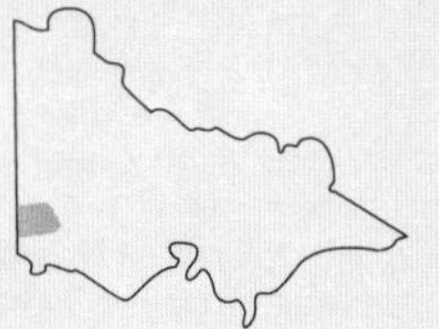

Casterton & Coleraine

The explorer Thomas Mitchell named this fertile region 'Australia Felix'; pioneer brothers, hearing of his praise, quickly established large sheep runs and became two of the earliest Australian wool barons. Wool remains an important industry, while visitors are drawn by the charm of small towns and tranquil fishing spots.

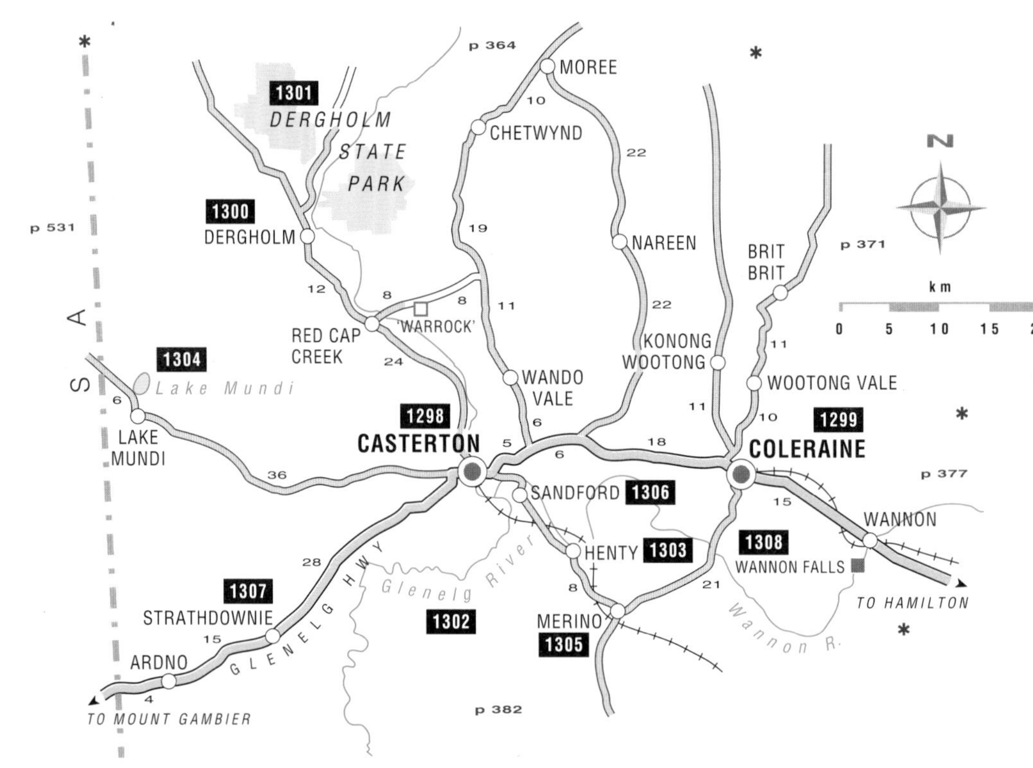

CASTERTON ■ 1298

So impressed was the busy explorer Sir Thomas Mitchell by this lush country, he named it 'Australia Felix', when he passed through here in 1836. To Mitchell it was 'champagne country', and on this rich soil, he exclaimed, 'British power and genius should plant…a little England'.

He went on to Portland and vividly described what he had seen to the Henty brothers who had settled there two years before. Edward, John and Francis, sons of Thomas Henty, an English merino breeder, soon after rode north and established four stations – 'Merino Downs', 'Muntham', 'Sandford' and 'Runnymede'. Several of the stations were to become known far and wide for their generous hospitality and lavish way of doing things, even though early guests were housed in sod huts. A weatherboard homestead built by Edward Henty for his 'Muntham' run can be seen south of the town.

A monument honouring Edward Henty stands on Muntham Hill which, along with Mickle Lookout, has panoramic views of the town and surrounding district. Poet and author Mary Gilmore lived in Casterton from 1907 to 1912 and taught at the local school. She moved to the town from nearby Strathdownie (see entry) where she spent five years after her return in 1902 from 'New Australia' – a settlement established in Paraguay by a group of high-minded Australians as an attempt to achieve an ideal state of socialism. While here she wrote for the *Bulletin*,

The highway runs conveniently close to the Wannon Falls where winter rains ensure a display for picnickers.

began the Woman's Page of the Sydney *Worker* newspaper – over which she presided for twenty-four years – and her first book of poems, *Marr'd* (1910) appeared.

Casterton was surveyed around 1840, and the first building, an inn, built about a year later. The hills surrounding the town enclose it like a wall, and its name, Casterton – after a similarly sited town in England – comes from an old Roman word meaning 'walled city'. A large fleur-de-lys, the Scout emblem, dominates the hillside above the town centre.

Modern Casterton is one of Victoria's most important stock marketing centres and many stud farms are found here. Dairying, woolgrowing, the raising of fat lambs, beef cattle and mixed farming are the main industries. An experimental sheepfarm for superfine wool is on the outskirts of Casterton. The surrounding district, particularly along the Wando River, is popular with gemstone fossickers. *Population 1810*

WARROCK HISTORIC HOMESTEAD This homestead complex – more like a medium-sized village of thirty original buildings, now listed by the National Trust – is north of Casterton. Built by George Robertson, a Scottish cabinet maker who settled here in 1843, each building has cleverly crafted detailing, particularly around the roofs and windows. One of the buildings is now a cottage museum and displays the tools used by George Robertson to build Warrock, handmade locks and keys, a wool bale stencil, shearing pieces and an old digital clock.

The cabinet-making background of the founder of 'Warrock', near Casterton, is evident even in the farm buildings where symmetry rules.

COLERAINE ■ 1299

John Bryan, a relative of the pioneering Henty family (see Casterton) – the first permanent European settlers in Victoria – took up a run here in 1839. He was displaced by the Whyte brothers who claimed some 23 000 hectares in 1840 and set up house at Wootong Vale, near Coleraine. The Whyte brothers divided their land into smaller stations and licensed these to new settlers at high prices.

By the mid-1850s, the Whytes had left the district but during the 1840s, the western districts of Victoria had been dominated by wool kings such as the Whytes, the Hentys and the Forlonges. Many of these large estates were sub-divided in the 1920s to allow for closer settlement, mainly by soldiers returned from the First World War.

One of the first serious conflicts between Aborigines and white settlers took place on a Whyte station in March 1840. Aborigines were massacred at a camping and corroboree spot by cannon loaded with nails, bolts and gravel, allegedly for stealing sheep. The spot became known as Murdering Flat, but today the peaceful countryside shows no sign of the violent events of the past.

Widespread bushfires in 1840 destroyed much native vegetation in the Coleraine district and an unseasonal and severe frost which came in 1844 killed off any new growth so that even today there are few mature native trees in the district.

Just outside town, is a monument to the poet, Adam Lindsay Gordon. Gordon raced horses, and wrote the famous poem, 'The Fields of Coleraine', after winning a maiden steeplechase here in 1865. Good trout fishing is found to the north, at the Konongwootong Reservoir. The reservoir, the banks of which are popular picnic locations, provides water storage for Coleraine, Casterton and the surrounding district. *Population 1090*

DERGHOLM ■ 1300

This small village still has the hotel, store and post office under the one roof. Settled in the 1860s and 1870s, the town was once a thriving centre with its own blacksmith and bootmaker. Little of this remains and today a handful of houses and the multifunctional hotel make up this tiny settlement.

Nearby is Red Cap Creek, named after Tommy Red Cap, a member of the Aboriginal cricket team which toured England in 1868 (see *Edenhope & Goroke*). A prodigious worker, he is supposed to have shorn ninety-one sheep in one day. Tommy Red Cap is buried under a wattle tree near the Dergholm cemetery.

DERGHOLM STATE PARK ■ 1301

North-west of Dergholm is this state park of the same name. The heathlands and woodlands of brown stringybark are typical of the vegetation which covered this part of Victoria before white settlement. No picnic facilities or running water are provided in the park which is generally used only by bushwalkers. Bailey's Rock to the north – a rare outcrop of dark green granite boulders – does have several picnic areas and scenic walks. Bilston's Tree, near Chetwynd, further north again, is said to be the biggest red gum in Australia. Gem fossickers find a great variety of stones such as agate, jasper, quartz and petrified wood in the Wando Vale, Carapook, Nareen and Chetwynd areas.

GLENELG RIVER ■ 1302

Rising in the Grampians, this river flows generally southward for 470 kilometres to Discovery Bay at Nelson, near the South Australian border. The Rocklands Reservoir on its upper reaches is part of the Wimmer–Mallee domestic and pastoral supply system, the largest of its kind in the world. The chief tributary of the Glenelg River is the Wannon River (see Wannon Falls) which also rises in the Grampians and joins the larger stream at Casterton.

Major Thomas Mitchell, who travelled down the river in 1836, described it in glowing terms '...picturesque limestone cliffs overhung the river, and cascades flowed out of caverns hung with stalactites...the shores were festooned with green dripping shrubs or creepers, or terminated in a smooth grassy bank...'. He named it after Lord Glenelg, Secretary of State for the Colonies.

HENTY ■ 1303

A road sign displaying the name 'Henty', a crumbling railway platform and goods shed and the local fire-truck shed are all that remain of this small hamlet. Henty was once a thriving village and, in 1883, became a railhead before the railway line was extended to Casterton in 1884. The railway line has long since been removed. Henty was named after the district's pioneers, the Henty family.

LAKE MUNDI ■ 1304

Now part of a wildlife reserve, this lake often appears more like a swamp covered with reeds. It is often bone dry in summer but can be up to twenty centimetres deep in winter. Wading birds are seen here and the lake is a habitat for the metallic sun orchid, a plant rarely found in western Victoria.

MERINO ■ 1305

This town is on the old Merino Downs Station where Francis Henty settled in 1837, and which became the most famously hospitable of the Henty stations (see Casterton). The town has a hotel, post office, four churches, a public hall and rifle, golf and tennis clubs.

SANDFORD ■ 1306

Records show this tiny hamlet was named by John Henty in 1857 after a place he knew in England. Early settlers claimed the settlement was named after a sandy ford which Major Mitchell used to cross the river at the northern boundary of the Sandford estate. The Land Act of 1861 brought an influx of new settlers to the area and the town began to grow. Business in the town transferred to nearby Casterton as it began to develop as the principal town of the district. For many years, Sandford had oil-burning street lights and was one of the last towns in Victoria to have electric street lighting installed.

STRATHDOWNIE ■ 1307

South-west of Casterton South is the tiny settlement of Strathdownie. The town was once the home of William Gilmore, who married young Mary Cameron while in Paraguay as part of William Lane's utopian 'New Australia' settlement. The couple came back to Australia in 1902 to live at the family property, 'Burnside'.

Mr Gilmore, a fencing contractor, was often away from home for long periods, and in her memoirs *Old Days, Old Ways*, (1934), Mary Gilmore vividly recounts being alone in a slab hut with her child, and listening to the wind whistle through the many cracks and the sound of snakes moving behind sheets of the *Sydney Morning Herald* which had been pasted on the walls as wallpaper. Other poems written by Mary Gilmore in this period include 'The Gilmore Chief', 'Casterton to Mount Gambier' and 'The Disinherited'. In the last poem, she expresses the limitations of life in a Strathdownie slab hut with some anguish. In 1907, the Gilmores moved into the relative comfort of Casterton (see entry).

WANNON FALLS ■ 1308

East of Coleraine, in red gum country on the Wannon River, are the Wannon Falls and the Nigretta Falls. The Wannon Falls, with a straight thirty-metre drop, are particularly spectacular in winter, when a curtain of spray often hangs over the valley. During summer, both locations provide good resting places for the traveller, with swimming in deep pools or fishing for trout or redfin.

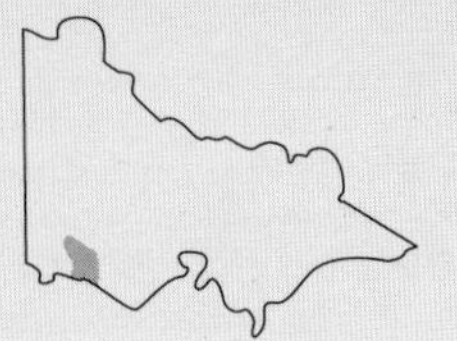

Warrnambool & Hamilton

The wild shores of the 'shipwreck coast', where the bones of many a seafarer lies in Davy Jones' locker, were bravely charted by English, French and perhaps even Portuguese navigators, and were for a time also the haunt of Bass Strait sealers and whalers. In the old ports and the farmlands they served, signs of the Scottish, Irish and Prussian origins of the European settlers can still be seen.

Warrnambool fishing boats wisely gather behind a seawall where the wild Southern Ocean scoops out Lady Bay.

ALLANSFORD ■ 1309
This quiet township on the Hopkins River serves a long-standing dairying industry based on the fertile plains of the district. Its butter co-operative, one of the few remaining in Victoria, was established in 1888 and the local Kraft factory is one of the largest cheese manufacturing plants in the world. The cheese connection is celebrated in the town with a display of early cheese- and butter-making equipment gathered from farms throughout the district.

Allansford was originally a private town established by the family of John Allan, one of the Allan brothers who settled in the area in the early 1840s. The pisé – rammed earth – schoolhouse they built was still being used in the early 1990s.

CARAMUT ■ 1310
The hamlet of Caramut grew up beside a crossing on Mustons Creek. Squatter John Muston was the first white settler in the area, staking out a run in 1839. The name 'caramut', thought to be an Aboriginal word for 'markings' was adopted in 1854.

DENNINGTON ■ 1311
Dennington has the unusual distinction of being home to what is believed to be the largest condensed milk factory in the Southern Hemisphere. The factory produces a wide range of dairy products for both domestic and overseas markets. The town is named after the birthplace in England of Charles Hotham, Governor of Victoria from 1854 to 1855.

GRIFFITHS ISLAND ■ 1312
Just offshore from Port Fairy (see entry), and now connected to it by a causeway, Griffiths Island was originally two islands. The eastern part, where the lighthouse now stands, was known as Rabbit Island. In the 1850s, when a breakwater was built, the two were joined, and riverbed silt dumped here enlarged the link.

The island was used in 1826 as a sealing base by brothers Charles and Captain John Mills. Ten years later, the whaling station established here by Portland Bay whaler John Griffiths was the impetus leading to the settlement at Port Fairy. The island came under the control of a James Atkinson in the early 1840s and the whalers were offered a fifty-year lease if they built a breakwater to protect Port Fairy harbour. This was agreed, but the wall, when only half-finished, was demolished by gale-driven winds so severe that a whale is reported to have been blown out of the sea!

The station ceased operations in the late 1840s, possibly as a result of this chain of events, although it may be that its supply of the southern right whale, whose great bones by this time thickly littered nearby East Beach, had been exhausted.

The island is a muttonbird sanctuary for the flocks which breed here from mid-October to late April.

PORT FAIRY LIGHTHOUSE The lighthouse stands on the eastern tip of Griffiths Island, once separated by water and known then as Rabbit Island. It dates from 1859, is built of bluestone quarried near its site and was originally painted red. The light is twelve-and-a-half metres above sea level and now runs on solar power. The massive stone risers of its spiral staircase are an integral part of the circular wall and are carried through as one slab of stone to the outside. Near the base of the lighthouse, century-old gardens still bloom in spring but the lightkeepers' cottages they embellished were demolished in the 1950s.

HAMILTON ■ 1313
In the grazing tradition of much of Victoria's Western District, Hamilton is renowned for its superfine merino wool. This region – and once upon a time, the nation with it – grew rich on the sheep's back, its pastures supporting record numbers per hectare, and the town lays claim to being the 'Wool Capital of the World'. This is still its economic base, although beef production has become increasingly important in recent years.

The area was settled in 1838 – after the wide-ranging explorations of the Surveyor-General Major Thomas Mitchell – by the Scottish Wedge brothers, who called their run 'The Grange'. By 1851, a web of rough tracks set out from Hamilton to Melbourne, Port Fairy and Portland. Thirty years later it had grown into a substantial town with a population of 3000 served by nine churches, publics offices, two colleges for boys and an academy for young ladies.

Lake Hamilton was created in 1977 by damming Grange Burn. Upstream on the banks of Grange Burn are some of the few remaining colonies of the eastern-barred bandicoot which, despite being one of the world's fastest breeding mammals – with a gestation period of less than two weeks – is an endangered species on the Australian mainland. Around Hamilton however, the creature survives in suburban gardens and nearby grasslands. A scientific research program is underway to ensure the bandicoot's long-term future. *Population 9750*

ABORIGINAL KEEPING PLACE MUSEUM This collection of Aboriginal art and artefacts of the Western District was created by the Department of Prehistory at La Trobe University and is housed in the old Mechanics' Institute in Hamilton. It includes a rare kangaroo tooth necklace, digging tools, emu egg carvings, grinding stones, stone scrapers and axe heads, and exhibits on the uses of fibres, fruits and grasses from local plants.

CITY OF HAMILTON ART GALLERY The Hamilton Gallery includes an extensive collection of watercolours by English painter Paul Sandby, Australian paintings from the nineteenth and twentieth centuries, a fifteenth-century carved duck from Germany, a Phoenician necklace from the fourth century BC and artefacts and tapestries from India, Tibet and Japan. The gallery was established under a bequest made by a local grazier Herbert Bucannan Shaw and opened to the public in 1961. Shaw's own fine art collection, now housed here, includes English silver, porcelain and fine Chinese ceramics.

FESTIVALS Wool Heritage Festival, late July.

HOPKINS RIVER ■ 1314

The Hopkins River rises in the Great Dividing Range near Ararat and on its journey south flows first through gentle hills, then cuts a deep valley across the lava plains of the Western District before plunging over the Hopkins Falls for its final leg to the sea. The falls are known for the annual migration of eels which takes place in early summer, when hundreds of tiny elvers can be seen fighting their way up the watery rockface. The river is tidal in its lower reaches and navigable for the last eight kilometres when it broadens before entering the sea through the estuary at Lady Bay, just east of Warrnambool. Fishing near the estuary may result in catches of bream, estuary perch, mulloway and mullet, as well as ocean fish such as salmon which move in with the tide. A feature of the river for more than a century is the ornate, timber boatshed complex near its mouth.

KOROIT ■ 1315

Descendants of this district's original Irish settlers still grow onions and potatoes here in the rich soil surrounding Koriot, one of the earliest farming villages in Victoria. It lies on the northern slopes of Tower Hill, halfway between Port Fairy and Warrnambool and is characterised by its tiny cottages, whitewashed fences, solid white-mullioned church and large presbytery and convent, all evidence of an Irish Roman Catholic community transplanted.

Many of the immigrants to Koroit and nearby Killarney were recruited by James Atkinson who 'owned' Port Fairy. They took up small farming blocks and grew prosperous supplying the huge market created by the 1850s gold rush. The novelist Henry Handel Richardson had an unhappy childhood association with this town. Her father, the model for her character 'Richard Mahony', died here in 1879 and is buried in nearby Tower Hill cemetery. To maintain the family, her mother was forced to take a position as Koroit's postmistress, an appointment noted by a plaque on the bluestone post office, a building classified by the National Trust.

One of the few things here which is not Irish is Koroit's name. That comes from the Aboriginal name of one of the islands in the crater lake of Tower Hill and is said to mean 'large male kangaroo'. *Population 970*

ROSEBANK This 'classical revival'-style house was built for David McLaws – Scottish, not Irish – the first publican of the Caledonian Inn in Port Fairy (see entry), and was his home for thirty years. Construction began in 1852 and substantial additions were made in 1880.

LADY JULIA PERCY ISLAND ■ 1316

This flat-topped volcanic island is surrounded by steep cliffs that rise almost fifty metres above sea level at its southern end. It shelters a colony of Australian fur seals, a remnant of

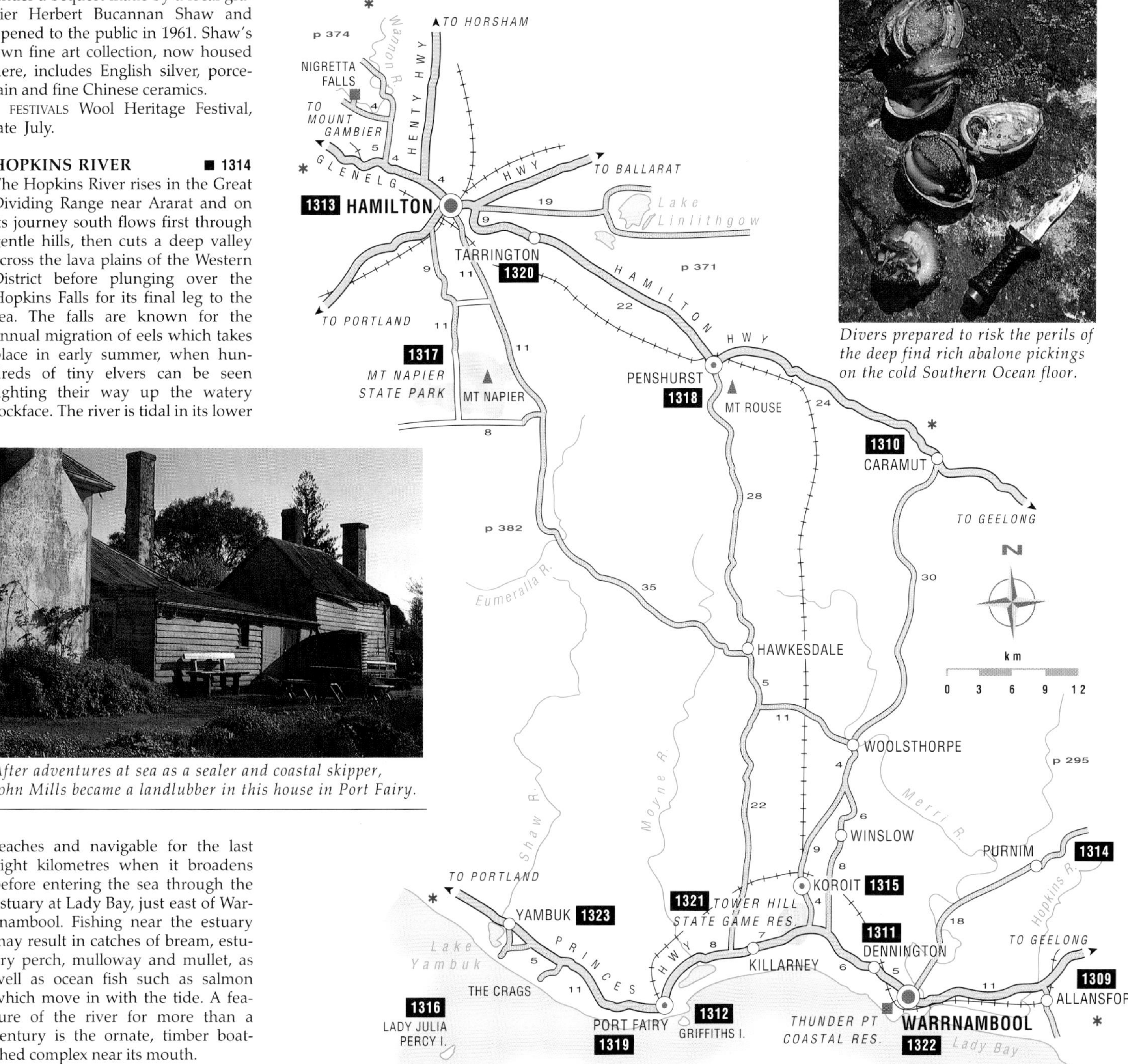

After adventures at sea as a sealer and coastal skipper, John Mills became a landlubber in this house in Port Fairy.

Divers prepared to risk the perils of the deep find rich abalone pickings on the cold Southern Ocean floor.

the huge herds that lived in Bass Strait and along the southern coastlines before the depredations of sealers. The island is a major breeding site for the diving petrel and the fairy prion – both are burrow-nesting birds, and it has been suggested that the fairy prion moves into burrows vacated by the earlier-breeding diving petrels. Muttonbirds also use the island to breed.

The island was named in 1800 by Lieutenant James Grant aboard the brig *Lady Nelson* after a member of the family of the Duke of Northumberland, Percy being the family name. Two years later, the French explorer Nicholas Baudin showed Gallic flair by naming it felicitously for its birds, `Île aux Alouettes' – Island of Larks.

MOUNT NAPIER STATE PARK ■ 1317

Outpourings of lava over thousands of years, built up layer upon layer, form the gently sloping cone of extinct volcano Mount Napier. At 440 metres above sea level, it is visible for many kilometres around and is surrounded by a rugged stony plateau. The quoll, once known as the tiger cat, is found here.

BYADUK CAVES These twelve caves, which look a little like railway tunnels, were formed when the outer crust of Mount Napier lava cooled and solidified while the inner part remained liquid and flowed on. They are difficult of approach and access but are of great interest to keen cave explorers. The caves are home to bent-wing bats.

The last remaining evidence of the long-demolished light-keeper's cottages on Griffiths Island are the irises (foreground) and other flowers gone wild.

PENSHURST ■ 1318

A tidy bluestone town serving the surrounding agricultural, and pastoral district, Penshurst numbered many Tasmanians among its first settlers, a reminder that in the days before reliable road links Launceston, across Bass Strait, was only a little more travelling time away than Port Phillip. The town lies at the foot of double-coned Mount Rouse, a traditional Aboriginal meeting place and in the 1840s site of an abortive attempt to establish an Aboriginal 'protectorate'. On its summit, 340 metres above sea level, is a fire-spotting lookout with panoramic views north towards the Grampians. *Population 480*

PORT FAIRY ■ 1319

In the 1850s, picturesque Port Fairy, in its sheltered cove at the mouth of the Moyne River, was one of the busiest shipping ports in Australia. Here, ocean-going vessels lying in the bay were loaded from the flat-bottomed lighters which swept across the shallow waters at the river mouth with cargoes of wool, potatoes and wheat, as well as gold wrested from the central highlands, to be shipped direct to England.

The anchorage here was discovered by chance about 1810 when Captain James Wishart of the cutter *Fairy* was blown across the sandbar at the mouth of the Moyne into the protected waters beyond. The settlement which grew up here around the whaling station on Griffiths Island (see entry) numbered some 100 whalers, boatbuilders and traders by 1840 but, because it had not been authorised or surveyed, was illegal in the eyes of the government. To sort matters out, leasehold to the entire area, including the island, was sold to a Sydney-based solicitor James Atkinson who renamed the town after his native Belfast – by which name it was known until 1887. The lease terms which then applied to the town's businesses, built up by independent effort and now suddenly tenants of a stranger, forced many of them to close. However, because of its location and good, safe anchorages – improved by the 1870s dredging of the river mouth which allowed access to the Gipps Street wharves upstream – the port remained popular with coastal and ocean-going ships until the 1880s when more competitive road and rail transport began to eat into its business. Even so, quite large ships continued to call until the 1930s. They turned in the basin that is now the yacht marina.

Between 1836 and 1876 more than thirty vessels were wrecked in the waters around Port Fairy, earning the shoreline the title of 'shipwreck coast'. A shipwreck walk guides visitors to the wrecks of four vessels which founderd here, perhaps the best known being the schooner *Thistle*, built in Calcutta in 1790 and bought to Australia in 1832 by the Henty brothers. She was driven ashore in 1837 while waiting to load a cargo of wattlebark.

Today shark, crayfish and abalone fishing are the main industries here, with dairying and potato and onion growing taking place on the surrounding farms. A pharmaceutical manufacturing plant is a major source of employment in the town. *Population 2470*

CALEDONIAN INN The simple, single-storey, bluestone Caledonian Inn has been in operation since 1844, when it was built for Scotsman David McLaws, and claims to be the oldest continuously licensed hotel in Victoria. The novelist Rolf Boldrewood (Thomas Alexander Browne) was superintendent of 'Squattlesea Mere', north of Port Fairy, from 1844 to 1858 and held horse sales in the inn's yard.

MOTTS COTTAGE, SACKVILLE STREET One of the oldest buildings in Port Fairy, the cottage bears the name of its first occupant, a Mr Sam Motts, a member of Captain James Wishart's whaling crew. The timber rooms at the front are the earliest, built most likely in the 1840s, the central two-storey, stone part was added in about 1860 and the rear timber section in 1890. The cottage is now owned by the National Trust and contains a collection of period furniture and other items from the Mott family. It is open for inspection.

JOHN MILLS COTTAGE, GIPPS STREET Captain John Mills moved into this cottage with his wife and two sons in the early 1840s, when it consisted of the central weatherboard section only. The rear kitchen was added several years later and the front section was built in 1853, after the captain retired from the sea and became Port Fairy harbour master.

MILLS REEF At the end of East Beach is the solidified remains of an ancient lava flow, probably from Tower Hill. According to local legend, southern right whales once used it to rub off their barnacles.

THE CRAGS Named for its spectacular rocky foreshore, The Crags, off the Princes Highway to the west of Port Fairy, is also of interest for the calcified roots of ancient trees and shrubs which can be seen in quantity here. The peak of the small islet adjoining the beach gives fine views of the coast in both directions.

FESTIVALS Folk Festival, March; Spring Music Festival, October.

TARRINGTON ■ 1320

The area around Tarrington was settled in the 1860s by German farmers from South Australia, exiled in the 1840s from Prussia, who were forced by drought to once again pack up and move on. The township was originally called 'Hochkirk'.

TOWER HILL STATE GAME RESERVE ■ 1321

Tower Hill is one of Victoria's youngest inactive volcanic remnants. The lake and its islands lie in a 'nested caldera', one of only three such craters in the world, which was formed when the central core collapsed down the throat of the volcano. The multi-coloured bands of volcanic ash clearly visible in the steep outer lake banks, once the lower slopes of the volcano, were laid down by a series of eruptions. Stone axeheads and other artefacts found in the banks indicate that men lived here at the time of the last eruptions some 7000 years ago.

The fertile soil of Tower Hill, formed by the lava and ash clouds, led to its clearing for pastoral purposes, from the 1860s, and for a while scoria quarried for road building. In 1892, Tower Hill was declared Victoria's first national park and the long job of repairing its damaged and denuded slopes began. Thousands of trees have been planted in an effort to recreate its pre-European vegetation cover.

The planting has encouraged the return of wild birds, and mammals once common in the area – koalas, kangaroos, wombats, bandicoots, sugar gliders and echidnas – have been re-introduced. An 1855 painting by Eugène von Guérard, depicting a densely vegetated Tower Hill, has been used as a guide to restoration and is on display in the reserve's Natural History Centre.

KILLARNEY In this very Irish village the brogue of the pioneer settlers can still be detected in the everyday

The bric-a-brac in Warrnambool's maritime museum is enough to bring a tear to an old salt's eyes.

The lacey bargeboards and friezes of the Hopkins River boathouse – most of it balanced on piers – identify it as a recreational relic of more leisurely times.

speech of their descendants. Killarney Beach is protected by offshore reefs and offers safe swimming and fine fishing, particularly for whiting. The village is on the old bullock track into Port Fairy, several kilometres of which is still in its original state.

WARRNAMBOOL ■ 1322

The fifth largest regional centre in Victoria, Warrnambool, with its boisterous maritime past, is now an important commercial and industrial centre with a woollen mill producing rugs and blankets, and a major garment manufacturing factory. As well, its moderate coastal climate, safe swimming beaches, rewarding fishing, historical attractions, proximity to the scenic 'shipwreck coast' and location at the junction of the Great Ocean Road and the Princes Highway have all contributed to its growth as a busy tourist destination.

Middens near Lady Bay are evidence that Aborigines have lived and hunted here for tens of thousands of years. The first accredited European sighting of these shores was by Matthew Flinders, in 1800, followed two years later by the French navigator Nicholas Baudin, but some say it is possible that this coast was first charted by the Portuguese explorer Mendonça (see box). The sheltered bay was used in the early 1800s by sealers and whalers to process their catch and repair their boats, and in the 1840s a settlement grew up at its western end near the mouth of the Merri River to provide a sea outlet for the farm products of the Western District. In its heyday, Warrnambool was also a major point of entry for immigrants. However miscalculations in the siting of the jetties and breakwaters caused both the river entrance and the town foreshore to silt up. *Population 23 950*

FLAGSTAFF HILL MARITIME MUSEUM Centred around the lighthouse, the lightkeeper's cottages and the 1887 fortifications – original features of the site – Flagstaff Hill helps recreate the atmosphere of an early coastal port. Historic ships moored here are the *Rowitta*, one of the few surviving Tasmanian steamers, and the *Reginald M.*, a restored sailing vessel. Also on display is some shipwreck booty including the gleaming, larger than life Minton earthenware peacock recovered from the ill-fated *Loch Ard* (see *Camperdown & Terang*), the *Schomberg* diamond and a bronze spike and an iron latch found near the site where the 'Mahogany' ship (see box) is supposed to be buried.

LOGANS BEACH WHALE NURSERY Each year, between late May and early August, southern right Whales come from the Antarctic to give birth at this beach. After a gestation period of nine to ten months, a single calf is born to each mother in a small number of shallow protected bays on the southern coasts of Australia, Africa and South America.

These whales were once hunted nearly to extinction for their oil and baleen plates, being regarded as the 'right' whale to pursue because they were slow moving, came into shallow water and floated, even when dead! Numbers are now slowly recovering, as evidenced by those that frolic in the 'nursery' here. A viewing platform has been built on the cliff tops overlooking the beach.

THUNDER POINT COASTAL RESERVE Some of the earliest anti-erosion, dune stabilisation work in Australia was carried out here when, in 1873, it was reserved for the 'Prevention of Irruption of Sand' because the dunes had become destabilised by overgrazing. Now pockets of the coastal vegetation once widespread along these shores survive here, providing an important range of habitats for some thirty species of sea bird. A small colony of fairy penguins live on Middle Island, near the mouth of the Merri River. The point and islands are the remains of a 100 000-year-old sand dune which has since become cemented in places to form the rock known as calcarentite.

FESTIVALS Warrnambool Wunta Festival, February.

YAMBUK ■ 1323

This village grew up on the banks of the Shaw River near where the first sheep run was taken up in 1840. Its old bluestone inn dates from the 1850s. Nearby Lake Yambook or Yambuk – the name indicates the variations in phonetic renderings of Aboriginal words by early European settlers – is rich in evidence of Aboriginal occupation; there are layers of shellfish remains which testify to past feasts and the bream, salmon and mullet still pulled from its waters provide many a fine meal today. Birdlife abounds, from sleek divers to the lumbering pelican.

On the white sand dunes which separate the lake from Yambuk Beach is a thirty-metre slippery dip, popular with children. The beach is not recommended for swimming as the deep water between here and Lady Julia Percy Island is crossed by dangerous rips and currents.

THE PORTUGUESE SHIPWRECK... HISTORY OR LOCAL LEGEND?

BENEATH the dunes west of Warrnambool may lie proof that Europeans sailed the south-eastern shores of Australia more than 250 years before James Cook arrived in the *Endeavour*. Was the 'mahogany' ship – said to lie some seven metres under the sands and a tantalising riddle for more than a century – a sixteenth-century Portuguese caravel that beached here or merely a nineteenth-century whaling punt?

The story dates from 1836 when two sealers whose boat was swamped at the mouth of the Hopkins River came upon the hull of a vessel on their arduous trek back along the coast (right) to the Port Fairy settlement. The wreck was subsequently investigated by the Port Fairy harbour master, Captain Mills, who noted its dimensions – its design seemed antiquated – and reported its timbers as being dark in colour, 'like mahogany', and different to any wood he was familiar with; his attempts to take a sample were defeated by its hardness.

There was no record of a ship being lost at sea in the area and according to Mills the Aborigines of the region said the wreck had always been there. Many locals examined it over the next few decades, some commenting on how far from the sea it was. Then, in 1880, storm-driven sands obliterated Hummocks Road, supposed to pass near the wreck, and apparently also covered the mysterious timbers. Some historians, both local and academic, say the 'mahogany' story is fanciful and that the timbers can be explained away as the remains of an old whaling punt which disappeared when it was burned by a Tower Hill farmer for its bronze and copper fittings.

Others believe that the wreck still lies beneath the hummocks and is in fact a Portuguese caravel lost in 1522 from a flotilla of three under the command of Cristovão de Mendonça. The Dauphin Map, produced in the sixteenth century by French cartographers and believed to be based on information gathered by Mendonça's expedition, could support this theory. It bears a resemblance to the coast of southern Australia, stopping abruptly in the vicinity of Warrnambool. Was Mendonça forced to turn back because he lost a ship? And were his explorations kept secret because he had crossed The Great Meridian – a division of the world into Spanish and Portuguese sections laid down by the Pope – into the forbidden Spanish half?

There is little doubt that a wreck in the sandhills was visible for several decades in the mid-nineteenth-century, yet none of the many attempts to relocate it have been successful and as there is nothing to prove its origin, the mystery remains. History may yet be rewritten to explain how close New Holland came to being New Portugal. □

Portuguese caravels (left) sailed to Timor, only 500 kilometres from Australia, in the early 1500s. Whether they ever reached the Port Fairy coast (right) will probably remain a matter for conjecture.

Portland & Heywood

Intrepid sealers, followed by whalers and wool barons, established Portland, Victoria's first European settlement, and Victorian mansions and whalers' lookouts testify to these pioneers. Walks past cliff, dune and lake give views of the spectacular coastline.

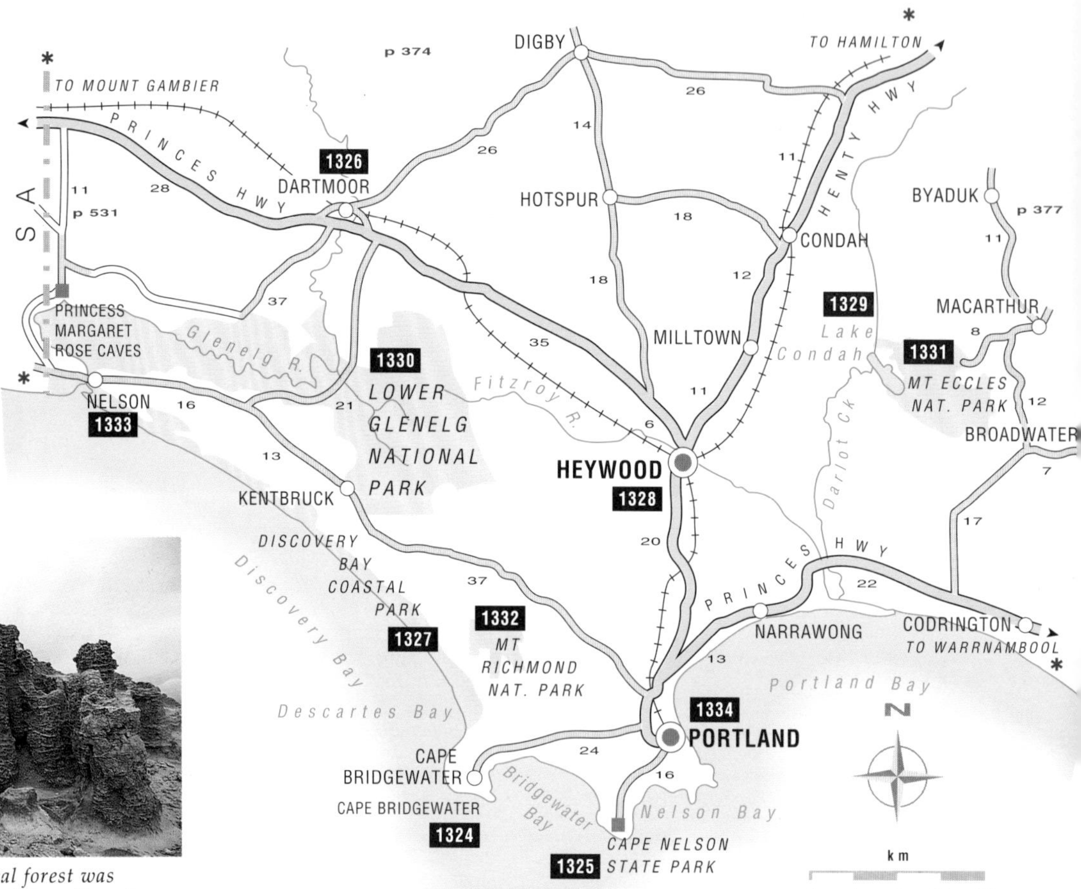

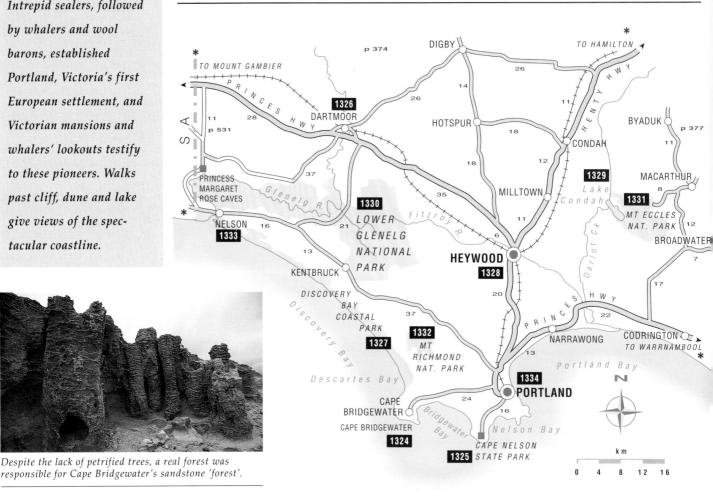

Despite the lack of petrified trees, a real forest was responsible for Cape Bridgewater's sandstone 'forest'.

CAPE BRIDGEWATER ■ **1324**
Once a volcanic island, Cape Bridgewater is now linked to the mainland by a sand spit. Bridgewater Bay has been the site of many shipwrecks – a cairn commemorates the ship, *Marie.* Other attractions of this coast are the Blowholes and the Petrified Forest. Soft scoria rock beneath the harder shoreline ridge has been eroded to create conduits through which water spouts into the blowholes. The petrified forest was formed when a forest was buried by a big sand dune thousands of years ago and water passing through this overlying sand helped form a sandstone crust around the trunks of the trees. At the same time, acid from the decomposing trees dissolved the accumulating sandstone from the inside, and in the process, 'pushed' the crust out to form the large petrified 'trunks' of sandstone.

CAPE NELSON STATE PARK ■ **1325**
Sea birds and animals such as kangaroos, echidnas, snakes and lizards can be seen on the three-kilometre Sea Cliff Nature Walk, one of two walks in this park. This 210-hectare park was formed to conserve the soap mallee, a tree found nowhere else in Victoria. A scenic drive follows the Nelson Bay coastline. Lawrence Rock, the site of one of the few gannet rookeries in the world, is off to the south. The rock was an early guano mining and sealing base.

DARTMOOR ■ **1326**
Early settlers named this small township Dartmoor, as it reminded them of their village on the River Dart in England. It is now surrounded by cool, green pine forests, and timber milling is an important industry. It is a popular holiday destination as it provides a good base for a fishing and bushwalking holiday on the Glenelg River.

DISCOVERY BAY COASTAL PARK ■ **1327**
Stretching around Discovery Bay to the South Australian border is a coastal park noted for its remote coastline and vast, undulating sand dunes, lakes, swamps and coastal heathlands. Swimming, boating and fishing are allowed on Bridgewater Lakes. Walks lead through the park to the ocean from Swan Lake and Lake Mombeong. A two-kilometre walking track from Lake Mombeong goes to Cape Montesquieu, which is an area of cliffs and rocky shore platforms. A pink and yellow blossomed eucalyptus tree, found nowhere else in Victoria, grows at Long Swamp, a large shallow tidal lagoon.

HEYWOOD ■ **1328**
Now an important sawmilling centre, this town was the first inland settlement in Victoria. It grew up around the Bush Inn, built in the early 1840s beside the Fitzroy River, which was the first resting place for travellers from Portland (see entry). A number of scenic drives from Heywood wind through forests of hardwood timber and fern gullies. *Population 1390*

LAKE CONDAH ■ **1329**
There is much of interest at Lake Condah. It was formed, along with the swamp to the north, when lava from Mount Eccles changed existing drainage patterns. Examples of Aboriginal fish traps at the lake's edge show Aboriginal technology and culture before white settlement. In the nineteenth century, this was also the site of an Aboriginal mission.

The Aborigines created canals and built a series of walls up to a metre high to harvest the eels which migrate annually between the lake and Darlot Creek. Fish swam into the dead-end stone traps and were then caught by nets stretched across gaps in the walls. Drainage of the wetlands for agriculture has left most of the traps in dry paddocks.

In 1868, an Anglican mission for Aborigines was established beside the Darlot Creek. By the 1880s, it was a sizeable settlement of approximately twenty-two buildings. The mission continued to grow until 1917 when the Lake Tyers Reserve became a

The second half of the 200-kilometre Great South West Walk takes in the full sweep of Discovery Bay's sandhills.

more important Aboriginal centre. The Lake Condah Aboriginal Mission Tourist Development now operates on the site, and invites visitors to learn more about the black history and culture of the region.

LOWER GLENELG NATIONAL PARK ■ 1330

The deep, long gorge of the Glenelg River in the Lower Glenelg National Park is ideal for exploring by canoe or boat. Access is provided from several landings along the route. Boats can be hired from Nelson and a passenger ferry runs from Nelson to the Princess Margaret Rose Caves.

An important discovery of ancient animal bones was made some years ago in McEachern's Cave, another of the many caves in the park. The remains of thousands of creatures were unearthed, including those of the long extinct marsupial lion, the giant kangaroo and the Tasmanian tiger and Tasmanian devil now extinct on the mainland. Kentbruck Heath to the east is noted for its wildflowers in spring. The Great South West Walk passes through a significant portion of this park. These spectacular limestone caves are open for inspection each day.

PRINCESS MARGARET ROSE CAVES One of the most attractive and accessible of the many limestone caves in the park, this complex has fine examples of stalactites and stalagmites.

MOUNT ECCLES NATIONAL PARK ■ 1331

In the crater of Mount Eccles in the national park, is a small, beautiful sheet of water aptly named Lake Surprise. It is apparently fed by underground rivers as the surface level rises after winter rain and falls during summer. Interesting features include a lava canal, lava cave and stoney rises. There are panoramic views of the lake from the lip of the crater, which is also the starting point for walking tracks around the lake and crater rim.

MOUNT RICHMOND NATIONAL PARK ■ 1332

Mount Richmond (230 metres) which lends its name to this park, is an extinct volcano. A lookout tower on its summit commands fine views of the countryside and coastline. The speciality of this national park is the 450 species of native plants growing here, including 50 varieties of wild orchids. Bird species that have been recorded here include the emu-wren and the tawny-crowned honey eater.

NELSON ■ 1333

Nelson, a holiday centre renowned for its river and estuary fishing, nestles at the mouth of the Glenelg River. River trips, beachcombing and forest walks are other popular pastimes. Mounds of shellfish identify Aboriginal camps, and are evidence of Nelson's long-standing popularity as a fishing spot.

THE GREAT SOUTH WEST WALK This testing walk winds around the coast to Cape Nelson finishing at Sheoke Road. The 200-kilometre track starts and finishes at the Portland Tourist Information Centre and meanders across the countryside to Nelson, and then doubles back to follow the coastline to Nelson Bay, five kilometres south of Portland. It takes about ten days to complete the walk and sixteen campsites are dotted along the route. The walk can be taken in easy stages and the Cape Grant section has been especially sealed and contoured for people in wheelchairs.

PORTLAND ■ 1334

Victoria's first permanent European settlement, Portland, was named by Lieutenant James Grant after George Betinck, Duke of Portland and Secretary of State for the Colonies.

Portland was initially a sealing station. About 200 sealers worked the seal colonies in the Bass Strait until the number of seals declined and whaling took over. The first European settler was a teenager, William Dutton, who visited the bay with a sealing gang in late 1828 and in the following year returned to build a hut and grow vegetables for himself and the visiting whalers and sealers. In 1833, he established a whale-fishery to boil down whale blubber and extract oil and baleen. At its peak, the fishery processed 280 tonnes of oil. Later that year, he was visited by Edward Henty, the son of Thomas Henty, a well-known merino sheep breeder in England, who was so impressed with the district that he established a house here in 1834.

The Hentys also established a fishery and owned some forty whaling boats in the bay. Spotters were posted at a lookout on the headland during the whaling season, and they would sound an alarm when a whale was sighted. Within minutes, dozens of boats would put to sea and the whale would be harpooned and towed back to shore. The blubber was cut out and boiled down in cauldrons. The industry declined, as did whale numbers, after 1840. However Portland's fortunes revived with the gold rushes of the 1850s as thousands of hopeful diggers landed here on their way to the fields. It was a bonanza for local business because the newcomers bought their goods and equipment in the port.

Fishing has always been an industry of some importance for Portland. A large lobster boat fleet and a number of abalone boats are based here. Portland is still an important shipping outlet for Victoria as it is the only deep water port between Melbourne and Adelaide. Development of the harbour in the 1950s added to the jetties and piers that had been built over the years. Ships from more than fifty countries use the four general shipping berths, an oil wharf, an all-purpose bulk berth, a fishing berth and a grain terminal.

Portland's many historic buildings, including the customs house, watch house, court house and the Steam Packet Inn tell much about its colourful past. *Population 10 120*

FESTIVALS Dahlia Festival, March.

Within 20 years of being founded, civilised Portland had a botanical gardens with a curator's cottage in the style of an English worker's house.

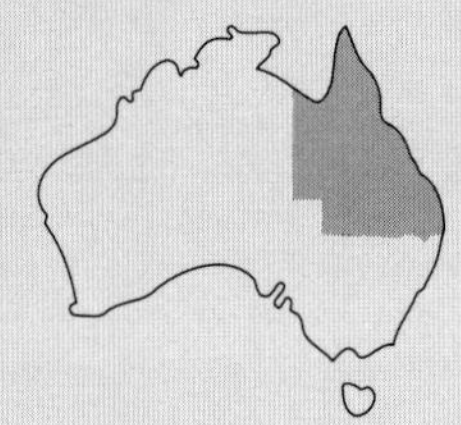

QUEENSLAND

Big, sunny Queensland, a giant region of contrasts covering twenty per cent of Australia's land surface, long ago shook off its rural image to become Australia's fastest growing state. The population is concentrated in the south-east corner and along the holiday-land of the coastal strip – with its exotic trim of the Great Barrier Reef – where tourism is the major earner while a sprinkling of inhabitants in the huge hinterland are at the grass roots of a substantial economy based on mining and food production.

SPECIAL FEATURES

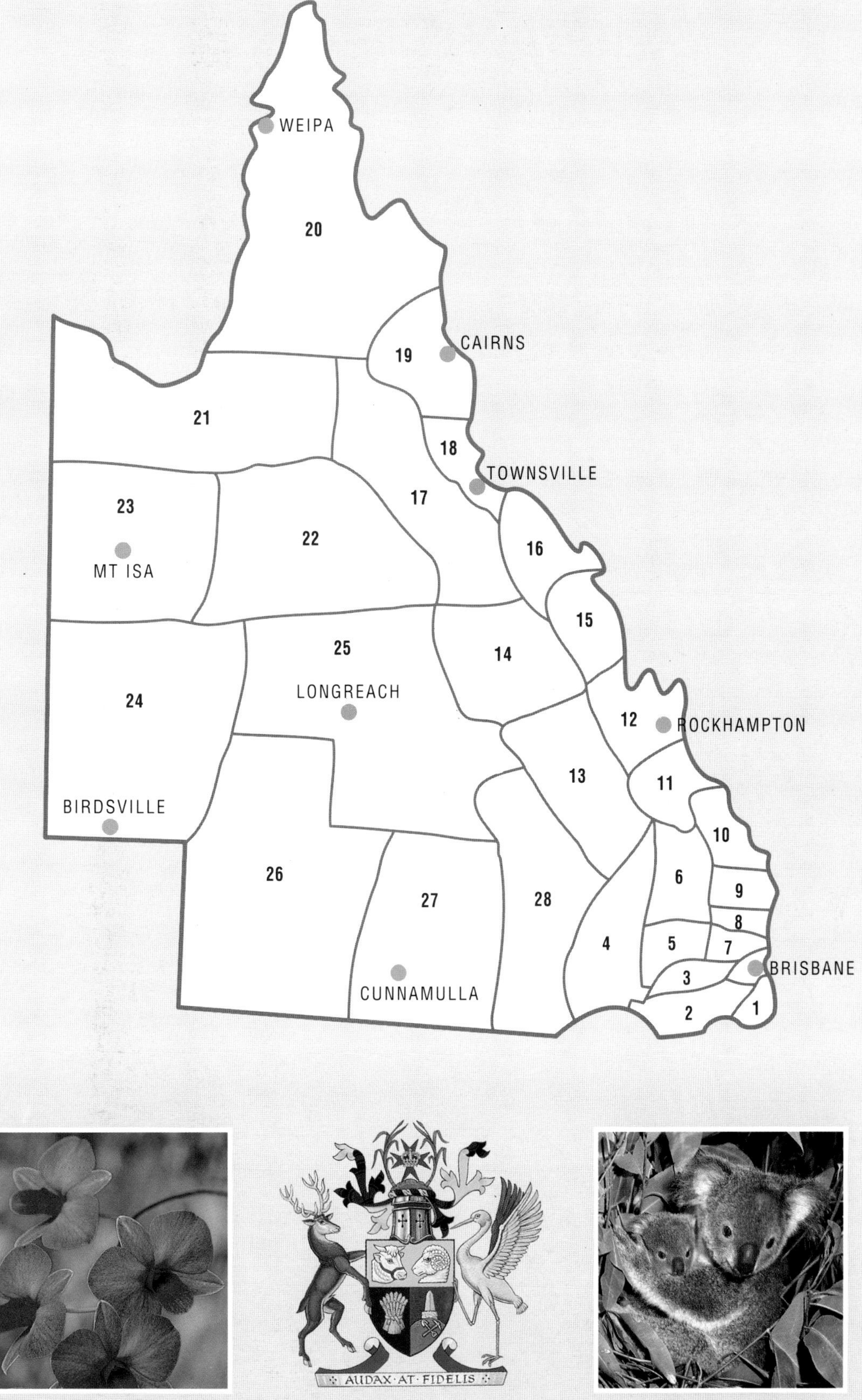

Queensland's coat of arms is the oldest in Australia; it was granted to the then colony in 1893. The flower and animal emblems came much later: the Cooktown orchid was adopted in 1959, the koala in 1971.

BRISBANE

In the south-eastern corner of a vast state almost as large as western Europe lies Brisbane, a subtropical river city growing at the same busy pace as the huge region it serves.

Despite the dramatic upwards and outwards expansion of both private and public building developments in the city centre and on the south bank there is still occasionally a touch of the 'big country town' about Brisbane. Part of the northern capital's charm lies in the fact that it is still the sort of place where the residents grumble about the humid summers – although there are few complaints during the mild winters when it is just cool enough to put on a sweater. Brisbane's population numbers well over 1 140 000 and possesses no shortage of civic pride: when the city launched a cane-toad eradication program, hundreds of citizens rolled up their sleeves and volunteered as 'toad-busters', helping scour parks and streets for the introduced pest.

Convict leg-irons at the Brisbane Museum are a symbol of the city's relatively brutal origins as a prison settlement 'for the worst class of offenders', as officialdom at the time so bluntly put it. The museum belongs to a city that developed from a convict outpost to service the huge hinterland to the west and the north and has as its heart a jigsaw of Victorian, Edwardian and glasshouse-modern architecture, held in a curve of the wide ribbon of the Brisbane River. The sprawl of the suburbs ripples out all around a city that seems at once more conservative, more mature, and more relaxed than the smaller but relentlessly showy Surfers Paradise, an hour's drive down the coast.

Brisbane gives the impression of not yet being caught up in the rat-race of southern capitals, even though high-rise office buildings now

Raft-sized water-lily leaves thrive in the domed glasshouse at the Mount Coot-tha Botanic Gardens. The classical facades of the University of Queensland's halls of learning (left) are shaded by the ferny foliage of subtropical jacarandas.

dwarf the imposing City Hall, begun in 1920 and officially opened ten years later. Until about 1960, this was Brisbane's tallest building, with its landmark clock tower – ninety-one metres above street level – visible from all around the town. Like many landmark buildings, the City Hall is in the compact central district which has stayed tidily defined because of the encircling loop of the Brisbane River.

Sandstone was used liberally in the construction of many of Brisbane's early buildings – much of it from the quarry at Helidon (see *Toowoomba & Gatton*). Upon its completion in 1885, the National Bank on the corner of Queen and Creek streets was considered one of the finest banks in the world. Its massive proportions, with tall Corinthian columns and pilasters of limestone, and an elaborate interior detailed with cedar and bathed in natural light from a leadlight dome above the banking chamber are a tribute to Victorian opulence. Though regarded as a fine example of Italian Renaissance architecture, the bank is trumped by the sheer architectural extravagance of the Treasury Building, with its palazzo – occupying an entire city block – considered the best example of such architecture in the Southern Hemisphere.

A much later addition to Brisbane's impressive sandstone architecture is the University of Queensland which has a central core of Helidon sandstone buildings set around a cloistered court. Carvings that decorate the main buildings and cloisters depict scenes from Queensland history, notable people and other universities' coats of arms. The projecting grotesque faces and animals around the courtyard, carved over a period of

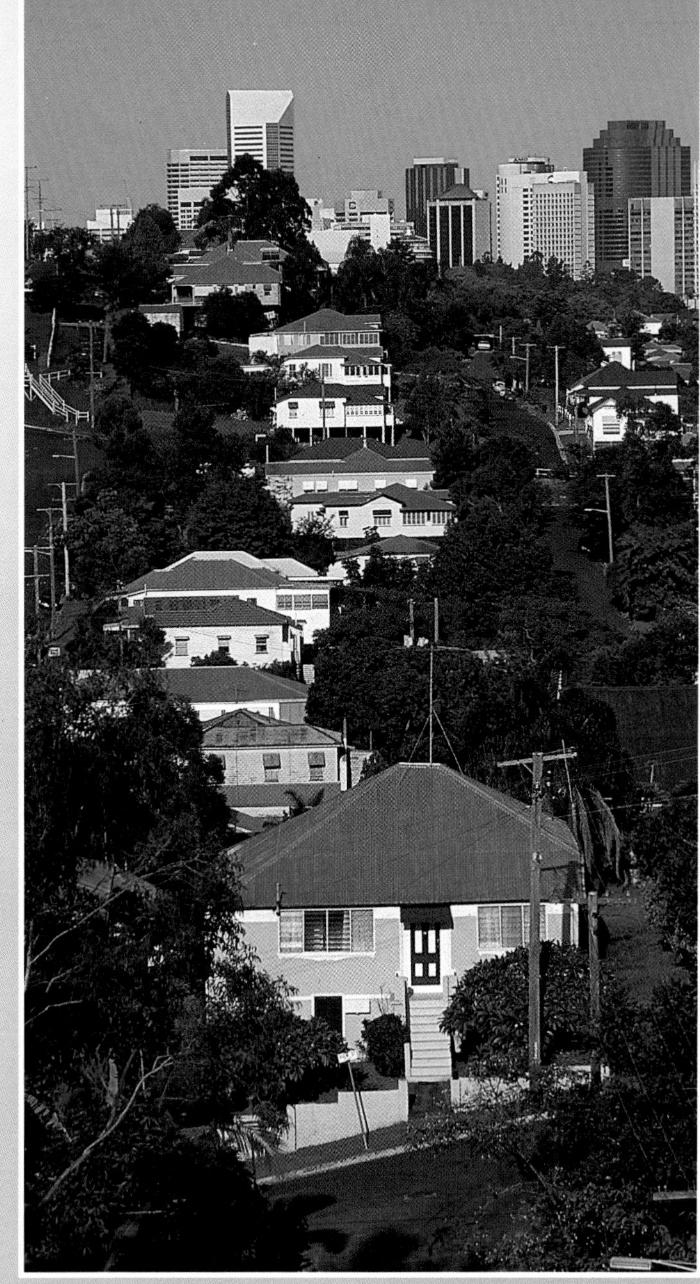

The stilted houses of suburbia run right up to the edge of Brisbane's commercial heart (above) where the landmark cantilevers of the Story Bridge link the city's northern end to the long neck of Kangaroo Point.

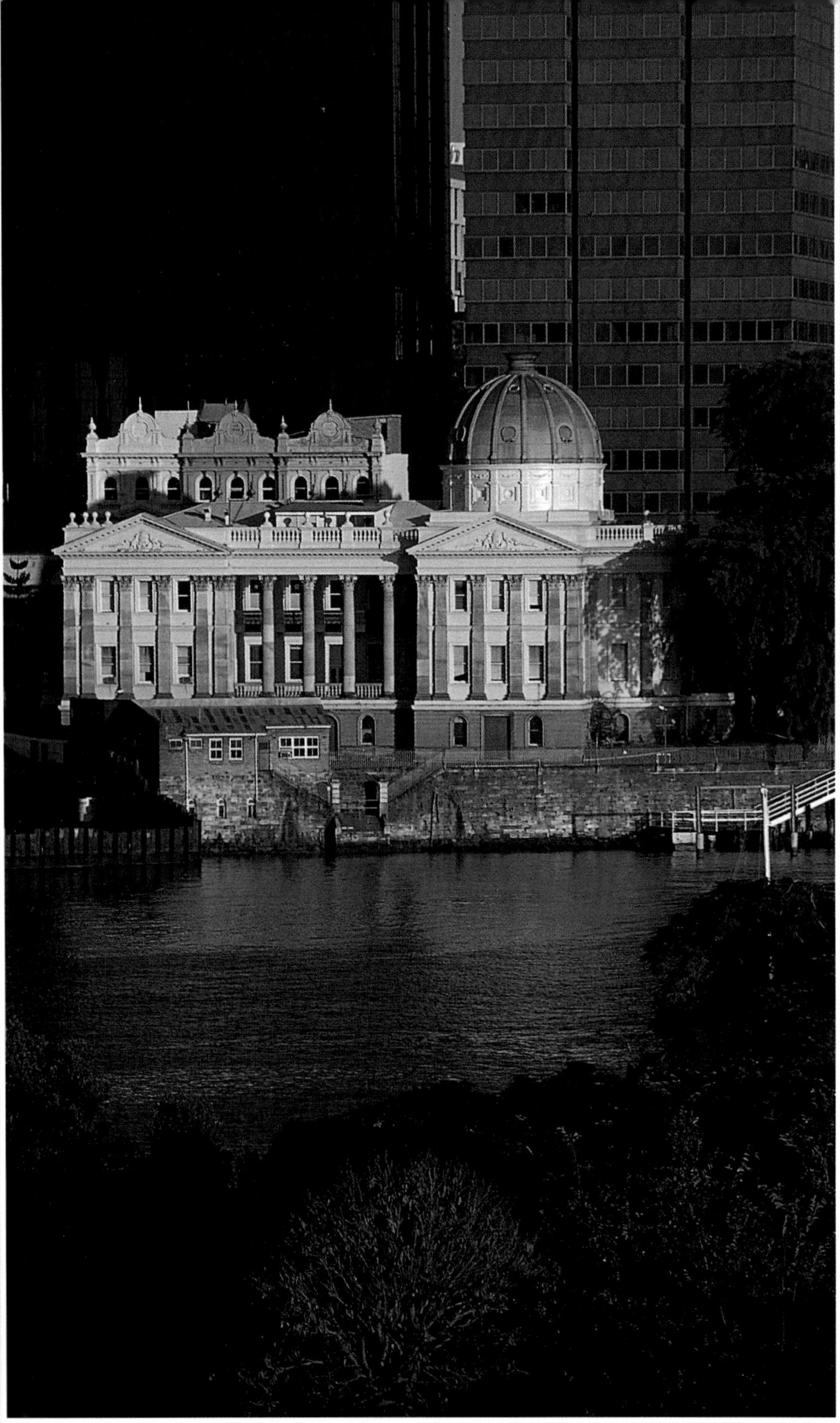

Despite the overshadowing, modern office towers, the Customs House is still the most commanding presence on the banks of the Brisbane River.

fourteen years, have imparted a sculptural elegance to the buildings. The university – it began the move from its original home in the Old Government House near the Botanic Gardens to its present St Lucia site in 1939 – is also the site of the Schonell Theatre, one of Brisbane's leading venues for non-mainstream films.

Bridges are part of the history and identity of Brisbane. Seven of them span the usually sluggish river, with the longest being the Gateway Bridge. Arguably the prettiest is the much older Story Bridge, the brainchild of Dr John Bradfield, the designer of Sydney Harbour Bridge. As with the Harbour Bridge, the main span of the Story Bridge was constructed in two halves, projecting from the north and south banks. The joining of these halves was an extremely delicate operation – thermometers were placed on each half to register temperatures, thus enabling the engineers to monitor the bridge's expansions and contractions. In the early hours of the morning of 28 October 1939, conditions proved just right. Construction teams were called immediately to the site and the joining of the main span proceeded perfectly. At night, the Story Bridge lights up like a Christmas tree, outlined by thousands of bulbs that were the city's gift for the celebration of the bridge's fiftieth anniversary in 1990.

Below, ferries cut through the water, zig-zagging cross-river and going up and down stream along with other craft as diverse as small motorised gondolas and huge coal barges. Brisbane uses its river like any other trafficway. Wooden paddlewheelers for sightseeing and dining glide along near-silently, while a thumping rock beat signals a colourful former vehicle ferry turned cruise barge, complete with fake palm trees and thatch-roof outhouses on deck.

In an afternoon on the water, visitors can enjoy an untrammelled view of the city while floating past the cluster of city office blocks, the Cultural Centre, Maritime Museum, University of Queensland, historic Newstead House and the Botanic Gardens. The Colonial Botanist, Walter Hill, who developed the gardens, introduced the jacaranda and poinciana trees which during spring and summer smother Brisbane suburbs with blossoms of pale blue and velvet red. In the early days, these gardens were more than a place of beauty. Tea, cotton, arrowroot, ginger and indigo were planted to see if they could be successful crops for Queensland and in 1862, a public experiment in the first manufacture of sugar in the state was conducted here.

At weekends, the Botanic Gardens are abuzz with picnickers, cyclists and rollerbladers while riverside cliffs, quarried by the convicts in the early days, are a weekend haunt for abseilers and rock-climbers. People take to the outdoors throughout the year in Brisbane where the average, year-round, minimum temperature is 15° Centigrade with a maximum of 25°. The imaginative riverside Cultural Centre brings together the state's art gallery, museum and reference library, as well as theatres, restaurants and gardens.

The river was explored in 1823 by John Oxley, Surveyor-General of the colony of New South Wales, who was sent north from Sydney to find a place for a convict settlement. When Oxley got to Bribie Island in Moreton Bay, he found two shipwrecked Europeans who told him they could show him a large river which they had crossed in a bark canoe.

So Oxley rowed up the Brisbane River. About eight kilometres downstream from the future site of Queensland's capital, he spotted a magnificent subtropical jungle and stopped for breakfast at the now commercial and industrial zone of Breakfast Creek. A landmark on one bank in modern times is the Breakfast Creek Hotel, dispensing beer and cheer since 1889 and largely unchanged. Across the creek is the Breakfast Creek boardwalk of restaurants and specialty shops, and Newstead House, the oldest surviving homestead in the city. The low-slung, stately house in Newstead Park, built in 1846, was where much of the administration of early Queensland was carried out.

City Hall has lost its height advantage but King George Square still displays the entrance to best effect.

Brisbane's newest botanic gardens, at Mount Coot-tha, are home to exotic rainforests, desert cacti, a tropical plant display dome and a butterfly house. Alongside the gardens, the more rugged Mount Coot-tha Reserve and lookout is the place many visitors drive to – and the hardy walk to – for the best views of Brisbane during the day or after sundown.

The 'Sunshine State's' most bountiful commodity inspires a run on shady hats at a riverside market.

Brisbane's French Renaissance-style Parliament House, where the state's decision-making has been done since 1868, overlooks the city's old Botanic Gardens and is the prize-winning design of the architect Charles Tiffin, who won an Australia-wide contest and 200 guineas for his concept.

In a glass-fronted hangar at Brisbane airport sits a famous Australian icon – Sir Charles Kingsford Smith's long-grounded Southern Cross. It was the first aeroplane to cross the Pacific from North America, the first to cross Australia non-stop, and the first to cross the Tasman to New Zealand.

On the fringe of Brisbane's business district is the suburb of Fortitude Valley – named after the ship that brought 256 immigrants in 1849. They settled in the area, which is now given over to mixed industry and shops with an attractive mall and a Chinatown. 'The Valley' also has a colourful reputation as a somewhat raffish, 'red-light district'.

On the heights of Wickham Terrace is the old Windmill, built by convicts in 1828. It failed as a windmill, and was converted to a convict-powered treadmill to punish prisoners and grind grain for their food. It was later a signal post, weather observatory, fire lookout and television transmission tower.

During the 1820s and 1830s no free settlers were allowed within eighty kilometres of Brisbane. Convicts were sent there from Sydney – thirty in the first shipment, with numbers eventually swelling to more than one thousand including thirty women. The hard-labour women built most of what is now Kingsford Smith Drive, the route from the airport to the city. But eventually the graziers who had opened up the rich Darling Downs to the west of Brisbane needed a port to bring in supplies and ship out their wool. That put an end to the convicts-only settlement and in 1842 the first Brisbane land was sold to free settlers and the true city's history began.

Convicts were sent out to one of Moreton Bay's most beautiful islands, St Helena, and the prison there became known as 'the hell-hole of the South Pacific'. Daytrippers now go out by launch to tour the ruins of this one-time Alcatraz, a prison from 1867 to 1932, built and then dismantled by the convicts incarcerated there. □

Beenleigh & Beaudesert

The southern coast of Queensland sets the tone for the holiday-oriented coastline that follows: balmy weather, golden sands and some of Australia's most expensive real estate combine to make a varied and busy starting point for the long corridor northwards.

Water and light burst through a break in the Natural Bridge in Springbrook Park to breathtaking, heavenly effect.

BEAUDESERT ■ **1335**
The Beaudesert district was explored in 1826 and 1827, and when settlement eventually began in 1842, one of the first properties to be established was called 'Beau Desert' after Henry Bayley's station near Mudgee in New South Wales. Bayley's forebears had links with an English family called Paget. Many hundreds of years before in the reign of King Stephen, the Cistercian monks established 'Beau Desir' monastery in England. When King Henry VIII dissolved the monasteries he gave 'Beau Desert' – as it had come to be known – to Sir Walter Paget. The version of the name that was transplanted to Australia was given to a town that grew on private land and was never officially gazetted.

Pioneer builders used whatever materials were to hand and here timber was plentiful. The historical museum complex in Jubilee Park includes a re-erected 1875 slab hut with a roof of shingles, peeled-log verandah posts and a timber-clad chimney, typical of the early building techniques in the district.

Beaudesert proudly lends its name to the 'Beaudesert Blue', a prince among pumpkins – it shares the Beaudesert Shire's coat of arms with a lyrebird – a rare distinction for a vegetable! Local farmers raise dairy and beef cattle, pigs and poultry, and use irrigated water from the Logan and Albert rivers for agriculture. The large meatworks near the town employs hundreds of people during peak times.

The remains of the Beaudesert Tramway can be seen on the way south to Tamrookum. From 1903 to 1944, the little steam-engines lugged food, medicine, tools and seed and brought news to the isolated towns in the southern part of the shire as far as Innisplain and Lamington.

There are two interesting cairns in the district commemorating people who worked there. One at Jerrys Downfall marks the spot where a South Sea Islander bullock driver, Jeremiah Hannant, dropped dead on 28 April, 1870. The other, at Christmas Creek, commemorates a group of Chinese migrants who were hired by wealthy pastoralists despite their unfamiliarity with sheep. The Christmas Creek area is also well known for its gemstones – agate, jasper, opal – and petrified wood. *Population 4030*

BOYS' TOWN The Beaudesert racecourse holds one meeting a year to help support Boys' Town which was established nearby in the early 1960s. It was modelled on the American institution which aimed to help wayward boys based on the dictum 'that there is no such thing as a bad boy'.

VERESDALE In the 1860s, the Veresdale area, near Beaudesert, was the site of Queensland's first cotton plantation established by Captain Robert Towns who brought in field workers from the South Sea Islands. There was a touch of *Gone With the Wind* about the scene – complete with implications of slave-like labour. The plantation revolved around the homestead called 'Townsvale' and had its own store and hospital. When the value of cotton slumped, the Veresdale settlers felled hoop pine for the Brisbane building market from the surrounding scrub.

BEENLEIGH ■ **1336**
Beenleigh's Aboriginal name was 'Wobbumarjoo' which meant 'boggy clay'. The town is situated in the Logan River Valley in low-fertility land and was the administrative centre for the Logan and Nerang districts in the nineteenth century. Many of the early settlers were of German descent.

Robert Johnson arrived in 1864 and began sowing arrowroot and sugarcane, two plants which liked the soil and the climate. Although arrowroot was an occasional ingredient in biscuits, the major part of the crop went to the pharmaceutical industry. The crop is so labour intensive that it became uneconomical in the early 1980s – today, Australia imports most of its arrowroot from underdeveloped countries.

The Beenleigh Rum Distillery, the oldest working distillery in Australia and one of three in the state, makes rum from sugar grown here. Francis Gooding and his brother-in-law, John Davy, established Queensland's second sugarcane plantation in 1865 and opened the Beenleigh Sugar Mill five years later. Beenleigh was the name of the family estate in England. In 1884, James 'Bosun' Stewart, who had a licence to produce rum on the *S.S. Walrus*, sold Gooding and Davey a copper still and so the Beenleigh Rum Distillery began. In 1885, there were forty sugar mills in the district but only one now survives at Woongoolba. *Population 16 390*

CANUNGRA ■ **1337**
Canungra is probably derived from the Aboriginal 'kerang-gum', said to mean 'place of the night owl'. The township was established by loggers and sawmillers over a century ago and nestles in a valley surrounded by mountains. It is part of a highly productive small-crop district which grows such vegetables as rhubarb and swedes.

The army's Land Warfare Centre – where Australian soldiers and personnel from overseas learn the techniques of jungle fighting – is on the outskirts of the town.

DUNWICH ■ **1338**
Dunwich, or Goompie as the Aborigines call it, was established in 1827 and has a history dating back to the days of convict settlement (see Stradbroke Island). The landward section of the present Dunwich jetty-ramp was built in two stages – the first in about 1828 by convicts supervised by Captain Logan and the second by prisoners from Peel Island. Cotton, planted in 1828, did not survive and nor did the stores depot which Governor Darling ordered to be built in 1827 – completed the following year, it was closed by 1831.

The first recorded Catholic Mission for Aborigines was established at Dunwich in 1843 and four Passionist Order priests came from Europe to run it. There were communication problems because only one of the priests spoke English; soon they were sent elsewhere and the Dunwich Mission was abandoned. In 1892, the Bribie Island Mission moved to Moongalba on Stradbroke.

In 1850, the vessel *Emigrant* with sixty-four cases of typhus aboard was quarantined at Dunwich and some years later the old quarantine buildings were turned into a benevolent asylum for old and infirm paupers, disabled people and drunkards. Many of Australia's old cemeteries record colonial history – the one at Dunwich is among Queensland's oldest and most historic. Dr Ballow and Dr Mitchell, who contracted typhus along with many of their patients, are buried there.

Visitors come to Dunwich for the history or to get away from it all. It is linked to the mainland by vehicular ferry from Cleveland or a twenty-minute journey by taxi-boat. There are also small settlements and facilities for holiday-makers to the north at Amity Point and Point Lookout. *Population 920*

EAGLE HEIGHTS ■ 1339

Eagle Heights is a resort on Mount Tamborine. It provides easy access to the circular track round Macdonald National Park and to other reserves in the area. The township has provided holiday accommodation for regulars and travellers for many years. *Population 1570*

HELENSVALE ■ 1340

Helensvale railway siding served the sugar plantation of the same name at the turn of the century. It was used to send cane to the Nerang Central Mill which was established in 1896 and managed to operate for almost twenty-five years despite often being less than profitable. The railway line continued to carry out dairy products to the markets until 1964 and for many years the area was prime grazing land for hundreds of dairy cattle.

In the 1990s, Helensvale is one of a number of rural areas transformed by the growth of residential settlements in the urban corridor between Brisbane and the Gold Coast and a significant number of people commute daily to the state capital. Despite its projected target population of 10 000, much of Helensvale still manages to suggest a rural lifestyle. Many of the locals are employed in the expanding tourist industry especially at the giant theme parks such as Dreamworld Park and Warner Brothers' Movie World. *Population 6050*

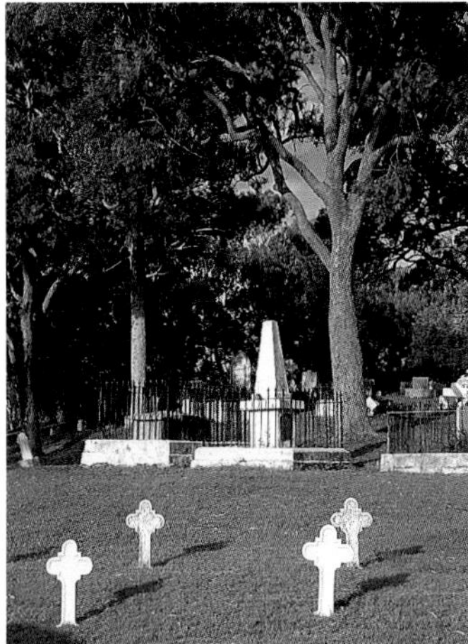

Graves at Dunwich recall the 1850s typhus sufferers destined never to leave Stradbroke's confinement.

JIMBOOMBA ■ 1341

Jimboomba is an important commercial centre for the rapidly developing rural-residential estates in northern Beaudesert Shire. Although not quite 500 people lived in Jimboomba proper in 1986, the town was already the site of a modern shopping centre – opened in 1985 and later extended; a reticulated water supply was connected to houses and businesses in 1988. *Population 790*

LAMINGTON NATIONAL PARK ■ 1342

The plateau within this park and the small sponge cakes coated in chocolate and coconut were both named in honour of the turn-of-the-century governor of Queensland, Lord Lamington. He visited the region only once and shot a koala – forty years later he remembered the 'terrible' sound of its dying cries.

Australia was second only to the United States in establishing national parks and Queenslanders figured importantly in the early days, first with parliamentarian Robert Collins and then with Romeo Lahey and Arthur Groom who campaigned for the preservation of wilderness areas – Lamington National Park, proclaimed in 1915, was the result of their special efforts. It is probably Queensland's most popular park and is not only the haunt of the Albert's lyrebird and the rare rufous scrub bird but is claimed to contain Australia's largest stand of subtropical rainforest – a remnant of vegetation from a much cooler era. Within its 20 200 hectares there are waterfalls, plunging streams and 160 kilometres of graded walking tracks. The spectacular Coomera Falls drop sixty-four metres and are representative of Lamington's awe-inspiring, hauntingly beautiful environment.

A twenty-one-kilometre track connects the two mountain resorts – Binna Burra and O'Reilly's, Green Mountains. The O'Reilly family took up selections in 1912 to clear the forest and were allowed to keep them when the national park was proclaimed in 1915. However they soon decided to drop farming and run a guesthouse which is now the gateway to the western side of the park.

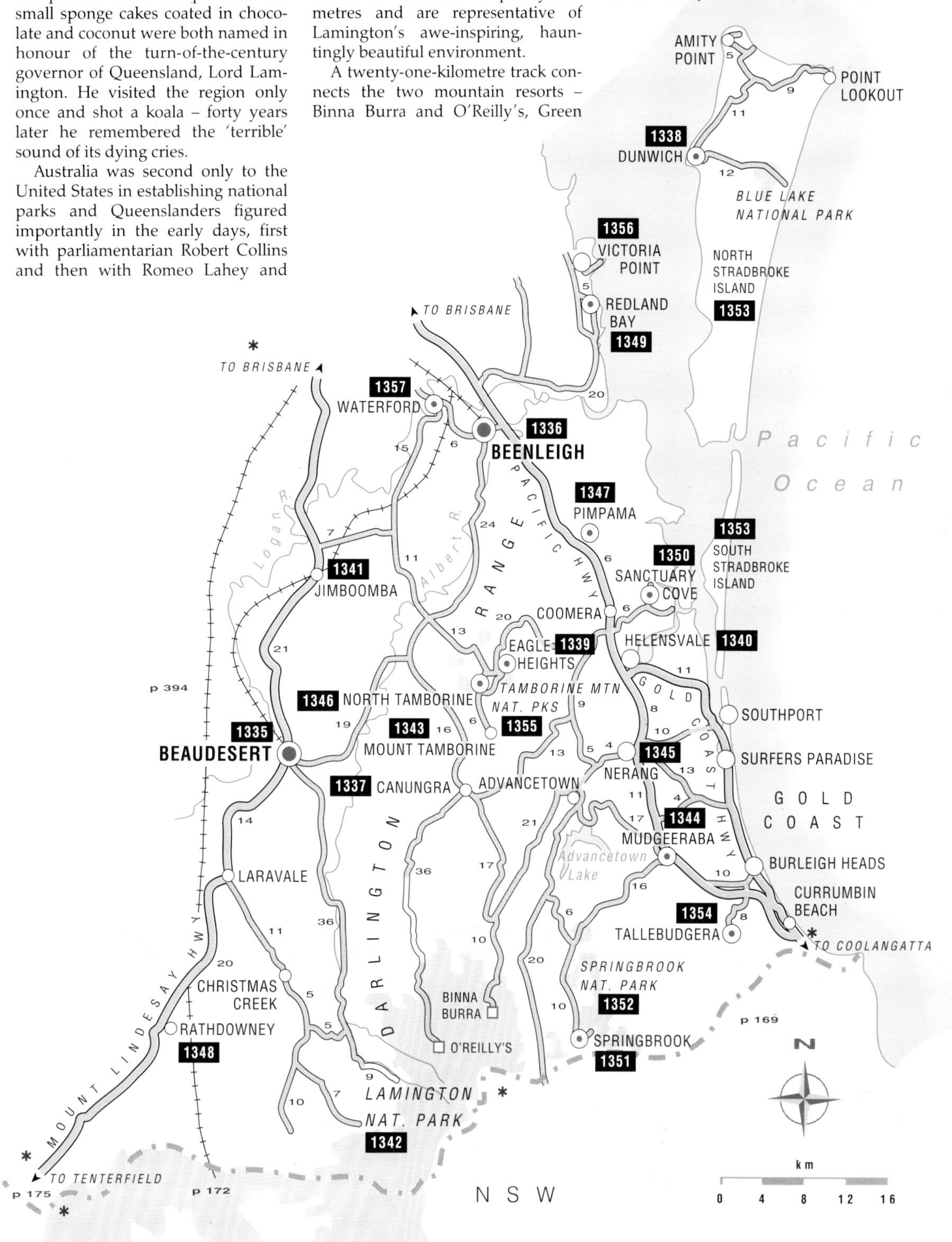

The late Bernard O'Reilly was an experienced local bushman. When the Stinson aircraft, 'City of Brisbane', crashed on the Lamington Plateau in 1937, he followed his hunch about the site of the disaster and found two survivors, John Proud and Joe Binstead, who had stayed with the plane and were barely alive after ten days in the rainforest. The story has become a legend in Australian aviation history and was made into a telemovie in 1988 with Jack Thompson playing the role of O'Reilly.

MOUNT TAMBORINE ■ 1343
Mount Tamborine is part of the Darlington Range which curves to the north from the McPherson Range between Queensland and New South Wales. It is, in fact, a plateau measuring about eight kilometres by five kilometres and encompassing the settlements of Eagle Heights, North Tamborine (see entries) and Mount Tamborine. The area was first opened up by loggers in the late 1800s who were attracted by the mighty beech, cedar, and blackbean trees – some of which still survive. The poet, Judith Wright, lived here for many years, and drew much inspiration from her environment.

Early settlers here were the four Curtis brothers – after whom Curtis Falls is named – who lived in the area in the 1880s and built a steam-driven timber mill which also incorporated a huge waterwheel. After forty years or so, when the wheel had served its purpose, they dismantled it and used the wood to make violins which they played at local dances. The Tamborine Mountain area is noted for its rich volcanic soil which not only sustains the native vegetation but also introduced crops like avocadoes – first planted here in the 1930s – rhubarb, kiwi fruit, lychees, tamarillos, and flower plantations which produce cut blooms for the florist industry.

MUDGEERABA ■ 1344
Two of the several explanations of the Aboriginal derivation of Mudgeeraba's name are 'place of sticky soil' or 'the place where someone told lies' – evidence that the European settlers' verbal communication with the region's original inhabitants was less than perfect! Dairying and beef cattle still persist but, like so many other places in this region, the town is now something of a rural retreat for Gold Coast commuters. New developments are planned to blend with Mudgeeraba's historic past. *Population 7000*

NERANG ■ 1345
This town beside the river of the same name, lies in the foothills of the MacPherson Range and is an out-of-town residential district of the Gold Coast. Surveyed in 1865, Nerang was once a terminus for supply ships and a centre for the sugar-farming community (see Helensvale). It retains its rural character and is surrounded by dairy pastures and natural bush.

The settlement was called Nerang after the river – 'neerang' meaning 'little or shovel-nosed shark'. Early reports suggest the site was once called 'birribi' after spirals of dead bark hanging from the eucalypt trees or 'eejung' meaning 'wet grassy flats'. *Population 10 170*

PIONEER HOUSE Shelter was the most urgent requirement of the early settlers when they arrived here and this simple but sturdy timber-getter's slab dwelling, beside the hotel at Advancetown near Nerang, is a reconstructed example of a typical home. The slabs of ironbark, cut with axe and adze, and the handmade original furniture emphasise the settlers' frugally practical lifestyle.

NORTH TAMBORINE ■ 1346
This tiny settlement on the plateau of Mount Tamborine claims to be the commercial heart of the mountain settlements but despite this, people here take life at the relaxed pace that is encouraged by such a beautiful environment. *Population 1010*

PIMPAMA ■ 1347
Pimpama is another town in the urban corridor between Brisbane and the Gold Coast which expects to expand rapidly by the early years of the twenty-first century. Traditionally a dairy cattle area, many farms still survive and bananas are grown in the district. *Population 1500*

RATHDOWNEY ■ 1348
Rathdowney on the edge of the 'scenic rim' – a spectacular arc of forest stretching from the northern New South Wales coast to Toowoomba – is the gateway to the wilderness areas of Mount Lindesay, Mount Barney and Mount Maroon national parks (see *Warwick & Boonah*). It is a town with an historic past which still presents an aura of pastoral tranquillity. Captain Patrick Logan, the Commandant of the Moreton Bay Settlement from 1826 to 1830, was one of the first Europeans to see the potential of the surrounding land from the top of Mount Barney. His journal records: 'This part of the country is the best I have seen, either for sheep or cattle, and is abundantly watered, each valley possessing a beautiful rivulet'. The Logan Lookout in Rathdowney honours this early explorer.

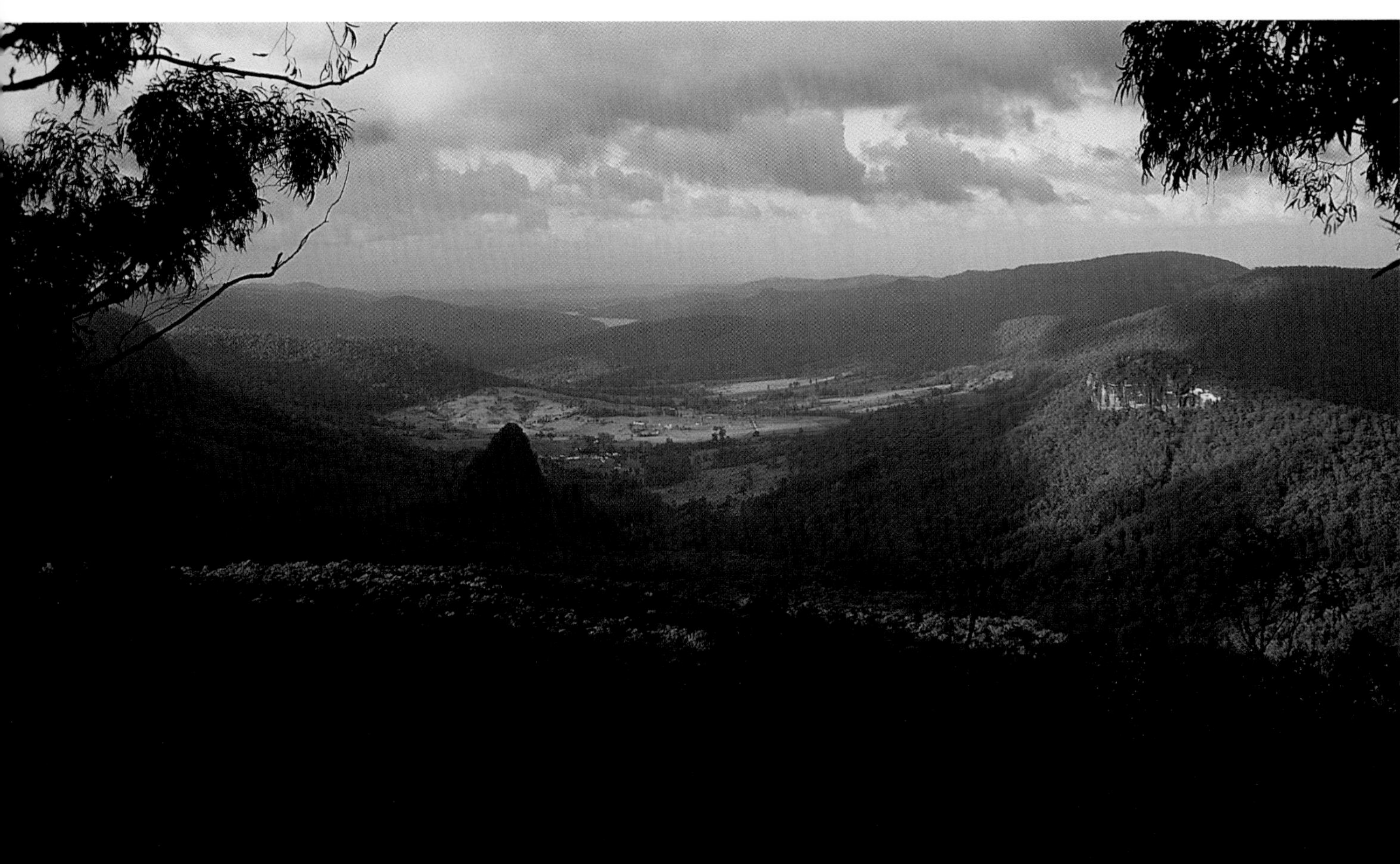

Egg Rock, in Lamington National Park, is the eroded remnant of the prehistoric volcano which helped contribute to the fertility of the Numinbah Valley.

REDLAND BAY ■ 1349

The area around Redland Bay has rust-coloured, fertile soil and is known as Brisbane's 'salad bowl'. The hillside market gardens grow crisp, green vegetables and tomatoes and are famous for winter strawberries, but residential development, creeping south from Brisbane, is slowly encroaching on the farmland. *Population 2580*

SANCTUARY COVE ■ 1350

The site of Sanctuary Cove was formerly Hope Island, named after Captain Louis Hope, who in 1867 was granted this land at the mouth of the Coomera River. In 1984, Albert Shire Council approved development of what was to all intents and purposes a new town – a residential-resort community to be built on 433 hectares. Sanctuary Cove officially opened in 1988 and expects to boast 2000 homes before the end of the century. Millions of dollars have been invested in recreational facilities for the residents including two championship golf courses, two bowling greens, a 332-berth floating marina and a recreation centre. *Population 600*

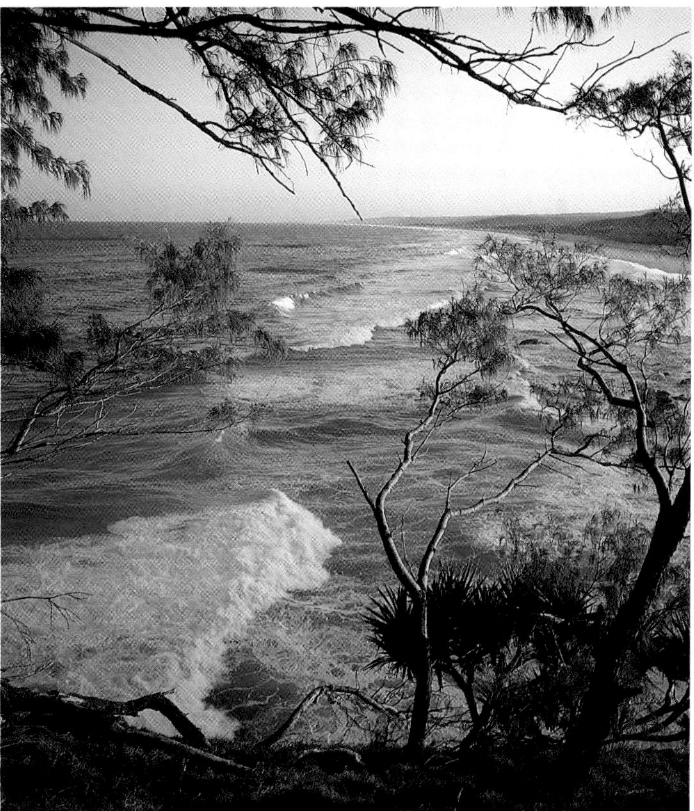

The abundant seafood resources of North Stradbroke Island attracted the Aborigines; nowadays its beaches are a favourite attraction for Brisbanites.

SPRINGBROOK ■ 1351

Springbrook is a mountain resort with only the atmospheric cries of whipbirds and lyrebirds to shatter the natural stillness. The town boasts Queensland's highest altitude holiday accommodation, purportedly the first buildings in Australia to catch the sunrise each morning

Springbrook, named Springwood then, was first selected in 1906 by a group of farming families from the south coast of New South Wales known collectively as the Springwood group. The 'wood' became 'brook' when the settlers found their mail was too often going to Springwood in the Blue Mountains, west of Sydney. *Population 500*

SPRINGBROOK NATIONAL PARK ■ 1352

Springbrook National Park contains three sections: Springbrook Plateau, Mount Cougal and Natural Bridge. It is near the state border in the McPherson ranges and protects 3000-year-old Antarctic beech trees and spectacular waterfalls, including the 109-metre drop of Purling Brook Falls. Mount Springbrook is a 730-metre-high mountain which offers panoramic views of the Pacific Ocean and the McPherson Ranges from its summit. Within the Natural Bridge area there is a glow-worm cave. Mount Cougal is an undeveloped wilderness which attracts only the most seasoned bushwalkers.

STRADBROKE ISLANDS (NORTH/SOUTH) ■ 1353

Called 'Minjerriba' ('Giant in the Sun') by the Aborigines, 'Straddie' by others, North and South Stradbroke islands form the eastern edge of Moreton Bay. The two were one island until 1896 when a storm battered a channel between them.

Captain Cook sighted Stradbroke Island on 17 May 1770 but Aborigines had lived on Minjerriba for thousands of years before that. They subsisted on the natural resources – plants, fish, shellfish and dugong. Saplings and teatree bark provided shelter, implements and weapons were fashioned from stones and trees and the women wove baskets from reeds. Canoes were made from swamp mahogany and box.

Poet Oodgeroo Noonuccal, who was previously known by her European name Kath Walker, grew up on North Stradbroke and lived at Moongalba. She wrote about her childhood and the traditional Aboriginal folklore of the region in *Stradbroke Dreamtime.*

Mineral sand and silica sand – used for making glass – are both shipped from North Stradbroke and money is also made from fishing, raising oysters, timber and tourism.

North Stradbroke is a nature reserve with a fascinating diversity of native plants and animals, especially round Eighteen Mile Swamp. Naturalists recognise sixteen different plant communities – including three carnivorous species – ferns, wattles and orchids – Australia's largest ground orchid, the swamp orchid lives here. The mangroves at Myora are home to the false water rat, a rare mammal.

TALLEBUDGERA ■ 1354

Tallebudgera is the name of the tidal creek between Southport and Coolangatta on the Gold Coast. It was first named Perry River after the New South Wales Assistant Surveyor-General, Captain S.A. Perry, in 1840. It is thought the name is derived from two Aboriginal words 'talle' meaning fish and 'budgerie' meaning 'good'. The latter word is believed to come from a Sydney-region dialect and was probably introduced by the cedar-getters who came to this region from the south.

Although Tallebudgera is developing a new character as a residential area for workers on the Gold Coast, the valley is still dotted with dairy farms and retains its rural charm. As elsewhere in these latitudes, bananas are grown here. *Population 1060*

TAMBORINE MOUNTAIN NATIONAL PARKS ■ 1355

There is a scattering of nine national parks on Tamborine Mountain and they conserve remnants of the original rainforests and eucalypt forests, preserve the habitats of native animals and provide easy-gradient walking tracks and pleasant picnic facilities so that visitors can enjoy the beauty of the countryside that has been protected.

JOALAH NATIONAL PARK These thirty-six hectares cover a zone of dense rainforest surrounding Curtis Falls and the upper reaches of Cedar Creek. Joalah is within easy walking distance of North Tamborine and Eagle Heights, and graded paths follow the creek downstream to a natural swimming pool.

PALM GROVE The 117 hectares of Palm Grove boast a varied vegetation, from dense stands of piccabeen palms to open eucalypt forest where staghorns, elkhorns, maidenhair ferns and orchids thrive in their natural habitat and whip birds, bowerbirds, bellbirds and scrub turkeys call. There is a track to Jenyns Falls and a wonderful view from Burrawang Lookout.

MACDONALD Subtropical rainforest and various strangler figs make a dense cover of these twelve hectares.

THE KNOLL This eighty-five-hectare park has a walk through eucalypt and rainforest to Sandy Creek and Cameron Falls.

CEDAR CREEK Cedar Creek's 230 hectares are easily reached from North Tamborine and consist mainly of eucalypt forest with a series of cascading waterfalls and deep rock swimming pools fed by Cedar Creek Falls. People go looking for gemstones in this area and those in luck find agate, chalcedony, common opal and thunder eggs.

WITCHES FALLS Queensland's first national park was proclaimed in 1908 after forestry officials declared the area 'unfit for any other purpose'. Here are giant figs, lagoons, a waterfall and superb valley and mountain views, all contained within a compact, 131-hectare-park.

MACROZAMIA GROVE These seven hectares protect a stand of uncommon, palm-like cycads – an ancient plant form dating back about 300 million years.

NORTH TAMBORINE ENVIRONMENT PARK Another small reserve of seven hectares which is open only to supervised groups.

PANORAMA POINT At five hectares, this is the smallest and newest park of the Tamborine Mountain group.

VICTORIA POINT ■ 1356

This small township, originally part of Redland Bay, has been known as Victoria Point since May 1882. The area was first settled because of its sugarcane potential and then found to be suitable for fruit. Victoria Point is now a centre for small crops and commercial flower growing – sending chrysanthemums and gladioli to interstate and overseas markets. It is the access point for Coochiemudlo Island. *Population 5360*

WATERFORD ■ 1357

The Waterford district, where dairy and beef cattle are still raised, was once part of the Logan Agricultural Reserve. Settlement began in 1842 and peaked in the 1860s. The Irish arrived first, bringing with them a famous homeland county name; German immigrants settled later. Many of Waterford's residents work in Brisbane. *Population 350*

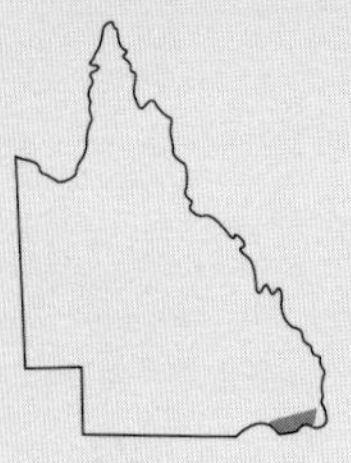

Warwick & Boonah

The discovery of the Darling Downs by the botanist and explorer Allan Cunningham fulfilled the dreams of many land-hungry pioneers. Since then, careful water management, the skilled husbandry of stock and sheer hard work have ensured a steady measure of prosperity.

ARATULA ■ 1358
Aratula, the gateway to Cunninghams Gap and the surrounding mountains, is tucked in the foothills of the Great Dividing Range in the shadow of Mount Edwards. Gemstones have been found nearby in the Reynolds Creek area including agate, jasper and chalcedony, as well as petrified wood.

FASSIFERN John Cameron named his run 'Fassifern' after his family's home in Scotland. By 1845, Bush Inn had opened at the junction of the Reynolds and Warrill creeks but an 1856 survey for a large town came to nothing and Fassifern is little more than the next rest area on the Cunningham Highway north of Aratula.

BOONAH ■ 1359
Boonah Shire is part of the 'Valleys of the Scenic Rim'. The region was first explored by the explorer and botanist, Allan Cunningham, Captain Patrick Logan, Commandant of the Moreton Bay penal colony, and Charles Fraser the Colonial Botanist. After 1842, it was opened for free settlement and 'Coochin Coochin' and 'Dugandan' runs were established.

In the 1870s, the district was more closely settled and a number of German immigrants took up selections. The Blumberg brothers opened a store and other businesses joined them. This small commercial centre became known as Blumbergville. The name was changed to Boonah in 1887 – 'buna' was said to be an Aboriginal word for 'bloodwood tree'. The railway arrived from Ipswich in the same year and Boonah became the railhead for the surrounding area and the centre of the shire; the trains continued running until 1964.

During the 1890s, this district relied on dairying and pigs and there was a co-operative butter factory in the town. Timber was also important. These industries declined gradually in the twentieth century and now much of the countryside is irrigated for grazing beef cattle and growing potatoes, carrots, soya beans, barley and lucerne. *Population 2100*

CUNNINGHAMS GAP ■ 1360
Allan Cunningham was born in Wimbledon near London in 1791 and worked as clerk to the curator of the Kew Botanic Gardens before coming to Australia. He joined John Oxley's expedition to central New South Wales in 1817 and accompanied Phillip King on his coastal survey. In 1827, Cunningham led an exploration of his own and discovered the Darling Downs which he named after Ralph Darling, the then Governor of New South Wales.

Cunningham entered the Great Dividing Range through the gap which bears his name and looked upon 'a beautiful and well-watered valley'. Cunninghams Gap was reserved as a national park in 1909 and there is a memorial to Cunningham at its highest point. The Crest carpark is the beginning of a number of walking tracks. The explorer is also remembered by a monument in Sydney's Botanic Gardens.

HARRISVILLE ■ 1361
Harrisville was the centre of the Ipswich Agricultural Reserve set aside by the new Queensland government in 1860 to grow cotton. This enterprise was to take advantage of the scarcity of supplies from the United States to British cotton mills during the American Civil War.

Cotton gins were established near the farms and the Harris brothers from Brisbane opened one on the corner of Robert Dunn's selection. Although this changed hands a few years later and then closed when the United States again became the world supplier, the Harris name was given to the small cluster of businesses that made up Harrisville.

The railway line from Ipswich reached the town in 1882 and was the first branch railway opened in Queensland. The line was extended to Mount Edwards in 1922 and was to be part of a planned rail route to Sydney – but the plan never went any further.

INGLEWOOD ■ 1362
There was a stand of native cypress pine trees on the northern bank of the Macintyre Brook when Allan Cunningham crossed it in 1827, near the site of the present town of Inglewood. The pioneering settlement, originally called Browns Inn, did not start to form until 1856.

After a survey the name was changed and is thought to be a derivation of 'ingol', the Aboriginal word for 'cypress pine'. Another explanation of the name says that the settlement developed in an angle of the brook and that 'Anglewood' was eventually corrupted to Inglewood.

The tobacco industry has declined in Inglewood Shire in recent years but now there are irrigated paddocks of lucerne, grain and fodder crops and irrigated pastures for fat lambs and beef cattle. Coolmunda Dam, twenty kilometres east of Inglewood, provides enough water to Macintyre Brook to supply up to 3200 hectares of farmland. It was completed in 1968 at a cost of seven million dollars. Apricots and grapes do well

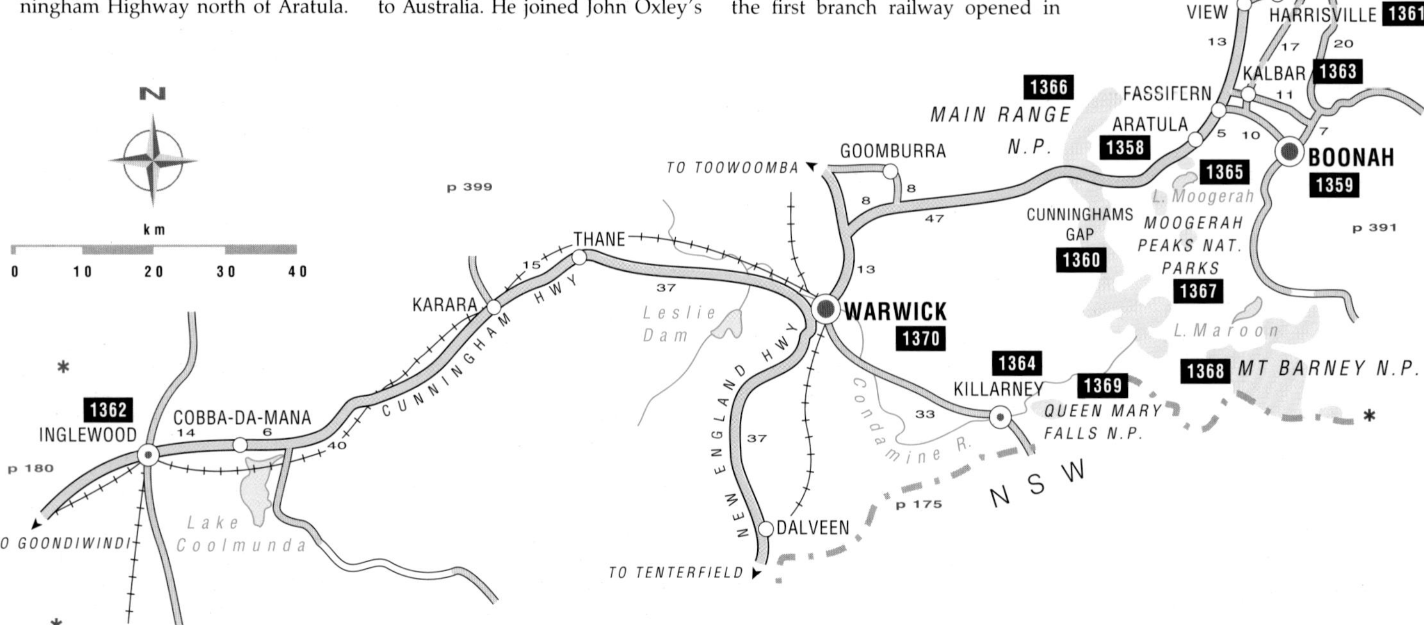

The Mount Edwards Gorge, overlooked by the mountain of the same name, is now Lake Moogerah, filled to the brim by the waters of Reynolds Creek.

where the soil is suitable and timber-cutting feeds the town's sawmill. *Population 1010*

KALBAR ■ **1363**
Originally this area was selected by German immigrants who carved prosperous farms out of the fertile, scrub-covered country by dint of sheer hard work. In the early 1870s, August Engels opened a store in his hut, a school was set up nearby and the town of Engelsburg began. Then during the First World War, there was widespread hostility to German place names and most of them were changed. Engelsburg became Kalbar after an Aboriginal word said to mean 'star' or 'shining place'.

Today, irrigation water from Lake Moogerah and the naturally rich soil make salad vegetables a profitable primary industry here.

KILLARNEY ■ **1364**
It is not difficult to guess the birthplace of the first settlers who came here: 'Named like so much else in Australia for a place on the far side of the globe that its founders meant to honour and were piously homesick for, Killarney bears no resemblance to its Irish original', wrote David Malouf in *Harland's Half Acre*. Although the green hills of southern Queensland were so unlike Ireland, most of the early pioneers soon adapted to their new environment.

In 1968, a freak cyclone swept through the village, killing one person and leaving eight hundred homeless, and there has been a vigorous building program in Killarney ever since. A winding, scenic mountain road with views of the southern Darling Downs leads to Queen Mary Falls National Park. Browns Falls, where it is possible to walk behind the curtain of water, is a short distance from the village. *Population 830*

LAKE MOOGERAH ■ **1365**
The name Moogerah is derived from the old Aboriginal name for this locality, which meant 'land of the thunderstorms'. The thin, arched concrete ribbon of the Moogerah Dam across Reynolds Creek in the Mount Edwards Gorge impounds a reservoir with a capacity of 91 000 million litres which provides a much-needed, regulated water supply to the surrounding farms as well as a fine, placid stretch of water for swimming and boating.

MAIN RANGE NATIONAL PARK ■ **1366**
The broad arc of mountains to the south-west, south and south-east of Brisbane forms Queensland's 'scenic rim' which is an almost continuous belt of protected forest or open countryside. Main Range National Park is one of the parks on the western limit. The vegetation varies from moist, sheltered rainforest to open eucalypt and mountain heath and giant spear lilies grow in some places in the park. In early summer, the lilies have branching spikes up to four metres tall covered in handsome scarlet flowers. Albert's lyrebirds, eastern bristlebirds and black-breasted button quail are among the birds that find shelter here; bellbirds frequent the Main Range picnic area to the west of Cunninghams Gap.

MOOGERAH PEAKS NATIONAL PARKS ■ **1367**
Like the 'collection' of small parks on Mount Tamborine, (see *Beenleigh & Beaudesert*) this is an area of almost 700 hectares comprising several national parks. The peaks are volcanic eruptions formed over twenty million years ago and include Mount French (579 metres), Mount Greville (770 metres), Mount Moon (784 metres) and Mount Edwards (632 metres). The vegetation is mainly open eucalypt forest with heathland on the exposed rock faces and some pockets of rainforest.

The Mount French 'Crack of Dawn' climb up a sheer stone cliff called Frog Buttress is one of Australia's most challenging rock climbs. It carries a difficulty rating of thirty-two – the highest rating on the international 'Ewbank' scale – and rivals the nation's most strenuous climb at the rugged Mount Arapiles in Victoria (see *Edenhope & Goroke*).

MOUNT BARNEY NATIONAL PARK ■ **1368**
Mount Barney East Peak (1360 metres) and Mount Barney West Peak (1362 metres), Queensland's second highest mountain, mark an area on the Queensland–New South Wales border held sacred by the Yagumbir Aboriginal people. In 1828, Patrick Logan made the first ascent of this rough terrain recorded by a European. Most of the park is wilderness with challenging tracks but the walk from the carpark to Lower Portals is suitable for the reasonably fit and leads to a beautiful pool on Barney Creek between sheer cliffs.

There are other rugged mountains in the park: Mount May (839 metres), Mount Ballow (1310 metres), Mount Maroon (965 metres), Mount Ernest (960 metres) and Mount Lindesay (1194 metres). Most of these mountains are remnants of a giant, ancient volcano but the slopes of Mount Barney are the result of an even earlier violent intrusion. The country supports some rare and restricted plant species and more than twenty different types of orchid have been identified on the drier slopes to the east of Mount Barney.

QUEEN MARY FALLS NATIONAL PARK ■ **1369**
Queen Mary Falls National Park is seventy-eight hectares of moist rainforest filled with the sound of water. Spring Creek, a tributary of the Condamine River, which rushes over steep cascades before plunging forty metres down through the bush surroundings of a gorge at Queen Mary Falls, is a home to platypuses and red spiny crayfish. To the north, Blackfellows Creek drops from a greater height but to less spectacular effect.

WARWICK ■ **1370**
The Moreton Bay penal colony was established in 1824 and free settlers were not permitted officially in the district until the convict settlement was closed but Patrick Leslie, enthused by the exploits of the explorer Allan Cunningham, could not wait (see Cunninghams Gap). In 1840, Leslie and others began grazing the fertile plains which are now dotted with horse and cattle stud farms. The early 'whip-cracking; oath-snapping;

joke-cracking; smoke-sucking' squatters – as an early grazier had it – were technically trespassers for they had no right to the land before the government released it for selection in 1842.

In 1847, Patrick Leslie chose a site on the banks of the Condamine River for the first town on the rolling expanse of the Darling Downs. This location was known as 'gooragooby' by the Aborigines.

Warwick began to take shape around 1849 and soon became the centre of Queensland's first pastoral area. Once they were established, these unofficial early 'Queenslanders' – Queensland did not become a separate colony until June 1859 – put up buildings to suit both their surroundings and their pockets. The excellent local sandstone and the prosperity of the times are reflected in the fine nineteenth-century churches and public buildings including St Mary's Church and the town hall.

In 1917, Prime Minister Billy Hughes travelled throughout Australia on a whistle-stop campaign to promote his government's conscription referendum. He had already been heckled at Stanthorpe and at Warwick railway station, he was hit on the hat by an egg. The local constable claimed he had no jurisdiction to arrest the missile thrower. The inaction of the Queensland police upset Hughes so much that it is said to have prompted him to establish the Commonwealth Police Force.

Wheat, barley, sorghum and most other grain crops are grown in the Warwick district. Livestock industries are dairying and cattle, sheep and pig raising. In the town itself there are bacon and butter and cheese factories, sawmills and stock-feed processing plants.

Warwick achieved city status in 1936 and has become known as the 'Rose and Rodeo' city. A red rose is its floral emblem and sometimes rosebushes spill over from private gardens into the city streets. The head office of the Australian Rough Riders Association is also located here and on the last weekend in October the bucking broncos reign supreme, throwing male and female competitors alike. Rodeos were first staged in 1929 and only war and, on one occasion, severe drought have prevented the annual rodeo being held. Colourfully named horses such as 'Knickerbockerbuckeroo' (1936), 'The Undertaker'(1948) and 'Banjo' (late 1960s and 1970s) have laid a lot of riders in the dust.

The monumental Warwick Town Hall takes account of the warm climate with its arcaded verandahs.

Outside the city, dirt of a different sort is popular with rockhounds and fossickers. The list of minerals and gems to be found is impressive. It includes gold, copper, silver, chalcopyrite, chalcedony, iris agate, citrine and quartz as well as fern fossils, shell fossils and petrified wood. Rare sapphires and zircons have been found round Goomburra in the Dalrymple Creek area. People come from as far away as the United States for the annual Rock Swap Festival. *Population 10 390*

LEICHHARDT'S TREE This old trunk is said to mark the spot where in 1848 Ludwig Leichhardt began the expedition from which he never returned. The tree stands near the entrance to Rosenthal Station on the outskirts of Warwick.

LESLIE DAM This dam outside Warwick was built to supply regulated water for farm irrigation but is also a popular venue for water sports and is kept well stocked with fish - especially eel-tailed catfish, silver and golden perch and Murray cod – for dallying anglers. The surrounding hills are at their most attractive in early spring when the wattle trees come into blossom.

FESTIVALS International Rock Swap Festival, January; Rose and Rodeo Festival, October.

CANNING DOWNS: MEMORIES OF BUCK JUMPERS, GUN SHEARERS AND JACKIE HOWE'S SINGLET

QUEENSLAND'S wool industry – and, briefly, a wool industry of a more exotic kind – had their start in paddocks now beneath the Warwick city streets. The original Canning Downs Station was established by Patrick and George Leslie in 1840. A third brother, Walter, trekked in shortly afterwards with 21 ticket-of-leave men and about 5000 sheep and so began Queensland's wool industry. The Leslies had excellent sheep connections; Patrick and George married two sisters – the nieces of John MacArthur, the major pioneer grower of the much sought-after merino fleece in New South

In the 1850s, the Leslies took part in a government-backed but short-lived experiment to start another kind of wool industry – they were to raise Peruvian llamas for their soft wool, in the hope of developing a industry to balance the low prices for sheep fleeces. The animals did not adapt to the warm climate and the scheme was abandoned. More recently, in 1984, a farm at Cooma in New South Wales imported four llamas and there has been renewed interest in these creatures for their wool. The price for a female llama in the early 1990s was around 11 000 dollars.

Canning Downs became one of the best known sheep stations in Queensland and there was rarely a dull moment in the old days. George Leslie is credited with organising the first professional buck-jumping contest in the district in the 1860s. He boasted that his station hand, Rory McLeod, could outride anyone. A Brisbane Valley squatter took up the challenge and wagered fifty pounds sterling – about a year's pay in those days – that his Mexican horse breaker would trounce McLeod. A large crowd gathered to see Leslie's man win the bet on a wild and cantankerous grey horse.

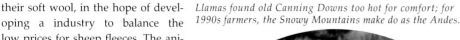

Llamas found old Canning Downs too hot for comfort; for 1990s farmers, the Snowy Mountains make do as the Andes.

A memorial in modern Warwick honours the gun shearer, Jackie Howe, born near Warwick in about 1861. He was the son of a circus acrobat and became an outstanding athlete. His father had the unpleasant task of shearing the ill-fated llamas which spat vile-smelling saliva. Jackie took to hand and machine shearing and set records for both in the large Central Queensland sheds – in 1892 he clipped an astonishing 321 sheep by blade in one day at 'Alice Downs' – an unbroken record, even by machine, for fifty-eight years. The Australian work singlet is still sometimes referred to as a 'Jackie Howe' because he ripped out his sleeves before going into action. Present-day Canning Downs Station, although much smaller than the original, carries on the tradition of excellence in animal husbandry and is one of the region's better known studs for thoroughbred horses and cattle. □

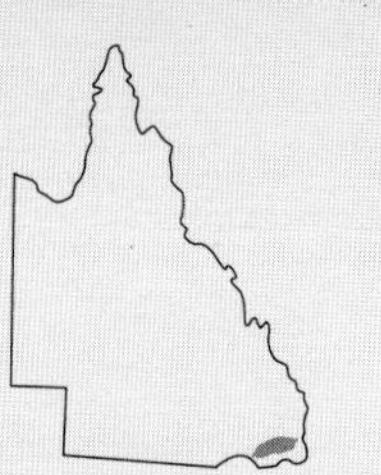

Toowoomba & Gatton

Queensland's largest market garden forms a multi-coloured patchwork over the fertile Lockyer and Brisbane valleys while to the 'golden' west, prodigious grain crops are produced from the legendary black-soil plains of the Darling Downs.

Outside the city limits, the soils that nourish Toowoomba's famous gardens produce serried ranks of capsicums.

ALLORA ■ 1371

Dalrymple Creek runs by one of Queensland's oldest inland towns, its calm waters complementing Allora's country-town tranquillity. Allora began as the site of an out-station of the old 'Goomburra' sheep station built in 1844 in the southern Darling Downs and by the mid-1850s it had been joined by a number of shepherds' huts. At the time, Dalrymple Creek was one of the many watercourses that had to be crossed on the route from the coast to the Darling Downs and in 1857 a hotel opened at the crossing point.

As the social and commercial focus of the district, the hotel was the centre of public life and a town site was surveyed around it in 1859. But it was the mid-1860s before the small cluster of bark huts and cottages took on a permanent appearance as a variety of businesses and public offices sprang up to serve the increasing number of settlers who had moved to the district to grow the first wheat crops.

For a while the little township looked set to become the busy centre of a large agricultural district, but such hopes were dashed when the main southern railway line from Toowoomba (see entry) to Wallangarra bypassed the town and it wasn't until 1897 that a branch line from Hendon connected the town to this main line. Allora was later compensated for this oversight when it became one of the links in the chain of the main Toowoomba–Warwick road, though it has still remained a small town.

Opinion differs as to the origin of the town's name, but the generally accepted theory is that Allora is from an Aboriginal word said to mean 'the place of the swamp'. *Population 900*

CAMBOOYA ■ 1372

'Steele Rudd', the author whose *On Our Selection* stories are described on a plaque at his birthplace in nearby Drayton, as having '...brought the rich gift of honest laughter – with undertones of the struggles and sorrows of the pioneers' to the nation, was probably better known in the Cambooya Shire by his real name, Arthur Hoey Davis, when he became its first shire council chairman in 1914. Famous authors aside, the small town of Cambooya is nowadays characterised by grain silos – giant vessels containing the harvest of wheat crops that grow in the fertile soil of the surrounding district.

CLIFTON ■ 1373

The small town of Clifton is at the centre of a rural district once dominated by the golden hue of ripening wheat crops – the extent of which once led it to be called, the 'million-bushel wheat district'. Nowadays, these extensive wheat fields have relinquished their grip on the Darling Downs to be replaced by other rural industries such as beef cattle- and pig-raising, small-crop cultivation and peanut-growing – one of the region's largest industries. At harvest time, the grading and shelling factory at Clifton processes the majority of the Darling Downs' peanuts, and tours of the factory can be arranged to see the activity.

The town takes its name from Clifton Station, one of three sheep stations taken up and stocked in the first year of settlement on the Darling Downs in 1840. With the arrival of the railway in 1869 and the division for closer settlement of the enormous areas of land held by the major stations, Clifton evolved from a single store and hotel next to the railway line to a thriving township by the turn of the century, where a contemporary report described some 'very presentable public buildings and private residences' gracing the town's streets. *Population 800*

GATTON ■ 1374

Gatton is the main agricultural town in the giant vegetable patch of the Lockyer Valley. The irrigated farmland surrounding the town is the fertile, black-soil resource which produces the region's abundance of primary produce. Small-crop farming, dairy-, beef cattle-, pig- and calf-raising and sawmilling constitute the region's major agricultural activities with potatoes, onions and lucerne rating highest in the small-crop division.

Like many small towns scattered throughout this region, Gatton began as a centre for several large stations that were established in the 1840s and as a changing point for horses on the Royal Mail coaches. Although the town was surveyed in 1859, it is thought that a village existed as early as 1846. Hard-working, sober Germans arriving in the 1850s, were the among the first of the valley's family farmers and by the 1880s, they had cleared the scrubland for the extensive agriculture that made the Gatton region so important throughout the nineteenth century as a food supplier for the developing colony at Brisbane. With such a history, it is not surprising that Gatton is the location for one of Australia's foremost agricultural institutions, the University of Queensland's Gatton College which specialises in agricultural- and rural-based tertiary courses, having been established in 1897 as the Queensland Agricultural College. *Population 5100*

FESTIVALS Potato Carnival, October.

GRANDCHESTER ■ 1375

The little hamlet of Grandchester is notable for two things: it is the terminus of Queensland's first railway line, which snaked out from Ipswich in 1865, and the location for one of the few sawmills that, in the early 1990s, was still operating under steam power.

The old weatherboard building at Grandchester railway station is the oldest station building in Queensland. The town's sawmill, though regarded as a tourist attraction, is still a viable commercial enterprise. The steam-engine used at the mill was purchased in 1962 after a succession of owners, having been imported from England in 1911 for use as a power plant in a milk factory. The power of the engine was boosted in

In Cambooya, where Steele Rudd was chairman of the shire council, selectors like those in On Our Selection *would have known this pub.*

1971 with the purchase of a locomotive boiler from the Queensland Railways and as this is fuelled mainly by sawdust generated by the mill, operating costs are said to be a mere two dollars a day.

HELIDON ■ **1376**

The natural mineral waters of the spa at Helidon well up at an icy-cold temperature from their deep, underground springs and are bottled as a refreshment or heated and piped into therapeutic mineral baths. The medicinal qualities of the spa were well-known to the local Aborigines long before European settlers sank the first bore in the early 1900s.

The early hydrotherapy baths were used by Sister Elizabeth Kenny, a pioneer in new treatments for sufferers of poliomyelitis (see Nobby) in the early part of this century. Since the 1940s, the baths have acted as a barometer for public attitudes towards hydrotherapy treatments, usage alternately waxing and waining. Nowadays the spa is enjoying a period of revival and has undergone extensive restoration.

Helidon is also known for its sandstone which is quarried north of the village and has been used in the construction of many of Brisbane's public buildings including the Queensland Parliament House, the Great Court of the University of Queensland and more recently, Jupiter's Casino and Bond University on the Gold Coast. *Population 580*

LAIDLEY ■ **1377**

The explorer and botanist Allan Cunningham crossed the Little Liverpool Range and probed the Lockyer Valley in 1829 coming upon a fertile plain where 'the soil appeared of a rich description partaking of a loam, with a decomposition of the Traprocks of the surrounding hills. This fine timbered land, which I have named Laidley's Plain (as a compliment to our present Deputy Commissary-General), would therefore produce very heavy crops of maize and other grain and is naturally clothed with an abundance of excellent pasture'. Cunningham's praiseworthy assessment of the land proved accurate and in the 1840s, squatters arrived to take up grazing runs in the valleys of the Darling Downs, some of them spilling over here into the Moreton region.

Lacking fences, the squatters were assisted in the management of their huge pastoral properties by new immigrants from England who were employed as shepherds to guard the flocks from dingoes and Aborigines. Such work guaranteed a hard and lonely existence and though the food supplied on a fortnightly basis by the station's ration courier – usually six kilograms of flour, two kilograms of sugar, a quarter-kilo of tea and seven kilograms of corned beef – might not have been much to look forward to, the company certainly was.

In those early days, Laidley, with its lagoon providing water for bullocks and horses and pub to quench the thirst of the teamsters and coach drivers, was a convenient resting place on the route from Ipswich to Drayton – in modern times a suburb of Toowoomba. A little settlement developed when the pub was joined by a blacksmith, butcher and grocer. With the arrival of the railway in 1866 however, a new settlement sprang up around the station and many of the old township's buildings switched their location.

A series of land acts passed from the 1860s onwards was the Queensland government's response to the increasing pressure from new immigrants for closer settlement. The squatters and their stock were forced further towards the edge of good agricultural land as farmers seeded the valley with vegetable crops transforming the valley floor into a huge 'market garden' which supplied fresh produce to the growing settlement of Brisbane during the late nineteenth century.

Nowadays, the region is still a market garden, its fertile soils irrigated to produce an even greater diversity of crops including lucerne, grain and oil seeds as well as a wide variety of vegetables. Ninety per cent of Queensland's beetroot crop is grown on the farms of the the Laidley Shire. *Population 2320*

DAS NEUMANN HAUS This colonial weatherboard building on the corner of William and Patrick streets was built in 1893 by the local carpenter and cabinetmaker, Herman Neumann. In 1983, the descendants of Neumann donated the building to the shire council and it now houses the tourist information centre and craft shops.

LAIDLEY PIONEER VILLAGE Located on the site of the original settlement of Laidley, this pioneer village is on the historic coach road to Drayton where teamsters made their first night's camp after crossing the Little Liverpool Range from the railhead at Grandchester. Established by the Laidley Historical Society in 1969, the village includes an original pioneer cottage, a nineteenth-century bush school, a museum with historic artefacts and photographic displays and early farming machinery.

ST SAVIOUR'S ANGLICAN CHURCH Built in 1910, this Gothic-style building in Ambrose Street is believed to be the first church in Australia to be built of reinforced concrete.

FESTIVALS Clydesdale and Heavy Horse Show, May; Chelsea Festival, September.

LOWOOD ■ **1378**

The small town of Lowood in the Brisbane Valley is surrounded by the 'market basket' fields of the Esk Shire where the traditional industries of fruit- and vegetable- and small-crop-growing have been complemented in more recent times by the profitable grazing of animals such as beef cattle, sheep, goats and even deer. This peaceful rural setting has made the town an increasingly popular escape for urban dwellers in Brisbane and Ipswich and Lowood is more and more the focus of rapidly developing rural-residential estates. *Population 1030*

FESTIVALS Lowood Hill and Valley Harvest Festival, September.

MARBURG ■ **1379**

Sheep – diversified with a little sly grog on the side – were the chief interest of Sam and Sally Owens – the first graziers to establish themselves in Marburg in 1842; the family is said to have become more famous in the region for its illegal alcoholic drinks than for its sheep. Later, another settler, Thomas Smith, cultivated a sugar plantation and established a mill to process it at his mansion, 'Woodlands' outside Marburg and by 1888 his rum distillery was producing copious quantities of the liquor. 'Woodlands' was later to become the property of Ipswich Grammar School.

Farmers nudged their way into the squatters' realm in the late 1860s and an influx of German settlers to

During her 30s – before she publicised her famous treatment for poliomyelitis – Sister Kenny worked as a nurse in the Darling Downs.

the area in the 1870s saw the land transformed into fields of maize and sugarcane while dairy herds and pigs were raised on the rich pasture lands. The surrounding Rosewood Scrub was exploited for its vast timber reserves. It was these German immigrants who named the settlement after the town in Germany. During the First World War, a few of the town's patriots caused the name to be changed to Townshend, after a British general, but by 1920 the residents had moved successfully to have Marburg reinstated as the official appellation.

The historic Marburg Hotel which opened in 1881, initially to serve the families of German background scattered throughout the district, still pays tribute to its Teutonic heritage when it hosts the annual 'Oktoberfest'. *Population 610*

FESTIVALS Oktoberfest, October.

MILLMERRAN ■ **1380**

The multi-coloured fields that surround Millmerran give a patchwork effect to the landscape and are a visual manifestation of the shire's

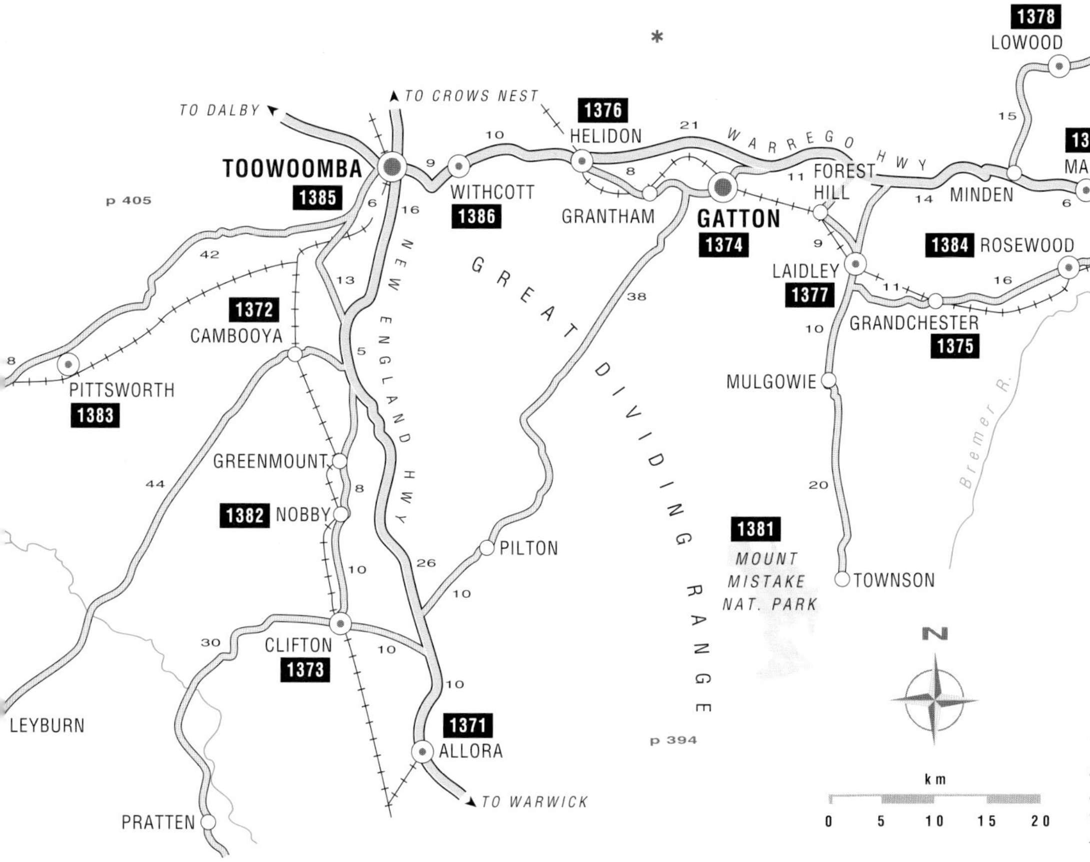

1378 LOWOOD
TO ESK
p 411
TO CROWS NEST
TO DALBY
1376 HELIDON
WARREGO HWY
1379 MARBURG
TOOWOOMBA 1385
WITHCOTT 1386
GRANTHAM
GATTON 1374
FOREST HILL
MINDEN
TO IPSWICH
p 405
1384 ROSEWOOD
LAIDLEY 1377
GREAT DIVIDING RANGE
NEW ENGLAND HWY
1372 CAMBOOYA
GRANDCHESTER 1375
PITTSWORTH 1383
MULGOWIE
Bremer R.
GREENMOUNT
1382 NOBBY
PILTON
1381 MOUNT MISTAKE NAT. PARK
TOWNSON
CLIFTON 1373
LEYBURN
1371 ALLORA
p 394
TO WARWICK
PRATTEN
km 0 5 10 15 20

The waste from Grandchester's steam sawmill is not wasted – it helps power the saws that turn wood into timber.

Passenger trains make a brief, sentimental return to Spring Bluff during Toowoomba's annual flower carnival.

agricultural diversity. The town grew up after the 1876 Crown Lands Alienation Act freed land previously used for grazing sheep and cattle for denser settlement by small farms. With the influx of farmers into the region, a social, business and commercial centre found its roots in the small settlement that grew up around Edward Walpole's store, which opened in 1881.

Originally known as Back Creek – named quite literally for the creek that ran at the back of the nearby Yandilla Station – the settlement was given the name Millmerran in 1895. The name derives from two Aboriginal words, 'meel', meaning 'eye' and 'merran', meaning 'to look out', as the place was once a lookout used by the local Aborigines. Today, the region's industries still include the grazing of beef cattle, sheep and pigs, poultry farming and the growing of irrigated crops such as cotton, grain and vegetables. Though the sheep may be fewer in number than they once were, the shire is still known for the fine quality of its wool. The foundations of Millmerran's sawmilling industry were also laid in the 1880s when cypress pine and hardwood forests were plentiful in the district. Nowadays, most of the timber is drawn from the Western Creek Forestry Reserve.

That unwelcome guest – the prickly pear – that choked the farmlands of south-east Queensland during the first quarter of this century (see *Chinchilla & Miles*) also visited Millmerran and was not eradicated – despite experiments with increasingly noxious chemical 'recipes' – until the cactoblastis moth was imported from South America in the 1920s; within fifteen months it broke the back of the plague and within fifteen years the cactus was eradicated.

Agricultural diversity aside, the district hoards other riches underground as was discovered in the 1970s when massive coal deposits were found a few kilometres from the town. Open-cut coal mining for the fuelling of power stations and coal liquefication plants to convert coal into synthetic fuel have been proposed as possible new industries in the region. *Population 1160*

ALL SAINTS' CHURCH This steep-roofed church adorned with three beautiful stained-glass windows in the nearby village of Yandilla is the oldest structure in Millmerran Shire. It was built in 1877 as a private chapel on the old Yandilla Station and was consecrated as All Saints' Anglican Church ten years later.

BRICK AND BOTTLE MUSEUM Millmerran's Brick and Bottle Museum in Mary Street has more than 2000 antique bottles. Handmade bricks and tiles dating back to the convict era are also on display.

MUSEUM The Millmerran Historical Society and Museum in Charlotte Street brings the past to life with pictorial displays and an impressive collection of artefacts dating from the last century.

MOUNT MISTAKE NATIONAL PARK ■ 1381

Visitors to the 5560-hectare wilderness park south of Laidley (see entry) must leave their vehicles behind and set off on foot along any of the unmarked bushwalking trails to enjoy the eucalypt forests and rainforest patches of Mount Mistake National Park. Until the 1960s, the open forests and rainforests of this spur running off Main Range were plundered sporadically for their timber and now the remnants of a former logging track lead keen bushwalkers up the steep ascent towards the park's high peak – Mount Mistake (1092 metres).

NOBBY ■ **1382**
Sister Elizabeth Kenny spent her childhood in Nobby before gaining world-wide recognition for pioneering a revolutionary treatment for poliomyelitis. She introduced her manipulative treatment at a time when doctors persisted in clinging to an unsuccessful method of immobilisation. After enduring years of strong medical opposition in Australia, Sister Kenny took her 'bush cure' to America and there was rewarded with the acclaim that was denied in her home country.

A film depicting Sister Kenny's life and starring American actress Rosalind Russell was released in 1946. Sister Kenny died in 1952 and is buried in Nobby's cemetery. At the entrance to the town, a small garden commemorates this famous nurse.

PITTSWORTH ■ **1383**
From the tender green shoots of newly planted grain crops to the yellow hues of ripened seed heads during harvest time, the irrigated farmlands surrounding Pittsworth present an ever-changing kaleidoscope of colour. The town is noted not only for the fertility of its blacksoil plains, but also for its cheeses, the 'Pittsworth Mild' having won a number of prizes including, in 1924, an invitation from the Australian Committee of the Empire Exhibition to produce a giant cheese for the exhibition in London. The patriotic citizens of Pittsworth duly produced a circular cheese weighing one-and-a-half tonnes!

One of the Darling Downs' best historical museums has a display from the Pittsworth Cheese Factory showing the complete cheese-making process. Also in the museum are the sash and trophy belonging to the Pittsworth-born 'Crimson Flash', otherwise known as Arthur Postle, who was acclaimed as the 'fastest man alive' when he was awarded the World Championship Cup for the 220-yard dash in 1906.

Modern Pittsworth is a pretty town, proud of its landscaped retirement village and streets that erupt with the colourful blooms of jacarandas and flowering silky-oaks during spring. Many residents commute daily to work in nearby Toowoomba.

Pittsworth is named for the family which held one of the downs' early stations, 'Goombungee' in 1854. Initially known as Beauaraba, the name was changed in 1915. *Population 2110*

PITTSWORTH HISTORICAL VILLAGE On Pioneer Way, this historical village captures the mood of the past with local sporting heroes, soldiers, pioneering settlers and Aborigines all honoured in a varied collection of historic artefacts.

ROSEWOOD ■ **1384**
After Moreton Bay became a free settlement in 1842, squatters flocked to the region; later came farmers who cleared the land to grow maize, cotton, and later, sugarcane. The river flats also supported dairy herds while the timber in the large forests provided the basis for a flourishing industry. The village of Rosewood appeared on the Moreton Shire map in the 1860s as a settlement on Queensland's first railway line, from Ipswich to Grandchester (see entry).

The village's most distinctive architectural structures are Saint Brigid's Catholic Church – a decorative timber building with fine detailing of handpainted frescoes – which is believed to be the largest timber church in the Southern Hemisphere, and the Rising Sun Hotel, with its unusual corner roof turret, designed by Ipswich architect Wil Haenke in 1908. *Population 1660*

TOOWOOMBA ■ **1385**
From its lofty position on the brow of the Great Dividing Range, Toowoomba celebrates its stature as the garden city of Australia with more than 1000 hectares of parks and gardens and two areas of bushland around the range escarpment.

Many of the city's parks have a special theme or focal point: Queens Park, alongside the Botanic Gardens, is the largest of the city's parks with twenty-six hectares of playing fields set amid clusters of massive, century-old, Northern Hemisphere trees, while Laurel Bank Park is planted with rare trees and has a scented garden for blind people. The lesser-known Webb Park is the setting for a broken pillar, built as a memorial to the poet, George Essex Evans, Toowoomba's poet laureate whose patriotic verses were inspired by his love of the countryside.

Toowoomba has the prodigious fertility of the Darling Downs to thank for its prosperity. Allan Cunningham's 'discovery' of the Darling Downs in 1827 led the way some thirteen years later for the squatters whose pastoralism was usurped by the more intensive industry of agriculture by the turn of the century. Wheat and other grain crops were grown by the downs' first farmers in the 1860s and dairy farming and pork-raising began in the 1890s with milk, butter and cheese factories soon dotting the landscape. The appearance of a store, blacksmith's shop and pub at Drayton in 1842 constituted the first settlement on the downs, but after a promising start, a lack of water prompted many of the town's residents to move to nearby marshy ground known as 'The Swamp'. By the 1860s, The Swamp had outstripped its neighbour and in time, Drayton became a Toowoomba suburb.

Exactly when, and how, Toowoomba acquired its name is not known. A popular theory has it that the local Aborigines in attempting to pronounce the name, called it 'tchwampa', which became modified to Toowoomba. Another is that it was Choowoom or Toowoomba, Aboriginal words meaning 'place where melons grow' or 'water sit down'. What *is* known, is that Thomas Alford settled in the vicinity in 1852 and named his house 'Toowoomba' and by the 1860s this had been adopted as the town's name.

With the arrival of the railway from Ipswich in 1867, Toowoomba's growth was assured and from the 1880s to the outbreak of the First World War the city consolidated its position as the major service centre for the downs' primary industries. This period also saw the construction of some of the city's finest public and private buildings, which have contributed so greatly to the perception of modern Toowoomba as a place of culture and stylish architecture.

Education has been the other hallmark of culture and prosperity and

The only part of the Darling Downs left unfurrowed are the roadways which frame the patchworked fields.

the private schools established during the thirty years before the First World War laid the foundation for the city's position as a scholastic centre, renowned for the quality of its private boarding schools and site of the University of Southern Queensland. *Population 75 990*

COBB & CO. MUSEUM This branch of the Queensland Museum in Lindsay Street, holds one of Australia's finest displays of horse-drawn vehicles including one on loan from the federal government – the Cobb & Co. coach 112 – which was the company's last horse-drawn coach to travel the roads as an official courier.

ROYAL BULLS HEAD INN Now fully restored by the National Trust, this historic inn in Brisbane Street, Drayton, is Toowoomba's oldest surviving building. Built in 1859 – an earlier structure dating from 1847 existed on the site prior to this, and only the slab kitchen remains – the inn was a meeting place for squatters and a watering hole for travellers. The first Church of England service held on the Darling Downs was held here in 1848 and for fifty years, one of the inn's rooms operated as the Drayton post office.

In the 1870s, the inn ceased to operate as a hotel and became a private residence until its acquisition by the National Trust in 1973.

SPRING BLUFF This little railway station tucked into the side of the Great Dividing Range just east of Toowoomba is famous for its gardens and picnic areas. Opened in 1867, the station is named after the spring that runs alongside the bluff and in earlier times, a guesthouse built on the hill overlooking the station was a popular haunt for honeymooners.

STEELE RUDD MEMORIAL 'Steele Rudd', or Arthur Hoey Davis, creator of those quintessentially Australian characters, Dad and Dave, and author of many humorous stories depicting the trials and tribulations of the district's early selectors, or family farmers, in *On Our Selection* and other books, is commemorated by a cairn here although he was born in Drayton in 1868 (see Cambooya).

FESTIVALS Gardenfest, May; Carnival of Flowers, September; Agricultural Show, September.

WITHCOTT ■ 1386

The relaxed style of rural living has lured many of Withcott's newer residents to this pleasant town in the Lockyer Valley. Close enough to Toowoomba (see entry) to avail themselves of the city's employment, cultural and commercial opportunities, the townspeople are able to take advantage of the best of both worlds. *Population 700*

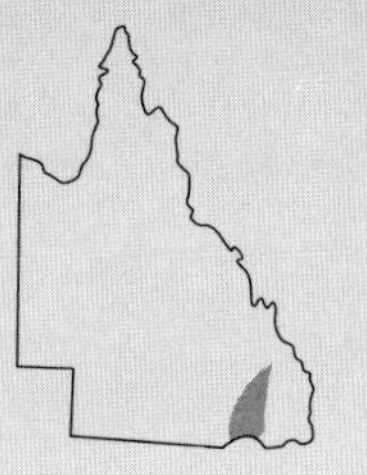

Chinchilla & Miles

The Darling Downs, one of the food bowls of Australia, is a great expanse of arable land dotted with small but prosperous country towns. It was not always so: in the early part of this century the fiercely spiky and seemingly unstoppable prickly pear cactus invaded the countryside.

City collectors of 'primitive' rustic artefacts would covet Miles' array of Condamine bells – bullock-size versions of the clanking, European cow bell.

ALTON NATIONAL PARK ■ 1387

Alton National Park protects 560 hectares of woodland containing smooth-barked apple, narrow-leafed ironbark and cypress pine. The sandplains and low ridges are covered by heath and hummock grass with occasional eucalypts and grass trees. The wildflowers put on a colourful show after winter and spring rain.

BENDIDEE NATIONAL PARK ■ 1388

These 930 hectares of national park bushland adjoin Bendidee State Forest and forest trees spill over into the protected brigalow and belah scrub. It is an area of low rainfall that supports acacias, casuarinas, teatree, wilga and vines. A good downpour quickly activates the flowering and fruiting plants which then attract birds and insects.

CHINCHILLA ■ 1389

Chinchilla was named by Ludwig Leichhardt in 1847 and is derived from 'jinchilla', said to be the Aboriginal word for 'cypress pine'. The Chinchilla Historical Museum has a fine collection of steam-powered traction engines and many exhibits recalling the pioneer days. In equestrian sporting circles, Chinchilla is known as the biggest polocrosse centre in Queensland.

The district relies on grazing, timber and grain growing with good crops of vegetables, melons, grapes and the more recently introduced strawberries. It contains one of the largest known petrified wood outcrops in the world and well-preserved shapes of ancient conifer and tree-fern trunks have been fossicked at Baking Board and Magic Stone. The wood – between 140 and 180 million years old – shares this location with specimens of agate and jasper. *Population 3150*

BOONARGA CACTOBLASTIS MEMORIAL HALL A few kilometres east of Chinchilla is Boonarga which may well have the only community hall in the world that honours an insect. Local graziers had good reason to be grateful to the cactoblastis moth from South America. In the early nineteenth century, the prickly pear cactus spread rapidly in south-east Queensland and by 1925 had choked more than 260 000 square kilometres of stock and crop land and ruined hundreds of farmers.

The problem originated when Captain Arthur Phillip brought the plant to Australia with the First Fleet; while loading food in Brazil, he gathered dye-yielding cochineal insects on their host plant, the prickly pear, to supply colour for his soldiers' red coats. Later, Darling Downs settlers planted cuttings to make stockproof hedges around their home steads and birds then proceeded to spread the seeds in their droppings.

The Commonwealth Prickly Pear Board investigated control methods and by 1925 large quantities of cactoblastis moth eggs had been released into the thickets and the larvae devoured the pear, miraculously controlling the plague within fifteen months. By 1935, the land was productive again, with the hollowed out shells of the plants mulching the soil.

BARAKULA STATE FOREST North of Boongara, this very large cypress pine plantation covers about 284 000 hectares and preserves spotted gum – popular with interior decorators and boatbuilders – narrow-leaf ironbark and Chinchilla white gum. The last is a quick-growing, hardy tree with silvery-white bark.

CONDAMINE ■ 1390

Present day Condamine grew where the river was most easily fordable by bullock and horse teams. The early residents had great hopes that the railway would come through the town but in 1878 the government decided to re-route it through Miles. One storekeeper expressed the community's bitter disappointment by inserting an obituary in the Roma newspaper: 'Died by Act Of Parliament, the township situated on the Banks of the Condamine River. It sprang into existence about AD 1860 and lingered, a sickly institution, till All Fools Day 1879 when it passed quietly away'.

The town's huge replica Condamine Bell is an unusual monument in honour of Samuel Jones, a Welsh blacksmith, who in the late 1860s, invented a bell suited, so it was said, specially to Australian conditions. Bullocks grazed vast unfenced pastures then and the teamsters located them at yoking time by the sound of the bells around their necks. Traditional European bells, made of brass, were scarce and expensive and their clanking sound did not carry far enough. Jones fashioned bells out of old crosscut saw blades, narrow at the mouth instead of flaring outwards. Later he used sheet metal. The words 'Bullfrog' or 'Jones' was stamped on the tongue and the bells are now sought after by collectors.

CONDAMINE RIVER ■ 1391

The Condamine River is the beginning of the longest river system in Australia. It rises at The Head, east of Queen Mary Falls (see *Warwick & Boonah*) in a beautiful valley best seen from Carrs Lookout, then cuts its way through the Condamine Gorge to flow lazily across the Darling Downs. Here the Condamine combines its forces with the Darling River which eventually flows into the Murray River. The Condamine River and its tributaries which drain the fertile, basalt soils of the Darling Downs have a heavy summer maximum flow but are sometimes a mere trickle in winter. Allan Cunningham named the river in 1827 after Governor Darling's private secretary.

DRILLHAM AND DULACCA ■ 1392

Drillham and Dulacca are only a few kilometres apart on the Warrego Highway and are surrounded by land devoted to growing grain and raising cattle. Dulacca, said to mean 'emu tracks', stands on a large holding of the same name and Drillham is built on part of that bygone run too. Drillham's name is colourfully explained as a distortion of Delirium Creek, so called because of the typhoid fever which killed many settlers when they were building the railway line. The towns were at their most prosperous during the railway construction period.

MEANDARRA ■ 1393

Meandarra began with a temporary school building in 1913, built at a cost to the Education Department of 197 pounds sterling. The township was surveyed in 1915 but little more than scrub grew there till work on the railway started in the early 1920s and farmers took up cattle instead of sheep. The district became prosperous grazing country, except for the years when the prickly pear ruled.

MILES ■ 1394

Miles was first known as Dogwood Crossing but was later renamed after William Miles, owner of Dulacca Station and member of parliament for the seat of Maranoa. The settlement grew up by chance when flooding in 1878 suspended the building of the railway line and Dogwood Crossing became the temporary terminal. Miles is now the commercial centre of the western Darling Downs. The country is tick-free and cattle studs produce Herefords and other top-value stock. The saleyards and wheat silos are focal points of the town, and the district's sawmills process cypress pine and hardwood. *Population 1260*

The sight of prickly pear can still send a shiver down the spine of old hands in rural Queensland – it once overran 25 million hectares of countryside (see Chinchilla).

FESTIVALS Back to the Bush Weekend, early September.

MOONIE OIL FIELD ■ 1395

Moonie was Australia's first commercial oil field. Oil-producing shafts were drilled here late in 1961 and more than eighteen wells were sunk between 1961 and 1964 with others being established until late 1967. Production began in February 1964 with the opening of a pipeline to Brisbane. After separation from the oil, the water which also gushes to the surface is pumped into a bore drain and used on adjoining properties; while the crude oil is held in storage tanks. The oil is piped to the Lytton Terminal in Brisbane in a once-weekly operation that takes a few hours.

SOUTHWOOD NATIONAL PARK ■ 1396

Southwood National Park is an undeveloped area of 7100 hectares which is fenced to keep stock out of the brigalow scrubland. Wilga, belah, cypress pine, casuarinas and eucalypts grow among the brigalow. Gilgai depressions are a feature of this reserve – they form when the clay soil swells in wet periods and then cracks as it dries out.

TARA ■ 1397

The early Tara district was made up of quite large leases. An 1863 map shows runs with names that still exist today: 'Weranga', 'Tara', 'Tartha', 'Culgara', 'Southwood', 'Cooroora', 'Canmaroo' and 'Undulla'. According to records, prickly pear was 'carefully nurtured' around 'Weranga' before its potential was realised and it became an uncontrollable pest – as early as 1870. By 1920, it had spoilt over twenty-four million hectares of this district. Before the Second World War, large patches of scrub were cleared for farming by ringbarking and burning off but after the war, bulldozers and ex-army tanks made scrub pulling much easier.

When the railway line reached Tara in 1911, dairying was the main occupation but sheep and beef cattle took over in time. The Queensland Government established a railway-sleeper mill at Tara in the 1920s and the timber industry provided employment during the lean depression years of the 1930s. Wheat growing began in the 1950s and there are four depots between Tara and Glenmorgan which handle a huge annual grain tonnage. *Population 880*

WANDOAN ■ 1398

The first Europeans to enter this region were Ludwig Leichhardt and his fellow explorers on their journey from Jimbour Station to Port Essington in 1844 and 1845 (see *Dalby & Oakey*). Wandoan's history begins with the settlement of Juandah Station in 1853. A wayside hotel was built there in the 1890s and the township expanded further with the completion of the rail link between Wandoan and Miles in 1914. The name Juandah was changed to Wandoan in 1927 to avoid confusion with a Queensland town called Jundah.

After the prickly-pear infestations in the first quarter of the twentieth century had come to an end (see Chinchilla), large areas of the brigalow country were cleared and sown with improved pasture grasses. After the Second World War, soldier-settlement boosted the farming community. Today, cattle and sheep raising are important industries and wheat and sorghum do well in the nitrogen-rich brigalow soil. Coal lies beneath Wandoan and the surrounding region, and petrified wood, petrified palm in many colours, as well as agate and jasper have also been found. *Population 480*

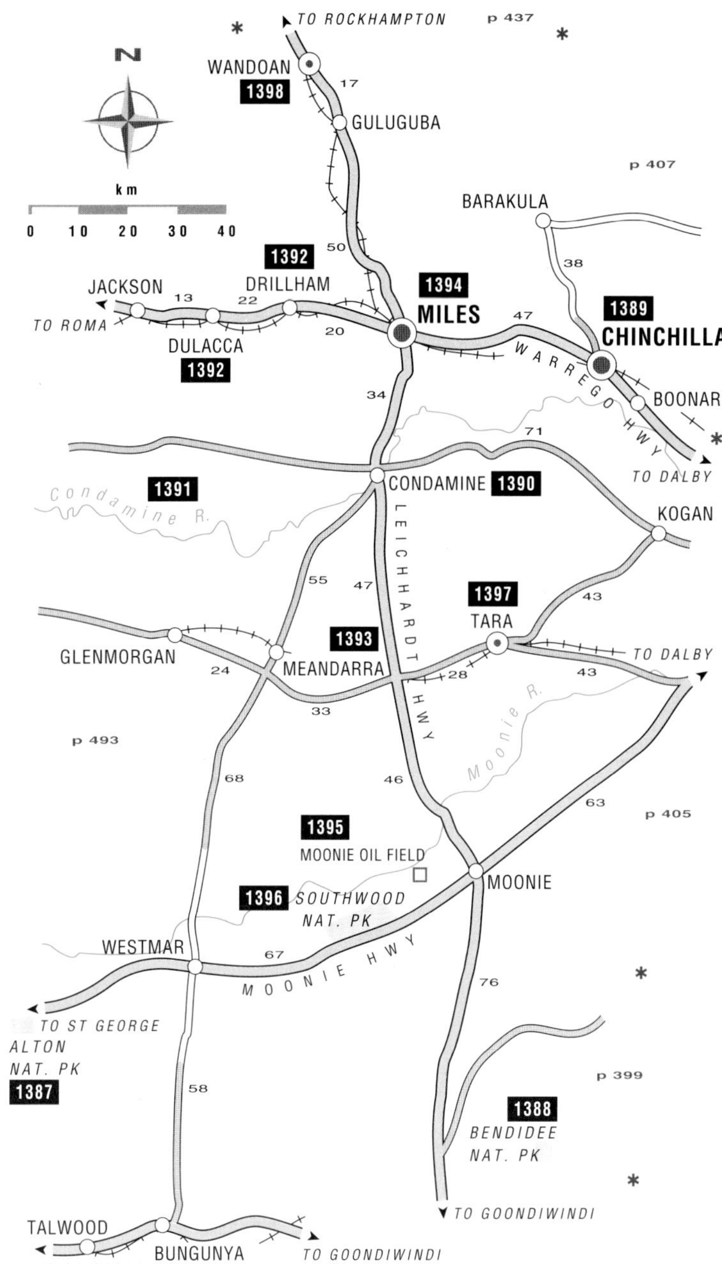

In a scene reminiscent of the 'good old days', this mob was herded to market across the Condamine River in 1992.

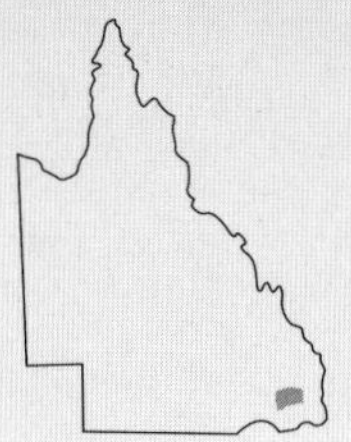

Dalby & Oakey

These plains and mountains supported Aboriginal Australians for many thousands of years before the European colonists drew on the soil, water and building materials for their most urgent needs. Now the region is known for its bountiful primary production.

The Aborigines carefully husbanded the majestic bunya pine for its nutritious, edible nuts (above) with good reason: they knew it grew only in this region and in a small section of the Atherton Tableland.

BELL ■ 1399

Bell is a peaceful little settlement at the foot of the Bunya Mountains (see entry) surrounded by sheep pastures and wheatfields. The grain silos which serve the fields dominate the village which also has an old hotel distinguished by its vine-clad verandah. Cattle and horses, especially high quality Arabian steeds, are bred at stud farms in the district.

BUNYA MOUNTAINS NATIONAL PARK ■ 1400

Geologists believe the Bunya Mountains were formed thirty million years ago when massive flows of volcanic basalt solidified. They are part of the Great Dividing Range and border the eastern rim of the Darling Downs. By 1878, the entire mountain area was opened up for selection and many stands of red cedar fell to the insatiable needs of the sawmills – the Great Bunya Sawmill began operating five years later, eliminating the need to transport the logs elsewhere for processing.

The Aborigines held the bunya pines which grow here as sacred and sometimes tried to chase off anyone they saw trying to cut them down. The timber-getters waited until the Aborigines left the rainforest before taking these trees.

Part of the range was given protection in 1908, making it the second national park in Queensland. The park's area has extended to more than 11 000 hectares and bunya pines and red cedars which escaped the logger's axe are now protected. There is rainforest, eucalypt forest and plains, known locally as 'balds', where botanical oddities such as bottle trees and grass trees grow.

The bunya pines, unique to Queensland, raise their graceful crowns above the rainforest canopy. The pineapple-shaped cones, weighing up to seven kilograms, protect nuts which take three years to mature and are about the size of a small hen's egg. They taste – so some say – like chestnuts when roasted and were considered a great delicacy. From the days of the Dreamtime, Aborigines hunted across the Darling Downs and every third autumn migrated to the Bunya Mountains where the ripening bunya nuts drew them to a special feast which was an occasion of celebrations and corroborees. Most of the trees were communally owned but it is thought that some belonged to families and were passed from father to son.

CECIL PLAINS ■ 1401

In 1841, 'Cecil Plains' was a successful cattle run taken up by Henry Stuart Russell and his brother, Sydenham. The land was thought to be cattle country only and useless for sheep and was not stocked with them until 1865, but since then great profits have been made from fat lambs and wool.

The above-ground 'ring' tanks for collecting water are a feature of the surrounding Darling Downs irrigation zone. Each tank looks like a big, square embankment where the stored water comes from flood run-off, normal wet-weather run-off or is pumped from the Condamine or North Branch rivers in flood periods. Irrigated crops include sorghum, soya beans, corn, sunflowers, wheat, barley and cotton.

The cotton gin at Cecil Plains, used by farmers from all over the Queensland south-west, is one of the largest in the state and works a twenty-four-hour day from April through to September. The gin processes between 100 000 and 120 000 bales of cotton each season and each bale weighs 225 kilograms. Here the seeds and leaves are stripped from the fibre which is then cleaned and baled and sent to Brisbane. From there ninety-five per cent is shipped overseas and the rest used for spinning into different grades of yarn, some of which will end up in the hands of clothing manufacturers within Australia. The seed is crushed and will eventually be used as stock meal or, combined with other waste products, as garden mulch by landscaping companies, for example.

CROWS NEST ■ 1402

Crows Nest began as an overnight stopping-place for the timber-haulers who dragged logs out of the Bunya Mountains. They rested near a large hollow tree which, according to legend, was the home of an Aborigine called Jimmy Crow who gave his name to the developing farming district. The tree is near the present town's police station. In 1969, the town council commissioned Fred Gardiner from Toowoomba to sculpt a life-size statue of Jimmy Crow from Helidon freestone and the completed work stands in Centenary Park together with a six-metre-high hollow tree stump.

Crows Nest is on the eastern slopes of the Main Range and has mild summers and bracing winters. The district is well watered and gold and tin have both been found in small quantities. The town is surrounded by agricultural land where shorthorn dairy cattle, pigs, potatoes, lucerne, wheat and corn are raised. There are also avocado and kiwi fruit orchards. *Population 1150*

CROWS NEST FALLS NATIONAL PARK ■ 1403

This is a reserved area of 1000 hectares where Perseverance Creek flows over a granite gorge to create Crows Nest Falls. There are deep swimming pools and short walking tracks within the park and excellent views over the Valley of Diamonds and Perseverance Dam. The ridges and high ground above the creek carry eucalypt forest and heathland which shelter many birds including a variety of honeyeaters.

DALBY ■ 1404

Henry Dennis was probably the first European to pitch camp near the present site of Dalby. That was in 1841 and the town began in a familiar way with a small pub built a few years later. The teams and waggons on their way to Jimbour Station (see entry) had to cross the Myall Creek here – historians agree that 'Jimbour' played an important role in the early development of the town which might never have existed without it.

It is not surprising that the settlement was first known as 'The Crossing' and then as Myall Creek; it was even Rochetown for a little while in honour of the first mayor, a storekeeper who apparently printed his own banknotes. Dalby became the official name from August 1863 when the municipality was officially proclaimed; the name was said to have been chosen for Dalby on the Isle of Man.

During the Second World War, industries began which continued to expand after 1945. Dalby services the surrounding district which produces wheat, cotton, maize and millet, cattle, sheep, pigs and poultry and has factories milling flour and timber and manufacturing agricultural implements, steel products, stock feed and butter. The Dalby Agricultural College was established in 1979.

An obelisk on the banks of the Myall Creek at Dalby pays tribute to the cactoblastis moth and the government scientists who introduced it to wage war on the dreaded prickly pear cactus (see *Chinchilla & Miles*). The creek runs through the town and offers sport to anglers with a chance to hook a mammoth Murray cod, or a golden or silver perch.

Rock fossickers in the Dalby area have found a colourless variety of opal called hyalite and 'thunder eggs' – fossil stones which according to Aboriginal legend were cast to earth by lightning – at Square Top Mountain, and olivine at Iron Pot Creek. Bottle trees, lifesavers for some parched early Queensland travellers, dot the landscape in Dalby State Forest. There is a compartment in the lower part of the trunk, between the inner bark and the wood, which holds a considerable amount of water, and the middle of the tree has another cavity filled with nourishing jelly. *Population 9380*

FESTIVALS Harvest Festival, October.

GOOMBUNGEE ■ 1405

Goombungee, the headquarters of Rosalie Shire, is a small township surrounded by beef and dairy farms. Some grain crops are grown in the district and pigs are also raised. The town economy is stimulated by a biscuit factory and a steelworks which manufactures sheds for farms and factories throughout Queensland and New South Wales. *Population 590*

HIGHFIELDS ■ 1406

In the 1860s, the whole district along the edge of the range stretching from Spring Bluff to Geham was known as Highfields. The present town was originally called 'koojarewon' – said

The smithy's anvil still rings to a beat at Jondaryan Woolshed where the museum pieces gather no dust.

to mean 'top of the range' – but later became known by the European name of Highfields. Sawyers were attracted by the magnificent trees, and steam sawmills were soon set up. When the timber and scrub was cleared, the land was divided into small holdings and dairying became the major industry. After the 1868 Lands Act, Highfields and nearby

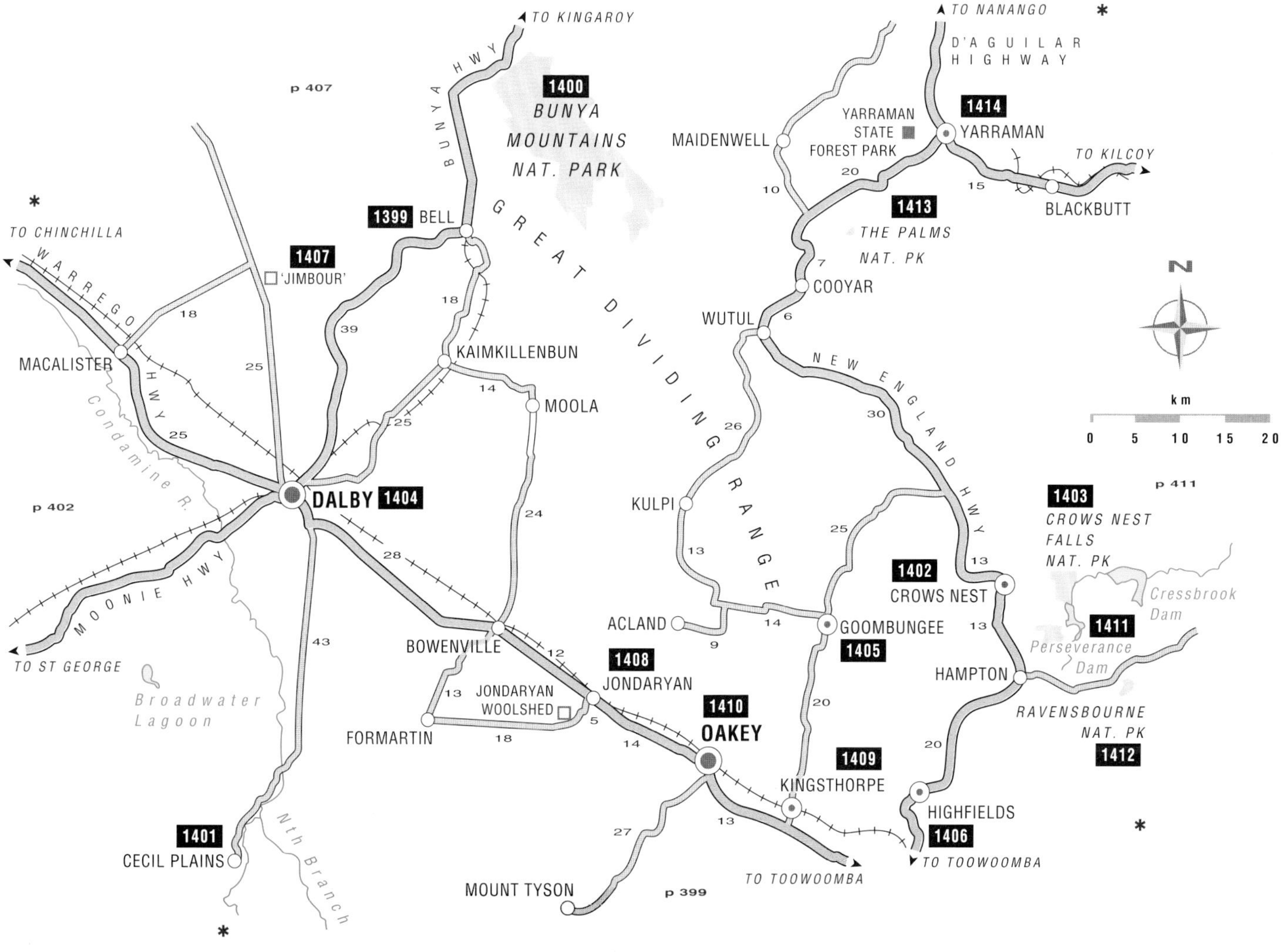

Geham attracted settlers, many of whom were from Ireland or Germany. At this time, Carbarlah was the centre of the rapidly developing district and boasted three hotels – the remaining Farmers' Arms claims to be the oldest hotel in Queensland.

The district has diversified into market gardens, plant nurseries and orchards. Dairy cattle are still raised and bulk milk is sent to the Downs Dairy Factory. Many of the Highfields farms have been subdivided to provide rural housing for the people of Toowoomba. *Population 1400*

'JIMBOUR' ■ 1407

Richard Todd Scougall established himself at Jimbour Station in 1842 – the area is said to have been called 'jimba' or 'gimba' by the Aborigines meaning 'bush grass'. Towards the end of 1844, Ludwig Leichhardt and nine companions, enthusiastically singing the chorus of *God Save the Queen*, set out from 'Jimbour' on a privately funded expedition to find an overland route to Port Essington at the northern tip of Arnhem Land. The naturalist, John Gilbert, lost his life on the way, the others continuing to reach their destination more than fourteen months later after a journey of over 4800 kilometres. In December 1846, the indefatigable German explorer again set out from Jimbour Station but returned disconsolately six months later having covered only 805 kilometres to the north-west in seven months. The character of Voss, in Patrick White's novel of the same name, is based on Ludwig Leichhardt and Jimbour Station became the fictitious 'Jildra'.

During this time of the opening up of Queensland, ownership of the property changed hands and in 1843 Thomas Bell of Sydney bought the station in partnership with his three sons. The eldest, Joshua, had most to do with 'Jimbour'. He was described as a squatter of high self-importance – one of the privileged 'pure merinos' who treated his employees well and invariably lunched alone with a bottle of champagne.

In 1867, the original dwelling, which had burnt down, was replaced by a two-storey bluestone house. In 1874, work began on a two-storey mansion of a grand and sophisticated design which is now the well-kept 'Jimbour House', one of Queensland's 'stately homes'. It was built entirely from local materials except for the Welsh roof slates. There was gaslight in the two dozen or so rooms, generated from coal mined on the property; water used in and around the mansion was pumped by what are believed to have been the first windmills erected in Queensland.

JONDARYAN ■ 1408

Jondaryan township is named after the huge run which was taken up in 1841 a year before free settlement officially began in Queensland. Some say the name is from the word 'yondaryan' meaning 'a long way off' because it was far from the Bunya Mountains on the Aboriginal triennial migration (see Bunya Mountains National Park).

Oakey held Bernborough in such high regard that the townspeople erected this statue to the horse which carried many a punter's flutter in the 1940s.

The timber St Anne's Church was originally built on Jondaryan Station in 1859 of hand-dressed, ironbark slabs. It was moved to its present site in 1893 and is the oldest surviving church on the Darling Downs. In 1868, His Royal Highness Prince Alfred, Duke of Edinburgh, visited Jondaryan to open the western terminal of the rail link with Brisbane and the townsfolk presented him with 'a damper the size of a flitch of bacon'. Like so many country towns, the fortunes of Jondaryan depended on the railway and between 1868 and the beginning of the First World War there was a period of growth. But the Railway Department's decision in 1912 to establish branch lines from Oakey instead of Jondaryan started a decline. From then on, Oakey took over as the hub of the region's pastoral industry.

JONDARYAN WOOLSHED This restored fifty-six-stand shed on Jondaryan Station, now used as a living museum of pioneer country life, has displays which explain the old method of hand shearing. The woolshed is a large structure of ironbark slabs and local red cedar with roof beams that came from England lashed precariously to the side of a ship because they were too long to fit on the deck! Building began in 1859 and took three years to complete.

FESTIVALS Woolshed Australian-Heritage Festival, late August–early September.

KINGSTHORPE ■ 1409

Kingsthorpe, west of Toowoomba, is one of the larger towns in Rosalie Shire and a rapidly developing satellite urban area. The small settlement is within commuting distance of Queensland's largest inland city and offers an aura of rural calm to escapees from the land of the tenth-of-a-hectare – or quarter-acre – block. *Population 1010*

FESTIVALS Farmfest, August.

OAKEY ■ 1410

In 1841, Tinker Campbell established Westbrook Station which included the area now occupied by the town of Oakey. Ludwig Leichhardt bought bullocks from Campbell for his second expedition and spent a night by a tree-lined creek which he called Oaky Creek. The 'e' seems to have been added when the first post office was established in 1869.

Oakey is home to the Australian Army Aviation Centre – the aircraft depot first opened to relieve the aerodrome at Amberley of overhaul work during the Second World War and as a forward depot for aircraft operating from New Guinea and Northern Australia. The Museum of Australian Army Flying has one of the best collections of flying memorabilia in the country, including a replica of Sir Charles Kingsford Smith's 'Southern Cross'.

A life-size bronze statue, weighing two tonnes, of the legendary 1940s racehorse Bernborough, takes pride of place in Jondaryan Shire Bicentennial Park in Oakey. The galloper was born at neaby Rosalie Plains. *Population 3430*

PERSEVERANCE DAM ■ 1411

A dam across Perseverance Creek has created an artificial lake officially named Lake Perseverance after the local council decided against calling it Lake Wilmoth after Geoffrey Wilmoth, the city engineer who chose the site. Instead, his name has been given to the park adjacent to the dam. The lake and its environs are home to many water birds and the natural habitat of platypuses and rock wallabies. Native violets, geebung, banksia and pink rock lilies flower prettily in their season.

The dam, which was completed in 1963, is unusual in that no cement was used in the retaining wall which has a centre zone of rock piled forty-six metres high and retaining walls of clay from the site, with a filter zone of rock to protect the clay from the ravages of the water.

RAVENSBOURNE NATIONAL PARK ■ 1412

This was a popular area with the early timber-getters who came to cut down the tall red cedars, blackbean and rosewood. These rainforest trees were once common on the eastern Darling Downs but the pioneer land developers valued their wood too much for buildings and furniture for them to survive. The 100-hectare Ravensbourne National Park preserves examples of these species together with eucalypt forest on the drier slopes and stands of piccabeen palms and corkwood. The walk to the higher of the two picnic grounds is rewarded with views of the 'scenic rim' mountains to the south.

THE PALMS NATIONAL PARK ■ 1413

Within this relatively tiny park – it covers barely twelve hectares – is an area which encloses a dense grove of piccabeen palms with a 500-metre nature trail winding through it. The trees are tall with slender trunks and have distinctive flower clusters that look like intricate filigree necklaces. Tree ferns grow among the palms and more complex rainforest begins at the edge of the park.

YARRAMAN ■ 1414

Yarraman settlement grew where hungry stockmen from 'Cooyar'and 'Taromeo' stations made their tea camp on mustering forays to separate the cattle from the two properties – a big job in those days of fenceless runs. It was hard work for your keep and a minimal wage. At the end of the nineteenth century, a head stockman earned one pound sterling a week and the Aboriginal hands were paid in twists of tobacco. It is said that the station dogs were terrified by dingo packs and some horses had already escaped to form mobs of brumbies.

In 1912, a big sawmill was built at Yarraman and the following year the Brisbane Valley railway line from Brisbane and Ipswich terminated there. The timber boom and the railway ensured the growth of the town and dairying, grazing and agricultural industries began. Today, timber is less important but the Yarraman State Forest is planted with hoop pines which are milled locally, and some Brazilian pines have been planted. Sapphires, topazes, and garnets have been found around the Googa Creek near Blackbutt. *Population 790*

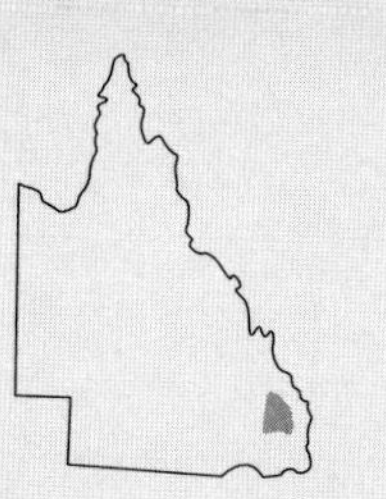

Kingaroy & Murgon

The rich lands which drew exploring sheepmen to this region now grow quality beef and dairy cattle, citrus fruit, peanuts and supply the crucial ingredient for the manufacture of an ever-popular staple – baked beans.

AUBURN RIVER NATIONAL PARK ■ 1415

In this rugged park, the Auburn River descends in a series of cascades and rock pools over extensive steps and boulders of pink granite rock. In places, the swirling waters have worn rocks into spheres and ovoids, such as the 'dinosaur eggs', two large rocks which lie cradled together in a smooth nest of stone. Walking tracks lead from the cascades to a lookout through a landscape of vine thicket and open ironbark forest.

BOONDOOMA DAM ■ 1416

Boondooma Dam's waters, on the headwaters of the beautiful Burnett River, extend twenty-five kilometres behind the dam wall. The dam was completed in 1980 and provides water for the Tarong Power Station as well as irrigation. Along its 160-kilometre shoreline are many inlets; there is a camping area, and opposite the dam wall, picnic facilities have been built. The waters are stocked with perch and bass.

The dam takes it name from nearby National Trust-listed Boondooma Homestead, built on the run taken up by the Lawson brothers in 1846. During restoration work in the 1970s, it was discovered that the old stone house had been built using metric rather than imperial measurements, the legacy of a Flemish builder working in the system to which he was most accustomed.

BURNETT RIVER ■ 1417

The Burnett River rises near Monto, on the western slopes of the Burnett Ranges, and turns east at Mundubbera to cut through the ranges. At Gayndah, it turns north-west to flow first through dairying country and then through the canefields to enter the sea at Burnett Heads, near Bundaberg, about 430 kilometres from its source. The Burnett is the major river of the Wide Bay–Burnett Region, its major southern tributaries are the Auburn and Boyne rivers, which join it near Mundubbera, and Barambah Creek, which meets the Burnett near Gayndah. In its upper reaches the river is home to the peculiar Queensland lungfish (see box).

CHERBOURG A few kilometres south of Murgon is an area of land set aside in 1904 for an Aboriginal settlement. Until the 1960s, its inhabitants worked for rations only, then wages were introduced. The settlement gained control of its own affairs in 1986 and is now managed solely by the Cherbourg Community Council. Harold Blair, the Aboriginal singer and teacher, was born here in 1924. The first emu farm in Queensland began operating at Cherbourg in 1989 to breed emus for their oil and leather. Carved eggs and other artefacts are on sale here.

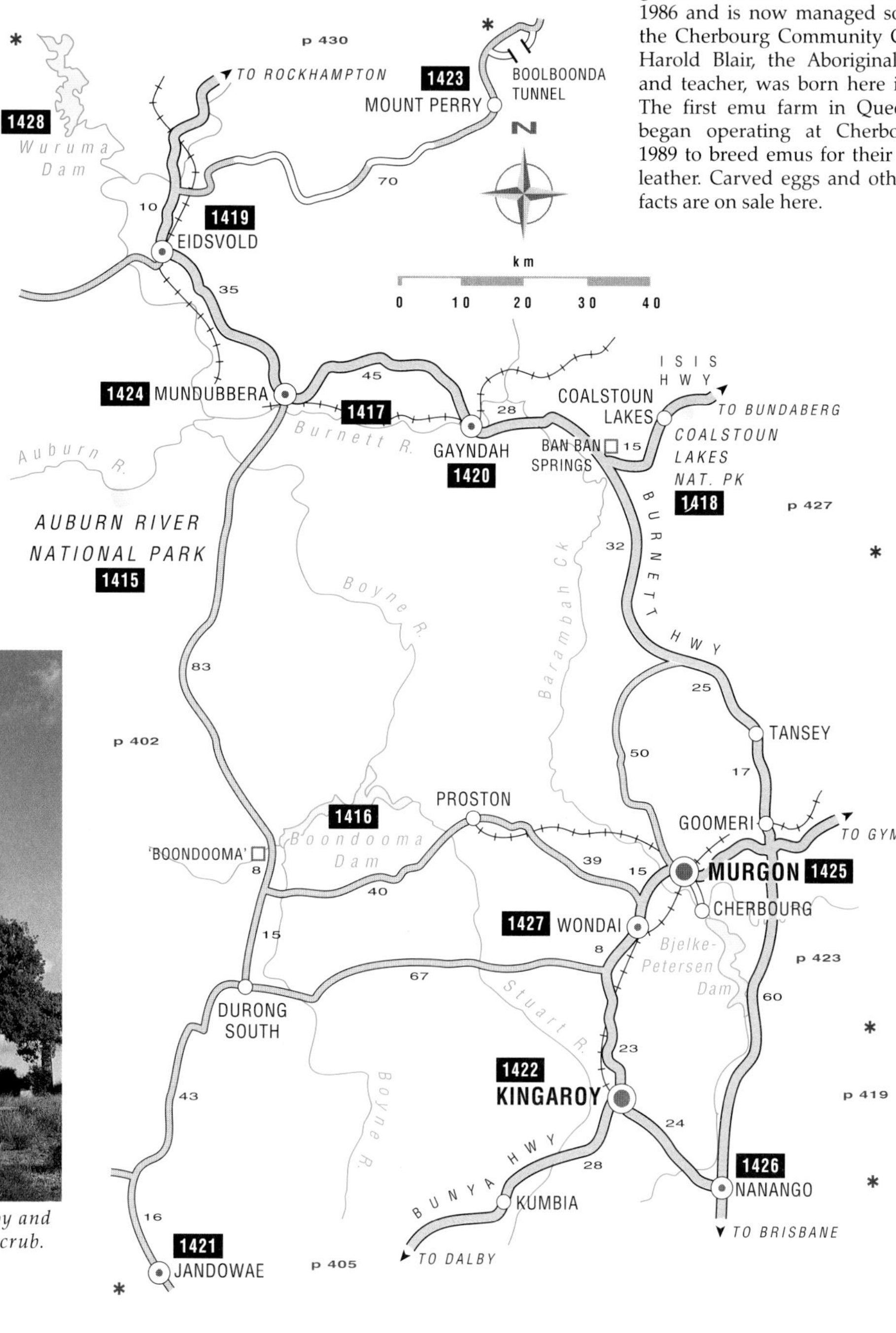

Drought-resistant bottle trees between Kingaroy and Murgon would once have been surrounded by scrub.

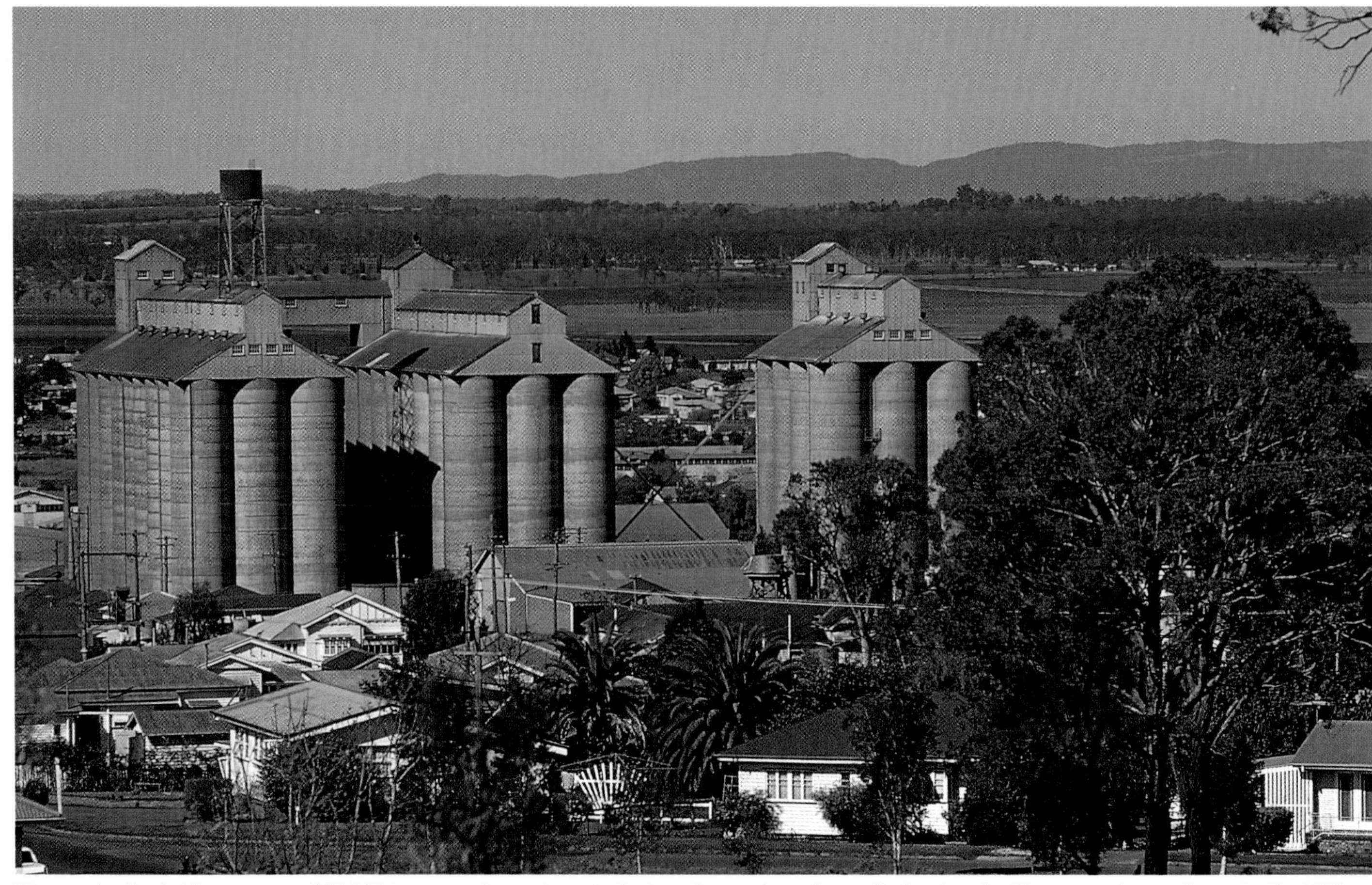

Kingaroy's silos hold an average of 35 000 tonnes – of peanuts, not wheat – a far cry from the small plantings by Chinese market gardeners in the 1890s.

COALSTOUN LAKES NATIONAL PARK ■ 1418

This small park protects twin crater lakes and the vine-covered slopes which surround them. They lie in the volcanic cone of Mount Le Brun and fill only after rain. The Mount Le Brun volcano was active until about 50 000 years ago; pumicestone lies along the lakeshores, as well as basalt fragments and volcanic 'bombs' – solidified lumps of ejected lava.

EIDSVOLD ■ 1419

Eidsvold is a centre for the breeding and sale of top-quality beef cattle, particularly fast-fattening store cattle – cattle bought lean to be fattened up for market. Each month, the saleyards here are packed with buyers from far and wide. The town takes its name from Eidsvold Station, settled in 1848 by Thomas Archer of the pioneering Archer brothers. Although born in Scotland the Archers were brought up in Norway, so Thomas called this homestead after the small Norwegian town where the constitution embodying the principles of that country's independence was signed in 1814. Initially he ran sheep, but soon turned to cattle which were better suited to the climate and terrain.

Gold was discovered in the 1850s but it was not until as late as 1887 that Eidsvold was opened up as a goldfield and serious mining began. Within a year the mining warden reported that the township had eight public-houses, eight stores, two bakers, two butchers, a Roman Catholic church, a Salvation Army barracks, one dance hall, two steam sawmills, and a population of 1200. Eidsvold still has a sawmill which processes and treats hardwood from nearby forestry reserves. *Population 590*

GAYNDAH ■ 1420

Gayndah is one of the oldest towns in Queensland, having been founded in 1848 beside a river crossing point used by the Archer brothers, the pioneering explorer-settlers of this region, who noted that 'the bed here consisted of a solid foundation of limestone'. Before long, there were four hotels and a blacksmith to cater to the travellers using the ford and within a decade, a substantial township with a population of some one thousand, to serve the increasingly prosperous surrounding pastoral district. The brick schoolhouse built in the 1860s in traditional English style still stands – with a crack in one wall caused by a 1935 earthquake.

Gayndah also prides itself as being the birthplace of the Queensland citrus industry; the orchards for which the district is now known date from the late nineteenth century, and are ideally suited to the sandy loam of the Burnett banks. A cotton industry which began here when the American Civil War dried up supplies from that source reached a peak in the 1920s and early 1930s; growers then turned to dairying on rich pastures of Rhodes grass, recently introduced from southern Africa. *Population 1750*

JANDOWAE ■ 1421

Jandowae is in the centre of a prosperous grain-growing region. During the 1930s, it was primarily a dairying town, with its own factory, now closed, producing butter and cheese, but since the 1950s wheat has been the mainstay of the local economy. Barley, oats, sorghum, millet and sunflower seed are also grown, and there are several timber mills in the district. The name is believed to derive from an Aboriginal word meaning 'camp', referring to a traditional site on Jandowie Creek, or 'waterhole'. *Population 800*

KINGAROY ■ 1422

The banks of silos that dominate the Kingaroy townscape – as in so many country centres – contain a surprise. They are filled with, not wheat, but peanuts for this is the centre of Australia's main peanut growing region, and the Peanut Marketing Board complex here takes in, tests, cleans, grades and distributes the bulk of both the local crop and also that from the Atherton tablelands in the far north. The first peanuts in the region were planted in the early 1900s from seed obtained from Chinese market gardeners in nearby Nanango (see entry). The industry expanded rapidly; the first silo and treatment plant was built in 1928 and by the early 1990s between 40 000 and 60 000 tonnes of peanuts were being delivered to the silos each year. Another abundant Kingaroy crop is the navy bean, often grown in rotation with peanut crops, and used in baked bean production. Maize, barley, oats and soya beans are also grown in the region.

The town's name is probably from an Aboriginal word meaning 'red ant', although 'King' was the surname of one of the early settlers. The homestead of Sir Joh Bjelke-Petersen, long-serving Queensland premier, is near the town. *Population 6670*

FESTIVALS Peanut Festival, April; Taabinga Spring Music Festival, October.

MOUNT PERRY ■ 1423

Although the high fields of Mount Perry were settled by sheepmen in the 1840s, the township owes its existence to the rich deposits of copper which were discovered here in 1869.

The substantial buildings here, many listed by the National Trust, are a result of the boom which followed and evidence of past mining activities can be seen in the slag heap and smelter dump on the outskirts. Today the town, now much reduced in size, services a wealthy pastoral area.

BOOLBOONDA TUNNEL Built in 1883, the Boolboonda Tunnel, at nearly 200 metres, is the longest, unsupported man-made tunnel in the Southern Hemisphere. Its construction took twelve months, with teams burrowing in from each end. It was built for the railway line which carried copper ore from the Mount Perry mines to Bundaberg, and in more recent times, timber and cattle.

The line was dismantled in the early 1960s and a dirt road now leads through the tunnel. Motorists braving its dark interior will encounter the large numbers of bats which live there and have given rise to the alternative name of Bat Tunnel.

MUNDUBBERA ■ 1424

Mundubberra, sited near the point where the Boyne, Auburn and Burnett rivers come together, is the centre of the most important citrus-growing region in Queensland. It is known particularly for its mandarins, especially the late-maturing 'Ellendale' which was developed here. Other industries include grain growing, dairying, sawmilling and beef cattle; peanuts are grown on the Gurgeena Plateau.

'Mundubbera' run, across the river from the present town, was taken up in 1848 for wool growing, however the unsuitability of the area for sheep soon became apparent and by the end of the 1880s the flocks had been replaced by cattle.

The name of the town is thought to derive from Aboriginal words for 'foot' and 'step', a reference to the footholds cut in the trunks of many tall trees by the Aborigines to make climbing them easier. *Population 1120*

MURGON ■ 1425

European settlement here dates from 1843 when Barambah Station was taken up. It was stocked with sheep until the hardships of scab, grass seed in the fleece and the difficulties of transporting the clip to market – problems common throughout the south Burnett region – were encountered, and the switch to beef cattle was made.

Teamsters hauling timber down the precipitous slopes of Boat Mountain – so-named because its shape resembled an upturned boat – rested their animals at the Murgon waterhole on 'Barambah', and it was from this rough camp that the town developed. This spot was also on the main droving path from the upper Burnett to the Brisbane Valley – the unusually wide main street results from its early use as a stock route.

Closer settlement took place in the early 1900s with new arrivals taking up farmsteads on the outskirts of the township. Murgon's position as the railhead for the surrounding district was strengthened by the construction of branch lines north and west to Windera and Proston in the early 1920s, which tapped the newly opened farmlands.

The meatworks in Murgon process meat from the area's flourishing beef-cattle industry, and dispatches frozen and chilled boneless beef to both domestic and overseas markets; hides and by-products are processed by a dry-rendering plant in the town.

Dairying has always been one of the region's important industries – the district produces award-winning cheddar cheeses – and agricultural products such as peanuts, navy beans, maize, sorghum and wheat also make a substantial contribution to Murgon's economy.

When the cascade over the stepped Joe Sippel Weir at Murgon runs dry local farmers rely on a 'top up' from the nearby Bjelke-Petersen Dam.

The secret of the peanut revealed (above); the nuts – actually seeds – mature underground before being harvested (right) between March and August. A large proportion of the Kingaroy crop is processed into peanut butter.

The town's name comes from an Aboriginal word for a type of water lily that grows here, once covering the surface of the now dried-out waterhole. *Population 2210*

NANANGO ■ 1426

Nanango is one of the oldest towns in Queensland. Its name comes from that of a sheep run taken up by pastoralist William Oliver at the end of 1842. Six years later, prospector Jacob Goode decided he had a better future selling liquor than digging for gold and with Oliver's blessing set up a hostelry on 'Nanango' at the point where the roads from the Brisbane Valley and Darling Downs met. He soon added slab stockyards for travelling sheep and cattle, later opened a general store as well and traded here with great success for many years. The township which grew up around him was first known as 'Goode's Inn'. In the 1860s, the discovery of gold nearby at what became known as Seven Mile Diggings, brought hundreds of hopeful gold seekers to the area, many of them Chinese.

Originally the properties ran only sheep, but problems with scab and grass seed because of the unsuitability of the pastures, led to a change to beef cattle in the 1880s. The area also grows beans and grain.

The discovery of substantial coal deposits here led to the establishment of a coal-fired power station – named after 'Tarong' cattle station – which became fully operational in 1986. Water for its operation comes from the Boondooma Dam (see entry). *Population 2570*

NANANGO ASTRONOMICAL OBSERVATORY Nanango lays claim to being the first observatory in the world to run on solar power; in addition, it has the only privately owned Remote-Access Automatic Patrol telescope; there is also a fully restored telescope dating back the 1870s. The observatory is open to the public.

WONDAI ■ 1427

Wondai serves an agricultural and pastoral district which produces beef and dairy cattle and grows peanuts and a variety of grains; forestry areas supply timber mills in the town. Gem fossicking is a popular activity in areas to the north and west of the town, where semi-precious stones such as agate, garnet and jasper and petrified wood and thunder rocks have been found. A feature of the district is large stands of bottle trees and clusters of grass trees.

The first European in the Wondai area was Richard Jones who took up 'Mondure' in 1844 and began grazing sheep. The town developed from a collection of humpies used by drovers and teamsters on the road from Nagango to 'Mondure'. With the coming of the railway in 1903, a siding was built here to serve the surrounding district; at the same time scores of new settlers moved into the area when land became available following the large-scale resumptions of older selections for closer settlement.

The name comes from an Aboriginal word thought to mean 'howling dogs'. *Population 1160*

WURUMA DAM ■ 1428

The Wuruma Dam stretches across the Nogo River, a major tributary of the Burnett River, in scenic, hilly country north-west of Eidsvold. The dam was completed in 1969 and its waters irrigate the surrounding farmlands. It is popular for waterskiing, sailing and powerboating, and for the variety of water birds that have come to live in its many inlets.

The lake has been stocked with bass and golden and silver perch; indigenous fish include the jewfish and spangled perch.

A TRUE SURVIVOR: HOW THE LUNGFISH DEFIED EVOLUTION AND WON

THE FIRST specimen of the strange creature briefly known as *Ompax spatuloides* to be captured was apparently served to a gullible naturalist for breakfast. He conveniently ate the evidence. Many years later it was revealed that this oddity, known only from a single specimen taken from a Burnett River waterhole in the 1870s, had been created by joining the body of a mullet, the tail of an eel and the head of a platypus!

Not surprising then that many suspected the platypus itself was a hoax. In 1884, a creature taken from the Burnett banks occasioned one of the most famous telegrams in zoological history. The brief 'monotremes oviparous, ovum meroblastic' cabled to the annual conference of the British Association for the Advancement of Science not only confirmed that the platypus did in fact lay eggs, but also described what sort of yolk the eggs had.

But the Burnett is probably best known as the home of the rare Queensland lungfish, a living fossil which has remained virtually unchanged for more than 100 million years. Although remains of larger ancestors dating from as long ago as 400 million years have been found in all parts of the continent and fossils of similar creatures have been found in Europe and America, all have died out or all have evolved into other forms; the Queensland fish, faced with a relatively stable environment, simply stayed as it was.

In the late 1860s, a local station owner, William Foster, saw fossil remains in the Sydney Museum of a fish labelled as being extinct. He had caught similar animals in the waters of the Burnett River, and was able to arrange for a specimen to be sent to Sydney for examination. This was found to be the same as the fossil, and the man who made the connection is remembered in its scientific name *Neoceratodus fosteri*.

The fish is unlike all other fish in that it has the ability to survive in oxygen-poor water by swallowing air directly into its single lung, gasping noisily when it surfaces to empty and refill the lung. It also has well-developed gills and if the water contains adequate oxygen it simply uses these in the way of all fish. Burnett River lungfish have been recorded coming to the surface to breathe at intervals of thirty to sixty minutes. The creatures can grow to more than one-and-a-half metres and weigh more than forty kilograms. They often 'walk' under water on their strong bottom fins and some scientists believe that ancient lungfish may have developed the ability to 'crawl' from one pool to another.

The first settlers are reported to have found the lungfish very good eating – they dubbed it the 'Burnett salmon'; it is now fully protected and its capture is prohibited. It is possibly the only example in Australia where European settlement has helped save a species from extinction rather than hastening it on its way. At the time of first European settlement, its natural range was limited to the Burnett and Mary river systems; the lungfish was successfully introduced into a number of south-eastern Queensland rivers from as early as the 1890s, but even so its range remains very restricted – the Tweed River, across the border in New South Wales, is too cold and in rivers further north the sluggish, dim-witted lungfish simply makes an easy meal for the crocodile.

Burnett farmers have developed a soft spot for this local curiosity and in times of severe drought have been known to move fish from drying pools to deeper stretches of river or to nearby dams. The slow-moving creatures are easy to catch and load into drums on the back of utility trucks for the life-saving trip overland. The important sounding Ceratodus, on the Burnett Highway north of Eidsvold, has the unchallengeable distinction of being the only railway siding in Australia to be named after a fish. □

The lungfish has two claims to fame. Not only has the species been around unchanged for about 100 million years but it is the second creature after the cactoblastis moth (see Chinchilla & Miles*) to lend its name to a building – the railway siding (left) is near Eidsvold.*

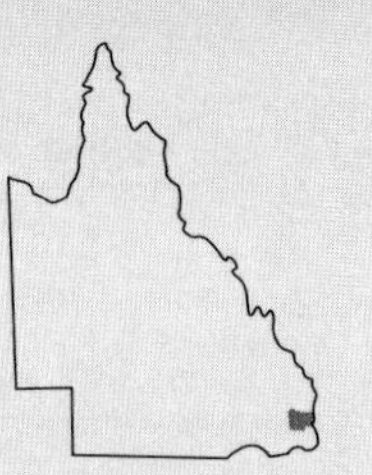

Redcliffe & Caboolture

Bora rings, middens, Aboriginal legends and the homesteads of pioneering pastoralists are all evidence of this area's long and rich human history. Now its string of national parks – onshore and offshore – provide breathing spaces for the citizens of Brisbane.

An average of 125 000 tonnes of spiky fruit is picked each year from Australia's main pineapple-growing region, between Cairns and Caboolture.

BEACHMERE ■ 1429

Fishing is a major preoccupation of the coastal village of Beachmere on Deception Bay near the mouth of the Caboolture River; there are public boat ramps at the river mouth and a sailing club is based here. A bora ground – an Aboriginal cermonial site used for initiations, formal fights and corroborees – north-east of the town, off the Bribie Island road, is one of the best-preserved of its type, with two well-defined rings connected by a pathway. *Population 2110*

BEERBURRUM ■ 1430

Near the township of Beerburrum, natural vegetation gives way to radiata pine tree plantations. On a ridge to the north, with sweeping views to the Glass House Mountains, is an Aboriginal bora ring where male initiation ceremonies were held. 'Beerburrum', an Aboriginal word meaning 'parrot' or 'the sound of parrots' wings', is also the name of one of the Glass House Mountains.

BEERWAH ■ 1431

This township takes its name from the bulging trachyte plug of Mount Beerwah, one of the Glass House Mountains. In Aboriginal legend, Beerwah was the pregnant mother, left by her cowardly son to fend for herself as floodwaters rushed onto the coastal plains. *Population 1090*

BONGAREE ■ 1432

Located on the mainland side of Bribie Island, Bongaree has still-water swimming beaches, boat ramps, sailing, windsurfing, an area for waterskiing and fishing in the channel near the bridge. The town lies near the entrance to Pumicestone Passage, a marine park where dugongs and dolphins play and more than 250 species of birds have been recorded. Matthew Flinders, who thought it a river, named it for the pumicestone, porous relics of ancient volcanic activity, which can still be collected along its shores. *Population 8430*

BRIBIE ISLAND ■ 1433

One hour's drive from Brisbane and linked to the mainland by a bridge over mangrove-lined Pumicestone Passage is Bribie Island, with white sand beaches – both surf and stillwater – sub-tropical bushland, holiday townships and flotillas of fishing, sailing and pleasure craft. Its northern foreshores are preserved within national parks which adjoin the protected waters of Pumicestone Passage, and in spring fields of fragrant pink boronia, bottlebrush,

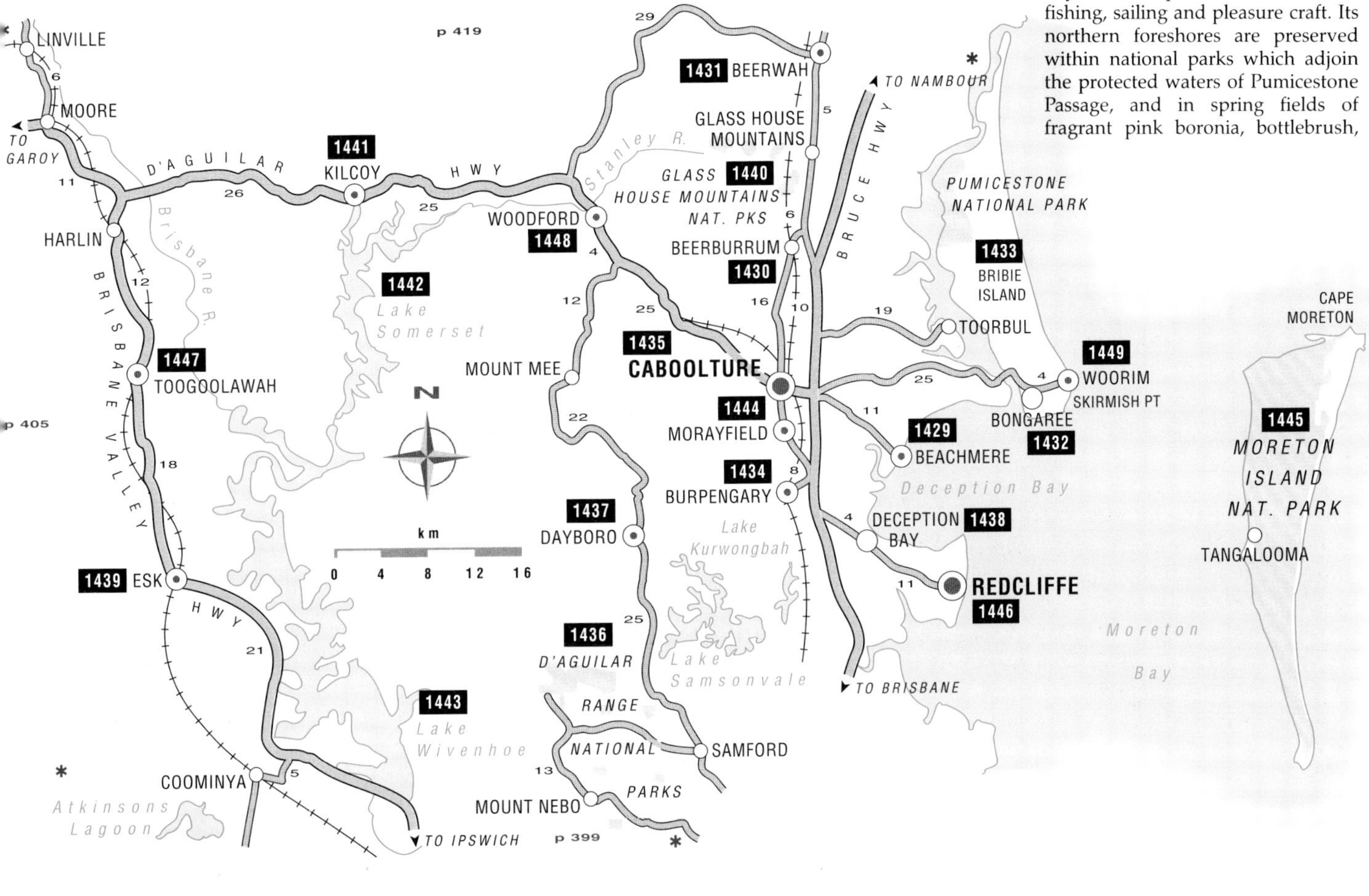

THE 'CATTLE-DOG' DOLPHINS OF BOUNTIFUL BAY

Muddy Moreton Bay, still a rich source of seafood, has been harvested of its bounty much longer than most people think, some of it herded ashore by dolphins for the benefit of their human 'masters'. The broad bay, indented with estuaries and edged with mangroves and mudflats, came into being with the melting of the polar icecaps some 6000 years ago.

When rising sea levels flooded the valley of the lower Brisbane River a fantastically rich source of marine foods was created, which since that time has fed the peoples – black and white – of these islands and shores. Huge middens contain the discarded remains of countless meals of fish, shellfish, turtle and dugong. Each winter, groups of Aborigines from far and wide gathered by the bay to feast on runs of sea mullet – in summer they trekked inland to the pines of the Bunya Mountains and the harvest of nutritious nuts.

The ancestors of these Moreton Bay dolphins may have worked together to drive fish towards waiting Aborigines.

Fish were caught by a variety of means. The most amazing fishing method and one which would leave modern fishermen slack-jawed with envy, was the use by the Aborigines of Moreton Bay of trained dolphins to drive schools of fish towards the shore where they could more easily be speared or caught in nets. Well-documented historical accounts speak of ownership of individual dolphins being claimed in much the same way as that of dogs, and when their herding services were required they were summoned by a distinctive call. Dolphins played another important role in the lives of these fishing peoples as they were regarded as custodians of the spirits of the dead. In modern times, more than 1000 dolphins are estimated to live in the waters of the bay and frolic near the shores of Bribie Island.

On the mainland, near the entrance to Pumicestone Passage and a kilometre or so south of the Bribie Island bridge, is a rare and well-preserved Aboriginal fish trap. This rock wall was built from the shore to encircle an area of about seventy-five metres by thirty-five metres. It filled at high tide, and the fish which entered it to feed on the mudflats inshore were stranded as the waters of the receding tide filtered back into the bay through the loosely packed stones. Collecting the catch was then a simple matter.

A short distance to the south-west, at Sandstone Point, below a wave-cut cliff with expansive views over the waters, is the richest coastal midden site on the bay. The people who gathered here for feasts and ceremonies have left behind 2000 years of bones and shells in a mound spread over 25 000 square metres. The extraordinarily high percentage of fish bones contained here is probably explained in part by the site's proximity to the stone trap. Also in the area was an almost limitless supply of oysters – there are beds here still, the word 'ningi', now applied to a township, creek and small island, means 'oyster' – and in the swamps and creeks eels and waterfowl were in abundant numbers.

Dugongs were reported in their thousands by the first European settlers who corned and smoked their flesh and used it as bacon. Dugong was also in the diet of Aborigines although, on the evidence of the middens, the marine mammals appear to be comparatively recent inhabitants of the bay – perhaps attracted there by the development in the last few hundred years of the seagrass beds on which they feed. The Aborigines caught dugongs in strong nets up to thirty metres long. When Matthew Flinders appropriated such a net he noted that its workmanship equalled that of European makers, and marvelled at the method used to get each mesh so square.

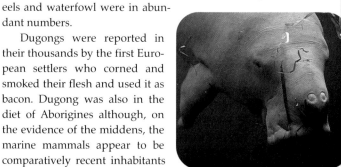

The sluggish dugong was such an easy catch for early settlers that it was almost wiped out.

The waterfowl and dugongs are nowadays protected in the Pumicestone Passage Marine Park, but there are still fish galore in the bay awaiting the keen angler. The area near Pumicestone Passage remains a particularly rewarding spot with bream, flathead, whiting and tailor. The bay is also well-known for its crabs – big, tasty swimmers much sought after by seafood gourmets – and many of today's locals set traps as a profitable hobby. Two species are fished commercially: the blue swimmer, also known as the sand crab, an inhabitant of the open, sandy-bottomed areas, and the larger mangrove or mud crab, found in the estuaries and inlets. □

A fleet of old dredges and barges scuttled off Moreton Island provides shelter for small craft.

wattle, and other wildflowers bloom. Artist Ian Fairweather lived and painted on Bribie for the last twenty years of his life.

Matthew Flinders landed here in July 1799 and named Point Skirmish after an incident – where he nearly lost his hat in an encounter with an Aborigine who tried to seize it. At sheltered White Patch on the island's north-eastern shore, he beached the *Norfolk* for repairs. Flinders reported that about 600 Aborigines lived in strong huts four to five metres long. In less than a century all these people were gone. On the mainland, near the western end of the bridge, is a monument honouring Kal-ma-Kutha, the last of Bribie's Aborigines, who died in 1897.

FESTIVALS Aquatic Festival, October; Powerboat Classics, November..

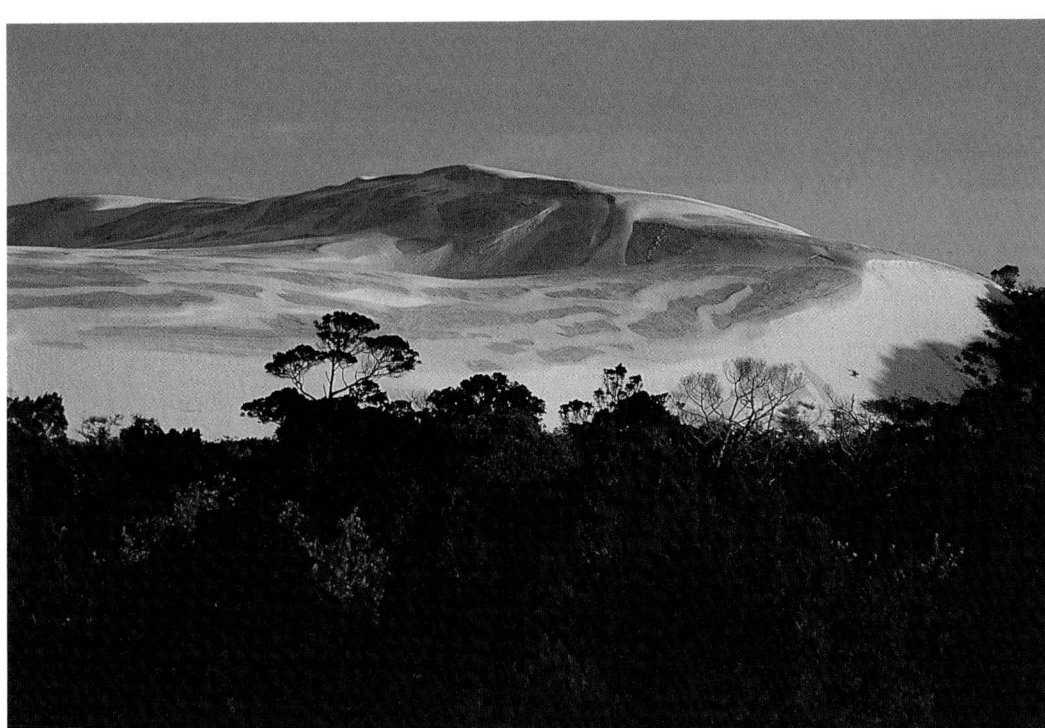

Opposite its busy, urban shore, Moreton Bay is buffered by the windswept dunes of Moreton Island's wilderness.

BURPENGARY ■ 1434
Now a suburb of Caboolture in one of the fastest growing regions of Queensland, the Burpengary area was first settled in the early 1840s. Early activities were timber-getting, and dairying – one of the first Jersey herds in Queensland was established here. Sugarcane was grown, and a crushing mill commenced operations in the early 1870s. The name comes from an Aboriginal word said to mean 'place of the green wattle tree'. *Population 5160*

CABOOLTURE ■ 1435
This country town in a region which has long been famous for its milk and cheese is now regarded as being part of the Brisbane urban area. On its rural outskirts there are still tropical fruit plantations where visitors can buy fruit direct from the growers at pineapple and banana ripening sheds. The district was opened up in the 1860s for grazing and the growing of sugar and cotton. Its name comes from an Aboriginal word thought to mean 'place of the carpet snake', and was given by the Reverend John Dunmore Lang to the bay into which the Caboolture River flows in 1848. *Population 12 720*

CABOOLTURE HISTORIC VILLAGE Most of the more than sixty buildings in the restored working village have been moved here from the surrounding Caboolture Shire. The buildings include a barbershop, post office and blacksmith, a general museum, the axeman's hall of fame and working antique farm machinery. Many of the cottages are furnished with period items donated by householders throughout the district.

D'AGUILAR RANGE NATIONAL PARKS ■ 1436
This string of parks beneath the peaks of the D'Aguilar Range, on the outskirts of Brisbane, are a popular recreation destination for the city. At Jollys Lookout there are picnic grounds and panoramic views over Samford Valley to the city and north to the Glass House Mountains. A walking track linking this site with Boombana passes through a variety of vegetation including hoop pines and forest oaks. Another track leaves the Manorina picnic area and winds through rainforest dominated by flooded gums, where bellbirds live, up to Mount Nebo Lookout; on a clear day the sandhills of Moreton Island stand out on the horizon. From Maiala more tracks lead through eucalypt and rainforest.

DAYBORO ■ 1437
What was originally a small country settlement north of Brisbane is now a rural outer suburb, popular for its houses set on large blocks and known for its regular craft markets. Timber-getters, attracted by cedar and beech, were among the first Europeans in the region, which for a time was known as Terror's Paddock, after a spirited stallion well known in the district who was regularly turned out to pasture here. Its present name comes from a Mr Day, a local police magistrate and sugar mill owner. *Population 820*

DECEPTION BAY ■ 1438
This bayside centre which is fast becoming an outer suburb of Brisbane offers many distractions including fishing, boating, swimming – when high tides cover the mudflats – and picnic areas. A memorial on Captain Cook Parade honours Dr Joseph Bancroft and his son Thomas Lane Bancroft, both scientists and early settlers of the district, who undertook important research while living in the neighbourhood, including experiments on rust-free wheat and pioneering work into the transmission of the disease filariasis, which causes elephantiasis. The rambling Bancroft house stood on a knoll overlooking the bay and the 640-hectare experimental farm where agricultural research was conducted, stretched inland towards Burpengary. *Population 10 340*

ESK ■ 1439
Nestled beneath protecting mountains this small town is the administrative centre of the shire with the same name. It has leafy gardens and broad streets lined with buildings typical of country Queensland in the late nineteenth and early twentieth centuries (see *Rockhampton & Yeppoon*). One such is the two-storey, timber Club Hotel, with verandahs and cast-iron balustrading on each floor. The town has a caravan park and camping facilities for visitors to nearby Lake Wivenhoe. *Population 880*

GLASS HOUSE MOUNTAINS NATIONAL PARKS ■ 1440
The series of huge 'pillars' which rise abruptly from the coastal plains are the eroded remnants of slow lava flows which millions of years ago solidifed in the throats of ancient volcanoes. Their outer surrounds are long gone. Around the base of four of them are small national parks: Mount Coonorwin is for climbers while Mount Berwah, Mount Tibrogargan and Mount Ngungun are for bushwalkers. The peaks caught the attention of James Cook when he sailed past them in 1770; they were glistening with rain and reminded him of the glass furnaces of his native Yorkshire. They are still used as landmarks by mariners today. The stance and shape of the plugs is explained in Aboriginal legend. They are a family group with Tibrogargan the father gazing far out to sea, Beerwah the mother, forever large with child, and Coonowrin (Crookneck) a cowardly son who got his wretched shape when struck a mighty blow by his father.

KILCOY ■ 1441
This is a town of tall timbers and tall tales set in the scenic hills of a cattle and dairy district near the northern end of Somerset Dam. Its attractive streetscapes are a fairly harmonious blend of old Queensland and modern architecture.

Local legend has the mysterious yowie, the Australian version of the Himalayan yeti or North American bigfoot, lurking in the hills around Kilcoy. Many sightings of the half-man, half-beast have been reported, one of the most celebrated being that made by two teenage boys in 1979. They claimed the creature stood about three metres high, had a kangaroo-like appearance, and took giant thumping strides. A statue based on their description stands in the town in Yowie Park.

Kilcoy Station, from which the town gets its name, was taken up by the Mackenzie brothers, recently arrived from Scotland, in 1841. In 1842, it was the scene of a maliciously murderous incident when about thirty Aborigines died after being given poisoned flour, apparently in retribution for the killing of two station hands and a prized bull. *Population 1420*

LAKE SOMERSET ■ 1442
The waters of Lake Somerset bank up behind Somerset Dam on the

Stanley River, a major tributary of the Brisbane River upstream from Lake Wivenhoe. There are boat ramps on the lake's western shore and waterskiing, powerboating, sailing, fishing – the lake is well stocked with perch and bass – swimming and camping are popular activities. Its name recalls Henry Plantagenet Somerset, who in 1890 built Caboonbah Homestead which still stands on its original site but with a completely different vista overlooking the waters of nearby Lake Wivenhoe. Somerset was a member of the Queensland parliament and an instrumental figure in the construction of the dam, which began in 1935.

LAKE WIVENHOE ■ **1443**
Formed by the construction of the Wivenhoe Dam in 1985, this vast body of water, three and a half times the size of Sydney Harbour and with a shoreline of 400 kilometres, has dramatically transformed the upper reaches of the Brisbane River. The dam serves as a major water storage for the Brisbane region and for hydro-electricity generation as well as greatly reducing the possibility of floods – especially important after the disastrous 1974 flood which inundated the Brisbane region. It is also a major recreational area: a growing population of birds, including ducks, pelicans and cormorants, is attracted to its shores and its waters have been stocked with bass and perch. The lake is popular for sailing and canoeing; power boats are not permitted.

BELLEVUE HOMESTEAD Between 1975 and 1985 the National Trust of Queensland moved Bellevue Homestead to Coominya, seven kilometres west of the Lake Wivenhoe, to save it from inundation. 'Bellevue' is a large, single-storey timber building with decorative woodwork above deep verandahs and it originally stood overlooking the Brisbane River on 'Wivenhoe', a run taken up in the early 1840s. The relocated main house and outbuildings date from the 1870s and on their new site maintain the same orientation and relative positions to each other.

MORAYFIELD ■ **1444**
The Morayfield area is notable for its dairying, pineapple plantations and citrus fruits. One of the first sugar plantations on the Queensland coast was established here in the early 1860s and named by its owner after Morayshire in Scotland. Other early industries were cotton growing, timber-getting – the logs were rafted down the Caboolture River – and in the early and mid-twentieth century, poultry farming. *Population 4000*

MORETON ISLAND NATIONAL PARK ■ **1445**
The island is part of the sand mass that includes the Cooloola coast and Fraser, Bribie and North Stradbroke islands. It forms much of the eastern side of Moreton Bay, sheltering it from the surge of the Pacific, and came into being when sands washed to the sea by the rivers of northern New South Wales came to rest against the volcanic outcrop now known as Cape Moreton. Over the ages these deposits stabilised into sand ridges which eventually sprouted vegetation – tree-clad Mount Tempest (280 metres) is reputedly the highest coastal dune in the world.

There is a number of changing habitats here. Stark white sands border verdant belts of casuarinas and pine trees, and trapped between high dunes in impervious saucers of cemented organic material are clear freshwater pools and lakes. There are heaths, swamps, open eucalypt forests and wind-blown dunes and along the eastern shore a surf beach runs virtually unbroken for more than thirty kilometres.

Although birdlife abounds, native mammal species on the island are small in size and few in number – without wings, they found it far more difficult to cross the waters! On Moreton's northern and western coasts there are huge middens, testimony to countless seafood feasts over the centuries and evidence that when the islands were inhabited by Aborigines they had a strong reliance on sea creatures as foodstuffs.

The island was sighted by James Cook in 1770 and the name Moreton given to the bay. Ninety per cent of it is wilderness national park, with unsealed roads suitable for four-wheel-drive vehicles only. There are few permanent residents and only one tourist resort, Tangalooma, on the western side, which from 1952 to 1962 was the site of Queensland's only whaling station. In the days of sail, many ships were wrecked on these shores and a twenty-three-metre-high sandstone lighthouse was built on Cape Moreton in 1857.

REDCLIFFE ■ **1446**
The bayside city of Redcliffe, on a peninsula of the same name, was the site of the first – though short-lived – settlement on Moreton Bay, when a military and convict camp was set up here in September 1824. In the following May, largely because of the activities of the Aborigines, it was abandoned in favour of a better watered site on the Brisbane River – the future Brisbane. The peninsula was then known as Humpybong, believed to derive from the Aboriginal 'oompie bong', meaning 'dead houses' a reference to the deserted, original settlement. Matthew Flinders was in the area in 1799, and noted in his journal the red cliffs after which the city and peninsula are now named.

Redcliffe is reached by a three-kilometre bridge across Bramble Bay and despite its large population, remains a quiet and popular fishing spot. The bridge replaced the Hornibrook Highway bridge in 1979, but the old structure has been retained for pedestrian use. *Population 47 800*

FESTIVALS First Settlement Festival, September.

TOOGOOLAWAH ■ **1447**
The township stands on part of the first sheep run in the Brisbane Valley, 'Cressbrook', which was taken up in 1841. The township itself was not laid out until 1904, following the movement towards closer settlement. The airfield here, headquarters of a skydiving and parachuting club, is named after Roderic Stanley Dallas, a legendary First World War fighter pilot from Queensland.

Bunya pines once grew throughout this area and huge corroborees were held when Aborigines from the surrounding districts came together to gather the bountiful triennial harvest of nuts. *Population 860*

CRESSBROOK HOMESTEAD This is the oldest building in the Brisbane Valley. Land was taken up here in 1841 and some of the ironbark slab-built parts of the original homestead date from two years later, with various additions between the 1870s and 1914. The Cressbrook Hereford Stud dates from the late 1880s.

WOODFORD ■ **1448**
Until the Closer Settlement Act, of 1842, it was illegal to take up land within an eighty-kilometre radius of the Moreton Bay penal settlement, an area known forbiddingly as the Prohibited Zone. So when the pioneering Archer brothers, David, Thomas and John, took up Durundur Station, near the present site of Woodford township, in 1841, they defied the law. They stocked the run with sheep from New South Wales, and lived off the land until their crops of potatoes, melons, pumpkins and cabbages were established. Ludwig Leichhardt spent some weeks at 'Durundur' during one of his expeditions. Cotton was grown here in the early 1860s. There is a co-operative dairy in Woodford, a township still surrounded by unspoilt rivers and forests. *Population 1140*

WOORIM ■ **1449**
The township of Woorim is on the ocean side of Bribie Island (see entry) at the southern end of its thirty-kilometre beach, the closest surfing beach to Brisbane. Gun turrets and bunkers still exist, a reminder that during the Second World War the island formed part of the front line of Brisbane's defences. *Population 1420*

The orchardist's cottage crouches diminutively in the shadow of Mount Beerwah, the tallest of the Glass House Mountains peaks.

THE GOLD COAST

The traditional summer-holiday resorts centred on the archetypal beach playground of Surfers Paradise have exploded into a booming city, second only in size to Brisbane.

For those who tire of the beach, one of Australia's largest casinos is only a dice throw from the Pacific.

Queensland's Gold Coast is a bustling, glittering built-up strip of residential and commercial development that stretches from South Stradbroke Island down to the New South Wales border towns of Coolangatta and Tweed Heads. The beach-hugging rows of high-rise apartments are part of a forty-two-kilometre string of towns on the edge of the Pacific, now all grown together and crowding their way inland.

Surfers Paradise is the busiest, most glittering segment and occupies centre stage. Visitors and neighbours either envy or despise its sometimes brittle raciness, depending on their personal taste and attitudes.

The Gold Coast/Tweed Heads population has risen to over 300 000 and growth is three or four times the national average. The region styles itself as the nation's tourist capital – a million overseas visitors go there each year, and several million Australians come to stay as well. Holidaymakers go for the more than 300 days of sunshine a year and sit on beaches that have the largest professional, life-saving staff in the country; the average sea temperature is a refreshing 22° Centigrade, the average daily shade temperature is 25° with a summer average maximum of 29° while the mercury hovers around a comfortable 22° in winter.

Fishing, boating, scuba diving, swimming and water-skiing are all popular, and the tourist centre claims more restaurants per square kilometre than any other Australian city – there are at least 500 eating houses. All around, the Surfers Paradise apartment buildings crowd down to the wide beach, and some people are still up in arms about the strips of shade the buildings cast. In an age of skin-cancer awareness, this afternoon choice between shadow and blinding sun has probably added just one more advantage to the already naturally well-endowed area.

The region has such a name for sun, sand and surf that tourism promoters are energetically trying to sell an image of a 'new' Gold Coast that has more to offer. They are less than keen on the foreign-inspired image conjured up by phrases such as 'just like Honolulu' or 'Miami without the vice'. There is more than a grain of truth in these descriptions, though a rising local crime rate has tarnished the gloss a little.

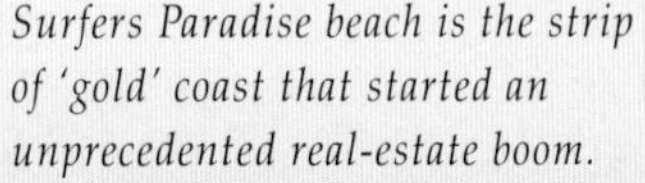

Surfers Paradise beach is the strip of 'gold' coast that started an unprecedented real-estate boom.

Cobb & Co. coaches started running three times a week from Brisbane to Southport and Coolangatta in 1884. Around that time the Gold Coast was already becoming quite a popular holiday spot for northern colonists. Development was greatly stimulated when a railway line came down from Beenleigh, just south of Brisbane, in 1889. The rail link was torn up in 1964.

In the 1920s, Surfers Paradise was the name of the local pub and the district was called Elston. Popular usage won out with a name-change in 1933. James Cavill built the hotel after coming as a visitor from Brisbane. He paid the then equivalent of about 200 dollars for the land and was once offered 370 000 dollars for his well-patronised pub, which was rebuilt in 1937 after a fire.

Now there is accommodation to suit all budgets, catering for campers and backpackers to those who prefer international hotels and resorts. Counting right down to camping grounds, this busy strip of humanity at play can make room for about 100 000 visitors all at once. Over the years, developers have turned quite a bit of the Gold Coast residential area into a maze of expensive 'canal' subdivisions. Some of these are genuinely navigable while low bridges make others unusable for anything much larger than a dinghy. The offshore Gold Coast waterways are a playground for pleasure boating. Few landlubbers realise that boats can pass practically all the way from Brisbane to Southport in calm, protected passages through the many islands and sandbanks. Thousands of boats ply these waters, especially at holiday times.

Captain John Bingle, in the 1840s, was the first seaman to take notice of the Southport bar and the large lagoon that seemed to be behind it. It was not realised that Stradbroke was an island, and the sea explorers of the time ventured south among the shallow channels and mudflats, thinking they were in 'the South River'.

It is said that every boating visitor to the area who strays outside the main channels will eventually find a mudbank or tidal sandbar to 'stick on'. The tortuous waterways – studded with quaint place-names like Tippler's Passage, Jumpinpin Bar, Jacob's Well, Tiger Mullet Channel and Crusoe Island – widen and deepen near Southport. Inland, away from the beach which started it all, there is a bewildering variety of attractions, the most famous of which are the 'theme' parks which vie for the tourist dollar. □

There is a boat in every garage in the little Venice of the canal estates behind the Broadbeach casino (top left). Performing dolphins (above) form the basis for one of the Gold Coast's most enduring attractions.

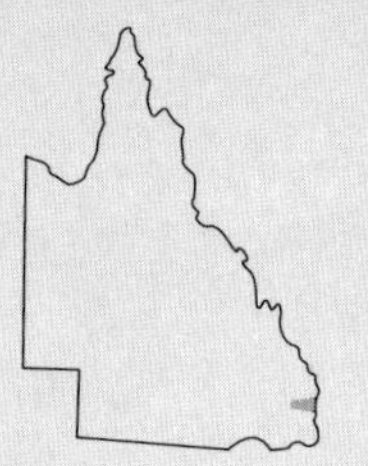

Caloundra & Maroochydore

A string of holiday resorts hang on the perfect shoreline of the Sunshine Coast while in the Blackall Range behind it there is beauty to rival any seaboard. In between, careful cultivation coaxes subtropical crops from the soil of the plains.

ALEXANDRA HEADLAND ■ 1450
Alexandra Headland and the Mooloolaba beaches sit side by side at the foot of the Buderim mountains. To the north are Cotton Tree and Maroochydore and the four resorts form a continuous strip of residential and holiday development along the Sunshine Coast. The patrolled beach at Alexandra Headland is popular with surfboard riders all year round. *Population 2780*

BLACKALL RANGE ■ 1451
The Blackall Range was named for Samuel Wesley Blackall, Governor of Queensland from August 1868 to his death in January 1871. The mountains were known to settlers by their Aboriginal name of 'bonyi bonyi', which referred to the tall, nut-bearing bunya pines. Every three years or so the Aborigines would collect the ripened kernels to roast as the high point of days of feasting and celebration (see *Dalby & Oakey*). The timber-getters arrived in the 1860s and began felling the forest giants – red cedar was most highly prized.

Once the land was cleared, farmers moved in to take advantage of the rich soil for orchards and pasture. They planted citrus and pineapples first and then, in more recent times, macadamias and avocadoes. Nowadays, rural-residential development encroaches on the hinterland (see Flaxton, Maleny, Mapleton and Montville).

The Baroon Pocket Dam – stocked with many varieties of freshwater fish – is the Sunshine Coast's major source of water.

BLI BLI ■ 1452
Bli Bli is a rapidly growing residential town, in effect a satellite suburb of Maroochydore. Aboriginal names used in the Maroochy district were often changed by the early settlers who could not pronounce what they heard and were writing them down for the first time. Variations in dialects between the Aboriginal groups compounded the problem. Bli Bli is considered by some to be a corruption of 'billai billai' which means 'swamp oak'. These trees are plentiful along the banks of the Maroochy River. 'Bli bli' may also mean 'twisting stream'. *Population 2390*

MAROOCHY WETLANDS SANCTUARY This 108-hectare zone of mangrove and melaleuca swamp containing a former canecutters' barracks has been turned into an education centre to display the history of the region's Aborigines. The project includes a boardwalk through the mangroves and a track which enable visitors to observe the wetlands. Mosquitoes are troublesome in this damp habitat and precautions are advised to repel them.

BUDERIM ■ 1453
Buderim Mountain was logged from 1862 onwards. John Kerle Burnett's restored cottage, where he lived with his wife and eight children, still stands where it has for almost 120 years and must be one of the few buildings of that era with an original front-door key in working order.

The sugar industry began in Buderim with imported labourers from the South Sea Islands and the first of two crushing mills opened in 1876. Very soon cane spread to many areas of the coastal flats. Ginger growing began in the late 1920s but the root did not become an important crop until the 1940s when supplies from Asia to Australia were stopped during the Second World War. The ginger factory set up during this time – the only one in Australia – is now at Yandina.

The gardens and streets of this village on the Buderim Plateau burst with flowering tropical trees, especially hibiscus, frangipani and bougainvillea. Kangaroos on the local golf course have refused to be driven from their habitat and tend to be more relaxed than the players. They lie about on the fairways, completely unperturbed by swinging mashie or niblick. *Population 7500*

FESTIVALS Freuhlingfest Spring Fair, August.

CALOUNDRA ■ 1454
The most common meaning attributed to Caloundra's name is 'beautiful place' but is also said to mean 'place of beech trees'. This seaside resort marks the beginning of the Sunshine Coast which stretches north to Noosa Heads. The Sunshine Coast is an industry in itself with everything geared to the needs of interstate and international holiday-makers and there is a proliferation of entrepreneurial tourist attractions.

Caloundra is usually described in superlatives – 'the most perfect weather', 'the safest beaches', 'the most spectacular surf', 'the most convenient accommodation', 'the best fishing'; it is also well placed for trips to the Glass House Mountains or to the beautiful national parks nearby.

A modern control station has replaced the old Caloundra Lighthouse which had been a landmark since 1896. The old lighthouse has been moved to Pumicestone Passage where it sits in restored splendour.

Some of the beaches around Caloundra have tales to tell. A drama was played out on Moffat Beach, in 1863, when a young woman died aboard the *Queen of the Colonies* and crewmembers came ashore to bury her. As they returned, they were caught in a sudden squall and had to swim back to the beach and tough it out until they were found, weak from hunger, weeks later. Dicky Beach is named after the *Dicky* which grounded there in 1893 and remains a rusting landmark. *Population 22 100*

FESTIVALS Art and Crafts Festival, late August; Festival of Gardens, early September.

CONONDALE NATIONAL PARK ■ 1455
This national park is a 2000-hectare zone of mountainous slopes, clothed in wet eucalypt and subtropical rainforest. The area is an undeveloped wilderness reserve which shelters tangled woody vines, palms and bunya pines. The edge of the park can be reached along rough backblock walking tracks but the dense undergrowth and the lack of facilities for bushwalkers ensure it stays pretty much undisturbed.

COOLUM BEACH ■ 1456
Coolum Beach is a rapidly growing coastal centre in the southern part of the Maroochy district, where the population nearly tripled in the ten years between 1976 and 1986 and gives all the signs of continuing to burgeon until well into the new century. The beach is patrolled and appeals to surfers while the small bays and rocky headlands attract fisher folk all year round. Nearby, Lows Lookout provides a 360-degree panoramic view over the surrounding countryside and the Pacific Ocean. *Population 5100*

EUMUNDI ■ 1457
Eumundi was named after an Aboriginal elder who helped rescue survivors from the shipwrecked *Stirling Castle* in 1836. The town's status was confirmed in 1891 when the railway station completed the rail link from Gympie to Brisbane. Beech and cedar attracted settlers and the railway made it all the more easy to freight out the timber. When most of the trees had fallen, the pioneers turned their attention to dairy farming and banana plantations.

The arrival of the car shifted the transport emphasis and Eumundi residents can now be on the beach at Noosa in about twenty minutes. This attraction no doubt contributes to the high rate of home building in the town; another stimulus to the town's development was the Eumundi Mini Brewery which was one of the largest employers in Maroochy Shire – before it moved its brewing operations to Yatala, near Beenleigh. The brewery specialises in distinctive 'designer' beers.

FLAXTON ■ 1458
Flaxton is a small mountain settlement in the Blackall Range on the edge of Kondalilla National Park. The permanent population is small but the village attracts some very adventurous visitors. At weekends, hang-gliders flock to Flaxton to launch themselves into space and ride the wind currents from a site on the Flaxton escarpment.

KAWANA WATERS ■ 1459
Kawana is thought to be an Aboriginal word meaning 'wildflowers'. They grow profusely behind the

The dyspeptic expression may mean this Kondalilla gastric-brooding frog has a stomach full of tadpoles.

A glimpse of the breakers at Alexandra Headland at dusk says more than a thousand glossy brochures about the attractions of the Sunshine Coast.

dunes that flank the eleven kilometres or so of beach. Kawana Waters is a collection of seven communities stretching from Currimundi Lake, north to the Mooloolah River estuary. In 1960, a lease was granted to develop the area for residential purposes and it has been growing ever since with some small industries now being established as well. *Population 14 400*

FESTIVALS Stewarts Kawana Prawn and Seafood Festival, January.

KENILWORTH ■ 1460

Kenilworth is on the Mary River in the west of the Maroochy district. Many local place names tend to have British or European associations and Kenilworth goes back to 1850, to the name of one of the earliest properties in the region. The wife of the first settler here was a great admirer of the novels of Sir Walter Scott, author of the historical romance *Kenilworth.* The town retains something of its pioneering atmosphere and is still a dairying and forestry centre. Bellbirds live in and around the little village and the mountain air rings all day with their fluting calls.

KONDALILLA NATIONAL PARK ■ 1461

Kondalilla National Park lies to the north of Montville on the outskirts of Flaxton and provides more than 200 hectares of great natural beauty where peace and tranquillity prevail. These reserved areas in the Blackall Range include the important environments of some of the giant rainforest and wet eucalypt forest trees that have been felled elsewhere. Kondalilla shelters red and white cedar, mahogany, hoop and bunya pine. Skenes Creek drops eighty metres into the valley below at Kondalilla Falls.

Skenes Creek is inhabited by the lungfish, a protected species which uses a lung to supplement its oxygen supply (see *Kingaroy & Murgon*). Another strange creature, the gastric-brooding frog, was discovered in 1972 at Picnic Creek. This rare amphibian keeps its tadpoles in its stomach and, luckily for them, stop the gastric juice flow so it does not inadvertently digest its own young!

LANDSBOROUGH ■ 1462

Landsborough, the gateway to the Blackall Range and the Mary Valley, is another historic township. Isaac Burgess selected Portion 1, Parish of Bribie, in 1871, at what was then called Mellum Creek. The town was later named after William Landsborough, who explored to the west of here. Cobb & Co. established a route through the district to the Gympie goldfields. Mellum Creek and Burgess's slab house became a stopover for refreshments and a change of horses. In 1877, he increased his property holdings and built a two-storey hotel, a store and a butcher's shop. The Mellum Creek school of 'sawn timber – hardwood and beech' was erected in August 1879 and opened a month later. *Population 1150*

MALENY ■ 1463

Maleny is the business centre of the Blackall Range and like all the small

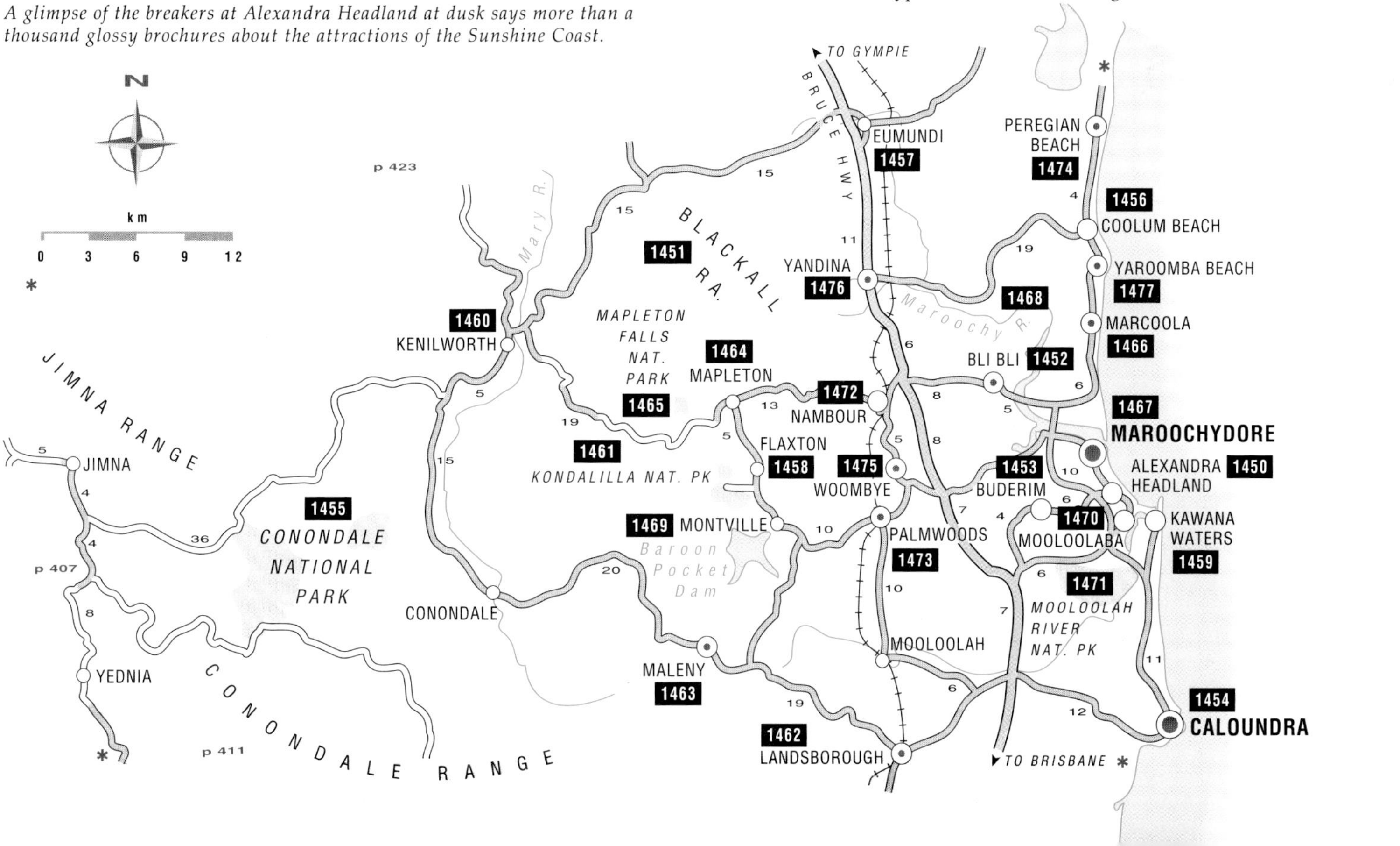

Maroochydore is the business centre of the district which shares its name and its relaxed, beach-oriented lifestyle.

towns in these mountains offers rural resort accommodation to holiday-makers. The streets are named for the indigenous mountain trees. The area is within easy driving distance of the Sunshine Coast and there are dramatic views over the Glass House Mountains from the Mary Cairncross Park.

In 1878, Isaac Burgess became the first selector in Maleny as well as in Landsborough (see entry). In 1886, he shipped a red cedar log to the Colonial and Indian exhibition in England. It was 6274 millimetres in diameter (247 inches) and a polished half of it still resides in the London Museum. This was an important dairying and cheesemaking area in the early 1900s. Nearby Witta, once known as Teutoborg, was settled by German migrants. *Population 780*

FESTIVALS Folk Festival, December.

MAPLETON ■ 1464

Mapleton, surrounded by forest in the most northerly part of the Blackall Range, is said to have taken its name from a town in an American novel. Australia's only thermometer manufacturing company is located here. The owner came for a holiday and liked the environment so much that he not only moved there himself but also persuaded his staff to join him! Artefacts from Aboriginal bunya nut ceremonies show that people appreciated the benefits of this location long before European settlers discovered its beauty.

FESTIVALS Yarn Festival, October.

MAPLETON FALLS NATIONAL PARK ■ 1465

This tiny park of twenty-six hectares is on the northern outskirts of Mapleton and includes the spectacular Pencil Creek waterfall which cascades 120 metres over the escarpment to the Mary River valley below and is at its best in the wet season. Three unusual species of frog have been recorded in the park – the pouched frog, the platypus frog and the Mount Glorious torrent frog. The park also offers a vestige of the region's natural environment to the red goshawk, the numbers of which have been seriously depleted by urban development.

MARCOOLA ■ 1466

Marcoola, a few kilometres north of Maroochydore, is another of the larger centre's satellite suburbs. It has many of the attractions of other coastal towns along this stretch and plenty of room to expand. As an 'offspring', it was appropriate that the name of this new settlement should have been coined from the first syllables of Maroochydore and Coolum. *Population 640*

MAROOCHYDORE ■ 1467

Maroochydore beaches are long stretches of clean white sand with tiny coves tucked between rocky headlands. The thirty kilometres between Mooloolaba and Peregian have become a well-patronised playground but Maroochydore is also within easy reach of the forest-clad hinterland and its alternatives to sun, surf and sand.

Maroochydore grew up on the site of the river-mouth timber mill where paddle steamers once loaded up on their way to Brisbane. The alluvial river flats are planted with sugarcane, avocados, macadamia nuts, lychees, strawberries, and even coffee. The town's name is believed to be derived from the Aboriginal words describing the region's black swans (see Maroochy River).

The early settlers had their work cut out to clear the land and secure a hold on it. By the turn of the century, settlement was well-established and around 1910 there was a demand for a variety of craftsmen including bag and bale makers, coach and carriage builders, coffee and spice mill hands, coopers, fellmongers – dealers in animal hides – portmanteau makers and curriers. *Population 19 000*

FESTIVALS Festival of Gardens, mid-September.

MAROOCHY RIVER ■ 1468

The Maroochy River system contains Coolum Creek and Petrie Creek as well as the Maroochy itself. It has been important to the development of the Nambour district ever since the first Europeans came to look for timber. Small craft are safe in the tidal Maroochy River for up to eighty kilometres upstream and one-metre draft boats can navigate the river for more than forty kilometres. The section from Yandina, on the Bruce Highway, to Maroochydore is canoeable – a distance of about thirty-five kilometres. The river is also used by anglers and waterskiers. The name Maroochy is made up of two Aboriginal words, 'muru' and 'kutchi', which mean 'red bill' and refer to the black swans of the river flats.

Flood plains stretch from Yandina to the coast and are dotted with the remains of several volcanic plugs. The volcanic soil is exceptionally rich and put to good use growing tropical and subtropical crops. In the early days, red cedar and other logs were floated downstream to the sea where they were rafted down to the Moreton Bay settlement.

MONTVILLE ■ **1469**
Montville was first settled in 1887 and retains an atmosphere of nineteenth-century charm complete with one of the few village greens in Australia. New buildings have managed to accommodate the old in architectural style and Montville has become the arts and crafts centre of the Blackall Range. Despite the British heritage of its founders, Montville was named after a town in the American state of Connecticut.

The 'senses trail' at the Razorback Lookout is designed to alert visitors to the natural beauty all about them. The air is crisp and invigorating and there are good views over a chequerboard of pineapple plantations to the blue Pacific Ocean.

FESTIVALS Christmas Lights, December/January.

MOOLOOLABA ■ **1470**
Mooloolaba harbour is said to be one of the safest on the east coast and provides a sheltered anchorage for a fleet of about sixty reef-fishing and prawning boats. Here the mouth of the Mooloolah River is protected by Alexandra Headland and Point Cartwright. Large quantities of prawns are hauled from the waters and make a handsome contribution to the town's economy. Mooloolaba is the site of the main pilot station for ships entering Moreton Bay.

The town's name comes from an Aboriginal word which is said to mean 'place of the schnapper fish' and shows that fishing was a common activity here even before Europeans arrived. Mooloolaba is also expanding rapidly as a resort and has one of the highest growth rates in residential housing in Maroochy Shire. *Population 9500*

FESTIVALS Prawn Festival, May.

Not a new hybrid but a potent tourist symbol at Nambour; the real pineapples are in the foreground.

MOOLOOLAH RIVER NATIONAL PARK ■ **1471**
This is an inland park of about 670 hectares to the south of Maroochydore, which is noted for its spring wildflowers. It flanks the eastern banks of the Mooloolah River which are backed by melaleuca swamps and marsh and then by low-lying sandflats which support wallum banksias, low scrub and heath. Scribbly gums, bloodwood and blackbutt grow on the northern edge. The undeveloped park preserves the type of vegetation that is fast disappearing from the coastal lowlands of south-eastern Queensland; this is the habitat of the rare ground parrot whose specialised wet heathland environment is threatened by burning off, clearing and drainage.

NAMBOUR ■ **1472**
Nambour, in the foothills of the Blackall Range, is the most southern of Queensland's sugar towns and the centre of the sugar industry on the Sunshine Coast. Small trains bring the cane from the surrounding fields to the Moreton Central Mill which crushes from June to November each year. Other crops grown locally are bananas, pineapples and citrus fruits and there is some dairying and sawmilling. Nambour – the name means 'red-flowering tea-tree' – is the administrative headquarters of Maroochy Shire.

The shire is expected to have nearly 110 000 residents by the year 2001. Approximately twenty-eight per cent of the present population is over fifty years old and the Sunshine Coast University of the Third Age, based on the French concept of learning in later life, has an enrolment of more than 1600 'retiree' students and is the largest institution of its kind in Australia. Nearly a hundred courses are offered, in such subjects as psychology, biology, languages, calligraphy and keyboard instruments. The weekly sessions are held in private homes, school classrooms and church halls all over the shire. Homework is rare, there are no examinations and the tutors donate their time.

Maroochy Shire residents are involved in diverse forms of employment including tourism as well as the more traditional agricultural pursuits of sugarcane growing and processing, fishing and prawning, forestry, dairying and milk processing, horticulture, cattle raising, honey production and fruit growing.

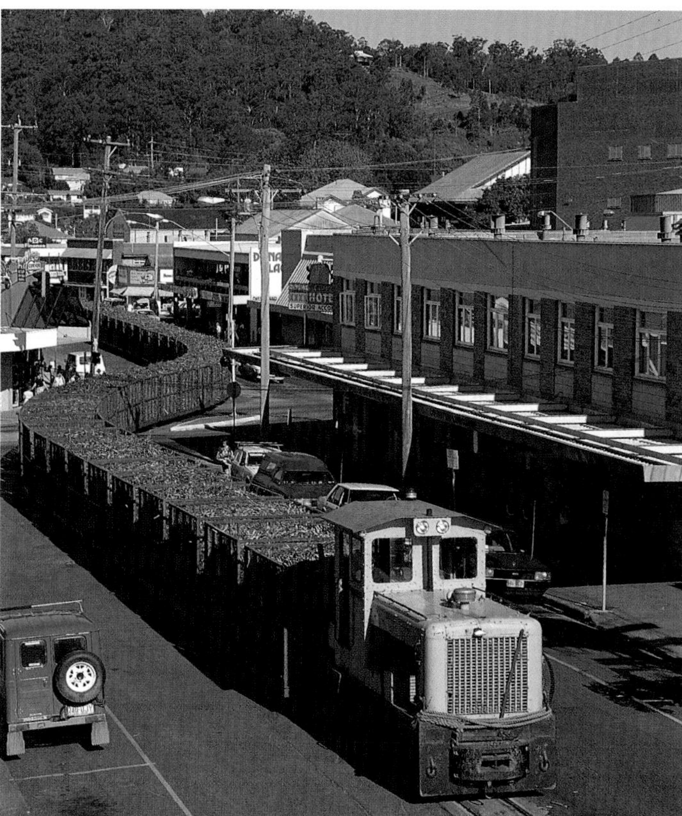

Nambour grew up around this track which has carried trainloads of sugarcane to the mill every July–November for more than 90 years.

The Sunshine Plantation, a few kilometres south of Nambour, is a productive twelve hectares of tropical fruits, nuts and spices – nearly sixty varieties in all. The fifteen-metre fibreglass pineapple at the entrance is one of the biggest and best known landmarks in a region that specialises in giant, tourist-stopping icons. *Population 10 360*

FESTIVALS Festival of Gardens, early-mid September.

PALMWOODS ■ **1473**
Palmwoods is a small township in the hinterland of the Maroochy district. By the turn of the century, timber was the main industry but fruit growing was becoming increasingly important. The town is now surrounded by a lush patchwork of exotic crops – pawpaw, pineapples, passionfruit, bananas, avocados and sugarcane. *Population 1170*

PEREGIAN BEACH ■ **1474**
Peregian, pronounced per-idg-ian, is named after an Aboriginal word for 'emu'. It is a fast-growing tourist resort and retirement town on a beautiful stretch of coast. A long strip of bushland lines the beachfront and the trees, which are mainly casuarinas, help to control erosion. Banksia trees are also plentiful here and attract lorikeets and honeyeaters. *Population 2290*

WOOMBYE ■ **1475**
Woombye is set inland behind Maroochydore. The settlement was originally known as 'Middle Camp' and then as 'Cobb's Camp', when around 1868, Cobb & Co. built a changing-post hotel there on its Brisbane–Gympie route. This was confusing to some travellers because many other coaching stops had the same name. Eventually the railway from Landsborough came through in 1891 and the station was called after the trees that grew close by – 'wumbai' – Aboriginal for 'black myrtle' or lilly pilly. The name Woombye has also been interpreted as 'place of the black snake'. *Population 660*

YANDINA ■ **1476**
Yandina, which gets its name from an Aboriginal word possibly meaning 'small water' or 'go on foot', was the first town surveyed in this region – in 1871 – and has grown into a light industrial and residential centre It is best known for its unique ginger factory which moved here from Buderim in the 1980s to allow for expansion. Forty per cent of the world's supply of sugar-processed ginger now comes from Yandina. *Population 710*

YAROOMBA BEACH ■ **1477**
Yaroomba Beach is another small and relatively new settlement on the popular Sunshine Coast, which will inevitably expand as long as the demand for more residential land continues to grow. Growth in the Yaroomba Beach locality is assured by the hamlet's enviable position close to the ocean and only a short distance from the Bruce Highway. *Population 1050*

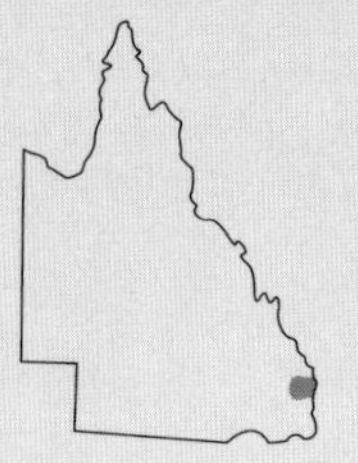

Gympie & Tewantin

Gympie gold helped save the colony of Queensland from bankruptcy in the last century; now a healthy boost to the state's cash flow comes from the cosmopolitan resort towns of the Sunshine Coast.

COOLOOLA NATIONAL PARK ■ 1478

The coastal wilderness of Cooloola National Park was the setting for a dramatic historic incident that over the years has become something of a legend – the capture by Aborigines and eventual rescue of Mrs Eliza Fraser, wife of the captain of the *Stirling Castle* which was shipwrecked on Swain Reef off the coast of Rockhampton in 1836.

After a journey by lifeboat to Fraser Island – then known as Great Sandy Island – the survivors were met by a group of Aborigines and there was an affray. Several of the party were killed, including the captain, and Mrs Fraser was taken to the mainland and made a servant of the Aboriginal women. Fortunately for her, some of the crew had escaped to the mainland and, making their way to Bribie Island, alerted soldiers stationed there to her predicament.

After some months, Mrs Fraser's exact location was pinpointed and an audacious rescue plan put together by John Graham, a convict who had lived with the Aborigines for some time and was familiar with their ways. He enlisted the help of an escaped convict who also knew the Cooloola area well, and together they successfully stole Mrs Fraser from under her captors' noses.

Cooloola National Park takes in a 55 000-hectare patch of hinterland heathlands, woodlands of banksia and scribbly gum, blackbutt forest, rainforest, lakes and waterways – all fringed by coastal cliffs.

A complex maze of mangrove-lined waterways that branch off the Noosa River, threading through swampy flats and interpersed with eyelets of lakes, forms the fabric of the southern part of Cooloola National Park, while the north is dominated by open heathlands that blossom with wildflowers in the summer, dense forests, and the towering, coloured sand dunes for which the region is famous. Much of the park is accessible only by four-wheel-drive vehicles or walking tracks that wind through the variegated coastal wilderness.

Tall, coloured sand cliffs stretch for thirty kilometres along the perimeter of the park forming a giant palette of more than seventy different shades of sand. Carbon tests have proved their age to be not less than 40 000 years but geologists are divided on the issue of colour. Some say that the colour comes from oxide which imparts various shades of red, yellow and brown to the sand while others think the sands have been dyed by decaying vegetable matter.

Aboriginal legend offers a more romantic explanation – a young woman fell in love with a spirit, Yiningie, who was represented by a rainbow. One day, an evil warrior captured the woman and was chased by Yiningie. In the ensuing fight, the warrior threw a giant boomerang at the rainbow spirit which smashed into the sand cliffs, dissolving into the colours we see today. The name of the park is also Aboriginal in origin: Cooloola is said to be the local Aborigines' word for the sound of the wind whistling through the cypress pines that grow on the coastal dunes.

COOROY ■ 1479

Darwin's theory of evolution by survival of the fittest explains neatly the rise and fall of a variety of primary industries during the course of Cooroy's history. The district was first settled in 1891, by pioneering timber-getters whose bullock teams took a week to haul their weighty cargo to Tewantin (see entry) for shipment to the southern markets. Railway transport linked Cooroy with Brisbane in the 1890s. The flourishing timber industry brought an influx of settlers to the region and the township that sprang up around the railway siding had two sawmills by 1908.

Dairying took precedence from 1900 to 1920 following a government decision to release timber lands for farming, while bananas and beans dominated during the 1920s – for years Cooroy was regarded as the best banana-growing district on the coast. But the 1930s brought depression and a plant disease, and the new crops took a back seat as dairying again became the dominant industry. This was supplemented by a new industry in 1951 when Finnish immigrants discovered suitable clay deposits near Cooroy and opened a brick-making factory in the town. Now Cooroy is one of the largest ceramic producers in Australia.

Today, Cooroy is a fast developing rural–residential area – the industrial and educational centre of the Noosa Shire – where dairying still holds its place as one of region's most profitable industries and the cultivation of crops has expanded to include a wide variety of fruit and vegetables. *Population 1780*

GYMPIE ■ 1480

During the mid-1860s, the fledgling colony of Queensland was about to fall headlong into bankruptcy – its agricultural base having been devastated by drought – when a gold prospector, James Nash, struck it rich at Gympie. He reported the find at the Maryborough Police Station in October 1867 and the great Gympie rush was on.

What drought had devastated, gold revived and a narrow bullock track, trodden by the constant traffic of hopeful diggers and drays bearing supplies, soon became the main street of a hastily assembled tent and bark-hut village that was named Nashville. By the time the licensed government surveyor completed his first survey of the main street in 1869, a number of substantial buildings had already appeared and he had no choice but to accommodate the irregular streetscape in his plan.

Subsequent building renovations have brought the street into greater alignment with his plan but to this day Mary Street, as the main street came to be known, adheres stubbornly to the meanderings of its bullock-track origins.

Residential developments dotted with exotic palm trees have turned the bush of Noosa Inlet into prime real estate.

The town acquired its present name after the diggers made painful contact with the stinging nettle bush that grew profusely along the banks of the Mary River, and adopted the Aboriginal word for the vegetative pest – 'gimpi gimpi' – as its name.

The extraction of gold from the Gympie fields went through three distinct phases: the easy pickings of alluvial gold were exhausted within a year and were followed by a period of shallow-reef mining with individual miners forming themselves into teams to sink shafts into the gold-bearing quartz reefs. This profitable period lasted until the mid-1870s when the miners hit a layer of extremely hard greenstone that was mistakenly believed to be the limit of the field's gold-bearing reefs and that, together with a lack of money, marked the end of the second phase.

By the mid-1880s, new capital became available and enterprising companies began to sink extremely deep shafts through the greenstone and into the slate strata below. They were rewarded handsomely for their efforts. These deeper layers yielded gold in quantities undreamed of in earlier years and over the next forty years more than 114 tonnes of gold were extracted from the goldfield.

That Gympie did not become a ghost town after the gold deposits were exhausted in the mid-1920s is largely due to its location. Surrounded by fertile land and cedar forests, its proximity to the coast placed it on the main rail and road route from Brisbane to all points north. The rail link to Maryborough was made in 1881, and to Brisbane ten years later.

The agricultural industries that now form the basis of the town's economy were preceded by short-lived ventures into wine production, sheep raising and sugarcane growing. By the 1920s, dairying, fruit- and vegetable-growing, and plantations established by the Forestry Depart-

A four-wheel-drive trip along the highway of the beach gives the best view of the variegated sandcliffs that trim the Cooloola Park's eastern fringe.

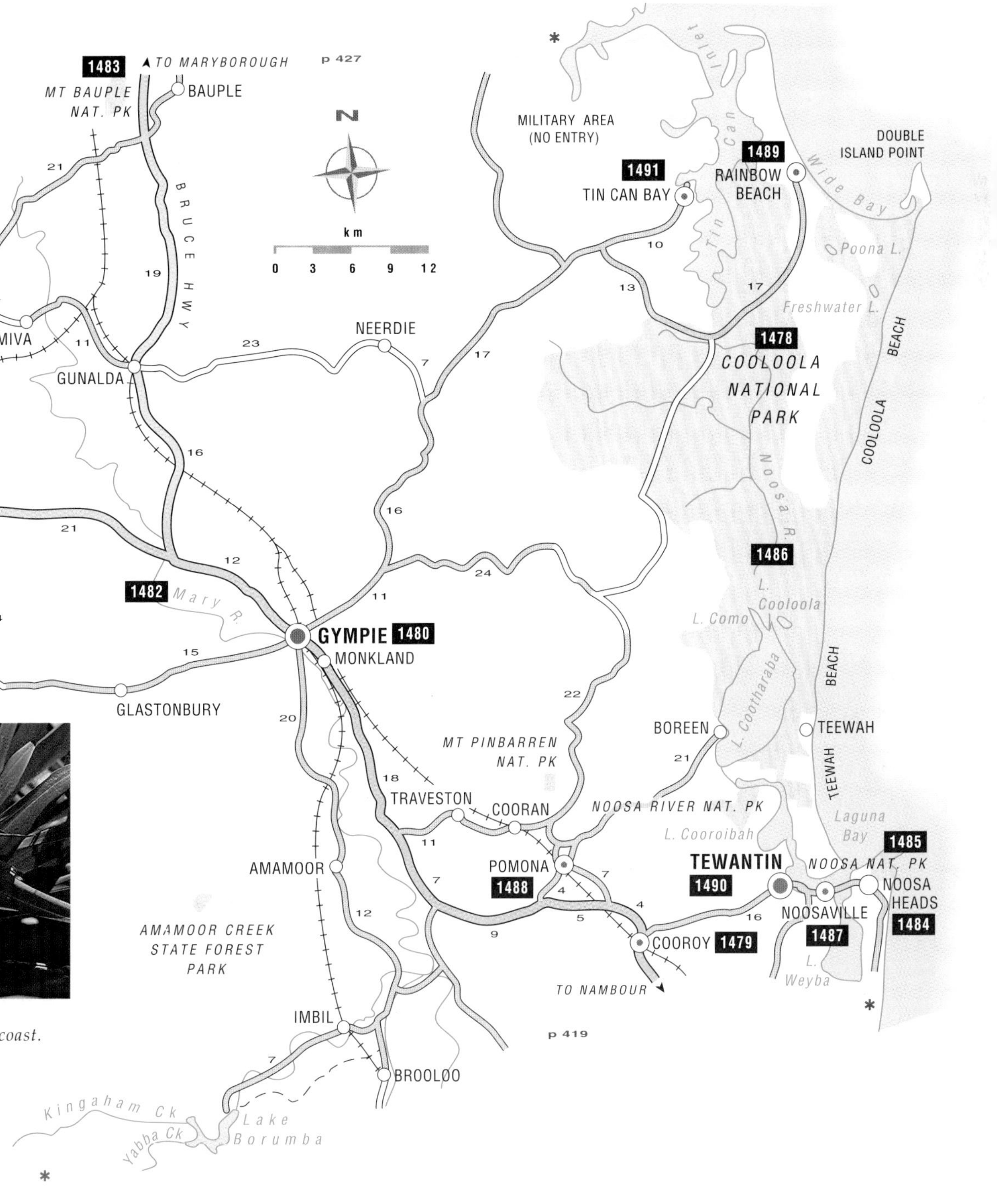

The prop-rooted pandanus, with its pineapple-like fruit, grows along this coast.

ment, became the district's growth industries. *Population 10 790*

DEEP CREEK GOLD FOSSICKING PARK This old goldmining site at Deep Creek gives visitors the chance to strike it lucky, if not rich, using pick, shovel and pan to fossick for gold in the traditional way – after obtaining a fossicking permit – just as the early miners did.

GYMPIE AND DISTRICT HISTORICAL AND MINING MUSEUM This historical museum on Brisbane Road, adjacent to Lake Alford, has a comprehensive display of old goldmining equipment that has been restored to working order, as well as agricultural and dairying exhibits.

In the grounds, there is a simple, four-room timber cottage with a verandah running the length of two sides which was once the home of Andrew Fisher, Australia's first Labor Prime Minister. Also in the grounds is the only remaining mine building from the goldmining days – the original retort house of the Scottish Gympie Gold Mining Company – where gold was extracted from the crushed quartz by a process of amalgamation with mercury. It was then separated from the mercury by heating in retorts.

WOODWORKS This timber and forestry museum on Gympie's northern outskirts has demonstrations of early timber-cutting techniques and a working steam-driven sawmill.

FESTIVALS Gympie Gold Rush Festival, October.

KILKIVAN ■ 1481

European graziers settled the Kilkivan district in the late 1840s and the town takes its name from 'Kilkivan', a property established to its north by a young Scot, J.D. MacTaggart. This pastoral scene remained undisturbed until 1868 when six diggers from New Zealand discovered payable gold at a site a few kilometres south of 'Kilkivan', which they named West Coast Creek after the district from which they hailed.

News of the find quickly spread through the district and almost overnight the first township of Kilkivan – an agglomeration of canvas tents – sprang up at the centre of the goldfield, populated by about 2000 people. At its height, the gold-rush population of Kilkivan numbered about 12 000 people.

The alluvial gold at West Coast Creek was soon exhausted and in 1874, the discovery of the nearby 'Rise and Shine' reef prompted a mass evacuation of West Coast diggers to the new goldfield, and with the miners went the town. As another settlement in Queensland was already named Rise and Shine, this new township took on the name of Mount Neurum, but only for a short time, the original 'Kilkivan' soon asserting its prior claim. The 'Rise and Shine' reef proved to be a rich find but an all too shallow one and was soon depleted.

Like Gympie (see entry), Kilkivan did not meet with the usual fate of gold-mining towns, most of which eventually became ghost towns after the gold dried up. From the late 1840s, pastoralism had flourished quietly in the surrounding countryside, interrupted only by a drought in 1882 that saw cattle replace sheep as the backbone of the grazing industry. The tough speargrass that took over as the dominant grass cover of the plains when the drought broke proved inedible for the sheep but nutritious for cattle, and cattle-raising is still the prime occupation of the farmers of the Kilkivan district.

The arrival of the railway in 1886 had a twofold effect. The township uprooted itself yet again and reformed around the railway station – a railway line extension built in 1902 prompted the town's final move to its present site – and the region's timber industry was boosted by the linking of Kilkivan with the busy sawmills at Gympie and the port of Maryborough. Now little remains of the original forests which were heavily populated with stands of hardwood before the sawyers arrived.

By the turn of the century, closer settlement boosted the dairy and agricultural industries and the excitement of the gold-rush days was long gone. Modern Kilkivan is essentially a government town where the local council and school are the main sources of employment.

CINNABAR Just west of Kilkivan is Australia's main 'quicksilver' field – Cinnabar – which was discovered in 1873. The field takes its name from the red, mercury-bearing mineral once mined here.

Two-thirds of Australia's total output of a mere twenty-four tonnes of mercury has come from this field. The industry has never flourished: the costs – both environmental and monetary – are considered too high and except for a brief period during the Second World War when mercury could not be obtained from overseas sources, the field has been little worked.

MARY RIVER ■ 1482

From its headwaters in the Conondale Range, the Mary River flows for more than 300 kilometres in a northerly direction through Gympie and Maryborough, before releasing its waters to the ocean through the estuary near Fraser Island (see *Bundaberg & Maryborough*). The river is renowned for major flooding, of which Gympie is the most freqent victim, at times having been inundated up to a depth of eight metres.

The river runs the length of the Mary Valley – a rich farming region where dairying, cattle raising and fruit- and vegetable-growing take place. Much of the valley has been cloaked with tree plantations, timber from which feeds the sawmilling industry. In recent years, the valley has also become the site of a new industry – deer farming for venison.

South of Gympie, Lake Borumba on Yabba Creek – a tributary of the Mary River – helps keep floodwaters in check and provides water for irrigation as well as the town's water supply. The lake was formed when the valley was inundated in 1965. The Borumba Fish Hatchery releases fingerlings to replenish depleted native fish stocks.

The first Europeans to 'discover' the Mary River were in a whaleboat party in 1842. It was later explored by the surveyor J.C. Burnett who named it after Lady Mary FitzRoy.

MOUNT BAUPLE NATIONAL PARK ■ 1483

Early confusion over place names has left Mount Bauple outside the boundaries of the national park after which it is named! The peak that

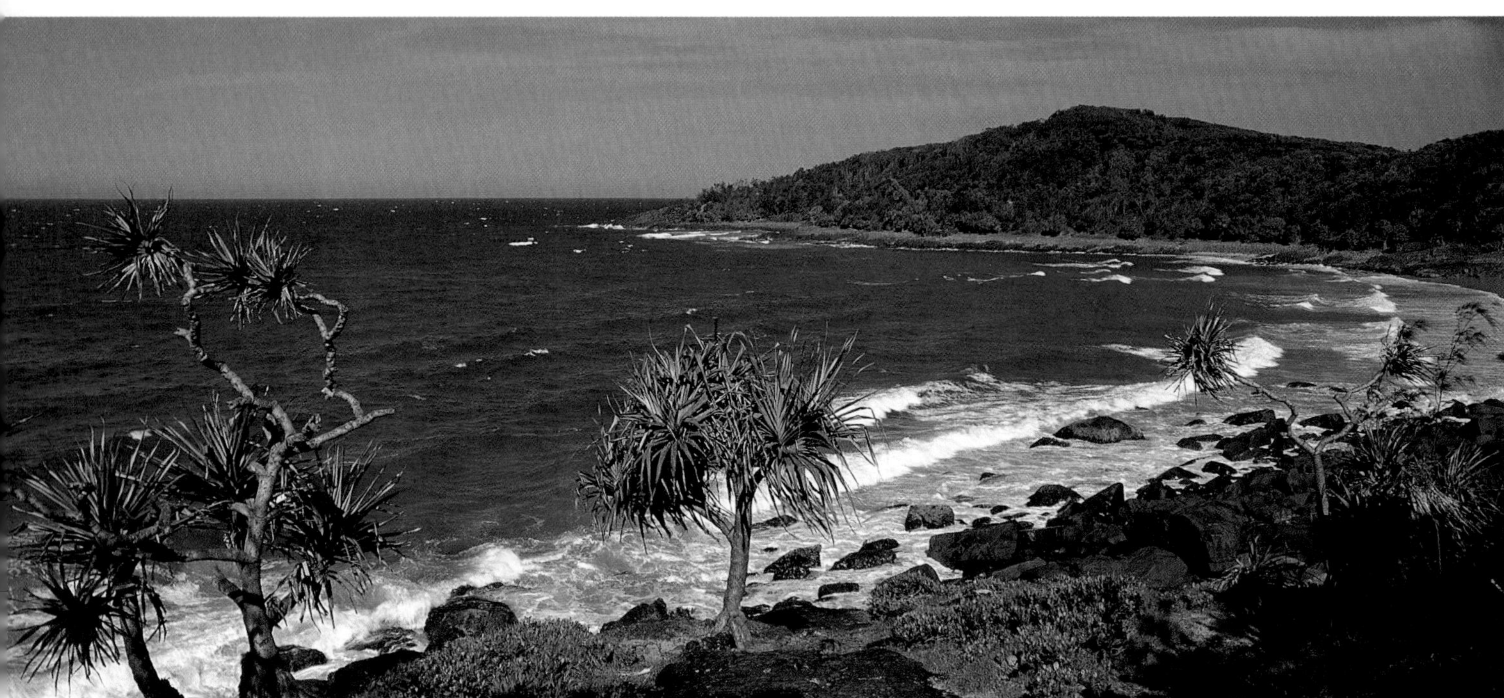

Pandanus palms (see previous page) cling to the thin soil of the Granite Bay shores, overlooked by Noosa Head proper, in Noosa National Park.

dominates the park is actually Mount Guyra (138 metres), the slopes of which are clad in a dense covering of eucalypts, vine thickets and some hoop pine rainforest, which in many places is difficult for even the hardiest of bushwalkers to penetrate. The park covers over 500 hectares and has no camping facilities.

NOOSA HEADS ■ **1484**

When the explorers, Andrew Petrie and Henry Russell, guided their whaleboat into the Noosa River estuary in 1842, looking for timber and good sheep-grazing country, they could not have foreseen that the region's other abundant commodities – sun, sand and surf – would in time eclipse the agricultural riches of the hinterland as the foundation of the local economy.

With its profusion of sidewalk cafes, restaurants, fashionable shops and luxury hotels – none of which compromise the town's strict edict that 'no building shall be higher than the trees' – Noosa Heads today is a far cry from the sleepy village of thirty years ago. The surfing boom of the 1960s was largely responsible for this cosmopolitan transformation. Noosa Heads occupies an enviable position, facing north on a beach along Laguna Bay and backed by the rainforests of Noosa National Park. The crystal clear waters of the bay and the rare – for Australia – northerly aspect of the beach with its perfect surfing waves, have made it an extremely popular place to 'hang ten'.

Noosa Heads was once known as Bracefield Cape, after the escaped convict who assisted in the daring rescue of Mrs Eliza Fraser after she was abducted by Aborigines in 1836 (see Cooloola National Park). Noosa comes from an Aboriginal word said to mean 'shade' or 'shadow'. *Population 9880*

FESTIVALS Jazz Party, September.

NOOSA NATIONAL PARK ■ **1485**

The 432-hectare patch of rainforest, open eucalypt forest, wallum heathlands, shrublands and grasslands that makes up Noosa National Park is an oasis of tranquillity in the intensely urbanised strip of the Sunshine Coast. That such a respite from the 'madding crowds' of coastal resorts exists is largely due to the foresight of the region's early settlers, whose 1879 declaration of the Noosa Town Reserve preserved this coastal ground for dedication as a national park in 1930.

The park's rocky headlands break the pounding ocean waves, leaving them to roll harmlessly into the sheltered beaches. A wide variety of plants and animals can be found in the park, including the pandanus tree – with its characteristic aerial 'prop' roots and plump, orange coloured fruit – brightly coloured honeyeaters, seagulls, terns, brahminy kites, mosaic-tailed rats and short-nosed bandicoots.

NOOSA RIVER ■ **1486**

Five major waterways – Lakes Cootharaba, Weyba, Cooroibah, Doonella and Como – broaden the length of the Noosa River as it flows from the high country north-west of Gympie to the Pacific Ocean. This complex system of tranquil coastal waterways forms the renowned Noosa 'lakes district', most of which is protected within Cooloola National Park (see entry).

More than fifty kilometres of navigable waterways have made the river, its many tributaries and the lakes an attractive haven for canoeists, who come in their thousands every year to glide over the dark water. A narrow, winding section of the river, aptly named, The Narrows, is renowned for its mirror-like reflections. Submerged logs here provide an excellent habitat for freshwater bass and the river has a reputation among anglers as being not only the best fishing river on the east coast of Australia, but also the best bass hunting-ground in the country! Several small islands dot the river's waters just upstream of Tewantin (see entry), and Goat Island, opposite Hilton Terrace, has been made into a nature reserve.

Beyond Lake Cootharaba, which covers an area of ninety square kilometres – making it the largest of the Noosa River lakes – is a very pretty spot known as the Everglades, which is popular with landscape photographers and naturalists.

The remains of old logging camps are still visible in the forests bordering the river. In the early days of timber-getting, kauri, hoop pine, cypress and beech were cut from the forests of the Upper Noosa River and floated downstream to the sawmills at Tewantin.

NOOSAVILLE ■ **1487**

Timber-getters and goldminers were the first holiday-makers in this relaxed family-style resort town on the sandy banks of the Noosa River between Tewantin and Noosa Heads.

In the early days, many miners from the Gympie goldfield built holiday homes at Gympie Terrace, as Noosaville was known then. From the 1940s, the district became an increasingly popular holiday destination and the simple timber blocks of flats and camping sites sprinkled with tents were soon replaced by modern resort architecture and caravan parks. *Population 4920*

POMONA ■ **1488**

Pomona – nestling at the base of the 438-metre-high Mount Cooroora in the hinterland of the Sunshine Coast – began life as a small timber and dairy town in the late nineteenth century. Despite the passage of time, the town's character has not changed greatly and as a small farming centre, Pomona has become a popular destination with those who are attracted by the measured pace of country living...and with jogging enthusiasts! Every year in July, the town hosts the annual 'king of the mountain' foot race up Mount Cooroora. While more active visitors are slogging it out up the steep mountain slopes, the town is busy with some less energetic festival activities that include a thong-throwing competition and billy-cart races.

The town's eighty-year-old picture theatre has the distinction of being the oldest continually running cinema in Queensland. *Population 890*

FESTIVALS King of the Mountain Festival, late July.

RAINBOW BEACH ■ **1489**

The developing resort of Rainbow Beach was originally a base for sand-mining operations in the Cooloola district and Fraser Island, but mounting pressure from conservationists led to a state government decision in the early 1970s to call a halt to all mining activities in the region, prompting the transformation of Rainbow Beach into a resort town.

Lying between the eastern side of Tin Can Bay and the Pacific Ocean and abutting Cooloola National Park, Rainbow Beach takes its name from the rock-strewn cliffs of coloured sands that form the township's magnificent backdrop. *Population 730*

TEWANTIN ■ **1490**

Tewantin was first settled in the late 1860s by cedar-getters who came to exploit the dense forests of the surrounding hills and valleys. In those early days, the Noosa River was the only thoroughfare to the hinterland's rich store of timber and Tewantin, on the shores of Lake Donella, developed as a river port. Much of the timber was rafted downstream from the Lake Cootharaba area to the sawmill at Tewantin from where it was shipped to Brisbane.

The discovery of gold at Gympie (see entry) in 1867 made Tewantin one of the access ports for miners headed for the goldfields and in 1870, the settlement was declared a town. By the 1880s, Tewantin had already acquired something of its present-day character as a holiday place, with goldminers returning to the riverside port for a rest. A popular day-trip at the time was a boat ride from the public wharf at Tewantin to Turtle Island.

The advent of the railway line in the late nineteenth century saw the decline of Tewantin as an important port and the town's development was soon eclipsed by that of the hinterland railway towns of Cooroy and Pomona. A scheme in 1913 to build a railway extension to Tewantin was put aside with the outbreak of the First World War, and never resurrected. But in 1893, the Queensland Government passed a Co-operative Communities Land Settlement Act – amended in 1895 – which allowed large tracts of land in the region to be developed as 'communes'. Although the venture ultimately failed and the co-operative communities were subdivided into plots for individual members, the end result was a boost to the region's population and the opening of several new sawmills in the hinterland. As the land was cleared, a new grass, paspalum, was introduced and many of the region's farmers turned to dairying.

Today, timber and dairy products along with sugar, pineapples and cattle are important to this region. Tewantin, as a starting point for exploration by houseboat or canoe of the famous Cooloola lakes district and the coloured sands at Teewah, forms part of the popular Noosa tourist area. *Population 5600*

Handsome brahminy kites glide above Noosa's tidal fringes searching for food cast up by the sea.

TIN CAN BAY ■ **1491**

Major fishing operations did not commence in Tin Can Bay until the 1950s when millions of prawns were harvested from the briny waters and the laid-back fishing village developed gradually into one of the main fishing centres on the Sunshine Coast. But Tin Can Bay has not lost sight of its simple origins and despite the prawning fleets and processing plants based beside the calm waters of the bay, the town has retained its easy-going character with many of the simplest pleasures – such as purchasing a just-caught fish direct from one of the trawlers – in no danger of losing their timeless appeal.

In May each year, the little town becomes the venue for the 'Bay to Bay' yachting classic with more than 200 sailors making the trip to Tin Can Bay for the sail up the Great Sandy Strait to Hervey Bay. *Population 1360*

FESTIVALS Easter Festival, April.

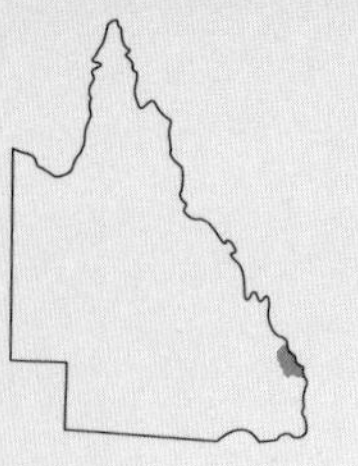

Bundaberg & Maryborough

The tree-lined beaches and sheltered waters in the lee of a great island of sand are a holiday playground where whales frolic and fish and birds abound. Canefields covering the fertile hinterland supply the mills of Bundaberg.

BARGARA ■ 1492
Reached by a road which runs past fields of lush sugarcane, this pretty, peaceful beach town is, like the other seaside resorts adjacent to Bundaberg, thankfully south of the limit of the fearful box jellyfish. There is rock fishing and a fine surfing beach here, and at Kellys Beach, six kilometres to the south, are two still water swimming areas, one, The Basin, was built by South Sea islanders brought to the area to work in the canefields. *Population 2700*

MON REPOS ENVIRONMENTAL PARK In the days before European settlement, Aboriginal tribes gathered at this beach north of Bargara to feast on turtles. It continues to be one of the most important rookeries in the Southern Hemisphere, with leatherback, loggerhead, and the rarer flatback turtles coming out of the ocean to nest from November to January. The hatchlings emerge from January to March, to make their frantic way to the sea. In order to protect the nesting and hatching, night viewing is now regulated by ticket.

THE HUMMOCK Inland from Bargara Beach is The Hummock – an extinct volcano that was formed by lava forced through a fault in the earth's surface. Lava near the fault cooled, creating the cone, the rest flowed over the surrounding country where it has weathered into the rocks and boulders, which in the nineteenth century provided building material for the many beachside and roadside walls of the district.

A freshly hatched batch of leatherbacks at Mon Repos prepares to slither to the safety of the Pacific.

BIGGENDEN ■ 1493
Europeans first pushed into the Burnett Valley in the 1840s, seeking pastures for sheep. Later, with the realisation that coastal Queensland was too hot and wet for sheep, and with the development of refrigeration – which allowed meat to be shipped to distant markets – graziers switched to beef cattle. Biggenden is now the centre of a premier beef cattle area. Farmers also grow grains, peanuts, and citrus fruits.

Gold was discovered in the area in the late 1880s bringing hundreds of prospectors to the goldfields of Paradise and Shamrock. On the western spur of Mount Biggenden, near the township, is Australia's only magnetite mine – the mineral is used in coal washing and water purification plants. *Population 690*

MOUNT WALSH NATIONAL PARK This rugged, 3000-hectare park is notable for its rock faces and gorges. Eucalypt forests grow on the slopes of Mount Walsh, which rises 450 metres above sea level, and dense pine and palm forests fill the valleys.

BUNDABERG ■ 1494
Europeans searching for timber first explored the Bundaberg district in the 1850s and 1860s. Recognising that the deposit of rich basaltic soil to the east of the present township would be suitable for sugarcane cultivation, the Stewart brothers took up selections in 1867.

A sawmill was operating by the end of 1868, with the timber being shipped down the Burnett River from the embryonic township, which then grew in importance as a port following the discovery of copper at Mount Perry. By the early 1870s, planters were raising sugar, coffee and a variety of fruit and vegetables. Despite some problems with rust in the mid-1870s, the district's sugar production grew rapidly. By the end of the 1880s, there were forty sugar mills, with rum an important byproduct. Today, the district produces approximately one-fifth of Australia's sugar and it is also an important market-garden centre.

Modern Bundaberg is a pleasant city, with tree-lined streets and colourful private gardens. *Population 38 100*

BOTANIC GARDENS As well as walking through these pleasant gardens, with their tropical, sub-tropical and cold-climate plants, visitors may tour on the restored steam tramway.

HINKLER HOUSE MEMORIAL MUSEUM AND BUNDABERG HISTORICAL MUSEUM The Bundaberg-born pioneer aviator Bert Hinkler developed his ambition from observing the flights of ibis at the nearby lagoons. After building a set of wings, he achieved unpowered flight at Mon Repos beach. Following service in the British air force in the First World War, he became, in 1928, the first person to fly solo from England to Australia. During 1983–84, Hinkler's house in England was dismantled and reconstructed in the Bundaberg Botanic Gardens, where flying artefacts are now displayed. The Historical Museum, also in the gardens, has period farm equipment and household appliances, Aboriginal artefacts, birds, and shells as well as Hinkler memorabilia.

BUNDABERG DISTILLERY The home of Bundaberg's famous rum, the distillery's many buildings cover three hectares. Guided tours are available.

BURNETT HEADS ■ 1495
This seaside resort at the mouth of the Burnett River is surrounded by small sugar farms. The lighthouse built here in 1873 and since replaced by an automatic unit, is now on display in the caravan park. For almost a century it guided vessels into the port of Bundaberg and was staffed twenty-four hours a day.

This district was first settled in the early 1870s – the first sugarcane was harvested in 1875. *Population 1360*

BURRUM HEADS ■ 1496
On the shores of Hervey Bay, north of Maryborough, this resort offers caravan, camping and boating facilities. The area is known particularly for its whiting fishing and the adjacent water supports a large dugong herd. *Population 770*

BURRUM RIVER NATIONAL PARK This 1618-hectare coastal wetland boasts a wealth of birdlife, especially swamp birds and waders, and an abundance of wildflowers.

CHILDERS ■ 1497
The first European settlers came to the Childers district in the 1850s in search of sheep and cattle runs. In the 1870s, selectors began cultivating sugarcane on the isolated deposit of rich basaltic soil adjacent to the present township. This has remained a major crop in the district, although avocados and vegetables are now also grown. Despite the fire which destroyed much of the town's shopping centre in 1902, a number of ornately decorated turn-of-the-century buildings still stand. Visitors may tour the Isis sugar mill to see the raw cane turned into the white crystals which sit on every dining-room table. *Population 1470*

Tall satinays – a form of turpentine growing to 60 metres – preside over Fraser Island's Pile Valley forest.

FRASER ISLAND ■ 1498
This is the largest sand island in the world. In the 1970s, a major battle between sandminers and conservationists, led by John Sinclair, resulted in a federal government ban on the mining of its sand. As this is one of the few places in the world were extensive rainforests grow on pure sand, there is also a strong crusade to ban logging as well. Fraser Island was the first site to be listed on the register of Australia's National Estate (see box).

The island takes its name as a consequence of the shipwreck of the *Stirling Castle* which struck a reef north of it in May 1836. A party including Mrs Eliza Fraser reached the island and her subsequent tales of their days spent there with the Aborigines meant that her name was soon applied to the area (see *Gympie & Tewantin*).

GREAT SANDY NATIONAL PARK Occupying a large part of Fraser Island, this 52 400-hectare reserve has all the features for which the whole island

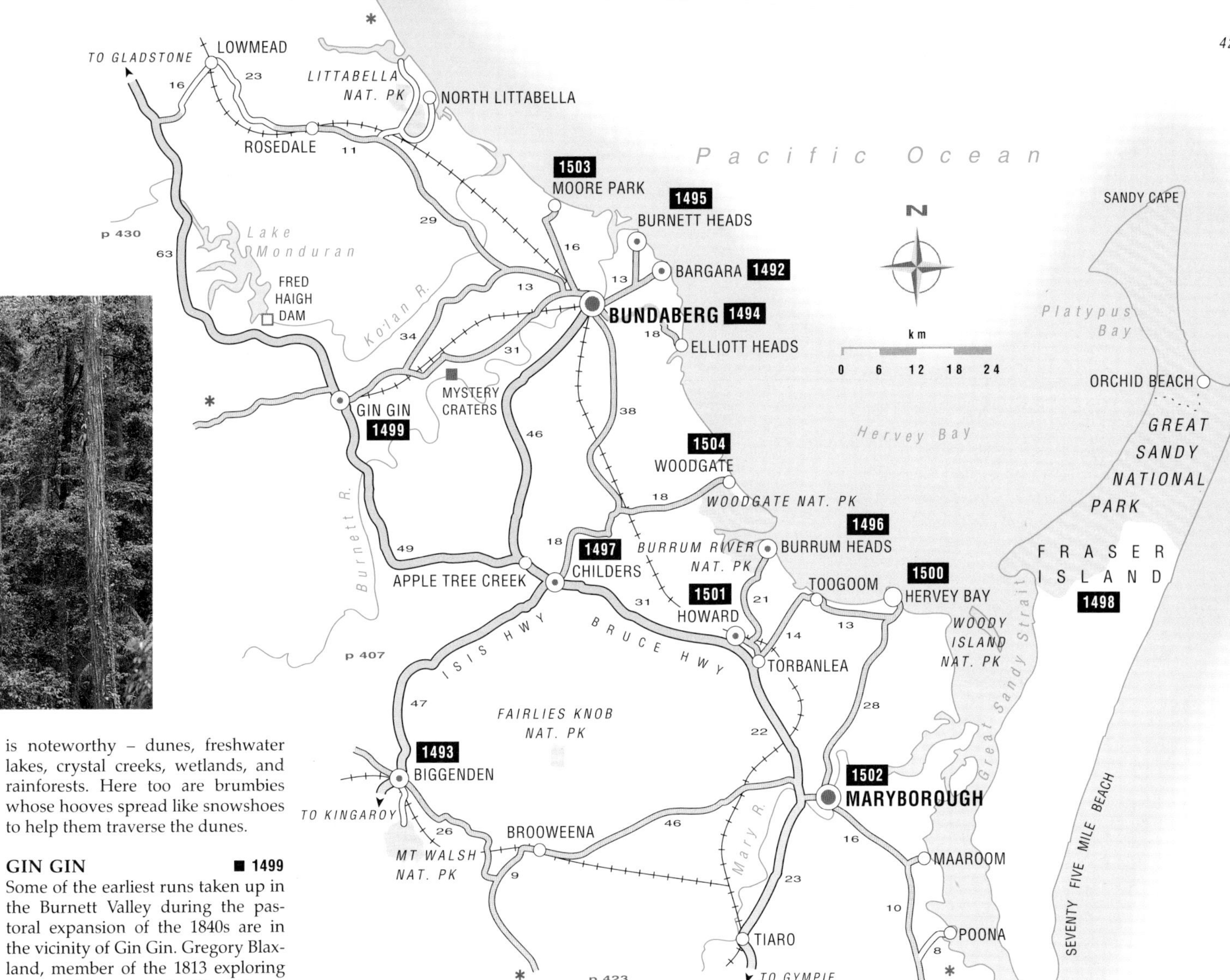

is noteworthy – dunes, freshwater lakes, crystal creeks, wetlands, and rainforests. Here too are brumbies whose hooves spread like snowshoes to help them traverse the dunes.

GIN GIN ■ 1499

Some of the earliest runs taken up in the Burnett Valley during the pastoral expansion of the 1840s are in the vicinity of Gin Gin. Gregory Blaxland, member of the 1813 exploring party which crossed the Blue Mountains, west of Sydney, settled here in 1846. In the 1860s, Queensland's only bushranger, James McPherson, also known as the 'Wild Scotchman', who on numerous occasions waylaid the Royal Mail in the Gin Gin and Burnett districts, had a letter published in the local newspaper disputing the accuracy of its reports concerning his deeds. *Population 910*

MYSTERY CRATERS East of Gin Gin on the Bundaberg road are the Mystery Craters, peculiar geological formations of uncertain age and origin.

HERVEY BAY ■ 1500

The resort city of Hervey Bay stretches along the tree-fringed shore of a bay with the same name, and takes in the beaches of Urangan, Torquay, Scarness, Pialba and Point Vernon. It is a major tourist destination – passenger cruisers and car ferries depart from here for Fraser Island and the bay is one of the best fishing grounds on the Queensland coast. From mid-August to mid-October families of southern humpback whales returning south to Antarctica after calving in northern waters stop in the bay to rest and play. Whale-watch boats sail among the huge mammals allowing tourists to view them at close range. The bay was named by Lieutenant James Cook in 1770. *Population 22 200*

FESTIVALS Whale Festival, August; Pier Festival, September.

HOWARD ■ 1501

The countryside around Howard was settled in the 1850s by timber-getters who cut logs for the Maryborough mills. Mining on the Burrum coalfields became the region's main industry from the 1860s.

The town is characterised by high-set, wide-verandahed timber houses, many with decorative woodwork. *Population 950*

BROOKLYN HOUSE Cedar and beech are the main materials in this gracious Queensland-style house, which was built in 1890 for William Rankin, general manager of the Queensland Colliery company.

MARYBOROUGH ■ 1502

The Brisbane official, Andrew Petrie, and party, with two escaped convicts who had lived with local Aborigines, explored the Wide Bay district in 1842, discovering areas of good grazing land. Pastoralists followed as soon as the Moreton Bay district was declared open to free settlement in 1842; and Maryborough developed as the port on the Mary River to service the runs from 1843 onwards. It received further impetus after gold was discovered at Gympie in 1867.

With the introduction of steam-driven machinery, the district's busy sawmills provided much of Queensland with timber from the then abundant forests of kauri, hoop and bunya pine. Sugarcane was cultivated from the mid-1860s onwards, and remains one of the district's principal products. Shipbuilding and the manufacture of industrial machinery at the Walker Brothers yards are also important activities. *Population 20 790*

WHARF STREET PRECINCT In the second half of the nineteenth century, Maryborough was a major point of entry for migrants from Europe. This history is reflected in the old buildings to be found in the Wharf Street area – the customs house, bond store, warehouses, banks and shops, and hotels and boarding houses – many of which are being restored to their nineteenth-century character.

MARYBOROUGH HERITAGE DRIVE This two-hour drive reveals former grammar school buildings, colonial houses in various styles – such as the classic 'Queenslanders' – hotels, workers' cottages, and gardens.

FESTIVALS Hermitage City Festival, September.

MOORE PARK ■ 1503

This resort's sixteen-kilometre-long beach is one of the last good surfing beaches before the Great Barrier Reef intrudes to break the Pacific Ocean's warm swell. Inland there are canefields, pineapple plantations, avocado orchards and aloe vera farms. *Population 560*

WOODGATE ■ 1504

Situated on the northern side of the Burrum River, this resort offers caravan, camping and boating facilities and has a notable surfing beach. *Population 620*

WOODGATE NATIONAL PARK A boardwalk meanders through lily-covered swamplands in this coastal reserve, which is home to many species of marsupials, birds and wildflowers.

BEHIND THE DUNES, THE TALL TIMBERS OF LAKELAND

THE NORTHERN rivers of New South Wales cut through the mountains along the coast, eroding the rocks of the Great Dividing Range and grain by grain carrying their sands down to the sea. Winds and currents then sweep this sand north, where it is built up against the continental shelf, there forming a series of exposed deposits off the southern Queensland coast. This process has been going on for so long that the sand grains have built up into a sandy chain of islands dominated by the vast Fraser Island, the world's largest sand island.

While there are the volcanic outpourings of Indian Head, Middle Rock and Waddy Point, Fraser Island is overwhelmingly of sand; and it is in this that its uniqueness lies. Shaped by a continuous process of formation and degeneration, the island is composed of dunes exhibiting five stages. Those next to the Pacific shoreline are the most sharply defined; and those on the western side are worn down to heathland. The dunes are highest at the island's centre, where the rainforests of palms, ferns, vines and massive kauri and hoop pines and satinay trees, and the lakes 'perched' above the water table are found.

Given its sand base, Fraser Island presents miracles of adaptation. There are trees that store nutrients in bulbous lumps on their trunks, and others that have aerial roots to accommodate sand movement. The ferns and palms are survivors from Gondwanaland of 250 million years ago, while 'sundew' plants use insects to obtain the nitrogen they cannot get from the sand.

At intervals along the eastern shoreline, such as at Cathedral Beach, there are eight-million-year-old deposits of 'Teewah' sands, rainbow-coloured by mineral leaching. Similar deposits occur at Cooloola, on the mainland opposite the island.

Lieutenant James Cook and his companions on the *Endeavour* were the first Europeans to see Fraser Island, in May 1770. Joseph Banks noted observantly: 'We could see through our glasses that the sands which lay in great patches of many acres each were moveable: some of them had been lately moved, for trees which stood up in the middle of them were quite green, others of a longer standing had many stumps sticking out of them which had been trees killed by the sand heaping about their roots'. The island was named after the shipwrecked Eliza Fraser (see Cooloola National Park, *Gympie & Tewantin*). □

Sand 'blows', like the giant moving dune (left) which threatens to engulf the 10-metre-deep Lake Wabby, are unvegetated patches of Fraser Island which shift as the wind wills. Elsewhere, such as at Wanggoolba Creek (above), forest colonises the nutrient-poor 'soil'.

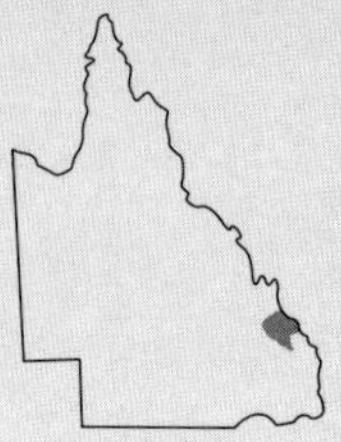

Gladstone & Biloela

From an unpromising start the now busy harbour city of Gladstone successfully blends tourism and industry. West, across the ranges, are coalfields and rich pastures; to the east, the shimmering coral-fringed islands of the Great Barrier Reef.

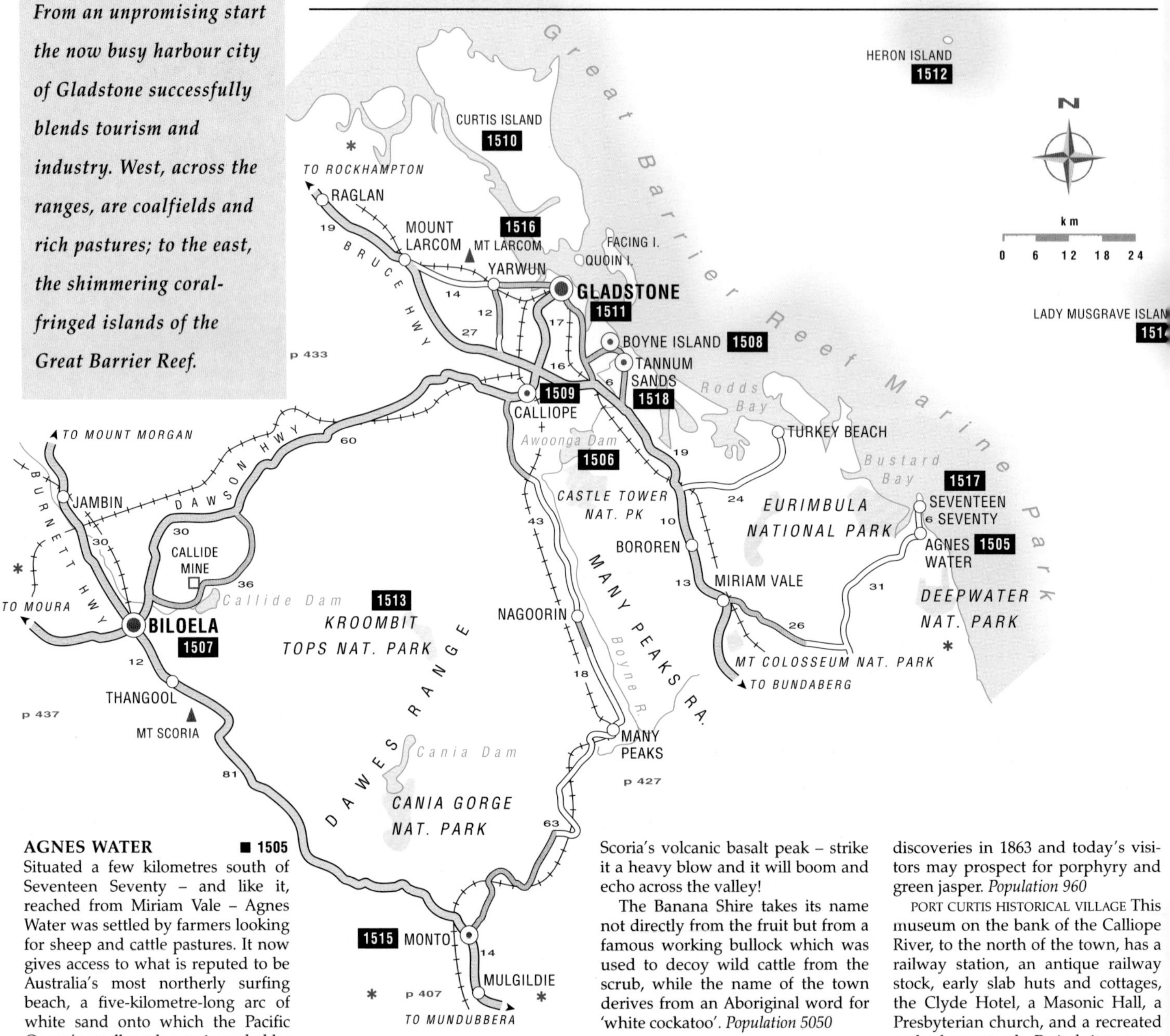

HERON ISLAND 1512
CURTIS ISLAND 1510
TO ROCKHAMPTON
RAGLAN
MOUNT LARCOM
MT LARCOM 1516
FACING I.
QUOIN I.
YARWUN
GLADSTONE 1511
BRUCE HWY
BOYNE ISLAND 1508
TANNUM SANDS 1518
CALLIOPE 1509
Rodds Bay
TURKEY BEACH
Awoonga Dam 1506
CASTLE TOWER NAT. PK
EURIMBULA NATIONAL PARK
Bustard Bay 1517
SEVENTEEN SEVENTY
AGNES WATER 1505
LADY MUSGRAVE ISLAN[D] 151[4]
Great Barrier Reef Marine Park
TO MOUNT MORGAN
JAMBIN
DAWSON HWY
BURNETT HWY
CALLIDE MINE
Callide Dam 1513
TO MOURA
BILOELA 1507
KROOMBIT TOPS NAT. PARK
NAGOORIN
BOROREN
MIRIAM VALE
DEEPWATER NAT. PARK
MANY PEAKS RA.
Boyne R.
MT COLOSSEUM NAT. PARK
TO BUNDABERG
THANGOOL
MT SCORIA
DAWES RANGE
Cania Dam
CANIA GORGE NAT. PARK
MANY PEAKS
1515 MONTO
MULGILDIE
TO MUNDUBBERA
km 0 6 12 18 24

p 433 p 437 p 427 p 407

AGNES WATER ■ 1505
Situated a few kilometres south of Seventeen Seventy – and like it, reached from Miriam Vale – Agnes Water was settled by farmers looking for sheep and cattle pastures. It now gives access to what is reputed to be Australia's most northerly surfing beach, a five-kilometre-long arc of white sand onto which the Pacific Ocean's swell crashes unimpeded by the Great Barrier Reef.

AWOONGA DAM ■ 1506
The Awoonga Dam has been raised progressively since 1965, and provides water for the city of Gladstone, for the Gladstone and Callide power stations, and for the huge alumina smelter on Boyne Island. The dam is now popular with fishing and watersports enthusiasts, and there are walking tracks about its perimeter.

BILOELA ■ 1507
The first European settlers in the Biloela district were pastoralists who arrived in the mid-nineteenth century. When the township of Biloela was surveyed in 1924, the old runs were made available for closer settlement and specialist farming. Now, the district produces both beef and dairy cattle, as well as cotton, sunflowers, grains and lucernes.

A museum of primary industries called Advance Australia Fair is located here and a number of the old homesteads in the district, including 'Greycliffe', offer visitors insights into the lives of the pioneers. Tours of the cotton ginnery are available from March to July. To the south is Mount Scoria's volcanic basalt peak – strike it a heavy blow and it will boom and echo across the valley!

The Banana Shire takes its name not directly from the fruit but from a famous working bullock which was used to decoy wild cattle from the scrub, while the name of the town derives from an Aboriginal word for 'white cockatoo'. *Population 5050*

BOYNE ISLAND ■ 1508
In the late 1800s, the island was used as a fishing and swimming place for miners working some nearby goldfields. Later it was a cattle run. By 1931, there was only one hut still standing on the island but a modern township has grown up to accompany the building of the huge alumina smelter which, by the early 1990s, was producing 220 000 tonnes of aluminium annually. *Population 2550*

CALLIOPE ■ 1509
Located at the entrance to the Boyne Valley, Calliope was the site of gold discoveries in 1863 and today's visitors may prospect for porphyry and green jasper. *Population 960*

PORT CURTIS HISTORICAL VILLAGE This museum on the bank of the Calliope River, to the north of the town, has a railway station, an antique railway stock, early slab huts and cottages, the Clyde Hotel, a Masonic Hall, a Presbyterian church, and a recreated early homestead. Period items are displayed in a large shed.

CURTIS ISLAND ■ 1510
Curtis Island and Facing Island form a barrier between Port Curtis and the Pacific Ocean, with the smaller Quoin Island located in the passage between them. All three are serviced by ferry from Gladstone.

Curtis Island has a lodge, store and campsites and is renowned for its fishing and for the turtles that nest on it from November to January. In the mid-nineteenth century, there was a quarantine station for immigrant ships at Sea Hill; the Grassy

At the heart of Gladstone's industrial machine and juxtaposed with an alluring coast, is this alumina refinery.

Hill lighthouse was built in 1886. Facing Island has weekend cabins and campsites; Quoin Island is a fauna reserve, where marsupials and birds wander unthreatened.

GLADSTONE ■ 1511
In 1847, following the end of convict transportation from Britain to New South Wales, an attempt was made to off-load convicts in Port Curtis. The advance party landed in January only to encounter the miserable conditions and myriads of mosquitoes associated with the height of the wet season. They were also attacked by local Aborigines and the venture was abandoned after three months.

By the mid-1850s, the expansion of sheep grazing in central Queensland underlined the need for a port on the coast. The town site of Gladstone was surveyed in 1853 and the Port Curtis pastoral district proclaimed in January 1854. But in the next few years, only a trickle of wool passed through the port for its immediate surrounds were infertile and the coastal ranges made arduous the routes to the inland runs.

Gladstone's importance increased from the 1920s as wheat and meat were shipped from it and after the Second World War, this importance grew rapidly, as it became a depot for petrol and oil, and a bulk-handling port for grain and coal from the vast Callide and Blackwater fields. The building of the alumina smelter and refining plant in the 1960s and 1970s led to Gladstone becoming one of the continent's busiest ports, with ten large wharves handling some thirty million tonnes of cargo annually. *Population 23 460*

GLADSTONE REGIONAL ART GALLERY AND MUSEUM Housed in a handsome colonial Georgian-style building, this institution has three exhibition areas – one devoted to touring displays, a second to local arts and crafts, and the last to photographs conveying the history of the region.

KULLAROO HOUSE Originally a bank, this grand building was built in 1911. Notable for the quality of its interior fittings, which have been preserved and restored, it is now a restaurant.

FESTIVALS Harbour Festival, April.

HERON ISLAND ■ 1512
This coral cay lies two hours by catamaran to the east of Gladstone. It has a scattering of holiday resort buildings, and a marine biology research station. A coral observatory is anchored on adjacent Wistari Reef and nearby Masthead Islet also provides good reef viewing. Heron Island is notable for the abundance and variety of its bird and reef life.

Heron Island was first seen by Francis Blackwood and Joseph Jukes in HMS *Fly* in 1843 and was later inspected by Owen Stanley and T.H. Huxley in HMS *Rattlesnake* in 1847–48. It was not settled until the 1920s, when a turtle-canning factory was established. In 1932, the factory buildings were converted into a tourist resort and the hulk of the old warship *Protector* scuttled to form a boat anchorage. The island was declared a national park in 1943.

KROOMBIT TOPS NATIONAL PARK ■ 1513
Situated in extremely rugged country in the Calliope Ranges, this 453-hectare reserve protects the weathered sandstone cliffs and deep gorges which support a cover of rainforest, hoop pine and eucalypt forest. After European pastoralists entered the area in the 1850s, the stockmen of Kroombit Station soon became legendary for their skill at combing the seemingly inaccessible hills and gullies for the brumbies and feral cattle that had taken refuge there. The park contains some of the finest remaining stands of hoop pine.

LADY MUSGRAVE ISLAND ■ 1514
This low island south-east of Gladstone marks the southern limits of coral formation and the edge of the continental shelf. It and Lady Elliott Island, further to the south-east (not shown on map), are coral cays, with vegetation cover predominantly of grass, pisonia and casuarina trees, and pandanus palms. Each is home to a myriad of seabirds and the surrounding reefs and waters offer good viewing and fishing.

Lady Elliott Island is named after the ship *Lady Elliott*, which passed by here in 1816. Goats released in the early 1900s caused great damage to the landscapes of both islands – a revegetation program began in the 1970s. The islands are also a nesting place for turtles as well as being well placed for watching the north–south migration of whales.

MONTO ■ 1515
The Monto district was first settled during the pastoral expansion of the mid-nineteenth century. The township itself dates from the mid-1920s, when closer settlement was encouraged. Graziers now run both dairy and beef cattle and the district also produces sorghum, wheat and other grains, sunflowers and lucerne. The name Monto derives from an Aboriginal word said to mean 'plains with ridges'. *Population 1340*

CANIA GORGE This break in a ridge of the Dawes Range, to the north of Monto, has colourful and spectacular rock and cave formations, sheer cliff faces, clear creeks and rock pools.

MOUNT LARCOM ■ 1516
This peak rising more than 630 metres to the north-west of Gladstone provides striking views of the hinterland, the coast, and the offshore islands. It is a favourite, but rugged, tourist climb.

The Mount Larcom homestead was the scene of an Aboriginal attack in December 1855, after which one writer, giving what for the time was an uncommonly balanced opinion, commented: 'Such a state of hostility is undoubtedly the natural consequence of the occupation of the soil by the white race'. Conflicts between Aborigines and new settlers continued to occur throughout the central Queensland region into the 1870s, although violent clashes began to diminish towards the end of the 1860s with some pastoralists adopting the policy of 'letting in' – allowing Aborigines to remain on their pastoral runs, either to work, or to hunt and gather in the traditional ways.

SEVENTEEN SEVENTY ■ 1517
This settlement on the spit that forms Bustard Bay, marks the site of James Cook's first landing on the coast of what is now Queensland, on 24 May 1770. He was little impressed with the dry and sandy soil but he noted the oysters, the mangroves and pandanus palms that fringed the land and sea. He saw fires but not the Aborigines who lit them, and remarked on the many birds, particularly ducks and 'Bustards such as we have in England...which occasioned my giving this place the name of Bustard Bay'. A cairn here commemorates Cook's landing.

TANNUM SANDS ■ 1518
Joined to Boyne Island by a high bridge, this resort suburb is only twenty minutes' drive from Gladstone and is notable for its beaches and for the variety of exotic flowering trees in its gardens. Since 1980, it has provided housing for the workforce of the nearby Boyne Island smelter. *Population 2460*

Bright patches of sunflowers – grown for their seed oil – face ever-skywards in the paddocks of Monto.

Rockhampton & Yeppoon

Lying to the north of the Tropic of Capricorn is gracious Rockhampton, the beef capital of the north; to the south is Mount Morgan, where fabulous wealth was dug from the ground. Nearby are limestone caves formed from ancient coral reefs, and offshore, a paradise of coral-ringed tropical isles.

Gnarled-trunk bougainvilleas of several varieties lend their support to the slab-walls of 'Gracemere's' 1858 homestead.

BYFIELD NATIONAL PARK ■ 1519

This reserve, little touched by human presence, is made up of dunes, wetlands, heaths and a rugged coastal range and is notable for its melaleuca forests and fauna. Natural history enthusiasts made important collections here in the late nineteenth and early twentieth centuries. The park is accessible only by four-wheel-drive vehicles or by boat. Canoe trees and tools and other artefacts in old campsites are all that remain of the Aboriginal people who once lived in this region.

CAPRICORN CAVERNS ■ 1520

In the hills north of Rockhampton there are limestone caves and caverns where over aeons of time, underground seepage and streams have created a variety of fascinating formations. A number of these caves can be reached from The Caves township, on the Bruce Highway.

The Capricorn Caverns' fascinating labyrinth of sixty-six dry caves hollowed out a limestone mountain was formed by rainwater percolating through cracks and crevices in the rock. They were discovered by John Olsen, also a Norwegian immigrant, in 1882. Particularly impressive is 'The Cathedral' cave, with its thirty-metre-high roof and rock formations reminiscent of a pulpit, choir stalls and font, in which church services and musical performances are sometimes held. The caves are privately owned, and there are guided tours.

CAMMOO CAVES This system of limestone caverns contains the fossilised remains of corals and primitive life forms dating from an age when this area was part of a coral reef. The caves were created by water permeating down through the limestone, building the formations drip by drip. Bats live here at certain times of the year and tree roots dozens of metres long thrust through the cave roof from the rainforest above. The caves had long been known to Aborigines but a thirteen-year-old Norwegian immigrant, Charlotte Kohn, is credited with finding the caves in 1881.

MOUNT ETNA NATIONAL PARK The caves in the small reserve encompassing Mount Etna and Limestone Ridge are home to the ghost bat and the bent-wing bat.

GANGALOOK HERITAGE VILLAGE Period buildings, furniture, transport and machinery are highlights of this pioneer village. There are tours and demonstrations designed to convey a sense of what life was like in the late nineteenth century, as well as an extensive collection of old clocks.

One hundred years of relentless digging and scraping for copper and gold – fifty of them by open-cut – left this crater at Mount Morgan in 1981.

EMU PARK ■ 1521

This settlement developed as a resort once the railway line was laid to it from North Rockhampton in 1888. It offers picturesque views to the Keppel Islands. The town's Singing Ship Memorial, which commemorates James Cook's 1770 voyage in the *Endeavour*, is a twelve-metre-high structure of pipes in the shape of a large sail which, with a strong breeze passing through it, is said to produce a sound similar to that of a sailing ship at sea. Nearby to the north, on the scenic coastal route, is the Coral Life Marine Land, where visitors may see turtles and stingrays; while to the south, on the lower bank of the estuary, is Koorna Crocodile Farm, where the hundreds of freshwater and saltwater crocodiles farmed here can be inspected safely from walkways elevated well above snapping jaw-height! *Population 1920*

GLENORA HISTORICAL COMPLEX This pioneer village near Emu Park is home to the old Glenora slab homestead, and has displays of period machinery and household items.

GRACEMERE ■ 1522

The central Queensland region has an old and well-deserved reputation as Australia's beef cattle heartland.

Tens of thousands of choice stock and hundreds of buyers come to the large saleyards at Gracemere. The first Europeans in the area were the Archer Brothers who took up a run in 1854, which they named 'Gracemere', and on a spit of land jutting onto the bird-rich lagoon they built their homestead. To Charles Archer the locality was 'a perfect paradise'. *Population 3400*

GREAT KEPPEL ISLAND ■ 1523

Great Keppel, the largest island in the Keppel group, is a high or continental island, one of nine hundred or so of varying sizes which occur off the Queensland coast – they are the remnants of mainland hills, ridges or mountains which were isolated gradually when the sea rose six to ten thousand years ago. Like other high islands Great Keppel is hilly and densely forested. A fringing reef protects its white sandy beaches. The resort on its western shore can be reached by ferry or hydrofoil from Rosslyn Bay Boat Harbour, north of Rockhampton. Visitors can observe marine life at an underwater observatory on nearby Middle Island.

KEPPEL GROUP NATIONAL PARK ■ 1524

James Cook reached Keppel Bay and its high islands on 26 May 1770 and described it thus: 'The Main land in this Latitude is tolerable high and Mountainous and the Islands which lay off it are the most of them pretty high and of a small circuit and have more the appearance of barrenness than fertility'.

The islands of the park together display all the usual features of Queensland's tropical continental islands. There is a camping site on North Keppel Island, where in season, visitors can see whales migrating and turtles nesting.

MOUNT HAY ■ 1525

On the fringe of the central Queensland gemfields, Mount Hay, the site of an ancient volcano, is renowned for its 'Thundereggs', 100-million-year-old, usually spherical stones which, when polished, display a great variety of colours. Some have hollows either totally filled with agate or lined with agate with a nest of amethyst, jasper or smoky quartz crystals at the core, and these are most spectacular when sliced across. Fossickers – picks, shovels and buckets are available – can have their 'eggs' cut while they wait.

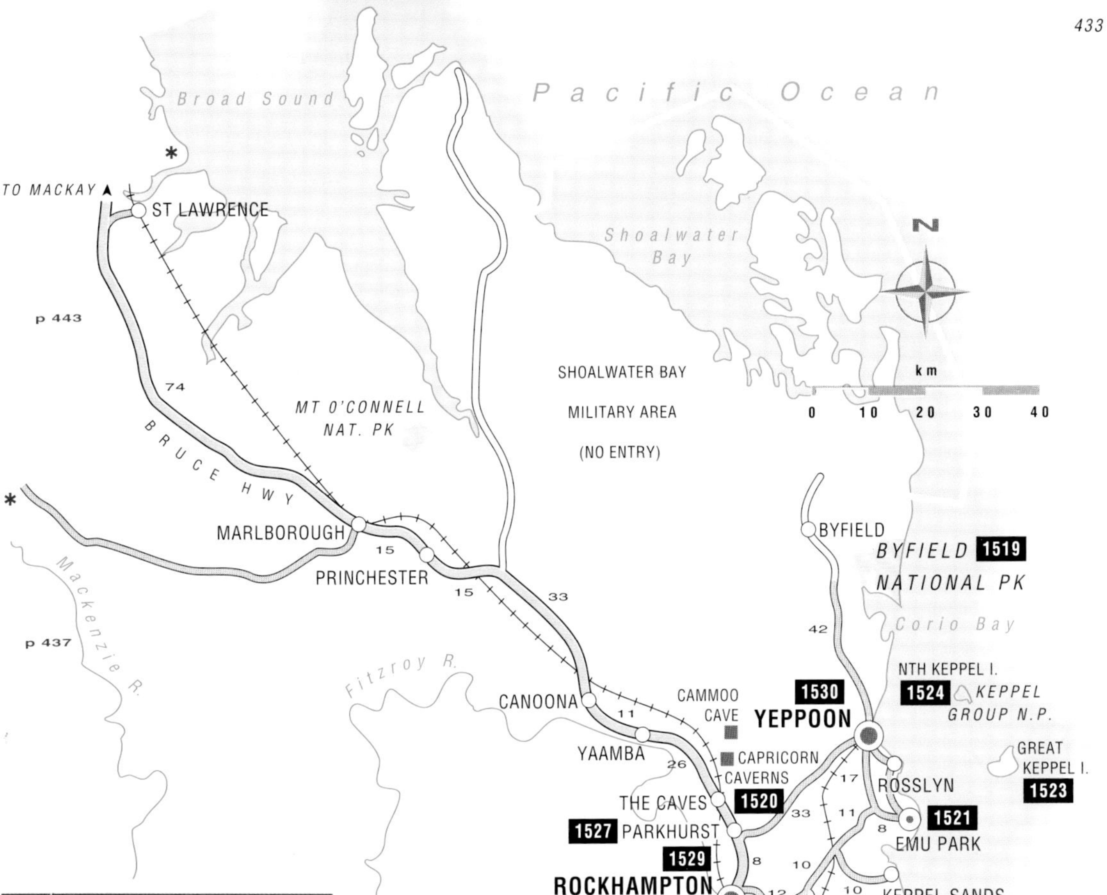

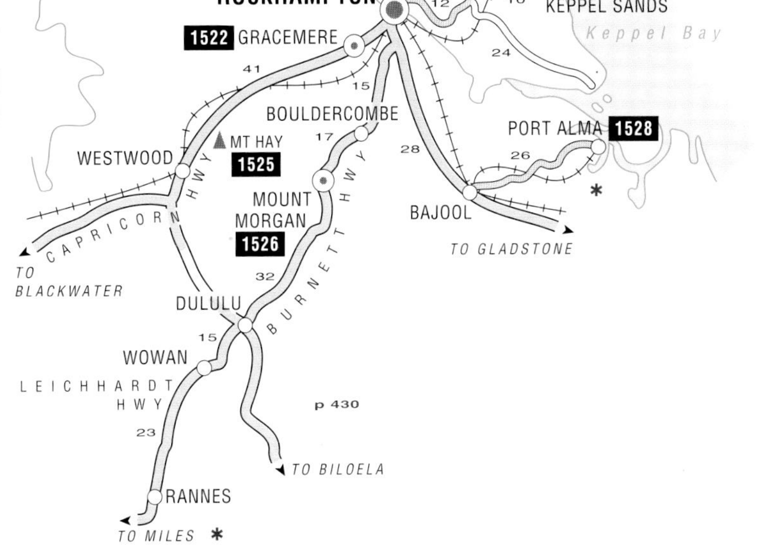

Rockhampton's cattle connection is underlined by the name and bull silhouette on this business house.

MOUNT MORGAN ■ 1526

Where once there was an ironstone mountain there is now a vast open-cut mine more than three hundred metres deep. One of the biggest holes dug by man, its mind-boggling proportions dwarf the township of Mount Morgan. The town was listed in the 1980s as an historical site by both the Australian Heritage Commission and the National Trust of Queensland and has many fine turn-of-the-century buildings, including civic and mining buildings, halls, hotels and churches. The historical museum has plaster casts of dinosaur footprints found in the area.

The Morgan brothers are credited with discovering gold on the mountain in 1882, but there is evidence that a local stockman, William Mackinlay had been quietly working a claim there since 1870. The Mount Morgan company was incorporated into Peko-Wallsend Investments Ltd in 1968. In a century of mining – operations ceased in 1981 – enormous quantities of gold and copper were taken from the mountain, first from shaft mines, then from the open-cut mine. In the twentieth century, the Mount Morgan company invested in coal exploration, which eventually became the major mining operation in the region. The hills surrounding the mine are bare, stripped of their timber to fuel the smelter. Wealth generated by the old mine helped to found the Walter and Eliza Hall Institute for Medical Research in Melbourne and it played a part in the formation of British Petroleum (BP) Company. *Population 2780*

FESTIVALS Golden Mount Festival, April–May.

PARKHURST ■ 1527

Behind the modern Parkhurst Industrial Estate and in dramatic contrast to its utilitarian structures, is the Glenmore Homestead, on the bank of the Fitzroy River. Begun by Samuel Birkbeck in 1858, this site now contains some of the oldest buildings in the Rockhampton district. There is the log hut, a rarity in Australia, which dates from 1859. In 1861, Birkbeck purchased and re-erected a slab cottage, which had been built in 1858 as a public house. Then, in 1862, he had a team of Mexican workmen build an adobe and slate house, completing the complex's architectural variety.

PORT ALMA ■ 1528

Port Alma, off the Bruce Highway from Bajool, is now the service harbour for the city of Rockhampton.

Along the Capricorn coast there is always an island floating dreamily offshore; the hump of Bluff Rock breaks a surfless sea at Rosslyn Bay, near Yeppoon.

The surrounding countryside is dotted with broad salt pans, from which salt is obtained through the evaporation of seawater.

ROCKHAMPTON ■ 1529

Ludwig Leichhardt was the first European to traverse the vast Fitzroy Basin, on his way up to Port Essington in 1844. He found the central river valleys scattered with areas of 'luxuriant grasses and herbs', and studded with 'fine' lagoons. He thought these plains and slopes comparable to the fertile Darling Downs, predicting that they 'would form a most excellent cattle station'.

In 1846, Leichhardt offered the Archer family, with whom he had stayed before beginning his trek, a 'peep behind the curtain' then veiling this part of Queensland. Drawn by dreams of pastoral empire, this remarkable family of nine brothers and assorted wives and children then moved progressively north into central Queensland. They had runs at Eidsvold in 1848; and in the early 1850s Charles and William Archer explored the valleys of the Dawson and Fitzroy rivers. In 1854, the Archers laid claim to the run they called 'Gracemere' (see entry), to the south-west of Rockhampton; dozens of other pastoralists soon followed.

Initially, the squatters ran sheep; but as they came to realise the unsuitability of the environment for these animals, they switched to beef cattle. The introduction and crossbreeding of several hardy species such as Hereford and Zebu, pasture improvement and water conservation measures have seen the Fitzroy Basin develop into the nation's premier beef cattle region, with herds now numbering more than two-and-a-half million.

In 1855, Colin Archer, bringing supplies for 'Gracemere', sailed up the Fitzroy River and unloaded on the site of the present town. This was the highest navigable point of the river – further upstream it is blocked by rocks. Thus began the inland port of Rockhampton. The township was proclaimed in 1857; and with the discovery of gold at nearby Canoona in the following year, the first wave of large-scale European immigration to central Queensland began.

Modern Rockhampton shows a pleasing mixture of colonial and modern architecture. The 'Quay Street' historical precinct preserves a large number of very impressive buildings, among them the city's second customs house – a sandstone edifice with a striking copper dome; the former headquarters of the historic Mount Morgan Gold Mining Company (now occupied by the Australian Broadcasting Corporation); the former Queensland National Bank Building; the former Union Bank of Australia building; and the Criterion Hotel. One block to the south are the imposing post office and supreme court buildings. *Population 55 770*

BOTANICAL GARDENS Proclaimed in 1869 and begun properly in 1872, these fine gardens spread over forty hectares beside the tranquil waters of Murray Lagoon. They contain Australian plants and a large range of exotics, including striking banyan figs and a variety of palms. There is an aviary, a small koala park and an orchid and fern house.

MOUNT ARCHER ENVIRONMENTAL PARK This park, on the north side of the Fitzroy River, within the city's boundaries, has interesting walking tracks. There are good views from the heights of the Berserker Range. The suburb of Frenchville – formerly Frenchman's Creek – at the foot of Mount Archer, commemorates the botanist Anthelme Thozet who established a garden there in the 1860s, which supplied squatters and settlers all over North Queensland with a great variety of plants and seeds. Thozet also planted a number of trees along the river bank at Quay Street, some of which remain.

PILBEAM THEATRE AND ART GALLERY The gallery possesses a good collection of Australian paintings and crafts, while the theatre has regular seasons of Australian and international works.

FESTIVALS Fieldfest, August; Capricana, September.

YEPPOON ■ 1530

For tens of thousands of years, the Yeppoon area was a meeting place for the Aborigines of the Fitzroy Basin. European settlers arrived in the 1870s, and in the 1880s and 1890s, sugarcane was grown here. By the 1930s, Yeppoon had become popular with the people of Rockhampton, and those of the inland, as a seaside resort. Now, it offers extensive holiday and boating facilities; there are attractive coastal walks, and even camel rides! *Population 7540*

FESTIVALS Pineapple Festival, late September.

QUEENSLAND'S TIN & TIMBER ELEGANCE – ACCIDENT OR DESIGN?

THE TIN-AND-TIMBER, high-set, old Queensland house is as identifiably Australian as the Digger's slouch hat, billy tea and the drover's dog. In style and building materials it was a convenient solution to practical problems for it was cheap, relatively quick and easy to erect and was suitable for hot climates.

The neat symmetry of this Townsville house is underlined by the skilled carpentry of the balustrade, entrance steps and fence.

Its main features are those traditionally associated with the Australian farmhouse – a basic bungalow shape with cool, wide verandahs – both doubtless a legacy of the many military men who found their way to Australian shores after service in India – a tin roof, usually in the shape of a low, four-sided, cropped pyramid, and a central corridor which served as a breezeway. But in Queensland were added several distinctive features – the screening off of the verandah to create an indoor–outdoor living area, the extensive use of decoration to enliven the basic simplicity of the design and, perhaps most distinctive of all, the whole was often perched head-high on stumps.

In the early days, timber usually arrived pre-cut and ready for use on site from southern centres as this was more efficient than transporting locally felled and milled timber over rough roads. This practice soon developed into the supply of complete prefabricated homes ready for assembly in remote parts of the north where many townships were semi-permanent, and it was of great advantage to many occupants if buildings could be easily dismantled for reuse at another site.

Tin proved especially versatile and came into its own when it was realised that the rolling machine which turned out corrugated-iron water tanks could be used just as well to produce curved and vaulted roofing iron.

Such were the materials that produced the housing style that is found from Brisbane to Cooktown, in both modest cottages and in grand homesteads. Deep verandahs, protected by wooden latticework or adjustable slatted blinds, cool the interior rooms by blocking off direct sun from the house, and at the same time taking advantage of any breeze. The cool and airy interior spaces created were used for informal living, with areas set aside for cooking, eating and laundering, as well as for relaxing. Cooking was usually done in a detached kitchen at the back of the house to reduce the fire risk. Any window not protected by the verandah usually had its own hooded shade.

In some places, verandahs have been added to verandahs to further protect users from sun and the torrential rains of the wet season. With increasing prosperity, the verandahs became more imposing, with elaborately carved decorative timber work and cast-iron balustrades. The entrance was often surmounted by a decorated triangular pediment – often a feature of the Rockhampton area – and approached by a double staircase. Some buildings had clerestories – a row of windows raised above the roof line and often shaded by wide eaves – to both admit light to the centre of the building and to catch any passing breeze.

Although 'high set' houses are found elsewhere in northern Australia – the first recorded was in 1838 at Port Essington near the present site of Darwin – it is the method of perching the building on tall hardwood stumps that is so peculiar to Queensland. Opinions vary as to whether the original reason for this was to escape the heat of the ground and allow cooling ventilation under the house, to rise above possible floodwaters or to thwart the white ant, whose progress could more easily be detected by exposing its skyward march to the floorboards. In any case a cool and useful understorey was created which was often also enclosed with lattice or slats to provide extra living or storage space.

The decoration that gives the old 'Queenslander' its charm is largely handcrafted to the personal caprice of the owner or the artisan - more likely the latter. Fretted balustrades, intricately carved pediment inserts, bargeboards and the infills of wooden lattices and slats give each house an individual character. Ornamentation extends to the roof, with many embellished with elaborate pressed metal ridge caps and crowned with fanciful ventilators. Until the 1940s, it was not usual to paint timber houses in Queensland, and despite the exhortations of paint manufacturers, some buildings remain unpainted to this day. □

Attention to detail can transform a weatherboard house into a tin-and-timber villa; despite their practical purpose, the ventilator, railing and awnings shown here have been given an extra, decorative dimension by a craftsman's attention.

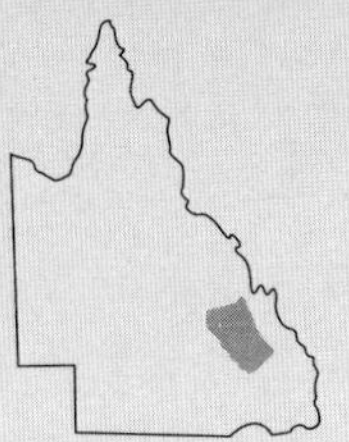

Blackwater & Emerald

With the bright yellow of harvested sunflowers, the blues and greens of sapphires, the white foam of spectacular waterfalls over bright green, moss-covered rocks and the rich blackness of coal, the physically colourful present of this inland region has emerged from an equally colourful past.

ANAKIE ■ 1531

Local Aborigines apparently used sapphires and a variety of other gemstones found around Anakie for bartering and Europeans knew of its existence from the 1870s, but it was not until the 1890s, after goldminers discovered economic quantities of sapphires that the field became commercially productive. Although the name Anakie comes from an Aboriginal word meaning 'twin peaks', the name is now synonymous with the world's largest sapphire field. Most of the sapphires are sent to Thailand for cutting. The Star of Queensland – the best black star sapphire in the world – was discovered at Anakie in 1935. It was cut as the Presidents' Heads Sapphire, and is kept at the Smithsonian Institution in Washington.

FESTIVALS Gemfest, August.

BLACKDOWN TABLELAND NATIONAL PARK ■ 1532

In the Blackdown Tableland, three ranges – Dawson Range, Expedition Range and Shotover Range – converge. The sandstone escarpment, rising to a height of 950 metres, has been folded and eroded to produce a series of gorges, overhangs and cliff faces over which tumble spectacular waterfalls.

This geologically old region with some superb Aboriginal stencil paintings was first proposed as a national park in the 1930s but the 23 800-hectare park was not finally gazetted until 1982. Within the park are some isolated and unique species of vegetation such as the striking blackdown stringybark, with its large bluish leaves and spherical seed capsules, and two species of wattle found nowhere else. Not all specimens of these species are protected within the park, which shares the tableland with a large state forest.

Some unique insects are also to be found within the park (see box).

BLACKWATER ■ 1533

From the late nineteenth century, Blackwater was a railway siding for a district noted for its beef cattle. The name Blackwater refers to the blackness of the sand in a nearby creek or to the blackness of the vegetation-stained water in local waterholes. It is, however, another blackness that catapulted Blackwater, in the late 1960s, from a quiet village with twenty-five people into a bustling town – the blackness of coal.

Although Ludwig Leichhardt first discovered coal in this region in 1844–45, early and sporadic attempts at mining were unsuccessful. The discovery of a seven-metre-thick coal seam, some twenty kilometres south-west of Blackwater in 1962, at what is now the Blackwater Mine (see sub-entry), sparked renewed interest and by the late 1960s three mining companies were operating in the vicinity. Branch lines from the mine sites to the railway siding at Blackwater gave direct access to the port facilities and power station at Gladstone.

There are a number of reminders of the early pioneering days around the town, from the original 1877 railway station, now used for arts and crafts, to the display of early mining equipment at the airport.

One of Australia's largest permanent displays of international flags flies in a local park, representing the workers of thirty-seven nationalities who pioneered the coal industry in and around the town. *Population 6760*

BLACKWATER MINE Opened by the United States Utah Development Company, this open-cut mine was the first of the post-1960s mines to be established south of Blackwater. The mining method used involves the removal of the so-called 'overburden' of sedimentary layers above the coal seam by drilling and the use of explosives followed by the use of a huge 'walking' dragline to extract the coal from the exposed seam. Coking coal, exported to Japan, Chile and a number of European countries for iron and steel mills and steaming coal for power generation are produced at the mine.

BLUFF ■ 1534

A few kilometres east of Blackwater, on the Capricorn Highway, Bluff is a mining village where most of the

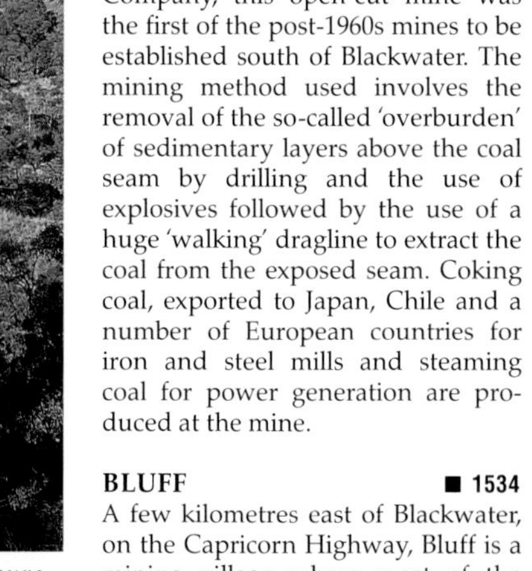

Mount Zamia – which lends its name to the park in which it stands – presents a raw, sandstone face to Springsure.

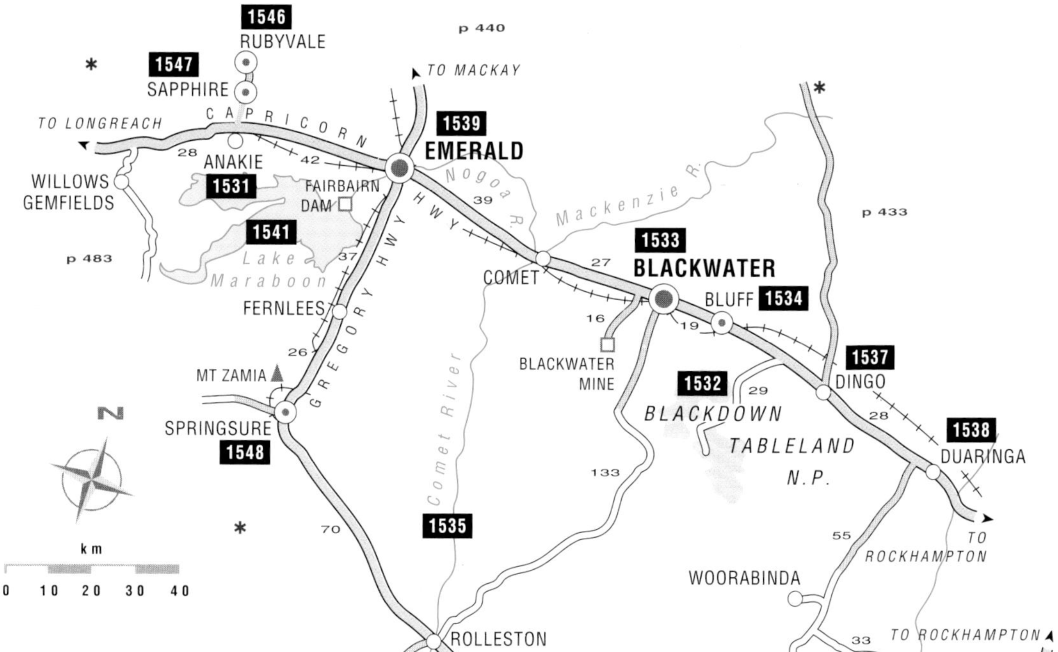

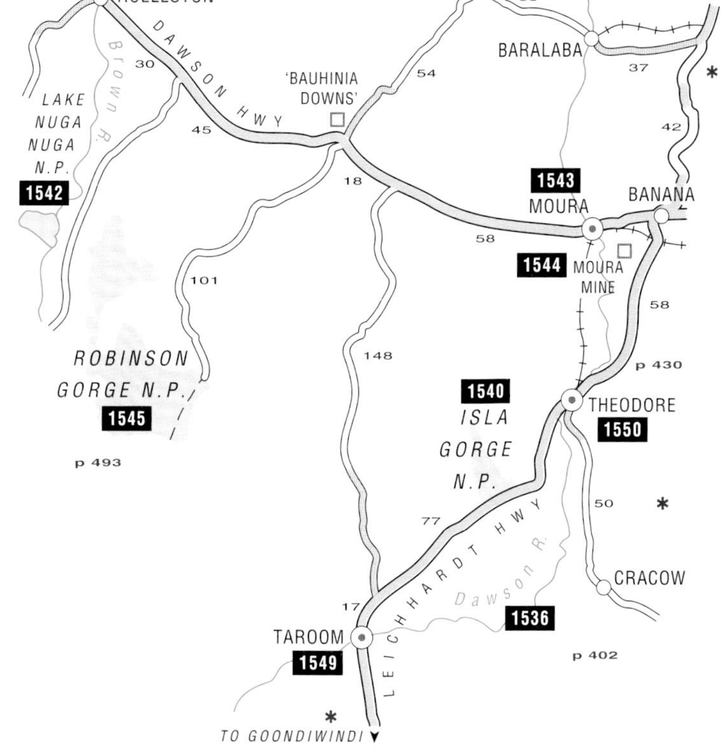

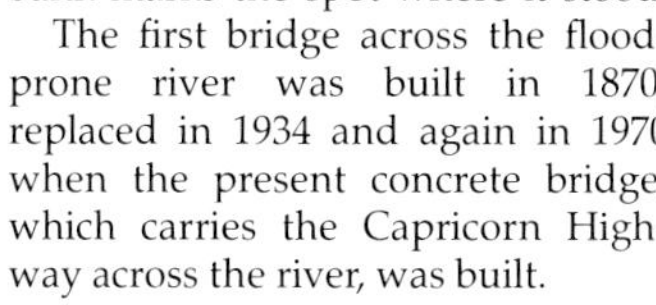

p 440
p 433
p 483
p 430
p 493
p 402

population earn their living, directly or indirectly, from the Blackwater mines. The Bluff Hotel has had twenty-five licensees since it was built in 1916, the high turnover of owners possibly a result of the stop-start nature of mining, which dates back to the early twentieth century.

The village sits at the foot of a hill once known as Arthur's Bluff and a truncated form of this name was adopted for the town.

COMET RIVER ■ **1535**

Rising as the Brown River, the short section of the river from Rolleston to where it joins the Mackenzie River, was given the name Comet River by Ludwig Leichhardt who spotted a comet while camping on its banks in 1844. Although not as famous as the 'Dig Tree' of Burke and Wills, a coolabah tree on the banks of the Comet was marked with the same instruction by Leichhardt – the tree itself is now in the Queensland Museum but a plaque on the river-bank marks the spot where it stood.

The first bridge across the flood-prone river was built in 1870, replaced in 1934 and again in 1970 when the present concrete bridge, which carries the Capricorn Highway across the river, was built.

DAWSON RIVER ■ **1536**

When Ludwig Leichhardt's party arrived at the Dawson River in 1844, they caught crayfish, jewfish and eels to supplement their paltry diet but the plants on the riverbanks which they hoped might prevent scurvy also caused diarrhoea.

The Dawson River, named after one of Leichhardt's supporters from Sydney, rises near Carnarvon Gorge, flows east for a short distance then heads north to join the Mackenzie and Fitzroy rivers near Duaringa (see entry). On its journey, the river passes through the cattle-grazing lands, crops and coalmining area on which the region's economy is based.

The tidy stacks of cotton in a field of bare stalks near Emerald are a result of irrigation from Lake Maraboon – and the harvester's neat efficiency.

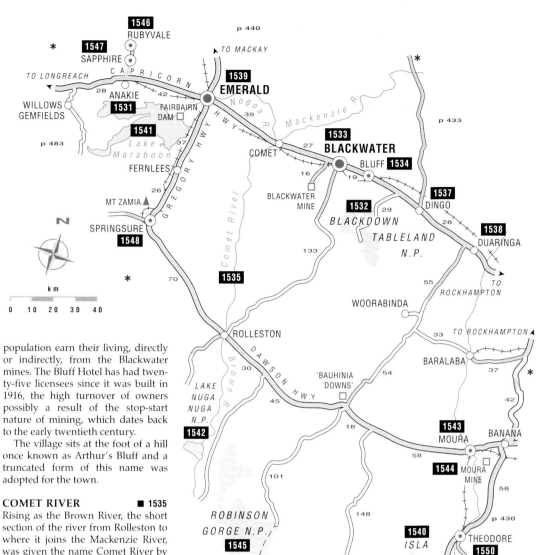

The elegantly Victorian portals of Emerald Station have welcomed passengers for almost 100 years.

The river has flooded dramatically on many occasions, most notably in 1875 when the backing up of the waters at the river's junction with the Mackenzie River caused the Dawson River to change direction and flow upstream for a number of days. In the 1920s, as part of an irrigation scheme, weirs were built on the Dawson River, including structures at Theodore and Moura (see entries), the two major towns on the river. The scheme supplies water for dairying and crops in the Dawson Valley.

DINGO ■ **1537**

The author Thea Astley, describing the distinctive features of Queensland, once wrote that 'Queensland means living in townships called Dingo and Banana and Gunpowder'. Dingo and Banana are near neighbours and Dingo, at least, did try to change its name in the 1930s but neither Remo, nor Lorraine nor Springton received sufficient votes so Dingo it remained.

This sawmilling town has, however, another claim to fame as the only remaining habitat of the bridled nail-tail wallaby (see box).

DUARINGA ■ **1538**

Duaringa was founded in 1875 as a base camp for workers building the railway west from Rockhampton. As the gangs moved on, it took on the responsibilities of a service centre for the surrounding beef-cattle district and a remnant preserved from that era is a section of the original timber slab hotel built here in the 1880s.

Since the 1890s, Duaringa has also had a sawmill, the original mill being built by James Norton who also owned a eucalyptus oil works in the town. Timber from the state forest on the Blackdown Tableland is still brought to Duaringa for sawing.

The rather obscure name possibly derives from 'djuaringe', 'to turn around' or is a gross corruption of 'd'wurra d'nanjie', 'meeting place of

Lake Nuga Nuga – with its floating beds of waterlilies which modestly close their petals at sundown – softens the harshness of the Central Highlands.

swamp oaks' although those who favour a more European origin say the original railway station was called 'Dear Inga's' after a popular resident, Inga Anderson, who later married the pioneer Moses Wafer.

EMERALD ■ 1539

Although in the centre of a gemfields district Emerald has nothing to do with the precious green stones. The bright green of new grass after fire and then a few days of rain led P.F. McDonald to name his 1860 station 'Emerald Downs'. Although the settlement that grew up on part of the station was initially a copper and goldmining town, Emerald's development was boosted in the late 1870s when it became the vital rail junction for the Central Highlands with three lines passing through the town.

The town's timber railway station (1900) has a romantic iron-lace portico and the retention of it in an undamaged state is fairly miraculous since a series of four devastating fires – 1936, 1940, 1954 and 1968 – ravaged most of the town's remaining old buildings. The 250-million-year-old fossilised tree, now standing outside the town hall was also spared, largely because it was safely buried until 1979, when it was unearthed during bridge building for the new Gregory Mine (see *Moranbah & Dysart*).

In the late 1940s, Emerald was one of the towns mooted as the capital for the proposed breakaway state of Capricornia with a substantial number of the 10 000 signatories to the petition favouring Emerald because of its prime position on road and rail. The Emerald Irrigation Scheme, based on water from Lake Maraboon (see entry), supplies water not only for wheat, sorghum, safflower, sunflower and cotton – the latter processed in the town's cotton gin – but also for local mining activities. *Population 6560*

ISLA GORGE NATIONAL PARK ■ 1540

The soft sandstone of this 7800-hectare national park has been eroded by creeks into a complex of gorges, sculptured arches, overhangs – sometimes with Aboriginal paintings – peaks and monoliths, cliffs and caves which often contain large bat colonies. Isla Gorge Lookout offers the best views of the park and its unusual structures, but the steep cliffs down to Isla Creek and the loose rubble on more gentle slopes, make access to the gorge floor difficult. Tracks are few and most of the streams are intermittent so stout boots and water supplies are vital. Vegetation is mainly eucalypt forest with some brigalow and bottle trees.

The park was first gazetted in 1964 and extended in 1990 to include the remains of a hand-paved road built in 1860 for transporting wool to the central Queensland coast and for the constant traffic of Cobb & Co. coaches. The road's stormwater culverts, which must have involved many hours of labour, have protected this section of the road for 130 years from erosion by floodwaters.

LAKE MARABOON ■ 1541

Fifteen kilometres upstream from Emerald (see entry) on the Nogoa River, sits Lake Maraboon, one of Queensland's largest water storages. The lake covers an area of 15 000 hectares and supplies one-and-a-half million megalitres of water, through two main irrigation channels, for the Emerald Irrigation Scheme.

The dam was completed in 1972, about twenty years after a report estimated that irrigation in the area would enable local farmers to grow pasture fodder crops and increase the region's revenue by 1000 per cent! There was some controversy over naming the reservoir and a compromise was eventually reached. The earth and rockfill dam wall was officially named Fairbairn Dam in recognition of David Fairbairn, federal Minister of National Development but the water impounded by it was named Lake Maraboon from an Aboriginal word said to mean 'where the black ducks fly'.

The beautiful setting of Lake Maraboon, with its backdrop of mountains and parks on its shore, make it popular for recreation, although it has a darker side to its history. The waters of the dam flooded part of 'Cullin-la-Ringo' station where nineteen Europeans were killed by Aborigines in 1861 – the tragic climax of a decade of abuse and indignities suffered by the Aboriginal people. In the subsequent white retribution, as many Aborigines died. A cairn on the lake shore commemorates the nineteen whose mass grave now lies under water.

LAKE NUGA NUGA NATIONAL PARK ■ 1542

Lake Nuga Nuga has long had a reputation among locals – and intrepid explorers – as an unspoilt sanctuary for water birds, especially black swans and pelicans. The lake and surrounding area, which contains some significant Aboriginal sites, were formally gazetted as a 2250-hectare national park in 1991.

Despite the thousands of dead trees peering up above the shallow water, Lake Nuga Nuga is not a man-made lake that flooded the forest floor but a natural lake fed by the Brown River (see entry).

MOURA ■ 1543

In 1936, there was only a shed, some trucking yards, and bush tracks 'rough enough to break a snake's back' at the railway siding at Moura. In that year, land on two Dawson Valley runs – 'Moura' and 'Kianga' – was resumed for closer settlement. Prickly pear leases, at less than one cent an acre, were cheaper than perpetual leases but their lease terms included clearing all the prickly pear within one year...and keeping it cleared thereafter. The early leaseholders used the railway line as a road in wet weather until passable roads were built. Cotton was the first cash crop but soon dairying, wheat and cattle grazing were added, especially after the release of irrigated blocks of land in the 1950s.

In 1962, the first two mines opened in the Moura–Kianga coalfield, the first field in the rich Bowen Basin to be exploited commercially, but operations soon concentrated on the Moura Mine (see entry). With the boost that came from mining activities, and despite its youth, Moura has emerged as a major centre and as the headquarters of Banana Shire. *Population 2370*

FESTIVALS Coal and Country Festival, August.

MOURA MINE ■ 1544

Both open-cut and underground mining have been conducted at Moura Mine, ten kilometres east of the town, since operations were begun by Thiess Peabody, a joint United States–Australian company formed in 1962. It was, however, the Japanese interest and investment that saw Moura take over from the earlier Kianga mine, Moura coal being more suitable for Japanese steel mill requirements. A pumping station brought water by pipeline from the Dawson River to the mine's washing plant. Ten kilometres of railway line connected the mine to Moura and what was at the time, the world's largest 'walking' dragline, with a 204-tonne bucket, made Moura a technological showpiece. Primitive housing conditions, however, led to the mine's first strike before living standards were raised.

ROBINSON GORGE NATIONAL PARK ■ 1545

The twelve-kilometre-long Robinson Gorge is the major attraction of this rugged, and relatively inaccessible, national park. Robinson Creek, a tributary of the Dawson River, has carved the gorge which varies in width from a few metres to several kilometres and passes between cliffs up to ninety metres high. The laconically named Cattle Dip is one of the more spectacular water holes in the gorge – 280 metres long and surrounded by totally sheer walls.

Vegetation varies from the ferns, mosses and cabbage palms of the numerous creeks which have cut side gorges in the main Robinson Gorge to the more resilient eucalypts of the hot, drier plateau regions. The fibrous bark of the budgeroo (*Lysicarpus angustifolius*) was used for burial cylinders and its flowers as a source of nectar by the Aborigines, evidence of whose occupation can be found in painting and burial sites within the park. There is also evidence of the oil drilling that was conducted in the park in the 1960s with land cleared for an airstrip and an oil drilling site.

Robinson Gorge National Park, which sits astride the Expedition Range, now covers 8900 hectares and is the second largest conserved area in the Central Highlands.

RUBYVALE ■ **1546**

Less than twenty kilometres north of Anakie, is another gemfields town – Rubyvale – where the prized black sapphire may be found.

As the world market for sapphires has waxed and waned, so has the population of Rubyvale where professional miners dig deep shafts, amateur fossickers use pick, shovel and sieve in shallower sapphire-bearing ground and less energetic tourists explore an underground sapphire mine. *Population 730*

SAPPHIRE ■ **1547**

Like Rubyvale (see entry), Sapphire is one of the two working sapphire-mining areas north of Anakie, which since the beginning of the century have produced most of Queensland's, and almost thirty per cent of the world's, sapphires. The yellow, blue and green sapphires were marketed by the government until the formation, in the 1930s, of the Rubyvale and Sapphire Gem Miners' Association, which took over the marketing. The latest moves in what is notably an up-and-down industry, are to cut the sapphires in Australia rather than send them to Thailand for processing.

Large-scale open-cut mining is still carried on at Sapphire and tourists may fossick in the unusually shallow washes dotted around the town – most are less than one metre deep. *Population 720*

SPRINGSURE ■ **1548**

Springsure is not only the Central Highlands' oldest settlement but has possibly the most attractive setting.

There were two shepherds' huts in what is now the town, as early as 1854 and the settlement developed as bullock waggons, carrying wool to the coast and produce from it, used Springsure as a stopping point. A slab-hut homestead, two historical museums and the nearby Rainworth Fort (see sub-entry) are constant reminders of these early days when sheep and wool reigned supreme.

Mount Zamia provides a dramatic backdrop to the town with its prehistoric-looking macrozamia palms providing a sharp contrast to the sunflower crops in the fields below. In a hollow near the top of Mount Zamia is the Virgin Rock, although the natural formation that was said to closely resemble the outline of the Virgin Mary and child has been eroded long ago and the likeness today is less obvious.

Springsure is now a centre for grain and beef; the volcanic opal found near the town is not of commercial value...but the permanent spring, which trickles down Mount Zamia flows as constantly as ever. *Population 730*

RAINWORTH FORT Built of adobe and basalt collected from the foot of the nearby mountains and using lime burned on the premises, the store-cum-fort was constructed on Burnside Station in 1861, the year after the massacre at Cullin-la-Ringo Station (see Lake Maraboon). The building, the only old stone building in the region, has been restored and other historic buildings have been moved and re-erected nearby to form an historic precinct.

FESTIVALS Springtime Festival, late October.

TAROOM ■ **1549**

The Aborigines ate the fruit and used the perfume from the taroom – 'wild lime tree' – but it is a coolabah tree for which Taroom is better known. When Ludwig Leichhardt carved 'L.L. 1844' in the tree, he could have had no idea that the tree was on the future main street of Taroom.

The early settlers, including the Fraser family who were killed by Aborigines in 1857 at nearby Hornet Bank Homestead, were sheep farmers. In retribution for the eleven Europeans massacred, 300 Aborigines were killed, indiscriminantly, leading to the decimation and dispersal of the local Jiman people and some of their allies. The homestead still stands but sheep have given way to beef cattle, wheat and sorghum, which now support this small town on the Dawson River. *Population 700*

FESTIVALS Flower Show and Festival, August.

THEODORE ■ **1550**

Theodore sits at the junction of Castle Creek and the Dawson River. Although the settlement was originally named Castle Creek, its position as one of the few towns on the Dawson River was ultimately to prove more relevant.

During the Great Depression, weirs were built near the town as part of the Dawson Valley Irrigation Scheme. The guarantee of work and the promise of prosperity that they brought led to the town of Castle Creek being renamed Theodore after E.G. Theodore, the Premier of Queensland (1919–25). *Population 500*

IN THE NICK OF TIME, HOMES FOR THE NAIL-TAILS & THE HAIRY-NOSES

WHEN A grazier caught an unusual wallaby while fencing a property near Dingo in 1973, the only means he had to identify the animal was an article in a women's magazine. The Queensland National Parks and Wildlife Service, with access to better scientific references, confirmed his tentative identification of the animal as a rare bridled nail-tail wallaby.

Although it had once been relatively common in many parts of New South Wales and southern and central Queensland, there had been no sightings of the wallaby since 1937 and the bridled nail-tail was thought to be extinct.

This medium-sized wallaby has a black-tipped tail with a distinctive horny spur, and two stripes – one white and one black – running fron the top of its head which give the animal its name. The small colony that was found around Dingo was living on two properties where brigalow scrub had survived despite extensive clearing since the 1880s, including a massive local clearance of four-and-a-half million hectares in the 1960s. The brigalow on both properties is now protected to secure a habitat for the wallaby.

In the neighbouring region of Moranbah & Dysart, the habitat of an even more endangered species is now protected within Epping Forest National Park. Charles, Wilfred and Harry Barnard, well-known local zoologists were commissioned by the Queensland government in 1937 to capture specimens of wombats whose tracks had been seen but who had never been sighted in the area. The specimen they captured was soft and furry right to the end of its blunt nose and was slightly smaller than the other species held by the Queensland Museum. The northern hairy-nosed wombat is one of the world's most endangered mammals; the world's last remaining colony at Epping Forest numbers around fifty animals and they are strenuously protected.

In Blackdown Tableland National Park, the unique species are rather smaller. The park is the only place in the world that plays host to the underground-dwelling, cricket-like insect commonly known as the 'dingo monster' (top left) and two as yet unnamed species of cicada. □

The clearing of bushland for agriculture has forced the hairy-nosed wombat and the nail-tail wallaby to retreat into isolated pockets of their former habitats.

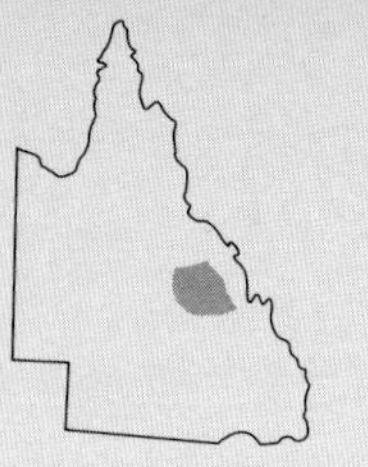

Moranbah & Dysart

In tropical climes, just above the Tropic of Capricorn, miners' helmets and hard hats are now more common than drovers' hats. On the land once devoted to cattle grazing and farming, men are delving deep below the old brigalow country to extract the rich, untapped coal seams of the downs.

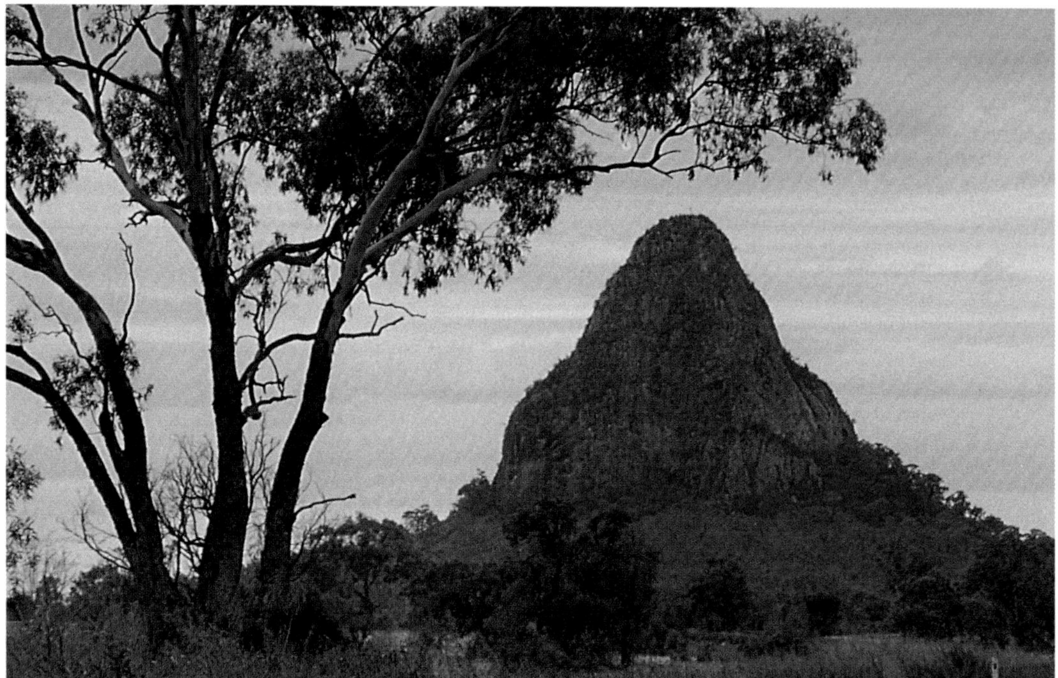

Jagged Wolfang Peak, in the park of the same name, was named by an early selector for its dog's tooth shape.

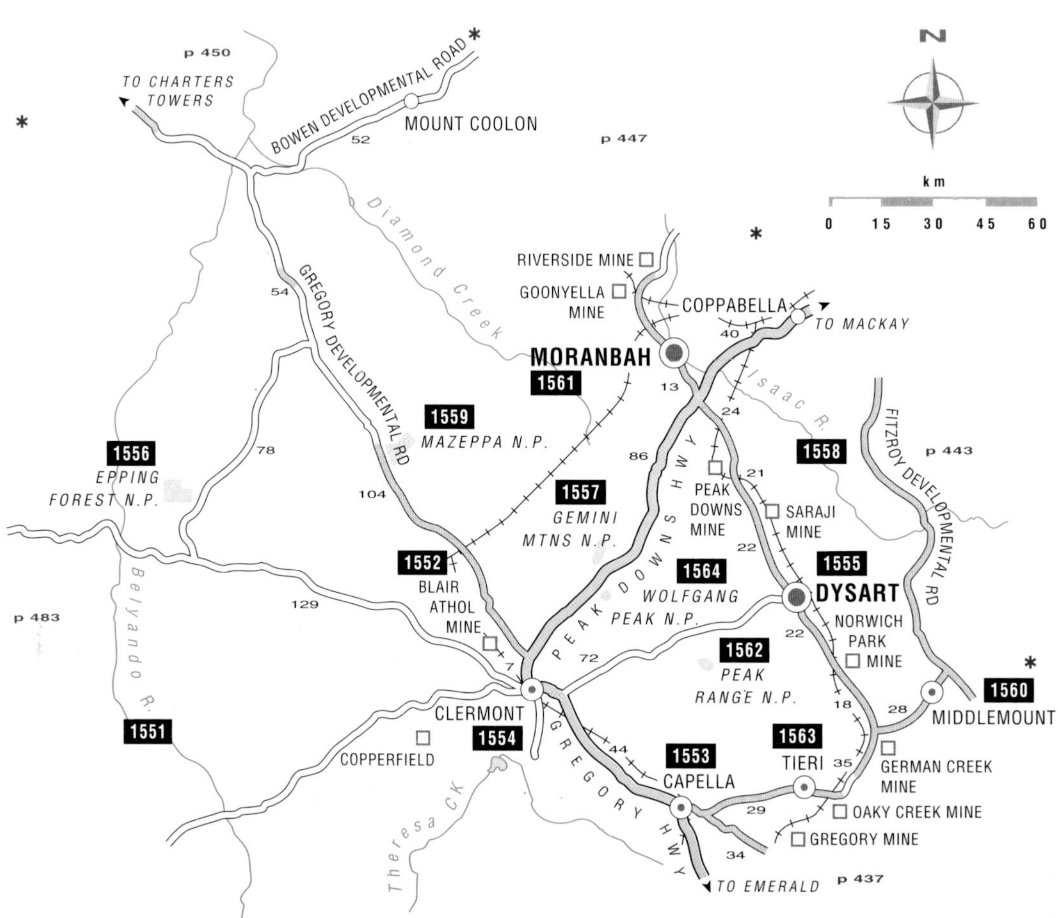

BELYANDO RIVER ■ 1551

One of the four major rivers draining the northern slopes of Queensland's Central Highlands, the Belyando rises in the Drummond Ranges and flows in a generally northerly direction to join the Suttor River and flow with it into the Burdekin. There are no towns, or even small townships on the river, which passes through sparsely populated high country and isolated properties.

The first bridge built across the Belyando River stood on huge ironbark piles, which had taken many weeks to find and fell in the Dawson Ranges. The river is now bridged by the Capricorn Highway and the railway line parallel to it.

BLAIR ATHOL MINE ■ 1552

When coal was discovered at Blair Athol in 1864, its remoteness meant that it lay ignored for another twenty-six years. Coal has been mined, more or less continuously at Blair Athol since 1890, making it the earliest of the mines in the Bowen Basin to start operating. The age of the coal seam, in peat bogs below prehistoric sedimentary layers, is similar to others in the basin.

The 'Big Seam' at Blair Athol Mine – a thirty-metre-thick seam of high-grade steaming coal – is the biggest such seam in the world. But world demand for such high-grade steaming coal remained low until the oil crisis of the 1970s and the output from Blair Athol was used primarily in local electricity generation and in the cement industry. In 1984, the first coal was exported from the open-cut Blair Athol Mine to Japan and the 270 million tonnes of reserves can now be fully exploited for this market.

CAPELLA ■ 1553

Named after the brightest star in the Auriga constellation, Capella was originally a coach stop on the route from the gold and copper mines at Clermont (see entry) to the coast. By the time the railway line reached Capella in 1882, the small settlement already had three pubs, three stores and a butcher's shop catering to the railway workers.

The town has long been a local centre for a farming and grazing district but, since 1979, Capella has become a residential and service centre for the nearby Gregory Mine from which coking coal is railed to Gladstone for export. With even more coal reserves to the south-west of the town, Capella's importance as a mining centre is likely to increase. *Population 870*

CLERMONT ■ 1554

Clermont is the oldest inland settlement in tropical Queensland. First settled in 1854 by a squatter, Jeremiah Rolfe, the town was originally known as Hood's Lagoon but, when surveyed in 1864, was renamed Clermont after Clermont-Ferrand in France, the birthplace of a pioneer and future state member of parliament, Oscar de Satge.

In 1861, a shepherd by the name of Sweeney discovered gold around Hood's Lagoon and, with the discovery of copper at nearby Copperfield, the twin frontier towns boomed. In 1867, the escorts of a load of gold bound for Rockhampton were murdered, not by bushrangers armed with guns but by the local gold commissioner armed with poison – he was later hanged for his crime.

With a major flood devastating the town in 1870 and the discovery of gold near Rockhampton, the goldfield lost much of its attraction although there was still some gold-mining activity as late as 1888 when Chinese miners were evicted from the field as the result of what was described diplomatically as 'trouble'. The 1870 flood was followed by an even worse flood in 1916 in which sixty-two people drowned. After two such floods of the Wolfang and Sandy creeks, the town was moved to higher ground. The traction engine which hauled homes, shops, the primary school and even a two-storey hotel to safer ground is on display in a local park.

By the time that the nearby Blair Athol coalfield was producing commercial quantities of coal, Clermont had already lived a number of lives. After its beginnings as a gold town, it became in turn, a centre for pastoral industry and the expanded coal industry. *Population 2730*

COPPERFIELD In 1862, a ten-metre high 'wall' of solid copper was found at Copperfield, six kilometres south-west of Clermont. Queensland's first copper mine attracted a population of almost 3000 and was declared a municipality in 1872. Within ten years, the town was dead and now some rusty machinery, a cemetery, a boarded-up shop and one solitary chimney are all that remain from those boom days.

DYSART ■ 1555

Dysart, built as a mining town by the BHP-Utah consortium in the early 1970s, was named after one of Scotland's earliest mining towns, which dates back to 1424. Built to service the Saraji Mine, north of the town, which has produced high-grade coking coal since 1975 and the Norwich Mine, to the south, which opened in 1979 and produces lower fluidity coking coal, this company town was carved out of the scrub on a section of what had been 'Tay Glen' cattle station. *Population 3920*

EPPING FOREST NATIONAL PARK ■ 1556

This national park was gazetted in 1971 to protect the last remaining group of northern hairy-nosed wombats, whose existence was known from the late 1930s (see *Blackwater & Emerald*). The flat and well-drained, sandy soil in the park is ideal for the wombats to dig their burrows.

The park, now expanded to cover an area of 3160 hectares around the wombat colony, was fenced in 1980 to exclude cattle from encroaching on the area. Human beings are also excluded from the park unless they are engaged in scientific research.

GEMINI MOUNTAINS NATIONAL PARK ■ 1557

Mount Castor and Mount Pollux, the twin volcanic peaks within Gemini Mountains National Park, rise above the surrounding plains to a height of 678 metres. The 787-hectare park, formerly part of Peak Range National Park (see entry) is of scenic and geological value. There are few facilities in the park so only well-equipped visitors wander among the sparse narrow-leaved ironbark and coolabah trees that vegetate the peaks.

ISAAC RIVER ■ 1558

Named by Ludwig Leichhardt in 1845 after a Darling Downs squatter, Frederick Isaac, the river held some painful memories for Leichhardt. Not only did he suffer lumbago while camping in the dry river bed but a threat to withold rations from his Aboriginal guide Charley Fisher for disobedience resulted in a punch in the mouth and two loose teeth for the German-born explorer!

The river, rising in the Denham Range, flows 300 kilometres through historic cattle and timber country to meet with the Mackenzie River west of Marlborough.

MAZEPPA NATIONAL PARK ■ 1559

This park, encompassing more than 4000 hectares of flat scrub on either side of Mazeppa Creek, was gazetted in 1972. The scrub contains not only brigalow, which before the extensive government-supported clearing during the 1960s covered much of the region, but also sandalwood, currant bush, Brown's box and gidgee. The gidgee is also known as stinking wattle because of the bad smell it gives off before rain.

MIDDLEMOUNT ■ 1560

Built in 1980, by the consortium CapCoal to service their German Creek mine, Middlemount sits on a former cattle run on Cockatoo Creek. The town, like the older and larger mining towns of Dysart and Moranbah (see entries), is totally self-contained but, unusually for this area where open-cut mines are the norm, both open-cut and underground mining are carried out at the town's German Creek Mine. *Population 2610*

MORANBAH ■ 1561

Equidistant from the two mines it was built to serve, the town of Moranbah was officially opened in 1971 when the first 400 mineworkers and their families moved in. Initial plans were for a self-contained township of 2500 people but, within five years, the populations had reached 4000 and the town had overtaken the older town of Clermont (see entry) as the major centre of population.

The new town does have one indirect link with an important historical event. The superb black charger ridden by King George V at the funeral of his father King Edward VII was bred at nearby 'Grosvenor Downs' and on what had been part of the old 'Moranbah' run. *Population 6530*

GOONYELLA, PEAK DOWNS AND RIVERSIDE MINES The establishment of the Goonyella Mine in 1971 and the Peak Downs Mine a year later were the catalysts for the building of Moranbah while the Riverside Mine is much newer having gone into production in 1984. The coking coal produced at the three mines is railed to Hay Point, south of Mackay, Australia's major coal-exporting port.

PEAK RANGE NATIONAL PARK ■ 1562

When Ludwig Leichhardt first saw the volcanic peaks of Peak Range in 1845, he was 'delighted and inspired' by the 'range of noble peaks', which were formed by volcanic action thirty-five million years ago.

A fragmented park enclosing most of the peaks was proclaimed in the early 1980s. In 1990, two sections of the park – Gemini Mountains and Wolfang Peak (see entries) became national parks in their own right and Peak Range National Park is now confined to the 784 hectares around the inaccessible Eastern Peak.

TIERI ■ 1563

Established in 1984 by Mt Isa Mines to house employees at their Oaky Creek Coal Mine, Tieri is one of only two major towns in the Peak Downs Shire and one of the newest towns in Queensland. The mine for which it was built exports two-and-a-half million tonnes of coal annually to steel mills overseas. *Population 1980*

WOLFANG PEAK NATIONAL PARK ■ 1564

Wolfang Peak proper is highly visible as it rises steeply from the surrounding plain of this 1990 national park at the side of the Peak Downs Highway. The park is popular with climbers and the views of the Peak Range and the cultivated plains from the top of Wolfang Peak are worth the climb. A cave within the park supports a large bat colony.

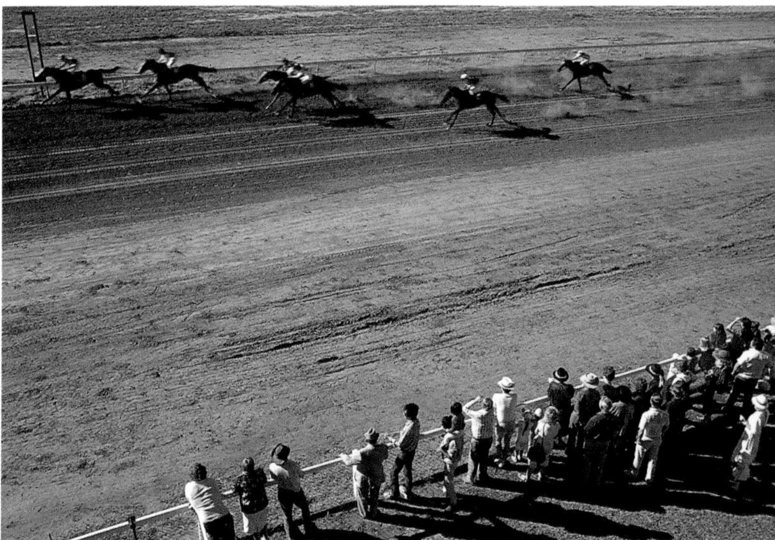

Runners have flashed past the winning post at Clermont's racecourse for eighty years – except when it was being used as a light-plane aerodrome.

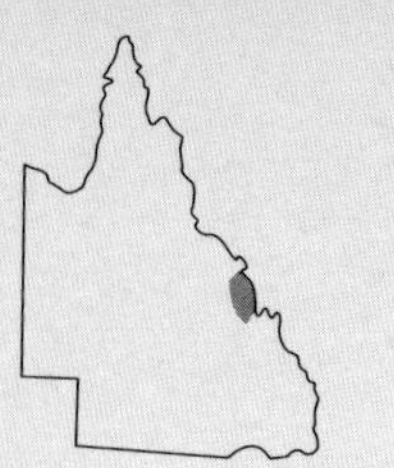

Mackay & Sarina

This region, where the rainforest reaches right down to the sea, likes to be known as the 'Hibiscus Coast'. Out to sea, holiday resorts nestle in sandy coves on islands little changed since Captain Cook picked his way through them in 1770.

BAKERS CREEK ■ 1565
Bakers Creek is named after Mackay's first police magistrate, J.T. Baker. Once the centre of a cane-growing district, an abattoir opened here in 1965 to process beef cattle from the surrounding district. It has an export licence and sends meat, offal, hides, tallow and meat meal through Mackay to markets in Japan, the United States, Canada, Sweden and Italy. *Population 670*

BLACKS BEACH ■ 1566
The first European use of this area was as a holiday beach for sugar plantation owners, onwards from the late 1870s. By the early twentieth century, the row of beach houses was surrounded by sugar fields, which stretched to the water's edge. Development of the town began in the early 1970s. The long, sandy stretches of Blacks Beach are popular with local people – many residents work in Mackay, only twenty minutes' drive away – and visitors alike. The beach was named for M.H. Black, the local member of state parliament in the 1880s and 1890s. *Population 630*

BUCASIA ■ 1567
This resort township built along a gently curved beach is approached through canefields and pineapple and paw paw plantations. Originally named Seaview, it became Bucasia in 1938, in recognition of Father Pierre Bucas who, showing a concern unusual for the time, helped to establish Marara – an orphanage for Aboriginal children – here in 1874. *Population 2010*

CAPE HILLSBOROUGH NATIONAL PARK ■ 1568
On a promontory to the north of Mackay, this park preserves rainforest, cave formations and striking rock outcrops. Its main headland is dominated by a steep-walled rock mass which rises to almost 300 metres. The long narrow beaches which wind round the shore can be walked at low tide and a series of tracks lead through dunes and mangroves, open eucalypt forest and rainforest to lookout points. Big brush turkeys are common around picnic areas and brush-tailed rock wallabies and sugar gliders can often be seen at night.

DIPPERU NATIONAL PARK ■ 1569
This 11 000-hectare reserve, about 100 kilometres south-west of Mackay, was created to preserve a pristine area of brigalow scrub and can be reached by four-wheel-drive vehicles only. The abundant birdlife found on its many permanent lagoons include jabirus, brolgas, royal spoonbills and the straw-necked ibis. There are no facilities for visitors in the park, but bush camping is possible.

EIMEO ■ 1570
This beachside resort with its avenue of mango trees, has been a popular recreation spot for more than a century. The area has both a wide, white-sand beach – where there is good beach fishing – and, at nearby Dolphin Heads, a lagoon. Eimeo offers fine views of the islands scattered between here and the Great Barrier Reef. *Population 920*

EUNGELLA NATIONAL PARK ■ 1571
Taking its name from an Aboriginal word said to mean 'Land of Cloud', this 51 000-hectare reserve west of Mackay is one of Queensland's most spectacular national parks. It extends thirty-five kilometres along the Clark Range overlooking the Pioneer Valley. Eungella's northern side is a largely inaccessible, high and rugged wilderness, but its southern borders can be reached by road. The park contains the high peaks of Mount Dalrymple (1277 metres), Mount William (1244 metres), and Mount David (1188 metres). Frequently shrouded by cloud and mist – hence its name – the park's deep gorges contain rainforests with a multitude of palms and ferns. There are also some areas of eucalypt forest.

FINCH HATTON GORGE Falls and creeks rush out of rainforests to wear away the rock of this gorge in Eungella National Park. A species of gastric-brooding frog was found here in 1983. There is a camping area.

HAY POINT ■ 1572
This port, at the terminus of the railway line from the Bowen Basin coal fields, is one of the biggest coal-exporting complexes in the world with a capacity of more than fifty million tonnes per year. Coal trains, two kilometres and more long, arrive daily with loads of up to 8500 tonnes, and from wharves stretching far out into the ocean massive bulk carriers are filled with coking coal for export.

MACKAY ■ 1573
Like many of Queensland's string of coastal cities, Mackay was founded as a port to export first wool, then tallow from boiled down sheep and cattle from the expanding stations of the hinterland, but eventually found its destiny in sugarcane.

Pushing up behind the coast from Rockhampton (see *Rockhampton & Yeppoon*), squatters took up a series of stock runs between 1856 and 1859. Then, in 1860, representing pastoralists on the New England tableland, Captain John Mackay led an exploration party inland up to the Fitzroy Valley and then along the Isaac River and Mebo Creek, over the Great Dividing Range then down the valley of the Pioneer River. The next year, Mackay returned to the valley with 1200 head of cattle, taking up a run at Greenmount, twenty kilometres inland.

By the end of 1863, there were eight large pastoral leases, stretching along the coast from Sandringham Bay north to St Helens Bay, and west to the Great Dividing Range. To meet these squatters' needs, Rockhampton merchants began supplying them by sea. Mackay was designated a port of entry and clearance in February 1863. Soon after, T.H. Fitzgerald surveyed the township, allowing space for its now graceful streets. A village quickly sprang up, with wharves, docks, warehouses, hotels, shops, houses and banks, a post office, a subcollector of customs, a police magistrate and a newspaper.

Sugar was first planted in 1865. Three plantations quickly assumed prominence – John Spiller's and John Crees' 'Pioneer', Fitzgerald's and J.E. Davidson's 'Alexandra', and J. Holmes' 'Pleystowe'. In March 1866, the editor of the district's newspaper, the *Mackay Mercury*, described what has become one of Queensland's quintessential scenes, when he wrote of Alexandra, 'for a mile along either side of the high road extend seas of waving green cane, stretching away in perfectly even lines'. This, he announced with considerable foresight, was 'not only pleasant to the eye', but also 'an earnest of future wealth to the district'. By the mid-1880s, there were thirty mills crushing cane and Mackay became the pre-eminent Australian sugar district, a position it has never lost. One-third of the Australian sugar harvest is produced in this region.

Between 1863 and 1906, South Sea Islanders formed the staple labour force in Queensland's sugar industry. Around 62 000 contracts were issued to mainly young males from eighty Melanesian islands. Many thousands of the islanders worked in the Mackay district, their labour supplemented by Singhalese, Chinese, Japanese and Malays. All worked as indentured labourers – usually for three-year periods – on the large sugar plantations, but also from the 1880s, on small farms that supplied co-operatively owned central mills.

When government policy changed, encouraging small holdings, and prohibiting non-European immigration, hundreds of Scandanavians, Italians, Spanish, Maltese and Greek labourers came into the northern sugar industry. North Queensland was multicultural 100 years before the word came into vogue. Modern Mackay reflects this varied history in the diversity of the names of its inhabitants, in their languages, and in their culture. *Population 40 250*

A forest of sturdy mooring poles marks a haven for small craft in Mackay's artificial harbour.

Near Eungella, hang gliders queue to float off the edge of the Clark Range into the blue yonder of Pioneer Valley.

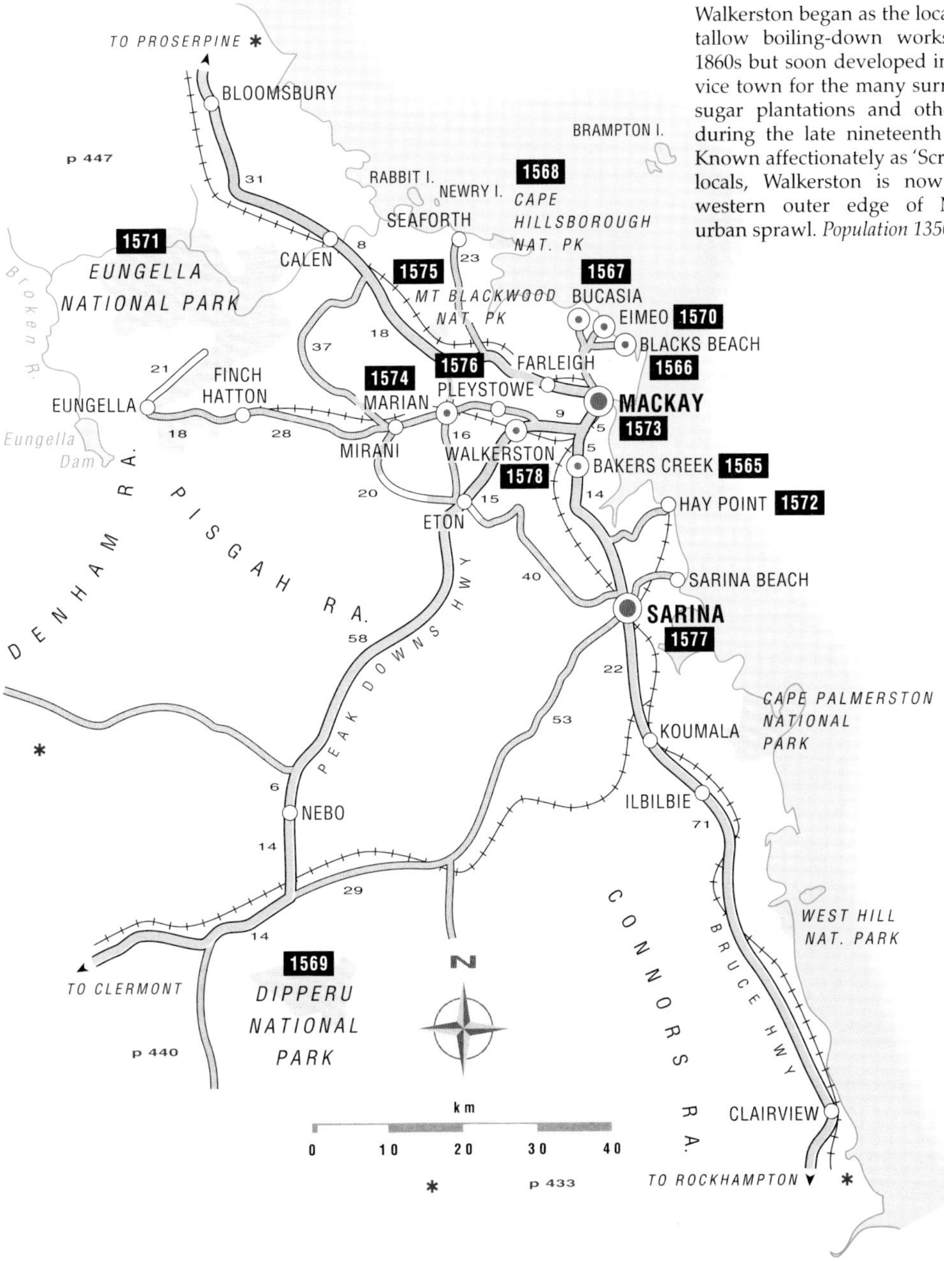

MARIAN ■ 1574

Marian is named after the daughter of George Smith, one of the investors in the first plantation mill built here in 1883. It was here that Helen Porter Mitchell, known later to the world as Nellie Melba, spent several miserable months in 1883. In an unhappy marriage with Charles Armstrong, the Marian mill engineer, and with the wet season lingering strangely into May, she wrote: 'My piano was mildewed; my clothes were damp; the furniture fell to pieces; spiders, ticks and other obnoxious insects penetrated into the house – to say nothing of the snakes, which had the habit of appearing under one's bed at the most inopportune moments'. *Population 590*

MOUNT BLACKWOOD NATIONAL PARK ■ 1575

Off the Bruce Highway north-west of Mackay, this rugged 1000-hectare reserve is accessible by foot only. Its slopes are precipitous but there are good views of the surrounding canefields from the peak.

MOUNT MANDURANA NATIONAL PARK

This small park preserves mountainous outcrops similar to those in Mount Blackwood Park. 'Black gin's Leap', also known as 'The Leap' is reputed to be the site of gruesome death and miraculous survival. It is said that in 1867, an Aboriginal woman with her baby in her arms, leapt from the precipice to escape the Native Police pursuing her people. She died, but her infant daughter survived and was raised by whites. This legend formed the basis of Thea Astley's 1974 novel *A Kindness Cup*.

PLEYSTOWE ■ 1576

This is the site of one of the Mackay district's earliest and most famous sugar plantations which in the 1870s was famous for both the quality of its production and the elegance of its proprietor's lifestyle.

Visitors may inspect the modern mill, which crushes the produce of the small holdings in the district.

SARINA ■ 1577

At the southern edge of the rich basaltic soils that mark the Mackay sugar region is the township of Sarina. Henry Bell took up the first pastoral lease here in 1865, and agricultural selections followed in the 1870s, but for some time sugar production was hindered by the lack of safe sea access to the region. The area continues to exhibit the mixed character of agriculture and pastoralism that grew out of its pioneer days. The township provides access to eight nearby beaches, including Half Tide, Salonika, Grasstree and Sarina; and to Cape Palmerston National Park. *Population 3090*

WALKERSTON ■ 1578

Walkerston began as the location of a tallow boiling-down works in the 1860s but soon developed into a service town for the many surrounding sugar plantations and other farms during the late nineteenth century. Known affectionately as 'Scrubby' by locals, Walkerston is now on the western outer edge of Mackay's urban sprawl. *Population 1350*

THE GREAT BARRIER REEF

Australia is the guardian of a unique natural wonder which literally and figuratively is part of the world's heritage – the unspoiled treasure of the sparkling Great Barrier Reef.

The seemingly endless chain of reefs that guards the eastern coast of Queensland is the world's biggest coral reef system – a massive skein of submerged beauty, studded with white sandbars and inviting green islands, that stretches 2300 kilometres from the Gulf of Papua to just beyond the Tropic of Capricorn at Lady Elliott Island. Reaching for the life-giving sunlight, the tiny coral animals, or polyps, which make up the reef constantly build up towards the surface through crystal-clear blue water which is rarely more than sixty metres deep – ironically, if it is exposed to the air for too long the beautiful coral dies.

The clown fish is allowed the privilege of hiding unharmed among poisonous anemone tentacles.

More than 2100 separate reefs make up the main barrier; some are up to 100 square kilometres in area, others are tiny. Together they total 230 000 square kilometres, while closer to shore, more than 500 islands have small fringing reefs. The reef is so big that James Cook sailed the *Endeavour* for 1000 kilometres inside it in 1770 before suspecting its existence.

The foundations of the Great Barrier Reef probably started to grow about eighteen million years ago, with many sections becoming established a mere one million years ago. The 'modern' reef is believed to have grown up in little more than the last 15 000 years, beginning with the inundation of the coastal valleys by the waters released in a great post-ice age thaw.

If the reef was not there, very little other life would be found in Australia's inshore tropical seas – such waters are not over-endowed with nutrients which is why they are so clear. Coral animals flourish because their cells evolved to contain algae, which uses sunlight to produce abundant food, just as plants do on land. The hard reef builds up on the calcium carbonate skeletons of dead coral polyps, with a thin veneer of live corals on top slowly but inexorably changing its shape.

Because the reef is there, billions of other creatures live on and around it. One coral head that would fit in a shopping trolley is likely to contain more than a thousand burrowing seaworms of 100 different kinds. The 400 different corals that form the reefs harbour more species of fish than any other place in the seas. The Great Barrier Reef has fish in an estimated 1500 variations of shape, colour and size. No place on land – not even the adjacent lush rainforests – have a greater variety of life.

Some of these fish may be a centimetre or less long. Others, like the constantly cruising tiger shark, grow to weigh a tonne or more. Then there are the mammals like whales, dolphins and dugong. Carnivorous predators such as mackerel, barracuda and tuna patrol the reef edges in schools to prey on the smaller denizens who leave the shelter of the coral and keep the waters clean by eating dead fish.

Turtles come to nest in huge numbers on many reef islands. The females come ashore in spring to dig out a sand nest and bury their eggs. Sometimes there are so many turtles that fresh nests are inadvertently dug up by a later arrival.

The reef is protected as a significant World Heritage site and as the largest marine park in the world. With such recognition, it is protected from any obvious threat of despoilation

Life is a constant event on the reef; the coral's nooks and crannies, which allow small fish to hide from predators, are colonised by creatures of every shape and colour.

The reef is an environment as exotic as its inhabitants: the fairy queen (left) lives on the reef edge where the 'wind' of the currents nudges the grass-like whip coral.

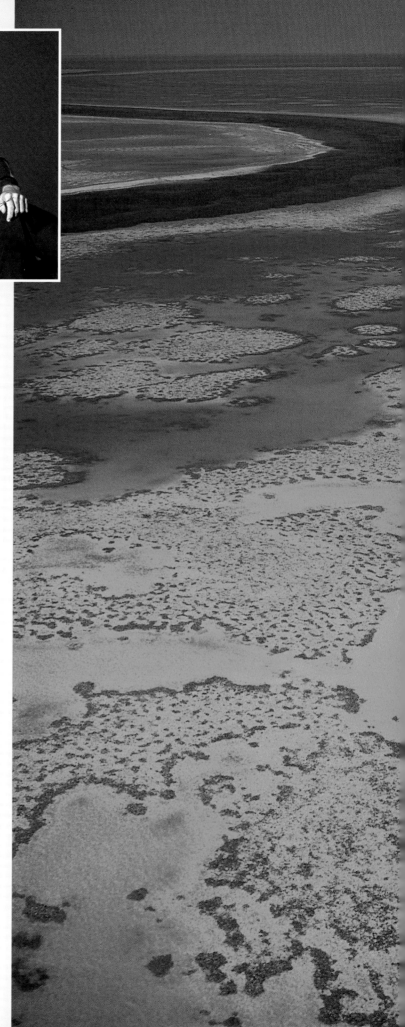

and is reserved as a recreational area. For the price of a simple face mask and snorkel, any visitor can 'fly' above an endless variety of colourful marine displays. The tide here may rise and fall six metres or more, creating fierce rips of up to ten knots in some channels. When the tide falls to expose the coral, visitors have a brief opportunity to examine at close hand the world's largest living structure.

But the highlight of reef displays is reserved for only a few nights each year, when it puts on a brilliant display of sexual activity. Cued by a full moon in late spring or early summer, the corals spawn, releasing millions of multi-coloured egg cells, creating an effect that has been described as like an 'upside-down snowstorm', that increases in intensity for up to a week.

People have been fishing the reef for at least 40 000 years and the Aborigines were in the region long before the sea rose and encouraged the growth of today's reef. There were once about forty tribal groups on this coast, with canoes to take them out to harvest the reef's food bounty, but most of them moved inland when settlement spread. European exploration has left the reef studded with wrecks and more than thirty barnacle-studded hulls beneath the surface are slowly decaying monuments to navigators who came to grief in a marine Garden of Eden. James Cook left the first detailed record of a navigational tussle with the reef, when, purposely hugging the coast to log its shape, he inadvertently wandered into the coral maze. Thirty years later, Matthew Flinders described his journey through the reef as 'threading the needle'. □

Early seafarers found the reef stressful: woe betide the vessel which wandered into the narrow channel between the Hook and Hardy reefs in the Whitsundays.

Ayr & Bowen

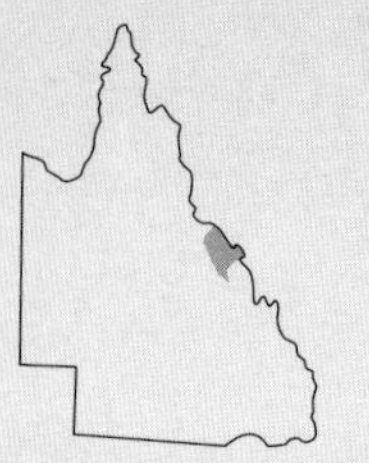

Sugarcane, mangoes and tomatoes grow on this fertile tropical coast while from further inland, tonnes of coal are hauled to modern port facilities. Offshore is the sailors' realm – the Whitsundays – a glimmering maze of reefs and rugged high islands where resorts and reserves sit side by side.

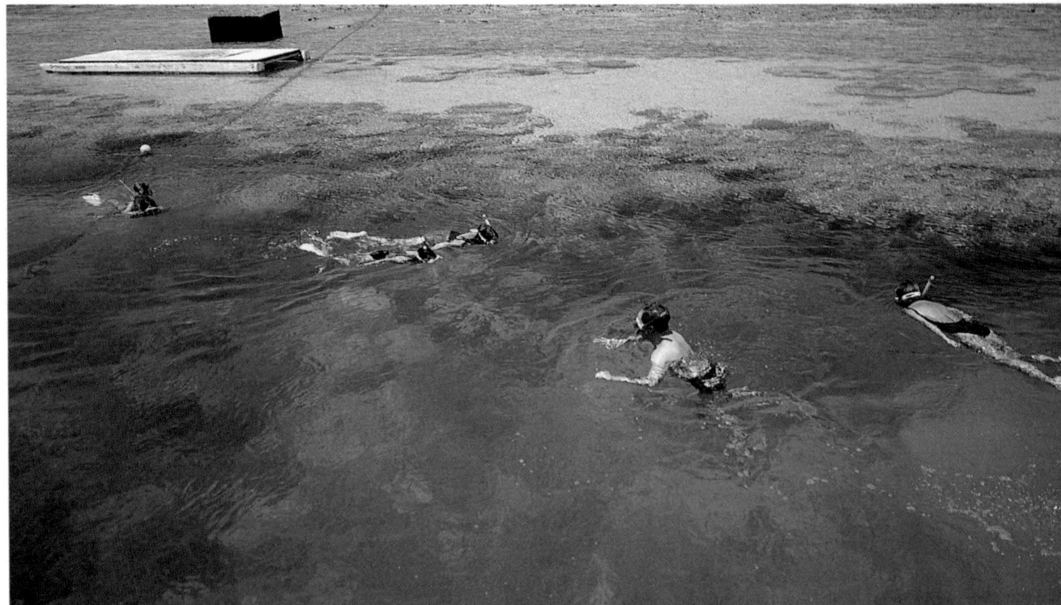

On the outer Barrier Reef, the coral-bedecked shoals of Hardy Reef attract day-trippers from the Whitsunday resorts.

AIRLIE BEACH ■ 1579
Palm trees give a South Sea island air to the waterfront resort of Airlie Beach. For visitors to the warm Whitsunday coast, it offers year-round swimming, snorkelling, fishing, boating, charter boat cruising of the reef and islands, hiking, shady picnic areas, bus tours of the rainforested hinterland and a wide variety of accommodation. There is a marina at nearby Able Point. And not all accommodation carries a five-star price tag. Many of the Whitsunday Islands are national parks with walking tracks and camping facilities. Camping permits are available from the Department of National Parks and Wildlife offices at Airlie Beach. *Population 2520*

AYR ■ 1580
Sugarcane has been grown here since 1879, and the first of the town's mills began crushing in 1883. Three mills still operate, and are open to the public during the sugar crushing season, June to December. Ayr's pioneer growers, with those of its sister town Home Hill, took advantage of the vast underground water supply here and used artesian wells to irrigate the canefields. The district also pioneered the commercial production of rice in Queensland.

The explorer Ludwig Leichhardt passed through this region in the early 1840s, naming its main river for Thomas Burkedin of Sydney, who had financially assisted the expedition. The first European to live permanently in the area was James Morrell a survivor of the shipwrecked *Peruvian*, lost off the coast in the mid-1840s. He spent a harrowing forty-two days on a raft before making landfall. For seventeen years, Morrell lived with the local Aborigines, becoming well-versed in their language, customs and hunting practices. He eventually made contact with stockmen on an outstation, settled down, and married in nearby Bowen, there becoming something of a local hero. Honouring a commitment made to the Aborigines who had adopted him, Morrell whenever possible tried to improve relations between the two peoples and this helped lessen the inevitable conflicts resulting from the advance of European settlement.

The town of Ayr was surveyed, proclaimed and named after the Scottish birthplace of the Queensland premier in the early 1880s, but had to be almost completely rebuilt following a disastrous cyclone in 1903. *Population 8640*

BURDEKIN BRIDGE The total absence of rock in the sandy river bed and banks created enormous difficulties in the building of this bridge, known locally as the 'Silver Link', which spans the Burdekin to join the towns of Ayr and Home Hill. Ten huge chambers of reinforced concrete had to be sunk more than thirty metres into the river before being filled with water and the tops and bottoms plugged. Construction took ten years and, ironically, the old low-level, timber bridge which had served the area through numerous floods over several decades was washed away in the first wet season after the new bridge opened in 1958.

FESTIVALS Festival of Water, late September.

BOWEN ■ 1581
Protected by a sheltering ring of islands and hills, Bowen, on the shores of Port Denison, is a happy, tropical mixture of business and pleasure. It is approached through tomato farms and mango orchards, and the bougainvillea-lined streets of the commercial and administrative centre end at the waters of Port Denison with its beach, boat harbour and deepwater jetty. The district has been dubbed 'the salad bowl of Queensland' and apart from mangoes and tomatoes – for which it is best known – it also produces crops of rockmelons, capsicums, beans, cucumbers and coffee beans. As well, there is a flourishing beef-cattle industry, with brahman and brahman-cross as the predominant breeds; Bowen is also the base for a large commercial fishing fleet which supplies fresh prawns, reef fish, mackerel, scallops and mudcrabs for both domestic and export markets.

Near the entrance to the town is a saltworks which uses evaporation to produce salt from a series of large seawater ponds – high, white stacks of salt can be seen from the main road. A short distance up the coast is Abbot Point, the most northerly deepwater coal-shipping port in Australia, where a long conveyor on a trestle jutting nearly three kilometres into sea loads coal from the Collinsville and Newlands fields.

Bowen – named after the first governor of Queensland, Sir George Bowen – was established in 1861 to help open and then service the fertile hinterland and was the first permanent settlement in north Queensland. It claims to have the best climate in Australia, with an average of eight hours sunshine daily throughout the year. *Population 8310*

FESTIVALS Coral Coast Festival, October–November.

BRANDON ■ 1582
In the late nineteenth century, Brandon was a serious rival to Ayr as the main service town for the surrounding sugar-growing district, but the construction of the tramway at Ayr in 1901 put Brandon out of the running. For many years it remained a chief sporting centre however, with field and track events such as foot races and caber tossing conducted by athletically minded residents in the main street! *Population 890*

CANNONVALE ■ 1583
Overlooking the Whitsunday Passage, midway between Proserpine and Shute Harbour, is the seaside town of Cannonvale. It provides tourist accommodation and facilities

for visitors to the Whitsunday coastal resort area and offers swimming, fishing, waterfront picnic areas and boats for hire. The town takes its name from a cannon and cannon balls said to have been found here in the early days. *Population 2400*

CAPE UPSTART NATIONAL PARK ■ 1584

The most distinctive feature of this park is the massive granite headland of Cape Upstart which rises steeply from the sea, its northern and eastern faces forming an unbroken rocky rampart. Upstart Bay, on its western shore, appears less forbidding, with small sandy beaches enclosed by narrow rocky promontories. Vegetation found here ranges from heathland to vine thicket.

COLLINSVILLE ■ 1585

Coal for both the Australian market and for export is produced here by open-cut and underground methods. Although the existence of the fields was known from as early as the 1860s – the area for many years was known as 'moongunya', the Aboriginal word for coal – mining did not begin until the rail link to Bowen opened in the 1920s, providing an outlet for the fields. The power station here supplies power to most of North Queensland. Gems and petrified wood are to be found in the surrounding district. *Population 2550*

CONWAY NATIONAL PARK ■ 1586

On the mainland edge of the Whitsunday Passage, where the coastal

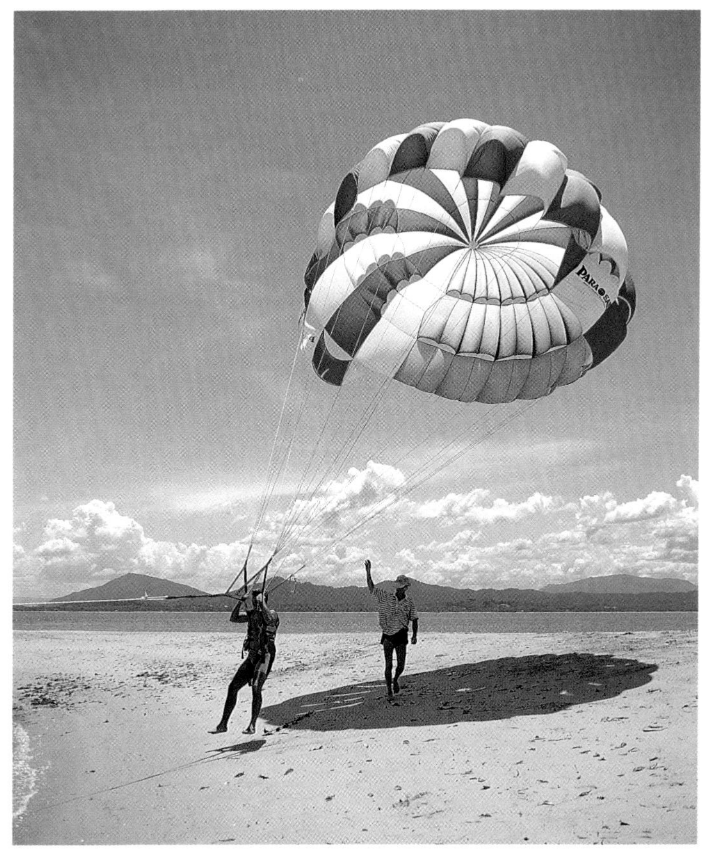

A bird's-eye-view shows the full glory of the green-on-blue necklace of the Whitsunday isles – parasailing is the most adventurous way to obtain one.

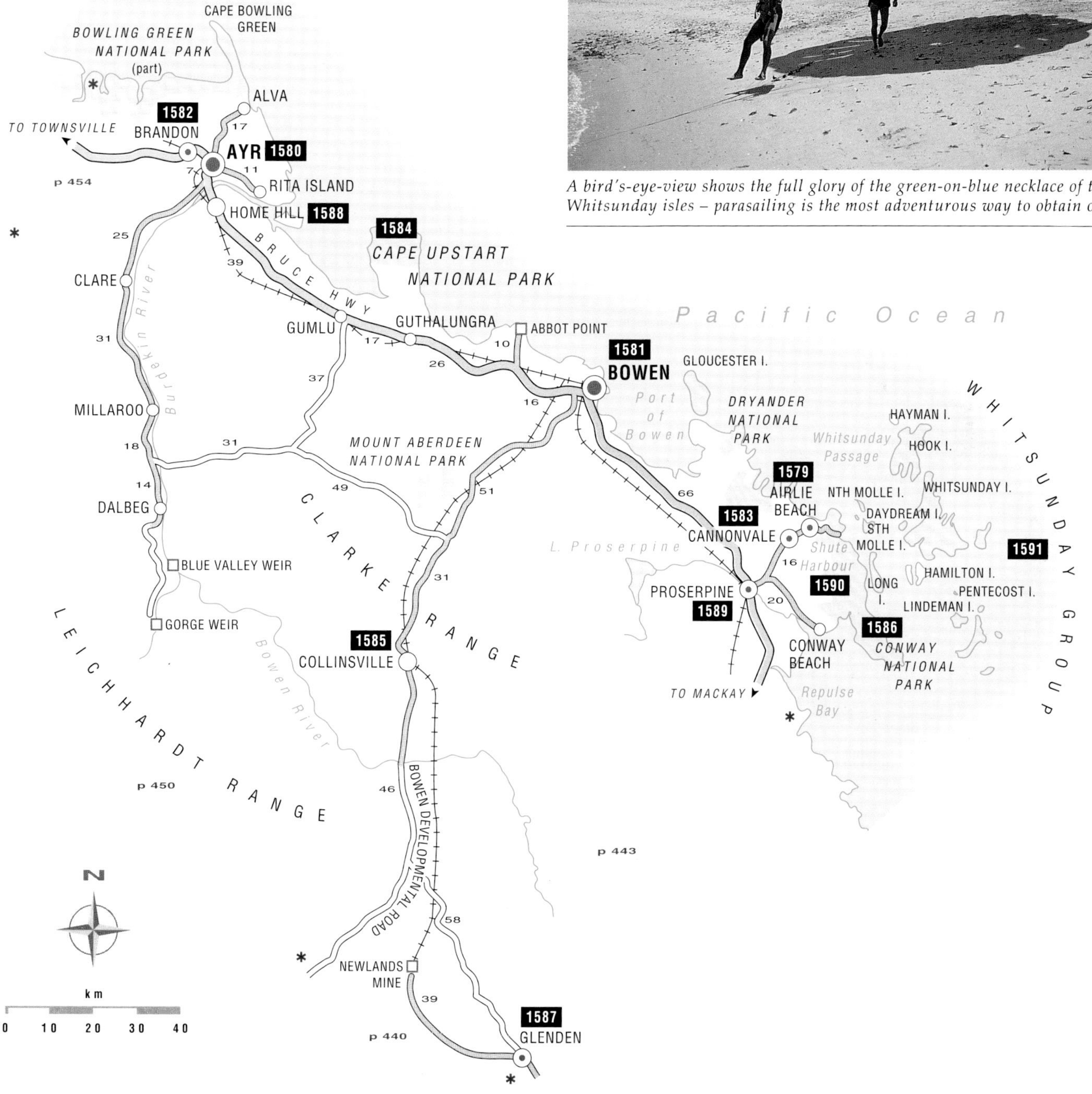

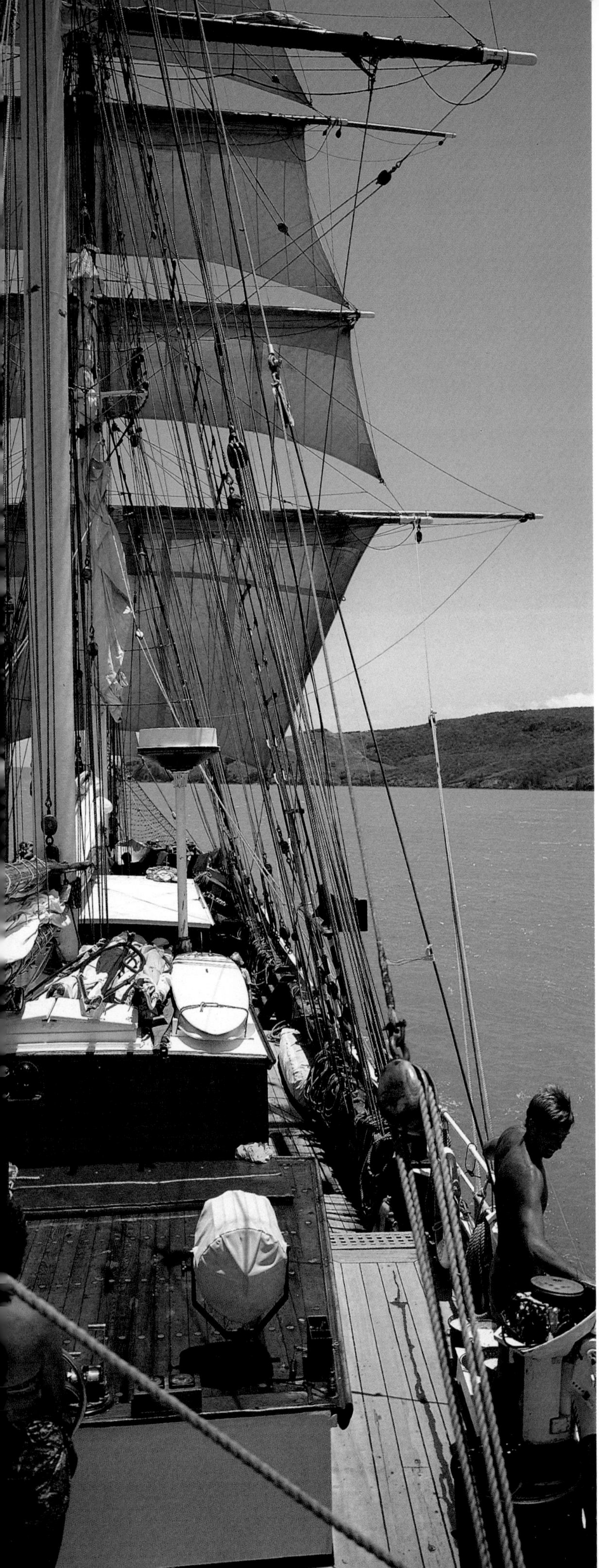

range plunges abruptly into the sea, the largely undeveloped Conway National Park preserves a stretch of coastline in its original state. Walking tracks on the northern end, near the camping area off the Airlie Beach–Shute Harbour Road, lead through many vegetation types from tall eucalypt and lowland rainforest to tangled mangrove clumps. Possums, gliders and bandicoots are common; birdlife includes brush turkey, scrub-fowl, waders and honey eaters, and dugongs and turtles breed in the quiet bays.

GLENDEN ■ **1587**

Glenden is a small coal-mining town which provides accommodation for workers from the nearby Newlands and Eastern Creek mines. Coal from here, extracted by open-cut, is taken by rail to the bulk carrier terminal at Abbot Point, north of Bowen, for shipment overseas and interstate. *Population 1680*

HOME HILL ■ **1588**

The vast artesian waters which lie under Home Hill, on the edge of the Burdekin delta, gave the security of a permanent water supply to the district's cane-growers and led to the area becoming the most intensively irrigated and productive sugarcane region in Australia. All farms in the surrounding region are irrigated by the underground supply, tapping it with 'spears'. These are lengths of pipe perforated with a series of holes which are covered with strong gauze to let the water in but keep the sand out; the end of the pipe, fitted with a cast-iron tip, is driven into the sand.

The myriad windmills which were originally used to pump water to the surface and were once a feature of the district have largely given way to diesel engines and electric motors. In the 1960s, several dry seasons led to an alarming fall in underground water levels and these supplies are now recharged by pumping from the river into natural and man-made channels from which the water can seep into the underground storage.

The town came into being in 1911 and four years later, when the railway lines from the north – which stopped at Ayr – and south – which stopped at Bobawaba – were joined, they ran through Home Hill. The Burdekin Bridge links it with its twin town, Ayr (see entry), on the north side of the Burdekin River. Groper Creek, to the south-east, is noted for its fish and giant mudcrabs and with its boat ramps and deepwater channel to the river mouth is the main outlet for professional fishermen and prawning trawlers. *Population 3200*

The close-set, mountainous islands and rocky outcrops of the Whitsunday Passage provide an alluring attraction for sailing boats of all sizes.

PROSERPINE ■ **1589**

This rich valley named by explorer George Dalrymple after the Roman goddess of fertility, Proserpina, is the centre of a prosperous sugar-growing region. There is also cattle-raising in the region. Fashions and furnishings worn and used by the district's pioneers are displayed in an historical museum, and a wildlife park on the road to Airlie Beach contains crocodiles, cassowaries, a reptile house and a walk-through aviary. Cedar Creek, in the rainforest hills of Conway Range, has hiking and swimming amid ferns and orchids. In the mountains to the west of the town is Peter Faust Dam and Lake Proserpine, both popular for skiiing and fishing. *Population 3030*

SHUTE HARBOUR ■ **1590**

The bustling jetty here is the departure point for a large number of the boats that ply the Whitsunday waterways. Vessels large and small leave each morning on trips to resort islands, cruises around uninhabited ones and to the outer reef – seventy kilometres to the east – and on specialised diving, snorkelling and fishing excursions, making Shute Harbour such a busy port that its passenger traffic is said to be second only to Sydney's Circular Quay. There are scenic flights over the area and helicopter services to the many resort islands. A glass-bottomed boat reveals the coral formations found within the harbour itself, and from its foreshores are magnificent views over Whitsunday Passage.

WHITSUNDAY GROUP ■ **1591**

Strictly speaking, the name Whitsunday Group should apply only to the islands at the top of the scattered string of island clusters named collectively by James Cook as the Cumberland Group, after his home county. It has come however, to cover all of the 100 or so islands which, in two chains separated by the Whitsunday Passage, stretch seventy kilometres along the coast from Mackay to Bowen. These islands are the peaks of a coastal range which became separated from the mainland when polar ice caps melted during the Ice Age, some 18 000–8000 years ago, raising sea levels and flooding the deep intervening valley. Known as high or continental islands, many are still forested with the pines that once extended from the Queensland–New South Wales border north to Cairns. They also have all the desirable traits that travellers have come to expect from Barrier Reef islands: rainforests, sheltered sandy beaches, warm, clear water and colourful coral reefs.

James Cook and his companions on the *Endeavour* were the first recorded Europeans to see these islands, coming upon them on Whit

Sunday, 1770. He wrote: 'The land both on the Main and Islands especialy on the former is tolerable high and distinguished by hills and Vallies which are deversified with woods and Lawns that look'd green and pleasent'. All but a handful of these 'emerald' islands were designated national parks by forward-thinking governments in the 1930s and 1940s and now form collectively the Whitsunday Islands National Park. Most are uninhabited and tourist development has been carefully controlled. Camping is permitted on a number, and there are developed holiday resorts on seven – Brampton, Lindeman, Hamilton, Long, South Molle, Daydream and Hayman. A leisurely cruise through the spectacularly beautiful Whitsunday Passage is regarded as one of the great tourist experiences, with the majority of the islands remaining very much as Cook saw them.

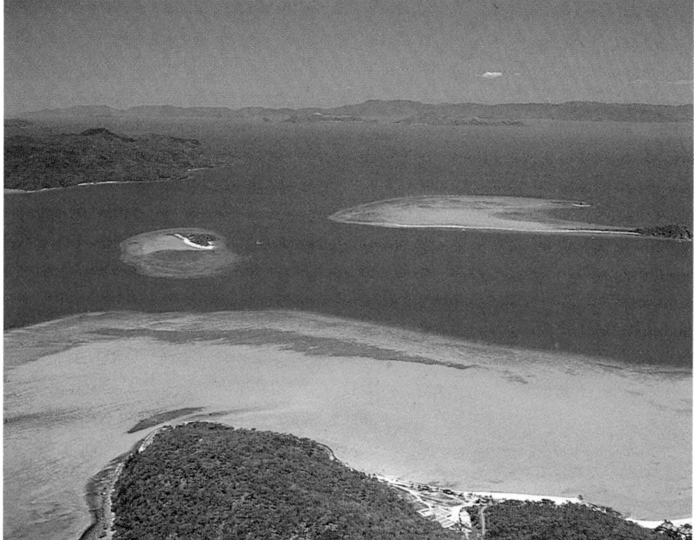

The coral on Black and Langford reefs, near Hayman Island, is constantly building on itself and these specks will one day graduate to island status.

Few yachtsman are able to resist the temptation to drop anchor in the tiny bays and deep inlets of the ruggedly beautiful and uninhabited Hook Island.

BRAMPTON ISLAND One of the southernmost of the Whitsundays, Brampton Island, most of which is national park, is reached by sea or air from Mackay, about thirty-two kilometres away. It is a continental island and features hilly terrain covered with hoop pines and some rainforest, white sand beaches, warm turquoise waters and fringing coral reefs. Walking tracks link sheltered bays with shallow swimming beaches, and from Brampton Peak there are panoramic views of the island-studded sea. Nearby Carlisle Island, a totally undeveloped reserve, can be reached at low tide across coral reefs. The tourist resort here opened as a holiday farm in 1933. The first guests stayed in empty shearing sheds – the island had earlier been used to breed horses for the Indian Army and to pasture livestock, an activity which has left some of its slopes bare.

DAYDREAM ISLAND Formerly called West Molle, Daydream is less than ten hectares in area and the smallest of the developed islands. It is encircled by a beach of coral sand and from it are views of either the neighbouring islands or the green hills of the mainland – Shute Harbour is only five kilometres away. The low-rise resort complex takes up much of the island. Access is by launch and day visitors are welcome.

HAMILTON ISLAND This is the most developed of the islands with a school, banks, post office, jet strip, man-made harbour and 400-berth marina, and a luxury resort which accommodates more than 1000 people each year. Catseye Bay is the focus for most of the island's activities and an excellent spot for both scuba diving and snorkelling on the reef, and for catamarans, sailboarding and surf skis. Hamilton was used for grazing before being developed as a resort in the early 1980s.

HAYMAN ISLAND Hayman, synonymous with the idea of a Barrier Reef resort holiday, is dominated by a thickly forested horseshoe-shaped mountain and was once leased to timber-getters. Hayman is the most northerly of the island chain and closest to the outer reef. It is fringed by the largest reef in the Whitsundays, making boat access difficult, and low tide exposes some 405 hectares of coral. The northern and western coasts are rugged and steeply cliffed and are home to numerous birds with some eighty species, including the satin drongo, nutmeg pigeons and dainty sunbirds recorded on the island. On the southern shore, a deep-water jetty behind the reef and overlooking a lagoon serves the resort. Hayman Island was named by Cook for a crew member on the *Endeavour*, as were Hook and Molle islands.

HOOK ISLAND This island is best known for the underwater observatory on its southern promontory where coral and other reef marine life can be seen in their natural habitat; nearby, glass-bottomed boats operate coral-viewing cruises. At the island's centre, a peak rises steeply to 460 metres; sheer-sided, fjord-like Nara Inlet, fringed with coral and surrounded by high timbered hills, is a magnet for yachts of all sizes.

LINDEMAN ISLAND With its rugged coastline softened here and there by small indented beaches, Lindeman stands at the southern entrance to the Whitsunday Passage. Before the establishment of the tourist resort in 1927, it was used to graze sheep, cattle and goats. The island is noted for its birdlife, especially lorikeets, and for its butterflies. Lindeman is covered with eucalypt forest with many kilometres of graded tracks leading to the scenic points. From the 210-metre peak of Mount Oldfield some seventy islands can be seen. There is a regular air service to Mackay, scenic flights over the Whitsundays and the outer reef and, from the deep-water jetty, cruises to other islands and to view coral formations and marine life.

LONG ISLAND A ridge crowded with wildlife runs the length of Long Island and is made accessible by graded walking tracks. On the northern shores, with views over the Whitsunday Passage, are the resorts of The Island and Palm Bay.

PENTECOST ISLAND Between Lindeman and Whitsunday is Pentecost, the steep-sided peak of a drowned mountain which rears sheer from deep waters for some 300 metres. Landings are rarely made here due to the inaccessability of the coastline.

SOUTH MOLLE High grasslands and eucalypts, with occasional rainforest pockets, cover the slopes of South Molle. The island lies in the heart of the Whitsunday Passage, close to Shute Harbour and the mainland, and from its peaks of Spion Kop and Mount Jefferies are breathtaking views of the waterway and surrounding islands. A village-style resort is located in wide bay on its northern side.

WHITSUNDAY ISLAND The largest of the chain at 10 930 hectares, this island has no tourist developments and is still much as described by Cook. It rises to a peak of 440 metres and, like its neighbour, Hook Island, has deep fjord-like inlets. Off its western shore is a sheltered expanse of water known as Cid Harbour which, during the Second World War, was an anchorage for United States' naval vessels.

The hilly landscape of Whitsunday Island proper indicates that it was once part of the mainland.

Charters Towers & Greenvale

This is a rugged region of strange geological formations where volcanic action has strewn basalt boulders and formed what are thought to be the world's longest, tubular tunnel-caves. Charters Towers, once so famous for its gold, now bases its continued prosperity solidly on the serious businesses of education and animal breeding.

BURDEKIN FALLS DAM AND LAKE DALRYMPLE ■ 1592

The 487-million-dollar Burdekin Falls Dam project consists of a main gravity dam across the river and three auxiliary earth and rockfill dams to the north. The main dam wall, completed in March 1987, is made from 630 000 cubic metres of concrete.

The storage capacity of Lake Dalrymple is 'four sydharbs' – at least four times the volume of Sydney Harbour. Its surface area is the largest of any dam in Queensland and water backs up for fifty kilometres along the Burdekin River. The system should satisfy industrial, urban, agricultural and recreational needs until the next century and irrigates the rice, sugarcane and other crops on the developing farms in the lower Burdekin River region.

CHARTERS TOWERS ■ 1593

Charters Towers was a pastoral area in the 1860s and 1870s, but the pastoralists soon found a ready meat market in the streams of goldminers who arrived from the 1870s onwards. During the so-called 'golden years' between 1872 and 1916 there were about 100 gold mines in the city and its environs, about the same number of hotels and taverns and a peak population of 30 000. The famous poet-soldier 'Breaker' Morant – real name Harry Harbord – lived here in 1884 and in March of that year married Daisy May O'Dwyer. He soon moved on leaving bad debts and his new wife behind him. In the boom times of the 1890s, residents called their town 'The World', a status that was sealed by the visit of Dame Nellie Melba who performed at the Theatre Royal.

Twentieth-century Charters Towers is best known for beef and boarding schools and has more National Trust properties than any other place in Queensland. The last city mine closed in 1926 and the last poppet head was dismantled in the early 1940s. During the Second World War, the United States Army Airforce had its airfield on the site of the present airport and 15 000 servicemen were stationed in the city.

Jupiter, a ten-year-old Aboriginal boy, first discovered gold at what was then called Charters Tors on Christmas Eve, 1871. He was with three prospectors from Ravenswood (see entry), Hugh Mosman, George Clarke and John Fraser. He went to retrieve the packhorses after they were frightened by lightning and came back to camp with gold from a nearby creek. This brought on a great rush to Queensland's most famous goldfield which produced 2000 tonnes of the yellow metal between 1872 and 1911. The town was named after the tors on the Dartmoor plain in England and William Skelton Eurbank Melbourne Charters, the Ravenswood, and later Charters Towers Gold Commissioner. Technological advances in gold recovery have made the old dumps and low-grade ore profitable again and there have been notable new discoveries to the south-east of the original workings.

Charters Towers is noted as the school education centre of northern Queensland. There are four secondary establishments catering for boarders mainly from northern Australia, Papua New Guinea and the Torres Strait Islands.

Cattle have long been a local industry. In 1875, when sheep had been discarded as unsuitable for the climate, graziers were receiving the equivalent of four dollars a head for their stock and rump steak was about ten cents a kilogram. Citrus trees, grapes and vegetables thrive on the fertile river flats and cotton,

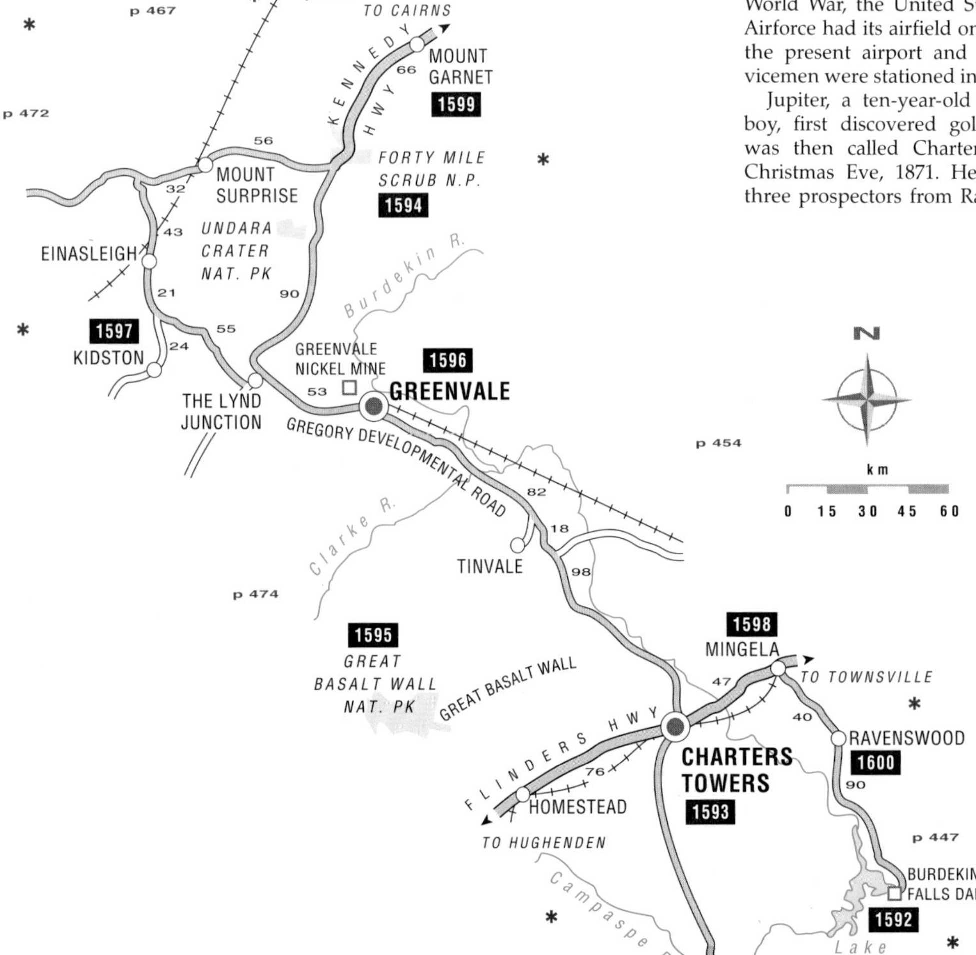

Stray cattle show little respect for Ravenswood's past glory – the elaborate facades are a legacy of a fleeting, 1860s gold boom.

tobacco, sorghum and millet are also grown. Charters Towers has a modern seismograph station which reports on earth tremors throughout the world and the Lands Department's Tropical Weeds Research Centre is based here. *Population 9020*

STOCK EXCHANGE In the 1890s, when Charters Towers was known as 'The World' to its residents, the local stock exchange remained open around the clock, seven days a week. A shopping arcade built in 1887–88 was adapted for use as the exchange, and three times a day stock quotations were called from a bridgeway set into the arch above the entrance passageway. The arcade has now reverted to its original function.

AUSTRALIAN BANK OF COMMERCE This grandiose building dates from 1891 when it was built as the Australian Joint Stock Bank.

CIVIC CLUB This club and its striking building had its origins in the all-male domain of the town's northern goldfields which spawned a group of businessmen who, from the late 1870s, met regularly at a local hotel. In 1900, they decided to build their own rooms in the manner of a well-appointed Queensland-style house, and this lattice-enclosed, high-roofed timber building was the result.

FESTIVALS Goldfield Ashes Cricket Carnival, Australia Day weekend; Country Music Festival, April/May.

Business confidence in Charters Towers' second gold boom is reflected in this monumentally solid, 1891 bank.

FORTY MILE SCRUB NATIONAL PARK ■ 1594

The distinctive, semi-evergreen vine thicket that grows here has similar characteristics to remnants of ancient flora found in Indonesia, Madagascar and Central and East Africa and is thought to go back 300 million years to the huge super-continent known as Gondwanaland. The hard, corky-barked vines shed their leaves in the winter dry season. The national park is an area of more than 4600 hectares, proclaimed in 1970, to preserve this unique vegetation and the largest continuous stand is known, despite the metric system, as the Forty Mile Scrub.

Nearby is another of the region's unusual features – the ancient lava tubes at Undara (see box).

GREAT BASALT WALL NATIONAL PARK ■ 1595

Volcanic activity up to three million years ago spewed out the lava beneath the Great Basalt Wall. More recent eruptions, which may have been watched by the region's Aboriginal inhabitants, left the actual wall, part of a 120-kilometre-long lava flow. The 30 500-hectare park, proclaimed in 1987, has basalt boulders and dense vegetation along much of its boundary but the confusing sameness of the countryside makes bushwalking a pastime best reserved for experts. The rocks contain many springs, lakes and small waterholes and the area is rich in animal and plant life.

GREENVALE ■ 1596

Copper was originally mined in the Greenvale area in the 1920s. Then in 1938, Harry Moss found traces of nickel but it was almost thirty years after that before a huge, workable deposit was discovered. Queensland's only nickel mine, costing 260 million dollars, opened in the 1970s and a railway line was built to carry the ore to the Yabulu refinery, north of Townsville. The ore supply is finite and as mining operations wind down, the future of this well-tended, modern township in the rugged northern hinterland will become more and more uncertain.

KIDSTON ■ 1597

Two mining eras can be compared at Kidston. Modern methods are in operation at the open-cut gold mine – one of the largest in the world – where high-technology machinery extracts the ore. Processing began in 1985 and the return for 1986–87 was more than seven tonnes. Remains of past mining activities are preserved nearby and a crushing battery in Kidston village shows how pioneer miners extracted the gold.

MINGELA ■ 1598

Mingela is a tiny town renowned in the region for its rodeo and picnic races that take place on May Day weekends. The town's site, with its series of waterholes, was a natural stopping place for travellers and was first called Cunningham's Waterholes. As Ravenswood Junction, it became a distribution point for food, and other supplies to Ravenswood, Charters Towers and the northern tin-mining settlement of Ewan, and the receiving depot for their ore.

Woodcutting and sawmilling were established in the 1920s but Ravenswood Junction always depended on the places around it, and when gold-mining stopped at Ravenswood and the Burdekin meatworks closed in 1928, the settlement declined. The railway line to Ravenswood closed in 1930 and the junction's name became Mingela which was said to come from 'min-illa', an Aboriginal word for 'a big waterhole'. Mingela railway station closed in December 1988 and now the town serves as a refreshment stop for visitors to Ravenswood and the Burdekin Falls Dam.

MOUNT GARNET ■ 1599

In 1883, lost horses led Albert Vollenweider to an outcrop of copper on Mount Garnet. As a result, the Mount Garnet Freehold Copper and Silver Mining Company was established in the late 1890s, employing hundreds of miners and smelters, many of whom died from typhoid fever. Until the railway was laid from Lappa to Mount Garnet in 1902, camels brought coke in for smelting and carried ore out along a forty-one-kilometre track known as the Camel Pad. When the copper was exhausted, an unusual geophysical phenomenon prompted the start of alluvial tin mining – huge slugs of tin from an unlocated source which were found on the hillside eventually became an important source of income. Nettle and Smith's creeks were dredged for many years and dry-mining, mobile plants were also used to extract alluvial tin from the creeks where the wash was too shallow for dredging. Mount Garnet also has gem-bearing topaz fields.

RAVENSWOOD ■ 1600

Ravenswood was the north's first major mining town for a short while after gold was discovered in the area in 1868. Forty-two pubs served the boom; today the town's remaining buildings are listed by the National Trust and include just two hotels. When the residents left Ravenswood, many of them took their homes with them on ox waggons.

Ravenswood was unlucky. Rich alluvial gold continued through to reef mining until the shafts reached the level of the water table. Then the precious metal became mineralised with sulphides of zinc and lead in 'mundic ore' and nobody knew how to extract the pure gold.

In January 1872, Hugh Mosman returned from Charters Tors with gold in his saddle-bags. People quickly deserted Ravenswood to hurry to the fresh fields. A few stayed to try to solve the extraction problem and the nearby Totley silver mine, opened in 1880, saved the town from complete collapse.

In 1893, the townspeople sent the manager of the John Bull mine to London to learn about the separation of concentrates from gold. After a second trip in 1897, special separating equipment was installed at the Mabel Mill and this propelled a second boom which lasted for about ten years. Then the 1912–13 industrial strike hastened the town's decline and in 1914 most of the remaining men enlisted in the services for the First World War.

In 1987, activity began again on Ravenswood's goldfields with a new open-cut mine. The operators used modern refining methods to process up to three-and-a-half tonnes of gold over five years.

A COOL, DANK LEGACY OF A FIERY PAST

MANY OF the strangely shaped rock formations which break Australia's relatively flat surface are the visible result of seething, volcanic turmoil. Although the lava tubes at Undara break the surface – literally – only when they collapse, they are unmistakeably the result of earth-shattering ruptures.

There are other lava-tube formations but Undara's claim to fame is that it is believed to be the longest system in the world. The Undara crater spewed forth its molten heart about 190 000 years ago and outer layers of the lava flow began to cool and solidify. Inside, the red-hot stream flowed on, until the eruptions stopped and the molten lava continued to drain out, leaving cavities behind.

The immensity of the earth-shaping eruptions of the past can be gauged by the size of this tunnel forged beneath Mount Surprise.

The dimensions of the huge, tubular caves give some idea of the grand scale of things. They wind like tunnels for about thirty-five kilometres underground with a further thirty kilometres of solid section; altogether the lava covered about 1550 kilometres and flowed in an unbroken stream for about 160 kilometres. Undara's rocks have been compared to basalt from the surface of the moon. The last fiery eruptions of Kinrara volcano, some twenty kilometres to the south-east, were between 18 000 to 70 000 years ago – in geological terms, a very short time indeed.

The thick outcrops of trees near Mount Surprise indicates where rainwater run-off has gathered in gullies formed by collapsed lava tubes.

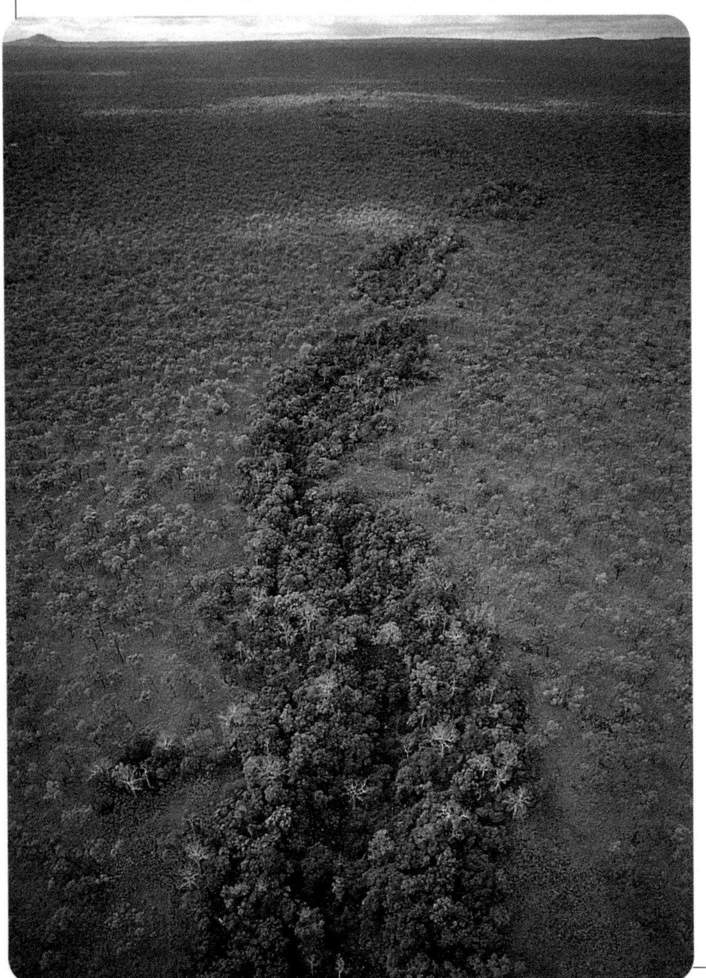

Bayliss tube, Undara's longest tunnel, is like a modern freeway underpass at twenty metres wide, nearly twelve metres high and stretching almost one-and-a-half thousand metres.

At intervals along the tube, weathering or earthquake activity have caused the roof to fall in so that there is access from the surface at various points. In many places, these collapses have created depressions where water has gathered and, protected from fire, they have developed their own micro-climate with a covering of semi-evergreen vines quite distinct from the surrounding dry, eucalypt-savannah country. The lines of dark green vegetation marking the course of the lava tubes are clearly visible from the air.

The cave walls are important roosting and nursery sites for horseshoe and other bat species. Lower lifeforms in this perpetually dark environment have evolved quite differently from their above-ground cousins. Centuries of adaptation have produced insects with small eyes and wings and pale bodies. These creatures have no need for colour to protect them from ultraviolet light or to camouflage them from predators. They feed on bat droppings and dead animals as well as the tree roots that push downwards into the caves to search for water. Fungi growing here have turned white too. The temperature of the caves can be up to 20° Centigrade cooler than on the surface and small marsupials use them for shelter.

Horseshoe bats take advantage of the kilometres of hanging space on the walls of lava tubes open to the surface.

Undara's tunnels were discovered about eighty to ninety years ago but public interest was not great until 1984 when they began to receive publicity. The Undara Crater National Park, proclaimed in 1989, covers the source point of the lava flow and an area of almost 600 hectares. The lava tubes are a protected 'biosphere' – several can be visited but only with an official guide. Some caves are reserved for scientific research and others are considered unsafe.

The sealed Undara Loop road circumnavigates the 164 craters of the system. Visitors can also take in the Forty Mile Scrub National Park (see entry), the gemfields at Mount Surprise, the Tallaroo Hot Springs, the goldmining town of Georgetown and many other historic and prehistoric sites in this mysterious landscape. □

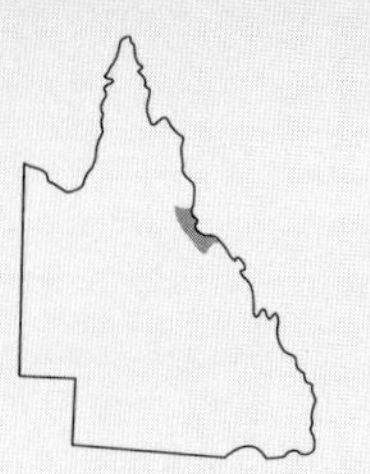

Townsville & Ingham

Leisure is big business on the reef coast and almost any kind of marine-centred holiday is possible in a region so well-endowed with offshore islands. The rainforest retreats of the national parks offer pleasures of a different kind. Townsville is the busy commercial and educational hub of this historically productive region and Thuringowa its newest 'city'.

Mount Bowen is part of the raw, eroded series of ridges that form the backbone and ribs of Hinchinbrook Island.

ALLIGATOR CREEK ■ 1601

This small settlement lies in the southern part of Thuringowa City (see box). The first Europeans in the area took up land at Alligator Creek, established a dairy farm at Toonpan Creek and grew tobacco and sugarcane in the Lower Burdekin. In 1880, a boiling down works was built in the town; it lasted for five years before being replaced by a meat-canning plant. At first the annual intake was about 12 000 head of cattle but in 1898 more than 50 000 beasts were processed. *Population 790*

BOWLING GREEN BAY NATIONAL PARK ■ 1602

The coastal section of Bowling Green Bay National Park is flanked by Cape Bowling Green, a long, low sandspit formed by the action of south-east winds on silt from the Burdekin River. Cape Cleveland to the north is a rugged, granite headland covered with eucalypts, vine forest and hoop pines. A variety of water birds live on the expanse of freshwater wetland which separates the coastal mangrove flats from Mount Elliot, a mountainous area just inland from Bowling Green Bay. The upper slopes and ridge tops are moist enough to support one of the mainland's southernmost stands of lush, tropical rainforest. Alligator Creek cascades over spectacular falls flowing from the rainforest down to drier woodland and provides a popular place for camping and swimming.

CARDWELL ■ 1603

'Cardwell-by-the-sea' is a popular fishing and holiday resort squeezed between rugged coastal mountains and the tropical ocean. It was established in the 1860s by George Elphinstone Dalrymple as an outlet for produce from the Upper Burdekin region. At the time, Cardwell was one of the first northern settlements and the only port between Bowen and Somerset at the tip of Cape York. Dalrymple hoped for speedy expansion, but the growth of Townsville overtook his dreams of 'churches, public buildings, streets, warehouses...spread far along the gleaming shore and back to the base of the mountains'. The settlement is named after Edward Cardwell who became Secretary of State for the Colonies in 1865.

The hinterland is used for cattle-raising and growing tea, sugarcane, bananas, watermelons, pumpkins and a veritable salad of tropical fruit. Logging serves the plywood mill at nearby Kennedy. The district has Australia's highest rainfall, a drenching average of about 500 centimetres a year. A road winds through the steamy rainforested ranges behind the village to a lookout with coastal vistas. Boats for Hinchinbrook Island leave from Cardwell. *Population 1290*

DEERAGUN ■ 1604

Deeragun is an adjacent suburb to Jensen Cordelia Estate – in the former Thuringowa City where the land has been subdivided for real estate to meet the needs of people wanting to escape from the city. A large proportion of the workforce is employed at the Yabulu nickel refinery, a short way north on Highway One. *Population 1290*

EDMUND KENNEDY NATIONAL PARK ■ 1605

In 1848, Edmund Kennedy crossed this area on his ill-fated expedition. His progress was hindered by the low-lying swampy areas of sedges, mangroves, melaleucas, fan palms, sword grass and dense rainforest but he battled through courageously to meet a violent death just before he reached Cape York. The going is easier these days as walking tracks and boardwalks provide a passage as they crisscross the park but some of the other dangers Kennedy faced have not gone away. In the summer months, mosquitoes are a problem and marine stingers – box jellyfish – appear in Rockingham Bay and the inland waterways. Estuarine crocodiles may lurk in or near the creeks and rivers.

FORREST BEACH ■ 1606

The wide, sandy sweep of Forrest Beach – originally known as Allingham – is within easy reach of Ingham. It is the site of beach carnivals and a marine stinger net encloses an area on the waterfront for safe swimming. There is access to the nearby reefs and the Palm Islands from the boat ramp. *Population 1040*

GIRU ■ 1607

Giru, a small, satellite township of Thuringowa City on the banks of the Haughton River, is named for an Aboriginal word meaning 'land of many waters'. It marks the southern boundary of Thuringowa City and is surrounded by canefields. The Invicta sugar mill established here in 1921 still employs many local people.

HALIFAX ■ 1608

Halifax is also a sugar town and was once a centre of trade for the Herbert River district, linked to the port of Lucinda by rail. As Ingham grew, so Halifax declined, and today it is a quiet country town with good fishing spots along the river banks. The town's main street is lined with mango trees and buildings that preserve memories of the nineteenth century. *Population 550*

HINCHINBROOK ISLAND ■ 1609

Hinchinbrook is Australia's largest island national park. This 39 350-hectare reserve is dominated by the formidable peaks of a precipitous and jagged mountain range. To the east, there are white sandy beaches, to the west, mangrove swamps. The island is within easy reach of Cardwell for a leisurely day trip and its only permanent buildings are a cluster of resort lodges at Cape Richards.

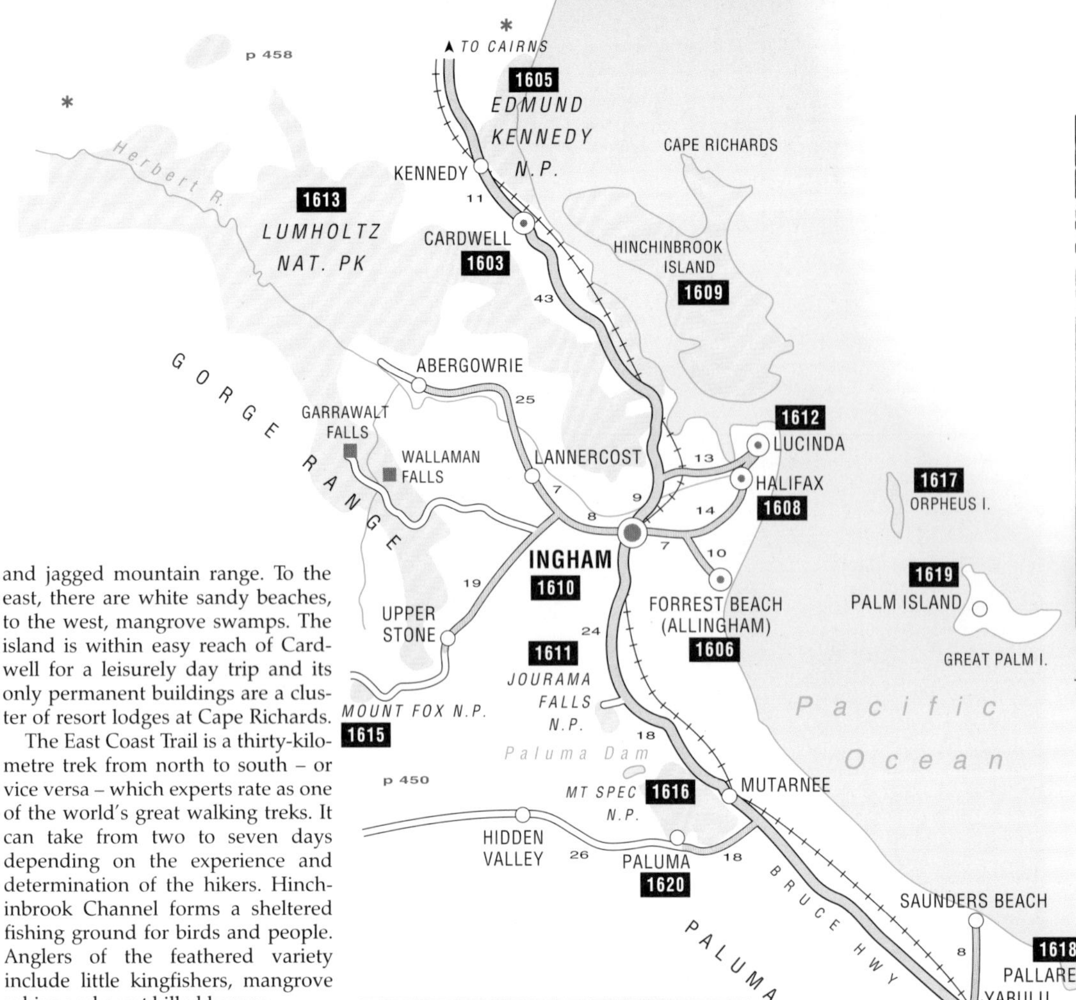

The East Coast Trail is a thirty-kilometre trek from north to south – or vice versa – which experts rate as one of the world's great walking treks. It can take from two to seven days depending on the experience and determination of the hikers. Hinchinbrook Channel forms a sheltered fishing ground for birds and people. Anglers of the feathered variety include little kingfishers, mangrove robins and great billed herons.

Ingham orchardists hope to see the juicy jack fruit gain a prominent spot on city greengrocers' shelves.

If the dry season 'winter' temperatures are cool enough, North Queensland's sugar produces graceful, plume-like flowers

INGHAM ■ 1610

Ingham's streets are wide and colourful and lined with lawns and gardens where plants of the tropics such as crotons, hibiscus and allamanda bloom. The town is named after William Bairstow Ingham, an early sugar planter and its prosperity is founded on sugar which was planted round Ingham in the early 1870s. The climate and soil suited it perfectly and the region has become one of the most prolific in the world, producing more than three million tonnes of sugarcane a year.

Macknade is the oldest continually operating mill in Northern Queensland and Victoria Mill is the largest crushing plant in the Southern Hemisphere – in 1989 the plant processed almost two-and-a-half million tonnes. The harvesting period lasts from July to December. Traditionally there was a pre-harvest burn-off to get rid of leaves and rubbish which interfered with harvesting and milling. Now the cane is often cut green and the debris left in the fields for its nitrogen value.

By-products of this crop include bagasse – cane fibre – which helps fuel the mills and is made into wallboard, molasses for stock feed and liquor distilleries, and ash which is used for fertiliser. The crushed sugar is sent in raw form to Lucinda – refining is done elsewhere in Australia or overseas.

The first Italian migrants arrived to work in the fertile Herbert Valley cane fields in 1891. Their numbers increased through individual sponsorship which stopped for the First World War and then became even stronger between 1920 and 1939. The dignified family mausoleums in Ingham cemetery demonstrate the early influence of Italian customs here.

Lee's pub in Ingham lays claim to being the original 'pub with no beer' immortalised in Dan Sheahan's ballad and sung by Slim Dusty. The story is that American troops, stationed here in 1942, drank it dry after victory in the Battle of the Coral Sea.

The district is well known for its cabinet timbers and is ranked by furniture makers as the 'veneer capital' of Australia. There is some horse and cattle breeding, and fishing, especially for prawns and crabs, is a growth industry. Hinchinbrook Shire supplies the southern states with huge quantities of pumpkins and watermelons. A developing tropical fruit industry specialises in some of the more exotic varieties including jack fruit, lychees, carambola and the sapota or sapodilla. *Population 5070*

FESTIVAL Maraka Festival, September/October.

JOURAMA FALLS NATIONAL PARK ■ 1611

Jourama Falls National Park, lying between Townsville and Ingham, has an attractive picnic and camping ground beside Waterview Creek at the base of the Seaview Range. The falls tumble over salmon-coloured granite slabs into refreshing, crystal-clear swimming holes and there is a mildly strenuous walk to the lookout above them. Palms, umbrella trees and figs fringe the creek and red-flowered weeping bottlebrushes attract butterflies. The moist, humid conditions encourage lush and vigorous plant growth and all manner of birds, reptiles and mammals find food and shelter here.

LUCINDA ■ 1612

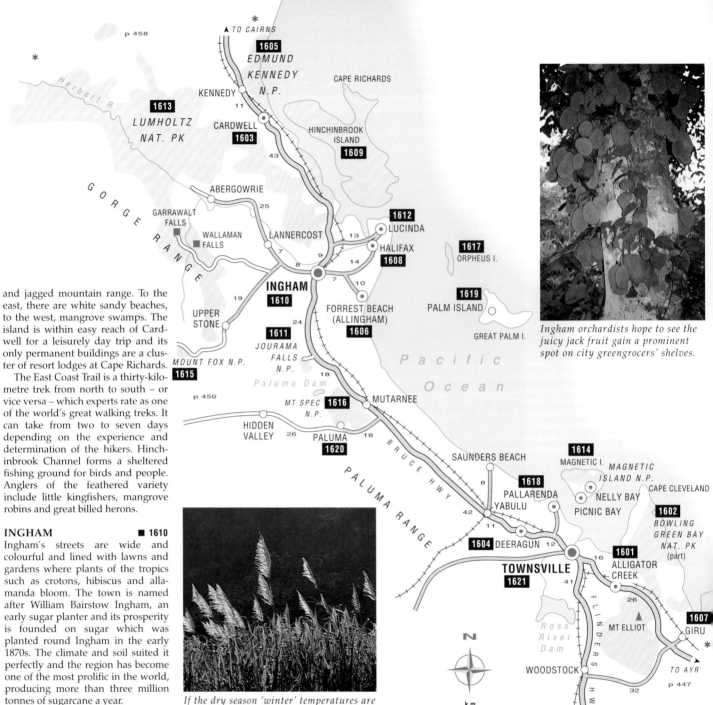

Lucinda provides access to Orpheus and Hinchinbrook islands and is famous for its beach and estuarine crabs, but its primary purpose is to provide the port facilities for Ingham's raw-sugar export. The three huge, bulk-storage sheds have the capacity to hold 231 000 tonnes of sugar before it is carried by conveyor belt to the wharf. The cyclone-resistant loading jetty stretches almost six kilometres in length. It was completed in 1979 with allowance made in the design for the curvature of the earth. *Population 780*

LUMHOLTZ NATIONAL PARK ■ 1613

This 150 000-hectare zone around the Herbert River and its tributaries comprises the old Herbert River Gorge and Falls, Wallaman Falls, Garrawalt Falls, Yamanie Falls, Hinchinbrook Channel, Herkes Creek Falls, Sword Creek Falls and Broadwater Creek Falls national parks, which were brought together in 1991 to form the new Lumholtz National Park.

The park extends from Hinchinbrook Channel through the Herbert Valley, and spans the Cardwell, MacAlister, Kirrama and Seaview ranges, taking in lowland and highland tropical rainforest, eucalypt forests and spectacular gorges and waterfalls. Much of this territory is inaccessible and even experienced bushwalkers must apply for an entry permit from the Queensland National Parks and Wildlife Service at Ingham.

The Yamanie Falls area is a World Heritage-listed wet tropics zone surrounding the ruins of Dalrymple, Australia's first inland town to be properly surveyed. Old mine sites remain and there is a memorial to Ludwig Leichhardt who passed this way on his first major expedition.

The area around Wallaman Falls is the most developed in the park. Here Stony Creek, often shrouded by rainbow-fringed mist, plunges in an unbroken drop of between 278 and 305 metres into a deep canyon to join the Herbert River. Some authorities say this is the longest single drop waterfall in Australia – others give the honour to Wollomombi Falls in New South Wales. The area is home to saw-shelled tortoises, black and green tree snakes, lace monitors and flightless cassowaries; water dragons and platypuses swim in the creek. The beautiful Owen Victoria's riflebird also inhabitats the park and performs intricate courtship dances high up in the canopy.

MAGNETIC ISLAND: NELLY BAY AND PICNIC BAY ■ 1614

Magnetic Island, one of the largest islands on the Great Barrier Reef, is only twenty minutes from Townsville city centre by fast catamaran en route to the Great Barrier Reef. Two passenger ferries and a vehicular ferry run every day and a helicopter service is available. In many respects the island is another satellite suburb of Townsville. The settlements of Picnic Bay, Nelly Bay, Arcadia, Alma Bay, Radical Bay and Horseshoe Bay dot the eastern side and house a mixture of permanent residents, daily commuters and holiday-makers in idyllic real estate – the island has a total permanent population of more than 1000. The remains of the Second World War army installations erected on the island as front-line defences can still be seen .

Stony Creek's metamorphosis into a 300-metre plunge at Wallaman Falls can be spectacular or modest depending on the Atherton Tableland rainfall.

Magnetic Island is rimmed with white, sandy beaches and crossed by a high spine of mountains covered by forests of eucalypts and wattles and strewn with granite boulders. More than half its area is national park and shelters koalas, wallabies, parrots, cockatoos and goannas. Fine walking tracks lead to exceptional views but there are some hazards in this other Eden. Tropical sunshine needs filtering through hats, protective clothing and sunscreen, and shoes are a must for reef-walking or strolling through muddy water. The netted swimming areas are free from most marine dangers except the deadly marine stinger (box jellyfish) during the November to March summer season.

The first recorded sighting of this region was made by Captain Cook in June 1770 when he sailed past in the *Endeavour*. He named Cleveland Bay and 'Magnetical' Island, recording in his log that the ship's compass 'did not traverse well' when near this land mass. No subsequent mariners have had problems with a swinging compass and the island is magnetic in name only.

MOUNT FOX NATIONAL PARK ■ 1615

The shape of Mount Fox is best seen from the air. This small national park of only 200 hectares preserves the well-formed, 811-metre cone around a long extinct volcanic crater which the Aborigines call 'yellerai'. Erosion is beginning to break up the southern rim and it is ankle-turning country where long grass conceals loose rocks. Sure-footed fossickers may find clear smoky quartz, black obsidian and petrified wood.

MOUNT SPEC NATIONAL PARK ■ 1616

Mount Spec National Park, named after a boat belonging to Robert Towns whose own name is commemorated in Townsville, protects a section of the Paluma Range northwest of Townsville. The foothills are covered with open eucalypt woodland which gives way to rainforest on the cool, moist mountain tops and in the creek valleys. The park is rocky in many places and ferns, palms and orchids grow there. It is the southernmost refuge for green ringtail and striped possums. The road from the Bruce Highway to Paluma (see entry) crosses an old

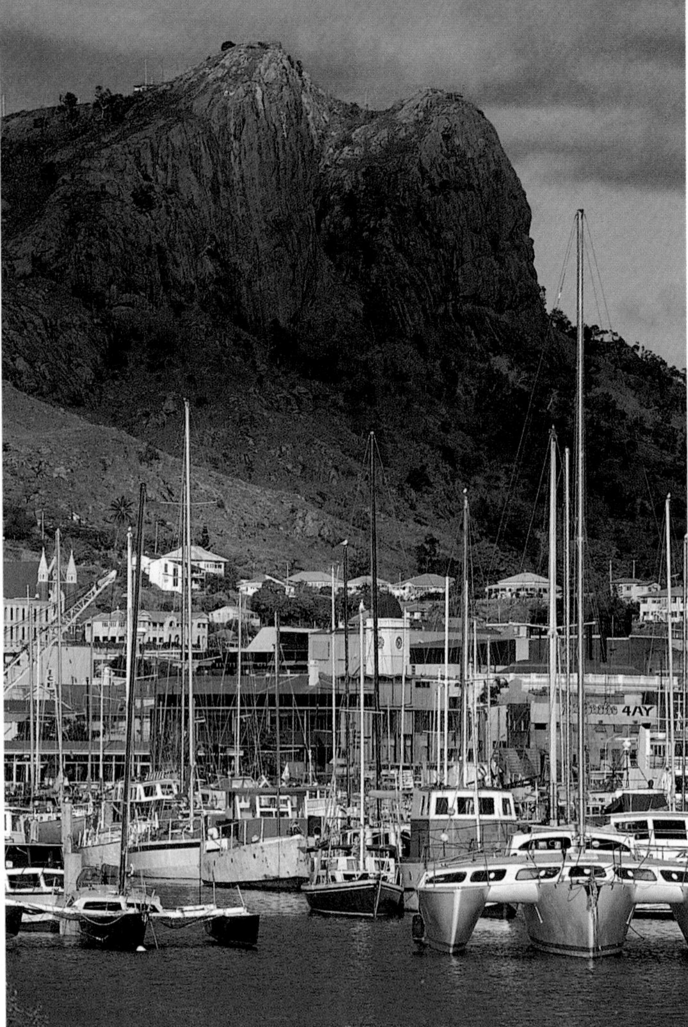

The brooding, inhospitable bulk of Castle Hill looms over Townsville, defying colonisation by the urban spread of Australia's major tropical city.

stone bridge at Little Crystal Creek which is a popular spot for swimming and picnicking.

ORPHEUS ISLAND ■ **1617**
Orpheus Island, one of the Palm Islands group, is a national park with on and offshore attractions which can be reached from Taylor's Beach and Lucinda. The island is fringed with coral reefs where snorkellers and scuba divers have almost unlimited access to a kaleidoscopic display of tropical marine life. Most of the waters around the island are zoned Marine National Park 'B' – this means they are in the 'look but don't touch' category. Fishing and shell collecting are not permitted. The walking track from Hazard Bay to the seaward side of the island crosses open grasslands, dry eucalypt woodland and cool, moist rainforested gullies and gives spectacular views from the rocky crags. Goats, introduced to the island in the nineteenth century to provide food for shipwrecked sailors, have depleted much of the native vegetation.

PALLARENDA ■ **1618**
Pallarenda, a six-kilometre drive from Townsville, is one of the city's newer suburbs. It lies almost on the point of Cape Pallarenda between the Townsville Town Common and Rowes Bay. A swimming area is enclosed in thick nylex mesh to protect bathers from sharks and the marine stinger, or box jellyfish, but drifting and still deadly poisonous tentacle pieces of the stingers may pass through the mesh and endanger swimmers in the November to March season. *Population 940*

PALM ISLAND ■ **1619**
Great Palm Island is the largest of the Palm Islands group of rocks and islands named by Captain Cook in 1770 after the cabbage palms that grew on them. Covering more than 6000 hectares, it contains mountains and sandy bays and is fringed with coral reefs. The island is the home of a community of Aborigines – some of whom can trace their families back to the original inhabitants and others whose forebears were brought to the island by force. The settlement was established in 1918 and supports itself with farming and boat-building. *Population 1980 (Palm Islands Group)*

PALUMA ■ **1620**
Paluma is a small mountain village retreat set in rainforest on the northwestern boundary of Thuringowa City. The settlement began as Cloudy Creek when tin was discovered there in 1875. Mining peaked in 1905 but then inevitably declined because of poor prices and the difficult terrain which discouraged travellers. McLellands Lookout is named for the overseer of the 1930s road gang who during the depression built the Paluma Road and the bridge that spans Little Crystal Creek. The water behind Paluma Dam contributes to Townsville's principal water supply.

TOWNSVILLE ■ **1621**
This busy international port is Australia's largest tropical city and the commercial, industrial and cultural hub of northern Queensland. Air and sea routes take sugar, minerals, beef, fresh tropical fruit, vegetables and seafood interstate and overseas. Limestone quarried from the nearby and aptly named Calcium feeds the local cement works. Townsville lies wholly within the tropical zone and receives three-quarters of its rainfall in the wet season between October and March. Cyclones are a regular threat in the region.

'Cattle would find here a tolerable abundance of nutritive food', said Matthew Flinders during his 1802 coastal survey, but it was not until 1864 that the town on Cleveland Bay at the mouth of Ross Creek began to grow. John Melton Black persuaded Robert Towns, a Sydney businessman, to provide financial backing for his plan for a boiling-down works to provide a market for the region's cattlemen. He named the settlement for his benefactor who made one brief visit to the area. By this time the early settlers were raising cattle and sheep and running cotton, sugar and coffee plantations with the help of labourers from the Pacific Islands – then known as Kanakas or South Sea Islanders. The discovery of copper at Einasleigh (1866) and gold at Cape River (1867), Ravenswood (1869) and Charters Towers (1871) gave a spurt to Townsville's growth, making it an important regional centre.

Aboriginal participants celebrate their culture at Townsville's annual festival, underlining the city's multicultural heritage.

Townsville was the terminus of the railway from the west, and had the region's first meat-freezing plant, at Ross River, from 1892. The establishment of the freezing works meant that cattle were good for more than just boiling-down and hides – frozen meat could be exported, and cattle from all over northern Queensland were brought to Ross River by rail.

A regional domestic architecture evolved to suit the climate with some regions displaying a progressive raising of houses on stilts – from approximately twenty centimetres in 1870 to a high of two metres in the 1920s (see *Rockhampton & Yeppoon*). The beautiful Buchanan's Hotel, burned to the ground in 1982, had an intricate, iron lacework facade and was immortalised in a 1973 ten-cent postage stamp – one of a series of four featuring Australian buildings – in company with the Sydney Opera House, Como House in Melbourne and St James' Church in Sydney.

Townsville's citizens have long had a sense of national and local identity. In 1901, the new Australian flag was officially unfurled here for the first time after Federation. Local workers have participated in three notable strikes shaping the north's political future – the 1891 shearers' strike, the 1919 meatworkers' strike and the 1948 railway workers' strike.

During the Second World War, Townsville was strategically close to the South Pacific arena and large numbers of Australian and American military and airforce personnel were based in the area. Japanese fighters bombed the town three times in 1942 but failed to do any damage.

This is the northern centre for higher education and research too. The Australian Institute of Tropical Medicine was set up in Townsville although it transferred to Sydney in 1930; Sister Elizabeth Kenny's well known polio clinic opened in 1933. The University College of Townsville became the James Cook University in 1970 and specialises in marine biology. There is also a tropical veterinary science post-graduate centre. The headquarters of the Australian Institute of Marine Science and the Great Barrier Reef Marine Park Authority are both in Townsville–Thuringowa. *Population 101 400*

TOWNSVILLE TOWN COMMON ENVIRONMENTAL PARK This refuge for wildlife is just five minutes' drive from the city centre. During the wet season, brolgas, jabirus and many other wetland birds fly in to this lowlying area. They move out again when the swamps turn into cracking claypans. Forest songbirds stay all year and wallabies, echidnas and goannas make the park their home.

FESTIVAL Pacific Festival, August.

THURINGOWA CITY: MORE CONCEPT THAN CONCRETE

TRAVELLERS familiar with sprawling, cheek-by-jowl city suburbs nudging the edges of arterial highways might be surprised to hear that Alligator Creek, Deeragun, Giru, Jensen (Cordelia Estate) and Paluma (see entries) are all suburbs of Queensland's newest city – Thuringowa – which completely surrounds Townsville. This city of thirty-five 'suburbs' was officially declared on 1 January 1986; a thirty-sixth, Thuringowa Central, had to be created later to provide a postcode for the official name.

The name Thuringowa goes back to 1879 when the Thuringowa Shire, or Division, covered an area of 7612 kilometres. Over the years, shire land was annexed by other authorities. In 1888, the forerunner of the present Burdekin Shire took a large slice, and ten suburbs were lost to Townsville between 1918 to 1936. Further bouts of land grabbing seemed inevitable, until in 1985 the shire council realised it had more than the requisite population numbers to apply for city status – even though the population was not gathered in one spot.

The local authorities knew that however much a shire might contribute to a region's prosperity, cities always had more clout. They successfully petitioned the Queensland government and immediately began promoting Townsville and Thuringowa as twin cities. There has been dramatic growth in recent years which undoubtedly owes much to Thuringowa's imaginative development plans. The suburbs of Kirwan, Condon, Ramussen and Kelso are still perceived by some to be suburbs of the older city but in fact the boundaries are drawn at the Bohle River, Dalrymple Road, Ross River and Mount Stuart.

Unlike most shire councils or other provincial local government bodies across Australia which have declared themselves 'cities' Thuringowa is beginning to appear on maps of Queensland – the dot, located slightly north-east of Townsville, shows the position of Thuringowa Central. The jurisdiction of this district-city extends over a population of more than 40 000 and an area stretching from Crystal Creek in the north to the Haughton River in the south, from the coastline to the Great Dividing Range in the west. Thuringowa now covers 4121 square kilometres and has 'suburbs' separated by canefields and pastures, pineapple plantations and orchards, national parks, a mining site and a refinery. □

Townsville's busy commercial centre and port, crowding the mouth of Ross Creek on Cleveland Bay, is surrounded by its twin 'city' of Thuringowa.

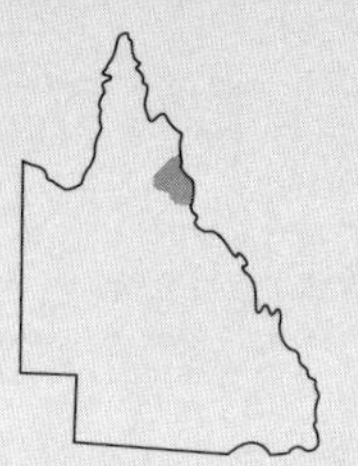

Cairns & Innisfail

Gold, tin and cedar drew early settlers here and they often stayed to plant the hillsides and valleys with sugar, bananas and tea. The unparalleled beauty of the far north's tropical forests and azure waters has spawned a major new industry – tourism.

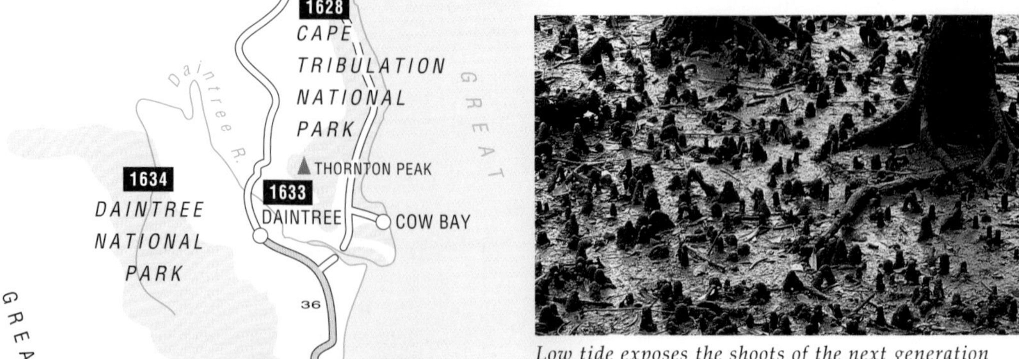

Low tide exposes the shoots of the next generation of mangroves crowding the nutrient-rich mud around the river estuaries of north Queensland.

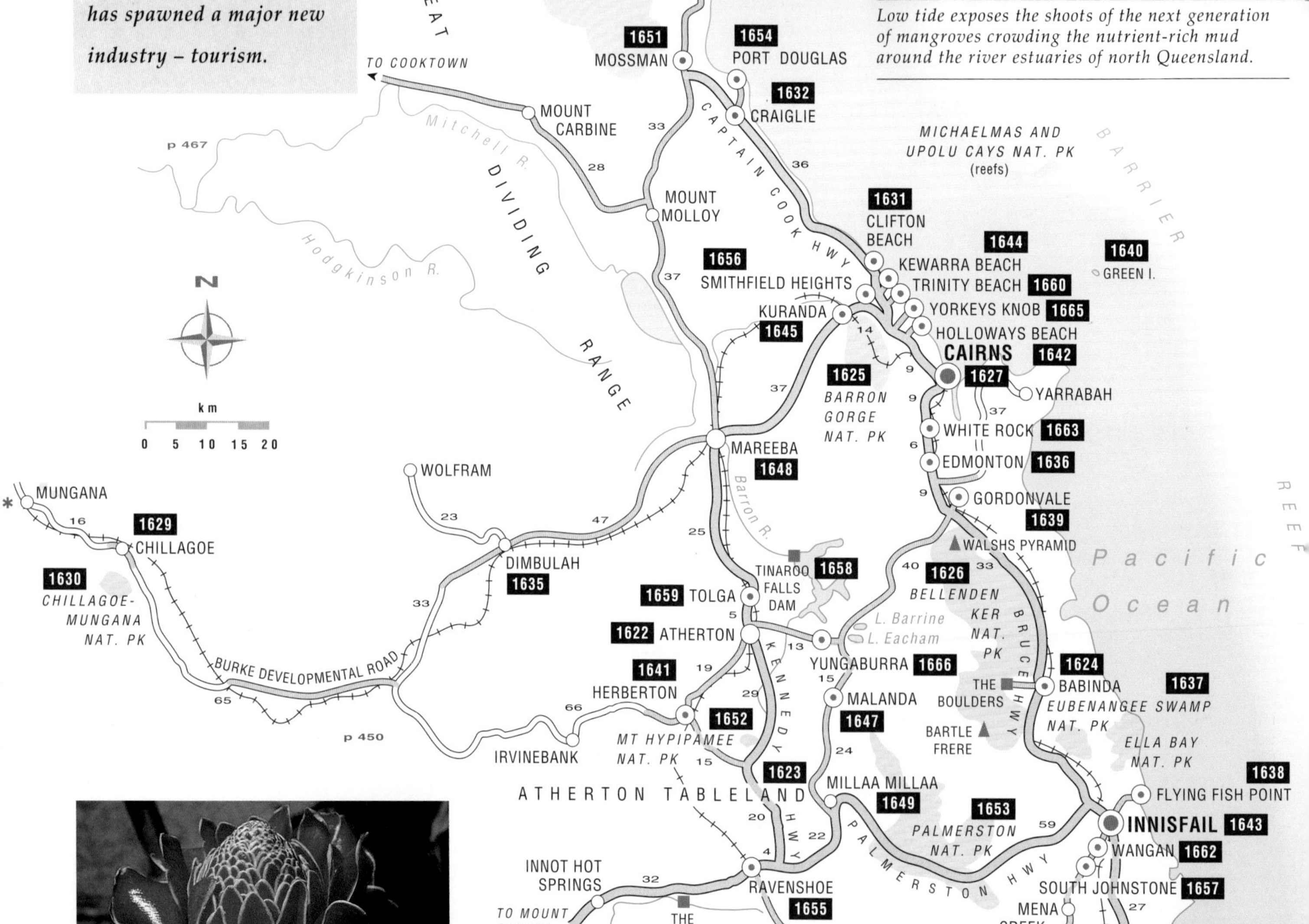

1628 CAPE TRIBULATION NATIONAL PARK
THORNTON PEAK
1634 DAINTREE NATIONAL PARK
1633 DAINTREE
COW BAY
GREAT BARRIER REEF
Daintree R.
1651 MOSSMAN
1654 PORT DOUGLAS
1632 CRAIGLIE
TO COOKTOWN
MOUNT CARBINE
Mitchell R.
GREAT DIVIDING RANGE
CAPTAIN COOK HWY
MICHAELMAS AND UPOLU CAYS NAT. PK (reefs)
MOUNT MOLLOY
1631 CLIFTON BEACH
1644 KEWARRA BEACH
1640 GREEN I.
1656 SMITHFIELD HEIGHTS
1660 TRINITY BEACH
1645 KURANDA
1665 YORKEYS KNOB
HOLLOWAYS BEACH
Hodgkinson R.
N
CAIRNS 1642
1627
1625 BARRON GORGE NAT. PK
YARRABAH
km 0 5 10 15 20
1663 WHITE ROCK
MAREEBA 1648
1636 EDMONTON
WOLFRAM
GORDONVALE
1639
Barron R.
MUNGANA
1629 CHILLAGOE
1630 CHILLAGOE-MUNGANA NAT. PK
DIMBULAH 1635
TINAROO FALLS DAM 1658
WALSHS PYRAMID
1626 BELLENDEN KER NAT. PK
Pacific Ocean
1659 TOLGA
1622 ATHERTON
L. Barrine
L. Eacham
BRUCE HWY
KENNEDY HWY
BURKE DEVELOPMENTAL ROAD
YUNGABURRA 1666
1624 BABINDA
1637 EUBENANGEE SWAMP NAT. PK
1641 HERBERTON
THE BOULDERS
MALANDA 1647
1652 MT HYPIPAMEE NAT. PK
BARTLE FRERE
ELLA BAY NAT. PK
IRVINEBANK
1623
ATHERTON TABLELAND
MILLAA MILLAA 1649
1653 PALMERSTON NAT. PK
1638 FLYING FISH POINT
INNISFAIL 1643
PALMERSTON HWY
WANGAN 1662
INNOT HOT SPRINGS
RAVENSHOE 1655
SOUTH JOHNSTONE 1657
MENA CREEK
TO MOUNT GARNET
THE MILLSTREAM FALLS
CARDSTONE
1646 KURRIMINE
TULLY FALLS
Tully R.
EL ARISH
1650 MISSION BEACH
L. Koombooloomba
1664 WONGALING BEACH
1661 TULLY
SOUTH MISSION BEACH
DUNK ISLAND
TO INGHAM

p 467
p 450
p 454

Cairns' emblem, the torch ginger, bears a striking resemblance to the waratah, the emblem of New South Wales.

ATHERTON ■ 1622

Nestling high on the Atherton Tableland between Innisfail and Cairns, Atherton is more than 760 metres above sea level and has what to most people is an idyllic climate. Named after John Atherton, an explorer and the first settler in the district, the town developed from cedar cutters' camps at what was called Prior's Pocket, in 1881–82. The town is now the centre of a rich agricultural district. Maize is the chief product but other fruit and field crops such as avocados, potatoes, macadamia nuts and peanuts are also grown. A legacy of the early Chinese inhabitants is the historic joss house (1900) near the Atherton Art Gallery. *Population 5210*

HALLORAN'S HILL ENVIRONMENTAL PARK A walking track leads up the slopes of this extinct volcanic crater from the Louise Street picnic area. The summit offers sweeping views of the Atherton Tablelands.

FESTIVALS Maize Festival, September; Tableland Folk Festival, October.

ATHERTON TABLELAND ■ 1623

One-hundred-and-fifty kilometres in length, the Atherton Tableland – actually comprising two tablelands, Atherton and Evelyn – is tucked away behind Cairns and Innisfail. The mountain range which divides the tablelands from the coast is one reason for the cool, subtropical climate within the tropics for which this region is famous. First Chinese, then European pioneers were drawn to the area by the promise of gold and tin and stayed to farm maize, potatoes, peanuts and coffee and establish beef and dairy herds. The tablelands have a wealth of natural treasures, which locals believe cannot be found in such concentration or with such an ideal climate, anywhere else in the world.

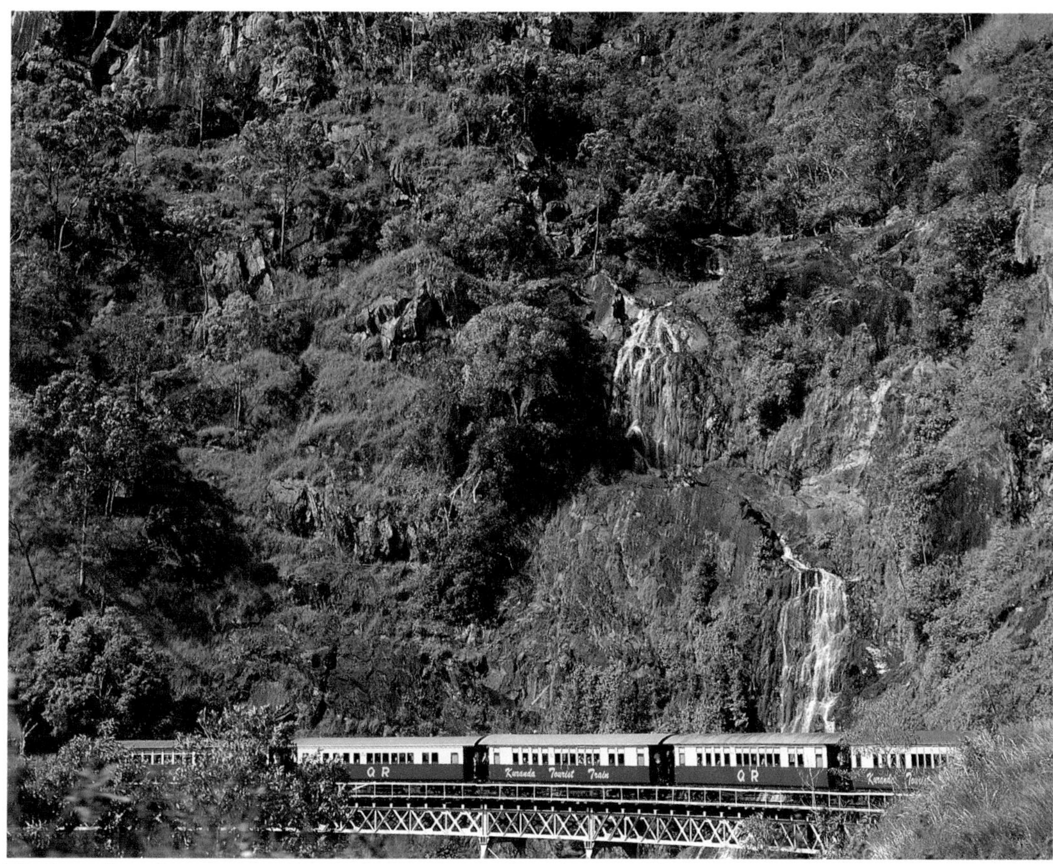

The Kuranda train sweeps tourists high above the jungle tree tops as it hugs the side of Stoney Creek Gorge.

BABINDA ■ 1624

Babinda is wet...very wet. This small settlement at the eastern foothills of Mount Bellenden Ker, holds a thirty-year record for the highest average annual rainfall – 4537 millimetres – in Australia. A sugar mill built here in 1914, now processes around a million tonnes of raw sugarcane each year. Babinda is made up of three Aboriginal words: 'Bana' for 'water', 'jindi' for 'rain' and 'bunda' for 'mountain'. *Population 1270*

THE BOULDERS Spectacular cascades of water rush by huge rocks lodged in the bed of the Babinda Creek. The Boulders are popular with tourists and locals, even though they have acquired something of a 'fatal attraction' reputation – since 1959, ten swimmers have drowned here.

FESTIVALS Harvest Festival, June.

BARRON GORGE NATIONAL PARK ■ 1625

Near Kuranda, the Barron River tumbles about 250 metres over the tall escarpment of the Atherton Tableland into a rainforest-covered gorge and forms this five-kilometre-long rugged, twisting break between the Macalister and Lamb ranges. Barron Gorge National Park has some of the finest examples of tropical rainforest close to Cairns fostering an unusual richness of flora and fauna within a relatively small area.

Aboriginal hunting routes passed through this area before white settlement when supply routes for the gold and tin fields were cut by miners from the rugged hillsides.

Work on a rail link through the gorge to the coast began in the 1880s. The thirty-four-kilometre line from Kuranda to Cairns was a formidable task for engineers, surveyors and construction workers because of the steep slopes, wet weather, landslides and dense rainforest. Fifteen tunnels and more than forty bridges were needed to negotiate the line's ninety-eight curves and provide grades suitable for steam locomotives as they gained another three-hundred-and-twenty metres in altitude. The line was finally opened in 1891.

Another project which stirred the imagination of engineers was the harnessing of the immense power of the Barron Falls. A small hydro-electric power station of just under four megawatts, built in 1935, was the first underground power station in Australia. A major irrigation project for the Atherton Tableland began in 1958 with the completion of the Tinaroo Dam on the Barron River, and a new sixty-megawatt station below the Barron Falls began to provide power to the Queensland electricity grid in 1963.

BELLENDEN KER NATIONAL PARK ■ 1626

This park contains the two highest mountains in the state, Mount Bartle Frere (1622 metres) and Mount Bellenden Ker (1580 metres). Covering 32 000 hectares on the eastern slopes of the Bellenden Ker Range, the park is largely undeveloped. A number of waterfalls and streams flow through the dense rainforest, the habitat for many mammals, birds and reptiles.

GOLDFIELDS TRACK Following an historic miners' pack-horse track of last century, this recently reopened ten-kilometre route crosses a low saddle in the Bellenden Ker Range to the Mulgrave Valley below. The track starts at Boulders Scenic Reserve, west of Babinda, and climbs through dense rainforest. It descends through the Goldborough State Forest ending at the East Mulgrave River causeway.

MOUNT BARTLE FRERE HIKING TRACK A fifteen-kilometre track climbs steeply to the summit of Mount Bartle Frere from the Josephine Falls car park. Rainforest is found on the lower slopes, changing to low scrub and open grasslands on the ridges. Water is available from a spring at the remains of an old hut near the summit. Cloud can cover the mountain peaks at short notice and sudden rainstorms are common. A shorter version of this walk leads to the dramatic Broken Nose cliffs on a spur of the main range. Permission to walk this track should be obtained from the ranger at Josephine Falls.

CAIRNS ■ 1627

By the 1860s, pioneer settlements were scattered intermittently along the coast but it took the lure of gold to populate the north. Cairns was established in 1876 as a port for the Hodgkinson River goldfields, but was overshadowed by Port Douglas until 1891, when Cairns became the terminus of the railway line to Kuranda (see entry). When the railway line from Brisbane was only extended as far as Cairns, in 1924, the rivalry was over and Cairns became the leading northern city.

The city today is a delightful blend of colonial architecture from the grand public and commercial buildings to the rambling country pubs. It is a handsome city, rich with history, character and charm.

During the Second World War, Cairns was the Australian Army's tropical training centre, one of the bases for the vital battle of the Coral Sea and headquarters for the under-cover 'Z force'. Cairns has grown

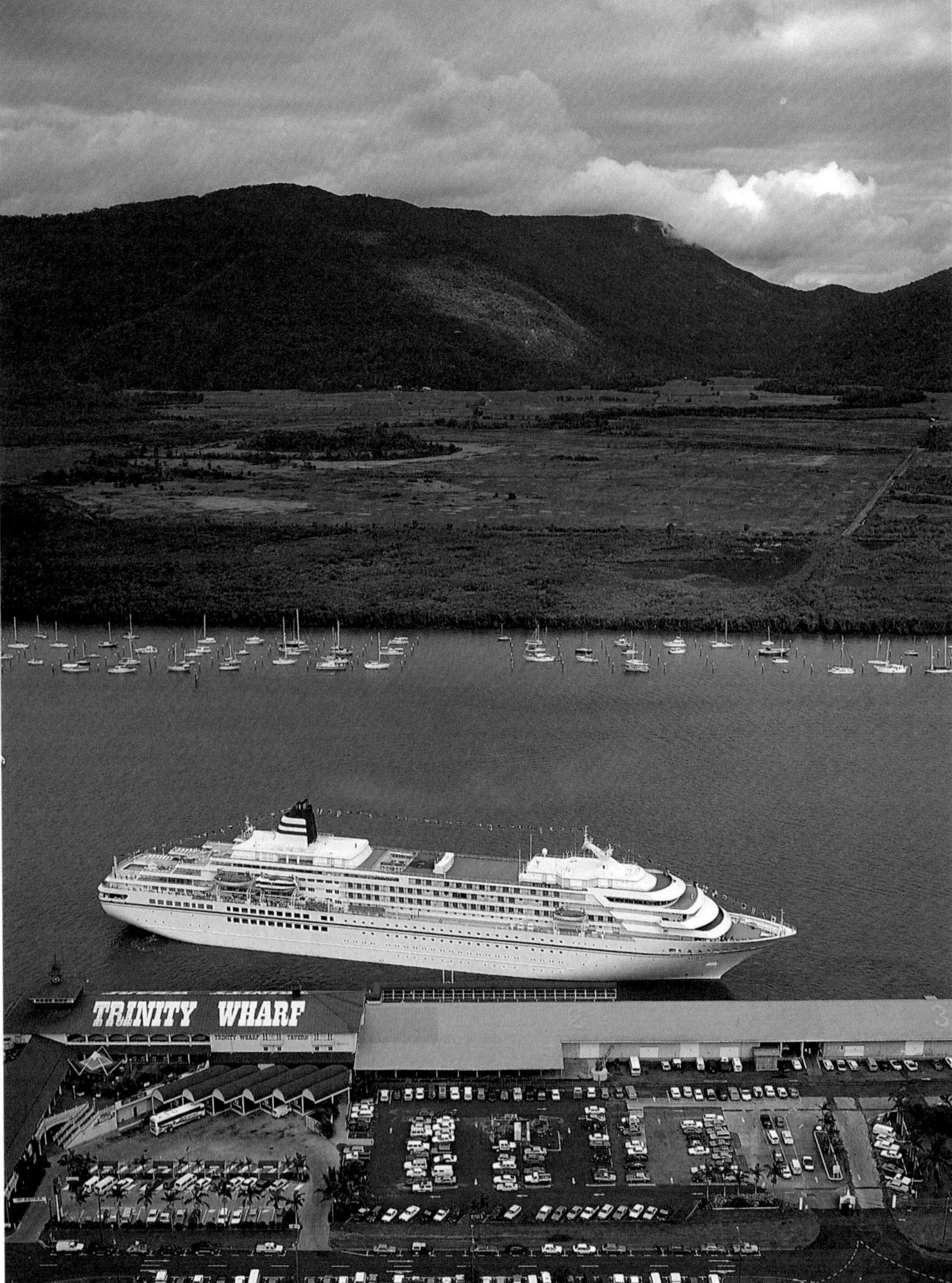

One section of Cairns' workaday waterfront wharves has been transformed into a terminal and shopping complex.

rapidly since 1979, and now earns around 400 million dollars a year from tourism and around the same amount from mining, fishing and agriculture. *Population 64 460*

THE PIER MARKET PLACE A high-quality craft market is held here on weekends in what is otherwise a popular and colourful local promenade and eating place. Boats leave daily from the Pier's Marlin Marina, bound for the Great Barrier Reef.

ANDERSON STREET ENVIRONMENTAL PARK A short boardwalk through the remains of this lowland tea-tree swamp provides a vivid illustration of the vegetation which once covered what is now Cairns.

FLECKER BOTANIC GARDENS Set up in the 1880s, these gardens have several distinct parts: the botanic garden in Collins Avenue, and the saltwater and freshwater lakes in Greenslopes Street. Between the lakes and the botanic garden is a forest of palms and paperbark trees, typical of the vegetation which once covered large swampy areas of the Cairns district.

FESTIVALS Fun in the Sun Festival, mid-October.

CAPE TRIBULATION NATIONAL PARK ■ 1628

Sweeping down from cloud-shrouded mountain tops, the rainforests of Cape Tribulation National Park meet the sea along a stretch of sandy beaches and rocky headlands.

The cape was named by Captain Cook after his ship the *Endeavour* was damaged on a reef in 1770. The 16 959-hectare park stretches along the coast between the Daintree and Bloomfield rivers and extends inland to the McDowall Range which forms the western boundary. Within these boundaries, there is a rich mosaic of vegetation of coastal and upland rainforest, mangroves, swamps and heathlands. Of great interest to botanists and amateur plant enthusiasts are the primitive species of flowering plants recently discovered in the park's rainforest.

A road which runs through the rainforest up to Cape Tribulation was bitterly opposed by conservationists who unsuccessfully set up a blockade across its proposed path in 1983. On a more modest scale, a 400-metre-long boardwalk leads from the Cape Tribulation car park to an observation platform overlooking the ocean, beach and mountains and an 800-metre track at Oliver Creek winds through rainforest and mangroves.

CHILLAGOE ■ 1629

Crowds pour into this former mining town each May for the annual rodeo and races. Things are then briefly reminiscent of the time when Chillagoe was a boom town with a mineral field among the richest in Queensland. By 1906, most of the state's lead, half its silver and much of its copper came from these mines. Gold, zinc, wolfram, fluorspar, tin and molybdenum were also mined.

As elsewhere, the mines became depleted, declined, and by 1943 the smelters were shut down. Mining is now confined to one quarry which crushes limestone, although digging of some rare blue marble deposits has again made Chillagoe a name on world markets. The town's museum of old copper smelters displays the machinery which was once the town's hub. *Population 500*

CHILLAGOE-MUNGANA NATIONAL PARK ■ 1630

Limestone outcrops in this park contain many spectacular caves, some of considerable size. Tours through five caves are conducted daily by the Queensland Parks and Wildlife Service. A number of the caves feature impressive stalactites and stalagmites as well as historic graffiti, in the form of names, initials and dates, from the turn of the century.

Various species of bats such as the bent-winged, sheath-tailed, and eastern horseshoe bats, roost and breed in these caves. The district is dotted with ant hills – brown earth formations constructed laboriously by these highly-organised insects. Pioneers found the crushed ant hills useful as natural 'cement' for their hut floors. To the north is Mount Molley, and Mount Carbine with its massive deposits of wolframite. To the east is the lush Julattan district.

CLIFTON BEACH ■ 1631

Clifton Beach is part of a twenty-six-kilometre stretch of coastline, north of Cairns, called the Marlin Coast. Now a residential suburb of Cairns, Clifton Beach is also a popular tourist spot. *Population 3730*

CRAIGLIE ■ 1632

A service station and a few houses are all that remains of this former logging town. *Population 2040*

DAINTREE ■ 1633

This small town is at the end of the sealed road and at the beginning of the wilderness to the north. It is a centre for the nearby dairy and cattle-farming district and a starting point for visitors heading for Cape York. A barge service from Daintree is the access for Cape Tribulation National Park; the turnoff for the barge is eleven kilometres before the town. Cruises on the Daintree River leave from the same point. There is a coffee plantation west of the town.

DAINTREE NATIONAL PARK ■ 1634
Mossman Gorge is at the southern end of the Daintree National Park, some eighty kilometres north of Cairns. Most of the park is covered by dense tropical rainforest with areas of open forest on its north-western side. Some of the most magnificent lowland rainforest in the world is found in this region, and the Daintree–Cooktown belt was given a World Heritage listing in 1989.

Many animals, such as Bennett's tree kangaroo, are unique to the area and they share the rainforest with the cassowary, the Cairns birdwing butterfly, the giant atlas moth, and more than 35 000 species of orchid!

Walking tracks from the picnic area, west of Mossman, go to forest-lined river banks and water holes. A suspension bridge high over Rex Creek is the start of a two-and-a-half-kilometre track through magnificent rainforest further up the gorge.

DIMBULAH ■ 1635
This tobacco-growing centre, west of Mareeba developed after the Chillagoe railway was built in 1900, and is today the gateway to the rugged, western regions of the Mareeba Shire. Dimbulah is said to be an Aboriginal word for 'long waterhole' and may refer to the nearby Walsh River. The Mareeba–Dimbulah irrigation schemes provide abundant irrigation water and the Dimbulah district is capable of further agricultural and pastoral development.

THE MAREEBA–DIMBULAH IRRIGATION SCHEME About 820 square kilometres between the towns of Walkamin, Biboohra, Mareeba and Dimbulah on the northern slopes of the Atherton Tableland are well watered by this scheme. The scheme consists of the Tinaroo Falls Dam, Lake Tinaroo and Barron Gorge hydro-electric station.

In the Daintree forest, board-like, stabilising buttress roots anchor tall trunks in the shallow soil.

EDMONTON ■ 1636
The largest sugar mill in the Cairns district closed down here in the early 1990s, but housing development has continued unabated in this former sugar town. *Population 3260*

EUBENANGEE SWAMP NATIONAL PARK ■ 1637
This 1520-hectare national park has a boardwalk – often impassable after rain – which provides cleverly sited vantage points to watch the park's abundant birdlife such as the black-necked stork or jabiru, herons, egrets, ibis, spoonbills and ducks. Rainforest and eucalypt forest at the edge of the wetlands are a habitat for the crimson finch, honey eater and butcherbird. An estuarine crocodile can occasionally be seen from a safely elevated position. The boardwalk is at the end of a one-and-half-kilometre walking track which leads from the parking area.

FLYING FISH POINT ■ 1638
This small but popular beach town near Innisfail has a boat ramp and jetty. To the north is Mount Maria, a 518-hectare national park. Sweeping views of the coastline are to be had from its steep slopes. Rainforest covers the lower portion of the park. *Population 640*

GORDONVALE ■ 1639
A sugar town in the Mulgrave Valley, south of Cairns, Gordonvale is surrounded by mountains, hills and rolling green canefields. The Mulgrave Sugar Mill, built in 1895, runs a steam locomotive to Orchid Valley and a museum depicting the history of the area has been built near the station. Walshs Pyramid dominates the landscape to the south and there are spectacular views from the summit. *Population 2660*

GREEN ISLAND ■ 1640
Most of this coral cay and its surrounding reef is a national park. There is a tourist resort on the island, the star attractions of which are two of the largest saltwater crocodiles in captivity, Oscar and Cassius. A walking track around the island passes through rainforest and open woodland and can be traversed in under half-an-hour.

MICHAELMAS AND UPOLU CAYS These two coral cays to the north-east of Green Island are the nesting grounds for thousands of sea birds. More than 30 000 birds may nest on Michaelmas Cay alone during summer. Common noddies, sooty terns, crested and lesser crested terns are the most common species. Visitors are advised not to move among the nesting sea birds as they are extremely sensitive to disturbance at this time of year.

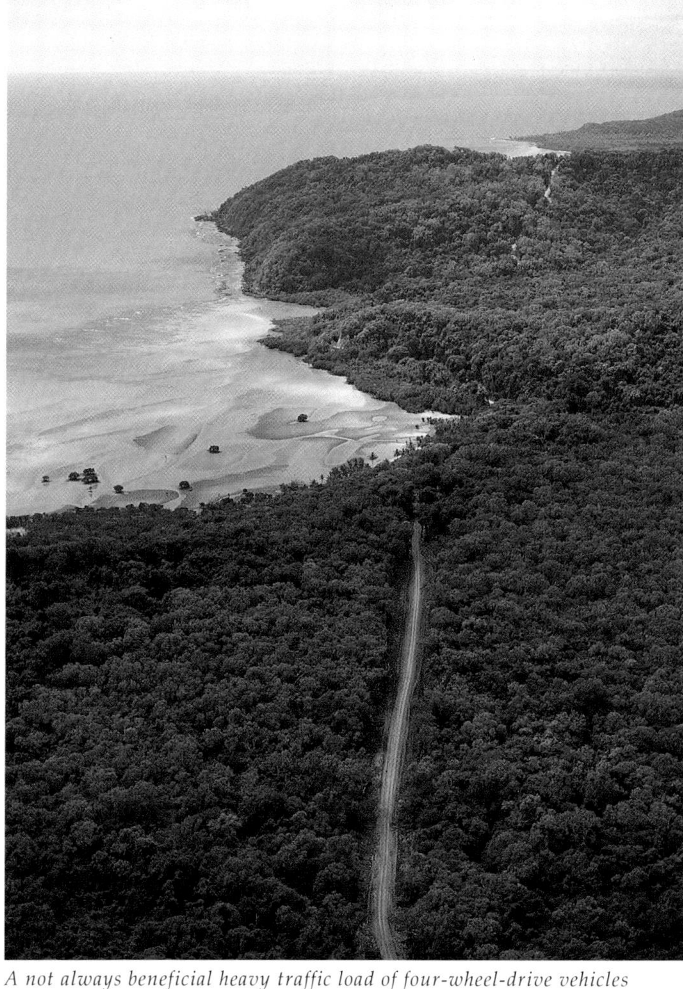

A not always beneficial heavy traffic load of four-wheel-drive vehicles followed after this road sliced through the Cape Tribulation rainforest.

HERBERTON ■ 1641
A centre for a lucrative tin field, Herberton is tucked among rolling hills which are honeycombed with mines, old and new. Irvinebank, a pioneer settlement established in 1883 by mining entrepreneur John Moffat is nearby. Some charming old buildings such as Moffat's house, the School of Arts, the National Bank and Loudon Mill, still stand. A plan of the original township shows how extensive it once was. *Population 950*

FESTIVALS Tin Festival, September.

HOLLOWAYS BEACH ■ 1642
This beach settlement on the popular Marlin Coast has picture-postcard looks. A sweep of clean white sand shaded by a palm fringe has encouraged residential development and made this a popular beachside suburb of Cairns. *Population 2460*

INNISFAIL ■ 1643
The Queensland Government expedition sent to investigate this region after the brig *Maria* was wrecked on a nearby reef generated much public interest in this, then unknown, coastline. The expedition, after exploring Mourilyan harbour, camped near the present Innisfail site in October, 1873. Nind's camp, as it was then known, became the base for exploration of all the Johnstone River lands. On his return to Rockhampton the leader of the expedition, George Elphinstone Dalrymple, put together a meticulous report in which he praised the future prospects of the region for tropical agriculture.

On the strength of his report, T.H. Fitzgerald formed a company which took up land on the Johnstone River. The biggest plantation was on the Innisfail Estate where the Innisfail Sugar Mill had its first crushing in 1881. Fitzgerald, although not the first permanent settler, laid the foundation for future prosperity and, as such, is considered the founder of Innisfail. His initial success generated interest and other groups set up plantations in the area. The small settlement which grew up at the original Nind's camp became known as the Junction, and this became part of the site reserved for a township in

1881. The first sale of town allotments took place in 1883 and local government was quickly established.

Many Chinese settled in the district after the depletion of the Palmer River goldfields in the 1870s. A slump in the sugar market at this time encouraged the cultivation of bananas, an industry largely carried on by the Chinese. A joss house still stands in Ernest Street.

Sugar growing was later revived and by the 1890s, a central mill system with cane supplied by small farmers replaced the old plantation system. The character of the district was finally determined by the influx of Mediterranean – mainly Italian – settlers after the First World War and the area has maintained a cosmopolitan mix ever since.

Fishing is an important industry with a substantial commercial prawn trawling fleet, mackerel boats and line fishing boats anchored near the mouth of the Johnstone River. Innisfail, at the junction of the North and South Johnstone rivers, remains a rural centre with older industries based on sugar, tropical fruits, timber, dairying and fishing joined by cattle fattening and tea. *Population 8520*

ETTY BAY ENVIRONMENTAL PARK One of the prettiest beaches in North Queensland, Etty Bay is a haven for local people who explore the rocky headlands or the rainforest which grows right down to the water's edge. The rainforest has attractive stands of fan palms and a road between Coquette Point and Etty Bay passes through the park.

JOHNSTONE RIVERS The modest North Johnstone river rises on the Atherton Tablelands and is joined by the relatively insignificant South Johnstone River east of Innisfail before it flows into the sea. The northern river was named by the explorer George Dalrymple after R.A. Johnstone, one of the men who discovered the river in 1872.

The river was once a busy transport route; a launch used to run regularly between Innisfail and small settlements upriver and many early settlers had their own boats. The only way of crossing the river near Daradgee was by punt, and travellers would ring a roadside bell for the service. Nowadays, the river is silted up but canoe trips are possible on the only navigable section of the North Johnstone River.

MENA CREEK Ruins of a Spanish-style castle still stand near this small centre, south of Innisfail on the old Bruce Highway to Mission Beach.

The towers, built by a Spanish migrant called Jose Paronella, are surrounded by hectares of rainforest, bamboo and kauri pine avenues. Walking tracks lead to Mena Creek and Teresa Falls.

NERADA TEA PLANTATION In the 1950s, Dr Alan Maruff proved that tea could be grown on a commercial basis in Australia when he harvested tea successfully from plants he had grown from seedlings at Nerada. A labour-efficient hedge technique for tea growing and special harvesting machinery was later developed. It is estimated that tea production at Nerada will rise from one to five million kilograms annually well before the year 2000.

WARRINA LAKES This seventeen-hectare stretch of parkland has lakes with islands, landscaped gardens, tropical surroundings and abundant wildlife, all of this encircled by a walking track. Visitors to the park can hire canoes and water bikes.

Two successful crops of the Innisfail region often end up together on the consumer's breakfast table; sugar (left) has been grown for more than 100 years, while tea (above) is a newcomer, first planted in the 1950s.

KEWARRA BEACH ■ 1644

With an enviable location on the Marlin Coast, Kewarra Beach underwent rapid residential development in the late 1980s and early 1990s after a number of cane farms were sold. The design of the Kewarra Beach resort – the first resort in town – is based on local Aboriginal design and art. *Population 1190*

KURANDA ■ 1645

One of the best train journeys in the world is from Cairns to Kuranda. Spectacular vistas of the coastline, Barron Gorge and Stoney Creek Falls flash into view as the steam locomotive skirts around the coast, then zigzags up the steep eastern slopes of the Lam Range. A 125-year-old A10 No.6 steam locomotive – said to be the oldest steam train still working in the Southern Hemisphere – makes the daily trip.

At Kuranda, visitors can enjoy the cool tropical gardens, lavish with ferns, for which the Kuranda Railway Station is famous. A walking track from the railway station leads to the Barron Falls Lookout, a vantage point with spectacular views of the falls and upper gorge.

Kuranda is the home of the much-acclaimed Tjapukai Aboriginal Dance Theatre which has toured in Australia and overseas, and the Ngoonbi co-operative, an Aboriginal arts and crafts shop, that sells artefacts made by various Aboriginal groups around Australia. Ngoonbi is an Aboriginal word for 'meeting place', and Kuranda was once the meeting place for coastal and mountain Aboriginal peoples during the wet season.

Kuranda also has a butterfly sanctuary, where many rare species of butterfly can be seen, and a wildlife nocturnal house which allows a glimpse of the rainforest nightlife.

Davies Creek National Park is nearby. An easy, six-kilometre drive off the highway leads to the crystal-clear mountain waters in a fine picnic setting. *Population 620*

FESTIVALS Folk Festival, May.

KURRIMINE ■ 1646

Once known as Murdering Point, Kurrimine has developed from a 'beachside shack' village of half-a-dozen houses to an established settlement. It was given its bloodthirsty name after bodies from the wrecked brig *Maria*, were discovered here in 1872. Kurrimine is the beach closest to the Great Barrier Reef and is part of a national park; a short sealed track suitable for wheelchairs provides a circuit of several hundred metres through mixed dune vegetation. *Population 770*

MALANDA ■ 1647

Malanda is the beginning of the longest milk run in the world: milk and dairy products from the Malanda dairy factory are transported to Townsville, Mount Isa, and other commercial centres throughout far North Queensland. Nearby is the old Boonjie goldfield which triggered much of the early settlement in the area. *Population 900*

LAKE BARRINE AND LAKE EACHAM Lake Eacham and its twin, Lake Barrine, to the north of Malanda, are crystal-clear volcanic crater lakes. The lakes are surrounded by rainforest, protected within a national park.

MALANDA FALLS ENVIRONMENTAL PARK Outside town is the Malanda Falls, with a natural swimming pool complete with starting blocks and diving pool fringed with rainforest and landscaped gardens. Walking tracks following the North Johnstone River overlook pools where platypuses may sometimes be seen.

MAREEBA ■ 1648

A huge concrete water tower is the landmark for this town near the

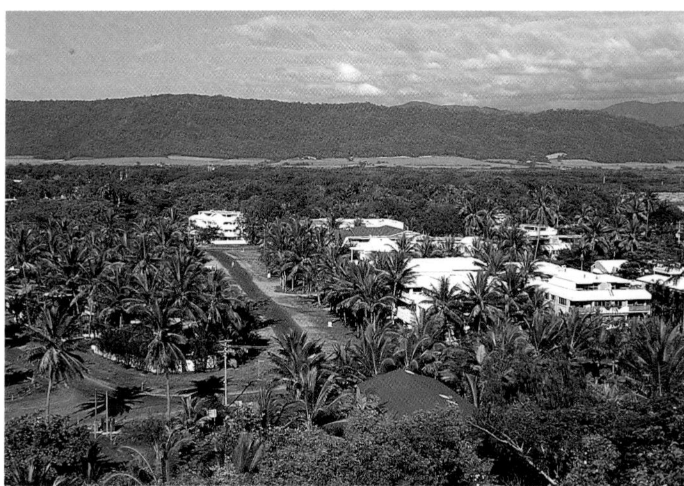

Palmy Port Douglas retains the air of a tropical outpost despite the disturbance of its 100-year, post-gold-rush slumber by tourists in the 1980s.

junction of the Barron River and Granite Creek. Mareeba is an Aboriginal word said to mean 'meeting of waters' or 'place to meet'.

Mareeba is the tobacco capital of Australia but it also produces commercial crops of avocadoes, coffee, mangoes, rice, sugarcane, pumpkins and sweet potatoes. The immensely popular annual rodeo has been immortalised in song by Slim Dusty.

Just south of Mareeba is the airport from which Allied aircraft set off to play a decisive part in the Battle of the Coral Sea. Thousands of American and Australian servicemen were based on the tablelands during the Second World War and former campsites are signposted throughout the region. *Population 6800*

GRANITE GORGE A walking track intrudes into this vast mass of jumbled grey stone, a wild and inhospitable landscape formed by an ancient volcanic upheaval. The gorge is hard to see from the road but once inside, walkers are surrounded by a two-and-a-half-square-kilometre zone of enormous boulders overlaying underground creeks. Rock wallabies are common in an environment tailor-made for them.

MILLAA MILLAA ■ 1649

Early this century, Millaa Millaa was a flourishing dairy and timber town but the district declined in the 1960s when farms were amalgamated and the railway and timber mill closed. The town remains the starting point for a popular waterfall circuit which leads from Palmerston Highway along Theresa Creek Road to the spectacular single drop of the Millaa Millaa Falls and then, through dense rainforest and rich farming land, on to the Zillie and Elinjaa falls. To the west is the turnoff to the Mungalli Falls, off the Innisfail road.

MISSION BEACH ■ 1650

A twenty-kilometre-long scenic drive through rainforest leads to this sweep of white sandy beaches. The Mission Beach area takes in some fourteen kilometres of coastline and includes Garners Beach, Bingil Bay, Narragon Beach, Clump Point and Wongaling Beach.

The Cutten brothers – James, Herbert, Leonard and Sidney – landed at Bingil Bay north of Mission Beach in 1882, and established a farming empire in the district. They introduced pineapple growing to North Queensland and established coffee and tea plantations. For more than twenty years, the Cuttens lived in isolation before they were joined by other pioneering farm families.

Mission Beach is named for the Aboriginal mission which was set up in 1912 at South Mission Beach. Settlements and farms in the district were devastated by the 1918 cyclone, which was reputed to be the 'cyclone of the century'.

Pearling was an early industry but in modern times bananas and sugarcane are among the chief products of the region. The unparalleled beauty of northern Queensland attracts millions of tourists in the dry season – and tourism is also a growth industry. *Population 810*

CLUMP MOUNTAIN NATIONAL PARK A two-kilometre walking track leads from Bingil Bay to a scenic lookout on Bicton Hill. Parts of the rainforest were flattened by a cyclone in 1986.

DUNK ISLAND Dunk Island – about four kilometres off Mission Beach – is one of Australia's best known resort islands. The author E.J. Banfield wrote about his life here in *Confessions of a Beachcomber*, first published in 1908. To the south is Bedarra Island with two of the most exclusive resorts in Australia, if not the world. Access to Bedarra is by water taxi from Dunk Island.

FESTIVALS Aquatic Festival, Great Tinnie Race, October; Banana Festival, July.

MOSSMAN ■ 1651

This small sugar town on the edge of the Daintree National Park is home to the Mossman Mill which began crushing sugar in 1897. The mill now runs a steam train for visitors and tours are conducted to show how sugar is produced.

George Dalrymple named the area in 1873 after Hugh Mosman, an early mineral explorer. The second 's' was added later to avoid confusion with the Sydney suburb of the same name. In the early 1870s, cedar-getters began operating, and the town dates from 1876. *Population 1770*

MOUNT HYPIPAMEE NATIONAL PARK ■ 1652

At the summit of Mount Hypipamee is the vast and unnerving cavity of the Crater. Here, thick rainforest suddenly gives way to sheer walls of granite which plunge more than sixty metres into a still and algae covered pool. Volcanic in origin, it was formed when the mounting pressure of gases and molten magma, having found no point of weakness through which to ooze, instead blasted away the rock. The rim of the crater can be reached by a walking track from the picnic grounds. The route back passes the Barron River at Dinner Falls, where swimming is possible.

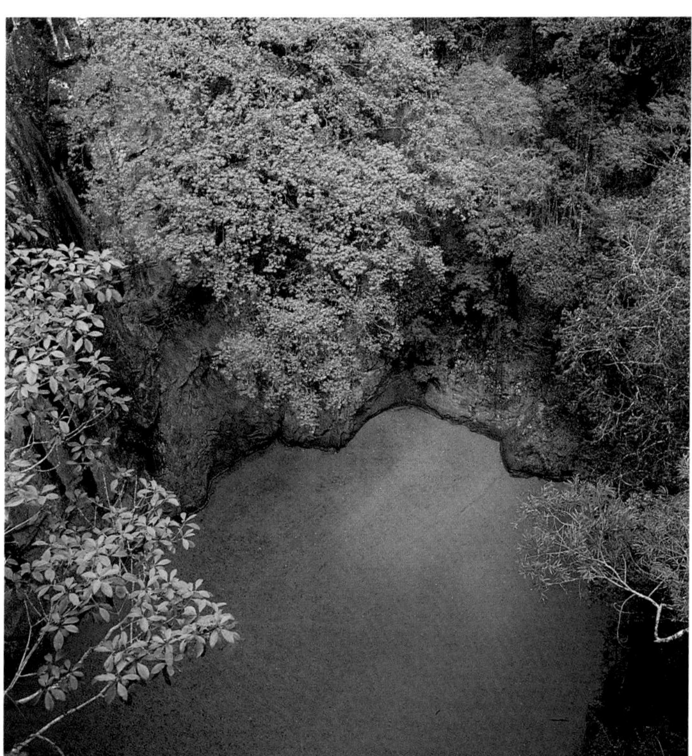

Far below the rim of the Mount Hypipamee crater, dense humidity and stagnant conditions encourage a thick carpet of algae on the water surface.

The dense rainforest vegetation of the park consists in the main of towering kauri and black pine. Some 300 bird species are found in the area.

PALMERSTON NATIONAL PARK ■ 1653

An average annual rainfall of around 3500 millimetres makes this area one of the wettest in Australia and thick rainforest covers most of this 14 200-hectare national park. The dense vegetation is a habitat for an abundance of wildlife.

Walking tracks at intervals along the highway lead to waterfalls in luxuriant leafy settings on the Johnstone River. Picnic areas are at Crawfords Lookout, the K-tree, Tchupala Falls and Henrietta Creek.

At Tchupala Falls, a constant mist has encouraged a prolific growth of mosses and ferns. This beautiful region is environmentally sensitive but potentially dangerous and visitors are advised to keep to the walking track. The musky rat-kangaroo is sometimes spotted on the walk to Henrietta Creek, and platypus and tortoises may be seen in the creek.

PORT DOUGLAS ■ 1654

Like Cairns, Port Douglas was established in the 1870s as a port for the Hodgkinson River goldfields. It was named Port Douglas after John Douglas, then premier of Queensland, and given a government allocation of two thousand pounds for road building. By 1882, Port Douglas had a population of 500, fourteen officially licensed hotels, several 'shanties' – unlicensed grog and boarding houses – and a Cobb & Co. coach service.

But its heyday was brief. In 1885, the Queensland Government decided that the long-requested railway line from the inland mining areas to the coast would go to Cairns. By 1901, the population of Port Douglas had shrunk to 331, and in 1911 a severe cyclone destroyed most of its buildings. When Cairns was made the terminus of the railway line from Brisbane in 1924, Port Douglas went into total decline.

Despite the shock-resistant, inflatable rubber rafts, riding the Tully River rapids is not for the faint-hearted.

By the early 1970s, Port Douglas' population had shrunk to 250 but in the 1980s it returned to the level of 100 years before tourists had discovered the pretty, peaceful, tropical village with its wide, tree-lined main street. Several large resorts have been built here. *Population 3660*

FESTIVALS Village Carnivale, June; Regatta, September.

RAVENSHOE ■ 1655

This dairy and timber town was initially hard hit by the World Heritage listing of the tropical rainforests (see box) which had supplied most of the timber for its sawmill. The mill has been converted to handle pine from the region's forestry plantations.

The Millstream and Little Millstream falls – the widest in Australia – are nearby. The steaming thermal waters of the Innot Hot Springs are to the west. Mount Garnet, further west again, hosts the Mount Garnet Rodeo and country race meeting every May Day weekend. The area is popular with gemstone fossickers. The local hotel displays some unusual historical items including a set of false teeth made of tin! *Population 870*

SMITHFIELD HEIGHTS ■ 1656

This predominantly residential centre north of Cairns is between the Kennedy and Captain Cook highways. Further south at the junction of the highways, is Smithfield, which has a large shopping complex that services the residents of both towns. The original Smithfield was at the mouth of the Barron River but was washed away by floods in 1879 and later rebuilt on the present, elevated site. *Population 1830*

SOUTH JOHNSTONE ■ 1657

This pretty sugar town on the South Johnstone River is the base for a research station of the Queensland Department of Primary Industries for the tropical coast. *Population 610*

TINAROO FALLS DAM ■ 1658

The Tinaroo Falls Dam on the Barron River – completed in 1958 – contains enough water to three-quarters fill Sydney Harbour. In Tinaroo township, a vantage point near the dam displays photographs and diagrams about the construction and statistics of the dam and irrigation area.

Spectacular vistas of Tinaroo come into view when crossing the bridge below the spillway and driving along the Danbulla Drive. Other highlights include the Platypus Rock Lookout, Downfall Creek and Kauri Creek picnic areas, Fong On Bay, Lake Euramo and Cathedral Fig tree. *Population 795*

TOLGA ■ 1659

Tolga is a centre for the peanut industry in North Queensland and regular tours of the Peanut Marketing Board's depot are held during harvest time from April to July. The woodwork showrooms display furniture and wood items made from rainforest timber.

The Tolga Hotel, once the Kulara Hotel, was moved from its original site before the Tinaroo Falls Dam was built and made a lake which flooded the Kulara townsite. *Population 840*

TRINITY BEACH ■ 1660

One of the most popular and attractive of the Marlin Coast beaches, this sandy cove has a Mediterranean feel with its casual seafront shops and restaurants. *Population 4420*

TULLY ■ 1661

Tully, a sugar town on Banyan Creek – a tributary of the Tully River – is noted for its river cruises which depart daily from the wharf.

Tully became a pastoral area in the 1870s and 1880s, originally called Banyan. Its sugar mill was built in 1924 and the townsite was surveyed and named Tully, after a surveyor in Dalrymple's 1864 expedition. Evening tours of the Tully Co-operative Sugar mill are conducted during harvest time from June to December.

The Kareeya State Forest and the hydro-electric power station to the north-west are reached through the wild Tully River Gorge – the river is famous for white-water rafting. The power station is open to the public *Population 2710*

FESTIVALS Rain Festival, August.

WANGAN ■ 1662

This small town on the old Bruce Highway that has declined with the closure of the timber mill and the construction of a new highway still supports an iron and brass foundry. *Population 510*

WHITE ROCK ■ 1663

This small residential centre south of Cairns and to the east of the Bruce Highway is named after the rocky outcrop to its east. *Population 3540*

WONGALING BEACH ■ 1664

Rapid tourist and housing development has turned this sleepy beachfront hamlet into a busy beachside suburb. Wongaling is between Mission and South Mission beaches, opposite Dunk Island. *Population 990*

YORKEYS KNOB ■ 1665

A popular tourist retreat, Yorkeys Knob, like other Marlin Coast beaches, is now an affluent residential suburb of Cairns. To the south is Yarrabah Aboriginal Settlement on Cape Grafton. *Population 2390*

YUNGABURRA ■ 1666

First known as Allumba, the name of this settlement was changed to avoid confusion with the town of Aloomba on the coast. Gold and tin were the lure for early settlers, then stands of red cedar, known as 'red gold', brought newcomers to the district. Many trees felled and left to rot on the mountains, because they were too difficult to drag out, were retrieved twenty-five years later from former cedar camps and taken by bullock team to Yungaburra. The scarcity of kauri, white beech, maple and cedar gave the loggers an added incentive. An old colonial pub in Yungaburra still displays its original gas-lamps and horse rail. Market day, on the last Saturday in the month, sees a wide range of tropical plants, fresh vegetables and cottage industry items for sale and has become a social as well as commercial occasion for the people of the surrounding district. *Population 810*

Motorists driving through the lowland rainforest near Mission Beach are warned of local traffic hazards.

A LIVING RAINFOREST 'MUSEUM' BECOMES PART OF THE WORLD'S HERITAGE

Chemicals derived from the seeds in the black bean tree's pods may have medical uses in fighting tissue rejection.

THE WORLD Heritage list is a unique international inventory, an elite register of outstandingly significant natural and man-made 'properties'. In 1988, the wet-tropic rainforests of Queensland had their distinction as the world's oldest such forests recognised when they were added to the list.

The listed rainforest area is a long and narrow coastal strip of approximately 900 000 hectares in area which stretches a green mantle for more than 500 kilometres between Townsville and Cooktown. It is of enormous scientific and ecological importance; as one of a shrinking list of intact rainforest areas it is a scientific storehouse for the planet with the potential to provide the raw materials from which new crops or pharmaceuticals can be developed – rice, taro and bananas came from rainforest, as did the source of one in four modern drugs.

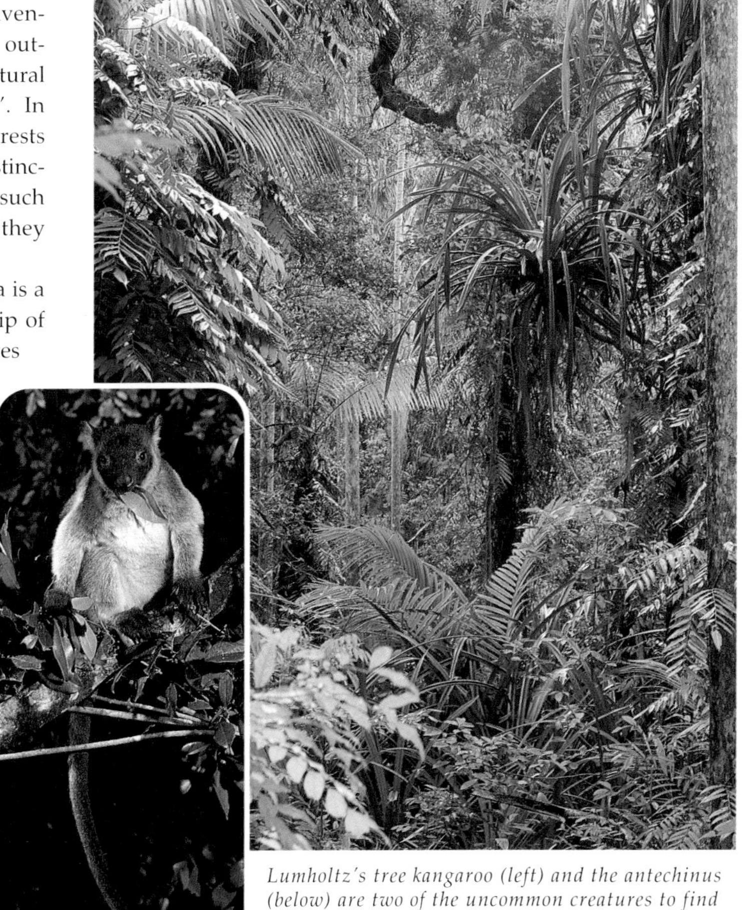

Lumholtz's tree kangaroo (left) and the antechinus (below) are two of the uncommon creatures to find an assured future in the World Heritage rainforests.

The Queensland wet tropics are also wildly and spectacularly beautiful. Here cloud-capped mountains drop into the sea in one of the wettest regions on earth. Frequent drenching showers keep the foliage always ashimmer with raindrops, and sparkling streams, having cut tunnels through steamy jungle, run across white beaches to the waters of the Coral Sea.

The forests here are fragments of those which one hundred million years ago clothed the supercontinent of Gondwana. This mighty landmass began to break up ninety million years ago to form the separate southern continents and, sixty million years ago, when the continent of Australia struck out on its own, it was covered by vegetation similar to that of the wet tropics. The major climatic changes since then have changed most of this to desert, and in the last heartbeat of time clearing by Europeans settlers for agriculture further reduced the forests to a tiny 0.1 per cent of the continent.

The rainforests still remain the richest animal habitat there is. They contain approximately 18 per cent of Australia's bird species, 23 per cent of the reptile species, 30 per cent of marsupial and frog species, 62 per cent of butterfly species, 60 per cent of bat species, an amazing 92 percent of known ferns; new species are being discovered all the time. More than 400 of these profoundly diverse plants and animals are in the rare or endangered category.

Because of their extraordinary antiquity, these wet tropic forests preserve a living record of the major stages in the earth's evolutionary history. Many survivors from the prehistoric world are in evidence – flowering plants that flourished when dinosaurs trod the earth bloom here, with a far greater concentration of families than anywhere else on earth. The forests contain the ancestors from which all the distinctive eucalypts, acacias and other 'natives' are descended. Here too are found a number of species believed to be relics of the creatures which inhabited the forests of Australia more than fifteen million years ago. These pockets of forest also withstood the ravages of the ice ages, some 15 000 years ago, and acted as a refuge, a sort of biological ark into which plant and animal species retreated to survive.

The tiny musky rat-kangaroo, considered to be the most primitive of all kangaroo-family creatures lives here. It is a descendant of tree-living ancestors, and retains some possum-like characteristics. Two species of tree kangaroo survive only in this region. The high, misty forests near Atherton are home to nine species of antechinus, members of a primitive group of carnivorous marsupials. Not surprisingly, the wet tropics have Australia's most diverse range of birds. There are more than 120 different species ranging from the lumbering southern cassowary, which stands up to two metres high, to colourful flocks of rainbow honey eaters, which congregate in coastal mangrove and casuarina groves, and the birds of the highlands, such as the golden bowerbird, the tooth-billed catbird and the Australian fern wren.

The large number of butterflies in the wet tropics includes the spectacular Atlas or Hercules moth, the largest in Australia and a contender for the world title. □

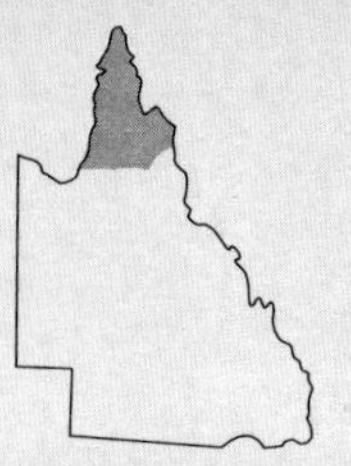

Weipa & Cooktown

The vast triangular promontory of Cape York has changed but little since 1644 when Abel Tasman called it Carpentaria Land. Its remoteness, rugged landscape and climate has meant that the cape remains a region of cattle stations dotted with Aboriginal communities.

Apart from its corporate label, Cooktown's 1891 bank remains unchanged.

ARCHER BEND AND ROKEBY NATIONAL PARKS ■ 1667

These neighbouring parks, to the east of Aurukun, make up a 457 000-hectare region which contains the Archer and Coen rivers, flowing from high in the rainforest-covered McIlwraith Range. Both rivers are annual and summer flooding over a wide area is common. As the river retreats in the dry season, water remains in the lagoons and swamps of the area's floodplain and these sustain an abundance of birdlife.

AURUKUN ■ 1668

Aurukun is one of a number of Aboriginal settlements on the cape that is administered by a resident council. Permission to visit the community must be obtained from the council. *Population 790*

BAMAGA ■ 1669

The Bamaga Aboriginal community, almost at the tip of Cape York, was established in 1948. Settled by islanders from Saibai in the Torres Strait, the region was named after their leader. The islanders moved here after high tides devastated the fields on their islands. Modern Bamaga has an Aboriginal Council and is the main access point for islands in the Torres Strait. The airfield is named after Jackey Jackey, the Aborigine who joined explorer Edmund Kennedy on his 1848 Cape York expedition. *Population 680*

CAPE MELVILLE NATIONAL PARK ■ 1670

The rugged granite range and coastline at the eastern edge of Princess Charlotte Bay, which borders the Normanby River delta, are preserved intact within Cape Melville National Park. The range is made up of caves, forest and heath dotted with vast boulders, while the coastal section consists of rocky headlands, dunes, mangroves and wetlands. The park is a significant flora and fauna protection zone.

CAPE YORK ■ 1671

The Australian mainland's most northerly point juts out into Torres Strait at 10 degrees 41 minutes south – a mere 150 kilometres from the coast of Papua New Guinea. The first attempt to reach the cape from the south was by Edmund Kennedy's ill-fated 1848 expedition – only three out of the party's original fourteen survived. Kennedy himself died of wounds inflicted by the spears of hostile Aborigines and only the Aboriginal member of the group, Jackey Jackey, reached a waiting vessel at the cape. Travelling the cape today is less hazardous and the region offers a wilderness lodge, where tourists can enjoy a truly remote holiday.

CEDAR BAY NATIONAL PARK ■ 1672

Cedar Bay National Park – south of Cooktown – marks the southern limit of tropical monsoonal vegetation and is a coastal wilderness of mangroves, paperbark swamps and salt pans complemented by a variety of forested regions.

COEN ■ 1673

Gold was discovered at Coen in 1876, but today the old Great Northern and Mount Wilson mines lie abandoned. The small town survives as a centre for the local Aboriginal population and several cattle stations.

COOKTOWN ■ 1674

In June 1770, during the journey north from Botany Bay, Captain Cook's ship, the *Endeavour*, was holed on the Great Barrier Reef. For seven weeks the ship was moored and repaired on the river which bears the vessel's name, at the site of present-day Cooktown. The town contains an 1887 memorial to James Cook, erected near the site of the *Endeavour*'s mooring.

Cooktown, named after the famed navigator and explorer, grew up during the 1870s as a result of the 1873 Palmer River gold rush. A need arose for both an access point for prospectors bound for the goldfields, and a port from which to ship the metal: Cooktown, or Cook's Town as it was originally known, was the logical answer. The settlement became a city of hundreds of tents, with the first buildings – including a police station and customs house – being erected in 1874, the year in which the town was officially proclaimed.

The town grew rapidly, with the population reaching 13 000 within the next few years. The miners were a thirsty lot: at one time Cooktown boasted sixty-five licensed premises, over thirty stores, three banks, several bakers and butchers, as well as a newspaper, and the settlement was Queensland's third busiest port.

Despite the decline of goldmining in the region, tin was discovered nearby during the 1880s and Cooktown continued to thrive as a port for mail steamers and the bêche-de-mer fishing industry, and as a base for the Burns Philp company's island trade and as the main access port for early traders in what was to become Papua New Guinea.

Contemporary Cooktown has settled for the existence of a tranquil tourist centre, set in the middle of lush coastal scenery. The town has a monument to Mary Watson, of Lizard Island fame (see entry) and the Cooktown cemetery is the site of her grave as well as those of many of the 18 000 or so Chinese who flocked into the region during the gold-rush days. *Population 1340*

FESTIVALS Cooktown Discovery Festival, June.

FLINDERS GROUP ■ 1675

This group of islands in Princess Charlotte Bay is of great interest to archaeologists because of its shell middens and painted rock shelters which indicate a long occupation of this region by Aboriginal people. Two of the islands – Blackwood and Denham – are important in Aboriginal mythology and contain a number of sacred burial sites.

HOPE VALE ■ 1676

This settlement at the centre of an Aboriginal reserve to the north-west of Cooktown is noted for its production of artefacts. Hope Vale welcomes visitors and derives a part of its income from the arts and crafts activities of its people. *Population 820*

IRON RANGE NATIONAL PARK ■ 1677

Iron Range National Park is considered to be of world significance because it has the largest remaining area of lowland rainforest in Australia. This coastal park, near the Lockhart River community, contains more than 300 large plant species, offers magnificent coastal scenery and is home to many types of butterfly, the cuscus and the spiny-haired bandicoot. Nearby is the small fishing community of Portland Roads, while offshore is Restoration Island, which was visited by Captain Bligh on his epic voyage to safety after the mutiny on the *Bounty*.

JARDINE RIVER NATIONAL PARK ■ 1678

Situated near the tip of Cape York, this 235 000-hectare region takes in the major portion of the catchment area of the Jardine River; Queensland's largest permanent waterway. The park contains areas of lush rainforest, heathland, eucalypt forest and swamplands, the last the habitat of countless crocodiles. The river and park are named after Frank Jardine, one of the peninsula's early explorers and settlers, who found the wetlands

N
km
0 20 40 60 80
1692
Torres Strait
1691 THURSDAY ISLAND
1671 CAPE YORK
1688
1687 POSSESSION I. N.P.
SOMERSET (ruins)
BAMAGA 1669
JARDINE RIVER NAT. PARK 1678
Jardine R.
PUDDINGPAN HILL
270
Shelburne Bay
1683 MAPOON
GREAT
91
Temple Bay
1677 IRON RANGE NAT. PK
RESTORATION I.
PORTLAND ROADS
DUYFKEN PT 1693
WEIPA
PENINSULA DEVELOPMENTAL ROAD
89
Albatross Bay
85
118
LOCKHART RIVER
1668 AURUKUN
46
13
33
DIVIDING
1667 ARCHER BEND NAT. PK
ARCHER RIVER ROADHOUSE
Archer R.
ROKEBY NAT. PK 1667
66
COEN 1673
CAPE YORK PENINSULA
FLINDERS GROUP 1675
CAPE 1670 MELVILLE NATIONAL PARK
108
Edward R.
MUSGRAVE ROADHOUSE
1680 LAKEFIELD NAT. PK
Normanby R.
LIZARD I. 1682
STARCKE NAT. PK 1690
PORMPURAAW 1686
236
63
RANGE
HANN RIVER ROADHOUSE
1684 MITCHELL & ALICE RIVERS NAT. PK
1679 KOWANYAMA
OLD LAURA
75
80
1676 HOPE VALE
COOKTOWN 1674
Hann R.
28
1681 LAURA
35
83
Alice R.
SPLIT ROCK
61
BLACK MTN
1685 PALMER RIVER GOLDFIELDS RES.
QUINKAN RESERVE
CEDAR BAY NAT. PK 1672
105
Palmer R.
31
LAKELAND
PALMER RIVER ROADHOUSE
MAYTOWN (ruins)
TO CAIRNS
BURKE DEVELOPMENTAL ROAD
Mitchell R.
1689
Staaten R.
STAATEN RIVER NATIONAL PARK
p 458
p 472
p 450

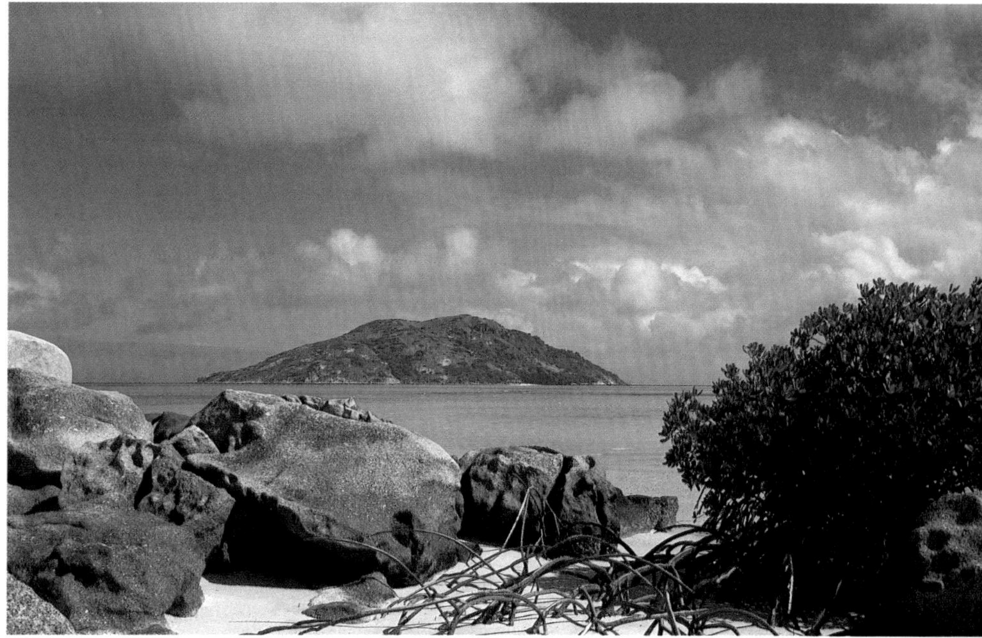

Barren Lizard Island drags several subsidiary rocky islets – 'continental' islands as opposed to coral cays – in its wake, including Palfrey Island, with a lighthouse on its western extremity.

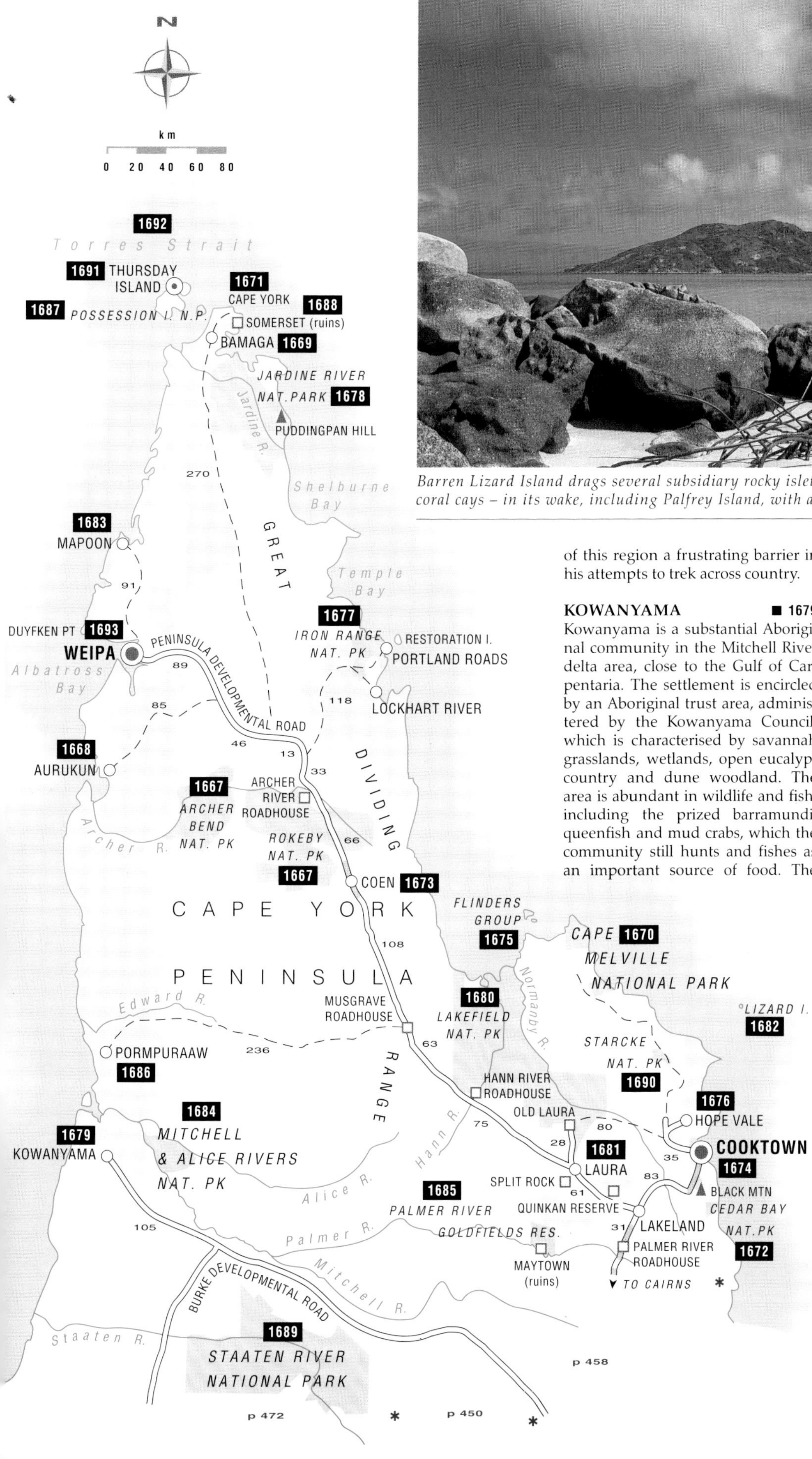

of this region a frustrating barrier in his attempts to trek across country.

KOWANYAMA ■ 1679

Kowanyama is a substantial Aboriginal community in the Mitchell River delta area, close to the Gulf of Carpentaria. The settlement is encircled by an Aboriginal trust area, administered by the Kowanyama Council, which is characterised by savannah grasslands, wetlands, open eucalypt country and dune woodland. The area is abundant in wildlife and fish, including the prized barramundi, queenfish and mud crabs, which the community still hunts and fishes as an important source of food. The Council's land resource policy was established to maintain wildlife for this purpose, and the Kowanyama community has appointed a ranger to oversee its lands.

Kowanyama favours the development of low-impact tourism and offers both guesthouse accommodation and camping facilities. As well as a post office, bank and shopping facilities, there is a hospital which is included in the Royal Flying Doctor Service network. *Population 1020*

LAKEFIELD NATIONAL PARK ■ 1680

This 537 000-hectare park, to the north of Laura, is one of Queensland's largest. Much of the park is covered with grasslands, woodland and mangrove-lined mudflats, with extensive floodplains that are crisscrossed by the North Kennedy, Morehead and Normanby rivers. From April to November, after the wet-season flooding, the region is covered with lagoons and permanent waterholes that are the habitat for a large and varied population of birds. Lakefield is also particularly important for its work in the conservation of estuarine crocodiles. The less aggressive freshwater crocodile is also present in large numbers in the inland waterways.

Lakefield offers a range of activities – bush camping, bushwalking and canoeing – for the adventurous; the easiest access to the park is from Laura, but the roads are generally impassable during the wet season.

LAURA ■ 1681

During the 1870s Palmer River gold rush, Laura developed as a major stopping place on the way to the

QUINKAN'S 10 000-YEAR-OLD DREAMTIME GALLERIES

ONE OF THE world's largest bodies of prehistoric art lies around the small township of Laura in Cape York Peninsula. The Quinkan Reserve contains cave and 'shelter' paintings in such concentration that to archaeologists at least, it is the most important cultural and historical Aboriginal site in Australia.

The area consists of a sandstone plateau which contains innumerable overhangs and caves that have been home to Aboriginal people for more than 13 000 years. Within these shelters is a treasure house of Aboriginal artwork, which was first explored by Percy Tresize, a local bush pilot, explorer, writer and artist, during the 1960s. Together with Dick Roughsey, an Aboriginal painter from Mornington Island, Tresize was the leading light in promoting and conserving the area's unique contribution to Aboriginal culture.The Quinkan Reserves Trust was established in 1977 and covers a wilderness region of 97 000 hectares.

The thousand or so art sites in the Laura region display a variety of styles and techniques, with the tens of thousands of paintings being most noteworthy for their large scale and liberal use of colour. At Split Rock, discovered by Europeans in 1960, there are a number of art sites depicting the region's wildlife and Quinkans – tall, angular figures with large staring eyes. Aboriginal people believe that these spirit beings live among the rocks, appearing occasionally to lure human beings to destruction. An Imjim spirit figure is also depicted here – this large-eared spirit was believed to hop around the countryside, living on frogs.

At nearby Guguyalangi, there are a dozen art sites including a variety of stencil paintings and engravings. The sinister-looking and ubiquitous Quinkans appear here also. Some of the largest and most dramatic scenes are depicted on the walls of the Giant Horse Gallery, between Split Rock and Laura. This 'gallery' has a dramatic, six-metre long, rendering of a horse – a creature with which Aborigines were not familiar until the coming of the white man. Other paintings depict human figures, stingrays and bush turkeys.

Although the reserve's main purpose is to preserve these important sites and protect them from vandals, several of the galleries are open for inspection in the company of Aboriginal rangers of the Quinkan Reserves Trust. Travellers brave enough to venture into this rugged region have a fine reward in store when they see the inspiring work of Australia's earliest artists. □

The walls of Split Rock – the reason for the name is obvious – bear rock art unknown to non-Aboriginal Australians until the 1960s.

goldfields and, when the railway from Cooktown arrived in 1888, it became the region's railhead. Some 20 000 people passed through the town each year in this boom era. In modern times, the small township on the Laura River supports only a meagre population; it has a hotel, a police station, camping ground and a few houses. There is also an Aboriginal art museum here, but Laura is best known as the starting point for visits to the famed Aboriginal rock paintings at nearby Quinkan Reserve – the settlement was the base for Percy Tresize's exploration of the area's rock art 'galleries' (see box). Percy Tresize and the Aboriginal artist Dick Roughsey have produced a number of children's books on Aboriginal legends.

Laura is also the location for the annual and very spectacular Cape York Aboriginal Dance Festival. As many as 3000 Aboriginal people from all over the peninsula congregate at this event to dance, sing and compete in traditional competitions such as boomerang and spear throwing.

LIZARD ISLAND GROUP NATIONAL PARK AND MARINE PARK ■ 1682

The granitic lump of Lizard Island is a six-hundred-hectare speck between the peninsula's east coast and the Great Barrier Reef. Aboriginals visited the islands for many thousands of years and have left extensive shell middens as a reminder of their long-term presence. James Cook and his companions camped overnight on the island in 1770, and named it after the large monitor lizards that they observed here.

Robert Watson and his wife, who were engaged in fishing for bêche-de-mer, were the first Europeans to settle on the island. In 1881, when Mr Watson was away, Mary Watson, her small son and a Chinese servant were attacked by Aborigines and fled the island in an iron tank. All three died of thirst on an uninhabited island only sixteen kilometres from the mainland and their remains were found the following year. The ruins of the Watson's stone cottage still stand, while Mary Watson's diary, covering the tragic episode, is in the John Oxley Library in Brisbane.

Lizard Island was declared a national park in 1939. The other four islands of the group were granted that status in 1987 and the surrounding waters and reefs are also protected as part of the Great Barrier Reef Marine Park. The islands are covered with grassland, heath, eucalypt woodland and dune vegetation and more than forty species of birds have been recorded here. There is also a wide variety of lizards, including the sand goanna.

Lizard Island contains an Australian Museum research station, a couple of campsites and a secluded, deluxe tourist resort, reached by a fifty-minute flight from Cairns. Fishing, snorkelling and diving around the coral reefs are the most pressing activities that take place on laidback Lizard Island.

MAPOON ■ 1683

At the mouth of the Wenlock River, north of Weipa, Mapoon was first established by missionaries from Moravia – later to become part of Czechoslovakia – in 1891. The Weipa mission was set up as an offshoot. Mapoon's mission closed in 1963 and the people moved to either Weipa or New Mapoon, near Bamaga. The settlement was officially returned to the Aboriginal people in 1989.

MITCHELL AND ALICE RIVERS NATIONAL PARK ■ 1684

Located to the east of Kowanyama, this 37 000-hectare park is a former pastoral property which protects the rainforested area at the junction of the two rivers.

PALMER RIVER GOLDFIELDS RESERVE ■ 1685

The Palmer River, south-west of Cooktown, was first reached in 1872 by William Hann who named it after Arthur Palmer, the Queensland Colonial Secretary. Gold was discovered here by the Hann expedition during the same year, and a find of payable alluvial gold by James Mulligan in 1873 turned the region into a hive of activity as great crowds of hopeful prospectors flocked north. Maytown, now in ruins, became the centre for the fields, while Cooktown was later established by the Queensland Government as the port for the region.

The miners in this particularly remote and rugged region had to contend with disease, lack of food, extreme heat and flooding. Interracial tension was also a major problem as the large Chinese and smaller European groups quarrelled over mining rights, and the Aborigines, who had been displaced from their hunting grounds, launched frequent spear attacks on miners of all races. Retaliation by the diggers led to widespread killings of the region's original inhabitants and the area has many placenames that attest to the twenty-five or so years of sporadic fighting between whites and blacks. Battle Camp Road and Hells Gate Track are just two such reminders of these bloody times.

Despite all of these deterrents, the goldfields boomed and there were up to 19 000 people mining in the district in 1877. The Palmer became known as the 'river of gold' and a railway line from Cooktown was proposed in 1882 – the line reached Laura in 1888 but it was never extended. By 1886, both alluvial and reef-mining operations had run into financial and other difficulties, and most of the prospectors moved on to other fields. Although its life was short, the Palmer River field produced gold worth more than five million pounds sterling.

To protect the historic mining sites, the region was designated as a reserve in 1986 and is administered jointly by the National Parks and Wildlife Service and the Queensland Department of Resource Industries.

PORMPURAAW ■ 1686

The township of Pormpuraaw, on the shores of the gulf, was once known as the Edward River Aboriginal Community. The local people derive most of their income from a cattle station and crocodile farming. Many of the skins produced here are exported to Japan and France for use in fashion items.

POSSESSION ISLAND NATIONAL PARK ■ 1687

This small island in Endeavour Strait, to the north of Bamaga, has great historical significance as the place where, in August 1770, the British flag was raised and the eastern coast of Australia, from Torres Strait to New South Wales, declared a British possession by Captain James Cook.

SOMERSET ■ 1688

Named after the Lord of the Admiralty, the Duke of Somerset, this was an early, but unsuccessful, attempt at settling the tropical north. Rockhampton Police Magistrate, John Jardine, along with settlers and a contingent of marines, established the township in 1863; it was the first on Cape York Peninsula and the continent's most northerly settlement. The optimistic intention was to set up a trading and defence post that would rival Singapore. In 1864–65, Jardine's sons, Frank and Alexander, made a remarkable five-month journey from Rockhampton to Somerset with 1000 head of cattle, intended to feed the outpost.

After peaking at a population of approximately 200, Somerset proved to be unworkable and was largely abandoned in 1877, when the inhabitants were transferred to Thursday Island. A cattle station established by Jardine's sons endured long after the evacuation. All that remains of the settlement today are the gravestones of Frank Jardine and his wife and a few other crumbling relics of long-abandoned buildings. Somerset also contains a memorial to the explorer Edmund Kennedy, who died while exploring the peninsula in 1848.

STAATEN RIVER NATIONAL PARK ■ 1689

The 467 000-hectare Staaten River National Park, at the southern end of the peninsula, includes large areas of floodplain vegetation, rainforest and an abundance of broad-leaved tea trees. This lowland park is also an important fauna reserve.

STARCKE NATIONAL PARK ■ 1690

Starcke National Park, to the north of Cooktown, preserves a rugged and mostly untouched region with a landscape ranging from heath-covered sandstone plateau to grassland and rainforest.

THURSDAY ISLAND ■ 1691

This small island – measuring about three kilometres by two kilometres – is Australia's most northerly settlement and the administrative and commercial centre of the Torres Strait Islands. It is reached by plane or a regular ferry service from Bamaga to Port Kennedy, the island's fine natural harbour. The local name is Waipen, but 'Thursday Island' first appeared in charts during the late 1840s – it is not known who bestowed this name, but it is possible that it may have been Captain William Bligh, of *Bounty* fame. Nearby are Wednesday and Friday islands – the latter has some fine beaches and an old pearling station.

The earliest European inhabitants here were the population of Somerset, which was relocated here in 1877 after the demise of that settlement (see entry). Thursday Island has been the headquarters of the region's pearling industry since the late 1870s and the cemetery contains the graves of a number of late nineteenth-century Japanese pearl fishermen, who contributed much to the industry in Australia. The island's other historic relics include Green Hill Fort, which was constructed at Battery Point in 1892 during Australia's Russian invasion scare, and Quetta Rock – the site of the sinking of the SS *Quetta* in February 1890. This ship struck an uncharted rock and sank within three minutes, with the loss of 133 lives. Port Kennedy's Quetta Cathedral also takes its name from the shipwreck. *Population 2650*

FESTIVALS The Coming of The Light Festival, July.

TORRES STRAIT ■ 1692

The strait's first European visit was in 1606 – by the Spanish navigator Luis Vaez de Torres, who had sailed here from Peru. The waterway was named in his honour by Alexander Dalrymple, the British cartographer, in the late 1760s. The region was later briefly visited by Captain Cook in 1770, with a more detailed exploration being carried out by Matthew Flinders in 1802.

Torres Strait stretches between Cape York and the southern Papua New Guinea coast and links the Arafura and Coral seas. The waters here are extremely shallow, criss-crossed by reefs and mud bars, and made even more treacherous by strong tidal currents – since 1884 the local islanders have provided a pilot service to guide vessels through the reef-dotted waterways.

The sixty-odd Torres Strait Islands are inhabited by several thousand people, who represent a wide variety of races and nationalities. In addition to the indigenous islanders, there are descendants of Melanesian, Malay, Chinese, Papuan, Polynesian and Japanese settlers. Many of these people came to work in the pearl and shell-fishing industries, which were first established in 1868, and the associated processing of cultured pearls. The latter industry still operates on a reduced scale, the main commercial activities being prawn and cray fishing, and a small amount of agriculture. Unemployment on the islands has led to many residents moving to mainland Queensland.

Christianity was brought to Torres Strait by missionaries during the 1870s, and the Queensland Government has administered most of the islands since 1872: a government resident and police magistrate were established on Thursday Island as early as 1877. Two distinct languages are spoken: a Papuan variety in the eastern section and Yagar-Yagar, an Aboriginal language, in the western isles. In the 1980s and 90s there were moves towards greater independence for the islands as well as efforts to give more emphasis to the islands' traditional culture.

Tourism is encouraged on Thursday Island, but most of the other islands in the group are Aboriginal reserves and permission must be obtained to visit them.

WEIPA ■ 1693

Located on the Gulf of Carpentaria, Weipa – said to be an Aboriginal word for 'hunting ground' – is one of this region's main ports, as well as being a major bauxite mining town and the home of a large Aboriginal community. The town was established in 1898 as a Presbyterian Church mission; bauxite, which is the essential mineral in the manufacture of aluminium, was discovered only a few years later. The deposits are regarded as the largest and richest in the world.

Despite this the deposit was not regarded as an economic proposition until the early 1960s when mining commenced. The mineral is extracted by the open-cut method and, once washed and graded, much of it is shipped to Gladstone (see *Gladstone & Biloela*) for export. Kaolin, a fine white clay used for paper coating, is also mined in the area.

The Weipa North mine township was established and constructed in the mid-1960s as a joint venture of the Comalco company and the Queensland Government, and it accommodates several hundred miners and their families. Weipa South, where the majority of the Aboriginal population lives, has been renamed Napranum, the Aboriginal name, and is part-funded by Comalco. The company has provided various community facilities and employment training schemes for the community.

There is a trickle of tourism to this isolated outpost, with mine inspections being one of the most popular attractions. The region also attracts a number of recreational fishermen. It was across Albatross Bay, close to the present township, that the Dutch explorer Willem Jansz made the first known European landing on Australian soil in 1606. Nearby Duyfken Point is named after the explorer's ship. *Population 2510*

SHELL MOUNDS This important Aboriginal site on the riverbanks near Weipa consists of more than 500 mounds of cockle shells, ranging from two to an extraordinary thirteen metres in height. Archaeological excavation has revealed that the middens, which also contain layers of charcoal, items such as bone and stone tools, and the barbs of fishing spears, mark the sites of Aboriginal meeting and eating places. Although located within the Comalco mining lease area, the mounds are under the protection of both the mining company and the Napranum Aboriginal Community Council.

Despite their size, the coral trout (top) and potato cod which patrol Lizard Island waters are docile enough not to bite the hand that feeds them.

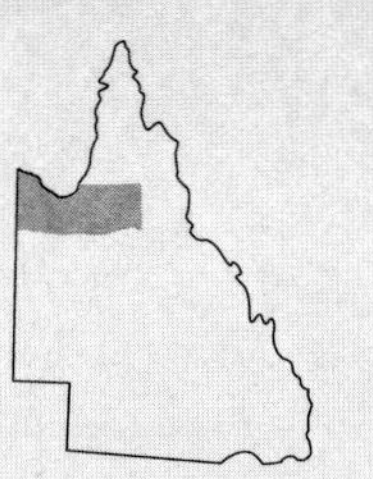

Normanton & Karumba

Normanton and Croydon are at the heart of the wild Gulf Country, a region characterised by flood-prone plains and grasslands that fringe the southern shores of the Gulf of Carpentaria. This wild country, first explored by Ludwig Leichhardt in the 1840s, has so far proved hospitable to few enterprises apart from immense cattle stations.

BURKETOWN ■ 1694

Originally known as Carpentaria Township, but later named after the explorer Robert Burke, who traversed the region in 1861 during his expedition's dramatic and ill-fated journey across the continent, this small western savannah settlement is located on the Albert River, inland from the gulf. The river was first sighted by Captain John Lort Stokes of the *Beagle* in 1841 and named in honour of Prince Albert, Queen Victoria's husband. Stokes envisioned the area becoming a major pastoral centre and described the southern grasslands as the 'Plains of Promise'.

This region marks the division between wetlands to the north and the drier grasslands to the south and was first settled during the early 1860s by pastoralists who established cattle runs. Burketown developed as a service centre for these properties and since the early days has had a reputation for lawlessness and once resembled an authentic 'wild west', gun-toting settlement. In 1866, an epidemic of 'Gulf Fever' – believed to be either yellow, typhoid or dengue fever – decimated the population and most of the survivors moved to Sweers Island and then Normanton.

Modern Burketown is the administrative centre for a region of vast cattle runs and a prosperous beef industry. The town's historic buildings include the verandahed 1887 timber post office and the Burketown Boiling Down Works. This enterprise was established in 1866 by Edward and Henry Edkins and became a major producer of cured meat, tallow, horns, hooves and hides.

CROYDON ■ 1695

Little evidence remains now, but in its heyday during the late nineteenth century, Croydon – named after nearby Croydon Downs Station – was a thriving town based on the gold-mining industry. Gas-lit streets, a foundry, police station, court house, numerous hotels, a multicultural population and notoriously riotous Saturday nights attested to the importance of this now almost desolate settlement.

Gold was discovered here in 1885 and the goldfields were proclaimed the following year. Subsequent finds of both gold and silver made the region one of outback Queensland's most eagerly sought after locations and initiated a thirty-year mining boom. The arrival of the railway line from Normanton (see Normanton) in 1891, boosted the town's fortunes considerably and at one stage four trains a week operated along the isolated stretch of track. The mines had ceased operating by 1925 and Croydon became a virtual ghost town. The present Croydon Historic Village contains the remnants of the much larger Croydon of yore. The court house dates from 1887 and an outdoor museum contains examples of mining machinery of the 1880s.

The nearby Golden Gate mines, once the main field of mining activity, have seen a recent resurgence of interest after being closed for many years. There are still gold deposits here and modern techniques have made extraction much easier.

The gulf plains fall so slightly towards their muddy seaward edge that the Norman River, here near Normanton, slides but sluggishly to its mouth.

DOOMADGEE ■ 1696

This substantial Aboriginal community, on the Nicholson River between Burketown and the Queensland–Northern Territory border, is a cattle industry centre and a base for Aboriginal arts and crafts. Doomadgee has a guesthouse, caravan park, bank and other services for travellers and can be reached by road or air. These tourist facilities are an outpost of the main village, which may be visited only with the permission of the community's council. *Population 1010*

FORSAYTH ■ 1697

This small settlement, earlier known as Charleston, sits at the end of the Cairns–Forsayth railway line: from Cairns it is a slow 24-hour journey of more than 420 kilometres. The town grew up during the 1880s gold boom and the line was built to transport gold ore from the nearby Etheridge Goldfields to crushing plants at Chillagoe. The railway has been a crucial factor in the survival of Forsayth, which somehow hangs on today despite the demise of gold mining.

GEORGETOWN ■ 1698

Georgetown was once the commercial centre for the booming Etheridge Goldfields and it was established in 1870, the same year gold was discovered. Although there was already some grazing in the region at this time, the establishment of cattle stations generally followed the mining boom. Georgetown once had a population of some 3000 but is now a much smaller settlement, located on a major beef-road intersection, which still supports cattle farming and mining operations.

The nearby, once abandoned Kidston Gold Mine was re-opened in 1985 and is one of Australia's richest gold outlets, producing up to six tonnes of the metal each year. In the last century, Kidston was a prosperous town in its own right.

AGATE CREEK MINERAL RESERVE To the south of Georgetown, surrounded by towering sandstone cliffs, Agate

Prawning trawlers tie up neatly in a row at Karumba – the only port along the fretted gulf coastline of tidal flats.

Creek contains some of the world's best quality coloured agates, varying from white to blue to red. The gems were first discovered here in 1887. The reserve includes a safari camp which offers tourists a chance to fossick for gems.

GULF OF CARPENTARIA ■ 1699

This region of warm, shallow waters was first visited by the Dutchmen Willem Jansz in 1606, and Jan Carstensz in 1623 and named after their countryman Pieter de Carpentier, Governor-General of what was then the Dutch East Indies. The region was later explored by Matthew Flinders in 1802 and 1803 and John Lort Stokes in 1841. The gulf is surrounded by low-lying shores which are criss-crossed by many rivers that become floodplains during the wet season. Karumba and Weipa, to the far north, are the region's major ports, while a number of Aboriginal communities are located in the Wellesley group of islands and in many Northern Territory settlements to the west. One of the gulf's most peculiar features is its spectacular 'Morning Glories' – tubular-shaped cloud formations which occur mainly from September to November.

HELLS GATE ■ 1700

This remote outpost, the location of which inspired its colourful name, was, during the late 1800s, a base for the Native Mounted Police. These Aboriginal people were employed to protect the grazing lands of the gulf region, and to safeguard travellers heading over the border to the new frontiers of the Northern Territory. Today, Hells Gate consists of little more than a roadhouse and is the base for ranger-guided safaris and fishing expeditions to the Gulf of Carpentaria's Macassan Coast.

KARUMBA ■ 1701

Located on the Gulf of Carpentaria at the mouth of the mangrove-lined Norman River, Karumba was named after a local Aboriginal tribe and is an important fishing port. The area is famous for its barramundi, which are caught from the creeks and inlets of the local delta system: these flat, treeless wetlands extend inland towards Normanton for around thirty kilometres and consist of tidal estuaries inhabited by a variety of birds and saltwater crocodiles.

The prawning industry developed in Karumba during the 1960s and the town was once Australia's biggest prawn processing centre. This activity has declined to some extent, but the many prawn trawlers which fish the gulf and the Arafura Sea still visit the port, particularly from April to June and August to December, when the town's population swells considerably. Karumba is now linked to Normanton by a sealed road, but for most of its history access was by the river only.

Karumba was for a long time used as a repair and refuelling stop for the Empire Flying Boats which once travelled between Australia and Britain. Karumba also became a RAAF Catalina flying boat base, and, during the Second World War, a military outpost. The town still has the old flying-boat slipway. *Population 710*

LAWN HILL NATIONAL PARK ■ 1702

Opened in 1985, this 10 000-hectare national park to the south of Burketown contains a number of important Aboriginal sites as well as creeks, waterfalls and a spectacular sandstone gorge system with walls up to seventy metres high. Lawn Hill's lush vegetation is a riot of tropical excess with livistona palms, paperbarks, pandanus, Leichhardt trees and figs all competing for space. It has been established that Aboriginal people occupied the region continuously for more than 35 000 years and two sections of the park contain Aboriginal sites with red, ochre-painted rock galleries, shell middens, campsites and tool 'factories'.

MORNINGTON ISLAND ■ 1703

The largest of the Wellesley group of islands was given its name by the navigator, Matthew Flinders in 1802, after the second Earl of Mornington, the Governor-General of India. As with the other islands in the Wellesley group, Mornington is Aboriginal land: visitors are welcome, but permission to land must be obtained from the Mornington Shire Council, based in the main town of Gununa. Mornington has a popular game and sport-fishing resort, operating from March to December, and an airstrip to cater for such tourists. The island was the home of Aboriginal artist Dick Roughsey.

NORMANTON ■ 1704

The region surrounding Normanton was first explored by Ludwig Leichhardt in 1844 when he travelled through the Gulf Country on his way to Arnhem Land from the Dar-

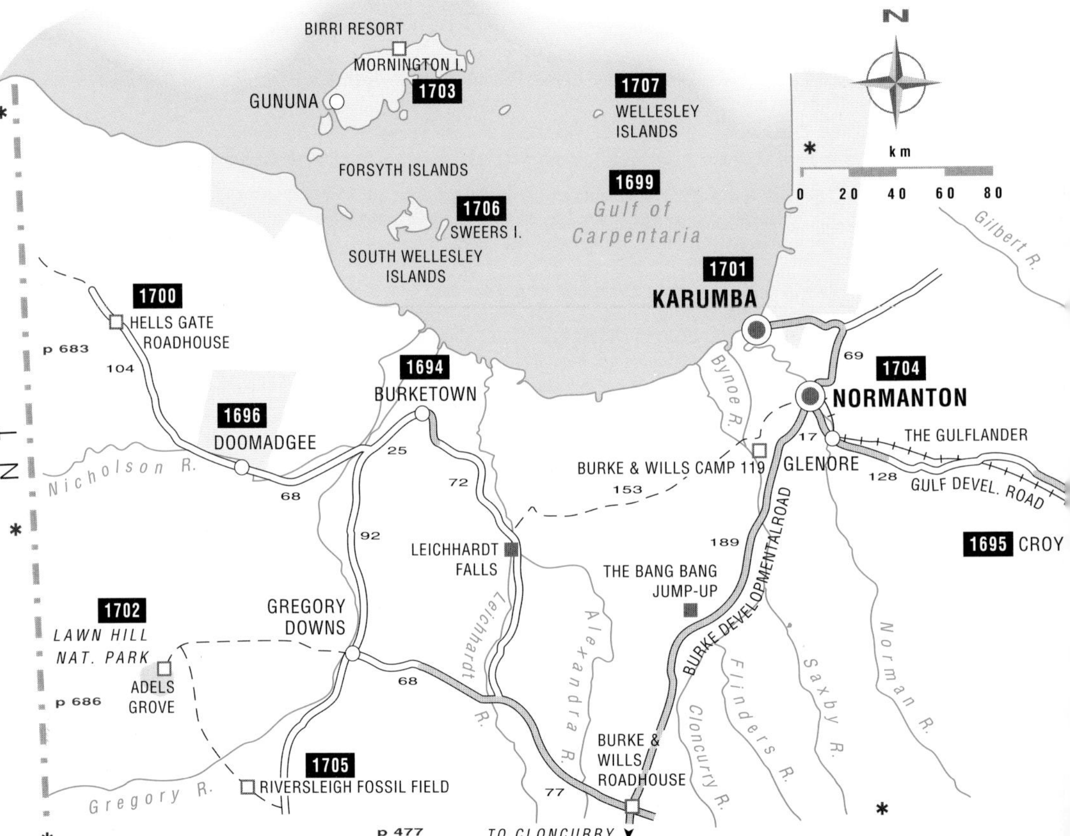

ling Downs. Leichhardt camped to the north of the present-day town and crossed the meandering Norman River nearby. Burke and Wills travelled through the region in 1861 and search parties for their 'lost' expedition, led by Frederick Walker and William Landsborough, later explored the region further.

A sea-going search was also carried out by Captain W.H. Norman, commander of HMCS *Victoria*, after whom both the river and town are named. Landsborough navigated the Norman River in 1867, in which year the town was founded, and selected the settlement's site. At this time, Normanton's population was boosted by the arrival of survivors of the 1866 Burketown gulf-fever epidemic, who were relocated here.

Although it is eighty kilometres upriver, Normanton became a major port for the surrounding cattle country and, during the 1880s, for the goldfields at Croydon and the copper and silver mines at Cloncurry, to the south-east. The town boomed during this era, and the port's strategic value became evident with the establishment of the Normanton–Croydon railway in 1889.

The impressive corrugated iron Normanton Railway Station dates from 1891. Other historic buildings include the 1896 Bank of New South Wales and the late 1800s penitentiary. Normanton is the gulf's administrative centre, serving the region's vast cattle stations and the Karumba fishing industry. *Population 1190*

Hidden in the gorges of the Barkly Tableland, pools fed by subterranean streams nourish palm groves.

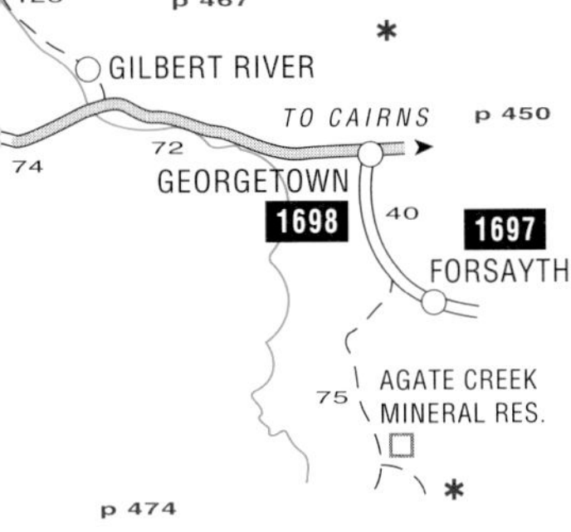

CAMP 119 To the south of Normanton there is a memorial to explorers Burke and Wills. This spot was the location of Camp 119, the 1861 expedition's last camping site before the explorers made their final weary push to reach the Gulf of Carpentaria, a feat they achieved on 11 February of that year.

THE GULFLANDER The Gulflander is probably Australia's most unusual train service, running along a completely isolated and unconnected 150-kilometre line between Normanton and Croydon. The line was first planned, in 1883, to operate between Normanton and Cloncurry, but the 1880s gold rush at Croydon led to its diversion to this destination. It never made it to Cloncurry. Work began in 1888 and the railway finally reached Croydon on 20 July 1891.

The line is served by the Gulflander, a diesel-run rail motor which runs from Normanton to Croydon each Wednesday and returns on the following day. The service takes around five hours for a one-way trip and offers both freight and passenger facilities.

RIVERSLEIGH FOSSIL FIELD ■ 1705

This major archaeological site of worldwide significance (see box) is a protected area to the south-east of Lawn Hill National Park and visitors should seek advice from a park guide before entering.

SWEERS ISLAND ■ 1706

The South Wellesley Group's Sweers Island, reached by air or boat from Karumba, was the site of Carnarvon, an early attempt at settlement, which was established by local police magistrate, William Landsborough in the 1860s. Sweers had been visited earlier by Matthew Flinders who named the island after Salamon Sweers, a member of the Batavia Council. The survivors of the 1866 Burketown gulf-fever epidemic were initially moved here before being transferred to Normanton. Sweers Island contains a small tourist resort which offers fine beaches and good fishing.

WELLESLEY AND FORSYTH ISLANDS ■ 1707

The Wellesley, South Wellesley and Forsyth groups of islands are Aboriginal Reserves, administered by the Mornington Shire Council. As with Mornington Island, permission is required for visitors to land on the islands. The name of Wellesley was bestowed by Matthew Flinders in 1802 in honour of the Marquis of Wellesley (see Mornington Island).

A FOSSIL MAUSOLEUM YIELDS UP ITS SECRETS

A HUGE, mass graveyard on a remote limestone plateau in the Gulf Country of northern Queensland has given up its secrets to explain what life was like here up to fifteen million years ago. The graveyard is a former string of lakes where animals came to drink and is a treasure trove of fossilised bones of prehistoric animals.

This land is now covered in spinifex and acacias but once upon a time it was lush rainforest. The water of the lakes contained massive amounts of dissolved limestone which crusted leaves and debris over its surface. Unwary animals coming to drink, fell through and were eaten by crocodiles and giant turtles. Their bones sank to the bottom and the fossilisation process began on their remains.

The owners of 'Riversleigh' cattle station first stumbled on fossils in 1901 but scientists did not examine them until 1963. Since the late 1970s, there has been an annual month-long pilgrimage to the site. Light blasting is used to loosen chunks of rock without damaging the fossils which are then freed from their limestone prison by treatment with diluted acetic acid in the University of New South Wales laboratories.

Extraordinary life-forms from three distinct periods have been identified. Fifteen million years ago, flesh-eating kangaroos mingled with the forebears of the Tasmanian tiger and dingo-sized marsupial lions kept company with rabbit-sized creatures known as 'thingodontas'. There were many species of possums, and three-metre-long lungfish and large platypuses swam in the pools. Birds and bats were abundant and seven-metre pythons, which some archaeologists refer to jocularly as 'montypythonoides', slithered through the trees.

By four million years ago, the rainforest had made way for grassy plains and open woodlands. An ancient cave site harbours carnivorous bats and other creatures of this time. The third period goes back a mere fifty thousand years to remains trapped in near-surface river gravels. In those times, huge red kangaroos grazed the diminishing grasslands and seven-metre-long crocodiles snacked on rhinoceros-sized diprotodons – the largest marsupial that ever lived. □

The bones of ancient animals, held in the grip of limestone on the Riversleigh Plateau (above), are being revealed by scientists (top).

Hughenden & Richmond

In good seasons, when drought or flood are not wreaking havoc, these open grasslands – once the domain of dinosaurs – provide nourishing pasture. Vast cattle stations are sliced by the Flinders and Landsborough highways, two long roadways punctuated by a string of small towns.

In winter, the hillsides of the Burra Range, near Torrens Creek, come alive with golden grevillea blooms.

HUGHENDEN ■ **1708**

The story of Burke and Wills' ill-fated expedition from Melbourne to the Gulf of Carpentaria and their death from starvation and exhaustion at Cooper Creek in 1861 has often been told, but few realise that they were indirectly responsible for opening up this region to Europeans. The men who searched for them across these vast tracts of north-west Queensland discovered fine cattle grazing land and also found gold.

In 1863, after William Landsborough had enthusiastically praised the grass-covered plains, four cattlemen raced to seize pastures in the Hughenden district. They were Ernest Henry, Hugh Walpole, Roger Sheaffe and Walter Hayes. Ernest Henry cautiously checked out the district before fetching his herd. Meanwhile the other three were on the move and were surprised, but generously admiring, when Henry drove his beasts past them and entered the Jardine Valley first. He called his station after Hughenden Manor, the home of his English maternal grandfather.

Flinders Shire is a vast area of more than 40 000 square kilometres. Hughenden is one of its three towns and the centre of local government. It lies on the Flinders River at the junction of the railway line from Townsville to Mount Isa and Winton and is at the heart of sheep and cattle country. Some farmers are growing small crops to supply livestock feed in the long, dry season. The wet season is from December to March and though the average annual rainfall is about 450 millimetres, it may reach as high as a sodden 1000 millimetres. The 'wet' and 'dry' are not the only extreme weather contrast – annual temperatures range from a very hot 49° Centigrade in mid-summer to a chilly minus 8° Centigrade in winter.

Hughenden has had some turbulent, vigorous and at times difficult history. During the shearers' strike in 1891 soldiers had to be brought from Townsville to keep the peace. Then 1895 was a year of affliction for humans and animals alike. Nineteen people died during a typhoid outbreak and later thirty serious cases of dengue fever were admitted to hospital. Pestilent cattle tick struck with a vengeance and most of the herds were wiped out. *Population 1590*

FESTIVALS Christmas Street Carnival, late December.

JULIA CREEK ■ **1709**

Donald Macintyre has been noted as the first European settler in north-west Queensland; one story says he named Julia Creek after his niece. Another story attributes the choice of name to Robert O'Hara Burke who, if the tale is true, sadly never had the chance to tell his sweetheart, actress Julia Matthews, how he had honoured her.

Julia Creek is an isolated township on the Flinders Highway set in a monotony of dusty plains broken only by acacias. The cattle retreat under the branches of these 'prickly trees' during the heat of the day. From here, in 1928, the first radio call went out to the flying doctor to bring medical aid to an injured stockman (see box, *Mount Isa & Cloncurry*).

This district's shale oil deposits are a major potential source of vanadium – a rare element used to toughen steel. If economical extraction methods are developed, Julia Creek may boom one day. As it is, the township is a very busy livestock trucking and saleyard centre with cattle now predominating over sheep. Most houses in Julia Creek have to install special cooling systems to deal with the hot water supplied by their artesian bores. *Population 570*

KYNUNA ■ **1710**

Kynuna – on the Diamantina stock route – is the watershed of Queensland's inland plains. It is a dot of a place in a vast landscape – more of a 'one dog' than a 'one-horse town'. The hotel's neon sign in the shape of a blue heeler dog with a flashing red tongue beckons passing travellers

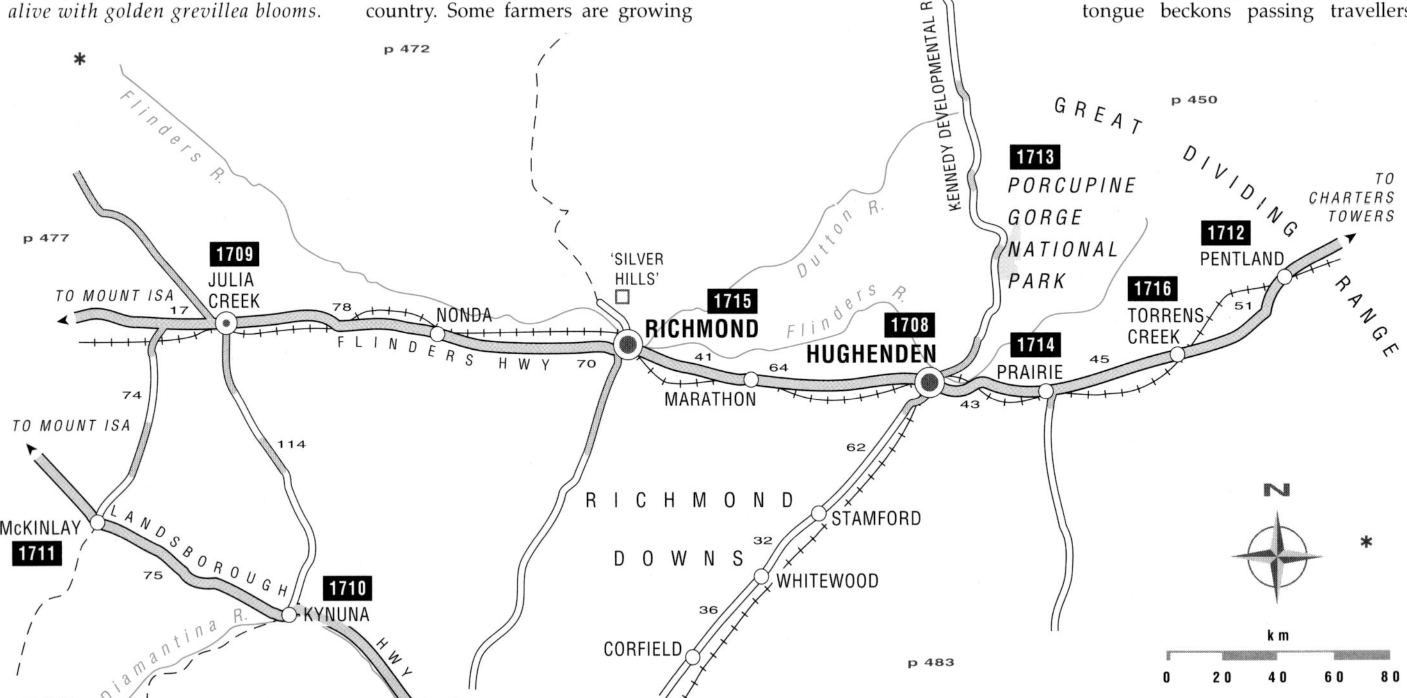

and modern transport trucks now stop where once Cobb & Co. coaches rested in the old days.

Banjo Paterson is said to have sat by a billabong – the Combo waterhole – 'under the shade of a coolabah tree' to write the words to *Waltzing Matilda*. Two incidents might have inspired him. During the shearers' strike in 1891, police were investigating arson at Dagworth Station and approached a man at a waterhole. He dived in to avoid them and subsequently drowned. The second tale tells of the hunt for a stockman wanted for murder. A swagman, who had just illegally killed a sheep for rations, feared the constabulary were after him and jumped into a nearby billabong where he drowned. Whatever the true source of Paterson's verse, the words have been debated and analysed almost from the first day he wrote them.

McKINLAY ■ **1711**

McKinlay bears the name of explorer John McKinlay who led one of the search parties looking for Burke and Wills in 1861–62. Not many people live in this tiny town but 'The Walkabout Creek Hotel' has epitomised outback life to filmgoers around the world. It appeared in the opening scenes of *Crocodile Dundee*, one of Australia's most successful films.

PENTLAND ■ **1712**

Dalrymple Shire is about the size of Tasmania and Pentland is a rail and communications centre for its most western part. The town was settled in 1881 on the site of Bett's Creek and was renamed sometime after the railway line was opened in October 1884. It was the centre of a district which included the Deep Lead and Cape River goldmining communities. When the gold ran out, a few prospectors stayed in the region and raised fruit and vegetables along the Cape River.

Richard and Lydia Pilcher emigrated here from England in 1890 and brought up ten children on their property called 'Eyethorne'. They sold produce to train passengers at Pentland. By 1890, the town's population was 250 Europeans and 150 Chinese. In good seasons, farmers grew such crops as maize and pumpkins. Now, with irrigation, the district produces vegetables, citrus fruits, grapes and avocados.

PORCUPINE GORGE NATIONAL PARK ■ **1713**

Porcupine Gorge is an impressive canyon scoured out by the Porcupine Creek between layered sandstone walls that are hundreds of millions of years old and up to 120 metres high. It is affectionately known locally as the 'little Grand Canyon' and at the bottom there are permanent deep pools fringed with casuarinas and melaleucas where tortoises lead a tranquil, undisturbed existence. In the wet season, the water courses strongly through the gorge. The Kennedy Development Road runs along the western edge of the park and gives access to lookouts with rewarding views. There are Aboriginal carvings and paintings on the walls and a large population of wallaroos and rock wallabies sleep in the gorge during the heat of the day. It is always cooler here than in the surrounding countryside but only the fit should venture on bushwalks.

Just outside the northern boundary of the park, in the wider section of the gorge, is an eye-catching geological feature – a pyramid-shaped monolith of coloured sandstone. This region is a likely place to pick up agate, thunder eggs and topaz, and there is peridot in gemstone quality at Cheviot Hills, about forty kilometres north of Porcupine Gorge. So far as anyone knows, Brazil is the only other place in the world where this unique stone is found. Topaz, sapphire and agate may also be found in the Cheviot Hills region.

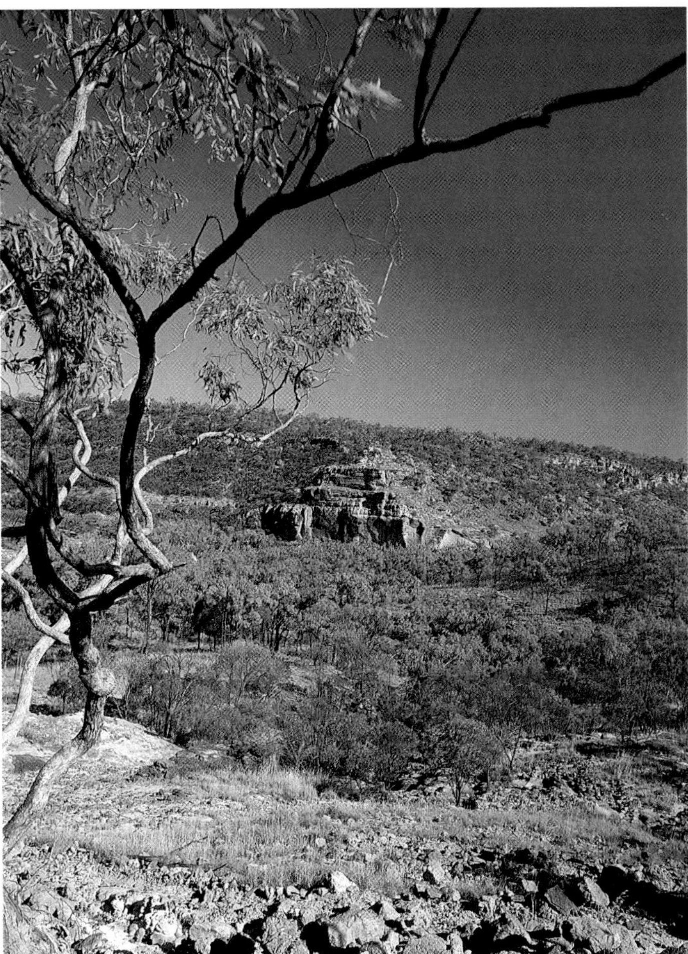

The constant flow of Porcupine Creek has worn away a channel in the middle of a broad plain to create this gorge which bears its name.

PRAIRIE ■ **1714**

The town's surroundings conjure up the flat, featureless North American countryside that inspired its name, for this is an Australian 'prairie' town. At the beginning of the century, the population of Prairie was about three hundred people and there was a boarding house, blacksmith's shop, two churches and two hotels. Now this whistle-stop on the Great Northern railway, which links Townsville and Mount Isa, is home to about fifty permanent residents. Nevertheless, Prairie has a reputation for making something truly Australian – barbecue sausages – and sends its snags all over the country.

The Rockies, north of Prairie, are thought to have once been part of an inland sea where marine dinosaurs cavorted, a theory borne out by the many fossils found in the area.

RICHMOND ■ **1715**

William Landsborough was the first European to set foot in this vast region in February 1862. Because of his glowing account of the possibilities of the land, pioneering settlers began driving cattle to the rich natural pastures which are still some of the best in Queensland. In good seasons, Mitchell and other species of grasses grow abundantly and the rivers provide ample water. 'Richmond Downs' was established by Walter Hayes after he lost the cattle-droving race against Ernest Henry (see Hughenden). The town grew up on a part of his vast property.

Richmond lies on the south bank of the Flinders River in the centre of Queensland's north-west. Though not quite what it was in the days of gold mining and Cobb & Co. coaches, it looks out on rolling sheep downs and the prime beef herds of gulf cattle country.

This is an ancient landscape where once prehistoric monsters trundled about foraging for food. Fossilised remains, millions of years old, have been found here. They include the skeletons of a kronosaurus, a plesiosaurus and a noto chelone or fossilised turtle. The bones and skin of an armoured ankylosaurus have also been found (see box, *Normanton & Karumba*). 'Moon rocks' lie around the countryside at Silver Hills to the north of the town. These are huge spherical rocks, like giant thunder eggs, enclosing fossilised remains of fish, shells and trees.

Richmond has an unusual export industry. Sandalwood trees grow in the area and the wood is sent to China where it is made into joss sticks and incense. *Population 630*

TORRENS CREEK ■ **1716**

In days gone by, this town on the Flinders Highway was a noted stop for bullock waggons and Cobb & Co. horse teams. Now Torrens Creek is little more than a refuelling station, but it has a monument to Jack Bunt, described as a carrier of 'resource and integrity'. East of the settlement are the Burra Ranges where bottlebrush and grevillea grow prolifically.

Nowadays, the wheels of giant road trains, not animal hooves, stir up the bull dust when cattle are driven – literally – through McKinlay to market.

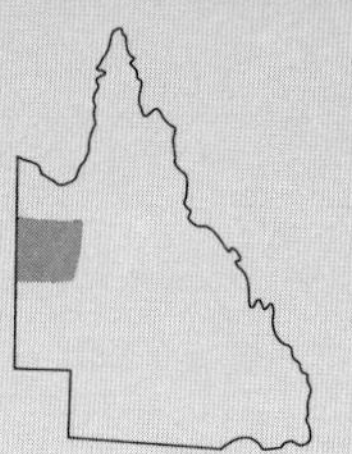

Mount Isa & Cloncurry

The dusty, red country at the isolated western limits of Queensland is a vast spinifex pasture for huge mobs of cattle. At its centre, and in dramatic contrast, is 'The Isa', the hub of the region and a thriving city which provides modern amenities and employment for thousands of people.

CAMOOWEAL ■ 1717

Camooweal is Queensland's westernmost town and has the Barkly Highway as its main street. Although it is almost 200 kilometres to the north-west of Mount Isa, it comes under the same city council. This makes the longest main street and the largest city area in the world (see Mount Isa). The Camooweal–Mount Isa section of the Barkly Highway is one of the inland defence roads built during the Second World War when about one thousand military vehicles used it every day. Now there is a solitary roadside rest area between the two isolated centres.

William Landsborough passed the site of Camooweal in early 1862 in his search for Burke and Wills. The town became established in 1884 and was important in those early droving days as a dipping centre for cattle entering or leaving the state. Camooweal's Shire Hall, built in 1922–23, and extended in 1938, is a fine colonial-style building classified by the National Trust.

CAMOOWEAL CAVES NATIONAL PARK ■ 1718

The Camooweal Caves National Park encloses 13 800 hectares of parched Barkly Tableland except where coolabah trees fringe Nowranie Creek. In the south, Mitchell grass plains predominate and to the north there are open woodland areas of turpentine wattle, western grey box, western bloodwood, and snappy gum among the spinifex. Sinkhole openings lead into a series of limestone caves which are some of the largest and least explored in Australia.

These underground chambers are roosting grounds for bats and owls and refuges for other birds and wildlife during the heat of the day. The Camooweal caves give up their secrets to properly equipped, experienced speleologists and potholers only; they are most accessible early in the dry season and completely off limits in the wet season when they fill with water. Great Nowranie Cave, about seventy metres by almost three hundred metres, is the largest in the park and can be reached only down a challenging eighteen-metre drop.

Although the major excavations are underground, Mount Isa and its mine are indivisible; where the mine workings stop, the oasis of suburbia begins.

CLONCURRY ■ 1719

Robert O'Hara Burke named the Cloncurry River after his cousin, Lady Elizabeth Cloncurry, and the town was subsequently called after the river. In 1861, explorer John McKinlay came this way looking for Burke and Wills and there is a monument commemorating their passing close to the Barkly Highway between Cloncurry and Mount Isa.

John McKinlay reported traces of copper in this district and six years later Ernest Henry discovered rich copper lodes. Cloncurry soon developed as the centre of a very rich mineral field. During the First World War it was supplying copper for shell cases and in 1916 was Australia's biggest exporter. The post-war copper slump prompted Cloncurry to divert its interests with beef cattle – the main industries are still cattle grazing and mining.

In 1974, twenty-two carat straw gold was discovered in the region for the first time. This lies near the surface, looks like strands of wire and is very rare – the only other place it has been discovered is in South Africa. Deserted mine workings in the surrounding hills still yield precious metals and semi-precious stones.

Cloncurry stands where four of inland Queensland's major roads meet and the town has a reputation for being very hot. The temperature of 51.1° Centigrade in the shade, recorded there on 16 January 1889, has never been topped anywhere else in Australia.

The railway line linked Cloncurry with Townsville in 1908 and there was another momentous transport and communication event in 1920 when a new QANTAS air service began between Cloncurry and Winton. The town subsequently clocked up two important firsts in the fields of outback health and education. The Royal Flying Doctor Service's first base was set up here in 1928 (see box) and in 1960, Queensland's first school of the air began from Cloncurry using the RFDS flying doctor radio network – it moved to Mount Isa four years later.

In the early years, 'ghantowns' – accommodating the 'Afghan' drivers and their camels who carried ore and supplies to places horses could not go – formed at Cloncurry and nearby Duchess. Dromedary camels did the job and their keepers were soon breeding them in Australia; the small number of imported, two-humped Bactrian camels proved unsuitable for pack work (see box, *Leigh Creek & Marree*). *Population 2310*

DAJARRA ■ 1720

This tiny town with its predominantly Aboriginal population, was once a very large cattle trucking depot. Huge herds were driven here from the Northern Territory and loaded aboard trains for markets in the east. It is said that Dajarra and Kajabbi (see entry) were second only to some Argentinian towns as cattle yarding centres. The town declined when the huge road trains took over the cattle-hauling business.

In a region rich in Aboriginal rock art sites, Dajarra has a particularly fine example of an Aboriginal spiral rock engraving.

GUNPOWDER ■ 1721

Gunpowder, to the north-west of Mount Isa, was originally named by the camel drivers. Once a prosperous copper-mining town, the re-opening of the mine has created a new settlement of about forty houses. The community now depends on mining, cattle and tourism.

There is holiday accommodation set in rugged, red hills not far from beautiful Lake Waggaboonyah – a stretch of water fringed with pandanus palms and covered in water lilies. This is an ideal environment to see Johnson River freshwater crocodiles in their natural habitat and to observe frill-necked lizards, red kangaroos, goannas and other native animals. Nearly 150 species of birds have been counted in the district.

KAJABBI ■ 1722

This small bush town, like so many others in the region, had its heyday as a railhead. Thousands of cattle ended up here after long weeks of cross-country droving.

Aborigines lived round Kajabbi for thousands of years before Europeans penetrated the area. The ochre-red sign of the emu foot marked the territory of the Kalkadoon people. They clashed bitterly with the early pastoralists as the latter pushed further into inland Queensland. In 1884, there was a battle between European settlers together with Queensland mounted native police and the Kalkatunga warriors on the slopes of

The infrequent run-off from the sun-baked Mount Godkin Range helps top up the waters of Lake Moondarra.

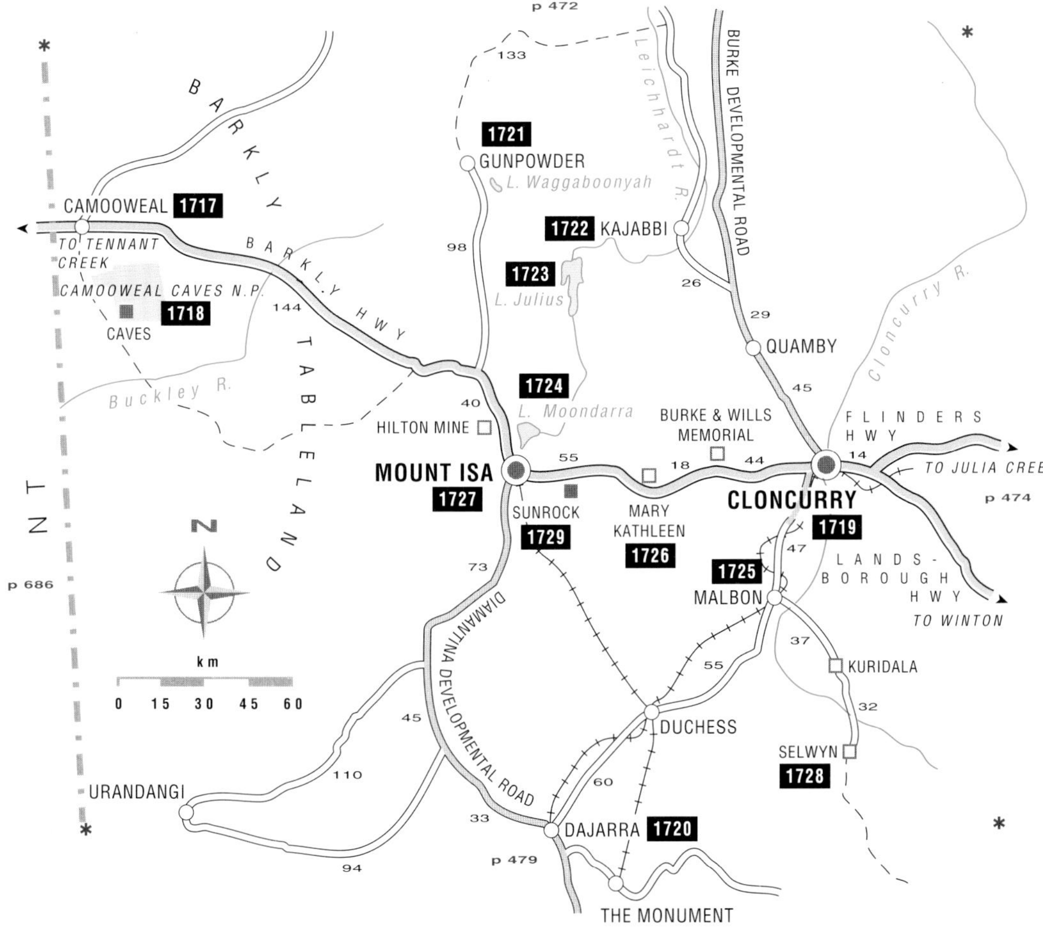

Battle Mountain, about twenty kilometres south-west of Kajabbi. What really happened is not very clear as there are no reliable reports, but certainly many of the Aborigines came off by far the worst and were slain. A hundred years later a memorial to them was unveiled in Kajabbi.

LAKE JULIUS ■ **1723**
The Lake Julius Dam, which is located downstream of Lake Moondarra (see entry), gives Mount Isa its second source of water. It was built in the 1970s at a cost of over twenty-one million dollars. Lake Julius, with its greater capacity than Moondarra, is the largest of northern Queensland's freshwater lakes and is used for fishing, waterskiing and boating.

LAKE MOONDARRA ■ **1724**
Much of the southern section of Lake Moondarra is a bird sanctuary which attracts pelicans, cormorants, ibis, storks, ducks, kingfishers and even seagulls, though the nearest coastline is more than 320 kilometres away. The lake, which was formed by the Leichhardt River Dam, is Mount Isa's regular water storage and provides an aquatic playground at the end of a sealed road only a few kilometres from the city.

MALBON ■ **1725**
Malbon, in the Cloncurry river bed, is the site of some well-preserved Aboriginal rock paintings that are unique in Queensland but are similar to some of the cave paintings in the deserts of central Australia. Their style is very different from other artwork at nearby Sunrock. The Malbon paintings decorate a twenty-metre-high quartzite outcrop and are red ochre designs on a yellow pigment background. Flood debris, up to two metres above them, shows they have survived immersion in water.

MARY KATHLEEN ■ **1726**
Mary Kathleen, named after the wife of Norman McConachy, one of the men who discovered uranium there in 1954, is the town that died in the early 1980s when Queensland's only uranium mine closed down. By then, mining was no longer economical, but already a total of 8898 tonnes of uranium oxide had been extracted from thirty-one million tonnes of ore. Allanite, the mineral in the tailings at Mary Kathleen, is a potential source of rare earth elements.

Mary Kathleen's buildings were sold and taken elsewhere. Some of them ended up on display in Cloncurry's Mary Kathleen Memorial Park. These include the police residence, the police station and the bank, which is now a museum. The most famous and poignant exhibit is Robert O'Hara Burke's water bottle which symbolises the privations of the early explorers and provides a vivid reminder of Burke's tragic end.

For two days every August, rodeo is king in Mount Isa as cattlemen from all over the world come to ride, rope – and sometimes bite the dust.

MOUNT ISA ■ 1727

Known affectionately by local people as 'The Isa', Mount Isa is thought to be named after John Campbell Miles' sister, Isabella. Others say its name may be a corruption of Mount Ida in Western Australia.

Mount Isa's boundaries enclose the largest geographic area of any city in the world. The city's administrative area of 40 977 kilometres is roughly the same size as Switzerland and twice as big as Israel. The population is not especially large by world standards, but were it not for Mount Isa and Cloncurry, to a much lesser degree, this region would be almost empty of people. Another fascinating Mount Isa statistic surfaced in 1973, during the golden jubilee celebrations. In that year, there were more than 2.5 vehicles for every one of its 28 000 residents – more vehicles per person than any other city except the United States city of Detroit.

Mount Isa, the site of Australia's largest underground mine, is the backbone of Queensland's mining industry and produces lead, zinc, silver and copper. The Hilton mine, north of Mount Isa, supplements the diminishing silver-lead-zinc ore from Mount Isa. Copper was extracted in the district from the early 1880s until prices slumped in the 1920s – there was a resurgence of interest in this metal in 1942 to help meet wartime demands. In 1923, John Campbell Miles discovered a silver-lead-zinc outcrop beside the old mail route from Duchess to Camooweal and sent a sample to Cloncurry to be surveyed. Soon 500 claims were staked out and the township was on its way.

In the 1950s, Mount Isa began to shed its frontier town image and grow towards the modern centre it is today. There has been a multicultural mix from its earliest days and fifty nationalities now work at the Mount Isa mines.

The people have done a great deal to overcome their isolation and the city is a pleasant oasis in a hot and monotonous landscape where spinifex and cattle predominate. However Mount Isa is still very much an outback settlement and has several institutions to cope with the remoteness. For example, there is a Royal Flying Doctor Service base (see box) and more than 200 of the region's children attend the Mount Isa School of Distance Education, learning by radio and correspondence papers.

The dingo fence is also a typical outback feature. This longest netting fence in the world was designed to keep the dingoes of central Australia from attacking sheep in the southern pasture areas. It runs for 9600 kilometres, from 35 kilometres north of Boulia to the Mount Isa road (see box, *Quilpie & Thargomindah*). The area close to Mount Isa is a rockhunter's treasure trove containing minerals and semi-precious stones, among them the rare Maltese crosses which are found here and around Cloncurry. *Population 23 670*

FESTIVALS Rotary Rodeo, August; Oktoberfest, mid-October.

SELWYN ■ 1728

Gold was first discovered in the Selwyn Ranges in the late 1860s. The find sparked a rush and like Kuridala, another former gold town a few kilometres to the north, Selwyn soon mushroomed into a rumbustious mining camp with a population of hard-living prospectors and the usual hangers-on. But once the minerals had gone, there was little to hold these pioneering people and Selwyn became one of Queensland's ghost towns with crumbling buildings and derelict mine equipment as evidence of former times.

SUNROCK ■ 1729

The Aboriginal fertility paintings at Sunrock, executed in red ochre on the rock face, are estimated to be up to 2000 years old. The fine-grained ochre has penetrated into minute cracks in the quartzite to produce a 'bonding' effect which preserves the surface against flooding and the elements. Because of the age of the paintings, the local Aboriginal people can no longer interpret their precise mythological meaning. The human figures and the prominent snake outline suggest that the site may be associated with the rainbow snake legend or have been an initiation place for the snake totem.

BY AIR & AIRWAVES: THE OUTBACK'S MANTLE OF SAFETY

SIR ROBERT MENZIES described the Royal Flying Doctor Service as 'perhaps the single greatest contribution to the effective settlement of the far distant country that we have witnessed in our time'.

The uniquely Australian service was the brainchild of a Victorian, John Flynn, who as an outback Presbyterian minister and missionary, saw the great need for medical services on the farms and stations in the isolated regions of Australia and decided to do something about it. He organised good doctors, aerial transport and radio communication and set up a service of 'flying' doctors.

Flynn chose Cloncurry for the first flying doctor headquarters because it had an established hospital, a QANTAS aerodrome and the essential telephone and telegraph network. Pedal wirelesses, developed by Adelaide electrical engineer, Alfred Traeger, were later installed in every remote homestead, as Flynn said, 'to make the dumb inland speak and its deaf distances hear'. Bicycle parts and footpower were used initially to drive the generators.

It became possible to diagnose many ailments and injuries and prescribe treatment over the airwaves. The writer Ernestine Hill tells of radioed advice 'for babies with gastritis, toddlers with measles and whooping cough, children with trachoma or sprained ankles, a lad badly burnt, a woman bitten by a red-backed spider, an old bushman in his camp crippled with sciatica – anything in the seven ages of man'. In emergencies, the doctor flew in to land on improvised runways – the first call was to an injured stockman in Julia Creek in 1928.

The flying doctor service now spreads a far-reaching 'mantle of safety' from bases at Mount Isa, Charleville and Cairns in Queensland, Wyndham, Derby, Port Hedland, Carnarvon, Kalgoorlie, Meekatharra and Jandkadot in Western Australia, Broken Hill in New South Wales, Port Augusta in South Australia, Alice Springs in the Northern Territory and Launceston in Tasmania. The service inspired a popular television series called, naturally enough, *The Flying Doctors*, and set in mythical, outback 'Cooper's Crossing'.

John Flynn Place opened in Cloncurry in 1988 as a Bicentennial tribute to a great Australian and a great institution. The museum section houses the first pedal radio and other such mementoes. □

In the early 1930s, before the Flying Doctor Service insignia (above left) found a place on the service's own planes, the infant QANTAS ferried doctor to patient on isolated outback stations.

Boulia & Birdsville

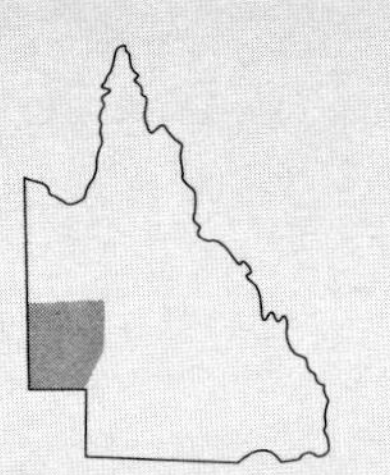

This region has been dubbed with many titles – 'Corner Country' because of its position in the far west corner of Queensland where three states meet; 'Channel Country' because of the intricate web of channels fed intermittently by fickle, desert-bound, outback rivers; and 'Kidman Country' because of the huge stations once owned by the cattle king.

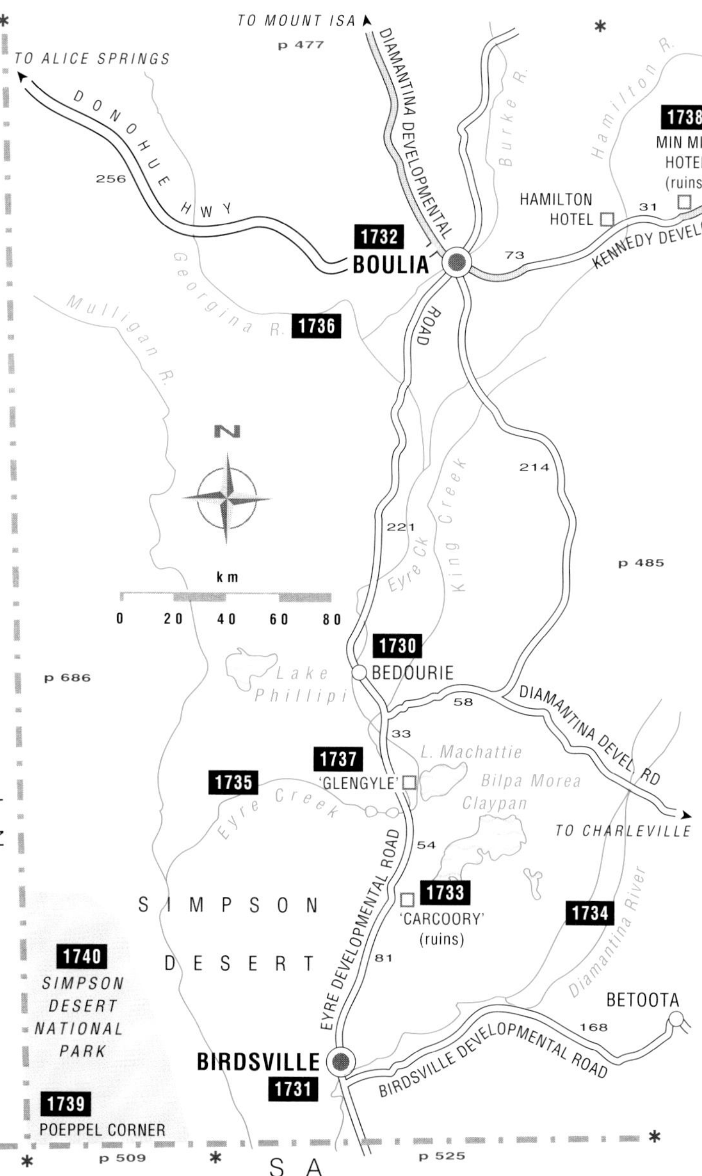

The dirt of the Donohue 'Highway' is an appropriately hot colour for a road which skirts the Simpson Desert as it connects Boulia with Alice Springs.

BEDOURIE ■ 1730

A 'Bedourie shower' does not bring rain, it brings red dust, the town's name being synonymous in this region with dust storms. Bedourie water, on the other hand, comes not in showers from above but from below the ground. The town sits on one of Queensland's largest sources of artesian water and its daily supply of millions of litres of lukewarm water comes from a 400-metre-deep bore dug in 1905.

Bedourie became a settlement for surrounding cattle properties in the 1880s. The local Royal Hotel dates back to these early days and the handmade adobe bricks, which took four years to make, were obviously meant to last although the thatched roof has had to be replaced by one of iron. The concrete crossing of the Eyre Creek in Bedourie may appear superfluous in the 'dry' but heavy rainfall in central or north-western Queensland can cause flooding here, cutting off the road for weeks.

Bedourie's population has always been tiny but it is the administrative headquarters for a shire that covers 95 000 square kilometres.

BIRDSVILLE ■ 1731

At Birdsville, it is not only the sun that is is fiercely hot, so is the artesian water, which is almost at boiling point when it reaches the surface from a 1200-metre-deep bore from which it passes into ponds to cool off. At the northern terminus of the famous Birdsville Track, the town has been on the Queensland–South Australia stock route since the late 1870s. The main – and only – street in the town is still broad enough to allow a mob of cattle to be driven through it although most cattle are now transported as passengers in a road train.

At what was then called Diamantina Crossing, because of its position on the Diamantina River (see entry), a number of stock routes from west and central Queensland converged and in 1882, a store was built to service stockmen and drovers. At its peak in the 1880s and early 1890s, the town had a population of about 400. A police magistrate, troopers and customs officials, who exacted a toll on stock and supplies crossing the border, were residents of Birdsville, which comprised several stores and three hotels to cater for their needs.

One of Birdsville's hotels, dating back to 1882, was, in 1923, to become the Australian Inland Mission hospital from which vital messages were transmitted to Adelaide by means of a pedal-powered radio. Another hostelry, the 1885 Birdsville Hotel with its air of a Mexican cantina, still operates in a town where the permanent population has hovered at around 100, since Federation put an end to the customs post and six years of drought put an end to the hopes of many pioneers.

Once a year, the Birdsville Hotel serves 4000–5000 people – the final number depending on whether rain has made the roads into the town impassable – during the Birdsville Races. The first race in 1882 attracted entrants and spectators from all over the district. With generous prize money, the races now attract amateur and professional riders who travel for thousands of kilometres to Birdsville's other 'track' – a grassless race course in the main street where dust raised by the winning horse can obscure those in second and third place. After three days, the racegoers vanish, leaving behind 80 000 empty

The second Birdsville track, after the famous stock route, is the Birdsville Cup racetrack where lack of turf fails to discourage the enthusiastic gallopers.

beer cans and a boost to funds for the Royal Flying Doctor Service.

FESTIVALS Birdsville Races, early September.

BOULIA ■ 1732

Boulia is the headquarters of a vast shire with a population of 530 people and, in a good year, 250 000 sheep and 75 000 cattle. The town at the centre of this 60 000-square-kilometre region has a population of 300...and a very long history.

The remains of pterosaurs – flying reptiles – have been found around the town, which was also a centre of Aboriginal spear- and shield-making before European settlement. Burke and Wills camped here in 1861 and the explorer, Ernest Henry, established a canvas store here in 1875 at a waterhole known as 'bulla bulla' from which the town that grew up around Henry's store got its name.

By the 1880s, Boulia had a police barracks, a telegraph station and a number of houses, one of which still stands and is used as a museum.

A crow flying from Sydney to Darwin would have covered half the required distance by the time it overflew Boulia, with its broad streets shaded by oleanders, neat irrigated lawns and air-conditioned school behind which stands the last known corroboree tree of the long-dispersed Aboriginal Pitta Pitta people.

WADDI TREES Ten kilometres from Boulia is a small patch of extremely rare waddi, a form of acacia which is also found near Birdsville. The slow-growing tree – it can take 150 years to grow 10 metres – has spiky leaves and dries to such hardness that it resists axes, saws and drills.

'CARCOORY' ■ 1733

Off the Eyre Developmental Road and beside the Oasis bore, lie the ruins of 'Carcoory', now preserved as an example of the many homesteads that once studded this region.

'Carcoory' was built of local limestone in the late 1870s and is very similar to cottages of a similar era in rural South Australia; it is thought to have been abandoned in 1906. The roofless house stands on a rise, its empty window frames and doorless entrance a poignant memorial to pioneers' dreams defeated by the twin conquerors of isolation and drought.

DIAMANTINA RIVER ■ 1734

When Burke and Wills were 'agreeably pulled up by a magnificent creek' on Christmas Day 1860, they failed to name it, assuming it was a continuation of Eyre Creek. John McKinlay named the river Mueller, after the botanist Baron von Mueller, when he crossed it in 1862 with his search party looking for Burke and Wills. Finally, it was the explorer William Landsborough who gave the river a name that stuck; he named it in 1866 after Lady Diamantina Roma, wife of Sir George Bowen, first Governor of Queensland.

One of the major Channel Country rivers (see box), the Diamantina never completely dries up and floods regularly. Its waterholes are popular for swimming and fishing for golden perch (yellow belly). The river rises in the ranges south-west of Cloncurry and flows for up to 900 kilometres into South Australia where it feeds the Goyder Lagoon and where, in flood seasons, it flows far enough south to feed the Warburton.

EYRE CREEK ■ 1735

Charles Sturt discovered this creek in 1845 and named it after his fellow explorer Edward John Eyre. In the year that Sturt followed the creek, all he found was a series of black, muddy holes and when he did come upon water, it was salty. In flood seasons, Eyre Creek, which rises as the Georgina River (see entry), changes character completely as it flows through Bedourie, flushes out the 300-square-kilometre saline waters of Lake Machattie, then crosses the state border to add its waters to Goyder Lagoon.

GEORGINA RIVER ■ 1736

The banks of the Georgina River were known to the Aborigines as the best source of pituri, a leaf containing more nicotine than chewing tobacco, a knowledge which gave the Aborigines around the river a strong trading currency. The river made the painless transition from being the male Herbert to the female Georgina in the 1860s. The first wave of settlers who used this name were, however, rapidly chased off by Aborigines and the land around the Georgina River was not resettled by Europeans until the 1870s.

Rising on the Northern Territory side of the dry Barkly Tableland, the Georgina River flows south-east to join with the Hamilton River and merge into Eyre Creek about 100 kilometres north of Bedourie. Unlike the Hamilton which flows – or trickles – through a catchment with little rainfall, the Georgina, like the other major rivers of the Channel Country (see box) has a monsoon catchment where heavy rainfall is just about the only form of precipitation known.

'GLENGYLE' ■ 1737

Sidney Kidman – the turn-of-the-century South Australian pastoralist who controlled cattle stations across more than 130 000 square kilometres – is supposed to have planned an expanding empire while camped under a coolabah tree on Glengyle Station in 1891. One of the Kidman family's major stations, 'Glengyle' sits on the west bank of Eyre Creek (see entry) about sixty kilometres south of Bedourie (see entry). The main house was built of pise – clay forced into frames to form sturdy walls – with a separate meathouse and kitchen wing, the whole complex protected from dust storms by a fence of galvanised iron. Kidman's linked chain of stations, enabled individual runs such as 'Glengyle' to survive as livestock was moved from property to property to beat the devastating droughts that ruined so many other cattle-farming ventures.

MIN MIN HOTEL ■ 1738

The Min Min hotel, east of Boulia, burnt down early in the twentieth century leaving a legacy of rubble, empty bottles, a graveyard in the nearby sandhills...and the mysterious Min Min light.

The light, sighted over the last seventy years by hundreds of people from drovers and stockmen to a local detective-sergeant and the district stock inspector, has been described as a strange oval light resembling a

The dusty cattle drovers who once crowded Birdsville's pub after bringing a mob up the track have been replaced by cattle-truck drivers and tourists.

car headlight or a luminous football, sometimes at a standstill, sometimes approaching and sometimes following or chasing the amazed witness. Some who see the light become terrified and hysterical while others are curious and pursue it.

One man who sighted the light on a pitch-dark night in the early 1900s said it was sufficiently bright that he could see the rising hairs on his forearm yet his usually nervous horse was unperturbed by it. In the 1950s, two men on the Barkly Tableland watched for ten minutes as the white light spiralled to a height of three hundred metres then disappeared.

Scientific explanations for the light include burning methane gas from a bore, a massive swarm of fireflies, an owl that has brushed against luminous fungus or the twin beams of car headlights bouncing off low cloud but none of the explanations satisfies those who swear by their sightings.

Poeppel Corner exists only on maps but a post marks where it would be if the state borders were fenced.

CAWNPORE HILLS The best view of the surrounding countryside is to be had from the top of the Cawnpore Hills – two peaked, almost perfectly circular hills which rise like tiny volcanoes from the flat plain north-east of the Min Min ruins.

POEPPEL CORNER ■ 1739

Poeppel Corner, in the dry Simpson Desert, is not a geographical reality but an imaginary corner – or upside-down T-junction – marked on maps. Where the Queensland, Northern Territory and South Australian borders meet on a map, there you will find Poeppel Corner.

Augustus Poeppel – government surveyor – surveyed the site with his chainman Henry just after Christmas in 1880. Their camel train came equipped with a two-metre-tall peg inscribed with the names of the three states and the latitude and longitude. Two natural features nearby – Lake Poeppel and Henry Hill – were used to take survey readings and accurately locate the 'corner'.

Unfortunately, the precise latitude and longitude of Adelaide was later amended, with the result that Poeppel's peg was moved 316.8 metres to the correct position in 1884 when the peripatetic Poeppel returned to do a more detailed survey of the Northern Territory border. The pastoralist, E.A. Colson was the next European to visit Poeppel Corner in 1936 and he added a tin plate with his initials to Poeppel's peg.

In 1962, a geologist found the peg rotted to a stump, marked the site with a large drum and brought the inscribed section of the peg back to Adelaide. The present monument was placed at Poeppel Corner in 1968 and Mr Poeppel might be amazed to know that, with a track now running the 150 kilometres from Birdsville to this out-of-the-way place, erosion caused by visitors threatens stability of even the solid 'new' monument.

SIMPSON DESERT NATIONAL PARK ■ 1740

The Simpson Desert National Park is the largest and most westerly of Queensland's national parks, covering more than half-a-million hectares – although this area is dwarfed by the even larger area of the desert conserved on the South Australian side of the border.

The distinctive desert and dunes, which vary in colour from white to iron-oxide red, run in a generally north-north-west to south-south-east direction. At around twenty metres in height and two hundred metres apart, the dunes can run unbroken for eighty kilometres. In the valleys between the dunes there are claypans, with their thin salty loam crusts overlying black sticky mud, and gibber-ironstone flats.

On the crests of the dunes, which are still subject to movement, sandhill cane grass grows while spinifex is found on the more stable lower section of the dunes. Gidgee and bladder saltbush are the most prominent species found in the valleys between the dunes. Summer rain, seldom more than 150 millimetres a year can result in sudden bursts of blooming as seeds dormant in the sand spring to life. In the 1960s, after light summer rain, eighty-five plant species were recorded in the park.

Bird species range from brown falcons, galahs and honeyeaters to crimson or orange chats and the rare Eyrean grasswren. A diversity of reptiles, more usually associated with this desert national park, include the desert death-adder, banded skinks, bearded dragons, sand goanna and the largest Australian lizard, the perentie. In recent years, two-legged visitors to the park have grown in such numbers that warnings are now issued for drivers going up and down the dunes to be cautious when approaching the crest in case they meet an oncoming vehicle.

CHANNEL COUNTRY: WHERE THE BONES OF DEAD MEN LIE

BURKE and Wills perished there, Charles Sturt almost came to final grief and Ludwig Leichhardt may have been a victim of its perverse climate and landscape. All of them challenged the no-man's land of the Channel Country, a wild land that inspired Barcroft Boake's chilling description:

Out where the grinning skulls bleach whitely
Under the saltbush sparkling brightly;
Out where the wild dogs chorus nightly –
That's where the dead men lie!

Channel Country was the ultimate in frustration not only for explorers and, later, pioneering cattlemen searching for a reliable supply of water but also for modern cartographers trying to follow the paths of errant rivers that appear, disappear, flood and trickle in a confusing web of ever-changing channels, which is almost impossible to map accurately.

The 780 000 square kilometres of the Channel Country are an almost totally flat, silt plain deposited and created by the major rivers – Diamantina, Georgina, Thomson, Barcoo and Cooper Creek – which, during the summer, carry the northern monsoon rains in an intricate network of arteries heading in the same south-westerly direction towards the arid inland. Dry, empty gutters become river channels and saltpans become lakes as the rivers meander sluggishly over hundreds of kilometres towards Lake Eyre in South Australia. The waters of the Channel Country rivers have succeeded in reaching Lake Eyre on three occasions only so far this century. More usually they dissipate in swampy regions long before reaching Australia's largest salt lake, where gravity tries desperately to take them. In years of heavy rainfall, the rivers of the Channel Country can be up to eighty kilometres wide and can join together in one vast 'super river'.

Channel Country, with its townships of Quilpie in the east, Birdsville in the west, Boulia in the north and Thargomindah in the south, may be an explorers' graveyard but it is reputed to be the best cattle-fattening country in the world – after rain – a claim upheld by families such as the Duracks and Kidmans who established stations in the area. But the 'wet' is notoriously unreliable and until the cattlemen were able to exploit the water in the Great Artesian Basin, the success or failure of stations and settlements depended on the few permanent waterholes and the vagaries of the unpredictable Channel Country landscape. □

After summer rains a thousand kilometres to the east, the Diamantina slithers slowly over its banks to create broad, marshy stretches.

Longreach & Blackall

This region is not only the birthplace of two national institutions – the Australian Labor Party and QANTAS – it also claims the distinctions of producing the world's fastest shearer, Australia's first museum to outback pioneers and a fashion item that has spread as far as the 'big smoke' – the navy-blue singlet.

Even tough acacias are defeated in their attempts to scramble up the soilless hills that dot the plains near Winton.

BARCALDINE ■ **1741**
Barcaldine was proclaimed in 1886 as the terminus of the Rockhampton railway, its position as the district's transport centre being enhanced by the Cobb & Co. coaches which ran from the town until 1914. The engineer in charge of the water supply for the new settlement struck artesian water at a mere 210 metres and Barcaldine became, in 1887, the first town in Australia to have a reliable, potable supply of artesian water. The district's citrus orchards, unexpected in this cattle and sheep region, owe their existence to artesian water.

The local bore water did have a few disadvantages – it made the beer brewed locally undrinkable. But the brewery proved useful in other ways by housing patients when the local hospital burned down.

Artful scientific deduction revealed the 65-million-year-old drama behind Lark Quarry's footprints.

Barcaldine earned its place in the history books during the historic six-month shearers' strike in 1891, when it became the strike headquarters. In May 1891, a thousand striking shearers camping in the town took part in the first May Day march in Australia. Troops arrested thirteen members of the strike committee, ten of whom were sentenced to hard labour. The pastoralists moved non-union labour into the shearing sheds.

The dramatic strike was far from being a failure since it was one of the catalysts that led to the formation of the Australian Workers' Party, the forerunner of the Australian Labor Party. Tommy Ryan, a member of the strike committee was to become, in 1892, the first Labor-endorsed candidate in the world to be elected when he entered the Queensland parliament. Barcaldine is the site for the new Australian Workers' Heritage Centre, the first stage of which was opened by the then Prime Minister Bob Hawke in 1991. *Population 1530*

'TREE OF KNOWLEDGE' A large gum tree, possibly more than 200 years old, near Barcaldine's railway station has been a meeting place since 1886 and because of its use by the Salvation Army, was once known as the 'Hallelujah Tree'. The organisers of the shearers' strike used to gather here and the tree became known as the 'Tree of Knowledge' as from beneath it 'emerged Australia's Labor Political Movement' – according to the plaque placed on the tree in 1958 and the granite shears erected as a memorial in 1987.

BARCOO RIVER ■ **1742**
Rising in the Warrego Ranges, the Barcoo River initially heads in a north-westerly direction past Blackall (see entry) then turns south-west to flow through the Channel Country (see *Boulia & Birdsville*) to become Cooper Creek in its lower reaches – a total distance of 480 kilometres.

The river's north-westerly direction led Sir Thomas Mitchell in 1846 into believing, and announcing to the world, that he had found the 'El Dorado of Australia' – a river he called the Victoria River heading inland towards the Gulf of Carpentaria and, hence, the Indian Ocean. His second-in-command, Edmund Kennedy, discovered the eventual direction of the river in 1847 and renamed it the Barcoo from an Aboriginal word.

The river has been mentioned in the works of both Henry Lawson and Banjo Paterson and has entered the Australian language but not always in a flattering context. A number of outback ailments such as Barcoo rot-scurvy and the Barcoo spews – caused by heat and an unvaried diet as well as the Barcoo salute – another anti-fly measure – have given the Barcoo a reputation very different from the one that Mitchell accorded it.

WILGA WATERHOLE This waterhole on the Barcoo, near Isisford, has been known to drive level-headed drovers to the point of hysteria. Sounds that are said to range from plaintive wailing to high-pitched shrieking have been heard at the waterhole since the 1860s. Local legend has it that animals are averse to dallying here although the noises are more likely to be wind in a subterranean channel than coming from some human or ghostly origin.

BLACKALL ■ **1743**
Named after Samuel Wensley Blackall, second governor of Queensland, Blackall established a reputation not only as a 'pedigree capital' because of the quality of the sheep and cattle from its stud farms, but also has a number of other claims to fame.

The sinking of the first artesian bore in Queensland was started at Blackall in 1885 but, because of the mineral content, water from the bore was undrinkable...though it may have been ideal for hot baths.

In December 1890, the constitution and rules of the Labor Party were drawn up at Blackall so that, like neighbouring Barcaldine (see entry) Blackall has some claim to assisting at the birth of the party. The extension of the railway to Barcaldine was to rob Blackall of its position as the main town in the west. But one achievement was not lost.

On Monday 10 October 1892, Jacky Howe of Blackall set a world shearing record by hand shearing 321 sheep in 7 hours and 40 minutes at the nearby Alice Downs Station. His record, using hand shears, has

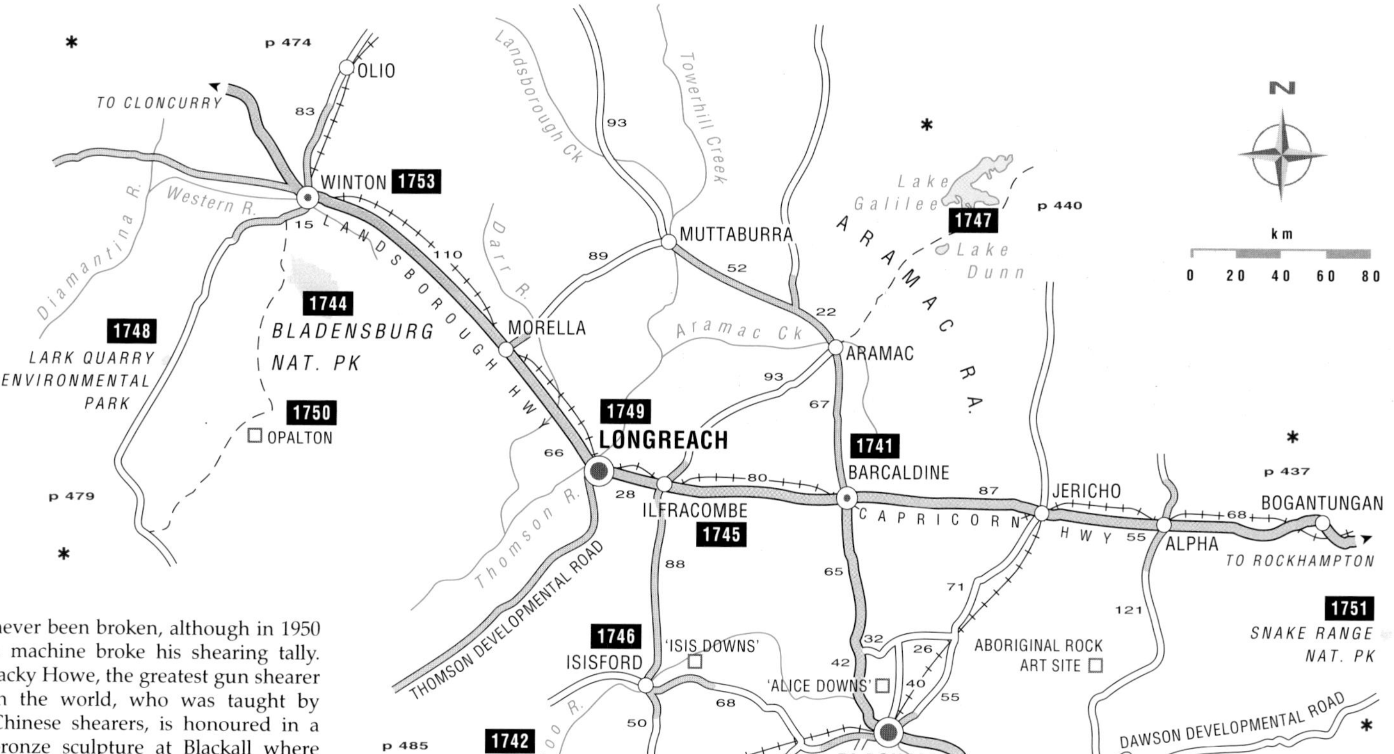

never been broken, although in 1950 a machine broke his shearing tally. Jacky Howe, the greatest gun shearer in the world, who was taught by Chinese shearers, is honoured in a bronze sculpture at Blackall where he was a publican for many years after giving up shearing and where he was buried in 1920. His name went into the dictionary as well as the record book for the 'Jacky Howe', the colloquial name for the sleeveless, dark navy singlet, which he 'invented' to give him ease of movement when shearing. *Population 1580*

ABORIGINAL ROCK ART SITE North-east of Blackall, in a small sandstone gorge, is the largest group of Aboriginal art sites in Queensland's central highlands. At more than forty sites there are stencils, engravings and paintings in the white sandstone of the cliffs. Between 9000 and 10 000 figures have been recorded so far.

BLACKALL WOOL SCOUR Beside an artesian bore on the Blackall to Jericho road stands the Blackall wool scour, built by a syndicate in 1906. The galvanised iron building operated as a wool scour until 1978 and is the most intact example of a mechanical scour in western Queensland.

BLADENSBURG NATIONAL PARK ■ 1744

Access to Bladensburg National Park, south of Winton, is by means of tracks through the private property of Bladensburg Station. There are no facilities within the 33 700-hectare park but it does preserve – in their undisturbed and ungrazed state – ridges of woodland, gidgee scrub and hummock grasslands. Around the rare waterholes and when the dry rivers fill after infrequent floods in the Channel Country (see *Boulia & Birdsville*), flowering plants and Cooper clover can also be seen.

ILFRACOMBE ■ 1745

Ilfracombe developed from a railway construction camp on a section of Wellshot Station – the biggest station in the region with 400 000 sheep on 6000 square kilometres. From the 1890s, fifteen teams carted wool to and supplies from the railhead at Ilfracombe, which had a number of urban conveniences including three hotels, a billiard saloon, an aerated water manufacturer and a dressmaker. But the ultimate innovation came in 1911 when the Cobb & Co. coach on the Ilfracombe to Isisford mail run was replaced by a truck – the first motorised mail run in Queensland.

In the Ilfracombe Folk Museum some of the transport that was so vital in the town's development has been preserved. Pride of place goes to one of the huge bullock waggons that required up to thirty bullocks or horses to pull it and which, before the advent of the railway, would transport 100 bales of wool to Rockhampton then return with supplies – a round-journey of six months.

Traditional materials such as stone and corrugated iron help shape the Stockman's Hall of Fame which enshrines and celebrates outback history.

ISISFORD ■ 1746

This very small town was founded in the 1870s by the brothers James and William Whitman, itinerant hawkers who broke an axle on their cart trying to cross the Barcoo River and decided to open a permanent store on the site. The brothers referred to the small settlement as Whittown but it was renamed Isisford in 1878 after the nearest property 'Isis Downs'.

For a while the small settlement prospered and the first mail to be delivered by truck, rather than the usual horse-drawn coach, attracted a crowd to Isisford in 1911. Only two of the five pubs of those days remain and the small historical museum can be visited by those travelling on the dry-weather road between Blackall and Longreach, which runs through the town.

'ISIS DOWNS' Isis Downs, named after the Isis River – a tributary of the Thames running through the English university town of Oxford – had the first all-electric shearing shed in Australia. The semi-circular shed with fifty shearing stands was manufactured in England and shipped in sections to Australia.

LAKE GALILEE AND LAKE DUNN ■ 1747

The Lake Galilee wetlands, comprising Lake Galilee and Lake Dunn, cover an area of 60 000 hectares and are the only large chain of permanent wetlands in Queensland's west.

The smaller of the two lakes, the freshwater Lake Dunn, is fed by four creeks and is popular for fishing and waterskiing. Lake Galilee is fed by more than twenty creeks and covers more than 15 000 hectares. It is shallow, seasonally flooded and often

The atmosphere of the 'outback' Australia of Waltzing Matilda *– heard first here in 1895 – survives in Winton.*

brackish. The lake's three islands – Dolphin, St Helena and Swan islands – are breeding and nesting sites for a variety of water birds. With almost 200 different kinds of plants around the lake providing a habitat for red and grey kangaroos and emus, Lake Galilee is an unexpected oasis in this arid region.

LARK QUARRY ENVIRONMENTAL PARK ■ 1748

A permanent roof over a triangular-shaped area of 210 square metres protects dinosaur footprints that tell the story of an ancient stampede, the principal attraction of Lark Quarry Environmental Park. From evidence gathered at the site in the 1970s, the Queensland Museum has been able to piece together what happened 95 million years ago.

Up to 200 small, non-carnivorous dinosaurs – hollow-boned coelurosaurs and bird-footed ornithopods – varying in size from bantam chickens to emus, were disturbed beside a lake by a large flesh-eating dinosaur. The large dinosaur pursued one animal while the others panicked and stampeded across the mud.

The ten sixty-four-centimetre-long footprints of the flesh-eater and the twelve hundred smaller footprints were left in the soft mud, which was then overlain with sand and silt and compressed to form layers of rock. Erosion of these covering layers revealed the fossilised footprints – the world's only physical evidence of a prehistoric stampede.

LONGREACH ■ 1749

Longreach started life as a teamsters' camp on a nine-kilometre-long reach of the Thomson River on 'Mount Cornish', an outstation of 'Bowen Downs'. It was from 'Mount Cornish' that a station hand, Harry Redford, on whom the fictional Captain Starlight from *Robbery Under Arms* was partly based, stole 1000 head of cattle and drove them on an awesome 2400-kilometre journey to South Australia where he sold them for 5000 pounds sterling.

The great wool boom in the early twentieth century brought rapid development to Longreach but the boom years from the 1920s did not come from wool but from wings. QANTAS – Queensland and Northern Territory Aerial Services Ltd – was based here from 1921–30 and the old galvanised iron hangar in which the company's aircraft were maintained and later built, has become a 'heritage' property.

The link between hospitals and aircraft was to continue when, in 1959, the Flying Surgeon Service, which sends specialist surgeons and anaesthetists to small outback hospitals, set up its first base at Longreach. *Population 3610*

THE AUSTRALIAN STOCKMAN'S HALL OF FAME AND OUTBACK HERITAGE CENTRE This national museum, opened by Queen Elizabeth in 1988, was the brainchild of the artist Hugh Sawrey, aided by others of like mind including Dame Mary Durack and clothing manufacturer R.M. Williams. The centre is a memorial to the early outback pioneers.

FESTIVALS Diamond Shears and South Pacific Shearing Championships, late July; Starlight's Stampede, September of even-numbered years.

OPALTON ■ 1750

Only the ruins of the old police lock-up are left in this ghost town. In the 1890s, up to 600 men were digging on what was one of Queensland's earliest opal fields. The carting of water over long distances and a drop in the market value of opals caused the field to be abandoned in 1915 although there are probably opals still to be found in the sandstone layer ten metres below the surface.

SNAKE RANGE NATIONAL PARK ■ 1751

In a remote area, fringed by sixty-metre-high cliffs is a hidden basin where the vegetation – isolated and, not surprisingly, undisturbed – is of interest to environmental scientists. A number of creeks flow from the one narrow opening into the basin and in the caves and overhangs around the basin are Aboriginal paintings. There is no public access to this small 1210-hectare park.

TAMBO ■ 1752

This township on the Barcoo River has some of the earliest buildings in western Queensland. Timber houses in the main street dating back to the 1860s include McLeod's house, constructed on a bed of logs laid on the ground rather than on stumps. The 'new' post office has been operating since 1904 while the 'old' post office, built in 1876, is now a museum displaying the old manual telephone exchange and postal memorabilia.

Since 1865, the year after the formation of the Great Western Downs Jockey Club, races have been run at the racecourse at Tambo, on the other side of the Barcoo River from the town.

WINTON ■ 1753

The village of Pelican Water Hole was established in 1875 around a store and hotel owned by Robert Allen, who was the first postmaster when the town was gazetted in 1880. Local legend has it that Pelican Water Hole had too many letters to fit on the rubber stamp used for hand-franking the letters so Robert Allen changed the name to the shorter Winton, a suburb of the English seaside town of Bournemouth where he was born.

The town was a centre for the sheep stations to the north and east and the cattle stations to the south and west. With the arrival of the railway from Townsville in 1899 and from Rockhampton in the 1920s, Winton became a major trucking centre and its position as an important road and rail centre for western Queensland persisted with the building of two major highways through the town.

Winton is known for the very high temperature of its artesian water – 83° Centigrade in the town and 99° Centigrade at the nearby Castle Hill Station, but the uncommon hybrid name of the local pioneer museum – Qantilda – commemorates the two major aspects of Winton's history.

The first registered office of QANTAS opened in Winton in 1920 and the first board meeting of the new company was held that year in the Winton Club. Although the office was moved to Longreach (see entry) the next year, Winton's role at the birth of QANTAS is commemorated with a cairn in the main street, unveiled in 1965 by Sir Hudson Fysh, one of the two founding partners of the pioneering airline.

The first public reading of *Waltzing Matilda* took place at Winton's North Gregory Hotel in May 1895. The Jolly Swagman Statue in Winton and the town's Bronze Swagman Award for bush verse commemorate Winton's role in the launching of Australia's unofficial anthem. *Population 1160*

'CARISBROOK' One of a number of cattle stations offering accommodation and the 'outback experience' to city-dwellers, 'Carisbrook' was where Lyndon B. Johnson and his fellow airmen made a forced landing in their Flying Fortress in 1942. The LBJ Historic Mine (opals), and an Aboriginal bora ground contribute to the property's historic interest.

FESTIVALS Outback Festival, September of odd-numbered years.

QANTAS long ago outgrew its original hangar at Longreach where six biplanes were built between 1926 and 1930 for the airline's early services.

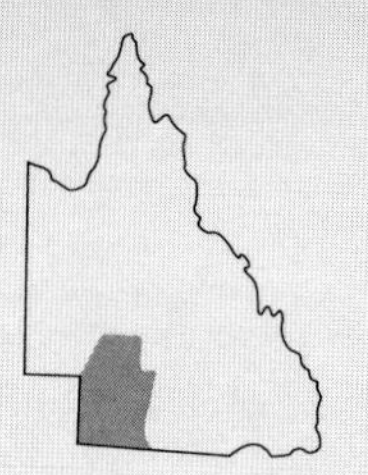

Quilpie & Thargomindah

The first Europeans to venture into this wide, brown land, where plains of pale Mitchell grass stretch into the far distance, were often driven to despair and even death. Fresh pastures, then the fiery opal, were enough to attract settlers and adventurers despite the fate of the early explorers.

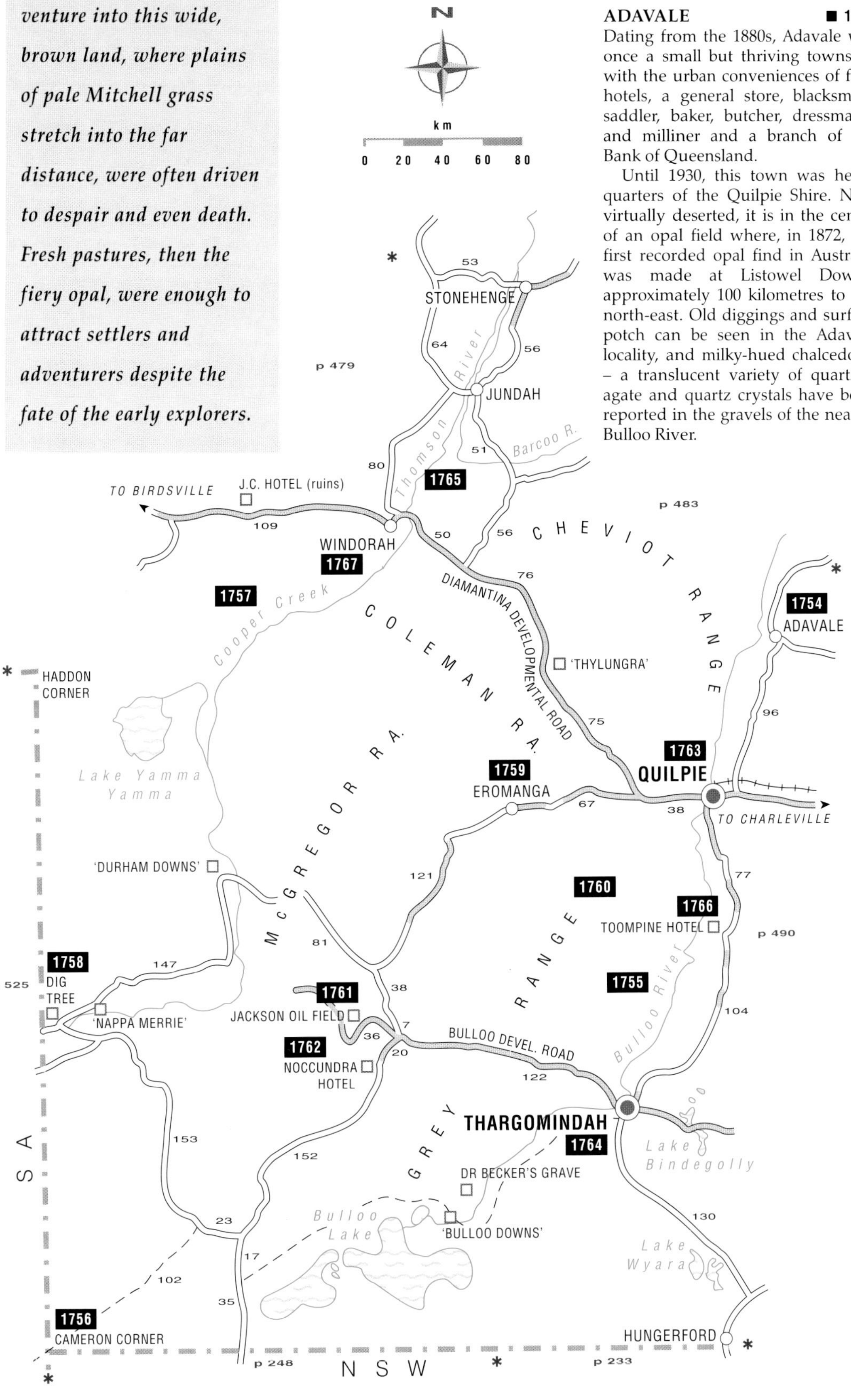

ADAVALE ■ **1754**
Dating from the 1880s, Adavale was once a small but thriving township with the urban conveniences of four hotels, a general store, blacksmith, saddler, baker, butcher, dressmaker and milliner and a branch of the Bank of Queensland.

Until 1930, this town was headquarters of the Quilpie Shire. Now virtually deserted, it is in the centre of an opal field where, in 1872, the first recorded opal find in Australia was made at Listowel Downs, approximately 100 kilometres to the north-east. Old diggings and surface potch can be seen in the Adavale locality, and milky-hued chalcedony – a translucent variety of quartz – agate and quartz crystals have been reported in the gravels of the nearby Bulloo River.

BULLOO RIVER ■ **1755**
The name of the Bulloo comes from an Aboriginal word for 'slow'. The often muddy waters of this river rise at the junction of the Grey and Gowan ranges and flow almost 500 kilometres in a westerly, then south-westerly direction into Lake Bulloo and a series of swamps. Along its course are the settlements of Adavale, Quilpie and Thargomindah.

'BULLOO DOWNS' There is an abundance of rich pastures covering the overflow plains along the river and in 1864 this run became the first to be taken up. It was later a link in the chain of stations owned by 'cattle king' Sir Sidney Kidman.

DR BECKER'S GRAVE On the western bank of the river is the grave of Ludwig Becker, a cultured German who was naturalist and artist with the Burke and Wills expedition. At fifty-two he was also the oldest member of the expedition, and succumbing to its rigours he died here of scurvy and dysentery in April 1861. A talented and sensitive artist, Becker depicted campsite activities and painted portraits of expedition members as well as meticulously recording the plants and animals he encountered. He was one of the first European artists to find beauty in the outback, and is regarded by some as the 'father' of Australia's desert painters.

CAMERON CORNER ■ **1756**
It is ironic that this wide, featureless brown land should also be a country of corners – Cameron, Peoppel and Haddon. They are the points where state lines meet. This one, pegged by surveyor John Cameron in 1880, is where the borders of New South Wales, South Australia and Queensland converge, and it is from here that the 'Corner Country' gets its name. Cameron's peg is long gone and the position is now marked by a white concrete post set deep into the ground in 1969. All around are red sandhills, broken only by the long line of the dingo fence.

COOPER CREEK ■ **1757**
With its strung-out headstreams, this irregularly flowing river is one of the longest watercourses in Australia. It is formed by the confluence of the Thomson (see entry) and Barcoo rivers, above Windorah, and flows 1300 kilometres south-west through the Strzelecki Desert, where its overflow supplies the sparkling Coongie Lake system, and then continues on towards the country's heart – the vast salt pan of Lake Eyre.

FENCING THE WORLD'S BIGGEST BACKYARDS

THE UNIMAGINABLY long mesh fences which stretch across some of the most forbidding tracts of outback Australia represent desperate attempts to control the movement of wild animals. The first fences were meant to stem the northward spread of the rabbit, and later barriers tried to prevent the southward ravages of the dingo.

The thousands of kilometres of mesh fencing which began going up in the late 1880s, eventually stretched from the Great Australian Bight in South Australia to the Darling Downs in south-eastern Queensland, some 5600 kilometres away. The longest fence in the world was more than twice the length of that other extraordinary barrier, the Great Wall of China. The fences required vigilant patrolling and constant work, and one by one they fell into disrepair as governments and owners of private properties fell into disagreement about who should pay for their maintenance.

Dingoes became the mainland's principal carnivorous animal after they arrived from Asia – perhaps as recently as 4000 years ago.

One of the earliest dingo fences was constructed in the north-west of Victoria in 1880. The New South Wales–South Australia fence started out as a rabbit fence, stubbornly erected in the late 1880s even though the animals already infested South Australia and New South Wales. Maintenance was lax and by 1910 long stretches had disappeared under drifting dunes. It was then agreed that part of the fence be converted into a 225-kilometre dingo fence running south from Cameron Corner in the direction of Broken Hill; it was impossible to reach agreement on ongoing repairs and in 1934 New South Wales assumed total control.

In the meantime, Queensland had been busy building its own fence, a mighty barrier that ran 1000 kilometres from Mungindi, in the south-east, westwards to Cameron Corner, and then up into the arid expanse of the Simpson Desert. As with the New South Wales–South Australia fence, rabbits were on both sides before building started and maintenance also soon became a problem, so the fence was handed over to a group of 'Corner' pastoralists who adapted it to protect sheep against dingoes from the Queensland cattle country – lambs were said to be easy prey for dingoes which are not fast enough to bring down kangaroos or emus. Their fence ran east from the 'corner' only as far as Hungerford – some 400 kilometres. Maintenance remained a problem and soon control of this stretch too was taken over by New South Wales.

But still the building continued. In the late 1950s, Queensland built the Dingo Barrier Fence, which at more than 5000 kilometres was the longest of the lot, indeed the longest single fence in the world. It ran from the New South Wales border up to the Cloncurry River at the base of the Gulf of Carpentaria and back. It was impossible to maintain. In the early 1980s, yet another fence was built in Queensland, this time a mere 2500 kilometres long, to enclose the very best of the western sheep country. It starts south of Thargomindah, runs north to Windorah, east to Adavale and then south-east to Jandowae. The Queensland government is responsible for its repair.

The wire-mesh dingo fences stand between one-and-a-half and two metres high and many things can happen to them. They may be damaged by kangaroos or emus and determined dingoes can tear their way through. They can be engulfed in one windy day by shifting red sands, or if the fence crosses an overflow, the posts and mesh can rust and rot away. The appropriate state governments employ a number of people to constantly patrol and repair the fences, and where first these fence menders used horses and camels, they now have four-wheel drive vehicles equipped with two-way radios. Ever-vigilant doggers on the New South Wales side set traps for rogue dingoes who manage to breach the defences of the great fence of Australia. □

Fence repairers – like this man fixing the Wompah Gate east of Cameron Corner in the 1920s – are a tough, independent breed.

Despite the success of eradication campaigns to the east and south of the dingo fence, there are still those who question whether the wild dog's depredations warrant the high maintenance costs of such a long barrier.

More often than not Cooper Creek's waters peter out long before reaching the lake basin, evaporated by the sun and soaked up by the sand. But if rainfall has been exceptionally heavy over more than one season the Cooper and other rivers of the extensive Channel Country drainage system may reach and on rare occasions even fill the usually dry Lake Eyre (see box, *Boulia & Birdsville*).

Sturt was the first of the inland bound explorers to meet the Cooper. In August 1845 he came upon 'a beautiful sheet of water' which he named Strzelecki Creek – an overflow of the Cooper. Three months later, after a frightful foray into the stony desert which now bears his name and in a last ditch effort to locate the phantom sea, he followed the Cooper upstream then struck north into 'heartless desert' where he was forced to finally admit defeat. The intense heat caused a thermometer to burst; two horses died and the exhausted party was lucky to regain the relative safety of the fast drying waterhole at Fort Grey several hundred kilometres to the south.

Not so fortunate were Burke and Wills. The Cooper featured largely in their tragic last days, and the Dig Tree (see entry), the site of Howitts Depot – a temporary camp set up in 1861 during the search for these explorers – and other memorials are on its banks. To a later explorer, Ernest Giles, the Cooper was a 'training ground', for here he prepared his party in the rigours of the outback before launching into his incredible inland expeditions of the 1870s.

The Cooper's channels can be 100 kilometres wide when in flood and until the construction of the Burke and Wills Bridge in 1992 – over the only feasible site at 'Nappa Merrie' – the crossing could be closed for up to ten months a year. This is the only bridge between Windorah and Lake Eyre, a distance of some 800 kilometres. The stream was named by Sturt after Charles Cooper, first judge of South Australia.

DIG TREE ■ 1758

One of the saddest stories in the history of Australian inland exploration was played out in the shade of this handsome coolabah on the western bank of Cooper Creek. This is the site of Depot LXV, established in November 1860, where Burke and Wills left a small group in the charge of German-born stockman William Brahe while Burke, Wills, King and Gray pushed further north to the Gulf of Carpentaria, 1200 kilometres away. They were successful in this quest, although mangrove swamps prevented them glimpsing the sea, but then began the desperate trek back to the Cooper Creek depot before their supplies – or the time limit before Brahe's group was to return to Menindee – ran out.

The little party faced the depths of despair when, ill, suffering from malnutrition and with one member, Gray, already dead, they reached the depot only to find that it had been abandoned just hours before. Burke recovered a cache of food left buried at the base of this tree on which Brahe had carved 'Dig', and replaced it with a letter telling of his decision to follow the Cooper south-west to the police outpost at Mount Hopeless. Tragically, not only did the party make the mistake of smoothing the ground so that it appeared undisturbed, they also failed to add a new blaze to the tree, so that when a worried Brahe returned a fortnight later he naturally assumed that his leaders had not returned.

Burke, Wills and King floundered westward down the Cooper, encountering great hardship and slowly starving to death in a land which provided its Aboriginal inhabitants with an abundant supply of food. It was only when King, who survived after being fed and sheltered by the Aborigines, was found by a rescue party two months later that the scale of the tragedy of errors associated with the 'Dig' tree was revealed.

EROMANGA ■ 1759

Eromanga has become a centre for oil exploration and the refinery here handles more than a million and a half barrels a year. It is also opal country. The Little Wonder mine, in the high ground some seventy kilometres to the north-west, is one of the first and most famous of Queensland's opal mines. It was here that the first parcel of Australian opals was bought for overseas sale. Gems of varying quality are still being recovered here by bulldozing the old mine workings.

The town claims to be the furthest from the sea in Australia and its name comes from an Aboriginal word meaning 'hot dusty plain'. The Royal Hotel was once a Cobb & Co. staging post.

GREY RANGE ■ 1760

This range of low hills runs for about 400 kilometres from south-western Queensland to the north-western corner of New South Wales where it peters out in the wilderness of Sturt National Park. It forms the divide between the waters of the Bulloo River, which end in the swamps of Bulloo Lake to the east of the range, and the streams which drain east towards the Barcoo and ultimately Lake Eyre.

Known as 'jump-up' country, the range landscape is a series of mesas – bare table-topped hills which rise abruptly some 150 metres above the plains. They are capped with an ancient soil layer which long ago hardened into the protective crust which now guards the softer strata below from erosion.

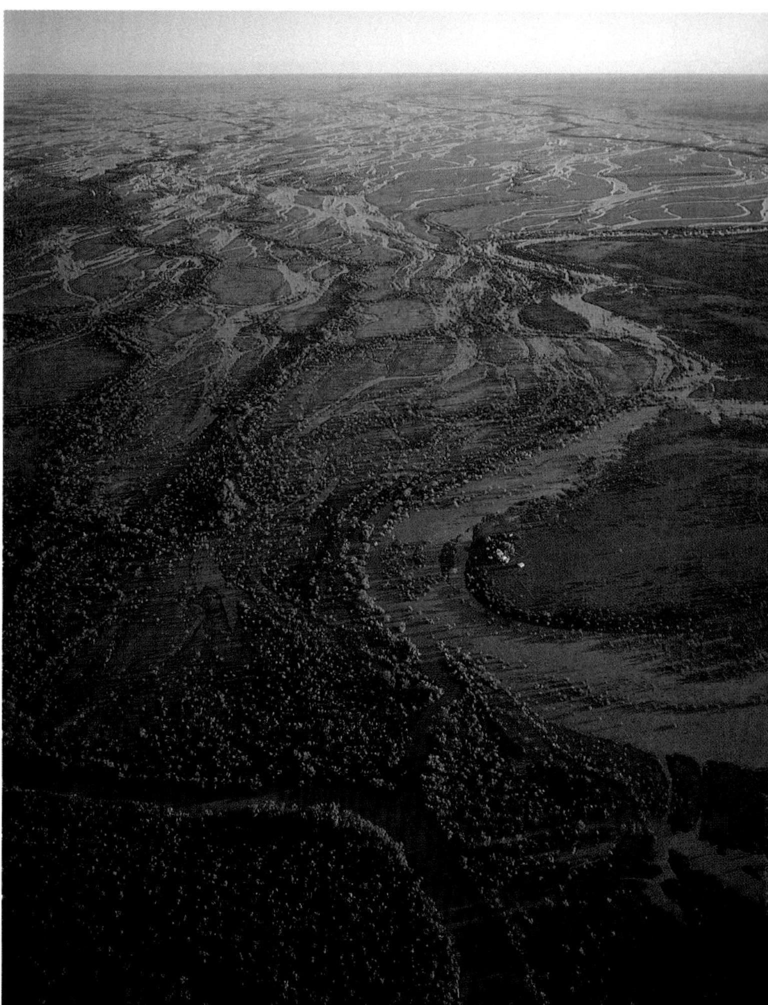

The flooded landscape that gives the Channel Country its name provides an instant if somewhat alarmingly close water view for a station homestead.

At its southern extremity, are Depot Glen, where explorer Sturt spent six weary months marooned near the only reliable water in the region, and Mount Poole, still topped with a stone cairn built by his men and named for his second-in-command, the unfortunate James Poole. Poole was buried with his face towards the interior near its base.

JACKSON OIL FIELD ■ 1761

The Jackson Oil Field, the largest land-based field in Australia, was discovered in 1981. Oil from here is pumped east through 800 kilometres of pipe to Moonie Downs, from where it goes to Brisbane through the Moonie-Brisbane pipeline.

NOCCUNDRA HOTEL ■ 1762

This single-storey stone hotel is one of the oldest buildings in south-west Queensland and is all that remains of a small isolated town established to cater for the workers at nearby Nockatunga Station. Three walls and a pile of stones to the west of the main building are the ruins of what was once the bar.

QUILPIE ■ 1763

Quilpie was established as a centre for the huge sheep and cattle properties of the region, but is better known for the boulder opal mined in the area. The local Catholic church even has panels of opal-bearing rock on the altar, font and lectern; special lighting brings out the rock's brilliant colours. There are opal dealers in town and opal workings can be seen on the outskirts.

The town's water comes from an artesian bore. Smelling strongly of sulphur it reaches the surface at a piping 75° Centigrade, eliminating the need for hot-water systems. The town's name, 'Quilpie' is an Aboriginal word thought to mean 'stone curlew'. *Population 620*

THARGOMINDAH ■ 1764

Thargomindah's goats are descendants of the herds which provided the town with milk in the days before the trucking in of pasteurised supplies. In 1908 they achieved the remarkable feat of eating into the town's Anglican church – it was a drought year and the building was made from thatched cane grass. The town's residents replaced the building with a considerably less tasty structure of wood and iron. In its heyday, in the 1890s, this dust-dry pastoral township had a brewery, three hotels and a soft-drink maker,

The Noccundra Hotel stands in splendid, unenvied isolation, a last oasis on the fringe of the fearful desert and the salt pans to the south and east.

and a decent fall of rain would bring the station men to town and set the champagne corks popping.

Modern Thargomindah showers and washes up with bore water, but it took two years and nearly 800 metres of digging before a good supply was struck in 1893, making Thargomindah the first place in Australia to have reticulated bore water. The same bore, which supplies the town today, was also the source of energy for Australia's first hydro-electric scheme when in 1893 the town was lit by means of a generator coupled to a water turbine driven by the bore's natural water pressure. This, the Sydney *Bulletin* told its readers, was one of the three great centres of electricity in the world – Paris, London and Thargomindah! The system remained in use until 1951.

THOMSON RIVER ■ 1765

The headstreams of the Thomson rise in the hills south of Hughenden and flow south to a point about 100 kilometres north of Longreach where they combine to form the river. The Thomson proper travels south-west through pastoral country to its junction with the Barcoo River north-east of Windorah, and their combined waters flow on as Cooper Creek (see entry). The system is characterised by braided streams – where numerous channels cut through the silt of the broad riverbed – caused by the infrequent flow of the rivers which range from practically nothing to sediment-laden floods that overflow their banks in the 'wet'.

TOOMPINE HOTEL ■ 1766

The historic Toompine Hotel in the Bulloo River district, is virtually all that remains of a once bustling settlement. It was constructed just before the turn of the century, was a Cobb & Co. changing station and remains a welcome watering hole in a parched and dusty land. This is an opal-mining area with Lushington and Copperella mines nearby where persistent fossickers may be lucky enough to find 'colour'.

WINDORAH ■ 1767

Many factors influence the siting of a town, but the reason claimed by some for the position of Windorah must surely be unique. It is said that a bullock waggon loaded with stores and rum became hopelessly bogged in Cooper Creek, so that anybody who wanted goods from the load had to come to the waggon to fetch it. The collection of shanties which sprang up at the scene became the township of Windorah. The Whitman brothers who feature in the town's early days are also associated with the establishment of Isisford (see *Longreach & Blackall*), to the north-east.

The pioneering pastoralists who settled this region were the Durack and Costello families. 'Thylungra', to the south-east, was the first of a number of Durack properties. It was taken up by Patrick Durack in the 1860s who, assisted by his brother Michael, overlanded cattle here from southern New South Wales. Patrick's granddaughter, Mary Durack, became well known as an historian, and playwright. The related Costello family settled to the north and west. They are remembered in the name of the old J.C. Hotel – now in ruins in the abandoned town of Canterbury, to the west of Windorah – which was named after John Costello.

Windorah was originally known as Stony Point. Its present name is an Aboriginal word thought to mean 'place of large fish'; a reference to the waterholes on nearby Cooper Creek.

The annual inundation from the Cooper Creek headwaters could quite suddenly transform this dune near Windorah into a riverbank.

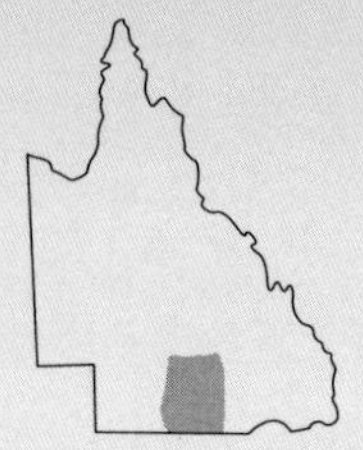

Charleville & Cunnamulla

In a region where the climate is rarely benevolent, the 'dry' can often turn into a drought but the people take a characteristically philosophical attitude to most events; they have also erected some unusual monuments to villainy as well as valour.

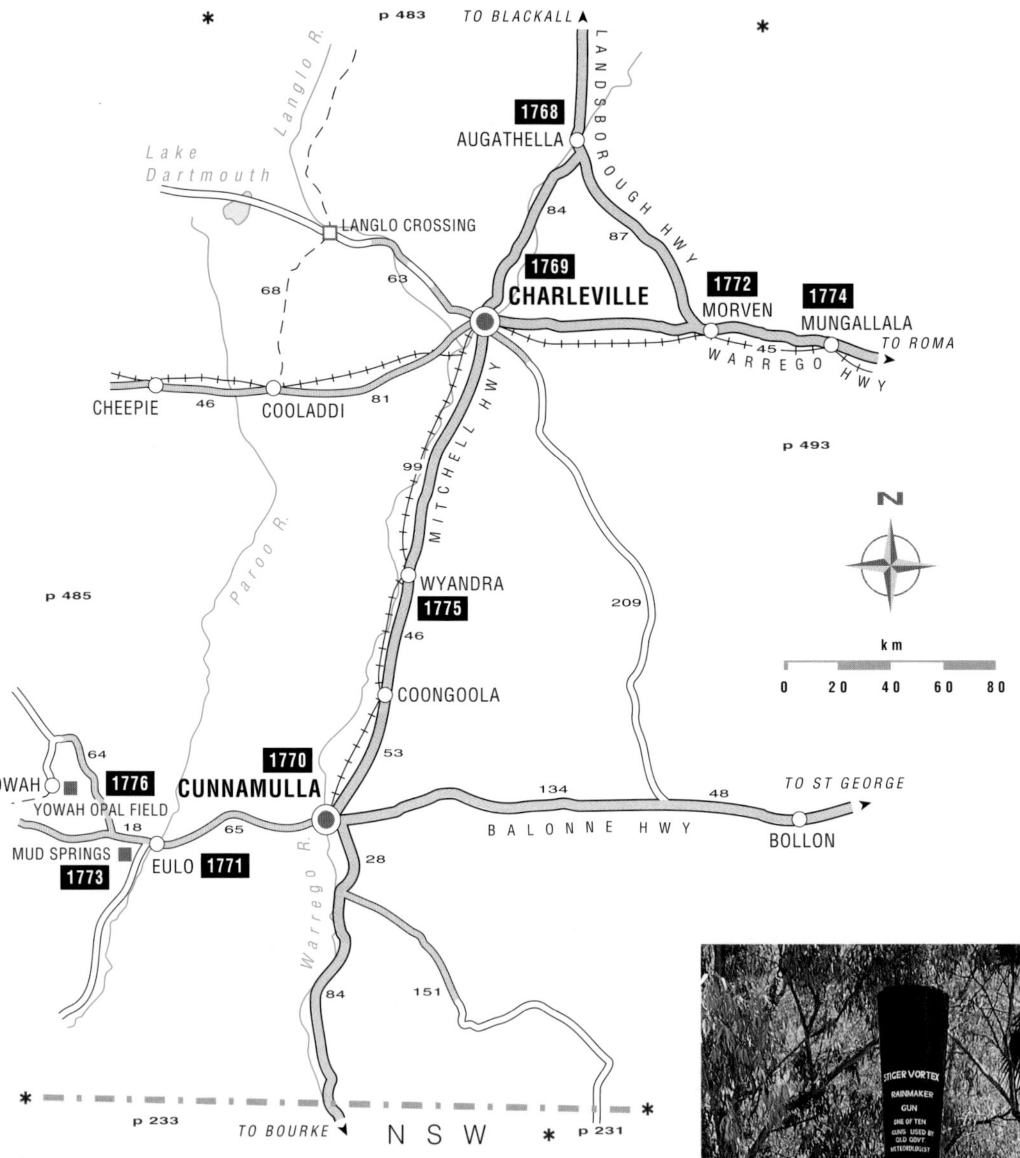

p 483 TO BLACKALL
LANDSBOROUGH HWY
1768 AUGATHELLA
Langlo R.
Lake Dartmouth
LANGLO CROSSING
84
87
1769 CHARLEVILLE
1772 MORVEN
1774 MUNGALLALA
TO ROMA
WARREGO HWY
45
68
63
CHEEPIE
46
COOLADDI
81
MITCHELL HWY
99
p 493
Paroo R.
p 485
WYANDRA
1775
46
COONGOOLA
209
km
0 20 40 60 80
64
YOWAH
1776
YOWAH OPAL FIELD
1770 CUNNAMULLA
53
134
48
TO ST GEORGE
BALONNE HWY
BOLLON
18
65
MUD SPRINGS
1773
EULO 1771
28
Warrego R.
84
151
p 233
TO BOURKE
NSW
p 231

AUGATHELLA ■ 1768

Augathella was known as Ellangowan when it was surveyed in 1880. It began as a bullock team camp on the banks of the Warrego River. Two tracks led to Burenda Station – one from Tambo and the other from Charleville. There was a time when the shearing sheds at 'Burenda', 'Nive Downs' and 'Oakwood' would keep itinerant shearers busy for most of the year. Now there is work at 'Oakwood' only but Augathella is still a centre for local graziers.

The Warrego River (see *Bourke & Hungerford*) flows placidly through the town except when in violent flood as in 1990. Warrego means 'river of sand' and Augathella's name is derived from an Aboriginal word said to mean 'waterhole'. There are several good ones nearby to excite the serious angler after Murray cod, catfish and golden perch.

CHARLEVILLE ■ 1769

Charleville is in the heart of Queensland's mulga country. It is a busy pastoral town built round a crossing over the Warrego River which was laid out in 1868 on the grid pattern that prevailed in town plans of that era. The Government Surveyor, William Alcock Tully, named it after his boyhood home in Ireland. There was great excitement when the first artesian water was tapped by bore in 1889. In the 1890s, before the railway came, 500 bullock waggons passed through each wool season. 'Weary Willie', a statue of the quintessential swagman, a survivor of outback hardships, stands in the main street; other streets are named for the explorers Burke, Wills, Eyre and Sturt.

In 1886, Cobb & Co. started an enterprise in Charleville, mainly for coach repairs. Then in 1893, the company consolidated their Charleville enterprise by moving their coachbuilding operations from Bathurst in New South Wales to 'Cobb & Co.'s Charleville Coach and Buggy Factory'. The coaches, which came to be known as the 'tall ships of Charleville', were especially designed for Australian conditions and did not reach their final form until after the advent of motor cars. Inevitably demand for such vehicles declined and the factory shut down in 1920 (see box, *Melton & Sunbury*).

In November 1922, QANTAS commenced its first regular flight service between Charleville and Cloncurry. Another aviation event is commemorated by a cairn outside the town. Here, Ross and Keith Smith were grounded with engine trouble in 1919 on the first UK–Australia flight made by Australians. The Royal Flying Doctor Service now bases its operations at the airport.

William Landsborough left his mark on a tree about fifteen kilometres downstream from the present township when he passed that way in 1862. There is another unusual monument alongside the highway, south of the town in the form of a Stiger Vortex gun, one of several which were part of an unsuccessful attempt to break the drought in 1902. The guns were supposed to make

The Stiger vortex gun, near Charleville, stands as a forlorn monument to a failed rain-making experiment.

Turned-up 'tiaras' on the guttering corners give an Oriental hint to the roof of this old Charleville bank – now a pioneer museum.

rain. They were tall cones, filled with gunpowder, which were fired into the air with no results at all.

The terrible dryness of 1902 has passed from living memory but not so the night of 20 April 1990, when continuous downpours were all too much for the region's rivers and Charleville was completely drowned. Bradley's Gully which runs through the town became a raging torrent. The roar and speed of the water is recalled with horror and there was widespread devastation. With characteristic outback resilience, people immediately began to repair the damage – prisoners from coastal jails helped in restoration – and Charleville has slowly recovered.

NATIONAL PARKS & WILDLIFE CENTRE A quiet conservation effort is being made by national parks officers in Charleville. A rabbit-sized marsupial, commonly referred to as the rabbit-eared bandicoot but properly called the bilby, once hopped over seventy per cent of the mainland. Now the bibly lives only in three small areas and is at constant risk from foxes, cats and land clearing. The Charleville Centre has set up a breeding program with funds from the World Wildlife Fund. *Population 3510.*

FESTIVALS Booga Woongaroo Festival, October.

CUNNAMULLA ■ 1770

The name Cunnamulla is said to be an Aboriginal word for 'long stretch of water' and in this case it refers to the tree-lined Warrego River on the banks of which Edmund Kennedy camped in 1847. Sir Thomas Mitchell had been there a year before him. By the 1880s, Cobb & Co. ran regular coaches through the growing town. In 1898, the Westlander narrow-gauge railway reached Cunnamulla – a distance of about 972 kilometres from Brisbane. In 1917, the Cobb & Co. Mail Service 45 left at six in the morning on Thursdays and Sundays, and after rattling across country, arrived at Thargomindah, 220 kilometres to the south, by five in the afternoon of the following day.

Sheep have always been important here and there are a lot of them – an estimated two million in good seasons when Cunnamulla becomes Queensland's biggest wool-loading rail centre. Beef cattle and angora goats are also raised in the district.

A tree at the southern end of Stockyard Street, enclosed by a fence, gives a local rogue a dubious immortality. It was here in 1880 that bank robber, Joseph Wells, holed up trying to escape the scene of his crime. He was so inept that he could not find his getaway horse! The tree's sparse branches were scant cover and the townspeople quickly spotted Wells, who was brought to justice.

Another tree takes pride of place in the civic centre – a yapunyah – the floral emblem of Paroo Shire. It was planted in the early 1970s by Princess Anne. Yapunyah trees bear heavy pollen and support a local honey industry. *Population 1680*

FESTIVALS Cunnamulla–Eulo Festival of Opals, late August.

EULO ■ 1771

Eulo, within working distance of the Yowah and Duck Creek opal fields, was once a vigorous mining centre. Isabel Robinson was known as 'Queen of Eulo' for many years spanning the turn of the century. She was born in England about 1851 and married Richard Robinson, a station manager at Surat, in 1871. They came to Eulo and ran several businesses including a hotel. Eulo was a three-hotel town and each hostelry had a dance every night of the week. It is said Mrs Robinson had a fine collection of opal jewellery, was a crack shot, a good horsewoman and an audacious gambler.

There's a unique racetrack at Eulo where the annual World Lizard Racing Championships are held. Nearby, a granite plinth and engraved bronze plaque commemorate the death of Destructo, a racing cockroach, who was accidentally trampled to death by an overexcited punter.

Palm Grove date farm, outside Eulo, was only the second commercial date farm to be set up in Australia – after two decades of research and preparation. The date palms cultivated here are descended from trees, believed to have come from Afghanistan, planted around the early church missions.

FESTIVALS World Lizard Racing Championships, August/September.

MORVEN ■ 1772

Morven, in Murweh Shire, is a small cluster of houses a few kilometres east of Charleville on the Warrego Highway with its own historical museum. In the early 1860s, this stop on the Cobb & Co. run was known as Saddler's Waterhole. The earliest official name was Victoria Downs Reserve which was later changed to Morven after a Scottish mountain. The settlement expanded temporarily when the railway was being built between Brisbane and Charleville and the railhead now serves a wide sweep of sheep and cattle country.

MUD SPRINGS ■ 1773

Beneath the surface of this dry land lies a huge body of water – the Great Artesian Basin. All through the area it releases near boiling water from bores that have been sunk to supply towns and properties. On the way to the Yowah opal fields, there are a series of springs by the roadside that were once the natural safety valves of the artesian basin. They belched hot mud into dome-shaped mounds. Few are still active but every now and then the pressure builds up to a mud-flinging high and the mudscape is arranged into new shapes.

MUNGALLALA ■ 1774

Mungallala began as a railway settlement and takes its name from the name of the creek that flows through the township. Mungallala is thought to be an Aboriginal word meaning 'emu' or 'food and water'. Either interpretation is possible, as emus are plentiful in the district and before the Europeans came, the land provided sustenance for the Aborigines.

WYANDRA ■ 1775

Like so many other dots on the map in this region, Wyandra, in Paroo Shire, also began as a camp for railway workers when the line was being driven through this outback territory. Despite its small size, this tiny settlement with a population of about fifty is served by a town hall, a hotel, a racecourse and an airport.

YOWAH OPAL FIELD ■ 1776

Queensland's opals lie in a belt of cretaceous sedimentary rock which stretches for about 900 kilometres in a north-westerly direction from the New South Wales border at Hungerford to Kynuna. They include the main fields near Eromanga, Kyabra, Yowah, Toompine, Quilpie and Winton. Experienced prospectors have been known to say, with straight-face, that these precious stones are found where the red-trunked minnaritchi trees grow.

Yowah township is home to about fifty miners. There have been people living here since opals were discovered but it is officially Paroo Shire's newest town – gazetted in 1984. This region is one of the hottest in the state with summer temperatures frequently reaching 42° Centigrade. The opal is found in boulders, sandstone, seams and pipes. Yowah is famous for a unique form of opal known as Yowah nuts which are the kernels of small ironstone nodules of rock.

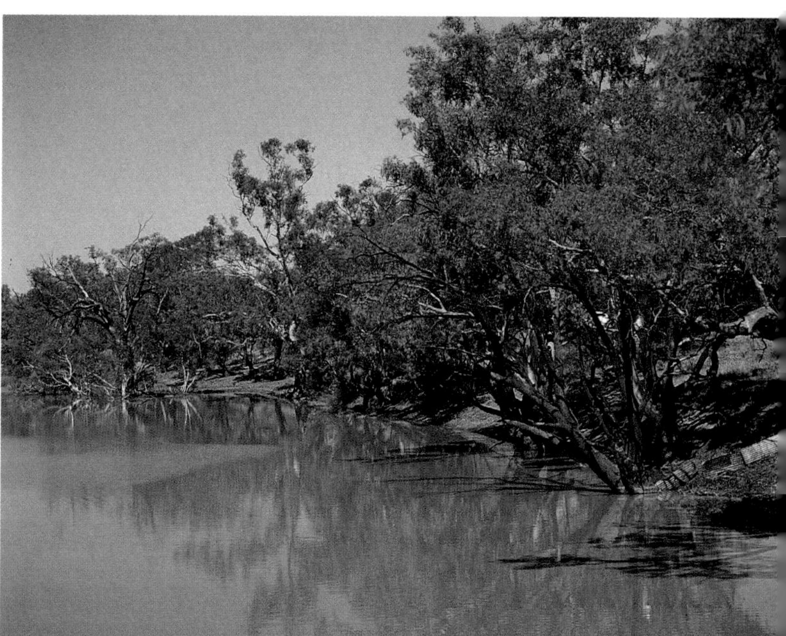

Despite its distance from the sea, Cunnamulla's position by a bend in the Warrego River means there is often fresh perch, cod or catfish for tea.

Roma & St George

This south-west corner of Queensland is a region of contrasts. Natural gas, hot artesian water and gemstones lie beneath the ground while to the north, the beautifully sculpted gorges and cliffs of Carnarvon National Park contain superb picture galleries of ancient Aboriginal rock art.

An artfully located tree fern on an outcrop in Carnarvon Creek completes the natural landscape as if by design.

BALONNE RIVER ■ 1777
The Balonne–Condamine River system has its headwaters about 1000 kilometres above St George and has a catchment area of around 70 000 square kilometres. The Balonne is fed primarily by the Condamine but is supplemented by at least eleven creeks and the Maranoa River. The annual rainfall over the catchment varies from 1270 millimetres on the Great Dividing Range to the east of Warwick to a low 490 millimetres around St George.

The river's name may be the result of one of the fairly frequent language misunderstandings between the pioneer explorers and the Aborigines. When Mitchell sighted the Balonne in 1846, he thought he was using the local name. However, it is possible that the man he questioned gave him the word for the tomahawk Mitchell was holding at the time. Even this story may be suspect, as 'balonne' is also said to mean 'pelican'.

Huge Murray cod have been taken from the river. Prime specimens of this fish of almost legendary status may grow nearly two metres long and weigh up to sixty-eight kilograms though such scaly superstars have not been seen for a while. A more usual catch is around a third that weight.

Behind the E.J.Beardmore Dam, the golden perch gives the man-made lake an extra attraction for anglers.

CARNARVON NATIONAL PARK ■ 1778
The Carnarvon National Park encloses about 251 000 hectares of land on the Consuelo Tableland which forms part of the Great Dividing Range. The dramatic Carnarvon Gorge, a twisting chasm more than thirty kilometres long, is relatively easy to reach. The vertical, white sandstone walls, fifty to four hundred metres apart, rise up to two hundred metres above the creek, which makes deep pools where platypus play. Cabbage palms, eucalypts, ancient macrozamia palms and she-oaks grow beside the water and mosses and ferns abound. Carnarvon Gorge was officially named in honour of Lord Carnarvon by Ludwig Leichhardt who traversed the area in 1844 and also called it 'Ruined Castle Valley'.

Carnarvon Gorge has some fifty Aboriginal sites which are thousands of years old. Most are decorated with engravings, paintings and especially stencils, and the biggest displays are in the shelters known as the Art Gallery and Cathedral Cave. There are spectacular geological features in the Mount Moffat region including Marlong Arch, Cathedral Rock and The Chimneys. The plentiful ochre deposits in Marlong Creek ensured that many of the rocks in this area were also decorated, notably the Kenniff cave, which is said to be the oldest site in the area, and 'The Tombs' where there is a complete stencilled human figure. Stencilled outlines include hands, feet, axes and boomerangs.

The park's other major features include Mount Salvator, Mount Ka Ka Mundi and the Moolyember Gorge. The township of Injune is the southern gateway to the park.

DIRRANBANDI ■ 1779
Dirranbandi is a small pastoral settlement and railhead on the Balonne River. The town reserve was proclaimed in August 1885 and a map a year later shows the priorities of nineteenth-century town planners. Housing came first with 100 allotments and then land was set aside for a police station – law and order; a state school – education; and a post office – communication. Dirranbandi is said to be an Aboriginal word for 'chorus of frogs in the swamp at night'.

E.J. BEARDMORE DAM ■ 1780
The E.J. Beardmore Dam and three weirs provide the water for the St George irrigation area (see entry). The dam was built between 1968 and 1972 and can store up to 101 000 megalitres of water on which crops and stock depend. The white gums along the banks attract a variety of birdlife and the dam waters are well stocked with yellowbelly. This delicious fish, more properly known as golden perch, is often called 'the barramundi of freshwater'.

LONESOME NATIONAL PARK ■ 1781
Lonesome National Park is appropriately named as it can be reached only by the Carnarvon Developmental Road. The park is a 3370-hectare sanctuary for many species of kangaroos and wallabies. A lookout on the rim of the ancient sandstone plateau gives panoramic views of the spectacular Arcadia and Dawson river valleys. The predominant vegetation is scrubland of bottlebrush, lancewood, brigalow, eucalypt, native bauhinia and wilga.

MITCHELL ■ 1782
Mitchell was named, of course, for the peripatetic explorer Major Thomas Mitchell, who came through the area in the 1840s. Mitchell Downs Station, taken up in 1854, is on its western fringes.

Mitchell is the birthplace of Francis Forde who became Prime Minister when John Curtin died on 6 July 1945, and was defeated by Ben Chifley in a caucus ballot on 12 July 1945. Thus, despite his significant political career, Frank Forde tends to be remembered for setting the unbroken record as Australia's shortest serving leader.

A monument in the vicinity of Arrest Creek commemorates the spot where Patrick and James Kenniff were finally apprehended by the police. They were said to be the last

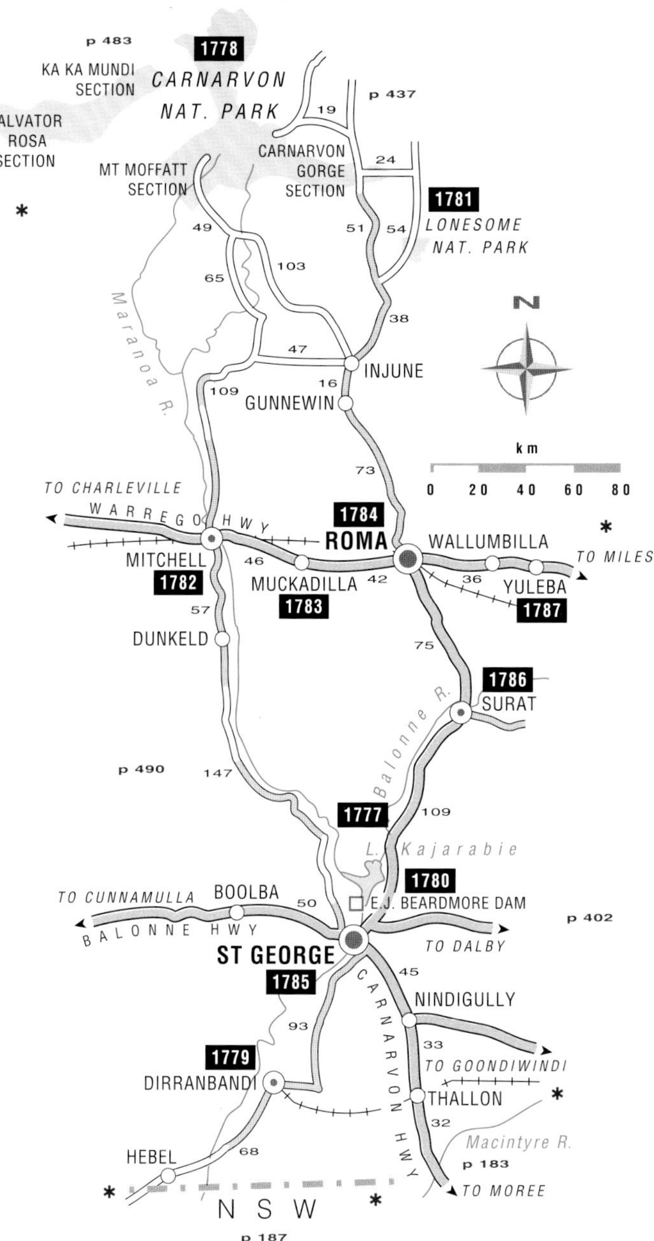

bushrangers, notorious horse and cattle thieves who killed a police constable and a station manager at Lethbridge Pocket in 1902, and had a cave hideout in the Mount Moffat area (see Carnarvon National Park). Patrick was subsequently hanged but James was released from prison in 1914 and worked as a station hand and miner until his death in 1940. *Population 1100*

MUCKADILLA ■ 1783

Muckadilla, on the Warrego Highway, is a village settlement in a district devoted mainly to wool production. It is noted for its hot springs which are fed from an artesian bore. The water, which has a distinct odour of hydrogen sulphide, is recommended to those with aches and pains for its healing properties.

ROMA ■ 1784

Roma was named after Lady Diamantina Roma Bowen, daughter of Count Roma, a Venetian nobleman. She was married to Queensland's first governor and Roma became the first gazetted settlement after the colony was separated from New South Wales in 1859. Roma is set on flat, featureless plains on the Bungil Creek which is prone to flooding but various proposals to move the town in its early days were rejected. Roma is the largest town in the Maranoa district and produces cattle, wool, sheep, grain, citrus fruit and timber. Vines were first planted in 1863, making 'Romavilla' the oldest winery in Queensland.

Arboreal avenues 'in memory' are not unusual in Australia and Roma's main street is lined with bottle trees, one for each of the local soldiers killed in the First World War. Ninety-three were planted and the first of these is known as the 'Tree of Knowledge' or the 'Tree of Wisdom' and is not to be confused with the ghost gum at Barcaldine (see *Longreach & Blackall*) where the striking shearers congregated in 1891.

Queensland's first petroleum was discovered as gas and condensate at Roma in 1900 but did not become commercially viable until the 1960s when a 450-kilometre gas pipeline was laid to Brisbane.

Roma is famous for an historic trial. On 11 February 1873, Harry Redford stood in the dock to answer charges of cattle duffing. Some years before, he had driven a large mob of stolen beasts through wild country from Bowen Downs Station in the Longreach area to Blanchewater in outback South Australia where he sold them for 5000 pounds sterling. A white bull had been recovered and was tethered outside the courtroom and inside one of Redford's accomplices spilled the whole story from the witness box.

It should have been an open and shut case, but such was the jury's admiration of Redford's droving feat that they acquitted him. The judge was furious, and the *Brisbane Courier* reported: 'They have a curious practice out in the far west of this Colony of "pulling" fellows for cattle stealing and taking them to Roma to be tried by a jury of their "peers"...who enjoy the fun amazingly and after going through a form of evidence and making a few bovine jokes... bring in a verdict of "Not Guilty"'. Harry Redford became something of a folk hero and an inspiration for Captain Starlight in Rolf Boldrewood's novel, *Robbery Under Arms*, published in 1888. *Population 5670*

ST GEORGE ■ 1785

St George, the administrative centre of Balonne Shire, lies at the junction of three major highways. Its annual rainfall is less than 500 millimetres and consequently this district, which produces a considerable proportion of Queensland's cotton, is heavily irrigated. Other crops include wheat, barley, maize, soybeans, sunflowers, grapes and citrus fruit and the traditional industries of wool growing and cattle grazing persist. The irrigation water is drawn from the large lake created by the E.J. Beardmore Dam (see entry).

The town site was named on St George's Day, 23 April 1846, when Thomas Mitchell forded the Balonne River. A cairn on the bank marks the spot. The early slab houses with their shingle and bark roofs were built from the cypress pines that grew thickly all around. *Population 2510*

SURAT ■ 1786

This neatly planned town was surveyed in 1850 by James Burrowes, who called it Surat after his former home in India. The main street bears Burrowes' name and his family is remembered in the names of the other streets.

The coach company Cobb & Co., which permeated so much of eastern Australia for so many years, ran its last service between Surat and Yuleba (see entry) on 14 August 1924. The Federal Government recognised this momentous event by purchasing the last coach for the sum of one hundred pounds sterling.

YULEBA ■ 1787

Yuleba, on the Warrego Highway, was a rail centre for St George and Surat until the line was extended in 1910. The town took the name of the old Yuleba Homestead and the meaning is thought to be 'the place of blue water lilies'. The area round Yuleba yields gemstones to dedicated fossickers – agate and petrified wood are most commonly found. There are several Aboriginal wells to the south of the township which were dug up to a metre deep in the rock hundreds of years ago. It is said they have never gone dry.

In the shadow of the Great Dividing Range, a dry climate and an altitude of 300 metres has encouraged distinctively regional wines around Roma.

SOUTH AUSTRALIA

South Australia has distinguished itself from its sister states ever since its founding in 1834 as the only Australian colony to be established without the aid of convict labour. It is the driest state in Australia with the bulk of its population pocketed in the fertile south-east corner where an agricultural cornucopia accounts for the major portion of the nation's wine production and where, in total contrast, the complex of steel mills and shipbuilding works at Whyalla forms one of Australia's biggest industrial plants.

SPECIAL FEATURES

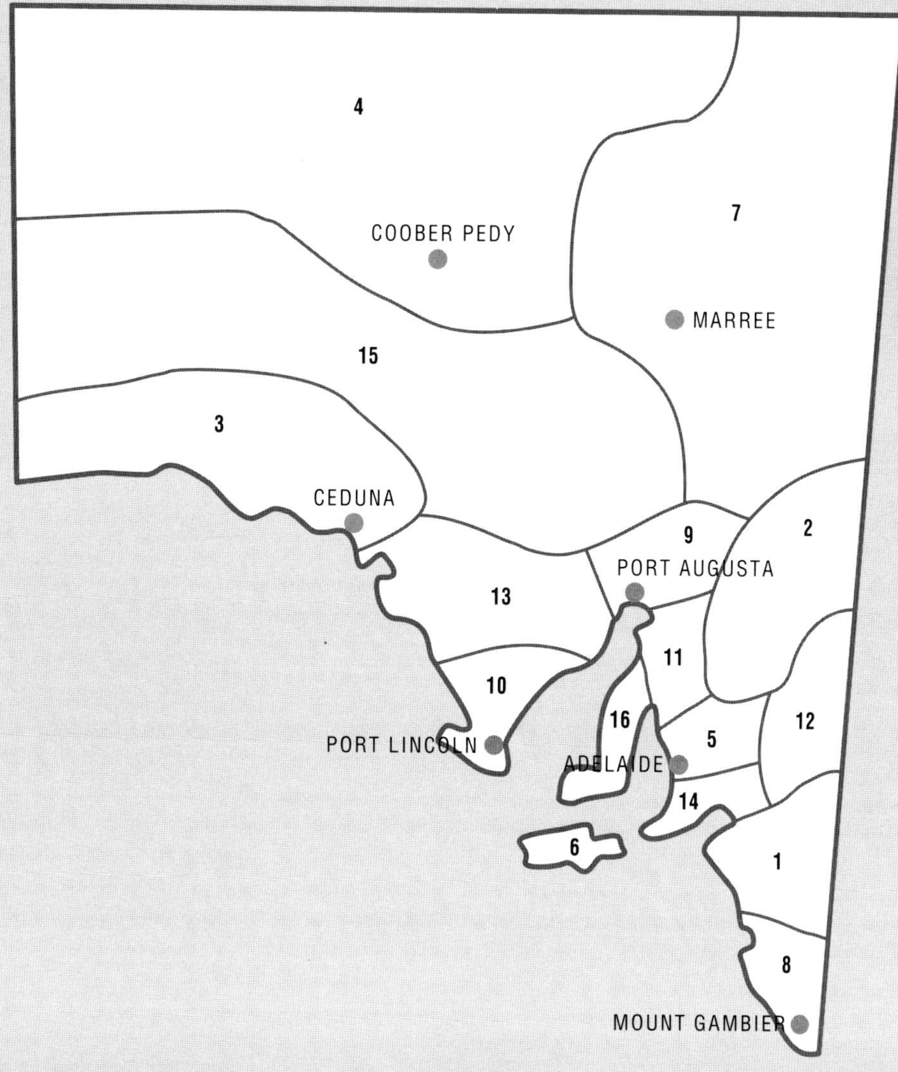

South Australia's floral emblem, Sturt's desert pea, is proudly displayed as the crowning glory of the coat of arms. Like Victoria's Leadbeater's possum, the southern hairy-nosed wombat is another endangered animal emblem.

ADELAIDE

Traffic-free Rundle Street mall provides an open-air stage for a modern generation of buskers.

South Australia's elegant, human-scale capital continues to stand as a monument to the vision and foresight of an imaginative founder whose grid system of streets and invigorating belts of parkland have remained inviolate in an age of freeways and urban sprawl.

As befits an orderly and civilised city which balances an international arts festival with world class sporting events, Adelaide has had its affairs steered by a formal city administration longer than any other capital.

Taking pride of place in the broad King William Street – a wider main thoroughfare than bisects any other Australian city – is the archetypically Victorian Town Hall, the headquarters of Australia's oldest municipal body. In 1836, only four years after the first governor, Hindmarsh, arrived in HMS *Buffalo* and Colonel William Light presented his grand city plan, the town fathers had formed a council to run Adelaide's affairs.

The city administrators could not afford their grand headquarters with its flamboyantly Victorian facade for another twenty-four years but it mattered not, for they had more important matters on their hands. In the financially strapped early days of the South Australian colony they established a gracious and civilised city using Light's master plan, a blueprint which, in the latter part of the twentieth century, would save their domain from the worst excesses of the motor-car age.

Sitting midway along the eastern shores of Gulf St Vincent, Adelaide is Australia's fifth largest city after Perth, with a population of just over one million and a metropolitan area that occupies an eighty-kilometre-long stretch of a fertile coastal plain from Gawler in the north to Willunga in the south. Five kilometres from the ocean and close enough to be cooled by a summer seabreeze stands the one-and-a-half square kilometre, grid-pattern city centre and another five kilometres beyond, the rounded foothills of the Mount Lofty Ranges rise up to provide the perfect city backdrop.

Residential development in the Adelaide hills has not been allowed to spread uncontrolled and the gentle slopes provide a wooded recreational retreat for Adelaide residents seeking

weekend relief from city and suburbia. The Mount Lofty Ranges have several good vantage points from which to view the city with perhaps the best of these at Windy Point near Belair. At night it offers breathtaking views of the city lights, stretching as far as the eye can see. Montefiore Hill, in the north, provides a close-up panorama of the city; this is 'Light's Vision' and the site for a dignified statue of Colonel William Light pointing towards a city that has matched his wildest expectations.

Adelaide enjoys all of the nightlife and other activities normally associated with a big city without the major traffic problems that so bedevil many of its contemporaries. At most times of the day, there is little difficulty driving into a city where freeways have been kept at bay and parking is rarely a problem. Much of the credit must go to Colonel Light. Light's plan for Adelaide was simplicity itself, a rectangular layout, set around five squares and bordered by the River Torrens. It is a design that dates back to Roman times but what made Adelaide unique among the many other grid-pattern towns of the nineteenth century was Light's sensitive adjustment of the street grids to match variations in terrain, his wide carriageways and the fact that he completely surrounded the town with the enviable breathing space of 850 hectares of parkland.

Settlement quickly followed Light's survey of the original town allotments in 1837 but the planner found himself under increasing attack from Governor Hindmarsh and others in the colony over the site. These attacks and Light's increasing debility from tuberculosis took their toll and he died a broken man in October 1839.

By 1840, the town at the centre of Australia's only colony to avoid the importation of British convicts was beginning to take shape, with brick buildings replacing tents and mud huts. The Corporation of the City of Adelaide found itself presiding over an 'instant' city bearing the name of Queen Adelaide by command of her husband, King William IV. Over the next decade about thirty small hamlets and villages, including Unley, Hindmarsh, Prospect, Thebarton, Burnside and Kensington, sprang up along the traffic routes or near water supplies, forming centres for further expansion and a basis for the suburbs of the twentieth century. Adelaide has continued to expand north and south across the plains and east into the hills and now covers an area of approximately 1924 square kilometres.

The city centre makes an impressive, symmetrical sight approached from the north along

'Light's Vision': on a hill above Adelaide a bronze Colonel Light looks out on his grand design.

More thought went into the siting of Adelaide than any other Australian capital and the modern city is a civilised, human-scale place where the ocean always beckons at the end of the Glenelg line (left).

After nightfall, the Elder Park precincts of the Festival Centre come alive with concert music.

The riverside rotunda and the steeples of the traditional 'city of churches' provide a contrast to the nearby modern Festival Centre.

the forty-two-metre-wide King William Street. St Peter's Cathedral, which boasts the finest and biggest bells in the Southern Hemisphere, announces the imminence of Adelaide Oval – one of the prettiest cricket grounds in the world and the scene of many a dramatic test-match encounter – and Elder Park, set on the banks of the River Torrens with its elegant 1882 rotunda as a decorative centrepiece.

Abutting Elder Park is the Festival Centre, a magnificent complex for the performing arts, which includes a multi-purpose concert hall, a lyric theatre and a drama theatre surrounded by a broad, open plaza. For three weeks in March every second year, the Festival Centre becomes the hub of Adelaide's world-renowned Festival of Arts, touted as the single most important cultural event in Australia.

The city's commercial centre begins where King Wiliam Street intersects with North Terrace, a sublime, tree-lined boulevard, boasting much of South Australia's architectural and cultural heritage. To the west along North Terrace is Parliament House. Completed in 1939, the building features imposing Corinthian columns fashioned in marble. Next door is the beautifully restored Old Parliament House. The parliament building was erected in 1855 as South Australia's original Legislative Council Chamber and now serves as a museum for the state's political history. It is flanked by the Adelaide Railway Station, a grandiose building that almost bankrupted the state when it was built in the railway heyday of the 1920s. Now the only bankruptcies are among the customers of the casino which has occupied the building since 1985.

North Terrace presents an impressive streetscape, lined with venerable edifices such as Government House, the National Soldier's War Memorial, the Mortlock Library and State Library of South Australia, the South Australia Museum – which boasts the world's largest collection of Aboriginal artefacts – the Art Gallery of South Australia and Adelaide University.

Rundle Mall, which runs parallel with North Terrace, is hallowed ground to Adelaide shoppers. Once a busy road, it has long been restricted to pedestrians and serves as a convenient and

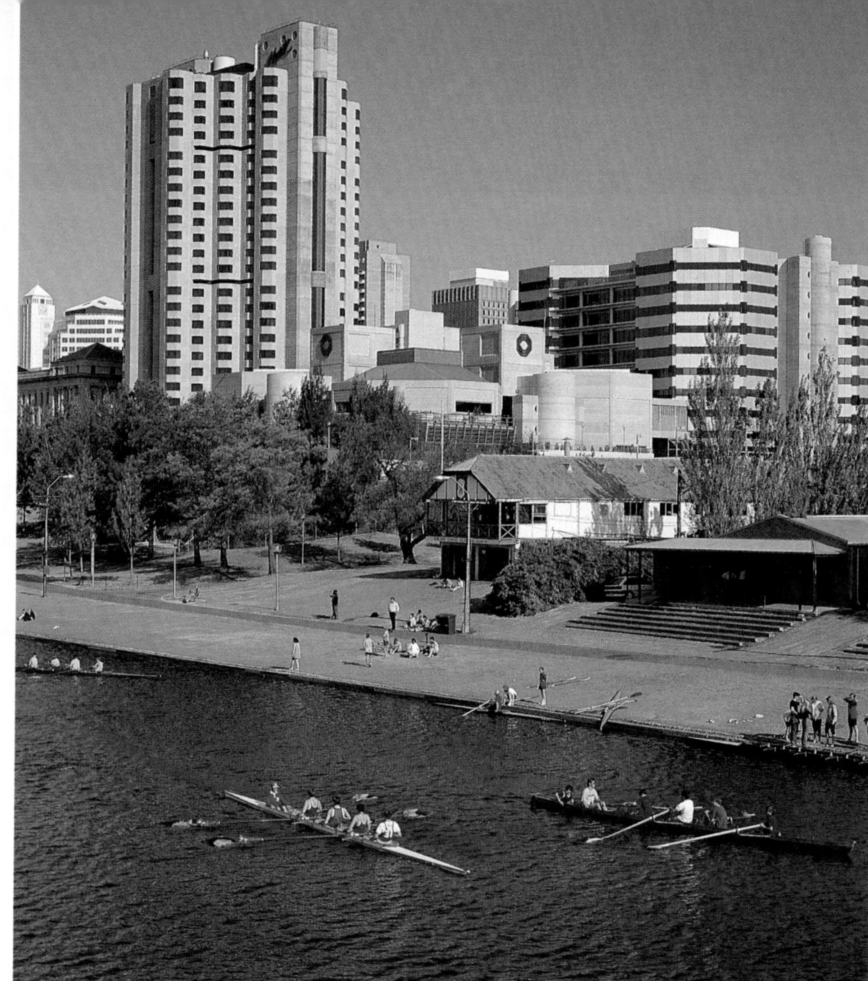

The River Torrens and its flanking green belts trim the northern edge of Adelaide's commercial sector.

attractive shopping precinct, with a number of large department stores and a network of arcades, filled with specialty shops and eateries. Hindley Street, which joins up with Rundle Mall at King William Street is a mecca for late-night revellers that buzzes with activity into the early hours of the morning and boasts nightclubs, hotels, discos, restaurants and coffee lounges.

In the very centre of the city, the invigorating open space of Victoria Square – which features Adelaide's most impressive fountain – is surrounded by government offices, with the law courts and police building on its southern side, and the General Post Office on its northern side, while just across the road from the GPO is the Adelaide Town Hall on the broad avenue of King William Street.

Thanks to the foresight of Colonel Light, the city has parks and gardens aplenty, including a traditional Japanese garden – the Adelaide Himeji Gardens in the south parklands – and the historic Adelaide Botanic Garden. Founded in 1855, the garden boasts a spectacular new addition in its Bicentennial Conservatory, the largest greenhouse in the Southern Hemisphere. The greenhouse contains a rainforest of 3000 to 4000 plants from Australasia and south-east Asia. Numerous other patches of green punctuate the outskirts of the inner city, including the Belair Recreation Park, the Cleland Wildlife Park, Mount Lofty Botanic Gardens and Warrawong Sanctuary, near Mylor.

For those with an eye to the past and an appetite for history, Adelaide offers a smorgasbord of museums and historic sites. In the city centre, there is the South Australian Police Museum, housed within the carefully restored, 1851 mounted police barracks, a Migration and Settlement Museum, the Adelaide University Museum of Classical Archaeology, the Tandaya Aboriginal Cultural Institute and a Telecommunications Museum. The old Adelaide Gaol with its grim Hanging Tower was once the scene of gruesome executions.

Port Adelaide, ten kilometres from Adelaide's city centre, is home to a number of other museums including the magnificent South Australian Maritime Museum - which displays a range of imaginative working exhibits – the Port Dock Station Railway Museum and the South Australian Historical Aviation Museum. At nearby Semaphore, Fort Glanville, built in 1878 to combat a feared Russian invasion, recreates colonial military life of last century, right down to the firing of one of the fort's massive guns. The National Motor Museum at Birdwood Mill, east of Adelaide, houses Australia's largest and most comprehensive collection of historic vintage, veteran and classic motor vehicles and motorcycles.

With the Barossa Valley and its cornucopia of produce only a short distance away, it is hardly surprising that good food and wine play an important part in the life of Adelaide. Tourist authorities have estimated that the city has more restaurants per head of population than any other Australian city. One of the best known restaurants is notable not only for its cuisine but for its novel location, being located in an accurate re-creation of the sailing ship, HMS *Buffalo*. The 'ship' is berthed on the Patawalonga Wharf at Glenelg, close to the very place where Governor Hindmarsh came ashore from the original HMS *Buffalo* in 1836 to found a new colony. □

Adelaide was the first city to host the Australian Grand Prix and each spring for 11 years its streets echoed to the roar of Formula One.

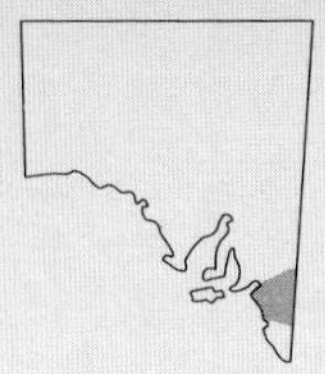

Bordertown & Keith

Despite the consolidation of European settlement after the coming of the railway, this is still a wilderness region characterised by the sand dunes and salty waters of the Coorong Coastlands and other tracts set aside for conservation.

BORDERTOWN ■ 1788
One might expect this town to be on the South Australia–Victoria border, but in fact it is almost twenty kilometres to the west, tucked firmly inside South Australia. The name, which first appeared as Border Town, was more appropriate in earlier times before disputes about the actual state boundaries were settled. Bordertown is in the Tatiara district – an Aboriginal word for 'good country'.

When the Victorian gold diggings opened in 1852, the gold escorts, led by Alexander Tolmer – South Australia's fourth police commissioner – came this way from Castlemaine and Bendigo to Adelaide. The town grew up on the banks of the Tatiara Creek where the men used to camp. Local legend has it that Tolmer expected the settlement to be named for him. He failed to achieve that immortality and Bordertown never became the main town of the south-east as some had predicted it would. There are, however, bronze plaques attached to granite boulders at various places along the escort's route, set up to remind contemporary travellers of those days gone by.

Bordertown lays claim to a more recent event that played a part in shaping Australia's history. On 9 December 1929, Robert James Lee Hawke, the Prime Minister of Australia between 1983 and 1991, was born here. He is honoured by a bronze sculpture outside the council chambers. His childhood home is now the Tatiara Employment Support service. *Population 2250*

FESTIVALS Clayton Farm Field Day, Ocotber.

COONALPYN ■ 1789
Coonalpyn is bisected by the Dukes Highway at the northern end of the Coonalpyn Downs. Museum records dourly attribute Coonalpyn's appellation to the Aboriginal word 'konangalpun' which is thought to mean 'place of mice excreta' and presumably refers to the periodic mice plagues which occur here.

The town is well placed for visits to the Mount Boothby and Carcuma conservation parks where native animals can be seen in their natural environment. Evidence of the old days is all around this area and at Tauragat Well, horse troughs recall the coaches that once clattered along the unsealed road.

COORONG NATIONAL PARK ■ 1790
The hauntingly beautiful Coorong Coast with its shifting dunes, shallow lakes and marshland, is secure within a national park encompassing almost 40 000 hectares, which was declared in 1966 (see box).

KEITH ■ 1791
Keith was originally known as Mount Monster and both the railway siding and the post office opened under that name. Later they both took the name of Sir Lancelot Stirling's eldest son. The segment of modern highway that forms Keith's main street has been renamed Heritage Street to focus attention on its historic buildings. The former Congregational Church, built of local stone in 1910, is now owned by the National Trust and the town also has a memorial to the men who conducted the gold escort service in the 1850s (see Bordertown).

Keith is roughly in the centre of what was once called the Ninety Mile Desert, now known as Coonalpyn Downs. In 1949, the Australian Mutual Provident Society financed a twenty-one-year project to turn sand dunes and mallee scrub into farming land, after the CSIRO had discovered ways of correcting soil deficiencies by applying traces of cobalt, copper, molybdenum and zinc. At the end of the 1960s, 280 000 hectares were being used to graze sheep and cattle and to grow wheat. An extensive area of infertile country had been transformed. *Population 1180*

TAILEM BEND–KEITH PIPELINE In this flat region there are no suitable sites for above-ground water storage reservoirs. Water is supplied by two main methods. The upper part of the south-east is supplied by the Tailem Bend–Keith pipeline and the more southerly area by aquifers which tap the artesian or sub-artesian groundwater. The pipeline, which serves thirteen townships including Coonalpyn, Tintinara and Meningie (see entries), began operating in 1973. Before that people had to rely on rainwater tanks, wells or bores for their water supply.

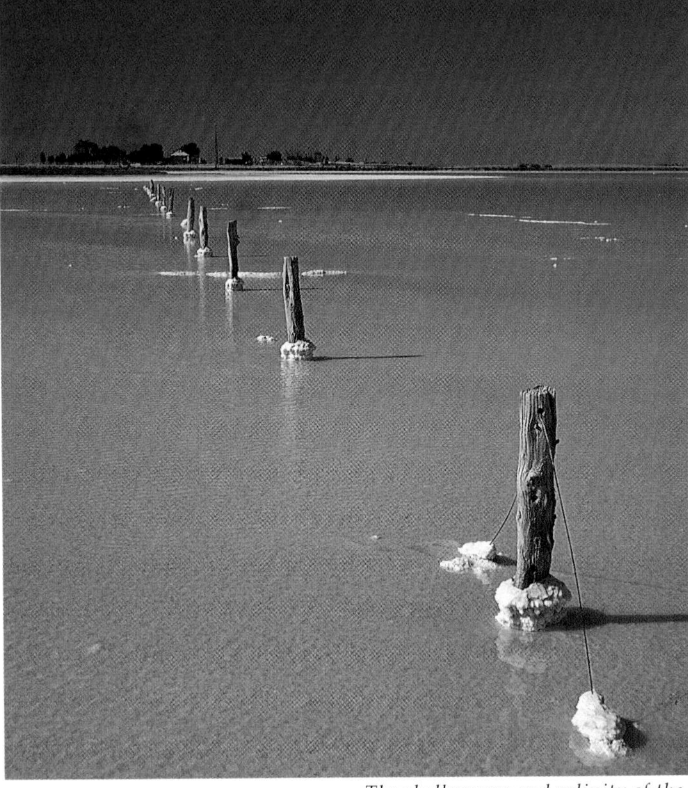

The shallowness and salinity of the lake north of Meningie can be gauged by the width of the salt collars around the neglected fence posts. To the south, the Coorong's vegetation (below) arranges itself to accommodate the prevailing wind coming off the Southern Ocean.

LAMEROO ■ 1792
Curiously, European settlers named Lameroo after a beach near Darwin but the Aborigines called the place 'wauwauwe' which means 'many kangaroos'. As with Pinnaroo (see entry), intensive settlement began after the railway arrived from Tailem Bend in 1906. The restored pug and pine hut which the Byrne family built in 1898 is three kilometres from the town on the old Yapara Road.

This quiet rural centre is a popular stopping place on the Ouyen Highway. The Pinnaroo–Lameroo area has plentiful sub-artesian water supplies which make the growth of feed and seed crops and vegetables possible and waters Lameroo's pleasant golf course. *Population 580*

MENINGIE ■ 1793
Meningie, called 'the gateway to the Coorong', is supposed to get its name from an Aboriginal word for

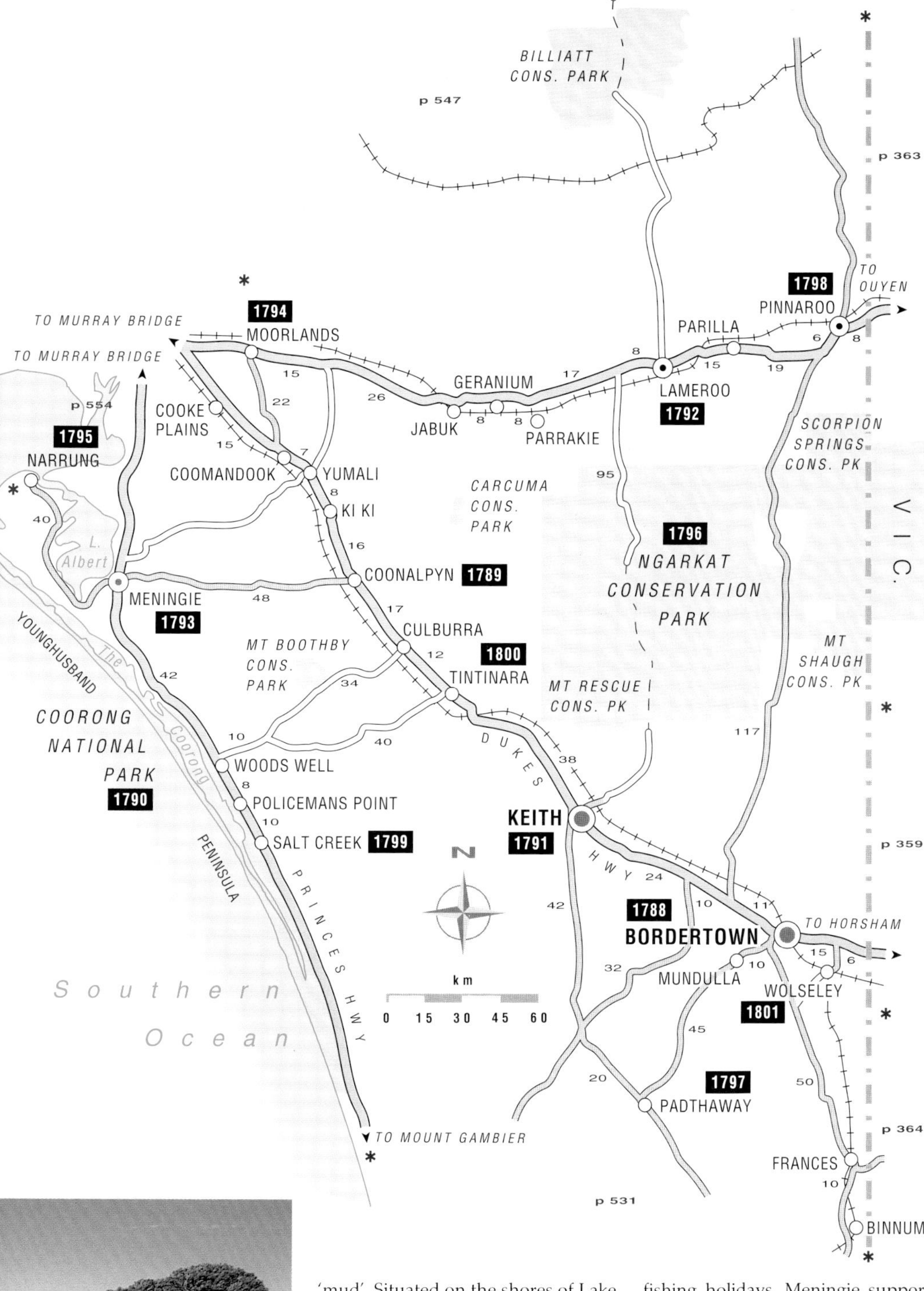

'mud'. Situated on the shores of Lake Albert, the site was probably very muddy in the early days of European settlement. Meningie was a port for travellers taking the lake route between Adelaide and Mount Gambier before going on to Melbourne and thus shortening the long overland trip.

Nearby Trig Hill breaks the unrelieved monotony of a remarkably flat landscape. In the pioneering years, trees between Meningie and Tailem Bend provided timber for the building industry, then fuel for the paddle steamers and after that firewood for the ever-voracious steam trains.

Lake Albert is a large body of fresh water which is home to a variety of waterbirds including pelicans, ibises, cormorants, ducks and swans. It is a popular location for watersports and fishing holidays. Meningie supports a commercial fishing fleet of some forty or so boats.

Many permanent residents are involved with the dairy industry and have invested in modern irrigation equipment. The rewards can make the hard work worthwhile – in the 1983–84 season fifteen dryland farmers in the Meningie district produced 310 569 kilograms of butter fat with a farm-gate price of five dollars per kilogram. *Population 820*

MOORLANDS ■ 1794

Moorlands is a small settlement along the Ouyen Highway which was named after Moorlands, near London. The district was first settled by John Whyte who formed the highly successful Whyte, Counsell and Co. which ran an Adelaide grocery business and a fleet of steamers on the River Murray – once it crosses the state border the great waterway becomes the 'River Murray' not the 'Murray River'.

Deposits of low-grade brown coal were found north of the town. This was mined between 1910 and 1925 and again shortly before the Second World War.

NARRUNG ■ 1795

Narrung lies between Lake Alexandrina and Lake Albert and the ferry service linking them is part of the South Australian highways system. The lighthouse at Point Malcolm, built in 1878 to mark the passage between the lakes, is the smallest inland lighthouse in Australia.

The town's name is a corruption of 'ngararung' said to mean 'place of the large she-oaks'. The Aborigines used the wood from these trees to make boomerangs and other weapons which were traded for stone axes and spears made from mallee wood. The Narrung district contributes to farming and dairying and is also noted for horse breeding.

NGARKAT CONSERVATION PARK ■ 1796

Ngarkat Conservation Park is a significant wilderness area which links the Scorpion Springs and Mount Shaugh conservation parks with Victoria's Big Desert region. The pygmy possum, which still thrives in Tasmania and on Kangaroo Island, is found in these parks but nowhere else on the mainland. The area is also a significant breeding ground for the rare mallee fowl (see box, *Ouyen*).

PADTHAWAY ■ 1797

This small settlement forms a centre for the Padthaway wineries. Here viticulturists' skills, the terra rossa soils and the region's climate have combined to produce some fine vintages. The old 'Padthaway' sheep station was leased by Robert Lawson in 1847. The name of the town is derived from an Aboriginal word meaning 'good water'.

PINNAROO ■ 1798

Pinnaroo is frequently described as a 'sleepy little township', perhaps as a result of its Aboriginal name, which is said to mean 'sleeping place' or 'place of the old men'. Though settlers first established themselves here in the 1860s, poor drainage inhibited agricultural development.

Pinnaroo struggled in the recession years of the 1890s and the community did not really get going until the railway pushed through from Tailem Bend in 1906 and the region, like so much of the Mallee country, began to attract farmers. Pinnaroo is part of the WOB – wheat, oats and barley – belt that stretches from western Victoria into South Australia, although agriculture

THE MAGIC OF THE COORONG, WHERE PELICANS RULE THE SKY

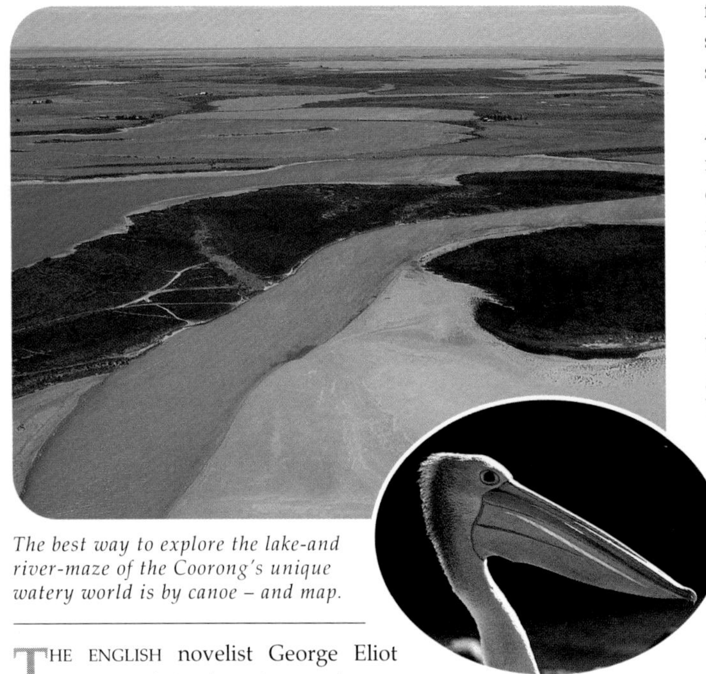

The best way to explore the lake-and river-maze of the Coorong's unique watery world is by canoe – and map.

THE ENGLISH novelist George Eliot suggested in the nineteenth century that 'there should always be some unknown regions preserved as hunting grounds for the poetic imagination'. Similar sentiments must have motivated the South Australian authorities who began to protect the magical Coorong coastline in 1966 – since then the Coorong National Park has grown to cover almost 400 000 hectares of water, dunes and marshland, while the 6840-hectare game reserve allows hunting for more than the 'poetic imagination' in the duck-shooting season.

In the way of so many rivers when they reach sea level, the mighty Murray dribbles into lakes Alexandrina and Albert and the shallow Coorong waterways. The two lakes are classified as freshwater but the lagoons of the Coorong region become progressively narrow, more silted and salty, until the marshy ponds at its southern end have three times the salt content of the sea.

Coorong – the name is like a sea bird's call – comes from the Aboriginal word 'kurangh' which means 'long neck of water'. This neck, which on average is only about two kilometres wide, stretches for more than one-hundred-and-thirty kilometres, and shelters from the relentless pounding of the Southern Ocean behind the high sand dunes of Younghusband Peninsula.

Middens of food scraps on this narrow spit record the lives of the people who lived in the Coorong for many thousands of years before Europeans intruded. An Aboriginal legend explains how a giant cod swam down the Murray Valley and carved out the river. When it reached the mouth, it was mortally speared and in its death throes made the lakes and lagoons. The later inhabitants were known as talented singers and good sportsmen – in 1885 an Aboriginal football team from the Coorong drew a crowd of 3000 in Adelaide.

There was always a plentiful supply of food to sustain a semi-permanent lifestyle. Younger Aborigines were forbidden to catch thirteen types of game that lived around their camps so that the older people could hunt more easily. There is still bream, salmon trout and Coorong mullet aplenty and flounder can be speared on calm, bright nights. More pelicans congregate in the Coorong than anywhere else in Australia. There are six islands in the protected area where the pelicans and other birds breed. Crested and fairy terns, albatrosses, cormorants, gulls and grebes are among at least 160 resident and visiting species.

The writer Colin Thiele made Australians aware of the Coorong with his acclaimed children's novel, *Storm Boy*. Made into a film, it told of a young boy who befriended an injured pelican he called 'Mr Percival'. □

The just-inland sea of the Coorong is home base for thousands of pelicans.

has lately diversified to sheep pellet production and market-gardening.

The D.A. Wurfel Cereal Collection at the Pinnaroo Institute houses a collection of more than 1000 varieties of grain and covers most of the grain crops currently grown in the world.

Pinnaroo is a short distance from various conservation parks. Billiatt is a 36 815-hectare mallee and broombush nesting ground for all sorts of birds including the western whipbird. Scorpion Springs and Mount Shaugh are the habitat for many birds and animals and a variety of native plants. *Population 640*

SALT CREEK ■ 1799

Salt Creek is little more than a handful of houses and two petrol stations clinging to the edge of the Princes Highway. In the early days of settlement, a mail coach ran between the town and Encounter Bay and all the tiny places along this stretch of bitumen had more importance.

CHINAMAN'S WELL Chinaman's Well, about twenty kilometres south of Salt Creek, is no longer on the road at all since upgrading has bypassed it. During the gold-rush days, Chinese migrants disembarked illegally along the stretch of coast between Encounter Bay and Robe. They then walked to the gold diggings in Victoria and New South Wales carrying their possessions in two large baskets slung across their shoulders. They set up circular wells along the track, hence the name Chinaman's Well.

TINTINARA ■ 1800

Tintinara is a small settlement surrounded by productive farming and grazing land which was once dominated by mallee scrub. This was cleared with the help of powerful machinery known as 'scrub rippers'. The town gets its name from an Aboriginal word, the meaning of which is a matter of debate. Some say it means 'boy' or 'youth', others link the name to 'tinlinyara', an Aboriginal name for the stars in Orion's belt.

The Tintinara Post Office dates back to the 1860s and the Tintinara Homestead was built about the same time. The grave of William Harding, one of the early settlers, can still be seen under a very old gum tree near the shearing shed. Tintinara Homestead was a watering stop for the gold escort. The local Tolmer Rocks might not have appeased Alexander Tolmer for failing to have a town named after him but at least they ensure his deeds are not forgotten in the district (see Bordertown).

Tintinara is well placed for access to the Mount Rescue Conservation Park where the sand plains shelter native plants and animals. There are also ancient Aboriginal campsites and burial grounds in the district.

WOLSELEY ■ 1801

First known as Tatiara, Wolseley was later named after Sir Garnet Joseph Wolseley, who was revered as a hero because he had won a great victory in Britain's Egyptian wars in 1882. Some time after this, he became Commander-in-Chief of the British Army. His younger brother, Frederick York Wolseley, went to New South Wales in 1854 and later patented a successful shearing machine which revolutionised the wool industry.

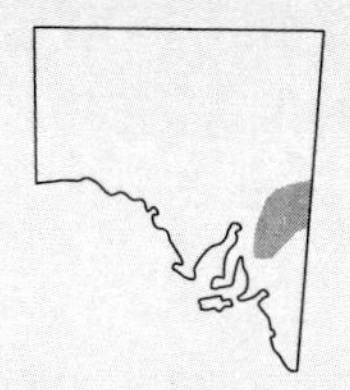

Peterborough & Burra

The ghost towns and crumbling farm buildings which litter the landscape of South Australia's mid-north testify to the fate of the brave and the foolhardy who attempted to farm this 'buffer' zone between the south-east and the arid northern lands.

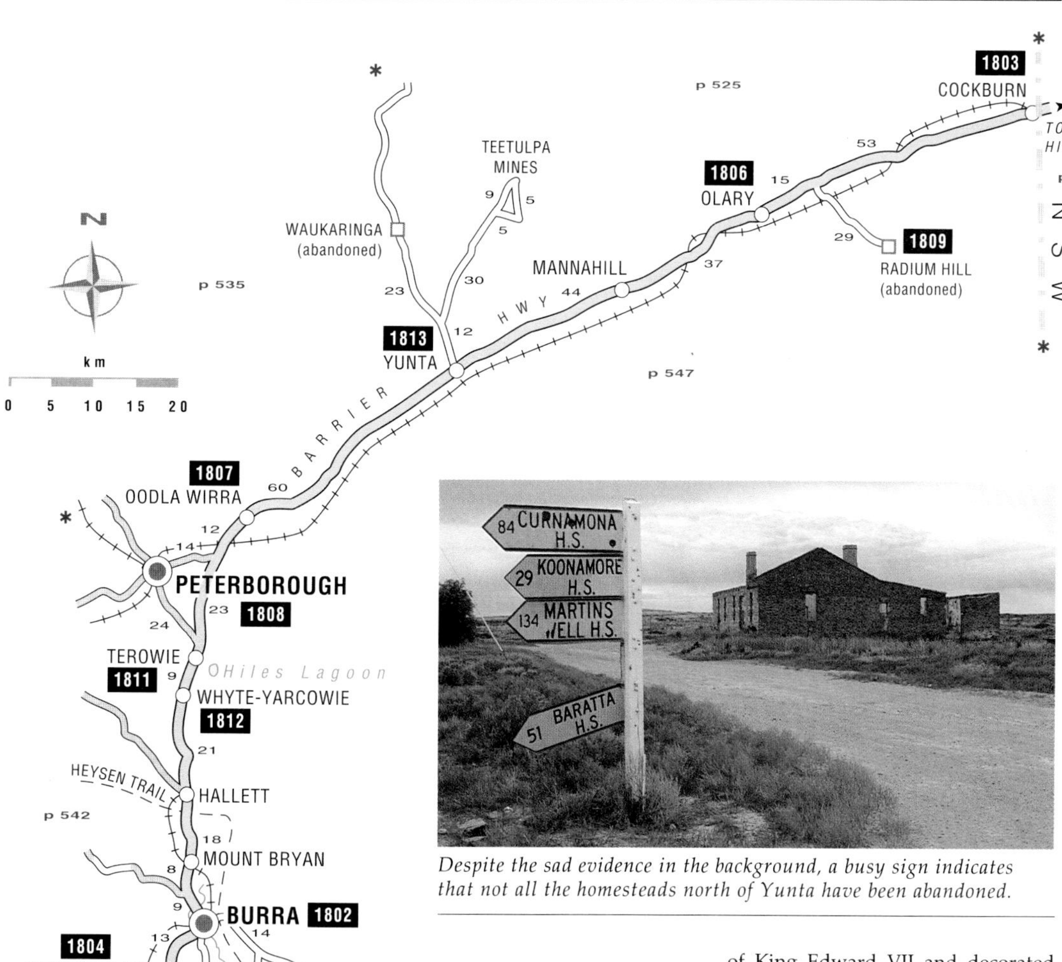

Despite the sad evidence in the background, a busy sign indicates that not all the homesteads north of Yunta have been abandoned.

BURRA ■ 1802

Burra nestles in the rolling hills 160 kilometres north of Adelaide, close to the creek which gave it its name and its reason for existence. The rich lode of copper which was discovered in the banks of the Burra Burra Creek in 1845 provided not only a much-needed financial stimulus for the infant colony of South Australia but also thirty years of regular employment for the thousands of Cornish miners and Welsh and German smelters who flocked to the region. In fact, this was the first of the mineral 'rushes', predating the gold fever of the east coast by almost a decade.

In those days before multiculturalism, the settlers all went their own national way; 'The Burra', as it was known, was made up of the original mining company town with an attendant group of government-sponsored villages, each with its own characteristics. The English lived in Hampton, the Scots in Aberdeen, the Welsh in Llywchwr, and the largest group, the Cornish – 600 came here from a single parish – in Redruth. In time, the villages merged to form Burra and Burra North.

Today, thanks to the no-nonsense craftsmanship of its original masons and carpenters, Burra survives as a living museum of the industrial and domestic architecture of the mid-1800s. The ruins of the mineshafts, chimneys, engine houses and powder magazines still stand today as stark monuments to the arrival of the Industrial Revolution in a peaceful rural setting. Two of the dugouts which once housed 1500 miners are preserved in the banks – the others were washed out during the floods of the 1850s – while the terraces of workers' cottages and the free-standing houses with their white quoins – all built of the same local stone as the mine buildings – testify to the Celtic origins of the original inhabitants. *Population 1190*

REDRUTH JAIL Built at a time when Burra was the largest country settlement in South Australia, Redruth Jail was the colony's earliest provincial prison. Behind its high walls and Georgian portals were three cells for males and three cells for females, a workroom, two large yards, and a residence for the jailer and turnkeys. It closed as a jail in 1894, and from 1897 to 1922 was used as a reformatory. Since the 1920s, it has been restored to order and figured prominently in the film *Breaker Morant.*

MINE VENTILATION CHIMNEYS Chimneys leading to shafts deep below the ground – square to a traditional Welsh design, round in the Cornish style – still stand starkly on the hills around Burra after 130 years.

PAXTON SQUARE This three-sided complex of thirty-three two-roomed and three-roomed cottages was built in the mid-1850s to house Cornish workers, the first example of company housing in Australia.

MARKET SQUARE The square, actually it is more of a triangle, is the centre of Burra, where roads from Adelaide, Morgan and Broken Hill meet. In its earliest days it consisted only of a standpipe and horse trough shaded by a single tree. Until as late as 1900 livestock was sold here on market days in the old, English village fashion. The square today is dominated by a traditional band rotunda, built in 1911 and dedicated to the memory of King Edward VII and decorated with cast-iron lacework. Other buildings include the National Trust folk and mining museum – which began life as a tailor's shop – and the 1847 Miners' Arms, now the Burra Hotel.

OPEN AIR MUSEUM The Mine and Enginehouse museums incorporate many of the restored and unrestored buildings of the original Burra copper mine including offices, cottages, enginehouses and the 1847 powder magazine, believed to be the oldest mine building in Australia.

COCKBURN ■ 1803

When travelling west along the Barrier Highway, Cockburn is the first South Australian town encountered by road travellers from New South Wales...but only just. This hamlet has the distinction of being sited so close to the state boundary line that many houses and outbuildings either straddle the border or have actually been built beyond it so that the occupants are technically subject to New South Wales jurisdiction.

Like other satellite towns of Broken Hill which have since become

Some Cornish miners lived literally 'on site', in dugouts gouged from the banks of Burra Burra Creek.

overshadowed by the 'Silver City', Cockburn was established – in 1886 – to service the mines which once flourished in the area. It has always been a railway town and the Australian National Railways is still the main employer here. The town was named after Sir John Cockburn, Premier of South Australia in 1889–90.

FARRELL FLAT ■ 1804

This hamlet between Burra and Mintaro began life as a crossroads settlement in the mid-1800s, servicing traffic on local stock routes and the copper and wool carriers on the intersecting road to the coastal ports. When the township was surveyed in 1870 it was named Hanson but the local epithet of Farrell's Flat persisted and in 1940 the powers that be finally acceded to common usage when the possessive 's' was dropped and 'Farrell Flat' replaced the imposed name on the map.

One story has it that Farrell Flat was named after James Farrell, a shepherd who worked on an early squatter's sheep run, but it is quite likely that the colony's second chaplain – who bore the same surname *and* Christian name and whose boat is said to have capsized in a local creek – is the Farrell to have been commemorated in this town's name.

MINTARO ■ 1805

In the 1840s, the drivers of the bullock teams and mule teams that hauled ore from the Burra mines to the coast found the site of what was to become Mintaro a handy place to halt for refreshment. But for a small and quite different type of mine of its own, this convenient watering hole would probably have slipped from the map when the railway took over the hauling of ore in 1870.

Slate is the secret of Mintaro's modest success; the town sits on top of a vast deposit of this perennially popular stone and its usefulness, originally as a paving material and more recently as durable flooring, has maintained the local quarry as one of Australia's major suppliers of a flagstone-like slate that equals the best in the world. On weekdays, it is possible to view the mining works, which have operated continuously for over 130 years, from a strategically located lookout.

The settlement has changed little since it was established and lives on in its own sleepy way as a 'heritage' town, where restored slate cottages in streets lined with eucalypts or ancient, gnarled Moreton Bay figs offer a 'get-away-from-it-all' retreat for jaded Adelaide city slickers. Slate blocks – readily broken from joints in the stratified deposits – were used to build most of the original buildings and the absence of 'unsympathetic' modern structures adds to Mintaro's period charm.

MARTINDALE HALL This grand, Georgian-style mansion a few kilometres east of Mintaro was built by a local pastoralist in 1879 in order to woo his intended bride in England – at least so says local legend. The lady in question must have been unimpressed for the pastoralist eventually married someone else and the couple went on to live in grand style; hunt club meets were held, the grounds were stocked with quail and a visiting English cricket team played on the property's own pitch.

Today, the atmosphere at Martindale Hall, while no less grand, is somewhat more egalitarian and the building must pay for its upkeep; it was used to represent a girls' school in the film *Picnic at Hanging Rock* and is open for public inspection, with overnight accommodation and dinner available for those wishing to experience the stately surroundings of a vanished era.

OLARY ■ 1806

This tiny community came into existence in the late 1880s to service the road and the railway on which it lies. Although the population declined sharply after the streamlining of railway operations between Adelaide and Broken Hill, it still has a hotel and general store to cater for travellers and the road and railway workers that are transient residents.

OODLA WIRRA ■ 1807

During the drought of 1865, the Surveyor-General, George Goyder drew a line – to become known as 'Goyder's Line' – around the regions of South Australia suitable for crop-growing (see *Whyalla & Port Augusta*). Land beyond the line was regarded as marginal at best and unsuitable for agriculture but almost thirty years later optimistic settlers were still pushing north and establishing settlements such as Oodla Wirra.

The town never became a pastoral centre but sprang briefly to life as a loading point for local ore going to Broken Hill or Peterborough until the standard-gauge line passed it by. Oodla Wirra is halfway between Adelaide and Broken Hill. Today it is a fruit-fly check point and also caters for road travellers. It is distinguished mainly by its unusual name – a version of an Aboriginal word for a curved, wooden weapon – which, although in everyday use, did not replace the bland, official appellation of 'Penn' until fifty years after the settlement's founding in 1890.

PETERBOROUGH ■ 1808

The Peterborough region, 530 metres above sea level and encircled by the outlying hills of the Flinders Ranges, was known as 'alta' or 'the circle', by its first inhabitants, the Ngadjuri Aboriginal people. The town at the centre of the circle – like a wheel hub – was to develop into a major railway junction radiating snaking lines of steel rails instead of spokes.

The newly-established town was named Petersburg in 1880, after Peter Doecke, a German immigrant landowner. Anti-German feeling during the First World War saw the name's Anglicisation in 1918. Within a year of Peterborough's founding the railway from Adelaide had arrived, and by 1888 the line from Broken Hill had intersected it. Eventually Peterborough was to become famous as one of the few places in the world to have three railway gauges, narrow, standard and broad, depending on whether the line was going north to Port Augusta, north-east to Broken Hill or south to Adelaide.

With the standardisation of the rail links to Alice Springs and Broken Hill, the tedious business of exchanging wheel assemblies on freight cars is a thing of the past but the railway heritage remains alive and well: Peterborough's Tourist Information Centre is a railway carriage which was honourably retired after operating on the transcontinental railway and the line to Alice Springs between 1917 and 1979.

The town's abbatoir – one of only two in Australia that is licensed to slaughter horses for human consumption – serves a vast grazing region stretching into south-west Queensland, while a more local service is provided by South Australia's only gold-extraction battery, where ore crushing has been continuous since 1897 – first under steam power and later diesel driven (see subentry). *Population 2140*

SAINT CECILIA This grand, twenty-roomed Federation-style mansion was built by the Roman Catholic Church as a bishop's palace. Named after the patron saint of music, it houses a collection of antique pianos and organs as well as a library and many fine paintings.

RAILWAYS ROUNDHOUSE This giant engine house, where more than twenty steam locomotives were once stabled around a central, three-gauge turntable, has fallen into disrepair but still houses restored engines and is planned as the centrepiece of a nostalgic display dedicated to Peterborough's railway heyday.

GOLD BATTERY After almost 100 years and more than 400 kilograms of gold – from 17 000 tonnes of ore – the Peterborough gold battery is still crushing ore. Ten piston-like heads crush the raw ore in water and the 'pulp' flows over a copper plate treated with mercury; the gold combines with the mercury from which it is readily separated and smelted to remove impurities. Inspections of the battery can be organised through the tourist office.

RADIUM HILL ■ 1809

Radium Hill, probably the first place in Australia where radioactive ores were discovered, is a modern ghost town, abandoned not once but three times as the volatile market for the ore fluctuated. Radioactive minerals – mainly davidite, a dark, shiny ore named for Edgeworth David, the distinguished geologist and Antarctic explorer – were discovered at the lonely site south of the Barrier High-

The symbolic crosses borne by the former bishop's palace of Saint Cecilia – now restored and open to the public – are echoed in the long garden path.

The bullocks and mules of the ore-transport days are long gone but the hills west of Burra are still grazed by working animals like these Clydesdales.

way in 1906 and mined – mainly for medical purposes – until the First World War.

Miners again took up residence in the settlement's huts in 1923, this time for an eleven-year burst of excavation and extraction but in 1934 the ghosts moved in once more. Radium Hill's final incarnation as a working mine town was between 1952 and early 1962 when, as a result of a purchase guarantee from a joint British–United States government authority, modern extraction methods made mining economical again. In 1961, the population peaked at 867 before a worldwide oversupply of uranium caused the diggings and the briefly thriving 'town' to be abandoned to the elements yet again.

ROBERTSTOWN ■ **1810**

Drovers and ore carriers seeking a stopping-off point on the road to Port Wakefield or Adelaide precipitated the growth of the settlement of Robertstown. Coming from the north on either side of the Burra Hills and the Scrubby Range, the junction where their paths met soon attracted entrepreneurs selling essential supplies such as food and drink.

One such man was John Roberts, who set up shop in 1871, and from 1874, as the first postmaster, stamped letters 'Roberts Town' – considered by some an improvement on the region's colloquial name of Emu Flats. The post office remained a Roberts family responsibility until 1926 by which time the town was established in its present role as a rail depot for the grain produced on the broad plains between the Murray River and the Barrier Highway.

TEROWIE ■ **1811**

There are two Terowies in Australia – the other one is a hamlet in the mid-west of New South Wales – but this is the only one to have had its name splashed across the front pages of the world's newspapers as the location chosen for one of the century's most famous declamations.

It was on the platform at Terowie railway station, in the darkest days of the Second World War, that General Douglas MacArthur conducted his first press conference after retreating from the Philippines and was able to formally repeat his famous promise, 'I shall return!'.

A plaque on the station wall commemorates the occasion when the famous general broke his journey from Darwin to Melbourne at what was then an important railway town, where the gauge changed from narrow to broad. After the war Terowie's role was to decline and its population slipped ever further away from its turn-of-the-century peak of more than 1000 citizens.

With the re-routing of the railway line to Alice Springs in the 1980s and the transfer of the break-of-gauge to Peterborough with standardisation in 1970, the railway connection was shunted into history. But in an age of mass tourism and heritage conservation, the lack of development in Terowie may well be considered the town's greatest asset for it is a nineteenth-century township preserved in a time capsule. The verandahed shopfronts facing the main street have changed little in 100 years and nowadays the click of the tourists' camera shutters echo the urgent sounds made by the newspaper photographers on the railway platform back in 1942.

WHYTE-YARCOWIE ■ **1812**

Whyte-Yarcowie has catered to the basic needs of the sheep-grazing properties which surrounded it since 1874. Then, it was known simply as Yarcowie and did not adopt the distinctive 'Whyte' – the name of the local railway station – until 1929.

As happened in many rural areas, the district population was swelled briefly in the 1920s by the arrival of First World War veterans taking advantage of the government-sponsored soldier-settlement scheme. But the influx was short-lived; small farms in such agriculturally marginal country (see box, *Whyalla & Port Augusta*) were not an easy proposition and most of the veterans eventually gave up the battle against the elements.

YUNTA ■ **1813**

The railway and the discovery of gold to the north put Yunta on the map. In the early 1890s, not long after the railway line to Broken Hill passed through, Yunta became the funnel through which more than 5000 miners poured on their way to the diggings – and possibly to making their fortunes – at either Teetulpa and Waukaringa.

In modern times, the railway line and its constant companion, the Barrier Highway, ensure that people continue to pass through Yunta but now they are tourists on their way to the northern Flinders Ranges and beyond – the tapping of the natural gas fields at Gidgealpa and Moomba resulted in a much improved access road to the state's arid north-east. Mileposts on the roads north are provided by the crumbling ruins of the gold settlements' stone buildings.

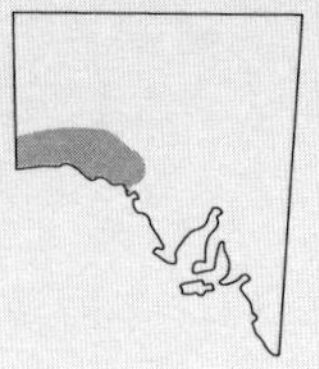

Ceduna

The vast, waterless Nullarbor, atop a limestone labyrinth of subterranean passages, meets the Southern Ocean at the mighty cliffs of the Great Australian Bight. At Ceduna, on its eastern fringe, great telecommunications dishes scan the heavens for television signals bounced across the world by satellite.

CACTUS BEACH ■ 1814
This stretch of remote coastal wilderness fringed with magnificent white sand dunes is a popular and internationally recognised surfing beach where hundreds of surfers gather each year during the hot summer months to test their skills in the pounding surf. Some devotees of the sport rate the three powerful 'breaks' off Cactus, one turning left and two turning right, as the best surf in Australia, and try to forget tales of white pointer sharks frequenting these waters to ride it.

CEDUNA ■ 1815
The shops, motels and caravan parks of Ceduna are a welcome sight for travellers who have made the long trip east over the Nullarbor; for those westward bound this is the last major outpost for stocking up on food and water and making final checks to the car before embarking on the crossing. Ceduna is also the centre for a large grain growing and pastoral area. Adjacent is the port of Thevenard (see entry).

The settlement on the shores of Murat Bay, which was established in the 1890s, was proclaimed a town in 1901. Local lore has it named after the police horse 'Ceduna', steed of Trooper Peter Hansberry, who in 1900 opened the Murat Bay police station here. However, this origin seems unlikely as the name 'Ceduna Plain' and 'Ceduna Hut and Well' first appeared on Lands Department maps in 1867 and derives ultimately from an Aboriginal word said to mean 'place to sit down and rest'. *Population 2750*

DENIAL BAY 'Mackenzie', as this small township was once known, was the site of the earliest settlement in the Ceduna region. The first European to settle here was pastoralist William McKenzie who built his homestead near the site of present day Denial Bay and there also established a small village, the ruins of which still stand.

The bay was given its name by the great cartographer, Matthew Flinders, during his detailed study of the South Australian coast in the *Investigator* in 1802, because the bay's aspect from the sea had raised hopes 'of penetrating by it some distance into the interior of the country'. As history was to show, this was denied.

OTC EARTH STATION The powerful Overseas Telecommunications Commission earth station, north-west of the town, was opened in 1970. Its giant 300-tonne antennae face west to provide links to the telephone and television networks of Asia, Africa and Europe through INTELSAT satellites orbiting high above the Indian Ocean. Telecom's east–west microwave repeater station, to the east of Ceduna, connects the earth station with the Australian domestic system.

FOWLERS BAY ■ 1816
The explorer Edward John Eyre pushed through the salty swamps here in November 1840 to replenish his supplies from the waiting government cutter *Waterwitch* before setting off on his arduous trek west. A stone on the foreshore commemorates his journey.

The first grazing run here was taken up by Robert Barr Smith, partner in the firm Elder, Smith & Co., in 1865. The town of Yalata (see Yalata Roadhouse) was proclaimed in 1890 and renamed Fowlers Bay in 1940. The bay was named by Matthew Flinders in 1802 for his First Lieutenant, Robert Fowler; the French navigator Louis de Freycinet, who was in these waters shortly after, named it Baie Denon.

GREAT AUSTRALIAN BIGHT ■ 1817
The bight is fringed by great limestone ramparts which rise sheer from the waters of the Southern Ocean to the vast plateau of the Nullarbor Plain (see entry). Ranging in height from ninety to one-hundred-and-thirty metres they form a mighty sea wall stretching for almost two hundred kilometres, believed to be the longest unbroken cliff line in the world. Clearly evident are the two broad bands of limestone of which the plain is composed. Near the base of the cliff wall are the pale chalky rocks laid down some forty million years ago, above them a grey line of rocks half that age.

There are access points from the Eyre Highway to high lookouts which afford not only spectacular views of this dramatic coastline but also, between June and October, the chance to witness the annual migration of the southern right whale.

NULLARBOR NATIONAL PARK ■ 1818
More than 230 000 hectares of the Nullarbor and its spectacular coastline are protected within this park.

Ceduna's dishes are Australia's eyes and ears, absorbing a constant flow of the world's images and chatter.

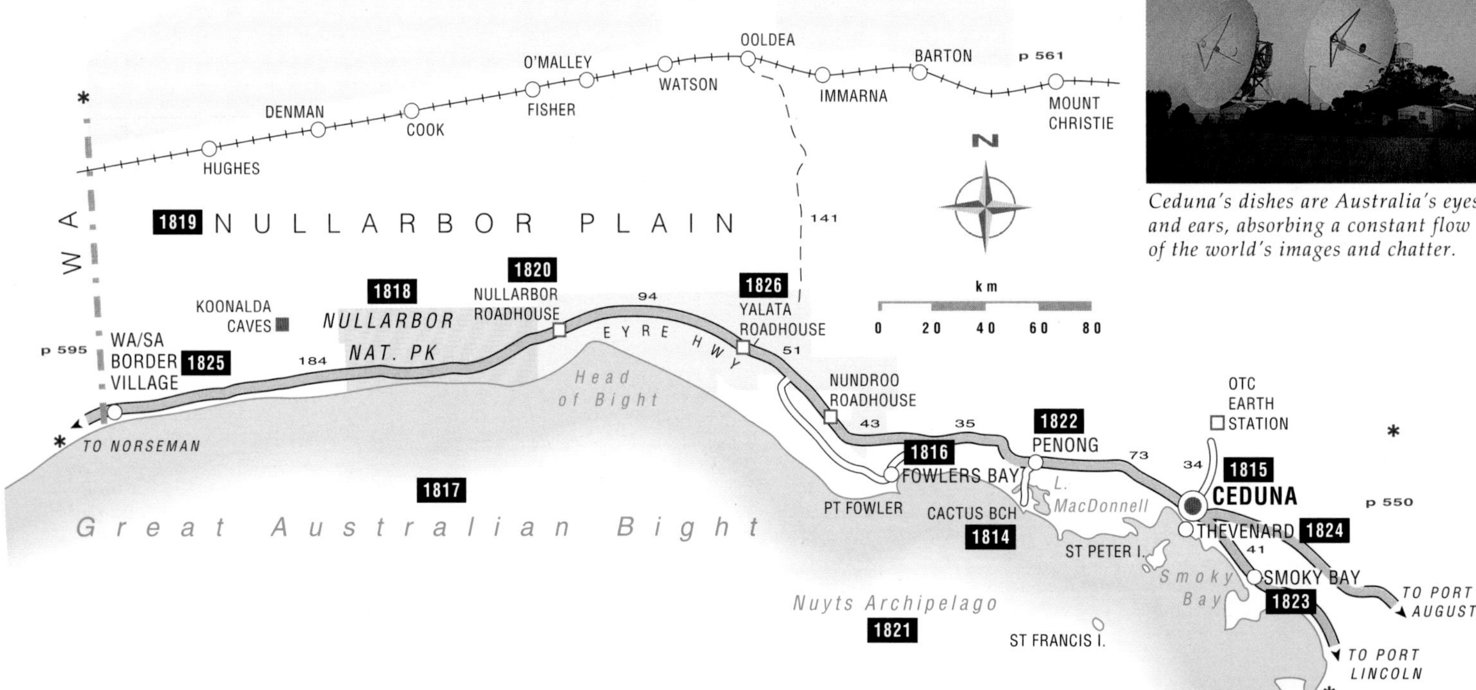

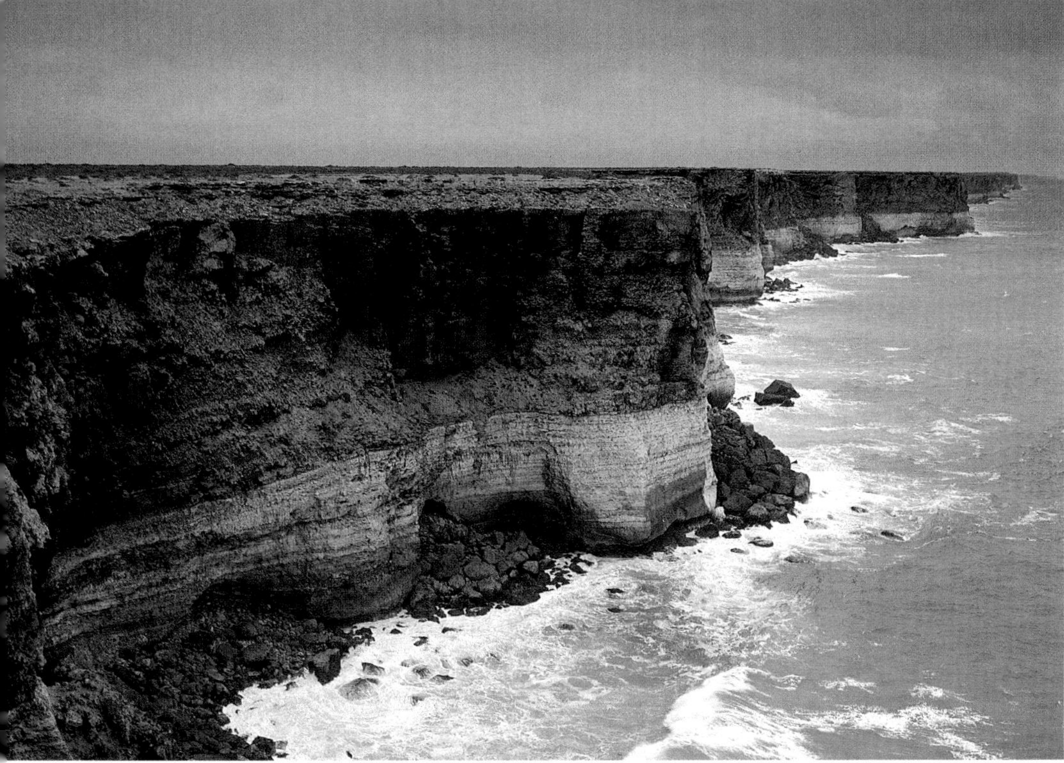

Few landscapes end so abruptly as where the Nullarbor collapses utterly before the might of the Southern Ocean.

Hidden in the caves beneath are well-preserved fossils of a number of extinct species which roamed a much greener plain 40 000 years ago. A discovery from more recent times – dated to some 2600 years ago – was the complete carcass of a Tasmanian tiger, or thylacine, still with a coat of fur, which had become mummified in the dry air.

KOONALDA CAVES Outside the park, near its western borders, is the Koonalda Cave system. The entrance is through a sinkhole and the main chamber lies nearly eighty metres below the plain. Evidence of human activity here dates back some 24 000 years; the chambers were prized highly both for their permanent water and for the deposits of flint-like chert and chalcedony used in the making of tools.

The caves were also used for ceremonial and ritual purposes. In the complete darkness of the inner passages are ancient engravings of grids, herringbones, lattices and concentric circles, made during the last ice age by the light of burning brush torches. Entry to the cave system by the public is prohibited.

NULLARBOR PLAIN ■ 1819

Twenty million years ago this nowadays flat, dry and empty region lay under a broad shallow sea, and the deposits on its floor formed a thick layer of dark grey limestone. This, the largest single slab of limestone in the world, was pushed upward by violent earth movements to form the plateau of the Nullarbor Plain. The plain stretches along and inland from the Great Australian Bight (see entry) and covers around 200 000 square kilometres, a formidable barrier between the major population centres of the south-eastern and south-western sides of the continent. Although the surface is waterless, below it are underground rivers and extensive cave systems, some with caverns the size of cathedrals, created over countless centuries by rain percolating through the Nullarbor's porous limestone.

In Aboriginal legend, a great snake called Ganba or Jeedara was said to live in this subterranean labyrinth and to move through its passages to the sea. He pushed up the great cliffs at the edge of the plain so that he could swim along beneath them, and the strange gurgling sounds which sometimes emanate from the blowholes near the base of the cliffs were the sounds of his breathing.

The name Nullarbor is not Aboriginal in origin, as is often assumed, but is derived from the Latin words 'nulla arbor' meaning 'no trees'. To the Aboriginal inhabitants the region was known as 'bunda bunda' – 'high cliffs'. The first European to cross the waterless plain was Edward John Eyre, who in 1840–41 travelled west across the Nullarbor, seeking a stock route from South Australia to the Swan River settlement. His harrowing and arduous journey followed the line of the Bight close to the route of the present highway which bears his name.

TRANS-AUSTRALIA RAILWAY Pushing across some of the most inhospitable parts of the Nullarbor Plain is the railway line which, in 1917, linked Port Augusta with Kalgoorlie, and thus Perth to the east of the continent (see box, *Esperance & Eucla*). Stations and sidings along its length honour a string of Australian leaders – in this section Barton, Watson, Fisher, Cook and Hughes, all former prime ministers, Denman – who as governor-general in 1912 turned the first sod in its construction – and O'Malley – who as Minister for Home Affairs was closely associated with the project. Immarna is an Aboriginal word meaning 'camp' and Ooldea, where gangs coming from opposite sides of the continent met was, because of a permanent water source, an Aboriginal meeting place for centuries past.

NULLARBOR ROADHOUSE ■ 1820

The needs of cross-Nullarbor travellers are catered for by this small settlement on the Eyre Highway. There is a hotel-motel, caravan park, restaurant and service station here. On both sides of the highway the plain lives up to its name and is not only completely treeless but bare of almost any distinguishing feature.

NUYTS ARCHIPELAGO ■ 1821

This scattered group of limestone capped granite islands and outcrops off Ceduna in the Great Australian Bight was sighted and named in 1627 by Pieter Nuijts aboard the Dutch ship *Gulden Zeepaard* – Golden Seahorse. This vessel, under François Thijssen, was separated during a storm from a convoy heading up the western coast of the continent, and then blown by fierce westerlies along the unknown southern shores. Nuijts, a high-ranking Dutch East India Company official, appears to have taken command and, as they ran before the gale, he charted the uninviting coast for fifteen hundred kilometres, reaching the vicinity of Ceduna before turning on his tracks and heading for the original destination of Batavia – modern Djakarta.

ST PETER ISLAND & ST FRANCIS ISLAND The almost unimaginable remoteness of these islands is said to have inspired the location where Gulliver, Jonathan Swift's fictional character, met with the tiny people of Lilliput. Nuyts Archipelago has the same longitude and latitude as the islands in the book – allowing for Swift's misreading of 32°S as 30°2' – and early editions of his book included a map clearly identifying the islands as 'St Pieter' and 'St Francot'.

PENONG ■ 1822

The tiny township of Penong serves an established farming community, the Lake MacDonnell gypsum works and the annual influx to the nearby surf beaches (see Cactus Beach) – a surfboard factory is now located here. Water is a severe problem and the town survives on ingenuity and water carted from Ceduna.

SMOKY BAY ■ 1823

Safe sandy beaches and fine fishing combine to make this a popular holiday spot for families and fishermen alike. The Aborigines of the area have known this for thousands of years. It was the smoke of their campfires along these shores in 1802 that caused Matthew Flinders to name the bay 'smoky'.

THEVENARD ■ 1824

Thevenard is the deep sea port for the Ceduna district, being on the peninsula separating Murat and Bosanquet bays. The jetty here has bulk-handling facilities for gypsum, grain and salt. The local fishing fleet is also located here with three factories processing catches of whiting, garfish, snapper, shark, prawns, lobster and abalone for South Australian and eastern states markets.

WA/SA BORDER VILLAGE ■ 1825

This tiny frontier outpost is a long way from anywhere and everywhere, a feeling reinforced by the cluster of signs here, giving distances and pointing not only in the general direction of Sydney, Darwin and Melbourne, but also to New York, Moscow and London. The timeline on the border gives forty-five minutes to those travelling west, and takes the same from those going east.

YALATA ROADHOUSE ■ 1826

As well as providing fuel, refreshments and the normal facilities, the village here is an outlet for a wide variety of artefacts made by local Aborigines. 'Yalata' is the Aboriginal name for Fowlers Bay (see entry), and is said to mean 'oyster place'.

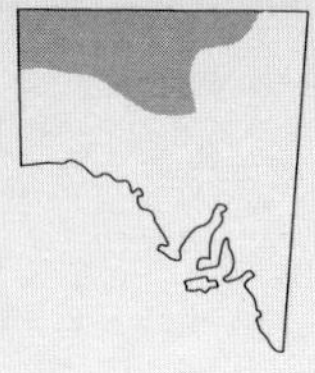

Coober Pedy & Marla

Fortune-seekers, tunnelling into the richest opal field in the world, have transformed the barren lands which repelled explorer and pastoralist alike into a moonscape, dotted with shafts and mounds of pale mullock. Both men and animals have adapted to an unrelentingly harsh climate by living in burrows.

COOBER PEDY ■ 1827

The mounds and mounds of pale mullock which surround the opal mining town of Coober Pedy have been deposited over the decades by successive waves of hopeful opal diggers trying their luck on Australia's richest field. Opal veins here occur as far as thirty metres below the surface, randomly distributed in clayey bands sandwiched between layers of sandstone. Anyone with a prospecting permit has a chance of striking it rich – either by serious shaft sinking, or by 'noodling' – sifting and searching through the piles of waste that dot the landscape.

The town lies in the low, flat-topped hills of the Stuart Ranges where the country is arid and the climate severe. The summer heat can reach 50° Centigrade and so, like the animals of the desert – long adapted to the region's harsh environment – the inhabitants of Coober Pedy retreat underground into dugouts unique to the town where the temperature is an even 24° year-round. Shafts provide air and some light. Shops and even churches are burrowed into the red earth.

The multicultural population here is a mixture of Aborigines, white Australians of European descent, and European migrants of various backgrounds – newspapers printed in several languages are available in the town, and there are a variety of Greek, Italian, Hungarian and Croatian eateries, bakeries, delicatessens and coffee lounges, lending an unexpectedly cosmopolitan air to this outback town. A solar desalination plant was constructed in 1967 to treat the saline bore water and Coober Pedy is now supplied with reticulated, desalinated water.

Although miners have been working and living here since the 1920s, their occupancy was under licence only and it was not until 1969 that Coober Pedy was proclaimed a town. Its name is derived from an Aboriginal word meaning, appropriately, 'hole in the ground'.

To the east and north of the town is the dog fence (see box, *Quilpie & Thargomindah*), which runs through to Queensland and just north of the fence is an area known as the 'moon plain' where fossilised shells can be found. *Population 2490*

THE BREAKAWAYS RESERVE This low range of exposed sandstone outcrops to the north of Coober Pedy is an isolated spur of the main Stuart Range with spectacular eroded mesas and buttes, which have provided the location for several Australian films including *Mad Max III*.

FESTIVALS The Glendie Festival, July; Coober Pedy Race Weekend, October.

ERNABELLA ■ 1828

Ernabella is the central settlement in the Pitjantjatjara Aboriginal Land which was handed back to its original owners in 1981. The Pitjantjatjara Land Rights Act gave freehold title to about one tenth of South Australia to the Pitjantjatjara people – a tract which escaped development largely because of its worthlessness for most European purposes, it is none-the-less significant as the object of the first negotiated land rights settlement in Australia. Around three hundred people – including fifty or so non-Aboriginal teachers – live in the town; within a radius of thirty kilometres there is a scattering of outstations – on each a small family group lives around a well dug into the aquifer from which water for houses and gardens is pumped by solar or wind power into an overhead tank.

Ernabella lies alongside a sandy creekbed in the floor of a valley fringed by gently sloping red granite hills. In the early years of the twentieth century, Ernabella came into existence as a short-lived sheep station and the original mud homestead is now the administrative centre. In 1936 the station was taken over by the Presbyterian Church so that a mission with a difference could be established – one that did not interfere with traditional ways, but instead provided a base to which the desert people came on their own terms. Ernabella ceased to be a mission in 1971, and the community is now controlled by an elected council. The Aboriginal name for the settlement is Pukatja. *Population 540*

Despite the relief from the above-ground heat, gouging opals deep beneath Coober Pedy is not for the claustrophobically inclined but some subterranean locations (right) may even be conducive to browsing.

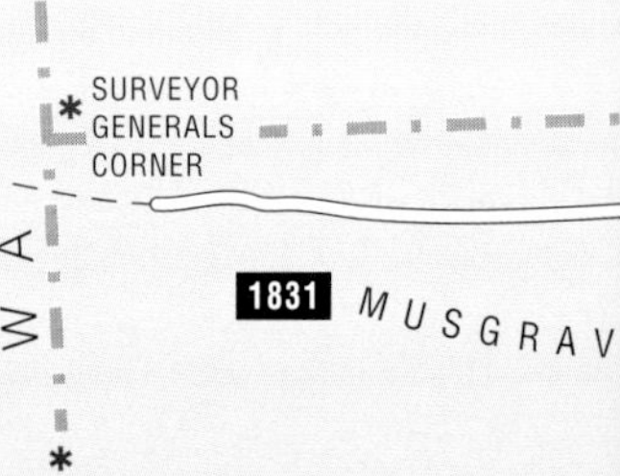

Heavily mineralised spring waters irrigate marshy patches of tough grass in the otherwise waterless Witjira Park.

MARLA ■ 1829

Sitting at the junction of the Oodnadatta Track (see entry) and the Stuart Highway, about 1000 kilometres north of Adelaide, the new town of Marla – proclaimed in May 1981 – marks the northernmost limits of 'civilisation' in South Australia's outback. It provides a base for road travellers through this sparsely populated region and is a centre for the government agencies which operate here. It is built beside a reliable water supply, the Marla Bore; the name probably comes from 'marlu', the Aboriginal word for kangaroo.

MINTABIE ■ 1830

This frontier mining camp on the opal fields of South Australia has recently outstripped Coober Pedy as the world's largest producer of precious, brilliantly coloured opals. Here the opal occurs in horizontal and angled seams down to a depth of twenty-five metres and is recovered by drilling, blasting, and the use of heavy-duty earth-moving equipment. Although many opal miners commute from Coober Pedy to work their Mintabie claims, some have now established permanent homes here. A permit is needed to cross Pitjantjatjara lands.

MUSGRAVE RANGES ■ 1831

The first Europeans to enter the granite hills of these ranges were probably the men of Ernest Giles' party, in late 1873, during the second of his three attempts to cross from the centre of South Australia to the west coast. Their thirsty horses emptied Aboriginal waterholes, and the men unthinkingly defaced sacred cave paintings by adding their own markings. The ranges had been named several months earlier by William Gosse who spied them from atop the monolith he called Ayers Rock, and labelled them in honour of Sir Anthony Musgrave, the then new Governor of South Australia.

The Musgraves extend east-west for about 180 kilometres and are up to 40 kilometres wide. Their steep, red sides rise 600 metres and more from well-grassed valley floors – the highest point is Mount Woodroffe, which at 1435 metres, is the highest point in South Australia. The ranges are part of the Pitjantjatjara lands.

OODNADATTA ■ 1832

In the 1870s, there was a busy depot here for the construction of the Overland Telegraph Line. The town itself was laid out in 1890 in anticipation of the arrival of the Central

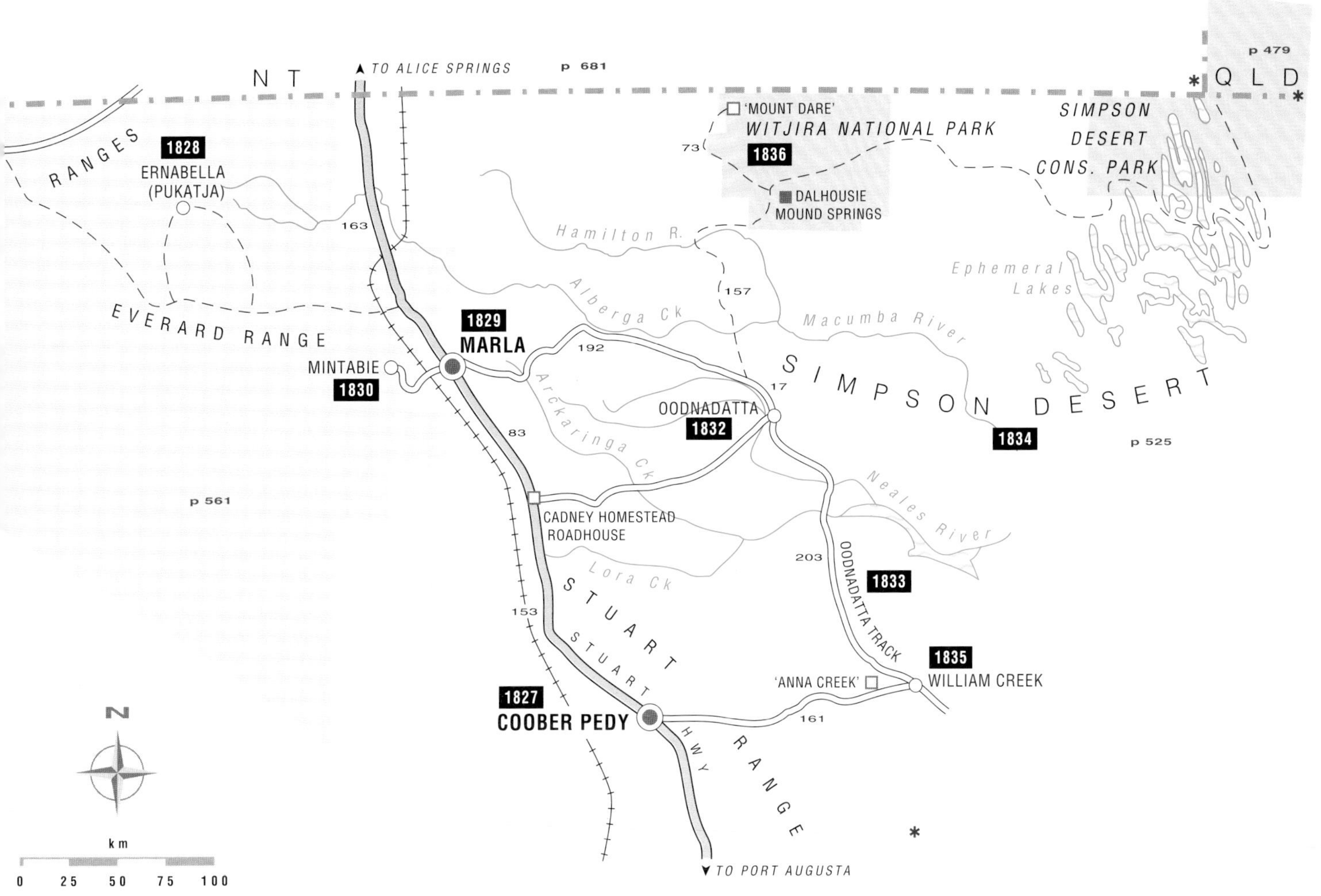

Australian Railway line, which came to Oodnadatta the following year, terminating here and making the town the railhead for central Australia. For the next four decades teams of camels operated by the town's Afghan community (see *Leigh Creek & Marree*) ferried freight from Oodnadatta to scattered sheep and cattle runs and when, in 1929, the line was extended across the 600-kilometre stretch of desert to Alice Springs the train it carried was dubbed 'the Ghan' (see sub-entry) in their honour.

THE GHAN The original Ghan carried its passengers from Port Pirie, through Oodnadatta and, after 1929, continued on to Alice Springs on the line that was originally intended to cross the continent from south to north. During the years of its operation it was one of the world's great railway journeys, crossing sand and saltbush plain and skirting dry lake beds. Sometimes heat buckled the rails or flash floods not only put the track under water but also washed away its foundations, stranding the train for weeks. When this happened camps were set up for the passengers, and with stewards and cooks to look after them, they sang around log fires and danced under the night skies, while up ahead navvies toiled to repair the track. In the 1970s, a standard gauge line was built 150 kilometres to the west, away from the flood prone area. The last old Ghan pulled out of Oodnadatta in 1980, but a section of the old line has been kept for historical purposes and as a tourist attraction.

An errant and deeply eroded spur of the Stuart Range called – appropriately – The Breakaways, intrudes into the desert near Coober Pedy.

OODNADATTA TRACK ■ 1833

Following in the 1861–62 tracks of explorer John McDouall Stuart and along the original route of the Ghan, the Oodnadatta Track heads north-west from Marree, skirting salt lakes that are part of the Lake Eyre basin, to the tiny township of William Creek, through to Oodnadatta and on to Marla. Along its course are the unmarked graves of the pioneer settlers and navvies who perished from heat exhaustion, dehydration and typhoid in the late 1880s during the building of the railway.

SIMPSON DESERT ■ 1834

The long, parallel dunes of the Simpson Desert lie aligned south-east to north-west across a 143 000-square-kilometre expanse of uninhabitable, arid country bounded by Lake Eyre, the Finke River and the MacDonnell Ranges. This harsh land repelled all attempts of the inland explorers to cross it, and it was not until 1929, when aerial surveys became possible, that the Simpson was first charted by geologist Dr Cecil Thomas Madigan who wrote 'every now and again we swooped down within a hundred feet of the ground, and felt its hot breath, escaping gladly again to the cooler air above'.

Dr Madigan named the barren expanse for the president of the South Australian branch of the Royal Geographical Society which had sponsored his expedition. The desert was not crossed on foot until 1973. Four years later, writer Robyn Davidson, with camels, made a lone trek over its sands, an experience recorded in her book *Tracks*.

There is very little wildlife here, but that which exists is admirably adapted to the incredibly harsh and usually waterless conditions. When

rain comes, plants and animals burst forth in a brief frenzy of activity, to feed and reproduce.

WILLIAM CREEK ■ 1835

The tiny township of William Creek is on Anna Creek Station, one of the biggest pastoral leases in the world, and is the closest settlement to Lake Eyre. It consists of little more than an outback pub, but has an enduring connection with the world of communications – in 1872 the Overland Telegraph Line passed through here and 115 years later it became the site of Telecom's Digital Radio Concentrator System (DRCS) which uses up-to-date digital radio transmission techniques to give some 400 remote subscribers in the surrounding 60 000 square kilometres access to modern telecommunications – and privacy – through an automatic exchange that has replaced the old manual switch.

Oodnadatta lingers listlessly on the desert's edge, bypassed by progress after 80 years as a rail town when the Ghan sought higher ground.

WITJIRA NATIONAL PARK ■ 1836

A unique complex of mound springs is protected in this arid region park which was declared in 1986. These outlets for the waters of the Great Artesian Basin are surrounded by the accumulated deposits of crystallised minerals left as the waters evaporate in the searing heat. Over the years these have combined with sand and clay to form the distinctive mounds. The springs are permanent sources of water in a region where rainfall is infrequent and summer temperatures extreme. They are home to rare fish and amphibians, and also support a large bird population.

FLINDERS RANGES

Native cranberry heath, labelled by homesick settlers, is a far remove from its old-world namesakes.

The Flinders' Arkaroola region was once a sheep station; now native vegetation reclothes the hills.

Once a mighty chain of mountains – reduced by millions of years of exposure to a modest range on an arid plain – the Flinders Ranges, from the hills and dales by Spencer Gulf to the worn, craggy peaks of the inland, possess a timeless, starkly beautiful attraction.

The Flinders Ranges combine the grandeur of a boldly undulating, upland landscape with the raw but beautiful harshness of the inland. This series of often purple-hued hills and ragged ranges – sometimes softening into rolling dales carpeted with wildflowers and interrupted by the slashes of red-cliffed gorges – is, like much of the inland, a captivating but unforgiving environment. Many explorers and early settlers found this to their tragic cost.

After the Great Dividing Range, the Flinders Ranges comprise the mainland's longest and most dramatic single upland region, an outcropping which brings character to and in some ways defines South Australia's fertile south-eastern corner – for beyond the hills there is little but desert for thousands of kilometres. These ranges of character rise in the south between Crystal Brook and Peterborough and extend for more than 400 kilometres in a northerly direction to a point between Lake Torrens and Lake Frome, about 160 kilometres east of Marree.

This ancient landscape had its origins in sediments that were laid down in the sea between 1400 million and 500 million years ago. Rocks were formed from these sediments and over time were lifted by enormous forces within the earth's crust to be buckled and fractured into a mountain range of Himalayan proportions. The mountains were gradually eroded but before they disappeared they were uplifted again to form a plateau, the forerunner of today's ranges.

In the south, the Flinders Ranges are a broad mass of ridges, cut by deep gorges on the western side. Travelling north, the terrain spreads out into gravel-filled basins and low, sandstone ridges, and then becomes more complex with curving parallel ridges and eroded domes and basins, steep cliffs and serrated skylines. The highest point in the Flinders, St Marys Peak (1200 metres), is part of the ridge enclosing the spectacular bowl-like depression in the earth's surface called Wilpena Pound. Further to the north, there are the isolated Gammon Ranges, riven by deep gorges, and finally in the north-east before the desert takes over, a tangled mass of rocky ridges

and gorges representing some of the wildest mountain scenery in Australia.

The climate of this region varies from temperate in the south, through semi-arid to extremely dry in the north. Rain is infrequent but can fall at any time of the year and often be heavy, causing dry creekbeds to quickly become gushing torrents. But when the rain subsides, its waters will have refreshed the cool oases hidden from the sun's harsh, evaporating rays in the ranges' shady gorges.

The first white man to see the ranges was Matthew Flinders during his circumnavigation of Australia between 1801 and 1803. As he sailed up Spencer Gulf in 1802, he sighted the southern part of the ranges which now bear his name. Flinders landed near where modern Port Augusta stands and named Mount Brown, nineteen kilometres to the east, after Robert Brown, the navigator aboard his ship, *Investigator*. Within a decade of South Australia's founding in 1836, pastoralists had reached Mount Remarkable in the Southern Flinders Ranges. By 1860, their leases extended over most of the ranges and mineral prospectors had soon followed in their train.

During the 1870s and 1880s, ambitious wheat farmers cultivated thousands of hectares of land in the ranges and many small towns sprang up. The farmers were unaware of the 'marginal' nature of this land and a succession of poor seasons, famine, disease and the hostility of the Aborigines combined to force many of them to give up in despair. Such factors also sounded the death knell for most of the towns. The ruins of such towns are now a tourist attraction, though visitors come mainly to see the scenery, most of it reserved in national parks. Aboriginal habitation of the Flinders Ranges dates back thousands of years and there are more than 100 recorded sites containing Aboriginal relics.

The ruggedness of this landscape holds a great attraction for film-makers and probably more people have seen the beauties of the Flinders – usually without realising it – than any other part of Australia. Despite their wildness, the ranges are relatively close to the civilised comforts of Adelaide and as such have provided a convenient and photogenic background – doubling as various parts of Australia or the Middle East – for such television and film photoplays as *Robbery Under Arms*, *Sunday Too Far Away*, *The Lighthorsemen*, *Gallipoli* and *The Shiralee*. □

The ruins of the Kanyaka Station homestead are a monument to an unrelentingly harsh environment.

The meagre rainfall of the Flinders Ranges is channelled into gorges where wildlife finds a green refuge.

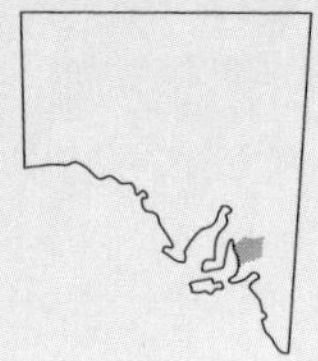

Gawler & Nuriootpa

The cultural influence of the early German settlers is still very much in evidence in the Barossa Valley, a place where the natural and cultivated landscape, regional history and taste sensations of all kinds demand leisurely consideration.

In Gawler, local bluestone and render was used for a town hall, institute and bank streetscape impervious to time.

ANGASTON ■ **1837**
Angaston was named officially when George Fife Angas lodged a plan of the town at the Adelaide Central Registry Office in 1857, but he had already held land in the area called 'German Pass' for fifteen years. The town, with handsome buildings and a main street lined with Moreton Bay fig trees, is ninety-two metres above the floor of the Barossa Valley and known as 'The Crown of the Valley'.

Samuel Smith, a churchgoing brewer from Dorset in England, founded the Yalumba Winery at Angaston in 1849. The name is an Aboriginal word meaning 'land all around'. His day job was gardener at Lindsay Park (see sub-entry) and he planted his first tiny vineyard by moonlight on land purchased from his employer, George Fife Angas.

Soon realising he needed capital, Smith set off for the flourishing Bendigo goldfields with characteristic determination, leaving his son, Sidney, to tend the vines. After digging sixteen back-breaking shafts, he returned to the village with three hundred pounds sterling. With this he purchased additional land, spent one hundred pounds on a plough, two horses and a harness and expanded his enterprise. In 1863, Samuel and Sidney Smith made 60 hogsheads of wine – approximately 14 000 litres.

William Salter established the Saltram vineyard in 1859 and by 1882 was successfully exporting wine, but Angaston has never been purely dependent on the wine trade. There are many stone-fruit orchards and the fruit is glazed and dried in the district. Quarrying was another local enterprise; some of the surrounding hills are almost pure marble. Slabs from the quarries were used for building both in Angaston itself and in Adelaide. The marble deposit also feeds a large cement works near the town. *Population 1820*

'COLLINGROVE' Collingrove Homestead, built in 1853 for John Howard Angas, was the home of several generations of the family until it was given to the National Trust in 1976. The house, in its parklike setting, retains the original workshop, coach house and stables. There is a beautiful little chapel which has always belonged to the estate. It was originally Baptist but was rededicated as Church of England in 1906.

LINDSAY PARK This house, built in 1847, belonged to George Fife Angas, John's father, and was also a family home until 1965. It is now a stud farm for racehorses and is famous as the home of the imported champion stallion 'Without Fear'. During the 1975–76 racing season, a world record of thirty two-year-old winners were his progeny. A 'Without Fear' filly was presented to Queen Elizabeth for her Silver Jubilee.

BALHANNAH ■ **1838**
There is some disagreement over the name of this town which appears as 'Belhannah' in early records. It was established by a Scotsman – James Turnbull Thompson – in the early 1840s. He chose the last part of the name to honour his mother and sister who were both called Hannah. The first syllable may be a corruption of 'belle' for 'beautiful' or from the Gaelic 'bal' which means 'town'.

Small deposits of gold, copper and bismuth were once mined in the district which also had a reputation for dairying. The economy is now based on potatoes, apples, poultry, sheep, cattle and horses. *Population 890*

BETHANY ■ **1839**
The first major Barossa settlement was at Bethany in 1842 when more than twenty German Lutheran families arrived from Silesia to escape religious persecution (see box). They called the area Neuschlesien – New Silesia – and a little later established a settlement at Langmeil on the banks of the River Para from which Tanunda grew (see entry). The name Bethany was taken from the Bible and means 'a fertile place'.

The original cottages stretched along the village street with farming strips reaching back behind them across the creek to the village common where the flocks were grazed. This was the way farming communities were set out in Silesia. The common is now the Bethany Reserve and some of the original thatched barns remain. The Pioneer Cemetery has many fine headstones engraved in German. The Lutheran Church has always been strong in this community and in 1875 a mission party left from the village to found the Hermannsburg Mission on the Finke River in central Australia (see *Alice Springs & Yulara*).

BIRDWOOD ■ **1840**
Birdwood was known as 'Blumberg', the German for 'hill of flowers', until the First World War when the name was changed to 'Birdwood' – after the Australian Forces Commander, General Sir William Birdwood (later Field Marshall Lord Birdwood) – because of strong anti-German feelings. Unlike other towns in the district, the original name was never restored. In the early days of settlement, gold was a major industry but the mining machinery is now rusting by the River Torrens. *Population 580*

BIRDWOOD FLOUR MILL This flour mill, which opened in 1852, is now a National Motor Museum and houses a steam car built at Mannum in 1898 and the Clement Talbot driven from Adelaide to Darwin by two pioneer motorists in 1908.

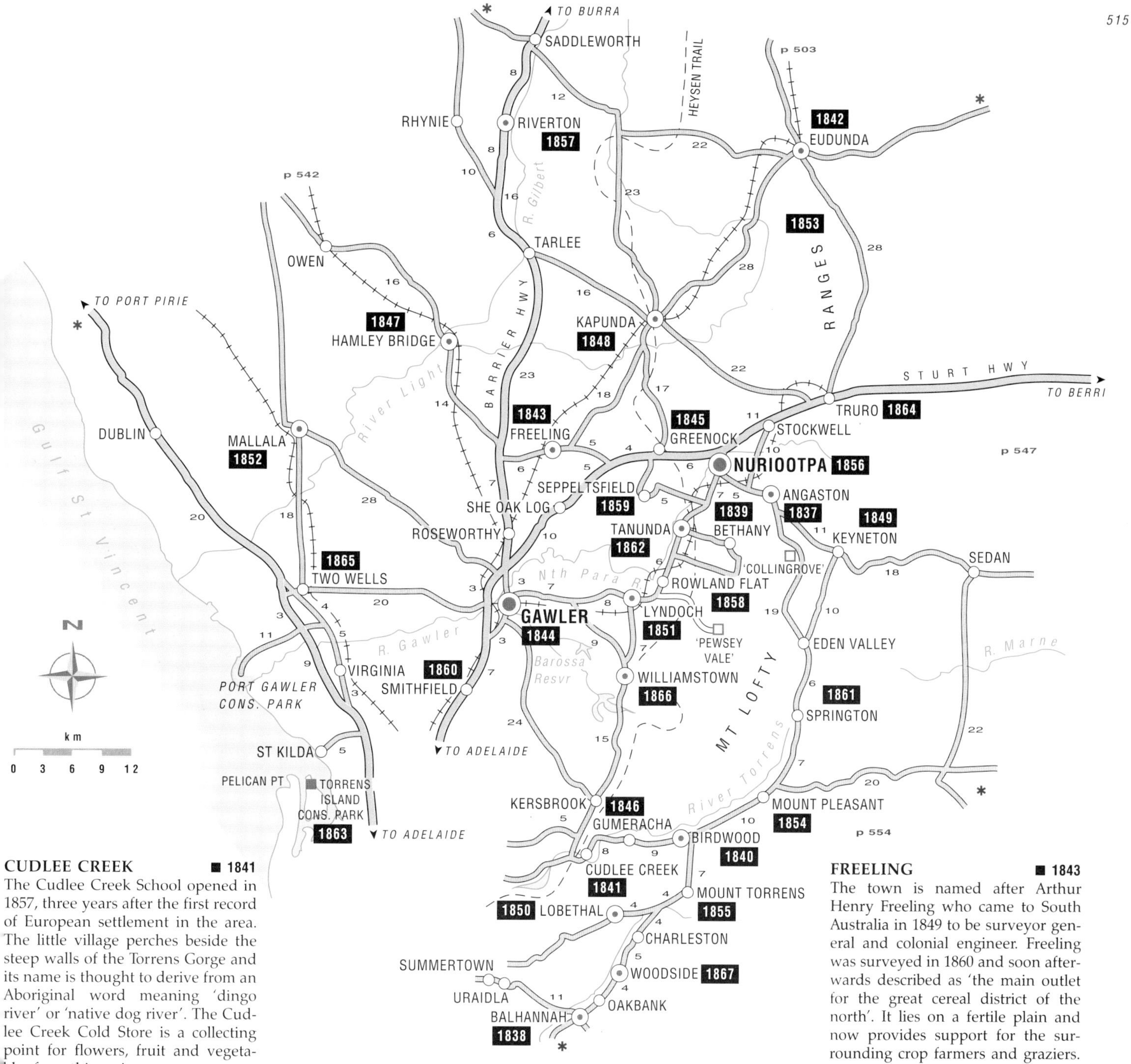

CUDLEE CREEK ■ 1841

The Cudlee Creek School opened in 1857, three years after the first record of European settlement in the area. The little village perches beside the steep walls of the Torrens Gorge and its name is thought to derive from an Aboriginal word meaning 'dingo river' or 'native dog river'. The Cudlee Creek Cold Store is a collecting point for flowers, fruit and vegetables from this region.

EUDUNDA ■ 1842

Eudunda, between the Barossa Valley and the Mallee plains, was surveyed in 1872 and named after a nearby spring which the Aborigines called 'eudana-cowie' meaning 'sheltered or hidden water'. The town serves the rural needs of the district. Many of its early settlers were German immigrants who concentrated mainly on mixed farming.

Poet and novelist Colin Thiele was born in Eudunda in 1920 and writes about the descendants of the original settlers in several of his books. He sums up the essence of his early family life in a few words from *The Quality of Experience*: 'It was...candlelight and oven bread, mealtime grace and family Bible, Christening font and graveside coffin'. *Population 650*

A thatched barn housing the workhorses' feed is an example of the central European village traditions transposed almost unchanged to Bethany.

FREELING ■ 1843

The town is named after Arthur Henry Freeling who came to South Australia in 1849 to be surveyor general and colonial engineer. Freeling was surveyed in 1860 and soon afterwards described as 'the main outlet for the great cereal district of the north'. It lies on a fertile plain and now provides support for the surrounding crop farmers and graziers. Many of the buildings are Victorian with iron lacework typical of architecture of that era. *Population 880*

GAWLER ■ 1844

In the early days, settlements were often named after governors and their relatives and South Australia was particularly punctilious in this practice; Gawler honoured George Gawler who led the colony from 1838–41. The town, began in 1839, is bounded by the South and North Para rivers and backed by hills. It was on the miners' route to the Yorke Peninsula, Burra and Kapunda, and bullock waggons and coaches rested there overnight.

Graced by many fine Victorian buildings, plentiful park space and three town squares, Gawler was planned by Colonel William Light with his characteristic vision. Later

Gawler came to be known as the 'colonial Athens'. When British Poet Laureate, Sir John Betjeman, visited in the 1970s, he said it 'was one of the most delightful country towns he had seen anywhere'.

The McKinley Memorial in Gawler honours 'Big John' McKinley who lived there after his marriage to Jeannie Pile in 1863. He led an expedition in 1861 to look for Burke and Wills (see *Hughenden & Richmond*) and died in 1872 in Gawler.

The railway connection between Gawler and Adelaide was completed in 1857 and the present station, built to replace the original limestone building in 1879, retains its tracery 'of the best quality Staffordshire iron'. Gawler became a prosperous industrial centre and a collection point for wheat and wool going to Port Adelaide. There were hundreds of jobs in the flour mills, foundries, brickworks and breweries.

Present-day Gawler serves a rich agricultural district and has become something of a dormitory town for many daily commuters to Adelaide. Primary produce includes fat lambs, wheat, wool, poultry and dairy products. *Population 13 840*

THE OLD TELEGRAPH STATION This is the oldest public building in Gawler, built of local stone soon after the Gawler–Adelaide railway link went through. The original gaslight still hangs over the front entrance. The building is owned by the National Trust and houses a telecommunications museum and rooms furnished in the style of bygone days.

DEADMAN PASS Up till 1849, the only southern access to Gawler was by way of the shallow ford across the Para Pass. William Light's diary entry for the day he camped there in 1839 reads: 'Having heard of a dead body being buried in an old tree here, we examined the spot and found it'. The dead man had perished from thirst in the bush and his body had been sealed with clay in the hollow tree. Light and his companion removed the corpse and buried it and ever since the ford has been known as Deadman Pass.

'KINGSFORD' This two-storey house, between Gawler and Turretfield at quaintly named Shea Oak Log, first belonged to a pastoral pioneer called Stephen King. It was built in 1856 from biscuit-coloured stone believed to have come out from England as ship's ballast. King's nineteen-year-old son, also called Stephen, joined John McDouall Stuart's exploring party across Australia. Kingsford's second owner was John Howard Angas who bred Hereford cattle there very successfully. A bull from his stud won the Grand Championship at the Melbourne Show for nine successive years.

ROSEWORTHY AGRICULTURAL COLLEGE Roseworthy Agricultural College, to the north of Gawler, has the distinction of being the oldest agricultural college in Australia. There was an experimental farm at Roseworthy from 1879 and superphosphate fertilisers were tried out there in 1881. The college was established in 1883 and took its first residential students two years later. Appropriately oenology and viticulture are now part of the program and offer scientific and practical training for people intending to work in the wine industry. Roseworthy has also been a major South Australian centre for breeding new wheat varieties.

FESTIVALS Gawler Three Day Event (dressage, cross-country riding and show-jumping), June.

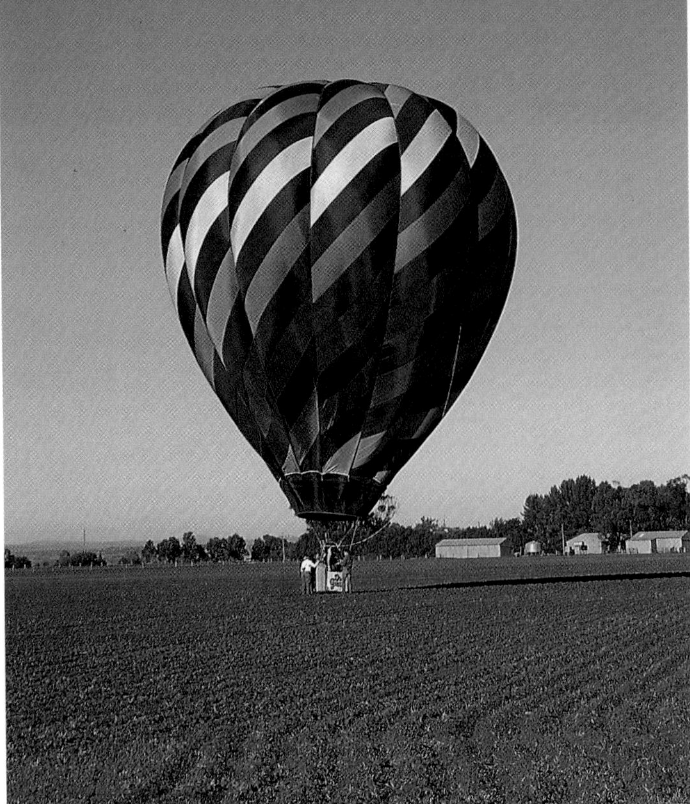

Conditions in the Barossa are so ideal for ballooning that Seppeltsfield has a balloon 'academy' where experts line up for an annual hot-air 'regatta'.

GREENOCK ■ 1845

Greenock sounds Scottish and it is generally thought the town is named after a Clydeside town but some say Colonel Light chose to remember his friend Lord Greenoch. Or the name might be a corruption of the German word 'gruneck' meaning 'green and verdant corner'.

The town experienced a brief period of copper mining when deposits were discovered in the 1850s, but on the whole Greenock's fortunes have always depended on cropping and grazing and the town's modern agricultural pursuits blend with its architectural past. The fine old cottages have verandahs laced with iron and some of the district's barns are still thatched.

GUMERACHA ■ 1846

The Aborigines named the deep pool at this site 'Umeracha'. The first European settler was William Beavis Randell, a miller by trade, who later laid out the town in 1860. His flour mill, constructed of solid bluestone in 1849, is now restored. In 1853, his two sons built the first River Murray steamer from red gums felled in the area (see box, *Swan Hill & Kerang*) and carried it in pieces over the ranges to the Murray flats at Mannum to reassemble and install an eight horsepower engine (see *Murray Bridge & Mount Barker*).

The main industries here are grazing, dairying and market gardening. Gold was found in reasonable quantities in the early days of settlement but mining activities now produce feldspar and talc.

HAMLEY BRIDGE ■ 1847

The small rural settlement of Hamley Bridge was established in 1868 and named for Lieutenant-Colonel Francis Hamley, Administrator of South Australia from 1868–69. It was the site of a bridge constructed over the River Light in the late 1860s to take the railway line from Adelaide to Balaklava. *Population 660*

KAPUNDA ■ 1848

By 1850, South Australia was known for its rich copper deposits and was dubbed the 'Copper Kingdom'. The accidental discovery of deposits of oxidised green and blue copper ore on a sheep run at Kapunda in 1842 was a major find. The Kapunda workings were the first significant metal mine in Australia and together with Burra (see *Peterborough & Burra*) accelerated the infant colony of South Australia's recovery from the economic crisis of 1841. Within ten years a prosperous mining town had developed near the site.

For the next thirty years, Kapunda was a major town and in 1871 was more populous than Gawler and Glenelg. However, the richest lodes were exhausted by the 1870s, and falling copper prices caused the closure of the mine in 1879. The town and mine area are now a part of the National Estate. Some of the buildings are decorated with exceptionally fine examples of intricately patterned iron lacework, which were wrought at the local foundries.

The celebrated pastoral landowner Sir Sidney 'Cattle King' Kidman once had his headquarters here and in 1921 donated his house to the education authorities. His local horse sales were reputed to be the largest in the Southern Hemisphere.

Kapunda also lays claim to a couple of unusual sporting 'firsts'. In 1868, Australia's first game of croquet was played in the town and in 1876 South Australia's first bowling green was established here.

Kapunda is believed to be a corruption of a local Aboriginal word, 'cappieoonda', which means 'jumping water', a reference to a spring that supplied the first settlers with water. *Population 1980*

'ANLABY' 'Anlaby' is one of the oldest stations in South Australia. Until quite recently it was owned by Geoffrey Dutton, poet and writer, who was born there on 2 August 1922. The property had been in his family since his great-great uncle took it up in the early 1840s. It bred some of South Australia's first merino sheep and Clydesdale horses.

KEYNETON ■ 1849

Keyneton is on the eastern side of the Barossa Ranges where Joseph Keynes established a sheep run in 1839. The early settlers called it the 'North Rhine' because it reminded them so much of that part of their homeland. The bell of St Peter's Lutheran Church was cast in Germany and hoisted up a convenient gum tree outside the door.

Barossa people talk about 'wine in the blood' and many of the oldest cellars have been in the one family for generations. Johann Henschke planted grapes in the vicinity of Keyneton in 1851, made wine in the 1860s and sold it in 1868. A family member still tends the vineyards – on the eastern uplands, over a hundred metres higher than the Barossa Valley proper and much more vulnerable to winter frosts – but the Mount Edelstone and Hill of Grace red wines have an international reputation. By 1980, Mount Edelstone shiraz variety had achieved twenty-five years of consecutive awards.

LOBETHAL ■ 1850

Pastor Gotthard Daniel Fritzsche led his congregation from Prussia to a place in the Mount Lofty Ranges where they could enjoy civil and religious freedom. The long journey to Australia aboard the *Skjold* was dogged by rough seas and appalling conditions and fifty-two emigrants died. Eighteen families settled on the Onkaparinga River and they held an open-air service of thanksgiving on 4 May 1842. The pastor quoted from the bible, Martin Luther's translation of the book of Chronicles: 'And on the fourth day [they] assembled themselves in Lobethal; for there they blessed the Lord. Therefore the name of the same place was called Lobethal unto this day'. In German 'Lobe' means 'love' and 'thal' means 'valley'. Lobethal is variously translated as 'Valley of Peace' or 'Valley of Praise'. Local residents fought hard to keep the town's original name during the anti-German hysteria of the First World War, but it was changed to 'Tweedvale' – ostensibly to recognise the local woollen industry (see Birdwood). Then in 1935, the name reverted to Lobethal.

The surrounding country is good for sheep and dairy cattle pasture and potatoes are grown. Dolomite is quarried locally. The Onkaparinga Woollen Mills, one of Australia's best known companies, have been in operation for well over 125 years in an imposing factory complex. They began in Hahndorf in 1869 but moved to their present site three years later. *Population 1520*

ST JOHN'S LUTHERAN CHURCH In 1843, the emigrants began building St John's Lutheran Church, now the oldest in Australia. All the settlers, including the women, took a hand in making the bricks and carrying them to the building site. Services are still held in the church, which was dedicated in 1845.

Despite its hollow centre, the sap still rises in the old Springton gum that once housed the Herbig family.

The garden setting of the handsome, bluestone winery at Seppeltsfield is famous for its tall palms (upper left).

LYNDOCH ■ 1851

In 1837, Colonel Light recorded in his diary: 'we came to a beautiful valley which I named Lynedoch Vale after my esteemed friend'. This was Light's fellow soldier, Lord Lynedoch, who led his men to victory at the Battle of Barrosa near Cadiz in the Spanish Peninsular War in 1811. Over the years, through carelessness or design, the 'e' was lost and the present version prevailed.

Lyndoch lies at the southern-most extremity of the Barossa Valley. The original Lutheran settlement was established at Hoffnungsthal – 'Valley of Hope' – in 1847 by emigrants from Posen. The local Aborigines warned them of winter rains swamping the valley but their advice was not heeded until a bad flood in 1854 forced the newcomers to move to higher ground. *Population 960*

'PEWSEY VALE' 'Pewsey Vale', near Lyndoch, was another vineyard cultivated around the middle of the last century. Joseph Gilbert planted the first vines there in 1847. He had arrived some years earlier and began constructing the stone Pewsey Vale Homestead around 1838. The lowest floor of the house is partly underground and there are deep shady verandahs on three sides.

MALLALA ■ 1852

The village's name is said to come from an Aboriginal word 'madlola', which is thought to mean 'place of the ground frog'. Phillip Butler and Thorold Grant were the first pastoral settlers in the district in 1846; the Mallala post office opened in 1865. The town itself was not laid out until five years later and is still the centre of a quiet rural district. *Population 590*

MOUNT LOFTY RANGES ■ 1853

Mount Lofty proper was named by Matthew Flinders as he sailed past in the HMS *Investigator* in 1802, after landing on Kangaroo Island. The ranges are a series of rounded hills to the east of Adelaide which stretch across 320 kilometres to the Peterborough region. They include the state capital's gently sloping backdrop of the Adelaide hills – which Colonel Light called 'the enchanted hills'. Many little settlements shelter in the valleys of the range (see Lobethal, Nuriootpa) and early settlers built cool, summer retreats on their slopes.

MOUNT PLEASANT ■ 1854

In 1843, a pioneer settler called James Phillis, whose mother's first name was Pleasant, drove sheep here to graze. He also grew the first crop of wheat on the hillside. The country around Mount Pleasant is still noted for its fine grazing qualities.

The town had a brief spurt of recognition when gold and copper were mined in the district in the early days. A mapped 'Scenic Wine Drive' winds for fifty kilometres through an attractive landscape between Mount Pleasant and Eden Valley. *Population 550*

MOUNT TORRENS ■ 1855

Mount Torrens township was laid out by George Dunn in 1853 and named in honour of Colonel Robert Torrens who had been Chairman of the South Australian Colonisation Commission and after whom the 'Torrens Title' is named. Dunn built a tavern which became a rest stop for teamsters from Mannum. The settlement became a substantial rural centre and many of the nineteenth-century buildings still stand.

NURIOOTPA ■ 1856

Nuriootpa is at the northern end of the Barossa Valley. The site was once an important barter centre for the Aborigines and one interpretation of the town's name is 'meeting place'. Another suggests it is derived from an Aboriginal word 'nuraitpa' meaning 'neck country' – apparently a reference to the low, narrow shape of the Mount Lofty Ranges at Nuriootpa which represented the neck of a giant in local legend.

European settlers arrived in the early 1840s and William Coulthard built the first hotel here out of slabs of red gum. Travellers stopped for rest and refreshment while passing through on their way to Kapunda and Burra and in the usual manner a town grew up around the watering hole. Nothing remains of that old building although there is still an inn on the site. Coulthard's home, the large, well-proportioned, bluestone 'Coulthard House' at the end of the main street, is now preserved as a National Trust museum. The unfortunate pioneer hotelier is said to have died of thirst in the fiercely hot summer of 1858 while out scouting for new pastoral land to the north of the town.

Kaiser Stuhl, the only co-operative winery in the Barossa Valley, opened in Nuriootpa in 1931. *Population 3320*

RIVERTON ■ 1857

Riverton is the largest town in the Gilbert Valley. James Masters was the first European arrival hereabouts, in 1840, and later asked his companion, John Jubb Horner, to help him name the place. Masters wanted 'Hornertown' but his friend suggested 'Gilberton'. This was rejected by the powers that be because it had already been given to an Adelaide suburb. Once again Masters insisted on 'Hornertown' to which his colleague is reported to have replied: 'If they will not accept Gilberton, call it Riverton'...and so it is.

Riverton has the familiar long, straight, main street of so many of Australia's country towns but this one is charmingly tree-lined and bordered with nineteenth-century stone cottages. The former blacksmith and wheelwright's shop has been turned into a museum, which houses a large

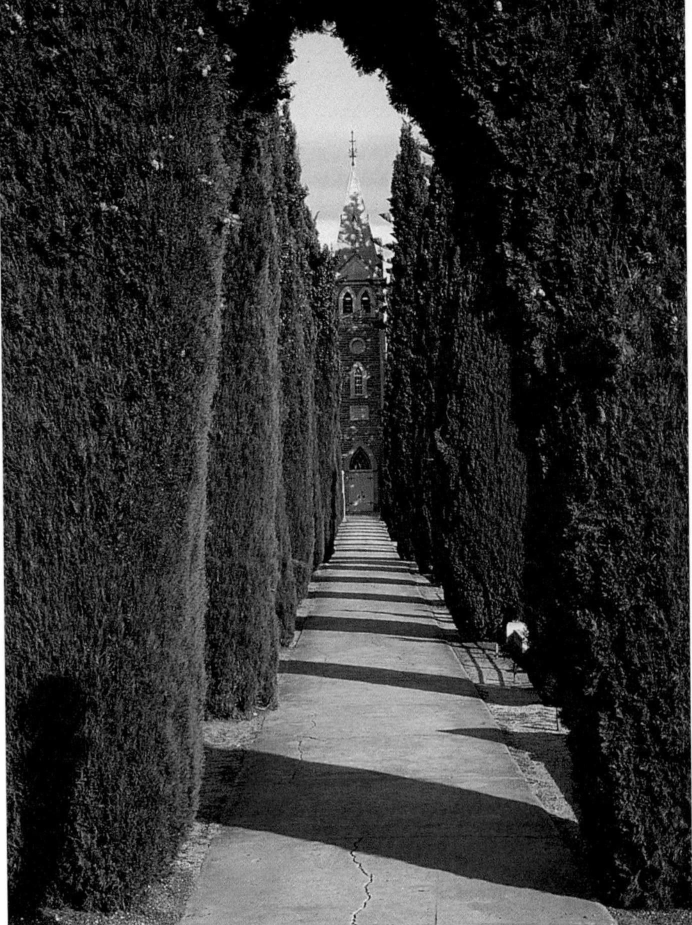

Perspective is employed to effect at Tanunda's Langmeil Lutheran Church where the cypress avenue focuses worshippers' attention on the bell tower.

collection of original tools and farming equipment. *Population 760*

ROWLAND FLAT ■ **1858**
In 1847, Johann Gramp – a German emigrant who had spent some years working for the South Australian Company – planted the Barossa Valley's first vines at Jacobs Creek near Rowland Flat. Three years later he bottled a white hock and founded the Orlando Winery. His son, Gustav, moved the business to Rowland Flat proper in 1877.

Hot-air ballooning has become a very popular sport in the area and Rowland Flat can offer the ultimate romantic tourist adventure – chicken and champagne at sunrise or sunset while drifting far above the fields and paddocks of the Barossa Valley.

SEPPELTSFIELD ■ **1859**
In 1850, Joseph Seppelt arrived from Germany and established Seppeltsfield a year later. Intending to grow tobacco, he put in a few vines at the same time. The tobacco plants failed and he shrewdly focused on the flourishing vines, which would become the basis of a large wine-producing venture. The Palm trees that form an avenue from Marananga to Seppeltsfield were planted during the Great Depression to provide work for staff who would otherwise have been laid off.

FESTIVALS Hot Air Balloon Regatta, mid-May.

SMITHFIELD ■ **1860**
Smithfield, named after John Smith, the first landowner in the area, evolved as a small farming centre. Early wheat crops were processed at the Yelki flour mill which was driven by a waterwheel. The railway line reached the settlement in the 1850s and the station and workmen's cottages, built around 1856, still stand. Smith settled here in 1848 and his hotel is still being used to this day.

SPRINGTON ■ **1861**
Springton is famous for the Herbig Tree, a large, old, hollow red gum on the main road, which once served as an unusual pioneer home. Johann Friedrich and Caroline Herbig began their married life here and two of their sixteen children were born in the tree. There are photographs and family records on display; a relic of this period stands opposite: a watering trough which can be filled by a hand pump.

Some attractive and valuable livestock graze in the paddocks about halfway between Springton and Mount Pleasant where an angora and cashmere goat farm greets each spring with the appealing bleat of newborn kids.

TANUNDA ■ **1862**
The name Tanunda comes from an Aboriginal word meaning 'waterhole' or 'abundance of wild fowl' or a combination of both: 'many birds upon a creek'. These derivations underlie the initial preoccupations of all new settlers – essential drinking water and a local, and preferably plentiful, source of food. Tanunda grew out of the village of Langmeil and has four Lutheran churches – Tabor Lutheran Church and its spire make a significant and graceful contribution to the townscape.

Tanunda falls about midway in the Barossa Valley and still maintains many of the traditions of the early settlers. When Friedrich Gerstaecker passed through the village in 1851, he found it 'a nice little place but entirely German. There are German public houses, a German drug store, German doctors, stores, blacksmith, carpenter, school, church, in fact everything is German. The traveller would believe himself in some little village of the old country between the Rhine and the Oder'. Goat Square was the common around which the town revolved. The atmosphere is preserved in the old hand pump and many of the original cottages, which are numbered rather than named.

Samuel Hoffmann was responsible for the first vineyards in the area. He arrived from Germany with his eight sons and one daughter intent on farming but he gradually switched to growing grapes and began producing wine with some considerable success. The district now produces wine, brandy, wool and wheat. *Population 3090*

FESTIVALS Oom Pah Festival, mid-January; Essenfest, March.

TORRENS ISLAND CONSERVATION PARK ■ **1863**
The Torrens Island Conservation Park encompasses a saltmarsh land system at the northern end of the island. The vegetation is a mix of white mangrove and low shrubland and more than thirty different kinds of salt-tolerant plants are known to thrive there. Marsh shrimps, worms and fish attract a great variety of birdlife and rare, long-legged waders visit during the summer months. These include whimbrels, bar-tailed godwits, terek sandpipers and eastern golden plovers.

TRURO ■ **1864**
This area was first developed in 1842 when Charles Flaxman purchased land to develop into pastoral leases. Copper was discovered by Charles Barton in 1846. Truro, the northern gateway to the Barossa, was founded in 1850 with the opening of a copper mine nearby and ore was mined for more than a century from the now disused Wheal Barton mine.

A December 1849 issue of the *South Australian* newspaper reported that 'the land is a rich garden mould, watered by ever flowing streams in the neighbourhood…limestone [is] easily procurable on the sections and in the immediate vicinity firewood without limit'. Three months later the paper stated 'the working of the mine has commenced with pre-eminent success'. Truro was laid out as a company town and was named by its Cornish settlers.

A Cornish skill is imprinted on the surrounding countryside. Solid stone walls instead of fences mark the divisions between the local properties which are engaged in the business of growing wheat and raising sheep, pigs and cattle.

TWO WELLS ■ **1865**
The town of Two Wells was laid out by John Bullock and Charles Farr around 1864. In the early days of settlement, two Aboriginal wells were used for domestic and stock water and the informal, descriptive name soon became official. The present township is a small settlement on the main highway with predominantly rural interests. *Population 520*

WILLIAMSTOWN ■ **1866**
According to local legend, the land around Victoria Creek was traded to a Scot called Lewis Johnstone for a mob of horses. He subdivided it for settlement and renamed it after his eldest son. The town is protected by the surrounding hills and nestles among tall gums, willows and pine trees. The Mount Crawford radiata pine forest on its eastern side is one of the largest in the state.

One of the earliest discoveries of gold was made about three kilometres from Williamstown in 1849 when a lump of gold-bearing quartz was unearthed during ploughing. Today, the district relies on agricultural pursuits such as grazing, wheat, fruit and dairy farming. *Population 850*

BAROSSA RESERVOIR This reservoir, built in 1898 in a landscape of tall pines, is the largest of its kind in South Australia. The shape and location of the dam creates an unusual acoustic phenomenon. Its retaining wall carries whispered words clearly from one side to the other. There are aquamarine, beryl, emerald, garnet, ruby and sapphire gemstones to be found by lucky prospectors in the local creeks and riverbeds.

WOODSIDE ■ **1867**
The first settler here was James Johnston, a brewer, who came from Woodside in Scotland. Other early residents were shepherds employed by the South Australian Company. Vegetable growing and dairying were soon established and several gold claims were worked. The town was built on slopes leading down to the Onkaparinga River and is now the local government and business centre for the surrounding rural district. The National Trust has classified the police station and the court house as being worthy of preservation. *Population 1090*

THE BAROSSA: WORTHY OF CELEBRATION!

SOUTH AUSTRALIA is the driest state in the driest continent with eighty-three per cent of its area receiving less than 250 millimetres of rain a year. Yet, without any assistance from irrigation, about a quarter of Australia's annual output of wine flows from 8000 or so hectares of grapes grown in one small region.

The Barossa Valley is blessed with hot dry summers, reliable winter rains and loamy soil which rarely feels the bite of frost. It is not just a huge vineyard but also produces wheat, fruit, eggs, vegetables and dairy goods and has flour mills and a cement works.

The fruitful 'Valley of the Vine' is about thirty kilometres long and varies in width from five to eleven kilometres. From Mengler Hill, the author Colin Thiele has described it eloquently and accurately as 'a halved bottle with its bottom upturned near Truro and its neck corked by Lyndoch'. It was named 'Barrosa' – hill of roses – in 1837 by Colonel William Light after a battle in the Spanish Peninsular War fought, coincidentally, in a well known wine region of Spain (see Lyndoch).

The story of how George Fife Angas, a director of the South Australian Company, helped Lutheran pastor August Ludwig Christian Kavel lead his congregation from civil and religious oppression in Silesia has often been told. Angas met Kavel in London, persuaded him to come to Australia and largely financed the cost of the refugees' emigration.

In 1840, Johann Menge, a German geologist, had gone into the hills to look for minerals. For a while he lived in a cave at Jacobs Creek and prophesied: 'I am quite certain we shall see flourishing vineyards and orchards and immense fields of corn throughout all New Silesia'. The first grapes were planted seven years later by a Silesian called Johann Gramp (see Rowland Flat).

The Barossa Valley presents a tidy pastoral landscape to the motoring visitor. All known varieties of wine grapes are on parade – stark brown for winter pruning; tender green in spring; mellow autumn colours at harvesting. Row upon row of bottles line the cellar shelves. The many well-tended towns have solid stone houses and small neat cottages, carefully cultivated gardens and straight, tree-lined main streets. The rising spires of meticulously kept churches dominate the landscape. Bells still ring sweetly and often. In Bethany, a dusk clangour on Saturdays symbolises the end of the working week. There are more than thirty Lutheran churches in the valley as well as those of other denominations.

Food as well as wine flows in the Barossa Valley and many old German recipes are alive and well and in everyday use. Restaurants serve delicious traditional dishes and shops sell sausages – blutwurst, bratwurst, mettwurst and leberwurst – pickled cabbage called sauerkraut and quarkstinkerkase – cottage cheese. The Barossa's bakers make a rich assortment off traditional cakes and biscuits such as apfel strudel – apple cake, streuselkuchen – crumble top cake, quarkkuchen – cheesecake and honigkuchen – honey biscuits. The Barossa's epicurian delights are celebrated in a Classic Gourmet Weekend held in August each year.

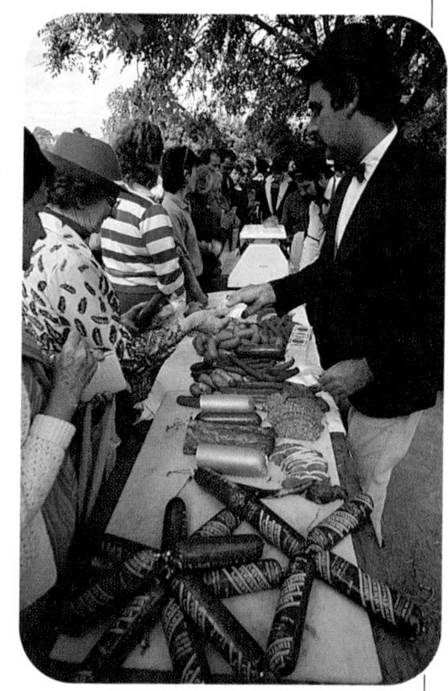

The varied meats and wursts of old Silesia grace the sausage table at the Barossa festival.

Though some of the early settlers came from Britain, German culture has always prevailed. Today there are signs of change, as machinery takes over and some customs are discarded. Young people are no longer fluent in the local patois known as Barossa Deutsch and few Lutheran brides wear traditional black. However, the Vintage Festival, first held in 1947, incorporates many of the old ways in a week of eating and drinking, fun and sport, music and pageantry (left and above). There are processions, grape-picking and grape-treading contests, dancing and performances by the 130-year-old Tanunda Liedertafel singing society so that the valley seems to ring with the sounds of its pioneers. □

The grapes from this last-of-the-vintage April harvest in the Barossa are being picked for a special destiny: they will be crushed by the bare feet of two local worthies as part of the biennial festival.

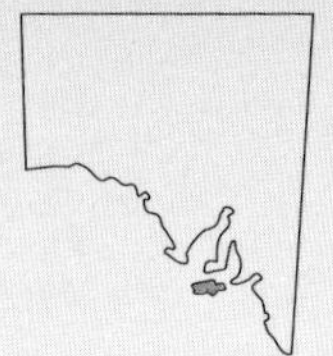

Kangaroo Island

Kangaroo Island is the perfect place to take a camera and a fishing line and simply revel in the undisturbed peace of a place where a rugged shoreline and eucalypt woodlands – undisturbed by feral predators – provide a wilderness backdrop for the gentle and often approachable native birds and animals.

AMERICAN RIVER ■ 1868

American River, now one of Kangaroo Island's main tourist resorts, was named after the American sealers who lived there for several months between 1803 and 1804 and built a thirty-five tonne schooner from local materials. Several of the pine trees near Pelican Lagoon became planking used in the construction of the *Independence* and there is a plaque to commemorate her launching.

American River is a sheltered tidal estuary which provides calm waters for pelicans and black swans. It is also a starting point for fishing cruises. Trolling for snook is popular all round the coastline and big game fishermen go after sharks which are reputed to be among the largest in the world.

KANGAROO HEAD The first European to record sailing past American River was the navigator, Matthew Flinders, in 1802. He came ashore at Kangaroo Head where his crew were able to kill several of the 'black substances' they had seen on the beach at twilight. They knocked them over the head with sticks. The distinctively dark furred island kangaroos, which are known as sooty kangaroos and which inspired Flinders' choice of name – he spelt it 'kanguroo' – were quite unafraid of human beings.

CAPE BORDA ■ 1869

Cape Borda was named by the French navigator, Nicholas Baudin, to honour John Charles Borda, mathematician, astronomer and fellow navigator. The unusual square, squat lighthouse first flashed here on 5 July 1858. It sits atop sheer, dark cliffs that rise 155 metres above the sea. The small cannon nearby stood in readiness to be discharged when ships were approaching danger.

Numerous wrecks, like barnacles sticking to these treacherous shores, are testimony to the fact that the warning systems were not fail-safe. In the early hours of a chilly June morning in 1885, the barque *Mars* ran aground near Cape Bedout and nine survivors eventually made it to Cape Borda. The lighthouse has become part of the network of South Australian meteorological stations.

CAPE GANTHEAUME CONSERVATION PARK ■ 1870

Most of this park is a limestone plateau clad in mallee scrub with some areas of shifting sand dunes. Hundreds of different bird species have been recorded here, the most commonly seen including wedgetail eagles, black cockatoos and willie wagtails. Part of the conservation park's coastline skirts the internationally famous Seal Bay (see entry).

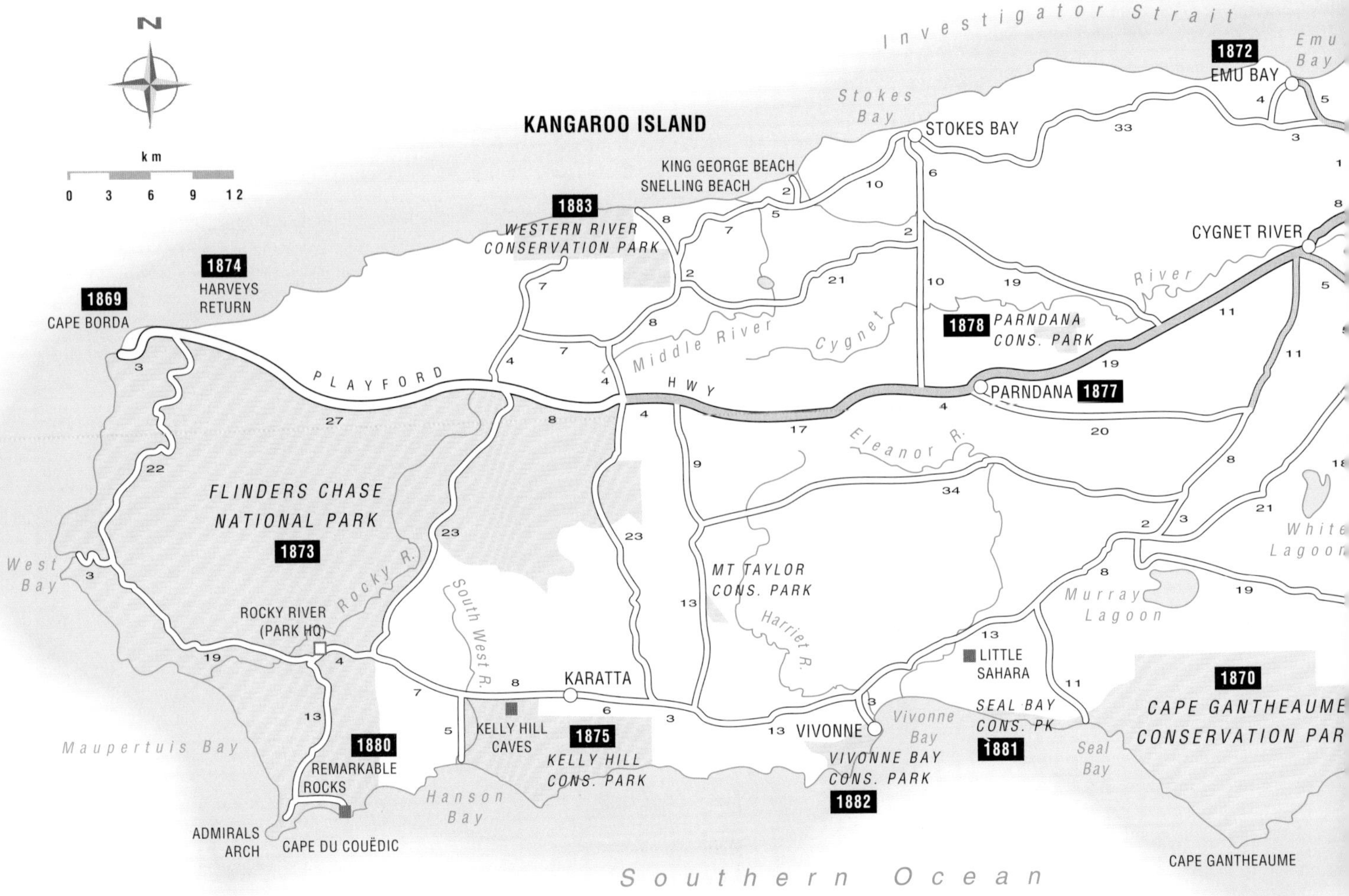

Kangaroo Island's wild shoreline is lashed by the sea to spectacular effect in the southern section of Flinders Chase National Park near Cape de Couedic; sea lions (right) have first claim to intermittent stretches of beach.

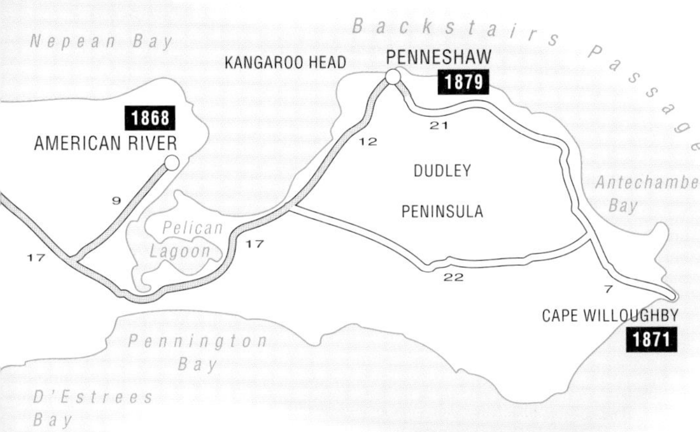

Kangaroo Island's namesake was a ready food source for its often piratically inclined early visitors.

Southern right whales – so named because their high oil yield made them the 'right' whale to hunt – regularly migrate to this part of the Southern Ocean and often pass by with their new-born calves in tow.

POINT TINLINE Sealers and whalers lived on the island during the first four decades of the nineteenth century. For some years there was a whaling station at Point Tinline and casks of whale oil were taken by bullock waggon to the jetty at American River for shipment to the mainland. All that remains of the industry is a small excavation in the cliff top which could have been for collecting water. Huge quantities of seal skins were salted and stored in the caves. In 1853 the steamer, *Osmanli*, went down off Point Tinline but happily, all passengers and crew struggled to the beach safely.

MURRAY LAGOON Murray Lagoon, in the north of the reserve, is the island's largest freshwater lagoon but there is evidence that its salinity is increasing due to increased surface runoff. As yet this does not seem to have affected the many waterbirds that gather there. Aboriginal artefacts, possibly dating back more than 30 000 years, have been found east of Murray Lagoon. What happened to Kangaroo Island's Aboriginal inhabitants is still a mystery, for they were long gone by the time Europeans first set foot on the island.

CAPE WILLOUGHBY ■ 1871

Cape Willoughby at the eastern end of the island was named by Matthew Flinders after the parish he came from in the English county of Lincolnshire. This beacon, which was originally called the Sturt light, first shone in January 1852. The twenty-seven-metre tower, the first to be built in South Australia, is made of local limestone and is seventy-three metres above sea level.

EMU BAY ■ 1872

Emu Bay, a popular swimming and fishing beach, was once the island's main port and was called Maxwell. In later years, shipping called at Kingscote to overcome the problems of shallow water and exposure to the winds. Before the jetty was built around 1916, cargo was taken off at Emu Bay by ketch. Ferrying it to and fro by long boat and slinging it aboard was a tricky process even in good weather. Grain had to be kept dry and livestock controlled. There was at least one instance of 'cow overboard' – she swam to shore and made her escape into the bush.

FLINDERS CHASE NATIONAL PARK ■ 1873

This reserve covers nearly seventeen per cent of Kangaroo Island. Within its boundaries there are representatives of almost all the native flora and fauna, spectacular geographical formations, two lighthouse sites and treacherous offshore points where many ships have foundered. The graves of David Kilpatrick from the *Loch Sloy*, which was wrecked in 1899, and an unknown victim from the *Loch Vennachar* (1905) are both within the park.

Bones of long-extinct animals have been found in swampy ground at Flinders Chase. Among them are the remains of very large kangaroos and rhinoceros-sized diprotodons – massive herbivorous creatures with some characteristics of the modern kangaroo and wombat.

There was no road access to Cape de Couedic in 1906, so the lighthouse's audacious builders winched all their materials up the cliff face by flying fox.

The island really lives up to its name at the Rocky River visitor area where kangaroos mob people and special enclosures are provided for picnickers to eat in peace. After Matthew Flinders' kangaroo kill in 1802, the numbers were drastically reduced over the following thirty years. The island's macropods are a larger, longer-haired, darker-coloured subspecies of the mainland western grey kangaroo and were lucky to escape extinction. Emus in the chase also vie for food scraps but these are introduced birds. The small Kangaroo Island native emus were wiped out by the sealers and whalers.

The absence of dingoes and feral predators is a bonus for the native animals and a number of mainland species have been successfully introduced to the island, including koalas, platypuses and brush turkeys. The island is free of foxes, rabbits and other European animal pests. It has also escaped takeovers by most introduced weeds and is a kaleidoscopic riot of heathland flowers in spring. There are more than fifty species of orchids and a great many other flowering plants and shrubs in all shades of the spectrum.

CAPE DU COUEDIC Cape du Couedic forms the southernmost extremity of Flinders Chase. An automatically controlled lighthouse was erected on this point in 1906. At nearby Weirs Cove the remains of a jetty, water tank and storeroom are all there is to show of the complicated arrangements for hauling building materials and stores up the precipitous cliffs by flying fox. Sleek New Zealand fur seals sun themselves at the base of Cape du Couedic on the rocks surrounding Admiral's Arch, an unusual limestone rock formation created by collapsed caves.

HARVEYS RETURN ■ 1874

This rugged cove was used by a gang of sealers, led by Joseph Murrell. They were just some of the tough characters known as 'sea rats' who unofficially occupied the island for about thirty years before the landing at Reeves Point. The place took the name of a man who came ashore there after his mates had given him up for dead. During the construction of the Cape Borda lighthouse, Harveys Return was the offloading spot for stores which were then hauled up the steep cliffs. The weathered headstones in the cemetery nearby are poignant reminders of the difficult lives of the pioneers.

KELLY HILL CONSERVATION PARK ■ 1875

The Kelly Hill Conservation Park covers about 6307 hectares of coastal dunes and limestone rises carpeted in a dense tangle of mallee and heath and some low-lying swampy patches. The reserve embraces excellent beaches and striking coastal scenery but is most visited for its caves.

These limestone chambers decorated with their interesting stalactites and stalagmites were literally stumbled upon in the 1880s when a stockman named Kelsy was riding his horse, 'Ned Kelly', through the thick scrub. His mount suddenly fell into a sinkhole. Kelsy went for help but when he returned the horse had disappeared. The local people tended to avoid the area until the caves were rediscovered in 1925.

KINGSCOTE ■ 1876

Kingscote, the main settlement on Kangaroo Island, is about 110 kilometres from Adelaide. It is where South Australia's first official white settlement began, and was named by Samuel Stephens, the first manager of the South Australian Company in July 1836. It has developed as a thriving holiday destination.

Kangaroo Island rates as the third largest island in Australia, smaller only than Tasmania and Melville Island. It has a surface area of 4350 square kilometres and 450 kilometres of coastline. Sheep and crops could not flourish on the island until it was discovered that the soil lacked cobalt and copper. Once traces of these essential elements were added, successful agriculture became possible. In 1906, the Kangaroo Island Eucalyptus Company was exporting its distinctive oil to England, thus establishing the first truly Australian export product (see box, *Heathcote & Nagambie*); oil is still produced in Kingscote in small quantities. Another early export which continues on a very small scale is the collection of yacca gum, cut from the yacca trees which are peculiar to the island. It is used in the manufacture of varnishes and explosives. Since the export of gypsum from Ballast Head ceased in the early 1990s, fishing and tourism have become Kingscote's predominant industries. *Population 1440*

REEVES POINT On 27 July 1836, the first colonists arrived from England aboard the *Duke of York* and disembarked at Reeves Point, just north of Kingscote, which is the site of South Australia's first official settlement. These emigrants were sponsored by the South Australian Company. Two-year-old Elizabeth Beare was the first emigrant to reach the shore, carried by a sailor to the water's edge. Years later, her niece laid the foundation stone of the Pioneers' Memorial, which was unveiled in 1936.

The Reeves Point settlement lasted less than four years, although about 300 people lived there at its peak and 42 buildings were completed. The location had three problems that were difficult for the pioneers to overcome: there was no fresh water, the soil was poor and the dense vegetation took too much effort to clear. But one of those first settlers planted a mulberry tree which, tied and propped, still produces enough fruit to be made into jam each year! The Reeves Point quarry once supplied basalt rock that was used in the construction of the road from Port Adelaide to Adelaide.

Despite the predations of sealers, New Zealand fur seals have reclaimed their Flinders Chase coast.

FESTIVALS Kangaroo Island Racing Carnival, late February.

PARNDANA ■ 1877

Parndana, 'the place of little gums', is the hub of a thriving farming community. It grew up as the service town for the surrounding soldier settlements, which were established after the Second World War when the island's soil deficiencies had been corrected. Logging to clear the land began in 1948, the first blocks were sown in 1950, the township started in 1951 and the following year families moved into the homesteads. Sheep and cattle grazing now predominate with some cereal growing.

PARNDANA CONSERVATION PARK ■ 1878

Parndana Conservation Park is dedicated to the preservation of native stringybark and banksias. The small area of 310 hectares has a hilly terrain on the edge of the Kohinoor Plateau which drops steeply to a tributary of the Cygnet River. The park is well stocked with island kangaroos and tammar wallabies and koalas have been introduced. With luck and some patience, several other nocturnal animals, including the bandicoot, may be spotted after dark.

PENNESHAW ■ 1879

The Dudley Peninsula is separated from the western part of the island by a narrow neck with the pleasant little town of Penneshaw on its north-east coast. Its name is derived from Dr Pennefather who was private secretary to Governor Jervois and Miss Flora Shaw, who was head of the Colonial Department of the London *Times*.

Some say the early sealers brought in pigs from Sydney and Van Diemen's Land, others claim the wild pigs on the island are descendants of domestic ones released by Captain Baudin. Either way, Freshwater Bay soon became known as Hog Bay, one of several porcine names to grace places on the peninsula. Fairy penguins patrol the Penneshaw foreshore after dark and during the day their young are tucked away in the rocks between Christmas Cove and Hog Bay.

In 1881, August Fiebig brought twelve hives of bees from the Italian province of Liguria and set them up in an apiary near Penneshaw where they lived on nectar and pollen from the native flora. No other breeds have since been imported to cross with these gentle natured, golden coloured Ligurian bees and the strain is thought to be genetically pure. Kangaroo Island queen bees are exported overseas and interstate for breeding purposes and the local swarms have so far remained free of mainland diseases.

FRENCHMANS ROCK At the end of the beach there is a replica of Frenchmans Rock, inscribed by a French sailor waiting for the ship's water casks to fill: 'expedition de decouverte par le Commendant Baudin, sur le Géographe, 1803' (Expedition of discovery by Captain Baudin in the *Geographe* 1803).

Captain Nicholas Baudin and his crew came ashore after meeting with Matthew Flinders in Encounter Bay and hearing his account of the island. The original rock is in the South Australian Art Gallery where it was moved in 1918 after a dome built over it in 1906 failed to provide adequate protection from the elements.

REMARKABLE ROCKS ■ 1880

This aptly named geographical feature is a group of granite boulders perched on the great granite dome of Kilpatrick Point within the domain of Flinders Chase National Park. Wind and water erosion has sculpted them into remarkable shapes. The headland was formed about 500 million years ago and the rocks are the result of the gradual wearing away of the softer limestone. Camera-toting visitors should beware; the weathering process has left a smooth, slippery surface across which strong winds often blow, so the rocks must be approached with caution.

SEAL BAY CONSERVATION PARK ■ 1881

From a conservation point of view, Seal Bay Conservation Park is one of the most optimistic places in Australia. It protects a breeding colony of sea lions whose forebears somehow escaped total annihilation by the early sealers. They were still being killed for shark bait after 1950 and the proclamation of this sanctuary in 1954 came just in time. Now the group of several hundred animals represents about ten per cent of the world's total number. Their food supply is further protected by an aquatic reserve which restricts fishing along the full length of the park and for one kilometre out to sea.

At Seal Bay it is all too easy to realise how these beautiful creatures were once slaughtered with such success. Relaxed family groups frolic in the water or loll about the beach soaking up the warm sun, apparently unperturbed by the presence of humans. Photographs can be taken at close quarters but protective mothers and jealous bull seals sometimes launch swift land attacks. Unlucky recipients will soon find a sea lion's bite is much worse than its bark.

VIVONNE BAY CONSERVATION PARK ■ 1882

Vivonne Bay is named in honour of Louis Victor Rochechouart, Duc de Mortemart et de Vivonne. The bay is as impressive as the grand name and title and one of the most beautiful places along the island's shores, but it has a strong, treacherous undertow in some parts and swimming is only safe around the jetty and boat ramp or at the mouth of the Harriet River.

Vivonne Bay is the only safe boat harbour on the south coast. The jetty was built in 1911 and decked with jarrah wood at an almost prohibitive cost for those days. It stretches for over 300 metres into the bay but a walk to the end of it is out of the question...during the Second World War, enthusiastic Local Defence Volunteers blew a huge gap in the centre to hinder possible Japanese invaders and the decking has never been replaced. Game fishing boats also leave from here and world-record tuna catches have been made in the surrounding waters.

LITTLE SAHARA Little Sahara is a collection of shifting white sand dunes just inland from Vivonne Bay, which can be reached from the South Coast Road. They do not have a beach frontage as might be expected but are completely surrounded by bush.

WESTERN RIVER CONSERVATION PARK ■ 1883

The Western River Conservation Park encloses more than 2300 hectares of coastal cliffs, steep gorges and hilly terrain which is covered with stringybark forest and woodland. Kangaroo Island kangaroos and tammar wallabies roam undisturbed and there is a population of feral pigs and goats. The pigs were responsible for nomenclature on Dudley Peninsula, and a goat, run wild, no doubt inspired the name for the park's Billygoat Falls.

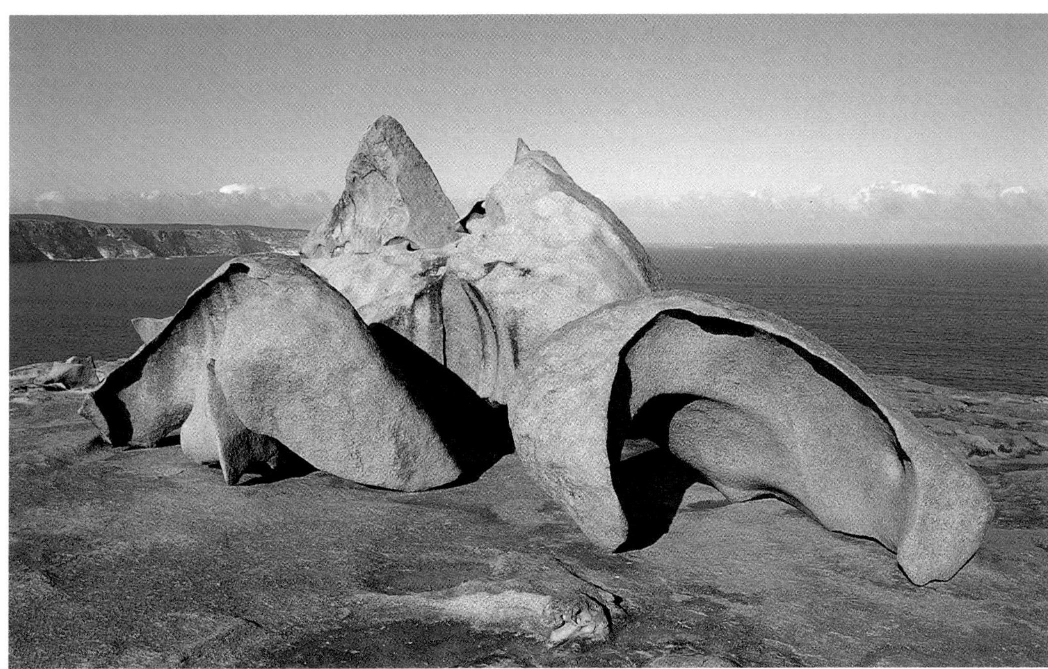
Constant exposure to salt-laden southerlies erodes Kangaroo Island's clifftop rocks into sculptural shapes.

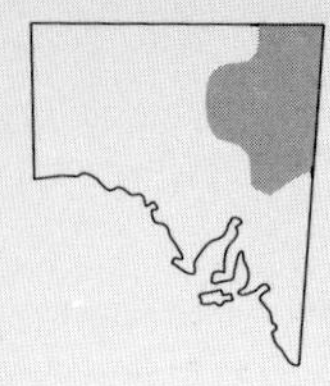

Leigh Creek & Marree

Only the hardiest explorers and settlers were able to withstand the rigours of the north-eastern corner of South Australia, but the Aborigines, who are still here, have a rich heritage of sacred sites and Dreamtime legends.

ANGORICHINA ■ 1884

Angorichina, constructed in 1927 as a sanatorium for returned servicemen suffering from tuberculosis, has been transformed into a holiday village for people visiting the central Flinders Ranges. It is in the Parachilna Gorge and is the starting point for walking tracks to locations such as Blinman Pools, Wild Dog Gap, Mount Falkland, Mount Mary and sections of the Heysen Trail (see *Port Pirie & Clare*). The name Angorichina comes from the Aboriginal word 'janaritjina', thought to mean 'open place'.

ARKAROOLA ■ 1885

The Arkaroola–Mount Painter wildlife sanctuary and resort village is a remote and starkly beautiful area of the Flinders Ranges, dotted with hot springs, gorges, waterholes, unusual mineral and gemstone deposits and some of the oldest land formations in the ranges.

Arkaroola takes its name from the Aboriginal legend of the Dreamtime serpent Arkaroo, which slithered down from the Gammon Ranges to slake its thirst. After drinking Lakes Frome and Callabonna dry, the serpent dragged its bloated body back to its mountain lair, carving out Arkaroola Gorge and Creek, and creating waterholes where it stopped to pass water. Frequent but minor earth tremors in the area are attributed to the gastric rumblings of the now dormant serpent.

RIDGETOP TRACK The rugged Ridgetop Track which runs past Mount Painter to a pinnacle called Siller's Lookout, provides a bird's-eye-view of the Flinders' prehistoric landforms, including Mount Gee, also known as Crystal Mountain because it is composed almost entirely of quartz crystals. The track is not open to private vehicles, but four-wheel-drive tours depart regularly from Arkaroola Village.

BOLLA BOLLANA SPRING AND NOOLDOONOOLDOONA WATERHOLE These waterholes west of Arkaroola Village are also associated with the legend of Arkaroo. Bolla Bollana waterhole – 'where the culprits got up and fled' – was the campsite for Dreamtime Aborigines who set out to ambush the serpent, Arkaroo, at Nooldoonooldoona waterhole – 'place of falling rocks'. Today, one huge boulder all but blocks off a nearby gorge. Nooldoonooldoona is considered the most spectacular of the waterholes in the region.

BOLLA BOLLANA SMELTER Copper ore was mined extensively in the area during the 1860s and ore from mines up to thirty kilometres away was carted to the Bolla Bollana smelter for treatment. The ruins of the old copper smelters, built by Cornish miners in 1871, are all that remain.

ECHO CAMP WATERHOLE One of the most beautiful waterholes in the Northern Flinders, the tranquil Echo Camp Waterhole is located at the mouth of Radium Creek.

STUBBS WATERHOLE This is a long expanse of still water set between towering layers of rocks and boulders formed from the debris shoved aside by melting glaciers more than 740 million years ago.

BELTANA ■ 1886

Beltana is a ghost town which has been restored to its colonial appearance. The town was gazetted in 1873 and was the base for pioneer pastoralists Thomas Elder and Robert Barr Smith, co-founders of the Elder Smith company. The camels used in the construction of the Overland Telegraph Line to Darwin in the 1870s came from the breeding farm established by Thomas Elder at Beltana Station (see box).

The town declined in the 1950s with the growth of the coal-mining centre at Leigh Creek but many of its public buildings, including the police station (1881), post and telegraph office (1875), bush hospital (1898) and school (1892) were privately purchased and have been preserved. Beltana Homestead, the oldest building in the district, is the original pastoral property from which the town took its name.

Remains of the campsites and tool manufacturing sites of the Aborigines who occupied the area before European settlement can still be seen in the area.

SLIDING ROCK Twenty-two kilometres from Beltana, Sliding Rock was the site of a copper mine in the 1870s. In 1877, the mine flooded and after several unsuccessful attempts to drain it, the water was put to good use and piped to Leigh Creek where it is still a secondary supply.

BIRDSVILLE TRACK ■ 1887

This notoriously rugged dirt track between Marree in South Australia and Birdsville in Queensland was developed in the 1880s as a stock

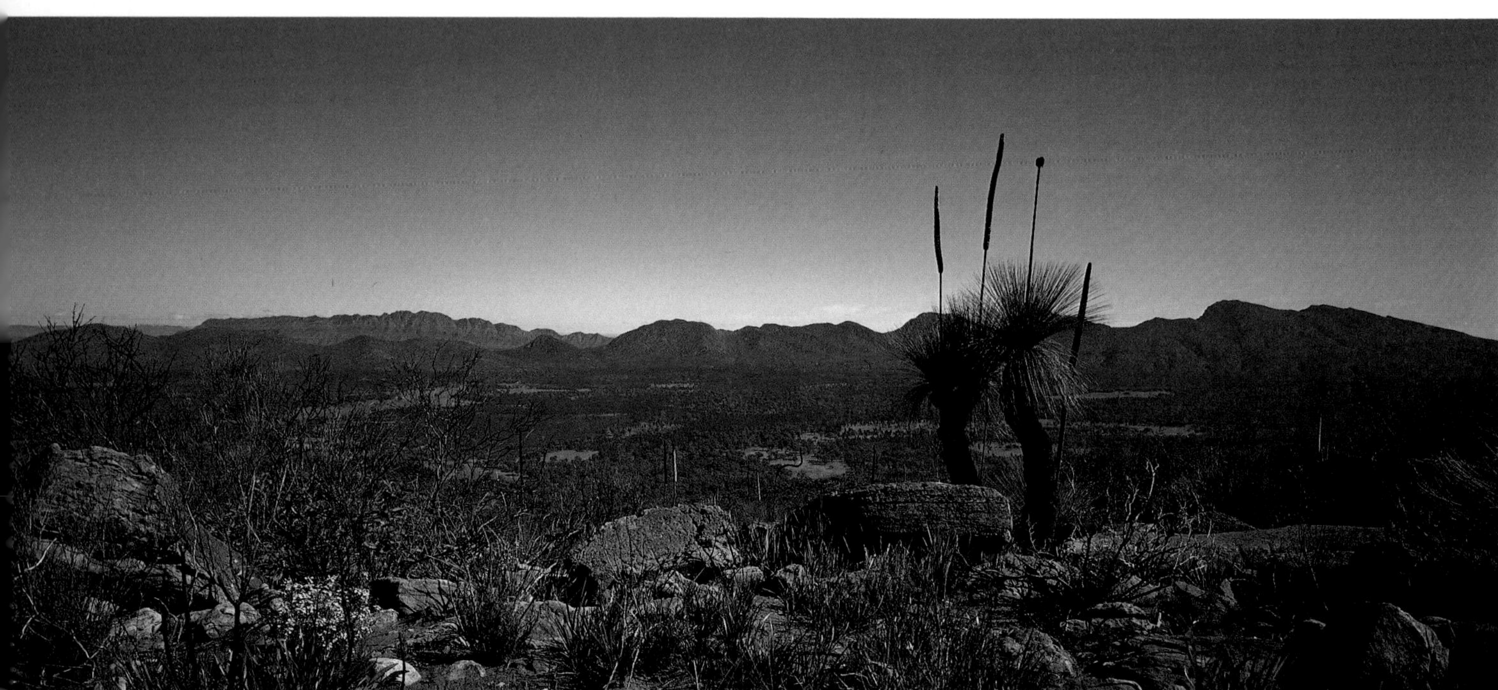

Deep within the time-scarred landscape of the Flinders Ranges, Wilpena Pound's sides provide a rainwater run-off bonus for its oasis-like, 'crater' floor.

Abandoned homesteads throughout the Flinders Ranges testify to a harsh landscape that did not yield readily to stock-grazing European settlers.

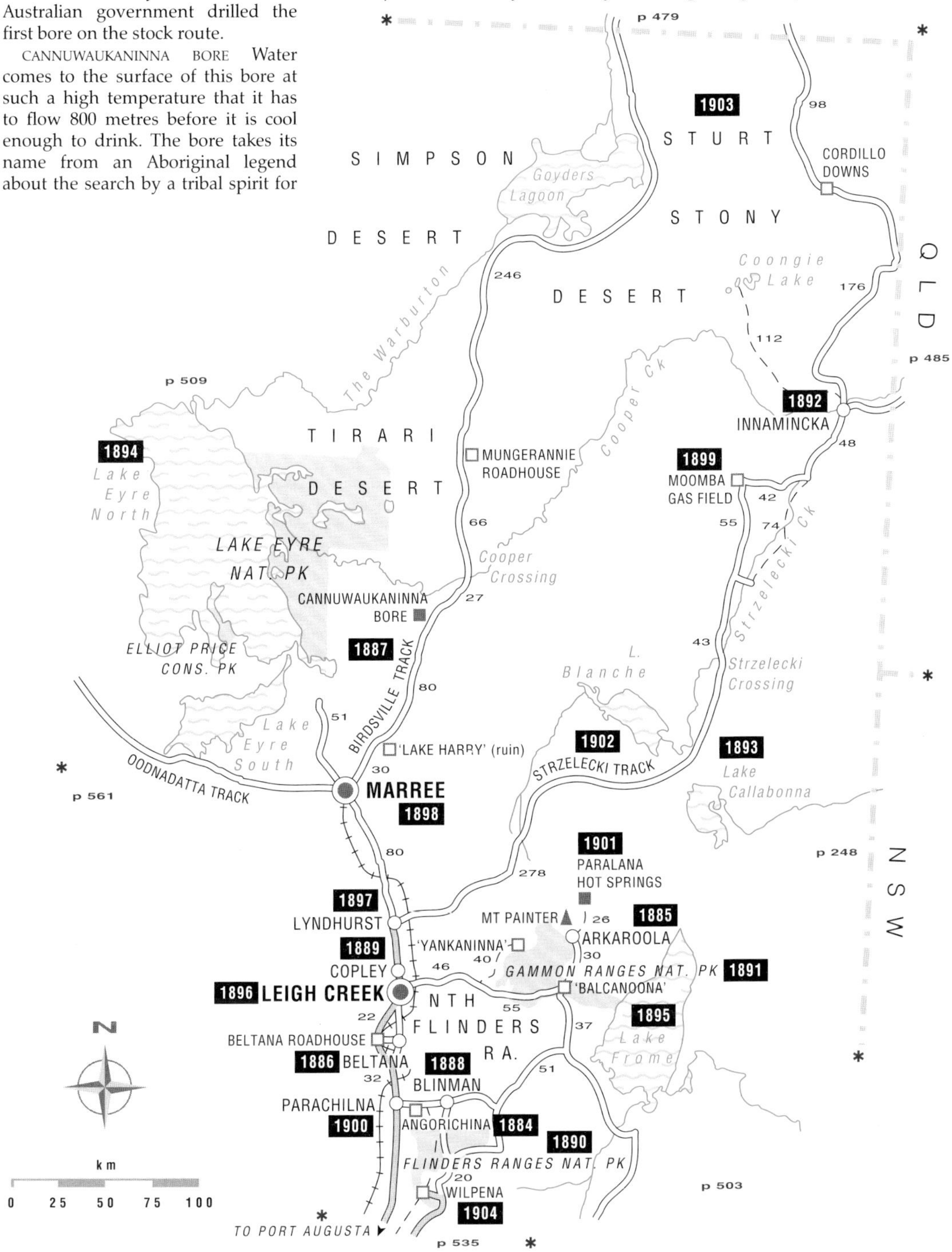

route for drovers bringing cattle – up to 10 000 head at a time – from south-west Queensland to the railhead at Marree. Artesian bores dug by the government provided water for the cattle along the way.

The track skirts some of the driest areas of Australia, passing between the Simpson Desert and the Sturt Stony Desert. Sudden – albeit infrequent – rain can cause the area to flood and the unsealed Birdsville Track to become impassable. Human habitation is limited to a scattering of remote homesteads.

LAKE HARRY RUINS Once a busy camel trading post, this old homestead has been deserted since 1951. Situated about thirty kilometres north-east of Marree, the homestead is near Lake Harry where the South Australian government drilled the first bore on the stock route.

CANNUWAUKANINNA BORE Water comes to the surface of this bore at such a high temperature that it has to flow 800 metres before it is cool enough to drink. The bore takes its name from an Aboriginal legend about the search by a tribal spirit for two dogs that escaped it at Beltana. The spirit tracked the errant dogs through difficult terrain, eventually reaching Cannuwaukaninna, which means 'place where the spirit complained of tired legs'. It continued to search until the dogs were found at Kiltallie-Oola, meaning 'two dogs'.

TOM BRENNAN BARGE–COOPER CROSSING The old barge, 'Tom Brennan', which was used up to 1956 to ferry travellers, stock and provisions over the flood prone Cooper Creek (see *Quilpie & Thargomindah*) is now on display at Cooper Crossing. A ferry is still used to transport vehicles during flood conditions.

BLINMAN ■ 1888

The discovery of copper in December 1859 resulted in the birth of Blinman. Robert 'Pegleg' Blinman, a one-legged shepherd employed at Angorichina station, was tending his sheep when he noticed signs of copper in an outcrop of rock. He secured a mineral lease but later sold out to a syndicate of Adelaide businessmen, which in turn sold the lease in 1862 to the Ydnamutana Copper Company for 70 000 pounds sterling.

Over the next thirty years, 10 000 tonnes of copper metal was extracted at Blinman. Nowadays there is little ore left and the only reminders of the town's bustling past are the mine workings in the hills and early dwellings such as the North Blinman Hotel – built in 1869 and now dramatically juxtaposed with an indoor swimming pool – the police station (1874) and the old miner's cottage dating from 1862.

GLASS'S, CHAMBERS AND BIG MORRO GORGES All routes to Blinman pass through one or other of these steep-walled gorges. In spring, their slopes are covered with spectacular displays of wildflowers. Ancient Aboriginal rock carvings adorn the walls of Chambers Gorge and at Big Morro there are limpid rock pools beneath the sheer cliffs.

GREAT WALL OF CHINA South of Blinman on the Wilpena Road is a ridge capped with remarkably flat, rocky outcrops of such evenness that they appear as though they have been man-made. The outcrop's more prosaic name is Mount Emily.

THE BLINMAN POOLS This secluded permanent waterhole, near the junction of the Parachilna and Blinman creeks, is reached by trekking along the winding creekbed between steep rock faces.

COPLEY ■ 1889

Originally a railway station called Leigh Creek, Copley was named in 1891 after William Copley, Commissioner of Crown Lands, and the railway settlement that had existed for ten years was simply absorbed into the new town. Some confusion over identity obviously resulted with having the Leigh Creek Railway Sta-

SIMPSON DESERT
STURT STONY DESERT
TIRARI DESERT
Goyders Lagoon
The Warburton
CORDILLO DOWNS
Coongie Lake
QLD
NSW
INNAMINCKA 1892
MOOMBA GAS FIELD 1899
MUNGERANNIE ROADHOUSE
Cooper Ck
Cooper Crossing
Strzelecki Ck
Strzelecki Crossing
L. Blanche
Lake Eyre North 1894
LAKE EYRE NAT. PK
CANNUWAUKANINNA BORE
1887
ELLIOT PRICE CONS. PK
Lake Eyre South
BIRDSVILLE TRACK
OODNADATTA TRACK
STRZELECKI TRACK
'LAKE HARRY' (ruin)
MARREE 1898
1902
Lake Callabonna 1893
1903
PARALANA HOT SPRINGS 1901
MT PAINTER
ARKAROOLA 1885
LYNDHURST 1897
'YANKANINNA'
COPLEY 1889
GAMMON RANGES NAT. PK 1891
1896 LEIGH CREEK
'BALCANOONA'
NTH FLINDERS RA.
Lake Frome 1895
BELTANA ROADHOUSE
1886 BELTANA
1888 BLINMAN
PARACHILNA 1900
ANGORICHINA 1884
1890
FLINDERS RANGES NAT. PK
WILPENA 1904
TO PORT AUGUSTA
p 479 p 485 p 509 p 561 p 248 p 503 p 535
km 0 25 50 75 100

tion and Post Office in the middle of the town of Copley. The early residents stubbornly adhered to the original name, even naming the local pub Leigh Creek Hotel.

RED GORGE HISTORIC RESERVE One of the largest concentrations of Aboriginal rock engravings in the Flinders Ranges is at Red Gorge, fifteen kilometres south-east of Copley. The motifs include representations of animals in the form of lizard, emu, kangaroo and dingo tracks as well as some of the few human figures found in South Australian Aboriginal engraving sites.

FLINDERS RANGES NATIONAL PARK ■ 1890

Flinders Ranges National Park is made up of a substantial (92 746 hectares) – and outstanding – portion of the central Flinders Ranges and is one of the best-known national parks in Australia (see special feature, pp. 512–13).

The park is a striking example of the semi-arid scenery typical of the region, with rugged, low ranges and rocky escarpments, deep gorges and grassy valley plains. The vegetation is sparse and shrubby with forests of native pines, casuarinas and wattles found in the valleys and river red gums along the creeks. In the spring masses of wildflowers, including the introduced Flinders Ranges hops, bloom on the slopes, colouring the hillsides with a profusion of reds, pinks, yellows, mauves and white. The park is home to a wide variety of wildlife including red kangaroos and wallabies, including the rare yellow-footed rock wallaby, as well as flocks of rosellas and galahs, emus and the wedge-tailed eagle.

At the heart of the park is Wilpena Pound, which is generally regarded as South Australia's most widely known landform (see sub-entry). To the north, the dominant peaks of the Heysen Ranges enclose the Bunyeroo and Aroona valleys where Sir Hans Heysen worked on many of his famous landscape paintings. Also within the Heysen Ranges is the Bookartoo Historic Reserve, site of a sacred Aboriginal ochre quarry.

WILPENA POUND Wilpena Pound is an immense, elevated, amphitheatre encircled by sheer cliffs of reddish quartzite and sandstone. Its apparent symmetry is the chance result of massive earth movements more than 450 million years ago which folded and lifted the compacted layers of an ancient sea. The softer shales weathered away leaving a precipitous rim of more resistant quartzite standing above the valley floor.

St Marys Peak (1200 metres) on the pound's northern rim is the highest point in the Flinders Ranges. There are walking tracks around its densely wooded slopes. Wilpena is an Aboriginal word meaning 'bent fingers of a cupped hand'; 'pound' comes from the basin's use as a stock run and enclosure in the nineteenth century.

SACRED CANYON Just outside the park, nineteen kilometres south-east of Wilpena, this rocky gorge displays ancient Aboriginal rock carvings and paintings which are thought to date back 20 000 years.

GAMMON RANGES NATIONAL PARK ■ 1891

Despite the spectacular scenery of the Flinders Ranges, the Gammon Ranges National Park is South Australia's chief mountain wilderness area. A major section of the park is made up of a flat quartzite plateau formation dissected by numerous deep gorges. The area is a rich source of Aboriginal legends and numerous stone etchings, painting sites and burial sites are located in the park.

From a humble camp at Italowie Gap, the famous bushman and grazier, R.M. Williams, began making the pack-saddles that were the basis of what eventually became a multi-million dollar business in quality stockmen's apparel. With his partner, 'Dollar' Mick – a colourful character wanted by the law for horse-theft – Williams developed a range of products including the now classic R.M. Williams' elastic-sided boots, which were supplied 'cash with order' to bushmen throughout Australia.

INNAMINCKA ■ 1892

The old Cooper Creek service town of Innamincka was built around a hotel which catered for the drovers bringing cattle down the Strzelecki Track from Queensland to the markets in Adelaide. Before 1901, the town also operated as a customs post on the South Australian–Queensland border when duty had to be paid on inter-colony transactions.

Charles Sturt passed this way in about 1845, and Burke and Wills traversed the area during their ill-fated expedition to the Gulf of Carpentaria in 1860–61 and, after the tragedy of missed chances played out under the Dig Tree (see *Quilpie & Thargomindah*), starved to death near this place in June 1861. Their remains were retrieved for Victoria's first state funeral which was held amid much

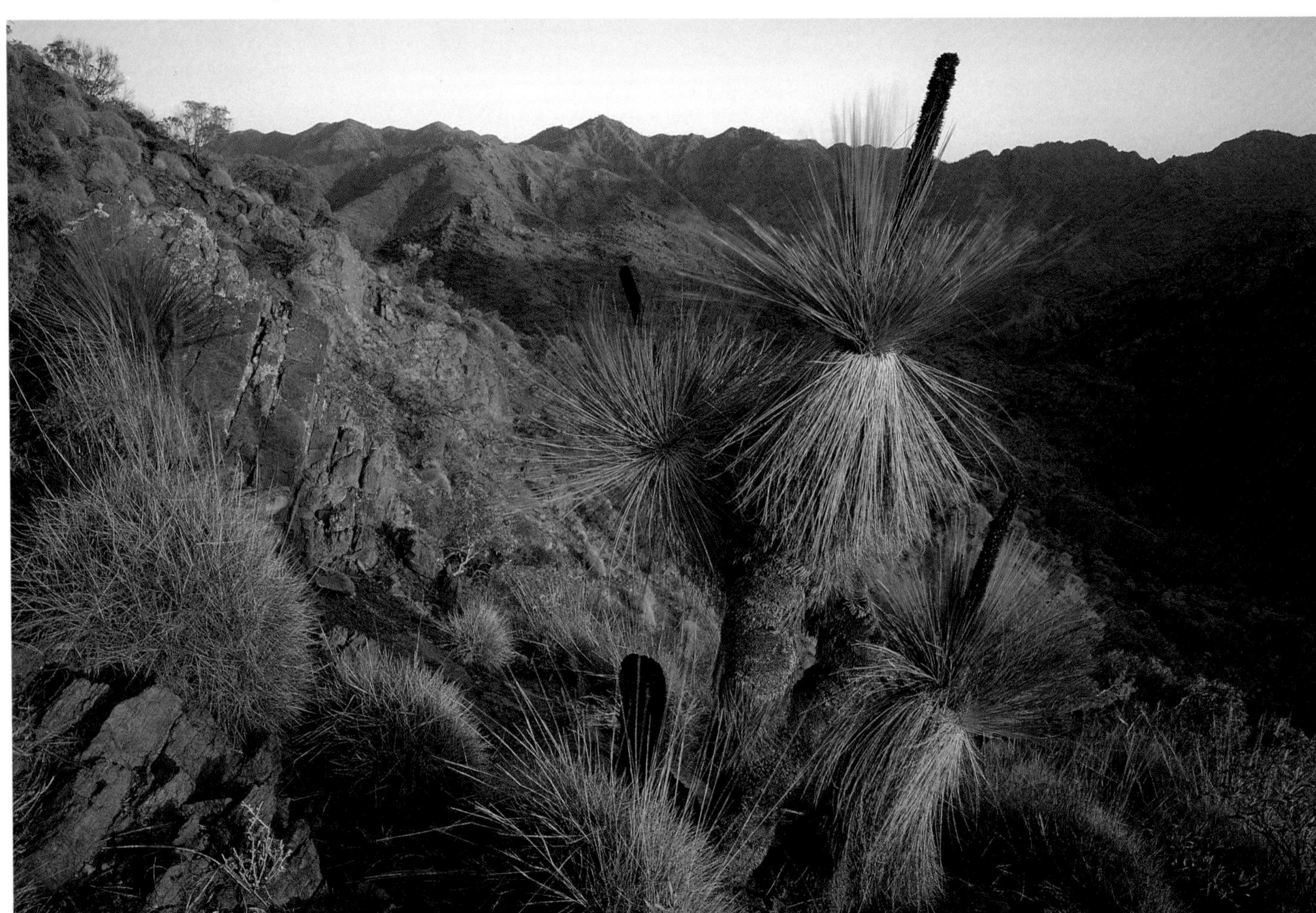

The Mount Lofty grass tree, with a stiffly flared skirt of dead stems, is found only on the rocky slopes of the Mount Lofty, Flinders and Gammon ranges.

At Lake Eyre, where daisies and wild hops spring up along the salty shore, skis offer a novel way of crossing an almost-dry surface.

pomp and ceremony in Melbourne in January 1863. John King, the only surviving member of the expedition, was found near Innamincka waterhole – a memorial, known as King's Marker, has been erected at the spot. King never fully recovered from his ordeal and died nine years later of tuberculosis at the age of thirty-three. A cairn with two memorial plaques commemorating both the Sturt and the Burke and Wills expeditions is located near the ruins of the Innamincka hostel.

Innamincka is a corruption of an Aboriginal word meaning 'you go into the hole there', referring to a legend when a Dreamtime spirit commanded a crocodile to disappear into a hole. The townsite was named Hopetoun in 1890 after Lord Hopetoun – the governor of Victoria who later took on the position of the first governor-general of Australia – but local preference for the Aboriginal name brought about the change to Innamincka in 1892.

COONGIE LAKES These permanent freshwater lakes located in the parched desert region 112 kilometres north-west of Innamincka support a huge variety of native wildlife. The frog community here is probably the most varied in central Australia. Despite the number and variety of wildlife, the lakes and surrounding wetlands form a fragile ecosystem sustained by one major river – Cooper Creek – in an area that averages less than 150 millimetres of rain each year. Without the overflow of flood water from Cooper Creek, Coongie Lake would dry up in 7–9 months – since European discovery in 1844, it has dried up only once.

CULLAMURRA WATERHOLE This natural pool on Cooper Creek lies within the Innamincka Historic Reserve and is surrounded by many hundreds of Aboriginal rock engravings.

LAKE CALLABONNA RESERVE ■ 1893

This reserve, 180 kilometres north-east of Leigh Creek, is the graveyard of prehistoric creatures that roamed what was once part of a vast inland freshwater lake and river system. Australia's largest fossil marsupial, the diprotodon – a creature about the size of a hippopotamus – found one of its last resting places in this unique reserve.

LAKE EYRE ■ 1894

Lake Eyre is the largest salt lake in Australia and the largest salt pan in the world. The lake is split into two parts, north and south, which are connected by the thirteen-kilometre long Goyder Channel. When full the two lakes cover almost 10 000 square kilometres. This happens only three or four times each century because, although the lake's massive catchment area of some 1.3 million square kilometres drains nearly one-sixth of Australia, it includes some of the most arid regions of the continent where the yearly rainfall is often less than 120 millimetres.

Lake Eyre last filled completely in 1989 and was topped up the following year when Cooper Creek again flooded. Overnight the lake was transformed into a haven for a wealth of birdlife such as gulls, pelicans, cormorants and black swans. In places, the lake can be almost six metres deep when full but its waters, if not replenished, will evaporate within two years to a saltpan.

At its lowest point the lakebed is sixteen metres below sea level, making it the lowest land in Australia. The salt-crust surface of the lake is dense enough to take the weight of a heavy vehicle and in 1964 Sir Donald Campbell set a world land speed record of 403.1 miles per hour (645 kilometres per hour) when he raced his jet-powered car, *Bluebird*, across the salt pan.

The lake, like many other landmarks in South Australia, is named in honour of Edward Charles Eyre, the drover turned explorer who devoted his considerable energies and money to the 'useful and honorable career' of exploring the unknown parts of Australia. The explorer led a number of expeditions to the north of South Australia in search of a route to the interior of the continent. In the last of these expeditions, in 1840, he became the first European to sight the lake – a disheartening view as its dry expanse blocked further progress to the north. Although Eyre did not succeed in breaking the 'horseshoe hoodoo' of the northern salt lakes, he nevertheless charted large areas of unexplored country in the arid north before turning his attention to the land lying west of Streaky Bay.

LAKE EYRE NATIONAL PARK Covering more than 1 225 000 hectares of arid desert wilderness, including all of Lake Eyre North and the adjoining Tirari Desert, Australia's dry heart is one of the world's great arid region national parks.

LAKE FROME ■ 1895

A dry salt flat for most of the year, Lake Frome is named after Edward Charles Frome, surveyor-general of South Australia, who abandoned an expedition to Central Australia in 1843 when he found his way blocked by the crusted salt bed of the lake. 'All our dreams of discovery of a large freshwater lake now vanished,' wrote Frome. 'We turned with disgust from this dreary spot'.

LEIGH CREEK ■ 1896

Leigh Creek is South Australia's only coal town. The original town of Leigh Creek ceased to exist when it was found to be in the way of the Leigh Creek coalmining operations. The entire town was moved thirteen kilometres south and the new town opened in 1980.

Leigh Creek now sits on undulating land surrounded by featureless plains. The town is owned by the Electricity Trust of South Australia: most breadwinners work in the coal mining or service industries. Hundreds of thousands of native trees and shrubs have been planted, making the town an oasis.

Coal-bearing shale was discovered near Leigh Creek railway siding in 1888, though mining did not start in earnest until the 1940s when a coal shortage prompted the South Australian Government to begin a search for the state's own deposits. Drilling began at the coalfields in 1941 and the mine produces more than two million tonnes of coal each year for the power stations at Port Augusta.

Settlement of the Leigh Creek area began around 1841 and the town is named after Harry Leigh, the head stockman for Alexander Glen, who took up a cattle run in this part of the country in 1856. *Population 1380*

YALPUNA VERI SITE The extensive collection of ancient Aboriginal rock art paintings found at Yalpuna Veri, south-east of Leigh Creek, are a very well-preserved example of the spectacular rock art galleries found in the Flinders Ranges.

LYNDHURST ■ 1897

As the starting point for the Strzelecki Track, the small town of Lyndhurst is an essential supply centre on the edge of the outback. In 1858, Mount Lyndhurst was named in honour of the British Lord Chancellor, Lord Lyndhurst. When entrepreneur and pastoralist Thomas Elder purchased a sheep run in the area in 1868, he adopted the name for his station. The name was perpetuated in 1896 when the township of Lyndhurst, surveyed around a new rail siding, was officially proclaimed.

MARREE ■ 1898

The tiny town of Marree sits at the junction of two major, but unsealed, outback routes – the Birdsville and Oodnadatta tracks. Despite its size, the town is historically significant, having been an important outback junction for more than a century.

In the late 1800s, Marree was a staging post for Afghan traders whose camel trains – often comprising seventy or more beasts – carried supplies to the isolated settlements of the outback (see box). When motorised transport supplanted their role many camels were turned loose to fend for themselves, in some places creating a major feral animal problem. More than 150 were shot near Marree on one day in the 1930s.

The Ghan train that runs from Adelaide to Alice Springs also took its name from these enterprising Asian traders. Once an important staging-point on the old Ghan route, Marree Station is now in a state of decay

Few regions are as pitilessly inhospitable as the Sturt Stony Desert, described bitterly by the explorer after whom it is named as 'the entrance into Hell'.

because the new standard-gauge line runs almost 200 kilometres to the west (see *Coober Pedy & Marla*).

MOOMBA GAS FIELD ■ 1899

The discovery of natural gas in this region in 1966 led to the establishment of Moomba and its pipelines which snake all the way to Adelaide and Sydney filled with gas. More recently a petroleum liquids pipeline has been laid to Port Bonython near Whyalla. The gas field was named after dry claypans in the area, actually known as Lake Moonba. Petrol company officials changed the name to 'Moomba' because they thought it was easier to pronounce. Moonba is an Aboriginal term meaning 'loud noise' or 'thunder'.

PARACHILNA ■ 1900

This tiny hamlet was first surveyed in 1864 some way east of the present town. It consisted of little more than an inn which provided basic fare for prospectors searching for minerals in the Flinders Ranges. After a few years the settlement declined, only to be revived when railway transportation reached the area in 1882 and a township developed around the Parachilna station, mainly to service the railway. Nowadays, Parachilna consists of a hotel and some railway workers' cottages.

PARALANA HOT SPRINGS ■ 1901

These hot springs are probably the last remnant of the days when Australia's surface was formed by volcanic eruptions. They are actively volcanic, with gases and near-boiling water issuing from a deep fissure in the earth's surface. In the 1920s, Paralana Springs was developed as a health resort for the treatment of rheumatism and related ailments, but the venture failed when the isolated location proved too difficult for prospective customers to reach.

STRZELECKI TRACK ■ 1902

The rough Strzelecki Track holds a colourful place in Australian outback lore. Running from Lyndhurst and passing through salt-lake country to the Moomba Gas Field and Innamincka, the track was pioneered by bushman and cattler duffer Harry Redford, believed to be the inspiration for Captain Starlight in Rolfe Boldrewood's novel *Robbery Under Arms*. In 1870, Redford drove a mob of stolen cattle from Queensland, along Cooper Creek, to Innamincka and from there through the arid lands to the markets in Adelaide.

Drovers followed in Redford's tracks for ten years until an alternative route which offered more watering points for cattle was found – this new route eventually became the southern section of the Birdsville Track. The Strzelecki Track was little used for a number of years until the discovery of natural gas at Moomba brought the historic gravel and earth road back into regular use by modern motor transport.

The track is named in honour of Polish-born explorer, Paul Edmund de Strzelecki, who named Mount Kosciusko and explored Gippsland in southern Victoria.

STURT STONY DESERT ■ 1903

This desolate area in north-eastern South Australia is named after Captain Charles Sturt, who crossed it in 1845 in search of an inland sea. The desert was a daunting terrain for the party to traverse – Sturt thought it 'looked like the entrance into Hell', with 'not a blade of anything for our horses'. Its unyielding surface was covered with gibber, a thick layer of hard, round stones ranging from small pebbles to large boulders. The desert crossing was a grim affair – the horses wore out their shoes on this stony surface and were reduced to shambling. Sturt wrote in his diary, 'My horses are worn out with fatigue and weariness. I myself begin to feel the effects of constant exposure, incessant riding, scarcity of food and anxiety of mind'.

Although inhospitable to humans, the gibber plains are a remarkable natural phenomena. Most of the stone lies on the surface because of the erosion of the finer material in which it was embedded.

WILPENA ■ 1904

This unlikely holiday resort at the foot of Wilpena Pound started as a small chalet in 1947 when the area was first opened to tourists. Since those early days, it has developed into a modern motel complex with a camping ground and caravan park.

THE 'AFGHAN' CONNECTION: FROM PAKISTAN TO THE OUTBACK

THE DEADPAN, indefatigable camel, which roams the outback in the world's last wild herds, is a lumbering monument to central Australia's least glamorous heroes.

These largely unsung pioneers were the camels themselves and their human attendants, the so-called 'Afghan' cameleers – most of whom in fact came from Pakistan, then part of British India – who carried first the explorers into the dry expanses of the interior and then ferried supplies to the settlers and miners who followed them. Sadly these hardworking teams of man and beast were frequently outcasts and generally distrusted – the camels were widely regarded as being nasty of nature and dangerous at both ends, while strange fears were sometimes held about the habits and morals of the cameleers who were forced to live, shunned and alienated, in shanty 'ghantowns' on the edges of isolated railhead settlements.

The western Queensland camel drivers recorded for posterity by a roving photographer in 1895 were clearly determined to illustrate the superior carrying power of the stoic camel on the left.

Camels were ideal for use in the outback. Their large feet were well-adapted to walking on sand and dust and they were able not only to survive on bitter desert plants and drought-withered grass but also to travel for days over waterless terrain, as could no other beast of burden. The first of these animals to reach Australia in any number were those of the team brought from Karachi to transport equipment on the Burke and Wills expedition. This exotic group of twenty-five animals and three cameleers landed in Melbourne in 1860. Six years later Thomas Elder imported 120 camels, mostly females, made up of large, hairy working beasts from Kandahar, fast riding camels from Mekrana, and versatile hill camels from the Sinde. Elder lent some for inland exploration expeditions, and then began breeding them as a commercial venture, forseeing their value in opening up the arid interior. The first stud was developed at Elder's Beltana Station in South Australia and it was here too that the first 'Afghan' settlement in Australia was established.

By the 1880s there were ghantowns of canvas and corrugated iron on the outskirts of a string of inland towns – Bourke, Broken Hill, Port Augusta, Marree, Oodnadatta, Cloncurry, Port Hedland and Marble Bar – and the control of the camel industry was firmly in the hands of the 'Afghan' camel merchants and handlers themselves. For more than fifty years these mysterious men and their strings of up to seventy pack camels – linked by a rope connecting the nosepeg of the animal behind to the tail of the one in front – carried farm equipment and other necessities over half the continent, to the arid lands where railways did not reach and horses could not work.

Camels did not need a made road, and came into their own in times of severest drought. They carted stores to outback pastoral and mining settlements, there loading wool and mineral ores for the return journey. In Cloncurry, they carried copper from mines inaccessible to wagons. In the 1870s, camels were used as transport during the construction of the Overland Telegraph Line from Port Augusta to Darwin and forty years later played a part in the construction across the Nullarbor of the Trans Australia Railway. Camels were also used for police work in northern South Australia from 1881 until the early 1950s.

The camels of Australia are all of the single-humped Arabian variety *Camelus dromedarius*, and this is the only country in the world where they run wild. The feral herds are descendants of the once indispensable teams which, no longer needed after the introduction of motorised transport in the 1930s, were cut loose in unoccupied desert regions. Their 'Afghan' masters also dispersed.

Those with sufficient capital set up small shops and a few returned to their homeland, but most, with few marketable skills, found jobs labouring on the railways or in the ports. They brought no women with them and although some of their part-European or part-Aboriginal descendants remained in the ghantowns of their fathers, their grandchildren, by and large, have disappeared into the great mass of Australian society. Apart from grave sites, the occasional remains of a bush mosque, and the name of a famous train, there are few tangible reminders of the cameleers so vital to the opening up of inland Australia. □

A herd of wild camels...a sight to be found no longer in their native lands but only in central Australia.

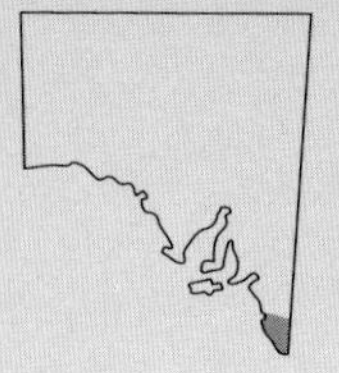

Mount Gambier & Millicent

South Australia's south-east is a region of thriving towns and farmlands, of radiata pine plantations and caverns , of treacherous coastlines and safe anchorages. Among its products are wines, cheeses and seafood to tempt the most jaded gourmet.

BEACHPORT ■ 1905

The Aborigines knew this place as 'wirmalngrang' – 'the cave of the mopoke' but the Acting-Governor of South Australia, Samuel Way, gave it a much more prosaic name in May 1878. This had nothing to do with the natural beach but was chosen to honour the current Secretary of State for the Colonies whose surname was Hicks-Beach. In the same year, the railway was laid between Beachport and Mount Gambier and the town began to attract holiday-makers. The trains no longer run but the erstwhile busy port is valued for its unspoiled natural beauty.

Beachport was settled in the 1830s by the Henty brothers and became the south-east's first whaling station. Today's local fleet goes out with lobster pots rather than harpoons while visitors fish from the beach or jetty with a good chance of catching whiting, mullet, tommy ruff, garfish or mulloway, and the reef areas of the 'Back Beach' are popular with skin and scuba divers. The Pool of Siloam, a lake with high enough salt content to make the water particularly buoyant, is a novel place to swim.

WOAKWINE CUTTING Off the Coastal Ports Highway between Beachport and Robe, there is a viewing platform which provides an interesting insight into the successful efforts of the early settlers to make the land productive. It overlooks the Woakwine Cutting, which was constructed by a local farmer and one helper, to drain a large area of swampland.

BOOL LAGOON ■ 1906

Though much of the south-east has been drained, Bool Lagoon, south of Naracoorte, is preserved as a large wetland drought refuge for waterbirds. It is carefully managed so that there is permanent water. More than seventy-five species of birds inhabit the area and at least half of them are known to breed there. The lagoon's ibis colony is the largest in South Australia and visitors can observe the inhabitants in comfort from the bird hide and board walks.

CANUNDA NATIONAL PARK ■ 1907

This park is a narrow sand barrier extending for about forty kilometres between Cape Buffon and Cape Banks, which traps the shallow fresh water of Lake Bonney and a stretch of flood-prone lowlands in a protected area of 9000 hectares. It has been called a 'miniature Coorong' (see *Bordertown & Keith*). The ever-shifting sand dunes make walking difficult and swimming is dangerous from all the park's beaches. The most frequent human visitors are fisherfolk and the sandhills and wetlands are mainly left for the birds to live in peace. Hair, fur and leopard seals occasionally rest on the beach.

COONAWARRA ■ 1908

The wine district of Coonawarra encompasses some fifteen wineries and the most southerly vineyards in South Australia. The success of the renowned vintages is said to come from the properties of the terra rossa soil. This small area of 'red earth' lies on top of deep limestone sub-soil in a cigar-shaped strip, north of Penola, about sixteen kilometres long and less than two kilometres wide. It was first planted with grapes in 1890 by John Riddoch who established the 'Coonawarra Fruit Colony' and built a winery three years later.

Not all varieties of grapes thrive in the relatively cool climate and the vineyards are planted with cabernet sauvignon, Rhine riesling, shiraz, malbec, semillon, sauvignon blanc, palomino and crouchen grapes. For many years, quality table wines were not much in demand and the viticulturists struggled to make a living. Respect for Coonawarra labels developed in the 1960s and has grown steadily since then.

South Australian museum records state that Coonawarra is derived from the Aboriginal 'kuneia-warama' meaning 'to light a fire'. Other sources prefer to translate it as 'honeysuckle rise'. An early settler saw that the local species of honeysuckle grew only in certain places and later discovered it marked the extent of the terra rossa soil.

FESTIVALS The Vignerons' Cup, November.

DINGLEY DELL CONSERVATION PARK AND MUSEUM ■ 1909

'Dingley Dell' is the name of the restored, whitewashed cottage, dating back to the 1860s, where Scottish poet and horseman, Adam Lindsay Gordon, lived for two years. Legend has it that the previous owner lost the building to Gordon in a card game. Some of his possessions are still on show there and visitors to the park can experience much the same environment of natural scrubland and wattle groves which once fired his imagination. Gordon later moved to Brighton in Victoria.

No blue could be more vividly indigo than the summer shade adopted by Mount Gambier's Blue Lake.

Kingston S.E.'s 'big lobster' may have been inspired by science fiction or a crayman's wishful thinking.

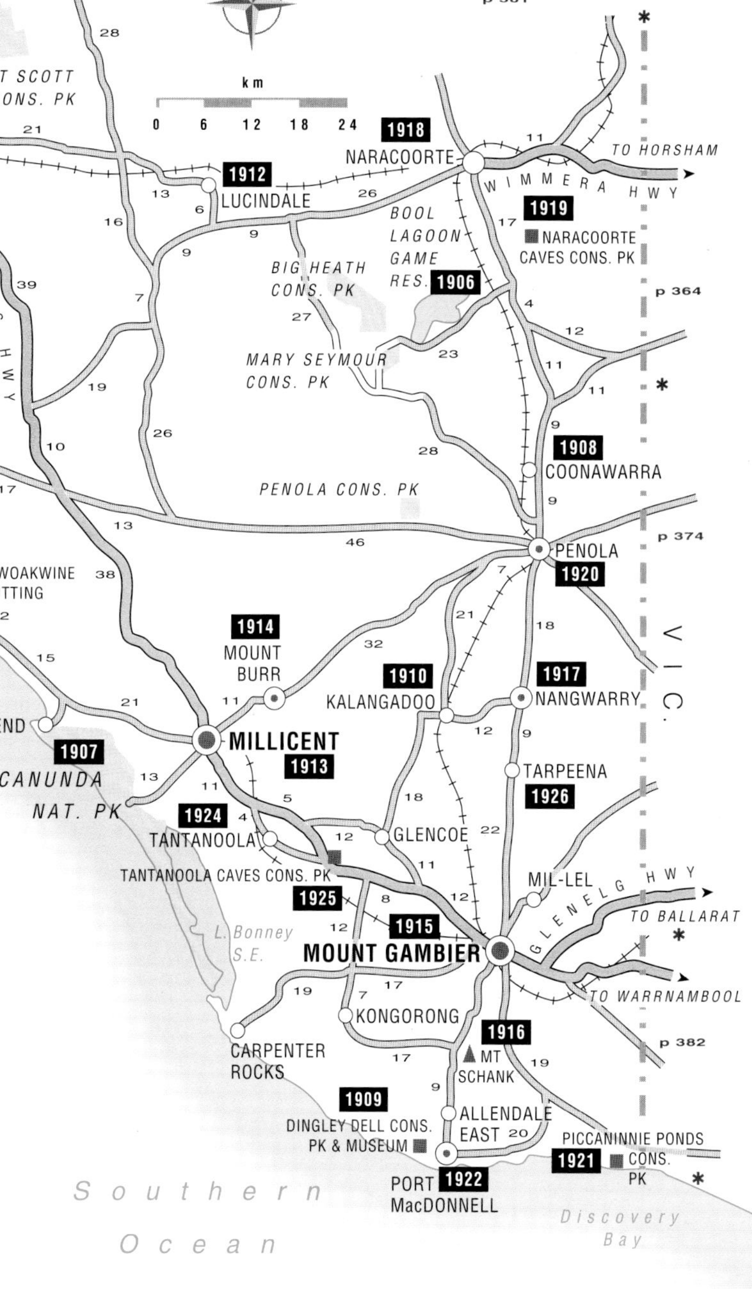

KALANGADOO ■ **1910**

Kalangadoo's economy is based on dairying, wool and vegetables. The original 'Kalangadoo Cattle Run' was taken up as early as 1846 but the town was not proclaimed as Kalangadoo East until 14 October 1891. The second part of the name was dropped fifty years later. The records state that the name either came from 'kalinerta', an Aboriginal word for 'dog watering place', or from 'kelenerte' meaning 'yabbie hole'.

KINGSTON S.E. ■ **1911**

James and Archibald Cooke first took up government grants near Maria Creek in 1856 intending to found 'Port Caroline' on the shores of Lacepede Bay. The name 'Kingston' was given by George Strickland Kingston, speaker of the House of Assembly, who built a house there at the beginning of the venture. The S.E., for south-east, is to avoid confusion with Kingston-on-Murray, also in South Australia.

The town is known locally as the 'Gateway to the Southern Ports' and marks the beginning of lobster territory, displaying a large crustacean rampant, and visible for many kilometres. 'Larry' is seventeen metres high and weighs four tonnes – well over the legal size limit! The first jetty here was very short and ended in water just over a metre deep at low tide so that big ships had to anchor offshore and load by ferry. In 1876, the jetty was extended to deeper water and Kingston's viability as a port improved, until modern road and rail transport put it out of business. The surrounding waters are a veritable 'fisherman's basket' and the spare-time angler can choose to fish from boat, jetty or the beach. Fish are important to the local economy and many people are employed at the town's fish factory.

Aboriginal Australians lived in this region for thousands of years before the first Europeans left their footprints on the sandy beach. A granite memorial by Maria Creek commemorates 'Queen Ethel' Watson, the last full-blooded Aborigine in the district, who died in 1954. *Population 1420*

CAPE JAFFA LIGHTHOUSE The thirty-three-metre tall iron lighthouse at Cape Jaffa should not be confused with the automatic light which now stands on Margaret Brock Reef. The new structure took over in the 1970s but the people of Kingston wanted to preserve this century-old part of their heritage and had the building moved to its present site.

CONSERVATION PARKS Three conservation parks lie within easy reach of Kingston S.E. Twenty kilometres east, the Mount Scott Conservation Park preserves brown stringybark forest inhabited by sugar gliders, wombats and the uncommon mallee fowl (see box, *Warracknabeal & Nhill*). Butchers Gap Conservation Park is a haven for birdlife. It is south-west of Kingston and encloses a seasonally flooded wetland and dense coastal vegetation. Jip Jip Conservation Park, about fifty kilometres north-east of Kingston, is full of large, unusually shaped granite boulders.

FESTIVALS Yachting Carnival, early January; Kingston Surf Fishing Competition, late January.

LUCINDALE ■ **1912**

Governor Musgrave named Lucindale after his second wife, Jeannie Lucinda Musgrave. In May 1877, the post office opened as 'Baker's Range' but that name only lasted a month. The town is small, well planned and proud of its parks and picnic spots. It is the geographical centre of the south-east and principally a rural service outlet with less than three hundred permanent residents.

MILLICENT ■ **1913**

George Glen settled in this district in 1851 and three years later married Millicent Sophia Short, daughter of

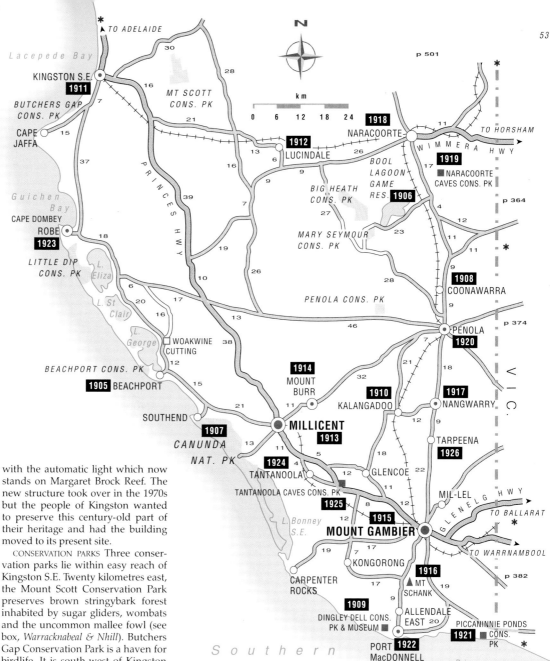

In Penola's side streets, the red-gum slab houses of the 1850s have been given fences and gardens to match their old-fashioned, cottagey appearances.

the first Anglican bishop of Adelaide. Her name was given to the town when it was surveyed in 1870. A farming community grew on the limestone ridge in the middle of the newly drained flats. The swampy land was interlaced with channels and turned into fertile paddocks for stock grazing and barley. At the beginning of this century, pine plantations were developed in the nearby ranges and a new settlement with a sawmill was established close by at Mount Burr (see entry). Two paper mills were later built at Snuggery, south of Millicent, and the population of the area began to expand in the 1960s with a high intake of European migrants. *Population 5120*

MILLICENT NATIONAL TRUST MUSEUM This museum has a reputation as one of the best regional museums in South Australia. The exhibits, which include sixteen restored horse-drawn vehicles, trace the development of farm implements and machines from the 1840s to more modern times.

MOUNT BURR ■ 1914

Mount Burr was named by Governor Grey in 1844 on a trip to Rivoli Bay. His companion on the expedition was one Thomas Burr and the name was chosen out of respect for his father. Mount Burr is a timber town tucked in among the pine trees that are its main source of income. It was not proclaimed until 1976, though the mill which pioneered large-scale softwood sawmilling opened in 1931. Its machinery was updated in 1986.

The south-east has eighty per cent of South Australia's radiata pine forests which are managed by the Woods and Forests Department of South Australia. Its duties include monitoring the sawmills at Mount Burr, Mount Gambier and Nangwarry, caring for many square kilometres of maturing trees, the replacement seedling program and the protection of native flora and fauna. Some of the logs from the pine plantations end up as house frames, floorboards, wall panelling and furniture, others are pulped for use in cardboard and other timber products. *Population 500*

MOUNT GAMBIER ■ 1915

Mount Gambier proper, an extinct volcano, is about mid-way between Melbourne and Adelaide and was the first part of South Australia to be named in 1800. James Grant chose to remember Admiral Gambier who commanded the British fleet at the second battle of Copenhagen in 1807. The Aboriginal name for the district was 'nerebalam' said to mean 'eagle's nest'; an Aboriginal myth told of two birds who were bitter enemies. The crow nested in the crater of the Blue Lake and the eagle's eyrie was on the mountain summit.

The first European to settle in the Mount Gambier district and to see the now famous Blue Lake was Stephen George Henty who arrived in 1839. When explorer Thomas Mitchell reached Mount Gambier a few years later he was surprised to meet him there. The city is built on the slopes of the mountain and is the largest settlement in the south-east.

In keeping with much of the region, Mount Gambier also has caves and holes in the bed of limestone rock beneath it. Among them are the open Umpherstone Cave which has been planted with terraced gardens, Town Hall Cave in the city centre and Engelbrecht Cave, a sinkhole used by divers.

Australia's largest softwood industry operates in Mount Gambier. The sawmill, which opened in 1959 and was modernised in 1980, is capable of processing enough timber each day to construct forty average-sized house frames. The Mount Gambier district also provides another building material in the huge deposits of coralline limestone which has been used for building for over a hundred years. The white stone is cut into blocks at the quarry face and is responsible for the solid, respectable look of many of the city's buildings. The city is the centre of a dairying region and has a reputation for fine cheeses, especially for extra-tasty cheddar. Wool, wheat, cereals and fat lambs are also produced.

Mount Gambier is very proud of its most famous son, Robert Helpmann, who was born there – with one 'n' – in 1909. Helpmann gained a considerable reputation overseas as a ballet dancer, actor and choreographer and has been honoured in his birthplace by an impressive theatre named after him. *Population 21 150*

BLUE LAKE The colour of Blue Lake, the main crater of Mount Gambier's four, is a curious phenomenon. In November each year, the lake turns from its pallid winter grey-green to an intense cobalt blue and remains this glorious colour until late March. Scientists have shown that the onset of warm weather precipitates countless particles of calcite from the waters of Blue Lake, which absorb all visible light except blue. When the water cools in autumn, the particles dissolve once more and the water resumes its less vibrant hue.

The town's domestic water supply is drawn from the lake. An obelisk commemorates Adam Lindsay Gordon's death-defying horseback leap over a post and rail fence onto a rocky ledge sixty metres above the lake. Leg of Mutton Lake, Valley Lake and Browne Lake are within the volcanic cone but remain the regular lake colour all year round.

MOUNT SCHANK ■ 1916

Mount Schank was also sighted and named by Lieutenant James Grant as he sailed past in the *Lady Nelson*. The volcano has been extinct for about 4700 years – a very short time in geological history – and walking tracks on the outside and inside of the crater allow the curious to get a thorough look at this formation. The views from the top are outstanding and to a far horizon because the surrounding plains are so flat.

NANGWARRY ■ 1917

Like Mount Burr, Nangwarry is a true timber town, constantly permeated by the fragrant smell of pine from trees cut close by for the large sawmill which was established in 1939; in the distance there is the snarl of the tree-felling chainsaws, which is not nearly as pleasant. The town was proclaimed in 1974 and took the name of the 'Nangwarry Run' which was established in the area in 1851. It comes from two Aboriginal words, 'naran' meaning 'cave' and 'wari' meaning 'cold'. *Population 640*

NARACOORTE ■ 1918

Settlers first reached this district in the 1840s and called it Mosquito Plains. Two private towns called Kincraig and Skyetown were established first and a hotel and store were built by William Macintosh around the middle of the last century. Naracoorte became the official name from 1869. It came from an Aboriginal word meaning 'large waterhole' or 'running water'. Several imposing limestone buildings from the 1870s and 1880s still grace the town. Today Naracoorte is a busy commercial centre for a rich agricultural and pastoral district which produces wool, fat lambs, beef cattle and seed crops. *Population 4710*

Inland divers at Piccaninnie Ponds roam where clear, subterranean spring water feeds into swamps and sinkholes.

NARACOORTE CAVES CONSERVATION PARK ■ 1919

The limestone rock of Cave Range conceals at least sixty caves decorated with delicate calcite structures. Sixteen of them are in the park and some of these are electrically lit so that visitors can enjoy the sculptures.

Fossil Cave, discovered in 1969, is one of the richest fossil deposits in the world. It contains the bones of animals that scientists believe lived in the Ice Age, up to two million years ago. A display has been set up in the cave so that specimens and excavations can be seen together in a working museum.

At night, one of the park's subterranean chambers disgorges living creatures. The bent-winged bats of Bat Cave move out to feed – a swarm of natural insect controllers. In the summer months, the population may be between one and two hundred thousand – the cave is a favourite breeding site. The numbers drop to a few thousand during winter.

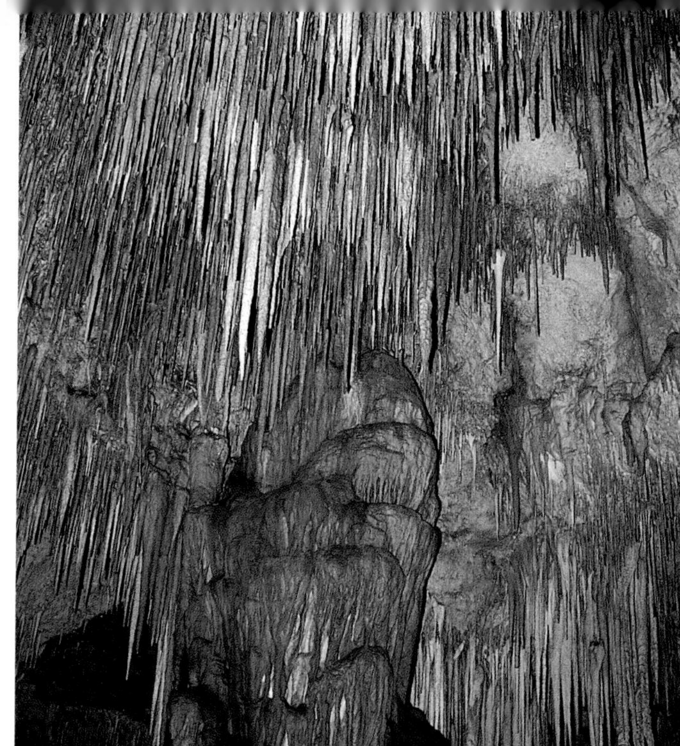

The main cave at Tantanoola, with its fearsome-looking ceiling, is open to the public; special tours are made of the 'wild' cave underground system.

PENOLA ■ 1920
Penola is the oldest town in the south-east region and cherishes its historical buildings such as the remains of a grand old railway station and several slab and hewn cottages from the 1850s. Petticoat Lane has a particularly interesting collection of these old buildings with landscaped gardens and red-gum guttering in the style of their humble beginnings. The 1857 Cobb & Co. office can also be visited.

In 1866, Mother Mary MacKillop established the first school to cater for children regardless of their parents' income or social class. She also founded the Congregation of The Sisters of St Joseph of the Most Sacred Heart of Jesus in South Australia. Her achievements are so highly regarded that she has long been seen as destined to become Australia's first saint.

Penola's name is derived from 'penaoorla' meaning 'big swamp' or from 'penaurla' meaning 'stringy bark forest' or from 'pano' meaning 'earthy'. The present interests of this town are based on pastoral and forestry industries. *Population 1150*

YALLUM PARK Yallum Park is a gracious, two-storey Victorian mansion built by John Riddoch who planted the first grapes in the Coonawarra district. In the early days, the Penola squattocracy were famous for their picnic race meetings and turf balls. Adam Lindsay Gordon was a guest at Yallum Park and in 1881 Prince Edward and Prince George – later King George V – spent a night there.

PENOLA CONSERVATION PARK This reserve lies west of the town and encloses a large seasonal swamp. It is particularly noted for its wildflowers and is home to western grey kangaroos and rock and Parma wallabies.

FESTIVALS The Penola Festival Poets' Week, August.

PICCANINNIE PONDS CONSERVATION PARK ■ 1921
The main feature of the Piccaninnie Ponds Conservation Park is a chain of deep ponds in a reed swamp. Cave divers are lured to challenge the depths but entry to the treacherous beauty of the sinkholes is limited to only those with the appropriate scuba-diving permits. The information about who can and cannot dive is available from the Cave Divers' Association in Mount Gambier.

PORT MacDONNELL ■ 1922
Port MacDonnell is the most southerly port in South Australia and was named in 1860 after Sir Richard Graves MacDonnell, the then Governor of South Australia. This one time bustling trading centre which sent freight to Adelaide and Melbourne in the second half of the nineteenth century is much changed, though the historic customs house is an imposing reminder of the past.

Contemporary Port MacDonnell has the atmosphere of a fishing village and is base to the state's largest rock lobster fleet. From October to May, pots are laid on the floor of the Southern Ocean to catch these marine delicacies, more commonly known as crayfish. *Population 680*

ROBE ■ 1923
Nicholas Baudin named Guichen Bay in 1802 and noted the rugged coastline, but did not stop to explore its secluded beaches. One of them, called simply Long Beach, is seventeen kilometres of enticingly clean sand. The sealers of the early 1830s were probably the first Europeans to enjoy it. In 1839, Charles Bonney and ten others drove three hundred head of cattle along a coastal stock route from New South Wales and focussed attention on the south-east region.

The Port of Robe, proclaimed in 1847, honoured Lieutenant-Colonel Frederick Holt Robe, Governor of South Australia between October 1845 and August 1848. The town grew gradually as an export centre for wool and horses, and was laid out around Royal Circus where enough space had to be left for a bullock team to turn round after unloading a wool dray. Many fine buildings from this period still stand.

By the mid 1800s, Robe had developed into one of South Australia's major ports. When the gold rush was at its peak in Victoria, about 16 000 Chinese prospectors and their families disembarked at the port to avoid paying the Victorian government's ten-pound poll tax. Entry through South Australia was free, though the locals collected substantial fees for rowing the immigrants ashore. The newcomers walked from Robe to their expected El Dorado.

In 1897, Robe and the surrounding area were shaken by a severe earthquake which damaged some of the stone buildings and made great fissures in the paddocks. These same paddocks were deficient in trace elements and grazing stock suffered from the mysterious 'coast disease' until minute quantities of copper and cobalt were added to the soil (see *Bordertown & Keith*).

Robe did not develop into a well known holiday resort until after the Second World War when motor cars made it possible for the general public to reach Guichen Bay. The town attracts its fair share of tourists and amateur fishermen. A professional crayfishing fleet operates from a sheltered anchorage in Lake Butler. The fleet is blessed in a special ceremony held on the last Sunday in September before the season begins the following month. Four fish factories are the focus of a major industry. *Population 730*

CALEDONIAN INN This restored inn was built several years before Adam Lindsay Gordon was confined there in 1862 after falling from his horse. The innkeeper's daughter, Margaret Park, became his nurse and then his wife. In 1865, Gordon was elected to the South Australian parliament as the representative for the Victoria district, which included Robe, but he resigned in 1866 because he had bought land in Western Australia.

TANTANOOLA ■ 1924
People argue about the origin of Tantanoola which some say comes from the Aboriginal name for the district, 'tentunola', which means 'boxwood hill' or 'boxwood camp'. Others have said it means 'meeting-place'. The latter is not particularly apt in these days as less than three hundred people live there but the town has a large reputation based on its 'Tiger' and its caves (see entry).

Round Kalangadoo there's a hullabaloo and panic at Penola;
From the Gulf to the Bight,
They're taking fright, at the thing they call the Tiger.

The aforesaid 'tiger' now lives in a glass case in the Tantanoola Tiger Hotel. Reports handed down over the years claim it terrorised the district killing sheep at the end of the last century, until it was hunted down and shot by a local farmer. The stuffed animal appears to be an Assyrian wolfhound, but just how it came to Tantanoola is not known. A likely explanation is that it jumped ship at one of the coastal ports .

TANTANOOLA CAVES CONSERVATION PARK ■ 1925
Tantanoola Caves Conservation Park contains two caves hollowed out of an ancient marine cliff overlooking the highway and decorated with a variety of impressive calcite formations. Access to them is much easier than to most cave systems; there are no stairs or ladders to negotiate and the pathways have been made suitable for wheelchairs.

The toy-like Cape Dombey obelisk at Robe once held rockets to carry rescue ropes to vessels in distress.

TARPEENA ■ 1926
Tarpeena township – the name is said to mean 'red gum tree' – dates back to 1860. In the following year, Laurence Egan constructed a hotel, boarding-house, store, school and blacksmith's shop and set up a changing post for coach horses and this became the nucleus of the little town. Contemporary Tarpeena is a small settlement that enjoys a quiet, uncluttered, rural lifestyle among the green pasture and pine plantation landscape of the south-east.

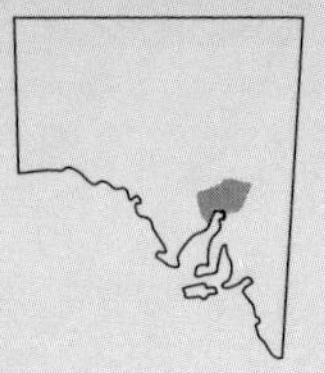

Whyalla & Port Augusta

On the north-western shores of Spencer Gulf, hills of iron feed a city of steel. Further inland are the crumbling remains of long-deserted towns which the hard-pressed 'marginal' lands could not sustain.

The sandstone ridges at the southern limits of the Flinders Ranges are in the Mount Remarkable National Park.

BOOLEROO CENTRE ■ 1927

If there was a competition for the nation's most exotic and unusual pioneers' memorial, the prize would surely go to Booleroo Centre, with its giant boulder, bristling with quartz and amethyst crystals and set firmly on a plinth in the centre of the town. This monument was hauled from a nearby amethyst deposit which was mined commercially for a few years at the beginning of the century and still produces occasional glistening finds for amateur gemologists.

The town was settled in the early 1880s, presumably during a very wet period, as the name means 'place of mud'. The 'centre' was added to indicate that it was the main settlement in the Hundred of Booleroo. (In 1846, a regional division system of 'Hundreds' – units smaller than counties and used in some parts of England – was introduced in South Australia. A Hundred was usually, but not always, 100 square miles – 260 square kilometres.)

The Booleroo Steam and Traction Society maintains what is thought to be Australia's largest collection of 'antique' tractors, stationary engines and farm implements.

FESTIVALS Steam and Traction Preservation Society Annual Rally, April.

CRADOCK ■ 1928

In the mid-1870s, when the South Australian government allowed settlers to go beyond Goyder's Line (see box) into the semi-arid lands of the colony's mid-north, the 'wheat rush' that resulted saw the establishment of many small service towns such as Cradock. Just as surely, when the climate asserted itself a few years later and the rush turned into a retreat, many of the towns were abandoned.

Cradock, laid out in 1878 on a 'grassy flat' of 'strong red loam', was a modest settlement from the start. By 1883 the optimism of its founding had been replaced by an increasing despair as the fourth poor crop in a row was harvested. The town has since weathered many droughts to survive as a welcome watering hole on the secondary road into the middle reaches of the Flinders Ranges.

HAMMOND ■ 1929

There are more buildings in a state of collapse in Hammond than there are still standing upright; the elements are gradually reclaiming the site of the old wheat settlement and it looks resigned to meeting the ghost-town fate that has befallen a dozen similar townships in this region of unpredictable rainfall.

Only a few residents remain in the town, which was founded in 1876. Despite this, Hammond has refused to lie down and die quietly – its centenary was marked by the siting of a plaque in the main street, 'To the pioneers of this community 1876–1976', and the old bank building is kept in good repair as a pioneers' museum.

HAWKER ■ 1930

This is the last outpost for tourists heading into the northern Flinders, where the ranges' best known attractions lie. If the climate was just a little kinder Hawker would still be the busy wheat town it started out to be in 1880. For a few years the settlement on the broad plain surrounded by handsome ranges was set in a sea of waving wheat, but in the end the region's erratic rainfall put paid to agriculture and all that remains are decaying buildings.

To the south, the evidence of two very different peoples, both long vanished, is still quite apparent: at Yourambulla the caves display the motifs and icons of the Aborigines who first roamed this land, while at the old Kanyaka Station, the homestead, outbuildings and stone walls of a once-vast property that offered work to seventy settler families are slowly being reduced to dust.

IRON BARON ■ 1931

Iron Baron is an iron-mining settlement, which in the tradition of such company towns is named after the mine that it was established to serve – one of many 'Irons' in the heavily excavated Middleback Range. Iron Baron township is a smaller sister to Iron Knob to the north but its mines have produced more ore than any other operation in the range.

IRON KNOB ■ 1932

The topography of the Middleback Range region was changed irrevocably when Australia's first iron-ore discovery was made there in the late 1870s – although the metallic outcrops had probably been noticed by explorer Edward Eyre some thirty years earlier. In less than a century, the two 350-metre-high hills known as Iron Knob and Iron Monarch have have been reduced to mere pimples of 200 metres. As their dark masses are open-mined and carried away to feed giant blast furnaces, not only at Whyalla but on the other side of the world as well, they will eventually disappear to be replaced by yawning pits more than 100 metres deep.

Iron Knob township, established at the same time as the mine in 1901, was set up to house mine workers and soon connected by tramway to Hummock Hill, later renamed Whyalla, on the coast. The Middleback Range region was Australia's major source of iron ore for almost sixty years – until the Western Australian deposits were opened up – and a whole series of nobly named open-cut 'Iron' mines – Iron Baron, Iron Queen, Iron Duke and Iron Prince – were carved out of the barren hillsides. So far more than sixty million tonnes of iron ore has been extracted from the mines.

MELROSE ■ 1933

Green streaks betraying the presence of copper in the bulk of Moun

ew clouds shade the summer sun round Orroroo where no building s complete without a verandah.

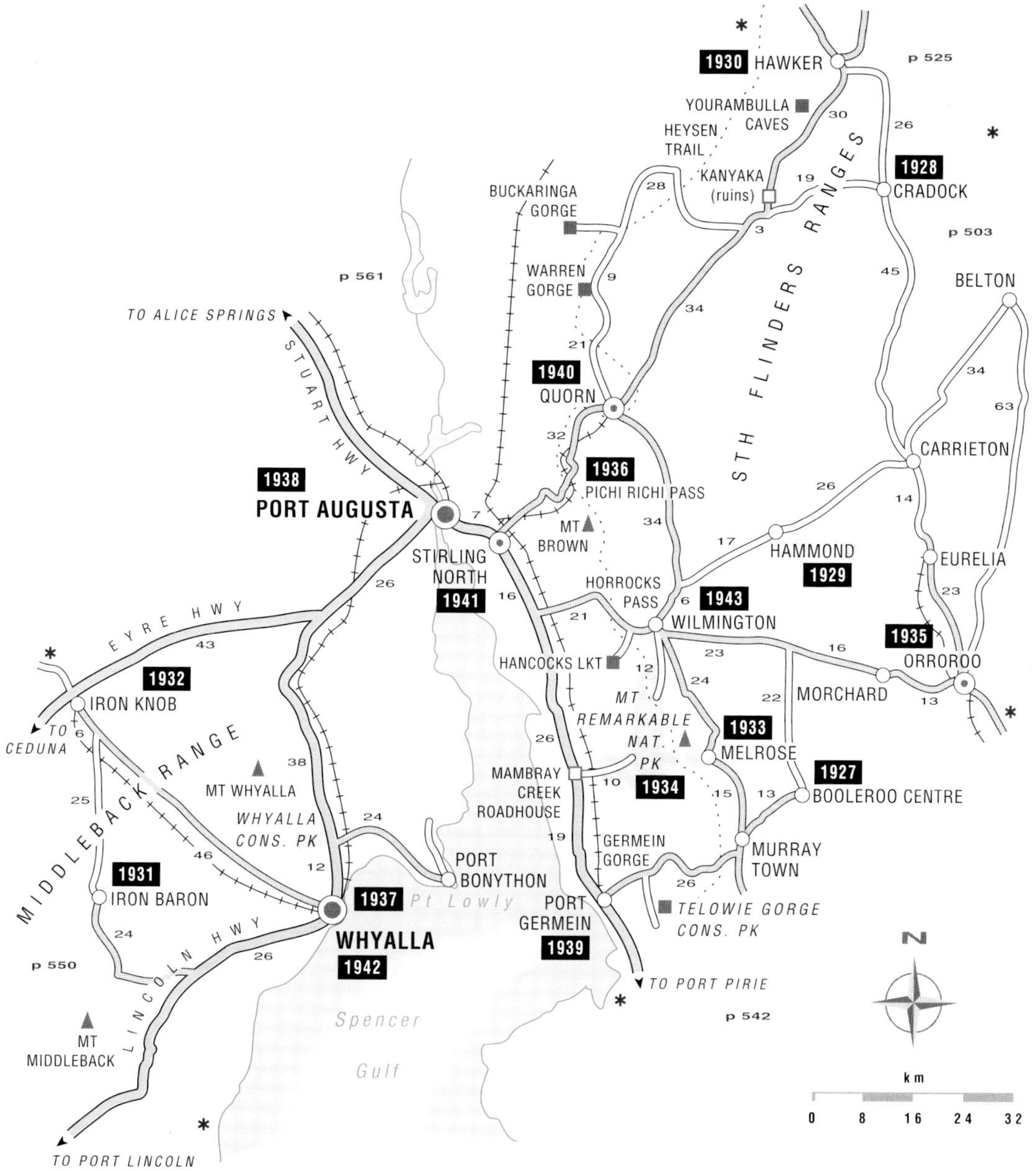

Remarkable were responsible for the establishment of this settlement – the oldest in the Flinders Ranges. The promise of the early copper discovery was never to be realised but in the 1850s, as the most northerly outpost of the South Australian colony, Melrose was the headquarters of one of the world's largest police districts, which stretched across the continent to the Arafura Sea.

The only reminder of those days is the police station and court house – now a museum – and the troopers' barracks and stables. The scattering of other old buildings which give the town its charm include Keating Cottage (1859), the post office (1865–66), the Mount Remarkable and North Star hotels (1881 and 1857 respectively) and the massive, five-storey, stone shell of Jacka's Brewery, which began life as a flour mill in 1879.

Melrose maintains its connection with Mount Remarkable as the main jumping-off point to the eastern section of the national park named after the mountain which towers almost 1000 metres above the town and the surrounding hills.

MOUNT REMARKABLE NATIONAL PARK ■ 1934

The low ranges which chaperone the dominant bulk of Mount Remarkable are not only responsible for the region's reasonable rainfall but also for channelling the run-off into the large, gurgling creeks which have cut their way deep into the red quartzite to form cool gorges.

Ferns and native orchids share the slopes with blue gums, sugar gums, wattles, mallees, she-oaks and grass trees, at times in almost rainforest-like abundance – an indication of the regeneration that has occurred since the wholesale clearance of hardwood trees during the last century for use as railway sleepers.

In the more-frequented western part of the park, cypress pines and river red gums vie for space along the banks of Alligator Creek as it runs through its spectacular gorge cut into a broad, shallow basin, similar to the more famous Wilpena Pound to the north. Red kangaroos, rock wallabies and emus are at home here where there is more room to roam than in the tiny eastern section of the park, dominated by Mount Remarkable (963 metres) itself.

ORROROO ■ 1935

Like many places given so-called Aboriginal names, the true meaning of the word 'orroroo' – 'rendezvous of the magpie', 'place of departure' or 'early start' depending on your source – may never be ascertained because the speakers of the language from which it is derived have long since departed from the region. What is known is that the name was bestowed by a pioneer who ran a coaching house to the south of the present town which served travellers on the Burra–Blinman track.

When the new town's generously broad streets were surveyed at the bottom of the rolling hills of the Flinders Ranges in 1875, this early settler was quickly on the spot as a wine dealer and shopkeeper in Orroroo's first building. His iron-walled shop no longer stands and the honour of oldest building goes to Solly's Hut, the town's first house – an 1875 clay-pugged log structure now used as a museum.

Orroroo has withstood the rigours of many droughts and the mockery of the 1870s postmaster-general – who, when a post office for the township was requested, is said to have responded: 'Dear me, there are only two letters in Orroroo, so what do you want a post office for?' – to survive as a centre for tourists and the surrounding pastoral district. It is also the birthplace of the poet Rex Ingamells, co-founder of the 1940s Jindyworobak movement, an influential affiliation of writers who believed that the Australian environment must be the inspiration for Australian culture. *Population 570*

PICHI RICHI PASS ■ 1936

After crossing the strip of coastal plain, the road from Port Augusta to Quorn and the north-east sets its course for the heart of the Flinders Ranges by winding through a gap in the Ranges' narrow lower extremities called the Pichi Richi Pass. Only a few kilometres long and of modest gradient, the pass climbs through rounded, lightly forested hills to a height of about 400 metres before descending to the Willochra Plain.

The way through the hills was found in 1853 by drovers moving their sheep north in search of new runs. Eventually the wool which their flocks produced was sent to market on the road built along the same route – the track it replaced

The restored steam trains of the Pichi Richi Railway have breathed new life into Quorn's officially retired station.

The harsh ridges of Buckaringa Gorge push through the foothills of the Southern Flinders near Quorn.

was described in horrific terms in 1853 by a grazier who bravely traversed it with his bullock drays: '...we had Flinder's Range [*sic*] to cross, some eight or ten miles of a gorge called Pichirichi, which I can hardly describe. It was so beset with blind creeks, winding, steep hills and the like ...We lamed the poor bullocks over the stony ground and smashed wheels and drays before we accomplished this pass ...'

The pass was also used by the original Central Australian railway line to Alice Springs until the standard gauge line was built on a different route in 1956 (see Quorn). The catchy name is said to come from 'pituri' or 'pitjuri', a plant with leaves which induce mild intoxication when chewed.

POINT LOWLY ■ 1937

The first white man to see Point Lowly was a disappointed Matthew Flinders who had hoped that the head of Spencer Gulf might end in a major river leading into the interior. On 9 March 1802, during his circumnavigation of Australia, he anchored off the wedge of land that juts into the gulf's northernmost reaches and noted: ' ...the furthest hummock seen from the anchorage ...stands on a projection of low sandy land, and beyond it was another similar projection to which I gave the name Point Lowly'. Beyond were mangroves and dangerous shoals.

A sleek white stone and concrete lighthouse built in 1882 – with its original lantern now illuminated automatically by electricity – marks the projection, which in fact has a shoreline more rocky than sandy.

PORT AUGUSTA ■ 1938

In the days when colonial settlements clustered around the coast and before long-distance road and rail transport had developed, sea transport often provided the only reliable travel and trade link between one place and another. Although it is now a port in name only, Port Augusta – sitting at the most northerly navigable point of Spencer Gulf – came into being as a major harbour settlement and survived as a railway and industrial centre because of its strategic location.

In 1802, when Matthew Flinders explored the gulf from its 80-kilometre-wide mouth to the narrow, mangrove-lined channel 320 kilometres to its north, he noted ' ...our oars touched mud on each side and it was not possible to proceed further ...' In spite of the unpromising beginning, a port developed on the site fifty years later and busily rode out the days of steam and sail as the funnel through which the produce of the wheatlands poured. The busy port became a base for the exploration of the arid regions to the north and the construction of the southern half of the Overland Telegraph Line.

The trans-continental railway line arrived in 1917 and by the time the city ceased to be a regular shipping port-of-call – in 1973 – it was long established as an important rail junction with trains coming and going from Perth, Adelaide, Sydney and Alice Springs. The vast Australian National Railways workshops are here as well as an equally vast power station complex, fuelled by coal from Leigh Creek, which supplies a large proportion of the state's electricity.

The modern city, the state headquarters of the School of the Air and the Royal Flying Doctor Service, sits astride the once mighty gulf, here no more than a pleasant, winding inlet which peters out only twenty kilometres from the salt flats of Lake Torrens; at one time some engineers even suggested that the two be connected by a canal. *Population 14 600*

HOMESTEAD PARK PIONEER MUSEUM South Australia's last pine-log station homestead was brought here, re-erected, and furnished in period style. It forms the centrepiece of a pastoral and railway museum.

WADLATA OUTBACK CENTRE This is a tourist information centre with a difference – it attempts to communicate an 'interpretive' experience of the outback from prehistoric times to the present day through the use of sound, video and imaginative, walk-through displays.

WATERWORKS BUILDING The troopers' barracks (1860) in Beauchamps Lane is a charming stone building virtually unaltered despite its chequered history; the rear section was added as a public bath house in 1875 and the residence added in 1881. The whole complex was used as a waterworks and store in 1882.

PORT GERMEIN ■ 1939

Like Port Augusta on a slightly smaller scale, Port Germein was most alive in the days when the grain clippers plied Spencer Gulf, delivering stores and loading wheat and wool for the mills of Australia and Britain.

The muddy, mangrove-encrusted stretch of shore was eminently unapproachable for vessels of almost any kind and loading and unloading was facilitated by the construction of Australia's longest jetty which needed to be more than one-and-a-half kilometres in length to reach deep water. It is built of huge, red gum piles and hardwood planking, which had to be hauled in across forty-five creeks from Wirraburra Forest, to the east. The jetty served the last of the square-rigged sailing ships – great windjammers loaded wheat here until the late 1930s. Today it is a tourist attraction, its maintenance provided for by such events as the Festival of the Crab, which heralds the New Year.

The waterfront, with its pub and woolshed, has changed very little since the last century when the town was named after the captain of the ship which carried supplies to the head of the gulf for Edward Eyre's 1840 expedition into the heart of the Flinders Ranges.

FESTIVALS Port Germein Festival of the Crab, early January.

QUORN ■ 1940

Like many towns and cities in 'mid-north' South Australia, Quorn is largely a child of the age of steam, when the railway lines from the south and the east snaked out to connect with far-flung settlements, their intersections and junctions forming the bases for busy railway towns.

The town – named for the town of Quorndon in England – sits at the northern end of the Pichi Richi Pass (see entry). Four years after it was established the Pichi Richi railway line was built to Port Augusta to carry ore from the busy mines to the north; today it is the only line that still operates here and it has the distinction of being one of the oldest intact railway systems in the world. So active is the Railway Preservation Society that it issues a detailed timetable listing the dates when it unleashes its barrage of historic, narrow-gauge engines, motor coaches and rolling stock on excursions to Woolshed Flat and back to Quorn.

The railway heritage is reflected in the expansive names of some of the old hotels – the Grand Junction and the Transcontinental are among the many unchanged historic buildings which are still in use. The elaborately gabled, limestone railway station (1914–16), the old, three-storey mill (1878), the town hall (1891) and an assortment of stone cottages and verandahed shops add to the period charm. *Population 1060*

Drilling and blasting and digging will eventually reduce the rugged spur of Iron Knob to nothing as its precious iron ore is carried off to Whyalla.

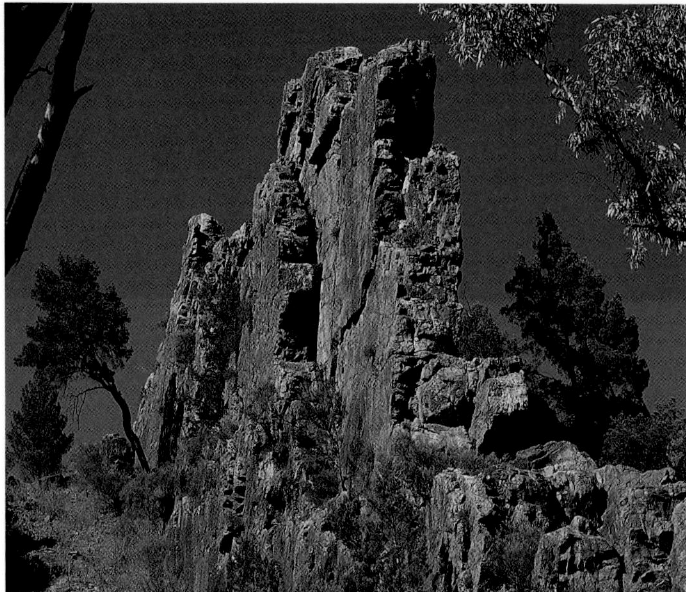

The sun-dried harshness of Warren Gorge , north of Quorn, is a sober signpost to the arid lands that rule the interior all the way to Arnhem Land.

STIRLING NORTH ■ **1941**
The town of Stirling North, now on the outskirts of Port Augusta, was laid out in 1859 by Robert Barr Smith, partner in the firm Elder, Smith & Co., and named by him after Edward Stirling, who for a few years was a member of the same firm. The site was previously known as Minchin Well for the well dug here in 1854 under the supervision of Henry Minchin, sub-protector of Aborigines. *Population 4120*

WHYALLA ■ **1942**
The largest provincial city in South Australia, Whyalla owes its development to the iron-ore deposits at nearby Iron Knob (see entry). First known as Hummock Hill, the name bestowed by Matthew Flinders in 1802, settlement here followed the building of a 'tramway' from the mines to enable iron ore to be loaded onto barges for transport across the waters of the gulf to the smelters at Port Pirie. In 1941, a blast furnace for the production of pig iron for the foundry market came into operation, and a major ship-building industry, which was to produce the largest ship ever built in Australia, began. Whyalla's most rapid spate of development followed the opening of the BHP steelworks in 1965. The shipyards are now defunct – their closure in 1978 and the subsequent cut in production at the steelworks resulted in unemployment and considerable social upheaval in the city.

Tourism is now a growth industry in Whyalla. Boating facilities and a pleasant beach are an easy walk from the city centre, and the seafront reserve has a caravan park, picnic area and a zoo. *Population 25 530*

WHYALLA MARITIME MUSEUM This museum is the home for the HMAS *Whyalla*, which in 1941 was the first ship to be built in the former shipyards. It now stands high and dry two kilometres from the sea near the city's northern highway entrance, and visitors can not only walk over its decks but also under its hull.

In the nearby Tanderra Building is a collection of artefacts relating to the *Whyalla*, ship models and models of the BHP shipyard as it functioned between 1940 and 1978, and what is believed to be the largest '00' gauge model railway in Australia.

FAUNA AND REPTILE PARK More than 100 hectares of undisturbed arid bushland – including myall trees up to 300 years old – have been enclosed and stocked with animals, reptiles and birdlife, most of them native to this area. Kangaroos and emus range free and a walk-through aviary houses some 200 birds, including rosellas, parrots and finches. The bushwalking section has a one-kilometre track where more than twenty native plant species are identified.

WILMINGTON ■ **1943**
The district here was once known as Beautiful Valley – inspired by the scenic hills of the Southern Flinders Ranges. The first land was taken up in 1851 by John Howard Angas – a member of a family notable in the public life of South Australia – and formed part of a string of properties which enabled him to get stock to market in the best possible condition.

The hotel dates from the 1850s; behind are coaching stables more than a century old. The town was named Wilmington in 1876 by Governor Musgrave because his wife had an association with a town of the same name in the United States.

FESTIVALS Wilmington Night Rodeo, late January.

GOYDER'S LINE: COMING TO GRIPS WITH THE 'HEARTBREAK' COUNTRY

GOYDER'S LINE is an imaginary line which wanders across South Australia's south-east. It was established more than 120 years ago to delineate those regions where the annual rainfall was reliable enough to support agriculture from the drier areas to the north. The path the line follows is often indicated by abrupt changes in the natural vegetation and it continues to exercise the public imagination as a constant reminder of the relatively small part of South Australia, some twenty per cent only, that can support farming.

Being next to the Goyder's Line marker near Port Pirie has not prevented this paddock from flourishing.

Beginning just north of Ceduna on the west coast, Goyder's Line heads in a south-easterly direction across Eyre Peninsula, striking Spencer Gulf between Arno Bay and Franklin Harbour. It starts again on the other side of the water near Moonta, curving north through Crystal Brook and then turning east around the dominant bulk of Mount Remarkable to Orroroo, where it cuts south along the eastern edge of the Mount Lofty Ranges before swinging in a south-easterly arc across to the border with Victoria near Peebinga.

Goyder's Line had its origins in a drought that hit South Australia in 1864–65. The fledgling colony's highly energetic and capable Surveyor-General, George Woodroffe Goyder, was instructed to travel to the north and map a line of demarcation to indicate exactly where the drought extended. Goyder set off into the wilds on horseback in 1865 and in the space of just two months completed his mammoth task.

Originally his line was intended to be used purely as a basis for reviewing pastoral leases and determining eligibility for drought relief, but it was soon firmly established as the northern boundary of country that was safe for crops. Inevitably, however, a run of good seasons led to a clamour for land in the scrub and saltbush country beyond Goyder's Line. While Goyder remained opposed to attempts to farm beyond his line, the government eventually gave in to these pressures, and the resulting 'wheat rush' had disastrous consequences when the droughts returned. The ruins of long-abandoned farms and small townships can be seen today, dotting the landscape in places like the Flinders Ranges.

Not that Goyder's Line has proved to be an infallible guide to farmers. Many of the state's best wheat-growing areas, using breeds of wheat developed for drier regions, are located north of the line and from an agricultural viewpoint it is less relevant today.

Goyder left an unmistakeable imprint on another, distant part of Australia. In 1869, he was sent to investigate the far northern coast of what was then South Australia where he selected the site of the capital, Palmerston, later to become Darwin, and surveyed extensive areas of agricultural land. □

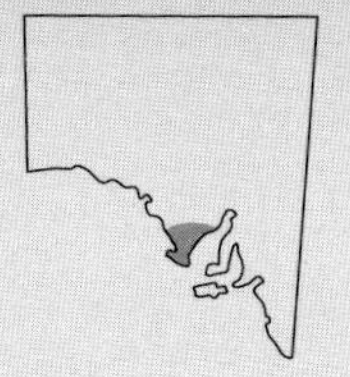

Port Lincoln & Tumby Bay

The explorer Edward John Eyre left both his name and his tracks on this peninsula where most of South Australia's cereal crops grow. The eastern coasts are scalloped with sandy beaches and fishing harbours, while the western shores have been sculpted by the full force of a never-ending barrage of Southern Ocean rollers.

It was along the rocky shoreline of today's Lincoln Park that crew members of Flinders' Investigator *drowned.*

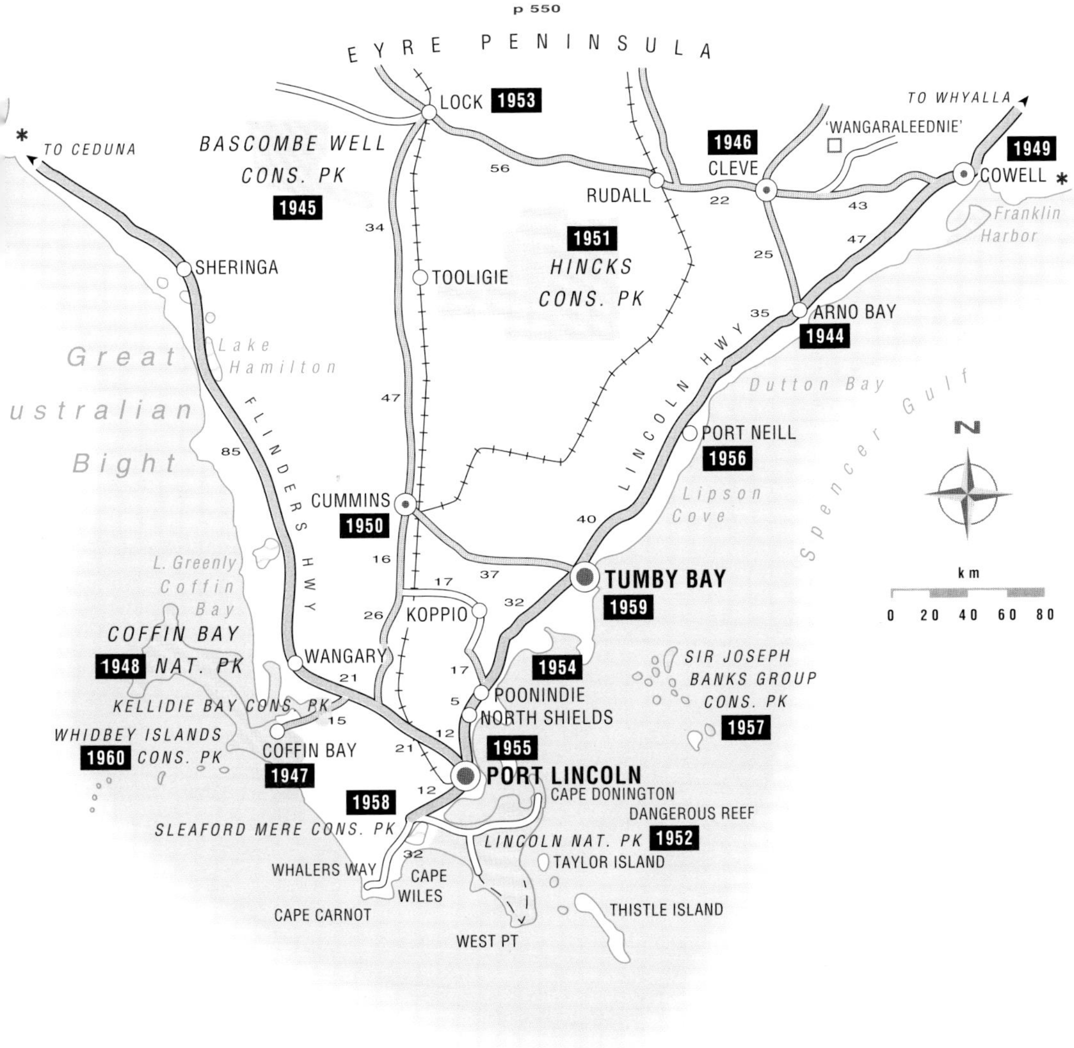

p 550

EYRE PENINSULA
TO CEDUNA
LOCK 1953
BASCOMBE WELL CONS. PK 1945
TO WHYALLA
'WANGARALEEDNIE'
1946 CLEVE
1949 COWELL
RUDALL
Franklin Harbor
SHERINGA
TOOLIGIE
1951 HINCKS CONS. PK
ARNO BAY 1944
Lake Hamilton
Great Australian Bight
FLINDERS HWY
LINCOLN HWY
Dutton Bay
Spencer Gulf
PORT NEILL 1956
Lipson Cove
CUMMINS 1950
L. Greenly
Coffin Bay
TUMBY BAY 1959
KOPPIO
COFFIN BAY 1948 NAT. PK
WANGARY
1954
SIR JOSEPH BANKS GROUP CONS. PK 1957
KELLIDIE BAY CONS. PK
POONINDIE
NORTH SHIELDS
WHIDBEY ISLANDS 1960 CONS. PK
COFFIN BAY 1947
1955 PORT LINCOLN
1958
CAPE DONINGTON
DANGEROUS REEF
SLEAFORD MERE CONS. PK
LINCOLN NAT. PK 1952
WHALERS WAY
CAPE WILES
TAYLOR ISLAND
CAPE CARNOT
THISTLE ISLAND
WEST PT
km
0 20 40 60 80

ARNO BAY ■ 1944

In the 1880s, this township was known as Bligh and was a small port which served the local farming district. Coastal trading vessels landed superphosphate – the shed which sheltered it still stands – and took out cargoes of grain. Ships too large to berth at the jetty anchored in the bay and flat-bottomed boats ran between them and the shore. The original jetty is now a favoured fishing spot for squid, whiting and mullet, and the nearby tidal creek also yields good catches.

BASCOMBE WELL CONSERVATION PARK ■ 1945

Protected in this large park of some 30 000 hectares are the diverse habitats of a wide range of birds – emus, quail, scrub robins, wrens, whistlers, thrushes, parrots and cockatoos – as well as kangaroos, echidnas and reptiles. The dominant vegetation is coastal mallee and broombush. In spring, the low ridges produce a fine display of orchids.

CLEVE ■ 1946

James, Donald and Peter McKechnie came to South Australia in 1853, enticed from their native Scotland by reports of the good life in the colony. They set up Wangaraleednie Station here – the original pine and pug homestead long ago fell into ruins; the present one dates from 1879. The nearby township was proclaimed in the same year as a service centre for the growing farming community. *Population 740*

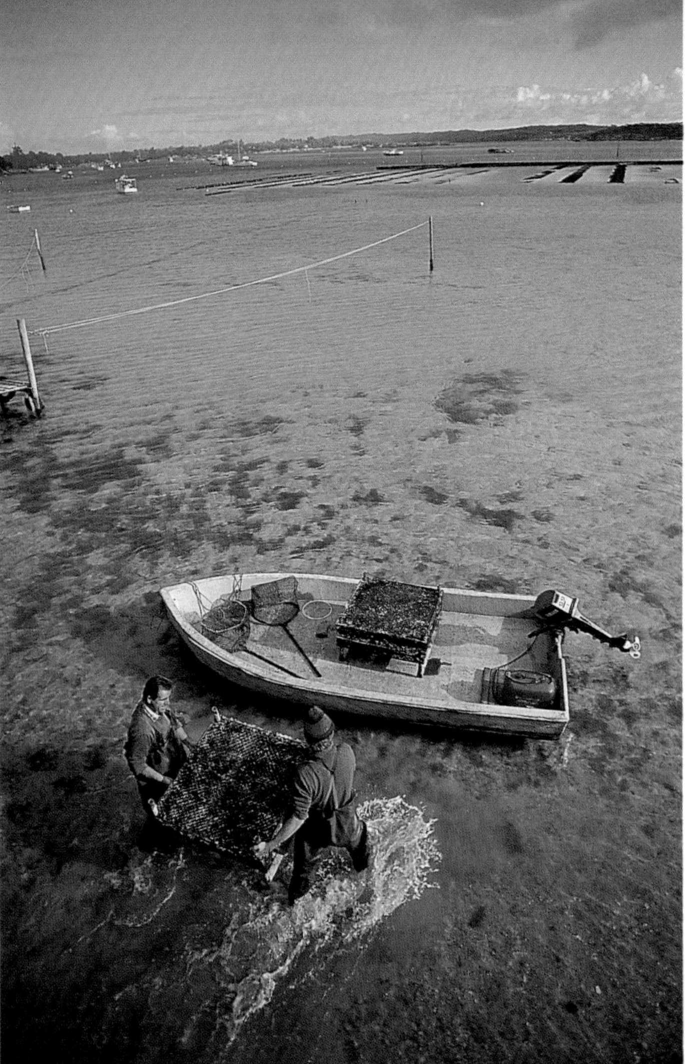

Seed oysters judged big enough to go it alone are ferried out to 'graze' and grow plump in the unpolluted waters in the middle of Coffin Bay.

COFFIN BAY ■ **1947**
At the head of a twisting estuary, some thirty kilometres from the full pounding force of the Southern Ocean, is the township of Coffin Bay, sheltered on the shores of a bay of the same name. These waters are renowned for their oysters – the oyster farm here is open to visitors during the summer holidays – and the shellfish has given its name to Oyster Walk, a graded track which winds for two-and-a-half kilometres around the foreshore.

North-west of the town, on Horse Peninsula, are several Aboriginal fish traps. Low semi-circular walls of stone, they are built on gently sloping beaches adjacent to rock ledges, and were designed to catch fish on a falling tide; a gap at the front was blocked when the trap was in use.

COFFIN BAY NATIONAL PARK ■ **1948**
The limestone and granite peninsula which makes up the bulk of this park protects the network of inlets on its lee side from the mighty westerly swells which roll in across the Great Australian Bight. Thus visitors have a choice between awesome booming surf or gentle landlocked waters. On the exposed western shores wind and water have worked the deposits of limestone into fantastic shapes and smoothed the great, hard shoulders of the tall, granite cliffs. The inner coves of the sheltered estuary are surrounded by woodlands and flower-covered heathlands. Walking and four-wheel drive trails lead to lookouts over the spectacular coastline. The park is popular with wilderness campers.

COWELL ■ **1949**
Mineral-rich hills loom behind the quiet township of Cowell on the sheltered shores of Franklin Harbor – in South Australia 'harbour' names are commonly spelt without the 'u'. In the early days of settlement, small-scale mining operations recovered silver and copper here, but in more recent years the hills have become famous for their deposits of jade, coloured marble and carving-quality talc.

Cowell, on one of this area's few stretches of swamp-free foreshore, came into existence in the 1880s as a shipping port where coastal vessels delivered supplies to, and took on produce from, the scattered sheep and wheat farms of the hinterland. It continues in this role of service centre, not only for the farmers, but also for the fisherfolk who work the harbour and gulf waters.

Matthew Flinders saw Franklin Harbor as a lagoon, an understandable error as it is almost completely landlocked and when the tide is on the turn waters rush through its narrow entrance like a fast-flowing river. The harbour is known for its wide variety of fish and night-time crabbing in the shallows can produce a rewarding catch. *Population 695*

COWELL JADE FACTORY The cutting and carving of some of the world's finest black and green jade can be seen here, and specimens purchased. The black variety is especially prized because of its rarity and its ability to take a high polish. The stone is mined in the hills behind the town.

CUMMINS ■ **1950**
This district was settled in the 1840s by pastoralists and sheep once grazed on the site of Cummins. Closer settlement and the extension of the railway from Port Lincoln in the early 1900s led to the growth of the town. The surrounding farms produce sheep, cattle, wheat and barley, and Cummins has the only flour mill on the peninsula. *Population 750*

HINCKS CONSERVATION PARK ■ **1951**
In the centre of Eyre Peninsula, this large (66 300 hectare) park consists in the main of a vast sand-dune system with minor sandstone outcrops supporting a surprisingly wide variety of animal and plant species. Mallee and broombush make up the predominant vegetation, but there are stands of mallee box and she-oak. Western grey kangaroos and emus are plentiful, and there are small populations of the dunnart, or fat-tailed marsupial mouse – a tiny marsupial which has a reserve of fat in its tail to carry it through lean times.

LINCOLN NATIONAL PARK ■ **1952**
Jutting into Spencer Gulf from the south-eastern tip of Eyre Peninsula and, but for a small neck of land, almost separated from the mainland, is the wild and beautiful Lincoln National Park. It takes up most of the Jussieu Peninsula and the waters that surround it are marine reserve. Its northern facing bays are sheltered, grassy and lightly wooded – here are sandy swimming beaches and in places the tall, coastal mallee grows right to the shoreline. Rising behind the shore is Stamford Hill, the highest point in the vicinity.

Matthew Flinders landed on Thistle Island, offshore from the park, in February 1802, naming it for his first mate and friend John Thistle, who had accompanied him with George Bass on the *Tom Thumb* and who on this occasion collected reptile specimens on the island. Later the same day Thistle and seven of the ship's company were dispatched to search for fresh water to replenish the dwindling supplies on the *Investigator*. They were never seen again.

The next day a badly damaged boat – apparently it had been dashed against the rocks – was recovered, as was a keg of water. In despair, Flinders named Cape Catastrophe, Thorny Passage and Memory Cove and the nearby islands that now bear the names – Taylor, Williams, Smith, Lewis, Hopkins, Little and Grindal – of the dead men.

FLINDERS MONUMENT, STAMFORD HILL Atop Stamford Hill there is a towering stone obelisk, raised in the 1840s to honour Matthew Flinders by his nephew and former midshipman on the *Investigator*, Sir John Franklin, by that time Governor of Tasmania. The stone of which the monument was built weathered so badly that by the late 1860s it needed restoration and so was faced with marble.

LOCK ■ **1953**
Requests for building blocks adjacent to a siding on the newly opened railway line through the Eyre Peninsula led to the proclamation, in 1918, of a township here. Its site is almost the geographical centre of the peninsula and it serves the surrounding sheep-farming and grain-growing district.

Like a number of small, country communities, Lock was deprived of many of its young men by the First World War and the town name honours Corporal Albert Lock, a local citizen who was killed in action in Belgium in 1917.

POONINDIE ■ **1954**
A mission station was established here in the early 1850s and work on the church began in 1854. The building is of granite quarried nearby and bricks fired on the site and, unusually for a church, it has twin chimneys. Massive beams of local eucalyptus hardwood support the upper floor which, equipped with fireplace, once housed the rector and his wife and

Port Lincoln's tuna fishermen roam the continent's southern coast to bring home a catch for the cannery.

was later used as a schoolroom. Old pictures show the building with a thatched roof. The ruins of other mission buildings are in the vicinity.

PORT LINCOLN ■ **1955**

On the sheltered blue waters of Boston Bay, a harbour several times the size of the one in Sydney, is busy Port Lincoln. It is the base for Australia's largest tuna fleet, handling point for the wool, fat lambs, live sheep and grain of the hinterland and centre for processing and export of local seafood – tuna, prawns and abalone. The writer Colin Thiele was a schoolteacher in the district, and his novel *Blue Fin* describes the tuna fishing industry of the bay, and the loss of a tuna boat in its waters.

The town site, named 'in honour of my native province' by Matthew Flinders in 1802, was used by whalers and fishermen and in 1836 was visited by Colonel William Light, who decided against a capital here largely because of worries about the arid interior. European settlement here dates from 1839, but faced many problems, including the lack of surface water and a natural hostility - oftimes leading to clashes – from the Aborigines. The town's first inn, the Lincoln Hotel, built in 1840, still stands on the waterfront. For explorer Edward Eyre the fledgling town was the starting point for his first westward trek. *Population 11 350*

MILL COTTAGE Pioneer settler Captain John Bishop built this house for his son Joseph in 1866. It is now owned by the National Trust, and in it is preserved more than one hundred years of Bishop family history and belongings.

MIKKIRA STATION This was the first sheep station on the peninsula and is nowadays open to the public and has picnic and barbecue facilities. The original homestead dates from the 1840s. It is a simple whitewashed, four-roomed, thatch-roofed dwelling and with its outbuildings, has been restored.

WHALERS WAY Whalers Way is a privately owned scenic drive and to enter it a key and permit must be obtained from the tourist office at Port Lincoln. The way winds along the clifftops above Sleaford Bay to the very tip of Eyre Peninsula giving dramatic panoramas of the rugged coastal scenery, with its capes, cliffs, caves, crevasses, blowholes and golden beaches. At the base of many of the limestone cliffs are platforms of harder granite where fur seals sometimes come ashore. The site of the old whaling station is in Fishery Bay, on the sheltered eastern side.

DANGEROUS REEF Off Port Lincoln are the windswept, rocky outcrops of Dangerous Reef, three sections of which are permanently above water. The reef supports the third largest breeding population of sea lions in Australia, as well as one of the largest colonies of black-faced cormorants in South Australia. This is the only exclusively marine cormorant in Australia, and it is restricted to the southern coasts where it breeds in nests of seaweed on islands and reefs. They feed by the hundreds in the waters of Spencer Gulf and to help with their ballast when swimming and diving, swallow pebbles so that they can stay under longer.

Regular services from Port Lincoln take tourists to the reef and a viewing platform anchored there has an underwater observatory, a large aquarium, and even a dive cage for those hoping for a close encounter with one of the great white sharks which frequent these waters.

FESTIVALS Adelaide to Port Lincoln Yacht Race, January; Tunarama Festival, January.

PORT NEILL ■ **1956**

The deepwater boat ramp and the breakwater, which allow all-weather fishing in any wind conditions, make Port Neill, on Dutton Bay, a haven for small boat fishermen, and the bay here is indeed bountiful with hauls of King George whiting, snapper and garfish to be expected. Swimming on the white sandy beaches, sailing, waterskiing and skin diving are also popular activities. From Port Neill Lookout, on a nearby hilltop, are sweeping views over Spencer Gulf, the coastline and rolling hinterland.

Port Neill came into existence in 1908, and was first known as Carrow, a derivation from its Aboriginal name. On the foreshore, there is the mighty anchor of the barque *Lady Kinnaird* which foundered off nearby Cape Burr in 1880.

SIR JOSEPH BANKS GROUP CONSERVATION PARK ■ **1957**

The offshore islands of the Eyre Peninsula, largely free of introduced predatory animals such as foxes or cats, are a last refuge for a number of native birds and animals which are endangered or extinct on the mainland. The islands of the Sir Joseph Banks Group Conservation Park have the largest breeding ground in Australia of the Cape Barren goose, a bird driven almost to extinction by sealers in the nineteenth century. These large, distinctive birds, unique to Australia, graze on the grassy swards and heaths of the islands, and nest and raise their young amongst the rocks and tussocks.

The rare Australian sea lion also finds a safe home here on English Island, where there is a breeding population. Births occur from mid-October to early January, the pups stay close to their mothers and are not weaned until about a year old. The sight of a bull sea lion guarding his lounging harem, whiskered dog-like face upturned, is a common one along the secluded beaches and wave-washed rocky platforms of this island chain. Dolphins are also frequently seen here in large numbers.

Neither man nor beast is present to disturb the breeding domain of the cormorants of Winceby Island, one of the Sir Joseph Banks Group.

The group was named in 1802 by Matthew Flinders for the botanist Sir Joseph Banks; individual islands he named for the parishes and villages of his own Lincolnshire home near Reevesby Abbey. In the nineteenth century, some of the islands were privately owned sheep stations – on Reevesby the original homestead has been restored and Spilsby still carries sheep on its rolling green pastures.

SLEAFORD MERE CONSERVATION PARK ■ **1958**

Sleaford Mere is a long coastal salt lake. On its flats is an expanse of grey-black mounds which are known as stromatolites. Almost brain-like in appearance, they vary in size from a few centimetres up to a metre high and consist of layer upon layer of fossilised algae. The mere was once a tidal inlet of the sea, but when drifting sand dunes closed its mouth its waters became increasingly saline, killing off its mollusc population but allowing a population explosion of the algae. The waving sticky sheaths of the microscopic algae picked up similarly minute particles of sand, mud and fragments of limestone which were bound together, layer upon layer, to form the stony mats and mounds of the mere.

Stromatolites are often called 'living fossils' because their surface consists of the current generation, while their bulk is made up of the remains of countless ancestors. Similar formations occur at Hamelin Pool in Western Australia (see *Carnarvon & Exmouth*).

TUMBY BAY ■ **1959**

The sheltered waters of this scenic bay harbour a flotilla of fishing and pleasure craft. The foreshores are lined with Norfolk Island pines, and at Tumby Bay township a boat ramp and breakwater provide all-weather access to the rich fishing grounds of Spencer Gulf. The town is the point of departure for vessels visiting the islands of the Sir Joseph Banks Group Preservation Park (see entry).

When sheep and wheat farms were established here the need for a port to take out produce became pressing, and Tumby Bay was an obvious site. The first of Tumby Bay's two jetties was built in the 1870s, replacing the cumbersome method of loading and unloading from drays into small boats which ferried cargoes to and from ketches anchored offshore. The township quickly grew as an important link with Adelaide and other ports.

Like most of this region, Tumby Bay owes its name to that tireless sailor Matthew Flinders, who here recalled yet another parish of his native Lincolnshire. For a period during the mid-nineteenth century, however, these shores were known as Harvey Bay, after a pioneer farmer. *Population 1150*

FESTIVALS Tumby Bay Lions Club Fishing Tournament, January.

WHIDBEY ISLANDS ■ **1960**

Virtually untouched because they are so difficult to land on, these stony islands lie in a scattered string off the south-west of Eyre Peninsula and are now officially protected within a conservation park. The islands furthest from the coast are rounded granite domes capped with grass; those nearer to shore are limestone, ringed by forbidding cliffs, their flat surfaces covered by low vegetation. There are colonies of sea lions here as well as a wide range of birds including breeding populations of rock parrots and fairy penguins.

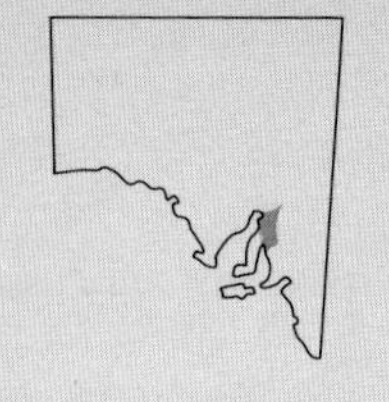

Port Pirie & Clare

Bullockies, winemakers, seamen, farmers, pastoralists and mining magnates all played a part in the development of South Australia's mid-north. Their legacy is a region of fine wine and historic towns juxtaposed with the largest lead-smelting and refining plant in the world.

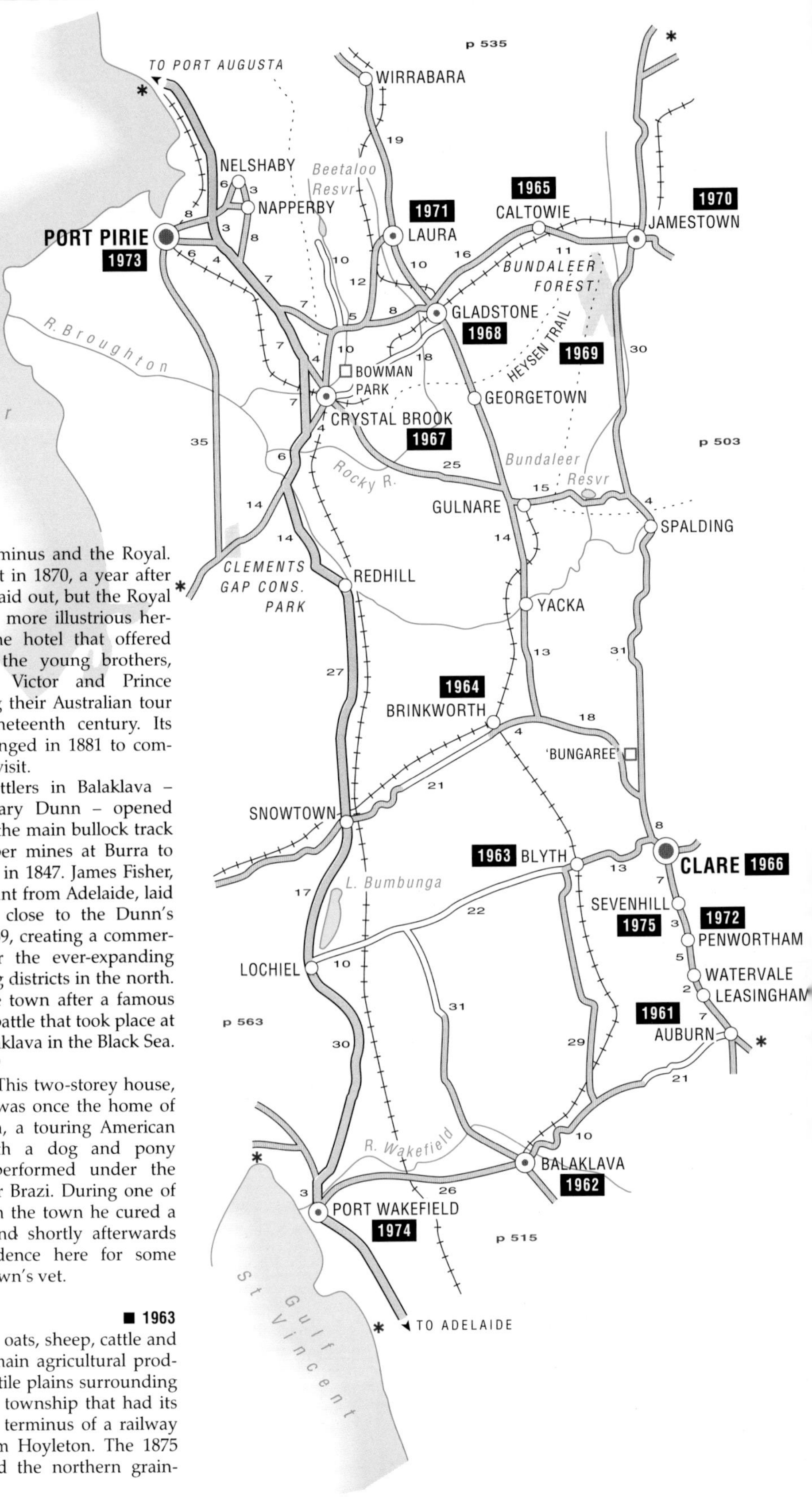

AUBURN ■ **1961**

Auburn is the birthplace of the poet C.J. Dennis (1876–1938), whose ear for the vernacular of ordinary Australians at the turn of the century was revealed in a series of humorous verses published in one of his best known works, *The Songs of a Sentimental Bloke*, in 1915. A birdbath and a drinking fountain commemorate his connection with the township.

Though a small place, Auburn is one of the oldest settlements in the Clare Valley, growing up around a resting place for the bullock teams hauling their loads of copper from the mines at Burra (see *Peterborough & Burra*) to Port Wakefield for shipment to Port Adelaide during the 1840s. This watering hole became permanent when the Rising Sun Hotel was built in 1849; more than a hundred years later, it was still one of the places where locals went to quench their thirst.

Charles Todd, South Australia's Postmaster-General and overseer of the construction of the Overland Telegraph Line, used the Rising Sun's stable – now converted to an entertainment area – as the venue for conducting the first tests of the colony's telegraphic system.

Despite its small size, Auburn has a high proportion of historic buildings that have survived more than a century of development virtually unscathed. Vincent Street is a 'heritage' street lined with buildings maintained by the National Trust.

BALAKLAVA ■ **1962**

There are two hotels in Balaklava that survive from the town's earliest days – the Terminus and the Royal. Both were built in 1870, a year after the town was laid out, but the Royal lays claim to a more illustrious heritage, being the hotel that offered hospitality to the young brothers, Prince Albert Victor and Prince George, during their Australian tour in the late-nineteenth century. Its name was changed in 1881 to commemorate the visit.

The first settlers in Balaklava – James and Mary Dunn – opened their hotel on the main bullock track from the copper mines at Burra to Port Wakefield in 1847. James Fisher, a grain merchant from Adelaide, laid out the town close to the Dunn's facilities in 1869, creating a commercial centre for the ever-expanding wheat-growing districts in the north. He named the town after a famous Crimean War battle that took place at the Bay of Balaklava in the Black Sea. *Population 1440*

'MATCHBOX' This two-storey house, built in 1906, was once the home of Frank Higham, a touring American showman with a dog and pony show, who performed under the alias, Professor Brazi. During one of his sojourns in the town he cured a sick animal and shortly afterwards took up residence here for some years as the town's vet.

BLYTH ■ **1963**

Wheat, barley, oats, sheep, cattle and pigs are the main agricultural products of the fertile plains surrounding Blyth, a small township that had its origins as the terminus of a railway extension from Hoyleton. The 1875 line connected the northern grain-growers and graziers with the markets at Adelaide. Agriculture is not the only interest in Blyth – the town is also the location of many well-preserved historic buildings including St Petri Kirche, built in 1886 as a Lutheran church, and now a private home. The town was named in honour of Arthur Blyth, the Premier of South Australia during the 1860s and 1870s.

BRINKWORTH ■ **1964**
Brinkworth is named after a farmer from the mid-north region, George Brinkworth, whose property at Magpie Creek became the site of a railway junction in 1892, the founding year of the town. One year later, a hotel opened its doors at the junction and the little township soon became the loading point and service centre for a prosperous grain-growing district – a role which it performs to this day.

A description of the town in the 20 October 1932 issue of the *Chronicle* noted: 'It consists of one main street about half a mile long, set in the centre of a vast wheat plain. I am certain it will be a big place one day'. The author's optimistic vision of the town's future was not completely unfounded – though not large, Brinkworth has remained an important grain collection point with bulk-handling facilities; its streets are lined with many well-preserved, original buildings

CALTOWIE ■ **1965**
Caltowie is typical of many of the small settlements in this region, having developed in the centre of a fertile alluvial plain, near a road, a river and a railway line, to serve the surrounding cereal-crop country. The town was established in 1871, its development unremarkable except for two historic highlights; in the 1920s, a local farmer, Gustav F. Petatz developed a new strain of wheat – 'Petatz Surprise' – that was awarded the champion prize at the Melbourne Royal Show, and then in 1970, as a result of various delays, the inaugural Indian–Pacific trains passed in Caltowie before speeding away in opposite directions.

CLARE ■ **1966**
Clare nestles in the 'valley of the vine' – the Clare Valley – surrounded by gently rolling hills that are dotted with the orderly lines of vineyards that were established in the nineteenth century. Of the twenty-odd wineries now operating in the valley, several of the oldest are based at Clare and the town has become famous for its 'gourmet weekend,' celebrated each year in May, during which each of the valley's wineries teams up with a restaurateur to combine their talents and tantalise the palates of visiting epicureans.

The valley's fertile soils, together with a high annual rainfall and hot, dry summers, provide the perfect conditions for grape-growing and the first settlers, initially intent on agriculture and pastoralism, soon realised the valley's potential for wine production. An Irishman, Edward Gleeson, established a sheep station in the valley in 1840 and by the end of that decade was making wine as well as growing fleece. Soon after, Gleeson laid out a village nearby, which he named Clare, after his home county in Ireland. Another Irishman to settle in the district at this time was John Hope whose property, 'Wolta Wolta', became one of South Australia's most successful sheep-breeding stations.

The discovery of substantial copper-ore deposits at Burra in 1845 gave impetus to the town's development, with the rapidly increasing mine population providing a ready-made market for the agricultural produce of the Clare district. Later, Clare found markets for its farm products in the rich copper mines that opened at the same time in the Yorke Peninsula.

The past lives on in Auburn where scores of old buildings – such as the Mechanics' Institute (above) – have been recycled into a new lease of life.

From its earliest days, Clare was promoted as a haven for tourists, its rustic pleasures offered as an antidote to the clamour and dust of the growing city of Adelaide. An 1850 issue of the *Mercury and Sporting Chronicle* described Clare in glowing terms: 'There is no prettier spot in the colony than the Village, and as there is plenty of game in the neighbourhood from Boomers down to Quail, it is as attractive a place for a fortnight's rustication or sport as the tired man of business or lover of the field could desire'.

During the 1870s, Clare's prosperity was boosted once again by events outside the district. The government's decision to open up vast tracts of land in the north for wheat growing, prompted a movement of farmers from the nutrient-depleted farming areas in the south through Clare to the new northern agricultural districts and the residents of Clare, quick to recognise an opportunity, built factories to meet the demand for farm implements. But the 1880s brought an end to growth; the colony was entering a long period of depression, years of intensive agriculture had left the once-fertile soils of the Clare Valley exhausted and many settlers abandoned their small farms to take up much larger selections in the north.

But by the early twentieth century, the town began to recover – wheat-growing in the Clare Valley was replaced by vineyard and orchard culture, for which the soils and climate were better suited and the widespread introduction of superphosphate fertiliser replenished the nutrient-depleted soil. By 1903, the basis of Clare's modern wine industry was firmly established. Later in the twentieth century, milk, pork and a variety of grains joined wine, wool and wheat as the valley's major products. *Population 2590*

'BUNGAREE' This historic sheep station near Clare was established on Christmas day 1841, by three brothers – George, James and Charles Hawker – whose search for good pastoral land led them to a place

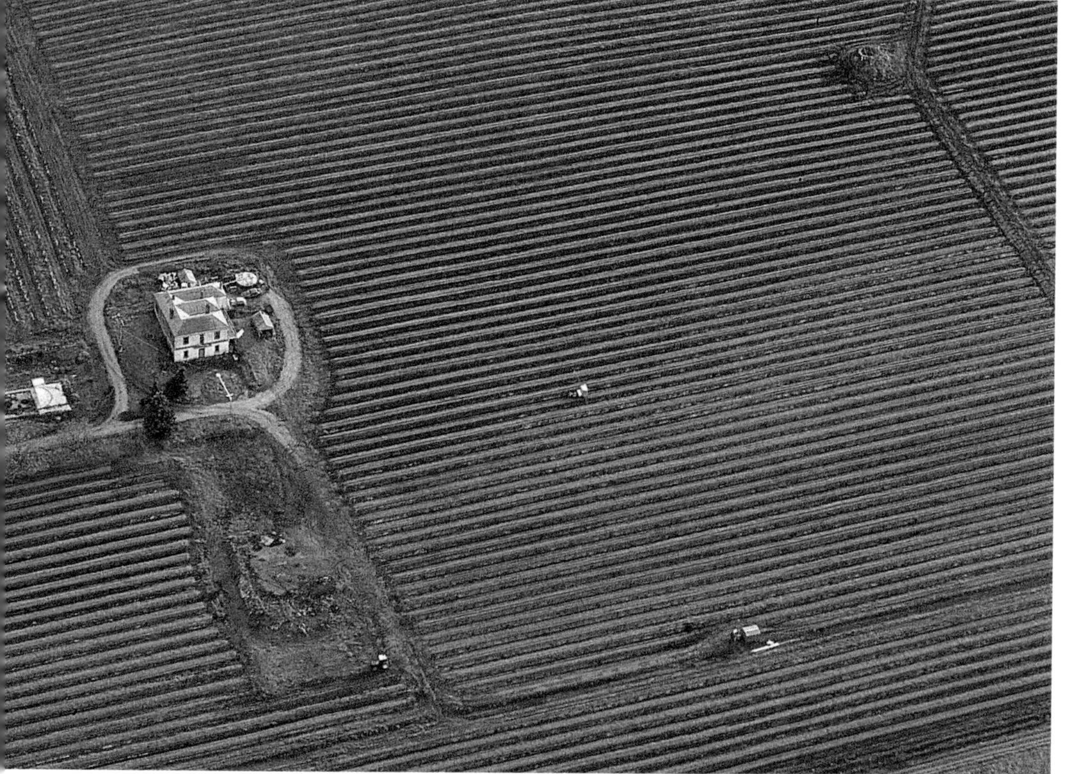

Wine grapes thrive in the cold winters and hot summers that so tried the patience of the Clare Valley's settlers.

where they sank a hole that yielded plenty of fresh water. The station was the first of many established by the Hawker brothers, who in time became the core of one of South Australia's most prominent pastoral and political families.

The woolshed is said to be haunted by the ghost of 'Bungaree' - said to be an Aboriginal word for 'my country' – supposedly an unhappy shearer who slit his throat in the woolshed in 1903. The blood-stained floorboards had to be replaced before the shearers would return to work and these 'new' boards are still clearly discernible.

POLICE STATION AND COURT HOUSE On the corner of Victoria Road and Neagles Rock Road, the former police station and court house built in 1850 was the first seat of local government in Clare. Edward Gleeson – the founder of Clare – was the first stipendiary magistrate. The building now houses the Clare district's historical museum.

'WOLTA WOLTA' This historic 1846 homestead has been restored after being almost completely destroyed in the terrible Ash Wednesday bushfire of 1983. The building still houses a fine collection of antique furniture – luckily spared by the fire – that was brought to Australia from Ireland.

As the fortunes of 'Wolta Wolta' increased, so to did the homestead building which was extended in 1869 and 1870. The additions included fretted bargeboards, unusual finials, and other elegant adornments.

FESTIVALS Clare Valley Gourmet Weekend, mid-May.

CRYSTAL BROOK ■ 1967

Edward Eyre set out from Adelaide on an exploratory expedition in 1840 and headed north, coming upon a creek which 'so forcibly reminded me of the beautiful bubbling brooks at home that I at once named it the Chrystal Brook'. And it is from this watercourse, flowing through the town's northern outskirts, that Crystal Brook takes its name.

The township was established officially in 1874 on land that the government resumed from the old 'Crystal Brook' run that was taken up in 1847. It developed as a service centre for the surrounding rural area which now produces grain, wool, milk and meat. A deviation of the main highway has excluded Crystal Brook from a constant traffic flow and since this beneficial innovation the town has resumed a quiet rural existence. *Population 1280*

BOWMAN PARK This forty-five-hectare reserve of bushland, located by Edward Eyre's 'Chrystal Brook' north of the town, is the site of the ruins of the Bowman Homestead – once the base for one of the largest sheep stations in South Australia.

A wide variety of native wildlife including rare birds such as the princess parrot and the nankeen night heron now finds shelter where sheep once grazed. The park has barbecue and picnic facilities and a lodge provides overnight accommodation for those energetic walkers who take on the hiking challenge of the 1500-kilometre-long Heysen Trail (see entry).

GLADSTONE ■ 1968

In its early days, Gladstone comprised two separate townships – Gladstone and Booyoolee – that faced each other across the railway lines that converged at Booyoolee Station. Gladstone was a private town established in 1871 and Booyoolee, named after the sheep station on its doorstep, was a government town, established in 1875. Eventually the two towns amalgamated but it was not until 1940 that Gladstone – named after the almost legendary British prime minister of the mid- to late nineteenth century – was adopted as the official name.

The clock tower of Port Pirie's elegantly formal station was destined never to show a true face due to turn-of-the-century bureaucrats' budget cuts.

The town developed as a major railway junction for local and interstate railway lines with three different railway gauges – narrow, standard and broad – all laid together in the one siding. Wheat and wool were the surrounding district's major products and the town became a loading point for the transportation of grain and later, the railway junction for trains carrying lead and zinc concentrates from Broken Hill for processing at Port Pirie. Gladstone has the largest inland grain-storage facilities in South Australia.

In 1870, 'Booyoolee' established the state's first meat-canning venture, as a means of putting the station's surplus sheep to profitable use. The preserved meat was a welcome addition to the bland diets of workers on the Overland Telegraph and local legend has it that these workers coined the term 'bully beef' – from 'Booyoolee beef'. In fact, the term is much older, coming from the French *bouilli*, meaning boiled beef. *Population 640*

GLADSTONE JAIL The first detainees in Gladstone Jail, which opened in 1881, were 'inebriates, debtors and other prisoners', but during nearly 100 years of operation, the jail was used as an internment camp during the Second World War, a military detention barracks and finally, as a medium-security jail.

HEYSEN TRAIL ■ 1969

The Heysen Trail is one of the longest walking tracks in the world. Extending for about 1500 kilometres from Cape Jervis in the Fleurieu Peninsula to Parachilna Gorge in the Flinders Ranges, the trail passes through much of South Australia's most spectacular country – a meandering line strung with places that recall the exploration and spread of settlement throughout the state.

From Cape Jervis it passes along the south coast of the Fleurieu Peninsula before turning north over the gum-covered ridges of the Mount Lofty Ranges. Through the Barossa Valley and over the Tothill Range, the trail links with Burra before entering the stark Flinders Ranges.

The trail is named after Sir Hans Heysen, the famous bush painter and conservationist who worked to preserve the plants of the Adelaide Hills. To trek its entire length would require the experience and stamina of a seasoned bushwalker, but the trail has been designed for a range of walkers with sections that can be completed in a day, a weekend, or several weeks.

JAMESTOWN ■ 1970

During the 1870s, the South Australian government encouraged the further spread of settlement into the colony's northern regions by resuming land held as part of vast pastoral stations, for the creation of new agricultural areas. Jamestown was one of the many agriculturally based settlements that sprang up as a result of this northward movement. The town was surveyed in 1871 and named after the then Governor of South Australia, Sir James Fergusson.

The arrival of the railway line gave impetus to the town's development and the Port Pirie–Broken Hill railway has long been an important factor in the town's growth. Sheep, wheat, barley and cattle still form the basis of the district's prosperity and the nearby Bundaleer Forest – the first government forest in Australia – yields large quantities of radiata pine. *Population 1360*

LAURA ■ 1971

The Australian poet C.J. Dennis lived for many years in Laura – a pretty town on the banks of the Rocky River and the eastern slopes of the Flinders Ranges. Laura held a special place in the poet's heart – his first poem was published in the *Laura Standard* in 1895. He said of the town: 'Of all country places I know, Laura still remains for me the place of most pleasant memory...' In 1932, Laura celebrated its Golden Jubilee and Dennis honoured the occasion with a poem, 'Laura Days', which ends with lines that clearly convey his affection for the town:

When the evening sun slants through the gums
By my forest-rimmed abode,
Once more the old clear picture comes,
And my mind drifts down the road;
Back to the town by Beetaloo,
Where the Rocky River strays;
Back to the old kind friends I knew
In the dear dead Laura days.

A copper sculpture of C.J. Dennis stands outside a gallery near the southern entrance to the town.

The town was established in 1872 and as a service centre for the surrounding farming district, Laura's early industries included market gardening, flax, dairying and brewing. In the late 1880s, Laura became the supply town for the nearby construction camp, the workers from which were building the Beetaloo Reservoir. Today, the district's rurally-based industries are complemented by a number of art and craft ventures including cottage crafts, art galleries, silver-smithing and pottery, many of which are housed in the town's historic, sensibly verandahed buildings. *Population 520*

BEETALOO RESERVOIR Surrounded by steep, forested hills, the tranquil waters of Beetaloo Reservoir, south-west of the town, are impounded by a thirty-three-metre-high concrete wall that was built in the late 1880s. Birds such as shags, black swans, cormorants and pelicans can be seen on

As a rail junction, Gladstone coped cleverly with a post-Federation nightmare: three different gauges.

the lake, while roads and walking tracks winding through the hillside forests offer the chance of a glimpse of the region's plentiful wildlife.

FESTIVALS Folk Fair, early April.

PENWORTHAM ■ 1972

The explorer John Ainsworth Horrocks founded Penwortham in 1840, naming the town after his home in England. By 1842, Penwortham had twenty-four residents including a blacksmith, innkeeper, carrier, shoemaker and two policemen. Horrocks' Hope Farm property was commonly referred to as 'The Manor'. It is not surprising then, that after his untimely death in 1846 at the age of twenty-eight, the village lost much of its developmental drive and people began to drift away.

On an expedition to the north in search of new pastures, Horrocks was injured when his bad-tempered camel, Harry, accidentally caused him to discharge his gun, injuring his right hand and his upper jaw. He survived long enough to be transported back to Penwortham where he died 'without a struggle' on 23 September 1846. Horrocks was buried in Penwortham cemetery and a cairn at its entrance honours the unlucky explorer.

PORT PIRIE ■ 1973

Port Pirie is the prince of provincial ports in South Australia, its maritime history a who's who of ships and sailors from around the world. It is also the site of the world's largest lead-smelting and refining plant and a huge bulk silo complex used for storing grain prior to export.

Its development from a simple jetty, a couple of woolsheds and a caretaker's cottage to South Australia's first provincial city began in the mid-1840s when the schooner *John Pirie* – after which the city is named – navigated the mangrove-lined estuary of Tarparrie Creek – later Pirie River – at the request of the region's pastoralists and transported sheep to new holdings near Port Lincoln (see *Port Lincoln & Tumby Bay*).

By the 1870s, farmers had settled throughout the colony's northern regions and Port Pirie became the funnel through which their produce flowed. Two townships named Port Pirie – one private, surveyed in 1848, the other government, surveyed in 1871 – faced each other across the creek. In time, this duplication resolved itself as the government town eventually developed ahead of the private settlement. In modern Port Pirie, up to one million tonnes of lead concentrates arrive from Broken Hill each year for export to other parts of the world or for treatment at the smelters.

Rail transport – essential for carrying the bulky raw materials of ore refining – has also played an important part in the development of the port to industrial-giant status. At one stage, three different railway gauges met at Port Pirie and trains rolled down the main street. Now, the city is an important railway centre for the nation's major east-west and north-south railway systems, providing servicing facilities for the Indian–Pacific and The Ghan trains.

Despite its industrial image, Port Pirie is not bereft of festivities and culture. On the second Sunday in September each year, the city's large Italian community perform the annual 'Blessing of the Fleet' ceremony, which starts with a church service followed by a procession to the fishing wharf where a statue of the Madonna Dei Martiri is carried aboard a decorated fishing trawler. Country music has made it big in Port Pirie and the annual Festival of Country Music draws sizeable crowds to the Northern Festival Centre each year. *Population 14 110*

'CARN BRAE' This majestic mansion in Florence Street, built in 1905, has exquisite stained-glass windows, an elaborate cast-iron fence and gates, old brass light fittings, delicately moulded ceilings and cornices and cedar venetian blinds. 'Carn Brae' is open to the public.

MEMORIAL PARK This city park is the final resting place of the original anchor of the schooner *John Pirie* – the first ship to navigate the Pirie River – which was wrecked off the Fleurieu Peninsula near Aldinga Bay. The anchor was salvaged from the seabed in 1968 and displayed in the park the following year.

FESTIVALS Blessing of the Fleet, late August–early September; Festival of Country Music, September/October; Athletic and Cycling Carnival, late November.

PORT WAKEFIELD ■ 1974

The discovery of substantial copper deposits in Burra in 1845 prompted the search for an outlet, closer than Adelaide, for the mine's copper ore – with Adelaide more than 160 kilometres away, the road cartage by bullock teams was hard-going and costly. A good natural harbour was discovered in 1849 at the head of Gulf St Vincent and the Patent Copper Company at Burra soon blazed a track across country to the newly established Port Henry at the mouth of the River Wakefield.

The town of Wakefield was established next to the port in 1850. Port Henry subsequently adopted the name Port Wakefield. In time, the name did service for both port and town though the two were, and still are, separate entities. The arrival of the railway line in the late 1850s brought an end to the copper trade but by this stage the port had become the major outlet for the region's agricultural exports. Port Wakefield died as a busy cargo centre when the trading ketches were phased out in 1930 – a waterfront monument reminds modern generations of those lively days. Wakefield's business and residential streets have survived the twentieth century very well with almost all of their original nineteenth-century buildings intact. *Population 510*

SEVENHILL ■ 1975

South-east of Clare and in the heart of the Clare Valley wine lands, this Jesuit settlement was established in 1851 by Father Aloysius Kranewitter and Brothers George Sadler and John Schreiner. They named their settlement after Rome – the 'city of the seven hills'. Vine clippings taken from Bungaree Station (see Clare) took root in the fertile Clare Valley soils and soon a vineyard was being cultivated for the production of sacramental wines for use in the colony and for export.

Father Kranewitter took leave of the community for a short while to accompany a band of Catholics bound for the Victorian goldfields. He was rewarded for his priestly duties with a bag of gold, donated by the diggers, and upon his return to Sevenhill he put it to good use building a boarding school to cater for the educational needs of the settlers' children. Construction of the impressive St Aloysius' Church commenced in 1864 but work on the final stage of the building – the south transept – did not commence until 1992. Since the 1950s, a range of table wines have joined the sacramental wines produced at Sevenhill Cellars – the oldest vineyard in the Clare Valley.

The faith of the Jesuits bore fruit in 1856 when the Clare's first grapes were used for altar wines; now the Sevenhill winery also makes fine table wines.

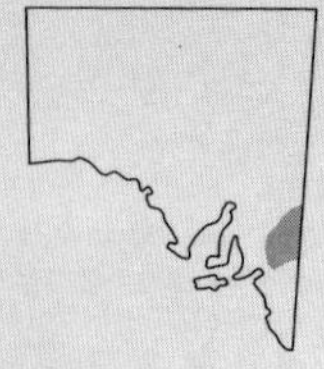

Berri & Renmark

The harnessing of the River Murray – not 'Murray River' in these parts – has transformed arid, mallee scrublands into a region dubbed the 'Riverland' – the biggest wine-producing region in Australia. The romance of the paddle-steamer days is relived aboard modern replicas that cruise between historic ports.

BARMERA ■ 1976

Barmera made the transition from bush camp to town after the First World War when the government, inspired by the success of the irrigation settlements at Renmark and Mildura, resurrected plans to create an irrigation area and provide blocks of arable land for soldier-settlers. Land clearing began in 1919 and the town, located on the shores of Lake Bonney – a large freshwater lake several kilometres from the river – was gazetted in 1921. Barmera is thought to come from an Aboriginal word for 'place of king spears' – referring to a javelin-style weapon – or an original name for Lake Bonney.

Although the youngest of the irrigation towns, Barmera has grown to become the centre of the Riverland's irrigation area with fruit-growing – particularly grapes for wine-making, drying and for the table – and tourism, as its main industries. The town is also acclaimed as the country music capital of South Australia.

Aborigines inhabited the area surrounding Barmera and Lake Bonney for at least 30 000 years before the drovers and their stock moved in – scattered artefacts and burial grounds are reminders of this pre-European heritage. *Population 1860*

DONALD CAMPBELL OBELISK Situated on the foreshores of Lake Bonney, this obelisk commemorates Donald Campbell's 1964 attempt to break the world water-speed record. Minor turbulence, causing dangerous rippling of the lake's surface, thwarted his attempt, despite his reaching a top speed of more than 347 kilometres an hour.

LAKE BONNEY The tranquil waters of Lake Bonney were sighted by overlander Joseph Hawdon in 1838 when droving the first mob of cattle from New South Wales to South Australia along the River Murray. After months of battling through unexplored country, the lake was a welcome sight to Hawdon, who named the lake after his companion, Charles Bonney.

Within months of this pioneering journey, the explorers Edward John Eyre and Charles Sturt drove cattle along much the same route, establishing the course of the Murray as the major overland route between the two colonies. By the 1870s, the area around the lake had become a huge camping ground for drovers and their stock going to Adelaide.

FESTIVALS South Australian Country Music Awards, early June.

BERRI ■ 1977

The name Berri is synonymous with fruit products, particularly wine and canned fruits, and the town is the economic and administrative centre of the abundantly productive Riverland region. The diversity and vast

West of Renmark, where the Murray has cut itself a channel through the limestone plains, the river appears to have slipped into a mountainous landscape.

quantity of fruit produced here is evidence of the success of the irrigation scheme developed in 1910 when the Berri Irrigation Area was proclaimed – the town of Berri was founded soon after, in 1911.

Prior to irrigation, the area was an undeveloped portion of the Cobdogla Station and Berri was little more than a woodpile for the paddle steamers and barges which plied the River Murray. Growth was spasmodic, relying largely on land settlement programmes after the two world wars. Then, in the 1950s, came the evolution of large co-operatives where owners controlled the packaging and marketing of their fruit products and Berri experienced a rapid growth in industry, commerce and tourism.

Surrounded by Australia's largest vineyards, the town is home to Berri Estates, which began operating as a co-operative winery and distillery in 1922 and was once the single largest operation of its kind in the Southern Hemisphere. In 1992 Berri merged to become part of Australia's second largest wine-producing group.

Some uncertainty surrounds the origin of the town's name – on early maps of the area, the name 'Beri Beri Hut' is shown – the irrigation area and the town of Berri were probably named after the hut, which may have derived from the Aboriginal word for a bush growing in this vicinity. *Population 3730*

WILABALANGALOO RESERVE Scrubland adjacent to the River Murray is protected in this 100-hectare reserve. Numerous walking tracks take in spectacular cliffs and a rich diversity of native animals and birds. The old Wilabalangaloo Homestead has an extensive collection of riverboat photographs. The PS *Roy* – the smallest paddle steamer to ply the Murray – has come to a permanent standstill in the grounds.

FESTIVALS Berri Easter Carnival, Easter Saturday; Riverland Special School Art & Craft Fair, November.

BLANCHETOWN ■ 1978

This pleasant and sleepy little town on the banks of the River Murray was named after Lady Blanche MacDonnell, the wife of Governor MacDonnell. Following an increase in river traffic, the settlement developed as a river port in 1856 and showed every sign of growing and prospering as a loading centre for riverboats and as a way-station on the overland route to the east. A customs house was built, followed by a hotel – constructed in 1858 and still operating – and later came a telegraph office and a police station.

In 1870, proposals for a railway connection with Gawler (see *Gawler & Nuriootpa*) were considered but never eventuated. Instead, the trains – and growth in trade – went to Morgan (see entry).

BLANCHETOWN HISTORIC RESERVE The river red gums in this reserve, east of Blanchetown, are some of Australia's best examples of Aboriginal canoe trees – so called because of the scars formed when sheets of bark were prised off to make canoes.

BROOKFIELD CONSERVATION PARK This 5530-hectare park, one of several established specifically to protect one of Australia's rarest animals – the hairy-nosed wombat – takes its name from the Brookfield Zoo in Chicago. The park was originally the site of a property which the owners sold to the Chicago Zoological Society – owners of the Brookfield Zoo – in 1971. Some years later, the park was donated to the South Australian government on the condition that it be maintained as a reserve.

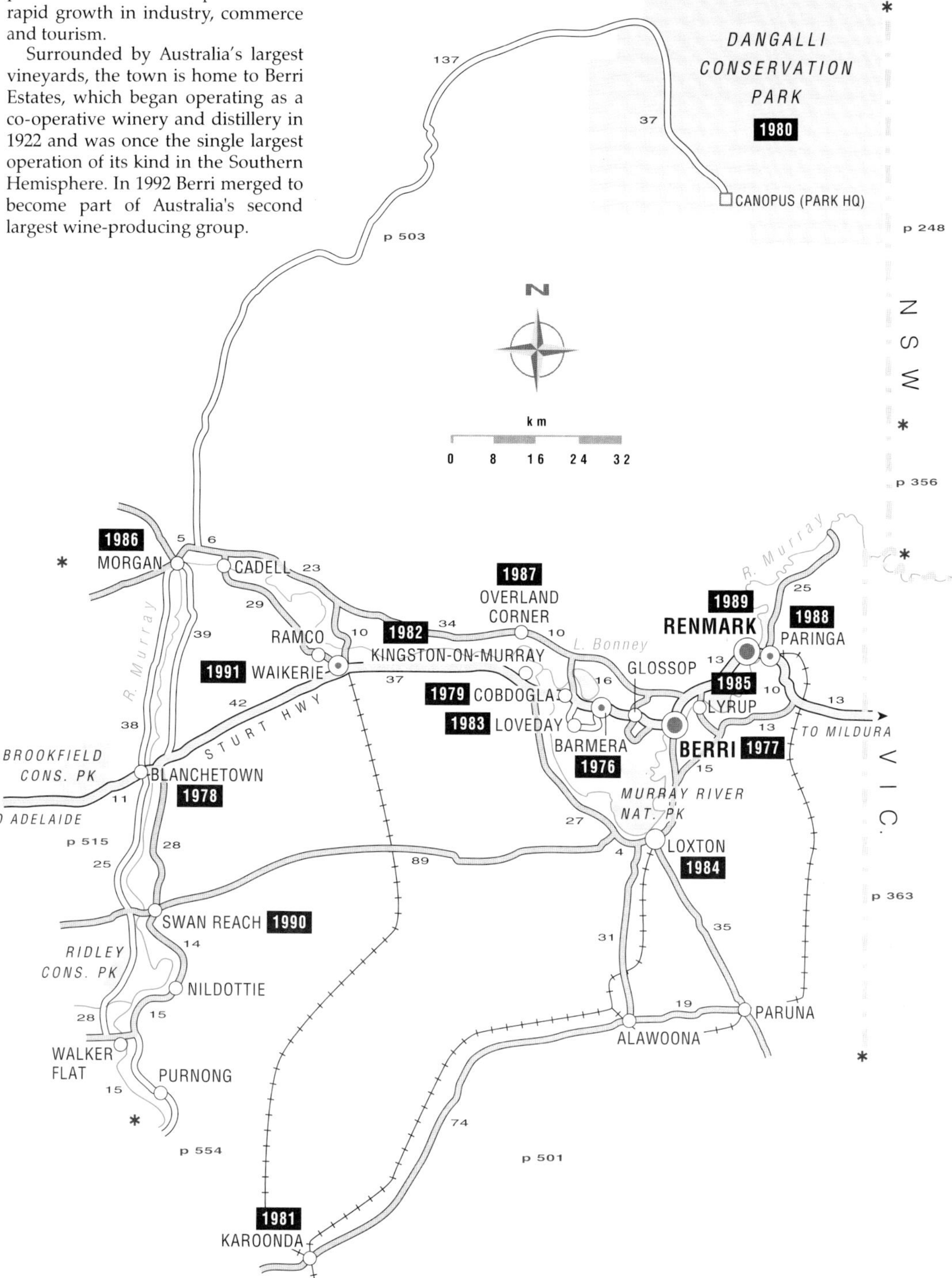

COBDOGLA ■ 1979

Cobdogla came into existence in 1919 as the best site for a unique gas-powered water pump that would supply water for a newly created irrigation area. The town and surrounding irrigation area are on what was once part of Cobdogla Station – for many years the focus of Riverland activity. 'Cobdogla' was the home of the original 'Greys' of the South Australian mounted police – horses famous for their quality and stamina. 'Cobdogla' is said to come from an Aboriginal word meaning 'land of plenty'.

The Humphrey pump – named for its inventor, Herbert Alfred Humphrey – was also known as the 'Big Thumper' and employed a revolutionary design to lift river water. Electrically powered pumps are used now with the world's only fully restored and working Humphrey pump taking pride of place at the Cobdogla Irrigation Museum.

DANGGALI CONSERVATION PARK ■ 1980

This vast and isolated park adjacent to the New South Wales border is in semi-arid mallee country with gently undulating sand dunes. Danggali is a botanist's delight with a number of rare or depleted plants thriving within its boundaries. Because of its great size, the park displays a gradual but distinctive change in plant life from north to south. Yorrell, red mallee, sand pine, desert poplar and emu bush growing in the south merge with a black-oak zone, which in turn gives way to blue bush and mulga in the drier, shallower soils of the north.

At Blanchetown, the canoeists have met their first obstruction – Lock No. 1,the first of 5 water 'steps' in Riverland.

KAROONDA ■ **1981**

Though less than forty kilometres from the River Murray, Karoonda and the surrounding district rely on bores for a water supply in country that is characterised by open stretches of agricultural land studded with pockets of mallee and periodic sand ridges – a reminder of the true nature of this semi-desert country.

A meteorite, weighing an estimated twenty-five kilograms, fell four kilometres east of the town in 1930; an obelisk in Railway Terrace commemorates the event.

KINGSTON-ON-MURRAY ■ **1982**

Kingston-on-Murray is the small service centre for a Riverland irrigation area that produces table and wine grapes, and citrus and stone fruits. The town tried and discarded several names before deciding that a variation of the original name given it in 1896 – with the addition of a suffix that leaves no doubt as to its location – would be most appropriate.

The first settlers arrived in the area in 1894 and camped on and around an old station house known as 'Thurk'. An area designated for settlement in 1896 was named the 'Kingston Village Association' but the community already established at Thurk Station moved instead to the cliffs above the river. The village that grew there was proclaimed in 1918 as the Town of Thurk; this name was changed in 1940 to honour Charles Kingston, the Premier of South Australia from 1893 to 1899. 'On-Murray' distinguishes the town from Kingston, in the south-east of the state.

LOVEDAY ■ **1983**

Loveday is one of the small satellite towns of the Berri Irrigation District and the centre of a busy fruit-growing area. The town was proclaimed in 1940 and is named after Ernest Alfred Loveday, the first superintendent surveyor of the Irrigation Department. Loveday's small population and its fruit and vegetable production were considerably boosted during the Second World War when an internment and prisoner-of-war camp was established here.

LOXTON ■ **1984**

Of all the irrigation towns along the Murray, the pleasant garden town of Loxton is perhaps most representative of the strong community spirit that was an essential ingredient in the Riverland's development.

Pastoral leases were taken up in the region in the 1850s and the town was founded on wool and wheat in the 1890s when German settlers, possessed of a strong work ethic, cleared the thick mallee scrub for grazing and farming. As the service centre for this rural industry, Loxton was proclaimed a village in 1907. But the real impetus to growth came after the Second World War when the state government made nearly 2500 hectares of irrigated land available for the largest soldier-settlement scheme in South Australia.

The scheme made Loxton a boom town, no longer solely dependent on wool and wheat for its economic well-being but a thriving community surrounded by many hectares of irrigated vineyards and fruit groves. The tradition of communal effort that supplied voluntary labour for a number of the town's public amenities continued with the formation of co-operative industries including a winery and distillery established in the early 1950s – which crushes more than 20 000 tonnes of grapes annually – as well as fruit packing sheds and a community-owned hotel.

The town is named after William Loxton, a boundary rider on the Bookpurnong Station, who lived in a pine and pug hut near the present site of Loxton. *Population 3320*

LOXTON HISTORICAL VILLAGE Much of the district's early history is captured in this recreation of an early 1900s farming town, built on the riverfront. A replica of William Loxton's hut is shaded by a giant pepper tree he planted almost 100 years ago.

PYAP RESERVE Just past Loxton, this quiet riverbank area is also known as the Daisy Bates Reserve – named for the remarkable woman who devoted her life to the Aboriginal cause. A commemorative plaque records the years she lived in a tent in this district, between 1936 and 1940.

ST PETER'S LUTHERAN CHURCH Voluntary labour supplied the workforce for this solidly built church – a tribute to the town's community spirit.

LYRUP ■ **1985**

The economic trough of the 1890s, partly brought on by the failure of crops on the northern frontier of the colony of South Australia in the 1880s, led the government to try some brave experiments in semi-communist-style settlements. Several hundred of Port Adelaide's dispossessed were transported to the dry mallee scrublands of the Riverland with the most basic of provisions and left to 'make a go of it'.

Individuals and families sought self-sufficiency on farming blocks, and purchases were made with coupons. Any earnings were paid into a village fund. Needless to say, the pioneering qualities of independence and individualism asserted themselves and the experiment in communal living largely failed.

Of eleven such settlements established along the River Murray in 1894, only Lyrup remains as a true communal village. Run by an association which holds 800 hectares of farming and grazing land under its control, Lyrup has a requirement that any person with more than one hectare of land must become a member of the association. The village takes its name from a boundary rider's rough shack – Lyrup Hut – that has long since disappeared.

MORGAN ■ **1986**

Paddle steamers plying the river trade gave South Australia an economic advantage over the colonies of Victoria and New South Wales during the 1850s. But by the end of the 1880s, trains had steamed into the inland river ports of the River Murray, the Murrumbidgee and the Darling, connecting them with the markets at Melbourne and Sydney, and Port Adelaide no longer held the upper hand.

It was against this background that Morgan – named after a premier of South Australia, Sir William Morgan – was surveyed in 1878 at that great bend in the River Murray where it cuts through a landscape of towering limestone cliffs and turns south. Connected to Adelaide by train, the port of Morgan linked the river and railway trade and by the turn of the century had become the busiest river port in South Australia – the massive old wharves jutting into the river still stand as a reminder of those bustling days. But success was short-lived; within a decade the battle between river and rail as the chief conveyor of colonial trade was over; the railway emerging as the victor.

Morgan's historic buildings make a charming cluster around the old railway station and wharves and the town is the starting point for a pipeline that carries water to Whyalla and its steel industry (see *Whyalla & Port Augusta*).

OVERLAND CORNER ■ **1987**

During the early nineteenth century, the grassy river flats at this 'corner' on the original overland stock route from New South Wales to the infant town of Adelaide, were a popular resting place for drovers and their livestock. By the mid-1850s, other travellers such as businessmen, station hands and gold-diggers had swollen the traffic on the overland route to such an extent that a small police station was established at Overland Corner to 'keep the peace'.

Built from local fossilised limestone, the Overland Corner Hote was the first stone dwelling in the Riverland and with walls up to half-a-metre thick, it is not surprising tha it has withstood the rigours of time to become a treasured property o the National Trust.

In the 1870s, the hotel also became a post and telegraph office and it was not until the turn of the century tha the growth of river and railway transport reduced the flow of over land traffic so much that the hote relinquished its role as a place of accommodation, although it continued as a post office until well into the twentieth century. The restored building now houses a museum.

PARINGA ■ 1988

The first South Australian town that drivers travelling along the Sturt Highway from Victoria reach is Paringa, a hamlet just a few kilometres from Renmark (see entry), on the opposite side of the Murray.

With its flotilla of houseboats moored under graceful willow trees at the council marina and pleasant riverside recreation areas, the town is popular as a holiday destination. Fine views of the surrounding irrigated farmlands and river cliffs are afforded by the town's two lookout towers while nearby is the massive root system and stump of the 'Black Stump' – all that remains of a river red gum thought to be nearly 600 years old.

In the mid-nineteenth century, the town site was a property on the River Murray named 'Paringa', an Aboriginal word said to mean 'land near or about the river'. The town of Paringa was not laid out until 1917, though a post office existed here in 1912. *Population 830*

RENMARK ■ 1989

Renmark is the largest town in the Riverland and the centre for South Australia's largest irrigation scheme, which covers nearly 7000 hectares of land along the River Murray and produces prodigious quantities of wine and table grapes, citrus, stone and dried fruits, vegetables, wheat and wool, for local and export markets. It is also the first of Australia's irrigation settlements – narrowly beating Mildura in Victoria to the claim (see box, *Mildura & Wentworth*).

The settlement was founded in 1887 by two noted experts on irrigation – the Canadian-born brothers, George and William Chaffey – who signed an agreement with the South Australian Government on 14 February of that year to establish an irrigation settlement on Chowilla and Bookmark stations (see box). Although the Chaffey brothers went bankrupt some years after the scheme was inaugurated, their place was taken by a local government trust – to this day housed in the original Chaffey brothers' office – which continued to administer the scheme.

Like many of the Riverland towns, Renmark was built on a strong foundation of community consciousness. The three-storey Renmark Hotel was the first community hotel established in the British Empire and is run by an elected board of management with the profits going towards community improvements. The first winery and distillery in Riverland was established here in 1910 and Australia's first co-operative winery was opened at Renmark in 1916.

Renmark's rich history is evident in its many old buildings and monuments. The Chaffey brothers' original homestead, 'Olivewood' – now classified by the National Trust – was built in 1887 in the style of a Canadian log cabin adapted for Australian conditions by the addition of wide verandahs all around the main house. An old hand-operated wine press and George Chaffey's original wood-burning, steam-operated irrigation pump are displayed in the main street while the paddle steamer *Industry*, built in Goolwa in 1911 (see *Murray Bridge & Mount Barker*), has found a permanent mooring as the town's floating museum.

The romance of the early days of paddle steamer trade is recreated in modern times through luxurious vessels such as the paddle steamer *Murray Princess* – the biggest sternpaddle steamer in the Southern Hemisphere – which sets out from Renmark for voyages along the river. On a smaller scale, houseboats provide a means of leisurely travel along the Murray, and Renmark, with its pretty riverfront parks and gardens, is a popular starting point for river excursions. *Population 4260*

FESTIVALS Renmark Show, late October.

SWAN REACH ■ 1990

Holiday shacks line the riverfront of the pleasant stretch of the Murray at Swan Reach, a small town popular as a holiday destination. Set against a backdrop of cliffs on the river's eastern bank, the town takes its name from the black swans that populated the waters here during the early days of settlement.

Swan Reach was never destined for major development, though it had some hopes of becoming a busy port town during its early years – a notion dispelled summarily by the intrepid paddle-steamer pioneer, Francis Cadell, during his journey up the River Murray in the *Lady Augusta* in 1853, when he wrote of the Swan Reach section of the river: 'We passed the Rhine (now the Marne) at 2 o'clock. Its waters seemed rather swollen. The last station we saw was Mr Tothill's; the house appears deserted. We reached Moorundie at 11 o'clock'.

The area was settled by Europeans during the late 1830s; the first pastoral lease was taken up in the area by Archibald Jaffray in 1845 on the 'right bank of Murray, eight miles below Moorundie'.

WAIKERIE ■ 1991

Waikerie was born as a communal settlement in 1894, when a government scheme created to relieve unemployment in Adelaide by decentralisation saw more than 200 people arrive by paddle steamer to establish a farming community on part of the old Waikerie Station.

Armed with government-supplied tools and a scant one month's provisions, these early settlers gradually transformed the dry mallee-scrub country into productive farmland, and now the Waikerie district, irrigated by the waters of the Murray, is the largest citrus-growing area in Australia – and the site of one of the world's largest co-operative fruit-packing sheds. *Population 1750*

FESTIVALS Waikerie Rotary International Food Fair, early March.

DOWN-MURRAY, THE PERILS OF SALT

SOUTH AUSTRALIA, the driest state in the world's driest continent, draws just over half of its total irrigation, stock, domestic and industrial water supply from the highly regulated River Murray, far and away its most important water source. But 'old man Murray' is rebelling against more than a century of heavy, and at times insensitive, demands on his waters – salinity levels have risen to the extent that the degradation of river waters and much of the irrigated landscape has become one of the most serious environmental problems facing the state today.

When the Canadian brothers, George and William Chaffey, (see box, *Mildura & Wentworth*) signed an agreement with the South Australian Government in 1887 to establish the first irrigation colony in Australia at Renmark, (see entry) they initiated a dramatic and imaginative transformation of the region into one of the major citrus- and grape-growing areas in Australia – fulfilling, to some extent, the optimistic declaration by the then Assistant Director of Kew Gardens in London, that 'from these sunny lands where our sons and daughters have made their homes, we shall draw our future supply of FRUIT, in quality and quantity probably exceeding that of any Fruit Industry the world has seen'. But the same dry-land irrigation schemes that have so magically brought the Riverland to horticultural life have been contributing gradually but surely to its degradation.

Rising levels of saline groundwater in irrigated areas have resulted from an increased infiltration of water brought about by the replacement of deep-rooted native plants with shallow-rooted crops and pastures, which absorb much less water. Surplus irrigation swells the water table, which then rises, transferring salty groundwater to the surface, which becomes an inhospitable environment for vegetation. Run-off from drainage channels then raises the salinity level of the river – and so the cycle continues.

Evaporation of drainage water from a near-river depression leaves a lifeless, salty surface.

Attempts to mitigate salinity, such as channelling drainage water into evaporation ponds before it runs into the Murray, controlling land use and improving irrigation practices on farms have helped, but the battle continues, with community involvement in water-resources management – particularly in South Australia – encouraged through advisory committees as well as specific projects such as the River Murray salinity program. □

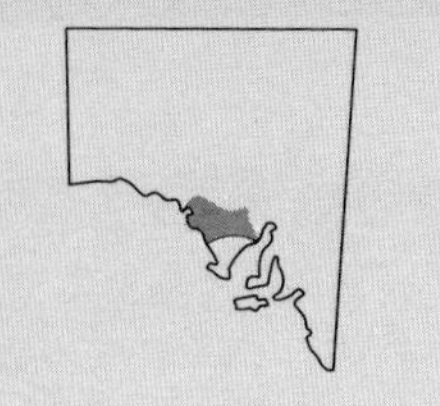

Streaky Bay & Kimba

Since the 1860s, the upper Eyre Peninsula has grown much of South Australia's wheat. In contrast, a series of arid-land parks protects examples of its plants and animals while outcrops of mound-shaped rocks dot the flat landscape.

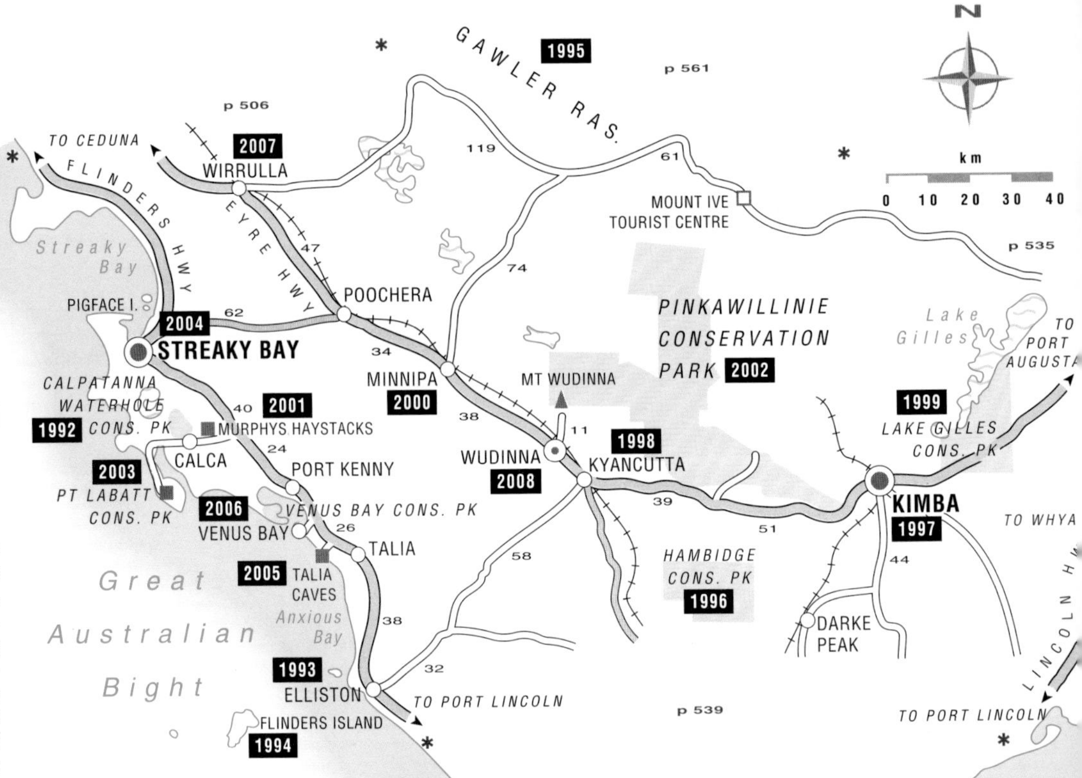

CALPATANNA WATERHOLE CONSERVATION PARK ■ 1992

The extensive system of salt lakes protected in this park fill with winter rains but, in the long hot summers, can dry to shimmering salt pans. They are fringed by low-growing semi-succulent plants, and surrounding them on sandy and stony ridges is an area of semi-arid scrub which is characteristic of the west coast of South Australia. In particular this includes salt paperbark and the multi-stemmed mallee. There are also stands of native cypress pine and, regenerating on those parts that had been cleared, tea-trees, wattles and she-oaks.

ELLISTON ■ 1993

Elliston is on the shores of Waterloo Bay, and is protected from the swells of the Southern Ocean within the arms of Wellington and Wellesley points – a naming spree of natural features here in 1865 celebrated the fiftieth anniversary of the British victory over Napoleon's forces in the Battle of Waterloo (appropriately, Wellington and Wellesley were brothers in fact as well as in arms). It is generally accepted that the town, though, was named for a local, Miss Ellen Liston, who was governess to the children of a local station owner, and that it is a combination of her first name and surname.

The town began as a port for the settlements of the inland, and coastal traders landed supplies and loaded produce here. Reaching its jetty was far from easy sailing, for a sandbar across the bay mouth had first to be negotiated. The jetty today is a popular fishing spot and at night is lit to improve anglers' chances.

On the clifftops near the town are numbers of small limestone formations which are unique to this coast and are known as 'clogs'. They are the fossilised cocoons of a large acacia-eating weevil and are believed to be up to 100 000 years old.

FLINDERS ISLAND ■ 1994

This 3750-hectare island, in the Great Australian Bight 35 kilometres off the coast from Elliston, was frequented by sealers in the 1820s and 1830s – tales of treasure buried somewhere here date from this lawless time. In later years the dingo-free pastures of the island attracted pioneering pastoralists and their flocks. It is still run as a sheep station but the original shearers' quarters have been restored for use as tourist accommodation.

GAWLER RANGES ■ 1995

The red granite hills of the Gawler Ranges, the result of volcanic activity 1500 million years ago, run east–west for some 160 kilometres, and rise 400 metres and more above the surrounding plains. They vary from gentle slopes which support low-density grazing, to steep bluffs. The highest point is Nukey Bluff (470 metres) in the eastern end. In spring, given the required rainfall, the hills are covered in colourful wildflowers, and it was here that the first observation was made – by explorer Edward Eyre in 1839 – of Sturt's desert pea, the floral emblem of South Australia.

Streaky Bay still lives up to the name given by Matthew Flinders in 1802, when he saw seaweed driven by an onshore breeze into long, 'streaky' bands.

The ranges were sighted by explorer Edward Eyre on his 1839 trek from Streaky Bay back east across the top of the peninsula which now bears his name. He named them for the Governor of South Australia, George Gawler. The area had been known to the Aborigines for thousands of years and within the ranges Yantanabie Historic Reserve protects an Aboriginal quarry where material for tools was obtained.

After 1500 million years of weathering, Murphys Haystacks' outer covering is now the soil on which they stand.

HAMBIDGE CONSERVATION PARK ■ 1996

This park preserves a large area of undisturbed arid country, an important example used in evaluating the impact of past land use in similar areas, and in understanding the processes which form various desert-region landscapes.

The scrub-covered limestone and sand ridges of Hambidge, rising usually six to twelve metres, run roughly parallel in a north-east, south-west direction. In the highest part of the park, at Prominent Hill, they are a towering sixty to ninety metres high. In the depressions and clay pans between the ridges grow tall mallees, and on the dune crests there are cypress pines. Its mammals include creatures which have adapted to the harsh desert life so that they can conserve moisture and survive climatic extremes. Among them are the fat-tailed dunnart, its tail a storehouse of food, Mitchell's hopping mouse and the western pigmy possum; there is even a possibility that the rare brush-tailed rat kangaroo exists in the park.

KIMBA ■ 1997

Kimba serves one of the major wheat regions in South Australia. European land use here dates from the 1870s, when sheep runs were taken up. Agricultural development dates from the early 1900s when the dense mallee was cleared and wheat and barley planted. The town was proclaimed in 1915. *Population 680*

KYANCUTTA ■ 1998

Kyancutta lies at the waterless heart of the Eyre Peninsula, a tiny township which serves the surrounding agricultural community. It came into being in 1917 when settlement here became possible due to the arrival of both the railway and the water pipeline. A weather station has operated from Kyancutta since 1928.

The town takes its name from an Aboriginal word meaning 'little night hawk', the name by which a nearby hill was known.

CORROBINNIE HILL CONSERVATION PARK North-east of the town a huge granite outcrop rises above the dusty mallee. This is Corrobinnie Hill, one of a number of similar formations scattered across the top of Eyre Peninsula and called 'inselbergs' – from the German words for 'island' and mountain'. The grooved and weathered slopes of Corrobinnie Hill often feature in Aboriginal legend. Wattle, broombrush and mallee grow near its base, and in spring the area is covered with wildflowers. Birds here include honey-eaters, scrub robins, and the black-faced cuckoo shrike.

LAKE GILLES CONSERVATION PARK ■ 1999

This park is known particularly for the variety of birds which can be easily seen here. The fifty-four species recorded include the Port Lincoln parrot, mallee fowl, peregrine falcon, orange chat, rufous tree creeper and turquoise wren.

On the park's north-west boundary lies the highly saline Lake Gilles which is considered unusual for the large crystals of gypsum which 'grow' in the mud. The lake and park are named for Osmond Gilles who introduced Saxon and Merino sheep to the colony of South Australia.

MINNIPA ■ 2000

Sheep have grazed here since the 1870s, and the town dates from 1915 and the opening of the railway. Before 1925, when the water pipeline reached Minnipa, farmers had to rely on the scanty rainfall collected in their own tanks and dams. Minnipa is now surrounded by wheatfields, and silos dominate the townscape.

Nearby are a number of granite outcrops known as inselbergs (see Kyancutta), remnants of the stony plateau which once covered this entire region. Yarwondutta Rock, to the north, is part of an agricultural reserve; Minnipa Hill, from which the town takes its name, is nearby; and just to the east is Tcharkulda Hill where each year students from the schools of Eyre Peninsula compete in a 5000-metre, cross-country event.

MURPHYS HAYSTACKS ■ 2001

These large granite boulders, with their weird and wonderful bulbous shapes, were a landmark on the old coach road. They are named for their supposed likeness to old-fashioned haystacks and for Patrick Murphy, whose 1930s land grant included the paddock in which they stand.

PINKAWILLINIE CONSERVATION PARK ■ 2002

A variety of desert birds, from tiny robins, wrens and honey-eaters – which flit and forage among the mallees – to the large, grazing emu, are found here as are the western grey kangaroo and a number of small arid-region mammals. Plants here are typical of desert environments and include the mallees, which conserve water in their roots and, as in some other slender-leafed species found here, further reduce moisture loss through minimising the leaf surface exposed to the sun. Wattles and tea-trees also grow here.

Transcontinental travellers going east-west or vice-versa receive a reassuring message at Kimba – either coast is a mere 1500 kilometres away.

POINT LABATT CONSERVATION PARK ■ 2003

This narrow coastal strip of rugged, limestone cliffs and smooth, wave-worn granite slabs protects the only known mainland colony of sea lions. Here they laze, frolic, swim and fish, diving repeatedly to feed on bottom-dwelling creatures such as crayfish, crabs and octopus. Seabirds – black-faced cormorants, red-necked stints and crested terns – keep them company on the rocks. A viewing area for visitors has been fenced off on the windswept cliffs above.

STREAKY BAY ■ 2004

It was in the vicinity of Streaky Bay, in 1627, that Dutch navigator Pieter Nuijts aboard the Dutch ship *Gulden Zeepaard* (Golden Seahorse), blown east along the unknown and desolate southern shores of Australia, hauled his vessel about and sailed back to the west. Had he continued to the more inviting coasts of the south-east the course of Australia's European settlement may well have been quite different. A monument on the foreshore remembers his efforts.

Nuijts did not name this bay. That task fell to Matthew Flinders who, in 1802, called it Streaky Bay because the 'water was much discoloured in streaks' – probably caused by bands of seaweed. To the Aborigines the area was 'cooeyana', by which name they also referred to the spring behind the beach.

As was the case all over the Eyre Peninsula life here for the first European settlers was far from easy. They were isolated from Adelaide by a rugged landscape and were forced to rely on sea transport for all supplies and for the taking to market of their produce. At Streaky Bay, as elsewhere, a jetty was built for the trading ketches that plied Spencer Gulf and the peninsula shores. Bales of wool then piled up on the waterfront awaiting the often-infrequent visits of the traders.

The jetty remains today much as it was then, a favoured fishing spot which carries Streaky Bay's history in its timbers. The township beyond the waterfront was surveyed in 1865 and called Flinders; in 1940, in a major reorganisation of South Australian place names, the town was renamed so as to agree with the name of the bay. *Population 960*

PIGFACE ISLAND CONSERVATION PARK On this small limestone and sand island, ten kilometres north of Streaky Bay, breeding colonies of silver gulls and black-faced cormorants thrive unmolested by predators.

THE GRANITES To the south of Streaky Bay township, The Granites is a popular picnic and recreation destination with a natural rockpool for swimming. The spectacular coastline can be viewed from High Cliff.

FESTIVALS Streaky Bay Family Fish Day Contest, January; Streaky Bay Racing Club Carnival Day, March.

TALIA CAVES ■ 2005

While most of the cliffs hereabouts are compacted sand dunes formed 100 000 years ago, along their bases, near sea level, is a far more ancient layer of pink coloured sandstone and conglomerate. Where the two layers meet, erosion of the softer, upper stratas has carved caverns, overhangs and tunnels under the cliffs.

THE TUB The continual erosion of the interior of a sandstone cave here left the roof so thin that eventually it gave way. The result is the large crater known as The Tub. A windswept monument nearby recalls a picnic which ended in tragedy when a cliff collapsed. Both are salutary reminders of the treacherous state of a soft cliffline honeycombed by caves and under constant onslaught from the sea below.

VENUS BAY ■ 2006

This little landlocked harbour was sighted from the mast head by Matthew Flinders in 1802, but its navigable entrance was not found until 1848 when the South Australian-built schooner *Venus*, became the first European vessel to sail through it. The harbour provided a sheltered anchorage for coastal trading vessels and for a time a whaling station was sited here.

Pastoral leases in the hinterland were taken up in the late 1850s and the town was surveyed in 1864. Originally it was called Parkin, but in the place-name rationalisation of 1940, its name was changed to agree with that of the bay.The township is on a sandy beach facing the placid waters of the harbour and behind it rises the rugged peninsula which protects it from the force of the Southern Ocean. The curved jetty is a base for a small prawning fleet.

VENUS BAY CONSERVATION PARK On the western side of Venus Bay is the long, limestone promontory of Cape Weyland, which, together with the islands it shelters in the bay, is a conservation park. On the exposed tops are stunted shrubs, pigface and spinifex. In the sandy interior, where western grey kangaroos graze, are mallee, tea-tree and candlebush, and a variety of birds including honeyeaters, red wattlebirds, spur-winged plovers and stubble quails.

The six islands of the bay are mostly limestone covered with low shrubs and fringed by narrow, sandy beaches. They were once used for grazing sheep and guano, or bird dung, was dug from them for use as fertiliser. Germein Island, a reclaimed sandbar, is often visited by mainland kangaroos at low tide.

WIRRULLA ■ 2007

Wirrulla township stands where once the horses of the early coastal settlers were wintered on plains of speargrass. Settlement here dates from the early nineteenth century and the township serves the surrounding agricultural community. Its name is derived from an Aboriginal word thought to mean 'waterhole'.

WUDINNA ■ 2008

In the Wudinna district there are many fine examples of the smooth granite platforms and domes which rise from the plains over a large part of the upper Eyre Peninsula. Properly termed inselbergs, they are commonly called 'whalebacks', and indeed some do closely resemble not only whales, but other creatures as well, presenting a vision of great animals of rock lumbering over a dusty landscape. One example is Turtle Rock, estimated to be between 1800 and 2400 million years old and which looks remarkably like its name. First leases were taken up here in the 1860s. The name Wudinna is derived from an Aboriginal word meaning, appropriately, 'hill with granite rocks'. *Population 570*

MOUNT WUDINNA ROCK Mount Wudinna Rock, ten kilometres north of the town, is one of a number of inselbergs in the area and is one of the largest monoliths in Australia, rising some 260 metres above the surrounding plains.

The relatively easy climb up the smooth, lower slopes of the rock gives a rewarding view over the plains, and from the summit can be seen hundreds of square kilometres of the Eyre Peninsula, bounded in the north by the undulating outline of the Gawler Ranges. The flattish top of the rock indicates the level of the ancient plateau of granite which once covered this region. Weathered away for the most part, remnants of it remain in the scattering of inselbergs which are found across the upper part of the peninsula.

From the stark intrusion of the Gawler Ranges to the sea, the altitude never rises beyond 150 metres.

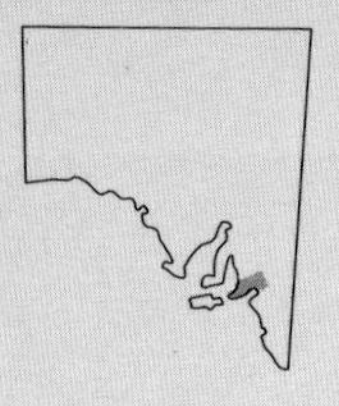

Murray Bridge & Mount Barker

The Murray lowlands stretch into South Australia's south-west where they give way to the high country that trims the tip of Fleurieu Peninsula. It is only a breath in time since Matthew Flinders and Nicholas Baudin met in Encounter Bay and Charles Sturt charted the mighty Murray – both features dotted with Aboriginal sites.

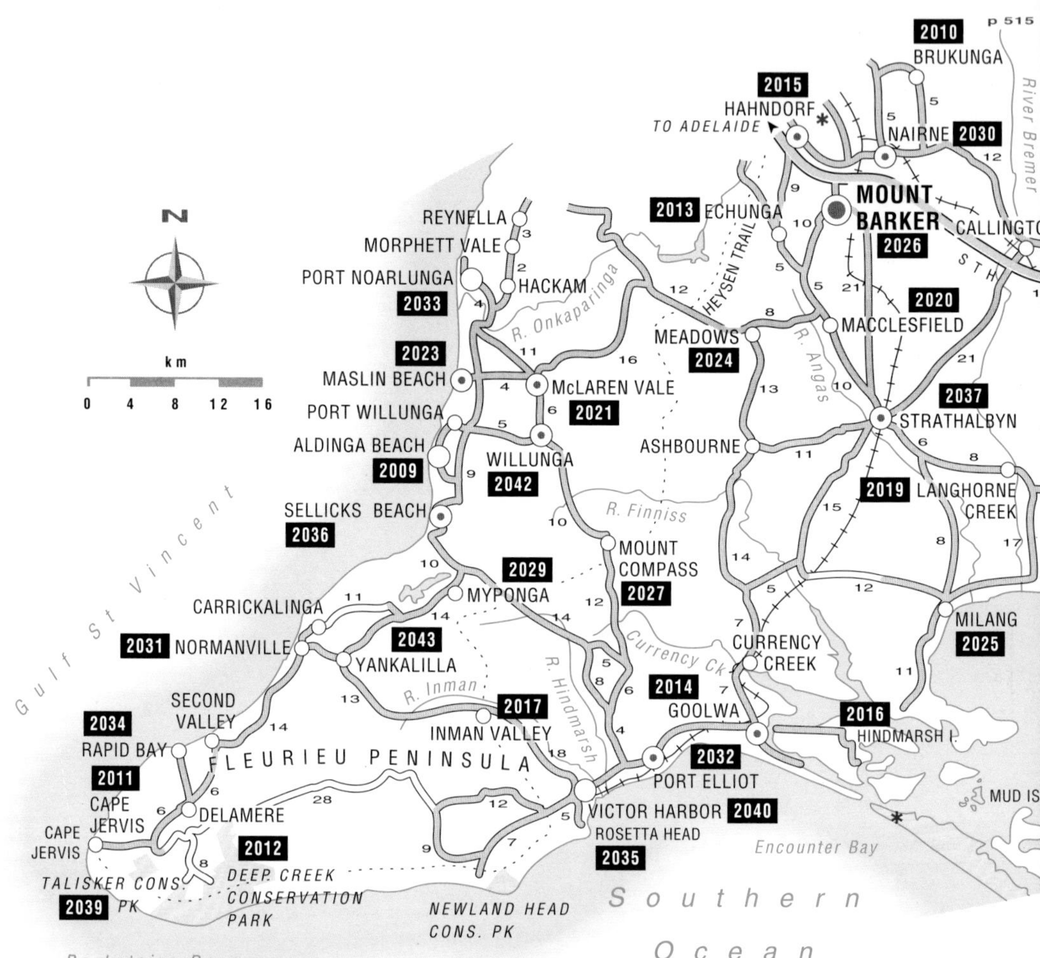

ALDINGA BEACH ■ 2009

The Fleurieu Peninsula is described as Adelaide's holiday playground. It encompasses stretches of white sand, pretty bush reserves, rural and seaside towns and tracts of arable land.

Tools and food remains from the days of Aboriginal occupation have been found in a five-hectare archaeological site about three kilometres south of Aldinga Beach. This land was once a hunting ground and the name means 'much water' or 'good place for meat' or 'open, wide plain' or 'tree district'. The coming of Europeans in the late 1860s transformed the area into a farming community and recently urbanisation has spread almost continuously along the north-western Fleurieu Peninsula coastline from Sellicks Bay to Port Willunga.

The area off Snapper Point is an aquatic reserve protecting a reef about 500 metres from the shore. No fishing is allowed and people can walk along a limestone platform and study the marine wildlife. At its far edge, seagrasses and sponges grow profusely in underwater caves. In 1888 the reef claimed the *Star of Greece*, a grain ship which foundered after leaving Port Willunga – seventeen lives were lost. *Population 3540*

BRUKUNGA ■ 2010

'Brukunga' means 'a place of stone to make fire by striking' which the Aborigines did with the iron pyrites available in this district. An open-cut mine and crushing and treatment plant operated here from 1955 to 1970, extracting sulphuric acid from the pyrite to make superphosphate. It was not an economical venture and the area is now being rehabilitated. Brukunga once had the oldest brickworks in South Australia with a nationwide reputation. It closed in 1983 after being owned and run by the same family for 120 years.

CAPE JERVIS ■ 2011

In 1802, Nicholas Baudin named the Fleurieu Peninsula for Charles Pierre Claret, Count of Fleurieu, the French navigator and Minister of Marine. A short while before him Matthew Flinders had named its most westerly tip Cape Jervis, after the family of the Earl of St Vincent, a Lord Commissioner of the Admiralty.

Cape Jervis had a boisterous history in the early nineteenth century as sealers and whalers plied their trade across Backstairs Passage to Kangaroo Island. Now car ferries do the same run. Two lighthouses have

Traditional skills were used to restore the half-timbered, Prussian-style farmhouse at Paechtown, near Hahndorf, to its original condition.

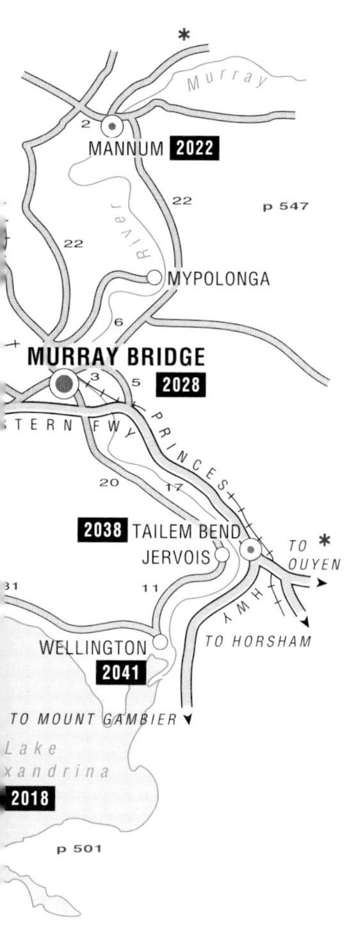

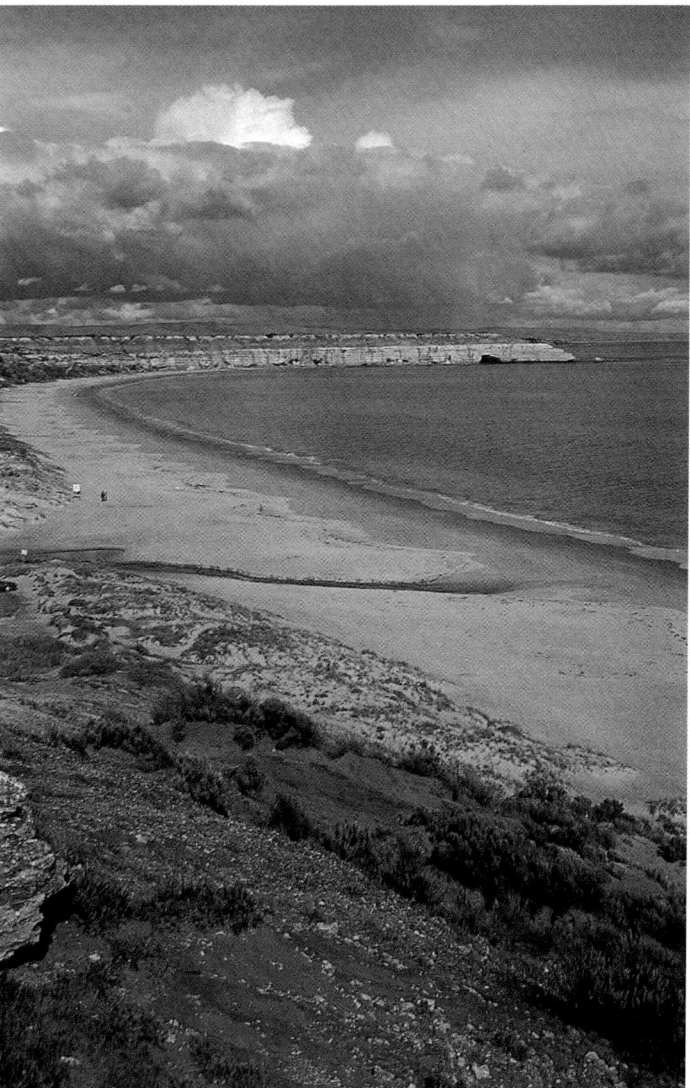
Swimmers can experience nature truly in the raw at the southern end of Maslin Beach where nude surfing does not attract the law's attention.

been erected on the point – the base of the 1871 structure sits beside its 1972 automated replacement. Today Cape Jervis is a quiet fishing village and a popular site for hang-gliders.

DEEP CREEK CONSERVATION PARK ■ 2012
This park on the southern Fleurieu Peninsula encloses some spectacular scenery within its 4184 hectares. Tall trees line the rugged coastal cliffs abutting on Backstairs Passage and pockets of the original forest vegetation cover the hills and steep-sided valleys inland. Moist gullies, fed by permanent creeks, shelter orchids and ferns. The park sustains western pygmy possums and one of South Australia's largest colonies of endangered short-nosed bandicoots. Rare peregrine falcons, southern emu wrens and elegant parrots have been sighted here and other bird species include white-breasted sea eagles, scaly thrushes, beautiful firetails and tawny frogmouths.

ECHUNGA ■ 2013
The first Europeans came to the Echunga district in 1839 and the name of the settlement is said to be derived from 'eechungga', an Aboriginal word for 'close by'. The town was established in 1849 when Jacob Hagen subdivided his property – the post office opened two years later.

William Chapman's discovery of payable gold in 1852 attracted about 4000 residents, who moved on when the alluvial ore ran out. Some diamonds have also been found in the Echunga area.

GOOLWA ■ 2014
Goolwa lies near the mouth of the Murray River on the Goolwa Channel. A barrage 632 metres long, one of five built between 1936 and 1940, helps separate the river water from the ocean and prevent seawater flowing into Lake Alexandrina, Lake Albert and the River Murray. Small craft can enter through a lock which forms part of the barrage network.

Sealers from Kangaroo Island were probably the first Europeans to visit Goolwa, around 1828. When Charles Sturt's whaleboat reached the site in 1830, he sent his men to bathe and they came back with cockles which must have been ambrosia to the exhausted explorers. Sturt suggested a settlement here and the first part of Goolwa was surveyed in 1840.

In the early 1850s, the competition for the Murray River trade began at Goolwa. Francis Cadell's *Lady Augusta* raced against William Randell's *Mary Ann* (see box, *Swan Hill & Kerang*). Cadell was given a hero's welcome when he arrived back in Goolwa and became a director of the River Murray Navigation Company which later foundered through disreputable trading practices.

By 1854, a horse-drawn railway was taking cargo from Goolwa to Port Elliot and the railway superintendent's house is still one of the town's most striking buildings. Goolwa became a busy port for the river trade and goods were sent downstream to be exported from Port Elliot and from 1864, Victor Harbor in Encounter Bay. This role diminished once the railway from Morgan to Adelaide opened in 1878 but the re-emergence of paddle steamers on the river as a tourist attraction is a link with Goolwa's past.

Early industries were ship building, milling and brewing and the town now depends on tourism and agriculture. Dairy cattle and sheep graze the river flats and wheat is grown. Goolwa's name is taken from an Aboriginal word meaning 'elbow'. It describes the shape of the last great bend in the river around Hindmarsh Island. *Population 3020*

HAHNDORF ■ 2015
Hahndorf is a quiet agricultural town which has retained the distinctive European character of its early German settlement and is the oldest surviving example of its kind in Australia. The local Aborigines called the site 'bukartilla' which is said to mean 'swimming place' but when the fifty-two German settler families arrived in 1839, they wanted to remember the captain of the Danish ship, *Zebra*, that brought them from their homeland.

Captain Dirk Hahn was highly impressed with his passengers and he determined to do everything he could to help them settle in their new land. He secured a lease on sixty hectares in a valley in the Adelaide Hills. The travellers trudged through the bush for more than two months, pushing handcarts loaded with precious seeds and their few belongings, before they reached Hahndorf – Hahn's Village – and slowly began to wrest a farming subsistence from the land. The name became Ambleside during the First World War but was restored in 1936. *Population 1660*

HAHNDORF ACADEMY This imposing two-storey structure opened as a school in 1857. The building was sold in 1916 and used for various purposes, barely escaping demolition. The academy is now an art gallery specialising in Hans Heysen's works.

THE CEDARS Hans Heysen, the celebrated bush watercolourist, lived in Hahndorf from 1908 to his death in 1968. In 1912 he bought 'The Cedars', a property on a hillside just outside Hahndorf. He modelled his studio on a Bavarian chalet and used it as a base for his painting expeditions into the Adelaide Hills and the Flinders Ranges, where he faithfully recorded the life he saw around him.

FESTIVALS Wooden Boat Festival, March in odd-numbered years; Blumenfest, November.

HINDMARSH ISLAND ■ 2016
With the establishment of the river trade on the Murray, dairy farmers took up selections on Hindmarsh Island. More recently it has become a

The original vegetation preserved in Newland Head's conservation park contrasts dramatically with the adjoining, shaved pastureland to the north.

popular holiday retreat where people come to see the river's mouth which trickles out through lagoons, lakes and sand-choked channels and needs barrages to stop seawater surging inwards from the Southern Ocean (see Goolwa). A monument honours the explorers Charles Sturt and Collet Barker who were among the first Europeans to set foot on the island. A ferry service to Goolwa began in 1858 (see entry).

INMAN VALLEY ■ 2017

Europeans first sighted the Inman River in 1837 and named it after Henry Inman who was South Australia's first Inspector of Police. The valley which is now given over to grazing and dairying was carved out from ancient mountains by glaciers about 250 million years ago. The huge boulder called Selwyn's Rock is believed to be twice that age and was the first recorded discovery of glaciation in Australia.

JERVOIS The 'green ribbon' across the river, between Wellington and Murray Bridge, is devoted to highly concentrated dairy farming. At the beginning of the 1880s the Jervois district was described as 'a large area of magnificent herbage' and today the quiet little settlement supports a modern cheese factory and is linked with Tailem Bend by vehicular ferry. The town itself was not proclaimed until 1929 and is named after Sir William Jervois, Governor of South Australia from 1877 to 1883.

LAKE ALEXANDRINA ■ 2018

Lake Alexandrina was discovered by sealers in 1828 and named by Captain Charles Sturt in February 1830. Princess Alexandrina later became Queen Victoria but although a name change for the lake was proposed, it never made it into common usage. The lake is flecked with the ten marshy islands of Mud Islands Game Reserve. They provide a 138-hectare breeding ground for waterbirds near the northern end of the Coorong (see box, *Bordertown & Keith*).

LANGHORNE CREEK ■ 2019

Langhorne Creek is a fertile area on the Bremer River supporting vineyards and mixed farming. Alfred Langhorne brought cattle here from New South Wales in 1841. The 1850 Bridge Hotel slaked many a South Australian's thirst on the road to the Victorian gold diggings.

Frank Potts, a former ship's chandler, purchased land in 1850, and set up the Bleasdale Winery where his redgum vats and enormous wooden winepress, built in 1892, are on show. The river floods from time to time and sometimes the grapes have even been harvested by boat.

MACCLESFIELD ■ 2020

George, Samuel and Robert Davenport were first here in 1842 and for a while the place was informally called 'Three Brothers'. The official name honours the Earl of Macclesfield who had employed their father. The Goats Head Inn, built in 1841, and now called the Davenport Arms, has been extended and rebuilt. In 1977 the South Australian Film Corporation used the slightly younger Macclesfield Hotel as part of the set for *Weekend of Shadows*.

The weeping willows, planted along the river bank by the Davenport brothers, are cuttings from those that grow near Napoleon's grave on the island of St Helena. They came to Australia slotted into potatoes and miraculously survived the journey.

Macclesfield marble has been used for Adelaide's War Memorial and sections of Canberra's War Memorial. The main pastoral activities of the area are dairying and sheep and the town services the rural community.

McLAREN VALE ■ 2021

McLaren Vale, a small community enfolded in the Mount Lofty Ranges, is the centre of the Fleurieu Peninsula's 'Wine Coast' and is named after John McLaren who surveyed it.

From the 1850s farmers grew wine grapes mainly for their own use until acceptance of Australian wines in London in the early 1900s led to a profitable market. There are over fifty wineries in the region which range from the very large to tiny family businesses. The soil is particularly well suited to red-wine grape varieties. *Population 1470*

FESTIVALS Wine Bushing Festival, throughout October.

MANNUM ■ 2022

The first Europeans to see Mannum were the crew of Sturt's whaleboat on their epic voyage down the Murray. The township was founded in 1852 by Captain William Randell of paddle steamer fame (see *Swan Hill & Kerang*). He skippered the *Mary Ann*, which left for Goolwa in 1853 (see entry). The settlement became a major port in the years of river trade, transporting wheat from the eastern Mount Lofty Ranges upstream to New South Wales and Victoria. The town is steeped in riverboat history and the site of a National Trust's Museum on the PS *Marion*; the Mannum Hotel occupies the site of Randell's original house built in 1854. Fishing, waterskiing and sailing are particularly popular recreational pastimes and houseboats and cruises find shelter along the river banks.

In 1877, David and John Shearer began making ploughshares and harvesters in Mannum. Later models went up and downstream to farmers in South Australia, Victoria and New South Wales. David also made one of Australia's first steam cars, which incorporated a precursor of today's differential. His car is now complete-

The southern brown bandicoot has found an unthreatened niche in the moist gullies of Deep Creek Park.

ly restored and preserved in the National Motor Museum at Birdwood (see *Gawler & Nuriootpa*).

Between Mannum and Blanchetown to the north lies 'Bunyip' country. The locals spin tales of this mythical creature who lurks in the swamps and shallows waiting to pounce on the unwary, most of the stories being richly embroidered over the years. *Population 2020*

COWIRRA HISTORIC RESERVE This historic reserve north-east of Mannum is important to the descendants of the Aborigines who once lived along the River Murray. A peppercorn tree marks the spot where a number of prominent community members are thought to be buried.

FESTIVALS River Festival, July.

MASLIN BEACH ■ 2023

Maslin Beach is named after the nearby Maslin Homestead. The little seaside town has its own art gallery which displays the works of local artists. The long sweep of sandy beach is backed by impressive cliffs and notched up a notable Australian first some years ago when nudity became legal here and the southern end was set aside as a nude-bathing area. *Population 860*

MEADOWS ■ 2024

The Aboriginal name for this place was 'battunga' which meant 'a forest of tall trees' but this became entirely inappropriate once the European settlers had cut them down to clear the land for cultivation. Until the 1860s, the settlement had the alternative name of Eden Bridge but then became known generally as Meadows. Some early buildings remain and the village is surrounded by dairy farms, orchards and apiaries. *Population 530*

MILANG ■ 2025

Milang, on the shores of the freshwater Lake Alexandrina, was settled in 1853 and preserves many old buildings from the pioneering era. Its name is said to be an Aboriginal word for 'place of sorcery'. At first Milang was important in the riverboat trade and cargoes destined for Adelaide were unloaded here to travel the rest of the way by bullock dray. Dairy and poultry farming are now established in the district and modern Milang has a flourishing tourist business.

MOUNT BARKER ■ 2026

Mount Barker was called 'wommamukurta' by the Aborigines which means 'hill on a plain'. Captain Collet Barker was the first European to recognise the peak in 1831. A year earlier Charles Sturt had taken bearings thinking Mount Barker and Mount Lofty were one and the same. When news of Barker's discovery reached him, Sturt decided the 'new' mountain should have his name. It is fitting that he is remembered here because he met his tragic end nearby before the year was over.

Mount Barker is the largest town in the Adelaide Hills, has tanning and tank-making factories, and is a service centre for the surrounding rural district. When wheat growing declined, farmers diverted to grazing, stock breeding, dairying, raising pigs, growing cucumbers for gherkins, strawberries and harvesting clover seed. *Population 6240*

THE MOUNT BARKER MILL Mount Barker was an important grain growing area before the northern regions of South Australia became productive and flour milling developed as a profitable trade. A wind-driven mill, erected in 1842 and in use until 1864, has been restored and is dedicated to the region's pioneers.

MOUNT COMPASS ■ 2027

If 'creeks' and 'paddles' were not so firmly entrenched in the national vocabulary, being 'up a mountain without a compass' might have caught on. Mount Compass took its name from a nearby hill where, according to local legend, Governor George Gawler is said to have lost his compass in 1840.

In the early years, market gardeners in the district supplied ships at Victor Harbor with fresh produce but dairy farming has taken over and, like many other towns in this region, Mount Compass has a major milk products factory. The Compass Cow Race, however, is probably the only one of its kind in Australia.

MURRAY BRIDGE ■ 2028

Captain Charles Sturt and his small band passed the site of Murray Bridge in 1830. Settlement did not begin until twenty-five years later and the town did not get its present name until 1924. Before that it was 'Coninba', 'Edward's Crossing', 'The Turnoff', and 'Mobilong'.

In the 1860s, travelling stock being overlanded to Adelaide from the eastern states swam the Murray River at this point. The impressive Swanport Bridge – 734 metres long – was built in 1979 about five kilometres downstream from the original cattle crossing. It spans the river on nine, rust-protected piers. Prior to that, crossing the river here could be frustrating. In 1864, Adelaide wool and wheat growers demanded a bridge to improve links with Victoria but it was fifteen years before one was opened. At this time the town was officially called Mobilong.

The 1879 bridge had no liftspan and irritated riverboat skippers had to unship high masts to pass under it. From 1886 to 1925, trains used the bridge too and road traffic came off worst. But even when a separate rail bridge was built, traffic to and from Adelaide was too heavy for the old structure and the locals welcomed

In 1842, real horsepower had an assured future and Nairne's flour mill was built to last; the original, sturdy timber walls were cased in stone by 1854.

the Swanport Bridge and the freeway which now bypasses the town.

The government began draining the swamps on the lower river near Murray Bridge and Tailem Bend in 1906. Since then the land has been irrigated with carefully controlled water from the river and supports dairy cattle, fruit and vegetables, cereal crops, sheep, pigs and poultry. Murray Bridge has flour mills and manufacturing industries and one of Australia's largest milk-products factories. Today modern milk tankers collect the output from the dairies, replacing the milk boats of earlier times. *Population 12 720*

MONARTO ZOO Ten kilometres west of Murray Bridge, this open-range zoological park specialises in African and Asian grassland and plains-dwelling animals such as giraffes and antelopes. Open on Sundays and public and school holidays.

FESTIVALS The Murray Bridge Big River Challenge Festival, November.

MYPONGA ■ 2029

Myponga is a corruption of the Aboriginal word 'Maipinga' meaning 'locality of high cliffs'. The area is now drained and irrigated and supports good dairy pastures and a cheese and milk factory. A few of the wattle, mud and brick cottages from the 1840s are still standing. Their damp, unhealthy conditions had a fearful reputation and there was high infant mortality from diphtheria, tuberculosis and typhoid fever.

MYPONGA CONSERVATION PARK This tiny, 166-hectare park south of the village is part of the 1500-kilometre-long Hans Heysen Trail which begins at Cape Jervis and ends at Parachilna Gorge in the Flinders Ranges. The area is very important as another habitat for the endangered short-nosed or southern brown bandicoot.

NAIRNE ■ 2030

Nairne, in hilly country on Nairne Creek, is one of South Australia's oldest settlements and many of the historic mid-1850s buildings have been restored to their original condition. The mill and the District Hotel are particularly good examples. The town was named for Elizabeth Corse Nairne who married Matthew Smillie, the first land purchaser in the area in 1839. Today the major industry is a factory producing bacon and smallgoods. *Population 1350*

NORMANVILLE ■ 2031

Normanville, with its long white beach stretching either side of the Bungala River mouth, is named after its founder, Robert Norman, and was once a thriving grain town with 2000 residents and a busy flour mill. A horse stud now occupies that land, called 'Comic Court' after the Melbourne Cup winner who was bred here in 1950. Like Nairne, Normanville still has some of its original buildings, built around the middle of the last century, but the first jetty was swept away by river flood waters in 1856. *Population 510*

PORT ELLIOT ■ 2032

Port Elliot, established on Encounter Bay in 1850, was named after Charles Elliot, a governor of Bermuda and friend of Governor Henry Young who tried to develop the port. The

The towers of 'Adare' at Victor Harbor – now, like many large Victorian houses, a conference centre – are topped wittily with 'clown' spires.

horse-drawn tramway which opened in 1854 to connect river traffic at Goolwa with Port Elliot was Australia's first public railway. When four ships foundered in the bay in 1856, Young's hopes that the port would become the 'New Orleans of the Australian Mississippi' foundered with them. Holiday-makers now use pretty Horseshoe Bay beach and a blue warning flag no longer flies from Freeman's Knob on days when port approaches are too rough for ships to reach safe harbour. *Population 1200*

PORT NOARLUNGA ■ 2033

Noarlunga comes from an Aboriginal word meaning 'fishing place', still an apt name. The private town was laid out in 1853 as a feeder port for Old Noarlunga but Port Noarlunga South was not gazetted until 1923. An early settler sang its praises: 'the luxury of deep water and a smooth beach for bathing…As a situation for a watering place this place is unequalled'. Port Noarlunga, which lies near the broad estuary of the Onkaparinga River, is now part of the well populated north-western coastal strip of the Fleurieu Peninsula. The river and the jetty are excellent 'fishing places' where fisherfolk of all ages angle for bream, salmon, sand whiting, mullet, mulloway, tommy ruffs, garfish and drummer. A reef, popular with scuba divers, extends on either side of the jetty. *Population 2470*

RAPID BAY ■ 2034

Rapid Bay is marked by a T-shaped jetty jutting 500 metres into Gulf St Vincent. The beach had long been popular as an Aboriginal camping ground before the Europeans came. The bay was named by Colonel William Light, whose brig, *Rapid*, dropped anchor here on 8 September 1836. It was his first landing on the South Australian mainland after a period of nearly three weeks on Kangaroo Island and his journal records: 'At 12.30 p.m. we came to anchor in 10 fathoms, a beautiful valley in view. At two, I went on shore and was enchanted with the appearance of the whole'.

Some of Light's passengers stayed at Rapid Bay until the end of January 1837 and the first white South Australians were born here – John Rapid Hoare on 7 November 1836 and Fanny Lipson Finniss on 2 January 1837. Rapid Bay is now owned by Broken Hill Proprietary Co. Ltd and a quarry supplies limestone for use as a purifier in steelmaking.

ROSETTA HEAD ■ 2035

The Rosetta Head promontory, a dominant feature of the Encounter Bay coastline also known as 'The Bluff' and 'Cape Victor', was a lookout point for whales in the early years of the nineteenth century. In 1902, a hundred years after the event, a plaque was fixed to a huge granite boulder to commemorate the meeting of Matthew Flinders' *Investigator* and Nicholas Baudin's *Le Géographe* in the waters of Encounter Bay. Although France and England were at war at the time, the two men met on the French ship to exchange explorers' notes. The promontory was named by Governor Gawler to honour Rosetta, wife of George Fife Angas. Freycinet charted it as 'C. [cape] de Caen' and the Aborigines called it 'kungkengguwar'.

SELLICKS BEACH ■ 2036

The small town of Sellicks Beach was named for William Sellick who had a land grant in the area in 1847. In 1925 George and Robert Herrick, farmers of Aldinga, subdivided some of their land into 'glorious large coastal bungalow sites'. The beach has been a popular venue for motor-cycle and car racing and the town is now the southern point of the expanding residential holiday strip. *Population 710*

STRATHALBYN ■ 2037

The township of Strathalbyn beside the Angas River was once a stopover on the Melbourne–Adelaide coach road. The Gaelic name was chosen by the Scottish settlers led by Doctor John Rankine of Glasgow who came to the district in 1839. 'Strath' meant 'wide valley' and 'albyn' is said to come from 'Albion'.

The tramway to Goolwa and Victor Harbor opened in 1869 and the railway line from Adelaide reached Strathalbyn in 1884. The original court house and police station is a National Trust Museum and so highly regarded are other old buildings that Strathalbyn is now a 'Heritage Town'. Copper was mined and smelted in the district from around 1848 to 1914 and other early industries included flour milling, brewing, a foundry and a gasworks. Strathalbyn's present prosperity is based on agricultural activities such as the production of butter, cheese and cereal crops. *Population 2620*

ANTHONYS HILL HISTORIC RESERVE

This reserve of about 150 hectares is located just a few kilometres north-west of Strathalbyn. It is the site of a small, sandstone rock shelter where human figures are painted in red ochre on the walls and ceiling. They are the most southerly example of cave decoration in the eastern Mount Lofty Ranges and are painted mainly in profile showing unusually strong movement. The style is unusual for this locality, being reminiscent of the 'Mimi' figures of northern Australia.

TAILEM BEND ■ 2038

Tailem Bend, proclaimed in 1887 in the Meningie District on the lower Murray, has railway workshops and marshalling yards and is a major road and railway junction. It is also the centre of a mixed farming district and has large silos which house grain from the Mallee region.

Some attribute the name 'Tailem Bend' to the stock that were tailed – herded – there in the early days of overlanding from New South Wales and Victoria to Adelaide. Others say it comes from Donald Gollen's run 'Taleam' or from the Aboriginal word 'Thealem' which may have meant 'bend'. But a fourth explanation suggests it derives from an Aboriginal word meaning 'to miss', from the legend of the giant Murray cod that carved out the great river (see box, *Bordertown & Keith*). This was the place where the great totemic being, Ngurunderi, failed for a second time to kill the fish. *Population 1500*

TALISKER CONSERVATION PARK ■ 2039

This park encloses 138 hectares of laterite plateau covered in stringybark open forest which also contains some very large grass trees. The remains of the silver-lead Talisker and Campbell Creek mines are scattered across the steep hillside. The ruined buildings and tunnels, which have heritage classification, are good examples of the skill of the early stonemasons.

VICTOR HARBOR ■ 2040

Victor Harbor is sheltered from the pounding waves of Encounter Bay by Granite Island. Like Goolwa (see entry), it was once tipped to become the capital of South Australia. Governor Hindmarsh declared it would be 'the port for the great River Murray' and with the failure of Port Elliot it was approved as a safe anchorage after extensive enquiries in 1861.

Victor Harbor enjoyed some status as a port until about the first decade

The gum exuded by the yacca grass trees around Yankalilla was used as a fixative in a variety of products at the turn of the twentieth century.

of the twentieth century but never gained its predicted importance, despite several schemes to connect it with Goolwa and so attract the River Murray trade. Victoria Pier was opened in 1864 and the occasion coincided with the railway's arrival from Port Elliot. In 1878, work began on a causeway and a breakwater which were intended to make the harbour suitable for boats of any draught. But when the eastern colonies developed efficient inland rail links, the River Murray was finished as a transport route.

Since the 1960s, Victor Harbor has been a steadily growing seaside and retirement resort and is now the unofficial capital of the Fleurieu Peninsula. It depends on fruit and dairy production as well as tourism. The town boasts a number of historic buildings including Warringa Guest House – a traditional guesthouse from the early years of the twentieth century, 'Adare' – a grand mansion from the 1890s – and St Augustine's Church of England (1869).

Whalers and sealers used the beach as early as 1819 but the whaling station was later moved to Granite Island. Captain Crozier, who anchored in the lee of the island in 1837 to survey the harbour, called it Port Victor after his ship, HMS *Victor*. A group of European settlers arrived in the following year and the name was later changed to its present form. *Population 5930*

NEWLAND HEAD CONSERVATION PARK This 945-hectare reserve, west of Victor Harbor, is an important habitat for the endangered hooded plover, a bird which nests on two wilderness beaches in the park.

GRANITE ISLAND This small island in Encounter Bay was called simply after the type of rock that forms it, but was known to the early Aborigines as 'nulcoowarra'. A causeway, which opened in 1882, joins Granite Island to the township of Victor Harbor and the journey across can still be made by horse-drawn tram pulled by huge and patient Clydesdales. A chairlift from the end of the causeway to the middle of the island gives magnificent views and a bird's-eye look at the sanctuary below where rock wallabies, kangaroos and fairy penguins live in peace.

WELLINGTON ■ 2041

Wellington, 'where the river meets the lake', was an overnight camp site for Captain Charles Sturt in 1830. It was then named for the hero of the Battle of Waterloo by John Morphett who set up a ferry crossing there in 1839. The original bell to call for service is still by the river. Alexander Tolmer used it on his gold shipment route from the Victorian diggings to Adelaide (see *Bordertown & Keith*).

By the late 1880s, Wellington had an unusual problem. It was in danger of being swallowed by sand. The tens of thousands of grazing animals passing through on the droving route from the south-east and Victoria had denuded the surrounding dunes causing the loosened sand to drift into the town. Travellers entering the Wellington Hotel through the front door were surprised to see drifts of sand up to the roof at the back. In 1889, an eye-witness wrote: 'Two houses were completely covered over so that no trace of them could be seen. This we could not believe until we dug down and found the tops of the chimneys'. It was not the sand, however, but the upstream railway bridge that eventually sent Wellington into decline.

WILLUNGA ■ 2042

Willunga's name is thought to come from 'willa-unga', an Aboriginal word for 'the place of green trees'. It was important in the early colony for slate from the nearby hills which was transported to Melbourne and Adelaide. The Delabole Quarry, which began in 1842 and operated for the next sixty years, is now on the register of the National Trust.

Wheat yields were high for twenty years or so from the 1850s but then over-exploitation of the soil caused crop failure. Willunga is now Australia's main almond-growing centre. The groves put on a wonderful show of delicate pink and white blossom at the end of July. *Population 1160*

FESTIVALS Almond Blossom Festival, July.

YANKALILLA ■ 2043

Yankalilla's name is linked to the Dreamtime story of Tjilbruke (see box) and is derived from 'jankalan' which means 'falling'. The town is a centre for local farmers who early on recognised a deterioration in pastures. James Porter of Victor Harbor pioneered topdressing with superphosphate and sowed new pasture crops such as subterranean clover which by the mid-1920s was common practice throughout the district.

Two local trees were the source of an income in the early years. By the end of the 1880s wattle bark was collected in great quantities. The tannin from it was in demand as a leather tanning agent and the industry lasted for about forty years. Later, yacca trees provided gum for paints, varnishes, explosives and many other products. The yacca, with its long nectar-bearing flower spike, grows in the high country of the southern Fleurieu Peninsula.

Christ Church, Yankalilla, built in 1857, is still used for services and babies are christened in the marble font which dates back to the Middle Ages and once stood in Salisbury Cathedral in England. It was presented to the rector at the turn of the century and so far all requests by the authorities to give it back to Salisbury have been politely refused.

WHY TJILBRUKE CRIED THE SPRINGS OF GULF ST VINCENT

AS ELSEWHERE around Australia's coastline, the coming of Europeans to the Fleurieu Peninsula in the nineteenth century disturbed the nomadic life of the Aboriginal people, interfered with their traditional hunting grounds and spread diseases among them to which they had no immunity. Although the descendants of the original inhabitants have long since gone from this region, their presence lingers on in lilting place names such as Noarlunga, Yankalilla, Carrickalinga, Willunga and many more. The origins of their Dreamtime legends, explaining the region's natural features, haunt the hills and valleys. Ngurunderi, a great totemic being, was responsible for forming many aspects of the Murray Valley (see Tailem Bend) and causing Granite Island and other islands to emerge from the sea. Another hero called Tjilbruke contributed to the people's future well-being along the east coast of Gulf St Vincent.

Tjilbruke rose from the ground near Mount Hayfield in Parawa where he camped with his friends, Lepuldawi and Watiriorn, who are represented by two hills in the region. One day he heard that his sister's son, Kulultuwi, had been put to death for violating a strict taboo near the Sturt River at Marion. The boy had killed an emu which was forbidden. His body was smoked according to the ancient custom of the Kaurna people; Tjilbruke carried his nephew from near Brighton to Cape Jervis, his final resting-place.

When Tjilbruke stopped along the way to mourn, clear springs bubbled up wherever his tears fell on the ground. These were important water sources for the Aborigines who later passed this way. There are freshwater springs at Hallet Cove, Port Noarlunga and near Red Ochre Cove. A few hundred metres south of the old Port Willunga jetty, Tjilbruke rested on the sand while the tide was out and wept again. To this day fresh water can be found here by digging at low tide. There are more springs on the beach near Sellicks Hill, just south of Carrickalinga Head and near a small creek at Second Valley.

Finally, Tjilbruke reached Cape Jervis and laid Kulultuwi's body in a cave at Rapid Bay. His grieving done, he then transformed himself into an ibis. The places where Tjilbruke rested on his journey are now marked by cairns and plaques which tell the part of the story for each locality along the route. □

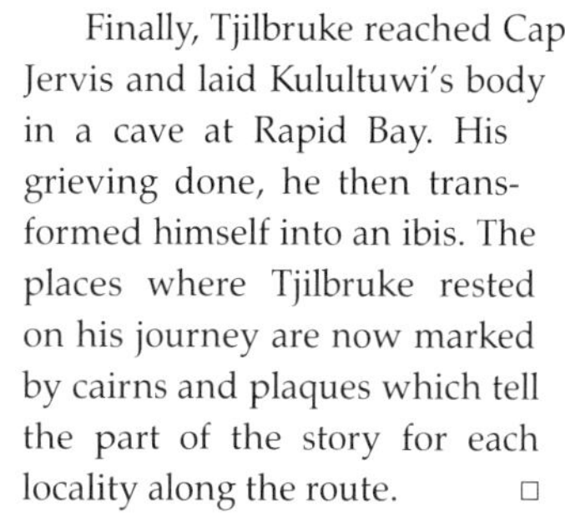

Tjilbruke, whose sorrow brought forth freshwater springs before he was transformed into an ibis, was one of the Kaurna people, like the warrior depicted here in an 1850s watercolour by George Angus.

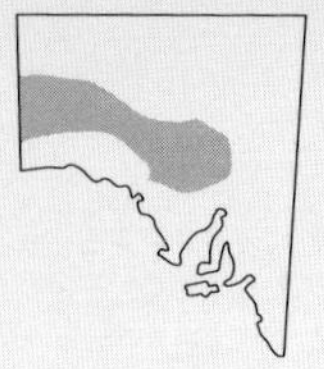

Woomera & Andamooka

A forty-year-old shadow – conjured up by secret tests of rockets and nuclear weapons – still hangs over this region of salt lakes and wind-driven sand dunes, inhospitable to all except the Aborigines, who have been handed back the stewardship of the western portion of their much-abused traditional lands.

While warm-blooded creatures rest where they can find shade, Gould's goanna patrols the Victoria Desert.

ANDAMOOKA ■ **2044**
Andamooka was originally known as 'Andamoka' which was the Aboriginal name for the large waterhole discovered by John McDouall Stuart in June 1858. Opal was first found at Andamooka in 1930. Local specimens are generally darker than Coober Pedy gemstones and are the hardest and most durable of the Australian opals. The 'Andamooka' opal, discovered here in 1946, was presented to Queen Elizabeth in 1954. Agate and jasper are also found in the area.

The town, gazetted in December 1976, is set in undulating gibber plain and the summer months are scorchingly hot. Some of the miners live in dugouts with only the roof above the ground. The community's water is supplied from bores or wells or is carted from Roxby Downs.

GLENDAMBO ■ **2045**
Glendambo, like Pimba (see entry), is a main service centre for travellers through South Australia's arid outback. It lies on the Stuart Highway, a sealed all-weather road which runs through more than 1240 kilometres of desert from Port Augusta to Alice Springs. Glendambo was proclaimed in 1982 and was called after Glendambo Homestead which is now within the limits of the town.

GREAT VICTORIA DESERT ■ **2046**
Ernest Giles was the first European to cross this great expanse of sandy terrain from east to west. The Great Victoria Desert takes its name from the Queen Victoria Spring which Giles named in honour of the reigning monarch in 1875. It is an area that extends across the state border, about 1100 kilometres east to west and some 500 kilometres north to south. It lies between the Musgrave and other ranges in central Australia and the Nullarbor Plain. Plateau country and dry lake beds form the western boundary and the black stretch of the Stuart Highway or the Tarcoola–Alice Springs railway line roughly mark the eastern boundary.

Large areas of the desert are owned by the traditional inhabitants – the Pitjantjatjara and Tjarutja people – or are part of the extensive two-and-a-half-million hectare Great Victoria Desert Nature Reserve. The 2 000 000-hectare unnamed park on its eastern edge is a unique arid-land sanctuary and a South Australian Biosphere Reserve.

The desert surface consists of parallel sand ridges sparsely covered with stabilising scrub which includes acacias, casuarinas and other mulga species. There is a scattering of herbs, swainsonas and Sturt's desert pea ready to break into gaudy red flowers after a reviving draught of late winter or spring rains.

Whatever moves across the sand, be it the smallest beetle, leaves a record of its passing until the wind erases the tracks. The area is well populated with kangaroos and emus, with shy nocturnal mammals, such as the spinifex hopping-mouse and the long-tailed dunnart, with many species of birds, some of which are brilliantly plumed, and with all manner of desert reptiles who, in the words of Noel Coward, 'go out in the midday sun'.

LAKE GAIRDNER ■ **2047**
The first Europeans sighted Lake Gairdner in 1857. In the same year Governor Sir Richard Graves MacDonnell named it after Gordon Gairdner who was Chief Clerk of the Australian Department of the Colonial Office. His description of the lake in his official despatch showed more excitement than his choice of name: 'Its size and remarkable cliffs projecting into a vast expanse of dazzling salt, here and there studded with islands, render it one of the most striking objects hitherto met with in Australian scenery'.

The irregularly shaped saline lake which covers thousands of square kilometres is now part of a national park. The rocky islands, mentioned by MacDonnell, rear up from the halite-encrusted bed which is surrounded by red hills, red beaches and crescent-shaped sand dunes and rimmed with pale green mulga and myall bushes. Salt weathering has formed holes and depressions in the shores of the lake and its islands.

LAKE TORRENS ■ **2048**
Lake Torrens was discovered by the explorer, Edward John Eyre, in October 1839, and named after Colonel Robert Torrens who was Chairman of the South Australian Colonization Commission. It stands about thirty-four metres above sea level and is overlooked by the dry sandstone Arcoona Plateau to the west. Mound springs arise on this side. These form as the heavily mineralised water of the Great Artesian Basin bubbles up through natural spring outlets, leaving deposits which build up over time with blown sand to form tranquil pools up to twenty-five metres above ground level.

The lake, the main feature of the Lake Torrens National Park, covers about 5830 square kilometres and is a parched and inhospitable salt pan for most of the time; but when there is heavy rain, the water can overflow the banks as far as Spencer Gulf. In a wet season the birds arrive and the lake becomes a short-term habitat for black swans and other species. Lake Torrens rarely fills to overflowing because its surface area is so large in comparison to its catchment; the first inundation of the lake in this century was early in 1989.

Fossils of a very ancient life form were found in the Flinders Ranges near Lake Torrens in 1946. These are the outlines of primitive jellyfish around 650 million years old.

LAKE DUTTON There are several other lakes in the region and Lake Dutton, west of the bottom of Lake Torrens, was the site of a tragedy in the early years of the colony. Eyre so inspired others with his tales of land to the north, that in July 1846, John Horrocks set off from Penwortham near Clare with a small expeditionary group whose members included the landscape painter, S.T. Gill. By September they had reached a salt lake which Horrocks named Lake Gill but later it was renamed Lake Dutton. Here the young man prepared to shoot 'a beautiful bird' for their collection. In a freak accident the camel – which had earlier revealed a truculent nature – lurched against him and the gun discharged into Horrocks's jaw and fingers. He

On the edge of the desert and a long way from anywhere, the nuclear-test outpost of Maralinga remains 'off limits' 30 years after it was abandoned.

died a few weeks later from infected wounds at the age of twenty-eight (see Penwortham, *Port Pirie & Clare*).

LYONS ■ 2049
Lyons can scarcely be described as a station – it is more of a siding on the Indian–Pacific railway line. Named after the Australian Prime Minister, Joseph Lyons, it is the first of a series of whistlestops along the line that honours past Australian leaders. As the train moves westwards, it passes Barton, Watson, Fisher, Cook and Hughes before crossing the South Australia–Western Australia border (see box, *Esperance & Eucla*).

MARALINGA ■ 2050
Three sites were used for British nuclear weapons testing in the 1950s. They were the Monte Bello Islands – some ninety kilometres from the north-west coast of Western Australia – a region about thirty-five kilometres north of Maralinga in the Great Victoria Desert, and Emu, about 250 kilometres west of Coober Pedy. The Maralinga village was established for the use of scientists.

The last of the twelve nuclear devices detonated in Australia was exploded in 1957 but for the next seven years there were trials at the Maralinga sites, several of which involved the dispersal of plutonium into the atmosphere. Some cleaning-up was undertaken before the area was abandoned in the late 1960s. Radioactive debris was sealed in concrete and buried in fenced pits. In 1979, the British removed some more plutonium and constructed a number of concrete plinths to mark the sites of the bomb explosions and some of the other experiments.

A 1985 Royal Commission found there was little radioactivity left on the Monte Bello Islands, the Emu site and at Maralinga but recommended further decontamination. A year earlier, the passing of the Maralinga Tjarutja Land Rights Act by the South Australian government gave the traditional owners, the Aboriginal people, freehold tenure over some state crown land in the area but they had to be excluded from a large section because of contamination. It is hoped that eventually the land will be given the 'all-clear' for repossession by its traditional owners. Negotiations concerning land repossession have been held with the Maralinga Tjarutja.

'Maralinga' is derived from an Aboriginal word which is said to mean 'thunder place'. The test sites are within the Woomera Prohibited Area and there is no public access.

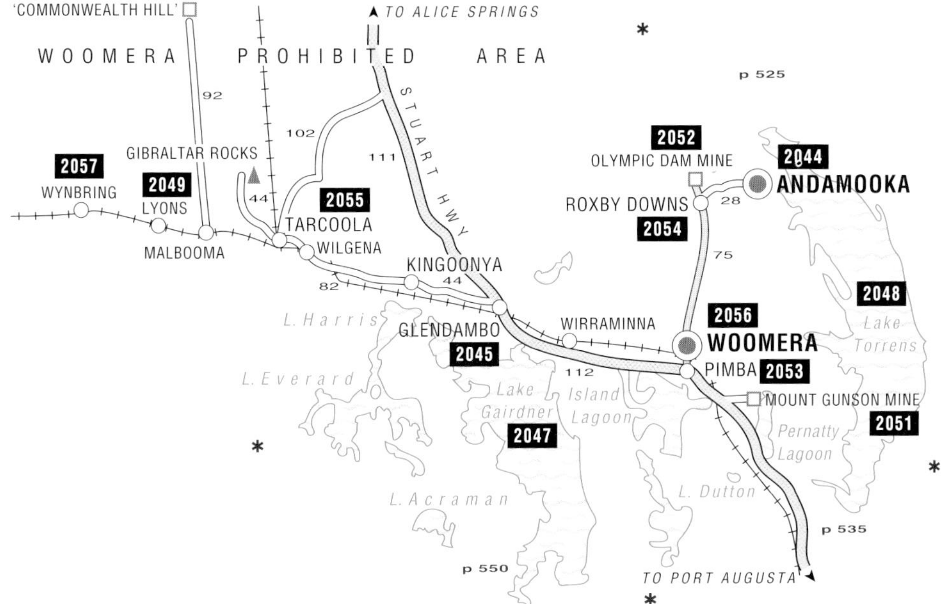

A sun-baked salt pan at Lake Harris, near Glendambo, is fringed by a sand range worthy of the Sahara.

MOUNT GUNSON MINE ■ 2051
Mount Gunson, dominating Pernatty Lagoon north-west of Port Augusta, was named in 1875 after Dr John Michael Gunson, who arrived in the colony of South Australia in 1852 and became a member of the Senate of Adelaide University and President of the Catholic Young Men's Society, and who endeared himself to the city's poor for what a contemporary described as 'his unassuming ways and charitable acts'.

Production of copper from the Mount Gunson area was first recorded in 1899 and a smelter was built there five years later. Mining went on intermittently until 1971. The Catlegrid copper deposit which was discovered close by was worked for twelve years, from 1974 until 1986.

OLYMPIC DAM MINE ■ 2052
The Olympic Dam Mine, reputed to be one of the world's biggest copper mines and probably its largest uranium mine, produces a range of metals including, high-quality copper, ura-

nium oxide, gold and silver. The orebody lies under the Roxby Downs pastoral lease and is a vast mineral resource of over 450 million tonnes which is expected to take many years to mine. It is named after a livestock watering dam which was built during the 1956 Melbourne Olympic Games. The deposit is embedded in granite rocks which are about 1600 million years old and are overlain by a 300-metre-thick layer of barren sedimentary rocks.

The underground mine is highly mechanised and access to it is down a steep, four kilometre roadway. By March 1992, more than fifty-five kilometres of underground roadway had been completed with a standard width of six metres and a height of nearly five metres. The presence of radioactive materials at the site is monitored and controlled.

Fifty-one per cent of the operation, which also includes a complex metallurgical treatment plant, is owned by Western Mining Corporation and forty-nine per cent by the BHP Group. The mine exports eighty per cent of its copper to Europe and has long-term uranium contracts with companies in Britain, Sweden, South Korea, Japan, Finland and the United States.

The Olympic Dam environment is harsh. The summers are hot, the rainfall is low and the soil quality is poor. Trees, mainly mulga and native pines, and grasses grow on the sand dunes and there are some small shrubs in the corridors or swales. In the twelve years between 1980 and 1992, attempts to green the semi-arid country have been made and more than 140 000 trees have been planted around the Olympic Dam mine site and the township of Roxby Downs (see entry).

PIMBA ■ 2053

Pimba is 176 kilometres north-west of Port Augusta. Its Aboriginal name comes from a word thought to mean 'pine trees'. Like Glendambo even further west, this tiny settlement is a stopover for passengers on the Indian–Pacific railway line and a petrol depot for motorists on the Stuart Highway as it snakes its way across millions of hectares of inhospitable landscape into the Northern Territory. It is also the turnoff point for Woomera, Roxby Downs, the massive Olympic Dam mining project and the Andamooka opal field.

ROXBY DOWNS ■ 2054

Roxby Downs is a purpose-built town which houses and supports the families of the Olympic Dam workforce. The community was set up in 1987 and will exist as long as the nearby mines are worked. There are commercial, sporting and educational facilities which include a Technical and Further Education College and a well-stocked public library.

The town taps the Great Artesian Basin for its water supply via a 110-kilometre pipeline. Drinking water is produced in a reverse osmosis desalination plant and water from treated sewage is used for irrigation. Clever landscaping and water use are beginning to green the semi-arid sand dunes and swales. *Population 2000*

TARCOOLA ■ 2055

Tarcoola took its name from the Tarcoola goldfield which was named after the winner of the 1893 Melbourne Cup. It is here that the Indian–Pacific railway line meets the line to Alice Springs which opened in November 1980. In 1974, the then Prime Minister Gough Whitlam travelled from Canberra to set off the blast to begin the new track. This big event for which a welcoming group of about a hundred outback people from a radius of many kilometres gathered at Tarcoola, turned out to be a false alarm as the contract for the new line's construction was not let until March 1975.

In earlier times, the mail travelled to Tarcoola from Port Augusta in strong, light, high-wheeled express waggons pulled by teams of mules, which despite their well known stubborn temperament, were chosen over horses for their superior constitutions. A contemporary magazine report described the coachman's lot as 'no sinecure...[he] has to be able to shoe all his horses, tire a wheel, put on a pole, and at a pinch manufacture an axle; to be a thorough bushman, man of iron nerve and endurance, and an expert driver'.

In the trackless northern depths of the Great Victoria Desert, the sand gives way to a quartzite deposit, eroded by the elements into a gibber plain.

WOOMERA ■ 2056

Woomera – the name comes from an Aboriginal word thought to mean a 'spear-throwing stick' – lies on a stony, treeless plateau just off the Stuart Highway, about 180 kilometres north-west of Port Augusta by road. The village and the rocket range were built by the British and Australian governments under an arrangement known as the UK/Australia Joint Project which lasted from 1947 to 1980. Water for local consumption is pumped by pipeline from Port Augusta.

Until 1982, Woomera was a prohibited area for travellers. It is now an open town but it is still administered by the Department of Defence. Residents are unable to stay there after they retire because there is no infrastructure to support retirees but the Department of Community Services and Health and the South Australia Housing Trust are investigating what is needed to lift this restriction. Numbers in the village are declining from a peak of over 6000 in the 1960s and more than a quarter of the present population are United States citizens.

The boundaries of the Woomera Prohibited Area have changed over the years. At present it extends some 130 000 square kilometres to the west of the town with its southern boundary running just above the long Indian–Pacific railway line to a point beyond the Maralinga test site. It is a sanctuary for wildlife and it is not unusual to see emus and kangaroos in the town itself together with flocks of screeching parrots.

Woomera has an eighteen-hole golf course about seven kilometres from the town centre which was established in 1955. The fairways are sandy shale, the greens, known as browns, are made from oiled sand and some local rules apply on the course. Like all good golf clubs, this one boasts a well-appointed nineteenth hole where visiting players are welcomed. *Population 1805*

WOOMERA ROCKET RANGE The range, which is about thirty-five kilometres north-west of Woomera, was set up to test experimental rockets and missiles of all types. Other countries besides Australia and Britain have used the site. Rocket trials at the range include those conducted by the European Launcher Development Organisation (ELDO) in the late 1960s and early 1970s and the United States National Aeronautics and Space Administration (NASA) used Woomera for space-tracking for a number of years.

Since the end of the joint launching project in 1980, the range has been kept at a care and maintenance level only and extra staff move in for trials when the need arises. At present the RAAF is the main user of the facilities for aircraft and weapons testing and the future of the Woomera Instrumented Range and the Woomera Prohibited Area is usually described by government authorities as 'always under review'.

COMMONWEALTH HILL An estimated seventy-five per cent of the Woomera range is leased by pastoralists. The 10 464 square kilometres of Commonwealth Hill comprise one of the properties within the prohibited area. In 1990, 70 000 sheep grazed within its boundaries and it was the largest sheep station in Australia.

WYNBRING ■ 2057

Wynbring is named after a rock waterhole discovered by Ernest Giles on 31 March 1875. It is a dot on the landscape and one of the tiny settlements (see Lyons, Pimba), some with lyrical Aboriginal names such as Wirraminna – 'gum tree water' – and Malbooma – 'wind' – that exist mainly because of the outstretched iron arm of the original Trans–Australia railway. Each one is testimony to the incredible skills of surveyors, engineers and tracklayers who crossed the desert from Port Augusta to Kalgoorlie and incidentally constructed the world's longest stretch of straight line – some 475 kilometres from a point between Ooldea and Watson to a point between Loongana and Nurina (see box, *Esperance & Eucla*).

'We'd have never built that line if it hadn't been for the camels', said one railway worker many years later. The stalwart beasts – originally imported from Afghanistan – carted materials and supplies for nearly ten years. When the east and west were joined on 17 October 1917, the work had cost 5 815 000 pounds sterling, considerably exceeding the predicted budget of one million pounds.

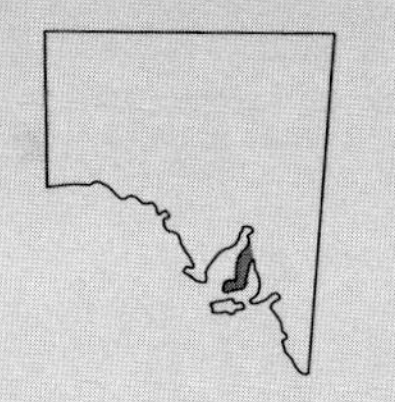

Kadina & Wallaroo

Pastoralists settled on the flat lands of Yorke Peninsula in the 1850s; later the land of their sheep and cattle runs was given over to the farming of cereals and now the peninsula is one of the world's leading barley-growing regions.

After ninety years at the tip of Yorke Peninsula, salt air has filleted the wreck of the unfortunate Ethel.

ARDROSSAN ■ **2058**
The silos and loading jetties here, comprising one of the largest grain receival centres in the country, came into existence as a by-product of the mining of dolomite. Dolomite – used as flux in steelmaking – is quarried by Broken Hill Proprietary Limited from a particularly pure deposit on the southern outskirts of Ardrossan. Although its presence was noted in 1918, the mineral was not exploited commercially until the 1940s when it was loaded from the one-thousand-metre-long jetty with its continuous belt which carries not only dolomite, but also wheat, barley and salt for export overseas. *Population 1010*

SMITH POWERHOUSE MUSEUM Now the venue for exhibits of agricultural machinery, this building was once at the core of the factory that produced the first stump-jump ploughs. This was an implement which made grain production possible, not only on the Yorke Peninsula, but in regions of mallee scrub around the continent.

CORNY POINT ■ **2059**
The Corny Point settlement grew up around the beach where farmers transferred their bagged grain from drays to barges to be ferried to waiting ketches. To the west, the jutting headland from which it takes its name is topped by a lighthouse built in the 1880s. It has operated automatically since the 1920s, but the keeper's cottage which once stood at its base has long since been removed.

Matthew Flinders named Corny Point in 1802; the French navigator Nicholas Baudin called it *Pointe des Soupirs* (Point of Sighs).

EDITHBURGH ■ **2060**
There are about one hundred salt lakes in the Edithburgh–Yorketown area. For more than a century their gleaming surfaces have been scraped in an industry which reached a peak between 1890 and 1900 when production rose to 40 000 tonnes of salt a year. To prevent the roads being damaged by heavily laden wagons, horse-drawn trucks piled high with bags were hauled to refineries in Edithburgh along a steel track which had been laid from the harvesting operations at Lake Fowler.

INNES NATIONAL PARK ■ **2061**
The tip of Yorke Peninsula is preserved in a magnificent national park of jutting headlands, rocky clifftops, wave-cut platforms and fine surfing beaches where waves roll in from the west. Vegetation ranges from stunted heath on the windswept heights of the coast, to mallee, which covers most of the interior.

In the 1880s, W. Innes – a Melbourne-based businessman – began gypsum-mining operations at the string of salt lakes to the west. At first the material was carted to Marion Bay, east of the park, for shipment, but after production from Inneston

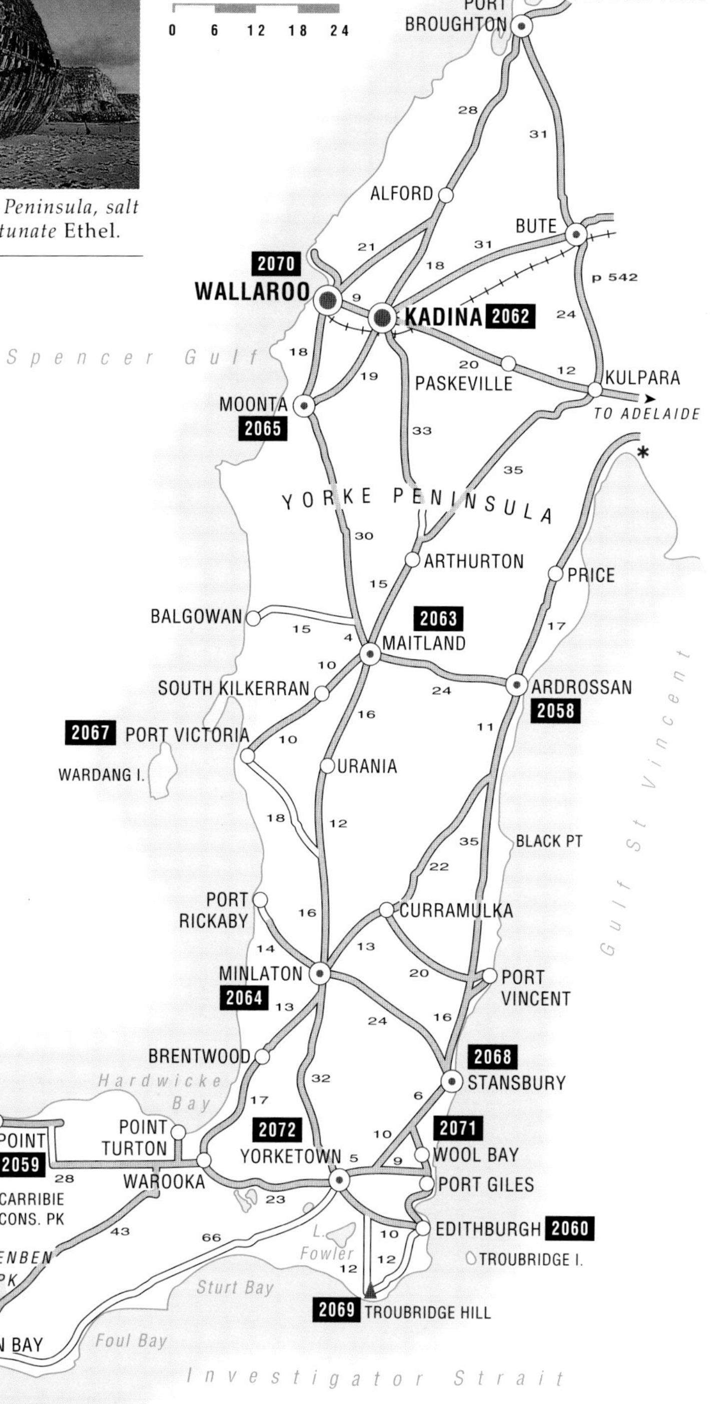

The Cornish engine in Moonta's old limestone pump house worked non-stop for 60 years with just minor repairs.

Lake began in 1913 the shipping point was moved to Stenhouse Bay. Marion, Snow and Spider lakes are excluded from the park because they are still being worked for their salt.

KADINA ■ **2062**
Although there was little to entice the pastoralist to this bleak and waterless part of the peninsula, Captain Walter Hughes, a former ship owner and opium trader, took on the challenge in the late 1850s when he leased Wallaroo Station. Aware of the rich copper mines not far to the east at Burra (see *Peterborough & Burra*), Hughes instructed his employees to bring in any promising stones they found – a shrewd move, for there were indeed rich mineral deposits hidden beneath the limestone crust here. The Wallaroo mine opened and soon grew large, even by today's standards. Veins were followed to depths of 800 metres and more by Cornish miners using techniques developed for similar deposits in their homeland.

Many Cornish traditions, such as the pasty, survive in Kadina. The pasty originated as an easy-to-carry meal in the tin mines of Cornwall. The crimped edge of pastry acted as a handle, so that the miner's dirty hand did not come into contact with the food. This part was thrown away uneaten (see box). *Population 3540*

MAITLAND ■ **2063**
European settlement started with pastoralist Samuel Rogers who took up Ynoo Station in 1851. Following the resumptions of the 1870s, the surrounding lands were surveyed for agricultural blocks, and the town proclaimed. As the geographical centre of the peninsula, Maitland today serves a large farming community. A museum in the former 1877 schoolrooms has a collection of agricultural machinery and memorabilia from the district. *Population 1070*

MINLATON ■ **2064**
Although Minlaton can claim, with much justification, to be the 'Barley Capital of the World', its beginnings, as with most of the settlements on the Yorke Peninsula, were pastoral. The first land lease here was the historic Gum Flat run, taken up in the early 1840s, which by the 1850s supported more than 40 000 sheep and hundreds of cattle.

Minlaton township is sited near natural springs and the original Gum Flat homestead and was surveyed in 1876. The town is now surrounded by sweeping fields of barley which supply malt for the brewing industry. *Population 800*

MOONTA ■ **2065**
Pastoral activity in this region dates from the 1840s, but it was the discovery of copper-bearing rocks near a wombat hole here in 1861 by shepherd Paddy Ryan which led to the growth of the town. Ryan worked for Captain Walter Hughes of Wallaroo Station, and the deposit he stumbled upon was the second to be located on the property. It proved, when mining began in the following year, to be even richer than the Wallaroo mine, and contained some of the purest copper ore ever mined.

Moonta is one of the three towns which make up the copper triangle at the top of the Yorke Peninsula. Thousands of immigrant Cornish miners poured into this area in the 1860s and 1870s (see box), coming either directly from their homeland, or from earlier mining settlements in South Australia. The town is now surrounded by wheatfields but its name derives from Aboriginal words thought to mean 'thick scrub'. *Population 2720*

MINER'S COTTAGE This National Trust-owned, restored cottage at Moonta is typical of those in which the Cornish miners lived. Featuring the local style of two rooms side by side topped by narrow pitched roofs with central gutters, it was built in about 1870. It is surrounded by a traditional stick fence and contains period furnishings.

HUGHES PUMP HOUSE This tall, rectangular structure was constructed in the mid-1860s of local limestone – small sea-shell fossils can be seen in some of the stones. The building houses a now silent pumping engine which operated twenty-four hours a day drawing water from the Hughes shaft to keep the underground mine workings dry.

PORT BROUGHTON ■ **2066**
When land became available for agricultural pursuits following the 1870s resumption of the pastoral holdings, wheat growers quickly established themselves across the top of the peninsula. To get their crops to market a small landing was constructed here in 1871 on a curving peninsula which creates a navigable waterway that looks more like a river than an inlet of the sea, and Port Broughton came into existence.

Today, Port Broughton is a fishing port noted especially for the hauls of deep-sea prawns which are landed at its long, T-shaped jetty. It is named in honour of the Reverend William Broughton, the first Bishop of South Australia. *Population 680*

PORT VICTORIA ■ **2067**
This peaceful seaside town calls itself 'the last of the windjammer ports' because it was from here that the last commercial passage to be undertaken by sailing ships began when the *Pamir* and *Passat*, their holds heavy with Yorke Peninsula grain, sailed for England in June 1949. On the waterfront adjacent to the head of the jetty is a maritime museum which has a display of the wrecks and relics of Port Victoria's sailing days.

WARDANG ISLAND Sheltering the waters of Port Victoria harbour is the land mass of Wardang Island. Pastoral leases granted in the 1850s and 1860s included a covenant which gave the local Aborigines and their descendants full and free access to the island. In 1884, control of the island was transferred to the Yorke Peninsula Aboriginal Mission. Permission to land here must be first obtained from the Point Pearce Community Council.

The Norfolk Island pines (left) suggest the waterfront, near-port location – important in the days of poor roads – of Wallaroo station – now a restaurant.

STANSBURY ■ 2068

Shellfish once abounded along these foreshores and for many years the area was known as Oyster Bay, although officially it has always been Stansbury, the name bestowed in 1873 by Governor Musgrave for a friend. It came into existence as a port to serve the needs of a growing farming community following the surveying and sale of inland agricultural blocks in the 1870s.

Kilns for burning limestone built on the waterfront here towards the end of the nineteenth century processed lime for the Adelaide market – later cement was produced and shipped from here as well. Limestone continues to be quarried at Kleins Point, between Stansbury and Wool Bay. *Population 510*

TROUBRIDGE HILL ■ 2069

Troubridge Hill, which rises from the sea at the heel of the peninsula, is surmounted by an unmanned light housed in a soaring, modern red-brick tower of classic lighthouse design. It replaced the earlier beacon which flashed its warning from Troubridge Island, across the channel, for these are dangerous straits where unexpected currents and winds have claimed many a ship. One such was the steamer *Clan Ranald* in 1911. Bound for South Africa laden with grain taken on only hours before at Port Adelaide, when she reached the waters off Troubridge Hill she began, inexplicably, to list, and before the night was out turned over completely and sank to the bottom of the sea. There she lies still, upside down in twenty metres of water. Forty lives were lost.

WALLAROO ■ 2070

This, the third point of the copper town triangle of 'Little Cornwall' at the top of the Yorke Peninsula (see box), was the first, in 1861, to be surveyed and was the port for the export of the ore and later for the grain produce of the area. It is to the west of the mines, at the place on the coast where Captain Walter Hughes built a landing soon after copper was discovered on his Wallaroo Station near the present site of Kadina (see entry) in December 1859. In 1861, Hughes established a smelting works on the Wallaroo waterfront to process the ore from both the Wallaroo Mine (in fact situated just outside Kadina) and the Moonta Mine.

Wallaroo was the entry port for many of the Cornish families heading to the mines, but the town itself had a sizable Welsh population. The Welsh were well known for their skills in the smelting and processing of ore – a number of them came here from the copper-smelting town of Swansea in South Wales – and it was Welsh masons who were responsible for the huge square stack of Hughes Chimney at the smelter – Cornish-built stacks were round. Copper mining ceased in the 1920s following a world slump in prices.

Wallaroo was one of the ports from which the majestic windjammers sailed in the days of the 'grain races' when, laden with wheat, they sped from the shores of South Australia to England. Five of the clippers which set sail from here won their races. The last square-rigged sailing ship left Wallaroo Bay in 1939.

Tall silos have now replaced the smelter stacks, and bulk carriers the windjammers. Wallaroo has become the main port for the export of wheat and barley and the import of phosphate rock. The latter is mixed with sulphuric acid to produce superphosphate fertiliser – this industry grew up here to utilise the excess sulphur that was a by-product of the smelting works. *Population 2460*

HERITAGE AND NAUTICAL MUSEUM

The whitewashed limestone building at the centre of this complex was Wallaroo's first post office and dates from 1865. It houses a display from the copper-smelting era, while in a nearby building the history of the port is explained by way of charts, old photographs, models of ships, documents, old record books and mementoes of the trading ketches that plied the waters of the gulfs.

BIRD ISLANDS CONSERVATION PARK

Two low-lying islands off Wallaroo are protected in a conservation park as breeding grounds for sea birds.

WOOL BAY ■ 2071

Bales of wool from adjacent Penton Vale Station were rolled from the clifftops here through a narrow opening to the waterfront below from where they were shipped out. Eventually a road was carved into the cliffside and a jetty built from which lime and grain were loaded.

Although always called Wool Bay by the local people the townsite was, in 1876, officially named Pickering for a parliamentarian of the time. This was dropped in the great rationalisation of place names which occurred in South Australia in 1940.

YORKETOWN ■ 2072

Because of the proximity of Yorketown to a number of salt pans it was once mooted that the settlement be named Salt Lake City. Originally it was called Weaners Flat because the meadows on the site of the present town were used by the early pastoralists for the weaning of lambs.

The town is now the commercial and administrative centre of the southern Yorke Peninsula. Many of its handsome stone buildings, some adorned with wrought-iron work, date from the 1880s and 1890s, including the old court house, the Uniting (formerly Methodist) church, the former Zion Lutheran church (now housing a kindergarten) and a number of hotels. *Population 740*

IN THE LAND OF PASTIES, PISKIES & COUSIN JACKS

A zig-zag roofline – rather than one roof – on this Moonta cottage was dictated by a scarcity of long timbers in a treeless landscape.

BECAUSE of the large movement of miners and their families from the valleys of Cornwall, in the far west of England, to settle near the South Australian copper mines in the 1860s, 1870s and 1880s, this region became known as 'Little Cornwall'. With earlier Cornish immigrants from the worked out Burra Mines the new arrivals formed solid communities where, with whitewashed stone cottages set in gardens of hardy geraniums, they re-created the villages they had left.

They maintained their Cornish identity fiercely with festivals, foods, religious observances, wrestling matches, choirs, brass, fife and drum bands, and building and mining methods. In 1909, the Scottish-born Australian politician W.G. Spence reflected that the people of the peninsula 'lived isolated from the rest of the colony, remaining more Cornish than Cornwall itself'.

The Cornish were renowned for their mining prowess. 'Wherever there's a hole in the ground you'll find a Cousin Jack at the bottom searching for metal', went an old saying, and indeed in mining methods, equipment and terminology their influence here was overwhelming (see Moonta).

Many mine names, too, echoed those of the homeland – Wheal Basset, Wheal Grenfell, Wheal Rose ('wheal' meaning 'a working'), Truro, Carn Brea and Crinnis. But while Cornishmen not only worked, but also managed, the mines, it was most unlikely that they would ever benefit by holding shares in the company. When the mines closed in 1923 some of the miners moved on to Broken Hill, but many remained, turning to farming. Today their descendants carry on many Cornish traditions.

Every second May a three-day festival, the Kernewek Lowender – literally 'Cornish happiness' – is held in Kadina, Moonta and Wallaroo. It features a maypole, the 'furry' (floral) dance, wheelbarrow races, highland games with caber tossing, haggis-eating competitions and quayside stalls. Swanky – a dark heavy beer developed here by the early miners – is brewed especially for the occasion and thousands of pasties are consumed. 'Piskies' – little folk akin to the Irish leprechaun who are ever ready to play tricks on the unwary – are abroad in force here during the Kernewek Lowender when, in their traditional pose – squatting with arms folded around the knees and head turned in a wide grin – they are captured in metal as lucky charms. □

WESTERN AUSTRALIA

Spanning the western third of the continent from north to south and stretching far into the arid interior, Western Australia is the giant of Australia's states. It was also the colony to start with probably the least amount of promise, only to realise its true potential after the discovery and exploitation of the minerals that lay beneath the desert's fringe; the boom which followed the nation's last great gold rush in the 1890s was equalled only by the twentieth-century boom in minerals ranging from iron ore to diamonds.

SPECIAL FEATURES

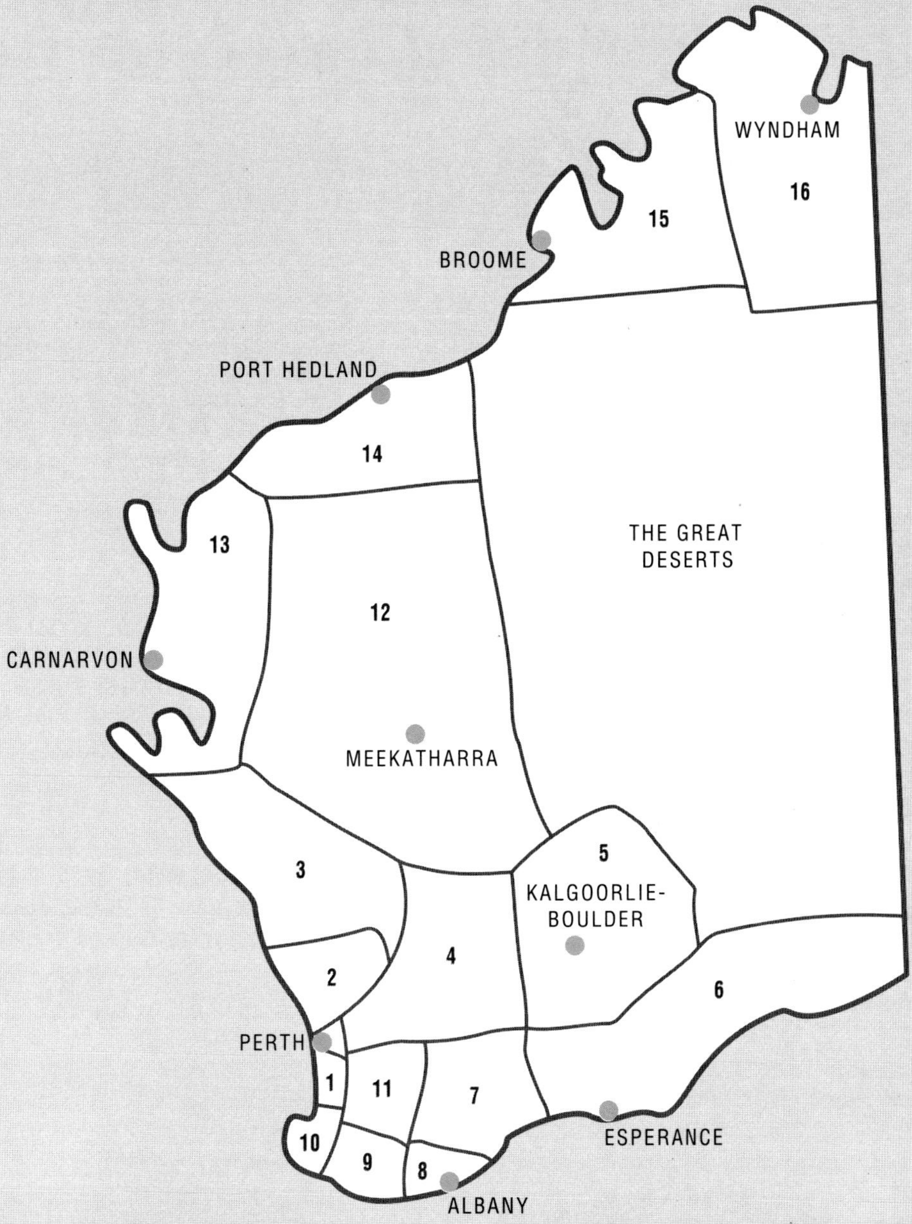

WYNDHAM
16
15
BROOME
PORT HEDLAND
14
13
THE GREAT DESERTS
12
CARNARVON
MEEKATHARRA
5
3
KALGOORLIE-BOULDER
4
2
6
PERTH
1
11
7
ESPERANCE
10
9
8
ALBANY

The black swan symbolises Western Australia on the state's coat of arms and as its bird emblem although it also occurs elsewhere. Its animal counterpart, the numbat, survives in diminishing numbers in the forests.

PERTH

After a slow start eventually hastened by the importation of convict labour, Australia's most isolated capital is now also its most modern, long ago leaving its 'poor cousin' image behind.

On 12 August 1829, on the birthday of His Britannic Majesty King George IV, a small party of soldiers and civilians travelled eighteen kilometres up the Swan River on Australia's western coast. On the river's bank the young wife of Lieutenant Dance made a symbolic mark on a tree. There were a few cheers, some speeches, a volley of musket shot, and thus Western Australia's capital city was founded.

It was not a unique founding ceremony and the event went almost unrecorded. There was nothing interesting about a group of private investors setting up a colony in what the English navigator and sometime pirate William Dampier called '...the barrenest spot on the Globe'.

Unlike other Australian colonies, Western Australia began as a free settlement, without the direct aid of the British Government. Britain's main concern was to establish a presence to thwart any French or Dutch interest in the west coast. Both administrators and settlers had set off '...without any greater preparation than if they had gone out upon a holiday excursion in the woods', as one observer recorded.

That Governor Stirling had finally made a choice for the site of his capital came as some relief for the several hundred settlers clinging to the sandhills of Fremantle. For several weeks they had been battered by north-west winds and pelting rain as a series of severe winter gales savaged the coast. Huddled behind a collection of rough, makeshift shelters they had time to reflect on their decision to become pioneers.

The colony's first surveyor had been given explicit directions by the British Home Office on the way the new townsite was to be laid out and for the first six months worked at a frantic pace to keep ahead of the demand for allotments. By the end of that first year, all the sites for the city's essential services had been surveyed – Government land, the burial ground, a number of hotels and the three monuments of a transplanted civilisation: the court house, the jail and the church.

Despite the planning, the town began like a scattered encampment and for the first few years most of the residents lived in tents and European versions of Aboriginal shelters made of brush and mud. '...a comfortless hole', wrote one early visitor to Perth. 'The soil is such that no human being can possibly exist. The miserable huts are built in a wood on a soil of dark-coloured sand, swarming with fleas and mosquitos; a more perfect purgatory cannot be devised'.

The site did appear to be a very poor choice indeed. It was bounded by swamps and lakes to the north, by Mount Eliza to the west, and by river mudflats to the south and east. By the end of the second year, most people believed that the decision to develop a colony in Western Australia was a blunder, and migration virtually stopped.

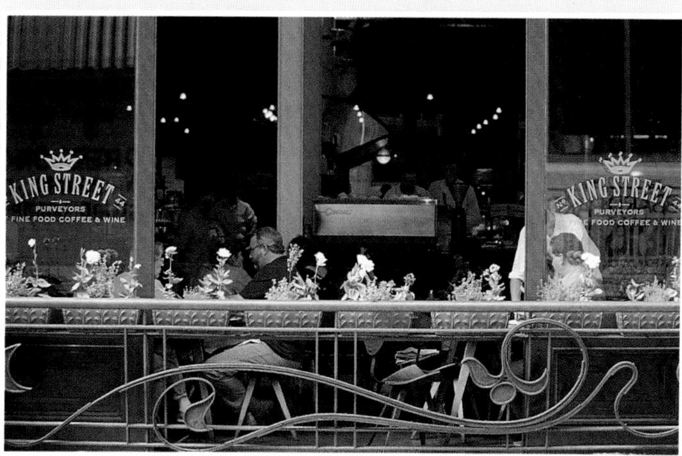

Perth's first two decades were marked by a stagnation which strangely enough had a direct influence on its appearance today. Unlike contemporary towns in the eastern colonies, it proceeded thoughtfully and was able to develop to a plan. Below the crest of the ridge, immediately above the open expanse of the Swan River, the surveyor John Septimus Roe laid out the wide strip of St Georges Terrace, which quickly became what it is today – Perth's financial and professional centre, and home to its government offices. On its western rise, he placed the army barracks which looked eastwards down the terrace to the Darling Range and the farmlands beyond. Two other streets – Hay and Murray – were laid on the crest parallel to the terrace. They were to be the town's retail centres.

Perth's skyline springs from the banks of the tranquil Swan River, bursting with the exuberance of the new in an exhilarating climate which its residents savour in such places as Kings Park (top), open-air cafes (centre) and the precincts of the Northbridge art gallery.

West of the city centre and facing Kings Park, Matilda Bay is part of the Swan's generous estuary.

Other streets were drawn at right angles to these main boulevards, running down to the river and cutting the area into blocks of about four hectares each. Today these dozen blocks are the heart of Perth, with St Georges Terrace the symbol of the state's modern wealth.

'The Terrace' is a long and grand line of monuments to this wealth, and to Western Australia's entrepreneurs and mining magnates. Like a modern Manhattan, its shining glass and concrete structures dominate the city's skyline. On its western rise, the old army barracks have gone, except for the impressive arch through which successive inhabitants of Parliament House can view the heart of their state's financial power. The other two tentative marks on Roe's survey map – Hay and Murray streets – have become busy shopping zones. Both are now traffic-free malls and are interlaced above and below ground with dozens of shopping arcades.

With the impoverishment of the first few decades, it would have been impossible for the early residents of Perth to imagine what would become of their encampment. In 1850, in a desperate attempt to ward off the seemingly inevitable demise of the fledgling colony, they asked that convicts be sent there. That unfortunate human cargo and the financial assistance that came with it ensured the colony's survival. Perth's Supreme Court buildings, its Town Hall and Government House remain as legacies of those short convict years.

But what sealed Perth's future as a significant city is the mineral wealth of Western Australia. The gold-rush years of the 1890s increased the state's population sevenfold in little over a decade. The impressive permanence of the Perth Mint erected at that time is a symbol of the enormous confidence felt by the grandchildren of the beleaguered settlers. Magnificent Victorian buildings appeared in the modest colonial capital and its position as a major centre was assured.

Unfortunately, most of these fine structures were in turn demolished by the next generation of grandchildren and replaced with more modern versions of permanence. The mineral boom of the 1960s and 1970s, and the oil and gas discoveries that followed, brought the state immense wealth in a short time. This is clearly reflected by Perth's centre, which has been almost completely rebuilt over the past twenty years.

Fortunately, that hectic urban development did not seriously affect the city's natural beauty. Regardless of the swamps and poor soils, Governor Stirling had chosen a uniquely attractive setting by the Swan's broad, estuary waters for this isolated capital. Because of the many lean years of the mid-1800s, the city was allowed time to develop in an orderly fashion. As it expanded in three great corridors to the north, south and east – with the older suburbs having followed the railway line west to the sea – large areas were set aside for parks and open spaces.

Mount Eliza – now Kings Park – which once obstructed the early town's westward movement, is one of Perth's greatest assets. Looking down on the city centre and much of metropolitan Perth's sprawl, it is 400 hectares of natural bushland blended with landscaped gardens and public recreational areas. In spring, Western Australia's kaleidoscopic range of wildflowers turn the park into a blaze of colour.

Kings Park also presents a microcosm of the state's animal and bird life. Euros, possums, snakes and eagles carry on their existence as they have for thousands of years – in the middle of a city of well over one million people. And every now and then a small flock of its noisy parrots will fly down to visit a busy street to remind the inhabitants of the bush.

Throughout Perth's area of more than 5500 square kilometres, broad tracts have been set aside as open land, particularly along the wetlands parallel to the coast. And eighty per cent of the river frontage has been kept as public space. Most visitors are surprised by the extent of Perth's sprawl and by what it has to offer. On a map it is a tiny dot in a huge, seemingly empty land. It is the most isolated city of its size in the world. Adelaide, the nearest equivalent centre, is more than 2100 kilometres away, and it is closer to Djakarta than to its own national capital.

As in many other cities, an architectural highlight of modern Perth is a Las Vegas-style casino.

In some ways, Perth's isolation is evident in the lifestyle of its residents. With the pristine white beaches running the full length of the city's western border, the enclosed waters of Cockburn Sound, the offshore islands and the open waters of the Swan River, it is easy to see why its people are pulled towards the physical. Add to this a mild winter, hot summer days and long, warm summer nights, and it would appear that nature has taken a very strong hand in dictating how Perth's residents are to live.

The result is a city of friendly people who welcome visitors, mix easily and spend a great deal of time out of their houses. What is also clear is that in Perth suburbia rules. The city's residential area is mostly a sprawl of Californian-style bungalows set amid lawns, exotic trees, native shrubs, palms, grass trees, swimming pools, solar heaters and television antennas.

It is an egalitarian city with large, readily accessible shopping centres, wide tree-lined streets, sporting fields and no traffic jams. And the comforts are evenly shared; the newly established northern suburbs have the same facilities as the older river suburbs of Peppermint Grove and Dalkeith, where many of Australia's super-rich have their multi-million dollar mansions.

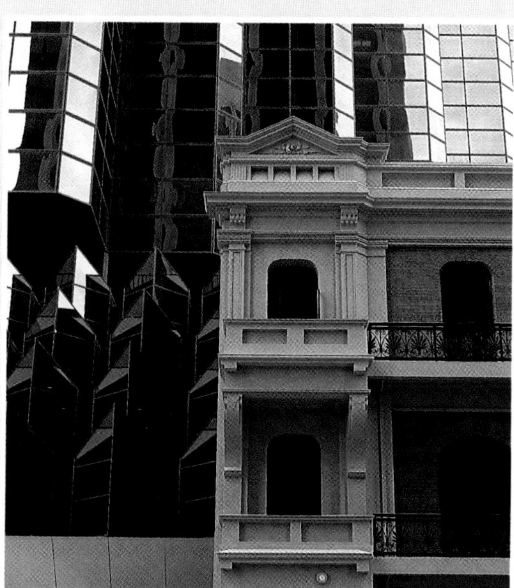

A potent symbol of modern Perth: the old Palace Hotel has been absorbed by a glossy office tower.

A modern restoration did the ornate, 1904 domed ceiling of His Majesty's Theatre proud.

Despite being dismissed by 'easterners' as a cultural desert in the past, modern Perth has a busy intellectual life. There is a fine concert hall, a regular festival of the arts, fine universities and an increasingly multicultural population of 'new Australians'. What Perth does lack, with two exceptions, are the Bohemian and cosmopolitan centres that characterise older cities in the world. But the two exceptions are significant. On the other side of the tracks from the city is Northbridge. Once referred to as 'little Italy', it is a major centre of Perth's migrant population and night life. When the city centre closes down for the day, Northbridge comes to life. Within its few streets it has one of the biggest concentrations of restaurants in the Australia.

Eighteen kilometres to the west of Perth proper is Fremantle. Once exclusively a port town and the domain of Italian fishermen, Australian wharfies and Irish factory workers, it has been invaded by professionals, artists and others escaping from life in the suburbs. Its cafes, elegantly restored old buildings and relaxed lifestyle have made it a significant creative centre.

Perth truly comes into its own on a Sunday afternoon. On the Swan River, armadas of pleasure launches jostle with the multi-coloured sails of yachts, the beaches at Leighton, Cottesloe, Scarborough and Swanbourne – the city's nudist beach – are strewn with bronzing bodies, and the sporting fields are crowded with future Denis Lillees, Greg Normans and Evonne Goolagongs. In the evening, the smell of barbecuing steak is mixed with the warble of magpies settling down for the night.

It is a strange mix for such a large city. Perhaps it is the isolation. But in bustling, 'state of excitement' Perth, with its skyscrapers and air of prosperity, there is still a strong sense of the past and of the bush being never far away. □

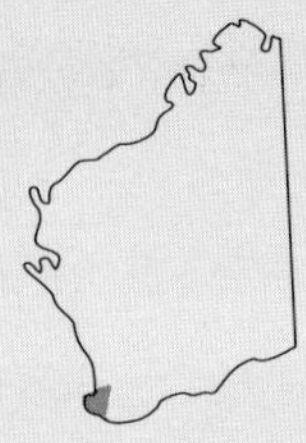

Rockingham & Fremantle

This populous region of Western Australia was first inhabited by black-skinned hunter-gatherers who were displaced by those who came to cultivate the fertile soil and log the stately jarrah forests. Mining and other modern industrial developments benefit from the convenient placement of ports along the coast.

After 70 years of wholesale selling, this building now houses a cosmopolitan collection of retail stalls.

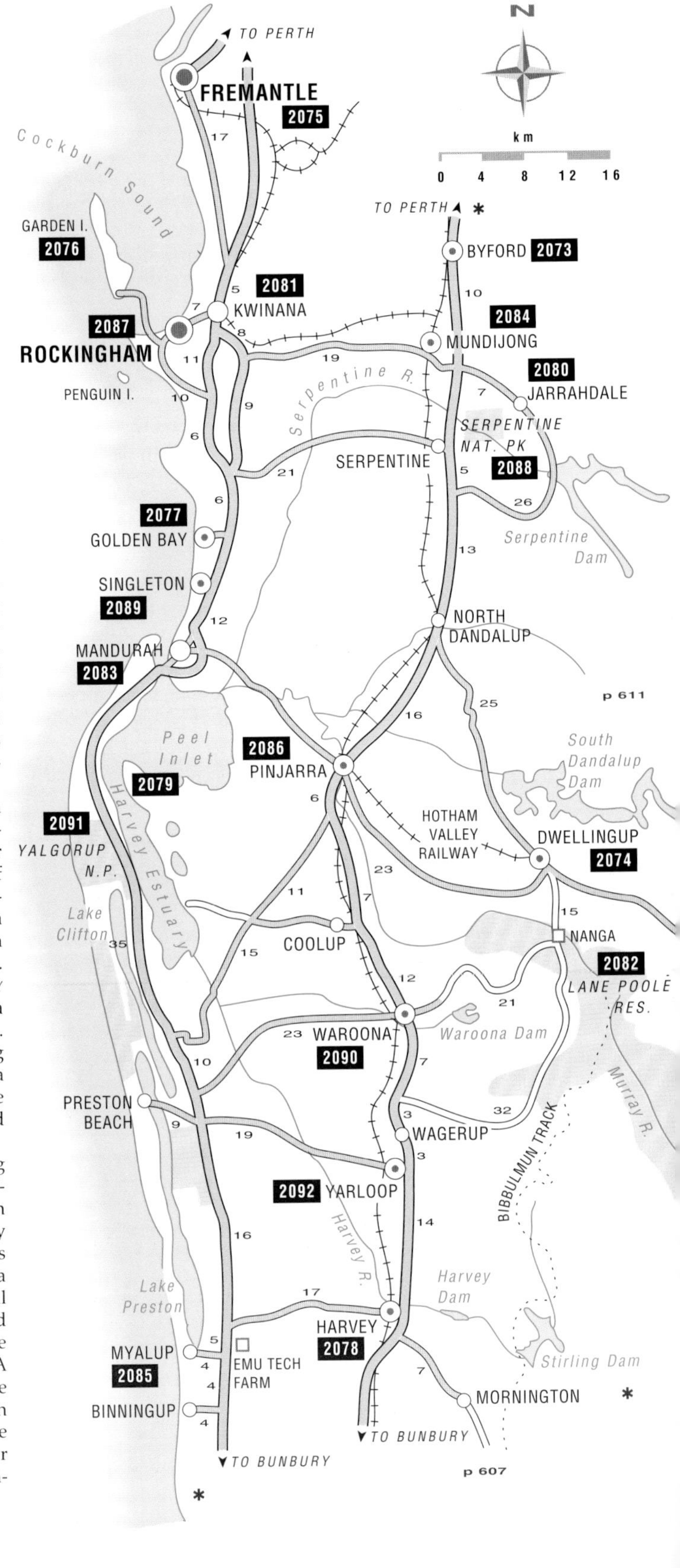

BYFORD ■ **2073**
Byford, known as Beenup until 1920, lies within the Serpentine–Jarrahdale Shire. Henry Mead arrived in the district in 1842 and soon cleared land south of here and built a two-storey house which he called 'Whitby Falls Estate' after his home town in Yorkshire. He raised cattle, supplied meat to other settlers and bred police and coach horses. The agricultural tradition persists in the shire and there are many fruit orchards here today.

The original town was planned west of the railway line but when a brickworks was established in 1913, the employees wanted their houses nearby and residential focus shifted to the east. The navy had an explosives depot at Byford during the Second World War. Much of the granite used for the causeway at Garden Island was extracted from the surrounding hills. *Population 1310*

DWELLINGUP ■ **2074**
The Dwellingup region was first settled at the turn of the century when it quickly became the centre of a booming timber industry. Mills at Holyoake, Marrinup, Nanga and Chadoora produced jarrah sleepers and other timber products which were railed from here to the docks at Rockingham. In 1918, after logging the jarrah forest became a state venture, Dwellingup became a base for forest management and research.

Towns in the forest are always at risk from fire and Dwellingup has twice been badly burnt. Hundreds of thousands of trees were consumed in 1951 and just ten years later lightning strikes started devastating bushfires. The flames raged for five days and destroyed most of Dwellingup and approximately 140 000 hectares around it. Only the hotel and a few houses escaped but the settlement has risen from the ashes to resume its place in the area's timber industry.

There are many milling roads in the forest where the magnificent jarrah trees can be seen in all their glory. They can grow to a height of forty metres and a girth of eight-and-a-half metres. Dwellingup serves as a convenient stopover for travellers on their way to the Lane Poole Reserve.

HOTHAM VALLEY TOURIST RAILWAY
The original line between Pinjarra and Dwellingup was built in 1910. The steam trains now running along the route have been restored by a band of enthusiastic volunteers. The track winds through farmland and jarrah forest.

MARRINUP NO. 16 POW CAMP During the Second World War, a prisoner-of-war camp for German and Italian prisoners was established at nearby Marrinup. In 1942, arrangements were made to ship POWs from Libya and India to supplement the rural workforce. The Marrinup compound was principally a transit stop where gardening was a favourite pastime. A fish pond and garden beds in the shape of playing cards suits remain on the site. The last prisoners were released in 1946 and some later returned to Australia through sponsored immigration.

Long, dry summers and short, wet winters ensure that there is no shortage of junior lifesaving recruits at Fremantle's three dazzling ocean beaches.

FREMANTLE ■ 2075

Fremantle attained city status when it turned 100 years of age in 1929 and though now merged with Perth's urban sprawl, still retains a separate identity. It has come a long way since Captain Charles Fremantle sailed into the sheltered waters of the harbour in HMS *Challenger* on 2 May 1829 with a political purpose. His mission was to hoist the Union Jack on the south head and claim the whole of the west coast of New Holland in the name of King George IV to prevent the French from taking the territory.

James Stirling was appointed Lieutenant-Governor of the new colony and landed on Garden Island early in June 1829 after a sea-journey from England that took almost four months. He named the settlement at the mouth of the Swan River after Captain Fremantle.

Early colonial life was not without incident. On 17 August 1832, Western Australia's only documented duel was fought over a business matter at a lonely spot near Fremantle. The combatants were William Clark, a solicitor, and George Johnson, a merchant, who died next day.

One Fremantle watcher observed in 1834 that there were among the colonists some 'cheerless dissatisfied people with gloomy looks, who plod through sand from hut to hut to drink grog and grumble out their discontent to each other'. The settlement developed slowly in the first two decades because of labour shortages. No doubt some of the gloomy colonists brightened a little when their request for assistance brought the first convicts to Western Australia in 1850 to help with the public buildings, roads and bridges. About 10 000 in all were transported to Western Australia in the next eighteen years.

Not everyone lived in abject servitude. In 1871, when Fremantle became a municipality, there were about 4000 people there. During the Western Australian gold rushes of the 1890s, thousands of miners passed through the port on their way to Kalgoorlie and Coolgardie. It was then necessary to pass a by-law 'restricting and regulating the driving of camels through the streets'.

In the middle of the 1890s, a rocky bar was blasted from the mouth of the Swan River making the harbour accessible to large ships. This was the imaginative idea of Engineer-in-Chief, Charles Yelverton O'Connor, whose statue now looks out over the harbour he made possible. There are four kilometres of docks at Fremantle and it is still very much a working port, though the new deepwater berths at industrial Kwinana (see entry) handle the very large tonnages. The investment boom of the 1960s and 1970s that transformed central Perth left Fremantle largely unchanged. However, much money was spent on smartening up the buildings and extending facilities for the international yachting crowd when the world sporting spotlight was turned on the city for the Royal Perth Yacht Club's unsuccessful defence of the America's Cup in 1987. *Population 17 400*

THE ROUND HOUSE The oldest public building in Fremantle is the original jail, designed by Henry Reveley, the colony's first civil engineer, and completed in January 1831. In fact, it is not round at all but a twelve-sided structure where up to fifteen prisoners at a time were crowded together in each of the eight cells.

FESTIVALS Fremantle Festival, mid-late November.

At Fremantle's maritime heart are four harbours: two for pleasure craft and two for fishing and cargo vessels.

GARDEN ISLAND ■ 2076

One of Louis de Freycinet's colleagues named this ten-kilometre-long, low, scrub island in Cockburn Sound 'Buache'. Lieutenant-Governor James Stirling renamed the island and he and Charles Fraser, the New South Wales colonial botanist, planted the first garden there – bananas and a selection of seeds. In 1829 settlers from HMS *Parmelia* sheltered there for two months before transferring to the mainland.

During the Second World War, 'underground' personnel trained on the island, including the crack 'Z' Force commando party. A stained-glass window in St Nicholas's Church, Rockingham and a memorial near the Palm Beach jetty pay tribute to them.

Garden Island is now linked to the mainland by a 4220-metre causeway built from 1.2 million tonnes – many thousands of truckloads – of limestone and granite, but public access by road has been forbidden since the Australian naval base HMAS *Stirling* was established in the 1970s.

GOLDEN BAY ■ 2077

Golden Bay lies to the north of Mandurah and is aptly named for its quality as a coastal resort – the beach frontage on the Indian Ocean is a stretch of clean golden sand beloved by holiday-makers. The locality is within easy reach of Perth and Fremantle and the jarrah forest reserves inland. *Population 500*

HARVEY ■ 2078

Harvey is the focal point of prosperous Harvey Shire. In 1829, Lieutenant-Governor Stirling selected land near the Harvey River and called it the Harvey River Settlement. He built a hunting lodge on the bank of the river near the site of the Harvey Agricultural School's farm. The floor was of beautifully fitted jarrah blocks cut across the grain. The tall pine tree known as Captain Stirling's tree was destroyed by fire in 1985.

Maurice B. Smith was one of the first landowners in the Harvey end of the shire and he established himself near Lake Preston in 1844. Five years later, Ephraim Clarke arrived and built a brick house at Jardup which has been restored as an art gallery. In those days, properties were largely unfenced except for small areas enclosed with split slabs to contain pigs or young vegetables. Mr Smith used heavy-gauge wire to enclose his land with two-strand post and rail fences. This earned him the nickname of 'Cast Iron Smith'.

The early settlers found the environment harsh and sometimes bare subsistence farming was all they could manage. However the good river-basin soil repaid their efforts and was soon being used for citrus orchards, vineyards and horticulture. Thomas Offer began growing potatoes at Benger Swamp in the 1890s.

A reliable water supply has usually been the main stumbling block in the struggle to farm in Australia and gravity irrigation first came to the Harvey–Brunswick area in 1916. In ironic contrast, the government set up the Harvey River Diversion and Drainage Scheme to divert the Harvey River to an ocean outlet near Myalup in order to keep arable land flood-free. The work was carried out in the depths of the Great Depression on a two-days-a-week for sustenance wages routine. There is a memorial to these hardy labourers in Harvey's Stirling Park.

Irrigation meant expansion in the dairy industry and a milk products factory was established at Brunswick Junction. Beef also became a major industry and Harvey's abattoir, one of the biggest in the country, is also Western Australia's largest meat exporter. Mining began in the 1960s with a titanium-dioxide plant at Australind. Bauxite mines feed the alumina refineries at Wagerup and Worsley. *Population 2600*

HARVEY ESTUARY – PEEL INLET ■ 2079

The double-armed inlet of Harvey Estuary and the Peel Inlet is fed by the Murray, Serpentine, Harvey and Dandalup rivers. Fishing, prawning and crabbing are popular with summer holiday-makers and the marine life that breeds in the estuary is so varied and prolific that the surrounding wetlands are always crowded with aquatic birds, especially in the nesting season.

JARRAHDALE ■ 2080

Jarrahdale, situated in the middle of jarrah forest in the Darling Range, is the centre of the Shire of Serpentine-Jarrahdale's timber industry. It is one of the region's oldest timber towns, dating back to 1872, and the mill is still a hub of activity. The district produces fruit and vegetables and is noted for tomatoes and pumpkins. Bauxite mining began nearby in the 1960s and is expected to continue for many years.

MILLBROOK COTTAGE Millbrook Cottage is an example of an early mill worker's cottage. It has been furnished in the style of the colonial era and contains a display of the town's early history.

FESTIVALS Jarrahdale Log Chop, early October.

KWINANA ■ 2081

Kwinana is said to be an Aboriginal word for 'young woman', a rather incongruous name for this strongly industrial town, but its choice is linked with local history. It was inspired by the freighter *Kwinana* – driven ashore in Cockburn Sound in 1922. The hulk was later filled with cement to anchor it and prevent it becoming a drifting marine hazard and the wreck rusts gently on.

Before 1951, most of this area south of Fremantle was coastal scrub, until an oil company decided to build a refinery on the shores of Cockburn Sound. They called the site after the stricken ship. The town is a well-planned industrial complex and is steadily expanding into residential suburbs.

There are three large plants in Kwinana processing iron ore, nickel and bauxite. About twenty million tonnes of bauxite a year is mined from the forested areas of the Darling Ranges and railed to the works in aluminium hopper waggons. This involves the clearing and subsequent rehabilitation of about 400 hectares of forested land each year. Processed alumina is exported to Geelong in Victoria and to Japan, the USA and Middle Eastern countries. Kwinana also has a large cement works, an enormous capacity for wheat storage (912 300 tonnes) and a shipping terminal. *Population 13 520*

LANE POOLE RESERVE ■ 2082

The Lane Poole Reserve is a relatively new protected area of more than 50 000 hectares declared in 1984 to protect conservation and recreation values. It was named after C.E. Lane Poole, one of the state's early Conservators of Forests who was himself a dedicated conservationist, and is within easy motoring distance of Perth. The reserve contains forested uplands, granite outcrops, steep valley slopes, rocky pools and open jarrah and wandoo woodlands. The Murray River is a delightful venue for holiday-makers and licence-holders can cast for trout, marron and freshwater cobbler. The site of the Nanga Mill which was completely destroyed in the fires of 1961 is now popular with bush-campers. Nearby Nanga Brook cascades down a trout ladder and into the Murray River.

MANDURAH ■ 2083

Mandurah, at the mouth of the Peel Inlet, and inland Pinjarra (see entry), were founded in the 1830s by Thomas Peel who took up 101 121 hectares – about 250 000 acres – of land in the area known as the Peel Estate. He had already missed an opportunity for land on the Canning River and made an unsuccessful attempt to settle on Cockburn Sound.

Mandurah is a popular summer holiday resort and doubles its population during peak months. Both locals and visitors tend to be understandably preoccupied with fishing. Blue manna crabs are the most sought after summer catch; in autumn the king prawns are 'running'. Herring, cobbler, pilchard, tailor and skipjack are among the fish caught regularly in the estuary and inlet, and pink snapper and cod are found in deeper waters.

Small freshwater lakes ornamented with happily inundated melaleucas dot the sandplain north of Mandurah.

The vegetation in the area ranges through coastal dune cover, tuart woodland, salt marsh plants and limestone with low heath growth of hakea, acacia, grevillea, melaleuca and templetonia. The noble jarrah trees grow on the high ground and at sea level close to the inlet there are swamp banksias, paperbarks, flooded gum, bulrushes, casuarina and peppermint trees. *Population 23 340*

FESTIVALS Foreshore Christmas Celebration, early December.

MUNDIJONG ■ 2084

This little town where the Serpentine-Jarrahdale shire offices are located was originally known as Manjedal, adopting its present name in 1897. The Rockingham-Jarrahdale railway, built in 1872, ran through it and the town's station was called Jarrahdale Junction until 1902 when it fell into line with the settlement. The Perth–Pinjarra railway was opened in 1893.

In the late 1830s, some 500 of Thomas Peel's settlers arrived in the district to farm and work in the timber industry. Dairy and beef farms are still important and the town has a cheese factory. Horse breeding is also a developing industry.

The fertile Pinjarra plain stretches between sand dunes and the Darling Scarp and supports forests and open woodlands of jarrah, marri and wandoo. Children call the urn-shaped fruit of the marri 'honkey nuts' and sometimes use them in playground games. *Population 730*

MYALUP ■ 2085

Myalup is a popular fishing spot with the local people, particularly at sunset when the gulls wheel overhead and the dying light turns the sea to a burnished metal colour. The beach is backed by towering sand dunes that attract hang-gliders and there are many good bush walks in the vicinity.

Nearby are the waters of Lake Preston which although much saltier than the sea, has several freshwater springs around its edge. Here birds find a haven within the protected area and the wildflowers are spectacular in the flowering season.

A short distance outside Myalup emus are raised commercially for their skins and other by-products at the Emu Tech Farm.

PINJARRA ■ 2086

Pinjarra, one of the oldest towns in the state, is the centre of Western Australia's Murray District, a region of magnificent waterways, immense jarrah trees, rolling expanses of grazing pastures, flocks of native birds and a colourful quilt of the southwest's famous wildflowers in season. Before Europeans arrived in the early 1830s, this district had long been inhabited by Aborigines who led a nomadic life in the bushland around the Murray River and lived on the bounty of the bush.

The first settlers, led by Thomas Peel, encountered significant resistance from the Aborigines who resented intruders in their hunting grounds. In 1834, upstream from a ford across the Murray, the 'Battle' of Pinjarra occurred when police and troops moved against the Aborigines. A soldier was speared; there were many deaths in retaliation, followed by a legacy of years of misunderstanding between the races.

Peel Inlet, Harvey Estuary and the Murray River had been explored by boat in 1829 and land assigned as far east as Coolup but it was not taken up until after the battle. The pioneers called the area Pinjarrup, adopting the Aboriginal name, which means 'place of the swamp'. With the fertility of the land and the easy water transport, it was not long before surplus produce was helping to feed the Swan River Colony as the Perth region was first called.

FAIRBRIDGE South African Rhodes Scholar, Kingsley Fairbridge, was invited by the Western Australian Government to set up a farm school at Pinjarra in 1912. He was the instigator of an immigration scheme for orphaned British children and set up other farms in South Australia, Tasmania and Canada. *Population 1780*

ROCKINGHAM ■ 2087

Rockingham, like Kwinana, is on Cockburn Sound and is also named after a wrecked ship, one of Thomas Peel's three, which blew aground there in a May gale in 1830. All the passengers scrambled ashore safely but then had to spend three cold, wet, uncomfortable days and nights on the beach. There is a cairn on the foreshore commemorating the *Rockingham* and papers about Peel's settlement scheme are on display in the town's museum, which also contains Sir John Forrest's telescope.

In the 1870s, Rockingham was a port and a coastal town but after the harbour fell into disuse when ships became larger it began to adopt a holiday atmosphere based on the access to good beaches along the Sound and at Shoalwater Bay. In the last few decades it has been feeling the pressures of Kwinana's industrial advance across the flat sand scrub. *Population 36 670*

PENGUIN ISLAND Penguin Island is situated off Mersey Point and supports many seabird species. This is about as far north as fairy penguins are prepared to go and about 400 of them visit the island every year for the breeding season.

FESTIVALS Cockburn Sound Regatta, December.

SERPENTINE NATIONAL PARK ■ 2088

The hilly Serpentine National Park in the shadow of the Darling Ranges is an area of more than 600 hectares extending up the steep slopes of the valley of the Serpentine River and enclosing a wide range of plant species. The slopes are covered in the justifiably famous wildflowers of Western Australia in the spring and early summer months between July and November and two rare protected species of eucalypt grow there. Salmon gums are found below the Darling Scarp and rare butter gums grow along the heights. Serpentine National Park has high conservation value in a region logged for the hardwood jarrah and extensively mined.

The restoration of Old Blythewood, built as a roadside inn south of Pinjarra in the 1860s, included the original kitchen and cottage garden.

SINGLETON ■ 2089

Singleton is named after one of the region's pioneers, Francis Singleton, who came here in 1839, about nine years after another early settler, Thomas Peel. Singleton left the Royal Navy resolving to become a landed gentleman in Western Australia but moved elsewhere in 1848.

Singleton lies between Mandurah and Golden Bay (see entries) and, like them, offers all the attractions of a coastal resort settlement. Though the resident population is small, it swells in the holiday season when people are seeking a tranquil place to 'get away from it all'. *Population 510*

WAROONA ■ 2090

Waroona, first settled in the 1890s, is the centre of a flourishing dairy and potato farming region which together with sheep and beef farming are the main agricultural pursuits. It too benefited from the Harvey River Diversion and Drainage Scheme built during the 1930s Depression (see Harvey). Forestry, a mainstay of the early days, is less important now and the nearby Wagerup Aluminium Refinery contributes to the town's prosperity. The Waroona Dam is popular for fishing, being stocked with rainbow trout and redfin perch, and has an area set aside for waterskiing. *Population 1830*

YALGORUP NATIONAL PARK ■ 2091

Yalgorup National Park lies south of Perth, between Mandurah and Myalup Beach. It spreads over more than 10 000 hectares – a chain of lakes and swamps between dunes and limestone ridges. Only certain hardy plants can resist the salt-laden wind and put down roots in the coarse sand. Tough spinifex grows near the shore and behind it wattle shrubs and patches of coastal heath take advantage of minimal shelter. More than 100 species of waterbirds have been identified in the region.

Part of Lake Clifton runs through the park, one of only three sites in Western Australia where the ancient formations known as stromatolites have been found. Stromatolites are 'rocks' made when micro-organisms such as bacteria, blue-green algae and unicellular algae trap sediment particles in layers. They are one of the first known lifeforms on earth and dominated shorelines throughout the world more than a billion years ago. They appear on the eastern edge of the lake between March and April.

YARLOOP ■ 2092

Yarloop has been a thriving timber community since the end of the last century but dairy farming and citrus orchards became important with the advent of irrigation. The original mills were built way out in the jarrah forest and this little railway siding was originally known as 'Yard Loop'. The construction of the South West railway began in 1893 and Yarloop too sent valuable jarrah wood to the ships at Fremantle and Bunbury for distribution all over the world.

The Yarloop timber mill has had modern machinery for many years now but the old workshops that spanned the eras of horse and steam power have been carefully restored to show visitors facets of the Victorian steam age. *Population 590*

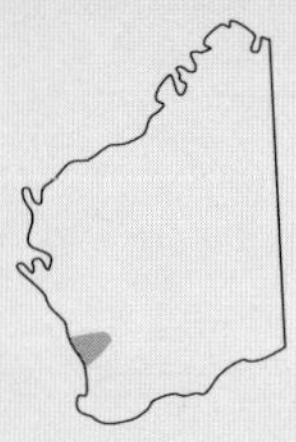

Wanneroo & Moora

North of Perth, along an urban coastal corridor, a series of sparkling new suburbs and marinas hug the shining shore. Inland are the towns where horses were bred for the Indian Army and Spanish monks left their architecturally distinctive mark.

Nambung National Park's dune landscape, cooled here by the sea, extends far beyond the coastal fringe.

BADGINGARRA NATIONAL PARK ■ 2093

This park protects the undulating hills and sandy valleys of one of the most prolific wildflower regions in Western Australia. Banksias, hakeas, dryandras, grevilleas, and outcrops of the rare black kangaroo paw – its bright green flowers held aloft on tall, felted black stems – grow here in rich profusion. A two-kilometre-long nature track takes in some of the best wildflower areas and leads to a lookout which gives a good view of the park and of the Darling Fault forty kilometres to the east.

WADDI WILDFLOWER AND EMU FARMS Located south of the park, the Waddi farms are licensed to farm emus as a commercial venture. There are guided tours of the emu-chick pens and a range of emu leather goods are on offer. Wildflowers occur naturally on the property and are also under cultivation for sale.

CERVANTES ■ 2094

This modern fishing and resort town was named after an island offshore from here, which in turn was named for the wreck of the American whaling ship *Cervantes*. Not only has the town the attractions of the coast, it is also the closest centre to Nambung National Park (see entry) and guided tours leave from here to both The Pinnacles and the area known as the Painted Desert. *Population 530*

DALWALLINU ■ 2095

The Dalwallinu region is, overwhelmingly, wheat country. Vast manicured plains of grain have almost entirely replaced the original vegetation cover. It lives on only in tiny pockets where the extraordinarily high concentrations of rare and localised plants of the region are protected – in springtime colourful orchids and everlastings cover the uncultivated areas. The whole region was once a granite plateau made up of ancient rocks. It has weathered over the ages into the sandplains which, with the long, dry summers and mild, wet winters, are eminently suitable for the growing of wheat.

Settlement here dates from 1912, and the first grain was sown a few years later. Sheep and cattle are also farmed. *Population 600*

PETRUDOR ROCKS This area of granite outcrops and native bushland, to the south-east of the town, is known for its spectacular wildflowers and is a popular picnic spot.

FESTIVALS Dalwallinu Agricultural Show, August.

DARLING RANGE ■ 2096

The Darling Range, also known as the Darling Scarp, runs roughly parallel to the coast from about 80 kilometres north of Perth to about 240 kilometres to the south of the city. The range rises from a line of foothills which mark the position of the Darling Fault, a great fracture in the earth's surface where the soft young sediments of the Perth region part company with the older volcanic rocks of the Great Western Plateau. Eastward the range extends inland across this plateau in a series of rolling hills broken here and there by the occasional granite-capped peak – remnants of an even more ancient and higher plateau – such as Mount Solus (574 metres), the highest point in the range.

The relatively steep slopes on the western side are cut deeply by rivers flowing to the sea, and there are some spectacular waterfalls. Bauxite mined on the uplands of the scarp is refined into alumina at Kwinana (see *Rockingham & Fremantle*).

The escarpment was given the name General Darling Range in 1827 by James Stirling, who became the first governor of Western Australia, for the then New South Wales governor, Ralph Darling.

DROVERS CAVE NATIONAL PARK ■ 2097

This is a park of caves. Drovers Cave, from which it takes its name, has spectacular stalactite formations bristling on the cave ceiling – but is not open to the public. On the sandy floor of Hastings Cave are deposits of animal bones up to 12 000 years old, and at least 40 different kinds of mammal have been identified here. The park is covered with a mixture of dry, sandplain heathlands and banksia woodlands.

GINGIN ■ 2098

European settlement around Gingin was among the earliest in Western Australia, dating from the 1840s. The township is built around a loop of Gingin Brook, a fern-fringed freshwater stream which rises from springs nearby and flows strongly all year round. On its course through the village green the brook turns a waterwheel, presenting a scene reminiscent of an English village.

Gingin still has many of its historic buildings including Jones' Shop (1854) and St Luke's Anglican Church (1861). The Granville Art Centre, built in the 1860s as a private home, operated as a hotel before being restored for its present use. The town serves a sheep, wheat and cattle area and is the site of a marron – freshwater crayfish – farm.

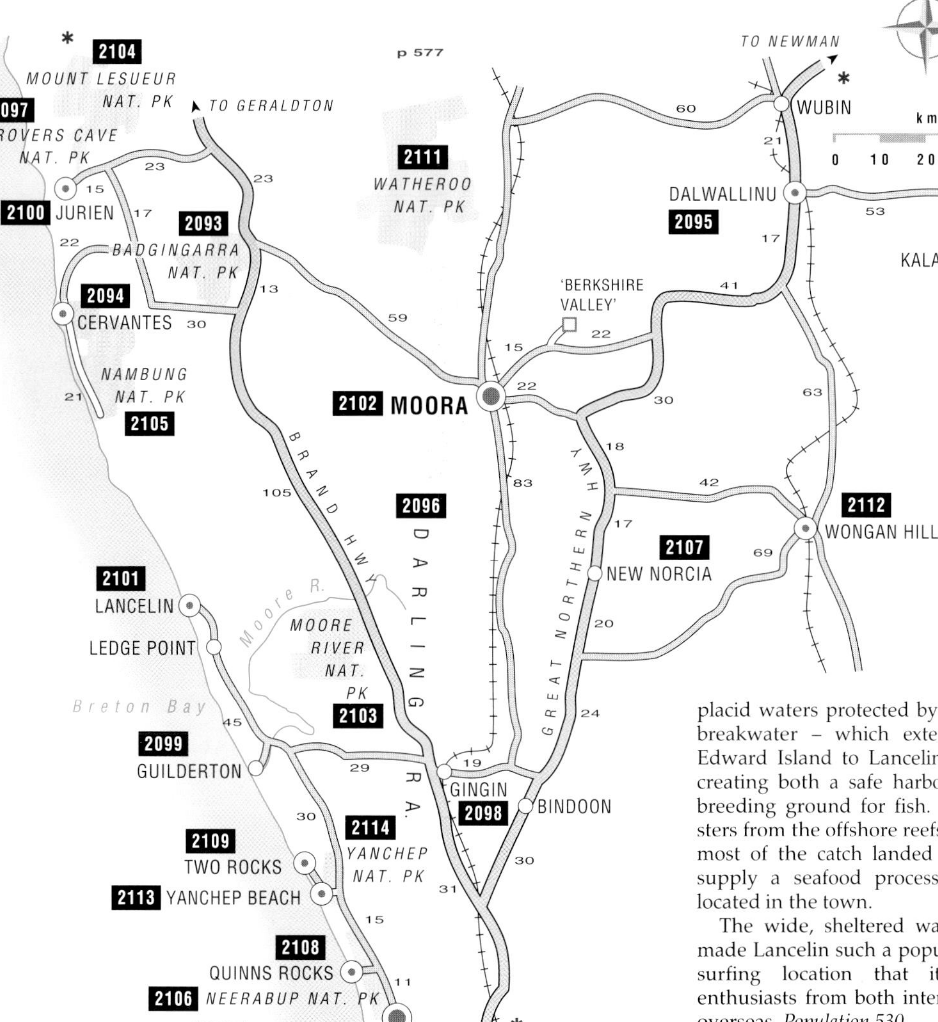

'BEEDAMANUP' The two-storey Beedamanup Homestead was built by the pioneering Dewar family in the mid-1850s from grey stone quarried on the site. It features three large chimneys and is a good example of early construction techniques.

MOONDAH BROOK ESTATE This vineyard, with more than 120 hectares of vines planted, is being developed as one of the largest in Australia.

GUILDERTON ■ 2099

This pleasantly situated coastal resort at the mouth of the Moore River has links with the Dutch ships which sailed these shores four centuries ago. In 1656, the vessel *De Vergulde Draeck* (Gilt Dragon), bound for the 'Spice Islands' of Indonesia and laden with treasure – eight chests stuffed with silver – was wrecked on a reef north-west of the present town. At least seventy crew members reached the shore, and seven of their number managed to sail to Batavia (now Djakarta) for help.

Rescue missions which were sent out found no trace of the men and their fate remains a mystery. Tales of sunken treasure, always common in the regions along this coast, received wider attention in 1931 when a local lad recovered some forty silver coins. The wreck was located in 1963 and though very little of the hull had survived the pounding waves, archaeologists from the Western Australian Museum have since recovered ammunition, cannons, domestic utensils, tools and more than 20 000 coins from the floor of the ocean.

JURIEN ■ 2100

All that remains of the nineteenth-century jetty from which goods were loaded for shipment to Fremantle and India are rows of timber piles. A new jetty is home to a large fishing fleet which brings in a catch that keeps two seafood processing plants in operation, largely for the export market. These waters, sheltered by the reefs that caused such problems for the early mariners, today attract holiday-makers who come to fish, swim and sail. *Population 600*

LANCELIN ■ 2101

The fishing town of Lancelin stands on the shores of a pretty bay, its placid waters protected by a natural breakwater – which extends from Edward Island to Lancelin Island – creating both a safe harbour and a breeding ground for fish. Rock lobsters from the offshore reefs make up most of the catch landed here and supply a seafood processing plant located in the town.

The wide, sheltered waters have made Lancelin such a popular windsurfing location that it attracts enthusiasts from both interstate and overseas. *Population 530*

FESTIVALS Lancelin Ocean Classic, early January.

MOORA ■ 2102

During the dark days of the Second World War, Moora was at the western end of a line, drawn across the continent from Brisbane and known as the 'Brisbane-line', north of which, it was suggested, would not be defended in the event of a Japanese invasion. Fortunately there was no need to put the proposal into action.

The district surrounding Moora has been settled since the 1840s, but the town itself was not gazetted until just before the end of the century. In the 1880s, much of the pastoral land taken up in the 1850s and 1860s was resumed for land concessions to the Midland Railway Company in return for their construction of the line from Perth, which opened in 1894. In 1905, the subdivision and sale of the company's lands to the north brought a flood of new settlers and greatly stimulated the growth of the town.

It was at this time that Moora's three Gothic-style churches, all of local stone, were built. Today the town is the centre of an important wheat- and sheep-farming district and is also known for its springtime wildflower display. *Population 1690*

BERKSHIRE VALLEY HOMESTEAD GROUP This well-integrated complex of farm buildings was constructed over a twenty-five-year period from 1847 by the early settler James Clinch who named it for Berkshire Valley in the Chilterns of south-east England. All the buildings are of local materials, mostly stone laid in uncoursed rubble because it was too difficult to work, bricks fired on the spot, adobe and pisé. The buildings – homestead, stables, flour mill, shearing shed, barn and manager's cottage – are arranged around a huge courtyard which is approached by a triple-arched brick bridge.

FESTIVALS Central Midlands Agricultural Show, September.

MOORE RIVER NATIONAL PARK ■ 2103

This national park preserves a section of the Swan Coastal Plain and is notable for its year-long display of wildflowers. The area here is not entirely untouched – parts of it were used as a stock route and resting place by the early settlers – but it is undeveloped, and contains a good example of the sandy heathlands of the northern coastal plain, including some dry dune systems and seasonal and permanent swamps.

The shifting sands in Nambung Park have been moved on by the wind to reveal thousands of craggy limestone pillars known as The Pinnacles.

The park is one of the few remaining natural habitats of the rose banksia which, with its pale yellow flowers and rose petal-like fruits, grows in the low woodlands amid other banksias, pricklybark and the Western Australian Christmas tree. In summer, when many other flowers have had their day, dense featherflowers turns the swamplands here pink with blossom.

Small birds are here in great numbers, drawn to the pollen and nectar of the blooms, and emus and grey kangaroos are also common.

MOUNT LESUEUR NATIONAL PARK ■ 2104

When the French ship *Naturaliste*, under the command of Baron Hamelin, charted this coast in 1801 the large, flat-topped mesa, which is a feature of the southern part of the park, was clearly visible from the sea and was named Mount Lesueur. The area was described by George Grey on his epic march south after being shipwrecked near Kalbarri (see *Geraldton & Kalbarri*), and in 1850, the Western Australian government botanist passed through the area to collect samples of its plants.

The scrub-covered sandplains surrounding Mount Lesueur are known by the Aboriginal name 'kwongan', and are remarkable for the fantastic diversity of wildflowers found on them – this is one of the richest flora areas in the world. Fortunately for later generations, the presence of poisonous plants and the ruggedness of the terrain deterred both pastoralists and farmers, and the region survived uncleared.

Among the many hundreds of species growing on the plain are a range of colourful orchids, including Cleopatra's Needle, found on the rocky summit of Mount Lesueur, and the Queen of Sheba and bronze orchid. The rare black kangaroo paw grows here, as does the one-sided bottlebrush and a number of relict species from an earlier era such as the kingia, cork mallee and trumpets.

NAMBUNG NATIONAL PARK ■ 2105

This large, undeveloped park, south of the township of Cervantes, preserves a region of dunefields and sandplains studded with fantastic, pinnacle-shaped formations (see subentry). Also within the park is an area of grey pillars known as the 'Painted Desert'. Along its twenty-six-kilometre coastline are safe, reef-protected, sandy beaches, accessible only by four-wheel-drive or on foot. The vegetation of the heath includes myrtles, banksias, wattles and legumes. Most of the park's animals are nocturnal, but during the day emus, western grey kangaroos and many sorts of reptiles and birds may be seen. The Nambung River makes a chain of waterholes through part of the park before disappearing into an underground cave system that is not open to the public.

PINNACLES DESERT Rising out of the drifting desert in the south-east corner of the park are the golden limestone pillars and knobs which gave the region its name. The craggy pillars have been sculpted smooth by wind-blown sand into a fantastic array of shapes – some lined up like tombstones, others resembling ominous figures hooded and hunched against the elements, and yet others a row of outsize milk bottles. Some are as small as a finger, others larger than a house.

The age of these strange formations is uncertain, probably between 15 000 and 80 000 years, and they were formed underground when rainwater seeping from above dissolved the lime in the rocks and cemented shafts of sand together into columns. But it is only in the past two centuries or so that the forms have been exposed by winds removing the overlying dunes.

NEERABUP NATIONAL PARK ■ 2106

This narrow strip of about 1100 hectares protects one of the last relatively undisturbed patches of coastal sandplain in the increasingly built-up Wanneroo (see entry) area. It stretches from near Lake Joondalup northwards to near Lake Carabooda and contains an unusually varied representation of plant communities, including open jarrah forest, banksia and casuarina in the south and in the north, massive grey-barked tuart trees with an understorey of heath plants or banksias. From July to September there are spectacular wildflower displays.

NEW NORCIA ■ 2107

Founded in 1846 by Benedictine monk Dom Rosendo Salvado as an Aboriginal mission, this exotic Spanish monastic complex stands on the fertile Victoria Plains, beside the Moore River, and was named after the Italian birthplace of St Benedict. Although fascinating for its architecture alone – a mixture of Classical, Byzantine and Gothic – it is also of note for its art gallery and museum and for its independent and relatively enlightened approach to the welfare of Aborigines during the nineteenth century.

Here efforts were made to not only minimise European impact but to also provide sufficient good land to support a community of Aboriginal farmers and artisans. The New Norcia routine of moral instruction, useful training and socialised leisure melded better with traditional Aboriginal ways than those followed at other missions and the result was a self-sufficient village based on wool-growing, agriculture, horse-breeding and the production of wine and olive oil. A flour mill which opened in 1879 is still going and is the oldest operating mill in Western Australia. It stands opposite an earlier mill which was built in 1854.

Contrasting styles, both firmly transplanted from Spain, are evident in St Gertrude's College and the still-operational 1879 flour mill at New Norcia.

During the 1880s New Norcia was known for its cultural achievements as well. Its string band, brass band and boys' choir all performed at Perth's Town Hall.

In the twentieth century, the focus of the mission changed to the education of European children and several ornate boarding colleges were built between 1904 and 1914. Salvado College, a co-educational secondary school, takes boarders from all over Western Australia.

New Norcia today is a small town ready to accommodate visitors of different intent: the Benedictine Abbey Guesthouse caters for those wishing to retreat and experience the monastic life while more conventional appointments are avilable at the historic New Norcia Hotel, with its imposing colonnaded verandahs and balconies, sweeping staircase and fine interior decorations.

MUSEUM AND ART GALLERY Housed in the original St Joseph's orphanage for Aboriginal girls, the museum details the history of the settlement and displays artefacts gathered during the first contacts between the monks and the Aborigines. In the same building is one of the greatest collections of religious art in Australia – original paintings by Spanish and Italian masters – and rare antiques. The museum is the starting point of a two-kilometre heritage trail through New Norcia.

QUINNS ROCKS ■ 2108

The residential beachfront development at Quinns Rocks is evidence of the rapid northward expansion of the Perth urban area which took place in the 1960s and 1970s. Along the foreshore is a recreational are where there is provision for th launching of small boats. The off shore reef from which the town ha taken its name is a breeding grounc for fish and a popular spot witl divers. There is a marina at Mindari Keys, to the south. *Population 2520*

WILDFLOWER COTTAGE This old-fash ioned rural cottage is surrounded by a sea of more than 100 large grasstrees; wildflowers can be pickec in season or purchased all yea round as dried everlastings.

TWO ROCKS ■ 210

In the early 1980s, the formerly quie coastal resort of Two Rocks becam briefly famous under the pseu donym of 'Yanchep Sun City', th base for Australia's preparation fo the America's Cup yachting chal lenge. The marina here has become major centre for every type of cra from cruising yachts to small fishin boats and small craft. *Population 126*

WANNEROO ■ 211

The area around Wanneroo is rich i Aboriginal heritage. Trees through out the region display scars wher their bark has been removed to mak canoes, shelters, shields, carryin baskets or other utensils. Many of th scars probably date from the earl years of European settlement a metal axeheads often appear to hav been used.

The first Europeans here wer members of a party chasing lost ca tle in the early 1830s, and the favourable reports on the lan brought permanent settlers aroun the shores of Lake Joondalup b 1837. There was a road to Wanner by the early 1840s and it was proba bly travelled by James Cockman an his family, who took up their run o the shores of Walluburnup Swam and there established a dairy far and market garden. Road access from Perth did not improve for many years and the district remained largely undeveloped until the 1930s when a road, which had been gazetted nearly seventy years earlier, finally reached Yanchep.

In the 1970s and 1980s, the Wanneroo region made up for lost time by becoming the fastest-growing local government area in Australia as Perth expanded to the north. It became a city in 1985. *Population 8720*

LAKE JOONDALUP WETLANDS HERITAGE WALKING TRAIL The name of this wetland area comes from an Aboriginal word meaning 'lake that glistens', and it is one of the few remaining in the south-west still being used as a breeding ground for birdlife. Musk ducks and great crested grebes may be seen as the trail winds along the edge of the lake through wetlands vegetation of paperbark, flooded gums and bulrushes.

MARMION MARINE PARK Covering an area from Trigg Island to Burns Rock, and out to sea for five kilometres, the waters of this marine park are warmed by the Leeuwin Current and contain thriving colonies of protected seals. Sea lions, dolphins and humpback whales frolic around the reefs and tiny islands here, and it is a popular spot for scuba diving. Just offshore from the outer wall of Hillarys Boat Harbour is Boyinaboat Reef – so named because of its appearance from shore – site of the first underwater nature trail in Western Australia. Underwater plaques give information about the rich ecosystem of the reef.

ORCHESTRA SHELL CAVE This is an Aboriginal site of great significance and can be visited only by special arrangement with the Aboriginal Heritage Authority. The limestone cave contains both rock art and prehistoric occupational deposits. On its walls are linear markings, some of which are similar to those at Koonalda, on the Nullarbor Plain (see *Ceduna*). It has been suggested that the parallel marks of Orchestra Shell may have been engraved when the limestone was softer, using a set of animal claws, such as those of the Tasmanian devil whose remains are also in evidence here.

YABEROO BUDJARA HERITAGE TRAIL This walking trail of almost thirty kilometres highlights a number of sites of Aboriginal, historic or natural significance, and takes in parts of Lake Joondalup and Neerabup and Yanchep national parks. It follows a traditional Aboriginal track linking the inland lakes with the coast and is said to have been carved out in the Dreamtime by the serpent, Waugal.

WATHEROO NATIONAL PARK ■ 2111

Much of this 45 000-hectare park is covered by quartz sand and the vegetation is scrubby heathland. A variety of wildflowers grow here, including some associated more with the south-west rather than the dry midlands plains. Occasionally there are shady outcrops of eucalypt woodland and tall banksia scrub.

WONGAN HILLS ■ 2112

The township of Wongan Hills is the centre of a large sheep and wheat farming district. It takes its name from a nearby range of hills – approximately 100 metres high but distinctive because of the flatness out of which they rise – which were sighted by Surveyor-General John Septimus Roe in 1836. To the Aborigines they were known as 'wongan katta', 'the talking – or whispering – hills', perhaps because of the gentle sighing sound the wind makes as it moves through the gullies.

The hills cover an area of some 3200 hectares and are the largest single area of natural vegetation in the area. Not only do a wide variety of wildflowers grow here, but the hills are also home to a small number of the mound-building mallee fowl.

Until the early 1900s, when the first settlers arrived, the only Europeans in the area were sandalwood cutters and monks driving their flocks from New Norcia (see entry). *Population 880*

YANCHEP BEACH ■ 2113

The chain of lakes which stretch north of Perth to the Yanchep area are believed to have once been an underground river system which flowed through a series of limestone caves, long since collapsed. For tens of thousands of years the Aborigines lived well off the rich resources of the land and waters. They called it 'yanjet' – from which its present name derives – for the bulrushes which fringe the lakes here.

Yanchep Beach today is a popular resort town which is rapidly being approached by the northern extremities of the Perth urban sprawl. Set among coastal sand dunes which back Yanchep Beach it offers swimming, good fishing, horse riding and hang-gliding. Yanchep Sun City is seven kilometres to the north at Two Rocks (see entry). *Population 1580*

YANCHEP NATIONAL PARK ■ 2114

This is a park of many parts. In 1905, the lands here were made a reserve to both protect a system of limestone caves and provide a recreational area. During the Great Depression of the 1930s, sustenance workers were given the task of building roads and landscaping a large part of the park – the Tudor-style buildings, manicured lawns, cultivated native gardens and the thriving colony of koalas imported from Victoria date from this period. The swampy, bulrush-fringed freshwater lake – originally called Lake Yanchep – was dredged and somewhat playfully renamed Loch McNess to honour philanthropist Sir Charles McNess who made a grant to assist the development of the reserve.

The park also has areas of natural bushland where the Swan Coastal Plain with its ancient sands and low-lying wetlands remains much the same as it was when the first European settlers arrived. Beneath the park is a vast network of limestone caves and underground streams – in the eastern section guided tours are available to view the drip formations of Crystal Cave.

There are two self-guided trails – the Boomerang Gorge Nature Trail, suitable for wheelchairs, and the Yanijidi Trail, which winds through the Loch McNess wetland at the western rim of the lake – and other walking tracks run through the park.

GLOUCESTER LODGE MUSEUM Built as a guesthouse during the 1930s, the handsome Gloucester Lodge building now houses exhibits tracing the history of the district, the park, and the building itself. Displays cover the geology, plants and animals of the area, the Aboriginal inhabitants, shipwrecks off the coastline of the Wanneroo–Yanchep coast, and early European settlement.

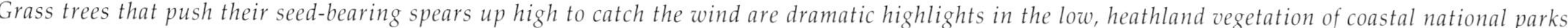

Grass trees that push their seed-bearing spears up high to catch the wind are dramatic highlights in the low, heathland vegetation of coastal national parks.

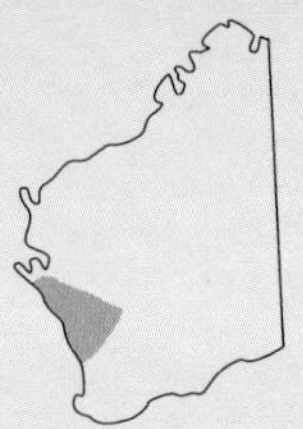

Geraldton & Kalbarri

The region along what Dutch mariners used to call the Batavia Coast – with its colourful history of shipwreck, mutiny, massacres, stranded sailors and sunken treasure – is these days the haunt of rock-lobster fishermen and holiday-makers.

ALEXANDER MORRISON NATIONAL PARK ■ 2115
Bisected by a little used road which links Coorow with the coast, this area is known for the brilliant drifts of late-blooming wildflowers which flourish on its sandplain heathlands. The 8500-hectare park is noted for its many different dryandras, with at least twenty species, some of them yet to be named, growing here.

CARNAMAH ■ 2116
European settlement started here with the MacPherson family, whose homestead, completed in 1880, stands on the eastern outskirts of the town. War-service farming schemes in the area in the 1920s and the 1950s, following both world wars, accelerated the growth of the town.

TATHRA NATIONAL PARK A variety of rare plants occur in this undeveloped reserve of rolling sandplain, heathlands and banksia woodlands.

YARRA YARRA LAKES This intermittent lake system is renowned for the colours of its waters, which range from blood red to pink, milky green and azure blue. It is a stopover for many interesting types of migratory birds including swans, pelicans, ducks, and the Siberian stilt.

FESTIVALS North Midlands Agricultural Show, September.

COOROW ■ 2117
The first European settlers in this district were William and Sara Long. The homestead the Longs built in the early 1860s stood just outside the present township, which did not really begin to develop until the arrival of the railway in 1894. In exchange for the construction of the line the Midland Railway Company was granted extensive tracts of land in the Coorow area – these it developed as individual farms which were then sold as going concerns. Local industries in Coorow today include wildflower cultivation, grain growing, wool, cattle and pigs.

AUSTRALIAN FLOWER FARMS About forty kilometres west of Coorow, what is believed to be the largest drip-irrigation wildflower farm in the world cultivates a variety of colourful Western Australian species for export to markets in Europe and the United States.

DONGARA ■ 2118
The first Europeans known in the area were George Grey and his party who crossed the Irwin River during their long march south after being shipwrecked near the site of Kalbarri (see entry). Dongara township, on the banks of the river, dates from the early 1850s when settlers arrived following favourable reports of fertile land and deposits of coal, gold and other minerals made by explorer and surveyor Augustus Gregory.

In 1846, Gregory discovered coal seams here and 'had the satisfaction of seeing the first fire of Western Australian coal burning cheerfully in front of the camp'. The district was soon growing wheat – Dongara's first flour mill was built in 1859.

Natural gas discovered near Dongara in the 1960s has been piped to Perth since 1971 to supply domestic and industrial markets. Gypsum mining and the development of the rock lobster fishing industry have also been added to the long established agricultural base of the town.

The Moreton Bay figs which are a feature of the town's main street – they are even listed by the National Trust – were planted in 1906. Sir David Brand, premier of Western Australia between 1959 and 1971, was born in Dongara. *Population 1680*

PORT DENISON South of the mouth of the Irwin River, sheltered Arurine Bay provides a picturesque site for Port Denison, originally called Irwin Port. Now a holiday resort with the attractions of windsurfing and diving on rocky reefs, it was here that a jetty was built in the 1860s to land supplies and take out produce for the Dongara farmers.

PRIORY LODGE Much altered in more than a century of different uses, sprawling Priory Lodge was built as a hotel by William Criddle in 1881. In 1902, the Dominican Sisters took over; they added a second storey and for almost seventy years the building was a girls' school before becoming a tourist hostel.

ROYAL STEAM ROLLER FLOUR MILL This grand four-storey stone building, now a shell, dates from 1894, and until 1935 the steam engines it housed ground the wheat from the surrounding farms. The mill's own branch line connected it with the Midland Railway Company line, and the bagged flour was then railed both north and south.

RUSS COTTAGE This building was acquired and restored by the local historical society as being typical of the dwellings of the district's early pioneers. It was built in the 1870s of limestone quarried from the Irwin banks by Titus Russ. After his death in 1874 his widow, who had been left with four young children, remarried and bore another four children. All lived under this roof. The crushed anthill kitchen floor was retained in the restoration.

FESTIVALS Craft Market Day, April; Country Music Festival, October; Blessing of the Fleet, November.

ENEABBA ■ 2119
The town exists largely as a centre for the mineral-sands mining business, which commenced in the early 1970s. Located within its vicinity is about eighty per cent of the world's known reserves of rutile, a dark mineral used in the manufacture of welding rods and paint. It was concentrated here by wave action at a time when sea levels were higher and the sands of Eneabba were on the shoreline.

GERALDTON ■ 2120
Known in the tourist brochures as 'Sun City' because of its climate and wide range of outdoor recreational activities, Geraldton's attractions for settlers in the 1840s were quite different: copper, lead and later gold in the lands nearby to the north and east. The townsite, on the shores of Champion Bay, was surveyed in 1851 by John Septimus Roe, Western Australia's first surveyor-general, and named Geraldton for the governor of the colony, Sir Charles Fitzgerald.

A jetty to ship out ore was built in 1860, and by 1879 a railway linked the town to the lead mines at Northampton (see entry). During the Second World War, Geraldton was a

The rock lobster is such a desirable commodity that fishermen set up seasonal sea-level camps above its haunts on the Houtman Abrolhos reefs.

Geraldton has theatres for all seasons: adjoining the conventional indoor auditorium is an amphitheatre with grass-seating for 500 people.

p 615
TO CARNARVON
BILLABONG ROADHOUSE
2136 ZUYTDORP CLIFFS
NORTH WEST COASTAL HWY
km 0 15 30 45 60
ZUYTDORP NATURE RES.
2125 KALBARRI NAT. PK
Murchison River 2130
2124 KALBARRI
GERALDINE MINE
WARRIBANNO CHIMNEY
HUTT RIVER PROVINCE
Hutt Lagoon
LYNTON (ruins)
2123 PORT GREGORY
2122 HORROCKS
2131 NORTHAMPTON
Bowes R.
2135 YALGOO
2129 MULLEWA
Houtman Abrolhos
2120 GERALDTON
WALKAWAY
GREENOUGH 2121
COALSEAM RES.
2118 DONGARA
PORT DENISON
Irwin R.
MINGENEW 2127
2128 MORAWA
2134 THREE SPRINGS
2133 PERENJORI
Indian Ocean
BRAND HWY
Yarra Yarra Lakes
2116 CARNAMAH
2119 ENEABBA
TATHRA N.P.
2126 LEEMAN
ALEXANDER MORRISON NAT. PK 2115
COOROW 2117
GREEN HEAD
TO PERTH
p 613
p 577
TO NEWMAN
2132 PAYNES FIND
GREAT NORTHERN HWY
Lake Moore
p 586
TO PERTH

base for United States submarines, flying boats and servicemen. Novelist and poet Randolph Stow was born in the town in 1935, and it and the landscape of the region inspired much of his poetry and are the setting for four of his seven novels, including the semi-autobiographical *The Merry-go-round in the Sea*.

Geraldton today is the administrative centre and main port of the mid-west of Western Australia, and is in the centre of an expanding industrial, mining, pastoral and fishing area. However it is tourism that is perhaps the fastest growing industry here – thousands of visitors come each year, attracted by the warm climate, scenery and recreational activities. Geraldton was proclaimed a city in 1988 during a visit by Queen Elizabeth. *Population 24 360*

GERALDTON MUSEUM This museum occupies two adjoining buildings – the Maritime Display Building, and the Old Railway Building. Relics of the many shipwrecks which occurred along this coast are housed in the former, including cannons, coins, navigational instruments, pottery and even the skeletons of some of the victims of the *Batavia* mutineers, recovered from the Houtman Abrolhos (see entry). In the Old Railway Building – built in 1879 – are displays covering the natural history of the region – the forces that shaped it, and its plants, animals and minerals – as well as the human history, from earliest Aboriginal occupation to the arrival of Europeans.

POINT MOORE LIGHTHOUSE This distinctive red and white lighthouse on the western extremity of Point Moore has operated continuously since 1879. It was shipped out from England in prefabricated form and was originally put up in the wrong place and so had to be moved.

ST FRANCIS XAVIER CATHEDRAL The foundation stone was laid in 1914, but construction of this cathedral, one of the most unusual in Australia, was plagued by technical and financial difficulties, and took more than twenty years to complete. It replaced an earlier church of the same name and incorporates in its structure the cornerstone of its predecessor.

The building was designed in Byzantine style by the English cleric Monsignor John Cyril Hawes, an interesting character whose on-off career as an architect and his devotion to the church – he practised architecture for fifteen years before becoming a priest – found some resolution after a chance meeting in Rome with the Bishop of Geraldton brought him to outback Western Australia. Hawes designed churches for a number of mid-west towns including Morawa, Mullewa, Perenjori and Yalgoo (see entries).

FESTIVALS Community Arts Exhibition, April of even-numbered years; Batavia Coast Fishing Classic, April.

Kalbarri's rocky shoreline is fretted by the same salt-laden winds that once drove sailing ships ashore.

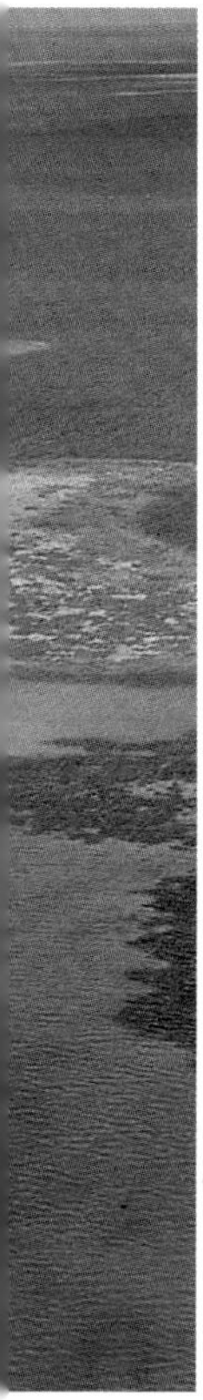

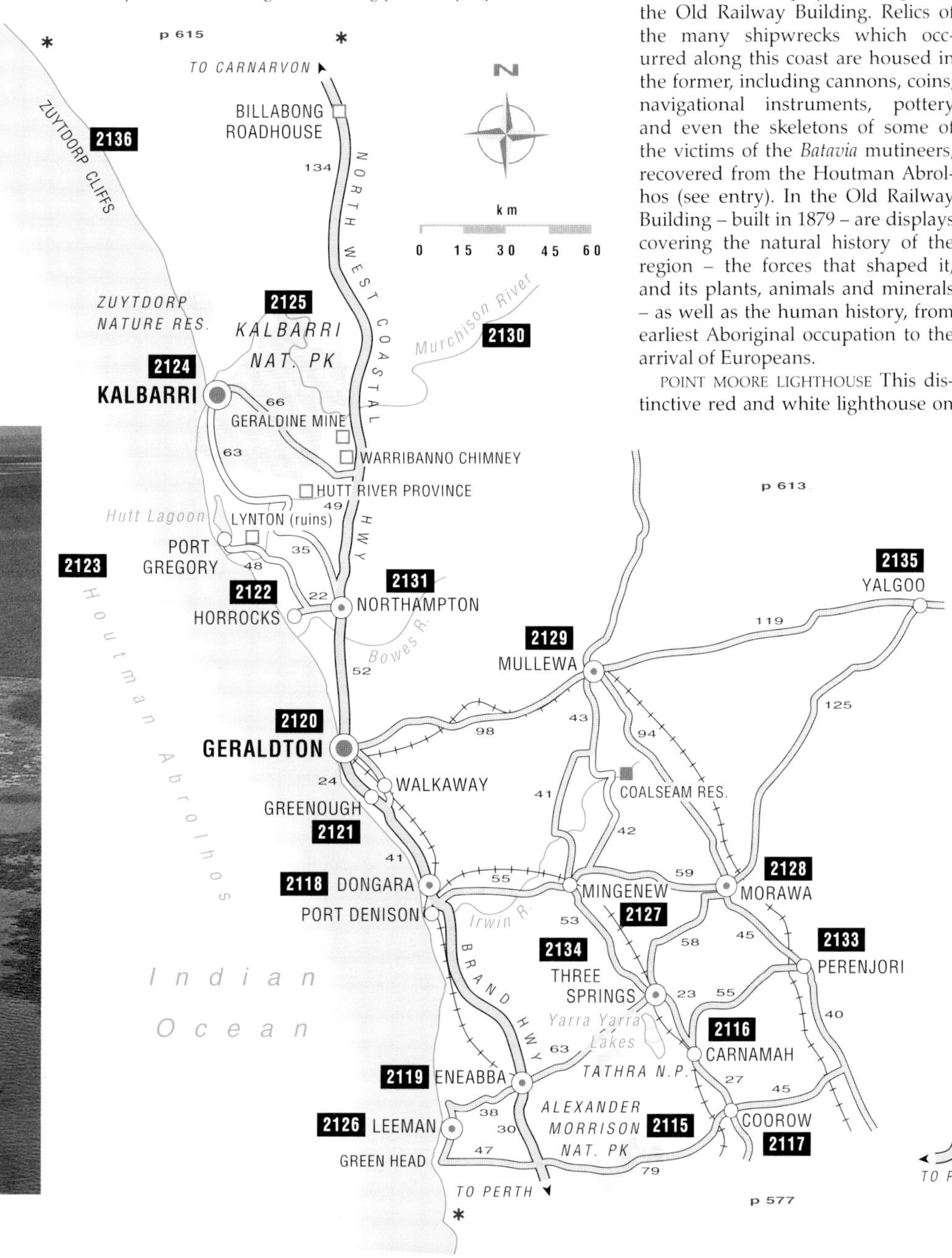

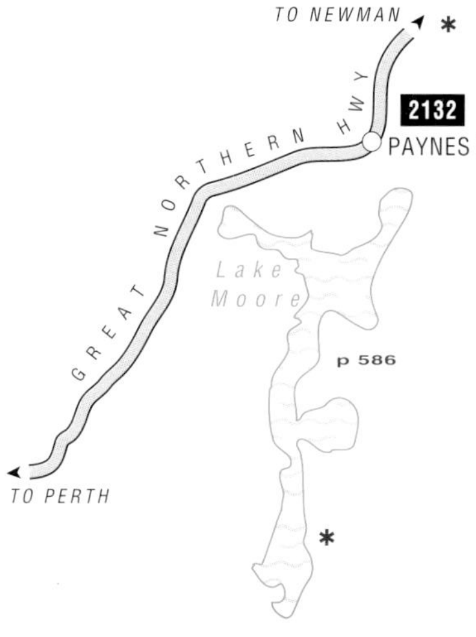

THE WHEAT FARM THAT BECAME A PRINCELY REALM

IN 1970, Geraldton wheat farmer Leonard Casley found himself locked into a seemingly unwinnable dispute with the Wheat Board over the introduction of a quota system which prevented him selling most of his crop. His novel solution was to gather his lands and family about him and secede from the Commonwealth of Australia.

On 21 April 1970, the 7475-hectare independent state of Hutt River Province was created by a Unilateral Declaration of Independence. Mr Casley styled himself first as the Administrator of the Province but, eventually aspiring to more regal status, later took on royal trappings as Prince Leonard, his wife becoming Princess Shirley.

What began as a humourous protest has stood the test of more than twenty years and now seems to be tacitly accepted by the authorities. The royal couple and their subjects – some thirty in all, mostly their own family – do not pay Australian taxes, nor do they vote in Australian elections. The province has its own system of welfare benefits and even its own peerages – earldoms and knighthoods have been conferred with some largesse. While the prince has been able to use the odd constitutional loophole to keep the bureaucrats at bay, he has also enjoyed a generous degree of forbearance on the part of both the Western Australian and the Commonwealth governments, who have drawn the line only at his bold attempt to buy three used jets from Mexico and establish his own airline.

The diplomatic passport issued by Prince Leonard's domain is accepted by a number of countries, including France, Greece, India, Lebanon and the Vatican, but both the British Commonwealth and the United Nations have refused pleas for recognition. Hutt River issues its own postage stamps and a great deal of its income comes from the sale of these as well as first-day covers for philatelists. It has its own currency and its coins are listed in the standard catalogue of world coins issued by the German Volksbank.

Although seldom mentioned in government tourist literature, Hutt River Province has none the less become established as a tourist destination which is visited by some 50 000 people each year. They can buy postage stamps and currency, have their visas stamped, look at the wildflowers or visit the Chapel of the Nain, built by His Highness, Prince Leonard and featuring paintings by Frank Pash, a Lord of the Principality. □

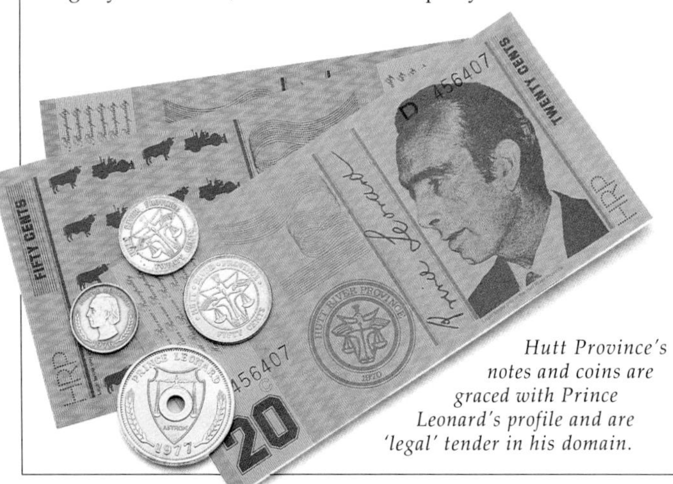

Hutt Province's notes and coins are graced with Prince Leonard's profile and are 'legal' tender in his domain.

GREENOUGH ■ 2121

This historic hamlet, south of Geraldton, was built in the early 1850s to serve the wheat-growing district which had been recently established on the rich black soil of the surrounding flats. Unfortunately, the farmers were unable to survive the double blow of both flood and drought and Greenough went into decline, but by the 1870s it had fought back to become part of a significant agricultural district. Eleven of its sandstone buildings have been fully restored by the National Trust. Also still standing is the 1860s convict-built McCartney Road bridge across the Greenough River.

Strong, salt-laden winds which blast off the ocean and across the low lying plains are responsible for the misshapen flood gums, some bent horizontally, that characterise the landscape of this region. These trees are represented on the official emblem of Greenough Shire.

HORROCKS ■ 2122

For a century and a half the coastal village of Horrocks, with soft white sands lining its crescent-shaped beach in a safe, reef-protected bay, has been a holiday resort. It was a popular spot with the early settlers of the inland and in more recent years it has drawn visitors from further afield as well. Horrocks is known particularly for the range of fish caught here – tailor, whiting, herring and garfish from the beach, octopus and rock lobster on the fringing reef, and snapper, cod and mackerel from boats on the bay. There is a jetty and boat ramp.

Joseph Horrocks, for whom the town is named, arrived in the early 1850s as medical attendant to the convicts at Lynton, near Northampton (see entry).

WILLIGULLI CAVE PAINTINGS This area was occupied for thousands of years by the Aborigines. Debris on the floors of four small rock shelters close to the mouth of Bowes River is evidence of many centuries use as camping places, but the sites are most significant for the paintings and stencils on their walls.

The caves have the largest concentration of motifs yet recorded in the south-west of Western Australia – human figures, lizards, emu feet, snakes, chains of dots and hand stencils of the type common across the continent – executed in red, black, yellow and white.

HOUTMAN ABROLHOS ■ 2123

Sixty kilometres offshore from Geraldton and prominent along an eighty-kilometre stretch of ocean are a chain of islands and reefs. Some 7000 years ago, before the sea rose, these islands were the edge of the prehistoric mainland. They support examples of rare vegetation unique to the Houtman Abrolhos, and are an important, and protected, breeding ground for huge colonies of terns, gulls, shearwaters and noddies, as well as some small mammals.

The fringing reefs, the largest coral system in the world so far from the equator, are washed by waters warmed in the tropics and carried south by the Leeuwin Current. Here flourish some eighty different types of coral.

There is no tourist accommodation on the islands, although there are seasonal camps for professional fishermen. This area is one of the most important fishing grounds in Western Australia and yields a substanial proportion of the state's rock-lobster catch. Excursions operate regularly from Geraldton and Kalbarri, allowing energetic visitors to dive and fish around the coral.

For early Dutch mariners battling their way off this coast from Java, these reefs and islands were a feared hazard in treacherous waters. Their name – 'abrolhos' is a Portuguese word for a heavily spiked, mediaeval war machine – was bestowed in 1619 by Dutch sea captain Frederik de Houtman as a reminder of the dangers lurking here for the unwary.

The dangers amply justified the warning which did not prevent the *Batavia* striking one of the coral reefs ten years later. Most of the vessel's passengers, with most of its provisions, managed to reach one or another of the islands, but were faced then with the problem of lack of water. The captain of the *Batavia*, François Pelsaert, took an open boat to search for supplies but, finding none, struck out instead for Batavia (now Djakarta) which he reached a month later in an extraordinary feat of navigation.

What unfolded on the islands after his departure was a desperate scene of mutiny, massacre and mayhem. A small group planned to recover chests of silver from the wreck and then, after killing all those who were either opposed or of no use to the enterprise, embark upon a career of piracy. Some one hundred and twenty-five men and women died. Still to be seen today are the stone barricades built by those who survived to meet the rescue vessel sailed south by the indefatigable Pelsaert.

The mutineers were captured and most were put to death immediately on a hastily erected gallows – the first executions to take place on Australian soil. Two spared the noose were left on the mainland near the present site of Kalbarri (see entry) at the mouth of the Murchison River and told to fend for themselves – thus becoming the first Europeans to live permanently on the continent. They were never seen again and although it has been suggested that they may have interbred with local Aborigines, it is more likely they drowned trying to sail to Indonesia.

Nature's Window provides the perfect frame for a spectacular view of the Murchison River in Kalbarri National Park, where the Diplolaena *(above) hangs its brush-like head of bright stamens each spring.*

Another Dutch vessel to come to grief here was the *Zeewijk*, wrecked in 1727. Most of the crew reached a nearby island and spent the next ten months arduously building a vessel from the ship's timbers and mangrove roots in which they then sailed on to Batavia. Both wrecks were located in the 1960s and some of the relics recovered are on show at the Maritime Display Building of the Geraldton Museum. Parts of the decayed timber hull of the *Batavia*, treated with polyethylene-glycol to preserve the ancient planks, are now housed in a special gallery of the Fremantle Maritime Museum.

The first marsupial to be recorded by Europeans, the Abrolhos Islands tammar wallaby, still roams near where the *Batavia* was wrecked; it was described by Pelsaert in 1629.

KALBARRI ■ **2124**

Kalbarri is the centre of one of Western Australia's most popular tourist areas. Situated by the smooth waters of the basin at the mouth of the Murchison River, it offers in the immediate vicinity good fishing, a boat ramp, safe, clear swimming water, surfing and diving, and further afield the spectacular Murchison River gorges, in Kalbarri National Park (see entry).

The rocky coasts of Kalbarri have claimed many a vessel over the centuries. The first known European contact with the district was in 1629 when the two *Batavia* mutineers were marooned near here – a cairn in Wittecarra Gully marks the place where it is believed this first landing of permanent European inhabitants on the Australian continent took place. There was no evidence of these men in 1696 when the Dutch navigator Willem de Vlamingh, in the course of charting this coastline, came ashore at almost the same spot to replenish his freshwater supplies.

The explorer George Grey was also wrecked near the mouth of the Murchison River in 1839. With his party, Grey was forced to reach the Swan River settlement on foot – a challenging 700-kilometre march that was ultimately responsible for the opening up of the pastoral land along the coast. Grey, although starving and exhausted, still managed to take note of the potential of the country he encountered.

It is believed that 'Kalbarri' was the name of a member of the local Aboriginal tribe as well as being used to describe an edible seed. Although European settlement of the Murchison dates from the late 1850s, the townsite was not surveyed until 1951. *Population 1520*

FESTIVALS Sports Fishing Classic, March.

KALBARRI NATIONAL PARK ■ **2125**

This park is famed for both the grandeur of the gorges created as the Murchison River (see entry) carves its way to the sea, and for the breathtaking views along its coast where giant waves pound the rugged cliffline. Earth movements some two million years ago forced upwards great rifts of rock, and the Murchison, which until that time had simply gently meandered over a flat sandstone plain, was forced to cut deeper and deeper to maintain its old course. This it did, and some eighty kilometres of dramatic red and white banded gorges, complete with meanders, are the result. These can be viewed from lookouts reached by road or by way of the river cruises and charter flights which operate out of Kalbarri township.

On the coast, the same ancient sandstone is overlain by a layer of softer sedimentary material and capped with limestone. Weathering here has produced an even more striking range of colours and erosion patterns and an extraordinary array of shapes.

More than 500 species of plants grow in this region, including banksias, grevilleas, grass trees, kangaroo paws and acacias. Euros, kangaroos and wallabies occur here, as do smaller mammals such as the little honey possum. Emus roam in great numbers on the sandplains and more than 170 different kinds of birds have been recorded.

NATURE'S WINDOW AND THE LOOP Multi-coloured ridges of sandstone high above the Murchison have been carved through by windblown sand into a natural window which frames a mighty loop of the river. It is the starting and finishing point for a six-hour walk which winds down to the floodplains and back up the ledges.

Z BEND Here the Murchison flows through a narrow ravine where banded cliffs plunge more than 150 metres to the river below.

LEEMAN ■ **2126**

The coastal fishing port of Leeman is a local centre for the coordination of ocean-rescue operations, and appropriately enough its name links it with one of several daring seventeenth-century rescue missions sent from Batavia (now Djakarta) to retrieve Dutch sailors wrecked along this coast. Abraham Leeman van Santwits, navigator on the ship *Waeckende Boey* which had been sent to find survivors of the *De Vergulde Draeck* (Gilt Dragon), wrecked in 1656 near Guilderton (see *Wanneroo & Moora*), was himself a victim of the coast. He was marooned near here and had to make the perilous return journey to Indonesia in an open boat. *Population 570*

DYNAMITE BAY South of Leeman, near Green Head, is this miniature bay with a sandy crescent-shaped beach, well protected by encircling rocky headlands. Although only one hundred metres or so across, its sheltered clear waters are a popular attraction offering safe swimming and snorkeling.

MINGENEW ■ **2127**

Mingenew township was established in the 1890s as a railhead for stock bound for southern markets. The exploring Gregory brothers, in the area in 1846, noted that the country was 'better adapted for cattle than sheep, but admirably adapted for agriculture, as the soil is very rich and there is scarcely a tree'. This glowing report and the presence of freshwater springs in the area soon attracted pastoralists who bred cattle for the colony's meat supply and horses for the Indian Army. Sheep farming was not practicable until closer settlement reduced the losses caused by marauding dingoes.

Mingenew's other major industry is wheat growing and the grain receival point here is the largest in inland Western Australia.

COALSEAM RESERVE This is the site where coal was first discovered by the Gregory brothers in 1846. The seam was later mined but the results were disappointing – the old shafts can still be seen.

MINGENEW HILL The town of Mingenew is dominated by the bulk of this tree-covered red monolith. At its summit are a lookout – with views across the Irwin Valley – and a memorial to the labours of the district's pioneers.

FESTIVALS Mingenew Cup, February; Mingenew Wildflower Display, September; Rural Expo, September.

MOROWA ■ 2128

Morawa is on the 'Wildflower Way', a route within easy reach of Perth which takes in not only some of the best wildflower regions in Western Australia, but also some of its most picturesque scenery. The Morawa district grows wheat and sheep and was settled from 1905. The town dates from 1913. *Population 620*

CHURCH OF THE HOLY CROSS This is one of the twenty or so buildings in the mid-west attributed to Father – later Monsignor – Hawes, designer of the cathedral at Geraldton (see entry). Behind it is a tiny stone room which Hawes used as the priest's lodge – possibly the smallest presbytery in the world.

FESTIVALS Music and Arts Spectacular, October.

MULLEWA ■ 2129

Situated on the mid-west 'Wildflower Way', the township of Mullewa is also the gateway to the Murchison pastoral and goldfields district. From July to September pink, white and yellow everlasting flowers carpet the plains; banksias, grevillias and hakeas also abound, as do a myriad of tiny orchids. Two flowers – the ground-hugging growing wreath flower, which blooms in a small-flowered halo around a leafy centre, and the orange and scarlet wild pomegranate – grow over a small area around Mullewa and nowhere else. Wheat growing is the major industry. *Population 740*

THE CHURCH OF OUR LADY OF MOUNT CARMEL AND SAINTS PETER AND PAUL Standing on the outskirts of the town, this extraordinary church – a mixture of Byzantine, Romanesque, Greek Orthodox and Spanish styles, with a Gothic gargoyle thrown in for good measure – is the creation of Monsignor John Cyril Hawes – who also designed the Geraldton cathedral – and was built in the 1920s, largely by his own efforts. Farmers brought in truckloads of rocks and sometimes gave days of labour, local businessmen donated cement and, under the eye and hand of the watchful priest–architect, the arches, white domes, columns, friezes and belfry gradually arose.

Its priesthouse, which is linked to the church by a colonnade, has been restored and is now a museum for a collection of memorabilia connected with Monsignor Hawes.

KEMBLA ZOO A large collection of native birds and animals wander under shady trees here, some of them in a 'free-range' area beside an ornamental lake.

FESTIVALS Mullewa Agricultural Show, September.

MURCHISON RIVER ■ 2130

The 800-kilometre-long Murchison River rises out of the southern slopes of the Robinson Range, near Meekatharra (see *Tom Price & Newman*), and flows west and south to enter the Indian Ocean at Kalbarri (see entry) on Gantheaume Bay. In its upper reaches it cuts through rich gold-bearing rocks where mining activity, both past and present, is much in evidence. The river then crosses a plateau of sedimentary rocks, today sheep-grazing country, and in its lower reaches makes the dramatic drop to sea level in which it carves out the spectacular eighty-kilometre gorge which is a feature of Kalbarri National Park (see entry).

The river was named for the British scientist Sir Roderick Murchison by explorer and future governor of South Australia George Grey, who was wrecked at its mouth in 1839.

Mullewa's rock-solid Church of Our Lady displays a varied mixture of Mediterranean influences.

NORTHAMPTON ■ 2131

Northampton, surrounded by gentle green hills in the valley of the Nokanena Brook, was originally settled as a mining town following the discovery here of copper and lead. In 1850 the Geraldine Mine – the first in Western Australia – began production on the site of the vein of lead found in 1848 in the bed of the Murchison River by the explorer Augustus Gregory.

Today, Northampton is the centre of a large and rich wheat and pastoral district. It is known in particular for its sheep studs which supply breeding stock to graziers throughout Western Australia. *Population 790*

CHIVERTON HOUSE FOLK MUSEUM Built between 1868 and 1875 by convict labour as a home for Captain Samuel Mitchell, the manager of the Geraldine Mine – and maternal grandfather of Sir David Brand, Premier of Western Australia between 1959 and 1971 – Chiverton House displays an extensive collection of relics of the pioneer settlers.

GWALLA CHURCH 'Dr' Joseph Horrocks came as a medical attendant with the convicts and stayed on to settle in the district (see Horrocks). He became manager and part-owner of the Gwalla Mine and was responsible for the building, in 1864, of Northampton's first church, the non-denominational Gwalla Church, on part of the mine property. Horrocks

THE CULTURE FROM THE RED LAGOON

IN A SERIES of clay-walled ponds built on the dry bed of Hutt Lagoon salt lake the microscopic plant known to scientists as *Dunaliella salina* flourishes in great quantity. This red algae is the richest known natural source of beta-carotene, a form of vitamin A, and as such forms the unlikely basis of an expanding multi-million dollar export industry.

Australia leads the world in the production of algal beta-carotene, which is extracted from this natural source in a process which is favoured over its manufacture by elaborate chemical synthesis. Most production takes place at two plants, here north of Geraldton, and near Whyalla, in South Australia.

Beta-carotene is used as a food colourant, in the cosmetics industry, and as a nutritional supplement – it is a source of dietary protovitamin A. As well, recent research indicates that it may help encourage remission of the disease in some types of cancers.

Hutt Lagoon won a state-wide 'suitability quest' to become the site of the algal ponds now installed here. Conditions were deemed to be almost ideal. The lake is free from water- and air-borne pollutants, and from pesticides. Cloudy days which cut down on the algae-stimulating sunlight are few, it has a supply of naturally occurring salty brine – a high salinity growing culture is necessary to deter the growth of competitor and predatory algae – rainfall, which would dilute the brine, is low, and the lake is within striking distance of Geraldton and its transport facilities.

Unlike the undesirable, river-borne algae all too common in some agricultural areas, this red 'bloom' is cultivated.

Ten five-hectare shallow ponds contain an algae soup of brine, seawater and fertilisers. The position of the pools was determined by the prevailing strong winds which are harnessed to naturally stir and aerate the rich mixture. The ponds are harvested every two to four weeks. Gravity flow channels feed the algae culture to harvesting equipment, which sifts out the vegetable matter at the rate of 100 000 litres per hour. The used growing medium is treated and recycled; the beta-carotene is concentrated and prepared for export, mainly to markets in Japan and the United States. □

is buried in the nearby Gwalla Cemetery. The old church complex has fallen into ruins.

LYNTON When convict labour was introduced to alleviate Western Australia's acute labour shortage Lynton, about forty kilometres roughly north-west of Northampton, was established as a depot where ticket-of-leave men could be hired to work in the mines, to build roads or to work as shepherds and farmhands. The depot operated from 1853 to 1856 only and was then allowed to fall into disrepair. The ruins of its stone buildings can still be seen.

PORT GREGORY The oldest port on the mid-west coast, Port Gregory began to be used after the 1848 discovery of lead ore. Today its reef-protected waters make it a popular spot for swimming, sailing, windsurfing and fishing. A beta-carotene production plant has been established on the dry bed of nearby Hutt Lagoon (see box).

WARRIBANNO CHIMNEY Constructed in 1851 to smelt lead from the Geraldine Mine, the Warribanno Chimney, restored in 1972, is an important relic of the earliest mining operations in Western Australia. Lead ore and brushwood were fed in at the top and the heat in the chimney, intensified by a strong draught introduced at its base, was sufficient to melt the ore and produce lead.

FESTIVALS Northampton Agricultural Show, September.

PAYNES FIND ■ 2132

Once a thriving goldmining centre, the biggest in the area, Paynes Find is now a tiny settlement which provides essential stopover facilities for travellers heading north along the highway. It is also popular with fossickers who are often rewarded with valuable pickings of gold.

LAKE MOORE Lake Moore is a large salt lake with a well-preserved, ceremonial stone formation, built by Aborigines and more than seventy-five metres long, on its bed. Several smaller, less-intact arrangements of stones can be seen nearby.

PERENJORI ■ 2133

Perenjori, in the middle of Western Australia's sheep-station country, is the main centre for an agricultural and pastoral district. It is also on both the 'Wildflower Way' and the fringes of the Murchison goldfields. Nearby are the old gold-mining centres of Rothsay, Warriedar and Paynes Find (see entry); Perenjori is also a good area for gemstone fossicking.

The surrounding terrain is typical of the eastern wheat belt – semi-arid plains which, when watered by the rains of winter and spring, are covered briefly with wildflowers. Flocks of waterbirds frequent the nearby salt lakes. Perenjori's name is said to be derived from an Aboriginal word meaning 'waterhole'.

FESTIVALS Perenjori Agricultural Show, early September.

THREE SPRINGS ■ 2134

George Grey and his starving men passed through this area in 1839 during their epic march south after having endured the drama of shipwreck on the coast near Kalbarri (see entry). Some seven years later the peripatetic Gregory brothers (see Mingenew and Northampton) were here, seeking out new runs for stock. In 1867, the surveyor C.C. Hunt, spying out the land for a possible road route, stood on the site of the present town and noted on his plans the 'three springs' here.

Wheat grown on the surrounding plains fills the towering silos which dominate Three Springs township. The fine talc which is mined by opencut on the eastern outskirts of Three Springs is exported for use in the ceramics industry.

YALGOO ■ 2135

Alluvial gold was discovered here in the 1890s and mining began almost immediately. By the turn of the century Yalgoo had five hotels, a court house – now the district museum – post office, police station, hospital, railway station and school. This was one of the many mid-west towns to benefit from the architectural skills of Monsignor Hawes (see Mullewa) – in 1919 he designed the chapel of the Dominican Convent which stands on a hill above the town to the west.

Today Yalgoo serves as the hub of the surrounding pastoral and mining communities. It still retains its popularity as a good spot for fossicking and a variety of gemstones and traces of gold are still found regularly in the area.

JOKERS TUNNEL This ironically titled tunnel, carved through solid rock by prospectors searching for gold, is a memorial to the powerful lure of gold in the 1800s. It is named after the Joker mining syndicate.

FESTIVALS Yalgoo Races, April.

ZUYTDORP CLIFFS ■ 2136

The wreck of the Dutch ship *Zuytdorp* has lain at the base of these wild cliffs since she was wrecked while sailing from Holland to the East Indies in 1712. Her fate was unknown until research in the 1950s identified relics found on the cliffs by a local stockman thirty years earlier as belonging to the *Zuytdorp*. Some survivors reached shore, but their ultimate fate is unknown. The sternpiece and coins from the vessel are now on display at the Geraldton Museum. The wreck lies just offshore from the Zuytdorp Cliffs Nature Reserve (see Houtman Abrolhos).

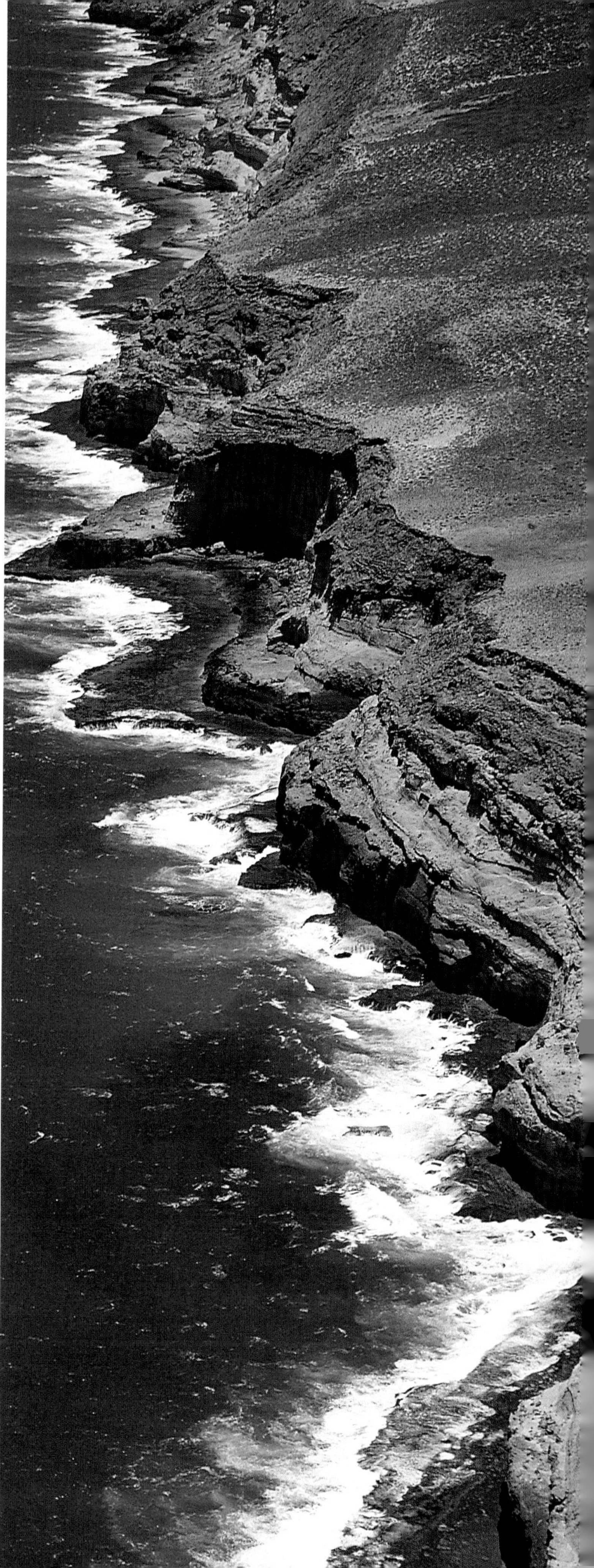

The wild Zuytdorp Cliffs are part of the Batavia Coast, both names inspired by early Dutch navigators.

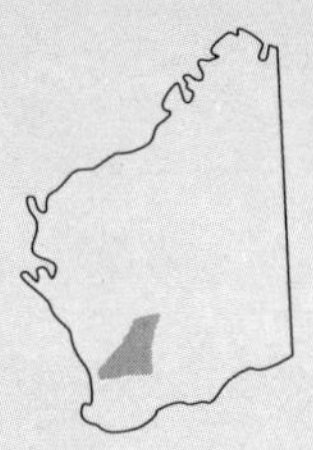

Northam & Merredin

Brilliant wildflowers interspersed with huge, oddly shaped granite monoliths are part of this region's ancient landscape. The wheat belt, intersected by pipelines, long stretches of rabbit-proof fences, major highways and three railway lines, represents an agricultural export from a more modern era.

Winter rains on the Darling Scarp provide a rush of water to thrill rafters on the Avon River rapids.

AVON VALLEY NATIONAL PARK ■ 2137

The largest of the national parks on the western scarp of the Darling Range – and one of the few wilderness national parks in Australia to have a railway line passing through it – Avon Valley National Park's 4400 hectares hold mainly jarrah–marri forest. The best views of the wild, steep-sided valley of the Avon can be seen from Bald Hill, preferably in winter when the river is in spate and the waterfalls are at their most dramatic. Winter is the preferred season for those interested in white-water canoeing – spring is a favourite time for those interested in the wildflowers, for which the park is famous.

BEVERLEY ■ 2138

The first settlers moved into the area around Beverley, as they did to the other Avon Valley towns, in the 1830s but it was only in the 1880s when it became a terminus on the privately sponsored Great Southern Railway that Beverley – from old English word meaning 'beaver stream' – was gazetted. Though Beverley is now a small village and the last passenger train ran in 1975, it was at one time one of the major Avon Valley towns and the location of the Avondale Research Station.

The grave of Billy Noongales, Sir John Forrest's Aboriginal companion on his arduous 1870 Perth to Adelaide trek, is in Beverley's Catholic cemetery. *Population 820*

BRUCE ROCK ■ 2139

This small settlement, surrounded by wheatfields, owes its development as a rural centre in the early twentieth century to not one but two railway lines. The appearance of the York–Merredin line in 1912, and the Narrogin–Merredin line the next year, brought a flurry of new settlers to join the few Scottish pioneers who had farmed in the area since the late nineteenth century. The name Bruce Rock, from a large granite outcrop east of the town used by sandalwood cutter John Bruce as a depot, was adopted for the new settlement.

Babakin, south-west of Bruce Rock, is one of only two places in the eastern wheatbelt where the rare Western Australian underground orchid is found. The orchid spends its entire life cycle under the ground where its small, flesh-pink flower blooms unseen. The flower is pollinated by burrowing insects, which are attracted by the the smell of a decaying fungus that is produced by the orchid. *Population 560*

CUNDERDIN ■ 2140

Number 3 pumping station – one of eight on the original goldfields water supply pipeline and now one of eighteen on the much extended agricultural water pipeline (see box) – was built at Cunderdin in 1902, at a time when only four families lived in the district. The old pumping station is now a museum dedicated primarily to wheat farming, although a display on the earthquake which destroyed nearby Meckering in 1968 is now also included.

This modern town, with an agricultural college and an airfield used by the RAAF during the First World War for training and now used by gliders, is at the centre of an agricultural district that is enlivened by the

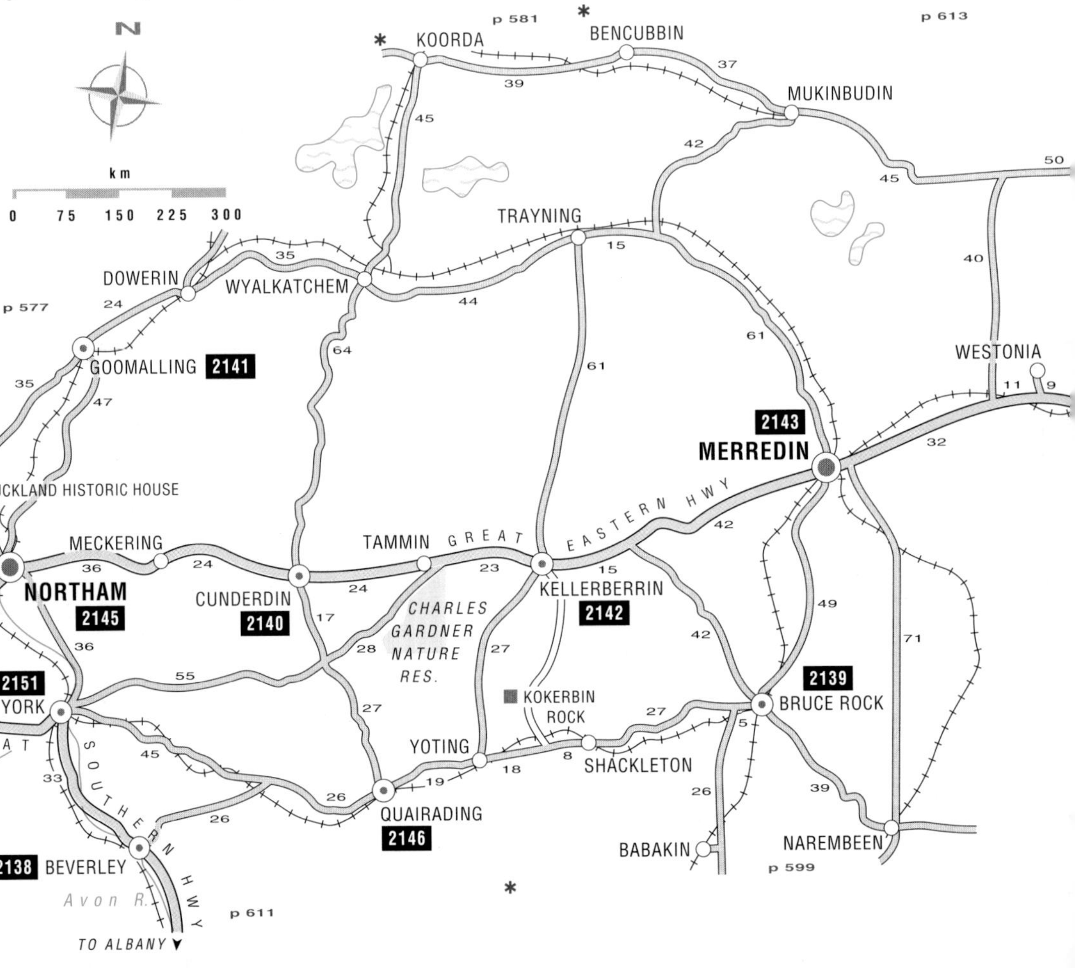

York's picture-book setting in the Avon Valley has made it a popular weekend retreat for residents of Perth.

unusual names of the farms and unmanned telephone exchanges such as Doodenanning, Honi Moni, Quelagetting, Youndegin, Bellakabella and Flowery Patch. *Population 690*

GOOMALLING ■ 2141

The Aborigines pointed out a spring at Goomalling to Robert Austin, the assistant surveyor, on his 1854 exploration, and several other Aboriginal waterholes or 'gnammas' can still be seen around the town.

In addition to agricultural pursuits, Goomalling had a successful aerated water factory for many years...and a more recent and less successful asbestos mine. Goomalling's population rose to 1400 in the 1970s and 1980s but has declined in recent years. *Population 530*

KELLERBERRIN ■ 2142

This wheatbelt town was one of the first settled areas on what is now the Great Eastern Highway. The early settlers concentrated on sheep and sandalwood with a little horsebreeding and wheat growing thrown in.

By the early 1890s, the railway arrived and the townsite that was gazetted in 1901 developed rapidly as a farming centre and as a stopping place for provisions and chaff for the teams heading for the goldfields. Using guano fertiliser and advanced mechanisation, the district's wheat crops increased rapidly in importance. *Population 920*

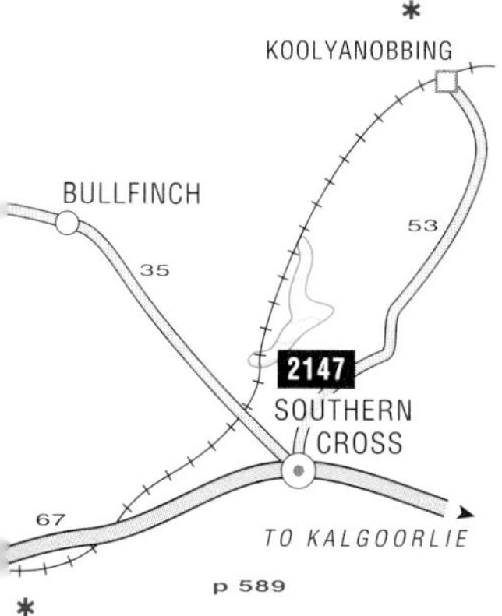

MERREDIN ■ 2143

Merredin, an attractive market town with jacaranda-lined streets, is the largest commercial centre in the eastern wheatbelt. In 1889, surveyor King found the natural water supply at Merredin Peak and camped there while surveying grazing leases.

If King gave the town its first boost, the coming of the railway four years later sealed its fate...and caused the entire town to relocate three kilometres south of King's site at the new railway line. Water for the steam trains was channelled from the natural water supply on Merredin Peak through a 100-metre-long channel to the railway dam and from there was pumped to the railway water tower with its advertisements for Kalgoorlie Bitter, brewed in Merredin. The huge silo at Merredin – the largest horizontal wheat storage in Australia, with a capacity of 220 000 tonnes – is used by a district which supplies forty per cent of the state's wheat. Although wheat remains the major cereal, barley for pig feed is also grown and the town is the site of Western Australia's busiest pig sales.

A grove of the trees from which the town got its name survive in the centre of the town: 'merritt-in', 'the place of the merritt trees', was the name given by the Aborigines to the area where good spear-making trees were to be found. *Population 3070*

CUMMINS THEATRE James Cummins, the owner of the Kalgoorlie Brewing and Ice Company, built the theatre in 1928 of bricks from old Coolgardie goldfields hotels, giving rise to the local rumour that the small amounts of gold dust in the bricks might now be of commercial value.

MUNDARING ■ 2144

'Mundaring' was the name given by the Jacoby family to their vineyard, bought from the Gugeri family who had established it in 1882. The name is Aboriginal, said to mean 'a high place on a high place' and is certainly appropriate for a settlement that sits in the wooded mountains, thirty kilometres east of Perth.

Mundaring is much closer to Perth – and much further from the goldfields – than the other settlements in this region but its contribution to the development of the goldfields was vital. In 1898–1902, Mundaring Weir and Number 1 pumping station were built as the start to the Goldfields Water Supply Scheme (see box). The weir dams more than seventy million cubic metres of water. *Population 1540*

NORTHAM ■ 2145

This, the largest town in the Avon (upper Swan) Valley, began developing in 1836. The first settler, John Morrell, built Morby Cottage in 1836 with the unheard-of luxury of glass windows. Morrell died of pneumonia after reputedly rescuing a man from drowning in the Avon River during the annual sheep washing but his simple mud house, which provided Northam's first schooling and church, still stands.

It was the decision that Northam should be the terminus for the goldfields railway in 1892 that led to the town overtaking the hitherto larger and older settlement of York. Until the railway was extended to the goldfields in the 1890s, prospectors disembarked at Northam and started the 450-kilometre trek to the goldfields, many on foot pushing their provisions in wheelbarrows.

The pedestrian suspension bridge across the Avon River in Northam is the longest in Australia, but it is the white swans for which the river at Northam is better known. Brought from England supposedly by the early Russian settler and later mayor, Oscar Bernard, the white swans have flourished and there are now over eighty birds in this unique natural breeding colony. *Population 6560*

BUCKLAND HISTORIC HOUSE At Irishtown, just north of Northam, stands Western Australia's stateliest home, acknowledged as one of the finest Victorian colonial homesteads in Australia. The two-storey home, set in landscaped gardens, houses a superb collection of antique furniture and silver, as well as a collection of old and contemporary paintings.

FESTIVALS The Avon Valley Arts Society Festival of Arts (Eisteddfod), August.

QUAIRADING ■ 2146

The district for which this small farming town is the centre was settled in the 1860s. Quairading sits just inside the nearer – to Perth – of the two rabbit-proof fences that run in a north-west to south-east direction through the region. The name Quairading, however, is associated with a different animal – one that predates the rabbit – since it comes from an Aboriginal word for the brush kangaroo. *Population 700*

SOUTHERN CROSS ■ 2147

After two days without water, Thomas Risely, Michael Toomey, Charles Crossland and their Aboriginal guide 'Wheelbarrow' were more desperate to find water than the gold they had originally set out to find. Using the stars of the Southern Cross as their compass, they came to a hill, above what is now the settlement of Southern Cross, and there they found gold in 1888. When the town was established in 1890, the role played by the Southern Cross was commemorated and the names of other constellations were used for the town's streets, which include Centaur, Leo and Scorpio, while a claypan outside the town was named Lake Polaris.

Tangible reminders of the brief gold-rush days can be seen in the old cemetery and at the Mining Registrar's Office and court house (1892), now the Yilgarn Historical Museum. *Population 900*

KOOLYANOBBING This is a ghost town with a difference: the streets are kerbed and sealed, the tennis and basketball courts stand silent and the club, halls and swimming pool have lain unused since the mine closed in 1983. Koolyanobbing was built as a private mining centre in the early 1950s and proclaimed a town in 1965.

A STEEL LIFELINE GOES OUT TO KALGOORLIE

IN MARCH 1902, the first water left Mundaring Weir in the Darling Range on its 557-kilometre journey by pipeline to Kalgoorlie. Ten months later it reached Kalgoorlie, where, on 24 January 1903, the former Premier Sir John Forrest officially opened the Goldfields Water Supply Scheme with the following words: '[It] will be said of us "They made a way in the wilderness and rivers in the desert"'. But the engineer responsible for what was the world's longest pipeline and one of its greatest hydraulic engineering feats was not present. Charles Yelverton O'Connor, exhausted by the constant criticism and complexities of constructing the pipeline, had shot himself on Fremantle Beach the month before the water started its long journey.

The earliest attempts at providing water for the goldminers had proved expensive and unreliable. Typhoid epidemics had already broken out at Coolgardie as desperate miners drank stale water during the drought. In 1895, O'Connor, the state's Engineer-in-Chief, proposed a solution that would capture water in a reservoir in the Darling Range near Perth and pump it, by means of eight pumping stations, to Kalgoorlie. The pumping engines and the boilers which produced the steam to work them were imported from Britain. The device that locked the steel pipes together came from a Melbourne inventor and the wood for the boilers came from farms on the pipeline route.

The scheme was even more successful than anticipated. Not only did O'Connor's scheme revolutionise life on the goldfields but, with extensions to the original pipelines from 1903 onwards, agriculture in the state's inland was also revolutionised. With the gradual replacement of the original pumps in the 1950s and 1960s by electrically operated pumps, the time it took for water to travel from Mundaring Weir (see Mundaring) to Kalgoorlie was reduced from four weeks to two weeks. Three million hectares of land and 130 towns receive water from what is now the Great Southern Towns and Goldfields Water Supply Scheme.

At Mundaring Weir, Number 1 pumping station has been converted to a museum where O'Connor's original models and diagrams, criticised by so many at the time, are now displayed. □

Behind the walls of Mundaring Weir, the waters of Helena River bank up in preparation for the long, forced journey to Kalgoorlie.

TOODYAY ■ 2148

The rich farmland of the Avon Valley attracted settlers from as early as the 1830s and the site of the original Toodyay, eight kilometres downstream from the present site, was one of the first settlements. The origin of the name (pronounced 'Too-jay') is the Aboriginal word 'duidgee', said to mean 'place of plenty'. There was certainly plenty of water – in fact too much – as the site was flood prone and, in 1860, the present site was chosen. The second settlement was called Newcastle until 1910, when it was renamed Toodyay and the original site became West Toodyay.

This historic town has a number of buildings dating back to the 1860s, twenty-five of which are listed by the National Trust. With the exception of the three-storey steam flour mill now used as a tourist centre, the old Newcastle jail is perhaps the best known of these preserved buildings. The small complex of shingled stone and brick buildings replaced the old lockup in 1865 when the increasing use of convict labour in the district made the seven-cell prison necessary.

The old lockup was never sufficiently secure to hold 'Moondyne Joe', Western Australia's most famous bushranger and escapologist extraordinaire. Joseph Bolitho Johns was sentenced for horse stealing in 1861 but escaped from the old lockup at Toodyay on three occasions. Some years later, he was sent to Fremantle jail on a different charge and again made a succesful escape from the exercise yard, after which a specially secure cell was built to hold him. *Population 600*

FESTIVALS Toodyay Folk Festival, October; Moondyne Festival, May.

WALYUNGA NATIONAL PARK ■ 2149

This park is perched on the steepest slopes of the Darling Range just north-east of Perth, and is deeply dissected by the Swan and Avon rivers. When swollen with winter rains the rivers attract canoeists to their upstream rapids. Further along the descent to the sea they level out and large pools, ideal for summer swimming, occur along smooth granite beds. The park takes its name from one of these pools, near which a large and ancient, seasonal Aboriginal campsite was used by groups who brought a variety of stone with them from a number of regions.

WUNDOWIE ■ 2150

Wundowie has a very recent history since, until the 1940s, it was a railway siding with a timber mill nearby. With the shortage of pig iron during the Second World War, the Western Australian Government decided to establish a charcoal-iron industry at Wundowie to supply local foundries. By the time the town was built and the plant opened in 1948, the war was over but until the 1970s Wundowie pig iron competed on the world market; with the development of Kwinana, Wundowie's star has faded. *Population 710*

Harnesses and bits have hung on the wall in York's Balladong Farm saddle room for 160 years.

YORK ■ 2151

A few years after the founding of the Swan River Colony, Ensign Dale of the 63rd Regiment, eager to discover what lay beyond the Darling Range, led several expeditions into the hinterland. As a result of Dale's third exploration in 1830, York, the earliest of the Avon Valley settlements and Western Australia's first inland town, was founded.

The early days were fraught with transport problems and labour shortages but within twenty years, the road to Fremantle was completed and convict labour was imported. By the 1860s, York had become the state's third largest town and the five-day York Fair attracted hundreds of people each year.

With the exception of the old jail, few buildings survive from the 1830s, but this most historic of towns has over two dozen restored and listed buildings, most of which date from the second half of the nineteenth century. These buildings range from the Residency (1843), the home of the resident magistrate and now a museum, the Church of the Holy Trinity (1856), with its stone from the fourteenth-century choir at York Minster in England, to Kairey Cottage (1850s), one of a group built for the British Army pensioners enlisted as convict guards. *Population 1560*

BALLADONG FARM Established in 1831 by Revett Bland, who accompanied Ensign Dale on one of his three explorations of the Avon Valley, Balladong Farm is the oldest settled farm in the state. It now operates as a working farming museum.

FESTIVALS Jazz Festival, September; Antique Fair, November.

Kalgoorlie-Boulder & Kambalda

Minerals have probably been more instrumental than any other product in shaping the fortunes of Western Australia and in this region ghost towns testify to the wealth wrung from the ground at the beginning of the century. The fabulous Golden Mile continues to produce but the economy now depends on nickel too.

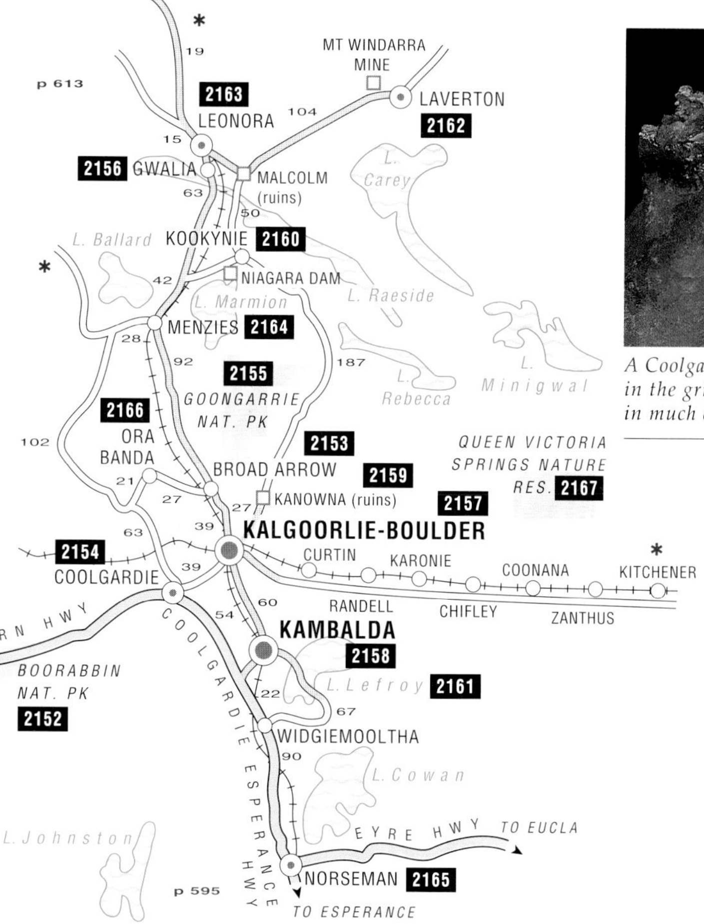

A Coolgardie gold find worth celebrating – still in the grip of the quartz where it formed – but in much cleaner form than when it was dug up.

It was into harsh country such as this, near Kalgoorlie, that prospectors 'rushed' to find gold in the 1890s.

BOORABBIN NATIONAL PARK ■ 2152

Boorabbin National Park covers an area of 26 000 hectares stretching for twenty kilometres on each side of the Great Eastern Highway between Southern Cross and Coolgardie. It is rolling country covered in the typical heathland of the sandplains east of the wheatbelt: various species of myrtle and banksia are the dominant plants and the park is at its best in spring when the low shrubs and smaller plants bloom with a colourful show of wildflowers.

BROAD ARROW ■ 2153

In 1900 there were 2400 people in Broad Arrow and the town had eight hotels and two breweries. There was also a stock exchange and a hospital. Today's permanent population is around the twenty mark but there is renewed mining activity in the district. One hotel, built in 1896, survives. It was renovated in 1971 and featured in the film *Nickel Queen* which starred Googie Withers.

Broad Arrow's name has nothing to do with the distinctive markings on the clothing of the lags of the early convict days. It was given its name around 1893 after a prospector scratched metre-long arrows in the dirt to make sure his mates could follow his trail.

COOLGARDIE ■ 2154

Arthur Bayley and William Ford discovered gold in the early 1890s on Fly Flat (see sub-entry) in the region now known as Coolgardie Shire and by 1898 there was a town near the site with a population of 15 000. 'Coolgardie' derives from an Aboriginal word thought to mean 'tree by the gnamma (watering) hole.' Coolgardie was once the third largest town in Western Australia – only

Lake Lefroy provides little joy for watersports-lovers – except sailors, who cruise the salty surface in wheeled land 'yachts' with no fear of drowning.

Perth and Fremantle were bigger. The telegraph line was established in 1894 and the railway line came through from Southern Cross and Northam in 1896.

Life, by anyone's standards, was very tough in this isolated region. Besides the illnesses associated with contaminated water, dust and lack of fresh food (see Kalgoorlie-Boulder), dysentery was also prevalent and the Coolgardie safe, designed to keep provisions cool and clear of flies, originated here. It was a primitive but relatively effective contraption – a box with hessian sides kept damp by dripping water put to hang in an air current. The evaporating water kept the food cool.

The Coolgardie area still produces exciting discoveries. The latest significant find in the area was the 'Happy New Year Nugget', weighing ninety-seven ounces (3000 grams), which was discovered by a lucky local married couple on 31 December 1990. *Population 1060*

FLY FLAT The first arrivals at Fly Flat were able to extract an amazing average of three kilograms of gold in a few hours from the surface alluvial ore. Many mining towns had a Fly Flat, probably so called for the clouds of ever-present bush flies. Today Coolgardie's field is covered with scattered trees and assorted mining relics, among them twenty-metre headframes, generators, tanks, boilers and dumps. Bayley's Reward Claim is marked by an obelisk.

MARBLE BAR HOTEL This is an opulent two-storey brick building from the turn of the century. Its architectural style typifies the exuberance of those early days – just one of Coolgardie's twenty-three hotels where triumphs were celebrated with gold sovereigns and champagne.

ERNEST GILES' GRAVE Ernest Giles, who is remembered in these parts for bringing camels from South Australia to Perth, joined the gold rush to Coolgardie and was there dogged with much the same bad luck he had on his journeys of exploration. He took a job in the mine warden's office in order to survive and died of bronchial pneumonia in 1897, aged sixty-two. His grave can be found in the local cemetery.

GOONGARRIE NATIONAL PARK ■ 2155

Goongarrie is a remote dry park, 100 kilometres north of Kalgoorlie. It is 49 878 hectares of genuine outback where mulga country meets mallee scrub and York gum woodlands. Emu bush – also known as poverty bush – and acacias grow among the groundcover of speargrass. Like many plants in these parts, the wildflowers put on a striking ephemeral show when there are soaking rains.

GWALIA ■ 2156

Gwalia, sister town to Leonora (see entry), is notable for the 'Sons of Gwalia' mine. It was discovered in 1896 and backed by Welsh finance – Gwalia is Welsh for Wales. Herbert Hoover, later thirty-first president of the United States, was manager there in 1897 and left to become the chief engineer for the Chinese Imperial Bureau of Mines. 'Sons of Gwalia' yielded gold until 1963, making it the largest and longest-producing mine outside the Golden Mile.

After 'Sons of Gwalia' closed, Gwalia quickly became a ghost town but recently the mine has re-opened with large, modern open-cut workings. The small township retains something of a deserted atmosphere and the galvanised iron buildings typify practical, turn-of-the-century Western Australian goldfields architecture. Nevertheless, Gwalia was once important enough to have the state's first electric trams and a regular double-decker service ran to Leonora, four kilometres away. The earlier lifestyle is impressively displayed in the town museum.

KALGOORLIE-BOULDER ■ 2157

In 1893, Thomas Flanagan, Dan Shea and 'Paddy' Hannan camped by Mount Charlotte, forty kilometres east of Coolgardie. They found 100 ounces of high-quality gold in a few days and began the last and most significant rush in Australia's history. A few months later there were 1400 prospectors at the site which was first known as Hannan's Find or Hannans and later as Kalgoorlie – 'Kal' to the local residents. The town's name comes from one of two Aboriginal words, 'kalgurli' thought to mean 'a twining vine-like plant' or 'koolgooluh', the word for an edible silky pear.

The town is surprisingly green because early on the streets were planted with trees for shade and protection against dust storms. Boulder took the name of the Great Boulder mine – its discoverers named it after 'The Boulder' they had unsuccessfully worked in South Australia. The two towns became one in modern times.

The gold rush increased Western Australia's population fourfold in ten years and brought thousands of people and hundreds of horses and camels to remote areas where water was an extremely scarce commodity (see sub-entry). Two years after Hannan's find, Kalgoorlie had six straight streets wide enough to accommodate turning camel trains and 6000 residents with another 1000 in nearby Boulder. In 1902, around 30 000 people lived in Kalgoorlie. There were more than forty hotels and eight breweries and the railway line to Boulder was the busiest in the state.

In September 1896 a much longer railway link was opened between the 'City of Gold' and Perth. Then on 12 February 1913, Prime Minister Andrew Fisher turned the first sod at Kalgoorlie for the Trans-Australia railway from Port Augusta in South Australia. This incredible engineering feat was completed in 1917 (see box, *Esperance & Eucla*). However, Kalgoorlie is still isolated enough to have a Flying Doctor base, one of seven such bases in Western Australia (see box, *Mount Isa & Cloncurry*).

Within 7 years of its founding, booming Kalgoorlie boasted substantial streetscapes punctuated by stylish hotels such as the Exchange.

Kalgoorlie has a rich architectural heritage. Public and commercial buildings were built of brick and stone and often were embellished with balconies, gables, towers and verandahs. Despite the use of corrugated iron as a building material for workers' homes, clever concessions to the climate were incorporated in their design. Most of the rather grand buildings in Kalgoorlie's racecourse complex, completed in the 1920s, are still in regular use.

Gold has fluctuated widely in price – 35 dollars an ounce in 1970 to 752 dollars an ounce in 1980 to 494 dollars in 1990, and the fortunes of Kalgoorlie-Boulder have fluctuated frequently too, but the rarest of Australia's mined minerals is still eagerly sought. Old tailings dumps near Kalgoorlie are being washed down and re-treated to recover valuable ore. Though nickel and gold are the mainstay of the region's economy, the Kalgoorlie-Boulder area is also noted as an important pastoral district. *Population 25 020*

MUNDARING–KALGOORLIE PIPELINE In its early days, Kalgoorlie's water situation was crucial with people paying eighteen pence to half-a-crown a gallon for drinking water that was often contaminated. This came from supplies carted in by horse and camel or from the huge condensers rigged up to distil it from bores sunk in the nearby salt lakes. These required fuel, and the landscape, which had supported stands of slow-growing tall trees, was quickly denuded. There was no water to wash out the gold and the dryblowing separation technique exacerbated the dust problem. Diseases such as typhoid, spread by the polluted water, barcoo rot – a form of scurvy – and inflammations of the eyes were rife.

The government sensibly recognised the goldfields' contribution to the state's economy. The inland population was mostly from the eastern colonies and were scornfully dubbed 't'othersiders' by the separatist and settled coastal colonists – it took the newcomers to tip the vote for Western Australia to become part of the Commonwealth of Australia in 1901. In 1896 the government announced plans to bring water to Kalgoorlie

LIMITED
& WESTERN ARGUS OFFICES
Kalgoorlie

from Mundaring 600 kilometres away through a pipeline and eight pumping stations (see *Northam & Merredin*). This incensed many Perth citizens who scoffed at Charles Yelverton O'Connor's daring plan which would cost 2.5 million pounds sterling. A prominent parliamentarian declared: 'it has never been done in the history of the world and it never will be done'. But it was – in January 1903 the first water trickled into the catchment of Mount Charlotte reservoir. Sadly, O'Connor, the brilliant visionary engineer, who had already proved himself by constructing the Fremantle harbour (see *Rockingham & Fremantle*) and making the state railways pay, could no longer stand the public ridicule and shot himself a few months before construction was completed.

PADDY HANNAN'S STATUE 'Paddy' Hannan, a slight, bearded Irishman who never made a great deal of money out of his momentous discovery, is remembered in Kalgoorlie by a three-quarter, life-sized bronze statue, a replica of the original one created in 1929 by John McLeod from ninety pieces of soldered copper which is now in the town hall for safekeeping from vandalism. He holds a waterbag in his hand which acts as a drinking fountain and a reminder that ultimately water is much more essential for human endeavour than gold.

GOLDEN MILE The prosperity of Kalgoorlie-Boulder is dependent on the Golden Mile, an area of one square mile rich in surface gold and underlain with a massive schistose lode discovered in 1893.

The Golden Mile has the reputation of being one of the richest gold-bearing areas in the world and was mined to a depth of 1300 metres. New treatments for low-quality lodes have now converted the area to a vast open-cut mine.

MUSEUM OF THE GOLDFIELDS This is partly housed in a converted pub, The British Arms. This was once the narrowest hotel in Australia and dates from 1899.

HAINAULT GOLD MINE The Hainault gold mine was one of the major mines on the Golden Mile in 1910 and produced 200 kilograms of gold. It closed in 1968 and five years later was restored as a tourist attraction and an opportunity to see an underground goldmine in safety.

FESTIVALS Kalgoorlie-Boulder Racing Round, October; Balzano Barrow Race, October.

Tach Mahomed, a cameleer, suffered the unfortunate distinction of being the goldfields' first murder victim.

KAMBALDA ■ 2158

The Red Hill Westralia mine flourished briefly but vigorously between 1897 and 1906 and yielded 30 000 ounces of precious gold. Kambalda served it well but there was nothing to keep the town alive once the mine closed. The site reverted to bush until sixty years later nickel was discovered and the Western Mining Corporation built a new modern town – Australia's first based on nickel. There are two centres, four kilometres apart, of which Kambalda West is the larger.

The original settlement was called Kambalda by the government surveyor W. Rowley because he thought it 'sounded a pleasant name' but its meaning is unknown. *Population 4260*

KANOWNA ■ 2159

Gold was discovered here in 1893 and by 1905 the population numbered 12 000 with sixteen hotels and two breweries to meet their needs. There were several churches and the train ran hourly to Kalgoorlie. Now little remains except rubble, and visitors would be hard put to imagine the town as it was in its heyday were it not for the 100-metre-long railway platform and the marker signs indicating where streets and major buildings once existed.

KOOKYNIE ■ 2160

At gold fever pitch in 1905, 1500 people lived in Kookynie and there were six hotels supporting a hard-worked local brewery. Today the place is a ghost town, the mines are abandoned and only a few of the buildings are still standing. Wood, stone, brick and iron were just too precious to leave lying around and when the miners moved on, the houses were often demolished and the materials used elsewhere.

The consumption of the locally brewed beer by thirsty miners was phenomenal and at one time there were more than a dozen breweries in the goldfields making two-and-a-half-million litres of beer a year. By all contemporary accounts, the local water had nothing to recommend it when available and it sometimes ran out. One observer wrote: 'crowds of men could be seen waiting around every waterstand, and not a drop to be had for love or money...men were walking around with their lips parched and cracked, too thirsty to speak...in the hotels the barman passed over the whisky bottle but kept a firm hold on the water jug.' Discarded bottles are strewn across hundreds of kilometres and the earliest clear glass ones have turned a deep purple in their prolonged exposure to sunlight. They are known as 'desert amethysts' and are highly prized by collectors.

NIAGARA DAM The Niagara Dam was built in 1897 as a water storage for the steam locomotives on the Kalgoorlie–Leonora run. The concrete wall is 250 metres long, 20 metres high and has an average thickness of 7 metres. It required vast amounts of cement which was carried in bags from Coolgardie by a long-suffering team of 400 camels.

LAKE LEFROY ■ 2161

Kambalda's nickel mine overlooks the large Lake Lefroy saltpan which covers an area of about 500 square-kilometres. It rarely contains water but the reflection of the sun's rays on the salt often creates a deceptive shimmering mirage.

Local residents enjoy land 'yachting' on this crusty expanse, an exhilarating sport adapted to the waterless conditions. The craft have a T-shaped frame with three wheels and a sail, and skim across the lake's salt crust at speeds over 100 kilometres per hour.

LAVERTON ■ 2162

In the skys above Laverton district wedgetail eagles hover nonchalantly over abandoned workings that once yielded rich rewards of payable ore, and camels, emus and kangaroos pass by without so much as a second glance. The first mineral lease here was called British Flag and the townsite was laid out north of the mine workings.

Laverton served a thriving mining district in the heady gold years and the name honours Dr Charles Laver, an early entrepreneur who held mineral leases here. It was considered due to his faith in the district and his untiring efforts to attract the attention of capitalists to it that the mines were given a chance. When the gold ran out, Laverton lapsed into obscurity, until Poseidon Limited's major nickel discovery at Mount Windarra in 1969 which sparked a famous share boom. Ore is extracted from the vast Windarra open-cut mine and Laverton has been reborn as a modern satellite town for the project. *Population 1200*

LEONORA ■ 2163

This area was first explored in 1869 when John Forrest and five companions set out to investigate the sighting of a white man's bones, thought to be the remains of Ludwig Leichhardt who had disappeared some twenty years before. The harsh environment failed to impress him and he wrote in disgust: 'What a native calls good country is where he can get a drink of water and a wurrong [desert rat]; and if there is an acre of grassy land they describe it as very extensive grassy country.' This same countryside now supports a widely distributed sheep population.

Leonora's main street and verandahed shop-fronts are little changed from its days as the largest centre in the north-eastern goldfields. It still maintains that role and is the railhead for copper from the northern copper mines and nickel from Leinster and Windarra. The success of the local pastoralists depends on the rainfall but a substantial woolclip leaves Leonora most years.

There is renewed goldmining activity in the district by the larger mining companies. New technology and mining techniques have made it economical to rework abandoned leases and open-pit mines and treatment plants have been established in the area. *Population 1200*

MENZIES ■ 2164

Menzies was named for Robert Leslie Menzies who discovered the area's main mine in 1894. It is presently a small mining and pastoral town but was once sizeable with camel races, cricket matches, a brewery and a forty-bed hospital. The substantial town hall which had a seating capacity of five hundred has a blank-faced tower. The ship bringing the clock from England sank and a replacement was never ordered.

Sandalwood is the 'timber gold' of the mulga scrub, north of Menzies. It is a small, shrubby, parasitic tree and cannot survive without a host plant usually a variety of acacia called the jam tree in these parts. The wood is prized in south-east Asia for carving and making incense sticks; it is also used to line chests and boxes and the strongly aromatic oil is a perfume and soap ingredient which, so far, cannot be synthesised.

Sandalwood exports were important to Western Australia from 1845, and by 1880 it was still the second most important export after wool. The sale of the aromatic wood helped many a prospector survive between small findings of gold and the wood is still being harvested.

NORSEMAN ■ 2165

This is the first town of any size reached by travellers crossing the Nullarbor from the east. Norseman was named after a miner's horse which is said to have stumbled over a large gold nugget in the 1890s and led his owner to the discovery of a gold reef. Before long, thousands of

THE TALE OF THE TOSS OF TWO COINS

TWO-UP GAMES were always popular with the miners at the Kalgoorlie corrugated-iron coliseum, set down the track in the scrub, a few kilometres from the town proper. In the early days the spice of illicit gambling added excitement to the play, but that changed a little while ago when a large police raid took place during Kalgoorlie race week. A number of notable personalities were caught in the net, and fearing a thoroughly embarrassing outcome, the state government decided to legalise the Kalgoorlie game. Its one proviso was that women, formerly barred from the excitement of the tin-walled ring, should now be allowed to participate in the game.

Two-up, also called 'swy' from the German 'zwei', can boast of a long – if humble – history. It is derived from the British game of pitch-and-toss which was played by the convicts. As with many of the best games, the rules are simple and experts say it is probably one of the fairest and least 'fixable' gambling games in the world – it requires no venue other than a piece of flat ground and a group of gamblers! The players gather in a circle and place their bets. With all eyes intent upon him, the spinner flicks two pennies from the small wooden bat (called a kip) so that they spin in the air before falling. The well-known and often impassioned call 'Come in, spinner!' urges this deciding action. If the coins land heads up, the spinner collects the bets. If they land tails, the players collect. If the fall is a mixed pair, the spin is on again.

To make things even more interesting, bets are also taken on possible long-term combinations of the toss, such as how many pairs of heads will be thrown in succession. Sometimes the heads of the pennies are highly polished to distinguish them from the tails, or marks are made on the coins for the same reason.

This unassuming game has always been associated with the goldfields of Kalgoorlie but many cities had two-up schools operating outside the law in the first half of the century. It is thought that Sydney's legendary 'Thommos', started in 1907 by professional boxer Joe Thomas, was still going in the 1970s. The game was adopted by soldiers in the Australian Imperial Force during the First World War and the 'diggers' continued to play in the second war, thus giving two-up a special place in Australian culture. Its popularity may have waned as it is now offered respectably in most Australian casinos and is legal throughout the land on Anzac Day when returned servicemen relive their army traditions. □

The spinner flicks the kip (top left) and another game of swy is underway at the comfortably appointed Kalgoorlie two-up arena in a 'traditional' atmosphere unlikely to be matched in any flashy city casino.

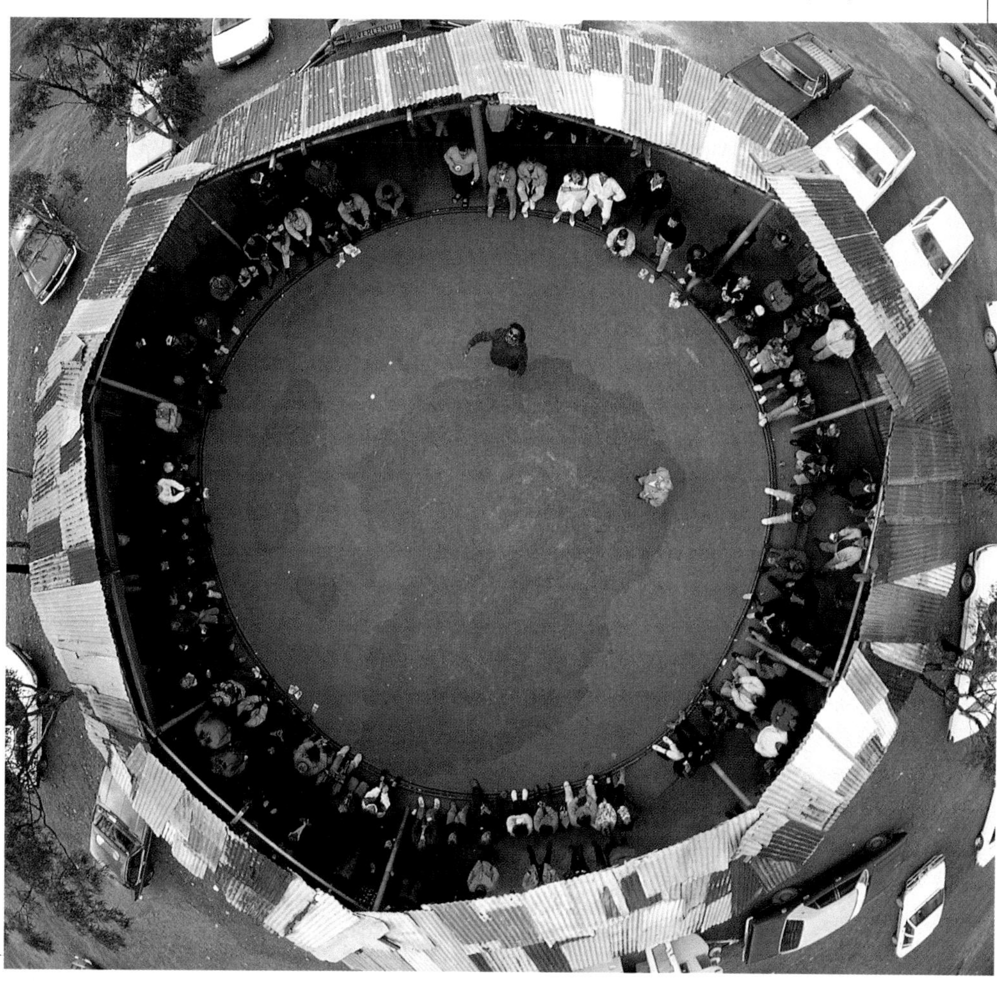

prospectors were flocking to the new field in search of their fortunes. The animal that started the rush is honoured by a statue in the main street.

Norseman's quartz reef is the richest in Australia and is still being mined. A tailings dump covering ten hectares is expected to produce millions of dollars' worth of ore. Large-scale prospecting goes on for gold, platinum, nickel, gypsum, lead, and zinc. *Population 1400*

HISTORICAL AND GEOLOGICAL MUSEUM This former School of Mines was built in 1940 and now houses a comprehensive collection of household items and mining tools from the gold-rush days.

ORA BANDA ■ 2166

Ora Banda's name – Spanish for 'band of gold' – reflects the optimistic hopes of those who flocked to the goldfields. In 1910, the place was humming with the daily lives of 2000 people in search of the elusive 'band of gold' – today there are less than fifty voices to be heard. In 1971, there was a brief moment of excitement for the residents when some scenes were shot here for Western Australia's first full-length feature film *Nickel Queen*. The historic Ora Banda inn, built in 1911, closed in 1945 but reopened in 1980 to cater to the tourist trade.

QUEEN VICTORIA SPRINGS NATURE RESERVE ■ 2167

This small soak on the western slope of a depression containing a claypan lies in a protected area of 340 000 hectares. It was named by Ernest Giles in 1875 and is an important sanctuary for desert plants and animals. The predominantly mulga vegetation is home to such animals as Mitchell's hopping-mouse and many species of inland birds.

Esperance & Eucla

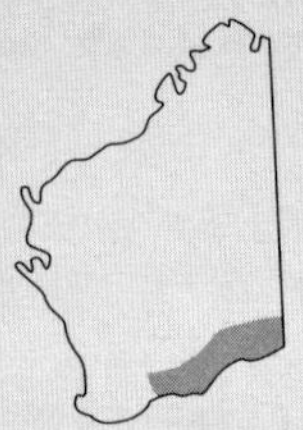

Along this wild southern coast are many names bestowed by early French navigators. One of them, Esperance, was the starting point for a stream of diggers; along the track north a string of small towns grew up to service their needs. Eastwards, a highway now approximates Edward Eyre's route across the Nullarbor.

Esperance's enviable green belt of parks and reserves includes rocky Thistle Cove, in the Cape Le Grand Park.

ARCHIPELAGO OF THE RECHERCHE ■ 2168

The Archipelago of the Recherche extends from Figure of Eight Island, south-west of Esperance Bay, to the northernmost rock of Eastern Group, about 240 kilometres eastwards, and covers an area of almost 4000 square kilometres. It comprises more than a hundred granite islands ranging in size from less than half a hectare to ten square kilometres, as well as innumerable reefs, rocks and shoals. Sixty or so of the larger islands have been named, but none are inhabited, although in the past they have been used as bases for sealers and in the early part of the twentieth century sheep were grazed on some.

The archipelago is now a nature reserve with wildlife of particular interest because it is more closely related to species found further to the east than those on the adjacent mainland. Only Woody Island is open to the public and can be reached by ferry from Esperance.

These barren islands were first recorded by Dutch mariner Pieter Nuijts in 1627 and then by George Vancouver in 1791; in the following year the French navigator d'Entrecasteaux gave the archipelago the name of his ship *Recherche*.

BALLADONIA ■ 2169

The high granite outcrop with a freshwater pool at its base fed by run-off was chosen in 1879 by brothers Stephen and William Ponton and their partner John Sharp as the homestead site for windy Balladonia sheep station. Rock quarried here was used for the original 1880 homestead and the later fourteen-roomed building, as well as for fencing.

'Balladonia' derives from an Aboriginal word which is thought to mean 'big rock by itself'. The name was also used for the now abandoned Telegraph Station, and more recently for the modern roadhouse and motel complex nearby on the Eyre Highway (see entry). It was into this area that Skylab, the United States' space station, made its fiery re-entry in July 1979.

CAIGUNA ■ 2170

This is another of the strategically placed roadhouses that cater for the needs of Eyre Highway overlanders who here must alter their watches to central time, gaining three-quarters of a hour if travelling west and losing the same if travelling east. The locality is named after Caiguna Rockhole, about 1500 metres to the west.

BAXTER CLIFFS About forty kilometres south of the highway a lonely memorial in what explorer Edward Eyre described as 'the wildest and most inhospitable wastes of Australia' honours John Baxter, who died here in Eyre's arms on a bitterly cold night in April 1841, shot by one of the party's three Aborigines. Because of the 'vast unbroken sheet of rock which extended … in every direction' it was impossible for Eyre to dig a grave, and instead Baxter's body, wrapped in a blanket, had to be left where he fell. The cliffs were named in Baxter's honour in 1968.

CAPE ARID NATIONAL PARK ■ 2171

This park is the starting point of a series of nature conservation areas which stretch east along the coast almost to the South Australian border. Here, between rocky headlands, are isolated beaches and from coastal vantage points there are sweeping views of the many islets of the eastern end of the Archipelago of the Recherche. Inland, the landscape is mainly sandplain and heathland

MOUNT RAGGED In the north of the park is the razorback ridge of Mount Ragged. Twenty million years ago it was an island, and on its upper slopes are clearly discernible wave-cut platforms where many species of orchids and several ferns grow. In 1930, a 'living fossil', the most primitive species of ant known in the world – more primitive even than those known from prehistoric times – was found alive and well here.

CAPE LE GRAND NATIONAL PARK ■ 2172

Windswept heaths and bulky granite outcrops characterise this park which has good swimming and fishing in its many sheltered coves, and inspiring views of the granite islands of the Archipelago of the Recherche from its hilly mallee scrublands.

Mount Le Grand (345 metres) is the highest of the park's granite peaks. Several natural features in this area are named for Le Grand, an ensign aboard *L'Esperance*.

ROSSITER BAY To his enormous surprise and relief, explorer Edward Eyre, on the desperate last leg of his 1841 east-west crossing, came over

The old sandstone telegraph station gradually melts back into the dunes ut modern Eucla is on higher ground, safe from the encroaching sands.

ıe ridge here to find the French ʻhaler *Mississippi* moored close to ıore. He and his Aboriginal companion, known as Wylie, were taken n board and that evening banqueted on the best the ship could offer. he sudden good luck of this chance ıeeting seemed to Eyre 'more like a ream than a reality', and in gratiıde he named the bay for his host, aptain Rossiter. Thirteen days later, den with supplies from the ship – ıcluding brandy and Dutch cheese the explorers resumed their trek ver the 400 kilometres between ıem and Albany.

A fifteen-kilometre full day hiking ack connects Rossiter Bay with Le rand Beach.

OCKLEBIDDY ■ 2173

modern roadhouse complex here hich has replaced the old roadside etrol pumps serves cross-Nullarbor avellers on the Eyre Highway.

COCKLEBIDDY CAVE Off the highway, north-west of the roadhouse, is a huge cavern with an underground lake in its depths. It is one of the network which riddles the plain here in a limestone labyrinth 100 metres and more below the surface. The subterranean system includes some of the longest underwater caves in the world and access to it is both difficult and dangerous. World diving records have been set here.

EYRE BIRD OBSERVATORY A track that turns off from the main road about seventeen kilometres east of the motel complex leads to the spot where explorer Edward John Eyre dug a lifesaving soak in March 1841. Local Aborigines told Eyre of a better supply a few kilometres to the west, and this water determined the siting of the old Eyre Telegraph Station, a fine stone building dating from 1897, which in the 1970s was restored for use as the Eyre Bird Observatory.

ESPERANCE ■ 2174

In 1792, French navigator d'Entrecasteaux took shelter here from a violent storm, and named the bay for *L'Esperance*, the first of the expedition's two vessels to enter its waters. Today Esperance is port for and centre of a prosperous wheat, sheep and beef district.

The first settlers in the district were the Dempster brothers, who drove their stock overland from Northam in 1863 to take up a huge land holding which included the present townsite. Boom times for the tiny port came in the 1890s with the opening of the Coolgardie goldfields, when Esperance became the starting point for prospectors from the eastern states who landed here, bought supplies at local shops, and then headed north. *Population 7070*

ESPERANCE DOWNS RESEARCH STATION Established in 1949 at Gibson, just north of Esperance, work here identified a deficiency of trace elements – in particular copper and zinc – in the surrounding sandplains which, when rectified, turned vast areas formerly only able to support mallee scrub into productive farmlands. This attracted investors from around Australia and from the United States, and now more than one million hectares has been transformed into a rich agricultural belt.

MUNICIPAL MUSEUM Skylab, the United States' first space station, fell to earth over south-western Australia in July 1979. Pieces of it were recovered throughout the Esperance region and now, on indefinite loan from the people who found them, they form a special display here. Other exhibits include early mining and agricultural machinery, seafaring relics, period clothes, household and business articles and fossils found in the surrounding area.

PINK LAKE As is the case with several other similarly named salt lakes, the colour of this Pink Lake is caused by a salt-tolerant algae which, in other parts of the continent, such as the Hutt River Lagoon (see *Geraldton & Kalbarri*), is harvested for the extraction of the food colourant beta-carotene. The salt is exceptionally pure – as first noted by Matthew Flinders after some of it was brought on board the *Investigator* in early 1802 – and has been gathered since the 1930s for use as table salt, butcher's salt and stock licks for animals. The first European here was the naturalist from the *L'Esperance* who in 1792, was separated from the vessel's main landing party while collecting specimens, and spent two days lost in this region.

WIND FARM, SALMON BEACH On a windy ridge above Salmon Beach, west of Esperance, stand a cluster of wind-powered generators, resembling peculiar slimline windmills, which are capable of producing one million kilowatt hours of electricity annually – equivalent to the energy needs of 200 homes. This, the first commercial operation of wind-generated electricity in Australia, began in 1987, and the machines – also known as aerogenerators – are linked to the State Energy Commission's local power grid to help offset the use of expensive fuel oil at the commission's diesel power station.

Esperance was chosen because of the reliability of strong winds here; it is the second windiest place in Western Australia – Cape Leeuwin is the windiest but it is already supplied with electricity from conventional, thermal power stations.

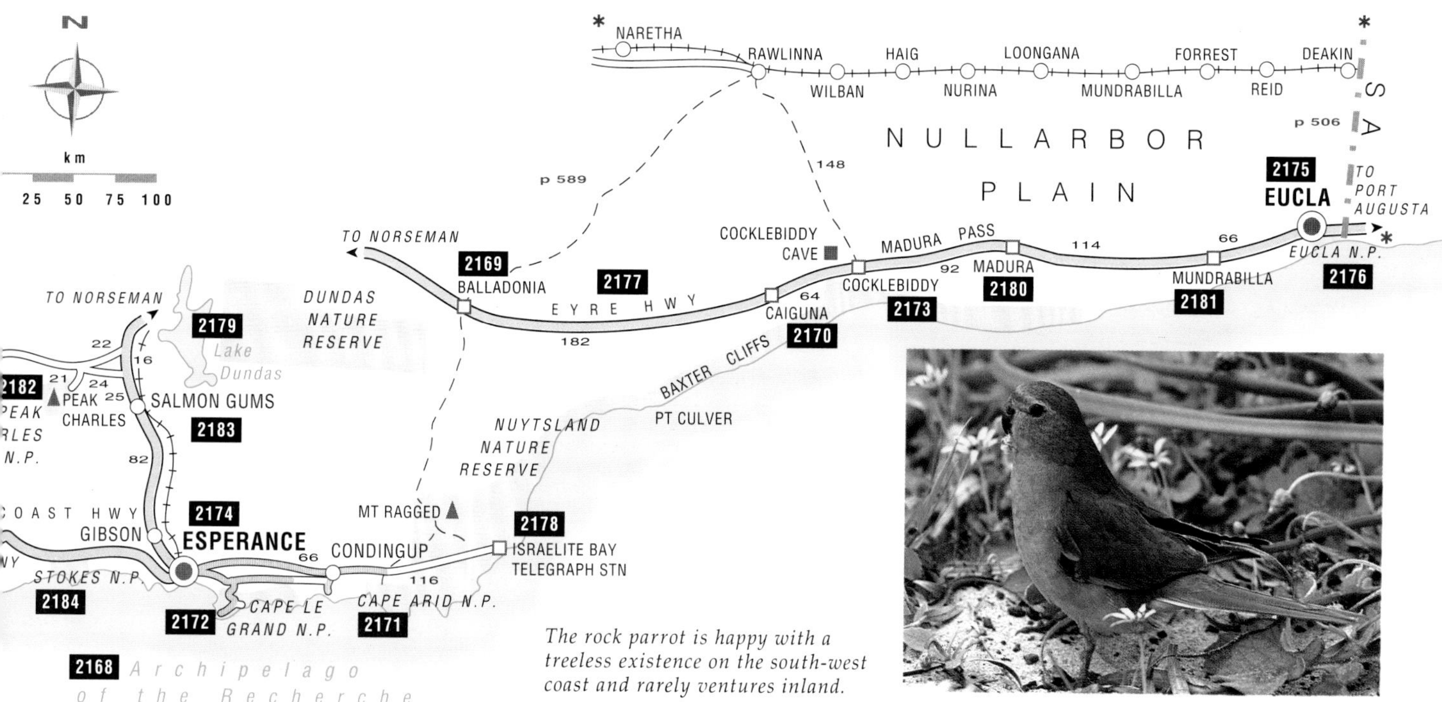

The rock parrot is happy with a treeless existence on the south-west coast and rarely ventures inland.

Near Cocklebiddy, 'sinkholes' provide a vertical entry into the underworld of the Nullarbor's huge limestone slab.

EUCLA ■ 2175

The 'new' settlement of Eucla stands atop an escarpment, overlooking the Roe Plains and the Southern Ocean above and some five kilometres away from the shifting white sands which have all but engulfed the old nineteenth-century buildings. It is the first of the Western Australian roadhouses encountered by the westward-bound traveller.

Quandong trees, whose fruit and the large pitted nut inside were an important part of the Aboriginal diet, grew in profusion just to the east of Eucla in an area now under the sands. Europeans, too, gathered the small, bright red 'native peach' for making into jam and jelly. The first rabbits in Western Australia were released here in 1894 – it is thought that prospectors and travellers assisted the spread of rabbits in this region in the 1890s – and the damage these creatures caused by overgrazing led to the destabilising of the dunes. A solution was sought in a shipment of cats – said to have been caught in the backstreets of Port Adelaide by urchins paid a shilling a head – whose hunting prowess, it was hoped, would bring rabbit numbers under control. The result, of course, was a plague of feral cats.

BUNDA CLIFFS Lookouts on the outskirts of Eucla give breathtaking views along the Bunda Cliffs. Rising sheer from the sea they are between forty and ninety metres high and stretch east from here for approximately 200 kilometres.

EUCLA TELEGRAPH STATION The telegraph line that linked Perth with the other Australian capital cities was built in the 1870s. The stone repeater station at Eucla, the midway point where the lines from east and west met, was built in 1877. Nearby were buildings for the operators and their families, a small community in the desert. There were two teams of telegraphists here, one from Western Australia and one from South Australia and, as each had their own version of the morse code, incoming messages had to be decoded and written out in full before being passed across the table to the other team for recoding and onward transmission. This duplication of work was not dispensed with until Federation in 1901.

In the years since the 1929 abandonment of the station – following the relocation of the telegraph line inland along the transcontinental railway – the empty buildings have gradually been buried as the massive coastal sandhills move inexorably inland. Not far from the ruins is the old jetty used by ships landing men and provisions.

EUCLA NATIONAL PARK ■ 2176

Mallee scrub, heathland and, on the coast, shifting dunes of white sand, characterise this region. From Wilson Bluff, a high limestone cliff which runs east-west across the park, are impressive views of the sheer cliffs of the Great Australian Bight.

EYRE HIGHWAY ■ 2177

To cross the fringe of the Nullarbor by road remains one of the great motoring experiences in Australia, even though it is no longer such a physical challenge because the Eyre Highway, the name given to the road between Norseman in Western Australia and Port Augusta in South Australia, is now not only completely sealed, but is also served by a string of roadhouses along the way. Coastal lookouts on the high cliffs take in the sweeping views along the Great Australian Bight.

The route follows a small part of the line trekked, in four months of unrelenting hardship, by explorer Edward Eyre in 1841. The first motor crossing of Australia was in 1912 when Francis Birtles made the trip between Fremantle and Sydney in a ten-horsepower car, following the rough telegraph-line track, at one stage winching the car from one telegraph pole to the next. Construction of the highway began in 1941 during the Second World War and was spurred on by the possible need to overland troops and equipment. It has been sealed since the late 1970s, and the average crossing time for car travellers is now three days or less.

ISRAELITE BAY TELEGRAPH STATION ■ 2178

Low scrub surrounds the roofless remains of the old Telegraph Station, opened in 1877, which was an essential link in communications between Perth and the rest of the continent. Until the relocation of the line in 1929, Israelite Bay was a small but bustling community, populated mainly by telegraphists and their families. Pioneer pastoralists established sheep runs in the countryside around the nearby Thomas River.

POINT MALCOLM It was here, to the west of Israelite Bay, that explorer Edward Eyre and his Aboriginal companion Wylie, without any food, weary and desperately weak, were able to spend a week rebuilding thei[r] strength feasting on fish, crab, an[d] kangaroo meat. Their horses, too benefited from the grass here, th[e] best they had eaten for months.

LAKE DUNDAS ■ 217[9]

Lake Dundas is a salt lake, surrounded by a parched and desolat[e] environment, and at its most spectacular at sunrise and sunset. When th[e] rains come, waterfowl soon appea[r] to breed on this ephemeral inlan[d] water, among them banded an[d] black-winged stilts. The food chain i[s] perfectly adjusted for the irregula[r] water supply. The rains allow brin[e] shrimp to breed which then becom[e] the stilts' principal sustenance.

There is one heart-tugging sign o[f] former European habitation on a sp[it] of land at the far edge of the lake. A lonely headstone marks the grave o[f] Stanley Arthur Whitehead who die[d] on 8 April 1897, aged seven months.

DUNDAS ROCKS The Dundas Rock[s] are twenty-two kilometres south o[f] Norseman off the Coolgardie–Espe[r]ance Highway and are 500 millio[n] years old. Gold was first discovere[d] on the Dundas goldfield in 1892 an[d] the ghost town of Dundas was th[e] original townsite for the area.

DUNDAS HILLS The Dundas Hills ar[e] the remnants of a vast range of fol[d]ed mountains, parts of which a[re] nearly 3000 million years old a[nd] among the oldest in the world.

MADURA ■ 218[0]

Situated at the bottom of the forme[r]ly notorious Madura Pass is [a] modern motel-service station with [a] camping area which serves the nee[ds] of the motorists on the Eyre Hig[h]way (see entry). In the past, the pa[ss] was considered the most dangero[us] section of the Nullarbor crossi[ng] with its steep cutting descendi[ng] from the low scrub of the Hampt[on] Tableland to the coastal plain belo[w].

Settlement here began wi[th] 'Madura', a small property esta[...]

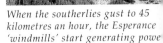

When the southerlies gust to 45 kilometres an hour, the Esperance 'windmills' start generating powe[r]

TRACKS ACROSS THE NULLARBOR

WHEN THE first transcontinental train rolled out of Port Augusta on 23 October 1917, five days after the triumphant meeting in the middle of the Nullarbor Plain of the line stretching from the east with that coming from the west, one man who must have been particularly gratified was King O'Malley, the flamboyant Commonwealth Minister for Home Affairs who, in the years after Federation, had been a vigorous champion of the project. Another who was pleased was Lady Ellison-Macartney, wife of the Governor of South Australia, who penned: 'East is east and west is west, and now the two have met' in a railway worker's autograph book.

In the late nineteenth century, the prospect of an overland railway had been used as an inducement to entice the western colony to the federation table even though the country to be crossed – waterless and largely uninhabited – would generate little or no profitable traffic for the constructing authority, the new Federal Government. But the new government, spurred on by the enthusiastic O'Malley, honoured the promise, and approved construction of the railway in 1911. The first sod was turned at Port Augusta in September 1914 by the Governor-General, Lord Denman, using a nickel-plated shovel, and deposited in a small barrow waiting alongside.

Because there was nothing in the entire 1690 kilometres to be crossed that would aid or support the construction teams, not even a single running stream, this was one of the most ambitious construction projects ever undertaken in the world. From an engineering point of view it presented few problems. By and large the featureless plain was so level that sleepers could almost be laid straight upon it, with very little needed in the way of ballast and support. The main problems were the logistical ones of transporting not only building materials to the centre of the desert, but also the infrastructure required to support the several thousand men and hundreds of working animals involved in the enterprise. There were no sources of water, no roads and certainly no settlements which could provide services and labour. Everything had to be taken with the two crews as they pushed into the desert, and each became a small town, with butcher, baker, bank, post office and hospital, all in railway cars, moving forward as the line pushed out. The men had to shift camp every two weeks or so to keep up near the work and provisions were sent out weekly from Port Ausgusta and Kalgoorlie in railway cars which became known as the 'Tea and Sugar Train'.

Originally the 2 432 000 sleepers in the line were timber, all cut from Western Australian jarrah. However, because they were subject to white ant and heat damage they had to be replaced every ten years. They have now given way to concrete sleepers that are expected to last five times as long.

Tiny isolated communities of railway maintenance workers are still scattered along the line. Many of the settlements are no more than a line of three or four houses set back from the rails. They have no shop, post office or bank, but still rely on the legendary 'Tea and Sugar' lifeline. It makes a weekly trip, starting from Port Augusta and takes three days to crawl across the plain, stopping at every station, siding and camp. Most eagerly awaited is the railway car which has been converted into a single-aisle supermarket, but the train also hauls tankers of fresh water and delivers goods ordered by phone or mail as well as general freight. Dust-caked workers push wheelbarrows loaded with provisions back to camp and rabbit-shooters in battered cars make round trips of a hundred or more kilometres to await the train. Items such as meat are pre-ordered and delivered frozen, but in the days before refrigerated vans, livestock carried in the butcher's van was slaughtered on the spot. In the old days, the train also had a medical van and a theatrette van. A fortnightly 'pay' van doubles as the bank and local post office. □

The 'Tea and Sugar' brings all the amenities of a small town to the sidings strung sparsely along an isolated, transcontinental thread.

ished in the 1870s near a hot spring, where horses were bred for the Indian Army and shipped out from the coast nearby. The old homestead stands alone a few kilometres from the motel complex.

MUNDRABILLA ■ 2181

The first European settlement in this region took place at Mundrabilla Homestead, established by William and Thomas Kennedy in the early 1870s. The motel complex beside the Eyre Highway was named after the historic homestead.

Scattered across this region are the remains of a huge meteorite which came down many thousands of years ago during the Ice Age. Fragments cover some sixty kilometres, making this one of the largest meteorite sites in the world.

PEAK CHARLES NATIONAL PARK ■ 2182

Protected here is an untouched area of dry woodlands, mallee-covered sandplain and salt-lake vegetation. The park takes its name from its highest peak, the ancient granite outcrop of Peak Charles (650 metres). Its precipitous cliffs are broken into numerous boulder-strewn shelves. Forty million years ago, when sea levels were much higher than this, Peak Charles and nearby Peak Eleanora (500 metres) were islands, and wave-cut platforms can be seen on their upper slopes. There are sweeping views of the sandplains and salt-lake systems from the tops.

SALMON GUMS ■ 2183

A cluster of buildings grew up here to service the needs of prospectors heading north to the Coolgardie goldfields. After the First World War it was proposed that the small settlement become the centre of the Mallee Region Farm Scheme, an ambitious agricultural project which aimed to turn the area into a wheat-growing district, and an advertising campaign was launched to attract settlers from interstate and overseas. Many of the selectors who took up their lots had little farming experience and this, combined with the economic depression of the 1930s, led to the collapse and abandonment of the scheme. A revival occurred in the 1950s and 1960s following the introduction to the soil of trace elements, the use of more modern methods of farming and the increase in area of individual farm units to a viable size.

SALMON GUMS RESEARCH STATION Established in 1926 to investigate the cereal-growing potential of the area, work at the station was later instrumental in the establishment and maintenance of legume pastures on the surrounding plains in the 1940s and 1950s.

STOKES NATIONAL PARK ■ 2184

A wide variety of waterbirds live in the low forests and wetlands of Stokes Inlet which are protected within this park. The calm waters here offer safe swimming, fishing and windsurfing, and are overlooked by a walking track which runs along the escarpment above.

'MORI' Roofless ruins are the only remains of this homestead, which dates from 1873.

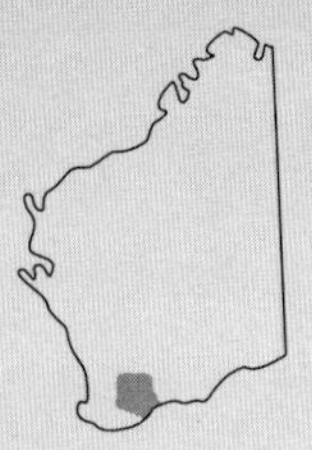

Katanning & Gnowangerup

Among the first Europeans to tread the endless plains now covered by fields of wheat were cutters seeking the aromatic timbers of the sandalwood tree. The lush grasslands in the north that beckoned pastoral pioneers were later trekked by hopeful prospectors from the southern coast headed for the goldfields.

BREMER BAY ■ 2185

Isolated Bremer Bay township is one of the two main access points for conventional vehicles into the huge Fitzgerald River National Park (see entry), the other is Hopetoun. It offers both still water and ocean-beach fishing – a small team of professional tuna fishermen operate from here – and the sheltered water of Wellstead Estuary is ideal for all types of watersports.

The bay is assumed to have been named by the Surveyor-General, John Septimus Roe in honour of Sir Gordon Bremer, captain of the HMS *Tamar*, after his visit to the region in 1831. The estuary is named for the Wellstead family who settled in the area in the 1850s and built Quaalap Homestead, now within the national park. The township grew up around the Old Telegraph Station, built at the mouth of the Wellstead Estuary in the 1870s.

CORRIGIN ■ 2186

The rolling wheat fields which surround Corrigin are the district's main industry, although sheep farming is also important. Gorge Rock, some twenty kilometres south-east of the town, is one of the few features to rise above the plains. The gorge has been dammed to form a large swimming area which was used before the building of an Olympic swimming pool in town. *Population 720*

DUMBLEYUNG ■ 2187

Near the shores of Lake Dumbleyung (see entry) is the town which was originally the railhead for the farming region to the east. Wheat, barley, oats, sheep and cattle are the main industries of the district.

The town is the starting point for the Dumbleyung Historic Schools Trail, four novel scenic drives which trace the development of schools in the district. The introduction of the school bus led to the disappearance of the one-teacher schools here which catered for children far from town centres. The chores that would be waiting no matter how late a child returned – sheep and cattle to be yarded and cows to be milked – were a compelling reason for wasting no time during school hours. As one former pupil recalled: 'We took great pride in that little country school of ours, and although we complained at times of the severity of the teacher we honoured him living and we honoured him dead'.

'WHEATFIELD' One of the first homsteads in the district, 'Wheatfield' dates from the 1870s and is built of locally produced mud bricks with a timber log frame.

The royal hakea's generous leaves are a cabbage-burst of lushness in the Fitzgerald River National Park.

FITZGERALD RIVER NATIONAL PARK ■ 2188

An extraordinarily high and varied number of plant species – nearly 1800, or about twenty per cent of the total number found in Western Australia – occur here. Some eighty of these, such as the graceful weeping gum, the prickly frilled royal hakea and the pink and delicate quaalup bell are found nowhere else. The park is large enough to provide a refuge for wildlife fast becoming rare or endangered in other parts.

In 1978 the park was designated a World Biosphere Reserve – this means it is regarded as a benchmark against which environmental change can be measured.

'QUAALUP' Within the park is Quaalup Homestead, with the small stone cottage built in 1858 by early settler John Wellstead as its core. The cottage is furnished with antiques, and memorabilia, and at night is lit by gas and oil lamps.

GNOWANGERUP ■ 2189

Gnowangerup is the centre of a major sheep-producing area where several important merino studs are located. Its name comes from an Aboriginal word thought to mean 'the place where the mallee hen made her nest', but at one time the townsfolk wished to change it because they felt there were too many names in the area ending in 'up' (meaning 'meeting place', usually a permanent water source – in this case a natural mineral spring), but officialdom won the day and 'Gnowangerup' stayed.

The first European to report on this area was the Surveyor-General, John Septimus Roe, who passed through here in 1835. In the late 1880s the meadows around the natural springs were grazed by horses used in the sandalwood trade. The township dates from the early 1900s, following the coming of the railway and the taking up of farmlands in the area. Soldier-settlement schemes in the area after both World Wars accelerated its growth. *Population 760*

HYDEN ■ 2190

European pioneers in this semi-arid area were searching for sandalwood. Settlement around Hyden dates from the early 1920s and today the town is the centre of a wheat-growing district. Nearby are a number of granite outcrops including the spectacular Wave Rock (see entry).

JILAKIN ROCK ■ 2191

The smooth granite rock which rises above the scrub-covered sandplain is the subject of an Aboriginal legend because of the stand of tall jarrah trees which grow at its base. Leftovers from an ancient forest, these trees are about 150 kilometres east of the main jarrah belt, but a stretch of fertile soil and the run-off from the rock has enabled them to persist.

The local Aboriginal legend tells of the meeting of two groups at the base of the rock. The band from the west, as a sign of friendship, placed their spears upon the ground and from these grew the trees.

KATANNING ■ 2192

Katanning, in the centre of a merino stud area, is one of the largest stock-selling centres in Western Australia. It is also, following the arrival of a Malay Muslim community in the early 1970s, one of Australia's most multicultural rural towns. The town had the first street lights in Western Australia, powered by that state's first machine-generated electricity. It also had the first free lending library in Western Australia, and one of the first inland swimming pools.

In the days before European settlement the natural springs here made it a regular meeting place for the Aborigines of the area and one of the many versions of the origin of the town name has it that 'Katanning' derives from an Aboriginal word meaning 'place to meet'. European exploration of the district dates from 1835 when James Stirling, the Governor, and John Septimus Roe, the Surveyor-General, travelled the country between Perth and Albany. Roe noted the 'good dark loam and grass as high as our knees'. In the 1840s, sheep were driven south into these grasslands and in the early 1850s the first grants were taken up. *Population 4140*

ROLLER FLOUR MILL Built in 1891 this mill was the site of the first electricity generating unit in Western Australia; it powered the mill as well as lighting Katanning's streets.

FESTIVALS Arts & Crafts Show, November; Caboodle Street Carnival, December.

KUKERIN ■ 2193

The small wheatbelt town of Kukerin is a major grain delivery centre fo

Freshwater crayfish, farmed in pond near Katanning, bring good prices from city restaurants.

the surrounding district and is the starting point for the Wheatbelt Wildflower Drive which takes in Tarin Rock Nature Reserve (see entry). The Vintage Fair in October attracts more than one hundred working farm machines, including forty vintage tractors dating from as far back as 1915.

LAKE DUMBLEYUNG ■ 2194

When full, salty Lake Dumbleyung is the largest natural lake in Western Australia. It is best-known as the place where Donald Campbell set the world water speed record in his boat *Bluebell* in 1964. A plaque on the rise local people call Pussy Cat Hill, overlooking the lake, honours Campbell's achievement. The lake is a sanctuary for birdlife and is a popular venue for watersports.

LAKE GRACE ■ 2195

This area was first explored in 1848 by John Septimus Roe, first Surveyor-General of Western Australia. The Inland Mission building, established in 1926 by John Flynn, is the last still operating in Western Australia.

The town stands to the east of the shallow salt lake from which it takes its name, which in turn was named in 1910 by District Surveyor Marshall Fox after Mrs Brockman – formerly Grace Bussell (see *Bunbury & Busselton). Population 600*

HOLLANDS TRACK This 400-kilometre track, which ran from Broomehill, south of Katanning, north-east to Coolgardie, follows the line laid down in 1893 by the enterprising prospector John Holland. Determined to find the fastest possible route to the goldfields he enlisted the aid of a small local party and cut this track which soon became an important route to goldfields.

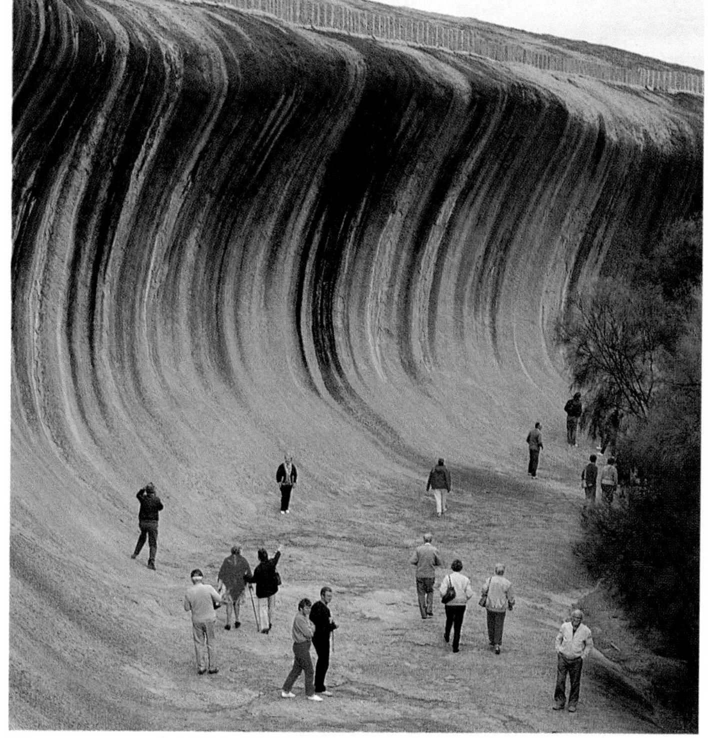

The awesome still life of Wave Rock is marred only by the man-made intrusion of the concrete reservoir wall behind the tip of the 'wave'.

TARIN ROCK NATURE RESERVE ■ 2196

To the Aborigines this type of undulating sandy country covered with low shrubby heath was known as 'kwongan'. It may not impress at first glance, but in fact it contains a fantastically rich and diversified range of plant species, all adapted to an environment where nutrients and rainfall are low.

Needle-thin leaves reduce to the minimum the surface area through which water can be lost. Some plants have long tap roots which probe deep for moisture, others sit on dense mats of nutrient gathering roots or have root nodules to convert hydrogen from the air into nutrients.

In the 1950s, the introduction of superphosphate fertiliser made agriculture possible on the sandplains, and vast tracts were cleared for wheat growing. The few natural areas that remain are preserved in reserves such as Tarin Rock.

WAVE ROCK ■ 2197

Fifteen metres high, and looking for all the world like a wave frozen just before it breaks, Wave Rock, near Hyden, is actually the overhanging north wall of Hyden Rock, an isolated granite hill, or 'inselberg'. The concave wave-like effect is the result of 3000 million years of weathering of the lower slopes. The bands of colour which streak its face – caused by minerals washed down the rock and deepened by the dark-coloured algae which grows upon them – heighten its resemblance to a wave.

Snaking across the top of the rock, above the lip of the 'wave', is a sixty-centimetre-high retaining wall built in the early 1950s to channel rainwater run-off into a reservoir which supplies the town of Hyden.

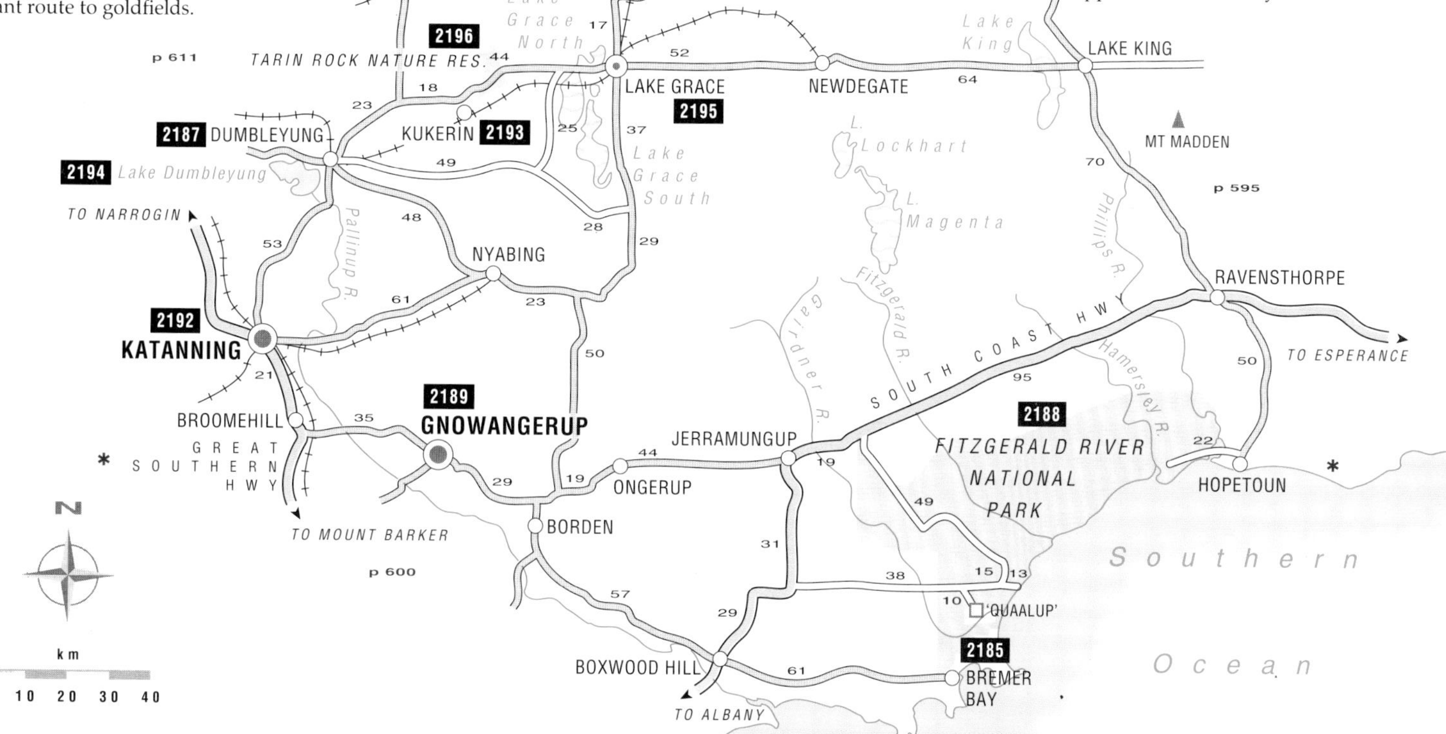

Albany & Mount Barker

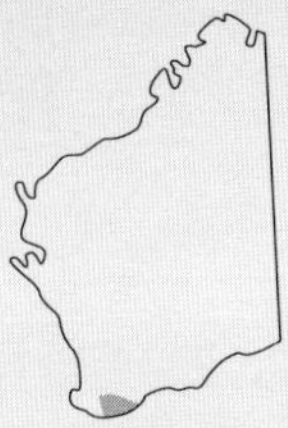

The leviathans of the deep have returned to waters off this southern coast where once they were hunted nearly to extinction. This is where the first European Western Australians settled before exploring the inland where they discovered wildflowers the equal of those they had left behind.

The Cheynes IV *goes whaling no more having literally turned its back on the sea in its role as an industrial artefact at the Albany Whaling Museum.*

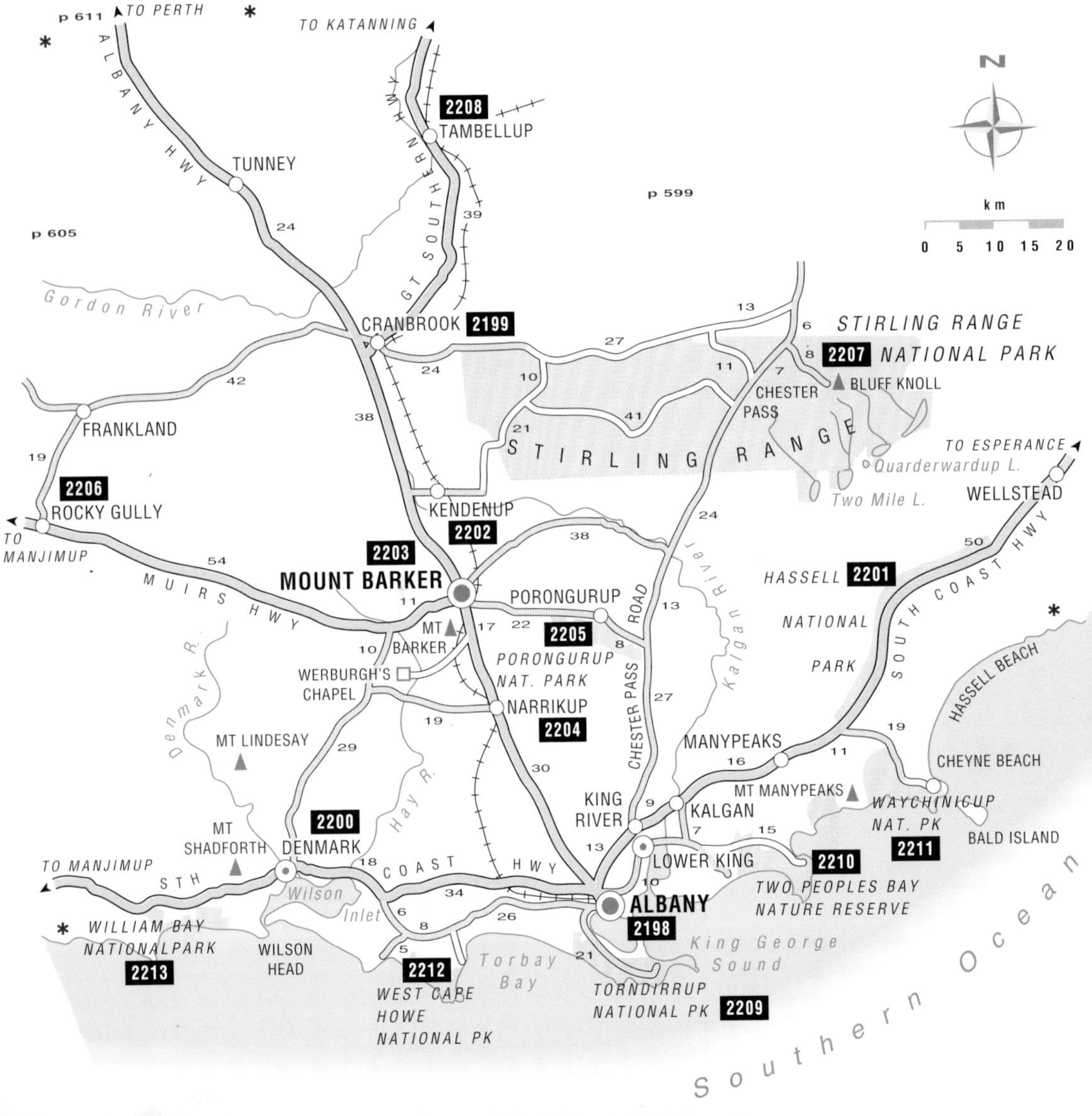

p 611 TO PERTH
TO KATANNING
p 599
p 605
ALBANY HWY
GT SOUTHERN HWY
2208 TAMBELLUP
TUNNEY
CRANBROOK 2199
Gordon River
STIRLING RANGE
2207 NATIONAL PARK
BLUFF KNOLL
CHESTER PASS
STIRLING RANGE
Quarderwardup L.
Two Mile L.
TO ESPERANCE
WELLSTEAD
FRANKLAND
2206 ROCKY GULLY
TO MANJIMUP
MUIRS HWY
KENDENUP 2202
2203 MOUNT BARKER
PORONGURUP
2205 PORONGURUP NAT. PARK
MT BARKER
WERBURGH'S CHAPEL
NARRIKUP 2204
HASSELL 2201 NATIONAL PARK
SOUTH COAST HWY
HASSELL BEACH
Kalgan River
CHESTER PASS ROAD
Denmark R.
MT LINDESAY
Hay R.
MANYPEAKS
MT MANYPEAKS
CHEYNE BEACH
WAYCHINICUP NAT. PK 2211
BALD ISLAND
KING RIVER
KALGAN
LOWER KING
2210 TWO PEOPLES BAY NATURE RESERVE
MT SHADFORTH
2200 DENMARK
TO MANJIMUP
STH COAST HWY
Wilson Inlet
ALBANY 2198
WILLIAM BAY NATIONAL PARK 2213
WILSON HEAD
2212 WEST CAPE HOWE NATIONAL PK
Torbay Bay
King George Sound
TORNDIRRUP NATIONAL PK 2209
Southern Ocean
N
km
0 5 10 15 20

ALBANY ■ 2198

Albany lies on Princess Royal Harbour, King George Sound and for a long time was the only port of call in Western Australia for mail steamers. Towards the turn of the century, as Fremantle flourished (see *Rockingham & Fremantle*), so Albany declined but its fine natural harbour and its strategic position made it valuable in the early days of colonisation.

The very first recorded European sighting of this southern shore was in late 1627 by the crew of the Dutch ship *Gulden Zeepaard,* accidentally separated from a convoy bound for Djarkarta. Fierce westerlies drove the ship as far as Ceduna. In September 1791, Captain George Vancouver sailed the new sloop, HMS *Discovery*, into sheltered water and reported 'one very excellent port which I have honoured with the name of King George the Third's Sound'. Then in December 1801, Matthew Flinders came to King George Sound in HMS *Investigator* on his voyage round Australia. This was probably the first ship to enter Princess Royal Harbour.

On Christmas Day, 1826, Major Edmund Lockyer arrived in King George Sound in the brig *Amity* with a detachment of soldiers, twenty-three prisoners and a quantity of sheep and pigs to claim the western part of the continent. The British flag was raised on 21 January 1827 and the site was called Fredericks Town in honour of the Duke of York and Albany but by the early 1830s everyone was calling it Albany.

Whalers soon took advantage of Albany's position and ships came from the USA, France and the eastern colonies to pursue the sperm whales. Cheynes Beach Whaling Co. became the town's leading industry and at one time killed up to 850 whales a season. It was Australia's last whaling station and finally closed in 1978. In a remarkably short time, whales have returned to calve in the waters off the Rainbow Coast. The main species sighted from the cliffs is the southern right whale.

Albany's industries include meat processing, fish trawling and processing, sawmilling, woollen milling and other manufacturing interests. The town is still an important business centre and port for the southern region and has a thriving tourist trade. *Population 18 820*

HORDERN MONUMENT The tall, red granite monument that stands at the top of York Street is a tribute to Anthony Hordern, the Sydney businessman who saw the potential for expanded settlement and raised the finance for the Great Southern Railway linking Albany with Beverley in the north. He went to London to set up the West Australian Land Company so that the line could be built by private enterprise sooner than the government could afford to do it. But he died before he could see his plans realised and is buried in the Pioneer Cemetery in Albany.

THE OLD JAIL A convict hiring depot existed on the site of the old jail up until 1868 when convict transportation ceased. The jail was built in 1872 and was used as a lock-up until the 1930s when the historic building became a storehouse. It was later converted to a museum.

ST JOHN'S ANGLICAN CHURCH This church, built in the 1840s and consecrated in 1848, is Western Australia's oldest consecrated church. It is a dignified stone building with notable stained-glass windows.

THE OLD FARM, STRAWBERRY HILL The original cottage on Strawberry Hill was built in 1831 for a visit to Albany by the new Governor of the Swan River colony, James Stirling. The present two-storey brick building, called the 'Old Farm', dates from the 1830s shortly after the Government Resident, Sir Richard Spencer, bought the property. In 1889 Francis Bird, an architect, bought the house and restored it. After more changes of fortune it passed safely into the hands of the National Trust in 1963.

FESTIVALS Strawberry Fair, March.

CRANBROOK ■ 2199

Cranbrook is a sheep and wheat town near the western foothills of the Stirling Range. It was initially a watering point on the Great Southern Railway and was named after Cranbrook in England. The townsite was declared in 1899. One of the earlier exports was sandalwood for Chinese temples but now the area has a reputation for vineyards, fine wool, and wildflowers. Botanists have recorded more than 500 flowering species in the district.

FESTIVALS Wildflower Show, September–October.

Plants descended from some of the original seeds and cuttings survive at Albany's 160-year-old Old Farm.

The rocky promontories above Jimmy Newhills Harbour, near Albany, are ideal vantage points for whale watchers.

DENMARK ■ 2200

Thomas Braidwood Wilson called the river after which this town takes its name, for a navy surgeon friend named Denmark. Development was slow because the density of the district's forest inhibited land clearing for agriculture. The settlement was not properly established until a mill was built in 1895 to process karri trees. Soon the timber was exported for paving blocks, telegraph poles, railway sleepers and wharf piles to places as far apart as Africa, Europe, China and South America.

Denmark is a few kilometres east of Mount Shadforth overlooking the Denmark River. A Group Settlement Scheme in 1922, designed to attract migrants to rural areas and to extend land settlement, boosted the town's economy. The local farmers produce beef and pork and grow potatoes and fruit but the most recent growth industry has been tourism with the town promoting itself as a quiet fishing resort. *Population 1590*

FESTIVALS Denmark Summer Arts Festival, January.

HASSELL NATIONAL PARK ■ 2201

Hassell National Park is a roadside reserve extending for 34 kilometres and a width 150 metres along the main Albany–Bremer Bay road. Its 1281 hectares are dense with wildflowers in the spring and early summer. Reptiles, especially snakes, are often seen and the tall flowering shrubs attract many birds including the New Holland, white-necked and singing honeyeaters.

KENDENUP ■ 2202

George Cheyne was the first European to take up land in this area in 1831. Then John Hassell purchased some grazing land from him and established a sheep farm which won acclaim for the quality of its wool. Kendenup was the site of Western Australia's first goldmine in 1874 but the yield never amounted to a significant quantity.

After the First World War, John de Garis came from Victoria to try to establish a 'Mildura of the West', based on his success with Sunraysia dried fruit (see *Mildura & Wentworth*) but his attempt to turn 20 000 hectares into orchards and vegetable farms was unsuccessful. Marketing and other problems plunged de Garis deeply into debt and he committed suicide.

Some farmers survived the crash and in the mid-1920s began to plant apples, pears and stone fruits. In the period before the Second World War, the orchards flourished and fruit was exported overseas. By the late 1950s, agriculture was encroaching on the orchards and the fruit industry has since steadily declined. Peas are now one of the area's best cash crops.

MOUNT BARKER ■ 2203

Like Mount Barker in South Australia (see *Murray Bridge & Mount Barker*), the mountain near this town was named in 1829 for Captain Collet Barker who was then the last military commandant at King George Sound (Albany). Two years later he discovered the site for Adelaide but his exploring days came to an untimely end when he disappeared in the sandhills at the mouth of the Murray River.

Mount Barker, once a staging post on the Perth–Albany road, is now a market town and the main administrative and general service centre for the Shire of Plantagenet. The land was settled when people from Albany came looking for new sheep pastures. They planted apple and pear trees and later the district between Mount Barker and Kendenup (see entry) became known for its orchards. Wool and apples are still important to the region's economy, together with fat lambs and beef cattle. There is also a local fresh and dried wildflower industry and a cheese factory.

Viticulture is the region's newest and most promising agricultural activity, with vineyards producing popular malbec, shiraz, cabernet sauvignon and riesling table wines. *Population 1520*

THE OLD POLICE STATION The Mount Barker police station was built by convict labour in 1868 of ironstone blocks cemented with mud with a split-shingled roof of jarrah wood which is now protected by corrugated iron. It did multiple duty as the post office and stables for stagecoach horses and was later the telegraph station as well. The building is now a district museum.

MOUNT BARKER LOOKOUT Mount Barker lookout, a short drive from the town, has a fine view from the top. It is a 360-degree panorama that takes in the Porongurup and Stirling ranges and looks out across Kendenup and Cranbrook to the north and westwards across the Hay River.

ST WERBURGH'S ANGLICAN CHAPEL St Werburgh's Chapel, built in 1872–73 on the St Werburgh Estate, has an ornamental chancel screen and altar rail of wrought iron, hand-beaten on the property. The chapel was dedicated in 1874 by the Right Reverend Matthew Hale, Bishop of Perth and services are still held there once every three months. Early settlers and members of the Egerton-Warburton family are buried in the cemetery adjoining the chapel grounds.

FESTIVALS Summer Wine Festival, mid-January.

NARRIKUP ■ 2204

This small village, south of Mount Barker, consists of half a dozen houses, a community hall and a store which dates back to 1922. Narrikup probably means 'place of the peat

In contrast to the low profiles of most Australian ranges, the Stirling Range – its eastern edge protected in a park – has some distinctively craggy peaks.

swamps'. It is also in the Plantagenet District but there is no written explanation of why Captain James Stirling chose this as the region's name in 1831, a year after George IV died. The British monarch was wont to boast of his Plantagenet blood and Stirling may have just followed the practice of naming places after royalty and their connections. Or he may have remembered the Plantagenet army's yellow broom insignia. The native broom bush grows profusely around Narrikup, Mount Barker, Kendenup and Rocky Gully.

PORONGURUP NATIONAL PARK ■ 2205

The Porongurup Range, formed from granite more than 1100 million years ago, is 12 kilometres long and 670 metres at its highest point. Slow weathering has exposed the peaks and the names of many of the rocky outcrops match their stark outlines – Castle Rock, Sheeps Head, Devils Slide and Balancing Rock.

Fossil pollen, found in the southwest, indicates an earlier, wetter era when karri forest would have been widespread. It now survives on the upper slopes of this 2400-hectare park where the heavy rainfall and deep red 'karri loam' support trees up to sixty metres high.

Porongurup is a colourful place – brilliant with wildflowers in the spring and summer months. Brightly plumed birds dart among the foliage all year round, including scarlet and yellow robins, western rosellas and purple-crowned lorikeets.

ROCKY GULLY ■ 2206

Rocky Gully is a small hamlet in the Plantagenet District, west of Mount Barker on the Muir Highway. The surrounding area was used for rough grazing from 1861 until land was taken up by a settler who came from South Australia seeking gold.

During the 1930s, when jobs were scarce, the district was surveyed for subdivision into dairy and mixed farms and unemployed men were paid a low wage to live at nine base camps and handclear the forest. Living conditions were poor, the work was impossibly hard and the scheme failed. The next major effort at land cultivation was made by the War Service Land Settlement Scheme in 1949 but it was not very successful either, largely because the soil was deficient in certain minerals. These have since been added, so that the area now produces quality wool and meat and oats, barley and lupins.

STIRLING RANGE NATIONAL PARK ■ 2207

The Stirling Range National Park encompasses an area of some 115 740 hectares with a wide diversity of native flora (see box). The mountains were first recorded by Matthew Flinders in 1802 and were named in 1835 by the Surveyor-General John Roe after Captain James Stirling, the first governor of Western Australia.

The range rises abruptly from the flat plain and runs for sixty-five kilometres from east to west. Bluff Knoll rises to 1073 metres above sea level and is the highest peak in the southwest region.

TAMBELLUP ■ 2208

Tambellup, beside the Gordon River, was declared a town in 1899. One of the earliest settlers in the district was William Clark who camped at what was then 'Slab Hut Gully', in 1840 and grazed sheep on land he noted as 'pastoral country comprised of gentle hills sloping into valleys'.

In 1870 Josiah Norrish arrived to fell the district's aromatic sandalwood trees which were in great demand by the Chinese for incense and carved ornaments. He established a family homestead that is still standing today.

TORNDIRRUP NATIONAL PARK ■ 2209

Torndirrup National Park is an area of 3906 hectares stretching across the southern section of Princess Royal Harbour. Windswept coastal heathlands, carpeted with wildflowers in spring, merge into steep sandy slopes and dunes, and massive granite outcrops and sheer cliffs are moulded into a dramatic landscape. The spectacular coastal rock formations of the Gap, Natural Bridge, the Blowholes and Peak Head resist the boisterous ocean swells.

The rare Albany woollybush has been found in the park and the dibbler, a marsupial feared to be extinct but rediscovered in 1967, was sighted in 1987. Whales and seals can be spotted from the cliffs.

TWO PEOPLES BAY NATURE RESERVE ■ 2210

This 4639-hectare reserve is also the last known natural habitat of a rediscovered endangered animal – the noisy scrub-bird. John Gilbert, an associate of British naturalist John Gould, likened its exceptionally raucous call to 'a shrill whistle blown in a small room'. The bird was first noticed by Europeans in 1842, in the jarrah forest at the foot of the Darling Scarp near Perth, and was last heard at Torbay in 1889 when it apparently disappeared. Seventy-two years later, noisy scrub-birds were found in the Two Peoples Bay area, a discovery so important that a proposed townsite was moved to another place. Breeding pairs have been transferred to the reserve at Mount Manypeaks and to Walpole-Nornalup National Park in attempts to establish new colonies for the species' survival. The park is managed largely as a wildlife sanctuary.

AN ANNUAL FLOWER SHOW BECOMES AN INDUSTRY

Australia's isolation from the rest of the world for tens of millions of years has had a profound effect on the development of its plants and animals. The uniqueness of mammals which lay eggs and have pouches is shared by many of the native plants. In Western Australia alone it is believed there are at least 8000 flowering species ranging from giant hardwood trees to tiny underground orchids. The proteas and ericas of South Africa's cape region are most like plants found here and share the formative conditions of an ancient land surface leached of major plant nutrients.

The parks of the south-west are special places, often set aside to preserve a particularly rare native plant or animal – the dibbler in Torndirrup National Park, the noisy scrub bird in Two Peoples Bay Nature Reserve, the Albany pitcher plant in West Cape Howe National Park (see entries).

The jagged peaks of the Stirling Range are 'ecological' islands with a climate and conditions very different from the surrounding lowlands and a rich diversity of plants. This park can justly claim to be one of the most outstanding botanic environments in the world and has more than a thousand species of which about sixty are thought to be endemic. Blooms may be seen at almost any time but the best wildflower show is between August and November.

On the slopes there are fuchsia grevillea and the scarlet-flowered *Grevillea wilsonii*, pink feather flower, lemon scented myrtle and rose coneflower shrubs (*Isopogon formosus*) with pale flower heads six centimetres wide. Higher up larger coneflowers (*Isopogon latifolius*) have wider, brighter pink blooms. At least six species of dryandra have been recorded and two of them (*Dryandra foliata* and *Dryandra concinna*) have not yet been seen outside the park. Then there are red-ink sundews and other varieties of sundews, lying in wait for insect prey, and over fifty orchid species – red spider, dwarf spider, cowslip, butterfly and others – and weirdly shaped kangaroo and cat's paws. Another common group is the beautiful and unusual Darwinias or mountain bells – several exclusive to this region. *Darwinia collina*, for example, grows only on Bluff Knoll. At least eighteen species of banksia inhabit these mountains and so far as anyone knows the Stirling Range banksia (*Banksia solandri*) grows nowhere else. It was named for Daniel Solander, the Swedish botanist who sailed with Joseph Banks on Captain Cook's *Endeavour*. Banksias are showy blooms much beloved by honeyeaters. Because of the flowers, Stirling Range National Park is also full of birds and insects. During the day the scarlet banksia (*Banksia coccinea*) attracts many of the park's fourteen species of honeyeaters and when the sun goes down, the nocturnal honey possum moves in to feed.

All kangaroo paw species, including the regal red and green, are cultivated enthusiastically as a cut-flower crop.

Wildflowers have been doing their bit for the Western Australian economy for quite some time. Tourist promoters have long recognised the potential of trips in the appropriate season to areas where the plants perform their show. More recently there has been increasing interest in commercial wildflower horticulture in several parts of the country. Western Australia leads the field and some failed wheat farms have been converted to wildflower plantations. The soil balance and climate are most important and research is being done into successful growth conditions for some of the showier species which include waratahs, banksias and dryandras. Glasshouse cultivation is also being investigated and Australia is developing a native cut-flower industry which could become a major export earner. □

The attractions of the west's native wildflowers are not restricted to small annuals that carpet paddocks in spring; many flowering shrubs – including (left to right) the cream-flowered riceflower, the purple calytrix, the feather flower and the scarlet banksia – lend themselves to cultivation.

WAYCHINICUP NATIONAL PARK ■ 2211

The partially declared Waychinicup National Park combines two new areas of national park in the Waychinicup area with the existing Mount Manypeaks and Arpenteur nature reserves. The next stage will extend the park's boundaries from the coast, inland across the trough of the main Waychinicup River valley up to the South Coast Highway – Cheyne Road Nature Reserve will also be included in this stage.

When all the various pieces of the park are amalgamated formally, Waychinicup will encompass around 14 000 hectares of country which includes unusual granite rock formations, wildflowers equal in diversity to those found in the larger Stirling Range National Park (see entry) and some of the most varied coastal heath in Western Australia.

WEST CAPE HOWE NATIONAL PARK ■ 2212

West Cape Howe has a superb coastline running from Forsyth Bluff, south of Cosy Corner, to Lowlands Beach. The park of the same name fringes a wild and untouched environment where a great variety of plants grow undisturbed. Among them is the unusual, insect-eating Albany pitcher plant. The park is one of the newest in the region and contains patches of karri forest set back from the granite and limestone cliffs.

WILLIAM BAY NATIONAL PARK ■ 2213

This park protects 1867 hectares of coastline and forest between Walpole and Denmark. A stretch of boulders and rocky shelves extends from Greens Pool to Madfish Bay and creates a reef which tempers the force of the relentless waves.

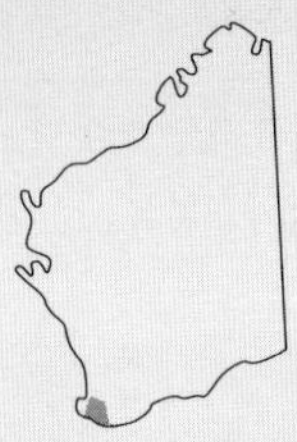

Manjimup & Bridgetown

Tall, majestic trees with uncharacteristically pretty names – marri and karri, jarrah and wandoo, tuart and tingle – dominate here. Though these are logged for their timber, stands of the giants are protected in several national parks.

BIBBULMUN WALKING TRACK ■ 2214

The Bibbulmun Track is a long-distance walk of some 650 kilometres from Kalamunda on the outskirts of Perth to Walpole in the south-west, through land once inhabited by the Bibbulmun Aboriginal people. For most of the way it follows old forestry roads and railway grades and winds through reserves of huge trees. This is Waugal's place, the creative spirit-serpent of the Bibbulmun people, and the way is marked with yellow metal triangles painted with stylised representations of this important figure of the Dreamtime.

BLACKWOOD RIVER ■ 2215

The Blackwood River is the longest river in this part of Western Australia. It winds over 290 kilometres through protected forests and fertile farmlands from its headwaters in the wheatbelt to the ocean at Augusta. This waterway is the venue for the Blackwood Classic Boat Race and canoeing is possible from above Bridgetown all the way to Augusta.

BOYUP BROOK ■ 2216

Names ending in 'up' are common in Western Australia's south-west. It is of Aboriginal origin, meaning 'place of' and may also suggest a 'watering-place' because the 'up' locations are so often on or near springs or ponds. The area's Aborigines named places with good food and water supplies and the first European settlers adopted some of these names.

Boyup Brook, the 'place of much smoke' or 'place of big stones', near the junction of Boyup Brook and the Blackwood River, is surrounded by neat farm houses, paddocks and tall forests. The first settlement was in 1854 but the town proper began in 1900 when the school and teacher's house were built. Boyup Brook is now a market centre for the surrounding rural district. *Population 590*

BRIDGETOWN ■ 2217

When John Blechynden was guided by the local Aborigines to pasture free from poison bush in 1857, he passed through timbered hills to the site of Bridgetown. The settlement, first known by its Aboriginal name 'Geejelup', later became Bridgetown because of the bridge and the ship, *Bridgetown*, the first ship to call at Bunbury to collect wool from the district. *Population 2020*

D'ENTRECASTEAUX NATIONAL PARK ■ 2218

D'Entrecasteaux National Park preserves isolated cliffs and beaches, sand dunes, coastal heath and swampland in an area of 114 000 hectares which stretches from Black Point near Augusta to Long Point, west of Walpole.

The Warren, Donnelly and Shannon are three of the six major rivers and streams that pass through the park to their ocean exits along its coastline. The annual average rainfall is among the highest in Western Australia and jarrah, bullich, yate and peppermint trees grow in some of the more sheltered places.

GREENBUSHES ■ 2219

Greenbushes gets its name from the distinctive green bushes that grow beside the highway. Teamsters and travellers called the place 'the green bushes well'. The town sprang up after tin was discovered in 1888. By the turn of the century, Greenbushes was a thriving mining town with jarrah wood houses instead of the usual tents and shanties.

Australia produces a substantial amount of tantalum, a co-product of tin used in electronic components and corrosion-resistant alloys and much of it comes from Greenbushes. In 1983 the mines began to produce lithium, the lightest of all metals.

MANJIMUP ■ 2220

In 1856, Thomas Muir set up the first timber camp in Manjimup – the 'place of edible bulrush root' The Giblett family moved into the district in the early 1860s and the Giblett sons eventually built up properties around Manjimup. The newcomers marvelled at the beauty of the jarrah and karri forests and recognised their potential as a cash resource. Back then timber-getters called both trees 'mahogany' and did not use the attractive Aboriginal names until the late 1860s. The timber made its way overseas and wooden blocks (see Nannup) from the local forests paved some of the streets of London.

In the late 1960s, despite strong opposition from environmentalists, a woodchipping industry was established to process defective and waste timbers. Other important activities are fruit growing, especially apples, mixed farming and dairying and there is a large potato-processing plant near Manjimup.

The conditions of the cool, well-watered south-west have produced magnificent forests between Manjimup and Walpole where the marri and the karri predominate. In spring, the grey-barked, gnarled marri trees are covered in white blossom and provide many hectares of bee pasture. The karris grow to more than eighty metres and are the world's third tallest tree. *Population 4350*

FONTYS POOL Fontys Pool is one of the more unusual items classified by the National Trust. This swimming pool, south-west of Manjimup, was created in 1925 when a local farmer threw a concrete dam across a creek to irrigate his vegetables.

FOUR ACES The Four Aces are magnificent karri trees that range in height from sixty-seven to seventy-nine metres and have been growing for around four hundred years. They stand in a row set back from Graphite Road and contain enough timber to build six houses.

DIAMOND TREE FIRE LOOKOUT This fire lookout is crowned with a four-legged wooden tower. The total height to the cabin floor is fifty-one metres. The lookout served its original purpose from 1941 to 1974 when it was superseded by spotter aircraft.

FESTIVALS Manjimup Chestnut Festival, April.

MOUNT FRANKLAND NATIONAL PARK ■ 2221

This 30 830-hectare park stretches about fifty kilometres east from the Southwestern Highway. There is tall karri forest near Deep River in the west and to the east the Frankland River is surrounded by jarrah woodland and swampy flats. Spectacular red-flowering gums grow naturally here. Mount Frankland itself is a large granite dome looming one hundred metres above the trees.

NANNUP ■ 2222

Nannup is a quiet township in the Blackwood Valley surrounded by lush pasture and jarrah and pine forests. The town developed where major stock routes from the south converged to ford the Blackwood River. In earlier times, convicts felled trees for 'Hampton's Cheeses' – the jarrah blocks that were used in road-building. Nannup has a sawmill and the local economy still depends on the timber industry. *Population 470*

PEMBERTON ■ 2223

The first European settler in the Pemberton area was Edward Brockman whose father was an early settler in Western Australia and first chairman of the Swan Roads Board. 'Warren House' remains much as he built it in 1872 with a tin roof added to protect the original shingles. The area was named after Pemberton Walcott, an early settler in the south-west.

The Pemberton–Northcliffe tramway with its replicas of 1907 trams runs through stands of huge trees and across timber bridges. Pemberton claims the tallest ever karri tree felled in the district – at over 104 metres it was equal to the height of a 35-storey building. *Population 930*

GLOUCESTER TREE This tree is the district's tallest fire lookout – the lookout platform, reached by 153 spiralling rungs, is 61 metres above ground. It was 15 metres taller before the crown was lopped off in 1946 to allow for the platform.

FESTIVALS King Karri Karnival, March long weekend.

PEMBERTON NATIONAL PARKS ■ 2224

Three reserves, known informally as the 'Pemberton National Parks', cluster around the forestry town of the

Untouched tracts of the tall timbers that brought wealth to this region stand in parks such as Beedelup.

same name. They are Beedelup National Park, Warren National Park and the much smaller Brockman National Park. The region is well watered by six rivers – the Beedelup tumbles over cascades, rapids and waterfalls and the Warren provides swimming holes and trout fishing.

SHANNON NATIONAL PARK ■ 2225

The 53 598-hectare Shannon National Park covers the entire basin of the Shannon River and contains some of the finest stands of tall timber in the south-west, preserved after a long battle between logging interests and conservation groups.

WALPOLE-NORNALUP NATIONAL PARK ■ 2226

This park of some 18 000 hectares, established in 1910, surrounds the Walpole and Nornalup Inlets where pelicans and black swans congregate. It is watered by the Frankland, 'river of perfect reflections', and the Deep River. Most trees common to the south-west are found in the reserve with the addition of the giant tingle, another slow-growing hardwood.

VALLEY OF THE GIANTS Along the wettest part of the coast – with an average annual rainfall of 1200 millimetres – are stands of huge karri and rare red and yellow tingle trees. A 400-metre walking track winds through this aptly named Valley of the Giants.

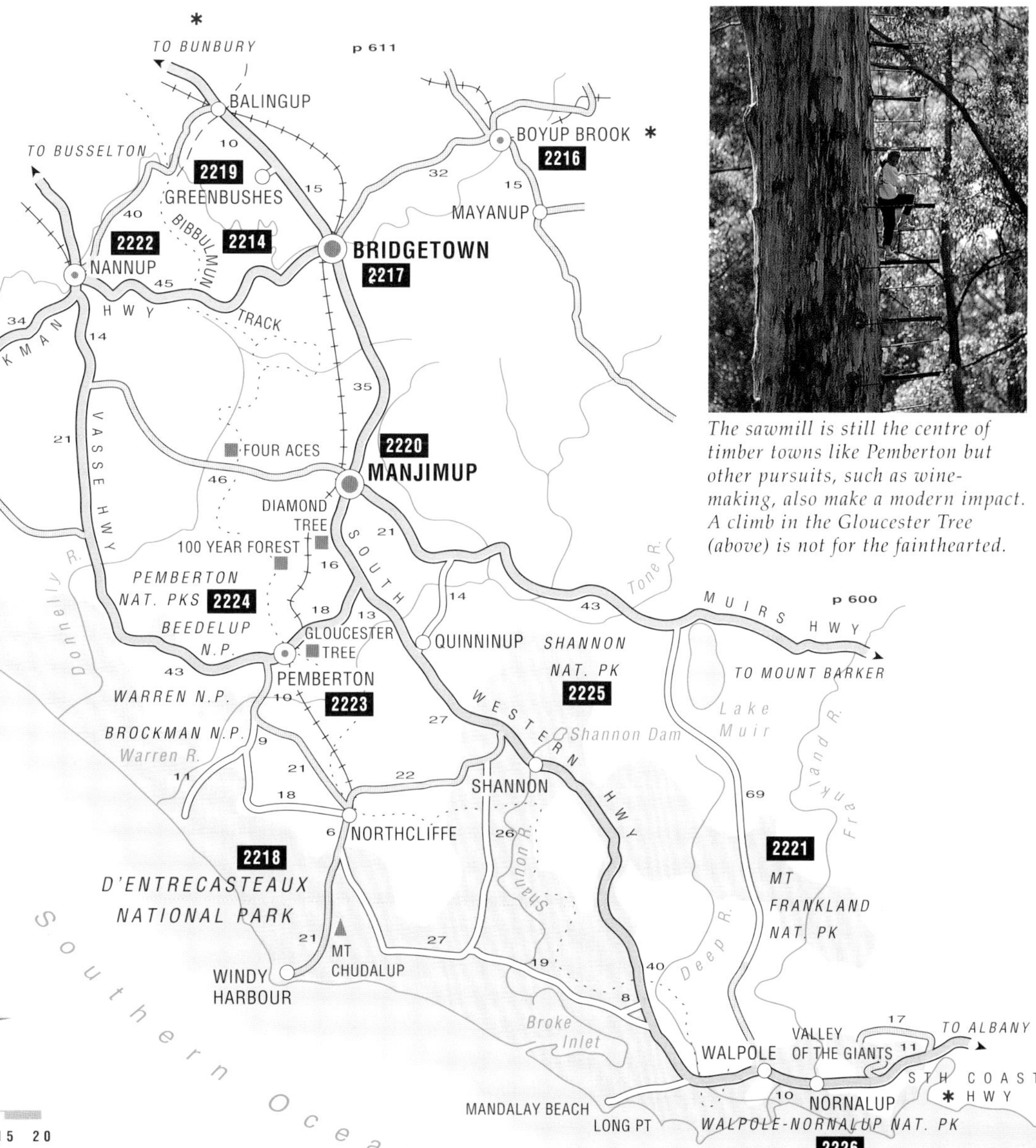

The sawmill is still the centre of timber towns like Pemberton but other pursuits, such as wine-making, also make a modern impact. A climb in the Gloucester Tree (above) is not for the fainthearted.

Bunbury & Busselton

The Indian Ocean crashes onto the beaches and rocky headlands of this most south-westerly outcrop of the continent, where the green of massive karri and jarrah forests is enlivened by the happy colours of wildflowers, particularly in the spring. Here, in a land of wine and honey, mineral sands are mined while closer to the shore, holiday-makers populate the beaches.

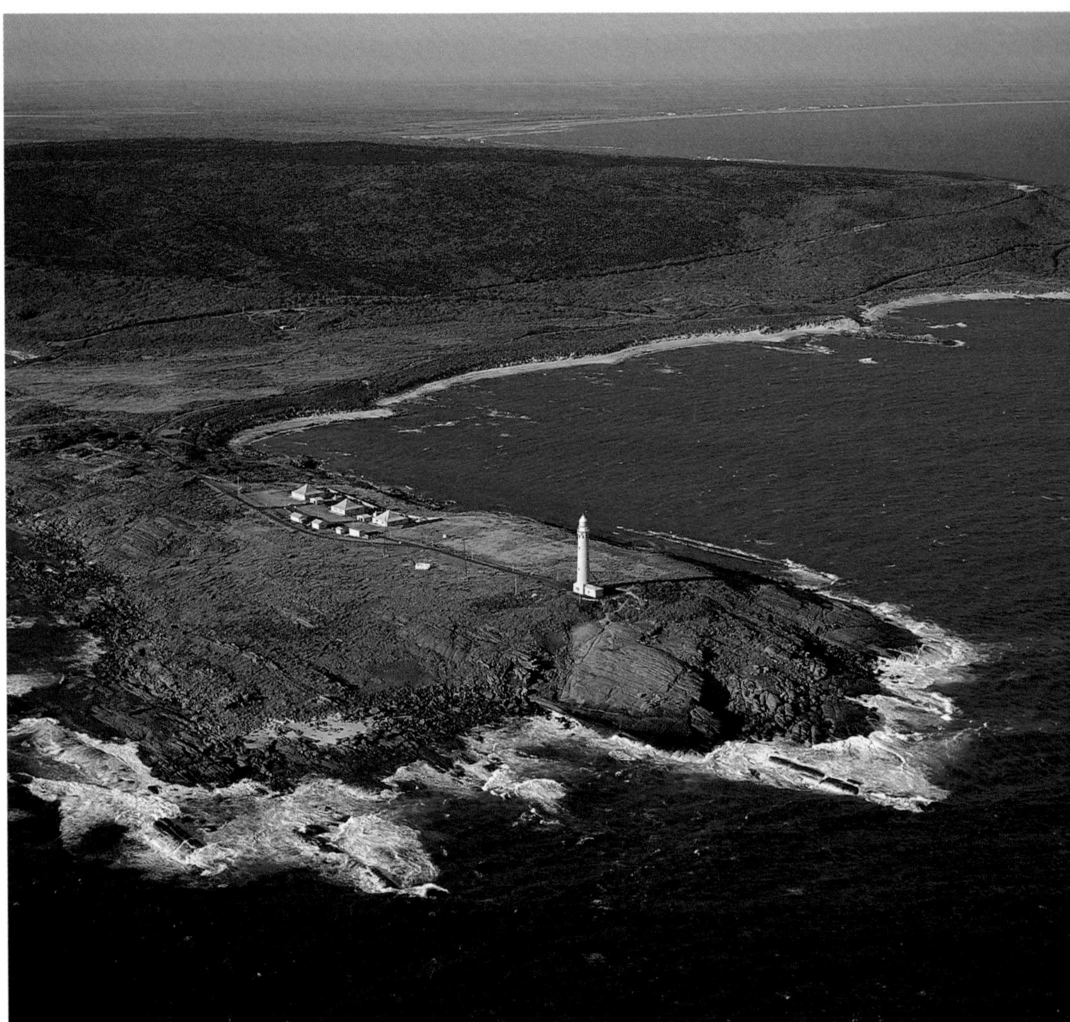

Beyond Leeuwin's lonely light it is a long way to anywhere – the next westward landfall is the coast of Africa.

AUGUSTA ■ 2227

Augusta has been protected from intensive development largely as a result of its inaccessibility. Located near the south-western tip of the continent, this small resort town is the third oldest settlement in Western Australia. The earliest settlers arrived in May 1830 having stopped first at Swan River; finding all the land taken, they sailed down the coast to Flinders Bay where they established the settlement of Augusta, named in honour of Princess Augusta Sophia, the second daughter of King George III and Queen Charlotte of England. Eventually, many of these pioneers abandoned Augusta and moved north to the Vasse River to begin again.

It was timber that finally gave the green light to development in the region and a flourishing timber trade based on exports of karri, marri and jarrah to overseas markets (see Karridale). Jetties were built at Flinders and Hamelin bays and settlers flocked to the district to work in the mills. The town's position on the estuary of Blackwood River, overlooking Hardy Inlet, has made it increasingly popular as a tourist and retirement destination.

In nearby Flinders Bay, a memorial commemorates one of the world's largest and most successful whale rescue operations. A school of 114 false killer whales were discovered stranding themselves on the town beach early on the morning of 30 July 1986. An army of volunteers was soon assembled, labouring for two days and nights in the bitterly cold surf to relaunch the whales, with the result that ninety-six of the giant mammals were successfully herded out of the bay. *Population 840*

JEWEL CAVE North of the town is the evocatively named Jewel Cave, with its fantastic cave formations including the jewel casket – a sparkling cluster of crystals from which the cave takes its name.

AUSTRALIND ■ 2228

The small settlement of Australind on the shores of Leschenault Inlet evolved from an ambitious land settlement scheme instigated by the Western Australian Company of London, in 1840. The company bought land adjacent to the inlet, drew up plans for a city and intensive farming district to be called Australind – a combination of Australia and India. But the scheme never got off the ground – the soil proved unsuitable for intensive agriculture and the company experienced financial difficulties. Now a monument to the ill-fated settlers' memory stands on the Old Coast Road overlooking the inlet. Other reminders of the land company's ill-considered scheme include St Nicholas' Church, which measures less than four metres by seven metres and is reputedly the smallest church in Australia.

Modern Australind is a pleasant dormitory suburb of Bunbury (see entry) and the site of a major titanium oxide plant, most of the output of which is exported for the manufacture of paints. *Population 4410*

BRUNSWICK JUNCTION ■ 2229

Brunswick Junction nestles in the foothills of the Darling Ranges, a small service centre for the surrounding dairy-farming district. The importance of dairying to Brunswick Junction's economy is acknowledged by a large statue of a Friesian cow, which takes pride of place in the town. *Population 830*

BUNBURY ■ 2230

Following the establishment of a settlement at Swan River in 1829, the Lieutenant-Governor Captain James Stirling, sent an exploration party down the south-west coast to search for good agricultural land. Lieutenant Preston and Doctor Collie

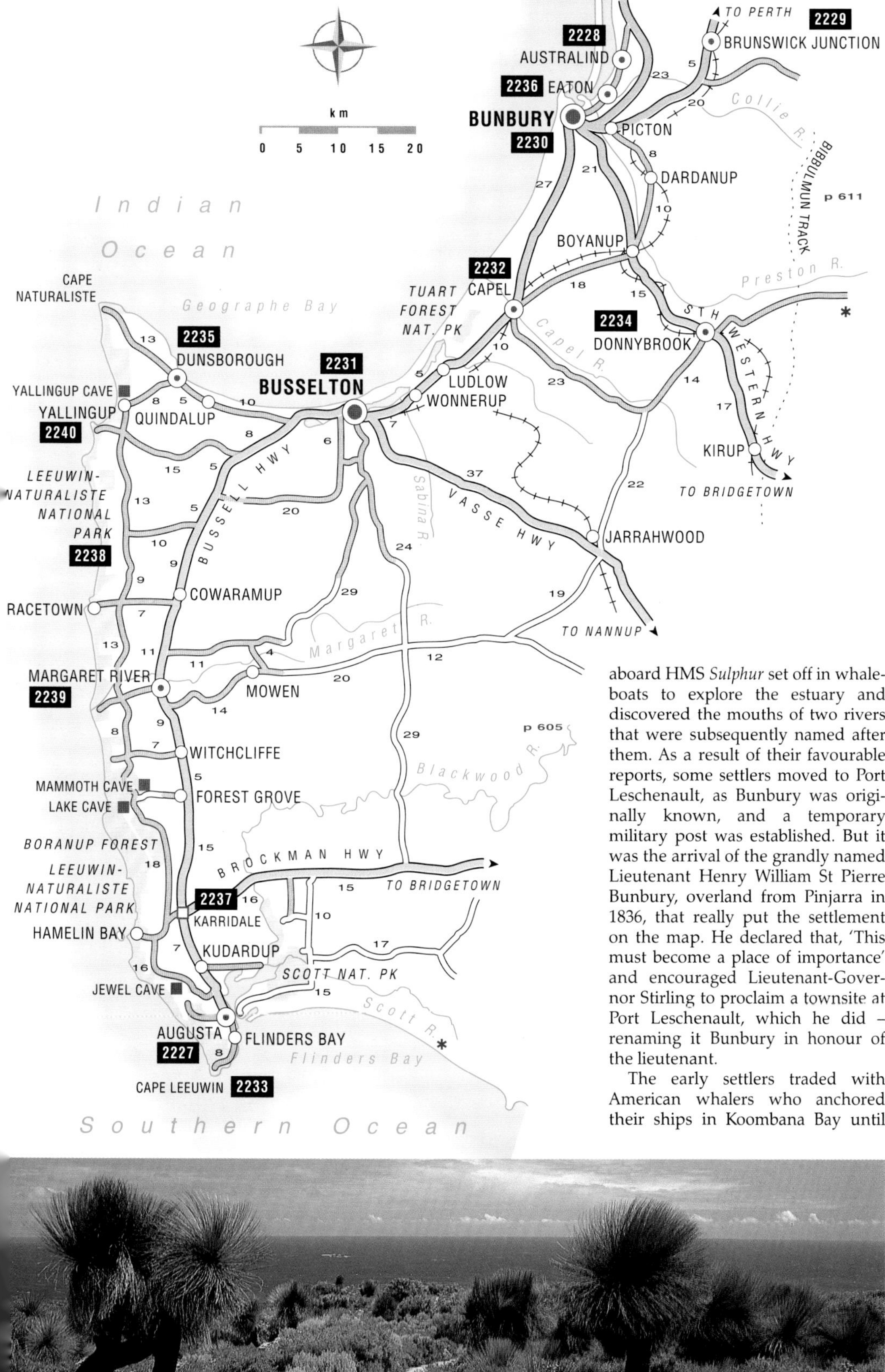

Grass trees dot the protected strip of limestone heathland flanked by the two great capes, Leeuwin and Naturaliste.

aboard HMS *Sulphur* set off in whaleboats to explore the estuary and discovered the mouths of two rivers that were subsequently named after them. As a result of their favourable reports, some settlers moved to Port Leschenault, as Bunbury was originally known, and a temporary military post was established. But it was the arrival of the grandly named Lieutenant Henry William St Pierre Bunbury, overland from Pinjarra in 1836, that really put the settlement on the map. He declared that, 'This must become a place of importance' and encouraged Lieutenant-Governor Stirling to proclaim a townsite at Port Leschenault, which he did – renaming it Bunbury in honour of the lieutenant.

The early settlers traded with American whalers who anchored their ships in Koombana Bay until the government slapped on a wharfage charge, prompting the whalers to move anchorage to 'free' Geographe Bay, off Busselton (see entry). With the disappearance of this ready market, development declined and it was not until the arrival of the railway from Boyanup in 1891, that new life was injected into the settlement.

Today, Bunbury is the major seaport and administrative centre of the south-western region – it was given official city status in 1979. The city's man-made, deep-water harbour, constructed in the 1970s, is bordered by bulk-storage and handling facilities that testify to the region's agricultural and mineral wealth. The rich deposits of mineral sands have been exploited since 1956 as have the district's extensive bauxite deposits.

Despite its major industrial role, tourism is the town's other important industry; its coastal location, temperate climate and proximity to the hinterland's historic towns make it a popular holiday destination. *Population 24 000*

KING COTTAGE MUSEUM Named in honour of its builder, Henry King, this cottage opened as a local history museum in 1968. Constructed in 1880, the five-roomed cottage has a comprehensive collection of colonial domestic artefacts.

'LESCHENAULT LADY' This vintage steam train, located at Bunbury Railway Station, began hauling timber from the south-western hardwood forests in 1898. It has been restored to take tourists on picnic excursions through the magnificent countryside of the south-west, stopping at neighbouring towns such as Busselton, Donnybrook (see entries) and Collie. Officially titled Locomotive G233 'G' Class 2-6-0, the 'Leschenault Lady' was renamed when it took on its more leisurely role in 1968.

SAINT MARK'S ANGLICAN CHURCH Saint Mark's Church, in nearby Picton, is the second oldest church in Western Australia. Built in 1842 from pit-sawn timber with wattle and daub filling, the church originally had a roof thatched with rushes from Leschenault Inlet. A bell salvaged from the wreck of the whaler *North America* still clangs in the church's miniature belfry.

TIMBER JETTY In bygone days, this six-berth jetty was a busy loading point. But the development of Bunbury's major inner harbour in the 1970s took the trade away and since 1982 the old timber jetty has proved a magnet for fishermen.

FESTIVALS Australia Day Celebrations, January; Bunbury Agricultural Show, February/March; Bunbury Fest, November.

BUSSELTON ■ 2231

The founders of Busselton were pioneering settlers from Augusta (see entry), who were defeated by the giant karri forests – which were difficult to clear – crop failure and isolation and took up land grants in the more gentle environment of the Vasse River–Geographe Bay area. John Garrett Bussell was one of the first settlers in the region, taking up a claim on the banks of the Vasse River in 1832 and moving his family there in 1834. The track he hacked through the bush to the river flats is now the town's main street.

Upon reaching the Vasse, he was greatly surprised to see one of his cows grazing contentedly on the river bank – having somehow wandered from the Augusta settlement through almost 100 kilometres of thick forest to the site where Bussell decided to take up his claim – and so he named his run 'Cattle Chosen'!

The town developed as a shipping outlet for agricultural produce and timber, the 1850s bringing more settlers, a convict workforce and an expansion of the dairying and timber industries. The increase in shipping led to the construction of Busselton's famous jetty – once the longest in Australia, the two-kilometre-long jetty has been eclipsed by a three-and-a-half-kilometre-long pier at Cape Lambert (see *Wickham*).

The end of the nineteenth century saw a number of significant developments in Busselton. The first butter factory in Western Australia opened in the town in 1893 and two years later the town was linked by rail to Perth through Boyanup. Its port suffered as a consequence, the ships were displaced by locomotives, and the town of Bunbury took over as the centre of trade. Unpredictably, it was the discovery of the state's rich goldfields in the 1880s and 1890s that provided the boost to the town's next phase of development.

Miners and engineers chose Busselton with its plentiful surf beaches and peaceful bays, scenic forests, nearby caves and temperate climate, as an ideal place for holidays and retirement. A century later, it is these same qualities that bring visitors flocking to the town every summer and the region's traditional industries of dairying, beef cattle and other agricultural products have been supplemented by the growth of a new industry – wine growing (see *Margaret River*). *Population 8940*

BALLARAT ENGINE Victoria Square, at the corner of Queen and Albert streets, is the final resting place of the Ballarat Engine – the first steam locomotive used in Western Australia. It ran from Yoganup to the mill at Wonnerup, hauling timber a distance of twenty kilometres.

OLD BUTTER FACTORY MUSEUM This red-brick building on the banks of the Vasse River in Peel Street is now a museum which pays tribute to the early days of the dairying industry of the south-west region. As well as its displays of old butter- and cheese-making equipment, the old factory houses an impressive collection of pioneering memorabilia.

ST MARY'S ANGLICAN CHURCH The foundation stone was laid in 1844, making St Mary's the oldest stone church in Western Australia. Roughly hewn blocks of local limestone were used for the walls and pit-sawn jarrah for the roof and floor. Many of the district's early pioneers, including John Garrett Bussell, are buried in the church's graveyard.

TUART FOREST NATIONAL PARK One of Western Australia's newest national parks, the 1786-hectare Tuart Forest, between Capel and the Sabina River, is the only remaining natural tuart forest. Its slow-growing hardwood trees are estimated to be between 300 and 400 years old and are unique to the south-west of Western Australia, growing only on the coastal limestone found either side of Perth.

WONNERUP HOUSE North of Busselton on Layman Road, this historic property was established by an early pioneer, George Layman, in 1835. Layman met an untimely end when he was speared by an Aborigine in 1841. The original thatched cottage was destroyed by fire in 1858 and the house that now stands on the farm was built by Layman's son in 1859. The property became one of the principal dairy farms in the area and has been gradually restored by the National Trust as an example of early rural living.

FESTIVALS Festival of Busselton, late January; Yachting Regatta, January; Beach Festival, January; Busselton Wildflower Show, September.

CAPEL ■ 2232

Roughly midway between Bunbury and Busselton, Capel is surrounded by a dairy and cattle district, but its chief importance is as the location of the south-western region's profitable mineral sands. Mining operations began in 1956 and two mining companies now process the mineral sands for the production of titanium and ziconium. Both the mineral sands and metals are exported through the nearby major port at Bunbury (see entry). *Population 2000*

CAPE LEEUWIN ■ 2233

In March 1622, the Dutch ship *Leeuwin* – Lioness – sailed past the rocky finger of Cape Leeuwin, her navigators naming this stretch of land, 't Landt van de Leeuwin'. It was after these early mariners that the cape was named by Matthew Flinders when he arrived at this extreme south-western point of the continent on 6 December 1801 to begin his eventual circumnavigation of the Australian coast.

The lighthouse that now overlooks this junction of two great oceans – the Southern and Indian – was opened in 1896 by the then Premier of Western Australia, Sir John Forrest, who dedicated it to the world's mariners. Though it presides over one of the busiest sea-traffic routes on the Australian coast – in the early days of settlement, most Australian-bound ships came via the Cape of Good Hope and Cape Leeuwin was often the first Australian landfall – the construction of the lighthouse commenced in 1893 only after the establishment of Western Australia's goldfields. Prior to then, the western colony simply could not afford to shoulder the entire cost of construction and the relatively affluent eastern colonies refused to share the expenditure.

Volcanic ironstone quarried locally was used to construct the thirty-nine-metre tower and cottages that make up the lighthouse complex, and its light – originally powered by kerosene – was visible for fifty kilometres on a clear night.

DONNYBROOK ■ 2234

Donnybrook is the home of the delicious and ubiquitous Granny Smith apple, which was introduced into the district at the turn of the century, though the first commercial plantings were not carried out until 1917. Now, the town is the centre of the biggest fruit-growing district in Western Australia and a very popular tourist destination in October each year, when the many hectares of apple orchards come into blossom.

The first settlers in the region were a group of Irishmen who established themselves on the banks of the Preston River in 1842, in an area known as Irishtown. Prior to this, the district was called Minninup but the name was changed to the unmistakeably Irish Donnybrook when the townsite was gazetted in 1894. The railway reached Donnybrook the next year.

In the early days, timber provided the major focus for development and railway sleepers were produced in their thousands. The discovery of gold in 1898 led to Donnybrook being gazetted as a goldfield, but the excitement died after a few years when it was realised that the district would never yield payable quantities of the precious metal. Now, along with apples and timber, the country surrounding Donnybrook produces a range of dairy products, potatoes and the decorative Donnybrook sandstone, which has been used extensively in the construction of many of Perth's fine historic buildings including the University of Western Australia. *Population 1570*

FESTIVALS Donnybrook Apple Festival, late March.

DUNSBOROUGH ■ 2235

Dunsborough is a popular holiday resort that is attracting an increasing number of permanent residents. Its location in the corner of Geographe Bay with its sheltered east-facing beach makes it ideal for swimming, boating and fishing, as well as being the starting point for the splendours of the rugged coastline and a wildflower-studded hinterland that is Leeuwin-Naturaliste National Park. Cape Naturaliste lighthouse – built in 1903 of local limestone – is a short distance from the town.

Dunsborough was not officially proclaimed as a townsite until 1879, but many settlers who populated the Vasse–Geographe Bay region in the early nineteenth century also took up land grants in Dunsborough and nearby Yallingup. American whalers anchored in Geographe Bay in the early 1800s were the first white visitors. The Castle Rock Whaling Company, which was established in 1846, operated for many years from Castle Bay. The manager of the company built himself a simple cottage – the oldest building in Dunsborough – which has since been moved and re-erected at the Old Mill near Yallingup (see entry).

It is generally accepted that the town was named after Dunn Bay. I was shown as 'Dunnsbro' on an 183

The limpid waters of Lake Cave's lake magically reflect the spotlit ceiling in a setting said by the Caves Board in 1901 to be one of 'sublime grandeur'.

map although not declared at that time. The Aborigines called the area 'quedjinup'. *Population 660*

EATON ■ 2236

Eaton – in fact a satellite town of Bunbury – is the largest town in the Dardanup Shire, a district that had its beginnings in 1831 when the first settlers took up land grants. Henry Prinsep, the son of the British agent general for the East India Company at Calcutta, managed property in the district for the company after he arrived in Western Australia in 1866. The intention was to create an export market of horses and timber railway sleepers to India. The horse market collapsed by 1871, but the timber industry continued until the completion of the Indian rail network.

Timber is still important to the shire, which is dominated by large stands of jarrah forest and pine plantations that are managed by Western Australia's Department of Conservation and Land Management. Other industries include fruit and vegetable growing, beef cattle, pig and sheep farming; because of the town's proximity to the south-western region's capital, Bunbury (see entry), hobby farming has also become increasingly popular.

Serving the surrounding agricultural district, the small settlement of Eaton was named after Mr Foster Eaton – the state's fisheries and game inspector – in recognition of the work accomplished by him in this region. *Population 3140*

KARRIDALE ■ 2237

Timber became a big business in the south-west during the last twenty years of the nineteenth century and this was almost solely due to the efforts of an enterprising timber merchant, Maurice Coleman Davies. In 1877, Davies applied for and was granted a lease for almost 19 000 hectares of almost untouched jarrah and karri forests between Hamelin and Flinders bays.

Davies' timber empire – centred at Karridale – developed quickly, eventually supporting 800 people. He built jetties at the two nearby bays, installed port facilities, built mills in the forests and connected the lot with more than sixty kilometres of railway lines.

Timber and timber products from the Karridale mills were successfully exported but by the turn of the century, the enterprise began to decline due to a slump in world markets. The Karridale mill closed in 1913 and a bushfire that swept through the region in 1961 destroyed the last remnants of this former timber town.

LEEUWIN-NATURALISTE NATIONAL PARK ■ 2238

Two capes – Leeuwin and Naturaliste – mark the extremities of the most south-western corner of the continent and the north–south limits of the Leeuwin-Naturaliste National Park. This 15 500-hectare national park comprises twenty-eight separate reserves, gazetted piecemeal since 1902, and protects a narrow strip of coastline that includes an extraordinary variety of native vegetation, rugged headlands, tranquil bays, long beaches, high windswept cliffs, caves and nearshore islets and reefs – a number of sailing vessels foundered on the latter in the early days of exploration.

The cool waters of the Indian Ocean crash onto beaches that are popular with surfers, while fishermen dangle their lines in the more tranquil waters of the park's many bays. Inland, water has percolated through the limestone ridge that stretches for eighty kilometres along the coast, to carve out hundreds of fascinating caves and rock formations – four of these are open to the public (see Augusta, Margaret River and Yallingup).

BORANUP KARRI FOREST Covering nearly 3200 hectares, this 100-year-old forest is the furthest west that the tall, pale-barked karri – the third tallest tree in the world – grows. Western Australia's main karri belt grows some 100 kilometres to the east, separated from Boranup Forest by grey, infertile sands. Boranup was originally plundered for its timber resource and it was not until the last mill closed in 1913 that the forest had a chance of regenerating.

The surf is always up at Yallingup where the westerlies give surfers one of their best chances in Australia of a ride on the elusive perfect wave.

MARGARET RIVER ■ 2239

The town of Margaret River was proclaimed in 1913, developing very slowly until the introduction of the Group Settlement Scheme in the 1920s, which was devised to attract migrants to the country and extend land settlement in the south-west. But members of the pioneering Bussell family had already established a property, 'Ellensbrook', north-west of the present townsite in 1854, and in 1865, the family moved to a new house near the mouth of the Margaret River – named after Margaret Wycher, a friend of the Bussells.

Closer settlement and extensive land clearing transformed the fertile countryside into a lush dairying region which was soon supplemented by thriving beef cattle and timber industries and cheese manufacturing for which the region is noted. Since the 1970s, vineyards have been cultivated successfully in the hinterland and now Margaret River is famous for its high-quality red and white table wines from more than fifty vineyards. Wine is not the only product that has made the town a popular holiday destination – sparkling beaches offering fine surfing, swimming, fishing and boating opportunities vie with the nearby limestone caves and the region's springtime profusion of brilliantly coloured wildflowers to offer a wide range of outdoor activities for holiday-makers. *Population 1720*

LAKE CAVE With its impressive natural entrance, Lake Cave lies at the bottom of a huge circular crater and takes its name from the lake which was formed by an underground stream. The cave is noted for its unique suspended table formation – originally two massive columns joined by a thin sheet of calcite on the cave floor which was washed away leaving just the columns and a calcite 'table' suspended a few centimetres above the lake.

MAMMOTH CAVE Mammoth Cave is aptly named – its massive proportions make it easily accessible to visitors and its caverns are filled with majestically shaped rock formations.

FESTIVALS Wine & Food Festival, February; Caves House Festival, late February.

YALLINGUP ■ 2240

Yallingup is mecca to surfing devotees. Day in, day out, its beach is pounded by huge waves that test the skills of the most experienced board-riders – an attraction that has made it the location for the annual Australian Surf Championships and many local surfing competitions.

But surfing is not all the town has to offer. The nearby Yallingup Cave has fascinating rock formations and its tourist potential was recognised at the turn of the century when the Western Australian Government constructed the Caves House Hotel in 1903. This accommodated visitors who made the two-and-a-half-hour journey along the dirt track from Busselton, in a horse-drawn buggy.

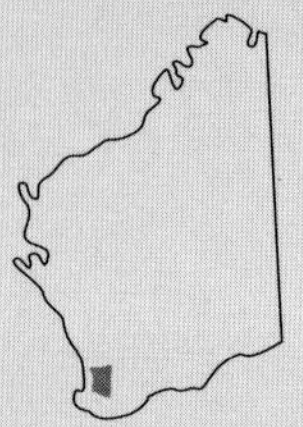

Collie & Narrogin

Lying between the settlement at Swan River and the port at Albany, this historic region, which today provides a rare sanctuary for the numbat, Western Australia's animal emblem, was much traversed by nineteenth-century coaches and steam trains. Today it produces coal to generate Western Australia's electricity.

The handsome numbat once roamed as far as western NSW but is now confined to small strongholds in the south-west such as the forest named after the showy and prickly-leaved dryandra shrub (below).

ARTHUR RIVER ■ 2241
One of the first settlements on the old 1850s coach route from Perth to Albany, Arthur River was bypassed by the main railway lines...and its historic buildings have also been bypassed by twentieth century development. The police barracks (1866) on the road south of Arthur River safeguarded travellers, James Spratt's Mount Pleasant Inn (1869) fed and watered them, while St Paul's Church (1882) satisfied their spiritual requirements. These and other old buildings at the settlement of Arthur River now attract travellers interested in the district's history.

BROOKTON ■ 2242
For almost twenty years after 1846, John Seabrook, in his homestead 'Brookton House', was the only settler in this district. In the 1860s, his son-in-law William Robinson also took up land in the district and several others followed suit. These early settlers survived on the proceeds of sandalwood pulling until their grain grew and was gristed (ground) at Seabrook's convict-built barn. Local brumbies were also broken and sold to the British Army in India.

The Great Southern Railway that now stretches from Northam to Albany reached Seabrook Siding, later renamed Brookton, in the late 1880s at about the same time that the eastern goldfields opened up with a consequent increase in the demand for agricultural produce. These two factors saw more rapid growth in settlements such as Brookton. The railway has now closed and the station is used for other purposes – a tourist information centre, arts and crafts shop and community newspaper office now share the premises. Brookton today is as well known for the wildflowers growing on its road verges and nature strips as it is for its grain. *Population 580*

FESTIVALS Old Time Motor Show, March of even-numbered years.

COLLIE ■ 2243
Dr Alexander Collie, naval surgeon and later Albany's first resident magistrate, discovered the Collie River in 1829 but although Collie owes him its name, its fortune was found by a shepherd, George Marsh. According to local legend, Marsh was camping by the Collie River in 1883 and used two large black stones to hold his billy steady on the campfire – only when the stones caught fire did Marsh realise they were coal. Collie was to provide the fuel for the state's railways and power stations, which made its industrial growth possible.

The ancient coal basin that makes up the Collie coalfields is isolated from Australia's other major coal deposits and remains Western Australia's only developed coalfield.

There is no working coal mine in the town itself and it is difficult for visitors to think of Collie, sitting as it does in the middle of wildflower-scattered jarrah forest, high in the Darling escarpment, as a coal-mining town. Lighting a campfire can, however, be dangerous since there are exposed pockets of coal on the surface that, if set alight, can smoulder as hot ash for months. Collie was also the site of a fuel-alcohol grain distillery. Funded by the Commonwealth government during the Second World War to make much needed fuel from alcohol distilled from wheat, the distillery was not completed until 1945, too late to help the war effort and therefore never operated. The more recent alumina refinery, built at Worsley – twenty kilometres from Collie – in the 1980s is more successful and one million tonnes of bauxite carried by conveyor belt from nearby Boddington is refined each year. *Population 7680*

ALL SAINTS ANGLICAN CHURCH When the Bishop of Bunbury preached in London requesting funds for building churches in his district, Nora Noyes, widow of Colonel Arthur Noyes, heard his plea. In 1912 she endowed All Saints Church at Collie, as well as donating a 400-year-old crucifix and brass candlesticks. Nora Noyes died in the 1940s without seeing 'her' church with its large mural of religious figures across the ages.

DRYANDRA STATE FOREST ■ 2244
In 1903, Dryandra was declared a state forest so that its plentiful supply of mallet bark, which had been found to contain large quantities of high-quality, water-soluble tannins, could be marketed. Since the 1960s, synthetic tannins have been used so 7500 hectares of mallets remain alongside the jarrah, marri, powderbark wandoo and jam trees – a

species of acacia smelling like raspberry jam when cut. It is the flora and the fauna that make Dryandra a priceless oasis in the midst of cultivated wheatfields. Rarest of all the inhabitants is the numbat – Western Australia's almost extinct animal emblem – with distinctive black and white bands on its reddish-brown body and a disproportionately long tongue for snaring termites.

KOJONUP ■ 2245
When Alfred Hillman was surveying the route from the Swan River settlement to the Port of Albany in 1837, a group of Aborigines directed him to

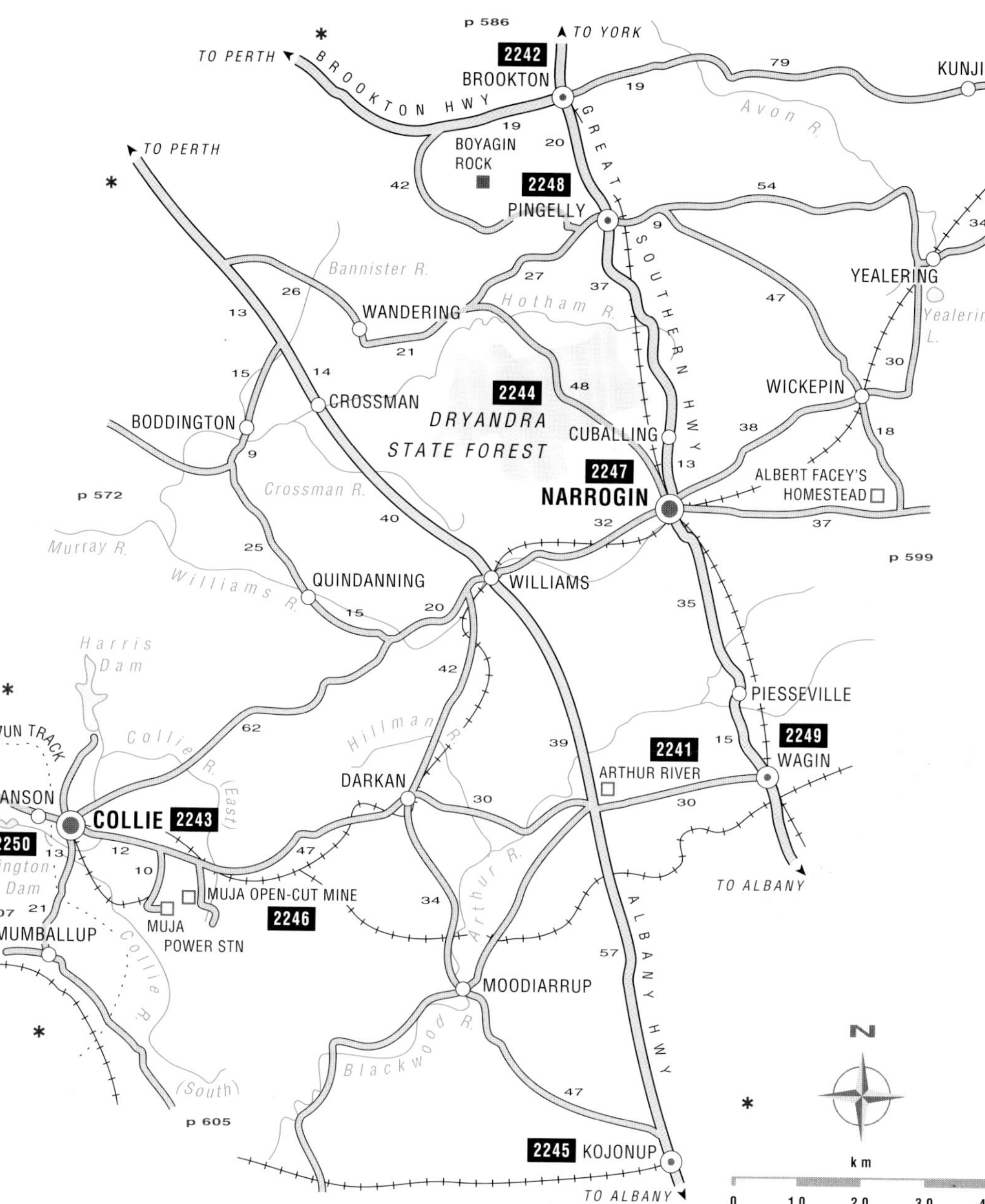

spring at a place they used to get stone for their axes. The 1845 barracks built to house the soldiers stationed here – and the life-saving spring – are still to be seen.

The coaching centre that grew up around the spring made Kojonup one of the earliest settlements in the south-west of the state. Hard work paid off for the pioneer pastoralists and Ion Idriess in *Across the Nullarbor* was to describe Kojonup as 'yet another prosperous little sheep town'. *Population 1020*

MUJA OPEN-CUT MINE ■ 2246

Opened in 1953, this mine 23 kilometres east of Collie (see entry) was an underground operation until 1965. The Muja Open Cut is the largest mine operating in the Collie coalfield...or indeed Western Australia. The coal, which produces little ash or sulphur, is ideal for power generation and all of the mine's output of 2.1 million tonnes goes to the nearby Muja Power Station. Water pumped from the mine – twelve million litres a day – goes to Muja Power Station for use as cooling water.

NARROGIN ■ 2247

The first lease in the district around Narrogin was granted in the 1860s but permanent residents were few and far between. The ruins of the first home near the town, thought to belong to John Stephens, can still be seen on Chuggamunny Hill. When the Great Southern Railway reached Narrogin in the 1880s, Anthony Hordern, the railway contractor, constructed the trackside Hordern Hotel and around it a new settlement developed quickly. The townsite was declared in 1897.

Narrogin is still a major rail junction and has become the largest commercial centre in this region of wheat, sheep and pig farming. The district around Narrogin also has a number of literary connections. Colin Johnson, the Aboriginal novelist, was born in the town, Dorothy Hewitt was born at nearby Wickepin in which she set her play *The Man from Muckinupin* and Albert Facey, whose autobiography *A Fortunate Life* was such a runaway success, had a homestead nearby (see sub-entry). *Population 4640*

ALBERT FACEY'S HOMESTEAD Albert Facey, who was granted land forty-four kilometres east of Narrogin as part of the soldier-settlement scheme after the First World War, described the twelve years he spent farming here in his autobiography, *A Fortunate Life*. The present homestead, built in 1924 by Facey to replace an earlier one that burnt down, was restored by volunteers in the 1980s.

FESTIVALS Narrogin Three Day Event, August; Spring Festival, October; Agricultural Show, October.

PINGELLY ■ 2248

Pingelly mornings are cold enough and its rainfall just sufficient to mimic a European climate and encourage the growth of the town's tulips. Wildflowers and flowering shrubs predominate, however, at the two reserves outside the town. Boyagin Nature Reserve north-west of the town comprises almost 5000 hectares of remnant natural bushland dominated by two very large granite monoliths, one of which, Boyagin Rock, is 360 metres high. Tutanning Flora and Fauna Reserve, east of the town, covers 2000 hectares, and the diversity of flora and fauna, according to a University of Western Australia survey, has not diminished since 1906 when a collection was made from the site.

When the Beverley to Albany railway line was built in the 1880s, many settlements developed at well sites along the route. Pingelly developed around one such well and the townsite, officially gazetted in 1898, is thought to have taken its name from an earlier siding on the Great Southern Railway. The town's original well was reconstructed in stone in 1980 by a community only too aware of water problems. Celebrations were held in 1957 when a piped water supply was connected. *Population 760*

WAGIN ■ 2249

Wagin, one of a number of service centres established on the Great Southern Railway, represents the halfway point on the railway. The land company that agreed to build the railway and settle migrants along its route in return for land had difficulty attracting settlers. In 1890, the government purchased the land and the townsite at Wagin – from an Aboriginal word said to mean 'place of emus' – was gazetted.

The local hotels proved very useful in the early days. Church services were held in the taproom of the Wagin Hotel (1896) and the school moved into the dining room of the Federal Hotel (1896) when it was unable to get a licence.

The giant merino ram, which sits in Giant Ram Park, is not a vain boast. Wagin today is the centre for a district that produces almost half of the state's wool. The annual Wagin Woolorama is Western Australia's most important sheep stud show after the Perth Royal. *Population 1290*

GEM THEATRE The old powerhouse, rebuilt in 1946 after a fire, was converted into a cinema in 1983. The Little Gem Theatre is one of the country's last – and most recently established – local picture houses.

FESTIVALS Woolorama, March.

WELLINGTON DAM ■ 2250

When Wellington Dam was built in 1933, it dammed the largest area of catchment in the Darling Range and was the main dam for domestic water for the Great Southern Towns scheme. Rising salinity in the 1970s and 1980s made the water unsuitable for domestic purposes and Harris Dam, completed in 1990, replaced it.

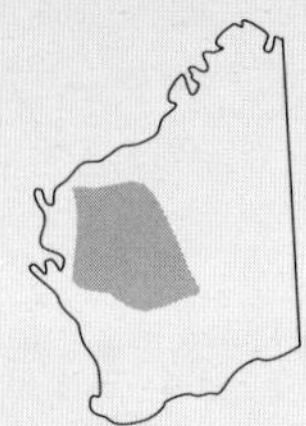

Newman & Tom Price

Some of the world's oldest known rocks are found in the Pilbara, a region with a complex geology and an equally fascinating human history. The many Aboriginal sites – set in the spectacular gorges and the semi-desert lands around them – evoke legends of the distant past.

Overwhelming the Hamersley's beauty is its geological novelty: the iron content of its ore is often over 60 per cent.

AGNEW ■ 2251

The hotel is all that remains of this small mining town, which once had a population of 500 but is now reduced to a mere 10 or so people. The hotel was built in 1945 around what was once a row of shops. To the west, just visible from the highway, are the poppet head and large dumps left from the East Murchison United gold mine.

COLLIER RANGE NATIONAL PARK ■ 2252

This undeveloped park lies between the upper reaches of the Ashburton and Gascoyne rivers. The ranges vary from low hills to high ridges often bounded by cliffs. The vegetation is mainly mulga and spinifex, with eucalpyts growing along many creeklines. The park is about 150 kilometres south of Newman on the Great Northern Highway.

CUE ■ 2253

Once the site of the richest goldfield in Western Australia, Cue at the peak of the boom had thirteen hotels. Today only two remain, however there is still much of interest to see. The main street is classified by the National Trust, and away from the street, buildings of note include the old jail (last used in 1930), the Masonic Lodge (dating from 1899), the primary school (1897) and the Catholic church. The town's bandstand rotunda is built over a well – sunk in 1892 – which was thought to have caused a typhoid epidemic in the settlement's early days.

Fossickers can search for gold in town or at Big Bell and Day Dawn mines nearby. Further evidence of goldmining days are the ghost towns nearby such as Austin, Cuddingwarra – once known as 'Dead Finish' – Reedy and Tuckanarra. Many Aboriginal rock paintings can be seen on Walga Rock, south-west of Cue.

GREAT NORTHERN HIGHWAY ■ 2254

This narrow sealed road that winds for 3206 kilometres through some of the most formidable country in Western Australia is the nation's longest highway. It starts at Midland outside Perth, approaches the Murchison goldfields, then meanders through the iron-ore country of the Pilbara, skirts around the Great Sandy Desert and climbs through the rocky gorges of the Hamersley Range and the ranges of the Kimberley before ending at Wyndham (see *Kununurra & Wyndham*). Travellers can obtain accommodation and fuel from roadhouses scattered along the route.

KARIJINI (HAMERSLEY RANGE) NATIONAL PARK ■ 2255

The scenery in this park is nothing short of spectacular, with mountains, gorges, rivers and plateaux. In the north, small creeks – dry for most of the year – plunge into dark, sheer chasms up to 100 metres deep. One of the park's features is Mount Bruce (1236 metres), the second highest mountain in the state.

The ranges are the traditional home of the Panyjima, Yinnawanjka and Injibaandi people and there is much evidence of their occupation. The surveyor Francis Gregory was the first European to explore the area, in 1861. He named the ranges after his friend Edward Hamersley. The park's name has now reverted to an Aboriginal word for the region – the three groups of Aboriginal people who claim kinship with this area banded together and chose the name Karijini, a word used by two of the language groups – Panyjima and Yinnawanjka – for the Hamersley Range region.

A wide range of wildlife habitats and plants and animals of the Pilbara are protected here in what is one of the largest national parks in Western Australia.

HAMERSLEY GORGES A series of deep gorges in the Hamersley Range are among Western Australia's most dramatic beauty spots. The gorges are spectacular but wild and visitors intent on hiking should notify a ranger first.

LEINSTER ■ 225

Leinster is a mining town that wa established to service the Agnev nickel mine. Nickel ore is processe here and then carried by road trai to Leonora where it is railed to smelter at Kalgoorlie. The Agnev mine and the treatment plant are nc open to visitors. *Population 990*

MEEKATHARRA ■ 225

Meekatharra is the centre for a ric mining, sheep-and-cattle raising dis trict and the name is thought to b an old Aboriginal word meanin 'place of little water'.

In its early days, Meekatharra wa a prolific gold producer, although was never as populous as towr such as Wiluna and Cue. Because its central position in an isolate area, the town has now become the regional centre for many services. The Royal Flying Doctor Service and School of the Air networks cover a wide area and many government departments have their regional bases here. There is a court house (1912) which is classified by the National Trust. Nearby Mount Gould is the site of the first police station in the Murchison district. The station, now classified by the National Trust, closed in 1902. *Population 1410*

MOUNT AUGUSTUS NATIONAL PARK ■ 2258

Two-and-a-half times larger than Uluru (Ayers Rock), Mount Augustus is the world's largest monolith. It lies at the end of a long ridge to the south of the upper Lyons River, towering 1106 metres above sea level. Mount Augustus is approximately 1750 million years old.

The rocks of Mount Augustus were deposited on an ancient sea floor as sand and boulders about one thousand million years ago. These deposits consolidated to form sandstone which was eventually uplifted and folded into an anticline – like an inverted 'V'.

The plants and animals in the park are just as fascinating as its geology. Several rare plant species such as the splendid native foxglove are known to grow only on the mountains.

Mount Augustus Station still runs beef cattle and is studded with more than seventy-two windmills.

MOUNT MAGNET ■ 2259

The Mount Magnet townsite was gazetted in 1895, taking its name from a nearby hill containing magnetic rocks that was named by the surveyor Robert Austin in 1854. The district was virtually untouched until gold was discovered in the 1890s. Nowadays, gold is still mined at the famous Hill 50 goldmine as well as at other sites. Mount Magnet is also renowned as an amateur gemstone hunter's paradise. *Population 1080*

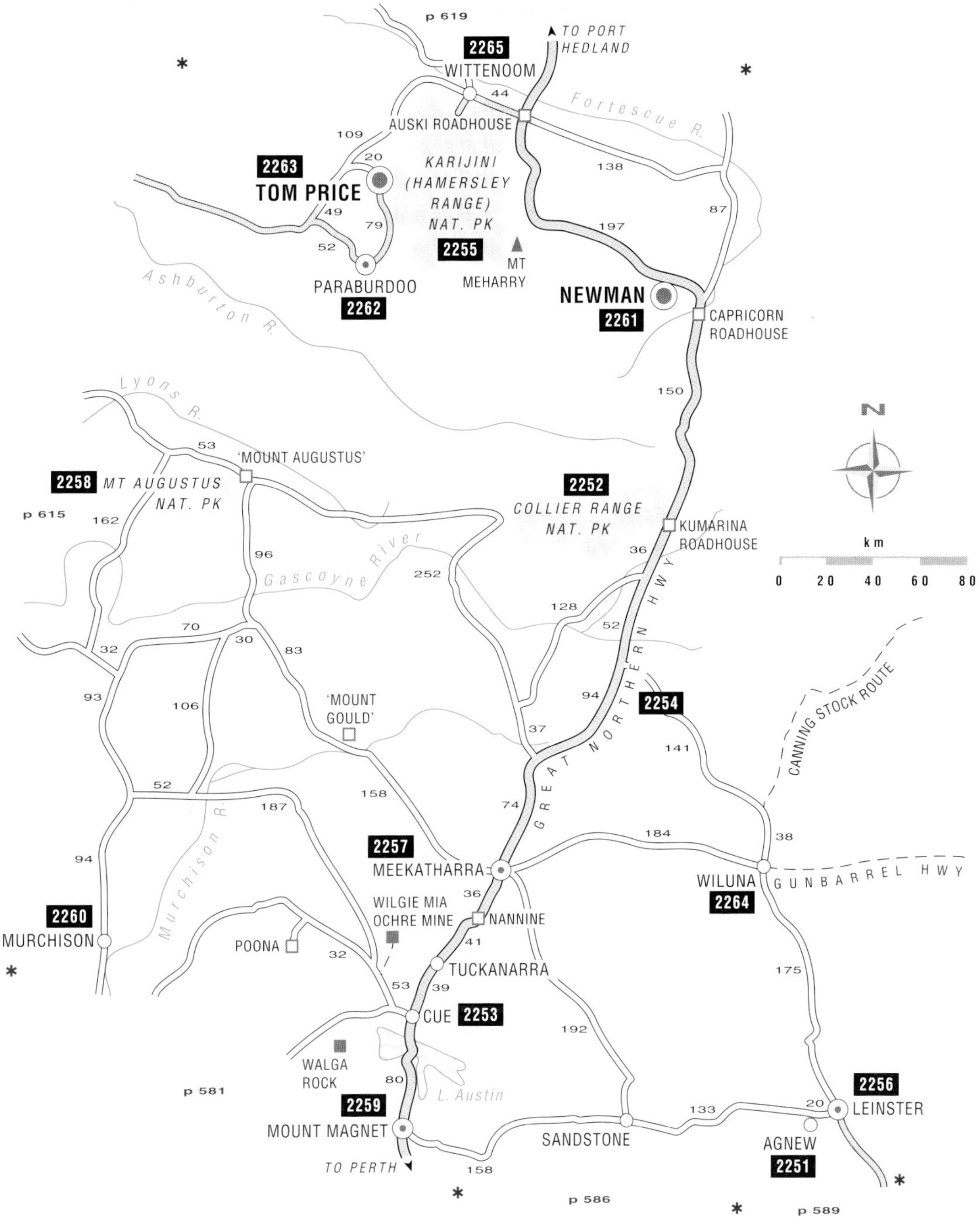

The imaginative artifice of a corrugated-iron Masonic Hall gives a hint of Cue's past greatness.

MURCHISON ■ 2260

Murchison is the only shire in Australia without a town. The settlement was proclaimed in June 1985 and only the shire office, museum and a single business, the Murchison Roadhouse and Caravan Park, are located there. The museum, built of rammed earth and timber, is designed in the style of a station homestead.

NEWMAN ■ 2261

Newman is an iron-ore mining town approximately 370 kilometres south of Port Hedland. The 200-million-dollar town was built in the late

At Wiluna's emu farm, workers display paternal care as they monitor the progress of soon-to-be-born chicks from the giant incubator.

THE OVERLANDERS: DROVING A MOB DOWN THE DUSTY CANNING

Once one of the world's longest and loneliest cattle tracks, the legendary Canning Stock Route is today nothing more than a set of well-worn wheel tracks that link Halls Creek in the Kimberley to Wiluna in the 'goldfields'.

The route through some of the most formidable desert country in the world was established by surveyor Alfred Wernam Canning in 1906 with the aim of delivering disease- and tick-free cattle to the goldfields as quickly as possible.

Within two years and at a cost of 25 000 pounds sterling the stock route was completed. Fifty-one watering points, including a number of wells dug by Canning's men, formed a thin lifeline through three deserts. Although his party would undoubtedly have perished without help from local Aborigines, Canning's treatment of them was often ruthless and inhumane, reflecting the attitudes of many Europeans of the time.

The stock route was completed in 1910 and was first used in 1911 by two drovers – Shoesmith and Thomson – who were killed by Aborigines at Well 37. The next drovers to attempt the route completed the drive successfully later in that same year.

Early mobs were 300 head strong, later on as many as 900 head were moved. Lack of maintenance made the route dangerous and about fifty years after the first mob, the last cattle were driven down and the track fell into disuse.

In 1942, the army sent a party along the route to try to reach the Kimberley. The party did not get far beyond Well 11, where the first sand beat them back. On the return journey to Wiluna, the group cut down a corkwood tree at Weld Spring which bore John Forrest's initials of 1874 and took it to Perth for preservation – it is now in the Western Australian Museum. Drovers were up in arms and the party's leader was reprimanded by the surveyor-general for the unauthorised removal of an 'official survey mark'.

It was 1968 before the stock route was traversed again and it took two four-wheel-drive vehicles a month to complete the trip. The route has since been discovered by holiday adventurers. □

Well 12, in the Little Sandy Desert, was once one of a string of oases that made a cattle-drive down the dry and dusty Canning route possible.

1960s by the Mount Newman Mining Company, which manages one of the world's largest iron-ore mining projects at Mount Whaleback, a few kilometres from the town. The ore is railed to Port Hedland and the shipping complex at Nelson Point. Newman is the largest town in the East Pilbara Shire. *Population 5630*

FESTIVALS Fortesque Festival, mid-August; Newman Open Bowls Carnival, August.

PARABURDOO ■ 2262

Paraburdoo was the second purpose-built town established by the Hamersley Iron company to serve its nearby mining operations. Named after Paraburdoo Station, the name comes from the local Aboriginal words 'piru' and 'pardu,' thought to mean 'meat' and 'feathers' respectively. *Population 2220*

FESTIVALS Paragala Trade Fair, November.

TOM PRICE ■ 2263

The mining town of Tom Price perches high in the Hamersley Range near one of the world's richest deposits of iron ore. Huge machines carve into the rich, red brown earth of Mount Tom Price while long, heavily laden ore trains snake down the range towards Dampier (see *Port Hedland & Karratha*). The mine was developed by Hamersley Iron in 1964 and the 'iron ore' town of Tom Price was established by the company in 1965. *Population 3630*

FESTIVALS Tom Price Annual Festival, early August.

WILUNA ■ 2264

Mining relics and fine old buildings recall the past prosperity of this former goldmining town. At the peak of the 1930s mining boom, the Wiluna mine was the largest in Western Australia and the town had four hotels serving a population of about 9000. Wiluna is now known for its commercial emu farm – run by the Ngangganawili Community Inc., a traditional Aboriginal community from central Western Australia – which produces leather and other by-products such as oil. The community also owns and runs an orchard.

The town is at the junction of access roads to the Gunbarrel Highway and the Canning Stock Route, two outback 'adventure' routes (see box). Permits are required for travel through Aboriginal communities.

WITTENOOM ■ 2265

Wittenoom, tucked high up in the Hamersley Range, was the site of a blue asbestos mine which was established in 1943 and closed in 1966 after years of government pressure to shut down because of health hazards.

A number of Wittenoom's former workers and residents eventually developed asbestosis and mesothelioma – degenerative diseases caused by breathing particles of asbestos, huge tailing mounds of which still loom above the mine site in the Wittenoom Gorge. Even though much of the excavated material has been covered with topsoil or asphalt, deadly fibres are still thought to be sometimes exposed to the wind. At its peak, the town had a population of about 2000 but less than fifty people remain and its fate hangs in the balance; there is pressure from the Western Australian government to evacuate the settlement.

WITTENOOM GORGE One of the largest gorges in the Karijini National Park, Wittenoom Gorge – a safe distance from the mine – has many swimming holes such as Cathedral, Town, Garden and Magazine pools, all of them surrounded by white-trunked trees and towering red cliffs topped by spectacular rock formations and outcroppings.

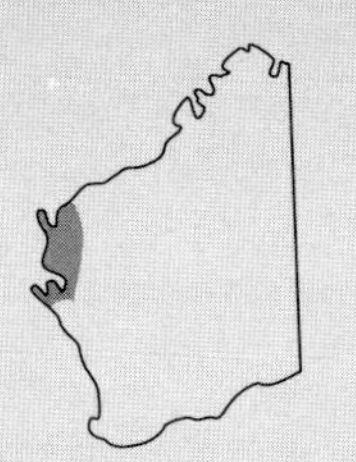

Carnarvon & Exmouth

French, Dutch and British explorers, Malay and Chinese pearlers, 'Afghan' cameleers and American sailors have all made a mark on this isolated, sometimes exotic landscape. Today, tourists come to see the coral reefs and feed the friendly dolphins.

Evidence of a huge – and ancient – colony of tiny molluscs lies metres deep and kilometres long on the shelly beaches of Denham Sound.

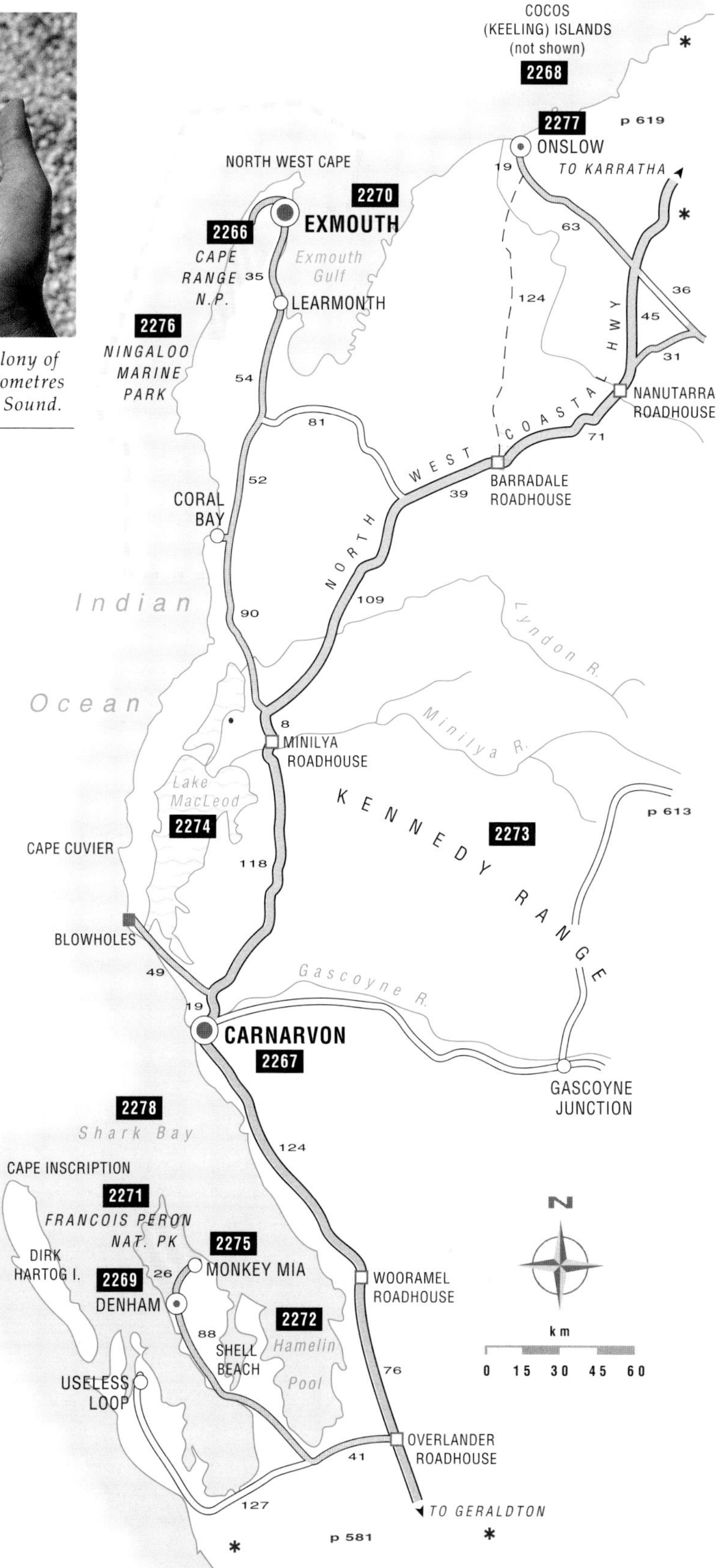

CAPE RANGE NATIONAL PARK ■ 2266

Cape Range is a low and almost inaccessible spine of limestone and sandstone hills running up the centre of North West Cape. Eroded by water and wind over millions of years into spectacular gulleys, caves and vertical-sided sinkholes, the range together with the slopes and narrow coastal plain to the west is now included within Cape Range National Park.

Expanded in 1974 to include the former Yardie Creek Station, Cape Range National Park now covers more than 50 000 hectares. Although there are four creeks in the park, only the largest, Yardie Creek, has water all year round and it flows through a beautiful gorge into a small estuarine lagoon.

Vegetation, mainly eucalypts and acacias, is sparse, as is to be expected in such arid conditions, although the occasional patch of Sturt's desert pea provides a pleasant surprise. A rare colony of yellow-footed rock wallabies live in the hilliest part of the park and within the caves there are specially adapted species of blind, colourless, freshwater eels, fish and shrimps. The park's spinifex bird was first discovered by the pastoralist and ornithologist Thomas Carter after whom Thomas Carter Lookout, one of the highest points in the park, is named.

Oil exploration in the 1950s is the main reason visitors can enter this relatively inaccessible park. During the unsuccessful search for oil in commercial quantities, the car park constructed at Shothole Canyon – so called because 'shots' were fired as part of the seismic survey – was a drill pad for the first exploratory well. The road was surveyed in order to gain access to the range for the large oil-drilling rigs.

CARNARVON ■ 2267

On the coast, where the region's major river, the Gascoyne, meets the Indian Ocean, stands this region's largest town, Carnarvon. With its broad streets planted with palms, bougainvillea and hibiscus, Carnarvon is a tropical outpost only two day's drive north of Perth.

In 1876, Aubrey Brown and John Monger, having driven 4000 sheep from York (see *Northam & Merredin*), became the first settlers at 'The Port'. By 1883, sufficient settlers had been attracted to the port for a town to be gazetted and named after the Secretary of State for the Colonies, Lord Carnarvon. On some of the country's largest stations thousands of sheep were raised and transport of stock and supplies was by boat…or by camel train. The town's forty-metre-wide roads, which allow for car parking on both sides and down the centre, were made to take in the turning-circle of a team of camels.

During the whaling years, Carnarvon was a land processing station but with the international ban on whaling in the early 1960s, the processing facilities were converted to packaging prawns.

In the 1920s, agriculture was developed in Carnarvon as bananas as well as other tropical fruit and vegetables began to appear on plantations on 1000 hectares of the Gascoyne river flats. The sole source of irrigation is the river, which is quite frequently empty.

The Gascoyne River has often been without visible water for months at a time but irrigation water can be tapped from below the sandy surface. When it rains inland, how-

COCOS (KEELING) ISLANDS (not shown) 2268
2277 ONSLOW p 619
TO KARRATHA
NORTH WEST CAPE
2270 EXMOUTH
2266 CAPE RANGE N.P.
Exmouth Gulf
LEARMONTH
2276 NINGALOO MARINE PARK
NANUTARRA ROADHOUSE
NORTH WEST COASTAL HWY
BARRADALE ROADHOUSE
CORAL BAY
Indian Ocean
Lyndon R.
Minilya R.
MINILYA ROADHOUSE
Lake MacLeod
2274
KENNEDY RANGE
2273
p 613
CAPE CUVIER
BLOWHOLES
Gascoyne R.
CARNARVON 2267
GASCOYNE JUNCTION
2278 Shark Bay
CAPE INSCRIPTION
2271 FRANCOIS PERON NAT. PK
2275 MONKEY MIA
DIRK HARTOG I.
2269 DENHAM
WOORAMEL ROADHOUSE
2272 Hamelin Pool
SHELL BEACH
USELESS LOOP
OVERLANDER ROADHOUSE
TO GERALDTON
p 581
N
km 0 15 30 45 60

Both humans and dolphins come to fish and frolic – sometimes together – in the shallow waters along the edge of the Peron Peninsula, on Shark Bay.

ever, the floods which follow are capable of submerging the 'Ten Mile Bridge' at Carnarvon.

But Carnarvon's history encompasses more than camels, whales and bananas. In the 1960s, part of Aubrey Brown's sheep station became the site of a NASA space-tracking station, which played a pivotal role in the Apollo space flights and in Neil Armstrong's moon landing. The station closed in 1975 and has since been used by Radio Australia for its transmissions to south-east Asia. On a site slightly further north in the Brown Range – named after Aubrey Brown – a satellite earth station operated for twenty years. The thirty-metre-wide satellite dish tracked satellites, transmitted the first satellite television program in Australia and was used by nine space agencies around the world before becoming technologically obsolete and closing in 1987. The big dish and memorabilia from the NASA and OTC stations can still be seen in Carnarvon.

With its spectacular beaches, blowholes and colourful everlasting daisies – not forgetting the almost complete absence of bothersome bushflies – Carnarvon is developing steadily as a tourist destination for visitors from the Pilbara and further afield. *Population 6900*

FESTIVALS Marari Tropical Festival, early May; Sun's Winter Home Bowling Carnival, June.

COCOS (KEELING) ISLANDS ■ 2268

Only two of the twenty-seven islands comprising the isolated Cocos group are inhabited: Home Island is the province of the true islanders who, through an elected council, run several coconut plantations, while on West Island a mainly temporary population supplies the workforce for government enterprises such as the animal-quarantine or meteorological stations (see box).

DENHAM ■ 2269

Denham is not only Australia's most westerly town but it sits opposite Dirk Hartog Island, the site of Australia's first known European landfall in 1616. The town was named after Captain H.M. Denham who charted and named many of the features of Shark Bay in 1858.

Freshwater soaks at Denham drew the first pastoralists and their sheep in the 1860s. They were closely followed by European pearlers and their indentured labourers from south-east Asia, shark fishermen and sandalwood 'pullers'. A salt mine at Useless Loop and the dolphins at Monkey Mia (see entry) have a more recent history and Denham remains the major town of the three Shark Bay settlements. *Population 940*

SHELL BEACH One of only two beaches in the world made up of non-fossilised shells, Shell Beach is formed from billions of tiny white coquina bivalves – molluscs that live in the extra salty water off Lharidon Bight. The shells on this stretch of coastline can reach ten metres in depth and where they have been compacted and fossilised into a solid mass, they are quarried and used as building blocks.

EXMOUTH ■ 2270

Although the North West Cape, on which Exmouth stands was visited by Dutch ships from as early as 1618, there was no settlement of any size here until the Second World War. Then, because of its strategic position so near to south-east Asian waters, Exmouth Gulf became a submarine refuelling base for allied submarines. Exmouth Gulf was also the starting point of Australian Z-force attacks on Japanese shipping in Singapore waters. The first operation on the *Krait* in 1943 was successful but the later Operation Rimau ended in death for all twenty-three Australians; all have had streets in Exmouth named after them.

In 1967, a $600 million joint US-Australian Naval Communications Station – the Harold E. Holt Base – was established and a support town was required to house naval personnel. Thus Exmouth was born, 350 years after the first European landing in the district. As one of a number of radio-relay stations sending and receiving messages to and from United States and Australian ships, the base has thirteen transmitter towers all taller than the Eiffel Tower. With no real wet season or winter and with access to beautiful beaches and Cape Range National Park (see entry), Exmouth is attracting an increasing number of tourists. *Population 3130*

VLAMINGH HEAD LIGHTHOUSE Built in 1912 on a 100-metre-high cliff, Vlamingh Lighthouse was named after Willem de Vlamingh, a Dutch East Indies Company captain who landed in the area in the seventeenth century. The lighthouse was manned until 1967 when the light was transferred to one of the Harold E. Holt station's transmitters. The 1907 shipwreck of the *Mildura*, the remains of an aircraft-warning radar that failed to prevent the three nights of Japanese bombing in 1943 and the museum in the lighthouse cover different aspects of the district's history.

FESTIVALS Exmo, July.

FRANCOIS PERON NATIONAL PARK ■ 2271

The Peron Peninsula and the newly established Francois Peron Park on 40 000 hectares of the peninsula are named after the French naturalist François Péron who was aboard the *Géographe* on an expedition to the area in 1801 and 1803. In addition to collecting specimens of flora and fauna, he wrote detailed descriptions of the life of the Aborigines.

The park was established to protect endangered wildlife and the wilderness and coastal environment within its boundaries. The most distinguishing features of the park are its many birridas – landlocked salt lakes or claypans with gypsum deposits – two of which have been swallowed by the sea, creating attractive, shallow, 'inland' bays.

Salt-tolerant shrubs grow beside the claypans while wattles are more common on the red sandy soils. The park is also the most northerly growing site for flowering plants, such as grevilleas and hakeas, common in the south-west of the state. The Shark Bay daisy, a purple-flowered

creeper, is as common now as it was in the days when William Dampier described it.

Much of the wildlife is nocturnal and therefore seldom seen but thorny devils, several small rodents, euros and many species of lizard are abundant as are brown snakes. The thick-billed grasswren has found sanctuary in the park, having been almost wiped out on the mainland. There are plans to reintroduce endangered species of mammals to Francois Peron Park, which because of its geography could quite readily be sealed off from the mainland by a vermin-proof fence.

For 100 years, until 1989, the Peron Peninsula was a sheep station and the old Peron Homestead with its 44° Centigrade artesian bore water is within the park boundaries. Dangers within the park therefore include possible burns at the bore as well as bogged vehicles on the birridas and crumbling cliffs at Cape Peron.

HAMELIN POOL ■ 2272

Named after the French captain of the *Naturaliste*, Hamelin Pool sits at the south-east end of Shark Bay. A shallow sandbar and a bank of sea grass limit tidal flushing of the pool, which, combined with high evaporation, makes Hamelin Pool twice as salty as seawater. This saltiness deters most life forms and has therefore protected the world's largest display of stromatolites from being eaten by other marine creatures.

To scientists, the discovery of the Hamelin Pool stromatolites is akin to finding a live dinosaur since stromatolites are the world's second oldest known fossil dating back some 3500 million years and most of those at Hamelin Pool are still alive and active. The stromatolites are spongy domes or matted sheets formed by tiny single-celled blue-green algae or cyanobacteria, one of the world's most primitive life forms. Unlike other fossils, which are the remains of parts of animals, stromatolites are the result of the active trapping and binding of sediments, and their size and shape are determined by waves and currents.

The stromatolites at Hamelin Pool vary from elongated ridges to club-shaped columns and huge mats. They are slow growing and, if damaged, never recover; camel-waggon tracks here are still visible many years after they were made. Tourists attracted to the pool are a modern threat to the stromatolites.

KENNEDY RANGE ■ 2273

Kennedy Range, a few hours drive from Carnarvon (see entry), is the flat-topped remnant of an eroded sandstone and limestone mountain range. On the south and west edges of the plateau, many steep-sided canyons and gulleys have been formed but the sandstone to the east, more erosion resistant, has formed into a distinctive cliff. With permanent springs on this eastern side and a road through to the cliffs, this is the part of the Kennedy Range most visited by tourists. Much of the rest of the 100-kilometre-long and 30-kilometre-wide range stretches across private property.

The fossils and gems in Kennedy Range, including ammonite fossils, petrified wood, chalcedony, opals and brightly coloured mookarite, are still washed down the Gascoyne River as far as Rocky Pool about fifty kilometres east of Carnarvon.

LAKE MacLEOD ■ 2274

Lake MacLeod is separated by a barrier ridge of high dunes from the Indian Ocean and most of the lake's surface lies between one and three metres below sea level. Despite its name this depression is normally dry although the ponds that surround it are constantly recharged with seawater, which wells up from caverns below them.

The salt lake has been the centre of a successful salt mining industry since 1965 when a huge plant was moved on to the 225 000-hectare lake surface. Brine is pumped on to the salt pans where evaporation by the sun crystallises the salt – with up to 3500 hours of sunshine each year, evaporation is guaranteed.

The salt is transported by road train to Cape Cuvier, a natural deep harbour where it is stockpiled on the clifftop before being bulldozed audaciously over the edge on to a long loading conveyer sixty metres below! At the end of the conveyor are ships bound for Japan, south-east Asia, Kenya or New Zealand. The wreck of one of these salt ships, the *Korean Star*, can be seen where it was broken in two by Cyclone Herbie in 1988.

It is estimated that up to 1.5 million tonnes of salt could be produced each year from Lake Macleod. In spite of this commercial activity, the Lake MacLeod area is a noted bird refuge and a resting place for thousands of migratory waders from south-east Asia.

MONKEY MIA ■ 2275

It is possible that a pearling boat called *Monkey* had its anchorage at this small bay, which has been called by the rather puzzling name of Monkey Mia since the late nineteenth century. The permanent population at Monkey Mia has always been small even during the years after 1912 when a fish canning and processing factory was based there.

Thousands of tourists from all over the world and many students of marine biology now visit Monkey Mia because of the dolphins which swim readily into the shallows to be handfed. From the early 1960s, a small group of dolphins, part of a much larger 'pod' of up to 300 animals, began swimming into the knee-deep water at Monkey Mia. This group of five adult females and two male calves would allow themselves to be touched and would accept fish from – and offer it to – willing humans.

The opening of a dolphin information centre in the 1980s encouraged more visitors but it was the completion of a sealed road in 1985 that caused numbers to escalate dramatically. The aim of the Department of Conservation and Land Management is to control the handfeeding so that the dolphins never become dependent but continue to come into Monkey Mia by choice.

NINGALOO MARINE PARK ■ 2276

Ningaloo Marine Park is the second of two national parks on the North West Cape peninsula and conserves the colourful aquatic environment here as Cape Range National Park (see entry) does the land. The park, proclaimed in 1987, runs along the full length of the beautiful Ningaloo coral reef and covers about 4000 square kilometres of ocean.

Ningaloo Reef is one of the world's major reefs and one of only two coral-reef systems found on a western coastline. It is Australia's longest continuous fringing coral reef at approximately 260 kilometres in length and the closest to land – 300 metres at its closest and 4 kilometres at its greatest distance from shore. The reef is made up of at least 220 varieties of coral and more than 500 different species of fish swim through the warm waters of the reef or the lagoon it protects.

The water within the park is clearly divided into sanctuary zones, recreational zones and general zones. No collecting or fishing is allowed in sanctuary zones, which preserve an undisturbed environment for visitors to observe rare starfish, dugongs, turtles which lay their eggs in protected beach rookeries and the world's largest fish, the whaleshark, which can reach weights of up to 40 000 kilograms. With an end to whaling, migrating humpback whales heading for their breeding grounds on the north-west shelf can be seen beyond the park boundaries.

Large areas of the coral have been eaten and killed by the *Drupella* snail and marine scientists are trying to establish whether this phenomenon is a natural part of the reef's cycle or is caused by human disturbance of the fragile ecology.

ONSLOW ■ 2277

For a small village in an isolated district, Onslow has had a fairly dramatic history. Originally established in 1885 as a port for inland sheep stations and as a centre for pearling and mining, the first townsite declined when most of the residents and as many buildings as possible were moved to a new site at Beadon Bay during 1925.

Although a series of cyclones had devastated the town prior to 1925, the relocation was prompted primarily by the need for better port facilities. But the deep-water jetty that opened in Beadon Bay in May 1925 was damaged by cyclones on

Since 1967, North West Cape's traditional beacon on Vlamingh Head has been overshadowed by the tall towers of a naval radio-relay base.

THE COCONUT ISLES...BARELY BREAKING THROUGH THE WAVES

The Clunies-Ross family's historic connection with the Cocos Islands is commemorated by the lonely gravestones on Home Island.

HALFWAY between Australia and Sri Lanka, about as isolated as it is possible to be on earth, lies a group of twenty-five uninhabited and two inhabited islands – perched on two low-lying coral atolls. The Cocos (Keeling) Islands were first settled in the mid-1820s – the two occupied islands were Pula Selma (later called Home Island) and Direction Island – but the most important arrival on the islands was that of John Clunies-Ross who spent a brief four days clearing land and planting seeds on Home Island before returning in 1827 to occupy his claim.

The settlement established by this Scottish seaman was to last for more than 150 years. With imported south-east Asian labourers – the forebears of the present residents of Home Island – the Clunies-Ross family established mills and workshops to process fresh coconuts from the plantations into oil and copra, the island's only source of income. In 1886, Queen Victoria granted George Clunies-Ross and his heirs, in perpetuity, all land above the high-water mark. Constitutional rights and administration, however, remained with the Crown.

Despite their isolation, the islands figured in the century's two great wars: the First World War saw a dramatic sea battle between the German warship *Emden* and HMAS *Sydney* off one of the islands. The Second World War brought a flying boat base and Allied troops. The end of the war saw 1600 Cocos islanders go to Christmas Island, Singapore or North Borneo (now Sabah) because the island's economy could no longer support them.

Australia's initial interest in these balmy tropical isles in 1951 was as an airport and refuelling base on the Australia–to–South Africa route. In 1955, the Cocos Islands became an Australian external colony, and in 1978 the Australian government bought the remaining Clunies-Ross assets on the islands for $6.25 million. By the mid-1980s, the Cocos islanders had voted, in a United Nations-supervised referendum, for Australian citizenship rather than independence.

The 400 Cocos islanders on Home Island now deal with local affairs through an elected Island Council and run the coconut plantations as a co-operative. The 200-odd population on West Island is employed in the animal-quarantine station for cattle being imported to Australia, in the meteorological station for aviation forecasts or as local-government administrators. □

three occasions and the damage sustained by the jetty during the third cyclone in 1963 led to its closure. By this stage, road haulage was making its impact felt in the north-west and the feasibility of repairing the thrice-damaged jetty was questionable.

Because cyclones are such regular visitors to this region, the houses in Onslow have special steel shutters and their iron roofs are cleated on in order to withstand any passing cyclonic wind.

Onslow airfield was bombed by the Japanese in 1943 and the town had a number of oil-storage bunkers for refuelling Allied ships. Ten years later, Onslow became the shore depot for the British nuclear tests on the Montebello Islands. It was also the main base for offshore oil and gas exploration and a supply depot for the Barrow Island field, eighty kilometres north of Onslow.

Things have quietened down considerably in recent years and even the shire headquarters has moved to Tom Price (see *Newman & Tom Price*). Now, a tourist industry – encouraged by the proximity of the ten offshore islands in the Mackerel Island group, a breeding place for turtles – is being developed. *Population 880*

SHARK BAY ■ 2278

Shark Bay is a series of semi-enclosed gulfs, inlets, bays and islands, split in two by Peron Peninsula. With 1500 kilometres of coastline and an area of 30 000 square kilometres – 55 per cent water and 45 per cent land – Shark Bay has a number of unique features such as the stromatolites at Hamelin Pool (see entry), the dolphins at Monkey Mia (see entry) and a number of islands providing sanctuary for endangered animals. These distinctive features led to its inclusion on the World Heritage list in 1991 (see box, *Cairns & Innisfail*).

Shark Bay was the site of the first known European landings on the Australian mainland. After Dirk Hartog landed in 1616 on the island later named after him, other French, Dutch and British explorers and naturalists – including Willem De Vlamingh, William Dampier and Nicolas Baudin – were attracted to Shark Bay. The names of many of these early explorers and the ships they came in were used to name features within Shark Bay.

Australia's first pearling industry started in Shark Bay in the 1870s and continued until the 1930s. The days of mining guano deposits – accumulated seabird excrement – on Shark Bay's many islands, whaling and turtle hunting are over but commercial fishing and trawling for scallops and prawns continue. The waters of the bay teem with turtles, dugongs, whales, sea snakes and sharks, mainly the small Shark Bay whaler and the tiger shark, which grows to over seven metres. It was the sight of some of these impressive creatures that led William Dampier to name the bay Shark Bay in 1699.

The main reason for this profusion of life is the huge quantity of seagrass, a flowering plant – not a seaweed – that pollinates underwater and covers 4000 square kilometres of the bay. One bank of this seagrass is almost 130 kilometres long, contains nine varieties of the plant and has matted together over approximately 5000 years aided by the prevailing winds and tidal currents. The 103 000 hectares of the Wooramel Seagrass Bank stretches along the eastern shore of Shark Bay almost to Carnarvon, providing a food supply, habitats and shelter for hundreds of different types of marine creatures.

FESTIVALS Great Nanga Fishing Competition, April.

No-one is quite sure who is watching whom at Monkey Mia, where inter-species socialisation is actively encouraged by dolphins as well as humans.

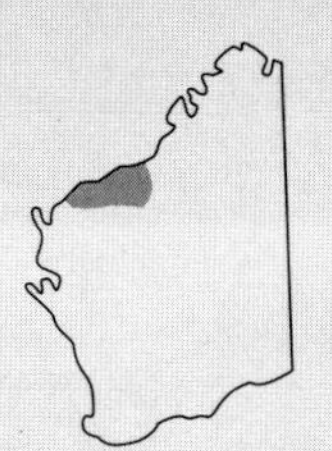

Port Hedland & Karratha

Early settlers were drawn here by vivid descriptions of fertile country, and many fine stone buildings still stand as testament to their pioneer industry. Over the years many people came chasing easy wealth from pearls or gold but it was the mineral boom of the 1960s which transformed small ports into bustling centres.

BARROW ISLAND ■ 2279

Barrow Island is the second biggest island off the Western Australian coast. First sighted by the French in the early 1800s, who thought it was part of mainland Australia, the island was named by Lieutenant Phillip Parker King in 1818, after Sir John Barrow, the Under Secretary to the Admiralty at the time.

Barrow Island was separated from the mainland of Australia about 6000 to 8000 years ago and is regarded by scientists as a living museum of the mainland before farming developed and introduced animals upset the balance of the habitats and landscapes of Western Australia.

Public interest in the island was generated after the naturalist John T. Tenney spent two months there in 1900 collecting birds and animals and it was declared a reserve in 1908.

A prickly spinifex covers almost the entire island while dispersed throughout it are big, dark green clumps of rock fig growing out of the limestone. Occasional native willows grow in the centre of the thickets. Nearly 300 species of native plants grow on Barrow, the biggest being a species of eucalypt. A valley that shelters an isolated group of these trees has been dubbed by local islanders as the Valley of the 'Giants' because the eucalypts there grow to a huge – by Barrow Island standards – eight metres.

WAPET CAMP Barrow Island was recognised as being a potential site for oil in the 1950s. By the end of the 1970s, about 280 wells were producing oil. Tankers load Barrow Island crude by anchoring about ten kilometres offshore at the end of a submarine pipeline.

In December, the Christmas Island shoreline turns crimson as land crabs make a lemming-like march to their primeval habitat in order to mate.

BURRUP PENINSULA ■ 2280

This 'island' was separated from the mainland by tidal mudflats until a causeway was built. It contains one of the richest sites for prehistoric rock engravings in Australia and probably the world: there are more than 10 000 Aboriginal engravings in over 500 recorded sites.

The rock etchings, shell middens, fish traps and hunting hides are thought to be the work of the Aboriginal people of the now-vanished Yapurrara language group who occupied the isolated Burrup Peninsula and neighbouring Dampier Archipelago long before white settlement.

The peninsula is the headquarters for an offshore drilling complex, its plant fed by an underwater pipeline on the sea floor from one of the world's largest gas-production platforms. The platform stands in 140 metres of water, tapping natural gas from beneath the continental shelf 135 kilometres offshore. Some of the

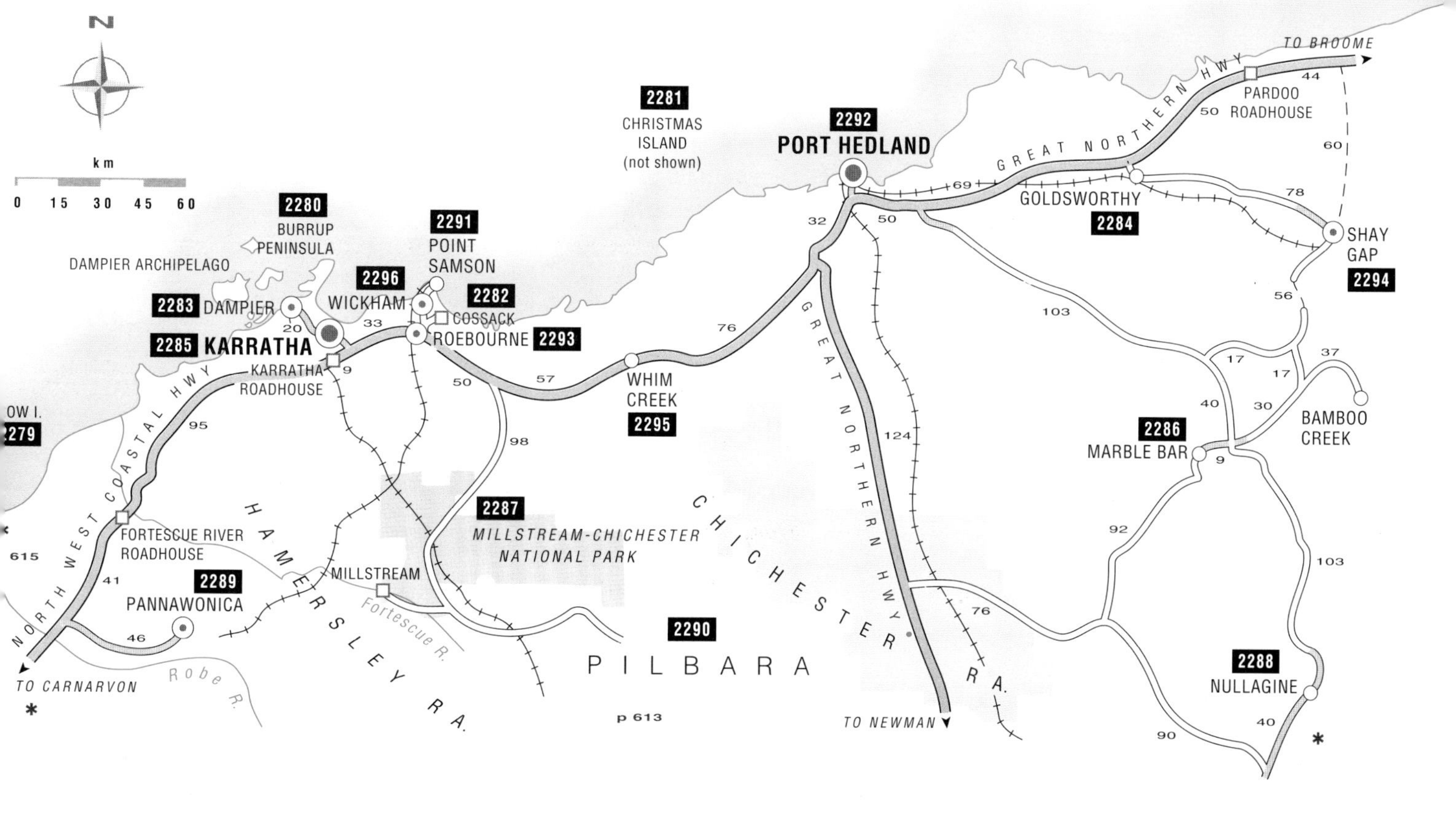

N
km
0 15 30 45 60
2280 BURRUP PENINSULA
DAMPIER ARCHIPELAGO
2283 DAMPIER
2285 KARRATHA
KARRATHA ROADHOUSE
2296 WICKHAM
2291 POINT SAMSON
2282 COSSACK
ROEBOURNE 2293
2281 CHRISTMAS ISLAND (not shown)
2292 PORT HEDLAND
TO BROOME
PARDOO ROADHOUSE
GREAT NORTHERN HWY
GOLDSWORTHY 2284
SHAY GAP 2294
WHIM CREEK 2295
BAMBOO CREEK
2286 MARBLE BAR
OW I. 2279
NORTH WEST COASTAL HWY
FORTESCUE RIVER ROADHOUSE
2289 PANNAWONICA
HAMERSLEY RA.
MILLSTREAM
Fortescue R.
Robe R.
2287 MILLSTREAM-CHICHESTER NATIONAL PARK
CHICHESTER RA.
2290
PILBARA
2288 NULLAGINE
TO CARNARVON
TO NEWMAN
p 613
615

gas is reserved for iron-ore plants in the Pilbara and an overland pipe carries an allotment south to Perth.

CHRISTMAS ISLAND ■ 2281

Christmas Island sits south of Java, closer to south-east Asia than Australia. Until recent times it was an important source for phosphate but the island's emphasis is now on tourism. A national park covers 8720 hectares, which is about two-thirds of the island as well as most of its fringing reef.

Included within the park is much of the island's remaining rainforest as well as the habitat of the endemic and endangered Abbott's Booby seabird. The island is also renowned for its land crabs; the world's largest remaining population of coconut, or robber, crabs is found on the island and, during the wet season, the migration of 130 million red crabs to the sea is a spectacular sight.

Walking and driving tracks provide access to the park's attractions and a picnic site and raised boardwalk have been constructed in the popular Dales section.

COSSACK ■ 2282

Walter Padbury and his party were the first settlers in the 'North District' arriving in Tien Tsin Harbour (now Port Walcott) in 1863. The harbour was named after the barque that carried the settlers to the region and similarly, Cossack was given its name in 1871 when Governor Weld visited in HMS *Cossack*.

As the first port in the North-West, Cossack played a vital role as a commercial and social centre for farms in the surrounding area, handling all supplies for the emerging region.

Cossack was also the base for an early pearling industry and up to fifty-seven luggers operated in the area by 1875, though a slump in shell and pearl prices after this date led to a decrease in the number of licensed boats. Many Asians arrived here as indentured labour and a reminder of this once-booming industry are the graves of many Japanese divers in the cemetery. Many others, including Aborigines who were employed as divers, were lost at sea.

By the 1880s, most of the pearling fleet had moved north to Broome, but discovery of gold at around the same time brought an influx of prospectors and maintained Cossack as the port of exit and entry for the region. By the turn of the century, the harbour had silted up so badly that it was no longer possible for large boats to enter and Point Samson became the major port after 1910.

EMMA WITHNELL TRAIL This fifty-two-kilometre driving route which retraces the settlement and development of the Roebourne district is named after the first European woman settler in the North-West. The trail begins at Roebourne, once the main town of the region, and features Cossack, the first port; Point Samson, established in 1909 as a deep-water port; and Wickham, an iron-ore mining town settled in 1971.

DAMPIER ■ 2283

Both the town and archipelago are named for William Dampier, the English explorer who landed on nearby Rosemary Island in 1699. The deepwater port and modern town were built by Hamersley Iron in the 1960s and it is here that the iron ore from mines at Tom Price and Paraburdoo is railed, stockpiled and loaded onto ships for export. Salt is also an important export.

Dampier is said to have more boats per capita than any other town in Australia and the busy harbour is a handy base for the popular fishing areas of the Dampier Archipelago. *Population 1810*

DAMPIER ARCHIPELAGO Over forty-two islands, islets and rocks make up the Dampier Archipelago which was formed by rising sea levels around 8000 years ago. The islands have been used for many different purposes such as pearling, grazing and whaling since white settlement, but today they are mainly for nature conservation and recreation areas.

The islands have been zoned to keep a balance between conservation and recreation, with areas set aside for visitors while seabird- and turtle-nesting sites are closed to the public.

A view of the mesas and buttes in the Millstream-Chichester Park reveals the rawness of a landscape where the only plants to survive in the thin topsoil are tough but alluringly – if briefly – flowered types like Sturt's desert pea (above).

GOLDSWORTHY ■ 2284

Mount Goldsworthy, the source of the iron ore for this mining town, was once a 132-metre peak that has been replaced by a deep pit after years of mining. Mining activities are centred at Shay Gap and people at Goldsworthy are employed to maintain the railway which takes ore to the Finucane Island shiploading facility, near Port Hedland.

KARRATHA ■ 2285

Karratha is an Aboriginal word said to mean 'good country'. The hills around Karratha are clothed in spinifex, but beautiful white-barked coolibahs line nearby creeks. The town is now the administrative centre for the Shire of Roebourne and regional centre for many businesses and government departments.

Many tourists use the town as a base when exploring the Pilbara and there is a modern shopping centre and caravan parks and motel accommodation. During early August, both Karratha and Dampier hold their annual festival, the tongue-twisting name of which is partly derived from the chemical symbols for the natural resources that have been the region's great asset. The FeNaClng Festival name has three elements: Fe – iron, NaCL – salt and LNG – liquefied natural gas! The festival includes a float parade, a fair and other activities. *Population 11 320*

MARBLE BAR ■ 228

A trio of prospectors – Ted Francis, Harry Jenkins and James Edmonson found alluvial gold here early in 1890, and a settlement sprang up as eager prospectors flocked quickly to the region. At the height of the gold boom, the population numbered in the thousands. Today a population of a few hundred makes a living from tin and manganese mining. The town takes its name from the immense band of jasper – not marble as was first supposed – that mark the site of the Coongan River approximately five kilometres away.

Of interest is Chinamans Pool, where legend has it a Chinese miner was hanged when he refused to disclose the secret location of his gold strike. The Bar, as it's affectionately called, is best known as the hottest town in Australia.

COMET MINE Gold was discovered in the district in mid-1930; the site was named after Halley's Comet and a once-in-a-lifetime strike it turned out to be. The mine began production in 1931, at one time providing employment for more than 100 workers during the lean years of the Great Depression. By the time the mine was closed, nearly five tonnes of gold had been extracted.

FESTIVALS Marble Bar Cup and Ball, June or July.

MILLSTREAM-CHICHESTER NATIONAL PARK ■ 2287

The Millstream-Chichester National Park protects almost 200 000 hectares of basalt ranges and clay tablelands in the central Pilbara district. Spinifex grass and white-barked snappy gums cover most of the Chichester Range with pale and graceful coolibahs and cajeputs growing along the edge of what are usually dry watercourses.

At Millstream, freshwater springs from an aquifer to create the lush tropical oasis of Chinderwarriner Pool. Afghan camel drivers in the late nineteenth century, carrying stores from Cossack to inland sheep stations and mining towns, then returning with the wool clips, planted date palms around this pool. The palms have now virtually taken over the native vegetation, which was once a majestic woodland of river gums and cajeputs.

Chinderwarriner is a very important site for the Yinjibarndi people of this region. They come to Millstream for important ceremonial rituals, to obtain a special acacia used for making spears, to catch fish and to eat other local foods.

NULLAGINE ■ 2288

This small copper and manganese mining town south-east of Port Hedland was gazetted just before the turn of the century, in 1899. The Nullagine Roads Board was created a few years prior to this to administer an area of 148 000 kilometres. The district has an interesting variety of gemstones and the one hotel is aptly named the 'Conglomerate'.

PANNAWONICA ■ 2289

Pannawonica is a mining town which was built to house the mine workers and their families employed in the Cliffs Robe River Iron Associates' open-cut, iron-ore mine. The name Pannawonica comes from an Aboriginal word said to mean 'the hill that came from the sea'. According to legend, two Aboriginal groups frequently had disputes over the hill. As a result, the sea spirit moved the hill inland to where it is today and the drag marks became the Robe River. *Population 820*

FESTIVALS Panna Regatta, June.

PILBARA ■ 2290

Some of the oldest rocks analysed by geologists are found in the Pilbara. These ancient rocks are covered in some areas by the rocks of a much younger geological age including the products of present-day erosion. Almost unlimited deposits of useful minerals are found here and this has made the region one of the busiest and most important mining centres in Australia.

There are also many historical sites, such as abandoned settlements and old mining towns. On the coast, vast tidal flats are interspersed with extensive mangrove thickets. Inland, the rugged uplands are intersected by steep river valleys. In the Hamersley Ranges, there are spectacular gorges where huge iron-ore extraction projects take place.

The Pilbara's arid climate has high temperatures with variable rainfall. Heavy rains and soaring temperatures are not uncommon, but there are often long periods without rain.

POINT SAMSON ■ 2291

This seaside town became the major port for the Roebourne district in 1910, after silting problems prevented large ships from entering Cossack harbour. It was the exit port for asbestos from Wittenoom until 1968, as well as receiving copper and wool exports from the district.

Traffic at the port declined when the mining companies established their own modern shipping facilities at Dampier (see entry). Point Samson supports a small fishing industry.

PORT HEDLAND ■ 2292

Once a quiet country town, Port Hedland grew rapidly with the mineral boom which began in the 1960s. Houses sprang up almost overnight, as the town spread and the new suburbs of South Hedland, Finucane and Cooke Point were built.

Port Hedland was named after Captain Peter Hedland who discovered the entrance to the shallow bay in 1863. Settlers were quick to follow; the first stock run was established on the banks of the DeGrey River in July of that year.

The town became a busy base for pearling luggers in the 1870s, but it was a gold strike at Marble Bar that brought settlers to the area in any number. Tin, copper, gold and manganese were mined over the years, but it was the discovery of an incredibly rich iron-ore body in the hinterland that provided the impetus for the modern mining industry and the development of the port.

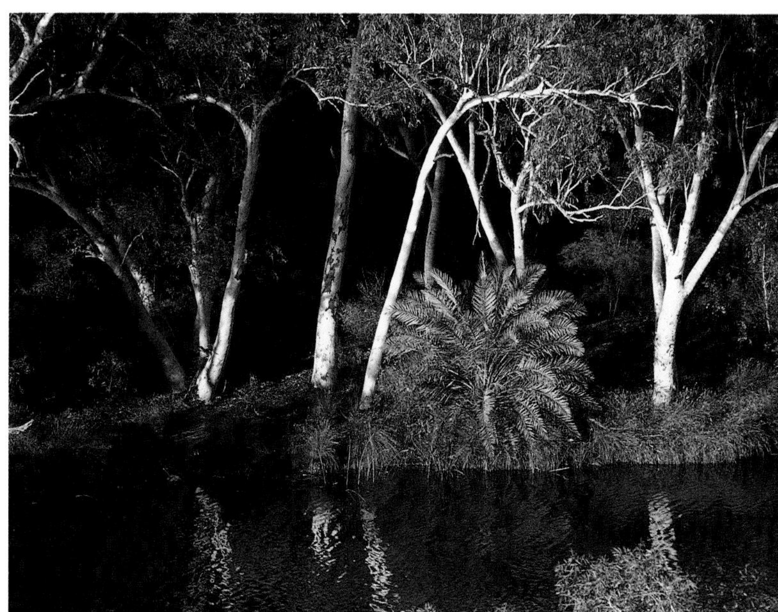

Date palms are an exotic intrusion into the oasis of Millstream, itself a green intrusion into a region which holds its breath for the annual 'wet'.

Today, Port Hedland is the major centre of a thriving industry. Some of the world's biggest ore carriers are seen here almost every day. Salt is also an important export and stark white dunes of the mineral waiting to be shipped overseas stand like salty, lunar landmarks along the North West Coastal Highway.

Many fine old buildings can still be seen in the town. Of interest is the police station and jail (1903), the court house (1900) – a former general store then men's quarters – and the Pier (1907) and Esplanade Hotels. There is a shipping observation lookout built with timber from old Port Hedland jetties.

The Port Hedland waters are an anglers paradise – they are reputed to have some of the best fishing in the world. On the turn of the tide, snapper, mullet, kingfish, bream, skippy and whiting can be caught almost anywhere along the beach. *Population 11 340*

ROEBOURNE ■ 2293

Named after John Roe, the Surveyor-General of the time, Roebourne was established as far back as 1866. First to explore the area was the surveyor Francis Gregory in 1861. Many settlers took up pastoral leases in the area after reading Gregory's inspiring descriptions of the fertile DeGrey River region.

In its early days, Roebourne was the administrative centre for the vast North-West region but, with the opening of the Port Hedland to Marble Bar railway line, the area declined until the mineral boom of the 1960s came along. In the old section of town there are a number of solidly built, stone public buildings still standing. *Population 1210*

SHAY GAP ■ 2294

Shay Gap takes its name from a nearby break in the hills. The town, designed specifically for Pilbara conditions, is operated and owned by the mining company which runs an iron-ore mine close by. As with Goldsworthy, there are no tourist facilities in Shay Gap, but fuel is available. *Population 820*

WHIM CREEK ■ 2295

The discovery of copper here by Nathaniel William Cooke in 1881 eventually led to mineral development of other areas in the Pilbara. Mining has since ceased and the area is now divided into large pastoral runs, with the old hotel the only reminder of the early mining days still standing.

WICKHAM ■ 2296

Built in the 1970s, this mining town is the sister settlement to Pannawonica. Iron ore mined at Pannawonica is processed and then exported from nearby Cape Lambert; Wickham is the town that houses the workers of the processing plant.

The town is still company owned and operated; it is named after Captain John Wickham who explored the north-west coast in HMS *Beagle*, also famous for carrying Charles Darwin on his round-the-world voyage.

There are fine community, sporting and shopping facilities and the Roebourne Golf Club hosts an annual Cossack-to-Wickham Golf Bash in September each year. *Population 1970*

CAPE LAMBERT The wharf here is one of the highest and longest open ocean wharves in Australia, sitting more than fourteen metres above the waves and stretching two-and-a-half kilometres out to sea.

THE GREAT DESERTS

In the Gibson Desert, the briefest of showers encourages plant growth in the crazy-paving surface.

The meagre run-off from 'mounts' Gordon and Everard trickles down to irrigate a ring of hardy scrub in the centre of the Gibson Desert.

Despite pastoral and mining intrusions into the so-called 'dead heart' of Australia, the great deserts remain steadfastly unconquerable. These parched zones – pocked with dry salt lakes, patched with stony desert or ridged with sand dunes – are the true, 'dead' interior.

In the 1870s, after struggling for almost half a century in a colony that most believed would fail, settlers in Western Australia felt secure enough to lift up their heads and look around at the land they had come to inhabit.

They were already aware that water was scarce and, because of that, there was very little land fertile enough to support a significant population. Unlike other large land masses in the world, Western Australia had no great rivers that flowed into the sea. With their knowledge of other continents, together with a good deal of wishful thinking, many reasoned that there must be great rivers, but that they flowed eastwards to an inland sea. In the early 1870s, the more adventurous headed inland. And they did find a sea – a vast ocean of rolling sand and endless wastes, three-quarters the size of Europe.

Viewed dispassionately, with the exception of the extreme south-west and north-east corners, Western Australia is largely desert. Almost two-thirds of the state is taken up by just three vast sandy deserts and their arid fringes.

But even the most desolate places are never totally barren. In every Australian desert there is enough occasional rain to maintain a variety of unique animals and plants. Add to that the cleansing emptiness of open spaces, cloudless skies, rugged ranges and startling gorges, and the vision of the arid expanse is transformed.

In the north of Western Australia, covering an area that could accommodate Italy and Great Britain, is the Great Sandy Desert. Stretching from the Northern Territory border to the Indian Ocean south of Broome, it is a boundless sea of red sand dunes – some of which are thirty metres high and several kilometres long – wind-blown in an east-west direction. In the centre of the desert, like a gleaming white skeleton, are the dried salt beds of the Percival Lakes.

To the south is the Gibson Desert – a searing desolate place with huge, open spinifex plains and great expanses of sand ridges running parallel to the horizon for hundreds of kilometres. Apart from a few eroded ridges that were once mountain ranges, the only feature of the Gibson Desert is the 150-square-kilometre waste of Lake Disappointment – a cracked, salty symbol of the shattered dreams of the early explorers.

Further south is the Great Victoria Desert. Covering an area the size of France, it stretches from Western Australia's goldfields far into South Australia. It too is a sea of rolling dunes, but stabilised by low scrub. At its narrow, eastern limits the desert territories balloon out again to create the awful, sandy void of the Simpson Desert.

Dusty earth, fiery red rock, unbearable heat, kilometre-high columns of 'dust devils' swirling menacingly on the horizon; it is difficult to believe that anything could live in such desolation. Then there is the darkness of a rain cloud and a stillness as the parched desert holds its breath. Large drops begin to fall, slowly at first, and a crack of thunder announces that a new cycle has begun. Millions of seeds that have lain in the dust for up to ten years awaken. Within days, a green mat covers the red sand. For one or two months the deserts are overwhelmed with the frenzied activity of those who know that their time is short. The sudden explosion of insects is welcomed by the few desert birds that endure the long drought. But within a few months the dryness will have returned.

Although the western deserts in particular have a special splendour of their own, what is most fascinating about them are the spectacular ranges on their mulga fringes. Their distant blueness, which turns to red in the morning sun, has a beauty that is enhanced by the arid desolation all around. On the western boundary of the Gibson Desert is the Hamersley Range, rugged blocks of ironstone carved over millions of years. It contains some of the oldest land formations on earth, and some extraordinarily beautiful gorges.

In this magnificent wasteland, where explorers colonial and modern alike have trekked in search of their personal El Dorados, lived the desert Aborigines. The Gibson Desert – the explorer Ernest Giles' 'terrible region' – was the home of the Gadudjara, the Ngadadjara and the Mandildjara. But by the mid-1970s it was virtually uninhabited as the nomads adopted a new lifestyle in settlements on the desert's edge.

Wiluna, now little more than a ghost town, is on the south-west edge of the Gibson. From there the Gunbarrel Highway begins its journey through the Gibson and Great Victoria deserts to Alice Springs. It is also the beginning of the Canning Stock Route – a 1600-kilometre track across the Gibson and the Great Sandy deserts to Halls Creek. Those who enter the deserts unprepared to bow to powerful natural forces, do so at their own peril. To those who go with respect and an open mind, the deserts reveal a great beauty. □

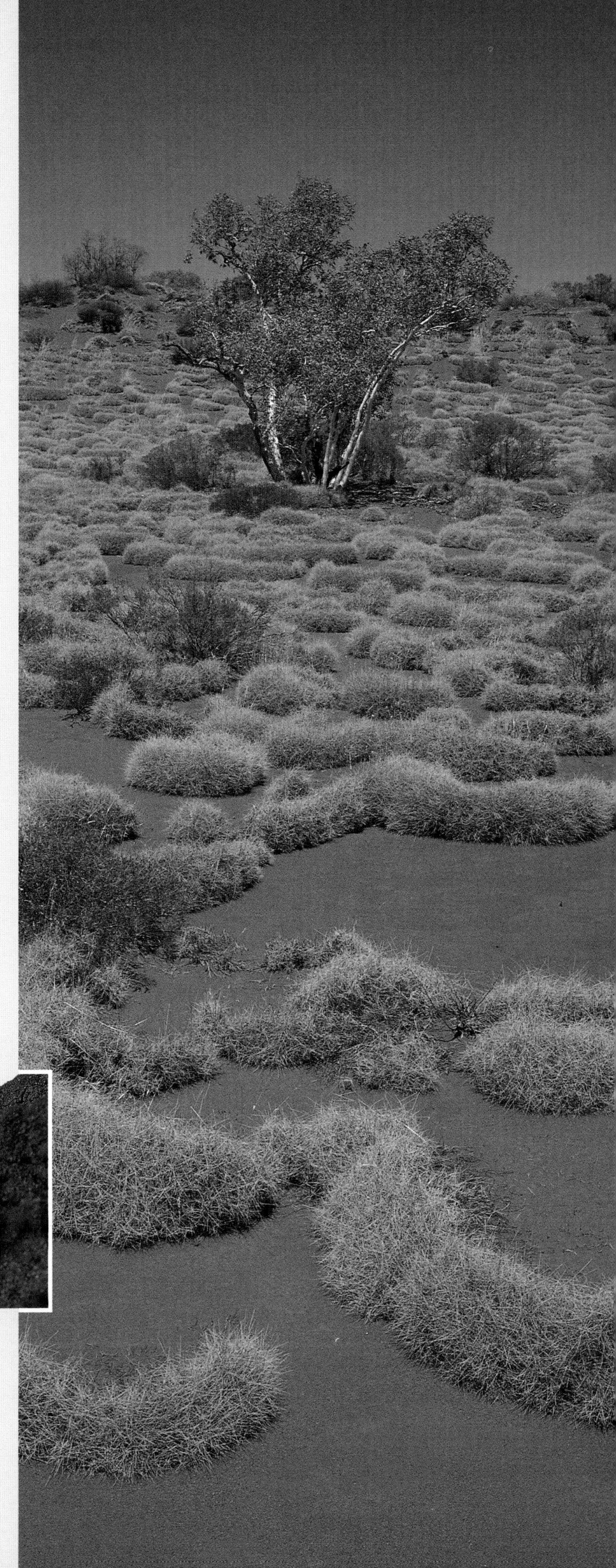

The neatly matching semi-circles of spinifex grow away from the direction of the prevailing wind in the Great Sandy Desert, home to many small, efficient forms of life such as the unlovely thorny devil.

Broome & Derby

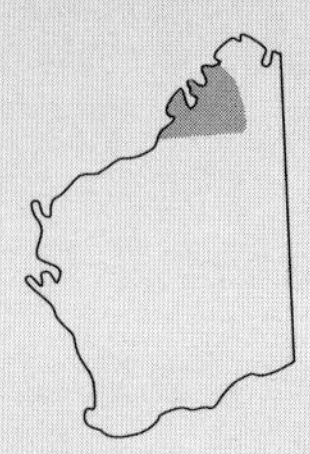

This is one of Australia's remotest corners, occupied continuously by Europeans since only 1879 and even in modern times still sparsely populated. Derby was the region's first town but Broome is its largest, despite a slump in its fortunes when the pearling boom days came to an end.

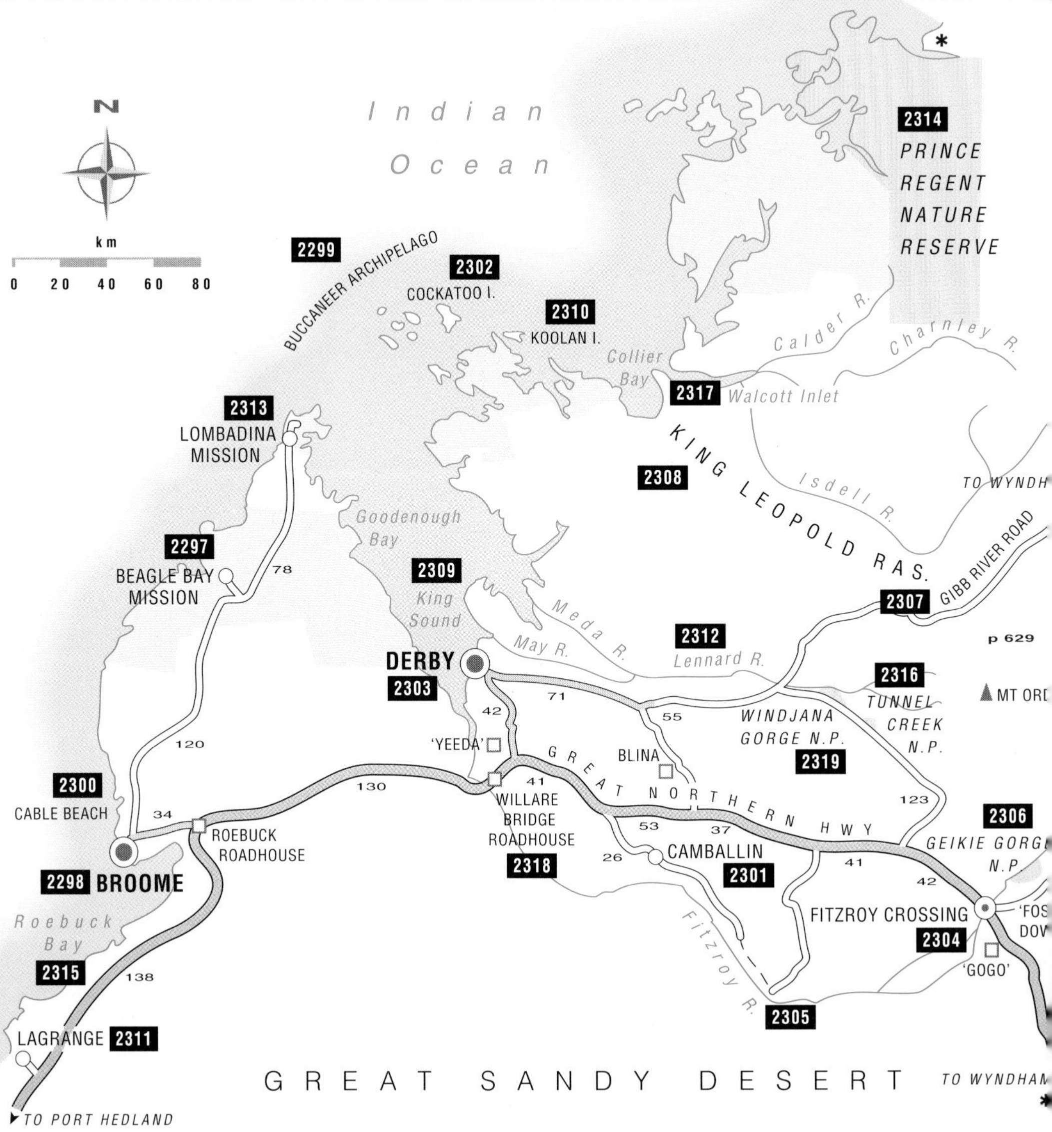

BEAGLE BAY ■ **2297**
Trappist monks established an Aboriginal mission at Beagle Bay, north of Broome, in 1890. The church was built during the First World War from 60 000 hand-made, double bricks and its altar is decorated with mother-of-pearl shell from local waters.

Permits are required for entry onto the Aboriginal land around both Beagle Bay and Lombadina Mission (see entry) to the north.

BROOME ■ **2298**
It seems fairly certain that William Dampier, the district's most famous early visitor, did not actually land at the present site of Broome, and although he certainly came ashore somewhere along this coast in search of water in 1699, the spot is thought to have been at Lagrange Bay, to the south of Roebuck Bay (see entry), around which the town of Broome is built. Roebuck Bay is named after Dampier's ship.

From their base at Cossack (see *Port Hedland & Karratha*) pearlfishers had been diving into the waters of Roebuck Bay since the early 1870s and a small settlement was founded here in 1883. The town was named in honour of Frederick Broome, Governor of Western Australia. In 1889, locals watched in amazement as an elaborate cable station (now the court house, see sub-entry) was erected in the settlement.

News of rich pearling grounds along this coast spread rapidly and by 1910, Broome was the pearling capital of the world, with a population of 5000, many of whom worked on the 400 luggers of the port. At first many of the divers were Aborigines, but as Japanese and Chinese businessmen took control of the industry, they were replaced by divers from Asia and the Pacific. Broome reached its peak population in the 1920s, a period that was also characterised by violence among rival ethnic groups.

Broome's gradual decline from those heady days began with the effects of the Great Depression of the 1930s and was exacerbated by the Second World War. There were several Japanese air raids on Broome – though these were organised to attack military installations rather than the town – and at least seventy people were killed in the strafing. At low tide the wrecks of some of the flying boats sunk in the harbour during these raids can still be seen. Japanese workers returned in 1953, and for a time it looked as though

The day of the working lugger is all but over in Broome where a cargo of tourists seeking a whiff of the past is more likely than a haul of pearl shell.

Tourism has helped revive Broome's commercial heart and Dampier Terrace is a match for the main street of any Queensland resort of a similar latitude.

the pearling industry might be revived. But this was not to be. A large part of the blame can be laid at the door of the humble plastic button which virtually wiped out the mother-of-pearl industry. A continuing demand for live shells to be seeded for cultured pearls, small sales of seed pearls, beef cattle and eventually, a growing tourist trade, combined to prevent Broome from becoming a ghost town.

The extremely low tides which occur between April and October are responsible for the natural phenomenon which is marked by the annual Staircase to the Moon Festival. The full moon reflected off the expanses of mudflats exposed at Roebuck Bay (see entry) creates a beautiful optical illusion resembling a grand staircase. *Population 8910*

COURT HOUSE The substantial court house on Frederick Street dates from 1889 and arrived in prefabricated form from England to be erected for use as the local cable station. In later years, it was suggested that the building had been shipped here by mistake and was actually intended for South Africa. The solid metal shutters with which it was equipped were supposedly designed to resist attacks by hostile Africans.

GANTHEAUME POINT The coloured, weathered rock and dinosaur footprints here attract many visitors. The footprints, believed to be those of a three-metre-high carnivorous reptile which lived 130 million years ago, are visible only at very low tide, but casts of them are embedded into the clifftop near the lighthouse.

JAPANESE CEMETERY The graves of more than 600 Japanese, many of them divers who lost their lives working in the pearling industry, can be seen in the cemetery at the end of Anne Street. Apart from the materials used to make the gravestones – weather-beaten rocks collected from the beaches – it is almost identical to cemeteries in Japan. In 1983, the cemetery underwent a major restoration that was financed by a Japanese syndicate, and many damaged headstones were replaced with traditional Japanese black granite.

PEARL COAST ZOO This zoo was built by a wealthy British businessman as an 'ark' for rare African plains animals, such as the cheetah, blackbuck antelope and the scimitar-horned oryx and also for a number of exotic parrot species. As well, 'common' kangaroos and uncaged birds live in landscaped grounds. All this is made possible by artesian water pumped from 800 metres below ground, treated at a desalination plant and piped into a series of artificial lakes.

FESTIVALS Staircase to the Moon, April; Shinju Matsuri (Pearl Festival), August; Mango Festival, November.

BUCCANEER ARCHIPELAGO ■ 2299

This scattering of reefs and low-lying islands stretches roughly south from Collier Bay to King Sound. The result of 40 million years of gradual erosion by tide and time of the northwest coastline, the islands were noted by Captain Read of the *Cygnet* in 1688. William Dampier was serving on the ship at the time, and the archipelago was named in his honour – and in recognition of his earlier buccaneering ways – by explorer Phillip Parker King when he charted these waters in 1821.

There are more than 800 islands in the archipelago which covers an area of approximately 50 square kilometres. Early pearling fleets often stopped at the islands of Yampi Sound to pick up ballast from the beaches and coves, little knowing that two of the islands – Cockatoo and Koolan (see entries) – would later be the source of one of the world's richest iron ore bodies and an early jewel in the crown of the BHP company. Although by 1984 reserves of ore were exhausted, townsfolk long departed and the school shut down, mining activities on Cockatoo Island are expected to resume with the reclamation of ore from the waste dumps left behind.

With the exception of Cockatoo and Koolan, the remaining islands are uninhabited save for the presence of crocodiles and birdlife and are little altered from the days when they were first observed by European eyes. Landing by sea or air is forbidden although chartered yachts negotiate the archipelago waters as part of their coastal tours. Due to the low height of the islands there are dramatic tidal ranges of up to 10 metres with the consequent hazards for unwary captains. Within one narrow passage between two islands measuring no more than the width of a boat, the fast approach of high tide produces a spectacular effect not unlike a horizontal waterfall.

CABLE BEACH ■ 2300

This twenty-kilometre-long, white, sandy beach was so named because it was the terminus of the original cable or telegraph line that linked Broome with Java. Whales and dolphins can be seen playing offshore here, and the fragile sandhills support a wide variety of vegetation.

CAMBALLIN ■ 2301

A barrage on the Fitzroy River east of the tiny township of Camballin was built to divert water into Uralla Creek for use in a local irrigation scheme – the only one on the river. When the river subsides at the end of the wet season, an interesting sight awaits those who visit the bar-

Derby was a rough-and-ready town of prospectors and sailors in the 1890s and a boab tree more bulbous than most made a handy overnight lock-up.

rage at night as thousands of freshwater prawns climb the structure under the cover of darkness.

COCKATOO ISLAND ■ 2302

Cockatoo Island was mined from 1951 for its high-grade ore reserves and at one stage the combined annual output of Cockatoo and nearby Koolan Island (see entry) was about three-and-a-half million tonnes. BHP's mining activities ceased in 1984 when the ore was exhausted.

DERBY ■ 2303

The first Europeans in this area were probably the members of an exploring party from HMS *Beagle* in March 1838. Their whaleboat was almost overturned by the rush of the tide as it lay anchored at the mouth of the Fitzroy River for the night.

The first official exploration by land took place in 1879 when Alexander Forrest led a party from the coast at Nickol Bay to a point near the mouth of the Fitzroy River, and then along it past the future site of Fitzroy Crossing, before heading north-west. He then continued through the east Kimberley to the Northern Territory.

After Forrest reported his findings in Perth, the government was keen to open up the Kimberley region and offered pastoral leases – the land was released by ballot to a range of lessees. First to stock allocated lands was the Murray Squatting Company, which established Yeeda Station – about thirty-five kilometres south of the present site of Derby – in 1881, on a nine-thousand-hectare parcel of land that comprised the leases of three of the company's shareholders. The owners brought sheep into the area by ship, landing them at Beagle Bay (see entry).

Derby grew up slowly as a small port serving the local pastoralists. It was officially declared a town in 1883 and was named for Lord Derby, Secretary of State for the Colonies. A jetty was built in 1885 – the year gold was discovered at Halls Creek (see *Kununurra & Wyndham*) – and many thousands of hopefuls flocked to the area, most of them arriving by ship through Derby and Wyndham – an en-route port closer to Halls Creek that was established in mid-1886. Derby's original jetty, even though it jutted way out over the mudflats, was not long enough to cope with the tidal range in the harbour – up to almost twelve metres – and ships which berthed here were often left high and dry.

Nowadays Derby is the administrative centre for the Shire of Derby–West Kimberley, though the Department of Marine and Harbours closed the port of Derby in 1983. Beef, cattle, grain and sorghum are thriving local industries and commercial quantities of oil have been discovered at Blina, to the east. *Population 3020*

PRISON TREE A huge, hollow boab with a girth of about fourteen metres stands beside the road just south of the town. It is thought to have been used in the 1890s as a lockup for prisoners – including the black guerrilla fighter Jandamarra (see Windjana Gorge National Park) – who were brought into Derby. Nearby is the 322-metre-deep Myall Bore, which feeds a 120-metre-long cattle trough – claimed to be the longest in the Southern Hemisphere.

FESTIVALS Boab Festival, July; Country Music Festival, July; Country Cattle Drive, July.

FITZROY CROSSING ■ 2304

The township of Fitzroy Crossing sits on the west bank of the Fitzroy River, its store, hotel, post office and hospital providing a service centre for people living in local Aboriginal communities and on nearby stations.

Members of explorer Alexander Forrest's party were probably the first Europeans to enter this area, in 1879. They were followed a few years later by pioneers such as the Duracks, then in 1886, William and Charles MacDonald founded Fossil Downs – one of the most famous outback properties in the north. Cattle for many of the properties were overlanded from the eastern states in audaciously ambitious migrations of men and animals. *Population 1120*

GOGO STATION FOSSIL FISH Stretching for nearly 400 kilometres north-east of Derby is part of an ancient coral reef which once formed a 1000-kilometre arc and was very much like the Great Barrier Reef, enclosing a warm, shallow sea between the reef and the shore. The part of the reef which crosses Gogo Station, south of Fitzroy Crossing, contains a remarkable profusion of fossilised skeletons of marine creatures – coral, shells, algae and a wide variety of fish. The weathering of the reef limestone has produced the spectacular landforms of Windjana Gorge National Park and Geikie Gorge National Park, and cave features such as Tunnel Creek National Park (see entries).

FITZROY RIVER ■ 2305

The Fitzroy River flows for about 620 kilometres from its headwaters in the Durack Range to enter the sea at King Sound, just south of Derby. Rainfall in the river's 85 000-square-kilometre catchment area varies enormously, with a dry season that extends from April to October, contrasting with very heavy falls in summer. When in flood it discharges at the rate of more than thirty-two million cubic metres of water an hour – enough to fill Sydney Harbour every sixteen hours. The river is well stocked with succulent freshwater prawns known throughout the district as 'cherabin'.

The Fitzroy was named by John Lort Stokes, its discoverer, in honour of Robert Fitzroy, who was captain of HMS *Beagle* during Charles Darwin's historic voyage of 1831–36.

GEIKIE GORGE NATIONAL PARK ■ 2306

This 3000-hectare national park centres around a spectacular gorge formed by the waters of the Fitzroy River which have carved deeply through an ancient barrier reef (see Fitzroy Crossing). A cross-section of fossil layers before the evolution of reptiles or mammals is exposed here. The park is accessible only in the summer dry season when the river ceases flowing and is reduced to a series of deep pools in which live the freshwater descendants of sawfish, barramundi, sharks and stingrays. Aeons ago these ocean fish strayed upstream and were stranded far from the sea.

The freshwater Johnston crocodile can often be seen basking on sandbanks in the river. Its normal diet is fish and it is not considered dangerous to humans. The gorge was named in honour of Sir Archibald Geikie, a British geologist.

GIBB RIVER ROAD ■ 2307

An increasing number of tourists are driving the wide, unsealed Gibb River Road, which runs 670 kilometres from Derby on the western Kimberley coast, north-east through the hinterland to Wyndham. It was initially built as a 'beef road' to transport cattle from inland stations to the coastal ports, and is still used as such, so motorists should beware of the huge road trains which roar and rumble out of the bulldust.

The road crosses broad tracts of unfenced terrain so that roving cattle and wildlife are an additional hazard. Turn-offs from the road lead to Windjana Gorge National Park and Tunnel Creek National Park (see entries) while briefly under or around it are the Lennard River and the King Leopold Ranges (see entries). Midway along its route between the coasts it forms a junction with the Kalumburu Road which runs north for some 260 kilometres to the isolated Kalumburu Mission on the coast.

JACKS WATERHOLE, DURACK RIVER STATION This large permanent waterhole on the Durack River has long been used as a stopover point and water

Rainbow bee-eaters wintering in the North-West gobble down bees and wasps with no ill effects at all.

ing place. Today there are camping and picnic facilities for those who stop to swim, fish or even go boating.

KING LEOPOLD RANGES ■ 2308

The King Leopold Ranges extend for approximately 600 kilometres in a horseshoe shape from Secure Bay to the Ord River near Kununurra and include the Lady Forrest, Sir John, Narrie, Durack, O'Donnell, Deception and Bandicoot ranges. There are fine views of the ranges, including the highest peak, Mount Ord (1000 metres), from the Gibb River Road (see entry) between Derby and Gibb River. The ranges were named in 1879 by Alexander Forrest for King Leopold II of Belgium 'in recognition of the great interest taken by His Majesty in exploration'.

KING SOUND ■ 2309

On 16 January 1688, the *Cygnet*, with William Dampier aboard, anchored in the outer extremity of what was later to become King Sound. He was rowed ashore and had the honour of becoming the first Englishman to set foot on Australian soil. He was not impressed: 'We saw no Trees that bore Fruit or Berries. We saw no sort of Animal, nor any Track of Beast, but once; and that seemed to be the Tread of a Beast as big as a great Mastiff-Dog. Here are a few small Land birds… and but few Sea-fowls. Neither is the Sea very plentifully stored with Fish…'

The next European visitor, after whom the sound was later named, was the explorer Phillip Parker King. During his voyage aboard the brig *Bathurst* in 1821–22 he landed in Goodenough Bay.

King Sound is 110 kilometres long and at its broadest point, about 60 kilometres wide. Its tidal range of almost twelve metres is the largest in Australia. The entrance is protected by the reefs and islands of the Buccaneer Archipelago (see entry) and most of the shores of the sound are lined with vast, mangrove-fringed, tidal mudflats. During the wet season many rivers, including the Fitzroy – which emerges near the town of Derby – discharge great quantities of silt into the sound.

KOOLAN ISLAND ■ 2310

Koolan Island in the Buccaneer Archipelago (see entry) is owned by BHP and has been mined for its iron ore since the 1930s. Huge machines are gradually eating through the deposits of ore, which is then crushed ready for shipment to steel mills in the eastern states. *Population 560*

LAGRANGE ■ 2311

This settlement – now home to two Aboriginal communities – evolved out of an Aboriginal ration depot which was established in 1912. The functions of the depot expanded,

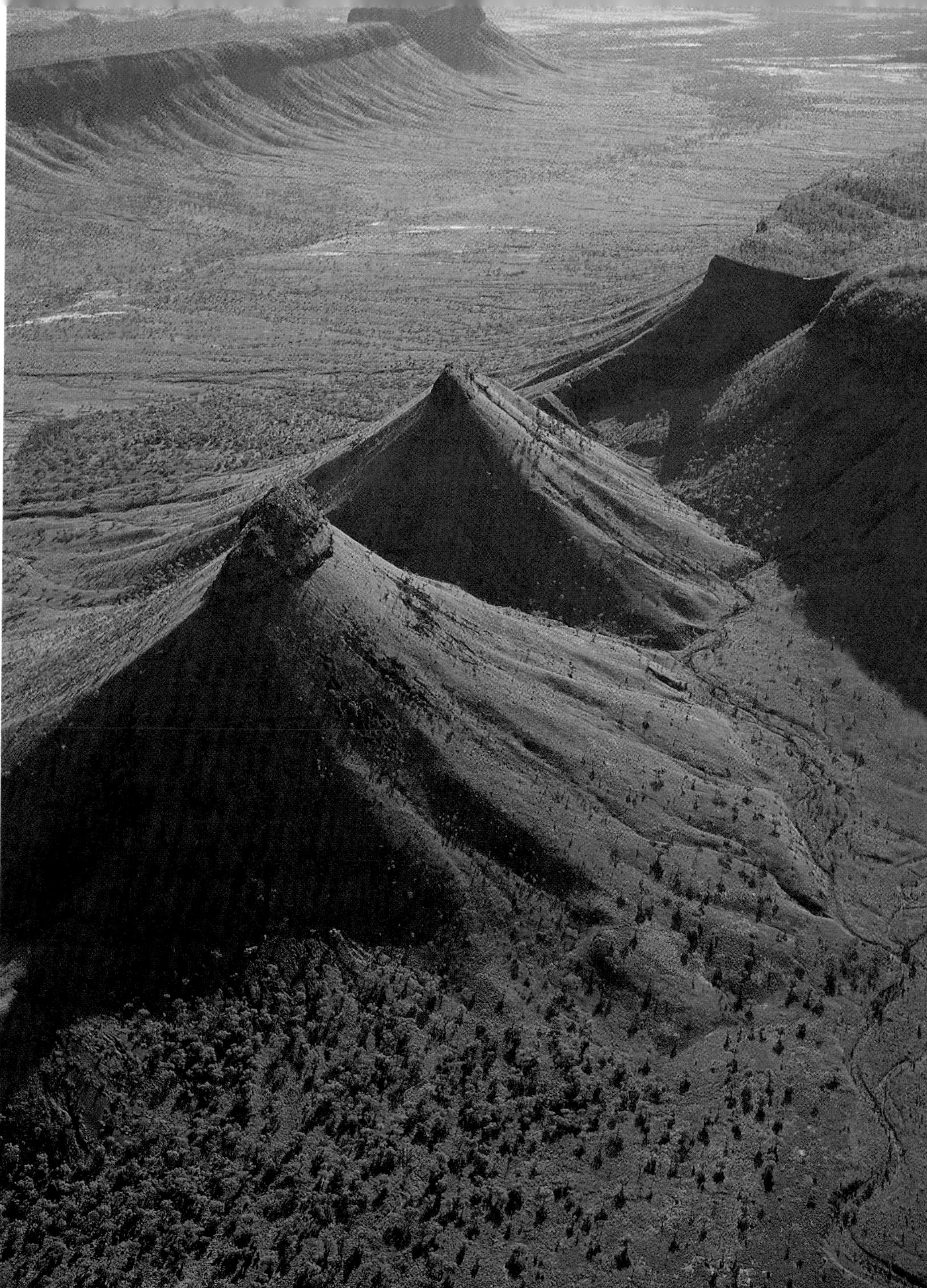

The majestic protrusions of the King Leopold Ranges trim the southern edge of the wild Kimberley landscape.

particularly in the 1930s and 1940s, and in 1955 the depot was placed under the control of the Pallotine Order, and became a mission.

The bay from which the community takes its name was sighted during the French Scientific Expedition of 1801–03, and named in honour of Joseph Louis Lagrange, a senior resident of the French Academy of Sciences and the most celebrated mathematician of the era.

LENNARD RIVER ■ 2312

The Lennard, on its course through the Napier Range, is responsible for scouring out the eighty-metre-high cliff walls which characterise Windjana Gorge National Park (see entry). The river rises on the southern slopes of Mount Ord, in the King Leopold Ranges (see entry), about 200 kilometres east of Derby. It is a seasonal river which, when swollen by the rains of the wet season, becomes a muddy torrent surging towards the coast. As it crosses the lowland cattle plain east of Derby, the river divides in two, becoming the Meda and the May, which both flow on to enter the sea at King Sound (see entry).

The river was named in 1879 by explorer Alexander Forrest for the Barrett Lennard family into which he would later marry.

LOMBADINA COMMUNITY ■ 2313

In 1892, Trappist monks established a mission station near Thomas Bay south of Cape Leveque as an adjunct to the Beagle Bay Mission (see entry). The present church was built in 1934 with local mangrove wood and was roofed with paperbark, to be covered by a layer of corrugated iron in 1942.

In modern times the local Aboriginal community manages and controls Lombadina where shellfishing venture, and the manufacture of dugout canoes, traditional artefacts, jewellery and bread are just some of the employment development projects they have initiated.

PRINCE REGENT NATURE RESERVE ■ 2314

This region, which has been declared a World Biosphere Reserve, contains most of the few pockets of rainforest that grow within conservation areas in Western Australia. The park protects a large saltwater crocodile population, the state's second largest mangrove area and populations of the endangered golden bandicoot.

Still discernible on the trunk of a large boab tree on the shore of Careening Bay are marks carved by the crew of the *Mermaid*, the ship used by Phillip Parker King to carry out hydrographic surveys between 1818 and 1820.

ROEBUCK BAY ■ 2315

The dense mangrove thickets which are returning to the shores of Roebuck Bay, on which Broome is located, provide the basis for the food chain of molluscs, crabs and fish which in turn support a large wading bird population. The huge tidal flow here necessitated the building, in 1966, of a new deepwater port. Ships at the old jetty were often beached by receding tides.

BROOME BIRD OBSERVATORY The food-rich mudflats of Roebuck Bay and nearby Eighty Mile Beach, one of the most important wading bird habitats in the world, are an essential stopover point for migratory birds during their long journeys from Siberia and Mongolia to the southern shores of Australia. Hungry and exhausted after flying over the Indian Ocean the birds recuperate here in September and October before continuing their journey south. In February, they return to spend a month or so building up their fat reserves before heading north. The observatory, established to witness this extraordinary congregation of birdlife, is one of only a handful of such facilities in Australia. It offers basic accommodation and conducts tours and educational courses.

TUNNEL CREEK NATIONAL PARK ■ 2316

This tiny park protects a 750-metre-long cavern carved by the waters of Tunnel Creek which follows a route formed along joint fractures through the prehistoric limestone reef of Oscar Range (see Fitzroy Crossing). Visitors can wade in the icy waters of the cave, but they need to be armed with a reliable torch. Near the halfway point, the roof has collapsed and this part of the cave is home to a large number of flying foxes.

On the limestone walls there are traces of Aboriginal paintings – red ochre crocodiles and white foot stencils – and in places stalactites occur. The cave was also used as a hideout by the so-called 'bushranger' 'Pidgeon' – his Aboriginal name was Jandamarra – in the 1890s (see Windjana Gorge National Park) and it was here that he was killed.

WALCOTT INLET ■ 2317

The mouth of Walcott Inlet is regarded as potentially one of the best tidal electric-power station sites in the world. Three large rivers – the Charnley, Calder and Isdell – disgorge into the eastern end of the inlet, and sixty kilometres away, at the western end, lies narrow Yule Entrance, which leads into Collier Bay and the open ocean. The Kimberley coast's massive tides – which can vary by up to eleven or twelve metres – race through the entrance creating powerful whirlpools and surging rips. The inlet was probably named for Pemberton Walcott, second-in-command of F.T. Gregory's 1861 expedition.

North-western Aborigines still maintain the cave paintings of the Windjana, executed hundreds of generations before the Pyramids were built.

WILLARE BRIDGE ROADHOUSE ■ 2318

The long, one-laned Willare Bridge across the Fitzroy River was built in 1968 to replace an old causeway downstream which became impassable in the wet season. The nearby roadhouse was built three years later. A 'no-go' zone near the river has been cordoned off in an effort to control the spread of the noogoora burr plant. As this spot is only 25 kilometres from the mouth of the Fitzroy, saltwater crocodiles are not uncommon and as pleasant as the location is, swimming is not recommended.

At Price Point, near Broome, the desert tumbles into broad shallows where the tidal range may reach 12 metres.

WINDJANA GORGE NATIONAL PARK ■ 2319

The narrow gorge of Windjana was carved by the Lennard River as it passes through the rugged Napier Range. Limestone walls up to thirty metres high rise above the deep pools left each summer after the river ceases to flow. The national park covers 2100 hectares and has several walking tracks for visitors.

In the 1890s, a former Aboriginal police tracker called Jandamarra – known to the Europeans as 'Pidgeon' (see Derby, Tunnel Creek National Park) – used caves in the gorge as a hideout from the police. In 1894, he killed a constable in a fracas at Lillimilura Police Station, the ruins of which can still be seen beside the road between Windjana Gorge and Tunnel Creek. Jandamarra - usually referred to inaccurately as a 'bushranger' – used guerrilla tactics in an effort to stem the spread of white settlement. He planned to lead an Aboriginal march on Derby in a campaign against settlement in the surrounding region but was killed by police in 1897.

Other caves in the park were once used as burial places by local Aborigines, and some are still decorated with paintings. According to Aboriginal legend the gorge was visited by the Wandjina, Dreamtime spirit figures that roamed the earth and at various points descended onto it leaving their image on rock faces to mark the spot. These paintings which have been carefully tended and repaired by countless generations of Aborigines, adorn the cliffs and rock shelters of the region.

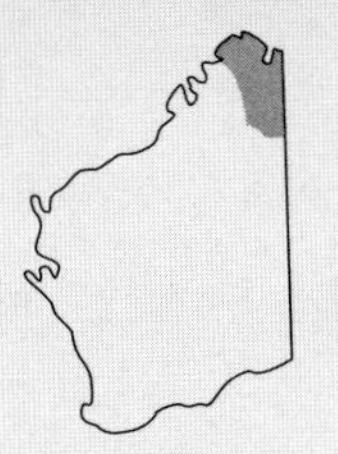

Kununurra & Wyndham

The wild and untamed north-western pocket of wilderness known as the Kimberley, cut off from the rest of the world by desert and ocean, contains some of Australia's least known natural wonders: the Bungle Bungle Range, a moon-worthy crater, pink diamonds and haunting Aboriginal rock art.

ARGYLE DIAMOND MINE ■ 2320

About eighty kilometres due south of Kununurra (see entry) is Australia's only diamond mine. Exploration in the Kimberley region began in the late 1960s but it was not until 1979 that the 1600-metre-long Argyle diamond 'pipe' was discovered in the Ragged Range. Previously, diamonds had been found in a rock called kimberlite but had never before been discovered in lamproite, the 'host' rock for these most sought-after gemstones at Argyle.

Operating since 1986, the open-cut mine now produces about forty million carats annually – one-third of the world's diamonds and the most carats; twenty million carats will be used in the jewellery industry. Although only five per cent of the output is of gem quality, it does include the lustrous pink diamonds that are unique to the Argyle mine.

ORYSDALE RIVER NATIONAL PARK ■ 2321

The only way to see this 436 000-hectare park is by helicopter, canoe or on foot – there is no road access. The park takes in the Ashton Range, the forty-eight-kilometre-long Carson Escarpment and a number of rivers including the Drysdale and the Carson as well as the headwaters of the King George River. With its pools, waterfalls, swamps, gorges and cliffs, all of which – for obvious reasons – have remained undisturbed, the park is of major interest to scientists as a pristine wilderness. An expedition was mounted in 1975 when plant and animal species were recorded, many of them previously undescribed or very rare. The beauty of the Morgan Falls, which crash into Worriga Gorge, and the Solea Falls – only 30 metres in height but a spectacular 100 metres in width – remain unseen except by scientists and the occasional intrepid canoeist, pilot or bushwalking expedition.

HALLS CREEK ■ 2322

On the edge of the Great Sandy Desert and at the northern end of the Tanami Track and the 1700-kilometre-long Canning Stock Route, geographically isolated Halls Creek is now served by the sealed Great Northern Highway. The settlement took its name from Charles Hall, who had the distinction of making

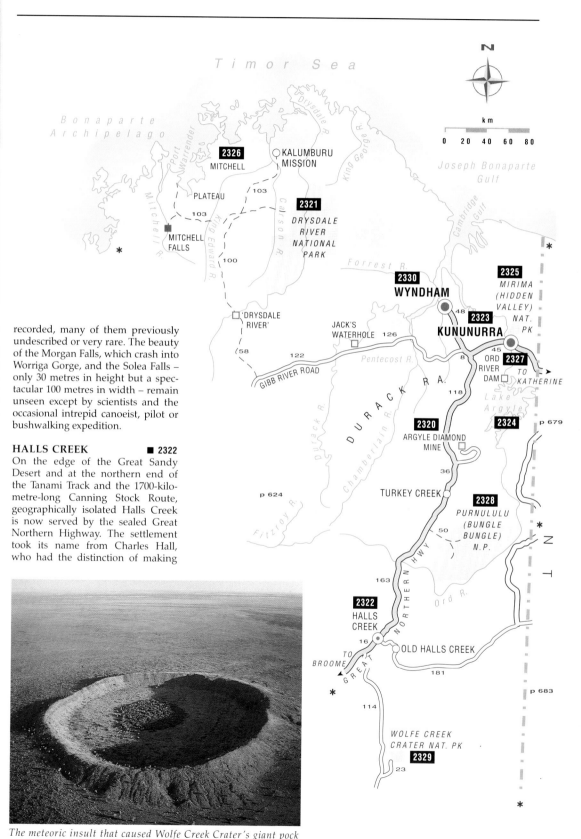

The meteoric insult that caused Wolfe Creek Crater's giant pock mark occurred long before Australia assumed its present shape.

Western Australia's first discovery of payable gold at Halls Creek in 1885.

The gold rush lasted for only three months – long enough for the tiny cemetery at old Halls Creek to become the last resting place of many prospectors who died of thirst and hunger. Not everyone had mates like Russian Jack whose statue now stands in the town. Local legend has it that in 1886, the heroic Jack walked the 300 kilometres to Wyndham pushing a handmade wheelbarrow containing a sick friend and enough food and water to keep the two of them alive until they found a doctor.

Another emergency medical situation, in 1917, was to lead to a more important lasting memorial – an Inland Mission hospital at Halls Creek. When James Darcy's horse rolled on him during mustering, the only available medical help was F.W. Tuckett, postmaster and magistrate, at Halls Creek. Tuckett, with the aid of a doctor in Perth who relayed detailed instructions to Halls Creek by means of a series of telegrams, operated on Darcy using a penknife, razor and a bag of Condy's crystals. The operation was a success but Darcy, weakened by malaria, died a short time later.

John Flynn used the case of James Darcy, who lies buried at Halls Creek, as an example to raise support for the Flying Doctor Service and years later Les A. Murray was to tell the tale in his poem 'Morse'.

The early goldmining town, which eventually became a trading centre for the surrounding cattle stations, mineral explorers and local Aboriginal communities, finally got its own aerodrome in 1948 and, building by building, during the 1950s, the settlement moved fifteen kilometres west, nearer the airfield. The ruins of a few old mudbrick buildings, disused mineshafts and plaques showing where other buildings once stood – along with a small cemetery – are all that remain of the original Halls Creek. The airfield at the 'new' settlement, the closest to Purnululu (Bungle Bungle) and Wolfe Creek Crater national parks (see entries), is now the centre of a growing tourist industry. *Population 1300*

CHINA WALL Stretching beyond Halls Creek and standing vertically above the surrounding land is a white 'wall', first glimpses of which may be reminiscent of the Great Wall of China. The wall is in fact a naturally occurring vertical quartz vein that has intruded into fractures in the softer sandstone. As the sandstone has been eroded, the harder quartz intrusion has been left, like a long wall meandering over hill and dale.

KUNUNURRA ■ 2323

Kununurra did not come into official existence until 1961. Purpose-built to house construction workers building the dams for the Ord River Irrigation Scheme and farmers who arrived to cultivate crops on the newly irrigated land, Kununurra's name derives from an Aboriginal word said to mean 'black soil'.

The town occupies part of what was the pioneering Durack family's Ivanhoe Station, where the initial small-scale experiments on irrigation were carried out (see sub-entry). With modern hotels, shops, and sports and other facilities common in less isolated towns, Kununurra sits beside Lake Kununurra, the smaller of the two reservoirs in the irrigation scheme. The diversion dam at Lake Kununurra, which carries the two-lane Duncan Highway across its crest, has crocodiles basking on its shores so swimming at the local Bandicoot Beach is not advisable.

After serious early problems with insect pests, an increased bird population attacking cultivated crops and Queensland farmers' objections to the growing of sugarcane, the irrigation farms now grow peanuts, soya beans, melons, cucumbers, bananas, mangoes, maize, sunflowers and sorghum – all of this transported from Kununurra to markets thousands of kilometres away. Sending produce to Perth where it is out of season and can therefore command higher prices helps overcome the economic disadvantage of distance. *Population 4060*

FRANK WISE INSTITUTE From a small experimental facility on Ivanhoe Station, initiated by the Durack family in 1941, the Western Australian Department of Agriculture and the CSIRO jointly developed the Kimberley Research Station in 1945. Research into irrigation and possible crops was conducted for almost twenty years before Kununurra came into being. Children from the town were bussed to the research station for schooling until the town's school was built. Since 1974, the research institute has been operated by the CSIRO on its own.

FESTIVALS Ord Festival, late August.

LAKE ARGYLE ■ 2324

Australia's largest man-made reservoir, Lake Argyle – nine times the size of Sydney Harbour – sits astride the Western Australia–Northern Territory border and is the key to the Ord River Irrigation Scheme. The lake inundated an 18 000-year-old Aboriginal campsite and many of the reef outcrops of red-striped zebra stone, unique to this region of the Carr Boyd Range. Argyle Downs homestead (see sub-entry) and many of the animals in the area flooded by Lake Argyle were, however, saved.

'Operation Noah' involved the rescue of much of the wildlife before the valley was drowned, however some short-eared rock wallabies and northern nail-tailed wallabies remain isolated on former hilltops now rising above the lake as isolated islands. The lake itself provides a habitat for almost sixty species of birds, the rarest being the radjah shellduck and the comb-crested jacana.

In the 1980s, a survey counted more than 180 000 birds, many of them formerly migratory but now seemingly permanent inhabitants.

'ARGYLE DOWNS' This was the second homestead built by the Durack family at Argyle between 1893 and 1895 – after their epic, two-year journey droving cattle 5000 kilometres from Cooper Creek. The homestead was dismantled and rebuilt in 1971 before it slipped beneath the waters of Lake Argyle. Now a museum to the Duracks and other pioneers of the Kimberley cattle industry, the building is surrounded by gardens re-created with the same plants, trees and creepers that were planted at 'Argyle Downs', one of four Durack stations in the district.

MIRIMA (HIDDEN VALLEY) NATIONAL PARK ■ 2325

The local Miriuwung Aborigines knew the Mirima region well for the variety of plant and animal food available in both the wet and the dry seasons. Evidence of Aboriginal culture can be seen within the park not only at rock art sites and at a natural amphitheatre which was a corroboree site, but also in dry creek beds where grooves formed by stone axe sharpening are still visible.

In winter, it is possible to walk along the network of dry, stony beds of Lily Creek and its tributaries, which pass through the gorges and valleys they have cut into the 300-million-year-old sandstone deposits. Because of the sandstone hills and ridges, rising up to 100 metres above the plain, the park is often described as a more accessible but smaller version of Purnululu (Bungle Bungle) National Park (see entry).

Vegetation includes yellow-flowered kapok around the sandstone outcrops, woolybutt and long-fruited bloodwood in the valleys and plants in fissures in rock faces and baobabs, which have yet to be given a proper description. The baobab tree, which so displeased the Dreamtime spirits that it was turned upside down with its roots in the air, has seeds that are too heavy to be transported by wind, yet small baobabs can be found high in sheer rock faces in the park. The seeds are carried in the droppings of wallabies, deposited on ledges and later encouraged to germination by the wet-season deluge.

MITCHELL PLATEAU ■ 2326

The Mitchell Plateau has been inhabited by Aborigines for thousands o years and is still home to th Wunambal people. It was only i 1954, when a road was put throug to Kalumburu Mission, that any sor of access to the Mitchell Plateau b vehicle became possible…although i still takes sixteen hours from th nearest settlement at Kununurra (se entry). An average rainfall figure o 1600 millimetres a year on th plateau makes even this basic eart road impassable for most of the yea

The valleys and gorges cut int the King Leopold sandstone of th plateau by the Mitchell and Lawle rivers are studded with fan palm many of them over 250 years old an nowhere else in the world found i such abundance. A list of the hun dreds of species of plants, from th

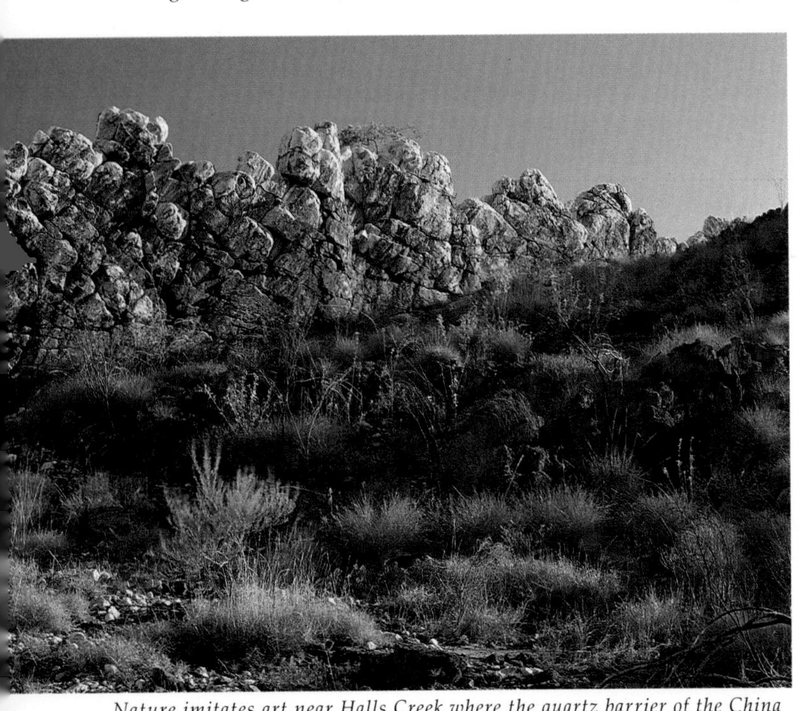

Nature imitates art near Halls Creek where the quartz barrier of the China Wall could readily be taken for an irregularly coursed, rubble farm wall.

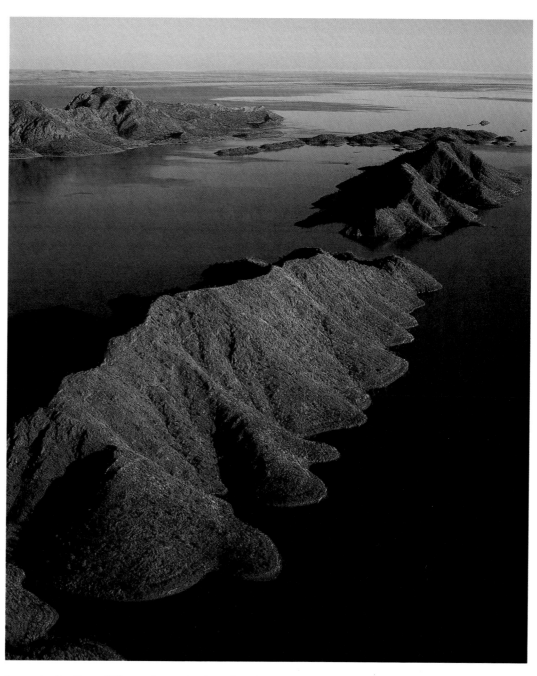

The waters of the artificial Lake Argyle – which made islands and promontories of some peaks of the Carr Boyd Range (right) - are siphoned off to water tropical crops such as chick peas (below).

tall spear grasses to the rare, submerged aquatic plants found at Mitchell Falls, was undertaken in the early 1980s, at the same time as the Mitchell Plateau Bauxite Company was formed.

The laterite that caps the plateau is also found extensively in the region around it and is a source of bauxite, the principal ore of aluminium. Both mining feasibility studies and environmental impact studies have taken place but with a downturn in the market in the 1980s, mining was postponed and half of the mining lease resumed for a possible conservation zone.

ORD RIVER DAM ■ 2327

Before it was dammed, the Ord River emptied fifty million litres of water each second into Cambridge Gulf during the wet season. Harnessing Australia's largest flow of water for irrigation was proposed as early as 1909 but it was not until 1972 that the Ord River Dam, the main dam in the Ord Irrigation Scheme, was opened.

The 'Top' dam – constructed about fifty kilometres upstream from Kununurra (see entry) – was a nightmare to build. Remoteness, heat, wet-season torrents and silt build-up caused by overgrazing all had to be tackled. The dam took two dry seasons to build, which meant that one wet-season flood had to pass over the half-completed dam wall.

The dam wall, rising almost sixty-eight metres above the river and plunging up to thirty metres below its surface, holds back the huge volume of water in Lake Argyle (see entry). The water is released over a spillway north-east of the dam wall to flow through Spillway Creek to the diversion dam at Lake Kununurra from which, taking advantage of a natural drop in the valley floor, it flows by gravity through irrigation channels in the Ivanhoe Plain.

PURNULULU (BUNGLE BUNGLE) NATIONAL PARK ■ 2328

It was only in the early 1980s, during the filming of a television series on the scenic attractions of Western Australia, that the existence of the spectacular Bungle Bungle Range became known to the general public. The aerial views of the tiger-striped, beehive-shaped domes stunned the world with its spectacular and distinctive beauty.

Aborigines of the Kimberley had used the region they called 'purnululu' ('sandstone') for thousands of years, particularly in the wet season, and every feature on the 'kawarra' – 'unclimbable cliffs' – was named. The park contains many sacred sites, burial sites and rock art.

The ancient Bungle Bungle massif has been protected within the confines of a 320 000-hectare national park and conservation area since 1987. The distinctive stripes of the 'beehives' are formed by the dark and light sediments of soft white sandstone covered by an outer skin of orange silica and black lichen. The fragile and easily eroded rock, laid down 350 million years ago, now rises up to 300 metres above the surrounding plain. Gorges, canyons and towering cliffs have been eroded in the distinctive structures, the best known at Piccaninny Creek where a large meteorite crater and an outcrop of Bungle Bungle fan palms sprouting on vertical cliff faces add to the primeval landscape.

The best views of the Bungle Bungles are from the air and this is how artists such as John Olson have portrayed the Bungle Bungle Range in their paintings. It can take five hours to make the fifty-five-kilometre trip on the only access road to the range and straying off existing tracks can threaten the fragile rock with erosion. The park is closed from January to March in an attempt to protect the soft sandstone during the wettest months when it is most susceptible to erosion.

WOLFE CREEK CRATER NATIONAL PARK ■ 2329

South of Halls Creek (see entry), in the Sandy Desert, lies a substantial 850-metre-wide and 50-metre-deep crater, protected within a national park. Wolfe Creek Crater was not officially 'discovered' and reported until 1947 and a reserve was gazetted for the protection of the crater in 1968. The national park dates from only 1977 – but the crater at its centre is at least one million years old.

Almost certainly caused by the impact and explosion of an iron meteorite weighing up to 50 000 tonnes, the crater has retained its perfect circular shape probably due to the arid conditions, which minimise erosion – sand and gypsum blown into the crater have started to fill the depression and made it substantially shallower today than it was a million years ago. Melaleuccas and large eucalypts now draw moisture from sinkholes in the gypsum surface layer to create a vegetated patch.

It is most unlikely that this huge crater – the second largest in the world – would have lain unnoticed by stockmen and gold prospectors in the region until it was 'discovered' by a geologist on an aerial survey in 1947, but none reported it. It was certainly well known to the Aborigines. There is an oft-told Dreamtime story of the 'kandimalal' – 'the crater' – which tells how one of the two Dreamtime snakes who created the sinuous routes of the two nearby creeks – Wolfe and Sturt – emerged from the earth at the crater.

WYNDHAM ■ **2330**

On Cambridge Gulf, at the mouth of the King River – named after Phillip Parker King who surveyed the coast in 1818 – is Wyndham, Western Australia's northernmost town and port. By the time that gold was discovered and Wyndham became an official settlement and the port of entry for thousands of prospectors in 1886, pastoralists had already been in the district for two years.

A jetty built in the 1890s at what was then Anthon's Landing was built in a 'T'-shape to facilitate the loading of cattle bound for Perth rather than for the convenience of prospectors passing through. This jetty survived until 1944 when it was burnt down but two old cemeteries in Wyndham, one of them devoted to Afghan cameleers, still survive, as does the 'prison tree' from the same era. Local legend has it that this large baobab, with a trunk fourteen metres in circumference, was used as an overnight 'lockup' for prisoners from the 1890s onwards and many of their names are supposedly carved on the tree trunk.

In 1919, a government freezing and meatworks was opened in Wyndham and was to remain the town's main industry until it closed down in 1985. This single but important industry encouraged the growth of Wyndham, not only in the old port area but also at Wyndham East – earlier a small settlement called 'Three Mile' that came into being with a hotel and camping area in 1886.

Saltwater crocodiles have long featured in Wyndham's history. They were attracted to the waters around the 'blood drain' at the meatworks after 1919 and live still in the waters and tidal mudflats of Cambridge Gulf as well as in the five rivers – Ord, Pentecost, Durack, King and Forrest – which empty into it. An enormous concrete and steel model of a crocodile greets visitors to the town, which was the scene of a fatal attack in 1980. *Population 860*

Purnululu's 'lost city' skyline of massed 'domes' and conical peaks pushes up through an arid plain.

TASMANIA

The island state, the apple isle, the holiday isle. Tasmania – Australia's smallest and second oldest state – has been ascribed many labels, none of them truly capturing a unique character which results from a landscape more diverse than any other state. The 'sunburnt country' does not extend this far south; here – in the island's isolated, western fastness of mountains, lakes and rivers – there are wild and impenetrable forests, while to the east, and in dramatic contrast, towns and villages dot a sea of lovingly cultivated, productive farmland.

SPECIAL FEATURES

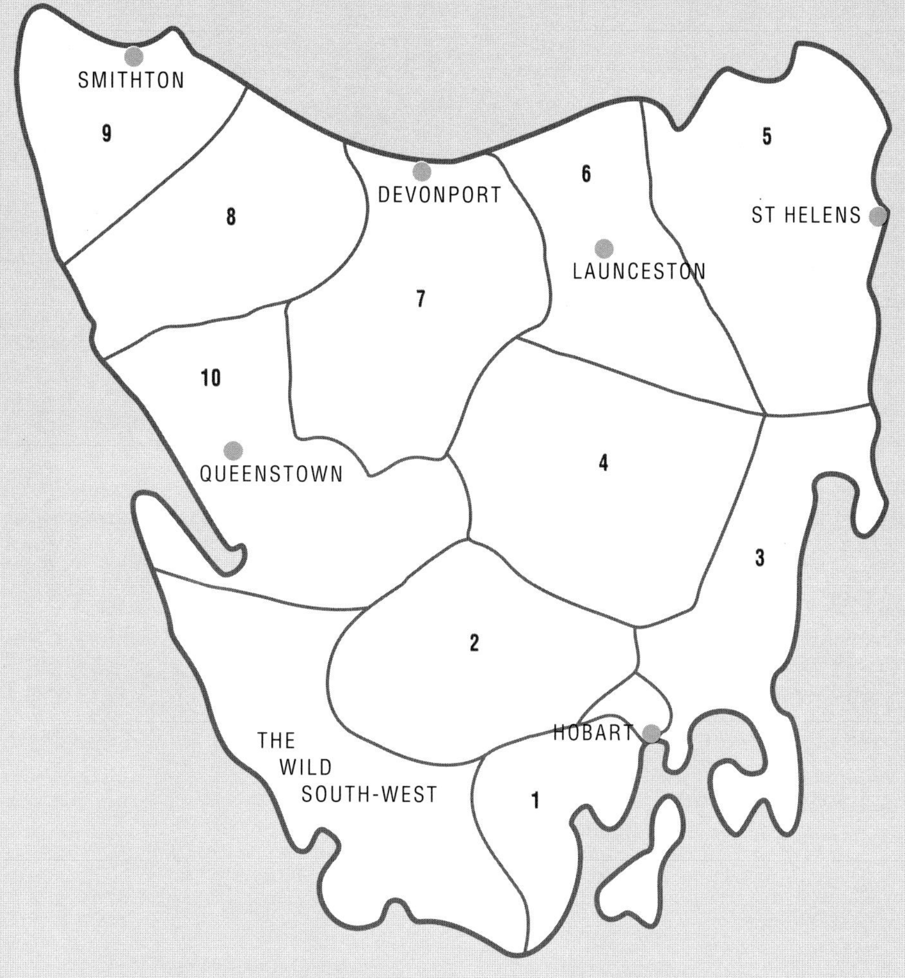

Only a few years after Tasmania adopted a coat of arms bearing matched thylacines the animals were seen for the last time in the wild. The blue gum is the state's floral emblem while the Tasmanian devil is an unofficial emblem.

HOBART

Hobart's twin attributes, its mountain and its river, combine to create an incomparable setting. Its other great strength is its preservation of the past – unspoilt colonial buildings are complemented, for the most part, by the more recent architecture.

Hobart, the southernmost and second oldest Australian capital, sits confidently and comfortably amid the splendour of its natural setting between a massive mountain and a deep river estuary.

The city lies approximately nineteen kilometres from the mouth of the River Derwent and extends about the same distance inland to Bridgewater. On a clear day the towering backdrop of Mount Wellington is visible from many points, rock solid against the sky or softened by a covering of snow. At other times it disappears altogether in a shroud of mist or driving rain.

The suburbs of Hobart scale the mountain's foothills, climb all over Mount Nelson and spread along both shores of the river. East and west are joined by the Tasman Bridge, a little less symmetrical than it was originally since a cargo vessel rammed one of its piers and severed the vital cross-city road link in 1975. The subsequent repairs to this graceful concrete structure took over two years to complete.

Hobart's maritime ties have always been strong and it shows its best face to travellers approaching from the sea. Once whaling ships crowded the port in the days when the great whales still ventured upriver. Much, much later freighters crammed the wharf space when they came to collect the annual apple harvest. Today, overseas ships berth almost in the city's heart, a stone's throw from the parliament, law courts, town hall, GPO, government offices, shopping mall, hospital and museum. Every year competitors in the Sydney to Hobart Yacht Race tie up at Constitution Dock at the foot of Argyle Street and the local people throw a huge New Year's Eve party to welcome them.

The first European settlement here was made on the eastern shore at Risdon Cove in 1803 but lasted only a few months. The following year Lieutenant-Colonel David Collins moved the site to Sullivans

Below Mount Wellington, the stylish architecture and leafy setting of the Cascades district – thus the name of the beer – suggest a grand chateau rather than Tasmania's famous brewery.

Cove and the settlement was soon named Hobart Town after Lord Hobart, then Secretary of State for the Colonies. Collins did well to choose one of the world's finest deepwater harbours but he was less adept at town planning. On his first visit in 1811, Governor Lachlan Macquarie 'observed with much regret' the haphazard development of the new community and issued orders for an orderly layout to be devised. He named the seven main streets and Georges Square and climbed a small hill about one-and-a-half kilometres south-west of the then town to nominate the place for Anglesea Barracks which is still occupied by the army.

The unusually high concentration of old sandstone and brick buildings, often the fruits of convict labour, is an abiding presence. The buildings are well-kept and hold their own against more modern architecture. The earliest surviving edifice is the Commissariat Store (1808–10), now part of the museum. The original part of Parliament House, at first the Customs House and constructed between 1835 and 1841, was designed by the notable architect John Lee Archer. The Cascade Brewery was built in 1832 and the Theatre Royal five years later. Laurence Olivier called it 'the best little theatre in the world'.

The splendid Georgian warehouses lining Salamanca Place rose commandingly between 1835 and 1860 and were the focus of commerce and trade for several decades. Many have made the transition to the twentieth century as shops, restaurants and art galleries and the Saturday open-air market in front of them echoes the bustle of bygone days. Battery Point, close by, is so called because of the battery of guns established there in 1818. Ten years later a tall mast went up to relay the exciting news of approaching ships from a similar signal station on Mount Nelson.

The beautiful St Davids Park was Hobart's first cemetery and it still preserves several headstones. Many notables are buried here including Lieutenant-Colonel Collins and Captain James Kelly, who circumnavigated Van Diemen's Land and later became the Hobart harbourmaster.

Hobart blends the old and the new with a remarkably sure touch and there is an absence of urban stress which is hardly surprising because the population is less than 130 000. The 'rush hour' is a mere thickening of traffic for much less than sixty minutes. There are no large industrial districts and little air pollution, though the city is not completely free of environmental problems; concerns for the purity of the Derwent waters have vexed the residents since the earliest times. □

Hobart's houses – especially the old terrace rows – traverse the contours of the River Derwent valley with grace and style.

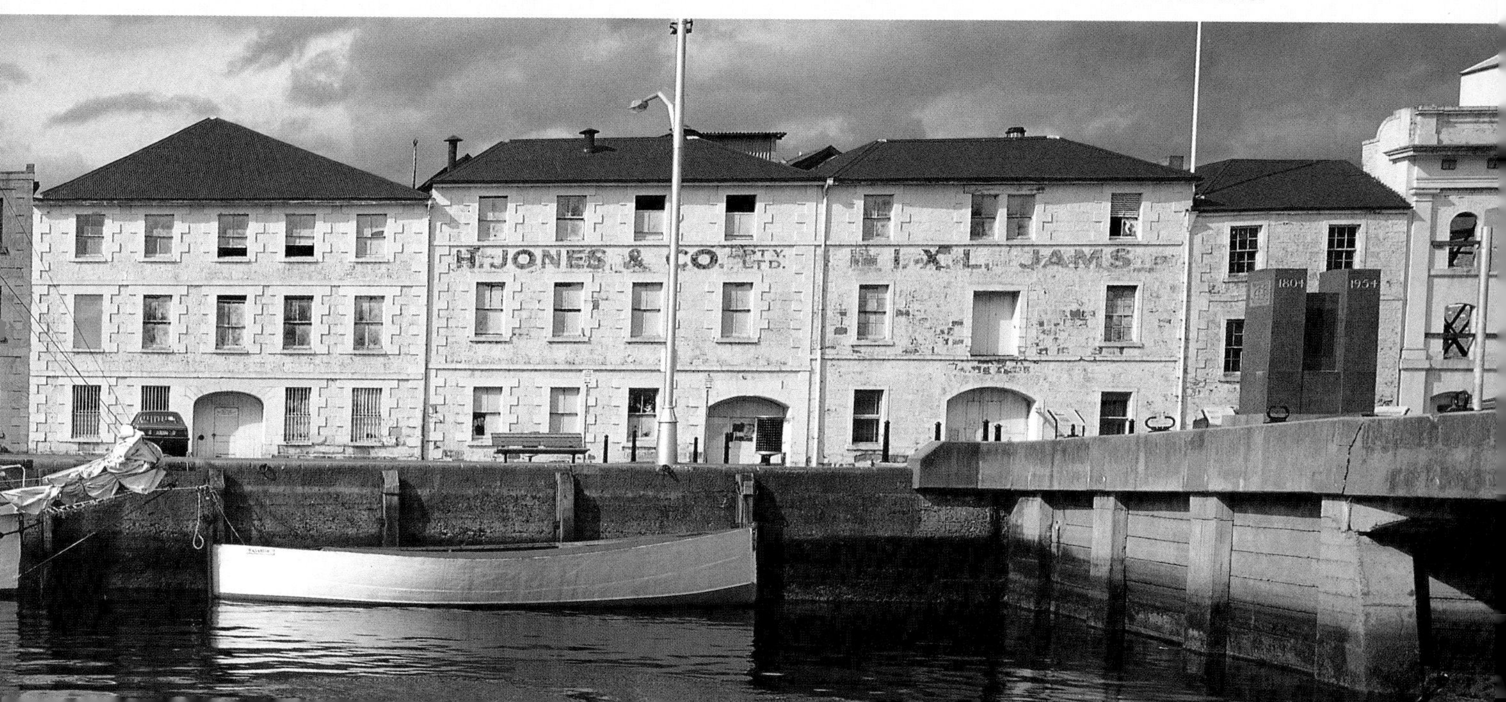

Victoria Dock is a part of the Hobart waterfront where the nineteenth-century streets come to life each January after the winner of the Sydney–Hobart Yacht Race trophy (left, opposite) sails into Sullivans Cove.

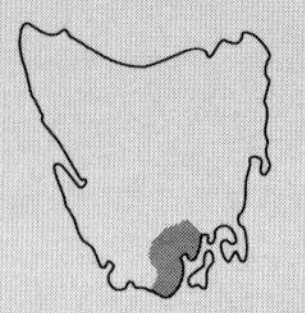

Kingston & Huonville

The D'Entrecasteaux Channel, once a haven for sealers and whalers, nowadays attracts boats used for more leisurely pursuits to its secluded bays. On shore, the trim farmlands of the Huon Valley have a backdrop of mountains that are often capped with snow.

Although Tasmania is no longer the 'Apple Isle', Huon Valley orchards still produce apples of a variety and quality hard to match on the mainland.

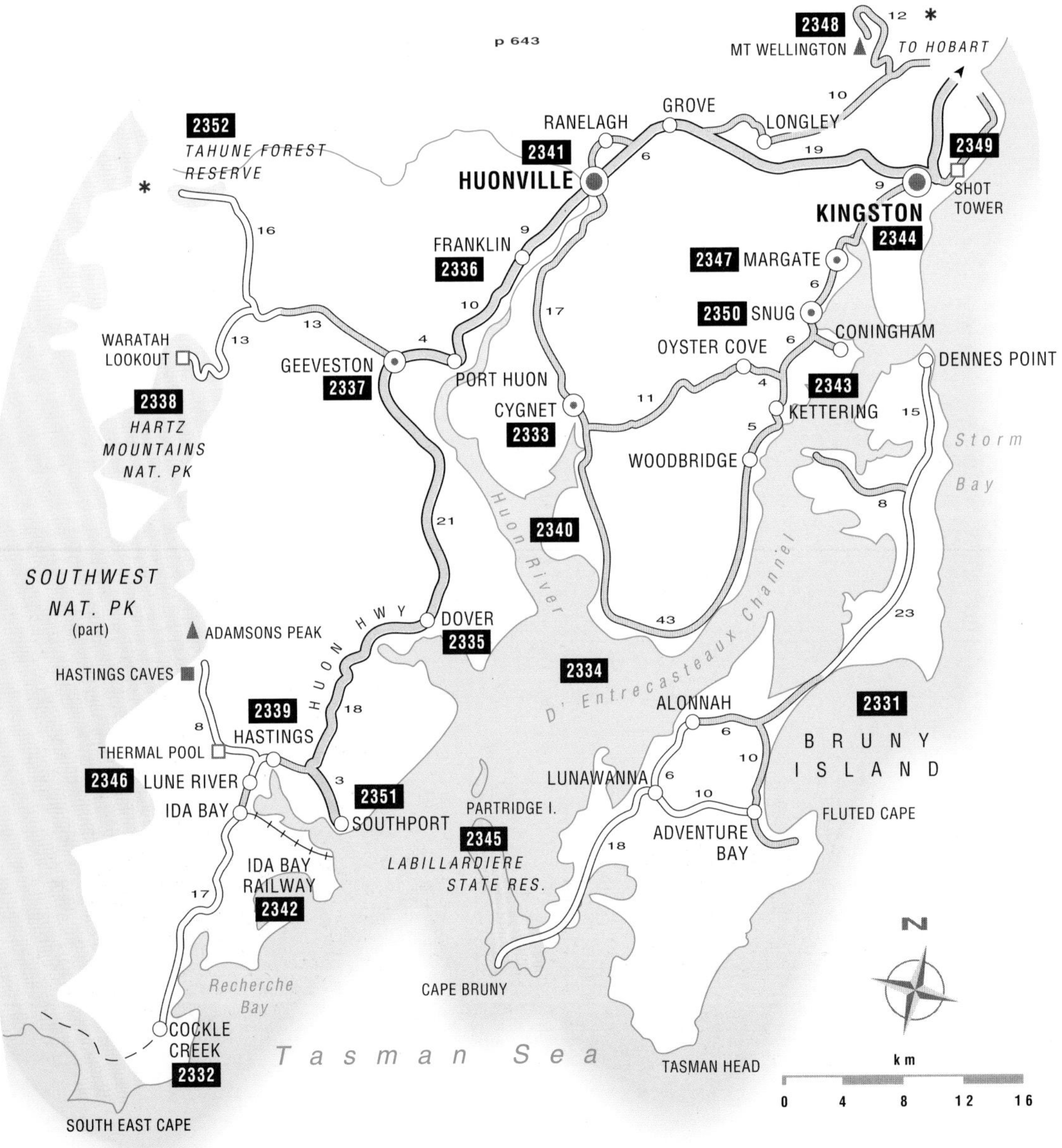

p 643
2348 MT WELLINGTON
TO HOBART
2352 TAHUNE FOREST RESERVE
RANELAGH
GROVE
LONGLEY
2341 HUONVILLE
2349 SHOT TOWER
KINGSTON 2344
FRANKLIN 2336
2347 MARGATE
2350 SNUG
CONINGHAM
WARATAH LOOKOUT
GEEVESTON 2337
PORT HUON
OYSTER COVE
DENNES POINT
2343 KETTERING
CYGNET 2333
2338 HARTZ MOUNTAINS NAT. PK
WOODBRIDGE
Storm Bay
Huon River
2340
D' Entrecasteaux Channel
SOUTHWEST NAT. PK (part)
ADAMSONS PEAK
HUON HWY
DOVER 2335
HASTINGS CAVES
2334
ALONNAH
2331
2339 HASTINGS
BRUNY ISLAND
THERMAL POOL
2346 LUNE RIVER
LUNAWANNA
IDA BAY
2351 SOUTHPORT
PARTRIDGE I.
ADVENTURE BAY
FLUTED CAPE
2345 LABILLARDIERE STATE RES.
IDA BAY RAILWAY 2342
N
Recherche Bay
CAPE BRUNY
COCKLE CREEK 2332
Tasman Sea
TASMAN HEAD
km
0 4 8 12 16
SOUTH EAST CAPE

BRUNY ISLAND ■ **2331**

The early written records of Bruny Island read like a maritime *Who's Who* of European explorers and navigators. Many of their names live on both in this region and in other parts of Tasmania and the mainland. In 1642, Abel Tasman sailed past but did not attempt to land. Tobias Furneaux stepped ashore in 1773. After Furneaux came a veritable scramble including James Cook (1777), William Bligh – four times between 1777 and 1809 – Matthew Flinders (1792 and 1798), John Cox (1789), Bruni D'Entrecasteaux (1792 and 1793) and Nicholas Baudin (1802). Bligh planted the first of Tasmania's apple trees on Bruny Island in 1788 and found one surviving when he returned four years later. He planted watercress too, and it still grows along many of the creeks.

Bruny Island is fifty-five kilometres long and is almost divided in two by a narrow, sandy isthmus. A part of the southern section of the island is now reserved in its natural state (see Labillardiere State Reserve). The local Aborigines knew it as 'lunawanna–alonnah' and settlements on the island still bear these names. They lived there for many years before they were either killed in clashes with sealers and whalers or decimated by European diseases. Island-born Truganini, who died in 1876, is thought to have been the last full-blooded Tasmanian Aborigine.

Whaling stations were established in 1827 and land was later cleared for sheep, cattle and apple orchards. Some Bruny Island timber was sent to Europe and stone from its quarries helped build Melbourne, including the city's GPO. The island is a nesting site for fairy penguins and migratory mutton birds, and the forty-spotted pardalote, an endangered bird, finds sanctuary here.

COCKLE CREEK ■ **2332**

Cockle Creek, notable as the almost abandoned, southernmost town in Australia, was settled by sealers and whalers and then by timber millers. Few people live there now and little survives except a sprinkling of cultivated flowers where gardens once grew and pieces of wooden-railed timber tramways. The area is used by campers who have access to the beautiful beaches of Recherche Bay and to the region's memorable walking country. The track to South Cape Bay is a starting point for the more adventurous to penetrate the southwest wilderness.

Cockle Creek is in the municipality of Esperance which is Australia's most southerly province and encompasses Macquarie Island – about 1300 kilometres further south. Sheltered Recherche Bay was named after the first European ship to sail there in 1792. Rusting relics beside the South Cape Road locate the abandoned towns of Leprena and Catamaran where once a huge sawmill and a coal mine supported many families.

CYGNET ■ 2333

Cygnet, on the Huon River estuary, was first named 'Port de Cygne Noir' by the French Admiral D'Entrecasteaux who was inspired by the number of black swans he saw there. There are still swans in the bay but 'Black Swanport' eventually became Cygnet. The town is now the centre of neat apple orchards, dairying and mixed farming; flower farms and vineyards are more recently developed agricultural enterprises. There is an abattoir and a sawmill and the significant number of tourists also contribute to the economy.

The old buildings in Cygnet are particularly interesting because stone was not used as a material and the timber dwellings recall the era when tree felling was dominant in the district. Newer houses keep faith with the prevailing architecture.

In 1834, William Nichols sailed round the coast from Browns River at Kingston to establish his family at what is now known as the misspelt Nicholls Rivulet. Others settled nearby and apple orchardists planted Ribstone Pippin, Stone Pippin and Prince Alfred varieties. In 1845, probation stations for convicts were established at Port Cygnet and nearby settlements. They did not last long but their occupants cleared much land and helped establish settlement. *Population 920*

FESTIVALS Huon Folk Festival, early January.

D'ENTRECASTEAUX CHANNEL ■ 2334

The French explorer Bruni D'Entrecasteaux charted many places in the vicinity and named this safe and beautiful waterway after himself in 1792. In early colonial days, D'Entrecasteaux Channel was frequented by whalers and formed a busy shipping lane between Hobart and the towns along its shores. It was later an important scallop fishery which collapsed in the mid-1960s and gave way to cray and scale fishing (see Margate, Kettering). Nowadays these sheltered waters are also greatly appreciated by yacht owners.

DOVER ■ 2335

Dover, settled in the 1850s, retains much of the atmosphere of a seaport village and is popular with holidaymakers. The beaches are unspoiled and the fishing always promising. The settlement nestles on the shore of Esperance Bay which enfolds three islands called Faith, Hope and Charity. The spectacular Adamsons Peak looms up from the bush behind it. Originally called Port Esperance after one of the ships in D'Entrecasteaux's 1792 expedition, Dover's economy has always been solidly fish-based. Two fish-processing plants deal with scale fish, lobsters and abalone and recently a lucrative Atlantic salmon industry has been established. This is the largest centre of salmon farming in the Southern Hemisphere and aquaculture is making a steadily expanding contribution to Tasmania's economy (see box). *Population 520*

FRANKLIN ■ 2336

There are good examples of early colonial buildings in Franklin, the settlement of which was encouraged by Lady Franklin and which is the oldest township on the Huon River. These include three churches constructed around 1860. The town's apple-processing factory produces bottled juice as well as 250 tonnes of dried apple rings annually.

There is some indefinable quality about the peaceful Huon Valley and the D'Entrecasteaux Channel which seems especially conducive to creative endeavour. Many craftspeople have studios tucked away in the bushland where the overheads are low and they can work in peace. Franklin is one of the shopfront outlets for locally made arts and crafts.

GEEVESTON ■ 2337

Originally known by the whimsical title of Lightwood Bottom, Geeveston became Geeves Town after William Geeves who took up land in 1849 and began clearing it the following year. He settled there in response to Lady Jane Franklin's request that someone should establish a church in the area.

Geeveston is the southern base for forestry management though the one-time flourishing timber industry has declined in recent years. The town is the starting point for trips to the Hartz Mountains National Park and the Tahune Forest Reserve (see entries) and there are fine views to be had from the nearby Waratah Lookout. *Population 820*

HARTZ MOUNTAINS NATIONAL PARK ■ 2338

The conqueror of Mount Everest, Sir Edmund Hilary, described the Hartz Mountains National Park as 'some of the wildest and most spectacular scenery I have ever seen'. A high ridge of dolerite peaks run north-south between the catchments of the Arve and Picton rivers and the 1254-metre-high Hartz Peak is often snow covered. The park encloses beech rainforests, tall eucalypts and alpine moorlands where heaths are interspersed with snow gums. The hardy alpine flora, winter snowfalls and rugged countryside attract enthusiastic photographers, cross-country skiers and bushwalkers.

HASTINGS ■ 2339

Hastings was once a prosperous logging town with a bustling wharf and a football team. There is almost nothing here now and the whole site might have been repossessed by the bush had not timber workers discovered three caves in 1917.

HASTINGS CAVES Newdegate, the largest of the three Hastings caves, was named after Sir Francis Newdegate, a governor of Tasmania. It was officially opened to the public in 1939 and attracts a steady stream of visitors. The cave makes imaginative use of electric light and a spiral staircase winds through stalactites, stalagmites, delicate shawls, columns and horizontal helictites.

HASTINGS THERMAL POOL The thermal pool, less than 100 metres from the road, is surrounded by fern glades. Hot springs keep the water temperature at about 27° Centigrade all year round.

HUON RIVER ■ 2340

To the Aborigines, this river was 'tahune-linah' and it did not acquire its present name until the French came in 1792. Bruni D'Entrecasteaux called the main river Huon after his colleague Captain Huon Kermandec; its tributary became the Kermandie.

An icy, glacier-carved lake allows bulky Mount Snowy to reflect on itself in the Hartz Mountains National Park.

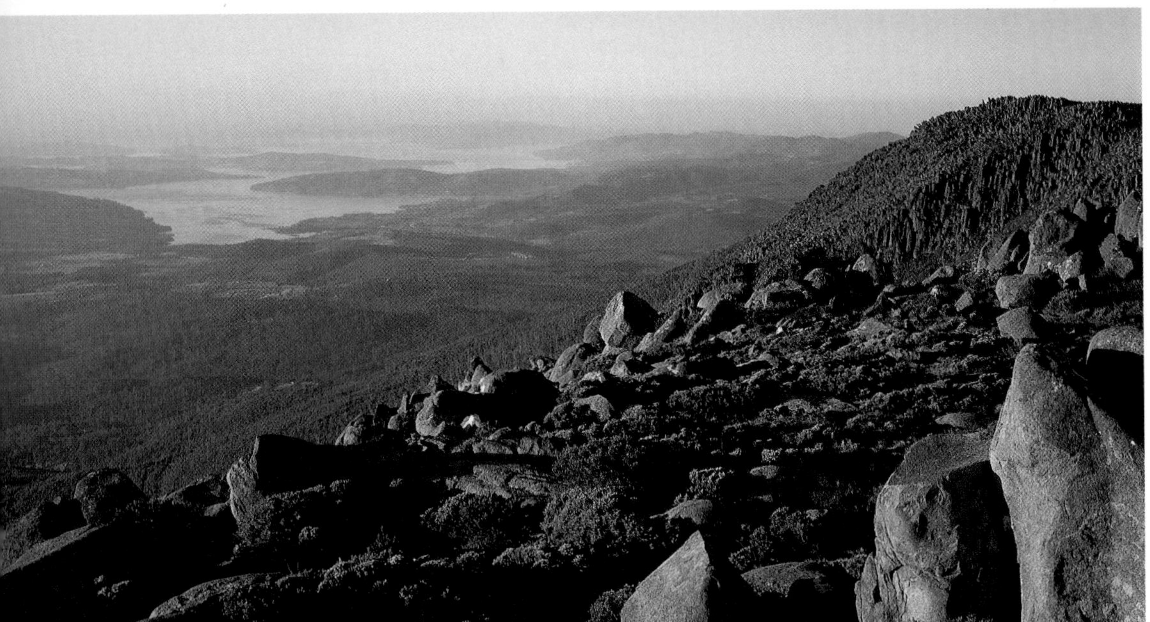

Mount Wellington looks south-west to the mouth of the Derwent and the craggy outposts of Storm Bay.

The Huon winds through an ordered landscape of orchards and pastures which are almost always lush green. So much tree clearing has been done that it is often difficult to believe that newcomers were daunted by the thickly timbered country. They were also impressed by some huge, unfamiliar trees along the river banks.

The Huon pine is peculiar to Tasmania although a similar species once grew in Chile. The pioneers called it 'green gold' and valued its durability for ship building but the wood is too rare and precious for such purposes nowadays. It is used mainly by craftspeople and carved or turned into ornaments and bowls. Huon pine sap has a distinctive aromatic smell which lingers long after a tree is felled. A few specimens survive in this area but the best are in a stand more than a thousand years old in the Truchanas Reserve, thirty kilometres from Strathgordon (see *Bridgewater & New Norfolk*).

HUONVILLE ■ 2341

Huonville is the main service centre for the Huon Municipality. From the main street there is a view of Mountain River Valley and the peak of Sleeping Beauty which resembles a woman's profile. Berry fruits, apples, pears and vegetables grow here and sheep and cattle are raised.

The Huon has become Tasmania's best known apple-growing district. Silas Parsons is credited with planting the first orchard at Huonville in 1841. Apples were soon established commercially and first shipped from the Huon River to India and New Zealand in 1849. In the 1850s, the increase in the gold-seeking mainland population caused a surge in the demand for fruit. As time went on, more orchards were planted in the Huon, the Derwent Valley and the north. The industry peaked between the two world wars when about 11 000 hectares of Tasmania's land surface was devoted to the fruit.

The area of land occupied by apple orchards is now much diminished. Several factors have brought about the decline including increases in freight rates, Britain's entry into the European Common Market and changing tastes. Once upon a time, 500 different varieties of apples were grown in the Huon Valley but the number of major varieties is now down to about eight. The 'Red Delicious' strain caters to the demand for a large, sweet, red apple. Despite all this, Huonville and the surrounding valley still produce plentiful crops of apples each year for juice, cider, pies and old-fashioned, keeping-the-doctor-away eating raw. *Population 960*

IDA BAY RAILWAY ■ 2342

The 600-millimetre gauge Ida Bay Railway was originally built to carry limestone trucks but like many other early Tasmanian enterprises, it now serves a completely different purpose. The line is owned by the government and leased to a private company which operates a newly designed train to take sightseers on a six-kilometre trip from Ida Bay to the Deep Hole. The train passes bushland, button grass plains and coastal inlets along the way. A forty-minute walk from the beach at Deep Hole ends at Southport Lagoon where there is a monument to those who went down with the convict transport ship *George III* in 1835 (see Labillardiere State Reserve).

KETTERING ■ 2343

The fishing port of Kettering is near the embarkation point for the car ferry to Bruny Island. It lies on the Channel Highway in a sheltered bay and is surrounded by neat orchards that spread across the hills and valleys. Fruit growing is an important industry and strawberries, raspberries, cherries, blackcurrants, loganberries, apples and pears can be bought – in season – from roadside stalls throughout this region.

OYSTER COVE The Tasmanian Aborigines lived in Oyster Cove near Kettering for many years before Europeans sighted its shores. Their way of life was substantially disturbed by the whalers and sealers and many died in the surrounding hills after being displaced from their near-shore settlements.

Between 1840 and 1847 Oyster Cove was a convict penitentiary but was abandoned for health reasons. After that the convict-built barracks became the last home of about forty full-blooded Aborigines who were brought back there from exile on Flinders Island. Truganini (see Bruny Island) requested that her ashes be scattered in the bay but it was not until 1976, a hundred years after her death, that her wish was granted.

The first berry fruits in Tasmania were planted at Oyster Cove. Raspberries and other small fruits soon became established throughout the Huon and Channel area.

KINGSTON ■ 2344

In 1802, the Scottish botanist Robert Brown slogged through the bush on foot from the site of present Hobart to the site of contemporary Kingston. Browns River is named after him. The first settlers built their homes of timber because it was in plentiful supply and stone was much harder to come by. Early transport was by boat but in 1835 the inland Proctors Road linked Hobart and Kingston. Ten years later, the coastal Bonnet Hill route was completed.

By the late 1800s, Kingston was a very popular holiday destination with beaches that are particularly good for safe swimming. Post-Second World War migration from the Netherlands resulted in a substantial Dutch community which maintains traditional festivities.

Kingston is the residential and administrative centre of the Municipality of Kingborough; with the building of a new expressway, it has become a major suburb of Hobart. There is some specialised manufacturing in the town and orcharding, cattle and sheep farming in the surrounding district. *Population 12 910*

ANTARCTIC DIVISION The research headquarters of the Antarctic Division of the Department of Science and Technology is just south of Kingston. Items from early Australian Antarctic expeditions are displayed together with the latest information about what is happening on the frozen continent.

FESTIVALS Kingborough Community Festival, March.

LABILLARDIERE STATE RESERVE ■ 2345

The Labillardiere State Reserve is named in honour of the naturalist who went with Bruni D'Entrecasteaux to Bruny Island. It is in the south of the island and consists of the peninsula and Partridge Island, which is accessible by boat. The entrance to the state reserve is marked by a cattle grid.

The Cape Bruny Lighthouse, standing 105 metres above the sea, is at the southernmost tip of the island, in the reserve. Governor Sir George Arthur suggested building a lighthouse on Actaeon Reef as early as 1825 but the port committee did not agree with this idea. In 1832, marker buoys were put in D'Entrecasteaux Channel but it took three wrecks in 1835 to encourage more constructive action. In April, 133 convicts and passengers died when the *George III* struck a submerged rock and the guards fired on the prisoners in the hold to prevent panic. In July, the *Enchantress* foundered and 17 drowned. A few weeks later Actaeon reef claimed the *Wallace*, mercifully with no loss of life. Convicts began work on the Cape Bruny Lighthouse in the following year, cutting the stone for it on the site. The ligh went on in 1838.

LUNE RIVER ■ 234

Lune River's post office has a unusual collectable prized by discerning philatelists – here they ca acquire Australia's most souther postmark. The town still supports limestone quarry which supplies th refineries at Risdon and Electron with raw material. The local gem fields are well known by fossicker and are renowned for their agate travertine and petrified manfern.

MARGATE ■ 234

Margate is a small agricultural an fishing village with a growing popu lation of 'out-of-towners' who hav chosen to live in this peaceful di trict. Many local people who do not work at the fish processing plant drive daily to jobs in Hobart.

Tasmania's last passenger train, the Tasman Limited, is now permanently stationed in Margate. The carriages have been turned into tourist shops and displays and the buffet car continues to serve its original purpose. *Population 740*

MOUNT WELLINGTON ■ 2348

In 1871, the distinguished English novelist and traveller Anthony Trollope pronounced Mount Wellington 'just enough of a mountain to give excitement to ladies and gentlemen in middle life'. Its broad dolerite summit is, in fact, 1271 metres above sea level and is often heavily snow-capped in winter. It forms a majestic backdrop to the city of Hobart. George Bass climbed Mount Wellington in 1798 as did botanist Robert Brown in 1804 after Hobart was established by Lieutenant-Colonel David Collins. Another distinguished climber was Charles Darwin who ascended the peak in 1836.

In the 1850s, the governor of Tasmania, Sir William Denison, ordered an icehouse to be built by convict labour on the mountain. This soon became a popular destination for riding parties. The road to the summit was opened in 1937. Building it was another government initiative; this time to provide work during the Great Depression.

SHOT TOWER HISTORIC SITE ■ 2349

This unusual landmark stands more than sixty metres tall beside the Channel Highway on the outskirts of Taroona. It was built by a Scottish architect, engineer and carpenter called Joseph Moir who, with the help of two masons, began assembling more than 8000 individually curved and tapered sandstone blocks in 1870. The base of the building is nearly eight metres in diameter and tapers to four metres at the top. Its principal purpose was to make lead shot. The molten metal was poured through perforations at the top of the tower and the droplets formed into perfectly spherical balls on the long drop to the water at the bottom. A 287-step climb to a viewing platform is rewarded with spectacular views of the district.

SNUG ■ 2350

Snug, proclaimed a township in 1908, may be so called because it provided a safe anchorage for the sailing vessels that navigated the Snug River from North West Bay. In 1967, the town was ravaged by fire and most of the buildings incinerated. On that horrifying day a pall of smoke hung over southern Tasmania, Hobart was encircled by flames and more than sixty people died. In kinder summers, the sheltered beach at nearby Coningham draws visitors and bushwalkers trek the rainforest near Snug Falls in the Snug Tiers. Many residents work at the calcium-carbide works at Electrona. *Population 770*

SOUTHPORT ■ 2351

Admiral D'Entrecasteaux named this spot 'Baie des Moules', which was translated by English geographers as Mussel Bay. The first settlers were sealers and whalers who called it Southport although the name Hythe appears on some early maps.

The place became a substantial timber town and provided a busy scene in the latter part of the nineteenth century when the shores were lined with wharves and jetties. Once the trees were gone Southport lost its central purpose, but a fishing fleet still uses the harbour and the resort is popular with holiday-makers.

TAHUNE FOREST RESERVE ■ 2352

The 102 hectares of Tahune Reserve preserve the heavily timbered rainforest that looked so inhospitable to the early European explorers that they condemned it as unsuitable for settlement. Several specimens of the famous Huon pine, blackwood, sassafras, myrtle and celery-top pine grow there and are relatively accessible from the Forestry Commission walking tracks and picnic areas. The reserve derives its name from an Aboriginal word for the Huon River.

SALMON 'PADDOCKS' & SHELLFISH BEDS OF THE SEAFOOD ISLE

THERE ARE those who express the opinion that 'the Salmon Isle' would nowadays be a much more appropriate nickname than 'the Holiday Isle' or 'the Apple Isle' for Australia's southern state. Aquaculture, or fish farming, has emerged as Tasmania's new environmentally friendly growth industry. There are at least a million dollars 'on the fin' at sea farms in Port Esperance at Dover (see entry) and in the Huon River near Geeveston.

Eggs imported from Nova Scotia 30 years ago are responsible for the plump Atlantic salmon which graze in sea pens (above,right) in the Tasman Sea's cool, unpolluted waters.

These modern farms raise Atlantic salmon in cool, sheltered, unpolluted waters with a high oxygen content and good current movements to disperse the natural waste. During the season, the fish are harvested daily and reach fishmongers and markets within twenty-four hours.

The fish are kept in netting cages suspended from circular pontoons from which they are fed a balanced diet of highly nutritious food. Every day divers give a cross-section of salmon in each 'paddock' a health check-up. In recent years Australians have wanted increasingly to eat fish both for health reasons and because of the gradual development of a more sophisticated national palate. Salmon is high in protein and low in calories and the carefully bred Tasmanian Atlantic variety contains more valuable omega-3 oils than other fish.

Tasmanian fish farming involves more than just salmon and successful farms have been established at several points around the coast with oysters, mussels, and abalone in readily harvestable positions. Trout have long been bred at Salmon Ponds for release into the inland waterways and are now raised at Macquarie Harbour on the west coast.

The experts hope for another success story with the highly popular scallop through a reseeding program being carried out at Triabunna on the east coast. These once-renowned Tasmanian shellfish are no longer harvested commercially and have become relatively scarce throughout the island's more readily accessible coastal waters but aquaculturists are confident they will soon be able to repair the damage done by dredging and starfish.

Plump Pacific oysters and tasty native flat oysters are raised on frames at Smithton and St Helens and bred artificially at Bicheno. Encouraged by progress so far, the aquaculturists are constantly looking for more marine species to cultivate on open-water farms. Sea farms have already been set up for stripey trumpeter, clams and seaweed. □

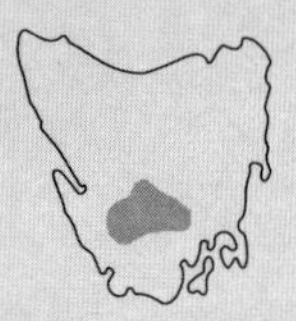

Bridgewater & New Norfolk

The Derwent Valley, criss-crossed with poplar windbreaks, has the tamed loveliness of a long-cultivated landscape. This contrasts starkly with the lakes and mountains to the south-west where hydro-electric power installations have not diminished the natural grandeur.

A 130-year-old tradition of hop drying continues at Bushey Park where the 1950s oast houses are in the old style.

BAGDAD ■ 2353

The naming of towns and villages in the days of early settlement was frequently a somewhat casual business: honouring friends and benefactors, assuaging homesickness, imperfectly listening to Aboriginal Australians and self aggrandisement were a few of the inspirations for labels still used today. A few southern Tasmanian names come from the Bible or *The Tales of the Arabian Nights*. Legend has it that explorer-soldier Hugh Germain and his friend, Jorgen Jorgenson, carried these two books on their meat-hunting forays from Hobart in 1806 and used them alternately for naming places. Bagdad, Jericho and the Jordan River are some of the few that survive. The apple and pear orchards that were to be planted in the surrounding valley have now been turned into pastures.

BRIDGEWATER ■ 2354

Bridgewater was originally known as Green Point and is the site of a causeway across the River Derwent with a lift-span section at one end and a large congregation of black swans on the surrounding water. Chain gangs of convict labour began building the first causeway in the 1830s. They carted more than two million tonnes of stone, some of which came from the mainland, and were punished for lagging by solitary confinement in a cell a claustrophobic two metres high and fifty centimetres square. The original causeway was finished in 1849 and the present structure dates from 1946.

Bridgewater, within easy commuting distance of Hobart, is now a large housing estate on the northern bank of the river. The site for the original town was on the opposite shore where the old watch-house – most recently a petrol station – still stands.
Population 8680

BRIGHTON ■ 2355

Brighton is an inland town not one bit like its English coastal namesake. New South Wales Governor Lachlan Macquarie named it in the early 1820s 'in honour of our present gracious sovereign's favourite place of residence'. At one stage, Brighton was intended as the capital of Van Diemen's Land – Macquarie thought it 'possessed all requisites of a town' but it never developed in the way he envisaged. A military post was established here in 1826 and today it is the location of the Brighton Military Camp. 'Cabbage-tree Ned' – Edward Devine – Cobb & Co.'s most famous driver, was born in Brighton (see *Melton & Sunbury*).

ELLENDALE ■ 2356

Ellendale, once known as Monto's Marsh, nestles in the foothills of Mount Field National Park (see entry) and was first settled by James Clark who lived to be 100 years of age. Mr Clark is buried in St Andrew's graveyard. A large hop-kiln is still a district landmark though hops have not been grown here since the 1970s. In the early part of the twentieth century, the village catered for visitors to nearby Russell Falls and it is still a good starting point for bushwalking and lake and stream trout fishing.

GORDON DAM ■ 2357

The high-arched, concrete Gordon Dam rises 140 metres out of the Gordon Gorge to intercept the Gordon River above its junction with the Serpentine River. It is overlooked by a viewing rotunda perched high above the structure. The impressive Gordon Power Station is underground and is accessible to visitors by a tunnel 183 metres below the surface of Lake Gordon.

GRETNA ■ 2358

Gretna was once a coaching stop of some importance between New Norfolk and Hamilton. It was most probably named after Gretna Green in Scotland but there are no written records to confirm this theory. In the mid-nineteenth century Mary Spode screwed up her courage, defied her father and eloped to be married in Gretna's St Mary's Anglican Church. She was a great-granddaughter of the English potter Josiah Spode, was happily married for many years, and lies by her true love in the cemetery. The Woolpack Inn, where the notorious bushranger, Martin Cash and his followers fought a fierce battle with the police in 1843, no longer exists but several examples of fine colonial stone buildings do remain between Gretna and Hamilton.

HAMILTON ■ 2359

Hamilton is classified as an historic town by the National Trust and is well endowed with charming buildings, among them St Peter's Church Rectory, Glen Clyde House and Emma's and McCauley's cottages, all constructed in the 1830s or 1840s. The Hamilton Inn Hotel is even older and had its origins as the family home of William Roadknight in 1826, not becoming the New Inn until 1838. There were ten other licensed inns in the town by the middle of the nineteenth century including the 'Hit or Miss', 'Bird in Hand' and 'Crooked Billet'.

The district built up a reputation for fine farming and grazing land which persists today; it once had a flour mill, brewery, coal mine, lime quarries and hop fields.

LAKE GORDON ■ 2360

About ninety billion tonnes of rain and snow fall on Tasmania each year and the island is therefore well endowed with rivers and lakes some of which have been reshaped on a grand scale to produce hydro-electricity. One such is Lake Gordon which was created by the Gordon Dam (see entry).

Water from Lake Gordon and Lake Pedder (see entry) is used in the underground Gordon Power Station. Together the two lakes form the largest water storage in Australia – their 514 square kilometres is one per cent of Tasmania's total surface and they hold twenty-seven times the volume of water in Sydney Harbour. Their capacity is three times that of Lake Eucumbene, the largest of the Snowy Mountains' lakes.

Fishing is a foregone expectation of any natural or artificial body of water in Tasmania. Between 197[illegible] and 1977, 500 000 rainbow trout fr[illegible] were released into Lake Gordon and consequently, it is now a popular location for anglers.

LAKE PEDDER ■ 236[illegible]

Building the Gordon River Power Development meant flooding Lake Pedder. This plan provoked vigorous opposition from many vocal conservationists who wanted to save rare plants in the surrounding enviro[illegible]

ake Gordon, formed by a slim concrete arc thrown across a gorge in 1974, s cradled by one of the world's few remaining impenetrable wildernesses.

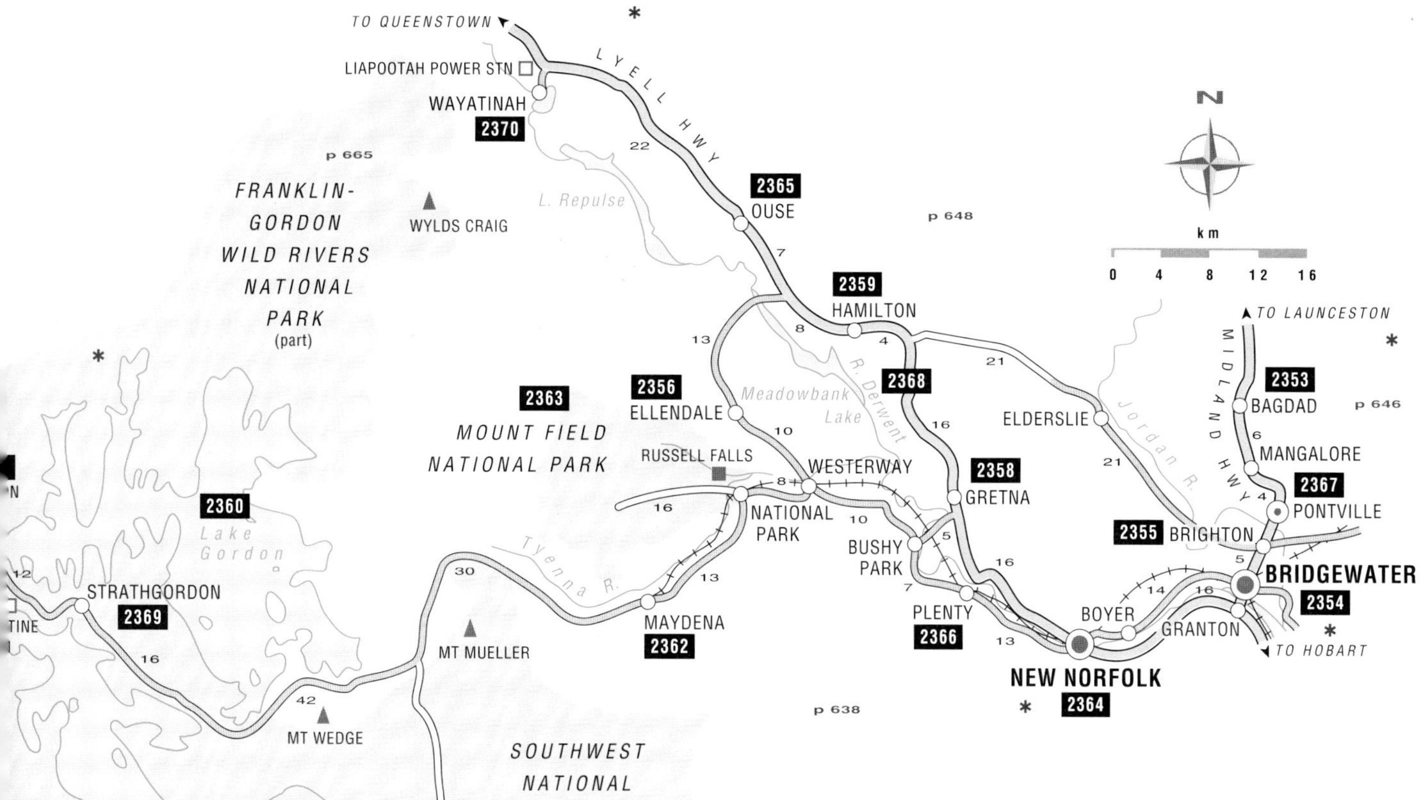

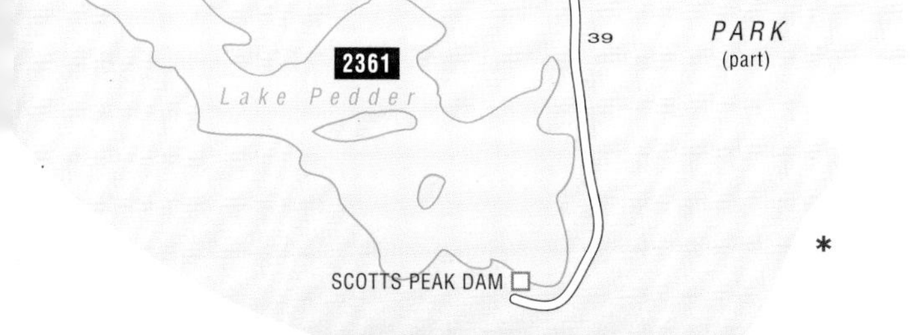

ment and the Pedder 'beach'. This sandy expanse was really the lake floor which appeared each year as the water level dropped and was a little more than three kilometres long and about seven-hundred-and-thirty metres wide in mid-summer. It was an incredibly beautiful strip of land which also provided a landing place in this rugged and remote region for light aircraft.

Olegas Truchanas, a Lithuanian emigrant who had worked for the Hydro-Electric Commission, was a spokesperson in the campaign. His landscape photographs had earned him many prizes and he made over thirty trips to Lake Pedder to record its moods in all seasons. Truchanas believed in preserving 'the unique, rare and beautiful' and asked if 'the ideal of beauty could not become an accepted goal of national policy?'. In January 1972, he set out to take more photographs of the Gordon River, for he knew this landscape would also soon be changed by power development. He never returned – a fatal slip on smooth, wet rocks plunged him into the river and he drowned. The Truchanas Nature Reserve in the south-west now protects a small part of the country he cherished.

Lake Pedder was flooded in the year Truchanas died and now has a surface area far greater than its original. In late 1972, the Inland Fisheries Commission released 350 000 brown trout fry. The rich nutrients in the water caused them to grow into giants and some say fish weighing up to twenty kilograms were caught in the early years.

Huge fish are not just ambitious anglers' dreams – the legendary Lake Pedder brown trout now average about four-and-a-half kilograms with some in excess of nine kilograms.

MAYDENA ■ 2362

Maydena is a forestry township at the beginning of the Gordon River toll road leading to Strathgordon (see entry). Once bullock teams used to haul the massive logs from the bush – work done now by huge log trucks. The spectacular mountain ash is one of the tallest of the eucalypts and take hundreds of years to grow to full maturity. 'The Big Tree', in a protected stand near Maydena, measures more than ninety metres and probably holds the record as the tallest Australian hardwood, even though its top has been slightly lopped by a fierce wind.

MOUNT FIELD NATIONAL PARK ■ 2363

It is no new thing for public voices to be raised in defence of Tasmanian wilderness. Mount Field National Park, one of the oldest and most popular reserves, was proclaimed in 1916 as a result of William Crooke's National Parks Association which lobbied the government of the day. It was named after Judge Barron Field from the New South Wales Supreme Court who came to Tasmania in 1819. A commercial trout farm and the camping ground sit side by side at the entrance, making it possible to enjoy a barbecued Tasmanian delicacy with very little effort.

The park is a massive highland plateau with several imposing peaks – Mount Field West rises 1434 metres. There are towering eucalypts and thick horizontal scrub. The weak stems of this curious plant bend horizontally to form its branches into a slippery, tightly-woven lattice and it is almost impossible to walk on or through. The last thylacine, or Tasmanian tiger in captivity was trapped in this region in the 1930s. A road ascends to Lake Dobson below the steep slopes of Mount Mawson (1310 metres) where skiing is popular in winter.

RUSSELL FALLS Russell Falls, most well known of the park's waterfalls, drops more than forty metres into a cool gorge and is more accessible than Lady Barron and Horseshoe Falls, being at the end of a track suitable for wheelchairs.

NEW NORFOLK ■ 2364

Lieutenant John Hayes explored the Derwent River (see entry) in a rowing boat as far as he could go upstream and landed slightly above the site of the present New Norfolk. A few years later, in 1803, Denis McCarty, an Irish convict who began his Australian life in New South Wales, was sent to Van Diemen's Land. Five years later he was police constable at New Norfolk and had built the first house there.

In 1811, McCarty entertained New South Wales Governor Lachlan Macquarie and his wife in his new home. Later McCarty made a road of sorts between Hobart and New Norfolk but drowned mysteriously before he was paid for it. New Norfolk was supposed to be called Elizabeth Town after Macquarie's wife but the name did not stick.

The evacuation of Norfolk Island, north-east of Sydney, occurred in 1806 and the next year the *Lady Nelson* arrived in Hobart with thirty-four Norfolk Islanders who were given land in the Derwent Valley. Within a year 544 people had arrived, much to the dismay of Lieutenant-Governor Collins who was already facing a famine in Van Diemen's Land. The local settlers were shooting kangaroos, ducks and swans, and clothing themselves in skins. Collins could not honour all the promises that had been made to the newcomers but they made good progress clearing their land grants around New Norfolk. The entire town has been registered by the National Trust and the buildings reveal much of this early history. *Population 5820*

ST MATTHEW'S ANGLICAN CHURCH St Matthew's Church, the oldest in Tasmania, is much changed since it was built in 1823 and only the walls and the flagged floor of the nave are from the original design.

THE BUSH INN The Bush Inn, constructed in 1815, claims to have the longest continuous licence in Australia, stretching back to 1825 but the Launceston Hotel's licence may be a few months older. Here William Vincent Wallace, the Irish composer, wrote his work *Maritana* in 1838, and here Dame Nellie Melba sang selections from the opera in the 1920s.

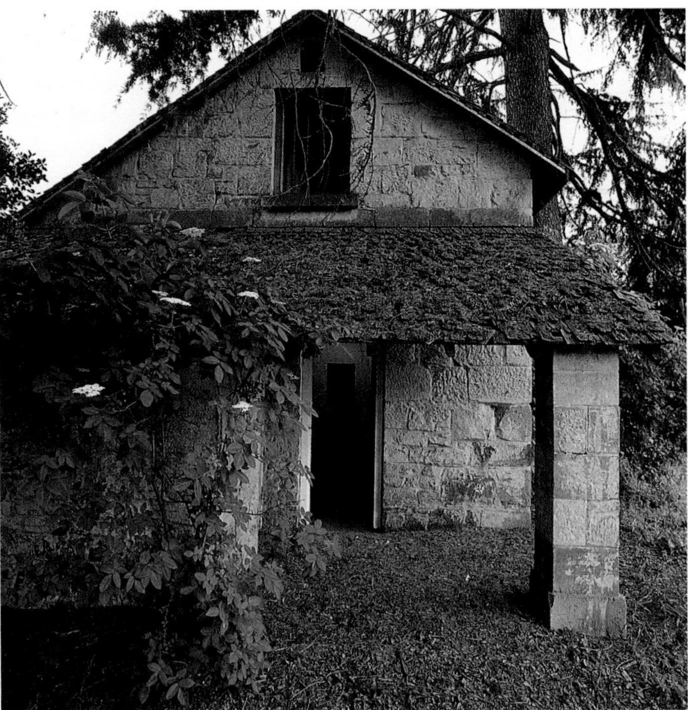

The 1830 stone coach house at the 'Valleyfield' homestead near New Norfolk doubled as a lock-up, necessitating bars on its upper-floor window.

DERWENT VALLEY Hops came to the Derwent Valley in the 1860s and row upon row of poplars were planted to shelter the wind-sensitive crop. In autumn these trees streak the river plain with gold and the disused oast houses add character to the landscape. The Australian Newsprint Mill has its Tasmanian plant at Boyer, near New Norfolk, and most Australian newspapers are printed on stock from here or from the other ANM factory in Albury, New South Wales (see *Albury & Wodonga*).

OUSE ■ 2365

Despite its closeness to Hamilton, Ouse has a very different character, mainly because most of the buildings have been built in twentieth-century weatherboard style. The settlement is overlooked by two hilltop churches – St John the Baptist and the Church of the Immaculate Conception. The former was built by convicts in 1843. The locals refer to their village as 'the Ouse', a reminder of the days when the site was a crossing on the river of the same name.

One of the early European settlers to live there was David Burn, Australia's first recorded playwright, but people inhabited the area long before he wrote his *Plays and Fugitive Pieces*. The river is geologically very old and was known to the Tasmanian Aborigines as 'the big river'.

PLENTY ■ 2366

The little village of Plenty is famous for its salmon ponds where the state's first brown and rainbow trout and salmon were raised in 1864. The fish eggs had a ninety-one day voyage from England in an ice chest and survived against incredible odds on a journey involving a clipper, a steam ship, a river steamer and horseback. The salmon failed to thrive but the descendants of the trout went on to stock Tasmanian, mainland and New Zealand waterways. The ponds and the piscatorial museum are set in attractive grounds planted with well-established European trees.

PONTVILLE ■ 2367

Pontville adjoins Brighton and during its early days was destined to be the centre of Tasmania's capital city. This early garrison town and staging post was established in 1830 and is now classified as an historic town. The Pontville quarries supplied a great deal of the sandstone used in Tasmanian buildings in the nineteenth century and two of them are still worked.

St Mark's Church of England was built around 1840 and has interesting headstones in the churchyard. It was designed by James Blackburn, an architect and engineer who was transported to Tasmania in 1833 and given a free pardon in 1841. No doubt his design for St Mark's Church earned him a measure of official approval. The former post office was once the officers' mess and 'The Row' housed the military overseers who supervised the early road-building works. *Population 1120*

RIVER DERWENT ■ 2368

In 1793, on an investigative voyage for the British East India Company, Lieutenant – later Commodore – John Hayes came upon a broad river estuary upon which he bestowed the name Derwent.

The river begins on the Central Plateau, rising in Lake St Clair almost 740 metres above sea level, and flows in a south-easterly direction to the Tasman Sea at Storm Bay. It is approximately 190 kilometres long, and drops to sea-level between New Norfolk and Granton. The estuary below Hobart is always crowded with yachts in the appropriate season and annual Sydney–Hobart Yacht Race contenders look with relief on this finishing stretch of the arduous course.

Work on harnessing the great hydro-electric potential of the Derwent's catchment area commenced in 1934 and the most recent power station was commissioned in 1968. Developments in the years between included sixteen dams, ten power stations and numerous weirs, flumes, canals, tunnels, pipelines and access roads. Tasmania's total hydro-electric capacity was just over 2315 megawatts in 1990. Water from the Derwent River and its tributaries, used over and over again as it flows downstream, generates millions of watts from Lake Echo Power Station to Meadowbank Power Station.

STRATHGORDON ■ 2369

Strathgordon, dating from the early 1970s, owes its existence to the Pedder-Gordon power scheme. It is one of Tasmania's numerous transitory 'hydro' villages where prefabricated bungalows house workers and their families and provide basic community facilities for the duration of the construction period. When the work is finished, buildings and people move out together.

A small band of permanent residents live here to maintain the Gordon Power Station and to cater to holiday-makers. Day-trippers come from Hobart and the district attracts a steady stream of trout fishermen and bushwalkers for longer sojourns. Strathgordon is surrounded by rugged mountain ranges which are spectacularly beautiful in all weathers and seasons.

WYATINAH ■ 2370

Wyatinah is an Aboriginal word thought to mean 'brook' or 'creek'. This village contains less than fifty permanent Hydro-Electric Commission houses for the staff who operate the six power stations on the Lower Derwent River.

Between 1952 and 1969 Wyatinah's population peaked at about two thousand. The construction sites included Catagunya Dam on Lake Repulse which was commissioned in 1962 and at the time was the largest pre-stressed concrete dam of its type in the world, and the simpler rockfill Wyatinah Dam.

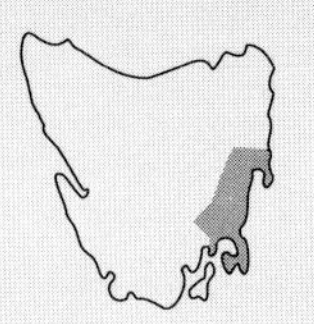

Lauderdale & Midway Point

Beaches sheltered from the westerly winds, warm offshore currents and good fishing prospects draw many people to Tasmania's east coast. In contrast, the Tasman Peninsula presents a dramatic coastline unrivalled for its ruggedness anywhere else in Australia.

COAL MINES HISTORIC SITE ■ 2371

These old coal mines were the first of four convict stations to be established on Norfolk Bay. They were opened in 1833 after a coal seam was discovered and were used as a punishment station for convicts from Port Arthur. They became a hellish place dreaded by all wrong-doers, for not only was the work underground in a cramped space but some solitary confinement cells were built in the mine galleries and any prisoner not completing an allotted task could find himself entombed.

Towards the end of 1848, the convicts were withdrawn; the coal mines were then leased and were finally abandoned in 1877. Later, they caught fire and burned for many years – now only ruins remain.

DODGES FERRY ■ 2372

The township of Dodges Ferry, like many of the settlements around Frederick Henry Bay, has long been a popular holiday resort with sandy beaches and rocky headlands close at hand. It lies at the entrance to the Pittwater estuary and has a reputation for safe fishing and boating. Until the 1960s, the buildings were mainly weatherboard holiday cottages but an influx of Hobart commuters has introduced brick bungalows and tall, A-frame houses. *Population 1550*

DUNALLEY ■ 2373

Dunalley, once known as East Bay Neck, is a small fishing village with its own cannery. Here a swing bridge crosses Denison Canal which provides a short cut for small boats on their way from the Derwent River to the east coast fishing grounds.

In 1942, two hundred years after the event, a memorial was erected on the foreshore to commemorate the landings by sailors from the Dutch ships *Heemskirk* and *Zeehan*. They were commanded by Abel Tasman who respectfully named the landmass in honour of Anthony Van Diemen, the then Governor-in-Chief of the Dutch East India Company in Batavia (Djakarta). It was not until December 1855 that Tasmania became the island's official name.

EAGLEHAWK NECK ■ 2374

The 410-metre-wide isthmus at Eaglehawk Neck isolates the Tasman Peninsula. It fitted it well for its grim role as a penal colony in the last century. Fierce dogs were tethered on chains across this strip with only a few centimetres between them. They were overlooked by zealous guards and formed an effective deterrent to any would-be escapers.

Eaglehawk Neck has become the main base for Tasmania's game-fishing charter fleet. Commercial fishing boats take bluefin tuna, trevally, crayfish and abalone. Colonies of fur seals inhabit the Hippolyte Rocks and other offshore sanctuaries and dolphins and occasional southern right whales patrol the Tasman Sea.

The Blowhole, Tasman Arch and the Devils Kitchen are three of a number of dramatic rock formations along this stretch of coast. They have formed over thousands of years as the soft sandstone capping has worn away. The Tessellated Pavement is a regularly patterned platform of mudstone which looks like the work of a skilled mason but is a freak formation caused by sea erosion.

FREYCINET NATIONAL PARK ■ 2375

The 13 000-hectare Freycinet National Park, declared in 1916, contains white sandy beaches, caves and rocky headlands, red granite peaks and eucalypt forests. There are Aboriginal middens in the dunes behind the beaches and an early settler, Silas Cole, first produced lime by burning oyster shells from the middens.

The resort shelters at the foot of mounts Dove, Amos and Mayson and is a good base for walking tours. Uninhabited Schouten Island, separated from the Freycinet Peninsula by a kilometre of water, was added to the park in 1967. Masons Downfall and Slaughterhouse Bay are sites of nineteenth-century whaling operations. The Chinese came here too, to extract tin from alluvial deposits in the area's creeks, but left after disputes with European miners.

WINEGLASS BAY Wineglass Bay is accessible only by walking track or boat. Its shimmering quartzite sand and sheltered position makes it a gem among swimming beaches. On a visit to Australia, the Royal yacht *Britannia* anchored in the bay and Queen Elizabeth was treated to an Australian-style barbecue in this secluded and beautiful place.

MOULTING LAGOON This lagoon, south of Bicheno and within the national park, is a natural sanctuary for waterfowl. Black swans breed here and the aquatic environment is a base for pelicans, ducks and various species of waders which include red-necked stints, red knots and bar-tailed godwits. Oysters are grown to maturity in the 512-hectare lagoon.

LAUDERDALE ■ 2376

Lauderdale is the main centre of the South Arm district, on the eastern shore of the Derwent. The canal across the isthmus was designed to provide a waterway for small craft between Ralphs Bay and Frederick Henry Bay but was never completed, silting up as it was built. Nearby Goat Bluff, where mutton birds nest, looks out over the Tasman Peninsula,

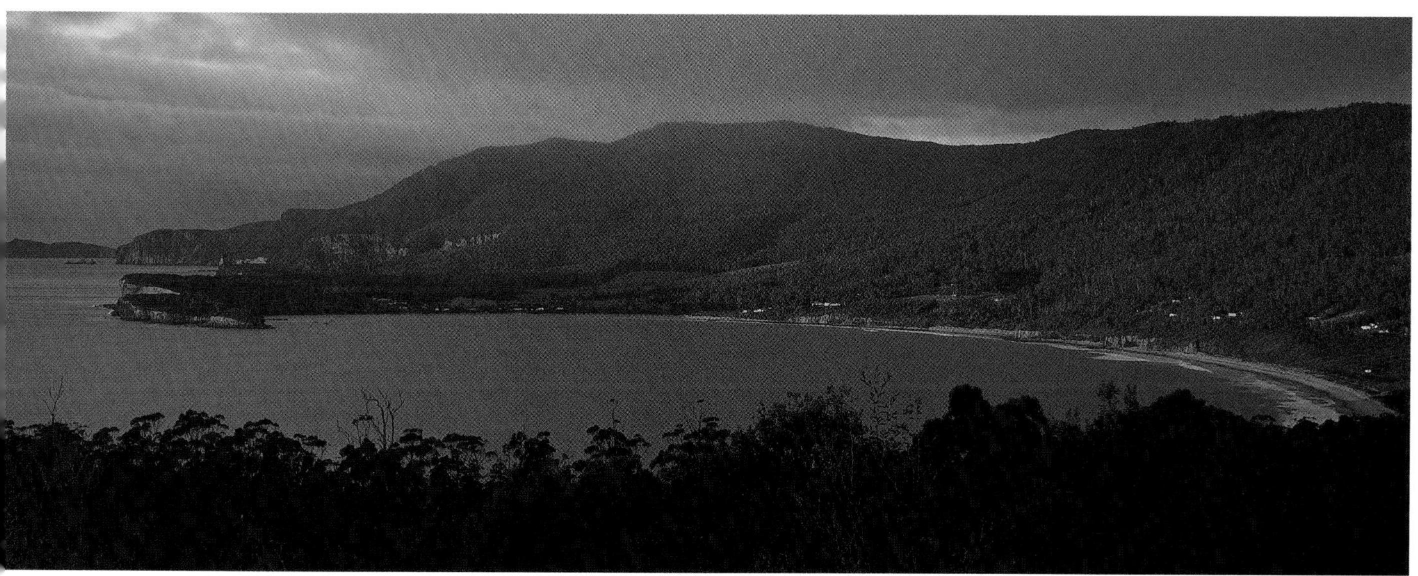

The waters of Pirates Bay wash onto the gentle sweep of Eaglehawk Neck, once a dreaded milestone on the road to Port Arthur and total incarceration.

Wineglass Bay provides a handsome trim for the eastern shore of the slim isthmus that broadens into a peninsula largely within the Freycinet Park.

Storm Bay, Bruny Island and the mouth of the Derwent River. The small township of South Arm, like Lauderdale, is a residential base for Hobart workers and a haven for retired people. *Population 2510*

MARIA ISLAND NATIONAL PARK ■ 2377

Abel Tasman sighted Maria Island in 1642 and named it after Anthony Van Diemen's wife (see Dunalley). Tobias Furneaux sailed past in 1773 and Englishman John Cox met with Aborigines there while he picked up water and firewood in 1789.

In 1825, Governor Arthur selected the northern end of the island for a penal settlement to relieve the numbers at Macquarie Harbour. Named Darlington in honour of the governor of New South Wales, it lasted less than seven years but during that time the prisoners put up buildings from locally made bricks. They also tanned leather, made convict clothing and farm implements and ran a sawmill and a smithy. In 1842, the island's second wave of penal occupation turned to growing things: wheat, flax, turnips, potatoes, vegetables and fruit trees.

After 1850, the island was leased to graziers until Diego Bernacchi landed in 1884 and found peaches on the abandoned trees. These gave him great hopes for his intended silk and wine industries. Darlington was renamed San Diego, and at one time supported 250 people and sent cement, marble, wine, fish, minerals and timber to the 1888 Melbourne Exhibition. Two years later, Bernacchi's business was failing and he abandoned the island in 1897. In 1918, he returned to set up a cement works but that too failed.

Maria Island was proclaimed a national park in 1972. It is a sanctuary for animals from the main island as well as Victorian emus. The sandstone cliffs south of Darlington are beautifully streaked and the limestone fossil cliffs are packed with shells. Mount Maria (709 metres) is the highest point on the island.

MIDWAY POINT ■ 2378

Midway Point gets its name from its position on a long spit which juts into Pittwater inlet at about the midpoint of the two halves of the Sorell causeway (see Sorell). The surrounding land is of rich, black, volcanic soil and the predominant rural activities are raising sheep for wool and mixed farming. The town is close enough to Hobart for daily commuters to travel with ease. *Population 2200*

ORFORD ■ 2379

Orford was an important port when the east coast's main means of transport was by sea. It lies on the Prosser River which was named for a prison escaper who was recaptured on its banks. Shelly and Spring beaches are within walking distance of the town.

The sharp-edged, prow-like 'cutwaters' facing the oncoming Coal River flow were added to Richmond Bridge in 1884 to stabilise the structure.

When Maria Island became a convict settlement in 1825, a shore station was established at Orford to serve the local garrison as well as passing whalers. Sandstone from the nearby quarry was used for building and some of the lifting equipment is still there. *Population 500*

PORT ARTHUR ■ 2380

In 1830, a new penal settlement opened on the Tasman Peninsula. It lasted until 1877. Its founder, Governor George Arthur, decreed the prisoners should undertake 'the most unceasing labour' with 'the most harassing vigilence'. The men in the chain gangs wore ill-fitting yellow uniforms and worked in silence from dawn to dusk.

Captain Charles Booth of the Twenty-first Fusiliers shaped Port Arthur from 1833 to 1844 and under his influence it gradually became an established town. He organised a railway from Norfolk Bay to Port Arthur and an elaborate hilltop semaphore system to transmit messages to and from Hobart. The convicts worked at all sorts of trades with timber being the main export.

After the convicts left, the place was shunned by the local community and renamed Carnarvon. Many hoped the fires that swept through the settlement would completely wipe out the stain of the shameful past. Some of the damaged buildings have been restored by the National Parks and Wildlife Service and sit mellowing among green grass and mature European trees. The site is now a leading historical attraction on the tourist route.

MODEL PRISON The Model Prison, built from 1848 to 1852, is one of the restored showpieces in the complex. It copied the Pentonville Prison system in England where silence and separation replaced corporal punishment. The prison's worst offenders were put in a tiny cell where they could neither see nor hear.

ISLE OF THE DEAD The cemetery on the Isle of the Dead is a short ferry trip away from Port Arthur. More than 1760 convicts were buried here in communal graves. Some of them may have helped carve the 180 headstones which mark the graves of free settlers, soldiers and prison officials.

RICHMOND ■ 2381

Richmond grew beside the crossing place on the Coal River used by early travellers to Sorell and the east coast and by the 1830s was the third largest town in the colony and major military post and convict station.

When the Sorell Causeway was completed in 1872, the Port Arthur traffic ceased to come through Richmond and it remained undeveloped. The village retained its colonial character and Georgian buildings. This historical past is now the essence of its attraction for modern visitors.

The cemetery behind St John's, Australia's first Roman Catholic church, has classic examples of early Tasmanian headstones, the oldest being that of Thomas Kearney who died on 13 December 1823. *Population 750*

RICHMOND JAIL The northern section of the jail predates Port Arthur by five years. Aborigines held there from late 1828 included Umarrah, the leader of the Stoney Creek people. Swindler Ikey Solomon, who was said to be the model for Charles Dickens' character Fagin in *Oliver Twist*, was briefly incarcerated here.

RICHMOND BRIDGE This bridge is the oldest in Australia and probably one of the most photographed with foreground ducks and St John's Roman Catholic Church on the hill framed by one of its arches. From 1823 to 1825 chain gangs hauled stones in handcarts from the quarry at Butchers Hill to create this sturdy four-span structure. Some believe the bridge is haunted by the ghost of a tyrannical overseer who was murdered during its construction.

FESTIVALS Country Music Festival, February; Village Fair, October.

SEVEN MILE BEACH ■ 2382

A line of pine trees backs the stretch of sand dunes along Seven Mile Beach in Frederick Henry Bay. Like other communities in this area, the small settlement of the same name is a mixture of resort cottages and more modern homes owned by people who work in Hobart. *Population 950*

SORELL ■ 2383

Sorell is one of the oldest settlements in Tasmania. The town site was set in 1805 and several small farms were established within three years. By 1815, wheat was being grown and milled, supplying the island colony and settlers in Sydney. In 1821, Governor Lachlan Macquarie named the growing township in honour of Colonel William Sorell, Lieutenant-Governor of Van Diemen's Land.

A brooding air hangs over Port Arthur where few of the tourists who enter the notorious prison and view the jailers' tools (right) could opine whether the most evil villains were the keepers or the kept.

This was bushranger territory in those early times. One December night in 1824, Matthew Brady and his gang carried out a daring raid on the town. They imprisoned the soldiers in their garrison and stole their weapons, released the prisoners and then surprised some of the citizens at table and helped themselves to a roast dinner. Brady's exploits were halted two years later when he was captured and hanged.

The first vehicles used the 3300-metre Sorell Causeway across the Pittwater shallows in 1872. The project was slow to get started after Sir William Denison suggested it in 1854. It took eight years to build and bankrupted several contractors. Little of their original work remains but there are many interesting old stone buildings in Sorell, which is still a busy country centre. *Population 880*

THE BLUEBELL INN The first Bluebell Inn was destroyed by fire in 1863. The present sandstone structure was then built and used for its original purpose until the second decade of this century. It then became an emergency hospital until 1945 when it was used as a private home.

SWANSEA ■ 2384

Swansea, named after Swansea in Wales by George Meredith, was first settled in 1821 as a military post. It is now a pleasant coastal resort and the centre of a grazing district. Abalone are bred and grown to market size in the waters just south of the town.

William Morey's black wattle bark mill was set up in the 1880s and has been fully restored. Tannin from the bark was a major ingredient in tanning heavy leathers. The three-storey Morris's General Store, built about 1838, is also in good condition. Its two freestone storeys are crowned with one of brick.

TASMAN PENINSULA ■ 2385

The Tasman Peninsula is the remains of a drowned mountain range joined to the mainland by Eaglehawk Neck (see entry). The waters off its southernmost tip are said to be as rough as those off Cape Horn and are called 'The Roll' by fishing and yachting crews. Prehistoric volcanic action threw up some dramatically shaped rock formations and sea erosion has further sculpted the coastline.

TRIABUNNA ■ 2386

Triabunna, named from an Aboriginal word for native hen, is the centre for the Spring Bay Municipality. A long tradition of dependence on the sea began in the last century with a whaling station. Now there is a base for commercial fishing boats and a fishmeal processing plant.

Stock herders first settled here in the 1820s; sandstone quarries and apple orchards are other industries that have come and gone. Much of the town's income now comes from a woodchip plant which processes timber from a large tract of low-grade eucalypt forests. *Population 830*

Campbell Town & Oatlands

The natural and artificial lakes of Tasmania's Central Plateau provide much of the island's power as well as superb challenges for fishermen. Nearer to sea level, the north-south link of the Midland Highway cuts through paddocks of sheep and cattle as it links many of Van Diemen's Land's earliest settlements.

A Roman Catholic steeple – built onto an old store – joined the Protestant spires of Church Street, Ross in 1918.

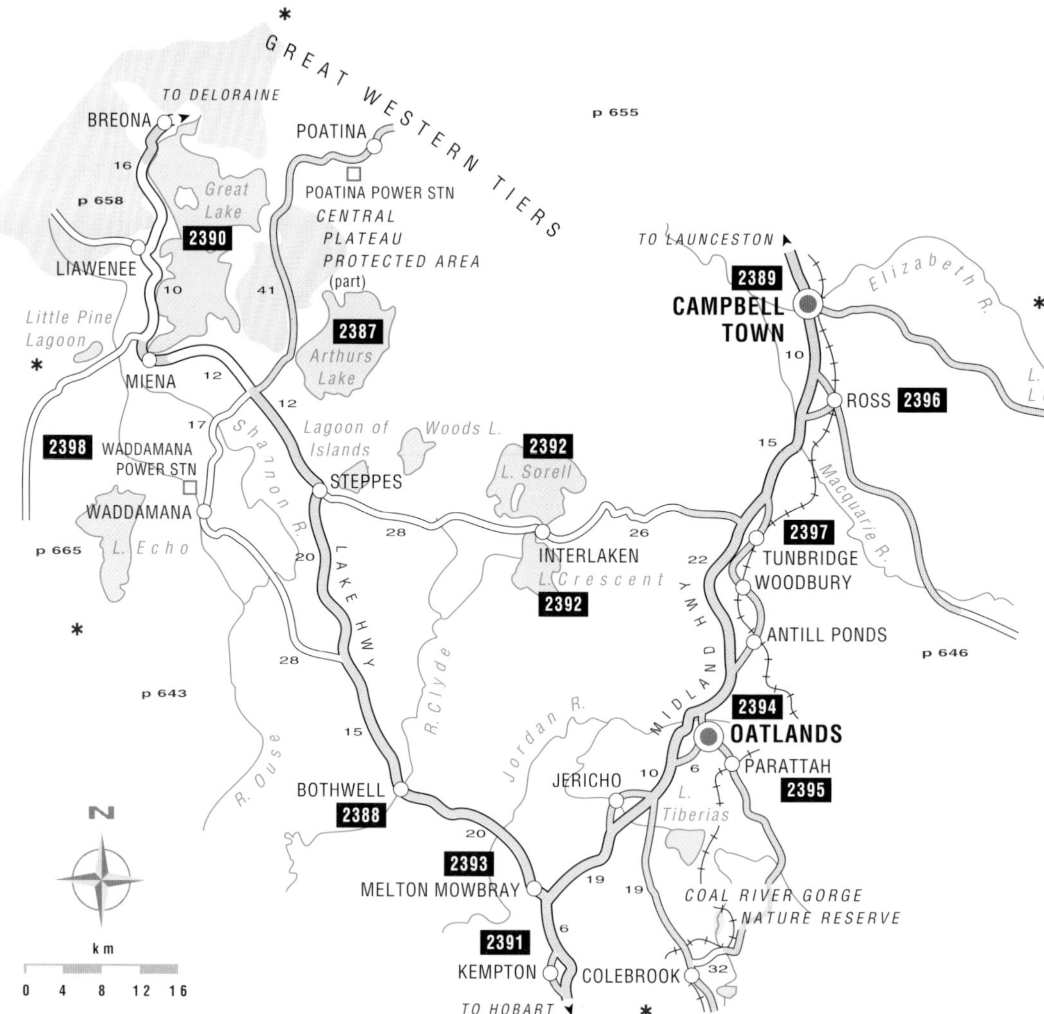

ARTHURS LAKE ■ 2387

The Central Plateau or the 'Lake Country' in the heart of Tasmania is strewn with several hundred glacial lakes and tarns. In the twentieth century, the water has been used for hydro-electric development which has created new lakes, increased the size of others and cut tunnels and canals through mountains.

The exact number of the district's lakes and waterways is unknown but they have been gaining a steady reputation with anglers since shortly after the first trout eggs were transported from Salmon Ponds in 1864 (see *Bridgewater & New Norfolk*) and released into the wild (see Bothwell). Just four years later, a trout weighing more than four kilograms was taken.

BOTHWELL ■ 2388

A number of Bothwell's pioneer settlers who took up land grants in about 1822 were wealthy Scots and the town was a district headquarters for the military. There are more than fifty buildings in the village that are either classified or recognised by the National Trust. They include several of Georgian style and the unusual Tudoresque 'Clifton Priory'. 'Wentworth House' (see box) was built by Captain D'Arcy Wentworth, the first Australian-born commissioned officer in the British Army and brother of the celebrated Blue Mountains explorer, William Charles Wentworth (see *Katoomba & Blaxland*).

Another legacy from Bothwell's founders is the excellent trout fishing in the lakes nearby. These include

Great Lake, Lake Sorell and Arthurs Lake (see entries). James Wilson established trout in the highland lakes. They carried the delicate fish eggs in billy cans by packhorse and dog cart all the way from Salmon Ponds in the south (see *Bridgewater & New Norfolk*).

Captain Patrick Wood, a retired Indian Army officer, is credited with establishing the first pedigree cattle herd in Australia. He successfully introduced Aberdeen Angus cattle and they are still bred in the district. Contemporary farming interests are not much changed from those of the first days, with sheep and cattle predominating.

CAMPBELL TOWN ■ 2389

Campbell Town – one of the few towns not bypassed by twentieth-century improvements to the Midlands Highway – is surrounded by fertile plains and has a good water supply which made it a certainty for rural development from the very beginning. It is a town with a reputation for 'riding on the sheep's back'. As early as 1847, Queen Victoria was presented with a fine merino wool carriage cloak, woven from the 'Wanstead' property clip.

Traditions are not lightly overthrown in the Tasmanian midlands. The early pastoralists held their first sheep show in 1838 and it has been an annual event ever since, making it the oldest agricultural show in Australia. The staples of the district's economy are still superfine merino wool, beef cattle and timber.

Campbell Town was first established as a garrison town in the 1820s (see Oatlands). In 1811, Governor Lachlan Macquarie, whose authority stretched from Cape York to Hobart Town, took five-and-a-half days to travel the route mapped out by his surveyor from Hobart to Port Dalrymple. Mrs Macquarie's maiden name was Elizabeth Campbell and in her honour Macquarie changed the name of Relief Creek to Elizabeth River and called the proposed settlement on the north bank of the waterway Campbell Town.

In 1821, Governor Macquarie despatched the Surveyoy-General, James Meehan, to peg out the road from Port Dalrymple (now George Town) to Hobart marking five towns along the track: Brighton, Oatlands, Ross, Campbell Town and Perth. By the time Melbourne was founded in 1835, the historic Midland Highway, stretching 200 kilometres from Hobart to Launceston, already passed through several closely settled districts cleared for agriculture of their native woodland.

The first known telephone call in the Southern Hemisphere was made between Launceston and Campbell Town in 1857. Schoolmaster Alfred Biggs made the pair of historic telephones from Alexander Graham Bell's drawings and they are now in Launceston's Queen Victoria Museum. *Population 820*

FESTIVALS Campbell Town Agricultural Show, June.

'ive-kilogram catches, descended 'rom trout eggs released 160 years go, are to be had in Arthurs Lake.

GREAT LAKE ■ 2390

Great Lake is on the Central Plateau, an area trimmed to the north and east by the 1300-metre range of mountains known as the Great Western Tiers. It is the largest of the region's lakes and has a 200-kilometre shoreline. In 1826, the Danish convict Jorgen Jorgenson, who earned a pardon exploring for the Van Diemen's Land Company, came upon the lake's southern end and reported 'a considerable extent of fine open country'. The harnessing of the waters of Great Lake in 1910 was the beginning of hydro-electric power in Tasmania.

KEMPTON ■ 2391

Kempton represents a short detour from the Midland Highway and was first settled around 1817 when Anthony Fenn Kemp was given a grant of land in the area. Kempton's original name was Green Water Holes, then it became Green Ponds and in the late 1830s was renamed Kemp Town after the Kemp family. The colony's first market place, which began trading in 1828, was set up here and at one time there were seven inns in the town.

LAKE CRESCENT AND LAKE SORELL ■ 2392

Lake Crescent and Lake Sorell were discovered early in the colony's history. Members of the New South Wales Corps were sent from Port Dalrymple to find an overland route to Hobart. In February 1807, the soldiers made 'a very fatiguing journey' to the Derwent passing lakes Crescent and Sorell on the way.

Lake Sorell is a wildlife sanctuary and has plentiful supplies of both brown and rainbow trout while Lake Crescent is not just another fishing lake...the experts declare that every specimen caught there is a trophy. In 1973, one trout catch weighed twelve kilograms – after being cleaned!

MELTON MOWBRAY ■ 2393

Melton Mowbray, at the junction of the Midlands and Lake highways, was once an important market town and was named for its counterpart in English fox-hunting country. Samuel Blackwell, who built the Melton Mowbray Hotel in 1849, also ran a pack of fox hounds. The hotel, which has been continuously licensed ever since, has one of the few remaining horse troughs in Tasmania.

OATLANDS ■ 2394

Governor Macquarie first passed through this district in 1811 but did not pronounce the site 'a very eligible situation for a town' until his second visit in 1821 when it reminded him of his native Scotland. By 1826, Oatlands was a key administrative centre of the new colony of Tasmania and Governor Arthur set up his headquarters here when he was directing the 'Black Line' against the Aborigines in 1829.

The district exports wool and live sheep. Beef cattle and cash cropping are the other two main farming activities. *Population 520*

PARATTAH ■ 2395

Parattah is a rail marshalling point at the highest point on the railway line between Hobart and Launceston. Semi-trailers offload logs onto rail trucks which then deliver them to sawmills and woodchip plants. The famous aviator, Sir Hudson Fysh, was a farmer at Parattah before he founded QANTAS.

ROSS ■ 2396

Governor Lachlan Macquarie named Ross in 1821 after the Scottish home of a friend of his. In the young colony, Ross was an important garrison town and a coaching stop where horses were changed at Sam Page's stables at 'Roseneath'. The town is steeped in colonial history and has been spared the main north-south traffic since 1971 when the Midland Highway was diverted to preserve its rural tranquillity.

In the heart of Ross, four street-corner buildings that face each other were said to represent aspects of the human condition: 'Temptation' (the Man-O-Ross Hotel), 'Salvation' (the Roman Catholic church), 'Recreation' (the town hall and council chambers!) and 'Damnation' (the jail – which is now a private home).

'SOMERCOTES' 'Somercotes', built by Captain Samuel Horton, stands just south of Ross. It was supposed to be impregnable to bushrangers. However, Martin Cash successfully raided the house in 1843 and graze marks from a bullet fired during the fracas remain on a wall.

FESTIVALS Ross Rodeo, November.

TUNBRIDGE ■ 2397

Tunbridge, on the northern end of an area originally called Salt Pan Plains, began life as the very English Tunbridge Wells when it was first settled in 1809. It soon became a stopover place for coaches travelling between Hobart and Launceston and there is a restored Royal Mail vehicle on show in the stables of the Tunbridge Wells Inn. Tunbridge does not have the same historical magnetism as Ross, and the business life of the town suffered greatly when it too was bypassed by alterations to the Midland Highway.

WADDAMANA POWER STATION ■ 2398

In 1990, Tasmania had twenty-six hydro-electric power stations. Waddamana, from an Aboriginal word meaning 'noisy water' or 'big river', was the rather apt name chosen for the first of these developments.

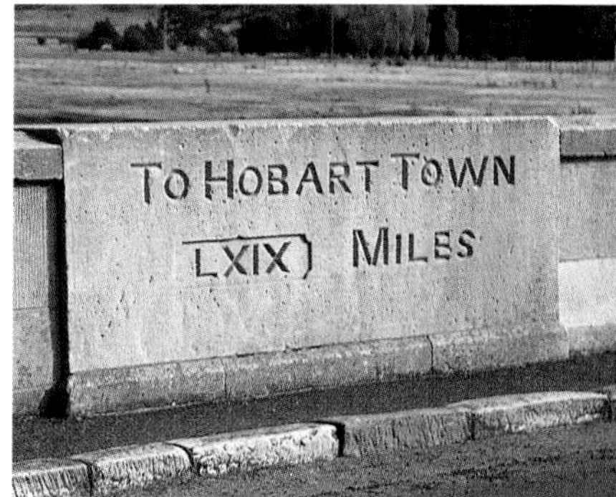

When Ross Bridge opened in 1836, the central milestone told the literate that it was 69 miles to Hobart.

In 1909, the Tasmanian government granted a concession to a private company to produce electricity. The plan was to divert water from the Great Lake and the Shannon River over a sheer drop into the Ouse River valley. In 1911, work commenced on a twenty-seven-kilometre wooden tramway from Red Gate near Bothwell to Waddamana, with fifteen draught horses pulling the loads. Advertisements for workers described the location as a 'comfortable two-day walk from Deloraine'. Wages were eight shillings a day and a tent and a sack of straw to sleep on were provided.

By 1914, the company was broke and the newly formed state Hydro-Electric Department took over. The Great Lake Power Scheme began operating commercially from Waddamana A station on 15 August 1916.

THREADED ALONG THE MIDLAND HIGHWAY: TASMANIA'S STRING OF ARCHITECTURAL PEARLS

Bothwell's magistrate built Wentworth House as a single-storey residence in 1833; his successor on the bench and in ownership courted bankruptcy with the grandeur of his renovations.

THE AUTHORITIES and citizens of substance in Van Diemen's Land wanted to build. They had the materials – a good supply of sandstone, bricks and timber; they had the labour – shackled convicts who were obliged to carry out any task required of them; they had the expertise – skilled professionals and artisans. The result was precincts and small-town groupings of houses and shops, bridges and churches, mills and taverns, which remain intact to delight the modern traveller. Some have enduring grace and stature, others are unique oddities.

Prosperous settlers and the convenience of the colony's early development of the north-to-south roadway ensured some finely crafted public and private works in villages and towns strung out along the Midland Highway, many of which have been lovingly preserved or restored. They represent a very small sample of Tasmania's varied historic architecture.

The work of convict masons decorates many early buildings; the Ross bridge is embellished with more than 180 carvings.

Ross has many beautiful buildings but the bridge spanning the Macquarie River is its most famous structure. Governor George Arthur ordered it in 1831 and opened it in 1836. The stonemason Daniel Herbert, was responsible for the 186 stone carvings on the arches depicting Celtic symbols, animals and human heads. He carved half of them himself. Governor Arthur gave Herbert a free pardon for his splendid contribution but never saw his cryptic social comment: on the keystones under the bridge is the figure of a judge in crown and wig with the paws and snout of a rat!

The Red Bridge at Campbell Town, built of convict-made bricks, is not nearly as lovely but has also solidly stood the test of time. Prisoners began constructing it in the year Ross Bridge was opened and it was completed in 1838 since when it has had no major repairs, stoutly withstanding the thundering road transports that use the Midland Highway regularly in modern times.

The Gothic–Tudor mansion called 'The Grange' at Campbell Town was the work of James Blackburn, originally transported to Van Diemen's Land for life in 1833. His crime was forging a cheque in England but by the mid-1840s he had his freedom and was recognised as a notable architect. 'The Grange' has Tudor-style chimneys, pointed Gothic gables and oriel windows.

'Wentworth House' at Bothwell was constructed in 1833. It has fine stone carving and a cantilever, floating staircase. When D'Arcy Wentworth – the brother of W.C. Wentworth of Blue Mountains fame – sold it to Major Charles Schaw, the new owner raised the roof and added another storey and a large central chimney. Smaller gems include 'Slate Cottage' – also in Bothwell – dating from 1836 and so called because of its roof. Kempton, closer to Hobart, has some beautifully proportioned colonial cottages.

The first settler on the Clyde near Bothwell was Edward Nicholas from Monmouthshire who built a cottage in 1821 which he called 'Nant', the Welsh word for 'brook'. It is a single-storey sandstone building with a verandah and a distinctive front door with fine joinery and a fanlight. The nearby mill is the second on the site, constructed in 1857, with a long-lasting iron wheel replacing the original wooden one. Although this waterwheel has not helped grind grain since the 1890s, it earned its keep by pumping domestic water to the main house until 1953, and is still in working order.

Lacey bargeboards of the English Gothic 'The Grange' at Campbell Town frame an oriel window based on brick corbels.

In 1977, stoneground wholemeal flour was again produced at the restored 'Thorpe Mill' using water power. This building, also near Bothwell, was well established by 1825 but ceased grinding wheat in 1906. □

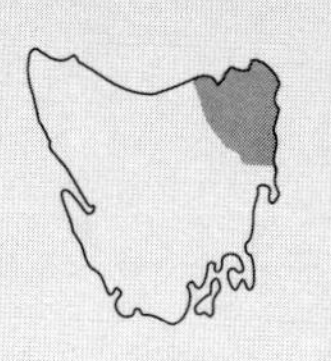

Scottsdale & St Helens

This somewhat overlooked north-east corner of Tasmania, early discovered but late to be settled, has a history based on Tasmania's 'tin rush'. Out to sea, the islands of the Furneaux Group were once the hunting grounds of sealers.

BEN LOMOND NATIONAL PARK ■ 2399

Colonel Patterson, a Scotsman, named Ben Lomond but this mountain – 1572 metres above sea level at its highest point – is considerably taller than its Scottish counterpart. The area was surveyed early in the nineteenth century and declared a national park about 140 years later, in 1947. Many prominent features have inspired colourful names – Misery Bluff, Plains of Heaven, Little Hell. The Ben Lomond plateau is usually covered with good snow in winter and attracts cross-country skiers to the alpine resort on the tallest peak, Legges Tor. Eucalypt woodlands clothe the lower slopes and above them grow two trees unique to Tasmania – the celery-top pine and the deciduous beech.

BICHENO ■ 2400

Sealers and whalers called this spot Waub's Harbour after Waubedebar, a brave Aboriginal woman who rescued two men from drowning. She died in 1832 and her tombstone reads 'erected in her memory by a few of her white friends'. Mary Harvey was another local woman of character. She saved her husband from a convict assault, survived snakebite and a fall from a horse and pulled a young man from the sea. She died in 1911, aged seventy-five.

James Ebenezer Bicheno was the well-liked Colonial Secretary of Van Diemen's Land from 1843 until his death in 1851. He was fond of good living and the arts and bequeathed his library of 2500 books to the people of Tasmania and his name to what was by then a little town known as The Old Fishery.

The port of Bicheno served various coal mines in the vicinity but production and transport costs eventually closed these and many people left for the Victorian goldfields. The settlement was almost forgotten until just before the Second World War when fishing was redeveloped and the mild climate and sandy beaches began to attract holiday-makers.

Today Bicheno's small commercial fishing fleet operates from the Gulch. Oysters are artificially bred and oyster spat is exported overseas (see box, *Kingston & Huonville*). Offshore, an underwater wilderness of coloured sponges and corals forms Tasmania's first marine reserve. *Population 700*

BRANXHOLM ■ 2401

Branxholm lies among valleys devoted to dairy farming and agriculture. The country, green and lush more often than not, supports contented milking cows and reliable cash crops including hops. Thick rainforests on the higher ground began the district's forestry and timber industries.

Payable tin in this region was first found by George Renison Bell in 1874 and later a small mining town on the west coast was named after him (see *Queenstown & Rosebery*). Between Bell's discovery and 1877 there were more important finds and for nearly thirty years the district enjoyed a mining boom, producing about 120 tonnes of tin each month.

Branxholm, declared a town in 1883, is just one of more than 100 mining settlements that were scattered throughout the district towards the end of last century.

MOORINA Moorina was an early mining boom settlement and had a large Chinese community. It was first called Krushka's Bridge for the crossing over the Ringarooma River. The name was changed in memory of the sister of Truganini, the last of Tasmania's full-blooded Aborigines (see *Kingston & Huonville).*

There is an altar and a conical-shaped oven in the Chinese part of the cemetery where relatives burned offerings for the souls of the departed. The largest sapphire ever found in Tasmania came from these parts.

PIONEER When the Pioneer Mine closed in the early 1930s, the workings were filled with water and Pioneer Lake now provides for water sports and trout fishing. The town was called Bradshaw's Creek until 1955 and for a while the school was run by Joseph Lyons, later Prime Minister of Australia. Small-scale tin mining still goes on round Pioneer.

WELDBOROUGH Weldborough was once known as Thomas Plains and during the tin rush most of its population were Chinese. Many of the emigrants later returned to their homeland and by the 1930s, Hee Jarm was the only Chinese person remaining. He feared for the gold-leaf decorations and treasures of the joss house and arranged for them to be taken to the Queen Victoria Museum in Launceston.

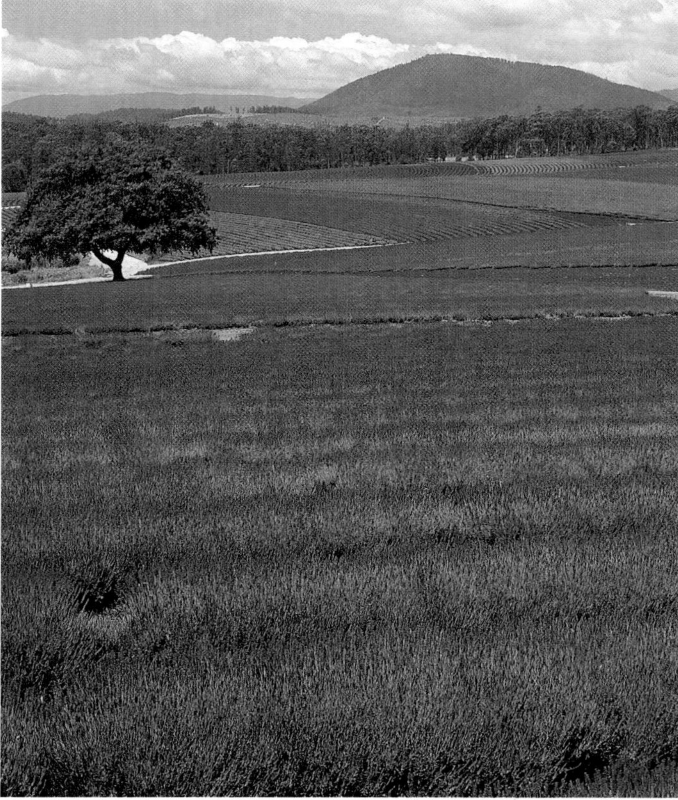

Midsummer travellers seeking the Nabowla lavender farm – based on seeds brought from the French Alps in 1922 – need only sniff the scented breeze.

BRIDPORT ■ 2402

Bridport is a resort town on the northern coast of Tasmania where the bush grows right down to the sheltered beaches that surround Andersons Bay, so called after the first settlers, Janet and Andrew Anderson, who arrived in 1833. A local factory processes crayfish tails for the lucrative United States market and there is a rainbow trout farm. *Population 1160*

CAPE BARREN ISLAND ■ 2403

Cape Barren, the second largest of the Furneaux Group (see Flinders Island), has an area of 445 square kilometres. In the past, sealers visited many of these islands and Kent Bay on Cape Barren became a base from which they competed fiercely against their American counterparts. They were a tough lawless band who became known as the 'Straitsmen'.

In the early 1800s, a seal pelt was worth fourteen shillings on the London market and the slaughter of the animals was wholesale with pups left to die after their mothers had been killed. Fur seals are now fully protected and have returned to repopulate the islands.

DERBY ■ 2404

Derby's Briseis Mine, called after the 1876 Melbourne Cup winner, became the richest tin mine in the north-east. Then on 4 April 1929, tragedy struck. Torrential rain smashed debris into the mine's concrete dam and a wall of water swept through, engulfing the town without warning. Fourteen people died and the flooded mine never went into full production again. Though tin is still worked, rural activity is now the district's first priority. Some of the mine buildings and the old school are used as a mining museum which presents the history of tin mining in the region from 1876 to 1940.

Flinders Island's first permanent European resident set up house at Palana, on the far northern side of Killiecrankie Bay, in 1888.

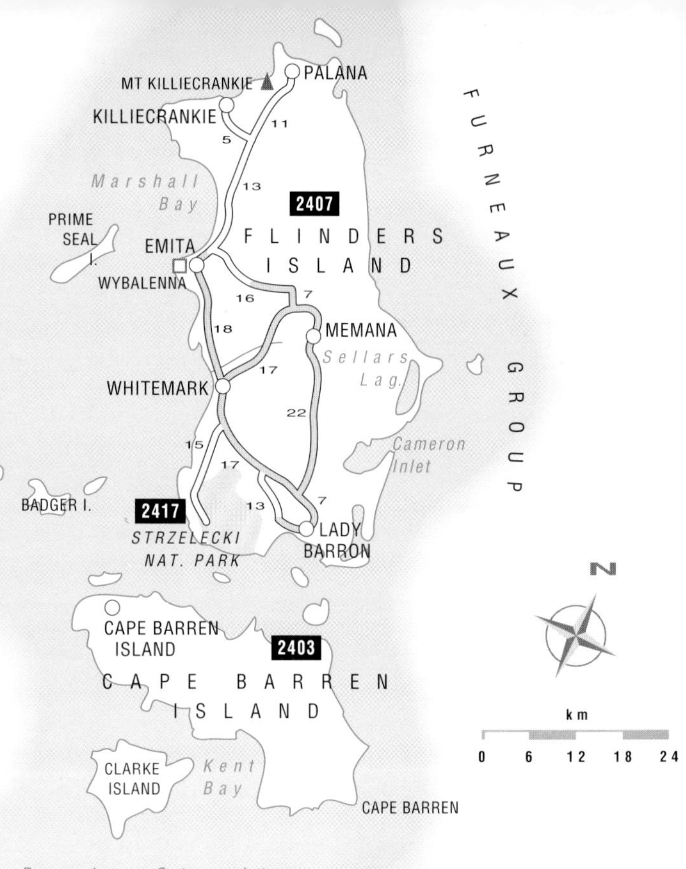

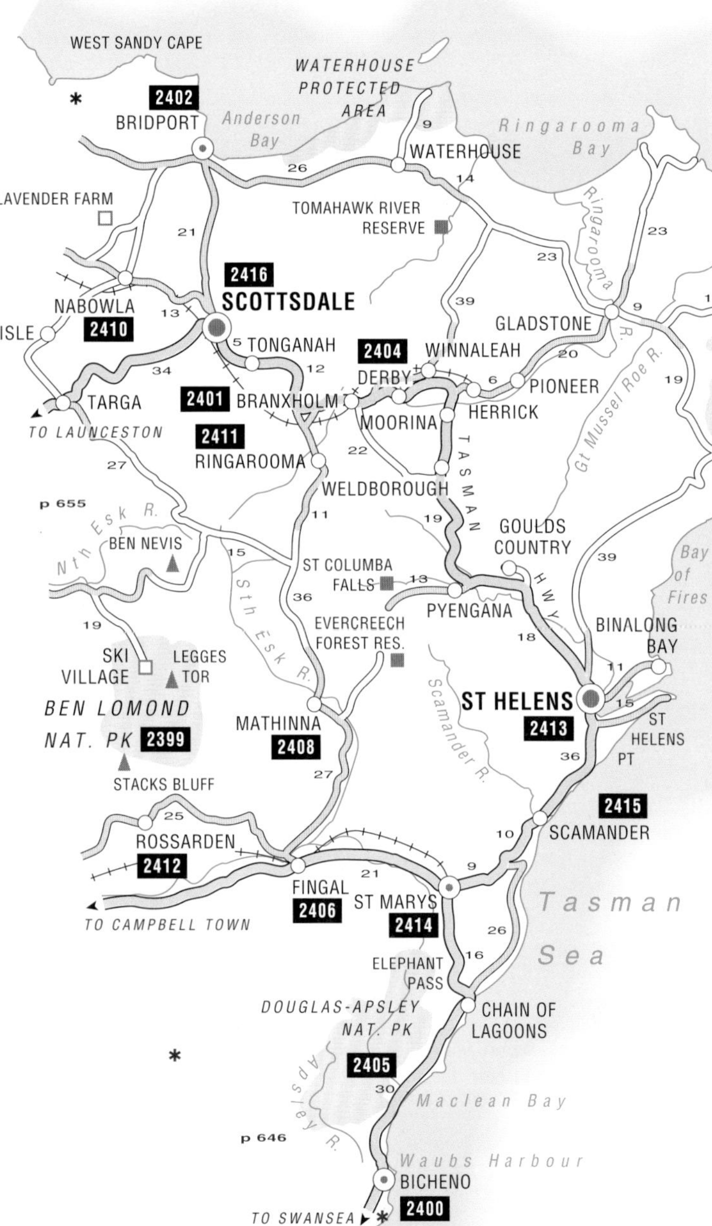

The dog-like Tasmanian devil's fierce appearance is mostly show; it prefers scavenging to killing.

DOUGLAS-APSLEY NATIONAL PARK ■ 2405

This national park was proclaimed in December 1989 and covers an area from Elephant Pass to the northern boundary of Bicheno which takes in streams, rivers, gorges and forested hills. Fourteen species of eucalypt are found in this reserve including five which grow only in Tasmania.

FINGAL ■ 2406

Fingal was named after the Irish town of the same name and was established as a convict station in 1827. The district's substantial homesteads were made possible with the cheap convict labour force. 'Killymoon', owned by Frederick Lewis von Stieglitz, dates from the 1840s. The first payable gold in Tasmania was found at 'the Nook' near Fingal in 1852. Fingal is now the main centre for the state's coal industry.

EVERCREECH FOREST RESERVE This reserve, gazetted in 1977, shelters what is believed to be the world's tallest white gum. It is eighty-nine metres tall with a girth of more than ten metres and is well above the normal height limit for this species. This tree and others near it, known as the White Knights, are estimated to be more than 300 years old and are registered by the National Trust.

FESTIVALS Fingal Valley Coal Shovelling Festival, February.

FLINDERS ISLAND ■ 2407

In 1773, Tobias Furneaux spotted some of the large group of islands that were named by Captain James Cook in tribute to him. Twenty-five years later, Matthew Flinders charted the Furneaux islands and the largest of them is called Flinders in his honour. The wild waters that lash the island's shores are part of the stormy strait named after his companion George Bass.

Lady Barron is the main fishing port on Flinders Island and farming and tourism are the other major industries. Farming first began in the 1890s, developing strongly in the 1950s with a post-war, soldier-settle ment program. Sheep by far outnumber the cattle. Flinders Island has a varied topography ranging from white beaches to mountain ranges. The decomposing granite rocks of Mount Killiecrankie are a source of topaz, known locally as Killiecrankie diamonds.

About 150 species of birds have been recorded in the Furneaux Islands including the rare forty-spotted pardalote, the green rosella and the black Tasmanian currawong. The Cape Barren goose, regarded as the world's second rarest goose species and wholly protected, was originally discovered here. About half the world's population live and breed on the islands.

WYBALENNA In 1833, George Robinson founded Settlement Point where he gathered the surviving Tasmanian Aborigines in order to educate them in European ways. Robinson's well-meaning attempts were tragically disastrous. Nearly half the displaced people died from what could only be described as homesickness for their own territory and this spelt the end of Tasmania's full-blooded Aborigines. In the late 1840s, old men and women were repatriated to Oyster Cove (see *Kingston & Huonville*). The chapel is all that remains of the buildings at Settlement Point. It has been restored by the National Trust and is rated as the third most historic building in Tasmania.

MATHINNA ■ 2408

Mathinna was named after a young Aboriginal girl who was found wandering in the bush and was later cared for by the governor, Sir John Franklin, and his wife. Once a gold-mining centre and for a time the third largest town in the state, Mathinna now relies on forestry activity in the district for its survival.

MOUNT WILLIAM NATIONAL PARK ■ 2409

Proclaimed in 1973, Mount William National Park takes in almost 14 000 hectares of the north-eastern tip of Tasmania and provides a sanctuary for Forester kangaroos, Bennet's wallaby, wombats and all kinds of birdlife. Mount William itself is 216 metres high. Eddystone Lighthouse, at the extreme south-east point of the park, is forty-two metres above sea level and is named after the famous light on England's south coast.

NABOWLA ■ 2410

This is a small township which depends mainly on farming and the nearby forestry industry at Lisle. The Bridestowe lavender farm a few kilometres to the west is the only one of its kind outside Europe. The lavender strain cultivated here is exceptionally pure because the bushes have not been cross-pollinated. The crop was first planted in 1922 from a few grams of seed imported from France and now covers fifty hectares. The fragrant harvesting period lasts for about three weeks from the end of December into January. The processing works supply flower oil for perfume manufacturers in Europe and the United States.

RINGAROOMA ■ 2411

The dense bush in this area hampered early settlement. In 1859, the government allocated 200 pounds for a road from Launceston to Ringarooma but most supplies to the scattered settlers came by ship from Launceston to Bridport. Like so many other towns in this region, Ringarooma's economy is based on timber milling and farming which began in the district in the late 1860s. The town enjoyed a brief period of excitement in the 1880s when gold was mined at nearby Alberton.

ROSSARDEN ■ 2412

In the 1870s, Chinese prospectors found rich lodes of tin and wolfram at Gipps Creek and Storeys Creek near Rossarden but these two places now show scant evidence of township status. Rossarden became a major producer of tin until 1982 when all the mines in the district were closed. The settlement now houses workers from the nearby underground mine which produces most of Australia's wolfram.

ST HELENS ■ 2413

St Helens, with its main street lined with elms, is the largest town on the east coast and derives most of its livelihood from tourism, fishing and timber. In holiday periods, visitors far outnumber the local residents.

At one time there were more than eighty sawmills between Launceston and St Helens and the north-east supplied great numbers of blue gum logs. Some have been used in the piles of Plymouth and Portsmouth harbours in England and along the Suez Canal. St Helens began as a whaling port and in 1834 a convict station was built at St Helens Point. Transport to the settlement was by sea until a coach service started in the 1870s. Chinese settlers came to St Helens in 1875 and trekked overland to Weldborough. *Population 1150*

ST MARYS ■ 2414

St Marys sits in the shadow of the Mount Nicholas Range at the head of the Fingal Valley. It was once a service town for coal mines and dairy farms and milk from the latter supplied two cheese factories. These are now closed and farmers have turned to wool and meat production. The road to St Helens includes St Marys Pass, a 300-metre winding descent through thick forest. *Population 630*

SCAMANDER ■ 2415

Scamander, initially called Yarmouth, lies almost exactly halfway between St Helens and St Marys. The surveyor John Wedge reached this part of the east coast in 1825. Bridging the Scamander River proved a challenge in the early days and there was no secure, permanent crossing until the present steel bridge was erected in 1936. One earlier model collapsed under a mob of cattle and others were weakened by borers or swept away by floods.

Scamander made its first serious attempt to attract the tourist trade in 1896 and it is still a popular holiday resort with access to good sea, beach and river fishing.

SCOTTSDALE ■ 2416

Scottsdale was named after the Government Surveyor, James Scott, who came to the district in the 1850s and explored the north-east hinterland. Thomas Cox, a miller from Launceston, settled near the present township and the settlement was known locally as 'Cox's Paradise'. The first official name was Ellesmere which became Scottsdale in 1863. The town is a centre for the district's pine-forest industry and there is a particle-board mill at Tonganah, to the east. There is also a large factory which processes locally grown vegetables; the headquarters of the Army Food Research Laboratories are nearby. *Population 2020*

STRZELECKI NATIONAL PARK ■ 2417

This park covers an area of more than 4000 hectares from the coast to the granite peaks of the Strzelecki Range. It was named after the Polish born explorer and scientist, Paul Strzelecki, who visited Flinders Island in 1842 and climbed the highest peak. Modern explorers can follow in his footsteps to experience magnificent views of the island and across the Franklin Sound to Cape Barren Island. The park's vegetation varies dramatically from thickly wooded slopes to heathland and damp gullies with prolific ferns.

Jacob's Ladder is the appropriate name given to the series of hairpin bends that skiers ascend on their way to the snowfields in Ben Lomond Park.

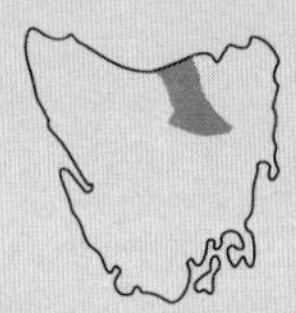

Launceston & George Town

Rural tranquillity and old-world charm hold sway in the fertile valley of the Tamar River where traditional apple orchards have now been joined by thriving vineyards. The broad estuary of the river provided a gateway to the north for the pioneers who came from Sydney to form the third oldest European settlement in Australia.

ASBESTOS RANGE NATIONAL PARK ■ 2418

Lying along a strip of the northern Tasmanian coast between Port Sorell and Greens Beach at the mouth of the Tamar River, this park's 4000-odd hectares range over coastal heathlands rich in wildflowers, sand dunes, a lagoon, woodlands, farmlands and virgin beaches separated by huge granite outcrops such as West Head. The northern point of the Asbestos Range, so named because of the asbestos once mined there, extends into the park.

The first European settlement in the area occurred in the 1820s at Bakers Beach, now a popular camping site. The Aborigines who lived here were known to the early settlers as the 'north tribe'. Their protection of their land was so vigorous that white settlement was suspended until they were removed to Flinders Island (see *Scottsdale & St Helens*). Now, the only records that remain of this people are shell middens.

BEACONSFIELD ■ 2419

Beaconsfield is the local-government centre for the surrounding municipality and received its present name in 1879, two years after it had been officially recognised as a town. It was named after the British Prime Minister Benjamin Disraeli, the Earl of Beaconsfield. This was considered a more dignified appellation than Cabbage Tree Hill or Brandy Creek, the names by which the locality had earlier been known although Cabbage Tree Hill survives, clinging on steadfastly as the name of a small village to the west of Beaconsfield.

In the 1820s, Beaconsfield's first industry was established – the quarrying of limestone for the building of nearby George Town. Quarrying led to small finds of gold, eventually discovered in substantial quantities, an event that finally established the area as a thriving town. By 1900, Beaconsfield was the third largest town in Tasmania. In contrast to other gold settlements, it had a reputation for sobriety and uprightness, with temperance societies said to outnumber pubs. Having produced more than twenty tonnes of gold, the mine closed in 1915 when pumping machinery was no longer able to control flooding. *Population 1090*

BEAUTY POINT ■ 2420

The town of Beauty Point on the western shore of the River Tamar is a popular fishing and boating resort. Its permanent population is boosted by students attending the Australian Maritime College, the nation's future seafarers and fishermen. The college's training ship *Wyuna* is berthed at the jetty here and one of the campuses – the other is in the town of Newnham – is located on the site of the town's original wharf.

Although the town's pleasant location and surroundings justify its name, they do not in fact reflect its origin. It is believed that the spot was named after Beauty, a prize bullock owned by a local farmer in the 1890s. *Population 1140*

BELL BAY ■ 2421

In 1912, the chief engineer of the Manchester Ship Canal Company was employed to investigate ways of developing the broad, transport corridor of the River Tamar, which empties into the waters of the Bass Strait. 'Bell Bay will be an inland port unexcelled in the world', were his prophetic words. And indeed, since the clearing of rock in its lower reaches, Bell Bay has become a busy industrial area, serving as Launceston's deepwater port. In 1947, it was chosen as the site of Australia's first aluminium refinery.

CARRICK ■ 2422

Carrick's bluestone flour mill, on the banks of the Liffey River, symbolises the connection between this small township and the city of Sydney. In the first half of the nineteenth century, when food supplies in Sydney were often scant, the early settlers on the farmland around Carrick grew the wheat which helped in saving Sydney's poulation from starvation. Other historic buildings of interest in Carrick include the original Plough Inn, licensed in 1841.

CRESSY ■ 2423

The small village of Cressy, in the Norfolk Plains district to the south of Launceston, is the gateway to an angler's paradise, with nearby creeks and rivers full of trout. This district was one of the earliest to be settled in northern Tasmania with a grazing property being established on the Lake River in 1826.

The township of Cressy dates officially from 1855 although the former Cressy Hotel was licensed in 1845. *Population 620*

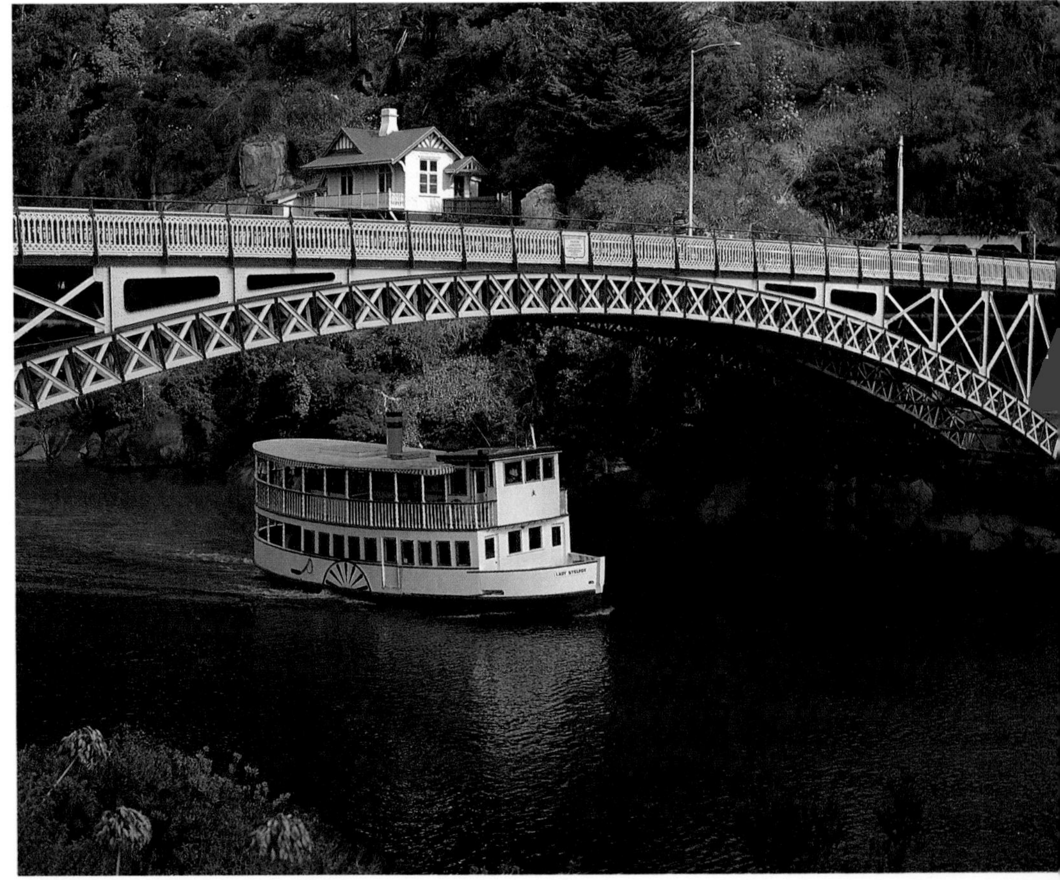

Alexandra Bridge spans the South Esk in one elegant leap where the river heads into Launceston's Cataract Gorge.

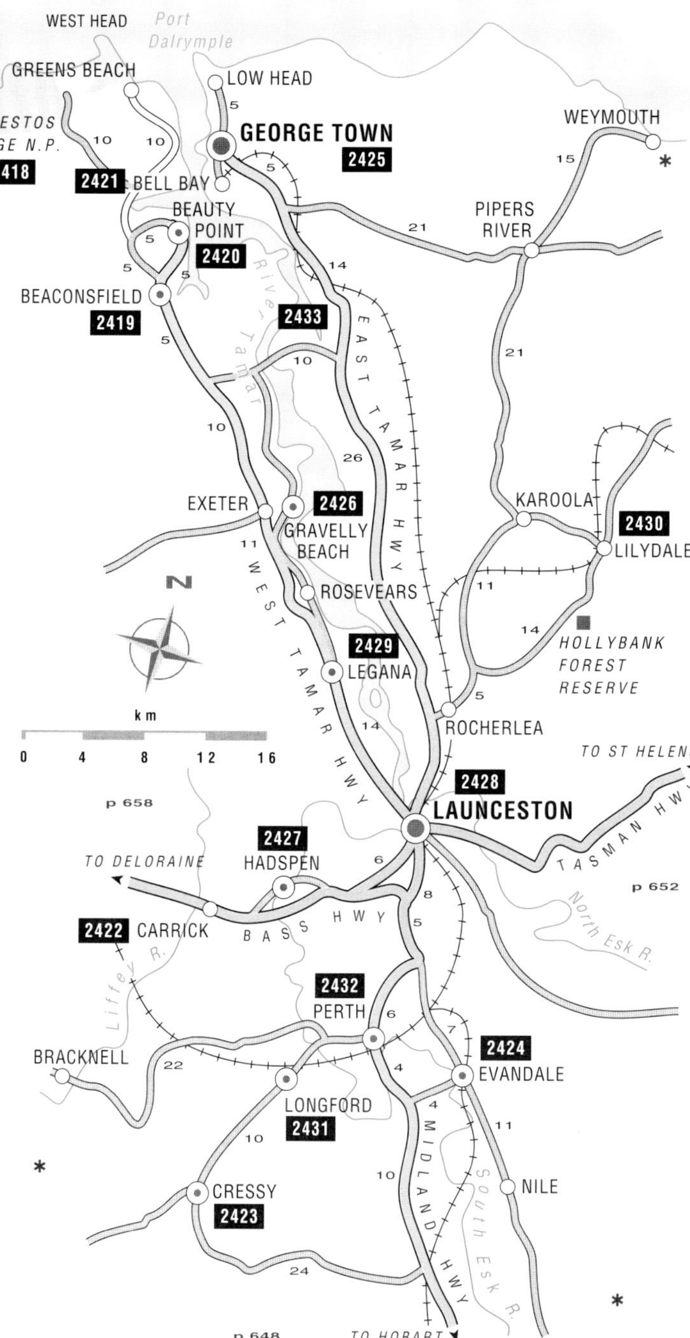

Entally House, near Hadspen, was the centre of its own small community in the 1820s, with outlying cottages, coach-house, chapel and glasshouse.

EVANDALE ■ **2424**

Evandale has more than one connection with the opening up of the fertile country to the west of the Blue Mountains in New South Wales in the early nineteenth century. It was named in honour of George Evans, the first surveyor-general of Van Diemen's Land, best known for his exploration work around Bathurst. As a reward for this, he was granted land in Van Diemen's Land. Similarly, James Cox, who built Clarendon (see below), was granted land in gratitude for the services of his father, William Cox, in building the first road across the once-impenetrable barrier of the Blue Mountains.

One of the many hundreds of convicts who laboured at Evandale in its early days was Ned Kelly's father.

Further away at Kingsford, near Ben Lomond, John Batman lived for fifteen years before he set out to found Melbourne in 1835. The renowned artist, Tom Roberts, who spent his honeymoon at 'Strathmore', one of the historic homes of the area, has his final resting place at the tiny bluestone church at Mount Ireh, near Longford. *Population 770*

'CLARENDON' This house is one of the finest examples of Regency architecture in Australia. The three-storey 'Clarendon' was constructed by John Richards for James Cox between 1830 and 1838 on land Cox had been granted in 1814. With its surrounding pasturelands and huge Ionic portico, 'Clarendon' brings to mind the gracious mansions of the southern United States.

GEORGE TOWN ■ **2425**

George Town has proud claims to be not only the site of the first European settlement in northern Tasmania but the oldest 'town' in Australia – the oldest town, that is, that has not developed into a city. As a monument on the town's Esplanade records, Lieutenant-Colonel William Paterson, having sailed from Sydney on HMS *Buffalo* with a commission from Governor King to establish a settlement in northern Van Diemen's Land, was driven ashore by a fierce gale and landed at the mouth of the river he called the Tamar on 5 November 1804.

The motley contingent comprised soldiers, administrators, about fifty convicts, a few ticket-of-leave men and one free settler. In 1811, Governor Lachlan Macquarie, on a tour of Van Diemen's Land, chose the original landing site as the centre for the colony's principal northern settlement and named it George Town. Paterson, in the meantime, had settled on what is now the site of Launceston. Plans for the town were laid out in 1813 but it did not become the real headquarters of northern Van Diemen's Land because of a shortage of fresh water.

The atmosphere of colonial times is recaptured at 'The Grove', built in the 1820s or 1830s as the house of the port officer, and now restored. The Old Watchhouse, built in 1843 as a jail, is a folk museum in modern times. *Population 5030*

GRAVELLY BEACH ■ **2426**

The name of this small town, with a mainly commuter or retired population, is slightly misleading. What was a sandy beach has now been largely taken over by couch grass. Its jetty, however, provides a setting-off point for fishing and boating on the midreaches of the River Tamar. The surrounding farming district boasts a blueberry farm as well as several boutique wineries, the produce of which may be tasted at a centre in nearby Exeter (see *Launceston & George Town). Population 590*

HADSPEN ■ **2427**

Hadspen has catered for travellers from its earliest days. The Red Feather Inn, built in the 1840s, is believed to have been the first coach station on the road from Launceston. Today it is joined by several hotels and a motel, making the town a holiday, entertainment and business convention centre. Its rural tranquillity is maintained by a modern bypass from the Bass Highway.

The town's history is intimately connected with that of the enterprising Reibey family, founded in Sydney by convict turned successful businesswoman, Mary Reibey. Her second son, Thomas II, was granted land along the river bank at Carrick, including the present site of Hadspen. After his death, his son, Thomas III, became the district's main landowner; his colourful life included being dismissed as first archdeacon of the Church of England at Launceston after he was accused of dubious moral behaviour. A few years later, in 1876, he bounded back to become premier of Tasmania. However, Hadspen long bore the scar of his fall from grace. At that time he withdrew his financial support for the construction of the Church of the Good Shepherd and the bluestone church stood an empty shell until 1961. *Population 1330*

ENTALLY HOUSE This gracious house stands across the South Esk River from the village of Hadspen. Built in 1820 by Thomas Reibey II, its heyday was in the time of Thomas III when grand entertainments were held for notable visitors such as the Duke of Edinburgh.

LAUNCESTON ■ **2428**

Tasmania's second city lies where the North and South Esk rivers unite to become the Tamar. The city nestles in the wide valleys formed by this marriage of rivers, with the rugged peaks of Mount Arthur, Mount Barrow and Ben Lomond in the distance. The third oldest town in Tasmania after Hobart and George Town, Launceston would not have become the hub of northern Tasmania if Governor Macquarie had had his way (see George Town).

The first buildings and shelters were erected between the Cataract Gorge (see below) and the present-day site of City Park. Paterson at first named the settlement Patersonia but later changed it to Launceston in honour of the birthplace in England, of Governor King. Between 1850 and 1890, the town became firmly established as a busy industrial and commercial centre, with new population and wealth brought by the mining boom. Its elegant Georgian facades became outnumbered by more ornate Victorian ones and in 1888, with a population of 17 000, it was proclaimed a city.

Launceston boasts a long and various list of 'firsts' in Australian history. These incude the first use of anaesthetic in Australia – in 1847 – the first production of an original Australian play – *The Bandit of the Rhine* in 1835 – and the hosting of an important sporting event, the first inter-colonial cricket match – between Tasmania and Victoria – in 1851.

What Patrick White described as Launceston's 'conventional Tasmanian-Gothic gloom' is seen by most visitors as quiet charm. The title of 'the Garden City' is justified by the city's many parks, providing tranquil, green oases between historic homes, churches and commercial buildings. *Population 66 750*

CATARACT GORGE With the neighbouring Cliff Grounds, spectacular Cataract Gorge is one of the most visited places in Tasmania. William Collins, the first European known to have visited the site where the South Esk River, confined in a narrow gorge, falls in a cataract to merge with the North Esk, recorded the following description in 1804: '...a huge fall of water over rocks, nearly a quarter of a mile up a straight gully between perpendicular rocks about 150 ft high. The beauty of the scene is probably not surpassed in the world'. There is a suspension bridge across the gorge, built in 1904, and those with a head for heights can cross the gorge in a chairlift which is believed to have the longest single chairlift span in the world.

FESTIVALS Sky Race, February; Targa International Car Rally, March; Garden Festival, September; Tasmanian Poetry Festival, October.

LEGANA ■ 2429

At the centre of a fruit-growing area to the north of Launceston, Legana has become a popular residential area. Legana Beach, a large subdivision on the River Tamar, was opened up in the 1980s. *Population 1400*

LILYDALE ■ 2430

Now known as the 'country garden' of Tasmania, the pleasant Lilydale district was an isolated area of seemingly impenetrable bush until late in the nineteenth century. Then came settlement and relentless clearing by itinerant workers travelling to the Midlands for shearing or to Longford for harvesting. In 1879, Lilydale became a base for transporting provisions to the Lisle goldfields. With the opening of the railway to Scottsdale in 1889, the establishment of the town was complete.

Waterfalls, forest reserves and rhododendron gardens are features of present-day Lilydale. The Falls Reserve boasts two oak trees grown from acorns from the Great Park at Windsor in England, planted in 1937 on King George VI's Coronation Day. A short distance away is the Hollywood Forest Reserve, managed jointly by the Forestry Commission and the Associated Pulp and Paper Mills company. The ash trees – which glow in golden rows in autumn – were planted in the early part of this century to supply timber for a Launceston tennis racquet and cricket bat manufacturing firm – a commercially unsuccessful venture.

LONGFORD ■ 2431

The neat, sweet-smelling hawthorn hedges, old farm houses and stately mansions of the Longford area bear witness to the desire of its early English and Irish settlers to carve the landscape of their homelands out of the alien Australian bush. Fed by the South Esk and Lake rivers, the area was initially called Norfolk Plains after it was explored in the early 1800s and populated with free settler refugees from Norfolk Island, who were given land grants by Governor Lachlan Macquarie.

The rollcall of the early settlers includes many names famous in Tasmanian history – Archer, Lawrence, Bell and Dumaresq. While these and other pioneer families were clearing land, planting crops and breeding stock, the town itself was founded by Launceston's first postmaster, Newman Williatt, who built an inn in 1827 and named it the Longford Hotel, after an Irish town. The hotel was followed by churches, schools and flour mills to process the area's prime crop, wheat. In modern times, wheat has been replaced by peas, poppies and grains and the municipality, of which Longford has been the local government centre since 1862, now carries the largest head of stock in Tasmania. *Population 2600*

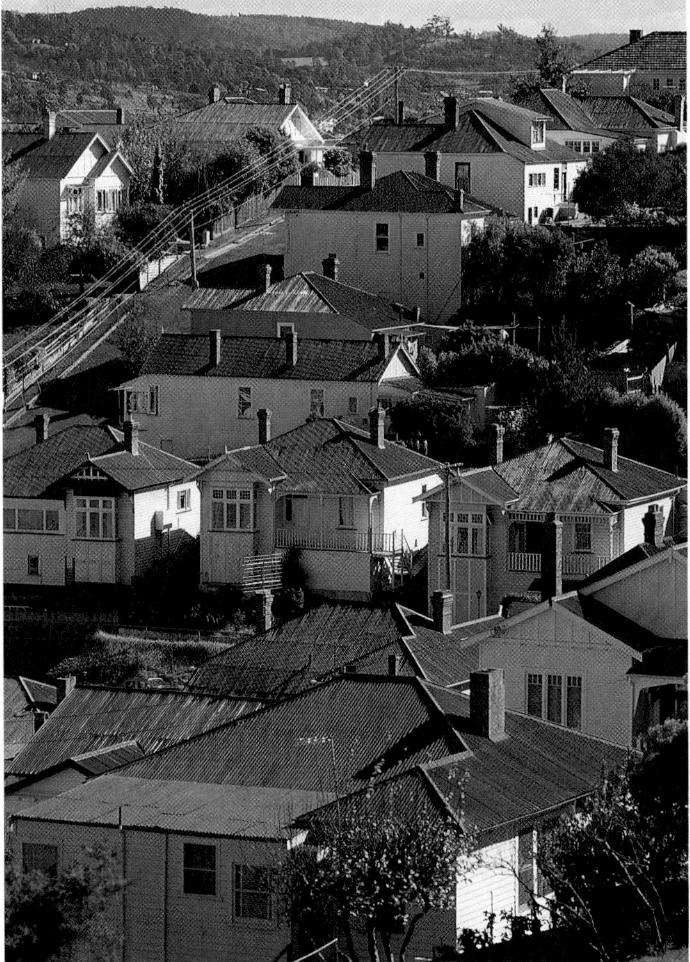

The number of chimneys in a Launceston roofscape suggest that in northern Tasmania's crisp winters the comforts of the hearth are still valued.

PERTH ■ 2432

Like the nearby towns of Cressy and Longford, Perth lies in the historic Norfolk Plains district. The area was first seen by Europeans in 1806 when Colonel Paterson sent officers from Launceston to explore the South Esk River. In 1811, Governor Macquarie viewed the present site of Perth when he toured the Norfolk Plains. Ten years later, he returned and decreed that a town should be laid out there and named it after Perth in Scotland, the birthplace of his friend David Gibson in whose Pleasant Banks house near Evandale the governor had recently stayed.

The Perth Bridge was built by convict labour between 1836 and 1840 close to the spot at which Macquarie had made his declaration. Its history has been chequered. Destroyed by floods in 1929, the bridge was rebuilt in 1931 only to be washed away again in 1971, when it was reconstructed yet again.

Perth's many historic buildings include the Queen's Head Hotel, dating from 1840; 'Eskleigh', a classical Victorian mansion built about 1870 and now a hospital; and a short distance to the south, 'Symmons Plains', a Georgian-style house built in 1830. *Population 1570*

RIVER TAMAR ■ 2433

The broad estuary of the Tamar, with its rivulets and reaches spreading like fingers into the hinterland, formed the pathway for the first European exploration and settlement of northern Tasmania. The river mouth was explored by Bass and Flinders in 1798 when they named it Port Dalyrymple after a distinguished British Navy hydrographer.

Further investigations were made by William Collins who named the river itself Dalrymple. It received its first group of settlers in 1804 when George Town (see entry) was founded. The leader of the expedition, Colonel Paterson, changed the name to Tamar, after the river in south-western England. Launceston, which soon took over from George Town as the major town of the area, stands at the Tamar's head and is united by it with its deepwater port, Bell Bay.

The Tamar is formed by the confluence of the North and South Esk rivers, both of which rise in the Ben Lomond range.

BATMAN BRIDGE The mid-reaches of the River Tamar – a few kilometres south of Beaconsfield (see entry) – are spanned and dominated by the distinctive Batman Bridge, opened in 1968. Its unusual design derives from the lack of a sound base on the east bank; a towering A-frame anchored securely in the west bank supports the whole structure with a system of tautly strung cables.

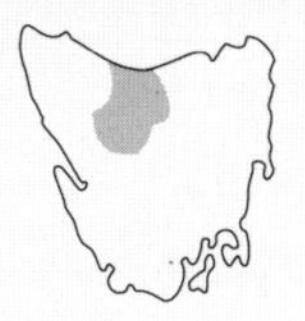

Devonport & Ulverstone

A string of towns along this coast is backed by fertile farming land while further inland a dramatic mountain presence changes with the weather. The noble peaks of national parks rise eerily from low-lying cloud, disappear in driving rain or fret the clear sky with wildly serrated outlines.

CENTRAL PLATEAU PROTECTED AREA ■ 2434

The rocky elevations of the Central Plateau range in height from 800 metres to more than 1400 metres and are interspersed with marshy areas and grassy plains. The north-western slopes were heavily scoured by glaciers during the ice age and this plateau was set aside as a protected area in 1978 to preserve the rugged environment, conserve water and catchment areas, promote public recreation and carry out scientific studies. The many lakes and rivers provide excellent fishing but crustaceans, aquatic insects and native fish have all suffered from the healthy appetites of the introduced brown, rainbow and brook trout.

CRADLE MOUNTAIN-LAKE ST CLAIR NATIONAL PARK ■ 2435

The Cradle Mountain-Lake St Clair National Park is vast – its 131 921 hectares, more than doubling in size in 1940, cover about a quarter of the central Tasmanian region. This reserve was listed by the World Heritage Committee in 1982. Cradle Mountain has an impressive outline and was named by Joseph Fossey in 1827 because he thought it looked like a miner's or perhaps a baby's cradle. Its alternative name in the early days was Rock Rib Crest.

The park's trees include several pine varieties – King William, pencil pine, chestnut pine, celery-top pine and creeping or strawberry pine – and there are alpine grasses and snow gums. Thickets of tanglefoot beech, Tasmania's only native deciduous species, gild the mountain slopes in autumn. Shrubs too are prolific and the perfume of lemon-scented boronia is memorable on summer days.

THE OVERLAND TRACK The eighty-three-kilometre-long Overland Track links Cradle Mountain in the north with Lake St Clair in the south and is Australia's most famous bushwalk. It is tackled by thousands each year taking, on average, about five days.

The landscape revealed to the walkers changes according to the season – snow in winter and brightly coloured wildflowers in the warmer months – and sometimes both at the same time! The weather is notoriously unpredictable and treacherous, with bouts of bitter cold in high summer; on many occasions the unwary have been trapped necessitating expensive rescue operations.

CRADLE VALLEY ■ 2436

The beauty of this place compelled Gustav Weindorfer, a keen field naturalist, to agitate for conservation. Although by no means the first there, he has long been considered the 'founder' of the Cradle Mountain-Lake St Clair National Park. The road he wanted made to Cradle Valley did not eventuate till after his death in 1932 but nearly half the area (63 990 hectares) of the present park was proclaimed a scenic reserve in 1927. Weindorfer, using axe and saw, built Waldheim Chalet from King Billy pine trees growing near the site and lived out his last years in the place he cherished. He is buried on a slope close to his 'forest home'.

DELORAINE ■ 2437

Thomas Scott, surveyor, named Deloraine from *The Lay of the Last Minstrel* by his kinsman, the romantic novelist and poet, Sir Walter Scott. This pretty country town, about equidistant between Launceston and Devonport, grew up in the 1840s beyond the ford where the present day bridge crosses the Meander River. The fertile surrounding countryside is framed against the majestic backdrop of Quamby Bluff (1226 metres) and the Western Tiers. Deloraine is classified as an historic town and has a charming range of well-preserved colonial buildings such as the Deloraine Hotel, in business since 1848, St Mark's Church and Bonney's Inn. A row of cottages which once housed army offices has been turned, appropriately, into a military museum. *Population 2100*

BOWERBANK MILL The Bowerbank flour mill, on the Bass Highway just outside Deloraine, is a three-storey Georgian stone building with a slate roof and windows set in arched openings. Originally powered by a waterwheel, the 1853 mill was used until the 1930s.

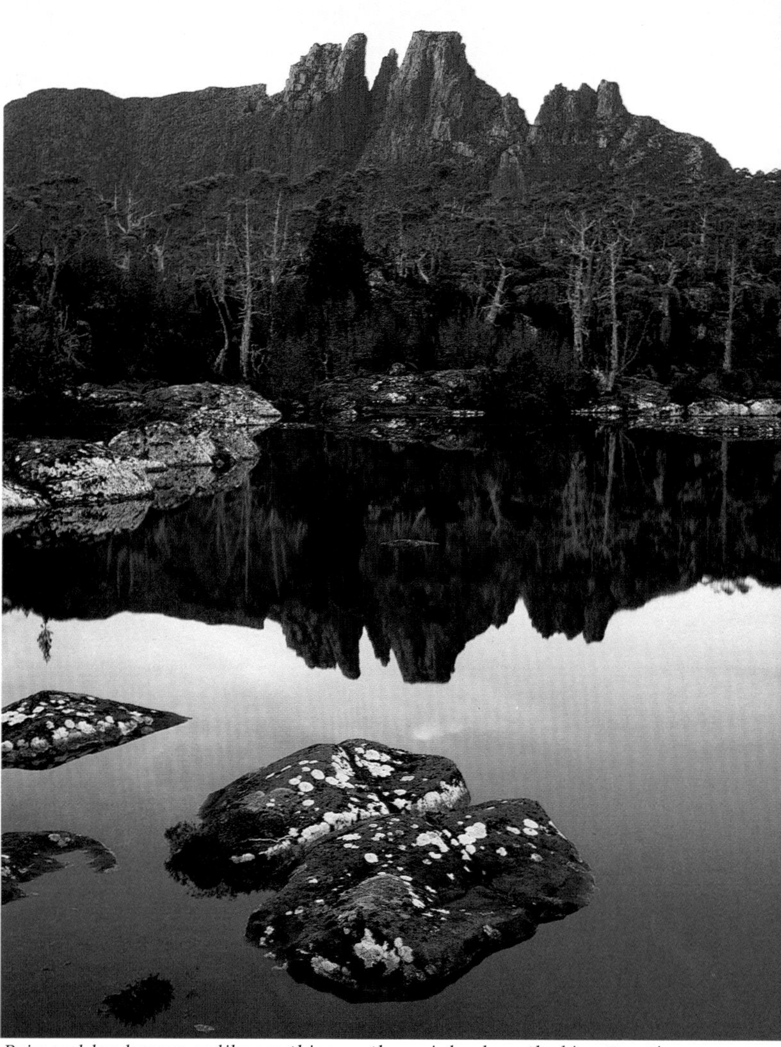

Primeval landscapes unlike anything on the mainland are the big attraction at Cradle Mountain; Mount Geryon looks into the Pool of Memories.

DEVONPORT ■ 2438

George Bass and Matthew Flinders sailed along the northern coastline of Tasmania in November 1798 and failed to notice the mouth of the Mersey River. In 1823, Captain Charles Hardwicke sailed past and reported gloomily: 'the land is mountainous, extremely barren and totally unfit for habitation'. But once the huge forests were cleared, the exceptionally fertile soil supported a remarkable variety of crops and large numbers of grazing animals.

The Mersey River was first known as Second Western River and the estuary settlement was originally called Port Frederick after Governor Arthur's son. In 1890, the towns of Formby on the west bank of the Mersey and Torquay on the east bank merged to become Devonport, now the youngest of Tasmania's five cities. The modern city is also the car- and passenger-ferry terminal for travellers crossing Bass Strait from Port Phillip Bay as well as being a busy cargo and port.

Devonport's original role as the service centre for a rich orcharding and agricultural district has taken on broader dimensions with the town's industrial growth. There are textile and timber mills and can and carpet making, metal fabrication and meat and dairy products factories, and the famous 'Ovaltine' is made at nearby Quoiba. *Population 22 660*

MERSEY BLUFF AND TIAGARRA The Tasmanian Aborigines lived and hunted along this stretch of coast for thousands of years before Europeans arrived. 'Tiagarra' – an Aboriginal word said to mean 'keep' – is the Tasmanian Aboriginal Cultural and Arts Centre display situated on Mersey Bluff; nearby there are Aboriginal rock carvings depicting patterns and objects from the landscape.

'HOME HILL' 'Home Hill' was built for the former Prime Minister, Joseph Lyons and his wife Dame Enid, in 1916. Dame Enid was one of the first two women members of the House of Representatives.

LAKE BARRINGTON ■ **2439**

The Mersey Forth Power Development covers an area of 2070 square kilometres and uses water originating on the Great Western Tiers augmented by the Fisher, Mersey, Wilmot and Forth rivers, passing it through seven power stations, seven large dams, three major tunnels and various penstocks, canals and flumes and several artificial lakes before it reaches Bass Strait. The construction of the eighty-four-metre-high Devils Gate Dam, a spectacular concrete arch, formed Lake Barrington and both are important parts of this complex engineering masterpiece.

LATROBE ■ **2440**

Latrobe has always prided itself on its sporting events. An English cricket team visited in January 1888 and the United Australian Axemen's Association was formed in Whitaker's Coffee Palace on 13 June 1891 to plan the first 'world champion' axemen's carnival to take place the following December. It merited viceregal patronage and drew a crowd of several thousand spectators. Though the carnival is no more, woodchopping events have since become part of the national culture and many Tasmanians have excelled in them.

Settled in the 1840s, Latrobe was once a major northern port and exported timber and produce to the mainland during the Victorian gold rush. It was a centre of consequence, shipyards lined the river banks and business was brisk but ferries have not come up this far for many a year. In the late 1800s the mouth of the Mersey River was dredged and Devonport became the main port; Latrobe focused on rural concerns.

The town's present economy is based on agriculture, orcharding and paper manufacturing. Opium poppies are one of Tasmania's more unusual crops and the fields round Latrobe, a blaze of colour in the flowering season, supply pharmaceutical manufacturers in Australia and overseas. Tasmania is the only state permitted to grow the plants and the crop is raised under strict security. *Population 2550*

FESTIVALS Latrobe Wheel and Latrobe Gift, December.

There is no 'Big Poppy' or guided tour to attract visitors to the paddocks near Latrobe planted with beautifully flowering poppies. On the contrary, visitors are discouraged while the poppies – the opium variety – are encouraged to run to seed so that their heads (below) might be used in drug production.

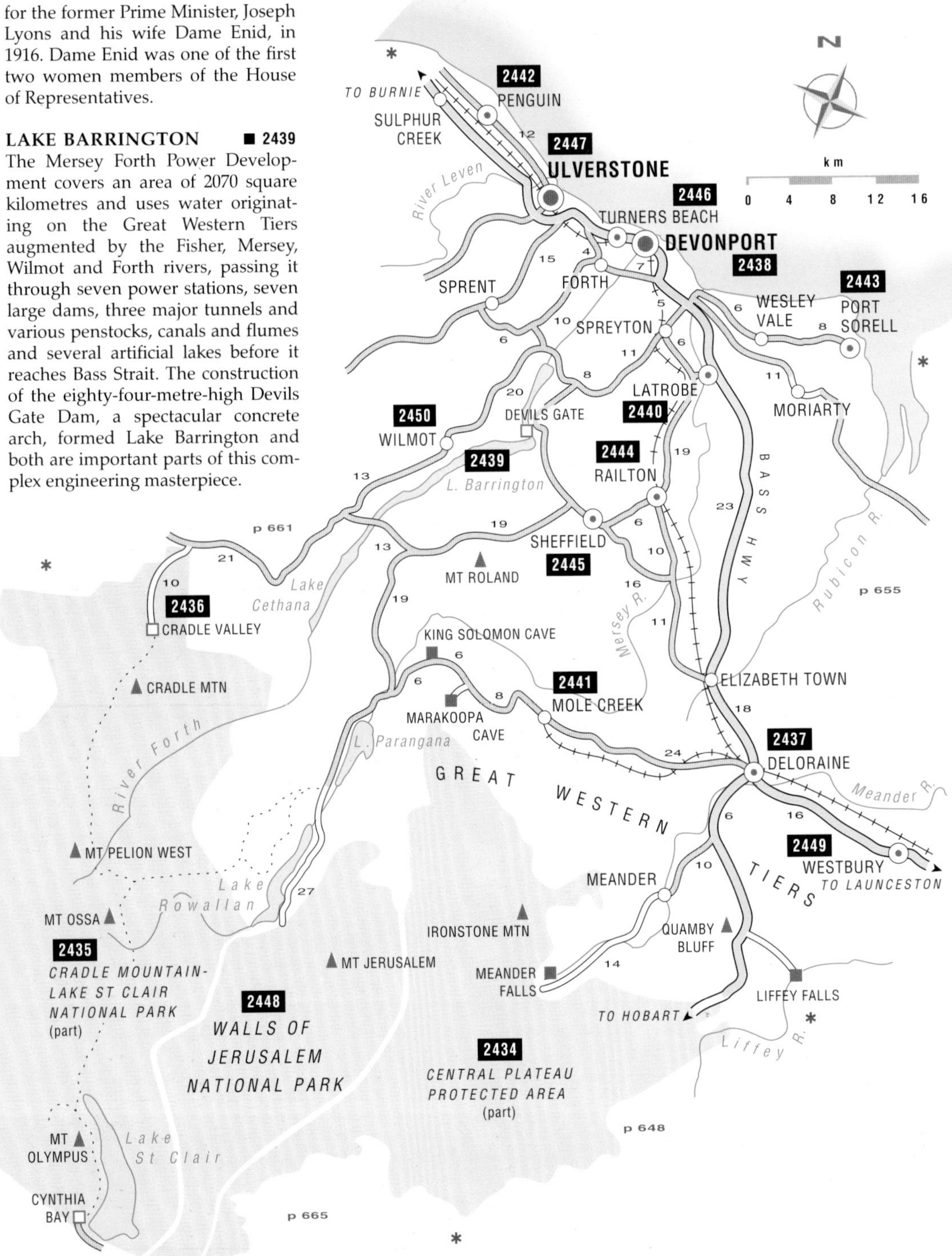

MOLE CREEK ■ **2441**

This unassuming little township supports a farming and forestry distric where an unusual breed of beef cattle called 'Belted Galloways' are raised. They are black with a broac white stripe around their middles Mole Creek gets its name from the nearby creek's habit of 'burrowing underground from time to time.

The town is also known for it leatherwood honey. For a few week every year the hives are transportec by semi-trailer to the west coast, s the bees can feast on the white wax flowers of the leatherwood trees and produce the strong-flavoured, ligh amber honey.

Mole Creek is well placed as th starting point for trips to the Grea Western Tiers and to the limeston caves where the year-round under ground temperature is 9° Centigrade King Solomon and Marakoopa cave only are open to the general public.

PENGUIN ■ **244**

Penguin is situated on three bay with sandy beaches and rocky clif tucked between Bass Strait and th

Dial Range. Ronald Campbell Gunn named the town in 1861 for the fairy penguins that nest along the coastline of north-western Tasmania. Like Ulverstone (see entry), it owes its early settlement to the insatiable demand for timber for home building across Bass Strait.

The area around Penguin, like much of the rest of the hinterland along this stretch of coast, is a major producer of vegetables for local and interstate markets. *Population 2880*

FESTIVALS Penguin Christmas Parade, December.

PORT SORELL ■ 2443
Port Sorell is a sheltered and well-established holiday resort set on the estuary of the Rubicon River. Fishermen and sealers frequented the area when the colony was young. Another early industry was the collection of wattle bark along the Rubicon River and Green's Creek for tannin extraction for use in leather tanning.

The settlement, first called Burgess, was named after Governor Sorell in 1822, and owes its early development to the Van Diemen's Land Company (see box *Smithton & Stanley*). *Population 1500*

RAILTON ■ 2444
The town site of Railton was marked out in 1853, but like many other places in this part of Tasmania, was slow to develop until the railway came through in 1914. In 1928, Goliath Portland Cement took over a small local concern and the town's future was assured from then on. The limestone and clay raw materials extracted from a huge quarry travel by overhead conveyor to the crusher, helping make cement production one of Tasmania's major industries. *Population 1000*

SHEFFIELD ■ 2445
Sheffield lies in the Kentish Plains, discovered by Nathaniel Lipscombe Kentish who was appointed government surveyor in Van Diemen's Land in 1841. He came upon the area while investigating the course of a road stretching from Deloraine to the north-west coast and pronounced it fine dry healthy ground, forming a much better winter than summer run for cattle'.

James Powlett built first in Sheffield – the Kentish Inn which was later called the Sheffield Inn was his. By 1877, a well-established village had developed. The present economy is rural-centred, supported by the Mersey Forth Power Scheme and the forestry industry.

Since 1986, the work of several artists, refugees from the mainland as well as Tasmanian painters, has earned Sheffield the nickname, 'Town of Murals'. There are twenty-three paintings in and around the township which depict the district's pioneer history. *Population 990*

TURNERS BEACH ■ 2446
Turners Beach is another well-established north coast resort. Like Port Sorell (see entry), it is conveniently placed for travellers passing through Devonport. The settlement fronts about two kilometres of good beach and has easy access to quiet fishing for mullet and salmon in the River Forth. *Population 900*

THE GABLES This building on the western bank of the river was first licensed as 'The Sailors' Return Inn' around 1850 but operated as a hotel for about ten years only. In 1853 it was raided by the bushrangers, Dalton and Kelly, who availed themselves of the landlord's whale boat and rowed it to Victoria. History does not record whether Kelly was related to the notorious Ned but he came to the same end. The pair of boat-nappers were soon caught, shipped back to Launceston to stand trial, and subsequently executed.

ULVERSTONE ■ 2447
Ulverstone is situated on the River Leven and is graced with beautiful beaches which attract holiday-makers in the warmer months. Log splitters worked in the area in the late 1840s, finding a ready market in Melbourne, across the strait. As the sawmills ate up the timber, attention turned to the rich volcanic soil and potatoes, beef cattle and milking cows were established. The irrigated, farmland now supports an expanded version of these industries including dairy produce, beef, mutton, wool and vegetables.

The very first challenge match between two local axemen in 1869 is claimed to be the forerunner of all subsequent chopping contests (see Latrobe). Timber milling continues to be important and a local blackwood furniture factory has won national awards for its designs.

Ulverstone, now the business and residential hub of a large agricultural district, grew slowly. The 1861 census recorded fifteen people living there and by 1870 there were only twenty-five. By 1880, the population had grown to 220 and the coming of the railway line from Launceston ten years later boosted settlement so that by the turn of the century the population just topped the thousand.

The town is dominated by the Second World War memorial clock tower which encloses the First World War memorial. Its three columns represent the RAN, AIF and RAAF: the chain links denote the strong bonds between the services and the torch of remembrance surmounts the structure. *Population 9920*

FESTIVALS Ulverstone Agricultural Show.

WALLS OF JERUSALEM NATIONAL PARK ■ 2448
The Walls of Jerusalem are a series of mountains on the western side of the Central Plateau forming forbidding sheer dolerite cliffs. The park encompasses an area of 11 510 hectares and includes several lakes and tarns. Grotesquely bent snow gums cling to the rocky ridges and the lower slopes are clothed in pencil pines. Subalpine heaths and wet grassland share the plateau.

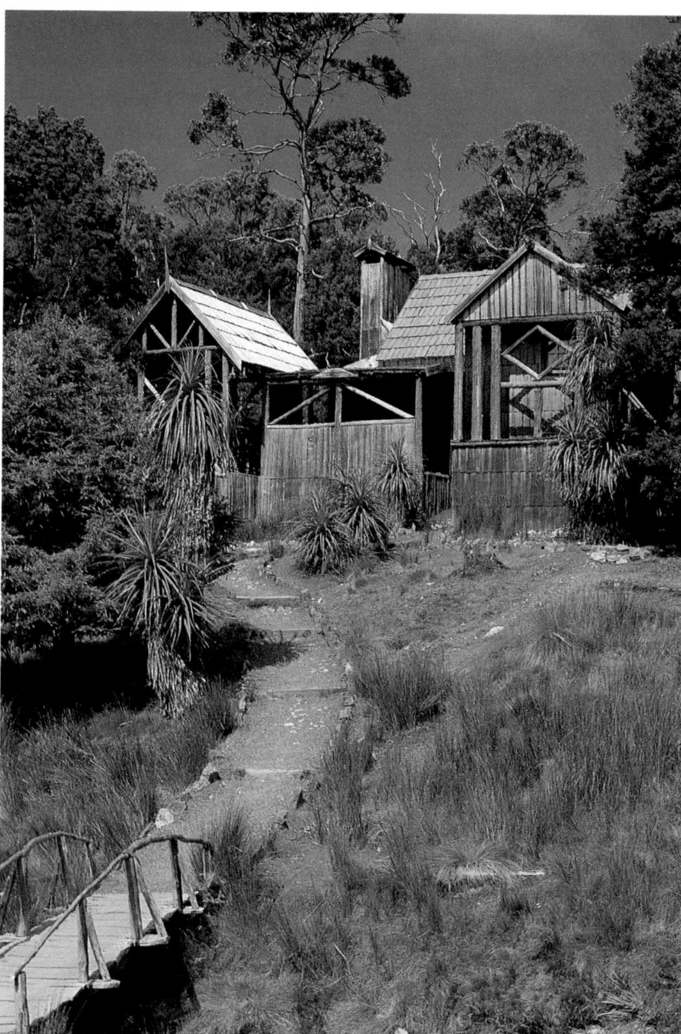

Austrian alpine and bushland rustic come together in the chalet built by Gustav Weindorfer, the forerunner of numerous Cradle Mountain lodges.

WESTBURY ■ 2449
Westbury is one of those colonial Tasmanian villages that prompt people to compare the island state with the British Isles. It lies in fertile pastoral, agricultural and timber country where the roads are lined with hawthorn hedges and the houses cluster round a village green with imported deciduous trees, such as oaks and elms. This is used in the traditional way for fetes and public occasions involving the townsfolk. It even has a maypole base for the maypole donated for the town's one hundred and fiftieth anniversary by the people of Westbury in the English county of Wiltshire.

The first settlers were the Field family who came to the area in 1823. An extensive town site was surveyed five years later by order of Governor Arthur and it was expected Westbury would become the gateway to the north-west which the Van Diemen's Land Company was developing at the time but the little town never grew to meet these expectations. *Population 1290*

'WESTFIELD' 'Westfield' lies at the end of a poplar-lined drive about three kilometres west of Westbury. It is a two-storey house, with symmetrically flanking, single-storey wings, which nestles in the lower foothills of the Western Tiers. The house was built in the 1850s by William Field who was one of Tasmania's earliest cattle barons, at one time owning more than 10 000 cattle.

WILMOT ■ 2450
Wilmot is a pretty country town on the Forth–Cradle Mountain road. In the early 1900s, George Coles, father of the founders of the G.J. Coles chain, ran a general store here which was still going strong in the early 1990s and which no doubt instilled good business principles in his sons. Edgar and Arthur Coles saw shopping systems in America on their way home from the First World War and soon started their first and very successful 'nothing over two shillings and sixpence' store in Melbourne.

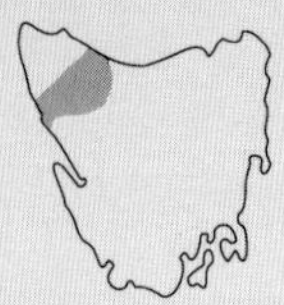

Burnie & Wynyard

The rugged north-west coast, famed for its rainforests, ferns and trout streams, has been mined for gold, tin and iron for more than a century. The bustling industrial city and port of Burnie is a stark contrast to the inland wilderness.

BOAT HARBOUR ■ 2451

A crescent-shaped, fine, white sand beach and clear water attracts both swimmers and skin divers to this popular coastal resort. Good fishing is to be had from the rocky points. As frosts are rare here it is possible for gardeners to grow plants normally only found in subtropical habitats.

The beach was originally known as Jacobs Boat Harbour, after either Captain John Jacobs, a skipper of the 1830s, or after a director of the Van Diemen's Land Company (see box *Devonport & Ulverstone*), also called John Jacobs.

BURNIE ■ 2452

A major manufacturing city, Burnie owes its rapid expansion in the 1970s and 1980s to the Associated Pulp and Paper Mills plant, one of the most important enterprises in Tasmania, which is situated on Emu Bay. Burnie's deepwater port also serves the west coast mining centres – the Emu Bay Railway, the only privately owned rail company in the state, runs to Rosebery and Zeehan (see *Queenstown & Rosebery*) and was built to haul minerals from the Mount Bischoff Mine near Waratah (see entry) to the coast.

The town's early links are with the Van Diemen's Land Company. In 1827 the site on Emu Bay was chosen by explorer and company surveyor Henry Hellyer as a suitable port for a proposed inland pastoral development. The town was laid out in the following year and named for William Burnie, a director of the company. For six years cattle and later sheep were raised in the region, but the depredations of the now extinct Tasmanian tiger, combined with the harsh winters, caused operations to cease in the mid-1830s. Emu Bay continued as a timber trading outlet and grew rapidly after the discovery of tin, as ore was carted here for shipment. *Population 20 500*

BURNIE INN This single-storey timber cottage, the oldest building in Burnie, dates from the late 1840s and was built by shipwright John Wiseman who operated it until his death in 1876. In 1973 the old inn was moved to Burnie Park and restored.

FESTIVALS Burnie Festival, late-September; Rhododendron Festival, mid-October; Christmas Festival, mid-December.

CORINNA ■ 2453

Corinna is now almost deserted and little remains of the gold rush of the late nineteenth century apart from old graves beside the Pieman River, marked by durable Huon pine headstones which have weathered for more than a century. The town is a base for wilderness cruises through the Pieman River State Reserve (see entry), and for trout fishing.

The name 'Corinna' is derived from an Aboriginal word for the thylacine or Tasmanian tiger which once roamed here, menacing the livestock of the early settlers to such an extent that a bounty was paid for each one killed. Now the creature which only a century ago was considered a menace is thought to be extinct – there have been no confirmed sightings for more than fifty years.

HELLYER GORGE STATE RESERVE ■ 2454

The road into the gorge winds for forty kilometres or so through farmlands and green rainforested hills where stands of sassafrass, giant myrtle, blackwood, leatherwood and huge ferns grow in profusion. It was named for Henry Hellyer, explorer and surveyor for the Van Diemen's Land Company, whose suicide in 1832 shocked the infant colony.

LEVEN CANYON ■ 2455

The River Leven winds in a great hairpin bend beneath the sheer, 120-metre-high walls of the canyon. A lookout – reached by a ten-minute walk from the picnic area – has sweeping views across to Black Buff (1340 metres). A walking track leads to a footbridge across the floor of the canyon. Other tracks lead to a lower cliff walk and Jean Brook Waterfall.

PIEMAN RIVER ■ 2456

There is some dispute as to just which pieman is remembered in the name of this river. Most commonly associated with the name is Alexander Pearce, a Hobart pieman jailed for selling food unsuitable for consumption. Pearce and several fellow convicts escaped into the wilds of the north-west and, when recaptured by this river, the pieman was found to be carrying some of the remains of his fellow escapees whom he had killed and eaten. The other claimant is tiny pastry-cook 'Little Tommy' Kent – he was less than a metre and a half tall – an absconder from Macquarie Harbour, who crossed the Pieman River and later reached the north-west coast, the first European known to have made this journey.

On the lower reaches of the river is Reece Dam – named after E.E.

Beyond the Donaldson River (below) are the inaccessible reaches of the Pieman Protected Area and just possibly – or so claim some bushmen – one of the holdouts of the tantalisingly elusive thylacine.

Reece, a former premier of Tasmania – and its associated power station.

PIEMAN RIVER STATE RESERVE ■ 2457

This 2330-hectatre reserve protects an 800-metre-wide rainforest strip along both banks of the Pieman River (see entry). Growing here are the most northerly stands of Huon pine as well as the rare and graceful Cunningham tree fern.

SAVAGE RIVER ■ 2458

This self-contained iron ore town, beside the fast-flowing Savage River in the forest country of the rugged west coast, was established in the 1960s to accommodate up to 1600 people. The ore deposits here had been discovered a century earlier, but were too low grade for economical extraction by methods available at the time. It was not until the construction of a pipeline which takes the crushed ore in slurry form to a pellet plant on the coast that mining operations here became worthwhile. *Population 540*

SOMERSET ■ 2459

The town of Somerset is a satellite of the city of Burnie, six kilometres to the east. It has extensive residential and light industrial development, including timber and plywood mills and a freezing and canning factory.

Somerset is on the Cam River and from the 1860s to 1880s was a busy port. Early settler Captain David Lewis built the Ferry House Hotel on the east bank in the late 1850s, and also ran a ferry across the river. On the west bank Thomas Wragg and his family established the settlement's first school and church, and were probably also responsible for naming it Somerset. *Population 3260*

TABLE CAPE ■ 2460

Table Cape is the almost circular plug of an ancient volcano, about one-and-a-half kilometres in diameter. On one side it borders the sea, where cliffs plunge 170 metres to the water, and on the other it rises 70 metres above the surrounding agricultural land of the rich volcanic plains. From the top there are panoramic views of both the coast and the hinterland.

In the 1850s, the convict Alexander brothers opened the Cable Cape Inn and a store nearby, and eventually became large landholders. The lighthouse here dates from 1888. Table Cape was named by George Bass and Matthew Flinders in 1798.

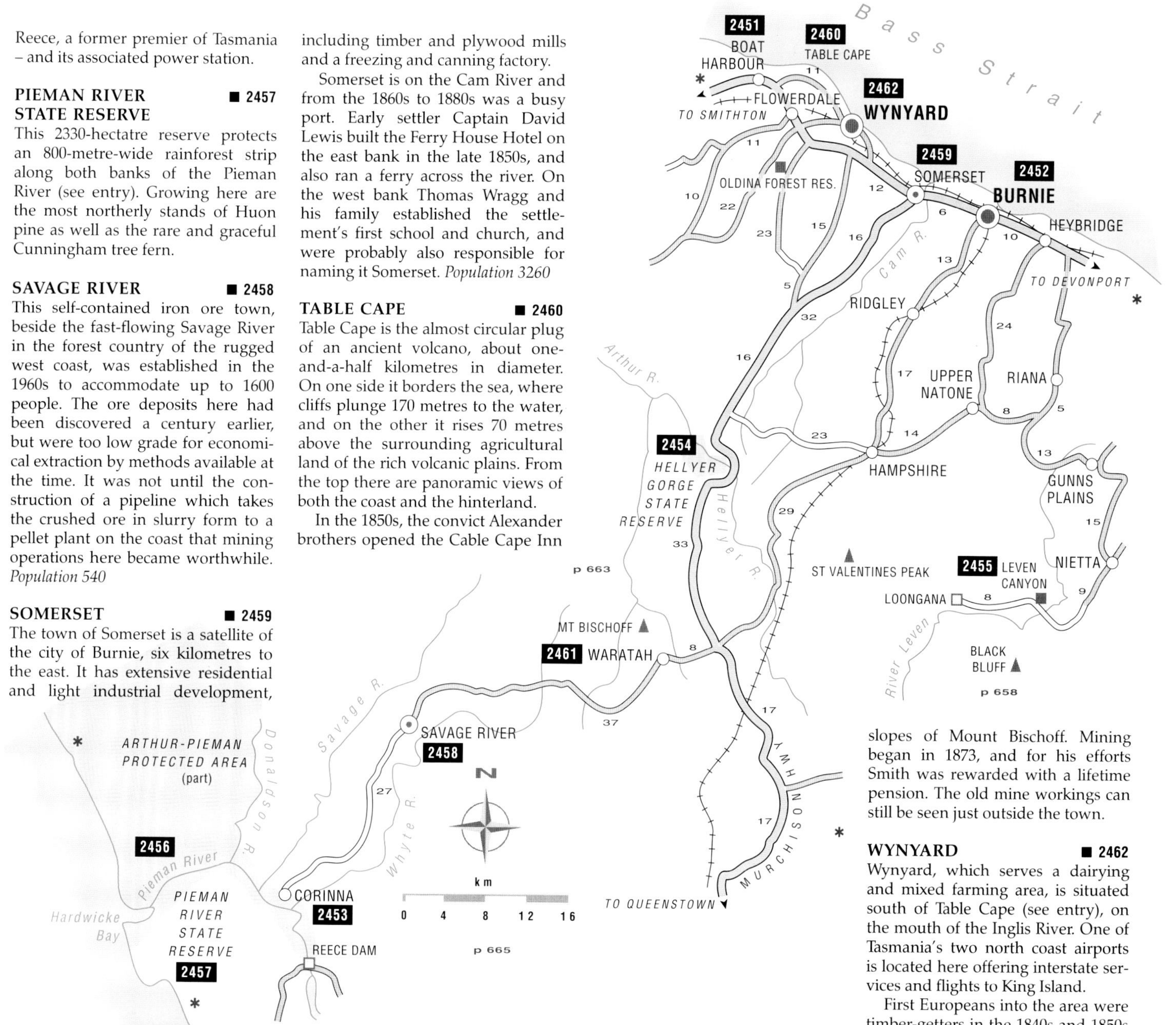

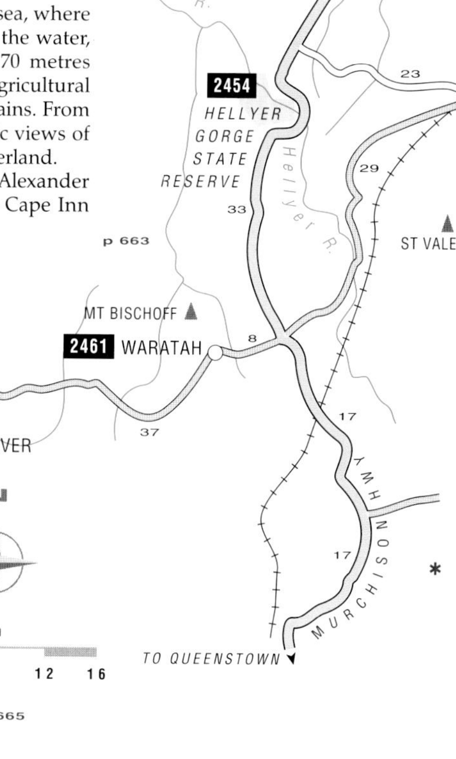

Tranquil Waratah basks in the glory of its turn-of-the-century days when its rich tin mine was the first 'plant' in Australia to use electric lighting.

WARATAH ■ 2461

This was the first mining boom town in Tasmania, for beneath the slopes of Mount Bischoff – once described as a 'mountain of solid tin' – was what in the 1890s was the richest tin deposit in the world. When it closed in the 1930s the mine had yielded more than 80 000 tonnes of ore, and in its heyday the town had more than 4500 residents.

Ore deposits here were discovered in 1872 by James Smith, a colourful character known locally as 'the Philosopher'. He joined the Victorian gold rushes in the 1850s, and when he returned to Tasmania continued prospecting, finding traces of various metals until his major find on the slopes of Mount Bischoff. Mining began in 1873, and for his efforts Smith was rewarded with a lifetime pension. The old mine workings can still be seen just outside the town.

WYNYARD ■ 2462

Wynyard, which serves a dairying and mixed farming area, is situated south of Table Cape (see entry), on the mouth of the Inglis River. One of Tasmania's two north coast airports is located here offering interstate services and flights to King Island.

First Europeans into the area were timber-getters in the 1840s and 1850s and the tiny settlement which arose here was named after Major-General Edward Buckle Wynyard of the New South Wales Corps. By the 1870s Wynyard had grown to be the main port on the north coast, outstripping nearby Burnie, and in the following decades a flour mill and butter factory were established.

Today the town serves a thriving dairy industry which supplies the United Milk Tasmania Company. Other activities are commercial fishing, sawmilling, and mixed farming. Table Cape Tulip Farm is occasionally open to the public. *Population 4680*

OLDINA FOREST RESERVE On the southern outskirts of Wynyard, this reserve features an aged log of Huon pine – because of its shape known locally as the 'dog bone' – which was used as a boom across the Pieman River to collect felled timber washed downstream by floodwaters.

FESTIVALS Tulip Festival, October.

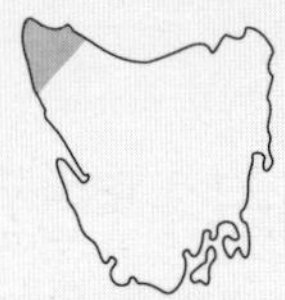

Smithton & Stanley

The north-west corner of the island state, with its fertile extension of King Island, is given over principally to agriculture. Though much of the shoreline is readily accessible by boat only, there are magnificent views from the windswept Nut at Stanley and other wild capes along the coast.

King Island fishing boats keep the Currie freezing works busy with a rich harvest from the wild Bass Strait waters.

CURRIE ■ 2463

Currie, on King Island's west coast, is its main settlement and commercial centre (see entry). It was named after Captain Archibald Currie, a leading Victorian citizen, who in the late 1800s salvaged the wreck of the *Netherby*. There is a beacon at the small harbour's entrance and the lightkeeper's house now functions as a local museum.

Kelp is harvested from the rocks and beaches and brought to a factory in Currie to be dried on racks. It is then kiln dried and crushed and exported to Scotland where it is used as an ingredient in a variety of products ranging from icecream to cosmetics. *Population 820*

DIP FALLS FOREST RESERVE ■ 2464

Dip Falls is a pretty, cascading double waterfall that plunges through rainforest in a first drop of twenty-eight metres and a second of about fourteen metres. Nearby several huge eucalypts, several hundred years old, stand impressively tall and safe from chainsaws. Their sheer size assured their survival in the era of axe logging before the reserve was declared – they were too big to be transported to the mills.

GRASSY ■ 2465

Grassy, King Island's mining township, is located on the south-east coast and is the port and docking point for the *Straitsman* roll-on, roll-off cargo vessel which links Stanley and Melbourne with the island. Modern stockyards are incorporated in the wharf design. Gold, tin, lead, slate and rutile have all been mined on the island at various times.

A Tasmanian prospector discovered a tungsten-bearing specimen on the beach near Grassy township in 1911 and this began scheelite mining operations. The level of activity has fluctuated with world prices and two underground mines have been producing ore.

KING ISLAND ■ 2466

King Island is fifty-eight kilometres long and has a total area of approximately 126 000 hectares. About half of this has been cleared for farming and few tall trees remain. The feathered population includes imported species such as pheasant and quail. The island has pasture grasses which do not grow elsewhere in Australia and are said to give a special flavour to the beef and cheese. The seeds are thought to have come from straw-filled mattresses washed ashore from stricken ships.

This explanation is backed up by the fact that there are more wrecks in the vicinity of King Island than in any other part of Australia. The worst of these was the immigrant ship *Cataraqui* which ran aground in 1845. About 400 passengers and crew were drowned and are remembered by a monument at Boggy Creek. The forty-eight-metre-high, granite Cape Wickham Lighthouse, the tallest in Australia, stands on the north end of the island and sends out radio signals which coordinate with those from Cape Otway and Cape Schank on the Victorian coast.

Some island names, such as Seal Rocks at the southern end and Sea Elephant Bay on the east coast, are reminders of first hunting sorties here by Europeans when the tally for seal pelts reached a bloodthirstily high level with elephant seals being hunted almost to extinction.

In 1801, the island was named Kings Island after Philip Gidley King, Governor of New South Wales. The following year Lieutenant Charles Robbins was sent from Sydney to claim it officially in the name of Great Britain. He anchored the *Cumberland* in Sea Elephant Bay alongside Nicholas Baudin's *Le Géographe*, borrowed dry gunpowder from the French, fired a salute over their bemused heads and hoisted the Union Jack upside down.

Some Europeans lived permanently on King Island as early as 1855 and settlement expanded from 1886. Gold and tin were mined in 1905 and scheelite was found a few years later (see Grassy). The Land Settlement Scheme after the Second World War gave a great boost to the economy and in modern times the main industries are grazing, tourism, fishing and kelp processing (see Currie); the island has a reputation for gourmet foods, among them cheeses and rich dairy cream.

NARACOOPA Naracoopa is a small settlement on the east coast which used to do duty as the island's second port. Bulk fuel tanks are still located here and are filled through a floating pipeline to tankers lying offshore. The old cable station which was the intermediate point linking Tasmania and the mainland across Bass Strait is also at Naracoopa.

MARRAWAH ■ 2467

Marrawah, at the extreme western point of the sealed highway, serves another farming region. This tamed landscape is within easy reach of the rugged coastline where the boisterous rollers of the Indian Ocean wash up skeletal driftwood on the beaches. Aboriginal carvings on nearby Mount Cameron West depict circle, dot, lattice and bird-track motifs gouged out of soft sandstone. They are the subject of sometimes controversial comparisons with similar artwork in the desert of central Australia. Most of the site is now covered with sand to protect it against erosion but there are slabs of the engraved rock-faces in the museums in Hobart and Launceston.

PORT LATTA ■ 2468

Port Latta is north of Savage River and the outlet for an eighty-five kilometre long pipeline which connects it to the mining town. The crushed iron ore is pumped through this as slurry, pelletised at the Port Latta plant and then carried on a conveyor belt to huge bulk-ore carriers.

ROCKY CAPE NATIONAL PARK ■ 2469

This 3000-hectare park covers about twelve kilometres of coastline from near Boat Harbour in the east to Rocky Cape in the west. It is the smallest of Tasmania's parks and was proclaimed in 1967 and enlarged in 1975. Bass and Flinders named Rocky Cape in 1798 during their circumnavigation of Tasmania.

At the time Aborigines were still sheltering in two caves which they had used for about 8000 years. The establishment of the Van Diemen's Land Company (see box) later drove them out of the area. The park is noted for its wildflowers including Christmas bells and two rare ground orchids – the leek orchid and the tailed spider orchid; it is also believed to be the only place in Tasmania where the saw banksia grows. Yellow-tailed black cockatoos are particularly fond of the banksia's seeds

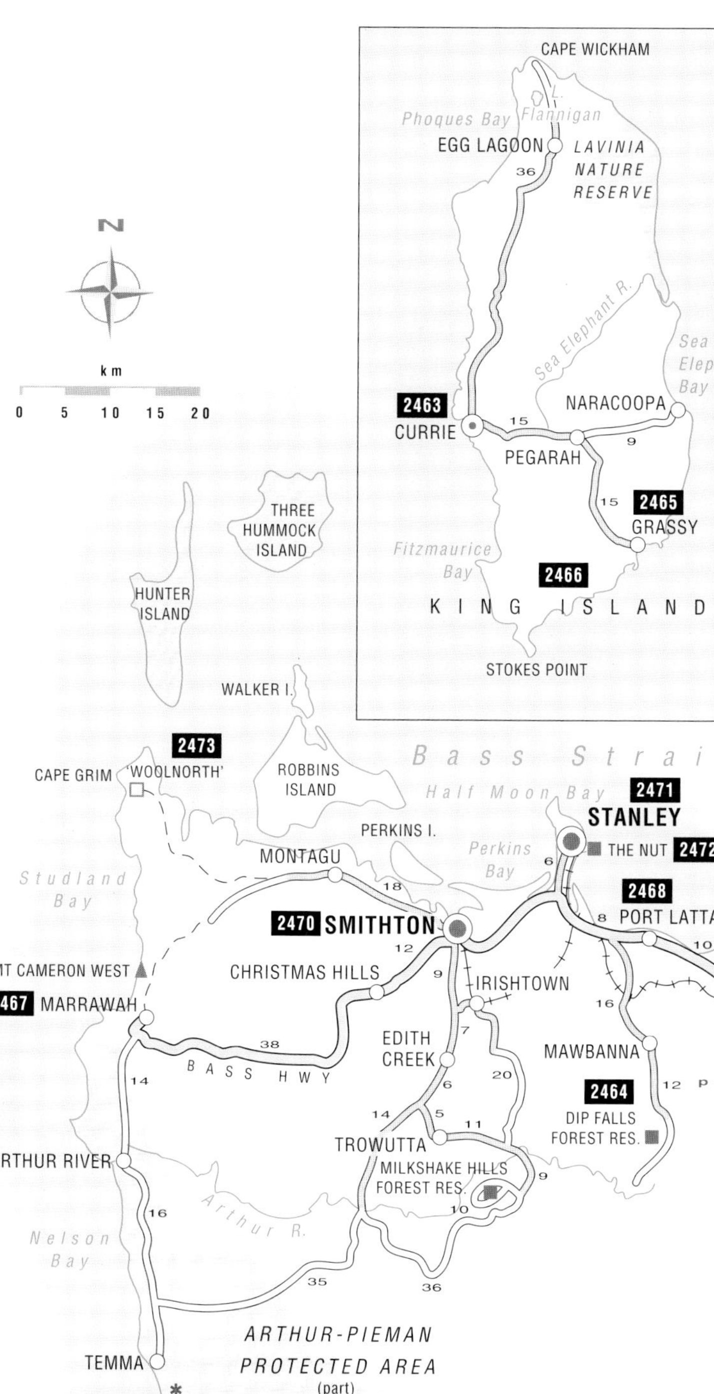

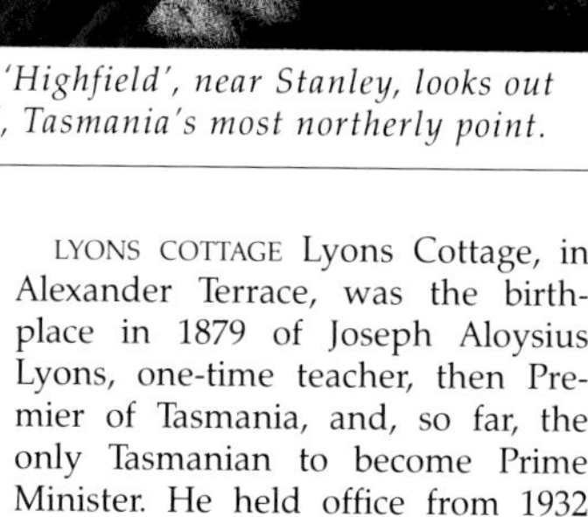

A ruined outbuilding at 'Highfield', near Stanley, looks out to the table-topped 'Nut', Tasmania's most northerly point.

SISTERS BEACH Sisters Beach, about two kilometres long, is an excellent bathing beach lying in a valley between the hills of the park. The slopes behind it are clad in a cross-section of native trees, some of which have been planted especially to attract native birds and dainty honeyeaters are frequent visitors.

SMITHTON ■ 2470

The main industries in Smithton are forestry, sawmilling, vegetable growing and freezing or canning, bacon curing, casein production and butter making. It is the headquarters of one of Tasmania's greatest forestry areas and has a specialist hardwood mill which processes blackwood for high-quality furniture.

The town is the municipal and industrial centre of Circular Head. Farmers draining and cultivating the swamps in the district found the fossil bones of creatures that roamed these parts – and the rest of Australia – about 37 000 years ago – clear evidence that Tasmania was once joined to the mainland. The bones are on show in the Hobart and Launceston museums. *Population 3500*

STANLEY ■ 2471

Stanley, a fishing port and tourist centre and now classified as an historic town, nestles at the foot of the Nut (see entry) and is connected to it by a narrow neck of land. It was the first settlement in north-western Tasmania and the Van Diemen's Land Company made its headquarters here (see box). The town was named Stanley in the early 1840s after Britain's then Secretary of State for the colonies. It is the site of the telegraphic cable linking the island with mainland Australia.

John Lee Archer, the Irish-born architect and engineer who designed many of Tasmania's colonial buildings, planned Stanley and was its magistrate for a time. He is buried in the local cemetery. Henry Hellyer, the surveyor and explorer who was first to investigate much of the wild country of the north-west, is also buried here.

The rugged section of coastline stretching eastwards from Circular Head past Rocky Cape and Sisters Beach (see sub-entry, Rocky Cape National Park) to Table Cape is most conveniently explored by small boat as access to the sheltered bays and cave-studded shoreline is not easy by land. *Population 580*

HIGHFIELD In 1832, Edward Curr, chief agent of the Van Diemen's Land Company (see box), wrote: 'The wooden house I live in will not stand 15 years: the stone one which I am building will stand a century'. The plans for 'Highfield' were drawn up by Henry Hellyer. It is flanked by outbuildings, stables, feed stores and there is a family chapel nearby. A deer park was established in 1836 with eight animals from England; by 1849 there was a herd of seventy-six.

LYONS COTTAGE Lyons Cottage, in Alexander Terrace, was the birthplace in 1879 of Joseph Aloysius Lyons, one-time teacher, then Premier of Tasmania, and, so far, the only Tasmanian to become Prime Minister. He held office from 1932 until his death in 1939.

THE NUT ■ 2472

The Nut at Stanley is a distinctive shape that rises abruptly from the ocean to a height of nearly 150 metres. This exposed lava plug, more than ten million years old, is one of several that dot Tasmania's northern coastline, reminders of the area's volcanic past. It was first sighted by Europeans when George Bass and Matthew Flinders rounded its rocky bulk on 6 December 1798 in the tiny ship *Norfolk*. It was this voyage that proved conclusively that Tasmania was separated from the mainland by the stretch of water later called Bass Strait. Matthew Flinders described the Nut as 'a cliffy round lump resembling a Christmas cake' and named the massive headland Circular Head. The Nut can be reached on foot or by the ease of a chairlift.

'WOOLNORTH' ■ 2473

The 'Woolnorth' property covers an area of approximately 22 000 hectares and is still owned by the Van Diemen's Land Company (see box). Several of the buildings date from the 1830s including an old jail which now houses the homestead's radio telephone. The last Tasmanian tigers to be captured are said to have been trapped at 'Woolnorth'. Cape Grim, which lies within the property, is the site of Australia's Air Monitoring Station and is a strategic point for breathtaking coastal views.

THE ONE-MILLION-POUND VAN DIEMEN'S LAND GAMBLE OF 1825

THE GIANT multi-national corporation of modern times is not without antecedents – similar ventures of ambitious and imaginative expansion were taking place more than 200 years ago.

In 1793, when the directors of the British East India Company decided to look for profitable lands south of the equator they sent young Lieutenant John Hayes to investigate the potential wealth of New Guinea. He ended up in Tasmanian waters instead, discovering and naming the Derwent River and fertile Risdon Cove (see *Bridgewater & New Norfolk*).

Hard in the lee of The Nut, the Van Diemen's Land Company store was the centre of a company town with 230 residents in 1848.

In 1835–1836, a joint-stock venture company was established to encourage investment – and to speed development – in the new British province of South Australia. The South Australian Company was influential in persuading many British families, farmers and agricultural labourers to migrate. Its South Australian affairs were finally wound up in 1949.

Between these two dates another company was formed, the Van Diemen's Land Company, which began in 1825 when a group of British businessmen – unaware that the days of the giant, London-based, British Empire land companies were numbered – wanted a source of fine colonial wool for the mills of the English Midlands. They saw such a source as cheaper and more dependable than the supplies from politically unsettled Europe.

'Woolnorth' – with the shorn and the unshorn at the shearing shed – is a modern activity of the 170-year-old Van Diemen's Land Company.

The British government granted the company more than 100 000 hectares of land in unexplored north-west Tasmania and the Colonial Secretary, Lord Bathurst, instructed its officers to settle an area of land 'beyond the ramparts of the unknown'. A Hobart merchant, Edward Curr, was hired as chief agent and with a capital of 1 000 000 pounds sterling the company was floated. Later, the amount of capital was reduced to 300 000 pounds sterling. Curr immediately sent out scouts to find the best area of the north-west. Other company explorers quickly followed including the successful Henry Hellyer who crossed overland to Circular Head and Jorgen Jorgensen who stumbled upon Great Lake (see *Campbell Town & Oatlands*).

Curr had a disagreement with Governor George Arthur about Lord Bathurst's intentions and the interpretation of 'remote' and the company finally took up a major grant of approximately 141 000 hectares at Cape Grim, on nearby islands and in the region near today's Burnie. Although the company story as an exploiter of new lands is by no means a happy one – it spent $500 000 over the next thirty-two years in development and paid only two small dividends – the whole colony benefitted from the exploratory expeditions which opened up unknown hinterland.

The history of Tasmania's north-west coast is inextricably linked with the fortunes of the Van Diemen's Land Company, despite the fact that the primary purpose of the venture failed. Many of the imported stud Cotswolds, Saxon Merino and Leicester sheep died and revenue from wool was under $40 000 between 1829 and 1852. Horses and cattle fared better but brought in little income.

Large shipments of agricultural machinery from England proved unsuitable in the antipodean conditions. Curr was assigned convict labour which caused much jealousy among free settlers. From the beginning, the company people were at complete variance with the culture of the few Aborigines still remaining in the area, who took aggressive action to repel them. Huts were burned and sheep speared but eventually the Aborigines were driven from the district and died in a forlorn exile.

From 1845 to 1858, the company tried to sell land to recoup its losses but managed to part with 4800 hectares only. In 1871, it benefitted from the discovery of tin at Mount Bischoff when Emu Bay became the port for the field. Later, company timber was exported and then supplied the paper mill at Burnie. Land continued to be sold and the much-diminished company – a unique link with the colonial past – now holds about 20 000 hectares of the 'Woolnorth' property (see entry) where cattle and sheep are raised. □

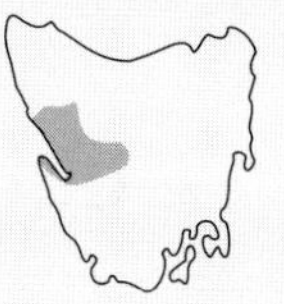

Queenstown & Rosebery

Tasmania's west is an isolated region of spectacular beauty where the communities, based on mining, are close-knit. They have all faced the hardships of an often inhospitable environment – where the high annual rainfall feeds rivers harnessed for hydro-electric power – and the uncertainties of fluctuating ore markets.

DERWENT BRIDGE ■ 2474

Derwent Bridge has long been a stopping place for travellers to the west coast and is within easy reach of good trout fishing waters. It lies at the southern end of the Cradle Mountain-Lake St Clair National Park between Lake King William and Lake St Clair. A sealed road leads to the latter which is the deepest natural freshwater lake in Australia, plunging in places to 190 metres.

Derwent Bridge is equidistant – approximately 170 kilometres – from Hobart *and* Launceston. West of the township, the scenery changes dramatically as the Lyell Highway enters mountain country where the peaks often disappear in a shroud of rain or mist. The region's high annual rainfall and numerous fast-flowing rivers provide perpetual moisture for a dense, rainforest environment.

FRANKLIN-GORDON WILD RIVERS NATIONAL PARK ■ 2475

This huge park of 181 075 hectares was created in 1981 by combining Frenchmans Cap National Park and the Lyell Highway and Gordon River state reserves with a portion of the Franklin River country. It boasts the white quartzite dome of the 1443-metre-high Frenchmans Cap and is a true wilderness, through which rush the unfettered waters of the Franklin River and its tributaries. The Franklin provides one of the world's most extraordinary white-water rafting experiences. Plans for hydro-electric development in the area were called off after a bitter controversy. The park was listed as a World Heritage Area in 1982 which ensures that its unspoilt beauty will be preserved undiminished for future generations.

LAKE MARGARET HYDRO-ELECTRIC STATION ■ 2476

The west coast has the highest rainfall of any part of Tasmania, and is the second wettest region in Australia after the tropics of northern Queensland. Lake Margaret is situated high on Mount Sedgwick where the catchment area is only twenty square kilometres but the annual rainfall approaches a drenching 4000 millimetres. It is the site of one of the first hydro-electric schemes in Tasmania, built in 1914 by the Mount Lyell Mining and Railway Company to provide power for its mines and associated townships.

Time is gradually erasing the scars of 30 years of wood-fired copper smelting as vegetation creeps back onto the denuded hills of Queenstown.

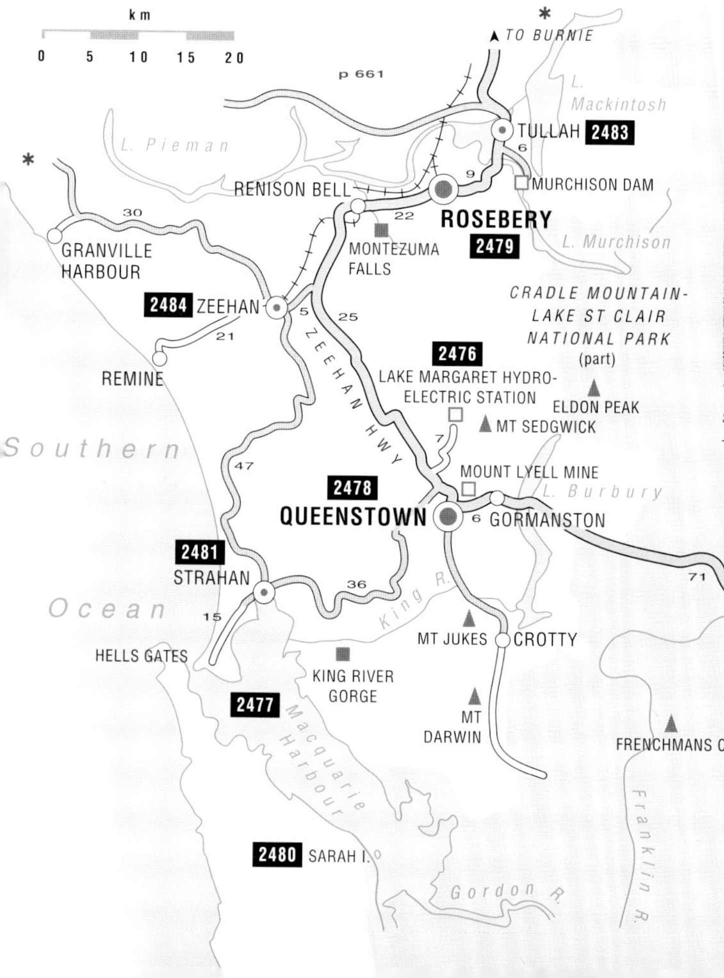

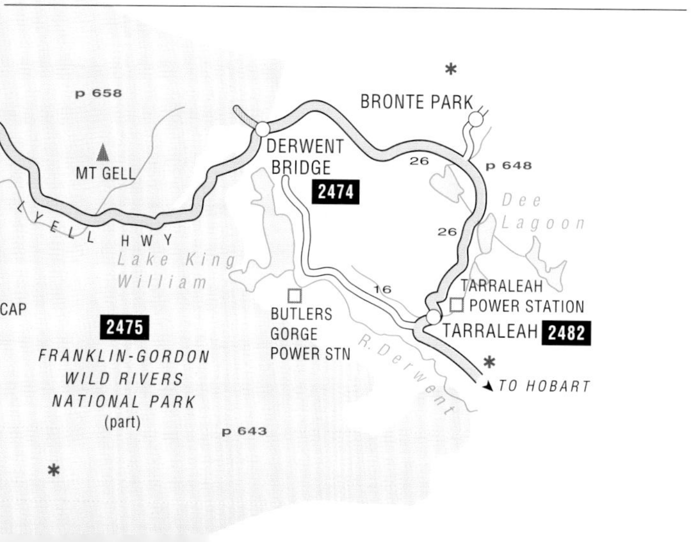

N
km
0 5 10 15 20
TO BURNIE
p 661
L. Mackintosh
L. Pieman
TULLAH 2483
MURCHISON DAM
RENISON BELL
ROSEBERY 2479
GRANVILLE HARBOUR
MONTEZUMA FALLS
L. Murchison
2484 ZEEHAN
CRADLE MOUNTAIN-LAKE ST CLAIR NATIONAL PARK (part)
REMINE
ZEEHAN HWY
2476
LAKE MARGARET HYDRO-ELECTRIC STATION
ELDON PEAK
MT SEDGWICK
Southern Ocean
MOUNT LYELL MINE
L. Burbury
2478 QUEENSTOWN
GORMANSTON
p 658
BRONTE PARK
2481 STRAHAN
King R.
MT GELL
DERWENT BRIDGE 2474
p 648
HELLS GATES
MT JUKES
CROTTY
LYELL HWY
Dee Lagoon
KING RIVER GORGE
Lake King William
2477
Macquarie Harbour
MT DARWIN
FRENCHMANS CAP
BUTLERS GORGE POWER STN
TARRALEAH POWER STATION
TARRALEAH 2482
2475
FRANKLIN-GORDON WILD RIVERS NATIONAL PARK (part)
R. Derwent
TO HOBART
Franklin R.
2480 SARAH I.
Gordon R.
p 643

A writhing catch of crayfish at Strahan will produce succulent tails bound for foreign dinner tables.

MACQUARIE HARBOUR ■ 2477

Macquarie Harbour is one of the largest natural harbours in the world. Its 285 square kilometres of water are enclosed by thick forested mountains and the entrance is through Hells Gates, aptly named for its treacherous sandbar and rips.

The first Europeans to find shelter in Macquarie Harbour were James Kelly and his crew of four in the open whaleboat, *Elizabeth*, in December 1815. He named it after Lachlan Macquarie, the governor of New South Wales. From the strong current, Kelly correctly deduced that 'there must be a large river in the southeast direction' and when he found it, he called it the Gordon after James Gordon who had lent him the whaleboat. Kelly recognised the value of the Huon pine growing along the river banks and returned often to harvest it.

Macquarie Harbour is the outlet for several other rivers including the Sorell and the King, which has had much of its marine life driven away by mining wastes and sewage.

QUEENSTOWN ■ 2478

The last few kilometres of the Lyell Highway from Hobart to Queenstown descend the slopes of Mount Owen in a series of hair-raising bends. All around are the renowned 'moonscape' bare hills, cleared of timber to feed the copper smelters and further denuded of vegetation by the smelters' noxious sulphur fumes. The copper smelters were the invention of an early mine manager, an American metallurgist called Robert Sticht, who perfected pyritic smelting. Now that the smelters have shut down, a few brave trees have started to grow on the hillsides.

This mining town built up around the Mount Lyell copper mine is situated on the Queen River. Gold was discovered to the south of Mount Lyell near Queenstown in 1881 and by 1888 the Mount Lyell Gold Mining Company was formed. The gold lasted only three more years and the company then looked to copper.

Queenstown has always been isolated and the local people have always maintained not only a resilient pioneer spirit but have had to be physically tough as well – the football oval is covered with a hard quartz-sand mixture instead of grass! It is undeniably wet and people often hang their washing under the front verandahs. The average rainfall is just over 2500 millimetres a year but the west coast can also have glorious summer sunshine and there are even some dry days in winter. Although most work still comes from mining, the future of this industry is by no means as assured as it used to be and tourism has become a modern growth industry. *Population 3370*

ROSEBERY ■ 2479

Gold was first discovered in Rosebery Creek in 1893. Lead and zinc on which the town now depends were subsequently found in the area. The building of the Murchison Highway in the 1960s eventually provided another outlet apart from The Emu Bay railway line.

Rosebery, named after Lord Rosebery, the then prime minister of England, is very much a company town and owes its existence to the massive Electrolytic Zinc Company which contributes to the various town amenities. The ore from the nearby mine at Williamsford is carried by a system of aerial buckets that cross the Murchison Highway to the Rosebery treatment plants where zinc, lead, copper, silver and gold are extracted. *Population 1640*

SARAH ISLAND ■ 2480

Sarah Island in Macquarie Harbour, or Settlement Island as it was first called, was operated as a penitentiary from 1821 until around 1834. It was a place for second offenders and feared above all prisons. There were many deaths in its short history and the convicts sent there worked very hard, cutting Huon pine in the forests round the Gordon and King rivers and building and repairing ships in the island's shipyards. The brutal regime is well described in Marcus Clarke's novel *For the Term of His Natural Life*. Incredibly, some prisoners did manage to escape only to perish in the bush, sometimes murdering each other with cannibalistic intent.

Matthew Brady was incarcerated on Sarah Island and made a daring getaway by sea to spend the next two years robbing homesteads and wealthy travellers with scrupulous courtesy. He was finally captured in 1826 by a party led by John Batman – later of Port Phillip settlement fame – and was hanged in Hobart Town, despite many pleas for leniency for the 'gentleman' bushranger.

There is not much left on Sarah Island to tell the sorry tale of its inglorious past. The once-extensive buildings have been allowed to decay into the ground but tourist launches take interested visitors to see what is left of the ruins.

STRAHAN ■ 2481

Strahan, on Macquarie Harbour, was a major port, established to support the early inland mining fields of the west coast. It was linked to them by a network of railways. There are some impressive buildings, including the customs house, built around the beginning of the twentieth century. For a while the Cascade Brewery operated in the town as well as in Hobart. Thomas Gratton Riggs, an American playwright and actor, died in Strahan and is buried in the local cemetery. He is known throughout the world, and particularly in the United States, as the founder of the Benevolent and Protective Order of Elks, a men-only benevolent society.

Strahan was named in honour of Major Sir George Cumine Strahan, a governor of Tasmania. The town's main industries are now cray-fishing, forestry and tourism. *Population 600*

GORDON RIVER Strahan is the main access point for cruises up the Gordon River, where the almost-perfect, mirror reflections in the rusty brown water so delight photographers. This brown-tinted water is characteristic of rivers in these parts and comes from the vegetable stains from the peat bogs and myrtle forests. The Gordon is Tasmania's largest river and is navigable for about forty-two kilometres of its length.

TARRALEAH ■ 2482

Tarraleah is derived from an Aboriginal word said to mean 'a forester kangaroo' and this hilltop village is yet another which owes its existence to hydro-electric power. The Tarraleah Scheme uses water from the upper Derwent catchment which is stored in Lake St Clair and the artificially made Lake King William. The Tungatinah Scheme uses the water from many rivers – the Clarence, Nive, Dee, Ouse and Little Pine. The village is the staff residential centre and control headquarters for the Tarraleah–Tungatinah power schemes.

TULLAH ■ 2483

Tullah, the mining town, first began with lead extraction in the 1890s. 'Wee Georgie Wood', a steam locomotive called after a famous Scottish comedian who once performed at Zeehan and Rosebery (see entries), was the settlement's only link with the outside world before the first road from the south reached it in the early 1960s.

Tullah, the hydro-electric construction village, is about a kilometre from the old township. Although an earlier hydro–power station at nearby Lake Herbert – completed in 1907 – was not a success, Tullah more recently housed the workers on the Pieman River Power Development which has created Lakes Murchison, Mackintosh, Rosebery and Pieman. It is now an administration centre for the scheme. *Population 720*

ZEEHAN ■ 2484

Mount Zeehan was named after one of the two ships in Abel Tasman's 1642 expedition and nearby Zeehan is another west coast settlement with a prosperous past, historically significant buildings and ever-changing fortunes, like so many other Australian mining towns.

The activity began in 1882 when prospectors, Frank Long and John Healey found silver-lead at Pea Soup Creek and by the end of the century the town was well established with a population of around 8000. The Gaiety Theatre here once seated audiences of 1000 who came to hear performers of the highest calibre such as Dame Nellie Melba and Enrico Caruso and to watch the magical tricks of Harry Houdini and the provocative dances of Lola Montez.

But within ten years the ore began to give out, mines closed and buildings were dismantled. By the late 1950s, the population had dwindled to less than 700 and Zeehan's status to almost that of a ghost town. In 1981, a fierce bush fire blazed through the town and many homes had to be rebuilt.

Zeehan's most renowned daughter was the famous pianist Eileen Joyce who was born here in 1912. She later moved to England to continue her studies and achieved international recognition.

Tin from nearby Renison Bell, the site of a large underground mine which produces a considerable percentage of Australia's ore, has given Zeehan new life as a residential centre. Tourism is also important and there are evocative displays of days gone by in the West Coast Pioneers' Memorial Museum. *Population 1130*

With more than 2000 millimetres of rain a year the Queenstown region boasts Queensland-like rainforest.

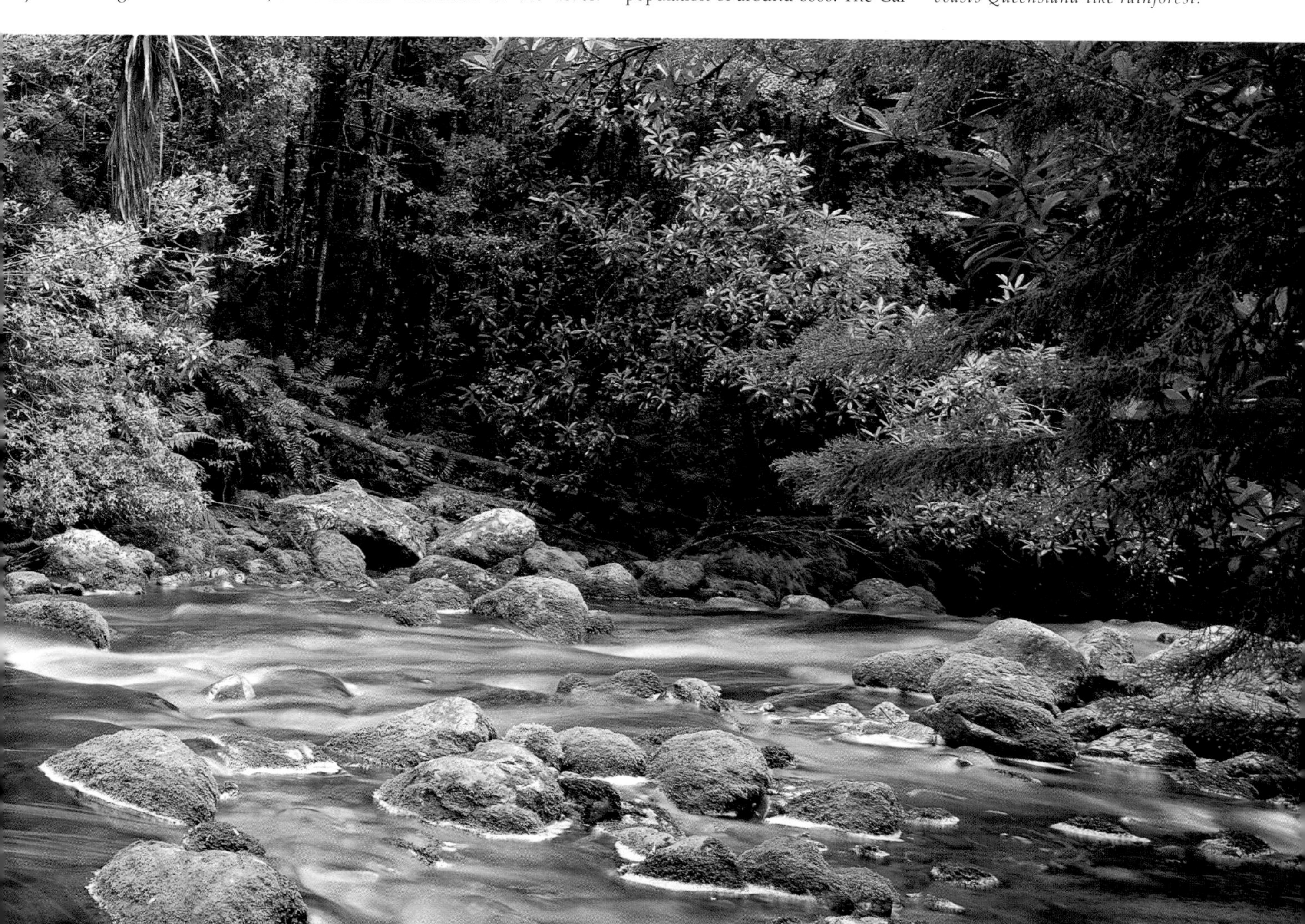

THE WILD SOUTH-WEST

An often inaccessible coastline backed by a hinterland with an equally wild terrain preserves a great natural realm which shrugs off attempts at human intervention.

The gloomy shores of the stormy south-west coast rebuffed all but the most intrepid early seafarers.

Rugged and often swept by storms, in parts almost inaccessible but always breathtakingly beautiful, Tasmania's south-west wilderness has become something of a national heirloom. It is a wild place that has earned the respect of men because it rebuffs their attempts to master it and as such has been granted the right to remain as forged by the elements. Internationally, the south-west takes its place on the World Heritage register because it is recognised as having outstanding natural, cultural and wilderness values.

At more than 600 000 hectares, the Southwest National Park is Tasmania's largest national park. Beyond it is yet another 'wild' area, the 340 000-hectare Southwest Conservation Area. The park's northern boundary loops around the shores of Lake Pedder where it joins the Franklin-Gordon Wild Rivers National Park, which is also generally regarded as an extension of the south-west wilderness. To the east, the park takes in the Arthur Range before closing its borders just beyond windy South East Cape.

It is only in recent years that this remote wilderness could be described as being fully explored. Until the mid-twentieth century there were tracts marked on maps as being 'unknown'. Abel Tasman's sighting of the Tasmanian west and south-west coasts during his voyage of discovery in 1642 signalled the end of 15 000 years of isolated occupation by the island's Aborigines.

The rare orange-bellied parrot breeds in southern Tasmania but flies north to escape the winters.

Almost 150 more years were to pass before Europeans again ventured into the south-west, with the voyages of exploration by the French and British. With British settlement in Tasmania in 1803, attention was again turned to the south-west and the whales waiting to be harvested off its shores. A little later, new settlers discovered what were then vast stands of excellent timber, notably Huon pine, which were cut and shipped to Hobart from the Gordon River and Port Davey.

In those days all transport was by sea around the stormy west and south-west coasts and very little was known about the south-west hinterland. Maps from the 1830s show the south-west marked, with a nervous hint of unease, as 'Transylvania'. The first major settlement in the inhospitable region was the notorious Sarah Island penal colony at Macquarie Harbour, which flourished during the 1820s and 1830s.

The first overland crossings of this wilderness were to provide routes back to civilisation for sailors shipwrecked in the gales of the Roaring Forties. Later there were concerted efforts to find and open up new stands of Huon pine and what were believed to be promising agricultural lands. From the 1840s, Tasmanian governments ordered systematic exploration and surveys. From late in the nineteenth century, major mineral deposits were discovered on the north-west coast and this exploration gradually extended into the south-west wilderness.

Tourism also came to the region with the first Gordon River cruises, while intrepid bushwalkers sought out and began traversing the old tracks cut by the pioneers. In the years following the Second World War, light aircraft provided easy access, bushwalking boomed and the south-west became an international hiking mecca.

It was also an era in which the south-west wilderness came under increasing threat, as pressure built up for hydro-electric development, forestry and mining activity. The first of the major battles, to save Lake Pedder from flooding, was lost, but it created world-wide attention and was the catalyst for the formation of large-scale conservation movements in Australia.

Lake Pedder National Park was the first in the region and it was extended in 1968. It was again extended, in association with declaration of the Franklin–Lower Gordon Wild Rivers National Park, in 1981. Along with other areas of Tasmanian wilderness, the south-west was listed on the World Heritage register in 1982.

The park encompasses much of Tasmania's temperate wilderness, with rugged mountains, dense rainforest, button-grass plains, swift flowing rivers and a rocky, isolated coastline. High peaks predominate, including mounts Anne (1425 metres) and Eliza (1289 metres), Federation Peak (1224 metres), Precipitous Bluff (1120 metres); the ranges, notably the Frankland and Arthur ranges, are particular favourites with experienced walkers and climbers.

Less strenuous sightseeing may be enjoyed by light aircraft from Hobart, Launceston and Strahan. The neighbouring Wild Rivers Park encompasses the Franklin River, the broad reaches of the Gordon, Frenchmans Cap – a striking white quartzite peak, with a sheer cliff face of 300 metres – and rainforest. The Franklin is the domain of the hardiest amateur explorers, with a reputation for providing some of the world's best white-water rafting. Civilisation is left behind here and all people entering the park should register with rangers or police. □

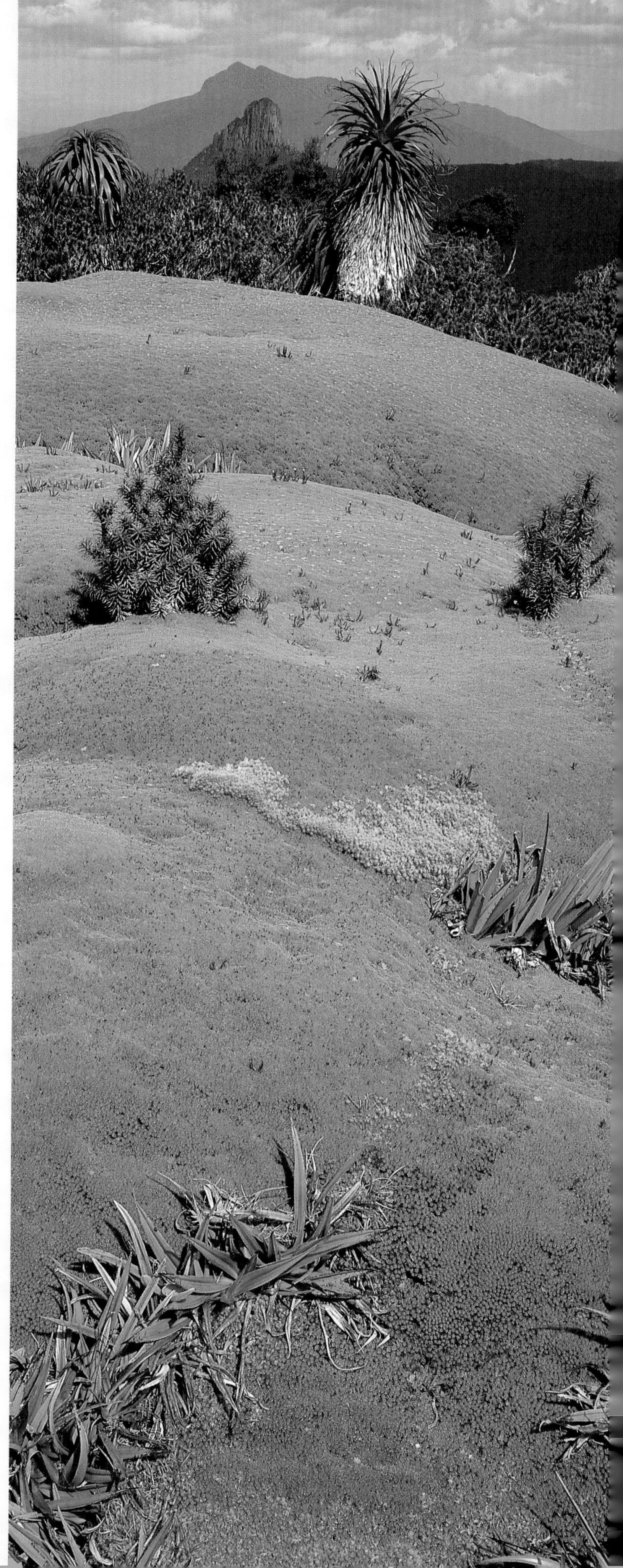

Botanical oddities such as cushion plants and tropical-looking pandani abound in the south-west.

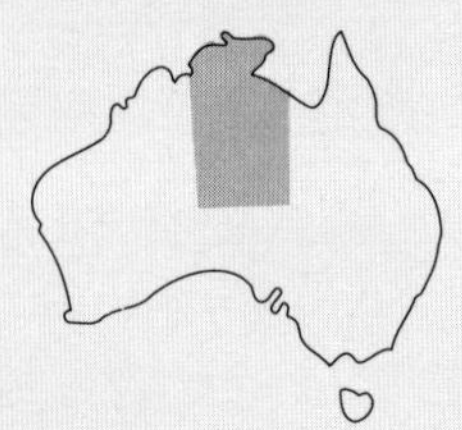

NORTHERN TERRITORY

Despite an uncompromising climate and a small population the Northern Territory – where the extremes of deluge and drought form a divide between the monsoonal 'Top End' and the arid 'Red Centre' – has progressed from a wild frontier to become a self-governing territory well advanced on the path to statehood and the heartland of Aboriginal Australia. Tourists – drawn by the wide, open spaces – and miners have joined pastoralists as the main generators of income.

SPECIAL FEATURES

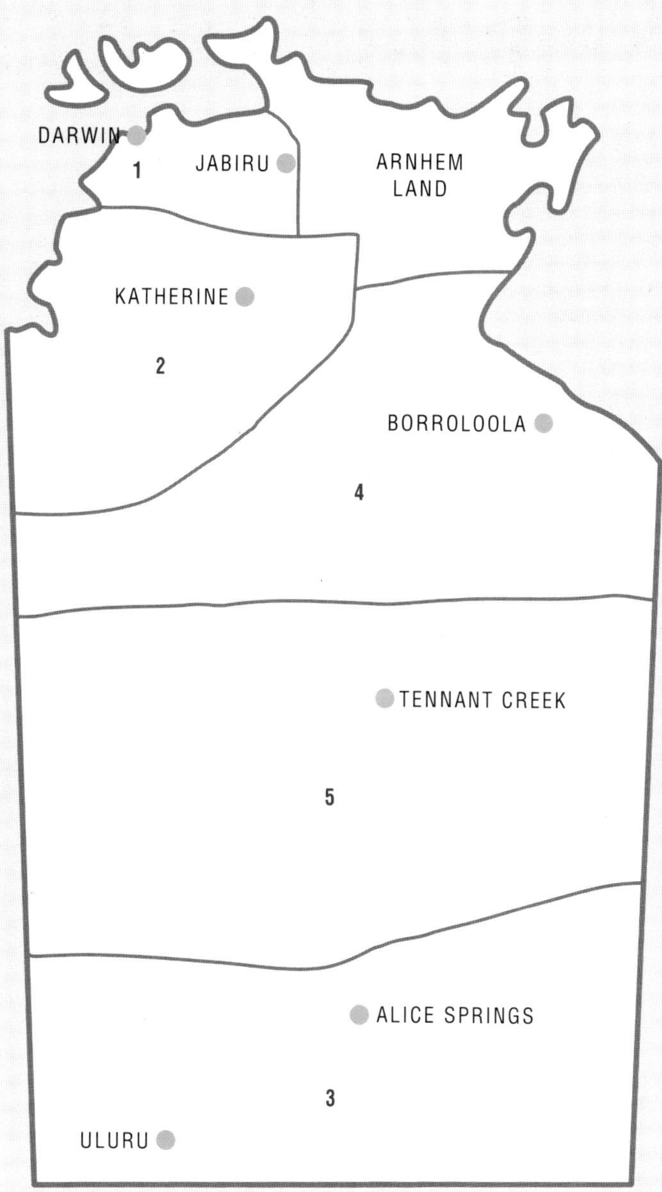

Two of the best known animals of the arid interior are the Northern Territory's emblems: the wedge-tailed eagle and the red kangaroo. Aboriginal motifs, including two sacred carvings, are given prominence on the coat of arms.

DARWIN

At the top of the 'Top End', Darwin is closer to Asia than it is to the cities of Australia's southern half. Its tropical climate and rich mix of races give it an exotic character which makes it difficult to compare the Northern Territory's largest centre with any of the state capitals.

Darwin's latitude is reflected in the drinks on offer at Mindil Beach market; coconut milk is a favourite.

Darwin sits at Australia's northern frontier, the last stop at the top end of 'The Track' – the Stuart Highway – that stretches across the continent's heart from South Australia to the Beagle Gulf. This is the isolated capital of the vast Northern Territory, where the closest large town, Katherine and its 6000 people, is a three-hour drive south, 'down the track'.

Darwin is the administrative centre of a territory that covers one-sixth of Australia but is home to just 144 000 people. Half of them live in Darwin, a multicultural city of more than forty ethnic groups. The city's exotic racial mix is on show at the sunset markets at Mindil Beach, where people set up folding chairs, watch the sun go down, and munch on food such as stuffed squid, laksa – a spicy noodle soup – or ice kachung, a concoction of beans, jelly and ice.

Present-day Darwin dates from 1869 and the first influx of migrants came during the gold rush of the 1880s when Chinese miners came seeking wealth. The Chinese remain the largest non-European ethnic group in modern times. In later years, the Japanese came for pearls, migrants arrived from post-war Europe and refugees from South-East Asia came to settle.

Darwin's modern appearance is not due just to the relatively late date of its founding. The city was bombed during the Second World War and almost completely blown off the map in 1974 during the worst cyclone ever to hit an Australian city. As a result many of the buildings are no more than fifty years old and often no more than twenty. Alongside the highway south of Darwin, a series of airstrips built during the Second World War are still visible and often signposted. Old plane wrecks from the conflict can still be stumbled upon in the bush south of the city.

Approximately 36 000 people were evacuated from Darwin after the 1974 Cyclone Tracy disaster, leaving 11 000 for the massive clean-up operation. Some classic buildings survived, such as the seven-gabled Administrator's Residence, with its colonial air. But there are many more new buildings than old and rental accommodation is often found in what is known locally as 'six-

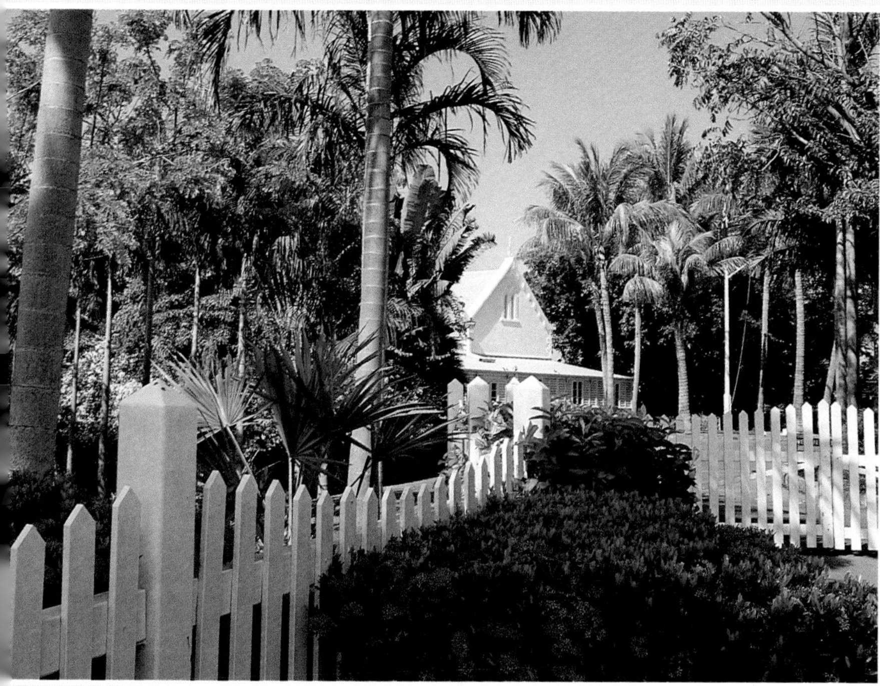

The Administrator's Residence in Darwin grew up around a single-roomed dwelling built in 1870.

packs' – the multi-unit concrete buildings of the 1970s. More interesting designs built to resist cyclone conditions include several international-standard hotels and the Diamond Beach Casino.

These attractions serve a city which is no longer an isolated outpost but has grown significantly as a business centre. The Northern Territory Government has set up a Trade Development Zone in Darwin which allows manufacturers to import raw materials and components with no customs duties, excise or sales tax payable if their products are exported. Despite some teething problems, the scheme has attracted wide interest in the Asia and Pacific region. Tourism is the fastest growing industry, recently overtaking agriculture to become second only to mining in overall economic terms.

Darwin celebrates its uniqueness with a number of attractions and celebrations that can be found nowhere else. An example is the thirty-four hectare Botanical Gardens which have a range of tropical plants – including about four hundred species of palms – unequalled in Australia. The Museum of Arts and Sciences includes a rich display of Aboriginal art and culture while the Cyclone Tracy exhibit at the Fannie Bay Gaol Museum gives a glimpse of devastation and shows how quickly the people regenerated their city. Nature-lovers need walk only a short distance from the city centre to see thousands of fish hand-fed each day at high tide at Doctors Gully. At the nearby Indo-Pacific Marine Exhibition beautiful tropical corals grow in tanks.

The old Darwin of prawn trawlers, buffalo shooters and crocodile hunters is becoming a place of the past but the famed Darwin thirst still exists and is celebrated in the annual Beer Can Regatta, an event matched only by the barefoot Mud Crab Tying Championship for its crazy, 'Top End' eccentricity. □

A view from the north-west shows Darwin's ultra-modern city centre and the greenery of the Esplanade fully recovered from the ravages of Cyclone Tracy. Exotic vessels made from a popular raw material compete in the annual Beer Can Regatta (right).

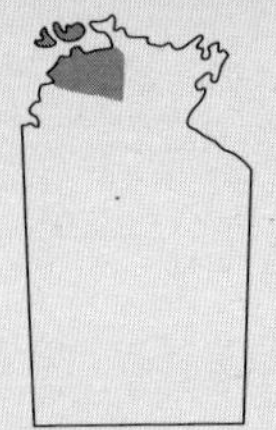

Jabiru & Batchelor

The Top End is a mixture of extremes – an ancient culture and an often raw, primitive landscape with a two-season, wet-dry climate juxtaposed with the totally up-to-the-minute intrusions of mining and tourism with their attendant technology.

ADELAIDE RIVER ■ **2485**
Adelaide River has long been a popular resting place for travellers headed north to Darwin. Before the railway reached the settlement in 1888, goldminers travelling by coach to the goldfields at Pine Creek stopped overnight at Adelaide River, which was located conveniently halfway between Darwin – then known as Palmerston – and Pine Creek. Today, many pleasant picnic areas line the banks of the river which gives the town its name.

Adelaide River was a major military centre during the Second World War and suffered heavy bombing by the Japanese. Nearly 500 servicemen and civilians killed in the Northern Territory and nearby islands during the air raids are buried in the peaceful, beautifully maintained grounds of the town's war memorial cemetery, while the 'Stone of Missing' lists 287 people missing during action. The cemetery is the only one of its kind on mainland Australia.

ADELAIDE RIVER John Lort Stokes of HMS *Beagle* discovered and named the Adelaide River in 1839 – in honour of Queen Adelaide, widow of King William IV – during his survey of the north coast of Australia. The river has long resisted attempts to harness its waters for agricultural uses. An early European settlement at Escape Cliffs, near the river's mouth, failed largely because of the region's remoteness, as did attempts to grow rubber, sugarcane and coffee on the fertile river flats in the 1880s.

During the Second World War, vegetables were successfully cultivated along the Adelaide's banks but the post-war Humpty Doo rice-growing scheme (see entry) was not successful. Now, a CSIRO research station on the middle reaches of the river continues experiments in beef-cattle raising and rice growing.

ALLIGATOR RIVERS ■ **2486**
If Captain Phillip King had known as much about zoology as he knew

When the wet-season rains top up the waters behind the Fogg Dam, the crowded, lush beds of sacred lotus send out flowers on metre-long stems.

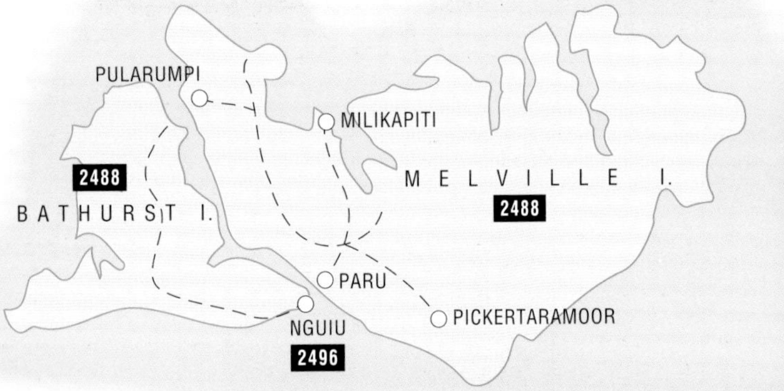

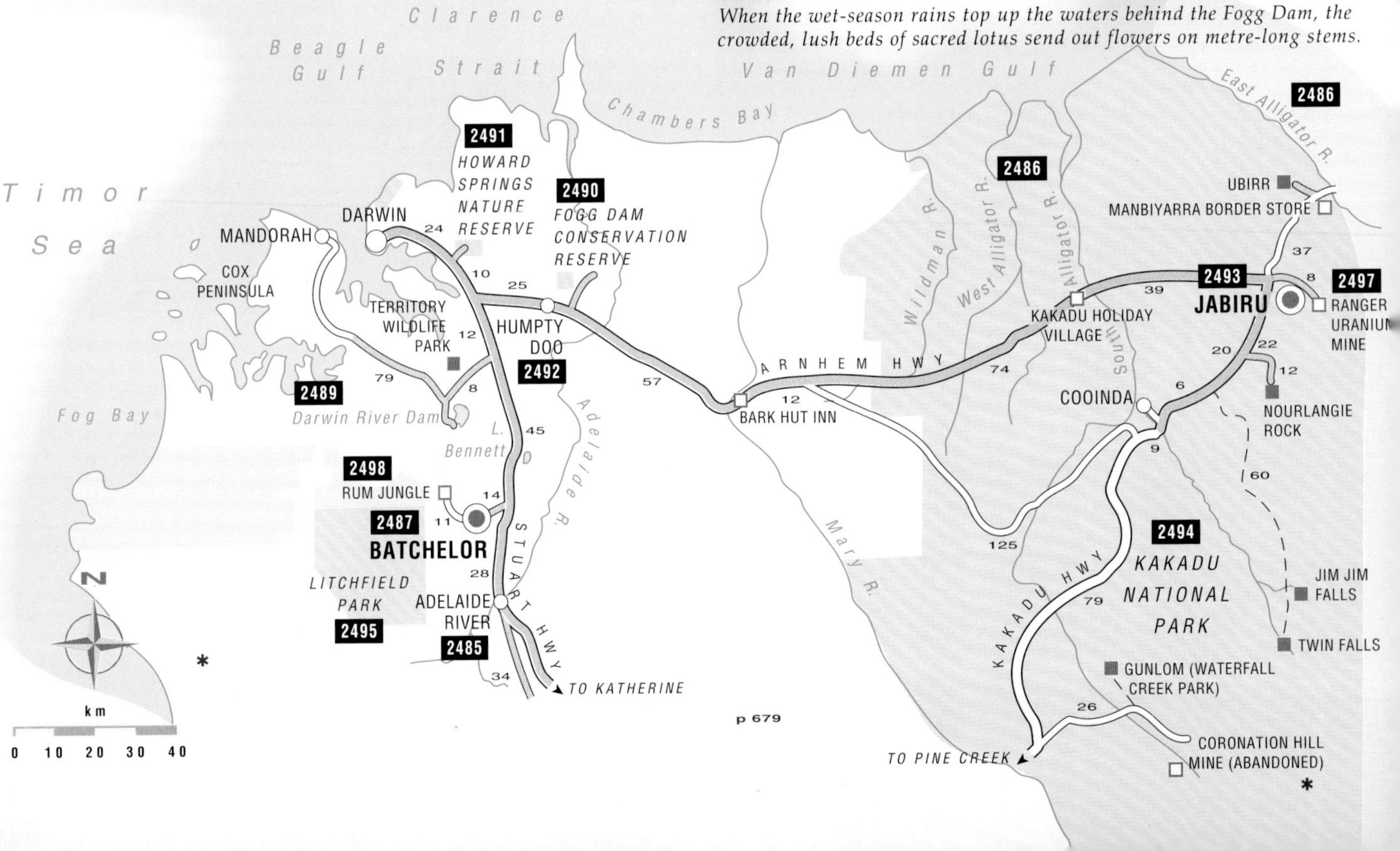

p 679

about surveying, the East, South and West Alligator rivers would probably be known now as the East, South and West Crocodile rivers. It was during his survey of Van Diemen's Gulf in 1818 that King saw hidden in the marshes of the three rivers, the saltwater crocodiles that he mistook for alligators and after which he named the perennial rivers.

The three rivers and the country through which they flow constitute the Alligator Rivers region, a two-and-a-half-million-hectare district of spectacular wilderness east of Darwin. Both the South and East Alligator rivers rise in the ancient sandstone bulk of the Arnhem Land Plateau and flow north-west to the massive 600-kilometre-long escarpment that rises in a rocky sweep from the wooded plains below.

When the heavy rains of the wet season inundate the plateau, the rivers, with their many tributary streams, cascade over the escarpment edge in a series of splendid waterfalls to meander through the lowlands before reaching the floodplains and the mangrove-lined tidal mudflats that fringe the coast – some 160 kilometres from their source.

During the long dry season, the rivers' waters recede from the floodplains into the main river channels and the tributary waterfalls of the plateau escarpment dry up leaving behind only a few permanent waterholes, billabongs and creeks.

Further west, the West Alligator River runs a somewhat less spectacular course, rising in the lowlands and flowing for eighty kilometres to the sea. The South Alligator River, lying between the East and West Alligator rivers, has a reputation for being a particularly fine river for anglers after the prized barramundi.

BATCHELOR ■ 2487

Batchelor was first settled in the late nineteenth century when the South Australian Government – then administering the central strip of the continent – distributed parcels of land for agriculture. The town is named after a South Australian and federal politician, Egerton Batchelor.

In the years leading up to the Second World War, Batchelor witnessed a variety of settlers and activities – Chinese market gardeners, small-scale tin and copper mining and a government experimental farm that was established in 1912. During the war, the town became an important Allied air force base and was bombed by the Japanese.

Batchelor really came to prominence in the early 1950s when a prospector called Jack White found uranium deposits at nearby Rum Jungle (see entry) and triggered the growth of a huge new mineral industry. Mining started in 1951 and a modern township was built at Batchelor in 1954 to house the mine workers. When the mine closed in 1963, stockpiles of ore continued to be treated at the plant until 1971 and since then this pleasant town with its poinciana- and bougainvillea-studded gardens has managed to endure without the stimulus of mining.

An export abattoir opened in 1972 and this industry, along with horticulture, aviation and education – this is the site of a multi-purpose Aboriginal tertiary institution – ensures the town's prosperity. Tourism is also important – the town is a short distance from Litchfield National Park (see entry). *Population 630*

BATHURST AND MELVILLE ISLANDS ■ 2488

Both Bathurst and Melville islands are owned by the Tiwi people, the occupants of these and smaller surrounding islands prior to European settlement in the early nineteenth century. The eighty-kilometre stretch of sea that separates the islands from mainland Australia left the Tiwi in splendid isolation for thousands of years, with the result that they have a substantially uniform language and culture that is quite distinct from that of Aborigines on the mainland.

The Dutch navigator Abel Tasman was the first European to sight the islands in 1644, though he and subsequent seventeenth-century Dutch explorers overlooked the narrow Apsley Strait that divides the two islands, assuming they were one land mass.

The British established the military outpost of Fort Dundas on Melville Island in 1824 – the first European settlement in northern Australia and almost inevitably doomed to failure. The monsoonal climate, disease, and opposition from the Tiwi people, whose land the soldiers had occupied, led to the abandonment of the settlement in 1829.

Legislation passed in the 1970s saw the ownership and control of both Melville and Bathurst islands returned to the traditional owners – the Tiwi – in 1978. Now, the four main settlements – Pirnupe (Garden Point), Milikapati (Snake Bay), Paru and Pickataramoor on Melville Island and Nguiu (see entry) on Bathurst Island – are increasingly popular tourist destinations as visitors from the mainland come to view the distinctive Tiwi arts and crafts.

On grand-final day, Australian Rules supporters at Melville Island can be just as enthusiastic as their counterparts at the Melbourne Cricket Ground.

A daredevil aviator zooms in for a close-up look at the post-wet season Twin Falls as they burst out of the confines of the Arnhem Land Plateau.

DARWIN RIVER DAM ■ 2489

The Darwin River Dam was completed in 1972 to supplement Darwin's principal water supply – Manton Dam – which no longer had the capacity to service the growing city's needs. The earth and rockfill dam has a capacity of nearly eleven times that of Manton Dam.

The dam's construction program was quite a show – in the process of clearing the soon-to-be flooded area to prevent rotting vegetation from contaminating the water supply, 3650 hectares of scrubland became a temporary battlefield as incendiary bombs dropped from an aircraft set the region ablaze with a smoke plume rising to 5500 metres.

FOGG DAM CONSERVATION RESERVE ■ 2490

Fogg Dam Conservation Reserve is a man-made, wetland habitat noted for its abundance of wildlife, particularly water birds, and its spectacular water plants which flower during the wet season. The dam, built in the late 1950s, was originally intended to provide water for an unsuccessful experimental rice farm at nearby Humpty Doo (see entry).

HOWARD SPRINGS NATURE RESERVE ■ 2491

A beautiful spring-fed swimming pool surrounded by a mixture of monsoon rainforest and open woodlands, with picnic areas and a shop and restaurant is one of the chief attractions of this 1009-hectare nature reserve.

William Auld was the first European to discover and name the Howard River in 1865, though the pool itself did not become known officially as Howard Springs until around 1936. The reserve's weir was built during the Second World War

MINE REGENERATION: HEALING OLD WOUNDS

THE OLD ADAGE 'don't soil your own nest' is an apt way of summarising the Northern Territory Government's increasingly enlightened approach to its management of natural resources and environmental protection.

Rum Jungle recovered: landscaping, replanting and the introduction of a lake has erased the scars of mining at the old uranium mine site.

In the territory's Top End a team of environmental 'plastic surgeons' is reconstructing the partially damaged, but still beautiful face of Kakadu National Park. Along with miners and engineers, the Ranger Uranium Mine employs environmental scientists and specialist consultants in order to see that its nest is not soiled.

Instead of the medical doctor's Hippocratic oath, their code of ethics involves the two underlying principles regarding pollution and degradation of the environment: ALARA – as low as reasonably achievable – and BPT – best practicable technology – the objective of the former achieved by the application of the latter.

In recent years, the onus has been placed on the Australian mining industry to restore mined areas to a condition comparable to that in which the land was first found. At Ranger, the rehabilitated land must meet the detailed conditions set down by two independent authorities as well as those of the land's Aboriginal owners – an arrangement that has existed since mining operations commenced in the park in 1979. The great number of 'watchdogs' guarding this World Heritage region makes Ranger one of the most highly regulated and intensively studied mines in the world.

When mining finishes, Ranger will be restored to blend with its open woodland surrounds, a self-sustaining ecosystem made up of local plants and animals, and created in accordance with the traditional owners' wishes for long-term land management. A massive trust fund of more than fifty million dollars is held by the Commonwealth Government as a rehabilitation guarantee.

Ranger's rehabilitation program is based on the assumption that an understanding of the physical, chemical and biological characteristics of the region is essential for formulating long-term procedures. The program incorporates extensive research and monitoring of water quality and flows, seepage control, the disposal of tailings (finely ground waste), air quality and dust concentrations, radioactivity emissions, as well as meteorological and biological observations such as toxicity testing and monitoring of birds and fish.

Every year native seeds are gathered and cultivated at the mine nursery for use as natural wetland filters and in landscaping. Disturbed areas are stabilised with matting and vegetation to protect against erosion, wildfire-prone sites undergo controlled burning, and irrigation and a hydro-mulch spray – a potent organic mixture of seed, fertiliser, pulped cardboard boxes and water – helps to green barren stretches of land. A constant war of eradication is waged on weeds and feral animals that damage the region's vegetation and waterways.

One of the first experiments in the new landscaping science of regeneration took place at the old Rum Jungle uranium mine (see entry) where the site has been transformed into a community recreation area, the great hole of the open cut now a pleasant lake and the scarred surrounds undergoing 'greening' with native tree planting and the reintroduction of native wildlife. □

to supplement Darwin's water supply (see Darwin River Dam).

HUMPTY DOO ■ 2492

Exactly how Humpty Doo came by its whimsical name is uncertain, but one local explanation has it that when the first white settler here made occasional trips to Darwin for supplies, he would reply 'Everything's humpty doo!' when asked how things were.

Humpty Doo came to national prominence in the 1950s when it became the site of an experimental rice farm. A joint Australian–American company received agricultural rights over 303 000 hectares in 1955 and 1956. But the project failed, dogged by the same problems – wild geese, buffalo, rats and alternate flooding and draining of the fields – that had defeated the Chinese farmers who had attempted to grow rice in the same area during the 1870s. The company forfeited the land to the government in 1962. Now, an agricultural research station occupies most of the area once taken up by the rice farm and speculation about the viability of growing rice in the region continues.

JABIRU ■ 2493

Jabiru is one of four major mining settlements in the Northern Territory and the centre for the uranium mines of the East Alligator River basin. The township was built in 1981 on a thirteen-square-kilometre lease within Kakadu National Park (see entry), and named after Australia's only native stork, which inhabits the waterways of the park.

Like many other mining centres, Jabiru is a brand-new, shiny presence in an ancient land, having been developed by the Northern Territory Government in three short years for the purpose of housing the workers and families of three uranium mines – Ranger, Jabiluka and Koongarra.

Apart from providing housing for the mine's workers and essential services such as shopping, medical and educational centres, Jabiru has an olympic swimming pool, an artificial lake and a luxury motel in the shape of an enormous crocodile. The town's location in Kakadu National Park has elevated the mining settlement to the status of a tourist centre.

Population 1730

FESTIVALS Jabiru Wind Festival, late August.

KAKADU NATIONAL PARK ■ 2494

Kakadu is the king among Australia's national parks – the 'jewel in the Top-End crown' is one description where the tourist brochure hyperbole gets it right. The park protects a large part of one of the nation's most ecologically complex regions.

Kakadu covers nearly 20 000 square kilometres of the Alligator Rivers Region (see entry), making it Australia's largest national park. The park is unique in encompassing almost the entire drainage basin of one major river – the South Alligator River – and within this wilderness are found most of the major habitat types of the Top End as well as a vast range of plants and animals. Kakadu is also one of the few places where descendants of the original Aboriginal inhabitants still maintain close physical and spiritual links with the land, sustaining a culture that dates back at least 25 000 years.

Controversy has raged sporadically over Kakadu ever since the idea of a national park for the Top End was broached by the Northern Territory Reserve Board in 1965. Aside from its ecological and cultural wealth, the park is the repository of rich reserves of uranium as well as other valuab minerals and a constant tug-of-war between preservation and exploitation has been a feature of its history (see box).

The park is jointly controlled by the traditional Aboriginal owners – most of whom are members of the Gagudju Association – and the Australian National Parks and Wildlife Service. In 1978, the Aboriginal owners agreed to lease the park to the service for ninety-nine years.

The only mining activity within the park takes place at the Ranger Uranium Mine (see entry). Development of other nearby ore bodies within the park – the Jabiluka and Koongarra mineral leases – depends upon the Commonwealth Government's uranium policy.

Aboriginal rock art found here spans more than 20 000 years and includes paintings of nineteenth-century Macassan boats, distinctive x-ray art that shows the internal features of animals as well as the conventional outline, European tall ships, and 'blue' art dating from the 1930s when the Aborigines inventively included Reckitt's Blue on their traditional palette.

Kakadu's main physical feature is the 600-kilometre-long sandstone escarpment that erupts from the woodlands to form the edge of the ancient Arnhem Land Plateau. Massive rocky outliers stud the plain below the escarpment – remnants of the eroded plateau which retreats from the plain at an estimated metre every 1000 years.

Kakadu is monsoon territory, subject to the extremes of a wet and dry season. During the 'wet' – November to March – when the park receives most of its 1400-millimetre average annual rainfall, water runs off the plateau, spilling over the escarpment in an array of spectacular waterfalls. During these months the floodplains become huge freshwater wetlands, a refuge for an enormous number and variety of migratory birds such as magpie geese, brolgas and jabirus.

The 'dry' – from May to September – brings a drop in humidity and temperature to a bearable average maximum of 30° Centigrade. This is the time when most visitors flock to the park. Waterfalls dry up, the waters of the floodplains recede to permanent rivers and billabongs and the main rivers are still.

The Aborigines have a more subtle appreciation of the seasons than Europeans: they recognise an annual cycle of at least six seasons, identifiable by the behaviour of particular plants and animals.

CORONATION HILL Coronation Hill, in the South Alligator River Valley, is the site of a controversial uranium mine and treatment plant that opened in 1956 and closed a few years later after it was mined out. It was the subject of one of the Top End's recent mining-versus-conservation debates, which resulted in the Commonwealth Government's 1991 decision to reject a proposal to reopen the mine for the extraction of gold, platinum and palladium. Now the old mine site and surrounding Conservation Zone is protected as part of Kakadu National Park.

Kakadu is two landscapes: the harsh plateau catchment area beyond the escarpment and the lushly vegetated wetlands below that run down to the sea, irrigated by its wet-season run-off to sustain huge colonies of water birds like the jabiru.

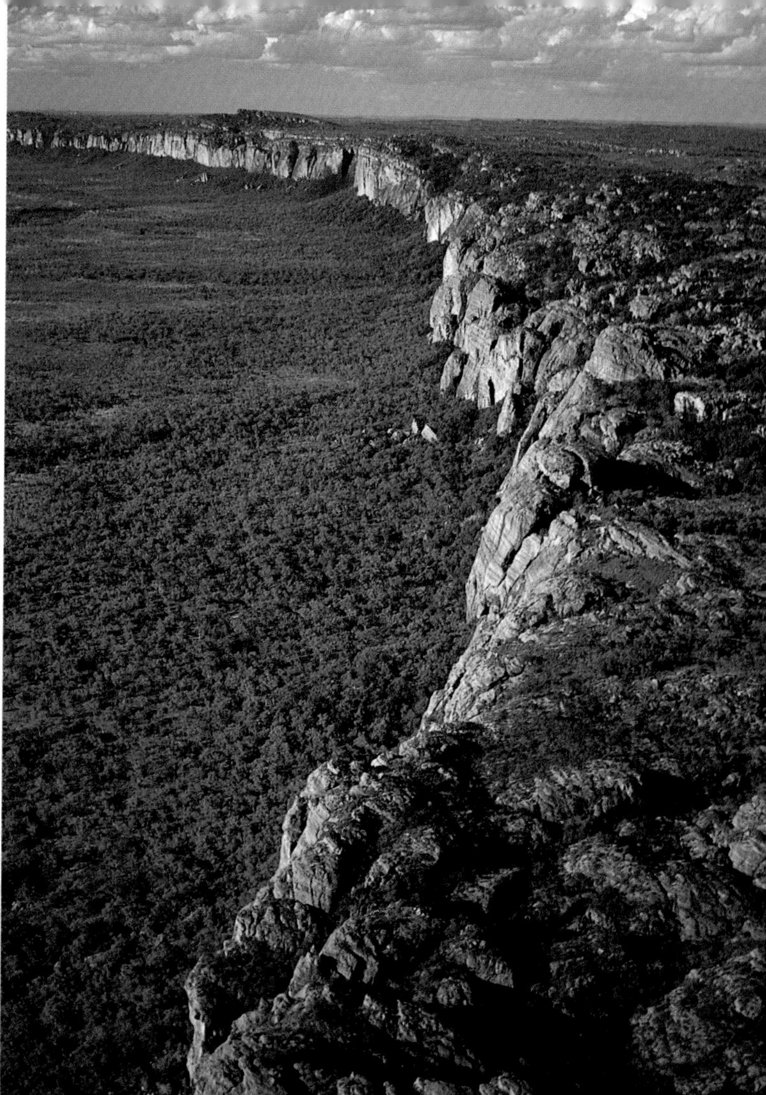

LITCHFIELD PARK ■ 2495

Litchfield Park, west of Batchelor (see entry) in the Tabletop Range, is a huge sandstone plateau cloaked with dry woodlands and forests. Close to the edge of the escarpment, springs bubble into creeks that have their ultimate destination within the rainforested valleys below. These creeks cascade over the escarpment in spectacular waterfalls, most notable of which are the Wangi, Florence, Tolmer and Sandy Creek falls, which flow throughout the year, spilling into crystal clear pools surrounded by lush rainforest.

Parts of the park are accessible in the dry season by two-wheel-drive tracks, while Sandy Creek Falls and the Lost City – an area of fantastic sandstone formations – are at the end of four-wheel-drive tracks.

NGUIU ■ 2496

Aside from its educative and religious functions, the Roman Catholic mission established at Nguiu on Bathurst Island (see entry) in 1911 has exerted a tremendous economic influence on the indigenous Tiwi people. Originally known simply as Bathurst Island Mission, the town was given its Tiwi name in 1974.

Nguiu is home to almost all the island's population, the place where its successful art–business ventures – all founded as part of the mission activities – are based.

The mission's role in running all important economic activities was greatly reduced in the 1970s with Tiwi-controlled organisations developing to take on many of the roles previously performed by the mission. The Tiwi people's gradual reclamation of autonomy was further enhanced in 1978 when the formal title of the island was transferred from the Crown to the Tiwi Land Council. Nowadays, Nguiu has taken on an increasingly touristic role as visitors come to see the range of art and crafts for which the Tiwi people are renowned. *Population 1050*

RANGER URANIUM MINE ■ 2497

The Ranger Uranium Mine, covering an area of approximately five square kilometres, lies, rather contentiously, in the Alligator Rivers Region within the boundaries of Kakadu National Park (see entry).

The mine site is part of seventy-nine square kilometres of leasehold land owned by the people of the Mirrar Gundjeibmi clan. It is the only uranium mill–mine in the Northern Territory and produces an average of 1300 tonnes of uranium oxide each year. In ten years it has generated more than three and a half billion dollars in export revenue. The mines' employees live in the nearby company town of Jabiru.

As a result of a government inquiry in 1975, the Commonwealth Government issued the mine's operators with an authority to mine in 1978, following which an agreement was reached with the land's traditional Aboriginal owners represented by the Northern Lands Council and mining operations commenced in 1981. Despite the mine's high level of environmental regulation, the issue of mining-versus-environment still simmers as a sometimes contentious subject of public debate (see box).

RUM JUNGLE ■ 2498

Uranium was first discovered in Australia in 1886 in the South Alligator River area but was not identified until 1950, a year after a prospector, Jack White, earned a 25 000 pounds sterling reward from the Commonwealth Government for his discovery of the Rum Jungle deposits.

The Federal Government offered incentives to private prospectors in the form of cash rewards – 1000 pounds sterling for every new discovery of uranium at Rum Jungle and double that amount for every tonne of extracted ore, with a limit of 25 000 pounds sterling.

Uranium was mined at Rum Jungle on behalf of the Commonwealth Government for twelve years from 1951. The old Rum Jungle uranium mine site has now been transformed into a pleasant recreation area, the great open-cut scar filled with water to form an artificial lake.

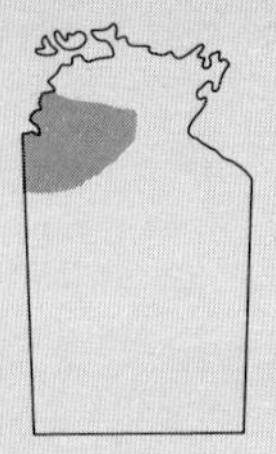

Katherine & Pine Creek

In a land where the European storybook 'Never-Never' has been cast into history by the advances of technology, tourism and Aboriginal land rights, visitors come to gaze at the walls of gorges which have been used as art 'galleries' for thousands of years.

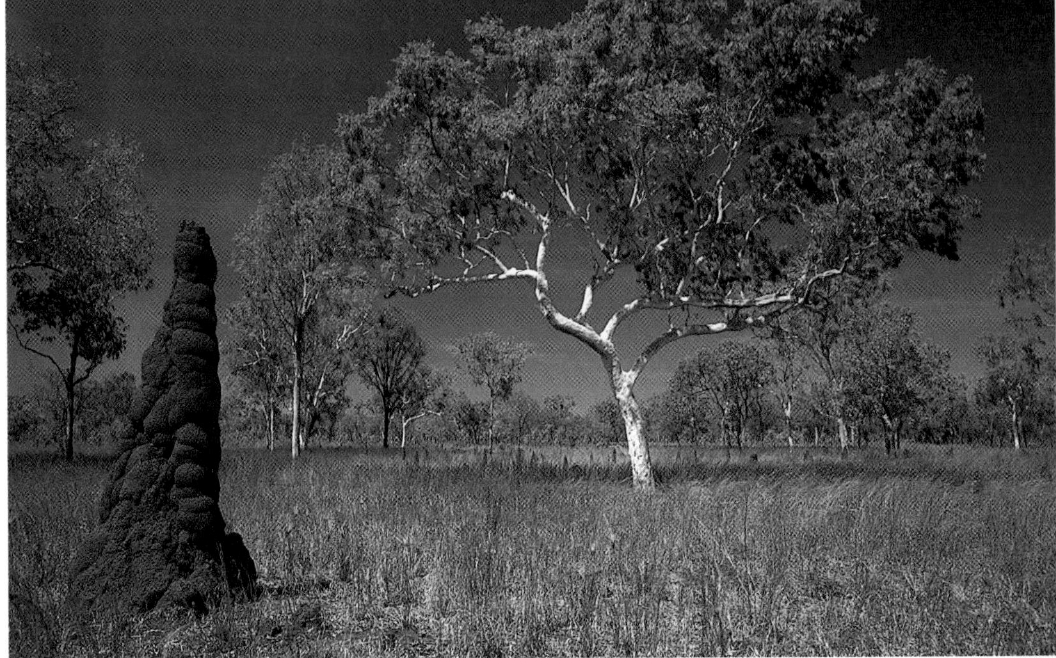

South of Katherine, ghost gums and termite nests are the only objects capable of rising above speargrass height.

CUTTA CUTTA CAVES NATURE PARK ■ 2499

Within this 1500-hectare park there are 500-million-year-old weathered limestone formations with weirdly shaped towers and a series of caves fifteen metres below the ground. The usual formations common in wetter and clammier caves can be found at Cutta Cutta but these tropical caves have limited seepage and are warm and mild all year round. But wet season rains do occasionally flood the caves, forcing the bat residents to temporarily relocate their quarters.

ELSEY CEMETERY ■ 2500

There were already five European graves in the old cemetery at Elsey Station before Aeneas Gunn, husband of Jeannie Gunn, the author of *We of the Never Never*, was buried there in 1903. The Gunns spent only thirteen months at Elsey Station before Aeneas Gunn's death from malaria and his wife's return to Melbourne. *We of the Never Never*, which chronicled life in the outback, was published in 1908 and became an Australian classic.

ELSEY NATIONAL PARK ■ 2501

One of the Northern Territory's most recently developed parks takes in almost 14 000 hectares of the headwaters of the Roper River and includes some pockets of rainforest and pandanus palms. The river passes through limestone and picks up calcium carbonate, which is carried in the water and deposited in natural dams around a number of springs.

But it is a thermal pool on the Waterhouse River that is the best known feature of Elsey National Park. Aborigines have been bathing in the warm waters of Mataranka thermal pool, surrounded by tall pandanus and cabbage tree palms, for thousands of years and it was protected within its own reserve from 1967, before becoming part of the new national park.

GREGORY NATIONAL PARK ■ 2502

This relatively new national park in the Victoria River region is named after Augustus Gregory who, with six companions, explored the river in 1855–56 and a tree on the boundary of the national park was inscribed by him (see sub-entry).

The Victoria River district contains some of Australia's largest and most significant Aboriginal cave paintings. Many engraving and art sites are now within the park as are ancient ovens, stone and ochre quarries, stone arrangements and hawk traps dating back thousands of years. The rock art depicts snakes, crocodiles, fish and mammals and humans, including Europeans and their cattle.

In the transitional zone between semi-arid and tropical, Gregory National Park has spectacular ranges and gorges. The Newcastle and Stokes ranges within the park rise to 300 metres above the plain. Of the gorges, the largest are Victoria River Gorge and Jasper Gorge whose waterfalls tumble 100 metres over cliff faces after the monsoon rains.

KATHERINE ■ 2503

The first Europeans in the district around Katherine were Ludwig Leichhardt who passed through in 1844 and John McDouall Stuart who named the Katherine River when he crossed it on his epic south-to-north crossing in 1862.

The first settlement on the Katherine River was at Knotts Crossing where the 1871 telegraph line ran across the river on tall pylons and where Frank and Kate Knott had a store with a licence to sell alcohol by the gallon. By 1902, when Jeannie Gunn passed through on her way to Elsey Station, the Sportsman's Arms had been established and according to her 'the Katherine settlement' consisted exclusively of the pub which 'seemed to be hanging on to its verandah posts for support'.

The railway superseded the telegraph line as the town focus and in 1917 a new but temporary settlement sprang up at the Emungalan railhead. The station was used as the school except on the one day a fortnight when the train came through. Katherine has been mainly a cattle centre but tropical fruit has been grown successfully and in recent years tourism and a RAAF base have been the town's major employers.

The base is the main tactical fighter base in northern Australia. The arrival of 75 Squadron brought hundreds of air-force personnel and their families to Katherine. *Population 7060*

FESTIVALS Katherine and District Show, July.

KEEP RIVER NATIONAL PARK ■ 2504

Keep River National Park, close to the Northern Territory–Western Australia borders is named after the Keep River which flows from coastal floodplains and mangrove swamps through sandstone gorges and open forest...but only in the wet season. In the dry season, it is possible to walk along the floor of the four-kilometre-long Keep River Gorge to view the Aboriginal art on the gorge walls.

There are many art sites in rock shelters and caverns used by the Miriwun people. One of these, in an outcrop with a huge archway made by the nose of Nganalang, the white cockatoo, is open to the public. The paintings and stencils are distinctive in style, vivid in colour and include a twenty-four-metre red, yellow and white snake, one of the longest paintings in Australia.

NITMILUK (KATHERINE GORGE) NATIONAL PARK ■ 2505

Most of those who visit Nitmiluk National Park, see only the first tw

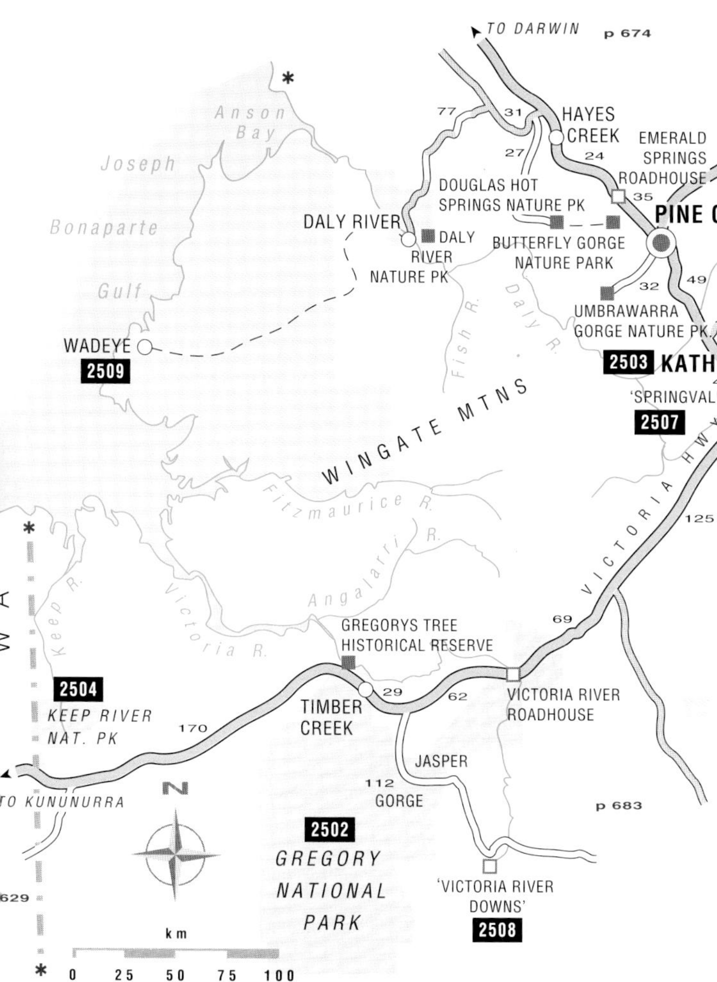

A timeless landscape meets modern technology in the form of Hornet jets at Katherine's RAAF base.

Elsey National Park contains the storybook oasis of the Mataranka thermal pool where the water has to cool down before travellers can cool off.

of the thirteen gorges gouged out of the sandstone of the Arnhem Plateau by the Katherine River twenty-five million years ago. In the dry season, the gorges are calm, clear and separated from each other by heaps of boulders, which prevent boats from continuing further up the eleven-kilometre stretch of river.

The first gorge passes through wooded hills which contrast sharply with the towering sandstone cliffs in the second gorge. In the wet season, when the river becomes a raging torrent, with whirlpools and waves sometimes up to two metres high breaking over the boulders between gorges, the water level may rise eighteen metres up the gorge walls.

Along the walls of the steep gorges and in the shelter of overhangs are Aboriginal paintings, ranging from larger-than-life human figures to crocodiles. This cultural heritage was returned to the Jawoyn people in 1988 and has since been leased back to the Northern Territory Government as a park.

PINE CREEK ■ 2506

It was a surveyor for the Overland Telegraph line who named the creek on which this settlement stands but it was the telegraph pole-hole diggers who came behind him who discovered the gold around the creek in 1872. Men and mining equipment arrived by ship in Darwin then made the overland journey to the fifteen mines in and around Pine Creek until the late 1880s when Pine Creek became the terminus for the North Australian Railway. The line was built largely by Chinese labour and scenes depicting the building of the railway appear in Aboriginal paintings in the district.

The railway closed in 1976 but the old railway complex remains and the station was used in the filming of *We of the Never Never* in 1981.

The opening of a large, open-cut gold mine at Pine Creek in 1985 has brought the town from oblivion. The six-metre-high anthills that greet approaching travellers are complemented by the man-made hills of the mine waste heaps.

'SPRINGVALE' ■ 2507

Springvale was the second station to be established in the Northern Territory and its homestead is the oldest still standing. Leased in 1876 by Dr W.J. Browne – brother of John Browne who accompanied Charles Sturt on his expeditions in the continent's south-east as medical adviser – Springvale was managed for many years by Alfred Giles who made an epic overland journey from Adelaide with stock for the station in 1878.

Giles and his party of forty men left Adelaide with 2000 cattle, 12 000 sheep, 300 thoroughbred horses, 'a score of good bulls and ninety brood mares'. On the nineteen-month journey, following the telegraph line, they even managed to shear some of the sheep and send back 200 bales of wool. The station's homestead and fortified barn with its commanding view and rifle slits in case of an Aboriginal attack are part of a tourist park where the Jawoyn people explain the region's history to visitors.

'VICTORIA RIVER DOWNS' ■ 2508

Established in 1883, Victoria River Downs – 'The Big Run' – once covered over 30 000 square kilometres and was the largest cattle station in the world. Now reduced to a mere 12 359 square kilometres, Victoria River Downs employs a fraction of the number who lived and worked there until the early 1970s when the station's Aborigines left to join those from Wave Hill Station in the campaign for land rights (see box).

Transport was a problem until the 1930s with no railway until 1929 and only rough tracks through to the station – it was on one of his mail trips to Victoria River Downs that Harry Peckham, the mailman immortalised in *We of the Never Never,* drowned in the Victoria River.

In its peak years, Victoria River Downs had a police station, an open-air cinema, a post office, workshops, and a number of houses for managers and employees, which together with the airstrip, now used by the mustering helicopters, gave the station the look of a small town.

WADEYE ■ 2509

This Aboriginal community, the largest and one of the oldest established in the region, officially gained freehold title to what had been the Port Keats Catholic Mission and the Daly River Reserve in 1976. The Aboriginal Land Rights (NT) Act granted control of the settlement at Wadeye to an Aboriginal Land Trust.

That there was abundant water and game on this coastal land was known to the Malag Malag people long before the arrival of whites and European influence on the Aboriginal community has been brief and largely irrelevant.

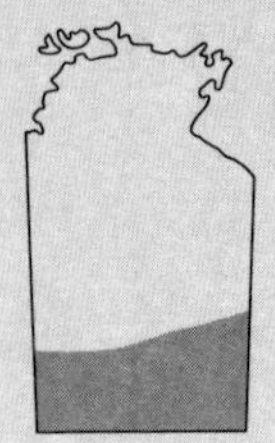

Alice Springs & Yulara

The red heart of Australia boasts a landscape of harsh, worn, rocky outcrops and narrow, shadowed gorges that has inspired many legends of the Dreamtime. They remain an inspiration to travellers who, in an age of resort accommodation, can afford to be a little less intrepid than last century's explorers.

Despite influences such as tourism, Territory Aborigines, like these Yuendumu men in ceremonial garb, vigorously maintain their traditional culture.

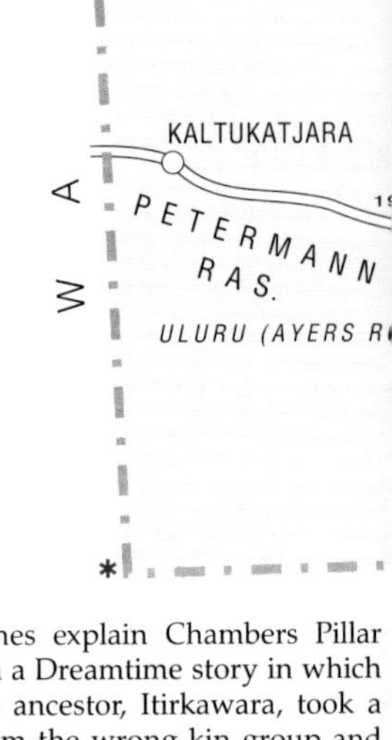

ALICE SPRINGS ■ 2510

John McDouall Stuart passed fifty kilometres west of where Alice Springs now stands on his great trek north in 1860. The site of the town was discovered by William Whitfield Mills in 1871 and in 1888 was surveyed and gazetted as 'Stuart' as a tribute to the explorer. When the original telegraph station (see subentry) was transferred to the town, its name came with it.

The 'Alice', located almost in the very centre of Australia, symbolises the traditional 'Red Centre' of the outback more than any other town. The 1950 novel by Neville Shute – made into a film and later a television mini-series – made a wide audience aware of the 'town like Alice'. Shute's image of rough and ready outback life persists, though the population of modern Alice Springs has increased more than fivefold since the 1960s and the town is modern and well maintained.

Though tourism is an important industry, the economy is also based on cattle, transport and communications and mining for gas, oil and gold. There is an export trade with Middle Eastern countries in camels and an enterprising former chemist has established a flourishing aridland vineyard.

The Royal Flying Doctor Service (see box, *Mount Isa & Cloncurry*) has a major base at Alice Springs and schoolchildren in the outlying districts do their lessons from the largest classroom in the world – by radio and correspondence course supervised by the South Australian Department of Education.

The annual Henley-on-Todd Regatta shows the local people's delight in the ridiculous, as teams race in bottomless boats, leg-propelled down the dry bed of the river. The Alice Springs Rodeo is one of the most highly regarded on the Australian roughriders' circuit and offers large sums in prize money. The third big day, the Lions Camel Cup Carnival, is also held in the Todd River bed and is a riotous event which has its origins in the spontaneous camel races which provided sport for the early cameleers. *Population 20 450*

TELEGRAPH STATION RESERVE The overland telegraph line across central Australia was designed to relay news from Adelaide to Darwin and from there on to London. The Morse keys tapped out messages in hours, where once it had taken months to send them by sea. The line was established in the 1870s and created a need for an Alice Springs settlement. Sir Charles Heavitree Todd, Postmaster-General of South Australia, was responsible for the construction of the line and his staff chose this place for a repeater station near springs on the Todd River and named it Alice Springs in honour of his wife. The Telegraph Station operated for over sixty years until the site became a school for Aboriginal children in 1932. A number of the early stone buildings have been restored and lie within a reserve.

EMILY AND JESSIE GAPS NATURE PARK This 695-hectare park enclosing two semi-permanent waterholes is readily accessible from Alice Springs along a track suitable for bicycles. Emily Gap, about ten kilometres east of Alice Springs, has one wall decorated with tall, caterpillar-like figures in vertical red and yellow stripes.

EWANINGA ROCK CARVINGS These ancient rock engravings are of complex designs so old that they are not recognised by the present-day Aborigines. They are protected in a reserve south of Alice Springs.

FESTIVALS Camel Cup Carnival, May; Alice Springs Rodeo, August; Henley-on-Todd Regatta, October.

ARLTUNGA HISTORICAL RESERVE ■ 2511

Arltunga is the site of an old mining town where gold was found in 1887 by a camel driver and his mate. There are ruins of old buildings, a restored jail and abandoned mining paraphernalia to give visitors a fragmented impression of what life must have been like in this isolated place. At its height, the area supported about 400 people and all their necessities of life had to be brought from the railhead at Oodnadatta – a journey of 650 kilometres. A number of miners later took up pastoral leases in the East MacDonnell Ranges district and some of their descendants still work these properties.

CHAMBERS PILLAR HISTORICAL RESERVE ■ 2512

This solitary sandstone column is all that remains of hills which have been gradually eroded over millions of years. It rises more than thirty metres above a twenty-five-metre-high pile of rubble. John McDouall Stuart sighted the pillar in 1860 on his first attempt to cross Australia and named it for one of his patrons. Aborigines explain Chambers Pillar through a Dreamtime story in which a gecko ancestor, Itirkawara, took a wife from the wrong kin group and was banished. He turned into the pillar while his shamed wife became Castle Rock, a low hill about 500 metres to the north-east.

FINKE GORGE NATIONAL PARK ■ 2513

The 46 000-hectare Finke Gorge National Park boasts dramatic gorge and river scenery and contains the world's only naturally occurring red cabbage palms which are most easily seen at Palm Valley oasis. The 3000 trees have taken several hundred years to grow to their present height and the species has been here for at least 10 000 years. The Finke River is one of the oldest watercourses in the world and once formed a major Aboriginal trade route. Its few nearly permanent waterholes and soaks are an emergency supply for fish and water birds in times of prolonged drought; heavy rain, though infrequent, makes the area inaccessible.

HENBURY METEORITE CRATERS CONSERVATION RESERVE ■ 2514

The land round Alice Springs is full of unusual formations. The Henbury meteorite craters lie approximately 130 kilometres to the south along an unmade road off the Stuart Highway in a conservation reserve. They are believed to have been formed when a single meteor weighing several tonnes and travelling at a speed of more than 40 000 kilometres an hour broke into fragments and struck the

p 686
TO TENNANT CREEK
PLENTY HWY
TO MOUNT ISA
HARTS RANGE
HARTS RA.
PAPUNYA
HAASTS BLUFF
ORMISTON GORGE & POUND N.P.
2521
REDBANK NATURE PK
2522
SIMPSONS GAP N.P.
2510
ALICE SPRINGS
2524
TREPHINA GORGE NATURE PK
2511
ARLTUNGA HISTORICAL RESERVE
RUBY GAP NATURE PARK
N'DHALA GORGE NATURE PARK
2519
2517
MacDONNELL RAS.
IWUPATAKA
TNORULA (GOSSE BLUFF) CONS. RES.
PINE GAP
2515
HERMANNSBURG
EWANINGA ROCK CARVINGS
SANTA TERESA
Todd R.
p 479
2513
FINKE GORGE NATIONAL PK
WATARRKA (KINGS CANYON) N.P.
2527
2514
HENBURY METEORITE CRATERS CONS. RES.
RAINBOW VALLEY NATURE PK
2520
2523
Hugh R.
Palmer R.
L. Amadeus
2512
CHAMBERS PILLAR HISTORICAL RESERVE
N
km
0 20 40 60 80
STUART HWY
2516
2528
KATJUTA (THE OLGAS)
YULARA
LASSETER HWY
ERLDUNDA ROADHOUSE
MOUNT EBENEZER ROADHOUSE
MAC CLARK CONSERVATION RESERVE
SIMPSON DESERT
ULURU (AYERS ROCK)
MT OLGA N.P.
2525
2526
CURTIN SPRINGS ROADHOUSE
MT CONNER
2518
Finke R.
FINKE
'OLD ANDADO'
'ANDADO'
LAMBERT CENTRE
KULGERA
p 509
TO COOBER PEDY
SA

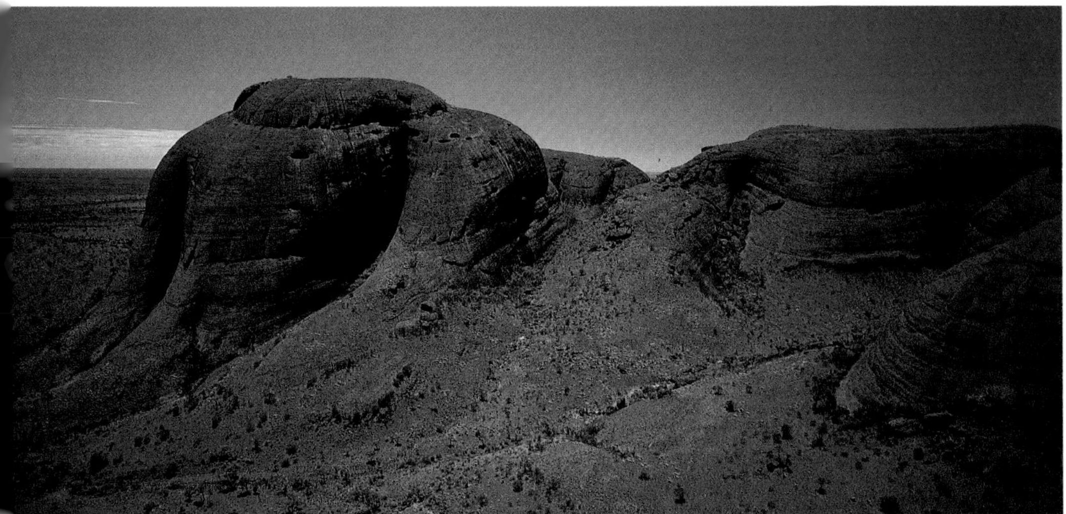

Katatjuta comes a close second to Uluru – Ayers Rock – as the most photographed landmark in the Uluru Park.

earth, gouging out great holes. The largest is 183 metres wide with its rim 6 metres above ground and its floor 12 metres below.

HERMANNSBURG ■ 2515

The Hermannsburg Mission on the north bank of the Finke River was one of the first settlements established by Europeans for Aborigines. It was set up in 1877 by Lutheran missionaries from the Barossa Valley (see *Gawler & Nuriootpa*). The date palms they planted survive as do many of their original buildings.

The school was completed in 1897 and for nearly a century missionaries looked after the settlement. In 1982, control of Hermannsburg passed to the traditional Aboriginal owners and it is now run as a cattle station (see box, *Borroloola & Elliott*).

NAMATJIRA MEMORIAL This memorial to Albert Namatjira, the first Aboriginal painter to be recognised by the European community, stands near Hermannsburg Mission, where he was born. It is inscribed: 'This is the landscape which inspired the artist'.

KATATJUTA (THE OLGAS) ■ 2516

Ernest Giles, the explorer, and his small band were the first Europeans to sight the Olgas in 1872. Giles likened them to 'monstrous pink haystacks'. Mightily impressed, Giles also wrote: 'The appearance of Mount Olga from this camp is truly wonderful; it displayed to our astonished eyes, rounded minarets, giant cupolas and monstrous domes. There they have stood as huge memorials from the ancient times of earth, for ages, countless aeons of ages since creation first had birth. Time, the old, the dim magician, has ineffectually laboured here…Mount Olga has remained as it was born'. He named Mount Olga after Queen Olga of Wurttemburg.

Aborigines know the Olgas as Katatjuta meaning 'many heads' and every feature of this collection of smooth domes, which changes colour with the weather and the light, is explained with a Dreamtime legend.

MacDONNELL RANGES ■ 2517

The conspicuous reddish ridges of the MacDonnell Ranges are formed from hard rock which is known to geologists as Heavitree quartzite. About 850 million years ago, the ranges' flat faces were layers of sand on the beach of a shallow sea.

STANDLEY CHASM The spectacular gap in the MacDonnell Ranges, known as Standley Chasm, is part of the Jay Creek Aboriginal reserve and is owned by the people of the nearby settlement of Iwupataka. The sheer cliffs rise almost 100 metres on either side of the gorge which is 9 metres across at its widest part.

JOHN FLYNN'S GRAVE The Reverend John Flynn established the Australian Inland Mission and the Royal Flying Doctor Service and has a special place in the history of the outback. His memorial is in a tiny reserve in the foothills of Mount Gillen where a grave is topped with a granite boulder brought from the Devils Marbles (see *Tennant Creek*).

MOUNT CONNER ■ 2518

Mount Conner is a characteristic mesa shape that rises more than 865 metres above the plain and has a level cap 3 kilometres long and 1200 metres wide. The soft layers at the base have eroded into honeycombed cliffs and rock shelters. It was named Mount Conner in 1873 after a South Australian parliamentarian; its Aboriginal name is Artula.

N'DHALA GORGE NATURE PARK ■ 2519

N'Dhala Gorge is a long and beautiful formation containing about 6000

Tourists come to stand and be overwhelmed by the awesomeness of Uluru's massive bulk at close hand.

Aboriginal engravings protected by the rugged walls of two gorges. They are said to be 30 000 years old and among the oldest in Australia. The artists showed a preference for decorating horizontal surfaces and almost all the engravings are pecked – a technique of indirect percussion, where a sharp, hard tool of bone or wood is hammered with a stone to make deep marks. Marine fossils are also embedded in the rocky faces.

RAINBOW VALLEY NATURE PARK ■ 2520
This is a region of 2480 hectares where spreading desert oaks and isolated claypans dot the spinifex sandplains. The bluffs and cliffs form part of the James Range and the park gets its name from their iron red and leached white bands of colour which are accentuated in the early morning and late afternoon.

REDBANK NATURE PARK ■ 2521
In this 1295-hectare park, ghost gums on the steep slopes beside the creek contrast with the shrubland and spinifex around the carpark area. A twenty-five-minute walk away, a long narrow cleft has been carved through the quartzite by Redbank Creek and several deep and icy-cold rock pools extend right through this narrow chasm. Progress through the gorge is easiest on an air mattress, for there are few footholds under the water and swimming is dangerous.

SIMPSONS GAP NATIONAL PARK ■ 2522
This park of 30 950 hectares begins only a few kilometres outside Alice Springs. The gap itself is a cleft in the red-stained quartzite of Rungutjirba Ridge through which runs the sandy bed of Roe Creek. It was one of the scenes painted by Albert Namatjira in the 1950s (see Hermannsburg).

TODD RIVER ■ 2523
The famous Todd River, named after Sir Charles Todd, rises – sometimes – in the heights of the MacDonnell Ranges to the north of Alice Springs and flows – sometimes – easterly through the centre of the town between the shopping centre and the casino and then south-easterly for about 320 kilometres until it disappears beneath the sands of the Simpson Desert just short of the South Australian border. In fact, for most of the time it neither 'rises' nor 'flows', because like most of the other rivers in central Australia, the Todd is a dry watercourse. However, in times of heavy rains, such capricious creeks can quickly turn into raging torrents with little warning. Before the new Todd River Bridge was built, Alice Springs would quickly be cut off at flood time.

TREPHINA GORGE NATURE PARK ■ 2524
Trephina Gorge, within this 1770-hectare nature park which was once a part of Undoolya Station, has quartzite walls and a sandy creek bed where huge ghost and river red gums grow amid semi-permanent waterholes. Trephina was the wife of William Benstead who opened the first hotel in Alice Springs. Rare black-footed rock wallabies shelter in the caves high up on the cliff face and Australia's largest lizard, the perentie, is common here.

ULURU (AYERS ROCK) ■ 2525
Uluru, or Ayers Rock, is a landmark of epic proportions, known throughout the world and probably more photographed at sunrise, sunset and all through the day than any other monolith. It rises 348 metres above the mulga plain and is almost 9 kilometres around at its base.

The rock is the tip of an underground sandstone mountain and, like the Olgas, has been around for about 600 million years. Its sides are grooved in deep gullies from constant wind and water erosion and there are many sculpted caves and overhangs. When it rains upon the rock, the water tumbles down the striated sides and a wildflower garden comes to life around its base.

The strenuous but much-climbed 346-metre route to the summit – a near-obligatory tourist pilgrimage – takes most people about forty-five minutes and the panoramic views from the top and the exhilarating sense of achievement make it a worthwhile climb. The rock's European name was chosen in 1873 to honour Sir Henry Ayers, the then Premier of South Australia.

Uluru, to give the rock its now commonly used Aboriginal name, is home to two groups of Western Desert Aborigines – the Yankunytjatjara and the Pitjantjatjara – and supplies their food and water. Uluru is a sacred place, vital to Aboriginal ritual life, and all its features have a special significance.

ULURU (AYERS ROCK/MOUNT OLGA) NATIONAL PARK ■ 2526
The 126 000-hectare Uluru National Park is managed jointly by the Aboriginal people who formally own the region and the Australian National Parks and Wildlife Service who have a leaseback agreement with them. It contains two of the most dramatically beautiful landmarks in the world – Uluru (Ayers Rock) and the Katatjuta (The Olgas; see entries). The park's rock formations are made all the more starkly impressive by the surrounding flat landscape and the ever-changing play of light and shadow on their round shapes. Solitary ghost gums suck a living from the run-off moisture at the base of the Olgas and are some of the few eucalypts found away from rivers in the Northern Territory.

WATARRKA (KINGS CANYON) NATIONAL PARK ■ 2527
The 72 200 hectares of Watarrka National Park, proclaimed in 1984, contain the western end of the curiously domed plateau of the George Gill Range, named after Ernest Giles' brother-in-law. Its main feature is Kings Canyon, central Australia's deepest and most beautiful gorge, the red walls of which rise up 270 metres. Despite Giles' efforts, the district was not fully explored by Europeans until 1960. There are waterholes that are never completely dry and palms, cycads, ferns, figs and cypress pines grow round the pools and in the moist gullies.

YULARA ■ 2528
This luxurious tourist resort, which opened in 1984, is about twenty-five kilometres from Uluru, outside the national park. Yulara is an Aboriginal word for 'place of the howling dingo' and its sole purpose is to cater to the needs of visitors to the 'Red Centre' with most of the permanent population employed in the hospitality trade. The resort was designed as a 'low-impact oasis' to blend in with the environment and no building is allowed to exceed the height of the tallest sandhill in the vicinity. The resort was built with the largest solar-energy system in Australia and has spectacular overhead sails to provide shade, encourage air circulation and help cut down the direct sunlight. *Population 2170*

The 'Alice' is marooned in a sea of cattle stations where everyday skills come into competition at the annual rodeo.

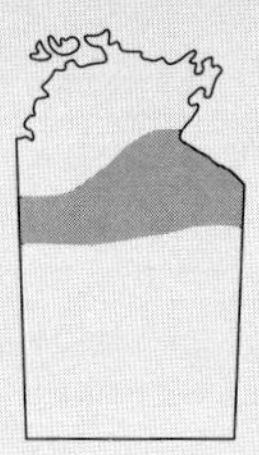

Borroloola & Elliott

When vast tracts of this isolated land were taken up by cattlemen in the 1880s, tiny frontier settlements grew up around the regular camps of the overlanders. Communications improved rapidly during the Second World War when the 'Territory' was a jump-off point to the front line.

BORROLOOLA ■ 2529

On the McArthur River, only ninety-five kilometres from the Gulf of Carpentaria, this once lawless frontier town is today the administrative capital of the Gulf of Carpentaria region and serves a fishing industry, the surrounding pastoral properties and a growing tourist trade.

By the mid-1880s, the small settlement was a wild place of horse and cattle stealing and sly-grog running – rum was smuggled from Thursday Island for illegal sale to overlanders droving the Queensland–Kimberley route. A contemporary observer remarked that Borroloola's greatest attraction was its distance from the Queensland police, but this lasted only until 1885 when a police outpost was established.

Somewhat at odds with its rowdy reputation was Borroola's substantial library, set up in the court house and operated as the McArthur River Institute – there was even a grant from the Carnegie Corporation in the United States. The local police acted as voluntary librarians. When the court house suffered cyclone damage in the late 1930s, the books were moved to a police cell. Northern Territory poet and bushman Bill Harney is said to have educated himself in the library while being held on cattle duffing charges.

Population 590

FESTIVALS Borroloola Barra Classic, April; Borroloola Rodeo, August.

CAPE CRAWFORD ROADHOUSE ■ 2530

The roadhouse complex, known throughout the region as 'Heartbreak Hotel', consists of a caravan park, motel and pub, and is situated at the intersection of the Carpentaria and Tablelands highways. It is a good base from which to explore the little known Gulf country to the north, including isolated landmarks such as the rock formations of The Lost City (see entry).

DALY WATERS ■ 2531

The fact that this tiny settlement was in the middle of nowhere gave it a vital role as an essential refuelling spot in the early days of Australian aviation. It was a centre of the London–to–Sydney Air race of 1926, a stopover for QANTAS flights during the 1930s – when passengers were fed at what became the Daly Waters pub – a link in Australia's airmail network and, during the Second World War, a refuelling base for fighters and bombers en route to Darwin and the battle zone of the Dutch East Indies - now Indonesia. Its airfield, so rich in history, was closed in the early 1970s. In 1992, the hangar was restored by the National Trust.

In 1862, the inland explorer John McDouall Stuart named the area here for Sir Dominick Daly, the newly appointed governor of South Australia – the colony then extended to the north coast. Following Stuart's reports of waterholes and 'splendidly grassed' country it was chosen as a site for an Overland Telegraph Station, with staff responsible for the maintenance of the line for 150 kilometres in either direction. Mail and supplies for Daly Waters and the surrounding stations were carted in once a year, in the 'dry', by camel and horse teams – epic journeys which took four to five months. Food often perished in the heat and shortages, especially of essential supplies such as flour, were common.

The waterholes here were also sites for camps for overlanders on the stock route from Queensland.

FESTIVALS Rodeo, September.

Southern sportsmen come north in search of a catch like this Roper River barramundi bounty.

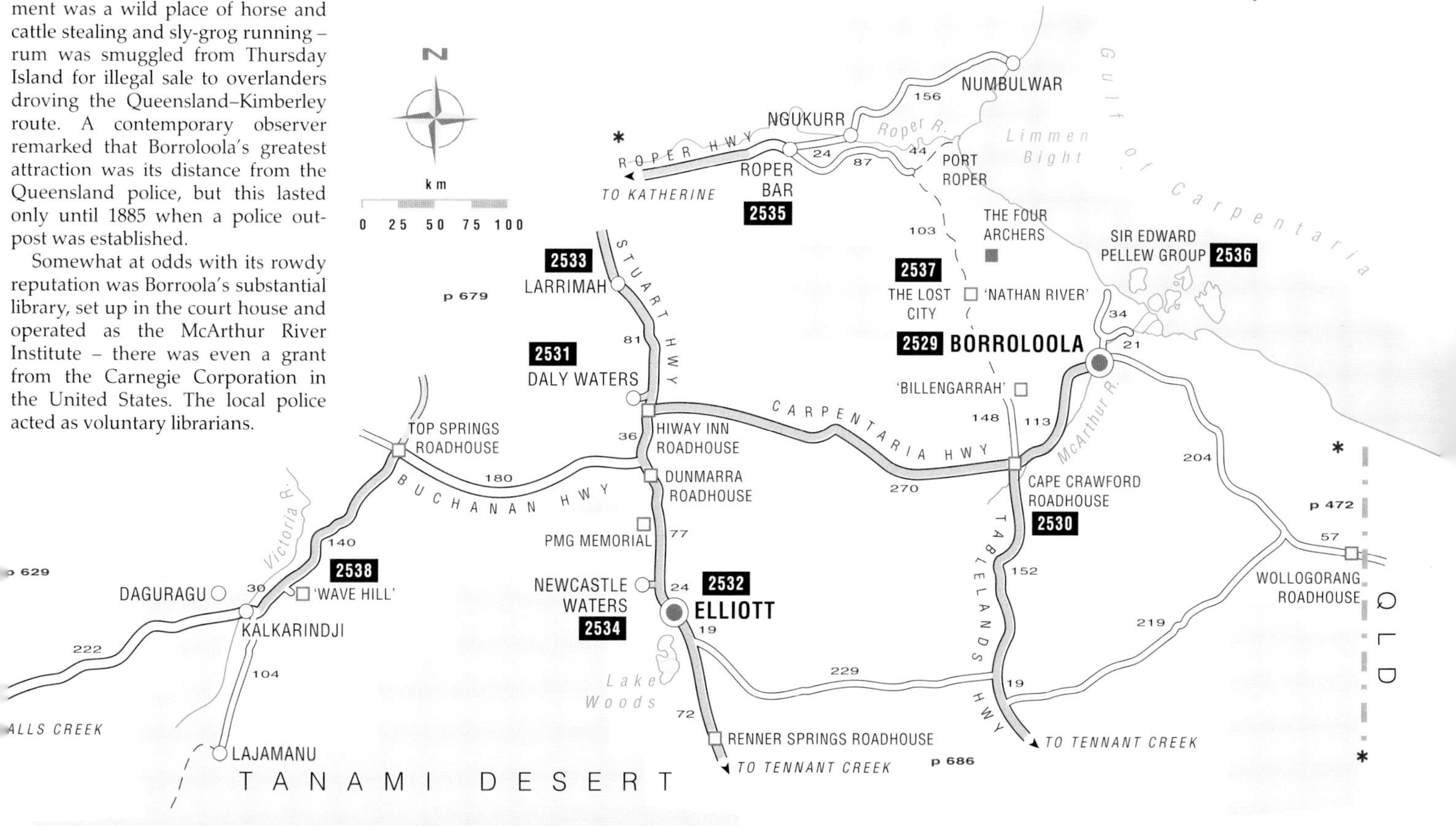

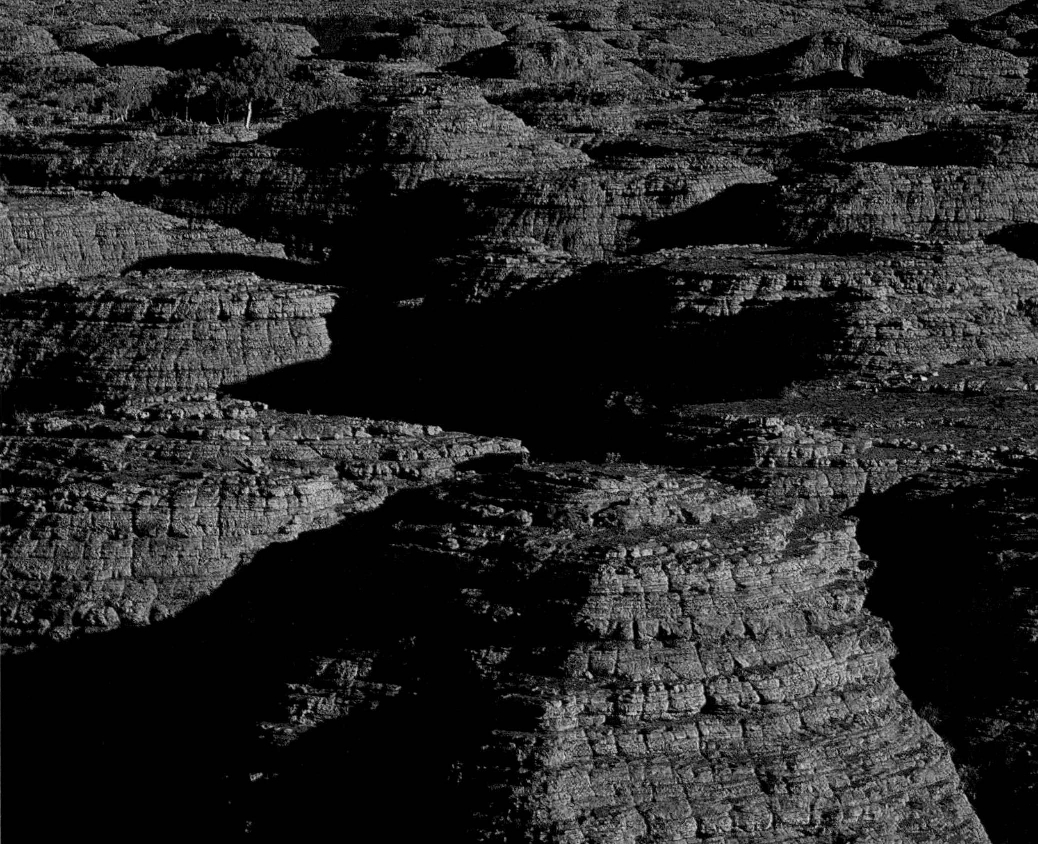

The Lost City sits in a landscape as cruelly raw as the setting of Purnululu (see Kununurra & Wyndham*).*

ELLIOTT ■ 2532

Before the construction of the Stuart Highway during the Second World War there was a dusty track winding along the route of the Overland Telegraph Line which was used in the main by the pony mail service and maintenance crews attending the line. A sealed highway – following roughly the route of the explorer whose name it bears – was constructed following the outbreak of the Second World War and it became an essential supply line to the north.

The small township of Elliott is one of several settlements along the highway, and offers travellers accommodation, including caravan parks, as well as fuel supplies. The highway here is lined with large, red-flowered bauhinia trees, which are home to noisy flocks of black cockatoos and white corellas.

PMG MEMORIAL Beside the highway between Elliott and Daly Waters, at almost exactly the spot where the northern and southern telegraph wires of the Overland Telegraph Line formed their historic link in 1872, is a memorial to Charles Todd, Postmaster-General of South Australia, who oversaw the line's construction.

LARRIMAH ■ 2533

Larrimah probably owes its existence to its position – during the Second World War – on the former North Australia Railway which made it the largest staging post in Australia, with more than 3000 servicemen stationed in the town

Birdum, just outside Larrimah, was the southern terminus of the North Australia Railway, a narrow-gauge line that meandered south from Darwin and was originally intended to reach Alice Springs to join The Ghan line and complete a north-south rail link. During the Second World War, when Japanese air attacks on coastal shipping prevented the movement of men and freight by sea, truck convoys carried troops and supplies to Larrimah from Alice Springs for transfer to the rail line and then on to Darwin and eventually, the war zone across the Timor Sea. The line closed in 1976 and most of the track has been removed.

Little remains at Larrimah to recall those days apart from the disused Gorrie airstrip, a few kilometres north of the town, the abandoned railway siding, and the building which housed the officers' mess, now the town pub.

NEWCASTLE WATERS ■ 2534

The water once described unflatteringly as being 'the colour and consistency of artichoke soup', fills this series of waterholes which sometimes come together to flow south into Lake Woods. The waterholes were named in 1861 by the explorer John McDouall Stuart for the Duke of Newcastle, Secretary of State for the Colonies.

A cattle station was established at Newcastle Waters in the late 1870s, but the tiny settlement was not recognised by officialdom until nearly a century later, in 1964. In more recent times it has declined to become a virtual ghost town; it has been classified by the National Trust, and the former Junction Hotel, housing a display of historical photos and documents relating to the region, is open to the public.

The notoriously difficult Murranji stock route pioneered by Nat Buchanan, founder of 'Wave Hill' (see entry), runs from the Victoria River area to Newcastle Waters, where it joins a second route to Queensland. In 1988, the township was the starting point for The Last Great Cattle Drive, in which a team of crack drivers took 1200 bullocks on a 2000-kilometre journey across the Barkly Tableland and over some of Australia's roughest terrain to Longreach in Queensland, re-creating the feats of the lengendary cattlemen of the pre-road-train days.

ROPER BAR ■ 2535

Roper Bar takes its name from the river it crosses which, in turn, honours John Roper, a member of Leichhardt's 1845 expedition, who sighted it when scouting ahead of the party for the best route. The bar divides the tidal section of the river from the freshwater channel, and marks the limit of navigation. The river was a main supply route during the construction of the Overland Telegraph in 1872 and thus a small settlement grew up at this point. The rock wall which reinforces the natural bar was built in the early 1900s.

LEICHHARDT PLAQUE In the grounds of the old Roper Bar police station there is a plaque commemorating the work of the explorer Ludwig Leichhardt who in 1845 made the arduous trek from the Darling Downs in Queensland to the shores of the Gulf of Carpentaria, and then on to the north-western tip of Arnhem Land.

SIR EDWARD PELLEW GROUP ■ 2536

Five untamed islands and several rocky islets at the entrance to the McArthur River make up this group, which was named by Matthew Flinders in 1802 'in compliment to a distinguished officer of the British Navy'. Sprawling Vanderlin Island, the largest of the group, was assumed by the Dutch to be part of the mainland when it was named Cape Vanderlin, probably by Abel Tasman in 1644.

The isolated beaches of the group were visited from the early 1700s by Macassan trepangers, who each December set out from Sulawesi (formerly called the Celebes) in eastern Indonesia, and headed for the northern coasts of Australia. They sought trepang, also known as sea slug or bêche-de-mer, a delicacy in some south-east Asian dishes. The creatures were collected from the shallow seabed and brought to a camp on the beach, where they were gutted, lightly boiled and then smoked to dry and preserve them. Stone hearths where mangrove logs were burned to heat the trepang pots can still be seen.

THE LOST CITY ■ 2537

In a region of barren and featureless desert so inaccessible that the only way in is by helicopter, rises a cluster of warm-hued sandstone turrets and towers which stand against the horizon like the outline of a fairytale city. These fantastic shapes were formed by water seeping into thin cracks in the sandstone walls which countless centuries of erosion has widened into canyons and stone corridors lined with rounded spires, domes and arches.

Known as 'Yalyalacomella' to the local Aborigines, this place was for thousands of years an important ceremonial site. The rocks in their various shapes and sizes are, it is believed, the body and eggs of the creative being Wallalu, the rainbow serpent. Ancient paintings can still be seen on the walls.

'WAVE HILL' ■ 2538

Wave Hill Station, named for its undulating terrain, was founded in 1883 by pioneer pastoralist and explorer Nat Buchanan, who was responsible for seeking out large areas of grazing country in Queensland and the Northern Territory and who pioneered the stock routes which linked many of them. Ironically, it was here, in another time, that the movement to return some of these lands to their original custodians had its beginnings with the dramatic 1966 strike of the Gurindji stockmen (see box).

LAND RIGHTS FOR THE FIRST TERRITORIANS

DEFIANT elders of the Gurindji clan blazed a trail that changed the course of history for their race. Their proud stand at the little settlement of Daguragu inspired the first broad public support for Aboriginal ownership of traditional lands.

Gurindji stockmen on Wave Hill cattle station abandoned their jobs in August 1966 and took their families to a camp by the Victoria River. Walk-offs in protest at poor living or working conditions in the rural north were not unprecedented, but this strike took on a deeper significance. The 200 Gurindji people rejected inducements to return for improved conditions in the form of better food and wages, insisting on nothing less than entitlement to land of their own. At the beginning of 1967 the group moved west to occupy an area on Wattie Creek, known to them as Daguragu.

Publicity of the dispute generated widespread sympathy for the Gurindji. It brought a sharp focus to a national referendum later in 1967, which gave overwhelming support for the Commonwealth Government to assume powers to legislate for Aboriginal advancement in all states and territories. But the government of the day made few attempts to tackle the issue of land rights. Ruling on a separate matter, the Supreme Court found no legal basis for tribal claims and made it clear that further legislation would be needed.

As Aborigines took control of their land, some continued to make a living from cattle raising. Pop music rang to the didgeridoo as groups like Yothu Yindi (below) used a land-rights message in their songs.

Gough Whitlam's Labor government, attaining office in 1972, lost little time laying the groundwork. The Gurindji were invited to identify what they considered to be the heartland of their traditional country. In 1975 – nine years after they began their campaign – they were granted a lease over more than 3000 square kilometres, bought on their behalf from the British owners of 'Wave Hill'. Soon the Gurindji, and thousands more of the Northern Territory's indigenous people, were to enjoy the long-awaited, freehold possession of property.

Recommendations of a Labor-appointed Aboriginal land rights commission had been incorporated in legislation tailored specifically for the Territory, where no complicating issues of states' rights would arise. The bill lapsed with the government's dismissal in 1975.

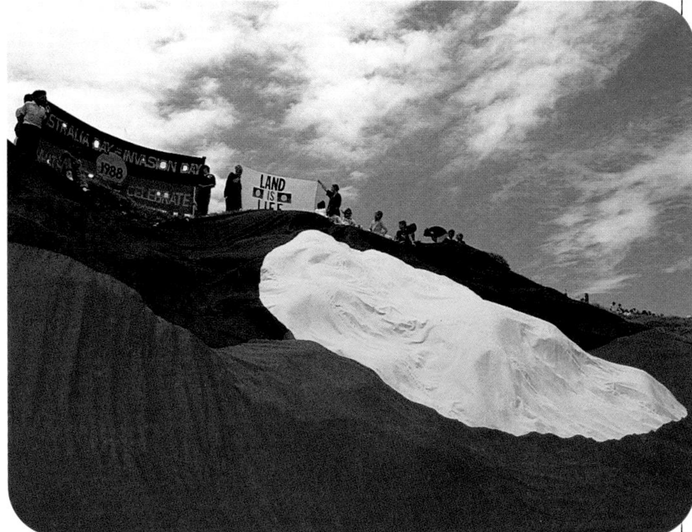

The Gurindji's success gave the land-rights movement new impetus; 1988 demonstrations included a Botany Bay Aboriginal flag unveiling.

But the incoming Liberal-National coalition revived it with some amendments, and the Aboriginal Land Rights (Northern Territory) Act was proclaimed on Australia Day 1977.

Existing Aboriginal reserves – nearly a fifth of the Territory's area – were promptly handed over to their occupants. And a mechanism was provided for other groups to lodge claims to vacant Crown lands on the grounds of traditional attachment. Successful applications increased the area under Aboriginal ownership to more than one-third by 1990, and are expected to take the proportion to roughly half by the time the process is complete. Aboriginal land includes all of the Northern Territory's national parks. Although the parks are administered by the Australian National Parks and Wildlife Service under leaseback arrangements, Aborigines have majority representation on their boards of management.

Titles are vested in community trusts with four land councils, based in Alice Springs, Darwin, Nguiu (for Melville and Bathurst Islands) and Alyangula (Groote Eylandt), acting as agents for the trusts. Land cannot be sold, though it may be leased to non-Aborigines subject to government approval. Mineral exploration and extraction can occur only with the owners' consent. Mining royalties are used to fund land council administration as well as compensate disrupted communities.

Travellers do not need permission to drive on public roads that cross Aboriginal land provided that they keep to their course but visitors driving west of Alice Springs should check with the Central Land Council before embarking on their journey. Travellers are expected to need no fuel or assistance. □

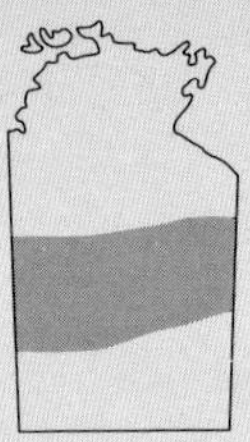

Tennant Creek

The communications lifeline of the Overland Telegraph, which linked Australia's population centres to the outside world – and a gold rush at Tennant Creek – were responsible for the first isolated European settlements in this ancient, eroded landscape.

Traditional Aborigines find a ready source of sugar in the bloated nectar sacs of honeypot 'storage' ants.

ATTACK CREEK HISTORICAL RESERVE ■ 2539

A memorial cairn to the explorer John McDouall Stuart marks the spot where, in June 1860, the expedition he led in an attempt to cross the continent from north to south was turned back by Aborigines. Stuart called them, '...tall powerful fellows...' who objected, '...in a great fury...', to the party moving across their lands. Stuart named the watercourse here Attack Creek.

Although Stuart and his men failed in their main objective, they had covered enough of the continent to disprove the popularly held theory of an inland sea. A year later, with a larger party, Stuart again headed north but it was not until the following year, on his third attempt, that he reached the waters of the Gulf.

In 1863, in large part as a result of these Adelaide-sponsored explorations, control of the Northern Territory passed from New South Wales to South Australia. The new route northward also made feasible the laying of the Overland Telegraph Line less than ten years later.

BARKLY TABLELAND ■ 2540

Flat and treeless in places, the 240 000-square-kilometre area of the Barkly Tableland slopes down to the edge of the warm waters of the Gulf of Carpentaria. The rivers which run off it follow no definite drainage pattern, and in the summer 'wet' they flood quickly, spilling onto the hard black soil of the plains, and turning it into an impassable quagmire.

The tablelands were named in 1861 by the explorer William Landsborough, for the then governor of Victoria, while he was searching for the missing Burke and Wills.

BARROW CREEK ■ 2541

The well-preserved buildings of one of the main repeater stations on the Overland Telegraph Line can be seen here. The site was chosen for its permanent freshwater spring, which was also an important water source for the local Aboriginal people and the animals they hunted. The sudden denial of access to the waterhole, when it was fenced off for stock grazing, may well have provoked a tragic incident in which a group of Aborigines attacked the lonely outpost, killing two Europeans.

The beleaguered technicians sent urgent SOS messages along the line, alerting Adelaide to their plight. Medical advice relayed directly from the Central Telegraph Station in Adelaide was unable to save the mortally wounded James Stapleton who tapped a poignant farewell message to his wife – 'God bless you and the children' – which was personally decoded by Charles Todd, Postmaster-General of South Australia.

CENTRAL MOUNT STUART HISTORICAL RESERVE ■ 2542

The geographical mid-point of Australia is the rounded red sandstone rise of Central Mount Stuart (845 metres). In 1860, John McDouall Stuart and his men, aware that they were in the centre of the continent, climbed to the summit of the nearest hill and raised the Union Jack and 'gave three hearty cheers for the flag'. Stuart named the hill for fellow explorer Charles Sturt but after Stuart's cross-continental journey, the South Australian Government renamed it in his honour.

CONNELLS LAGOON CONSERVATION RESERVE ■ 2543

Formerly part of a cattle lease, this area is now closed to grazing so that regeneration can take place. The thick grasses are a breeding ground for small mammals, including the long-haired rat, plains birds such as the once-widespread kori bustard and tiny seed feeders such as the brightly coloured yellow chat.

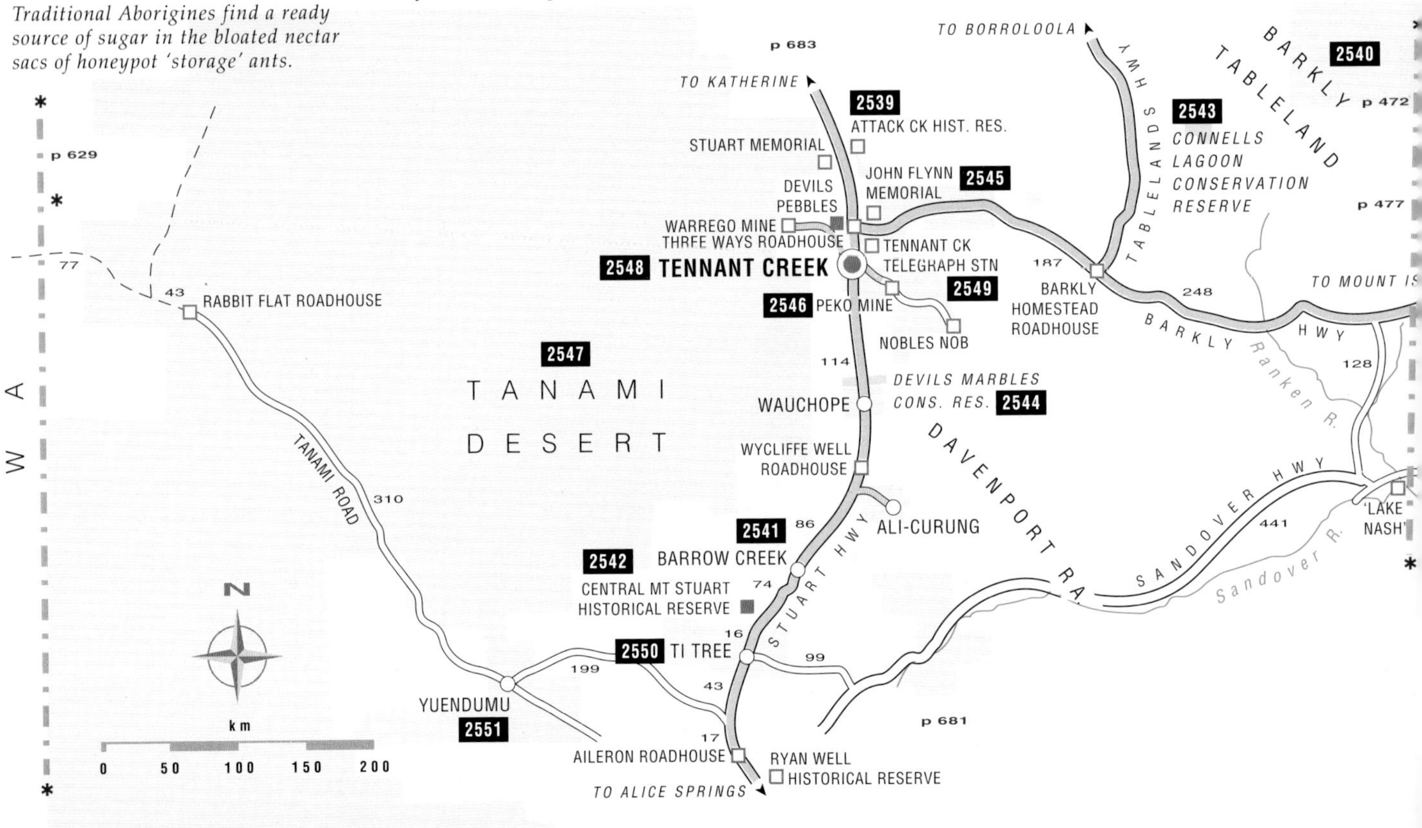

TO BORROLOOLA
p 683
TO KATHERINE
2539 ATTACK CK HIST. RES.
STUART MEMORIAL
DEVILS PEBBLES
JOHN FLYNN MEMORIAL 2545
WARREGO MINE
THREE WAYS ROADHOUSE
2548 TENNANT CREEK
TENNANT CK TELEGRAPH STN 2549
2546 PEKO MINE
NOBLES NOB
BARKLY HOMESTEAD ROADHOUSE
2540 BARKLY TABLELAND
2543 CONNELLS LAGOON CONSERVATION RESERVE
TABLELANDS HWY
p 472
p 477
TO MOUNT IS
BARKLY HWY
Ranken R.
p 629
WA
RABBIT FLAT ROADHOUSE
2547 TANAMI DESERT
TANAMI ROAD
DEVILS MARBLES CONS. RES. 2544
WAUCHOPE
WYCLIFFE WELL ROADHOUSE
ALI-CURUNG
DAVENPORT RA.
2541 BARROW CREEK
2542 CENTRAL MT STUART HISTORICAL RESERVE
STUART HWY
SANDOVER HWY
Sandover R.
LAKE NASH
2550 TI TREE
YUENDUMU 2551
AILERON ROADHOUSE
RYAN WELL HISTORICAL RESERVE
TO ALICE SPRINGS
p 681
N
km
0 50 100 150 200
77 43 310 114 187 248 128 441 86 74 16 199 99 43 17

In a land where time is of no account, even the solid granite of the Devils Marbles is reduced to submission by the inexorable erosive power of the elements.

DEVILS MARBLES CONSERVATION RESERVE ■ 2544

These massive granite boulders, piled one upon the other, are the last stages in the weathering process of a single outcrop of 1500-million-year-old granite. Water seeping into horizontal and vertical fault lines caused the rock to crack into huge regular blocks up to seven metres square which, following the gradual removal of the covering soil, were exposed to the elements.

Erosion along the joints, together with a process known as 'spalling' – in which thin 'skins' of weathered surface, loosened by the daily expansion and contraction of the rock, flake from the boulders – have smoothed and shaped the giant tors. The formation is most spectacular at sunrise and sunset, when the low rays of the sun highlight the warm tones of the brown and red iron minerals in the granite. The area is protected in an 1800-hectare conservation park.

The Devils Marbles form part of an Aboriginal sacred site. In traditional belief, the boulders are the eggs of the Rainbow Serpent, a creative being who travelled over the land forming its features. A boulder from here has been transported some 480 kilometres south, to the base of Mount Gillen, outside Alice Springs, where it forms a memorial over the grave of John Flynn, the founder of the Flying Doctor Service.

JOHN FLYNN MEMORIAL ■ 2545

At Three Ways, at the junction of the Barkly and Stuart highways, there is a huge brick obelisk built to commemorate the contribution made by John Flynn to the lives of the people of outback Australia. Flynn established the Australian Inland Mission and the Royal Flying Doctor Service (see box, *Mount Isa & Cloncurry*).

PEKO MINE ■ 2546

'Peko' was the pet dog of a prospector who discovered gold here in 1935. The old Peko mine closed in 1972, but its name lives on in Peko Wallsend, part of the North Broken Hill Group, with mining operations in many parts of Australia.

TANAMI DESERT ■ 2547

Sandy and tufted with spinifex, the wide and waterless band of the Tanami stretches west of Tennant Creek to the Western Australia border and beyond. In the 1930s, gold lured hardy souls into this vast and inhospitable place, and small mines still operate here.

RABBIT FLAT ROADHOUSE A service station and general store, which claims to be the most isolated in Australia, caters for motorists who brave the unsealed track across the Tanami.

TANAMI WILDLIFE SANCTUARY Covering some 3 750 000 hectares, this region of dry spinifex is home to numerous desert birds. In the early 1980s it was returned to its traditional Aboriginal owners.

TENNANT CREEK ■ 2548

Tennant Creek, one of the largest, and also one of the most isolated towns in the Northern Territory, is not actually on the creek which explorer John McDouall Stuart described in glowing terms and where the Tennant Creek Overland Telegraph Line Station (see entry) was built, but on a waterless plain more than ten kilometres distant.

According to local legend, the reason for this confusion was that a waggon loaded with beer and building supplies for the construction and stocking of a hotel was destined for the telegraph station and broke an axle here in 1933. To save further carting, the Tennant Creek Hotel was simply erected on the spot, and a shanty town quickly grew up around it to meet the needs of the gold miners who were then arriving in droves. The more likely but less lively explanation is that the Overland Telegraph Station was on government land, where private buildings were not allowed.

When gold was found in the early 1930s, Tennant Creek became the site of Australia's last gold rush and for ten years was a bustling town. One of the largest mines was the El Dorado which yielded almost 175 000 grams of gold. *Population 3480*

NOBLES NOB Worked from 1945 to 1985 Nobles Nob, which began operations underground, was converted to open-cut mining after the collapse of the crown pillar in 1967. It then became the largest open-cut gold mine in Australia.

DEVILS PEBBLES Smaller than the Devils Marbles (see entry), are the granite formations of the Devils Pebbles which are strewn over a wide area to the north of the town.

FESTIVALS Goldrush Folk Festival, July; Goldrush Festival, October; Desert Harmony, September.

TENNANT CREEK TELEGRAPH STATION ■ 2549

After the opening of the Tennant Creek Post Office in 1937 the old telegraph station complex was leased to various pastoral companies until 1986. Four of the station's original eleven buildings are still standing and are protected in a conservation area. In 1860, John McDouall Stuart named the watercourse, which had what he described as 'excellent feed', for John Tennant of Port Lincoln.

TI TREE ■ 2550

Ti Tree was an extremely important stop for early travellers on the Stuart Highway as its well was the only source of clean water for approximately 150 kilometres in either direction. In the 1930s, the hamlet became the location of one of the first roadhouses in the Northern Territory and it still offers travellers fuel, food and accommodation.

YUENDUMU ■ 2551

The Aboriginal settlement here was established in 1946 when Aborigines who had been living at what was then called the Tanami Native Settlement sought a more reliable water supply. The inverted 'L' shape of the Yuendumu land results from a dispute in the early 1950s with a grazier who had possession of a lease on the eastern side. *Population 670*

FESTIVALS Yuendumu Festival, early August.

The overland telegraph line had 11 repeater stations like the one at Tennant Creek – now preserved as a reminder of pre-satellite age communications.

ARNHEM LAND

Apart from the intrusion of mining activity in the 1970s, Arnhem Land has managed to remain an unsullied region of wild splendour still occupied by its traditional inhabitants.

The wildly primeval, ancient landscape of Arnhem Land can justly be seen as forming one of Australia's last frontiers. This is a spectacular scenic region that few people get to see. The entire north-eastern half of the Top End of the Northern Territory, beyond the widely visited Kakadu National Park, is Arnhem Land Aboriginal Land Trust which – apart from one town – cannot be visited without special permission.

Extending from Gove Peninsula in the north-east to Cobourg Peninsula in the north-west, and including the western shore of the Gulf of Carpentaria, Groote Eylandt and the smaller offshore islands, Arnhem Land was first declared Aboriginal land – as a reserve – in 1931.

Aborigines are believed to have lived here for at least 40 000 years, possibly much longer. The world's oldest archaeological evidence for the use of axes with ground-stone heads is found in Arnhem Land, where there are also the earliest known sites of Aboriginal occupation in northern Australia. Around 1500 'cave galleries' of rock art have been found there. As well as illustrating the relationship of the Aborigines to the land and the region's plants and animals, the rock walls show evidence of overseas visitors – the Macassans – who, from the seventeenth century, sailed their praus from Sulawesi to fish for bêche-de-mer along the Arnhem coast. Tamarind trees believed to have been planted on the coast by the Macassans are still growing today.

Aboriginal rock artists also recorded the arrival of European sailing ships, and of Ludwig Leichhardt, who, in 1845, led the first expedition into Arnhem Land. The explorer discovered to his dismay that the waterless plateau surfaces of Arnhem Land that look level from a distance are in fact stony, rugged and difficult to cross.

The Arnhem Land region received its Dutch name in 1803, when Matthew Flinders named it after the off-course ship *Arnhem,* whose crew had sighted the northern coastline in the 1620s. European settlement of this region has had a stop-start history. A township which began at Raffles Bay on the north shore of Cobourg Peninsula in 1827 was abandoned after two years. Another attempt, in 1837, to establish a settlement at nearby Port Essington lasted ten years with the residents struggling against isolation, hunger and disease.

With its floodplains, escarpments and rainforest, Arnhem Land supports a huge range of wildlife. At least 1000 different plants have been identified together with more than 50 mammals, 75 reptiles, 25 kinds of frogs and 55 fish. In the wetlands alone there are 275 known bird species and new species are still being discovered.

Arnhem Land's greatest glory is its spectacular scenery. Over thousands of years, rivers

In Arnhem Land, time-honoured customs are still observed and the cave-painting tradition continues; the region's teeming wetlands have inspired this depiction of a sea creature and a lotus (above).

Dancers from Arnhem Land's Lake Evella helped celebrate the hand-over of the Nitmiluk National Park to its traditional owners. Jim Jim Falls (right) pour from the Arnhem cliffs, swelling the wetlands below.

swollen by wet-season rains have cut steep-sided gorges and dramatic escarpments, over which magnificent waterfalls cascade during summer downpours. The 500-kilometre-long Arnhem Land escarpment began forming about 2000 million years ago when huge layers of compressed sand were slowly carved into the cliff that now marks the escarpment's edge.

Except for mission stations, white settlement in Arnhem Land was forbidden until the 1970s. Since then mining has been allowed by the Aboriginal community in exchange for royalty payments and mining has become big business. Nhulunbuy, at the north-eastern tip of Arnhem Land is the only part of the reserve the public can visit without obtaining a permit. Australia's third largest bauxite mine is here on the Gove Peninsula. In a year, nearly one-and-a-half million tonnes of alumina go out to countries such as Germany, Japan, the United States and Venezuela.The fourth largest manganese mine in the world is on Groote Eylandt.

Mission stations such as Yirrkala, Oenpelli and Maningrida have been the main population centres for the Aborigines of Arnhem Land, but since the 1970s many extended family groups have returned to their traditional homelands. The Gove Peninsula is home to many of these traditional Aboriginal groups whose art, especially bark painting, has become world famous. With the rapid growth of tourism in the Northern Territory and increased visitor interest in Aboriginal culture, tours into some parts of Arnhem Land have been organised by the Aborigines, giving small groups of visitors an insight into a timeless culture. □

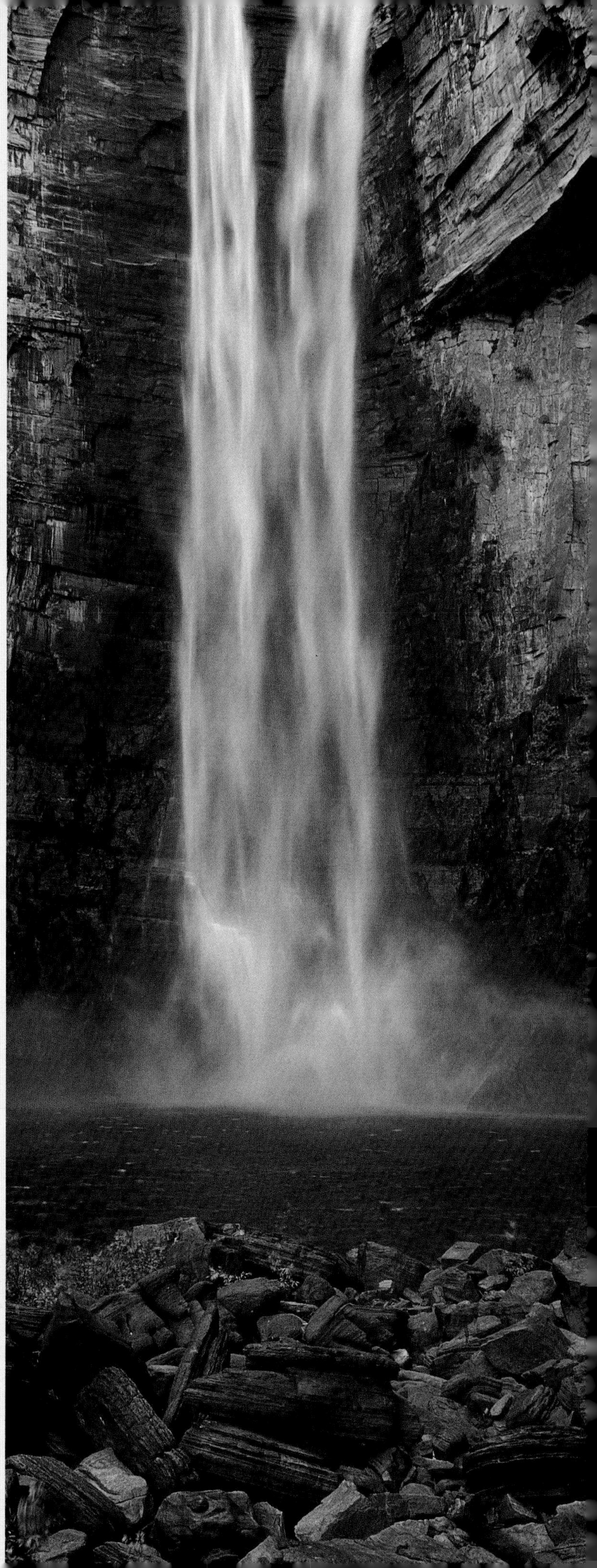

Index

Places described in detail are listed in the book as entries in numerical order, ■1 to ■2551. **Bold** type here indicates these places, their entry number and page number. Non-geographical places such as buildings are listed with the name of the entry under which they appear. Page numbers in *italics* denote an illustration while square brackets refer to an expanded box reference (see legend, bottom of page). Abbreviations: National Park N.P., Conservation Park C.P.

A

B

Place, entry number and main reference page number: ABERDEEN NSW ■196 78 Illustration: *48* Box story: [40]

D

E

F

G

H

I

J

K

L

M

Place, entry number and main reference page number: **ABERDEEN** NSW ■ **196 78** **Illustration:** *48* **Box story:** [40]

N

O

P

Q

R

U

V

W

Y

Z

Acknowledgments

The publishers are indebted to the many state and regional tourist authorities, as well as local tourist committees, associations and tourist or visitor information centres and bureaux, who provided generous assistance during the preparation of this book. Particular thanks are also due to the following individuals and organisations:

NEW SOUTH WALES Australian Heritage Commission; Ballina Shire Council; Ballina Shire Promotions Association; Bland Shire Council; Brewarrina Aboriginal Cultural Museum; Brewarrina Shire Council; Byron Shire Marketing Committee; Cabonne Shire Council; Central Darling Shire Council; Cobar Regional Museum; Coffs Harbour City Centre Mall Management; Coffs Harbour City Council; Coolah Shire Council; Cooma–Monaro Shire Council; Cootamundra Advancement Corporation Ltd; Copmanhurst Shire Council; CSIRO Radiophysics Laboratory (NSW); Culcairn Shire Council; Department of Lands; Department of Sport, Recreation & Racing; Department of Water Resources; Dungog Shire Council; Forbes Shire Council; Forestry Commission of New South Wales; Geographical Place Names Board of NSW; Gilgandra Shire Council; Goondiwindi Town Council; Goulburn City Council; Gunning Shire Council; Harden–Murrumburrah Shire Council; Hay Shire Council; Holbrook Shire Council; Kyogle Shire Council; Lachlan Shire Council; Lake Macquarie City Council; Madura Tea Estates Pty Ltd; Merimbula Area Promotions Inc.; Mudgee Shire Council; National Parks & Wildlife Service; The National Trust of Australia (NSW); NSW Council of Tourist Associations (Inc.); Oberon Shire Council; Port Stephens Shire Council; Queanbeyan City Council; Ralph & Amy Reid; Richmond River Shire Council; Roads & Traffic Authority; Eve Robinson, ASMP Species Co-ordinator, Western Plains Zoo; Rutherglen Development Association; State Library of NSW; Tumbarumba Shire Council; Tumut Shire Council; Uralla Shire Council; Wakool Shire Council; Walgett Shire Council; Warren Shire Council; Weddin Shire Council; Wellington Shire Council; Winemakers of Rutherglen; Wingecarribee Shire Council; Wyong Shire Council; Yass Shire & Development Association; Yallaroi Shire Council; Young Shire Council. AUSTRALIAN CAPITAL TERRITORY Aboriginal & Torres Strait Islander Commission; Australian Bureau of Statistics; Australian Heritage Commission; Australian National Parks & Wildlife Service; National Trust of Australia. (ACT). VICTORIA Bacchus Marsh Chamber of Commerce; Ballarat Begonia Festival Association Inc.; Barrabool Shire Council; Beechworth Chamber of Commerce; Bendigo Trust; Bet Bet Shire Council; Birchip Shire Council; Boort Traders Association; Bower Bird's Nest Museum; Brits Four-wheel-drive Rental; Warren Bunker, Mulgrave Shire Council; Camperdown & District Promotions Group; Terry Carroll, *Australasian Post*; Central Victorian Promotions; Coal Corporation of Victoria; Corbang Shire Council; Creswick Motel; CSIRO Radiophysics Laboratory; Daylesford & District Chamber of Commerce; Department of Conservation & Environment; Donald Shire Council; Doncaster & Templestowe City Council; Euroa Shire Council; Falls Creek Chamber of Commerce; Frankston City Council; Giant Worm Tourist Attraction; Gippsland Regional Information Bank; Glenelg Shire Council; Golden Triangle Promotions Group; Gordon Shire Council; Gourmet Deli Tourism; Hamilton City Council; Stephen Harding, CEO, Wentworth Shire; Heywood Shire Council; Bob Holschier; Horsham Promotions Committee; Jeparit Promotions Committee; Kaniva Shire Council; Kerang Shire Council; Lorne, Birregurra, Winchelsea Promotion & Development Association Inc.; Lorne Promotions Association; Lowan Shire Council; Mansfield Chamber of Commerce; Ministry of Finance; Moe City Council; Mooroopna Chamber of Commerce; Mornington Shire Council; Mount Beauty & District Chamber of Commerce; Mount Hotham Chamber of Commerce; Peter Musgrove, Department of Conservation and Environment, Victoria; Myrtleford Chamber of Commerce; Narracan Shire Council; National Trust of Australia (Victoria); North East Victorian Regional Council; Otway Scenic Circle Association Inc.; Packenham Shire Council; Pecan Deli (Healesville); Jill Peters, Johnstone Shire Council; Place Names Committee; Ponderosa Cabin; Pyramid Hill Traders Inc.; Rainbow Traders Association; Ripon Shire Council; Rochester Shire Council; Romsey Shire Council; Rosedale Shire Council; Rural Waters Commission of Victoria; Sale City Council; Seymour Shire Council; Shepparton City Council; Shepparton, Kyabram, Rodney Development Association; Snow Road Promotions Association; Stawell & Grampians Development Association Inc.; Strathfieldsaye Shire Council; Sun Country Playground Promotions Group; Swan Hill Promotion & Development Corporation Inc.; Swan Hill Shire; Tatura Chamber of Commerce & Industry; Upper Yarra Shire Council; Victorian Eastern Development Association; Vic. Roads; Walpen–Ouyen Shire Council; Wannon Shire Council; Whittlesea City Council; Winchelsea Shire Council; Woorayl Shire Council; Wycheproof Shire Council; Yea Shire Council. QUEENSLAND Albert Shire Council; Alpha Shire Council; Aramac Shire Council; Atherton Shire Council; Banana Shire Council; Barcoo Shire Council; Bauhinia Shire Council; Beaudesert Shire Council; Belyando Shire Council; Booringa Shire Council; Boulia Shire Council; Bowen Shire Council; Broadsound Shire Council; Bulloo Shire Council; Bungil Shire Council; Burdekin Shire Council; Caloundra City Council; Carpentaria Shire Council; Charters Towers City Council; Chinchilla Historical Museum; Clifton Shire Council; Cloncurry–Mary Kathleen Memorial Museum & Park; Cloncurry Shire Council; Cook Shire Council; Cooloola Regional Development Board; Council of the Shire of Esk; Croydon Shire Council; Dalby Shire Council; Dalrymple Shire Council; Department of Environment & Heritage; Department of Family Services & Aboriginal & Islander Affairs; Department of Lands; Department of Primary Industries; Department of Resource Industries; Department of Transport; Diamantina Shire Council; Duaringa Shire Council; Etheridge Shire Council; Flinders Shire Council; Gatton Shire Council; Goondiwindi Town Council; Gulf Local Authorities Association; Hinchinbrook Development Council; Hinchinbrook Shire Council; Inglewood Shire Council; Johnstone Shire Council; Kingaroy & District Development Board; Laidley Shire Council; Kathleen Laurie; Livingston Shire Council; Mareeba Shire Council; Maroochy Shire Council; McKinlay Shire Council; Miriam Vale Shire Council; Mount Morgan Shire Council; Murgon Shire Council; Murilla Shire Council; The National Trust of Queensland; Nebo Shire Council; Noosa Shire Council; Paroo Shire Council; Peak Downs Shire Council; Pioneer Shire Council; Queensland Mineral Resources; Queensland National Parks & Wildlife Service; Queensland Place Names Board; Quilpie Shire Council; Reef Adventureland; Richmond Shire Council; Roma Town Council; Sarina Shire Council; Sunshine Coast Economic Development Board Ltd; Tambo Shire Council; Tara Shire Council; Thuringowa City Council; Torres Shire Council; Water Resources Commission; Woongarra Shire Council. SOUTH AUSTRALIA Department of Environment & Planning; Department of Lands; Department of Mines & Energy; Engineering & Water Supply Department; Geographical Names Board of South Australia; Mintaro Slate Quarries Pty Ltd; National Parks & Wildlife Service; The National Trust of South Australia; Royal Automobile Association of South Australia (Inc.); Woods & Forests Department. WESTERN AUSTRALIA Albany Town Council; Coorow Shire Council; Corrigin Shire Council; Cranbrook Shire Council; Dandaragan Shire Council; Department of Conservation & Land Management; Department of Land Administration; Department of Mines; Department of Planning & Urban Development; Department of Regional Development and the North West; Department of State Development; East Pilbara Shire Council; Geographic Names Committee; Geraldton Mid-West Development Authority; Goldfields–Esperance Development Authority; Great Southern Development Authority; Kent Shire Council; Koorda Shire Council; Kulin Shire Council; Laverton Shire Council; Leonora Shire Council; Meekatharra Shire Council; Midlands Travel Association; Mid West Travel Association; Moora Shire Council; Morawa Shire Council; Mount Magnet Shire Council; Murchison Shire Council; Narembeen Shire Council; Narrogin Town Council; The National Trust of Western Australia (WA); Nungarin Shire Council; Pingelly Shire Council; Plantagenet Shire; Quairading Shire Council; Sandstone Shire Council; Serpentine–Jarrahdale Shire Council; Shark Bay Shire Council; South-West Development Authority; Trayning Shire Council; Wagin Shire Council; Water Authority; West Australia Heritage Commission; West Australia Petroleum Pty Ltd; Western Australia Water Resources Council. TASMANIA Beaconsfield Municipal Council; Bothwell Municipal Council; Brighton Municipal Council; Bruny Island Municipal Council; Burnie City Council; Campbell Town Municipal Council; Clarence Municipal Council; Deloraine Municipal Council; Department of Parks, Wildlife & Heritage; Department of Resources & Energy; Department of Tourism; Devonport Municipal Council; Esperance Municipal Council; Evandale Municipal Council; Fingal Municipal Council; Flinders Municipal Council; Forestry Commission; George Town Municipal Council; Glamorgan Municipal Council; Hamilton City Council; Huon Municipal Council; Hydro-Electric Commission; King Island Municipal Council; Kingsborough Municipal Council; Latrobe Municipal Council; Launceston City Council; Longford Municipal Council; Names Board of Tasmania; National Trust of Australia (Tasmania); New Norfolk Municipal Council; Oatlands Municipal Council; Penguin Municipal Council; Port Cygnet Municipal Council; Portland Municipal Council; Richmond Municipal Council; Ringarooma Municipal Council; Ross Municipal Council; St Helens Municipal Council; Scottsdale Municipal Council; Sorell Municipal Council; Spring Bay Municipal Council; Ulverstone Municipal Council; Waratah Municipal Council; Westbury Municipal Council; Wynyard Municipal Council. NORTHERN TERRITORY Borroloola Community Government Council; Conservation Commission of the Northern Territory; Coomalie Community Government Council; Daguragu Community Government Council; Department of Mines & Energy; Jabiru Town Council; Litchfield Shire Council; National Trust of Australia (NT); Nauiyu Nambiyu Community Government Council; Northern Land Council; Pine Creek & Community Government Council; Place Names Committee of the Northern Territory; Yuendumu Community Government Council; Yugul Mangi Community Government Council.

Maps in book or sheet form produced by the following organisations were an invaluable source of reference:
AUSLIG; Australian Geographic; BP Australia; Central Mapping Authority of NSW; Gregory's; National Roads and Motorists' Association; Northern Territory Automobile Association; Northern Territory Tourism Commission; Queensland Transport; RA Broadbent; Reader's Digest; Royal Automobile Association of South Australia; Royal Automobile Club of Queensland; Royal Automobile Club of Tasmania; Royal Automobile Club of Victoria; Royal Automobile Club of Western Australia; Sunmap Queensland; Survey & Mapping Victoria; Travelog Publications; Tropical Publications; UBD; Universal Press.

The following books and periodicals were consulted for reference:
Aboriginal Place Names A.W. Reed (Reed); *Albany and the Whalers* Les Johnson (Albany Travel Centre); *Archaeology of the Dreamtime: The Story of Prehistoric Australia and its People* Josephine Flood (Collins); *Arts of the Dreaming: Australia's Living Heritage* Jennifer Isaacs (Weldon); *Australia! Australia! The Pioneer Years* R.M. Younger (Rigby); *Around Australia on Highway 1* Robert Wilson (Weldon); *Australia's Great River* R.M. Younger (Horizon); *Australia's Heritage Sketchbook* Keith Norris (Lansdowne Press); *Australia's Railway Days: Milestones in Railway History* Brian Carroll (Macmillan); *Australia's Waterways* Nevill Drury (Rigby); *Australia's Wilderness Heritage (Vols 1 & 2)* Penelope Figgis/Geoff Mosley (Weldon); *Australian Album: The Way We Were* Daniel O'Keefe; *The Australian Colonists* K.S. Inglis (Melbourne University Press); *The Australian Encyclopaedia* (Australian Geographic Society/The Grolier Society of Australia); *The Australian House: Homes of the Tropical North* Balwant Saini/Ray Joyce (Weldon); *Australian Medicinal Plants* E.V. Lassak/T. McCarthy (Mandarin Australia); *Australian National Dictionary* (Oxford University Press); *The Australian People* (Angus & Robertson); *Australian Place Names* Brian & Barbara Kennedy (Hodder & Stoughton); *Australian Sea Mysteries* Jack Loney (Maritime History Publications); *Australians: Events and Places* (Fairfax, Syme & Weldon Associates); *Australians: A Guide to Sources* (Fairfax, Syme & Weldon Associates); *Australians: A Historical Atlas* (Fairfax, Syme & Weldon); *Bailliere's New South Wales Gazetteer and Road Guide* R.P. Whitworth (Bailliere) *The Barossa Valley* Nola Totham (Macmillan/Golden Fleece); *Barossa Valley Sketchbook* Colin Thiele (Rigby); *Out of the Big Scrub, Bangalow* L.C. Furnell; *Blood on the Wattle* Bruce Elder (Child & Associates); *Borroloola, Isolated & Interesting 1885–1985* J.A. Whitaker; *Braidwood, Dear Braidwood* Netta Ellis (N.N. & N.M. Ellis); *Bridges and Ferries of Australia* Valmai Phillips (Bay Books); *The Brunswick: Another River and its People* J. Brokenshire (Brunswick Valley Historical Society); *Building Queensland's Heritage* Janet Hogan (Richmond Hill Press); *Burnum Burnum's Aboriginal Australia: A Traveller's Guide* (Angus & Robertson); *Burra in Colour* Peter Inch/Ian Auhl (Investigator Press); *Bushwalking in North-East New South Wales* Bob Blanch/Vince Kean (Artrand Pty Ltd); *Camels and the Outback* H.M. Barker (Rigby); *Canberra and the Australian Capital Territory* T. Aslanides/J. Stewart (Kangaroo Press); *The Canberra Handbook* (Australian National University Press); *Central Goldfields of Australia* Howard Tanner (MacMillan); *Central Goldfields of Victoria* Howard Tanner (Macmillan/Golden Fleece); *In the Centre on a Budget* Brian Sheedy (Viking O'Neil); *Clare: A District History* Robert J. Noye (Investigator Press); *The Concise Encyclopaedia of Australia* (2 Vols) (Horwitz); *Coorong* Colin Thiele (Rigby); *Country Australia* (Reader's Digest); *Crossing Australia's North* Julia Thorn (Kangaroo Press); *Cruising the NSW Coast* Alan Lucas (Castle Books); *Darling Downs Sketchbook* Kevin Jopson/Peter Newell (Rigby); *Discover Australia* (Reader's Digest); *Discover Australia: Our Highways and Byways* Robert Wilson (Runaway Publications); *Discover Australia's Great Country Towns* Frances Cook (Child & Associates); *Discover Victoria, Australia* (Decalon); *Discovering Historic Australia* Douglass Baglin/Barbara Mullins (Ure Smith); *Discovering Kangaroo Island* Neville Cordes (Island Press); *The Exploration of Australia* Michael Cannon (Reader's Digest); *Explore Australia* (Viking O'Neil/BP); *Explore Australia's Great Rivers* Bill Andrews (Child & Associates); *Explore Historic Australia* Margaret Barca (Currey O'Neil/BP); *Explore Tasmania* Jennifer Pringle-Jones (Kingfisher Books); *Exploring the ACT and Southeast New South Wales* J. Kay Donald (Kangaroo Press); *Exploring Australia's Southeast* Bary Dowling (Kangaroo Press); *Exploring the Golden West* J. Kay Donald (Kangaroo Press); *Exploring Historic New South Wales* Katherine Bell/Ian Wigney (Child & Henry); *Exploring the Hunter Region* J.K. Donald/M.E. Hungerford (Kangaroo Press); *Exploring the North Coast and New England* J. Kay Donald (Kangaroo Press); *Exploring Outback Australia* Meryl Brown Tobin (Kangaroo Press); *Exploring Queensland's Central Highlands* Charles Warner (Charles Warner); *A Field Guide to the National Parks of Victoria* Alan Fairley; *Folklore of the Australian Railwaymen* Patsy Adam-Smith (Rigby); *From Dusk till Dawn: A History of Australian Lighthouses* Department of Transport and Communications (Macmillan); *From Squatter's Hut to City: Traralgon 1840 to 1976* Jean Court/Bert Thompson (Back to Traralgon Festival Committee); *From Steamhorse to Power: A History of Morwelltown* Prue McGoldrick; *Frontier Country: Australia's Outback Heritage (Vols 1 & 2)* (Weldon Russell); *Ghost Ports of Australia* Jeff Toghill (Macmillan); *Gippsland Sketchbook* Desmond Norman/K.A. Austin (Rigby); *Oldtown Railway: History of Moe to Walhalla Railway* Stephen Watson; *Goulburn and Environs* Timoshenko Aslanides/Jenny Stewart (Olive Press); *The Grampians* Jane Calder (Victorian National Parks Association); *Grand Goulburn* Stephen J. Tazewell (Goulburn City Council); *Gregory's Touring Australia* (Universal Press); *Handbook of Central Australia* Wendy Kirke (Alice Springs Regional Tourist Association); *The Heritage of Australia* Robin Smith/Cedric Flower (Viking O'Neil); *The Heritage of Australia: The Illustrated Register of the National Estate* (Macmillan); *Historic Towns of Australia* Cox/Stacey (Lansdowne Press); *A History of Berrima District 1798–1973* James Jervis (Berrima County Council); *A History of Goulburn* R.T. Wyatt (Lansdowne Press); *A History of Maryborough* (Maryborough City Council); *A History of Neerim (Vols 1 & 2)* Dorothy Hunt (Neptune Press); *History Tours in and around Canberra* Bill Waterhouse (Australian National University Press); *The Hume: Australia's Highway of History* Brian Carroll (Kangaroo Press); *The Hunter Valley* Philip Cox/Howard Tanner/Meredith Walker (Macmillan/Golden Fleece); *The Illustrated A–Z of Australian Towns and Cities* Robert Wilson (Weldon); *The Iron Road to Walhalla: A History of the Moe–Walhalla Railway* Marc Fiddian (Pakenham Gazette); *Jeff Toghill's Boating Guide to the NSW North Coast* (Reed); *Journeys into History* (Weldon Russell); *Jeff Toghill's Guides to the Australian Coastline* (Hodder & Stoughton); *Keep the Billy Boiling* R.M. Brennan/G. White (Warren Shire Council); *Lakes and Rivers of Australia* Vincent Serventy/Robert Raymond (Summit); *Land of the Pelican: The Story of Yarram and District* Kenneth Cox; *Land Worth Saving* Nancy Schumann (The Sunnyland Press); *The Last Coach* John Bird; *Lismore* (The Currawong Press); *Little Hills* Max Thomson (Narre Warren State School); *The Macquarie Book of Events* (Macquarie Library); *Maffra: The History of the Shire to 1975* Doris Kemp (Maffra Shire); *The Mallee Pioneers of Hopetoun* Agnes Hilton; *Manning's Place Names of South Australia* (Geoffrey H. Manning); *On McGuire's Punt:* Ron Michael (City of Shepparton); *McIvor* J.O. Randell (McIvor Shire); *Memories of Diggora, its School and its People* Patricia Jean Coughlin; *Mid North and Yorke Peninsula* Stuart Nicol (RAA); *Mingenew 1846–1986* (Hesperian Press); *Mount Gambier: The City around a Cave* Les R. Hill (Investigator Press); *Under Mount Lofty* Robert Martin (District Council of Stirling); *With Mud on Their Boots* Ine Vale/Neil Everitt (Toora Centenary Committee); *Museums & Historical Buildings of NSW & ACT* (NRMA); *Myrtleford: Gateway to the Alps* Kay Robertson (Rigby); *Names on the Omeo Highway* P.D. Gardner (Ngarak Press); *The National Trust in South Australia* M. Colwell/P. Finch (Rigby); *New Classic Wines* Oz Clarke (Mitchell Beazley); *New Crossing Place* Niall Brennan (Shire of Seymour); *New England Sketchbook* Unk White/Peter Newell (Rigby); *North Stradbroke Island* Ellie Durbridge/Jeanette Covacevich (Imprint Pty Ltd Brisbane); *The Observer's Book of National Parks of Australia* Alan Fairley (Frederick Warne); *Outback Heroes* Patsy Adam-Smith (Collins, Angus & Robertson); *The Oxford Literary Guide to Australia* (Oxford University Press); *Parkes: One Hundred Years of Local Government* (Parkes Shire Council); *Pastures of Peace: A Tapestry of Mortlake Shire* (Shire of Mortlake); *Pictorial History of Australia's Little Cornwall* Philip Payton (Rigby); *A Pictorial History of Moe and District* (Moe City Council); *Pioneer Pageant* John Kerr (Pioneer Shire Council); *Pioneering East Gippsland* Denis O'Bryan; *Place Names of Australia* A.W. Reed (Reed); *Place Names of Victoria* Les Blake (Rigby); *Portrait of Tasmania* Cedric Emanuel (Rigby); *Ravensthorpe – Then and Now* A.W. Archer; *Reader's Digest Book of Historic Australian Towns*; *Reader's Digest Guide to the Australian Coast*; *Reader's Digest Motoring Guide to Australia*; *Reflections 1879–1979* Sue Wallace (Shepparton Shire); *Rich River* Allan Morris (*Colac Herald*); *The Riches of Ancient Australia* Josephine Flood (University of Queensland Press); *Road to the Murchison* Marion Nixon/R.F.B. Lefroy (Shire of Murchison); *Rockingham Looks Back* Nora Taggart (Rockingham District Historical Society); *The Rush That Never Ended* Geoffrey Blainey; *Salisbury South Australia* H. John Lewis (Investigator Press); *Saltbush Country: History of the Deniliquin District* John E.P. Bushby (Library of Australian History); *Scenic Wonders of Australia* (Reader's Digest); *The South Coast of New South Wales* Jean Stranger (The Jacaranda Press); *South Coast of New South Wales* Philip Cox (Macmillan/Golden Fleece); *Spanning Two Centuries: Historic Bridges of Australia* Colin O'Connor (University of Queensland Press); *The Story of Australia* Don Watson (Penguin); *Story of the Dandenongs* Helen Coulson (F.W. Cheshire); *A Story of Horsham* B. Brooke/A. Finch (City of Horsham); *The Story of Stokers Siding: A Village in the Tweed Valley* Laine Langridge (Artrand Pty Ltd);*Tasmania: A Guide* Sally Farrell Odgers (Kangaroo Press); *They Came to a Plateau (The Stanthorpe Saga)* Jean Hasslett/Mervyn Royle (International Colour Productions); *Thunderbolt Country* G. Powell (Robert Brown & Associates); *Tin Mosques and Ghantowns* Christine Stevens (Oxford University Press); *Touring the Eyre Peninsula* (RAA); *Touring the Flinders Ranges* (RAA); *Touring the Murray* (RAA); *Tours from Adelaide* (RAA); *Traralgon, a Tableau Through Time* (Traralgon & District Historical Society); *Travel Guide to New South Wales: Sydney and ACT, Australia* (Blair's Guides); *Travel Guide to Victoria and Melbourne* (Suzanne Jacobe Blair); *Tunnels on Australian Railways* William A. Bayley (Austrail Publications); *25 Family Bushwalks in and around Canberra* Graeme Barrow (Dagraja Press); *Victor Harbor and District Sketchbook* Bob Muir/V.M. Branson (Rigby); *The Victorians* (Volumes 1, 2 & 3) Richard Broome, Tony Dingle, Susan Priestley (Fairfax, Syme & Weldon Associates); *A Vital Link: Eucla and the Eyre Highway* Jessie White (Median Man); *West Australian Goldfields Sketchbook* Arthur Evan Read/Kim Lockwood (Rigby); *When We Rode the Rails* Patsy Adam-Smith (Lansdowne Press); *Where the Whirlwinds Rise Tall* A.M. Connor; *Wild Australia* (Reader's Digest); *Wongan–Ballidu: Pioneering Days* R.R.B. Ackland (Wongan–Ballidu Shire Council); *The World of Olegas Truchanas* Max Angus (OBM).

Special thanks are due to the regional historical societies, associations, committees and museum groups in the following cities, towns, districts or shires: NEW SOUTH WALES Albury; Bathurst; Batlow; Berrima; Berry; Bingara; Bland; Bourke; Braidwood; Brewarrina; Brisbane Water; Brunswick Valley; Bundanoon; Casino; Cessnock; Clyde River & Batemans Bay; Cobar; Condobolin; Cooma–Monaro; Coonabarabran; Coutts Crossing & Nymboida; Cowra; Dubbo; Dungog; Eden; Forbes; Gerringong; Glen Innes; Gloucester; Goulburn; Grenfell; Gulgong; Gunnedah; Harden–Murrumburrah; Hastings; Hawkesbury; Hills; Illawarra; Jerilderie; Lake Cargelligo; Lake Macquarie; Lockhart; Maclean; Macleay River; Maitland; Manning Valley; Merimbula–Imlay; Millthorpe; Mudgee; Murrurundi; Muswellbrook & Upper Hunter; Nandewar; Narrandera & Sturt; Nepean; Nyngan; Parkes; Port Stephens; Port of Yamba; Queanbeyan; Quirindi; Raymond Terrace; Richmond River; Scone & Upper Hunter; Shoalhaven; Stroud; Tamworth; Tathra; Temora; Tenterfield; Tumut; Walcha; Walgett; Warialda; White Cliffs; Wilcannia; Yass; Young. VICTORIA Ararat; Beaufort; Bellarine; Benalla; Berwick–Pakenham; Broadford; Cape Clear; Cobram Shire; Colac; Coleraine; Cranbourne; Creswick; Donald; Dromana; Echuca; Euroa; Geelong;

Halls Gap & Grampians; Healesville; Hopetoun; Horsham; Inglewood; Katamatite; Kerang; Kiewa Valley; Koroit; Korong; Korumburra; Kyneton; Linton; McIvor; Maffra; Mallacoota; Mansfield; Marysville; Melton; Midlands; Minyip; Mirboo North; Moe; Monbulk; Mornington Peninsula; Mortlake; Morwell; Mount Macedon; Murchison; Murtoa; Myrtleford; Newstead; Nhill; Numurkah; Orbost; Phillip Island; Portland; Queenscliff; Rochester; Rupanyup; Rutherglen; St Arnaud; Seymour; Shepparton; Skipton; Stawell; Stratford; Sunbury; Swan Hill; Tambo Shire; Tatura; Traralgon; Warracknabeal; Warragul; Warrandyte; Warrnambool; Whittlesea; Winchelsea; Wodonga; Wonthaggi; Woodend; Woomelang; Woorayl; Yackandandah; Yarram; Yarrawonga & Mulwala. QUEENSLAND Allora; Banana Shire; Barcaldine; Beaudesert; Biggenden; Blackwater; Brisbane Valley; Broadsound; Buderim; Bundaberg; Byfield; Caboolture; Charleville; Clifton; Crows Nest; Cunnamulla; Eacham; Eidsvold; Eumundi; Fassifern; Gayndah; Gin Gin; Goondiwindi; Gympie; Hervey Bay; Ilfracombe; Innisfail; Ipswich; Isis; Kenilworth; Kilkivan; Kumbia; Laidley; Landsborough; Logan Village; Mackay; Maryborough, Wide Bay & Burnett; Miles; Millmerran; Monto; Mount Morgan; Mulgrave; Mundubbera; North Stradbroke Island; Nundah; Oakey; Redcliffe; Rockhampton; Samford; Sandgate; Stanthorpe; Tara; Texas; Toowoomba; Torres Strait; Townsville; Warrego & Southwest Queensland; Warwick; Winton; Woocoo. SOUTH AUSTRALIA Kapunda; Mount Gambier; Mount Horrocks; Murray Bridge; Pinnaroo; Port Broughton; Salisbury; Waikerie; Yankalilla Inc. WESTERN AUSTRALIA Albany; Armadale–Kelmscott; Augusta; Beverley; Brookton; Broomehill; Broome; Busselton; Cunderdin; Esperance Bay; Gascoyne; Goomalling; Irwin; Kalamunda; Kellerberrin; Kojonup; Mandurah; Manjimup; Merredin; Mingenew; Moora; Narrogin; Northampton; Plantagenet; Ravensthorpe; Rockingham; Southern Cross; Swan–Guildford; Wongan–Ballidu; Yalgogrin North. TASMANIA Bothwell; Devon; St Helens; Tasman Peninsula. NORTHERN TERRITORY Katherine.

The following organisations and individuals provided photographs and illustrations and gave permission for them to be reproduced:
(Abbreviations: ANT Photo Library = Australasian Nature Transparencies Photo Library; APL = Australian Picture Library; Auscape = Auscape International; IPL = International Photographic Library; RD = Reader's Digest; The Photo Library = The Photographic Library of Australia. Positions of photographs and illustrations on the page are given as: t – top; b – bottom; l – left; r – right; c – centre.) Front cover APL. Back cover t–b: Auscape, Philip Quirk/Wildlight Photo Agency, Mark Lang/Wildlight Photo Agency, APL. Endpapers Photo Index. 1 Bill Bachman. 3 John Peel. 5 Bill Bachman. 7 Philip Quirk/Wildlight Photo Agency. 8 l, The Photo Library; r, Jean-Paul Ferrero/Auscape. 9 l, Otto Rogge/Stock Photos; r, Mark Lang/Wildlight Photo Agency. 10 Jane Eliza Currie, 1830–2/Mitchell Library, State Library of NSW. 11 t, Matthew Flinders/Mitchell Library, State Library of NSW; b, IPL. 12 IPL. 13 t, John Oxley 'Journals of Two Expeditions'/Mitchell Library, State Library of NSW; b, IPL. 14 t, National Library of Australia; b, John Oxley Library/Stock Photos. 15 t, Kathy Grant; b, Frederick Strange c1807–73, Brisbane St, Launceston, May 1848/Collection, Queen Victoria Museum and Art Gallery, Launceston. 16 t, David Barnes/Peter Luck Productions/NSW Dept Mineral Resources; b, John Oxley Library/Stock Photos. 17 t, Hans Weverling/Kent Town Pro Lab; b, John Oxley Library/Stock Photos. 18 t, *Australasian Sketcher* 19 June 1880/National Library of Australia; b, John Oxley Library/Stock Photos. 19 t, 9712P/Passey Collection, Battye Library; b, John Oxley Library/Stock Photos. 20 t, Tarac Industries; b, John Oxley Library/Stock Photos. 21 John Oxley Library/Stock Photos. 22 t, Battye Library 816B/TB7495; b, IPL. 23 John Oxley Library/Stock Photos. 24 John Rae, ZML244/Mitchell Library, State Library of NSW. 25 t, John Oxley Library/Stock Photos; b, Australian National Railways. 27 l, Jaime Plaza van Roon/Auscape; r, Jean-Paul Ferrero/Auscape. 28 t, John Peel. 28–9 Lance Nelson/Stock Photos. 29 Lance Nelson/Stock Photos. 30 t, Lance Nelson/Stock Photos; b, John Peel. 31 t & c, Lance Nelson/Stock Photos; b, Otto Rogge/Stock Photos. 32 Austral-International. 33 John Carnemolla/APL. 34 APL. 35 l, IPL; r, Brett Gregory/Auscape. 37 t, John Carnemolla; bl, Jonathan Marks/APL; br, IPL. 38 t & c, IPL; b, Owen Wilson/Austral-International. 40 John Carnemolla/APL. 41 t, IPL; b, APL. 42–3 Barry Smith. 44 t, Austral-International; b, IPL. 45 Noeline Kelly/APL. 46 l, The Photo Library; r, IPL. 47 Robin Morrison/Auscape. 48 Allan Fox/Auscape. 49 t, John Carnemolla/APL; b, Ross W. Barnett/Auscape. 50 John Baker/APL. 51 l, Jaime Plaza van Roon/Auscape; r, Elke Oelrichs/APL. 52 John Carnemolla. 52–3 Susan Burry/APL. 53 l, NSW Government Printing Office Collection, State Library of NSW; r, Augustus Earl/National Library of Australia (detail). 55 t, Noeline Kelly/APL; b, IPL. 56–7 Austral. 57–8 John Carnemolla/APL. 59 l, IPL; tr, R. Garwood/APL; br, Austral-International. 60–1 The Photo Library. 61 Fritz Prenzel/APL. 62 IPL. 63 t, The Photo Library; b, Michael Lees/APL. 64 John Peel. 64–5 R. Fretwell/APL. 65 l, Rick Altman, Stock Photos; r, Don Skirrow. 66 IPL. 67 t, IPL; b, John Carnemolla/APL. 68 Douglass Baglin/APL. 69 t, Leigh Hemmings/APL; b, Noeline Kelly/APL. 70 Fritz Prenzel/APL. 71 John Carnemolla/APL. 72 IPL. 73 John Carnemolla/APL. 74 Jaime Plaza van Roon/Auscape. 75 Jonathan Marks/APL. 76 t, Brett Gregory/Auscape; b, IPL. 77 Noeline Kelly/APL. 78 John Carnemolla/APL. 79 IPL. 80 The Photo Library. 81 IPL. 82 t, Steve Hynes/APL; bl, The Photo Library; br, John Carnemolla/APL. 83 John Carnemolla/APL. 84 IPL. 85 t, IPL; b, Milton J. Brady/IPL. 86 t, IPL; b, Graham Smith/APL. 87 Douglass Baglin/APL. 88 Brian Carroll *Australia's Railway Days*/Macmillan 1976. 89 The Photo Library. 90 l, J. Marks/APL; r, John Baker/APL. 91 t, Michael Jensen/Auscape; b, John Carnemolla/APL. 92–3 Ross Ellis. 94 Brian Scott/APL. 95 Adrian Seaforth/IPL. 96 t, Noeline Kelly/APL; b, APL. 97 t, John Carnemolla/APL; b, APL. 98 John Baker/APL. 99 t, Fritz Prenzel/IPL; b, IPL. 101 t, APL; b, Jocelyn Burt/IPL. 102 APL. 103 t, John Baker/APL; b, David Moore/Wildlight Photo Agency. 104 Nick Rains/APL. 105 t, Fritz Prenzel/APL; b, John Baker/APL. 106–7 John Baker/APL. 108 t, Owen Hughes/APL; b, John Baker/APL. 109 t, Ann Ronan Picture Library; b, Barbara Todd/ANT Photo Library. 110 APL. 111 Robir Morrison/RD. 112 M. Lees/APL. 113 t, Kerrie Ruth/Auscape; b, Jean-Paul Ferrero/Auscape. 114 t, John Carnemolla/APL; b, Esther Beaton/Auscape. 115 t, The Photo Library; b, Scienceworks Collection, Museum of Victoria. 116 t APL; b, Auscape. 117 l, APL; r, John Baker/APL. 118 t, Otto Rogge/Stock Photos; b, M. Pugh/APL. 119 t, Lance Nelson/Stock Photos; b, Paul Steel/Stock Photos. 120 John Carnemolla/APL. 121 t, Robin Morrison/RD; b, Johr Carnemolla/APL. 122–3 David Moore/Wildlight Photo Agency. 124 Robin Morrison/RD. 125 t, Australian War Memorial Neg. No. 067180; l & r, APL. 126 l–r: Tony Rodd, Murray Fagg, Murray Fagg, Stirling Macoboy; b, Johr Carnemolla/APL. 127–8 IPL. 130 t, Michael Jensen/Auscape; b, Jean-Paul Ferrero/Auscape. 131 Wayne Lawler/Auscape. 132 The Photo Library. 133 t, APL; b, John Carnemolla/APL. 134 Ken Griffiths/ANT Photo Library. 135 Ross W. Barnett/Auscape. 136 t, IPL; b, The Photo Library. 137 Garry Hansen/Auscape. 138 tl, IPL; cl, The Photo Library; tr & bl, APL; b, John Carnemolla/APL. 139 John Carnemolla/APL. 140 The Photo Library. 141 IPL. 142 The Photo Library. 143 l, APL; c, The Photo Library; r, *The Northern Daily Leader*. 144 APL. 145 The Photo Library. 146–7 Mark Lang/Wildlight Photo Agency. 147 l, APL; r, R. King/APL. 148 APL. 149 Jaime Plaza van Roon/Auscape 150 l, The Photo Library; r, Glen Threlfo/Auscape. 151 Leo Meier/APL. 152 t, Susan Burry/APL; cl & bl, Robin Morrison/RD. 153 l, IPL; r, Leo Meier/APL. 154 Ken Griffiths/APL. 155 t, APL; b, The Photo Library. 156 l, R Bisson/APL; r, Graham Robertson/Auscape. 157 IPL. 158 l, The Photo Library; r, John Baker/APL. 159 APL. 160 The Photo Library. 161 APL. 162 l & c, Wayne Lawler/Auscape; r, Kathie Atkinson/Auscape. 163 APL. 164 t, Fritz Prenzel/APL; c, APL; r, Michael Cannon/*Australia: A History in Photographs*. 165 P. Morton/APL. 166 John Peel. 167 Dick Hoole/APL. 168 t, Kev Deacon/Auscape; b, John Baker/APL. 169 IPL. 170 Graeme Chapman/Auscape. 170– The Photo Library. 172 J. Vissel/The Photo Library. 173 APL. 174 Esther Beaton/Auscape. 175 t, Kathie Atkinson/Auscape; b, Robin Morrison/RD. 176 APL. 176–7 Philip Quirk/Wildlight Photo Agency. 177 t, Craig La Motte/APL c, John Peel; b, John Baker/APL. 178 t, Robin Morrison/RD; b, NSW Tourism Commission. 179 John Tregartha. 180–1 APL. 181 tr, The Photo Library; c, APL. 182 Moree Shire Council. 183 t, Australian Museum; b, IPL. 184– Grenville Turner/Wildlight Photo Agency. 185 Robin Morrison/RD. 186 t, Robin Morrison/RD; b, '*Chronicles of Crime*, London 1841' (detail) 187 IPL/National Library of Australia. 188–9 The Photo Library. 190 tc, The Photo Library; b, Fritz Prenzel/APL. 191 APL. 192 t, APL; b, National Sound & Film Archives. 193 Courtesy G. & B. Ferguson. 194–5 The Photo Library. 196 Colin Beard. 197 APL. 198 Wayne Lawler/Auscape. 199 APL. 200 CSIRO. 202 t Raglan Gallery, Manly; b, John Baker/APL. 203 l, *Sydney Mail*, 1935: Mitchell Library, State Library of NSW; r, Young Historical Society. 204 Hans & Judy Beste/Auscape. 204–5 Michael Lees/APL. 205 John Fairfax Group Pty Ltd 206 John Carnemolla/APL. 207 t, APL; b, The Photo Library. 208 APL. 208–9 The Photo Library. 210 Jean-Paul Ferrero/Auscape. 211 t, Jean-Paul Ferrero/Auscape; b, APL. 212 t, Nick Rains/APL; b, J. Marks/APL. 213 l, Bicentennia Copying Project, State Library of NSW; c & r, Snowy Mountains Hydro-Electric Authority. 214 J.P. & E.S. Baker/APL. 215 Ross Barnett/Auscape. 216 The Photo Library. 217 t, The Photo Library; b, APL. 218 t, *Sydney Mail*, 10 July 1935: Mitchell Library, State Library of NSW; b, IPL. 219–20 Nick Rains. 221 Robin Morrison/RD. 222–3 Nick Rains. 224 John Peel. 225 Nick Rains. 226 The Photo Library. 227 Nick Rains. 228 Noeline Kelly/APL. 229 Mar Lang/Wildlight Photo Agency. 230 Bicentennial Copying Project, State Library of NSW. 231 G. Vines, Melbourne's Living Museum of the West. 231 John Peel. 232 APL. 233 Douglass Baglin/APL. 234 t, Esther Beaton/Auscape; b APL. 235 l, The Photo Library; r, APL. 236–7 Grenville Turner/Wildlight Photo Agency. 237 t, Otto Rogge/ANT Photo Library; c, The Photo Library. 238–9 Otto Rogge/ANT Photo Library. 240 t, John Peel; b, Leo Meier/APL. 241 C. Bento/Australian Museum; r, Peter Schouten/Angus & Robertson. 242–3 John Baker/APL. 243 The Photo Library. 244 l, J.W. Kelly/ANT Photo Library; r, F.S. Falkiner & Sons Pty Ltd. 245–6 Ralph & Daphne Keller/ANT Phot Library. 247 t, APL; b, Nick Rains/APL. 248 Nick Rains/APL. 249 t, APL; b, Philip Quirk/Wildlight Photo Agency. 251 l, Jean-Paul Ferrero/Auscape; r, Otto Rogge/ANT Photo Library. 252 Lance Nelson/Stock Photos. 252–3 Ott Rogge/Stock Photos. 253 t, R. Della-Piana/Stock Photos; b, Roger Du Buisson/Stock Photos. 254 t, R. Gordon/The Photo Library; b, The Photo Library. 255 t, P. Steel/Stock Photos; b, Bill Bachman. 257 The Photo Library. 258 Philip Quirk/Wildlight Photo Agency; r, Frank Park/ANT Photo Library. 259 Bill Bachman/ANT Photo Library. 260 J.P. & E.S. Baker/ANT Photo Library; b, Ralph & Daphne Keller/ANT Photo Library. 261 The Photo Library. 26 Philip Quirk/Wildlight Photo Agency. 263 The Photo Library. 264 t, Otto Rogge/ANT Photo Library; l, Dave Watts/ANT Photo Library; r, Otto Rogge/ANT Photo Library. 265–7 t, The Photo Library. 267 T. & P. Gardner/AN Photo Library. 268 P. & M. Walton/ANT Photo Library. 269 t, Robin Morrison/RD; b, J. O'Neil/ANT Photo Library. 270–1 Roger Du Buisson/Stock Photos. 272 Ralph & Daphne Keller/ANT Photo Library. 273 A. Bartel/APL. 274 J.P. & E.S. Baker/ANT Photo Library; b, The Photo Library. 275 Otto Rogge/Stock Photos. 276 J.P. & E.S. Baker/APL. 277 t, The Photo Library; b, APL. 278 J.P. & E.S. Baker/ANT Photo Library. 279 Bill Bachman. 280 Nick Rains.28 APL. 283 t, Fredy Mercay/ANT Photo Library; b, Frank Park/ANT Photo Library. 284–5 J. Lauritz/Stock Photos. 286 t, L.A. Frances/Stock Photos; b, William Ford, 'Picnic party at Hanging Rock, near Mount Macedon' N6V2255. (detail)/National Gallery of Victoria. 287 t, F.W. Niven Lithographer after S.T. Gill, La Trobe Collection, State Library of Victoria (detail); b, La Trobe Collection, State Library of Victoria. 288 The Photo Library. 289 Natfoto/AN Photo Library. 290 t, Robin Morrison/RD; b, G. Lewis/APL. 291–2 J.M. La Roque/Auscape. 293 L.A. Frances/Stock Photos. 294 t, The Photo Library; b, L.A. Frances/Stock Photos. 295 The Photo Library. 296–7 Eugène vo Guérard, Koort Koort-nog Homestead, Reg Nan Kivell Collection NK4017 (detail)/National Library of Australia. 297 Bill Bachman. 298 t, Ralph & Daphne Keller/ANT Photo Library; b, Philip Quirk/Wildlight Photo Agency. 29 APL. 300 Lance Nelson/Stock Photos. 301 t, Collection, Ballarat Fine Art Gallery; c, Government Printer, Victoria; b, *Illustrated Australian News*, Mitchell Library. 302 Robin Morrison/RD. 303 t, Lance Nelson/Stock Photos; b Robin Morrison/RD. 304 James Lauritz/Stock Photos. 305 The Photo Library. 306 Nick Rains. 307 Philip Green. 308 Lance Nelson/Stock Photos. 309 t, Don Skirrow; b, Robin Morrison/RD. 310 t, APL; b, Nick Rains. 311 Nic Rains. 313 t, Bill Bachman/ANT Photo Library; b, Otto Rogge/ANT Photo Library. 314–15 Otto Rogge/Stock Photos. 316 Dave Watts/ANT Photo Library. 317 APL. 318 Esso Australia. 319 J. Burt/ANT Photo Library. 320 Robi Morrison/RD. 321 The Photo Library. 322 APL. 323 t, P. & M. Walton/ANT Photo Library; b, J. Burt/ANT Photo Library. 324 John Baker/APL. 325 t, The Photo Library; b, T. & P. Gardner/ANT Photo Library. 326 l, Ott Rogge/Stock Photos; r, Lance Nelson/Stock Photos. 327 P. & M. Walton/ANT Photo Library. 328 t, Colin Beard; b, Nick Rains. 329 Nick Rains. 330 l, A.J. Stopps, hand col. lithograph after a daguerrotype by Acley and Rochlet Rex Nan Kivell Collection NK1335/S, National Library of Australia; r, J.M. La Roque/Auscape. 331 t, S. Paintin/Winterlight; b, J.M. La Roque/Auscape. 332–3 Philip Quirk/Wildlight Photo Agency. 333 t, The Photo Library; b, Joh Peel. 334–5 M. Hampton/Winterlight. 336–8 Nick Rains. 339 t, APL; b, The Photo Library. 340 Otto Rogge/Stock Photos. 341 t, Nick Rains; b, Leo Meier/APL. 343 t, Lance Nelson/Stock Photos; b, R. Thwaites/ANT Photo Librar 344 APL. 345 l, Lance Nelson/Stock Photos; r, Robin Morrison/RD. 346–7 J.M. La Roque/Auscape. 348 Gunther Schmida. 348–9 Philip Quirk/Wildlight Photo Agency. 349 t, Ross W. Barnett/Auscape; c, R. Garstone/National Phot Index. 350 t, T. & P. Gardner/ANT Photo Library; b, Don Skirrow. 351 Don Skirrow. 352 t, Lincoln Fowler; c, P.J. Phillips Collection, National Library of Australia; b, H.A. Godson Collection, State Library of South Australia. 353 H & J. Beste/Auscape. 354 APL. 354–5 Excitations/Stock Photos. 356 H. & J. Beste/Auscape. 357 t, Bill Bachman/Stock Photos; b, K. Uhlenhut/ANT Photo Library. 358 t, The Photo Library; b, Excitations/Stock Photos. 359 Ott Rogge/ANT Photo Library. 360 Otto Rogge/Stock Photos. 361 The Photo Library. 362 C.A. Henley/Auscape. 363 t, Otto Rogge/ANT Photo Library; b, APL. 364 J.W. Kiely/ANT Photo Library. 365 t, Nicholas Chevalie Australia/New Zealand 1828–1902, Mount Arapiles and the Mitre Rock 1863, oil, Collection, Australian National Gallery, Canberra; b, J. Chester/ANT Photo Library. 366 Wild Nature/ANT Photo Library. 367 Don Skirrow. 368 L Trobe Collection, State Library of Victoria. 369 Ron Ryan/Coo-ee Picture Library. 370 t, James Lauritz, Stock Photos; b, Don Skirrow. 372 The Photo Library. 373 t, Otto Rogge/ANT Photo Library; b, Philip Quirk/Wildlight Pho Agency. 374–6 The Photo Library. 377 l, Robin Morrison/RD; r, Guy Lamothe/Auscape. 378 l, Robin Morrison/RD; r, The Photo Library. 379 The Photo Library. 380 Science Museum, London. 380–1 Otto Rogge/Stock Photos. 38 The Photo Library. 383 t, J.M. La Roque/Auscape; b, Robin Morrison/RD. 385 l, Peter McDonald/ANT Photo Library; r, C. & S. Pollitt. 386 t, Lance Nelson/Stock Photos; c, John Baker/APL. 386–7 Otto Rogge/Stock Photos. 387 t- Lance Nelson/Stock Photos. 389 t, APL; b, Lance Nelson/Stock Photos. 390–2 Nick Rains. 393 APL. 395 Nick Rains. 396 t, Nick Rains; b, APL. 397 Ken Straiton/Stock Photos. 398 l, John Peel; r, Minneapolis Star and Tribune. 3 Nick Rains. 400–1 David Hancock/Auscape. 402 Nick Rains. 403 t, Nick Rains; b, Geoff Frame. 404 l, Esther Beaton/Auscape; r, Nick Rains. 405–6 Nick Rains. 407–8 Shaughn Lowry/APL. 409 tl, M. Viard/Auscape; tr, Lan Nelson/Stock Photos; b, Fraser Coast, South Burnett Tourism Board. 410 t, Jean-Paul Ferrero/Auscape; c & b, G.E. Schmida/ANT Photo Library. 411 APL. 412 t, R.J. Tomkins/ANT Photo Library; c, D. Parer & E. Pare Cook/Auscape; b, Fritz Prenzel/APL. 413 C. & S. Pollitt/ANT Photo Library. 414–15 APL. 416 Pelton/WL/APL. 416–17 Otto Rogge/Stock Photos. 417 l, John Carnemolla/APL; r, D. Parer & E. Parer-Cook/APL. 418 D. Parer & Parer-Cook/Auscape. 419 Don Skirrow. 420 John Peel. 421 t, APL; b, Lance Nelson/Stock Photos. 422 John Peel. 423 t, Don Skirrow; b, Jean-Paul Ferrero/Auscape. 424 Bill Bachman/ANT Photo Library. 425 Leo Meier/APL. 426 Sauvanet/Auscape. 426–7 Bill Bachman/ANT Photo Library. 428–9 John Carnemolla/APL. 429 Robin Morrison/RD. 431 t, Natural Images/ANT Photo Library; b, Lance Nelson/Stock Photos. 432 t, Robin Morrison/RD; b, APL. 4 Robin Morrison/RD. 434 Fritz Prenzel/APL. 435 t, Robin Morrison/RD; bl, Ray Joyce/Weldon trannies; bc, Robin Morrison/RD; br, Ray Joyce/Weldon trannies. 436 Bill Bachman/ANT Photo Library. 437 t, Bill Bachman; b, B Bachman/Stock Photos. 438 Gerry Whitmont. 439 l, Rentz/CSIRO; c, H. & J. Beste/Auscape; r, J. Cancalosi/Auscape. 440–1 Meg Farmer. 442 Lance Nelson. 443 Don Skirrow. 444 t, Rudie Kuiter/ANT Photo Library; c, Linco Fowler; b, Paddy Ryan/ANT Photo Library. 445 t, Alby Ziebell/Auscape; r, Don Skirrow. 446 Ron Gale/Stock Photos. 447 Lincoln Fowler. 448 C. Copeland/APL. 449 Don Skirrow. 450 Ron Gale/Stock Photos. 451 Rob Morrison/RD. 452 t, Craig Lamotte/APL; l, Bill Bachman/ANT Photo Library; r, G.B. Baker/ANT Photo Library. 453 Ted Mead/ANT Photo Library. 454 t, Frith Foto/ANT Photo Library; b, Don Skirrow. 455 Otto Rogge/Sto Photos. 456 l, John Peel; r, Lincoln Fowler. 457 Otto Rogge/Stock Photos. 458 t, Otto Rogge/Stock Photos; b, Don Skirrow. 459 N. Kelly/APL. 460 Lincoln Fowler. 461 t, Leo Meier/APL; b, Otto Rogge/Stock Photos. 462 l, Linco Fowler; r, Lance Nelson/Stock Photos. 463 t, Lance Nelson/Stock Photos; b, Otto Rogge/Stock Photos. 464 t, Lincoln Fowler; b, Ralph & Daphne Keller/ANT Photo Library. 465 l, Jean-Paul Ferrero/Auscape; tr, Leo Meier/APL; M. Cianelli/ANT Photo Library; br, Frith Foto/ANT Photo Library. 466 Otto Rogge/Stock Photos. 467 Grenville Turner/Wildlight Photo Agency. 468 Leo Meier/APL. 469 Lance Nelson/Stock Photos. 470 Jean-Paul Ferrero/Auscap 471 Otto Rogge/Stock Photos. 472 Bill Bachman. 473 tr, Otto Rogge/Stock Photos; c, John Carnemolla/APL; b, Reg Morrison/Auscape. 474 Don Skirrow. 475 t, Ron Gale/Stock Photos; b, Don Skirrow. 476 Robin Smith/The Pho Library. 477 Bill Bachman/Stock Photos. 478 t, Don Skirrow; c, APL; b, John Oxley Library/Stock Photos. 479 Otto Rogge/Stock Photos. 480 Diana Calder/Stock Photos. 481 l, Jocelyn Burt/The Photo Library; r, Grenvi Turner/Wildlight Photo Agency. 482 t, Otto Rogge/Stock Photos; b, Reg Morrison/Auscape. 483 Don Skirrow. 484 t, John Carnemolla/APL; b, Bill Bachman. 486 t, The Photo Library; c, John Gerritson; b, Dave Watts/ANT Pho Library. 487 Robin Smith/The Photo Library. 488 Nick Rains. 488–9 Nick Rains/APL. 490 Nick Rains. 491 t, Nick Rains; b, IPL. 492 t, Bill Bachman; b, G.E. Schmida/ANT Photo Library. 493 Nick Rains. 495 l, The Photo Library; Jean-Paul Ferrero/Auscape. 496 t, Segments Photo Library. 496–7 Philip Quirk/Wildlight Photo Agency. 497 t, John Carnemolla/APL; c, Lance Nelson/Stock Photos. 498 t, Segments Photo Library; b, Lance Nelson/Stock Phot 499 t, John Carnemolla/APL; b, APL. 500 APL. 500–1 Reg Morrison/Auscape. 502 t, The Photo Library; c, Philip Green; b, Leo Meier/APL. 503 P. Holden/APL. 504 t, Robin Morrison/RD; b, David Hoile/Saint Cecilia. 505 B Bachman/Stock Photos. 506 Otto Rogge/ANT Photo Library. 507 IPL. 508 t, Philip Green; b, Grenville Turner/Wildlight Photo Agency. 509 Otto Rogge/Stock Photos. 510–11 Otto Rogge/Stock Photos. 511 The Photo Library. 5 Otto Rogge/ANT Photo Library. 512–13 Grenville Turner/Wildlight Photo Agency. 513 l, APL; r, Robin Morrison/RD. 514 Robin Morrison/RD. 515 Philip Green. 516 IPL. 517 Don Skirrow. 518 Robin Morrison/RD. 519 t, Jean-Pa Ferrero/Auscape; c, Philip Green; b, Jean-Paul Ferrero/Auscape. 521 tl, Jean-Paul Ferrero/Auscape; r, J.R. Brownlie/ANT Photo Library; b, Philip Green. 522 Philip Green. 523 t, Kelvin Aitken/ANT Photo Library; b, APL. 5 Grenville Turner/Wildlight Photo Agency. 525 Otto Rogge/ANT Photo Library. 526 Ted Mead/ANT Photo Library. 527 Bill Bachman. 528 Grenville Turner/Wildlight Photo Agency. 529 t, IPL; b, Diana Calder/Stock Photos. 5 The Photo Library. 531 t, Don Skirrow; b, Rosalie Potter. 532 R. & V. Taylor/ANT Photo Library. 533 l, Don Skirrow; r, Robin Morrison/RD. 534 Robin Morrison/RD. 535 Bill Bachman. 536 t, The Photo Library; b, APL. 537 IPL. 5 t, Geoff Higgins/The Photo Library; b, D. & T. O'Byrne/ANT Photo Library. 539 Bill Bachman/Stock Photos. 540 t, Bill Bachman; b, Gunther Deichmann/Auscape. 541 Bill Bachman. 543 t, Don Skirrow; b, Bill Bachman/AN Photo Library. 544 Robin Smith/The Photo Library. 545 t, Don Skirrow; b, Bill Bachman. 546 Rosalie Potter. 548 Don Skirrow. 549 D. & T. O'Byrne/ANT Photo Library. 550 Otto Rogge/Stock Photos. 551 t, Mark Lang/Wildlig Photo Agency; b, Don Skirrow. 552–3 L. & B. Hemmings/APL. 554 Robin Morrison/RD. 555 Don Skirrow. 556 t, Robin Smith/The Photo Library; b, Dave Watts/ANT Photo Library. 557 Don Skirrow. 558 t, Geoff Higgins/T Photo Library; b, Don Skirrow. 559 George French Angus (painting) AA8 Kaurna Man/South Australian Museum. 560 Michael Cermak/ANT Photo Library. 561 t, Gary Hansen/Auscape; b, Bill Bachman. 562 Jean-Pa Ferrero/Auscape. 563 Excitations/Stock Photos. 564 t, Robin Smith/The Photo Library; b, Rosalie Potter. 565 Robin Smith/The Photo Library. 567 l, The Photographic Library; r, D. Whitford/ANT Photo Library. 568–70 Phc Index. 571 tl, Paul Steel/Stock Photos; tr, Robin Morrison/RD; b, Photo Index. 572 Robin Morrison/RD. 573 t, David Dare Parker/Auscape; b, Photo Index. 574 J.P. & E.S. Baker/ANT Photo Library. 575 The Photo Library. 576 E Bachman. 577 Otto Rogge/Stock Photos. 578 Robin Smith/The Photo Library. 579 Bill Bachman. 580 Natural Images/ANT Photo Library. 581 t, Otto Rogge/Stock Photos; b, Don Skirrow. 582 Brian Geach/Polperro Pictures. 58 Bill Bachman; r, Robin Morrison/RD. 584 t, Robin Smith/The Photo Library; b, Bill Bachman. 585 Leo Meier/APL. 586 A. Burbidge & J. Raines/ANT Photo Library. 587 Robin Morrison/RD. 588 t, Robin Morrison/RD; b, Phc Index. 589 t, Otto Rogge/Stock Photos; b, Photo Index. 590 John Baker/APL. 591 John Peel. 592 David Dare Parker/Auscape. 593 t, David Dare Parker/Auscape; b, Western Australia Tourism Commission. 594 John Baker/APL. 5 t, Evan Collis/APL; b, T. & P. Gardner/ANT Photo Library. 596 t, Gary Hansen/Auscape; b, Natfoto/ANT Photo Library. 597 David Dare Parker/Auscape. 598 t, Robin Morrison/RD; b, Bill Bachman. 599 Gary Lewis/The Phc Library. 600 Geoff Higgins/The Photo Library. 601 t, Wayne Stead/APL; b, Robin Morrison/RD. 602 Leo Meier/APL. 603 t, Laurie Brackley; bl & c, The Photo Library; br, Rosalie Potter. 604–5 David Dare Parker/Auscape. 606 T Photo Library. 607–8 Bill Bachman. 609 David Dare Parker/Auscape. 610 t, D. Whitford/ANT Photo Library; b, I.R. McCann Photo/ANT Photo Library. 612 The Photo Library. 613 t, Auscape; b, Reg Morrison/Auscape. 614 J.M. Roque/Auscape. 615 David Dare Parker/Auscape. 616–7 Bill Bachman. 617 Don Skirrow. 618 t, John Hicks/ANT Photo Library; b, David Dare Parker/Auscape. 619 Jan Aldenhoven/Auscape. 620 l, Reg Morrison/Auscape; r, I Bachman/Stock Photos. 621 Philip Green. 622 t, M.W. Gillam/Auscape; b, J.M. La Roque/Auscape. 623 Jean-Paul Ferrero/Auscape. 624 APL. 625 The Photo Library. 626 l, The Photo Library; r, Bill Bachman. 627 APL. 628 b, T Photo Library; t, J. Burt/ANT Photo Library. 629–30 Leo Meier/APL. 631 l, Bill Bachman/Stock Photos; r, Owen Hughes/APL. 632–3 Owen Hughes/APL. 635 l, Dave Watts/ANT Photo Library; r, I.R. McCann Photo/ANT Phc Library. 636 l, Cruising Yacht Club of Australia; r, Dennis Harding/Auscape. 636–7 Auscape. 637 The Photo Library. 638 Bill Bachman/ANT Photo Library. 639 Dennis Harding/Auscape. 640 Otto Rogge/Stock Photos. 6 Auscape. 642 R. Eastwood/APL. 643–4 The Photo Library. 645 R. Eastwood/APL. 646 t, Jean-Paul Ferrero/Auscape; b, Robin Morrison/RD. 647 t, Stock Photos; b, Philip Green. 648 Robin Morrison/RD. 649 l, Bill Bachman/AN Photo Library; r, Don Skirrow. 650 Robin Morrison/RD. 651 J.P. & E.S. Baker/ANT Photo Library. 652 l, Esther Beaton/Auscape; r, Dave Watts/ANT Photo Library. 653 Grant Dixon/ANT Photo Library. 654 K. Stepnell/The Phc Library. 655 Don Skirrow. 656 Owen Highes/APL. 657 Dennis Harding/Auscape. 658 l, Esther Beaton/Auscape; r, Auscape. 659 J.P. & E.S. Baker/ANT Photo Library. 660 t, Dave Watts/ANT Photo Library; b, Ted Mead/ANT Phc Library. 661 Gary Hansen/Auscape. 662 Robert Della Piana/Stock Photos. 663 J.P. & E.S. Baker/APL. 664 t, Dennis Harding/Auscape; b, Van Diemen's Land Company. 665 J.P. & E.S. Baker/APL. 666 Jean-Paul Ferrero/Ausca 666–7 R. Eastwood/APL. 668 Dave Watts/ANT Photo Library. 668–9 Gerry Whitmont. 669 Ted Mead/ANT Photo Library. 671 l, Dave Watts/ANT Photo Library; r, John Cancalosi/Auscape. 672 David Hancock/Skyscans. 67 Terry Knight/Terry Knight & Associates. 673 t, The Photo Library; c, Frank McGuinness/The Photo Library. 674 Don Skirrow. 675 t, Matt Jones/Auscape; b, David Hancock/Skyscans. 676 David Hancock/Skyscans. 677 l, D Skirrow; r, Jean-Paul Ferrero/Auscape. 678 Bill Bachman. 679 t, Bill Bachman; b, Rosalie Potter. 680 David Hancock/Skyscans. 681 Otto Rogge/Stock Photos. 682 t, John Peel; b, David Hancock/Skyscans. 683 Bill Bachman. 6 Jean-Paul Ferrero/Auscape. 685 t, Jean-Paul Ferrero/Auscape; c, Nick Rains/APL; b, Lorrie Graham/Wildlight Photo Agency. 686 Reg Morrison/Auscape. 687 t, Mark Lang/Wildlight Photo Agency; b, Philip Green. 688 t, Rosa Potter; b, Gunther Deichmann/Auscape. 689 l, David Hancock/Skyscans; r, Leo Meier/APL.